*The Consumer Credit and Sales
Legal Practice Series*

CONSUMER BANKRUPTCY LAW AND PRACTICE

VOLUME ONE: CHAPTERS AND INDEX

Tenth Edition

See *page ix* for information about the companion website.

Henry J. Sommer

John Rao, Editor and Contributing Author

Contributing Authors: Susan A. Schneider (for Chapter 17),
Tara Twomey, Geoff Walsh

National Consumer Law Center®
7 Winthrop Square, 4th Floor   Boston, MA 02110

www.nclc.org

About NCLC®	The National Consumer Law Center®, a nonprofit corporation founded in 1969, assists consumers, advocates, and public policy makers nationwide who use the powerful and complex tools of consumer law to ensure justice and fair treatment for all, particularly those whose poverty renders them powerless to demand accountability from the economic marketplace. For more information, go to www.nclc.org.
Ordering NCLC Publications	Order securely online at www.nclc.org, or contact Publications Department, National Consumer Law Center, 7 Winthrop Square, 4th Floor, Boston, MA 02110, (617) 542-9595, FAX: (617) 542-8028, e-mail: publications@nclc.org.
Training and Conferences	NCLC participates in numerous national, regional, and local consumer law trainings. Its annual fall conference is a forum for consumer rights attorneys from legal services programs, private practice, government, and nonprofit organizations to share insights into common problems and explore novel and tested approaches that promote consumer justice in the marketplace. Contact NCLC for more information or see our website.
Case Consulting	Case analysis, consulting and co-counseling for lawyers representing vulnerable consumers are among NCLC's important activities. Administration on Aging funds allow us to provide free consulting to legal services advocates representing elderly consumers on many types of cases. Massachusetts Legal Assistance Corporation funds permit case assistance to advocates representing low-income Massachusetts consumers. Other funding may allow NCLC to provide very brief consultations to other advocates without charge. More comprehensive case analysis and research is available for a reasonable fee. See our website for more information at www.nclc.org.
Charitable Donations and Cy Pres Awards	NCLC's work depends in part on the support of private donors. Tax-deductible donations should be made payable to National Consumer Law Center, Inc. For more information, contact Gerald Tuckman of NCLC's Development Office at (617) 542-8010 or gtuckman@nclc.org. NCLC has also received generous court-approved *cy pres* awards arising from consumer class actions to advance the interests of class members. For more information, contact Robert Hobbs (rhobbs@nclc.org) or Rich Dubois (rdubois@nclc.org) at (617) 542-8010.
Comments and Corrections	Write to the above address to the attention of the Editorial Department or e-mail consumerlaw@nclc.org.
About This Volume	This is the Tenth Edition of *Consumer Bankruptcy Law and Practice*. Discard all prior editions and supplements. This book includes a companion website. Continuing developments can be found in periodic supplements to and revised editions of this volume, on the companion website, and in NCLC eReports.
Cite This Volume As	National Consumer Law Center, Consumer Bankruptcy Law and Practice (10th ed. 2012).
Attention	*This publication is designed to provide authoritative information concerning the subject matter covered. Always use the most current edition and supplement, and use other sources for more recent developments or for special rules for individual jurisdictions. This publication cannot substitute for the independent judgment and skills of an attorney or other professional. Non-attorneys are cautioned against using these materials to conduct a lawsuit without advice from an attorney and are cautioned against engaging in the unauthorized practice of law.*
Copyright	© 2012 by National Consumer Law Center, Inc. National Consumer Law Center and NCLC are registered trademarks of National Consumer Law Center, Inc. All rights reserved. ISBN: 978-1-60248-114-5 (this volume) ISBN: 978-0-943116-10-5 (Series) Library of Congress Control Number: 2012953645

About the Authors

Henry J. Sommer, the author, is supervising attorney at the pro bono Consumer Bankruptcy Assistance Project in Philadelphia. Previously, he was the head of the Consumer Law Project at Community Legal Services in Philadelphia, where he worked for over 21 years. He has also served as a lecturer-in-law at the University of Pennsylvania Law School and is an adjunct professor at Temple University School of Law. He is the author of the ten editions of this treatise and editor in chief of *Collier on Bankruptcy* and the entire Collier line of bankruptcy publications published by Matthew Bender and Co. He is also the author of *Consumer Bankruptcy: The Complete Guide to Chapter 7 and Chapter 13 Personal Bankruptcy* (John Wiley & Sons, 1994), numerous articles on bankruptcy law, and co-author of *Collier Family Law and the Bankruptcy Code* (Matthew Bender). He is a former member of the Federal Judicial Conference Advisory Committee on Bankruptcy Rules and the Federal Reserve Board Consumer Advisory Council. He is a past president of the National Association of Consumer Bankruptcy Attorneys and former chairman of the Eastern District of Pennsylvania Bankruptcy Conference. He is president of the National Consumer Bankruptcy Rights Center, a member of the National Bankruptcy Conference, a Fellow of the American College of Bankruptcy, and a member of the American Law Institute. He was the first recipient of the Vern Countryman Consumer Law Award and has also received the National Conference of Bankruptcy Judges' Excellence in Education Award.

John Rao, the editor and a contributing author, is an NCLC attorney with a focus on consumer bankruptcy, foreclosures, and credit law. He is co-author of *Foreclosures* and *Bankruptcy Basics*. He is also a contributing author to *Collier on Bankruptcy* and the *Collier Bankruptcy Practice Guide*. For 18 years, he had a bankruptcy and consumer law focus at Rhode Island Legal Services and was a managing attorney there. He is vice-president of the National Association of Consumer Bankruptcy Attorneys, a conferee of the National Bankruptcy Conference, a fellow of the American College of Bankruptcy, a member of the editorial board of Collier on Bankruptcy, and former board member for the American Bankruptcy Institute. He is a former member of the federal Judicial Conference Advisory Committee on Bankruptcy Rules, appointed by Chief Justice John Roberts in 2006.

Susan A. Schneider, a contributing author for the family farmer bankruptcy chapter, is a professor of law and director of the LL.M. Program in Agricultural and Food Law at the University of Arkansas School of Law. Her private practice and consultation experience include agricultural law work with firms in Minnesota, North Dakota and Washington, D.C. She served as a staff attorney at Farmer's Legal Action Group, Inc. (FLAG), working on financial distress and farm bankruptcy issues and currently serves on the FLAG Board of Directors. She has published numerous articles on agricultural and food law subjects and authored the new agricultural law casebook, *Food Farming & Sustainability: Readings in Agricultural Law* (Carolina Press, 2010). She was the 2010 recipient of the American Agricultural Law Association (AALA) Distinguished Service Award and the 2011 recipient of the AALA Professional Scholarship Award.

Geoff Walsh has been a legal services attorney for over twenty-five years. He is presently a staff attorney with NCLC, and before that he worked with the housing and consumer units of Community Legal Services in Philadelphia and was a staff attorney with Vermont Legal Aid in its Springfield, Vermont office. His practice has focused upon housing and bankruptcy issues. He is a co-author of *Foreclosures* and a contributing author to *Student Loan Law* and *Access to Utility Service*.

Tara Twomey is of counsel with NCLC. She was formerly a clinical instructor at the Legal Services Center of Harvard Law School and a lecturer-in-law at Harvard Law School, Stanford Law School, and Boston College Law School. She is co-author of *Bankruptcy Basics, Foreclosures,* and *Mortgage Lending* and a contributing author to *Repossessions* and *Collier on Bankruptcy*.

Acknowledgments

We are particularly grateful to Vivian Abraham for editorial supervision; Kim Calvi for editorial assistance; Erika Barber for legal research; Shirlron Williams and Allen Agnitti for assistance with cite checking; Shannon Halbrook for the companion website; Xylutions for typesetting services, and Mary McLean for indexing. This Tenth Edition is based on the contributions of the many individuals who have worked on the prior nine editions and also on the twenty-one supplements to those editions. We want to thank all of these individuals, even though they are too numerous to list individually here. But special mention must be made of Gary Klein, for his numerous contributions over the years to prior editions and supplements.

What Your Library Should Contain

The Consumer Credit and Sales Legal Practice Series contains 20 titles, updated annually, arranged into four libraries, and designed to be an attorney's primary practice guide and legal resource in all 50 states. Titles are available individually or as part of the complete 20-volume series. Each title includes free access to a companion website containing sample pleadings, primary sources, and other practice aids, allowing pinpoint searches and the pasting of text into a word processor. Access remains free as long as purchasers keep their titles current.

Debtor Rights Library

2012 Tenth Edition (Two Volumes) and Companion Website

Consumer Bankruptcy Law and Practice: the definitive personal bankruptcy manual, from the initial interview to final discharge, including consumer rights when a company files for bankruptcy. This practice package contains the leading expert analysis of individual bankruptcy law and such practice aids as over 150 pleadings and forms, a client questionnaire and handout, the latest Bankruptcy Code, Rules, and fee schedules, a date calculator, and means test data.

2011 Seventh Edition (Two Volumes), 2012 Supplement, and Companion Website

Fair Debt Collection: the basic reference covering the Fair Debt Collection Practices Act and common law, state statutory and other federal debt collection protections. Thousands of unique case summaries cover reported and unreported FDCPA cases by category. The companion website contains sample pleadings and discovery, the FTC Commentary, an index to and the full text of *all* FTC staff opinion letters, and other practice aids.

2012 Fourth Edition and Companion Website

Foreclosures: examines RESPA and other federal and state requirements placed on mortgage loan servicers, and details on loan modification and mediation programs implemented by federal and state governments. The volume features standing and substantive and procedural defenses to foreclosure and tactics after the foreclosure sale. Special chapters cover tax liens, land installment sales contracts, manufactured home and condominium foreclosures, and other topics.

2010 Seventh Edition, 2012 Supplement, and Companion Website

Repossessions: a unique guide to motor vehicle and mobile home repossessions, threatened seizures of household goods, statutory liens, and automobile lease and rent-to-own default remedies. The volume examines UCC Article 9 and hundreds of other federal and state statutes regulating repossessions.

2010 Fourth Edition, 2012 Supplement and Companion Website

Student Loan Law: collection harassment; closed school, disability, and other discharges; tax intercepts, wage garnishment, and offset of social security benefits; and repayment plans, consolidation loans, deferments, private student loans, and non-payment of loan based on school fraud.

2011 Fifth Edition and Companion Website

Access to Utility Service: consumer rights as to regulated and unregulated utilities, including telecommunications, terminations, billing errors, low-income payment plans, utility allowances in subsidized housing, LIHEAP, and weatherization.

National Consumer Law Center ■ (617) 542-9595 ■ FAX (617) 542-8028 ■ publications@nclc.org
Order securely online at www.nclc.org

Credit and Banking Library

2012 Eighth Edition (Two Volumes) and Companion Website

Truth in Lending: detailed analysis of *all* aspects of TILA, the Consumer Leasing Act, the Fair Credit Billing Act, the Home Ownership and Equity Protection Act (HOEPA), and the Credit CARD Act, including the major 2010 amendments. Appendices and the website contain the Acts, Reg. Z, Reg. M, and their official staff commentaries, numerous sample pleadings, rescission notices, two programs to compute APRs, TIL legislative history, and a unique compilation of *all Federal Register* notices and supplementary information on Regulation Z since 1969. The text references to both FRB and CFPB versions of Regulation Z.

2010 Seventh Edition, 2012 Supplement, and Companion Website

Fair Credit Reporting: the key resource for handling any type of credit reporting issue, from cleaning up blemished credit records to suing reporting agencies and creditors for inaccurate reports. Covers the new FACTA changes, identity theft, creditor liability for failing to properly reinvestigate disputed information, credit scoring, privacy issues, the Credit Repair Organizations Act, state credit reporting and repair statutes, and common law claims.

Superseded

The Cost of Credit is replaced by two new titles, *Mortgage Lending* and *Consumer Credit Regulation*. Responding to major changes in the nature and regulation of mortgage lending and other consumer credit, these two new titles expand upon, update, and re-organize *The Cost of Credit* material.

2012 First Edition and Companion Website, replacing The Cost of Credit

Mortgage Lending: covers federal and state regulation (and federal preemption) of the origination and the terms of mortgage loans, including ability to pay, steering, churning, flipping, appraisals, loan broker compensation, insurance, adjustable rates, negative amortization, interest rate limitations, late fees, reverse mortgages, holder-in-due course, mortgage litigation, and claims against failed banks.

2012 First Edition and Companion Website, replacing The Cost of Credit

Consumer Credit Regulation: examines federal and state regulation (and federal preemption of state regulation) concerning credit cards, payday loans, automobile finance and installment sales, auto title pawns, rent-to-own, refund anticipation loans, "sale" of the consumer's future income stream and other non-mortgage lending. Special chapters on credit math, what is interest, and credit insurance.

2009 Fourth Edition, 2012 Supplement, and Companion Website

Consumer Banking and Payments Law: covers checks, telechecks, electronic fund transfers, electronic check conversions, money orders, and credit, debit, payroll, unemployment, and stored value cards. The title also covers banker's right of setoff, electronic transfers of federal and state benefit payments, and a special chapter on electronic records and signatures.

2009 Fifth Edition, 2012 Supplement, and Companion Website

Credit Discrimination: analysis of the Equal Credit Opportunity Act, Fair Housing Act, Civil Rights Acts, and state credit discrimination statutes, including reprints of all relevant federal interpretations, government enforcement actions, and numerous sample pleadings.

Consumer Litigation Library

2011 Second Edition, 2012 Supplement, and Companion Website

Collection Actions: a complete guide to consumer defenses and counterclaims to collection lawsuits filed in court or in arbitration, with extensive discussion of setting aside default judgments and limitations on a collector's post-judgment remedies. Special chapters include the rights of active duty military, and unique issues involving medical debt, government collections, collector's attorney fees, and bad check laws.

2011 Sixth Edition, 2012 Supplement, and Companion Website

Consumer Arbitration Agreements: successful approaches to challenge arbitration agreements' enforceability and waivers of class arbitration, the interrelation of the Federal Arbitration Act and state law, class actions and punitive damages in arbitration, implications of NAF's withdrawal from consumer arbitrations, the right to discovery, import of recent Supreme Court rulings, and other topics.

National Consumer Law Center ■ (617) 542-9595 ■ FAX (617) 542-8028 ■ publications@nclc.org
Order securely online at www.nclc.org

2010 Seventh Edition, 2012 Supplement, and Companion Website

Consumer Class Actions: makes class litigation manageable even for small offices, including numerous sample pleadings, class certification memoranda, discovery, class notices, settlement materials, and much more. Includes a detailed analysis of the Class Action Fairness Act, class arbitration, state class action rules and case law, and other topics.

Website and 2012 Index Guide: ALL pleadings from ALL NCLC treatises, including Consumer Law Pleadings Numbers One through Eighteen

Consumer Law Pleadings: over *2000* notable pleadings from all types of consumer cases, including predatory lending, foreclosures, automobile fraud, lemon laws, debt collection, fair credit reporting, home improvement fraud, student loans, and lender liability. Finding aids pinpoint desired pleading in seconds, ready to paste into a word processor.

Deception and Warranties Library

2012 Eighth Edition and Companion Website

Unfair and Deceptive Acts and Practices: the only practice manual covering all aspects of a deceptive practices case in every state. Citations to tens of thousands of state UDAP and FTC cases. Special sections on automobile sales, unfair insurance practices, unfair and deceptive credit practices, third party liability, attorney fees, and many other topics.

2011 Fourth Edition and Companion Website

Automobile Fraud: examination of title law, "yo-yo" sales, odometer tampering, lemon laundering, sale of salvage and wrecked cars, undisclosed prior use, and prior damage to new cars. The website contains numerous sample pleadings and title search techniques.

2010 Fourth Edition, 2012 Supplement, and Companion Website

Consumer Warranty Law: comprehensive treatment of new and used car lemon laws, the Magnuson-Moss Warranty Act, UCC Articles 2 and 2A, mobile home, new home, and assistive device warranty laws, FTC Used Car Rule, tort theories, car repair and home improvement statutes, service contract and lease laws, with numerous sample pleadings.

2012 First Edition and Companion Website

Federal Deception Law: new treatise covering FTC and CFPB rulemaking, special chapters on the FTC Holder and Telemarketing Sales Rules, federal restrictions on unwanted calls and texts, junk faxes and spam, federal and state RICO, the federal False Claims Act, federal and state regulation of debt relief services, and more.

NCLC's Companion Websites

Every NCLC manual includes a companion website, allowing rapid access to appendices, pleadings, primary sources, and other practice aids. Search for documents by category or with a table of contents or various keyword search options. All documents can be downloaded, printed, and copy-pasted into a word processing document. Pleadings are also available in Word format. Web access is free with each title ordered and remains free as long as a title is kept current.

Website continually subject to update

Consumer Law on the Web: combines *everything* from the 20 other NCLC companion websites. Using *Consumer Law on the Web*, instead of multiple individual companion websites, is often the fastest and most convenient way to pinpoint and retrieve key documents among the thousands available on our individual companion websites.

Other NCLC Publications for Lawyers

Over 100 articles a year

NCLC eReports: a web-based newsletter (currently free to those on automatic subscription to updates to NCLC treatises) containing over 100 articles a year, with the latest consumer law developments, novel ideas, innovative tactics, and key insights from NCLC's experienced consumer law attorneys. Articles can be cut/pasted into a word processor, web links are live, and past articles are easily searchable. Optional free e-mail alerts announce new articles and list the latest new regulations, statutes, and key court decisions.

National Consumer Law Center ■ (617) 542-9595 ■ FAX (617) 542-8028 ■ publications@nclc.org
Order securely online at www.nclc.org

First Edition and Companion Website

Bankruptcy Basics: A Step-by-Step Guide for Pro Bono Attorneys, General Practitioners, and Legal Services Offices: provides everything attorneys new to bankruptcy need to file their first case, with a companion website that contains software, sample pleadings, and other practice aids that greatly simplify handling a bankruptcy case.

First Edition

Instant Evidence: A Quick Guide to Federal Evidence and Objections: facilitates objection by rule number and includes common objections and motions at every stage of a case—all in under 20 pages! Spiral-bound to lay flat, all pages are laminated, allowing new notations for each trial with a dry-erase pen.

Second Edition with CD-Rom

The Practice of Consumer Law: Seeking Economic Justice: contains an essential overview to consumer law and explains how to get started in a private or legal services consumer practice. Packed with invaluable sample pleadings and practice pointers for even experienced consumer attorneys.

National Consumer Law Center Guide Series are books designed for consumers, counselors, and attorneys new to consumer law:

2010 Edition

NCLC Guide to Surviving Debt: a great overview of consumer law. Everything a paralegal, new attorney, or client needs to know about home foreclosures and mortgage modifications, debt collectors, managing credit card debt, whether to refinance, credit card problems, evictions, repossessions, credit reporting, utility terminations, student loans, budgeting, and bankruptcy.

First Edition

NCLC Guide to the Rights of Utility Consumers: explains consumer rights concerning electric, gas, and other utility services: shut off protections, rights to restore terminated service, bill payment options, weatherization tips, rights to government assistance, and much more.

First Edition

NCLC Guide to Consumer Rights for Domestic Violence Survivors: provides practical advice to help survivors get back on their feet financially and safely establish their economic independence.

> Visit www.nclc.org to order securely online or for more information on all NCLC publications and companion websites, including the full tables of contents, indices, and **web-based searches of the publications' full text**.

National Consumer Law Center ■ (617) 542-9595 ■ FAX (617) 542-8028 ■ publications@nclc.org
Order securely online at www.nclc.org

About the Companion Website, Other Search Options

The Companion Website

Purchase of any title in NCLC's consumer law practice series includes free access to its companion website. Access remains free if you subscribe or continue to purchase updates to that title. Frequently updated, NCLC companion websites offer the treatises' appendices plus hundreds of additional documents in PDF and Microsoft Word formats—pleadings, forms, statutes, regulations, agency interpretations, legislative and regulatory history, and much more—all easily located with flexible, powerful search tools. Documents can be electronically searched, printed, downloaded, and copy-pasted into a word processor.

We highly recommend reading the Help page on the website, found at the top of the left toolbar once you are logged in.

Accessing the Companion Website

One-time registration is required to access the companion website. Once registered, a user subsequently logging in will be granted immediate access to all the companion websites he or she is authorized to use.

To register for the first time, go to **www.nclc.org/webaccess** and click "Register as a New User." Enter the Companion Website Registration Number[1] found on the packing statement or invoice accompanying this book. Then enter the requested information to create your account. An e-mail address may be used for the username, or a different username may be chosen.

Users do *not* need to register more than once.[2] If you subsequently purchase additional NCLC titles, you will automatically be given access to the corresponding companion websites. Registering a second time with the same registration number overrides a prior username and password.

Once registered, go to www.nclc.org/webaccess, enter your username and password, and click the Login button. Then select a companion website from the list.

An alternative log-in method may be particularly useful for libraries, legal aid offices, or law firms that subscribe to the entire set of NCLC treatises. Simply send an e-mail to publications@nclc.org with a list or range of static IP addresses for which access should be permitted. Users from those addresses can then go to www.nclc.org/ipaccess to be granted access *without* entering a username and password.

Once logged in, users can click the Preferences link located on the top toolbar to change their account information.

Locating Documents on the Companion Website

The companion website provides three ways to locate documents:

1. The search page (the home page) uses keyword searches to find documents—full text searches of all documents on the website or searches of just the documents' titles. Enter text in the appropriate field and click the Search button.

- Narrow the search to documents of a certain type (for example, federal regulations or pleadings) by making a selection from the "Document Type" menu, and then perform a full text or document title search.
- To locate a specific appendix section, select the appendix section number (for example, A.2.3) or a partial identifier (for example, A) in the search page's "Appendix" drop-down fields.
- When searching documents' full text, each entry in your search results will include excerpts of the document, showing your search terms highlighted in context.
- Click on the "Search Hints" link for a quick reference to special search operators, wildcards, shortcuts, and complex searches. Read this information closely, as syntax and search operators may be slightly different from those used by other search engines.

2. The contents page (click the "Contents" tab at the top of the page) is a traditional nested table of contents. Click a branch to expand it into a list of sub-branches or documents. Each document appears once in this contents tree.

3. The pleading finder page (click the "Pleading Finder" link at the top of the search page, if available) allows pleadings to be located using one or more menus, such as "Type of Pleading" or "Subject." **Select more than one item from a menu, or deselect items, by holding the Ctrl key while clicking.** For example, make one selection from "Type of Pleading–General," one from "Subject," and three from "Legal Claims" to locate all pleadings of that type and subject that contain one or more of the three legal claims selected. If this search produces insufficient results, simply broaden the search by deselecting "Subject" and/or "Legal Claims" to find pleadings of that type in any subject area or based upon any legal

---

1 If you cannot locate this number, contact NCLC Publications at (617) 542-9595 or publications@nclc.org.
2 If you have not updated *any* of your NCLC treatises for some time, your account may be deleted; if this happens, you must re-register if you subsequently purchase a book.

claim. This page also includes optional fields to specify terms to be found in the documents' text or titles, to further narrow search results.

How to Use the Documents, Find Microsoft Word Versions, and Locate Additional Features

Click a document title in your search results or on the contents page to view the document in your web browser. Text may be copy-pasted directly from the page or the full document may be downloaded as a PDF file. (You will need a PDF reader to open PDF documents; the free Adobe Reader is available at www.adobe.com.) Additionally, pleadings and certain other documents can be downloaded in Microsoft Word format, enabling the opening of entire documents in a word processing program. Icons to download PDF and Word versions are found at the top of the page.

Links on the left-hand toolbar bring you to credit math software, search tips, other websites, tables of contents and indices of all NCLC treatises, and other practice aids. Links to especially important new developments will be placed toward the bottom of the "Search" page.

Documents Found on the Website

The companion website to *Consumer Bankruptcy Law and Practice* is packed with useful information, including the current Bankruptcy Code, up-to-date rules and rule changes, sample completed official forms with committee notes and annotations, and a survey of state exemption laws. Also available are hundreds of pleadings, plus other tools for practitioners such as a date calculator and current means testing data.

Locating Topics in This Treatise

NCLC offers a handy online utility to search the full text of our publications. This free search utility is found at www.nclc.org/keyword and requires no registration or log-in. While the chapters' text is not available online, this web-based search engine will find a word or phrase, which can then easily be located in this printed treatise. Select this book, enter a search term or combination of search terms—such as a case name, a regulation citation, or other keywords—and the page numbers containing those terms will be listed. Search results are shown in context, enabling selection of the most relevant pages.

Locating Topics in Other NCLC Manuals or NCLC eReports

The search utility found at www.nclc.org/keyword can also be used to search other NCLC publications, including NCLC eReports. Simply perform the search as described above and select the publication to be searched.

Current tables of contents, indices, and other information for all twenty titles in the NCLC *Consumer Credit and Sales Legal Practice Series* can be found at www.nclc.org/shop. Click the "For Lawyers" link and scroll down to the book you are interested in. The PDF-format documents found there can be quickly searched for a word or phrase.

The Quick Reference, found at www.nclc.org/qr, is an alphabetical index spanning all twenty NCLC treatises. It lists over 1000 subjects and indicates the book(s) and section(s) where each subject is discussed.

Finding Pleadings

Pleadings relating to this title are found in PDF and Word format on the companion website; search options are discussed above at "Locating Documents on the Companion Website." Over 2000 pleadings are also available at NCLC's *Consumer Law Pleadings* website using the same search techniques discussed above. Pleadings can also be located using *Consumer Law Pleadings*' index guide, which lists pleadings organized by type, subject area, legal claim, title, and other categories identical to those on the website.

Summary Contents

Volume 1

Contents xiii

Chapter 1	About This Treatise	1
Chapter 2	What Is Bankruptcy? Some General Concepts	17
Chapter 3	Chapter 7 Bankruptcy (Straight Bankruptcy): The Basic Steps	33
Chapter 4	Chapter 13 Bankruptcy: The Basic Steps	47
Chapter 5	Getting All the Necessary Facts	57
Chapter 6	Counseling the Consumer Debtor: Does Bankruptcy Provide the Best Solution and, If So, How and When?	65
Chapter 7	Preparing and Filing the Papers	81
Chapter 8	After the Papers Are Filed	109
Chapter 9	Automatic Stays and Turnover of Property	135
Chapter 10	Exemptions	191
Chapter 11	Dealing with Secured Creditors	257
Chapter 12	Issues Arising in Chapter 13 Cases	307
Chapter 13	Dismissal or Conversion of a Bankruptcy Case	359
Chapter 14	Litigating in the Bankruptcy Court	387

xi

Chapter 15	The Discharge: Protecting It and Using It	451
Chapter 16	Attorney Fees for Debtor's Counsel and Attorney Duties in Consumer Bankruptcy Cases	541
Chapter 17	Chapter 12 Bankruptcy: Family Farmer and Family Fisherman Reorganization	571
Chapter 18	Consumers As Creditors in Bankruptcy: Selected Topics	629
	Bibliography	691
	Index	695

Volume 2

Appendix A	Bankruptcy Statutes	725
Appendix B	Federal Rules of Bankruptcy Procedure	883
Appendix C	Bankruptcy Regulations, Fees, and Agency Notices	957
Appendix D	Official Bankruptcy Forms with Annotated Samples	969
Appendix E	Director's Procedural Forms	1115
Appendix F	Bankruptcy Questionnaire	1177
Appendix G	Sample Bankruptcy Pleadings and Other Forms	1201
Appendix H	Practice Aids	1331
Appendix I	Means Test Data	1355
Appendix J	Summaries of State Exemption Laws	1377
Appendix K	Bankruptcy Client Handouts	1413
Appendix L	Helpful Websites	1427
Appendix M	Finding Pleadings and Primary Sources on the Companion Website	1429

Contents

Volume 1

About the Companion Website, Other Search Options ix

Chapter 1   About This Treatise

1.1 Bankruptcy As a Remedy for Consumer Debtors. 1
    1.1.1 Overview. 1
    1.1.2 The Bankruptcy Reform Act and Subsequent Amendments. 1
        1.1.2.1 Passage of the Bankruptcy Reform Act 1
        1.1.2.2 Consumer Bankruptcy Amendments of 1984. 2
        1.1.2.3 Bankruptcy Judges, United States Trustees, and Family Farmer
                Bankruptcy Act of 1986 2
        1.1.2.4 The Bankruptcy Reform Act of 1994. 2
        1.1.2.5 The 2005 Bankruptcy Amendments. 3
        1.1.2.6 Other Amendments to the Code 4
    1.1.3 Bankruptcy's Past As Neglected Remedy. 5
    1.1.4 Making Bankruptcy Available to Consumer Clients. 5
1.2 The Focus of This Treatise—Bankruptcy Practice for Consumer Debtors and
Family Farmers 6
1.3 How to Use This Treatise 6
    1.3.1 Purpose of the Treatise. 6
    1.3.2 Organization of the Treatise 6
    1.3.3 Web-Based Text Search Feature. 8
    1.3.4 Using This Treatise As a Research Tool 8
        1.3.4.1 This Treatise Does Not Contain Citations to Every Relevant Case 8
        1.3.4.2 NCLC Case Consulting and Other NCLC Treatises 8
1.4 The Governing Law. 8
    1.4.1 Statutory Materials 8
        1.4.1.1 The Bankruptcy Code 8
        1.4.1.2 Other Relevant Statutes 9
    1.4.2 The Federal Rules of Bankruptcy Procedure. 9
    1.4.3 The Official Bankruptcy Forms 10
    1.4.4 Other Issues Concerning Sources of Law. 10
        1.4.4.1 Pending Legislation and Amendments to the Rules. 10
        1.4.4.2 Local Bankruptcy Rules. 11
        1.4.4.3 Case Law Under the Code 11
1.5 Other Resources for Practicing Under the Bankruptcy Code 11
    1.5.1 Legislative History. 11
        1.5.1.1 The Bankruptcy Reform Act of 1978 11
        1.5.1.2 The 1984 Amendments 12
        1.5.1.3 The 1986 Amendments 13
        1.5.1.4 The Bankruptcy Reform Act of 1994 13

	1.5.1.5 The 2005 Amendments	13
	1.5.2 Rules Advisory Committee Notes	13
	1.5.3 Treatises and Texts	13
	1.5.4 Reporting Services	15
	1.5.5 Periodicals	15
	1.5.6 Citator	16
	1.5.7 Computer Assisted Legal Research	16

Chapter 2 What Is Bankruptcy? Some General Concepts

2.1 A Definition	17
2.2 Relief Available in Bankruptcy	17
2.3 Purposes of Bankruptcy	17
2.4 The Bankruptcy Court	18
2.4.1 Status Under the Bankruptcy Reform Act As Amended in 1984	18
2.4.2 Jurisdiction	18
2.4.3 Appeals	19
2.5 The Bankruptcy Estate	20
2.5.1 Contents of the Estate	20
2.5.2 Pensions and Spendthrift Trusts	24
2.5.3 Education Savings Accounts	27
2.5.4 Pawned Personal Property	27
2.5.5 Tax Refunds and the Earned Income Tax Credit	27
2.6 The Bankruptcy Trustee	30
2.7 The United States Trustee	31

Chapter 3 Chapter 7 Bankruptcy (Straight Bankruptcy): The Basic Steps

3.1 General Explanation of Chapter 7 Bankruptcy	33
3.2 Commencement of the Case	33
3.2.1 Who May File?	33
3.2.1.1 General Rules, Including Credit Counseling Requirement	33
3.2.1.2 Effect of Prior Bankruptcy Cases on Eligibility to File	34
3.2.1.3 Eligibility to File a Case Does Not Assure Discharge of Debts	35
3.2.1.4 Credit Counseling Briefing Requirement	36
3.2.1.5 Dismissal for Abuse and the Means Test	37
3.2.2 The Initial Forms	37
3.2.3 Proper Venue for Bankruptcy Case	38
3.3 First Steps After Filing	39
3.4 The Section 341(a) Meeting (Meeting of Creditors)	39
3.5 After the Meeting of Creditors	40
3.5.1 Exempt and Encumbered Property; Abandonment of Property	40
3.5.2 Liquidation of Nonexempt Property	42
3.5.3 Filing and Allowance of Claims	42
3.5.4 Distribution of Property to Creditors	42
3.6 The Discharge and Discharge Hearing	44

Chapter 4 Chapter 13 Bankruptcy: The Basic Steps

4.1 General Explanation of Chapter 13 Bankruptcy	47
4.2 Commencement of the Case	47
4.2.1 Who May File?	47
4.2.1.1 General Rules	47
4.2.1.2 Individuals with Regular Income	47
4.2.1.3 Debt Limitations	48

Contents

	4.2.1.4 Effect of Prior Bankruptcy Cases	48
	4.2.1.5 Availability of a Discharge	48
4.2.2	The Initial Forms	48
4.2.3	Conversion from a Chapter 7 Case	49
4.3 First Steps After Filing		50
4.4 The Meeting of Creditors and Other Preconfirmation Activities		51
4.5 The Confirmation Hearing		52
4.6 Modification of the Plan and Postpetition Transactions		52
4.7 Options in the Event of Failure to Complete the Plan		53
4.7.1 Overview		53
4.7.2 Hardship Discharge		53
4.7.3 Modification		54
4.7.4 Conversion to Chapter 7		54
4.7.5 Dismissal		54
4.8 Discharge		55

Chapter 5 Getting All the Necessary Facts

5.1 Introduction to the Treatise's Second Part	57
5.1.1 Purpose of These Four Chapters	57
5.1.2 Roles for Non-Attorneys	57
5.1.3 Use of the Materials in the Treatise	57
5.2 The Importance of Getting All the Facts	57
5.3 Methods of Gathering Information	58
5.3.1 The Initial Interview	58
5.3.2 Filling in the Complete Picture	58
5.3.3 Frequently Missed Information	58
5.3.3.1 Introduction	58
5.3.3.2 Property	59
5.3.3.3 Liabilities	60
5.3.3.4 Expenses	61
5.3.3.5 Other Aspects of Financial Affairs	62
5.3.4 Other Sources of Information	62
5.4 Impressing upon Clients the Need for Full and Accurate Information	63

Chapter 6 Counseling the Consumer Debtor: Does Bankruptcy Provide the Best Solution and, If So, How and When?

6.1 Introduction	65
6.1.1 Explaining the Options to Clients	65
6.1.2 Methods of Explaining Bankruptcy	65
6.2 Advantages and Disadvantages of Bankruptcy	66
6.2.1 Advantages: The Uses of Bankruptcy	66
6.2.1.1 Discharge of Most Debts	66
6.2.1.2 Protection of Property and Income from Unsecured Creditors	66
6.2.1.3 Tools for Eliminating or Modifying Secured Debts	67
6.2.1.4 Automatic Stay	67
6.2.1.5 Other Protections Available Through Bankruptcy	67
6.2.1.6 Litigation Advantages of the Bankruptcy Forum	67
6.2.2 Disadvantages: Reasons for Not Filing a Bankruptcy Case	68
6.2.2.1 Overview	68
6.2.2.2 Loss of Property in Bankruptcy	68
6.2.2.3 Effect on Credit and Reputation	68
6.2.2.4 Possible Discrimination After Bankruptcy	69
6.2.2.4.1 The available protections	69

xv

Consumer Bankruptcy Law and Practice

	6.2.2.4.2 Medical debts	69
	6.2.2.5 Clients' Feelings of Moral Obligation	70
	6.2.2.6 Cost of Filing a Bankruptcy Petition	70
	6.2.2.7 Is Bankruptcy Necessary?	70
	6.2.2.8 When Bankruptcy Offers No Help or Is Unavailable	71
	6.2.2.8.1 When bankruptcy will not help	71
	6.2.2.8.2 Clients who have filed prior bankruptcy cases	71
6.3	Choosing the Type of Bankruptcy Case to File	72
	6.3.1 Introduction	72
	6.3.2 Considerations Favoring Chapter 7	72
	6.3.3 Considerations Favoring Chapter 13	72
	6.3.4 Use of Chapter 11 by Consumer Debtors	74
6.4	Should Both Spouses File?	74
6.5	Considerations of Timing and Events Prior to Filing	75
	6.5.1 Reasons to File Quickly	75
	6.5.2 The Effects of Prebankruptcy Transfers or Other Actions	76
	6.5.2.1 Fraudulent Acts, Conveyances, and Preferences	76
	6.5.2.2 Exemption Time Periods and Exemption Planning	77
	6.5.3 Other Reasons for Delaying a Petition	78
	6.5.3.1 Anticipation of Further Debt	78
	6.5.3.2 Paying Favored Creditors	79
	6.5.3.3 Delay of a Petition As a Strategy to Forestall Harm to Clients	79
	6.5.3.4 Tax Reach Back Periods	79
	6.5.3.5 Delay to Obtain More Favorable Treatment of Certain Secured Debts in Chapter 13	79
	6.5.3.6 Timing the Petition to Avoid a Presumption of Abuse in Chapter 7 or to Lower Disposable Income in Chapter 13	80
	6.5.3.7 Timing the Petition to Avoid Automatic Stay Limitations	80
	6.5.3.8 Less Common Reasons for Delaying a Petition	80

Chapter 7

Preparing and Filing the Papers

7.1	Introduction	81
	7.1.1 Some General Principles	81
	7.1.2 Obtaining the Forms	81
	7.1.3 Computer Programs	82
	7.1.4 Electronic Filing of Documents	82
7.2	The Papers Necessary to Start a Case	83
	7.2.1 Forms Usually Filed	83
	7.2.2 The Emergency Bankruptcy, or How to Prepare a Bankruptcy Case in Under One Hour	84
	7.2.3 Timing the Filing of Multiple Cases	85
7.3	Forms at the Outset of the Case	85
	7.3.1 Official and Unofficial Forms	85
	7.3.2 The Bankruptcy Petition (Official Form 1)	85
	7.3.3 Statement of Social Security Number (Official Form 21)	86
	7.3.4 List of Creditors, Codebtors, and Parties to Executory Contracts	87
	7.3.5 Credit Counseling Statement, Certificate from Counseling Agency, and Debt Management Plan (If Any)	87
	7.3.6 Notice of Chapters Under Which Relief Is Available and Other Information	87
	7.3.7 The Bankruptcy Schedules (Official Form 6)	87
	7.3.7.1 Overview	87
	7.3.7.2 Schedules A, B, and C: The Debtor's Property	87
	7.3.7.2.1 Schedule A—real property	87
	7.3.7.2.2 Schedule B—personal property	88

Contents

	7.3.7.2.3 Schedule C—property claimed as exempt	90
7.3.7.3	Schedules D, E, and F: Information About Creditors	91
	7.3.7.3.1 In general	91
	7.3.7.3.2 Schedule D—secured debts	93
	7.3.7.3.3 Schedule E—priority debts	93
	7.3.7.3.4 Schedule F—general unsecured debts	94
7.3.7.4	Schedule G: Unexpired Leases and Executory Contracts	94
7.3.7.5	Schedule H: Codebtors	95
7.3.7.6	Schedules I and J: Income and Expenses	95
7.3.7.7	Declaration Concerning Debtor's Schedules	96
7.3.7.8	The Summary of Schedules and Statistical Summary of Certain Liabilities	96

- 7.3.8 The Statement of Financial Affairs (Official Form 7) ... 96
- 7.3.9 Statement of Current Monthly Income, Means Test, and Chapter 13 Calculations (Official Forms 22A and 22C) ... 99
- 7.3.10 Filing Debtor Payment Advices ... 100
- 7.3.11 The Statement of Intention with Regard to Property Securing Consumer Debts (Official Form 8) ... 101
- 7.3.12 The Chapter 13 Plan ... 102
  - 7.3.12.1 Introduction ... 102
  - 7.3.12.2 Form of Plan ... 102
  - 7.3.12.3 Required Provisions and Confirmation Standards ... 102
  - 7.3.12.4 Other Plan Provisions Permitted ... 104
  - 7.3.12.5 Formulating the Plan ... 104
- 7.3.13 Other Forms ... 105
  - 7.3.13.1 Overview ... 105
  - 7.3.13.2 Disclosure of Fees ... 105
  - 7.3.13.3 Application to Pay Filing Fee in Installments ... 106
  - 7.3.13.4 Application for Waiver of Filing Fees in Whole or in Part ... 106
  - 7.3.13.5 Motion for Extension of Time to File Required Documents ... 106
  - 7.3.13.6 Forms Required by Local Rules or Practice ... 106

7.4 Signing, Verification, and Filing ... 106

Chapter 8 After the Papers Are Filed

- 8.1 Introduction ... 109
- 8.2 Advice to Clients ... 109
- 8.3 Events Which May Occur Prior to or After the Section 341 Meeting of Creditors ... 110
  - 8.3.1 Notice of the Automatic Stay and Turnover Requirement ... 110
  - 8.3.2 Amendments to Statements or Schedules ... 111
  - 8.3.3 Personal Financial Management Course ... 111
  - 8.3.4 Production of Tax Returns or Transcripts ... 112
    - 8.3.4.1 Providing Tax Return or Transcript to Trustee and Creditors ... 112
    - 8.3.4.2 Filing Tax Returns or Transcripts with the Court ... 113
    - 8.3.4.3 Privacy Concerns and Safeguards ... 114
  - 8.3.5 Annual Statements of Income and Expenditures in Chapter 13 Cases ... 114
  - 8.3.6 Avoiding Transfers of Exempt Property ... 115
  - 8.3.7 Redemption and Assumption of Leases of Personal Property in Chapter 7 Cases ... 115
    - 8.3.7.1 Redemption ... 115
    - 8.3.7.2 Assumption of Personal Property Leases ... 115
  - 8.3.8 Proceedings Regarding Dischargeability of Particular Debts ... 116
  - 8.3.9 Objections to Claims of Creditors ... 116
  - 8.3.10 Other Disputes That May Arise ... 116
  - 8.3.11 Retaining Nonexempt Property in Chapter 7 Cases ... 117

	8.3.12	Commencement of Payments in Chapter 13 Cases	117
		8.3.12.1 Plan Payments	117
		8.3.12.2 Adequate Protection Payments and Payments to Personal Property Lessors	118
		8.3.12.3 Graduated Plan Payments	118
	8.3.13	Proof of Insurance in Chapter 13 Cases	118
	8.3.14	Filing of Tax Returns with Taxing Authorities in Chapter 13 Cases	119
	8.3.15	Audits and Rule 2004 Examinations	119
		8.3.15.1 Debtor Audits	119
		8.3.15.2 Rule 2004 Examinations	120
8.4	The Meeting of Creditors	120
	8.4.1	Preparation	120
	8.4.2	Document Requirements	120
	8.4.3	Procedure at the Meeting of Creditors	121
	8.4.4	Attendance of Creditors Seeking Reaffirmation Agreements	122
	8.4.5	Examination of Chapter 7 Debtors' Awareness of Bankruptcy Information—Bankruptcy Information Sheet	123
	8.4.6	Checking Claims That Have Been Filed	123
8.5	Chapter 7 Cases—After the Meeting of Creditors	124
8.6	Chapter 13 Confirmation Hearing	124
8.7	Administration of the Chapter 13 Plan	125
	8.7.1	Trustee Payments to Creditors	125
	8.7.2	Postpetition Claims	126
	8.7.3	Postpetition Mortgage Payments	127
	8.7.4	Modification of the Plan	127
	8.7.5	Debtor's Inability to Complete the Plan	128
		8.7.5.1 Failure to Make Plan Payments	128
		8.7.5.2 Plan Modifications That Enable the Debtor to Complete the Plan	129
		8.7.5.3 Obtaining a Hardship Discharge	129
		8.7.5.4 Conversion to Chapter 7	129
		8.7.5.5 Dismissal	129
8.8	The Discharge and the Discharge Hearing	130
	8.8.1	Overview	130
	8.8.2	Reaffirmation of Debts	131
	8.8.3	Procedure When There Is a Discharge Hearing	132
8.9	After Discharge	132

Chapter 9 Automatic Stays and Turnover of Property

9.1	Introduction	135
9.2	Purpose of the Automatic Stay	135
9.3	Duration of the Stay	135
	9.3.1 In General	135
	9.3.2 Duration If No Prior Case Was Dismissed in Year Before Petition	136
	9.3.3 Duration If a Prior Case Was Dismissed in Year Before Petition	136
	9.3.3.1 Overview	136
	9.3.3.2 One Prior Case Dismissed Within Previous Year	137
	9.3.3.2.1 General application	137
	9.3.3.2.2 Demonstrating good faith for extension of stay past thirty days	137
	9.3.3.2.3 Overcoming the presumption that case was not filed in good faith	138
	9.3.3.3 Two or More Cases Dismissed Within Previous Year	139
	9.3.3.4 Order Confirming Stay Termination	139
	9.3.3.5 Codebtor Stay Still Applicable	140

Contents

- 9.3.3.6 Filings in Violation of Section 109(g) or a Prior Court Order—Section 362(b)(21) ... 140
- 9.4 Scope of the Automatic Stay ... 140
  - 9.4.1 Introduction ... 140
  - 9.4.2 Legal Proceedings ... 141
  - 9.4.3 Acts Directed at the Debtor's Property ... 143
  - 9.4.4 Other Acts Prohibited by the Stay ... 146
  - 9.4.5 The Automatic Stay Protecting Codebtors in Chapter 13 ... 149
  - 9.4.6 Exceptions to the Automatic Stay ... 151
    - 9.4.6.1 Overview ... 151
    - 9.4.6.2 Criminal Proceedings ... 151
    - 9.4.6.3 Family Law Exceptions ... 152
    - 9.4.6.4 Continued Withholding of Income for Loans from Retirement Funds ... 153
    - 9.4.6.5 Provisions Based on Prior Bankruptcy Case Filings by Debtor or Related Parties ... 153
      - 9.4.6.5.1 In general ... 153
      - 9.4.6.5.2 *In rem* orders ... 153
    - 9.4.6.6 Exceptions to Stay of Residential Tenant Evictions ... 154
      - 9.4.6.6.1 Overview ... 154
      - 9.4.6.6.2 Prepetition judgment for possession ... 154
      - 9.4.6.6.3 Illegal use of controlled substances or endangerment to the property ... 155
    - 9.4.6.7 Transfers Not Avoidable Under Section 549 ... 156
    - 9.4.6.8 Setoff of Tax Refunds ... 156
    - 9.4.6.9 Other Exceptions Sometimes Applicable in Consumer Cases ... 156
  - 9.4.7 Non-Automatic Stays ... 157
- 9.5 Notice of the Automatic Stay ... 158
- 9.6 Enforcing the Stay ... 159
  - 9.6.1 Actions Taken in Violation of the Stay Are Void ... 159
  - 9.6.2 Cause of Action for Damages, Punitive Damages, and Attorney Fees ... 160
  - 9.6.3 Notice Issues ... 161
    - 9.6.3.1 Giving Notice ... 161
    - 9.6.3.2 Effect of 2005 Amendments on Notice Requirements ... 162
      - 9.6.3.2.1 Introduction ... 162
      - 9.6.3.2.2 Deletion of safe harbor in section 342(c) ... 162
      - 9.6.3.2.3 Creditor notice request given prepetition ... 162
      - 9.6.3.2.4 Notice request in particular case ... 162
    - 9.6.3.3 Effective Notice Under Section 342 ... 163
  - 9.6.4 Contempt Remedies ... 163
  - 9.6.5 Other Possible Remedies ... 165
  - 9.6.6 Remedies Against State and Federal Government ... 165
  - 9.6.7 Procedural Issues ... 166
- 9.7 Proceedings Seeking Relief from the Stay ... 166
  - 9.7.1 Proceedings Must Be Commenced by Motion ... 166
  - 9.7.2 Time Limits for Court Actions ... 167
  - 9.7.3 Defending Against Motions for Relief from the Stay ... 168
    - 9.7.3.1 Procedural Questions ... 168
      - 9.7.3.1.1 Parties ... 168
      - 9.7.3.1.2 Discovery ... 170
      - 9.7.3.1.3 Defenses and counterclaims ... 170
      - 9.7.3.1.4 Burden of proof ... 171
      - 9.7.3.1.5 Effect of prior bankruptcy cases involving the same debtor ... 171
    - 9.7.3.2 Grounds for Relief ... 174
      - 9.7.3.2.1 For cause ... 174
      - 9.7.3.2.2 Lack of adequate protection ... 175

Consumer Bankruptcy Law and Practice

	9.7.3.2.3 Lack of equity or necessity for effective reorganization	177
	9.7.3.2.4 Leases involving residential property	179
	9.7.3.3 Tactics in Stay Litigation	180
	9.7.3.3.1 Valuation problems	180
	9.7.3.3.2 Other tactics	181
	9.7.3.3.3 Stays pending appeal	181
9.8	Utility Services in Bankruptcy Cases	182
9.8.1	No Utility May Deny Service Within Twenty Days After Bankruptcy	182
9.8.2	A Utility May Be Able to Discontinue Service If the Debtor Does Not Furnish Adequate Assurance of Future Payment	183
	9.8.2.1 Procedure	183
	9.8.2.2 Adequate Assurance of Future Payment	183
	9.8.2.2.1 Methods of adequate assurance	183
	9.8.2.2.2 Adequate assurance not always required	184
	9.8.2.2.3 Amount necessary for adequate assurance	184
	9.8.2.2.4 Postpetition termination procedures	185
	9.8.2.2.5 Possible special protections for customers of governmental utilities	185
9.9	Turnover of Property Under Section 542	186
9.9.1	The General Rule	186
9.9.2	Questions of Scope: Secured Parties in Possession	186
9.9.3	Procedure	187
9.9.4	Issues of Possession After Turnover	188

Chapter 10 Exemptions

10.1	Introduction	191
10.1.1	Importance of the Exemption Provisions	191
10.1.2	Definition of Exempt Property	191
10.1.3	Purposes of Exemptions	192
10.2	What Property Is Exempt?	192
10.2.1	The Choice of State or Federal Exemptions	192
	10.2.1.1 In General	192
	10.2.1.2 Determining the Applicable Exemption Law	194
10.2.2	The Federal Bankruptcy Exemptions	195
	10.2.2.1 In General	195
	10.2.2.2 Homestead—§ 522(d)(1)	196
	10.2.2.3 Motor Vehicle—§ 522(d)(2)	196
	10.2.2.4 Household Goods, Household Furnishings, Wearing Apparel, Appliances, and Similar Items—§ 522(d)(3)	197
	10.2.2.5 Jewelry—§ 522(d)(4)	197
	10.2.2.6 Any Property—§ 522(d)(5)	198
	10.2.2.7 Tools of the Trade—§ 522(d)(6)	198
	10.2.2.8 Unmatured Life Insurance—§ 522(d)(7)	199
	10.2.2.9 Accrued Dividend, Interest, or Loan Value of Life Insurance— § 522(d)(8)	199
	10.2.2.10 Health Aids—§ 522(d)(9)	199
	10.2.2.11 Disability, Retirement, and Other Benefits Replacing Wages— § 522(d)(10)	200
	10.2.2.12 Rights to Compensation for Injury or Losses, and Payments for Lost Earnings—§ 522(d)(11)	203
	10.2.2.13 Pensions and Retirement Accounts—§ 522(d)(12)	204
	10.2.2.13.1 Overview	204
	10.2.2.13.2 Guidelines for exempt retirement funds	205
	10.2.2.13.3 Cap on certain IRA accounts	205

Contents

10.2.3 Using the State and Federal Nonbankruptcy Exemptions 206
    10.2.3.1 Federal Bankruptcy Modifications of These Exemptions 206
    10.2.3.2 Exemption of Property Not Subject to Process 208
    10.2.3.3 Special Retirement Exemptions Available to Debtors Who Utilize State and Federal Nonbankruptcy Exemptions 211
    10.2.3.4 Limitations on State Homestead Exemptions 211
        10.2.3.4.1 In general 211
        10.2.3.4.2 Scope of the new restrictions 211
        10.2.3.4.3 Homestead limitation based on fraudulent conversion of nonexempt property 212
        10.2.3.4.4 Cap on homestead property acquired during 1215-day period before filing 213
        10.2.3.4.5 Homestead cap based on certain criminal or wrongful conduct 213
            10.2.3.4.5.1 Introduction 213
            10.2.3.4.5.2 Felony conviction 213
            10.2.3.4.5.3 Debts arising from certain wrongful conduct 214
            10.2.3.4.5.4 Standing to bring objection to exemption 214
            10.2.3.4.5.5 No cap if homestead reasonably necessary for support 214
            10.2.3.4.5.6 Delay of discharge 215
            10.2.3.4.5.7 Application of homestead caps in joint cases 216
10.3 Procedure for Claiming Exemptions 216
    10.3.1 The Initial Claim 216
    10.3.2 Amending the Claim of Exemption 217
    10.3.3 Objections to Exemptions 218
    10.3.4 Absent Successful Objections, the Exemptions Are Allowed 220
10.4 Making the Most of Exemptions 221
    10.4.1 Exemption Planning 221
    10.4.2 Avoiding Powers of the Debtor 222
        10.4.2.1 General Principles 222
        10.4.2.2 Procedure for Use of Avoiding Powers 223
        10.4.2.3 Power to Avoid Judicial Liens—§ 522(f)(1)(A) 224
            10.4.2.3.1 Extent of the power to avoid judicial liens 224
            10.4.2.3.2 Limitations on power to avoid judicial liens 227
            10.4.2.3.3 Avoidance of liens on property which may be claimed as exempt under § 522(b)(2)(B) 229
        10.4.2.4 Power to Avoid Nonpossessory, Nonpurchase-Money Security Interests in Certain Items—§ 522(f)(1)(B) 229
        10.4.2.5 Power to Exempt Property Recovered by Trustee—§ 522(g) 232
        10.4.2.6 Debtor's Right to Utilize Trustee's Avoiding Powers—§ 522(h) 234
            10.4.2.6.1 Overview 234
            10.4.2.6.2 The "strong-arm clause"—§ 544 234
            10.4.2.6.3 Statutory liens—§ 545 237
            10.4.2.6.4 Preferences—§ 547 238
                10.4.2.6.4.1 In general 238
                10.4.2.6.4.2 Exceptions to preference avoiding power 240
                10.4.2.6.4.3 Debtor's use of preference avoiding power 242
            10.4.2.6.5 Fraudulent transfers—§ 548 244
            10.4.2.6.6 Postpetition transfers—§ 549 247
            10.4.2.6.7 Setoff—§ 553 248
            10.4.2.6.8 Liens securing fines, penalties and forfeitures—§ 724(a) 251
        10.4.2.7 Other Limitations on Debtor's Use of Trustee Avoiding Powers 251
        10.4.2.8 Recovery of Property After Transfer Is Avoided 251
        10.4.2.9 Preservation of Avoided Transfers or Recovered Property 252

Consumer Bankruptcy Law and Practice

          10.4.2.10 Limits on Availability of Debtor's Avoiding Powers As Applied to Liens Predating the Bankruptcy Reform Act 253
  10.5 Protection of Exempt Property After Discharge 254

Chapter 11   Dealing with Secured Creditors

  11.1 Introduction 257
  11.2 Determination of the Allowed Secured Claim 257
      11.2.1 The Concept of the Allowed Secured Claim 257
          11.2.1.1 General Principles 257
          11.2.1.2 Limitations on Claim Bifurcation in Chapter 7 258
          11.2.1.3 Claim Bifurcation Alive and Well in Other Chapters 258
      11.2.2 Procedure for Determining the Allowed Secured Claim. 259
          11.2.2.1 Overview of the Process 259
          11.2.2.2 Date of Valuation. 261
              11.2.2.2.1 In general 261
              11.2.2.2.2 Statutory rules for some personal property 261
          11.2.2.3 Method of Valuation. 262
              11.2.2.3.1 Valuation standard 262
              11.2.2.3.2 Valuation of motor vehicles 263
              11.2.2.3.3 Property other than automobiles 264
              11.2.2.3.4 Computation of value 265
  11.3 Creditors' Efforts to Obtain Security After Bankruptcy Commenced 265
      11.3.1 Overview 265
      11.3.2 Reclamation of Property 266
      11.3.3 Abandonment of Property by the Trustee 266
      11.3.4 Disposition by the Trustee Under Section 725 267
      11.3.5 Holding of Cash Collateral by Creditors. 267
  11.4 Statement of Intention with Respect to Property Securing Consumer Debts and with Respect to Personal Property Leases 268
      11.4.1 Overview 268
      11.4.2 Effect of 2005 Amendments to Section 521(a)(2) and Related Provisions 269
          11.4.2.1 In General 269
          11.4.2.2 No Material Change to the Statutory Language. 269
          11.4.2.3 Section 362(h) 270
          11.4.2.4 Section 521(a)(6) 271
              11.4.2.4.1 Overview 271
              11.4.2.4.2 Requirement of allowed claim 271
              11.4.2.4.3 Requirement of claim for the purchase price 272
              11.4.2.4.4 Rights of creditors and debtors when section 521(a)(6) applies 272
          11.4.2.5 Section 521(d). 273
          11.4.2.6 Legislative History of the 2005 Amendments 273
          11.4.2.7 Bankruptcy Policies Supporting the Retain and Pay Option. 273
          11.4.2.8 Practice Tips. 274
  11.5 Right of Redemption in Chapter 7 Cases. 274
      11.5.1 Purpose. 274
      11.5.2 Limitations on the Right to Redeem. 274
      11.5.3 Redemption by Payment in Installments 275
      11.5.4 Secured Creditors Who Refuse to Agree to Continued Installment Payments . . 275
      11.5.5 Uses in Practice 276
  11.6 Using Chapter 13 to Deal with Secured Creditors. 277
      11.6.1 Modification of Secured Creditors' Rights in Claims Not Secured Only by Real Estate That Is the Debtor's Principal Residence 277
          11.6.1.1 In General 277

Contents

  11.6.1.2 Limitations on Modifying Certain Debts Secured Only by Real Estate That Is Debtor's Principal Residence 278
    11.6.1.2.1 In general 278
    11.6.1.2.2 Security interests in the debtor's residence that are not protected by section 1322(b)(2) 278
      11.6.1.2.2.1 Overview 278
      11.6.1.2.2.2 Strip off of wholly unsecured junior mortgages 278
      11.6.1.2.2.3 Short-term and balloon payment mortgages 279
      11.6.1.2.2.4 Mortgages with additional security 280
      11.6.1.2.2.5 Mortgages on multi-family residences 281
      11.6.1.2.2.6 Liens that are not security interests in real property 281
    11.6.1.2.3 Right to cure defaults is not impaired by section 1322(b)(2) 282
  11.6.1.3 Provisions Dealing with Allowed Secured Claims Provided for by the Plan 282
    11.6.1.3.1 Overview 282
    11.6.1.3.2 Creditor acceptance of plan or debtor's surrender of collateral 282
    11.6.1.3.3 Payment of allowed secured claim through plan when creditor does not accept plan 283
      11.6.1.3.3.1 Lien retention and present value of payments— the chapter 13 cramdown 283
      11.6.1.3.3.2 Payments in equal monthly amounts and provision of adequate protection 284
      11.6.1.3.3.3 Filing of the secured claim 285
      11.6.1.3.3.4 Plan need not provide for all secured claims 285
      11.6.1.3.3.5 Determination of allowed secured claim 286
      11.6.1.3.3.6 Trustee's fee and present value interest 287
      11.6.1.3.3.7 Plans not complying with section 1325(a)(5) may be confirmed 288
  11.6.1.4 Different Rules for Secured Claims Described in Paragraph at End of Section 1325(a) 289
  11.6.1.5 Voluntary Loan Modifications in Conjunction with Bankruptcy 291
 11.6.2 Right to Cure Defaults on Long-Term Debts Including Mortgages on Debtor's Residence 292
  11.6.2.1 Overview 292
  11.6.2.2 Cure of Mortgages After Acceleration or Foreclosure Judgment 293
  11.6.2.3 Cure of Mortgages That Mature Before the Bankruptcy Case or Before the End of the Plan 294
  11.6.2.4 Cure Permitted Even If Debtor Has No Personal Liability 294
  11.6.2.5 Length of Time Permitted for Cure 295
  11.6.2.6 Method of Maintaining Current Payments on Debts Being Cured 295
  11.6.2.7 Amount Necessary to Effectuate Cure 295
    11.6.2.7.1 Attorney fees and costs 295
    11.6.2.7.2 Interest on arrears 297
  11.6.2.8 Effect of Cure 298
    11.6.2.8.1 Overview 298
    11.6.2.8.2 Use of Rule 3002.1 to ensure cure is effectuated 299
      11.6.2.8.2.1 Application of Rule 3002.1 299
      11.6.2.8.2.2 Notice of payment change—Rule 3002.1(b) 299
      11.6.2.8.2.3 Notice of postpetition fees—Rule 3002.1(c) 300
      11.6.2.8.2.4 Fee dispute procedure—Rule 3002.1(e) 300
      11.6.2.8.2.5 Notice of final cure payment—Rule 3002.1(f) and Rule 3002.1(h) 300

		11.6.2.8.2.6 Sanctions for noncompliance—Rules 3001(c)(2)(D) and 3002.1(i)	301
		11.6.2.8.2.7 Rule 3002.1 and the attorneys general settlement with major servicers	301
11.7	Use of Section 506 to Reduce Liens That Are Not Paid Under Section 1325(a)(5)		302
11.8	Rent-to-Own Transactions in Bankruptcy		303
11.9	Automobile Title Pawn Transactions in Bankruptcy		304

Chapter 12 Issues Arising in Chapter 13 Cases

- 12.1 Introduction ... 307
- 12.2 Eligibility for Chapter 13 ... 307
  - 12.2.1 Introduction ... 307
  - 12.2.2 Individuals with Regular Income ... 308
  - 12.2.3 Debt Limitations ... 309
    - 12.2.3.1 Determining Whether Debts Are Secured or Unsecured ... 309
    - 12.2.3.2 Determining Whether Debts Are Liquidated and Non-Contingent ... 310
    - 12.2.3.3 Procedure for Determining Eligibility ... 311
    - 12.2.3.4 Strategies for Avoiding Eligibility Problems ... 311
- 12.3 What Amount Must Be Paid to Unsecured Creditors? ... 312
  - 12.3.1 Overview ... 312
  - 12.3.2 The Best Interests of Creditors Test ... 312
  - 12.3.3 Use of the Good Faith Test Prior to the Enactment of the Section 1325(b) Disposable Income Test ... 314
  - 12.3.4 The Ability to Pay (Disposable Income) Test ... 316
    - 12.3.4.1 Introduction ... 316
    - 12.3.4.2 Procedure for Objections Based upon Section 1325(b) ... 317
    - 12.3.4.3 Full Payment Test ... 317
    - 12.3.4.4 Disposable Income Test ... 317
      - 12.3.4.4.1 Use of "current monthly income" ... 317
      - 12.3.4.4.2 Exclusions from disposable income ... 319
        - 12.3.4.4.2.1 Overview ... 319
        - 12.3.4.4.2.2 Child support, foster care, and similar payments ... 320
        - 12.3.4.4.2.3 Payments on domestic support obligations ... 320
        - 12.3.4.4.2.4 Repayments of pension loans and pension contributions ... 320
      - 12.3.4.4.3 Use of means test expense calculations for debtors with incomes above median income ... 320
      - 12.3.4.4.4 Administrative expenses ... 322
      - 12.3.4.4.5 Calculation of expenses for debtors below median income ... 322
      - 12.3.4.4.6 Applicable commitment period and plan length ... 324
    - 12.3.4.5 Postconfirmation Modification of Plan Based Upon Change in Circumstances ... 326
  - 12.3.5 Use of the Good Faith Test After the 1984 Amendments ... 327
  - 12.3.6 Payments to Unsecured Priority Creditors ... 328
    - 12.3.6.1 Priority Claims ... 328
    - 12.3.6.2 Required Filing of Tax Returns ... 330
    - 12.3.6.3 Postpetition Domestic Support Obligation Payments ... 331
- 12.4 Classification of Claims ... 331
  - 12.4.1 In General ... 331
  - 12.4.2 Claims with Cosigners ... 332
  - 12.4.3 Other Classifications ... 332
  - 12.4.4 Payments Directly to Creditors ... 334
  - 12.4.5 Payments to Former Chapter 7 Trustees ... 335
  - 12.4.6 Practical Considerations ... 335
- 12.5 Feasibility of the Plan ... 336

Contents

12.6 Other Plan Provisions	336
12.6.1 Payment of Debtor's Income Directly to Trustee	336
12.6.2 Payment of Interest and Penalties	337
12.6.3 Length of Plan	338
12.6.4 Adjustments in Trustee's Charges	338
12.6.5 Liquidation of Property in Chapter 13	339
12.6.6 Refinancing a Property During a Chapter 13 Case	340
12.7 Do the Section 1325(a) Standards Set Mandatory Requirements?	340
12.8 Use and Possession of Property of the Estate and Adequate Protection	341
12.8.1 Continuing Use of Property	341
12.8.2 Adequate Protection	342
12.8.2.1 Overview	342
12.8.2.2 Adequate Protection Payments	342
12.8.2.2.1 When payments required	342
12.8.2.2.2 Determining the amount and timing of payments	343
12.8.2.2.3 Remedy for failure to make payments	343
12.8.3 Payments to Personal Property Lessors	343
12.8.4 Proof of Insurance	344
12.8.5 Vesting of Property Upon Confirmation	344
12.9 Unexpired Leases and Executory Contracts	344
12.9.1 Definition of Executory Contract	344
12.9.2 Assumption of a Lease or Executory Contract in Chapter 13	346
12.9.3 Rejection of Leases or Executory Contracts	348
12.9.3.1 Overview	348
12.9.3.2 Residential Leases	348
12.9.3.3 Credit Insurance	349
12.9.4 Procedure and Tactics	350
12.9.5 Assumption or Rejection of Personal Property Leases by Chapter 7 Debtor	351
12.9.5.1 2005 Amendments	351
12.9.5.2 Effect of Lease Rejection in Chapter 7	351
12.9.5.3 Lease Assumption by the Debtor in a Chapter 7 Case	351
12.10 Chapter 13 Cases After Prior Bankruptcies	352
12.10.1 Availability of a Discharge	352
12.10.2 Determining Whether a Prior Discharge Was Under Chapter 7 or Chapter 13	352
12.10.3 Repeat Filing Still Permissible Even If Discharge Unavailable	353
12.11 Confirmation of Plan Binds Debtor and All Creditors	354

Chapter 13   Dismissal or Conversion of a Bankruptcy Case

13.1 Introduction	359
13.2 Voluntary Dismissal of Bankruptcy Cases	359
13.3 Typical Causes and Effects of Involuntary Dismissal or Conversion to Chapter 7	360
13.3.1 Reasons for Dismissal or Conversion	360
13.3.2 "Automatic" Dismissal Under Section 521(i)	363
13.4 Involuntary Dismissal for Abuse of the Provisions of Chapter 7	364
13.4.1 In General	364
13.4.2 Section 707(b) Applicable Only to Debtors with Primarily Consumer Debts	364
13.4.3 Limits on Section 707(b) Motions for Debtors with Incomes Below State's Median Income	365
13.4.3.1 Overview	365
13.4.3.2 Determining the Debtor's Current Monthly Income	366
13.4.3.2.1 A six-month average normally used	366
13.4.3.2.2 Payments toward household expenses of debtor or dependents on a regular basis	366

Consumer Bankruptcy Law and Practice

- 13.4.3.2.3 Treatment of spouse's income.................... 366
- 13.4.3.2.4 Treatment of business income.................... 367
- 13.4.3.2.5 Treatment of capital gains and losses............... 367
- 13.4.3.2.6 Withdrawals from an IRA or pension plan........... 367
- 13.4.3.2.7 Explicit statutory exemptions from current monthly income... 368
- 13.4.3.2.8 Other possible types of income................... 368
- 13.4.3.3 Determining Whether Current Monthly Income Is Above State's Median Family Income.................................. 369
- 13.4.4 Safe Harbor for Disabled Veterans, Reservists, and National Guard Members... 370
- 13.4.5 The Means Test Formula................................... 370
  - 13.4.5.1 Introduction.. 370
  - 13.4.5.2 Deduction of IRS Expense Allowances................. 371
    - 13.4.5.2.1 General....................................... 371
    - 13.4.5.2.2 IRS national standards for food, clothing, housekeeping supplies, personal care, and miscellaneous expenses....... 371
    - 13.4.5.2.3 IRS national standard for out-of-pocket health care expenses....................................... 372
    - 13.4.5.2.4 IRS local standards for transportation expenses........ 372
    - 13.4.5.2.5 IRS local standards for housing and utilities.......... 373
    - 13.4.5.2.6 Other necessary expenses allowed under IRS standards..... 373
  - 13.4.5.3 Other Expenses That May Be Deducted................. 374
    - 13.4.5.3.1 In general..................................... 374
    - 13.4.5.3.2 Deduction for secured debts..................... 374
    - 13.4.5.3.3 Deduction for priority debts..................... 375
    - 13.4.5.3.4 Deduction for health insurance................... 376
    - 13.4.5.3.5 Deduction for expenses to maintain safety from domestic violence.. 376
    - 13.4.5.3.6 Deduction for support of elderly and disabled family members.. 376
    - 13.4.5.3.7 Deduction for administrative expenses.............. 376
    - 13.4.5.3.8 Deduction for education expenses................. 376
    - 13.4.5.3.9 Deduction for charitable contributions............. 377
- 13.4.6 Application of the Means Test Formula........................... 377
  - 13.4.6.1 Presumption of Abuse................................ 377
  - 13.4.6.2 Rebutting the Presumption of Abuse.................... 377
  - 13.4.6.3 Discretionary Dismissal............................... 378
- 13.4.7 Other Changes in the Abuse Standard Under Section 707(b)............. 378
  - 13.4.7.1 No Challenges Based on Ability to Pay for Debtors with Incomes Below Median Income................................. 378
  - 13.4.7.2 Substantial Abuse Standard Changed to Abuse Standard.......... 379
  - 13.4.7.3 Elimination of Explicit Presumption Favoring the Debtor.......... 379
  - 13.4.7.4 Dismissal for Bad Faith or Based on a Totality of Circumstances Showing Abuse...................................... 379
  - 13.4.7.5 Dismissal for an Abusive Rejection of an Executory Contract....... 381
- 13.4.8 Procedures for Means Testing Under Section 707(b).................. 381
- 13.5 Chapter 7 Involuntary Dismissal Based on Certain Crimes................... 382
- 13.6 Effect of Dismissal... 382
- 13.7 Conversion of a Bankruptcy Case................................... 383
  - 13.7.1 Conversion from Chapter 7 to Chapter 13......................... 383
  - 13.7.2 Conversion from Chapter 13 to Chapter 7......................... 383
  - 13.7.3 Effect of Conversion.. 385

Chapter 14   Litigating in the Bankruptcy Court

14.1 Introduction 387
14.2 Bankruptcy Court Jurisdiction Under the 1984 Amendments 387
    14.2.1 A Brief History 387
    14.2.2 Initial Referral of Bankruptcy Matters to the Bankruptcy Courts 389
    14.2.3 The Bankruptcy Case 390
    14.2.4 Types of Proceedings 390
        14.2.4.1 Adversary Proceedings, Contested Matters, and Applications 390
        14.2.4.2 Core and Non-Core Proceedings 390
        14.2.4.3 Court's Determination of Jurisdictional Questions 391
        14.2.4.4 Procedure in Non-Core Proceedings 394
    14.2.5 Withdrawal to the District Court 395
        14.2.5.1 In General 395
        14.2.5.2 Mandatory Withdrawal 395
        14.2.5.3 Discretionary Withdrawal 396
    14.2.6 Personal Injury and Wrongful Death Claims 397
    14.2.7 Jury Trials in the Bankruptcy Court 397
    14.2.8 Contempt Powers of the Bankruptcy Courts 399
14.3 Advantages of the Bankruptcy Court As a Forum 399
    14.3.1 Possibilities of a Fairer Result for the Consumer Client 399
    14.3.2 Avoidance of Substantive or Procedural Difficulties 400
        14.3.2.1 *In Personam* Jurisdiction, Venue and Service Requirements 400
        14.3.2.2 Sovereign Immunity 401
        14.3.2.3 Overcoming Barriers to Federal Court Access 404
        14.3.2.4 Recoupment Claims in Bankruptcy After Expiration of Limitations Periods 405
        14.3.2.5 Avoiding Mandatory Arbitration Agreements 405
        14.3.2.6 Avoiding Standing and Judicial Estoppel Problems 407
            14.3.2.6.1 In general 407
            14.3.2.6.2 Standing 407
            14.3.2.6.3 Judicial estoppel 408
14.4 Bringing a Matter Before the Bankruptcy Forum 409
    14.4.1 Removal 409
        14.4.1.1 In General 409
        14.4.1.2 Procedure for Removal 410
        14.4.1.3 Procedure After Removal 410
        14.4.1.4 Remand of Removed Actions 411
    14.4.2 Litigation of Other Claims Commenced by the Debtor 412
    14.4.3 Objections to Claims 413
        14.4.3.1 Overview 413
        14.4.3.2 Claims Filed After Bar Date for Claims 413
        14.4.3.3 Claims Not Enforceable Against the Debtor 415
        14.4.3.4 Objecting to Claims Filed by Mortgage Creditors and Challenging Servicing Abuses 416
            14.4.3.4.1 In general 416
            14.4.3.4.2 Escrow overcharges 418
            14.4.3.4.3 Interest overcharges 419
            14.4.3.4.4 Late charge abuses and other mistakes in crediting payments 420
            14.4.3.4.5 Bankruptcy monitoring fees and other bankruptcy fees 420
            14.4.3.4.6 Undisclosed fees and payment changes 423
            14.4.3.4.7 Standing challenges to proofs of claim based on securitized mortgage debt 424
            14.4.3.4.8 Responding to mortgage servicer abuses by making use of section 524(i) 425

Consumer Bankruptcy Law and Practice

    14.4.3.5 Objecting to Claims Filed by Debt Buyers.................... 427
    14.4.3.6 Objecting Based Upon Prepetition Settlement Attempts—Section
        502(k).. 430
    14.4.3.7 Reconsideration of Claims..................................... 431
  14.4.4 An Example: Truth in Lending Claims of the Debtor.................... 431
  14.4.5 Habeas Corpus.. 433
 14.5 Abstention.. 433
  14.5.1 In General.. 433
  14.5.2 Mandatory Abstention.. 433
  14.5.3 Discretionary Abstention.. 435
 14.6 *In Forma Pauperis*—Filing Fee Waivers in Bankruptcy Cases and Proceedings..... 435
  14.6.1 General Principles... 435
  14.6.2 Statutory Authority of Bankruptcy Courts to Waive Fees................. 436
    14.6.2.1 Chapter 7 Filing Fee... 436
    14.6.2.2 Other Filing Fees... 437
 14.7 Class Actions in Bankruptcy Court.. 438
 14.8 Involuntary Bankruptcy Cases... 439
 14.9 Bankruptcy Appeals... 442
  14.9.1 Appeals from the Bankruptcy Court...................................... 442
  14.9.2 Direct Appeal from Bankruptcy Court to Court of Appeals................ 443
  14.9.3 Appeals from the District Court or Appellate Panel..................... 444
  14.9.4 What Is a Final Order?.. 445
  14.9.5 Procedure on Appeals.. 447

Chapter 15 The Discharge: Protecting It and Using It

 15.1 Introduction... 451
 15.2 Objections to Discharge in Chapter 7 Cases................................... 451
  15.2.1 How They Arise.. 451
  15.2.2 Grounds for Objecting to Discharge...................................... 453
    15.2.2.1 Debtor Is Not an Individual—11 U.S.C. § 727(a)(1)............... 453
    15.2.2.2 Intentional Concealment, Transfer or Destruction of Property—
        11 U.S.C. § 727(a)(2)... 453
    15.2.2.3 Unjustified Failure to Keep Books or Records As to Finances—
        11 U.S.C. § 727(a)(3)... 454
    15.2.2.4 Dishonesty in Connection with the Bankruptcy Case—11 U.S.C.
        § 727(a)(4)... 455
    15.2.2.5 Failure to Explain Loss or Deficiency of Assets—11 U.S.C.
        § 727(a)(5)... 456
    15.2.2.6 Refusal to Obey Court Orders or to Testify—11 U.S.C. § 727(a)(6)... 456
    15.2.2.7 Commission of Prohibited Acts in Connection with Another
        Bankruptcy Case Concerning an Insider—11 U.S.C. § 727(a)(7)..... 456
    15.2.2.8 Prior Discharge in Chapter 7, Chapter 11, or Their Predecessors—
        11 U.S.C. § 727(a)(8)... 457
    15.2.2.9 Prior Discharge Under Chapter 13—11 U.S.C. § 727(a)(9).......... 457
    15.2.2.10 Written Waiver of Discharge—11 U.S.C. § 727(a)(10)............. 457
    15.2.2.11 Failure to Complete Course in Personal Financial Management—
        11 U.S.C. § 727(a)(11).. 458
    15.2.2.12 Delay of Discharge to Determine Homestead Exemption
        Rights—11 U.S.C. § 727(a)(12).................................. 458
 15.3 Revocation of Discharge—11 U.S.C. § 727(d)................................... 458
 15.4 Exceptions to Discharge.. 459
  15.4.1 Differences Between Chapter 7 and Chapter 13........................... 459
  15.4.2 How Exceptions to Discharge Are Raised................................. 461
  15.4.3 Which Debts Are Excepted from Discharge?............................... 463

Contents

15.4.3.1 Taxes—11 U.S.C. §§ 523(a)(1), 1328(a)(2)................. 463
    15.4.3.1.1 Taxes that cannot be discharged 463
    15.4.3.1.2 Analyzing tax debts to determine dischargeability 467
15.4.3.2 Debts Incurred Through False Pretenses, Fraud, or False Financial Statements—11 U.S.C. § 523(a)(2) 469
    15.4.3.2.1 Overview 469
    15.4.3.2.2 Elements which must be proved by the creditor in cases of alleged false financial statements................... 469
        15.4.3.2.2.1 Generally 469
        15.4.3.2.2.2 The debtor obtained money, property, services, or an extension, renewal, or refinancing of credit..... 470
        15.4.3.2.2.3 The statement was materially false and in writing .. 471
        15.4.3.2.2.4 The statement concerned the financial condition of the debtor or an insider 472
        15.4.3.2.2.5 The creditor reasonably relied upon the false statement 472
        15.4.3.2.2.6 The debtor's intent to deceive 473
    15.4.3.2.3 Debts incurred through false pretenses or fraud........... 473
        15.4.3.2.3.1 Generally 473
        15.4.3.2.3.2 Credit cards and other credit use with no intent to pay 475
        15.4.3.2.3.3 Public benefits overpayments 479
    15.4.3.2.4 Tactics in cases under 11 U.S.C. § 523(a)(2) and award of attorney fees under 11 U.S.C. § 523(d) 479
15.4.3.3 Creditors Not Listed or Scheduled by the Debtor—11 U.S.C. § 523(a)(3)... 482
15.4.3.4 Fraud As a Fiduciary, Embezzlement, or Larceny—11 U.S.C. § 523(a)(4) 485
15.4.3.5 Domestic Support Obligations—11 U.S.C. § 523(a)(5)............ 486
    15.4.3.5.1 In general 486
    15.4.3.5.2 Support debts owed to governmental units 487
    15.4.3.5.3 Determination of whether debt is a domestic support obligation 487
15.4.3.6 Willful and Malicious Injury—11 U.S.C. §§ 523(a)(6), 1328(a)(4) 490
15.4.3.7 Fines and Penalties—11 U.S.C. §§ 523(a)(7), 1328(a)(3).......... 493
15.4.3.8 Student Loans—11 U.S.C. § 523(a)(8)...................... 495
    15.4.3.8.1 In general 495
    15.4.3.8.2 Student loan dischargeability tests.................... 498
        15.4.3.8.2.1 Former seven-year test.................... 498
        15.4.3.8.2.2 Undue hardship test 499
    15.4.3.8.3 Procedure for dischargeability determination............. 503
    15.4.3.8.4 Pursuing student loan defenses and nonbankruptcy alternatives 504
    15.4.3.8.5 Special issues regarding student loans in chapter 13....... 505
    15.4.3.8.6 Health education assistance loans and other special loan programs 506
15.4.3.9 Debts Incurred Through Drunk Driving—11 U.S.C. § 523(a)(9)...... 507
15.4.3.10 Debts Not Discharged in Prior Bankruptcy Case—11 U.S.C. § 523(a)(10), (b) 508
15.4.3.11 Debts Emerging from Responsibilities to Federal Depository Institutions—11 U.S.C. § 523(a)(11), (12)................... 508
15.4.3.12 Federal Criminal Restitution—11 U.S.C. § 523(a)(13) 509
15.4.3.13 Debts Incurred to Pay Nondischargeable Taxes or to Pay Federal Election Law Fines or Penalties—11 U.S.C. § 523(a)(14A), (14B) ... 509
15.4.3.14 Marital Property Settlement Debts—11 U.S.C. § 523(a)(15) 510

Consumer Bankruptcy Law and Practice

15.4.3.15 Debts for Condominium, Cooperative, or Home Owner Association Fees—11 U.S.C. § 523(a)(16)	510
15.4.3.16 Costs and Fees in Prisoner Litigation—11 U.S.C. § 523(a)(17)	511
15.4.3.17 Pension Loans—11 U.S.C. § 523(a)(18)	511
15.4.3.18 Debts Arising from Securities Violations—11 U.S.C. § 523(a)(19)	512
15.4.3.19 Debts Made Nondischargeable by Other Statutes	512
15.4.3.20 Debts That Were Nondischargeable in a Previous Bankruptcy Case—11 U.S.C. § 523(b)	512
15.4.4 Res Judicata and Collateral Estoppel in Dischargeability Cases	512
15.5 The Protections of the Discharge	516
15.5.1 Effects on Discharged Claims	516
15.5.1.1 Definition of Claim for Discharge Purposes	516
15.5.1.2 Elimination of Personal Liability and Protections for Property	517
15.5.1.3 Voiding of Judgments	517
15.5.1.4 The Discharge Injunction	518
15.5.2 Reaffirmation and Security Interests Which Survive Bankruptcy	521
15.5.2.1 Reaffirmation by Agreement Only	521
15.5.2.2 Disclosure Requirements	523
15.5.2.3 Form of the Reaffirmation Agreement	523
15.5.2.4 Protective Provisions	524
15.5.2.5 Abusive Creditor Reaffirmation Practices	525
15.5.2.6 The Undue Hardship and Best Interests Tests	526
15.5.2.7 Factors to Be Considered by Attorneys Validating Reaffirmation Agreements	527
15.5.3 Secured Debts Without Reaffirmation	528
15.5.4 Protection Against Discrimination Based on Bankruptcy	529
15.5.5 Particular Problems Relating to Discharge Protections	532
15.5.5.1 Drivers' Licenses	532
15.5.5.2 Student Loans and College Transcripts	533
15.5.5.3 Public and Private Housing	534
15.5.5.4 Social Security, Welfare, and Other Governmental Benefits	535
15.5.5.5 Criminal Proceedings, Fines, and Incarceration	535
15.5.5.6 Tax Consequences of the Discharge	536
15.5.5.7 Enforcement of the Discharge Protections	537

Chapter 16   **Attorney Fees for Debtor's Counsel and Attorney Duties in Consumer Bankruptcy Cases**

16.1 Introduction	541
16.2 Initial Fee Arrangements with Clients	541
16.2.1 The Basic Fee	541
16.2.2 Amounts Typically Charged	542
16.2.3 Method of Payment	543
16.3 Court Supervision of Bankruptcy Attorney Fees	546
16.3.1 Introduction	546
16.3.2 Disclosures Required	546
16.3.3 Bankruptcy Court Review of Fee Disclosures and Requests	547
16.3.4 Making a Record on Fee Issues	549
16.4 Payment of Attorney Fees Through the Chapter 13 Plan	550
16.4.1 Fees Which Can Be Paid Through a Plan	550
16.4.2 Procedure for Obtaining Payment of Fees Through the Plan	551
16.5 Other Sources of Attorney Fees in Bankruptcy Cases	552
16.5.1 Overview	552
16.5.2 The Civil Rights Attorney's Fees Awards Act of 1976	553
16.5.3 Consumer Protection Statutes	553

Contents

16.5.4 The Equal Access to Justice Act	554
16.5.5 Fees As Sanction for Violation of Bankruptcy Rules	555
16.5.5.1 Rule 9011	555
16.5.5.2 Rules 3001 and 3002.1	556
16.5.6 Other Fee-Shifting Provisions	556
16.5.7 Limitations on Fee Awards Against Governmental Units	557
16.6 Services Provided by Petition Preparers and Other Non-Attorneys	557
16.7 Duties of Debtors' Counsel Under Bankruptcy Rule 9011 and Related Provisions	562
16.7.1 Federal Rule of Bankruptcy Procedure 9011	562
16.7.2 Section 707(b)(4)	562
16.7.2.1 Costs and Attorney Fees for Successful Section 707(b) Motions—§ 707(b)(4)(A)	562
16.7.2.2 Civil Penalties Under Bankruptcy Rule 9011—§ 707(b)(4)(B)	563
16.7.2.3 Attorney Certifications—§ 707(b)(4)(C)	563
16.7.2.4 Attorney Certification As to Schedules—§ 707(b)(4)(D)	563
16.8 Debt Relief Agency Provisions	564
16.8.1 Applicability of Debt Relief Agency Provisions to Debtor's Attorney	564
16.8.1.1 Definition of Debt Relief Agency	564
16.8.1.2 Persons Specifically Excluded from the Definition of Debt Relief Agency	564
16.8.2 Restrictions on Debt Relief Agencies	565
16.8.3 Disclosures Required of Debt Relief Agencies	565
16.8.3.1 Relationship Between Section 527 and Section 342(b)(1) Disclosures	565
16.8.3.2 Disclosures Concerning the Bankruptcy Process	566
16.8.3.3 Required Statement About Bankruptcy Assistance Services	566
16.8.3.4 Disclosures Required of Non-Attorney Agencies That Prepare Bankruptcy Documents	567
16.8.4 Written Contract Under Section 528(a)	567
16.8.5 Advertising Requirements Under Section 528(a)	568
16.8.6 Remedies for Failure to Comply with Debt Relief Agency Provisions	568

Chapter 17 — Chapter 12 Bankruptcy: Family Farmer and Family Fisherman Reorganization

17.1 Overview	571
17.1.1 Evolution and Historical Background of Chapter 12	571
17.1.1.1 Current Status of Chapter 12	571
17.1.1.2 Purpose of Chapter 12	571
17.1.2 Special Bankruptcy Code Protections Outside of Chapter 12	572
17.1.3 Farmer Reorganizations Under Chapters Other Than Chapter 12	573
17.1.3.1 Overview	573
17.1.3.2 Problems Under Chapter 13 for Farmers	573
17.1.3.3 Problems Under Chapter 11 for Farmers	574
17.1.4 The Unique Nature of Farm Finance	574
17.1.4.1 Overview	574
17.1.4.2 The Farm Credit System	574
17.1.4.3 The Farm Service Agency Loan Programs	575
17.1.4.4 The Federal Farm Programs	575
17.1.4.4.1 Treatment in bankruptcy	575
17.1.4.4.2 Basic attributes of federal farm programs	576
17.1.5 Timing a Chapter 12 Filing	577
17.2 Commencement of a Case	578
17.2.1 Introduction	578
17.2.2 Eligibility for Chapter 12 Relief	578
17.2.2.1 In General	578

- 17.2.2.2 The Regular Annual Income Requirement 579
- 17.2.2.3 The "Engaged in a Farming Operation" Requirement 579
- 17.2.2.4 Definition of "Family Farmer" and "Family Fisherman" 581
  - 17.2.2.4.1 Overview 581
  - 17.2.2.4.2 Debt ceiling 581
  - 17.2.2.4.3 Debt arising from the farm operation or commercial fishing operation 581
  - 17.2.2.4.4 Income arising from the farming operation or the commercial fishing operation 582
  - 17.2.2.4.5 Eligibility requirements for partnerships and corporate farmers 584
- 17.2.2.5 Joint Chapter 12 Filings 584
- 17.2.3 Initial Schedules, Forms, and Fees 585
  - 17.2.3.1 Schedules 585
  - 17.2.3.2 Appointment of Counsel 585
  - 17.2.3.3 Costs and Attorney Fees 585
  - 17.2.3.4 Other Reports and Documentation 586
- 17.2.4 Voluntary Conversion from Other Chapters to Chapter 12 586
- 17.2.5 What to Expect at the Meeting of Creditors 586
- 17.3 The Family Farmer As Debtor-in-Possession 587
  - 17.3.1 What Is a Debtor-in-Possession? 587
  - 17.3.2 Removal of the Farmer As a Debtor-in-Possession 587
- 17.4 General Principles 587
  - 17.4.1 The Chapter 12 Trustee 587
    - 17.4.1.1 Role and Standing of the Trustee 587
    - 17.4.1.2 Payments Made Through the Chapter 12 Trustee and Trustee Compensation 588
      - 17.4.1.2.1 General 588
      - 17.4.1.2.2 Challenges to variations in trustee costs paid by different debtors 588
      - 17.4.1.2.3 Avoiding the trustee commission for certain payments 589
      - 17.4.1.2.4 Does the trustee receive a fee on its fee? 589
    - 17.4.1.3 Role of the Chapter 12 Trustee upon Removal of the Family Farmer As a Debtor-in-Possession 590
  - 17.4.2 What Constitutes Property of the Estate 590
  - 17.4.3 Exemptions, Lien Avoidance, and Recapture Powers 590
    - 17.4.3.1 Exemptions Available to Family Farmers Under Chapter 12 590
    - 17.4.3.2 Exemptions for "Tools of Trade" and "Livestock" 591
    - 17.4.3.3 Lien Avoidance Under Section 522(f) 592
    - 17.4.3.4 Section 552 Lien Dissolution 592
    - 17.4.3.5 Other Avoidance and Recapture Powers of the Family Farmer Debtor-in-Possession 593
      - 17.4.3.5.1 In general 593
      - 17.4.3.5.2 Recovery of property as a fraudulent transfer 593
      - 17.4.3.5.3 Preferential transfers 594
      - 17.4.3.5.4 Avoidance of improperly perfected security interests 594
      - 17.4.3.5.5 Redemption and cure 594
  - 17.4.4 The Automatic Stay and Codebtor Stay in Chapter 12 Cases 595
    - 17.4.4.1 The Automatic Stay 595
    - 17.4.4.2 The Codebtor Stay 595
    - 17.4.4.3 Grounds for Relief from the Automatic Stay 595
  - 17.4.5 Objections to Discharge 596
  - 17.4.6 Dismissal and Conversion 597
    - 17.4.6.1 Voluntary Dismissal 597
    - 17.4.6.2 Involuntary Dismissal 598

Contents

- 17.4.6.3 Voluntary Conversion from Chapter 12 to Other Chapters 599
- 17.4.6.4 Involuntary Conversion from Chapter 12 to Chapter 7 599
- 17.4.7 Executory Contracts and Unexpired Leases 599
  - 17.4.7.1 Overview 599
  - 17.4.7.2 Federal Farm Program Contracts As Executory Contracts 600
  - 17.4.7.3 Installment Land Contracts As Executory Contracts 600
  - 17.4.7.4 Unexpired Equipment Leases 600
  - 17.4.7.5 Unexpired Farmland Rental Agreements 600
- 17.4.8 Use of Cash Collateral 600
- 17.4.9 New Financing and Its Approval 601
- 17.4.10 Sale of Property Free and Clear of Liens 602
- 17.4.11 Adequate Protection Under Chapter 12 602
- 17.4.12 Creditors' Right to Set Off 603
- 17.5 The Chapter 12 Reorganization Process 604
  - 17.5.1 Introduction 604
  - 17.5.2 Procedure and Timing in Chapter 12 Cases 604
  - 17.5.3 Determining the Value of the Creditor's Claims: The Allowed Secured Claim 605
  - 17.5.4 Chapter 12 Plan Requirements: Secured Claims 606
    - 17.5.4.1 In General 606
    - 17.5.4.2 Amortization and Extending Plan Payments Beyond the Plan's Life 607
    - 17.5.4.3 Interest Rates for Secured Creditors 609
    - 17.5.4.4 Return or Surrender of Property to Secured Creditors 609
    - 17.5.4.5 Sale of Property Free and Clear of Liens 610
    - 17.5.4.6 Replacement Liens 610
  - 17.5.5 Chapter 12 Plan Requirements: Unsecured Claims 611
    - 17.5.5.1 In General 611
    - 17.5.5.2 The Liquidation Test 611
    - 17.5.5.3 The Disposable Income Requirement 611
    - 17.5.5.4 Treatment of Priority Unsecured Creditors 614
  - 17.5.6 Classification of Claims 615
    - 17.5.6.1 Introduction 615
    - 17.5.6.2 Classification of Codebtor Claims 615
    - 17.5.6.3 Classification of the Claims of Unsecured Creditors 615
    - 17.5.6.4 Classification of the Claims of Secured Creditors 616
  - 17.5.7 Other Chapter 12 Plan Requirements 616
    - 17.5.7.1 Good Faith Test 616
    - 17.5.7.2 The Feasibility Requirement 617
      - 17.5.7.2.1 General observations 617
      - 17.5.7.2.2 Determination of feasibility 618
    - 17.5.7.3 Trustee Fees and the Direct Payment Issue 620
  - 17.5.8 Additional Protections for Domestic Support Obligations 621
  - 17.5.9 Other Plan Provisions 621
- 17.6 Denial of Confirmation 623
- 17.7 The Chapter 12 Discharge and Its Operation 623
  - 17.7.1 Scope of the Chapter 12 Discharge 623
  - 17.7.2 The Hardship Discharge 624
  - 17.7.3 Revocation of Discharge 624
- 17.8 Postconfirmation Issues 625
  - 17.8.1 Postconfirmation Modification of the Chapter 12 Plan 625
  - 17.8.2 Postconfirmation Indebtedness 626
  - 17.8.3 Revocation of Confirmation 627

| Chapter 18 | Consumers As Creditors in Bankruptcy: Selected Topics |

18.1 Introduction 629
18.2 Prebankruptcy Strategy 629
    18.2.1 Preparing for the Debtor's Voluntary Bankruptcy 629
    18.2.2 Putting the Debtor into Involuntary Bankruptcy 630
18.3 The Automatic Stay 631
    18.3.1 Introduction 631
    18.3.2 Relief from the Stay 632
    18.3.3 Practical Considerations Applicable to Stay Relief Issues 634
    18.3.4 Tenants' Counterclaims Against a Bankrupt Landlord 634
18.4 Filing a Proof of Claim 635
    18.4.1 For Individual Consumer Creditors 635
    18.4.2 Class Proofs of Claim 636
18.5 Strategies to Increase the Chance of Recovery 639
    18.5.1 General 639
    18.5.2 Property Which Is Not Part of the Bankruptcy Estate—Trust Funds 639
        18.5.2.1 General 639
        18.5.2.2 Determining the Existence of a Trust 640
        18.5.2.3 Tracing Trust Funds 643
    18.5.3 Postpetition Claims As Administrative Expenses 644
    18.5.4 Challenging Dischargeability 645
        18.5.4.1 General 645
        18.5.4.2 Individual Debtors in Chapters 7, 11, and 12 645
            18.5.4.2.1 Grounds for a finding of nondischargeability 645
            18.5.4.2.2 Procedures for obtaining a determination of
                        nondischargeability 648
        18.5.4.3 Chapter 13 650
        18.5.4.4 Corporate or Partnership Debtors 650
    18.5.5 The Consumer Priority 651
    18.5.6 Equitable Subordination 653
    18.5.7 Seeking Defendants Not in Bankruptcy 654
    18.5.8 Rule 2004 Examinations 655
18.6 *In Forma Pauperis* 655
    18.6.1 Need for Consumers As Creditors to Proceed *In Forma Pauperis* 655
    18.6.2 Seeking *In Forma Pauperis* Relief 655
18.7 Chapter 11 657
    18.7.1 Introduction 657
    18.7.2 General Role of Creditors and the United States Trustee 658
        18.7.2.1 Creditors' Right to Vote on the Debtor's Plan 658
        18.7.2.2 Creditors' Right to Participate in the Chapter 11 Plan 658
        18.7.2.3 The United States Trustee 658
    18.7.3 Appointment of a Creditors' Committee 659
    18.7.4 Appointment of a Trustee or an Examiner 660
        18.7.4.1 Introduction 660
        18.7.4.2 General Standards 661
        18.7.4.3 Grounds for Appointment of a Trustee Under Section 1104(a)(1) ... 661
        18.7.4.4 Grounds for Appointment of a Trustee Under Section 1104(a)(2) ... 662
        18.7.4.5 Appointment of a Trustee for Fraud, Dishonesty or Criminal
                Conduct by Insiders 663
        18.7.4.6 Appointment of an Examiner 663
        18.7.4.7 Practice and Procedure 664
    18.7.5 Objection to Compensation Paid to Debtor's Principals 665
    18.7.6 Transfer Avoidance Actions 666
    18.7.7 Objections to the Debtor's Disclosure Statement 666
    18.7.8 Objections to the Debtor's Plan of Reorganization 667

Contents

  18.7.9 Creditor's Plan of Reorganization 668
  18.7.10 Special Provisions Applicable to Small Business Bankruptcies 669
  18.7.11 Seeking Dismissal or Conversion of a Chapter 11 Case 670
  18.7.12 Representing Employees and Other Industrial Stakeholders in Chapter 11
    Proceedings 671
    18.7.12.1 Introduction 671
    18.7.12.2 Employee Priority Claims 671
    18.7.12.3 Job Retention Strategies in Chapter 11 Proceedings 673
      18.7.12.3.1 Introduction 673
      18.7.12.3.2 Right to intervene............................ 673
      18.7.12.3.3 Opposing a chapter 11 liquidation 673
      18.7.12.3.4 Placing conditions upon approval of a sale of the
        debtor's business 674
      18.7.12.3.5 Other job retention strategies 674
18.8 Special Problems of Tenants 674
  18.8.1 General 674
  18.8.2 Maintaining Services When Private Landlords File Chapter 7 Bankruptcy 675
    18.8.2.1 Abandonment by a Chapter 7 Trustee 675
    18.8.2.2 Legal Theories to Prevent Abandonment 675
    18.8.2.3 Loss of Services Without Abandonment 676
    18.8.2.4 Steps to Take 677
    18.8.2.5 Forcing Abandonment to the Lender 678
    18.8.2.6 Maintaining Services in the Event the Property Has Been
      Abandoned 679
  18.8.3 Pursuing Opportunities for Tenant Ownership in a Chapter 7 Bankruptcy 679
  18.8.4 Preventing Evictions in Chapter 11 and 13 Proceedings 680
  18.8.5 Security Deposits 681
18.9 Representing Consumers When Lenders File Bankruptcy 684
  18.9.1 Lender Bankruptcies 684
  18.9.2 Automatic Stay Issues for Consumer Borrowers 684
  18.9.3 Loan Company Sales of Assets Under 11 U.S.C. § 363 687
  18.9.4 Filing a Proof of Claim for a Consumer Borrower 687
  18.9.5 Third-Party and Successor Releases and Injunctions 688
18.10 Other Mechanisms to Protect Consumers in Business Bankruptcies 690

Bibliography 691

Index 695

Volume 2

Appendix A Bankruptcy Statutes

  A.1 Selected Provisions of the Bankruptcy Code, 11 U.S.C. §§ 101–1532 725
  A.2 Selected Provisions of Title 28 of the United States Code 829
  A.3 Selected Provisions of Other Titles of the United States Code 841
  A.4 Selected Uncodified Provisions of Bankruptcy Acts 871
    A.4.1 Selected Provisions of Title IV [Transition] of Bankruptcy Act of 1978 (as
      amended by the Bankruptcy Amendments and Federal Judgeship Act of
      1984) 871
    A.4.2 Selected Provisions of the Bankruptcy Amendments and Federal Judgeship
      Act of 1984 872

Consumer Bankruptcy Law and Practice

	A.4.3 Selected Provisions of Title III [Transition and Administrative Provisions] of Bankruptcy Judges, United States Trustees, and Family Farmer Bankruptcy Act of 1986 (as amended by the Judicial Improvements Act of 1990)	873
	A.4.4 Provisions Related to Effective Date of 1990 and 1991 Student Loan Dischargeability Issues	875
	A.4.5 Selected Provisions of the Judicial Improvements Act of 1990	876
	A.4.6 Selected Provisions of the Bankruptcy Reform Act of 1994	876
	A.4.7 Selected Provision of the National Defense Authorization Act for Fiscal Year 2000	877
	A.4.8 Selected Provision of the Federal Courts Improvements Act of 2000	877
	A.4.9 Selected Provisions of the Bankruptcy Abuse Prevention and Consumer Protection Act of 2005	877

Appendix B — Federal Rules of Bankruptcy Procedure ... 883

Appendix C — Bankruptcy Regulations, Fees, and Agency Notices

- C.1 Final Rule on Credit Counseling Agencies, 28 C.F.R. Part 58 ... 957
- C.2 Debtor Audits ... 963
  - C.2.1 Debtor Audit Standards, 71 Fed. Reg. 58,005 (Oct. 2, 2006) ... 963
  - C.2.2 Information on Debtor Audits ... 964
  - C.2.3 Debtor Audit Document Request Form ... 964
- C.3 Miscellaneous Fees ... 966
- C.4 Electronic Public Access Fee Schedule ... 968

Appendix D — Official Bankruptcy Forms with Annotated Samples

- D.1 How to Complete the Official Bankruptcy Forms ... 969
  - D.1.1 Introduction ... 969
  - D.1.2 The Initial Forms ... 969
  - D.1.3 Permitted Alterations to the Official Forms ... 969
  - D.1.4 Electronic Case Filing (ECF) ... 970
    - D.1.4.1 Overview ... 970
    - D.1.4.2 Converting Documents to PDF Format ... 971
- D.2 Annotated and Completed Bankruptcy Forms to Institute a Case ... 971
- D.3 Other Official Bankruptcy Forms Filed Later in the Case ... 1064

Appendix E — Director's Procedural Forms

- E.1 Introduction ... 1116
- E.2 Notice to Individual Consumer Debtor Under § 342(b) of the Bankruptcy Code ... 1118
- E.3 Statement of Attorney Compensation Under Bankruptcy Rule 2016(b) ... 1120
- E.4 Disclosure of Compensation of Attorney for Debtor ... 1121
- E.5 Adversary Proceeding Cover Sheet ... 1123
- E.6 Summons ... 1125
  - E.6.1 Summons and Notice of Trial in an Adversary Proceeding ... 1125
  - E.6.2 Summons in an Adversary Proceeding ... 1127
  - E.6.3 Third-Party Summons ... 1129
- E.7 Subpoenas ... 1131
  - E.7.1 Subpoena for Rule 2004 Examination ... 1131
  - E.7.2 Subpoena in an Adversary Proceeding ... 1133
  - E.7.3 Subpoena in a Case Under the Bankruptcy Code ... 1135
- E.8 Discharge Orders ... 1137
  - E.8.1 Order Discharging Joint Debtors in Chapter 7 Case ... 1137

Contents

E.8.2 Order Discharging One Joint Debtor in Chapter 7 Case	1139
E.8.3 Order Discharging Debtor After Completion of Chapter 13 Plan	1141
E.8.4 Order Discharging Debtor Before Completion of Chapter 13 Plan	1143
E.8.5 Order Discharging Debtor After Completion of Chapter 12 Plan	1145
E.8.6 Order Discharging Debtor Before Completion of Chapter 12 Plan	1147
E.9 Disclosure of Compensation of Bankruptcy Petition Preparer	1149
E.10 Reaffirmation Agreement	1150
E.11 Appearance of Child Support Creditor or Representative	1159
E.12 Statement of Military Service	1170
E.13 Required Lists, Schedules, Statements and Fees	1171
E.14 Chapter 13 Debtor's Certifications Regarding Domestic Support Obligations and Section 522(g)	1175

Appendix F — Bankruptcy Questionnaire ... 1177

Appendix G — Sample Bankruptcy Pleadings and Other Forms

G.1 Introduction	1201
G.2 Pre-Filing Forms	1204
G.3 Initial Forms	1208
G.4 Automatic Stay	1230
G.5 Turnover of Property	1242
G.6 Utilities	1244
G.7 Steps After Filing	1246
G.8 Claims	1254
G.9 Exemptions and Lien Avoidance	1269
G.10 Litigation	1276
G.11 Privacy Protection	1290
G.12 Discharge and Reaffirmation	1291
G.13 Conversion, Dismissal, and Modification of Plan After Confirmation	1311
G.14 Consumers As Creditors	1318
G.15 Family Farmer Reorganization	1324

Appendix H — Practice Aids

H.1 Date Calculator	1331
H.2 Obtaining Tax Returns or Transcripts from the Internal Revenue Service	1332
H.3 Interim Guidance Regarding Tax Information	1346
H.4 Helpful Resources from the United States Trustee Program	1347
H.5 Best Practices for Consumer Bankruptcy Cases (including Commentary)	1347
H.6 Interim Procedures Regarding the Chapter 7 Fee Waiver Provisions	1350
H.7 Best Practices for Document Production Requests by Trustees in Consumer Bankruptcy Cases	1351

Appendix I — Means Test Data

I.1 Median Income by State	1355
I.2 Internal Revenue Service Standards As to Allowable Expenses	1357
I.2.1 Internal Revenue Manual (IRM) Provisions Regarding Allowable Expenses	1357
I.2.2 National Standards for Allowable Living Expenses	1368
I.2.3 Local Housing and Utilities Expense Standards	1369
I.2.4 Local Transportation Expense Standards	1370
I.2.5 Out-of-Pocket Health Care Expense Standard	1375
I.2.6 Administrative Expenses Multipliers	1375

Consumer Bankruptcy Law and Practice

Appendix J	Summaries of State Exemption Laws............................	1377

Appendix K	Bankruptcy Client Handouts

K.1 Introduction... 1413
K.2 Answers to Common Bankruptcy Questions 1414
K.3 Your Legal Rights During and After Bankruptcy: Making the Most of Your Bankruptcy Discharge.. 1419
K.4 Using Credit Wisely After Bankruptcy................................. 1422

Appendix L	Helpful Websites..	1427

Appendix M	Finding Pleadings and Primary Sources on the Companion Website

M.1 Introduction 1429
M.2 Pleadings and Primary Sources Found on the Companion Website............ 1429
M.3 How to Access the Website... 1430
M.4 Locating Documents on the Website.................................... 1431
M.5 How to Use the Documents, Find Microsoft Word Versions, and Locate Additional Features 1434
M.6 Electronic Searches of This and Other NCLC Titles' Chapters 1434
M.7 Finding Additional Pleadings... 1434

Chapter 1 About This Treatise

1.1 Bankruptcy As a Remedy for Consumer Debtors

1.1.1 Overview

The past thirty years have seen an explosive increase in the already easy availability of consumer credit in the United States.[1] The significantly higher debt loads carried by more and more American consumers, particularly those of low and moderate income, render them and their families vulnerable to enormous financial difficulties when they suffer income interruptions.[2] Exorbitant interest rates and fees that quickly accumulate upon a default have left more families than ever vulnerable to a financial death spiral when they experience even a short term drop in income or an emergency expense that disrupts their debt payments. Aggressive creditors regularly threaten to throw debtors' lives into chaos, through foreclosures, repossessions, levies, executions, garnishments, collection harassment, and utility shut-offs.

In many cases bankruptcy is the only option that will bring order, rational planning and permanent or at least temporary relief to people who are under immense financial pressure. Bankruptcy provides an effective means of leveling the playing field between debtors and creditors, and it can profoundly improve the well-being of individuals and families.

It should come as no surprise, then, that approximately one and one-half million families file consumer bankruptcy cases each year.[3] As credit expands and bankruptcy becomes increasingly central to our economic and legal systems, ever larger numbers of consumers and businesses seek bankruptcy relief. Bankruptcy gives them an opportunity to reorder their finances and obtain a fresh start. Although the 2005 bankruptcy legislation enacted by Congress made bankruptcy more cumbersome, more costly and, in some cases, less effective, it did not change the stark economic realities that drive people to file bankruptcy cases. Consumers continue to need bankruptcy relief and will continue to seek it in large numbers.

It has become impossible to ignore bankruptcy. Not only is bankruptcy an important option to offer a client with financial difficulties, but it also frequently affects individuals and corporations with whom a client may be involved through employment, marriage, a tenancy, a consumer relationship, or as party to a lawsuit. Bankruptcy can eliminate both long and short term debts, with a minimum of effort in many cases, and can upset the firmest of expectations about consumer, landlord-tenant, and even marital relationships. Large municipal governments, like Orange County, California, have filed bankruptcy cases with potentially significant implications for all residents.

As the importance of bankruptcy increases, so does the need for low and moderate income clients to have access to the bankruptcy system. Unfortunately, though, because of high filing and attorney fees, it is those with low and moderate incomes who have had the least access to bankruptcy and will have an even more difficult time due to the 2005 bankruptcy amendments. This book is intended to serve as a guide for those interested in providing high quality bankruptcy representation to consumers, particularly for those serving consumers with low and moderate incomes.

1.1.2 The Bankruptcy Reform Act and Subsequent Amendments

1.1.2.1 Passage of the Bankruptcy Reform Act

On October 1, 1979, a new and far-reaching consumer protection law went into effect.[4] That law, the federal Bankruptcy Code,[5] may well be the most important federal legislation ever passed, in terms of its benefits for consumers. From its

---

1 See Lawrence M. Ausubel, *Credit Card Defaults, Credit Card Profits and Bankruptcy*, 71 Am. Bankr. L.J. 249 (1997).

2 See Elizabeth Warren & Amelia Warren Tyagi, The Two-Income Trap: Why Middle Class Mothers & Fathers are Going Broke (2003); Teresa A. Sullivan, Elizabeth Warren & Jay Lawrence Westbrook, The Fragile Middle Class: Americans in Debt (2000).

3 After the effective date of the 2005 amendments to the Bankruptcy Code, the number of bankruptcy cases filed fell precipitously. The number of filings has since increased to pre-2005 levels, even though those amendments raised serious barriers to access through burdensome and costly new requirements.

4 The effective dates of different portions of the Bankruptcy Reform Act, Pub. L. No. 95-598, 92 Stat. 2549 (1978) are established by section 402 of that Act, as amended by the 1984 amendments. The Bankruptcy Reform Act of 1978 as a whole consisted of four titles. Title 1 enacted a new title 11 of the United States Code, the Bankruptcy Code, which went into effect on October 1, 1979. Title II contained amendments to title 28 of the United States Code. Title III contained amendments to other acts and title IV contained transitional provisions.

5 The new title 11 is commonly referred to as the Bankruptcy Code, in contrast to the prior law, which was known as the Bankruptcy Act. In this treatise that distinction will be maintained: "the Code" will refer to the law now in effect, and "the Bankruptcy Act" will refer to prior law.

§ 1.1.2.2   *Consumer Bankruptcy Law and Practice*

first years, the Code has demonstrated its enormous potential as an area for creative advocacy on behalf of low and moderate income people, as well as its utility as a source of quick, concrete, and far-reaching relief in the day-to-day circumstances of financially troubled individuals. The burgeoning number of bankruptcies was matched by a tidal wave of interpretive case law.

1.1.2.2 Consumer Bankruptcy Amendments of 1984

The significant benefits of the Bankruptcy Code for consumer debtors were noted early on by creditors as well. Within a year after the Code's effective date, the consumer credit industry mounted a drive to drastically cut back on the relief obtainable in bankruptcy and, in some ways, to tilt the law in creditors' favor even more than it had been under the prior Bankruptcy Act.

Despite an intense lobbying and public relations campaign, the credit industry's efforts were largely rebuffed. Congress did pass, in the Bankruptcy Amendments and Federal Judgeship Act of 1984,[6] a package of consumer bankruptcy amendments. But those amendments were mere shadows of the creditors' original proposals, narrowly tailored to meet the few abuses of the Code that might actually be occurring.[7]

While they did have important effects, usually detrimental, in the cases of a minority of debtors, the 1984 amendments did not alter the basic rights of consumers to bankruptcy relief. Indeed, in several ways the 1984 amendments clarified and strengthened consumer rights.[8] Their net effect in most cases was probably a slight increase in the paperwork required and nothing more. Hence, the importance of bankruptcy law to low and moderate income consumers, and the opportunities for its development on their behalf, continued unabated.

1.1.2.3 Bankruptcy Judges, United States Trustees, and Family Farmer Bankruptcy Act of 1986

In 1986, Congress again made substantial changes in the Bankruptcy Code, passing the Bankruptcy Judges, United States Trustees, and Family Farmer Bankruptcy Act of 1986.[9] Besides adding a substantial number of new bankruptcy judgeships in many judicial districts, the 1986 Act made the many changes necessary to institute a phased-in United States trustee system to handle many administrative functions formerly handled by the court. It also created a new chapter 12 of the Bankruptcy Code especially tailored to meet the needs of family farmers in financial distress in ways that neither chapter 11 nor chapter 13 could offer.[10] Chapter 12 is discussed at length in Chapter 17, *infra*. The 1986 amendments also made a number of other changes, mostly minor, affecting consumer bankruptcies. The most significant of these changes was the elimination of a mandatory discharge hearing in most cases.[11]

1.1.2.4 The Bankruptcy Reform Act of 1994

In the waning hours of the 103d Congress, lawmakers addressed bankruptcy once more, passing the Bankruptcy Reform Act of 1994.[12] That Act, the culmination of four years of legislative efforts, made changes to numerous parts of the Bankruptcy Code, more changes than any legislation since the original enactment of the Bankruptcy Reform Act of 1978. In addition, after substantially amending the Code, Congress created a National Bankruptcy Review Commission to study whether further changes should be made.[13] The Commission issued its report on October 20, 1997.[14] The report recommended a variety of controversial changes to the provisions of the Code governing consumer bankruptcy cases, but these recommendations were almost totally ignored by Congress.[15]

Among the many changes made by the 1994 Act in the area of consumer bankruptcy were some which benefited consumers and some which were detrimental to them. On the positive side, the amounts of the federal exemptions under Code section 522(d), as well as most other dollar amounts in the Code, were doubled, and a mechanism was built into the Code for automatic cost-of-living adjustments in the future.[16] The dollar limits for chapter 13 eligibility were also substantially increased, with similar adjustments to be made in the future.[17] The fifth of these adjustments became effective on April 1, 2010, and the adjusted numbers are used throughout this treatise. Future adjustments will be reflected in the annual supplements to this treatise.

---

6   Pub. L. No. 98-353, 98 Stat. 333 (1984).
7   For a short review of the 1984 amendments specifically directed at consumer bankruptcies, see Henry J. Sommer, *Consumer Bankruptcy Amendments of 1984*, 31 Prac. Law 45 (Jan. 1985).
8   See, for example, 11 U.S.C. § 525(b), prohibiting discrimination by private employers, discussed in Chapter 15, *infra*.
9   Pub. L. No. 99-554, 100 Stat. 3088 (1986).
10 Chapter 12 of the Bankruptcy Code was originally a temporary measure, which expired and was renewed numerous times. It was made permanent, and amended to include family fishermen, by the 2005 amendments. See § 17.1.1.1, *infra*.
11 11 U.S.C. § 524, as amended in 1986, made the discharge hearing discretionary with the court unless the debtor intends to reaffirm a debt. See § 8.8, *infra*.
12 Pub. L. No. 103-394, 108 Stat. 4106 (generally effective with respect to cases filed on or after October 22, 1994). The bill's provisions dealing with the effective date of the amendments are reprinted in Appendix A.4.6, *infra*. The amendments themselves have been integrated into the revised Bankruptcy Code reprinted in Appendix A.1, *infra*.
13 Bankruptcy Reform Act of 1994, Pub. L. No. 103-394, tit. VI, 108 Stat. 4106.
14 Nat'l Bankruptcy Review Comm'n, Bankruptcy: The Next Twenty Years, Final Report (Oct. 20, 1997), *available at* http://govinfo.library.unt.edu/nbrc/reporttitlepg.html.
15 For a discussion of the Review Commission's recommendations, see Gary Klein, *Consumer Bankruptcy in the Balance: the National Bankruptcy Review Commission's Recommendations Tilt Toward Creditors*, 5 Am. Bankr. Inst. L. Rev. 293 (1997).
16 11 U.S.C. §§ 104, 522(d) (as amended by the Bankruptcy Reform Act of 1994, Pub. L. No. 103-394, 108 Stat. 4106). See § 10.2.2, *infra*.
17 11 U.S.C. §§ 104, 109(e) (as amended by the Bankruptcy Reform Act of 1994, Pub. L. No. 103-394, 108 Stat 4106). See § 12.2.3, *infra*.

In addition, the 1994 amendments overruled (but only for future mortgages) the Supreme Court's misguided decision in *Rake v. Wade*,[18] which had required debtors curing mortgage arrears to pay thousands of dollars of additional interest, and reinstated the law most circuits had followed before that decision.[19] Congress also partially overruled the Court's decision in *Nobelman v. American Savings Bank*,[20] which had prohibited the stripping down of many mortgage liens in chapter 13, by creating additional categories of mortgages which could be modified.[21]

The 1994 amendments also clarified the law in areas in which there had been conflicting court decisions, such as those concerning when a debtor loses the right to cure a default on a mortgage,[22] how to determine whether a lien impairs an exemption,[23] how to determine property of the estate when a case is converted from chapter 13 to chapter 7,[24] whether a late-filed claim should be allowed,[25] whether a student loan grantor can discriminate against a debtor based on a bankruptcy filing or a discharged debt,[26] and whether condominium and cooperative fees are dischargeable.[27]

Unfortunately, the amendments contained a number of provisions detrimental to consumers as well, including a weakening of the protections with respect to reaffirmation,[28] several new exceptions to discharge, including an additional exception to the chapter 13 discharge,[29] and procedural changes that have increased the time and costs necessary to process consumer bankruptcy cases.[30]

Finally, the many other changes made by the amendments included a broad abrogation of sovereign immunity, intended to reverse the result in two harmful Supreme Court cases which had limited the Code's original waiver of sovereign immunity,[31] a package of amendments intended to strengthen the rights of a debtor's dependent spouse, former spouse, or children to receive alimony, maintenance, support and, in some cases, property settlements,[32] tough new provisions to regulate non-attorney bankruptcy petition preparers,[33] and procedural provisions concerning jury trials[34] and appeals.[35]

1.1.2.5 The 2005 Bankruptcy Amendments

On April 20, 2005, the President signed the "Bankruptcy Abuse Prevention and Consumer Protection Act of 2005" (the 2005 Act).[36] The Act, 512 pages in length, made significant changes to the Bankruptcy Code and other bankruptcy statutes, and affects nearly every aspect of bankruptcy cases. The Act in general took effect on October 17, 2005. Several provisions, however, became effective upon enactment, while other provisions had individualized effective dates.[37]

From its Orwellian title (the Act is clearly *not* a "Consumer Protection Act") to the last of its 512 pages, the 2005 Act presents numerous challenges to attorneys who represent consumer debtors. How such terrible legislation could be passed by Congress is a story of money, political mean-spiritedness, and intellectual dishonesty, as detailed in a number of media and law review articles.[38]

The changes made by the 2005 legislation are too numerous even to summarize here; they are described throughout this treatise. They affected, to some degree, most aspects of consumer bankruptcy, in almost every instance reducing consum-

---

18 508 U.S. 464, 113 S. Ct. 2187, 124 L. Ed. 2d 424 (1993).
19 11 U.S.C. § 1322(e) (as enacted by the Bankruptcy Reform Act of 1994, Pub. L. No. 103-394, 108 Stat. 4106). See § 11.6.2.7, *infra*.
20 508 U.S. 324, 113 S. Ct. 2106, 124 L. Ed. 2d 228 (1993).
21 11 U.S.C. § 1322(c)(2) (as enacted by the Bankruptcy Reform Act of 1994, Pub. L. No. 103-394, 108 Stat. 4106). See § 11.6.1.2, *infra*.
22 11 U.S.C. § 1322(c)(1) (as enacted by the Bankruptcy Reform Act of 1994, Pub. L. No. 103-394, 108 Stat. 4106). See § 11.6.2.2, *infra*.
23 11 U.S.C. § 522(f)(2) (as enacted by the Bankruptcy Reform Act of 1994, Pub. L. No. 103-394, 108 Stat. 4106). See §§ 10.4.2.2, 10.4.2.3, *infra*.
24 11 U.S.C. § 348(f) (as enacted by the Bankruptcy Reform Act of 1994, Pub. L. No. 103-394, 108 Stat. 4106) (this change was partially reversed by the 2005 amendments). See § 4.7.4, *infra*.
25 11 U.S.C. § 502(b)(9) (as enacted by the Bankruptcy Reform Act of 1994, Pub. L. No. 103-394, 108 Stat. 4106). See § 14.4.3, *infra*.
26 11 U.S.C. § 525(c) (as enacted by the Bankruptcy Reform Act of 1994, Pub. L. No. 103-394, 108 Stat. 4106). See § 15.5.5.2, *infra*.
27 11 U.S.C. § 523(a)(16) (as enacted by the Bankruptcy Reform Act of 1994, Pub. L. No. 103-394, 108 Stat. 4106) (this section was further amended by the 2005 amendments). See § 15.4.3.14, *infra*.
28 11 U.S.C. § 524(c), (d) (as amended by the Bankruptcy Reform Act of 1994, Pub. L. No. 103-394, 108 Stat. 4106) (the reaffirmation provisions were further revised by the 2005 amendments). See § 15.5.2, *infra*.
29 11 U.S.C. §§ 523(a)(14)–(16), 1328(a) (as enacted and amended by the Bankruptcy Reform Act of 1994, Pub. L. No. 103-394, 108 Stat. 4106). See §§ 15.4.1, 15.4.3.12–15.4.3.14, *infra*.
30 11 U.S.C. §§ 341(d), 342(c) (as enacted or amended by the Bankruptcy Reform Act of 1994, Pub. L. No. 103-394, 108 Stat. 4106); Fed. R. Bankr. P. 7004. See §§ 1.4.2, 8.4.3, *infra*.

31 11 U.S.C. § 106 (as amended by the Bankruptcy Reform Act of 1994, Pub. L. No. 103-394, 108 Stat 4106) (effective with respect to cases pending on or after October 22, 1994) (overruling Hoffman v. Connecticut Dep't of Income Maint., 492 U.S. 96, 109 S. Ct. 2818, 106 L. Ed. 2d 76 (1989) and United States v. Nordic Vill., 503 U.S. 30, 112 S. Ct. 1011, 117 L. Ed. 2d 181 (1992)). See § 14.3.2.2, *infra*. However, some of the 1994 amendments have been found to be unconstitutional. See § 14.3.2.2, *infra*.
32 11 U.S.C. §§ 362(b)(2), 507(a)(7), 522(f)(1), 523(a)(15), and 547(c)(7) (as amended or enacted by the Bankruptcy Reform Act of 1994, Pub. L. No. 103-394, 108 Stat. 4106) (these sections were further amended by the 2005 amendments). See §§ 3.5, 9.4.6.3, 10.4.2.3, 10.4.2.6.4, 15.4.3.13, *infra*.
33 11 U.S.C. § 110 (as enacted by the Bankruptcy Reform Act of 1994, Pub. L. No. 103-394, 108 Stat. 4106) (this section was further amended by the 2005 amendments). See § 16.6, *infra*.
34 28 U.S.C. § 157(e) (as enacted by the Bankruptcy Reform Act of 1994, Pub. L. No. 103-394, 108 Stat. 4106). See § 14.2.7, *infra*.
35 28 U.S.C. §§ 158, 1334(c)(2) (as amended by the Bankruptcy Reform Act of 1994, Pub. L. No. 103-394, 108 Stat. 4106). See §§ 2.4.3, 14.9.1, *infra*.
36 Pub. L. No. 109-8, 119 Stat. 23 (2005).
37 Most of the provisions affecting consumer bankruptcies took effect on or after October 17, 2005, except for several of the exemption changes discussed in Chapter 10, *infra*, which went into effect on April 20, 2005. Provisions concerning audits of certain debtors' cases became effective October 20, 2006.
38 See Henry J. Sommer, *Causes of the Consumer Bankruptcy Explosion: Debtor Abuse or Easy Credit?*, 27 Hofstra L. Rev. 33 (1998) for some earlier views on this subject.

ers' rights. Although substantial relief continues to be available to debtors, the amendments made it almost always more expensive and more cumbersome. The 2005 amendments did make chapter 12 a permanent part of the Bankruptcy Code and extended it to family fishermen.[39] They also enacted a new chapter 15 of the Code to deal with international bankruptcies.

There is no doubt that bankruptcy relief has become more expensive for almost all debtors,[40] less effective for many debtors, and totally inaccessible for some debtors as a result of the new law. At the same time, a minority of debtors, often the higher-income individuals whose "abuses" of bankruptcy the Act was ostensibly aimed at, have found themselves better off than before because of generous new exemptions for retirement and education savings accounts and a means test which can be turned to the debtor's advantage, in both chapters 7 and 13, by the careful planning that only higher income debtors can afford to do.

One of the chief problems that practitioners have confronted is atrocious drafting, especially in many of the consumer provisions of the Act. In contrast to the 1978 legislation, which was crafted with extensive assistance from many of the finest minds in the bankruptcy world, the consumer provisions of the 2005 legislation were largely drafted by lobbyists with little knowledge of real-life consumer bankruptcy practice.[41] It is perhaps a credit to the bankruptcy bar that no true expert in bankruptcy participated in drafting the consumer provisions sought by the financial services industry; apparently the industry did not trust any experienced bankruptcy attorneys, even creditor attorneys, to carry out its mission of defacing the Code. Or perhaps it is just an indication of the arrogance of the Act's drafters, who throughout the legislative process steadfastly resisted even the smallest technical corrections to their handiwork.

The silver lining is that the Act is so poorly drafted that it did not accomplish much of what its financial backers wanted it to accomplish. It has been interesting to see courts that have been instructed to strictly follow the plain language of the statute adhere to that rule in interpreting the new provisions, leaving it to Congress to fix any mistakes.[42] Of course, some judges who profess to follow that method of statutory interpretation seem to do so only when it brings about the result they desire.[43]

Another redeeming fact is that the amendments are not interpreted or implemented by those who wrote them, but rather by judges, trustees, United States trustees, and attorneys for both debtors and creditors, individuals who want to see the bankruptcy system work and serve its intended purposes, not come to a grinding halt. Some provisions have been largely ignored due to their sheer silliness. Amended section 342(b)(1) of the Bankruptcy Code requires the clerk to give the debtor a notice[44] that another provision, new section 527(a)(1), seems to require others to give to the debtor.[45]

It is no secret that the Act's proponents sought to limit the discretion of bankruptcy judges who, they said, are "not real judges."[46] However, despite such efforts, there are many areas in which judicial discretion remains. In addition, one should never underestimate the inertia of local legal culture. After all, there still remain many districts where courts "require" chapter 13 plans to pay a minimum percentage to unsecured creditors, despite statutory amendments over twenty-five years ago and numerous appellate decisions making clear that the Code contains no such requirement.

There is no question that the provisions of the Bankruptcy Code have been changed in many significant respects. There is also no question that many debtors, especially those priced out of bankruptcy relief due to increased costs, will be adversely affected by those changes. And there is no question that some debtors will have to pay more to some creditors. However, debtors and creditors alike have found that some of the supposedly pro-creditor changes in the Code can benefit some consumer debtors, that the credit industry did not accomplish all that it may have thought it did, and that practices have not changed nearly as extensively as many people anticipated. As judges, attorneys, and trustees have worked together to try to make sense out of some of the bizarre language enacted by Congress, consumer bankruptcy has remained a lifeline, albeit a bit frayed, for most of the millions of families who so desperately need it.

1.1.2.6 Other Amendments to the Code

Over the years, Congress has occasionally made other amendments to the Bankruptcy Code, usually tucked away in appropriations bills that received little scrutiny. Some of these amendments, for example, have greatly limited the dischargeability of student loans,[47] family support obligations owed to governmental units,[48] and criminal restitution.[49] Despite much talk about a

---

39 See § 17.1.1.1, infra.
40 See Lupica, Lois R., The Consumer Bankruptcy Fee Study: Final Report (Dec. 1, 2011), available at http://ssrn.com/abstract=2132913.
41 See Rehfeld, Top Creditor Lobbyist Tassey Goes for Broke, The Am. Banker, May 17, 2001, at 1 (lobbyist-produced report became framework for bill); McAllister, Reopening Chapter 7, Wash. Post, Jan. 1, 1998, at A23 (early version of bankruptcy bill was "similar" to bill drafted by George J. Wallace for American Financial Services Association).
42 See Lamie v. United States Tr., 540 U.S. 526, 124 S. Ct. 1023, 157 L. Ed. 2d 1024 (2004).
43 See BFP v. Resolution Trust Corp., 511 U.S. 531, 549, 114 S. Ct. 1757, 128 L. Ed. 2d 556 (1994) (Souter, J. dissenting) (rejecting the holding of the majority opinion written by Justice Scalia that

"value" means foreclosure sale price is as easy as plain language interpretation is likely to get).
44 A similar provision in existing section 342(b), requiring the clerk to give a notice to debtors (who rarely appear at the clerk's office) before the case is filed, is widely ignored.
45 See § 16.8.3.1, infra.
46 Peter G. Gosselin, Judges Say Overhaul Would Weaken Bankruptcy System, L.A. Times, Mar. 29, 2005, at A1 (quoting creditor lobbyist Jeff Tassey).
47 See § 15.4.3.8, infra.
48 See § 15.4.3.5.2, infra.
49 See § 15.4.3.7, infra.

bankruptcy overhaul in 1998, largely instigated by a consumer credit industry media and lobbying campaign,[50] only one set of changes to the Bankruptcy Code actually became law in the first few years after the report of the National Bankruptcy Review Commission. This was the Religious Liberty and Charitable Donation Protection Act of 1998.[51] The amendments made by this Act protect bona fide and reasonable religious and charitable contributions[52] from being attacked and recovered from the donee as fraudulent transfers.[53] In addition, the amendments permit debtors to continue to make such contributions after bankruptcy in cases filed under chapter 7 and chapter 13.[54]

Since the passage of the 2005 legislation, there have been only minor changes to the Code. After at least one court had ruled that the disposable income test, as amended in 2005, did not permit some debtors to make religious and charitable contributions,[55] Congress quickly amended section 1325(b) to permit such expenses for all chapter 13 debtors.[56] Several other amendments, not affecting consumer cases, were made at the behest of the bond industry.[57] Congress also twice amended section 1930 of title 28, raising bankruptcy filing fees to their current levels.[58] Congress passed limited exclusions from the chapter 7 means test for certain members of the armed forces in 2008.[59] In 2009, Congress changed several time periods in several sections of the Code to conform to time period changes being made in the Bankruptcy Rules.[60] And in 2010, Congress passed The Bankruptcy Technical Corrections Act of 2010.[61] That legislation made changes in the 2005 bankruptcy amendments that were almost entirely technical corrections to drafting errors.

1.1.3 Bankruptcy's Past As Neglected Remedy

Despite its potential importance to consumer clients, the use of bankruptcy law is avoided by some attorneys. These practitioners see bankruptcy as an intimidating maze of paperwork in an unfamiliar and sometimes (for rural offices) inconvenient forum. And, perhaps, a touch of the old-time stigma still remains from the early days of consumer debtor representation, which saw bankruptcy as a lazy cop-out, either for client or lawyer, if not just a bit immoral.

In legal services offices, the disfavored status of bankruptcy has sometimes been officially announced as a principle of office priorities, bankruptcy being a matter which could be left to the private attorneys who traditionally handled bankruptcies in their community. More troubling, though, is the narrow view of bankruptcy which such policies evince—bankruptcy only as an easy way out for judgment-proof debtors.

Offices which have excluded bankruptcy from their practice have excluded a remedy which often can be used to better or more easily deal with those problems which they traditionally handle in other ways. To say "we don't do bankruptcies" is basically not much different than saying "we don't file complaints." In many cases bankruptcy is the best way to prevent loss of housing, utility service, income, a car or driver's license necessary to maintain or gain employment, or even freedom, as imprisonment may result from failure to comply with orders to pay support or other indebtedness.[62] Bankruptcy has certainly provided millions of people with relief from the incessant collection calls, letters, and other harassment tactics that accompany unpaid debts. Yet, presumably, the clients of some attorneys do not have that remedy available to them.

1.1.4 Making Bankruptcy Available to Consumer Clients

It is incumbent upon those who represent financially troubled clients to have a basic knowledge of what can be accomplished through the use of bankruptcy. Not only may such knowledge save a client thousands of dollars, a home, a car, or a job, but it may accomplish these desired results better, faster, and with less expenditure of attorney and client resources than any other means. The bankruptcy court may be a more favorable forum for the raising of affirmative claims and may dispose of them more quickly. Moreover, it may be malpractice not to make available to clients the powerful tools available in bankruptcy for solving their problems.

Probably even more important is the impact of bankruptcy practice on creditor behavior in a particular community. The use of bankruptcy when appropriate often makes a lasting impression, and the ever-present threat of bankruptcy in subsequent cases causes many creditors to become a lot more

---

50 See § 1.4.4.1, infra.
51 Pub. L. No. 105-183, 112 Stat. 517. The amendments made by this Act affect cases pending on or after the date of the Act (June 19, 1998).
52 The contributions must be made to a qualified donee under the Internal Revenue Code. The amount may not exceed fifteen percent of the debtor's gross income unless a larger contribution is consistent with the debtor's past pattern of contributions.
53 Protections from avoidance have been added to both 11 U.S.C. §§ 544 and 548. The law overrules cases such as In re Newman, 203 B.R. 468 (D. Kan. 1996) and In re Gomes, 219 B.R. 286 (Bankr. D. Or. 1998) which had found charitable contributions to be constructive fraudulent transfers within the meaning of the Bankruptcy Code. See §§ 10.4.2.6.2, 10.4.2.6.5, infra.
54 See §§ 12.3.3, 13.4, infra.
55 In re Diagostino, 347 B.R. 116 (Bankr. N.D.N.Y. 2006).
56 Religious Liberty and Charitable Donation Clarification Act of 2006, Pub. L. No. 109-439, 120 Stat. 3285.
57 Pub. L. No. 109-390, 120 Stat. 2692 (2006).
58 Pub. L. No. 109-13, § 325, 119 Stat. 231 (2005); Pub. L. No. 109-171, § 10101, 120 Stat. 4 (2006).
    See §§ 3.2.2, 4.2.2, infra, for further discussion of filing fees.
59 Pub. L. No. 110-438, 122 Stat. 5000 (2008). These provisions were extended until December 19, 2015, by Pub. L. No. 112-64 (2011). See § 13.4.4, infra.
60 Pub. L. No. 111-16, 123 Stat. 1607 (2009).
61 Pub. Law No. 111-327 (2010).

---

62 Such debt-related imprisonment still exists in some places. See, e.g., Judice v. Vail, 430 U.S. 327, 97 S. Ct. 1211, 51 L. Ed. 2d 376 (1977). Moreover, virtually every state imposes imprisonment for failure to pay child or spousal support.

reasonable than they were before in settling cases and in dealing with their customers. Practitioners have sometimes found regular and skillful use of bankruptcy remedies to have greater deterrent effect than a dozen class actions. The creditor facing an attorney known for filing class actions usually is of the firm belief that it has little to worry about because it firmly believes all of its practices are legal (at least in the particular case involved). But the creditor facing an attorney known to be well-versed in bankruptcy will know, or soon learn, that it stands to lose money in almost every case the bankruptcy attorney handles and that every case is one in which it can be forced to be reasonable, if indeed bankruptcy leaves any claim to be reasonable about.

Of course, bankruptcy is not always the preferable remedy and consumer attorneys should not hesitate to bring class actions whenever appropriate. The well-rounded advocate should know how to use all kinds of remedies, often in conjunction with each other, as tools to effect clients' objectives.

1.2 The Focus of This Treatise— Bankruptcy Practice for Consumer Debtors and Family Farmers

This treatise provides the basic information needed to best utilize the tools that bankruptcy provides to consumer debtors. Of necessity, most of what follows is also applicable to debtors who have had small businesses; many consumer clients are, after all, simply businesspeople who have fallen upon hard times and no longer operate their businesses. However, while this treatise may be of some use in cases in which debtors seek to continue operating their businesses, advocates will have to look elsewhere for assistance in handling the more complex problems which can arise in such an undertaking.

Chapter 17, *infra*, deals extensively with the issues and problems arising in the representation of family farmers and family fishermen under chapter 12 of the Bankruptcy Code. Although most of the concepts and strategies involved in such representation are similar to those applicable to chapter 13, there are a number of provisions and subjects which are either more akin to chapter 11 principles or unique to chapter 12.

Although this treatise is primarily oriented toward representing debtors, Chapter 18, *infra*, provides a basic outline for representing consumers as creditors: for example, when a merchant, landlord, lender, or other entity with whom an individual consumer is involved files bankruptcy. The treatment of this topic provided in Chapter 18, *infra*, is far from exhaustive, and anyone seeking to aggressively represent a creditor in the bankruptcy process is encouraged to utilize other resources.

Although this treatise contains a thorough discussion of those substantive issues which are most common and important, it is neither exhaustive nor comprehensive on all of bankruptcy law. In general, for the issues discussed, only a few leading cases, along with the applicable statutes and rules, are cited. Because it is now possible to find at least one bankruptcy court opinion taking almost any position on a given issue, lower court decisions contrary to the text of this treatise are not always noted. Appellate decisions normally are cited, however, whether or not they agree with the author. Again, for further research, the sources at the end of this Chapter and in the Bibliography should be consulted.

1.3 How to Use This Treatise

1.3.1 Purpose of the Treatise

This treatise is intended to serve as a basic resource to advocates, both attorneys and paralegals working with attorneys, handling bankruptcy cases. It is meant to provide an introduction for the novice considering her first bankruptcy case and also a useful tool for the expert who has handled many such cases. It should be serviceable both as a quick reference in offices with substantial libraries as well as a fairly complete basic resource in those offices which maintain only a minimal library immediately accessible.

Naturally, offices doing many bankruptcies will wish to purchase other comprehensive texts on the subject, as well as a subscription to at least one bankruptcy reporting service. Suggestions for these are listed at the end of this Chapter. Those offices may also wish to develop forms, checklists, and other materials tailored to their own particular needs, for use in addition to or instead of those in this treatise.

1.3.2 Organization of the Treatise

Volume 1 contains the text chapters, bibliography, and index, while Volume 2 contains the appendices. This treatise's companion website includes a search engine, over 170 pleadings and other forms from Appendix G, *infra*, additional bankruptcy forms, a client questionnaire (in English and Spanish), and client handouts. Many of the documents are available in both Adobe Acrobat (PDF) and Microsoft Word formats. The website also includes software to complete the initial forms and to compute look-back dates, PDF versions of all bankruptcy forms relevant to consumer cases, as well as the Code, other statutes, the Bankruptcy Rules, and many other practice aids.

To facilitate Volume 1's use by the various constituencies to which it is addressed, it is divided into several parts. Although there are frequent cross-references, each part has a different purpose.

The first part, consisting of the first four chapters, is intended to provide an introductory "nuts and bolts" understanding of how bankruptcy works. To keep these chapters relatively non-technical, they contain many references to later chapters for in-depth discussion of particular topics.

The next four chapters contain a step-by-step practice guide on how to handle a case from the moment that bankruptcy is first considered until events that occur after the case is over. Together, the first eight chapters should provide the reader with a basic knowledge of what happens in a typical consumer bankruptcy. The remaining chapters may then be consulted as necessary.

Chapters 9 through 16, *infra*, contain a more detailed discussion of the legal issues frequently arising in consumer bankruptcy cases. As these issues are so often present, those who practice regularly in bankruptcy courts should become knowledgeable in the areas covered by these chapters as well as the chapters preceding them.

Finally, Chapter 17, *infra*, contains a discussion of issues involved in representing family farmers and family fishermen in cases under chapter 12 of the Bankruptcy Code and Chapter 18, *infra*, addresses issues related to representing consumers as creditors when a merchant, landlord, or other entity is in bankruptcy.

Volume 2 consists of a set of appendices that contain basic bankruptcy reference materials. These materials have been substantially updated and revised for this Ninth Edition. They should be used in preference to older editions and supplements which no longer present accurate versions of current law. As new supplements are published, they should be consulted for the most current available materials. And because the supplements are published yearly, interim materials such as *NCLC REPORTS* should also be consulted. The companion website will also be updated throughout the year.

Appendix A, *infra*, reprints the text of the United States Bankruptcy Code[63] as well as selected provisions of other relevant statutes. Changes made by the 2005 amendments, as well as subsequent amendments, are included.[64] Appendix B, *infra*, reprints the Federal Rules of Bankruptcy Procedure as amended through December 2011. Appendix C, *infra*, contains a listing of bankruptcy filing fees and reprints the United States Judicial Conference's Bankruptcy Court Miscellaneous Fee Schedule.

Appendix D, *infra*, includes those Official Forms promulgated by the federal Judicial Conference which are generally relevant to consumer bankruptcy practice, as amended through December 2012. These forms are regularly changed, so it is important not to rely on old forms, including those reproduced in prior editions of this treatise. The forms required to institute a case are included as sample completed bankruptcy schedules illustrating how to prepare an initial filing. Many commonly occurring issues encountered in filling out the official forms are addressed. Other Official Forms are included in blank. To complete the forms, practitioners can use either a specialized bankruptcy document preparation program or the Adobe Acrobat (PDF) format fillable forms available for download on the website of the Administrative Office of the U.S. Courts.[65]

Appendix E, *infra*, contains some other reproducible forms which, though not "official," are in common use. Although they may be filed as is in most jurisdictions, local practice may impose different requirements. These may also be printed out from this treatise's companion website.

Appendix F, *infra*, is a sample bankruptcy interview form which can be filled out either by an advocate or by clients directly. It may need to be edited to accommodate local practice. The form is found on this treatise's companion website in both Adobe Acrobat (PDF) and Microsoft Word format, to facilitate adapting the interview form to individual needs. A Spanish version is also available on the companion website in both PDF and Word formats.

Appendix G, *infra*, contains more than 170 model pleadings and form letters for representing consumer debtors. The Appendix includes a number of new pleadings specially adapted to respond to the 2005 Bankruptcy Code changes, and also includes pleadings commonly used by consumers as creditors. These forms are intended to serve as a guide for addressing issues which commonly arise in consumer bankruptcy practice. A listing of these forms can be found both in the table of contents and at the beginning of Appendix G, *infra*. All these forms are available on this treatise's companion website, in both Adobe Acrobat (PDF) and Microsoft Word format, so that they can be edited for actual use.

Appendices H and I, *infra*, contain several useful practice aids. This treatise's companion website contains a "Date Calculator" that assists practitioners in computing the time periods for critical prepetition events that may affect the debtor's decision when to file a bankruptcy petition. Appendix H.1, *infra*, contains a sample of this calculator with a detailed description of the prepetition events. Appendix H, *infra*, also contains information and Internal Revenue Service (IRS) forms that can facilitate obtaining a client's tax returns or tax transcripts, which may have to be filed in a bankruptcy case. Again, the IRS forms are available on this treatise's companion website to facilitate printing them for actual use. Appendix I, *infra*, contains Census data, IRS standards, and other information that relates to the application of the means test mandated by sections 707(b)(2) and 1325(b)(3) of the Code.[66]

Appendix J, *infra*, is a summary of state exemption laws. The Appendix includes information to help determine the applicable exemption law in a bankruptcy proceeding based on the domiciliary provisions found in Code section 522(b)(3)(A).

Appendix K, *infra*, contains sample handouts for clients, which answer many common bankruptcy questions. These handouts are available on this treatise's companion website in Adobe Acrobat (PDF) format so that they can be printed out and distributed to clients, and also in Microsoft Word format, so that they can be edited for individual use.

Appendix L, *infra*, lists a number of official and unofficial websites which provide useful information for the bankruptcy practitioner. Another helpful resource is the bibliography of

---

[63] The full Code is reprinted with the exception of chapters 9 and 15 and subchapters III and IV of chapter 7, which are not relevant to consumers.

[64] A red-lined version of the Code showing the changes made by the 2005 amendments is available on this treatise's companion website.

[65] The Official Bankruptcy Forms are available at www.uscourts.gov/FormsAndFees/Forms/BankruptcyForms.aspx. Not all of the forms are available in a fillable PDF format.

[66] These figures are updated at various times each year, so it is important to check the current amounts at www.usdoj.gov/ust/eo/bapcpa/meanstesting.htm. Most commercial bankruptcy software programs are updated by their vendors when new figures are put into effect.

articles and books on consumer bankruptcy which precedes the appendices.

As stated above, these practice aids are included on this treatise's companion website, allowing rapid computer searches, editing of pleadings with word-processing software, and copying source materials directly into briefs. The companion website contains all the material found in *Consumer Bankruptcy Law and Practice*'s appendices, and much additional information as well. In particular, it contains software to complete bankruptcy look-back dates.

1.3.3 Web-Based Text Search Feature

NCLC offers a unique web-based text search feature for this and all its treatises. The search engine is located at www.nclc.org. Clicking on "Keyword Search" brings up a screen that allows the user to search for any term or phrase in NCLC's treatises. The search can be confined to a single treatise, or can extend to all NCLC's treatises. The search engine will indicate the pages in the treatise where the term or phrase appears, and display the text on both sides of the search term.

This function is not only the best way to locate the discussion of a particular topic, but is also an excellent way to find out where a particular case, statute, regulation, or rule is discussed in this or other NCLC treatises. The search instructions explain how to use wildcards in search terms, how to search for phrases, how to search for one term that is near another term, how to search for either of two terms, and how to search for one term that is not on the same page as another term.

1.3.4 Using This Treatise As a Research Tool

1.3.4.1 This Treatise Does Not Contain Citations to Every Relevant Case

The number of reported cases on consumer bankruptcy issues has far outstripped the space in this treatise to catalogue them. The text of the treatise discusses a wide variety of issues that may arise in consumer cases. The footnotes contain case law which will serve as a starting point for research. We have attempted, whenever possible, to include the relevant court of appeals decisions on the topics discussed as well as other cases which support the arguments a consumer may wish to make. However, do not expect to find all relevant cases on any topic or cases in each jurisdiction. Further research into case law is likely to be necessary.

This treatise identifies arguments which support the consumer position on most issues. For this reason, the footnotes contain many more cases which provide support for the consumer debtor than cases which support creditors. However, when there are court of appeals cases on both sides of an issue, we have attempted to be inclusive.

Because many bankruptcy issues overlap more than one bankruptcy topic, this book contains many cross references. Careful attention to the cross references will often yield additional relevant case law. Other valuable research tools are discussed at the end of this Chapter.

1.3.4.2 NCLC Case Consulting and Other NCLC Treatises

Consumer law questions on issues other than bankruptcy often arise in the context of a bankruptcy case. For example, bankruptcy clients are often the victims of debt collection abuses and may have causes of action to remedy those abuses. Similarly, creditor overcharges can often result in overstated claims. Many of these issues are covered at length in other books in this NCLC series. The *Consumer Credit and Sales Legal Practice Series* contains books on, for example, fair debt collection, fair credit reporting, foreclosures, repossessions, the cost of credit, truth in lending, access to utility service, student loans, arbitration agreements, unfair and deceptive practices, and automobile fraud, which are as exhaustive as this treatment of bankruptcy.

NCLC also publishes a guide for attorneys just starting out in bankruptcy, *Bankruptcy Basics: A Step-by-Step Guide for Pro Bono Attorneys, General Practitioners, and Legal Services Offices*. It is intended as a companion to this treatise to assist attorneys in handling their first bankruptcy cases.

In addition, NCLC has established a low-cost case consulting service. NCLC can provide additional research, pleadings, briefs, or other litigation support on a wide variety of consumer issues. More information about this service is available on a card in the front of this treatise or by calling (617) 542-8010.

1.4 The Governing Law

1.4.1 Statutory Materials

1.4.1.1 The Bankruptcy Code

The most important source of law in bankruptcy cases is, of course, the statute itself. The Bankruptcy Code, which is title 11 of the United States Code, was meant to be a comprehensive body of law, gathering from other parts of the United States Code all those provisions dealing with the substantive law of bankruptcy.

As with any comprehensive code, frequent reference to the definitions is critically important. The definitions applicable throughout the Bankruptcy Code are contained in section 101 of the statute. Among the many terms defined are "claim," "consumer debt," "creditor," "current monthly income," "debtor," "domestic support obligation," "entity," "governmental unit," "judicial lien," "lien," "statutory lien," "security interest," "person," and "transfer." In addition to these general definitions, various other chapters of the Code contain definitions of other terms applicable only to those chapters.

The first chapter of the Code also contains rules of construction.[67] Most important among these is the use of the phrase "after notice and a hearing." Depending on the circumstances, this phrase may not mean that a hearing will actually take place. Other rules explain use of the words "or," "includes," and "order for relief."

Chapter 1 also provides an explanation of the Code's structure. One should always remember that chapters 1, 3, and 5 of the Code are applicable to all proceedings under any chapter of the Code, except chapter 15, unless a provision of that specific chapter provides otherwise.[68] In contrast, chapters 7, 9, 11, 12, 13, and 15 are only applicable to cases brought under those chapters respectively.

The Bankruptcy Judges, United States Trustees, and Family Farmer Bankruptcy Act of 1986[69] enacted amendments to the Bankruptcy Code to phase-in the United States trustee program. The United States trustee program has now become operative in every district, except those in North Carolina and Alabama.[70]

1.4.1.2 Other Relevant Statutes

Other statutory materials relevant to bankruptcy cases are found outside the Bankruptcy Code itself. Most importantly, the jurisdictional provisions relevant to bankruptcy are found in title 28 of the United States Code.[71] Additionally, a small number of military and other government benefit programs now have their own bankruptcy dischargeability provisions that have been codified with the program authorization rather than in the Bankruptcy Code itself.[72] Similarly, some taxation provisions relevant to bankruptcy cases and debts discharged in bankruptcy are found in title 26, generally known as the Internal Revenue Code.[73]

Finally, some bankruptcy law, particularly portions of statutes which provide implementation dates, is not codified at all. These provisions can only be found by reviewing the enacted public laws themselves, relevant portions of which are included in Appendix A, *infra*.[74]

Throughout this treatise, full citation to this material is provided to the best source available. With few exceptions, relevant statutory material is also reprinted in Appendix A, *infra*.

1.4.2 The Federal Rules of Bankruptcy Procedure

Complementing the statute's mostly substantive provisions are the Federal Rules of Bankruptcy Procedure, also known as the Bankruptcy Rules, which were promulgated by the Supreme Court in 1983 and amended at various times since then.[75] These rules provide detailed guidelines in numerous areas not specifically covered by the Code. They cover the procedures not only for administering the bankruptcy petitions themselves, but also for proceedings within or related to the principal bankruptcy case.[76]

The rules' distinction between a "case" and a "proceeding" is important to keep in mind. Although nowhere specifically defined, the word "case" encompasses the bankruptcy petition itself, seeking the relief provided by the Code, and includes within its scope all controversies which arise as to that petition.[77] A "proceeding," on the other hand, concerns a dispute which arises within a case, or which is related to a case.[78]

"Proceedings" are themselves divided into two categories. Those which are considered more significant or complex are classified as "adversary proceedings" and governed by Part VII of the rules. Rule 7001 contains a list of the matters that fall in this category, including proceedings to recover money or property (with certain exceptions), to determine the validity or priority of a lien or interest in property (*except* proceedings to avoid judicial liens or non-possessory non-purchase money security interests under section 522(f)), to obtain approval pursuant to section 363(h) for a sale of joint property by the trustee, to object to or revoke a discharge (*except* if the objection is based on the case having been filed too soon after an earlier case), to obtain an injunction or other equitable relief, to determine the dischargeability of a debt, to obtain most declaratory judgments, and to determine a claim or cause of action removed to a bankruptcy court.

Generally, the adversary proceeding rules, Rules 7001–7087, provide for a lawsuit within the bankruptcy case. With some exceptions (such as service of process which can be done by mail more easily),[79] these rules conform closely to the Federal Rules of Civil Procedure and are numbered to correspond to those rules.[80] For example, Rule 7004 corresponds to Federal Rule of Civil Procedure 4. All of the federal discovery rules,

---

67 11 U.S.C. § 102.
68 11 U.S.C. § 103.
69 Pub. L. No. 99-554, 100 Stat. 3088.
70 Pub. L. No. 99-554, § 302, 100 Stat. 3088. *See* § 2.7, *infra*.
71 *See* Appx. A.2, *infra*.
72 *See, e.g.*, Appx. A.3, *infra*.
73 *See* Appx. A.3, *infra*.
74 *See, e.g.*, Appx. A.4.1–A.4.9, *infra*.

75 The Federal Rules of Bankruptcy Procedure, as most recently amended in 2011, appear in Appendix B.3, *Infra*. The Rules are now to be formally cited as the Federal Rules of Bankruptcy Procedure (Fed. R. Bankr. P.) as opposed to the "Bankruptcy Rules" under prior law. Fed. R. Bankr. P. 1001.
76 The Bankruptcy Rules cover proceedings in bankruptcy cases even when those proceedings are before district court judges. Fed. R. Civ. P. 81(a)(1); Fed. R. Bankr. P. 1001. See Hedges v. Resolution Trust Corp., 32 F.3d 1360 (9th Cir. 1994) (Fed. R. Civ. P. 11 does not apply when district court is reviewing bankruptcy decision; proper authority is Fed. R. Bankr. P. 9011).
77 Fed. R. Bankr. P. 1002; 11 U.S.C. §§ 301, 303.
78 1 Collier on Bankruptcy ¶ 3.01[3][d] (16th ed.).
79 The procedures for service under Fed. R. Bankr. P. 7004 were amended by the Bankruptcy Reform Act of 1994, Pub. L. No. 103-394, 108 Stat. 4106, to require service on insured depository institutions by certified mail in most cases. *See* Fed. R. Bankr. P. 7004(h); § 14.3.2.1, *infra*.
80 Certain other Federal Rules of Civil Procedure, applicable to all bankruptcy matters, and not just adversary proceedings, are incorporated in Part IX of the Bankruptcy Rules. *See, e.g.*, Fed. R. Bankr. P. 9024 (incorporating Fed. R. Civ. P. 60).

including the disclosure requirements contained in Federal Rule of Civil Procedure 26, are applicable in every district and bankruptcy court.[81]

Disputes which are not considered adversary proceedings, such as requests for relief from the automatic stay,[82] are called "contested matters" and are governed by Rule 9014.[83] Generally, this rule provides for a more summary procedure akin to motion practice, to which only certain of the adversary proceeding rules apply, and in which an answer is not always required, depending on local rules and practice. However, it is important to note that the applicable rules do incorporate various adversary proceeding rules including most of those governing discovery,[84] default, and summary judgment.[85] Further, the applicability of the various adversary proceeding rules in contested matters may be expanded or restricted by the court.[86]

Even with the detailed statute and rules, however, there are many procedural questions to which there are no clear answers. Moreover, any rule which is in conflict with the statute is not valid.[87]

Under the Federal Rules of Bankruptcy Procedure, it continues to be important to determine whether there are also supplemental local rules or unusual local procedural practices, which are typically published on the court's website.[88] When in doubt as to procedure, it is best to check with the clerk of the local bankruptcy court, who will usually be quite cooperative. A failure to be aware of such rules could have dire consequences, because their force and effect equal those of the Bankruptcy Rules.[89] Because the rules specifically provide authority for supplemental local rules,[90] it may also be useful to suggest to the local bankruptcy court that it promulgate particular rules which would codify or improve current practices.

An additional Interim Rule 1007-I has been released to implement the National Guard and Reservists Debt Relief Act of 2009 excluding certain military and former military members from means testing.

1.4.3 The Official Bankruptcy Forms

Lastly, official bankruptcy forms have been promulgated for use in bankruptcy cases. These are detailed examples of what various documents in a case are to contain. The Bankruptcy Rules provide that the official forms must be "observed and used with alterations as may be appropriate," including the combination or rearrangement of their contents to permit economies in their use.[91]

The official bankruptcy forms were substantially amended in recent years to make many of the forms clearer and more understandable, to conform them to statutory changes, and to protect somewhat the privacy of debtors and their dependents.

The Official Bankruptcy Forms, as most recently amended in 2012, appear in Appendix D, *infra*. They may all be found on the website of the Administrative Office of the U.S. Courts.[92]

1.4.4 Other Issues Concerning Sources of Law

1.4.4.1 Pending Legislation and Amendments to the Rules

Nearly every year there are a variety of efforts to amend the Bankruptcy Code, rules, and official forms. Some of these efforts come to fruition and others do not. Careful attention to the progress of those amendments and their effective dates is required.

In addition, potential changes to the rules and forms are almost always percolating through the system. The progress of proposed amendments can be tracked at the United States Courts' website.[93]

Finally, the Executive Office for United States Trustees has proposed regulations governing various subjects within the ambit of its authority, including requirements for credit counseling agencies and providers of financial education. Interim final rules can be found in Appendices C.1 and C.2, *infra*.

Changes are made to this treatise through annual supplements reflecting changes in the law as of their publication deadlines. Significant amendments are also reported in our bimonthly publication, *NCLC REPORTS Bankruptcy and Foreclosures Edition*.

---

81 However, Fed. R. Bankr. P. 9014(c) provides that the mandatory disclosure requirements of Fed. R. Civ. P. 26, as incorporated by Fed. R. Bankr. P. 7026, do not apply in contested matters.

82 The automatic stay obtained by filing a bankruptcy petition is discussed in detail in Chapter 9, *infra*.

83 Fed. R. Bankr. P. 9014 advisory committee's note.
   The only exceptions to this principle are those few matters specifically designated as "applications" in particular rules, which normally do not give rise to actual disputes. *See, e.g.*, Fed. R. Bankr. P. 1006(b) (application to pay filing fee in installments).

84 Fed. R. Bankr. P. 7028–7037.

85 Fed. R. Bankr. P. 7055, 7056.

86 Fed. R. Bankr. P. 9014(c).

87 28 U.S.C. § 2075.

88 *See* § 1.4.4.2, *infra*.

89 *See, e.g., In re* Adams, 734 F.2d 1094 (5th Cir. 1984) (failure to properly list creditor's address on mailing matrix required by local rule resulted in debt being excepted from discharge as not "duly scheduled").

90 Fed. R. Bankr. P. 9029.

91 Fed. R. Bankr. P. 9009. *See In re* Orrison, 343 B.R. 906 (Bankr. N.D. Ind. 2006) (unique forms developed by debtor's attorney deviated too substantially from Official Forms and could not be used).

92 The Official Bankruptcy Forms are available at www.uscourts.gov/FormsAndFees/Forms/BankruptcyForms.aspx. Not all of the forms are available in a fillable PDF format.

93 Proposed changes and their status may be found at www.uscourts.gov/rules/index.html.

1.4.4.2 Local Bankruptcy Rules

In addition to the Bankruptcy Rules, practitioners should refer to any local rules[94] and local practice to fill in gaps in interpretation. Pursuant to the policy of the federal Judicial Conference, local bankruptcy rules are generally numbered to correspond to the Federal Rules of Bankruptcy Procedure to which they relate. Some courts may also promulgate local "procedural orders" applying to all cases before that court. Many courts have local forms which are to be used in particular situations, including forms for chapter 13 plans (although any such form that abridged statutory rights would be invalid). Consequently, in each jurisdiction, attorneys should consult the court's website and, if necessary, the clerk of court concerning all local rules, forms, orders, and customs.[95]

In some instances, there may be important ways in which the local rules conflict with the national rules or even with the Bankruptcy Code. When necessary, these conflicts should be pointed out to the local committee which drafted the rules or to the judges who adopted them.[96] When clients' rights are affected, it is appropriate to challenge the rules and they should certainly be invalidated when they are inconsistent with the national rules, the official forms, or the Code.[97]

1.4.4.3 Case Law Under the Code

Over the years, many bankruptcy cases under the Code have reached the United States Supreme Court. Although the Supreme Court's definitive holdings reach only limited specific issues in bankruptcy law, two important guiding principles have been enunciated on several occasions. First, as expected, the plain language of the statute controls.[98] Second, the Court has repeatedly held that it will not find congressional intent to overrule law under the prior Bankruptcy Act absent a clear statement by Congress to that effect.[99] Because of the latter principle, it is important to review precedent under the Bankruptcy Act as well as cases under the Bankruptcy Code in researching unresolved bankruptcy questions. Since 1978, a substantial body of case law from the bankruptcy courts has been reported. In addition, appellate decisions in each jurisdiction have created a pool of binding precedent which must be examined before advocating on bankruptcy issues. In a bankruptcy court, it is generally only circuit court precedent which is considered binding. District court decisions and bankruptcy appellate panel decisions[100] have *stare decisis* effect in bankruptcy, but because of the potential for inconsistent decisions from different judges of the same district court, they are generally not considered binding even on bankruptcy judges in the district in which they arose.[101]

Additionally, state courts have ruled on issues directly or indirectly related to bankruptcy, most notably in the areas of state exemptions, dischargeability of certain debts, and lien rights of secured creditors. As is discussed more fully below, many bankruptcy issues turn on questions of state law. The body of bankruptcy case law continues to grow and careful research will generally uncover helpful decisions, if not binding precedent, on virtually any issue.

1.5 Other Resources for Practicing Under the Bankruptcy Code

1.5.1 Legislative History

1.5.1.1 The Bankruptcy Reform Act of 1978

In dealing with legal questions about bankruptcy, the first places to look, of course, are the statute itself and the Federal Rules of Bankruptcy Procedure, the relevant parts of which are

---

94 Fed. R. Bankr. P. 9029.
95 Courts are empowered to charge fees for copies of their local rules commensurate with the cost of printing. *See* United States Judicial Conference, Bankruptcy Court Miscellaneous Fee Schedule ¶ 18 (reprinted following 28 U.S.C.A. § 1930 and in Appx. C.3, *infra*). Obviously, the fee, if any, varies from jurisdiction to jurisdiction. Local rules and forms are also available on local courts' websites, accessible through www.uscourts.gov.
96 Local rules also must be promulgated by the district court judges (rather than the bankruptcy court) with appropriate opportunity for notice and comment. Fed. R. Bankr. P. 9029.
97 *See, e.g.*, Fed. R. Bankr. P. 9029 (local rules may not be "inconsistent with" the national rules or "prohibit or limit the use of the Official Forms"); *In re* Petro, 276 F.3d 375 (7th Cir. 2002) (striking down local rule requiring chapter 13 debtors to file affidavit every six months listing income along with copies of paycheck stubs); *In re* Wilkinson, 923 F.2d 154 (10th Cir. 1991) (striking down local rule requiring district court permission to move for rehearing as inconsistent with Fed. R. Bankr. P. 8015); *In re* Steinacher, 283 B.R. 768 (B.A.P. 9th Cir. 2002) (invalidating local rule requiring short cure period for any debtor who had previous chapter 13 case pending within six months before current case).
98 *See, e.g.*, Lamie v. United States Tr., 540 U.S. 526, 124 S. Ct. 1023, 157 L. Ed. 2d 1024 (2004); Toibb v. Radloff, 501 U.S. 157, 111 S. Ct. 2197, 115 L. Ed. 2d 145 (1991); Johnson v. Home State Bank, 501 U.S. 78, 111 S. Ct. 2150, 115 L. Ed. 2d 66 (1991); Pennsylvania Dep't of Pub. Welfare v. Davenport, 495 U.S. 552, 110 S. Ct. 2126, 109 L. Ed. 2d 588 (1990); United States v. Ron Pair Enter., Inc., 489 U.S. 235, 109 S. Ct. 1026, 1030, 103 L. Ed. 2d 290 (1989). However, whether some of the Supreme Court's recent decisions purporting to rely on the Code's plain language have actually comported with that language is quite debatable. *See, e.g.*, Rake v. Wade, 508 U.S. 464, 113 S. Ct. 2187, 124 L. Ed. 2d 424 (1993) (a mortgage arrearage is an allowed secured claim that must be paid interest under 11 U.S.C. § 1325(a)(5)(B)).
99 *See, e.g.*, Dewsnup v. Timm, 502 U.S. 410, 112 S. Ct. 773, 116 L. Ed. 2d 903 (1992); Kelly v. Robinson, 479 U.S. 36, 107 S. Ct. 353, 93 L. Ed. 2d 216 (1986); Midlantic Nat'l Bank v. New Jersey, 474 U.S. 494, 106 S. Ct. 755, 88 L. Ed. 2d 859 (1986).
100 See § 2.4.3, *infra*, for discussion of bankruptcy appellate panels.
101 *See In re* Rheuban, 128 B.R. 551 (Bankr. C.D. Cal. 1991) (bankruptcy judge in multi-judge district need not follow decisions of the district court); *In re* Johnson-Allen, 67 B.R. 968 (Bankr. E.D. Pa. 1986) (bankruptcy court should make every effort to follow decisions of district court where it is sitting). Similarly, bankruptcy appellate panel decisions are not binding on district or bankruptcy judges in districts of the circuit other than where the panel sits. *In re* Selden, 121 B.R. (D. Or. 1990). *See* Bank of Maui v. Estate Analysis, Inc., 904 F.2d 470 (9th Cir. 1990) (bankruptcy appellate panel decisions do not bind the district courts).

included in Appendices A and B, *infra*, as well as relevant case law. Often, these will not provide sufficient answers, and other sources must be consulted.

Generally, the most important indicator of what Congress meant in a particular section of the Code is the legislative history. Because of the long gestation periods which produced both the final law and the later amendments, there are a number of parts to the legislative history.[102]

The first major document in the evolution of the 1978 Bankruptcy Code was the report of the Commission on the Bankruptcy Laws.[103] The Commission, a special body set up by Congress, proposed a precursor to the final legislation and in its report explained its reasons for the provisions contained in its proposed bill. In the many areas in which the Bankruptcy Reform Act is identical or similar to the Commission's proposal, the report of the Commission is an excellent explanatory authority.

Even more important are the House[104] and Senate[105] reports which accompanied the bills first passed by those two bodies (H.R. 8200 and S. 2266 of the 95th Congress). As these bills were in most respects identical to the final Act, the reports accompanying them are the most comprehensive and definitive explanation of congressional intent for many provisions.

Unlike most legislation, the Bankruptcy Reform Act never went to a conference committee of the two houses, so there is no conference report regarding how the differences between the House and Senate bills were reconciled. Instead, there are long and detailed floor statements by the sponsors in each house, who had met and worked out the differences among themselves. The floor statement of Representative Edwards[106] explains each change in the House bill which resulted from the compromises reached, and similarly the statement of Senator DeConcini[107] explains each change in the Senate bill.

Thus, in using the legislative history, the floor statements, which are the latest explanations, must be consulted first to see if there was any change from the previous bills, and if so whether any explanation for the change was given. Next, the report of each house and finally the Commission report should be checked. For very detailed research the many volumes of hearings,[108] reflecting the views of numerous parties on various provisions, are also available, as well as some congressional debate on earlier versions of the bill.[109]

1.5.1.2 The 1984 Amendments

Like the Bankruptcy Reform Act, the 1984 amendments, particularly those concerning consumer bankruptcy, evolved through a lengthy process of hearings and reports followed by a last minute frenzy of compromises. As with the 1978 Act, there is no formal conference report and no explanation of many of the final provisions other than in statements on the floor of Congress by their sponsors.

The jurisdictional sections of the 1984 amendments, in particular, were determined almost entirely on the floor and in unreported conferences. Therefore, to the extent that there is legislative history, it is to be found in the floor statements of June 29, 1984[110] and in the earlier statements and debates concerning the amendment offered by Representative Kastenmeier to the original House Bill,[111] as that amendment in large part formed the basis of the final enactment.

The other provisions of the 1984 amendments emerged from a variety of sources. The consumer bankruptcy amendments were the result of successive revisions of a bill originally proposed by the consumer finance industry. A weakened version of that bill passed the Senate in 1983, and the Senate report[112] on that version is helpful in interpreting provisions that were not substantially changed in the final bill. However, many provisions of the Senate bill were further altered in a later compromise in the House, which produced the final language of the consumer amendments. There are only floor statements, particularly those of Representative Rodino,[113] who sponsored the compromise, to explain those changes, though for a few sections other portions of the legislative history are also relevant.[114] Again, for further research, there are several volumes of hearings as well as earlier versions of many provisions of the amendments which may be consulted.[115]

---

102 A good discussion of the Code's legislative history is found in Kenneth N. Klee, *Legislative History of the New Bankruptcy Code*, 54 Am. Bankr. L.J. 275 (1980).

103 Report of the Commission on the Bankruptcy Laws of the United States, H.R. Doc. No. 93-137 (1973) (hereafter "Commission Report"). The Commission Report is available, among other places, in Collier on Bankruptcy App. vol. B (16th ed.).

104 H.R. Rep. No. 95-595 (1977).

105 S. Rep. No. 95-989 (1978).

106 124 Cong. Rec. H11,089–H11,116 (daily ed. Sept. 28, 1978).

107 124 Cong. Rec. S17,406–S17,434 (daily ed. Sept. 7, 1978).

108 *Hearings on H.R. 31 and H.R. 32 Before the Subcomm. on Civil and Constitutional Rights of the House Comm. on the Judiciary*, 94th Cong. (1975–1976); *Hearings on S.235 and S.236 Before the Subcomm. on Improvements in Judicial Machinery of the Senate Comm. on the Judiciary*, 94th Cong. (1975); *Hearings on S.2266 and H.R. 8200 Before the Subcomm. on Improvements in Judicial Machinery of the Senate Comm. on the Judiciary*, 95th Cong. (1977); *Hearings on H.R. 8200 Before the Subcomm. on Civil and Constitutional Rights of the House Comm. on the Judiciary*, 95th Cong. (1977).

109 Large portions of the legislative history are reprinted in Collier on Bankruptcy App. (16th ed.) along with a detailed description of the legislative process, and in 1978 U.S.C.C.A.N. 5786–6573.

110 130 Cong. Rec. H7471–H7497 (daily ed. June 29, 1984); 130 Cong. Rec. S8887–S8900 (daily ed. June 29, 1984).

111 130 Cong. Rec. E1107–E1110 (daily ed. Mar. 20, 1984); 130 Cong. Rec. H1832–H1854 (daily ed. Mar. 21, 1984).

112 S. Rep. No. 98-65 (1983).

113 130 Cong. Rec. H1721, H1722 (daily ed. Mar. 19, 1984); 130 Cong. Rec. H1807–H1832 (daily ed. Mar. 21, 1984); 130 Cong. Rec. H1941, H1942 (daily ed. Mar. 26, 1984).

114 For example, the amendments to 11 U.S.C. § 1325(b) and 11 U.S.C. § 1329 were adopted virtually verbatim from a proposal made and explained by the National Bankruptcy Conference in hearings on the amendments. *See Oversight Hearings on Personal Bankruptcy Before the Subcomm. on Monopolies and Commercial Law of the House Comm. on the Judiciary*, 97th Cong. 181–222 (1981–1982).

115 *See Oversight Hearings on Personal Bankruptcy Before the Subcomm. on Monopolies and Commercial Law of the House Comm. on the Judiciary*, 97th Cong. (1981–1982).

1.5.1.3 The 1986 Amendments

The legislative history of the 1986 amendments is somewhat less ample. The United States Trustee Program, first conceived and discussed in the legislative history of the 1978 Bankruptcy Reform Act, was the subject of several competing bills in the House and Senate. Similarly, the plight of family farmers led to the hurried introduction of a number of bills to remedy their situation. There were hearings[116] and reports[117] in both houses of Congress and a final conference report resolving differences between the two houses.[118]

1.5.1.4 The Bankruptcy Reform Act of 1994

Like much other bankruptcy legislation, the Bankruptcy Reform Act of 1994 was passed in a flurry of last minute activity, so there is no conference report detailing the final compromises between the House and Senate versions of the bill. Instead, these compromises were worked out as the bill was being considered in the House Judiciary Committee and during the time between its passage out of that committee and its consideration on the House floor. The final explanation of the bill is contained in floor statements made when it was considered on the House floor.[119] This explanation is mostly identical to the House report on the bill,[120] except as to those provisions that were changed after the bill was voted out of the House Judiciary Committee. A comparison of the final bill to the bill which had previously passed the Senate[121] and its accompanying committee report[122] sheds further light on the decisions and compromises that were made in the legislative process.

1.5.1.5 The 2005 Amendments

The tortuous legislative process leading to the 2005 amendments lasted over eight years. There were numerous versions of the bankruptcy bill that reflected changes as the legislation evolved.[123] There were also various committee reports explaining many of these bills. The final legislation is explained, to some degree, in the House Judiciary Committee Report issued before the bill went to the House floor.[124] To the extent the language of the amendments is not clear, reference to the House report and to the prior versions of the bill which may have had different wording can be illuminating. However, for some of the provisions in the legislation, there is very little, if any, explanation in the legislative history.

1.5.2 Rules Advisory Committee Notes

The Federal Rules of Bankruptcy Procedure were accompanied by advisory committee explanatory notes, as was each amendment to those rules. These notes are available on this treatise's companion website and in a number of published versions of the rules[125] and, like the legislative history, are the most authoritative explanation of the drafters' intent. On questions of rule interpretation, therefore, they should be the first source consulted.

1.5.3 Treatises and Texts

Collier on Bankruptcy. Of the many treatises and texts on bankruptcy law which have been available, one has become by far the most frequently used and is a bible to many judges and practitioners.[126] Any office doing a substantial amount of bankruptcy work should have access to *Collier on Bankruptcy*,[127] which includes among its Board of Editors one of the principal congressional staff persons who worked on drafting the legislation.[128]

---

116 *Hearings on H.R. 4128 and H.R. 4140 Before the Subcomm. on Monopolies and Commercial Law of the House Comm. on the Judiciary,* 99th Cong. (1986); *Hearings on H.R. 1397 and H.R. 1399 Before the Subcomm. on Monopolies and Commercial Law of the House Comm. on the Judiciary,* 99th Cong. (1985); *Hearings on S. 705, S. 1342, S. 1516, and H.R. 2211 Before the Subcomm. on Admin. Practice and Procedure and the Subcomm. on Courts of the Senate Comm. on the Judiciary,* 99th Cong. (1985); *Hearings on S. 1923 Before the Senate Comm. on the Judiciary,* 99th Cong. (1985).

117 H.R. Rep. No. 99-764 (1986); H.R. Rep. No. 99-178 (1985); S. Rep. No. 99-269 (1986).

118 H.R. Rep. No. 99-958 (1986).

119 140 Cong. Rec. H10,752–H10,773 (daily ed. Oct. 4, 1994).

120 H.R. Rep. No. 103-835 (1994), *reprinted in* 1994 U.S.C.C.A.N. 3340.

121 S. 540, 103d Cong. (1994).

122 S. Rep. No. 103-168 (1993).

123 For a description of the legislative process and citations to previous versions of the bill, see Susan Jensen, *A Legislative History of the Bankruptcy Abuse Prevention and Consumer Protection Act of 2005,* 79 Am. Bankr. L.J. 485 (2005).

124 H.R. Rep. No. 109-31 (2005) (available on this treatise's companion website).

125 The Federal Rules of Bankruptcy Procedure are published as a part of the *United States Code Annotated,* and in paperbound form. Collier Pamphlets (2009 ed.) (three volumes, including Code, rules, and portable pamphlet). In addition to sections of the legislative history and the Rules Advisory Committee Notes, this edition now includes a brief editorial commentary on each Code section and rule as well as some case annotations and a smaller, portable version of the Code and rules. A one-volume compilation of the Code and rules, along with the Federal Rules of Civil Procedure and Federal Rules of Evidence, is published by West Group Publishing Co. Norton Quick Reference (2009 ed.). A two-volume paperback version containing the Code, rules, forms and commentary is available from West Group. Norton Bankruptcy Code and Rules (2008–2009 ed.). A smaller sized "Mini-Code" (2009 ed.) and "Mini-Rules" (2009 ed.) are available from AWHFY Publishing, 545 E. Cimarron St., Colorado Springs, Colorado 80903.

126 Authors' disclaimer: This sentence is taken verbatim from the first edition of this treatise, written several years before one of this treatise's authors became a contributing author, and then Editor-in-Chief, of *Collier.*

127 This treatise is published by Lexis/Matthew Bender, with a sixteenth edition being rolled out gradually. It is available on-line on Lexis. Lexis/Matthew Bender bankruptcy publications' prices vary depending upon the publications purchased.

128 Richard B. Levin, who served on the staff of the House subcommittee which put a large portion of the new law into its final form, is a member of the Board of Editors of the 16th edition.

§ 1.5.3   *Consumer Bankruptcy Law and Practice*

Numerous other treatises, texts, and handbooks are also available. Some of the most popular and useful ones include, in alphabetical order by author:

Richard I. Aaron, *Bankruptcy Law Fundamentals*. This text, another one-volume general treatment of bankruptcy, contains an often interesting, but sometimes uneven discussion of some of the issues arising in consumer and business bankruptcies.[129] It is supplemented by an annual maintenance service.

Arnold Cohen & Mitchell W. Miller, *Consumer Bankruptcy Manual* (2d ed.). A one-volume practice manual for attorneys handling chapter 7 and chapter 13 cases, it competently but somewhat less comprehensively covers many of the same topics as this treatise. As the Cohen and Miller volume provides guidance for those who represent creditors, it would be an excellent addition to any library wishing to expand its materials on consumer bankruptcy.[130]

Collier Bankruptcy Manual (3d ed. revised). A shorter version of the treatise, this three-volume set is less comprehensive than the treatise and it is not in the library of many judges who have the full *Collier* treatise instead. An accompanying two-volume *Collier Consumer Bankruptcy Forms Manual* may also be purchased, which contains the forms in the standard *Collier* treatise.[131]

W. Homer Drake, Jr., *Bankruptcy Practice for the General Practitioner* (3d ed.). This text offers little discussion of consumer bankruptcy issues and would not add a great deal to what is contained in this treatise.[132]

Nancy C. Dreher, Joan M. Feeney, *Bankruptcy Law Manual* (5th ed.). This text is still another two-volume work, not focused particularly on consumer bankruptcy, attempting to emphasize practical aspects of bankruptcy.[133]

David G. Epstein, *Bankruptcy and Related Law in a Nutshell* (7th ed.). This short text is a very good, easy-to-read, and concise explanation of much substantive bankruptcy law with especially helpful discussions of trustees' avoiding powers.[134]

Herzog's Bankruptcy Forms and Practice (9th ed.). A two-volume form book covering all aspects of bankruptcy practice, this work is the latest edition of a longstanding bankruptcy reference.[135]

Morgan D. King, *Discharging Taxes in Bankruptcy*. A one-volume text on the intersection of tax law and bankruptcy, this book contains useful information about Internal Revenue Service procedures and forms, as well as sample forms and pleadings.[136]

Richard B. Levin, *Fundamentals of Bankruptcy Law* (6th ed.). A one-volume overview of bankruptcy law.[137]

Keith M. Lundin, *Chapter 13 Bankruptcy*. The five-volume third edition of this text by a respected bankruptcy judge contains much practical information, presented in a coherent, accessible form. It is primarily a practical guide, so that the case citations are not extensive, and some general bankruptcy topics are discussed only to a limited degree.[138]

Patrick A. Murphy, *Creditors' Rights in Bankruptcy* (2d ed.). A good one-volume text which, while oriented to creditors, contains useful information.[139]

Norton Bankruptcy Law and Practice (3d ed.). This service consists of a thirteen-volume treatise, soft-cover versions of the Code and rules, a monograph binder, and a monthly newsletter.[140] It contains sections written by a large number of respected bankruptcy practitioners and other authorities who provide a discussion of many areas of the law. It also seems to be gaining some degree of acceptance as a recognized authority.

Alan N. Resnick, Henry J. Sommer, & Contributing Authors, *Collier Bankruptcy Practice Guide*. This six-volume work is intended to be the practice manual counterpart to the *Collier* treatise.[141] It is primarily oriented toward business bankruptcies although it contains some material on consumer cases.

Alan N. Resnick, Henry J. Sommer, *Collier Consumer Bankruptcy Practice Guide*.[142] This one-volume practice guide is devoted to the nuts and bolts of representing consumers and creditors in consumer bankruptcy cases. It contains some material that is similar to that in this treatise, as well as other material, including material pertaining to representing creditors, that is not found in this treatise. It may also be purchased on a CD-ROM that contains other Matthew Bender publications including *Collier Family Law and the Bankruptcy Code*, *Collier Consumer Bankruptcy Forms*, the *Collier Bankruptcy Manual*, and the *Collier Exemption Guide*.

Alan N. Resnick, Henry J. Sommer & Margaret Dee McGarity, *Collier Family Law and the Bankruptcy Code*. This one-volume text is the only comprehensive treatment of the growing areas of intersection between bankruptcy and family law, going far beyond the limited discussion possible in this treatise. It is essential for practitioners doing significant amounts of work in family law areas in which bankruptcy may arise, as well as for bankruptcy practitioners who must confront family law issues in their practices.[143]

---

129 Publisher is West Group (1984).
130 Publisher is West Group (2d ed. 1991).
131 *Collier Bankruptcy Manual*'s publisher is Lexis/Matthew Bender (3d ed. 1997).
132 Publisher is West Group (3d ed. 2002).
133 Publisher is West Group (5th ed. 2002).
134 Publisher is West Group (7th ed. 2005).
135 Publisher is West Group (9th ed. 1991).
136 Publisher is Kings Press, Suite 222, 7080 Donlon Way, Dublin, California 94568, or www.bankruptcybooks.com (2009 ed.).
137 Publisher is American Law Institute–American Bar Association (6th ed. 2006).
138 Publisher is Bankruptcy Press, Inc., 2300 21st Ave. South, Nashville, Tennessee 37212, (615) 385-2752, or http://bankruptcypress.com/home_body_order.htm.
139 Publisher is West Group (2d ed. 1988).
140 Publisher is West Group (3d ed. 2008). A monthly newsletter, the *Norton Bankruptcy Law Advisor*, is also available.
141 Publisher is Lexis/Matthew Bender (2005).
142 Publisher is Lexis/Matthew Bender (1997).
143 Publisher is Lexis/Matthew Bender (1991).

Rosemary E. Williams, *Bankruptcy Practice Handbook* (2d ed.). Another one-volume how-to-do-it guide for relatively inexperienced attorneys, this text contains a number of useful tips, but virtually no discussion of substantive bankruptcy law.[144]

Harvey J. Williamson, *Attorney's Handbook on Consumer Bankruptcy and Chapter 13* (33d ed.). An inexpensive paperbound volume, this handbook is oriented to private attorneys representing consumers. Although it contains some useful information and forms, on the whole it is considerably less comprehensive than this treatise.[145]

Another useful resource, particularly for debtors seeking to handle their own cases, is *How to File for Chapter 7 Bankruptcy*.[146] It is published by Nolo Press, which is a nonprofit organization dedicated to assisting non-lawyers with self-help legal remedies. While there are numerous self-help guides to bankruptcy presently flooding the market, *How to File for Chapter 7 Bankruptcy* is probably the best, most detailed and easiest to understand. Note that it is important, if the book is recommended to a client, to point out the need for the most recent edition, incorporating recent amendments, updated forms, and commentary. Many bookstores stock older versions of self-help manuals and forms which do not include current versions of necessary documents. Clients should also be advised of the many pitfalls of proceeding *pro se*, which should be recommended only in the simplest cases and only when there is no possibility of legal representation.

Potential *pro se* debtors, as well as other debtors and non-attorneys interested in learning more about bankruptcy, may also be referred to the United States Courts' website, which has an explanation of bankruptcy for consumers.[147]

1.5.4 Reporting Services

Because much of the initial case law developed under the Code is found in decisions of the bankruptcy courts, which are not reported in the *Federal Supplement* or other standard reporters, and because federal district court bankruptcy decisions are no longer reported in the *Federal Supplement*, access to a bankruptcy reporting service is essential.[148] Several competing services are available.

West Bankruptcy Reporter (B.R.). A product of the mammoth Thomson/West system, this reporter publishes full text opinions of the bankruptcy courts. It offers the advantage of being tied into the West Digest and the West keynote system. The weekly advance sheets also offer a newsletter of very recent cases and a bibliography of recent articles on bankruptcy.[149] According to *The Bluebook: A Uniform System of Citation*,[150] the *West Bankruptcy Reporter* should be cited if a case is reported therein, with other reporting services cited only if a West reporter citation is not available.

Bankruptcy Court Decisions (Bankr. Ct. Dec. (LRP)). Also a full-text service, this publication is often more current than West. Containing some bankruptcy news beyond its reprints of decisions and a calendar of bankruptcy seminars, it comes out every two weeks. One useful feature is a table of cases based upon different sections of the statute.[151]

Collier Bankruptcy Cases 2d (Collier Bankr. Cas. 2d (MB)). Another full-text service, similar to *Bankruptcy Court Decisions*, this reporter also appears biweekly but contains fewer decisions. Besides a table of cases keyed to statute sections and to *Collier* treatise sections, it also contains a useful Shepard's-like citator for cases it reports.[152]

BNA Bankruptcy Law Reporter. This weekly newsletter does not contain full text opinions. It is often the most current journal and contains news articles about bankruptcy developments and pending legislation. A daily version is available through legal research services such as Westlaw and Lexis.[153]

Collier Bankruptcy Case Update. This newsletter is delivered weekly by e-mail or monthly in hard copy to its subscribers. It contains summaries of all recent bankruptcy decisions, helpfully organized by the Code sections to which they pertain.[154]

Consumer Bankruptcy Abstracts & Research. This monthly electronic newsletter discusses both published and unpublished bankruptcy court opinions. It offers subscribers access to a website with topical and circuit-by-circuit compilations of cases.[155]

1.5.5 Periodicals

From time to time articles on bankruptcy appear in the various law reviews and other periodicals. Many appear in the *American Bankruptcy Law Journal*,[156] in the *American Bankruptcy Institute Law Review*,[157] or in the *Annual Survey of Bankruptcy Law*.[158] In addition, a *Bankruptcy Developments Journal* is published by Emory Law School[159] and there is a

---

144 Publisher is West Group (2d ed. 1995).
145 Publisher is Argyle Publishing, 630 Front St., Louisville, Colorado 80027 (33d ed. 2009).
146 Publisher is Nolo Press, Berkeley, California (15th ed. 2008). It is available at a discount in many bookstores.
147 The information is located at www.uscourts.gov/bankruptcycourts/bankruptcybasics.html.
148 Federal court of appeals decisions concerning bankruptcy continue to be reported in the *Federal Reporter*, as well as in the *Bankruptcy Reporter*.
149 Publisher is West Group. The *West Bankruptcy Digest*, which was formerly provided free of charge with the *West Bankruptcy Reporter*, now must be purchased separately.
150 Table 1 (18th ed.).
151 Publisher is LRP Publications, 360 Hiatt Drive, Palm Beach Gardens, Florida 33418.
152 Publisher is Lexis/Matthew Bender.
153 Publisher is the Bureau of National Affairs, Washington, D.C.
154 Publisher is Lexis/Matthew Bender.
155 Subscription information may be found at www.bankruptcyabstracts.com/subscription.html.
156 Publisher is the National Conference of Bankruptcy Judges, 241 Aristides Dr., Irmo, South Carolina 29063.
157 Publisher is West Group.
158 Publisher is West Group.
159 This publication is also available on the Internet at www.law.emory.edu/

commercial publication, *The Journal of Bankruptcy Law and Practice*,[160] which contains some articles pertaining to consumer bankruptcy. A selected bibliography of recent bankruptcy articles is contained at the end of the text of this treatise.

Another useful publication for updated news on consumer bankruptcy issues is the biweekly publication *Consumer Bankruptcy News* which contains articles and reports of recently decided cases.[161]

And last, but hardly least, six times a year the National Consumer Law Center distributes a *Bankruptcy and Foreclosures Edition* of *NCLC REPORTS* to each neighborhood legal services office and to other subscribers.[162] The report contains new developments, new ideas, model forms, and reprints of important source materials, keeping this treatise and its bound supplements current with the latest developments.

1.5.6 Citator

Fortunately, with all the different reporting services providing multiple citations for most opinions, there is a citator that allows easy cross-referencing, *Shepard's Bankruptcy Citations*.[163]

---

student-life/law-journals/emory-bankruptcy-developments-journal.html.
160 Publisher is West Group.
161 Publisher is LRP Publications, 360 Hiatt Drive, Palm Beach Gardens, Florida 33418.
162 NCLC REPORTS *Bankruptcy and Foreclosure Edition* is one of four NCLC REPORTS editions (also including the *Consumer Credit and Usury Edition*, the *Debt Collection and Repossession Edition*, and the *Deceptive Practices and Warranties Edition*). The full set includes twenty-four issues annually.
163 Seven-volume set published by Lexis.

1.5.7 Computer Assisted Legal Research

One of the fastest and most thorough methods of bankruptcy research is use of any of the several computer assisted legal research services that are now available, for example, Lexis and Westlaw. These systems contain a full-text database of bankruptcy cases, and usually also contain many unreported decisions, as well as a citator. The Lexis and Westlaw databases also contain public record information that may be necessary, including UCC filings, bankruptcy records, and various bulletins, law reviews, and newsletters. These services are now available over the Internet. A useful entry point for Lexis is the bankruptcy practice page at www.lexis.com which offers easy access to cases, statutes, rules, forms, the Collier publications, Shepard's, public records, news articles, and other secondary materials. Another recent entrant to the field of electronic legal research is Fastcase.com. Although it is not as robust, complete or current as Lexis or Westlaw, it is available free to all members of the National Association of Consumer Bankruptcy Attorneys (NACBA).[164] Google Scholar is also a free internet search tool that can be used to find court opinions.

Finally, the text of the Bankruptcy Code, like the rest of the United States Code, the Federal Rules of Bankruptcy Procedure, and local bankruptcy court rules are available on the Internet.[165] Many other useful materials, such as court decisions and law review articles, are also available through various websites offering free legal resources.

---

164 Information about joining NACBA is available at www.nacba.org.
165 For example, the Bankruptcy Code and Rules are available at the Cornell Law School Legal Information Institute, www.law.cornell.edu.

Chapter 2   What Is Bankruptcy? Some General Concepts

2.1 A Definition

In essence, a voluntary[1] bankruptcy case is a legal proceeding, brought by a debtor, that seeks relief specifically provided for by a federal statute, the Bankruptcy Code.[2] The bankruptcy case must be brought in the United States District Court, which has jurisdiction over all bankruptcy cases, but bankruptcy cases are normally automatically referred to the bankruptcy court for the district, a unit of the district court.[3] Therefore, the actual bankruptcy petition is filed with the bankruptcy court.

2.2 Relief Available in Bankruptcy

For individuals, there are two types of relief that are usually used. The first is liquidation under chapter 7 of the Code. In a liquidation case, sometimes referred to as a straight bankruptcy, any substantial nonexempt[4] assets of the debtor are converted to cash and distributed to creditors according to certain statutory rules. The individual debtor ordinarily receives a discharge, which absolves him or her from any responsibility to pay most debts and also provides various other protections.[5]

The second type of relief is a reorganization,[6] or adjustment, of the debtor's financial affairs. Although such a reorganization may be available to individuals under both chapters 11[7] and 13 of the Code, chapter 13 is more beneficial for almost every consumer debtor.[8] Although chapter 13 has become a somewhat less attractive alternative as a result of the 2005 amendments to the Bankruptcy Code, it remains less expensive and it also offers a number of protections not found in chapter 11.[9] In a chapter 13 case, the debtor proposes a plan for payment of some or all of his or her debts, within certain statutory guidelines.[10] The plan is then carried out under court supervision with the court protecting the debtor, and usually all of the debtor's property, from creditors. At the end of the case, as in a chapter 7 case, the debtor receives a discharge from personal liability on most debts, as well as other protections.

Neither discharge by itself protects the debtor's property from creditors with valid liens on the property. However, the Code offers a number of ways, particularly in chapter 13, for debtors to obtain full or partial relief from secured claims in most cases.[11]

2.3 Purposes of Bankruptcy

The purposes of bankruptcy are usually described as twofold: (1) a fresh start for the debtor and (2) equity among creditors. In most cases involving consumer debtors, the first is by far the more significant, because there are typically few assets to be distributed, equitably or otherwise, to the creditors involved.

The "fresh start" concept encompasses the statutory goal of allowing individuals who have become mired in debt to free themselves from that morass and to engage in newly productive lives unimpaired by their past financial problems. It avoids the kind of permanent discouragement that would prevent a person from ever becoming reestablished as a hard-working member of society, striving to find the good life and fulfill the American

---

1 Most bankruptcies are voluntary petitions filed by debtors. The Bankruptcy Code also provides for involuntary bankruptcy cases filed by creditors. 11 U.S.C. § 303. These are quite rare in consumer cases and are discussed in Chapter 14, *infra*.
2 11 U.S.C. §§ 101–1532.
3 28 U.S.C. §§ 157(a), 1334(a).
4 Many assets, called exempt assets, may be retained by individual debtors in bankruptcy. A detailed discussion of exemptions is contained in Chapter 10, *infra*.
5 See Chapter 15, *infra*, for a detailed discussion of discharge protections and the limited circumstances in which no discharge is granted.
6 Although chapter 13 functionally offers much the same type of reorganization relief as chapter 11, the term "reorganization" is often used as a term of art to refer to chapter 11. This term will therefore be avoided herein in referring to chapter 13, which will be referred to simply as "chapter 13."
7 The Supreme Court has held that individual debtors may file under chapter 11, whether or not they have an ongoing business. Toibb v. Radloff, 501 U.S. 157, 111 S. Ct. 2197, 115 L. Ed. 2d 145 (1991). A discussion of the relief available to debtors under chapter 11 is, for the most part, beyond the scope of this treatise. See § 6.3.4, *infra*.

8 Individual family farmers and fishermen may also file under chapter 12, discussed in Chapter 17, *infra*.
9 For example, chapter 13 provides for a somewhat broader discharge and a stay of most actions against codebtors. It also does not allow creditors to propose, vote on, or approve the debtor's plan. Chapter 11 is normally used in business reorganization cases, but in some circumstances may offer advantages to high income individuals. If an individual cannot utilize chapter 13 or does not wish to proceed under that chapter, the lack of an ongoing business does not bar chapter 11 relief. See Toibb v. Radloff, 501 U.S. 157, 111 S. Ct. 2197, 115 L. Ed. 2d 145 (1991); § 6.3.4, *infra*.
10 The requirements for a chapter 13 plan are discussed in Chapters 7 and 12, *infra*.
11 See Chapters 10 and 11, *infra*, for discussion of the debtor's rights with respect to secured creditors.

Dream. The Supreme Court has described the fresh start as "a new opportunity in life, unhampered by the pressure and discouragement of pre-existing debt."[12] Functionally, then, bankruptcy serves to grease the wheels of a capitalist economy, offering a safety valve that somewhat tempers its harshness for those who do not fare well in free-market competition. At the same time, it adds to the dynamism of the society, encouraging risk-taking and expansion of new enterprises by limiting the risk involved and by offering a new start to those who fail.

The goal of equity among creditors is achieved by the fair distribution of the debtor's assets according to established rules, set forth in the statute, which guarantee identical treatment to similarly situated creditors. This guarantee, and various provisions that require creditors to disgorge certain assets obtained by them shortly before bankruptcy,[13] are meant to discourage creditors from rushing to be the first to execute on or to repossess property from a struggling individual or business. Thus, the specter of bankruptcy sometimes causes creditors to negotiate with debtors, because the aggressive dismemberment of debtors' assets could force those debtors to seek relief from the bankruptcy court.

Both of these purposes were somewhat undermined by the 2005 amendments to the Bankruptcy Code. Those amendments created obstacles that prevent some debtors from obtaining a fresh start, and also contained numerous special interest provisions that give some types of creditors special treatment, detracting from the goal of equity among creditors.

2.4 The Bankruptcy Court

2.4.1 Status Under the Bankruptcy Reform Act As Amended in 1984

Under the 1984 amendments to the Bankruptcy Reform Act, the bankruptcy court is a "unit" of the federal district court in each judicial district.[14] Its powers, however, are greatly diminished compared to those that were originally contemplated by the drafters of the 1978 Act. Bankruptcy judges are appointed for terms of fourteen years by the courts of appeals that have jurisdiction over the various districts;[15] the judges have a status and power roughly equivalent to United States magistrate judges. Because the bankruptcy court is a part of the district court, statutes applicable to the federal district courts, as well as the Federal Rules of Evidence, generally are applicable in bankruptcy proceedings.

The records of the bankruptcy court are kept by the clerk of the court. Typically, there is a case docket listing all filings and orders in each bankruptcy case. The case docket notes the filing of each adversary proceeding, which then has its own separate docket. In addition, there is a separate claims docket, listing the claims filed in the case. All of these dockets—and, usually, the complete contents of all documents filed in a case—are accessible electronically over the Internet through a system called PACER.[16] The fees for such access are set forth in the Judicial Conference's Electronic Public Access Fee Schedule.[17] They may be waived by the court in order to avoid unreasonable burdens and to promote public access to the information. Courts have used the power to waive fees to give free PACER access to legal services and pro bono programs.

2.4.2 Jurisdiction

A principal goal of the 1978 Bankruptcy Reform Act had been to simplify a jurisdictional scheme which had caused endless litigation for the previous eighty years under the Bankruptcy Act of 1898. This simplification was to be accomplished by giving the bankruptcy court broad and pervasive jurisdiction over all matters related in any way to the bankruptcy case.[18] But granting such broad jurisdiction to a non-Article III court was found unconstitutional by the United States Supreme Court.[19]

The 1984 amendments attempted to meet the Supreme Court's objections in a variety of ways, most of which involved removing matters from the jurisdiction of the bankruptcy court. Under the amendments, all matters arising under the Bankruptcy Code (title 11 of the United States Code), or arising in or related to cases under title 11, are initially referred by the district court to the bankruptcy court,[20] or may arrive in the bankruptcy court by removal from another court.[21] However, some matters will not stay in the bankruptcy court. The statute provides for a complex system of mechanisms to transfer cases or proceedings to the district court or to state courts, often depending upon the type of proceeding involved. These include devices such as discretionary abstention and mandatory abstention, discretionary withdrawal to the district court and mandatory withdrawal to the district court, and referral to bankruptcy judges as masters.[22] In some proceedings bankruptcy judges are permitted to enter final orders, and in others they are allowed only to submit

---

12 Local Loan Co. v. Hunt, 292 U.S. 234, 244, 54 S. Ct. 695, 78 L. Ed. 1230 (1934). *See also* H.R. Rep. No. 95-595, at 117, 118 (1977) (fresh start is the "essence of modern bankruptcy law"; chapter 13 designed to ensure "the debtor is given adequate exemptions and other protections to ensure that bankruptcy will provide a fresh start"; whether debtor uses chapter 7 or 13, premise of the Code is that "bankruptcy relief should be effective, and should provide the debtor with a fresh start").

13 These provisions, termed the "avoiding powers," are discussed in Chapter 10, *infra*.

14 Pub. L. No. 98-353, 98 Stat. 343 (1984). *See* Appx. A.4.2, *infra*.

15 28 U.S.C. § 152.

16 Information about accessing PACER may be obtained at http://pacer.psc.uscourts.gov/ or by calling (800) 676-6856.

17 Reprinted in Appx. C.4, *infra*.

18 See the sources cited in § 1.5.1.1, *supra*, for a discussion of the evolution of the 1978 Act.

19 N. Pipeline Constr. Co. v. Marathon Pipe Line Co., 458 U.S. 50, 102 S. Ct. 2858, 73 L. Ed. 2d 598 (1982).

20 28 U.S.C. § 157(a).

21 28 U.S.C. § 1452.

    It is assumed that cases removed under this section to the district court will initially be referred to the bankruptcy court handling the related bankruptcy case. *See* Fed. R. Bankr. P. 9027(f).

22 *See* 28 U.S.C. § 157.

proposed findings of fact and conclusions of law to the district court.[23] The procedures effectuating this jurisdictional scheme are discussed elsewhere in this treatise.[24]

These jurisdictional complexities added in 1984 did not affect most routine bankruptcy cases, which are resolved entirely in the bankruptcy court. However, for more unusual matters, the statute's many twists and turns have caused considerable confusion and litigation, not unlike that which existed before 1978, thus ending the hopes of many that such wasteful expenditures of time and money could finally be eliminated.

Corresponding to the court's broad initial jurisdiction are provisions for nationwide service of process. Most proceedings arising in or related to a bankruptcy case may be commenced in the court where that case is pending even if that court is in Maine and the defendant is in Hawaii.[25] However, a case or proceeding may be transferred to another district in the interest of justice or for the convenience of the parties.[26]

Furthermore, proceedings already commenced elsewhere may be removed by a party to a district court that has bankruptcy jurisdiction.[27] This provision can be of tremendous assistance in obtaining a better forum or other procedural advantages in a particular case. It should be noted, though, that the receiving court may choose to remand the proceeding, and that such a decision is not reviewable by appeal or otherwise except by the district court.[28]

Finally, assuming a matter is properly referred to it, the bankruptcy court, in some circumstances, may conduct jury trials in cases in which the right to a jury trial exists.[29] The district court in a bankruptcy case may issue writs of habeas corpus[30] and the bankruptcy court may issue any other order, process, or judgment necessary to carry out its functions.[31] The bankruptcy court generally has all the powers of a court of equity, law, and admiralty.[32]

2.4.3 Appeals

There are several possible avenues for appeals from the bankruptcy court. The path to be taken depends upon the wishes of the parties, the practice adopted by the federal district court and judicial circuit where the bankruptcy court is located and, in some cases, the consent of an appellate court.

In the case of a final judgment, order or decree, when a bankruptcy court is authorized to enter one, an appeal is normally taken to the district court.[33] Further appeals from the district court decision may then be taken to the court of appeals, provided the district court's order is also a final order.[34] However, there is no statutory provision explaining what is or is not a final judgment, order, or decree, and some uncertainty remains.[35]

The principal exception to this general rule is when a bankruptcy appellate panel service (BAPS) has been established by the judicial council of the circuit to hear appeals arising in the district where the case is pending.[36] An appeal from a bankruptcy court order may be taken to a panel of three bankruptcy judges appointed to a bankruptcy appellate panel (BAP) instead of to the district court only if (1) all parties consent and (2) the district judges for the district, by majority vote, have authorized referral of appeals to the appellate panel.[37]

---

23 28 U.S.C. § 157(b), (c). One aspect of this scheme, allowing bankruptcy judges to enter final judgments on certain counterclaims against creditors who file claims, was found unconstitutional in *Stern v. Marshall*, 131 S. Ct. 2594, 180 L. Ed. 2d 475 (2011). This issue is discussed further in Chapter 14, *infra*.
24 See Chapter 14, *infra*, for further discussion of jurisdictional issues.
25 28 U.S.C. § 1409.
    There are, however, certain venue limitations on actions for small amounts of money or property, on postpetition claims brought by or against a trustee, and on actions brought by a trustee as successor to the debtor or creditors. 28 U.S.C. § 1409(b)–(e).
26 28 U.S.C. § 1412.
27 28 U.S.C. § 1452.
    Exceptions to this principle are proceedings in the United States Tax Court and civil actions by governmental units to enforce their police or regulatory powers. Removed proceedings will normally be referred to bankruptcy judges like all other proceedings. Fed. R. Bankr. P. 9027(f). See Chapter 14, *infra*, for discussion of removal.
28 28 U.S.C. § 1452(b). *But see* Pacor Inc. v. Higgins, 743 F.2d 984 (3d Cir. 1984) (decision may be reviewed if jurisdictional issues involved).
29 28 U.S.C. §§ 157(e), 1411. See § 14.2.7, *infra*, for further discussion of jury trials in the bankruptcy court.
30 While 28 U.S.C. § 2256, specifically permitting bankruptcy courts to issue writs of habeas corpus, was repealed in 1984, the issuance of such writs could possibly be delegated to bankruptcy courts pursuant to 28 U.S.C. § 157. *See* § 14.4.5, *infra*.
31 11 U.S.C. § 105(a).
32 While 28 U.S.C. § 1481, specifically conferring these powers upon the bankruptcy court, was repealed in 1984, 28 U.S.C. § 151 grants bankruptcy judges "the authority conferred under this chapter with respect to any action suit or proceeding . . . except as otherwise provided by law or by rule or order of the district court." United States v. Energy Res., Inc., 495 U.S. 545, 549, 110 S. Ct. 2139, 109 L. Ed. 2d 580 (1990) (bankruptcy courts, as courts of equity, have broad power to modify creditor-debtor relationships). See generally Chapter 14, *infra*, for further discussion of bankruptcy jurisdiction.
33 28 U.S.C. § 158(a).
34 28 U.S.C. § 158(d)(1).
35 See Chapter 14, *infra*, for discussion of what orders are final orders.
36 *See* 28 U.S.C. § 158(b).
    The courts of appeals for the First, Sixth, Eighth, Ninth, and Tenth Circuits have established appellate panels for all or some of the districts within their circuits. The First, Ninth, and Tenth Circuit panels hear appeals from all districts in the circuit. The Sixth Circuit appellate panel hears appeals arising only in the Northern and Southern Districts of Ohio. The Eighth Circuit panel hears appeals arising anywhere in the circuit except those arising in the District of South Dakota.
37 28 U.S.C. § 158(b).
    Parties required to consent probably include all those with any adversarial interest in the proceeding. *See In re* Odom, 702 F.2d 962 (11th Cir. 1983).
    Under the statute as amended, if a bankruptcy appellate panel is authorized to hear appeals, consent is presumed unless the appellant elects, at the time of filing the appeal, to have the appeal heard in district court, or any other party so elects, by a separate writing, within thirty days after service of the notice of appeal. 28 U.S.C. § 158(c)(1).

The 2005 amendments added a second exception, permitting a direct appeal from the bankruptcy court to the court of appeals in certain circumstances.[38] The court of appeals must agree to hear the appeal, which will not occur frequently. And that court may only be asked to hear a direct appeal from the bankruptcy court if either the court where the case is pending certifies,[39] or all of the parties jointly certify, that the case:

- Involves a question on which there is no controlling court of appeals or Supreme Court authority;
- Involves a matter of public importance;
- Involves a question of law requiring resolution of conflicting decisions; *or*
- May be materially advanced by a direct appeal.[40]

Appellate procedure for interlocutory orders and decrees is somewhat different. An appeal to either a three-judge bankruptcy appellate panel or the district court (whichever is applicable) is permitted only with the leave of that panel or district court.[41] At least one bankruptcy appellate panel has held that only a showing of exceptional circumstances will justify the granting of such leave to appeal.[42] In addition, the procedures for direct appeals to the court of appeals also apply if such an appeal is sought. When the district court or appellate panel takes an appeal of an interlocutory order, there is then a further right of appeal to the court of appeals for that circuit.[43]

The procedure for appeals to a district court or bankruptcy appellate panel is governed by the Federal Rules of Bankruptcy Procedure.[44] These rules are similar to the Federal Rules of Appellate Procedure, but they differ in several significant respects, most notably in the fourteen-day time limit for such appeals.[45] Procedures for seeking a direct appeal to the court of appeals are set forth in Bankruptcy Rule 8001(f). The Federal Rules of Appellate Procedure govern cases appealed to the court of appeals.[46]

2.5 The Bankruptcy Estate

2.5.1 Contents of the Estate

The term *bankruptcy estate* describes the aggregation of property rights that can be administered by the court in a bankruptcy case. The estate is created upon the commencement of the case and it generally consists of all interests of the debtor in any kind of property as of that time.[47] It includes interests in community property, entireties property, and other property which cannot be attached under state law, such as the right to receive various kinds of income in the future.[48] Moreover, property comes into the bankruptcy estate free from restrictions

---

38 28 U.S.C. § 158(d).

This statute also provides that a direct appeal to the court of appeals may be made while an appeal from the bankruptcy court is still pending in the district court or bankruptcy appellate panel, prior to a decision by the district court or bankruptcy appellate panel, at least in certain circumstances. See generally Chapter 14, *infra*, for further discussion of direct appeals to the court of appeals.

39 The court may make the certification on its own motion or upon request of a party, but must make the certification if it receives a request from the majority of the appellants and the majority of the appellees (if any). 28 U.S.C. § 158(d)(2)(B).

40 28 U.S.C. § 158(d)(2)(A); Fed. R. Bankr. P. 8001(f).

41 28 U.S.C. § 158(a), (b); Fed. R. Bankr. P. 8001(e). See § 14.9.1, *infra*.

42 *In re* Nat'l Shoes, 20 B.R. 672 (B.A.P. 1st Cir. 1982).

43 28 U.S.C. § 1292; Conn. Nat'l Bank v. Germain, 503 U.S. 249, 112 S. Ct. 1146, 117 L. Ed. 2d 391 (1992).

44 Fed. R. Bankr. P. 8001–8019.

See Chapter 14, *infra*, for further discussion of appellate procedure in bankruptcy cases.

45 Fed. R. Bankr. P. 8002(a).

As the fourteen-day period includes intervening holidays and weekends, a decision on whether to appeal has to be made relatively quickly. See Fed. R. Bankr. P. 9006(a).

46 Fed. R. Bankr. P. 8001 advisory committee's note.

47 11 U.S.C. § 541. See, *e.g.*, *In re* Nejberger, 934 F.2d 1300 (3d Cir. 1991) (even though debtor's liquor license had expired prepetition, right to make late renewal application comes into the estate); Miller v. Shallowford Cmty. Hosp., Inc., 767 F.2d 1556 (11th Cir. 1985) (debtor's right to receive insurance benefits existing on date bankruptcy was filed held property of the estate even though right to benefits became apparent under state law only after that date); NLT Computer Servs. v. Capital Computer Sys., 755 F.2d 1253 (6th Cir. 1985) (fact that monies had been paid into registry of district court in interpleader action did not prevent them from becoming property of the estate in a subsequent bankruptcy).

However, property belonging to a debtor's children is not property of the estate. *In re* Biancavilla, 173 B.R. 930 (Bankr. D. Idaho 1994).

48 Parks v. Dittmar (*In re* Dittmar), 618 F.3d 1199 (10th Cir. 2010) (stock appreciation rights received from employer postpetition were property of the estate because debtor had contingent entitlement to them pursuant to prepetition collective bargaining agreement). See, *e.g.*, *In re* Parsons, 280 F.3d 1185 (8th Cir. 2002) (real estate commissions attributable to prepetition contracts were property of estate); *In re* Yonikus, 996 F.2d 866 (7th Cir. 1993) (contingent right to receive workers' compensation in the future was property of the estate); *In re* Lonstein, 950 F.2d 77 (1st Cir. 1991) (debtor's vested interest in bequest under will was property of the estate); Sierra Switchboard Co. v. Westinghouse Elec. Corp., 789 F.2d 705 (9th Cir. 1986) (emotional distress claim was property of the estate); *In re* Wicheff, 215 B.R. 839 (B.A.P. 6th Cir. 1998) (debtor's right to receive insurance commissions after bankruptcy based upon prepetition sales of insurance was property of estate); Smoker v. Hill & Assoc., Inc., 204 B.R. 966 (N.D. Ind. 1997) (contingent interest in employer's profit-sharing plan was property of estate to extent attributable to prepetition earnings); Morris v. Philadelphia Elec. Co., 45 B.R. 350 (E.D. Pa. 1984) (fuel assistance grants to which debtor was entitled on date of bankruptcy held property of estate despite the fact that they were to be paid directly to utility); *In re* Dibiase, 270 B.R. 673 (Bankr. W.D. Tex. 2001) (stock options were property of estate even though they were subject to forfeiture if debtor's employment terminated prior to one year of employment); *In re* Lawton, 261 B.R. 774 (Bankr. M.D. Fla. 2001) (stock options property of estate, but not to the extent they were attributable to work performed postpetition); *In re* Edmonds, 273 B.R. 527 (Bankr. E.D. Mich. 2000) (contingent interest in employer's profit-sharing plan was property of estate to extent attributable to prepetition earnings); *In re* Scanlon, 10 B.R. 245 (Bankr. S.D. Cal. 1981) (right to receive sales commission is property of estate). But see *In re* Chappo, 257 B.R. 852 (E.D. Mich. 2001) (employment bonus received postpetition not property of estate when employer retained right to modify or terminate bonus plan at any time before distribution); *In re* Fess, 408 B.R. 793 (Bankr. W.D. Wis. 2009) (under tribal law, debtor had no right to tribal casino revenue distribution

conditioned on insolvency or the filing of a bankruptcy case.[49]

The estate also includes property recovered by the trustee,[50] proceeds or rents of property already in the estate,[51] prepetition causes of action or claims possessed by debtor,[52] interests in insurance policies,[53] and various other interests set forth in 11 U.S.C. § 541. Generally, except when the trustee brings property into the estate through the use of an avoiding power, the estate's interest in such property is no greater than the debtor's interest at the time of the filing of the bankruptcy petition.[54] And, in addition to the debtor's interest in property, if only one spouse in a community property jurisdiction files a petition, the estate may sometimes include the other spouse's share of all community property.[55]

Although most property acquired by the debtor after commencement of the case does not come into the estate,[56] there are

---

until it was actually paid, so postpetition payment was not property of estate).

49   11 U.S.C. § 541(c)(1)(B). See *In re* Knapp, 137 B.R. 582 (Bankr. D.N.J. 1992) (when only reason that creditor revoked debtor's credit card was the filing of a bankruptcy case, that revocation was invalid under the Code, and chapter 13 debtor had right to continue using card).

50   The bankruptcy trustee is discussed in § 2.6, *infra*. The trustee may recover property from other parties in various ways, discussed in Chapter 10, *infra*, along with the debtor's power to recover exempt property.

51   *See, e.g.*, Bradt v. Woodlawn Auto Workers Fed. Credit Union, 757 F.2d 512 (2d Cir. 1985) (insurance payment for collision repairs to automobile that was property of the estate was also property of the estate because payment constituted proceeds of property of the estate). See also *In re* Bumper Sales, Inc., 907 F.2d 1430 (4th Cir. 1990) (section 552(b) protects security interests in after-acquired property when such property constitutes proceeds of property already in the estate). *Cf. In re* Jones, 908 F.2d 859 (11th Cir. 1990) (postpetition increases in value of property created by postpetition payments do not constitute proceeds within the meaning of section 552(b)).

52   *See* Bracewell v. Kelley, 454 F.3d 1234 (11th Cir. 2006) (crop disaster payment not property of estate because statute authorizing entitlement to payment was not passed until after date of petition), *cert. denied*, 127 S. Ct. 1815 (2007); *In re* Burgess, 438 F.3d 493 (5th Cir. 2006) (en banc) (although right to crop disaster payment was rooted in prebankruptcy past, it was not property of estate because statute authorizing payment not passed until after petition date); Wieburg v. GTE Southwest, Inc., 272 F.3d 302 (5th Cir. 2001) (employment discrimination claim was property of estate); *In re* Crysen/Montenay Energy Co., 902 F.2d 1098 (2d Cir. 1990) (debtor's right to collect accounts receivable is property of the estate); *In re* Cottrell, 876 F.2d 540 (6th Cir. 1989) (personal injury action is property of the estate even though action is not assignable under state law and may be prosecuted by chapter 7 trustee); Jones v. Harell, 858 F.2d 667 (11th Cir. 1988); Krank v. Utica Mut. Ins. Co., 109 B.R. 668 (E.D. Pa.) (once cause of action becomes property of the estate, debtor may not bring suit unless that property is abandoned by the trustee), *aff'd*, 908 F.2d 962 (3d Cir. 1990) (table). *See also* § 2.6, *infra*. *But see In re* Witko, 374 F.3d 1040 (5th Cir. 2004) (Florida legal malpractice action did not accrue to debtor until postpetition resolution of lawsuit, so was not property of estate).

53   *See In re* Titan Energy, Inc., 837 F.2d 325 (8th Cir. 1988) (bankruptcy court has jurisdiction over suit to determine scope of insurer's liability to the debtor, but may abstain from hearing dispute).

The estate does not normally include the proceeds of an insurance policy, unless the debtor is the beneficiary presently entitled to the proceeds of the policy. Wornick v. Gaffney, 544 F.3d 486 (2d Cir. 2008) (beneficiary has no legal or equitable interest in life insurance policy on living individual (which is subject to change by policy's owner) that could be made part of the property of the beneficiary's bankruptcy estate); *In re* Edgeworth, 993 F.2d 51 (5th Cir. 1993) (malpractice policy proceeds were not property of estate); First Fid. Bank v. McAteer, 985 F.2d 114 (3d Cir. 1993) (credit life insurance proceeds not property of the estate; proceeds belong to creditor/beneficiary rather than estate); Counties Contracting & Constr. Co. v. Constitution Life Ins. Co., 855 F.2d 1054 (3d Cir. 1988) (debtor's interest in reinstating lapsed policy during policy's "grace period" is property of the estate and is extended by operation of 11 U.S.C. § 108, but unless policy is reinstated, debtor cannot collect benefits). *But see In re* Baird, 567 F.3d 1207 (10th Cir. 2009) (trustee had right to sell debtor doctor's rights in malpractice policy to plaintiffs in suit against debtor).

54   *See In re* Bergman, 467 F.3d 536 (6th Cir. 2006) (estate's interest in personal injury claim did not include amount subject to subrogation rights of insurer that had paid debtor's medical expenses); Universal Bonding v. Gittens & Sprinkle Enter., Inc., 960 F.2d 366 (3d Cir. 1992) (when monies paid to contractor had to be held in trust for laborers and materialmen, estate could gain only legal title to those funds, which would be held in trust for benefit of laborers and materialmen); *In re* Crossman, 259 B.R. 301 (Bankr. N.D. Ill. 2001) (trustee could not sell right to future payments under structured personal injury settlement when such sale was prohibited by state law and settlement agreement); *In re* Thompson, 253 B.R. 823 (Bankr. N.D. Ohio 2000) (trustee could not compel turnover of pro rata refund for future months' rental fees, which debtor would have been able to obtain if she had moved from residence, when debtor had not elected to move).

55   11 U.S.C. § 541(a)(2). *See In re* Fingado, 995 F.2d 175 (10th Cir. 1993) (property acquired by married couple through an instrument indicating joint ownership was community property under New Mexico law and therefore was property of the bankruptcy estate); *In re* Petersen, 437 B.R. 858 (D. Ariz. 2010) (although nondebtor spouse was required to turn over to trustee his share of community property, turnover was subject to recoupment of amounts he was to receive from community property pursuant to prepetition divorce decree, because trustee takes property subject to rights of recoupment). *Cf. In re* LaNess, 159 B.R. 916 (Bankr. S.D. Cal. 1993) (estate did not include community property not yet divided after couple's divorce, because section 541(a)(2) refers to property of the debtor and the debtor's spouse, and the couple was no longer married when the bankruptcy case was filed).

It is unclear what happens under this provision and other similar provisions in the Code with respect to community property of domestic partners or spouses who are of the same gender, because the federal Defense of Marriage Act, 1 U.S.C. § 7, provides that in interpreting all federal statutes "spouse" refers "only to a person of the opposite sex who is a husband or wife." *See* Collier on Bankruptcy ¶ 541.13[5] (16th ed.); Robert F. Kidd & Frederick C. Hertz, *Partnered in Debt: The Impacts of California's New Registered Domestic Partner Law on Creditors' Remedies and Debtors' Rights under California Law and under Federal Bankruptcy Law*, 28 Cal. Bankr. J. 148 (2006).

56   11 U.S.C. § 541(a)(6); Patrick A. Casey, P.A. v. Hochman, 963 F.2d 1347 (10th Cir. 1992) (patent on device invented by debtor after bankruptcy petition filed was not property of the estate); *In re* Clark, 891 F.2d 111 (5th Cir. 1989) (salary paid postpetition pursuant to a prepetition contract not property of the estate in chapter 7); *In re* Swanson, 36 B.R. 99 (B.A.P. 9th Cir. 1984). *But see In re* Froid, 109 B.R. 481 (Bankr. M.D. Fla. 1989) (postpetition renewal commissions for insurance policies sold prepetition are property of the

exceptions for certain types of property acquired within 180 days of filing. These exceptions include property acquired by bequest or inheritance,[57] through a spousal property settlement or divorce decree,[58] or as a beneficiary of life insurance. The 180 days runs from the date the original bankruptcy petition is filed, even if a case is converted from one chapter to another.[59] Also, in a chapter 13 case, all property and earnings acquired during the pendency of the case (unless the case is converted to another chapter) are property of the estate.[60]

Even very limited and remote property interests are included in the debtor's bankruptcy estate. For example, bare legal title to property, as a trustee or as a convenience co-tenant, brings an interest in that property into the estate.[61] Property of the debtor in the hands of a creditor after repossession also comes into the estate, subject to the creditor's lien.[62] Similarly, a mere possessory interest without legal title is sufficient to bring property into the estate.[63] Such property may not be available for actual administration by the trustee however, as the estate's interest is

---

estate because no postpetition services were performed by the debtor).

57 11 U.S.C. § 541(a)(5). *See In re* Newman, 903 F.2d 1150 (7th Cir. 1990) (distribution from spendthrift trust within 180 days of petition is not property of the estate under section 541(a)(5) because it is not acquired by bequest, devise or inheritance); Bakst v. Miller (*In re* Miller), 441 B.R. 154 (Bankr. S.D. Fla. 2010) (debtor's right to take elective share of deceased spouse's estate was not property of estate, because it was not property under state law, and share of estate debtor received when he exercised election more than 180 days after petition was not property of estate); *In re* Roth, 289 B.R. 161 (Bankr. D. Kan. 2003) (postpetition distribution from an *inter vivos* trust that occurred after settlor's death and within 180 days of petition was not "bequest, devise, or inheritance"); *In re* Hendricks, 22 B.R. 572 (Bankr. W.D. Mo. 1982) (rights accruing to the debtor within 180 days under wrongful death statute held property of the estate).

Courts interpreting various state laws have held that funds a debtor receives from a "payable on death" account, "transfer on death" deed, or other contractual relationships are not received by bequest, devise, or inheritance. Williamson v. Hall (*In re* Hall), 441 B.R. 680 (B.A.P. 10th Cir. 2009); *In re* Kilstrom, 2011 Bankr. LEXIS 955 (Bankr. N.D. Iowa Mar. 17, 2011); *In re* Holter, 401 B.R. 372 (Bankr. W.D. Wis. 2009) and cases cited therein.

A debtor's effort to disclaim an interest in an inheritance may not be effective. *See In re* Kolb, 326 F.3d 1030 (9th Cir. 2003) (prepetition disclaimer was invalid because debtor had already "accepted" interest in trust by listing it as an asset in a loan application); *In re* Chenoweth, 3 F.3d 1111 (7th Cir. 1993) (debtor who inherited property within 180 days after bankruptcy case filed could not disclaim inheritance and thereby keep property out of estate; debtor became entitled to acquire property, for purposes of 11 U.S.C. § 541(a)(5), when testator died, not when will was probated); *In re* Cornell, 95 B.R. 219 (Bankr. W.D. Okla. 1989). *See also In re* Stevens, 112 B.R. 175 (Bankr. S.D. Tex. 1989) (prepetition disclaimer of interest in estate is avoidable by the trustee as a fraudulent transfer); §§ 10.4.2.6.2 n.431, 10.4.2.6.5 n.505, *infra*. *Cf. In re* Simpson, 36 F.3d 450 (5th Cir. 1994) (prebankruptcy disclaimer of any interest in deceased father's estate was not a fraudulent transfer because the debtor never had a state law interest in the disclaimed property); *In re* Atchison, 925 F.2d 209 (7th Cir. 1991) (prepetition disclaimer of inheritance prevents property from vesting in the debtor or her estate).

58 *See In re* Fritch, 2011 WL 2181661 (Bankr. S.D. Ind. June 3, 2011) (debtor became entitled to property settlement when divorce was filed, even if final decree was more than 180 days after petition). However, several courts have held that alimony or support rights, as opposed to property settlements, are not included within this provision. *In re* Wise, 346 F.3d 1239 (10th Cir. 2003); *In re* Jeter, 257 B.R. 907 (B.A.P. 8th Cir. 2001).

Several courts have also held that rights to child support belong to the child and not to the divorcing spouse. *In re* Perry, 2009 WL 367079 (Bankr. D.S.D. Feb. 13, 2009) (child support payments owed to debtor as trustee for children). *See, e.g., In re* Poffenbarger, 281 B.R. 379 (Bankr. S.D. Ala. 2002).

For conflicting decisions on whether entireties property of which a debtor becomes sole owner pursuant to a divorce within the 180 days may still be exempted under 11 U.S.C. § 522(b)(2)(B), see § 10.2.3.2, *infra*. *See also In re* Etoll, 425 B.R. 743 (Bankr. D.N.J. 2010) (upon death of debtor who is an entireties co-tenant with a nondebtor, estate's interest ceases to exist).

59 *In re* Carter, 260 B.R. 130 (Bankr. W.D. Tenn. 2001).

60 11 U.S.C. § 1306(a). *See* § 12.8.1, *infra*. *But see In re* Key, 465 B.R. 709 (Bankr. S.D. Ga. 2012) (property excluded from estate by § 541, other than wages and income specifically mentioned in § 1306(a) is not brought into estate by § 1306(a)). *Cf. In re* Meade, 84 B.R. 106 (Bankr. S.D. Ohio 1988) (wages earned by chapter 7 debtor prepetition are property of the estate even if unpaid, but wages earned postpetition are not).

However, social security benefits received by the debtor, whether prepetition or postpetition, are not property of the estate based on 42 U.S.C. § 407. *See In re* Carpenter, 614 F.3d 930 (8th Cir. 2010).

61 *See* Ga. Pac. Corp. v. Sigma Serv. Corp., 712 F.2d 962 (5th Cir. 1983) (debtor had interest in property subject to constructive trust). *See also In re* Crabtree, 871 F.2d 36 (6th Cir. 1989) (under Florida law, debtor owns property in fee although deed named debtor as trustee, when no beneficiary is named and no declaration of trust recorded). *Cf.* Parker v. Handy (*In re* Handy), 624 F.3d 19 (1st Cir. 2010) (creditor had no *in rem* interest in property merely because it had asserted an unadjudicated claim seeking constructive trust); T & B Scottdale Contractors, Inc. v. United States, 866 F.2d 1372 (11th Cir. 1989) (debtor had no interest in funds being held in joint account when funds were clearly deposited to satisfy secured claim of third party); *In re* Newcomb, 744 F.2d 621 (8th Cir. 1984) (debtor had no interest in escrowed funds when, at time of petition, condition of escrow agreement had been fulfilled); *In re* Vitta, 409 B.R. 6 (Bankr. E.D.N.Y. 2009) (civil forfeiture proceeding did not eliminate debtor's ownership rights under New York law because the order was only a provisional remedy). *But see In re* Thena, 190 B.R. 407 (D. Or. 1995) (property seized under criminal forfeiture statute was not property of estate even though no criminal charges had yet been brought).

62 United States v. Whiting Pools, Inc., 462 U.S. 198, 103 S. Ct. 2309, 76 L. Ed. 2d 515 (1983); *In re* Knaus, 889 F.2d 773 (8th Cir. 1989). *But see In re* Lewis, 137 F.3d 1280 (11th Cir. 1998) (under Alabama law, debtor no longer has possessory right or title to an automobile after repossession so that only a right of redemption comes into the estate).

The *Lewis* decision fails to explain its inconsistency with *Whiting Pools*. Numerous courts have disagreed with it. *See* § 9.9.2, *infra*.

63 *In re* Atl. Bus. & Cmty. Corp., 901 F.2d 325 (3d Cir. 1990); *In re* 48th St. Steakhouse, Inc., 835 F.2d 427 (2d Cir. 1987); *In re* Preston, 428 B.R. 340 (Bankr. W.D.N.C. 2009) (employer travel advance is not estate property); *In re* Mumpfield, 140 B.R. 578 (Bankr. M.D. Ala. 1991) (vendee in contract for sale of real property who became chapter 13 debtor had a property interest that became property of the estate even though vendor had terminated contract and sought eviction, because debtor was still in possession of the property).

usually limited to the debtor's interest.[64] The nature of that interest is generally determined under state law.[65] If the debtor has no right under state law to transfer the property, the trustee usually does not have that right either.

Significant issues may arise when two or more people jointly own property and only one of the co-owners files a bankruptcy case.[66] Although the debtor's partial interest in the property clearly comes into the estate, the Code mandates some protection of the interests of the non-debtor co-owner.[67]

Counsel must exercise care in identifying and listing a debtor's various interests in property. Failure to properly list property of the estate in the debtor's schedules may be grounds to deny or revoke the debtor's discharge[68] and may give rise to claims by creditors or the trustee against the unlisted property.[69]

---

[64] *See, e.g.,* Davis v. Cox, 356 F.3d 76 (1st Cir. 2004) (debtor had only contingent interest in funds held in escrow account pursuant to divorce court order and, based on equities and preliminary injunction issued upon filing of divorce, IRA funds were held by debtor in constructive trust); *In re* Baum, 22 F.3d 1014 (10th Cir. 1994) (although debtor was settlor and trustee of trusts for his children, he did not have power to revest property in himself, so trust assets were not property of bankruptcy estate); Chiu v. Wong, 16 F.3d 306 (8th Cir. 1994) (constructive trust imposed upon debtor's homestead so that equitable interest of trust beneficiary was not property of bankruptcy estate); *In re* Columbia Gas Sys., Inc., 997 F.2d 1039 (3d Cir. 1993) (estate's interest did not include property subject to constructive trust created by federal common law, to extent that trust property can be traced when commingled with other property); Mid-Atlantic Supply v. Three Rivers Aluminum Co., 790 F.2d 1121 (4th Cir. 1986) (property held in trust belongs to beneficiary); *In re* N.S. Garrott & Sons, 772 F.2d 462 (8th Cir. 1985) (estate's interest in property subject to constructive trust); *In re* Schmitt, 215 B.R. 417 (B.A.P. 9th Cir. 1997) (property granted to debtor in a revocable trust did not become property of estate because state law deemed such property to belong to grantors of trust); *In re* Catenaccio, 2010 WL 5207586 (Bankr. D.N.J. Dec. 16, 2010) (trustee did not rebut state law presumption that depositors owned funds in joint account in proportion to their deposits to account); *In re* Dally, 202 B.R. 724 (Bankr. N.D. Ill. 1996) (money in custodial accounts for debtor's children established under Uniform Gifts to Minors Act not property of estate); *In re* Amos, 201 B.R. 184 (Bankr. N.D. Ohio 1996) (van titled in debtor's name was property of her boyfriend, who paid for it and was beneficial owner pursuant to express trust). *See also In re* Corrigan, 93 B.R. 81 (Bankr. E.D. Va. 1988) (estate has no interest in portion of military retirement pay awarded to ex-wife under final decree of divorce). *But see In re* Kemp, 52 F.3d 546 (5th Cir. 1995) (prepetition commissions purportedly escrowed by debtor's employer were property of estate); *In re* First Capital Mortgage Loan Corp., 917 F.2d 424 (10th Cir. 1990) (en banc) (escrow funds recovered by the trustee pursuant to avoiding powers become property of the estate and escrow depositor holds only a general unsecured claim); *In re* Beatrice, 296 B.R. 576 (B.A.P. 1st Cir. 2003) (property that debtor claimed to have put in trust for children was property of the estate because debtor retained incidents of ownership including power to terminate trust); *In re* Ross, 162 B.R. 863 (Bankr. D. Idaho 1993) (debtor's power to revoke "living trust" was property of bankruptcy estate and trustee could exercise revocation power).

In some cases, the trustee's avoiding powers may defeat the unrecorded interest of the beneficiary of a constructive trust. *Compare In re* Omegas Group, 16 F.3d 1443 (6th Cir. 1994) (constructive trust is a legal fiction which, absent prebankruptcy judicial action impressing a trust on property, does not create a property interest in the party who claims a constructive trust interest) *and* Belisle v. Plunkett, 877 F.2d 512 (7th Cir. 1989) (equitable ownership could be defeated by bona fide purchaser under state law) *with In re* Howard's Appliance Corp., 874 F.2d 88 (2d Cir. 1989) (contra).

The holding of *Omegas Group* has been substantially narrowed in subsequent cases. *See In re* Morris, 260 F.3d 654 (6th Cir. 2001). *See generally* 11 U.S.C. § 544; § 10.4.2.6.2, *infra.*

[65] *See, e.g., In re* Yeary, 55 F.3d 504 (10th Cir. 1995) (chapter 13 debtors' prepetition settlement agreement had not effectuated a transfer of stock but merely created a security interest under state law, so stock was property of the estate); *In re* Crysen/Montenay Energy Co., 902 F.2d 1098 (2d Cir. 1990). *See also* W. United Life Assurance Co. v. Hayden, 64 F.3d 833 (3d Cir. 1995) (debtor had no interest in periodic payments made to her under structured settlement of lawsuit, because she had executed prepetition assignment of her rights that was valid under state law); Goldberg v. N.J. Lawyer's Fund, 932 F.2d 273 (3d Cir. 1991) (issue of whether trust exists is determined under state law). *Cf. In re* Bowden, 315 B.R. 903 (Bankr. W.D. Wash. 2004) (purported pledge of military benefits did not create express trust because law did not permit assignment of such benefits).

[66] *See In re* Mantle, 153 F.3d 1082 (9th Cir. 1998) (proceeds of sale of house which was community property are also community property and therefore proceeds were property of estate).

[67] 11 U.S.C. § 363(h). *See In re* Persky, 893 F.2d 15 (2d Cir. 1989) (although state law allows execution on one spouse's interest in a tenancy by the entireties, bankruptcy court must evaluate detriment of sale to non-debtor spouse under section 363(h)(3)); Lovald v. Tennyson (*In re* Wolk), 451 B.R. 468 (B.A.P. 8th Cir. 2011) (significant harm to co-owner outweighed minimal, if any, benefit to creditors from sale); *In re* Ziegler, 396 B.R. 1 (Bankr. N.D. Ohio 2008) (trustee could sell all remainder interests in property to realize value of debtor's one-sixth remainder interest, but could not sell interest of life tenant under section 363(h)); *In re* Hajjar, 385 B.R. 482 (Bankr. D. Mass. 2008) (life estate owner's interest could not be sold under section 363(h)); *In re* Nelson, 129 B.R. 427 (Bankr. W.D. Pa. 1991) (jointly owned property could not be sold under section 363(h) when co-owning non-debtor spouse had occupancy rights for the duration of her life). *See also In re* Heinze, 418 B.R. 576 (Bankr. M.D.N.C. 2009) (costs assessable against co-owner under section 363(j) do not include trustee's attorney fees).

On remand, the bankruptcy court in *In re* Persky, 134 B.R. 81 (Bankr. E.D.N.Y. 1991) held that retroactive application of section 363(h) to sell the interest of a non-debtor spouse who was not involved in any debtor-creditor relationship would violate the takings clause of the Fifth Amendment to the United States Constitution because it was not a public use that would justify a taking. *See also In re* Flynn, 418 F.3d 1005 (9th Cir. 2005) (attorney fees and trustee compensation could not be deducted from proceeds of jointly owned property payable to non-debtor co-owner when property sold by trustee); *In re* Lyons, 995 F.2d 923 (9th Cir. 1993) (proceeding by trustee seeking authority to sell property pursuant to section 363(h) must be adversary proceeding and not a motion).

[68] 11 U.S.C. § 727(a)(2), (4), (5), 727(d). *See* §§ 15.2, 15.3, *infra.*

[69] *See* Krank v. Utica Mut. Ins. Co., 109 B.R. 668 (E.D. Pa. 1990), *aff'd,* 908 F.2d 962 (3d Cir. 1990) (debtor may not enforce prepetition cause of action not listed in his schedules without reopening bankruptcy case and allowing trustee an opportunity to enforce or abandon the claim). *See also* Vreugdenhill v. Navistar Int'l Transp. Corp., 950 F.2d 524 (8th Cir. 1991) (claim belonging to debtor was not abandoned back to debtor at close of case, even though trustee knew of claim, because debtor had not formally scheduled it as property).

Most consumer debtors will find that they can exempt all or almost all property of their estate.[70] Even property which cannot be exempted is often of little interest to the trustee, because of the cost of liquidation, including payment of liens and taxes, and is therefore abandoned or sold back to the debtor.[71]

2.5.2 Pensions and Spendthrift Trusts

Particularly thorny issues arise in evaluating whether the beneficiary's interest in pensions, retirement funds, certain employee benefit accounts, and spendthrift trusts come into the estate. Section 541(c)(2) of the Bankruptcy Code provides that "[a] restriction on the transfer of a beneficial interest of the debtor in a trust that is enforceable under applicable nonbankruptcy law is enforceable in a case under this title." This provision means that when the beneficiaries of a trust cannot lose their interests in that trust to a creditor outside of bankruptcy, they are equally protected in the bankruptcy case.[72]

For many years, courts reached various conclusions about whether section 541(c)(2) protects ERISA-qualified pension plans by excluding them from a debtor's bankruptcy estate. The issue was whether the "anti-alienation" provision protecting ERISA-qualified pensions[73] constituted "applicable nonbankruptcy law" such that those pensions could not be transferred to a debtor's bankruptcy estate.[74]

Fortunately, in 1992 the Supreme Court cleared up the morass of case law in the area and concluded that ERISA does protect debtors' pensions.[75] The Court held that a debtor's interest in an ERISA-qualified pension is outside the estate based on section 541(c)(2).[76] The entire plan, including after-tax contributions, is excluded from the estate, because the entire plan is subject to the anti-alienation language.[77] If a plan is an ERISA plan and has the anti-alienation language, it does not matter whether the plan is also tax-qualified.[78]

The importance of determining whether a retirement plan is excluded from the estate was greatly reduced by the 2005 amendments. New subsections 522(b)(3)(C) and (d)(12) permit a debtor to exempt, usually without any limitation, all funds in most types of retirement plans.[79] In addition, new provisions made clear that any amounts withheld or received by employers for retirement plans or employee benefit plans are not property of the estate.[80]

For those few pension plans that cannot be exempted, some issues nevertheless remain. Debtors who have filed bankruptcy cases while in the process of rolling over their pension funds into another plan have been faced with claims that the funds were not in an ERISA plan on the date of bankruptcy and were therefore not excluded from the estate.[81] The policy of protect-

---

A debtor's failure to schedule a prepetition cause of action may also bar the debtor from pursuing that cause of action under the doctrine of judicial estoppel. *See* §§ 7.3.7.2.2, 14.3.2.6, *infra*.

Funds in bank accounts on the petition date, because debtors have written checks that have not yet been cashed, are property of the estate. The cases are split regarding whether debtors have an obligation to provide such funds to the trustee, to the extent they are not exempted, when the checks have been cashed after the petition is filed. *See* § 5.3.3.2 n.5, *infra*.

70 11 U.S.C. § 522. *See* Ch. 10, *infra*.
71 11 U.S.C. § 554. *See* §§ 3.5, 8.3.11, *infra*.
72 *See In re* Frank-Hill, 300 B.R. 25 (Bankr. D. Ariz. 2003) (funds held in trust in Individual Indian Money Account by U.S. Dep't of Interior subject to restrictions on transfer and not property of estate).
73 29 U.S.C. § 1056(d)(1).
"ERISA" is the Employee Retirement Income Security Act of 1974.
74 *Compare In re* Harline, 950 F.2d 669 (10th Cir. 1991) (ERISA anti-alienation provision constitutes "applicable nonbankruptcy law") *with In re* Dyke, 943 F.2d 1435 (5th Cir. 1991) (ERISA does not protect pensions because "applicable nonbankruptcy law" encompasses only state law protections).
75 Patterson v. Shumate, 504 U.S. 753, 112 S. Ct. 2242, 119 L. Ed. 2d 519, *motion granted*, 505 U.S. 1239 (1992).
Based on this holding, it would seem that a claim that can be secured by a debtor's ERISA plan, such as a tax claim, cannot be an allowed secured claim, because an allowed secured claim is secured by property of the estate. *See* Internal Revenue Serv. v. Snyder, 343 F.3d 1171 (9th Cir. 2003) (tax lien on ERISA plan cannot create an allowed secured claim); *In re* Wingfield, 284 B.R. 787 (E.D. Va. 2002).

76 *But see In re* Harshbarger, 66 F.3d 775 (6th Cir. 1995) (funds that chapter 13 debtors wished to use to repay prepetition loan from ERISA plan were not excluded from the estate).
77 *In re* Conner, 73 F.3d 258 (9th Cir. 1996).
78 *In re* Sewell, 180 F.3d 707 (5th Cir. 1999) (ERISA plan excluded from estate even if acts of employer rendered plan not tax-qualified); *In re* Craig, 204 B.R. 756 (D.N.D. 1997); *In re* Bennett, 185 B.R. 4 (Bankr. E.D.N.Y. 1995) (ERISA plan need not be tax-qualified; Supreme Court's decision had looked only to non-alienation provisions); *In re* Hanes, 162 B.R. 733 (Bankr. E.D. Va. 1994) (pension plan need not be tax-qualified to be "ERISA-qualified"). *See also* Raymond B. Yates, M.D., P.C. Profit Sharing Plan v. Hendon, 541 U.S. 1, 124 S. Ct. 1330, 158 L. Ed. 2d 40 (2004) (working owner of business that has at least one non-owner employee who is not owner's spouse can be employee protected by ERISA); *In re* Stern, 345 F.3d 1036 (9th Cir. 2003) (when plan covered only owner and his spouse, owner was not protected by ERISA); *In re* Baker, 114 F.3d 636 (7th Cir. 1997) (ERISA violations did not render ERISA inapplicable, even if debtor violated his duties as trustee and exposed employer to extra taxes). *But see* Morlan v. Universal Guar. Life. Ins. Co., 298 F.3d 609 (7th Cir. 2002) (unlike ERISA pension benefits, ERISA welfare plan benefits are assignable); *In re* Adams, 302 B.R. 535 (B.A.P. 6th Cir. 2003) (ERISA exempts 403(b) plans from trust requirement so they are included in property of estate).
79 *See* §§ 10.2.2.13, 10.2.3.3, *infra*.
There is a $1,171,650 cap, waivable by the court, only with respect to IRA accounts that were never rolled over from another type of plan. 11 U.S.C. § 522(n).
80 11 U.S.C. § 541(b)(7); *In re* Braulick, 360 B.R. 327 (Bankr. D. Mont. 2006) (amounts in employers' hands were not property of estate).
81 *See In re* Toone, 140 B.R. 605 (Bankr. D. Mass. 1992) (funds were not in ERISA plan during rollover process and were property of estate even though tax law treated them as if they were in a plan during that period). *See also In re* Barshak, 106 F.3d 501 (3d Cir. 1997) (decided under Pennsylvania state exemption laws).
The *Barshak* result was subsequently overruled by an amendment to Pennsylvania's exemption laws. *Cf. In re* Goldman, 182 B.R. 622 (Bankr. D. Mass. 1995) (funds being rolled over could be exempted under state law, even though amount rolled over to IRA exceeded

ing pension plan benefits should prevail in this situation, but it is better to avoid such situations if at all possible by deferring either the bankruptcy case or the rollover so that the bankruptcy case is filed while the funds are in a qualified plan.[82] It does seem clear, though, that a plan does not lose its ERISA protections simply because it is funded in whole or in part by an employee debtor[83] or because the debtor has the right to receive a lump-sum distribution.[84]

There are also issues with respect to non-ERISA plans. For example, the *Patterson* Court pointed out that at least two types of retirement accounts do not qualify under ERISA and therefore are not entitled to its protection. These accounts are certain pensions established by governmental entities or religious organizations and individual retirement accounts (IRAs).[85] The treatment of these types of retirement accounts for purposes of determining whether they are property of the estate, along with other employee benefit plans not subject to ERISA's anti-alienation language, must still be analyzed on a case-by-case basis.[86]

However, it should be noted that government and church pensions qualify as exempt under subsections 522(b)(3)(C) and 522(d)(12).[87] In addition, they may have been established with provisions similar to the anti-alienation provisions in ERISA plans or may qualify for protection under state law.[88] And if the debtor has no right to reach the funds in a plan, the estate can have no greater rights. Thus, for example, when a county employee could not reach the funds in his retirement plan while he was still employed by the county, the trustee had no right to compel turnover of those funds.[89] Similarly, IRAs qualify as exempt under subsections 522(b)(3)(C) and (d)(12) (with a $1,171,650 waivable cap for funds that were never rolled over from another plan)[90] and may also be protected from alienation under state law.[91] Therefore, with these expanded protections for retirement savings, it will be rare for a debtor to lose such funds in a bankruptcy case.

Generally, other employee benefit plans are also protected, assuming they come within the ambit of section 541(b)(7),[92] ERISA's anti-alienation language, or alternative protections of the plan or state law. The benefits under some plans may not be vested so that they cannot be reached by debtors or their estates. One critical issue may be whether receipt of the funds is contingent upon additional services from the debtor or some other future event.[93]

---

amount that could be deposited to qualify for exemption), *aff'd*, 192 B.R. 1 (D. Mass. 1996); *In re* Nudo, 147 B.R. 68 (Bankr. N.D.N.Y. 1992) (state exemption statute protecting plan funds also protected funds to which debtor had access upon terminating employment, but which could be rolled over into another exemptible qualified account).

82 *See In re* Latta, 189 B.R. 222 (N.D. Ga. 1995) (pension plan proceeds withdrawn for purpose of rollover after chapter 7 case filed were not property of the estate).

83 *In re* Rueter, 11 F.3d 850 (9th Cir. 1993) (employee-funded plan excluded from bankruptcy estate); *In re* Conner, 165 B.R. 901 (B.A.P. 9th Cir. 1994) (plan excluded despite fact that it included employee after-tax contributions), *aff'd*, 73 F.3d 258 (9th Cir. 1996).

84 Whetzal v. Anderson, 32 F.3d 1302 (8th Cir. 1994) (retired debtor's right to immediate distribution did not become estate property).

85 Patterson v. Shumate, 504 U.S. 753, 112 S. Ct. 2242, 2249, 119 L. Ed. 2d 519, *motion granted*, 505 U.S. 1239 (1992).

86 *See, e.g., In re* Walker, 959 F.2d 894 (10th Cir. 1992) (plans not containing anti-alienation language were not excluded from estate, but could be exempted under Oklahoma law).

87 The exemptions for retirement benefits are discussed in §§ 10.2.2.11, 10.2.2.13, 10.2.3.3, *infra*.

88 Skiba v. Laher (*In re* Laher), 496 F.3d 279 (3d Cir. 2007) (university retirement plan was protected trust under New York law); *In re* Moses, 167 F.3d 470 (9th Cir. 1999) (medical group retirement plan was spendthrift trust under California law and therefore excluded from estate under section 541(c)(2)); Morter v. Farm Credit Serv., 937 F.2d 354 (7th Cir. 1991) (teacher's retirement account qualifies as spendthrift trust under state law and is excluded from estate); *In re* Tykla, 353 B.R. 437 (Bankr. W.D. Pa. 2006) (state law prohibiting alienation of employee's interest in state deferred compensation plan required plan to be treated as spendthrift trust excluded from estate); *In re* Fink, 153 B.R. 883 (Bankr. D. Neb. 1993) (teacher's retirement annuity plan was a trust and also subject to restrictions on transfer enforceable under nonbankruptcy law, so it was not property of the estate). *But see In re* Swanson, 873 F.2d 1121 (8th Cir. 1989) (teacher's retirement fund is property of the estate).

89 *In re* Sanders, 969 F.2d 591 (7th Cir. 1992).

90 IRAs that do not qualify as exempt under section 522(d)(12) may nevertheless qualify as exempt under section 522(d)(10)(E). *See* Rousey v. Jacoway, 544 U.S. 320, 125 S. Ct. 1561, 161 L. Ed. 2d 563 (2005). For cases filed before April 1, 2010, the dollar amount for the cap is $1,095,000.

91 *In re* Yuhas, 104 F.3d 612 (3d Cir. 1997) (state law deemed IRA to be a trust and exempted it from claims of creditors); *In re* Meehan, 102 F.3d 1209 (11th Cir. 1997) (IRA excluded from estate because state law prohibited garnishment of debtor's interest). See Velis v. Kardanis, 949 F.2d 78 (3d Cir. 1991) (IRA included in estate because debtor had reached age allowing free withdrawal); *In re* Nelson, 180 B.R. 584 (B.A.P. 9th Cir. 1995) (ERISA did not preempt state law exempting IRAs); *In re* Kramer, 128 B.R. 707 (Bankr. E.D.N.Y. 1991) (IRA does not qualify as spendthrift trust under New York law); *In re* Howerton, 21 B.R. 621 (Bankr. N.D. Tex. 1982) (individual retirement annuity contracts property of the estate).

92 *In re* Leahy, 370 B.R. 620 (Bankr. D. Vt. 2007) (section 403(b) retirement plan excluded from estate by 11 U.S.C. § 541(b)(7)).

93 *In re* Parsons, 280 F.3d 1185 (8th Cir. 2002) (real estate commissions earned prior to petition were property of estate); *In re* Ryerson, 739 F.2d 1423 (9th Cir. 1984) (severance pay sufficiently rooted in prebankruptcy past considered property of estate); *In re* Haynes, 679 F.2d 718 (7th Cir. 1982) (future military retirement pay conditioned upon performance of future obligations is not property of estate); Denedai v. Preferred Capital Markets, Inc., 272 B.R. 21 (D. Mass. 2001) (interest in stock options was property of estate to extent options resulted from prepetition efforts); *In re* Edmonds, 263 B.R. 828 (E.D. Mich. 2001) (contingent interest in employer's profit sharing plan was property of estate); *In re* Chappo, 257 B.R. 852 (E.D. Mich. 2001) (bonus awarded after bankruptcy petition was filed not property of estate because employer could have decided not to grant bonus); *In re* Jokiel, 447 B.R. 868 (Bankr. N.D. Ill. 2011) (execution of non-compete agreement and release of claims against former employer were not future obligations that excluded severance pay from property of estate, but severance pay should be pro-rated to exclude from estate amount for four months of postpetition services); *In re* Siverling, 72 B.R. 78 (Bankr. N.D. Ga. 1987) (debtor subject to future military recall); *In re* Kervin, 19 B.R. 190 (Bankr. S.D. Ala. 1982) (renewal premiums earned by debtor's postbankruptcy servicing of old insurance policies not property of estate).

Alternatively, other plans may qualify as state law spendthrift trusts, so that they cannot be alienated for purposes of bankruptcy.[94] Generally, though, a spendthrift trust cannot be created by its beneficiary and such "self-settled" trusts are usually not protected under state laws.[95] However, two states, Alaska and Delaware, have recently changed their laws to permit protection of self-settled spendthrift trusts if the assets in those trusts were not generated through fraudulent transfers.[96]

The laws regarding other spendthrift trusts vary widely from jurisdiction to jurisdiction. However, most states allow trusts to be established that protect the beneficiary's interest from creditors, as long as the beneficiary has no right to obtain trust funds whenever she desires. Those trusts are excluded from the debtor's bankruptcy estate under section 541(c)(2).[97] However, once funds are distributed or withdrawn from any qualified trust account, they presumably lose their protection.[98]

Another situation that can arise is that of the debtor whose pension has been divided in a divorce proceeding, usually pursuant to a Qualified Domestic Relations Order (QDRO). Most courts have held that such an order divests the debtor of any property rights in the pension rights that were transferred by the QDRO to the debtor's former spouse.[99] If the former spouse who received such a transfer later becomes a bankruptcy debtor, that spouse's interest should be deemed a pension interest with the same protections as the debtor would have had with respect to that interest.[100]

The debtor must list pensions and other trust interests in Schedule B of the bankruptcy schedules whether or not they come into the estate.[101] Any argument that the interest is outside the estate should be carefully noted on Schedule B with a reference to subsections 541(c)(2) or 541(b)(7). And nothing prevents a debtor from claiming that property is outside the estate (on Schedule B), but nevertheless listing an applicable exemption (on Schedule C) in the alternative.[102]

---

94 *Compare In re* Lowenschuss, 171 F.3d 673 (9th Cir. 1999) (pension plan not a spendthrift trust under Pennsylvania law because debtor was settlor, administrator, and sole beneficiary of the pension plan, exercised control over the pension plan, and had the power to terminate the pension plan and distribute the proceeds to himself); *In re* Kaplan, 97 B.R. 572 (B.A.P. 9th Cir. 1989) (pension plan in which debtor is sole beneficiary as well as trustee is property of the estate); *In re* Davis, 125 B.R. 242 (Bankr. W.D. Mo. 1991) (profit-sharing plan not valid spendthrift trust under state law); *In re* Council, 122 B.R. 64 (Bankr. S.D. Ohio 1990) (trustee can reach debtor's deferred compensation plan when plan allows distribution in the event of unforeseeable emergency); *In re* Klayer, 20 B.R. 270 (Bankr. W.D. Ky. 1981) (retirement plan is property of estate when trust held invalid) *with In re* Wilcox, 233 F.3d 899 (6th Cir. 2000) (anti-assignment provision in city charter was enforceable restriction on alienation); *In re* Johnson, 191 B.R. 75 (Bankr. M.D. Pa. 1996) (tax-deferred annuity, though not ERISA plan, contained spendthrift trust clause enforceable under state law); *In re* Kleist, 114 B.R. 366 (Bankr. N.D.N.Y. 1990) (employee savings plan meeting certain IRS Code requirements is spendthrift trust under New York law even though debtor could withdraw funds at any time); SSA Baltimore Fed. Credit Union v. Bizon, 42 B.R. 338 (D. Md. 1984) (when government employee had no choice in connection with government's contribution to Civil Service Retirement and Disability Fund and would not currently receive annuity, fund was spendthrift trust under state law and excluded from bankruptcy estate).
To the extent that some of these cases involved ERISA plans, the issue of whether the plan is a spendthrift trust is no longer significant after the Supreme Court's decision in *Patterson v. Shumate*, discussed above. However they continue to be instructive on the principles for determining whether a retirement plan is a spendthrift trust.

95 *See In re* Lowenschuss, 171 F.3d 673 (9th Cir. 1999) (pension plan not a spendthrift trust under Pennsylvania law because debtor was settlor, administrator, and sole beneficiary of the pension plan, exercised control over the pension plan, and had the power to terminate the pension plan and distribute the proceeds to himself); *In re* Shurley, 115 F.3d 333 (5th Cir. 1997) (assets placed in spendthrift trust by debtor were not protected from creditors by Texas law applicable to spendthrift trusts, but other trust assets were protected).

96 In response to these laws, Congress enacted 11 U.S.C. § 548(e), permitting avoidance of some transfers to self-settled trusts made within ten years before the bankruptcy. *See* § 10.4.2.6.5, *infra*.

97 *See* Wetzel v. Regions Bank, 649 F.3d 831 (8th Cir. 2011) (debtor's interest in the net income from spendthrift trust was subject to a restriction on transfer under applicable nonbankruptcy law and excluded from bankruptcy estate); Drewes v. Schonteich, 31 F.3d 674 (8th Cir. 1994) (trusts created for benefit of debtor's caretaker and charitable institution were spendthrift trusts excluded from bankruptcy estate); *In re* Neuton, 922 F.2d 1379 (9th Cir. 1990) (percentage of trust which qualifies as valid spendthrift trust under California law is not property of the estate); *In re* Newman, 903 F.2d 1150 (7th Cir. 1990) (trustee cannot reach valid spendthrift trust under Missouri law); *In re* Fitzsimmons, 896 F.2d 373 (9th Cir. 1990) (forfeiture on alienation provision in land trust prevents beneficiary's interest in trust from passing to bankruptcy trustee and may be given effect under section 541(c)(2)); *In re* Robbins, 826 F.2d 293 (4th Cir. 1987). *See also In re* Moody, 837 F.2d 719 (5th Cir. 1988) (postpetition distribution from spendthrift trust may be attached by postpetition creditors). *Cf.* Hoff v. McConnell (*In re* Hoff), 644 F.3d 244 (5th Cir. 2011) (estate included amount that debtor was entitled to withdraw from trust); *In re* Brown, 303 F.3d 1261 (11th Cir. 2002) (Florida law did not protect funds in self-settled spendthrift trust from creditors); *In re* Jordan, 914 F.2d 197 (9th Cir. 1990) (trust established by debtor's employer as compensation for personal injury not spendthrift trust under Washington law); *In re* Meyers, 139 B.R. 858 (Bankr. N.D. Ohio 1992) (fact that state held debtor's lottery winnings to be paid annually in the future did not create spendthrift trust).

98 *See* Velis v. Kardanis, 949 F.2d 78 (3d Cir. 1991) (pension and Keough plans are included in the bankruptcy estate to the extent of any distribution). *But see In re* Coumbe, 304 B.R. 378 (B.A.P. 9th Cir. 2003) (income distributions were property of estate but *corpus* distributions were not); *In re* Bresnahan, 183 B.R. 506 (Bankr. S.D. Ohio 1995) (funds distributed from pension plan and placed in debtor's bank account were property of estate, but could be exempted under Ohio law protecting pension funds).

99 *See* § 15.4.3.5, *infra*.

100 *In re* Nelson, 322 F.3d 541 (8th Cir. 2003); *In re* Lalchandani, 279 B.R. 880 (B.A.P. 1st Cir. 2002) (interest in ERISA plan obtained by debtor through QDRO was not property of estate); *In re* Farmer, 295 B.R. 322 (Bankr. W.D. Wis. 2003); *In re* Satterwhite, 271 B.R. 378 (Bankr. W.D. Mo. 2002) (anti-alienation provisions of Uniform Services Spouse's Protection Act caused interest in pension of debtor's former spouse to be excluded from estate).

101 *See* § 7.3.7.2.2, *infra*.

102 A pension or other trust interest may be exempt under either state or federal law. Such exemptions are not preempted by ERISA. *In re*

2.5.3 Education Savings Accounts

The 2005 amendments added new exclusions from the bankruptcy estate for certain education savings accounts. Specifically, funds in an education IRA and funds in a section 529 tuition savings program are excluded from the estate.[103] However, to the extent funds were placed in either type of account within 365 days before the petition was filed they are not excluded, and to the extent they were placed in such an account between 365 and 720 days before the petition was filed the exclusion is limited to $5850 per beneficiary.[104]

The funds are also not excluded from the estate if the beneficiary, during the tax year the funds were deposited, was not the child, stepchild, grandchild, or stepgrandchild of the debtor, or if they are attributable to excess contributions to an education IRA.[105]

Section 521(c) requires the debtor to "file with the court a record" of any interest the debtor has in an education IRA or a section 529 plan, apparently regardless of whether it is property of the estate. This requirement is to be carried out, it appears, in addition to listing the account in the designated portion of Schedule B on Official Form 6.[106]

2.5.4 Pawned Personal Property

Another exclusion from the bankruptcy estate added in 2005 concerns pawned property. Section 541(b)(8) excludes from the estate tangible personal property the debtor has pledged or sold as collateral for a loan from a licensed lender if the property is in the possession of the lender, there is no obligation to repay the loan or redeem the property, and neither the debtor nor trustee has redeemed in a timely manner.[107] Because the provision requires possession of the tangible personal property involved, it is clear it would not apply to an automobile title pawn if the debtor retains possession of the vehicle.[108]

While section 541(b)(8) excludes the collateral for certain pawn transactions from the estate, it is unclear whether it permits a pawnbroker to actually sell the property. To the extent that selling the property is an act to collect a prepetition claim against the debtor, it is stayed by section 362(a)(6).[109] Moreover, the provision is prefaced by the language that it is "subject to subchapter III of chapter 5," which includes the turnover provisions of section 542, requiring turnover of property that the debtor may use, sell, or lease.[110] To the extent that the pawn transaction may be avoided under sections 544, 545, 547, 548, 549, and 553, the pawned property is property of the estate.[111] Further, there does not appear to be any prohibition against the debtor providing for such a claim in a chapter 13 plan. It seems likely that determinations of whether a debtor has any interest in the property on the petition date will continue to be guided by state law.

2.5.5 Tax Refunds and the Earned Income Tax Credit

The right to receive a tax refund for a tax year that has ended before the petition date is clearly property of the estate.[112] The debtor may also have a property interest in excessive withholding by an employer for the then-current tax year which becomes a part of a refund due after the filing of the bankruptcy.[113] When such withholdings do result in a refund, the refund is often prorated over the entire year, with the prebankruptcy portion considered property of the estate.[114] Courts have also differed

---

Schlein, 8 F.3d 745 (11th Cir. 1993). See § 10.2.2.10, *infra*, for a discussion of pension exemptions.

103 11 U.S.C. § 541(b)(5), (6).

The new provisions do not determine whether the debtor has an interest in such funds that would otherwise be property of the estate, so the debtor may still argue, to the extent funds are not excluded by those provisions, that the funds belong to the beneficiary and not to the debtor. *See In re* Cheatham, 309 B.R. 631 (Bankr. M.D. Ala. 2004).

104 11 U.S.C. § 541(b)(5), (6). *See In re* Bourguignon, 416 B.R. 745 (Bankr. D. Idaho 2009) (funds contributed to section 529 plan established by debtors two weeks before petition were property of estate, even though funds were not contributed by debtors).

For cases filed before April 1, 2010, the dollar amount is $5475.

105 11 U.S.C. § 541(b)(5), (6).

106 Schedule B was amended to require the listing, in item 11, of "Interests in an education IRA . . . or a State tuition plan" but also to state "(File separately the record(s) of any such interests.)" Federal Rule of Bankruptcy Procedure 1007(b)(1)(F) requires that the debtor file a record of an account described in section 521(c) in addition to the schedules. It is not clear what the statute, rule, or form mean by a "record" of such interests. Presumably, a statement describing the interest would qualify as a "record."

107 *In re* Martin, 418 B.R. 710 (Bankr. S.D. Ohio 2009) (pawned property not property of estate because debtor failed to redeem within time period set under state law, as extended under section 108(b) for an additional 60 days).

108 *In re* Moore, 448 B.R. 93 (Bankr. N.D. Ga. 2011).

109 *In re* Mosher, 2007 WL 1487399 (Bankr. D. Mont. May 17, 2007) (granting stay relief motion and finding pawned property not property of the estate under section 541(b)(8)). See § 9.4.3, *infra*.

110 See § 9.9, *infra*.

111 *In re* Boudouvas, 2009 WL 693624 (Bankr. E.D.N.Y. Mar. 5, 2009) (property pledged under pawn agreement which court found to be usurious and void was property of estate and subject to turnover under section 542). *See* § 10.4.2.6, *infra*.

112 *In re* Barowsky, 946 F.2d 1516 (10th Cir. 1991). *See In re* Canon, 130 B.R. 748 (Bankr. N.D. Tex. 1991) (when trustee made proper demand for tax refund constituting property of the estate, IRS is required to pay trustee, even though it had paid the refund to the debtors). *See also* United States v. Michaels, 840 F.2d 901 (11th Cir. 1988) (IRS can recoup tax refund paid to debtor which should have been paid to trustee as property of the debtor's estate).

113 Turshen v. Chapman, 823 F.2d 836 (4th Cir. 1987); *In re* Doan, 672 F.2d 831 (11th Cir. 1982). *Cf. In re* Christie, 233 B.R. 110 (B.A.P. 10th Cir. 1999) (tax refund attributable to overpayment made after bankruptcy petition was filed, from postpetition earnings and borrowings, was not property of estate).

114 *In re* Meyers, 616 F.3d 626 (7th Cir. 2010) (adopting generally "pro rata by days" method to calculate portion of tax refund that is property of the estate, except that debtors permitted to present evidence that method is not appropriate in particular cases, such as when income fluctuates widely from month to month throughout the year); *In re* Barowsky, 946 F.2d 1516 (10th Cir. 1991); *In re* Rash, 22 B.R. 323 (Bankr. D. Kan. 1982); *In re* Koch, 14 B.R. 64 (Bankr.

about how to treat a refund on a joint return, with some courts holding that it must be prorated according to the spouses' incomes and others holding that it must be divided equally or using some other formula.[115]

However, in many jurisdictions, trustees do not check whether there has been excessive withholding from the debtor's pay during the tax year in which the bankruptcy case is filed, probably because it is usually eligible for exemption. Debtors' counsel should be sure to be familiar with local practices on this issue.

Debtors' rights to various tax credits which arise prepetition have also been held to come into the estate,[116] but there is some precedent for distinguishing the right to an earned income tax credit.[117] The courts that have concluded that the earned income tax credit is always excluded from the estate base their decision on a belief that a debtor can have no legal or equitable interest in the credit prior to receiving it, or at least claiming it by filing a return. Similarly, the child tax credit, to which a debtor becomes entitled only after a full tax year ends, can be considered property not acquired until January 1 of the following year, at the earliest.[118]

Because the right to a credit cannot be determined at least until the end of the tax year, the argument that it should not be included in the estate is strongest when bankruptcy is filed prior to the end of the relevant tax year.[119] A slightly weaker argument can be made when the debtor files bankruptcy before claiming the credit by filing a return. In that event, the debtor can argue that there is not yet a cognizable entitlement to the credit.[120]

It is also plausible to argue that the mere filing of the return does not create an interest in the credit, because the credit does

---

D. Kan. 1982). *See In re* Aldrich, 250 B.R. 907 (Bankr. W.D. Tenn. 2000). *See also In re* Lambert, 283 B.R. 16 (B.A.P. 9th Cir. 2002) (prepayment of current year refund pursuant to special provision in tax legislation treated as refund for current year, not prior year, even though amount of prepayment was calculated based on income for prior year).

However, a trustee may not demand turnover of a tax overpayment from the debtor when the debtor has not yet received a refund because a debtor cannot be required to turn over property not in the debtor's possession. *In re* Graves, 396 B.R. 70 (B.A.P. 10th Cir. 2008), *aff'd as modified,* 609 F.3d 1153 (10th Cir. 2010).

115 *Compare In re* Barrow, 306 B.R. 28 (Bankr. W.D.N.Y. 2004) (trustee failed to rebut presumption that refund was due to submission of joint return and joint deductions) *and In re* Bading, 154 B.R. 687 (Bankr. W.D. Tex. 1993) (estate entitled to prorated portion of return calculated based on one-half of joint refund even through debtor was unmarried on petition date) *with In re* Carlson, 394 B.R. 491 (B.A.P. 8th Cir. 2008) (spouse who had not paid any withholding had no ownership interest in refund) *and In re* Kleinfeldt, 287 B.R. 291 (B.A.P. 10th Cir. 2002) (joint income tax refund not divided between husband and wife because husband earned all of the income on which return was based). *Cf. In re* McCrory, 2011 WL 4005455 (Bankr. N.D. Ohio 2011) (since homebuyer tax credit was not based on taxes owed or withheld, it was equally owned by nonearning spouse); *In re* Glenn, 430 B.R. 56 (Bankr. N.D.N.Y. 2010) (presumption of fifty-fifty ownership, absent evidence of financial practices warranting different result); *In re* Garbett, 410 B.R. 280 (Bankr. E.D. Tenn. 2009) (property acquired during marriage presumptively held by the entireties under state law); *In re* Spina, 416 B.R. 92 (Bankr. E.D.N.Y. 2009) (presumption of fifty-fifty ownership based on harmonizing state law, bankruptcy law, and tax law).

In re Kleinfeldt was held not applicable to a case where both spouses had income, and the bankruptcy appellate panel instead based the division of the tax refund on a formula taking into account the withholding, taxes, and credits that would be applicable to each spouse if separate returns were filed. Crowson v. Zubrod (*In re* Crowson), 431 B.R. 484 (B.A.P. 10th Cir. 2010). *Accord* Hundley v. Marsh, 944 N.E.2d 127 (Mass. 2011) (adopting "separate filings rule" for bankruptcy purposes in response to certified question from First Circuit, in case in which only one spouse had income but refund included tax credits applicable to both spouses); *In re* Palmer, 449 B.R. 621 (Bankr. D. Mont. 2011).

116 Segal v. Rochelle, 382 U.S. 375, 86 S. Ct. 511, 15 L. Ed. 2d 428 (1966).

Although *Segal* was decided under the Bankruptcy Act rather than the Code, the language of Code section 541(a)(1) is at least as broad as the language on which the *Segal* holding is based. *See In re* Prudential Lines, Inc., 928 F.2d 565 (2d Cir. 1991) (debtor's prepetition net operating loss carry forward is property of the estate). *See also In re* Andrews, 386 B.R. 871 (Bankr. D. Utah 2008) (stimulus payment under Economic Stimulus Act not part of bankruptcy estate when debtor's petition was filed prior to Act's enactment).

117 *In re* Searles, 445 F. Supp. 749 (D. Conn. 1978); *In re* Hurles, 31 B.R. 179 (Bankr. S.D. Ohio 1983). *See also In re* Hankerson, 133 B.R. 711, 717 (Bankr. E.D. Pa. 1991), *rev'd on other grounds,* 138 B.R. 473 (E.D. Pa. 1992) (earned income tax credit does not arise until a tax return is filed).

Even if the earned income tax credit is deemed to be property of the estate, it usually may be exempted, either by using a wild card exemption, or an exception for public assistance benefits under the federal bankruptcy exemptions, or state exemption law. *See* § 10.2.2.11, *infra*.

118 *In re* Schwarz, 314 B.R. 433 (Bankr. D. Neb. 2004). *See also In re* Donnell, 357 B.R. 386 (Bankr. W.D. Tex. 2006) (refund based on additional child tax credit was not estate property, because debtor had no prepetition earned income). *But see In re* Law, 336 B.R. 780 (B.A.P. 8th Cir. 2006).

119 *See* Official Comm. of Unsecured Creditors of Tousa, Inc. v. Citicorp N. Am., Inc. (*In re* TOUSA, Inc.), 422 B.R. 783, 877 (Bankr. S.D. Fla. 2009) (debtor has no right to refund until end of tax year because debtors cannot claim refund before end of tax year), *aff'd,* 680 F.3d 1298 (11th Cir. 2012); *In re* Pratavadi, 281 B.R. 816 (Bankr. W.D.N.Y. 2002) (ruling on related issue that taxes due from debtor are not prorated unless debtor elects to file a split-year return in year bankruptcy case was filed). *But see In re* Johnston, 222 B.R. 552 (B.A.P. 6th Cir. 1998), *aff'd,* 209 F.3d 611 (6th Cir. 2000); *In re* Montgomery, 219 B.R. 913 (B.A.P. 10th Cir. 1998), *aff'd,* 224 F.3d 1193 (10th Cir. 2000) (earned income tax credit is available to the debtor and becomes property of the estate during the tax year not at year end). The rationale of the *Johnston* and *Montgomery* cases is no longer valid, because individuals can no longer receive advance payments of the earned income tax credit.

These cases require proration of the earned income tax credit on the same basis as the balance of the refund.

120 *In re* Hankerson, 133 B.R. 711, 717 (Bankr. E.D. Pa. 1991) (earned income tax credit does not arise until a tax return is filed), *rev'd on other grounds,* 138 B.R. 473 (E.D. Pa. 1992). *See also In re* Meza, 243 B.R. 538 (Bankr. M.D. Fla. 1999) (earned income credit not property of estate because on date bankruptcy petition was filed, dependent child had not lived with debtors for requisite six months). *But see In re* Luongo, 259 F.3d 323 (5th Cir. 2001) (date of filing return irrelevant).

not come into existence until it is determined by the government. It follows, then, that the credit does not come into the estate unless it is actually mailed or received prepetition.[121]

Prior to commencing a bankruptcy case, counsel should consider how a tax refund will be treated in the bankruptcy process. Careful efforts should be made to set up the case in a way that maximizes the debtor's ability to obtain the benefit of the refund.

When possible, the simplest way of ensuring that a debtor will retain control over a tax refund, whether or not it includes an earned income tax credit, is to wait for the refund to be received before filing bankruptcy. Most debtors are easily able to use such funds prepetition for attorney fees, consumable necessities, or tangible property that can be exempted once bankruptcy is filed.[122] Even if the debtor is in a court that prorates the current year's anticipated refund, the amount of the prorated refund will be very small and likely to be exemptible or abandoned if the case is filed early in the calendar year. Alternatively, debtors can choose to change the amount of withholding by filing a new W-4 form with their employer, so that there will be no anticipated tax refund.

Obviously, this strategy of delaying the filing pending receipt of a tax refund may not be appropriate if the tax refund is subject to prepetition interception by the Internal Revenue Service on a government claim. In certain circumstances, the government can seize both an overpayment of withholding taxes and the earned income tax credit.[123] The potential interception of a tax refund can be a consideration in favor of filing sooner rather than later. An earlier filing may also make sense if the petition can be filed before January 1 and the practice in the debtor's jurisdiction is to consider tax refunds as property of the debtor only after January 1.

If the refund is seized by a creditor either before or after filing, the preference,[124] postpetition transfer,[125] and setoff[126] provisions of the Code may apply in some cases, enabling the debtor to reverse the transfer.[127]

Another way of protecting the right to a tax refund may be to elect to apply it to the following year's taxes. It has been held that when debtors have made an irrevocable election to apply a tax overpayment to their next year's taxes they no longer have an overpayment or a right to a refund, and therefore no longer have a property interest in the funds.[128] Similarly, the debtor may choose to assign the tax refund to pay the bankruptcy attorney fees, at least for any prepetition services.[129] Once the refund is assigned in a contemporaneous payment for the attorney's services, it no longer belongs to the debtor and will not become property of the estate.

Whether or not there is an argument that the refund or tax credit is not part of the estate, it is always a good idea to evaluate whether there is an applicable exemption. In many cases a debtor can assert an exemption to protect a tax refund or the earned income tax credit based on the federal or state wild card exemption, or some other state exemption.[130] Similarly, the earned income tax credit may qualify for exemption based on state or federal exemptions for public assistance benefits.[131]

---

121 Some support for this argument can be derived from *In re* Searles, 445 F. Supp. 749 (D. Conn. 1978) and *In re* Hurles, 31 B.R. 179 (Bankr. S.D. Ohio 1983). *But see* Segal v. Rochelle, 382 U.S. 375, 86 S. Ct. 511, 15 L. Ed. 2d 428 (1966) (prepetition business-generated loss carry-back tax refund comes into the estate).

122 For a discussion of exemption planning, see § 10.4, *infra*.

123 *See* Sorenson v. Sec'y of the Treasury, 475 U.S. 851, 106 S. Ct. 1600, 89 L. Ed. 2d 855 (1986) (earned income tax credit can be intercepted to recoup welfare payments made in default of the taxpayer's child support obligations).

124 11 U.S.C. § 547. *See* § 10.4.2.6.4, *infra*. *But see* Kleven v. Household Bank, 334 F.3d 638 (7th Cir. 2003) (transfer of tax refund pursuant to refund anticipation loan (RAL) was not voidable as preference); *In re* Swartz, 119 B.R. 219 (Bankr. D. Idaho 1990) (transfer of tax refund pursuant to refund anticipation loan (RAL) was not voidable as preference).

125 11 U.S.C. § 549. *See* § 10.4.2.6.6, *infra*.

126 11 U.S.C. § 553. *See* §§ 10.4.2.6.7, 14.3.2.2, *infra*. Compare *In re* Hankerson, 133 B.R. 711 (Bankr. E.D. Pa. 1991) (prepetition tax intercept set aside pursuant to section 553(b)) *with In re* Stall, 125 B.R. 754 (Bankr. S.D. Ohio 1991) (tax intercept not set-aside).

In re Hankerson was reversed. Hankerson v. Dep't of Educ., 138 B.R. 473 (E.D. Pa. 1992). The district court held that the recovery of a prepetition set-off from the federal government was barred by sovereign immunity, which would no longer be true under the amended version of 11 U.S.C. § 106.

127 New limits on use of these powers against governmental units based on the Eleventh Amendment and sovereign immunity have emerged from recent Supreme Court decisions. *See* § 14.3.2.2, *infra*.

128 Weinman v. Graves (*In re* Graves), 609 F.3d 1153 (10th Cir. 2010) (because debtors could not obtain funds by revoking their election to apply refund to following year's taxes, trustee had no greater rights and debtors had no duty to turn over funds they did not have, but trustee had reversionary interest in any refund for following year's taxes that was attributable to prepetition earnings); *In re* Block, 141 B.R. 609 (N.D. Tex. 1992) (debtors no longer had interest in $11,000 tax refund when they had elected to apply it to estimated taxes); *In re* Simmons, 124 B.R. 606 (Bankr. M.D. Fla. 1991) (once debtor made election it was irrevocable, and overpayment of taxes no longer existed). *But see* Nichols v. Birdsell, 491 F.3d 987 (9th Cir. 2007) (though election was irrevocable, right to credit on future taxes was an asset).

129 *See* § 16.2.3, *infra*.

130 11 U.S.C. § 522(d)(5). *See In re* Benn, 491 F.3d 811 (8th Cir. 2007) (statute exempting property not subject to attachment did not create exemption for tax refunds); § 10.2.2.6, *infra*. However, an exemption may not protect a right to a tax refund from a prepetition right to setoff, at least absent the ability to avoid the right to setoff. *In re* Luongo, 259 F.3d 323 (5th Cir. 2001).

131 *See* § 10.2.2.11, *infra*. *See also In re* James, 406 F.3d 1340 (11th Cir. 2005) (Alabama exemption for "public assistance" payments applies to earned income tax credit); *In re* Goldsberry, 142 B.R. 158 (Bankr. E.D. Ky. 1992) (earned income credit exempt as "public assistance" under Kentucky law); *In re* Jones, 107 B.R. 751 (Bankr. D. Idaho 1989) (state exemption for federal public assistance benefits); *In re* Taylor, 99 B.R. 371 (Bankr. S.D. Ohio 1989) (state exemption for "poor relief" payments). *But see In re* Wooldridge, 393 B.R. 721 (Bankr. D. Idaho 2008) (stimulus payment under Economic Stimulus Act not exempt as public assistance under Idaho law).

However, the federal exemption of certain wages from garnishment does not extend to wages withheld for taxes even if they are still in the hands of the employer. Kokoszka v. Belford, 417 U.S.

2.6 The Bankruptcy Trustee

In every case under chapter 7 or chapter 13 of the Code, a trustee is appointed by the United States trustee, or if no United States trustee exists in the district, by the court.[132] The trustee's basic role is to represent the interests of the unsecured creditors.[133]

The trustee's duties in carrying out this role are set forth in the statute. They can include collecting property of the estate, invalidating certain transfers made by the debtor, objecting (if appropriate) to a claim of exemption, objecting to discharge, liquidating any nonexempt property and distributing it to creditors with valid claims, and making a final accounting to the court and to the United States trustee.[134] In addition, if there is a claim for a domestic support obligation[135] with respect to the debtor, the trustee must send two separate notices to the claimant regarding the claimant's rights.[136] The trustee may sue or be sued as the representative of the estate in order to determine claims by or against the estate.[137]

In a typical chapter 7 consumer case, there is no nonexempt property, so the trustee's duties are limited. In such cases, she evaluates the debtor's schedules, statements, and exemption claims, and ensures that the debtor carries out the stated intentions with respect to property securing consumer debts.[138] The trustee participates in and, in most districts, presides at the meeting of creditors, reviewing documents that the debtor is required to provide.[139] The trustee also may make inquiries of the debtor to determine whether to file objections to discharge or whether the filing of the case is otherwise improper.

Trustees, often at the urging of the United States trustee, have increased their efforts in this regard, sometimes making unreasonable and burdensome requests for information from the debtor above and beyond the documents required by the statute and the rules. While the debtor, under 11 U.S.C. § 521(a)(3), has a duty to cooperate with the trustee, the debtor does not have a duty to do the trustee's work nor to expend significant funds or do substantial work (such as obtaining documents not already in the debtor's possession) to comply with such requests. In many cases, the appropriate response to a request for documents or information the debtor does not possess is to give the trustee information about where they may be obtained and a release authorizing the trustee to obtain them. A directive from the Executive Office of United States Trustees concerning best practices for trustees makes clear that blanket requests for documents that go beyond the rules and official forms, and questionnaires that go beyond the official forms, are not proper, and therefore this directive may be helpful in this regard.[140] On the other hand, active obstruction of the trustee's tasks may lead to sanctions against the debtor.[141] In some places, the trustee also files a report with the court stating any objections to the discharge or to exemption claims.

The chapter 13 trustee has considerably more to do. Unlike in chapter 7 cases, in which the trustee is one of a number who can be chosen from a panel in each district, there is usually only one trustee, a "standing trustee," to handle all chapter 13 cases in a particular district or part of a district.[142] In addition to most of the duties of a chapter 7 trustee, including sending notices to domestic support creditors, a chapter 13 trustee must attend all hearings on the value of property subject to liens or on confirmation or modification of the debtor's plan, receive and disburse payments (including, in some judicial districts, adequate

---

642, 94 S. Ct. 2431, 41 L. Ed. 2d 374 (1974) (construing 15 U.S.C. § 1671).

A different result might be reached based on state law restrictions on garnishment. *In re* Davis, 136 B.R. 203 (Bankr. D. Iowa 1991) (earned income tax credit exempt in Iowa as public assistance). *But see In re* Collins, 170 F.3d 512 (5th Cir. 1999) (earned income tax credit not exempt as public assistance under Louisiana law); *In re* Wallerstedt, 930 F.2d 630 (8th Cir. 1991) (Missouri protection for "earnings" does not apply to tax refund); *In re* Rutter, 204 B.R. 57 (Bankr. D. Or. 1997) (earned income tax credit not exemptible public assistance); *In re* Goertz, 202 B.R. 614 (Bankr. W.D. Mo. 1996) (same).

132 11 U.S.C. §§ 701, 1302. Sections 701 and 1302 were amended, effective upon the United States trustee program becoming operational in a district, to provide that the United States trustee appoints the chapter 7 interim trustee and the chapter 13 trustee. There is a now a United States trustee in every judicial district except for those in Alabama and North Carolina, where a court-appointed Bankruptcy Administrator performs most United States trustee functions.

133 *But see In re* Andrews, 49 F.3d 1404 (9th Cir. 1995) (chapter 13 trustee represents all creditors).

134 11 U.S.C. § 704(a).
The trustee lacks standing, however, to object to the dischargeability of particular debts. *See, e.g., In re* Dunn, 83 B.R. 694 (Bankr. D. Neb. 1988).

135 "Domestic support obligation" is defined in 11 U.S.C. § 101 to include primarily claims in the nature of alimony, maintenance, or support.

136 11 U.S.C. § 704(a)(10), (c).

137 Wieburg v. GTE Southwest, Inc., 272 F.3d 302 (5th Cir. 2001) (trustee should have been allowed to join or ratify debtor's employment discrimination case); Tanenbaum v. Smith, Friedman & Assoc., 289 B.R. 800 (D.N.J. 2002) (settlement of debtor's prepetition personal injury claims reached without consent of chapter 7 trustee voided). *See, e.g.*, Bellini Imports v. Mason & Dixon Lines, Inc., 944 F.2d 199 (4th Cir. 1991) (failure to name trustee as defendant when pursuing administrative claims precludes enforcement of those claims against the estate). See also § 14.3.2.6, *infra*, for discussion of standing to pursue prepetition claims by the trustee and the debtor.

138 This duty, set forth in 11 U.S.C. § 704(a)(3), is discussed in § 11.4, *infra*.

139 Federal Rule of Bankruptcy Procedure 2003(b)(1) provides that the United States trustee shall preside at the meeting of creditors. In most places, the interim trustee is designated by the United States trustee to preside at the meeting. In chapter 13 cases, the designee will generally be the standing chapter 13 trustee. See Chapters 3 and 8, *infra*, for discussion of the meeting of creditors and document production requirements.

140 *See* Best Practices for Document Production Requests by Trustees in Consumer Bankruptcy Cases (May 14, 2012), Appx. H.7, *infra*.

141 *See, e.g., In re* Onubah, 375 B.R. 549 (B.A.P. 9th Cir. 2007) (upholding court order surcharging debtor's exemptions due to debtor's obstruction of trustee's sale of debtor's property).

142 11 U.S.C. § 1302(d) was replaced by 28 U.S.C. § 586(b) in the 1986 amendments, providing for appointment of standing chapter 13 trustees by the United States trustee when a United States trustee has been appointed.

protection payments) according to the debtor's plan, make sure the debtor is making payments,[143] advise the debtor on non-legal matters, and assist the debtor in performance of the plan.[144] In the past the diligence of chapter 13 trustees in performing the last two duties of advice and assistance has varied widely among districts.

Both chapter 13 and chapter 7 trustees are accountable for the performance of their statutory duties and may generally be held liable for failure to perform them.[145] Courts have differed on the extent of a bankruptcy trustee's immunity from suit.[146] Most chapter 13 trustees have websites on which debtors, creditors, and their attorneys may track plan payments by debtors and disbursements by the trustee.

However, it is clear that the bankruptcy trustee is not a judicial officer with the power to resolve disputed issues arising in a bankruptcy proceeding. The trustee is a party with equal status to other persons interested in the outcome of the case. If there is a disputed issue, the trustee may file or respond to a contested matter or an adversary proceeding and seek resolution by the court. The trustee, like other parties, is also required to take and respond to discovery. *Ex parte* communications between the trustee and the bankruptcy judge are prohibited.[147]

Some trustees have claimed a right as successor-in-interest to control an individual debtor's attorney-client privilege, based on the Supreme Court's holding that a trustee may do so in the case of a corporate debtor in *Commodity Futures Trading Comm'n v. Weintraub*.[148] The better reasoned cases reject this claim in individual cases because, unlike in a corporate case, the individual remains a separate entity from the bankruptcy estate the trustee represents.[149] The court in *Weintraub* itself made clear that it did not apply to individual cases: "Under our holding today, [the attorney-client privilege] passes to the trustee because the trustee's functions are more closely analogous to those of management outside of bankruptcy than are the functions of the debtor's directors. *An individual, in contrast, can act for himself; there is no 'management' that controls a solvent individual's attorney-client privilege. If control over that privilege passes to a trustee, it must be under some theory different from the one that we embrace in this case.*"[150]

Depending on the type of matter involved, then, the trustee may be either a friend or a foe of the debtor. Naturally, it is important to distinguish these situations carefully and to be familiar with how the trustee sees her role. An active trustee may closely scrutinize the debtor's affairs, sometimes to help the debtor and sometimes to help the creditors. Some trustees may be interested in asserting the debtor's counterclaims or defenses,[151] while others may not. As will be seen in the following chapters, knowing the predilections of a particular trustee may be of considerable help in choosing the correct bankruptcy strategy.

2.7 The United States Trustee

Every judicial district, with the exception of those in Alabama and North Carolina, is part of a larger United States Trustee District, served by a United States trustee and one or more assistant United States trustees.[152] For political reasons, neither Alabama nor North Carolina has a United States trustee.[153]

---

143 Many chapter 13 trustees post their records of payments by debtors and of payments to creditors on the Internet, where they can be accessed by debtors, creditors, and their counsel.

144 11 U.S.C. § 1302(b), (d).

145 *See, e.g., In re* Gorski, 766 F.2d 723 (2d Cir. 1985) (chapter XIII trustee in case under Bankruptcy Act ordered to pay $500 or other compensation to creditors damaged by his failure to act when debtors made no plan payments for thirty-three months); *In re* Nash, 765 F.2d 1410 (9th Cir. 1985) (chapter 13 trustee held liable to debtors for distributing funds to creditors after receiving notice of voluntary dismissal of case).

146 *Compare* Conn. Gen. Life Ins. v. Universal Ins. Co., 838 F.2d 612 (1st Cir. 1988) (trustee liable for willful and deliberate violation of fiduciary duties); Yadkin Valley Bank & Trust Co. v. McGee, 819 F.2d 74 (4th Cir. 1987) (no absolute immunity from civil damages for negligence in performing duties) *with* Gregory v. United States, 942 F.2d 1498 (10th Cir. 1991) (trustee has absolute immunity for executing bankruptcy judge's orders); Bennett v. Williams, 892 F.2d 822 (9th Cir. 1989) (trustee acting within scope of authority has quasi-judicial immunity from suit for discretionary acts); Mullis v. United States Bankruptcy Court, 828 F.2d 1385 (9th Cir. 1987) (trustee has absolute quasi-judicial immunity from civil damages for acts within the scope of official duties).

147 Fed. R. Bank. P. 9003(a).

148 471 U.S. 343, 348, 105 S. Ct. 1986, 85 L. Ed. 2d 372 (1985).

149 McClarty v. Gudenau, 166 B.R. 101 (E.D. Mich. 1994); *In re* Bounds, 443 B.R. 729, 733 (Bankr. W.D. Tex. 2010).

150 Commodity Futures Trading Comm'n v. Weintraub, 471 U.S. 343, 356–57, 105 S. Ct. 1986, 85 L. Ed. 2d 372 (1985) (emphasis added).

151 As successor-in-interest to property of the estate, the trustee has full power to raise claims of the debtor. *See, e.g., In re* Scaife, 825 F.2d 357 (11th Cir. 1987). *See also* Bauer v. Commerce Union Bank, 859 F.2d 438 (6th Cir. 1988) (trustee is properly substituted as party plaintiff for debtor when cause of action becomes property of estate); Tanenbaum v. Smith, Friedman & Assoc., 289 B.R. 800 (D.N.J. 2002) (court could deem debtor's postpetition settlement of prepetition cause of action void because trustee did not participate in settlement).

However, if a case is in chapter 13, or is converted to chapter 13, the debtor has the right, pursuant to 11 U.S.C. § 1306(b), to control litigation on behalf of the estate. *In re* Wirmel, 134 B.R. 258 (Bankr. S.D. Ohio 1991) (chapter 7 trustee lost control of debtor's civil rights case upon conversion of debtor's bankruptcy case to chapter 13).

152 The United States Trustee Program is part of the Executive Branch's Department of Justice.

153 Under Pub. L. No. 99-554, § 302(d)(3), 100 Stat. 3088 (1986), as amended by Pub. L. No. 106-518, 114 Stat. 2410 (2000), the judicial districts in North Carolina and Alabama do not have a United States trustee unless they opt to have one. The six federal judicial districts in North Carolina and Alabama have not opted for a United States trustee and instead participate in the Bankruptcy Administrator program administered by the Administrative Office of the U.S. Courts. The exclusion of districts in only two states from the program was held to be an unconstitutional violation of the bankruptcy uniformity clause of the United States Constitution by the Ninth Circuit Court of Appeals. St. Angelo v. Victoria Farms, Inc., 38 F.3d 1525 (9th Cir. 1994). However, as the districts without a United States trustee are not in the Ninth Circuit, the court ordered no remedy for the violation.

The Bankruptcy Rules require notice to the United States trustee, either by the clerk or by the parties, in numerous areas of bankruptcy practice. The rules should be checked carefully to avoid overlooking these service requirements.

The function of the United States trustee is to oversee administrative matters, leaving the court to perform its primary function of resolving disputes that arise among parties in the bankruptcy case and related proceedings. Thus, the United States trustee carries out such functions as appointing and supervising trustees, convening the meeting of creditors, and monitoring fees charged by bankruptcy attorneys.[154]

The United States trustee is also given the right to move for dismissal of a case under chapter 7 for "abuse" of that chapter, and for dismissal of cases under all chapters for undue delay in filing required documents.[155] The 2005 amendments appear to contemplate that the United States trustees will be the primary enforcers of the new means test provisions imposed by section 707(b), placing a number of new duties on their shoulders.[156]

The 2005 amendments also provide that the United States trustee for each district shall contract with auditors who will conduct random audits of the schedules and other information provided by debtors and, if advisable, shall take appropriate action in cases in which audit reports indicate there has been a material misstatement.[157]

The United States trustee's role in a bankruptcy case beyond the duties enumerated in the statute remains unclear.[158] Although the United States Trustee Program was intended to provide neutral administration of the system, it has in recent years focused almost exclusively on scrutinizing and challenging debtors' cases, and has failed to expend any significant resources on curbing abuses by other parties, such as creditors and trustees. In any event, the United States trustee is prohibited from *ex parte* contacts with the court concerning particular cases[159] and, like the bankruptcy trustee, must submit disputes, in the appropriate manner, to the court for resolution.

---

154 *See In re* Plaza de Diego Shopping Ctr., Inc., 911 F.2d 820 (1st Cir. 1990) (district court abused its discretion by selecting a trustee because such duty is exclusive responsibility of the United States trustee).
   In Alabama and North Carolina judicial districts, many of these duties are performed by a court official called the bankruptcy administrator.
155 11 U.S.C. §§ 707(a)(3), 707(b), 1307(c)(9), 1307(c)(10). *See* Fed. R. Bankr. P. 1017; Ch. 13, *infra*.
156 11 U.S.C. § 704(b).
157 28 U.S.C. § 586(f); Pub. L. No. 109-8, § 603, 119 Stat. 23 (2005). *See also* Ch. 16, *infra*.
158 *See* United States Tr. v. Price Waterhouse, 19 F.3d 138 (3d Cir. 1994) (United States trustee has standing to appeal); *In re* Revco, 898 F.2d 498 (6th Cir. 1990) (United States trustee has standing to appeal the bankruptcy court's refusal to appoint an examiner in a chapter 11 case; under certain circumstances the appointment of an examiner is required upon request of the trustee).
159 Fed. R. Bankr. P. 9003(b).

Chapter 3 Chapter 7 Bankruptcy (Straight Bankruptcy): The Basic Steps

3.1 General Explanation of Chapter 7 Bankruptcy

When most people think of bankruptcy, they think of the type of bankruptcy provided for in chapter 7 of the Code, a liquidation proceeding sometimes called straight bankruptcy. This type of bankruptcy has by far been the most popular type of proceeding for individuals. Although the percentage of debtors choosing chapter 7 has diminished somewhat since enactment of the Code because of the advantages that chapter 13 offers, chapter 7 continues to be the chapter most frequently utilized, and it remains a lifeline for over a million consumer debtors each year.

This Chapter describes the routine steps in a typical liquidation case, from beginning to end, with emphasis on the procedures in "no-asset" cases. (A "no-asset" case is one in which none of the debtor's assets are available to be sold for the benefit of unsecured creditors because all of the debtor's significant assets are exempt[1] or encumbered by liens[2] to the full extent of their value.) Chapters 5 through 8, *infra*, then provide a detailed practical guide on how to prepare and handle a bankruptcy case.

In a liquidation case, all of the debtor's nonexempt assets that have significant value are distributed to creditors and the debtor normally receives a bankruptcy discharge. From the beginning of the case until its conclusion, each step in the process is directed toward one or both of these ends.

3.2 Commencement of the Case

3.2.1 Who May File?

3.2.1.1 General Rules, Including Credit Counseling Requirement

Any individual residing, domiciled, or having property or a place of business in the United States may file a chapter 7 bankruptcy.[3] To be eligible, the individual must, with certain limited exceptions, have received a credit counseling briefing from an approved nonprofit budget and counseling agency within the 180 days before filing the bankruptcy petition.[4] The individual need not be insolvent. A person, whether a citizen or not, may file a bankruptcy case even if the person does not reside in the United States, as long as the person has assets in the United States.[5] In very limited circumstances a chapter 7 case may be dismissed by the court for "abuse," and an individual whose income is above certain standards is subject to a means test to determine whether there is a presumption of abuse based on the debtor's ability to repay creditors.[6]

Although a debtor may file on her own behalf, an individual generally may not file as trustee on behalf of some other person.[7] This rule may cause occasional problems in cases in which parents have title to encumbered property in trust for their children. However, the child may be able to file, claiming as exempt her interest as beneficiary of the trust.[8] It may also be possible for the trustee of a trust, by filing a case, to secure the benefits of the automatic stay and to prevent loss of the property, if adequate protection is provided to the secured creditors involved.[9] An incompetent person has also been held

---

1 Exempt property is property that the debtor may retain in a liquidation case. See generally Ch. 10, *infra*.

2 Property fully encumbered by a valid lien not voided by the trustee or the debtor during the bankruptcy through use of their various powers (see Chapter 10, *infra*), is not considered an asset available to unsecured creditors as the secured party has superior rights to the property.

3 11 U.S.C. § 109.
 Subject to certain limitations, corporations and partnerships may also file under chapter 7, because they are within the definition of "person" under the Code. 11 U.S.C. § 101(41).

4 11 U.S.C. § 109(h).
 This requirement is discussed in detail in § 3.2.1.4, *infra*.

5 See, e.g., Bank of Am., N.T. & S.A. v. World of English, N.V., 23 B.R. 1015 (N.D. Ga. 1982) (bank account in United States); *In re* McTague, 198 B.R. 428 (Bankr. W.D.N.Y. 1996) (resident of Canada with $194 bank account).

6 11 U.S.C. § 707.
 See Chapter 13, *infra*, for discussion of dismissal and the abuse provisions added by the 1984 and 2005 amendments.

7 *In re* Kirby, 9 B.R. 901 (Bankr. E.D. Pa. 1981).
 Similarly, an individual's attorney-in-fact may not commence a bankruptcy case or sign a bankruptcy petition on behalf of the individual. See *In re* Vitagliano, 303 B.R. 292 (Bankr. W.D.N.Y. 2003) (bankruptcy case dismissed when petition was signed by mother of incarcerated individual as his attorney-in-fact).

8 See *In re* Nesset, 33 B.R. 326 (Bankr. D.N.M. 1983).

9 See *In re* Foster, 19 B.R. 28 (Bankr. E.D. Pa. 1982) (trustee's bare legal title sufficient to invoke automatic stay). See also Fed. Home Loan Mortgage Corp. v. Wynn, 29 B.R. 679 (Bankr. D.N.J. 1983).
 See generally § 2.5, *supra*, for a discussion of trust property as property of the trustee's bankruptcy estate.

eligible to file a case under the Code.[10] The rules provide that an attorney or relative may file the petition as "next friend" to the debtor, or for a court-appointed guardian to file the petition.[11] Bankruptcy may also be filed for an incompetent person pursuant to a sufficiently broad valid power of attorney, when evidence of the power of attorney is filed with the petition.[12] If there is a court appointed guardian, only that person has the authority to file for the debtor[13] and one court has held that an appointed conservator cannot file a bankruptcy case on behalf of an absent debtor whose whereabouts are unknown.[14]

Although an executor or administrator of an estate cannot file a bankruptcy petition because a probate estate is not an entity eligible to file a bankruptcy case, if the debtor dies during the case, especially if the case is a chapter 7 case, the case will usually continue. Federal Rule of Bankruptcy Procedure 1016 provides that death or incompetency of the debtor shall not abate a chapter 7 case. In such circumstances, the rule requires that the estate is to be administered and the case concluded, to the extent possible, as if the death or incompetency had not occurred. The debtor's interests may have to be represented by a personal representative with the legal authority to represent the debtor's estate.[15]

3.2.1.2 Effect of Prior Bankruptcy Cases on Eligibility to File

One limitation exists on the broad right to file under chapter 7. An individual is not eligible to file a petition if, within the preceding 180 days, (1) she was the debtor in a bankruptcy case dismissed for willful failure to abide by orders of the court or to appear before the court in proper prosecution of the case or (2) she requested and obtained voluntary dismissal of a bankruptcy case following the filing of a request for relief from the automatic stay provided by section 362.[16]

In interpreting this provision with respect to involuntary dismissals, it is important to note that filing a petition within 180 days of an involuntary dismissal does not render a debtor ineligible unless the failure to abide by court orders or to appear was willful.[17] Because this determination is not one that the clerk can normally make upon filing of the later case, such a dismissal should occur only if, after a motion to dismiss by some party in interest, the court finds the requisite willfulness as a matter of fact.[18] Absent a specific court order issued for cause, involuntary dismissals do not preclude the debtor from filing a new case under the Code, unless they fall within the parameters of section 109(g).[19]

---

10 In re Sapp, 2011 WL 2971048 (Bankr. E.D. Mo. July 20, 2011) (collecting cases).

11 Federal Rule of Bankruptcy Procedure 1004.1 provides that a legally appointed representative may file a petition on behalf of an infant or incompetent person. If no such representative exists, such a person may file a petition by next friend. In re Myers, 350 B.R. 760 (Bankr. N.D. Ohio 2006) (wife appointed as next friend for joint debtor husband with dementia, except for matters in which there might be conflict of interest).

Prior case law had generally been consistent with these rules. In re Murray, 199 B.R. 165 (Bankr. M.D. Tenn. 1996) (parent could file petition on behalf of seven-year-old debtor as "next friend" of debtor); In re Smith, 115 B.R. 84 (Bankr. E.D. Va. 1990) (power of attorney does not allow wife to file on behalf of her incapacitated husband; however incapacitated person may file through court-appointed guardian); In re Jones, 97 B.R. 901 (Bankr. S.D. Ohio 1989) (guardian for incompetent debtor may file chapter 13); In re Zawisza, 73 B.R. 929 (Bankr. E.D. Pa. 1987) (attorney filed as "next friend"). Cf. In re Brown, 163 B.R. 596 (Bankr. N.D. Fla. 1993) (petition filed on behalf of debtor by his wife, who signed it without indicating that signature was in representative capacity, was a nullity).

12 In re Gerholdt, 2011 WL 4352353 (Bankr. N.D. Iowa Sept. 16, 2011); In re Hurt, 234 B.R. 1 (Bankr. D.N.H. 1999). See also In re Benson, 2010 WL 2016891 (Bankr. N.D. Ga. Apr. 30, 2010) (guardian ad litem appointed for debtor by bankruptcy court pursuant to Rule 1004.1 because authority under two powers of attorney signed by debtor prepetition was uncertain). But see In re Eicholz, 310 B.R. 203 (W.D. Wash. 2004) (power of attorney was not specific enough to authorize filing of bankruptcy); In re Curtis, 262 B.R. 619 (Bankr. D. Vt. 2001) (general power of attorney is insufficient to authorize filing case for another person); In re Harrison, 158 B.R. 246 (Bankr. M.D. Fla. 1993) (petition on which debtor's name was signed by another, purportedly based upon later-submitted power of attorney, was a nullity, because there was no indication on petition that it was signed based on power of attorney and there were no exigent circumstances making it impossible for debtor to sign his own petition).

13 It is unclear whether a state conservatorship may deprive a debtor-ward of the right to file a bankruptcy case. See In re Kjellsen, 53 F.3d 944 (8th Cir. 1995) (if a guardian has been appointed for an incompetent person, only the guardian has authority to file a bankruptcy petition); In re Woods, 248 B.R. 322 (Bankr. W.D. Tenn. 2000) (petition dismissed for cause when not authorized by conservator). See also In re Blumeyer, 297 B.R. 577 (Bankr. E.D. Mo. 2003) (incarcerated person could file chapter 11 case despite existence of statutory trustee appointed by state court).

14 In re King, 234 B.R. 515 (Bankr. D.N.M. 1999) (distinguishing the situation of an absent debtor from one who is otherwise incapacitated).

15 See In re Lucio, 251 B.R. 705 (Bankr. W.D. Tex. 2000) (debtor's daughter could not appear for deceased debtor at meeting of creditors; personal representative of estate could appear).

16 11 U.S.C. § 109(g).

See Chapter 9, infra, for further discussion of this provision and the automatic stay.

17 Given the language of the statute and its purpose of preventing abuse, it seems clear that a failure to appear before the court must be "willful" to justify dismissal of a subsequent petition filed within 180 days. See In re Arena, 81 B.R. 851 (Bankr. E.D. Pa. 1988). But see In re Smith, 851 F.2d 747 (5th Cir. 1988) (subsequent petition precluded when first petition dismissed for lack of proper prosecution, apparently without consideration of willfulness).

18 In re Montgomery, 37 F.3d 413 (8th Cir. 1994) (issue of willfulness is to be decided when later bankruptcy is filed, but debtor has burden of showing that earlier dismissal was not due to willful failure to prosecute case). See also In re Arena, 81 B.R. 851 (Bankr. E.D. Pa. 1988) (party moving for dismissal has burden of proof); In re Quinones, 73 B.R. 333 (Bankr. D. P.R. 1987) (same). But see In re Bigalk, 813 F.2d 189 (8th Cir. 1987).

Regardless of when the determination of willfulness is made, it is clear that the debtor must receive notice and an opportunity to introduce evidence that the conduct in question was not willful before the court may dismiss a new petition under section 109(g). In re Bradley, 152 B.R. 74 (E.D. La. 1993).

19 11 U.S.C. § 349(a).

Simply failing to make payments of filing fees, or plan payments in a prior chapter 13 case, should not, without more, be considered willful so as to preclude a successive filing for 180 days.[20] Nor should failure to appear at the meeting of creditors in a prior case, by itself, be grounds for dismissal of a subsequent filing.[21] A new petition may even be proper while a prior petition is still pending.[22]

There is also some question concerning the scope of the subsection covering voluntary dismissals[23] "following" requests for relief from the automatic stay.[24] The obvious purpose of this provision is to prevent debtors from repeatedly filing new bankruptcy cases and obtaining new automatic stays after relief was requested or granted in previous cases.[25] With this purpose in mind, it is not unreasonable to read the word "following" to imply some causal connection between the request for relief and the new filing.[26] Surely the provision was not meant to apply when there is a voluntary dismissal and a new case after a request for relief from the stay is denied,[27] withdrawn, or settled favorably to the debtor.[28] These situations were not among Congress's concerns when it passed section 109(g). Similarly, the provision should not apply when the voluntary dismissal and new case are remote in time from the request for relief from the stay, for example, when a request for relief was filed several years before the dismissal and has nothing to do with the new case. Nor should debtors who requested dismissal before the filing of a motion for relief from stay, but who did not obtain a dismissal order until after such a motion, be considered within the scope of the bar to refiling.[29] Moreover, the existence in the Code of specific limitations on refiling strongly suggests that courts are precluded from issuing more general injunctions precluding future filings.[30]

Nonetheless some courts do enter dismissal orders, not based directly on section 109(g), that prohibit a debtor from filing another case for a period of time, usually 180 days.[31] In extremely rare cases, courts may dismiss a bankruptcy case with prejudice, which precludes a debtor from ever discharging the debts involved in that case.[32] It is important to distinguish between these two types of dismissal, because courts sometimes use "with prejudice" language when they intend only to preclude refiling for a period of time.[33]

3.2.1.3 Eligibility to File a Case Does Not Assure Discharge of Debts

Apart from eligibility to file a chapter 7 case, however, there are also certain requirements for obtaining a chapter 7 discharge. Because the discharge is usually the main goal of filing, few people who do not meet these requirements should voluntarily[34] start a chapter 7 case. The various bars to discharge are listed in section 727(a) of the Code. Most are discussed at greater length elsewhere in this treatise.[35] The provisions which

---

20 See In re Howard, 134 B.R. 225 (Bankr. E.D. Ky. 1991) (debtors who fell behind in payments and did not attend dismissal hearing not precluded from refiling when failure to pay was due to job loss); In re Dodge, 86 B.R. 535 (Bankr. S.D. Ohio 1988); In re Samuel, 77 B.R. 520 (Bankr. D. Pa. 1987). See also In re Hollis, 150 B.R. 145 (D. Md. 1993) (pro se debtor's failure to follow rules, due to ignorance of them, does not warrant dismissal of case with prejudice or a finding of willfulness under section 109(g)); § 9.7.3.1.5, infra. But see In re McIver, 78 B.R. 439 (D.S.C. 1987).

21 In re Dodge, 86 B.R. 535 (Bankr. S.D. Ohio 1988); In re Arena, 81 B.R. 851 (Bankr. E.D. Pa. 1988).

22 See In re Saylors, 869 F.2d 1434 (11th Cir. 1989) (second bankruptcy may be filed while first case still pending in some situations); In re Cormier, 147 B.R. 285 (Bankr. D. Me. 1992) (court could consider whether change in circumstances justified filing of second case); In re Strause, 97 B.R. 22 (Bankr. S.D. Cal. 1989) (filing of chapter 13 case was not barred by pending chapter 7 case when debtor's discharge would have been granted but for court's administrative delays).

23 Failing to respond to a motion to dismiss in the prior case does not make the dismissal voluntary. In re Gamble, 72 B.R. 75 (Bankr. D. Idaho 1987). See also In re Walker, 171 B.R. 197 (Bankr. E.D. Pa. 1994) (section 109(g) did not apply to debtor who did not actively seek a voluntary dismissal but rather had consented to the court's dismissal of his case).

24 11 U.S.C. § 109(g)(2).

25 This provision was enacted prior to the 2005 amendments, which limit the application of the stay in cases filed within one year of previously dismissed cases. 11 U.S.C. § 362(c)(3), (4). See also Ch. 9, infra.

It does seem clear that the 180 days cannot be measured from date creditor obtained relief from stay. In re Berts, 99 B.R. 363 (Bankr. N.D. Ohio 1989).

26 See In re Luna, 122 B.R. 575 (B.A.P. 9th Cir. 1991) (application of section 109(g) is discretionary with the court); In re Patton, 49 B.R. 587 (Bankr. M.D. Ga. 1985) (when new case begun two weeks after voluntary dismissal caused no prejudice to creditor, it was not abusive filing prohibited by section 109(g)). See also § 9.7.3.1.5, infra. But see Kuo v. Walton, 167 B.R. 677 (M.D. Fla. 1994) (when section 109(g) applies, dismissal is mandatory and not discretionary); In re Keziah, 46 B.R. 551 (Bankr. W.D.N.C. 1985) (application of section 109(g) not limited to abusive filings after voluntary dismissal).

27 In re Jones, 99 B.R. 412 (Bankr. E.D. Ark. 1989).

28 See, e.g., In re Milton, 82 B.R. 637 (Bankr. S.D. Ga. 1988) (motion for relief which was settled between the parties does not preclude subsequent filings within 180 days).

29 In re Hicks, 138 B.R. 505 (Bankr. D. Md. 1992).

30 In re Frieouf, 938 F.2d 1099 (10th Cir. 1991) (bankruptcy court could not enjoin all access to bankruptcy court beyond 180 day period provided in section 109(g), but it could bar discharge of particular debts listed in prior bankruptcy case for a longer period). See also § 9.7.3.1.5, infra.

The question of willfulness related to the dismissal of the prior bankruptcy should not be confused with issues of good faith in the existing bankruptcy. See generally In re Chisum, 847 F.2d 597 (9th Cir. 1988).

31 See 11 U.S.C. § 349(a).

Note that an order barring a future case can only be entered "for cause." Presumably, as a due process matter, a finding of cause can only be entered after notice and a hearing. Thus, the practice of barring future cases for 180 days whenever a case is dismissed is improper.

32 See 3 Collier on Bankruptcy ¶ 349.02[2] (16th ed.).

33 See In re Tomlin, 105 F.3d 933 (4th Cir. 1997) (although court used words "with prejudice," it intended only to prohibit refiling for 180 days).

34 Involuntary bankruptcies, rare in consumer cases, are provided for in 11 U.S.C. § 303. See Ch. 14, infra.

35 See Ch. 15, infra.

most commonly present problems are those that deny a discharge when the debtor has received a bankruptcy discharge in a chapter 7 case filed less than eight years earlier or, with some exceptions, a chapter 13 case filed less than six years earlier,[36] or when the debtor has committed certain acts with an intent to hinder, delay, or defraud a creditor.[37] In addition, in order to receive a chapter 7 discharge, the debtor must (with certain limited exceptions) complete an instructional course in personal financial management and file a statement certifying completion of the course.[38]

3.2.1.4 Credit Counseling Briefing Requirement

The 2005 amendments to the Code added a new eligibility requirement for all individual debtors, with very limited exceptions. Section 109(h) provides that a debtor shall not be eligible for relief if the debtor has not received, within 180 days before the petition, a briefing from an approved nonprofit budget and credit counseling agency.[39] The agency providing the briefing must be one that has been approved by the United States trustee or by the bankruptcy administrator to render counseling in the judicial district in which the case is filed. A list of the approved counseling agencies may be found on the website of the United States Trustee Program[40] and on the websites of most bankruptcy courts.[41]

Many agencies provide counseling over the telephone or over the Internet, and an in-person briefing may be obtained in most areas. The United States Trustee Program's website states that certain agencies provide briefings in various foreign languages. However, if the debtor is unable to obtain a briefing in a language the debtor can understand, there are strong arguments that the requirement should be waived.[42]

Credit counseling agencies typically charge $35 to $50 for the briefing, but must waive their fee for debtors who are unable to pay it.[43] At least one credit counseling agency offers the counseling at no charge for all debtors.[44] Most attorneys choose an agency with which they are comfortable. They are then able to make arrangements for the debtor's fee to be paid through the attorney's office, which expedites the availability of counseling.

Some counseling agencies are able to provide the briefing immediately in an emergency case. At the counseling session, which usually takes less than an hour, the agency will prepare a budget that reviews the debtor's income and expenses. Based on this budget, the agency will review possible options available to the debtor in credit counseling. In most cases, agencies confirm the debtor's assessment that no viable options exist for addressing the debtor's financial problems other than the filing of a bankruptcy petition.

Some bankruptcy courts have erroneously held the counseling requirement to be jurisdictional, even though eligibility requirements are not jurisdictional.[45] In any event, the failure to obtain the required briefing prior to the case will usually lead to dismissal of the case unless an exception to the pre-filing counseling requirement is successfully claimed.[46] However some courts have held that the requirement of a prepetition briefing can be waived and that the lack of a briefing does not necessarily require dismissal.[47] A few others have held that the petition may be "stricken" rather than dismissed.[48] But some

---

36 11 U.S.C. § 727(a)(8), (9). See §§ 15.2.2.8, 15.2.2.9, infra.
37 11 U.S.C. § 727(a)(2). See § 15.2.2.2, infra.
38 11 U.S.C. § 727(a)(11). See § 8.3.3, infra.
39 In addition, section 521(b) of the Code requires an individual debtor to file a certificate from the approved counseling agency stating that the debtor has received the briefing. The certificate may be filed with the debtor's statement of compliance with the credit counseling requirement, which is Exhibit D to the petition. See Official Form 1 (reprinted in Appx. D, infra); § 7.3.5, infra.
40 The website is located at www.usdoj.gov/ust.
41 Bankruptcy court websites are accessible through www.uscourts.gov.
42 See In re Petit-Louis, 344 B.R. 696 (Bankr. S.D. Fla. 2006).
43 11 U.S.C. § 111(c)(2)(B).
    Based on regulations issued by the Executive Office of the United States Trustee, credit counseling agencies must not withhold a certificate of counseling completion because of a debtor's inability to pay. See 28 C.F.R. § 58.15(3) (reprinted in Appendix C.1, infra).
    Credit counseling agencies that willfully or negligently fail to comply with any Code requirements with respect to a debtor shall liable for actual damages, costs, and attorney fees. See 11 U.S.C. § 111(g)(2).
44 www.consumerbankruptcycounseling.info/cbcp/start.html. It may take slightly longer to obtain a credit counseling certificate from this agency than from some others. And this agency now charges $5 for the credit counseling certificate.
45 Adams v. Zarnel (In re Zarnel), 619 F.3d 156 (2d Cir. 2010) (credit counseling requirement is not jurisdictional); 2 Collier on Bankruptcy ¶ 109.01[2] (16th ed.). See also In re Tomco, 339 B.R. 145 (Bankr. W.D. Pa. 2006); In re Ross, 338 B.R. 134 (Bankr. N.D. Ga. 2006).
46 See, e.g., In re Ingram, 460 B.R. 904 (B.A.P. 6th Cir. 2011) (case properly dismissed when counseling not completed before petition filed); In re Mitrano, 409 B.R. 812 (E.D. Va. 2009) (bankruptcy court had no discretion to waive counseling requirement).
47 See, e.g., In re Mendez, 367 B.R. 109 (B.A.P. 9th Cir. 2007); In re Fiorillo, 455 B.R. 297 (D. Mass. 2011) (denying, on judicial estoppel grounds, debtor's motion to dismiss his own case); In re Nichols, 362 B.R. 88 (Bankr. S.D.N.Y. 2007); In re Manalad, 360 B.R. 288 (Bankr. C.D. Cal. 2007); In re Kernan, 358 B.R. 537 (Bankr. D. Conn. 2007); In re Hess, 347 B.R. 489 (Bankr. D. Vt. 2006). See also In re Anderson, 391 B.R. 758 (Bankr. S.D. Tex. 2008) (debtor permitted to complete counseling after petition and to file amended petition); In re Vollmer, 361 B.R. 811 (Bankr. E.D. Va. 2007) (incarcerated debtor granted permanent waiver of counseling and education course requirements, even though ineligible for statutory waiver, because of debtor's inability to access computer, make collect calls, and participate in course classes); In re Bricksin, 346 B.R. 497 (Bankr. N.D. Cal. 2006) (although initial counseling session occurred more than 180 days before petition was filed, ongoing counseling during debt management plan continued to within 180 days before petition). But see In re Anderson, 397 B.R. 363 (B.A.P. 6th Cir. 2008) (incarcerated debtor not eligible for waiver of counseling); In re Bristol, 61 Collier Bankr. Cas. 2d (MB) 37 (E.D.N.Y. 2009) (same).
48 In re Thompson, 344 B.R. 899 (Bankr. S.D. Ind. 2006), vacated by 249 Fed. Appx. 475 (7th Cir. 2007); In re Rios, 336 B.R. 177 (Bankr. S.D.N.Y. 2005), overruled by Adams v. Zarnel (In re Zarnel), 619 F.3d 156 (2d Cir. 2010) (credit counseling requirement

of these latter courts also unnecessarily held that a stricken petition never triggers the automatic stay, a holding that could potentially be very detrimental to debtors, who would lose the stay's protections.[49]

Prior to 2010, a few courts had held that the language of section 109(h) required that the credit counseling briefing be obtained no later than the day before the bankruptcy petition was filed. The 2010 technical amendments to the Code clarified that this is not necessary, by changing the language to state that the briefing must be obtained during the period ending on the date of filing. Indeed, this language appears to permit the briefing to occur on that date, even if the petition is filed earlier in the day.[50] However, caution dictates obtaining the briefing before the petition is filed if at all possible, as it almost always is.

The only exception to the counseling requirement is contained in section 109(h)(4). That section permits the court to waive the requirement if the debtor is incapacitated, disabled, or on active military duty in a combat zone. Incapacity is defined as being so impaired by reason of mental illness or mental deficiency as to be incapable of realizing and making rational decisions regarding financial responsibilities.[51] Disability is defined as being so physically impaired as to be unable after reasonable effort to participate in an in-person, telephone, or Internet briefing.[52]

A debtor may also seek to defer the credit counseling briefing until after the petition is filed, but the statute permits delay of the briefing only if the debtor must file immediately due to exigent circumstances, the debtor requested a briefing from an approved agency,[53] and the debtor was not able to obtain a briefing within seven days after making the request.[54] If the debtor's request to defer the briefing is granted, the briefing must occur within thirty days after the petition is filed.[55] It is almost never advisable to seek a delay of the briefing under this provision. Usually the briefing can be completed over the telephone or Internet within an hour or two. And some courts have been ridiculously strict in interpreting the exigent circumstances requirement,[56] so if a delay is sought there is always a risk that it will not be granted and the case will be dismissed.

3.2.1.5 Dismissal for Abuse and the Means Test

Although not an eligibility requirement, section 707(b) permits a bankruptcy court to dismiss a chapter 7 case, after notice and a hearing, if the court finds that granting relief under chapter 7 would be an abuse of its provisions. Section 707(b) applies only to debtors whose debts are primarily consumer debts. A means test, found in section 707(b)(2) of the Code, determines whether there is a presumption of abuse based on the debtor's ability to repay creditors. This test does not apply to debtors whose income is below certain standards. Chapter 13, *infra*, provides a detailed discussion of dismissals for abuse.

3.2.2 The Initial Forms

Although the bankruptcy filing process may seem intimidating at first, a voluntary case is actually started by the debtor[57] filing a simple three-page petition, which includes a statement of compliance with the prebankruptcy credit counseling brief-

---

is not jurisdictional and automatic stay comes into effect even if requirement has not been met).

49 *See In re* Rios, 336 B.R. 177 (Bankr. S.D.N.Y. 2005) (filing of petition later stricken does not give rise to automatic stay). The *Rios* case was overruled by *Adams v. Zarnel (In re Zarnel)*, 619 F.3d 156 (2d Cir. 2010), which held the credit counseling requirement is not jurisdictional and that the automatic stay comes into effect even if the requirement has not been met.

50 *But see In re* Lane, 2012 WL 1865448 (Bankr. N.D. Okla. May 22, 2012) (amended language does not permit credit counseling requirement to be fulfilled after the petition is filed); *In re* Soohyun Koo, 2012 WL 692578 (Bankr. D. Col. Mar. 2, 2012) (same).

51 *See, e.g., In re* Jarrell, 364 B.R. 899 (Bankr. N.D. Tex. 2007) (mental illness was incapacity).

52 *See, e.g., In re* Dumas, 397 B.R. 883 (Bankr. N.D. Ill. 2008) (debtor found to be exempt from credit counseling based on dyslexic condition); *In re* Howard, 359 B.R. 589 (Bankr. E.D.N.C. 2007) (debtor had been hospitalized; suffered from memory loss, hearing loss, and limited mobility). *See also In re* Patasnik, 425 B.R. 916 (Bankr. S.D. Fla. 2010) (court could not waive requirement, but it could order prison officials to allow telephone call to counseling agency). *But see In re* Anderson, 397 B.R. 363 (B.A.P. 6th Cir. 2008) (incarcerated debtor is not "disabled" based solely on his imprisonment); *In re* Larsen, 399 B.R. 634 (Bankr. E.D. Wis. 2009) (same); *In re* Hubel, 395 B.R. 823 (N.D.N.Y. 2008) (same).

53 A few courts have erroneously held that the briefing cannot be obtained on the same day as the petition, and presumably these holdings would similarly apply to a request for a briefing made on the petition date. *See, e.g., In re* Gossett, 369 B.R. 361 (Bankr. N.D. Ill. 2007). See *also In re* Warren, 339 B.R. 475 (Bankr. E.D. Ark. 2006) (explaining why these decisions are wrongly decided).

54 11 U.S.C. § 109(h)(3)(A).

The debtor must certify the exigent circumstances on Exhibit D to the petition. *See* § 7.3.5, *infra*. Any dispute regarding the issue will usually be raised by a challenge to the debtor's certification.

55 11 U.S.C. § 109(h)(3)(B).

56 *See, e.g., In re* Dixon, 338 B.R. 383 (B.A.P. 8th Cir. 2006) (no abuse of discretion by bankruptcy court in denying motion for deferral based on finding that debtor had been given sufficient twenty-day advance notice of pending foreclosure under Missouri law); *In re* LaPorta, 332 B.R. 879 (Bankr. D. Minn. 2005). Most decisions have been more reasonable. *See, e.g., In re* Giambrone, 365 B.R. 386 (Bankr. W.D.N.Y. 2007) (foreclosure sale constituted exigent circumstances, even if debtor delay contributed to emergency); *In re* Romero, 349 B.R. 616 (Bankr. N.D. Cal. 2006) (fact that garnishment was predictable did not preclude it from being exigent circumstances); *In re* Childs, 335 B.R. 623, 630–631 (Bankr. D. Md. 2005) (imminent sale of property at foreclosure and imminent eviction from residence are exigent circumstances); *In re* Cleaver, 333 B.R. 430, 435 (Bankr. S.D. Ohio 2005) (pending foreclosure sale "exactly the sort of exigent circumstance contemplated by the statute").

57 *See In re* Carter, 285 B.R. 61 (Bankr. N.D. Ga. 2002) (case could be converted after discharge without vacating discharge order).

Under the Bankruptcy Code, the person filing the petition is called the "debtor" rather than the "bankrupt" as the latter term was thought to have a pejorative meaning.

ing requirement,[58] along with a statement of the debtor's Social Security number or lack thereof.[59] The debtor must also submit a list of creditors and other entities listed in the schedules (sometimes called the "mailing matrix").[60] All of the documents in a bankruptcy case may be, and in some districts must be, filed electronically, as discussed in a later chapter.[61]

The fee for filing the petition, comprising a statutory filing fee of $245 and other fees imposed by the courts, is currently $306,[62] which is normally paid at the time of filing. The fee for a husband and wife filing together as a joint case is the same as for an individual filing alone.[63] The court will accept the petition without the fee if it is accompanied by an application to pay the fee in installments over the next 120 days.[64] Alternatively, the petition will be accepted if the debtor files an application to waive the filing fee.[65] If the fee is required and not ultimately paid, or if the required forms are not filed, the case will normally be dismissed.[66]

A number of other forms must also be filed either concurrently with the petition or shortly thereafter.[67] These include the debtor's statement of affairs and schedules,[68] a statement of current monthly income and means test calculation,[69] a disclosure of attorney fees,[70] copies of "payment advices" from employers,[71] a certificate from a credit counseling agency evidencing completion of a prepetition credit counseling briefing,[72] and a statement of intention with respect to property securing consumer debts.[73] If the debtor has an interest in an education savings account, a "record" of that interest must also be filed.[74] In many districts local rules or administrative orders may prescribe another form or two, such as a verification of the list of creditors.[75]

3.2.3 Proper Venue for Bankruptcy Case

Under section 1408 of title 28 of the United States Code, a debtor may commence a bankruptcy case in any federal judicial district in which the domicile, residence, principal place of business, or principal assets of the debtor have been located for 180 days prior to the petition, or for a longer portion of that 180 days than any other district. The language of the statute referring to the district meeting the test for "the longer portion of such one-hundred-and-eighty-day period" suggests that only one district can satisfy the requirement for residence.[76] However, there may be more than one venue that fits the statute's description, for example, if the debtor's residence and principal place of business have been in two different districts for 180 days. Occasionally, debtors file in an incorrect venue, either

---

58 Fed. R. Bankr. P. 1002(a). *See* Official Form 1 (reprinted in Appx. D, *infra*).

Relief under chapter 7 may also be obtained by a debtor who converts from another chapter, such as chapter 13. *See* § 4.7.2, *infra*.

59 Fed. R. Bankr. P. 1007(f). *See* Official Form 21 (reprinted in Appx. D, *infra*).

Technically, this statement is not filed, but rather "submitted" to the clerk, because it is not included in the documents that are docketed and kept in the public court file for the case.

60 Fed. R. Bankr. P. 1007(a)(1). An extension of time for the filing of the list may be granted only on motion for cause shown. Fed. R. Bankr. P. 1007(a)(5).

61 *See* § 7.1.4, *infra*.

62 28 U.S.C. § 1930(a).

In addition to the $245 filing fee provided by 28 U.S.C. § 1930(a), the federal Judicial Conference decided to assess an additional noticing fee of $46 in connection with all chapter 7 and chapter 13 filings pursuant to 28 U.S.C. § 1930(b). The federal Judicial Conference also decided to add yet another $15 fee to be paid at the outset of a chapter 7 case to provide the funds necessary for additional compensation to chapter 7 trustees mandated by 11 U.S.C. § 330(b)(2), as amended by the Bankruptcy Reform Act of 1994, Pub. L. No. 103-394, 108 Stat. 4106 (1994). *See* Appx. C.3, *infra*. The noticing fee and trustee fee, like the filing fees, can be paid in installments, and the form application to pay the filing fee in installments has been modified to accommodate this possibility. *See* Official Form 3A (reprinted in Appx. D, *infra*); Fed. R. Bankr. P. 1006.

63 11 U.S.C. § 302. *But see In re* Allen, 186 B.R. 769 (Bankr. N.D. Ga. 1995) (gay couple could not file joint petition unless legally married).

One court has ruled that the federal Defense of Marriage Act precludes legally married gay couples from filing a joint bankruptcy petition. *In re* Kandu, 315 B.R. 123 (Bankr. W.D. Wash. 2004). *But see In re* Balas, 449 B.R. 567 (Bankr. C.D. Cal. 2011) (DOMA is unconstitutional violation of equal protection clause); *In re* Somers, 448 B.R. 677 (Bankr. S.D.N.Y. 2011) (denying motion to dismiss joint case filed by same sex married couple because cause for dismissal had not been shown).

64 28 U.S.C. § 1930(a); Fed. R. Bankr. P. 1006(b). See Official Form 3A (reprinted in Appx. D, *infra*).

Under the rule, the time for payment of any installment may be extended for cause until up to 180 days from the petition filing date.

65 A debtor whose income is less than 150% of the federal poverty level may seek a waiver of the chapter 7 filing fee under 28 U.S.C. § 1930(f). *See* Official Form 3B (reprinted in Appx. D, *infra*); § 7.3.13.4, § 14.6 *infra*.

66 11 U.S.C. § 707(a); Fed. R. Bankr. P. 1017(b), (c).

67 Federal Rule of Bankruptcy Procedure 1007(c) deals with the filing date for these forms.

68 Fed. R. Bankr. P. 1007(a)(1), (b).

See completed Official Forms 6 and 7 in Appendix D, *infra*. This rule also requires a statement of executory contracts and unexpired leases. That statement is Schedule G of Official Form 6.

69 Fed. R. Bankr. P. 1007(b)(4).

See completed Official Form 22A in Appendix D, *infra*. A chapter 7 debtor whose debts are not primarily consumer debts need not file Official Form 22A. Fed. R. Bankr. P. 1007(b)(4); *In re* Moates, 338 B.R. 716 (Bankr. N.D. Tex. 2006).

70 Fed. R. Bankr. P. 2016(b). *See* Forms 31, 32, Appx. G.3, *infra*.

71 11 U.S.C. § 521(a)(1)(iv). *See* § 7.3.10, *infra*.

In some districts, courts have adopted local rules requiring the copies of payment advices to be provided to the trustee at or before the meeting of creditors, rather than filed. Some districts require a debtor to file a certificate that no such documents exist if that is the case.

72 11 U.S.C. § 521(b); Fed. R. Bankr. P. 1007(c).

73 11 U.S.C. § 521(2)(A). See completed Official Form 8 in Appendix D, *infra*.

74 11 U.S.C. § 521(c); Fed. R. Bankr. P. 1007(b)(1)(F).

75 The bankruptcy court's website or the clerk of the local bankruptcy court may be consulted as to these requirements. *See also* Ch. 7, *infra*.

76 *In re* Handel, 253 B.R. 308 (B.A.P. 1st Cir. 2000).

inadvertently or intentionally, especially if that venue is more convenient or offers some other advantage.

Incorrect venue does not deprive the bankruptcy court of jurisdiction over the case. However, the court may dismiss or transfer the case to a proper venue if a party files a motion for it to do so.[77] Some courts have held that they also have discretion to retain a case filed in an improper venue.[78] Sanctions may be assessed against an attorney who knowingly files a case in an improper venue.[79] The court may also transfer a case from a proper venue to a different venue in the interest of justice or for the convenience of the parties.[80]

3.3 First Steps After Filing

The filing of a voluntary chapter 7 petition "constitutes an order for relief" under that chapter.[81] This means that the process of granting the relief requested is automatically set in motion.

An interim trustee, chosen from the panel of trustees established in the district,[82] is immediately appointed.[83] However, in most cases, this trustee will have little to do until later in the case except, perhaps, to peruse the papers filed. If the debtor has sought a waiver of the filing fee, the court typically rules upon that request within a few days after the filing of the petition. If the debtor has filed an application to pay the filing fee in installments, the court issues an order setting the dates for those payments.

The filing of the petition, except in cases in which two prior bankruptcy cases have been dismissed within the preceding year,[84] operates to effectuate the automatic stay provided for in section 362 of the Code.[85] With a number of exceptions, the stay prevents further proceedings or acts against the debtor or the debtor's property by anyone, except in the bankruptcy court, with respect to any claims arising before commencement of the case. The stay has the general purpose of freezing the debtor's property so that it may be examined and administered in the bankruptcy case, and therefore usually remains in place throughout the case unless the court orders otherwise.[86] The statute also requires any entity holding property that the trustee[87] may use, sell, or lease, or that the debtor may exempt, to deliver that property to the trustee forthwith.[88]

Normally, within a few weeks after filing, the court mails to all creditors, the debtor, and the debtor's attorney, a notice of the stay and of the date and place set for the section 341(a) meeting, also known as the meeting of creditors.[89] This meeting is normally scheduled for a date twenty-one to forty days after the filing of the petition[90] and must occur at least twenty-one days after the notice.[91] It may be held at the court or at any other place that the United States trustee or bankruptcy administrator deems to be convenient to the parties.[92]

The notice also contains deadlines for creditors who wish to file claims, objections to exemptions,[93] or complaints raising objections to discharge[94] or to the dischargeability of a particular debt.[95] Under the rules, the deadline for complaints objecting to discharge or requesting determination of certain dischargeability issues is sixty days after the first date set for the meeting of creditors.[96] The deadline for filing objections to exemptions, with limited exceptions, is thirty days after the conclusion of the meeting of creditors or the filing of any amendment to the exemptions.[97] If the case appears to be a no-asset case, the court will notify creditors that claims should not be filed unless they later receive notice that there are assets.[98]

3.4 The Section 341(a) Meeting (Meeting of Creditors)

The debtor's first, and often only, appearance at any kind of a hearing usually occurs at the section 341(a) meeting (meeting of creditors).[99] This proceeding is intended to give the various parties a chance to examine the debtor and her affairs. In practice, the meeting allows the trustee to learn whatever she

---

77 *Id.*
78 *See, e.g., In re* Jordan, 313 B.R. 242 (Bankr. W.D. Tenn. 2004), *rev'd by* Thompson v. Greenwood, 507 F.3d 416 (6th Cir. 2007).
79 *In re* Pannell, 253 B.R. 216 (S.D. Ohio 2000).
80 28 U.S.C. § 1412.
81 11 U.S.C. § 301.
82 This panel is established by the United States trustee if one exists, otherwise by the bankruptcy administrator for the court. 28 U.S.C. §§ 586(a), 604(f).
83 The appointment is made by the United States trustee if one exists, otherwise by the court. 11 U.S.C. § 701.
84 11 U.S.C. § 362(c)(4). *See* § 9.3.3.3, *infra.*
85 *See* Ch. 9, *infra.*
86 The primary exception is found in 11 U.S.C. § 362(c)(3), which provides that the stay terminates with respect to the debtor thirty days after the petition if the debtor has had a prior bankruptcy case dismissed in the year preceding the petition, unless the court extends the stay after finding that the case was filed in good faith. *See* § 9.3.3.2, *infra.*

87 Under chapter 13, the debtor may exercise the trustee's power to use, sell, or lease property. 11 U.S.C. §§ 1303, 1304. *See generally* Ch. 12, *infra.*
88 11 U.S.C. §§ 542, 543. *See* § 9.9, *infra.*
89 See Official Form 9, reprinted in Appendix D, *infra*, for the commonly used versions of these forms. Like all notices, this notice is sent by e-mail, rather than mailed, to attorneys who are enrolled in the court's electronic filing system.
90 Fed. R. Bankr. P. 2003(a).
  If the meeting is not at a location staffed by the United States trustee, it may be held up to sixty days after the filing. *Id.*
91 Fed. R. Bankr. P. 2002(a)(1).
92 Fed. R. Bankr. P. 2003(a).
93 *See* § 10.3.3, *infra.*
94 There are various grounds upon which a party may object to the debtor's discharge. 11 U.S.C. § 727(a). *See* Ch. 15, *infra.*
95 A creditor may contest the discharge of a particular debt in certain circumstances. 11 U.S.C. § 523. *See* Ch. 15, *infra.*
96 Fed. R. Bankr. P. 4004(a), 4007(c). The same deadline applies to a motion to dismiss a case under § 707(b) or (c), except as provided in § 704(b). Fed. R. Bankr. P. 1017(e).
97 Fed. R. Bankr. P. 4003(b).
98 Fed. R. Bankr. P. 2002(e).
99 This meeting is provided for in 11 U.S.C. § 341.

feels is necessary to perform the trustee's duties.

The Code and Bankruptcy Rules set forth a number of document production requirements with respect to the meeting of creditors. The debtor must provide to the trustee, at least seven days before the meeting, copies of the debtor's federal income tax return, or a transcript thereof, for the tax year ending immediately before the petition date and for which such a return was filed, or provide a written statement that such documents do not exist.[100] The debtor must also produce, at the meeting: (1) a governmental picture identification or other personal identifying information establishing the debtor's identity, (2) evidence of the debtor's Social Security number or a written statement that such documentation does not exist, (3) evidence of current income, (4) copies of statements from depository and investment accounts covering the date of the petition, and (5) if required by the means test provisions, documentation of certain monthly expenses claimed by the debtor.[101] With respect to the evidence of current income, bank statements or monthly expense documentation, the debtor may alternatively file a statement that the documentation does not exist or is not in the debtor's possession.

Despite the name, creditors rarely appear at the meeting of creditors in a consumer bankruptcy case. Some of those who do attend are there only because they are unsophisticated and believe that the notice they received compels their attendance. Others may occasionally come to ask questions for discovery purposes.[102] And a few creditors (particularly retail stores whose credit card agreements give them questionable purchase money security interest claims) have sometimes attended in order to coerce debtors to enter into inadvisable reaffirmation agreements.[103]

The meeting itself is usually conducted by the interim trustee or the United States trustee.[104] It may last from three to thirty minutes and consists of a series of routine questions,[105] generally covering most of the information in the statement of affairs and schedules.[106] These are typically propounded to the debtor by the interim trustee,[107] who also reviews the documents provided by the debtor. However personnel from the United States trustee's office sometimes appear at meetings of creditors to propound questions in addition to those of the panel trustee.

The interim trustee normally becomes the permanent trustee.[108] The bankruptcy judge is not permitted to attend the meeting, so that she is not influenced by any information brought out there.[109] It is somewhat unclear whether evidentiary rules apply, and the trustee (who, in essence, is another party to the case) does not have the authority to compel testimony or resolve any disputes that arise other than disputes about how to conduct the meeting.[110] Any dispute or challenge to the trustee's procedures must be resolved by the judge, much like a dispute arising in a deposition, if any party feels strongly enough about the issue to pursue it. Although creditors new to bankruptcy may not realize it, it is clear that the trustee has no power to rule on any question concerning the stay, discharge, or any other dispute between a creditor and the debtor.

The trustee has an additional duty to perform at the meeting of creditors. The trustee is required to "orally examine" the debtor to assure that the debtor is aware of several things, including the potential consequences of seeking a discharge in bankruptcy, its effects on the debtor's credit history, the debtor's ability to file under a different chapter of the Code, the effect of receiving a discharge, and the effect of reaffirming a debt.[111] In practice, most trustees give much of this information in writing and ask if the debtor has read it.[112] Although it is a good idea, naturally, to prepare the debtor to respond appropriately to these questions, there are no apparent consequences if the debtor expresses a lack of awareness in response to the trustee's inquiries, except perhaps that the debtor will be asked to read or reread the written information provided by the trustee.

3.5 After the Meeting of Creditors

3.5.1 Exempt and Encumbered Property; Abandonment of Property

What happens after the meeting of creditors depends to some extent on whether there are substantial assets in the bankruptcy estate that are neither exempt[113] nor encumbered, and that are thus available for the unsecured creditors.

In all cases, unless some party successfully objects, the debtor retains property claimed as exempt.[114] Although aban-

---

100 11 U.S.C. § 521(e)(2)(A); Fed. R. Bankr. P. 4002(b)(3). See Ch. 8, infra.
101 11 U.S.C. §§ 521(h), 707(b)(2); Fed. R. Bankr. P. 4002(b)(1), (2). See Ch. 8, infra.
102 See Ch. 8, infra.
103 It is usually a bad idea to agree to these reaffirmation agreements at the meeting of creditors. See § 15.5.3, infra; Helping Your Client Do the Wash: The Effect in Bankruptcy of PMSI Claims Created by Revolving Credit Accounts, 12 NCLC REPORTS Bankruptcy and Foreclosures Ed. 37 (Jan./Feb. 1994).
104 See Fed. R. Bankr. P. 2003(b).
105 The questions recommended by the United States Trustee Program are set out in Forms 61, 64, Appx. G.7, infra.
106 See completed versions of the forms in Appendix D, infra. Blank versions may be found on this treatise's companion website.
107 The interim trustee has been previously appointed under 11 U.S.C. § 701.
108 Creditors may vote to elect a trustee if a sufficient number of creditors are present. 11 U.S.C. § 702. A sufficient number is almost never present in consumer cases, so the interim trustee then becomes the permanent trustee. 11 U.S.C. § 702(d).
109 11 U.S.C. § 341.
110 The questions typically propounded, as well as other guidelines set for section 341(a) meetings and administration of chapter 7 cases by the Executive Office of the United States Trustees, can be found in the Chapter 7 Trustee Handbook published by that office, available at www.usdoj.gov/ust/library/trusteelib.htm. See also Form 62, Appx. G.7, infra.
111 11 U.S.C. § 341(d).
112 A sample form used by many trustees is reprinted in Form 63, Appendix G.7, infra.
113 Exempt property is property that the debtor may retain in a liquidation case. See generally Ch. 10, infra.
114 11 U.S.C. § 522(l); Taylor v. Freeland & Kronz, 503 U.S. 638, 112

donment of property by the trustee may be sought before the case ends, on motion by the trustee, debtor, or some other party, it usually occurs automatically at the end of the case.[115] The trustee generally abandons all property in which there is little or no nonexempt equity by declining to administer the property and simply closing the case.[116] When the property is abandoned, the trustee in effect disclaims interest in it, and ownership status reverts to whatever it was prior to the bankruptcy. Ordinarily, once property is abandoned by the trustee, that decision is irrevocable.[117] However, property which has not been scheduled is not deemed abandoned and the trustee may reopen the case to administer such property if it is later discovered. Rights to such property therefore may not revest in the debtor at the closing of the case.[118] Moreover, when abandonment is sought by motion, the parties must comply with the procedural requirements of the rules.[119]

Various other proceedings may sometimes take place, such as motions to avoid liens on exempt property.[120] In cases in which there is property securing a consumer debt,[121] or personal property subject to an unexpired lease, and the debtor has filed a statement of intention[122] to redeem the property,[123] surrender it, or reaffirm the debt,[124] or to assume the lease on personal property,[125] that intention normally must be performed.[126] The normal deadline for the debtor's performance is thirty days after the first date set for the meeting of creditors, but the court may extend that deadline for cause if the debtor so requests before it expires.[127] And, in any case, the debtor's substantive rights with regard to the property should not be affected by the debtor's failure to meet the deadline, except that in certain circumstances the automatic stay may terminate with respect to the property.[128]

In cases in which property remains in the estate, it is normally administered by the trustee, except when the property has little value. In such cases, called "nominal asset cases," if it appears that the trustee intends to administer the property, the debtor may request that the property be abandoned[129] on the grounds that it would not provide any meaningful distribution to creditors after the costs of administration were paid.[130] A

S. Ct. 1644, 118 L. Ed. 2d 280 (1992). *See* § 10.3, *infra*.

115 A sample motion by the debtor for abandonment is reprinted in Form 108, Appendix G.10, *infra*.

116 11 U.S.C. § 554. *See In re* Kane, 628 F.3d 631 (3d Cir. N.J. 2010) (disclosure of divorce action was sufficient to disclose inchoate interest in possible equitable distribution, which trustee acknowledged, so asset was abandoned at closing of case).

Once the trustee has filed a final report certifying that the estate has been fully administered, if no objection is filed within thirty days, there is a presumption that full administration has taken place regardless of whether the case is closed. Fed. R. Bankr. P. 5009. Once the presumption is in place, all property scheduled which has not been administered is deemed abandoned unless the court orders otherwise. 11 U.S.C. § 554(c). *See In re* Potter, 228 B.R. 422 (B.A.P. 8th Cir. 1999) (court could order that contingent remainder interest remain part of estate as unadministered asset when case was closed).

117 *In re* Tadlock, 338 B.R. 436 (B.A.P. 10th Cir. 2006) (abandonment may not be revoked because property has higher value than trustee previously believed, absent lack of disclosure by debtor); *In re* Wornell, 70 B.R. 153 (W.D. Mo. 1986); *In re* Pioch, 2010 WL 3701593 (Bankr. E.D. Mich. Sept. 1, 2010) (fact that asset may have appreciated or may have been valued incorrectly by trustee was not grounds for revoking abandonment); Murray v. Nagy (*In re* Nagy), 432 B.R. 564 (Bankr. M.D. La. 2010) (although debtors did not exempt their interest in real estate they disclosed, abandonment after case was closed would not be revoked just because trustee failed to accurately determine value of property); *In re* Bast, 366 B.R. 237 (Bankr. S.D. Fla. 2007); *In re* Johnson, 361 B.R. 903 (Bankr. D. Mont. 2007); *In re* Enriquez, 22 B.R. 934 (Bankr. D. Neb. 1982). *But see In re* Woods, 173 F.3d 770 (10th Cir. 1999) (court may revoke deemed abandonment of property under section 554(c) pursuant to Fed. R. Bankr. P. 9024); *In re* Alt, 39 B.R. 902 (Bankr. W.D. Wis. 1984) (revocation of mistaken abandonment permitted).

The revocability of an abandonment often turns on whether the debtor fully disclosed the interest in property involved. *Compare* Donarumo v. Furlong (*In re* Furlong), 660 F.3d 81 (1st Cir. 2011) (causes of action sufficiently disclosed), *and In re* Bryson, 53 B.R. 3 (Bankr. M.D. Tenn. 1985) (abandonment irrevocable when trustee knew of debtor's interest in lawsuit that, after abandonment, resulted in large recovery, and no objection was filed at time of abandonment), *with In re* Schmid, 54 B.R. 78 (Bankr. D. Or. 1985) (abandonment revoked when debtor's interest in lawsuit was insufficiently listed in the schedules).

118 11 U.S.C. § 554(d). *See In re* Baudoin, 981 F.2d 736 (5th Cir. 1993) (lender liability claim scheduled as "any possible claim against creditor for actions taken against debtor," with value listed as "undetermined" was not properly scheduled and therefore was not deemed abandoned at end of case); Vreugdenhill v. Navistar Int'l Transp. Corp., 950 F.2d 524 (8th Cir. 1991). *See also* § 14.3.2.6, *infra*.

119 Fed. R. Bankr. P. 6007. *See* Seward v. Devine, 888 F.2d 957 (2d Cir. 1989) (abandonment without notice to creditors is ineffective). *See also In re* Killebrew, 888 F.2d 1516 (5th Cir. 1989) (assets had never been abandoned by trustee).

120 See § 10.4.2, *infra*, for discussion of lien avoidance motions.

121 "Consumer debt" is defined at 11 U.S.C. § 101(8).

122 The statement of intention is required by 11 U.S.C. § 521(a)(2). *See* § 11.4.1, *infra*.

123 Redemption is provided for in 11 U.S.C. § 722. See § 11.5, *infra*, for discussion of redemption.

124 Reaffirmation of debts is permitted in some circumstances by 11 U.S.C. § 524(c). See § 15.5.2, *infra*, for discussion of reaffirmation.

125 See § 12.9.5, *infra*, for discussion of assumption or rejection of personal property leases.

126 11 U.S.C. § 521(a)(2)(B).

127 11 U.S.C. § 521(a)(2)(B).

The intention clearly need not be performed before the thirtieth day. *See, e.g., In re* Grace, 85 B.R. 464 (Bankr. S.D. Ohio 1988) (sanctions imposed against creditor that prematurely repossessed car that debtor intended to surrender).

128 11 U.S.C. §§ 362(h), 521(a)(2)(C). *See* § 11.4.1, *infra*.

129 Any party in interest may request that the court order the trustee to abandon property if the trustee does not do so voluntarily. 11 U.S.C. § 554(b). See § 8.3.11, *infra*, for further discussion of abandonment of property. See also Form 108, Appendix G.10, *infra*, for an example of a motion for abandonment.

130 Any sale of estate assets involves some administrative expense to the trustee, and these costs must be paid before creditors receive anything. If only a small amount of property can be sold, all of the proceeds would likely go to the trustee and none to creditors, thus defeating the purpose of the sale, which is to benefit creditors. Congress specifically disapproved of the sale of assets in nominal-asset cases. H.R. Rep. No. 95-595, at 93 (1977). The amount of assets considered to be nominal varies from district to district, and

motion to abandon may also be necessary if a trustee simply sits on property in hopes of eventually being able to sell it or extract some money from the debtor.

3.5.2 Liquidation of Nonexempt Property

If the estate has more than nominal assets, they must be turned over to the trustee at or after the creditors meeting.[131] Usually, the debtor is offered the option of paying their value to the trustee instead.[132] If the trustee declines to abandon property, it ordinarily becomes the trustee's responsibility to pay costs of maintaining the property and insuring it.[133] The trustee then collects any other property of the estate that is neither exempt nor abandoned, and liquidates the estate, that is, converts it to cash. The trustee must normally give twenty-one days' notice of intent to sell the property.[134] Any party, including the debtor, may object within specified time limits to the proposed sale, which may be a private sale or a sale by public auction.[135] If an asset is partially exempt, the debtor's exemption should be paid in cash from the proceeds prior to distribution of any proceeds to creditors or for administrative expenses.[136]

3.5.3 Filing and Allowance of Claims

While the nonexempt assets of the estate are being liquidated, the trustee receives and evaluates all claims filed by creditors, objecting to them if they are improper.[137] Unless an objection is filed, a proof of claim in proper form is deemed allowed.[138] Any objections filed commence contested matters under Rule 9014[139] and are ruled upon by the court. Once the status of the claims has been determined and the deadline for filing claims has expired, the distribution to creditors is made.

3.5.4 Distribution of Property to Creditors

After the estate has been liquidated and the amounts of the claims have been determined, the trustee is in a position to make distributions of the estate's property to creditors. The distribution to creditors is carried out according to priority rules in the Bankruptcy Code, which serve to effectuate various policy decisions of the drafters regarding which creditors should be paid first. Distributions to creditors are generally known as "dividends."

Under the statutory distribution scheme, to the extent that any asset is partially encumbered, the claims of creditors with liens on that asset are paid from the proceeds of sale prior to distribution to unsecured creditors. Briefly, the order of distribution is as follows (although many of these categories are rarely applicable in consumer cases):

(1) Senior liens granted to secure credit obtained by the trustee or the debtor during the case under 11 U.S.C. § 364(d) (normally for operation of the debtor's business), in the amount of the allowed secured claim.

(2) Secured claims of creditors in the amount of their allowed secured claims[140] and in order of lien priority,[141] in property

---

ranges from under $500 to about $3000. *See, e.g., In re* Kusler, 224 B.R. 180 (Bankr. N.D. Okla. 1998) (criticizing trustee for selling encumbered property which would not realize significant dividends for creditors); *In re* Maropa Marine Sales Serv. & Storage, Inc., 92 B.R. 547 (Bankr. S.D. Fla. 1988) (trustee's sale of asset subject to lien of undersecured creditor would be abusive). *See also In re* Nelson, 251 B.R. 857 (B.A.P. 8th Cir. 2000) (granting motion compelling trustee to abandon real estate in which there was no equity); *In re* Luban, 2011 Bankr. LEXIS 3507 (Bankr. S.D. Fla. Sept. 15, 2011) (permitting conversion where trustee threatened to charge rent to the debtors and stating that trustee should not cause mortgages to go into default in order to pay unsecured creditors).

131 Although 11 U.S.C. § 521(a)(4) literally requires debtors to turn all property of the estate over to the trustee, such a transfer does not occur in practice. The trustee normally takes constructive possession of estate property in a consumer bankruptcy case, not actual possession. *In re* Figueira, 163 B.R. 192 (Bankr. D. Kan. 1993).

Generally, all of the property is exempt or encumbered and therefore not available for distribution to creditors, so there would be no purpose served by physical transfer of assets to the trustee. *See also* 4 Collier on Bankruptcy ¶ 521.16 (16th ed.).

132 *In re* Bailey, 234 B.R. 7 (Bankr. D.R.I. 1999) (approving compromise in which debtor paid trustee slightly less than amount that sale of debtor's home would have generated under "best case scenario").

The debtor may use exempt assets or property which does not belong to the estate for this purpose. Most practically, because postpetition income is not part of the chapter 7 estate, a debtor can use postpetition savings to buy back nonexempt property interests from the trustee.

133 *See In re* Wait, 2010 WL 2667413 (Bankr. N.D. Iowa June 24, 2010) (nothing in the Code allows trustee to shift to debtor the costs of maintaining estate property).

134 Fed. R. Bankr. P. 6003.

135 Fed. R. Bankr. P. 6004.

136 *See* 11 U.S.C. § 522(k).

137 The debtor usually has no interest in whether particular creditors are paid in a chapter 7 case, but in rare cases may wish to object to a claim if the disallowance of a particular creditor's claim would mean that more funds will be available to pay a nondischargeable debt or that the debtor would receive estate property in excess of the amount necessary to pay all allowed claims with interest. *See* 11 U.S.C. § 726(a)(6).

138 11 U.S.C. § 502(a).
Objections to claims are discussed in Ch. 14, *infra*.

139 A claim objection should not include a claim for relief of a kind specified in Federal Rule of Bankruptcy Procedure 7001 (for example, bringing into question the validity of a lien), but rather the objection should be included in an adversary proceeding. Fed. R. Bankr. P. 3007(b).

140 The allowed secured claim may be less than the debt owed to the creditor. It cannot exceed the creditor's interest in the collateral. 11 U.S.C. § 506. *See* Ch. 11, *infra*.

141 *See In re* Darnell, 834 F.2d 1263 (6th Cir. 1987); Pearlstein v. United States Small Bus. Admin., 719 F.2d 1169 (D.C. Cir. 1983).

Secured creditors' claims may be equitably subordinated in some cases to those of other secured or unsecured creditors under either bankruptcy or state law. *See* 11 U.S.C. § 510; Small v. Beverly Bank, 936 F.2d 945 (7th Cir. 1991) (equitable subordination considered under Illinois law). There is also an exception under which tax liens can be subordinated to certain priority claims under 11 U.S.C. § 724(b) in some cases. *See* § 6.6.3, *infra*.

not abandoned (when there is a nonexempt interest in the property which can be liquidated by the trustee).

(3) Junior liens granted to secure credit under 11 U.S.C. § 364(d), in the amount of the allowed secured claim.

(4) Allowed unsecured claims for domestic support obligations[142] owed to or recoverable by a spouse, former spouse, or child of the debtor or such child's parent, guardian or responsible relative on the petition date, subject to payment of the trustee's administrative expenses to administer assets to pay the claims. 11 U.S.C. § 507(a)(1)(A), (C).

(5) Allowed unsecured claims for domestic support obligations[143] owed to or recoverable by a governmental unit on the petition date, subject to payment of the trustee's administrative expenses to administer assets to pay the claims. 11 U.S.C. § 507(a)(1)(B), (C).

(6) "Super priority" unsecured claims granted to creditors who have been harmed by failure of the debtor or trustee to provide adequate protection[144] of their interests in property during the case. 11 U.S.C. § 507(b).

(7) Other administrative expenses, including costs of preserving the estate, taxes incurred by the estate,[145] payments to the trustee, attorneys, accountants, and so forth, and certain specified expenses of creditors helping the estate. 11 U.S.C. §§ 507(a)(2), 503(b).[146]

(8) Certain unsecured claims incurred in involuntary cases. 11 U.S.C. § 507(a)(3).

(9) Allowed unsecured claims for wages, salaries, vacation, severance, or sick pay earned from the debtor within 180 days before the filing of the petition or cessation of a debtor's business, whichever occurred first, up to $11,725[147] per claimant. 11 U.S.C. § 507(a)(4).

(10) Allowed unsecured claims for contributions to employee pension or benefit plans arising from services within 180 days before the filing of the petition or the cessation of business, whichever occurred first, up to $11,725[148] times the number of employees, minus the amount paid under (7) above. 11 U.S.C. § 507(a)(5).

(11) Allowed unsecured claims of persons engaged in the production or raising of grain, for grain or its proceeds, against debtors who own or operate grain storage facilities, or of United States fishermen, up to $5775[149], against debtors operating fish produce storage or processing facilities. 11 U.S.C. § 507(a)(6).

(12) Certain allowed unsecured claims from the deposit of money by consumers who had deposited money for the purchase, lease, or rental of property or services not provided, up to $2600[150] per individual. 11 U.S.C. § 507(a)(7).[151]

(13) Certain allowed unsecured claims of governmental units, for example, taxes, specified in 11 U.S.C. § 507(a)(8).[152] However, tax penalty claims are given this priority only if they are in compensation for actual pecuniary loss.[153] As in cases concerning dischargeability of taxes, there is sometimes an issue regarding whether a particular claim is a tax at all.[154]

---

142 "Domestic support obligation" is defined in 11 U.S.C. § 101 and generally includes claims in the nature of alimony, maintenance, or support. *See* § 15.4.3.5, *infra*.

143 "Domestic support obligation" is defined in 11 U.S.C. § 101 and generally includes claims in the nature of alimony, maintenance, or support. *See* § 15.4.3.5, *infra*.

144 See Chapter 9, *infra*, for explanation of adequate protection of creditors' interests in property during the case. *See also In re Campbell*, 205 B.R. 288 (Bankr. D. Colo. 1997) (payments that were to be made pursuant to chapter 13 plan and that were denominated as "adequate protection payments" were not in fact true adequate protection payments, but rather simply plan payments, and therefore failure to make payments did not create super priority claim).

145 Postpetition interest on postpetition tax claims also appears to be a priority claim. *In re* Mark Anthony Constr. Co., 886 F.2d 1101 (9th Cir. 1989); *In re* Allied Mech. Serv., Inc., 885 F.2d 837 (11th Cir. 1989).

146 Administrative expenses include only debts for services to the extent they are actually utilized by the trustee or the estate. *In re* Subscription Television of Greater Atlanta, 789 F.2d 1530 (11th Cir. 1986); *In re* Thompson, 788 F.2d 560 (9th Cir. 1986).

147 For cases filed between April 1, 2007, and April 1, 2010, the amount is $10,950.

148 For cases filed between April 1, 2007, and April 1, 2010, the amount is $10,950.

149 For cases filed between April 1, 2007, and April 1, 2010, the amount is $5400.

150 For cases filed between April 1, 2007, and April 1, 2010, the amount is $2425.

151 *See* § 18.5.5, *infra*.

The deposit may be part or all of the price for the purchase, lease, or services. *In re* Salazar, 430 F.3d 992 (9th Cir. 2005). It has been held that tenants' security deposits fall within this priority. *In re* River Vill. Assoc., 161 B.R. 127 (Bankr. E.D. Pa. 1993), *aff'd*, 181 B.R. 795 (E.D. Pa. 1995).

One court has held that debts owed by a money order issuer to stores that sold money orders to consumers do not fall within this priority, even though the store had obtained assignments of the consumers' rights. *In re* Northwest Fin. Express, Inc., 950 F.2d 561 (8th Cir. 1991).

152 Prepetition and postpetition interest on priority tax claims have also been held to constitute priority claims. *In re* Garcia, 955 F.2d 16 (5th Cir. 1992) (prepetition interest on priority tax claim entitled to same priority); *In re* Bates, 974 F.2d 1234 (10th Cir. 1992) (same). *See In re* Hanna, 872 F.2d 829 (8th Cir. 1989) (postpetition interest on prepetition taxes).

Language at the end of section 507(a)(8) provides that any time period in that subsection is suspended for any period during which a governmental unit was stayed from collecting by a prior bankruptcy case, plus ninety days. That provision superseded the Supreme Court's decision in Young v. United States, 535 U.S. 43, 122 S. Ct. 1036, 152 L. Ed. 2d 79 (2002). The time periods are discussed further in § 15.4.3.1, *infra*.

Finally, in an involuntary bankruptcy case, the three-year period dictated by section 507(a)(8) is counted from the date the involuntary petition is originally filed. *In re* Rassi, 140 B.R. 490 (Bankr. C.D. Ill. 1992).

153 *In re* Mako, Inc., 135 B.R. 902 (E.D. Okla. 1991); *In re* Hovan, 172 B.R. 974 (Bankr. W.D. Wash. 1994), *aff'd*, 96 F.3d 1254 (9th Cir. 1996).

154 *See In re* DeJesus, 243 B.R. 241 (Bankr. D.N.J. 1999) (motor vehicle surcharge debt was not an excise tax). *See also* § 15.4.3.1.1, *infra*.

(14) Certain allowed unsecured claims based on responsibilities to the government related to its oversight of the banking industry. 11 U.S.C. § 507(a)(9).[155]

(15) Allowed claims for death or personal injuries resulting from debtor's operation of a motor vehicle or vessel that was unlawful because of the debtor's intoxication from alcohol, a drug, or other substance. 11 U.S.C. § 507(a)(10).

(16) Timely-filed general unsecured claims and certain tardily-filed claims. 11 U.S.C. § 726(a)(2).

(17) Other general unsecured claims filed after the deadline for filing claims. 11 U.S.C. § 726(a)(3).[156]

(18) Allowed claims for fines, penalties, forfeitures, or multiple, exemplary, or punitive damages. 11 U.S.C. § 726(a)(4).

(19) Interest at the legal rate on all claims paid, from the date of filing. 11 U.S.C. § 726(a)(5).

(20) The debtor. 11 U.S.C. § 726(a)(6).

If there are certain types of community property involved,[157] distribution follows a somewhat different order. That community property is segregated from other property of the estate and the estate is distributed in several stages. Within each stage, except the first two stages, the order set forth above is applied. The stages are:

(1) The claims set out in (1), (2), (3), (6) and (7) above, in that order from property to which they are applicable.

(2) Claims for administrative expenses, which can also be paid from other property of the estate, as justice requires. 11 U.S.C. § 726(c)(1).

(3) Community claims[158] against the debtor or the debtor's spouse, from community property in the estate, except to the extent that the community property is solely liable for debts of the debtor. 11 U.S.C. § 726(c)(2)(A).

(4) Community claims against the debtor not paid under (3) above, from community property in the estate that is solely liable for debts of the debtor. 11 U.S.C. § 726(c)(2)(B).

(5) Claims against the debtor, including community claims not paid under (3) and (4) above, from property of the estate other than the community property involved. 11 U.S.C. § 726(c)(2)(C).

(6) Community claims against the debtor or the debtor's spouse not already paid, from all remaining property of the estate. 11 U.S.C. § 726(c)(2)(D).

After distribution, the trustee makes a final report and accounting to the court, which then concludes the case.

In most cases involving consumer debtors, of course, no distribution is made to any of the parties listed above, because there are no assets to distribute. In such cases, depending upon local practice, the trustee may or may not make a report to the court,[159] setting forth the lack of any objections to discharge or the claim of exemption.[160]

3.6 The Discharge and Discharge Hearing

The final step in a chapter 7 bankruptcy is usually the granting of the debtor's discharge. To become eligible to receive a chapter 7 discharge a debtor must, with very limited exceptions, complete a personal financial management instructional course offered by an approved provider, which can be taken in person, on the telephone, or over the Internet.[161] Under the Bankruptcy Rules, the debtor must file a statement certifying completion of the course within sixty days after the first

---

155 This provision was added to the Code to assist the government's attempts to recover assets from individuals involved with failed banks and savings and loans.

156 Prior to the 1994 amendments, some courts had held that the failure to mention tardily-filed priority claims in this section meant that tardily-filed priority claims could be paid ahead of timely-filed nonpriority claims. *In re* Century Boat Co., 986 F.2d 154 (6th Cir. 1993) (late-filed priority claim should receive priority in distribution, at least if the priority creditor did not receive notice of the case and files its claim before the trustee makes any distribution of estate, provided that there is no bad faith on the part of the priority claimant and no undue prejudice to other creditors). Other courts rejected this reasoning, holding that late-filed priority claims had to be paid after timely-filed claims. *In re* Mantz, 151 B.R. 928 (B.A.P. 9th Cir. 1993), *rev'd*, 33 F.3d 59 (9th Cir. 1993). The 1994 amendments resolved this issue, amending 11 U.S.C. § 726(a)(1) to provide that tardily-filed priority claims are to be paid before general unsecured claims in chapter 7 cases, as long as the priority claims are filed before the trustee commences distributions to creditors.

However, only tardily filed claims filed by creditors under § 501(a) can be paid and, at least if a party objects, not those filed by the debtor or trustee under § 501(c). *In re* Davis, 430 B.R. 62 (Bankr. W.D.N.Y. 2010) (sustaining debtor's objection to use of surplus estate funds to pay claims tardily filed by trustee).

157 The bankruptcy estate includes all community property of the debtor and the debtor's spouse that is (1) under sole, equal, or joint management or control of the debtor, or (2) liable for an allowable claim against either the debtor or the debtor and the debtor's spouse. 11 U.S.C. § 541(a)(2).

It is unclear what happens under this provision and other similar provisions in the Code with respect to community property of domestic partners or spouses who are of the same gender, because the federal Defense of Marriage Act, 1 U.S.C. § 7, provides that in interpreting all federal statutes "spouse" refers "only to a person of the opposite sex who is a husband or wife." It would appear that community property owned by the debtor and someone who is not a spouse of the opposite gender would not be subject to distribution by the trustee. *See* Collier on Bankruptcy ¶ 541.13[5]; Robert F. Kidd & Frederick C. Hertz, *Partnered in Debt: The Impacts of California's New Registered Domestic Partner Law on Creditors' Remedies and Debtors' Rights under California Law and under Federal Bankruptcy Law*, 28 Cal. Bankr. J. 148 (2006).

158 A "community claim" is defined at 11 U.S.C. § 101(7).

159 In some districts, it is presumed that if the trustee does not object to exemptions a report is unnecessary because the exemptions will be granted under 11 U.S.C. § 522(*l*) without the filing of a report.

160 The procedures for litigating the objections are discussed in Chapters 8 and 15, *infra*. The current Federal Rules of Bankruptcy Procedure do not provide for the trustee's report required by prior rules, stating only that any objections to exemptions must be filed within thirty days after the conclusion of the meeting of creditors or the filing of any amendment to the exemptions and any objection to discharge must be raised by an adversary proceeding. Fed. R. Bankr. P. 4003(b), 7001.

161 11 U.S.C. §§ 111(d), 727(a)(11). *See* § 8.3.3, *infra*.

date set for the meeting of creditors.[162]

The discharge is effective as to all debts except: certain taxes, some debts not listed by the debtor in the schedules, debts for domestic support obligations,[163] most fines and penalties owed to governmental units, most student loans, debts which were or could have been listed in a prior bankruptcy in which discharge was denied or waived, certain debts incurred by driving while intoxicated, certain debts of individuals involved in the banking or savings and loan industry, and debts which have been ruled nondischargeable during the case.[164] Other exceptions to the discharge include federal criminal restitution debts, debts incurred to pay nondischargeable taxes, marital property settlement debts, certain condominium, home owner association and cooperative fees,[165] certain court fees and costs owed by prisoners,[166] and debts for repayment of loans from pension plans. Also, to the extent a secured creditor's lien has not been disallowed, avoided, or satisfied, that creditor normally will retain the right to bring an *in rem* action to enforce its lien.[167]

In any case in which the debtor wishes to reaffirm a debt and the debtor was not represented by an attorney in negotiating the reaffirmation agreement, the court is required to hold a discharge hearing.[168] The court may, in its discretion, hold discharge hearings in other cases, and will often do so if the reaffirmation documents raise a presumption of undue hardship.

Because of the strong policy against reaffirmation agreements, which are unfairly coerced by some creditors, the Code requires a careful explanation of reaffirmation to the debtor by the court at the discharge hearing, or by an attorney if the debtor is represented in connection with the proposed reaffirmation.[169] Unless the debt is secured by real property of the debtor, or an attorney representing the debtor in the reaffirmation agreement files a written declaration that the agreement is a fully informed and voluntary act of the debtor that does not impose undue hardship on the debtor or the debtor's dependents, the reaffirmation agreement is not valid until it is approved by the court.[170] In addition, the court must review the reaffirmation agreement, even when signed by an attorney representing the debtor or secured by real property, if a presumption of undue hardship arises because the debtor's budget does not have sufficient funds available to make the reaffirmation agreement payments.[171] The court may only approve the agreement if it (1) does not impose undue hardship on the debtor or the debtor's dependents and (2) is in the best interest of the debtor.[172]

Once the discharge order has been entered, a no-asset chapter 7 case is complete, except for a notice of discharge sent out by the court to the debtor and all creditors.[173] Unless new property comes into the estate within 180 days of the filing of the original petition,[174] there is nothing further to be done by the court and the case is closed.[175] Once a case is closed, further action may still be possible in the bankruptcy court, including actions to provide relief for the debtor, but reopening the case will usually be a prerequisite.[176]

---

162 Fed. R. Bankr. P. 1007(b)(7), (c). *See* Official Form 23 (reprinted in Appx. D, *infra*).
   If the statement is not filed, the case may be closed without entry of a discharge.
163 "Domestic support obligation" is defined in 11 U.S.C. § 101 and generally includes claims in the nature of alimony, maintenance, or support.
164 11 U.S.C. §§ 523, 727(b). See Chapter 15, *infra*, for discussion of debts which are not discharged. Certain types of debts, listed in 11 U.S.C. § 523(a)(2), (4), and (6) are discharged unless a creditor files an adversary proceeding during the bankruptcy case to have them found nondischargeable.
165 *See* §§ 15.4.3.12, 15.4.3.13, 15.4.3.15, *infra*.
166 *See* § 15.4.3.16, *infra*.
167 *See* § 15.5.3, *infra*. *See also* Estate of Lellock v. Prudential Ins. Co. of Am., 811 F.2d 186 (3d Cir. 1987); Chandler Bank of Lyons v. Ray, 804 F.2d 577 (10th Cir. 1986).
168 *See* § 15.5.2, *infra*.
169 See § 15.5.2, *infra*, for detailed discussion of reaffirmation agreements.
170 11 U.S.C. § 524(d).
   Under the 1994 amendments, the affidavit must also state that the attorney fully advised the debtor of the legal effect and consequences of the reaffirmation and of a default on the reaffirmation agreement.
171 11 U.S.C. § 524(m).
   However, court review is not required if the debt is owed to a credit union.
172 11 U.S.C. § 524(d).
173 If there are assets being administered, the discharge is usually entered before distribution occurs and the case remains open until administration of the assets is completed by the court's approval of the trustee's final report.
174 11 U.S.C. § 541(a) provides that certain property acquired after filing becomes part of the estate. See § 2.5, *supra*.
175 Closing of the case is an administrative act which occurs separately from the entry of discharge. Courts vary widely in how quickly this occurs. Occasionally, the debtor will want the case closed more quickly than the normal course (for example, to commence a new case in a jurisdiction which does not allow a debtor to maintain two open cases simultaneously). An informal request to the clerk may be sufficient or, if necessary, a motion can be filed. In asset cases, the discharge does not await the completion of administration of the estate. Filing of claims and distribution to creditors may continue after discharge, and the case is closed only after the trustee has filed a final report on this process.
176 11 U.S.C. § 350(b); Fed. R. Bankr. P. 5010. For a sample motion to reopen case, see Form 159, Appx. G.13, *infra*.

Chapter 4   Chapter 13 Bankruptcy: The Basic Steps

4.1 General Explanation of Chapter 13 Bankruptcy

Chapter 13 bankruptcy gives the debtor the opportunity to adjust his or her financial affairs without having to liquidate current assets. Rather than being designed to pay debts out of those assets, a chapter 13 case usually involves payment of debts out of future income (although the debtor may also choose to make some payment out of current assets). The debtor is allowed to keep and use all property, whether exempt or not, and to pay some or all debts according to a plan approved by the court. At the completion of this plan (or, in some cases, earlier) the debtor receives a discharge which, with several significant exceptions, is similar to the discharge received in a chapter 7 case.

This Chapter describes the sequence of events in a typical chapter 13 case. Many of these events are quite similar to those in a chapter 7 bankruptcy. Chapters 5 through 8, *infra*, will then provide a detailed guide to the steps the debtor's counsel must take in preparing and handling the case.

4.2 Commencement of the Case

4.2.1 Who May File?

4.2.1.1 General Rules

Chapter 13 is available to "individual[s] with regular income"[1] who reside, are domiciled, or have a place of business or property in the United States. An infant or incompetent person may be a debtor in a chapter 13 case.[2] As in chapter 7 bankruptcies, to be eligible the individual must also, with certain rare exceptions, have received a credit counseling briefing from an approved nonprofit budget and counseling agency within the 180 days before filing the bankruptcy petition.[3] This counseling requirement is discussed in detail in § 3.2.1.4, *supra*.

4.2.1.2 Individuals with Regular Income

To qualify as an "individual with regular income," one must be "any individual whose income is sufficiently stable and regular to enable such individual to make payments under a plan under chapter 13."[4] This definition was clearly intended to encompass not only wage earners, but also recipients of government benefits, alimony or support payments, or any other regular type of income.[5] The question of how regular the income must be is left to case law but, as types of income such as commissions are meant to be included, it is clear that the debtor need not receive payments at particular or rigid intervals.

It is clear that the spouse of an individual with regular income may file a joint case with that individual.[6] Probably, a spouse or other living partner of a person with regular income, who has no independent source of income, may also file a petition without the other spouse or partner. As the definition is directed toward whether the debtor will have funds available for a plan, if such a debtor can show a regular allowance from the living partner for expenses, she should be eligible to file chapter 13.[7] Regular payments from friends or other family members, who do not live with the debtor, should also qualify as regular income, although problems related to documentation may arise. A letter or affidavit from the friend or family member would satisfy most trustees, but when disputes arise, testimony and documentary evidence in the form of canceled checks may be required.

---

1   11 U.S.C. § 109(a), (e).
2   Fed. R. Bankr. P. 1004.1 provides that a legally appointed representative may file a petition on behalf of an infant or incompetent person. If no such representative exists, such a person may file a petition by "next friend." The bankruptcy court may appoint a guardian *ad litem* for a debtor who is not otherwise represented. Prior case law had generally been consistent with these rules. See *In re* Kjellsen, 53 F.3d 944 (8th Cir. 1995) (guardian has authority to file); *In re* Murray, 199 B.R. 165 (Bankr. M.D. Tenn. 1996) (parent could file chapter 13 petition on behalf of seven-year-old debtor as "next friend" of debtor); *In re* Smith, 115 B.R. 84 (Bankr. E.D. Va. 1990) (guardian may file on behalf of incapacitated debtor, although wife by virtue of power of attorney may not); *In re* Jones, 97 B.R. 901 (Bankr. S.D. Ohio 1989) (guardian for incompetent debtor may file chapter 13).

In *In re* Zawisza, 73 B.R. 929 (Bankr. E.D. Pa. 1987), an attorney, as "next friend," filed on behalf of an incompetent, who had no validly appointed guardian or representative. *See also* § 3.2.1.1, *supra*. However, a trust is not "an individual with regular income." *In re* W.F.C. Real Estate Trust #1, 236 B.R. 90 (Bankr. S.D. Fla. 1999). See § 3.2.1.1, *supra*, for discussion of whether a trustee may file a case.
3   11 U.S.C. § 109(h).
4   11 U.S.C. § 101(30).
5   H.R. Rep. No. 95-595, at 119 (1977).
6   11 U.S.C. § 109(e). *See also* 11 U.S.C. § 302.
7   *In re* Rowe, 110 B.R. 712 (Bankr. E.D. Pa. 1990) ($200 monthly contribution from son is sufficient as regular income for purpose of eligibility for chapter 13).

See § 12.2.2, *infra*, for further discussion of the regular income requirement.

4.2.1.3 Debt Limitations

Besides the requirement of regular income, a second limitation on eligibility to file a chapter 13 case, not present in chapter 7, is the amount of debt. Although the debt limits do not pose problems for most consumer debtors, chapter 13 is not available to debtors (or debtor couples) with over $360,475 of non-contingent, liquidated, unsecured debts or over $1,081,400 of non-contingent, liquidated, secured debts.[8] As in chapter 7, though, the debtor need not be insolvent. The chapter 13 debt limitations are discussed in detail in Chapter 12, *infra*.

4.2.1.4 Effect of Prior Bankruptcy Cases

Also, as in chapter 7 bankruptcies, an individual whose prior bankruptcy was dismissed within the previous 180 days may not be eligible for chapter 13 relief. Code section 109(g) bars a debtor from filing a new case if the prior case was (1) dismissed for willful failure of the debtor to abide by orders of the court or to appear before the court in proper prosecution of the case or (2) voluntarily dismissed following a request for relief from the automatic stay of section 362 of the Code.[9]

A major advantage of chapter 13 as compared to chapter 7 is the difference in the bars to discharge between the two chapters.[10] A chapter 13 discharge may be obtained by some debtors who have received a chapter 7 discharge within the eight years before filing, or who would not be granted a discharge due to some other provision in chapter 7.[11] A chapter 13 discharge may be obtained by a debtor unless the debtor received a chapter 7 discharge in a case filed within four years before filing the new petition, or received a chapter 13 discharge in a case filed within two years before filing the new petition.[12]

4.2.1.5 Availability of a Discharge

The only impediments to discharge in a chapter 13 case are normally the requirements for a plan, the requirement that the debtor certify that domestic support obligation payments are current,[13] the requirement of completion of a credit education course, discussed in Chapter 8, *infra*, and the possibility that the discharge could, in some cases, be revoked on the grounds that it was fraudulently obtained.[14] It is important to recognize that it is possible, and at times advisable, for a debtor to file a chapter 13 case even if a discharge cannot be granted.[15] For example, a debtor may file a chapter 13 case to cure a mortgage default or other default. Circumstances in which a bankruptcy filing can be useful even if a discharge cannot be granted are discussed in Chapter 12, *infra*.

4.2.2 The Initial Forms

A chapter 13 bankruptcy case is commenced by the filing of a three-page petition which in form is identical to a chapter 7 petition but which is completed somewhat differently.[16] The petition must be accompanied by $281 in fees whether the petition is individual or joint (including a $235 filing fee and a $46 noticing fee imposed by the federal Judicial Conference),[17] or an application to pay the fees in installments.[18] If an application to pay in installments is filed, the debtor need not pay the fees at the time of filing; the fees may be paid over a period up to 120 days, which the court can extend to 180 days for cause.[19]

---

8   11 U.S.C. § 109(e).
    The debt limits are subject to the inflation adjustments provided under 11 U.S.C. § 104 and are discussed further in § 12.2.3, *infra*. The amount of secured debt may be measured by the value of the security rather than the amount of the claim. Compare *In re* Day, 747 F.2d 405 (7th Cir. 1984) *with In re* Morton, 43 B.R. 215 (Bankr. E.D.N.Y. 1984). *In re* Belknap, 174 B.R. 182 (Bankr. W.D.N.Y. 1994), holds that a debt is a secured debt for the purpose of calculating the debt limits even if it is secured by property that is not property of the debtor, though there are strong arguments to the contrary. The debt limitations of section 109 are not jurisdictional. They do not, for example, preclude conversion of a case to a chapter under which the debtor qualifies. Rudd v. Laughlin, 866 F.2d 1040 (8th Cir. 1989); *In re* Wenberg, 94 B.R. 631 (B.A.P. 9th Cir. 1988), *aff'd*, 902 F.2d 768 (9th Cir. 1990).

9   11 U.S.C. § 109(g).
    See § 3.2.1, *supra*, and § 9.7.3.1.5, *infra*, for further discussion of this provision and of the automatic stay.

10 11 U.S.C. § 727(a).
    However, section 727(a)(11) and (a)(12) have counterparts in section 1328(g) and (h). See § 15.2.2, *infra*, for discussion of objections to discharge.

11 See § 12.10, *infra*, for discussion of chapter 13 cases after prior bankruptcies.

12 11 U.S.C. § 1328(f). *See In re* Ybarra, 359 B.R. 702 (Bankr. S.D. Ill. 2007) (time period depends on chapter under which discharge ultimately granted); § 12.10, *infra*.

13 11 U.S.C. § 1328(a).
    This certification need not be made when the debtor seeks a hardship discharge under section 1328(b).

14 11 U.S.C. § 1330. *See In re* Hicks, 79 B.R. 45 (Bankr. N.D. Ala. 1987) (discussing requirements for revoking confirmation); *In re* Scott, 77 B.R. 636 (Bankr. N.D. Ohio 1987) (debtor fraudulently concealed identity).
    See § 15.3, *infra* for further discussion of revocation of discharge.

15 *See In re* Bateman, 515 F.3d 272 (4th Cir. 2008) (inability to receive a discharge did not make a debtor ineligible for chapter 13 relief). *See also* § 12.10.1, *infra*.

16 Fed. R. Bankr. P. 1002(a). *See* Official Form 1 (reprinted in Appx. D, *infra*).
    The venue rules for chapter 13 are the same as for chapter 7. *See* § 3.2.3, *supra*.

17 The initial fee for chapter 13 is now somewhat lower than for chapter 7, because there is no $15 trustee surcharge at the outset of the case. In the long term, though, the total fees for chapter 13 are likely to be higher, because trustee's fees will be collected on payments made under the plan.

18 Fed. R. Bankr. P. 1006; Official Form 3 (reprinted in Appx. D, *infra*).
    The noticing fee may also be paid in installments. Fed. R. Bankr. P. 1006. A form for an application to waive the noticing fee can be found at Form 17 in Appendix G.3, *infra*. See modified application to pay fees in installments. Official Form 3 (reprinted in Appx. D, *infra*). See also § 3.2.2, *supra*, and § 14.6, *infra*, for further discussion of filing fee issues, including waiver of filing fees and recent fee increases.

19 Fed. R. Bankr. P. 1006(b)(2) states that the fee is ordinarily payable within 120 days of filing, but that this period may be extended to 180 days from filing for cause shown.

However, no waiver of the $235 filing fee is permitted.[20] The debtor must also submit a list of creditors, codebtors, and parties to executory contracts (sometimes called the "mailing matrix")[21] and a statement of compliance with the prebankruptcy credit counseling briefing requirement, included with the petition as Exhibit D.

In addition to the petition, the debtor must file a statement of Social Security number,[22] schedules,[23] a statement of financial affairs,[24] a statement of current monthly income and calculation of commitment period and disposable income,[25] a certificate from the credit counseling agency that provided the debtor's prebankruptcy briefing,[26] and any payment advices or other evidence of payment from employers received by the debtor in the sixty days before the date of the petition.[27] A disclosure of attorney fees[28] and chapter 13 plan are also required.[29] If the debtor has an interest in an education savings account, a "record" of that interest must also be filed.[30] Except for the list of creditors and statement of Social Security number, if these documents are not filed with the petition they may be filed within fourteen days afterward.[31] The schedules and statement of financial affairs for a chapter 13 filing are identical to those required in chapter 7. There are only three significant differences in the filings required under the two chapters. First, chapter 13 debtors need not file a statement of intention with regard to property securing consumer debts.[32] Second, a different version of the current monthly income form, Form 22C rather than Form 22A, is used. Third, a chapter 13 plan is required.[33]

The debtor is given great leeway in formulating the plan, subject to only a few requirements. The most important of the provisions usually required, which are discussed in greater detail elsewhere[34] in this treatise, are listed below:

- All claims given priority by 11 U.S.C. § 507[35] must be paid in full, with very limited exceptions;[36]
- The present value[37] of payments on unsecured claims must be at least equal to what would be paid in a chapter 7 liquidation;[38]
- With respect to each allowed secured claim provided for by the plan, either (1) the holder of the claim must accept the plan, (2) the plan must provide for payments with a present value[39] in the amount of the claim and continuance of the lien until full payment of the claim or discharge, or (3) the debtor must surrender the property securing the claim to the creditor;[40] and
- If a party in interest objects to the plan, the plan must either commit all of the debtor's disposable income for the applicable commitment period (three or five years) or pay unsecured claims in full.[41]

Lastly, local rules or practice may require certain other papers to be filed, either with the petition or shortly thereafter. All documents in a case may (and in some districts must) be filed or submitted electronically, as discussed in a later chapter.[42]

4.2.3 Conversion from a Chapter 7 Case

Another way of obtaining chapter 13 relief is through conversion from a chapter 7 case. Any debtor who has begun a chapter 7 case may convert it to a chapter 13 case at any time during the case provided the debtor is eligible for relief under chapter 13.[43]

The Supreme Court has held that the right of a debtor to convert from chapter 7 to chapter 13 is not absolute, and can be denied for bad faith.[44] The Court held that in the rare situation when a case would be subject to immediate dismissal or conversion back to chapter 7 under section 1307(a) for bad faith, a bankruptcy court may deny a conversion to chapter 13.

---

20 28 U.S.C. § 1930(a).
21 Fed. R. Bankr. P. 1007(a)(1).
22 Fed. R. Bankr. P. 1007(f).
   Technically, this statement is not filed, but rather "submitted" to the clerk, because it is not included in the documents that are docketed and kept in the public court file for the case.
23 Fed. R. Bankr. P. 1007(b)(1); Official Form 6 (reprinted in Appx. D, *infra*).
24 Fed. R. Bankr. P. 1007(b)(1); Official Form 7 (reprinted in Appx. D, *infra*).
25 Fed. R. Bankr. P. 1007(b)(6); Official Form 22C (reprinted in Appx. D, *infra*).
26 11 U.S.C. § 521(b)(1); Fed. R. Bankr. P. 1007(a)(1); Fed. R. Bankr. P. 1007(b)(2); Official Form 1, Exh. D (reprinted in Appx. D, *infra*).
   The counseling requirement, and certain limited exceptions to the requirement, are discussed in § 3.2.1.4, *supra*. If the counseling agency developed a debt repayment plan, that plan must also be filed. 11 U.S.C. § 521(b)(2).
27 11 U.S.C. § 521(a)1)(B)(iv); Fed. R. Bankr. P. 1007(b).
   This requirement, like others in 11 U.S.C. § 521(a)(1)(B), can be waived if the court orders otherwise. In some districts courts have adopted local rules requiring the copies of payment advices to be provided to the trustee at or before the meeting of creditors, rather than filed. Some districts require a debtor to file a certificate that no such documents exist if that is the case.
28 Fed. R. Bankr. P. 2016(b).
29 Fed. R. Bankr. P. 3015.
30 11 U.S.C. § 521(c); Fed. R. Bankr. P. 1007(b)(1)(F).
31 Fed. R. Bankr. P. 1007(c), 2016(b), 3015(b).
32 See §§ 7.3.11, 11.4.1, *infra*; Official Form 8 (reprinted in Appx. D, *infra*).
33 See generally Chapters 7 and 12, *infra*, for a detailed discussion of the chapter 13 plan.

34 *See generally* §§ 11.6–11.8, 12.3–12.9, *infra*.
35 These types of debts are listed in § 3.5, *supra*.
36 11 U.S.C. § 1322(a)(2), (4). See § 12.3.6.1, *infra*.
37 The concept of present value arises from the language "value as of the effective date of the plan" in 11 U.S.C. § 1325(a)(4). Basically, it envisions a total of payments which equals the amount creditors would receive in a liquidation case plus interest over the term of the plan. See discussion in § 12.3.2, *infra*.
38 11 U.S.C. § 1325(a)(4). See § 12.3.2, *infra*.
39 *See* 11 U.S.C. § 1325(a)(4); § 12.3.2, *infra*.
   For these purposes, the total of payments to the creditor would be the allowed secured claim plus interest.
40 11 U.S.C. § 1325(a)(5). See § 11.6, *infra*.
41 11 U.S.C. § 1325(b). See § 12.3.4, *infra*.
42 *See* § 7.1.4, *infra*.
43 11 U.S.C. § 706(a).
44 Marrama v. Citizens Bank of Mass., 549 U.S. 365, 127 S. Ct. 1105, 166 L. Ed. 2d 956 (2007).

A court determination that debts are nondischargeable in chapter 7 does not preclude conversion and, in fact, conversion may be the best strategy in such a situation, given the somewhat broader discharge available in chapter 13.[45] Similarly, any person who has commenced a chapter 13 case may elect to convert it to a chapter 7 case.[46] A debtor may convert a case from chapter 7 to chapter 13 as of right only if the case was commenced as a chapter 7 case; if the case had previously been converted to chapter 7, a second (or third) conversion may occur only with the court's permission.[47] Case conversions are discussed in detail in § 13.7, *infra*.

4.3 First Steps After Filing

As in a chapter 7 case, the filing of a petition operates as an order for relief and sets the bankruptcy process in motion.[48] A trustee, usually the standing trustee for the district,[49] is appointed and, if the debtor has applied for it, an order is entered for payment of the filing fee in installments.

The filing of a petition immediately puts into effect the automatic stay,[50] which with limited exceptions prevents creditors from taking any further actions against the debtor or the debtor's property with respect to claims arising prior to commencement of the case. The filing of a chapter 13 case also effectuates a stay of most actions against non-filing codebtors who are obligated to pay claims against the debtor.[51] Creditors must obtain the permission of the bankruptcy court before proceeding with any of the acts prohibited by either stay.[52] With respect to the stay of actions against codebtors, this permission may be granted to the extent that:

- The codebtor was the principal debtor who received the consideration on the claim; or
- The debtor's plan proposes not to pay the claim; or
- The creditor would be irreparably harmed by the stay.[53]

The statute requires that, as of the commencement of the case, any entity holding property that the trustee[54] may use, sell, or lease, or that the debtor may exempt, must deliver that property to the trustee.[55] Because the debtor in a chapter 13 case generally has a right to possess[56] all property of the estate, the trustee must then deliver the property to the debtor.

The debtor must begin making plan payments within thirty days after filing of the petition unless the court orders otherwise.[57] This requirement makes possible quicker payment to creditors and also gives the court some evidence of the debtor's ability to pay, a consideration in confirmation of the plan.[58] At the debtor's request, the court will issue a wage deduction order to cover the plan payments.[59] These payments are retained by the trustee pending confirmation of the plan and, if a plan is not confirmed, they are returned to the debtor after deduction of administrative costs.[60] The failure to commence payments as required may be grounds for dismissal of the case.[61]

The debtor must also begin making "adequate protection" payments to creditors whose debts are secured by purchase money security interests in personal property and to personal property lessors. The statute requires these payments to commence within thirty days after filing of the petition, but such payments need only be made to holders of allowed claims, so no payments need be made to secured creditors until a proof of claim is filed.[62] The payments must be made directly to the creditor or lessor with evidence of payments provided to the trustee unless the court orders otherwise. In some districts courts have ordered that the payments be made through the trustee, in order to ease the accounting issues that direct payments cause for the trustees; in those districts a portion of the preconfirmation payments to the trustee will be paid before confirmation to creditors entitled to adequate protection payments.

---

45 *Compare* 11 U.S.C. § 727 *with* 11 U.S.C. § 1328. See § 13.7, *infra*.
One court has held that a case may be converted for this reason even after the debtor's chapter 7 discharge is granted. *In re* Caldwell, 67 B.R. 296 (Bankr. E.D. Tenn. 1986). See *also In re* Starling, 359 B.R. 901 (Bankr. N.D. Ill. 2007) (case could be converted after discharge if court granted debtors relief from discharge order prior to conversion). After discharge, however, it may be less problematic to simply refile under chapter 13, because such filing is not barred by any provision of the Code. *See* § 12.10, *infra*.

46 11 U.S.C. § 1307(a).

47 11 U.S.C. § 706(a), (b). See *In re* Masterson, 141 B.R. 84 (Bankr. E.D. Pa. 1992); *In re* Walker, 77 B.R. 803 (Bankr. D. Nev. 1987) (section 706(a) constitutes an absolute ban on reconversion); *In re* Hollar, 70 B.R. 337 (Bankr. E.D. Tenn. 1987).

48 11 U.S.C. § 301.

49 *See* § 2.6, *supra*.

50 11 U.S.C. § 362. *See generally* Ch. 9, *infra*.

51 11 U.S.C. § 1301.
The codebtor stay applies only to individuals liable on "consumer debts" and does not apply if the cosigner became liable in the ordinary course of her business. *See* Ch. 9, *infra*.

52 11 U.S.C. §§ 362(d), 1301(c).
However, if neither the debtor nor codebtor makes a written objection to a request for relief from the codebtor stay that is sought because the plan does not propose full payment of the claim, the stay is automatically modified as requested. 11 U.S.C. § 1301(d). See Chapter 9, *infra*, for further discussion of this procedure.

53 11 U.S.C. § 1301(c).

54 In a chapter 13 case, the debtor exercises most of the trustee's powers to use, sell, or lease property. 11 U.S.C. §§ 1303, 1304.

55 11 U.S.C. §§ 542, 543. See § 9.9, *infra*.

56 11 U.S.C. § 1306(b).

57 11 U.S.C. § 1326(a)(1).
Payments may not be made to the debtor's attorney rather than the trustee unless the court so orders. *See In re* Barbee, 82 B.R. 470 (Bankr. N.D. Ill. 1988).

58 11 U.S.C. § 1325(a)(6).

59 See Forms 20 and 21, Appendix G.3, *infra*, for a sample request for a wage order. Some courts have local rules and forms governing requests for wage orders. See § 12.6.1, *infra*, for further discussion of payment orders.

60 11 U.S.C. § 1326(a)(2). See *In re* Brown, 118 B.R. 1008 (Bankr. E.D. Mo. 1990). *But see In re* Beam, 229 B.R. 454 (D. Or. 1998) (Internal Revenue Service could levy on debtor's funds in hands of trustee and receive funds that would otherwise be returned to debtor upon dismissal), *aff'd*, 192 F.3d 941 (9th Cir. 1999).

61 11 U.S.C. § 1307(c)(4).

62 11 U.S.C. §§ 502(a), 1326(a)(1)(C).
The requirement of adequate protection payments is discussed further in § 8.3.12.2, *infra*.

A chapter 13 debtor must also file with taxing authorities any tax returns that were required to be filed for tax years ending in the four years before the date of the filing of the petition and that were not previously filed. If such returns are not filed, the meeting of creditors may be held open for a period of time and, ultimately, the case may be dismissed.[63]

Within a relatively short time after the petition is filed, the clerk issues the notice of the section 341(a) meeting of creditors.[64] This form also provides notice to creditors of the automatic stay and of the deadlines for filing their claims, objections to exemptions, or complaints to determine the dischargeability of a particular debt with the court.[65] Usually it also gives notice of the date set for the confirmation hearing and the deadline for objections to confirmation.[66]

4.4 The Meeting of Creditors and Other Preconfirmation Activities

The meeting of creditors, required in each case by section 341(a) of the Code, is normally scheduled between twenty-one and fifty days after the date the bankruptcy petition is filed.[67] If the meeting is to be held at a place not regularly staffed by the United States trustee's office, it may be held as many as sixty days after the order for relief.[68]

The 2005 amendments to the Code and Bankruptcy Rules set forth a number of document production requirements with respect to the meeting of creditors. The debtor must provide to the trustee, at least seven days before the meeting, copies of the debtor's federal income tax return, or a transcript thereof, for the tax year ending immediately before the petition date and for which such a return was filed, or provide a written statement that no such documents exist.[69] At the meeting the debtor must also produce a governmental picture identification or other personal identifying information establishing the debtor's identity, evidence of the debtor's Social Security number or a written statement that such documentation does not exist, evidence of current income, copies of statements from depository and investment accounts covering the date of the petition, and, if certain monthly expenses are claimed by the debtor, documentation of those expenses as required by the means test provisions.[70] With respect to the evidence of current income, bank statements, or monthly expense documentation, the debtor may alternatively file a statement that the documentation does not exist or is not in the debtor's possession.[71]

The primary purpose of the section 341(a) meeting (the meeting of creditors), as in a chapter 7 case, is to provide the trustee and the creditors the opportunity to examine the debtor and determine whether there are any grounds for objecting to the plan. The trustee inquires generally into the information presented in the statement and plan, including the debtor's ability to make the proposed payments. Despite the popular name for the proceedings, creditors rarely appear in most judicial districts, and the bankruptcy judge is not permitted to be present.[72]

The meeting is likely to last between five and thirty minutes, generally following the pattern of routine questions asked in a chapter 7 case.[73] In some districts, the proceeding serves as an opportunity for the debtor to negotiate with creditors or the trustee in order to obviate any objections to the plan.

During or after the meeting, the trustee must decide whether to object to any of the claims filed. The debtor may also object to the amount, validity, secured status, or any other aspect of a claim.[74] Ultimately all disputes on these matters must be resolved by the bankruptcy judge, who sometimes considers them in conjunction with the confirmation hearing.

The debtor may wish to file claims on behalf of certain creditors who have not filed claims themselves, in order to protect the purposes of the plan.[75] For example, a debtor who wants a secured or nondischargeable claim to be paid through the plan should file a claim on behalf of that creditor if the creditor does not file its own claim. This filing must be done within thirty days after the expiration of the time for the creditor to file a claim, usually ninety days after the meeting of creditors, but longer in the case of governmental units.[76]

In many jurisdictions, absent such a filing, the debtor's plan payments will be distributed to other creditors who do file claims. Such a result can frustrate the purpose of the bankruptcy entirely. It thus is crucial to check the claims docket at

---

63 11 U.S.C. §§ 1307(e), 1308, 1325(a)(9).
    See § 8.3.14, *infra*, for further discussion of the tax return filing requirement.
64 Fed. R. Bankr. P. 2002(a), 2003.
    Like all notices, this notice is sent by e-mail, rather than mailed, to attorneys who are enrolled in the court's electronic filing system.
65 Official Form 9I (reprinted in Appx. D, *infra*).
    The deadline for filing complaints requesting determination of certain dischargeability issues is sixty days after the first date set for the meeting of creditors. Fed. R. Bankr. P. 4007(c). *See also* 11 U.S.C. § 1328(a); Ch. 15, *infra*.
66 Fed. R. Bankr. P. 2002(b).
67 Fed. R. Bankr. P. 2003(a).
68 *Id.*
69 11 U.S.C. § 521(e)(2)(A); Fed. R. Bankr. P. 4002(b)(3). *See* Ch. 8, *infra*.
70 11 U.S.C. §§ 521(h), 707(b)(2); Fed. R. Bankr. P. 4002(b)(1),(2). *See* Ch. 8, *infra*.
71 Fed. R. Bankr. P. 4002(b)(1),(2). For a sample statement, see Form 60, Appx. G.7, *infra*.
72 11 U.S.C. § 341(c).
73 *See* § 3.4, *supra*.
    A sample list of questions asked in creditors meetings is found in Form 64, Appendix G.7, *infra*.
74 Under 11 U.S.C. § 502(a), a "party in interest" may object to a claim. The advisory committee note to Fed. R. Bankr. P. 3007 recognizes both that parties other than the trustee may object and that a counterclaim may be joined with such an objection. The procedure for filing and objecting to claims is discussed in Chapters 8 and 14, *infra*.
75 11 U.S.C. § 501(c); Fed. R. Bankr. P. 3004.
    See §§ 8.4.1–8.4.6, 14.4.3, *infra*, for discussion of claims filed by the debtor.
76 Fed. R. Bankr. P. 3004, 3002(c); Fed. R. Bankr. P. 3002(c).

regular intervals to make sure that the necessary claims are submitted and, when required, to submit them within the deadline on a creditor's behalf.

Various other proceedings may take place as well, such as motions to avoid liens on exempt property of the debtor,[77] or creditors' motions for relief from the automatic stay.[78]

4.5 The Confirmation Hearing

The confirmation hearing may occur on the same day as the meeting of creditors or sometime within the next forty-five days, depending upon local practice.[79] In either case, the court must give at least twenty-eight days' notice of the date of the hearing.[80] The purpose of the hearing is to provide a basis for ruling on whether the plan will be confirmed, to inquire into whether the requirements of chapter 13 are met,[81] and to hear any objections to confirmation and any evidence or argument that is necessary. Objections to confirmation must be timely filed and served on the debtor, trustee, and any other entity ordered by the court, as well as transmitted to the United States trustee.[82] Local rules often set specific deadlines for such objections.[83] The hearing may also encompass other matters related to confirmation, such as objections to claims or disputes about valuation of property.

Under local practice in some jurisdictions, the debtor and/or her counsel may not be required to attend the confirmation hearing if the standing trustee is recommending confirmation. Although the court often rules on confirmation at the hearing, there is no requirement that it do so. In some cases the hearing may have to be continued to a later date to resolve various types of issues. If confirmation is denied, the debtor is normally allowed an opportunity to amend the plan to meet the court's objections.[84]

The effect of confirmation is to bind the debtor and all creditors of the debtor to the terms of the plan.[85] The trustee then begins payments to creditors under the plan. Confirmation also revests title to all property of the estate in the debtor, free and clear of any creditor's claim, except as otherwise provided in the plan or order confirming the plan.[86] If the plan is completed successfully, there are rarely any possible impediments to the debtor's discharge.[87] However, in very limited circumstances, the court may revoke an order of confirmation, if a party in interest can show that the confirmation order was procured by fraud.[88]

4.6 Modification of the Plan and Postpetition Transactions

For various reasons, the debtor may wish to modify the plan that was originally submitted. Such modifications can usually be accomplished with little difficulty. Before confirmation, the plan may be modified as a matter of course, as long as the modified plan meets the requirements of chapter 13. If a claim holder has filed an acceptance of the plan (a consideration only relevant in the case of some secured or priority claims),[89] the acceptance is deemed to apply to the modified plan unless the

---

77 See § 10.4.2, *infra*, for discussion of lien avoidance motions.
78 See § 9.7, *infra*, for discussion of motions for relief from the stay.
79 11 U.S.C. § 1324 provides that the meeting may not be held before twenty days after the meeting of creditors unless the court so orders and no party objects.
80 Fed. R. Bankr. P. 2002(b).
     The procedure for the confirmation hearing and objections to confirmation is governed by Fed. R. Bankr. P. 3015.
81 Issues concerning these requirements are discussed in Chapter 12, *infra*. See generally *In re* Dues, 98 B.R. 434 (Bankr. N.D. Ind. 1989).
82 Fed. R. Bankr. P. 3015(f).
83 *See In re* Dorn, 315 B.R. 68 (E.D. Ark. 2004) (no abuse of discretion in dismissing objection not timely filed under local rule); *In re* Carbone, 254 B.R. 1 (Bankr. D. Mass. 2000) (objection not timely because it was not received by clerk within time period allowed by local rule); *In re* Duncan, 245 B.R. 538 (Bankr. E.D. Tenn. 2000) (objection not timely filed under local rule even though filed before confirmation).
84 11 U.S.C. § 1323.
85 11 U.S.C. § 1327(a). *See* United Student Aid Funds, Inc. v. Espinosa, 130 S. Ct. 1367 (2010); *In re* Bonnano, 78 B.R. 52 (Bankr.

E.D. Pa. 1987) (discussing the effects of confirmation). See *also* § 12.11, *infra*.
86 11 U.S.C. § 1327(c). See also § 12.8.5, *infra*.
87 11 U.S.C. § 1328(a).
     However, if the debtor is subject to an order to pay a domestic support obligation, the debtor must certify that all required payments on the obligation have been made. Also, if the debtor has claimed a homestead exemption under section 522(b)(3)(A) in excess of the amount set out in section 522(q)(1), the debtor must file a statement concerning whether any civil and criminal proceedings described in section 522(q)(1) are pending. See Fed. R. Bankr. P. 1007(b)(8); § 10.2.3.4.5.6, *infra*. A form statement is provided at Form 135 in Appx. G.12, *infra*.
     The objections to discharge available in chapter 7 cases under 11 U.S.C. § 727(a) are not available in chapter 13 proceedings. 11 U.S.C. § 103(b). *See also In re* Kelly, 358 B.R. 443 (Bankr. M.D. Fla. 2006) (trustee could not evade requirements for revocation of confirmation by moving to reopen case so that he could file a motion to convert case to chapter 7); *In re* Daniels, 163 B.R. 893 (Bankr. S.D. Ga. 1994) (creditor could not have chapter 13 case reopened and discharge revoked based upon creditor's mistake in filing proof of claim). *But see In re* Escobedo, 28 F.3d 34 (7th Cir. 1994) (confirmation of plan that did not pay priority claims in full was "nugatory" and case could be dismissed even though there was no appeal of confirmation order and debtor had completed plan payments).
88 11 U.S.C. § 1330(a). *See In re* Valenti, 310 B.R. 138 (B.A.P. 9th Cir. 2004) (180-day deadline for complaint to revoke confirmation enforced).
     Even if the order of confirmation is revoked, the debtor should generally have an opportunity to propose a modified plan. 11 U.S.C. § 1330(b). *But see In re* Scott, 77 B.R. 636 (Bankr. N.D. Ohio 1987).
     Simply failing to list a creditor is not, without more, grounds for revoking an order of confirmation. *See In re* Hicks, 79 B.R. 45 (Bankr. N.D. Ala. 1987) (failure to inform court of new obligations incurred during case is not fraud sufficient to revoke confirmation).
89 Holders of general unsecured claims have no right to accept or reject the plan, but acceptance by the holder of a priority or secured claim may be necessary under 11 U.S.C. § 1322(a)(2) or § 1325(a)(5) if the provisions of those sections are not otherwise met.

holder's rights are modified and the holder withdraws its acceptance.[90]

After confirmation, the procedure is slightly different. The plan may be modified by the debtor unless, after notice and a hearing, the modification is disapproved.[91] A creditor may not object to a modification if its rights would not be altered by the modified plan.[92] Given the Code's definition of "notice and a hearing,"[93] it is unlikely that disapproval could occur without a hearing, provided the debtor or some other party requests one. In most cases, an uncontested modification is approved without a hearing. Any objection to a postconfirmation modification is resolved by the court after a hearing. Although there is no requirement that a debtor establish good cause for modification,[94] the plan as modified must, of course, meet the requirements of the Code.[95]

One of the most common reasons for modification is to cure postpetition mortgage defaults.[96] Another reason, expressly permitted by the Code, is to purchase reasonably necessary health insurance for the debtor and the debtor's dependents which the debtor, perhaps, could not previously afford.[97] The debtor may also wish to provide for postpetition transactions that arise from an unforeseen emergency or change in the debtor's circumstances. Postpetition claims may generally be provided for in the initial plan, but will be disallowed if the claimant knew or should have known that the trustee's prior approval of the debtor's incurring the obligation was practicable and was not obtained.[98] Postpetition obligations may also be incurred with the trustee's permission and paid outside the plan.[99]

Because a postpetition claim may only be filed by the holder of the claim and not by the debtor,[100] and because a postpetition claim may be paid through the plan only if the plan provides for it, which is the debtor's choice,[101] the inclusion of postpetition claims in a chapter 13 plan occurs only when both the debtor and the creditor agree to that procedure. If a postpetition claim is filed and provided for by the plan, unless the claim is of a type that is not dischargeable, it is discharged along with other debts when the debtor completes the plan or receives a hardship discharge whether or not it has been paid in full.[102] Otherwise, a postpetition claim survives the chapter 13 discharge at the end of the case.

The holder of an unsecured claim or the trustee may also move for modification of the plan.[103] The principal reason for such a motion would be a change in the debtor's income or expenses that would enable the debtor to make larger payments for the remainder of the plan.[104] Normally, a modification of the plan at a creditor's request should not be granted without a hearing unless the debtor consents. As the Bankruptcy Rules are not fully clear on the procedure for postconfirmation modification, local practice may vary. Debtors should be sure to oppose any plan modification to which they do not fully consent.

4.7 Options in the Event of Failure to Complete the Plan

4.7.1 Overview

In some cases, usually due to loss of income, the debtor is unable to complete the plan as proposed. In such situations four options are available—a hardship discharge, a plan modification, conversion to chapter 7, or dismissal—each of which has somewhat different consequences.

4.7.2 Hardship Discharge

The Code provides for a hardship discharge if the debtor's problems are caused by circumstances for which the debtor is not justly accountable.[105] Such circumstances need not be catastrophic; they need only be circumstances that make it impossible for the debtor to complete the plan.[106] Such circumstances may include the debtor's death or a serious deterioration in the debtor's financial circumstances.[107] However a chapter

---

90 11 U.S.C. § 1323(c).
91 11 U.S.C. § 1329.
   The procedure for modification of a plan after confirmation is governed by Fed. R. Bankr. P. 3015(g). See § 8.7.4, *infra*, for further discussion of plan modification.
92 *In re* Eason, 178 B.R. 908 (Bankr. M.D. Ga. 1994) (doctrine of res judicata bars the litigation of issues already decided by confirmation of plan).
93 11 U.S.C. § 102(1).
94 *In re* Davis, 34 B.R. 319 (Bankr. E.D. Va. 1983). *See* 8 Collier on Bankruptcy ¶ 1329.02 (16th ed.).
95 *See In re* Farquhar, 112 B.R. 34 (Bankr. D. Colo. 1989) (modified plan which discriminates among unsecured creditors may not be approved).
96 *In re* Mendoza, 111 F.3d 1264 (5th Cir. 1997); *In re* Hoggle, 12 F.3d 1008 (11th Cir. 1994) (debtor could modify plan to cure postconfirmation default); *In re* McCollum, 76 B.R. 797 (Bankr. D. Or. 1987). *See* § 11.6.2, *infra*.
97 11 U.S.C. § 1329(a)(4).
98 11 U.S.C. § 1305.
99 Payments outside the plan are not made through the trustee. *See* Ch. 12, *infra*. See *also In re* Edwards, 190 B.R. 91 (Bankr. M.D. Tenn. 1995) (overruling creditor's objection to debtor incurring postpetition debt because debtor would still be able to complete payments under confirmed plan, to which creditor had not objected).
100 11 U.S.C. § 1305(a). *See* § 8.7.2, *infra* (discussion of postpetition claims).

101 11 U.S.C. § 1322(b)(6).
102 *See* 8 Collier on Bankruptcy ¶ 1305.03 (16th ed.).
103 11 U.S.C. § 1329(a).
104 See § 12.3.4, *infra*, for discussion of motions to increase plan payments.
105 11 U.S.C. § 1328(b). *See also* § 8.7.5.3, *infra*.
106 *In re* Bandilli, 231 B.R. 836 (B.A.P. 1st Cir. 1999) (circumstances need not be catastrophic, but temporary relapse of medical condition which did not affect income was insufficient); *In re* Edwards, 207 B.R. 728 (Bankr. N.D. Fla. 1997).
107 *In re* Graham, 63 B.R. 95 (Bankr. E.D. Pa. 1986); *In re* Bond, 36 B.R. 49 (Bankr. E.D.N.C. 1984). *See also* Fed. R. Bankr. P. 1016. *But see In re* Roberts, 279 F.3d 91 (1st Cir. 2002) (no abuse of discretion in denying hardship discharge to debtor who made no attempt to modify the plan or to sever her case from her husband's, actions that in all likelihood would have been allowed by the

13 case can sometimes continue after the debtor's death, when that is practicable.[108] A hardship discharge may be granted at any time after confirmation, provided that unsecured creditors have received as much as they would have received in a chapter 7 liquidation.[109] Unlike the full compliance discharge, the hardship discharge does not require the debtor to certify that all domestic support obligation payments have been made. Thus there need not have been the full payment of priority claims normally required in a chapter 13 case.

The hardship discharge also permits a debtor to maintain the benefits of having paid an allowed secured claim through the plan. This is a significant advantage as compared to dismissal or conversion, because to be assured of confirmation a plan must provide that the holder of an allowed secured claim will retain its lien until the earlier of payment of the full underlying debt or discharge. Thus, absent a discharge, the lien would continue to secure the remainder of the debt as calculated under nonbankruptcy law.[110] Therefore the plan may provide that the lien is eliminated when the debtor receives a discharge, and such language would apply in cases of a hardship discharge. Presumably, if a creditor has retained its lien under the plan and the case is dismissed or converted, the creditor will continue to have a lien in the full amount remaining due under nonbankruptcy law.[111] As to other claims the debtor receives a discharge equivalent to that granted in a chapter 7 case, and not the somewhat broader chapter 13 discharge that the debtor would have received upon completion of the plan.[112]

A hardship discharge may be granted only if modification of the plan is not practicable.[113] Thus, the Code seems to prefer modification whenever possible. In some cases the debtor, too, may have good reason to prefer that remedy.

4.7.3 Modification

It is often possible to modify the plan, under the provisions discussed above, to accommodate new problems as they arise.[114] The payments under the plan may be reduced, or even terminated, if the plan, as modified, still complies with the requirements of chapter 13.

The advantages of modification are that the broader "full compliance" discharge of chapter 13 is preserved, and the hardship discharge tests need not be met. Normally, however, the priority claims and allowed secured claims provided for in the plan must still be paid, and if they cannot be paid modification may be impracticable. Modification is discussed in more detail elsewhere in this treatise.[115]

4.7.4 Conversion to Chapter 7

The debtor has an absolute right to convert a case to chapter 7,[116] without any showing of hardship, and in many respects such a conversion provides the same relief as the hardship discharge. A new set of schedules generally need not be filed; however, a statement of intention must be submitted within thirty days after the order of conversion is entered or before the first date set for the meeting of creditors, whichever is earlier.[117] A chapter 7 means test calculation form may also be required after conversion.[118]

The debtor must also file a supplemental schedule of debts arising since the chapter 13 case was initially filed.[119] These will be treated as if they arose prior to the commencement of the case.[120] Thus, when applicable, the automatic stay prevents creditor action on these debts, and they may be discharged.[121] After the conversion, the debtor's nonexempt property, if any, is liquidated, and the debtor receives a chapter 7 discharge. Case conversions are discussed in more detail elsewhere in this treatise.[122]

4.7.5 Dismissal

Occasionally, dismissal may be preferable to any of the other options. The debtor may at any time obtain dismissal as of right unless the case was previously converted from another chapter.[123] This route may be particularly attractive if it appears that

---

bankruptcy court and might have permitted her to obtain a discharge).
108 *In re* Perkins, 381 B.R. 530 (Bankr. S.D. Ill. 2007).
109 11 U.S.C. § 1328(b).
  Again, the present value as of the effective date of the plan is the relevant figure. *See* 11 U.S.C. § 1325(a)(4); § 12.3.2, *infra*.
110 11 U.S.C. § 1325(a)(5)(B)(i)(I).
111 11 U.S.C. § 1325(a)(5)(B)(i)(I). *See also* 11 U.S.C. § 348(f)(1)(C).
112 The exceptions to discharge found at 11 U.S.C. § 523(a) are applicable to a hardship discharge. 11 U.S.C. § 1328(c)(2). See Chapters 6 and 15, *infra*, for a discussion of the differences between chapter 7 and chapter 13 discharges.
113 11 U.S.C. § 1328(b)(3).
114 *See* § 4.6, *supra*.
115 *See* §§ 8.7.4, 8.7.5.2, 12.3.4.5, *infra*.
116 11 U.S.C. § 1307(a); Nady v. Defrantz (*In re* Defrantz), 454 B.R. 108 (B.A.P. 9th Cir. 2011) (no bad faith exception to right to convert). *See also* §§ 8.7.5.4, 13.7.2, *infra*. *But see In re* Spiser, 232 B.R. 669 (Bankr. N.D. Tex. 1999) (case could not be converted after both debtors had died).
  The Bankruptcy Rules provide that the debtor need only file a notice of conversion, and that no court order is necessary to effect the conversion. Fed. R. Bankr. P. 1017(d).
117 Fed. R. Bankr. P. 1019(1). *See* Official Form 8 (reprinted in Appx. D, *infra*).
  Additional (postpetition) debts to existing creditors, such as utilities, should be listed to ensure that they are discharged.
118 Official Form 22A (reprinted in Appx. D, *infra*). *See In re* Kellett, 379 B.R. 332 (Bankr. D. Or. 2007) (new Official Form 22 required, may be waived upon motion); *In re* Fox, 370 B.R. 639 (Bankr. D.N.J. 2007) (new Official Form 22 not required after conversion); *In re* Edwards, 367 B.R. 921 (Bankr. S.D. Ga. 2007) (new Official Form 22 not required for below-median income debtors because information would be unchanged from original Form 22C). *See also* § 13.4.1, *infra*.
119 Fed. R. Bankr. P. 1019(5).
120 11 U.S.C. § 348(d); *In re* Fickling, 361 F.3d 172 (2d Cir. 2004); *In re* Deiter, 33 B.R. 547 (Bankr. W.D. Wis. 1983).
121 It is not uncommon, for example, for postpetition utility arrearages to be discharged following conversion from chapter 13 to chapter 7.
122 *See* § 13.7, *infra*.
123 11 U.S.C. § 1307(b).

the case may be converted to chapter 7 against the debtor's will and if the debtor has nonexempt property that she does not wish to see liquidated. It is doubtful whether the right to a dismissal continues after the case has been converted.[124] Voluntary dismissals and those ordered against the debtor's will are discussed in more detail elsewhere in this treatise.[125]

4.8 Discharge

The final step in a successfully completed chapter 13 case, or in one ended under the hardship provisions,[126] is the discharge. A discharge must be granted by the court "as soon as practicable" after completion of all payments under a confirmed plan.[127] However, there are several other prerequisites that must be met to obtain the chapter 13 discharge. If the debtor is required to pay a domestic support obligation, the debtor must certify that all amounts due on the obligation, including prepetition arrears only to the extent provided for by the plan, have been paid.[128] The debtor, with very limited exceptions, also must certify completion of an instructional course in personal financial management.[129] And, if the debtor has claimed a homestead exemption in excess of $146,450,[130] the debtor must file a certification regarding the pendency of any proceeding in which the debtor could be found guilty of a felony described in section 522(q)(1)(A) or liable for a debt described in section 522(q)(1)(B).[131] Lastly, if a mortgage has been cured under the plan, the debtor or trustee should obtain the creditor's agreement or a court determination that the mortgage is fully cured.[132]

There is no possibility of any further objection to discharge at this point. Thereafter, the discharge is revocable only if it was obtained by fraud, and then only if the fraud first came to an objector's attention after the discharge and is raised within a year of the discharge.[133]

A few courts have limited the right to dismiss a case in situations where the debtor has acted in bad faith. See § 13.2, *infra*, for further discussion of the right to dismiss a chapter 13 case.

124 The relevant section, 11 U.S.C. § 1307(b), permits dismissal of "a case under this chapter." It is likely that after conversion the case would no longer be under chapter 13 and the right to dismiss would be lost.

125 See §§ 13.2, 13.3, *infra*.

126 11 U.S.C. § 1328(b).

127 11 U.S.C. § 1328(a).

128 11 U.S.C. § 1328(a).

129 11 U.S.C. § 1328(g); Fed. R. Bankr. P. 1007(b)(7); Official Form 23 (reprinted in Appx. D, *infra*). Bankruptcy Rule 1007(c) provides that the debtor must file the statement certifying completion of the course no later than the date of the last payment made as required by the debtor's plan or the filing of a motion for a hardship discharge under section 1328(b).

130 For cases commenced between April 1, 2007, and April 1, 2010, the amount is $136,875. For cases commenced before April 1, 2007, the amount is $125,000.

131 Fed. R. Bankr. P. 1007(b)(8). See 11 U.S.C. § 1328(h).

The dollar amount listed in section 522(q) is adjusted for inflation every three years.

132 Fed. R. Bankr. P. 3002.1(f). See § 11.6.2.8.2, *infra*.

133 11 U.S.C. § 1328(e).

The discharge hearing provisions of section 524 apply to chapter 13 cases as well as to chapter 7.[134] Thus, the debtor must seek court approval for any reaffirmation agreement on a consumer debt which is neither secured by real property nor negotiated by an attorney who certifies that it is fully informed, voluntary, and does not pose any hardship for the debtor or the debtor's dependents.[135] The debtor must also receive the "Miranda warnings" about the consequences of reaffirmation at a discharge hearing in every case in which there is a reaffirmation agreement, if the reaffirmation was not negotiated by the debtor's attorney who advised the debtor of those consequences.[136] In addition, unless the creditor is a credit union, the court must review the reaffirmation agreement, even when signed by an attorney representing the debtor, if a presumption of undue hardship arises because the debtor's budget does not have sufficient funds to make the reaffirmation agreement payments.[137]

The discharge received in a chapter 13 case is often broader than that received in a chapter 7 case. It includes all debts "provided for"[138] by the plan, except:

- Long-term debts with final payments due after the completion of the plan that are cured in the plan;
- Tax debts described in section 507(a)(8)(C), or section 523(a)(1)(B) or (C);
- Debts incurred through false pretenses or fraud, as described in section 523(a)(2), if the court has found such debts nondischargeable in a timely proceeding brought by the creditor;
- Debts not listed in the bankruptcy, as described in section 523(a)(3), if the creditor had no actual notice of the case and was prejudiced by the lack of notice;
- Debts for fraud as a fiduciary, as described in section 523(a)(4), if the court has found such debts nondischargeable in a timely proceeding brought by the creditor;
- Domestic support obligations;
- Most unpaid student loan debts;
- Certain drunk driving debts;
- Certain criminal fines and restitution debts ordered in connection with a criminal sentence; and
- Debts for restitution or damages awarded in a civil action as a result of willful or malicious injury by the debtor that caused personal injury or death.[139]

Thus, the chapter 13 discharge may eliminate liability on certain debts not dischargeable in a chapter 7 case, including

---

See § 15.3, *infra*, for further discussion of revocation of discharge.

134 11 U.S.C. § 103(a). See § 3.6, *supra*.

135 11 U.S.C. § 524(c).

See Chapter 15, *infra*, for further discussion of reaffirmation agreements.

136 11 U.S.C. § 524(d).

137 11 U.S.C. § 524(m).

138 11 U.S.C. § 1328(a).

See Chapter 15, *infra*, for further discussion of the chapter 13 discharge.

139 11 U.S.C. § 1328(a).

willful and malicious injuries to property, marital property settlements, and certain fines or penalties. However, as in chapter 7, to the extent that a secured creditor's lien has not been disallowed, avoided, or satisfied, that creditor most likely will retain the right to bring an *in rem* action to enforce its lien.[140]

Promptly after the discharge, a notice of discharge is mailed to all creditors and the trustee.[141] The debtor and the debtor's attorney also receive a copy of this notice. Notice of the discharge order normally marks the last activity in the case, although the case may be formally closed later. However, even after the case is closed, the debtor has a broad right to have a case reopened if additional relief is necessary.[142]

---

[140] *See* § 15.5.3, *infra*. *See also* Estate of Lellock v. Prudential Ins. Co. of Am., 811 F.2d 186 (3d Cir. 1987); Chandler Bank of Lyons v. Ray, 804 F.2d 577 (10th Cir. 1986).

[141] Fed. R. Bankr. P. 4004(g).

[142] 11 U.S.C. § 350(b); Fed. R. Bankr. P. 5010. For a sample motion to reopen case, see Form 159, Appx. G.13, *infra*.

Chapter 5 — Getting All the Necessary Facts

5.1 Introduction to the Treatise's Second Part

5.1.1 Purpose of These Four Chapters

Chapters 5 through 8 of this treatise, unlike the first four chapters, are intended primarily to be a practice guide for practitioners handling consumer bankruptcy cases. To put the practices outlined into a meaningful context, the reader should have a general grasp of the basic concepts of bankruptcy set out in Chapters 1 through 4, *supra*.

These next four chapters describe all of the necessary steps involved in representing consumer debtors in bankruptcy cases. They can serve as a "cookbook" for bankruptcy novices and also a useful self-checkup for those who have already handled many bankruptcy cases. As most of the steps involved in chapter 7 and chapter 13 cases are identical or at least similar, both types of cases are considered together.

5.1.2 Roles for Non-Attorneys

As will quickly become apparent, most of the tasks involved in handling a bankruptcy case can be ably accomplished by non-attorney legal workers with a relatively small amount of training. This situation presents a significant advantage to busy offices. Of course, an attorney involved in a case prepared by non-attorneys must supervise and take ultimate responsibility for handling the case. The attorney should review the case prior to filing and at various points thereafter, with particular attention to ascertaining that non-routine circumstances are handled properly.

5.1.3 Use of the Materials in the Treatise

To facilitate thorough and competent preparation of bankruptcy cases, this treatise also contains a number of other materials in Volume 2. Appendix D.2, *infra*, contains sample completed bankruptcy schedules and statements illustrating how to prepare an initial filing. Blank versions of other official forms are also included. All the forms in Appendix D, *infra*, as well as blank versions of the forms to institute a case, can also be printed from the companion website to this treatise and used in actual cases. However, it will usually be more efficient to use either a specialized bankruptcy document preparation program or the Adobe Acrobat (PDF) fillable forms available for download on the website of the Administrative Office of the U.S. Courts.[1]

Appendices E through G, *infra*, contain annotated forms, pleadings, and checklists which should prove useful in most cases. All of these documents may also be found on this treatise's companion website. Appendix K, *infra*, contains form brochures for clients that answer common bankruptcy questions. These materials can and should be altered as necessary to meet the needs of particular clients and offices.

Each office or program must decide for itself the exact division of labor between attorney, legal worker, and client that best serves its purposes. While one office may choose to have a paralegal bankruptcy specialist handling most aspects of the case, another may decide that it is appropriate to have many of the details attended to by a secretary or outsourced to a private service provider or a group with whom the office works. Still others may wish to require clients to do much of the leg work of obtaining necessary information, relying on a detailed questionnaire to guide them. Finally, some will prefer the more traditional method of having most steps taken by an attorney.

5.2 The Importance of Getting All the Facts

Before a bankruptcy case can be filed, it is necessary that a decision be made that bankruptcy is, in fact, the best vehicle for dealing with the problems facing a particular client. Indeed, most of the legal analysis that occurs in a typical consumer bankruptcy case involves comparing bankruptcy with other possible avenues of relief.

An absolutely necessary prerequisite to such consideration, just as in most other legal analysis of real world problems, is knowledge of all the relevant facts. Although it may sometimes be possible to rule out bankruptcy based upon knowledge of only a few facts (for example, that the client does not wish to lose certain property that cannot be saved in bankruptcy), it is never possible to recommend bankruptcy safely without a thorough knowledge of the facts. Without such knowledge, unknown property (such as the right to a tax refund) may be lost in bankruptcy, major debts may turn out to be nondischargeable or unaffected because of security interests, the debtor may be ineligible to receive a discharge or the benefit of the automatic

---

1 The Official Bankruptcy Forms are available at www.uscourts.gov/FormsAndFees/Forms/BankruptcyForms.aspx. Not all of the forms are available in a fillable PDF format.

stay because of a prior case, or undervalued property might be determined to be nonexempt and lost.

Of equal importance is the fact that, without complete information, an attorney may not be able to utilize fully the bankruptcy for the debtor's maximum benefit. Substantial hardship may be caused, for example, if a creditor is not notified of the automatic stay before the debtor's car is repossessed because no one checked to see if the debtor was behind in payments to that secured creditor. The debtor's right to avoid or modify a lien may be lost because the existence of the lien is not discovered in the fact-gathering stage of the case. Moreover, debts not listed in the bankruptcy papers might survive a discharge;[2] even if they are discovered during the pendency of the case and can be included, they may lead to additional fees for the debtor and more work for the debtor's attorney.[3]

Finally, much of the information which should be sought early is necessary in any case for proper completion of the bankruptcy forms. It makes sense, then, to obtain this information before, rather than after, there is a commitment to pursue a bankruptcy instead of other possible strategies.

5.3 Methods of Gathering Information

5.3.1 The Initial Interview

The steps necessary to assure complete information will vary somewhat from case to case. For example, if no real estate is involved, a title search might not be necessary; if a client has clearly kept organized and complete records counsel may often rely upon them with little risk.

Normally, the first step is an interview with the client. In addition to the establishment of a relationship, this interview will usually serve to quickly identify most cases in which bankruptcy is not appropriate. Regardless of whether the possibility of a bankruptcy is first broached by a client who believes it is necessary or an attorney whose initial reaction to the case leads in that direction, a few questions will usually reveal the most likely impediments to a successful bankruptcy.

These initial questions should be asked early to get an overview of the client's problems:

- What types of debt are causing the most trouble?
- How were the debts incurred and are they secured?
- What significant assets does the client have?
- How much income does the debtor have available which is not committed to unavoidable expenses?
- How imminent is creditor action which may limit the client's options?

---

2   11 U.S.C. § 523(a)(3).
    See § 15.4.3.3, *infra*, for discussion of dischargeability of unscheduled debts.

3   The fee currently set by the Administrative Office of the United States Courts for an amendment adding a creditor is $30. It may be waived upon application to the court in cases of indigent debtors. See § 14.6, *infra*, for discussion of filing documents *in forma pauperis*.

The answers to these general questions (which, of course, must be put in terms the client understands) will reveal not only the likelihood of relief in a bankruptcy but also many other dimensions of the client's problems: their causes, their scope, whether they are likely to continue or recur, and whether other solutions seem obviously preferable. They can lead naturally into a broad discussion of the problems most troubling to the client.

5.3.2 Filling in the Complete Picture

Once bankruptcy is being seriously considered, and has perhaps been tentatively decided upon, much more information is necessary. Only after all of this information is gathered can bankruptcy be finally recommended. Again, the principal source of information is usually the client, but methods of tapping this source may vary.

Many bankruptcy specialists have clients do much of the information assembly on their own, through use of a detailed questionnaire phrased in easily understandable terms. One such questionnaire is suggested in Appendix F, *infra*. Practitioners using questionnaires cite two principal advantages. First, they save time, and encourage the client to gather much information prior to a detailed interview. Second, use of a form questionnaire, even if it is completed by the attorney or by the attorney's staff, minimizes the possibility of any later misunderstanding (or malpractice claim) concerning whether the client was asked a particular question.

Whether or not a questionnaire is used, it is important to conduct a careful interview to assure the completeness and accuracy of the data obtained. Even the simplest written questions may not be understood by some clients, and clients may be confused about the purpose of others. They may fail to list debts they wish to pay, or property they do not consider "really" theirs.

The oral and written questions to clients should always be supplemented and checked by obtaining every shred of documentation the client possesses regarding his or her financial situation. Consumer debtors may not realize that security interests have been taken in their property; they may also be unaware of defenses and counterclaims available to them. In addition, the documents will usually provide precise information on the amounts due and the addresses of creditors.

5.3.3 Frequently Missed Information

5.3.3.1 Introduction

Certain types of information, in particular, are frequently overlooked in the handling of bankruptcy cases, especially by practitioners who rely exclusively on questions in the official forms as their interview guide. Given the broad definitions of property and claims in the Code, the forms by themselves are not adequate as a means of inquiring into nontraditional types of assets and debts.

Some of the most commonly missed items in the cases of consumer debtors are listed below. Regardless of the method used to elicit information from a client, inquiry should always be made into the following matters.

5.3.3.2 Property

Among the types of property clients often forget in reporting their assets are long-dormant accounts with savings institutions, such as banks and credit unions. Especially in the case of the latter, the client may not have access to a share balance (deposit) that was required to secure a loan. Nonetheless, such a balance belongs to the client and may become important to the case. Similarly, pledged goods, such as those in the hands of pawnbrokers, are often not considered by clients to be "their own."[4] In each of these cases, as much property as possible should be withdrawn from the hands of others prior to bankruptcy. Not only can this property be converted to exempt assets, if necessary,[5] but the return of the property will avoid later difficulties caused by reluctance of the holding party to relinquish it after the bankruptcy.[6]

Other types of property that clients may not recognize include entitlement to tax refunds or credits,[7] rights to alimony or support arrearages or marital property settlements,[8] rights to inheritance or life insurance proceeds from someone who has recently died or may soon pass away,[9] security deposits given to landlords or utilities, accrued vacation pay, possible rights to severance pay,[10] future commissions from sales positions, salary or pension rights, legal claims against third parties,[11] leasehold interests which are of value,[12] shares in housing, shopping, agricultural or other cooperatives, the right to collect money owed to the debtor, a joint bank account or other property that is nominally in the client's name but not considered by the client to be his or her property,[13] interests in education savings such as section 529 plans and education IRAs for children or other relatives,[14] and entitlements to government grants such as energy assistance grants.[15] It is crucial to know about all of these interests, both to ensure that they will not be lost and to take full advantage of them. Depending on the circumstances, a bankruptcy petition might be postponed until a tax refund is received or vacation pay or other entitlements are exhausted.[16]

Lastly, insurance interests are often overlooked. Clients may have life insurance with a cash value or credit insurance that can be terminated and "cashed in" at the time of bankruptcy.[17] On the other hand, whether clients have fire or automobile insurance may be an important factor in providing "adequate protection"[18] to creditors who might otherwise be entitled to

---

4 See § 2.5.4, *supra*, for a discussion of pawned personal property that may come into the bankruptcy estate.

5 See Chapter 6, *infra*, for discussion of such "exemption planning." Goods constituting security for a debt should not be transferred, because doing so may risk objections under 11 U.S.C. § 727(a)(2) or 11 U.S.C. § 523(a)(6). *See generally* §§ 15.2.2.2, 15.4.3.6, *infra*.

6 See § 9.4.4, *infra*, for discussion of banks freezing debtors' accounts after a bankruptcy case is filed and § 9.9, *infra*, for discussion of the duty to turn over property of the debtor after filing.

A few banks have adopted policies of freezing all debtor accounts, at least until a trustee relinquishes the estate's rights in the account. Such policies are questionable at best. *Compare In re Mwangi*, 432 B.R. 812 (B.A.P. 9th Cir. 2010), *subsequent appeal*, 473 F. Supp. 2d 802 (D. Nev. 2012), *with In re Calvin*, 329 B.R. 589, 601 (Bankr. S.D. Tex. 2005). The only major bank to engage in this practice is Wells Fargo, which has now extended it to Wachovia, which it acquired. Such freezes can extend to funds in accounts that really belong to others, for which debtor is simply a convenience signer. However, if there is any possibility a depository institution may have such a policy, funds should be withdrawn prior to the filing of the petition.

Similarly it is best to avoid, if possible, filing a case when there are outstanding checks drawn on the debtor's account on the petition date, to avoid arguments that the funds in the account are property of the estate, at least if such funds could not be exempted. *See In re Pyatt*, 486 F.3d 423 (8th Cir. 2007) (rejecting holdings of some other courts that debtor had to turn over such funds after payees on checks had already cashed them); *Shapiro v. Henson (In re Henson)*, 449 B.R. 109 (D. Nev. 2011) (turnover could not be required if debtors no longer possessed funds); *In re Ruiz*, 440 B.R. 197 (Bankr. D. Utah 2010) (debtors had no duty to stop payment on prepetition checks or to turn over funds). *But see* Jubber v. Ruiz *(In re Ruiz)*, 455 B.R. 745 (B.A.P. 10th Cir. 2011) (debtors had duty to turn over funds); *In re Minter-Higgins*, 399 B.R. 34 (N.D. Ind. 2008) (debtor ordered to turn over funds). Alternatively, if exemptions are available, the debtor can exempt amounts equal to the unpaid checks.

7 See § 2.5.5, *supra*.

8 Property acquired as a result of a marital settlement or divorce decree within 180 days *after* a bankruptcy case is filed is considered property of the bankruptcy estate. 11 U.S.C. § 541(a)(5). *See* § 2.5, *supra*.

9 If the debtor acquires such rights within 180 days after a bankruptcy is filed, the rights become property of the bankruptcy estate. 11 U.S.C. § 541(a)(5). *See* § 2.5, *supra*.

10 *In re Ryerson*, 739 F.2d 1423 (9th Cir. 1984).

11 Such legal claims, if not disclosed in the bankruptcy schedules, may later be barred by the doctrine of judicial estoppel. *See* §§ 7.3.7.2.1, 14.3.2.6.3, *infra*.

12 *See In re* Santiago-Monteverde, 466 B.R. 621 (Bankr. S.D.N.Y. 2012) (discussing exemptability of rent stabilized Manhattan lease).

13 *See In re* Carstens, 2011 WL 869748 (Bankr. D. Neb. Mar. 10, 2011) (account in debtor's name was owned by his parents under state law).

14 Most interests in education savings accounts are excluded from the bankruptcy estate by 11 U.S.C. § 541(b)(6) and (7). However, a "record" of the debtor's interest in such accounts must be filed with the court. 11 U.S.C. § 521(c); Fed. R. Bankr. P. 1007(b)(1)(F). *See* § 2.5.3, *supra*.

15 *See In re* Thompson, 253 B.R. 823 (Bankr. N.D. Ohio 2000) (debtor's right to partial refund of monies paid to move into retirement community if she moved out within one-hundred months was property of the estate, but trustee had no right to require debtor to move in order to liquidate property). *But see In re* Ball, 201 B.R. 210 (Bankr. N.D. Ill. 1996) (trustee not entitled to cash payment received postpetition in lieu of debtor's accrued sick and vacation days, because payment was discretionary with employer and debtor had no right to receive the money).

See § 2.5, *supra*, for further discussion of unusual property interests that may come into the bankruptcy estate.

16 More information concerning the appropriate timing of a bankruptcy filing is contained in § 6.5, *infra*. A more complete discussion of tax returns and their impact on timing a bankruptcy may be found in § 2.5.5, *supra*.

17 See § 12.9.3.3, *infra*, for the possibilities of rejecting executory contracts for credit insurance.

18 Creditors are entitled to "adequate protection" of their interests in

possession of their security.[19] Local practice usually determines the extent to which the trustee or court will inquire into such nontraditional assets, but there is no excuse for the debtor's counsel being less than fully informed and prepared for all possible problems that might arise.

5.3.3.3 Liabilities

Naturally, the opportunity for discharge of debts in bankruptcy should be used to its fullest, and every conceivable liability should be searched out and considered in weighing the advantages of a petition. Clients do not always realize that they have certain types of debts, especially if payment has not been demanded. Just as a legal claim may be a form of property, so too may a legal claim give rise to a liability if the client is the potential defendant. The terms of a lease or land installment sales contract may be important, especially if it is possible to modify them in a chapter 13 case,[20] or if an unfair lease or rent-to-own contract is found.[21] Debts of others for whom clients have cosigned are not usually considered by clients as their own liabilities. Similarly, clients are rarely aware of possible deficiencies remaining after property is repossessed in satisfaction of secured debts, or after vacating a rental property, voluntarily or involuntarily, before the expiration of a lease.

In many states a person is automatically liable for necessaries provided by a third party to an individual's dependents, or for welfare payments provided; few clients are aware of such liabilities. Divorce-related debts, such as money owed on a property settlement, division of marital liabilities, or alimony and child support may also be overlooked. Utility bills paid regularly may be omitted by a client because they are not perceived as comparable to a loan or other long-term debt, or because the client is current on a payment agreement to cure a long-term arrearage. A client may not think it necessary to mention that a driver's license was revoked because of an old tort judgment or fines which may be dischargeable.[22] Likewise, if public benefit overpayments are being deducted from current benefits, a client may feel that fact has little to do with bankruptcy and fail to list such overpayments as debts.[23] A debtor who has been involved in running a business may not realize that sales or payroll taxes which the business failed to pay may become the debtor's liability.

Special care must also be taken to inquire into debts likely to be treated differently in bankruptcy. Unpaid taxes must be carefully analyzed to determine their dischargeability and priority status.[24] Are there large liabilities for student loans, support, or alimony?[25] Has there been recent, improvident use of credit cards, in excess of the credit limits imposed by the card agreements or the amounts set out in section 523(a)(2) for triggering a presumption that the debts were incurred through false pretenses?[26] Clients should be advised, at the same time, of the likely loss of their credit cards due to a bankruptcy.[27]

Bankruptcy clients also may not always recognize when a debt is or may be a secured debt. Some clients, for example, co-sign on debts for others and offer their own property as collateral. This practice is particularly common among elderly clients who are looking for a way to help their adult children. Similarly, clients may forget about second or third mortgages which have not been aggressively collected. And most clients rarely understand (and in some cases may never even know) when a judgment lien has been entered. Often, judgment liens secure a debt after a consumer has been sued or after a divorce property settlement.

As the presence of a security interest greatly affects the impact of bankruptcy,[28] looking for these types of liens on real property, if necessary by ordering a title search, is very important. Similarly, cars may be used as collateral for lenders other than those making the loan that allowed the client to purchase the car. And debtors may have made assignments of rights, such as future pension payments or lawsuit recoveries, that have the effect of security interests.[29]

Unfortunately, related issues arise with credit card debts and finance company loans. Several retailers claim to have security interests in property purchased with their credit cards. Similarly, some finance company loans which appear to be unsecured have provisions which purport to take personal property as collateral.[30] As discussed elsewhere in this treatise, many of

---

collateral as a condition of maintaining the automatic stay. *See* Ch. 9, *infra*.

19 In a chapter 13 case, a debtor who is retaining personal property subject to a lease or security interest must provide the lessor or creditor with proof of insurance coverage. *See* 11 U.S.C. § 1326(a)(4); § 12.8.4, *infra*.

20 See Chapter 12, *infra*, for a discussion of tenants' rights in chapter 13 cases and executory contracts.

21 See § 11.8, *infra*, for discussion of rent-to-own contracts and § 12.9, *infra*, for a general discussion of leases in bankruptcy.

22 See § 15.5.5.1, *infra*, for discussion of restoring drivers' licenses through bankruptcy.

23 See § 15.5.5.4, *infra*, for discussion of discharging public benefit overpayments.

24 See § 15.4.3.1, *infra*, for discussion of taxes that are not dischargeable and methods of obtaining a debtor's tax records.

25 These debts are all usually nondischargeable and support and alimony claims are usually priority claims. 11 U.S.C. §§ 507(a)(7), 523(a). *See* §§ 12.3.6.1, 15.4, *infra*.

26 This behavior may cause problems if the creditor claims the debts were incurred under false pretenses and that they are nondischargeable. 11 U.S.C. § 523(a)(2). *See* § 15.4.3.2, *infra*.

27 See § 8.4.3, *infra*, for discussion of the practice of requiring debtors to give up their credit cards.

28 *See* Ch. 11, *infra*.

29 *See, e.g., In re* Terry, 687 F.3d 961 (8th Cir. 2012) (prepetition recovery of retroactive Social Security disability benefits by insurance company based on assignment in long-term disability policy was voidable preference; insurance company permitted to withhold from debtor's future benefits preference amount paid to trustee under recoupment doctrine).

Such assignments may be invalid. *See* Structured Invs. Co., L.L.C. v. Dunlap (*In re* Dunlap), 458 B.R. 301 (Bankr. E.D. Va. 2011) (assignment of military pension rights prohibited).

30 Other creditors, most notably credit unions, may assert that a credit card account is secured by the debtor's automobile or home based on a cross-collateral clause in the card agreement or in other loan

those interests are worthless or cannot be documented by the lender.[31] Nevertheless, it is important to be aware of whether these interests exist in formulating an appropriate bankruptcy strategy.[32]

Finally, many debtors ask that certain debts be omitted from their bankruptcy papers because of embarrassment about notifying particular creditors, or because of a continuing intent to repay. The answer to this request must always be that every existing liability has to be listed (including personal debts to family members and friends). The debtor's signature on the schedules is a certification under penalty of perjury that the information provided is complete and accurate. Upon learning this fact, some debtors may instead choose to pay off a particular debt prior to filing so that there is no liability to be listed, although they should be advised of the ramifications if a creditor receives an avoidable preference.[33]

5.3.3.4 Expenses

Determining debtors' expenses is particularly problematic in many cases, for two reasons. First, most debtors do not keep very good records of their expenses and may have only a vague idea of what they are spending for food, clothing, transportation, and other necessities that do not involve a monthly bill. The expenses they list in many cases seem to be a good deal less than their incomes, yet it is clear that they are not saving money. In such cases it is often effective to ask the debtors where they are depositing the surplus income each month in order to bring home the reality that they are spending more than they have stated.

Second, most debtors are so financially strapped by the time they come in for bankruptcy advice that they are skimping on many necessities and other reasonable expenses, often spending nothing on them. For example, debtors often defer home maintenance when they are short of funds, so their homes may need painting or even repairs to plumbing or electrical systems. Similarly, many debtors do not receive regular dental care or medical checkups, especially if they have no health insurance.

Particularly for debtors with higher incomes, it is important to fully explore not only what the debtor is spending but also the needs that are not being met, so that Schedules I and J of Official Form 6, the debtor's statements of income and expenses, do not show a large surplus of income over expenses. Generally, expenses that total approximately the amount allowed by the chapter 7 means test should be considered a presumptively reasonable standard of living. In particular, Congress has made very clear through the enactment of section 1329(a)(4) that debtors have a right to maintain or obtain health insurance for themselves and their families.

Thus, in reviewing debtors' expenses, it is important to look not only at current expenses but also at unmet needs in order to determine a reasonable budget going forward. In some cases the simple fact is that debtors' incomes are insufficient to meet all reasonable needs, and the budget may show a net monthly deficit. But in others, when debtors have more middle-class income levels, debtors should be sure to list all of their reasonable expenses. Expenses that are often overlooked or underestimated include:

- Health insurance—debtors who do not have adequate insurance should consider obtaining it prior to filing the bankruptcy case;
- Uninsured medical expenses—these often include co-pays and deductibles, nonprescription drugs and vitamins, contact lenses and fluid, and checkups;
- Dental care—many debtors need dental work which they have deferred because they cannot afford it;
- Eye care—regular vision checkups and glasses or contact lenses are not covered by most insurance plans;
- Child care—debtors may have been imposing on family members out of necessity, and can consider whether their children would be better off in day care;
- Home maintenance—an amount should be budgeted for home maintenance, including both unexpected repairs or replacement of old systems and appliances, and tasks such as painting and roof repairs that may occur only once every four or five years, as well as lawn care, snow removal, and other necessary services a debtor cannot perform herself;
- School expenses and children's activities—children have expenses for a variety of school activities, school lunches, and sometimes uniforms, at most schools; other activities, such as music lessons, scouting expenses, or sports fees, should be allowed if reasonable;
- Automobile maintenance—debtors with no immediate repair needs often ignore the fact that maintenance of an older car usually exceeds $1000 per year—even with a newer car, oil changes and other maintenance add up to a significant amount annually;
- Alarm service—in many urban areas, a burglar alarm is considered a reasonable expense;
- Pest control—in some areas pest control is a necessity;
- Personal care—haircuts and the like, especially for a family with children, add up to a considerable amount each month;
- Baby supplies—diapers and clothes for a small child constitute a large monthly expense;
- Summer camp for children—camp would usually be considered a reasonable expense, especially for working parents;
- Cigarettes—for debtors who are addicted to smoking, most courts have allowed this considerable expense as reasonable, especially because the only reasonable alternative may be smoking cessation programs at even greater expense;

---

agreements the debtor has with the creditor. *See* § 15.5.3, *infra*.
31 *See* § 15.5.3, *infra*.
 It is likely to cost the creditor more to repossess and resell the property than the property is worth. These claimed "interests" are thus used more for their threat value, than for their real economic worth.
32 *See* §§ 10.4.2.4, 11.4.1, 11.5, 15.5.2, *infra*.
33 *See* § 10.4.2.6.4, *infra*.

- Charitable donations—the Code clearly allows for debtors to make reasonable religious or charitable donations, which they may have been unable to make before filing the bankruptcy petition due to financial stress;
- Tax return preparation fees—courts will generally allow debtors to pay reasonable amounts for tax return preparation;
- Pet expenses—reasonable expenses for pets, including food and occasional visits to a veterinarian, are rarely questioned, however, debtors should be sure to list the pets as assets on Schedule B;
- Bank charges—ATM fees and other bank charges, such as monthly account fees, are often forgotten;
- Christmas and birthday gifts for family members—few judges would begrudge debtors the ability to give modestly priced presents to their children;
- Work expenses—debtors may have to pay for uniforms or tools, or for parking at work, and there may be reasons debtors must purchase meals at work;
- Annual automobile registration and license expenses—these expenses are sometimes considerable, and are often forgotten because they are paid only once a year;
- Life insurance—if debtors have any dependents and do not have life insurance, the purchase of term insurance would clearly be considered reasonable.

5.3.3.5 Other Aspects of Financial Affairs

Finally, careful inquiry must be made into other areas of the client's affairs that are likely to generate issues if a bankruptcy case is filed. For example:

- Are payroll deductions being made, such as to a credit union, that the client can terminate? Similarly, are there electronic fund transfers and preauthorized payments to creditors that the client can stop? If so, that step usually prevents later complications of trying to recover money deducted after a bankruptcy is filed. It also increases the client's available income.
- Has the client made any prebankruptcy transfer or disposition of property which could cause problems?[34]
- Has the client acquired an interest in homestead property during the 1215-day period preceding any anticipated bankruptcy filing?[35]
- Does the client remember giving a financial statement to any creditor which was not completely true?[36]
- Has there been recent excessive or unusual use of a credit card?[37]
- Are there any criminal prosecutions pending related to bad checks, theft of utility service, conversion of collateral, or other liabilities on debts?[38]
- Is any property that the debtor owns or possesses hazardous or alleged to be hazardous, giving rise to potential liabilities or a diminution in the property's value?[39]

5.3.4 Other Sources of Information

Depending upon the complexity of a client's debt situation, and the completeness of the information obtained from the client, it may be necessary to seek further information elsewhere. One source which should not be overlooked is the creditor to whom a debt is or may be owed. Especially if they think it may be to their benefit, as in a chapter 13 case, creditors are usually quick to respond to inquiries regarding the balance due and the security interests they have. And the same letter which requests this information can also serve notice upon the creditor that it must henceforth communicate only with the attorney and not with the client.[40]

In addition, a credit report, which can be used to check or supplement previous information, should normally be obtained. It can be accessed by the client at no cost or for a small fee.[41] Tax returns, recent pay stubs, and bank statements also will provide information useful in handling the case. A federal tax return or transcript thereof, as well as recent pay stubs, will be needed in any event once the case is filed.[42] Similarly, past appraisals, lien or title searches, or previous years' tax returns may be necessary or helpful. If there are likely to be tax issues, records should be obtained from taxing authorities to ensure that the potential for discharging taxes is maximized by delaying the petition until expiration of an applicable reach back

---

34 These transfers may be preferences or fraudulent transfers avoidable by the trustee or may give rise to an objection to discharge. *See* Ch. 6, *infra*.

35 An interest that has been acquired during this period may give rise to an objection to any exemption claimed on the property. *See* § 10.2.3.4.3, *infra*.

36 If so, that statement may be grounds for a claim that the debt is nondischargeable under 11 U.S.C. § 523(a)(2). *See* § 15.4.3.2, *infra*.

37 This behavior can give rise to claims under 11 U.S.C. § 523(a)(2) (A) for fraud. Particular attention should be paid to the presumption of fraud based on prepetition purchases of luxury items within ninety days of bankruptcy or use of a credit card for cash advances within seventy days of bankruptcy. 11 U.S.C. § 523(a)(2)(C). *See* § 15.4.3.2, *infra*.

38 *See* §§ 9.4.6.2, 15.5.5.5, *infra*.

39 If property owned or possessed by the debtor poses or is alleged to pose a threat of imminent and identifiable harm to public health or safety, that fact must also be disclosed in Exhibit C to the bankruptcy petition.

40 *See* Form 2, Appx. G.2, *infra*.

41 Consumers can obtain one free copy of a credit report per year from each of the national reporting agencies. The three nationwide consumer credit reporting agencies have set up one central website, toll-free telephone number, and mailing address through which free annual reports can be ordered. The client can visit www.annualcreditreport.com, call (877) 322-8228, or complete the Annual Credit Report Request form and mail it to: Annual Credit Report Request Service, P.O. Box 105281, Atlanta, Georgia 30374-5281. Usually, reports can also be obtained over the Internet directly from consumer reporting agencies and it may be wise to obtain one while the debtor client is in the attorney's office if a recent report is not already available. For more information on obtaining reports from reporting agencies see National Consumer Law Center, Fair Credit Reporting § 3.4 (7th ed. 2010 and Supp.).

42 *See* §§ 7.3.10 and 8.3.4, *infra*, for discussion of the requirement that these documents be filed or provided to the trustee.

period if necessary.[43] In a few districts, aggressive trustees have been known to use their section 544 "strong arm" powers to avoid unperfected security interests in property such as automobiles and homes,[44] creating equity in the property which the debtor cannot exempt and thereby creating a risk that the debtor could lose the property. A lien search may also indicate other liens which the debtor does not remember or know about, and which may be avoided or otherwise dealt with in the bankruptcy.[45] If the value of real property is of significant importance, checking local records or Internet listings of real estate sales, a letter from a real estate broker stating her opinion of the property's value, or even a current appraisal may be required to get a full picture of the case. Information about recent sales is available from websites such as www.domania.com, www.zillow.com, www.eppraisal.com, www.bankofamerica.cyberhomes.com, and www.homegain.com. In addition, multiple listings of homes currently on the market can be accessed through www.realtor.com and many realtors' websites that list recent sales in the neighborhoods they cover.

If valuation of an automobile is an issue, the average wholesale and retail values for most models can be obtained from industry guides, such as the Kelley Blue Book and the NADA Used Car Guide. In addition, wholesale values are available on the Internet through the Kelley Blue Book at www.kbb.com, and also at www.autopricing.com or www.carprices.com. Uniform Commercial Code filing information often may be obtained through LexisNexis or other electronic databases.

If there are questions about previous bankruptcy cases filed by the debtor, such as the case number, date filed, date of any prior dismissal, or number of earlier cases, information on prior bankruptcy filings may be obtained from the bankruptcy court. Normally, this information is available electronically, through the PACER system[46] or another automated system. In addition, a national database of bankruptcy filings is available through LexisNexis. Prior bankruptcy filings within the previous ten years should also appear on a client's credit report. Because it is now so easy to electronically check on prior filings, it is a good idea to have some verification of the debtor's prior bankruptcy cases, or lack of them, in every case.

5.4 Impressing upon Clients the Need for Full and Accurate Information

No matter what method is used to inquire into the client's situation, it is crucial that the client understand the importance of providing every detail requested. A lack of trust or other feeling on the part of a client that something should be concealed must be dispelled.

Usually the best way to do this is to paint a vivid picture of the worst consequences which can result from less than full disclosure, while at the same time emphasizing the confidentiality of the attorney-client relationship. It should be made clear that property not listed as exempt may be lost and that debts not reported may not be discharged. It should also be pointed out that there is often a filing fee for amending the papers, that bankruptcy cases may be audited,[47] and (in a non-threatening manner, of course) that by giving incomplete or false information under oath on the bankruptcy forms the debtor risks not only losing the bankruptcy discharge but also criminal prosecution.

More than anything else, though, it should be emphasized that representation in the client's case may suffer if counsel has less than the whole story and that the real loser in that case will be the client. Once they understand this reality (which indeed is the central point of this Chapter) most clients realize the importance of a real effort on their part to help develop the facts of the case.

---

43 See § 15.4.3.1.2, *infra*, for discussion of the dischargeability of taxes and the availability of federal tax records.
44 See § 10.4.2.6.2, *infra*, for discussion of the "strong arm" powers.
45 See Chapters 10 and 11, *infra*, for discussion of ways to deal with secured creditors.
46 Access to the PACER system, administered by the courts, is available at www.pacer.psc.uscourts.gov. A national search of bankruptcy filings can be made on PACER using the "U.S. Party/Case Index" by selecting "All Courts" for the region in the bankruptcy search index. The search may be done using the debtor's full name entered under "Party Name," as well as by using the debtor's Social Security number or tax identification number, or the prior case number, if known. PACER can be also used to identify missing information about a known previous filing such as the case number, date filed, date of discharge or dismissal, among other things. Documents from the previous filing may also be obtained. PACER access to court documents costs ten cents per page. However, the service is effectively free for occasional users because the Judicial Conference policy provides that usage of less than $15 in a quarterly billing cycle is waived. In addition, the Judicial Conference Policy provides that courts may, upon a showing of cause, exempt court-appointed pro bono attorneys and not-for-profit legal services organizations from payment of PACER fees. *See* Judicial Conference Electronic Public Access Fee Schedule, *reprinted at* Appendix C.5, *infra*.
47 See § 8.3.15.1, *infra*.

Chapter 6   Counseling the Consumer Debtor: Does Bankruptcy Provide the Best Solution and, If So, How and When?

6.1 Introduction

6.1.1 Explaining the Options to Clients

Whether, how, and when to file a bankruptcy petition is probably the most important single decision made in a bankruptcy case. Like most questions of legal strategy, it is rarely simple. It involves the interplay of a number of factors. Many of these are unique to each client; others turn on state law, custom, or practice in a community, or the provisions of the Bankruptcy Code. This chapter describes the considerations and alternatives that should be explored in the representation of consumer debtors, as well as steps that could improve the debtor's position before a bankruptcy case is filed.

Naturally, it is important early on to explain to clients the options being considered, and what they would entail. In cases in which bankruptcy is a serious possibility, the general principles and procedures involved should be discussed.[1] Often, it is necessary to dispel some of the common myths that exist about bankruptcy, for example, that debtors will lose all of their property, or that the law prohibits the acquisition of property or credit after bankruptcy.

In many cases, it is also crucial to deal with the perceived stigma of bankruptcy. The moral overtones of not paying one's debts (which, of course, are constantly reinforced by those to whom debts are owed) are frequently forgotten by those who deal with such problems on a daily basis. The idea of bankruptcy, which represents a declaration of sorts that a debtor does not intend to pay, may be difficult for clients to accept at first, especially if they have been continually and sincerely insisting to creditors that they do intend to make good on their obligations.

For these clients, some counseling is especially helpful. They should be reminded that bankruptcy is their right under the law, provided for in the Constitution, intended to provide a fresh start for those in precisely their situation, and that big corporations, like Chrysler, General Motors, Kmart, Texaco, Macy's, United Airlines, and Penn Central, and famous people, such as Jerry Lewis, Mickey Rooney, Tammy Wynette and even former Treasury Secretary John Connally, have not hesitated to utilize this right. It might help to point out that the "stigma" of bankruptcy is largely a creation of creditors who have every reason to make bankruptcy appear unattractive, and that bankruptcies are not generally publicized in newspapers or elsewhere, although they are a matter of public record. Some clients might find comfort in the fact that the Bible itself provides for periodic release from debts: "At the end of every seven years thou shalt make a release. And this is the manner of the release: every creditor shall release that which he has lent unto his neighbor and his brother; because the Lord's release hath been proclaimed."[2]

Lastly, the alternatives to bankruptcy must be explained. What are the likely results of doing nothing? Are there other ways available to defend against the largest and most troublesome debts? What would be the consequences of waiting until later before filing a bankruptcy petition?

6.1.2 Methods of Explaining Bankruptcy

Certainly the most common method of explaining these subjects is through a face-to-face discussion during the client interview. Not surprisingly, many bankruptcy specialists have found that doing this job can be both time-consuming and repetitive. For that reason, some have chosen to give most of this general information in written form and to supplement that information in the interview. A model client information brochure, *Answers to Common Bankruptcy Questions*, is provided in Appendix K, *infra*.[3] Some bankruptcy practice manuals contain similar materials. Clients seeking further information

---

1 The 1984 Bankruptcy Amendments specifically require a debtor's attorney to certify that the debtor has received an explanation of the relief available under the different chapters of the Code. The required certification is now incorporated into the bankruptcy petition form. *See* Official Form 1 (reprinted in Appx. D, *infra*).

    The 2005 amendments added 11 U.S.C. § 527, which mandates various other disclosures (some of which are inaccurate) that must be made by "debt relief agencies," as defined in 11 U.S.C. § 101(12A) (definition may include attorneys). *See* § 16.8.3, *infra*.

2 *Deut.* 15:1–2.

3 Two other brochures, *Your Legal Rights During and After Bankruptcy: Making the Most of Your Bankruptcy Discharge* and *Using Credit Wisely After Bankruptcy*, are also provided in Appendix K, *infra*. In addition, the American Bar Association publishes a booklet entitled "Your Legal Guide to Consumer Credit" which contains a seven-page section on bankruptcy and other alternatives for dealing with debts ($2.00). The federal judiciary's website has a section entitled "Bankruptcy Basics," located at www.uscourts.gov/bankruptcycourts/bankruptcybasics.html.

may also be referred to books about bankruptcy for lay audiences, which are available in most public libraries.[4] They may also be able to access a wealth of information on the Internet at websites like www.uscourts.gov/library/bankbasic.pdf, but they should be cautioned that the Internet can also be a source of misinformation.[5]

The National Consumer Law Center's *NCLC Guide to Surviving Debt*[6] is a good introduction for individual consumers to a variety of strategies for dealing with consumer debt. The *NCLC Guide to Surviving Debt* includes chapters on dealing with debt collectors, setting priorities for debt payments, raising defenses to debt collection lawsuits, preventing evictions, and negotiating mortgage workout agreements among other things. Basic bankruptcy information is also included.

The *NCLC Guide to Surviving Debt* was written by NCLC staff for use by individual consumers and their advocates. The book thus provides a useful supplement to what you can offer in a basic bankruptcy or debt counseling consultation.[7]

6.2 Advantages and Disadvantages of Bankruptcy

6.2.1 Advantages: The Uses of Bankruptcy

6.2.1.1 Discharge of Most Debts

In a sense, most of this treatise is devoted to describing the advantages of bankruptcy for consumer debtors and showing how to make the most of those advantages. Before a client can make an intelligent decision on a course of action, the advantages applicable to that client's case, and the disadvantages, if any, must be explained.

The principal goal of most bankruptcies is to achieve the total discharge of most unsecured debts. Bankruptcy is a relatively quick and easy way to end the creditor harassment (though, of course, there are other ways to curtail this),[8] hardship, anxiety, and marital stress normally associated with debt overload.

6.2.1.2 Protection of Property and Income from Unsecured Creditors

Bankruptcy is often the only sure way to protect a debtor's property from execution by unsecured creditors. Bankruptcy may provide total protection for a home, car, or other vital property. The amount of property debtors are allowed to protect from creditors through use of exemptions in bankruptcy is, in many states, far greater than the amount they can protect in state law execution processes.[9]

Even when state exemptions from execution are similar to or better than the federal bankruptcy exemptions or when the federal exemptions are not available, bankruptcy allows the debtor to avoid having to assert the exemptions repeatedly in response to the execution attempts of different creditors. Once a bankruptcy case is filed, an unsecured creditor holding a dischargeable claim, including a dischargeable tax claim, is ordinarily stayed from ever obtaining a lien on the debtor's property, even a lien that, had it been obtained prior to bankruptcy, could not have been eliminated by the bankruptcy.[10] Normally bankruptcy also serves to prevent any garnishment of wages or other income after the petition is filed. This result, in turn, may protect a client's job if the client's employer does not favor multiple wage garnishments.[11] Even recoupment of Social Security or other public benefit overpayments should be preventable by a timely bankruptcy petition.[12]

---

4 *See, e.g.*, Nathalie Martin & Stuart Paley, J.K. Lasser's The New Bankruptcy Law and You (2005); Stephen Elias et al., How to File for Chapter 7 Bankruptcy (13th ed. 2006).

Because some of these sources may not reflect the most recent changes to the Code, rules and forms, clients should be advised that they may not be entirely accurate. Clients should also be advised that books published prior to late 2005 are outdated in some respects. A useful book for clients who decide to file a bankruptcy case is John Ventura, Fresh Start!: Surviving Money Troubles, Rebuilding Your Credit, Recovering Before or After Bankruptcy (1992). Another resource, available for use by bankruptcy attorneys at no charge from King's Press at www.bankruptcybooks.com is Morgan D. King & Nancy Finley-King, How to Rebuild Your Credit (4th ed. 1998).

5 For example, the website www.bankruptcy.com contains creditor propaganda urging people not to file bankruptcy cases.

6 (2006 ed.).

7 The *NCLC Guide to Surviving Debt* can be ordered for $19 per copy (with discounts for bulk orders) by calling NCLC at (617) 542-9595.

8 Harassment by collection agencies and by certain attorneys acting as debt collectors is regulated by the Fair Debt Collection Practices Act (FDCPA), 15 U.S.C. §§ 1692–1692*o*. Actions of creditors may violate state tort law on the grounds of intentional infliction of emotional distress or invasion of privacy, as well as state statutes dealing with unfair and deceptive practices. *See* National Consumer Law Center, Fair Debt Collection § 4.2.8 (7th ed. 2011 and Supp.). In some cases a "stop contact" or "cease communication" letter from the client to the debt collector may provide relief from upsetting and harassing debt collection efforts. The FDCPA requires collection agencies and attorneys to stop dunning consumers after receiving a written request asking the collector to cease collection contacts or stating that the debt is not owed. 15 U.S.C. § 1692c(c). Creditors collecting their own debts are not covered by the FDCPA, but they often comply with such requests. Both creditors and debt collectors may be subject to state debt collection laws which often contain a similar provision. A sample letter is provided in NCLC's *Bankruptcy Basics* and the *NCLC Guide to Surviving Debt*.

9 The federal and state exemption laws are discussed in Chapter 10, *infra*.

10 This issue is complicated in some cases when tax lien creditors have a prepetition interest in the debtor's property pursuant to state law that may be perfected postpetition. 11 U.S.C. § 362(b)(3). *See In re Parr Meadows Racing Ass'n, Inc.*, 880 F.2d 1540 (2d Cir. 1989).

11 Garnishments are limited by the Consumer Credit Protection Act, 15 U.S.C. § 1674, as is the employer's right to discharge employees due to garnishment. The laws of many states further restrict the extent to which wages may be garnished.

12 *See* § 15.5.5.4, *infra*, for discussion of the discharge of debts arising out of public benefits programs.

6.2.1.3 Tools for Eliminating or Modifying Secured Debts

Under the Code, bankruptcy gives debtors mechanisms to deal with most secured creditors. Many types of liens may be eliminated, either because they impair exemptions,[13] or because they are in reality undersecured.[14] In a chapter 13 case, payments on most other secured debts can be lowered,[15] and a reasonable time can be gained to cure any defaulted secured debt.[16] Often, one or more of these aspects of bankruptcy will make it possible for a client to retain a home, car, or other property that would otherwise be lost.

6.2.1.4 Automatic Stay

Sometimes, the most valuable feature of a bankruptcy is the automatic stay, usually gained instantaneously upon the filing of a petition. The stay forces an abrupt halt of most creditor actions against the debtor, including repossessions, garnishments or attachments, utility shut-offs, foreclosures, and, in many cases, evictions.[17] Many of these collection actions can thereafter be permanently prevented.[18] The stay is also an effective way (though, again, hardly the only way) to end creditor collection efforts, with contempt, or money damages, and attorney fees as available remedies for violations of the stay.[19] Furthermore, the stay affords the debtor a breathing spell—a chance to sort things out—through the additional time gained to solve problems.

In addition to the automatic stay available in every bankruptcy case, chapter 13 provides a special automatic stay of creditor actions against most people who are codebtors with the debtor.[20] This codebtor stay, which can relieve creditor pressure on friends or relatives of the debtor, may be an important reason to file a chapter 13 case.

6.2.1.5 Other Protections Available Through Bankruptcy

Bankruptcy may offer the only possible way for a client to keep or regain a driver's license subject to revocation because of an unpaid accident judgment.[21] Keeping the license, in turn, may mean employment and income for the client's family. Bankruptcy may, in some cases, literally mean freedom for a debtor who might otherwise be incarcerated for failure to pay support obligations,[22] or as a result of a contempt proceeding involving some other debt.[23] Even for some tax debts that cannot be discharged in chapter 7, a chapter 13 case may save the debtor thousands of dollars in interest and penalties.[24] The Code also protects the debtor from many types of discriminatory action by governmental units and private employers on the basis of unpaid debts discharged in bankruptcy.[25] Nor can a private party take any action intended to coerce payment of such debts.[26]

6.2.1.6 Litigation Advantages of the Bankruptcy Forum

An important factor to consider in opting for bankruptcy is the opportunity to litigate disputes with creditors in a federal court, which has at least initial jurisdiction over such disputes after a case has been filed.[27] In some places the bankruptcy court may provide a far more sympathetic forum than the local state court, and it may be far more familiar with the applicable law. It may also offer procedural advantages, such as greater discovery rights[28] or the ability to serve distant defendants.[29] Other rights, such as statutes of limitations[30] or sovereign immunity,[31] may also be affected to the client's advantage.

---

13 See § 10.4.2, *infra*, for discussion of liens which impair exemptions.
14 See Chapter 11, *infra*, for discussion of liens which can be modified because they are undersecured.
15 See Chapter 11, *infra*, for discussion of the right to modify secured claims in chapter 13 cases.
16 See § 11.6.2, *infra*, for discussion of the right to cure defaults within a reasonable time in chapter 13 cases.
17 See Chapter 9, *infra*, for discussion of the automatic stay.
18 The creditor normally may not have the stay lifted prior to the end of the case, except in certain specified circumstances. 11 U.S.C. § 362(d),(h). *See* Ch. 9, *infra*.
  If the debt is discharged during the case, 11 U.S.C. § 524(a) prevents any act to collect it after the case is over, though some liens may survive bankruptcy.
19 11 U.S.C. § 362(k).
  For discussion of remedies for violation of the stay order, see § 9.6, *infra*.
20 See § 9.4.5, *infra*, for discussion of the codebtor stay, which is also available in chapter 12 cases.
21 Normally, such revocation cannot be continued after discharge of the judgment. Perez v. Campbell, 402 U.S. 637, 91 S. Ct. 1704, 29 L. Ed. 2d 233 (1971). *See* § 15.5.5.1, *infra*.
22 Dischargeability of these obligations is discussed in Chapter 15, *infra*. See also Chapter 12, *infra*, for discussion of use of chapter 13 in support cases.
23 *See, e.g.*, Judice v. Vail, 430 U.S. 327, 97 S. Ct. 1211, 51 L. Ed. 2d 376 (1977).
  The bankruptcy court or district court may exercise its habeas corpus powers to end a debt-related incarceration. *See also* Ch. 14, *infra*.
24 Generally, no postpetition interest need be paid on unsecured tax claims that are paid through a chapter 13 plan if they are dischargeable under 11 U.S.C. § 1328(a). *See* § 12.3.6.1, *infra*.
25 11 U.S.C. § 525. *See* § 15.5.4, *infra*.
26 11 U.S.C. § 524(a). *See* Ch. 15, *infra*.
27 28 U.S.C. § 1334(a), (b), (d). *See* § 14.2, *infra*.
28 Basically, the Federal Rules of Bankruptcy Procedure incorporate the liberal federal discovery rules. *See* Fed. R. Bankr. P. 7026–7037, 9014.
29 The venue provisions of 28 U.S.C. § 1408 essentially provide for nationwide service of process in most proceedings. *See* § 14.3.2.1, *infra*.
30 *See* 11 U.S.C. § 108.
31 *See* 11 U.S.C. § 106. *See also* § 14.3.2.2, *infra*.

In sum, then, bankruptcy may be the best way, if not the only way, to save a home, a job, a car, or thousands of dollars for a client. It may even mean a debtor's freedom, literally as well as figuratively.

6.2.2 Disadvantages: Reasons for Not Filing a Bankruptcy Case

6.2.2.1 Overview

Despite all of the possible advantages that bankruptcy may provide, there are many valid reasons for choosing not to file a petition. Some of these concern problems in the cases of particular clients, and others relate simply to the fact that bankruptcy is not the only means to address a client's legal problems and may not be necessary.

6.2.2.2 Loss of Property in Bankruptcy

One consequence of a chapter 7 bankruptcy may be the loss of nonexempt property (or its value in cash). For most consumer clients this potential loss is not a problem because consumer debtors rarely have any nonexempt property. Except in those few states which not only have low exemptions but also have opted out of the federal exemptions,[32] the amount of property a debtor is allowed to keep is relatively generous; only debtors with equity substantially over $21,625 per debtor in a home, $3450 in a car, or $11,525 in household goods and certain other property are likely to have any problems under the federal exemptions.[33] Many states have more generous exemptions. Even when a debtor has nonexempt property, a chapter 13 bankruptcy often presents a viable alternative through which debtors may retain everything that they own.

6.2.2.3 Effect on Credit and Reputation

It is likely that a bankruptcy will be part of a debtor's credit history for as long as the law allows, which is ten years under the Fair Credit Reporting Act.[34] The effect this notation will have on future credit is less predictable, but it is an understandable concern to many clients.[35]

There is no definite response to this concern. However, clients should be reminded that if they have substantial debts, and especially if they are in default, their credit histories are already poor. In the eyes of some creditors, a bankruptcy that wipes the slate clean will be an improvement. Not only will the potential customer be free of other financial obligations, but she will also be unable to obtain a chapter 7 discharge, in most cases,[36] for another six or eight years. For these reasons, some creditors have been known to actively solicit recent bankruptcy debtors.

In any case, the available research on the subject is inconclusive.[37] It is fair to say is that each credit decision turns on the bias of the individual creditor and that most creditors look more to a potential customer's current income situation, and its stability, than anything else.[38] Most creditors have chosen not to exclude automatically all of the millions of people who have filed a bankruptcy case, especially if a few years have passed since the filing.[39] Indeed, as credit standards loosened in recent years, bankruptcy debtors were regularly offered new credit, even while they are still in bankruptcy, though often on fairly unfavorable terms. And clients should also be reminded that they always have the option of voluntarily paying a favored creditor with whom they wish to maintain a line of credit, either before the bankruptcy (though preferences of over $600 within ninety days should be avoided if possible)[40] or afterward.[41] It is

---

32 See § 10.2.1.1, *infra*, for discussion of states' rights to opt out of the federal exemptions. Summaries of state exemptions are provided in Appendix J, *infra*.

33 See § 10.2, *infra*, for discussion of the interplay of the dollar limits among the federal exemption provisions.

34 15 U.S.C. § 1681c(a)(1). *See also* § 8.9, *infra*.

Although the FCRA permits bankruptcy filings to be reported on a debtor's consumer report for a ten-year period beginning with the petition date, the three major credit reporting agencies have policies which provide that chapter 13 cases are reported for a shorter period, typically the seven-year period used for other credit information.

35 *See* Declaring Bankruptcy Can Improve Your Credit Score, www.smartmoney.com/debt/advice/index.cfm?story=boostscore.

36 *See* 11 U.S.C. § 727(a)(8), (9). *See also* § 15.2.2, *infra*.
However, the earlier availability of a chapter 13 discharge may be understood by some creditors. *See* 11 U.S.C. § 1328(f); § 12.10, *infra*.

37 One study, albeit somewhat dated, is contained in D. Stanley & M. Girth, Bankruptcy: Problem, Process, Reform 62–65 (1971). This study found wide regional variations in ability to obtain credit. However seventy percent of those interviewed had made major purchases on credit since filing bankruptcy, and only about one-third found credit harder to get after bankruptcy. A similar number found no change and eight percent found getting credit easier; twelve percent had not tried to obtain credit.

38 Each creditor uses its own mix of closely guarded criteria including income, assets, job stability, and so forth.

39 Mortgage creditors often rely upon the underwriting guidelines adopted by Fannie Mae. These guidelines require a four-year "waiting period" from the discharge or dismissal in a chapter 7 case before a debtor is eligible for a loan saleable to Fannie Mae. In a chapter 13 case, the waiting period is two years from the discharge date or four years from the dismissal date. The four-year waiting periods may be reduced to two years if extenuating circumstances can be documented. For a debtor with more than one bankruptcy filing within the past seven years, a five-year waiting period is required, measured from the most recent dismissal or discharge date. This may be reduced to three years if extenuating circumstances can be documented. *See Selling Guide: Fannie Mae Single Family*, Section B3-5.3-07, May 15, 2012, available at www.efanniemae.com/sf/guides/ssg/.

40 *See* § 10.4.2.6.4, *infra*, for a discussion of preferences. While there is nothing illegal or immoral about a debtor making a preferential transfer before bankruptcy, the trustee may avoid many such transfers if she chooses. Therefore, if the property to be transferred can be claimed as exempt in the bankruptcy, the debtor may be advised to transfer it after the bankruptcy to eliminate the risk of avoidance of the transfer by the trustee.

41 These debts may or may not be reaffirmed. A debtor may choose to continue payments after bankruptcy without reaffirming the obligation. *See* § 15.5.2, *infra*.

often possible for a client to pay off a low balance on at least one credit card prior to bankruptcy, so that the creditor need not be listed on the schedules. In most such cases, the creditor will then permit continued use of the credit card after bankruptcy.[42]

As discussed earlier, the effect of a bankruptcy on a client's reputation in the community is almost always imperceptible. However, in a small town, especially if debts are owed to local people, the stigma of bankruptcy cannot be entirely discounted. The potential harm can only be evaluated locally, on a case-by-case basis, and weighed against the advantages that bankruptcy has to offer. Again, the possibility of voluntarily paying selected debts should not be overlooked if that would ameliorate the problem.

6.2.2.4 Possible Discrimination After Bankruptcy

6.2.2.4.1 The available protections

Closely related to the problem of reputation is that of discrimination against debtors who have filed bankruptcy cases. To a large extent, the Bankruptcy Code alleviates this problem.

Under the Code, governmental units[43] generally may not discriminate on the basis of a bankruptcy filing.[44] Thus, a housing authority or student loan agency cannot deny benefits to a client based upon the filing of a bankruptcy case or a previously discharged debt.[45] Similarly, utilities may not deny service based upon a bankruptcy or discharged debts.[46] Nor may any private employer discriminate with respect to employment or terminate employment based upon bankruptcy or debts discharged in bankruptcy.[47] Clients can be assured that the law protects them in this regard and that they will be able to enforce their rights in court, if necessary.

However, the distinction between discrimination based upon bankruptcy or debts discharged in bankruptcy and discrimination based upon future financial responsibility or ability should be carefully explained.[48] That is, a client should be told that even creditors who are precluded from discrimination based on bankruptcy may refuse new credit or other services if the refusal is properly based on other considerations.[49] Also, a client seeking new employment should be told that the protection against employment discrimination may not extend to hiring decisions due to the courts' interpretation of ambiguous statutory language in section 525(b).[50] It may be advisable for such a client to delay the bankruptcy filing until after employment in the new job has begun.

The law regarding discrimination by other private entities, such as creditors who provide essential services, is not as clear. It should be pointed out that this type of discrimination is extremely rare, especially in more urban areas where many providers of goods and services are available to a client. It would be most likely to occur in a small town, where only one merchant offers a particular product or service. In that case, at least if it can be shown that later discrimination was an attempt to coerce payment of a debt, the client would also have a remedy.[51]

Again, the situation can best be assessed locally, on a case-by-case basis. Normally discrimination against debtors who have filed bankruptcy cases is not a problem, but if a practitioner is in doubt, the chapter 13 standing trustee or a more experienced bankruptcy attorney may be consulted.

6.2.2.4.2 Medical debts

Medical debts to doctors or hospitals with whom a patient would like to have a continuing relationship are often a source of concern. Particularly in small communities where there may not be many health care providers, clients may worry that a discharge will leave them with few options for future care.

One response is that, if the client cannot pay the debts anyway, the doctor or hospital involved may have little concern about a bankruptcy discharge. Often a frank discussion with a sympathetic doctor about inability to pay will allay any concern about future refusal to provide service.

A second option is for the debtor to agree to make voluntary payments after the bankruptcy.[52] In extreme cases, even reaffirmation of a particular debt may be appropriate.[53] Before taking such drastic action, however, the debtor should be reminded that the ethical obligations of doctors and hospitals should preclude their refusal to provide service to patients who are in extreme need. Moreover, even the most recalcitrant doctor will generally provide care if cash payments or medical

---

42 Indeed, it has been held that, at least in the case of a chapter 13 debtor, a creditor has no right to revoke a non-delinquent credit card based solely on a bankruptcy filing, because under 11 U.S.C. § 541(c)(1)(B) the prepetition property rights of the debtor become property of the bankruptcy estate notwithstanding any contractual provision that gives an option to terminate the contract upon a bankruptcy filing. *In re* Knapp, 137 B.R. 582 (Bankr. D.N.J. 1992).
43 The term "governmental unit" is defined in 11 U.S.C. § 101(27).
44 11 U.S.C. § 525(a). *See* § 15.5.4, *infra*.
45 *In re* Stolz, 315 F.3d 80 (2d Cir. 2002). *See also* 11 U.S.C. § 525(c) (clarifying that discrimination in the granting of student loans is prohibited).
46 11 U.S.C. § 366.
   However, utilities may be able to demand adequate assurance of future payments. *See* § 9.8, *infra*.
47 11 U.S.C. § 525(b). *See* § 15.5.4, *infra*.
48 The legislative history makes clear that it is not prohibited discrimination to take into account such factors as financial responsibility and ability to repay, if this is done with all people and not just those who have filed bankruptcy cases. H.R. Rep. No. 95-595, at 81 (1977). *See* Ch. 15, *infra*.

49 As with any discrimination issue, questions may arise about whether a creditor's articulated reason for refusing credit or services is a pretext for bankruptcy discrimination.
50 *See* Burnett v. Stewart Title, Inc. (*In re* Burnett), 635 F.3d 169 (5th Cir. 2011) (section 525(b) does not extend to hiring); Myers v. TooJay's Mgmt. Corp., 640 F.3d 1278 (11th Cir. 2011) (same); Rea v. Federated Investors, 627 F.3d 937 (3d Cir. 2010) (same).
51 11 U.S.C. § 524(a) prohibits any act to collect a discharged debt. *See* § 15.5, *infra*.
52 11 U.S.C. § 524(f).
   As discussed above, a refusal to provide service which is directed at coercing payments on a discharged debt is an actionable violation of the discharge injunction.
53 11 U.S.C. § 524(c). *See* §§ 8.8.2, 15.5.2, *infra*.

coverage is offered, and many hospitals have a legal obligation under state or federal law to provide free medical care to people who cannot afford to pay.[54]

In summary, there is no completely satisfactory answer to questions about future health care because a doctor has no legally enforceable obligation to provide care to a debtor who has discharged prior medical debts. However, the problem should rarely affect access to needed care.

6.2.2.5 Clients' Feelings of Moral Obligation

Another factor mitigating against bankruptcy may be the client's personal feelings on the subject. This difficult subject, which is generally outside a lawyer's training, must be discussed carefully and with understanding. Remember, it is not easy for clients suddenly to decide to seemingly discard those values which may have guided them since childhood.

Usually, it is best to remind the client of other values which must also be considered. Besides the fact that bankruptcy is a right guaranteed by law and provided for in the Constitution[55] and even the Bible,[56] a client should consider the hardship bankruptcy may avoid for her family. It may be the only way to provide the family with food, clothing, and shelter in hard times. Very often, clients decide that the moral obligation to provide for loved ones outweighs the obligation to pay their creditors.

It may also be possible to explore chapter 13 with clients who wish to pay some or all of their debts. In some cases, a chapter 13 bankruptcy may provide a viable mechanism for repaying creditors as well as solving other problems, if the debtor has sufficient income. Lastly, clients should be reminded that filing a bankruptcy case does not prevent them from voluntarily paying their debts at a later time if they wish.[57] This realization, too, provides comfort to those who cannot come to terms with the idea of turning their backs on their creditors forever.

6.2.2.6 Cost of Filing a Bankruptcy Petition

Besides any attorney fees, bankruptcy carries an out-of-pocket cost for the filing fee, normally $306 in a chapter 7 case and $281 in a chapter 13 case.[58] The chapter 7 filing fee may be waived by the court for a debtor unable to pay it.[59] Debtors must also pay the costs of a consumer credit counseling briefing and a personal financial management education course, usually totaling $50 to $100, unless those costs are waived due to inability to pay.[60] Occasionally, other fees may raise these figures somewhat. And in a chapter 13 case the trustee is usually entitled to a commission of up to ten percent of the payments made through the plan.[61] Also, in some cases, various utilities may require security deposits to ensure future service.[62]

These costs, like those other tangible costs, must be weighed in deciding whether to file a bankruptcy case. Usually, however, the other factors discussed in this Chapter are considerably more important.

6.2.2.7 Is Bankruptcy Necessary?

The question of fees leads back to a more basic issue. In some states, there are debtors who are totally judgment-proof at the time they seek advice. Legally, creditors can do virtually nothing to harm these clients.

In such cases, several other factors must be considered. Is the client likely to fall further into debt? For some clients the answer is no; their debts arose before they lost a job because of layoff, disability, or retirement. For many, though, there is a prospect of medical bills, or other continuing financial problems which will result in greater debt. For most, there is also a slight possibility of a motor vehicle accident or other incident creating a large liability.

Some debtors have only a few debts and have strong defenses to each. For those debtors, the best avenue might be either litigation or settlement outside of bankruptcy court. This decision may also depend on whether resources are available to make the alternative of vigorous litigation a possibility.

Still others, if they have more than modest incomes, may be able to avoid bankruptcy by reevaluating their lifestyle or the budget choices they make. In extreme cases, if such debtors choose to file, they will be vulnerable to a claim of bad faith or "abuse" of chapter 7.[63] When appropriate, such debtors might be referred to a reputable credit counseling agency.

---

54 For example, the Hill-Burton uncompensated care assurance requirements apply to hospitals which have received federal funds. See 42 C.F.R. §§ 124.501–124.518. Hospitals are also limited in turning away patients with medical emergencies by the Emergency Medical Treatment and Women in Active Labor Act, 42 U.S.C. § 1395dd, and may have other obligations to serve the community due to their charitable status.

55 U.S. Const. art. I, § 8 (Congress given power to establish uniform bankruptcy laws).

56 See Deut. 15:1–2.

57 11 U.S.C. § 524(f).

58 The filing fee for chapter 7 under 28 U.S.C. § 1930(a) is $245 and for chapter 13 it is $235. Under 28 U.S.C. § 1930(b), the federal Judicial Conference decided to assess an additional noticing fee of $46 in connection with all chapter 7 and chapter 13 filings, so that the initial fee for a chapter 13 case now totals $281. In addition, the federal Judicial Conference has mandated a $15 fee for chapter 7 debtors to pay compensation to chapter 7 trustees. The noticing fee and trustee fee, like the filing fees, can be paid in installments, and the form application to pay the filing fee in installments has been modified to accommodate this possibility. Fed. R. Bankr. P. 1006. See Appx. D, infra. Moreover, these two fees should be waivable by the courts for indigent debtors, if the total chapter 7 fee has not been waived under 28 U.S.C. § 1930(f), because they are imposed under 28 U.S.C. § 1930(b). See § 14.6, infra. See Form 17, Appendix G.3, infra, for an application to waive administrative fees. See also § 3.2.2, supra, for discussion of recent fee changes.

59 28 U.S.C. § 1930(f). See § 14.6, infra.

60 See Chapters 7 and 8, infra, for discussion of the prepetition credit counseling and postpetition credit education requirements.

61 However, debts paid outside the plan in a chapter 13 case may not be subject to the commission. See Ch. 12, infra.

62 11 U.S.C. § 366(b). See § 9.8, infra.

63 See § 13.4, infra.

In all of these cases, a client should be advised to bear in mind that the same relief in bankruptcy will almost always be available later,[64] but that filing a bankruptcy case now may impair the right to obtain bankruptcy relief in years to come.[65] Thus, unless a judgment-proof debtor expects to soon acquire nonexempt property, the client may wish to wait.

Ultimately, the client must make a choice. Do the advantages of bankruptcy outweigh the disadvantages? Will bankruptcy in some way have a positive effect on that client's life? Obviously, for many consumer clients who face real threats that bankruptcy can eliminate, the answer is yes. But even those clients who are not in danger of sustaining a tangible loss may value the peace of mind that comes from having their burden of debt lifted. Whether they arise from the hope of someday making it out of a life of poverty, or simply from the anxiety of constantly feeling pressure to pay what is owed, these feelings should not be discounted. Thus, the decision of an informed client as to whether to file a bankruptcy petition should almost always be respected.[66]

6.2.2.8 When Bankruptcy Offers No Help or Is Unavailable

6.2.2.8.1 When bankruptcy will not help

Finally, there are some cases in which bankruptcy is the wrong tool to use and in which none of the advantages listed above will be realized.

One such situation is that of the debtor whose debts are fully secured by security interests or other liens that cannot be eliminated or modified through bankruptcy, and who does not have sufficient income to remedy a default even with all of the help bankruptcy provides. Unless there is some special advantage to litigating in bankruptcy court, bankruptcy will not solve the basic problems this debtor faces. At most, it may discharge the debtor's personal liability for the debts and gain the advantage of the automatic stay for a month or more.[67] Although in some cases these results could be worthwhile, in many such cases bankruptcy will not ultimately benefit the client.

The problem of clients in these predicaments is often that their current expenses exceed their income. Because bankruptcy (except for chapter 13's ability to stretch out or reduce certain types of short-term expenses) basically deals with assets and liabilities, it does not directly address this problem in most cases.

The opposite situation can also sometimes cause problems. If a debtor has substantial and valuable unencumbered property which cannot be exempted, a premature bankruptcy will generally hasten loss of the property rather than prevent it. Because unsecured creditors would have to obtain judgment liens or levies on the debtor's property under state law, execution outside bankruptcy may be quite slow. On the other hand, liquidation of nonexempt property generally occurs relatively quickly in the bankruptcy process. And, as unsecured creditors are entitled to the present value of nonexempt property in chapter 13, a case under that chapter could be quite costly. In this situation, the best option is probably to advise the client to wait at least until execution on the property appears imminent, unless the client can afford the necessary chapter 13 case.

Another potentially difficult situation arises when a client holds property in trust for children or other relatives. Because a trust may not file a bankruptcy petition, it may be difficult to gain the protection of bankruptcy for such property. However, in some cases relief may be possible if the beneficiaries of the trust file cases on their own behalf, which could protect their beneficial interests in the property. Alternatively, a trustee's bare legal title may be sufficient to invoke the automatic stay while a creditor secured by the property in question is paid through the trustee's chapter 13 plan.[68]

6.2.2.8.2 Clients who have filed prior bankruptcy cases

Some clients may be barred from filing a bankruptcy case altogether for some period of time. If a client was the debtor in a bankruptcy dismissed in the previous 180 days, and that dismissal was (1) for willful failure to abide by court orders or to appear in court in proper prosecution of the case or (2) a voluntary dismissal following a request for relief from the automatic stay of section 362, then that client is not eligible to be a debtor until 180 days after the dismissal.[69] Occasionally, a court has entered, or a client has agreed to, an order that bars the client from filing a new case for some specified period of time or that purports to limit the client's protection under the automatic stay. Such an order or agreement may sometimes be reconsidered, or challenged in a later case, but otherwise it may be a significant hurdle.[70] In addition, a recent dismissal of a bankruptcy case may make it difficult to maintain or, in some cases, even to obtain, the automatic stay.[71] In any event, if a client has filed prior bankruptcy cases in the recent past, the situation must be examined carefully to determine whether a new case is likely to succeed or whether it will fail for the same reasons that the prior cases failed. Debtors' attorneys should not become participants in their clients' efforts to abuse the bankruptcy process by filing repeated cases that have no chance of success.

---

64 A warning should be added, however, that if the client's situation changes greatly, or if the law changes (if, for example, the state opts out of the federal exemptions), bankruptcy may not be as attractive in the future.

65 11 U.S.C. §§ 727(a)(8), (9), 1328(f).
   See §§ 12.10, 15.2.2.8, *infra*, for discussion of the bar to future cases.

66 However, an attorney is not necessarily obligated to represent the client in the course of action chosen.

67 See Ch. 9, *infra*.

---

68 *See In re Foster*, 19 B.R. 28 (Bankr. E.D. Pa. 1982).
   See also § 2.5, *supra*, for discussion of trust property.

69 11 U.S.C. § 109(g). *See* § 3.2.1, *supra*. *See also* § 9.7.3.1.5, *infra*.

70 *See* § 9.7.3.1.5, *infra*.

71 11 U.S.C. § 362(c)(3), (4) curtails automatic stay protection when a prior case was dismissed within the year before filing of the new petition. *See* Ch. 9, *infra*.

Lastly, some clients may stand to gain little from a chapter 7 bankruptcy because they cannot receive a discharge due to a prior bankruptcy.[72] For these clients the prospect is somewhat brighter. In many cases, a chapter 13 case is still available to provide significant relief.[73] Even if a discharge cannot be obtained, the filing of a chapter 13 case may help clients in other ways, such as by providing the opportunity to cure a mortgage default or by providing a respite from creditor collection actions.[74]

When a client is advised not to pursue bankruptcy or makes that choice after consultation, additional counseling may be necessary. For example, such clients are likely to need advice about nonbankruptcy approaches to debt problems and their consumer rights. Much of that information is collected in NCLC's publication the *NCLC Guide to Surviving Debt*.[75]

6.3 Choosing the Type of Bankruptcy Case to File

6.3.1 Introduction

Bound up with the decision of whether to file a bankruptcy case is the question of which type of bankruptcy offers the greatest benefit to a client. Although this decision may normally be changed at least once by converting the case after it is filed, it is nonetheless of obvious importance to ultimately settle upon the chapter offering the greatest advantages for the debtor.

6.3.2 Considerations Favoring Chapter 7

For many consumer debtors, "straight bankruptcy," provided for in chapter 7 of the Code, has traditionally been the remedy chosen. There are a number of reasons why chapter 7 usually meets the needs of the low-income debtor in particular.

First, one of the main factors leading to a chapter 13 case—the desire to protect nonexempt property—is rarely present. A low-income debtor in most states will rarely have any nonexempt property. Nor will she be likely to have any excess income, over and above that necessary for living expenses, with which to pay unsecured creditors through a chapter 13 plan.[76]

Thus, unless a chapter 13 petition is necessary for some specific reason, such as those discussed below, many consumer debtors will not desire it. They can obtain a quick and easy fresh start in life through a chapter 7 case which will discharge most of their debts. Even if the debtor has one or two secured creditors who must be dealt with, a chapter 13 plan may not be necessary. Debtors can handle some secured creditors as well, or better, in a chapter 7 case, by utilizing the devices for reducing or eliminating liens that are available in that type of case,[77] or by dealing with the claims outside the bankruptcy court.[78]

A small number of consumer debtors have a different problem. The amounts of their debts exceed the limitations for eligibility to file a chapter 13 case. If a debtor's secured non-contingent liquidated debts exceed $1,081,475, or unsecured non-contingent liquidated debts exceed $360,475, the Code denies that debtor access to chapter 13.[79] As these limits are not doubled for a husband and wife filing together, the debt limits may sometimes dictate that only one spouse, or each spouse separately, file a chapter 13 case if the individual spouse's debts alone are within the statutory limits.[80]

Moreover, an important factor to remember is that a subsequent chapter 13 case may be filed at any time after a chapter 7 case.[81] Thus, if a chapter 13 case is not necessary at the time the debtor wants to file, it may still be possible to take advantage of many chapter 13 benefits later if circumstances change.

6.3.3 Considerations Favoring Chapter 13

Probably the most common reason for filing a chapter 13 case on behalf of a consumer client is the presence of one or more secured creditors who cannot be satisfactorily handled in any other way. One frequent example is a bank or finance company that is about to repossess a client's car. Few legal

---

72 11 U.S.C. § 727(a)(8) and (9) bar a chapter 7 discharge within eight years after the filing of a prior chapter 7 case resulting in discharge or, usually, within six years after the filing of a prior chapter 13 case resulting in discharge.

73 11 U.S.C. § 1328(f)(1) and (2) bar a chapter 13 discharge within four years after the filing of a prior chapter 7 case resulting in discharge or within two years after the filing of a prior chapter 13 case resulting in discharge. *See* § 12.10, *infra*.

74 *See* § 12.10.3, *infra*.

75 The *NCLC Guide to Surviving Debt* can be ordered for $20 per copy (with discounts for bulk orders) by calling NCLC at (617) 542-9595.

76 One requirement of chapter 13 is that all priority claims, including the trustee's fees, domestic support obligations (with a limited exception), and priority taxes, must be paid in full. 11 U.S.C. § 1322(a)(2); § 12.3.6, *infra*.

77 11 U.S.C. §§ 506, 522, 722. *See* Chs. 10, 11, *infra*.

78 However, even if the debtor does not invoke the bankruptcy court's jurisdiction, the creditor may shift litigation to the bankruptcy court by filing a proceeding to lift the automatic stay or for reclamation of property, or by removal. *See* Chs. 9, 11, 14, *infra*.

79 11 U.S.C. § 109(e). *See* Ch. 12, *infra*.

80 Alternatively, they may choose to file a chapter 11 case. *See* § 6.3.4, *infra*.

81 *See* Johnson v. Home State Bank, 501 U.S. 78, 111 S. Ct. 2150, 115 L. Ed. 2d 66 (1991).

However, the debtor is not eligible for a discharge in a chapter 13 case filed within four years after the filing of a chapter 7 case resulting in discharge or, within two years after the filing of a prior chapter 13 case resulting in discharge. 11 U.S.C. § 1328(f). *See* § 12.10, *infra*.

Moreover, it is not clear whether a chapter 13 case may be filed while a chapter 7 case is still pending. Normally, conversion would be appropriate in those circumstances. *See* Ch. 4, *supra*. *But see In re* Saylors, 869 F.2d 1434 (11th Cir. 1989) (chapter 13 case may be filed while chapter 7 case still pending if debtor has received discharge and only lack of trustee's administrative acts delays closing of case); *In re* Strause, 97 B.R. 22 (Bankr. S.D. Cal. 1989) (filing of chapter 13 case not barred by pending chapter 7 case when discharge would have been granted but for court's administrative delays); § 12.10, *infra*.

steps prevent repossession as quickly and effectively[82] as a chapter 13 petition and plan, which can also usually lower the monthly payments and perhaps the balance due.[83] Similarly, a chapter 13 case can be used to halt a mortgage foreclosure, giving the client time to cure a default and, in some cases,[84] a chance to lower the payments or principal due. And in limited circumstances, a tax lien on the debtor's property that can be avoided, or subordinated to certain priority claims, by a chapter 7 trustee under section 724(b) may dictate a chapter 13 case to prevent the loss of the property.[85]

As mentioned above, other reasons to file a chapter 13 case spring from deficiencies in the relief available under chapter 7. If the debtor does have nonexempt property, it is protected in chapter 13, though its present value must usually be paid to unsecured creditors over the course of the plan.[86] And, if the debtor has obtained a chapter 7 discharge in a case filed within the previous eight years or a chapter 13 discharge in a case filed within the previous six years, it is likely that the only real option in bankruptcy is chapter 13.[87]

Another feature of chapter 13 which may sometimes be important is the somewhat broader discharge it provides. Some debts that are not dischargeable in chapter 7 may be discharged in chapter 13. These include willful and malicious torts causing injury to property or not yet reduced to a judgment or restitution award; marital property settlement debts that are not in the nature of support; condominium or home owner association fees; certain fines or restitution obligations; and debts with respect to which a previous bankruptcy discharge was denied or waived.[88]

High income debtors may sometimes find chapter 13 advisable to avoid a motion to dismiss based upon the "abuse" provisions of section 707(b). That section creates a formula to determine whether there is a presumption of abuse, but the United States trustee or a creditor may allege abuse even if the presumption of abuse does not arise.[89]

Even for the nondischargeable debts, such as alimony, maintenance, or support arrearages, or for debts like taxes which must be paid in a chapter 13 case because they are priority debts,[90] a chapter 13 plan may still benefit the debtor by allowing her to stretch out the payments over a longer period than would otherwise be possible and perhaps avoid interest and penalties. In addition, most of the possible objections to a chapter 7 discharge, such as fraudulent transfer, concealment of property, or inability to explain loss of assets, may not be raised in a chapter 13 case.[91]

A decision to file under chapter 13 sometimes depends on how likely it is that these questions will arise. Some debts are dischargeable in chapter 7 unless the creditor affirmatively files a complaint seeking a declaration of their nondischargeability.[92] When a motion to dismiss for alleged abuse or an objection to discharge or dischargeability is not predictable, it may be preferable to commence a chapter 7 case and later convert to chapter 13, if necessary.

Another reason to file a chapter 13 case is to help a client who does want to pay her debts but needs the protection of the bankruptcy court and, perhaps, the "discipline" of a chapter 13 plan. Chapter 13 usually offers this client, in addition, an end to finance charges and late charges on unsecured claims, and possibly less detriment (when there is any) to the debtor's credit history[93] and reputation. However, such a client should be reminded that most of these advantages are available without a chapter 13 case; she may pay all or part of any debt voluntarily after a chapter 7 case, without the deadlines and extra costs of a chapter 13 plan.

Occasionally, the filing of a chapter 13 case is required because a client cannot afford to pay her bankruptcy attorney fees except by installments as part of a chapter 13 plan.[94]

---

82 The repossession is ordinarily prohibited upon filing by the automatic stay provided for in 11 U.S.C. § 362. *See* Ch. 9, *infra*.

83 However, if the value of the collateral is substantially less than the debt, the debtor could choose to redeem the property in a chapter 7 case, which would also stay a repossession. 11 U.S.C. § 722. *See* § 11.5, *infra*.

84 A claim for which there is a security interest in the debtor's principal residence may only be modified by a chapter 13 plan in certain circumstances. 11 U.S.C. § 1322(b)(2), (c)(2). *See* § 11.6.1, *infra*.

85 11 U.S.C. § 724(a) permits a chapter 7 trustee to avoid a tax penalty lien, but the debtor can exempt the property subject to such lien under section 522(g) if the debtor could otherwise exempt such property. The debtor may also avoid a tax penalty lien under section 522(h) if the property is exemptible. *See* § 10.4.2.6.8, *infra*. 11 U.S.C. § 724(b) permits a chapter 7 trustee to liquidate property subject to a tax lien in order to pay holders of claims described in section 507(a)(1), (2), (3), (4), (5), (6) or (7). A tax lien should not be avoided if the only claim to be paid is for the trustee's administrative expenses or the taxes secured by the lien, because the purpose of section 724(b) is to elevate the other types of priority debts over the tax lien. *But see* Sheehan v. Posin, 2012 WL 1413020 (N.D. W. Va. Apr. 23, 2012) (permitting trustee to liquidate property to pay tax lien).

86 11 U.S.C. § 1325(a)(4). *See* § 12.3.2, *infra*.

87 11 U.S.C. § 727(a)(8), (9).

The time bar cannot be evaded by filing a chapter 13 case within the proscribed time period after an earlier petition and then converting the case to chapter 7 after the time period has run. *In re Burrell*, 148 B.R. 820 (Bankr. E.D. Va. 1992).

When a chapter 13 case is impossible for some reason, exempt property may nevertheless be protected from most creditors in a chapter 7 case even if a discharge is not available. 11 U.S.C. § 522(c). 11 U.S.C. § 727(a)(8) and (9) prohibit another chapter 7 discharge within this period. Those subsections do not bar the filing of another chapter 7 case, in which exemptions would still be available. For at least a few debtors, that may be the best alternative as they would receive the benefit of the automatic stay and their exempt property would thereby be preserved despite the lack of a discharge.

88 Discharge of these debts is barred by 11 U.S.C. § 523(a) in a chapter 7 case. *See* Ch. 15, *infra*.

89 11 U.S.C. § 707(b). *See* Ch. 13, *infra*.

90 11 U.S.C. § 1322(a)(2).

91 However, a court may well consider outrageous behavior to be violative of the "good faith" requirement of 11 U.S.C. § 1325(a)(3). *See* § 12.3.3, *infra*.

92 11 U.S.C. § 523(c) specifies these types of debts.

93 The evidence as to this point is mixed. *See* § 6.2.2.3, *supra*.

94 *See* § 16.4, *infra*, for further discussion of payment of attorney fees through the chapter 13 plan.

Attorneys should be careful not to abuse this device; the bankruptcy courts and United States trustees are giving greater scrutiny to chapter 13 cases which seem to have been filed primarily so that the debtor's attorney could "use the chapter 13 trustee as his collection agent."[95]

Finally, if there is significant doubt as to whether any bankruptcy is the right solution, but for some reason the debtor must file a petition before that doubt is finally resolved, chapter 13 usually offers a safer course than chapter 7. The debtor may voluntarily dismiss a case commenced under chapter 13 at any time as a matter of right.[96] The same is not true of a case commenced under chapter 7 (or later converted to chapter 7). In a chapter 7 case, dismissal may occur only with leave of the court, and may be denied if it appears to prejudice the rights of creditors.[97]

6.3.4 Use of Chapter 11 by Consumer Debtors

In *Toibb v. Radloff*,[98] the Supreme Court held that individual debtors may file under the reorganization provisions of chapter 11 of the Bankruptcy Code. While even a cursory review of the chapter 11 process is beyond the scope of this treatise, some basic information about chapter 11 from the perspective of consumer creditors is available in Chapter 18, *infra*.

For the great majority of consumer debtors, chapter 11 is not the right choice. Most of the relief available in chapter 11 is available for individuals in chapter 13 at a much lower cost in time and money.

However, a limited number of debtors might choose chapter 11 over chapter 13 in the following situations:

- The debtor is ineligible to file under chapter 13 because of non-contingent, liquidated, secured debt in excess of $1,081,475 or non-contingent, liquidated, unsecured debt in excess of $360,475.[99]
- The debtor cannot pay priority tax claims within the five-year period permitted under chapter 13, but could do so within the time permitted under chapter 11.[100]
- The debtor will save a very substantial amount of money due to the absence of a limit on reducing claims secured by motor vehicles purchased within 910 days before bankruptcy.
- The debtor is permitted to modify a mortgage, but cannot pay the entire present value of the allowed secured claim during the term of a five-year plan, but could pay a restructured claim over a longer period.[101]

In addition some practitioners find that, without a chapter 13 trustee scrutinizing the debtor's plan, a high-income debtor is allowed more leeway in plan provisions and living expenses than would be likely in chapter 13.

Chapter 11 cases tend to be expensive[102] and complicated. Unlike a chapter 13 case, a chapter 11 case may not be dismissed as of right;[103] a plan may ultimately be proposed by creditors over the debtor's objection;[104] creditors generally must vote on the plan;[105] there is no codebtor stay;[106] and the same exceptions to discharge found in chapter 7 apply.[107] For this reason, it is advisable to perform a thorough review to make certain that chapter 11 is necessary. It also may be helpful to obtain expert assistance or a practice manual which covers chapter 11 in some detail.

6.4 Should Both Spouses File?

In cases in which both a husband and wife are represented, an additional question presents itself—whether both spouses should file, or only one of them. The answer to this question is that it is usually preferable for both to file. The filing fee is the same for joint cases as for an individual case and can provide both spouses the advantages of a bankruptcy discharge.[108] Most often, many debts are jointly owed; a spouse who does not file thus remains liable as a codebtor, and may continue to be pursued by creditors.[109]

When a joint bankruptcy case is filed, the debtors file joint schedules, statements and other papers, reducing the amount of work necessary as compared to the filing of two separate cases. However, the filing of a joint bankruptcy does not automatically consolidate the cases of the two debtors; such consolidation,

---

95 *See, e.g.*, Berliner v. Pappalardo (*In re* Puffer), 674 F.3d 78 (1st Cir. 2012) (discussing chapter 13 cases where only attorney fees are paid and rejecting a per se rule against such plans); *In re* San Miguel, 40 B.R. 481 (Bankr. D. Colo. 1984).
96 11 U.S.C. § 1307(b). *See In re* Eddis, 37 B.R. 217 (E.D. Pa. 1984). *See also In re* Nash, 765 F.2d 1410 (9th Cir. 1985); § 13.2, *infra* (discussion of voluntary dismissal and a few erroneous decisions limiting the right to dismiss).
97 Voluntary dismissal of a chapter 7 case is sometimes denied. *See* § 13.2, *infra*.
98 501 U.S. 157, 111 S. Ct. 2197, 115 L. Ed. 2d 145 (1991).
99 11 U.S.C. § 109(e). *See* § 12.2.3, *infra*.
100 *Compare* 11 U.S.C. § 1322(a)(2), (c) *with* 11 U.S.C. § 1129(a)(9)(C) (which permits six years after the date of assessment).
  This situation would be very rare. In chapter 11 present value payments on the priority tax debts would be required.
101 *See* § 11.6.1.3.3.1., *infra*, for a discussion of modification of a secured claim in a plan.
102 The filing fee for chapter 11 is currently $1213. 28 U.S.C. § 1930(a)(3).
  In addition, fees to the United States trustee of at least $250 per quarter are required until the case is closed, converted, or dismissed. 28 U.S.C. § 1930(a)(6). There are also other costs, including those of preparing and mailing disclosure statements and ballots for creditor voting.
103 *Compare* 11 U.S.C. § 1112 *with* 11 U.S.C. § 1307.
104 11 U.S.C. § 1121.
105 11 U.S.C. §§ 1125, 1129.
106 *See* § 9.4.5, *infra*. *Cf.* 11 U.S.C. § 1301.
107 11 U.S.C. § 523(a).
108 *See* Appendix D, *infra*, for a sample completed application to waive the chapter 7 filing fee and Form 17, Appendix G.3, *infra*, for an application to waive the noticing fee. See also § 3.2.2, *supra*, for discussion of other issues relating to filing fees.
109 However, in many chapter 13 cases, such pursuit is at least temporarily prohibited by 11 U.S.C. § 1301, which stays actions against codebtors. See Chapter 9, *infra*, for discussion and exceptions.

which would consolidate the bankruptcy estates of the debtors, must be ordered by the court.[110] This issue is significant primarily in cases in which one spouse has nonexempt property that will be distributed (or much more nonexempt property than the other spouse) and some or all of the debts are not joint debts. In such cases, the creditors of the spouse with more nonexempt property have an interest in opposing consolidation so they do not have to share that spouse's nonexempt property with creditors of the other spouse.[111]

The decision to file jointly, if appropriate, must be made at the outset of the case. Numerous courts have held that a spouse cannot be added to an existing bankruptcy petition after it is filed.[112] If an existing debtor's spouse seeks to file shortly after the initial spouse's petition, the best option might be a separate filing under the same chapter and a request for joint administration of the two cases.[113]

There are several exceptions to the general rule that both spouses should file. The most obvious is the situation in which one spouse does not wish to participate. After an explanation of the disadvantages of such a course of action to that spouse, most of the advantages of bankruptcy can still be obtained by filing a petition on behalf of the willing spouse.

A second exception is the case in which one spouse is barred from filing by a prior bankruptcy or, if the case proposed is a chapter 7 case, is likely to face an objection to discharge or an allegation of "abuse" under section 707(b). Similarly, if a chapter 13 case is advisable, some debt of the non-filing spouse,[114] for example, a very large priority debt which must be paid, or a debt above the chapter 13 debt limitations, might make a viable case impossible.

Probably the most important case in which it is necessary to deviate from the general rule is the situation in which filing for only one spouse would protect property. Occasionally, this may mean not filing for a spouse with nonexempt property. However, creditors can then usually continue to proceed against that property.[115] The more likely reason is the presence of substantial amounts of entireties property or other jointly owned property in excess of the federal exemption levels, which under state law are not reachable by a creditor of only one spouse. In such cases, if only one spouse files, and the state, rather than federal, exemptions are chosen, all of that spouse's interest in such property may be claimed as exempt, at least as to creditors of only the filing spouse.[116] Then, after the bankruptcy, those creditors[117] will be unable to reach the joint property because their claims have been discharged.[118] The advantages of one spouse filing in such situations, then, are obvious.

Finally, it is necessary to remember the effects of the bankruptcy on community debts and community property in community property states. Although the considerations involved will vary with the different community property laws, most community property generally becomes a part of the estate, and most community claims usually are discharged with respect to any community property, including community property acquired after the bankruptcy, even if only one spouse files.[119] Thus, most or all of a spouse's property and debts may be affected by the bankruptcy regardless of whether he or she joins in the petition. This factor may be either advantageous (debts may be discharged) or disadvantageous (property may be lost) to a non-filing spouse, and should be considered carefully.

6.5 Considerations of Timing and Events Prior to Filing

6.5.1 Reasons to File Quickly

A final factor to be considered in deciding on a course of action is the timing of the petition. Even after the debtor decides that a bankruptcy should be filed, in many cases it is advisable to wait before filing.

Of course, in some cases, a debtor has no choice but to file immediately. Prompt action may be necessary to forestall a repossession, eviction, execution sale, or utility shut-off. In some cases, a debtor may wish to file immediately before, or even after, foreclosure, if there is a possibility that the debtor will be able to effectuate a cure of a mortgage default through a chapter 13 plan.[120] It may also be the only way to stay a state court proceeding and thereby avoid much unnecessary work therein. Filing before the expiration of a statute of limitations or a period for redemption can provide the debtor with an extension of the

---

110 11 U.S.C. § 302(b).
111 *See In re* Reider, 31 F.3d 1102 (11th Cir. 1994) (substantive consolidation is abuse of discretion in case in which creditor can show it will thereby inequitably receive lesser share of assets because it relied on credit of one spouse); Robert B. Chapman, *Coverture and Cooperation: The Firm, the Market, and the Substantive Consolidation of Married Debtors*, 17 Bankr. Dev. J. 105 (2000).
112 *See, e.g., In re* Morgan, 96 B.R. 615 (Bankr. N.D. W. Va. 1989); *In re* Kirkus, 97 B.R. 675 (Bankr. N.D. Ga. 1987).
113 Fed. R. Bankr. P. 1015(b).
114 11 U.S.C. § 1322(a)(2).
115 *But see* 11 U.S.C. § 1301 (staying actions against codebtors in chapter 13 cases); Ch. 9, *infra*.
116 11 U.S.C. § 522(b)(2)(B). *But see* Sumy v. Schlossberg, 777 F.2d 921 (4th Cir. 1985); *In re* Grosslight, 757 F.2d 773 (6th Cir. 1985); Napotnik v. Equibank, 679 F.2d 316 (3d Cir. 1982) (limiting the exemption possible under 11 U.S.C. § 522(b)(2)(B)).
    Title to property may not always be clear and must sometimes be investigated. *See In re* McKain, 455 B.R. 674 (Bankr. E.D. Tenn. 2011) (discussing whether various assets held by entireties under Virginia law). Some courts have held that even in a joint case, the entireties exemption may be claimed with respect to non-joint creditors. For discussion of the joint property exemption, see § 10.2.3.2, *infra*.
117 An exception is the secured creditor whose rights were not impaired by the bankruptcy.
118 In a few jurisdictions, courts have also ruled that even when there are joint creditors, a bankruptcy filed by one spouse who chooses the exemption for entireties property can protect the entireties property from their claims. *See* § 10.2.3.2, *infra*.
119 11 U.S.C. §§ 524(a)(3), 541(a)(2). *See In re* Morgan, 286 B.R. 678 (Bankr. E.D. Wis. 2002) (trustee permitted to liquidate home where debtor's estranged wife and children lived because, as community property, it had become property of the estate and it had not been exempted by debtor); § 2.5.1, *supra*.
120 *See* § 11.6.2.2, *infra*.

§ 6.5.2   Consumer Bankruptcy Law and Practice

time period to commence a lawsuit or take other action.[121] Another occasional reason for a quick bankruptcy is an expectation[122] of soon acquiring nonexempt property. Such property does not usually become part of the estate after filing.[123] In all of these cases, a bankruptcy case can be filed almost instantaneously, if necessary, under the current rules.[124] However, the debtor must, with certain rare exceptions, receive a credit counseling briefing from an approved nonprofit budget and counseling agency within the 180 days before the petition is filed.[125]

6.5.2 The Effects of Prebankruptcy Transfers or Other Actions

6.5.2.1 Fraudulent Acts, Conveyances, and Preferences

One of the prime reasons for a delay before filing stems from the possible effects, both negative and positive, of prebankruptcy transfers. Some transfers already made may dictate a delay in filing, and it may be advisable to take time to make others before filing in order to gain maximum advantage from the case.

Several types of acts fall into the class of transfers that dictate delays; some of these may affect a discharge in chapter 7 proceedings. If the debtor, with intent to hinder, delay or defraud creditors, has transferred, removed, destroyed, mutilated or concealed her property within one year prior to the filing of a petition, a successful objection to a chapter 7 discharge may be brought.[126] This definition may include the transfer of specific property subject to a security interest in favor of a creditor, but only if the requisite intent existed.[127] If it seems likely that such an objection will be raised, it may be prudent to delay filing a chapter 7 case, if possible, until a year has passed since that act. Even after that year, a trustee may still seek to recover a fraudulent transfer,[128] and a secured creditor may still raise a claim of willful and malicious conversion of the collateral, but only to seek an exception to the discharge of that particular creditor's claim in a chapter 7 case.[129]

Usually less serious are two other types of transfers. These are preferences and those types of fraudulent conveyances made without actual intent to defraud creditors. The worst possible result of these transfers is a reversal of the transfer by the bankruptcy trustee.[130] Briefly, an avoidable preference in an individual bankruptcy is a transfer of property worth more than $600 from an insolvent debtor to a creditor on account of an antecedent debt, that allows that creditor to receive more than it would otherwise receive in a chapter 7 liquidation case, made within ninety days before filing (or one year before filing if the creditor is an insider, such as a relative).[131] Thus, large payments to some creditors prior to bankruptcy may be set aside by the trustee if they were made within the stated time periods.[132] If the client cares, as she may if the payment was made to a friend or relative, it may be better to delay filing until after the applicable preference period has passed.[133] However, it should be stressed that there is nothing improper or illegal about making a preferential payment. The only possible negative consequence is avoidance of the transfer by the trustee.

A fraudulent transfer may also be set aside by the trustee. Basically, the trustee's power extends to a transfer or obligation made within two years before filing, either (1) for the purpose of hindering, defrauding, or delaying creditors, or (2) for which the debtor did not receive reasonably equivalent value at a time that the debtor was insolvent or was about to incur debts beyond her ability to pay.[134] In addition, a transfer which could be set aside under a state fraudulent transfer statute can usually be set aside by the trustee at any time within the period allowed by that statute (usually longer than two years).[135] Again this possibility may be of no concern to the debtor, but if it is it may be advisable to wait, if possible, before filing.

On the other hand, some preferences and fraudulent transfers may be set aside by the debtor within the same time periods allowed the trustee. Generally, if the transfer was involuntary, the debtor did not conceal the property, and the debtor could have exempted the property involved, then the debtor may set aside the transfer.[136] Thus, if the debtor plans to make use of this power, it may be crucial to file the petition *before* the time period has run.

---

121 11 U.S.C. § 108(b). See Thomas v. GMAC Residential Funding Corp., 309 B.R. 453 (D. Md. 2004) (right of rescission under Truth in Lending Act extended by sixty days after filing of bankruptcy petition).

122 This expectation would have to be something less than an entitlement, as the latter would probably be property of the estate under 11 U.S.C. § 541.

123 Certain property acquired within 180 days of filing does become a part of the estate, for example, property acquired by inheritance or marital property settlement. 11 U.S.C. § 541(a)(5).

In addition after-acquired property becomes part of the estate in a chapter 13 case. 11 U.S.C. § 1306. See § 2.5, supra.

124 See § 7.2, infra.

125 11 U.S.C. § 109(h). See § 7.3.8, infra.

126 11 U.S.C. § 727(a)(2).

127 See § 15.2, infra.

128 The trustee may be able to avoid a fraudulent transfer under 11 U.S.C. §§ 544 or 548. See § 10.4.2.6.2, infra.

129 11 U.S.C. § 523(a)(6). See Ch. 15, infra.

130 11 U.S.C. §§ 544, 547, 548.

However, in some states, some types of fraudulent conveyances constitute crimes as well.

131 11 U.S.C. § 547.

The terms "transfer," "insider," and "insolvent," are all defined in 11 U.S.C. § 101. In most districts, a trustee will not pursue a preference avoidance unless the transfer is substantially more than $600. See § 10.4.2.6.4, infra, for further explanation of preferences.

132 See, e.g., State Compensation Ins. Fund v. Zamora (*In re* Silverman), 616 F.3d 1001 (9th Cir. 2010) (avoiding transfer of large criminal restitution payment made by debtors, possibly subjecting them to obligation to pay it again).

133 The longer one-year preference period before filing applies in the case of a payment to a relative, based on the definition of "insider" provided in 11 U.S.C. § 101(31)(A).

134 11 U.S.C. § 548. See § 10.4.2.6.5, infra.

135 11 U.S.C. § 544. See § 10.4.2.6.2, infra.

136 11 U.S.C. § 522(h).

See § 10.4.2.6.5, infra, for examples and further discussion.

Finally, section 523(a)(2)(C) of the Code creates a rebuttable presumption that consumer debts of more than $600 in the aggregate owed to a single creditor for "luxury goods and services" obtained within ninety days before a bankruptcy case was filed, or for cash advances of more than $875 in the aggregate obtained within seventy days before filing, were fraudulently incurred.[137] If the debtor plans to file a bankruptcy case and has recently incurred these types of debt, it is usually better, if possible, to wait until the applicable period has passed. Creditors do not always challenge the dischargeability of such debts, but the absence of the presumption will make creditor challenges to dischargeability less likely. However, waiting out this period does not guarantee dischargeability if the creditor can otherwise show fraud or false pretenses.

6.5.2.2 Exemption Time Periods and Exemption Planning

The 2005 amendments made it much more likely that exemptions will have to be considered in deciding when to file a bankruptcy case. The time period during which a debtor must be domiciled in the debtor's current state in order to claim that state's exemptions was extended from ninety days or less to two years.[138] If a debtor's state of domicile has changed in the two years before bankruptcy, the laws of the debtor's prior domicile will usually govern. Depending on which state's exemption laws are more favorable for the debtor, this change may dictate filing a case quickly, before the two-year period expires, in order to take advantage of the prior domicile's laws, or waiting so that the laws of the debtor's current domicile will govern.

In addition, the 2005 amendments added limitations on homestead exemptions in states that permit large or unlimited homestead exemptions.[139] If the debtor acquired the homestead property within 1215 days before filing for bankruptcy, except to the extent that the debtor used proceeds received from the sale of another home in the same state, the homestead exemption is limited to $146,450. In such cases it may be advantageous to wait, if possible, until the 1215-day period has run.

There are also steps a debtor can sometimes take prior to filing to improve her ability to retain property. Most of these come under the general rubric of exemption planning. Basically, exemption planning means arranging the debtor's affairs so that a maximum amount of property can be claimed under the exemption provisions, and a minimum amount is lost to creditors in the bankruptcy. It is much akin to tax planning, which is the way people arrange their affairs to take maximum advantage of the tax laws. In the opinion of most commentators, it is perfectly legal under present law, at least if not done to excess.[140]

A number of steps can be taken to take advantage of the exemption provisions. For example, some states require the debtor to file a homestead deed in order to claim the state homestead exemption. Assets that are not exempt, such as cash above the amounts allowed, can be spent on food, household goods, and clothing (each item must be worth less than $550 if the federal exemptions are used), life insurance, or other items in categories in which the debtor has unused exemptions (assuming the federal exemptions or similar state exemptions are available). If there is nonexempt equity in a debtor's home, the possibility of obtaining a second mortgage (again using the money to purchase exempt assets) should be weighed against

---

137 See § 15.4.3.2.3.2, infra.
138 See Chapter 10, infra, for discussion of exemption domicile requirements.
139 See Chapter 10, infra, for discussion of homestead limitations.
140 In re Addison, 540 F.3d 805 (8th Cir. 2008) (conversion of nonexempt assets to exempt assets not made with intent to defraud creditors); In re Stern, 345 F.3d 1036 (9th Cir. 2003) (purposeful conversion of nonexempt assets to exempt assets on eve of bankruptcy not fraudulent per se); In re Carey, 938 F.2d 1073 (10th Cir. 1991) (no intent to defraud found when debtor mortgaged nonexempt equity in residence and fully disclosed transaction); In re Bowyer, 932 F.2d 1100 (5th Cir. 1991) (use of assets to create exempt equity in home not improper when debtors had not yet formed plan to file bankruptcy); In re Armstrong, 931 F.2d 1233 (8th Cir. 1991); In re Holt, 894 F.2d 1005 (8th Cir. 1990) (conversion of nonexempt assets into exempt assets on eve of bankruptcy is not necessarily fraudulent); In re Johnson, 880 F.2d 78 (8th Cir. 1989) (mere fact of conversion of property into exempt assets does not establish fraud); In re Bradley, 294 B.R. 64 (B.A.P. 8th Cir. 2003) (conversion of nonexempt assets to exempt assets permissible under Arkansas law); In re Channon, 424 B.R. 895 (Bankr. D.N.M. 2010) (transfer of virtually all of insolvent debtor's assets into Roth IRA was not made with intent to defraud creditors, so exemption allowed under New Mexico law); In re Wadley, 263 B.R. 857 (Bankr. S.D. Ohio 2001) (debtor's sale of motorcycle and use of proceeds to acquire exempt assets was permissible).

H.R. Rep. No. 95-595, at 361 (1977) states that this practice is not fraudulent with respect to creditors, and permits the debtor to make full use of the exemptions to which she is entitled under law. For a discussion of prior law, see Resnick, *Prudent Planning or Fraudulent Transfers: The Use of Non-Exempt Assets to Purchase or Improve Exempt Property on the Eve of Bankruptcy*, 31 Rutgers L. Rev. 615 (1978).

However, some courts have held that transfers designed to maximize exemptions are fraudulent even under the Code. Clients must be advised that there is a risk that the transfers will be avoided, and that there is even a risk to their discharge. Most of these cases have involved state exemption law, large amounts of money, and conduct intended to conceal the transfers. See, e.g., In re Sholdan, 217 F.3d 1006 (8th Cir. 2000) (ninety-year-old's conversion of virtually all assets into exempt homestead found fraudulent and exemption denied); In re Tveten, 848 F.2d 871 (8th Cir. 1988) ($700,000 transfer to exempt assets found fraudulent and discharge denied); Ford v. Poston, 773 F.2d 52 (4th Cir. 1985) (conversion of nonexempt property to exempt property is normally permissible, but a court may find extrinsic evidence of an attempt to defraud creditors); In re Reed, 11 B.R. 683 (Bankr. N.D. Tex. 1981), aff'd, 700 F.2d 986 (5th Cir. 1983) (debtor denied discharge due to prebankruptcy rearrangement of property). See also In re Levine, 134 F.3d 1046 (11th Cir. 1998) (transfer of assets into exempt annuities was fraudulent transfer under Florida law).

11 U.S.C. § 522(o), added in 2005, provides that a homestead exemption shall be reduced to the extent its value is attributable to property that a debtor disposed of within ten years prior to the bankruptcy with the intent to hinder, delay, or defraud a creditor. See Ch. 10, infra. It is unclear whether this more specific direction from Congress will take the place of prior judicially fashioned rules in this area.

loss of that equity (or against paying that amount in a chapter 13 case).[141] All of these steps are nothing more than a rearrangement of a debtor's assets. Unless there is established case law in a jurisdiction finding them not permissible, these steps should be relatively free from risk.[142]

It is also important to remember property owed to the debtor. Tax refunds due[143] are always considered part of the estate and are often claimed by the trustee if they are not exempt.[144] Thus, if the refund due is greater than the debtor's unused exemptions, it may be better to wait until it arrives and spend it on exempt assets before filing the bankruptcy petition. In some areas, exemption planning may even come down to waiting until the debtor's payday to file, as careful trustees may seek out any nonexempt wages or vacation pay owed the debtor for the previous few days.[145] If no unused exemptions remain, prepaid rent could also pose a problem; in a few areas trustees and judges may consider the remaining portion of a month's prepaid rent, as well as any security deposits to landlords or utilities, to be assets.[146] Arrangements for a temporary refund may be worked out if no money is presently owed to the utility companies. Similarly, trustees have occasionally even been known to claim bank deposits as assets because checks which have been written have not yet cleared by the date of filing.[147] Local practice regarding these types of property varies greatly and should be investigated. In most areas, trustees do not inquire into these small amounts due the debtor. And, of course, if the debtor has significant unused exemptions to cover these amounts, there is no cause for concern.

A debtor may also take steps to ensure that no new nonexempt property comes into the bankruptcy estate after filing. Such property could come into the estate, for example, if the debtor receives or becomes entitled to acquire it by bequest, devise, or inheritance, as a result of a marital property settlement or divorce decree, or as a beneficiary of a life insurance policy or death benefit plan. If the situation warrants, it may be advisable to temporarily change the will or insurance policy giving rise to the possible entitlement, and to arrange marital settlements accordingly. As most of these steps involve the acts of persons other than the debtor (for example, the testator or owner of an insurance policy), there is little likelihood that they could adversely affect the debtor's case.[148]

Finally, exemption planning should be distinguished from a process by which debtors transfer property completely out of their estate. It is not permissible, for example, for a debtor to give valuable property to a spouse or other relative shortly before bankruptcy, without return of fair consideration, in order to keep it from coming into the bankruptcy estate.[149] Such conduct may be considered an effort to defraud the estate and may give rise to a challenge to discharge, to avoidance of the transfer as fraudulent or even, in serious cases, to criminal prosecution.[150]

6.5.3 Other Reasons for Delaying a Petition

6.5.3.1 Anticipation of Further Debt

It is sometimes said that a bankruptcy should not be filed until a client's debt load has peaked. If the client anticipates further unavoidable liabilities, such as medical bills, the bank-

---

141 See 11 U.S.C. § 1325(a)(4); § 12.3.2, infra.

142 In the unlikely event a court finds the property nonexempt because of such actions, the debtor will still be able to save it through payment of its value in a chapter 13 plan, or perhaps by voluntary dismissal of the case. Therefore, if there is doubt about whether a transfer might be considered fraudulent, a chapter 13 case should be seriously considered from the outset.

143 See § 2.5.5, supra, for further discussion of tax refunds and withholdings.

144 United States v. Michaels, 840 F.2d 901 (11th Cir. 1988) (Internal Revenue Service permitted to recoup tax refunds paid to debtors because they should have been paid to chapter 7 trustee).

145 See, e.g., In re Grimes, 2009 WL 1117654 (Bankr. S.D. Ind. Apr. 22, 2009) (state garnishment exemption for wages available in bankruptcy); In re Jones, 318 B.R. 841 (Bankr. S.D. Ohio 2005) (federal garnishment protection available to exempt earnings in employer's hands); In re Sexton, 140 B.R. 742 (Bankr. S.D. Iowa 1992); In re Meade, 84 B.R. 106 (Bankr. S.D. Ohio 1988) (wages earned by debtor but not yet paid on date of petition were property of the estate).

In many states, most or all of a debtor's accrued wages are exempt from garnishment, and wages are also protected from garnishment by the Consumer Credit Protection Act. 15 U.S.C. §§ 1671–1677. Such exemptions may also be applicable if the state and federal nonbankruptcy exemption scheme is utilized by the debtor in a bankruptcy case. See In re Irish, 303 B.R. 380 (Bankr. N.D. Iowa 2003), aff'd, 311 B.R. 63 (B.A.P. 8th Cir. 2004); In re Maidman, 141 B.R. 571 (Bankr. S.D.N.Y. 1992). See generally § 10.2.3, infra. Some states also have specific exemptions for accrued wages applicable to bankruptcy cases.

146 It should be possible to exempt prepaid rent under 11 U.S.C. § 522(d)(1), the federal homestead exemption, which is broadly worded to permit exemption of an interest in property used as a residence or a similar state exemption. Indeed, if such an exemption is available the debtor may use nonexempt cash to prepay rent and claim that asset as exempt. See In re Casserino, 290 B.R. 735 (B.A.P. 9th Cir. 2003) (prepaid rent could be exempted under Oregon homestead exemption), aff'd, 379 F.3d 1069 (9th Cir. 2004); In re Coffey, 339 B.R. 689 (Bankr. N.D. Ind. 2006) (Indiana homestead exemption could be used to protect prepaid lease interest).

In a few states, prepayments to utilities may be exempt. See In re Ward, 2010 WL 447326 (Bankr. D. Ariz. Feb. 9, 2010) (prepayment to energy utility exempt under provision protecting "all food, fuel and provisions ... for debtor's individual or family use for six months" but prepayment for telephone/Internet was not).

147 See, e.g., In re Pyatt, 486 F.3d 423 (8th Cir. 2007); § 5.3.3.2 n.5, supra.

148 But see In re Green, 986 F.2d 145 (6th Cir. 1993) (in unusual situation of debtor who, having a contractual right to receive property under a will, agreed to give up that right, the exercise of a power of appointment to terminate the debtor's rights under a will was found to be a fraudulent transfer).

149 See, e.g., In re White, 28 B.R. 240 (Bankr. E.D. Va. 1983) (absent consideration, prebankruptcy transfer from one spouse to another not permitted).

However, a fair trade of property for consideration should be allowed. See In re Armstrong, 931 F.2d 1233 (8th Cir. 1991) (transfer of home to father found proper when father paid fair consideration).

150 11 U.S.C. § 727(a)(2); 18 U.S.C. § 152. See § 15.2, infra.

ruptcy should, if possible, be delayed until after these are incurred. The object of this delay, of course, is to gain maximum benefit from the discharge.

However, this delay must be carefully distinguished from another type of behavior—that of obtaining goods or services under false pretenses with no intent of paying for them. Debts incurred in this manner may be declared nondischargeable in a chapter 7 case.[151] Fortunately, the line between these two courses of action is not as difficult to draw as it might at first seem. In general, the courts have found nondischargeable only the most obvious examples of debts incurred with no intent to pay, for example, prebankruptcy vacation trip and credit card shopping spree debts.[152] Expenses for medical bills and other necessities are rarely challenged.

6.5.3.2 Paying Favored Creditors

Clients may wish to delay a bankruptcy until after they have paid creditors whose claims they do not want to see discharged, for example friends or the grantors of credit cards they hope to keep. As noted above, such payments, if over $600 and within the applicable preference period, could be set aside by the bankruptcy trustee. Thus, if a client wants to pursue this course of action, and ensure that the creditor retains the payment, the petition must be delayed until after the preference period has run.[153]

In most cases, it is preferable not to delay a bankruptcy for this purpose, but rather to pay the creditor after the petition is filed, using either exempt assets or postpetition income. There is no impediment to this course of action in a chapter 7 case and usually it will not be questioned in a chapter 13 case.[154]

6.5.3.3 Delay of a Petition As a Strategy to Forestall Harm to Clients

There will be occasions when, for purposes of litigation strategy, a bankruptcy petition should be delayed. For example, a client defending against an eviction or mortgage foreclosure may also desire a bankruptcy. By waiting to file the petition until delay of eviction or foreclosure is no longer possible in state court litigation, a good advocate can take advantage of the automatic stay arising from the bankruptcy to gain additional time during which the client may remain in her residence.[155] This additional time can be invaluable to a client who may later be able to settle the housing problem, either outside the bankruptcy or in a chapter 13 case. At the least, the client will have more time to find another place to live. There is certainly nothing unethical about timing a legitimate and necessary bankruptcy to obtain the maximum advantage for the client. Of course, filing a bankruptcy petition solely for the purpose of delay is quite a different matter and would likely be found unethical,[156] or cause for sanctions against the debtor, the debtor's counsel, or both.[157]

6.5.3.4 Tax Reach Back Periods

The dischargeability of certain taxes and their possible treatment as priority debts (which must be paid in full in chapter 13 cases) will depend on various time periods having passed.[158] Investigation concerning the exact date of expiration of these time periods is essential if discharging taxes is an objective of the case.[159] Many debtors have been disappointed by an attorney's miscalculation of the relevant dates, which can be complicated by tolling periods and special tax rules. Possible malpractice claims can result.

Delay until the date of expiration of the periods is appropriate if there will not be other harmful consequences in the interim. If delay creates other risks, those risks must be weighed against the benefit of discharging the taxes involved.

On the other hand, if the debtor has not filed tax returns for past tax years, it may be advantageous for the debtor to file the missed tax returns and to file bankruptcy more quickly so that the taxes are priority debts. If the debtor then files a chapter 13 case, the debtor can pay the priority tax debts before paying other unsecured creditors, thereby devoting more of the debtor's disposable income to paying debts that would otherwise be nondischargeable.

6.5.3.5 Delay to Obtain More Favorable Treatment of Certain Secured Debts in Chapter 13

The 2005 amendments added a new provision to chapter 13 that may impair the debtor's right to "cramdown" certain debts secured by purchase money security interests in personal property.[160] The provision applies if a motor vehicle was purchased for the debtor's personal use within the 910 days before the bankruptcy petition was filed or if other property was purchased within one year before the petition was filed.[161] If the debtor is

---

151 *See* § 15.4.3.2, *infra*.
152 *Id*.
153 Further discussion of preferences is found in § 10.4.2.6.4, *infra*.
154 However, paying more to one creditor than to another while a chapter 13 case is pending, even outside the plan, could be considered an unfair classification of debts or evidence that the debtor can afford to pay more under the disposable income test. *See* §§ 12.3, 12.4, *infra*.
155 However, 11 U.S.C. § 362(b)(22), enacted in 2005, limits the applicability of the stay after an eviction judgment in some circumstances. *See* Ch. 9, *infra*.
156 *See* Model Rules of Prof'l Conduct R. 3.1; Fed. R. Bankr. P. 9011(a).
157 Cinema Serv. Corp. v. Edbee Corp., 774 F.2d 584 (3d Cir. 1985).
158 *See* § 15.4.3.1, *infra*, for detailed discussion of ways to obtain and analyze tax information.
159 In some cases, returns must be filed to first start the clock running. *See* § 15.4.3.1, *infra*.
160 Language added at the end of 11 U.S.C. § 1325(a) makes section 506 inapplicable to these debts for purposes of section 1325(a)(5). See Chapter 11, *infra*, for discussion of the right to cramdown and the limitations on that right.
161 This treatise's companion website contains a "Date Calculator" that assists practitioners in computing the time periods for prepetition events that may affect the debtor's decision when to file a bankruptcy petition. Appendix H.1, *infra*, contains a sample of the

filing a chapter 13 case in which the debtor can benefit from the bifurcation of such secured claims to reduce the amount that must be paid to secured creditors, it may be important to wait until the requisite time periods have run.

6.5.3.6 Timing the Petition to Avoid a Presumption of Abuse in Chapter 7 or to Lower Disposable Income in Chapter 13

The means test and the new method of calculating disposable income in chapter 13 cases add yet another timing issue that must be considered in some cases. The debtor's "current monthly income" upon which both the chapter 7 means test and chapter 13 calculation of disposable income are based is an average of the debtor's income (with certain exclusions and additions) over the six calendar months preceding the filing of the petition.[162] If the debtor's income has increased during that period, the current monthly income will become higher each month after the increase because the calculation will include more months at a higher income level. If the debtor's income has decreased during that period, the current monthly income will become lower if the debtor delays the petition.

In most chapter 7 cases, the timing may not make a difference because the debtor will be below the applicable median income threshold that brings the means test into play, even at the higher income level.[163] However, in some cases, delaying or expediting the petition may drop the debtor below that threshold, or may change the result of the means test calculation so that a presumption of abuse does not arise. Other factors that might change in the near future, such as expenses permitted under the means test or the debtor's household size for purposes of the means test, must also be taken into account in deciding when to file the case.

In chapter 13 cases, current monthly income is the basis for calculating the debtor's payments to unsecured creditors in every case. Although some debtors may have insufficient funds to pay unsecured creditors even at the higher income level, for many debtors an increase in current monthly income will lead to higher required payments in the chapter 13 plan, unless their expenses have also increased commensurately. If the debtor's current monthly income changes from above to below the applicable median income level stated in section 1325(a)(4) or vice versa, the "applicable commitment period" determining total payments to unsecured creditors also is changed, from sixty to thirty-six months or vice versa. Thus, careful planning of the timing of a chapter 13 petition may make a significant difference in the amount a debtor is required to pay.

6.5.3.7 Timing the Petition to Avoid Automatic Stay Limitations

The dismissal of prior bankruptcy cases within one year before filing a new petition may result in early termination of the automatic stay with respect to the debtor or, in some cases, prevent the stay from taking effect altogether.[164] Delaying the bankruptcy filing beyond the one-year period may ensure the debtor gains the full protection of the automatic stay and eliminates the need to file a motion for extension or imposition of the stay in the new case.[165]

In the case of an eviction proceeding, delaying the bankruptcy filing could prevent the debtor from gaining the protection of the automatic stay. If a bankruptcy is filed after a judgment for possession against the debtor has entered in an eviction case, proceedings to obtain possession of the property are not automatically stayed; in some such cases, the debtor may be able to take certain steps to obtain the full protection of the automatic stay, but in others the stay will be permanently lost.[166]

6.5.3.8 Less Common Reasons for Delaying a Petition

The situations described above are the most common scenarios in which the timing of the bankruptcy case can work to the debtor's advantage or disadvantage. They are not the only ones. For example, if debtors have recently placed substantial amounts in education savings accounts, the amounts excluded from the bankruptcy estate under subsections 541(b)(5) and (b)(6) may be affected by a delay in filing. A quickly rising real estate market may dictate filing a bankruptcy case sooner rather than later so that the debtor's home equity does not increase to an amount that cannot be exempted. Ultimately, only a thorough knowledge of all of the Code provisions that may be relevant to a particular debtor, especially those containing time periods, can ensure the optimal timing of a petition.

---

results produced by this calculator, with a detailed description of the prepetition time periods.
162 11 U.S.C. § 101(10A).
   See Chapters 12 and 13, *infra*, for discussion of current monthly income, the chapter 7 means test, and disposable income under chapter 13.
163 11 U.S.C. § 707(b)(7). *See* Ch. 13, *infra*.
164 11 U.S.C. § 362(c)(3), (4). *See* § 9.3.3, *infra*.
165 The one-year period runs from the date the order dismissing the prior case is entered, even if the case remains open for administrative purposes after that date. *See In re* Moore, 337 B.R. 79 (Bankr. E.D.N.C. 2005).
166 11 U.S.C. §§ 362(b)(22), 362(l)(1). *See* § 9.4.6.6, *infra*.

Chapter 7 Preparing and Filing the Papers

7.1 Introduction

7.1.1 Some General Principles

Once it has been decided that bankruptcy is appropriate in a particular case, most of the remaining work is relatively routine. A good deal of it involves preparation of the necessary papers for the initial filing. This Chapter provides a detailed step-by-step description of how to prepare and file the forms used in a typical bankruptcy case.

Preparing a bankruptcy case is mostly a matter of gathering documents and filling in the blanks on a standard set of forms. As with all legal documents, an important goal of this exercise is to convey information as clearly and completely as possible. If necessary, the preparer should not hesitate to supplement the answers given with notes indicated by asterisks or otherwise. The annotated forms in Appendix D, *infra*, provide an example of the completed papers, but need not (and should not) be followed verbatim in any particular case. It is reassuring to remember that mistakes made in completing the forms may ordinarily be corrected later without great difficulty by amendment.[1]

In answering the various questions posed in the Official Forms, it is important to have a general understanding of the purpose of those questions. The overall purpose is to give the court, the trustee, and the creditors a full and accurate picture of the debtor's case. Knowing the reason for a question enables the debtor's attorney to ensure that the question is answered in a way that provides the necessary information.

Knowing the purpose of a question is also important in presenting the client's case in the best possible truthful light. For example, in questions of property valuation, estimates on the low side of a possible range of values (often forced-sale value) are usually used to maximize the amount of property that can be claimed within the dollar limits of the exemptions allowed.[2] Similarly, it is often important to give a low estimate of the amount of a claim against the debtor, taking into account all possible defenses and setoffs, if it may not be fully eliminated by the discharge. However, these general rules cannot be applied in every case. In some instances it may be advantageous to give a higher estimate of the value of an encumbrance on a piece of property if the strategy is ultimately to have the trustee decide to abandon the property because it has no equity available for creditors.[3] In other cases, property should be given a higher estimated value to preclude a creditor that is likely to seek relief from the stay from arguing that the debtor has admitted to having no equity in the property.[4]

In every case it should be borne in mind that the trustee and creditors will have an opportunity (of which they may or may not make good use) to examine the client concerning the information given. However, these parties do not usually have a great interest in going over the affairs of the typical consumer debtor with a fine-tooth comb, as they might in the case of a higher-income debtor or business person who is far more likely to have something of significance to hide.

7.1.2 Obtaining the Forms

A few bankruptcy practitioners who do not handle many cases, as well as *pro se* debtors, may make use of bankruptcy forms printed by various commercial suppliers. They are usually available from sellers of legal stationery for about eight to fifteen dollars a set. These preprinted forms are easily obtained and they follow the required format.

However, there are also many inconveniences in using the preprinted forms in an era of computerized word processing. The spaces provided for answers to some questions may be much larger or smaller than necessary in most consumer cases. Moreover, the problem of obtaining the money to pay for the forms from either the client or the office's funds may create more inconvenience in bookkeeping and other ways than it is worth.

For these reasons, offices doing more than one or two bankruptcy cases generally use computer programs as described in the next section of this treatise. For offices which do not currently have ready access to such a program, the simplest alternative is to use the blank Official Forms that are available for download in Adobe Acrobat (PDF) fillable format on the website of the Administrative Office of the U.S. Courts.[5] Using the interactive fillable PDF format, some fields on the forms are automatically populated after information has been typed.

---

1 Fed. R. Bankr. P. 1009.
    See Chapter 8, *infra*, for discussion of amendment procedures.
2 See Chapter 10, *infra*, for a detailed discussion of exemptions.
3 See § 3.5, *supra*, for discussion of abandonment.
4 See § 9.7.3.2, *infra* (discussion of grounds for relief from the automatic stay).
5 The Official Bankruptcy Forms are available at www.uscourts.gov/FormsAndFees/Forms/BankruptcyForms.aspx. Not all of the forms are available in a fillable PDF format.

7.1.3 Computer Programs

It is common for offices that handle significant numbers of bankruptcy cases to use word processing programs, or to purchase special computer programs, that generate bankruptcy forms based on input data. There are a wide range of such programs now on the market and, of course, they vary in cost and quality.

Every office desiring to computerize bankruptcy practice should make its own decision about which program works best for the needs of its clients. Most of the programs are marketed through demonstration versions and it is useful to obtain as many as possible before making a final decision.[6]

There are a number of considerations to keep in mind in selecting the appropriate program. Most importantly, the program must work well with the configuration of computer equipment available in a particular office. Certain programs are designed to work best with particular systems, software or printers, so each office should try to obtain a good match.

In addition all judicial districts permit, and many require, electronic filing of bankruptcy forms, which can be a great convenience, especially for offices located at some distance from the courthouse. Every program is compatible with the standards for electronic filing set by the relevant bankruptcy court clerks' offices, but some have features that may make the process easier in various ways. For example, some programs can automatically incorporate information from credit reports or other downloaded information.

Also importantly, some programs print forms which comply more closely with the Official Forms than others. It is a good idea to obtain a set of completed forms from the contemplated program or to print sample forms from the demonstration version. If they vary significantly from the Official Forms, prior approval for their use should probably be obtained from the clerk of the local bankruptcy court. Similarly, it is important to determine whether the forms generated will meet the requirements of local rules, administrative orders, or community custom. For example, many districts have model chapter 13 plans that practitioners are strongly encouraged to use.

Another consideration, and one which is sometimes more difficult to evaluate, is the degree to which the forms allow entry of complete information. On some programs it is difficult to input anything but the most routine information, to edit the actual forms, or to modify the standard bankruptcy plan, making it difficult to handle complicated cases. A large degree of flexibility is optimal.

A final consideration is whether adequate support will be available from the publisher of the program. The ability to get assistance is often crucial in getting the program to run well. It is sensible to check on the availability of help, including the hours help is available and the number of technical support personnel, before buying any sort of expensive software. The vendor should be asked for references that can be called for their views about the program.

7.1.4 Electronic Filing of Documents

All of the bankruptcy courts have adopted procedures and systems to permit the electronic filing of documents.[7] In some districts electronic filing is required of all bankruptcy attorneys. It is also possible to access any electronically filed document (and sometimes other documents) over the Internet and thereby obtain a copy of the document without a trip to the bankruptcy court or paying for copies. (There is, however, usually a charge of ten cents a page for accessing documents over the court's PACER system, which may be waived for indigent clients.) Unfortunately, there are some variations in the procedures that the various courts are adopting, which are generally set forth in local rules. However, all of the courts appear to require that the documents be filed in Adobe Acrobat's PDF format,[8] and

---

6 Most of the leading software providers exhibit their products and provide demonstrations at national consumer bankruptcy conferences, such as those of the National Association of Consumer Bankruptcy Attorneys.

7 Information on courts that have adopted electronic filing can be obtained from the local courts' websites, accessible through www.uscourts.gov or from the PACER website at http://pacer.psc.uscourts.gov.

8 An Adobe Acrobat (PDF) file is a kind of electronic photograph of the original file. First, the attorney prepares the bankruptcy petition and schedules using their software program: for example, Microsoft Word, or a specialized bankruptcy program. When finished, the file must be converted into Acrobat, if not created in an interactive fillable PDF format. The Acrobat PDF file is then sent to the bankruptcy court via the Internet.

The principal method of creating PDF files is to use the "full" Adobe Acrobat program (not the free Acrobat Reader). When the full Adobe Acrobat program is installed on a computer, any file can be duplicated as an Acrobat (PDF) file. Besides using Adobe Acrobat to create the PDF version, there are other methods. Recent versions of Microsoft Word have an internal PDF generator. The specialized bankruptcy programs typically include a PDF converter to save the petition as a PDF document for you. However, most users will likely find that they still need to use Adobe Acrobat or other software for pleadings not covered by the bankruptcy forms software, such as custom motions, complaints, and adversary proceedings. Free and low-cost third party (non-Adobe) PDF converters may be found on the Internet. For example, see www.primopdf.com for a free PDF print driver which creates Acrobat PDF files. For best quality on screen however, the full Adobe Acrobat program is better than the free converters.

Scanning is another method of creating a PDF file, by using Adobe Acrobat or some other software program. However, the attorney generally needs a scanner only to make PDF versions of exhibits which exist only on paper, such as a mortgage or a contract. In general, bankruptcy petitions and pleadings are not scanned; the PDF copies are created using Adobe Acrobat software (or some third-party PDF generator). In the most progressive bankruptcy courts, nothing in the initial bankruptcy filings needs to be scanned, and the court accepts signatures in the format of "S/Attorney Signature" and "S/Debtor Signature" as a certification that the original document was signed. However, other courts require the page with the debtor's signature to be scanned. This is a matter to be checked in the local bankruptcy rules, available at www.uscourts.gov. *See In re* IFC Credit Corp., 663 F.3d 315 (7th Cir. 2011) (when petition of corporation lacked signature of attorney that was necessary, defect could be remedied by amendment and petition was not a nullity); *In re* Patasnik, 425 B.R. 916 (Bankr. S.D.

attorneys who file documents (or at least documents requiring a filing fee) must provide a credit card to which filing fees may be charged.[9]

There are obvious advantages to electronic filing of documents for virtually all attorneys who file any significant number of bankruptcy cases, particularly those whose offices are not near the courthouse. Much travel time and expense can be saved by avoiding trips to the courthouse to file documents or by avoiding fees of couriers who perform that task. Emergency cases or other documents can be filed from any location with Internet access, even when the clerk's office is not open.

All of the major commercial bankruptcy software programs now may be used to file documents electronically. For most offices, electronic filing requires some investment in computer hardware or software compatible with the courts' systems. Standard office procedures are also necessary to deal with receipt of electronic notices, accounting for credit card payments to the court, and storage of electronic files.

7.2 The Papers Necessary to Start a Case

7.2.1 Forms Usually Filed

Normally, a bankruptcy case is started by filing several documents at once. In a chapter 7 case the documents usually required are:

- The petition, which is the pleading that actually starts the case;
- A statement of the debtor's Social Security number;
- A list of names and addresses for all creditors and certain other entities (sometimes known as the mailing "matrix");[10]
- A certificate from an approved counseling agency that the debtor received a credit counseling briefing;
- The debtor's statement of financial affairs and schedules; and
- A statement of current monthly income.

Other documents which may be required include:

- An application to waive the filing fee or to pay it in installments;
- The means test calculation (included as a part of the statement of current monthly income);
- A statement of intention with respect to personal property securing consumer debts or personal property leases;
- Any payment advices the debtor received in the sixty days before filing the petition; and
- A disclosure of attorney fees paid or promised.[11]

In a chapter 13 case, the documents normally required are quite similar:

- The petition;
- A statement of the debtor's Social Security number;
- A list of names and addresses for all creditors and certain other entities;
- A certificate from an approved counseling agency that the debtor received a credit counseling briefing;
- The debtor's statement of financial affairs and schedules; and
- A statement of current monthly income and commitment period.

Other documents which may be required include:

- An application to pay the filing fee in installments;
- A calculation of disposable income (included on the same form as the statement of current monthly income);
- Any payment advices the debtor received in the sixty days before filing the petition;
- The chapter 13 plan; and
- The attorney fee disclosure.[12]

The documents filed in a chapter 13 case are the same as those that are filed in a chapter 7 case, with the exception that a statement of intention is not filed in a chapter 13 case and a chapter 13 plan is not filed in a chapter 7 case.

In addition, local rules may require one or two other papers. Also commonly mandated is a form summarizing the plan in a chapter 13 case. Some courts require a certification that no

---

Fla. 2010) (neither sanctions nor dismissal of case were warranted when attorney instructed office to file case in sincere, but incorrect, belief that debtors had signed documents and had promptly rectified the error); *In re* Wenk, 296 B.R. 719 (Bankr. E.D. Va. 2002) (attorney sanctioned for electronically filing petition with debtor's electronic signature when debtor had not signed petition).

9 Exceptions to this rule are sometimes made for legal services or pro bono programs that do not have a credit card available.

10 The failure to properly list a creditor's address on such a form could lead to a debt being excepted from discharge as not "duly scheduled." *In re* Adams, 734 F.2d 1094 (5th Cir. 1984). See § 15.4.3.3, *infra*, for further discussion of this exception to discharge.

11 11 U.S.C. § 521(a)(1),(2); Fed. R. Bankr P. 1007(b), (c), (f).
 Fed. R. Bankr. P. 2016(b) requires the fee disclosure to be filed within fourteen days after the filing of the petition unless the court orders otherwise. The easiest practice is probably to file it with the schedules and statement of affairs at the outset of the case. Section 521(a)(1)(B)(iii) also requires a certification that the debtor has received the disclosures under section 342(b), but such a certification is included in the petition form. Similarly, the statement of monthly net income and statement regarding anticipated increases in income or expenses required by section 521(a)(1)(B)(v) and (vi) are included in Schedules I and J. However, Bankruptcy Rule 1007(b)(1)(F) may require filing a separate "record" of an interest in education savings, even though such an interest is listed on Schedule B.

12 Fed. R. Bankr. P. 1007(b), (c), (f).
 Section 521(a)(1)(B)(iii) also requires a certification that the debtor has received disclosures under section 342(b), but such a certification is included in the petition form. Similarly, the statement of monthly net income and statement regarding anticipated increases in income or expenses required by section 521(a)(1)(B)(v) and (vi) are included in Schedules I and J. However, Bankruptcy Rule 1007(b)(1)(F) may require filing a separate "record" of an interest in education savings, even though such an interest is listed on Schedule B.

payment advices exist if that is the case,[13] or a certification in a chapter 13 case that all required tax returns for the prior four tax years have been filed by the debtor.[14]

The Bankruptcy Rules do not state the number of copies of the petition, statements, and schedules to be filed, leaving that matter to local rules. Because most cases are now filed electronically, this issue rarely arises. For cases that are still filed on paper, the rules require only one copy of the chapter 13 plan and fee disclosure statement,[15] though local rules may impose additional requirements. Usually, again possibly excepting documents required by local rule, all of the paper forms may be filed in a single package. Many courts require two holes to be punched at the top of paper forms. However, local practices regarding these procedures vary and should be checked. In any event, the clerk is not permitted to reject the filing of any paper because it is not presented in proper form.[16] Regardless of how the case is filed, the court may require that a defective filing be corrected.

Lastly, the initial filing must be accompanied by a filing fee of $245 for chapter 7 or $235 for chapter 13, plus a $46 noticing fee. The total filing fee in chapter 13 cases is thus $281. In addition, in chapter 7 cases, the debtor must also pay an extra $15 to be used for trustee compensation, raising the total filing fee in chapter 7 cases to $306. If the debtor cannot pay all of these fees at the time of filing, she may instead file an application requesting permission to pay the filing fee in installments. This application is normally granted as a matter of course.[17] If filed in hard copy, only one copy of the application and a proposed order need be filed.[18]

If a chapter 7 debtor's income is below 150% of the poverty level and the debtor is unable to pay the filing fee even in installments, the debtor may file an application for a waiver of the fee.[19] The application, Official Form 3B,[20] must be completed and submitted with the petition. If the schedules are also submitted with the petition, designated portions of Form 3B containing duplicative information need not be completed.

Prior to the 2005 amendments, some courts waived the noticing fee upon the filing of an affidavit of indigency and a request for a waiver because the fees are imposed under 28 U.S.C. § 1930(b).[21] Such a waiver should no longer be necessary in chapter 7 cases, because all filing fees may be waived, but requests for a waiver may still occasionally be appropriate in chapter 13 cases.

7.2.2 The Emergency Bankruptcy, or How to Prepare a Bankruptcy Case in Under One Hour

It is sometimes necessary to file bankruptcy immediately in order to utilize the automatic stay[22] to stop some possibly imminent harm from befalling a client. In such cases, it is often impossible to gather the necessary information and prepare all of the required papers quickly enough.

Fortunately, the Bankruptcy Rules provide a solution for this problem. They allow a debtor to commence a case by filing only the three-page bankruptcy petition (and attached Exhibit D, which includes the debtor's statement of compliance with the credit counseling briefing requirement, and may request a deferral of the briefing or be accompanied by a motion for waiver of the briefing requirement),[23] a list of names and addresses for all creditors and certain other entities,[24] and a statement of the debtor's Social Security number.[25] If filed on paper, the number of copies of these forms required is the same as in a bankruptcy in which all the forms are filed together. The filing must also include the filing fee, an application for waiver of the fee (available only in chapter 7), or an application to pay the fee in installments.

After these few documents are filed, the rules require that the remainder of the usual forms be filed within fourteen days.[26]

---

13 See Form 13, Appx. G.3, infra.
14 See § 8.3.14, infra.
15 Fed. R. Bankr. P. 3015, 2016.
16 Fed. R. Bankr. P. 5005(a).
17 Fed. R. Bankr. P. 1006(b).
   Note that all installments of the filing fee must be paid in full before debtor's counsel may receive any further payments from the debtor or chapter 13 trustee for services rendered in the case. Fed. R. Bankr. P. 1006(b)(3). In a few districts, contrary to the express language of the rule, courts require part of the filing fee to be paid when a petition is filed with an application to pay the fee in installments. Appellate challenges to such practices should be considered.
18 Official Form 3A. See Appx. D, infra.
19 28 U.S.C. § 1930(f). See § 14.6, infra.
20 See Appendix D, infra, for a completed sample of this form.
21 See § 14.6, infra, and Form 17, Appendix G.3, infra, for an application to waive administrative fees.
22 See Chapter 9, infra, for discussion of the automatic stay.
23 If the debtor does not request a deferral or waiver of the required briefing, the debtor must also file a certificate from the credit counseling agency that provided the debtor the required briefing, but it may be filed within fourteen days after the petition date if it is not filed with the petition. Fed. R. Bankr. P. 1007(c).
   Although the statute provides for deferral of the prebankruptcy credit counseling briefing in limited circumstances, as discussed in § 3.2.1.4, supra, it is always preferable for the client to complete the briefing before filing. The briefing can usually be obtained almost instantly over the telephone or on the Internet.
24 Fed. R. Bankr. P. 1007(a)(1). An extension of time for the filing of the list may be granted only on motion for cause shown. Fed. R. Bankr. P. 1007(a)(5).
   The failure to properly list a creditor's address on such a form could lead to a debt being excepted from discharge as not "duly scheduled." In re Adams, 734 F.2d 1094 (5th Cir. 1984). See § 15.4.3.3, infra, for further discussion of this exception to discharge.
25 Fed. R. Bankr. P. 1007(a), (c), (f), 3015. See also Appx. E, infra.
   This right to file minimal documentation is not meant to be used routinely for debtors when there is no emergency. A number of bankruptcy courts have indicated their displeasure with attorneys who regularly fail to file the complete package of documents at the outset of the case, especially when the later documents are not promptly filed. See, e.g., In re Waddell, 21 B.R. 450 (Bankr. N.D. Ga. 1982).
26 Fed. R. Bankr. P. 1007(c), 3015.
   The statement of intentions with regard to property securing

Preparing and Filing the Papers § 7.3.2

The court may further extend the deadline for all of the forms to be filed upon application, for cause shown.[27]

If the remaining required forms are not filed, the case is usually dismissed.[28] Dismissal may be acceptable to the debtor, if bankruptcy later proves to be the wrong course of action,[29] as the dismissal is normally without prejudice.[30] However, a dismissal may affect the availability of the automatic stay in a later case,[31] and it cannot be assumed that the case will always be dismissed. A chapter 13 case may be involuntarily converted by the court to chapter 7.[32] And, if creditors or the trustee object to dismissal of a chapter 7 case, the court may require the case to proceed, possibly affording creditors the equivalent of an involuntary bankruptcy case without requiring them to satisfy the normal prerequisites for such a proceeding.[33]

7.2.3 Timing the Filing of Multiple Cases

Offices filing several bankruptcies during a short time period may wish to check with the clerk of the bankruptcy court as to how the date of filing affects the dates of later proceedings, such as the section 341 meeting of creditors. Especially when the site of the meeting is located at some distance from the office, it is obviously a more efficient use of resources to have more than one meeting scheduled for a single date. Such scheduling can often be accomplished by filing several bankruptcy cases simultaneously. Even if the cases cannot be filed together, however, it is worthwhile to check with the court, the trustee, or the United States trustee on the possibility of having several meetings scheduled for the same day. (Such inquiry must be made promptly, however, because the notice of the meeting of creditors is usually sent out shortly after the case is filed.)

---

consumer debts has a somewhat different deadline. *See* § 7.3.11, *infra*. The deadlines may not be strictly enforced in all jurisdictions. *But see In re* Casteel, 85 B.R. 741 (Bankr. W.D. Mich. 1988) (court to strictly enforce deadline prospectively).

27 Fed. R. Bankr. P. 1007(c), 3015.

The rules provide that the application for extension must be made on notice to the United States trustee and the trustee in the case. Fed. R. Bankr. P. 1007(c), 3015.

28 11 U.S.C. § 521(i) provides for "automatic" dismissal if various forms are not filed within forty-five days of the petition. Courts have struggled with what this provision means. *See* § 13.3.2, *infra*. Most courts provide the debtor with some notice that the papers filed are incomplete prior to this deadline, giving the debtor the chance to correct the deficiency.

29 Of course, a case should not be filed if there is no intention of proceeding, because that type of a filing solely for delay would not be in good faith as required by Fed. R. Bankr. P. 9011.

30 11 U.S.C. § 349(a).

But see 11 U.S.C. § 109(g), discussed in § 3.2.1, *supra*, and § 9.7.3.1.5, *infra*, which bars a new case within 180 days after involuntary dismissal for willful failure to appear before the court to prosecute the case. It is doubtful that failure to file papers is a failure to appear before the court. In most cases failure to file papers is also not "willful" within the meaning of the Code.

31 11 U.S.C. § 362(c)(3), (4). *See* Ch. 9, *infra*.

32 11 U.S.C. § 1307(c).

33 *See* § 14.8, *infra*, for discussion of involuntary bankruptcy.

7.3 Forms at the Outset of the Case

7.3.1 Official and Unofficial Forms

Most of the forms filed at the outset of the case are Official Forms promulgated by the Judicial Conference of the United States and are reprinted in Appendix D, *infra*. A few forms, such as the attorney fee disclosure[34] are not officially promulgated, but nevertheless are standardized forms in common use. Those forms are reprinted in Appendix E, *infra*.

The Advisory Committee note to Federal Rule of Bankruptcy Procedure 9009 states that the forms used should substantially comply with the Official Forms. The Introduction and General Instructions for the Official Forms states that a form will be in substantial compliance if it contains the complete substance of the information required by the Official Forms. Thus, for example, typefaces can be changed and the instructions in the forms can be deleted. Of course, when necessary, continuation sheets may be attached to provide complete information.

The instructions state that courts may not reject forms because they are presented in novel or unfamiliar formats.[35] The only requirements other than complete substantive information are that, for forms not filed electronically, the forms be printed on one side only, with two pre-punched holes at the top of the document and an adequate top margin so that the caption and text are not obscured. In many localities, the requirement of pre-punched holes is waived. Local practice should be checked.

In filling out the forms, it is important to check boxes which state "none," if "none" is the appropriate answer. Additionally, if the answer to a question is "none" or "not applicable" it is necessary to so indicate. However, when multiple choices are contained in the Official Form, it is acceptable to file a form which contains only the choice selected.

It is also acceptable, especially in emergency situations, to file legible handwritten forms or to indicate that required information is the most complete available and that it will be supplemented by amendment or otherwise.[36]

All of the official bankruptcy forms include the information which must be provided by non-attorney bankruptcy petition preparers under Bankruptcy Code section 110. The failure to provide this information will lead to serious sanctions against a petition preparer.[37]

7.3.2 The Bankruptcy Petition (Official Form 1)

The actual bankruptcy petition, which is the document that officially begins a case, is a three-page form with boxes for

---

34 *See* § 7.3.13, *infra*.
35 *But see In re* Orrison, 343 B.R. 906 (Bankr. N.D. Ind. 2006) (unique forms developed by debtor's attorney deviated too substantially from official forms and could not be used).
36 Fed. R. Bankr. P. 1009 allows amendments to be made as a matter of course, at any time before the case is closed. *See* § 8.3.2, *infra*.
37 11 U.S.C. § 110. *See* § 16.6, *infra*.

information to be filled in as appropriate and an attached Exhibit D.[38] Its content is prescribed by the Official Forms.[39]

The petition must include all names, including fictitious or trade names, that the debtor has used over the previous eight years and the last four digits of the debtor's Social Security number.[40] In a similar vein, the petition requests basic information about the chapter chosen by the debtor, the type of case being filed (individual, joint, partnership, corporate, or otherwise), an estimate of the the number of creditors and the amount of the debtor's assets and liabilities, an estimate as to whether funds will be available for distribution to unsecured creditors, the nature of the debts (whether primarily consumer or business debts), bankruptcy cases filed by the same debtor within the prior eight years,[41] and pending related[42] cases. It sets forth that the debtor(s) meets the basic venue[43] and jurisdictional prerequisites for the chapter selected. The debtor must certify on Exhibit D, which is attached to the petition, that she has obtained consumer credit counseling from an approved agency within 180 days before the petition or that the debtor is seeking a deferral or waiver of such counseling.[44] The debtor must also state whether the full filing fee will be paid when the petition is filed or whether an application to waive the filing fee or to pay it in installments will be filed.[45] The averments of the petition must be verified by the debtor's signature, under penalty of perjury.[46]

The petition in every consumer chapter 7 case must also contain an averment by the debtor that she is aware of and understands the choice available between relief under chapter 7, chapter 11, chapter 12, and chapter 13 of the Code. This averment is contained in the box in which the debtor signs the petition.

In addition, to reinforce the importance of an informed choice of chapter, every consumer chapter 7 bankruptcy petition must contain a separately signed declaration by the debtor's attorney that she has explained the relief available under chapters 7, 11, 12, and 13.[47] The same declaration includes a certification that the attorney has given the debtor the disclosures required by section 342(b). In addition, the petition contains language below the attorney signature line informing the debtor's attorney that in a case in which section 707(b)(4)(D) is applicable, the attorney's signature is a certification that "the attorney has no knowledge after an inquiry that the information in the schedules is incorrect."[48]

If, and only if, the debtor is a residential tenant against whom a judgment for possession has been obtained, the debtor must give the name and address of the landlord holding the judgment and indicate whether the debtor asserts a right to cure the monetary default leading to the judgment and whether the debtor is depositing with the court any rent that becomes due within thirty days.[49]

Lastly, the debtor must state on the petition whether or not she owns or possesses property that poses or has been alleged to pose an imminent threat of identifiable harm to public health or safety. If the debtor does own or possess such property, the possible harms must be identified on Exhibit C to the petition in order to notify the trustee, who might be responsible for the property, and other parties who might be affected.[50]

The petition must be filed with the clerk of the bankruptcy court, who transmits a copy to the United States trustee.[51] Except for occasional problems concerning venue, or whether a particular debtor is eligible for chapter 13, the petition itself rarely gives rise to any issue in a case. Even with respect to the latter problem, the court normally refers to the schedules rather than to the petition in deciding the issue.

7.3.3 Statement of Social Security Number (Official Form 21)

The debtor must submit to the clerk, with the petition, a verified statement that sets forth the debtor's full Social Security number or states that the debtor does not have a Social Security number.[52] This statement is not made a part of the official court file, so the debtor's Social Security number is not

---

38 Exhibit A pertains to certain business cases, so is not included in individual cases. Exhibit B is included in the three-page petition, and Exhibit C is attached only if the debtor has potentially hazardous property. Exhibits B and C are discussed below.
39 Official Form 1.
   A copy of this form is included in Appendix D, *infra*, as well as in interactive fillable Adobe Acrobat (PDF) format on this treatise's companion website.
40 Fed. R. Bankr. P. 1005.
41 This information is requested because a discharge in a prior case could bar a discharge in the present case. 11 U.S.C. §§ 727(a)(8), 727(a)(9), 1328(f). See §§ 15.2.2.8, 15.2.2.9, *infra*. Additionally, dismissal of the prior case within 180 days of the present case may render the debtor ineligible for relief. 11 U.S.C. § 109(g). See § 3.2.1, *supra*; § 9.7.3.1.5, *infra*.
42 A case is defined as related if filed by a spouse, partner, or affiliate of the debtor.
43 See Chapter 14, *infra*, for discussion of venue. Venue problems occur most often with debtors who have recently moved or who are employed in a judicial district other than that in which they reside.
44 If the debtor is not seeking a deferral or waiver of the counseling, the debtor must attach to Exhibit D a certificate from the credit counseling agency that provided the debtor's briefing and a copy of any debt repayment plan, if developed, or file those documents within fourteen days after filing the petition. Fed. R. Bankr. P. 1007(b)(3), (c).
45 See §§ 7.3.13.3, 7.3.13.4, 14.6, *infra*.
46 See *In re* Harrison, 158 B.R. 246 (Bankr. M.D. Fla. 1993) (petition on which debtor's name was signed by another, purportedly based upon later-submitted power of attorney, was a nullity, because there was no indication on petition that it was signed based on power of attorney and there were no exigent circumstances making it impossible for debtor to sign his own petition).

47 This declaration is incorporated into Official Form 1 in Exhibit B. See Appx. D, *infra*.
48 See § 16.7.2, *infra*.
49 This information relates to whether the automatic stay exception for certain eviction proceedings is applicable. See § 9.4.6.6, *infra*.
50 This declaration is incorporated into Official Form 1, and a form for Exhibit C, if necessary, is part of that Official Form. See Appx. D, *infra*.
51 Fed. R. Bankr. P. 1002.
52 Fed. R. Bankr. P. 1007(f).

available to the general public or over the Internet. However, the Social Security number is included in the notice of the section 341(a) creditors meeting that is mailed to creditors.[53]

7.3.4 List of Creditors, Codebtors, and Parties to Executory Contracts

Federal Rule of Bankruptcy Procedure 1007(a)(1) requires each debtor to file a list of all creditors listed on Schedules D, E, and F of Official Form 6, as well as parties to executory contracts and unexpired leases listed on Schedule G, and codebtors listed on Schedule H of the same official form.[54] This list must be filed with the petition in every case.[55] Some districts require particular formatting of the list, which is often called the "mailing matrix."[56]

7.3.5 Credit Counseling Statement, Certificate from Counseling Agency, and Debt Management Plan (If Any)

Section 521(b) of the Code requires an individual debtor to file a certificate from an approved credit counseling agency stating that the debtor has received the briefing required by section 109(h).[57] If that agency developed a debt management plan for the debtor, the debt management plan must be filed as well. The certificate and the debt management plan, if any, should be attached to the debtor's statement of compliance with the credit counseling requirement, which is Exhibit D to the petition.[58] If these documents are not attached to Exhibit D and filed with the petition, Bankruptcy Rule 1007(c) requires that they be filed within fourteen days after the petition is filed.

7.3.6 Notice of Chapters Under Which Relief Is Available and Other Information

Section 342(b) of the Code requires the clerk of the bankruptcy court to give each consumer debtor a notice describing each chapter under which such individual may proceed, the services of credit counseling agencies, and the possible consequences of bankruptcy fraud prior to the filing of the petition. To meet this requirement, some courts require the debtor to submit a certification that this notice was received. However, somewhat confusingly, section 521(a)(1)(B)(iii) requires the debtor's attorney or bankruptcy petition preparer to file a certification that the attorney or petition preparer delivered the notice to the debtor. This certification is part of Exhibit B in Official Form 1, the bankruptcy petition.

Based upon these provisions, the debtor's attorney should deliver the notice to the debtor and sign the certification to comply with section 521(a)(1)(B)(iii).[59] The Administrative Office of United States Courts has promulgated a form of notice, so it is safest simply to use that form.[60]

In any event, the failure to file or receive the acknowledgment of notice, even in those places where it is still required, does not invalidate a bankruptcy petition.[61] However, failure to file the required certification could lead to dismissal of the case under section 521(i), unless the court orders that the filing is excused.[62]

7.3.7 The Bankruptcy Schedules (Official Form 6)

7.3.7.1 Overview

Each individual debtor who files a bankruptcy case, under any chapter, must submit schedules A through J (Official Form 6). The main purpose of these schedules is to give an exact picture of the debtor's assets, liabilities, and budget, as of the date of filing, in a uniform manner that facilitates administration of the case. This section describes generally how the schedules are to be completed, but local rules may impose additional requirements, such as a requirement to alphabetize creditors.

7.3.7.2 Schedules A, B, and C: The Debtor's Property

7.3.7.2.1 Schedule A—real property

Schedule A is the list of the debtor's real property. In this schedule the debtor must list all legal, equitable, and future interests in real property. As with all the schedules, if the debtor has no such interests, the schedule should state "none." Lease-

---

The statement should be made on Official Form 21, reprinted in Appendix D, *infra*.
53 Fed. R. Bankr. P. 2002(a)(1).
54 Although the debtor's Schedules D, E, and F arguably satisfy the requirement to file a "list of creditors" found in section 521(a)(1)(A), some courts have held that the statute imposes a separate document requirement consistent with Bankruptcy Rule 1007(a)(1). *See In re* Wilcox, 463 B.R. 143 (B.A.P. 10th Cir. 2011) (debtor's failure to file separate list of creditors resulted in automatic dismissal of case under § 521(i); *In re* Young, 2006 WL 3524482 (Bankr. S.D. Tex. Dec. 6, 2006) (same). Moreover, Fed. R. Bankr. P. 1007(a)(1) provides that the list should include all entities included on debtor's Schedules D, E, F, G and H.
55 An extension of time for the filing of the list may be granted only on motion for cause shown. Fed. R. Bankr. P. 1007(a)(5).
56 *See* Fed. R. Bankr. P. 1007 advisory committee's note (2005).
57 The credit counseling briefing requirement is discussed in detail in § 3.2.1.4, *supra*.
58 *See* Official Form 1 (reprinted in Appx. D, *infra*).

59 To the extent not covered by the section 342(b)(1) notice, and within three days of first providing bankruptcy assistance to the debtor, section 527(a)(2) requires a debt relief agency to also provide a notice to the debtor containing various other disclosures about the bankruptcy process. *See* Ch. 16, *infra*. Attorneys may want to provide the notices required by these sections to the debtor at the same time. See sample notice, Form 11, Appx. G.3, *infra*.
60 The form is reprinted in Appx. E.2, *infra*.
61 *See In re* Bryant, 51 B.R. 729 (Bankr. N.D. Miss. 1985).
62 See Chapter 13, *infra*, for discussion of involuntary dismissal of cases.

hold interests must be listed separately in Schedule G.[63] If the debtor's interest in a particular property is other than a full possessory interest in fee simple (as in the case, for example, co-ownership or ownership of a life estate or the beneficial interest in property held in trust), a careful description of the debtor's actual interest should be provided.[64] Similarly, if there are limits on the debtor's access to the property (as, for example, in some divorce agreements), the nature of the limitation should be described. The question may arise whether a mobile or manufactured home should be listed as real property on this schedule or as personal property on Schedule B. This decision will depend upon applicable state law and, in some cases, whether the debtor has taken steps under state law to convert the interest to real property.[65]

It is more important to list accurately the nature of the interest, than to fit it into the available space. Footnotes or supplemental pages should be supplied when necessary.

If the debtor is married, the schedule must indicate whether the property is owned by the husband, the wife, jointly, or as community property, regardless of whether the petition is filed jointly. If the property is owned jointly, whether or not by spouses, the box describing the nature of the debtor's interest should so indicate and an appropriate adjustment reflecting the extent of the debtor's ownership interest should be made to the value.

The value of the property interest should be given without deduction for any secured debts, such as mortgages, which are listed in the last column and described more fully in Schedule D. As noted earlier,[66] value should be listed at the amount most helpful to the debtor's case that can truthfully be given. Usually, if the property is to be claimed as exempt or if it may be worth less than the amount of any liens affecting it, the best valuation will be on the low side of the possible range. If the property is likely to be the subject of a motion for relief from stay, a higher choice may be preferable. If the value seems to be above the exemption amount, it may be appropriate to give a value that takes into account liquidation costs, such as a broker commission, trustee fees, trustee's professionals' fees, transfer taxes, and the interest and escrow portions of the mortgage payments that would not be made while the house is awaiting sale. If such items are deducted, that fact should be noted on the schedules to avoid any confusion.

Sometimes, there may be uncertainty as to how to estimate the value of one spouse's undivided and unalienable interest in certain types of joint property which cannot be sold without the consent of both spouses. In such cases, as the trustee may have a right to partition the property,[67] it is probably best to indicate the value of a one-half ownership as one-half the total value of the property, but with a note explaining that the debtor could not sell his or her share for that amount.[68] The same approach is appropriate for other interests in jointly held property when the joint owner is not a debtor.[69] Similarly, if the debtor has a life estate or other non-fee-simple interest in the property, the value assigned should account for the limited nature of the interest.[70]

Lastly, courts vary regarding the specificity they demand in the description of real property. Usually, the address and a brief description are sufficient. Courts in some districts, however, may require a full legal description including the metes and bounds from the deed.

7.3.7.2.2 Schedule B—personal property

Schedule B is a list of the debtor's personal property. Schedule B should contain a list of all of the debtor's interests in personal property together with a description and the location of the property. In addition to tangible possessions, all other types of interests should be set out in this schedule, including causes of action, eligibility for government grants such as energy assistance, security deposits with landlords or utilities, support or alimony owed to the debtor, education savings accounts, earned income tax credits, retroactive Social Security awards, and so forth.[71] Property the debtor is purchasing under a rent-to-own agreement should also be listed if the debtor wants to treat the rent-to-own agreement as a credit sale rather than an executory contract.[72] If a debtor has only a nominal interest in an asset, such as the bank account of an elderly relative for which the debtor is a convenience co-signer, that interest should be disclosed with an explanatory note. Because of the potential consequences of failing to list property in the

---

63 See § 7.3.7.4, infra.
64 The Internal Revenue Service produces a table for valuation of life estates in its Publication 1459, available at www.irs.gov. A review of some of the unusual types of property interests which may come into the debtor's estate is provided in § 2.5, supra. Frequently overlooked property interests are discussed in § 5.3.3.2, supra.
65 For a discussion of these state conversion statutes, see National Consumer Law Center, Foreclosures § 12.2.3 (4th ed. 2012).
66 See § 7.1.1, supra.
67 11 U.S.C. § 363(h).
   Under section 363(h), the appropriate inquiry is whether the benefit to the estate accruing from sale of the property would outweigh the detriment to the co-owner occurring due to partition. Courts may apply a variety of factors in making such a determination. Compare, e.g., In re McCoy, 92 B.R. 750 (Bankr. N.D. Ohio 1988) (partition refused because of psychological and emotional stress on mentally handicapped co-owner); In re Coombs, 86 B.R. 314 (Bankr. D. Mass. 1988) (partition denied on ground of psychological stress to handicapped co-owner); In re Ray, 73 B.R. 544 (Bankr. M.D. Ga. 1987) (partition refused) with In re Vassilowitch, 72 B.R. 803 (Bankr. D. Mass. 1987) (partition authorized). See § 2.5, supra.
68 See Appendix D, infra, for an example of completed Schedules.
69 The co-owners, however, may lack standing to object to the disposition of the debtor's interest in the jointly held property even if it is liquidated and sold without their knowledge to a third party. See In re Globe Inv. & Loan Co., 867 F.2d 556 (9th Cir. 1989).
70 Actuarial tables found in Internal Revenue Service Pub. 1459 may be used for this purpose.
71 A review of some of the less common types of property interests which may come into the debtor's estate is provided in § 2.5, supra. Frequently overlooked property interests are discussed in § 5.3.3.2, supra.
72 See § 11.8, infra.

Preparing and Filing the Papers § 7.3.7.2.2

schedules,[73] it is always better to be over-inclusive, rather than under-inclusive. It is especially important to list all claims or causes of action the debtor may have so that the debtor is not prevented from pursuing them after bankruptcy under the doctrine of judicial estoppel.[74] And debtors who are entitled to tax refunds should be sure to list that entitlement on Schedule B. If the refund cannot be claimed as fully exempt, and it is not practical to delay the case until after the refund is received, the debtor should be instructed not to spend the refund, because the trustee may demand it.[75]

Although the categories of property set out in schedule B are quite detailed, it is not critical to list each piece of property in the right category as long as it is listed somewhere. Note that the instructions also require that an "x" be placed in any category for which the debtor has no property and that, for married debtors, the property be listed as that of the husband, or wife, or as joint or community property.

Once more, there is considerable variation among courts as to the degree of specificity they require in descriptions of property. In view of the small values involved, some might allow low-income debtors to group property broadly in categories such as "used clothing" or "assorted household goods, each item worth under $550." Others require much more specific lists. One frequently used compromise is to list major appliances and furniture, with the latter designated more or less by room, for example, "2 bedroom sets," "kitchen set," and so forth.[76] It is normally a good idea also to include a catchall of "miscellaneous household goods," to cover all of the other items with values too small to warrant individual listings.

As for valuation, there is quite a bit of leeway. Usually, the value given takes into account the proposed method of liquidation by distress sale,[77] without deduction for liens or exemptions.[78] A good way to convey this concept to clients is to ask them for the "tag sale" or "garage sale" value of specific items. In completing this schedule it is important to bear in mind the very low sale value of most used furniture and appliances. Because of this low value, the trustee will have little interest in the personal property of consumer clients, except perhaps for a few more valuable items.

Some categories of property present more tricky problems of valuation. The value of a cause of action, for example, should be discounted for the likelihood of success and ultimate ability to collect any judgment.[79] These considerations should be explained by a short note. Sometimes a similar note can explicate a seemingly low valuation on other property. For example, a relatively new car given a low value might be described as "inoperable, 120,000 miles" if those were the facts. In every case, of course, the trustee and creditors will have an opportunity to demand more detail later. Amendments to the schedule are also possible.[80] Therefore, the consequences of an innocently imperfect description of assets are not grave.

Alternatively, if the value of property is truly unknown, it is often best to simply state the value as "unknown," leaving it to the trustee and creditors to assess the value on their own. This treatment of a cause of action has the advantage of ensuring the debtor will not be accused of undervaluing it, and has been deemed sufficient by the Supreme Court.[81]

---

73 In egregious cases of omitted assets, criminal prosecution is possible. 18 U.S.C. § 152. In addition, counsel may be sanctioned. *See* Orton v. Hoffman (*In re* Kayne), 453 B.R. 372 (B.A.P. 9th Cir. 2011) (sanctions under Fed. R. Bankr. P 9011 and § 707(b)(4)(D)). Similarly, an exemption may be denied if the debtor conceals assets. *In re* Yonikus, 996 F.2d 866 (7th Cir. 1993) (contingent right to receive workers' compensation in the future not disclosed in schedules could not be exempted when court found intentional and bad faith concealment of asset).

Also, failure to schedule property that is not exempted will preclude that property from being deemed abandoned at the close of the case pursuant to 11 U.S.C. § 554(c). *See* Vreugdenhill v. Navistar Int'l Transp. Corp., 950 F.2d 524 (8th Cir. 1991); *In re* Shondel, 950 F.2d 1301 (7th Cir. 1991) (debtor's failure to list liability policy as an asset justified reopening bankruptcy case for benefit of tort liability claimant); Krank v. Utica Mut. Ins. Co., 109 B.R. 668 (E.D. Pa. 1990), *aff'd*, 908 F.2d 962 (3d Cir. 1990) (once cause of action becomes property of the estate, debtor may not bring suit unless that property is abandoned by the trustee). *See* § 3.5.1, *supra*.

74 *See* § 14.3.2.6, *infra*.

75 *See In re* Bailey, 380 B.R. 486 (B.A.P. 6th Cir. 2008) (trustee could demand tax refund from debtor even though debtor no longer had money); § 15.2.2.6, *infra* (discussing possible denial of discharge to debtors who fail to obey orders to turn over tax refunds).

76 Failure to give a description which at least puts the trustee on notice of the likely value of the property (and of the wisdom of further inquiry) may be cause for denying an exemption of property not properly disclosed. Payne v. Wood, 775 F.2d 202 (7th Cir. 1985) (debtors could not exempt insurance proceeds received after destruction of certain property not fairly disclosed in schedules).

77 Section 527(a)(2) has caused some confusion with respect to valuation. It requires a debt relief agency to give assisted persons a notice that "the replacement value of each asset as defined in section 506 must be stated in [the documents filed to commence a case] where requested." This disclosure is not applicable to the schedules for several reasons. First, the document that commences a case is the petition. Second, the replacement value is not "requested" in the schedules. Third, section 506 pertains to replacement value only with respect to personal property securing an allowed claim, and at the time the schedules are filed no claim is likely to have been allowed. It is also unclear whether a notice that debt relief agencies are supposed to give to assisted persons (and is therefore not given to debtors who are not represented by debt relief agencies) could control how property is to be listed on the schedules, especially because other provisions to which the schedules pertain more directly, such as the exemption provisions, speak of fair market value (see 11 U.S.C. § 522(a)(2)), and the primary purpose of the property schedules is to determine whether there is nonexempt property for the trustee to liquidate.

78 Security interests and exemptions should be listed separately in Schedule D and C respectively.

79 *See In re* Polis, 217 F.3d 899 (7th Cir. 2000) (Truth in Lending cause of action was fully exempt because, when discounted for contingency of success, it was within exemption limits).

80 Fed. R. Bankr. P. 1009. *See* § 8.3.2, *infra*.

81 Taylor v. Freeland & Kronz, 503 U.S. 638, 112 S. Ct. 1644, 118 L. Ed. 2d 280 (1992) (cause of action described but valued as "unknown" was sufficient to put trustee on notice of the exemption). *See also In re* Adair, 253 B.R. 85 (B.A.P. 9th Cir. 2000) (debtors had no duty to volunteer information about settlement offer on cause of action listed in schedules and ultimately abandoned by trustee when settlement offer was received after schedules were filed and

As with real estate, it is important to describe the nature of the debtor's interest accurately if it is other than a full ownership interest in fee simple. A legal or beneficial interest in a trust, for example, should be explained with as much detail as possible. Similarly, in a divorce scenario, a non-filing spouse's interest in property under a state law equitable distribution provision should be described. Footnotes to the schedule or supplemental pages should be filed if necessary to provide full and complete information. Some care is also required in valuing property in which the debtor holds an unusual interest. Legal restrictions on use or access to property can lower its value.

Bank accounts and other deposit or investment accounts must also be handled carefully. The debtor is required by Bankruptcy Rule 4002(b)(2), in most cases, to bring to the meeting of creditors copies of statements for such accounts showing their balance on the date of filing. Often debtors can obtain this balance over the Internet, from an automated teller machine (ATM), or by a telephone call, and debtors' attorneys should document the information obtained in this manner for their files in case any questions arise later. The reported balance will not always reflect checks that are paid on the date of filing, but that simply means the scheduled amount could be higher than the statement will later reflect, which should not be a problem. The debtor should be instructed not to make any deposit on the date of filing that could increase the balance above the amount listed. If, for some reason, the debtor cannot obtain the balance on the date the petition is filed, and assuming excess exemptions are available, it is preferable to err on the high side in any estimate of the balance, taking into account checks that may not yet have been deposited by the payees, so that there can be no claim that the debtor understated her assets.[82]

One other question which sometimes arises in connection with Schedule B is how to treat property in which the debtor has an interest, but which does not become property of the bankruptcy estate.[83] An example of this kind of property is the debtor's interest in certain ERISA-qualified pensions.[84] Because Schedule B is a list of all the debtor's property interests and not just those which come into the estate, the best practice is to list the debtor's interest with a notation that it is excluded from the estate, together with a statutory reference. In the case of a pension and most other non-estate property, the appropriate reference will be 11 U.S.C. § 541(c)(2). Often the claim that property is not part of the estate should be coupled with an exemption claim, raised in the alternative in Schedule C.[85]

7.3.7.2.3 Schedule C—property claimed as exempt

Schedule C is the debtor's list of property claimed as exempt. Normally, it is permissible to incorporate by reference much of the listing in Schedules A and B in order to avoid repetition, and most bankruptcy software programs are designed to avoid the need to re-enter the debtor's assets.[86] As always, though, local practice should be checked.

Schedule C must, first of all, state whether the debtor is utilizing the state exemptions or the federal bankruptcy exemptions. (Often, there is no choice because the state has opted out of the federal exemptions.) The debtor must also state on Schedule C, by checking the applicable box, if the debtor claims a homestead exemption in excess of $146,450.[87] Because a detailed explanation of this and other exemption issues follows in a later chapter,[88] only a few other points need be made here regarding completion of this schedule.

Obviously, the goal in completing this schedule is to exempt as much as possible, preferably all of the client's property. In the case of most low-income clients, that is not difficult. If all property cannot be exempted, the debtor should consider exemption planning prior to filing the petition.[89]

Another strategy that is effective, if the debtor has a relatively small amount of property that cannot be exempted, is to claim exemptions in a manner that will discourage the trustee from liquidating any particular item. For example, if the debtor has five valuable household items and a car, with a total value of $2400 over the amount that can be exempted, the debtor may exempt all but $400 in value of each item, assuming the exemptions afford that flexibility, either through a wild card exemption or a total exemption amount for a variety of personal property items. The trustee would then be less likely to liquidate these items than if one item worth $2400 was not exempted.

Similarly, if not all property can be exempted, it is better to leave as nonexempt the property which the trustee is least likely to liquidate, such as a cause of action which would involve litigation expenses, or all or part of a joint interest in real estate. For example, if a debtor using the federal exemptions has an interest in real estate worth $21,625 and $3000 in cash or other liquid assets, the debtor might exempt only $19,625 worth of

---

trustee never sought further information during case).

82 See *In re* Pyatt, 486 F.3d 423 (8th Cir. 2007) (rejecting holdings of some other courts that debtor had to turn over such funds after payees on checks had already cashed them) for the types of issues that can arise when debtor did not take into account outstanding uncashed checks drawn on a bank account. *But see In re* Minter-Higgins, 399 B.R. 34 (N.D. Ind. 2008).

Alternatively, if exemptions are available, the debtor can exempt amounts equal to the unpaid checks. Other cases on this issue are cited in § 5.3.3.2 n.5, *supra*.

83 See § 2.5, *supra*.
84 See § 2.5.2, *supra*.

85 However, if the debtor owes a domestic support obligation, claiming non-estate property as exempt may not be advisable, because the claim could make the property vulnerable to execution after bankruptcy under section 522(c). *See* § 10.5, *infra*.

86 However, any cross reference should be to specific items listed, because a general claim of exemption for "assets of the petitioner" probably does not satisfy the requirements of the statute. *In re* Andermahr, 30 B.R. 532 (B.A.P. 9th Cir. 1983).

87 A claim of exemption in excess of $146,450 could in limited circumstances give rise to an objection based on the homestead limitations in section 522(p) and 522(q). *See* Ch. 10, *infra*.

88 *See* Ch. 10, *infra*.

89 *See* Ch. 6, *supra*.

the real property interest, using the remainder of the exemption for the liquid assets under the wild card provisions of section 522(d)(5).[90] Although a trustee probably would demand the nonexempt cash from the debtor, it is unlikely that he or she would invest the time and expense necessary to liquidate a $2000 interest in real estate.

The items listed in Schedule C should be checked against Schedules A and B to be sure nothing has been inadvertently omitted. For each item, the specific applicable exemption statute should be listed. Most often, the value given in Schedule C for the exemption equals the value given in Schedules A and B, except that lien amounts can and should be deducted. If the federal exemptions are available (and under some state statutes as well), property which would not normally appear to be exempt may be exempted under the "wild card" exemption.[91] When exemptions contain monetary limits, two or more different exemptions that are applicable to the same property can be combined. Therefore, it should be fairly rare to completely omit any property interest from Schedule C unless it is an interest which the trustee is unlikely to liquidate or an interest which the debtor is willing to surrender.

It is also important to exempt property as to which the right of redemption is to be exercised. Otherwise, unless the property is sure to be abandoned, the right to redeem may be jeopardized.[92] Similarly, if property is subject to liens or transfers avoidable under section 522,[93] the property should be claimed as exempt before the avoiding powers are exercised.[94]

There is no need to use exemptions on property the trustee cannot reach, that is, to the extent property is subject to a non-avoidable lien. Only equity in the property over and above the lien need by exempted. For example, if a debtor owns a $50,000 home subject to a $46,000 mortgage, only the debtor's interest—the $4000 equity above the mortgage—need be claimed as exempt. However, the debtor should still exempt the interest, giving its value as nominal, because valuing the exemption at zero may be interpreted as not claiming the exemption.

Finally, the importance of careful attention to Schedule C is underscored by 11 U.S.C. § 522(*l*) which provides that property listed as exempt is exempt unless a party-in-interest objects. As there is a strictly enforced deadline for objecting to exemptions, it is to the debtor's advantage to be certain that all good faith exemptions are listed.[95] Such listing shifts the burden to the trustee and creditors to raise timely objections if any are available.[96]

It is important, in light of a recent Supreme Court decision, to specify that the debtor is exempting the debtor's entire interest in the property listed, that is, the full market value of the debtor's interest in the property.[97] In *Schwab v. Reilly*, the Supreme Court held that a debtor who listed an asset as having a certain dollar value and then exempted that same dollar value had not made clear her intent to exempt the entire asset if it turned out to be worth more than that dollar value. To address this problem, particularly with respect to exemptions that are capped at a specific dollar amount, the Supreme Court provided language that may be used on Schedule C to make absolutely clear the debtor's intent to exempt the entire asset. The debtor should list the exempt value as "full fair market value (FMV)" or "100% of FMV" in the "Value of Claimed Exemption" column on Schedule C.[98]

It should be remembered, however, that Schedule C (and all the debtor's schedules) may be amended as of right at any time before the close of the case so that mistakes and oversights are easily corrected.[99] Amended exemption schedules are then subject to objection for the time period provided in the rules.[100]

7.3.7.3 Schedules D, E, and F: Information About Creditors

7.3.7.3.1 In general

Schedules D, E, and F divide all of the client's liabilities into three categories: those to secured creditors, those to unsecured creditors entitled to priority, and those to unsecured creditors without priority.

In filling out these schedules, it is of critical importance to list the correct name and address of the creditor.[101] If the correct

---

90 See § 10.2.2.6, *infra*.
91 11 U.S.C. § 522(d)(5). See § 10.2.2.6, *infra*.
92 See § 11.5, *infra*, for discussion of right to redeem.
93 See § 10.4, *infra*, for discussion of lien avoidance.
94 Because section 522(h) allows avoidance of liens on property "which the debtor could have exempted," it may not be necessary to list the property as exempt before the lien is avoided under that section. *See* Botkin v. Dupont Cmty. Credit Union, 432 B.R. 230 (W.D. Va. 2010) (section 522(f) refers to property to which debtors would have been entitled), *aff'd*, 650 F.3d 396 (4th Cir. 2011); *In re* Morais, 2009 WL 3054059 (Bankr. D. Mass. Sept. 18, 2009) (same).However, it is safer as a general practice to claim the debtor's interest in the property as exempt, with an explanatory note about planned lien avoidance if appropriate.

95 Fed. R. Bankr. P. 4003(b) provides that, with limited exceptions, objections to exemptions must be made within thirty days of the conclusion of the meeting of creditors unless more time is sought within that period and the court grants the request. *See* § 10.3.3, *infra*.
96 Taylor v. Freeland & Kronz, 503 U.S. 638, 112 S. Ct. 1644, 118 L. Ed. 2d 280 (1992).
97 *See* Schwab v. Reilly, 130 S. Ct. 2652 (2010). *See also* § 10.3.3, *infra*.
98 130 S. Ct. 2652, 2668 (2010). *See In re* Moore, 442 B.R. 865 (Bankr. N.D. Tex. 2010) (overruling trustee's objection to claim of exemption based solely on debtor's use of *Schwab's* "100% of FMV" suggested language). *But see In re* Massey, 465 B.R. 720 (B.A.P. 1st Cir. 2012) (finding debtor's use of "100% of FMV" to be "facially invalid" in case where debtor did not also list a value for the asset).
99 Fed. R. Bankr. P. 1009.
100 Fed R. Bankr. P. 4003(b) allows objections within thirty days after amendment. *See* § 10.3.3, *infra*.
101 If an incorrect address is listed on a filed schedule, the Bankruptcy Rules provide a simple procedure for amending the schedule to correct the error. *See* § 8.3.2, *infra*. The $30 filing fee for an amendment to the filed schedules will not be charged if the debtor amends the schedules to change the name and address of a creditor

name or address is not listed and, consequently, the creditor fails to receive notice, the dischargeability of a debt may be affected.[102] With respect to state and federal government creditors, and local agencies responsible for tax collection, the clerk of the bankruptcy court is required to maintain a register of addresses at which agencies wish to receive notice.[103] Other creditors may also register their addresses with the court pursuant to Code section 342(f) in order to receive notices to be provided by the court in all cases, except if a different address is requested by the creditor for a particular case. The courts then attempt to use matching software to provide notice to the registered address. If an agency has listed its address in that registry, that address should be used, because it provides a safe harbor from any later claims that the wrong address was used.[104] Also, if the debtor knows that a person to be included on a list of creditors or in the schedules is an infant or incompetent person, the debtor should include, in addition, the name, address, and legal relationship of any person who would be served with process in an adversary proceeding brought against the infant or incompetent person in accordance with Federal Rule of Bankruptcy Procedure 7004(b)(2).[105] Normally, this person would be the parent or guardian of the infant or incompetent person. The instructions for the schedules direct that only the initials of a minor child should be given.

The other information, regarding the account number (which is optional, except for the last four digits), the amount of debt, the date incurred,[106] whether there are codebtors, and the consideration for the claim is usually less crucial but, of course, should be answered as accurately as possible. When accurate information is unavailable, the debtor's best estimate is usually sufficient as long as it is made in good faith. In most consumer cases the amount listed in the schedules has little relevance, because if assets are available, they are paid according to the creditor's proof of claim rather than according to the debtor's schedules.[107]

For joint petitions only, the debtor must list whether the debt is owed by the husband, the wife, or as a joint or community debt. The schedule should note the existence of a co-obligor (other than a spouse with whom the debtor has filed jointly) by a check in the appropriate box labeled "codebtor" and by providing the necessary information about the codebtor in Schedule H.[108]

If there is any chance that the amount of a debt will continue to be relevant after bankruptcy (as with secured or nondischargeable debts) or in a claim allowance proceeding in the bankruptcy case,[109] the schedules should not contain an admission of a debt larger than the debtor will later maintain to be due. If the amount of the debt is contingent, unliquidated, or in dispute, that should be noted in the appropriate place. Whether a debt is contingent or unliquidated may be important if the debtor has large debts that could make her ineligible for chapter 13.[110] A debt is usually considered contingent if payment is not yet due and will not become due unless a particular event occurs in the future. An example of a contingent debt is a guarantor's obligation to pay a debt only if the principal obligor does not pay. A debt is unliquidated when the debtor has a legal obligation to pay some amount of money, but the amount has not yet been fixed. An example of an unliquidated debt is an auto accident claim for which the debtor acknowledges liability, but the amount of the liability has not yet been fixed. By listing such debts and having them discharged, the debtor can often avoid having to fight over the details concerning the validity or amount of the debt.

It is always wise to check the column which lists a debt as disputed if there is any doubt about the validity of the debt or the amount the creditor claims due. For example, a debtor who has been contacted by an entity that claims to have purchased a debt should mark any debt to such entity as disputed unless the debtor has been provided proof of the purchase. Noting the debt as disputed should prevent a later claim by the creditor that the schedules constitute an admission by the debtor of the validity or extent of the creditor's claim.[111]

---

or an attorney for a creditor. *See* Judicial Conference of the United States, Bankruptcy Court Miscellaneous Fee Schedule ¶ 4 (reprinted in Appx. C.3, *infra*).

102 11 U.S.C. §§ 523(a)(3), 1328(a), (c). *See* § 15.4.3.3, *infra*.

Dischargeability may be similarly affected by failure to list a correct address in the mailing matrix. *In re* Adams, 734 F.2d 1094 (5th Cir. 1984). *See* § 15.4.3.3, *infra*. Section 342(c)(2) has caused some confusion with respect to listing of addresses. That section is applicable only to "any notice required by [title 11] to be sent by the debtor to [a] creditor." The schedules are not a notice. Similarly, section 342(f) pertains only to notices the court sends, and not the schedules. It may, however, cause the courts' noticing center to send notices to a creditor at a different address than the one listed in the schedules, either in addition to, or instead of, the listed address.

103 *See* Fed. R. Bankr. P. 5003(e).

104 *See* Fed. R. Bankr. P. 5003(e).

105 Fed. R. Bankr. P. 1007(m).

106 For many credit accounts, listing of "charges incurred on various dates" or similar language should be sufficient.

107 There may occasionally be an issue under 11 U.S.C. § 109(e) concerning debt limits for eligibility for chapter 13 to which such estimates are relevant. *See* § 12.2, *infra*. There also may be issues which arise under section 707(b) or section 1325(a)(3), (4), or (b) concerning whether debts are primarily consumer debts, the debtor's purposes in filing, good faith, or the amount which must be paid to unsecured creditors under a chapter 13 plan. *See* §§ 13.4 and 12.3, *infra*, respectively. At most, the amounts listed in Schedule D are evidence of the debtor's belief about what such creditors are owed at the outset of the case. They should not be conclusive proof of the amount of the debt even against the debtor. However, some courts have treated debts scheduled as undisputed as admitted for purposes of claims allowance in chapter 13 cases, even though schedules are not filed for that purpose except in chapter 11 cases pursuant to 11 U.S.C. § 1111(a). *See, e.g., In re* Dove-Nation, 318 B.R. 147 (B.A.P. 8th Cir. 2004); *In re* Cluff, 313 B.R. 323 (Bankr. D. Utah 2004), *aff'd*, 2006 WL 2820005 (D. Utah Sept. 29, 2006); § 14.4.3.5, *infra*.

108 *See* § 7.3.7.5, *infra*.

109 The schedules, however, are not filed for the purposes of claim allowance except in chapter 11 cases. *See* 11 U.S.C. § 1111(a) (not applicable in other chapters); § 14.4.3.5, *infra*.

110 *See* § 12.2.3.2, *infra*, for further discussion of contingent and unliquidated debts.

111 *See* § 14.4.3.5, *infra*.

Because debts that are not listed are sometimes not discharged, it is of obvious importance to list every conceivable claim against the client so that the discharge may be used to maximum advantage. As discussed above in a previous chapter, this may necessitate prompting the client to remember various types and categories of frequently overlooked debts.[112] It may also mean listing debts that appear on a client's credit report, even if the client does not recognize them and they appear to be erroneously reported. There is ordinarily no disadvantage to listing these debts and noting that they are disputed.

7.3.7.3.2 Schedule D—secured debts

Schedule D lists all secured creditors. This schedule should include all creditors that hold liens, even if they are undersecured, and even if their liens can later be avoided by the debtor or trustee.[113] Creditors holding security deposits also should be listed here, as well as creditors holding less noticeable types of security interests, such as those in the refunds of credit insurance. Similarly, banks and other savings institutions with a right of setoff against the debtor's accounts should be considered secured for the amounts in such accounts. (But normally, with good planning, all money will be withdrawn prior to bankruptcy and therefore these creditors will be unsecured.)[114] Again, if the debtor intends to treat a rent-to-own contract as a credit sale of property subject to a security interest, the rent-to-own debt should be included in this schedule.[115] There is a box in the Official Form for the debtor to check if there are no secured creditors at all.

If the debtor disputes whether a claim is secured, it should be listed in Schedule D, along with the fact that the security interest is disputed. Again, as with all of the forms, the goal should be clarity in depicting the client's affairs. As long as clarity is achieved, even errors as to placement in the proper schedule will not be of great importance.

Finally, some care should be taken in Schedule D to identify undersecured creditors, particularly in chapter 13, and to list the amount of the unsecured portion in the appropriate box. These figures may help in a later attempt to determine the creditor's allowed secured claim.[116]

7.3.7.3.3 Schedule E—priority debts

Schedule E lists the different categories of debt that may have priority under the Code. The Official Form has boxes that should be checked to designate the types of priority debt or to note that the debtor has no priority obligations.

In order to complete this schedule, the practitioner must first determine which claims, if any, fall into the priority categories set out in 11 U.S.C. § 507.[117] If the creditor has a lien, the debt should be placed in Schedule D whether or not the creditor would otherwise be entitled to a priority.[118] (If there is neither a lien nor an applicable priority, the debt belongs in Schedule F as unsecured, non-priority.) In some cases, only part of a debt will be entitled to priority status. With respect to each priority debt, the amount entitled to the priority and the amount not entitled to priority should be listed separately in the appropriate column on the schedule. In other words, the non-priority portion of the debt is listed on Schedule E, not Schedule F.

The most common type of priority debt owed by consumer clients is taxes. It should be noted, however, that not all tax claims are entitled to priority, and only those which are at least partially priority claims and also are unsecured should be listed in Schedule E. This determination is especially important because priority tax claims must be paid in full in chapter 13 and they are nondischargeable in chapter 7 and sometimes in chapter 13. If there will be any payments to creditors in the case, it is important to make sure that such nondischargeable tax debts are listed as priority claims, so that they will be paid first.[119] However, if there are no assets in a chapter 7 case, and if there is any doubt as to priority status, the taxes should be listed in Schedule F (unless secured by a lien) so as not to make any admission as to nondischargeability.

Other types of priority debts sometimes found in consumer cases are those for domestic support obligations,[120] wages or consumer deposits, which sometimes exist if the client had a small business, and certain debts incurred through drunk driving. As in the case of taxes, if there is any doubt whether a debt to a spouse or former spouse is in the nature of nondischarge-

---

112 See § 5.3.3.3, supra.
113 See Ch. 10, infra.
114 See § 6.5, supra.
115 See § 11.8, infra.
116 See In re Gabor, 155 B.R. 391 (Bankr. N.D. W. Va. 1993) (claim of creditor holding security interest in debtor's car was treated as totally unsecured under section 506(a) because debtor's wife had absconded with car, debtor had no knowledge of her whereabouts, and therefore estate's interest in the car was worthless); § 11.2, infra.

The same issues also may be relevant to a determination of whether a chapter 13 debtor meets the debt limitations under section 109(e). See § 12.2.3, infra.

117 See § 3.5, supra.
118 11 U.S.C. § 507(a) which defines types of priority debts is applicable only to unsecured claims.
119 It is also important to make sure a timely proof of claim is filed on behalf of the creditor, by the debtor if not by the creditor, because a trustee can pay an unsecured claim in chapter 7 only if a proof of claim has been filed. See § 8.5, infra.
120 There may be issues regarding whether a debt owed is in the nature of alimony, maintenance, or support and thus a domestic support obligation priority debt, or in the nature of a property settlement and therefore not entitled to priority. For discussion of this dichotomy, see § 15.4.3.5, infra. A debtor in a particular case, depending upon the circumstances, may wish to argue that a debt is not a priority debt, but is rather a property settlement (which is a dischargeable general unsecured claim in chapter 13 cases), or that a debt is in the nature of alimony, maintenance, or support, so that it will be accorded priority treatment if assets of the estate are liquidated. See generally Henry J. Sommer & Margaret Dee McGarity, Collier Family Law and the Bankruptcy Code (1992). The treatment of the debt in the debtor's schedules should be consistent with the strategy desired.

able alimony, maintenance, or support,[121] the debtor in a chapter 13 case should claim the debt to be a dischargeable property settlement[122] and list it on Schedule F (unless it is likely to be paid in full during the case).

Because wages and consumer deposit claims are normally dischargeable, there need be no hesitation about listing any such possible priority claims on Schedule E in chapter 7 cases. In chapter 13, however, more care should be exercised because an admission of priority status will carry a requirement that the particular debt be paid in full under the debtor's plan.[123]

7.3.7.3.4 Schedule F—general unsecured debts

All of the client's remaining debts are included on Schedule F. The general principles stated above apply here with equal force, and all possible claims should be listed. Often forgotten are the contingent subrogation claims which may be available to codebtors who later pay off a claim, including those on mortgages guaranteed by the Veterans Administration or Federal Housing Administration and those on guaranteed student loans.[124] Though such entities are often unlikely to pursue the client, or even know they have a right to do so, it is good practice to list them as creditors as well, with an indication that the debt is not a separate one to be added to the total amount owed.[125] If such listing is done, codebtors will be given notice of the case, and any possible claims they have will be extinguished.

Another frequently overlooked category of debt is a continuing obligation to pay prorated amounts on a prepetition contract for services. When the contract calls for deferment of a lump sum balance due at the outset of the agreement, such as with many condominium assessments, those debts may be dischargeable.[126]

Courts vary on the specificity required in completing the section of the form detailing the consideration for the debt and the date the debt was incurred. In the case of credit card debts, courts will usually accept a general description such as "credit card" or "miscellaneous purchases" made on "various dates."

Finally, even though the Official Form is not formatted to easily input an obligation that is owed to two separate creditors, it is a good idea to include both creditors in the schedule. Probably, the easiest way to do so is to enter the creditors' names separately in the same box, or in two boxes with a notation that it is the same debt so that it does not affect the total.[127] This approach is also useful with respect to an obligation assigned to another entity or to a collection agency for purposes of collection. Including both the original creditor and the collection agency or assignee in both the schedule and the mailing matrix ensures that both get notice of the bankruptcy and that any claim of either of them is discharged. An attorney representing the creditor may be listed in the same way so she receives notice of the case from the court.[128]

7.3.7.4 Schedule G: Unexpired Leases and Executory Contracts

Schedule G, the schedule of unexpired leases and executory contracts, is required in all cases. It is designed primarily to put the trustee on notice of leases or other executory contracts which might be assumed or rejected because of their potential benefit or cost to the estate.[129] Although the issues which might be raised by the schedule are rarely of great importance in consumer cases, the schedule is not difficult to complete.

An executory contract is broadly defined as one for which significant aspects of performance remain due on both sides. An unexpired lease is one that has not yet terminated by its terms.[130] If, as is common, the debtor has no unexpired leases or executory contracts, the debtor should check the box marked "none."

For most consumer debtors, a residential lease will be the only entry on this form. These should probably be listed even if the lease is only a month-to-month oral agreement. Occasionally, the debtor may have an automobile lease, an ongoing employment contract, or a pending sale agreement for goods or real estate. These should be listed as well.

In those cases which include unexpired leases or other executory contracts, the listing must include a statement of the debtor's interest. The other party to the contract may also be listed as a creditor in the applicable schedule, particularly if there has been a default on the contract. All entities listed on Schedule G must be included in the list of creditors filed at the outset of the case to ensure they receive notice.[131]

---

121 See § 15.4.3.5, infra.
122 Marital property settlements are dischargeable in chapter 13 cases if the debtor completes the plan, but are not dischargeable in other cases. See Ch. 15, infra.
123 11 U.S.C. § 1322(a)(2).
124 See Appendix F, infra, for example of completed form. See also In re Barnett, 42 B.R. 254 (Bankr. S.D.N.Y. 1984) (debt to guarantor of student loan must be scheduled); In re McCrady, 23 B.R. 193 (Bankr. W.D. Ky. 1982) (codebtor who paid note could not sue debtor who had given him notice of bankruptcy).
125 Though government guarantors of mortgages rarely pursue a debtor after foreclosure, the failure to discharge the personal liability to the Veterans Administration (VA), for example, may leave a debtor ineligible for a new veteran's mortgage. If the debt is discharged, the VA may not discriminate based on previous nonpayment. 11 U.S.C. § 525(a). See § 15.5.4, infra.
126 See In re Rosteck, 899 F.2d 694 (7th Cir. 1990) (condominium assessments falling due postpetition on a prepetition contract are dischargeable).
Dischargeability of condominium assessments is now addressed by 11 U.S.C. § 523(a)(16) and is discussed in § 15.4.3.14, infra.
127 See completed Official Forms found in Appendix D, infra.
128 The $30 filing fee for an amendment to the filed schedules will not be charged if the debtor amends the schedules to add the name and address of an attorney for a creditor. See Judicial Conference of the United States, Bankruptcy Court Miscellaneous Fee Schedule ¶ 4 (reprinted in Appx. C.3, infra).
129 See § 12.9, infra.
130 See § 12.9, infra, for a fuller discussion of the Code's treatment of unexpired leases and executory contracts.
131 Fed. R. Bankr. P. 1007(a)(1).

Preparing and Filing the Papers

One other issue that may occasionally arise is how to treat a rent-to-own contract for consumer goods. For the reasons discussed in a later chapter, there is a significant advantage and considerable precedent for treating these contracts as security agreements rather than executory contracts.[132] Consequently, the rent-to-own obligation should generally be listed in Schedule D as a secured debt.

7.3.7.5 Schedule H: Codebtors

The debtor's codebtors, other than a spouse in a joint case, should be listed in Schedule H. The instructions for the Official Form provide that, in community property states, a married debtor not filing a joint case should always report the name and address of the non-debtor spouse, together with any other names used by the non-debtor spouse within the previous eight years. As discussed above, codebtors may also be listed as creditors in Schedule F due to any potential subrogation claims that could arise if the codebtors later pay off the obligation. However, even if they are not listed in that schedule, they must be listed in the list filed for notice purposes at the outset of the case and their claims are ordinarily discharged as long as they receive notice of the case.[133]

7.3.7.6 Schedules I and J: Income and Expenses

The last two parts of Official Form 6 are schedules I and J which require a complete disclosure of the debtor's income and expenses. In chapter 7 cases, these schedules are intended to provide information that could help a bankruptcy court to determine whether a chapter 7 case might be an "abuse" and therefore subject to dismissal under 11 U.S.C. § 707(b).[134] In chapter 13 cases, schedules I and J allow the trustee and interested creditors to determine whether the debtor's plan is feasible and whether it is in compliance with statutory requirements.[135] Creditors and the trustee may look to these schedules to decide whether to object to confirmation under 11 U.S.C. § 1325(b), the "ability-to-pay" (also known as "disposable income") test.[136]

The court may also look to these schedules to decide whether the plan is the debtor's best effort,[137] and whether there is cause for extending the plan beyond the usual three years.[138]

Schedule I must include income for both spouses in a joint case and also when one spouse files a case individually, unless the spouses are separated and a joint petition is not filed. Income contributions to the debtor by persons not married to the debtor should generally be listed separately in the schedule as "other monthly income." This listing is of particular importance in chapter 13 cases in which the income contributions are necessary to meet the regular income eligibility requirement or to make the plan feasible.[139]

When income from a business or farm is included, a detailed statement of the business revenues must be attached. When expected income is not likely to be received, such as alimony or support payments that have not historically been paid, this circumstance should be noted in order to present a realistic picture. Although food stamps and certain other public benefits are not treated as income for many purposes, they could nevertheless be considered income for the purpose of the bankruptcy filing. The existence of food stamps in Schedule I, for example, will be offset by the debtor's food expense in Schedule J, and may explain what otherwise appears to be an unrealistic budget.

Schedule J requires information about the expenses of the debtor and the debtor's family. A box is provided on the Official Form to be checked by spouses who have filed a joint case but keep separate households. Such debtors are instructed to file separate schedules of expenditures, with the second schedule labeled "spouse." When household expenses are paid by persons whose income or contributions are not included in Schedule I, it is best to list the expense as zero with an appropriate note about how it is paid.

When there are regular expenses for operation of a farm or business, a detailed statement of those expenses must be attached.

In listing the debtor's income and expenses, particularly the latter, the purposes of the forms should be kept in mind. A good faith effort to be accurate is always required, but budgets are flexible and budgeting for the future is an inexact science. Many debtors have only a vague idea of what they spend for various items, and have often spent less than necessary for things like home maintenance and clothing because they were trying to make debt payments they no longer will have to make. The debtor's expenses usually can be estimated, within the limits of realistic planning, in a way that presents the case in a favorable light. In chapter 7, for example, it is not wise to show a great deal of income not needed for reasonable living expenses of the debtor and the debtor's dependents if that can truthfully be avoided, because some courts might find the

---

132 *See* § 11.8, *infra*.

133 Unscheduled creditors' claims are discharged if they receive notice of the case. *See* § 15.4.3.3, *infra*. The rules ensure that they receive notice by including codebtors listed on Schedule H on the list of creditors filed at the outset of the case. *See* Fed. R. Bankr. P. 1007(a)(1).

134 *See* § 13.4, *infra*, for discussion of the "abuse" test and the limited relevance of Schedules I and J under the 2005 amendments to section 707(b). Because different income amounts are listed on Official Form 22, *see*§ 7.3.9, *infra*, the instructions for Schedule I inform the debtor that the monthly income reported on the form may differ from the current monthly income amount calculated on Official Form 22.

135 *See* § 7.3.12 and Chapter 12, *infra*, for a fuller discussion of chapter 13 plans and the limited relevance of Schedule I and J under the 2005 amendments to section 1325(b). Because different expense amounts are listed on Official Form 22, *see* § 7.3.9, *infra*, the instructions for Schedule J inform the debtor that the monthly expenses reported on the form may differ from the deductions from income allowed on Official Form 22.

136 *See* § 12.3.4, *infra*, for discussion of the "ability to pay" test.

137 *See* § 15.2.2.9, *infra*, for discussion of the "best effort" requirement, relevant under 11 U.S.C. § 727(a)(9).

138 *See* § 12.6.3, *infra*, for discussion of the requirements for extending a plan over more than three years when the applicable commitment period under section 1325(b)(4) is three years.

139 *See* §§ 12.2.2, 12.5, *infra*.

availability of such income to dictate a dismissal for "abuse" of chapter 7. A catchall category, such as "miscellaneous expenses" can be added to reflect the various items not specifically listed, and other categories, such as the substantial expenses for school expenses and haircuts in a large family may also need to be added. Similarly, expenses such as needed dental care or home repairs that a debtor has been unable to pay for in the recent past because of debts that will be discharged may be listed as part of the debtor's projected budget going forward.[140] However, "excess" income is rarely likely to be a problem; the overwhelming majority of debtors filing chapter 7 bankruptcies have barely enough income to meet the most basic family expenses.[141]

In chapter 13, the debtor's income and expenses must support the debtor's position that sufficient disposable income is available to fund the proposed plan. If, for example, the debtor's income is only barely sufficient to fund the necessary payments required under chapter 13, some care may be necessary to use the lowest possible reasonable estimates of the debtor's expenses so that the plan will not appear infeasible. In other cases, it will be to the debtor's advantage to list greater expenses so that it does not appear that there is unused income which could otherwise be paid to unsecured creditors.[142] In that event, the maximum good faith estimate of anticipated necessary expenses should be used. Generally, expenses that do not exceed those permitted by the chapter 7 means test will not be questioned as unreasonable.[143]

It is not uncommon for debtors to estimate poorly their expenditures on items such as food, clothes, and transportation. Counsel should make every effort to get an appropriate good faith estimate that supports the debtor's goals for the case. Items frequently overlooked on the expense side are child care costs (including diapers), home maintenance costs, dental care the debtor has been unable to afford, and irregular expenses such as schoolbooks and auto maintenance.[144] Because the income and expense information requested are estimates of future income and expenses, there is some latitude to go back to the debtor to obtain good faith estimates consistent with the debtor's objectives. There is probably little need for concern that a low-income client's expenses will appear too high, as bankruptcy judges are more accustomed to middle-class debtors who typically have much higher expenses.

Because Schedules I and J require information about anticipated increases or decreases in income and expenses in the year following the filing of the petition, any significant non-speculative expected changes should be listed.[145] For example, if unemployment benefits are due to terminate within a year of the petition, the date of termination should be given. A statement of monthly net income, reflecting the income and expenses listed in Schedules I and J, is included as the final item on Schedule J so that the debtor may satisfy the document filing requirement of section 521(a)(1)(B)(v).

7.3.7.7 Declaration Concerning Debtor's Schedules

The Official Form schedules include a separate "declaration" page. This page contains the debtor's oath under penalty of perjury that the debtor has read the schedules and that they are true and correct to the best of her knowledge, information, and belief. Joint debtors must each sign the declaration page.

The meeting with the debtor to review the schedules is another opportunity to explain the bankruptcy process as well as the purposes of the information contained in the schedules. It is a good idea to allow the debtor as much time as the debtor needs to read over all the schedules and statements and also to double-check the balances in deposit accounts. A practitioner can then spend some time with the debtor to explain the meeting of creditors and anything else anticipated concerning future progress of the case.[146]

7.3.7.8 The Summary of Schedules and Statistical Summary of Certain Liabilities

Accompanying the schedules is a form summarizing debts, property, income, and expenses. The form is self-explanatory. After the summary is filled out, it is usually inserted at the front of the schedules for filing, or elsewhere if required by local practice. An additional form, entitled Statistical Summary of Certain Liabilities, is used by the courts solely to gather statistics mandated by law.[147] It requires the debtor to compute the total of amounts listed for certain types of debts that are often nondischargeable.

7.3.8 The Statement of Financial Affairs (Official Form 7)

The statement of financial affairs (Official Form 7) is also required in both chapter 7 and chapter 13 cases. Every question must be answered, but the form is simple to fill out. Each question has a box labeled "none" which should be checked if that is the appropriate response to a given question.

Spouses filing a joint petition may file a single statement. In cases under chapter 12 or 13, married debtors must provide information for both spouses whether or not a joint petition is filed, unless the spouses are separated and a joint petition is not

---

140 A discussion of frequently overlooked expenses can be found in § 5.3.3.4.1, *supra*.
141 Of course, there is no requirement that a chapter 7 debtor show a positive cash flow. It is therefore quite common for chapter 7 debtors to schedule substantially greater expenses than income. Having greater expenses than income is, after all, how they got into substantial debt before the bankruptcy case.
142 See § 12.3.4, *infra*.
143 See § 13.4.5, *infra*, for discussion of expenses permitted by the means test.
144 See § 5.3.3.4 *supra*.

145 Because these statements satisfy the document filing requirement of section 521(a)(1)(B)(vi), the debtor should state "none" if no change in income or expenses is anticipated.
146 See Ch. 8, *infra*.
147 See 28 U.S.C. § 159.

filed. Debtors engaged in business must provide the requested information for all unincorporated businesses as well as for their personal affairs.

Questions 1 to 18 must be answered by every debtor, but questions 19 to 25 are required only for debtors who have been engaged in business[148] within the six years preceding bankruptcy.

The first two questions on the statement of financial affairs address the debtor's income history. The information to be included in response to these questions goes back two years and therefore may be different from the expected future income included in Schedule I.[149] The income figures provided should be in terms of gross income, not take-home pay. Although income is usually not important in a chapter 7 case, which deals primarily with assets and liabilities, a statement of high income or one which does not fit in with other information provided may prompt further investigation. It may also trigger an inquiry by the United States trustee or the court as to whether the filing of a chapter 7 case is an abuse of that chapter.[150]

The next eight questions concern recent transfers or losses of property by the debtor. Using the responses to these questions, the trustee can sometimes avoid transfers or seek proceeds due the debtor.[151] Because debtors themselves may exercise avoiding powers,[152] especially with respect to executions on their property, accurate information here is important to protect these rights. Lastly, the answers to these questions could indicate possible impediments to discharge, such as transfers to hinder or defraud creditors.[153]

The first part of question 3 requests information from consumer debtors about loans and other debts on which more than $600 was repaid within the ninety days prior to the bankruptcy. Payments made for a domestic support obligation or as part of a debt management plan to a counseling agency approved under section 111 are to be identified with an asterisk.[154] The second part is not applicable to consumer debtors. The third part deals with payments made to or for the benefit of creditors who were "insiders"[155] within the year prior to the bankruptcy, regardless of the amount.[156] The trustee may be able to recover these payments as preferences.[157] Again, in most cases, the trustee will not be interested in pursuing small amounts of money, even if they are somewhat above the $600 threshold, especially if they are not easily collectible. Local practice varies as to the specificity required in answering this question. In some places it may be sufficient to state that "monthly payments" or "several payments" of a particular amount were made to some or all creditors if the aggregate to any single creditor is under $1000 or so. If the trustee is interested, she may then inquire further. The question seeks information about payments to secured creditors, such as mortgagees and car lenders, as well as to unsecured creditors, even though such payments would not ordinarily be avoidable as preferences.

Question 4 seeks information about all lawsuits and administrative proceedings involving the debtor which are pending or were terminated within the previous year. It also seeks the details of any execution, seizure, or garnishment in the previous year.[158] The information required is minimal; the debtor need only provide the caption, case number, nature of proceeding, court, and status of the case. Such information may help uncover creditor actions which can be set aside by the trustee or debtor. It also may lead to a further source of information about the debtor's affairs. In addition, property seized or levied upon may still belong to the debtor and may come into the estate if it has not been sold. The question also recognizes that lawsuits brought by the debtor may, in fact, be assets of the debtor that can benefit the estate. When such claims of the debtor are listed, they should also be included in Schedule B as property of the debtor and in Schedule C as exempt, if possible.

Question 5 requests information about repossessions, foreclosures, deeds in lieu of foreclosure, and returns of property. These events may also give the trustee an opportunity to recover property for the estate.

Question 6, concerning assignments and receiverships, is rarely applicable to consumer cases, as those mechanisms normally concern business insolvencies in the few situations when they are still used. Like the preceding questions, this question is intended to identify property that might be recovered by the trustee.

Question 7 seeks information about large gifts or charitable contributions in the year before bankruptcy. Because gifts, by definition, are without consideration, the trustee reviews the answer to this question to determine whether recoverable property may have been lost to the estate.[159] Charitable contributions are generally protected in trustee avoidance proceedings,[160] and if the debtor's budget and, if applicable, Form 22 calculations, assert ongoing charitable or religious contribu-

---

148 Being "in business" is defined for the purposes of Official Form 7 in the Official Form. It includes debtors who are officers, directors, managing executives, or persons in control of a corporation; partners other than limited partners; sole proprietors or self-employed. Family farmers are included.

149 Note that the two-year period is not identical in questions 1 and 2. Question 1 refers to the present calendar year and the "two years immediately preceding this calendar year." Question 2 refers to the "two years immediately preceding the commencement of this case."

150 See § 13.4, infra, for discussion of the "abuse" test.

151 See § 10.4, infra, for discussion of avoiding powers.

152 See § 10.4, infra.

153 11 U.S.C. § 727(a)(2). See § 15.2.2, infra.

154 Such payments may not be recovered by the trustee as preferences. 11 U.S.C. § 547(c)(7), (h).

155 Insider is defined as it is in the Bankruptcy Code, 11 U.S.C. § 101(31). It includes relatives and certain business relations of the debtor. Relative is in turn defined in 11 U.S.C. § 101(45) and includes an "individual related by affinity or consanguinity within the third degree by the common law, or individual in a step or adoptive relationship within such third degree."

156 A consumer debtor should not answer the second part of question 3, which pertains only to non-consumer debtors.

157 See § 10.4, infra, for discussion of avoiding powers.

158 Such transfers may be preferences or fraudulent transfers. 11 U.S.C. §§ 547, 548.

159 See § 10.4.2.6.5, infra, concerning fraudulent transfers.

160 11 U.S.C. §§ 544(b)(2), 548(a)(2). See §§ 10.4.2.6.2, 10.4.2.6.5, infra.

tions the answer to this question should be consistent with the debtor's assertions on those forms. The debtor need not list ordinary and usual gifts to family members (such as birthday or holiday gifts) if they total less than $200 per recipient. Similarly, charitable contributions aggregating $100 or less to a single recipient need not be listed.

Question 8, seeking information as to gambling, theft, or fire losses, is designed to explain lost assets. It is also sometimes used to smoke out dishonest debtors who use this section to account for the sudden disappearance of large amounts of property. In some cases, this question will help the trustee discover the availability of a claim to insurance proceeds which might substitute for the lost property.

Question 9 seeks disclosure of payments made for debt counseling or bankruptcy within one year before the case by or on behalf of the debtor. In addition to payments made to third party debt counselors and prior attorneys, payments made in connection with the debtor's existing case should be included, including any attorney fees and charges for the credit counseling briefing. Payments made by persons other than the debtor must also be disclosed. The question's purpose is to assist in court supervision of attorney fees paid to debtors' counsel and occasionally to turn up exploitative debt counseling or other bankruptcy related scams.[161]

The next question, number 10, again looks for transfers which can be set aside, including fraudulent transfers.[162] Any transfers made within two years before filing the petition that were not in the ordinary course of the business or financial affairs of the debtor (such as payments for normal household expenses) and that are not listed elsewhere in the statement should be listed in response to Part A of question ten. It is important to remember that the granting of a security interest is a transfer within the meaning of this question,[163] as is any payment to any entity not listed in answering the previous questions. Also included are involuntary transfers other than repossessions and returns.[164] Part B of the question also requires the debtor to list all property transferred within ten years before filing the petition to a self-settled trust or similar device of which the debtor is a beneficiary.

Questions 11 and 12 concerning closed financial accounts and safe deposit boxes are designed to determine if the debtor has hidden or transferred any assets that could potentially benefit the estate. The answers to these questions, in some cases, are also used to trace the debtor's assets. Closed financial accounts must be listed, whether they were in the debtor's name or for the benefit of the debtor. They may include bank accounts, certificates of deposit, credit union accounts, pension funds, brokerage accounts, and other types of financial accounts. Safe deposit boxes must be listed only if they contained cash, securities, or other valuables within the year prior to the bankruptcy. In some jurisdictions, trustees will routinely request additional information about the contents of safe deposit boxes or statements from the closed accounts.

Question 13 requests information about setoffs by a bank or any other entity within the ninety days preceding the case, again because the trustee or debtor may have the option to recover the setoff.[165] Debtors who have had setoffs against their accounts during that period must list the name and address of the creditor, the date of the setoff, and the amount of the setoff.

Question 14 deals with property held by the client but belonging to another person. Especially if large amounts of such property exist, or if the property seems to encompass things that most people would own themselves, such as household goods or clothing, the trustee might inquire further. Property held in trust for another or in a Uniform Transfer to Minors account should also be listed here.

Question 15 requires prior addresses of the debtor within the previous three years. The answer to this question sometimes provides a clue to the trustee or a suspicious creditor of additional interests of the debtor in real estate or a way to begin an investigation of potential hidden assets. It may also help these parties verify the identity of the debtor and determine whether the debtor's claim of exemptions is proper under the domiciliary requirements of section 522(b)(3)(A).[166]

Question 16 requests information concerning spouses and former spouses, but only for debtors who have lived in community property states in the previous eight years. Such debtors must list the name of the debtor's spouse or any former spouse who resided with the debtor in a community property state. This information is necessary because the community property provisions of the Bankruptcy Code[167] often will cause a debtor's bankruptcy case to affect the property and debts of a spouse or former spouse in a community property state, even if the spouse or former spouse has not joined in the bankruptcy case.

Question 17 seeks information concerning potential environmental liabilities of the debtor. Although few debtors have such liabilities, any debtor who has received a notice that she may have an environmental violation, or who is subject to a judicial or administrative proceeding under an environmental law, must provide information in response to this question.

Question 18 is intended to identify debtors who have been in business in the previous six years. Every debtor must either answer the question or check the box marked "None." If the debtor has been in business, information identifying the business must be provided and questions 19–25 must be answered.

---

161 *See generally* Ch. 16, *infra*.

   This question should help the court and the trustee identify issues involving petition preparers under 11 U.S.C. § 110, but there is evidence that some less scrupulous petition preparers are failing to list their fees in filling out the answer to this question. Failure to disclose the fee is a violation of section 110(h). *See* § 16.6, *infra*.

162 11 U.S.C. §§ 544, 548. *See* Ch. 10, *infra*.

163 11 U.S.C. § 101(54).

164 However, because question 5 asks about certain types of involuntary transfers and only looks back one year, it appears that the types of transfers listed in that question need not be listed if they occurred more than one year before the petition was filed.

165 11 U.S.C. § 553. *See* § 10.4.2.6.7, *infra*.

166 *See* Ch. 10, *infra*.

167 11 U.S.C. §§ 524(a)(3), 541(a)(2). *See* § 2.5, *supra*; § 15.5.1.4, *infra*.

Questions 19–25 are applicable to debtors who have owned or operated businesses, including family farms, partnerships, and sole proprietorships, within the six years prior to the case. Information must be provided about the business, the business books and records, inventories, present and former business partners, officers, directors, and shareholders, as well as withdrawals or distributions made to insiders.

The debtor's statement of financial affairs, like the schedules, must be signed by the debtor or debtors under penalty of perjury. For almost all consumer debtors, the responses to the questions in the statement of financial affairs are routine. It is likely that the trustee will engage in little more than a cursory review of the statement and it will have little impact on the case. Obviously, though, thorough answers are appropriate, because any attempt to obfuscate is only likely to lead to problems and perhaps a claim that the debtor is seeking to hide assets. To the extent that the debtor intends to seek to recover exempt property from creditors, the answers in the statement should be consistent with the debtor's theory for that recovery.[168]

7.3.9 Statement of Current Monthly Income, Means Test, and Chapter 13 Calculations (Official Forms 22A and 22C)

In order to provide the information necessary to make the determinations concerning the presumption of abuse in chapter 7 and concerning disposable income in chapter 13, the debtor must file the appropriate version of Official Form 22. These forms, though lengthy and complicated, are largely self-explanatory. Although the mechanics of the presumption of abuse and disposable income determination are explained elsewhere in this treatise,[169] some instructions concerning these forms are in order.

The first part of the form for chapter 7 debtors, Form 22A, is a declaration that can be made by a disabled veteran whose indebtedness occurred primarily during the period in which the debtor was on active duty or performing homeland defense activity. The miniscule number of debtors who meet this definition can check the box in this part and are excused from completing almost all of the remaining parts of the form. This section is followed by a declaration that should be made by any debtor whose debts are not primarily consumer debts. Such debtors are similarly excused from completing the rest of the form.[170] The final portion of this section includes a declaration that can be made by certain reservists and National Guard members who were called to active duty during specified periods, again exempting them from completing the balance of the form.

Part II of Form 22A is the calculation of monthly income for the purposes of section 707(b)(7), which creates a safe harbor from the means test for lower income debtors. As discussed elsewhere, Form 22A erroneously takes the position that both a husband and wife's income must always be included in this calculation unless the spouses are separated, not filing jointly, and living in separate households for purposes other than evading the means test.[171] In a case in which this issue is important, the debtor's counsel should understand that the form is not determinative of whether that position is correct. Part I of Form 22C is similar, except that it requires a non-debtor spouse's income in all cases. Obviously, some debtors simply do not have such information if they are separated from their spouses, and will have to state on the form that the information is unknown.

Neither form takes a position on whether unemployment compensation is a benefit under the Social Security Act that is excluded from the income calculation.[172] If the debtor does not include such benefits in the calculation, the compensation must nonetheless be disclosed on line 9 of Form 22A and line 8 of Form 22C.

Part III of Form 22A determines whether, according to the form's methodology, the section 707(b)(7) safe harbor from the means test applies. The income calculated in Part II is compared to the applicable median family income for the debtor's state and household size.[173] As discussed earlier, the debtor may disagree with that methodology to the extent it includes the income of a non-debtor spouse.

Part II of Form 22C uses a similar calculation to determine the applicable commitment period under section 1325(b)(4), comparing the amount computed in Part I to the applicable median family income for the debtor's state and household size. However, unlike Form 22A, Form 22C allows a debtor to choose to make the comparison after subtracting the income of a non-debtor spouse.

Part IV of Form 22A and Part III of Form 22C both calculate the debtor's "current monthly income," as that term is defined in Code section 101. If a non-debtor spouse's income was previously included in the prior income calculations, that income is subtracted, except to the extent it has been paid for household expenses of the debtor or the debtor's dependents. Part III of Form 22C then compares the resulting figure to the applicable median family income for the debtor's state and household size to determine whether the chapter 13 debtor must calculate expenses using the methodology of section 707(b), as incorporated by section 1325(b)(3).

Having completed these parts of the forms, most debtors may proceed to the last part and sign the verification. Only debtors whose incomes listed in Part III of each form are above the applicable state medians must complete the other portions of

---

168 *See* Ch. 10, *infra*.
169 *See* Chs. 12, 13, *infra*.
170 *See* § 13.4.2, *infra*.

171 *See* Ch. 13, *infra*.
172 *See* Ch. 13, *infra*.
173 See § 13.4.3.3,*infra*.
   State median income figures by family size can be found in Appendix I.1, *infra*, and at the United States Trustee Program's website, www.usdoj.gov/ust.

the form. Chapter 7 debtors whose incomes in part III are below the median income must also check the box labeled "The presumption does not arise" at the top of the first page of the form. Chapter 13 debtors must check the appropriate boxes at the beginning of Form 22C concerning the applicable commitment period and whether, according to the calculations on the form, disposable income is determined under section 1325(b)(3).

Those debtors who must complete the other sections of the form must consult the Internal Revenue Service living expense standards to answer the first few questions in Part V of Form 22A and Part IV of Form 22C. These expense standards, discussed in more detail elsewhere in this treatise,[174] can be found on the United States Trustee Program website.[175] For the most part the questions in this part of the form are self-explanatory. Certain deductions are permitted on lines 54 and 55 in Part V of Form 22C that are not permitted on Form 22A, because those deductions are allowed only in chapter 13 cases.

The calculations in Form 22A will determine whether, at least according to the form, the chapter 7 debtor is subject to the presumption of abuse. If the calculations in Part VI of the form result in a number above the presumption threshold, the debtor must check the box on the front of the form stating that the presumption arises according to the calculations on the form. Otherwise, the debtor should check the box stating that the presumption does not arise. In any event, the debtor is free to argue that the form does not accurately reflect the statute, and that the presumption does not arise under the statute, if that is the debtor's position.

For example, the forms have no place to deduct some of the "other necessary expenses" permitted by the Internal Revenue Service expense standards.[176] Additional expense claims of the debtor may be listed at the end of the form, but they are not included in the calculations.[177] The deduction of such expenses may eliminate the presumption of abuse in a chapter 7 case. It may also change the calculation of the debtor's disposable income in a chapter 13 case.

Some disputes may arise regarding completion of the form. For example, the United States Trustee Program takes the incorrect position that payments on a 401(k) loan are not mandatory payroll deductions, even when the loan contract clearly provides they are. There may also be disputes about the number of members of the debtor's household.

However, the debtor should not be compelled to change how the form is completed based on such disputes over the meaning of the law. If a party contends that the form is incorrectly completed in a way that makes a substantive difference in the case, for example by causing a presumption of abuse to arise or changing the debtor's disposable income, then that party may press its position based on its own interpretation of the form.

7.3.10 Filing Debtor Payment Advices

The 2005 amendments added section 521(a)(1)(B)(iv) to the Code, which requires, unless the court orders otherwise, that the debtor file copies of all payment advices or other evidence of payment received from employers within sixty days before the petition was filed.[178] Bankruptcy Rule 1007(b)(1)(E) and (c) requires that the payment advices be filed within fourteen days after filing the petition (although the court can extend the time) and that all but the last four digits of the debtor's Social Security number should be redacted from these documents. If a debtor has not received any payment advices or documentation of payment from an employer during the relevant period, neither the statute nor the rule requires anything to be filed.[179] However, some courts have adopted local rules requiring the debtor to file a declaration that no such documents were received.[180]

Because section 521(a)(1)(B) applies only if the court does not order otherwise, some courts have used their power to "order otherwise" to adopt local rules or general orders providing that payment advices are to be delivered to the trustee at the meeting of creditors rather than filed with the court.

The same power of the court to order otherwise also provides a remedy for a debtor who has not retained the payment advices or other evidence and cannot obtain them.[181] Although the debtor or the debtor's attorney can often obtain from an employer a statement of compensation paid in the form of a letter, some debtors may be reluctant to let their employers know they are filing bankruptcy cases. In other cases, the debtor may no longer be employed by the same employer or may not be on good terms with an employer or former employer. A short motion explaining the circumstances may be filed seeking to

---

174 See Ch. 13, infra.
175 The website is located at www.usdoj.gov/ust. Selected expense items from the Internal Revenue Service standards are reprinted in Appendix I.2, infra.
176 See Chapter 13, infra, for discussion of "other necessary expenses."
177 The inclusion of such expenses on the form at least permits the debtor to alert other parties of the expenses, which may also be a basis for claiming special circumstances under section 707(b)(2)(B). See Chs. 12, 13, infra.
178 When debtors had not provided every pay stub for the sixty-day period, but missing information could be deduced from year-to-date figures on later pay stubs and the earlier pay stubs that were supplied, debtors had provided "other evidence of payment" and complied with statutory requirement. Cmty. Bank v. Riffle, 617 F.3d 171 (2d Cir. 2010) (adopting a "payment-focused" interpretation of the statutory requirement and finding that the debtor provided adequate information by filing the most recent payment advice which included his year-to-date earnings and a "Sales Earnings Report" from his employer); In re Tay-Kwamya, 367 B.R. 422 (Bankr. S.D.N.Y. 2007) (cumulative information on pay stubs provided by debtor was sufficient); In re Luders, 356 B.R. 671 (Bankr. W.D. Va. 2006). See also In re Reynolds, 370 B.R. 393 (Bankr. N.D. Okla. 2007) (year-to-date information on pay stub sufficient).
179 In re LaPlante, 354 B.R. 648 (Bankr. W.D.N.Y. 2006) (vacating dismissal of case because debtor's only income was from Social Security and workers' compensation).
180 See Form 13, Appx. G.3, infra, for a sample declaration.
181 See In re Ackerman, 374 B.R. 65 (Bankr. W.D.N.Y. 2007) (granting trustee's motion to excuse filing of missing payment advices).

excuse the filing of some or all of the payment advices.[182] Such a motion will usually be granted, especially if the debtor offers to provide some evidence of wages, such as a recent pay stub with year-to-date figures, or a recent W-2 form. Debtors may also seek to prevent disclosure on the Internet of sensitive information in the payment advices by filing a form motion under section 107(c) of the Code[183] in every case or by advocating a general order or local rule that would prevent those documents from being available to the public, perhaps by requiring them to be instead provided to the trustee at the meeting of creditors as some courts have done.

7.3.11 The Statement of Intention with Regard to Property Securing Consumer Debts (Official Form 8)

Another required document in chapter 7 cases is the statement of intention regarding debts secured by property of the estate and leased personal property.[184] This document must state certain intentions of the debtor, as of the date of its filing, with regard to any property, real or personal, that serves as collateral for a debt. In addition, Official Form 8 requires the debtor to state the debtor's intentions with respect to leases of personal property. The statement must be filed within thirty days after the debtor files a petition under chapter 7, or on or before the date of the section 341 meeting of creditors, whichever is earlier, unless the court, for cause, extends the deadline for filing.[185] As a practical matter, it is normally filed with the statement of affairs and schedules in a chapter 7 case.

The Bankruptcy Rules provide that the statement of intention must be prepared as prescribed by Official Form 8.[186] That form requires a listing of all property subject to security interests securing consumer debts, and the names of the creditors holding liens on the property, as well as all leased personal property and the lessors' names. The rules also require that the statement be served on the trustee and each creditor named in the statement on or before the date the statement is filed.[187]

It is important to note what section 521(a)(2) does and does not require. With respect to secured debts, it requires only that the debtor state (1) whether the property will be surrendered or retained, (2) whether the debtor intends to redeem the property,[188] (3) whether the debtor intends to reaffirm the debt secured by the property,[189] and (4) whether it will be claimed as exempt.[190] The Official Form[191] offers the debtor the option of indicating such intentions, if applicable.

But there is no requirement that the debtor choose one of the options or reaffirm or redeem.[192] A debtor may choose to retain the property subject to the creditor's security interest and state law rights whatever they may be.[193] Or the debtor may intend to avoid the creditor's lien in the bankruptcy case.[194] When such options are chosen, the debtor should ordinarily check the box indicating an intent to retain the property and should include a note that makes clear the debtor's intention to continue payments in the space the Official Form provides for "other" intentions.

There is also nothing in section 521 stating that a debtor may not change her intentions. Like other statements and schedules, this statement may be amended at any time before the time period for performance of the intention expires.[195] Although it is unclear whether any negative consequences result from failing to act in accordance with the statement of intention,[196] it is normally advisable to file amendments to the statement when the debtor's plans change and to serve them, as required, on the trustee and any affected creditors.[197]

The debtor is normally required to follow through on the stated intention within thirty days after the first date set for the meeting of creditors, but that deadline should be seen more as a guideline for when redemption or reaffirmation should occur, if they are going to happen. The Code makes clear that the statement of intention does not alter any of the debtor's substantive rights as they previously existed, although relief from the stay may be granted in some circumstances.[198]

In most chapter 7 cases, completion of the statement of intention is quite simple. Generally, chapter 7 debtors retain all of their property, as they claim their interests in all of it as exempt. (If there is significant nonexempt property the debtor usually chooses chapter 13 rather than chapter 7.)[199] The fact that the property is encumbered by a secured creditor's lien does not prevent the debtor from claiming her interest, subject to the lien, as exempt. In many cases the lien may be partially

---

182 See Form 12, Appx. G.3, *infra*, for a sample of such a motion.
183 11 U.S.C. § 107(c) provides that the court, for cause, may protect an individual with respect to information that would create an undue risk of identity theft or other unlawful injury.
184 11 U.S.C. § 521(a)(2). *See* Official Form 8 (reprinted in Appx. D, *infra*).
185 11 U.S.C. § 521(a)(2)(A).
186 Fed. R. Bankr. P. 1007(b)(2).
    A completed form is included in Appendix D, *infra*.
187 Fed. R. Bankr. P. 1007(b)(2).
    The enhanced service requirements under Fed. R. Bankr. P. 7004(h) for insured depository institutions are not applicable, because the filing of the statement does not arise in a contested matter or adversary proceeding.
188 *See* § 11.5, *infra*.
189 *See* § 15.5.2, *infra*.
190 11 U.S.C. § 521(a)(2).
    With respect to a personal property leases, Official Form 8 requires the debtor to state whether the debtor intends to assume the lease pursuant to 11 U.S.C. § 362(h)(1)(A). *See* 11 U.S.C. § 365(p); Ch. 10, *infra*.
191 Official Form 8. *See* Appx. D, *infra*.
192 For discussion of debtors' rights to retain property without reaffirming, see § 11.4.1, *infra*.
193 *See* § 15.5.2, *infra*.
194 Lien avoidance is discussed in Chapters 10 and 11, *infra*.
195 Fed. R. Bankr. P. 1009(b). *See* § 8.3.2, *infra*.
196 *See* § 11.4.1, *infra*.
197 Fed. R. Bankr. P. 1009(c).
198 11 U.S.C. §§ 521(a)(2)(C), 362(h). *See In re* Eagle, 51 B.R. 959 (Bankr. N.D. Ohio 1985) (debtors who stated intention to reaffirm debt not barred from redeeming property instead); Ch. 11, *infra*.
199 *See* § 6.3, *supra*, for discussion of this choice.

§ 7.3.12   Consumer Bankruptcy Law and Practice

or totally avoidable in bankruptcy.[200] Few debtors reaffirm their debts[201] or redeem more than one or two items under section 722.[202]

Probably the greatest uncertainty about section 521(a)(2) when it was enacted was whether a statement of intention had to be filed in a chapter 13 case as well as in a chapter 7 case. The text of the section, requiring filing "within thirty days after the date of the filing of a petition under chapter 7 of this title or on or before the date of the meeting of creditors, whichever is earlier," strongly indicates that it is meant only to apply to chapter 7, and neither the rules nor the courts have required the form in chapter 13 cases.[203]

In any case, the function of the statement of intention is simply one of notice.[204] It is intended to meet creditors' complaints at congressional hearings that they could not get necessary information from debtors' attorneys and were not permitted to contact *pro se* debtors at all. Except in those courts that hold that the form requires a debtor to either reaffirm, redeem, or surrender the collateral, it should impose little burden on debtors, because it changes none of their substantive rights.[205]

7.3.12 The Chapter 13 Plan

7.3.12.1 Introduction

The most important document filed in a chapter 13 case is usually the debtor's proposed plan. This plan, which only the debtor can propose, sets out how the debtor wishes to reorganize her financial situation. Its purpose, then, is to make clear how the debtor desires payments and distributions to be made in the case. The plan may be modified as of right before confirmation and also, with the court's permission, after confirmation in certain circumstances.[206]

7.3.12.2 Form of Plan

The form of the plan is not prescribed by the rules or the statute. As long as the plan meets all of the requirements of the statute, and clearly describes how creditors will be paid, its form should be acceptable.[207] Most practitioners draft a standard plan that may then be modified to suit the needs of each case. Several examples are contained in Appendix G, *infra*.

In some jurisdictions, chapter 13 trustees promulgate form plans, which are sometimes even "required" by local rules. This procedure is probably not objectionable, as long as it does not in any way impair the debtor's flexibility in utilizing all of the options provided by chapter 13.[208] Practitioners in a jurisdiction with a form plan should take care to add, delete or modify form provisions, as necessary, to create a chapter 13 plan which meets the debtor's objectives. The need to comply with a form should never be a basis for limiting a chapter 13 debtor's substantive rights.

7.3.12.3 Required Provisions and Confirmation Standards

There are only a few plan provisions that are required by the statute. First, with one limited exception, the plan must provide for full payment of all claims entitled to priority under section 507 of the Code, unless the holder of such a claim agrees otherwise.[209] Notably, these claims must be paid even if they would have been discharged in a chapter 7 case filed by the debtor. Most important among them are usually those for administrative expenses, which include the trustee's commission and, in cases handled by private attorneys, any unpaid portion of the debtor's attorney fee as approved by the court. The trustee's commission, to cover both compensation and expenses, can vary from two to ten percent of the payments although it may occasionally be reduced in unusual cases.[210] Some courts have held that the trustee's percentage fee must be calculated as a percentage of amounts the trustee receives from the debtor and disburses to creditors, and not on the total amount the trustee receives from the debtor including the percentage fee,[211] but the fee is not always calculated that way. The Code sets a minimum trustee's commission of five dollars

---

200 See § 10.4, *infra*, for discussion of avoiding liens.
201 See §§ 8.1 and 15.5.2, *infra*, for discussion of reaffirmation.
202 See § 11.5, *infra*, for discussion of redemption.
203 Bankruptcy Rule 1007(b)(2) requires the filing of such a statement only in chapter 7 cases, and no one has argued otherwise. However, the 1984 amendments also amended 11 U.S.C. § 1302(b)(1) to incorporate among the chapter 13 trustee's duties the chapter 7 trustee's duty under section 704(3) (now section 704(a)(3)), to "ensure" the debtor's performance of the intentions in the statement.
204 *In re* Price, 370 F.3d 362 (3d Cir. 2004).
205 See § 11.4.1, *infra*, for a discussion of the requirement in section 521(a)(2)(B) that the debtor perform the stated intentions within a specified time, the other provisions related to section 521(a)(2), and the conflicting case law on these provisions.
206 See § 8.7.4, *infra*, for discussion of modification procedure.
207 *See In re* Maloney, 25 B.R. 334 (B.A.P. 1st Cir. 1982) (plan not meeting requirement that it provide for submission of earnings or income to trustee as necessary for the plan was not adequate).
208 *See In re* Walat, 89 B.R. 11 (E.D. Va. 1988) (upholding local rule requiring form chapter 13 plan when form did not impinge on debtor's substantive rights to devise plan provisions).
209 11 U.S.C. § 1322(a)(2), (4).
See Chapter 12, *infra*, for further discussion including the exception to the rule, and Chapter 3, *supra*, for a list of these claims. However interest on those claims is not required by section 1322(a)(2). *See In re* Hageman, 108 B.R. 1016 (Bankr. N.D. Iowa 1989).
If a plan pays more than the debtor would otherwise be required to pay in order to pay all expected priority claims, the plan can later be modified to provide for lower payments if some priority claim holders never file claims. When the debtor does not choose to file a claim for a non-filing priority creditor, there seems to be no reason why the debtor could not argue that unfiled priority claims should not be looked to under this section, as they would not be paid even if the higher plan payments continued. *See In re* Int'l Horizons, Inc., 751 F.2d 1213 (11th Cir. 1985) (late-filed claims may not be paid).
210 *See, e.g., In re* Eaton, 1 B.R. 433 (Bankr. M.D.N.C. 1979) (fees can be adjusted for equitable reasons). *See also* 8 Collier on Bankruptcy ¶ 1302.05[1][a] (16th ed.).
211 *See, e.g.,* Pelofsky v. Wallace, 102 F.3d 350 (8th Cir. 1996). *But see In re* BDT Farms, Inc., 21 F.3d 1019 (10th Cir. 1994).

per month unless the court orders otherwise.[212] Therefore, if the debtor wishes to pay less than that amount, perhaps because five dollars per month would constitute a disproportionate part of the payments in a low-payment plan, the plan should include a provision permitting a lower trustee's fee. The confirmation order could then serve as the order required for an exception to the general rule.[213]

A second requirement is that the plan provide for submission of "all or such portion" of the debtor's future income as is necessary for the execution of the plan.[214] Conceivably, in an exceptional case, a debtor might propose to make no payments through the trustee and therefore submit no income. Whether such a plan would be deemed to meet this requirement is unclear;[215] there is little to be lost in making the attempt if it seems appropriate, as a disapproved plan can normally be modified as necessary to gain confirmation.

Third, if the plan classifies claims, it must provide the same treatment for each claim in a particular class. This provision is intended to prevent unfair discrimination against disfavored creditors. As discussed later in this treatise,[216] the courts have not agreed as to which classifications are fair. While it is clear that secured claims, priority claims, claims with codebtors, and possibly claims that are nondischargeable may be treated separately, there is considerable difference of opinion as to discrimination between other groups of unsecured claims. Some potential classifications, which on their face appear discriminatory, may in fact be allowable based on principles of equitable subordination.[217]

With the exception of the above mentioned requirements, chapter 13 generally provides total flexibility as to the order of distribution. No particular scheme is required, although most plans call for payment of priority and secured debts before other debts, and a secured creditor may demand that plan payments be made to it in equal monthly payments and be sufficient to provide adequate protection.[218] Some debtors may wish to have priority administrative expenses paid first so that the debtor's attorney can be paid.[219] Sometimes, it might be advisable to pay some priority claims later in the event that the case is converted to chapter 7, in which event those claims would be discharged. In such a case, it would be to the debtor's advantage to pay first the secured creditors holding non-avoidable liens that would remain in existence after a chapter 7 case, rather than unsecured dischargeable priority claims. However, such a plan would likely meet with loud objections from the trustee, at least if her claim for administrative expenses were deferred, especially because section 330(c) requires trustee compensation of five dollars per month from any plan distribution. Generally, however, priority status does not entitle a claim to payment before all others, but merely to full payment as provided in section 1322(a)(2), sometime during the plan.[220]

The payments made to the trustee need not be equal. The plan may provide for graduated payments over time, or annual payments,[221] or even a lump sum payment from the debtor's property. However, the court may disapprove such a plan if it finds it to be not in good faith or not feasible.[222] The plan may provide for payments over any period of time up to five years,[223] although specific court approval, upon good cause shown, is needed for plans that last longer than three years unless the debtor's current monthly income is above the applicable median family income stated in section 1322(d).[224]

The court may[225] also disapprove a plan if it does not meet certain standards as to allowed secured claims provided for in the plan. Unless the holder of such a claim has accepted the plan, the court may require that the debtor either surrender the property securing the debt or propose in the plan to make payments having a present value at least as great as the amount of the allowed secured claim, with the creditor retaining its lien.[226] In order to achieve the latter result, unless the full amount of the allowed secured claim is paid immediately, the plan should provide for interest on the amounts outstanding. Although the Supreme Court has set guidelines for deciding the issue, there may still be some dispute regarding the appropriate rate of interest, so at least in courts which have not already decided the issue the plan may provide for the lowest arguably proper rate.[227]

---

212 11 U.S.C. § 330(c) actually sets the minimum trustee compensation at $5.00 per month. Although the trustee's commissions in the aggregate are designed to cover both compensation and expenses of the trustee, 28 U.S.C. § 586(e), there is no requirement that the fee in any particular case include expenses. Therefore, the minimum compensation is also the minimum commission.
213 *See* 8 Collier on Bankruptcy ¶ 1302.02[5][a] (16th ed.).
214 11 U.S.C. § 1322(a)(1).
215 See § 12.4, *infra*, for further discussion of plan requirements.
216 *See* Ch. 12, *infra*.
217 *See* 11 U.S.C. § 510(c). *But see* United States v. Noland, 517 U.S. 535, 116 S. Ct. 1524, 134 L. Ed. 2d 748 (1996) (non-pecuniary loss tax penalties may not be subordinated to other unsecured claims in derogation of legislatively established priority scheme).
218 11 U.S.C. § 1325(a)(5)(b)(iii). *See* Ch. 11, *infra*.
219 *In re* Tenney, 63 B.R. 110 (Bankr. W.D. Okla. 1986).

220 11 U.S.C. § 1322(a)(4) is a narrow exception to the full payment rule. 11 U.S.C. § 1322(b)(4) gives the debtor flexibility to pay priority claims concurrently with other unsecured claims.
221 *In re* Fiegi, 61 B.R. 994 (Bankr. D. Or. 1986).
222 *See* 11 U.S.C. § 1325(a)(3), (a)(6). *See also* § 12.5, *infra*.
223 It should be noted that although the plan must call for payments to be made within a period not to exceed five years, the five-year limitation may run from the date the first payment under the plan becomes due following confirmation, rather than from the date of bankruptcy filing. *See* West v. Costen, 826 F.2d 1376 (4th Cir. 1987); *In re* Endicott, 157 B.R. 255 (W.D. Va. 1993). *See also In re* Martin, 156 B.R. 47 (B.A.P. 9th Cir. 1993); *In re* Black, 78 B.R. 840 (Bankr. S.D. Ohio 1987) (Bankruptcy Code contains no provision for dismissing a chapter 13 case because payments extend over sixty-six months, if the plan complied with the duration limitations of the Code at the time of confirmation); *In re* Eves, 67 B.R. 964 (Bankr. N.D. Ohio 1986) (modification which could have been effective before five years following first payment after plan confirmation was timely, even though proposed modification was filed more than five years after first plan payment was made).
224 11 U.S.C. § 1322(c).
225 The court has discretion to approve such a plan. *See* § 12.7, *infra*.
226 See discussion of present value in § 11.6.1.3, *infra*.
227 *See* § 11.6.1.3, *infra*, for discussion of present value interest rate.

Similarly, the court may refuse to confirm a plan[228] if it does not meet both of two tests requiring payments in some circumstances to unsecured creditors.[229] The first is the "best interests of creditors" test and is set out in 11 U.S.C. § 1325(a)(4). This test requires the property to be distributed under the plan to unsecured creditors to have a present value not less than the amount those creditors would receive in a chapter 7 liquidation. Put another way, the present value of payments under the plan must be at least equal to the value of the debtor's nonexempt property (minus hypothetical costs of administration in a chapter 7 case) in order to satisfy the test.[230] The second test is based on the debtor's ability to pay and is set out in 11 U.S.C. § 1325(b). It requires, if the trustee or an unsecured creditor objects to confirmation, that unsecured creditors be paid in full or that the debtor commit to unsecured creditors all of her "disposable income" for the applicable commitment period of three or five years, depending on the debtor's income. Disposable income is defined by complicated statutory rules that are discussed in detail elsewhere in this treatise.[231]

7.3.12.4 Other Plan Provisions Permitted

In addition to the criteria set forth above, the Code offers some guidance as to what the plan may do but establishes few limitations. Under section 1322(b), the plan may classify claims (as long as it does not unfairly discriminate), modify the rights of holders of secured claims except some claims secured only by a security interest in real property that is the debtor's principal residence,[232] provide for curing or waiving any default, provide for payments on unsecured claims to be concurrent with those on secured claims, provide for curing defaults on long-term debts, provide for postpetition claims, provide for payment of claims through the sale of property, and provide for assumption or rejection of any executory contract or unexpired lease.

Moreover, the plan may include any other appropriate provision not inconsistent with title 11. Thus, except when there is an express provision of the Code, practically the only limitation on a chapter 13 plan is the advocate's imagination. Such provisions might[233] include liquidation of property by the debtor to pay certain claims;[234] higher payments on debts which are nondischargeable in chapter 13;[235] payment of some debts outside the plan;[236] priority status for postpetition utility defaults (to be deemed adequate assurance of future payment under section 366);[237] rejection of leases or executory contracts for credit insurance, health spas and other dubious bargains;[238] exemption of all property recovered by the trustee unless the applicable exemption is exhausted; avoidance of liens under section 522;[239] liquidation of property by the debtor to pay certain claims;[240] vesting of all property of the estate and the right to use it in the debtor;[241] and so forth. Many provisions that may be appropriate in a particular case are included in the annotated forms in Appendix G, *infra*.

7.3.12.5 Formulating the Plan

As a practical matter, when formulating a chapter 13 plan, practitioners should keep several broad principles in mind. A strategy must be designed for priority, secured, and unsecured debts which meets the debtor's objectives, consistent with the Code and the debtor's available income. Legitimate priority debts generally must be paid in full, unless the creditor agrees otherwise. A secured debt may be treated in one of five ways, depending on the circumstances: 1) pay the allowed secured claim (usually the value of the creditor's collateral) in full in the plan with interest, 2) cure the default, 3) treat it outside the plan and let the lien ride through unaffected by bankruptcy, 4) avoid the lien and treat the debt as unsecured, or 5) surrender the property securing the debt. Unsecured creditors are entitled to at least what they would receive if the debtor's estate were liquidated in chapter 7 (the "best interest of the creditors' test"). All of these options and requirements of the Code are discussed above and elsewhere in this treatise.

The debtor must have sufficient income to pay at least the amounts necessary to meet these standards for secured, priority, and unsecured debts as the plan is designed, plus the trustee's commission. In so providing, there is no need to accept any creditor's proof of claim as a given. It is possible to object to a creditor's characterization of a claim as priority or secured, to the amount that the creditor is claiming, or to the creditor's right to any claim at all.[242]

Once the amounts listed above are committed to the plan, it is necessary to return to the debtor's disposable income calculation under section 1325(b) to check whether the debtor has additional disposable income. If so, the trustee or a creditor will

---

228 See § 12.7, *infra*.
229 See § 12.3, *infra*.
230 Because in both a chapter 7 and a chapter 13 case administrative expenses would be paid, the deduction for those expenses in either type of case must be taken into account. For further discussion of the best interests of the creditors test, see § 12.3.2, *infra*.
231 11 U.S.C. § 1325(b)(2), (3).
  For further discussion of the ability to pay test, see § 12.3.4, *infra*.
232 Under 11 U.S.C. § 1322(c) the rights of certain residential mortgage holders may be modified. See § 11.6.1.2, *infra*.
233 It should be noted that some of the provisions discussed have never been contested in court. It is likely that some would not be allowed in some bankruptcy courts, given those courts' decisions under chapter 13.
234 See § 12.6.5, *infra*.
235 See § 12.4, *infra*.
236 See § 12.4.4, *infra*.
237 See § 9.8.2.2, *infra*, for discussion of adequate assurance to utilities.
238 See § 12.9, *infra*, for discussion of executory contracts and leases.
239 *But see In re* McKay, 732 F.2d 49 (3d Cir. 1984) (under Rules of Bankruptcy Procedure, lien avoidance under 11 U.S.C. § 522(f) must be by motion).
  See Chapter 10, *infra*, for discussion of lien avoidance procedures.
240 See § 12.6.5, *infra*.
241 See § 12.8.5, *infra*.
242 See § 14.4.3, *infra*.

probably object if that income is not paid to the unsecured creditors under the ability to pay test.[243]

Unless there are only one or two debts, it is usually impossible to specify the precise amounts that will actually be paid to different creditors under the plan. In most cases, the ultimate distribution is dependent on a number of events that occur only after formulation of the plan. For example, the amount of a secured claim may be disputed. If the plan provides for a certain level of payments to the trustee, the amount to be distributed to claims paid after the disputed claim is calculable only after the amount of the disputed secured claim has been determined. Moreover, not all creditors file claims; nationally, forty percent do not. Thus the amount each unsecured creditor receives from the total allocated to unsecured claims depends upon how many other unsecured creditors file their claims.

For these reasons, the plan need not specify how much each creditor will receive;[244] it may simply describe the order of distribution in sufficient detail so the trustee will know how to proceed once the amounts of all allowed claims are known. So long as the amounts paid into the plan by the debtor appear to be sufficient to meet the requirements outlined above, the plan should be confirmed. In any case, as mentioned earlier, modifications are freely allowed if a problem does arise.

A plan formulated as prescribed above, which does not specify how much each general unsecured creditor will receive, is known as a "pot plan" or a "base plan" because it simply provides a residual pot of money for unsecured creditors after all other claims have been paid.[245] Its advantages, which stem from its flexibility in dealing with the unpredictability of claims, are described above.

Some practitioners, however, prefer to file a "percentage plan." This type of plan specifies that each general unsecured creditor will receive a certain percentage of its claim. The advantage of this type of plan, which is typically calculated on the assumption that all creditors will file claims, is that the debtor may not have to pay all of her disposable income if not all creditors file claims. Precisely because of this possibility, some courts refuse to approve percentage plans if the trustee or a creditor objects to the plan.[246] Percentage plans also leave the debtor uncertain regarding how much the ultimate plan payments will be until all secured claims and priority claims have been determined, and until the claims deadline has passed. In addition, a percentage plan may require the debtor to object to unsecured claims filed in excessive amounts, because such claims would increase the debtor's payments.[247] (If a pot plan has been filed, the debtor is not concerned if one unsecured creditor files an excessive claim, because that will simply reduce the other creditors' share of the pot.) And, for the same reason, if an unscheduled creditor files a claim or is later discovered, many percentage plans cannot provide for that creditor's claim except through amendment of the plan, which would probably be necessary to obtain its discharge at the end of the case under section 1328.

7.3.13 Other Forms

7.3.13.1 Overview

Aside from the papers already described, there are one or two other forms which usually must be filed. These rarely require much work to prepare.

7.3.13.2 Disclosure of Fees

In every case, under Federal Rule of Bankruptcy Procedure 2016(b), a disclosure of fees paid to the debtor's attorneys must be filed. The purpose of this form is to allow the court and the United States trustee, who also must receive a copy, to monitor fees to make sure they are reasonable. A form for this disclosure comes with most commercially printed sets and is included in bankruptcy software programs.[248] Because no fee is paid to legal services or pro bono attorneys by their clients, completion of this form should pose little difficulty for them. Attorneys charging fees must provide some specificity about the services to be provided. The degree of specificity required varies to some extent based on local rule, the preferences of the United States trustee or local judges, and community custom.[249] If the debtor was assisted by a non-attorney bankruptcy petition preparer, as defined in section 110 of the Bankruptcy Code, the preparer must file a similar statement, required by section 110(h)(1).[250]

---

243 As discussed above, in some cases it may be appropriate to reevaluate the budget at this stage and to increase certain expenses, if possible in good faith, in order to minimize the necessary payments to unsecured creditors. See § 7.3.7.6, supra. It is also appropriate to withhold payments under the "ability to pay" (disposable income) test pending an objection by a party-in-interest. The test only applies to preclude confirmation if there is an objection by the trustee of the holder of an allowed secured claim. See § 12.3.4, infra.

244 See In re Parker, 21 B.R. 692 (E.D. Tenn. 1982) (plan need not describe exactly how trustee would make payments).

245 These terms are used to describe different things in different places. In some places, the "pot" refers only to money that will be paid to unsecured creditors.

246 In re Bass, 267 B.R. 812 (Bankr. S.D. Ohio 2001).

247 See In re Roberts, 279 F.3d 91 (1st Cir. 2002) (plan which provided that debtor would pay fixed amount to trustee but also provided specified percentage return to unsecured creditors required debtor to pay larger of the two amounts); In re Rivera, 177 B.R. 332 (Bankr. C.D. Cal. 1995) (chapter 13 case dismissed, even though debtors had made all payments required under plan, because payments did not provide unsecured creditors sixty-five percent return provided for in plan).

This problem might be avoided in a carefully drafted plan by including a provision which automatically decreases the percentage paid to each unsecured creditor to the extent that claims exceed the total anticipated by the debtor.

248 See discussion of this form in Chapter 16, infra, and a copy of the form itself in Appendix E, infra.

249 A more complete discussion of this issue is contained in § 16.3, infra. See also Appendices E and G, infra, for sample forms.

250 A form for this statement has been promulgated by the Administrative Office of the United States Courts. See Appx. E, infra.

7.3.13.3 Application to Pay Filing Fee in Installments

If the filing fee is not paid in full at filing or has not been waived in a chapter 7 case, the debtor must file an application to pay it in installments. The form for this application is provided in Official Form 3A.[251] The form also contains a proposed order for payments in installments. If the debtor seeks to pay the filing fee in installments, Bankruptcy Rule 1006(b)(3) prohibits additional payments to an attorney before the filing fee is paid.

7.3.13.4 Application for Waiver of Filing Fees in Whole or in Part

A chapter 7 debtor whose income is below 150% of the poverty level may apply for a waiver of all filing fees.[252] The form for the application is Official Form 3B, which also contains a proposed order. The form requests information about the debtor's income, expenses, major assets, and payments for bankruptcy services. Parts of the form need not be completed if the debtor's schedules are filed with the petition and copies of the requested completed schedules are attached to the form.

The clerk must accept a petition filed with an application for waiver of the filing fee. If the court denies the waiver, the debtor is then given an opportunity to pay the fee in installments.

As discussed above, it may sometimes be possible to file an application to waive some of the filing fees, even if the debtor has not filed a chapter 7 case.[253]

7.3.13.5 Motion for Extension of Time to File Required Documents

If the schedules, statements, plan, or other documents required to be filed within fourteen days of the petition cannot be filed on time, a motion for additional time must be filed or the case may be dismissed.[254] A simple form for this purpose can easily be prepared for repeated use.[255] Such an application should show cause for the extension and be served on the trustee, if any, and the United States trustee.[256] Most courts routinely grant a two to three week extension of time if requested before the papers are due.[257] Some courts require proposed orders to be attached to these papers and local practice should be checked.

7.3.13.6 Forms Required by Local Rules or Practice

Finally, local practice may require other papers, and may dictate the size of the paper to be used for non-electronic filings and so forth. Practitioners should consult local rules or the clerk's office for these and any other requirements.

7.4 Signing, Verification, and Filing

Once all of the forms are prepared and reviewed, they must be signed by the attorney of record, the debtor(s), or both, depending on the form, and some forms must be verified by the debtor(s). In appropriate circumstances, a petition may be signed and filed by another on behalf of a debtor pursuant to a power of attorney.[258]

The attorney normally signs two documents—the petition (including a separate signature on Exhibit B to the petition in cases involving primarily consumer debts) and the disclosure of attorney fees. Those signatures, like any other signatures on pleadings, constitute certifications that the documents meet the requirements of Federal Rule of Bankruptcy Procedure 9011.[259] The debtor verifies the petition, credit counseling statement, schedules and statement of financial affairs, and signs the statement of intention. If an application to pay the fee in installments is filed, the debtor must sign the application. If an application for waiver of the filing fee is filed, the debtor must verify that application. Either the attorney or the debtor may sign the chapter 13 plan. Under federal law, a notarized signature to a verification is not necessary if the signer certifies its truth under penalty of perjury.[260]

Every document prepared by a non-attorney bankruptcy petition preparer, as defined by section 110 of the Code, must contain the signature and printed name and address of the preparer.[261] It must also contain the Social Security number of the preparer and the printed names and Social Security numbers of all other individuals who prepared or assisted in preparation of the document, and attach separate certifications by each person who prepared the document.[262] The failure to comply with these requirements will render the violators subject to serious sanctions.[263]

---

251 See Appendix D, *infra*, for a reproducible form.
252 For a more complete discussion of this issue see § 14.6.2, *infra*.
253 See § 7.2.1, *supra*.
254 See Fed. R. Bankr. P. 1007(c).
   Failure to file timely schedules without an extension of time could lead to loss of substantive rights such as exemptions, even if the case is not dismissed. *See* Petit v. Fessenden, 80 F.3d 29 (1st Cir. 1996) (debtor's exemptions disallowed when schedules not timely filed).
255 *See, e.g.*, Forms 9–11, Appx. G.3, *infra*.
256 Fed. R. Bankr. P. 1007(c).
257 *Id. See* § 7.2.2, *supra*.
258 *In re* Ballard, 10 Bankr. Ct. Dec. (LRP) 1328 (Bankr. N.D. Cal. 1987). *See* § 3.2.1, *supra*.
259 *See In re* Jerrels, 133 B.R. 161 (Bankr. M.D. Fla. 1991) (attorney sanctioned pursuant to Rule 9011 for falsely certifying that he had explained debtor's choices of various bankruptcy chapters).
   In a chapter 7 case, section 707(b)(4) contains slightly different certifications made by an attorney in signing a petition or other documents. *See* Ch. 16, *infra*.
260 28 U.S.C. § 1746 provides that an unsworn declaration "under penalty of perjury" shall have the same force and effect as a sworn statement.
261 11 U.S.C. § 110(b), (c).
   Spaces for this information have been added to each official bankruptcy form in which it is likely to be required.
262 11 U.S.C. § 110(c)(2).
   See the various official bankruptcy forms.
263 11 U.S.C. § 110(b), (c), (i), (j); 18 U.S.C. § 156. *See* § 16.6, *infra*.

It is always important to have a client carefully review the documents and point out any inaccuracies before signing. This review serves as a final check on their correctness, and also prevents any later misunderstanding in which the client might claim that the forms were not properly prepared.

Once the papers have been signed and verified, they are ready for filing.[264] With the filing of the complete set of documents, or just the petition (including Exhibit D), statement of Social Security number, and list of creditors with the required fee (or application to waive or pay the filing fee in installments if necessary), the bankruptcy case is officially commenced.

---

[264] Local rules typically require documents containing original signatures that are electronically filed to be stored in paper form by the debtor's attorney for a period of two to five years following expiration of all time periods for appeals after entry of a final order terminating the case or proceeding. Documents should never be filed electronically before they are signed, as such conduct constitutes a misrepresentation that the documents have been signed and may subject the attorney to sanctions. *See, e.g.*, *In re* Phillips, 433 F.3d 1068 (8th Cir. 2006) (attorney sanctioned for relying upon client signatures obtained in an earlier case in electronically filing second case).

Chapter 8 After the Papers Are Filed

8.1 Introduction

Once the decision to file a bankruptcy has been made and acted upon by commencement of the case, the remainder of many a routine bankruptcy case seems anticlimactic. Although numerous complications can occur, and significant steps must sometimes be taken on behalf of the debtor, quite often only a few formalities are left after the filing of the initial papers. This Chapter describes those events which occur in every case, and also how to handle some of the other proceedings that may arise during the pendency of the case.

8.2 Advice to Clients

It is important to advise the client immediately about what will occur. The client should understand what has happened and what will happen next. She should be told about the notices that will be issued by the court. These include the Notice of Appointment of a Trustee and the Notice of the Section 341(a) Meeting of Creditors, which is normally combined with other notices of deadlines, and so forth.[1] The client should also be advised of all documents that must be provided at or before the meeting of creditors, so that she will retain current payment advices and bank statements and gather whatever other documents are necessary.[2]

Any obligations to make payments, including installment payments of the filing fee,[3] payments under a chapter 13 plan and outside the plan,[4] adequate protection payments and proof of insurance if required in chapter 13,[5] and security deposits for utility service,[6] should be carefully explained and set forth in writing.[7] In most cases any or all of these payments will be due within a month or two after the case is filed. Chapter 13 plan payments must begin within thirty days after the order for relief (normally the filing of the petition),[8] unless the court orders otherwise.[9]

The debtor should also be advised of the financial education course requirement and given information about how to take the course.[10] Attorneys often urge their clients to take the course before the meeting of creditors, at least in chapter 7 cases, so that they can know that the work of handling the case is, in many cases, essentially over after the meeting. Because many chapter 13 trustees conduct their own courses, and the deadline for completing the course is much later in chapter 13,[11] advice to chapter 13 debtors may be different.

Clients also should know their rights under the automatic stay provisions—that creditors are not permitted to seek payment of any debts,[12] and that any creditor that does take any action should be advised of the bankruptcy, with the creditor's contact reported to the person handling the case. In general, debtors should be advised not to pay any prebankruptcy debt (except in cases in which debts will remain after bankruptcy or in which they are being paid outside a chapter 13 plan). Debtors should not enter into new credit transactions without consultation, especially in chapter 13, as the trustee's permission is usually needed.[13]

As in any case, clients must advise their attorneys of any change in address. The court should then also be advised, because all notices will otherwise go to the debtor's old address.[14] Similarly, any property acquired that would become a part of the estate, for example, inheritances, marital property settlements or life insurance proceeds,[15] should be reported so

---

1 Fed. R. Bankr. P. 2002, 4004(a), 4007(c); Official Form 9 (reprinted in Appx. D, *infra*).
2 See sample letters which may be sent to clients advising them of documents needed for the meeting of creditors. Forms 26, 27, Appx. G.3, *infra*.
3 *See* § 3.2.2, *supra*.
4 See Chapter 12, *infra*, for discussion of payments outside the plan.
5 11 U.S.C. § 1326(a)(1),(4).
   See Chapter 11, *infra*, for discussion of adequate protection payments and providing proof of insurance to some secured creditors and personal property lessors.
6 See § 9.8, *infra*, for discussion of utility deposits.
7 See sample letters which may be used in chapter 7 and chapter 13 cases. Forms 26, 27, Appx. G.3, *infra*.

8 The petition constitutes the order for relief. 11 U.S.C. § 301(b). If a case is converted, the conversion is the order for relief. 11 U.S.C. § 348(a).
9 11 U.S.C. § 1326(a)(1).
10 The financial education course is discussed in § 8.3.3, *infra*.
11 In a chapter 7 case, the debtor must file a certification of course completion within sixty days after the first date set for the meeting of creditors. In a chapter 13 case, the debtor must file the certification no later than the date of the last plan payment or the filing of a motion for a hardship discharge under section 1328(b). *See* Fed. R. Bankr. P. 1007(b)(7), (c).
12 For further discussion of the automatic stay, see Chapter 9, *infra*.
13 *See* 11 U.S.C. §§ 1305(c), 1328(d).
   As a practical matter, most large creditors will be aware of these provisions and will not usually grant credit without the trustee's approval.
14 Fed. R. Bankr. P. 4002(a)(5) requires the debtor to file a statement of any change of address.
15 Under the law of some states, the debtor may be able to disclaim an inheritance, with retroactive effect, to keep that inheritance from

the schedules filed with the court can be amended[16] if necessary. And, of course, a chapter 7 debtor should not dispose of any property that is not exempt, because the trustee can, and often will, demand that it be turned over to her.[17] In some places local practice may require the trustee's permission even to use property of the estate, although this practice is questionable and may be successfully challenged if a chapter 13 case has been filed[18] or if the property is exempt.[19]

8.3 Events Which May Occur Prior to or After the Section 341 Meeting of Creditors

8.3.1 Notice of the Automatic Stay and Turnover Requirement

Although all creditors should receive a notice of the automatic stay as part of the notice of the meeting of creditors, that notice may not be sufficient to protect the debtor's rights. It may not be mailed until weeks after the petition is filed; in the meantime, creditors without notice might take action harmful to the debtor. A creditor without notice of the case will normally not be found to have willfully violated a stay it knew nothing about.

Thus, if there is any chance that a creditor might act to the debtor's detriment soon after the case is commenced, notice should be given by the debtor's counsel that the stay is in effect.[20] Certainly such notice should be given, by certified mail if possible and if necessary preceded by a telephone call or facsimile transmission, to forestall any threatened foreclosure, repossession, execution, or utility shut-off. When time is especially short, such as when a bankruptcy is filed immediately before a scheduled foreclosure sale, a special effort to provide notice should be made. This effort might include advance notice of the filing to the creditor or the creditor's attorney as long as threatened action cannot be taken early to thwart the debtor's purpose in filing bankruptcy.[21] If a utility shut-off or repossession is imminent, the debtor may choose to provide personal notice to the repossessing agent or utility employee by waiting at or near the property involved. Similarly, posting notice of the bankruptcy on a car which is about to be repossessed should be sufficient. If any of these latter actions are taken, a witness is helpful in the event of a later case based on a creditor's violation of the stay.

Special notice may also be appropriate in cases involving creditors prone to harassing collection efforts and those filing legal proceedings in state courts. And it may be necessary to notify courts where actions against the debtor are pending as well. In chapter 13 cases, the letter should also mention the stay of actions against codebtors, if it is applicable.[22]

If, after notice, a creditor or judicial officer acts in violation of the stay, debtor's counsel may file a proceeding under section 362(k) to have that party held in contempt of court, including claims for damages and attorney fees.[23] It is well established that the stay is automatic, that no further court order is necessary to restrain a creditor, and that actual notice of the bankruptcy, even without official notice from the court, is sufficient.[24] Appropriate sanctions that can be sought from the bankruptcy court include actual damages, punitive damages, and orders to pay the attorney fees and costs of the party enforcing the stay.[25] The debtor is also entitled to an order undoing the action that violated the stay.

Additionally, the filing of a case puts into effect the automatic turnover provisions of sections 542 and 543 of the Code. Under these sections, any entity holding property the trustee may use, sell, or lease (powers exercised by the debtor in chapter 13 cases),[26] or that the debtor may exempt, must turn over such property to the trustee. Because the debtor may exempt equity in property subject to a lien, or even an interest in property when there is no measurable equity,[27] this turnover should include any property held by creditors which has been repossessed or is subject to a possessory lien.[28] Here, too, notice by e-mail, facsimile, and certified mail of the property-holder's obligation is appropriate, followed up by court action if necessary.[29]

---

becoming property of the estate. *See In re* Andrade, 2010 WL 5347535 (Bankr. E.D.N.Y. Dec. 21, 2010) (refusing to treat lender claiming assignment of rights in lawsuit as secured creditor). See 11 U.S.C. § 541(a)(5) for a list of properties acquired after filing which may come into the estate. In a chapter 13 case generally property acquired after bankruptcy filing is property of the estate, but it is not necessary to amend the schedules of assets to reflect that property unless it is property that is also within the scope of section 541(a)(5) and therefore deemed to be property held as of the commencement of the case.

16 Federal Rule of Bankruptcy Procedure 1007(h) requires amendment within fourteen days after the information comes to the debtor's knowledge or such further time as the court allows. For amendment procedures, see § 8.3.2, *infra*.

17 Technically, the trustee can demand such turnover immediately. 11 U.S.C. § 521(a)(4).

18 See § 12.8.1, *infra*, for a discussion of property use in chapter 13 cases.

19 See Chapter 10, *infra*, for a discussion of exempt property after filing.

20 See sample letter to creditor, Form 33, Appx. G.4, *infra*.

21 Advance notice might also provide a later basis to challenge unnecessary costs, such as an auctioneer's fee for a canceled sale. Early notice of a bankruptcy case should cause the creditor to eliminate any avoidable costs related to a stayed proceeding or sale in order to minimize the claim which will later be filed in the case.

22 See Chapter 9, *infra*, for discussion of the automatic stay and the stay against codebtors.

23 *See* § 9.6, *infra*; Forms 34, 35, Appx. G.4, *infra*.

24 *See, e.g.*, Fid. Mortgage Investors v. Camelia Builders, 550 F.2d 47 (2d Cir. 1976).

25 11 U.S.C. § 362(k).
    Cases and issues relating to stay violations are discussed in § 9.6, *infra*.

26 See § 12.8.1, *infra*, for further discussion of the debtor's power to use, sell, or lease property in chapter 13.

27 See Chapter 10, *infra*, for further discussion of what property may be exempted.

28 See § 9.9, *infra*, for further discussion of the turnover provisions and examples.

29 *See* Forms 50, 51, Appx. G.5, *infra*.

8.3.2 Amendments to Statements or Schedules

When an amendment is necessary, whether due to inadvertence, mistake, on an unexpected change in circumstances, the procedure is quite simple. Under current Bankruptcy Rules, the debtor may amend the initial papers as a matter of course at any time before the case is closed.[30] The procedure requires the filing of an amended document verified by the debtor.[31] The amended document should be filed with the same number of copies as the original document, if filed in hard copy, and signed or verified in the same manner as the document being amended.[32]

The rules also provide that "[t]he debtor shall give notice of the amendment to the trustee and to any entity affected thereby."[33] Generally, notice of an amendment to the debtor's exemptions should be sent to all creditors. Notice should also be sent to creditors added by amendment so that they may protect their rights (although other creditors may be affected as well). Notices to creditors added by amendment should include the debtor's name, address, and Social Security number, but any copy of the notice filed with the court should not include the first five digits of the Social Security number.[34] In certain cases, the late filing of an amendment adding a creditor could prejudice the right to discharge a debt.[35] Therefore, the debtor's counsel should make sure that the creditor receives notice of the amendment and a copy of the notice of the meeting of creditors as soon as possible. There is a $30 fee for filing amendments to the schedules, list of creditors, or mailing list, other than amendments changing the address of a creditor or attorney for a creditor and amendments adding an attorney for a creditor. However, this fee can be waived upon application to the court for good cause.[36] For all other amendments, there is no fee.

Adding a creditor to the schedules may not be sufficient to bring about the discharge of the creditor's claim in a chapter 13 case if the deadline for filing proofs of claims has already passed, because a chapter 13 case discharges only those claims provided for in the plan.[37] If the debtor's plan is worded in such a way that a tardily filed claim is provided for, the debtor may be able to file a claim on behalf of the creditor under Federal Rule of Bankruptcy Procedure 3004 or seek an extension of time to file such a claim.[38] If the debtor or the creditor files a late proof of claim and no party objects that the claim is tardy, the claim is allowed.[39]

8.3.3 Personal Financial Management Course

To receive a discharge in a chapter 7 or chapter 13 case, the debtor must, with limited exceptions, submit proof of completion of an instructional course concerning financial management.[40] The Bankruptcy Rules provide that the certification of course completion will be submitted by the debtor using Official Form 23.[41] This certification must be filed within sixty days after the first date set for the section 341 meeting in a chapter 7 case, and no later than the date of the last payment made by the debtor as required by the plan or the date of filing of a motion for hardship discharge in a chapter 13 case.[42] If it appears the debtor will not be able to meet the deadlines, a motion to extend the deadline should be filed, preferably before the time has expired. Most courts will grant such a motion routinely if any good reason is alleged.

Similar to the credit counseling requirement, there are very limited exceptions for debtors whose disability or incapacity renders them unable to complete the course, or who are on active military duty in a combat zone, or if the courses are not available in the debtor's district.[43] The restrictive definitions of

---

30 Fed. R. Bankr. P. 1009(a); *In re* Olson, 253 B.R. 73 (B.A.P. 9th Cir. 2000). *See also In re* Kaelin, 308 F.3d 885 (8th Cir. 2002) (while a debtor may be barred from amending to exempt property that has been concealed, or in other circumstances of bad faith, debtor who promptly amended to exempt cause of action after he first learned about it was permitted to claim exemption even though he intended to abandon cause of action that would have benefited creditors). *But see In re* Hannigan, 409 F.3d 480 (1st Cir. 2005) (it was not abuse of discretion to deny leave to amend schedules to debtor who in bad faith had omitted real estate he knew he was supposed to schedule); § 10.3.2, *infra* (citing a few cases holding that the claimed exemptions may not be amended after a certain time).

The rules are not so liberal that they allow a single spouse's petition to join the other spouse, creating a joint case, by amendment. A spouse who has not joined in the petition originally must file a new petition, which would commence that spouse's case as of the date of its filing. *In re* Austin, 46 B.R. 358 (Bankr. E.D. Wis. 1985); *In re* Perkins, 51 B.R. 272 (Bankr. D.D.C. 1984).

31 *See* Forms 29, Appx. G.3, *infra*.
32 Fed. R. Bankr. P. 1008.
33 Fed. R. Bankr. P. 1009. *See In re* Govoni, 289 B.R. 500 (Bankr. D. Mass. 2002) (order granting amendment to exemption schedule vacated because notice not provided to judicial lienholder).
34 11 U.S.C. § 342(c)(1).
35 *See* 11 U.S.C. § 523(a)(3); § 15.4.3.3, *infra*.
36 Judicial Conference of the United States, Bankruptcy Court Miscellaneous Fee Schedule ¶ 4 (reprinted in Appx. C.3, *infra*). *See* Form 101, Appx. G.10, *infra*.
37 11 U.S.C. § 1328(a) (incorporating 11 U.S.C. § 523(a)(3)).
38 *In re* Moore, 247 B.R. 677 (Bankr. W.D. Mich. 2000).
39 11 U.S.C. § 502(a).
40 11 U.S.C. §§ 727(a)(11), 1328(g).
41 *See* Fed. R. Bankr. P. 1007(b)(7); Official Form 23 (reprinted in Appx. D, *infra*).
42 Fed. R. Bankr. P. 1007(c).

There is some question whether this rule is in conflict with the statute, and therefore invalid, with respect to a case in which the debtor files the certificate before the discharge would have been entered, because the only basis for denying the discharge under 11 U.S.C. §§ 727(a)(11) and 1328(g) is the failure to complete the course. However the better course of action is to seek an extension of the deadline to avoid having to litigate this issue.

43 11 U.S.C. §§ 727(a)(11), 1328(g) (incorporating 11 U.S.C. § 109(h)(4)). *See In re* Trembulak, 362 B.R. 205 (Bankr. D.N.J. 2007) (requirement waived when debtor died before completing course); *In re* Gates, 2007 WL 4365474 (Bankr. E.D. Cal. Dec. 12, 2007) (incarcerated debtor who was not permitted Internet access and could make only collect telephone calls found to be "disabled" within the meaning of section 109(h)(4)); *In re* Hall, 347 B.R. 532 (Bankr. N.D. W. Va. 2006) (course requirement waived for debtor

"disability" and "incapacity" provided in the Code have made it difficult for some debtors to obtain a waiver of the requirement.[44] Because there are approved national providers offering courses over the telephone and Internet in every district, the exception dealing with course availability will not normally apply. In most districts there are also in-person courses available, although transportation costs and time may be an issue in rural areas. However, there are occasional issues concerning the unavailability of courses in foreign languages for debtors who do not understand English or Spanish, and such debtors should be excused from the requirement if no course they can understand is available to them.[45]

The Unites States Trustee Program has approved a large number of courses, based on the vague statutory criteria provided in section 111(d) of the Code, and they are listed both on local court websites and on the United States Trustee Program's website, along with information about foreign language counseling availability.[46] In the regulations, application forms, and related instructions developed by the United States trustee for those seeking approval of an instructional course, the United States trustee has stated that the agencies shall provide, at a minimum, written information and instruction on the following topics: budget development, money management, wise use of credit, and consumer information.[47] The United States trustee has also determined that the course should be a minimum of two hours in length.[48] If a fee is charged for an approved course, the entity providing the course must provide services without regard to ability to pay.[49]

Chapter 7 debtors, at least, should be encouraged to take the course as soon as possible. Bankruptcy Rule 4004(c)(1)(H) provides that the discharge will not be entered if the debtor has not filed a statement regarding completion of the required course.[50] If one spouse in a joint case does not complete the required course or is denied a waiver of the requirement, this should not delay entry of the discharge as to the other spouse who has filed a statement of course completion.[51] The advisory committee note to this rule states that the clerk will close the case without entry of a discharge if the debtor fails to file the required statement. A court would probably reopen a bankruptcy to grant a discharge if a course was subsequently taken and Official Form 23 submitted, but obviously it is best to avoid the risk that the court would decline to reopen, as well as the extra work and expense a motion to reopen the case would entail.[52] The current policy of the Judicial Conference is to charge a new filing fee when a case is reopened for this purpose.[53]

Chapter 13 debtors have more time to complete the course, and often it will be offered to them at no charge by the chapter 13 trustee. They should be advised about the procedures for taking the course and urged to take it as soon as it is available to them. In some cases, the information gained in the course may help debtors with budgeting and make it more likely that they will understand chapter 13 requirements and complete their plans.

8.3.4 Production of Tax Returns or Transcripts

8.3.4.1 Providing Tax Return or Transcript to Trustee and Creditors

At least seven days before the section 341 meeting the debtor must provide the trustee with a copy of the debtor's federal income tax return (or tax transcript thereof) required under applicable law for the most recent tax year ending immediately before the commencement of the case and for which a federal income tax return was filed.[54]

This language is somewhat unclear. The better view is that it appears to require a tax return or transcript only for the most recent year, and not require it if no return was required or if no return was filed in that year.[55] If read to require a return or transcript for the most recent tax year in which a return was required or filed, it could require a return or transcript from many years before the case, which would offer no useful information and might be impossible to obtain. Bankruptcy

---

who had serious health issues including hearing impairment, impaired mental capacity, and limited mobility).

44 See 11 U.S.C. § 109(h)(4); In re Ferrell, 391 B.R. 292 (Bankr. D.S.C. 2008) (although debtors' medical conditions made it difficult for them to obtain the financial management course in person, they failed to establish that their medical conditions rendered them unable to participate in a telephone or Internet course); In re Cox, 2007 WL 4355254 (Bankr. M.D. Ga. Nov. 29, 2007) (incarcerated debtor not eligible for waiver of course).

45 In re Petit-Louis, 338 B.R. 132 (Bankr. S.D. Fla. 2006) (waiver of prepetition credit counseling requirement based on debtor's limited English language skills and lack of Creole speaking credit counselors).

46 The website is located at www.usdoj.gov/ust.

47 See Instructions for Application for Approval As a Provider of a Personal Financial Instructional Management Course § 4(2), available at www.usdoj.gov/ust/bapcpa/ccde.htm. See also Interim Final Rule, Application Procedures and Criteria for Approval of Nonprofit Budget and Credit Counseling Agencies and Approval of Providers of the Personal Financial Management Instructional Course by United States Trustees (reprinted in Appx. C.1, infra).

48 Instructions for Application for Approval As a Provider of a Personal Financial Instructional Management Course § 4(3), available at www.usdoj.gov/ust/bapcpa/ccde.htm.

49 11 U.S.C. § 111(d)(1)(E).

50 See Appx. B, infra.

51 See In re Cox, 2007 WL 4355254 (Bankr. M.D. Ga. Nov. 29, 2007) (closing of joint case without discharge as to incarcerated debtor did not prevent entry of spouse's discharge).

52 See In re Knight, 349 B.R. 681 (Bankr. D. Idaho 2006) (reopening case but refusing to waive filing fee for reopening).

53 See Judicial Conference Schedule of Miscellaneous Bankruptcy Fees, item (11) (reprinted in Appx. C.3, infra).

54 11 U.S.C. § 521(e)(2)(A).
    At least one court has required the Internal Revenue Service to provide transcripts directly to the trustee in chapter 13 cases. See In re Guidry, 354 B.R. 824 (Bankr. S.D. Tex. 2006).

55 In re Wandvik, 2009 WL 909260 (Bankr. S.D. Iowa Apr. 2, 2009) (construing statute to require federal tax return for the tax year ending just before commencement of the case). But see In re Mixon, 2011 WL 1587123 (Bankr. D. Col. Apr 26, 2011).

Rule 4002(b)(3) implements this requirement by providing that the debtor shall provide the tax return or transcript for the most recent tax year "ending immediately before the commencement of the case and for which a return was filed."[56]

At the same time as the return or transcript is provided to the trustee, it must be provided to any creditor that timely requests it.[57] By the plain words of the statute, if the return has already been provided to the trustee, a request from a creditor is not timely.[58] Bankruptcy Rule 4002(b)(4) states that the debtor must comply with a creditor's request for a tax return that is to be provided if the request is made at least fourteen days before the first date set for the section 341 meeting, thereby requiring creditors to meet an earlier deadline than the deadline for the debtor.[59] The rule does not appear to compel production to a creditor of a tax return that has previously been provided to the trustee, because it speaks only of a return "to be provided." Thus, debtors who are concerned that a creditor may request a copy of the tax documents may want to provide them to the trustee immediately after the commencement of the case. However, few creditors bother to make such requests. In any event, if a creditor does not timely request a copy of the return or transcript, it is doubtful that the trustee is authorized to show the return to the creditor. Trustees are given no authority to disclose to third parties the information in the returns or transcripts they receive, and could incur liability by improperly disclosing such information.

If the debtor fails to provide a required return or transcript to the trustee or to a creditor that timely requests it, the case must be dismissed, unless the debtor shows that such failure is due to circumstances beyond the debtor's control.[60] The most likely qualifying circumstance, at least in a case in which the debtor has counsel, would be the debtor's inability to timely obtain a copy of a return or transcript from the Internal Revenue Service (IRS) if the debtor has not retained a copy of the return.[61] The IRS may be deluged with additional requests for returns or transcripts[62] and it is not always quick to respond. A debtor with an emergency bankruptcy case may not be able to obtain the transcript in time. In such a case the debtor may wish to send a copy of the debtor's request to the IRS for the return or transcript to the United States trustee so that the United States trustee knows that the debtor is not providing the return for reasons beyond the debtor's control. Similarly, a copy of such a request might also be sent to the trustee and any requesting creditor. If this procedure is followed, a motion to dismiss filed by a United States trustee or creditor with such knowledge and without reasonable inquiry into whether the request has been fulfilled might be deemed to be a sanctionable abuse, as the motion would not be well grounded in fact or law. Even if this procedure is not followed and the debtor does not submit the tax returns in a timely manner, dismissal under section 521(e)(2) is not automatic. The filing of a motion by an interested party seeking dismissal would be required, and a United States trustee or trustee may exercise "prosecutorial discretion" to refrain from filing such a motion if the delay has caused no harm.[63]

8.3.4.2 Filing Tax Returns or Transcripts with the Court

The debtor may also be required to file with the court copies of tax returns that are filed with the IRS during the bankruptcy case or for tax years ending during the case, or transcripts of those returns, if requested appropriately.[64] At the request of the court, the United States trustee, or a party in interest, an individual debtor must file with the court:

- A copy of the debtor's federal income tax return (or at the election of the debtor a transcript of the return) for a tax year ending during the time the case is pending, at the same time it is filed with the taxing authority;
- A copy of any tax return (or transcript) that had not been filed with the taxing authority before the commencement of the case but was subsequently filed for a tax year ending in the three years before the petition, at the same time it is filed with the taxing authority; and
- A copy of any amendments to such returns.

It is unclear what will happen if the case has already been closed when such returns are filed with a taxing authority. The bankruptcy court is not likely to accept them for filing, as documents are not normally accepted for filing in closed cases. And what would the remedy be if they were not filed with the court, once a discharge has already been entered?

---

56 *See* Appx. B, *infra*.
57 11 U.S.C. § 521(e)(2)(A)(ii).
58 *In re* Fontaine, 397 B.R. 191 (Bankr. D. Mass. 2008); *In re* Collins, 393 B.R. 835 (Bankr. E.D. Wis. 2008).
59 *See* Appx. B, *infra*.
 Bankruptcy Rule 4002(b)(4) also provides that, in the alternative, the debtor may provide at least seven days before the first date set for the section 341 meeting a written statement that the tax documentation does not exist. See sample tax return statement, Form 60, Appx. G.7, *infra*.
60 11 U.S.C. § 521(e)(2)(B). *See In re* Ring, 341 B.R. 387 (Bankr. D. Me. 2006) (trustee has discretion in deciding whether to move for dismissal based on lack of return or transcript).
61 Bankruptcy Rule 4002(b)(3) also provides that the debtor may provide at the section 341 meeting a written statement that the tax documentation does not exist. *See* Appx. B, *infra*.
62 Forms and procedures for requesting tax transcripts are discussed in Appendix H.2, *infra*. Transcripts may be ordered online at https://sa2.www4.irs.gov/irfof-tra/start.do.

63 *See In re* Grasso, 341 B.R. 821 (Bankr. D.N.H. 2006) (trustee not required to file motion to dismiss; failure to timely provide tax return was beyond debtor's control as debtor's attorney was unaware of production deadline); *In re* Ring, 341 B.R. 387 (Bankr. D. Me. 2006); *In re* Duffus, 339 B.R. 746 (Bankr. D. Or. 2006) (ordinary procedures under Bankruptcy Rule 9014 requiring filing of motion and notice apply to all proceedings in which dismissal may result, except as specified in section 521(i)(1)). *See also In re* Satinoff, 2006 WL 1206492 (Bankr. S.D. Fla. May 3, 2006) (reinstating case dismissed for failure to timely provide tax return to trustee).
64 11 U.S.C. § 521(f)(1)–(3).

In any event, it is clear that this provision is only applicable if a proper request is made. The privacy requirements for such a request are discussed below.

8.3.4.3 Privacy Concerns and Safeguards

The requirement to provide tax returns or transcripts to the trustee, and in some cases to the court and interested parties, raises enormous privacy concerns. The new tax return requirements are subject to procedures established by the Director of the Administrative Office of the United States Courts to safeguard the confidentiality of tax information, including restrictions on creditor access to the information.[65] The procedures require that tax information provided under section 521 be redacted to show only the last four digits of Social Security numbers, only the initials and not the names of minor children, only the year of any date of birth, and only the last four digits of any financial account number. In addition, the procedures do not permit tax returns filed with the court to be accessible to the public.

The privacy procedures also require that a motion be filed with the court and that cause be shown, including inability to get needed information in any other manner, before a United States trustee, trustee, or party in interest, including a creditor, can obtain tax information under section 521(f).[66] The procedures limit further disclosure of tax information by any entity that receives it.[67] Because Bankruptcy Rule 4002(b)(5) provides that information provided to the trustee is also subject to the procedures promulgated by the Director of the Administrative Office for safeguarding the confidentiality of tax information, a similar motion may well be necessary if a creditor seeks a copy of tax information provided to the trustee.

To prevent further invasion of the debtor's privacy, debtors may wish to provide or file tax transcripts, rather than tax returns, because transcripts generally include less personal identifying information. Typically, transcripts are also quicker and easier to obtain than tax returns.[68] There are several different types of tax transcripts that can be requested from the Internal Revenue Service, and section 521 does not specify which type of transcript is to be used. Due primarily to privacy concerns, in most cases the preferred transcript will be the Return Transcript, which is the simplest one.[69]

8.3.5 Annual Statements of Income and Expenditures in Chapter 13 Cases

A chapter 13 debtor may also be required to file annual statements of income and expenditures, but only if they are requested by the court, the United States trustee, or a party in interest.[70] The statements must be filed beginning one year after the case is filed or ninety days after the end of "such tax year," whichever is later, and annually after the plan is confirmed (at least forty-five days before the anniversary of confirmation). It is somewhat unclear which tax year is referred to by "such tax year" as the preceding paragraphs refer to multiple tax years. Presumably, as the language applies only before confirmation, the reference is to the first tax year that ends after the case is commenced.

The sworn statement required by section 521(f)(4) must disclose:

- The debtor's income and expenditures in the preceding tax year and the debtor's monthly income, showing how those numbers are calculated;
- The amounts and sources of the debtor's income;
- The identity of any person responsible with the debtor for support of any dependent of the debtor; and
- The identity of any person who contributes support to the household in which the debtor resides, and the amounts contributed.[71]

The statement is to be available to the United States trustee, bankruptcy administrator, trustee, or any party in interest.[72]

Not all chapter 13 trustees make a practice in every case of requesting annual tax returns and income and expense statements. If they do so, they presumably will then review all of the documents, which requires a great deal of additional resources. Likewise, a chapter 13 debtor's attorney will have to devote a great deal of resources to assembling these materials every year, which will lead to larger attorney fees for an annual consultation with the debtor and for preparation of the documents. Ultimately, in most cases, these administrative costs will come from the pockets of unsecured creditors, raising serious questions about whether they will increase or decrease the distributions to those creditors, and whether they will render chapter 13 less affordable for lower income debtors.

---

65 Section 315(c) of the 2005 Act requires that the Administrative Office of the United States Courts "shall establish procedures for safeguarding the confidentiality of any tax information provided," which "shall include restrictions on creditor access." Pub. L. No. 109-8, § 315(c), 119 Stat. 23 (2005). These procedures are set forth in a Director's Interim Guidance that is reprinted in Appx. H.3, *infra*. Courts have generally protected debtors' privacy interests from unnecessary intrusions. *See* McCready v. Becker (*In re* Becker), 2010 WL 3119903 (Bankr. W.D. Tex. Aug. 6, 2010) (denying creditor access to Social Security records).

66 *In re* Pullen, 2007 WL 7143080 (Bankr. N.D. Ga. July 9, 2007) (denying dismissal of case where creditor's request for tax returns failed to state cause as required by Director's privacy procedures and was intended to harass the debtor).

67 The Director's Interim Guidance recommends that the order granting a motion for tax information should include language advising the movant that the tax information obtained is confidential and that sanctions may be imposed for improper use, disclosure, or dissemination of the tax information.

68 For information about requesting tax returns and transcripts, and copies of the relevant Internal Revenue Service forms, see Appx. H.2, *infra*.

69 Other transcripts, such as the "Account Transcript" (MFTRA-X), IMF MCC SPECIFIC or TXMOD, contain more information and are useful in determining the dischargeability of tax debts, or their secured or priority status. *See* Appx H.2, *infra*.

70 11 U.S.C. § 521(f)(4).

71 11 U.S.C. § 521(f)(4), (g)(1).

72 11 U.S.C. § 521(g)(2).

8.3.6 Avoiding Transfers of Exempt Property

As discussed in detail below, the Code gives debtors a wide range of powers to avoid transfers, including various liens on property.[73] Many of these powers are intended to protect the full use of the exemptions provided by the Code or by state and federal nonbankruptcy law.

In some cases in which a transfer, such as a lien, may be avoided by the debtor, it may save time to attempt to obtain a stipulation from the lienholder or transferee that the transfer is null and void. Occasionally a letter to the creditor, accompanied by a proposed stipulation,[74] will accomplish this stipulation. The letter might also let the creditor know that if court action is necessary, the losing party is sometimes liable for costs.[75]

If a stipulation is not obtained, the safest course of action is to seek avoidance of the transfer by the court prior to discharge. The language of sections 522(f) and 522(h) indicates that lien avoidance is not self-executing, and must be initiated by the debtor. The best practice is to do so before the case is closed.[76] In that way, there will be no loose ends or possibility of later problems once the discharge is granted at the end of the case.

The Federal Rules of Bankruptcy Procedure set out the procedure for lien avoidance. When a debtor seeks to avoid a lien under section 522(f) (applicable to judicial liens and certain non-purchase money security interests), a motion should be filed in accordance with Rule 9014 (governing contested matters).[77] For all other types of lien avoidance, or other exercises of avoiding powers, an adversary proceeding is required.[78] Some courts may permit lien avoidance to be done through a provision in the debtor's chapter 13 plan, but many do not.[79]

Regardless of the method chosen, it is good practice to follow through once an order has been obtained. The order proposed to the court may include a provision requiring the lienholder or transferee to take all steps necessary to terminate the lien.[80] Once it has been signed, it can be forwarded to the lienholder accompanied by a request that termination of the lien be recorded in all necessary records offices, and that evidence of such action be sent to the debtor's counsel. However, in most cases it may be more expeditious for the debtor's attorney simply to file the bankruptcy court order in the appropriate records offices. The latter procedure ensures that a client's rights are fully protected and does not require waiting for the lienholder to act.

8.3.7 Redemption and Assumption of Leases of Personal Property in Chapter 7 Cases

8.3.7.1 Redemption

Another important right that the debtor may exercise against secured creditors in a chapter 7 case is the right to redeem certain personal property by paying the lienholder the value of the property.[81] As with lien avoidance, it is probably easiest to attempt a stipulated settlement regarding redemption prior to filing for judicial enforcement. Of course, such a settlement must involve the lienholder's agreement on the value of the property. It could also involve an agreement by the lienholder not to seek to enforce the lien as long as the stipulated amount is paid in agreed-upon installments, either with or without reaffirmation of the debtor's personal liability.[82] A few courts have held that redemption agreements are subject to court review and therefore should be filed with the bankruptcy court.[83]

If an agreement cannot be reached, debtor's counsel should seek judicial enforcement of the right to redeem. It is unclear whether the rules require that this enforcement be done by complaint, as a "proceeding . . . to determine the validity . . . or extent of a lien,"[84] or whether it may be done by motion.[85] If there is a dispute about valuation, preparations for proof of value at trial must be made.[86] For the reasons stated above, and also because the protection of the automatic stay is lost thereafter[87] as to lien enforcement, the redemption proceeding should be filed before the discharge is granted. To meet the requirements of section 521(a)(2)(B), redemption should normally be initiated within thirty days after the first date set for the meeting of creditors, unless the court extends that deadline.

8.3.7.2 Assumption of Personal Property Leases

Section 365(p) provides that a chapter 7 debtor may assume a personal property lease if it is not assumed by the trustee. The debtor must notify the lessor in writing that the debtor seeks to assume the lease, and, if the debtor does so, the lessor at its option may notify the debtor that it is willing to have the lease assumed and condition assumption on cure of any outstanding

---

73 See Chapters 10 and 11, *infra*, for discussion of these powers.
74 *See* Form 95, Appx. G.9, *infra*.
75 Although their authority to do so is somewhat unclear, some courts have provided by local rule that creditors who unsuccessfully oppose lien avoidance proceedings are also liable for attorney fees. Additionally, Federal Rule of Bankruptcy Procedure 9011 may provide a basis to claim fees and costs if opposition to a lien avoidance is unfounded. Such a motion may be enhanced if the creditor had an opportunity to assent to the relief requested and refused.
76 11 U.S.C. § 546(a)(2) may preclude certain lien avoidance proceedings once a case has been closed. See § 10.4.2.2, *infra*, for discussion of lien avoidance after discharge.
77 Fed. R. Bankr. P. 4003(d).
78 Fed. R. Bankr. P. 7001.
79 For further discussion of lien avoidance in a chapter 13 plan, see § 10.4.2.2, *infra*.
80 *See* Form 93, Appx. G.9, *infra*.

81 See § 11.5, *infra*, for further discussion of redemption.
82 See §§ 8.8.2, 15.5.2, *infra*, for further discussion of reaffirmation.
83 *See* § 11.5.5, *infra*.
84 Fed. R. Bankr. P. 7001.
85 Fed. R. Bankr. P. 6008.
86 For a discussion of valuation problems, see Chapter 11, *infra*.
87 The automatic stay is terminated by the discharge, except as to property of the estate, in which case the stay continues until the case is closed (usually on or soon after the date of discharge in a no-asset case). 11 U.S.C. § 362(c).

    When the case is closed, unadministered property is deemed abandoned and is no longer part of the estate. 11 U.S.C. § 554(c).

default.[88] If, within thirty days after the first notice, the debtor notifies the lessor in writing that the lease is assumed, the lease is assumed by the debtor and the debtor has the right to retain the property if payments are maintained.[89] Court review and approval of the lease assumption are not required.[90]

The most common use of this provision is for automobile leases. Most courts have held that assumption of a lease under section 365(p) does not, by itself, constitute a reaffirmation of personal liability.[91]

8.3.8 Proceedings Regarding Dischargeability of Particular Debts

On occasion, it may be advisable for strategic reasons for the debtor to seek a determination regarding the dischargeability of a particular debt.[92] Such action can resolve the issue of whether a debt is being discharged once and for all, in the forum of the debtor's choice, and the debtor may obtain specific injunctive relief as well.[93] For example, if a particular tax is to be discharged, having the bankruptcy court specifically order the taxing authority to cease collection attempts may be preferable to raising the discharge as a defense later in some other forum. Similarly, it is always a good idea to obtain a determination in bankruptcy court on the dischargeability of a student loan when undue hardship is an issue, as some courts have held that such a determination may not be sought after the bankruptcy case is concluded.[94]

The procedure for seeking a determination of dischargeability is governed by the adversary proceeding rules.[95] Thus, a complaint stating the relief sought must be filed and served. Unlike complaints of creditors raising the nondischargeability of certain debts,[96] such a complaint may be filed by the debtor at any time, and a case may be reopened for that purpose without payment of an additional filing fee.[97]

8.3.9 Objections to Claims of Creditors

In those cases in which creditors do file claims, and particularly when they file secured or priority claims, an objection to a claim may be crucial to the debtor's case. Such an objection may mean the difference between success and failure of a chapter 13 plan or the reduction of a secured debt by thousands of dollars.[98] An objection may allege that the claim has not been timely filed or that it is improper or excessive for some other reason.[99]

An objection to a claim may raise any defense the debtor has against the creditor who filed the claim. It may also seek a determination that the claim is only partially secured, or not secured at all because the value of the property encumbered is less than the amount of the claim.[100]

Under current rules, there is no fixed deadline for filing an objection, but as the claim is allowed unless an objection is filed, the objection should be filed by the debtor[101] before distribution of dividends begins in a chapter 7 or 13 case.[102] The rules stipulate that the objection must be in writing[103] and must be mailed or delivered to the claimant, the trustee, and the debtor at least thirty days prior to a hearing on the objection.[104] A claim objection should not include a claim for relief of the kind specified in Rule 7001, but rather the objection may be included with the relief sought in an adversary proceeding.[105] Otherwise, a claim objection is a contested matter governed by Rule 9014. In either case, discovery should be available and the matter can be treated as fully contested litigation between the debtor and creditor.

8.3.10 Other Disputes That May Arise

Various other types of disputes may occur between the debtor and creditors before (or after) the meeting of creditors. Perhaps the most common dispute putting the debtor on the defensive is a creditor's motion for relief from the automatic stay. Strategies for defense of these actions are discussed in a later chapter.[106] Occasionally, a creditor may file a complaint seeking reclamation of property from the estate.[107] If the debtor was a debtor in one or more dismissed cases pending within the year before the filing of this petition, the debtor may need to file

---

88 11 U.S.C. § 365(p)(1)(A). *See* § 12.9.5.3, *infra*.
89 11 U.S.C. § 365(p)(1)(B).
90 *In re* Ebbrecht, 451 B.R. 241 (Bankr. E.D.N.Y. 2011).
91 *See, e.g.,* Thompson v. Credit Union Fin. Group, 453 B.R. 823 (W.D. Mich. 2011); *In re* Farley, 2011 Bankr. LEXIS 1237 (Bankr. E.D.N.Y. Apr. 6, 2011).
92 See § 15.4, *infra*, for a more complete discussion of dischargeability issues.
93 The provisions of 11 U.S.C. § 523(c), however, make clear that it would not be in the debtor's interest to raise dischargeability issues under 11 U.S.C. § 523(a)(2), (4), or (6), because if the creditor fails to assert nondischargeability under these sections, the debt is automatically rendered dischargeable.
94 See § 15.4.3.8, *infra*, for a discussion of the dischargeability of student loans.
95 Fed. R. Bankr. P. 4007(e); 7001.
96 See § 15.4, *infra*, for a discussion of such complaints.
97 Fed. R. Bankr. P. 4007(b).
98 See Chapters 11 and 12, *infra*, for a discussion of objections to secured claims and the treatment of such claims in a chapter 13 plan. See also Forms 75–85, Appendix G.8, *infra*, for examples of objections.
99 See § 14.4.3, *infra*, for further discussion of timeliness and other requirements for claims.
100 11 U.S.C. § 506. *See* Ch. 11, *infra*.
101 In some places a trustee will file an objection if the debtor alerts her to existing defenses, but the debtor should not rely on the trustee unless the trustee's filing is certain to achieve the debtor's goals.
102 Theoretically an objection could be resolved even after the distribution begins, with a return of any dividends wrongfully paid. *See* Fed. R. Bankr. P. 3007 advisory committee's note. However, recovery of such funds may be difficult. In some courts, the trustee files a motion to allow claims that have been filed, and any objection must be raised in response to that motion.
103 Fed. R. Bankr. P. 3007(a).
104 *Id.*
105 Fed. R. Bankr. P. 3007(b).
106 *See* § 9.7, *infra*.
107 See § 11.3.2, *infra*, for a discussion of reclamation complaints.

a motion to maintain, or obtain, the full protections of the automatic stay, which is otherwise limited or nonexistent in such situations.[108] All of these types of proceedings usually bring disputes regarding secured claims to a head early in the case.

Occasionally, a creditor files a complaint objecting to discharge or seeking a determination that a particular debt is nondischargeable.[109] It is also possible (1) that a motion to dismiss will be filed if there has been some procedural defect or if the debtor has not made required chapter 13 plan payments, or (2) that a motion may be filed alleging that a chapter 7 case constitutes an "abuse" of the Code.[110]

There may also be other issues that the debtor should bring to the court's attention. One method of doing so is by filing a complaint seeking declaratory relief regarding the issue in dispute. If the issue is one which frequently recurs, a class action should be considered. Further discussion of such litigation is contained in Chapter 14, *infra*.

8.3.11 Retaining Nonexempt Property in Chapter 7 Cases

In consumer chapter 7 bankruptcies, although the trustee pretty clearly has a right to take possession of totally nonexempt property prior to the section 341 meeting of creditors,[111] this turnover rarely occurs. All parties involved usually recognize that when such property is of more than nominal value the simplest method of disposition is to sell it back to the debtor, who may purchase it with exempt assets or postpetition income. For example, the debtor's automobile may be worth three thousand dollars more than the amount that can be exempted. Usually, terms can be arranged for a payment to the trustee in lieu of turning over the car for a sale in which the debtor would receive the exempted amount in cash. That payment should normally be something less than three thousand dollars in order to reflect the trustee's avoided liquidation costs.[112] As long as the case will not be delayed, the trustee should also be willing to accept the payment in installments. If difficulties do arise, the case can be converted to chapter 13, in which the debtor has the absolute right, in essence, to do the same thing—to pay the value of the nonexempt property over time.[113]

If the total value of the nonexempt property in a chapter 7 case is small, for example, less than two or three thousand dollars, it should also be possible to argue that the property should not be sold because the proceeds of a sale would be largely or totally consumed by administrative expenses and thus would be of little or no benefit to creditors, especially if the assets are not liquid assets such as a bank account. In many cases, even if the debtor does not pursue such an argument, the trustee either declines to administer (that is, sell) such property or formally abandons it.[114] Under the prior Bankruptcy Act many courts dealt with nominal-asset cases by ordering abandonment of the property back to the debtor and Congress made clear its desire that this practice should continue under the Code.[115] The Executive Office of the United States Trustees also has policies discouraging the administration of assets worth only small amounts.[116]

8.3.12 Commencement of Payments in Chapter 13 Cases

8.3.12.1 Plan Payments

Pursuant to 11 U.S.C. § 1326(a), the debtor must commence making payments pursuant to her plan within thirty days after the petition is filed.[117] Payments to the trustee must be retained by the trustee until the plan is confirmed or confirmation is denied. If the plan is confirmed, the payments are distributed in accordance with the plan.[118]

If confirmation is denied, the trustee, after deducting allowed administrative expenses, must return to the debtor any payments to the trustee "not previously paid and not yet due and owing to creditors under [section 1326(a)(3)]."[119] This language is hard to decipher. To whom were the payments not yet paid? Unless the court has ordered otherwise, the trustee would not have been paying adequate protection payments, at least with respect to creditors secured by personal property who are to be paid directly by the debtor.[120] The payments returned to the debtor must also be not yet due and owing under section 1326(a)(3).[121] However, the trustee may have no way to know what payments are due and owing. There is no indication of what the trustee is to do with the money not returned to the

---

108 See Chapter 9, *infra*, for discussion of limitations on the stay in various situations. See also Forms 46, 47, Appendix G.4, *infra*, for examples of motions.
109 See Chapter 14, *infra*, for a discussion of these types of complaints.
110 See §§ 13.2–13.4, *infra*, for discussion of dismissal proceedings.
111 11 U.S.C. § 521(a)(4).
112 The source of the payment may be exempt property of the debtor or property which does not come into the estate such as postpetition wages in a chapter 7 case. A postpetition gift to the debtor also may provide cash which the debtor can use to pay the trustee.
113 See Chapters 11 and 12, *infra*, for further discussion of chapter 13 cases. See § 13.7, *infra*, for discussion of conversion.
114 11 U.S.C. § 554.
115 See H.R. Rep. No. 95-595, at 93–95 (1977).
    For further discussion of abandonment of property under 11 U.S.C. § 554, see § 3.5, *supra*.
116 See Executive Office, United States Trustee Program, Handbook for Chapter 7 Trustees at 8-3 ("Property should be abandoned when the total amount to be realized would not result in a meaningful distribution to creditors or would primarily redound to the benefit of the trustee and professionals."), *available at* www.usdoj.gov/ust/eo/private_trustee/library/chapter07/docs/7handbook1008/Ch7_Handbook.pdf.
117 In a case converted to chapter 13, the deadline would be thirty days after the case is converted.
118 11 U.S.C. § 1326(a)(2).
119 11 U.S.C. § 1326(a)(2).
120 See discussion of adequate protection payments in Chapter 11 and § 8.3.12.2, *infra*.
121 Section 1326(a)(3) provides that the court may, upon notice and hearing, modify, increase, or reduce the payments required pending confirmation of the plan.

debtor after paying administrative expenses. There is no authorization to distribute it to anyone else. Ordinarily, after administrative claims are paid, trustees will return such funds to the debtor.

Often, payments to the trustee are made through wage deductions forwarded by the debtor's employer. A court order, normally obtained by motion of the debtor or the trustee depending on local practice, is necessary to effectuate such payments pursuant to section 1325(c).[122] If such an order is sought, the debtor should be advised that it sometimes takes several weeks for the employer to begin making the deductions and that the debtor must pay directly to the trustee any plan payments that become due before the deductions begin.

If the plan proposes to cure a default on a secured claim (usually a mortgage) or other long-term debt and to maintain current payments to be paid directly to the creditor, the debtor also must make regular payments to that creditor as they come due.[123] In most jurisdictions this obligation can be fulfilled by payments made directly to the secured creditor, thereby avoiding a trustee's commission, but in some places such payments are usually made through the chapter 13 trustee.[124] Local practice should be reviewed.

8.3.12.2 Adequate Protection Payments and Payments to Personal Property Lessors

Section 1326(a)(1) also imposes a separate requirement that a chapter 13 debtor must make adequate protection payments directly to a creditor holding an allowed claim secured by personal property to the extent that it is "attributable to the purchase of such property by the debtor for that portion of the obligation that becomes due after the order for relief." Similarly, regular payments must be paid to lessors on personal property leases (primarily automobile leases). These payments are to commence within thirty days after the filing of the plan or the order for relief, whichever is earlier.[125] Plan payments are to be reduced by the amount of the adequate protection payments and the trustee is to be provided evidence of payments made, including the amounts and dates of the payments.[126] This requirement creates bookkeeping headaches for the debtor, debtor's attorney, and chapter 13 trustee, who must keep track of this separate set of payments and integrate the amounts with the plan's payment requirements.

Some courts have ordered, pursuant to their section 1326(a)(3) power to modify the adequate protection payments, that adequate protection payments are to be made through the trustee in order to ease the bookkeeping nightmare the payments otherwise create if they are made directly by the debtor to the secured creditor. Such procedures simplify life for the debtor, the trustee, and the creditor.

When such procedures have not been adopted, for ease of administration, the debtor's attorney may wish to make one payment, directly through the attorney's office, to facilitate bookkeeping and provide evidence to the trustee. There would appear to be no disadvantage when such a payment for the preconfirmation period is less than a full plan payment (as will usually be the case), as the amount paid will be deducted from the plan payments due.[127]

8.3.12.3 Graduated Plan Payments

In some cases, the first months of a chapter 13 plan create a significant hardship for a debtor because of the confluence of required utility deposits, installment payments on the filing fee, and the need to commence plan payments and sometimes adequate protection payments. One potential solution is to propose a plan featuring graduated payments to the trustee, with lower payments in the first several months and higher payments thereafter. As long as the monthly payments and the total to be paid over the life of the plan meet the requirements of the Code,[128] the plan is feasible,[129] and the payments in each given month commit the debtor's full disposable income,[130] graduated payment plans should be confirmed without a problem.[131]

8.3.13 Proof of Insurance in Chapter 13 Cases

A debtor who is retaining personal property subject to a lease or securing a purchase money claim is required, within sixty days after the petition, to provide the lessor or creditor reasonable evidence of the maintenance of any required insurance coverage.[132] Normally, such creditors or lessors already will know if insurance lapses, as they are named as loss payees in the policy. Only when insurance has lapsed will such evidence be important to creditors or lessors. If insurance is in force, the creditor is not likely to move for relief from the stay because the debtor has not notified it of facts it already knows.

The debtor is required to continue to provide evidence of coverage "for as long as the debtor retains possession of the property."[133] The Code provision does not specify how often such evidence should be provided. Should it be annually, monthly, hourly? Creditors and lessors will not really have a concern, because they will be notified if insurance lapses. It is

---

122 See § 12.6.1, infra.
123 See § 11.6.2, infra.
124 See § 12.4.4, infra.
125 11 U.S.C. § 1326(a)(1).
126 11 U.S.C. § 1326(a)(1)(C).

127 Section 1326(a)(1)(C) provides that the plan payments are to be reduced by the amount of the adequate protection payments.
128 See § 7.3.12, supra; Ch. 12, infra.
129 See § 12.5, infra.
130 See § 12.3.4, infra.
131 Payments to certain secured creditors can be required to be in equal monthly amounts, however, at least during the period in which they are being paid. 11 U.S.C. § 1325(a)(5)(B)(iii). See Chapter 11, infra, for discussion of this confirmation standard.
132 11 U.S.C. § 1326(a)(4).
133 11 U.S.C. § 1326(a)(4).

8.3.14 Filing of Tax Returns with Taxing Authorities in Chapter 13 Cases

Chapter 13 debtors are required to file with the appropriate taxing authorities, by the day before the first scheduled section 341 meeting, all tax returns that the debtor was required to file for all taxable periods ending in the four years before the petition.[134] If the debtor was not required to file a return for a particular tax year, no return need be filed for that year to meet this requirement. Presumably this provision applies only to returns that were not already filed, although it does not say so.

If returns are not filed by this deadline, the trustee may hold the section 341 meeting open for a period of up to 120 days or, in the case of a return that was not past due on the petition date, until the latest automatic extension date.[135] The debtor may also move for an extension of time to file returns beyond the time established by the trustee, but not more than thirty days after the trustee's deadline or, if a return was not past due on the petition date, beyond the latest automatic extension date. The debtor must demonstrate that the failure to file returns as required by this section occurred for reasons beyond the debtor's control.[136]

Section 1307(e) of the Bankruptcy Code provides a new ground for dismissal or conversion of a chapter 13 case if the debtor does not file the tax returns required by section 1308.[137] As a practical matter chapter 13 debtors will often have to expend funds to have tax returns prepared in order to qualify for chapter 13 relief, even if they do not owe any taxes, further increasing the cost of bankruptcy. Again, if the returns are prepared after the petition is filed, such funds should be either an administrative expense (if prepared by the debtor's attorney) or an "other necessary expense" to be deducted in the disposable income test[138]—so the expenses will often reduce payments to unsecured creditors.

8.3.15 Audits and Rule 2004 Examinations

8.3.15.1 Debtor Audits

The 2005 amendments added new provisions for audits to determine the accuracy, veracity, and completeness of debtors' petitions, schedules, and other information required by sections 521 and 1322 of the Code.[139] Most of the audits are conducted in random chapter 7 and chapter 13 cases, except that not less than one out of every 250 cases in each judicial district shall be selected for audit.[140] There are to be other targeted audits of the schedules of income and expenses for those with unusually high income or expenses.

Since the audit provisions became effective, the procedures for audits have become somewhat more clear.[141] The audit begins with a letter from the auditor requesting extensive documentation.[142] Other documents may also be requested, but debtors should not be obligated to obtain documents that they do not have. The principal purpose of the audit is to determine whether the debtor has made a "material misstatement," but the United States trustees have refused to divulge their instructions to auditors regarding what constitutes a material misstatement.[143] In practice, auditors have claimed material misstatements existed with respect to statements that were either not material, and had no effect on the outcome of the case, or were not misstatements. In some cases the "misstatement" stemmed from an auditor's different view of the law, and in others from simple mistakes on the part of the auditor. Although auditors are instructed to seek an explanation from the debtor prior to filing a report of a material misstatement, they have not always done so. Such a report has no impact on the case unless it is followed up with a motion or adversary proceeding seeking specific consequences, but a debtor may nonetheless wish to challenge the report, which is a publicly filed document that, at a minimum, strongly suggests the debtor engaged in wrongdoing. Possible methods of challenging the report could include a motion to strike the report or service of a motion for sanctions under Rule 9011, perhaps on both the auditor and the United States trustee on whose behalf the auditor has acted. The failure of the debtor to satisfactorily explain a material misstatement in an audit or to satisfactorily explain a failure to make necessary papers or property available for inspection can be grounds for revocation of a discharge under section 727(d)(4) of the Code.[144]

---

134 11 U.S.C. § 1308(a). *See In re* Cushing, 401 B.R. 528 (B.A.P. 1st Cir. 2009) (return must be filed even if not yet due under tax law unless trustee affirmatively holds meeting open or court extends time before it has expired; there is a good argument that this decision is erroneous insofar as it required the debtor to file tax returns that were not yet required to be filed under nonbankruptcy law).

135 11 U.S.C. § 1308(b)(1).

136 11 U.S.C. § 1308(b)(2).

137 *In re* Chassie, 2011 WL 133007 (Bankr. D. Mass. Jan. 14, 2011) (court lacked discretion under § 1307(e) to take action other than dismissal or conversion and therefore granted IRS' motion to dismiss).

138 See Chapter 12, *infra*, for discussion of the disposable income test.

139 *See* Pub. L. No. 109-8, § 603(a), 119 Stat. 23 (2005); 28 U.S.C. § 586(f).

140 Due to funding shortfalls for the United States Trustee Program, the number of audits has sometimes fallen below this level.

141 A copy of the Debtor Audit Standards, 71 Fed. Reg. 58,005 (Oct. 2, 2006), issued by the Executive Office of the United States Trustees, is reprinted in Appx. C.2, *infra*.

142 A copy of the document request form approved by the Executive Office of the United States Trustees is reprinted in Appx. C.2.3, *infra*.

143 *See* Debtor Audit Standards, 71 Fed. Reg. 58,005 (Oct. 2, 2006).

144 If there is a material misstatement of income, expenses, or assets in an audit report, the United States trustee shall report the material misstatement to the United States Attorney and "if advisable, take appropriate action," which may include the filing of an adversary

There is no similar provision in chapter 13, perhaps because the audit will be completed before discharge.

8.3.15.2 Rule 2004 Examinations

In rare instances in consumer cases, either before or after the meeting of creditors, the debtor may be ordered by the court to attend an additional examination. A creditor, the trustee, or any party in interest can seek an examination of the debtor (or any other entity) pursuant to Federal Rule of Bankruptcy Procedure 2004. The permissible scope of such an examination is broad, but not unlimited.[145] Motions[146] for such examinations are rare in consumer cases, but sometimes occur due to the desire of credit card companies to pursue nondischargeability claims based on fraud. A motion for an examination can be opposed (and a subpoena can be quashed) on the ground that it would not serve a legitimate purpose consistent with the scope of examination defined in the rule.[147] The examination cannot be used for the purpose of abuse or harassment.[148]

In situations in which a creditor comes to court unprepared with evidence to establish a dischargeability case or when a complaint is filed without the sufficient grounds required by Federal Rule of Bankruptcy Procedure 9011, the creditor's failure to conduct a Rule 2004 examination can be used by the debtor as a sword. By failing to avail itself of the opportunity to examine the debtor, a creditor is open to the argument that the reasonable inquiry requirements of Rule 9011 have not been met, or that attorney fees should be awarded to the debtor under section 523(d) in a nondischargeability action.[149]

8.4 The Meeting of Creditors

8.4.1 Preparation

In many a routine chapter 7 bankruptcy, the only real event of any importance between filing and discharge is the meeting of creditors, sometimes colloquially called the "first meeting of creditors" or the "section 341(a) meeting" in honor of the relevant statutory provision. While it may pose occasional problems, this proceeding is usually routine and uneventful.

Despite the attorney's knowledge that the meeting of creditors is rarely anything to worry about, most debtors cannot believe that it will all be so simple; many expect their creditors to turn out in force to grill them about why they are not paying their just obligations. Therefore, it is important to give the client a detailed explanation of the procedure, and the questions that are likely to be asked, in much the same manner one would use in preparing for a trial or deposition.

Usually this preparation will not be difficult, as most trustees tend to ask the same questions in every case.[150] Because the questions center on the schedules and statements already filed, it is essential to review these carefully with the client, paying particular attention to the items claimed as exempt and the values given them. It is sometimes a good idea to give the debtor a copy of all or part of these documents to take home and review, although doing so may only heighten the anxiety of some clients.

8.4.2 Document Requirements

It is also necessary to assemble whatever documents are required to be brought to the meeting under local practice or the Bankruptcy Rules. In all jurisdictions, the trustee will wish to see picture identification issued by a governmental unit, or other identifying information establishing the debtor's identity,[151] as well as a Social Security card or other documentary proof of the debtor's Social Security number.[152]

In addition, the Bankruptcy Rules require the debtor to provide evidence of current income, such as a recent payment advice and, unless the trustee or United States trustee instructs otherwise, statements for each of the debtor's depository and investment accounts for the time period that includes the date of the petition.[153] If the debtor has claimed expenses under the means test calculation that require documentation, such documentation must also be provided.[154] However, the rules provide that if documentation described in this paragraph does not exist or is not in the debtor's possession, the debtor may provide a written statement to that effect.[155]

In some districts, the trustee may request deeds, titles to motor vehicles, tax returns, pay stubs, rent receipts, bank statements, real estate tax assessment documents, etcetera. These requests are often made in a notice sent to the debtor before the meeting. In a few places, local rules list documents that must be brought to the meeting. If an advocate is in doubt about these requirements, local practice can usually be easily checked. In any event, it is a good idea to bring the entire file in case something is needed. If a trustee's request is overly burdensome, the debtor

---

proceeding to revoke a debtor's discharge pursuant to section 727(d). See 28 U.S.C. § 586(f)(2)(B).

145 The examination "may relate only to the acts, conduct, or property or to the liabilities and financial condition of the debtor, or to any matter which may affect the administration of the debtor's estate, or to the debtor's right to a discharge." The scope of examination if the debtor operates a business may include inquiries about the operation of the business. Fed. R. Bankr. P. 2004(b).

146 Some courts have local rules which allow examinations to be held on notice subject to objection by the party being examined. See 9 Collier on Bankruptcy ¶ 2004.01[2] (16th ed.).

147 In re Eagle-Picher Indus., Inc., 169 B.R. 130 (Bankr. S.D. Ohio 1994).

148 In re Fearn, 96 B.R. 135 (Bankr. S.D. Ohio 1989).

149 In re Chinchilla, 202 B.R. 1010 (Bankr. S.D. Fla. 1996).

150 The questions required by the United States Trustee Program in chapter 7 cases are reprinted in Form 62, Appx. G.7, *infra*.

151 Fed. R. Bankr. P. 4002(b)(1)(A).

152 Bankruptcy Rule 4002(b)(1)(B) requires evidence of the debtor's Social Security number or a written statement that such documentation does not exist.

153 Fed. R. Bankr. P. 4002(b)(2).

154 The means test expenses and documentation requirements are discussed in Chapter 13, *infra*.

155 Fed. R. Bankr. P. 4002(b)(2).
    See sample statement, Form 60, Appx. G.7, *infra*.

may choose to take the position that only the documents required by national and local rules are required to be produced.

8.4.3 Procedure at the Meeting of Creditors

The debtor must attend the meeting of creditors.[156] If the debtor cannot or does not attend, it is often possible to obtain at least one postponement of the meeting. However, failure to attend or to obtain a postponement will ordinarily lead to dismissal, unless a reasonable excuse is provided.[157] In exceptional cases of hardship, including illness or incarceration, the personal appearance of the debtor may be excused, upon a motion filed by the debtor, and the debtor may be examined by telephone or by written interrogatories.[158]

The proceeding is likely to be short and informal in the case of a typical consumer debtor. Despite its name, it is rarely graced by the presence of any creditors. Indeed, neither trustees nor creditors show much interest in the cases of most consumer debtors.

There are several reasons for this lack of interest. Probably paramount is the feeling that there are rarely any assets worth pursuing in such cases and that the cost in time and effort required of the trustee and creditors is not justified by the benefits achieved. Unless the trustee can obtain property for the estate worth thousands of dollars, her fee will not be significantly increased in a chapter 7 case.[159] Most creditors realize that there is little they can accomplish at the meeting other than perhaps some discovery. Some creditors will appear to find out the location of their collateral and to attempt to negotiate its future disposition. Often, though, the only ones to show up are unsophisticated creditors who are under the misimpression that they are required to attend.

Local practice does, however, vary from jurisdiction to jurisdiction. In a few localities, for example, it is relatively common for creditors to appear in chapter 13 cases in order to negotiate with the debtor's counsel and the trustee concerning various provisions of the plan. If this occurs, it is important to remember that the trustee has no power to make a final decision on whether a particular plan will be confirmed. When issues are contested, the trustee or a creditor may file an objection, and the debtor may present opposition if necessary and obtain judicial resolution.[160] Frequently, even when issues are raised at the meeting of creditors, neither the trustee nor any creditor will go to the effort necessary to formally raise the appropriate objection.

The purpose of the meeting is to obtain further information about the debtor's case, particularly regarding the debtor's assets and liabilities. This information is obtained through a set of routine questions usually propounded by the presiding officer, who may be the trustee or the United States trustee depending on local rules. In a few jurisdictions, the debtor's attorney may pose questions as in a direct examination.

The questions typically seek to check the accuracy of the schedules and statements filed and, in a chapter 13 case, the debtor's ability to perform under her plan.[161] It is not uncommon for information somewhat inconsistent with the previously filed documents to come out, but it is rare that any serious problems arise. Usually any discrepancies can be cured by amendment.[162]

The questions may also go to the right to a discharge. These questions are rarely very detailed unless a particular creditor has appeared to seek information on a debt that it claims is nondischargeable. Then the proceeding may become, for all practical purposes, a deposition by that creditor.

By and large though, the questions asked parallel those in the official forms that the debtor has already answered, and have similar purposes.[163] They seek information concerning fraudulent transfers, preferences, former bankruptcies and, usually, how the debtor fell into financial difficulty. Unless an answer arouses suspicion, the questions are rarely followed up. In many districts, though, trustees are careful to ask about types of property frequently not listed by debtors, such as tax refunds, security deposits, and the like. If the procedures suggested in this treatise have been followed, no surprises should surface. However, even if new property is uncovered, it usually can still be claimed as exempt by amendment of the schedules.

As the bankruptcy judge is not present at the meeting, disputes may occasionally arise either between the debtor and

---

156 11 U.S.C. § 343.
157 *But see In re* Dinova, 212 B.R. 437 (B.A.P. 2d Cir. 1997) (case could not be dismissed without notice and a hearing after debtor failed to attend section 341 meeting, notwithstanding legend in notice of meeting that "failure by the debtor(s) to appear . . . shall result in dismissal of the case upon *ex parte* order").
158 *See In re* Seitz, 430 B.R. 761 (Bankr. N.D. Tex. 2010) (joint debtor whose spouse died after the petition was filed and who was personal administrator of his estate could appear on behalf of his estate at creditors meeting to satisfy debtor's obligation to appear under 11 U.S.C. § 343); *In re* Bergeron, 235 B.R. 641 (Bankr. N.D. Cal. 1999) (debtor with severe dementia and other medical problems excused from testifying when wife had already testified); *In re* Vilt, 56 B.R. 723 (Bankr. N.D. Ill. 1986); *In re* Sullivan, 30 B.R. 781 (Bankr. E.D. Pa. 1983) (debtor's brother, who had the debtor's power of attorney, could appear in debtor's place); *In re* Edwards, 2 B.R. 103 (Bankr. S.D. Fla. 1979) (debtor in military service in Philippines and wife available to testify). *See also In re* Oliver, 279 B.R. 69 (Bankr. W.D.N.Y. 2002) (debtor's failure to appear because he had died prior to meeting was not cause for dismissal because Fed. R. Bankr. P. 1016 provides that a chapter 7 case in which the debtor dies should ordinarily proceed to its conclusion). *But see In re* Davis, 275 B.R. 864 (B.A.P. 8th Cir. 2002) (bankruptcy court did not abuse its discretion in dismissing case of incarcerated debtor who made no attempt to make arrangements to conduct creditors meeting by means other than personal appearance).
   See also the cases on attendance at discharge hearings cited in § 8.8.2, *infra*. In many cases, it may be a good idea to request that the trustee agree to such a procedure in advance. Form pleadings may be found in Forms 66 and 67, Appendix G.7, *infra*.
159 The amount of the trustee's compensation is set by 11 U.S.C. §§ 326(a) and 330(b).

160 *See* § 8.6, *infra*.
161 See sample lists of questions in Forms 58 and 61, Appendix G.7, *infra*.
162 See § 8.3.2, *supra*, on procedure for amending.
163 The purposes of the questions are discussed in Chapter 7, *supra*.

creditors, or between the debtor and the trustee. For example, the debtor's counsel may object to certain questions for any one of several reasons, such as privilege, the Fifth Amendment,[164] relevance, or repetitiousness. Although neither the statute nor the rules address how such disputes are to be resolved, it is clear that neither the trustee nor the United States trustee can issue enforceable orders. The procedure usually followed is similar to that of a deposition—an instruction to the client not to answer, if necessary, with the dispute reserved for the court's decision if a party seeks to compel an answer.

Similarly, there is sometimes confusion about how much a debtor may consult counsel during the examination. In most jurisdictions, the practice is quite liberal; the client is allowed to confer with counsel before answering a question and counsel is allowed to interject clarifying remarks when necessary.

Occasionally a debtor cannot produce photo identification, a Social Security card, or some other document demanded by a trustee. If the document is not produced the only thing the trustee can do is move to dismiss the case, and in that event it is for the court to decide whether the document is required. Nothing in the Bankruptcy Code or the Federal Rules of Bankruptcy Procedure requires a debtor to produce either photo identification or a Social Security card in every case; the Bankruptcy Rules, as described above, require only some personal identifying information and any evidence of the Social Security number, allowing exceptions if the debtor submits a statement that documents do not exist or are not in the debtor's possession. Indeed, the Code does not even require that the debtor have a Social Security number.[165] Therefore, unless there is a legitimate question about the debtor's identity or Social Security number, especially if the documents demanded by the trustee do not exist or are not in the debtor's possession, there is little likelihood that a court would require them. Often, a trustee may back down without even filing a motion. Of course, in some cases, the course of least resistance and expense may be to have the debtor obtain the documents demanded by the trustee.

One practice that has arisen in some bankruptcy courts is a request that debtors surrender all credit cards still in their possession at the time of the meeting of creditors. Although most debtors are quite willing to relinquish the cards, if they have not already done so, some may have legitimate objections to this procedure, especially regarding necessary accounts which may not even be in default. If the debtor wishes to retain possession of the cards the request for their surrender should be opposed. Most judges and trustees admit that they lack specific authority for the turnover of the cards absent a request by the creditors involved, and they will not pursue the issue, especially if the debtor has shown good reason for retaining the cards. Indeed, it has been held that, at least in the case of a chapter 13 debtor, a creditor has no right to revoke a non-delinquent credit card based solely on a bankruptcy filing and the debtor may continue to use the card.[166]

8.4.4 Attendance of Creditors Seeking Reaffirmation Agreements

Another issue that has cropped up in some jurisdictions, but seems less prevalent in recent years, involves creditors who attend meetings seeking to pressure debtors into signing reaffirmation agreements. These creditors often threaten the debtor with repossession of items of personal property pursuant to questionable or nonexistent security interests.[167] For the reasons discussed more fully later in this treatise, reaffirmation of debts is rarely a good idea.[168] Clients may need to be reassured, however, that repossession is unlikely, and that if the clients simply refuse to allow a creditor to enter their homes to repossess, the creditor will need to obtain a court order permitting repossession.[169] It may also be necessary to assure clients that representation will be provided in any postbankruptcy action filed by the creditor seeking to obtain possession of the claimed collateral. However, few creditors take the trouble to pursue the matter that far. In the unusual instance in which that occurs, a vigorous defense raising issues concerning the validity of the security interest, and perhaps its use to circumvent the bankruptcy discharge, normally results in the creditor finding a graceful way to end the proceeding and deciding it will seek to concentrate its future efforts on debtors represented by less diligent attorneys.

Past class action cases filed against certain major retailers concerning their reaffirmation practices turned up some horror stories about creditor behavior at meetings of creditors. In some cases, creditor representatives (who earned commissions for each reaffirmation) convinced debtors to sign reaffirmation

---

164 Discharge cannot be denied for refusal to answer a question on this ground unless the debtor has first been granted immunity with respect to the matter involved. 11 U.S.C. § 727(a)(6).
    Trustees are also constrained by other constitutional protections. *See, e.g., In re* Truck-A-Way, 300 B.R. 31 (E.D. Cal. 2003) (*ex parte* order allowing trustee's entry, search, and seizure of debtor's property without probable cause or a warrant violated Fourth Amendment).

165 *In re* Merlo, 265 B.R. 502 (Bankr. S.D. Fla. 2001).
    The Statement of Social Security Number submitted with the petition and schedules provides that the debtor may check a box indicating that she does not have a Social Security number. *See* Official Form 21 (reprinted in Appx. D, *infra*).

166 *In re* Knapp, 137 B.R. 582 (Bankr. D.N.J. 1992) (under 11 U.S.C. § 541(c)(1)(B) the prepetition property rights of the debtor become property of the bankruptcy estate notwithstanding any contractual provision that gives an option to terminate the contract upon a bankruptcy filing).

167 Very often the creditors involved have claimed that they have a security interest pursuant to a credit card agreement. These security interests, if they exist, are difficult, if not impossible, to enforce. They are generally based on an adhesion contract which is mailed to the debtor with the card and in the case of a revolving charge, it is often impossible to determine whether the secured claims have been paid off.

168 *See* §§ 8.8.2, 15.5.2, *infra*.

169 For a more complete discussion of the issues, see National Consumer Law Center, Repossessions (7th ed. 2010 and Supp.).
    See also Helping Your Client Do the Wash: The Effect in Bankruptcy of PMSI Claims Created by Revolving Credit Accounts, 12 NCLC REPORTS *Bankruptcy and Foreclosures Ed.* 37 (Jan./Feb. 1994).

agreements without the knowledge of the debtor's attorney, often because the attorney was in the meeting room with other clients and the trustee. As the agreements were never filed with the court, neither the attorney nor the court system was aware of the existence of these agreements. Debtors nevertheless paid under the agreements when billed after bankruptcy.

Practices such as these require educating clients prior to the meeting of creditors concerning the disadvantages of reaffirmation agreements. Perhaps even more importantly clients should be told to report any direct contact by a creditor, not only for advice before making a decision, but also so that sanctions against the creditor may be considered.

8.4.5 Examination of Chapter 7 Debtors' Awareness of Bankruptcy Information—Bankruptcy Information Sheet

In chapter 7 cases only, the trustee must orally examine the debtor to "ensure" that the debtor is aware of several things.[170] The legislative history makes clear that the sole purpose of this examination is informational.[171] Thus, there should be no consequences if the debtor expresses lack of awareness or confusion in the face of the trustee's examination.

The first subject of the required examination is the debtor's awareness of the potential consequences of bankruptcy on a person's credit history. However, other than the fact that bankruptcy appears on a credit report for ten years, it is hard to see what a trustee can say on this topic. If the idea was to convince a debtor not to file a bankruptcy case, the information would come too late; the bankruptcy has already been filed by the time of the meeting and cannot be removed from a credit history. Moreover, as the legislative history states,[172] the trustee cannot and should not prognosticate about how bankruptcy will affect future credit, or that dismissal would improve the debtor's chances of obtaining credit. Some creditors give credit to recent bankruptcy debtors. Indeed, if the debtor's income is freed from payment on numerous obligations, the debtor may have a better chance of obtaining credit. And, because many creditors do not distinguish between chapter 7 and chapter 13 cases on credit reports, the trustee cannot and should not predict that the debtor's credit will be better if the case is converted to chapter 13.

The second topic is the debtor's ability to file a petition under a different chapter. This information is presumably to ensure the debtor knows that chapter 13 is also available. However, the debtor will already have been informed of that fact both by counsel (who must certify in the petition that this information was given) and in the notice of the chapters available that must be given to every debtor.[173]

The third topic is the effect of receiving a discharge of debts under the Code. This information includes not only the fact that the discharge eliminates liability on most debts, but also the risks of and procedures for reaffirming debts.[174] In this context, the debtor should be informed that a debt may be paid voluntarily after discharge without a reaffirmation which waives the protections of the discharge.[175] As the legislative history points out,[176] most debtors who reaffirm debts will no longer receive the warnings about the dangers of reaffirmation given by the court, so it is important that this information be given by the trustee.

The normal procedure is that trustees will attempt to minimize the time necessary for this examination by giving out the information in written form, the "Bankruptcy Information Sheet," and then inquiring whether the debtor has read it.[177] If the debtor is given such a handout and has questions about it, the time following the creditors' meeting is a good time for the debtor's attorney to answer these questions.

8.4.6 Checking Claims That Have Been Filed

The meeting of creditors is a good time to check which creditors have filed proofs of claim in cases where claims will be paid, and to set up a tickler for any claims that the debtor may wish to file on behalf of creditors. Because generally the only creditors that will be paid in a chapter 13 case (or in those few chapter 7 cases in which there are dividends) are those for whom proofs of claim are filed, a debtor's counsel should make sure to file claims on behalf of any creditors who have not filed and whom the debtor wants to pay.[178] The debtor may file such claims at any time during the thirty days after the deadline for the creditor to file a claim.[179] In addition, it is useful to check the claims filed at this time, as well as shortly after the deadline for filing claims,[180] to determine whether there are any claims

---

170 11 U.S.C. § 341(d).

171 H.R. Rep. No. 103-835, at 43 (1994), *reprinted in* 1994 U.S.C.C.A.N. 3340.

172 *Id.*

173 *See* Official Form 1 (reprinted in Appx. D, *infra*); 11 U.S.C. §§ 342(b), 521(a)(1)(B)(iii).

174 H.R. Rep. No. 103-835, at 43 (1994), *reprinted in* 1994 U.S.C.C.A.N. 3340.

175 11 U.S.C. § 524(f).

176 11 U.S.C. § 524(f).

177 11 U.S.C. § 524(f).

   A sample of this form is reprinted as Form 63, Appendix G.7, *infra*. Versions of this form reprinted in Spanish, Vietnamese, French, Chinese, Korean, Hmong, Tagalog, and Arabic are available on the United States Trustee Program's website, www.usdoj.gov/ust.

178 Because secured debts, nondischargeable debts, or debts that were cosigned by friends or relatives often have to be paid by the debtor or others even after the discharge, it is to the debtor's advantage to make sure the maximum amount possible is paid on these debts during the bankruptcy case. See Chapter 15, *infra*, for a discussion of nondischargeable debts in chapters 7 and 13.

179 Fed. R. Bankr. P. 3004.

   Notice of such a claim is given to the creditor and trustee. Although the rules do not provide for a creditor to respond to such a claim, some courts have allowed a creditor to amend a proof of claim filed by the debtor on the creditor's behalf. *See, e.g., In re Kolstad*, 101 B.R. 492 (Bankr. S.D. Tex. 1989), *aff'd*, 928 F.2d 171 (5th Cir. 1991).

180 This deadline is ninety days after the first date set for the meeting of creditors. Fed. R. Bankr. P. 3002(c).

to which the debtor wishes to object.[181] The rules do not set a time limit for objections to claims. However, local rules and practice should be checked because some courts set deadlines for claim objections in chapter 13 cases.[182]

8.5 Chapter 7 Cases—After the Meeting of Creditors

In the typical no-asset bankruptcy, there is little to be done between the meeting of creditors and the discharge. If the debtor has not yet completed the financial education course, that must be accomplished so that the certification of completion may be filed by sixty days after the first date set for the meeting of creditors. Proceedings commenced by the debtor, such as for lien avoidance or redemption, may be litigated, as well as proceedings concerning dischargeability of debts and other matters. Amendments to the schedules or statement of affairs may be necessary. However, amendments that add creditors may not always be of value after the deadline for filing a nondischargeability complaint has passed.[183]

If the debtor has more than nominal nonexempt assets, of course, they are turned over or their value is paid to the trustee who, as described in an earlier chapter, liquidates them.[184] Such events rarely occur because consumer debtors with nonexempt assets usually opt for chapter 13. However, when this does occur, it is important for the debtor to check to make sure that claims are filed for debts that may be nondischargeable, in order to maximize the amount that is paid toward those debts from the assets of the estate.[185]

In some districts, the trustee files a report to the court concerning whether she objects to the exemptions claimed or to the discharge of the debtor. The necessity of this report, which was required under a provision of the prior rules not included in the current rules,[186] is questionable because under the Code the exemptions are self-executing if no objection is filed.[187]

The trustee or any creditor who wishes to object to the exemptions claimed must file such objections in writing and serve them within thirty days after the conclusion of the meeting of creditors (or, if later, the date of any amendment to the exemptions claimed).[188] Thereafter, there must be a hearing on the objections, at which the objecting party has the burden of proving the exemptions are not properly claimed.[189]

8.6 Chapter 13 Confirmation Hearing

In a chapter 13 case, the next step after the section 341 meeting is normally the confirmation hearing, which may be scheduled on the same day or any time up to forty-five days later.[190] In many cases the confirmation hearing will not be concluded on that date, however. Often it is not possible to conclude the confirmation hearing until many months after the meeting of creditors, pending determination of the claims that are filed or the court's decision on various issues, such as objections to priority or secured claims. Without such decisions there may be no way to determine whether the plan pays such claims the amount to which they are entitled,[191] as is usually required for confirmation.[192]

The procedures followed at the confirmation hearing vary greatly. If neither the trustee nor any creditor objects to confirmation, the hearing usually takes only a few minutes, and the court simply enters an order of confirmation finding that the plan complies with all of the provisions of chapter 13.[193] The debtor's attendance may not be necessary. In fact, some bankruptcy judges actively discourage counsel from bringing their clients to the confirmation hearing, so that the debtors will not

---

However, governmental units are given 180 days from the date of the order for relief (normally the date the petition was filed) to file their claims, and sometimes longer if the debtor files a tax return during the case pursuant to section 1308. 11 U.S.C. § 502(b)(9).

181 This should include a review of the Mortgage Proof of Claim Attachment form that is attached to a mortgage creditor's proof of claim in a chapter 13 case in which the debtor is curing a mortgage default. *See* Fed. R. Bankr. P. 3001(c)(2)(C); Official Form 10 (Attachment A), *reprinted in* Appx. D, *infra*; § 11.6.2.8.2, *infra*. *See also* § 14.4.3, *infra* (discussing claims objections).

182 It is not clear that such deadlines are valid, especially if the resolution of the objection is not necessary to the chapter 13 plan confirmation process, as the Federal Rules of Bankruptcy Procedure do not set a deadline. *See* § 14.4.3.1, *infra*.

183 See Chapter 15, *infra*, for a discussion of creditors not listed in the schedules prior to the creditors meeting. Some courts have allowed the addition of creditors even after the closing of the case in no-asset chapter 7 cases. *In re* Rosinski, 759 F.2d 539 (6th Cir. 1985); *In re* Stark, 717 F.2d 322 (7th Cir. 1983); *In re* Adams, 41 B.R. 933 (D. Me. 1984); *In re* Soures, 19 B.R. 798 (Bankr. E.D. Va. 1982) (permission to add creditor after discharge granted when no prejudice to creditor in no-asset case). *But see In re* Swain, 21 B.R. 594 (Bankr. D. Conn. 1982) (debtors denied permission to amend schedules to add creditor after discharge).

184 *See* Ch. 3, *supra*.

185 *See In re* Danielson, 981 F.2d 296 (7th Cir. 1992) (debtor not permitted to file untimely claim for Internal Revenue Service, which would have allowed distributions from the estate that would have reduced nondischargeable tax liability).

This decision may have been overruled by amendments to section 726 permitting distributions on late-filed claims.

186 *Compare* Fed. R. Bankr. P. 4003 *with* former R. Bankr. P. 403(b).

187 11 U.S.C. § 522(*l*).

For further discussion of exemption practices, see Chapter 10, *infra*.

188 Fed. R. Bankr. P. 4003(b).

189 Fed. R. Bankr. P. 4003(c).

190 11 U.S.C. § 1324(b) provides that the confirmation hearing must be held between twenty and forty-five days after the meeting of creditors unless the court finds it is in the best interests of creditors and the estate to hold it earlier and no party objects. Under prior law, some courts waited until three months after the meeting of creditors had passed before holding the confirmation hearing so that all claims (except perhaps governmental claims) were filed by the date of the hearing.

191 See § 14.4.3, *infra*, for further discussion of objections to claims.

192 See Chapters 11 and 12, *infra*, for discussion of confirmation requirements.

193 *See In re* Hines, 723 F.2d 333 (3d Cir. 1983) (trustee's recommendation is sufficient basis for confirming plan); *In re* Dues, 98 B.R. 434 (Bankr. N.D. Ind. 1989) (absent objection, full evidentiary hearing is not required).

lose another day's pay. Other judges do not even require that counsel be present when there is no objection; they simply sign the confirmation order in chambers. Local practice in this regard should be checked.

If there are objections or if the court has questions of its own, testimony and argument may be taken regarding the debtor's income, ability to pay, and other matters.[194] Normally, objections are filed prior to the hearing,[195] but they may be filed as late as the hearing itself if the court sets that deadline for their filing.[196] A creditor that has not filed a proof of claim generally does not have standing to object to the plan.[197] The substantive issues likely to be raised by objections are discussed in later chapters.[198]

Lastly, in some districts the court may require counsel to present a proposed order of confirmation[199] or an application for confirmation. As is required in other proceedings, inquiry should be made into local practice on these matters prior to the date of the hearing. The day of the confirmation hearing is a good time to determine what claims have been filed, especially if the hearing has been continued to a date on which the deadline for filing claims has already expired. If only a few claims have been filed, the plan may provide more than enough payments to pay all filed claims in full. If that is the case, it is obviously in the debtor's interest to modify the plan to lower either the amount or the number of payments. Otherwise, because of the way some trustees' computers are programmed, the debtor may continue to make payments to the trustee even after all claims have been paid.

Because the debtor has the absolute right to modify the plan prior to confirmation,[200] it may be wise to file a modified plan to deal with anticipated objections to confirmation that are not likely to be rejected by the court. Usually, if the court denies confirmation, the debtor is also given an opportunity to file a modified plan. Once the debtor files a modified plan, the court must base its confirmation decision on that modified plan.[201]

8.7 Administration of the Chapter 13 Plan

8.7.1 Trustee Payments to Creditors

Once the chapter 13 plan has been confirmed, the trustee usually takes over the administrative details. Although the debtor may have been making payments for some time, no distribution is made until after confirmation unless the trustee has been distributing adequate protection payments. If the time for filing claims has not yet elapsed,[202] there may be further delays before all claims are determined and allowed. In the interim, objections to other claims, as well as other disputes that arise, may be litigated.

It is a good idea to monitor the trustee's payments periodically once distribution has begun. Most trustees allow convenient access to their records, often on the Internet or by other electronic means, and some mail computer printouts to debtors or their counsel. It is not uncommon for computer-ordered payments from a trustee's office to deviate from either the plan or the claims actually filed. In that event, it is important to bring the problem to the trustee's attention before incorrect amounts have been paid.[203] An occasional check on the progress of the plan can also reveal any other budding problems, such as a delinquency in the debtor's payments. Similarly, it is important to make sure that employer wage withholding for payments to the trustee end when the plan is completed.[204]

Finally, it is common for creditors to credit payments received from the trustee in a manner which is inconsistent with the debtor's plan. For example, current payments of principal and interest may be lumped together with payments made on the arrears and credited in ways that will not lead to reinstatement of a mortgage debt upon completion of the plan. All amounts paid may be credited exclusively to the interest arrears so that there is no principal reduction commensurate with the debtor's payments and new late charges may continue to accrue. It is therefore a good idea to monitor the debtor's account

---

194 At this hearing the burden of proof and the burden of going forward concerning an objection should be placed on the objecting party. *In re* Mendenhall, 54 B.R. 44 (Bankr. W.D. Ark. 1985); *In re* Flick, 14 B.R. 912 (Bankr. E.D. Pa. 1981).

195 The objections must consist of more than simply checking a box on the proof of claim form rejecting the plan. They must state specific grounds for objections. *In re* DeSimone, 17 B.R. 862 (Bankr. E.D. Pa. 1982).

196 Federal Rule of Bankruptcy Procedure 3015(f) provides that objections to confirmation must be filed and served upon the debtor and the trustee, as well as transmitted to the United States trustee, prior to confirmation. A local rule may set an earlier deadline for such objections. *See In re* Turner, 2010 Bankr. LEXIS 3300 (Bankr. D.S.C. Sept. 21, 2010) (creditor could not object to confirmation of debtor's amended plan when creditor failed to object to original plan within deadline set in local form plan and amendments to plan did not change treatment of creditor's claim); *In re* Dorn, 315 B.R. 68 (E.D. Ark. 2004); *In re* Gaona, 290 B.R. 381 (Bankr. S.D. Cal. 2003) (objections untimely under local rule); *In re* Harris, 275 B.R. 850 (Bankr. S.D. Ohio 2002) (objections filed after deadline established in clerk's notice were untimely); *In re* Carbone, 254 B.R. 1 (Bankr. D. Mass. 2000) (objection not timely because it was not received by clerk within time period allowed by local rule); *In re* Duncan, 245 B.R. 538 (Bankr. E.D. Tenn. 2000) (objection not timely filed under local rule even though filed before confirmation).

197 *In re* Stewart, 46 B.R. 73 (Bankr. D. Or. 1985). *See In re* Hansel, 160 B.R. 66 (S.D. Tex. 1993) (holder of untimely filed proof of claim lacks standing to object to confirmation).

198 *See* Chs. 11, 12, *infra*.

199 *See* Form 19, Appx. G.3, *infra*.

200 11 U.S.C. § 1323.

201 *In re* Nielsen, 211 B.R. 19 (B.A.P. 8th Cir. 1997).

202 Fed. R. Bankr. P. 3002(c) allows the filing of claims up to three months after the first date set for the meeting of creditors.

203 Although a trustee is probably liable for such improper payments and can often recoup them from improperly paid creditors, it is far better to avoid having to litigate that issue.

204 *See* Nowlin v. RNR, L.L.C. (*In re* Nowlin), 2009 WL 2872916 (Bankr. M.D. Tenn. Aug. 27, 2009) (employer sanctioned for continuing to withhold wages from debtor to recover money it was ordered to pay to bankruptcy trustee).

statements in order to catch these problems before the plan is completed,[205] and to include a provision in the plan directing how payments are to be applied.[206] Alternatively, pre-discharge or post-discharge litigation may be necessary based on the creditor's failure to comply with the confirmed plan.[207]

8.7.2 Postpetition Claims

Once distribution has begun, events normally flow smoothly for the duration of the plan, with the debtor or the debtor's employer[208] sending payments regularly to the trustee for distribution. The Code provides for incorporation of certain postpetition claims (debts incurred after the petition) into the plan;[209] however, such debts may also be paid outside the plan. Allowable postpetition claims may include debts for postpetition taxes[210] and consumer debts for property or services necessary for the debtor's performance under the plan.[211] Regardless of whether the postpetition claims are to be paid through the plan or outside it, creditors often require the trustee's approval before any significant obligation is incurred.[212] Such approval is rarely difficult to obtain,[213] though local practices may vary.

When the debtor, trustee, and creditor do not agree that a postpetition claim should be paid through the plan, there may be different results. Only a creditor may file a postpetition claim, so that a debtor may not force a postpetition creditor into the plan involuntarily.[214] If a creditor does not choose to file a claim, the postpetition claim will survive the bankruptcy and can be enforced in nonbankruptcy courts to the extent that it is not paid.[215] Similarly, the debtor may choose not to provide for postpetition claims in the plan for a variety of reasons, including the inability to control which postpetition claims are filed and the possibility that they may exceed what the debtor can pay.[216] However, if the plan provides for payment of a postpetition claim and a postpetition claim is filed, the trustee must pay the claim.[217]

If a creditor and the debtor both want the claim to be treated under the plan, and the claim is filed and allowable under 11 U.S.C. § 1305(a)(2) and § 1305(c),[218] a modification of the plan may be necessary to accommodate the claim. Modification may be accomplished either by increasing the payments or the length of the plan and perhaps separately classifying the claim so it is paid in full. At least one court has held that, if the debtor refuses to apply for the necessary modification, the claim cannot be allowed and it will be retained by the creditor for enforcement outside the bankruptcy.[219] This result seems clearly correct, as Code section 1322(b)(6) is a permissive provision. The debtor may provide for postpetition claims in the plan, but is not required to do so.

Postpetition claims that are filed and allowed are normally discharged by a chapter 13 discharge if they are provided for in the plan. However, if the trustee's approval of a postpetition debt could have been obtained by the debtor but was not obtained, that debt survives the discharge to the extent it has not been paid.[220]

---

205 When a debtor suspects that payments have not been credited properly, a "qualified written request" under the Real Estate Settlement Procedures Act (RESPA) may be sent to the creditor which will trigger an obligation on the part of the creditor (or servicer) to provide information relating to the account and to correct account errors. See 12 U.S.C. § 2605(e). See also Little Known RESPA Provision Offers Relief from Servicer Problems, 15 NCLC REPORTS Consumer Credit and Usury Ed. 21 (May/June 1997); National Consumer Law Center, Foreclosures Ch. 9 (4th ed. 2012).
For a sample request form, see Form 87, Appx. G.8, infra.
206 For sample plan provisions, see Form 18, Appx. G.3, infra.
207 Fed. R. of Bankr. P. 3002.1 provides procedures that can be followed to resolve such issues. See §§ 11.6.2.8.2, 12.11, infra.
A creditor's willful failure to apply payments in accordance with the plan may give rise to a claim under section 524(i). See § 14.4.3.4.4, infra.
208 See § 12.6.1, infra, for discussion of wage orders requiring employers to remit a portion of the debtor's paycheck to the trustee.
209 11 U.S.C. § 1305.
210 See In re Ripley, 926 F.2d 440 (5th Cir. 1991) (income tax is payable postpetition, when return is due, rather than prepetition when quarterly payments were due, for the purpose of determining whether postpetition claim for taxes is timely). But see In re Joye, 578 F.3d 1070 (9th Cir. 2009) (taxes incurred before petition date were prepetition claims once tax year ended, even if return was not yet due). Postpetition taxes are not entitled to administrative expense status, regardless of whether the governmental entity files an allowable postpetition claim. In re Gyulafia, 65 B.R. 913 (Bankr. D. Kan. 1986).
211 See 11 U.S.C. § 1305(a); In re Roseboro, 77 B.R. 38 (Bankr. W.D.N.C. 1987). But see In re Farquhar, 112 B.R. 34 (Bankr. D. Colo. 1989) (claims based on fire damage to debtor's property are not allowable as postpetition claims).
212 See 11 U.S.C. § 1305(b).
213 See Form 91, Appx. G.8, infra; 11 U.S.C. §§ 1305, 1328(d).

214 In re Seyden, 294 B.R. 418 (Bankr. S.D. Ga. 2002) (debtor did not have standing to file postpetition tax claim); In re Benson, 116 B.R. 606 (Bankr. S.D. Ohio 1990) (debtor could not file claim for postpetition rent-to-own creditor); In re Hester, 63 B.R. 607 (Bankr. E.D. Tenn. 1986); In re Pritchett, 55 B.R. 557 (Bankr. W.D. Va. 1985); In re Nowak, 17 B.R. 860 (Bankr. N.D. Ohio 1982).
215 In re Dunn, 83 B.R. 694 (Bankr. D. Neb. 1988) (postpetition claims not discharged because they were not provided for in the plan); In re Lewis, 33 B.R. 98 (Bankr. W.D.N.Y. 1983) (leave of court obtained to sue debtor in state court while chapter 13 case pending).
If the case is converted to chapter 7 and the claim is dischargeable, a postpetition claim is discharged. 11 U.S.C. § 348(d). See § 8.7.5, infra.
216 See In re Owens, 2010 WL 730717 (Bankr. E.D.N.C. Feb. 25, 2010) (debtor not required to pay in plan IRS claims filed after debtor had completed plan payments).
217 In re Woods, 316 B.R. 522 (Bankr. N.D. Ill. 2004) (debtor successfully argued that plan providing for payment of all priority claims provided for payment of postpetition tax claim).
218 The trustee or debtor may object to allowance of the claim under this section if the creditor knew or should have known that obtaining the trustee's approval of the debt was practicable and that approval was not obtained.
219 In re Nelson, 27 B.R. 341 (Bankr. M.D. Ga. 1983). See also In re Smith, 192 B.R. 712 (Bankr. E.D. Tenn. 1996) (local rule providing that postpetition claim must be paid one-hundred percent unless creditor affirmatively consents otherwise and payments on other claims may not be reduced due to postpetition claim unless debtors comply with local rule procedures).
220 11 U.S.C. § 1328(d).

8.7.3 Postpetition Mortgage Payments

It is helpful to monitor whether changes in the ongoing, postpetition mortgage payments are being implemented in cases in which the debtor is curing mortgage defaults. Bankruptcy Rule 3002.1(b) requires the mortgage creditor to notify the trustee, debtor, and debtor's attorney of any change in the payment amount no later than twenty-one days before the new amount is due.[221] If the plan provides for the postpetition payments to be paid by the debtor directly to the mortgage creditor, and the mortgage has a variable interest rate or escrow account, the debtor should be advised to anticipate receiving such notices and to begin making payments at the new amount on the effective date of the change listed in the notice. If the trustee is making the postpetition mortgage payments under the plan, it is advisable to periodically check whether the trustee is disbursing the changed payment amount. However, if it appears that the payment change is not authorized by the contract or nonbankruptcy law, a determination by the court should be sought promptly.

Similarly, the mortgage creditor in such cases must notify the trustee, debtor, and debtor's attorney of any fees that are charged on the account, within 180 days after they are incurred.[222] It is advisable to consult with the debtor, at least on an annual basis during the plan, about how the debtor intends to respond to such notices. If the fees are disputed, the debtor may file a motion within one year after service of the notice requesting that the court determine whether the fees are required by the underlying contract or applicable nonbankruptcy law to cure the default or maintain ongoing payments.[223] If the debtor does not dispute the fees and is unable to pay them by making payments outside the plan in addition to the required plan payments, it may be advisable for the debtor to seek a modification of the plan to provide for payment of the fees under the plan.

8.7.4 Modification of the Plan

Debtors often need to modify their plans after confirmation, either to raise payments to accommodate postpetition claims or to lower the payments because the debtor has had a change of circumstances. One such change of circumstances may occur if the debtor loses use of a car that serves as collateral for a secured claim being paid under the plan, through its destruction, repossession, inoperability, or other cause, or if the debtor no longer needs the vehicle. Although some courts have erroneously refused to permit a debtor to modify a plan in order to surrender a vehicle and treat the secured creditor's claim as unsecured,[224] others have permitted such modifications.[225] The Code permits modification of the "amount of the distribution to a creditor" to "take into account any payment of such claim other than under the plan,"[226] which should include surrender or repossession of the vehicle. In addition, a court may reconsider a claim under Code section 502(j) and, under Federal Rule of Bankruptcy Procedure 3008, the court's reconsideration may allow or disallow a claim, increase or decrease the amount of a prior allowance, accord the claim a different priority, or give rise to any other appropriate order.[227] A court reconsidering a claim can reclassify a secured claim as unsecured and grant a motion modifying the amount of payments to the creditor accordingly.[228] Alternatively, the debtor may wish to modify a plan to use insurance proceeds available due to a car's destruction (which typically serve as additional collateral because the creditor is named as loss payee) to purchase a new vehicle that can serve as substitute collateral for the creditor's claim.[229]

Alternatively, a debtor may seek to modify the plan in order to complete plan payments through a sale of property or refinancing of a mortgage. The issues surrounding such modifications are discussed later in this treatise.[230] The trustee or a holder of an unsecured claim may also seek plan modification, if the debtor's financial circumstances have improved since confirmation.[231] However, the debtor probably need not prove

---

221 *See* § 11.6.2.8.2, *infra*.
222 *See* Fed. R. Bankr. P. 3002.1(c); § 11.6.2.8.2, *infra*.
223 *See* Fed. R. Bankr. P. 3002.1(e); § 11.6.2.8.2, *infra*.
224 *See, e.g., In re* Adkins, 425 F.3d 296 (6th Cir. 2005); *In re* Nolan, 232 F.3d 528 (6th Cir. 2000). *But see In re* DeAvila, 431 B.R. 178 (Bankr. W.D. Mich. 2010) (when debtors surrendered property to creditor they had been paying directly and did not seek in modified plan to change creditor's classification to unsecured, reduction in plan payments was consistent with *Nolan*).
225 *In re* Bowles, 2009 WL 2601131 (Bankr. M.D.N.C. Aug. 19, 2009) (debtors permitted to surrender vehicle and treat claim formerly secured by vehicle as unsecured when one debtor lost job, causing drop in income that made retention of vehicle impossible). *See, e.g.,* Bank One v. Leuellen, 322 B.R. 648 (S.D. Ind. 2005); *In re* Lane, 374 B.R. 830 (Bankr. D. Kan. 2007) (debtors permitted to modify after destruction of vehicle, and classify as unsecured the deficiency remaining after payment of "910" car claim); *In re* Mellors, 372 B.R. 763 (Bankr. W.D. Pa. 2007) (debtors permitted to modify after discovering structural damage to vehicle); *In re* Mason, 315 B.R. 759 (Bankr. N.D. Cal. 2004); *In re* Zieder, 263 B.R. 114 (Bankr. D. Ariz. 2001); *In re* Townley, 256 B.R. 697 (Bankr. D.N.J. 2000). *See also In re* Hernandez, 282 B.R. 200 (Bankr. S.D. Tex. 2002) (debtor could modify plan to surrender collateral to secured creditor in payment of secured claim); *In re* Morris, 289 B.R. 783 (Bankr. S.D. Ga. 2002) (establishing procedure requiring that creditors who obtain relief from stay to repossess chapter 13 debtors' vehicles file amended claims, to which parties could object, or else their allowed secured claims would be deemed paid in full).
226 11 U.S.C. § 1329(a)(3).
227 Fed. R. Bankr. P. 3008 advisory committee's note.
228 *In re* Zieder, 263 B.R. 114 (Bankr. D. Ariz. 2001).
However, a trustee cannot unilaterally reduce the creditor's secured claim. *In re* Davis, 314 F.3d 567 (11th Cir. 2002).
229 *See In re* Guthrie, 2009 WL 2208334 (Bankr. D. Kan. July 20, 2009) (debtors permitted to use insurance proceeds to finance another vehicle if they gave replacement lien to creditor secured by original vehicle).
230 *See* § 12.6.6, *infra*.
231 See discussion of the "ability-to-pay test" in Chapter 12, *infra*. *See In re* Gronski, 86 B.R. 428 (Bankr. E.D. Pa. 1988) (substantial change in circumstances necessary to permit creditor to impose modification on debtor requiring increase in payments). *See also* 8 Collier on Bankruptcy ¶ 1329.03 (16th ed.). *But see In re* Witkowski, 16 F.3d 739 (7th Cir. 1994) (plan could be modified on motion of trustee even though there was no change in circumstances

changed circumstances to establish grounds for a modification.[232] The requirements for modification are set out in 11 U.S.C. § 1329, and basically provide that the modified plan must meet most of the tests for confirmation of the original plan.[233] The procedure, prescribed by Federal Rule of Bankruptcy Procedure 3015(g), requires the filing of a motion,[234] along with the proposed modification, and at least twenty-one days' notice to the debtor, the trustee, and all creditors of the time for filing objections and of a hearing to consider any objections.[235] A copy of the notice is also transmitted to the United States trustee, and all notices must be accompanied by a copy of the modification or a summary thereof.[236] Any objection to the proposed modification gives rise to a contested matter under Federal Rule of Bankruptcy Procedure 9014, and must be served on the debtor, the trustee and any other entity designated by the court, and transmitted to the United States trustee.[237] If a modification sought by the debtor is unopposed, no hearing is normally held[238] and the modification is approved. Once approved, it binds all parties.[239]

In some courts, a hearing is held on any request for modification by a party other than the debtor, unless the debtor expressly agrees to the modification; in others, no hearing is held absent a request for a hearing.[240] However, as with many issues that affect a debtor's rights, it is best to affirmatively file an objection to the relief requested, because a response guarantees that the debtor will obtain a hearing.

8.7.5 Debtor's Inability to Complete the Plan

8.7.5.1 Failure to Make Plan Payments

Unfortunately, many debtors encounter difficulties of various sorts in completing their chapter 13 plans as originally confirmed. These difficulties may arise due to loss of income, unexpected expenses, marital problems, or other causes.

Sometimes financial problems prevent debtors from making required plan payments as they come due. When the debtor misses payments, the debtor should be encouraged to catch up if possible. Most trustees are quite willing to accept delinquent plan payments as long as the debtor does not fall too far behind. However, in serious cases the trustee may request dismissal based upon the debtor's failure to comply with the plan.[241]

In other cases the debtors are unable to keep up with current mortgage payments that must be made outside the plan. Generally this problem will give rise to a motion by the secured creditor for relief from the stay to commence or continue foreclosure proceedings.[242] In the event of such a motion the best response, if possible, is for the debtor to catch up before the motion is heard. Most secured creditors will agree to allow a debtor to catch up because they know that, if the debtor brings the delinquent payments to a hearing on a motion for relief from stay, the bankruptcy judge will probably deny relief. Other creditors will agree not to foreclose immediately and to allow the debtor an opportunity to catch up on payments, if the debtor in return agrees to future relief from the stay if the postpetition payments are not brought current. In general, it is a good idea to avoid such agreements, except as a last resort when no modification of the plan or defense to relief from stay is possible.[243]

When these issues come to a head, either by motion to dismiss or motion for relief from stay, several options must be considered if the debtor cannot cure payment defaults within a

---

since confirmation); *In re* Perkins, 111 B.R. 671 (Bankr. M.D. Tenn. 1990) (changed circumstances not statutory prerequisite to trustee's motion to modify).

The court may not order a particular modification of the plan. *In re* Muessel, 292 B.R. 712 (B.A.P. 1st Cir. 2003).

232 *See In re* Larson, 122 B.R. 417 (Bankr. D. Idaho 1991) (no requirement of proof of changed circumstances by debtor required for modification). *See also* 8 Collier on Bankruptcy ¶ 1329.02 (16th ed.).

233 *See In re* Black, 292 B.R. 693 (B.A.P. 10th Cir. 2003) (debtor could not circumvent sixty-month maximum plan period by modification that labeled payments made over first twenty-eight months as "lump sum contribution"); *In re* Jourdan, 108 B.R. 1020 (Bankr. N.D. Iowa 1989) (debtor may modify plan to change treatment of creditor when plan as amended meets all requirements of Code); *In re* Perkins, 111 B.R. 671 (Bankr. M.D. Tenn. 1990) (trustee's proposed modified plan may not be confirmed when it does not pass the feasibility test for confirmation). *See also In re* Sunahara, 326 B.R. 768 (B.A.P. 9th Cir. 2005) (debtor may modify plan to provide for early plan termination without full payment of all claims, because plain language of section 1329(b) does not require application of disposable income test with respect to modified plans). Modification based upon a change in the debtor's ability to pay is discussed in more detail in § 12.3.4.5, *infra*.

234 *See* Forms 149, 150, Appx. G.13, *infra*.

235 *In re* Franklin, 459 B.R. 463 (Bankr. D. Nev. 2011) (less than 21 days' notice violates rules).

The notice must be specific in describing the modification. *See In re* Friday, 304 B.R. 537 (Bankr. N.D. Ga. 2003).

The court may limit the notice required to include only creditors affected by the proposed modification. Fed. R. Bankr. P. 3015(g). Otherwise, all creditors, including those that have not filed claims, must be given notice of the motion. *In re* Arnold, 2010 WL 3810862 (Bankr. N.D.N.Y. Sept. 27, 2010).

236 Fed. R. Bankr. P. 3015(g).

237 *Id.*

238 The phrase "after notice and a hearing" is construed in accordance with 11 U.S.C. § 102(1).

239 *In re* Bailey, 425 B.R. 825 (Bankr. D. Minn. 2010) (trustee could not obtain modification increasing plan period to 60 months because earlier modification reducing period to 36 months, to which trustee had not objected, was binding); *In re* Rincon, 133 B.R. 594 (Bankr. N.D. Tex. 1991) (creditor which had not objected to modified plan lost right to amend proof of claim in a manner inconsistent with the modified plan).

In some courts, no order approving the modification is necessary and it becomes effective immediately, subject only to disapproval upon a timely objection. *See In re* Taylor, 215 B.R. 882 (Bankr. S.D. Cal. 1997).

240 *See* 8 Collier on Bankruptcy ¶ 1329.06 (16th ed.).

241 If the debtors can catch up at any time before the hearing on a dismissal motion based on missed payments, it is unlikely that the court would actually dismiss the case.

242 The creditor may also seek to have the case dismissed pursuant to 11 U.S.C. § 1307(c).

243 *See* § 9.7, *infra*, for a discussion of defenses to motions for relief from stay.

reasonable time. Often, if not always, the debtor can still obtain full or partial bankruptcy relief by utilizing one of the strategies discussed below.

8.7.5.2 Plan Modifications That Enable the Debtor to Complete the Plan

The most preferable option when addressing a problem in completing the plan is often modification, following the procedure described above.[244] Modification may allow the chapter 13 plan to proceed to conclusion by lowering the payments to a level the debtor can afford or by extending the payments. It may also be possible to modify the plan to terminate earlier than originally proposed. As long as all of the requirements of chapter 13 are met, such as full payment of priority debts and payment of all postpetition domestic support payments, this type of modification should be allowed. However, if the claims of secured creditors have not yet been satisfied, the termination of the plan may pose difficulties unless arrangements can be made with those creditors. If the plan is modified, the debtor preserves the right to the somewhat broader chapter 13 discharge, which is important in cases in which there are unsecured debts that are not dischargeable in chapter 7.[245]

8.7.5.3 Obtaining a Hardship Discharge

A second possibility is to apply for a hardship discharge. This discharge is granted when the failure to complete payments is "due to circumstances for which the debtor should not justly be held accountable,"[246] but only if modification is impracticable and the value of payments to unsecured creditors, as of the effective date of the plan, is not less than the amount they would have received had the case originally proceeded as a chapter 7 liquidation.[247] In most consumer cases these tests should not be difficult to meet.[248] The debtor need not pay all priority claims or be current on postpetition domestic support payments to obtain a hardship discharge; however, secured creditors that have not yet been fully paid normally retain their liens for the unpaid amounts of their claims, thus possibly posing problems that must be resolved. Lastly, the hardship discharge is not as broad as the normal chapter 13 discharge, but rather is coextensive with the chapter 7 discharge, which may mean that fewer debts will be discharged. However, if seventy percent of the unsecured claims have been paid, a hardship discharge will not bar a subsequent chapter 7 discharge within eight years, as would a chapter 7 discharge.[249]

The procedure for obtaining a hardship discharge is set forth in Federal Rule of Bankruptcy Procedure 4007(d). If the debtor files a motion for a hardship discharge, the court gives notice to all creditors of the motion and of the deadline for filing a complaint to determine the dischargeability of a debt under Code section 523(c)(6). If a hardship discharge is granted, the court then determines the issues raised if a complaint is filed.

8.7.5.4 Conversion to Chapter 7

A third choice when addressing failure to complete a chapter 13 plan is conversion of the case to a chapter 7 case. Conversion may be accomplished by the debtor as of right,[250] and may also be requested by creditors for various reasons.[251] The procedure for a debtor to convert a case to chapter 7 is set forth in Federal Rule of Bankruptcy Procedure 1017(d), which provides that the conversion is effectuated when the debtor files a notice of conversion with the clerk.[252] The conversion is deemed to take place when the notice is filed. The effect of conversion is discussed elsewhere in this treatise.[253]

8.7.5.5 Dismissal

A final option is dismissal, also available to a chapter 13 debtor as of right in any case not previously converted from another chapter.[254] Pursuant to Federal Rule of Bankruptcy Procedure 1017(d), the debtor may obtain a voluntary dismissal by filing a motion stating the debtor's entitlement to dismissal. An involuntary dismissal may also occur on motion of the chapter 13 trustee, the United States trustee, or a creditor.

---

244 See § 8.7.4, supra.
245 See § 15.4.1, infra, for discussion of the difference between the chapter 7 and chapter 13 discharges.
246 11 U.S.C. § 1328(b).
   At least one court has found that death is such a circumstance. In re Bond, 36 B.R. 49 (Bankr. E.D.N.C. 1984). However a chapter 13 case can sometimes continue after the debtor's death, when that is practicable. In re Perkins, 381 B.R. 530 (Bankr. S.D. Ill. 2007).
247 11 U.S.C. § 1328(b).
248 In re Bandilli, 231 B.R. 836 (B.A.P. 1st Cir. 1999) (circumstances need not be catastrophic, but temporary relapse of medical condition which did not affect income was insufficient); In re Edwards, 207 B.R. 728 (Bankr. N.D. Fla. 1997) (hardship need not involve catastrophic circumstances). But see In re Roberts, 279 B.R. 396 (B.A.P. 1st Cir. 2000) (no abuse of discretion in denying hardship discharge to debtor who made no attempt to modify the plan or to sever her case from her husband's, actions that in all likelihood would have been allowed by the bankruptcy court and might have permitted her to obtain a discharge).

249 11 U.S.C. § 727(a)(9).
250 11 U.S.C. § 1307(a); Nady v. Defrantz (In re Defrantz), 454 B.R. 108 (B.A.P. 9th Cir. 2011) (no bad faith exception to right to convert). See also § 4.7.4, supra, § 13.7.2, infra. But see In re Spiser, Bankr. N.D. Tex. 1999) (case could not be converted after both debtors had died).
251 11 U.S.C. § 1307(c). See also § 4.7.2, supra.
   For example, unsecured creditors may request conversion if there are nonexempt assets that could be liquidated for their benefit when required plan payments are not being made.
252 A sample form for this notice is provided in Form 154, Appx. G.13, infra.
253 See § 13.7.3, infra.
254 11 U.S.C. § 1307(b).
   Voluntary dismissal, and a few erroneous decisions limiting the right to dismiss, are discussed in § 13.2, infra. If the case was originally filed under another chapter, dismissal by leave of court may be obtainable by motion. 11 U.S.C. § 1307(c). See § 13.2, infra.

Dismissal may be preferable if the debtor cannot meet the hardship test or "best interests" test[255] for a hardship discharge and if the debtor stands to lose significant nonexempt property in a conversion to chapter 7. Dismissal, to the extent possible, returns the parties to the status quo prior to the bankruptcy, negating many benefits that the debtor might already have obtained, such as the avoidance of liens.[256] Nonetheless, the debtor might find it preferable to deal with creditors outside of bankruptcy rather than subject nonexempt assets to immediate liquidation. If the case is dismissed, all trustee payments to creditors immediately cease, and property in the hands of the chapter 13 trustee should be promptly returned to the debtor.[257]

Once the case is dismissed, the debtor has the option to file again under either chapter 13 or chapter 7. However, if this option is in the debtor's interest, some care should be taken that the anticipated subsequent case will not be barred by section 109(g),[258] and the possible limitations on the automatic stay under section 362(c)(3) or (4) must also be considered.[259]

It should be noted that both the right to dismiss and the right to convert may be lost by the debtor who does not exercise them in a timely manner. Once the case is converted to a chapter 7 case, perhaps on request of creditors, the chapter 13 right to dismiss the case ceases to exist. Similarly, once a case is dismissed over the debtor's objection, no further right to convert exists. Thus it is important to exercise these rights before an involuntary conversion or dismissal. Although a new chapter 7 petition could usually be filed after a chapter 13 case is dismissed,[260] it would entail needless effort and a new filing fee. The consequences of an involuntary conversion can be worse; conversion may mean the loss of nonexempt property that is critical to the debtor's affairs.

8.8 The Discharge and the Discharge Hearing

8.8.1 Overview

Once the time for objecting to a discharge has passed in a chapter 7 case and the debtor has certified completion of a financial education course, with a few limited exceptions, the debtor is entitled to a discharge.[261]

Similarly, once the debtor has completed the payments required by a confirmed chapter 13 plan, even if the payments are completed early by a lump sum payment, the debtor is entitled to seek a discharge.[262] Once the payments are completed, it is too late for any party to move for modification of the plan.[263] However, the debtor must take additional steps to obtain the discharge. First, the debtor must file, no later than the time the last plan payment is made, a certification of completion of the personal financial management course.[264] Second, if the debtor has claimed a homestead exemption of more than the amount stated in section 522(q)(1) (currently $146,450) the debtor must file, not earlier than the time the last plan payment is made, a statement as to whether there is pending any proceeding in which the debtor might be found guilty of, or liable for, the kind of bad acts or debts listed in section 522(q)(1)(A) and (B).[265] Third, if the debtor is required by a court or administrative order or by statute to pay a domestic support obligation, and the debtor is seeking a full compliance discharge under section 1328(a), the debtor must file a certification that all amounts payable that were due before the certification was filed have been paid, except to the extent the plan provided that prepetition arrearages need not be paid.[266]

Although the Code as originally enacted required that the court hold a discharge hearing in every case, a discharge hearing is now required only when the debtor desires to reaffirm

---

255 See Chapter 12, *infra*, for discussion of the "best interest of creditors" test in chapter 13.
256 11 U.S.C. § 349. See *In re* Sadler, 935 F.2d 918 (7th Cir. 1991) (once case is dismissed, avoided preferences are reinstated irrespective of whether a new case is contemplated or filed).
  However, if limitations periods on avoidance have not expired, collateral estoppel may apply in the subsequent case.
257 *In re* Nash, 765 F.2d 1410 (9th Cir. 1985); *In re* Tran, 309 B.R. 330 (B.A.P. 9th Cir. 2004) (upon voluntary dismissal of case chapter 13 debtor was entitled to receive mortgage refinancing proceeds that were in hands of trustee), *aff'd*, 177 Fed. Appx. 754 (9th Cir. 2006); *In re* Inyamah, 378 B.R. 183 (Bankr. S.D. Ohio 2007) (funds must be returned notwithstanding creditor's service of garnishment order on trustee); *In re* Bailey, 330 B.R. 775 (Bankr. D. Or. 2005) (trustee required to distribute funds despite service of state court garnishment because Supremacy Clause invalidated state law which conflicted with federal law); *In re* Slaughter, 141 B.R. 661 (Bankr. N.D. Ill. 1992). *But see In re* Brown, 280 B.R. 231 (Bankr. E.D. Wis. 2002) (funds in hands of trustee subject to levy by Internal Revenue Service); *In re* Witte, 279 B.R. 585 (Bankr. E.D. Cal. 2002) (when debtor's house had been sold pursuant to court order prior to dismissal, proceeds held by trustee were not plan proceeds that had to be returned to debtor, and had to be turned over to holders of liens on house).
258 See § 3.2.1, *supra*, and § 9.7.3.1.5, *infra*, for a discussion of 11 U.S.C. § 109(g) and other issues connected with serial bankruptcy filings. Additionally it should be noted that, unless there is some change in circumstances, a subsequent chapter 13 case may be alleged to be filed in bad faith. *See generally* § 12.3.3, *infra*.
259 See Chapter 9, *infra*, for discussion of section 362(c)(3) and (4).
260 A new petition is expressly barred after an involuntary dismissal only if the debtor willfully disobeyed court orders or willfully failed to appear to prosecute the case, and then only for 180 days. 11 U.S.C. § 109(g). See § 3.2.1, *supra*.
  However, the automatic stay in a new case could be limited by section 362(c)(3) or (4).
261 Fed. R. of Bankr. P. 4004(c) (stating exceptions such as nonpayment of filing fee, pendency of an objection to discharge, motion to dismiss for abuse, or motion to extend time for filing of such objection or motion).
262 11 U.S.C. § 1328(a); *In re* Celeste, 310 B.R. 286 (Bankr. D. Md. 2004) (debtor entitled to discharge after payments completed even if trustee had not yet disbursed all funds); *In re* Smith, 237 B.R. 621 (Bankr. E.D. Tex. 1999); *In re* Bergolla, 232 B.R. 515 (Bankr. S.D. Fla. 1999).
263 11 U.S.C. § 1329(a); 8 Collier on Bankruptcy ¶ 1329.08 (16th ed.).
264 11 U.S.C. § 1328(g); Fed. R. Bankr. P. 1007 b)(7), (c); Official Form 23 (reprinted in Appx. D, *infra*).
265 11 U.S.C. § 1328(h); Fed. R. Bankr. P. 1007(b)(8), (c).
  See sample statement in Form 136, Appx. G.12, *infra*.
266 11 U.S.C. § 1328(a).
  See sample certification in Form 135, Appx. G.12, *infra*.

a debt and was not represented by an attorney in negotiating the reaffirmation agreement.[267] Otherwise, it is discretionary with the court and few courts now hold discharge hearings when there is no reaffirmation involved.

When a discharge hearing is held, the Code clearly provides that the debtor must attend.[268] If the discharge hearing is not one which involves a reaffirmation agreement, it should be possible to convince a court to waive the required appearance of the debtor when attendance at the hearing would cause real hardship.[269] Indeed, several courts have announced that Congress did not really mean what it said, and that the debtor need not attend in all cases.[270]

Whether or not a discharge hearing is held, the debtor ultimately receives a discharge order from the court, which in chapter 7 cases conforms in general to Official Form 18. The chapter 7 discharge order contains a general explanation of the discharge and is mailed by the clerk as a matter of course to the debtor, the debtor's attorney, and all creditors. The debtor can move to delay the granting of the discharge for thirty days to negotiate a possible reaffirmation agreement with a creditor.[271] The debtor should be encouraged to keep a copy of the discharge order, a list of creditors scheduled in the bankruptcy, a list of property claimed as exempt,[272] and copies of any orders entered during the course of the proceedings in a safe place in case issues arise later about the disposition of the case.

8.8.2 Reaffirmation of Debts

The principal stated purpose of the discharge hearing is to advise debtors of their rights, especially with regard to reaffirmation of debts. In a well-handled case, this counsel should already have been provided by the debtor's attorney. Without doubt, the best advice in this regard is simply that reaffirmation is rarely a good idea. Reaffirmation, which in essence is a promise to pay a debt despite its discharge, effectively waives the benefits of discharge as to that particular debt[273] and should be advised only in exceptional circumstances.[274] Perhaps, if a debtor is in economic default, that is, behind in payments on a secured debt, and does not wish to pursue chapter 13 to deal with the problem, reaffirmation might be appropriate in exchange for a creditor's forbearance. Similarly, if it is unlikely that any recovery of a deficiency would be sought after foreclosure on a mortgage, either because the value of the collateral far exceeds the debt or because deficiency judgments are barred in the jurisdiction, then little harm can be done by reaffirming that debt. In either case, the debt should not be reaffirmed in an amount exceeding the value of the collateral;[275] there may also be ways to save the debtor's property without reaffirmation.[276]

Many debtors (and some attorneys) are under the misimpression that no payment may be made to a creditor after bankruptcy unless the debt is reaffirmed. This is not correct.[277] Usually, the results sought by reaffirmation of a debt can be obtained just as well by simply continuing to make regular voluntary payments on a debt. For example, a creditor will rarely foreclose on its collateral or pursue a cosigner if payments on a debt are current.[278] Although it is reassuring for the debtor to have a promise from the creditor that it will not exercise the right to foreclose given it by the common "bankruptcy clause"[279] in consumer contracts, this agreement can often be negotiated without a reaffirmation which again obligates the debtor personally. The debtor usually has some leverage in negotiating such an agreement, because there may be issues as to defenses the debtor may raise, or a dispute as to the value of the security.[280]

In any case, creditors should be put on notice that they risk substantial litigation if they threaten to exercise their rights under bankruptcy clauses to foreclose or pursue cosigners either to force a reaffirmation or to obtain valuable collateral. Bankruptcy clauses are obviously adhesion clauses, never really bargained over between debtor and creditors. As such their use can probably be challenged as unconscionable and as unfair and deceptive acts.[281] Indeed the law of some states specifically prohibits repossession from a debtor who is current in pay-

---

267 11 U.S.C. § 524(d).
268 See Chapter 15, *infra*, for further discussion of this requirement.
269 *In re* Mensch, 7 B.R. 804 (Bankr. S.D.N.Y. 1980) (debtor suffered disabling stroke); *In re* Keefe, 7 B.R. 270 (Bankr. E.D. Va. 1980) (debtor suffered mental breakdown); *In re* Garber, 4 B.R. 684 (Bankr. C.D. Cal. 1980) (use of "shall" in section 524 is directory, not mandatory); *In re* Killett, 2 B.R. 273 (Bankr. E.D. Va. 1980) (debtor in England serving in U.S. Air Force).
270 See § 15.5.2, *infra*, for further discussion of reaffirmation agreements.
271 Fed. R. Bankr. P. 4004(c)(1).
272 Such property is not liable for any debt that arose before commencement of the case, with certain limited exceptions. 11 U.S.C. § 522(c). See § 10.5, *infra*.
   It is somewhat unclear whether exempt property can be reached by a creditor whose debt is reaffirmed. Because the better view is that a reaffirmed debt does not first arise after the petition, such property should still be protected from liability on that debt.
273 Fed. R. Bankr. P. 4004(c)(2).
   See § 15.5, *infra*, for a discussion of reaffirmation agreements.
274 Preprinted materials, such as the handout reprinted in Appendix K, *infra*, may assist the attorney in conveying this information to the client. See Appx. K.2, *infra*.
275 See Chapter 11, *infra*, for methods to reduce the debt to equal the value of the collateral.
276 See § 15.5.2, *infra*, for a more detailed discussion of reaffirmation.
277 11 U.S.C. § 524(f).
278 Section 524(j) provides that certain actions of creditors holding security interests in real property of the debtor, such as seeking regular payments, do not violate the discharge injunction. See Ch. 15, *infra*.
279 This clause usually provides that the filing of a bankruptcy case constitutes a default under the contract.
280 See Chapter 11, *infra*, for further discussion of how such disputes arise.
281 The use of other similar boilerplate clauses, neither bargained over nor understood by most debtors, has been found to be unfair by the Federal Trade Commission (FTC). *See* Am. Fin. Servs. Ass'n v. Fed. Trade Comm'n, 767 F.2d 957 (D.C. Cir. 1985).
   See also National Consumer Law Center, Unfair and Deceptive Acts and Practices § 4.3.4 (7th ed. 2008 and Supp.) for a fuller discussion of the FTC's unfairness analysis as it applies to adhesion contracts.

ments. The debtor often will have a strong argument that a default under any such clause has been waived by acceptance of postpetition payments by the creditor.[282] Repossession might also be found to violate the good-faith requirements of section 1-203 of the Uniform Commercial Code. And finally, the exercise of such rights can be swiftly prevented or reversed by converting the case to a chapter 13 bankruptcy, or by filing a new chapter 13 case if the previous case has already ended. Because chapter 13 provides both that a plan may waive a default[283] and that a prior bankruptcy is no bar to filing,[284] debtors are fully within their rights to utilize a new chapter 13 case to prevent such creditor abuses.

Despite its clear disadvantages, many debtors agree to reaffirmation, especially if they do not have counsel in negotiating with the creditor. It is in these situations that the discharge hearings can serve an important purpose. The judge's main duty is to advise debtors of the dangers of reaffirmation, of the fact that reaffirmation is not required, and of the debtor's right to rescind the reaffirmation within sixty days after it is filed with the court or, if later, up to the date of the discharge.[285]

An attorney who represents a debtor in negotiating a reaffirmation agreement on a consumer debt[286] must also counsel the debtor about the advisability of reaffirmation. The attorney must then file a declaration with the court stating that the reaffirmation is a fully informed and voluntary agreement that does not impose an undue hardship on the debtor or a dependent of the debtor.[287] If the debtor's budget shows that the debtor does not have sufficient funds to make the reaffirmation agreement payments, the attorney must also certify that in the attorney's opinion the debtor is nonetheless able to make the payments.[288] The attorney's declaration must also state that the attorney fully advised the debtor as to the legal effect and consequences of the agreement and of any default under the agreement. Attorneys should think carefully about possible malpractice liability before signing such a declaration, in view of the uncertainties of most debtors' future income and expenses.

In all reaffirmations of consumer debts not negotiated by an attorney for the debtor, except those secured by real property, the court has the duty to decide whether to approve the reaffirmation agreement. In addition, except if the creditor is a credit union, the court must review any reaffirmation agreement in which a presumption of undue hardship arises under section 524(m) because the debtor's budget does not have sufficient funds to make the reaffirmation agreement payments. Such agreements may be approved only if they do not impose an undue hardship on the debtor or a dependent of the debtor and they are in the best interests of the debtor.[289]

8.8.3 Procedure When There Is a Discharge Hearing

If the court decides to have a discharge hearing even though there will be no reaffirmation of debts, the discharge hearing is usually a very brief affair, with nothing to be said by the debtor or the debtor's counsel. In fact, in many jurisdictions, debtors' counsel are not required to attend the hearing in such cases. The court usually warns the debtor about creditors trying to collect their debts or obtain reaffirmations in the future, and lets the debtor know that bankruptcy is a serious business. Generally, the court then advises prudence in future credit transactions and wishes the debtor good luck. Given the potential for mind-numbing repetition, some judges give this message to all the debtors scheduled on a particular day *en masse*. Others give it once, to the first debtor to appear, and then simply ask the debtors appearing later whether they heard what was said to the first debtor, saying that the same applies to them. A few judges do, however, repeat the message, with slight variations, for each debtor who appears.

If a reaffirmation agreement is proposed for approval, most courts require pre-hearing filing, or the filing at the hearing, of a motion and a proposed order.[290] The court may (and should) then examine the debtor closely to determine if she understands what reaffirmation means and whether reaffirmation is really in the debtor's best interest. If it is not, the reaffirmation should not be approved.[291]

8.9 After Discharge

Once the discharge has been granted and all related litigation has ended, one or two steps normally remain to be taken in representing the debtor. These final details may be quite important in particular cases and should not be neglected.

Public records must often be modified to reflect what has occurred in the bankruptcy. For example, liens may no longer exist or may have been modified. Debtor's counsel should be sure that any record of such liens has been corrected or that

---

282 *See* § 11.4.2.5, *infra*.
283 11 U.S.C. § 1322(b)(3).
284 11 U.S.C. § 1322(f) only bars a chapter 13 discharge within certain periods after an earlier case, but not the filing of a chapter 13 case to pay a secured creditor over time. *See* Ch. 12, *infra*.
285 11 U.S.C. § 524(c)(2).
    If court approval is required, the agreement normally becomes effective only when the approval is granted. In all other cases, unless the agreement provides otherwise, the effective date is the date of filing with the court. 11 U.S.C. § 524(c)(3).
    After discharge and passage of sixty days from the date of the reaffirmation agreement it may be difficult to rescind a reaffirmation agreement. *See In re* Jones, 111 B.R. 674 (Bankr. E.D. Tenn. 1990) (discharge may not be revoked in order to create additional opportunity to rescind reaffirmation agreement).
286 Consumer debt is defined in 11 U.S.C. § 101(8).
287 11 U.S.C. § 524(c)(3).
288 11 U.S.C. § 524(k)(5).

289 11 U.S.C. § 524(c)(6). *See* § 15.5.2, *infra*.
290 Part E of the form reaffirmation agreement issued by the Administrative Office of the Courts contains a "Motion for Court Approval" which must be completed by an unrepresented debtor, as required by section 524(k)(3) and (4). *See* Appx. E.10, *infra*.
    Fed. R. Bankr. P. 4008 requires a motion for approval of reaffirmation to be filed before or at the hearing.
291 *See* § 15.5.2, *infra*, for further discussion of standards for approval of reaffirmation.

bankruptcy court orders modifying or avoiding liens are properly recorded in the appropriate registry. Normally, this has been done as part of the lien avoidance process,[292] but it is important to check the records when closing a case.

In some jurisdictions it is a matter of practice to notify courts where proceedings have been pending that the discharge has been granted or that certain judgments are void or satisfied by payment.[293] Technically, this notice is not necessary, because the effect of the discharge is automatic, but local practice or the dictates of court etiquette may make it advisable.

Credit reports should also be checked thirty to sixty days after discharge to verify whether creditors are properly reporting information about discharged debts as required by the Fair Credit Reporting Act.[294] All debts discharged in the bankruptcy case should show a zero balance and be noted as having been included in the bankruptcy.[295] If the client's credit reports still show balances owed on discharged debts, steps should be taken to have the client send letters demanding correction of the report, with letters sent to both the creditor furnishers of information and the credit reporting agencies. If the report is not corrected, it may be necessary to initiate litigation to enforce the debtor's rights under the Fair Credit Reporting Act.[296]

Finally, there is some very important advice to be given to clients. They should be made fully aware of the meaning of their discharge so they are not misled into paying discharged debts. They should be told to report any contacts by creditors so that advice can be given and steps taken against those creditors if necessary. Debtors should also be advised of the other protections arising from their discharge, particularly against any governmental and employer discrimination.[297]

Most importantly, clients must be told not to ignore legal actions brought against them after bankruptcy. Many clients are under the impression that the bankruptcy makes any further action to protect their interests unnecessary. While perhaps technically true with respect to some debts,[298] as a general rule it is advisable for a client to seek the advice of counsel if sued by a creditor after discharge. Some creditors may wrongfully institute legal actions to collect a discharged debt and, while this type of action can usually be rectified, early intervention and assertion of the bankruptcy discharge can prevent later complications, such as harm caused by a wrongful execution. Other creditors may seek to foreclose on a valid lien or to collect a debt that a creditor claims was not discharged, such as a student loan. In these cases, the debtor needs counsel as much as ever. The solution may be a new chapter 13 bankruptcy or any one of numerous other defensive strategies. These strategies may include the possible reopening of the bankruptcy case for a proceeding to determine dischargeability of the debt or, in some jurisdictions, to schedule a creditor not previously listed.[299]

Preprinted materials or a form letter may save time and assure that these warnings are clearly conveyed.[300] Regardless of the method used (interview, letter, or both), it is appropriate to ensure that there are no new or undiscovered legal problems and to give the client a clear understanding of the new post-bankruptcy situation.[301] Normally, that situation should be a good deal better than that which existed when the client first came into your office.

---

292 See Chapters 10 and 11, *infra*, for further discussion of lien avoidance.

293 See Chapter 15, *infra*, for further discussion of the discharge.

294 For detailed discussion of the Fair Credit Reporting Act (FCRA), 15 U.S.C. §§ 1681–1681x, see National Consumer Law Center, Fair Credit Reporting (7th ed. 2010 and Supp.).

295 Fed. Trade Comm'n, Official Staff Commentary to the Fair Credit Reporting Act § 607 item 6. *See also* National Consumer Law Center, Fair Credit Reporting § 4.3.2.4 (7th ed. 2010 and Supp.).

296 The credit reporting agency must first be notified that the information is disputed before an action may be brought under the FCRA against the creditor furnisher. *See* National Consumer Law Center, Fair Credit Reporting § 10.2.4 (7th ed. 2010 and Supp.).

The inaccurate reporting of a prepetition debt with the intent to coerce a debtor into paying the debt may also pursued as an automatic stay or discharge injunction violation. *See, e.g., In re* Goodfellow, 298 B.R. 358 (Bankr. N.D. Iowa 2003) (reporting of discharged debt as ninety days past due violated discharge injunction); *In re* Singley, 233 B.R. 170 (Bankr. S.D. Ga. 1999); *In re* Sommersdorf, 139 B.R. 700 (Bankr. S.D. Ohio 1992) (bank's actions in placing notation of debt charge-off on codebtor's credit report violated stay). *See also* §§ 9.4.4, 9.4.5, 15.5 *infra*.

297 See § 15.5, *infra*, for further discussion of these protections.
298 *See* Ch. 15, *infra*.
299 *See* § 8.5, *supra*, and § 15.4.3.3, *infra*, for discussion of this possibility.
300 *See* Form 139, Appx. G.12, *infra*.
301 Debtors may also appreciate receiving information on how to avoid credit problems after bankruptcy. *See* Appx. K.3, *infra*.

Chapter 9   Automatic Stays and Turnover of Property

9.1 Introduction

Simply by filing a bankruptcy petition, a debtor brings to his or her aid an instrument of awesome breadth and power—the Bankruptcy Code's automatic stay. Few other legal steps that may be taken on behalf of a consumer can bring about relief so simply, so effectively, and so dramatically. The stay provisions of the Code,[1] along with the other related provisions that are discussed in this Chapter, take effect the instant a case is filed, from that moment placing the debtor and the debtor's property under the protection of the bankruptcy court.

The power of these provisions extends to many sorts of actions that may be taken against consumers, including some that at first glance do not appear to be debt-related. These actions are stopped, totally and immediately, by the filing of a three-page bankruptcy petition.[2] Indeed, the certainty of obtaining such relief is often a prime factor in the decision to file a case. In some situations, there may be no other remedy as effective, and usually none is as simple. For clients who have come to an attorney's office at the last possible minute before some serious adverse action, the automatic stay may provide the only practical solution. And for other clients, for whom all other legal steps have failed, it may provide one last way to at least postpone a crisis while the debtor seeks relief in the bankruptcy court.

9.2 Purpose of the Automatic Stay

The basic purpose of the stay is to protect the debtor and his or her property. As stated in the House Report on the Bankruptcy Code:

> The automatic stay is one of the fundamental debtor protections provided by the bankruptcy laws. It gives the debtor a breathing spell from his creditors. It stops all collection efforts, all harassment, and all foreclosure actions. It permits the debtor to attempt a repayment or reorganization, or simply to be relieved of the financial pressures that drove him into bankruptcy.[3]

Functionally, the stay also freezes the debtor's assets as of the date of filing, preventing individual creditors from picking away at them for their own benefit and to the detriment of the ultimate goals of the bankruptcy. In chapter 7 liquidation cases, the stay guarantees the protection of the debtor's property or equity therein, both so it can be exempted to provide a fresh start and so nonexempt property can be fairly distributed to creditors. In chapter 13, the stay ensures protection of property that may be necessary not only for the debtor's fresh start but also for the success of the debtor's plan.

Along with other provisions governing property of the estate, the stay permits the bankruptcy court to deal with all aspects of the debtor's situation in an orderly manner. It prevents, at least until such time as the bankruptcy court allows, other courts and parties from interfering with or complicating the bankruptcy process. Virtually all activity concerning the debtor and the debtor's property thus comes into a single forum to be handled in accordance with the (usually) overriding purposes of the bankruptcy.

9.3 Duration of the Stay

9.3.1 In General

The duration of the automatic stay can vary significantly depending upon the circumstances. Theoretically it can be ended almost immediately, if the circumstances require, by the court granting relief to affected parties. Such circumstances, usually dealing with very perishable property, are almost never present in cases involving consumer debtors.[4] As a practical matter, the stay usually is not lifted by the court in much less than thirty days; and it may last for the duration of the case, a matter of three to six months in a no asset chapter 7 case and up to five years in a chapter 13 case.[5]

---

1   11 U.S.C. § 362.
2   The bankruptcy petition which commences a case may be filed before most of the schedules and statements that usually accompany it, if necessary. See § 7.2, *supra*. The automatic stay goes into effect even if there is a defect in the petition. Wekell v. United States, 14 F.3d 32 (9th Cir. 1994) (stay went into effect with respect to individual listed as a debtor, even if her spouse lacked authority to file bankruptcy case on her behalf).
3   H.R. Rep. No. 95-595, at 340 (1977). See *In re* Ionosphere Clubs, Inc., 922 F.2d 984 (2d Cir. 1990) (breathing spell from creditors is a principal purpose of automatic stay).
4   See *In re* Delaney-Morin, 304 B.R. 365 (B.A.P. 9th Cir. 2003) (reversing stay relief order entered based on grounds not alleged in motion at hearing debtor did not attend because *ex parte* relief not appropriate in case in which mortgage creditor alleged defaults).
5   Some courts have held that the stay is supplemented or supplanted by the chapter 13 plan after confirmation, because 11 U.S.C. § 1327(a) makes the plan binding upon all creditors. These courts have held that after confirmation even a lack of adequate protection

9.3.2 Duration If No Prior Case Was Dismissed in Year Before Petition

Technically, if no prior case was dismissed in the year before the filing of the petition, the statute[6] provides that the stay continues until the following dates.

To the extent the stay is based upon provisions barring an act against property of the estate,[7] the earlier of:

- The date such property is no longer property of the estate (usually the date property is abandoned, or the date it is deemed abandoned at the close of the case under 11 U.S.C. § 554(c));
- The date on which an order of the court terminating the stay becomes effective,[8] or by inaction of the court upon a request for relief from the stay.[9]

To the extent the stay is against any other act, the earliest of the following:

- The date the case is closed;[10]
- The date the case is dismissed;[11]
- The date a discharge is granted or denied;
- The date on which an order of the court terminating the stay becomes effective.[12]

Practically, however, the benefits of the stay may last a good deal longer. A lazy or inefficient opponent may not pay attention to when the bankruptcy ends, and thus may not reinstitute actions promptly (assuming there remains an action to reinstitute after the stay is terminated). While the court notifies all parties that the stay is in effect, usually as part of the notice of the meeting of creditors,[13] and debtor's counsel may also give a notice of the stay, there is normally no specific notice that the stay is terminated at the end of the case. In the interim a creditor may give up on or simply forget the course of action originally planned. In either case, much additional time may pass, sometimes years, to the benefit of the debtor. Indeed, a statute of limitations, which is extended, if necessary, until thirty days after termination of the stay,[14] may run before any action is taken.

9.3.3 Duration If a Prior Case Was Dismissed in Year Before Petition

9.3.3.1 Overview

Generally, if a case is dismissed, and a new filing is appropriate, a new automatic stay comes into effect.[15] However, counsel should take care that the subsequent filing is in good faith and not barred by the 180 day limit of 11 U.S.C. § 109(g).[16] If relief from the stay is granted or the stay is terminated during

---

or other grounds which would be available to lift the section 362 stay would not be sufficient to obtain court permission to proceed against the debtor. *See In re* Schewe, 94 B.R. 938 (Bankr. W.D. Mich. 1989) (stay continues in force after confirmation of debtors' chapter 13 plan); *In re* Lewis, 8 B.R. 132 (Bankr. D. Idaho 1981). *See also* Sec. Bank of Marshalltown, Iowa v. Neiman, 1 F.3d 687 (8th Cir. 1993) (property acquired by chapter 13 debtor during case continues to be property of the estate protected by the stay after it vests in the debtor upon confirmation); *In re* Harlan, 783 F.2d 839 (9th Cir. 1986); *In re* Ellis, 60 B.R. 432 (B.A.P. 9th Cir. 1985); *In re* Evans, 30 B.R. 530 (B.A.P. 9th Cir. 1983) (section 362 inapplicable after confirmation, absent postconfirmation default in carrying out plan); *In re* Brock, 6 B.R. 105 (Bankr. N.D. Ill. 1980); §§ 9.4.3, 12.8.5, 12.11, *infra*. *Cf. In re* Mann Farms, Inc., 917 F.2d 1210 (9th Cir. 1990) (confirmed plan may bind parties on some issues, but not on others).

Additionally, some courts have held that a preconfirmation termination of the stay does not override the binding effect of a confirmed chapter 13 plan. *In re* Sullivan, 321 B.R. 306, (Bankr. M.D. Fla. 2005); Green Tree Fin. Corp. v. Garrett (*In re* Garrett), 185 B.R. 620 (Bankr. N.D. Ala. 1995); § 12.11 *infra*. *But see In re* Thomas, 91 B.R. 117 (N.D. Ala. 1988) (creditor which did not file proof of claim entitled to relief from stay because confirmed plan does not provide for its claim).

See also discussion of Federal Rules of Bankruptcy Procedure 3003, 3004 in § 11.6.1.3, *infra*.

6   11 U.S.C. § 362(c)–(e).

If the court does not act within specified time periods after the filing of a motion seeking relief from the stay, the stay may terminate automatically. 11 U.S.C. § 362(e). *See* § 9.7.2, *infra*.

7   *See* United States v. White, 466 F.3d 1241 (11th Cir. 2006) (income tax assessment was not act against property of estate).

8   Unlike many orders, an order granting relief from the stay does not take effect until fourteen days after it is entered, so that a debtor or other party may seek a stay pending appeal. However, the order granting relief from the stay can specifically provide otherwise. Fed. R. Bankr. P. 4001(a)(3).

For a discussion of stay pending appeal, see §§ 9.7.3.3.3, 14.9.5, *infra*.

9   11 U.S.C. § 362(e). *See* § 9.7.2, *infra*.

10   *See In re* Bryant, 95 B.R. 856 (Bankr. M.D. Ga. 1989) (court will not reopen closed case to consider motion for relief from stay).

11   *In re* Lomagno, 429 F.3d 16 (1st Cir. 2005) (even though order dismissing case was later reversed, stay was not in effect during time appeal was pending because debtors had not obtained stay of bankruptcy court's order pending appeal); *In re* Sewell, 345 B.R. 174 (B.A.P. 9th Cir. 2006) (bankruptcy court did not abuse discretion in reinstating stay upon entry of order reinstating previously dismissed case on the docket, and in not invalidating foreclosure that had occurred before docketing of order); *In re* Barnes, 119 B.R. 552 (S.D. Ohio 1989) (same).

12   An order granting relief from the stay does not take effect until fourteen days after it is entered. Fed. R. Bankr. P. 4001(a)(3). *But see In re* Duran, 483 F.3d 653 (10th Cir. 2007) (section 362(e) takes precedence over Fed. R. Bankr. P. 4001(a)(3) so creditor did not have to wait ten days (the time period stated in Rule 4001(a)(3) at the time) after order granting stay relief when time period in section 362(e) ended earlier).

For a discussion of stay pending appeal, see §§ 9.7.3.3.3, 14.9.5, *infra*.

13   *See* Official Form 9 (reprinted in Appx. D, *infra*).

14   11 U.S.C. § 108(c). *See, e.g.*, Valley Transit Mix of Ruidoso, Inc. v. Miller, 928 F.2d 354 (10th Cir. 1991).

15   *See In re* Cont'l Airlines, 928 F.2d 127 (5th Cir. 1991) (automatic stay implemented in second case precludes appeal of claim denied in prior case).

The new stay will even bar actions allowed by the court pursuant to relief from stay proceedings in the prior case. Carr v. Sec. Sav. & Loan Ass'n, 130 B.R. 434 (D.N.J. 1991).

16   *See* §§ 3.2.1, 4.2.1, *supra*; § 9.7.3.1.5, *infra*.

a case, conversion of the case to another chapter does not create a new stay.[17]

9.3.3.2 One Prior Case Dismissed Within Previous Year

9.3.3.2.1 General application

Section 362(c)(3) of the Bankruptcy Code, added by the 2005 amendments, limits the stay under section 362(a) of the Code in an individual chapter 7, 11, or 13 case if the individual was a debtor in a case dismissed within the year before the filing of the petition.[18] Because the provision applies to each debtor individually, the expiration or inapplicability of the stay as to one debtor does not apply to a joint debtor who has not filed a prior case.[19] For debtors covered by this new restriction, the automatic stay under section 362(a) terminates with respect to the debtor thirty days after the petition is filed, unless it is extended by the court upon a showing by the debtor that the case was filed in good faith.

This provision does not apply if the prior case was dismissed under section 707(b) of the Code and the new case is not a chapter 7 case. Because the stay terminates under this provision only with respect to the debtor and only as to actions taken[20] in relation to "a debt or property securing such a debt or to any lease," the automatic stay provided under section 362(a) of the Code continues to apply in the later case to property of the estate and to actions not taken in relation to a debt.[21]

In addition, section 362(c)(3) does not prevent the application of the codebtor stay provided under section 1301 of the Code.[22] Finally, this stay limitation does not apply in a case brought by a family farmer under chapter 12.

9.3.3.2.2 Demonstrating good faith for extension of stay past thirty days

On the motion of a party in interest, after notice and a hearing held before the thirty-day period expires, the court may extend the stay as to all or some creditors upon a showing that the case was filed in good faith.[23] If the court extends the stay, it may impose conditions or limitations upon it. The provision does not define good faith for purposes of this stay limitation, but good faith with respect to the filing of a case has been given a recognized meaning by existing case law.[24] Most cases should be found to have been filed in good faith under this standard.

Section 362(c)(3), while not defining good faith, sets forth several circumstances in which a case is presumed not to be filed in good faith.[25] Under section 362(c)(3)(C), a case is presumptively not filed in good faith, as to all creditors in the case, if any of the following is true:

- More than one prior case involving the debtor was pending in the year preceding the filing of the petition.
- A case was dismissed within the preceding year for failure to file required documents without substantial excuse. The subsection specifies that inadvertence or negligence of the debtor is not such an excuse, but negligence of the debtor's attorney can be a substantial excuse.[26]
- The debtor failed to provide adequate protection as ordered by the court. This provision would not include adequate protection payments made under section 1326 unless the court ordered them.[27] This provision should not affect many debtors, as failure to provide adequate protection has not been a common problem or cause for plan failure under prior law.
- The debtor failed to comply with the terms of a confirmed plan. This provision does not apply if the debtor defaulted before confirmation of the plan, but it will apply to the common case of a debtor who, well into the plan period, suffers an interruption in income or a large unexpected expense. It should not be difficult, however, to overcome the presumption in such a case.
- There has not been a substantial change in circumstances

---

17 *In re* State Airlines, Inc., 873 F.2d 264 (11th Cir. 1989).
18 In computing the one-year period, the time should be counted from dismissal of the prior case rather than from when the case was closed. *In re* Lundquist, 371 B.R. 183 (Bankr. N.D. Tex. 2007) (case was "pending" only until dismissal despite filing of motion to vacate dismissal); *In re* Williams, 363 B.R. 786 (Bankr. E.D. Va. 2007); *In re* Moore, 337 B.R. 79 (Bankr. E.D.N.C. 2005). However, to be safe, it is probably wise to wait until one year after the prior case was closed.
19 *In re* Parker, 336 B.R. 678 (Bankr. S.D.N.Y. 2006).
20 *In re* Stanford, 373 B.R. 890 (Bankr. E.D. Ark. 2007) (prepetition state court replevin action is the type of formal, judicial proceeding described in section 362(c)(3)(A)); *In re* Paschal, 337 B.R. 274 (Bankr. E.D.N.C. 2006) ("action taken" language construed to mean that stay termination under section 362(c)(3) applies only as to creditors who have taken some type of prepetition formal action against the debtor, such as a "judicial, administrative, governmental, quasi-judicial, or other essentially formal activity or proceeding"). *But see In re* James, 358 B.R. 816 (Bankr. S.D. Ga. 2007).
21 *In re* Holcomb, 380 B.R. 813 (B.A.P. 10th Cir. 2008); *In re* Jumpp, 356 B.R. 789 (B.A.P. 1st Cir. 2006); *In re* Scott-Hood, 473 B.R. 133 (Bankr. W.D. Tex. 2012); *In re* Rinard, 451 B.R. 12 (Bankr. C.D. Cal. 2011) (refusing to follow Ninth Circuit B.A.P.'s *Reswick* decision); *In re* Stanford, 373 B.R. 890 (Bankr. E.D. Ark. 2007); *In re* McFeeley, 362 B.R. 121 (Bankr. D. Vt. 2007); *In re* Murray, 350 B.R. 408 (Bankr. S.D. Ohio 2006); *In re* Harris, 342 B.R. 274 (Bankr. N.D. Ohio 2006) (noting contrasting language of section 362(a)(4) that precludes application of stay entirely unless imposed by court); *In re* Jones, 339 B.R. 360 (Bankr. E.D.N.C. 2006) (same); *In re* Johnson, 335 B.R. 805 (Bankr. W.D. Tenn. 2006). *But see* Reswick v. Reswick (*In re* Reswick), 446 B.R. 362 (B.A.P. 9th Cir. 2011) (stay also expires with respect to property of estate); *In re* Daniel, 404 B.R. 318 (Bankr. N.D. Ill. 2009); *In re* Jupiter, 344 B.R. 754 (Bankr. D.S.C. 2006).
22 *See* § 9.3.3.5, *infra*.
23 11 U.S.C. § 362(c)(3)(B); *In re* Acevedo, 2012 WL 2062399 (Bankr. D.N.M. June 7, 2012).
24 *See In re* Baldassaro, 338 B.R. 178 (Bankr. D.N.H. 2006) (good faith found based on changed circumstances); §§ 9.7.3.1.5, 12.3.3, 12.3.4, 12.10, *infra*.
25 11 U.S.C. § 362(c)(3)(C).
26 11 U.S.C. § 362(c)(3)(C)(i)(II)(aa).
27 *See* 11 U.S.C. § 1326(a)(1)(C); Ch. 12, *infra*.

since the dismissal of the prior case[28] or some other reason to expect that the new case will be successfully concluded with a discharge or with a confirmed plan that will be fully performed.

In addition, a case is presumptively not filed in good faith as to a particular creditor in the case if the creditor's request for relief from the automatic stay in a prior case was still pending when the case was dismissed or the request was resolved with an order terminating, conditioning, or limiting the stay.[29] If the presumption under this subsection as to a particular creditor is not rebutted and section 362(c)(3) is otherwise applicable, the stay would terminate only as to the creditor who had sought relief from the stay in the prior case.

The presumption of a bad faith filing does not arise if the prior case was dismissed due to the creation of a "debt repayment plan," often referred to as a debt management plan.[30] Unlike the prepetition credit counseling requirement found in section 109(h) of the Code, or the claim reduction provision found in section 502(k) of the Code, section 362(i) does not require that the debt repayment plan be proposed or negotiated by an approved nonprofit budgeting and credit counseling agency.[31] Indeed, it would appear that a plan to repay debts created by the debtor would suffice. This provision also does not require that the debtor successfully complete the debt repayment plan.

9.3.3.2.3 Overcoming the presumption that case was not filed in good faith

A presumption that a case was not filed in good faith can be overcome by clear and convincing evidence.[32] There is no reason to think that the evidence required to show good faith under section 362(c)(3) should be any different than that necessary to show good faith under current law. Under the existing body of law defining "good faith" in the bankruptcy context, an honest debtor making a second attempt to save a home or obtain other bankruptcy relief would be considered to have filed in good faith by most courts.[33] A showing by the debtor of a change in personal or financial circumstances or other reason why the current case will be successful is generally sufficient to rebut the presumption.[34]

Whenever possible, the debtor's motion to extend the automatic stay beyond the initial thirty days should be filed with the petition or immediately thereafter,[35] because a hearing on the motion, if held by the court, must be completed within the thirty-day period before the partial termination of the stay.[36] The motion should set forth the details of the prior filing, including dates of filing and dismissal and case number, whether the motion seeks a stay as to all or only certain creditors, and the reasons why the new case is filed in good faith and is likely to lead to a discharge, including any change in circumstances that has occurred.[37] The motion should be served on all creditors who would be affected by the stay.[38] As courts have made clear their intentions about how such issues are to be resolved, most such motions to extend the automatic stay have not been contested. Many courts allow such uncontested motions to be granted without a hearing, or establish other procedures through standing orders or local rule that help debtors avoid unnecessary added expenses in seeking extensions of the stay.[39]

If the court does not extend the stay, it expires at the end of the thirty-day period to the extent described in section 362(c)(3). Nothing in the 2005 Act, however, prevents the court from granting a section 105 injunction reimposing the stay after the

---

28 *See In re* Castaneda, 342 B.R. 90 (Bankr. S.D. Cal. 2006) (although debtor's personal and financial circumstances not much different between current and prior case, presumption did not arise under this provision because substantial change did exist "since the dismissal" of debtor's prior case, at which time she had lost her daughter's contribution to household expenses).

29 11 U.S.C. § 362(c)(3)(C)(ii).

30 11 U.S.C. § 362(i).

31 *See* 11 U.S.C. § 111.

32 11 U.S.C. § 362(c)(3)(C).

33 *See In re* Metz, 820 F.2d 1495 (9th Cir. 1987) (filing of successive bankruptcies does not necessarily show bad faith and may be perfectly proper); *In re* Smith, 43 B.R. 319 (Bankr. E.D.N.C. 1984) (plan confirmed, with conditions, even though there had been three prior unsuccessful chapter 13 cases); §§ 9.7.3.1.5, 12.3.3, 12.3.4, 12.10, *infra*.

34 *See* 1200 Buena Vista Condos. v. Young (*In re* Young), 467 B.R. 792 (Bankr. W.D. Pa. 2012) (debtor found in good faith due to change in circumstances even though debtor's attempt to strip off lien would not be successful); *In re* Hardman, 2008 WL 4107488 (Bankr. S.D. Tex. Aug. 29, 2008); *In re* Elliott-Cook, 357 B.R. 811 (Bankr. N.D. Cal. 2006); *In re* Castaneda, 342 B.R. 90 (Bankr. S.D. Cal. 2006); *In re* Whitaker, 341 B.R. 336 (Bankr. S.D. Ga. 2006).

35 For a sample Motion for Continuation of Automatic Stay in Case Filed Within One Year After Dismissal of Prior Bankruptcy Case, see Form 46, Appx. G.4, *infra*.

36 11 U.S.C. § 362(c)(3)(B). *See* Capital One Auto Fin. v. Cowley, 374 B.R. 601 (W.D. Tex. 2006); *In re* Norman, 346 B.R. 181 (Bankr. N.D. W. Va. 2006); *In re* Berry, 340 B.R. 636 (Bankr. M.D. Ala. 2006) (court lacks authority to extend stay under section 362(c)(3)(B) because debtor's motion filed more than thirty days after petition). *See also In re* Furlong, 426 B.R. 303 (Bankr. C.D. Ill. 2010) (termination of stay under § 362(c)(3)(A) does not divest court of authority to consider motion for stay extension filed within 30 days after petition, to conduct hearing on stay extension after 30-day period has expired, and to reimpose and extend stay prospectively); *In re* Toro-Arcila, 334 B.R. 224 (Bankr. S.D. Tex. 2005) (motion for stay extension filed on thirtieth day after petition, and therefore not permitting timely hearing under section 362(c)(3)(B) before stay termination, may nevertheless be heard under section 362(c)(4)(B) and stay may be reimposed).

37 *See In re* Wilson, 336 B.R. 338 (Bankr. E.D. Tenn. 2005) (setting forth that court's requirements).

Although the *Wilson* court required an affidavit, many courts would not require an affidavit and no affidavit is required by the Federal Rules of Bankruptcy Procedure. A sample motion for extension of the stay can be found in Form 46, Appx. G.4, *infra*.

38 *In re* Collins, 334 B.R. 655 (Bankr. D. Minn. 2005).

39 *See In re* McMinn, 452 B.R. 247 (Bankr. D. Kan. 2011) (no hearing necessary if motion not opposed and debtor has pleaded necessary facts).

thirty-day period.[40] Alternatively, the terms of a confirmed chapter 13 plan can provide equivalent relief.[41]

9.3.3.3 Two or More Cases Dismissed Within Previous Year

If an individual debtor has had two or more cases dismissed within the year before the petition is filed, section 362(c)(4) of the Code provides that the automatic stay under section 362(a) does not go into effect upon the filing of any case, other than a case refiled under section 707(b).[42] Because the provision applies to each debtor individually, the expiration or inapplicability of the stay as to one debtor does not apply to a joint debtor who has not filed a prior case.[43] On a motion filed by a party in interest within thirty days after the filing of the latest case, and after notice and a hearing, the court may order the stay to take effect as to all or some creditors, subject to such conditions or limitations as the court may impose.[44] The motion may have to be filed on an emergency basis, with a shortened notice period, due to imminent impending creditor actions.[45] Unlike the language of section 362(c)(3)(B), however, section 362(c)(4)(B) does not require that a hearing on the debtor's motion to impose the stay be completed within the thirty-day period.[46] The movant must demonstrate that the case has been filed in good faith as to the creditors whose actions are to be stayed.[47] If the debtor misses the thirty-day deadline, an injunction to stay creditor actions must be sought under the court's equitable powers instead.[48] Alternatively, the terms of a confirmed chapter 13 plan can provide equivalent relief.[49]

If the debtor or another party in interest seeks an order imposing a stay, a presumption may arise that the case was not filed in good faith based on circumstances similar to those that apply to a debtor who had a single case dismissed in the previous year.[50] This presumption is subject to rebuttal by clear and convincing evidence to the contrary.[51]

9.3.3.4 Order Confirming Stay Termination

Section 362(j) of the Code provides that, on request of a party in interest, the court shall issue an order under section 362(c) confirming that the automatic stay has been terminated. A similar provision is found in section 362(c)(4)(A)(ii), stating that the court shall promptly enter an order confirming that no stay is in effect as a result of the application of section 362(c)(4). These provisions do not require the order to be entered upon notice and a hearing, but Bankruptcy Rule 9013 provides that a request for an order be made by motion and served on affected parties, initiating a contested matter under Rule 9014, which ensures that the court has sufficient information to determine whether the stay has been terminated or is not in effect based on the conditions set forth in section 362(c).[52] Section 362(j) gives the court authority simply to confirm that the stay has terminated under section 362(c) and no other relief

---

40 *In re* Radson, 462 B.R. 911 (Bankr. S.D. Fla. 2011) (finding authority to reimpose stay, but denying request after applying the factors considered in *Whitaker* and *Franzese*); *In re* Furlong, 426 B.R. 303 (Bankr. C.D. Ill. 2010); *In re* Franzese, 2007 WL 2083650 (Bankr. S.D. Fla. July 19, 2007) (reimposing stay under § 105(a) based on good faith of debtors, lack of objection, and inadvertence of counsel in failing to timely seek stay extension); *In re* Reed, 370 B.R. 414 (Bankr. N.D. Ga. 2006) (permitting debtor to proceed with request for injunction under section 105(a), noting that evidentiary standards for issuance of injunction and for rebutting a presumption that case was not filed in good faith under section 362(c)(3)(C) were comparable); *In re* Williams, 346 B.R. 361 (Bankr. E.D. Pa. 2006) (stay may be invoked under section 105(a) even though debtor did not file timely motion for stay extension under section 362(c)(3)(B)); *In re* Whitaker, 341 B.R. 336 (Bankr. S.D. Ga. 2006) (same). See also § 9.4.7, *infra*.

41 *In re* Hileman, 451 B.R. 522 (Bankr. C.D. Cal. 2011) (creditor bound by confirmed plan even though the stay had expired under § 362(c)(3)(A)); *In re* Carlton, 2011 WL 3799885 (Bankr. N.D. Ala. Aug. 26, 2011) (although stay terminated pursuant to § 362(c)(3)(A), contempt sanctions were imposed on mortgage creditor for publishing foreclosure sale notices in violation of confirmed plan providing for cure of mortgage default); *In re* Murray, 350 B.R. 408 (Bankr. S.D. Ohio 2006); *In re* Murphy, 346 B.R. 79 (Bankr. S.D.N.Y. 2006) (creditor may be bound by plan confirmation even after stay has terminated under § 362(c)(3)(A)); *In re* Kurtzahn, 342 B.R. 581 (Bankr. D. Minn. 2006) (debtor waived rights under plan by failing to assert them in state court). See also §§ 9.7.3.2.1, 12.11, *infra*.

42 Bates v. BAC Home Loans (*In re* Bates), 446 B.R. 301 (B.A.P. 8th Cir. 2011).

The phrase "other than a case refiled under § 707(b)" was probably intended to mean, as under section 362(c)(3), that the stay limitation does not apply in a case filed under a chapter other than chapter 7 following the dismissal of a prior chapter 7 case under section 707(b). In addition, when section 362(c)(3) and (c)(4) are read together, it should also mean that in counting whether there have been two or more prior dismissed cases, a prior dismissed case that was filed under chapters 11, 12, or 13 following a chapter 7 dismissal under section 707(b) should not be considered.

43 *In re* Parker, 336 B.R. 678 (Bankr. S.D.N.Y. 2006).

44 11 U.S.C. § 362(c)(4)(B).

For a sample Motion to Invoke Automatic Stay in Case Filed Within One Year After Dismissal of Two Prior Bankruptcy Cases, see Form 47, Appx. G.4, *infra*.

45 See *In re* Frazier, 339 B.R. 516 (Bankr. M.D. Fla. 2006) (short notice was sufficient given exigencies of the case).

46 See *In re* Norman, 346 B.R. 181 (Bankr. N.D. W. Va. 2006).

47 See *In re* Chapman, 2008 WL 873641 (Bankr. E.D.N.C. Mar. 27, 2008) (finding debtor rebutted presumption of bad faith); *In re* Payen, 2008 WL 545001 (Bankr. D. Md. Feb. 21, 2008) (same); *In re* Ferguson, 376 B.R. 109 (Bankr. E.D. Pa. 2007) (presumption of bad faith rebutted even though debtor's circumstances had not changed since dismissal of second case due to failure to obtain prepetition counseling); *In re* Sarafoglou, 345 B.R. 19 (Bankr. D. Mass. 2006) (discusses good faith standard under section 362(c)(4)(B)). But see *In re* Thornes, 386 B.R. 903 (Bankr. S.D. Ga. 2007) (debtor failed to rebut presumption of bad faith because he did not establish a "substantial change" in his financial condition).

48 See *In re* Schroeder, 356 B.R. 812 (Bankr. M.D. Fla. 2006).

49 *In re* Fleming, 349 B.R. 444 (Bankr. D.S.C. 2006). See also § 9.7.3.2.1, *infra*.

50 11 U.S.C. § 362(c)(4)(D). See § 9.3.3.2.3, *supra*.

51 See *In re* Washington, 2012 WL 602182 (Bankr. S.D. Tex. Feb. 23, 2012) (presumption rebutted by evidence debtor had income to make plan payments).

52 *In re* Rice, 392 B.R. 35, 39 (Bankr. W.D.N.Y. 2006).

should be granted.[53] For example, orders should not be entered under section 362(j) to confirm that the stay has terminated under section 362(h) based on the debtor's failure to timely carry out an intention listed on the statement of intention.[54]

9.3.3.5 Codebtor Stay Still Applicable

The 2005 Act did not amend any of the provisions of section 1301 of the Code, and no mention of the codebtor stay is made in the revised versions of subsections 362(c)(3) or (c)(4). Thus, the stay limitations under these subsections discussed above do not prevent the application of the stay provided under section 1301 as to any actions taken against a codebtor on a consumer debt of the debtor.[55] Section 362(c) therefore would not prevent the codebtor stay from arising if the first case was a joint case and the second case was filed by only one spouse. This arrangement may also dictate that, if there is no strong reason to file a joint case, it may sometimes be advisable for only one spouse of a debtor couple to file an individual case, especially in the common situation in which a chapter 13 case is filed in order to cure a default on a joint mortgage. By proceeding in this way no issue will arise under section 362(c)(3) or (c)(4) about the application of the stay if the first case fails and circumstances later compel the filing of another case by the other spouse.

Indeed, because section 1301 protects "any individual that is liable on [the] debt with the debtor," and does not distinguish between codebtors who are also bankruptcy debtors and those who are not, there is a very good argument that in a joint chapter 13 case each debtor is protected by the codebtor stay created by the other joint debtor's case, even when section 362(c)(40) applies.[56]

9.3.3.6 Filings in Violation of Section 109(g) or a Prior Court Order—Section 362(b)(21)

Another provision of the 2005 Act affects the automatic stay for two subcategories of repeat filers, but only as to the enforcement of real property liens. Section 362(b)(21) of the Code renders the automatic stay inapplicable to enforcement of a lien on, or a security interest in, real property when the debtor is ineligible for relief under section 109(g) of the Code or has filed the case in violation of a prior court order limiting new bankruptcy case filings.

If there are codebtors on a real estate secured debt this stay exception would not apply in a case filed by one of the codebtors if that codebtor is not ineligible under section 109(g) or was not named in the prior court order, and in a chapter 13 case the stay under section 1301 would protect the interest of the joint debtor.[57] In a joint case this provision would apply as to real property jointly held by both debtors only if both debtors are ineligible under section 109(g) or subject to the prior court order.[58] This provision also does not affect the codebtor stay under section 1301.[59]

Under section 109(g) a debtor is not eligible for relief under the Code if, within 180 days before the filing of the petition, the debtor had a prior case dismissed for willful failure to abide by orders of the court or to prosecute the case, or the debtor requested and obtained the voluntary dismissal of the case following the filing of a request for relief from the automatic stay.[60] However, it is often not clear whether section 109(g) applies to a case filed after a prior case. Courts rarely make express findings that the debtor willfully failed to prosecute the case or willfully failed to obey a court order.

Thus it is not likely that real estate secured creditors will rely upon this stay exception if the debtor's filing status is unclear. A creditor who proceeds with enforcement of a real property lien in reliance on the exception based on section 109(g) may act at its peril. There may be factual or legal disputes about whether the debtor is eligible for relief and whether section 109(g) applies. If the debtor prevails, the creditor's action is likely to be found a willful violation of the stay, as a mistake does not vitiate the willfulness of an action in violation of the stay.[61]

9.4 Scope of the Automatic Stay

9.4.1 Introduction

The acts prohibited by the automatic stay are set out in a series of overlapping statutory provisions.[62] This section dis-

---

53 *See In re* Murphy, 346 B.R. 79 (Bankr. S.D.N.Y. 2006) (court may not include in "comfort order" under section 362(j) provision declaring that creditor will not be bound by any subsequent chapter 13 plan confirmation or a provision which awards attorney fees to the creditor).

54 *In re* Hill, 364 B.R. 826 (Bankr. M.D. Fla. 2007) (car creditor denied "comfort order" for alleged stay termination under section 362(h)); *In re* Dienberg, 348 B.R. 482 (Bankr. N.D. Ind. 2006) (same). *See also* § 11.4.2.3, *infra*.

55 *See In re* Lemma, 393 B.R. 299 (Bankr. E.D.N.Y. 2008) (although automatic stay applicable to debtors was terminated by operation of section 362(c)(3)(A), mortgage creditor's scheduling of foreclosure sale violated codebtor stay under section 1301); *In re* King, 362 B.R. 226 (Bankr. D. Md. 2007) (although no stay went into effect as to debtor based on prior dismissed case, postpetition foreclosure sale violated the codebtor stay under section 1301 and was therefore void).

For discussion of the codebtor stay, *see* § 9.4.5, *infra*.

56 *In re* Lemma, 393 B.R. 299 (Bankr. E.D.N.Y. 2008) (codebtor stay under section 1301 was applicable to each debtor even though automatic stay entered in joint case had terminated by operation of section 362(c)(3)(A)).

57 *See* § 9.4.5, *supra*.
58 Section 362(b)(21) should be compared with the refiling provision in section 362(c)(3), which expressly states that the provision is applicable in a single or joint case filed by an individual debtor.
59 *See* § 9.4.5, *supra*.
60 *See* § 3.2.1.2, *supra*; § 9.7.3.1.5, *infra*.
61 *See* § 9.6, *infra*.
62 11 U.S.C. § 362(a).

cusses those provisions, which are subject to a variety of exceptions.

9.4.2 Legal Proceedings

The stay bars "the commencement or continuation, including the issuance or employment of process, of a judicial, administrative, or other action or proceeding against the debtor that was or could have been commenced before the commencement of the case . . . or to recover a claim against the debtor that arose before the commencement of the case."[63] Thus, almost all forms of civil legal actions are brought to an abrupt halt.[64] The only possible exceptions to this provision, other than those enumerated in section 362(b), are actions that do not arise out of circumstances existing prior to the case and do not pertain to a claim[65] that existed prior to the case.[66] However, many of those actions may still be barred by a different provision of section 362(a).

One illustrative issue, which arises with more frequency in business bankruptcy cases, is how to treat tort claims in cases in which the acts giving rise to liability occur prepetition, but in which no injury is discovered until after the commencement of the tortfeasor's bankruptcy case. Many courts have held that the victim has a prepetition claim which is subject to the automatic stay.[67]

Among the many types of legal proceedings affected by the automatic stay are attachments,[68] garnishments[69] and executions, evictions,[70] and some family-related court proceedings, including some divorce[71] and support cases.[72] A proceeding against the debtor commenced in the federal district court or court of appeals is stayed, notwithstanding the fact that they are "higher" courts than the bankruptcy court.[73] Even proceedings in which the debtor is sued solely in a fiduciary capacity,[74] and proceedings based on admittedly nondischargeable debts,[75] are

---

63 11 U.S.C. § 362(a)(1).
64 11 U.S.C. § 362(a)(1); *In re* Miller, 397 F.3d 726 (9th Cir. 2005) (state court order and judgment entered after petition was void despite earlier prepetition oral ruling, as was order of a different bankruptcy court against debtor entered after debtor's petition); Sunshine Dev. Inc. v. Fed. Deposit Ins. Corp., 33 F.3d 106 (1st Cir. 1994) (Federal Deposit Insurance Corp. (FDIC) is not exempt from stay when acting as receiver or conservator because it is not exercising regulatory powers excepted by 11 U.S.C. § 362(b)(4)); *In re* Colonial Realty Co., 980 F.2d 125 (2d Cir. 1992) (provisions of Federal Deposit Insurance Act giving FDIC rights superior to a bankruptcy trustee did not make automatic stay provisions inapplicable to FDIC). *But see* Rexnord Holdings Inc. v. Bidermann, 21 F.3d 522 (2d Cir. 1994) (ministerial act of a court clerk in entering judgment which had been ordered prior to bankruptcy filing did not violate stay because it was not a continuation of a legal proceeding); *In re* Roxford Foods, Inc., 12 F.3d 875 (9th Cir. 1994) (automatic stay does not prohibit lawsuits filed in bankruptcy court where debtor's bankruptcy case is pending); *In re* Geris, 973 F.2d 318 (4th Cir. 1992) (stay does not prevent foreclosure on real estate not owned by debtor even if debtor has personal liability on debt secured by mortgage).
65 "Claim" is defined extremely broadly in 11 U.S.C. § 101(5), to include contingent, unmatured, non-monetary and many other types of rights. *See* Ohio v. Kovacs, 469 U.S. 274, 105 S. Ct. 705, 83 L. Ed. 2d 649 (1985).
66 One court of appeals has held that claims arising directly from the act of filing a petition in bankruptcy, such as a cause of action for abuse of process under state law, are not covered by the stay. However, according to that court such claims are within the exclusive federal bankruptcy jurisdiction and may not be litigated in state court. Gonzalez v. Parks, 830 F.2d 1033 (9th Cir. 1987).
67 *See* Grady v. A.H. Robins Co., 839 F.2d 198 (4th Cir. 1988). *Cf. In re* Cent. R.R. Co. of N.J., 950 F.2d 887 (3d Cir. 1991) (claim does not exist until claimant discovers injury and knows, or has reason to know, its cause).
68 *In re* Matthews, 184 B.R. 594 (Bankr. S.D. Ala. 1995) (IRS levy notices and tax refund seizures violated stay and discharge injunction).
69 *See In re* Roberts, 175 B.R. 339 (B.A.P. 9th Cir. 1994) (state franchise tax board violated stay by continuing to accept payments from debtor's employer pursuant to prepetition garnishment).

However, certain wage garnishments or attachments for domestic support obligations are permitted by section 362(b)(2). *See* § 9.4.6.3, *infra*.
70 *In re* Smith Corset Shops Inc., 696 F.2d 971, 976 (1st Cir. 1982); *In re* Butler, 14 B.R. 532 (S.D.N.Y. 1981); *In re* Lowry, 25 B.R. 52 (Bankr. E.D. Mo. 1982). *See also In re* Goodman, 991 F.2d 613 (9th Cir. 1993) (unlawful detainer action against sublessee debtor's sublessor by owner of property violated stay).

However, some evictions are permitted by section 362(b)(22), (23). *See* § 9.4.6.6, *infra*.
71 While it is clear that such actions are stayed to the extent they seek division of property, 11 U.S.C. § 362(b)(2)(A)(iv), the stay will often be lifted by the court, upon a proper request, for cause. *See* § 9.7, *infra*. One case discussing the stay of a divorce action, and refusing to lift the stay, is *In re* Pagitt, 3 B.R. 588 (Bankr. W.D. La. 1980). *See also* H.R. Rep. No. 95-595, at 343, 344 (1977). *See generally* Henry J. Sommer & Margaret Dee McGarity, Collier Family Law and the Bankruptcy Code ¶ 5.03 (1992).
72 Various actions to collect domestic support obligations or pursue certain family law issues are permitted by section 362(b)(2). *See* § 9.4.6.3, *infra*.

For cases under prior law, see Carver v. Carver, 954 F.2d 1573 (11th Cir. 1992) (action seeking to collect divorce obligations from chapter 13 debtor's wages violated automatic stay); *In re* Kearns, 161 B.R. 701 (D. Kan. 1993) (contempt proceedings in a support case may violate the automatic stay); *In re* Farmer, 150 B.R. 68 (Bankr. N.D. Ala. 1991) (state court order to incarcerate chapter 13 debtor unless support payments are made from wages violates automatic stay); *In re* Tweed, 76 B.R. 636 (Bankr. E.D. Tenn. 1987) (petition for contempt of child support order violated stay); *In re* Marriage of Lueck, 140 Ill. App. 3d 836, 489 N.E.2d 443 (1986) (child support contempt proceedings violated automatic stay). The reasoning of these cases must be examined to determine whether it remains valid with respect to section 362(b)(2) as amended in 2005.

See generally Henry J. Sommer & Margaret Dee McGarity, Collier Family Law and the Bankruptcy Code ¶ 5.03[3]–[6] (1992).
73 *See* Constitution Bank v. Tubbs, 68 F.3d 685 (3d Cir. 1995) (district court judgment was void, and therefore court of appeals had no jurisdiction, when it was entered in violation of stay, even though district court purported to enter judgment *nunc pro tunc* to date prior to bankruptcy filing).
74 *In re* Panayotoff, 140 B.R. 509 (Bankr. D. Minn. 1992) (proceeding to remove debtor as personal representative of decedent's estate violated stay); *In re* Colin, 35 B.R. 904 (Bankr. S.D.N.Y. 1983) (suit against debtor in his capacity as a trustee was stayed).
75 *See In re* Merchant, 958 F.2d 738 (6th Cir. 1992) (actions to collect nondischargeable student loan violate stay); *In re* Arneson, 282 B.R.

prohibited unless an exception to the stay applies or the court grants relief from the stay. Also enjoined in most cases are administrative proceedings such as those to revoke drivers' licenses,[76] to intercept tax refunds,[77] or to determine and collect overpayments of public benefits,[78] as well as arbitrations and other less formal proceedings.[79] Appeals of all proceedings against the debtor are also stayed.[80]

No further steps may be taken in any stayed proceedings without the permission of the bankruptcy court.[81] Thus, the act of continuing the date of a foreclosure sale violates the stay, although several appellate courts have held otherwise on the theory that such a postponement merely preserves the status quo.[82] Ongoing discovery must also be discontinued. Similarly, civil contempt proceedings for alleged discovery order violations are stayed. Counsel bringing an action against the debtor has a duty to take action to halt a non-bankruptcy court's actions.[83] However, the provision pertaining to legal proceedings is subject to several limited exceptions, discussed below.[84]

It is important to note that 11 U.S.C. § 362 bars only actions against the debtor, and not those brought by the debtor.[85] The

---

883 (B.A.P. 9th Cir. 2002) (stay applies to bar enforcement of debt found nondischargeable in earlier bankruptcy case); In re Parker, 334 B.R. 529 (Bankr. D. Mass. 2005) (actions to collect nondischargeable student loan violate stay). But see In re Cady, 315 F.3d 1121 (9th Cir. 2002) (after creditor obtains judgment of nondischargeability, it may proceed against property of the debtor but not property of the estate); In re Embry, 10 F.3d 401 (6th Cir. 1993) (once creditor obtained determination that debt was nondischargeable in chapter 7 case due to false pretenses, creditor could proceed against property that was not property of the estate without violating the automatic stay).

Note, however, that exempted property is protected during and after the case. 11 U.S.C. § 522(c). See § 10.5, infra.

76 In re Duke, 167 B.R. 324 (Bankr. D.R.I. 1994) (stay prohibited state from suspending debtor's driver's license for failure to pay judgment).

However, section 362(b)(2)(D) permits revocation for failure to pay child support. See § 9.4.6.3, infra.

77 In re Herron, 177 B.R. 866 (Bankr. N.D. Ohio 1995) (student loan creditor's failure to act to reverse postpetition tax refund intercept after notice of bankruptcy was willful stay violation); In re Stucka, 77 B.R. 777 (Bankr. C.D. Cal. 1987).

However, section 362(b)(2)(F) permits tax intercepts for failure to pay child support. See § 9.4.6.3, infra.

78 Lee v. Schweiker, 739 F.2d 870 (3d Cir. 1984). See § 9.4.4, infra.

79 See, e.g., Acands, Inc. v. Travelers Cas. & Sur. Co., 435 F.3d 252 (3d Cir. 2006) (arbitration was stayed, even if initiated by debtor); In re King Mem'l Hosp., 5 B.R. 192 (Bankr. S.D. Fla. 1980) (state certificate of need process for hospital stayed).

80 See, e.g., Raymark Indus. v. Lai, 973 F.2d 1125 (3d Cir. 1992) (appeal stayed even though debtor had posted deposit to stay execution prepetition); Sheldon v. Munford, Inc., 902 F.2d 7 (7th Cir. 1990) (appeal stayed even when appellant-debtor had filed supersedeas bond).

81 Dean v. Trans World Airlines, 72 F.3d 754 (9th Cir. 1996) (involuntary dismissal of action against debtor violated the stay); Ellis v. Consol. Diesel Elec. Corp., 894 F.2d 371 (10th Cir. 1990) (dismissal of case against debtor violates stay); Pope v. Manville Forest Prods. Corp., 778 F.2d 238 (5th Cir. 1985) (dismissal of case against debtor is precluded by the stay); In re Westwood Lumber, Inc., 113 B.R. 684 (Bankr. W.D. Wash. 1990) (voluntary dismissal of case against debtor to allow state court case to go forward against others violates stay); In re Weed, 6 Bankr. Ct. Dec. (LRP) 606, 2 Collier Bankr. Cas. 2d (MB) 994 (Bankr. S.D. Iowa 1980) (discovery in district court case not allowed without lifting of stay). See In re Knightsbridge Dev. Co., 884 F.2d 145 (4th Cir. 1989) (postpetition entry of arbitration award violates stay when arbitrators had not completed their deliberations before the petition was filed); In re Tampa Chain Co., 835 F.2d 54 (2d Cir. 1987) (appeal of defendant in adversary proceeding cannot be dismissed after that defendant became debtor in his own bankruptcy case). But see Picco v. Global Marine Drilling Co., 900 F.2d 846 (5th Cir. 1990) (subsequent blanket order granting relief from stay validates prior dismissal of action against debtor in violation of stay).

82 Taylor v. Slick, 178 F.3d 698 (3d Cir. 1999) (postponement of foreclosure sale to new date does not violate stay); In re Peters, 101 F.3d 618 (9th Cir. 1996) (creditor did not violate stay by continuing foreclosure sale date after plan confirmation). Cf. In re Derringer, 375 B.R. 903 (B.A.P. 10th Cir. 2007) (filing and serving notice of foreclosure was more than mere postponement or continuance of sale so it violated stay); In re Lynn-Weaver, 385 B.R. 7, 11 (Bankr. D. Mass. 2008) (while a one-time postponement is permitted as a temporary place-holding measure, repeated rescheduling of sale violated stay).

83 Eskanos & Adler, Prof'l Corp. v. Leetien, 309 F.3d 1210 (9th Cir. 2002) (failure to dismiss or stay pending collection action against debtor was willful violation of stay); In re Scroggin, 364 B.R. 772 (B.A.P. 10th Cir. 2007) (creditor willfully violated stay when it waited twelve weeks before it sent release of wage garnishment to employer); Sroge v. Sloan (In re Sroge), 2010 Bankr. LEXIS 1310 (Bankr. N.D. Ind. May 6, 2010) (creditor had duty to cease court proceedings that resulted in arrest warrant for debtor); In re Daniels, 316 B.R. 342 (Bankr. D. Idaho 2004) (creditor and creditor's counsel assessed actual and punitive damages for failing to take action to withdraw an arrest warrant based upon unpaid debt issued at creditor's request); In re Braught, 307 B.R. 399 (Bankr. S.D.N.Y. 2004) (creditor willfully violated stay by failing to take affirmative action to vacate state court judgment entered in violation of stay); In re Atkins, 176 B.R. 998 (Bankr. D. Minn. 1994) (creditors' attorney was in contempt of automatic stay injunction when he failed to abort a prepetition process that led to the debtor's postpetition arrest on a bench warrant for contempt of discovery order after attorney had notice of the debtor's bankruptcy). See also In re St. Vincent, 2011 WL 1258479 (Bankr. N.D. Ill. Apr. 1, 2011) (stay violation motion based on wrongful continuation of bank account hold obtained by creditor should be brought against creditor, not bank).

84 See § 9.4.6, infra.

85 In re U.S. Abatement Corp., 39 F.3d 563 (5th Cir. 1994) (creditor's motion with respect to debtor's counterclaim did not violate stay because counterclaim was not claim against the debtor); Koolik v. Markowitz, 40 F.3d 567 (2d Cir. 1994) (debtor's appeal of judgment on counterclaim against debtor was stayed because counterclaim was an action or proceeding against debtor); Brown v. Armstrong, 949 F.2d 1007 (8th Cir. 1991) (automatic stay does not apply to the debtor's action against the Farmers Home Administration); Mar. Elec. Co. v. United Jersey Bank, 959 F.2d 1194 (3d Cir. 1991) (automatic stay can preclude claims against the debtor without staying debtor's counterclaims; claims and counterclaims could be disaggregated so that a defendant-debtor's counterclaims could proceed); Martin-Trigona v. Champion Fed. Sav. & Loan Ass'n, 892 F.2d 575 (7th Cir. 1989) (automatic stay inapplicable to debtor's lawsuit); Carley Capital Group v. Fireman's Fund Ins. Co., 889 F.2d 1126 (D.C. Cir. 1989) (debtor's appeal of judgment in action filed by debtor not stayed); In re Bryner, 425 B.R. 601 (B.A.P. 10th Cir. 2010) (party sued by debtor in state court was permitted to file motion to set aside default judgment). See also In re Mann Farms, Inc., 917 F.2d 1210 (9th Cir. 1990) (debtor's lawsuit not affected by

debtor's actions may be continued after commencement of the case, although the trustee may acquire an interest in the action and a party may be able to remove the action to the bankruptcy court.[86] Occasionally it is not clear whether an action is against the debtor or brought by the debtor, for example, when a debtor's counterclaim predominates or when a defendant/debtor has filed an appeal. The answer to this question turns on whether the action was brought initially by or against the debtor.[87] When the original action was brought against the debtor, the action may be stayed, even if the debtor would prefer that it go forward.[88]

It is also quite clear that, except as provided in 11 U.S.C. § 1201 or § 1301,[89] the stay does not affect acts against codebtors.[90] However, a creditor cannot pursue community property or entireties property owned jointly by the debtor and a codebtor, even if acquired after the bankruptcy, because section 362(a)(1) prohibits any legal action to recover a prepetition claim against the debtor and a "claim against the debtor" includes a claim against the debtor's property.[91]

9.4.3 Acts Directed at the Debtor's Property

Several provisions protect, in various ways, the property owned by the debtor at the time of filing. They also protect community property that is brought into the estate under section 541(a)(2).[92] They prohibit, subject to the exceptions found in section 362(b):

- The enforcement, against the debtor or against property of the estate, of a judgment obtained before the commencement of the case under title 11;[93]
- Any act to obtain possession of property of the estate or property from the estate or to exercise control over property of the estate;[94]
- Any act to create, perfect, or enforce any lien against property of the estate;[95] and
- Any act to create, perfect, or enforce any lien to the extent that such lien secures a claim that arose before the commencement of the case under title 11.[96]

These provisions have slightly different effects depending upon whether a judgment or a lien is involved. A judgment obtained prior to filing cannot be enforced against either the debtor or property of the estate. This bar covers most injunctive as well as monetary judgments.[97] And because legal proceedings are also stayed as to prepetition claims, only a judgment which

---

pendency of bankruptcy case except to the extent debtor bound itself under confirmed plan). *But see* Acands, Inc. v. Travelers Cas. & Sur. Co., 435 F.3d 252 (3d Cir. 2006) (arbitration was stayed, even if initiated by debtor).

Even counterclaims against the debtor in the bankruptcy court may be barred. *In re* Lessig Constr., Inc., 67 B.R. 436 (Bankr. E.D. Pa. 1986).

86 See Chapter 14, *infra*, for discussion of removal of litigation to bankruptcy court.

87 TW Telecom Holdings Inc. v. Carolina Internet Ltd., 661 F.3d 495 (10th Cir. 2011); *In re* Delta Airlines, 310 F.3d 953 (9th Cir. 2002) (but appeal could proceed in cases of non-debtor co-defendants); Delpit v. Comm'r Internal Revenue Serv., 18 F.3d 768 (9th Cir. 1994) (appeal from Tax Court proceeding was stayed because it was continuation of what was originally an administrative proceeding to collect taxes from the debtor); Nielsen v. Price, 17 F.3d 1276 (10th Cir. 1994) (stay did not apply to appeal in adversary proceeding initiated by debtors in prior bankruptcy); Alpern v. Lieb, 11 F.3d 689 (7th Cir. 1993) (appeal from dismissal of suit originally filed by debtor was not stayed); Farley v. Henson, 2 F.3d 273 (8th Cir. 1993) (debtor's appeal in action brought against debtor was stayed); Carley Capital Group v. Fireman's Fund Ins. Co., 889 F.2d 1126 (D.C. Cir. 1989) (debtor's appeal of judgment in action filed by debtor not stayed); Ingersoll-Rand Fin. Corp. v. Miller Mining Co., 817 F.2d 1424 (9th Cir. 1987); Commerzanstalt v. Telewide Sys., Inc., 790 F.2d 206 (2d Cir. 1986); Teachers Ins. & Annuity Ass'n of Am. v. Butler, 803 F.2d 61 (2d Cir. 1986); Freeman v. Internal Revenue Serv., 799 F.2d 1091 (5th Cir. 1986); Cathey v. Johns-Manville Sales Corp., 711 F.2d 60 (6th Cir. 1983); Ass'n of St. Croix Condo. Owners v. St. Croix Hotel Corp., 682 F.2d 446 (3d Cir. 1982). *See also* Ellison v. Northwest Eng'g Co., 709 F.2d 681 (11th Cir. 1983). *But see* Koolik v. Markowitz, 40 F.3d 567 (2d Cir. 1994) (appeal by debtor plaintiff from adverse judgment on defendant's counterclaim was stayed); Accredited Assocs., Inc. v. Shottenfeld, 292 S.E.2d 417 (Ga. Ct. App. 1982) (result turns on which party filed appeal); Kessel v. Peterson, 350 N.W.2d 603 (N.D. 1984) (appeal by debtor plaintiff from adverse judgment on defendant's counterclaim was stayed).

88 *See In re* Hoffinger Indus., Inc., 329 F.3d 948 (8th Cir. 2003) (appeal by debtor in action in which debtor was defendant was stayed); Borman v. Raymark Indus., Inc., 946 F.2d 1031 (3d Cir. 1991) (debtor's appeal of judgment against it is stayed).

Nothing prevents the debtor from seeking relief from the stay for cause, in order to allow the appeal to go forward. *See* § 9.7.3.2.1, *infra*.

89 *See* § 9.4.5, *infra*.

90 Queenie, Ltd. v. Nygard Int'l, 321 F.3d 282 (2d Cir. 2003) (appeal stayed as to defendant who had filed a bankruptcy case and his wholly owned corporation, but not as to other defendants); Credit Alliance Corp. v. Williams, 851 F.2d 119 (4th Cir. 1988); Fortier v. Dona Anna Plaza Partners, 747 F.2d 1324 (10th Cir. 1984); Williford v. Armstrong World Indus., 715 F.2d 124 (4th Cir. 1983); Wedgeworth v. Fibreboard Corp., 706 F.2d 541 (5th Cir. 1983); Austin v. Unarco Indus., 705 F.2d 1 (1st Cir. 1983); Pitts v. Unarco Indus., 698 F.2d 313 (7th Cir. 1983); HBA East, Ltd. v. JEA Boxing Co., 796 S.W.2d 534 (Tex. App. 1990). *See also In re* Am. Hardwoods, Inc., 885 F.2d 621 (9th Cir. 1989) (court lacks power to institute non-automatic stay pursuant to 11 U.S.C. § 105 to protect non-debtor guarantors). *Cf. In re* Replogle, 929 F.2d 836 (1st Cir. 1991) (determinations made in non-stayed case which affect the estate's interests because of debtor's guarantee are not binding in the bankruptcy case).

91 11 U.S.C. § 102(2).

92 *See In re* Thongta, 401 B.R. 363 (Bankr. E.D. Wis. 2009) (creditor of non-debtor spouse violated stay by docketing tort judgment against her because judgment created lien on community property); *In re* Passmore, 156 B.R. 595 (Bankr. E.D. Wis. 1993) (creditor could not attach postpetition wages of debtor's spouse, as they were community property in which debtor had an undivided interest); § 2.5.1, *supra*.

93 11 U.S.C. § 362(a)(2).

94 11 U.S.C. § 362(a)(3).

95 11 U.S.C. § 362(a)(4).

96 11 U.S.C. § 362(a)(5).

97 Certain judgments obtained by governmental units to enforce police or regulatory powers may be enforced. 11 U.S.C. § 362(b)(4). *See* § 9.4.6.9, *infra*. *But see In re* Watson, 78 B.R. 232 (B.A.P. 9th Cir.

arose solely out of postpetition claims can be enforced against the debtor without violation of the stay.[98]

The provisions prohibiting acts to obtain possession or to utilize liens against property of the estate apply regardless of when the claim arose, as property of the estate is essentially frozen, to be administered only by the bankruptcy court.[99] In a chapter 13 case, this freeze can be very important because, generally, all property the debtor acquires during the entire time the case is pending becomes property of the estate.[100] Thus, the imposition of fees or charges added to a mortgage that are not authorized by a chapter 13 plan can violate the stay.[101] The prohibition of acts to obtain possession also applies to property not owned by, but in possession of, the estate, such as leased property, even if the lease was terminated prior to the case.[102] And it applies to any other property in which the debtor has any interest,[103] to intangible property rights as well as to tangible property.[104]

1987) (judgment held nondischargeable may be executed without relief from stay).

98 See Taylor v. First Fed. Sav. & Loan Ass'n of Monessen, 843 F.2d 153 (3d Cir. 1988); In re Petruccelli, 113 B.R. 5 (Bankr. S.D. Cal. 1990).

Note that such judgments cannot be enforced against property of the estate. However, some postpetition claims can be collected only as administrative claims in the context of the debtor's bankruptcy proceeding. See 11 U.S.C. § 503. See also In re Creative Cuisine, Inc., 96 B.R. 144 (Bankr. N.D. Ill. 1989) (lessor cannot collect claim for postpetition rent in state court).

And creditors may not use the subterfuge of claiming that payments extracted from the debtor are for postpetition services when they are really applied to prepetition debts. In re Lansdale Family Restaurants, Inc., 977 F.2d 826 (3d Cir. 1992).

99 Similarly, the provision against exercising control over property of the estate prevents third parties from attempting to enforce claims which have come into the bankruptcy estate. See In re Sherk, 918 F.2d 1170 (5th Cir. 1990) (non-debtor wife may not bring fraudulent transfer action outside bankruptcy based on claim which had passed, in part, into husband's bankruptcy estate); In re Crysen/Montenay Energy Co., 902 F.2d 1098 (2d Cir. 1990); §§ 12.8.1, 12.8.5, infra. See § 2.5, supra, for a discussion of what property comes into the estate.

However, postpetition transfers of estate property may be authorized by the court pursuant to 11 U.S.C. § 363. The relevant portions of this provision are made applicable to debtors in chapter 13 by 11 U.S.C. § 1303. In addition it is not clear that a voluntary transfer of property by the debtor is stayed, although such a transfer, if not authorized, may be subject to avoidance under section 549. See In re Tippett, 542 F.3d 684 (9th Cir. 2008) (voluntary transfer of real estate to good faith third-party purchaser did not violate stay); § 10.4.2.6.6, infra.

100 11 U.S.C. § 1306(a); Sec. Bank of Marshalltown, Iowa v. Neiman, 1 F.3d 687 (8th Cir. 1993) (property acquired by chapter 13 debtor during case continues to be property of the estate protected by the stay after it vests in the debtor upon confirmation); In re Kolenda, 212 B.R. 851 (W.D. Mich. 1997) (automobile acquired postconfirmation was property of the estate protected by stay); In re Jackson, 403 B.R. 95, 101 (Bankr. D. Idaho 2009) (postpetition creditor could not obtain lien on property debtors inherited during chapter 13 case). But see In re Fisher, 203 B.R. 958 (N.D. Ill. 1997) (vesting of property of estate in debtor at confirmation deprives that property of stay protection afforded to property of the estate), rev'g 198 B.R. 721 (Bankr. N.D. Ill. 1996); In re Sak, 21 B.R. 305 (Bankr. E.D.N.Y. 1982); In re Adams, 12 B.R. 540 (Bankr. D. Utah 1981) (all of debtor's property except that used to fund plan is no longer property of the estate after confirmation, under 11 U.S.C. § 1327(b)).

One possible way to avoid the potential problem of property losing its character as property of the estate in jurisdictions in which that is at issue is to provide in the plan for such property to vest in the debtor at the end of the case, because section 1327(b) provides that confirmation vests estate property in the debtor only if the plan does not provide otherwise. This provision will extend the protection of the stay. For an example of such plan language, see Form 18, Appendix G.3, infra. See In re Clark, 207 B.R. 559 (Bankr. S.D. Ohio 1997) (postconfirmation wages were property of estate protected from IRS levy for postpetition taxes when plan clearly provided that property of estate did not revest in debtors upon confirmation); In re Lambright, 125 B.R. 733 (Bankr. N.D. Tex. 1991); In re Petruccelli, 113 B.R. 5 (Bankr. S.D. Cal. 1990); In re Denn, 37 B.R. 33 (Bankr. D. Minn. 1983). See also § 9.3, supra; §§ 12.8.5, 12.11, infra.

101 See § 14.4.3.4.5, note 350, infra.

102 In re Convenient Food Mart No. 144, Inc., 968 F.2d 592 (6th Cir. 1992); In re Atl. Bus. & Cmty. Corp., 901 F.2d 325 (3d Cir. 1990) (mere possessory interest in property triggers stay); In re 48th St. Steakhouse, 835 F.2d 427 (2d Cir. 1987) (same); In re Sudler, 71 B.R. 780 (Bankr. E.D. Pa. 1986); In re Gibbs, 9 B.R. 758 (Bankr. D. Conn. 1981); In re A.L.S. Inc., 3 B.R. 107 (Bankr. E.D. Pa. 1980). See also In re Di Giorgio, 200 B.R. 664 (C.D. Cal. 1996) (declaring unconstitutional state statute which permitted execution on writ of possession despite tenant's bankruptcy filing), appeal dismissed as moot, 134 F.3d 971 (9th Cir. 1998). But see In re Pinetree, Ltd., 876 F.2d 34 (5th Cir. 1989) (debtor's interest in property by unrecorded deed from related entity not protected by automatic stay when debtor did not assert its interest prepetition).

However, if a lessor has obtained a prepetition judgment for possession, the stay applies only to the extent provided in section 362(b)(22). See § 9.4.6.6, infra. Also, the protection of possessory interests after lease termination does not apply to some leases of non-residential real property. 11 U.S.C. § 362(b)(10).

103 In re Chesnut, 422 F.3d 298 (5th Cir. 2005) (stay extends to property as to which the debtor has any arguable claim of right); Missouri v. United States Bankruptcy Court, 647 F.2d 768 (8th Cir. 1981); In re Levenstein, 371 B.R. 45 (Bankr. S.D.N.Y. 2007) (under New York Domestic Relations Law debtor had marital property interest in property titled in name of his estranged wife). See also Borman v. Raymark Indus., 946 F.2d 1031 (3d Cir. 1991) (section 362(a)(3) protects property of the estate even if it is not in the debtor's possession); In re McCall-Pruitt, 281 B.R. 910 (Bankr. E.D. Mich. 2002) (state violated stay by accepting funds arising from prepetition tax garnishment after bankruptcy case was filed). But see United States v. Inslaw, 932 F.2d 1467 (D.C. Cir. 1991) (party's use of property in its possession under claim of right does not violate stay); In re Lockard, 884 F.2d 1171 (9th Cir. 1989) (surety bond to protect debtor's creditors not property of the estate so that state court action to collect on bond not stayed).

104 See In re Gaskin, 120 B.R. 13 (D.N.J. 1990) (postpetition termination of "interest credit agreement" by Farmers Home Administration violates automatic stay); Scrima v. John Devries Agency Inc., 103 B.R. 128 (W.D. Mich. 1989) (purported postpetition cancellation of insurance policy void); In re R.S. Pinellas Motel P'ship, 2 B.R. 113 (Bankr. M.D. Fla. 1979).

Even a debtor's interest in a liability insurance policy is property subject to the automatic stay. In re Minoco Group of Companies, Ltd., 799 F.2d 517 (9th Cir. 1986) (prepaid policy may not be canceled by the issuing company without relief from the stay); Tringali v. Hathaway Mach. Co., 796 F.2d 553 (1st Cir. 1986).

Similarly, it is a violation of the stay to unilaterally terminate a license or a contract with the debtor. In re Computer Communica-

The stay also prevents any action to create, perfect or enforce a lien against property of the estate.[105] Although this provision prevents renewal or extension of most expiring liens while the stay is in effect,[106] another provision of the Code effectively extends an existing lien until at least thirty days after the stay expires if renewal or extension of the lien is stayed.[107]

Finally, these provisions generally prevent the creation, perfection, or enforcement of any lien against the debtor's property, even if it is not property of the estate, for example, most property acquired after the filing of the bankruptcy case or property abandoned in a chapter 7 case, if the lien secures a prepetition claim.[108]

Thus, repossessions and sales of repossessed property are clearly enjoined.[109] If relief from the stay is subsequently granted to allow the sale of estate property to go forward, the creditor may be required to re-advertise and provide new notice of the sale to all interested parties including the debtor.[110]

The applicability of the stay to acts against property of the estate often turns on difficult questions about whether the debtor had a property interest at the time the case was filed.[111] Generally, however, even a very limited interest brings the stay into effect. For example, probate proceedings concerning an estate from which the debtor may inherit property are stayed.[112] The stay may halt even evictions, foreclosures, or other transactions that are nearly complete, depending upon the state law as to the debtor's interest.[113]

---

tions, Inc., 824 F.2d 725 (9th Cir. 1987). *See also In re* Carroll, 903 F.2d 1266 (9th Cir. 1990) (termination of management agreement postpetition violates stay); *In re* Nejberger, 120 B.R. 21 (E.D. Pa. 1990) (postpetition termination of liquor license due to failure to pay prepetition taxes violates stay), *aff'd*, 934 F.2d 1300 (3d Cir. 1991); *In re* North, 128 B.R. 592 (Bankr. D. Vt. 1991) (suspension of chiropractor's license for failure to pay prepetition taxes violates stay); *In re* Pester Ref. Co., 58 B.R. 189 (Bankr. S.D. Iowa 1985). *Cf.* Hazen First State Bank v. Speight, 888 F.2d 574 (8th Cir. 1989) (stay does not prevent contract from expiring by its own terms); Holland Am. Ins. Co. v. Succession of Roy, 777 F.2d 992 (5th Cir. 1985).

105 *In re* Avis, 178 F.3d 718 (4th Cir. 1999) (section 362(a)(5) prevented attachment of federal tax lien to property acquired by estate due to inheritance of property by the debtor); *In re* Glasply Marine Indus., 971 F.2d 391 (9th Cir. 1992) (stay prohibits creation of new property tax liens after petition filed); Makoroff v. City of Lockport, 916 F.2d 890 (3d Cir. 1990) (perfection of tax lien postpetition violates stay); *In re* Parr Meadows Racing Ass'n, Inc., 880 F.2d 1540 (2d Cir. 1989); *In re* Ozenne, 337 B.R. 214 (B.A.P. 9th Cir. 2006) (owner of storage unit who sold debtor's stored property to satisfy unpaid fees violated stay).

A 1994 amendment to the Code added 11 U.S.C. § 362(b)(18), which overrules these cases. That section creates an exception to the stay for the creation or perfection of a statutory lien for an *ad valorem* property tax that comes due after the filing of the bankruptcy petition. *But see* Mann v. Chase Manhattan Mortgage Corp., 316 F.3d 1 (1st Cir. 2003) (mortgage company adding charges to debtor's account in its internal bookkeeping, absent any overt attempt to collect the fees, did not violate automatic stay); *In re* Stanton, 303 F.3d 939 (9th Cir. 2002) (increase in lien on debtors' home due to new advances on loan to corporation that they had guaranteed did not violate stay); *In re* Knightsbridge Dev. Co., 884 F.2d 145 (4th Cir. 1989) (creditor did not violate stay by amending its *lis pendens* postpetition).

106 *In re* Lobherr, 282 B.R. 912 (Bankr. C.D. Cal. 2002) (renewal of judgment violated stay and was void).

A 1994 amendment to 11 U.S.C. § 362(b)(3) permits acts to maintain or continue perfection of a lien in certain limited circumstances.

107 *See* 11 U.S.C. § 108(c); *In re* Hunter's Run Ltd. P'ship, 875 F.2d 1425 (9th Cir. 1989); *In re* Morton, 866 F.2d 561 (2d Cir. 1989).

Additionally, note that perfection of certain types of liens which relate back to an event occurring prepetition is permitted under 11 U.S.C. § 362(b)(3). *See* Equibank v. Wheeling Pittsburgh Steel, 884 F.2d 80 (3d Cir. 1989). *But see In re* Larson, 979 F.2d 625 (8th Cir. 1992) (stay did not prohibit a filing of mortgage addendum to extend duration of existing lien).

108 *In re* Brooks, 871 F.2d 89 (9th Cir. 1989) (creditor cannot re-record deed after bankruptcy to perfect interest in debtor's property by changing incorrect property description); *In re* Sedgwick, 266 B.R. 185 (Bankr. N.D. Cal. 2001) (creditors could not obtain lien on debtor's property after confirmation of plan, regardless of whether property was still property of estate); *In re* Passmore, 156 B.R. 595 (Bankr. E.D. Wis. 1993) (creditor could not attach postpetition wages of debtor's spouse, even though they were not property of the estate, because they were community property in which debtor had an undivided interest).

109 *In re* Suggs, 377 B.R. 198 (B.A.P. 8th Cir. 2007) (local rule purporting to allow repossession before stay relief if debtor did not have insurance was invalid); *In re* Reed, 102 B.R. 243 (Bankr. E.D. Okla. 1989) (postpetition sale of repossessed collateral violates automatic stay); *In re* Koresko, 91 B.R. 689 (Bankr. E.D. Pa. 1988) (debtor retains right to redeem vehicle after repossession; postpetition sale violates stay).

The refusal of an auto creditor to remove or disable a device that prevents the debtor from starting a vehicle upon payment default may give rise to a stay violation. *See In re* Garner, 2010 WL 890406 (Bankr. M.D.N.C. Mar. 9, 2010) (creditor violated stay by not promptly removing "On Time Payment Protection System"); *In re* Peterkin, 2009 WL 1076816 (Bankr. E.D.N.C. Apr. 16, 2009) (refusal to remove payment protection system that deactivated the vehicle's electrical system or to provide debtor with code to disable it was a willful stay violation); *In re* Crawford, 2008 WL 5427713 (Bankr. S.D. Ill. Dec. 24, 2008) (actual damages, punitive damages, and attorney fees awarded to debtor for creditor's refusal to repair disabling device); *In re* Dawson, 2006 WL 2372821 (Bankr. N.D. Ohio Aug. 15, 2006).

110 *See also* § 9.4.2, *supra*.

111 *See* United States v. Pelullo, 178 F.3d 196 (3d Cir. 1999) (debtor had no interest in assets which had been divested by a criminal forfeiture order prior to bankruptcy petition).

112 *In re* Molitor, 183 B.R. 547 (Bankr. E.D. Ark. 1995) (probate proceedings that occurred without relief from the stay were void; stay protected trustee's right to be involved in distribution of probate estate).

113 *See, e.g., In re* 48th St. Steakhouse, 835 F.2d 427 (2d Cir. 1987) (notice of lease termination to debtor's sublessor violated stay); *In re* Aponte, 82 B.R. 738 (Bankr. E.D. Pa. 1988) (tenant's bare possessory interest triggers stay); *In re* Evans, 22 B.R. 608 (Bankr. D. Neb. 1982) (debtor retained interest in pawned goods during redemption period); *In re* Jones, 20 B.R. 988 (Bankr. E.D. Pa. 1982) (debtor retained interest in home after sheriff's sale); *In re* Gambogi, 20 B.R. 587 (Bankr. D.R.I. 1982) (post-eviction possessory interest in leased property sufficient to activate stay); *In re* Jenkins, 19 B.R. 105 (D. Colo. 1982) (debtors retained interest in property subject to deed of trust foreclosure until redemption period had run).

See also cases cited above in this subsection and in § 9.7.3.2.4, *infra*.

However, if a lessor has obtained a prepetition judgment for

In particular, the relationship of the stay to rights of redemption from foreclosure sales under state law has been the subject of frequent litigation. Here, too, the applicable state law may be critical, especially if the creditor must take some further action, such as obtaining a deed, after the redemption period runs.[114] When a creditor need take no affirmative act to assert its rights after the redemption period, the debtor's only protection may come from section 108 of the Code, which extends a redemption period to sixty days after the petition is filed if it would otherwise have expired earlier.[115] It is unclear whether this period can be further extended under the broad powers granted to the bankruptcy court under 11 U.S.C. § 105.[116] However, even when the right of redemption expires, the creditor must seek relief from the stay to file an action against the debtor for possession of the property.[117]

Similar issues arise with respect to property in the possession of pawnbrokers. Section 541(b)(8) excludes from the bankruptcy estate an interest of the debtor in tangible personal property that has been pledged or sold as collateral for a loan and is in possession of the pledgee or transferee, if the debtor has no obligation to repay the loan or redeem the collateral and the debtor has not redeemed in a timely manner under state law or section 108(b). However, while exclusion from the bankruptcy estate may prevent certain portions of section 362(a) from going into effect, nothing in the language of this provision overrides other provisions that prohibit acts to collect a prepetition debt, or acts to enforce a lien securing a prepetition debt against property of the debtor.[118] Therefore, section 541(b)(8) does not necessarily eliminate the automatic stay with respect to such property.

9.4.4 Other Acts Prohibited by the Stay

The automatic stay also prohibits, subject to the exceptions found in section 362(b):

- Any [other] act to collect, assess or recover a claim against the debtor that arose before the commencement of the case;[119]
- The setoff of any debt owing to the debtor that arose before the commencement of the case against any claim against the debtor;[120] and
- The commencement or continuation of a proceeding before the United States Tax Court concerning the tax liability of an individual debtor for a prepetition taxable period.[121]

These provisions round out the stay's protections. Creditors may not engage in any collection activity, nor in any other acts to try to force the debtor to pay a prepetition claim.[122] This

---

possession, the stay applies only to the extent provided in section 362(b)(22). See § 9.4.6.6, infra.

114 In re Brown, 126 B.R. 767 (N.D. Ill. 1991) (nonbankruptcy law determines whether IRS levy terminates debtor's interests in bankruptcy); In re Lambert, 273 B.R. 663 (Bankr. N.D. Fla. 2002) (postpetition issuance of tax deed based on prepetition sale of tax certificate violated stay because it was not mere ministerial act); In re Cooper, 273 B.R. 297 (Bankr. D.D.C. 2002) (resale of debtor's property after first foreclosure sale purchaser failed to comply with terms of sale was stayed by bankruptcy petition filed before resale occurred because debtor had right of redemption); In re Davenport, 268 B.R. 159 (Bankr. N.D. Ill 2001) (action of tax sale purchaser in seeking tax deed violated stay because debtor still had equitable and beneficial interest in property after tax sale). See Fish Mkt. Nominee Corp. v. Pelofsky, 72 F.3d 4 (1st Cir. 1995) (stay prevented state court order terminating debtor's right of redemption during bankruptcy case); In re Garber, 129 B.R. 323 (Bankr. D.R.I. 1991) (state law right of redemption comes into the estate precluding sale of seized property by creditor). But see In re Rodgers, 333 F.3d 64 (2d Cir. 2003) (when right to redemption from tax sale expired before bankruptcy petition was filed, automatic stay did not prevent delivery of deed to tax sale purchaser).

115 11 U.S.C. § 108; In re Canney, 284 F.3d 363 (2d Cir. 2002) (Vermont strict foreclosure); In re Tynan, 773 F.2d 177 (7th Cir. 1985); Johnson v. First Nat'l Bank of Montevideo, 719 F.2d 270 (8th Cir. 1983) (automatic transfer of property under Minnesota law would not violate stay). See also Counties Contracting & Constr. Co. v. Constitution Life Ins. Co., 855 F.2d 1054 (3d Cir. 1988) (statutory grace period for payment on insurance policy is extended sixty days by bankruptcy filing; at end of sixty days policy expires); In re McCallen, 49 B.R. 948 (D. Or. 1985) (stay applied when further creditor action required to complete foreclosure); In re Jenkins, 19 B.R. 105 (D. Colo. 1982) (stay applies when further action required of creditor or third party after running of redemption period).

Neither the requirement of a ministerial act by a court clerk after the running of the redemption period nor the retention of greater rights by the debtor during the redemption period is sufficient to bring the automatic stay into effect. In re Carver, 828 F.2d 463 (8th Cir. 1987); In re Manum, 828 F.2d 459 (8th Cir. 1987).

However, other courts have found the stay applicable regardless of the necessity of further creditor action. See, e.g., In re Dohm, 14 B.R. 701 (Bankr. N.D. Ill. 1981).

Also, if a creditor fails to object to a chapter 13 plan extending the right to redemption, he may be bound by that confirmed plan. See In re Bennett, 29 B.R. 380 (W.D. Mich. 1981).

116 Compare Johnson v. First Nat'l Bank of Montevideo, 719 F.2d 270 (8th Cir. 1983) with Bank of Ravenswood v. Patzold, 27 B.R. 542 (N.D. Ill. 1982).

117 11 U.S.C. § 362(a)(3).
118 See Cash Am. Advance, Inc. v. Prado, 413 B.R. 599 (S.D. Tex. 2008) (sale of pawned property that was not property of the estate (and was property of the debtor because it was exempted) violated section 362(a)(5) as act to enforce lien against property of the debtor). See also In re Spinner, 398 B.R. 84, 94 (Bankr. N.D. Ga. 2008) (title pawn lender could not obtain benefit of pawnbroker statute because it did not comply with all statutory requirements).
119 11 U.S.C. § 362(a)(6).
120 11 U.S.C. § 362(a)(7). But see In re Holford, 896 F.2d 176 (5th Cir. 1990) (certain recoupments allowed if they arise from the same transaction).
121 11 U.S.C. § 362(a)(8).

For corporate debtors, Tax Court proceedings are stayed with respect to the debtor's tax liability for any taxable period that the bankruptcy court may determine. But see Cheng v. Comm'r Internal Revenue Serv., 938 F.2d 141 (9th Cir. 1991) (automatic stay does not apply to appeal of tax court proceeding).

122 See In re Diamond, 346 F.3d 224 (1st Cir. 2003) (threat to take action at real estate commission to have broker's license revoked could violate stay); In re Flynn, 143 B.R. 798 (Bankr. D.R.I. 1992)

prohibition encompasses all types of collection attempts: by mail, by phone, in person or through third parties.[123] As noted earlier, the word "claim" is broadly defined to include not only rights to payment, regardless of whether they are liquidated, contingent, matured, disputed, or secured, but also many rights to equitable remedies.[124] It includes mortgage escrow payments that were due from the debtor prior to the petition, so that a lender's recalculation of escrow in a way that caused postpetition demands for the payments outside the claim process violated the stay.[125] Administrative recoupments of public benefits, such as Social Security or welfare, based upon a claim of overpayment or fraud, are not allowed.[126] If a collection motivation is shown, the withholding of a student's transcript or other benefits normally provided to non-debtors is also prohibited.[127] Denying the debtor the right to register a vehicle based on prepetition debts is prohibited for the same reason.[128]

Similarly, creditors may not exercise a right of setoff against the debtor's property, such as bank accounts, without violating

---

(credit union violated stay by communicating with debtor to seek reaffirmation when it knew she was represented by counsel); *In re* Guinn, 102 B.R. 838 (Bankr. N.D. Ala. 1989) (termination of credit union membership and refusal to accept mortgage payments violate stay); *In re* Sechuan City, Inc., 96 B.R. 37 (Bankr. E.D. Pa. 1989) (creditor's posting of signs in lobby of hotel that debtor restaurant does not pay its bills violates automatic stay; creditor's first amendment arguments rejected).

Even revocation of a debtor's probation motivated by desire to coerce payment of a prepetition restitution debt has been held to violate the stay. See § 9.4.6.2, *infra*. *But see In re* Duke, 79 F.3d 43 (7th Cir. 1996) (erroneously holding that a non-threatening, non-coercive letter to the debtor seeking reaffirmation of a debt did not violate the stay); Brown v. Pa. State Employees Credit Union, 851 F.2d 81 (3d Cir. 1988) (credit union's letter informing debtor that it would not do further business with her unless she reaffirmed debt does not violate stay); Morgan Guar. Trust Co. v. Am. Sav. & Loan, 804 F.2d 1487 (9th Cir. 1986) (a holder in due course's presentment of prepetition notes executed by the debtor does not violate the stay).

The *Duke* decision was narrowly construed by at least one bankruptcy court, which found a creditor in contempt for simply mailing a proposed reaffirmation agreement directly to a debtor who was represented by counsel. *In re* Seelye, 243 B.R. 701 (Bankr. N.D. Ill. 2000).

Communications seeking reaffirmation of debt may also violate other consumer protection laws, regardless of whether they violate the stay. *See* Sears, Roebuck & Co. v. O'Brien, 178 F.3d 962 (8th Cir. 1999) (state law prohibiting creditor from communicating with debtor represented by counsel was not preempted by federal bankruptcy law); Greenwood Trust Co. v. Smith, 212 B.R. 599 (B.A.P. 8th Cir. 1997) (creditor's direct communication with debtor represented by attorney violated state consumer credit laws); Sturm v. Providian Nat'l Bank, 242 B.R. 599 (S.D. W. Va. 1999) (state law claims for unfair debt collection not preempted by automatic stay provisions).

123 *See* Butz v. People First Fed. Credit Union (*In re* Butz), 444 B.R. 301 (Bankr. M.D. Pa. 2011) (statement that creditor claimed was purely informational violated stay because it contained the language "Your account is 10 or more days past due. Please remit the amount due immediately."); *In re* King, 396 B.R. 242, 248 (Bankr. D. Mass. 2008) (placing tax lien on property of debtor's parents to collect debtor's tax debts could be act to collect debt); *In re* Crudup, 287 B.R. 358 (Bankr. E.D.N.C. 2002) (letter sent to debtor's in-laws was attempt to collect debt); *In re* Draper, 237 B.R. 502 (Bankr. M.D. Fla. 1999) (repeated invoices requesting payment and sent to debtor with payment coupon and return envelope violated the stay even though they acknowledged bankruptcy filing and stated that they were for "informational purposes only"). *But see* Redmond v. Fifth Third Bank, 624 F.3d 793 (7th Cir. 2010) (mortgage payoff letter issued at debtor's request was not attempt to collect); Knowles v. Bayview Loan Servicing, L.L.C. (*In re* Knowles), 442 B.R. 150 (B.A.P. 1st Cir. 2011) (same; sending annual tax statement not an attempt to collect).

124 11 U.S.C. § 101(5).

125 *In re* Rodriguez, 629 F.3d 136 (3d Cir. 2010).
126 Lee v. Schweiker, 739 F.2d 870 (3d Cir. 1984); Crabtree v. Veterans Admin., 31 B.R. 95 (Bankr. S.D. Ohio 1983). However, some types of "recoupment" may be allowed if previous payments to a debtor reduce or eliminate any entitlement to future benefits and are not otherwise considered as collectible debts. *In re* Kosadnar, 157 F.3d 1011 (5th Cir. 1998) (employer could reduce debtor's paychecks to recoup prior advances that were overpayments to debtor); *In re* Mullen, 696 F.2d 470 (6th Cir. 1983) (military readjustment allowance not considered a debt). *See also In re* Malinowski, 156 F.3d 131 (2d Cir. 1998) (state agency could not reduce debtor's unemployment benefits to repay overpayment on prior claim; reduction was setoff and not recoupment because two unemployment claims covered separate periods and were not same transaction); *In re* Univ. Med. Ctr., 973 F.2d 1065 (3d Cir. 1992) (Department of Health and Human Services (HHS) not permitted to withhold Medicare payments to hospital based upon prepetition debts of hospital to HHS); *In re* O'Neil, 408 B.R. 823 (D. Neb. 2008) (state could recoup unemployment benefits overpaid in prior period from benefits due for current period); *In re* Beaumont, 586 F.3d 776 (10th Cir. 2009) (recoupment of veterans benefits permitted); *In re* Gullett, 230 B.R. 321 (Bankr. S.D. Tex. 1999) (recoupment of erroneously paid workers' compensation benefits violated stay when recoupment was not permitted by state law); *In re* Gaither, 200 B.R. 847 (Bankr. S.D. Ohio 1996) (recoupment of unemployment compensation overpayment from postpetition benefits does not violate stay as claims arise out of same transaction); *In re* Howell, 4 B.R. 102 (Bankr. M.D. Tenn. 1980) (administrative determination of overpayments not stayed but overpayments themselves were simply unsecured claims to be treated as others).
127 *In re* Kuehn, 563 F.3d 289 (7th Cir. 2009) (withholding transcript violated stay and discharge injunction); *In re* Merchant, 958 F.2d 738 (6th Cir. 1992) (although student loan debt found nondischargeable, school's refusal to release transcript violates stay); *In re* Gustafson, 934 F.2d 216 (9th Cir. 1991) (refusal to release transcript violates stay, but state university held immune from money damages); Loyola Univ. v. McClarty, 234 B.R. 386 (E.D. La. 1999) (damages imposed for refusal to release transcript); *In re* Mu'min, 374 B.R. 149 (Bankr. E.D. Pa. 2007) (withholding of transcript was intended to compel payment); *In re* Walker, 336 B.R. 534 (Bankr. M.D. Fla. 2005) (violation to withhold transcript regardless of dischargeability); *In re* Parker, 334 B.R. 529 (Bankr. D. Mass. 2005) (preventing debtor from registering for class and from graduating violated stay); *In re* Scroggins, 209 B.R. 727 (Bankr. D. Ariz. 1997) (parochial school's withholding of transcript to collect debt violated stay); *In re* Carson, 150 B.R. 228 (Bankr. E.D. Mo. 1993) (threats to prevent student from attending graduation and to withhold transcript violated stay); *In re* Parham, 56 B.R. 531 (Bankr. E.D. Va. 1986) (student transcript); *In re* Olson, 38 B.R. 515 (Bankr. N.D. Iowa 1984) (refusal of medical services until prepetition debt paid was contempt); *In re* Ware, 9 B.R. 24 (Bankr. W.D. Mo. 1981).
128 Bererhout v. City of Malden (*In re* Bererhout), 2011 WL 2119007 (Bankr. D. Mass. May 24, 2011).

the stay,[129] nor may they garnish the debtor's wages,[130] or collect their debts from property of the debtor, such as energy assistance payments, that comes into their hands.[131] The reporting of a debt to a credit bureau is a violation of the stay if done with the intent to coerce a debtor into paying a prepetition debt.[132] Even the acceptance of payroll deductions or continuing bank account withdrawals authorized by the debtor before the bankruptcy on payments for a prepetition debt constitutes an act to collect that debt and thus is a violation of the stay.[133]

The interception of tax refunds to pay student loans or other debts being collected by the government is another example of an act that is stayed.[134] Although it is sometimes not easy to determine the date the intercept actually occurred, if it occurred after the bankruptcy case was filed it is normally possible to have the intercepted funds returned to the debtor.[135]

However, the Supreme Court has held that a "freeze" on a debtor's bank account, by a bank to which the debtor owes money, does not constitute a setoff prohibited by the stay.[136] The court held that a temporary freeze, while a creditor seeks relief from the stay in order to exercise a right of setoff is permissible.[137] However, a more permanent freeze should be considered differently. If a creditor does not promptly seek relief from the stay in order to set off its debt, the Supreme Court's decision should not be considered applicable.[138] Moreover, cases prohib-

---

129 *See In re* Adomah, 340 B.R. 453 (Bankr. S.D.N.Y. 2006) (bank could not refuse to turnover funds in bank account subject to prepetition creditor restraining notice and require debtor to obtain creditor's consent to release of funds), *aff'd*, 368 B.R. 134 (S.D.N.Y. 2007); *In re* Jimenez, 335 B.R. 450 (Bankr. D.N.M. 2005) (bank to which debtor owed no money violated stay when it froze debtor's account upon learning of bankruptcy, but did not turn account balance over to trustee), *rev'd*, 406 B.R. 935 (D.N.M. 2008); *In re* Scharff, 143 B.R. 541 (Bankr. S.D. Iowa 1992) (creditor violated stay by withholding pension checks to repay debt to pension plan); *In re* Figgers, 121 B.R. 772 (Bankr. S.D. Ohio 1990) (creditor's set-off rights are fixed as of date of filing despite conversion from one chapter to another).

See also § 10.4.2.6.7, *infra*, for discussion of rights to setoff a creditor may later exercise. *But see In re* McMahon, 129 F.3d 93 (2d Cir. 1997) (utility's application of prepetition deposit to prepetition debt was not prohibited setoff because it was recoupment under New York law).

130 *In re* Warren, 7 B.R. 201 (Bankr. N.D. Ala. 1980). *See also In re* Carlsen, 63 B.R. 706 (Bankr. C.D. Cal. 1986).

However, actions to withhold wages to pay domestic support obligations are permitted by 11 U.S.C. § 362(b)(2)(C). *See* § 9.4.6.3, *infra*.

131 *In re* Morris, 45 B.R. 350 (E.D. Pa. 1984). *See also In re* Farmers Mkts., Inc., 792 F.2d 1400 (9th Cir. 1986) (state could not condition transfer of liquor license it held on payment of prepetition taxes).

132 Carriere v. Proponent Fed. Credit Union, 2004 WL 1638250 (W.D. La. July 12, 2004); *In re* Wynne, 422 B.R. 763 (Bankr. M.D. Fla. 2010); *In re* Weinhoeft, 2000 WL 33963628 (Bankr. C.D. Ill. Aug. 1, 2000) ("even if it is shown that the Bank's reports to the credit-reporting agencies contain truthful information, such a report, if made with the intent to harass or coerce a debtor into paying a prepetition debt, could be deemed a violation of the automatic stay"); *In re* Singley, 233 B.R. 170 (Bankr. S.D. Ga. 1999); *In re* Sommersdorf, 139 B.R. 700 (Bankr. S.D. Ohio 1991) (bank's actions in placing notation of debt charge-off on codebtor's credit report violated stay).

However, credit reporting by a child support creditor is permitted by 11 U.S.C. § 362(b)(2)(E). *See* § 9.4.6.3, *infra*.

133 *In re* Hellums, 772 F.2d 379 (7th Cir. 1985); *In re* Krivohlavek, 405 B.R. 312 (B.A.P. 8th Cir. 2009) (credit unions continuing to collect automatic loan payments from debtor's paycheck deposits violated stay); *In re* Juliano, 2012 WL 760312 (Bankr. N.D.N.Y. Mar. 2, 2012) (damages awarded for continuing preauthorized withdrawals from bank account); *In re* Briggs, 143 B.R. 438 (Bankr. E.D. Mich. 1992) (credit union's notice to debtor that it would continue to apply postpetition earnings to prepetition debt unless requested not to do so constituted violation of stay); *In re* Brooks, 132 B.R. 29 (Bankr. W.D. Mo. 1991) (refusal to disgorge payroll deductions on demand constitutes willful violation of stay). *See also In re* O'Neal, 165 B.R. 859 (Bankr. M.D. Tenn. 1994) (retention of loan payment automatically withdrawn from checking account violated stay).

However, actions to withhold wages to pay domestic support obligations are permitted by 11 U.S.C. § 362(b)(2)(C). *See* § 9.4.6.3, *infra*.

134 *In re* Blake, 235 B.R. 568 (Bankr. D. Md. 1998) (Department of Education violated stay by causing setoff of tax refund to pay student loan).

However, intercepting tax refunds to pay domestic support obligations and prepetition tax debts is permitted by 11 U.S.C. § 362(b)(2)(F), (b)(26). *See* §§ 9.4.6.3, 9.4.6.8, *infra*.

135 *See In re* McCall-Pruitt, 281 B.R. 910 (Bankr. E.D. Mich. 2002) (state violated stay by accepting funds arising from prepetition tax garnishment after bankruptcy case was filed).

If the intercept was for a loan held by the United States Department of Education, a refund may be obtained by contacting the U.S. Department of Education, Debt Collection Service. If the loan is held by a guarantor contact the guarantor, or the guarantor and the Department of Education. If these contacts fail, the Department of Education's General Counsel should be contacted and, of course, an action can be brought in the bankruptcy court for turnover of the property, damages, and attorney fees.

136 Citizens Bank of Md. v. Strumpf, 516 U.S. 16, 116 S. Ct. 286, 133 L. Ed. 2d 258 (1995).

See § 10.4.2.6.7, *infra*, for a discussion of the implications of such a freeze on the creditor's right of setoff.

137 A few banks have adopted policies of freezing all debtor accounts even when a right to setoff does not exist, arguing that section 542 authorizes this at least until a trustee relinquishes the estate's rights in the account. Such policies are questionable and may result in a violation of the automatic stay. *See In re* Mwangi, 473 B.R. 802 (D. Nev. 2012); § 5.3.3.2, *supra*.

138 *In re* Radcliffe, 563 F.3d 627 (7th Cir. 2009) (even if creditor had a right to setoff, *Strumpf* exception did not apply when creditor waited six months to seek relief from stay); *In re* Holden, 217 B.R. 161 (D. Vt. 1997) (IRS could not permanently hold debtors' refund to coerce payment of much smaller debt already addressed in debtors' chapter 13 plan); *In re* Okigbo, 2009 WL 5227844 (Bankr. D. Md. Dec. 30, 2009) (credit union not permitted to hold deposit account when it did not seek stay relief until well after debtor complained about freeze; in addition, credit union had not obtained valid security interest that would except it from Regulation Z prohibition on setoff for credit card accounts); *In re* Cullen, 329 B.R. 52 (Bankr. N.D. Iowa 2005) (credit union violated stay by not seeking relief until forty days after debtors complained about setoff); *In re* Schafer, 315 B.R. 765 (Bankr. D. Colo. 2004) (credit union willfully violated stay by freezing debtor's accounts and making repeated requests for reaffirmation for period of six weeks before seeking stay relief); *In re* Orr, 234 B.R. 249 (Bankr. N.D.N.Y. 1999) (credit union violated stay by freezing funds and not seeking relief from stay for over two months); Town of Hempstead Employees Fed. Credit Union v. Wicks, 215 B.R. 316 (Bankr. E.D.N.Y. 1997)

iting a setoff or freeze in contravention of a confirmed plan providing for different treatment of the creditor's claim remain good law.[139] In addition, there is no right to setoff prepetition debts against postpetition deposits in an account.[140] And any freeze or setoff for credit card debts or overdrafts on consumer lines of credit is usually prohibited by non-bankruptcy law.[141]

Usually, the best way to prevent such a freeze from occurring is to ensure that the debtor has no money deposited, at the time the bankruptcy petition is filed, with any institution that is a creditor. When possible, the debtor should also try to make sure that all checks written on such accounts have cleared prior to the petition date. If that cannot be done, the debtor may want to consider withdrawing all funds from the account, advising the payees on the undeposited checks not to deposit those checks, and paying the payees with cash, money orders, or replacement checks drawn on a different account.

The Internal Revenue Service (IRS) has been one of the most frequent adversaries in litigation regarding these issues. An exception to the stay permits the IRS or other taxing authority to set off a prepetition tax refund against a prepetition tax debt.[142]

This amendment at least delineates clearly those tax refunds with respect to which setoff is permitted. With respect to cases not within the exception, the IRS now appears to give some recognition to the necessity that it seek relief from the stay before it can set off a tax refund arising from a tax year ending after the petition against a prebankruptcy tax debt, perhaps because, in several instances, the IRS has been held in contempt for setting off tax refunds without getting relief from the stay.[143]

However, despite these cases, it is often difficult to have tax refunds released to a debtor, because the IRS claims a right to "retain" them;[144] in some districts, questionable standing orders of the court have given the IRS blanket relief from the automatic stay for the setoff of mutual debts.[145]

9.4.5 The Automatic Stay Protecting Codebtors in Chapter 13

In chapter 13 cases, another type of automatic stay also goes into effect. This stay prohibits any act or civil legal action to collect all or part of a consumer debt of the debtor from any codebtor.[146] The codebtor need not be personally liable on the debt; it is sufficient that the codebtor put up security for the obligation.[147] Congress found this provision to be necessary because in many instances under the old Chapter XIII codebtors were pursued by creditors as soon as a debtor filed a case, leading ultimately to the failure of the Chapter XIII plan.[148] As discussed throughout this chapter, the codebtor stay has become much more important after the enactment of the 2005 amendments, because almost none of the limitations to the section 362 automatic stay apply to the codebtor stay.

One problem which arises not infrequently is the reporting of a bankruptcy on the credit report of a codebtor, even though the codebtor has not filed a bankruptcy case. Although creditors have argued that such a report accurately reflects that the particular debt is being paid in a bankruptcy plan, the report may be actionable if it inaccurately appears from the report that the codebtor has filed a bankruptcy case.[149] Even if the report

---

(four-month administrative freeze without filing of motion for relief from automatic stay violated stay).

139 *In re Cont'l Airlines*, 134 F.3d 536 (3d Cir. 1998) (reaffirming principles in earlier chapter 13 decision prohibiting IRS setoff after confirmation of plan providing for payment of tax debt through plan).

140 *In re Dunning*, 269 B.R. 357 (Bankr. N.D. Ohio 2001) (punitive damages awarded when bank admitted setoffs of prepetition debts against postpetition deposits as a matter of course); *In re Harris*, 260 B.R. 753 (Bankr. D. Md. 2001); *In re Orr*, 234 B.R. 249 (Bankr. N.D.N.Y. 1999) (credit union had no right to setoff except as to funds on deposit on petition date which were not withdrawn after the petition was filed); *In re Schwartz*, 213 B.R. 695 (Bankr. S.D. Ohio 1997).

141 The Fair Credit Billing Act prohibits such setoffs. 15 U.S.C. § 1666h(a). *See Bank Setoffs: Federal Prohibition on Credit Card Debt Often Ignored*, 20 NCLC REPORTS Bankruptcy and Foreclosures Ed. 5 (Sept./Oct. 2001).

142 11 U.S.C. § 362(b)(26). *See* § 9.4.6.8, *infra*.

143 *In re Price*, 103 B.R. 989 (Bankr. N.D. Ill. 1989) (that notice was sent out inadvertently by IRS computer is no defense), *aff'd*, 42 F.3d 1068 (7th Cir. 1994); *In re Hebert*, 61 B.R. 44 (Bankr. W.D. La. 1986) (IRS in contempt for attempting to collect interest on its claim outside chapter 13 plan); *In re Cudaback*, 22 B.R. 914 (Bankr. D. Neb. 1982) (IRS action to enforce prebankruptcy tax lien is contemptuous); *In re Hackney*, 20 B.R. 158 (Bankr. D. Idaho 1982) (IRS in contempt for refusing to release refund when confirmed plan gave debtors right to pay debt in installments); *In re Holcomb*, 18 B.R. 839 (Bankr. S.D. Ohio 1982) (IRS required to turn over tax refunds to chapter 13 trustee). *See also United States ex rel. Internal Revenue Serv. v. Norton*, 717 F.2d 767 (3d Cir. 1983) (IRS may not offset money due to debtors against prepetition claim which was provided for in confirmed chapter 13 plan; section 362 also bars such setoff before

confirmation); *United States v. Holden*, 258 B.R. 323 (D. Vt. 2000) (debtors awarded damages for IRS's administrative freeze of tax refund that was contrary to terms of confirmed chapter 13 plan).

In seeking damages or an injunction for violation of the stay against the IRS, issues related to federal sovereign immunity or the Anti-Injunction Act may arise. *See* §§ 9.6, 14.3.2.2, *infra*.

144 Both the Third and Fourth Circuit Courts of Appeals have held that, perhaps depending in some cases on state law, an IRS "freeze" on a debtor's tax refund is a setoff that is prohibited by the automatic stay. *United States v. Reynolds*, 764 F.2d 1004 (4th Cir. 1985); *United States ex rel. Internal Revenue Serv. v. Norton*, 717 F.2d 767 (3d Cir. 1983). *Cf. In re Murry*, 15 B.R. 325 (Bankr. E.D. Ark. 1981) (retention by IRS was not a prohibited setoff).

145 Such orders have not always withstood scrutiny. *See In re Internal Revenue Serv. Liabilities & Refunds in Chapter 13 Proceedings*, 30 B.R. 811 (M.D. Tenn. 1983) (vacating standing order allowing *ex parte* relief from stay); *In re Willardo*, 67 B.R. 1014 (Bankr. W.D. Mich. 1987) (local rule violated due process clause as well as Bankruptcy Code).

146 11 U.S.C. § 1301. *See In re Holder*, 260 B.R. 571 (Bankr. M.D. Ga. 2001) (perfection of lien was an act to collect barred by codebtor stay and therefore was void); *In re Sommersdorf*, 139 B.R. 700 (Bankr. S.D. Ohio 1992) (bank's actions in placing notation of debt charge-off on codebtor's credit report violated stay).

147 *In re Harris*, 203 B.R. 46 (Bankr. E.D. Va. 1994) (conveyance of jointly held property to foreclosure sale purchaser violated codebtor stay even though non-debtor spouse's personal liability on joint mortgage had been discharged in prior bankruptcy case).

148 H.R. Rep. No. 95-595, at 122 (1977).

149 For a discussion of claims brought under the Fair Credit Reporting

is accurate, it may be a violation of the codebtor stay if it is made with the intent to coerce payment by the codebtor.[150]

There are several limitations upon this stay. It applies only to "consumer debts,"[151] and it does not apply to codebtors who became obligated in the ordinary course of their business.[152] It ends automatically if a chapter 13 case is closed, dismissed, or converted to a chapter other than chapter 12.

In several situations, the stay is effective as of the filing of the case, but may be lifted by the court upon request of a creditor or other party in interest. Such a request could be grounded upon the fact that the chapter 13 debtor was really the cosigner, and the non-filing individual received the consideration for the claim.[153] However, the issue in such cases is not whether the cosigner is the primary obligor or secondary obligor; cosigners are protected if they are also liable, along with the debtor, on a debt which provided a benefit to the debtor.[154] Relief from the codebtor stay is also available upon a showing of irreparable harm to the creditor caused by the stay.[155]

In addition, the codebtor stay will be lifted upon a creditor's motion to the extent that the proposed plan does not provide for full payment of the claim.[156] Thus, if a plan proposes to pay ten percent of a claim, relief from the stay may be granted as to the remaining ninety percent.[157] As discussed in a following chapter, the need to retain the codebtor stay justifies separate classification of debts involving codebtors in a chapter 13 plan so that those debts will receive full payment even when the debtor cannot afford to pay other creditors in full.[158]

The fact that a creditor will be paid late does not by itself justify relief from the stay if payment will be made in full.[159] Less clear is what happens when unearned interest is involved. Normally, unearned interest is not considered part of an unsecured claim in chapter 13,[160] and not paid in a plan. Therefore, it should not be taken into account in deciding whether the "claim" is paid in full.[161] However, some courts have held otherwise, stating that a codebtor may be pursued to the extent that postbankruptcy interest is not paid in the plan.[162]

The procedure by which creditors may obtain relief from the codebtor stay is similar to that followed for relief from the section 362 automatic stay, discussed below, except in a few respects. A creditor that files a motion for relief from the

---

Act, see National Consumer Law Center, Fair Credit Reporting (7th ed. 2010 and Supp.).

150 In re Singley, 233 B.R. 170 (Bankr. S.D. Ga. 1999); In re Sommersdorf, 139 B.R. 700 (Bankr. S.D. Ohio 1992) (bank's actions in placing notation of debt charge-off on codebtor's credit report violated stay). See also § 15.5.1.4, infra, for a discussion of whether such actions violate the discharge injunction.

151 Consumer debt is defined at 11 U.S.C. § 101(8). The term includes legal fees incurred for a non-business purpose. Patti v. Fred Ehrlich, Prof'l Corp., 304 B.R. 182 (E.D. Pa. 2003) (state court action to collect divorce legal fees violated codebtor stay).

The term probably does not include a tax debt. See In re Westberry, 215 F.3d 589 (6th Cir. 2000) (tax debt not a consumer debt); In re Pressimone, 39 B.R. 240 (N.D.N.Y. 1984); In re Stovall, 209 B.R. 849 (Bankr. E.D. Va. 1997) (personal property tax not a consumer debt); In re Goldsby, 135 B.R. 611 (Bankr. E.D. Ark. 1992); In re Reiter, 126 B.R. 961 (Bankr. W.D. Tex. 1991).

It also may not include tort liability. In re Alvarez, 57 B.R. 65 (Bankr. S.D. Fla. 1985). See also § 13.4.1, infra, for cases concerning definition of "consumer debt."

152 11 U.S.C. § 1301(a)(1).

153 11 U.S.C. § 1301(c)(1). See, e.g., In re Jones, 106 B.R. 33 (Bankr. W.D.N.Y. 1989).

However, this principle is a narrow one. Even if a debtor's non-filing spouse also benefited from the debt and that debt was a community claim against community property of both spouses, the non-filing spouse did not receive the consideration for a debt rather than the spouse in bankruptcy. In re Lopez Melendez, 145 B.R. 740 (D. P.R. 1992).

Only if all the consideration at the time of the original transaction went to the codebtor does this exception apply. In re Motes, 166 B.R. 147 (Bankr. D. Mo. 1994) (codebtor stay applied because loan to purchase mobile home benefited both debtor and spouse when it was made, even though non-debtor spouse had obtained full title to mobile home by time of bankruptcy).

154 In re Lemma, 394 B.R. 315, 320 (Bankr. E.D.N.Y. 2008) (stay applies when both debtor and codebtor received consideration); In re Zersen, 189 B.R. 732 (Bankr. W.D. Wis. 1995).

155 11 U.S.C. § 1301(c)(3). See, e.g., In re Case, 148 B.R. 901 (Bankr. W.D. Mo. 1992) (creditor would suffer irreparable harm if not permitted to file a timely claim against deceased codebtor's estate).

156 11 U.S.C. § 1301(c). See In re Fink, 115 B.R. 113 (Bankr. S.D. Ohio 1990) (student loan creditor entitled to relief from stay to pursue codebtors because plan did not provide for full payment of claim). But see In re Bonanno, 78 B.R. 52 (Bankr. E.D. Pa. 1987) (chapter 13 plan providing that stay would continue throughout plan was binding upon creditors who did not object to it despite plan's failure to provide for full payment); In re Weaver, 8 B.R. 803 (Bankr. S.D. Ohio 1981) (same); 8 Collier on Bankruptcy ¶ 1327.02[1] (16th ed.).

Other courts have refused to give effect to such plan provisions. In re Britts, 18 B.R. 203 (Bankr. N.D. Ohio 1982) (creditor not bound by such a clause unless it specifically adopts plan after notice of clause); In re Rolland, 20 B.R. 931 (Bankr. W.D.N.Y. 1982) (such a clause is inconsistent with provisions of chapter 13).

157 However, the codebtor is required to pay the amounts not paid under the plan only as they fall due, and not immediately, if there has been no prior acceleration of the debt. In re Matula, 7 B.R. 941 (Bankr. E.D. Va. 1981); Int'l Harvester Employee Credit Union, Inc. v. Daniel, 13 B.R. 555 (Bankr. S.D. Ohio 1981). But see In re Jacobsen, 20 B.R. 648 (B.A.P. 9th Cir. 1982) (creditor could sue comaker immediately for amount not included in plan).

The stay should not be lifted if the only reason a claim is not being paid under the plan is the creditor's own failure to file a timely claim. In re Humphrey, 310 B.R. 735 (Bankr. W.D. Mo. 2004) (refusing to grant relief when creditor failed to file timely proof of claim); In re Francis, 15 B.R. 998 (Bankr. E.D.N.Y. 1981).

158 11 U.S.C. § 1322(b)(1). See § 12.4.2, infra.

159 Harris v. Fort Oglethorpe State Bank, 721 F.2d 1052 (6th Cir. 1982); In re Lemma, 394 B.R. 315, 320 (Bankr. E.D.N.Y. 2008).

160 11 U.S.C. § 502(b)(2).

161 In re Alls, 238 B.R. 914 (Bankr. M.D. Ga. 1999).

For discussion of whether a plan may separately classify cosigned debts and pay postpetition interest on such debts, see § 12.4.2, infra.

162 Southeastern Bank v. Brown, 266 B.R. 900 (S.D. Ga. 2001) (creditor may pursue codebtor for postpetition interest, but debtor may prevent this claim by separately classifying creditor and paying interest through plan); In re Leger, 4 B.R. 718 (Bankr. W.D. La. 1980). See also In re Bradley, 705 F.2d 1409 (5th Cir. 1983) (holding codebtors could be pursued for interest as it came due; debtor apparently did not argue that unearned interest was not part of the unsecured claim).

codebtor stay based upon allegations that the plan will not pay its claim in full need not obtain a court order terminating the stay, if that motion is not opposed. If the debtor or codebtor does not file a response to the motion and serve it upon the creditor within twenty days, the codebtor stay is terminated to the extent requested by the creditor.[163] It is important to note that this exception applies to only one of the grounds for relief from the codebtor stay (failure to propose payment in full), and it has no effect if a response to the creditor's motion is timely filed and served. Also, the time limits set forth in section 362(e) for court determination of a motion for relief are not made applicable to the section 1301 codebtor stay.[164] Finally, the burden of proof should be on the party seeking relief from the codebtor stay to prove that the grounds for relief exist.[165]

9.4.6 Exceptions to the Automatic Stay

9.4.6.1 Overview

The breadth of the automatic stay is narrowed by twenty-eight exceptions listed in section 362(b). Many of these exceptions have little bearing in consumer cases (such as those concerning commodity futures or Department of Housing and Urban Development foreclosures on multi-family dwellings). Some, though, are significant in particular cases.

9.4.6.2 Criminal Proceedings

The stay does not automatically prohibit commencement or continuation of criminal proceedings.[166] Thus, a criminal case based upon a bad check can continue without violation of the stay.[167] This exception, however, does not necessarily protect a private creditor who instigates such proceedings in an attempt to collect a debt.[168] The exception also does not include the collection of a monetary liability imposed as part of a probation program or as restitution in a criminal case.[169] However, it is less clear whether a court could, under the guise of continuing a criminal case, substitute jail time for unpaid restitution as an element of the punishment for the crime. The Supreme Court did not fully resolve this issue in the *Davenport* case, holding restitution to be a debt but implying that restitution orders may not be enforced during bankruptcy at all. At least two courts have so held.[170] However, if the debtor does not pay according to the restitution order and then fails to either pay the order during the case or obtain a discharge of the debt,[171] the consequences may be severe.

It is unclear whether contempt proceedings are stayed. The answer may turn on the distinction between civil and criminal contempt.[172] When the contempt proceeding is intended to coerce payment of a debt, as opposed to upholding the dignity of the court, the stay almost certainly applies.[173]

---

163 11 U.S.C. § 1301(d).

164 11 U.S.C. § 362(e).

165 *In re* Root, 203 B.R. 55 (Bankr. W.D. Va. 1996) (creditor failed to meet burden of showing irreparable harm); *In re* Burton, 4 B.R. 608 (Bankr. W.D. Va. 1980); 5 Collier on Bankruptcy ¶ 1301.03[1] (16th ed.). *Cf.* 11 U.S.C. § 362(g).

166 11 U.S.C. § 362(b)(1); *In re* Gruntz, 202 F.3d 1074 (9th Cir. 2000) (en banc) (criminal child support proceeding was not stayed); *In re* Bartel, 404 B.R. 584, 590 (B.A.P. 1st Cir. 2009) (stay exception also applies to actions against property of estate). *See In re* Sims, 101 B.R. 52 (Bankr. W.D. Wis. 1989) (incarceration of debtor for failure to pay fine imposed in lieu of jail sentence does not violate stay); § 9.4.7, *infra*.

167 However such a case may be enjoined by the court under 11 U.S.C. § 105. *See* § 9.4.7, *infra*. *See also In re* Bicro Corp., 105 B.R. 255 (Bankr. M.D. Pa. 1989) (creditor enjoined from participating in criminal proceeding against debtor when central purpose of creditor's participation had been to procure payment on a debt).

168 *In re* Brown, 213 B.R. 317 (W.D. Ky. 1997) (creditor violated stay and discharge injunction by filing criminal complaint to collect debt); *In re* White, 2010 WL 2465340 (Bankr. E.D.N.C. June 11, 2010) (creditor violated stay by reporting bad check to police); *In re* Pearce, 400 B.R. 126 (Bankr. N.D. Iowa 2009) (creditor violated stay and discharge injunction by contacting police to instigate criminal proceedings against debtor to collect debt); *In re* Muncie, 240 B.R. 725 (Bankr. S.D. Ohio 1999) (creditor violated stay when it initiated criminal charges, its attorney prosecuted charges, and its motive was to collect the debt); *In re* Barboza, 211 B.R. 450 (Bankr. D.R.I. 1997) (state and creditor sanctioned for using probation hearing to collect debt). *But see* Dovell v. The Guernsey Bank, 373 B.R. 533 (S.D. Ohio 2007) (preliminary injunction vacated as automatic stay does not prevent creditor from reporting bad check violation to the police).

169 Pennsylvania Dep't of Pub. Welfare v. Davenport, 495 U.S. 552, 110 S. Ct. 2126, 109 L. Ed. 2d 588 (1990); *In re* Carlin, 274 B.R. 821 (Bankr. W.D. Ark. 2002) (arrest intended solely to collect debt not within exception); *In re* Washington, 146 B.R. 807 (Bankr. E.D. Ark. 1992). *See also In re* Gandara, 257 B.R. 549 (Bankr. D. Mont. 2000) (section 549 could be used to invalidate payment made in exchange for dismissal of criminal bad check case, even if payment was not prohibited by automatic stay).

But see 11 U.S.C. § 1328(a)(2) making restitution obligations imposed as part of a criminal sentence nondischargeable in chapter 13. *See* §§ 15.4.3.7, 15.5.5.5, *infra*.

170 *In re* Rainwater, 233 B.R. 126 (Bankr. N.D. Ala. 1999) (granting writ of habeas corpus to debtor imprisoned for failure to pay criminal restitution that was provided for in chapter 13 plan), *vacated*, 254 B.R. 273 (N.D. Ala. 2000); *In re* Walters, 219 B.R. 520 (Bankr. W.D. Ark. 1998) (municipality violated stay by arresting debtor to coerce payment of restitution debt). *See also In re* Coulter, 305 B.R. 748 (Bankr. D.S.C. 2003) (state probation department was bound by debtor's chapter 13 plan and was enjoined from holding probation hearing based on nonpayment of restitution provided for in plan).

171 Many criminal restitution orders are nondischargeable in either chapter 7 or chapter 13. *See* §§ 15.4.3.7, 15.4.3.11, *infra*. *See also In re* Gruntz, 202 F.3d 1074 (9th Cir. 2000) (en banc) (criminal child support proceeding not stayed).

172 One court has held, however, that a federal district court civil contempt proceeding is not stayed. *See* U.S. Sprint Communications Co. v. Buscher, 89 B.R. 154 (D. Kan. 1988).

173 Small v. McMaster (*In re* Small), 2011 WL 2604820 (S.D. Tex. June 30, 2011) (order for support order enforcement was in the nature of civil contempt and was stayed); *In re* Goodman, 277 B.R. 839 (Bankr. M.D. Ga. 2001) (arrest warrant arising out of contempt proceeding to coerce compliance with discovery was not part of a criminal proceeding and was stayed; creditor had duty to ensure that warrant was not enforced after bankruptcy filed); *In re* Foster, 100 B.R. 174 (Bankr. D. Del. 1989) (contempt proceeding against debtor for failing to pay a judgment is stayed). *But see* Miller v. Miller, 813 P.2d 353 (Idaho 1991) (state court contempt proceeding

9.4.6.3 Family Law Exceptions

The 2005 amendments to the Code created exceptions to the automatic stay provisions for proceedings concerning child custody, visitation rights, domestic violence, and divorce (to the extent the divorce proceeding does not seek to divide property of the estate).[174] These exceptions are common sense corrections for proceedings that do not have an impact on bankruptcy. Many people had probably assumed they were not stayed, though in fact they usually were, because they were legal proceedings that could have been commenced prior to petition. Due to these amendments there will be fewer void divorces and technically bigamous marriages.

Also excepted from the automatic stay is the collection of a domestic support obligation[175] from property that is not property of the estate.[176] Thus, in a chapter 7 case, postpetition income can be collected and retained by an obligee for this purpose, but property of the estate cannot be collected (at least until it has gone out of the estate because it is exempt or abandoned).[177] In a chapter 13 case, on the other hand, all property acquired by the debtor is property of the estate unless the plan or confirmation order provides otherwise.[178] Therefore, all actions to collect domestic support obligations are usually stayed, unless permitted by another specific provision of section 362(b)(2) discussed below.[179] Notably, unlike other exceptions, section 362(b)(2)(B) does not permit "the commencement or continuation of a proceeding" to collect a domestic support obligation, even with respect to property that is not property of the estate.[180] It permits only the collection of payments.

Some judicial proceedings with respect to domestic support obligations are permitted under more narrow exceptions. Section 362(b)(2)(A) of the Code provides an exception to the stay for the commencement or continuation of proceedings to establish paternity or to establish or modify an order for a domestic support obligation.[181] This exception is carefully worded so that it does not permit proceedings to enforce such orders.[182] However, once an order for current support is entered by a state family court, the bankruptcy court is likely to permit relief from the stay in most cases in which the debtor does not comply with it.[183]

Section 362(b)(2) of the Code was augmented in 2005 to provide an exception to the stay with respect to the withholding of income from property of the estate or property of the debtor for payment of a domestic support obligation.[184] Notably, this exception also does not mention the commencement or continuation or an action or proceeding. In addition, the following methods of enforcement of at least some support obligations, as authorized under the Social Security Act or comparable state laws, are now excepted from the stay:

- The withholding, suspension, or restriction under state law of a driver's license, a professional or occupational license, or a recreational license, as provided in 42 U.S.C. § 666(a)(16);[185]
- The reporting of overdue support owed by a parent to any consumer reporting agency, as provided in 42 U.S.C. § 666(a)(7);[186]

---

against chapter 13 debtor to coerce payment of postpetition support arrearage does not violate stay). *See generally* Henry J. Sommer & Margaret Dee McGarity, Collier Family Law and the Bankruptcy Code ¶ 5.03[3][iii] (1992).

174 11 U.S.C. § 362(b)(2); Marino v. Seeley (*In re* Marino), 437 B.R. 676 (B.A.P. 8th Cir. 2010) (creditor's initiation of domestic violence proceeding did not violate stay).

175 The term "domestic support obligation" is defined in section 101(14A) to include any obligation in the nature of support other than obligations not assigned to certain designated entities. See § 15.4.3.5, *infra*, for discussion of this definition.

176 11 U.S.C. § 362(b)(2)(B). *But see In re* Stringer, 847 F.2d 549 (9th Cir. 1988) (prior to 1994 amendments, exception applied only to collection of support that has been awarded by a prepetition order and action to modify order is not within exception). *See generally* Henry J. Sommer & Margaret Dee McGarity, Collier Family Law and the Bankruptcy Code ¶ 5.03[3]–[6] (1992).

177 11 U.S.C. § 522(c)(1) allows exempt property to be pursued for these debts.

178 11 U.S.C. § 1306(a).

179 Carver v. Carver, 954 F.2d 1573 (11th Cir. 1992) (action seeking to collect divorce obligations from chapter 13 debtor's wages violated automatic stay); *In re* Clouse, 446 B.R. 690 (Bankr. E.D. Pa. 2010) (postnuptial agreement that required payments to debtor's spouse from chapter 13 debtor's estate violated stay and was void); *In re* Steenstra, 280 B.R. 560 (Bankr. D. Mass. 2002) (revenue department's attempt to attach chapter 13 debtor's wages and causing debtor's arrest to compel payment violated stay); *In re* Price, 179 B.R. 209 (Bankr. E.D. Cal. 1995) (refusal to terminate wage assignment and continued collection of payments after notification of chapter 13 case violated stay); *In re* Farmer, 150 B.R. 68 (Bankr. N.D. Ala. 1991) (state court order to incarcerate chapter 13 debtor for failing to pay support would violate automatic stay). *See also* Sec. Bank of Marshalltown, Iowa v. Neiman, 1 F.3d 687 (8th Cir. 1993) (property acquired by chapter 13 debtor during case continues to be property of the estate protected by the stay even after it vests in the debtor upon confirmation of a plan). *But see In re* Bernstein, 20 B.R. 595 (Bankr. M.D. Fla. 1982) (only property necessary to fund the plan is property of the estate after confirmation, and that other property can be pursued for alimony, maintenance or support, unless the plan provides otherwise); *In re* Adams, 12 B.R. 540 (Bankr. D. Utah 1981) (same). *See also* § 9.4.3, *supra*; § 12.8.5, *infra*. *See generally* Henry J. Sommer & Margaret Dee McGarity, Collier Family Law and the Bankruptcy Code ¶ 5.02 (1992).

180 Small v. McMaster (*In re* Small), 2011 WL 2604820 (Bankr. S.D. Tex. Nov. 23, 2010) (support creditor and her attorney violated stay by seeking to have chapter 7 debtor incarcerated for failure to pay support); *In re* Lori, 241 B.R. 353, 355 (Bankr. M.D. Pa. 1999). *But see In re* Johnston, 321 B.R. 262 (D. Ariz. 2005) (collection includes court enforcement).

181 11 U.S.C. § 362(b)(2)(A). *See* Allen v. Allen, 275 F.3d 1160 (9th Cir. 2002) (appeal of dissolution proceeding not stayed to extent it sought to modify support); *In re* Peterson, 410 B.R. 133 (Bankr. D. Conn. 2009) (stay exception permitted proceeding to seek support order but not to determine division of property).

182 *In re* Gresham, 2008 WL 3484318 (Bankr. N.D. Ga. Aug. 8, 2008) (contempt proceeding violated stay).

The exception thus does not affect the holdings in the cases cited above.

183 *See generally* Henry J. Sommer & Margaret Dee McGarity, Collier Family Law and the Bankruptcy Code ¶ 5.03[3] (1992).

184 11 U.S.C. § 362(b)(2)(C).

185 11 U.S.C. § 362(b)(2)(D).

186 11 U.S.C. § 362(b)(2)(E).

- The interception of tax refunds, as provided in 42 U.S.C. §§ 664 and 666(a)(3), or under analogous state law;[187] and
- The enforcement of medical obligations, as provided in 42 U.S.C. §§ 601–687.[188]

These new provisions largely give support creditors the ability to ignore the automatic stay and render the bankruptcy court process subservient to proceedings concerning support in the state courts. However, a support creditor remains bound by a confirmed plan, at least as long as current support is being paid and the debtor is performing under the plan.[189] Even then, a support creditor may seek to modify current support. But presumably the support creditor could not seek to collect additional monies by an income withholding or tax intercept for past support that is provided for under the plan.

9.4.6.4 Continued Withholding of Income for Loans from Retirement Funds

Another exception enacted in 2005 authorizes the continued withholding of wages for repayment of retirement fund loans.[190] The wage withholding must be for repayment of a loan from a plan under section 408(b)(1) of the Employee Retirement Income Security Act (ERISA) or that is subject to section 72(p) of the Internal Revenue Code, or from a thrift savings plan in the Federal Employee's Retirement System.

This provision is part of the enhanced protection of retirement accounts provided by the 2005 Act,[191] and dovetails with the new section 1322(f) provision which states that funds used for such loan repayments are not considered part of disposable income in a chapter 13 case.[192] By permitting wage withholding without interruption this stay exception will prevent the triggering of tax penalties through default on such loans.

9.4.6.5 Provisions Based on Prior Bankruptcy Case Filings by Debtor or Related Parties

9.4.6.5.1 In general

In addition to section 362(c)(3) and (4), discussed above,[193] two exceptions to the automatic stay enacted in 2005 limit its application based upon prior bankruptcy case filings. Under section 362(b)(21), discussed above,[194] the stay of section 362(a) is inapplicable to enforcement of a lien on, or security interest in, real property when the debtor is ineligible for relief under section 109(g) of the Code or has filed the case in violation of a prior court order limiting new bankruptcy case filings.

9.4.6.5.2 In rem orders

Another provision added by the 2005 Act allows creditors with claims secured by real property to seek *in rem* stay relief in certain limited circumstances.[195] If the court enters an *in rem* order under new section 362(d)(4), and the order is properly recorded, section 362(b)(20) provides that the stay does not apply with respect to the particular property covered by the order in a later case filed within two years after the date of the order.[196]

An *in rem* order may be granted if the secured creditor proves that:

- The filing of the petition was part of a scheme to hinder, delay, or defraud creditors;[197] and
- The scheme involved either (1) transfer of full or partial interests in the property without creditor or court approval, *or* (2) multiple bankruptcy filings involving the same property.[198]

Because the provision requires specific factual findings by the court, an *in rem* order should not be entered by default.[199]

Prior to the enactment of section 362(d)(4), the phrase "hinder, delay or defraud" a creditor was found in various sections of the Code,[200] and this same phrase was also used in two other provisions added at the same time as section 362(d)(4) by the 2005 amendments.[201] It can be expected that the phrase will be given a similar meaning in section 362(d)(4).

If an *in rem* order is sought based on the provision regarding multiple filings involving the same property, the order cannot be imposed during the first bankruptcy filing involving the property, given the "multiple" filing requirement. However, the new filing could be used as the basis for an order if a spouse, co-owner, or former owner of the property had recently filed for bankruptcy. A filing in the more distant past would not likely be considered part of a scheme to hinder, delay, or defraud creditors.

For the exception to the automatic stay to be binding in a later case, section 362(d)(4) requires that the *in rem* order from

---

187 11 U.S.C. § 362(b)(2)(F).
188 11 U.S.C. § 362(b)(2)(G).
189 See § 12.11, *infra*.
190 11 U.S.C. § 362(b)(19).
   This provision also states that nothing in section 362(b)(19) may be construed to provide that either a loan made under a governmental plan under section 414(d) of the Internal Revenue Code, or a contract or account under section 403(b) of the Internal Revenue Code, constitutes a claim or a debt for purposes of a bankruptcy proceeding.
191 See, e.g., 11 U.S.C. §§ 522(b)(3)(C), (d)(12). See also H.R. Rep. No. 109-31, at 63–64 (2005) (available on this treatise's companion website); Ch. 10, *infra*.
192 Section 1322(f) of the Bankruptcy Code also provides that a chapter 13 plan may not alter the terms of a pension loan described in section 362(b)(19).
193 See §§ 9.3.3.2, 9.3.3.3, *supra*.
194 See § 9.3.3.6, *supra*.
195 11 U.S.C. § 362(d)(4). See In re McCray, 342 B.R. 668 (Bankr. D. Col. 2006) (relief under section 362(d)(4) not available to purchaser of property at foreclosure whose claim is not secured by interest in real property).
196 11 U.S.C. § 362(b)(20).
197 In re Smith, 395 B.R. 711, 719 (Bankr. D. Kan. 2008) ("scheme" refers to a "a plan or design or an 'artful plot' ").
198 11 U.S.C. § 362(d)(4).
199 In re Knight, 2009 WL 6499237 (Bankr. N.D. Ga. Dec. 16, 2009).
200 See 11 U.S.C. §§ 101(23), 548(a), 727(a)(2).
201 See 11 U.S.C. §§ 522(o), 548(e).

the prior case be recorded in compliance with state laws for recording liens or interests in property.[202] It is not clear whether the order must be recorded before the later case is filed. If it need not be, the purpose of recording would seem to be defeated and an innocent purchaser may be unable to file a bankruptcy case to protect the property.

While section 362(b)(20), which creates the exception to the automatic stay, does not mention the recording requirement, if courts do not read the recording requirement into section 362(b)(20) then the recording requirement of section 362(d)(4) would be mere surplusage.

Another potential problem is that the new *in rem* orders do not appear to be limited in scope to the creditor that sought the order in the first place. Thus a predatory lender who extended credit after the order was recorded could take advantage of it. Nothing in section 362(d)(4) or section 362(b)(20), however, prevents the court from limiting application of the order to the creditor that requested it.[203]

A debtor in a later case may move for relief from the order based on changed circumstances or other good cause.[204]

As the Code now sets a bright line rule for *in rem* stay relief, courts should not grant such orders in other circumstances.[205] Certainly, such an order should not be granted in the first bankruptcy filing involving a property, unless an unapproved transfer is involved. Nor should such an order be granted in a later bankruptcy case unless the case meets the requirement of being part of a scheme to hinder, delay, and defraud creditors.

The stay exception in section 362(b)(20) also does not affect the applicability of the section 1301 codebtor stay.

9.4.6.6 Exceptions to Stay of Residential Tenant Evictions

9.4.6.6.1 Overview

The 2005 Act created two new limitations on the automatic stay in landlord-tenant matters. These are likely to cause hardship to some tenants seeking to avoid homelessness by curing rent arrearages through chapter 13 bankruptcy. They are also likely to cause confusion among landlords and lead to violations of the automatic stay.

The first limitation applies when the lessor has obtained a prepetition judgment in an eviction, unlawful detainer, or similar action for possession of the residential real property where the debtor resides.[206] The second limitation applies if the landlord files a certification regarding illegal use of controlled substances on the property or endangerment of the property.[207]

9.4.6.6.2 Prepetition judgment for possession

Under section 362(b)(22), the eviction of a debtor from residential property in which the debtor resides as a tenant under a lease or rental agreement is not stayed by section 362(a)(3) if the lessor has obtained a judgment for possession prior to the filing of the bankruptcy petition, unless the debtor meets certain conditions. If a prepetition judgment for possession has been obtained for property in which the debtor resides, the debtor must so indicate on the bankruptcy petition, and state the name and address of the lessor.[208]

The prepetition judgment for possession must relate to rental property in which the debtor resides under a lease or rental agreement. It does not apply, for example, to an eviction judgment obtained by a purchaser of property at foreclosure who does not have a lease or rental agreement with a debtor occupying the property.[209] A judgment that the debtor has appealed and that is subject to a trial de novo is not a judgment for purposes of this subsection.[210]

This stay exception is limited to the continuation of proceedings stayed under section 362(a)(3), which are actions seeking to obtain possession of property of the estate or of property from the estate, or to exercise control over property of the estate.[211] If the lessor has obtained a judgment for possession that includes a money judgment against the debtor for back rent owed, the lessor must still seek relief from the stay under section 362(a)(6) in order to enforce the judgment against the debtor, or at least the portion of the judgment representing the claim for back rent. Section 362(b)(22) also does not apply to judicial actions stayed under section 362(a)(1) to recover a prepetition claim against the debtor, including further proceedings that may be necessary to enforce the judgment for possession.[212]

---

202 *In re* Lee, 467 B.R. 906 (B.A.P. 6th Cir. 2012).
   Section 362(d)(4) of the Code provides that federal, state, or local governmental units that accept notices of interests or liens in real property shall accept for indexing and recording any certified copy of an order entered under the subsection.

203 *In re* Lee, 467 B.R. 906 (B.A.P. 6th Cir. 2012) (remanding overly broad order entered by bankruptcy court that improperly granted a permanent injunction against anyone having a possessory interest in the property, rather than only those having a claim derived from the debtor).

204 11 U.S.C. § 362(d)(4).
   For a sample Motion for Relief from *In Rem* Order Entered in Prior Case, see Form 48, Appx. G.4, *infra*.

205 Some of the grounds used to justify such orders in decisions prior to the 2005 amendments may no longer be valid. *See In re* Barner, 597 F.3d 651, 654 (5th Cir. 2010) (specific rules for applying stay relief in prior case to subsequent case did not apply when prior case was filed before effective date of section 362(d)(4)); *In re* Johnson, 346 B.R. 190 (B.A.P. 9th Cir. 2006) (in rem order was not valid under either pre- or post-2005 Code law); § 9.7.3.1.5, *infra*.

206 *See* § 9.4.6.6.2, *infra*.
207 *See* § 9.4.6.6.3, *infra*.
208 11 U.S.C. § 362(*l*)(5).
   Official Form 1 provides a space for this information. Presumably, if a judgment has been resolved by a cure of any default and the lessor is no longer seeking to evict the debtor based on the judgment, it need not be listed. Otherwise, listing of judgments that are years old and no longer valid would be required.

209 *See In re* McCray, 342 B.R. 668 (Bankr. D. Col. 2006).
210 Dupree v. Tucker, 2011 WL 1237936 (S.D. Tex. Mar. 30, 2011); *In re* Alberts, 381 B.R. 171 (Bankr. W.D. Pa. 2007).
211 Ward v. Edwards, 2007 WL 3046133 (N.D. Ill. Oct. 10, 2007) (section 362(b)(22) does not permit landlord to remove evicted debtor's personal property that was part of the bankruptcy estate).
212 *See* Alan M. Ahart, *The Inefficacy of the New Eviction Exceptions*

Notwithstanding the stay exception under new section 362(b)(22), the debtor may obtain an automatic stay for a period of thirty days by filing and serving on the lessor a certification under penalty of perjury that:

- The debtor has a right to cure the monetary default under applicable non-bankruptcy law;[213] and
- The debtor, or an adult dependent of the debtor, has deposited with the clerk of the bankruptcy court all rent that would become due during the thirty days after the filing of the petition.[214]

If no certification is filed with the petition, the clerk must "immediately" serve on the debtor and the lessor a certified copy of the docket indicating the lack of a certification and the applicability of the exception to the stay.[215] If the debtor files a certification with the petition and makes the required deposit with the clerk, the clerk is to promptly transmit the deposit to the lessor.[216]

The debtor may obtain a stay under section 362(a)(3) beyond the initial thirty days if the debtor files, within thirty days after the petition, a further certification that the monetary default upon which the eviction is being sought has been completely cured.[217]

The lessor has the right to contest either the initial certification seeking a thirty-day stay or the certification that the monetary default has been cured.[218] If the lessor files an objection to either certification and serves it on the debtor, the court must hold a hearing within ten days to determine if the certification is true.[219]

If the stay under section 362(a)(3) is terminated by section 362(b)(22), and the lessor has not enforced the prepetition judgment for possession prior to confirmation in a chapter 13 proceeding or objected to confirmation, the lessor may be bound by the terms of a confirmation order which provides for the curing of the default.[220]

9.4.6.6.3 Illegal use of controlled substances or endangerment to the property

A second new exception to the automatic stay under section 362(a)(3) applies if the lessor files and serves on the debtor a certification under penalty of perjury that:

- An eviction action has been commenced based on endangerment of the property or illegal use of controlled substances on the property; or
- The debtor has within thirty days before the certification either endangered the property or illegally used or allowed to be used controlled substances at the property.[221]

If the landlord files such a certification the debtor has fifteen days to file and serve on the lessor an objection to the truth or legal sufficiency of the lessor's certification before the stay exception goes into effect.[222] If the debtor files an objection challenging the truth or legal sufficiency of the lessor's certification, the exception to the stay does not go into effect, if at all, until after the court rules on it. The court must hold a hearing within ten days of the filing of the debtor's objection to determine whether the circumstances described in the lessor's certification existed or have been remedied.[223] It is not clear when the debtor may remedy the circumstances, but presumably it may occur at any time prior to the hearing. If the court rules in favor of the debtor, the stay under section 362(a)(3) remains in effect.

If no objection to the lessor's certification is filed, or if the court rules against the debtor, the clerk must "immediately" serve a certified copy of the docket on the lessor and the debtor, indicating the failure to object or the court's order.[224]

It appears that, if the certification is based on the commencement of an eviction action, the eviction must specifically have been based at least in part on the endangerment of the property or illegal use of controlled substances on the property. In addition, because this stay exception is limited to the stay provided under section 362(a)(3), the lessor may not proceed with any eviction that seeks to recover on a prepetition claim against the debtor, such as a property damages claim or a rent claim, without obtaining relief from the stay provided under section 362(a)(6), or with any judicial action that could have

---

to the Automatic Stay, 80 Am. Bankr. L.J. 125 (2006) for discussion of this and other issues related to the eviction exceptions. *But see In re* Williams, 371 B.R. 102 (Bankr. E.D. Pa. 2007).

213 *In re* Paul, 473 B.R. 474 (Bankr. S.D. Ga. 2012) (debtor may not request stay under section 362(l) if prepetition judgment for possession was based upon a non-monetary default); *In re* Griggsby, 404 B.R. 83 (Bankr. S.D.N.Y. 2009) (same).

214 11 U.S.C. § 362(l)(1); *In re* Harris, 424 B.R. 44 (Bankr. E.D.N.Y. 2010) (debtor who failed to file certifications under section 362(l) and was evicted day after the petition was filed based on prepetition judgment for possession cannot invoke automatic stay retroactively by filing amended petition with certifications); *In re* Griggsby, 404 B.R. 83 (Bankr. S.D.N.Y. 2009) (debtor was not permitted to make use of section 362(l) safe harbor precluding termination of stay under section 362(b)(22) because prepetition judgment for possession was based upon a non-monetary default); *See also In re* Weinraub, 361 B.R. 586 (Bankr. S.D. Fla. 2007) (court waived requirements of section 362(l) and reimposed stay terminated under section 362(b)(22) to prevent enforcement of state court eviction judgment obtained against debtor as part of foreclosure rescue scam); *In re* Kelly, 356 B.R. 899 (Bankr. S.D. Fla. 2006) (section 525(a) eliminates need for public housing debtor to cure prepetition default in order to prevent stay exception under section 362(b)(22) from taking effect).

The form petition, Official Form 1, has been modified to include a statement that contains the required certification. *See* Appx. D, *infra*.

215 11 U.S.C. § 362(l)(4)(A).
216 11 U.S.C. § 362(l)(5)(D).
217 11 U.S.C. § 362(l)(2).
218 11 U.S.C. § 362(l)(3).
219 11 U.S.C. § 362(l)(3)(A).

220 *See, e.g., In re* Sullivan, 321 B.R. 306 (Bankr. M.D. Fla. 2005); Green Tree Fin. Corp. v. Garrett (*In re* Garrett), 185 B.R. 620 (Bankr. N.D. Ala. 1995). *See also* § 12.11, *infra*.

221 11 U.S.C. § 362(b)(23).
222 11 U.S.C. § 362(m).
223 11 U.S.C. § 362(m)(2)(A), (B).
224 11 U.S.C. § 362(m)(2)(D), 362(m)(3).

been commenced prior to the petition, without obtaining relief from the stay under section 362(a)(1).

9.4.6.7 Transfers Not Avoidable Under Section 549

Another provision enacted in 2005 creates an exception from the automatic stay for postpetition transfers that are not avoidable under sections 544 and 549 of the Bankruptcy Code.[225] Generally, section 549 allows avoidance of voluntary and involuntary postpetition transfers, absent authorization of the transfer by the court. An exception to this rule is found in section 549(c),[226] but the exception is limited to voluntary transfers of real property because section 549(c) concerns transfers to "a good faith purchaser," and "purchaser" is defined in section 101(43) of the Code to mean a transferee of a voluntary transfer. The 2005 Act also amended the definition of the term "transfer" in section 101(54) to make clear that the creation of a lien is a transfer for purposes of the Bankruptcy Code.[227]

9.4.6.8 Setoff of Tax Refunds

Section 362(b)(26) permits taxing authorities to set off tax refunds for prepetition tax periods against prepetition tax debts. If there is a pending action to determine tax liability, the taxing authority may hold the refund pending the outcome of the action. However, on motion by the trustee and after notice and a hearing, the court may order turnover of the refund, but only if the taxing authority is granted adequate protection for any secured claim it has under section 506(a) of the Code based on its setoff rights. Moreover, the setoff may still be prevented by the provisions of a confirmed chapter 13 plan.[228]

It is important to note that this provision does not allow setoff of refunds for tax years ending after the petition or for setoffs to pay taxes for tax years that end after the petition is filed. The specificity of this exception to the stay should clarify that these other types of setoffs are improper without relief from the automatic stay granted by the court.

9.4.6.9 Other Exceptions Sometimes Applicable in Consumer Cases

Among the twenty-eight listed exceptions, several others can apply in consumer bankruptcy cases. Certain acts to perfect or continue perfection of security interests in property, mainly Uniform Commercial Code (UCC) filings which relate back to their creation, are also permitted,[229] as are proceedings and enforcement of some non-money judgments pursuant to governmental regulatory powers.[230] Courts have disagreed regarding whether some or all criminal or non-criminal forfeiture proceedings come within the latter exception.[231] Even when

---

225 11 U.S.C. § 362(b)(24).

226 Section 549(c) protects the transfer of real property to a good faith purchaser who pays present fair equivalent value and lacks knowledge of the bankruptcy case, unless a copy of the petition was recorded in the land records office.

227 The legislative history indicates that the stay exception in section 362(b)(24) and the amendment to the definition of "transfer" in section 101(54) were intended to respond to the outcome in Thompson v. Margen (In re McConville), 84 F.3d 340 (9th Cir. 1996), in which a voluntary deed of trust was invalidated. See H.R. Rep. No. 109-31, at 75–76 (2005) (available on this treatise's companion website).

228 See § 12.11, infra.

229 11 U.S.C. § 362(b)(3). See Reedsburg Util. Comm'n v. Grede Foundries, Inc. (In re Grede Foundries, Inc.), 651 F.3d 786 (7th Cir. 2011) (stay exception did not permit municipal utility to place lien on debtor's property when it had not taken steps required under state law to create a property interest prior to petition); Equibank v. Wheeling Pittsburgh Steel, 884 F.2d 80 (3d Cir. 1989); In re Yobe Elec., Inc., 728 F.2d 207 (3d Cir. 1984) (filing of mechanics lien permitted when, under state law, it related back to date materials installed); In re Boggan, 251 B.R. 95 (B.A.P. 9th Cir. 2000) (mechanic did not have to turn over debtor's car, held pursuant to mechanic's lien because maintaining possession of car was necessary to preserve existence of lien). See also In re Parr Meadows Racing Ass'n, Inc., 880 F.2d 1540 (2d Cir. 1989) (prepetition but not postpetition tax lien interests may be perfected). Cf. United States v. ZP Chandon, 889 F.2d 233 (9th Cir. 1989) (maritime lien for seaman's wages may be enforced notwithstanding the automatic stay).

The result in the Parr Meadows case was overruled, for property tax liens only, by the enactment of 11 U.S.C. § 362(b)(18) in 1994.

230 11 U.S.C. § 362(b)(4).

11 U.S.C. § 362(b)(4) was enacted by Pub. L. No. 105-277, 112 Stat. 2681 (1998) to replace former 11 U.S.C. § 362(b)(4) and (5). Although the language is slightly different, adding entities enforcing the Chemical Weapons convention and references to section 362(a)(3) and (6), it appears that the new language has substantially the same meaning as the former language. Fed. Reserve Bd. v. MCorp, 502 U.S. 32, 112 S. Ct. 459, 116 L. Ed. 2d 358 (1991) (Federal Reserve Board administrative action to enforce banking regulation is within exception to the stay); In re McMullen, 386 F.3d 320 (1st Cir. 2004) (disciplinary proceeding against real estate agent was within scope of stay exception); Alpern v. Lieb, 11 F.3d 689 (7th Cir. 1993) (a proceeding to impose Rule 11 sanctions on debtor was exempt from stay as an exercise of police or regulatory powers); In re Wade, 948 F.2d 1122 (9th Cir. 1991) (state bar's disciplinary action against attorney may proceed under the police power exception to the automatic stay); In re Bevelle, 348 B.R. 812 (Bankr. N.D. Ala. 2006) (condemnation proceeding). But see In re PMI-DVW Real Estate Holdings, L.L.P., 240 B.R. 24 (Bankr. D. Ariz. 1999) (condemnation proceeding was not within exception for police and regulatory actions).

231 Compare In re James, 940 F.2d 46 (3d Cir. 1991) (state forfeiture action involving alleged proceeds of criminal activity comes within police power exception); In re Chapman, 264 B.R. 565 (B.A.P. 9th Cir. 2001) (civil forfeiture action was within exception to stay to extent government sought money judgment or possession of property, but government could not enforce money judgment without relief from stay) and In re Smith, 176 B.R. 221 (Bankr. N.D. Ala. 1995) (same) with In re Finley, 237 B.R. 890 (Bankr. N.D. Miss. 1999) (forfeiture proceeding against debtor charged with drunk driving was civil proceeding and not within police and regulatory powers exception); In re Bell, 215 B.R. 266 (Bankr. N.D. Ga. 1997) (in rem civil forfeiture proceeding directed at debtor's property was not permitted by exception for police and regulatory actions); In re Thomas, 179 B.R. 523 (Bankr. E.D. Tenn. 1995) (postpetition non-criminal forfeiture proceeding that could not have been brought prepetition was stayed) and In re Goff, 159 B.R. 33 (Bankr. N.D. Okla. 1993) (civil forfeiture action that had no remedial purpose and

there is a regulatory action, courts look carefully to determine whether the real goal of the proceeding is to collect money from the debtor.[232]

Another exception to the automatic stay allows negotiation of checks which were delivered prepetition.[233] However, this exception does not cover debits to the debtor's account that do not qualify as the presentment of a check, and thus the exception does not protect all preauthorized debits obtained by payday lenders.[234] And yet another permits taxing authorities to conduct an audit to determine tax liability, issue a notice of deficiency, make a demand for tax returns, and make an assessment for any tax along with a notice and demand for payment.[235] Similarly, there is an exception to the stay which permits the creation of postpetition statutory liens for property taxes.[236] Still other exceptions to the stay exist, but they are rarely applicable in consumer bankruptcy cases.[237]

Finally, it is clear that proceedings and actions pursued by the debtor against others are not stayed.[238] Although this situation may occasionally become complicated when there are claims and counterclaims in one action or multiple parties, the distinction can and should be made; the debtor's action should be permitted to proceed.[239]

9.4.7 Non-Automatic Stays

None of the inclusions or exceptions to the automatic stay in any way limits the general injunctive power of the court, under section 105(a) of the Code, to stay other actions.[240] Thus, if the automatic stay is found to be not applicable to a criminal proceeding based upon a bad check, the court may nonetheless be persuaded that the purpose of the action is really to collect the liability and thus to circumvent the bankruptcy. Some bankruptcy courts have held that when restitution is a likely result, the prosecution of criminal actions can be enjoined.[241]

---

232 *See Ohio v. Kovacs*, 469 U.S. 274, 105 S. Ct. 705, 83 L. Ed. 2d 649 (1985); *In re* Mystic Tank Lines Corp., 544 F.3d 524, 527 (3d Cir. 2008) (government can seek judgment for clean-up costs for hazardous waste site but cannot enforce judgment); *In re* Berg, 230 F.3d 1165 (9th Cir. 2000) (court's imposition of sanctions on attorney was exercise of regulatory power); *Nat'l Labor Relations Bd. v. Cont'l Hagen Corp.*, 932 F.2d 828 (8th Cir. 1991) (NLRB order may be enforced by court of appeals except that back pay award must be enforced in bankruptcy proceedings); *In re* Commonwealth Companies, Inc., 913 F.2d 518 (8th Cir. 1990) (government may pursue debtor to obtain judgment, but not enforcement of judgment, under False Claims Act notwithstanding automatic stay); *In re* Commerce Oil Co., 847 F.2d 291 (6th Cir. 1988) (state can establish liability for violation of pollution control law as long as it does not seek to collect); *Equal Employment Opportunity Comm'n v. McLean Trucking Co.*, 834 F.2d 398 (4th Cir. 1987) (EEOC can proceed against debtor for injunction including claim for back pay, but would be subject to automatic stay if its monetary claims were reduced to judgment); *Brock v. Morysville Body Works*, 829 F.2d 383 (3d Cir. 1987) (OSHA citation enforceable against debtor to extent it ordered abatement of safety violations, but not to extent it imposed monetary penalty); *In re* Corp. de Servicios Medicos Hospitalarios, 805 F.2d 440 (1st Cir. 1986) (action to enforce government's contractual rights does not qualify as an exercise of "police power"); *Nat'l Labor Relations Bd. v. Edward Cooper Painting, Inc.*, 804 F.2d 934 (6th Cir. 1986); *United States v. Jones & Laughlin Steel Corp.*, 804 F.2d 348 (6th Cir. 1986); *Cournoyer v. Town of Lincoln*, 790 F.2d 971 (1st Cir. 1986); *Equal Employment Opportunity Comm'n v. Rath Packing Co.*, 787 F.2d 318 (8th Cir. 1986) (automatic stay does not apply to Title VII actions brought by the EEOC); *In re* Dunbar, 235 B.R. 465 (B.A.P. 9th Cir. 1999) (state agency proceedings to revoke contracting license of debtor if he did not pay restitution to home owners and pay for state's costs violated stay), *aff'd*, 245 F.3d 1058 (9th Cir. 2001); *In re* Reyes, 2011 WL 1522337 (Bankr. W.D. Tex. Apr. 20, 2011) (creditor's complaint with state real estate commission was attempt to collect debt); *In re* Berkelhammer, 279 B.R. 660 (Bankr. S.D.N.Y. 2002) (removal of physician debtor from list of Medicaid-eligible physicians based on nonpayment of prepetition debts was based on pecuniary motivations and therefore violated stay); *In re* Massenzio, 121 B.R. 688 (Bankr. N.D.N.Y. 1990) (license revocation against insurance agent violates stay when government unit uses the sanction in attempt to enforce prepetition monetary claim). *But see Eddleman v. United States*, 923 F.2d 782 (10th Cir. 1991) (exception in section 362(b)(4) allows the government to take actions which affect property of the estate).

233 11 U.S.C. § 362(b)(11). *See In re* Roete, 936 F.2d 963 (7th Cir. 1991).

Even though the postpetition presentment of a check and the creditor's receipt of funds from the debtor's account may fall within this exception to the automatic stay, the debtor should be able to recover the funds as the postpetition transfer is avoidable under section 549. *See In re* Meadows, 396 B.R. 485 (B.A.P. 6th Cir. 2008); *In re* Webb, 432 B.R. 234 (Bankr. N.D. Miss. 2010); *In re* Thomas, 311 B.R. 75 (Bankr. W.D. Mo. 2004), *aff'd*, 428 F.3d 735 (8th Cir. 2005). *See also* § 10.4.2.6.6, *infra*.

234 *In re* Snowden, 422 B.R. 737, 743 (Bankr. W.D. Wash. 2009) (electronic debit by payday lender did not qualify as presentment within stay exception).

235 11 U.S.C. § 362(b)(9). *See Reedsburg Util. Comm'n v. Grede Foundries, Inc.* (*In re* Grede Foundries, Inc.), 651 F.3d 786 (7th Cir. 2011) (exception not applicable to municipal utility bills, which are not taxes). However, no lien may attach as a result of an assessment unless the tax is a debt of the debtor that will not be discharged in the case and the property or its proceeds are transferred out of the estate to, or otherwise revested in, the debtor. 11 U.S.C. § 362(b)(9).

236 11 U.S.C. § 362(b)(18).

237 *See* 11 U.S.C. § 362(b).

238 *In re* Berry Estates, Inc., 812 F.2d 67 (2d Cir. 1987).

239 *See* § 9.4.2, *supra*.

240 *In re* Gruntz, 202 F.3d 1074 (9th Cir. 1999) (en banc) (bankruptcy courts have injunctive power under section 105 to impose stay on actions excepted from the automatic stay).

However, the Anti-Injunction Act of the Internal Revenue Code may limit the court's power. *See Laughlin v. Internal Revenue Serv.*, 912 F.2d 197 (8th Cir. 1990) (Anti-Injunction Act precludes entry of order requiring additional specificity in levy served on chapter 13 trustee to collect amounts due under confirmed chapter 13 plan); *In re* Am. Bicycle Ass'n, 895 F.2d 1277 (9th Cir. 1990) (Anti-Injunction Act precludes a bankruptcy court from enjoining IRS levy of non-debtor attorney's receipts under a chapter 13 plan); *In re* Becker's Motor Transp., Inc., 632 F.2d 242 (3d Cir. 1980).

241 *In re* James, 10 B.R. 2 (Bankr. W.D.N.C. 1980) (criminal case based upon alleged worthless checks enjoined because it would frustrate bankruptcy process). *See Howard v. Allard*, 122 B.R. 696 (W.D. Ky. 1991) (preliminary injunction may issue against county attorney preventing prosecution of bad faith bad check charges); *In re* Cancel, 85 B.R. 677 (N.D.N.Y. 1988) (debtor entitled to injunction preventing state from taking action to enforce restitution during

However, several appellate decisions have not looked favorably on such injunctions, holding them violative of the principles of federal-state court comity.[242] One possible alternative method is an injunction that prevents a creditor from receiving or profiting from any restitution order.[243] If such orders against creditors became a predictable response to the initiation of bad check prosecutions for collection purposes, such prosecutions would soon be few in number.

Similarly, the action of a private employer in discharging an employee,[244] or of some other entity that would affect the debtor's income or expenses, might well be enjoined under section 105 if such an injunction is necessary for success of a chapter 13 plan. An injunction in such cases is not automatic upon filing; it must be specifically sought.[245] A court may also occasionally be persuaded that an injunction against a creditor collecting from a non-debtor third party is necessary for the success of the plan.[246]

Furthermore, the court may use its powers under section 105 to reinstitute the automatic stay if it has previously been terminated.[247] Thus, if the stay was allowed to terminate through inadvertence, or if a substantial change in circumstances has occurred since a court order lifting the stay, the court may renew all or some of its protections. There is no reason such an order may not also be entered if the stay has terminated under section 362(c)(3) or (4), and section 362(b)(22).[248] An order granting relief from the stay may also be superseded by the provisions of a confirmed chapter 13 plan, at least if the creditor has had fair notice that the plan proposes to alter the order.[249]

9.5 Notice of the Automatic Stay

Creditors are notified officially of the automatic stay in the notice of the meeting of creditors.[250] Unfortunately, from the debtor's perspective, this notice is not always adequate for several reasons. First, the notice is not mailed until weeks after the petition is filed. Second, when it is mailed, it goes only to creditors listed in the schedules or statement. Entities to whom no debts are owed, or who are not lessors or parties to executory contracts with the debtor, may not be included in these lists.[251] Although the notice mailed to creditors by the court explains the automatic stay to some extent, few unsophisticated creditors who receive it have a clear understanding of all of the acts that are prohibited.

---

pendency of chapter 13 case); *In re* Reid, 9 B.R. 830 (Bankr. M.D. Ala. 1981); *In re* Caldwell, 5 B.R. 740 (Bankr. W.D. Va. 1980).

242 *In re* Fussell, 928 F.2d 712 (5th Cir. 1991) (refusal to enjoin criminal prosecution for "hindering enforcement of security interest" as bad faith attempt to collect dischargeable debt); *In re* Heincy, 858 F.2d 548 (9th Cir. 1988) (court should not enjoin collection of restitution without examining other remedies available to allow restitution payments in the context of chapter 13 plan); *In re* Davis, 691 F.2d 176 (3d Cir. 1982) (injunction not proper, but possibility of later relief from restitution order, if not overturned on state court appeal, left open); Barnette v. Evans, 673 F.2d 1250 (11th Cir. 1982); United States v. Carson, 669 F.2d 216 (5th Cir. 1982); Pennsylvania v. Barone, 23 B.R. 761 (E.D. Pa. 1982) (injunction not proper when prosecution stated it would not seek restitution).

243 *See In re* Redenbaugh, 37 B.R. 383 (Bankr. C.D. Ill. 1984); *In re* Holder, 26 B.R. 789 (Bankr. M.D. Tenn. 1982); *In re* Lawson, 22 B.R. 100 (Bankr. S.D. Ohio 1982). *See also In re* Bicro Corp., 105 B.R. 255 (Bankr. M.D. Pa. 1989) (creditor enjoined from participating in criminal proceeding against debtor when central purpose of creditor's participation was to procure payment on a debt). *Cf. In re* Roussin, 97 B.R. 130 (D.N.H. 1989) (refusal to enjoin state court contempt proceeding for failure to comply with state court order in aid of execution on prepetition debt because creditor would not profit from remedy).

244 A discharge or other employment discrimination based upon the bankruptcy or a prepetition debt is specifically prohibited. 11 U.S.C. § 525(b). *See* Ch. 15, *infra*.

245 However, section 105 permits the court to act *sua sponte* notwithstanding any provision of the Code providing that a party in interest must raise an issue.

246 *See In re* Drexel Burnham Lambert Group, Inc., 960 F.2d 285 (2d Cir. 1992).

247 *In re* Martin Exploration Co., 731 F.2d 1210 (5th Cir. 1984); *In re* Twenver, Inc., 149 B.R. 950 (D. Colo. 1993) (four-part test to establish grounds for injunctive relief must be met); *In re* Bailey, 111 B.R. 151 (W.D. Tenn. 1988); *In re* Casner, 302 B.R. 695 (Bankr. E.D. Cal. 2003) (court issued preliminary injunction under section 105 enjoining mortgage foreclosure to allow debtors time to complete refinancing and modify chapter 13 plan); 9 Collier on Bankruptcy ¶ 4001.03 (16th ed.). *See also In re* Gledhill, 76 F.3d 1070 (10th Cir. 1996) (reimposition of stay may be sought by motion under Fed. R. Bankr. P. 9024; adversary proceeding seeking injunction not necessary). *See also In re* Miles, 436 F.3d 291 (1st Cir. 2006) (affirming district court's order reimposing stay based upon changed circumstances when debtor appealed order denying reconsideration of bankruptcy court order granting relief from stay).

The best practice is to continue to proceed on both tracks because the standard for relief from judgment under Bankruptcy Rule 9024 and the showing required to obtain a stay under 11 U.S.C. § 105 are not necessarily the same. *See also In re* Krueger, 88 B.R. 238 (B.A.P. 9th Cir. 1988) (court can reinstate case so as to void subsequently held foreclosure sale when case was dismissed in violation of debtor's right to notice and hearing).

248 *In re* Weinraub, 361 B.R. 586 (Bankr. S.D. Fla. 2007) (court may invoke authority under section 105 to reimpose stay terminated under section 362(b)(22) to prevent enforcement of state court eviction judgment obtained against debtor as part of foreclosure rescue scam); *In re* Williams, 346 B.R. 361 (Bankr. E.D. Pa. 2006) (stay may be invoked under section 105(a) even though debtor did not file timely motion for stay extension under section 362(c)(3)(B)); *In re* Whitaker, 341 B.R. 336 (Bankr. S.D. Ga. 2006) (same). *See also* §§ 9.3.3.2.1, 9.3.3.3, *supra*.

249 *In re* Hileman, 451 B.R. 522 (Bankr. D. Cal. 2011) (confirmed plan prevented foreclosure even though stay had expired under § 362(c)(3)); *In re* Sullivan, 321 B.R. 306 (Bankr. M.D. Fla. 2005); *In re* Garrett, 185 B.R. 620 (Bankr. N.D. Ala. 1995). *See also In re* Simpson, 240 B.R. 559 (B.A.P. 8th Cir. 1999) (failure of creditor to appeal confirmation of plan that provided for cure of mortgage default rendered mortgage creditor's appeal of order denying relief from stay moot); § 12.11, *infra*. *But see* New Hampshire v. McGrahan (*In re* McGrahan), 459 B.R. 869 (B.A.P. 1st Cir. 2011) (plan did not address right to intercept tax refunds specifically enough to be binding on support creditor).

250 Official Form 9 (reprinted in Appx. D, *infra*).

251 If the debtor does not list certain entities on the schedules, such as an attorney representing a creditor, it may still be possible to add these entities to the mailing matrix filed with the case. *See* § 7.3.4, *supra*. If included on the matrix, these entities will be sent Official Form 9.

The only solution to this problem is for the debtor's advocate to give additional notice of the stay, at least as to creditors and others who might violate the stay without prompt, clear notice. This notice should be sent by certified mail, return receipt requested, immediately after the petition is filed.[252] If time is a critical factor, a telephone call, e-mail, or facsimile preceding the mailed notification may be appropriate. The debtor's notice can be much more specific than the official notice, tailored to the action the recipient is likely to take. Copies of the notice should be sent to both the party stayed and the party's attorney, so no excuse of communication problems is possible. In the case of the Internal Revenue Service, to suspend or forestall collection actions such as a wage levy, notice should be given to the Revenue Officer on the case as well as to the IRS Special Procedures Staff in the District Office collection branch for the relevant jurisdiction. Lastly, if appropriate, the notice can advise that the debtor will seek to have violators of the stay held in contempt and held liable for unfair practices, with damages and attorney fees assessed against them.

9.6 Enforcing the Stay

9.6.1 Actions Taken in Violation of the Stay Are Void

It has long been held that actions taken in violation of the stay are void.[253] This principle means that any actions taken after the bankruptcy filing, including foreclosure sales, repossessions and judgments, are without effect.[254] This rule applies whether or not the violator acted with knowledge of the stay, though there are limited exceptions to this general rule.[255]

Courts have the power to undo violations of the stay by injunction, by avoiding postpetition transfers under 11 U.S.C. § 549,[256] and, if appropriate, by ordering other statutory and equitable remedies as discussed below. Numerous courts have held, for example, that postpetition credit union deductions or repossessed automobiles must be returned.[257]

---

252 *See In re* Calder, 907 F.2d 953 (10th Cir. 1990) (failure to provide notice together with debtor's continued litigation activity in the stayed action equitably precludes the debtor from later claiming the protection of the automatic stay with regard to that action).

253 Kalb v. Feuerstein, 308 U.S. 433, 60 S. Ct. 343, 84 L. Ed. 370 (1940). *See, e.g., In re* Knightsbridge Dev. Co., 884 F.2d 145 (4th Cir. 1989) (arbitration award entered in violation of stay is void); *In re* La. Ship Mgmt. Inc., 761 F.2d 1025 (5th Cir. 1985); *In re* Posner, 700 F.2d 1243 (9th Cir. 1983); Borg-Warner Acceptance Corp. v. Hall, 685 F.2d 1306 (11th Cir. 1982); Butzloff v. Quandt, 397 N.W.2d 159 (Iowa 1986). *See also In re* Smith, 876 F.2d 524 (6th Cir. 1989). *But see In re* Coho Res., Inc., 345 F.3d 338 (5th Cir. 2003) (violations are merely "voidable" and are subject to discretionary "cure" through annulment of stay); Riley v. United States, 118 F.3d 1220 (8th Cir. 1997) (responsible party tax assessment was not invalid due to notice of proposed assessment that was issued in violation of stay); Matthews v. Rosene, 739 F.2d 249 (7th Cir. 1984) (when debtor inexcusably and unreasonably delayed contempt petition for almost three years, ordinary rule that orders issued in violation of stay are void would not be applied due to laches).

254 *See, e.g.*, 40235 Wash. St. Corp. v. Lusardi, 329 F.3d 1076 (9th Cir. 2003) (tax foreclosure auction in violation of stay was void even though bankruptcy case later dismissed); *In re* Schwartz, 954 F.2d 569 (9th Cir. 1992) (IRS violation of stay was void, not voidable); *In re* 48th Street Steakhouse, Inc., 835 F.2d 427 (2d Cir. 1987); *In re* Shamblin, 878 F.2d 324 (9th Cir. 1989) (tax sale held in violation of the stay is void); *In re* Ward, 837 F.2d 124 (3d Cir. 1988) (foreclosure sale occurring in violation of the stay is void). *See also* Lampe v. Xouth, Inc., 952 F.2d 697 (3d Cir. 1991) (legal action commenced in violation of the stay is void and cannot be referred to the bankruptcy court); *In re* Ebadi, 448 B.R. 308 (Bankr. E.D.N.Y. Mar. 30, 2011) (foreclosure sale on mortgage guaranteed by debtor violated stay even though debtor failed to file required documents after bankruptcy petition was filed). *But see In re* Paxton, 440 F.3d 233 (5th Cir. 2006) (authority to set aside sale conducted in violation of stay derives from section 549, assuming requirements of that section are met); *In re* Siciliano, 13 F.3d 748 (3d Cir. 1994) (court had authority to annul stay in proper circumstances, validating acts taken in violation of stay); Easley v. Pettibone Mich. Corp., 990 F.2d 905 (6th Cir. 1993) (actions in violation of stay are voidable and shall be voided absent limited equitable circumstances); Fed. Deposit Ins. Corp. v. Shearson-Am. Express, Inc., 996 F.2d 493 (1st Cir. 1993) (even if an attachment violated the stay, an unappealed bankruptcy court order finding that the stay had not been violated was not subject to collateral attack, so that the attachment was deemed valid).

255 *See, e.g., In re* Smith, 876 F.2d 524 (6th Cir. 1989) (postpetition sale of repossessed car is void even though bank had no notice of stay; debtor found not to have remained "stealthily silent"); Zestee Foods, Inc. v. Phillips Foods Corp., 536 F.2d 334 (10th Cir. 1976). *See generally* Kennedy, *The Automatic Stay in Bankruptcy*, 11 U. Mich. J.L. Reform 177 (1978).

See also cases cited in § 9.4.7, *supra*.

256 *See* § 10.4.2.6.6, *infra*.

Although a debtor or trustee may not, under section 549(c), be able to avoid a transfer of real property to a good faith purchaser without knowledge of the bankruptcy and for fair equivalent value (unless a copy or notice of the bankruptcy petition has been filed in the county recording office before the transfer has become so far perfected that it could not be overturned by bona fide purchaser) most courts have held that section 549(c) does not protect a transfer that violated the automatic stay. *See In re* Cueva, 371 F.3d 232 (5th Cir. 2004) (section 549(c) does not create exception to protect transfers that are void under section 362(a)); 40235 Wash. St. Corp. v. Lusardi, 329 F.3d 1076 (9th Cir. 2003) (same); *In re* Ford, 296 B.R. 537 (Bankr. N.D. Ga. 2003). *See also In re* Ward, 837 F.2d 124 (3d Cir. 1988) (sale not perfected and therefore not within exception).

When a trustee or debtor does not seek to avoid a transfer of property under section 549(c), a non-debtor party having an interest in the property may have standing to seek avoidance of an action in violation of the stay. *In re* Donovan, 266 B.R. 862 (Bankr. S.D. Iowa 2001) (holder of first mortgage on debtor's home had standing to seek declaratory judgment that issuance of tax deed violated automatic stay because tax deed, if not voided, would extinguish its mortgage).

257 Thompson v. GMAC, L.L.C., 566 F.3d 699 (7th Cir. Ill. 2009) (refusal to return car that was repossessed prepetition is violation of stay); *In re* Knaus, 889 F.2d 773 (8th Cir. 1989) (property seized in violation of the stay must be returned; failure to return it constitutes an actionable violation of the stay); *In re* Smith, 876 F.2d 524 (6th Cir. 1989) (postpetition sale of repossessed car is void); *In re* Hellums, 772 F.2d 379 (7th Cir. 1985) (postpetition payroll deductions must be returned); *In re* Sharon, 234 B.R. 676 (B.A.P. 6th Cir. 1999) (damages awarded for willful violation of stay when creditor refused to return car after tender of adequate protection); *In re* Berscheit, 223 B.R. 579 (Bankr. D. Wyo. 1998) (adequate protection not required as a prerequisite to turnover).

Some courts have required adequate protection of the creditor's

9.6.2 Cause of Action for Damages, Punitive Damages, and Attorney Fees

The Bankruptcy Code in section 362(k)[258] contains a specific cause of action against a creditor who causes injury[259] to an individual[260] by a willful violation of the section 362 stay.[261] A willful violation is one committed knowingly; no malice need be shown.[262] Even when a violation begins innocently, refusal to rectify it after notice of the case renders it willful.[263] Similarly, a willful violation occurs when a creditor fails to act affirmatively to prevent an action prohibited by the stay, for example, by failing to prevent the sheriff from selling the debtor's property at a postpetition sheriff's sale.[264] In such cases, section 362(k) provides for actual damages,[265] costs and

---

interest as a prerequisite to return of automobiles repossessed prior to the petition. These issues are discussed in § 9.9.3, infra. *In re Taylor*, 7 B.R. 506 (E.D. Pa. 1980); *In re Brooks*, 132 B.R. 29 (Bankr. W.D. Mo. 1991) (postpetition payroll deductions); *In re Fry*, 122 B.R. 427 (Bankr. N.D. Okla. 1990) ($25,000 in punitive damages awarded for failure to return repossessed mobile home); *In re Miller*, 10 B.R. 778 (Bankr. D. Md. 1981), aff'd, 22 B.R. 479 (D. Md. 1982); *In re Newman*, 1 B.R. 428 (Bankr. E.D. Pa. 1979).

258 Prior to the 2005 amendments, section 362(k) was designated as section 362(h).

259 *See In re Roman*, 283 B.R. 1 (B.A.P. 9th Cir. 2002) (injury can be as minimal as costs expended in going to an attorney's office).

260 Several courts have held that use of the term "individual" in the statute does not preclude an award of damages under section 362(k) to a corporate debtor. *See, e.g., In re Chateaugay Corp.*, 112 B.R. 526 (S.D.N.Y. 1990); *In re Bair Island Marina & Office Ctr.*, 116 B.R. 180 (Bankr. N.D. Cal. 1990).

261 *See Pettitt v. Baker*, 876 F.2d 456 (5th Cir. 1989).

In 1998, Congress enacted 26 U.S.C. § 7433(e) which provides a damage remedy against the United States for willful stay violations by the IRS in situations not covered by section 362(k). This provision primarily benefits non-individual debtors, because damages for willful violations with respect to individuals are available under section 362(k). The provision, specifically 26 U.S.C. § 7433(e)(2)(B), also contains some confusing language which provides that administrative and litigation "costs," even in an action under section 362(h) (now codified as section 362(k)), may only be awarded under 26 U.S.C. § 7430, which may mean that exhaustion of administrative remedies is required to recover such costs. Thus, a debtor may have to show exhaustion of administrative remedies in order to recover attorney fees. *See Kuhl v. United States*, 467 F.3d 145 (2d Cir. 2006). Although IRS regulations define these costs to include "legal fees," Treas. Reg. § 301.7433-1(b) (1992), this provision mentioning only "costs" should not be read to limit the right to "attorney fees" under section 362(k). Alternatively, the language could be read to simply limit the hourly rate for attorney fees to that found in section 7430. It is unclear how the fact that section 362(h) no longer governs such cases will affect application of this provision.

262 *See In re Johnson*, 501 F.3d 1163 (10th Cir. 2007) (no specific intent to violate stay necessary); *Fleet Mortgage Group, Inc. v. Kaneb*, 196 F.3d 265 (1st Cir. 1999) (willfulness does not require intent to violate stay); *In re Lansdale Family Restaurants, Inc.*, 977 F.2d 826 (3d Cir. 1992) (willfulness does not require an intent to violate the stay, it requires only that acts which violate the stay be intentional acts); *In re Ketelsen*, 880 F.2d 990 (8th Cir. 1989); *In re Bloom*, 875 F.2d 224 (9th Cir. 1989); *In re Webb*, 470 B.R. 439 (B.A.P. 6th Cir. 2012) (good faith belief that action was permitted does not vitiate willfulness); Green Tree Servicing, L.L.C. v. Taylor, 369 B.R. 282 (S.D. W. Va. 2007) (knowledge of counsel imputed to creditor); *Haile v. New York State Higher Educ. Servs. Corp.*, 90 B.R. 51 (W.D.N.Y. 1988); *In re Coons*, 123 B.R. 649 (Bankr. N.D. Okla. 1991) (knowledge of bankruptcy case makes action taken by creditor willful). *Cf.* 11 U.S.C. § 523(a)(6) (referring to willful *and* malicious acts); *In re Lafanette*, 208 B.R. 394 (Bankr. W.D. La. 1996) (IRS did not willfully violate stay when it diverted debtor's tax refund to child support agency, because IRS had no notice of bankruptcy case). *But see In re Skinner*, 90 B.R. 470 (D. Utah 1988) (actions not willful when creditor received notice of stay, but did not read it; nonetheless creditor could be held in civil contempt), aff'd, 917 F.2d 444 (10th Cir. 1990).

263 *In re Carrigg*, 216 B.R. 303 (B.A.P. 1st Cir. 1998) (creditor's failure to return repossessed vehicle after notice of case sanctioned as willful violation of stay even though creditor had not had notice of case when vehicle was repossessed); *In re Abrams*, 127 B.R. 239 (B.A.P. 9th Cir. 1991) (retention of repossessed automobile after receiving notice of the stay is willful); *America's Servicing Co. v. Schwartz-Tallard*, 438 B.R. 313 (D. Nev. 2010) ($40,000 emotional distress damages and $20,000 punitive damages upheld in part because creditor failed to void foreclosure sale in violation of reinstated stay, even after it discovered its mistake); *Nissan Acceptance Corp. v. Baker*, 239 B.R. 484 (N.D. Tex. 1999) ($23,000 damages for refusal to turn over vehicle and applying proceeds of canceled extended service contract to debt); *Carr v. Sec. Sav. & Loan Ass'n*, 130 B.R. 434 (D.N.J. 1991) (refusal to return repossessed automobile); *Tyson v. Hunt (In re Tyson)*, 450 B.R. 754 (Bankr. W.D. Tenn. 2011) (damages against third party purchaser at foreclosure sale who refused to reconvey property after notice of bankruptcy); *In re Coats*, 168 B.R. 159 (Bankr. S.D. Tex. 1993) (county and constable liable for $36,000 damages and attorney fees for refusal to release property which had been seized pursuant to prepetition execution for forty-one days after they received notice of bankruptcy); *In re Brooks*, 132 B.R. 29 (Bankr. W.D. Mo. 1991) (refusal to return postpetition payroll deductions); *In re Holman*, 92 B.R. 764 (Bankr. S.D. Ohio 1988); *In re Stephen W. Grosse, Prof'l Corp.*, 84 B.R. 377 (Bankr. E.D. Pa. 1988), aff'd, 96 B.R. 29 (E.D. Pa. 1989), aff'd, 879 F.2d 857 (3d Cir. 1989) (table); *In re Maas*, 69 B.R. 245 (Bankr. M.D. Fla. 1986).

See § 9.9, infra, for a further discussion about recovering property after bankruptcy which was repossessed prior to the date of the petition.

264 *In re Webb*, 470 B.R. 439 (B.A.P. 6th Cir. 2012); *In re Galmore*, 390 B.R. 901 (Bankr. N.D. Ind. 2008) (creditor that failed to request recall of civil bench warrant after receiving notice of bankruptcy willfully violated stay); *In re Mims*, 209 B.R. 746 (Bankr. M.D. Fla. 1997) (creditor had duty to dismiss garnishment proceeding after bankruptcy filed).

265 In addition to recovery of any payments made to the creditor that violated the stay, loss of use damages are available if property is repossessed or retained in violation of the stay. Similarly, lost wages should be recoverable for time that the debtor must spend in court. *In re See*, 301 B.R. 549 (Bankr. N.D. Iowa 2003) (debtor awarded actual damages consisting of lost wages and travel expenses).

Emotional distress damages are also available. *In re Dawson*, 390 F.3d 1139 (9th Cir. 2004); *Fleet Mortgage Group, Inc. v. Kaneb*, 196 F.3d 265 (1st Cir. 1999); *In re Rijos*, 263 B.R. 382 (B.A.P. 1st Cir. 2001) (debtors must be given opportunity to put on evidence of damages); *In re Flynn*, 185 B.R. 89 (S.D. Ga. 1995); *In re Griffin*, 415 B.R. 64 (Bankr. N.D.N.Y. 2009) (emotional distress damages available against Social Security Administration); *In re Come*, 2008 WL 2018280 (Bankr. D.N.H. May 8, 2008) (awarding $1000 for emotional distress where debtor's children were upset by witnessing wrongful repossession); *In re Lofton*, 385 B.R. 133 (Bankr. E.D.N.C. 2008) ($1500 emotional distress damages for willful stay violation which caused debtor to get someone to cover his job while he

attorney fees[266] as well as, if appropriate, punitive damages.[267] The only exception stated in the provision is for creditors who act in a good faith belief that section 362(h) applies to the debtor, in which case the recovery against the creditor is limited to actual damages.[268] An action for damages based on violation of the automatic stay survives the dismissal of the underlying bankruptcy case and the bankruptcy court has continuing jurisdiction to decide it.[269] There is no time limitation on such an action.[270] If a willful violation of the automatic stay is proven, the bankruptcy court must afford the debtor an opportunity to present evidence at a hearing in support of a claim for damages.[271]

9.6.3 Notice Issues

9.6.3.1 Giving Notice

An issue in some cases is whether the creditor has received actual notice. For damages to be available, the debtor must prove notice of the stay to the party enjoined.[272] A telephone call or fax to a creditor or its counsel provides such notice,[273]

---

266   responded to improper lawsuit, thus revealing his financial problems to employer); *In re* McLaughlin, 2007 WL 3229166 (Bankr. D. Ariz. Oct. 30, 2007) (emotional distress damages of $3000 per debtor for false threats of arrest that aggravated husband's preexisting physical illness, caused him to miss work, forced him to request removal from supervisory position, and caused wife to fall behind in schoolwork because of inability to concentrate); *In re* Dawson, 346 B.R. 503 (Bankr. N.D. Cal. 2006) (debtor awarded $20,000 damages for emotional distress); *In re* Covington, 256 B.R. 463 (Bankr. D.S.C. 2000) (emotional distress damages awarded without need for medical testimony); *In re* Lohbauer, 254 B.R. 406 (Bankr. N.D. Ohio 2000) ($3000 emotional distress damages based on debtors' testimony); *In re* Johnson, 253 B.R. 857 (Bankr. S.D. Ohio 2000) (same); *In re* Lord, 270 B.R. 787 (Bankr. M.D. Ga. 1998) (lost wages due to lack of wrongfully held car, plus wages improperly garnished after petition filed due to failure to end garnishment, plus attorney fees); *In re* Holden, 226 B.R. 809 (Bankr. D. Vt. 1998). *But see In re* Aiello, 239 F.3d 876 (7th Cir. 2001) (debtor could not recover for "purely emotional injury" when there were no other damages); Duby v. United States (*In re* Duby), 451 B.R. 664 (B.A.P. 1st Cir. 2011) (emotional distress damages unavailable against federal government).

266   If the court finds a willful violation of the stay, the debtor is entitled to all reasonable attorney fees and costs; the court does not have discretion to award less. Young v. Repine (*In re* Repine), 536 F.3d 512 (5th Cir. Tex. 2008) (attorney fees incurred in prosecuting 362(k) proceeding available to any individual injured by willful violation); Lopez v. Consejo De Titulares Del Condominio Carolina Court Apartments (*In re* Lopez), 405 B.R. 24, 26 (B.A.P. 1st Cir. 2009) (fees should not be reduced simply because damages are small); *In re* Stainton, 139 B.R. 232 (B.A.P. 9th Cir. 1992); Small v. McMaster (*In re* Small), 2011 WL 2604820 (S.D. Tex. June 30, 2011) (creditor and her attorney jointly liable for fees of over $42,000).

    Attorney fees should include any fees necessary to obtain or protect an award under section 362(k) on appeal. Duby v. United States (*In re* Duby), 451 B.R. 664 (B.A.P. 1st Cir. 2011) (attorney fees are a form of actual damages); *In re* Roman, 283 B.R. 1 (B.A.P. 9th Cir. 2002); *In re* Parker, 419 B.R. 474 (M.D. Ala. 2009) (attorney fees should be awarded for resisting appeal of § 362(k) award). *But see* Sternberg v. Johnston, 595 F.3d 937 (9th Cir. Ariz. 2009) (attorney fees under § 362(k) available only for proceedings to remedy the violation and not for obtaining damages under § section 362(k)).

    The *Sternberg* decision is wrongly decided but, in any event, leaves open the possibility of attorney fees for obtaining contempt damages. Sternberg v. Johnston, 595 F.3d 937, 946 n.3 (9th Cir. Ariz. 2009). *See* § 9.6.4, *infra*.

    Attorney fees and costs may be awarded against the Internal Revenue Service under section 362(k), at least if it has filed a proof of claim. Taborski v. Internal Revenue Serv., 141 B.R. 959 (N.D. Ill. 1992). *See also In re* Walsh, 219 B.R. 873 (B.A.P. 9th Cir. 1998) (debtor also entitled to attorney fees for work done on appeal); *In re* Seal, 192 B.R. 442 (Bankr. W.D. Mich. 1996) (debtor can recover damages from payments due to the creditor in other chapter 13 cases, if necessary).

    The Tax Reform Act of 1998 establishes that the filing of a proof of claim by the Internal Revenue Service is not required for an award of costs and attorney fees in an action under section 362(k). *See* 26 U.S.C. § 7433(e). However, the Act limits the hourly rate that can be recovered for attorney fees. 26 U.S.C. § 7430.

267   *In re* Repine, 536 F.3d 512 (5th Cir. 2008) (punitive damages for refusal of attorney to consent to release from contempt imprisonment until attorney fees were paid); *In re* Ocasio, 272 B.R. 815 (B.A.P. 1st Cir. 2002) (ratio of 9-to-1 between punitive damages and compensatory damages was not excessive); *In re* Panek, 402 B.R. 71, 77 (Bankr. D. Mass. 2009) ($10,000 in punitive damages awarded against creditor that failed to cooperate in returning debits to debtor's bank account that continued after bankruptcy was filed); *In re* Henry, 266 B.R. 457 (Bankr. C.D. Cal. 2001) ($65,700 in punitive damages awarded against mortgage holder who contacted debtors ninety-three times postpetition); *In re* Kaufman, 315 B.R. 858 (Bankr. N.D. Cal. 2004) (total damages, including punitive damages, of $570,000 awarded against mortgage company that auctioned personal property that was in debtor's residence, in violation of stay); *In re* Kortz, 283 B.R. 706 (Bankr. N.D. Ohio 2002) ($51,000 punitive damages and equitable subordination of mortgage to remedy mortgage company's "belligerent" violations of stay); *In re* Shade, 261 B.R. 213 (Bankr. C.D. Ill. 2001) (punitive damages may be awarded even if there are no compensatory damages); *In re* Meeks, 260 B.R. 46 (Bankr. M.D. Fla. 2000) ($35,000 punitive damages for repossession with notice of automatic stay); *In re* Timbs, 178 B.R. 989 (Bankr. E.D. Tenn. 1994) (punitive damages awarded against attorney who failed to take affirmative steps to end wage garnishment; actions were willful even if attorney had not understood the law). *But see* Duby v. United States (*In re* Duby), 451 B.R. 664 (B.A.P. 1st Cir. 2011) (sovereign immunity not waived for punitive damages).

268   11 U.S.C. § 362(k)(2).

269   *In re* Johnson, 390 B.R. 414, 419 (B.A.P. 10th Cir. 2008), *aff'd*, 575 F.3d 1079 (10th Cir. 2009); *In re* Williams, 323 B.R. 691 (B.A.P. 9th Cir. 2005).

270   Stanwyck v. Bogen (*In re* Stanwyck), 450 B.R. 181 (Bankr. C.D. Cal. 2011).

271   *In re* Vazquez Laboy, 647 F.3d 367 (1st Cir. 2011).

272   *See* Price v. Rochford, 947 F.2d 829 (7th Cir. 1991) (commencing lawsuits without notice of the stay is not actionable under section 362(h) (now section 362(k)); *In re* Abt, 4 B.R. 527 (Bankr. E.D. Pa. 1980) (repossession of automobile by several creditors without notice of stay was not contempt).

    For further discussion of notice of the stay, see § 9.5, *supra*.

273   *In re* Johnson, 501 F.3d 1163 (10th Cir. 2007) (car dealer had duty to investigate if it had doubts about representations of debtor's counsel); Green Tree Servicing, L.L.C. v. Taylor, 369 B.R. 282 (S.D. W. Va. 2007) (knowledge of counsel imputed to creditor); *In re* Carter, 16 B.R. 481 (W.D. Mo. 1981) (stating that if creditor's counsel had doubts about representations of debtor's counsel, it was incumbent upon creditor's counsel to verify filing with bankruptcy court), *aff'd*, 691 F.2d 390 (8th Cir. 1982); *In re* Coons, 123 B.R. 649 (Bankr. N.D.

§ 9.6.3.2

though later problems of proof could arise when the notice is not in writing. Similarly, if the filing occurs at the last minute to prevent a foreclosure sale, repossession, or utility termination, it may be a good idea to tell the client to inform the creditor or the creditor's agent directly, at the location of the threatened action. Even posting a copy of the petition on property that is likely to be repossessed should be sufficient notice to the creditor and the repossessing agent.

9.6.3.2 Effect of 2005 Amendments on Notice Requirements

9.6.3.2.1 Introduction

The 2005 Act added complicated and confusing notice requirements by making amendments to section 342 with which both debtors' counsel and the courts must comply. While some of the new language is terribly drafted and confusing, the amendments to section 342 have little practical effect.[274]

9.6.3.2.2 Deletion of safe harbor in section 342(c)

Section 342(c)(1), as renumbered, was amended to delete language in the section which had stated the failure to provide a debtor's name, address, and taxpayer identification (Social Security) number (now only the last four digits) does not invalidate the legal effect of a notice. It is unclear what deletion of this language means. Presumably effectiveness of notice will be determined by otherwise applicable law. In any event this subsection only applies to notices that the debtor is required to give by statute, rule or order of court—a limited number of notices which are primarily notices of motions, amendments of schedules, and similar events.

9.6.3.2.3 Creditor notice request given prepetition

Section 342(c)(2) requires that notice from a debtor to a creditor be sent to the address specified by the creditor for receipt of correspondence, and include the account number, but only if the creditor has supplied both the address request and the account number in at least two communications sent to debtor in the ninety days before the petition was filed.

This wording leaves open the question of what is a creditor request to receive correspondence under this provision. Language such as "send billing error notice to . . ." would not appear to be a request for correspondence.[275] Presumably the provision would not apply to communications from collection agencies, who are not "the creditor." The use of the word "sent" also precludes oral requests. Moreover if only the address is supplied, or only an account number, the provision is not operative.

If the creditor was precluded by law from sending any communications to the debtor in the ninety days before the petition was filed, the provision would apply to the last two communications, no matter when they were sent.[276] Such a restriction might occur if the creditor had knowledge that the debtor was represented by an attorney or had been subject to the automatic stay in a prior case. For this exception to apply, the creditor must have been precluded from sending communications for the entire ninety-day period.

Importantly, the requirements of section 342(c)(2) only apply to notices the debtor is required to send by title 11 itself. This provision therefore has no relation to addresses to be used on schedules, because those addresses are not used in notices that the debtor is required to send the creditor. Similarly service of documents required by the Federal Rules of Bankruptcy Procedure is not within the scope of this provision. However if a debtor sends notice of the addition of a creditor to the schedules, the notice to the creditor must include the full taxpayer identification (Social Security) number, though it should not be included in the copy filed with the court.[277]

9.6.3.2.4 Notice request in particular case

Section 342(e) allows a creditor to file with the court and serve on the debtor an address which it wants to be used for notices in a particular chapter 7 or chapter 13 case. Any notice provided by the court or the debtor more than seven days after such an address request is made must use the requested address. This provision appears to override the more general address provision of section 342(c)(2), though it does not expressly so state. This provision also neglects to include any coverage of notices from other parties, such as the trustee, United States trustee, or other creditors. Apparently, these parties, and participants in chapter 9, 11, and 12 cases, to which the provision does not apply, do not have to follow the dictates of this subsection. In any event, with the advent of electronic filing and noticing, most notices are provided electronically and available to any creditor in a particular case.

An entity may also file with any bankruptcy court an address request that is to be used by all bankruptcy courts or by particular bankruptcy courts, as specified by the entity, to provide notice in all chapter 7 and chapter 13 cases.[278] This standardization already occurs to the extent the Bankruptcy Noticing Center uses address matching software to send notices. All notices required

---

Okla. 1991) (phone call from debtor's attorney to creditor is sufficient notice of stay to make subsequent violations willful).

274 These requirements appear to override Bankruptcy Rule 7004, as incorporated in Bankruptcy Rule 9014, with respect to notices to governmental officers and agencies, and insured depository institutions. See § 14.3.2.1, infra. It is not clear whether a summons in an adversary proceeding is considered notice as it is service of process but, if this provision applies, it also overrides Bankruptcy Rule 7004 with respect to service of process on such entities. See also In re Sawyer, 373 B.R. 454 (Bankr. D.S.C. 2007) (section 342(c)(2)(A) does not determine manner of service of process in adversary proceedings or contested matters, which continues to be addressed by Fed. R. Bankr. P. 7004 and 9014(b)).

275 Such language is routinely found in monthly statements sent on credit card accounts in order to comply with the billing error notification requirements found in the Truth in Lending Act. See 15 U.S.C. § 1637(a)(7).
276 11 U.S.C. § 342(c)(2)(B).
277 11 U.S.C. § 342(c)(2).
278 11 U.S.C. § 342(f).

to be sent by the court more than thirty days after such a request must be sent to the requested address, unless a creditor makes a request under section 342(e) in a particular case for use of a different address.[279] Courts may wish to require creditors to file requests of the addresses they want used, to ensure that they give effective notice as defined by section 342(g).

9.6.3.3 Effective Notice Under Section 342

Section 362(g)(2) provides that a "monetary penalty" may not be imposed on a creditor under section 362(k) for violation of the stay if the creditor has not received "effective notice" of the order for relief as defined in section 342(g)(1). This provision, when it applies, precludes only the recovery of punitive damages under section 362(k)(1), so actual damages, which by the terms of section 362(k)(1) include costs and attorney fees, may still be obtained.

However, this limitation should rarely be a problem for debtors. First, it applies only to awards against creditors and not against others, such as their attorneys or agents. Second, it applies only if "effective notice" as defined in section 342(g)(1) has not been received.

Section 342(g)(1) states that notice provided to a creditor other than in accordance with section 342 is not "effective notice" unless "brought to the attention of" the creditor. The first question to resolve in order to determine the applicability of this provision is when is notice not given in accordance with section 342? With respect to notice given by a debtor, especially early in the case to alert the creditor to the petition, nothing in section 342 applies to such notices. They do not come within the ambit of section 342(c) or (e) because they are not notices that are required by the Code, rules, court order, or other applicable laws, and the other provisions of section 342 apply only to notices from the court. For example, notice from a debtor to a creditor that is given to prevent an imminent foreclosure or repossession is not required by any rule or Code provision.[280]

Thus, such a notice is provided in accordance with section 342 because the section does not set any particular requirements for this type of notice. Read any other way, section 342 would not provide any way for such notice to a creditor to be given by the debtor in accordance with section 342, as the section simply does not apply to such notices. It is almost inconceivable that courts would adopt a reading that makes it impossible for debtors to effectively notify creditors about the automatic stay. Because a notice sent by the debtor for purposes of notifying creditors of the automatic stay is not a notice required to be sent by the debtor, the provision in section 342(c)(2) regarding the address at which a creditor requests correspondence is simply not applicable.

The next question concerns the language "brought to the attention of" the creditor, which is not defined, except by exclusion.[281] Under section 342(g)(1), if a creditor has established reasonable procedures to deliver notices to a responsible person or department, then notice is not considered "brought to the attention of such creditor" until it reaches that person or department. This provision will provide fertile ground for discovery into a creditor's "reasonable procedures," including whether the creditor has given an address to the Bankruptcy Noticing Center for notices, whether it uses BANKO (an on-line service that notifies creditors of bankruptcy filings)[282] to check on filings, whether the creditor receives notices of case events electronically, and what mechanisms are in place to transmit timely notices to appropriate departments. If a debtor gives reasonable notice, a creditor should have procedures that transmit it almost instantly. It is hard to imagine how a creditor that does not have a procedure for immediate transmission of notices received by its attorneys, collection staff, repossession agents, and collection agents could be deemed to have reasonable procedures.[283] And presumably, by negative implication, if such reasonable procedures do not exist, any actual notice given to a creditor should be deemed brought to the creditor's attention. So, in the end, any reasonable notice should be sufficient to be effective notice for purposes of section 342(g). This conclusion is buttressed by Bankruptcy Rule 2002(g)(5), which provides that a creditor may treat a notice as not having been brought to its attention only if, prior to issuance of the notice, the creditor has filed a statement that designates the name and address of the person or organizational subdivision responsible for receiving notices under the Code and that describes the procedures established by the creditor to cause such notices to be delivered to that person or subdivision. Needless to say, very few, if any, creditors have filed such statements.

With respect to notices from the court, although creditors do not usually receive the official notice of the case filing until ten to twenty days after the petition, if a notice is received in accordance with section 342(e) there can be no doubt that the creditor has received effective notice. Many creditors have arranged with the court system's noticing facilities to receive electronic or mail notices at a certain address. Having given that address for notice, they obviously cannot complain about lack of notice when it is used.

9.6.4 Contempt Remedies

In addition to remedies under section 362(k), the debtor also has remedies for violation of the automatic stay as contempt of

---

279 11 U.S.C. § 342(f)(2).
280 See Form 33, Appx. G.4, infra.
281 See In re Crawford, 476 B.R. 83 (S.D.N.Y. 2012) (rejecting creditor defense under section 342(g) where creditor's agent attended foreclosure sale at which it was announced that debtor had filed bankruptcy); In re Tillett, 2010 WL 1688016 (Bankr. E.D. Va. Apr. 26, 2010) (no monetary penalty imposed on creditor who violated stay because notice of commencement of case was not mailed to address required by § 342(c)(2) and debtor had not alleged that notice was "brought to the attention of" creditor).
282 Information on BANKO is available at www.banko.com.
283 In re Harvey, 388 B.R. 440, 447 (Bankr. D. Me. 2008) (creditor whose procedure was to discard correspondence sent to billing address did not have reasonable procedures).

§ 9.6.4   Consumer Bankruptcy Law and Practice

a court order.[284] The legislative history of section 362(k) (formerly designated as section 362(h)) makes clear that Congress was granting an additional remedy to debtors beyond those already in existence.[285] Neither remedy may be available, however, if it was unclear whether an act was barred by the stay.[286]

Contempt sanctions can be imposed regardless of whether the violation is in willful disregard of the stay.[287] So long as the enjoined party knows of the stay, it is responsible for the consequences.[288] The duty is on creditors, especially those regularly involved with bankruptcy cases, to establish procedures that ensure compliance with the stay, in order that bankruptcy cases proceed smoothly.[289] Indeed, if either a creditor or its collection agent has knowledge of the case, the creditor may be held in contempt for any postpetition collection attempts by its agent.[290] Additionally, reliance in good faith on the advice of an attorney that actions are not barred by the stay is no defense.[291] Nor is "computer error" a valid defense.[292]

The sanctions that may be imposed for contempt are similar to those available under section 362(k), except that punitive damages are not available.[293] They may include fines and attorney fees, in appropriate cases, against both the violator and any attorneys who advised such violations.[294] Many courts have held that damages for contempt may also be awarded.[295]

The Court of Appeals for the Ninth Circuit has held that contempt must be sought by a motion, rather than an adversary proceeding.[296] Because Rule 7001 appears to dictate that damages under section 362(k) are to be sought by an adversary proceeding, this may mean that both a motion and an adversary

---

284 It is quite clear that a violation of the stay's prohibitions constitutes contempt of court. Jove Eng'g Inc. v. Internal Revenue Serv., 92 F.3d 1539 (11th Cir. 1996) (contempt remedy available when section 362(h) not applicable); *In re* Pace, 67 F.3d 187 (9th Cir. 1995); *In re* Carter, 691 F.2d 390 (8th Cir. 1982); Fid. Mortgage Investors v. Camelia Builders, 550 F.2d 47 (2d Cir. 1976).

Contempt proceedings in bankruptcy cases are governed by Federal Rule of Bankruptcy Procedure 9020. *See* § 14.2.8, *infra*. *See also In re* Del Mission Ltd., 98 F.3d 1147 (9th Cir. 1996) (state found in contempt for failing to promptly return taxes it had been ordered to repay debtor after violation of stay).

285 130 Cong. Rec. H1942 (daily ed. Mar. 26, 1984) (remarks of Rep. Rodino). *See also In re* Skinner, 917 F.2d 444 (10th Cir. 1990); *In re* Wagner, 74 B.R. 898 (Bankr. E.D. Pa. 1987).

286 United States *ex rel.* Internal Revenue Serv. v. Norton, 717 F.2d 767 (3d Cir. 1983).

287 McComb v. Jacksonville Paper Co., 336 U.S. 187, 191, 63 S. Ct. 497, 93 L. Ed. 599 (1949); Perry v. O'Donnell, 759 F.2d 702 (9th Cir. 1985); Vuitton et Fils S.A. v. Carousel Handbags, 592 F.2d 126 (2d Cir. 1979); *In re* Demp, 22 B.R. 331 (Bankr. E.D. Pa. 1982), *aff'd*, 17 Clearinghouse Rev. 1129 (E.D. Pa. 1983). *See also In re* Skinner, 90 B.R. 470 (D. Utah 1988) (actions not willful when creditor received notice of stay, but did not read it; nonetheless creditor could be held in civil contempt), *aff'd*, 917 F.2d 444 (10th Cir. 1990); *In re* Womack, 4 B.R. 632 (Bankr. E.D. Tenn. 1980) (filing fee and attorney fees awarded even though no contempt found).

288 *See, e.g., In re* Kilby, 100 B.R. 579 (Bankr. M.D. Fla. 1989) (landlord responsible for property lost during eviction in violation of the stay), *aff'd*, 130 B.R. 259 (N.D. Ill. 1991).

289 *In re* Perviz, 302 B.R. 357 (Bankr. N.D. Ohio 2003) (creditor must assure that bankruptcy notices sent to an internally improper, but otherwise valid, corporate address are forwarded in a prompt and timely manner to the correct person/department); *In re* Price, 103 B.R. 989 (Bankr. N.D. Ill. 1989) (IRS threat to levy against debtor violates stay even though notice was generated by computer; IRS had no procedures in place to prevent notices from being sent out in violation of the stay); *In re* Stucka, 77 B.R. 777 (Bankr. C.D. Cal. 1987) (failure to adopt procedures to prevent stay violations rendered violations "willful" and "wanton"); *In re* Stalnaker, 5 Bankr. Ct. Dec. (LRP) 203 (Bankr. S.D. Ohio 1978).

290 *In re* Mauck, 287 B.R. 219 (Bankr. E.D. Mo. 2002) (notice to mortgage servicing agent at payment address sufficient to render later notice of foreclosure a willful violation by both servicing agent and mortgage holder); *In re* Fultz, 18 B.R. 521 (Bankr. E.D. Pa. 1982) (creditor had notice); *In re* Fowler, 16 B.R. 596 (Bankr. S.D. Ohio 1981) (agent's knowledge imputed to creditor).

291 *In re* Taylor, 884 F.2d 478 (9th Cir. 1989).

However, under such circumstances punitive damages may not be available. *In re* Ketelsen, 880 F.2d 990 (8th Cir. 1989).

292 *In re* Campion, 294 B.R. 313 (B.A.P. 9th Cir. 2003) (failure of debt collector's computer to match debtor's name with name in its database did not render violation non-willful); *In re* Rijos, 263 B.R. 382 (B.A.P. 1st Cir. 2001) (creditor's "computer did it" defense allegedly caused by installation of new software system rejected); *In re* Chateaugay Corp., 112 B.R. 526 (S.D.N.Y. 1990); *In re* McCormack, 203 B.R. 521 (Bankr. D.N.H. 1996) (computer error defense called a "non-starter").

293 *In re* Dyer, 322 F.3d 1178 (9th Cir. 2003) (although attorney fees may be awarded and mild non-compensatory fines may be necessary under some circumstances, serious punitive penalties not available for civil contempt).

294 *See* Hubbard v. Fleet Mortgage Co., 810 F.2d 778 (8th Cir. 1987) (upholding imposition of $7649 fine, plus attorney fees, plus cancellation of mortgage); Borg-Warner Acceptance Corp. v. Hall, 685 F.2d 1306 (11th Cir. 1982); *In re* Gustafson, 111 B.R. 282 (B.A.P. 9th Cir. 1990) (attorney fees awarded to recompense debtor for action necessary to obtain school transcript withheld in violation of stay); *In re* Timbs, 178 B.R. 989 (Bankr. E.D. Tenn. 1994) (punitive damages awarded against collection agency's attorney); *In re* Stephen W. Grosse, Prof'l Corp., 84 B.R. 377 (Bankr. E.D. Pa. 1988) (sanctions against attorney upheld), *aff'd*, 96 B.R. 29 (E.D. Pa. 1989), *aff'd*, 879 F.2d 857 (3d. Cir. 1989) (table).

295 *In re* Zartun, 30 B.R. 543 (B.A.P. 9th Cir. 1983); *In re* Batla, 16 B.R. 392 (Bankr. N.D. Ga. 1981); *In re* Reed, 11 B.R. 258 (Bankr. D. Utah 1981); Springfield Bank v. Caserta, 10 B.R. 57 (Bankr. S.D. Ohio 1981); *In re* Walker, 7 B.R. 216 (Bankr. D.R.I. 1980).

However, damages may be denied when no notice of the stay is given. *In re* Smith Corset Shops, 696 F.2d 971 (1st Cir. 1982). *See In re* Ketelsen, 880 F.2d 990 (8th Cir. 1989) (no damages proved in case in which Farmers Home Administration seized the debtor's tax refund in violation of the stay; however attorney fees awarded). *But see In re* Walters, 868 F.2d 665 (4th Cir. 1989) (award for damages for emotional distress resulting from contempt is impermissible).

Disallowance of a secured claim may also be an appropriate sanction. *In re* Carrigan, 109 B.R. 167 (Bankr. W.D.N.C. 1989) (secured creditor's prepetition arrearage claim of nearly $5000 disallowed and punitive damages awarded). The debtor may wish to argue against such a sanction when the only benefit would be to other unsecured creditors.

296 Barrientos v. Wells Fargo Bank, 633 F.3d 1186 (9th Cir. 2011). *See also* Std. Indus. v. Aquila Inc. (*In re* C.W. Mining Co.), 625 F.3d 1240 (10th Cir. 2010) (contempt *may* be sought by motion, at least if movant seeks only return to status quo and attorney fees).

proceeding must be filed, especially because the same court of appeals has limited attorney fees under section 362(k).[297]

9.6.5 Other Possible Remedies

The same actions which can be penalized as violations of the automatic stay might also be unfair trade practices under state law or violations of federal debt collection protections.[298] In some cases it may be a good idea to seek this remedy in the alternative because of the availability of enhanced damages. But, in any event, the bankruptcy court has exclusive jurisdiction over sanctions for violation of the automatic stay itself.[299]

9.6.6 Remedies Against State and Federal Government

Another issue which unfortunately often arises concerns the remedies available against government entities for violations of the stay. If the stay is violated through state action as defined for purposes of the civil rights laws, remedies under 42 U.S.C. § 1983 may be available against the officials who violate the stay under color of law.[300] Such remedies may be available because a violation of 11 U.S.C. § 362 may be considered a denial of rights secured by federal law for purposes of section 1983.[301] If such an action were successful, then attorney fees would also be proper under the Civil Rights Attorney's Fees Awards Act of 1976, 42 U.S.C. § 1988.[302]

In light of Supreme Court cases taking a narrow view of the Bankruptcy Code's original provisions regarding waiver of sovereign immunity,[303] there had been some doubt about whether damages are available against state and federal governmental entities for violating the automatic stay. Such issues should no longer arise with respect to the federal government, because the 1994 amendments to the Code specifically abrogated sovereign immunity with respect to section 362.[304] Although the same amendment attempted to abrogate states' Eleventh Amendment immunity, the Supreme Court has found that it was unnecessary for Congress to do so under its Article I powers.[305]

Several courts have held that when the government violates the stay in attempting to collect a tax claim, the debtor's claim for damages and attorney fees under section 362(k) arises out of the same transaction or occurrence as the government's claim, so that sovereign immunity is waived.[306] And, at least if the state government has filed a claim in the bankruptcy case, the state should be deemed to have submitted itself to the bankruptcy court's jurisdiction.[307]

Even if any remedies are precluded under section 362(k) based on the Supreme Court sovereign immunity decisions,[308] contempt remedies may remain available.[309] However, punitive damages may not be authorized.[310]

---

297 See § 9.6.2, note 254, supra.
298 See In re Aponte, 82 B.R. 738 (Bankr. E.D. Pa. 1988).
   Relief under other theories should also be considered. See Randolph v. IMBS, Inc., 368 F.3d 726 (7th Cir. 2004) (claim under Fair Debt Collection Practices Act (FDCPA) is not preempted by Bankruptcy Code provisions providing other remedies for stay violations); Vahlsing v. Commercial Union Ins. Co., 928 F.2d 486 (1st Cir. 1991) (damages for abuse of process, negligence and other theories unsuccessfully sought); In re Panek, 402 B.R. 71, 77 (Bankr. D. Mass. 2009) (awarding damages under FDCPA as well as section 362(k)); In re Gunter, 334 B.R. 900 (Bankr. S.D. Ohio 2005) (claim under FDCPA is not preempted by Bankruptcy Code provisions providing other remedies for stay violations). But see Hyman v. Tate, 362 F.3d 965 (7th Cir. 2004) (collection agency could assert bona fide error defense under FDCPA because it reasonably relied on creditor not to forward accounts of debtors in bankruptcy).
299 Halas v. Platak, 239 B.R. 784 (N.D. Ill. 1999) (because state court had no jurisdiction to sanction stay violations, prior state proceeding could not be res judicata on issue of whether sanctions for such violations were proper). See also E. Equip. & Serv. v. Factory Point Nat'l Bank, 236 F.3d 117 (2d Cir. 2001) (actions based upon stay violations must be brought in bankruptcy court and state law tort claims for same acts were preempted by federal law); Carnes v. IndyMac Mortg. Servs., 2010 WL 5276987 (D. Minn. Dec. 17, 2010) (stay violation claims should be brought in bankruptcy court, but district court retained jurisdiction over Telephone Consumer Protection Act claims).
300 Judges and similar officials, however, have immunity for their violations of the stay. See In re 1736 18th Street, N.W., 97 B.R. 121 (Bankr. D.D.C. 1989) (city rent administrator has judicial immunity for conducting rent proceeding in violation of the stay).
301 Maine v. Thiboutot, 448 U.S. 1, 100 S. Ct. 2502, 65 L. Ed. 2d 555 (1980).
302 Id. See also § 16.5.2, infra.
303 United States v. Nordic Vill., 503 U.S. 30, 112 S. Ct. 1011, 117 L. Ed. 2d 191 (1992); Hoffman v. Connecticut Dep't of Income Maint., 492 U.S. 96, 109 S. Ct. 2818, 106 L. Ed. 2d 76 (1989).
304 11 U.S.C. § 106(a).
   However, punitive damages may not be awarded under this provision, and there are limitations on attorney fees, at least against the federal government. See § 14.3.2.2, infra.
   In addition, the Tax Reform Act of 1998 provides for claims against the Internal Revenue Service for damages based on willful violations of section 362. 26 U.S.C. § 7433(e).
305 See Cent. Va. Cmty. College v. Katz, 126 S. Ct. 990, 163 L. Ed. 2d 945 (2006) and § 14.3.2.2, infra, for discussion of sovereign immunity and Eleventh Amendment issues. See also Florida Dep't of Revenue v. Omine (In re Omine), 485 F.3d 1305 (11th Cir. 2007) (proceeding to enforce automatic stay seeking sanctions against state for contempt, which may include award of attorney fees, not barred by Eleventh Amendment).
306 In re Lile, 161 B.R. 788 (S.D. Tex. 1993); In re Boldman, 157 B.R. 412 (C.D. Ill. 1993); Taborski v. Internal Revenue Serv., 141 B.R. 959 (N.D. Ill. 1992).
307 11 U.S.C. § 106(b); In re Burke, 200 B.R. 282 (Bankr. S.D. Ga. 1996).
308 See § 14.3.2.2, infra.
309 See Small Bus. Admin. v. Rinehart, 887 F.2d 165 (8th Cir. 1989) (affirming award of actual damages, costs and attorney fees); In re Colon, 114 B.R. 890 (Bankr. E.D. Pa. 1990) (Hoffman case bars damages under section 362 but not under court's contempt power); In re Price, 103 B.R. 989 (Bankr. N.D. Ill. 1989) (IRS not immune from suit for violations of the stay), aff'd, 130 B.R. 259 (N.D. Ill. 1991). See also United States v. McPeck, 910 F.2d 509 (8th Cir. 1990) (section 106(b) waives sovereign immunity to the extent of the government's claim); In re Fernandez, 132 B.R. 775 (M.D. Fla. 1991) (waiver of sovereign immunity under section 106(a) found). But see In re Gustafson, 934 F.2d 216 (9th Cir. 1991) (governmental units are immune from money damages for violating stay); In re Pearson, 917 F.2d 1215 (9th Cir. 1990) (same).
310 See Small Bus. Admin. v. Rinehart, 887 F.2d 165 (8th Cir. 1989).

9.6.7 Procedural Issues

One further issue is the best way to go forward procedurally in seeking a remedy for a violation of the stay. Although several courts have held that relief under section 362(k) is available by motion,[311] it may be preferable to proceed by complaint pursuant to the adversary proceeding rules, especially if injunctive relief or a contempt remedy is sought.[312] This procedure will eliminate any potential issues about the due process rights of the defending party. In many, if not all cases, careful practice requires seeking statutory remedies together with relief for contempt in the alternative.[313]

Expeditious action to protect the debtor's rights is generally advisable, especially if damages may be mitigated, but a remedy is available even after the bankruptcy case is terminated.[314] Prompt action is particularly important if the stay violation involves proceedings in a state court. It is almost always better to seek to enforce the stay in the bankruptcy court, which is usually more familiar with and sympathetic to the stay than a state court, than to allow the state court to rule on whether the stay applies. Although the Ninth Circuit has held that the bankruptcy court can still find such a state court ruling to be erroneous and therefore void as a violation of the stay,[315] other courts have ruled otherwise and refused to overturn a state court's decision.[316]

9.7 Proceedings Seeking Relief from the Stay

9.7.1 Proceedings Must Be Commenced by Motion

While the scope of the stay is broad and the sanctions to enforce it are powerful, the duration of its protections may be short-lived. A common creditor response to the bankruptcy petition is to file a proceeding seeking relief from the automatic stay. The court may grant relief, upon motion of a party, terminating, annulling,[317] modifying, or conditioning the stay. Only the bankruptcy court has the power to grant relief from the automatic stay.[318]

Federal Rule of Bankruptcy Procedure 4001(a) specifically provides that the proper method of proceeding "shall" be by motion under Bankruptcy Rule 9014.[319] Indeed, the stay may

---

311 Fed. R. Bankr. P. 9014. *See In re* Zumbrun, 88 B.R. 250 (B.A.P. 9th Cir. 1988); *In re* Karsh Travel, Inc., 102 B.R. 778, 780, 781 (N.D. Cal. 1989); *In re* Hooker Invs., 116 B.R. 375, 378 (Bankr. S.D.N.Y. 1990); *In re* Forty-Five Fifty-Five, Inc., 111 B.R. 920, 922, 923 (Bankr. D. Mont. 1990). *See also In re* Rijos, 263 B.R. 382 (B.A.P. 1st Cir. 2001) (debtors denied due process when bankruptcy court denied motion for stay sanctions without conducting evidentiary hearing); *In re* Elegant Concepts Ltd., 67 B.R. 914, 917 (Bankr. E.D.N.Y. 1986) (court, approving procedure of filing motion for sanctions, suggested that adversary proceeding might be more appropriate, but noted that adverse party raised no procedural objections and thereby waived any procedural irregularity); *In re* Herbert, 61 B.R. 44, 45 (Bankr. W.D. La. 1986) (because creditor was properly served under Rule 9014 and creditor failed to raise any procedural objections, motion for sanctions was appropriate, even if, as court suggested, adversary proceeding was more appropriate).

312 Fed. R. Bankr. P. 7001–7087.

313 *See, e.g.*, Forms 34, 35, 37, Appx. G.4, *infra*.
See also § 14.2.8, *infra*, concerning the contempt power of the bankruptcy court.

314 Price v. Rochford, 947 F.2d 829 (7th Cir. 1991); *In re* Johnson, 575 F.3d 1079 (10th Cir. 2009) (dismissal of underlying chapter 13 case did not divest bankruptcy court of jurisdiction over adversary proceeding seeking damages under § 362(k) for stay violations); *In re* Davis, 177 B.R. 907 (B.A.P. 9th Cir. 1995).
In some instances the case may need to be reopened pursuant to 11 U.S.C. § 350(b).

315 *In re* Gruntz, 202 F.3d 1074 (9th Cir. 2000) (en banc); *accord In re* Rainwater, 233 B.R. 126 (Bankr. N.D. Ala. 1999), *vacated*, 254 B.R. 273 (N.D. Ala. 2000). *See also In re* Dunbar, 245 F.3d 1058 (9th Cir. 2001) (administrative agency ruling).

316 *See, e.g., In re* Singleton, 230 B.R. 533 (B.A.P. 6th Cir. 1999). *See also In re* Coho Res., Inc., 345 F.3d 338 (5th Cir. 2003) (state courts have jurisdiction to determine whether a pending action is stayed by a ruling of the bankruptcy court, but should consider deferring close questions involving the applicability of the automatic stay to the bankruptcy court).

317 Annulment of the stay is usually sought by parties seeking to validate an innocent violation of the stay in circumstances in which relief from the stay would have been granted, if it had been sought. *See In re* Soares, 107 F.3d 969 (1st Cir. 1997) (annulment should not be granted to validate foreclosure when mortgagee knew of bankruptcy and failed to inform state court); Franklin v. Office of Thrift Supervision, 31 F.3d 1020 (10th Cir. 1994) (power to annul stay should rarely be used, probably only in cases of claimants who were honestly ignorant of stay); *In re* Siciliano, 13 F.3d 748 (3d Cir. 1994) (court had authority to annul stay in proper circumstances); *In re* Bright, 338 B.R. 530 (B.A.P. 1st Cir. 2006) (no abuse of discretion in annulling the stay to retroactively validate foreclosure sale when the debtor found in bad faith because she failed to disclose her ownership interest in the property in her bankruptcy filings, failed to inform the bankruptcy court and the chapter 13 trustee of her claim to the sale proceeds, and did not promptly invoke the automatic stay); *In re* Melendez Colon, 265 B.R. 639 (B.A.P. 1st Cir. 2001) (decision to annul stay made without request from creditor or opportunity for debtor to argue issue was abuse of discretion); *In re* Brown, 251 B.R. 916 (Bankr. M.D. Ga. 2000) (party seeking annulment of stay has burden of proving that annulment would not negatively impact any other creditors); *In re* Adams, 215 B.R. 194 (Bankr. W.D. Mo. 1997) (although creditor innocently violated stay, annulment not granted when relief from the stay would not have been granted had it been sought). *See also In re* Williams, 323 B.R. 691, 702 (B.A.P. 9th Cir. 2005) (although stay was annulled retroactively to validate a foreclosure sale, creditor may still be liable for damages under section 362(k) for conducting sale before the annulment order), *aff'd*, 204 Fed. Appx. 582 (9th Cir. 2006); Emigrant Sav. Bank v. Rappaport, 20 A.D.3d 502, 799 N.Y.S.2d 533 (2005) (only bankruptcy court, not state court, has jurisdiction to annul the automatic stay retroactively and validate a foreclosure sale that took place while stay was in effect).

318 *In re* Gruntz, 202 F.3d 1074 (9th Cir. 2000) (en banc).

319 Fed. R. Bankr. P. 4001(a)(1).
Normally this motion should be heard in the bankruptcy court where the bankruptcy case is pending, although other courts may have concurrent jurisdiction over some of the issues that arise. *In re* Baldwin-United Corp. Litig., 765 F.2d 343 (2d Cir. 1985). *See In re* LPM Corp., 300 F.3d 1134 (9th Cir. 2002) (prior order directing debtor to pay rent was not order granting relief from stay, so execution on debtor's bank account when debtor did not pay

not be eliminated without court approval even if the parties agree to relief.³²⁰ The trustee and, if the court orders, other creditors are entitled to notice of any agreement to terminate the stay before it is approved, if a motion for relief from stay was not previously served.³²¹ For the same reason, a prepetition agreement by the debtor that the stay will not apply to a particular creditor cannot be enforced.³²²

The rule dictating that a motion be filed to seek relief reflects the view that, due to the expedited treatment that the Code affords to stay litigation, a request for relief from the stay should be a discrete proceeding that can be disposed of quickly, without the trappings of a full adversary proceeding. A request for relief from the stay may not be honored if it is filed as an adversary proceeding commenced by a complaint, or joined with any claim for relief that would require an adversary proceeding.³²³ At a minimum, the party seeking relief from the stay in that fashion should be deemed to have waived the right to a prompt hearing, because the normal timetable for an adversary proceeding does not accommodate the deadlines of Code section 362(e).³²⁴ If such ancillary claims are permitted at all, they should normally be deferred until after the creditor's right to relief from the stay has been determined, so that the debtor does not lose discovery rights and other rights available in adversary proceedings.

Rule 9014 provides that no answer is required to a motion, unless the court directs otherwise.³²⁵ Nonetheless, it is often useful to file an answer in order to frame the issues to be presented as defenses to the motion. Moreover, some courts grant relief by default when answers are not filed, despite the clear contrary language of the rules.³²⁶ Because Rule 9014 provides only that there be "notice and opportunity for hearing," it is usually wise to file at least a request for a hearing on the motion. Local rules and practice should be checked carefully in this regard.

9.7.2 Time Limits for Court Actions

The Code sets out strict time limits for stay litigation involving stays of acts against property. Section 362(e)(1) provides that at least a preliminary hearing on a request for relief from the stay must be held within thirty days; if that hearing is not held, the stay is automatically terminated as to property of the estate.³²⁷ If the court at the preliminary hearing finds that there is a "reasonable likelihood that the party opposing relief" from the stay will prevail in the stay litigation, the stay can be continued until the conclusion of a final hearing. This finding may sometimes be made without the taking of evidence,³²⁸ but there must be at least an opportunity for the movant to be heard.³²⁹

Under a 1994 amendment to the Code, the final hearing must be concluded within thirty days after the conclusion of the preliminary hearing. If it is not, the stay of acts against property of the estate is terminated unless the thirty day period is extended with the consent of the parties or for a specific time that the court finds is required by compelling circumstances.³³⁰

Section 362(e)(2), added in 2005, creates additional deadlines, applicable in all chapter 7, 11, or 13 cases in which the debtor is an individual. If a party in interest files a motion for relief from the automatic stay, the stay automatically terminates sixty days after the motion is filed, unless:

- The court decides the motion before that time; or
- The time period is extended by agreement of the parties or by the court for a specific period of time for good cause based on findings of the court.³³¹

---

violated stay). *See also* NLT Computer Servs. Corp. v. Capital Computer Sys., Inc., 755 F.2d 1253 (6th Cir. 1985) (fact that monies had been paid into district court registry did not remove them from jurisdiction of bankruptcy court once a bankruptcy was filed).

One court of appeals has held that, at least in some cases when a motion for relief has been filed, an oral order granting relief from the stay is sufficient, even if it is not memorialized by a subsequent written order. Noli v. Comm'r of Internal Revenue Serv., 860 F.2d 1521 (9th Cir. 1988).

320 *In re* Fugazy Express, 982 F.2d 769 (2d Cir. 1992).
321 Fed. R. Bankr. P. 4001(d).
322 Farm Credit of Cent. Fla., ACA v. Polk, 160 B.R. 870 (M.D. Fla. 1993). *See also In re* Riley, 188 B.R. 191 (Bankr. D.S.C. 1995) (prepetition agreement to waive protections of automatic stay could not be enforced after cure of default that gave rise to agreement); *In re* Madison, 184 B.R. 686 (Bankr. E.D. Pa. 1995) (prepetition agreement not to file a bankruptcy case for 180 days was void because it violated public policy).
323 These types of claims for relief are listed in Federal Rule of Bankruptcy Procedure 7001. *See, e.g., In re* Harvey, 13 B.R. 608 (Bankr. M.D. Fla. 1980) (stay proceeding dismissed when commenced in improper form). *But see* Pursifull v. Eakin, 814 F.2d 1501 (10th Cir. 1987) (relief from stay proper on motion to abstain in adversary proceeding when trustee had notice such relief would be sought).
324 *In re* Med. Plaza Assocs., 67 B.R. 879 (W.D. Mo. 1986). *See* 9 Collier on Bankruptcy ¶ 4001.02[1] (16th ed.).
325 The rule previously required a specific court order that an answer be filed, but was amended so courts could require answers to motion by local rule. *See In re* Allstar Bldg. Prods., 809 F.2d 1534 (11th Cir. 1987) (decided under prior wording of rule), *rev'd on other grounds*, 834 F.2d 898 (11th Cir. 1987) (en banc).

In most other respects, proceedings under Rule 9014 are covered by the same rules as adversary proceedings, which in general conform to the Federal Rules of Civil Procedure. *See* Fed. R. Bankr. P. 9014, 7001–7087; § 1.4.2, *supra*.

326 It is, of course, also inappropriate for a court to enter relief from the stay on the basis of an *ex parte* affidavit, except in the limited circumstances described in Federal Rule of Bankruptcy Procedure 4001(a)(2) [formerly Rule 4001(a)(3)]. *See* First Republicbank Dallas v. Gargyle Corp., 91 B.R. 398 (N.D. Tex. 1988).
327 *In re* Wedgewood Realty Group, Ltd., 878 F.2d 693 (3d Cir. 1989); *In re* River Hills Apartments Fund, 813 F.2d 702 (5th Cir. 1987). *See also In re* Looney, 823 F.2d 788 (4th Cir. 1987) (overcrowded docket does not excuse failure to meet time limits).
328 Satter v. KDT Indus., 28 B.R. 374 (S.D.N.Y. 1982).
329 *In re* Looney, 823 F.2d 788 (4th Cir. 1987).
330 11 U.S.C. § 362(e)(1). *See In re* Duran, 483 F.3d 653 (10th Cir. 2007) (section 362(e) takes precedence over Fed. R. Bankr. P. 4001(a)(3) so creditor did not have to wait ten days (fourteen days under current rule) after order granting stay relief when time period in section 362(e) ended earlier).
331 11 U.S.C. § 362(e)(2).

It is unlikely that this provision will significantly change practice with respect to stay relief motions. Under pre-2005 Act practice, stay motions were normally decided within sixty days. In the few cases in which they were not, the delay beyond sixty days was usually based on an agreement of the parties or was for good cause. However, attorneys should be careful not to allow the sixty-day period to run through inadvertence.

These time limits were meant to prevent a bankruptcy judge from simply ignoring a motion to lift the stay and thus denying the moving party an appealable order through which to seek review. However, there still may be ways in which the time limits can be avoided by a court that is determined to take longer to decide a stay motion. Parties may be pressured into "consenting" to a continuance of the hearing; few litigants can refuse a judge's strong suggestion that they agree to a postponement. And a court can always find cause for taking longer to decide the motion if it wishes to do so.

Several important points must be remembered with respect to these time limits. First, they apply only to the automatic stay. A judge may always reinstitute that stay by order, or issue a separate injunction staying certain acts.[332] Second, while the section 1301 stay of actions against codebtors in chapter 13 cases may also be challenged under the rules by a motion,[333] the time limits in section 362 do not apply to such a proceeding,[334] nor do they apply to any other request for relief joined with a request for relief from the stay. For such other relief, which might require a more extensive final determination of rights, a slower pace is permitted for the remainder of the proceedings. Finally, the time limits may be waived by the party seeking relief, either explicitly or implicitly.[335]

A number of bankruptcy courts have created loss mitigation programs that are available to debtors faced with motions for relief from the stay filed by mortgage holders or servicers.[336] These programs typically require face-to-face meetings involving creditor representatives with authority to modify the mortgage. The courts' authority to order such programs has been upheld when it was challenged.[337]

9.7.3 Defending Against Motions for Relief from the Stay

9.7.3.1 Procedural Questions

9.7.3.1.1 Parties

Normally, any proceeding must include as parties all persons who will be ordered by the court to do something or whose interests will be seriously affected if the action is successful. Thus, both Federal Rule of Civil Procedure 19 and Federal Rule of Bankruptcy Procedure 7019 generally provide that such indispensable parties must be joined. While these rules are not specifically incorporated in Federal Rule of Bankruptcy Procedure 9014, that rule does provide that notice shall be given to the party against whom relief is sought.[338]

In a proceeding for relief from the stay it seems clear that joinder of the debtor and the trustee is almost always necessary. The former typically has possession of property, or will be the defendant in legal proceedings if the stay is lifted, and usually has a strong interest in continuation of the stay. The latter also has at least a possible interest in almost every case involving property. Indeed, because of the chapter 13 trustee's important role, the Code expressly provides that she appear and be heard at any hearing that concerns the value of property subject to a lien, a frequent issue in stay litigation.[339]

Thus, one of the first issues that can be raised is whether the court should dismiss the proceeding for lack of an indispensable party. A request to dismiss on these grounds may be necessary when a motion for relief from the stay has been filed only against the trustee or only against the debtor.[340] In such a case, a good argument can be made that the proceeding must be dismissed so that the thirty-day time limit will begin to run only when all of the proper parties have been notified and joined in the proceeding. Any other result would allow a party seeking relief from the stay to sue only some of the necessary parties, and then to add others when the thirty days is about to run, giving those others inadequate time to prepare a defense.

In some cases there may also be questions about the standing of the moving party to seek relief from the automatic stay. Some courts have held that a mortgage servicing company with no beneficial interest in the underlying mortgage does not have standing to file a motion for relief from the stay and that only the holder of the note and mortgage may file such a motion.[341]

---

332 *In re* Wedgewood Realty Group, Ltd., 878 F.2d 693 (3d Cir. 1989) (stay can be reimposed on grounds similar to those which would warrant a preliminary injunction); *In re* Kozak Farms, 47 B.R. 399 (W.D. Mo. 1985). *See, e.g., In re* Fulghum Constr. Corp., 5 B.R. 53 (Bankr. M.D. Tenn. 1980) (preliminary injunction issued by court prior to automatic expiration of stay prevented order of possession to creditors); *In re* Walker, 3 B.R. 213 (Bankr. W.D. Va. 1980) (stay renewed on assumption it had expired due to time limits); *In re* Feimster, 3 B.R. 11 (Bankr. N.D. Ga. 1979). *See also* § 9.4.7, *supra*.
333 Fed. R. Bankr. P. 4001(a).
334 By its terms, section 362(e) applies only to requests for relief from the section 362(a) stay and section 362(e)(1) is further limited to the stay of acts against property of the estate. *See In re* Small, 38 B.R. 143 (Bankr. D. Md. 1984).
335 *In re* Alderson, 144 B.R. 332 (Bankr. W.D. La. 1992) (creditor waived benefit of time limits when it set the hearing date beyond thirty days itself and because its motion sought additional relief—abandonment—in addition to relief from stay); *In re* Small, 38 B.R. 143 (Bankr. D. Md. 1984) (party who files discovery requests due beyond the thirty-day period and seeks other relief implicitly waives thirty-day hearing requirement); *In re* Wilmette Partners, 34 B.R. 958 (Bankr. N.D. Ill. 1983).
336 *See* § 11.6.1.5, *infra*.

337 *In re* Sosa, 443 B.R. 263 (Bankr. D.R.I. 2011).
338 *See In re* Ctr. Wholesale, 759 F.2d 1440 (9th Cir. 1985) (cash collateral order allowing debtor's use of sale proceeds subject to lien of junior secured party was void when inadequate notice was given to that party and adequate protection was not provided).
339 11 U.S.C. § 1302(b)(2).
340 *See In re* DiBona, 7 B.R. 798 (Bankr. E.D. Pa. 1980) (joinder of trustee ordered on grounds that he was indispensable party).
341 *In re* Miller v. Deutsche Bank Nat'l Trust Co., 666 F.3d 1255 (10th

Similar issues arise when courts review the standing of a party to file a proof of claim.[342]

As the selling and securitization of mortgages has become commonplace, it has become harder for mortgage holders and servicers to keep track of which party holds the mortgage. Bankruptcy courts have become increasingly aware of such issues and have more frequently denied motions for relief from stay based upon lack of standing.[343] In some instances courts have denied motions for relief when the movant failed to provide true copies of documents establishing assignment of the note.[344] To comply with federal court standing and real party in interest requirements,[345] the creditor must have been assigned the note and have the right to enforce it at the time a motion for relief from the stay is filed.[346] Any entity making an assignment must comply with state law requirements for a proper assignment. Proof of these requirements is often obscured by the use of the Mortgage Electronic Registration System (MERS), which is an electronic database for recording mortgage assignments independently of local land records systems.[347] In such cases MERS is named as the mortgagee, typically as "nominee" for the original creditor and its assigns. However, because MERS is merely a recording service with no enforceable ownership rights in the underlying obligation, several courts have held that it does not have standing to seek relief from the stay.[348]

Cir. 2012) (bank did not have standing when note was payable to original holder and bank did not prove possession of note); Veal v. Am. Home Mortg. Servicing, Inc. (*In re* Veal), 450 B.R. 897 (B.A.P. 9th Cir. 2011) (lack of possession of note or assignment of note fatal to standing to enforce note); *In re* Jackson, 451 B.R. 24 (Bankr. E.D. Cal. 2011) (no standing where there was no evidence movant was holder of note by endorsement of possession of note); *In re* Alcide, 450 B.R. 526 (Bankr. E.D. Pa. 2011) (servicer had no standing to bring stay motion absent evidence that it was authorized to do so on behalf of note holder); *In re* Weisband, 427 B.R. 13 (Bankr. D. Ariz. 2010) (servicer had no standing because unaffixed allonge was ineffective, MERS had no standing to assign note, and there was no evidence that servicer's alleged principal owned note); *In re* Shapoval, 441 B.R. 392 (Bankr. D. Mass. 2010) (indorsement of note set forth in allonge was not valid if allonge was not affixed to note); *In re* Minbatiwalla, 424 B.R. 104 (Bankr. S.D.N.Y. 2010) (in addition to establishing rights of the mortgage holder, a servicer seeking stay relief must show it has authority to act as the holder's agent); Deutsche Bank Nat'l Trust Co v. Tarantola (*In re* Tarantola), 2010 WL 3022038 (Bankr. D. Ariz. July 29, 2010) (allonge allegedly transferring note to holder was attached to copy of note rather than original as represented, was not attached until after holder sought relief from stay, and was executed by party who had no authority to transfer note); *In re* Box, 2010 WL 2228289, at *1 (Bankr. W.D. Mo. June 3, 2010) (movant presented no evidence it was holder of note and therefore had no standing); *In re* Canellas, 2010 WL 571808 (Bankr. M.D. Fla. Feb. 9, 2010) (servicer claiming to be owner and holder of note and mortgage did not present credible evidence that this was true); *In re* Jones, 2010 WL 358494 (Bankr. E.D.N.C. Jan. 21, 2010) (party seeking relief did not present evidence it was note holder entitled to enforce note and deed of trust); *In re* Morgan, 225 B.R. 290 (Bankr. E.D.N.Y. 1998), *vacated on other grounds sub nom. In re* Nunez, 2000 WL 655983 (E.D.N.Y. Mar. 17, 2000). *See also* Banks v. Kondaur Capital Corp. (*In re* Banks), 457 B.R. 9 (B.A.P. 8th Cir. 2011) (party must prove possession of bearer note to be entitled to enforce it).

For a detailed discussion of standing to enforce a note and mortgage, including the right to foreclose or seek stay relief in bankruptcy, see National Consumer Law Center, Foreclosures, § 5.1 (4th ed. 2012).

342 *See* § 14.4.3, *infra*.
343 *See, e.g., In re* Alcide, 450 B.R. 526 (Bankr. E.D. Pa. 2011) (collecting decisions on servicer standing to file stay relief motions and proofs of claim in bankruptcy cases; *In re* Hayes, 393 B.R. 259 (Bankr. D. Mass. 2008) (trustee of securitized trust who submitted documents which failed to establish it was holder of mortgage lacked standing to file stay relief motion or proof of claim); *In re* Maisel, 378 B.R. 19 (Bankr. D. Mass. 2007) (assignee who filed motion before mortgage was assigned to it did not have standing).
344 *In re* Jacobson, 402 B.R. 359 (Bankr. W.D. Wash. 2009) (servicer's declaration did not establish that it had beneficial interest in note); *In re* Lee, 408 B.R. 893 (Bankr. C.D. Cal. 2009) (attorney sanctioned for pursuing stay relief motion knowing that named party lacked ownership interest in note); *In re* Hwang, 396 B.R. 757 (Bankr. C.D. Cal. 2008) (servicer who is not holder of the note may not seek relief from stay in its own name), *rev'd*, 438 B.R. 661 (C.D. Cal. 2010); *In re* Vargas, 396 B.R. 511 (Bankr. C.D. Cal. 2008) (evidence by written declaration and from clerical staff testimony not admissible to establish mortgage holder's standing); *In re* Hayes, 393 B.R. 259 (Bankr. D. Mass. 2008). *See also In re* Nosek, 386 B.R. 374 (Bankr. D. Mass. 2008) (imposing sanctions on creditor for misrepresenting status of holder of note during protracted litigation), *aff'd in part, rev'd in part*, 406 B.R. 434 (D. Mass. 2009), *aff'd in part, modified in part*, 609 F.3d 6 (1st Cir. 2010).
345 *See* Fed. R. Civ. P. 17(a) (made applicable in bankruptcy by Fed. R. Bankr. P. 7017).
346 *In re* Miller v. Deutsche Bank Nat'l Trust Co., 666 F.3d 1255 (10th Cir. 2012) (bank did not have standing when note was payable to original holder and bank did not prove possession of note); *In re* Jackson, 451 B.R. 24 (Bankr. E.D. Cal. 2011) (movant failed to show had right to enforce promissory note under any category of U.C.C. § 3-301); *In re* Maisel, 378 B.R. 19 (Bankr. D. Mass. 2007) (servicer bringing stay relief motion failed to document standing as of time motion filed). *See also In re* Foreclosure Cases, 521 F. Supp. 2d 650 (N.D. Ohio 2007).
347 *See* National Consumer Law Center, Foreclosures § 5.9 (4th ed. 2012).
348 Mortgage Elec. Registration Sys. v. Mitchell (*In re* Mitchell), 423 B.R. 914 (D. Nev. 2009) (servicer could not produce note or written authority from note holder and therefore did not have standing to seek stay relief); *In re* Lippold, 457 B.R. 293 (Bankr. S.D.N.Y. 2011) (MERS was never holder of note, so its assignment of note to party moving for relief did not assign the note); *In re* Wilhelm, 407 B.R. 392 (Bankr. D. Idaho 2009) (MERS lacked authority to transfer note; stay relief denied); *In re* Jacobson, 402 B.R. 359, 367 n.9 (Bankr. W.D. Wash. 2009) (finding "problematic" MERS' identification as the beneficiary of obligation "solely as nominee"; denying motion for relief from stay); *In re* Fitch, 2009 WL 1514501 (Bankr. N.D. Ohio May 28, 2009) (MERS was never in chain of title for mortgage note and had no standing); *In re* Sheridan, 2009 WL 631355 (Bankr. D. Idaho Mar. 12, 2009) (MERS failed to show standing to bring motion); *In re* Vargas, 396 B.R. 511 (Bankr. C.D. Cal. 2008) (motion of MERS to obtain relief for its successors and assigns improperly sought relief for undisclosed parties). *See generally* Landmark Nat'l Bank v. Kesler, 216 P.3d 158 (Kan. 2009) (by labeling itself a "mortgagee" in boilerplate language of mortgage MERS does not become mortgagee under state law and necessary party to foreclosure action); Bellistri v. Ocwen Loan Servicing, L.L.C., 284 S.W.3d 619 (Mo. Ct. App. 2009) (MERS' assignment of deed of trust without note had no legal effect).

9.7.3.1.2 Discovery

Either party may take discovery in connection with a motion for relief from stay.[349] Although the full range of federal discovery opportunities is available, the short time limits require that discovery be completed with great speed to be meaningful. The normal time period allowed by the rules to provide discovery is in every case too long a period to wait unless the parties agree that the stay can continue pending discovery. Thus an order for expedited discovery must be sought if any discovery is needed, and it should be granted by the court. Such discovery can then be pursued just as it would be in any other contested proceeding.

9.7.3.1.3 Defenses and counterclaims

To the extent there are defenses or counterclaims which reduce or eliminate the right of the party seeking relief from the stay to proceed after the stay is lifted, they should be relevant to stay litigation and raised therein.[350] For example, if a debtor claims that a lien does not exist because it was rescinded under the Truth in Lending Act, the stay should not be lifted to permit enforcement of that lien.[351] Or, if a debtor's defenses and counterclaims reduce the balance owing on an automobile loan to an amount that does not justify lifting of the stay,[352] then evidence of those defenses should be allowed.

Notwithstanding these points, a number of questions existed under the prior law as to whether counterclaims could be raised and determined in stay litigation, due to the narrow jurisdiction of the bankruptcy courts.[353] These questions have not been totally laid to rest under the Code despite the fact that the bankruptcy court's expanded jurisdiction includes such counterclaims.[354]

Thus, a problem can arise when one of the parties to the case does not feel ready to engage in an extensive trial of the counterclaim. The party seeking relief from the stay may protest that the counterclaims have nothing to do with the stay litigation.

The legislative history of the stay provision points to a compromise solution. The House Report states that the hearing "will not be the appropriate time at which to bring in other issues, such as counterclaims against the creditor *on largely unrelated matters*. Those counterclaims are not to be handled in the summary fashion that the preliminary hearing under this provision will be."[355]

Thus Congress contemplated that counterclaims and defenses on related matters should be considered in stay litigation. The rules should be read consistently with this approach. While they do foreclose the actual pleading of counterclaims in response to a motion, they certainly do not preclude the debtor from raising the existence of defenses and counterclaims in defending against the motion. If the counterclaims and defenses are related to the creditor's claim, they can then be considered to the extent it is necessary to determine whether they are reasonably likely to be successful, as might be done in a preliminary injunction proceeding.[356] However, the final litigation of the issues raised would ordinarily be deferred until later in the case.[357]

---

349 Fed. R. Bankr. P. 9014.

350 *See In re* Allstar Bldg. Prods., Inc., 809 F.2d 1534 (11th Cir.), *rev'd on other grounds*, 834 F.2d 898 (11th Cir. 1987) (en banc); United Companies Fin. Corp. v. Brantley, 6 B.R. 178 (Bankr. N.D. Fla. 1980) (defenses and counterclaims striking at the heart of plaintiff's lien should be considered); 9 Collier on Bankruptcy ¶ 4001.02[2] (16th ed.). *See also In re* Errington, 52 B.R. 217 (Bankr. D. Minn. 1985) (Farmers Home Administration not entitled to adequate protection when it was enjoined from foreclosing by court orders totally unrelated to automatic stay).

351 *In re* Gurst, 75 B.R. 575 (Bankr. E.D. Pa. 1987).

352 The question of how value can play a role in stay litigation is discussed below, in § 9.7.3.3.1, *infra*.

353 *See* Kennedy, *The Automatic Stay in Bankruptcy*, 11 U. Mich. J.L. Reform 230–232 (1978).

354 See generally § 14.2, *infra*, for discussion of bankruptcy court jurisdiction.

355 H.R. Rep. No. 95-595, at 344 (1977) (emphasis supplied).
The Senate Report, S. Rep. No. 95-989, at 55 (1978), is somewhat more restrictive, but should not be considered meaningful because the Senate Bill did not include the expanded jurisdiction of the final statute. *See also In re* Montgomery, 262 B.R. 772 (B.A.P. 8th Cir. 2001) (transfer avoidance claims must be litigated in separate proceeding, and failure to have filed such proceeding may have influenced court to grant relief from stay).

356 Payment Plans, Inc. v. Strell, 717 F.2d 25 (2d Cir. 1983) (fact that creditor's lien was unperfected considered in denying relief from stay); *In re* Bialac, 694 F.2d 625, 627 (9th Cir. 1982) (when debtor's defenses and counterclaims directly involve question of debtor's equity, they should be heard in stay proceeding); *In re* Hubbel, 427 B.R. 789 (N.D. Cal. 2010) (debtor's assertion of Truth in Lending rescission claim created doubt about whether creditor had valid lien, so bankruptcy court properly denied relief from stay); Societa Internazionale Turismo v. Lockwood, 14 B.R. 374 (Bankr. E.D.N.Y. 1981) (creditor denied relief on ground that it had "no real claim" even though it had state court default judgment). *See also In re* Rice, 82 B.R. 623 (Bankr. S.D. Ga. 1987) (relief from stay must be denied if evidence supports conclusion that lien will be held invalid in a collateral proceeding); *In re* Gellert, 55 B.R. 970 (Bankr. D.N.H. 1985) (continuing the stay on the ground of an available defense to the claim requires a showing analogous to the showing necessary for a preliminary injunction including "likelihood of success on the merits"). *But see* Farm Credit Bank of Omaha v. Franzen, 926 F.2d 762 (8th Cir. 1991) (counterclaims previously concluded in state court proceeding cannot be considered). *See generally Using Consumer Defenses In Response to a Motion for Relief From Stay in Chapter 13*, 12 NCLC REPORTS, Bankruptcy and Foreclosures Ed. 29 (Sept./Oct. 1993).

357 3 Collier on Bankruptcy ¶ 362.08[6] (16th ed.) seems to interpret the legislative history similarly, stating that a res judicata determination on counterclaims should not be made when the court decides on relief from the stay, but that they may be raised and considered by the court at that time. *See* Grella v. Salem Five Cent Sav. Bank, 42 F.3d 26 (1st Cir. 1994) (relief from stay determination did not have preclusive effect with respect to trustee's preference claim); Estate Constr. Co. v. Miller & Smith Holding Co., 14 F.3d 213 (4th Cir. 1994) (failure to raise fraud claim at hearing on relief from stay did not preclude raising it in a later proceeding); D-1 Enters., Inc. v. Commercial State Bank, 864 F.2d 36 (5th Cir. 1989) (order granting relief from stay did not resolve debtor's lender liability claim against creditor); *In re* Vigil, 250 B.R. 394 (Bankr. D.N.M. 2000) (determination that debt was in nature of alimony, maintenance or support in stay proceedings was not binding in later dischargeability proceeding).

9.7.3.1.4 Burden of proof

The Code provides that the burden of proof in stay litigation is on the party seeking relief from the stay as to the issue of the debtor's equity in property and on the party opposing relief on all other issues.[358] While this provision is not as clear as it might be, it apparently means that whenever equity is at issue, the party seeking relief must prove it. Thus, if the question of equity is central to whether a creditor's interest is adequately protected from harm because of the stay, the creditor probably must prove that the debtor lacks sufficient equity to provide adequate protection.[359] If a debtor asserts that equity in a property by itself provides adequate protection, as discussed below, and the creditor fails to offer sufficient evidence on the question of equity, the debtor should prevail.[360]

Regardless of which party has the ultimate burden of proof on a motion for relief from stay, the creditor always must carry an initial burden of production on the grounds alleged for the motion. A creditor's failure to carry this burden of going forward to show grounds for relief should result in a decision for the debtor.[361] In many cases, due to their lack of proper accounting for payments and their imposition of illegal charges, mortgage companies bring motions for relief from the stay when the debtor is not in default or when they cannot prove that the debtor is in default.[362] Problems often go undetected due to the separation of functions and lack of communication between mortgage creditors and the national default service firms and local law firms they hire to file stay relief motions.[363] Courts have properly sanctioned creditors who bring such motions and their attorneys.[364] Courts have also sanctioned the common practice of filing relief from stay motions in chapter 7 cases, apparently with the purpose of running up attorney fees, when there can be no showing of cause for relief from the stay because the stay is already likely to expire imminently with the closing of the case.[365]

9.7.3.1.5 Effect of prior bankruptcy cases involving the same debtor

One problem that has received substantial judicial attention is the repetitious filing in bad faith of new bankruptcy petitions by debtors seeking to reinvoke the automatic stay after it has been lifted in their earlier cases. In their zeal to prevent this

---

358 11 U.S.C. § 362(g); Chizzali v. Gindi (*In re* Gindi), 642 F.3d 865 (10th Cir. 2011) (relief should have been granted when party opposing relief did not even attempt to prove that stay was necessary to effective reorganization). See *In re* Allstar Bldg. Prods., Inc., 834 F.2d 898 (11th Cir. 1987) (en banc) (party opposing creditor's motion for relief has burden on claim that security interest is not properly perfected).

359 *In re* Carroll, 2012 Bankr. LEXIS 1164 (Bankr. E.D.N.C. Mar. 19, 2012) (creditor failed to meet burden of showing it was not adequately protected by equity cushion); *In re* DaRosa, 442 B.R. 173 (Bankr. D. Mass. 2010) (neither internet valuation nor tax assessment met burden to prove value, but drive-by appraisal was sufficient absent contrary evidence); 3 Collier on Bankruptcy ¶ 362.10 (16th ed.). *But see In re* Gauvin, 24 B.R. 578 (B.A.P. 9th Cir. 1982) (debtor always has burden on adequate protection).

360 *In re* Raymond, 99 B.R. 819 (Bankr. S.D. Ohio 1989); *In re* Boisvert, 4 B.R. 664 (Bankr. D. Mass. 1980).

361 *In re* Anthem Communities/RBG, L.L.C., 267 B.R. 867 (Bankr. D. Colo. 2001) (court denied relief *sua sponte* to creditor who failed to meet initial burden of production). *See, e.g., In re* Sonnax Indus., Inc., 907 F.2d 1280 (2d Cir. 1990).

362 *See, e.g., In re* Vargas, 396 B.R. 511 (Bankr. C.D. Cal. 2008) (low level clerk who simply compared declaration to computer screen was not competent to testify to anything relating to stay motion).

363 *See In re* Taylor, 407 B.R. 618 (Bankr. E.D .Pa. 2009) (local law firm which filed stay relief motion lacked access to servicer's software system, including account loan history used by national default service firm to prepare proof of claim), *aff'd*, 655 F.3d 274 (3d Cir. 2011); *In re* Parsley, 384 B.R. 138 (Bankr. S.D. Tex. 2008) (inaccuracies regarding account arrears alleged in motion not detected in part because national default service firm's engagement letter with local law firm specifically prohibited any communication between local firm and its client, the mortgage servicer).

364 *In re* Haque, 395 B.R. 799 (Bankr. S.D. Fla. 2008) (attorney fined total of $95,130.45 for filing forty-five false affidavits); *In re* Schuessler, 386 B.R. 458 (Bankr. S.D.N.Y. 2008) (sanctions for filing unwarranted stay motion in chapter 7 case); *In re* Fagan, 376 B.R. 81 (Bankr. S.D.N.Y. 2007) ($10,000 plus attorney fees awarded to debtor when creditor's own records showed debtor was not in default); *In re* Osborne, 375 B.R. 216 (Bankr. M.D. La. 2007) (attorney sanctioned for filing affidavit alleging debtor defaulted on agreement despite attorney's lack of personal knowledge); *In re* Ulmer, 363 B.R. 777 (Bankr. D.S.C. 2007) (awarding sanctions and finding that affidavits of default related to motions for relief from stay were not executed before a notary public and may not have been reviewed and signed by attorney whose signature appeared on the affidavits); *In re* Martin, 350 B.R. 812 (Bankr. N.D. Ind. 2006) (sanctions imposed on attorney who alleged inaccurately that debtor had no equity in property despite lack of reasonable inquiry into the facts); *In re* Szymanski, 344 B.R. 891 (Bankr. N.D. Ind. 2006) (sanctions imposed on attorney who filed stay relief motion but could produce no evidence at hearing); *In re* Rivera, 342 B.R. 435 (Bankr. D.N.J. 2006) (sanctions imposed on foreclosure law firm for filing default affidavits using "blanks" that were presigned by employee who no longer worked for servicer), *aff'd*, 2007 WL 1946656 (D.N.J. June 29, 2007); *In re* Porcheddu, 338 B.R. 729 (Bankr. S.D. Tex. 2006) (foreclosure law firm sanctioned for filing false fee applications and misrepresenting that fee statements were based on contemporaneous time records); *In re* Brown, 319 B.R. 876 (Bankr. N.D. Ill. 2005) ($10,000 sanction imposed on mortgagee for groundless stay relief motion); *In re* Gorshtein, 285 B.R. 118 (Bankr. S.D.N.Y. 2002); *In re* Williams, 2001 WL 1804312 (Bankr. D.S.C. Nov. 19, 2001) (actual damages for lost wages, additional blood pressure medication, and emotional distress, plus punitive damages and attorney fees, awarded to debtor based on mortgage servicer's violation of the automatic stay by filing a false affidavit accusing debtor of noncompliance with consent order and triggering relief from the stay when debtor was not in default); *In re* Kilgore, 253 B.R. 179 (Bankr. D.S.C. 2000). *See also In re* Thompson, 350 B.R. 842 (Bankr. E.D. Wis. 2006) (damages and attorney fees awarded to debtors under Real Estate Settlement Procedures Act and Bankruptcy Rule 9011 based on servicer's failure to properly credit payments and identify missed payments on affidavit of default).

365 *In re* Cabrera-Mejia, 402 B.R. 335 (Bankr. C.D. Cal. 2008) (law firm fined $21,000). *See also In re* Biazo, 314 B.R. 451 (Bankr. D. Kan. 2004) (because chapter 7 consumer cases generally conclude in a short time period, creditor's filing of a stay relief motion is unnecessary and does not satisfy reasonableness standard for award of attorney fees and costs).

abuse, a few bankruptcy courts ruled that a determination between two parties in a prior proceeding for relief from the automatic stay was res judicata as to all future stay litigation between those parties.[366] These courts went so far as to hold that the prior determination prevented a new stay from even coming into effect in a new case.[367] According to those decisions, the only possible remedy for a debtor seeking to invoke the stay in a new or converted case would be to obtain relief from the prior judgment under Federal Rule of Bankruptcy Procedure 9024, which incorporates the standards of Federal Rule of Civil Procedure 60.[368]

Such holdings were incorrect and have largely been rejected or overruled.[369] The principles of res judicata apply only if a later proceeding involves the same transactional facts.[370] Yet, under the cases discussed above, a debtor would be forever barred from invoking the stay by a new petition, even in a new case several years later when the debtor's circumstances had changed dramatically and the prior default with the creditor had been totally cured. When there is any change of circumstances, res judicata is not applicable.[371]

The appropriate principles to look to in this situation are those of collateral estoppel (also known as issue preclusion). To the extent that the facts and the law have been actually litigated and determined, were essential to the judgment in the previous case, and have not changed since then, the parties are bound by those determinations.[372] However, if factual or legal issues were not previously litigated, either because of changed circumstances or because a default judgment was entered in the previous proceeding,[373] those issues must be decided in the second proceeding for relief from the stay.

A few courts, mostly located in the Central District of California, concluded that they have power to make and enforce *in rem* orders as to the property against which relief from the stay is requested if there has been a consistent pattern of abusive refiling.[374] Such orders purported to grant stay relief to the creditor with respect to the property involved such that no new automatic stay could arise that affects that property. The grounds for this practice were questionable for many of the same reasons discussed above because, when entering such an order, the court might determine the rights of unknown parties not present in the bankruptcy process. The enactment in 2005 of specific provisions authorizing *in rem* orders in limited circumstances[375] should deal with such issues. The provisions provide for notice to third parties who might be affected by the order, as well as ways to obtain relief from the order, and delineate the situations in which Congress deemed such an order appropriate. The court has ample sanctions, strengthened by the Federal Rules of Bankruptcy Procedure,[376] to discourage abuses in other situations.

Congress in 2005 also addressed the applicability of the automatic stay when there have been repeat bankruptcy filings.[377] It has also provided specific criteria for when a stay can

---

366 In a related development, some creditor attorneys have attempted to obtain stipulations from debtors in one bankruptcy which preclude the same debtors from invoking the automatic stay in future bankruptcies. Although it should go without saying that such stipulations should be assiduously avoided in the first instance, when they have been entered it should be argued that they are void. Among the arguments against the validity of such stipulations are that the provisions of 11 U.S.C. § 362 are mandatory upon filing and specifically address the application of the stay when there have been repeat bankruptcy filings, and that the benefits of the stay cannot be waived. Allowing waiver would encourage creditors to attempt to impose a prebankruptcy waiver in many form contracts, in which there is a significant imbalance in bargaining power. Farm Credit of Cent. Fla., ACA v. Polk, 160 B.R. 870 (M.D. Fla. 1994) (prepetition agreement by debtor not to contest motion for relief from stay in any later bankruptcy was not self-executing or binding on the debtor). *See also In re* Pease, 195 B.R. 431 (Bankr. D. Neb. 1996) (prepetition contractual provision that waived automatic stay was unenforceable). *But see In re* Franklin, 802 F.2d 324 (9th Cir. 1986) (bankruptcy court has jurisdiction to construe stipulation entered in prior bankruptcy).
367 *In re* Bystrek, 17 B.R. 894 (Bankr. E.D. Pa. 1982).
368 *In re* Durkalek, 21 B.R. 618 (Bankr. E.D. Pa. 1982).
369 *In re* Taylor, 77 B.R. 237 (B.A.P. 9th Cir. 1987); *In re* Norris, 39 B.R. 85 (E.D. Pa. 1984); *In re* McClam, 2012 WL 526297 (Bankr. E.D.N.C. Feb. 16, 2012); *In re* Artishon, 39 B.R. 890 (Bankr. D. Minn. 1984).
370 Restatement (Second) of Judgments § 24 cmt. f (1982); *accord In re* Darling, 141 B.R. 239 (Bankr. M.D. Fla. 1992) (stay motion in chapter 11 case involved different issues than previously granted stay motion of same creditor in same debtor's prior chapter 7 case).
371 *In re* Bumpass, 28 B.R. 597 (Bankr. S.D.N.Y. 1983). *See also In re* Metz, 820 F.2d 1495 (9th Cir. 1987) (filing of successive bankruptcies does not necessarily show bad faith and may be perfectly proper); *In re* Johnson, 708 F.2d 865 (2d Cir. 1983) (court must inquire into facts to determine if change of circumstances occurred before concluding that second chapter 13 case is improper after dismissal of earlier case); *In re* Chisum, 68 B.R. 471 (B.A.P. 9th Cir. 1986) (filing four successive bankruptcies was not in bad faith when changed circumstances explained each filing), *aff'd*, 847 F.2d 597 (9th Cir. 1988). *Cf. In re* Strause, 97 B.R. 22 (Bankr. S.D. Cal. 1989)

(existence of pending chapter 7 case when chapter 13 case is filed is not automatic ground for relief from stay; court must determine whether chapter 13 case is in bad faith).
372 Restatement (Second) of Judgments § 27 (1982).
373 A default judgment does not meet the requirement that issues be actually litigated, so collateral estoppel does not apply. Restatement (Second) of Judgments § 27 cmt. e (1982).
374 *See In re* Fernandez, 212 B.R. 361 (Bankr. C.D. Cal. 1997), *aff'd on other grounds*, 227 B.R. 174 (B.A.P. 9th Cir. 1998).
375 *See* § 9.4.6.5.2, *supra*.
376 Fed. R. Bankr. P. 9011(a); *In re* Eisen, 14 F.3d 469 (9th Cir. 1994) (history of prior bankruptcy filings and dismissals justified dismissal of debtor's petition as one filed in bad faith; sanctions imposed on debtor for frivolous filing). *See also In re* Ulmer, 19 F.3d 234 (5th Cir. 1994) (Rule 9011 sanctions imposed on counsel for filing improper petition in violation of section 109(g)); *In re* Taylor, 884 F.2d 478 (9th Cir. 1989) (Rule 9011 sanctions may not be imposed on debtor or attorney for multiple filings absent finding that successive petitions were filed in bad faith); *In re* Jones, 41 B.R. 263 (Bankr. C.D. Cal. 1984) (sanctions of $500 against debtor and attorney filing debtor's fifth and sixth bankruptcy petitions); *In re* Eck, 34 B.R. 11 (Bankr. M.D. Fla. 1983) ($500 attorney fees awarded when debtor dismissed and filed new case on date of stay hearing).
  For a general discussion of the propriety of chapter 13 after previous bankruptcy cases see § 12.10, *infra*.
377 *See* § 9.3.3, *supra*.

have *in rem* effect in a subsequent bankruptcy involving the same property.[378] Because Congress has again delineated very specific rules governing such cases, there is no reason for courts to decide them on some basis other than that dictated by the statute.[379]

In addition, as to the question of whether a new bankruptcy case can be filed at all, Code section 109(g) provides statutory guidelines which explicitly articulate the standard for determining when repeat filings are not permissible. That section renders ineligible for relief under the Code any individual who within the previous 180 days has (1) suffered dismissal of a case for *willful* failure to abide by orders of court or to appear before the court or (2) requested and obtained *voluntary* dismissal "following" the filing of a request for relief from the section 362 stay. A companion provision in section 349(a) makes clear that, except as provided in section 109(g), the dismissal of a case, whether voluntary or involuntary, does not prejudice the debtor with regard to the filing of a subsequent petition.[380] These provisions strongly suggest that a court does not have authority to enjoin debtors from filing future cases or to dismiss repeat filings except under the terms specified in the statute.[381]

Section 109(g) was intended to be carefully targeted only at the types of repetitive filings in which there is rarely a justification for the new bankruptcy. Its precise language should be strictly construed, with careful attention paid to the statute's distinction between voluntary and involuntary dismissal. Thus, an involuntary dismissal following a request for relief from the stay does not bar a new case (unless it was for willful failure to abide by court orders or to appear). And a voluntary dismissal may be willful, but it does not bar a second filing unless it follows a request for relief from the stay.

The limitations on new bankruptcy cases after an involuntary dismissal, including the stay exception of section 362(b)(21),[382] do not apply if that dismissal was for reasons other than the debtor's willful malfeasance as specified in section 109(g). As the issue of willfulness is usually not litigated when the first case is dismissed, it normally must be raised by a motion to dismiss the second case;[383] the initial filing of the second petition cannot be barred because the court clerk has no way of knowing whether the previous case met the willful malfeasance test. For the same reason, it may be difficult for a secured creditor to argue that the automatic stay does not come into being in the second bankruptcy case based simply on an alleged violation of section 109(g),[384] and the operation of section 362(b)(21). It also would be improper for the court in the earlier case to enjoin a new filing within 180 days, especially if there had been no showing of willfulness in the earlier case, nor any notice that the right to refile would be considered at the dismissal hearing.[385]

Courts have generally recognized that willful malfeasance means more than inadvertence or even reckless disregard for the duties involved.[386] Thus, a dismissal for failure to make payments, or to appear in court, should not by itself bar a new case within 180 days.[387] However, the addition of other facts in a particular case may prove willfulness.[388] The debtor must be permitted an opportunity to introduce evidence that the conduct in question was not willful before the court may dismiss a new petition under section 109(g).[389]

Debtors' attorneys have had to litigate how broadly to construe the prohibition of filings after voluntary dismissals when there has been a request for relief from the stay. If read literally, it could prevent a new case even if the debtor had successfully defended against a request for relief from the stay in the first bankruptcy, or if the creditor who had requested relief had subsequently been paid in full.[390] Moreover, there is no time

---

378 *See* 11 U.S.C. § 362(d)(4); *In re* Barner, 597 F.3d 651, 654 (5th Cir. 2010) (specific rules for applying stay relief in prior case to subsequent case did not apply when prior case was filed before effective date of section 362(d)(4)). *See also* § 9.4.6.5.2, *supra*.

379 *In re* McClam, 2012 WL 526297 (Bankr. E.D.N.C. Feb. 16, 2012).

380 11 U.S.C. § 349(a) currently refers to section 109(f) rather than section 109(g). This reference is to a prior codification and is thus purely a technical error.

381 *See* § 3.2.1, *supra*. *See also In re* Frieouf, 938 F.2d 1099 (10th Cir. 1991) (court may not enjoin filings by a debtor beyond the statutory 180-day limit but may enjoin discharge of debts listed in prior dismissed case for a three-year period); *In re* Jones, 192 B.R. 289 (Bankr. M.D. Ga. 1996); *In re* Friend, 191 B.R. 391 (Bankr. W.D. Tenn. 1996). *But see In re* Casse, 198 F.3d 327 (2d Cir. 1999) (court has power to enjoin future filings for period longer than 180 days).

382 *See* § 9.3.3.6, *supra*.

383 *In re* Montgomery, 37 F.3d 413 (8th Cir. 1994) (debtor has burden of showing that prior dismissal was not for willful failure to attend or prosecute case). *See also* § 3.2.1, *supra*.

384 *In re* Flores, 291 B.R. 44 (Bankr. S.D.N.Y. 2003).

385 *In re* Surace, 52 B.R. 868 (Bankr. C.D. Cal. 1985). *But see In re* Tomlin, 105 F.3d 933 (4th Cir. 1997) (interpreting bankruptcy court order dismissing case "with prejudice" as one imposing a bar to refiling within 180 days).

386 *In re* Lewis, 67 B.R. 274 (Bankr. E.D. Tenn. 1986); *In re* Fulton, 52 B.R. 627 (Bankr. D. Utah 1985); *In re* Morris, 49 B.R. 123 (Bankr. W.D. Ky. 1985).

387 *In re* Howard, 134 B.R. 225 (Bankr. E.D. Ky. 1991) (failure to make plan payments debtors were unable to make and failure to appear at creditors' meeting not willful); *In re* Chmura, 63 B.R. 12 (Bankr. D.N.J. 1986); *In re* Glover, 53 B.R. 14 (Bankr. D. Or. 1985); *In re* Fulton, 52 B.R. 627 (Bankr. D. Utah 1985); *In re* Nelkovski, 46 B.R. 542 (Bankr. N.D. Ill. 1985). *See also In re* Hollis, 150 B.R. 145 (D. Md. 1993) (*pro se* debtor's failure to follow rules, due to ignorance of them, does not warrant dismissal of case with prejudice or a finding of willfulness under section 109(g)).

388 *In re* Correa, 58 B.R. 88 (Bankr. N.D. Ill. 1986) (dismissal warranted when, during previous bankruptcy, debtor had "voluntarily and intentionally" abused cocaine resulting in failure to comply with directives of the court); *In re* Patel, 48 B.R. 418 (Bankr. M.D. Ala. 1985) (the debtor's two prior chapter 13 petitions had been dismissed for failure to make payments).

389 *In re* Bradley, 152 B.R. 74 (E.D. La. 1993).

390 Most courts have taken a sensible approach to this aspect of section 109(g). *See In re* Richter, 2010 WL 4272915 (Bankr. N.D. Iowa Oct. 22, 2010) (second petition in no way thwarted creditors' rights when stay motion in prior case had been resolved by surrender of vehicle); *In re* Beal, 347 B.R. 87 (E.D. Wis. 2006) (provision not applicable when order granting motion for relief from stay in prior case had been vacated); *In re* Jones, 99 B.R. 412 (Bankr. E.D. Ark. 1989) (voluntary dismissal after unsuccessful motion for relief from stay in first case does not trigger 180-day limitation on subsequent filing); *In re* Milton, 82 B.R. 637 (Bankr. S.D. Ga. 1988) (motion for

limit as to how long before the dismissal the request for relief may have been filed. Thus, the section could be applicable even when the request for relief was filed five years before the voluntary dismissal and was based upon circumstances totally different than those existing when the second case is filed. In view of the potential unfairness of such results, courts have read a causal relationship into the word "following" in section 109(g), which was used instead of the more common "after" or "subsequent to," and have refused to dismiss a second bankruptcy when the rights of the party who sought relief from the stay in the first case have not been prejudiced.[391]

Finally, some courts have held that if a repeat bankruptcy case is dismissed under section 109(g), the 180-day period from the prior case may either be renewed for an additional 180 days[392] or tolled during the period that the automatic stay in the later case was in effect.[393] In any event, it is clear that section 109 eligibility requirements are not jurisdictional, and can be waived if they are not timely raised.[394]

9.7.3.2 Grounds for Relief

9.7.3.2.1 For cause

The first of the grounds listed in the statute for relief from the stay is a catchall. It provides that the stay may be lifted "for cause." While it is clear that a lack of adequate protection, as discussed below, is one such cause, the provision is meant to allow courts considerable discretion to grant relief for other reasons. Thus, legal proceedings against the debtor that have nothing to do with bankruptcy would ordinarily be allowed to go forward. Similarly, the court may lift the stay with respect to other activities that will have no effect on the bankruptcy. As a catchall provision, this ground for relief is also used to remedy a variety of other situations in which the stay is not deemed necessary by the court.[395] On the other hand, prepetition bad faith does not necessarily constitute cause for relief from the stay.[396]

Conversely, when the bankruptcy case may affect the debt, stay relief is normally denied.[397]

This section is also sometimes used by parties seeking to proceed with litigation that does affect the debtor's financial condition. In some cases, creditors argue that litigation on a nondischargeable debt should be allowed to proceed. Courts may consider various factors in deciding such matters, including whether the debt would clearly be nondischargeable if the plaintiff prevailed and how far the proceedings elsewhere had progressed.[398] When state court litigation is already in progress,

---

relief from stay which was settled between the parties does not preclude new filing for 180 days).

391 *In re* Sole, 233 B.R. 347 (Bankr. E.D. Va. 1998) (§ 109(g) not applicable when no connection between stay motion and dismissal); *In re* Duncan, 182 B.R. 156 (Bankr. W.D. Va. 1995) (same); *In re* Santana, 110 B.R. 819 (Bankr. W.D. Mich. 1990) (dismissal denied when second case filed within five days of prior voluntary dismissal because motion for relief filed in previous case had been withdrawn); *In re* Patton, 49 B.R. 587 (Bankr. M.D. Ga. 1985) (dismissal denied when creditor was not prejudiced and refiling was not "abusive"). See 2 Collier on Bankruptcy ¶ 109.08 (16th ed.). See also *In re* Eason, 166 B.R. 793 (E.D.N.Y. 1994) (section 109(g) inapplicable when debtors requested dismissal prior to motion for relief from stay even though dismissal order was entered after motion was filed); *In re* Hutchins, 303 B.R. 503 (Bankr. N.D. Ala. 2003) (refusing to apply strict language of statute when it would lead to absurd results); *In re* Bates, 243 B.R. 466 (Bankr. N.D. Ala. 1999) (section 109(g) not applicable when dismissal order was entered by mistake); *In re* Hicks, 138 B.R. 505 (Bankr. D. Md. 1992) (section 109(g) inapplicable when debtors requested dismissal prior to motion for relief from stay even though dismissal order was entered after motion was filed). *But see* Kuo v. Walton, 167 B.R. 677 (M.D. Fla. 1994) (court has no discretion to create exceptions to section 109(g)).

392 *In re* McIver, 78 B.R. 439 (D.S.C. 1987).

393 *In re* Carty, 149 B.R. 601 (B.A.P. 9th Cir. 1993) (period may be tolled as a matter of court's discretion, but would not be in this case because creditor sat on his rights by doing nothing until ten months after the second bankruptcy was filed).

394 *In re* Lewis, 392 B.R. 308, 314 (E.D. Mich. 2008). See § 12.2.3.3, *infra*.

395 *See, e.g.*, Claughton v. Mixson, 33 F.3d 4 (4th Cir. 1994) (relief from stay granted to permit effectuation of state court equitable distribution order which had distributed marital assets prior to bankruptcy in light of fact that debtor's estate had sufficient assets to pay all creditors even after distribution); *In re* Robbins, 964 F.2d 342 (4th Cir. 1992) (stay lifted to permit state court to enter equitable distribution judgment, with bankruptcy court retaining jurisdiction to determine allowance of claim created by state court judgment); *In re* White, 851 F.2d 170 (9th Cir. 1988) (stay lifted to allow divorce proceeding to continue in state court; state court may determine spouses' respective property rights but not enforce them); Casperone v. Landmark Oil & Gas Corp., 819 F.2d 112 (5th Cir. 1987) (relief granted to liquidate claim but not to decide dischargeability); Pursifull v. Eakin, 814 F.2d 1501 (10th Cir. 1987) (stay lifted to allow determination of lease validity under state law by state court); *In re* Busch, 294 B.R. 137 (B.A.P. 10th Cir. 2003) (relief granted to allow state divorce court to determine debtor's equity in former marital home); *In re* Pieri, 86 B.R. 208 (B.A.P. 9th Cir. 1988) (stay lifted to allow landlord to pursue cross-complaint against debtors in state court, because landlord could appropriately set off her claim against those of the debtors); *In re* Roberge, 188 B.R. 366 (E.D. Va. 1995) (court granted relief to allow determination of vested equitable distribution rights of debtor's spouse in state court), *aff'd*, 95 F.3d 42 (4th Cir. 1996); *In re* Hohenberg, 143 B.R. 480 (Bankr. W.D. Tenn. 1992) (relief from stay granted to pursue divorce, custody, alimony and support in state court, but other unsecured creditors given leave to participate in state court proceedings concerning property of the estate and bankruptcy court retained jurisdiction to control disposition of property of the estate); *In re* Palmer, 78 B.R. 402 (Bankr. E.D.N.Y. 1987) (relief granted to adjudicate state law matrimonial rights, but not to enforce them).

396 *In re* Ramkaran, 315 B.R. 361 (D. Md. 2004).

397 *See, e.g., In re* Kasco, 378 B.R. 207 (Bankr. N.D. Ill. 2007) (stay relief denied because debtor had right to pay off tax sale redemption amount through plan). *See also* Salta Group, Inc. v. McKinney, 380 B.R. 515 (C.D. Ill. 2008) (debtor could pay off redemption amount through chapter 13 plan).

398 *See, e.g., In re* Bogdanovich, 292 F.3d 104 (2d Cir. 2002) (stay should not have been lifted to permit entry of judgment on jury verdict and appeals because it was not clear whether debt was nondischargeable); *In re* Wilson, 116 F.3d 87 (3d Cir. 1997) (relief from stay granted to allow creditor to appeal adverse judgment in state proceeding alleging what would have been willful and malicious injury, because appeal was sole means for creditor to pursue

the bankruptcy court may grant relief from the stay on facts similar to those which would justify abstention under the statute.[399] On the other hand, the bankruptcy court may well be persuaded to determine a dischargeability issue itself before allowing the debtor to be subjected to proceedings in other courts.

Other grounds that might constitute cause may exist when the debtor is only a nominal party in litigation involving others.[400] However, if the debtor's interests are significantly involved, or if there is a possibility of duplicative or burdensome litigation for the debtor, the stay should not be lifted because that would undermine the purpose of the bankruptcy.[401] Such an action could, though, proceed as to all other parties.[402]

One other type of cause averred in a number of cases is the failure of a debtor to make current payments on a mortgage or other secured obligation. Generally, if the creditor's interest is adequately protected (as discussed in the next subsection), the stay should not be lifted solely for this reason.[403] Obviously, a creditor's refusal to accept payments or inaccuracies in crediting payments also should preclude it from obtaining relief under this theory.[404] Another common response, as discussed in a prior chapter, is to modify the plan to include a cure of the postpetition default.[405] However, if the failure to pay is prolonged or the collateral is depreciating, and there is no prospect for cure, a court may decide that there is no purpose in maintaining the stay.[406] Often, in chapter 12 or chapter 13 cases, the court articulates the reason for relief from stay as "failure to comply with the plan."[407]

The failure to make postpetition payments might also in some circumstances result in the creditor being allowed a claim for a priority administrative expense.[408] However, this claim is important only if assets of the estate are ultimately liquidated under chapter 7 or if the debtor ultimately fails to cure the delinquency, but still wishes to complete a chapter 13 plan.

On the other hand, if the debtor is in compliance with a confirmed plan, the grounds for a creditor to obtain relief from the stay are extremely limited. Courts have generally held that confirmation of the plan is res judicata on issues such as adequate protection and that a creditor is bound by the terms of the plan.[409] Even if the creditor's motion would have been granted prior to plan confirmation, the creditor is usually deemed to have waived its rights by not raising them in opposition to confirmation of a plan that did not protect them.[410]

9.7.3.2.2 Lack of adequate protection

Many motions seeking relief from the stay are based on the grounds that the movant does not have "adequate protection" for an interest in property. The provision of adequate protection is a basic concern of the Code, and thus what is meant by that term is of critical importance.

---

case without bankruptcy court effectively sitting as appellate court for state court judgment); *In re* Loudon, 284 B.R. 106 (B.A.P. 8th Cir. 2002) (relief granted allowing state court to determine liability and damages but limiting enforcement of any judgment); *In re* Dixie Broad., 871 F.2d 1023 (B.A.P. 11th Cir. 1989) (debtor's apparent bad faith in filing bankruptcy considered a factor in allowing state court specific performance lawsuit to go forward); *In re* Harris, 4 B.R. 506 (S.D. Fla. 1980) (action allowed to proceed after declaratory judgment that judgment for plaintiff would be res judicata on all facts necessary to show nondischargeability).

399 *See, e.g., In re* Kissinger, 72 F.3d 107 (9th Cir. 1995) (relief granted for completion of trial on large claim which needed to be determined before chapter 11 reorganization could be completed).

See § 14.5, *infra*, for a further discussion of mandatory and discretionary abstention. *See also In re* Tucson Estates, Inc., 912 F.2d 1162 (9th Cir. 1990).

400 *See In re* Fernstrom Storage & Van Co., 938 F.2d 731 (7th Cir. 1991) (relief from stay allowed for creditor to proceed against debtor's insurers); *In re* Holtkamp, 669 F.2d 505 (7th Cir. 1982) (personal injury action allowed to go forward when insurer assumed full financial responsibility); *In re* Traylor, 94 B.R. 292 (Bankr. E.D.N.Y. 1989) (relief from stay granted to allow accident victims to proceed against debtor's insurer even though their claim against the debtor had been discharged); *In re* Honosky, 6 B.R. 667 (Bankr. S.D. W. Va. 1980) (stay lifted to extent necessary to proceed with suit against debtor which would be defended by insurance company that would be liable for a judgment).

401 *Compare In re* Hawaiian Mini Storage Sys., Inc., 4 B.R. 489 (Bankr. D. Haw. 1980) *with In re* Cloud Nine, Ltd., 3 B.R. 202 (Bankr. D.N.M. 1980).

402 *See, e.g.*, Stone's Pharmacy, Inc. v. Pharmacy Accounting Mgmt., Inc., 875 F.2d 665 (8th Cir. 1989) (debtor not a necessary party to lawsuit; lawsuit allowed to go forward as to other parties).

403 *See In re* Nichols, 440 F.3d 850 (6th Cir. 2006); Household Fin. Corp. v. Adams, 27 B.R. 582 (D. Del. 1983); *In re* Mathews, 208 B.R. 506 (Bankr. N.D. Ill. 1997) (stay relief inappropriate after debtor missed two postpetition mortgage payments, especially given an $8000 equity cushion); *In re* Mannings, 47 B.R. 318 (Bankr. N.D. Ill. 1985); *In re* Davis, 11 B.R. 680 (Bankr. E.D. Pa. 1981). *See also In re* Can-Alta Properties, Ltd., 87 B.R. 89 (B.A.P. 9th Cir. 1988) (when creditor is protected by equity, debtor must be given a reasonable opportunity to propose and implement a confirmable plan); *In re* Raymond, 99 B.R. 819 (Bankr. S.D. Ohio 1989) (sporadic postconfirmation payments alone is not ground for relief from stay when no evidence established amount of postconfirmation arrears or value of collateral); *In re* Heath, 79 B.R. 616 (Bankr. E.D. Pa. 1987) (relief denied when creditor protected by equity cushion).

404 *In re* Alvarez, 101 B.R. 176 (B.A.P. 9th Cir. 1989); *In re* Schuessler, 386 B.R. 458 (Bankr. S.D.N.Y. 2008) (creditor created default by refusing to continue to accept payments at branch bank, equity cushion was sufficient to deny relief in case of minor payment default).

405 *See* §§ 8.7.4, 8.7.5, *supra*.

406 *See, e.g., In re* Wieseler, 934 F.2d 965 (8th Cir. 1991).

407 *See, e.g.*, Reinbold v. Dewey County Bank, 942 F.2d 1304 (8th Cir. 1991).

408 Grundy Nat'l Bank v. Rife, 876 F.2d 361 (4th Cir. 1989).

409 *See, e.g., In re* Wellman, 322 B.R. 298 (B.A.P. 6th Cir. 2004); Chevy Chase Bank v. Locke, 227 B.R. 68 (E.D. Va. 1998). *See also In re* Carvalho, 335 F.3d 45 (1st Cir. 2003) (bifurcation of a creditor's claim into secured and unsecured portions is not annulled by the mere act of granting relief from the automatic stay); *In re* Ealy, 392 B.R. 408 (Bankr. E.D. Ark. 2008) (no cause for granting relief from stay allowing Internal Revenue Service (IRS) to set off against tax refund when IRS debt was being paid in accordance with confirmed plan); *In re* Sullivan, 321 B.R. 306 (Bankr. M.D. Fla. 2005) (confirmation order was binding on creditor even though creditor had obtained relief from stay prior to confirmation); § 9.4.7, *supra*; § 12.11, *infra*.

410 *See* § 12.11, *infra*.

Yet adequate protection is not defined, except by example in section 361. We are told what does not provide adequate protection—the granting of a priority status as an administrative expense claim.[411] Thus, even if the assets of the estate clearly would cover such priority claims, an offer to allow such status is not sufficient. Examples of what can be sufficient include cash payments to compensate for a decrease in value of collateral due to use or depreciation, or providing an additional or replacement lien that is clearly sufficient to compensate any loss due to the stay or other situations in which adequate protection is required.[412]

Adequate protection is probably best described by the Code's language stating that it must insure the protected party's realization of the "indubitable equivalent" of that party's interest in the property in question.[413] While there is no definition of "indubitable equivalent" either, the concept is apparent. In a situation involving the automatic stay, adequate protection has been provided if there is no reasonably foreseeable way that the protected party's interest in the property can be economically harmed by continuation of the stay. Ultimately, whether adequate protection has been provided is a question of fact to be decided by the bankruptcy court.[414]

In general, the Code contemplates that the debtor will propose methods of providing adequate protection that are intended to satisfy a party who might seek relief from the stay. The only exceptions to this rule are embodied in section 1326(a)(1) and (a)(4), which mandate a method of adequate protection: periodic payments to certain secured creditors prior to plan confirmation and proof of insurance (although the payment provision is subject to the court ordering otherwise under section 1326(a)(3)).[415] Besides those methods of adequate protection mentioned above, others might include a cash security deposit, procurement of a guarantor, obtaining insurance,[416] or anything else that protects the interests of the other party. There are no limits on what might satisfy this requirement except those of the imagination.

One of the most common and important examples of adequate protection for a secured creditor is the existence of an equity "cushion." For example, in the case of a $60,000 mortgage on a $150,000 house, the existence of $90,000 in equity provides protection to the creditor. Even if the stay is continued for quite a while, the creditor should still easily be able to fully satisfy its claim, by foreclosure if necessary, when the stay is terminated.[417] In other words, unless the collateral is worth less than the claim or will depreciate so much that it might not fully satisfy the claim, adequate protection is normally provided by an equity cushion. If the possibility of destruction is eliminated, usually by insurance, real estate collateral values will, in most cases, remain high enough to provide adequate protection. With depreciating collateral, such as motor vehicles, it may also be necessary to provide, through a chapter 13 plan or by agreement with the creditor, for periodic cash payments which will reduce the claim at least as fast as the value of the collateral decreases.[418] The court may monitor or reconsider the situation at later dates to ensure that the creditor is protected.[419]

There is sometimes a question as to how much of an equity cushion the creditor is entitled to have. It seems clear from the statute that it is not necessarily the amount originally bargained for in the transaction, but rather can be considerably less. The purpose of the provision is to allow the court to decide what is adequate to protect the creditor's interest, even if the creditor once had better than adequate protection.[420]

---

411 11 U.S.C. § 361(3).

412 *See In re* Besler, 19 B.R. 879 (Bankr. D.S.D. 1982). *See also* 11 U.S.C. § 361(1), (2).

    Adequate protection does not include protection against lost "opportunity costs" incurred by not being able to immediately foreclose on collateral and reinvest the proceeds. United Sav. Ass'n of Tex. v. Timbers of Inwood Forest Assocs. Inc., 484 U.S. 365, 108 S. Ct. 626, 98 L. Ed. 2d 740 (1988). That decision must be applied retroactively. *In re* Cimarron Investors, 848 F.2d 974 (9th Cir. 1988).

    A guaranty by a non-debtor party may serve as adequate protection when that guaranty is secured by sufficient collateral. *See, e.g., In re* T.H.B. Corp., 85 B.R. 192 (Bankr. D. Mass. 1988).

    Adequate protection is also required in other situations besides stay litigation. *See* 11 U.S.C. § 364(d)(1)(B). However, the discussion here will concentrate on automatic stay cases.

413 11 U.S.C. § 361(3).

414 *In re* O'Connor, 808 F.2d 1393 (10th Cir. 1987) (whether adequate protection provided was a question of fact subject to review under "clearly erroneous" standard).

415 *See* Chapter 12, *infra*, for discussion of chapter 13 adequate protection payment requirements.

416 The courts are divided as to whether Federal Housing Administration insurance or Veterans Administration guarantees on home mortgages can constitute adequate protection. *Compare In re* Roane, 8 B.R. 997 (Bankr. E.D. Pa.), *aff'd*, 14 B.R. 542 (E.D. Pa. 1981), *with In re* Britton, 9 B.R. 245 (Bankr. E.D. Pa. 1981).

417 Cases applying this principle include: *In re* Schuessler, 386 B.R. 458 (Bankr. S.D.N.Y. 2008); *In re* Heath, 79 B.R. 616 (Bankr. E.D. Pa. 1987) (thirty-nine percent equity cushion in property appraised at $32,000); *In re* Shockley Forest Indus., 5 B.R. 160 (Bankr. N.D. Ga. 1980) (additional security provided collateral which far exceeded claim); *In re* Breuer, 4 B.R. 499 (Bankr. S.D.N.Y. 1980) (debtor's agreement to cure default promptly plus cushion of $21,000 were adequate protection); *In re* Rogers Dev. Corp., 2 B.R. 679 (Bankr. E.D. Va. 1980) (fifteen percent to twenty percent equity cushion gave adequate protection); *In re* McAloon, 1 B.R. 766 (Bankr. E.D. Pa. 1980) ($20,000 mortgage on $28,000 property has adequate protection). *See also In re* McKillips, 81 B.R. 454 (Bankr. N.D. Ill. 1987) (adequate protection payments necessary when equity cushion eroding, but only to the extent of the erosion).

418 *See* 11 U.S.C. § 361(1); *In re* Stembridge, 287 B.R. 658 (Bankr. N.D. Tex. 2002) (adequate protection payments must be credited towards amounts to be paid under section 1325(a)(5)(B) to satisfy allowed secured claim), *rev'd*, 394 F.3d 383 (5th Cir. 2004).

419 *See In re* Pitts, 2 B.R. 476 (Bankr. C.D. Cal. 1979) (small equity cushion with court monitoring every few months sufficient to provide adequate protection). Adequate protection for interests in personal property is also required by sections 1325(a)(5) and 1326(a)(1). *See* chapters 11 and 12, *infra*.

420 *In re* San Clemente Estates, 5 B.R. 605 (Bankr. S.D. Cal. 1980). *See also In re* Ahlers, 794 F.2d 388 (8th Cir. 1986) (considering the extent to which a creditor is entitled to adequate protection for potential delays associated with foreclosure), *rev'd on other grounds*, 485 U.S. 197 (1988). *But see In re* Tucker, 5 B.R. 180 (Bankr. S.D.N.Y. 1980) ($6500 cushion on $88,000 property inadequate

This consideration in turn raises the question of whether equity encumbered by soon-to-be-avoided liens should be counted in calculating amounts of equity available as a cushion.[421] The better view is that the equity should be considered unencumbered, once the court is satisfied that the liens will be avoided, because the main determinant is the amount of equity that will actually be available to satisfy the creditor seeking relief from the stay.[422] For the same reason, liens junior to that of the party seeking relief should not be considered in determining adequate protection.[423]

Perhaps the most useful concept of adequate protection in the foreclosure or repossession context, because the debtor will often have little or no equity in the property at issue, is the concept of cash payments to compensate the creditor for the collateral's depreciation.[424] This provision of the Code allows the debtor to propose a plan in a chapter 13 case which, in effect, cures or pays off the debt on a car or home. As long as the debtor makes the plan payments, the creditor is adequately protected within the meaning of the Code.

Alternatively, when the debtor cannot afford the necessary plan, it may occasionally be an option to provide an additional or replacement lien which can constitute adequate protection.[425] For example, if the debtor owns two cars and only one is encumbered, a lien on the second may be offered to the secured creditor as adequate protection. Of course, the risk in doing so is that the creditor will then have a security interest in both automobiles rather than just one. If payments cannot be made the debtor might lose both. For this reason, the strategy is advisable only in the most extreme cases.

Thus, in opposing a creditor's claim that adequate protection has not been provided, it is necessary to show that the creditor will not be economically harmed by continuation of the stay. Even if no equity can be shown, the stay may be continued if the creditor's then-current interest is protected.[426] For example, a tenant may offer to make payments on a lease equivalent to what the lessor would receive by renting the property at that time to another tenant,[427] or a debtor may propose payments on an automobile loan that protect the creditor against depreciation.

Finally, it should be pointed out to the court that section 362(d) does not require termination of the stay when there is no adequate protection. The stay may be modified to provide a time limit for some action, or conditioned, for example, upon monthly payments being made or other risks to the property being eliminated.[428] Partial relief may be granted to allow the litigation of certain rights to proceed in state court, with the final issue of the property's disposition to remain with the bankruptcy court. In short, even if there is no possibility of providing adequate protection, every effort should be made to salvage some of the benefits of the stay for the debtor.

9.7.3.2.3 Lack of equity or necessity for effective reorganization

Section 362(d)(2) sets forth one other basis for relief from the automatic stay that is applicable to consumer cases.[429] This ground is limited to acts against property and requires proof of two coexisting facts. These are:

- That the debtor does not have an equity interest in the property; and
- That such property is not necessary for an effective reorganization.

The purpose of this provision is to allow creditors to proceed against property that is of no value to either the debtor or the estate insofar as the bankruptcy case is concerned. If there is no equity in property that can be exempted by the debtor or sold by the estate and if the property is not needed in a reorganization of the debtor's affairs, there is no reason that the property is needed for bankruptcy purposes.[430]

Conversely, the stay should not be lifted if it protects some interest in property that the debtor may exempt under section 522, because allowing a creditor to proceed outside the bankruptcy court could jeopardize the exemption and thus the debtor's fresh start. Similarly, if there is equity in property that is not exempt, the court usually prefers that it be disposed of in the normal bankruptcy liquidation process.[431] And if the prop-

---

when liens increasing at $25 per day, no payments were offered, no insurance was in existence, and no successful plan was likely); *In re* Lake Tahoe Land Co., 5 B.R. 34 (Bankr. D. Nev. 1980) (dicta stating that for land a forty percent to fifty percent cushion is necessary); *In re* Pitts, 2 B.R. 476 (Bankr. C.D. Cal. 1979).

421 For discussion of lien avoidance, see § 10.4, *infra*.
422 Although the decision is vague, *In re* McAloon, 1 B.R. 766, 768 n.12 (Bankr. E.D. Pa. 1980), indicates that the court considered the fact that liens were avoided under 11 U.S.C. § 522(f).
423 *In re* Indian Palms Assocs., Ltd., 61 F.3d 197 (3d Cir. 1995) (junior liens are disregarded in determining senior lienholder's equity cushion for adequate protection purposes); *In re* Mellor, 734 F.2d 1396 (9th Cir. 1984).
424 11 U.S.C. § 361(1).
When the creditor's interest in the property is declining because of the accrual of more senior liens, such as property taxes, adequate protection may consist of payments in the amount of the debtor's monthly property tax liability. *In re* Busconi, 135 B.R. 192 (Bankr. D. Mass. 1991).
425 11 U.S.C. § 361(2).
426 *In re* Alyucan Interstate Corp., 12 B.R. 803 (Bankr. D. Utah 1981).
427 *In re* Dabney, 45 B.R. 312 (Bankr. E.D. Pa. 1985) (lease payments constituted adequate protection).
428 *See, e.g., In re* Polvino, 4 B.R. 677 (Bankr. W.D.N.Y. 1980) (stay modified to continue, provided debtors obtained confirmation of plan, paid back real estate taxes, mortgage payments, and arrearages, and avoided other liens within six weeks).
429 11 U.S.C. § 362(d)(3) is applicable only to single asset real estate cases, which are defined under section 101 to exclude cases involving residential real estate with fewer than four units.
430 For purposes of this subsection, equity is the difference between the value of the property and the total value of the liens on the property. Stewart v. Gurley, 745 F.2d 1194 (9th Cir. 1984). However, it probably can be successfully argued that invalid or avoidable liens should not be counted.
431 However, this process could include a release to a secured creditor later in the case if that was deemed in the interest of the estate. 11 U.S.C. § 725. See § 11.3.4, *infra*.

erty is necessary for an effective reorganization, the purposes of the bankruptcy reorganization provisions are protected by the continuation of the stay even when the debtor has no equity.

Because of poor drafting, a threshold question has arisen over whether these provisions are even applicable to consumer cases. Generally, the term "reorganization" is applied only to cases under chapter 11 of the Code, usually used for business reorganization. A few courts have interpreted the use of this term to mean that section 362(d)(2) is only partially applicable or not applicable at all to chapter 13 cases, in which the process is usually described as "rehabilitation" or "adjustment of debts" rather than "reorganization."[432] One such court thus found that the stay may be lifted only upon the grounds stated in section 362(d)(1).[433]

An alternative result based upon a finding that section 362(d)(2)(B) is inapplicable would be that the party seeking relief from the stay in a chapter 13 or chapter 7 case need only meet the lack-of-equity ground of section 362(d)(2)(A), because there is no "reorganization" at all. While for most purposes the determination of a lack of equity would also be a determination of a lack of adequate protection, such is not always the case. There may be significant equity over and above the lien of the creditor seeking relief from the stay that would protect that creditor's claim, even if that equity is encumbered by junior liens.[434] Moreover, because adequate protection can be provided by other means, for example, by periodic payments, permitting the stay to be lifted upon a simple showing of no equity would seriously undermine the concept of adequate protection, by not allowing use of these other means specifically mentioned in the statute.

The more accepted and better view is that chapter 13 cases, at least, were meant to be included within the term "reorganization."[435] This view also received some Congressional recognition by clarifying amendments proposed in both the House and Senate versions of technical amendments to the Code.[436] In terms of the purpose of the stay, it is just as necessary to protect completion of a chapter 13 plan as it is to protect completion of a corporate reorganization, and the term "reorganization" should be deemed to include such cases.[437]

In cases in which relief is sought under these provisions, questions of how property is to be valued necessarily become crucial. Should the property be given a liquidation value, a wholesale value, or a replacement-cost value?[438] As of what date should the property be valued? The answers to these questions, in many cases, will determine whether relief from the stay is granted.

Generally, at this stage of the case it is in the debtor's interest that a high value, such as the replacement value, be placed on the property, to show that equity exists and that the creditor is adequately protected.[439] It can be argued that section 362(d)(2) is at least partially concerned with the possibility of the debtor having to replace property necessary for a reorganization if the stay were lifted and that, therefore, the replacement value is the proper criterion for determining the debtor's equity in stay proceedings.

On the other hand, the debtor's counsel should be careful to assess what effect a high valuation could have later in the case. For example, that same high value might well be the amount found necessary to redeem the property from a lien under section 722 or to satisfy an allowed secured claim under section 1325(a)(5).[440] Although it can be argued that different values should be used in those situations because the purpose of the valuation is different,[441] it is likely that the court's earlier determination of value in the stay proceedings will be of great importance.

In chapter 13 cases, the debtor's testimony is usually sufficient to prove the necessity of assets for a reorganization. If the property is a house in which the debtor lives, the burdens and expense of a forced move, along with higher housing costs, can easily be shown to have enough disruptive potential to cause failure of a chapter 13 plan. Similarly, if the property in question is an automobile necessary for transportation to work or other important family business, it is not difficult to prove the deleterious effects on a plan that would be caused by its loss. As for "luxury" items, such as entertainment equipment or a second car not needed for work, the test is somewhat more

---

432 *In re* Feimster, 3 B.R. 11 (Bankr. N.D. Ga. 1979).
433 *Id.*
434 *See In re* Indian Palms Assocs., Ltd., 61 F.3d 197 (3d Cir. 1995) (although junior liens are disregarded in determining senior lienholder's equity cushion for adequate protection purposes, they are counted in determining equity under section 362(d)(2)).
435 *In re* Pittman, 8 B.R. 299 (D. Colo. 1981); *In re* McAloon, 1 B.R. 766 (Bankr. E.D. Pa. 1980); *In re* Zellmer, 6 B.R. 497 (Bankr. N.D. Ill. 1980). *See also In re* Purnell, 92 B.R. 625 (Bankr. E.D. Pa. 1988).
436 A technical amendments bill, S.658, was passed by both the House and Senate in the 96th Congress, but died at the end of that Congress without being passed into law. Later technical amendments in 1984 did not ultimately include the clarifying language.
437 This view is also adopted by 3 Collier on Bankruptcy ¶ 362.07[4][b] (16th ed.).

438 *See* Assocs. Commercial Corp. v. Rash, 520 U.S. 953, 117 S. Ct. 1879, 138 L. Ed. 2d 148 (1997) (replacement value must be used in valuing creditor's allowed secured claim for purposes of 11 U.S.C. § 1325(a)(5) if automobile is to be retained by debtor during term of plan).
   Although the valuation issues are not identical under sections 1325 and 362, a debtor may be able to use this case to advantage in the context of arguing for a higher valuation of property for the purposes of automatic stay litigation. *See generally* § 11.2, *infra*.
439 *But see In re* George Ruggiere Chrysler-Plymouth, 727 F.2d 1017 (11th Cir. 1984) (corporate debtor successfully argued for lower value when it wished to remit that amount to creditor to provide adequate protection).
440 See Chapter 11, *infra*, for a discussion of these provisions and the valuation approaches they have engendered.
441 In determining the amount of an allowed secured claim under section 506(a), value is determined "in light of the purpose of the valuation and of the proposed disposition or use of such property." *See also In re* George Ruggiere Chrysler-Plymouth, 727 F.2d 1017 (11th Cir. 1984) (value for stay litigation purposes was amount particular secured creditor could realize upon sale after deduction of expenses in its usual course of disposing of property); 3 Collier on Bankruptcy ¶ 361.04 (16th ed.).

difficult. When it can be shown that saving the property is a prime motivation for the plan, and that its loss will cause the debtor to give up on the plan, it should be possible to argue that this property, too, is necessary for an effective reorganization.[442] Of course, all of these possibilities are based upon the assumption that an effective reorganization or plan can otherwise be accomplished. If it cannot, then logically the property cannot possibly be necessary for an effective reorganization.[443]

9.7.3.2.4 Leases involving residential property

Special problems are posed under the stay provisions in cases that involve leases of residential property.[444] While it may be quite possible for a debtor to give a lessor adequate protection, perhaps in the form of a security deposit, it is usually difficult to argue that the debtor has equity in the leased premises unless the debtor has a long-term lease at a rate below current market values, or receives other benefits from remaining in possession, such as the special rights available in public housing or in a rent-control jurisdiction. Also, as to the property's necessity for an effective reorganization, it is usually somewhat harder to argue that moving to other leased premises is as great a hardship as losing a home owned by the debtor, because the lease usually guarantees only a short term of residency in any case. (Again, if rent control laws include eviction controls, stronger arguments can be made.)[445]

The greatest problems of persuasion arise because the debtor, by means of the stay, could, in effect extend a lease beyond the term to which she was otherwise entitled, and in some cases retain possession of property in which she otherwise had no rights whatsoever still in existence.

The most difficult cases are those in which the debtor's tenancy and right of possession, but not actual possession, are validly terminated before the bankruptcy is filed. In such cases, many bankruptcy courts had been loath to continue the stay, holding that the debtor had no legal interest in the property and there was no lease that the debtor or trustee might assume under section 365.[446] According to these courts, if the debtor and the estate had no legal interest in the property, then cause exists for lifting the stay, just as it would if the debtor were simply a squatter who had moved in after the commencement of the bankruptcy. They had held that if the debtor cannot assume the lease, perhaps because it is impossible to cure a default promptly as required by section 365, then there is no reason to allow the stay to continue.[447]

This issue was partially addressed by amendments to section 362 with respect to cases in which lessors have obtained a judgment of possession prior to the bankruptcy petition.[448] When these amendments do not apply, there are several reasons why the stay should be continued as to a leased property, even if the tenancy has ended or will soon end. These arguments are most convincing in cases in which the lessor has adequate protection and the continuation of the stay is necessary to an effective reorganization. The stay's provisions are meant to allow use by the debtor of property, such as collateral which would otherwise be repossessed, including property which the debtor does not technically "own."

Even if this argument is not accepted, as long as adequate protection is provided, there is no economic harm to the lessor, compared to what could otherwise be realized by renting the property. The substitution of money for the right of possession is in accord with a long line of recent cases holding that residential rental real estate is a fungible consumer good and not a unique interest for which money is no substitute.[449] This argument is especially compelling in the bankruptcy court, which as a court of equity must consider the "balance of hurt." When a lessor cannot show any real harm resulting from the stay, and protests only the continued occupancy by people to whom she does not choose to rent, the bankruptcy court should not feel compelled to lift the stay preventing eviction of the debtors.

For the same reasons, the fact that there is no lease for the debtors to assume is also not in itself cause for the stay to be lifted. Section 362 need not be read as limited by section 365, because the latter has other purposes. In a business case, for example, a long-term lease may be a valuable asset and the right to assume the lease may mean continued occupancy at below-market rents or the ability to assign the lease in exchange for a large cash payment. Such is not likely to be the case in a consumer case. If there is not an assumable lease, continued occupancy may still be allowed, but only with adequate protection, for example, rent payments at the market rate the lessor could otherwise receive.

---

442 Grundy Nat'l Bank v. Stiltner, 58 B.R. 593 (W.D. Va. 1986) (when debtor's primary purpose in filing bankruptcy is to save home, an "irrebuttable presumption" is created that the home is necessary to effective reorganization). *See also In re* Poissant, 405 B.R. 267 (Bankr. N.D. Ohio 2009) (property necessary to debtor's rehabilitation); *In re* McAloon, 1 B.R. 766 (Bankr. E.D. Pa. 1980) (court found property necessary upon debtor's testimony that he would not remain in chapter 13 if it were lost).

443 *In re* Canal Place Ltd. P'ship, 921 F.2d 569 (5th Cir. 1991) (creditor entitled to relief from stay when chapter 11 debtor has no prospect of reorganizing within a reasonable period of time); *In re* Sutton, 904 F.2d 327 (5th Cir. 1990); *In re* Sun Valley Ranches, 823 F.2d 1373 (9th Cir. 1987); *In re* Aries Enters., 3 B.R. 472 (Bankr. D.D.C. 1980).

444 *See generally In re* Reice, 88 B.R. 676 (Bankr. E.D. Pa. 1988).

445 *See In re* Gibbs, 9 B.R. 758 (Bankr. D. Conn. 1981), *later proceeding at* 12 B.R. 737 (Bankr. D. Conn. 1981).
See also discussion of leases in Chapter 12, *infra*.

446 See § 12.9.2, *infra*, for discussion of lease assumption under section 365.

447 *In re* GSVC Restaurant Corp., 10 B.R. 300 (S.D.N.Y. 1980); *In re* Mimi's of Atlanta, Inc., 5 B.R. 623 (Bankr. N.D. Ga. 1980); *In re* Greco, 5 B.R. 155 (Bankr. D. Haw. 1980); *In re* Racing Wheels, 5 B.R. 309 (Bankr. M.D. Fla. 1980); *In re* Aries Enters., 3 B.R. 472 (Bankr. D.D.C. 1980).

448 11 U.S.C. § 362(b)(22). *See* § 9.4.6.6, *supra*.

449 *See* Javins v. First Nat'l Realty Corp., 428 F.2d 1071 (D.C. Cir. 1970) (warranty of habitability implied through comparison of leased housing with other consumer goods); Centex Homes Corp. v. Boag, 128 N.J. Super. 385, 320 A.2d 194 (Super. Ct. Ch. Div. 1974) (specific performance of sales agreement denied because realty not unique); Case Note, 48 Temple L.Q. 847 (1974).

Lessors sometimes argue that the automatic rejection of a lease by a chapter 7 trustee under Code section 365(d)(1), which occurs in virtually every case involving a tenant, terminates the lease. This argument is incorrect, because the rejection simply abandons the lease back to the debtor.[450] Therefore, rejection of a residential lease under section 365 does not necessarily mean that the lessee may not continue in possession. It only means that the court must consider the lease in light of bankruptcy law provisions such as the right to adequate protection.[451]

These arguments are significantly strengthened by the 1984 amendments to the Code, which for the first time recognized the differences between residential and nonresidential leases. Section 365(c)(3) prohibits the assumption of a lease terminated prior to a bankruptcy only in the case of a nonresidential lease. Section 365(d)(4) provides that property be immediately surrendered to a lessor after rejection only if the lease is a nonresidential lease. And section 362(b)(9) makes clear that the stay applies even when a residential lease has expired, by excepting from the stay only nonresidential leases which have expired. The obvious implication of these provisions pertaining to nonresidential leases is that residential tenants are not bound by them, and may be allowed to remain in a property even when a lease has been rejected or terminated.[452] Similarly, section 362(b)(22) and (b)(23) create exceptions to the stay for residential leases only in very limited circumstances.[453] These provisions thus underline that, when a lessor is adequately protected, nothing in the Code requires granting the lessor relief from the automatic stay and imposing the hardships of eviction on a bankruptcy debtor.

Thus, although some early case law was not encouraging, there are strong arguments for the continuation of the stay with respect to leased property even after the lease terminates. However, the doubt about the case law and the provisions reducing a debtor's rights after a prepetition judgment for possession has been made militate in favor of filing before the debtor's rights under the lease are terminated under state law whenever that is possible.[454]

9.7.3.3 Tactics in Stay Litigation

9.7.3.3.1 Valuation problems

Necessarily, the tactics to be followed in litigating to preserve the automatic stay vary from case to case. Certain issues, however, are likely to recur frequently, and certain strategies are likely to be repeatedly useful.

One problem that will very often arise is that of proving the value of property.[455] Although the party seeking to lift the stay has the initial burden on the question of equity, it will normally be necessary to have evidence ready to rebut that party's proof. Obtaining such evidence is not always easy.

In some cases the debtor's testimony may be sufficient. If property was recently purchased at arms-length, the price may be a good indication of value. The debtor may also have knowledge (supplemented by certified copies of deeds or other sale documents presented in evidence) of recent sale prices of similar properties. Neighbors or friends may be able to offer testimony about the value of their properties. Generally, a landowner's testimony as to the value of his or her land is admissible without further qualification.[456] The debtor should usually testify to the basis for her opinion, such as review of recent sales, asking prices, or industry guides on the Internet,[457] discussions with possible brokers or dealers, or discussions with neighbors. In the case of a life estate or remainder interest, the debtor can cite Internal Revenue Service tables.[458]

More common is the use of experts in property appraisal. Their expertise, of course, allows them to render opinions regarding the value of property. In most places real estate appraisers are available to testify; in larger cities they may be employed full time in that profession, while in other areas they are usually real estate brokers. In either case, paying their fees may be a real hardship for some clients. In cases in which appraisers are necessary, however, this relatively small investment may save thousands of dollars for a client.

For appraisals of property other than real estate, obtaining an expert may be difficult. In cases involving motor vehicles or mobile homes, standard industry guides may be acceptable as evidence, and in many areas, auctioneers are willing and able to testify to the value of consumer goods. When property such as an automobile is worth less than the standard value for that model based on, for example, mechanical problems, testimony of a mechanic or used car dealer may be necessary.

One way to ease the problem of proof, and in some cases shift the costs, is to engage in pre-trial discovery on issues of value. If a request for an admission of value is denied by an

---

450 See cases cited in § 12.9.1, *infra*.
451 *In re* Braniff Airways, 783 F.2d 1283 (5th Cir. 1986) (when there is a lease, adequate protection consists of reasonable value of debtor's use and occupancy). *But see In re* Miller, 103 B.R. 353 (Bankr. D.D.C. 1989) (once lease is rejected, landlord is entitled to relief from stay when debtor proposes to pay only current monthly rent).
452 *But see In re* Williams, 144 F.3d 544 (7th Cir. 1998) (bankruptcy court did not abuse discretion in granting relief from stay for lessor to continue eviction proceedings in which state court could better assess debtor's defenses); Robinson v. Chicago Hous. Auth., 54 F.3d 316 (7th Cir. 1995) (relief from stay appropriate if lease terminated and the debtor has no way to revive lease under state law).
453 *See* § 9.4.6.6, *supra*.
454 *See* Bennett v. St. Steven Terrace Apartments, 211 B.R. 265 (N.D. Ill. 1997) (lease does not terminate until judgment is entered in forcible detainer case; no stay relief appropriate because debtor retains rights in the leased property).

455 Valuation issues arise in many different bankruptcy contexts. It is important to think through how valuation in one context may impact other valuation issues which are likely to arise in the case. *See* § 9.7.3.2.3, *supra*; §§ 10.3.3, 11.2, 11.5.5, *infra*.
456 Joe T. Dehmer Distribs. Inc. v. Temple, 826 F.2d 1463 (5th Cir. 1987); United States v. 3698.63 Acres of Land, 416 F.2d 65, 67 (8th Cir. 1969); United States v. Sowards, 370 F.2d 87 (10th Cir. 1966); *In re* Saucier, 353 B.R. 383 (Bankr. D. Conn. 2006).
457 Some of these guides are listed in § 5.3.4, *supra*.
458 Such tables are available at www.irs.gov/pub/irs-pdf/p1459.pdf.

opposing party and that value is later proved, the party denying the request can be required to pay for the costs of proof on that issue, including attorney fees.[459] Thus, it may be possible to obtain a written appraisal inexpensively and request that its authenticity and correctness be admitted, or even to simply request that a specific valuation be admitted. If the valuation is not admitted, then the cost of successful testimony can usually be shifted.

Similarly, if there may be a problem of admissibility, a request for admissions can demand that an opponent admit or deny the accuracy of sources such as the NADA used car guides, and the fact that they are regularly used as indicators of value in the trade.[460] Especially given the costs and expenses of proving disputed issues at trial, a request for admissions can result in a stipulated value which meets the debtor's needs and, on occasion, to withdrawal of a poorly grounded motion.

9.7.3.3.2 Other tactics

Discovery may be helpful, as always, in narrowing the issues or pointing up flaws in an opponent's case. In any case, because of the time deadlines involved in stay litigation, a motion for expedited discovery is usually necessary to complete discovery within the thirty days before the preliminary hearing. One positive result of such a motion is often a quick stipulation from the party seeking relief from the stay agreeing that the hearing (and the stay) can be continued beyond the thirty-day deadline.

Discovery may also demonstrate that the motion for relief from the stay is frivolous. It has become increasingly common for mortgage servicing companies to make errors in crediting bankruptcy debtors' payments and to file motions for relief from the stay when a debtor is current in postpetition payments.[461] In such cases, sanctions against the moving party and its attorney may be warranted.[462]

Other aggressive litigation strategies in fighting to preserve the stay may pay similar dividends. As discussed earlier, counterclaims and defenses probably can be considered and they definitely should be asserted. Many parties seeking relief from the stay expect little in the way of defense, and when faced with strong opposition, may decide they are getting more than they bargained for. If their motions meet answers raising questions of equity, laches, Truth in Lending or other consumer statutes,[463] they may well choose not only to delay the initial hearing but also to agree to a settlement favorable to the debtor. Alternatively, it is common for parties to agree to continue or dismiss a motion for relief from stay until an underlying question about the validity of a counterclaim or defense can be resolved in a separate proceeding.

In any case, it is unlikely that the court will want to decide a complicated case within the short time provided for the preliminary hearing. The debtor can then take advantage of the section 362(e) provisions allowing the preliminary hearing to be continued for up to thirty days, arguing that the pleadings and discovery to date show a reasonable likelihood that she will prevail at the final hearing. Of course, if the party seeking relief from the stay has not cooperated in discovery, additional grounds exist for continuing the hearing. It should always be pointed out that that party will have another day in court, that the continuation of the stay is only like a preliminary injunction, and that the harm to that party is relatively slight in comparison to the potential for harm to the debtor.

Finally, it should be remembered, and argued forcefully, that while the statute provides that relief from the stay may be granted in certain circumstances, that relief need not be complete lifting of the stay. Lesser relief, such as conditioning the stay on certain actions of the debtor or modifying it to give the debtor a reasonable period of time to relinquish property or get other affairs in order, is expressly contemplated by section 362(d) and should be granted, when appropriate, under the court's equitable powers.[464] In such cases, the debtor should be sure to oppose, if possible, the addition of attorney fees for the creditor's action, especially if such action was unnecessary because the matter could have been resolved without court intervention, or if the debt is undersecured.[465] The debtor also must monitor the creditor's subsequent actions to be sure they do not exceed those permitted by the limited relief from stay that was ordered.[466]

9.7.3.3.3 Stays pending appeal

If an appeal is contemplated after the automatic stay is terminated by order of the court or otherwise, it may be

---

459 Fed. R. Bankr. P. 7037 (incorporating Fed. R. Civ. P. 37(c)); *In re Sweeten*, 56 B.R. 675 (Bankr. E.D. Pa. 1986).
  See Form 111, Appx. G, *infra*, for a sample Request for Admissions on valuation of property.
460 See § 11.2.2.3.2, *infra*.
461 *See, e.g., In re Webber*, 314 B.R. 1 (Bankr. N.D. Okla. 2004) (lender had misapplied payments and there was no basis for motion).
462 *In re Wilson*, 2011 WL 1337240 (Bankr. E.D. La. Apr. 6, 2011) (sanctioning mortgage processor for submitting false and deceptive purported affidavits). See § 9.7.3.1.4, *supra*.
463 *See* § 9.7.3.1.3, *supra*; Form 42, Appx. G.4, *infra*.
464 Courts also should not grant requests in stay litigation for relief beyond the issue of whether, and to what extent, the stay remains in place. *See In re Van Ness*, 399 B.R. 900 (Bankr. E.D. Cal. 2009) (court denied creditor's request for bans on filing of future bankruptcy cases by other persons, bans on automatic stays in future cases, and authorization for sheriff to ignore a future bankruptcy case when conducting an eviction).
465 *See In re Kamai*, 316 B.R. 544 (B.A.P. 9th Cir. 2004) (challenge to creditor's attorney fees for stay motion on which debtor largely prevailed could not be raised for first time on appeal); *In re Nair*, 320 B.R. 119 (Bankr. S.D. Tex. 2004) (creditor sanctioned for seeking fees on undersecured claim), *aff'd*, 202 Fed. Appx. 765 (5th Cir. 2006); *In re Cox*, 251 B.R. 446 (Bankr. W.D.N.Y. 2000) (bankruptcy court adopted policy which discouraged stay motions by oversecured lenders unless lenders gave debtors notice of opportunity to cure default in postpetition payments).
466 *In re Morris*, 2008 WL 4949892 (Bankr. N.D. Tex. Nov. 19, 2008) (domestic relations creditor and his attorney sanctioned for taking actions beyond those permitted by relief from stay order). *See also In re Wardrobe*, 559 F.3d 932, 934 (9th Cir. 2009) (denying preclusive effect to state court judgment for purposes of dischargeability litigation because relief from stay to obtain the judgment had been only for purpose of pursuing parties other than the debtor).

essential to obtain a stay pending appeal. The rules provide a fourteen-day delay in the effectiveness of an order granting relief from stay in order to provide time to seek a stay pending appeal, but a court may order otherwise.[467] Therefore, if a possible appeal is contemplated, a debtor should argue against any language in the court's order changing the normal fourteen-day delay of relief from the stay. Absent a stay pending appeal, property may be sold, litigation terminated unfavorably, or both.[468] In that event, an appeal may be rendered moot.[469]

9.8 Utility Services in Bankruptcy Cases

9.8.1 No Utility May Deny Service Within Twenty Days After Bankruptcy

Closely akin to the automatic stay provisions of Code section 362 are the provisions regarding refusal to provide utility service in section 366. While the general purpose of this section closely parallels that of the automatic stay, its operation and effect are somewhat different.

The first part of section 366 sets forth a general rule for at least the first twenty days after the petition is filed. No utility[470] may "alter, refuse, or discontinue service or discriminate against" the debtor solely on the basis of an unpaid prepetition debt or the filing of a bankruptcy case during that time period.

This subsection clearly prohibits a utility with notice of the case from shutting off the debtor's utility service in the first twenty days after the bankruptcy petition is filed. Thus, what was said earlier in this Chapter about giving notice to creditors and sanctions for violations of the automatic stay[471] applies equally in the utility context. Swift court relief, as well as possible fines and attorney fees, should be available for illegal shut-offs.[472]

One problem that may occasionally arise is a shut-off which is ostensibly based not merely on the unpaid debt, but rather on defective equipment, an illegal hookup by the customer, or some other reason. Naturally, such cases boil down to a problem of proof, with special attention being given to why the utility happened to terminate service immediately after bankruptcy.[473] If the utility has at any time stated that a payment of money will cure the problem, it should not be hard to show that the shut-off was an attempt to collect money, rather than to protect the public from unsafe equipment.

More complicated is the question of obtaining service if it was discontinued prior to the bankruptcy. Section 366(a) requires that the utility service be reinstated, because it cannot be "refused" solely on the basis of the unpaid debt. If service is refused due to an unpaid debt, section 366 is violated.[474] However, a clever utility may argue that it requires an initial deposit from all customers and therefore is not refusing service based upon the unpaid debt.[475] The answer to this contention lies in whether the utility is "discriminating" on the basis of that debt. Under the utility's normal practices, would a deposit have been required of a new customer, or to effectuate a reinstatement of service if a customer had paid the back bill in full? In most cases the answer to this question is no, and in fact many state or local utility regulations provide that service can

---

467 Fed. R. Bankr. P. 4001(a)(3); *In re* Derringer, 375 B.R. 903 (B.A.P. 10th Cir. 2007) (mailing and filing foreclosure notice within former ten-day stay period violated stay); *In re* Banks, 253 B.R. 25 (Bankr. E.D. Mich. 2000) (damages awarded against creditor who proceeded to evict debtor before expiration of former ten-day stay from order granting relief from stay). *But see In re* Duran, 483 F.3d 653 (10th Cir. 2007) (section 362(e) takes precedence over Fed. R. Bankr. P. 4001(a)(3) so creditor did not have to wait former ten-day stay period after order granting stay relief when time period in section 362(e) ended earlier).
468 *See* Fish Mkt. Nominee Corp. v. Pelofsky, 72 F.3d 4 (1st Cir. 1995) (automatic stay ended immediately upon dismissal of case).
469 *In re* Nat'l Mass Media Telecomm. Sys., Inc., 152 F.3d 1178 (9th Cir. 1998) (when foreclosed property was sold to nonparty, appeal from order granting relief from stay to permit foreclosure became moot). *See also In re* Highway Truck Drivers & Helpers Local 107, 888 F.2d 293 (3d Cir. 1989); *In re* Weston, 110 B.R. 452 (E.D. Cal. 1989) (foreclosure sale occurring after dismissal held valid because debtor had not obtained stay pending appeal); § 14.9.5, *infra*.
470 The term "utility" covers any supplier of utility services with a monopoly position. The legislative history of section 366 states: "This section is intended to cover utilities that have some special position with respect to the debtor, such as an electric company, gas supplier, or telephone company that is a monopoly in the area so that the debtor cannot easily obtain comparable services from another utility." S. Rep. No. 95-987, at 60 (1978), *reprinted in* 1978 U.S.C.C.A.N. 5846.
 The cases have given the term a similarly broad reading. *In re* Gehrke, 57 B.R. 97 (Bankr. D. Or. 1985) (electric co-operative association is a utility); *In re* Hobbs, 20 B.R. 488 (Bankr. E.D. Pa. 1982) (condominium owners association that sells electricity to condominium owner treated as a utility for purposes of section 366); *In re* Good Time Charlie's Ltd., 25 B.R. 226 (Bankr. E.D. Pa. 1982) (shopping mall providing electricity is a utility). *But see In re* Darby, 470 F.3d 573 (5th Cir. 2006) (cable television not a utility when it was not a necessity).
 Another purpose of the section is to assure that a debtor can obtain vital services, so that the elimination of monopolies by deregulation should not free providers of services such as water, gas, electricity, and telephone from the requirements of section 366. *See* 3 Collier on Bankruptcy ¶ 366.05 (16th ed.). *Accord* One Stop Realtour Place, Inc. v. Allegiance Telecomm, Inc., 268 B.R. 430 (Bankr. E.D. Pa. 2001) (deregulated local telephone service provider was "utility" under section 366).
471 *See* §§ 9.5, 9.6, *supra*; Forms 53–55, Appx. G.6, *infra*.
472 *See, e.g., In re* Smith, 170 B.R. 111 (Bankr. N.D. Ohio 1994) (actual damages and attorney fees awarded for willful disconnection of telephone service after notice of bankruptcy).
473 *See, e.g., In re* Parks, 2008 WL 2003163 (Bankr. N.D. Ohio May 6, 2008) (evidence suggested that debtor's receipt of unbilled service resulted from utility's oversight or negligence in failing to complete shut off years earlier rather than tampering by debtor).
474 *In re* Whittaker, 882 F.2d 791 (3d Cir. 1989); *In re* Parks, 2008 WL 2003163 (Bankr. N.D. Ohio May 6, 2008) (actual damages and attorney fees awarded for gas utility's willful stay violation in demanding payment for one year of prepetition service as condition to restoration of debtor's service); *In re* Tarrant, 190 B.R. 704 (Bankr. S.D. Ga. 1995) (city utility ordered to pay damages and attorney fees for violating sections 362 and 366 by demanding prepetition debt repayment as condition of reconnection).
475 *See In re* Roberts, 29 B.R. 808 (E.D. Pa. 1983) (deposit required before service provided when nonbankruptcy customer would be required to post deposit).

be reinstated if even a part of the prior bill is paid, with an agreement to pay the rest in installments. If such is the case, then a refusal to reinstate when the bill has not been paid should be considered discrimination solely on the basis of the unpaid debt.[476] Similarly, if service was terminated prepetition solely for nonpayment, a reconnection fee that would not have been charged to someone had been current in payments when service was terminated would be prohibited as discrimination based solely upon nonpayment of the prepetition debt.

9.8.2 A Utility May Be Able to Discontinue Service If the Debtor Does Not Furnish Adequate Assurance of Future Payment

9.8.2.1 Procedure

Section 366(a) is significantly limited by section 366(b) which provides that a utility may "alter, refuse or discontinue service" if the debtor does not, within twenty days after filing a voluntary petition, furnish adequate assurance of future payment.

The statutory section cited above reads, at first glance, as if it is self-executing, and it is generally understood to mean that the utility may terminate service after twenty days without special permission from the court if it does not believe adequate assurance has been provided.[477] If that is the local understanding, then it behooves the debtor to come to some agreement with the utility as to what is adequate assurance before the twenty days has run. Counsel should become familiar with local practice regarding adequate assurance because, for example, some utilities do not require deposits or other forms of adequate assurance except in extraordinary cases. If there is any doubt about local practice, counsel may wish to send a letter to all utilities, immediately upon filing the bankruptcy petition, stating that the debtor is prepared to provide adequate assurance, but that none will be provided unless a request is made by the utility.[478] In cases in which there is a dispute, the debtor must seek the court's intervention along with preliminary relief if the utility will not agree to continue service.

However, a utility may take substantial risks in terminating service when the debtor has tendered what she believes to be adequate assurance. The second sentence of section 366(b) states that "[o]n request of a party in interest and after notice and a hearing, the court may order reasonable modification of the amount . . . necessary to provide adequate assurance." Thus, the "parties in interest" required to seek court modification of a deposit or security with which they do not agree include the utility providers.

At least one court has suggested that there is a presumption that the deposit terms permitted by state utility regulations set the maximum a utility can demand without court modification.[479] If a utility does not seek a determination regarding adequate assurance before altering service, it can be strongly argued that it is in contempt of the requirements of section 366(b) if a court later determines the amount that had been tendered by a debtor to be sufficient for adequate assurance.[480] This reading, which places utilities terminating service without court permission at risk of contempt, more closely parallels the operation of the automatic stay provisions, as well as the executory contract provisions,[481] as section 366 was intended to do.[482]

9.8.2.2 Adequate Assurance of Future Payment

9.8.2.2.1 Methods of adequate assurance

The term "adequate assurance" is not defined in the Code, except to the extent that examples are given. Those examples are a "deposit or other security."[483] Certainly, the former of these is the most common in consumer cases. However, it is clear from the statute that there are other possibilities, including the voluntary granting of a lien on property of the debtor to be available in the event of a postpetition delinquency. In some states it may be possible to have a prepetition security deposit applied to provide postpetition adequate assurance.[484] Still another way of giving adequate assurance, at least in a chapter 13 plan in which significant payments are being made, would be the granting of priority status to any delinquent debt for postpetition utility service. This result is clear both from the legislative history,[485] and because there is no specific exclusion of the granting of an "administrative expense" (and thus priority status) in section 366 similar to that in section 361.[486]

---

476 *See In re* Whittaker, 882 F.2d 791 (3d Cir. 1989); *In re* Kiriluk, 76 B.R. 979 (Bankr. E.D. Pa. 1987).

477 *See, e.g.*, 3 Collier on Bankruptcy ¶ 366.03 (16th ed.). *See also In re* Stagecoach Enters., Inc., 1 B.R. 732 (Bankr. M.D. Fla. 1979).

478 *See In re* Am. Investcorp & Dev. Co., 155 B.R. 300 (Bankr. D.R.I. 1993) (section 366 places burden on debtor to furnish adequate assurance within twenty days).

479 *In re* Kiriluk, 76 B.R. 979 (Bankr. E.D. Pa. 1987). *See also In re* Cannon, 2008 WL 2553475 (Bankr. E.D. Wis. June 23, 2008) (debtor cannot be charged greater deposit than state regulations permit).

480 *See, e.g., In re* Tabor, 46 B.R. 677 (Bankr. S.D. Ohio 1985) (utility fined $250 as sanctions for contempt of court and $526 in damages for applying amount tendered to prepetition debt and requesting excessive amount as adequate assurance).

481 See § 12.9, *infra*, for a discussion of section 365.

482 3 Collier on Bankruptcy ¶ 366.06 (16th ed.).

Sending an improper termination notice can also be a violation of the automatic stay. Bedford Town Condo. v. Wash. Gas Light Co. (*In re* Bedford Town Condo.), 2010 WL 3777826 (Bankr. D. Md. Sept. 20, 2010).

483 11 U.S.C. § 366(b).

484 *In re* Cole, 104 B.R. 736 (Bankr. D. Md. 1989) (prepetition security deposit which constituted exempt property of the estate could be used as postpetition adequate assurance).

This strategy may not be available when the deposit secures a prepetition delinquency.

485 H.R. Rep. No. 95-595, at 350 (1977).

486 Va. Elec. & Power Co. v. Caldor, Inc., 117 F.3d 646 (2d Cir. 1997) (availability of administrative expense claim can be a component of adequate assurance; court need not order a security deposit or other assurance). *See In re* Hennen, 17 B.R. 720 (Bankr. S.D. Ohio 1982)

The enactment of such an exclusion in section 366(c), limited to chapter 11 cases only, reinforces this result.[487] In short, adequate assurance may be given in any way that protects the utility from an unreasonable risk of nonpayment, even if it falls short of an absolute guarantee.[488] Once a utility accepts a deposit as adequate assurance, it cannot later terminate service based on the deposit being paid more than twenty days after the petition.[489]

9.8.2.2.2 Adequate assurance not always required

Other questions also arise as to the necessity for adequate assurance. Several of these concern the interplay of section 366 with state customer service regulations which govern the utilities. One question is whether normal shut-off procedures required by such regulations can be omitted by the utility. While the utility may argue that section 366(b), which allows termination after twenty days, overrides state regulations, there are several reasons that this argument should not prevail. The first is that the overriding effect of the Supremacy Clause comes into effect only if there is a conflict between the state and federal law. Section 366(b) says only that the utility "may" discontinue service, not that it "shall" do so. If there are other reasons why, under state laws, the utility cannot discontinue service, then there is nothing which requires that those reasons be ignored.

For example, it is clear in most places that service cannot be terminated if the bill is fully current. The mere filing of a bankruptcy petition should not suddenly give the utility the right to terminate in such a case. Another indication that it was not the intent of Congress to give the utilities greater rights than they already have under state law is that "discrimination," prohibited in section 366(a), is conspicuously omitted from the actions allowed in section 366(b) if adequate assurance is not provided.[490] This conclusion is also supported by statements in the original Report of the Bankruptcy Commission that the term "adequate assurance," in a slightly different context, is not intended to give the non-debtor party greater rights in a case than it would otherwise have.[491]

Thus, if the state regulations do not require any deposit for continuance of service to someone who pays a prior utility bill before termination, it can also be argued that it would be discrimination to require a deposit from a debtor in bankruptcy whose utility bills are current.[492] Alternatively, the debtor's past record of prompt payments should be considered, in itself, adequate assurance.[493] Similarly, if a utility never requires a deposit from a new customer, then it should not be able to require one from a bankruptcy debtor, because that would be discrimination based upon the unpaid debt.[494]

A 1984 amendment to the Bankruptcy Code clarified these principles, by adding to section 366(a) an explicit prohibition of discrimination with respect to service based merely upon the filing of a bankruptcy. There is no exception in section 366(b) to this prohibition.[495]

9.8.2.2.3 Amount necessary for adequate assurance

Utilities often demand a deposit equal to the amount required of new customers under state utility regulations. Such regulations should set an upper limit on the amount of a deposit required.[496] While it is clear that the bankruptcy court has the power to set a lower deposit than required by such regulations for reinstatement,[497] the utility should have a heavy burden to

---

(every chapter 13 plan to include provision setting aside deposit out of initial payments to the trustee, to be held in reserve as adequate assurance for future service); *In re* George C. Frye Co., 7 B.R. 856 (Bankr. D. Me. 1980). *See also In re* Steinebach, 303 B.R. 634 (Bankr. D. Ariz. 2004) (debtors delinquent in utility payments could provide for deposit in plan, for which utility could file proof of claim); *In re* Epling, 255 B.R. 549 (Bankr. S.D. Ohio 2000) (approving plan provision requiring any utility seeking a deposit to file an administrative claim to be paid by the trustee).

487 *In re* Astle, 338 B.R. 855 (Bankr. D. Idaho 2006) (section 366(c) applies only in chapter 11 cases and therefore does not prevent chapter 12 debtor from providing adequate assurance of payment by extending to utility a first position, secured lien on the debtor's cattle).

488 *In re* Keydata Corp., 12 B.R. 156 (B.A.P. 1st Cir. 1981). *See* Form 57, Appx. G.6, *infra*.

489 *In re* Weisel, 428 B.R. 185 (W.D. Pa. 2010).

490 *In re* Cannon, 2008 WL 2553475 (Bankr. E.D. Wis. June 23, 2008).

491 Bankruptcy Commission Report, vol. 2, at 156, 157.

The term "adequate assurance" in the Commission's original bill was derived from section 2-609 of the Uniform Commercial Code, and thus the comments and interpretations of that section may be useful in determining its meaning.

492 *See In re* Heard, 84 B.R. 454 (Bankr. W.D. Tex. 1987); *In re* Coury, 22 B.R. 766 (Bankr. W.D. Pa. 1982); Form 56, Appx. G.6, *infra*.

However, in a case in which a previous security deposit was applied to pay the prebankruptcy debt, a utility may argue that it has the right to maintain the security deposit it would have been holding had the debt been paid in full.

493 *In re* Steinebach, 303 B.R. 634 (Bankr. D. Ariz. 2004) (utility has no unreasonable risk of nonpayment from debtor current in payments); *In re* Demp, 22 B.R. 331 (Bankr. E.D. Pa. 1982).

The enactment of an exclusion of this method in section 366(c), limited to chapter 11 cases only, makes the appropriateness of this approach even more clear.

494 *But see* Hanratty v. Philadelphia Elec. Co., 907 F.2d 1418 (3d Cir. 1990) (utility may require adequate assurance in bankruptcy even if it does not normally require security deposits from its new non-corporate customers).

Again, the enactment of section 366(c), excluding consideration of lack of a prior deposit in chapter 11 cases only, supports its consideration in cases under other chapters.

495 *In re* Coury, 22 B.R. 766 (Bankr. W.D. Pa. 1982); *In re* Shirey, 25 B.R. 247 (Bankr. E.D. Pa. 1982). *See also In re* Begley, 41 B.R. 402 (E.D. Pa. 1984), *aff'd*, 760 F.2d 46 (3d Cir. 1985).

496 *See In re* Steinebach, 303 B.R. 634 (Bankr. D. Ariz. 2004) (when utility not entitled to deposit under state regulations, those regulations provide guidance supporting decision that no deposit necessary under section 366(b)); *In re* Kiriluk, 76 B.R. 979 (Bankr. E.D. Pa. 1987).

For a discussion of utility deposit regulations, see National Consumer Law Center, Access to Utility Service §§ 5.2, 5.3 (5th ed. 2011).

497 3 Collier on Bankruptcy ¶ 366.03 (16th ed.). *See also* Sharon Steel Corp. v. Nat'l Fuel Gas Distrib. Corp., 871 F.2d 1217 (3d Cir. 1989) (court, not local regulating authority, has power to set terms under

show its entitlement to a deposit higher than the legal limit under state law deemed reasonable by the state regulatory body for even the worst cases.[498] Adequate assurance need not be the equivalent of a guaranty of payment.[499] When the prepetition debt is small, the debtor and utility may also agree that the debtor will pay the prepetition debt as adequate assurance and waive the automatic stay with respect to that debt.[500] However, it should be added that there seems to be nothing which would prevent the bankruptcy court from ordering continued service conditioned on prompt payments and specifically allowing a waiver of normal state termination procedures, with or without an additional court order, if those payments are not made.[501] The debtor may, in fact, propose such a solution as a last resort if it is impossible to otherwise provide adequate assurance. Obviously, such a waiver of state protections involves significant risk to the client and should be considered only with the greatest caution.

The guidelines to be used in determining the amount necessary for adequate assurance have slowly emerged from case law. Although the precise amount varies from case to case, the courts have tended to look to "all of the circumstances" including the prebankruptcy history of the debtor, the nature of the debtor, how much was owed, the previous course of dealing and conduct on the part of the utility, the stability of the debtor's present circumstances, the speed with which the utility may terminate service, the frequency of payments, and the likely usage of the utility in months to come.[502] Other factors that might be considered include the time of year (a deposit of one average monthly payment could pay for six months' heating service in non-winter months), the possibility of sureties, and the likely availability of energy assistance for some consumers. One reported case that considered the matter used most of these factors and finally set a deposit approximately equal to one upcoming winter month's bill, payable in three monthly installments by the debtor, with the utility to refund half of the deposit, with interest, a year later, and the other half according to its normal practice. The court also provided for speedy termination in the event of nonpayment.[503]

9.8.2.2.4 Postpetition termination procedures

Once the debtor has provided adequate assurance to a utility, the involvement of the bankruptcy court normally ends. Absent a contrary procedure specifically ordered by the court or agreed to by the debtor as part of the adequate assurance, state law will govern the treatment of postpetition debts.[504] Thus, any termination procedures required by state law or consumer rights provided by state law are applicable to debts arising after adequate assurance has been provided.[505] However, if the debtor converts a case from chapter 13 to chapter 7, the preconversion postpetition usage is treated as a prepetition debt that is dischargeable debt.[506] The debtor may be required to again provide adequate assurance if there is a new delinquency, but cannot be required to pay for the preconversion usage to maintain service.[507]

9.8.2.2.5 Possible special protections for customers of governmental utilities

Finally, there is a significant question as to the interplay of section 366 with section 525 of the Code, which prohibits discrimination by a governmental unit with respect to the granting of a "license, permit, charter, franchise, or other similar grant," solely because of bankruptcy or because of nonpayment of a debt discharged in bankruptcy. Assuming that the right to use normally monopolized utility service is some sort of license or grant, there is a good argument that the two sections must be read together in those frequent cases in which utilities are also "governmental units."[508] Reading these two sections together would mean that there could be no discrimination by such utilities based upon dischargeable debts and that bankruptcy debtors should be treated the same as persons who never had a debt to the utility.[509] Because consumers in the latter category need not supply a deposit for continued service, bankruptcy debtors should not be required to do so either. Following the same rationale, for a reinstatement of service, debtors should have the same rights as someone who had no previous debt to the utility or to any of the other creditors listed in the petition. If such persons need not pay a deposit to obtain service under the utility's normal practices, then debtors should be given the same treatment.[510]

In support of this argument, it should be noted that nothing in section 366 requires the utility to demand a deposit. Therefore, there is no contradiction between section 366 and section

---

which service must be provided); In re Cunha, 1 B.R. 330 (Bankr. E.D. Va. 1979).

498 See In re Hennen, 17 B.R. 720 (Bankr. S.D. Ohio 1982) (utility could not demand deposit in excess of that set by state regulation without violating section 366(a)).

499 In re Adelphia Bus. Solutions, Inc., 280 B.R. 63 (Bankr. S.D.N.Y. 2002).

500 In re Wells, 280 B.R. 701 (Bankr. S.D. Ala. 2001).

501 Va. Elec. & Power Co. v. Caldor, Inc., 117 F.3d 646 (2d Cir. 1997) (availability of administrative expense claim can be a component of adequate assurance; court need not order a security deposit or other assurance beyond remedies already available to utility under bankruptcy law).

502 In re Cunha, 1 B.R. 330 (Bankr. E.D. Va. 1979).

503 Id.

504 Begley v. Philadelphia Elec. Co., 760 F.2d 46 (3d Cir. 1985).

505 Id. See also In re Jones, 369 B.R. 745 (B.A.P. 1st Cir. 2007) (utility need not seek stay relief in chapter 13 case before terminating service based on a debtor's failure to pay for postpetition service).

506 11 U.S.C. § 348(d). See § 13.7, infra.

507 In re Davis, 311 B.R. 922 (Bankr. M.D. Ga. 2004).

508 "Governmental unit" is defined at 11 U.S.C. § 101(27).

509 See discussion of section 525 in Chapter 15, infra.

510 See, e.g., Fed. Communications Comm'n v. Nextwave Personal Communications, Inc., 537 U.S. 293, 123 S. Ct. 832, 154 L. Ed. 2d 863 (2003) (termination of licenses is contrary to section 525(a) if Commission would have allowed purchaser to retain licenses had it made timely installment payments on debt).

525, and normal rules of statutory construction require that every effort be made to read the two sections harmoniously.

9.9 Turnover of Property Under Section 542

9.9.1 The General Rule

The commencement of the case also activates two other automatic provisions relating to the debtor's property—sections 542 and 543. These sections require turnover to the trustee of property in which the debtor has an interest. Both of these sections have similar provisions; section 543 applies to "custodians,"[511] such as sheriffs or receivers legally appointed to take charge of the debtor's property,[512] and section 542 applies to all other "entities."[513]

Very simply, section 542 requires that any entity, other than a custodian, in possession, custody, or control of property that the trustee[514] may use, sell, or lease, or that the debtor may exempt, must immediately deliver to the trustee such property or the value of such property, unless the property is of inconsequential value or benefit to the estate. Its purpose is to assist in the gathering up of all property of the estate for the liquidation or reorganization that will take place in bankruptcy, as well as to effectuate the debtor's right to claim exemptions.

This general rule has few exceptions, stated in later subsections and not often applicable in consumer cases. Except for these, the rule normally applies to all property of the estate, because an individual debtor may usually choose to exempt any property of the estate,[515] that is, any property in which the debtor has any legal or equitable interest.[516] It applies no matter where the property is located and no matter how it was acquired by the entity in possession.[517] The rule also applies to recorded information, such as records subject to an attorney's lien.[518]

Another issue that has arisen is whether the turnover requirement applies once an entity no longer has possession of the property. Some trustees have demanded that debtors "turn over" funds that were in their bank accounts as of the filing of the petition because checks drawn on those funds had not yet been cashed, even though the checks were cashed before the trustee's turnover demand. The better reasoned decisions have held that a debtor has no obligation to turn over property the debtor does not have, and that the trustee's remedy is to seek avoidance of a postpetition transfer under section 549.[519] An additional issue is whether section 542 is the appropriate section to look at in this situation, because a more specific section provides merely that the debtor "surrender" property to the trustee.[520] "Surrender" is a term that indicates that the debtor not oppose the trustee taking property, but does not carry the affirmative requirement that property be delivered to the trustee, which in many cases of property having insignificant value the trustee would not desire. In addition, it makes no sense for a debtor to turn over to the trustee property that the debtor may exempt, as section 542 would require if applied to a debtor.

9.9.2 Questions of Scope: Secured Parties in Possession

Unfortunately, due to poor drafting of the statute, a question arose as to whether an entity must surrender property in which the debtor's present interest does not include a possessory interest but only something less, such as a right of redemption, for example, an automobile validly repossessed just prior to the bankruptcy. Noting that only property of the estate can be used, sold, or leased under section 363, some courts concluded that the estate's property was only the right of redemption in such cases, and not the right of possession, so that turnover was not required.[521]

This interpretation was unduly narrow, in that little would remain of section 542 if it were adopted. The principal purpose of section 363 is to allow the debtor to continue to use, sell, or lease property that the creditor could otherwise repossess due to its security interest in the property. Indeed, even "cash collateral," such as bank deposits subject to a right of setoff by the bank, may be used if adequate protection is provided.[522] Thus,

---

511 "Custodian" is defined at 11 U.S.C. § 101(11).
512 *In re* Skinner, 213 B.R. 335 (Bankr. W.D. Tenn. 1997) (sheriff who seized debtor's truck based upon writ of execution was custodian required to turn over truck to trustee).
513 "Entity" is defined at 11 U.S.C. § 101(15).
514 In a chapter 13 case the debtor exercises most of these trustee powers. *See* § 12.8.1, *infra*.
515 See Chapter 10, *infra*, for a discussion of what property may be exempted.
516 11 U.S.C. § 541. *But see In re* Charter Co., 913 F.2d 1575 (11th Cir. 1990) (debtor may not obtain turnover of funds claimed due on a disputed contract claim).
  The debtor's right to the property, however, must be more than a contingent claim on it. *In re* Graves, 396 B.R. 70 (B.A.P. 10th Cir. 2008) (trustee had no right to turnover from debtors' funds of the amount of tax refund they had applied to current year's taxes because debtors did not possess the funds), *aff'd as modified*, 609 F.3d 1153 (10th Cir. 2010).
517 *But see In re* James, 940 F.2d 46 (3d Cir. 1991) (court may not order turnover of currency confiscated as proceeds of drug transaction).
518 11 U.S.C. § 542(e).
  It should be noted that section 543 requires custodians to turn over "any property of the debtor transferred to" them, probably a broader collection of property interests than that covered by section 542.
519 *In re* Pyatt, 486 F.3d 423 (8th Cir. 2007); Shapiro v. Henson (*In re* Henson), 449 B.R. 109 (D. Nev. Mar. 29, 2011). *See also* § 5.3.3.2, note 5, *supra* and § 10.4.2.6.6, *infra*. *But see* Jubber v. Ruiz (*In re* Ruiz), 455 B.R. 745 (B.A.P. 10th Cir. 2011) (debtors required to turn over funds); Brubaker v. Jensen (*In re* Brubaker), 443 B.R. 176 (M.D. Fla. 2011) (debtors had duty to turn over funds).
520 11 U.S.C. § 521(a)(4). *See* § 3.5.2, note 130, *supra*.
521 *See, e.g., In re* Avery Health Ctr., 8 B.R. 1016 (W.D.N.Y. 1981), *overruled by* United States v. Whiting Pools, Inc., 462 U.S. 198 (1983). *Cf. In re* Smith, 921 F.2d 136 (8th Cir. 1990) (IRS not required to turn over tax overpayment when no timely claim for a refund was made by taxpayer before the bankruptcy).
522 11 U.S.C. § 363(c). *But see In re* Lyons, 957 F.2d 444 (7th Cir. 1992) (trustee could not compel turnover of retirement funds, even

it is evident that the debtor need not have a right to retain possession as of the commencement of the case in order to use, sell or lease property. For the same reason, if a debtor claims as exempt an equity interest in a repossessed vehicle, it is hard to see how that interest could be delivered except by return of the entire vehicle.

Most courts and commentators accepted this interpretation and found that turnover of property is required whenever the estate has any interest in that property.[523] For chapter 11 cases, the Supreme Court has explicitly held that, at least when the debtor has more than bare legal title, turnover is required.[524] Although the Court expressly declined to rule on the issue with respect to non-chapter 11 cases,[525] the logic employed in its decision also dictates turnover in chapter 13 cases in which property is necessary for the debtor's rehabilitation[526] and perhaps in chapter 7 cases in which the right of redemption could be exercised.[527] Thus, the turnover provisions should be very useful in regaining possession of repossessed automobiles, pledged goods,[528] goods subject to garagemen's, warehousemen's or artisans' liens, and any other property seized legally or illegally by an entity prior to the bankruptcy.[529] A willful failure to turn over assets seized prepetition may constitute an actionable violation of the automatic stay.[530] Additionally, failure to turn over property in a timely fashion may result in disallowance of a creditor's claim.[531]

Similarly, even if property has been legally seized after the filing of the petition, there is a duty to turn it over if it is property of the estate.

9.9.3 Procedure

Theoretically, a party obligated to turn over property should do so immediately upon notice of the case. Sometimes this turnover happens, especially when courts have made clear that it is required. Thus, the first step which should be taken on behalf of the debtor is to give the creditor or other party in possession notice of the case, both informal and formal, in a manner similar to that used to give notice of the automatic stay.

In practice, however, many holders refuse to turn over property. Many simply do not believe that they are required to do so, because these provisions are not nearly as clear as those

---

though they were estate property, when debtor had no right to withdraw them or use them).

523 *In re* Pester Ref. Co., 845 F.2d 1476 (8th Cir. 1988); Carr v. Sec. Sav. & Loan Ass'n, 130 B.R. 434 (D.N.J. 1991) (repossessed collateral must be returned). *See* 5 Collier on Bankruptcy ¶ 542.02 (16th ed.) (secured creditor in possession must turn over property).

524 United States v. Whiting Pools, Inc., 462 U.S. 198, 103 S. Ct. 2309, 176 L. Ed. 2d 515 (1983). *See also In re* Challenge Air Int'l, Inc., 952 F.2d 384 (11th Cir. 1992) (third party required to turn over to chapter 11 debtor funds subject to IRS levy).

525 United States v. Whiting Pools, Inc., 462 U.S. 198, 208 n.17, 103 S. Ct. 2309, 76 L. Ed. 2d 515 (1983).

526 *In re* Curry, 509 F.3d 735 (6th Cir. 2007); *In re* Gaimo, 194 B.R. 210 (E.D. Mo. 1996) (funds in bank account subject to prepetition IRS levy subject to turnover power in chapter 13 case); *In re* Attinello, 38 B.R. 609 (Bankr. E.D. Pa. 1984); *In re* Robinson, 36 B.R. 35 (Bankr. E.D. Ark. 1983). *But see In re* Kalter, 292 F.3d 1350 (11th Cir. 2002) (following prior *Lewis* decision, repossessed vehicle not property of the bankruptcy estate based on operation of Florida certificate of title statute); *In re* Lewis, 137 F.3d 1280 (11th Cir. 1998) (under Alabama law, debtor no longer has possessory right or title to an automobile after repossession so that only a right of redemption comes into the estate).

The *Lewis* and *Kalter* decisions fail to explain their inconsistency with United States v. Whiting Pools, Inc., 462 U.S. 198, 103 S. Ct. 2309, 76 L. Ed. 2d 515 (1983) and have not been followed by other courts. *See In re* Moffett, 356 F.3d 518 (4th Cir. 2004) (repossession did not terminate debtor's interest under Virginia law and turnover required); *In re* Robinson, 285 B.R. 732 (Bankr. W.D. Okla. 2002).

They have also not been followed in the 11th Circuit with respect to other types of liens. Tyree v. Guzman (*In re* Tyree), 2010 WL 4008300 (Bankr. N.D. Ga. Sept. 27, 2010) (turnover of property that had been seized by sheriff pursuant to levy was required; failure to turn over property violated automatic stay).

Indeed, even the Eleventh Circuit appears to be backing away from the decision, distinguishing a case under Georgia law based upon an opinion of the Georgia Supreme Court. *In re* Rozier, 376 F.3d 1323 (11th Cir. 2004), *relying upon answer to certified question*, Motors Acceptance Corp. v. Rozier, 278 Ga. 52, 597 S.E.2d 367 (2004).

527 *See In re* Gerwer, 898 F.2d 730 (9th Cir. 1990) (trustee may obtain turnover from secured party in possession in chapter 7 case).

528 *In re* Dunlap, 143 B.R. 859 (Bankr. M.D. Tenn. 1992) (property in possession of pawnbroker must be turned over to chapter 13 debtors if debtors provide adequate protection).

Although in some circumstances section 541(b)(8) provides that pledged goods are not property of the estate, that does not necessarily mean that they are not property that the debtor may use, sell, or lease if adequate protection is provided, nor does that provision limit a debtor's other rights, such as the right to cure a default in chapter 13.

529 *See, e.g., In re* Stage, 85 B.R. 880 (Bankr. M.D. Fla. 1988) (engagement ring held by debtor was conditional gift under state law in which the debtor had a cognizable interest). *But see In re* Hayden, 308 B.R. 428 (B.A.P. 9th Cir. 2004) (because holder of a lien by towing company depended on possession under state law, section 362(b)(3) exception to stay applied and retention of property did not violate stay); *In re* Boggan, 251 B.R. 95 (B.A.P. 9th Cir. 2000) (mechanic did not have to turn over debtor's car, held pursuant to mechanic's lien because maintaining possession of car was necessary to preserve existence of lien, and maintaining possession was therefore within exception to stay provided by section 362(a)(3)).

530 Thompson v. GMAC, L.L.C., 566 F.3d 699 (7th Cir. 2009) (refusal to return car that was repossessed prepetition is violation of stay); *In re* Knaus, 889 F.2d 773 (8th Cir. 1989) (refusal to turn over property lawfully seized prepetition after being given notice of the stay constitutes violation of the automatic stay remediable pursuant to section 362(h) (now 362(k)); *In re* Yates, 332 B.R. 1 (B.A.P. 10th Cir. 2005) (damages mandated under section 362(h) (now section 362(k))); *In re* Abrams, 127 B.R. 239 (B.A.P. 9th Cir. 1991) (retention of repossessed automobile after receiving notice of the bankruptcy is a willful violation of the stay); Mitchell v. BankIllinois, 316 B.R. 891 (S.D. Tex. 2004) (awarding damages and attorney fees of over $15,000). *See In re* Diviney, 211 B.R. 951 (Bankr. N.D. Okla. 1997) (compensatory damages and $40,000 in punitive damages awarded when lender failed to return repossessed automobile after the dismissal of debtors' chapter 13 case was vacated), *aff'd*, 225 B.R. 762 (B.A.P. 10th Cir. 1998). *See also* § 9.6, *supra*.

531 11 U.S.C. § 502(d). *See In re* Davis, 889 F.2d 658 (5th Cir. 1989) (IRS entitled to a reasonable time to turn over property before its claim is disallowed).

setting out the automatic stay. In such cases, there is no alternative but to obtain a court order for turnover, seeking immediate interlocutory relief if necessary.[532] Continuing to exercise control over property of the estate is a violation of the automatic stay as well as section 542.[533] Sanctions under section 362(k) or a contempt order, including damages and attorney fees, are also available.[534]

Some creditors (primarily automobile lenders) have claimed that adequate protection payments are a prerequisite to turnover. Courts are divided on this issue.[535] In jurisdictions which do require adequate protection payments prior to turnover, negotiation of the value of the property and the amount of appropriate adequate protection may be necessary.[536] In chapter 13 cases, adequate protection will often consist of payments under the plan.[537] If that is the case, the only required showing should be that plan payments are being made.

Finally, it is important to give notice of the case promptly to any holder of property not only to obtain a turnover, but also to prevent the complications that could arise from a transfer to a third party by a holder without notice. It is clear that the holder incurs no special liability for such a transfer,[538] and thereafter the property may not be recoverable, although there are good arguments that it does remain property of the estate because rights were frozen as of the filing of the case.[539]

Some creditors resisting turnover may claim that their actions are justified by a lack of "effective notice" under section 342(g). As discussed above,[540] this provision applies only to notices that a debtor is required to send. A notice advising a creditor that a petition has been filed and that the creditor must turn over property is not such a notice. In any event, the lack of effective notice would not relieve a creditor of the turnover requirement, because the only consequence for lack of effective notice stated by the statute is to protect a creditor from a monetary penalty above actual damages and attorney fees.[541] However, if a proceeding must be brought against the creditor to enforce the turnover requirements, the debtor should give notice of the proceeding as described in section 342 in order to preclude any creditor argument based upon that section.

9.9.4 Issues of Possession After Turnover

It must be noted that section 542 requires turnover of property to the trustee, and not to the debtor.[542] Nowhere does the Code clearly spell out the procedure that should be used to transfer such property to the debtor in cases in which it seems clear the debtor should have possession of it. Thus, for example, if property that the debtor may exempt in a chapter 7 case is turned over to the trustee, the trustee may not feel free to relinquish it immediately to the debtor before the exemptions are approved.

It seems fairly obvious that the intent of the Code is that debtors should have possession of exempt property during the case; they are not expected to relinquish their household goods pending approval of the exemptions claimed. In fact, the exemptions are approved automatically if there is no objection to them.[543] Moreover, such goods are rarely of any use to the trustee who would incur needless expense in storing and preserving them. In view of all these considerations, and the general purpose of the exemptions to allow the debtor to maintain a modest standard of living, there can be little doubt that property claimed as exempt should be immediately relinquished to the debtor by a trustee to whom it is turned over under section 542, at least absent a serious dispute about the exemption claim.

Until this issue is definitively resolved, however, it is best to avoid having to litigate it. As much exempt property as possible should be in the debtor's possession on the date the case is commenced. All monies should be withdrawn from bank accounts, so that access to them is not prevented because they were turned over to the trustee or frozen. If possible, the filing should be delayed until after receipt of a tax refund, because the Internal Revenue Service also frequently pays such refunds to the trustee rather than to the debtor.

In chapter 13 cases, the situation is somewhat more clear. Because section 1306 provides that the debtor is to remain in possession of all property of the estate, there is no reason for the trustee to retain any property turned over to him or her. Such

---

532 *See* Form 51, Appx. G.5, *infra*.
   A complaint rather than a motion is required by Rule of Bankruptcy Procedure 7001. *In re* Estes, 185 B.R. 745 (Bankr. W.D. Ky. 1995); *In re* Riding, 44 B.R. 846 (Bankr. D. Utah 1984). Under 28 U.S.C. § 157(b)(2)(E) the matter is a core proceeding.
533 *In re* Hill, 174 B.R. 949 (Bankr. S.D. Ohio 1994).
534 *See* Gen. Motors Acceptance Corp. v. Ryan, 183 B.R. 288 (M.D. Fla. 1995) (retention of property was stay violation; creditor cannot wait until debtor files turnover complaint after receiving request for turnover); *In re* Cordle, 187 B.R. 1 (Bankr. N.D. Cal. 1995) (failure to turn over insurance proceeds violated stay and justified sanctions); *In re* LaTempa, 58 B.R. 538 (Bankr. W.D. Va. 1986); §§ 9.6, 9.9.2, *supra*.
535 *Compare In re* Nash, 228 B.R. 669 (Bankr. N.D. Ill. 1999) (creditor could retain automobile; adequate protection required as a prerequisite to turnover); *In re* Fitch, 217 B.R. 286 (Bankr. C.D. Cal. 1998); *In re* Young, 193 B.R. 620 (Bankr. D.D.C. 1996) *and In re* Richardson, 135 B.R. 256 (Bankr. E.D. Tex. 1992) (in failing to adequately insure repossessed automobile, chapter 13 debtor failed to satisfy the adequate protection precondition for turnover) *with In re* Sharon, 234 B.R. 676 (B.A.P. 6th Cir. 1999) *and In re* Berscheit, 223 B.R. 579 (Bankr. D. Wyo. 1998) (adequate protection not required as a prerequisite to turnover).
536 *See* §§ 8.2.7.3, 8.7.2.1, *supra*.
   Proof of insurance may also be required.
537 *See* § 9.7.3.2.2, *supra*.
   For chapter 7 cases, other forms of adequate protection may be necessary.
538 11 U.S.C. § 542(c).
539 See discussion as to voidability of postpetition transfers under 11 U.S.C. §§ 549 and 550 in § 10.4.2.6.6, *infra*.
540 *See* § 9.6.2.1, *supra*.
541 *Id.*
542 At least one court has held that creditors may not request turnover when the trustee fails to do so. *In re* Perkins, 902 F.2d 1254 (7th Cir. 1990).
543 11 U.S.C. § 522(*l*). *See* § 10.3.4, *infra*.

property should be promptly delivered to the debtor. Indeed, it is unfortunate that there is no provision requiring turnover directly to the debtor to obviate the necessity for any trustee involvement, because in most cases, the right to use, sell, or lease property is that of the debtor, exclusive of the trustee.[544]

Finally, it should be noted that much of what has been said above applies equally to property obtained by the trustee through use of other powers. The trustee has a wide range of ways to gather property into the estate and to avoid prebankruptcy transfers of property. Many of these are discussed in the context of the debtor's exemptions, in the next chapter of this treatise.

---

[544] 11 U.S.C. § 1303. *See* § 12.8.1, *infra.*

Chapter 10   Exemptions

10.1 Introduction

10.1.1 Importance of the Exemption Provisions

For most consumer debtors, no section of the Bankruptcy Code is more important than section 522, which governs the debtor's rights in relation to exempt property. It is a section that has resulted in enormous advances in debtors' rights. With a few exceptions, the exemption provisions in the Code make bankruptcy much more attractive to consumers than the previous law, and give better protection to their property than can be had under the law governing execution in most states.

Indeed, the availability of exemptions is usually key to the determination of whether to file a bankruptcy in the first place, and also the determination as to which type of bankruptcy case to file.[1] If the debtor has significant amounts of property that are not exempt, and thus would be lost in a chapter 7 liquidation, a chapter 13 case is usually preferable. And in a chapter 13 case, the value of nonexempt property may determine the minimum that must be paid to unsecured creditors;[2] if that amount cannot be paid through the plan, then a chapter 13 case may not be feasible.

The exemption provisions are closely related to other parts of the Code. For example, they give the debtor many of the trustee's powers to avoid prepetition transfers of property, as well as some additional powers over and above those of the trustee, all of which are discussed in this Chapter. The turnover provisions of section 542 specifically require that property that is in the possession of a third party and that the debtor can exempt must be turned over to the trustee.[3] Similarly, the right to redeem certain types of property from liens under section 722 applies only to exempt or abandoned property.[4] And many of the protections after discharge bear a direct relationship to what property has been exempted.[5]

10.1.2 Definition of Exempt Property

The Code contains no formal definitions of "exemption" or "exempt property." Fundamentally, these are the designations given to the property that the trustee is not permitted to liquidate and the debtor is permitted to retain in a chapter 7 liquidation.[6] Other than the exempt property, virtually all of the debtor's interests in property that have significant value are transferred to the trustee for the benefit of creditors.

With some exceptions, discussed later in this Chapter, exemptions do not affect valid security interests or other liens on property of the debtor.[7] A debtor must usually pay the secured creditor the amount of its secured claim to eliminate a lien. As the lien can be thought of as diminishing the debtor's interest in the encumbered property, only the value of the interest remaining after subtraction of the lien amount need be claimed as exempt.

The procedure for claiming exemptions is not fully spelled out in the Code. Although section 522(*l*) states that the debtor shall "file a list" of property claimed as exempt, the questions of when, where, and how this list is to be filed are left to the Rules of Bankruptcy Procedure. The rules require the debtor to file the list of property claimed as exempt in the schedules at the outset of a case.[8]

Exemptions are claimed and determined with respect to the debtor's property at the outset of the case, except to the extent additional property becomes property of the estate under section 541 thereafter, in which case the value of property is determined on the date the property becomes property of the estate.[9] Ordinarily, if a case is converted to chapter 7 from

---

1 For a general discussion of these decisions, see Chapter 6, *supra*.
2 11 U.S.C. § 1325(a)(4).
   See discussion of the "best interests of creditors" chapter 13 test in § 12.3.1, *infra*. This test is also applicable in chapter 12 cases. *See* § 17.5.5.2, *infra*.
3 See § 9.9, *supra*, for discussion of the turnover provisions.
4 See § 11.5, *infra*, for discussion of the right to redeem property.
5 11 U.S.C. § 522(c). *See* § 10.5, *infra*.

6 Exempt property also may not be used to pay any costs of administration, except if the trustee brings additional property into the estate through use of avoiding powers, in which case the exempt portion of such property may be charged its aliquot share of the costs and expenses of the transfer avoidance. 11 U.S.C. § 522(k).
7 *In re* Sloma, 43 F.3d 637 (11th Cir. 1995) (debtor's claim that annuity payments were exempt did not affect bank's security interest in annuity, which debtor had assigned as collateral for loan).
8 Fed. R. Bankr. P. 4003(a); Official Form 6, Sch. C (reprinted in Appx. D, *infra*).
9 11 U.S.C. § 522(a)(2); Lowe v. Sandoval (*In re* Sandoval), 103 F.3d 20 (5th Cir. 1997).
   Property of a corporation is not property of a debtor who owns stock in the corporation, even if the debtor is the owner of all the stock. The debtor's property is the stock in the corporation. Fowler v. Shadel, 400 F.3d 1016 (7th Cir. 2005) (debtor could not claim as exempt equitable interest in vehicles owned by closely held corporation if corporation had not been dissolved as of petition date).

chapter 13, property acquired since the filing of the petition need not be claimed as exempt as it is not property of the estate in the converted case unless it would have been property of the estate on the date the chapter 13 petition was filed.[10]

The Code also does not specify when exempt property loses its previous character as property of the estate. Is it when the list is filed (at the commencement of the case in most instances)?[11] At the latest, it should be when the time for objections[12] has passed.[13]

Similarly, the Code does not address the question of who shall possess exempt property during the period before the time for objections has run. Courts have generally assumed that the debtor has the right to remain in possession of exempt property throughout the case;[14] it is hard to imagine debtors delivering all of their household goods to the trustee. In any event, the fact that a debtor has relinquished possession of property to the trustee does not waive the debtor's right to exempt that property.[15] However, if the property comes into the hands of the trustee, because of a turnover or avoidance of a transfer, there are no guidelines as to when the trustee must deliver it to the debtor in a chapter 7 case. Presumably, in view of the purposes of exemptions discussed below, this turnover should be accomplished promptly.[16] It is clear in a chapter 13 case that prompt delivery to the debtor is required, because the debtor is entitled to possession of all property of the estate.[17]

10.1.3 Purposes of Exemptions

Historically, the purpose of exemption laws has always been to allow debtors to keep those items of property deemed essential to daily life. Without this bare grubstake, it was feared that debtors could not retain the minimum of dignity and self-respect to which all members of a society are entitled. Perhaps more importantly to some, it was feared that stripping debtors of all of their property would increase the chances of their becoming public charges, unable to maintain themselves without assistance.

In the bankruptcy context, exemptions serve the overriding purpose of helping the debtor to obtain a fresh start. They allow the debtor to come out of the process with not only a minimum amount of dignity, but also the essentials upon which to build a new life. They leave at least the basic necessities, chosen by the debtor from the possessions that the debtor has acquired over a lifetime, so that the debtor may proceed to move forward, rather than spend time struggling simply to exist.

These policies have been judged, by state legislatures and by Congress, to be more important than satisfying the claims of unsecured creditors (and, in bankruptcy, some secured creditors) out of certain items of the debtor's property. The Bankruptcy Code gave new strength and protection to these principles, and eliminated many of the creditor practices which, over the years, had come to undermine them. While the 2005 amendments placed limits on some large homestead exemptions, expanded exemptions for retirement savings, and made other minor changes, they did not change these fundamental policies.

10.2 What Property Is Exempt?

10.2.1 The Choice of State or Federal Exemptions

10.2.1.1 In General

In many states, a debtor may choose from two sets of exemptions. As under the prior law, a debtor in any state may choose to utilize the exemptions provided by state law, as enhanced by section 522(b)(3)(C), and the exemptions provided by federal nonbankruptcy law (for example, laws protecting Social Security benefits and veterans benefits, and so forth). If the debtor chooses the state exemptions, then certain other property of the estate not normally subject to process under state law may also be claimed as exempt.[18]

The Code also provides a comprehensive list of special federal exemptions that are applicable only in bankruptcy cases. Debtors may choose these exemptions as an alternative to the traditionally available exemptions, as long as their state has not "opted out" of the federal exemption scheme.[19] The

---

See § 2.5, *supra*, for a discussion of the limited types of property which may come into the estate after filing.

10 11 U.S.C. § 348(f)(1) (with exception for bad faith conversions in section 348(f)(2)). *See* § 13.7.3, *infra*.

11 *In re* Peterson, 897 F.2d 935 (8th Cir. 1990) (exemptions are fixed and vested at the time of petition, so debtor's death eight months after filing the petition does not constitute an abandonment of the debtor's homestead exemption or cause the exemption to lapse back into the estate).

12 Objections to exemptions are discussed in § 10.3.3, *infra*.

13 *In re* Gamble, 168 F.3d 442 (11th Cir. 1999); *In re* Hahn, 60 B.R. 69 (Bankr. D. Minn. 1985). *See* Kennedy, *Automatic Stays Under the New Bankruptcy Law*, 12 U. Mich. J.L. Ref. 3, 38 n.158 (1978); § 10.3.4, *infra*. *See also* Wissman v. Pittsburgh Nat'l Bank, 942 F.2d 867 (4th Cir. 1991); Christy v. Heights Fin. Corp., 101 B.R. 542 (C.D. Ill. 1987).

14 However, a debtor must be careful in using property, especially cash, the exemption of which might ultimately be in dispute. *See In re* Walker, 83 B.R. 14 (B.A.P. 9th Cir. 1988) (order may be entered denying debtor use of funds in pension plan when the exempt character of those funds is in dispute). *See also* 11 U.S.C. § 363 (insofar as it relates to use of property by a debtor).

15 *In re* McKain, 325 B.R. 842 (Bankr. D. Neb. 2005).

16 *But see In re* Salzer, 52 F.3d 708 (7th Cir. 1995) (erroneously holding that Indiana execution procedures permit a bankruptcy trustee to hold property after the deadline for objecting to exemptions has run until the trustee obtains an appraisal of the property; *pro se* debtor waived argument that commercial property in question was totally exempt); Greene v. Balaber-Strauss, 76 B.R. 940 (S.D.N.Y. 1987) (trustee could wait until she completed her administrative duties; decision is poorly reasoned, confusing the issue of discharge with that of exemptions, which are provided regardless of discharge).

17 11 U.S.C. § 1306(b). *See* § 12.8.1, *infra*.

18 *See* § 10.2.3, *infra*, for discussion of using state and federal nonbankruptcy exemptions.

19 11 U.S.C. § 522(b)(1).

"opt out" provision, adopted as a last-minute compromise to secure passage of the Code, allows any state to pass a law prohibiting the use of the special federal bankruptcy exemptions. While this concept is unusual, it has not been successfully challenged.[20] Currently, thirty-four states have such a law,[21] and in those states, debtors may utilize only the state and federal nonbankruptcy exemptions, except that the debtor using the state exemptions may also exempt under section 522(b)(3)(C) certain retirement funds.[22] (A state may also opt out of the federal bankruptcy exemptions and pass its own bankruptcy exemptions, which may be different from its normal exemptions from execution.)[23] By repealing these laws, of course, those states can opt back into the federal exemptions.[24] In any case, even when a state has opted out of the federal bankruptcy exemptions, the remaining provisions of section 522 remain applicable to enhance the exemptions that are available to the debtor; a state may not opt out of those provisions.[25]

Assuming that the debtor's state has not opted out, the debtor must choose the applicable exemptions. In some states, the state exemptions may be more liberal than the federal exemptions, particularly with respect to homesteads and insurance interests.

The choice between state and federal exemptions is normally made by designation in Schedule C, the schedule of exemptions that is filed with the debtor's other bankruptcy schedules.[26] The designation is sufficient if one set of statutory references is used rather than the other. Under the rules, that schedule can later be amended, including presumably to change from federal to state exemptions or vice versa.[27] In a joint filing of a husband and wife, both spouses must choose the same exemption scheme.[28] If the spouses cannot agree upon which exemptions to choose, they are deemed to have chosen the federal exemptions.[29] They also, however, have the option of filing two separate petitions,

---

When a state opts out after the petition is filed, federal exemptions are available. *See* Hollytex Carpet Mills v. Tedford, 691 F.2d 392 (8th Cir. 1982) (law in effect on date of petition governs exemptions throughout the case); *In re* Boozer, 4 B.R. 524 (Bankr. N.D. Ga. 1980).

20 A fairly strong argument can be made that the provision allowing states to opt out is unconstitutional. Article 1, section 8 of the Constitution gives Congress the power to establish "uniform laws on the subject of bankruptcy" and it could be argued that the opt-out provision is a non-uniform law. While the previous Act's complete deference to state exemption laws was upheld against such a challenge, there may be a difference now that there is a federal standard for exemptions which states may reject. Put another way, may Congress delegate to the states the right to deprive citizens of federal rights applicable only in bankruptcy cases? *See* Michael Terry Hertz, *Bankruptcy Code Exemptions: Notes on the Effect of State Law*, 54 Am. Bankr. L. J. 339, 341–344 (1980).

The argument that the opt-out provision violates the Constitution's requirement for a uniform bankruptcy law has been rejected in several cases. *In re* Storer, 58 F.3d 1125 (6th Cir. 1995) (also holding that opt-out did not violate privileges and immunities, due process, supremacy, or equal protection clauses of Constitution); *In re* Sullivan, 680 F.2d 1131 (7th Cir. 1982).

However, several opt-out statutes have been found unconstitutional for other reasons. State exemptions provided by Maryland have been found to so greatly discriminate against non-home owners that they thwart the Congressional policy of nondiscrimination and thus violate the Supremacy Clause. *See In re* Locarno, 23 B.R. 622 (Bankr. D. Md. 1982). But this reasoning has been rejected by at least one court of appeals. Rhodes v. Stewart, 705 F.2d 159 (6th Cir. 1983). In addition, the Maryland statute required, as a condition precedent to claiming a homestead exemption, that the debtor attempt to negotiate payment agreements with creditors. This provision has also been found to violate federal bankruptcy policy and thus the Supremacy Clause. *In re* Smith, 23 B.R. 708 (Bankr. D. Md. 1982); *In re* Davis, 16 B.R. 62 (Bankr. D. Md. 1981). Indiana's exemption scheme making certain property available to tort creditors in bankruptcy, but not to contract creditors was upheld, however, without express consideration of the Supremacy Clause. *In re* Ondras, 846 F.2d 33 (7th Cir. 1988).

21 The following states have opted out: Alabama, Alaska, Arizona, California, Colorado, Delaware, Florida, Georgia, Idaho, Illinois, Indiana, Iowa, Kansas, Louisiana, Maine, Maryland, Mississippi, Missouri, Montana, Nebraska, Nevada, New York, North Carolina, North Dakota, Ohio, Oklahoma, Oregon, South Carolina, South Dakota, Tennessee, Utah, Virginia, West Virginia and Wyoming. Arkansas and New Hampshire, which previously had opted out, subsequently repealed their opt-out laws. *See In re* Gardner, 139 B.R. 460 (Bankr. E.D. & W.D. Ark. 1991).

A summary of state exemption laws, including citations to state opt-out statutes, is contained in Appx. J, *infra*.

22 When a state has opted out, the argument that the federal bankruptcy exemptions may in some way limit a more expansive state law exemption has been rejected. *In re* Thompson, 867 F.2d 416 (7th Cir. 1989); *In re* Taylor, 861 F.2d 550 (9th Cir. 1988).

The exemptions available are those in effect on the date of the bankruptcy petition. Amendments to the state exemptions cannot be retroactively applied to bankruptcies pending before the effective date of the state statute, even when the petition was involuntary. *In re* Peacock, 119 B.R. 605 (Bankr. N.D. Ill. 1990), *aff'd*, 125 B.R. 526 (N.D. Ill. 1991). Similarly, if a state repeals its opt-out law, exemptions are governed by the law in effect on the date of the petition. *In re* Gardner, 139 B.R. 460 (Bankr. E.D. & W.D. Ark. 1991).

23 *See In re* Bloom, 5 B.R. 451 (Bankr. N.D. Ohio 1980).

Challenges to the ability of states to enact special exemptions applicable only in bankruptcy have, for the most part, been rejected. *See* Sheehan v. Peveich, 574 F.3d 248 (4th Cir. 2009); *In re* Applebaum, 422 B.R. 684 (B.A.P. 9th Cir. 2009); *In re* Morrell, 394 B.R. 405 (Bankr. N.D. W. Va. 2008). *See also* § 10.2.3.1, *infra*. But *see In re* Regevig, 389 B.R. 736 (Bankr. D. Ariz. 2008).

24 *See In re* Gardner, 139 B.R. 460 (Bankr. E.D. & W.D. Ark. 1991).

25 Owen v. Owen, 500 U.S. 305, 111 S. Ct. 1833, 114 L. Ed. 2d 350 (1991) (section 522(f) treats federal and state exemptions equally and a state cannot opt out of the Code's lien avoidance provisions by passing exemption statutes which purport to exclude property subject to liens).

26 *See In re* Pierce, 214 B.R. 550 (Bankr. E.D.N.C. 1997) (in court statement by the debtor does not reflect a choice of exemptions particularly as mentioning a "wild card" exemption could reflect either state or federal law), *rev'd on other grounds*, 231 B.R. 890 (E.D.N.C. 1998).

27 *See* § 10.3.2, *infra*.

28 11 U.S.C. § 522(b). *See* Seung v. Silverman, 288 B.R. 174 (E.D.N.Y. 2003) (requiring New Jersey debtor to use New York exemptions rather than federal exemptions in joint case because her New York domiciliary husband could only choose New York exemptions, a questionable result). *But see In re* Connor, 419 B.R. 304 (Bankr. E.D.N.C. 2009) (spouses could utilize separate exemption schemes when state exemptions were not available to one spouse who had moved from another state in preceding 730 days).

29 11 U.S.C. § 522(b).

§ 10.2.1.2   Consumer Bankruptcy Law and Practice

with each spouse electing the exemptions of his or her choice.[30] Even when a state has opted out of the federal exemptions, it may be possible to assert the state exemptions separately for each debtor,[31] as section 522(m) of the Code provides that each debtor's exemptions must be treated separately.

10.2.1.2 Determining the Applicable Exemption Law

In an apparent attempt to discourage debtors from moving to states with more generous exemption laws before filing bankruptcy, the 2005 Act substantially changed the domiciliary provision found in former section 522(b)(2)(A). The new requirements are found in section 522(b)(3)(A). These domiciliary requirements also determine which state law will be used to determine whether the debtor may elect to claim the federal bankruptcy exemptions.

The state exemption law that applies to a debtor is determined by the state in which the debtor's domicile has been located for the 730 days immediately preceding the petition filing date, rather than the ninety-one-day period used under former law. If the debtor's domicile has not been located in a single state for the 730-day period, the applicable state exemption law is that of the state in which the debtor was domiciled for the 180 days immediately preceding the 730-day period, or in which the debtor was domiciled for the longer portion of such 180-day period than in any other place.[32] Notably, however, the domicile rules do not apply to exemptions under section 522(b)(3)(B) for entireties interests not subject to process, which are based on the law of the state where the property is located.[33] It is also possible that the debtor was not domiciled in any state during that 180 days, either because the debtor was abroad or, as domicile includes an intent to stay, because the debtor did not have that intent.

If the effect of section 522(b)(3)(A) is to render the debtor ineligible for any exemption, the debtor may elect to exempt property as specified under section 522(d).[34] The debtor is therefore permitted to exempt property under the federal exemption scheme in this situation even if the state of the debtor's domicile as determined by section 522(b)(3)(A) is an opt-out state. This situation could arise if the exemption law of the state deemed to be the debtor's domicile requires the debtor to reside within the state to claim exemption rights[35] or if the law does not permit an exemption to be claimed on property located outside the state.[36] The statute is somewhat ambiguous with respect to the situation of a debtor who qualifies for some, but not all, exemptions under a state's laws, because the phrase "ineligible for any exemption" could mean either ineligible for all exemptions or ineligible for any particular exemption. The better view is that the latter was intended. Otherwise, a debtor could be limited to only one or two particular exemptions that are worded differently than most of a state's exemptions.[37]

The amendments to section 522(b) have produced many court decisions on the extraterritorial application of state exemption laws. Courts are currently divided on this issue when state exemption law is silent as to its extraterritorial effect.[38]

---

30 *But see* Fed. R. Bankr. P. 1015(b) (court may order joint administration of husband's and wife's individual petitions and fix time in which they must choose same set of exemptions).

If the husband and wife filed under different chapters, such joint administration would be far less likely.

31 *In re* Cheeseman, 656 F.2d 60 (4th Cir. 1981); *In re* Bartlett, 24 B.R. 605 (B.A.P. 9th Cir. 1982); *In re* Smith, 27 B.R. 30 (Bankr. D. Ariz. 1982); Manufacturers & Traders Trust Co. v. Borst, 128 Misc. 2d 691 (Sup. Ct. 1984). *See also* John T. Mather Mem'l Hosp. v. Pearl, 723 F.2d 193 (2d Cir. 1983) (based upon interpretation of state law); § 10.2.3.1, *infra*. *But see In re* Talmadge, 832 F.2d 1120 (9th Cir. 1987) (California's exemption scheme allowing spouses single set of exemptions does not violate Equal Protection and can be enforced despite section 522(m)); Stevens v. Pike County Bank, 829 F.2d 693 (8th Cir. 1987) (state could limit couple to one homestead exemption in bankruptcy); *In re* Granger, 754 F.2d 1490 (9th Cir. 1985) (state exemption scheme which did not provide separate exemptions for husband and wife enforced in bankruptcy); First Nat'l Bank v. Norris, 701 F.2d 902 (11th Cir. 1983) (section 522(m) does not create separate state exemptions for joint debtors). *See also In re* Pruitt, 829 F.2d 1002 (10th Cir. 1987) (when only one homestead is allowed to a couple, value of single debtor's interest is computed by taking one half of the difference between value of property and homestead exemption).

32 11 U.S.C. § 522(b)(3)(A). *See In re* Urban, 375 B.R. 882 (B.A.P. 9th Cir. 2007) (domicile rules were constitutional); *In re* Varanasi, 394 B.R. 430 (Bankr. S.D. Ohio 2008) (same).

33 *In re* Garrett, 435 B.R. 434 (Bankr. S.D. Tex. 2010) (debtors who formerly lived in North Carolina could not claim entireties exemption in Texas property); *In re* Holland, 366 B.R. 825 (N.D. Ill. 2007); *In re* Zolnierowicz, 380 B.R. 84 (Bankr. M.D. Fla. 2007); *In re* Schwarz, 362 B.R. 532 (Bankr. S.D. Fla. 2007).

34 11 U.S.C. § 522(b)(3)(A); Zebley v. Karavias (*In re* Karavias), 438 B.R. 86 (Bankr. W.D. Pa. 2010); *In re* George, 440 B.R. 164 (Bankr. E.D. Wis. 2010); *In re* Adams, 375 B.R. 532 (Bankr. W.D. Mo. 2007) (because Florida law was construed to provide exemptions only to residents, debtor could claim federal exemptions); *In re* West, 352 B.R. 905 (Bankr. M.D. Fla. 2006) (debtors who had moved from Indiana to Florida within 730 days before petition could claim federal exemptions); *In re* Jewell, 347 B.R. 120 (Bankr. W.D.N.Y. 2006) (debtor who moved from Colorado to New York within 730 days before petition could claim federal exemptions); *In re* Crandall, 346 B.R. 220 (Bankr. M.D. Fla. 2006) (debtors who had moved from New York to Florida within 730 days before petition could claim federal exemptions).

35 *In re* Camp, 631 F.3d 757 (5th Cir. 2011) (debtor permitted to claim federal exemptions because Florida opt-out statute applicable only to residents of Florida); *In re* Rody, 468 B.R. 384 (Bankr. D. Ariz. 2012) (Arizona opt-out applicable only to Arizona residents); *In re* Chandler, 362 B.R. 723 (Bankr. N.D. W. Va. 2007) (Georgia opt-out statute is not applicable to non-residents); *In re* Underwood, 342 B.R. 358 (Bankr. N.D. Fla. 2006) (debtor whose domicile is Colorado for purposes of section 522(b)(3)(A) but who resides in Florida may claim exemptions under section 522(d) because Colorado exemptions apply only to residents).

36 *In re* Adams, 375 B.R. 532 (Bankr. W.D. Mo. 2007) (Florida's exemptions are not applicable to property located out of state).

37 *See, e.g., In re* Katseanes, 2007 WL 2962637 (Bankr. D. Idaho Oct. 9, 2007) (although the Utah homestead exemption does not have extraterritorial effect, debtors were not "ineligible for any exemption" under other Utah exemption law and therefore debtors were prevented from using any homestead exemption on Idaho property).

38 *Compare In re* Drenttel, 403 F.3d 611 (8th Cir. 2005) (debtors who moved to Arizona but whose domiciliary state was Minnesota permitted to claim Minnesota homestead exemption on property

The longer look-back period will mean that debtors who have moved from another state within two years before an anticipated bankruptcy filing may want to delay or speed up a filing, if possible, in order to maximize the available exemptions.[39] It will also require bankruptcy attorneys to become familiar with exemption laws in states other than where they practice.[40]

Occasionally a debtor who is deemed to be domiciled or who resides in an opt-out state may still utilize the federal exemptions in other situations, depending upon the precise wording of the opt-out statute. Because "domicile" is usually defined as a permanent home, from which a person may be away for a period of time but to which the person intends to return, a person may be domiciled in a different state than that in which the person resides temporarily.[41] Thus, a debtor who has been domiciled for two years in a state that has opted out for its *residents* may reside in a second state temporarily, even if it is an opt-out state, file in the first state (the debtor's domicile) within ninety days after the move,[42] and claim the federal bankruptcy exemptions because the debtor is not a resident of the first state and the state opted out only for residents.[43]

Conversely, if a state has opted out only for persons domiciled in the state, some debtors who are residents but intend to return to another permanent domicile may be able to claim the federal exemptions.[44] Similarly, if a debtor is subject to the laws of such a state under the domiciliary requirements of section 522(b)(3)(A), but is no longer domiciled in the state, the debtor is not subject to the opt out provision.[45] And a debtor who is subject to the exemption laws of a state and who no longer resides in that state is not subject to a state's statute opting out of the federal exemptions only for its residents.[46]

10.2.2 The Federal Bankruptcy Exemptions

10.2.2.1 In General

The property that can be claimed as exempt under the federal bankruptcy exemptions (in states that have not opted out) is listed in section 522(d) of the Code. The list itself, adopted originally by the Bankruptcy Commission, was later generally followed in the Uniform Exemptions Act.[47] Although Congress made some changes in drafting the Code and in later amendments, the commentary to the Uniform Act, therefore, is a good place to look for interpretive assistance.

Because the exemptions may be claimed by each debtor individually,[48] a husband and wife filing a joint case are each entitled to the full exemption amounts listed for each category of property in section 522(d), effectively doubling those amounts for jointly held property. (In many states there is a presumption that property acquired during the marriage is jointly owned.) However, the same provisions would probably prevent the application of one spouse's unused exemption amount to the separate property of the other spouse.[49]

---

purchased in Arizona); *In re* Arrol, 170 F.3d 934 (9th Cir. 1999) (debtor domiciled in California entitled to claim California homestead exemption on residence located in Michigan); Stephens v. Holbrook (*In re* Stephens), 402 B.R. 1 (B.A.P. 10th Cir. 2009) (Oklahoma resident could claim Iowa homestead exemption in proceeds of former Iowa home); *In re* Fernandez, 2011 WL 3423373 (W.D. Tex. Aug. 5, 2011) (permitting use of Nevada homestead exemption on property located in Texas despite Nevada exemption law requirement that homestead be recorded in county where property located); *In re* Varanasi, 394 B.R. 430 (Bankr. S.D. Ohio 2008) (Ohio debtor could claim New Hampshire homestead exemption with respect to Ohio home); *In re* Jevne, 387 B.R. 301 (Bankr. S.D. Fla. 2008) (Rhode Island exemptions had extraterritorial effect) *and In re* Williams, 369 B.R. 470 (Bankr. W.D. Ark. 2007) (debtor could use Iowa homestead exemption for Arkansas property) *with In re* Sipka, 149 B.R. 181 (D. Kan. 1992) *and In re* Ginther, 282 B.R. 16 (Bankr. D. Kan. 2002) (relying upon state court decisions holding that Kansas exemption laws do not have effect in other states, court held that debtor may not exempt Colorado property under Kansas homestead exemption).

A summary of the states' rules on this issue, to the extent they are known, can be found in Appx. J, *infra*.

39 This treatise's companion website contains a Date Calculator program that performs the task of computing the 730 and 180-day periods, after the user types in the expected petition filing date. A detailed description of the program and of the twenty-one other prepetition date-sensitive events that it can compute is set out in Appx. H.1, *infra*.

40 For a summary of state exemption laws, see Appx. J, *infra*.

41 *In re* Porvaznik, 456 B.R. 738 (Bankr. M.D. Pa. 2011) (debtor's domicile did not change even though she resided in various other places while husband was in military).

42 *In re* Battle, 366 B.R. 635 (Bankr. W.D. Tex. 2006) (debtors who moved from Florida to Texas within 730 days before petition could claim federal exemptions because Florida opted out for residents only).

Venue for a case is determined by 28 U.S.C. § 1408.

43 *See In re* Underwood, 342 B.R. 358 (Bankr. N.D. Fla. 2006) (debtor who is resident of Florida, even if eligible to claim Colorado exemptions, may claim federal exemptions because Colorado opt-

out statute only applies to residents); *In re* Schultz, 101 B.R. 301 (Bankr. N.D. Fla. 1989); *In re* Hawkins, 15 B.R. 618 (Bankr. E.D. Va. 1981) (as Virginia exemptions were available for residents only, opt-out could not apply to nonresident).

44 *In re* Arispe, 289 B.R. 245 (Bankr. S.D. Fla. 2002) (resident alien who was not domiciled in Florida or any other state was not subject to Florida exemption laws, including opt-out, and could claim federal exemptions).

45 *In re* Chandler, 362 B.R. 723 (Bankr. N.D. W. Va. 2007).

46 Camp v. Ingalls (*In re* Camp), 631 F.3d 757 (5th Cir. 2011); *In re* Footen, 2012 WL 669849 (Bankr. D. Or. Feb. 29, 2012); *In re* Long, 470 B.R. 186 (Bankr. D. Kan. 2012).

47 13 U.L.A. 371–406.

48 11 U.S.C. § 522(m).

49 *In re* Cunningham, 8 Bankr. Ct. Dec. (LRP) 863, Bankr. L. Rep. (CCH) ¶ 68,578 (Bankr. D. Mass. 1980) (husband's exemption may not be used for wife's property); *In re* Crum, 6 B.R. 138 (Bankr. M.D. Fla. 1980) (tax refund allocated between spouses according to monies withheld); *In re* Colbert, 5 B.R. 646 (Bankr. S.D. Ohio 1980) (wife could not claim exemption on joint tax refund if she had no earnings that year).

When some or all property is held as tenants by the entirety under some state laws, it may be possible for one spouse to exempt the full value of such property, which would permit the use of the other spouse's exemptions on other property. *See In re* Brannon, 476 F.3d 170 (3d Cir. 2007) (entireties co-tenant had interest in full value of property under Pennsylvania law and could exempt full value, not

As a result, problems occasionally arise from the wording of some of the exemptions. For example, if there are two jointly held motor vehicles, each worth $3450, each joint debtor could only exempt one-half of the value of one car because the motor vehicle exemption applies to the debtor's interest in one motor vehicle.[50] This result would leave the equivalent of one vehicle not exempted under that subsection. One simple solution to this problem would be a prebankruptcy trading of interests so that each spouse owned one car in full. Then each could exempt the full $3450 value of his or her car. Thus, prebankruptcy exemption planning may be especially important in joint filings.

The list of federal exemptions was amended in 1994 to double the previous dollar amounts of exemptions permitted, most of which had gone unchanged since 1978. Under Code section 104, the dollar amounts of the federal bankruptcy exemptions are now adjusted every three years to take into account changes in the cost of living. The most recent of these adjustments was effective on April 1, 2010.

10.2.2.2 Homestead—§ 522(d)(1)

The largest specific dollar amount applicable to particular property is the $21,625 that each debtor may claim as a homestead exemption.[51] This exemption, like all of the other exemptions, applies only to the debtor's interest in property, that is, the equity over and above liens. Hence, a debtor with a one-half interest in a $60,000 jointly-owned home encumbered by a $30,000 mortgage, has a $15,000 interest in that home (1/2 x [$60,000–$30,000]). Being not more than a $21,625 interest, the debtor's interest would be fully exempt. However, it is important to remember that in subtracting liens to determine equity, precomputed but as yet unearned interest should not be included. Only the current "payoff figure" due on the lien can properly be considered owing.[52]

As discussed earlier, two joint owners may exempt an interest of $43,250 under this exemption. In fact, they may add an additional $2300 to that figure (or to any other exemption) because a different subsection permits each to exempt an interest of $1150 in "any property."[53] If the property is titled in only one name, a joint debtor may still be able to exempt some residual interest such as dower rights if such interests exist under state law.[54]

The homestead exemption is applicable to interests in either real or personal property, and therefore it clearly includes mobile homes, houseboats, shares in a cooperative, and so on.[55]

It also clearly includes non-ownership interests such as leases.[56] The property must be a residence of the debtor or a dependent of the debtor, though it does not appear necessary that it be the principal residence.[57] The debtor need not necessarily be occupying the property on the date of the petition.[58] A burial plot may also be exempted under this subsection.

Unlike some state exemption schemes, the federal bankruptcy homestead exemption does not explicitly apply to proceeds of the sale of a homestead.[59] However, when a home is sold after bankruptcy is filed, the exemption is preserved because section 522(a)(2) explicitly states that exemptions are to be determined as of the date the bankruptcy petition was filed.[60] It is less clear whether a debtor may use the federal homestead exemption to exempt proceeds of a sale of a home that occurred prior to filing. This uncertainty can frequently be avoided with careful prebankruptcy exemption planning.[61]

10.2.2.3 Motor Vehicle—§ 522(d)(2)

A debtor may exempt an interest of up to $3450 in one motor vehicle under section 522(d)(2). It is important to note the

---

just one half of value); *In re* Pyatte, 440 B.R. 893 (Bankr. M.D. Fla. 2010) (same). *See also In re* Browning, 2010 WL 1541629 (Bankr. C.D. Ill. Apr. 19, 2010) (same result for Illinois joint tenants with right of survivorship).

50 11 U.S.C. § 522(d)(2).
51 11 U.S.C. § 522(d)(1).
52 *In re* Parenteau, 23 B.R. 289 (B.A.P. 1st Cir. 1982).
53 11 U.S.C. § 522(d)(5).
54 *See In re* Wycuff, 332 B.R. 297 (Bankr. N.D. Ohio 2005) (debtor could claim separate state exemption for dower rights).
55 *See In re* Meola, 158 B.R. 881 (Bankr. S.D. Fla. 1993) (travel trailer qualified as exempt under Florida homestead exemption for a "dwelling house"). *See also In re* Murphy, 367 B.R. 711 (Bankr. D. Kan. 2007) (debtors' breach of implied warranty claim for defects in mobile home and UDAP claim for deceptive sales practices were exempt under Kansas homestead statute).
56 *In re* Rutland, 318 B.R. 588 (Bankr. M.D. Ala. 2004) (prepaid rent could be exempted under Alabama homestead exemption); *In re* Princiotta, 49 B.R. 447 (Bankr. D. Mass. 1985) (debtor's interest in land installment sale contract could be exempted under this section). *See* Unif. Exemption Act, § 4, cmt. 4, 13 U.L.A. 379. *See also In re* Casserino, 290 B.R. 735 (B.A.P. 9th Cir. 2003) (Oregon homestead exemption applied to prepaid rent on leasehold interests), *aff'd*, 379 F.3d 1069 (9th Cir. 2004); *In re* Coffey, 339 B.R. 689 (Bankr. N.D. Ind. 2006) (Indiana homestead exemption could be used to protect prepaid lease interest). *Cf. In re* Moody, 862 F.2d 1194 (5th Cir. 1989) (debtor's attempt to fraudulently transfer residence prepetition does not deprive the debtor of homestead exemption under Texas law when the property is brought back into the estate). *But see In re* Johnson, 375 F.3d 668 (8th Cir. 2004) (lien on former marital residence was not a property interest under Minnesota law); *In re* Schuhmann, 2010 WL 5125321 (Bankr. D. Or. Dec. 9, 2010) (prepayments on month to month tenancy that debtors could have returned to them if they terminated tenancy could not be exempted).
57 *But see In re* Tomko, 87 B.R. 372 (Bankr. E.D. Pa. 1988) (exemption not allowed in vacation home because debtors lived elsewhere most of the year).
58 *In re* DeMasi, 227 B.R. 586 (D.R.I. 1998) (debtor who owned a remainder interest in home, had resided there previously and intended to reside there again was permitted to claim property as exempt).
59 *See In re* Healy, 100 B.R. 443 (Bankr. W.D. Wis. 1989) (debtors not entitled to exemption in proceeds of prepetition sale of homestead absent evidence that proceeds would be reinvested in residence which debtors planned to occupy). *See also, e.g., In re* Williamson, 844 F.2d 1166 (5th Cir. 1988) (proceeds of sale of exempt property exempt under Mississippi homestead provision).
60 *See* § 10.3.3, *infra*. *See also In re* Reed, 940 F.2d 1317 (9th Cir. 1991) (when property is sold prior to abandonment by trustee, debtors are entitled to exemption from the proceeds, but trustee may claim balance).
61 *See* § 6.5.2.2, *supra*.

limitation in this provision to one vehicle per debtor. Again, the exemption need be applied only to the debtor's interest over and above any security interest or other lien.[62] And an interest in excess of the $3450 amount may sometimes be picked up using another exemption, such as the exemption for any property,[63] or in some cases, the exemption for tools of a trade.[64]

10.2.2.4 Household Goods, Household Furnishings, Wearing Apparel, Appliances, and Similar Items—§ 522(d)(3)

Section 522(d)(3) allows a debtor to exempt an interest of up to $550 in value in any item of household furnishings, household goods, wearing apparel, appliances, books, animals, crops, or musical instruments held primarily for the personal, family or household use of the debtor or the debtor's dependents. Like the other exemptions, this exemption may be doubled in a joint case to include items of up to $1100 in value if jointly owned by the debtors.[65] There is an aggregate dollar limit of $11,525 per debtor on the property that can be exempted under this subsection. The dollar values in this provision are adjusted for inflation every three years.[66] Thus, especially in joint cases in which the limit is doubled, all of the household belongings of most debtors may be saved under this provision.

One question which may occasionally arise concerns the definition of the term "item." When several related pieces of property may be considered a "set" worth over $550, disputes could occur as to whether that set is an item. For example, it is not clear whether each chair in a dining room set, or each spoon in a set of silver, or each speaker in a stereo system, should be considered to be an item apart from the set as a whole.[67] Common sense should prevail in dealing with these issues and, except in cases in which the debtors have a great deal of valuable property, trustees have little interest in litigating about the exemption of a few household goods.

The scope of the subsection may also raise questions. It will not generally include motor vehicles, though a lawn tractor might be an exception.[68] Similarly, most items specifically listed elsewhere in the exemption provisions, such as jewelry,[69] are not usually included. Other items, such as guns, may be subject to a dispute because it is unclear whether they are household goods.[70] Although the provision is not specifically limited to personalty, it may be hard to use section 522(d)(3) to have real property exempted (except possibly for some fixtures and the like).

Finally, items used *primarily* for business purposes are not meant to be included.[71] The language limiting the exemption to items used *primarily* for "personal, family, or household use," derived from the Truth in Lending Act,[72] does make this limitation clear. However, under that Act, the case law and Federal Reserve Board interpretations and staff opinions have given that phrase a fairly broad meaning, and should be consulted if questions arise.[73] The same phrase is used in the Code's definition of "consumer debt," discussed elsewhere in this treatise.[74]

It seems safe to say that, except for debtors who conduct a business in their home, this exemption should be applicable to just about all of the personal property normally kept at the debtor's residence that is not specifically mentioned in other exemptions.[75] It is clear that the scope of the exemption extends beyond necessities, as it does not include, as do some others,[76] only amounts "reasonably necessary for the support of the debtor." The section is concerned only with how the property is used, and not whether it might be considered a luxury.

10.2.2.5 Jewelry—§ 522(d)(4)

Each debtor is allowed to exempt up to $1450 worth of jewelry, as long as it is held primarily for personal, family, or household use of the debtor or a dependent. As with the household goods exemption, unused exemptions applicable to "any property" may be used to increase this amount. For example, a jewelry item worth $1525 may be exempted using the $1450 jewelry exemption plus $75 worth of the exemption

---

62 *See In re* Browning, 2010 WL 1541629 (Bankr. C.D. Ill. Apr. 19, 2010) (when property is owned by joint tenants with right of survivorship in Illinois, each debtor's interest extended to whole of vehicle, so one debtor could use his exemption to exempt entire value of joint tenants' equity in vehicle).
63 11 U.S.C. § 522(d)(5).
64 11 U.S.C. § 522(d)(6). *See* § 10.2.2.7, *infra*.
65 *In re* Lambert, 10 B.R. 11 (Bankr. N.D. Ind. 1980).
66 11 U.S.C. § 104.
67 *See In re* Wahl, 14 B.R. 153 (Bankr. E.D. Wis. 1981) (each knife, fork or spoon in a set of silver considered an item; court looked to *Webster's Dictionary* for guidance).
68 *See In re* Jones, 5 B.R. 655 (Bankr. M.D.N.C. 1980) (garden tractor exempt as household good).
  There has also been some litigation about whether a mobile home can be considered a household good for the purposes of the lien avoidance provision applicable to nonpossessory, nonpurchase-money security interests in exempt household goods. *See* § 10.4.2.4, *infra*.

69 11 U.S.C. § 522(d)(4).
70 Most of the litigation on this issue had taken place in the context of lien avoidance motions. *See* § 10.4.2.4, *infra*.
71 *See In re* Reid, 757 F.2d 230 (10th Cir. 1985) (debtor's "classic religious paintings," worth $187,000 and pledged as collateral for business loans, were primarily used for business and are not household furniture exemptible under Oklahoma law).
72 15 U.S.C. § 1602(h).
73 *See* National Consumer Law Center, Truth in Lending § 2.2.3 (8th ed. 2012).
74 11 U.S.C. § 101(8). *See* § 13.4, *infra*.
75 *See In re* Ratliff, 209 B.R. 534 (Bankr. E.D. Okla. 1997) (computer and printer were household goods for purposes of Oklahoma exemptions); *In re* Beard, 5 B.R. 429 (Bankr. S.D. Iowa 1980) (stereo components and Betamax are household goods); *In re* Coleman, 5 B.R. 76 (Bankr. M.D. Tenn. 1980) (stereo system constitutes household furnishings).
  The Fourth Circuit has adopted a slightly more limited definition, finding "household goods" to mean those items of personal property typically found in or around the home and used by a debtor or the debtor's dependents to support and facilitate day-to-day living within the home. *In re* McGreevy, 955 F.2d 957 (4th Cir. 1992).
76 *See, e.g.*, 11 U.S.C. § 522(d)(11)(B), (C), (E).

applicable to any property (sometimes referred to as the "wild card" exemption).

Some questions may arise under this provision concerning whether a particular item is classified as jewelry or wearing apparel.[77] If the item is worth under $550, it is usually to the debtor's benefit for it to be considered the latter, because a larger total exemption is available for wearing apparel worth less than $550 per item. On the other hand, if the debtor has items worth more than $550, the debtor's use of other exemptions will determine which interpretation is more favorable in a particular case. If none of the exemption for "any property" has been used and all of the jewelry exemption has been used, then it is preferable to argue that the items are wearing apparel so that on each item any value in excess of the $550 available for wearing apparel may be exempted (until the wild-card exemption is exhausted). However, if the jewelry exemption has not yet been used, it is preferable to argue that the item is jewelry so that the amount available only for jewelry can be used and the wild-card exemption can be saved for some other property. In any event, case law developed under the various state exemption laws pertaining to jewelry and wearing apparel will be relevant to the argument.

A common issue under this subsection arises with respect to wedding rings, engagement rings and other jewelry with great sentimental value. The monetary value of those items can sometimes exceed the amount of the available exemptions. Most trustees do not make a practice of taking a debtor's personal jewelry unless it is very valuable, but there is no way to make this guarantee about a particular item to a nervous debtor contemplating bankruptcy. In such situations, it may make sense to obtain an appraisal, because it is not uncommon for debtors to have an inflated opinion about the value of jewelry which is based in sentiment rather than reality. After appraisal, if the jewelry still cannot be exempted under any combination of available provisions, local practice should be checked. In some jurisdictions, given the practice of trustees, there may be little cause for worry. Further, as discussed in an earlier chapter, a trustee who is interested in selling valuable jewelry may be willing to sell it to the debtor or a relative of the debtor in order to avoid liquidation costs and the hardship caused by sale of a highly personal item.[78] Finally, if a sale cannot be avoided, the debtor will receive the amount of the exemption in cash, and that cash can be used to purchase a substitute item.

10.2.2.6 Any Property—§ 522(d)(5)

One of the most important of the federal exemptions is the exemption which can be applied to "any property," sometimes called the "wild card." The amount of this exemption is $1150 per debtor, plus any unused amount of the homestead amount from subsection (d)(1) up to $10,825 per debtor. The applicability of the unused homestead exemption to any property, sometimes called the "homestead pourover," was originally intended to equalize home owners and renters but was significantly reduced when a $3750 limit was added in 1984. That limit was raised in 1994 and is adjusted every three years to take into account changes in the cost of living.[79] It gives tremendous flexibility to both home owners and renters, as many home owners may not choose to or need to use the entire homestead exemption for their residences. And as there is no requirement that any portion of the homestead exemption be used on a home as a prerequisite to qualifying for the homestead pourover, renters can get the benefit of a total wild card exemption worth $11,975.[80]

As noted above, this exemption can be used in conjunction with any other specific exemption to pick up value in excess of the amount provided by the particular exemption, for example, the remaining $50 on a $3500 car.[81] It can also be applied to any possible property interest, including intangibles, non-liquid property, causes of action, tax refunds, cash, public benefits already received, and so forth.[82] If the wild card exemption is not used in the debtors' initial exemption claim, it remains available to be raised by way of amendment to protect property which the trustee unexpectedly contends is to be nonexempt.[83]

10.2.2.7 Tools of the Trade—§ 522(d)(6)

Each debtor may exempt up to $2175 worth of implements, professional books, or tools of the trade that belong to the debtor or a dependent of the debtor. This exemption, too, may overlap with some of the others. For example, a motor vehicle sometimes can be claimed as exempt under this subsection as well as subsection (d)(2) if it is used by the debtor in his or her work (beyond normal commuting.)[84] Thus, a vehicle worth

---

77 See, e.g., In re Fernandez, 855 F.2d 218 (5th Cir. 1988) (under Texas law jewelry may be exemptible as clothing); In re Hazelhurst, 228 B.R. 199 (Bankr. E.D. Tenn. 1998) (jewelry could be considered wearing apparel under Tennessee exemptions).
78 See § 8.3.11, supra.
79 11 U.S.C. § 104.
  The most recent adjustment became effective on April 1, 2007.
80 See In re Martin, 140 F.3d 806 (8th Cir. 1998) (no requirement that the debtor use any portion of the homestead exemption on a home in order to qualify for the homestead pourover).
81 Augustine v. United States, 675 F.2d 582 (3d Cir. 1982) (section 522(d)(5) exemption may be used to exempt tools of trade in excess of $750 limit applicable at that time).
82 4 Collier on Bankruptcy ¶ 522.09[5] (16th ed.); In re Smith, 640 F.2d 888 (7th Cir. 1981) (Truth in Lending claim could be exempted under 11 U.S.C. § 522(d)(5)); In re Laird, 6 B.R. 273 (Bankr. E.D. Pa. 1980) (arbitration award); In re Collins, 5 B.R. 675 (Bankr. N.D. Cal. 1980) (credit union account); In re Nichols, 4 B.R. 711 (Bankr. E.D. Mich. 1980) (wage withholdings and tax refunds); In re Cramer, 3 B.R. 428 (Bankr. D. Ariz. 1980) (business inventory).
83 See § 10.3.2, infra.
84 Compare In re Breen, 123 B.R. 357 (B.A.P. 9th Cir. 1991) (carpenter may avoid nonpossessory, nonpurchase-money security interest on pick-up truck considered to be tool of the trade), In re McNutt, 87 B.R. 84 (B.A.P. 9th Cir. 1988) (truck used in dry-wall business exempt as tool of debtor's trade), In re Lyall, 191 B.R. 78 (E.D. Va. 1996) (if car was necessary for debtor's work as an architect, it was tool of trade under Virginia law even if it was a luxury car), In re Sackett, 394 B.R. 544, 545 (Bankr. D. Colo. 2008) (high-end sports utility vehicle was nurse's tool of trade under Colorado law because it was used to get from place to place in her work), In re Graettinger,

$5625 per debtor could be claimed by combining these sections. Three way combinations, including the wild card exemption, are also possible.[85] Additionally, the spouse of a debtor may claim jointly-owned equipment as exempt tools of the trade even if that spouse only handles the business end of the enterprise.[86] As with jewelry, it may be preferable to argue that a particular item falls within the household goods exemption, that is, is held primarily for personal, non-business use, if its value is under $550, or if the tools of trade exemption has been exhausted on other property.

There are often significant questions as to whether farm equipment or livestock are included within this exemption or similar exemptions under state law. Although the importance of the issue is diminished in the federal scheme by the relatively low amount of the exemption, it has been raised in a number of reported cases.[87] Similar issues may arise in connection with home office equipment.[88]

10.2.2.8 Unmatured Life Insurance—§ 522(d)(7)

The subsection providing an exemption for unmatured life insurance, as distinguished from the subsection following it, is for those interests in life insurance owned by the debtor which do not have a cash or loan value. Thus, any interest in term insurance can be exempted in full under this subsection.

Credit life insurance is specifically excluded from the coverage of this subsection. And, if the debtor is merely the beneficiary of a policy insuring the life of a living person and owned by someone other than the debtor, no exemption need be used, because generally the debtor has no property interest in that policy. (However, if the insured dies within 180 days after the bankruptcy petition is filed, the debtor's interest in the proceeds does become property of the estate,[89] and can be exempted under section 522(d)(11), discussed below.)[90] It is important to note that the debtor need not be the person insured by the life insurance contract for this exemption to apply.

10.2.2.9 Accrued Dividend, Interest, or Loan Value of Life Insurance—§ 522(d)(8)

Interests in life insurance policies which do have a cash value may be exempted to the extent of $11,525 per debtor under subsection (d)(8). From this amount must be subtracted any amounts that are used by the insurance company to continue premium payments under a contract which provides for automatic payments out of the accrued value.[91]

Unlike the exemption provided by the previous subsection, this exemption may only be applied to policies insuring the life of the debtor or someone of whom the debtor is a dependent. Nonetheless, because life insurance can be a relatively liquid type of property, if a debtor has excess liquid assets prior to filing a case that cannot be otherwise exempted, this exemption provides a way to exempt a substantial additional amount through a prebankruptcy purchase of life insurance.[92]

10.2.2.10 Health Aids—§ 522(d)(9)

A debtor may exempt an unlimited amount of professionally prescribed health aids for the debtor or a dependent of the debtor. This exemption clearly covers such items as wheelchairs and artificial limbs. Arguably, it is much broader, and could include specially equipped automobiles, or even normal automobiles essential to receiving medical treatments.[93] It is also possible that property prescribed for therapy, such as swimming pools, could be included.[94]

---

95 B.R. 632 (Bankr. N.D. Iowa 1988) (pick-up truck is tool of trade in debtor's business as grain bin salesperson), *and In re* Dubrock, 5 B.R. 353 (Bankr. W.D. Ky. 1980) (real estate broker and salesman may claim automobile as tool of the trade), *with In re* Johnston, 842 F.2d 1221 (10th Cir. 1988) (pick-up truck used only for commuting not tool of trade under Wyoming law), *and In re* Damron, 5 B.R. 357 (Bankr. W.D. Ky. 1980) (mechanic and factory worker may not claim automobile as tool of the trade if they could carry on occupation without car).

85 *See* § 10.2.2.6, *supra*.
86 *In re* Meckfessel, 67 B.R. 277 (Bankr. D. Kan. 1986). *See also In re* Lampe, 331 F.3d 750 (10th Cir. 2003) (wife-debtor had joint ownership interest in farm equipment so her exemption could be added to husband's exemption).
87 *See In re* Heape, 886 F.2d 280 (10th Cir. 1989) (breeding livestock are tools of a livestock farmer's trade under Kansas law); *In re* Stewart, 110 B.R. 11 (Bankr. D. Idaho 1989) (horses necessary for debtor's work as a yardman were tools of trade under Idaho law); *In re* Siegmann, 757 P.2d 820 (Okla. 1988) (tractor, front-end loader and flat-bed trailer are tools of farmer's trade under Oklahoma law). *Compare In re* Walkington, 42 B.R. 67 (Bankr. W.D. Mich. 1984) (cattle found tools of trade under federal law) *with In re* Patterson, 825 F.2d 1140 (7th Cir. 1987) (cattle and farm machinery not tools of trade).
88 *See In re* Clifford, 222 B.R. 8 (Bankr. D. Conn. 1998) (facsimile machine used to submit bids and keep in touch with clients is a tool of the trade).
89 11 U.S.C. § 541(a)(5)(C).
90 *See also* BancOhio Nat'l Bank v. Walters, 724 F.2d 1081 (4th Cir. 1984) (when debtors claimed unmatured life insurance policies as exempt under section 522(d)(7), proceeds of policy acquired within 180 days of petition were included in that exemption).
91 Such payments are also specifically excepted from the turnover requirements of section 542. 11 U.S.C. § 542(d).
92 *See In re* O'Brien, 67 B.R. 317 (Bankr. N.D. Iowa 1986). *But see In re* Mueller, 867 F.2d 568 (10th Cir. 1989) (purchase of insurance policy three days before bankruptcy when debtor already had insurance contained badges of fraud on creditors so as to make it nonexempt under Kansas law).
93 *See In re* Reardon, 403 B.R. 822 (Bankr. D. Mont. 2009) (van with wheelchair conversion kit was health aid exempt under Montana law); *In re* Allard, 342 B.R. 102 (Bankr. M.D. Fla. 2005) (van with wheelchair lift was health aid exempt under Florida law); *In re* Hellen, 329 B.R. 678 (Bankr. N.D. Ill. 2005) (customized van treated as health aid). *But see* Unif. Exemption Act § 5, 13 U.L.A. 380 (which has different wording limiting exemption to aids necessary to enable individual to work or sustain health).
94 *See In re* Man, 428 B.R. 644 (Bankr. M.D.N.C. 2010) (modifications to condominium necessary to meet debtor's health needs could be exempted as health aids under North Carolina law); *In re* Johnson, 101 B.R. 280 (Bankr. W.D. Okla. 1989) (water treatment system recommended by physician qualifies as professionally prescribed health aid under Oklahoma law), *aff'd*, 113 B.R. 44 (W.D. Okla. 1989).

Some guidance on these issues may be obtained from the income tax cases dealing with the medical expenses deduction. These cases have allowed deductions for a home elevator[95] and automobile modifications to accommodate a disabled person.[96] However, the deductions are allowed only to the extent they do not increase the value of the property on which they are installed.[97] A good argument can be made that the bankruptcy exemption should be more broadly construed due to its different purpose. First, the tax cases are also concerned with distinguishing expenses from capital expenditures, and that concern is what led to the limitation on deductions which increase the value of property. In addition, the exemption's principal purpose is to preserve for the debtor that property necessary because of health problems. It would do little good to preserve the special automobile equipment without the automobile, so arguably the entire specially equipped vehicle can be claimed as exempt. Moreover, there is no reason in bankruptcy to only allow part of the value of a home improvement to be exempted because the rest can later be recouped upon sale of the house. If the home and improvement are lost because of such an interpretation, the purpose of the exemption would be defeated.

10.2.2.11 Disability, Retirement, and Other Benefits Replacing Wages—§ 522(d)(10)

Because of the Code's broad definition of property of the bankruptcy estate,[98] a debtor's entitlement to receive various benefits in the future has for the first time become subject to the claims of creditors.[99] Rights to such entitlements must therefore be exempted if they are to be saved for the debtor's future use. Thus, section 522(d)(10) exempts the right to receive, in the future, Social Security, unemployment, welfare, disability, and illness benefits.[100] Alimony and support payments are also exempt but only to the extent reasonably necessary for the support of the debtor and any dependents of the debtor.[101] (In some states that have opted out of the federal exemptions, there may be a question with respect to whether alimony payment arrearages are exempted.)[102]

Similarly, payments under most pension plans and many employee benefit plans are exempt under this provision to the extent reasonably necessary for the support of the debtor and the debtor's dependents.[103] As discussed below, the enactment

---

95 Hollander v. Comm'r of Internal Revenue, 219 F.2d 934 (3d Cir. 1955).
96 Rev. Rul. 70-606, 1970-2 C.B. 66.
97 Rev. Rul. 59-411, 1959-2 C.B. 100.
98 11 U.S.C. § 541. See Ch. 2, supra.
99 A cause of action to enforce such an entitlement should be exempt under this provision. In re Daly, 344 B.R. 304 (Bankr. M.D. Pa. 2005).
100 11 U.S.C. § 522(d)(10)(A), (B), (C).
 Severance pay based upon years of service may be exempted under section 522(d)(10)(C) as an unemployment benefit or under section 522(d)(10)(E) as a contract payment based upon years of service. In re Gonsalves, 2010 WL 5342084 (Bankr. D. Mass. Dec. 21, 2010).
 Worker's compensation benefits probably fall within this category or within section 522(d)(11)(D) or (E) (payments on account of personal injuries or in compensation for loss of future earnings). See In re Cain, 91 B.R. 182 (Bankr. N.D. Ga. 1988); In re Evans, 29 B.R. 336 (Bankr. D.N.J. 1983); In re LaBelle, 18 B.R. 169 (Bankr. D. Me. 1982). See also In re Jones, 446 B.R. 466 (Bankr. D. Kan. 2011) (annuity obtained in settlement of FELA claim supplanted disability pension, and therefore was based on disability). But see In re Sanchez, 362 B.R. 342 (Bankr. W.D. Mich. 2007) (debtor who had received settlement for workers compensation did not have right to receive benefits exemptible under section 522(d)(10), but could claim exemption under section 522(d)(11)(D) and (E)).
 Benefits under privately purchased disability policies may be able to be exempted only under section 522(d)(10)(E), which limits the exemption to amounts reasonably necessary for support. In re Wegrzyn, 291 B.R. 2 (Bankr. D. Mass. 2003). But see In re Lambert, 9 B.R. 799 (Bankr. W.D. Mich. 1981). Similarly a Federal Employers' Liability Act settlement for an injury that led to disability was determined by one court to be exempt under section 522(d)(10)(C). In re Albrecht, 89 B.R. 859 (Bankr. D. Mont. 1988).
 However, the mere fact that a debtor is in bad health does not transform unrestricted lottery winnings paid as an annuity into an annuity paid on account of illness. In re Skog, 144 B.R. 221 (Bankr. D.R.I. 1992). And benefits that bear no relation to lost income normally do not fall within this provision. In re Chavis, 207 B.R. 845 (Bankr. W.D. 1997) (proceeds of accidental death or dismemberment policy not eligible to be claimed as exempt under section 522(d)(10), but were eligible for exemption under section 522(d)(11)).
 When in doubt, a debtor should claim all possible exemptions.
101 11 U.S.C. § 522(d)(10)(D).
 It is unclear whether the court can examine an award to determine whether its true purpose is support as it can do in determining dischargeability under section 523(a)(5). See In re Milligan, 342 F.3d 358 (5th Cir. 2003) (because § 522(d)(11)(D) did not have language contained in section 523(a)(5) regarding true purpose of award, court could not look behind labels in decree); In re Tennihill, 2012 WL 293633 (Bankr. M.D. Fla. Jan. 15, 2012) (court could look behind language of decree to determine true purpose of award); In re Miller, 424 B.R. 171 (Bankr. M.D. Pa. 2010) (despite discussion in property division portion of master's report, divorce award was clearly founded on debtor's need for support and could be exempted); In re Ellertson, 252 B.R. 831 (Bankr. S.D. Fla. 2000) (divorce decree payments not exemptible because they were not in nature of support despite labels in divorce decree); In re Bentley, 245 B.R. 684 (Bankr. D. Kan. 2000) (court cannot look behind state court label); In re Sheffield, 212 B.R. 1019 (Bankr. M.D. Fla. 1997) (life insurance proceeds that debtor received from policy that former husband was required by divorce decree to maintain did not constitute alimony because insurance requirement in decree was reciprocal and therefore not in the nature of support); § 15.4.3.5.3, infra.
 It seems fairly clear that child support and awards for the benefit of someone other than the debtor need not be exempted because they can be considered to be held in trust for the real intended beneficiary. See Hughes, Code Exemptions: Far-Reaching Achievement, 28 DePaul L. Rev. 1025, 1033 n.57 (1979) and cases cited therein.
 It is the trustee's burden to show that the right to payments belongs to the parent who is the debtor rather than the child. In re Green, 423 B.R. 867 (Bankr. W.D. Ark. 2010).
102 See In re Poffenbarger, 281 B.R. 379 (Bankr. S.D. Ala. 2002) (while right to child support arrearages was in reality property of debtor's children, there was no exemption for alimony arrearages under Alabama law).
103 11 U.S.C. § 522(d)(10)(E); Rousey v. Jacoway, 544 U.S. 320, 125 S. Ct. 1561, 161 L. Ed. 2d 563 (2005) (exemption of IRAs allowed under section 522(d)(10)(E)); In re Lightbody, 240 B.R. 545 (Bankr. E.D. Mich. 1999) (county deferred compensation plan was a "similar plan" even though debtor could withdraw money for unforeseen

of section 522(d)(12) in 2005 should greatly reduce the need to litigate such issues.[104] When section 522(d)(12) does not apply for some reason, a determination of whether a pension is reasonably necessary for the support of a debtor and any dependents requires an examination of the debtor's age, health, earning capacity, present and future financial needs and ability to reestablish a retirement fund.[105] Some courts have rejected exemptions under section 522(d)(10) in cases of middle-income and upper-income debtors with no present need for support or right to receive the payments,[106] but such decisions are of questionable validity after the Supreme Court's decision in *Rousey v. Jacoway*.[107] In such cases, the state exemptions may provide superior protection.[108] An issue has also arisen about whether this provision protects only distributions under such plans or the funds in the plan as a whole.[109] This issue should be resolved in favor of the debtor's position because there would be no value to protecting payments under a plan, when the funds in the plan itself can be liquidated, and because the exemption is for the debtor's prospective "right to receive" the payment.[110]

It is important to note that the Supreme Court has ruled that ERISA-qualified pension and employee benefit plans do not come into a debtor's bankruptcy estate at all.[111] When benefit plans are not in the estate, the debtor need not claim them as exempt.[112] However, if there is any doubt about whether the plan is excluded from the estate, there is no reason not to claim all available exemptions in the alternative, while also asserting the property is not property of the estate. When a plan does not qualify under ERISA, whether or not it may be claimed as exempt under section 522(d)(10)(E), it is still likely to be eligible to be claimed under section 522(d)(12).[113] If it is not, applicable nonbankruptcy law restrictions on transfer[114] may result in the plan being excluded from the estate. Alternatively, state law exemptions,[115] which are sometimes more generous than section 522(d), may be available.[116]

Except in the case of Social Security and SSI benefits,[117] property traceable to benefits already received may have to be

---

emergency); *In re Miller*, 33 B.R. 549 (Bankr. D. Minn. 1983) (court looked to future retirement needs in exempting interest in profit-sharing plan). *See also In re Andersen*, 259 B.R. 687 (B.A.P. 8th Cir. 2001) (annuity purchased with lump sum from inheritance for purpose of retirement income could be exempted under section 522(d)(10)(E)). *But see* Weidman v. Shapiro, 299 B.R. 429 (E.D. Mich. 2003) (annuity bequeathed to debtor by her mother not replacement for lost income or future earnings); *In re Collett*, 253 B.R. 452 (Bankr. W.D. Mo. 2000) (payments under annuity established by testamentary trust not within scope of exemption because not under plan on account of illness, disability, death, age, or length of service).

104 See § 10.2.2.13, *infra*.
105 *In re Hamo*, 233 B.R. 718 (B.A.P. 6th Cir. 1999); *In re Fisher*, 63 B.R. 649 (Bankr. W.D. Ky. 1986).
106 *See In re Moffatt*, 959 F.2d 740 (9th Cir. 1992) (annuity established in contemplation of bankruptcy with quarterly payments of $4370 beginning immediately after bankruptcy was not reasonably necessary to debtor when he and his wife had income in excess of $90,000 per year); *In re Kochell*, 732 F.2d 564 (7th Cir. 1984) (pension plans not necessary to support of forty-four-year-old physician); *In re Clark*, 711 F.2d 21 (3d Cir. 1983) (funds not needed by forty-three-year-old therapist).
107 Rousey v. Jacoway, 544 U.S. 320, 125 S. Ct. 1561, 161 L. Ed. 2d 563 (2005). *See In re Krebs*, 527 F.3d 82, 86 (3d Cir. 2008) (overruling *Clark* based on *Rousey*).
108 See cases cited later in this subsection.
109 Patterson v. Shumate, 504 U.S. 753, 112 S. Ct. 2242, 2249 n.5, 119 L. Ed. 2d 519, 530 n.5 (1992).
110 *In re Carmichael*, 100 F.3d 375 (5th Cir. 1996) (debtors could exempt both right to receive current payments from IRA and right to receive payments in the future); *In re Marsella*, 188 B.R. 731 (Bankr. D.R.I. 1995); *In re Yee*, 147 B.R.624 (Bankr. D. Mass. 1992).
111 Patterson v. Shumate, 504 U.S. 753, 112 S. Ct. 2242, 119 L. Ed. 2d 519 (1992).
   The Supreme Court pointed out, however, that at least two types of retirement accounts do not qualify under ERISA and, therefore, are not entitled to its protection. These are certain pensions established by governmental entities or religious organizations and individual retirement accounts (IRAs). Protection for those plans will have to be sought under section 522(d)(10)(E), section 522(d)(12), section 522(b)(3)(C), state law exemptions, or claims that they are not property of the estate because under applicable nonbankruptcy law they have the same inalienability as the Supreme Court found in ERISA plans. For further discussion of the latter issues, see § 2.5.2, *supra*.
112 In addition to ERISA-qualified plans, funds placed in an education individual retirement account, as defined in section 530(b)(1) of the Internal Revenue Code, and funds contributed to a tuition program, as defined in section 529(b)(1) of the Internal Revenue Code, before the filing of the petition, may be excluded from property of the estate pursuant to section 541(b)(5) and (b)(6) if certain conditions are met. See § 2.5.3, *supra*.
113 For debtors who are claiming state and federal nonbankruptcy exemptions in an opt-out state, such a plan is also likely to be exemptible under section 522(b)(3)(C). *See* § 10.2.3.3, *infra*.
114 Applicable nonbankruptcy law restrictions on transfer of pensions and employee benefit plans are enforceable by all debtors through 11 U.S.C. § 541(c)(2) whether or not state exemptions are chosen. *See* § 2.5.2, *supra*. *See generally* Patterson v. Shumate, 504 U.S. 753, 112 S. Ct. 2242, 119 L. Ed. 2d 519 (1992).
115 State law exemptions (as opposed to restrictions on transfer) are available only to those who claim state exemptions under 11 U.S.C. § 522(b)(2). *In re MacIntyre*, 74 F.3d 186 (9th Cir. 1996) (section 403(b) plan fully exempt under California law); *In re Schlein*, 8 F.3d 745 (11th Cir. 1993) (Florida exemption for employee benefit plans protected debtor's SEP-IRA accounts and was not preempted by ERISA); *In re Walker*, 959 F.2d 894 (10th Cir. 1992) (Oklahoma exemption provisions protected debtor's non-ERISA retirement plans and were not preempted by ERISA); *In re Buzza*, 287 B.R. 417 (Bankr. S.D. Ohio 2002) (Ohio exemption covering self-settled IRA not preempted by ERISA). *See* § 10.2.1.1, *supra*.
116 In jurisdictions where both federal and state law exemptions are available, state exemptions may offer superior protection if section 522(b)(3)(C) does not apply for some reason. Such would be the case when state exemptions are not limited to amounts reasonably necessary for the support of the debtor or the debtor's dependents. *See, e.g.*, Hovis v. Wright, 751 F.2d 714 (4th Cir. 1985) (employee contributions to teacher retirement fund held exempt under South Carolina law).
117 Since the Bankruptcy Code was passed, Congress has amended the Social Security Act to make clear that benefits thereunder are not subject to the bankruptcy laws and thus should not become property of the estate. 42 U.S.C. §§ 407, 1383(d). *See In re Buren*, 725 F.2d 1080 (6th Cir. 1984). Therefore, they need not be exempted to be preserved for the debtor. This protection should apply not only to

exempted under other provisions of the federal exemptions. If so, this requirement is a departure from some of the federal nonbankruptcy laws protecting income benefits such as veterans benefits, under which accrued benefits were also exempt from execution.[118] Thus, a debtor who has saved from such benefits a substantial amount of money that cannot all be claimed as exempt, perhaps because of a large retroactive payment, may be better off choosing the alternative of the state and federal nonbankruptcy exemptions.[119]

As noted above, some types of property covered by this provision, for example, alimony, child support, and private retirement plans, are exempt only to the extent reasonably necessary for the support of the debtor and the debtor's dependents. This limitation was included primarily to prevent wealthy people with enormous amounts of income from such sources from protecting all of that income in bankruptcy. With this purpose in mind, the courts are likely to be relatively liberal in deciding what amounts are reasonably necessary for support. Although the statute gives no guidance, judges who see mostly middle-class debtors usually approve a living standard that supports a middle-class lifestyle.[120]

Another question likely to arise concerns the definition of the term "public assistance." Obviously, welfare cash payments are included. It also seems clear that supplements such as food stamps and energy assistance should come within this category.[121] The question becomes slightly closer with housing subsidies. Payments under Section 8, which reduce a family's rent to a certain percentage of income, can be analogized to food stamps, which reduce food costs to a certain percentage of income. And from there it should not be difficult to extend the principle to mortgage interest subsidies and the subsidy inherent in living in public housing, where rent is limited to a certain percentage of income. Similar issues arise with regard to the federal earned income tax credit, other tax credits, and other subsidy programs.[122] The argument is more difficult when a

---

the right to receive benefits, but also to the benefits already received. See Philpott v. Essex County Welfare Bd., 409 U.S. 413, 93 S. Ct. 590, 34 L. Ed. 2d 608 (1973); In re Carpenter, 408 B.R. 244 (B.A.P. 8th Cir. 2009) (Social Security Act protects benefits already received by debtor), aff'd, 614 F.3d 930 (8th Cir. 2010); In re Hildestad, 2010 WL 320362 (Bankr. D. Ariz. Jan. 20, 2010) (lump sum Social Security payment deposited in bank and commingled with other funds could be exempted if reasonably traceable); In re Spolarich, 2009 Bankr. LEXIS 3059 (Bankr. N.D. Ind. Sept. 30, 2009) (tax refund that consisted of funds withheld from Social Security benefits was exempt under 42 U.S.C. § 407); In re Frazier, 116 B.R. 675 (Bankr. W.D. Wis. 1990) (exemption covers not only future benefits but also lump sums received prior to bankruptcy filing). See also In re Sparks, 410 B.R. 602 (Bankr. S.D. Ohio 2009) (tax refunds traceable to retirement, unemployment, and Social Security benefits exempt under state law were exempt).

Similar protections are likely to be found for veterans benefits and perhaps other federal benefits with statutory language similar to the anti-alienation provisions of the Social Security Act. See Meyer v. Scholz (In re Scholz), 447 B.R. 887 (B.A.P. 9th Cir. 2011) (railroad retirement benefits excluded from any availability in bankruptcy by similar language in 45 U.S.C. § 231m(a)).

118 Compare In re Treadwell, 699 F.2d 1050 (11th Cir. 1983) (decided prior to the amendment discussed above), In re Wyman, 437 B.R. 478 (Bankr. D. Mass. 2010) (lump sum unemployment benefit received before petition could not be exempted), and In re Moore, 214 B.R. 628 (Bankr. D. Kan. 1997) (retirement funds already received were not exempt but Social Security funds received were exempt), with In re Donaghy, 11 B.R. 677 (Bankr. S.D.N.Y. 1981) (recently received lump sum payments could be exempted under section 522(d)(10)(E) even though "right to receive" no longer technically existed).

119 See Philpott v. Essex County Welfare Bd., 409 U.S. 413, 93 S. Ct. 590, 34 L. Ed. 2d 608 (1973) (Social Security benefits in bank account could not be attached); In re Smith, 242 B.R. 427 (Bankr. E.D. Tenn. 1999) (veteran's benefits received by widow of veteran exempt even though they were used to purchase a certificate of deposit); In re Crandall, 200 B.R. 243 (Bankr. M.D. Fla. 1995) (debtor's bank account, which consisted solely of Social Security benefits, exempt under Social Security Act); In re Bresnahan, 183 B.R. 506 (Bankr. S.D. Ohio 1995) (retirement fund distribution deposited in debtor's bank account was still exempt under Ohio exemption law).

120 See, e.g., In re Hendricks, 11 B.R. 48 (Bankr. W.D. Mo. 1981); In re Lambert, 9 B.R. 799 (Bankr. W.D. Mich. 1981). But see In re Thurston, 255 B.R. 725 (Bankr. S.D. Ohio 2000) (under similar state exemption court found $14,000 support arrearages not necessary for support of debtor with no dependents earning $38,000); Hughes, Code Exemptions: Far-Reaching Achievement, 28 DePaul L. Rev. 1025, 1033 nn.60, 61 (citing cases which have set varying standards). See also Vukowich, The Bankruptcy Commission's Proposal Regarding Bankrupts' Exemption Rights, 63 Cal. L. Rev. 1439, 1461–1462 (1975) (citing cases and recommending amount "reasonably essential or needed by an average and reasonable person"); Plumb, The Recommendations of the Commission on the Bankruptcy Laws—Exempt and Immune Property, 61 Va. L. Rev. 1, 94–95 (1975).

The language "reasonably necessary for support," also contained in section 1325(b), is discussed further in § 12.3.4, infra.

121 See Morris v. Philadelphia Elec. Co., 45 B.R. 350 (E.D. Pa. 1984) (energy assistance).

122 See In re James, 406 F.3d 1340 (11th Cir. 2005) (earned income credit exempt as public assistance under Alabama law); Flanery v. Mathison, 289 B.R. 624 (W.D. Ky. 2003) (earned income credit exempt as public assistance under Kentucky law); In re Lee, 415 B.R. 518 (Bankr. D. Kan. 2009) (Kansas food sales tax refund was local public assistance benefit); In re Wilson, 305 B.R. 4 (Bankr. N.D. Iowa 2004) (federal commodity program payments based on determination of need were public assistance under Iowa law); In re Koch, 299 B.R. 523 (Bankr. C.D. Ill. 2003) (child tax credit available to affluent taxpayers not in nature of public assistance, but refundable child tax credit available only to lower income taxpayers was); In re Tomczyk, 295 B.R. 894 (Bankr. D. Minn. 2003) (federal earned income credit and state equivalent were "relief based on need" and therefore exempt under Minnesota law); In re Longstreet, 246 B.R. 611 (Bankr. S.D. Iowa 2000) (earned income credit exempt as public assistance under Iowa law); In re Fish, 224 B.R. 82 (Bankr. S.D. Ill. 1998) (earned income credit exempt as public assistance under Illinois law); In re Barnett, 214 B.R. 632 (Bankr. W.D. Okla. 1997) (earned income credit exempt under Oklahoma law protecting earnings from personal services); In re Goldsberry, 142 B.R. 158 (Bankr. E.D. Ky. 1992) (earned income credit was public assistance under Kentucky law); In re Jones, 107 B.R. 751 (Bankr. D. Idaho 1989) (earned income tax credit is exempt as public assistance payment under Idaho law); In re Murphy, 99 B.R. 370 (Bankr. S.D. Ohio 1988) (earned income tax credit is exempt as a "poor relief" payment under Ohio law). But see In re Collins, 170 F.3d 512 (5th Cir. 1999) (earned income credit not exemptible under Louisiana law protecting public assistance payments); In re Trudeau,

right to a government payment is not based upon need.[123]

It is usually not necessary to claim all of these benefits as exempt, although it may often be safer to do so. Trustees are unlikely to show much interest in such benefits, other than tax refunds, because they are probably not transferable. If a trustee does show interest, the schedules and claim of exemption can be amended at that time. Also, there are questions about the appropriate value to assign to these benefits. Should the right to receive welfare be valued as if it will continue through the close of the case? Or is it value only nominal, as it is not really transferable and may end the next day if other income appears or if durational limits apply? Must all workers who have paid Social Security taxes list a vested or non-vested contingent right to receive Social Security benefits when they retire or become disabled? Local practice, which usually does not require the listing of such assets, generally provides a guide as to such questions. In general, because of the contingencies involved, when benefits are listed as an asset, listing the value as "unknown" makes the most sense.

10.2.2.12 Rights to Compensation for Injury or Losses, and Payments for Lost Earnings— § 522(d)(11)

Another exemption covers the right to receive, and property traceable to, payments for various types of injury or loss.[124] These include crime-victim reparations awards, as well as payments, not to exceed $21,625, on account of bodily injury of the debtor or a person upon whom the debtor is dependent (but not including pain and suffering or pecuniary loss).[125] They also cover wrongful death awards based upon the death of someone of whom the debtor was a dependent, payments on life insurance that insured the life of someone of whom the debtor was a dependent, and payments in compensation for loss of future earnings of the debtor or one upon whom the debtor was a dependent.[126]

It is important to note, first, that this exemption category does include property that can be traced to the listed benefits, as well as the benefits themselves.[127] This inclusion may pose difficult problems of tracing past payments, but to the extent exemption planning can maximize traceability, it should be carefully considered. Second, some but not all of the payments listed are limited to amounts reasonably necessary to the support of the debtor and the debtor's dependents.[128] The comments made with respect to this limitation in section 522(d)(10) are equally applicable here.[129] Debtors should be careful in preparing their schedules to detail all their normal expenses for this analysis, even if they cannot currently pay them.[130]

One category has a specific dollar limit: $21,625 on account of personal bodily injury.[131] This category not only explicitly excludes pain and suffering and compensation for pecuniary

---

237 B.R. 803 (B.A.P. 10th Cir. 1999) (earned income credit not personal services earnings exempt under Wyoming law); In re Annis, 229 B.R. 802 (B.A.P. 10th Cir. 1999) (earned income credit not public assistance or earnings exempt under Oklahoma law); In re Rutter 204 B.R. 57 (Bankr. D. Or. 1997) (earned income credit not exemptible public assistance); In re Goertz, 202 B.R. 614 (Bankr. W.D. Mo. 1996) (earned income credit not exempt under Missouri law). See generally § 2.5.5, supra.

State exemption law may also explicitly provide an exemption for the earned income credit or child tax credit. See Borgman v. Cohen (In re Dunckley), 452 B.R. 241 (B.A.P. 10th Cir. 2011) (interpreting Colorado exemption for child tax credit); In re Sanderson, 283 B.R. 595 (Bankr. M.D. Fla. 2002) (citing newly enacted Florida exemption for earned income credit). But see In re Zingale, 693 F.3d 704 (6th Cir. 2012) (non-refundable portion of child tax credit not exempt under Ohio law).

123 See In re Hutchinson, 354 B.R. 523 (Bankr. D. Kan. 2006) (distributions made to all tribe members from casino revenues were not public assistance benefits).

124 Because section 541(a)(5) of the Code brings life insurance proceeds acquired within 180 days of the bankruptcy filing into the estate, one court has held that such insurance proceeds must be exempted under this subsection, notwithstanding the fact that the unmatured policy was properly claimed as wholly exempt at the time the bankruptcy was initiated. Cyrak v. Poynor, 80 B.R. 75 (N.D. Tex. 1987).

Other courts have found that properly the insurance policy protects any subsequent proceeds. See BancOhio Nat'l Bank v. Walters, 724 F.2d 1081 (4th Cir. 1984).

125 Because this exemption provision, unlike subsections 522(d)(1), (3), (4), (5), (6) and (8) does not refer to the debtor's aggregate interest, the debtor may exempt an amount up to the statutory dollar limit for each accident giving rise to exemptible damages. In re Daly, 344 B.R. 304 (Bankr. M.D. Pa. 2005); In re Comeaux, 305 B.R. 802 (Bankr. E.D. Tex. 2003); In re Chavis, 207 B.R. 845 (Bankr. W.D. Pa. 1997) (proceeds of accidental death or dismemberment); In re Marcus, 172 B.R. 502 (Bankr. D. Conn. 1994). But see In re Christo, 192 F.3d 36 (1st Cir. 1999) (dollar limit applies to personal injury claims in the aggregate rather than to each claim).

126 See In re Jackson, 593 F.3d 171 (2d Cir. 2010) (holding, erroneously, that loss of future earnings encompasses only earnings that would have been earned after bankruptcy petition date); In re Marble, 2010 WL 3198901 (E.D. Mich. Aug. 12, 2010) (annuity traceable to loss of consortium claim not exempt); In re Lewis, 406 B.R. 518, 520 (E.D. Mich. 2009) (right to payments from Ford buyout program that gave debtor option of educational benefits or cash payout could be exempted under section 522(d)(11)(E)), aff'd, 387 Fed. Appx. 530 (6th Cir. 2010).

127 See In re Miller, 36 B.R. 420 (Bankr. D.N.M. 1984) (real estate lot traced to payment for loss of future earnings; party objecting to exemption had burden of proof on tracing).

128 In re Collins, 281 B.R. 580 (Bankr. M.D. Pa. 2002) (life insurance proceeds reasonably necessary for young widowed mother); In re Cramer, 130 B.R. 193 (Bankr. E.D. Pa. 1991) (personal injury award of $20,000 reasonably necessary for support of disabled debtor whose only other income is Social Security disability); In re Gallo, 49 B.R. 28 (Bankr. N.D. Tex. 1985) (life insurance proceeds of $275,000 reasonably necessary for support of unemployed, possibly disabled debtor with two young children). See also In re Collopy, 99 B.R. 384 (Bankr. S.D. Ohio 1989) ("dependent" under Ohio exemption scheme may include someone physically, but not financially dependent on the insured).

129 See § 10.2.2.11, supra.

130 See In re Jackson, 593 F.3d 171 (2d Cir. 2010) (court based analysis of amount reasonably necessary on debtor's schedules, which may have shown reduced expenses due to reduction in debtor's income).

131 This amount is adjusted every three years pursuant to 11 U.S.C. § 104.

loss (the latter being covered by a separate provision), but also implicitly seems to exclude punitive damages. Courts have disagreed whether this exemption can be claimed only for one injury incident or whether a separate exemption can be claimed for each incident.[132] It is unclear how the bankruptcy court will be able to divide lump sum awards or settlements into these component parts.[133] Because the burden of proof in objections to exemptions is on the party objecting to the exemptions,[134] the exemption should be allowed unless the objector can demonstrate that a specific portion of the award is not exempt.[135] It is also unclear to what extent damage recoveries, or the right thereto, for non-bodily injuries such as discrimination or invasion of privacy, may be protected.[136] While these may not be covered by subsection (D) of section 522(d)(11), which is limited to personal bodily injuries, some portions of them may be deemed compensation for loss of future earnings, and thus exempt under subsection (E).[137] As with the personal injury exemption, it is the trustee's burden to show what portion of an unallocated personal injury award is not for loss of future earnings.[138] Because of these uncertainties, and because there is often an element of lost earnings in a personal injury award, such awards should usually be exempted under both section 522(d)(11)(D) and (E), and the wild card exemption of section 522(d)(5) to the extent it is available. In any event, the debtor's exempt share of any award should not be reduced to pay a pro-rata portion of the attorney fees incurred to obtain the funds.[139]

In light of these considerations, it may be also worthwhile to attempt to obtain a favorable designation of a damage award or settlement, if possible, prior to bankruptcy for the purposes of exempting as much property as possible under these provisions when permissible.

Similarly, it may be a good idea prior to bankruptcy to structure settlements or to place the proceeds of awards in spendthrift trusts which are valid under state law, in order to exclude them from the debtor's estate.[140]

10.2.2.13 Pensions and Retirement Accounts— § 522(d)(12)

10.2.2.13.1 Overview

The 2005 amendments added a broad new category of property that may be claimed as exempt when the debtor claims exemptions under the federal bankruptcy exemption scheme. Section 522(d)(12) permits the debtor to exempt retirement funds to the extent they are in a fund or account that is exempt from taxation under sections 401, 403, 408, 408A, 414, 457, or 501(a) of the Internal Revenue Code.[141] These sections of the Internal Revenue Code deal with all common types of pension, profit-sharing, and stock bonus plans; employee annuities; individual retirement accounts (including Roth IRAs); deferred compensation plans of state, local government, and tax-exempt organizations; and certain trusts.[142]

---

132 *Compare* Christo v. Yellin, 192 F.3d 36, 39 (1st Cir. 1999) (section 522(d)(11)(D) limited to one exemption, regardless of the number of incidents of bodily injury) *with In re* Daly, 344 B.R. 304 (Bankr. M.D. Pa. 2005).

133 *See In re* Scotti, 245 B.R. 17 (Bankr. D.N.J. 2000) (award is exemptible unless it was for pain and suffering with no bodily injury). *See also* n. 124, *supra*.

134 Fed. R. Bankr. P. 4003(c).

135 *See In re* Reschick, 343 B.R. 151 (Bankr. W.D. Pa. 2006) (exemption allowed when trustee offered no evidence); *In re* Barner, 239 B.R. 139 (Bankr. W.D. Ky. 1999) (trustee had burden of proving purpose of award); *In re* Blizard, 81 B.R. 431 (Bankr. W.D. Ky. 1988) (objecting trustee failed to meet his burden of proving portion of award attributable to personal bodily injury exceeded available exemption amount); *In re* Harris, 50 B.R. 157 (Bankr. E.D. Wis. 1985) (under Fed. R. Bankr. P. 4003(c), objectors had burden of showing how much of insurance settlement was attributable to pain and suffering). *See also In re* Sidebotham, 77 B.R. 504 (Bankr. E.D. Pa. 1987) (pain and suffering damages excluded only if clearly separable and far out of proportion to injuries). *But see In re* Patterson, 128 B.R. 737 (Bankr. W.D. Tex. 1991) (debtor failed to meet court ordered burden to establish basis for undivided settlement payment); *In re* Hill, 5 B.R. 518 (Bankr. S.D. Ohio 1980) (under similar Ohio exemption debtor has burden of proof that award claimed exempt was for trauma or injury rather than pain and suffering or pecuniary loss).

136 Several courts have concluded, probably erroneously, that a "personal bodily injury requirement" in a state law exemption precludes use of that exemption to protect proceeds of a sexual harassment lawsuit. *In re* Hanson, 226 B.R. 106 (Bankr. D. Idaho 1999); *In re* Ciotta, 222 B.R. 626 (Bankr. C.D. Cal. 1999). These courts assume that personal bodily injury can only be manifested by actual physical injury and that the basis on which damages are calculated (lost wages) establishes the nature of the injury. *See In re* Graves, 464 B.R. 225 (Bankr. E.D. Pa. 2012) (loss of consortium derives from bodily injury); *In re* Lynn, 13 B.R. 361 (Bankr. W.D. Wis. 1981) (award for loss of consortium with spouse arising out of personal injury to spouse is an award on account of injury exempt under 11 U.S.C. § 522(d)(11)(D)).

137 *In re* Jackson, 593 F.3d 171 (2d Cir. 2010) (proceeds from employment claim could be exempted under section 522(d)(11)(E) to extent necessary for support); *In re* Flattery, 444 B.R. 501 (Bankr. D. Mass. 2011) (employment discrimination damages based on postpetition wages exemptible under § 522(d)(11)(E) if funds reasonably necessary for support); *In re* Meyer, 433 B.R. 739 (Bankr. D. Minn. 2010) (annuity based on automobile accident injuries compensated debtor for loss of earning ability even though she had not worked for three years before accident). *See* Plumb, *The Recommendations of the Commission on the Bankruptcy Laws—Exempt and Immune Property*, 61 Va. L. Rev. 1, 94–95 (1975).

138 *In re* Whitson, 319 B.R. 614 (Bankr. E.D. Ark. 2005).

139 11 U.S.C. § 522(k); *In re* Harrington, 306 B.R. 172 (Bankr. E.D. Tex. 2003).

140 11 U.S.C. § 541(c)(2). *See* § 2.5.1, *supra*. *See also* Walro v. Striegel, 131 B.R. 697 (S.D. Ind. 1991) (annuity contract containing proceeds of personal injury action does not constitute valid spendthrift trust under Indiana law).

141 26 U.S.C. §§ 401, 403, 408, 408A, 414, 457, 501(a).

142 Section 521(c) requires a debtor with an interest in an education IRA to file with the court a record of such interest. *See also* Fed. R. Bankr. P. 1007(b)(1)(F). No similar requirement is imposed for other IRAs. Presumably this document filing requirement for education IRAs serves a notice function because such IRAs are excluded in whole or in part from property of the debtor's estate. 11 U.S.C. § 541(b)(5).

This exemption right is apparently intended to supplement similar, but more limited, rights found in section 522(d)(10)(E), because Congress did not amend section 522(d)(10) when this additional category of exempt funds was added in 2005. One significant advantage in exempting retirement funds under section 522(d)(12), as compared to section 522(d)(10)(E), is that the debtor does not have to prove that such funds are necessary for the support of the debtor and the debtor's dependents.[143] However, section 522(d)(10)(E) still remains important as it permits the debtor to exempt payments from retirement plans that do not qualify for tax-exempt status under the Internal Revenue Code, subject to the exception in section 522(d)(10)(E)(i) for plans established by an insider that employed the debtor.[144]

Section 522(d)(12) was one of several changes in the Code intended by Congress to expand the protection of certain tax-exempt retirement plans that would not otherwise be protected as property excluded from the debtor's estate under section 541(c)(2).[145]

10.2.2.13.2 Guidelines for exempt retirement funds

If the debtor's funds are in a retirement fund that has received a favorable tax determination (under section 7805 of the Internal Revenue Code), and that determination is in effect when the debtor's petition is filed, the funds are presumed to be exempt for purposes of section 522(d)(12).[146] If such funds are in a retirement fund that has not received a favorable tax determination, they are exempt if the debtor demonstrates that:

- No prior unfavorable determination has been made by a court or the Internal Revenue Service (IRS); and
- The retirement fund is either in substantial compliance with applicable IRS requirements or the debtor is not materially responsible for any failure of the retirement fund to be in substantial compliance with applicable IRS requirements.[147]

In addition, retirement funds continue to qualify for exemption under section 522(d)(12) if they are directly transferred from a tax-exempt fund or account into another qualifying fund or account.[148] The debtor's exemption rights under section 522(d)(12) also continue to apply if there has been a distribution that qualifies as an eligible rollover distribution within the meaning of section 402(c) of the Internal Revenue Code, or is a distribution from a fund or account that is exempt from taxation and is deposited to the extent allowed in such fund or account not later than sixty days after the distribution.[149]

10.2.2.13.3 Cap on certain IRA accounts

Section 522(n) imposes a $1,171,650[150] cap on the value of an individual debtor's aggregate interest that may be exempted under either section 522(d)(12) in individual retirement accounts (IRAs) established under section 408 or 408A of the Internal Revenue Code, other than a simplified employee pension account under section 408(k) or a simple retirement account under section 408(p) of the Internal Revenue Code.[151] The limit does not apply to amounts attributable to rollover contributions, and any earnings thereon, made under sections 402(c), 402(e)(6), 403(a)(4), 403(a)(5), and 403(b)(8) of the Internal Revenue Code.[152] Although this dollar limit is set quite high and should protect most debtors' IRAs, section 522(n) also provides that the cap may be increased "if the interests of justice so require." And the exemption applies to an IRA that has been inherited by the debtor.[153]

---

143 Another point of comparison relates to the scope of the exemptions. Although courts have generally held that section 522(d)(10) permits the debtor to exempt not only the right to distributions from a retirement plan but also the funds in the plan itself (see, for example, *In re Carmichael*, 100 F.3d 375 (5th Cir. 1996)), section 522(d)(12) resolves this issue by making clear that funds held in the account for future distribution are exempt. *See* § 10.2.2.11, *supra*.
144 *See* § 10.2.2.11, *supra*.
145 *See* H.R. Rep. No. 109-31, at 63–64 (2005) (available on this treatise's companion website).
 Pension and benefit plan contributions are also excluded from the estate and from disposable income by 11 U.S.C. § 541(b)(7). In addition, section 1322(f) provides that amounts required to repay loans from qualified pension plans shall not constitute disposable income under section 1325(b). *See* Ch. 2, *supra*; Ch. 12, *infra*.
146 11 U.S.C. § 522(b)(4)(A). *See In re Daley*, 459 B.R. 270 (Bankr. E.D. Tenn. 2011) (trustee rebutted presumption that Merrill Lynch IRA was exempt based on favorable tax determination by showing that debtor, through no fault of his own, indirectly engaged in prohibited transaction under 26 U.S.C. § 4975 simply by signing Client Relationship Agreements granting Merrill Lynch a lien on all of his accounts); *Willis v. Menotte*, 2010 WL 1408343 (S.D. Fla. Apr. 6, 2010), *aff'd*, 424 Fed. Appx. 880, 2011 WL 1522383 (11th Cir. Apr. 21, 2011).
147 11 U.S.C. § 522(b)(4)(B).
148 11 U.S.C. § 522(b)(4)(C).
149 11 U.S.C. § 522(b)(4)(D). *See* 414 B.R. 103 (Bankr. N.D. Tex. 2009) (exemption disallowed because rollover was to an unqualified account); *In re Patrick*, 411 B.R. 659 (Bankr. C.D. Cal. 2008) (Internal Revenue Code's rule that only one tax free rollover can be made in a one-year period rendered debtor's second and third rollover distributions nonexempt).
150 This amount will be periodically adjusted pursuant to section 104 of the Bankruptcy Code to reflect changes in the Consumer Price Index. The next adjustment will occur April 1, 2013.
151 The debtor may not need to claim an exemption, or may do so in the alternative, for funds placed before the filing of the petition in an education individual retirement account (as defined in section 530(b)(1) of the Internal Revenue Code), as such funds are excluded from property of the estate if certain conditions are met pursuant to section 541(b)(5). *See* § 2.5.3, *supra*.
 Section 529 education accounts and many retirement accounts are also excluded from the estate. *See* §§ 2.5.2, 2.5.3, *supra*.
152 *In re Dixon*, 2009 WL 5110664 (Bankr. N.D. Cal. Dec. 18, 2009).
153 *Chilton v. Moser*, 674 F.3d 486 (5th Cir. 2012); *Mullen v. Hamlin (In re Hamlin)*, 465 B.R. 863 (B.A.P. 9th Cir. 2012); *In re Nessa*, 426 B.R. 312 (B.A.P. 8th Cir. 2010); *In re Stephenson*, 2011 WL 6152960 (E.D. Mich. Dec. 12, 2011); *Bierbach v. Tabor (In re Tabor)*, 433 B.R. 469 (Bankr. M.D. Pa. 2010).

10.2.3 Using the State and Federal Nonbankruptcy Exemptions

10.2.3.1 Federal Bankruptcy Modifications of These Exemptions

In cases in which the federal bankruptcy exemptions are either not chosen or not available, debtors may use the exemptions in effect on the date the bankruptcy case is filed[154] provided to them by the state[155] or local law deemed applicable to them,[156] by federal nonbankruptcy law,[157] and by section 522(b)(3)(C).[158] The term "local law" presumably includes Indian Tribal law, and any other provisions applicable to a particular locality. (For convenience, this collection of exemptions will sometimes be referred to simply as the "state exemptions.") Some states have special state exemptions applicable only in bankruptcy cases.[159] Most courts have rejected constitutional challenges to these bankruptcy-specific state exemption laws.[160] The property that the debtor may exempt in bankruptcy under a state exemption scheme probably also includes any property that is not subject to execution under state law, such as contingent tort claims.[161] In some states, such property is specifically made exempt. State law may also determine whether a debtor whose non-debtor spouse's interest in community property has been brought into the estate[162] can utilize that spouse's exemptions to protect that interest.[163] And state exemption rights are significantly enhanced by the Bankruptcy Code in several ways.

First, debtors have available to them all of the other protections of section 522. Any waiver of exemptions is unenforce-

---

154 *In re* Wolf, 248 B.R. 365 (B.A.P. 9th Cir. 2000) (debtor could not take advantage of exemption enacted after petition, even if property interest not acquired until after enactment).

155 It is not totally clear what effect state law exceptions to general exemption statutes have in bankruptcy (for example, when exemptions are not applicable to executions by certain creditors). It is likely that these exceptions will not be preserved in bankruptcy, at least in part based on the preemptive effect of section 522(c). *In re* Weinstein, 164 F.3d 677 (1st Cir. 1999) (exceptions to homestead exemption under Massachusetts law do not apply in bankruptcy); *In re* Kim, 257 B.R. 680 (B.A.P. 9th Cir. 2001) (state procedural law permitting court to consider debtor's postpetition use of property cannot override bankruptcy principle that property of estate and exemptions are determined on petition date), *aff'd*, 35 Fed. Appx. 592 (9th Cir. 2002); *In re* Evans, 362 B.R. 275 (Bankr. D.S.C. 2006) (amendment to South Carolina's homestead exemption increasing amount from $5000 to $50,000 applies to debts incurred prior to the change, despite state law exception to exemption for existing contracts); *In re* Scott, 199 B.R. 586 (Bankr. E.D. Va. 1996) (state law exception to exemption making it inapplicable to debts arising from intentional torts is not applicable in bankruptcy). *See In re* Cooley, 72 B.R. 54 (N.D. Ala. 1987), *aff'g* 67 B.R. 229 (Bankr. N.D. Ala. 1986); Michael Terry Hertz, *Bankruptcy Code Exemptions: Notes on the Effect of State Law*, 54 Am. Bankr. L.J. 339, 353, 354 (1980); Stern, *State Exemption Law in Bankruptcy: The Excepted Creditor as a Medium for Appraising Aspects of Bankruptcy Reform*, 33 Rutgers L. Rev. 70 (1980). *See also* § 10.3.3, *infra*. *But see In re* Ondras, 846 F.2d 33 (7th Cir. 1988) (Indiana permitted to opt for exemption scheme treating tort and contract claims differently).

156 See § 10.2.1.2, *supra*, for discussion of how to determine the applicable state law.

157 Such federal nonbankruptcy exemptions include Social Security benefits, 42 U.S.C. § 407; veterans benefits, 38 U.S.C. § 5301; Railroad Retirement Act annuities and pensions, 45 U.S.C. § 231m; civil service retirement benefits, 5 U.S.C. § 8346; Foreign Service retirement and disability payments, 22 U.S.C. § 4060; compensation payments for injury or death from war risk hazards, 42 U.S.C. § 1717; wages of master and seamen, 46 U.S.C. § 11109; Longshoremen's and Harbor Worker's Compensation Act death and disability benefits, 33 U.S.C. § 916; government employees' benefits for work-related injuries leading to disability or death; 5 U.S.C. § 8130; military survivors' benefits, 10 U.S.C. § 1450(i); student assistance, 20 U.S.C. § 1095a(d); and military annuities, 10 U.S.C. § 1440.

It has been held that the federal protection of certain wages from garnishment under 15 U.S.C. § 1673 is not an exemption available in bankruptcy. *In re* Bloomstein, 2010 WL 4607525 (Bankr. D. Mass. Nov. 5, 2010).

However, similar state statutes have been found to protect wages. Yaden v. Robinson (*In re* Robinson), 241 B.R. 447 (B.A.P. 9th Cir. 1999) (Oregon); *In re* Jones, 318 B.R. 841 (Bankr. S.D. Ohio 2005) (Ohio).

The Supreme Court has held that pension plans covered by ERISA do not come into the estate at all. Patterson v. Shumate, 504 U.S. 753, 112 S. Ct. 2242, 119 L. Ed. 2d 519 (1992). Note that this holding is applicable regardless of whether the debtor utilizes state or federal bankruptcy exemptions. *See* § 2.5.2, *supra*.

158 See § 10.2.3.3, *infra*.

159 *See, e.g., In re* Reaves, 285 F.3d 1152 (9th Cir. 2002) (prior determination that debtor could not exempt car under regular state law exemptions did not preclude exemption under special state exemptions for bankruptcy cases); *In re* Sassak, 426 B.R. 680 (E.D. Mich. 2010) (use of special Michigan state bankruptcy exemptions did not preclude use of other state exemptions). *Cf. In re* Williams, 280 B.R. 857 (B.A.P. 9th Cir. 2002) (debtor could not claim normal state exemption in property when state court had denied claim of same exemption).

160 *See In re* Schafer, 689 F.3d 601 (6th Cir. 2012) (Michigan's bankruptcy-specific exemption statute does not violate the Bankruptcy Clause or Supremacy Clause of the Constitution); Sheehan v. Peveich, 574 F.3d 248 (4th Cir. 2009) (West Virginia's bankruptcy-specific exemption scheme held to be constitutional); *In re* Applebaum, 422 B.R. 684 (B.A.P. 9th Cir. 2009) (special state exemptions for bankruptcy debtors held constitutional); *In re* Westby, 473 B.R. 392 (Bankr. D. Kan. 2012) (special bankruptcy exemption for Earned Income Tax Credit was constitutional). *But see In re* Cross, 255 B.R. 25 (Bankr. N.D. Ind. 2000) (Indiana's bankruptcy-specific exemption for entireties property violates Supremacy Clause of Constitution).

161 *In re* Williams, 293 B.R. 769 (Bankr. W.D. Mo. 2003) (unliquidated personal injury claims exempt). *But see* Howe v. Richardson, 193 F.3d 60 (1st Cir. 1999) (fact that property could not be attached was not equivalent to being exempt under Rhode Island law; issue depended on state law); *In re* Wishcan, 77 F.3d 875 (5th Cir. 1996) (debtor's personal injury claim could not be exempted under Louisiana state exemptions; debtor does not appear to have argued that property was exempt because it was not subject to process under state law); Tignor v. Parkinson, 729 F.2d 977 (4th Cir. 1984) (property not exempt though not subject to process because of specific provisions of state law). *See also In re* Ford, 638 F.2d 14 (4th Cir. 1981).

162 *See* § 2.5.1, *supra*.

163 *See, e.g., In re* Perez, 302 B.R. 661 (Bankr. D. Ariz. 2003) (non-debtor spouse's exemptions could be used to protect her interest in community property).

able, regardless of whether exemptions could be waived under state law.[164] The extensive powers to avoid prebankruptcy transfers of exempt property all are applicable to the state as well as the federal exemptions, because the sections providing them refer to exemptions claimed under section 522(b), which includes both sets of exemptions.[165] And exempt property is permanently protected after the bankruptcy under section 522(c), as discussed later in this Chapter.[166]

Certain states, however, have narrow limitations in their exemption schemes which apply under some conditions to prevent property from being exempt. Some courts had given effect to these limitations by concluding that liens may not be avoided on such property because the property is not exempt in the first instance.[167] Those decisions were overruled by the United States Supreme Court.[168]

In addition, debtors in bankruptcy may be able to take advantage of section 522(m) which provides that the exemption section applies separately with respect to each debtor in a joint case. In states where a single exemption is granted to a household, this provision could mean that each debtor is entitled to claim that exemption, especially if a two separate bankruptcy cases are filed.[169]

Lastly, debtors have the right to redeem property claimed as exempt, through use of section 722. As discussed in a later chapter,[170] this right can be extremely important in dealing with purchase money or possessory security interests in chapter 7 cases.

However, debtors may still have to comply with state procedural requirements for claims of exemptions. For example, in states that require debtors to file a declaration of homestead prior to the use of that exemption, courts are split on the question of whether that requirement is also a prerequisite to claiming a state homestead exemption in bankruptcy.[171] The precise wording of the state statute involved and previous state case law interpreting it may be determinative.[172]

Debtors may also occasionally have problems in proving that they have been domiciled in a state where they have recently moved for the requisite period of time to claim that state's exemptions—the two years preceding the petition.[173] When it appears that debtors have recently moved to take advantage of more generous exemptions in a particular state, courts may closely scrutinize whether they have actually changed their domicile.[174] However, considering the longer

---

164 11 U.S.C. § 522(e); *In re* Thompson, 884 F.2d 1100 (8th Cir. 1989) (waiver of state law exemptions by voluntary encumbrance of property does not preclude lien avoidance); *In re* Howell, 51 B.R. 1015 (M.D.N.C. 1985). *See also* § 10.4.1, *infra*.

165 *See* Owen v. Owen, 500 U.S. 305, 111 S. Ct. 1833, 114 L. Ed. 2d 250 (1991).

166 *In re* Cunningham, 513 F.3d 318, 323 (1st Cir. 2008). *See* § 10.5, *infra*.

167 *See In re* Owen, 877 F.2d 44 (11th Cir. 1989) (when homestead exemption does not attach under state law to residence, because liens arose before homestead attached, liens on residence may not be avoided); *In re* McManus, 681 F.2d 353 (5th Cir. 1982) (state scheme which renders all personal property subject to chattel mortgages nonexempt precludes lien avoidance).

168 Owen v. Owen, 500 U.S. 305, 111 S. Ct. 1833, 114 L. Ed. 2d 250 (1991). *See also In re* Betz, 273 B.R.313 (Bankr. D. Mass. 2002) (state law could not limit lien avoidance on increased exemption amounts). *But see* Owen v. Owen, 961 F.2d 170 (11th Cir. 1992) (on remand, court concluded lien could not be avoided because it had not attached to a preexisting interest of the debtor in property); *In re* Pederson, 230 B.R. 158 (B.A.P. 9th Cir. 1999) (same).

169 *In re* Cheeseman, 656 F.2d 60 (4th Cir. 1981) (each spouse could claim householder exemption when both were employed). *But see In re* Talmadge, 832 F.2d 1120 (9th Cir. 1987) (California's exemption scheme upheld allowing spouses only a single set of exemptions); Stevens v. Pike County Bank, 829 F.2d 693 (8th Cir. 1987) (state could limit couple to one homestead exemption in bankruptcy); *In re* Granger, 754 F.2d 1490 (9th Cir. 1985) (Oregon exemption scheme did not permit doubling exemptions for husband and wife); First Nat'l Bank of Mobile v. Norris, 701 F.2d 902 (8th Cir. 1983); *In re* Rabin, 359 B.R. 242 (B.A.P. 9th Cir. 2007) (California registered domestic partners were entitled to only one homestead exemption under state law); *In re* Thompson, 4 B.R. 823 (E.D. Va. 1980) (husband and wife could not both claim householder exemption when they were living together and only husband was employed), *rev'g* 2 B.R. 380 (Bankr. E.D. Va. 1980). *See also* § 10.2.1.1, *supra*.

170 Redemption is discussed in § 11.5, *infra*.

171 *See also In re* Nguyen, 211 F.3d 105 (4th Cir. 2000) (debtors had complied with procedural requirements for claiming homestead exemption under Virginia law, which was construed liberally in favor of debtor); *In re* Niland, 825 F.2d 801 (5th Cir. 1987) (homestead declaration upheld); Smoot v. Wolfe, 271 B.R. 115 (W.D. Va. 2001) (debtors required to file Virginia homestead declaration within five days after first date set for meeting of creditors); *In re* Govoni, 289 B.R. 500 (Bankr. D. Mass. 2002) (right to amend state law declaration of homestead terminated as of petition filing date); *In re* Collins, 24 B.R. 485 (Bankr. E.D. Va. 1982) (Virginia debtors required to file claim of property to be exempted on or before date of petition). *Cf. In re* Michael, 49 F.3d 499 (9th Cir. 1995) (debtors could claim Montana homestead exemption after petition filed); *In re* Renner, 822 F.2d 878 (9th Cir. 1987) (homestead declaration defective and therefore exemption disallowed); Zimmerman v. Morgan, 689 F.2d 471 (4th Cir. 1982) (homestead not exempt); *In re* Martin, 20 B.R. 235 (B.A.P. 9th Cir. 1982) (debtor could file postpetition claim for homestead).

172 *See* Danduran v. Kaler (*In re* Danduran), 657 F.3d 749 (8th Cir. 2011) (reversing decision that proceeds of personal property sold with homestead qualified for exemption under North Dakota law); *In re* Zibman, 268 F.3d 298 (5th Cir. 2001) (debtors who had sold Texas homestead before bankruptcy and had not reinvested proceeds in another homestead within six months as required by Texas exemption law could not claim proceeds as exempt even though six months had not run as of date of petition); *In re* Stanton, 457 B.R. 80 (Bankr. D. Nev. 2011) (debtor may file homestead declaration after date of bankruptcy petition because Nevada exemption statute permits filing of declaration at any time before sale of property).

173 11 U.S.C. § 522(b)(3)(A).

174 *See, e.g., In re* Ring, 144 B.R. 446 (Bankr. E.D. Mo. 1992) (rejecting claim that debtors had changed their domicile to Florida in view of evidence that they intended to remain in Missouri). *See also In re* Drenttel, 403 F.3d 611 (8th Cir. 2005) (debtors who lived in Arizona for less than ninety days before filing petition in Minnesota allowed to use Minnesota homestead exemption on property purchased in Arizona); *In re* Tanzi, 297 B.R. 607 (B.A.P. 9th Cir. 2003) (debtors not permitted to use Florida homestead exemption because section 522(b)(2)(A) (now designated as section 522(b)(3)(A)) must be applied no differently in involuntary case; 180-day period runs from petition date rather than date on which order for relief was entered).

§ 10.2.3.2   Consumer Bankruptcy Law and Practice

domiciliary periods enacted in 2005, this issue is less likely to arise.[175]

10.2.3.2 Exemption of Property Not Subject to Process

Debtors who claim the state exemptions in bankruptcy may also be able to take advantage of another special provision that protects certain jointly owned property. This provision[176] allows the debtor to claim as exempt "any interest in property in which the debtor had, immediately before the commencement of the case, an interest as a tenant by the entirety or joint tenant to the extent such interest as a tenant by the entirety or joint tenant is exempt from process under applicable nonbankruptcy law."[177]

The intent of this provision is to protect that property which a creditor of only the debtor (and not of both joint tenants) could not have levied upon as of the date that the bankruptcy was filed. In this way it duplicates what the debtor could have kept out of the estate under the 1898 Bankruptcy Act; there the trustee only had rights in that property of the debtor which a creditor of that debtor alone could attach. One example of such property is property owned as tenants by the entireties, in states where such property can be levied upon only by a joint creditor of the cotenants.[178] If one cotenant files a bankruptcy and claims the state exemptions, then such an interest in entireties property may be claimed as exempt, at a minimum from creditors holding claims against only that cotenant.[179]

Presumably, joint property could be claimed under this exemption even if the co-owner also files a bankruptcy.[180] Indeed, the two co-owners should both be able to claim their interests in entireties property as exempt, even in a joint case, because section 522(m) states that this provision should apply separately to each debtor.[181] However, because courts have not agreed on these issues, it is safer to file a petition for only one of two co-tenants if that will suffice to effectuate the relief sought.

It is important to note several other aspects of this subsection:

- It applies to both real and personal property;
- It is unlimited in value;
- It is applicable to any interest;
- It is not subject to the homestead limitations in section 522(*o*), (p), or (q);[182]
- It is based upon the law of the state where the property is located and not the exemptions available to the debtor under the domicile rules of section 522(b)(3)(A).[183]

Thus, debtors with significant amounts of property that fall within these provisions may be far better off choosing the state rather than the federal exemptions. However, as discussed below, the case law in the jurisdiction in which the case is filed should be carefully researched before that step is irrevocably taken.

The original purpose of this subsection was to preserve the protection given under the previous Bankruptcy Act to certain

---

175 See § 10.2.1.2, supra.
176 11 U.S.C. § 522(b)(3)(B).
177 If the property is not located in the state where the debtor resides, the applicable law is the law in the state where the property is located. *In re* Gillette, 248 B.R. 845 (Bankr. M.D. Fla. 1999). *See also In re* Bellingroehr, 403 B.R. 818 (Bankr. W.D. Mo. 2009) (placing entireties property in revocable trust did not end entireties status).
178 These states are Delaware, District of Columbia, Florida, Indiana, Michigan, Maryland, Missouri, Montana, Mississippi, North Carolina, Pennsylvania, Rhode Island, Vermont, Virginia, and Wyoming. In other states, such as Massachusetts, tenancies by the entirety may be partially exempt from claims of one spouse's creditors. Courts have come to sometimes strange results in attempting to effectuate those exemptions, as nearly as possible, under the Bankruptcy Code. *See In re* McConchie, 94 B.R. 245 (Bankr. D. Mass. 1988) (trustee given rights of a hypothetical creditor, under 11 U.S.C. § 544(a)(1) to attach but not sell debtor's interest). *But see* United States v. Craft, 535 U.S. 274, 122 S. Ct. 1414, 152 L. Ed. 2d 437 (2002) (federal tax lien may attach to entireties interest).
    The *Craft* decision should not alter the debtor's rights as to creditors other than those making claims under federal law. *See In re* Sinnreich, 391 F.3d 1295 (11th Cir. 2005) (*Craft* not applicable to bankruptcy exemption under section 522(b)); *In re* Hutchins, 306 B.R. 82 (Bankr. D. Vt. 2004) (applying *Craft* to two liens securing federal criminal fines); *In re* Dahlman, 304 B.R. 892 (Bankr. M.D. Fla. 2003) (federal criminal obligation); *In re* Greathouse, 295 B.R. 562 (Bankr. D. Md. 2003) (*Craft* did not give trustee greater powers); *In re* Knapp, 285 B.R. 176 (Bankr. M.D.N.C. 2002) (*Craft* did not enhance trustee's rights).
    Additionally, in those states where a tenancy by the entireties may be subjected to execution by a creditor of either spouse, the bankruptcy court must nevertheless apply the provisions of 11 U.S.C. § 363(h) before property is liquidated for the benefit of creditors of one joint tenant only. *See In re* Persky, 893 F.2d 15 (2d Cir. 1989); *In re* Davis, 403 B.R. 914 (Bankr. M.D. Fla. 2009) (separate judgments against each spouse cannot be combined to create a joint debt); § 12.6.5, *infra*.
179 *In re* Ford, Jr., 638 F.2d 14 (4th Cir. 1981), *aff'g* 3 B.R. 559 (D. Md. 1980); *In re* Thacker, 5 B.R. 592 (Bankr. W.D. Va. 1980) (all applying the exemption language); *In re* Shaw, 5 B.R. 107 (Bankr. M.D. Tenn. 1980). *See also In re* Martin, 269 B.R. 119 (Bankr. M.D. Pa. 2001) (exemption allowed even though debtor became sole owner of property within 180 days pursuant to divorce decree, because entireties tenant always was seized of the whole of the property as of petition date). *Cf. In re* Steury, 94 B.R. 553 (Bankr. N.D. Ind. 1988) (separate chapter 7 cases of husband and wife consolidated to the extent necessary to allow trustee to liquidate property held by the entireties for the benefit of joint creditors). *But see In re* Weiss, 4 B.R. 327 (Bankr. S.D.N.Y. 1980) (because creditor could reach one spouse's interest in New York entireties property, exemption was not applicable).
180 *But see* Ragsdale v. Genesco, 674 F.2d 277 (4th Cir. 1982) (joint debtors could not exempt or avoid lien on entireties property subject to judgment lien of creditor).
181 *In re* Bunker, 312 F.3d 145 (4th Cir. 2002), *aff'g* Thomas v. Peyton, 274 B.R. 450 (W.D. Va. 2001) (entireties property claimed as exempt in joint case could be administered only for benefit of joint creditors).
182 *See* § 10.2.3.4, *infra*.
183 *In re* Holland, 366 B.R. 825 (N.D. Ill. 2007); *In re* Zolnierowicz, 380 B.R. 84 (Bankr. M.D. Fla. 2007); *In re* Schwarz, 362 B.R. 532 (Bankr. S.D. Fla. 2007).

property which could not be levied upon under state law.[184] Under the Act such property was usually not considered a part of the bankruptcy estate. Without the new subsection, debtors utilizing the state exemptions, either by choice or because their state had opted out, would have been worse off than before the Code was enacted. Their interests in property such as entireties property or other property not subject to state law process would have, for the first time, been brought into the estate under section 541's broadened definition of property of the estate.[185] Such property, then, would have been available to their creditors, even though it had not been under state law, unless it could be exempted. And as it never had been available to creditors under state law, state exemption laws did not take such property into account, so that state exemption provisions were insufficient to protect it. Section 522(b)(2)(B) was meant to fill this breach.

But section 522(b)(3)(B) does more than simply duplicate the results under the prior Act. Under the Act the debtor's interests in property which could not be levied upon did not come into the estate or were abandoned by the trustee.[186] However, to a large degree the effect of the bankruptcy on joint debts had been vitiated by judicially created law which allowed joint creditors to obtain a stay of the discharge to pursue entireties property.[187] The Code, which gives these property interests the same status and protections as all other exempt property, intended to preclude this result. Thus, as discussed below, pursuit of such property during or after the case by a prebankruptcy creditor should be prohibited by section 522(c), and any judicial lien obtained by such creditor should be avoidable by the debtor under section 522(f).[188]

Despite the history and intent of section 522(b)(3)(B), most courts of appeals have interpreted that section far more restrictively. Ignoring early decisions and other authorities which had discussed the issue,[189] the Third Circuit Court of Appeals refused to avoid a lien on entireties property claimed as exempt under section 522(b)(3)(B).[190] The court held that as the property as a whole could be reached by the lien creditor, it did not fall within the exemption provision, even though the *debtor spouse's interest*, which the language of the statute actually looks to, could not be reached by any creditor. Citing no legislative history to support its views, or to refute the analysis of legislative history in an earlier Fourth Circuit decision,[191] the court strongly implied that it would refuse to find property exempt under section 522(b)(2)(B) whenever (but perhaps only to the extent that) a husband and wife had joint creditors.[192]

The Third Circuit's decision was subsequently followed by the First, Fourth, Sixth, and Eighth Circuit Courts of Appeals.[193] The Sixth Circuit cases have held that entireties prop-

---

184 It is less clear what happens to property not subject to process, which is not within the scope of section 522(b)(3)(B) but which is brought into the bankruptcy estate, when the state exemptions are applicable. The answer may depend on the particulars of state law. See In re Benn, 491 F.3d 811 (8th Cir. 2007) (property not specifically listed as exempt in Missouri statute is not exempt despite fact that it is not subject to attachment or execution); Howe v. Richardson, 193 F.3d 60 (1st Cir. 1999) (fact that property could not be attached was not equivalent to being exempt under Rhode Island law; issue depended on state law); Tignor v. Parkinson, 729 F.2d 977 (4th Cir. 1984) (property not exempt though not subject to process due to specific provisions of state law).

185 See § 2.5, *supra*, for a discussion of property of the estate. However, if a debtor who owns property as tenant by the entireties with a nondebtor spouse dies during the bankruptcy case, the nondebtor spouse becomes sole owner and the estate no longer has any interest in the property. In re Etoll, 425 B.R. 743 (Bankr. D.N.J. 2010).

186 See § 3.5, *supra*, for a discussion of abandonment of property.

187 Phillips v. Krakower, 46 F.2d 764 (4th Cir. 1931), was the first of these cases, most of which were in the Fourth Circuit. The correctness of their result had been questionable even under the Act and Rules, which required the discharge to be granted "forthwith." Former R. Bankr. P. 404(d). See In re Cantwell, 7 Bankr. Ct. Dec. (LRP) 807 (E.D. Pa. 1980), *appeal dismissed as moot* 639 F.2d 1050 (3d Cir. 1981).

188 See S. Rep. No. 95-989, at 76 (1978), H.R. Rep. No. 95-595, at 362 (1977) ("The debtor may avoid [any] judicial lien on any property to the extent that the property could have been exempted in the absence of the lien.").

However, notwithstanding the fact that the theoretical underpinnings of *Krakower* have disappeared with the inclusion of entireties property interests in the estate, some courts (mostly in the Fourth Circuit) have continued to follow *Krakower* even under the Code. See, e.g., Chippenham Hosp. Inc. v. Bondurant, 716 F.2d 1057 (4th Cir. 1983); In re Menefee, 22 B.R. 425 (Bankr. E.D. Va. 1982). See also Paeplow v. Foley, 128 B.R. 429 (N.D. Ind. 1991) (although creditor could pursue lien on property held by entireties during bankruptcy case, failure to do so prior to discharge precludes that option), *aff'd*, 972 F.2d 730 (7th Cir. 1992). As discussed in the text, this result is contrary to express provisions of 11 U.S.C. § 522.

189 See Ray v. Dawson, 14 B.R. 822 (E.D. Tenn. 1981), *aff'g* 10 B.R. 680 (Bankr. E.D. Tenn. 1981); In re Gibbons, 17 B.R. 373 (Bankr. D.R.I. 1982); In re Buck, 17 B.R. 168 (Bankr. D. Haw. 1982); In re Phillos, 14 B.R. 781 (Bankr. W.D. Va. 1981); In re Lunger, 14 B.R. 6 (Bankr. M.D. Fla. 1981); In re Woolard, 13 B.R. 105 (Bankr. E.D.N.C. 1981); Marc S. Cohen & Kenneth N. Klee, *Caveat Creditor: The Consumer Debtor Under the Bankruptcy Code*, 58 N.C. L. Rev. 681, 690–691 (1980); R.L. Hughes, *Code Exemptions: Far Reaching Achievement*, 28 DePaul L. Rev. 1025, 1028 (1979); Douglas R. Rendleman, *Liquidation Bankruptcy Under the '78 Code*, 21 Wm. & Mary L. Rev. 575, 596 (1980); William T. Vukowich, *Debtor's Exemption Rights Under the Bankruptcy Reform Act*, 58 N.C. L. Rev. 769, 792 (1980).

190 Napotnik v. Equibank, 679 F.2d 316 (3d Cir. 1982).

191 In re Ford, 638 F.2d 14 (4th Cir. 1981).

192 The *Napotnik* court did not explain how this entireties property would be distributed once it did come into the estate. Would it be distributed only to joint creditors who might have reached it outside of bankruptcy? The Code provides no basis for believing that such a bifurcated system of distribution was contemplated. Yet, if all creditors shared in the property, then those who could not have reached it otherwise would receive a windfall.

193 In re Edmonston, 107 F.3d 74 (1st Cir. 1997); In re Garner, 952 F.2d 232 (8th Cir. 1991), *rev'g* Garner v. Strauss, 121 B.R. 356 (W.D. Mo. 1990); Sumy v. Schlossberg, 777 F.2d 921 (4th Cir. 1985); In re Grosslight, 757 F.2d 773 (6th Cir. 1985).

These cases should perhaps be reevaluated, based on federal preemption, in light of the Supreme Court's decision in Owen v. Owen, 500 U.S. 305, 111 S. Ct. 1833, 114 L. Ed. 2d 350 (1991). See In re Weinstein, 164 F.3d 677 (1st Cir. 1999) (exceptions to state law exemption do not apply in bankruptcy). But see In re Tyree, 116 B.R. 682 (Bankr. S.D. Iowa 1990) (trustee could not liquidate homestead held jointly by debtor and non-debtor spouse).

erty not protected from joint creditors by other exemption provisions can be liquidated in the bankruptcy for the benefit of joint creditors.[194] They also held, however, that when a joint creditor does not timely object to the use of the section 522(b)(3)(B) exemption, it is barred from pursuing the entireties property after the bankruptcy.[195] Only the Seventh Circuit Court of Appeals, interpreting an Indiana statutory exemption of entireties property, has come to the result that was intended by Congress.[196]

The net result of the decisions limiting the use of section 522(b)(3)(B) is that, when they are applicable, the principal use of this exemption may be in those cases in which all or almost all of the debts involved are debts of only one spouse.[197] In such cases, at least, the entireties property is protected from liquidation or (if there are small joint debts) only a small portion of it may be found nonexempt under section 522(b)(3)(B).[198] It seems clear from language of section 522(b)(3)(B), as well as the case law that, when there are joint creditors, only that amount of the property that is equal to the amount of the joint unsecured debts is not exempt.[199] This result should occur even if both spouses file a joint bankruptcy case, because their exemptions are claimed individually and no consolidation of the estates occurs in a joint case unless it is specifically ordered.[200] Ordinarily, such consolidation would be improper, as it would seriously diminish the rights of joint creditors to the benefit of other creditors. After the bankruptcy, the exempt property is protected because the debt of the cotenant who filed the bankruptcy has been discharged. Even if the other entireties cotenant dies during or after the bankruptcy, leaving the bankruptcy debtor as the sole owner, the exemption protects the property.[201] And it is also important to remember that even if the debtor's interest in joint property is not exempt, the trustee may still be prohibited from liquidating it for the benefit of creditors by 11 U.S.C. § 363(h) which requires the court to consider the hardship to the non-debtor spouse that would be caused by liquidation.[202]

Thus, the state exemptions, as enhanced by the Code, may have a great deal to offer to some debtors, even in states where they have relatively low dollar limits. Of course, debtors in

---

194 *In re* Grosslight, 757 F.2d 773 (6th Cir. 1985). *See also In re* Oberlies, 94 B.R. 916 (Bankr. E.D. Mich. 1988) (Michigan law requires that property be liquidated for the benefit of joint creditors only). *But see In re* Ballard, 65 F.3d 367 (4th Cir. 1995) (when non-debtor spouse dies during the bankruptcy case, the bankruptcy estate becomes sole owner of the property and joint creditors no longer have the right to be paid ahead of non-joint priority creditors from the proceeds of the property).

195 *In re* Dembs, 757 F.2d 777 (6th Cir. 1985). *See* Taylor v. Freeland & Kronz, 503 U.S. 638, 112 S. Ct. 1644, 118 L. Ed. 2d 280 (1992) (extending the holding in *Dembs*). *But see In re* Williams, 104 F.3d 688 (4th Cir. 1997) (even though no objection to exemption was filed within time permitted, debtor's interest in entireties property not protected from joint creditors).

196 *In re* Hunter, 970 F.2d 299 (7th Cir. 1992).

The same result, prohibiting an *in rem* proceeding by a joint creditor against the entireties property claimed as exempt after an Indiana debtor had discharged his indebtedness in a non-joint case, was reached in *In re* Paeplow, 972 F.2d 730 (7th Cir. 1992). *See also* Great S. Co. v. Allard, 202 B.R. 938 (N.D. Ill. 1996) (applying Illinois law and permitting debtor to avoid judicial lien on interest in entireties property claimed as exempt under section 522(b)(2)(B) (now section 522(b)(3)(B)).

197 Despite the restrictive holdings cited above, it may nonetheless be worthwhile to claim the entireties exemption as to all creditors, because that exemption will be allowed if no party timely objects. Taylor v. Freeland & Kronz, 503 U.S. 638, 112 S. Ct. 1644, 118 L. Ed. 2d 280 (1992); *In re* Dembs, 757 F.2d 777 (6th Cir. 1985).

Certainly, as there are strong arguments that restrictive holdings are wrong, there is nothing unethical about doing so and there may be little risk of adverse consequences when a chapter 13 case is filed that may be dismissed as a matter of right or when there is no alternative to bankruptcy in any case. *But see In re* Williams, 104 F.3d 688 (4th Cir. 1997) (even though no objection to exemption was filed within time permitted, debtor's exemption of interest in entireties property construed to mean only exemption from non-joint creditors).

198 Somerset Sav. Bank v. Goldberg, 166 B.R. 776 (D. Mass. 1994) (debtor could claim property held as tenant by entireties as exempt because creditor was not permitted to execute on property under Massachusetts law); *In re* Pernus, 143 B.R. 856 (Bankr. N.D. Ohio 1992) (all of debtor's interests in entireties property were exempt when debtor had no unsecured joint creditors).

However, even if the debtor's interest is not exempt under section 522(b)(3)(B), there remains the issue of valuing that interest. A number of courts, particularly in New York, have used a method of subtracting the value of the non-debtor spouse's life and survivorship interests from the total value of the property, leaving a very small value for the estate in most cases. *Cf. In re* Van der Heide, 164 F.3d 1183 (8th Cir. 1999) (one half of value of property became property of estate and debtor was entitled to one half of state homestead exemption). *But see In re* Cordova, 73 F.3d 38 (4th Cir. 1996) (when debtor acquired, through divorce decree within 180 days of petition, full ownership of property previously held by entireties, debtor's full ownership interest became property of estate subject to claims of all creditors pursuant to section 541(a)(5)(B) and not exemptible under section 522(b)(2)(B) (now section 522(b)(3)(B))). *See generally In re* Persky, 893 F.2d 15 (2d Cir. 1989).

199 *See, e.g., In re* Edmonston, 107 F.3d 74 (1st Cir. 1997); Sumy v. Schlossberg, 777 F.2d 921, 922 (4th Cir. 1985) (debtor loses benefit of exemption to the extent of joint claims); *In re* Grosslight, 757 F.2d 773, 776 (6th Cir. 1985) (debtor's interest in portion of entireties property reachable by joint creditors not exempt). *See also In re* Eads, 271 B.R. 371 (Bankr. W.D. Mo. 2002) (if entireties property not fully exempt due to existence of joint creditor, proceeds of sale of property must first be divided—with non-debtor spouse's share distributed to her—and then joint creditors could be paid from debtor's share, with any remaining funds from that share distributed to debtor), *later opinion at* 307 B.R. 219 (Bankr. W.D. Mo. 2004) (administrative expenses must be paid from amount set aside for joint creditors).

200 11 U.S.C. § 302(b). *See In re* Bunker, 312 F.3d 145 (4th Cir. 2002); *In re* Eichhorn, 338 B.R. 793 (Bankr. S.D. Ill. 2006) (trustee could not circumvent this principle through use of section 544).

201 *In re* Birney, 200 F.3d 225 (4th Cir. 2000); *In re* Bradby, 455 B.R. 476 (Bankr. E.D. Va. 2011) (death of cotenant during case did not affect exemption, which is determined as of petition date).

202 *See In re* Persky, 893 F.2d 15 (2d Cir. 1989); Henry J. Sommer & Margaret Dee McGarity, Collier Family Law and the Bankruptcy Code ¶ 2.06[3] (1992); § 12.6.5, *infra. But see In re* Morgan, 286 B.R. 678 (Bankr. E.D. Wis. 2002) (equitable factors of § 363(h) do not apply to former community property because, as entire asset in debtor's bankruptcy estate, no interest of the non-debtor spouse was being sold).

states which have opted out of the federal bankruptcy exemptions have no choice but to make the most of the state provisions. But all other debtors' advocates should carefully consider that option as well, as in some cases it may provide greater benefits than the federal exemption provisions.

10.2.3.3 Special Retirement Exemptions Available to Debtors Who Utilize State and Federal Nonbankruptcy Exemptions

Sections 522(b)(3)(C) permits a debtor claiming the state exemptions to exempt retirement funds to the extent they are in a fund or account that is exempt from taxation under sections 401, 403, 408, 408A, 414, 457, or 501(a) of the Internal Revenue Code.[203] These sections of the Internal Revenue Code deal with pension, profit-sharing, and stock bonus plans; employee annuities; individual retirement accounts (including Roth IRAs); deferred compensation plans of state and local government, and tax-exempt organizations; and certain trusts. The debtor may claim these funds as exempt regardless of whether they may be claimed as exempt under state law.[204] And the exemption applies to an IRA that has been inherited by the debtor.[205]

The property that can be exempted under section 522(b)(3)(C) is exactly the same property as can be exempted under section 522(d)(12). Similarly, the limitations on the exemption, including the $1,171,650 dollar cap on funds that have always been in an individual retirement account (IRA),[206] are equally applicable. Therefore, readers should refer to the discussion of section 522(d)(12) for further guidance.[207] Both section 522(b)(3)(C) and section 522(d)(12) were intended by Congress to expand the protection of certain tax-exempt retirement plans that would not otherwise be protected as property excluded from the debtor's estate under section 541(c)(2).[208]

10.2.3.4 Limitations on State Homestead Exemptions

10.2.3.4.1 In general

The 2005 Act added three new subsections to section 522 that prevent the debtor from taking full advantage of state homestead exemptions under certain circumstances. These provisions deal with the prepetition conversion of nonexempt property with fraudulent intent (section 522(o)), the acquisition of homestead property within 1215 days before the bankruptcy filing (section 522(p)), and the commission of certain bad acts by the debtor (section 522(q)).

10.2.3.4.2 Scope of the new restrictions

All three subsections apply only to homestead property similar to the kind described in section 522(d)(1). The property interest must fall within one of the following categories:

- Real or personal property that the debtor or a dependent of the debtor uses as a residence;
- A cooperative that owns property that the debtor or a dependent of the debtor uses as a residence;
- A burial plot for the debtor or a dependent of the debtor; or
- Real or personal property that the debtor or dependent of the debtor claims as a homestead.

Subsections 522(o), (p), and (q) apply only when the debtor seeks to exempt homestead property under section 522(b)(3)(A) by claiming an exemption under state law or federal law other than section 522(d). The new homestead limitations therefore do not restrict the ability of the debtor to exempt homestead property under section 522(b)(2) by making use of the federal homestead exemption found in section 522(d)(1), or to exempt homestead property held as a tenant by the entirety or by joint tenancy under section 522(b)(3)(B)[209] to the extent that the interest is exempt from process under nonbankruptcy law.[210]

It is important to note that both section 522(p) and (q) use language different than what is found in section 522(o) in describing when the limitations apply. Sections 522(p) and (q), unlike section 522(o), state that the provisions apply only "as a result of electing under subsection (b)(3)(A) to exempt property under State or local law." Thus, in order to give meaning to the plain words of the phrase "as a result of electing," one court has held that sections 522(p) and (q) are applicable only

---

203 26 U.S.C. §§ 401, 403, 408, 408A, 414, 457, 501(a); *In re* Daley, 459 B.R. 270 (Bankr. E.D. Tenn. 2011) (trustee rebutted presumption that Merrill Lynch IRA was exempt based on favorable tax determination by showing that debtor, through no fault of his own, indirectly engaged in prohibited transaction under 26 U.S.C. § 4975 simply by signing Client Relationship Agreements granting Merrill Lynch a lien on all of his accounts). *See* Willis v. Menotte, 2010 WL 1408343 (S.D. Fla. Apr. 6, 2010), *aff'd*, 424 Fed. Appx. 880, 2011 WL 1522383 (11th Cir. Apr. 21, 2011).

204 *See In re* Orr, 2008 WL 244168 (Bankr. C.D. Ill. Jan. 28, 2008) (exemption under section 522(b)(3)(C) for retirement funds available independent of, and in addition to, state law exemptions); *In re* Braulick, 360 B.R. 327 (Bankr. D. Mont. 2006).

205 Chilton v. Moser, 674 F.3d 486 (5th Cir. 2012); Mullen v. Hamlin (*In re* Hamlin), 465 B.R. 863 (B.A.P. 9th Cir. 2012); Clark v. Rameker (*In re* Clark), 466 B.R. 135 (W.D. Wis. 2012); *In re* Stephenson, 2011 WL 6152960 (E.D. Mich. Dec. 12, 2011); *In re* Nessa, 426 B.R. 312 (B.A.P. 8th Cir. 2010); *In re* Thiem, 443 B.R. 832 (Bankr. D. Ariz. 2011); *In re* Kuchta, 434 B.R. 837 (Bankr. N.D. Ohio 2010); *In re* Tabor, 433 B.R. 469 (Bankr. M.D. Pa. 2010).

206 11 U.S.C. § 522(n).

207 *See* § 10.2.2.13, *supra*.

208 *See* H.R. Rep. No. 109-31, at 63–64 (2005) (available on this treatise's companion website).

209 11 U.S.C. § 522(b)(3)(B) (formerly designated as section 522(b)(2)(B)). *See* § 10.2.3.2, *supra*.

210 *In re* Davis, 403 B.R. 914 (Bankr. M.D. Fla. 2009) (homestead limitation in section 522(o) does not apply to debtor's tenancy by the entireties exemption); *In re* Hinton, 378 B.R. 371 (Bankr. M.D. Fla. 2007) (same); *In re* Buonopane, 359 B.R. 346 (Bankr. M.D. Fla. 2007) (entireties property claimed as exempt under section 522(b)(3)(B) is not subject to dollar limit in § 522(p)); *In re* Jacobs, 342 B.R. 114 (Bankr. D. Colo. 2006) (debtor's claim of exemption under section 522(d) not subject to section 522(q)).

in states which have not opted out of the federal exemption scheme, because non-opt out states are the only states where such an election is available.[211]

The homestead limitations apply only to limit the exemption a debtor can claim in a bankruptcy case. They do not affect creditors' ability to obtain a lien against a homestead under state law.[212]

10.2.3.4.3 Homestead limitation based on fraudulent conversion of nonexempt property

Section 522(*o*) provides that the value of the debtor's interest in certain homestead property shall be reduced to the extent that it is attributable to any nonexempt property that the debtor disposed of within ten years before the filing of the petition with the intent to hinder, delay, or defraud a creditor.[213] This restriction on the debtor's homestead exemption is therefore limited to the conversion of nonexempt property into exempt homestead property with fraudulent intent.[214] If there is no equity in the homestead, the provision is inapplicable, because the value of the debtor's interest cannot be reduced below zero.[215]

The language of section 522(*o*) requires the court to look at whether the converted property could be exempted "if on such date the debtor had held the property so disposed of." Because the only other date in the subsection that could be referenced by the phrase "on such date" is the "10-year period ending on the date of the filing of the petition," it is the petition date that controls the determination of whether the interest may be claimed as exempt. This interpretation also gives meaning to the remaining words in the phrase "if . . . the debtor had held the property so disposed of," as there would be no need to include this language if the relevant timeframe was the time of disposition, which is a time when the debtor would have held the property. Thus, if the property converted within the ten-year look-back period could be exempted under any applicable provision of section 522(b) at the time the petition is filed, then the debtor's interest in the homestead that may be claimed as exempt should not be reduced under this provision.

The statutory language also requires that the debtor intended to hinder, delay, or defraud some creditor at the time the property was disposed of. Because section 522(*o*) uses the identical "intent to hinder, delay or defraud a creditor" language found in section 727(a)(2), courts are likely to construe the required intent in a similar manner.[216] Thus, a party in interest objecting to the debtor's homestead exemption should have to prove that the conversion of nonexempt property was done with a specific intent on the part of the debtor to defraud a creditor, and this intent must involve actual rather than constructive intent.[217]

Another question raised by the provision is whether section 522(*o*) would be applicable if no creditor who may have been hindered, delayed, or defrauded is a "creditor" of the debtor at the time the petition is filed. Because "creditor" is defined in section 101(10) as an entity that has a claim against the debtor or the debtor's estate, a trustee or other party in interest should not prevail on an exemption objection under section 522(*o*) if the debts of the defrauded creditors have been satisfied prepetition. This interpretation is consistent with the apparent purpose of the provision, which is to protect the ability of defrauded creditors to recover on their claims.

Prior to the enactment of the 2005 amendments, courts had uniformly held that the scope of an exemption created under state law and claimed in a bankruptcy proceeding was determined by state law.[218] This rule meant that, depending upon the applicable state law, the issue of conversion with fraudulent intent could not be asserted in some bankruptcy cases. For example, the Florida Supreme Court concluded in *Havoco of America, Ltd. v. Hill*, on a question certified to it by the Eleventh Circuit in a bankruptcy case,[219] that conversion of nonexempt assets into an exempt homestead with the intent to hinder, delay, or defraud creditors does not defeat the unlimited Florida homestead exemption because such a transfer is not an exception provided for in the Florida Constitution.[220] New section 522(*o*) overrules the outcome in *Havoco* and permits

---

211 *In re* McNabb, 326 B.R. 785 (Bankr. D. Ariz. 2005). *But see In re* Virissimo, 332 B.R. 201 (Bankr. D. Nev. 2005).

212 Smith v. HD Smith Wholesale Drug Co. (*In re* McCombs), 659 F.3d 503 (5th Cir. 2011).

213 "Disposed of" does not include designation of property as a homestead, because debtor does not transfer any property interest to another. *In re* Lyons, 355 B.R. 387 (Bankr. D. Mass. 2006).

214 *In re* Mathews, 360 B.R. 732 (Bankr. M.D. Fla. 2007) (section 522(o) not applicable because debtor transferred exempt property into other exempt property).

215 Soulé v. Willcut (*In re* Willcut), 472 B.R. 88 (B.A.P. 10th Cir. 2012).

216 *In re* Addison, 540 F.3d 805 (8th Cir. 2008); *In re* Stanton, 457 B.R. 80 (Bankr. D. Nev. 2011).

217 *See* § 15.2.2.2, *infra*. *See also In re* Addison, 540 F.3d 805 (8th Cir. 2008) (section 522(o) did not change standard for consideration of prebankruptcy conversions of nonexempt property other than to extend look back period to ten years); Clark v. Wilmoth (*In re* Wilmoth), 397 B.R. 915 (B.A.P. 8th Cir. 2008) (using badges of fraud analysis but finding insufficient extrinsic evidence of intent); *In re* Cook, 460 B.R. 911 (Bankr. N.D. Fla. 2011) (creditor did not prove fraudulent scheme); *In re* Anderson, 386 B.R. 315 (Bankr. D. Kan. 2008) (substantial evidence of prebankruptcy planning to pay down a mortgage on a homestead using nonexempt assets is not sufficient to show fraudulent intent); *In re* Presto, 376 B.R. 554 (Bankr. S.D. Tex. 2007) (several badges of fraud indicated fraudulent intent); *In re* Agnew, 355 B.R. 276 (Bankr. D. Kan. 2006) (objecting party has burden under section 522(o) to establish actual fraud by preponderance of evidence; debtor's transfer of nonexempt farm assets to mother's trust in exchange for exempt homestead property was done for legitimate estate planning purposes and not with intent to hinder, delay, or defraud a creditor); *In re* Maronde, 332 B.R. 593 (Bankr. D. Minn. 2005) (debtor's prepetition sale of nonexempt truck and trailer for purpose of paying down equity line of credit on debtor's home found subject to limitation in section 522(*o*)). *But see In re* Lacounte, 342 B.R. 809 (Bankr. D. Mont. 2005) (use of nonexempt $42,000 by insolvent debtors to pay down mortgage was intended to protect money from creditors in bankruptcy).

218 *See, e.g., In re* Johnson, 880 F.2d 78 (8th Cir. 1989).

219 Havoco of Am., Ltd. v. Hill, 255 F.3d 1321 (11th Cir. 2001).

220 Havoco of Am., Ltd. v. Hill, 790 So. 2d 1018 (Fla. 2001).

the issue of fraudulent conversion to be raised despite contrary state law.

10.2.3.4.4 Cap on homestead property acquired during 1215-day period before filing

Under new section 522(p)(1), the debtor may not exempt "any amount of interest that was acquired by the debtor" in homestead property by the debtor during the 1215-day period before the filing of the petition that exceeds the amount of $146,450.[221] The monetary cap imposed by section 522(p)(1) does not apply to any interest transferred from a debtor's previous principal residence to the debtor's current principal residence, if the debtor's previous residence was acquired before the 1215-day period and both the previous and current residences are located in the same state.[222] In addition, the limitation does not apply to an exemption claimed on a principal residence by a family farmer.[223]

A significant question to be decided by the courts will be how to interpret the phrase "interest that was acquired by the debtor." Given that the apparent legislative intent for enacting section 522(p) was to discourage prebankruptcy exemption planning in which some debtors have taken advantage of unlimited or substantial homestead exemption laws, it would seem that the phrase should be construed as applying to the actual purchase or acquisition of an ownership interest in homestead property, an interest that the debtor gains though his or her own affirmative actions or efforts.[224] Under this view, section 522(p) should not apply to an interest attributable simply to an increase in the market value of the debtor's homestead during the 1215-day period, because that is not an interest "acquired" by the debtor, but rather an increase in the value of the debtor's existing interest.[225] Similarly, this provision should not prevent the debtor from claiming as exempt an interest in a homestead resulting from the application of mortgage payments, or from home improvements, because neither changes the property interest that the debtor holds.[226] Nor should designation of property as a homestead be considered acquiring an interest.[227]

10.2.3.4.5 Homestead cap based on certain criminal or wrongful conduct

10.2.3.4.5.1 Introduction

The final restriction on homestead exemptions imposed by the 2005 Act applies to debtors who have been convicted of felonies or who owe debts arising from certain unlawful conduct.[228]

10.2.3.4.5.2 Felony conviction

The debtor may not exempt an interest in homestead property that exceeds $146,450 if the debtor has been convicted of certain criminal conduct. Under section 522(q)(1)(A), the cap applies if the court determines, after notice and a hearing on an objection to the exemption, that the debtor has been convicted of a felony (as defined by 18 U.S.C. § 3156),[229] "which under the circumstances, demonstrates that the filing of the case was an abuse" of the bankruptcy provisions. Based on the language of the provision, the felony conviction probably must occur prior to the filing of the petition, and any criminal activity of the debtor that takes place postpetition, such as during the three to five year pendency of a chapter 13 case, cannot provide the basis for an objection to a homestead exemption under section 522(q)(1)(A).

Although the statutory language is not clear, it would seem that the objecting party would need to prove a connection between the felony conviction and the bankruptcy filing such that the filing would be deemed an abuse. This connection might be shown with proof that the debtor is attempting discharge civil liability owing to victims of the crime, or that the bankruptcy filing may affect the debtor's obligation to pay restitution related to the felony.

---

221 This dollar limit is subject to automatic adjustment every three years pursuant to Code section 104 to account for changes in the cost of living.
222 11 U.S.C. § 522(p)(2)(B). See In re Wayrynen, 332 B.R. 479 (Bankr. S.D. Fla. 2005) ("safe harbor" in section 522(p)(2)(B) found to be applicable because phrase "previous principal residence" includes an interest transferred from a previous residence acquired before the 1215-day period, even if that residence is not most immediate prior residence).
223 11 U.S.C. § 522(p)(2)(A).
224 See In re Aroesty, 385 B.R. 1 (B.A.P. 1st Cir. 2008) (change in debtor's interest in property during 1215-day period from beneficial interest to owner of legal title was acquisition of interest); In re Presto, 376 B.R. 554 (Bankr. S.D. Tex. 2007) (actively acquiring former spouse's interest in property was acquisition of interest); In re Rasmussen, 349 B.R. 747 (Bankr. M.D. Fla. 2006) (equity resulting from rollover of equity from sale of prior homestead was not an interest "acquired by the debtor" during the 1215-day period).
225 In re Sainlar, 344 B.R. 669 (Bankr. M.D. Fla. 2006) (increase in value due to appreciation is not interest acquired within meaning of section 522(p)); In re Chouinard, 358 B.R. 814 (Bankr. M.D. Fla. 2006) (passive market appreciation is not interest acquired); In re Blair, 334 B.R. 374, 376 (Bankr. N.D. Tex. 2005) (one does not "acquire" equity in a home; one acquires title).
226 In re Burns, 395 B.R. 756 (Bankr. M.D. Fla. 2008). But see Parks v. Anderson, 406 B.R. 79, 95 (D. Kan. 2009) (equity resulting from $240,000 lump-sum pay-down of mortgage shortly before bankruptcy was interest acquired subject to limitation under section 522(p)).
227 In re Greene, 583 F.3d 614 (9th Cir. 2009) (perfection of a homestead exemption by recording homestead or moving onto property does not constitute acquisition of property interest for purposes of section 522(p)(1)); In re Rogers, 513 F.3d 212 (5th Cir. 2008) ("interest" as used in section 522(p)(1) refers to property interests having some economic value; although homestead acquired after debtor occupied inherited property during 1215-day period is a legal interest under Texas state law, it is not an economic interest of the kind contemplated by section 522(p)(1)); In re Lyons, 355 B.R. 387 (Bankr. D. Mass. 2006).
228 11 U.S.C. § 522(q)(1).
229 The term "felony" is defined as an "offense punishable by a maximum term of imprisonment of more than one year." 18 U.S.C. § 3156.

10.2.3.4.5.3 Debts arising from certain wrongful conduct

A $146,450 cap on the debtor's homestead interest that may be claimed as exempt may also be invoked under new section 522(q)(1)(B) if the debtor owes a debt arising from certain wrongful conduct. The debt must arise from one of the following four specified categories:

- Any violation of state or federal securities laws (as defined in section 3(a)(47) of the Securities Exchange Act)[230] or any regulation or order issued under state or federal securities laws;
- Fraud, deceit, or manipulation in a fiduciary capacity or in connection with the purchase or sale of any security registered under sections 12 or 15(d) of the Securities Exchange Act of 1934 or under section 6 of the Securities Act of 1933;[231]
- Any civil remedy under the Racketeer Influenced and Corrupt Organizations (RICO) Act;[232] or
- Any criminal act, intentional tort, or willful or reckless misconduct that caused serious physical injury or death to another individual in the preceding five years.[233]

10.2.3.4.5.4 Standing to bring objection to exemption

Section 522(q)(1) does not specify who has standing to initiate a proceeding under the subsection, so presumably it would include any party in interest who timely files an objection to the debtor's exemption based on the procedures in Bankruptcy Rule 4003(b) and (c).[234] However, a creditor or other party having no relation to the felony conviction may have a difficult time proving that the bankruptcy filing was an "abuse," particularly if the crime victim has not objected to the debtor's exemption claim. In fact, a crime victim who has a related civil judgment or claim against the debtor may oppose an objection to the debtor's homestead exemption, preferring instead to pursue a nondischargeability action.[235] Similar standing and proof problems might exist if a party other than the creditor who is owed a debt listed in section 522(q)(1)(B) asserts an exemption objection, particularly if the debt is unliquidated and the debtor offers defenses to owing the debt.

A related question is whether a court has jurisdiction in chapter 13 cases, before the completion of the plan, to adjudicate an exemption objection based on a debt owing under section 522(q)(1)(B), if the debtor is proposing to pay the debt in full as part of the chapter 13 plan.[236] The Bankruptcy Rules avoid this issue by providing in Rule 4003(b)(3) that an objection to a claim of exemption based on section 522(q) may be filed at any time before the closing of the case.[237]

10.2.3.4.5.5 No cap if homestead reasonably necessary for support

Section 522(q)(2) provides that the dollar limitation contained in section 522(q)(1) shall not apply to the extent that the amount of any interest in homestead property is reasonably necessary for the support of the debtor and any dependent of the debtor.[238] This provision would permit the court to decline to apply the $146,450 cap on the debtor's homestead interest that may be claimed as exempt based on a reasonably necessary test like that found in other subsections of section 522,[239] and other sections of the Code, which generally consider whether the questioned item is a "luxury."[240] For no apparent reason, this exemption from the homestead cap may be asserted by the debtor only in response to an objection to a claim of exemption based on section 522(q) and not an objection based on section 522(p). Congress was apparently more sympathetic to a debtor who commits securities fraud or criminal acts causing serious personal injury than to a debtor who may have innocently acquired homestead property within 1215 days before filing the petition.

A determination as to whether the homestead interest in question is reasonably necessary, based on court interpretations of identical language found in other provisions of section 522 (such as section 522(d)(10)), would therefore require the court to consider the debtor's (and dependents) age, health, earning capacity, present and future financial needs and ability, other

---

230 The term "securities laws" means the Securities Act of 1933 (15 U.S.C. §§ 77a–77aa), Securities Exchange Act of 1934 (15 U.S.C. §§ 78a–78nn), Sarbanes-Oxley Act of 2002, Public Utility Holding Company Act of 1935 (15 U.S.C. §§ 79a–79z-6 (repealed 2005), Trust Indenture Act of 1939 (15 U.S.C. §§ 77aaa–77bbbb), Investment Company Act of 1940 (15 U.S.C. §§ 80a-1–80a-64), Investment Advisers Act of 1940 (15 U.S.C. §§ 80b-1–80b-21), and the Securities Investor Protection Act of 1970 (15 U.S.C. §§ 78aaa–78lll). See 15 U.S.C. § 78c(a)(47).

231 In re Presto, 376 B.R. 554 (Bankr. S.D. Tex. 2007) (debtor violated fiduciary duty to former spouse by concealing and failing to turn over her share of tax refund).

232 See 18 U.S.C. § 1964.

233 Unlike section 522(q)(1)(A) which requires a criminal conviction, this provision refers to a "criminal act" and may not require a conviction if it can be shown that the act giving rise to the debt is a crime. See In re Larson, 513 F.3d 325 (1st Cir. 2008) (although charge against debtor was continued without conviction, homestead limitation applied to debt arising from negligent operation of motor vehicle because debtor's admission of guilt in criminal proceeding was equivalent of guilty plea under state law).

234 See Fed. R. Bankr. P. 4003(b)(2) (reprinted in Appx. B, infra).

235 The crime victim might prefer that the debtor keep his or her homestead, even though it is protected under section 522(c), so that the debtor would be in a better position to satisfy the nondischargeable debt.

236 See, e.g., In re Campbell, 313 B.R. 313 (B.A.P. 10th Cir. 2004).

237 See Fed. R. Bankr. P. 4003(b)(3) (reprinted in Appx. B, infra).
If an exemption is first claimed after a case is reopened, an objection under section 522(q) must be filed before the reopened case is closed.

238 Section 522(a)(1) defines "dependent" as including the debtor's spouse, whether or not actually dependent. This definition is ordinarily not relevant to the application of state exemption laws. However it should apply in any consideration of whether section 522(q)(2) prevents the application of the $146,450 cap on a state homestead exemption.

239 See, e.g., 11 U.S.C. § 522(d)(10), (11).

240 See, e.g., 11 U.S.C. § 1325(b)(2)(A).

assets, future financial obligations such as alimony and child support, and any special needs of the debtor and dependents.[241] In the context of the debtor's potential loss of homestead property if the monetary cap were to be applied, the debtor may wish to present additional evidence on matters such as any potential difficulty the debtor may have in finding suitable and affordable replacement housing, the length of time the debtor has lived in the community, the costs of relocation, the safety of the debtor's current neighborhood as compared to any potential replacement housing's surroundings, and the impact relocation may have on the debtor's future income and the education of the debtor's children.

10.2.3.4.5.6 Delay of discharge

The 2005 Act added new subsections 727(a)(12), 1141(d)(5)(C), 1228(f), and 1328(h), which provide that the entry of the debtor's discharge in a chapter 7, 11, 12, or 13 case may be delayed pending the outcome of any criminal and civil proceedings against the debtor referred to in section 522(q)(1). If a motion to delay or postpone discharge is filed under section 727(a)(12),[242] and after notice and hearing held ten days before the date discharge would otherwise enter, the court shall not grant the discharge if it finds that there is reasonable cause to believe that (1) section 522(q)(1) may be applicable, and (2) there is a pending proceeding in which the debtor may be found guilty of a felony described in section 522(q)(1)(A) or liable for a debt described in section 522(q)(1)(B). These provisions are not intended to provide grounds for the denial of a discharge, but simply provide a procedural mechanism for delaying the entry of discharge until the events that could trigger a potential exemption objection under section 522(q) are resolved.[243]

Given that the first condition is that section 522(q)(1) must be applicable, a debtor's discharge may not be delayed if the debtor is not claiming homestead property as exempt, has not claimed a homestead interest in excess of $146,450 as exempt, or if the debtor is claiming homestead property as exempt under section 522(b)(2) or (b)(3)(B).[244] In addition, there should be no delay of discharge if the potential felony conviction did not cause the debtor's bankruptcy filing to be abusive, the debt alleged to be owed is not of the type described in section 522(q)(1), or the homestead property is reasonably necessary for the support of the debtor and any dependent of the debtor.[245]

The second condition requires that the court, if a motion to delay is filed, have reasonable cause to believe that one of the identified types of proceedings is pending against the debtor and that the debtor may be found guilty or liable in such proceeding. The debtor should therefore have the right to be heard on any claims or defenses asserted in the proceeding that would establish that the debtor may not be guilty or liable. However, to avoid the possibility of the debtor making self-incriminating statements, this would not likely occur if a criminal proceeding is pending. Moreover, even as to a pending civil matter, the bankruptcy court may prefer to abstain and permit the court in which the proceeding is pending to determine the underlying debt. In such cases, the entry of the debtor's discharge will be delayed until resolution of the criminal or civil proceeding.

A problem with the drafting of these new delay in discharge provisions is that they conflict with the language used in section 522(q) in regard to a criminal conviction. Section 522(q)(1)(A) provides that the homestead cap may apply if "the debtor *has been convicted* of a felony." Because exemptions are determined on the date the petition is filed,[246] this language should mean that no objection may be brought under section 522(q) if the debtor has not been convicted of a felony prior to the filing of the petition. However, the delay in discharge provisions, as in section 727(a)(12) for example, provide that the discharge may be delayed if there is a pending proceeding in which "the debtor *may be found guilty* of a felony," suggesting that the conviction could occur postpetition. Given the conflict between these provisions, and because section 522(q) is the more specific provision which controls a debtor's substantive rights under the Code relating to exemptions rather than procedural matters relating to the timing of the entry of discharge, section 522(q) probably should control. One could read section 727(a)(12) to deal only with post-conviction cases that are on appeal or somehow not yet final on the date of the petition. Thus, the discharge should not be delayed if the debtor had not been convicted of a felony prior to the filing of the petition.

The new potential barrier to the granting of a discharge under these provisions could mean that some debtors will have to wait months or even years before their bankruptcy cases are concluded and they obtain a discharge. This result is particularly troublesome in chapter 7 cases in which debtors ordinarily are granted a discharge approximately three to four months after the filing of the petition. It could place some debtors in an extended period of uncertainty about their financial situation, during which time they will be effectively locked out of the financial marketplace and denied a fresh start. While courts are

---

241 *See, e.g., In re* Cramer, 281 B.R. 193 (Bankr. E.D. Pa. 2002); *In re* Mann, 201 B.R. 910 (Bankr. E.D. Mich. 1996). *See also* § 12.3.3, *infra*.

242 *See* Fed. R. Bankr. P. 4004(c)(1)(I).
  If a debtor in a chapter 11, 12 or 13 has claimed a homestead exemption under section 522(b)(3)(A) in excess of the amount set out in section 522(q)(1), Fed. R. Bankr. P. 1007(b)(8) provides that the debtor must file a statement concerning whether any civil and criminal proceedings described in section 522(q)(1) are pending. A sample statement is provided in Appx G.12, *infra*.

243 These provisions are found in section 330 of Pub. L. No. 109-8, which is entitled: "Delay of Discharge During Pendency of Certain Proceedings." Presumably Congress sought to include these provisions because of the implications under section 522(c) of the entry of a discharge before a section 522(q) exemption objection is resolved.

244 *In re* Buonopane, 359 B.R. 346 (Bankr. M.D. Fla. 2007) (entireties exemption claimed under section 522(b)(3)(B)); *In re* Jacobs, 342 B.R. 114 (Bankr. D.D.C. 2006) (federal exemptions claimed under section 522(b)(2)). *See* § 10.2.3.4.2, *supra*.

245 *See* §§ 10.2.3.4.5.2, 10.2.3.4.5.3, 10.2.3.4.5.5, *supra*.

246 *See, e.g.,* Lowe v. Sandoval (*In re* Sandoval), 103 F.3d 20 (5th Cir. 1997).

generally not inclined to grant a motion for voluntary dismissal of a chapter 7 case in response to an exemption objection, courts may be more willing to do so under these circumstances.

10.2.3.4.5.7 Application of homestead caps in joint cases

If the homestead cap under section 522(p) (for property acquired within the 1215-day period before filing) or section 522(q) (for certain criminal or wrongful conduct) is imposed, it is applicable to interests that exceed "in the aggregate" $146,450 in value in homestead property. The use of the word "aggregate" in referring to the debtor's interest, consistent with its application in other subsections such as section 522(d)(6),[247] suggests Congress intended the dollar limit to be applied to the combined interests of the debtor in the various forms of property listed in section 522(p)(1)(A) through (D). It is not intended to impose an overall $146,450 cap on the amount both debtors in a joint case may exempt in a homestead under a state exemption law. This construction is supported by the fact that the 2005 Act did not amend section 522(m), which states that section 522 applies separately with respect to each debtor in a joint case.

Thus, the dollar limit of sections 522(p) or (q), if applicable, should apply separately to each debtor's homestead interest and exemption claim.[248] Sections 522(p) or (q), if applicable, will not prevent each debtor in a joint case from claiming as exempt a homestead interest up to the amount of $146,450. For example, if the cap under section 522(q) were imposed in a joint case as to each debtor's homestead interest, the debtors could claim as exempt their total interest in homestead property up to the amount of $292,900 or, if lower, the amount state law provides that the joint debtors may exempt in homestead property.

In addition, in a joint case the dollar limit of sections 522(p) or (q) would not apply to both debtors' homestead interests if only one of the debtors has been convicted of a felony or is liable on a debt specified in section 522(q)(1)(B).

10.3 Procedure for Claiming Exemptions

10.3.1 The Initial Claim

The Bankruptcy Code itself says little regarding the procedure for claiming exemptions, other than that the debtor or a dependent shall "file a list" of property claimed exempt.[249] If the debtor does not file such a list, a dependent of the debtor may do so.[250] The procedure for a dependent claiming exemptions is set out in Federal Rule of Bankruptcy Procedure 4003(a), which sets the deadline for filing as thirty days after the debtor's deadline for filing. It is not clear whether the debtor may thereafter amend or object to the exemptions to alter the dependent's claim.[251]

The Bankruptcy Rules require this list to be filed by a debtor as part of the schedules of property. As discussed in Chapter 7, *supra*, the list is to be set forth on Schedule C of Official Form 6.[252] Failure to file a timely schedule of exemptions may be a basis for an objection to the exemptions.[253] The property must be at least fairly specifically described.[254] If it is not, the debtor may later encounter problems in protecting property that was not specifically listed, or the proceeds of such property.[255]

---

247 Section 522(d)(6) provides that a debtor who elects federal exemptions may exempt "[t]he debtor's aggregate interest, not to exceed $2175 in value, in any implements, professional books, or tools, of the trade of the debtor or the trade of a dependent of the debtor." 11 U.S.C. § 522(d)(6).

248 *See* Dykstra Exterior, Inc. v. Nestlen (*In re* Nestlen), 441 B.R. 135 (B.A.P. 10th Cir. 2010); *In re* Limperis, 370 B.R. 859 (Bankr. S.D. Fla. 2007); *In re* Rasmussen, 349 B.R. 747 (Bankr. M.D. Fla. 2006).

249 11 U.S.C. § 522(*l*).

250 11 U.S.C. § 522(*l*). *But see In re* Alexander, 288 B.R. 127 (B.A.P. 8th Cir. 2003) (debtor's spouse could not assert exemption in property that had already been found nonexempt after debtor's claim of exemption).

It has been held that even when the debtor files a list, a dependent of the debtor may supplement that list if other exemptions are available and unclaimed. *In re* Crouch, 33 B.R. 271 (Bankr. E.D.N.C. 1983). However, a non-debtor dependent may not supplement an incomplete list of federal exemptions with state exemptions. *In re* Homan, 112 B.R. 356 (B.A.P. 9th Cir. 1989).

251 A debtor may also be able to assert a non-debtor spouse's exemptions in community property, depending on state law. *See In re* Perez, 302 B.R. 661 (Bankr. D. Ariz. 2003) (debtor could assert community's exemptions in community property).

252 *See* § 7.3.7.2.3, *supra*.

253 *See* Petit v. Fessenden, 80 F.3d 29 (1st Cir. 1996) (debtor's exemptions disallowed when schedules not timely filed).

If the schedule of exemptions is not timely filed, a motion for enlargement of time may be filed on the basis of excusable neglect under Federal Rule of Bankruptcy Procedure 9006(b)(1). *See In re* Fetner, 218 B.R. 262 (Bankr. D. Colo. 1997) (requiring procedure to file late exemptions which meets the requisites of the rule).

254 *In re* Andermahr, 30 B.R. 532 (B.A.P. 9th Cir. 1983); *In re* Wenande, 107 B.R. 770 (Bankr. D. Wyo. 1989) (exemption denied when property not listed with sufficient particularity); *In re* Hill, 95 B.R. 293 (Bankr. N.D.N.Y. 1988) (same); *In re* Elliott, 31 B.R. 33 (Bankr. S.D. Ohio 1983).

255 *See* Preblich v. Battley, 181 F.3d 1048 (9th Cir. 1999) (trustee's time for objecting to exemptions only began to run when debtor clarified that exemption claim covered escrow accounts as well as wages); *In re* Yonikus, 996 F.2d 866 (7th Cir. 1993) (debtor's exemption for workers' compensation claim denied after debtor had initially fraudulently concealed existence of the claim); Payne v. Wood, 775 F.2d 202 (7th Cir. 1985) (debtors not permitted to exempt insurance proceeds of property not listed; intent to conceal property inferred); *In re* Bauer, 298 B.R. 353 (B.A.P. 8th Cir. 2003) (clearly untruthful and bad faith disclosure of home's value as $80,000, when it was worth over $200,000, justified sustaining objection to exemption amendment filed only after trustee determined true value of property); *In re* Bogert, 104 B.R. 547 (Bankr. M.D. Ga. 1989) (trustee permitted to withdraw no asset report after learning debtor did not adequately describe his pension plan). *But see* Massey v. Pappalardo (*In re* Massey), 465 B.R. 720 (B.A.P. 1st Cir. 2012) (debtor could not simply state "100% of FMV" on Schedule C); Rossi v. Westenhoefer (*In re* Rossi), 2012 WL 913732 (B.A.P. 6th Cir. Mar. 20, 2012) (debtors entitled to hearing to explain why values on schedules should not estop them from later claiming higher amount when property was destroyed by fire); *In re* Rutherford, 73 B.R. 665 (Bankr. W.D. Mo. 1986) (debtor entitled to insurance proceeds

If there is any conceivable doubt regarding whether the entire value of an asset is exemptible, debtors should make clear that they are claiming their entire interest in that asset as exempt. If the debtor fails to do so, and the asset is worth more than the amount listed as exempt, a trustee may argue that the debtor has only exempted the asset up to amount listed, and that the excess value over that amount may be liquidated for creditors. The Supreme Court in *Schwab v. Reilly* accepted this argument, but also provided suggested language the debtor may use to make clear the debtor's intent to exempt the entire asset. The debtor may list "full fair market value (FMV)" or "100% of FMV" in the "Value of the Claimed Exemption" column on Schedule C.[256]

10.3.2 Amending the Claim of Exemption

Under the rules, any part of the schedules, including the exemption claim, may be amended as a matter of right before the case is closed.[257] Presumably, an amendment may include a change from the state to the federal exemption scheme or vice versa.[258] Under similar language in the prior rules, some courts had imposed time limitations on the right to amend the exemption claim, holding that the claim became "finalized" after the time for objections to exemptions had passed.[259] However, the current rules' provision for extending the time for objections to thirty days after any amendment[260] lays those decisions to rest.

A debtor may sometimes even be allowed to reopen the case after discharge to amend the exemptions.[261] It has been held, however, that a debtor cannot exempt property which has been knowingly concealed from the trustee.[262] Additionally, some courts have held that a trustee's or creditor's detrimental reliance on the debtor's original claim of exemption may limit later amendment.[263] These courts do not fully address why prejudice to the creditor in the absence of bad faith[264] on the part of the debtor should be sufficient to affect the right to amend nor why there should be an exception that does not exist in the Federal Rules of Bankruptcy Procedure.[265] Other courts have required the debtor who amends to include property brought into the estate by the trustee to pay the fees and costs of expended by the trustee in obtaining the property.[266] At least with respect to property obtained by the trustee under the turnover and avoiding powers, the Code specifically provides that the exempted

---

when exempt property destroyed by fire despite undervaluation on schedules).

The debtor may encounter similar problems in not specifically describing property in an amended exemption. However, the description need only be sufficient to put the trustee on notice of the nature of the property and the amount of the exemption. Taylor v. Freeland & Kronz, 503 U.S. 638, 112 S. Ct. 1644, 118 L. Ed. 2d 280 (1992) (cause of action described but valued as "unknown" was sufficient to put trustee on notice of the exemption).

256 Schwab v. Reilly, 130 S. Ct. 2652, 2668 (2010). *See also* § 10.3.3, *infra*. Some courts had taken the view before *Schwab v. Reilly* that the debtor must list a dollar value for the interest claimed to be exempt.

257 Fed. R. Bankr. P. 1009; *In re* Michael, 163 F.3d 526 (9th Cir. 1998) (debtors had right to amend even after discharge if case not yet closed); *In re* Williamson, 804 F.2d 1355 (5th Cir. 1986). *See also* Lucius v. McLemore, 741 F.2d 125 (6th Cir. 1984); *In re* Shirkey, 715 F.2d 859 (4th Cir. 1983); Redmond v. Tuttle, 698 F.2d 414 (10th Cir. 1983) (exemptions may be amended at any time before case is closed); *In re* Doan, 672 F.2d 831 (5th Cir. 1982) (reversing a denial of debtor's motion to amend schedules to add exemption claim).

258 *In re* McComber, 422 B.R. 334 (Bankr. D. Mass. 2010); *In re* McQueen, 21 B.R. 736 (Bankr. D. Vt. 1982).

259 *In re* Mertsching, 4 B.R. 519 (Bankr. D. Idaho 1980) (debtor forced to pay trustee $50 costs in order to modify exemptions to meet previous objection of trustee which was sustained); *In re* Lyon, 6 Bankr. Ct. Dec. (LRP) 343, 2 Collier Bankr. Cas. 2d (MB) 561 (Bankr. D. Kan. 1980) (local rule provided that exemption finalized if no objection within fifteen days after section 341 meeting); *In re* Duggan, 4 B.R. 709 (Bankr. N.D. Tex. 1980) (debtor could not change to federal exemptions fifteen days after trustee's statement of exempt property filed).

Objection time limits are discussed in § 10.3.3, *infra*.

260 Fed. R. Bankr. P. 4003(b); 9 Collier on Bankruptcy ¶ 4003.02[2] (16th ed.).

261 *In re* Goswami, 304 B.R. 386 (B.A.P. 9th Cir. 2003); *In re* King, 27 B.R. 754 (Bankr. M.D. Tenn. 1983).

262 *In re* Ford, 492 F.3d 1148 (10th Cir. 2007); *In re* Wood, 291 B.R. 219 (B.A.P. 1st Cir. 2003); *In re* Dorricott, 5 B.R. 192 (Bankr. N.D. Ohio 1980). *See also* Payne v. Wood, 775 F.2d 202 (7th Cir. 1985); *In re* Trudell, 424 B.R. 786 (Bankr. W.D. Mich. 2010) (debtors allowed to amend schedules to list tax refund as asset and exempt it; no bad faith because, at time schedules were prepared, debtors did not know they were entitled to refund); *In re* Ruiz, 406 B.R. 897, 902 (Bankr. E.D. Cal. 2009) (amendment allowed when trustee introduced no evidence that debtors intended to hide property). *But see In re* Moody, 862 F.2d 1194 (5th Cir. 1989) (attempted fraudulent transfer of property did not preclude debtor from later claiming homestead exemption under Texas law).

263 *See In re* Kaelin, 308 F.3d 885 (8th Cir. 2002) (debtor could exempt recently discovered cause of action because debtor had acted promptly to amend exemptions after learning of its existence); *In re* Osborn, 24 F.3d 1199 (10th Cir. 1994) (stating that a limited exception to the general permissibility of amendments could exist if the debtors were equitably estopped, but declining to find exception applicable when misrepresentations relied upon by creditors were not made by both husband and wife debtors); Hardage v. Herring Nat'l Bank, 837 F.2d 1319 (5th Cir. 1988) (creditor may change litigation posture in reliance on debtor's initial exemption claim resulting in prejudice precluding amendment); *In re* Ardrey, 316 B.R. 531 (B.A.P. 8th Cir. 2004) (mere fact that trustee had obtained order that debtor turn over tax refund did not preclude amendment that claimed refund as exempt); *In re* Goswami, 304 B.R. 386 (B.A.P. 9th Cir. 2003) (debtors had right to amend exemptions for purpose of lien avoidance absent bad faith or prejudice).

264 *Cf. In re* Hannigan, 409 F.3d 480 (1st Cir. 2005) (affirming denial of right to amend to debtor who in bad faith originally valued real property at less than half its true value); *In re* Barrows, 408 B.R. 239 (B.A.P. 8th Cir. 2009) (affirming denial of right to amend schedules that initially listed $300 in bank account when true amount was over $13,000).

265 The Bankruptcy Rules contemplate that exemptions may be claimed in a reopened case. *See* Fed. R. Bankr. P. 4004(b)(3) (providing that if an exemption is first claimed after a case is reopened, an objection must be filed before the reopened case is closed).

266 *In re* Arnold, 252 B.R. 778 (B.A.P. 9th Cir. 2000); *In re* Myatt, 101 B.R. 197 (Bankr. E.D. Cal. 1989) (when trustee conducts litigation based on belief that litigation costs and fees would be paid from recovery of nonexempt property, debtor's later amendment of exemptions to include recovered property may be conditioned on payment of trustee's expenses).

property is liable for its aliquot share of the costs and expenses of recovering the property.[267] And a debtor may not, after the case is filed, convert nonexempt property into exempt property to claim it as exempt.[268]

One type of situation in which an amendment may be necessary is the case in which property acquired after the petition is filed becomes property of the estate.[269] The debtor is permitted to amend the exemption schedules to exempt such property if it fits within applicable exemption limits, regardless of whether a discharge has already been entered.[270]

Any amendment, of course, should comply with Bankruptcy Rule 1009 which requires service on all parties affected by an amendment; in the case of amended exemptions, service should presumably be made on the trustee and all creditors, except creditors already being paid in full.[271] Perhaps also, if the time for filing claims has run, the amendment need not be served on creditors who did not file claims. Failure to make proper service may extend the deadline for objections.[272]

10.3.3 Objections to Exemptions

The Code allows objections to claims of exemption by "a party in interest," again specifying no procedure.[273] The procedure is provided by Bankruptcy Rule 4003(b), though the rule does not prescribe any particular form for the objection.[274] In most cases the party who would be likely to object is the trustee. However, the rules make clear that any creditor has standing to file objections to exemptions.[275]

In some districts, trustees still file reports of any objections to exemptions as well as a recommendation concerning discharge. In any case, with four exceptions discussed below, all objections to exemptions must be filed within thirty days after the conclusion of the meeting of creditors or the filing of any amendment to the exemption list, unless a motion for an extension of the deadline is filed within that period and the court grants the motion.[276] Bankruptcy Rule 1009 requires that notice of any amendment of the exemptions be given to any entity affected by it, which usually would include the trustee and all creditors, so that they have an opportunity to object.[277] Objections that are not timely filed cannot be considered.[278] If a case is converted to chapter 7, a new objection deadline is set thirty days after the conclusion of the chapter 7 meeting of creditors, unless (1) the case was converted to chapter 7 more than one year after entry of the first order confirming a chapter 11, 12, or 13 plan or (2) the case had previously been converted from chapter 7 after the deadline for exemption objections had expired in the original chapter 7 case.[279]

However, the time for objecting to a claim for exemption may not prevent a trustee from attempting to liquidate an asset if the debtor does not clearly state the interest that the debtor intends to exempt. In *Schwab v. Reilly*[280] the Supreme Court held that a debtor who listed an asset as having a certain dollar value and then exempted that same dollar value had not clearly manifested her intent to exempt the entire asset if it turned out

---

267 11 U.S.C. § 522(k)(1).
268 *In re* Blue, 5 B.R. 723 (Bankr. S.D. Ohio 1980).
269 Certain types of property acquired within 180 days after the petition is filed, such as inheritances, life insurance proceeds and property settlements, become property of the bankruptcy estate. 11 U.S.C. § 541(a)(5).
270 *In re* Notargiacomo, 253 B.R. 112 (Bankr. S.D. Fla. 2000); *In re* Magness, 160 B.R. 294 (Bankr. N.D. Tex. 1993). See also Fed. R. Bankr. P. 4003(b)(2) (dealing with amendments in case that is reopened).
271 See *In re* Casani, 214 B.R. 459 (D. Vt. 1997) (all creditors should be served); *In re* Govoni, 289 B.R. 500 (Bankr. D. Mass. 2002) (order granting amendment to exemption schedule vacated because notice not provided to judicial lienholder).
272 Compare *In re* Woodson, 839 F.2d 610 (9th Cir. 1988) (creditor's objection to amendment was timely on thirty-first day after amendment because creditor had not been served with debtor's amendment, even though the creditor had actual knowledge of the asset about which the amendment was made) and *In re* Robertson, 105 B.R. 440 (Bankr. N.D. Ill. 1989) (deadline for objecting to amended exemption did not apply when trustee had no notice of amendment) with *In re* Peterson, 929 F.2d 385 (8th Cir. 1991) (objection to amended exemption untimely when creditor had actual notice of the amendment by virtue of service of the trustee's objection ten months earlier).
273 11 U.S.C. § 522(*l*).
274 See *In re* Spenler, 212 B.R. 625 (B.A.P. 9th Cir. 1997) (objection to exemption was timely even though it did not conform to local rule).
275 Fed. R. Bankr. P. 4003(b).

276 *Id.*; Fed. R. Bankr. P. 9006(b)(3); *In re* Bernard, 40 F.3d 1028 (9th Cir. 1994) (creditors meeting is not concluded until after two adjournments caused by debtors' failure to cooperate, so objection was timely); *In re* Kahan, 28 F.3d 79 (9th Cir. 1994) (trustee's objection to amendment was timely objection, because amendment was not merely a clarification of prior schedule).

Rule 4003(b) was amended in 2000 to overrule cases that had held that the court had to grant the extension prior to the expiration of the thirty days. See, e.g., *In re* Laurain, 113 F.3d 595 (6th Cir. 1997); *In re* Stoulig, 45 F.3d 957 (5th Cir. 1995).

An objection to an amended exemption claim may only raise issues concerning the amendment if the time for objecting to the initial claim has run. *In re* Kazi, 985 F.2d 318 (7th Cir. 1993); *In re* Payton, 73 B.R. 31 (Bankr. W.D. Tex. 1987). See also *In re* Alderton, 179 B.R. 63 (Bankr. E.D. Mich. 1995) (grant of extension of time to file dischargeability complaint did not extend deadline for objecting to exemptions).
277 See *In re* Banke, 267 B.R. 852 (Bankr. N.D. Iowa 2001) (creditor had until thirty days after actual notice of amended exemption to object). See also § 10.3.2, supra.
278 Taylor v. Freeland & Kronz, 503 U.S. 638, 112 S. Ct. 1644, 118 L. Ed. 2d 280 (1992). See also *In re* Bush, 346 B.R. 523 (Bankr. E.D. Wash. 2006) (objections must be served, as well as filed, within thirty-day period). But see *In re* Young, 806 F.2d 1303 (5th Cir. 1986) (objection allowed when debtor had notice of trustee's objection prior to deadline even though actual objection filed after deadline).

Some courts had held, incorrectly, that an untimely objection to an exemption could be sustained when the exemption claim has "no statutory basis" or no "good faith statutory basis." See, e.g., *In re* Peterson, 920 F.2d 1389 (8th Cir. 1990); *In re* Sherk, 918 F.2d 1170 (5th Cir. 1990). Those decisions have been overruled by the United States Supreme Court. Taylor v. Freeland & Kronz, 503 U.S. 638, 112 S. Ct. 1644, 118 L. Ed. 2d 280 (1992). See § 10.3.4, infra.
279 Fed. R. Bankr. P. 1019(2)(B).
280 130 S. Ct. 2652 (2010).

to be worth more than that dollar value.[281] The court set forth a very simple solution to this problem: the debtor need only make absolutely clear the debtor's intent to exempt the entire asset by listing the exempt value on Schedule C as "full fair market value (FMV)" or "100% of FMV."[282] Then the trustee will know that she must object within the time set by Rule 4003 or else the entire asset will be exempted.[283]

The only exceptions to the thirty-day rule for filing objections to exemptions are contained in Bankruptcy Rule 4003(b)(2) and (3). Rule 4003(b)(2) permits the trustee, and only the trustee, to object to a fraudulently asserted exemption within one year after the case is closed. This exception is unlikely to be utilized often, because a trustee seldom devotes any attention to a case after it is closed. It would probably come into play only if some third party alerted the trustee to an alleged fraudulent exemption claim. Presumably, the usual standards for proving fraud would determine whether this extended deadline could be used by a trustee.

Rule 4003(b)(3) governs exceptions under section 522(q), which limits a state homestead exemption to $146,450 for debtors who have been convicted of certain crimes or are liable for certain bad acts.[284] This type of objection, which can only be made if the debtor claims a state homestead exemption in excess of that amount, will be rare. If made, it must be filed before the closing of the case. However, if the case is reopened, it may be made at any time before the reopened case is again closed.

The next exception is for objections when a debtor first claims an exemption after a case is reopened, and also requires that this type of objection be filed before the close of the reopened case. This exception, provided in Rule 4003(b)(3), is only a minor variation on the general rule contained in Rule 4003(b)(1), which give parties thirty days after such a new claim of exemption to file an objection. Usually, if the case is only reopened for purposes of making the amended exemption claim, the date of closing will not be long after the case is reopened. Indeed, it could be less than the thirty days after the exemption claim that is permitted for objections to amended exemptions.

The final exception permits a creditor to challenge a claim of exemption in a lien avoidance proceeding even though a timely objection to the exemption was not filed.[285] Rule 4003(d) provides that, notwithstanding Rule 4003(b), a creditor may object to a motion filed by the debtor to avoid a lien on exempt property under section 522(f) by challenging the validity of the exemption asserted to be impaired by the lien. This exception under Rule 4003(d) is limited to an objection to a claim of exemption in property that is the subject of the lien avoidance proceeding and only permits the creditor to object to the exemption insofar as it is necessary to defeat the lien avoidance motion.[286]

Copies of the objections must be served on the trustee, the person filing the exemption claim (usually the debtor), and that person's attorney.[287] At the hearing on the objections, the objecting party has the burden of proof.[288] Exemption statutes should be construed liberally in favor of the debtor.[289]

As in other areas of bankruptcy procedure, questions of value may be critical in objections to exemption claims. In general, the discussion in Chapter 9, *supra*, of methods to prove value for stay litigation purposes is equally relevant here.[290] However, while the goal in that type of litigation may be to prove a high value for property, in exemption claims the debtor usually attempts to prove the property to have a low value, within the exemption limits. While it can be argued that the different purposes of the valuations should lead to different values in each case, it is certainly preferable to try to be consistent, which means carefully planning strategy from the outset. In fact, at least if value is determined in one proceeding and the purpose of valuation is the same in a subsequent proceeding, collateral estoppel may bar the debtor from relitigating the question of value.[291]

In any case, the debtor usually should argue that for exemption purposes the "fair market value" of section 522(a)(2) is liquidation value, because the purpose of the valuation is to see if liquidation of the property will produce cash in excess of the exemption amount.[292] There is no point in selling the debtor's property if all of the proceeds after the costs of sale will go back to the debtor.

The value should be determined as of the date the petition was filed, and any appreciation since then should be considered property acquired postpetition that is not a part of the estate.[293]

---

281 See also Gebhart v. Gaughan (*In re* Gebhart), 621 F.3d 1206, 1210 n.4 (9th Cir. 2010) (similar holding, expressly noting that debtor, like debtor in *Schwab*, did not claim full fair market value of property as exempt).

282 130 S. Ct. 2652, 2668 (2010).

283 *In re* Moore, 442 B.R. 865 (Bankr. N.D. Tex. 2010); *In re* Winchell, 2010 WL 5338054 (Bankr. E.D. Wash. Dec. 20, 2010). But see *In re* Massey, 465 B.R. 720 (B.A.P. 1st Cir. 2012) (finding debtor's use of "100% of FMV" to be "facially invalid" in case where debtor did not also list a value for the asset); *In re* Salazar, 449 B.R. 890 (Bankr. N.D. Tex. 2011) (objection by trustee to a "100% of FMV" exemption claim treated as a "facially valid objection" thus requiring the debtor to amend the schedule and list a value for the exemption); *In re* Stoney, 445 B.R. 543 (Bankr. E.D. Va. 2011) (Virginia exemption statute requires debtor to claim an exemption amount rather than use "100% of FMV"). These cases should not prevent a debtor from both listing a value and claiming one hundred percent of FMV as exempt.

284 *See* § 10.2.3.4.5.2, *supra*.

285 Lien avoidance under section 522(f) is discussed in § 10.4.2.3, *infra*.

286 *See* Fed. R. Bankr. P. 4003 advisory committee's note (2008).

287 Fed. R. Bankr. P. 4003(b).

288 Fed. R. Bankr. P. 4003(c); *In re* Green, 423 B.R. 867 (Bankr. W.D. Ark. 2010) (in absence of evidence on critical factual issues, objection denied).

289 *See, e.g., In re* Wallerstedt, 930 F.2d 630 (8th Cir. 1991).

290 *See* § 9.7.3.3.1, *supra*.

291 *In re* Bohrer, 19 B.R. 958 (Bankr. E.D. Pa. 1982).

292 *In re* Walsh, 5 B.R. 239 (Bankr. D.D.C. 1980).
But see *In re* Windfelder, 82 B.R. 367 (Bankr. E.D. Pa. 1988) and cases cited therein.

293 11 U.S.C. § 522(a)(2); *In re* Rappaport, 19 B.R. 971 (Bankr. E.D. Pa. 1982). *See also In re* Harris, 886 F.2d 1011 (8th Cir. 1989) (debtors could not claim exemption in proceeds of property of estate, when apparently property of the estate had not previously been claimed as exempt, when proceeds came into existence under

§ 10.3.4 Consumer Bankruptcy Law and Practice

However, this may depend upon whether the debtor's entire interest in the property has been claimed as exempt.[294] Conversion of a case from one chapter to another does not change the relevant date for calculating value for the purpose of determining exemptions.[295] Similarly, a change in the applicable exemption law following the filing of the case does not apply; the law in effect at the time of filing determines the property which may be exempted.[296] Even if the property would no longer be considered exempt, the same principle applies.[297] Exemptions are determined as of the filing of the petition.

Of course, if the property is sold during the bankruptcy case, the sale price is normally the best evidence of its value, unless a change in value since the petition date can be proved.[298] When property is sold by the bankruptcy trustee during the bankruptcy case and unexpected proceeds are realized, the debtors should be allowed at a minimum to amend the exemption claim and thereby obtain the maximum exempt share of the funds raised.[299]

10.3.4 Absent Successful Objections, the Exemptions Are Allowed

If no timely and successful objection to the debtor's exemptions is made, the exemptions listed by the debtor are automatically allowed.[300] Untimely objections cannot be entertained by the court, whether or not the original exemption was proper.[301]

This rule means that the trustee or a creditor can dispute an exemption only by affirmatively filing a timely objection. For this reason, debtor's attorneys should not acquiesce to a request to turn over to the trustee property which the debtor claims as exempt. In practice, as often as not, the trustee never files the necessary objection. In those instances in which an objection is actually filed on time, the debtor can then litigate the question of whether the property is actually exempt.

Debtors should also beware of trustees' attempts to indefinitely extend the time for objections. Some trustees have indefinitely "adjourned" the meeting of creditors to prevent the conclusion of the meeting, from which the time period begins to run. Such adjournments should not be permitted, because they render the deadline for objections meaningless.[302] They

---

state law only because of event occurring postpetition); *In re* Finn, 151 B.R. 25 (Bankr. N.D.N.Y. 1992) (property valued as of filing date for lien avoidance purposes). *But see In re* Alsberg, 68 F.3d 312 (9th Cir. 1995) (erroneously holding that, even though debtor's interest was totally exempt at time of filing, when debtor first claimed exemption long after the petition was filed, trustee could object that appreciation of interest above exemption amount was not exempted); *In re* Hyman, 967 F.2d 1316 (9th Cir. 1992) (when debtor's interest was not totally exempt at time of petition, appreciation could not be exempted).

Both *Alsberg* and *Hyman* should be distinguishable from the more typical situation in which the debtor promptly claims the entire equity as exempt at the time of the petition and no timely objection is filed. At that point the estate has no interest that can appreciate. *See In re* Polis, 217 F.3d 899 (7th Cir. 2000) (TILA claim should be valued for exemption purposes based on fair market value, discounted for contingency, on date of bankruptcy petition). Both cases also rely on the peculiar wording of the California homestead exemption statute.

However, the Ninth Circuit subsequently refused to limit the *Alsberg* and *Hyman* holdings to an interpretation of the California exemption statute. *See In re* Gebhart, 621 F.3d 1206 (9th Cir. 2010).

294 *See In re* Orton, 687 F.3d 612 (3d Cir. 2012); *In re* Gebhart, 621 F.3d 1206 (9th Cir. 2010).

This problem should be resolved by the Supreme Court's decision in *Schwab v. Reilly*, 130 S. Ct. 2652 (2010). If the debtor clearly states an intent to exempt the entire asset, then a trustee must object to the exemption within the time provided by Fed. R. Bankr. P. 4003, or else the trustee is precluded from claiming any interest in the asset is not exempt.

295 11 U.S.C. § 348(a). *See In re* Hall, 1 F.3d 853 (9th Cir. 1993) (value of property in converted case is determined as of date of original bankruptcy petition filing); *In re* Kaplan, 97 B.R. 572 (B.A.P. 9th Cir. 1989).

It is unclear whether the *Hall* decision is still valid precedent. The decision was withdrawn and then subsequently reaffirmed by the Ninth Circuit without reissuing the decision. *See In re* Hall, 41 F.3d 502 (9th Cir. 1994) and 42 F.3d 1399 (9th Cir. 1994). *See also In re* Alsberg, 68 F.3d 312 (9th Cir. 1995). It would appear that the reasoning of the court, albeit limited, nevertheless continues to have persuasive value.

296 *In re* Marcus, 1 F.3d 1050 (10th Cir. 1993).

297 *In re* Alexander, 239 B.R. 911 (B.A.P. 8th Cir. 1999) (homestead determined as of petition date); *In re* Beshirs, 236 B.R. 42 (Bankr. D. Kan. 1999) (property that was exempted as tool of trade was still exempt after conversion even though no longer used as tool of trade).

298 Fitzgerald v. Davis, 729 F.2d 306 (4th Cir. 1984).

299 Armstrong v. Hursman, 106 B.R. 625 (D.N.D. 1988). *See* § 10.3.2, *supra*.

300 11 U.S.C. § 522(*l*). *See* Taylor v. Freeland & Kronz, 503 U.S. 638, 112 S. Ct. 1644, 118 L. Ed. 2d 280 (1992); *In re* Sadkin, 36 F.3d 473 (5th Cir. 1994) (even if exemption is without merit, failure of any party to file a timely objection results in allowance of exemption); *In re* Green, 31 F.3d 1098 (11th Cir. 1994) (if no party challenges debtor's valuation of asset claimed as fully exempt, debtor is entitled to exempt the entire asset regardless of what the value ultimately proves to be); *In re* Morgan-Busby, 272 B.R. 257 (B.A.P. 9th Cir. 2002) (deadline for objections includes objections based on valuation of property clearly claimed as exempt); *In re* Chaparro Martinez, 293 B.R. 387 (Bankr. N.D. Tex. 2003) (court has no jurisdiction over debtors' personal injury settlement proceeds, even though in excess of claimed exemption, because debtors claimed one-hundred percent of claim as exempt and trustee failed to file timely objection). *But see In re* Wick, 276 F.3d 412 (8th Cir. 2002) (erroneously holding that, even though debtor listed value of stock options as unknown and trustee did not object to exemption, property was only partially exempt because trustee expressed interest in asset and debtor supposedly made statements suggesting she "understood" options to be only partially exempt); Petit v. Fessenden, 80 F.3d 29 (1st Cir. 1996) (if exemption claim is not filed timely, automatic allowance after objection period does not occur); *In re* Clark, 266 B.R. 163 (B.A.P. 9th Cir. 2001) (ambiguous exemption claim construed against debtor when debtor claimed as exempt "five lots listed in qualified retirement plan" and plan did not exist).

301 Fed. R. Bankr. P. 4003(b); Taylor v. Freeland & Kronz, 503 U.S. 638, 112 S. Ct. 1644, 118 L. Ed. 2d 280 (1992). *See* § 10.3.3, *supra*.

302 *In re* Smith, 235 F.3d 472 (9th Cir. 2000) (trustee could not adjourn section 341 meeting indefinitely; rules required specific place and time); Newman v. White (*In re* Newman), 428 B.R. 257 (B.A.P. 1st Cir. Apr. 26, 2010) (when trustee adjourned meeting without announcing date for continuation, and had all necessary information within ten days thereafter, objections filed after second meeting held months later was not timely); *In re* Clark, 262 B.R. 508 (B.A.P. 9th

also violate Bankruptcy Rule 2003(e), which specifically requires the trustee to promptly file a statement specifying the date and time to which the meeting is adjourned. Trustees have also attempted in other ways to keep their options open without litigating an objection.[303]

Given the burden on the trustee and the creditors to raise timely objections, the debtor should be careful to make all appropriate exemption claims at the outset of the case, when possible.[304] It is to the debtor's advantage to fully describe the property, including its value and any features which would decrease its value if it were sold, and then to list the basis for the exemption. Obviously, the limit on this principle is one of good faith. Bad faith exemption claims that are not grounded in fact or law not only create the risk of a successful objection, but also expose debtors and their counsel to the risk of sanctions.[305]

Once property is exempt by virtue of the expiration of the deadline for objections, nothing prevents the debtors from using or otherwise disposing of their exempt interest.[306] When a single piece of property is only partially exempt, the debtor may retain the entire property until the trustee pays the value of the exemption to the debtor in cash.[307] Importantly, this rule means that the debtor can continue to reside in property which the trustee may liquidate without responsibility to the trustee for rent or other payments.[308] The fact that the estate must pay months of mortgage payments and other postpetition expenses prior to sale of the property may sometimes discourage an objection to an exemption. Moreover, under section 522(k), the trustee must pay the entire exemption amount to the debtor before the trustee can use the proceeds of the sale to pay any costs or fees in connection with the sale.[309]

10.4 Making the Most of Exemptions

10.4.1 Exemption Planning

Section 522 of the Code provides many protections and powers in connection with debtors' exemption rights. The exemptions, whether state or federal, are non-waivable for bankruptcy purposes, even if state law would normally allow a waiver of exemptions.[310] And the debtor's powers to enhance the exemptions, to be discussed below, are also non-waivable.[311] In essence, the exemption provisions federalize all of the law applying to bankruptcy exemptions, except for the actual items which can be claimed as exempt by a debtor utilizing the state exemptions.[312] Under this uniform bank-

---

Cir. 2001) (trustee must announce date of continued creditors meeting within reasonable time, not to exceed thirty days); *In re* Hurdle, 240 B.R. 617 (Bankr. C.D. Cal. 1999) (trustee could not adjourn meeting with no new date scheduled to avoid deadline); *In re* Levitt, 137 B.R. 881 (Bankr. D. Mass. 1992) (trustee's failure to announce an adjourned date and time within thirty days of the initial meeting of creditors means that meeting must be deemed closed as of the initial date). *See also In re* Dutkiewicz, 408 B.R. 103 (B.A.P. 6th Cir. 2009) (at a minimum, trustee must announce meeting is being held open); 3 Collier on Bankruptcy ¶ 341.02[5][g] (16th ed.). *But see In re* Peres, 530 F.3d 375 (5th Cir. 2008) (adopting case-by-case approach, court held that repeated continuances were permitted, when several continuances were requested by debtors and debtors never sought to conclude meeting); *In re* DeCarolis, 259 B.R. 467 (B.A.P. 1st Cir. 2001) (adjournment without setting new date could extend time for objections if amount of extension reasonable under circumstances).

303 *In re* Thomas, 236 B.R. 573 (Bankr. E.D.N.Y. 1999) (trustee could not file "no asset report," close case, and still retain right to reopen if cause of action proved to have unexpected value).

304 Note, however, the right to amend. *See* § 10.3.2, *supra*.

305 *See* Fed. R. Bankr. P. 9011.

It is unclear whether sanctions for bad faith exemptions are possible after the time for objecting to the actual exemption has passed.

306 Wissman v. Pittsburgh Nat'l Bank, 942 F.2d 867 (4th Cir. 1991) (debtors may pursue an exempt cause of action in order to recover their exemption); Ball v. Nationscredit Fin. Serv. Corp., 207 B.R. 869 (N.D. Ill. 1997) (exempt property revests in debtor when time to object to exemptions expires); Seifert v. Selby, 125 B.R. 174 (E.D. Mich. 1989) (absent timely objection, exempt property revests in the debtor and is no longer property of the estate). *Cf. In re* Reed, 940 F.2d 1317 (9th Cir. 1991) (although debtor is entitled to exemption when no one timely objects to the exemption, the trustee is entitled to proceeds of sale to the extent they exceed the actual dollar value of the exemption); *In re* Salzer, 52 F.3d 708 (7th Cir.) (reading Indiana law to delay revesting of exempt property in debtor), *aff'd*, 68 F.3d 312 (9th Cir. 1995).

307 *In re* Szekely, 936 F.2d 897 (7th Cir. 1991); *In re* Aldeir, 2010 WL 1656953 (N.D. Ill. Apr. 21, 2010) (trustee could not demand partially exempt automobile from debtor until exemption amount paid to debtor in cash). *But see In re* Salzer, 52 F.3d 708 (7th Cir. 1995) (erroneously holding that Indiana execution procedures permit a bankruptcy trustee to hold property after the deadline for objecting to exemptions has run until the trustee obtains an appraisal of the property; *pro se* debtor waived argument that commercial property in question was totally exempt); Greene v. Balaber-Strauss, 76 B.R. 940 (S.D.N.Y. 1987) (trustee could wait until she completed her administrative duties).

The *Greene* decision is poorly reasoned, confusing the issue of discharge with that of exemptions, which are provided regardless of discharge.

308 *In re* Szekely, 936 F.2d 897 (7th Cir. 1991); *In re* Rolfes, 307 B.R. 59 (Bankr. E.D. Tenn. 2004) (trustee could not retain exempt proceeds of sale to pay for postpetition rent).

309 *In re* Allen, 203 B.R. 925 (W.D. Va.), *aff'd sub nom.* Scott v. United States Trustee, 133 F.3d 917 (4th Cir. 1997) (table).

310 11 U.S.C. § 522(e); *In re* Howell, 51 B.R. 1015 (M.D.N.C. 1985). *See In re* Scrivner, 535 F.3d 1258, 1265 (10th Cir. 2008) (court could not use section 105 to override exemption protections by surcharging exemptions when debtors failed to turn over property); Dominion Bank of Cumberlands v. Nuckolls, 780 F.2d 408 (4th Cir. 1985). *But see* Latman v. Burdette, 366 F.3d 774 (9th Cir. 2004) (court could surcharge the debtor's wildcard exemption to compensate for cash that debtors did not disclose and no longer had in order to ensure that debtors did not retain property in excess of the amount permitted by exemption laws).

311 11 U.S.C. § 522(e). *See In re* Hebert, 301 B.R. 19 (Bankr. N.D. Iowa 2003) (waiver of homestead exemption unenforceable due to section 522(e)).

312 *See* Owen v. Owen, 500 U.S. 305, 111 S. Ct. 1833, 114 L. Ed. 2d 250 (1991). *But see In re* Golden, 789 F.2d 698 (9th Cir. 1986) (giving effect to substantive limitation on California homestead exemption which requires that proceeds of sale of homestead be reinvested in new home within six months to maintain exemption).

It should be noted that California's exemption is thus broader than the federal exemption. *See also* § 10.2.1.1, *supra*.

ruptcy system, dependents of the debtor may claim exemptions if the debtor does not,[313] and the exemptions are automatically allowed if no objection is filed.[314]

As discussed in an earlier chapter,[315] the amount of property that may be claimed as exempt can be greatly increased, if necessary, by careful exemption planning. For example, cash in a bank account which cannot be claimed as exempt can be used to pay down a mortgage to create home equity which may be claimed as exempt.[316] Similarly, contributions within the limitations of tax law may be made to a retirement plan that will be claimed as exempt. Although there was some question as to the propriety of exemption planning under the prior Act, the federalization of most bankruptcy exemption law should somewhat ease those doubts. However some courts have found the movement of very large amounts of money into exempt property to be fraudulent, at least with respect to state exemptions.[317]

10.4.2 Avoiding Powers of the Debtor

10.4.2.1 General Principles

One of the most far-reaching and exciting changes made by the Bankruptcy Reform Act was its grant to the debtor of the power to avoid (nullify) many types of prebankruptcy transfers of exempt property. This set of powers, contained in section 522, opened up an entirely new area in which debtors can greatly expand upon the exemption rights given to them by state or federal law. Because this area was new, it was largely uncharted when the Code was enacted. Since then, numerous courts, including the Supreme Court on several occasions, have interpreted the lien avoidance provisions of section 522(f).

The power to avoid transfers is expansive due, in part, to the broad definition of the word "transfer." Section 101(54) includes within this term any lien, execution sale, setoff, or any other mode of disposing of or parting with an interest in property, whether voluntarily or involuntarily, including foreclosure of the debtor's equity of redemption.

The debtor, with certain limitations, may thus invalidate numerous types of transfers, and recover valuable interests in property, as long as those interests can be claimed as exempt. Put another way, if the interest in property involved fits within the exemption scheme utilized by the debtor and if the interest is impaired by a transfer of a type covered by section 522, then that transfer may be avoided.[318] But if only a portion of the transferred property may be claimed as exempt, the transfer may be avoided only to that extent.[319]

Resolving a dispute in the case law,[320] Bankruptcy Rule 4003(d) was amended in 2008 to provide that a creditor can challenge the eligibility of property for exemption in a lien avoidance proceeding even if the creditor did not object to the exemption of the property within the normal deadline for exemption objections under Rule 4003(b). Rule 4003(d) now gives the creditor a second bite at the apple, stating that the creditor can defend a lien avoidance motion by challenging the validity of the exemption that the debtor claims is impaired by the lien.[321] The advisory committee note to this change makes

---

313 11 U.S.C. § 522(*l*).

314 11 U.S.C. § 522(*l*); Taylor v. Freeland & Kronz, 503 U.S. 638, 112 S. Ct. 1644, 118 L. Ed. 2d 280 (1992).

In fact, a creditor's failure to file a timely objection can preclude that creditor from later challenging the debtor's exemptions when the debtor attempts to use the Bankruptcy Code's avoiding powers. *In re* Hahn, 60 B.R. 69 (Bankr. D. Minn. 1985). *See also* 9 Collier on Bankruptcy ¶ 4003.03[3] (16th ed.); § 10.3.4, *supra*. However, Bankruptcy Rule 4003(d) provides that a creditor who does not file a timely objection may nevertheless object to a motion filed by the debtor to avoid a lien on exempt property under section 522(f) by challenging the validity of the exemption asserted to be impaired by the lien.

315 See § 6.5.2.2, *supra*, for a discussion of exemption planning and its legitimacy.

316 *In re* Bowyer, 932 F.2d 1100 (5th Cir. 1991); *In re* Bradley, 294 B.R. 64 (B.A.P. 8th Cir. 2003) (use of nonexempt assets to purchase exempt homestead did not constitute fraud necessary to deny Arkansas homestead exemption). *See also In re* Carey, 938 F.2d 1073 (10th Cir. 1991) (debtor's negotiation of a mortgage which prepaid a prior mortgage and created exemptible home equity does not constitute fraud).

However, payments in an amount greater than that permitted by section 522(p) may raise an issue under that provision. See § 10.2.3.4.4, *supra*.

317 *Compare* Hanson v. First Nat'l Bank in Brookings, 848 F.2d 866 (8th Cir. 1988) *with In re* Sholdan, 217 F.3d 1006 (8th Cir. 2000) (ninety-year-old's conversion of virtually all assets into exempt homestead found fraudulent and exemption denied) *and* Norwest Bank Neb. v. Tveten, 848 F.2d 871 (8th Cir. 1988).

The *Hanson* and *Tveten* decisions were issued on the same day. They reach different conclusions based on facts which on close reading are not meaningfully distinguishable. If anything, the two decisions illustrate the care necessary in exemption planning and the potential for fact-intensive decision-making by courts finding a debtor's manipulation of Code provisions unpalatable. *See also In re* Stern, 345 F.3d 1036 (9th Cir. 2003) (conversion of assets from nonexempt forms into exempt forms is not, in and of itself, sufficient to establish fraud absent other facts showing fraud); *In re* Armstrong, 931 F.2d 1233 (8th Cir. 1991) (exemption planning which is legitimate under state law is legitimate for bankruptcy purposes).

318 *See In re* Snyder, 279 B.R. 1 (B.A.P. 1st Cir. 2002) (debtor could avoid lien that impaired state homestead exemption even though debtor had amended exemptions after having originally claimed federal exemptions and having lost lien avoidance motion based on those exemptions); *In re* Dardar, 3 B.R. 641 (Bankr. E.D. Va. 1980) (section 522(f) only applicable to property claimed exempt).

319 *In re* Jordan, 5 B.R. 59 (Bankr. D.N.J. 1980).

As the issue is whether property may be claimed as exempt, and exemptions are determined as of the petition date, property is valued as of the petition date for purposes of the debtor's avoiding powers. 11 U.S.C. § 522(a)(2); *In re* Finn, 151 B.R. 25 (Bankr. N.D.N.Y. 1992).

320 *Compare In re* Tofani, 365 B.R. 338 (Bankr. D. Mass. 2007) *and In re* Chinosorn, 248 B.R. 324 (N.D. Ill. 2000) *with In re* Schoonover, 331 F.3d 575 (7th Cir. 2003).

321 *See also In re* Willett, 544 F.3d 787, 793 (7th Cir. 2008) (erroneously holding that value of interests acquired by chapter 13 estate postpetition under section 1306 must be included in calculation).

The *Willett* decision fails to recognize that exemptions are deter-

clear that this right to object applies only in the lien avoidance proceeding and does not give the creditor the right to object to any other claims of exemption.[322]

The avoiding powers may be invoked even if the debtor has no equity in a particular property, as long as the debtor can claim some interest in that property as exempt, even a mere right to possession or to redemption.[323] Nor is it necessary to show that the debt upon which a transfer is based is a dischargeable debt before the transfer can be avoided. The statute seems clear that, with the exception of transfers for domestic support obligations in certain circumstances, nondischargeability of an underlying debt is no defense to an otherwise proper action to avoid a transfer that impairs an exemption.[324] And, despite a few early lower court decisions to the contrary, it is clear that the avoiding powers are equally available in chapter 7 and chapter 13.[325]

10.4.2.2 Procedure for Use of Avoiding Powers

The Federal Rules of Bankruptcy Procedure prescribe the procedure to be followed for lien avoidance by the debtor. Rule 4003(d) provides that lien avoidance under 11 U.S.C. § 522(f) shall be by motion in accordance with Bankruptcy Rule 9014.[326]

However, transfer or lien avoidance under 11 U.S.C. § 522(h), which is often a more complicated matter, requires an adversary proceeding initiated by complaint.[327]

At least some avoidance actions carry with them a right to trial by jury. The Supreme Court has made clear that a defendant to a fraudulent conveyance action who has not filed a proof of claim in the bankruptcy case has a right to jury trial that is protected by the Seventh Amendment.[328]

It is the debtor's burden to file a lien avoidance proceeding; if none is filed, all liens on the debtor's property, including otherwise exempt property, will normally survive the bankruptcy.[329]

The statute does not specify whether lien avoidance under section 522(f) has to take place prior to discharge, and as exemptions are afforded continued protection after the bankruptcy, they could continue to be impaired after the bankruptcy by an otherwise avoidable lien. Most courts have held that a proceeding to avoid a lien may be filed after the discharge.[330]

---

mined as of the date of the petition and that interests acquired postpetition need not be exempted (other than those within the scope of section 541(a)(5)) so that their value is irrelevant to lien avoidance provisions intended to prevent impairment of exemptions.

322 Fed. R. Bankr. P. 4003 advisory committee's note (2008).

323 *In re* Bland, 793 F.2d 1172 (11th Cir. 1986) (en banc); *In re* Brown, 81 B.R. 432 (N.D. Ohio 1985); *In re* Lovett, 11 B.R. 123 (W.D. Mo. 1981), *opinion vacated on other grounds*, 23 B.R. 760 (W.D. Mo. 1982); *In re* Kursh, 9 B.R. 801 (Bankr. W.D. Mo. 1981); *In re* Van Gorkom, 4 B.R. 689 (Bankr. D.S.D. 1980). *See also In re* Sherwood, 94 B.R. 679 (Bankr. E.D. Cal. 1988) (debtor could avoid lien on household goods destroyed by postpetition fire and thereby obtain insurance proceeds held by the creditor). *Contra In re* Boteler, 5 B.R. 408 (Bankr. S.D. Ala. 1980).

Section 522(f) was clarified in 1994 to eliminate any doubt on this issue, so that cases like *Boteler* can no longer be considered as valid precedent. *See* § 10.4.2.3, *infra*.

324 Walters v. U.S. Nat'l Bank of Johnstown, 879 F.2d 95 (3d Cir. 1989) (debtor may avoid lien of creditor whose claim is nondischargeable on ground of fraud); *In re* Liming, 797 F.2d 895 (10th Cir. 1986); *In re* Krajci, 7 B.R. 242 (Bankr. E.D. Pa. 1980), *aff'd*, 16 B.R. 462 (E.D. Pa. 1981); *In re* Gantt, 7 B.R. 13 (Bankr. N.D. Ga. 1980). *See also In re* Clark, 217 B.R. 943 (Bankr. M.D. Fla. 1998) (debtor had lien avoidance powers even though he was denied a discharge); *In re* Sullivan, 83 B.R. 623 (Bankr. S.D. Iowa 1988) (although general rule is that lien avoidance is not dependent on dischargeability of underlying debt, under Iowa law homestead property could not be exempted to the extent impaired by child support judgment).

325 *In re* Hall, 752 F.2d 582 (11th Cir. 1985). *See also* James B. McLaughlin, Jr., *Lien Avoidance by Debtors in Chapter 13 of the Bankruptcy Reform Act of 1978*, 58 Am. Bankr. L. J. 45 (1984).

326 For a sample motion to avoid judicial lien, see Form 92, Appendix G.9, *infra*. As in all contested matters under Bankruptcy Rule 9014, however, the adversary proceeding service rules that apply have special requirements for serving insured depository institutions. *See* Fed. R. Bankr. P. 7004(h); *In re* Hamlett, 322 F.3d 342 (4th Cir. 2003) (judgment properly vacated when officer of institution not served); *In re* Villar, 317 B.R. 88 (B.A.P. 9th Cir. 2004) (default

order avoiding lien reversed because service did not comply with Fed. R. Bankr. P. 7004(b)(3) or due process).

327 Fed. R. Bankr. P. 7001. *See, e.g.,* Connelly v. Marine Midland Bank, 61 B.R. 748 (W.D.N.Y. 1986) (proceeding by motion deprives the bankruptcy court of jurisdiction).

328 Granfinanciera, S.A. v. Nordberg, 492 U.S. 33, 109 S. Ct. 2782, 106 L. Ed. 2d 26 (1989). *See* § 14.2.7, *infra*.

329 Fed. Deposit Ins. Corp. v. Davis, 733 F.2d 1083 (4th Cir. 1984). *But see In re* Penrod, 50 F.3d 459 (7th Cir. 1995) (default rule in chapter 11, based on language of section 1141(c), is that if confirmed plan provides for creditor but is silent about whether creditor retains its lien, that lien is automatically extinguished).

The *Penrod* rationale should apply equally in chapter 13 under section 1327(c). Of course, if liens are paid off in a chapter 13 plan, they are also eliminated, and there are other options for treatment of liens under the Code as well. *See* Ch. 11, *infra*.

330 *In re* Wilding, 475 F.3d 428 (1st Cir. 2007) (debtor permitted to avoid judicial lien under section 522(f) two years after discharge even if he has satisfied the lien prior to filing a motion to avoid, so long as the lien in question impaired an exemption as of the bankruptcy petition date); *In re* Goswami, 304 B.R. 386 (B.A.P. 9th Cir. 2003) (debtors have right to amend exemptions after case closing for purpose of lien avoidance absent bad faith or prejudice); *In re* Ricks, 89 B.R. 73 (B.A.P. 9th Cir. 1988) (creditor's action to execute on lien after bankruptcy does not constitute sufficient prejudice to bar reopening of case to avoid lien); *In re* Yazzie, 24 B.R. 576 (B.A.P. 9th Cir. 1982) (post discharge avoidance allowed when no prejudice to creditor from delay); *In re* McDonald, 161 B.R. 697 (D. Kan. 1993) (local bankruptcy rule that required lien avoidance motions to be filed at least five days before date set for discharge was invalid and court could allow reopening of case for motion to avoid lien unless equitable considerations dictated otherwise); First Nat'l Bank of Park Falls v. Maley, 126 B.R. 563 (W.D. Wis. 1991); Hassler v. Assimos, 53 B.R. 453 (D. Del. 1985) (creditors not prejudiced by delay in failing to move to avoid lien until after discharge and thus lien avoidance not barred by laches); Beneficial Fin. Co. of Va. v. Lazrovitch, 47 B.R. 358 (E.D. Va. 1983) (debtors entitled to reopen cases after discharge to avoid liens); *In re* Orr, 304 B.R. 875 (Bankr. S.D. Ill. 2004) (case could be reopened for lien avoidance four years after case was closed even though debtor no longer had interest in property); *In re* Mailhot, 301 B.R. 774 (Bankr. D.R.I. 2003) (debtor allowed to avoid judicial liens seven years after discharge); *In re* Baskins, 14 B.R. 110 (Bankr. E.D.N.C. 1981); *In re* Smart, 13 B.R. 838 (Bankr. D. Ariz. 1981). *See also In re* Goydoscik, 94 B.R. 72 (Bankr. W.D. Pa. 1988) (section 550(e) does not prevent reopening case to avoid a lien); *In re*

Similarly, the granting of relief from the automatic stay to the lienholder does not preclude an avoidance motion.[331] Unlike many of the other Bankruptcy Rules, the Rules providing for debtor lien avoidance set no time limits. And because lien avoidance is a personal right which does not affect the administration of the bankruptcy case, there is no need for the bankruptcy case to be reopened in order for the debtor to avoid a lien.[332]

Contrastingly, most actions to avoid transfers under section 522(h) are subject to a statute of limitations.[333] They must be brought within two years of the order for relief (the date a voluntary petition is filed) or by the date the case is closed or dismissed, whichever is earlier. If a trustee is first appointed or elected within two years of the order for relief, the limitations period may be extended (beyond two years after the order for relief) until the expiration of one year after the appointment of that trustee or until the case is closed or dismissed, whichever is earlier. To be safe, it is better to avoid liens and other transfers within the limitations period and prior to discharge whenever possible.

It may also be possible to include in a chapter 13 plan provisions which effectuate the avoidance of transfer upon confirmation.[334] Although the Rules provide that a motion or complaint are necessary in a "proceeding" to avoid a lien, it can be argued that when the lien is avoided in the plan, no separate "proceeding" is necessary. Otherwise, the Rules might conflict with section 1322(b)(11) which allows plans to incorporate any appropriate provision not inconsistent with the Code.[335] Although one provision of chapter 13 appears to indicate that the plan cannot modify the rights of a creditor secured only by a security interest in the debtor's residence, it was held under the prior rules that at least those transfers that do not come within the narrow definition of "security interest," defined as "a lien created by agreement,"[336] can be avoided through the plan.[337] However, to avoid doubt on these issues, the best practice is to seek to avoid the lien in a separate proceeding rather than to rely on a plan provision.[338]

Whatever the method used, the debtor's counsel should be sure to obtain an order giving complete relief, including a requirement that the transferee (usually a creditor) take all steps necessary to reflect the avoidance of the transfer in state and local recording offices,[339] or else an order suitable for filing in those offices by the debtor's counsel. Keep in mind as well that if a separate action is necessary to recover property subsequent to avoidance of a transfer of that property, it must be brought within one year.[340]

10.4.2.3 Power to Avoid Judicial Liens—§ 522(f)(1)(A)

10.4.2.3.1 Extent of the power to avoid judicial liens

Section 522(f)(1)(A) gives the debtor an unqualified right to avoid any judicial lien that impairs an exemption, subject only to an exception for domestic support obligation[341] debts. As the term "judicial lien" is defined broadly[342] to include levies, judgment liens (including confessed judgments)[343] and liens obtained by sequestration or any other legal or equitable proceeding,[344] this section provides a powerful tool for the debtor.

Babineau, 22 B.R. 936 (Bankr. M.D. Fla. 1982) (liens can be avoided after confirmation of chapter 13 plan). *But see* Hawkins v. Landmark Fin., 727 F.2d 324 (4th Cir. 1984) (court has discretion to refuse to reopen a case for amendment of exemptions and lien avoidance).

A postbankruptcy transfer of property may cut off the right to avoid a lien as to that property. *In re* Vitullo, 60 B.R. 822 (D.N.J. 1986); *In re* Carilli, 65 B.R. 280 (Bankr. E.D.N.Y. 1986). However, a debtor could argue that all exemption rights are fixed as of the date of the petition so a postpetition transfer is irrelevant. *See In re* Chiu, 304 F.3d 905 (9th Cir. 2002) (judicial lien may be avoided even after property sold as debtors owned property when lien fixed upon it); *In re* Sheckard, 394 B.R. 56 (E.D. Pa. 2008) (debtors could avoid lien two years after case closed, even though property had been transferred after bankruptcy).

331 *In re* Ginter, 349 B.R. 193 (B.A.P. 8th Cir. 2006).
332 *In re* Keller, 24 B.R. 720 (Bankr. N.D. Ohio 1982); *In re* Schneider, 18 B.R. 274 (Bankr. D.N.D. 1982). *But see In re* Bianucci, 4 F.3d 526 (7th Cir. 1993) (debtors could not reopen bankruptcy case to avoid lien two years after closing of case, and five months after they became aware of the lien, when creditor had been prejudiced by payment of expenses to enforce lien); Hawkins v. Landmark Fin., 727 F.2d 324 (4th Cir. 1984).
333 11 U.S.C. § 546(a). *See* § 10.4.2.6.8, *infra*. *See also* Zilkha Energy Co. v. Leighton, 920 F.2d 1520 (10th Cir. 1990) (two-year limitation period runs from date of filing and applies to successor to chapter 11 debtor).
Note that the limitations period does not apply to transfers avoidable under sections 522(f), 549, or 724(a).
334 McLaughlin, *Lien Avoidance by Debtors in Chapter 13 of the Bankruptcy Reform Act of 1978*, 58 Am. Bankr. L. J. 56 (1984). *But see In re* Commercial W. Fin. Corp., 761 F.2d 1329 (9th Cir. 1985) (Bankruptcy Rules require individual proceedings against investors whose security interests trustee wished to avoid in chapter 11 case); *In re* McKay, 732 F.2d 44 (3d Cir. 1984) (chapter 13 lien avoidance must be by motion).
335 *But see In re* Commercial W. Fin. Corp., 761 F.2d 1329 (9th Cir. 1985); *In re* McKay, 732 F.2d 44 (3d Cir. 1984) (lien avoidance must be by motion rather than in plan).
336 11 U.S.C. § 101(51).
337 *In re* Jordan, 5 B.R. 59 (Bankr. D.N.J. 1980).
338 Further doubt on this issue was created by the Supreme Court's decision in *United Student Aid Funds, Inc. v. Espinosa*, 130 S. Ct. 1367, 176 L. Ed. 2d 158 (2010), in which the court stated that it was improper to seek dischargeability of a student loan through a plan provision rather than an adversary proceeding provided for in the rules).
339 *See* Form 93, Appx. G.9, *infra*.
340 11 U.S.C. § 550(f). *See* § 10.4.2.7, *infra*.
341 "Domestic support obligation" is defined by 11 U.S.C. § 101(14A), generally, as debts in the nature of support. *See* Ch. 15, *infra*.
342 11 U.S.C. § 101(36).
343 *In re* Gardner, 685 B.R. 106 (3d Cir. 1982); *In re* Bensen, 262 B.R. 371 (Bankr. N.D. Tex. 2001) (garnishment lien on bank account avoided). *See also In re* Bistansin, 95 B.R. 29 (Bankr. W.D. Pa. 1989) (lien created by sheriff's levy is avoidable judicial lien). *Cf. In re* Duden, 102 B.R. 797 (D. Colo. 1989) (lien which would impair the debtor's ability to alienate property postpetition is avoidable even though it may not presently attach to debtor's property as a judicial lien because of state homestead exemption).
344 *In re* Thomas, 215 B.R. 873 (Bankr. E.D. Mo. 1997) (debtor could

To the extent a creditor's lien is avoided, the creditor becomes an unsecured creditor and the lien cannot attach to property that the debtor acquires after the petition is filed.[345]

Occasionally there is a dispute as to whether a particular lien is a judicial lien,[346] sometimes involving liens granted in divorce proceedings.[347] In such cases, careful analysis of the Code's definition is required. However, some of the difficult questions about whether certain divorce-related liens are judicial liens have been rendered moot by the Code provision that makes divorce-related liens non-avoidable if they are liens for domestic support obligations.[348]

The power to avoid judicial liens extends to every type of exempt property, without limitation, including property exempted under a wild card provision.[349] Unlike some of the other avoiding powers, the lien need not have been obtained within a certain time period before the bankruptcy petition.[350] The lien may also be avoided if it was obtained after the filing of the petition on a prepetition debt.[351] Even if the lien has caused the property to have been removed from the debtor's possession or the debtor has transferred the property after the petition, it can be avoided, forcing the return of the property.[352]

---

avoid garnishment lien on wages in employer's possession); *In re Waltjen*, 150 B.R. 419 (Bankr. N.D. Ill. 1993) (debtor could avoid garnishment lien on wages still in employer's possession). *But see In re Lucas*, 21 B.R. 794 (Bankr. W.D. Mich. 1982) (lien given to secure appeal bond held security interest and not judicial lien).

345 *In re Marshall*, 204 B.R. 838 (Bankr. S.D. Ga. 1997).

However, the holder of a nondischargeable claim might be able to pursue nonexempt property acquired after the bankruptcy.

346 *See, e.g., In re Schick*, 418 F.3d 321 (3d Cir. 2005) (New Jersey motor vehicle surcharge lien was a statutory lien because clerk's ministerial act of docketing the debt did not render it a lien arising from judicial process); *In re Ingram*, 431 B.R. 307 (B.A.P. 6th Cir. 2010) (mortgage foreclosure did not transform mortgage into judicial lien); *In re Nichols*, 265 B.R. 831 (B.A.P. 10th Cir. 2001) (foreclosure decree did not transform mortgage into judicial lien); *In re James*, 304 B.R. 131 (D.N.J. 2004) (lien arising from unpaid motor vehicle insurance surcharges was non-avoidable statutory lien); *In re Concrete Structures, Inc.*, 261 B.R. 627 (E.D. Va. 2001) (Virginia mechanics' lien, though enforced judicially, is a statutory lien); *In re Liberman*, 244 B.R. 557 (E.D.N.Y.) (mortgage foreclosure judgment not avoidable), *aff'd*, 225 F.3d 646 (2d Cir. 2000) (table); *Mozingo v. Pennsylvania Dep't of Labor & Indus.*, 234 B.R. 867 (E.D. Pa. 1999) (lien for overpayments of unemployment compensation was statutory lien that simply became choate upon recordation); *In re Washington*, 238 B.R. 852 (M.D. Fla. 1999) (Florida attorney's charging lien not a judicial lien), *aff'd in relevant part*, 242 F.3d 1320 (11th Cir. 2001); *In re McHenry*, 2010 WL 1571174 (Bankr. D. Conn. Apr. 19, 2010) (stipulated entry of prejudgment attachment was judicial lien); *In re Morais*, 2009 WL 3054059 (Bankr. D. Mass. Sept. 18, 2009) (judgment lien obtained under § 548 by trustee in another bankruptcy case was judicial lien); *In re Gregory Rockhouse Ranch*, 380 B.R. 258 (Bankr. D.N.M. 2007) (transcript of judgment was judicial lien under New Mexico law, but *lis pendens* was not); *In re Felizardo*, 255 B.R. 85 (Bankr. S.D. Fla. 2000) (Florida attorney's charging lien, though reduced to judgment, was not judicial lien); *In re Rouse*, 145 B.R. 546 (Bankr. W.D. Mich. 1992) (tax refunds intercepted for payment of support delinquency and held by "Friend of the Court" considered subject to judicial lien); *In re Frost*, 111 B.R. 306 (Bankr. C.D. Cal. 1990) (California tax lien avoided as judicial lien); *In re MacLure*, 50 B.R. 134 (Bankr. D.R.I. 1985) (landlord's lien, though statutorily authorized, required resort to judicial process and was thus judicial lien); *In re Barbe*, 24 B.R. 739 (Bankr. M.D. Pa. 1982) (lien for overpayments of unemployment compensation held judicial lien due to requirement of recordation).

347 *In re Pederson*, 875 F.2d 781 (9th Cir. 1989) (lien granted in divorce proceedings was judicial lien), *aff'g* 78 B.R. 264 (B.A.P. 9th Cir. 1987); *Maus v. Maus*, 837 F.2d 935 (10th Cir. 1988) (property settlement agreement incorporated into divorce decree gives rise to an avoidable judicial lien); *Boyd v. Robinson*, 741 F.2d 1112 (8th Cir. 1984) (lien awarded by court in marital dissolution action held not a judicial lien); *In re Rittenhouse*, 103 B.R. 250 (D. Kan. 1989) (lien awarded in divorce decree is not avoidable); *In re Duncan*, 85 B.R. 80 (W.D. Wis. 1988) (lien granted in divorce proceedings constitutes avoidable judicial lien); *In re Scott*, 400 B.R. 257 (Bankr. C.D. Cal. 2009) (attorney's lien granted by divorce decree was avoidable); *In re Wicks*, 26 B.R. 769 (Bankr. D. Minn. 1982) (lien granted in marital dissolution agreement held a security interest and not judicial lien), *aff'd*, 741 F.2d 1112 (8th Cir. 1984). *See also Mead v. Mead*, 974 F.2d 990 (8th Cir. 1992) (holding lien created by fraud judgment to be a reinstatement of divorce lien not avoidable under holding of *Farrey*); *In re Borman*, 886 F.2d 273 (10th Cir. 1989) (debtor's wife entitled to nondischargeable, non-avoidable equitable lien based on divorce decree); *In re Donahue*, 862 F.2d 259 (10th Cir. 1988) (divorce decree which awarded former spouse money judgment and awarded debtor real property subject to the money judgment creates a lien in favor of the former spouse; bankruptcy court must determine whether lien is avoidable).

This issue was not resolved by the Supreme Court decision in *Farrey v. Sanderfoot*, 500 U.S. 291, 111 S. Ct. 1825, 114 L. Ed. 2d 337 (1991). However the *Farrey* decision does limit the avoidance of liens arising in domestic relations proceedings when they are created in connection with transfer of the property to which the lien simultaneously attaches. *See* § 10.4.2.3.2, *infra*. *See generally* Henry J. Sommer & Margaret Dee McGarity, Collier Family Law and the Bankruptcy Code ¶ 7.04[3] (1992).

348 11 U.S.C. § 522(f)(1)(A). *See In re Lowe*, 250 B.R. 422 (Bankr. M.D. Fla. 2000) (lien could be avoided because it secured property settlement debt rather than debt for alimony, maintenance or support).

Although the wording of this provision is confusing, its intent is clear. *See* § 10.4.2.3.2, *infra*.

349 *In re Groff*, 223 B.R. 697 (Bankr. S.D. Ill. 1998) (debtors could avoid lien that impaired their equitable interest in property being purchased under land installment sales contract); *In re Garcia*, 149 B.R. 530 (Bankr. N.D. Ill. 1993) (wages in the hands of an employer can be exempted under Illinois wild card provision so that lien giving rise to the wage garnishment can be avoided), *aff'd*, 155 B.R. 173 (N.D. Ill. 1993).

350 *In re Naples v. London*, Bankr. L. Rep. (CCH) ¶ 67,422 (Bankr. D. Conn. 1980).

However, the avoiding power may not extend to liens that were already on a property when the debtor acquired it. *See* § 10.4.2.3.2, *infra*.

351 *In re Vaughan*, 311 B.R. 573 (Bankr. 10th Cir. 2004).

352 *In re Bagley*, 1 B.R. 116 (Bankr. E.D. Pa. 1979) (sheriff ordered to return automobile seized under a levy). *See also In re Chiu*, 304 F.3d 905 (9th Cir. 2002) (debtor could avoid lien on escrowed proceeds of sale of homestead that had been claimed as exempt in schedules and sold after petition date); *In re Brown*, 734 F.2d 119 (2d Cir. 1984) (debtor could exempt and avoid judicial lien on cash proceeds of execution sale of property when proceeds were still in hands of state court commissioner); *In re Fairchild*, 285 B.R. 98 (Bankr. D. Conn. 2002) (debtor need only have interest in property at time of fixing of lien and not when motion to avoid is filed); *In*

In some cases, courts had refused to avoid liens because of provisions in state exemption laws which they read to prevent the debtor from claiming any exemption in bankruptcy which could be impaired.[353] For the reasons discussed earlier, these cases ignored clear congressional intent and the Supremacy Clause.[354] For the most part these decisions have been overruled by the Supreme Court.[355] In *Owen v. Owen* the Court held that a state law limiting exemptions from execution to property that is not subject to certain liens does not preclude avoidance of those liens under section 522(f).[356]

In 1994, responding to several cases which had misconstrued the lien avoidance provisions, Congress amended section 522(f) to specifically set forth a general arithmetic formula for determining whether a lien could be avoided under that section.[357] Section 522(f)(2) specifies that a judicial lien is avoidable to the extent that the lien, plus all other liens on the property, plus the amount of the exemption that the debtor could claim[358] if there were no liens on the property exceeds the value that the debtor's interest in the property would have in the absence of any liens.[359] The liens used in the calculation should be those that existed on the date of the bankruptcy petition.[360] Similarly, the value of the property should be determined as of the petition date.[361] However, when the property is owned jointly with a

---

re Carroll, 258 B.R. 316 (Bankr. S.D. Ga. 2001) (lien avoidance based on interests held on date of petition).

In a development necessitated in part by the limitation on avoiding preferences worth less than $600, discussed in § 10.4.2.6.4, *infra*, debtors in some states have successfully recovered garnished wages still in the hands of their employers by avoiding the lien which gave rise to the garnishment. Bryant v. Gen. Elec. Credit Corp., 58 B.R. 144 (N.D. Ill. 1986); *In re* Lafoon, 278 B.R. 767 (Bankr. E.D. Tenn. 2002) (debtor could avoid lien on garnished wages despite procedural waiver caused by failure to claim state law exemption at time of garnishment); *In re* Buzzell, 56 B.R. 197 (Bankr. D. Md. 1986). *See also In re* Rowell, 281 B.R. 726 (Bankr. N.D. Ala. 2001) (debtor could avoid lien on garnished funds, even those paid erroneously by court clerk to creditor, because state court had not entered condemnation order terminating debtor's interest in wages).

353 *See In re* Dixon, 885 F.2d 327 (6th Cir. 1989) (Ohio exemption scheme does not contemplate any homestead exemption absent execution on judgment; therefore liens may not be avoided in bankruptcy as impairing a debtor's exemption); *In re* Owen, 877 F.2d 44 (11th Cir. 1989) (when homestead exemption does not attach under state law to residence as against judicial liens which attached first, liens on residence may not be avoided).

The *Dixon* decision has been overruled by the 1994 amendments to the Bankruptcy Code which now define what it means to impair an exemption. 11 U.S.C. § 522(f)(2); *In re* Holland, 151 F.3d 547 (6th Cir. 1998). *See* H.R. Rep. No. 103-835, at 53 (1994), *reprinted in* 1994 U.S.C.C.A.N. 3340, 3362.

354 *See* § 10.2.1.1, *supra*.

355 Owen v. Owen, 500 U.S. 305, 111 S. Ct. 1833, 114 L. Ed. 2d 250 (1991); *In re* Maddox, 15 F.3d 1347 (5th Cir. 1994) (prior case law of circuit on this issue had been overruled by *Owen*). *See also In re* Snow, 899 F.2d 337 (4th Cir. 1990) (debtors entitled to avoid judicial lien on personal property based on back rent even though state law provided that exemption does not apply to claims for rent); *In re* Kinnemore, 181 B.R. 516 (Bankr. D. Idaho 1995) (landlord's lien could be avoided despite state statute excluding exempt property from protection with respect to claims for unpaid rent).

356 *In re* Henderson, 18 F.3d 1305 (5th Cir. 1994) (judicial lien could be avoided even though no execution on the lien was possible because lien was unenforceable as to homestead); *In re* Coats, 232 B.R. 209 (B.A.P. 10th Cir. 1999) (same); *In re* Shafner, 165 B.R. 660 (Bankr. D. Colo. 1994) (lien impaired exemption even though it did not technically attach to exempt property, because of its practical effects on debtor's ability to encumber or dispose of property). *See also In re* Watts, 298 F.3d 1077 (9th Cir. 2002) (California law limiting judicial liens to surplus equity did not prevent lien from attaching and thereby becoming avoidable). Some of these cases may no longer be good law after the decision in *Botkin v. DuPont Cmty. Credit Union*, 650 F.3d 396 (4th Cir. 2011), which held that it is not necessary to have claimed property as exempt as a precondition to avoiding a lien.

This principle may not apply, however, to debtors who fail to meet the condition for declaring the state law exemption in the first instance. *See In re* Amiri, 184 B.R. 60 (B.A.P. 9th Cir. 1995) (failure to timely file for homestead exemption under state law precludes avoidance of lien); *In re* Wall, 127 B.R. 353 (Bankr. E.D. Va. 1991) (same). *See also* § 10.2.3.1, *supra*. *Cf. In re* Johnson, 184 B.R. 141 (Bankr. D. Wyo. 1995) (lien could be avoided as long as homestead exemption existed on date of bankruptcy petition); *In re* Pinner, 146 B.R. 659 (Bankr. E.D.N.C. 1992) (failure to claim property as exempt at time creditor obtained judgment did not preclude avoidance of creditor's lien).

The *Owen* decision should invalidate state laws that purport to exclude from exempt status wages that are subject to a garnishment lien. *But see In re* Youngblood, 212 B.R. 593 (Bankr. N.D. Ill. 1997) (discussing such a statute in case in which debtor apparently did not argue that statute was invalid under *Owen*).

357 The 1994 amendments generally apply in cases filed on or after October 22, 1994. However, as the new section was intended to clarify rather than change existing law, liens should be avoidable based on the formula contained in the amendment regardless of when the case was filed. As a clarification of what Congress believed existing law to be, this result should apply even if application of the amendment is required to overrule case law of a jurisdiction which had previously limited judicial lien avoidance. *See* 140 Cong. Rec. H10764 (daily ed. Oct. 4, 1994).

358 The amount the debtor could claim as exempt is the full amount of the debtor's available exemption, not the amount claimed as exempt on the schedules. *In re* Scannell, 453 B.R. 36 (Bankr. D.N.H. 2011).

359 *See In re* Brinley, 403 F.3d 415 (6th Cir. 2005) (debtor could avoid lien even though it was senior to nonavoidable liens); *In re* Kolich, 328 F.3d 406 (8th Cir. 2003) (formula required avoidance of lien even though it was senior to non-avoidable lien of subsequent mortgagee); *In re* Silveira, 141 F.3d 34 (1st Cir. 1998) (applying formula to partially avoid lien); *In re* Charnock, 318 B.R. 720 (B.A.P. 9th Cir. 2004) (debtor could avoid lien even though it was senior to nonavoidable liens); *In re* DaRosa, 318 B.R. 871 (B.A.P. 9th Cir. 2004) (lienholder could not evade formula by arguing that joint debtors were subrogated to each other); *In re* Hanger, 217 B.R. 592 (B.A.P. 9th Cir. 1998), *aff'd* 196 F.3d 1292 (9th Cir. 1999) (same).

360 *In re* Salanoa, 263 B.R. 120 (Bankr. S.D. Cal. 2001) (first trust deed taken into account even though it was paid in full after the petition). *See also In re* Smith, 315 B.R. 636 (Bankr. D. Mass. 2004) (unrecorded mortgage was a lien against property that had to be included in calculation).

The lien amount used in the calculation should include all amounts the debtor would be contractually obligated to pay to satisfy the lien on the petition date. *In re* Barrett, 370 B.R. 1 (Bankr. D. Me. 2007) (five percent prepayment amount counted in total of mortgage claim).

361 *In re* Thigpen, 374 B.R. 374 (Bankr. S.D. Ga. 2007).

non-debtor, courts have not agreed on whether the total value of the property should be used in the statutory formula.[362]

Once a lien has been avoided, it is not counted for the calculation of whether other liens impair exemptions.[363] And the formula does not apply to judgments arising out of mortgage foreclosures.[364]

As the legislative history makes clear, this language adopts the conclusion of those cases holding that a debtor who has no equity in a property may still avoid liens on the property.[365] It also overrules cases which had held that a partially secured creditor could protect against lien avoidance that portion of its lien which exceeds the value of the collateral, and similar cases which had held that a debtor could not avoid a lien to the extent that the amount of the lien exceeded the debtor's exemption.[366] Finally, by focusing on the dollar amount of the exemption in defining when an exemption is impaired, the amendment overrules cases that had held that a debtor's exemption was not impaired unless the creditor was executing on that lien.[367]

10.4.2.3.2 Limitations on power to avoid judicial liens

As with the other avoiding powers, if the lien only partially impairs the exemption, only that part may be avoided. Thus, if a $3000 judgment lien encumbers an otherwise unencumbered house worth $17,000, in which an interest of $15,000 can be claimed as exempt and in which an interest of $2000 is not exempt, only $1000 worth of the lien can be avoided.[368] The other $2000 is deemed an encumbrance on that interest in the house which may not be claimed as exempt. In such cases the debtor should, if at all possible, obtain an order specifying the amount of the creditor's remaining lien, so that any postbankruptcy appreciation inures to the benefit of the exempt interest and not to the creditor.

On the other hand, when the total value of the liened property can be claimed as exempt, then any amount of liens can be avoided, because even if only a few dollars' worth of liens remained, they would impair the exemption. Hence, if a house with $15,000 of equity in excess of a mortgage is claimed as totally exempt, all judgment liens on that house may be avoided under this section no matter what their amount.[369] When only

---

[362] See also In re Coley, 437 B.R. 779 (Bankr. E.D. Pa. 2010) (applying Miller decision to entireties property). Compare In re Cozad, 208 B.R. 495 (B.A.P. 10th Cir. 1997) (in applying formula to jointly-held property when only one debtor is in bankruptcy, formula must be followed literally and total of liens and exemption must be subtracted from only debtor's one-half interest in property), and In re White, 337 B.R. 686 (Bankr. N.D. Cal. 2005) (same), with In re Brinley, 403 F.3d 415 (6th Cir. 2005) (interest of one entirety cotenant valued at total value of property); In re Miller, 299 F.3d 183 (3d Cir. 2002) (total value of property used even though only one co-owner filed); In re Lehman, 205 F.3d 1255 (11th Cir. 2000) (total value of property used even though only one co-owner filed); In re Nelson, 192 F.3d 32 (1st Cir. 1999) (despite language of statute, lien avoidance formula applied only to debtor's fifty percent interest in property) and In re Snyder, 249 B.R. 40 (B.A.P. 1st Cir. 2000) (value of one entireties cotenant's interest deemed to be one-hundred percent of value of property), aff'd, 2 Fed. Appx. 46 (1st Cir. 2001).

[363] It is not clear whether liens must be avoided in reverse order of priority, that is, the most junior judicial lien first, as some courts have held. See, e.g., In re Hanger, 217 B.R. 592 (B.A.P. 9th Cir. 1998), aff'd 196 F.3d 1292 (9th Cir. 1999); In re Jochum, 309 B.R. 327 (Bankr. E.D. Mo. 2004).

An earlier version of the statute would have required this ordering, but the priority language was deleted from the final version. See S.540, 103d Cong. § 303 (1994).

[364] 11 U.S.C. § 522(f)(2)(C). See In re Maxwell, 2010 WL 4736206 (Bankr. E.D. Tenn. Nov. 16, 2010) (deficiency judgment was based on note, and was not foreclosure judgment).

Because judgments arising out of mortgage foreclosures are not normally considered to be avoidable judicial liens, this provision will have little impact. Courts have held that deficiency judgments are not protected by this provision. See In re Hart, 328 F.3d 45 (1st Cir. 2003) (deficiency judgment not a lien arising out of mortgage foreclosure); In re Been, 153 F.3d 1034 (9th Cir. 1998) (section 522(f)(2)(C) did not protect judgment lien obtained by creditor's suit on note after its junior lien on another property was extinguished by senior lienholder's foreclosure sale); In re Carson, 274 B.R. 577 (Bankr. D. Conn. 2002) (deficiency judgment not a lien arising out of a mortgage foreclosure); In re Smith, 270 B.R. 557 (Bankr. W.D.N.Y. 2001) (same); In re Pascucci, 225 B.R. 25 (Bankr. D. Mass. 1998) (deficiency judgment lien was not a judgment arising out of a mortgage foreclosure).

[365] In re Higgins, 201 B.R. 965 (B.A.P. 9th Cir. 1996); In re McQueen, 196 B.R. 31 (E.D.N.C. 1995) (prior Fourth Circuit case law overruled by 1994 amendments); In re Thomsen, 181 B.R. 1013 (Bankr. M.D. Ga. 1995); H.R. Rep. No. 103-835, at 52–54 (1994), reprinted in 1994 U.S.C.C.A.N. 3340, 3361–3363.

The legislative history also states that the law overruled In re Simonson, 758 F.2d 103 (3d Cir. 1985), in which the court had held that a judicial lien could not be avoided if it was senior to a non-avoidable mortgage and the non-avoidable mortgages on the property exceeded the value of the property. See also In re Holloway, 81 F.3d 1062, 1069 n.10 (11th Cir. 1996) (recognizing that prior case law not applicable to post-amendment cases). But see In re Soost, 262 B.R. 68 (B.A.P. 8th Cir. 2001) (court, seemingly confused by irrelevant fact that debtor claimed $1.00 exemption in property, found it "difficult to fathom" how debtor could avoid lien on property in which he had no equity).

[366] H.R. Rep. No. 103-835, at 52–54 (1994), reprinted in 1994 U.S.C.C.A.N. 3340, 3361–3363. See In re Toplitzky, 227 B.R. 300 (B.A.P. 9th Cir. 1998) (formula in 1994 amendments precluded creditor from retaining its lien by paying debtor amount of equity in property above senior lien).

[367] H.R. Rep. No. 103-835, at 52–54 (1994), reprinted in 1994 U.S.C.C.A.N. 3340, 3361–3363; In re Holland, 151 F.3d 547 (6th Cir. 1998).

[368] See In re Silveira, 141 F.3d 34 (1st Cir. 1998) (explaining partial lien avoidance).

[369] See In re Galvan, 110 B.R. 446 (B.A.P. 9th Cir. 1990) (unsecured portion of undersecured judicial lien is avoidable as it impairs debtor's right to fully realize homestead exemption); In re Sajkowski, 49 B.R. 37 (Bankr. D.R.I. 1985). See also In re Magosin, 75 B.R. 545 (Bankr. E.D. Pa. 1987) (discussing lien avoidance methodology).

The Supreme Court in Owen specifically cited two bankruptcy court decisions which clearly set forth this method of determining which liens could be avoided. 111 S. Ct. at 1838, n.5 (citing In re Brantz, 106 B.R. 62, 68 (Bankr. E.D. Pa. 1989) and In re Carney, 47 B.R. 296 (Bankr. D. Mass. 1985)).

Decisions to the contrary have also been specifically overruled by legislation. See, e.g., In re Wrenn, 40 F.3d 1162 (11th Cir. 1994); In re Sanders, 39 F.3d 258 (10th Cir. 1994); In re Menell, 37 F.3d 113 (3d Cir. 1994). See also § 10.4.2.3.1, infra.

some liens may be avoided, the most junior avoidable liens are presumably the ones which impair the debtor's exemption.[370]

In *Farrey v. Sanderfoot*,[371] the Supreme Court held that section 522(f)(1) can only be used to avoid the fixing of a lien on a debtor's preexisting interest in property. Unless the debtor had an interest in the property *before* the lien attached to the property, the lien cannot be avoided. In applying this principle to a lien granted in a divorce decree that conveyed jointly held property to the debtor, the Court found that the divorce decree extinguished the debtor's preexisting undivided half-interest in the marital home and granted him a new fee simple interest. The Court therefore concluded that the simultaneously created lien for the benefit of the debtor's former spouse did not attach to a preexisting interest of the debtor in property and that section 522(f)(1) was not available to avoid the lien. The Court assumed without deciding that the divorce decree did create a judicial lien. It also left open the possibility that a divorce decree lien could be avoided if it attached to property that had previously been titled only in the name of the debtor spouse.[372]

The Eleventh Circuit extended the *Farrey* rationale to a debtor who obtained a homestead in a jurisdiction where an unsatisfied judgment had previously been recorded against him.[373] The judgment automatically fixed as a lien on property in that jurisdiction when it was acquired by the debtor. The court concluded that the lien could not be avoided because it did not fix on a preexisting interest of the debtor in property. While this ruling seems on the surface like a reasonable extension of *Farrey*, it is inconsistent with the congressional purpose in allowing the avoidance of judicial liens[374] and illogically gives more protection to a judgment lien creditor that had no lien when it obtained a judgment than to one with a judgment lien interest in the debtor's property that arose at the time it obtained its judgment.[375]

Similarly, a few courts had refused to avoid judicial liens that were senior to non-avoidable liens to the extent that the junior non-avoidable liens exceed the debtor's exemptions.[376] As discussed above,[377] these decisions were overruled by Congress in the Bankruptcy Reform Act of 1994.

The 1994 amendments also added an exception to the power to avoid judicial liens, which was expanded by the 2005 amendments. In order to better protect a spouse, former spouse, child, governmental unit or other specified entity that is owed a domestic support obligation, section 522(f)(1)(A) now provides that liens securing such debts cannot be avoided.[378]

---

370 *In re* Hoffman, 28 B.R. 503 (Bankr. D. Md. 1983). *See* Owen v. Owen, 500 U.S. 305, 111 S. Ct. 1833, 114 L. Ed. 2d 250 (1991) (if property would be exempt "but for" the lien, then lien can be avoided).

371 500 U.S. 291, 111 S. Ct. 1825, 114 L. Ed. 2d 337 (1991).

372 *See In re* Parrish, 7 F.3d 76 (5th Cir. 1993) (divorce lien attaching to debtor's preexisting separate property could be avoided); White v. Commer. Bank & Trust Co. (*In re* White), 460 B.R. 744 (B.A.P. 8th Cir. 2011), *aff'd*, 470 Fed. Appx. 538 (8th Cir. 2012) (lien obtained before entireties property divided upon divorce by mutual quitclaim deeds attached before debtor acquired interest in property); *In re* Stoneking, 225 B.R. 690 (B.A.P. 9th Cir. 1998) (debtor could avoid lien which first attached to property when it was held with spouse as community property despite fact that it later became debtor's separate property, because lien fixed on property at time debtor had interest in property). *See also In re* Lawton, 2010 WL 147913 (Bankr. N.D. Cal. Jan. 12, 2010) (lien in favor of former spouse could be avoided because it attached to debtor's preexisting community property interest); *In re* McFee, 2009 WL 1383290 (Bankr. D. Neb. May 14, 2009) (under Nebraska law, lien attached immediately after debtor acquired interest in property). *See generally* Henry J. Sommer & Margaret Dee McGarity, Collier Family Law and the Bankruptcy Code ¶ 7.04 (1992).

373 Owen v. Owen, 961 F.2d 170 (11th Cir. 1992).

Interestingly, this decision is the Court of Appeals' decision following the Supreme Court's remand in Owen v. Owen, 500 U.S. 305, 111 S. Ct. 1833, 114 L. Ed. 2d 250 (1991). *See also In re* Scarpino, 113 F.3d 338 (2d Cir. 1997) (same result under New York law); *In re* Pederson, 230 B.R. 158 (B.A.P. 9th Cir. 1999) (same result under California law). *Cf. In re* Kuehnert, 271 B.R. 434 (Bankr. D. Conn. 2001) (debtor who owned real property as joint tenant with non-debtor husband and who became owner of entire property through postpetition divorce transfer could avoid lien on entire property because she had always held undivided interest in entire property); *In re* Ulmer, 211 B.R. 523 (Bankr. E.D.N.C. 1997) (debtor who had owned property as entireties cotenant before lien attached had interest in property when lien attached due to transmutation of debtor's interest at divorce); *In re* Cooper, 197 B.R. 698 (Bankr. M.D. Fla. 1996) (debtor could avoid lien that attached after she had title to property even though she had not established homestead exemption before lien attached); *In re* Conyers, 129 B.R. 470 (Bankr. E.D. Ky. 1991) (relying on the Supreme Court decision in *Owen* to avoid a lien based on a judgment which arose before the debtor acquired the otherwise exempt homestead).

374 Congress enacted section 552(f)(1)(A) to protect the debtor's right to exempt property and to eliminate an otherwise unsecured creditor's "race to the courthouse" to obtain a lien before the debtor declared bankruptcy. *See* Farrey v. Sanderfoot, 500 U.S. 291, 111 S. Ct. 1825, 1830, 114 L. Ed. 2d 337 (1991).

375 The decision also goes beyond the Supreme Court's expressed concern in *Farrey* with protecting against fraudulent transfers of property which is already subject to a lien to a third person who could avoid that lien in bankruptcy. Farrey v. Sanderfoot, 500 U.S. 291, 111 S. Ct. 1825, 1830, 114 L. Ed. 2d 337 (1991). *Cf. In re* Garcia, 155 B.R. 173 (N.D. Ill. 1993) (debtor could avoid lien obtained by creditor on wages prior to bankruptcy if wages were claimed as exempt and state court had not yet entered final wage deduction order).

376 *See, e.g., In re* Duncan, 43 B.R. 833 (Bankr. D. Alaska 1984). *See also In re* Simonson, 758 F.2d 103 (3d Cir. 1985) (when non-avoidable junior mortgages, when added to senior mortgage, exceeded the value of the property, intervening judicial liens not avoidable because even if judicial liens did not exist property would still be fully encumbered; court did not discuss the possible operation of section 506(d) to render the junior mortgages void, and ignored dissent's application of section 522(i)(2) to preserve avoided judicial liens for the benefit of the debtor); *In re* Patterson, 139 B.R. 229 (B.A.P. 9th Cir. 1992) (permitting judicial lienholder to prevail over debtor's claim of exemption because judicial lien was senior to a consensual lien; court ignored section 522(i)(2)).

377 *See* § 10.4.2.9, *infra*; § 10.4.2.3.1, *supra*.

378 *See In re* Kestella, 269 B.R. 188 (Bankr. S.D. Ohio 2001) (divorce lien on debtor's retirement plan secured alimony or support obligations and could not be avoided); *In re* Allen, 217 B.R. 247 (Bankr. S.D. Ill. 1998) (debtor could not avoid liens for support and attorney fees deemed in nature of support); *In re* Willoughby, 212 B.R. 1011 (Bankr. M.D. Fla. 1997) (husband who owed support to former wife not permitted to avoid lien on residence owned jointly with new

Exemptions § 10.4.2.4

However, this exception does not apply if the debt has been assigned to another entity, other than a governmental unit, unless it is assigned solely for the purpose of collection.[379]

10.4.2.3.3 *Avoidance of liens on property which may be claimed as exempt under § 522(b)(2)(B)*

A final issue which may arise under this section is whether a lien may be avoided if that lien is on joint property, such as property owned as tenants by the entireties when, but for the lien, the property could be claimed as exempt under section 522(b)(2)(B). Creditors have argued that because the lien made such property subject to process immediately before the commencement of the case, the property could not be claimed as exempt in the first place under section 522(b)(2)(B), and that therefore the avoiding powers do not even come into play. This argument is refuted by the legislative history, which states that the "debtor may avoid a judicial lien on any property to the extent that the property could have been exempted in the absence of the lien."[380] Hence, if the interest in joint property is subject to process and is thus nonexempt only because of a judicial lien, then that judicial lien should be avoidable to the extent the property could otherwise be exempted.[381] In any case, there should be no doubt that, to the extent a creditor has a judicial lien on the interest of only one of two entireties cotenants, and that interest may be claimed as exempt under section 522(b)(2)(B), the creditor's lien is avoidable.[382]

10.4.2.4 Power to Avoid Nonpossessory, Nonpurchase-Money Security Interests in Certain Items—§ 522(f)(1)(B)

Another potent avoiding power is that provided by section 522(f)(1)(B)[383]—the power to avoid nonpossessory, nonpurchase-money security interests in the following items:

- Household furnishings, household goods (as defined in section 522(f)(4), discussed below) wearing apparel, appliances, books, animals, crops, musical instruments, or jewelry that are held primarily for the personal, family, or household use of the debtor or a dependent of the debtor;[384]
- Implements, professional books, or tools of the trade of the debtor or the trade of a dependent of the debtor; and
- Professionally prescribed health aids for the debtor or a dependent of the debtor.[385]

As the above list illustrates, this avoiding power extends to most, but not quite all, exempt tangible personal property of the debtor that is not in the creditor's possession.[386] It is not limited to necessities,[387] nor is it limited to those items encompassed

---

wife, but new wife entitled to avoid lien to extent it impaired her interest because she did not owe support).

379 See definition of "domestic support obligation" in 11 U.S.C. § 101(14A).

380 H.R. Rep. No. 95-595, at 362 (1977).

This reading of the statute is also supported by the concern in the legislative history that the debtor not be harmed by losing the "race to the courthouse," H.R. Rep. No. 95-595, at 126 (1977). *But see* Napotnik v. Equibank, 679 F.2d 316 (3d Cir. 1982). See § 10.2.3.2, *supra*, for discussion of *Napotnik*. See also Ragsdale v. Genesco, Inc., 674 F.2d 277 (4th Cir. 1982) (joint debtors could not exempt or avoid lien on entireties property subject to judgment lien of joint creditor).

381 This argument is greatly enhanced by the similar rationale for the Supreme Court decision in Owen v. Owen, 500 U.S. 305, 111 S. Ct. 1833, 114 L. Ed. 2d 250 (1991). The issues might be relitigated even in those jurisdictions with binding appellate case law, based on an argument that those cases were overruled by *Owen*. *See* Massie v. Yamrose, 169 B.R. 585 (W.D. Va. 1994) (judicial lien held by creditor of only one of two entireties tenants was avoidable, even though it was not presently enforceable, because it could at some future date attach to the debtor's interest, and thereby impair it, if the entireties tenancy ended). *But see In re* Arango, 992 F.2d 611 (6th Cir. 1993) (lien on the debtor's rights in entireties property did not impair his ability to exempt those rights because the creditor could not execute on the lien).

This case was overruled by the 1994 amendments, creating section 522(f)(2), as discussed in § 10.4.2.2, *supra*. *See In re* Holland, 151 F.3d 547 (6th Cir. 1998).

382 *See In re* Wansor, 346 B.R. 147 (Bankr. W.D. Pa. 2006) (judgment that was inchoate lien against real estate owned by judgment debtor as tenant by entirety could be avoided); *In re* Tolson, 338 B.R. 359 (Bankr. C.D. Ill. 2005) (debtor could avoid lien even though, as lien against only one cotenant, it was not presently enforceable); *In re* Patenude, 259 B.R. 481 (Bankr. D. Mass. 2001) (judicial lien on only debtor's interest in property held as tenants by entireties impaired exemption even though creditor had no present right to execute on lien). *See also In re* Alexander, 2012 Bankr. LEXIS 2656 (Bankr. E.D.N.C. June 12, 2012) (lien avoided as to debtor's interest in entireties property claimed as exempt under state exemption law).

383 This provision, formerly designated as section 522(f)(2), has been upheld against a constitutional challenge based on the takings clause of the Fifth Amendment. *In re* Thompson, 867 F.2d 416 (7th Cir. 1989).

384 A mobile home has been held not to be a household good within the meaning of this provision. *In re* Coonse, 108 B.R. 661 (Bankr. S.D. Ill. 1989). *Cf. In re* Rhines, 227 B.R. 308 (Bankr. D. Mont. 1998) (rifle, shotgun, computer and VCR were household goods); *In re* Crawford, 226 B.R. 484 (Bankr. N.D. Ga. 1998) (rifle and computer were household goods); *In re* DiPalma, 24 B.R. 385 (Bankr. D. Mass. 1982) (mobile home is a household good).

A gun has also been held not to be a household good. *In re* McGreevy, 955 F.2d 957 (4th Cir. 1992) (defining household goods as those items of personal property typically found in or around home and used by debtor or his dependents to support and facilitate day-to-day living within the home); *In re* Barrick, 95 B.R. 310 (Bankr. M.D. Pa. 1989). *See also* § 10.2.2.4, *supra*.

385 A water treatment system recommended by a doctor has been held to be a professionally prescribed health aid within the meaning of this provision. *In re* Johnson, 101 B.R. 280 (Bankr. W.D. Okla.), *aff'd*, 113 B.R. 44 (Bankr. W.D. Okla. 1989).

386 It may also be possible to recover property that was repossessed by a creditor who had held a nonpossessory, nonpurchase-money security interest. *In re* White, 203 B.R. 613 (Bankr. N.D. Tex. 1996) (debtor could avoid security interest even though creditor had obtained possession through judicial proceedings); *In re* Vann, 177 B.R. 704 (D. Kan. 1995) (debtors allowed to avoid lien on tool of trade and recover it from creditor even though tool had been repossessed prior to bankruptcy filing).

387 Fraley v. Commercial Credit, 189 B.R. 398 (W.D. Ky. 1995) (stereo and camcorder were household goods); *In re* Doss, 298 B.R. 866 (Bankr. W.D. Tenn. 2003) (fifty-inch television was household good); *In re* Gebhart, 260 B.R. 596 (Bankr. S.D. Ga. 2000) (forty-inch television was household good; no exception for luxury items).

within the restrictive definition of household goods used by the Federal Trade Commission in its Credit Practices Rule.[388]

The 2005 amendments added a definition of "household goods," that by its terms is applicable only in section 522(f)(1) lien avoidance proceedings, and thus not in determining what is a household good under section 522(d)(3) or state exemption laws.[389] Section 522(f)(4)(A) provides that, for purposes of lien avoidance under section 522(f)(1)(B), the term "household goods" means:

- Clothing;
- Furniture;
- Appliances;
- One radio;
- One television;[390]
- One VCR;
- Linens;
- China, crockery, and kitchenware;
- Educational materials and educational equipment primarily for the use of minor dependent children of the debtor;
- Medical equipment and supplies;
- Furniture exclusively for the use of minor children, or elderly or disabled dependents of the debtor;
- Personal effects (including the toys and hobby equipment of minor dependent children and wedding rings) of the debtor and the dependents of the debtor;[391] and
- One personal computer and related equipment.

Section 522(f)(4)(B) provides that the term "household goods" does not include:

- Works of art (unless by or of the debtor, or any relative of the debtor);
- Electronic entertainment equipment with a fair market value of more than $600 in the aggregate (except one television, one radio, and one VCR);
- Items acquired as antiques with a fair market value of more than $600 in the aggregate;[392]
- Jewelry with a fair market value of more than $600 in the aggregate (except wedding rings); and
- A computer (except as provided for in section 522(f)(4)(A)), motor vehicle (including a tractor or lawn tractor), boat, or a motorized recreational device, conveyance, vehicle, watercraft, or aircraft.

One problem with the dollar limits in this subsection is that finance companies which make loans secured by personal property often have consumers sign a personal property list that includes inflated values. While this practice is often engaged in by such lenders to support the charging of higher premiums on personal property insurance sold in connection with these loans, such finance companies will now have another reason to engage in this practice.

Like many provisions of the 2005 Act that were drafted many years before its passage, when the first bill was introduced, and which were not amended or updated prior to passage, this subsection refers to a "VCR" even though most consumers have replaced this item with a DVD player. Of course, this illustrates the problem of having a laundry list of items in a statutory provision that will inevitably become obsolete. Hopefully, courts will expand the list to include reasonable substitutes for the listed items.[393]

However, the new definition should not pose much of a problem for debtors because no other changes were made to section 522(f)(1)(B). Some of the categories of items that continue to be listed in section 522(f)(1)(B) are broad and provide for overlapping coverage. To the extent that an item is excluded from the household goods category based on the definition in section 522(f)(4), the debtor should still be able to avoid a nonpossessory, nonpurchase-money lien on the item if it falls within another category listed in section 522(f)(1)(B), such as "appliances,"[394] "household furnishings," or "jewelry."

The items with respect to which lien avoidance may be obtained need not be within the value limitation set forth in section 522(d)(3), as long as they have been validly claimed as exempt under some subsection or combination of subsections in section 522(d) or other applicable exemption law (including a wild card provision).[395] Thus, if a motor vehicle is claimed as

---

388 *In re* Reid, 121 B.R. 875 (Bankr. D.N.M. 1990) (Federal Trade Commission definition at 16 C.F.R. § 444.1(i) rejected as too restrictive).

389 For other purposes, the definition should continue to be that developed by pre-amendment case law, under which the term "household goods" was construed broadly under this section to include all items kept in or around the home and used to facilitate the day-to-day living of the debtor and the debtor's dependents (*In re* McGreevy, 955 F.2d 957, 960 (4th Cir. 1992)), all items normally used by the debtor or the debtor's dependents in or about a residence (*In re* Barrick, 95 B.R. 310 (Bankr. M.D. Pa. 1989); *In re* Bailey, 74 B.R. 450 (Bankr. N.D. Ind. 1987)), or personal property normally found in or around a home which allows the debtor or the debtor's dependents to live in a convenient or comfortable manner or has entertainment or recreational value (*In re* Courtney, 89 B.R. 15 (Bankr. W.D. Tex. 1988); *In re* Bandy, 62 B.R. 437 (Bankr. E.D. Cal. 1986)).

390 Presumably the debtor can choose which of several televisions the debtor owns (probably the most valuable) as the one on which a lien will be avoided. Liens on other televisions or on a radio other than the one designated under this provision may be avoided either under the electronic entertainment equipment category, or as liens on appliances.

391 Because the term "including" is not exclusive, 11 U.S.C. § 102, hobby equipment of adults is also included.

392 This provision would appear not to include items that become an antique after being acquired by the debtor.

393 *See In re* Zieg, 409 B.R. 917, 920 (Bankr. W.D. Mo. 2009) (allowing avoidance of lien on DVD player, "recogniz[ing] that technology has changed since BAPCPA was drafted").

394 The term "appliances" is listed in both the definition of household goods in section 522(f)(4)(iii) and in the list of items in section 522(f)(1)(B)(i). *See In re* Zieg, 409 B.R. 917 (Bankr. W.D. Mo. 2009) (lawn mower and weed eater held to be "appliances" under section 522(f)(4)(iii)).

395 *In re* Liming, 797 F.2d 895 (10th Cir. 1986); First Nat'l Bank of Park Falls v. Maley, 126 B.R. 563 (W.D. Wis. 1991) (lien may be avoided on optometrist's equipment exempt under combination of

exempt using the motor vehicle exemption, but is also used as a tool of the debtor's trade,[396] a nonpossessory, nonpurchase-money lien on that vehicle may be avoided.[397] The dispute in such cases often centers on the definition of "tools of trade" under state or federal law, because many states have an exemption for tools of trade that is large or unlimited in amount.[398]

Disputes concerning tools of the trade will only be increased by an incomprehensible 1994 amendment which purports to create an exception to the power to avoid nonpossessory non-purchase-money security interests on tools of the debtor's trade, farm animals, or crops in certain cases. Section 522(f)(3) states that if certain conditions are met and the items in question exceed $5850 in value, such a lien cannot be avoided. However, among the conditions which must be met are that the state either permits the debtor to claim exemptions that are unlimited in amount, except to the extent that property is encumbered by a consensual lien, or the state prohibits avoidance of consensual liens. Because no state has unlimited exemptions, and no state could have had, consistent with the Supremacy Clause, a law prohibiting avoidance of liens in bankruptcy, it is not clear that the exception can be invoked in any state.[399] The legislative history does make clear that the exception applies only to exemptions claimed under state exemption schemes, and has no applicability to a debtor choosing the federal bankruptcy exemptions.[400] It also states that the $5850 limit, if it is ever applicable, is calculated separately for each debtor in a joint case.[401] When the exception is applicable, the $5850 limit is designed to free $5850 of equity in tools of the trade from liens, not to limit the amount of the lien that could be avoided to $5475.[402]

Issues may also arise as to whether or not a purchase-money security interest exists.[403] For example, the debtor may have entered into a series of credit purchases with cross-collateral clauses. These clauses secure each purchase with property previously purchased, even if that property had been fully paid for, through language stating that the property purchased in each transaction is security for subsequent purchase transactions. In such cases, it has been held that no purchase-money security interest exists, even as to the last item purchased. Under the former provisions of the Uniform Commercial Code, the term purchase-money security interest had been narrowly defined to exclude any transactions in which the agreement purports to make collateral secure a debt other than its own price.[404] The revised Uniform Commercial Code takes no position on the issue, leaving it for courts to decide, presumably in light of prior case law.[405] Thus, whenever such clauses exist, stating that the collateral will secure future indebtedness, it should be held that no purchase-money security interest exists, even if there has been no later indebtedness.[406] Certainly, when

---

tool of trade and wild card exemptions). *See also In re* Reid, 757 F.2d 230 (10th Cir. 1985) (valuable paintings pledged as collateral for business loans not household furniture that is exempt under Oklahoma law so that nonpossessory, nonpurchase-money liens on those paintings could not be avoided).

It is possible, however, for some goods to be exempted under state law, yet not held for the personal, family, or household use of the debtor. *See In re* Thompson, 750 F.2d 628 (8th Cir. 1984).

396 *See* § 10.2.2.7, *supra*.

397 *See* Dominion Bank of Cumberlands v. Nuckolls, 780 F.2d 408 (4th Cir. 1985) (restaurant equipment exempted with homestead exemption is subject to lien avoidance as tool of trade); *In re* Graettinger, 95 B.R. 632 (Bankr. N.D. Iowa 1988) (liens could be avoided in pick-up truck exempted as motor vehicle, because truck was a tool of debtor's trade); *In re* Meyers, 2 B.R. 603 (Bankr. E.D. Mich. 1980) (motor vehicle used only for commuting not a tool of trade, but if it were, lien could be avoided). *But see In re* Moore, 5 B.R. 669 (Bankr. S.D. Ohio 1980) (vehicle must be claimed exempt under tool-of-trade exemption to avoid lien using tool-of-trade avoidance power).

Even a mobile home, exempted under section 522(d)(5), may be considered as household goods or furnishings, according to one court. *In re* Dipalma, 24 B.R. 385 (Bankr. D. Mass. 1982).

398 *See* § 10.2.2.7, *supra*. *See also In re* Heape, 886 F.2d 280 (10th Cir. 1989) (lien avoided in debtors' breeding livestock on ground that livestock is tool of breeder's trade); *In re* Thompson, 867 F.2d 416 (7th Cir. 1989) (debtor's state law exemption of tools of trade is not in any way limited by federal limitation of that exemption to $750); *In re* Taylor, 861 F.2d 550 (9th Cir. 1988) (logging equipment worth $50,000 could be freed from nonpossessory, nonpurchase-money security interest); *In re* Erickson, 815 F.2d 1090 (7th Cir. 1987) (baler and haybine were tools of trade so security interest therein could be avoided); *In re* La Fond, 791 F.2d 623 (8th Cir. 1986) (Bankruptcy Code's definition of "farmer" given at 11 U.S.C. § 101(20) is not determinative for the purpose of avoiding nonpossessory, nonpurchase-money lien on farm equipment as tool of trade); Dominion Bank of Cumberlands v. Nuckolls, 780 F.2d 408 (4th Cir. 1985) (lien may be avoided on restaurant equipment used to operate business out of home); *In re* Cleaver, 407 B.R. 354 (B.A.P. 8th Cir. 2009) (lien could be avoided on semi-tractor truck if it was tool of trade under state law); *In re* Taylor, 73 B.R. 149 (B.A.P. 9th Cir. 1987) (liens on log truck and trailer avoidable), *aff'd*, 861 F.2d 550 (9th Cir. 1988).

399 *Compare In re* Ehlen, 202 B.R. 742 (Bankr. W.D. Wis. 1996) (section 522(f)(3) inapplicable in Wisconsin), *aff'd* 207 B.R. 179 (W.D. Wis. 1997) *and In re* Zimmel, 185 B.R. 786 (Bankr. D. Minn. 1995) (Minnesota did not allow unlimited exemptions or permit debtors to waive exemptions, so section 522(f)(3) was inapplicable) *with In re* Parrish, 186 B.R. 246 (Bankr. W.D. Wis. 1995) (Wisconsin law prohibited the avoidance of consensual liens, so debtor could only avoid security interest to extent of $5000 interest in tractor).

400 H.R. Rep. No. 103-835, at 56, 57 (1994), *reprinted in* 1994 U.S.C.C.A.N. 3340, 3365, 3366.

401 *Id.*

402 *In re* Duvall, 218 B.R. 1008 (Bankr. W.D. Tex. 1998) (also holding that $5000 limit does not apply to each tool individually).

403 See National Consumer Law Center, Repossessions Ch. 3 (7th ed. 2010 and Supp.) for a detailed discussion of the existence and duration of purchase money security interests.

404 *In re* Freeman, 956 F.2d 252 (11th Cir. 1992) (security interest lost its purchase money character when debt consolidated with other debts under Alabama law); *In re* Manuel, 507 F.2d 990 (5th Cir. 1975); *In re* McCombs, 126 B.R. 611 (N.D. Ala. 1989); *In re* Johnson, 1 Bankr. Ct. Dec. (LRP) 1023 (Bankr. S.D. Ala. 1973). *See* National Consumer Law Center, Repossessions § 3.8.5 (7th ed. 2010 and Supp.).

405 Unif. Commercial Code § 9-103 cmt. 8.

406 Southtrust Bank v. Borg-Warner Acceptance Corp., 760 F.2d 1240 (11th Cir. 1985); *In re* Jones, 5 B.R. 655 (Bankr. M.D.N.C. 1980). *But see* Pristas v. Landaus of Plymouth, 742 F.2d 797 (3d Cir. 1984) (Pennsylvania Goods and Services Statute provided a method of

a refinancing has occurred, and the collateral in fact secures indebtedness other than its price, any possible purchase money character should be extinguished.[407] And similarly, if a loan involves other funds besides the purchase price (perhaps even those used to buy insurance), then property purchased using only some of the proceeds should not be considered subject to a purchase money security interest.[408]

In addition, it should be noted that the Federal Trade Commission has promulgated a rule which makes the taking of certain nonpossessory, nonpurchase-money liens in certain personal property an unfair trade practice.[409] The rule can be used in litigation asserting the unfair practice, and in at least one instance has been used in bankruptcy to avoid otherwise non-avoidable liens.[410]

10.4.2.5 Power to Exempt Property Recovered by Trustee—§ 522(g)

A power of the debtor utilized somewhat less often is provided in section 522(g). This provision allows the debtor to exempt any property that the trustee recovers using the various trustee powers to recover property.[411] Thus, if such property comes into the trustee's hands, the debtor may claim it as exempt, as long as the prebankruptcy transfer of the property from the debtor was not voluntary and the debtor did not conceal the property. The debtor may also exempt the property, under section 522(g)(2), if the debtor could have avoided the transfer because the transfer was pursuant to a nonpossessory, nonpurchase-money security interest.[412]

In some cases, under both section 522(g)(1) and section 522(h), an issue may arise as to whether the transfer avoided by the trustee was a voluntary transfer.[413] For example, there is no question that a debtor who pays money with a gun to his or her head has made an involuntary transfer. Would it be much different if the debtor paid a large utility arrearage upon the threat of a shut-off of heating or water service to a home in which the debtor's children live (or perhaps an elderly or sick relative)? What about a debtor threatened with lesser evils, for example, repossession of property necessary for daily existence, such as a refrigerator?[414] Thus, a seemingly voluntary transfer made under threat of foreclosure or based on misrepresentations about the circumstances of the transfer may be found to be involuntary for purposes of section 522(g) or (h).[415]

It is also a little unclear whether section 522(g) is really an expansion of the debtor's powers to exempt property or rather, in fact, a limitation. Because under section 522(b) the debtor already may claim exempt property from any property of the estate, and because property of the estate under section 541(a)(3) and (4) includes property recovered by the trustee under sections 543, 550, 551, 553 and 723, section 522(g) seems to add only a right to exempt property recovered by the trustee under sections 510(c) and 542.[416] But section 522(g) does not

---

apportioning payments so purchase-money character retained even if later sales made); *In re* Mattson, 20 B.R. 382 (Bankr. W.D. Wis. 1982) (purchase-money character not lost if consolidation agreement provides clear and fair way to apportion payments among items of collateral).

407 *In re* Matthews, 724 F.2d 798 (9th Cir. 1984); *In re* Freeman, 124 B.R. 840 (N.D. Ala. 1991), *aff'd*, 956 F.2d 252 (11th Cir. 1992); *In re* Cameron, 25 B.R. 410 (Bankr. N.D. Ga. 1982); Rosen v. Assocs. Fin. Servs. Co., 17 B.R. 436 (Bankr. D.S.C. 1982). *But see In re* Billings, 838 F.2d 405 (10th Cir. 1988) (when purpose of refinancing substantially appears to be to allow the debtor more favorable repayment terms, almost no new money advanced, and agreement stated specific intent to continue purchase-money status, refinancing may not extinguish purchase money character of original lien).

408 *In re* Mulcahy, 3 B.R. 454 (Bankr. S.D. Ind. 1980). *But see In re* Griffin, 9 B.R. 880 (Bankr. N.D. Ga. 1981) (fact that collateral secured finance and insurance charges did not render security interest nonpurchase money).

409 16 C.F.R. § 444. *See* National Consumer Law Center, Unfair and Deceptive Acts and Practices § 6.13.1 (7th ed. 2008 and Supp.).

410 *In re* Raymond, 103 B.R. 846 (Bankr. W.D. Ky. 1989).

411 Most of these powers are discussed below in the context of the debtor's right to use them under section 522(h). Sections 542 and 543 are discussed in § 9.9, *supra*. Although the avoiding powers of sections 544 through 549 are not specifically enumerated in section 522(g), they are encompassed by the inclusion of section 550 under which the trustee actually recovers the property transferred in an avoided transfer.

412 *In re* Vasina, 337 B.R. 684 (Bankr. D. Neb. 2006) (debtor could avoid under section 522(f)(1)(B) unperfected lien on car that was tool of trade and exempt the property even though trustee could also

have avoided lien); *In re* Flitter, 181 B.R. 938 (Bankr. D. Minn. 1995) (debtor may exempt property recovered by trustee if debtors could have avoided transfer under section 522(f), even if transfer was voluntary).

It appears that this subsection would allow the debtor to recover goods repossessed pursuant to a nonpossessory, nonpurchase-money security interest if that repossession was first avoided by the trustee, because there are really two transfers being avoided—the repossession and the granting of the original security interest. The repossession, being involuntary, fits within section 522(g)(1); the original grant of the security interest does not, because it was voluntary, but it does come within section 522(g)(2). Thus, the debtor, who could have avoided the security interest, would not lose the right to exempt such property simply because the trustee avoided the transfer first. *But cf. In re* Vann, 177 B.R. 704 (D. Kan. 1995) (security interest could be avoided through simply using section 522(f) even after goods had been repossessed); *In re* Meadows, 75 B.R. 357 (W.D. Va. 1987) (same).

413 *See, e.g.*, Berman v. Forti, 232 B.R. 653 (D. Md. 1999) (although consent to judgment against debtors was voluntary, transfer effected by judgment itself was involuntary); *In re* Pfiester, 449 B.R. 422 (Bankr. D.N.M. 2011) (funds paid to credit card company from sale of debtor's home were paid voluntarily because debtor had agreed to payment in marital settlement agreement); *In re* Rollins, 63 B.R. 780 (Bankr. E.D. Tenn. 1986) (property transferred pursuant to insurance policy required by mortgage is voluntary transfer).

414 *See In re* Via, 107 B.R. 91 (Bankr. W.D. Va. 1989) (payment made to creditor to avoid garnishment was involuntary), *aff'd*, Clearinghouse No. 45,232 (W.D. Va. 1990); *In re* Taylor, 8 B.R. 578 (Bankr. E.D. Pa. 1981) (threat of sheriff sale of home forced involuntary transfer); *In re* Reaves, 8 B.R. 177 (Bankr. D.S.D. 1981) (creditor applied unfair pressure).

415 *In re* Davis, 169 B.R. 285 (E.D.N.Y. 1994) (sale/leaseback agreement in which debtor executed a deed to avoid a threatened foreclosure was set aside as a fraudulent transfer under 11 U.S.C. § 548).

416 One possible exception to this statement is property claimed under section 522(b)(3)(B), which can only be claimed exempt to the

allow the property to be exempted if it was transferred voluntarily or concealed by the debtor. This provision could mean that property which could be otherwise claimed as exempt under section 522(b) may not be claimed as exempt because of the limitations in section 522(g).[417] On the other hand, the legislative history states that the several provisions of section 522 are cumulative,[418] and therefore if property can be exempted under section 522(b), section 522(g) should not impair that right.[419] In any event, if the trustee acquires property other than through use of the provisions listed in section 522(g), section 522(g) does not prevent the debtor from exempting the property.[420]

It is not very likely that such disputes will arise often under section 522(g), as it will be a rare case in which the trustee bothers to avoid a transfer of property that the debtor may claim as exempt.[421] Indeed, it is unusual for trustees to avoid the small transfers involved in consumer cases at all; when the only result will be more exempt property for the debtor rather than proceeds for the creditors, trustees have no incentive to do so.[422] Except in cases in which the trustee would recover a substantial amount of nonexempt property along with the exempt property, the trustee's avoiding powers, and thus section 522(g), are not likely to be used often in consumer cases. When they are used though, prejudgment interest may be available to enhance the award.[423] And when the trustee does avoid a transfer, the debtor's exempt share of the property recovered can be reduced by a pro rata share of the costs and expenses of avoiding the transfer.[424]

Occasionally, when the trustee does move to avoid an unperfected lien on a car or other property, however, it may cause problems for the debtor by creating equity in the property which may not be claimed as exempt. (For example, the trustee may avoid a security interest of $6000 on an $8000 vehicle. The debtor usually would not be able to exempt the equity created because a security interest is typically a voluntary transfer of property and because applicable law may not permit an exemption in that high an amount.) In such cases, the trustee may attempt to liquidate the property if the debtor does not pay the trustee its value.[425] The debtor should argue that the trustee

---

extent of "any interest the debtor had immediately before commencement of the case."

417 *In re* Kuhnel, 495 F.3d 1177 (10th Cir. 2007); *In re* Sullivan, 387 B.R. 353 (B.A.P. 1st Cir. 2008) (debtor could not claim homestead exemption in property interest trustee obtained by avoiding unrecorded mortgage for benefit of estate under section 551); *In re* Arzt, 252 B.R. 138 (B.A.P. 8th Cir. 2000) (debtors could not exempt property recovered by trustee because transfer of property had been voluntary); *In re* Milcher, 86 B.R. 103 (Bankr. W.D. Mich. 1988); *In re* Lamping, 8 B.R. 709 (Bankr. E.D. Wis. 1981); *In re* Lanctot, 6 B.R. 576 (Bankr. D. Utah 1980) (debtors could not claim property recovered by trustee avoidance of unperfected conventional security interests). *See In re* Wilson, 694 F.2d 236 (11th Cir. 1982) (section 522(g) is a limitation on general power to exempt any property of estate, and does not apply to property not brought into estate by trustee avoiding powers enumerated therein). *See also In re* Duncan, 329 F.3d 1195 (10th Cir. 2003) (debtor not entitled to homestead exemption in property recovered by trustee as fraudulent transfer to tenancy by entireties based on section 522(g) even though trustee failed to object to debtor's claim of exemption in property within thirty-day period under Fed. R. Bankr. P. 4003(b); trustee recovered, and debtor could not exempt, all interests in property that had been transferred under Wyoming law); *In re* Glass, 60 F.3d 565 (9th Cir. 1995) (trustee need not have first recovered property transferred by debtor in order to object to exemption under section 522(g)); *In re* Kelsey, 270 B.R. 776 (B.A.P. 10th Cir. 2001) (when debtor withdrew money from joint account with wife he became owner of funds, so all of the funds later transferred to her were his property); *In re* McDaniel, 2012 WL 174370 (Bankr. N.D. Ala. Jan. 20, 2012) (provision not applicable when trustee did not recover property using avoiding powers and transfer to relatives was not intentional or fraudulent concealment).

One solution to the problem of obtaining possession of property recovered by the trustee when it cannot be claimed as exempt is to convert to chapter 13 wherein the debtor has a right to possession of all property of the estate. *See* § 12.8.1, *infra*.

418 S. Rep. No. 95-989, at 77 (1978); H.R. Rep. No. 95-595, at 363 (1977).

419 In some cases, there may be an issue regarding whether the trustee recovered property or whether it was in the estate all along. *See In re* Moody, 862 F.2d 1194 (5th Cir. 1989) (attempted fraudulent transfer of property did not preclude debtor from later claiming homestead exemption under Texas law); *In re* Pancratz, 175 B.R. 85 (D. Wyo. 1994) (transfer of property to self-settled spendthrift trust was invalid, so property was property of the estate at outset of case and section 522(g) was inapplicable).

420 McFatter v. Cage, 204 B.R. 503 (S.D. Tex. 1996). *But see In re* Kuhnel, 495 F.3d 1177 (10th Cir. 2007) (debtor could not exempt property interests created when creditor released lien upon trustee's request); *In re* Glass, 164 B.R. 759 (B.A.P. 9th Cir. 1994) (debtor could not exempt property that had been voluntarily transferred to

son, even though trustee had recovered property without using avoiding powers enumerated in section 522(g)), *aff'd*, 60 F.3d 565 (9th Cir. 1995); *In re* Dorricott, 5 B.R. 192 (Bankr. N.D. Ohio 1980) (holding under 11 U.S.C. § 522(g)(1) that debtor could not exempt concealed property even in case in which trustee never recovered property for estate). *See also In re* Hill, 562 F.3d 29, 35 (1st Cir. 2009) (section 522(g) inapplicable to property that was reconveyed back to debtor prior to petition).

421 However, in those cases in which the trustee does move to avoid a transfer, the debtor may be obligated to intervene in that action to protect his or her rights. *See* H.R. Rep. No. 95-595, at 362 (1977). *Cf.* Wellman v. Wellman, 933 F.2d 215 (4th Cir. 1991) (debtor-in-possession in chapter 11 case precluded from avoiding transfer when avoided transfer would not benefit bankruptcy estate). This result should be different when the debtor can exempt an interest in the property once it is brought into the estate, even if there is no additional benefit to creditors.

422 In fact, when the amount recovered by the trustee can be substantially exempted so that the balance will pay only trustee fees, the trustee may be required to abandon the property in favor of the debtor. *In re* Melvin, 64 B.R. 104 (Bankr. W.D. Mo. 1986). *But see In re* Myatt, 101 B.R. 197 (Bankr. E.D. Cal. 1989) (when trustee conducts litigation based on belief that litigation costs and fees would be paid from recovery of nonexempt property, debtor's later amendment of exemptions to include recovered property could be conditioned on payment of trustee's expenses).

423 *In re* Chattanooga Wholesale Antiques, Inc., 930 F.2d 458 (6th Cir. 1991).

424 11 U.S.C. § 522(k)(1). *But see In re* Breen, 123 B.R. 357 (B.A.P. 9th Cir. 1991) (section 522(k)(1) not applicable when trustee recovers property through methods other than avoiding powers).

425 *See In re* Bagnato, 80 B.R. 655 (Bankr. E.D.N.Y. 1987) (although debtor did not properly preserve her rights in exempt property,

has merely stepped into the shoes of the former holder of the avoided lien, because the lien is preserved for the benefit of the estate under section 551, in which case the trustee has no greater rights than the former lienholder.[426]

10.4.2.6 Debtor's Right to Utilize Trustee's Avoiding Powers—§ 522(h)

10.4.2.6.1 Overview

More likely to be used are the provisions of section 522(h), which give the debtor the wide panoply of avoiding powers available to the trustee under sections 544, 545, 547, 548, 549, 553 and 724(a) in cases in which the trustee does not choose to avoid a transfer.[427]

The use of these powers is subject to the same limitations as section 522(g); the transfer to be avoided cannot have been a voluntary transfer, and the debtor may not use these powers to exempt property that was concealed by the debtor. The discussion above regarding voluntariness under section 522(g) is equally applicable to this subsection.[428]

In some cases, especially under chapter 13, a debtor may be able to convince a trustee to exercise an avoiding power the debtor cannot use because the transfer was voluntary, especially if it will mean greater dividends for unsecured creditors. It may even be possible to provide that the trustee will do so as part of the chapter 13 plan[429] or to provide in the plan that the debtor shall have the right to exercise the trustee's avoiding powers.[430] The debtor has a right to possession of any property recovered in this manner (though it cannot be exempted).[431] When a plan does provide for the trustee to avoid a transfer, the trustee's prior concurrence in such a provision should be sought if possible. Because the recovery of such property for use in funding the plan can also be enormously helpful to the debtor in paying priority or secured claims, debtor's counsel might even offer to draw up all of the necessary papers for use by the trustee. Perhaps because such methods of invoking the chapter 13 trustee's powers are available, some courts have held that all chapter 13 debtors, as debtors in possession, have full use of the trustee's powers without the limitations in section 522(h).[432] However, other courts disagree.[433]

The debtor's powers under section 522(h) are otherwise the same as those of the trustee.[434] To use them, it is therefore first necessary to understand what powers the trustee has. The discussion below briefly describes each of the trustee's powers as well as the debtor's possible use of them.

10.4.2.6.2 The "strong-arm clause"—§ 544

Through the use of section 544, the trustee (and thus the debtor in many instances) is able to avoid a wide variety of transfers. Section 544(a) allows the trustee to avoid any transfer or obligation[435] incurred by the debtor that is voidable by:

- A creditor that extends credit to the debtor at the time of commencement of the case, and that obtains at that time and with respect to such credit a judicial lien on all property on which a creditor on a simple contract could have obtained such a judicial lien, whether or not such a creditor exists;
- A creditor that extends credit to the debtor at the time of the commencement of the case, and obtains, at such time and with respect to such credit, an execution against the debtor that is returned unsatisfied at such time, whether or not such a creditor exists;
- A bona fide purchaser of real property other than fixtures from the debtor against whom applicable law permits such transfer to be perfected, that obtains the status of a bona

---

trustee's failure to avoid lien prior to discharge prevented trustee from preserving lien to benefit the estate).

426 See Rodriguez v. Drive Fin. Servs. L.P. (In re Trout), 609 F.3d 1106 (10th Cir. 2010) (trustee had same rights as holder of lien that was avoided); In re Carvell, 222 B.R. 178, 180 (B.A.P. 1st Cir. 1998) (preservation for the benefit of the estate puts the estate in the shoes of the creditor whose lien was avoided, the trustee assumes the position that the lienholder previously held, and the mortgage is treated as if it had not been avoided, as between the debtor and the trustee).

427 See Deel Rent-A-Car v. Levine, 721 F.2d 750 (11th Cir. 1983) (debtor may avoid transfer that trustee could have avoided even though transfer was pursuant to prebankruptcy execution on property that would not otherwise have been exempt due to liens eliminated by the execution). Cf. In re Merrifield, 214 B.R. 362 (B.A.P. 8th Cir. 1997) (debtor could not use trustee's powers to avoid voluntary transfer that trustee had already sought to avoid).

428 See § 10.4.2.5, supra.

429 In re Johnson, 36 B.R. 381 (Bankr. D. Colo. 1982) (plan could provide for chapter 13 trustee to avoid fraudulent transfer).

430 In re Hearn, 337 B.R. 603 (Bankr. E.D. Mich. 2006).

431 11 U.S.C. § 1306. See § 12.8.1, infra. See also In re Walls, 17 B.R. 701 (Bankr. S.D. W. Va. 1982) (opinion is confusing as to why the debtor could not himself avoid the transfer).

432 In re Dickson, 655 F.3d 585 (6th Cir. 2011) (court can grant chapter 13 debtor derivative standing to assert trustee's avoiding powers); In re Cohen, 305 B.R. 886 (B.A.P. 9th Cir. 2004); In re Freeman, 72 B.R. 850 (Bankr. E.D. Va. 1987); In re Ottaviano, 68 B.R. 238 (Bankr. D. Conn. 1986); In re Boyette, 33 B.R. 10, 11 (Bankr. N.D. Tex. 1983). See also In re Hearn, 337 B.R. 603 (Bankr. E.D. Mich. 2007) (creditor bound by provision in confirmed plan giving debtor right to exercise trustee's avoiding powers).

433 See, e.g., In re Stangel, 219 F.3d 498 (5th Cir. 2000); In re Hansen, 332 B.R. 8 (B.A.P. 10th Cir. 2005); Hollar v. United States, 174 B.R. 198 (M.D.N.C. 1994) (chapter 13 debtor may not directly avoid transfer under section 548, case remanded to determine if requirements of section 522(h) are met); In re Mast, 79 B.R. 981 (Bankr. W.D. Mich. 1987); In re Driscoll, 57 B.R. 322 (Bankr. W.D. Wis. 1986).

434 See In re Saults, 293 B.R. 739 (Bankr. E.D. Tenn. 2002) (debtor's procedural waiver of state exemption rights in bank account during state execution process did not prevent use of section 522(h) to recover funds).

435 Section 522(h) only speaks of incorporating the trustee's power to avoid transfers, not obligations. It is not clear whether it would be carried over to section 522(h) despite the failure to mention it specifically. Generally, unsecured obligations of the debtor are eliminated by the discharge, so that there would be no need to avoid them, and secured obligations involve a transfer of an interest in property that can be avoided. (The trustee may wish to avoid an obligation to prevent other creditors from being prejudiced.).

fide purchaser and has perfected such transfer at the time of the commencement of the case, whether or not such a purchaser exists.

In addition, section 544(b) bestows the power to avoid any transfer or obligation that is avoidable under applicable law by an actually existing creditor holding an unsecured claim.[436]

All of these rights depend on the powers given to creditors or purchasers under state or local law. They carry forward, mostly unchanged,[437] the powers the trustee had under the former Bankruptcy Act, so reference to case law under the Act continues to be useful. They make clear that the first three powers, relating to a "hypothetical" creditor, rather than actual existing creditors, assume that the hypothetical creditor had no knowledge of the transfer, to the extent that knowledge might otherwise bar the avoidance of a transfer.[438]

The most frequent use of the section 544(a) powers is the avoidance of unrecorded security interests and other liens. Section 9-301(1)(b) of the Uniform Commercial Code (UCC) gives a lien creditor priority over the holder of an unperfected UCC security interest.[439] A close examination of the nature and manner of perfection of a creditor's security interest may turn up avoidable transfers.[440] In many cases trustees have successfully asserted these rights when financing statements were incorrectly filed, thus rendering the security interest unperfected, or when a transaction denominated as a lease was found to be a disguised security interest with no financing statement filed.[441] (In these cases the debtor usually cannot exempt the equity created by the trustee's lien avoidance because the lien avoided was a voluntary transfer.) Similarly, the law in most states gives judicial lien creditors and bona fide purchasers priority over unrecorded or improperly recorded mortgages and many other unrecorded liens on real estate.[442] Depending upon state law, the power to avoid transfers that are not enforceable against a bona fide purchaser of real estate may permit the debtor to avoid foreclosure sale transfers that have not been completed by the filing of a deed.[443]

---

436 *See In re* Bushey, 210 B.R. 95 (B.A.P. 6th Cir. 1997) (open credit card account maintained by debtor qualified as existing creditor, even though balance was zero at some time between date of transfer and bankruptcy petition).

437 One change is the addition of bona fide purchaser status of section 544(a)(3).

438 *But see In re* Hamilton, 125 F.3d 292 (5th Cir. 1997) (remanding case to determine whether reasonably diligent inquiry could have given hypothetical bona fide purchaser inquiry notice that would defeat right to avoid trustee's deed); *In re* Weisman, 5 F.3d 417 (9th Cir. 1993) (under California law, bona fide purchaser is deemed to be on notice of and obligated to determine ownership status of persons who occupy real estate); *In re* Prof'l Inv. Properties, 955 F.2d 623 (9th Cir. 1992) (involuntary bankruptcy petition put trustee on constructive notice of creditor's interest under unrecorded instrument, so trustee could not invoke strong-arm powers); Watkins v. Watkins, 922 F.2d 1513 (10th Cir. 1991) (when hypothetical purchaser would have constructive notice of debtor's former wife's security interest granted by divorce decree of record, lien could not be avoided); *In re* Hagendorfer, 803 F.2d 647 (11th Cir. 1986) (constructive knowledge of mutual mistake will permit reformation of a security interest); McCannon v. Marston, 679 F.2d 13 (3d Cir. 1982) (trustee is charged with constructive knowledge that would be charged to any purchaser under state law).

439 *In re* Freeman, 72 B.R. 850 (Bankr. E.D. Va. 1987).

An exception in the Uniform Commercial Code exists for purchase money security interests perfected within ten days. Similar exceptions exist in various other state lien statutes.

440 *See, e.g., In re* Crawford, 274 B.R. 798 (B.A.P. 8th Cir. 2002) (improperly perfected security interest in annuity); *In re* Ware, 59 B.R. 549 (Bankr. N.D. Ohio 1986). Compare *In re* Wuerzberger, 284 B.R. 814 (Bankr. W.D. Va. 2002) (no amendment to mobile home certificate of title required if assignor remains as servicing agent for assignee securitization trust; court adopts "conduit" theory that assignor/servicer can provide information to those inquiring about status of lien) with *In re* Wuerzberger, 271 B.R. 778 (Bankr. W.D. Va. 2002) (assignment by mobile home lender of all its interest to securitization trust extinguished its lien).

Problems with perfection of automobile and mobile home security interests may occur when the loans are securitized.

441 *See, e.g., In re* Merritt Dredging Co., 839 F.2d 203 (4th Cir. 1998) ("rental" agreement creates avoidable unperfected security interest).

442 *See, e.g., In re* Deuel, 594 F.3d 1073 (9th Cir. 2010) (unrecorded deed of trust avoided); *In re* Biggs, 377 F.3d 515 (6th Cir. 2004) (improperly acknowledged mortgage subject to avoidance); *In re* Burns, 322 F.3d 421 (6th Cir. 2003) (improperly witnessed mortgage subject to avoidance); *In re* Kroskie, 315 F.3d 644 (6th Cir. 2003) (mortgage on permanently affixed mobile home that was recorded at registry of deeds but not properly perfected under state mobile home statute may be avoided by trustee); *In re* Bridge, 18 F.3d 195 (3d Cir. 1994) (trustee's rights as hypothetical bona fide purchaser of real estate prevailed under New Jersey law over equitable lien created when mortgage was satisfied by refinancing but new mortgage was not recorded); *In re* Ryan, 851 F.2d 502 (1st Cir. 1988); *In re* Sandy Ridge Oil Co., 807 F.2d 1332 (7th Cir. 1987); *In re* Pac. Express, Inc., 780 F.2d 1482 (9th Cir. 1986); Mortgage Elec. Registration Sys. v. Agin, 2009 WL 3834002 (D. Mass. Nov. 17, 2009) (mortgage that was not properly notarized avoided under Mass. law); Thacker v. United Companies Lending Corp., 256 B.R. 724 (W.D. Ky. 2000) (defective mortgage avoidable even though it was recorded); *In re* Check, 129 B.R. 492 (Bankr. N.D. Ohio 1991) (trustee may avoid mortgage to debtor's attorney which was improperly certified by the attorney so as to be invalid under state law); *In re* Consol. Southeastern Group Inc., 75 B.R. 102 (Bankr. N.D. Ga. 1987) (unrecorded lien for utility services). *See also In re* Robertson, 203 F.3d 855 (5th Cir. 2000) (trustee could not avoid prepetition divorce decree transfer of interest in house because judgment of divorce had been recorded in appropriate conveyance records); *In re* Seaway Express, 912 F.2d 1125 (9th Cir. 1990) (unrecorded security interest may be avoided by trustee even though failure to record could be blamed on the debtor). *But see In re* Donahue, 862 F.2d 259 (10th Cir. 1989) (unrecorded equitable lien held by debtor's wife pursuant to divorce decree could not be avoided due to unjust enrichment which would result); Nesse v. GMAC Mortg., L.L.C. (*In re* Barnes), 2012 WL 1378449 (Bankr. D. Md. Apr. 19, 2012) (trustee could not avoid transfer of entireties property when only one spouse was debtor, because bona fide purchaser from debtor alone or lien creditor of debtor alone could not reach property).

The trustee probably cannot avoid liens which were properly recorded as of the date of bankruptcy, but which subsequently lose that status under state law because no continuation statements were properly filed. *See* Gen. Elec. Credit Corp. v. Nardulli & Sons, Inc., 836 F.2d 184 (3d Cir. 1988).

443 *In re* Gomez, 388 B.R. 279, 291 (Bankr. S.D. Tex. 2008); *In re* Elam, 194 B.R. 412 (Bankr. E.D. Tex. 1996).

The "bona fide purchaser" power also allows the cutoff of other rights (in real property only), such as equities created by fraud, unperfected or constructive trusts,[444] and in most states, unrecorded deeds.[445] In such proceedings, most often, one issue is whether the trustee can be considered a bona fide purchaser or whether she must be deemed to have constructive notice.[446]

Under section 544(b) certain other transfers may also be totally avoided, if they could have been avoided, even in part, by an actually existing unsecured creditor.[447] This provision allows the trustee to make use of applicable state laws to avoid fraudulent conveyances, bulk transfers in which the notices required by Article 6 of the Uniform Commercial Code were not given, and other types of transfers avoidable under state law by existing creditors.[448]

However, in 1998 Congress enacted a restriction on the trustee's right to use state fraudulent conveyance laws, and indeed upon creditor's rights to use such laws outside of bankruptcy, to recover religious or charitable contributions of the debtor. The Religious Liberty and Charitable Donation Protection Act of 1998[449] amended section 544(b) to provide that charitable contributions[450] to qualified religious or charitable entities or organizations,[451] are protected from avoidance under section 544 and under state law.[452] As discussed below,[453] section 548(a)(2) protects from avoidance religious or charitable contributions within the two years prior to bankruptcy of up to fifteen percent of the debtor's gross income in the year they were made, or even more if consistent with past giving. Under the language of the provision, the fifteen percent limit applies to each transfer individually, even if the aggregate in a single year exceeds fifteen percent. However, at least one court has read the language to mean that if the fifteen percent limit is exceeded and there was no past giving no part of the contribution is protected.[454]

The debtor's rights to use the section 544 powers are somewhat limited by the incorporation of language from section 522(g) into section 522(h) excluding voluntary transfers. Many security interests and other transfers of property are voluntary, and those transfers will not be avoidable by the debtor even if they are avoidable by the trustee.[455]

The powers of section 544(a) can be used by the debtor to avoid various types of unperfected or improperly perfected[456] involuntary liens,[457] such as mechanics' or repairmen's liens, and tax liens,[458] if they are subordinate to judicial liens or the rights of bona fide purchasers under state law. These powers can also be used to cut off various equitable rights in real property, such as constructive trusts, if those rights were not created voluntarily by the debtor.[459]

---

444 *In re* Seaway Express, 912 F.2d 1125 (9th Cir. 1990) (claim of constructive trust beneficiary can be avoided); Belisle v. Plunkett, 877 F.2d 512 (7th Cir. 1989) (leasehold interest held by debtor in constructive trust for others can be brought into estate by trustee); *In re* Tleel, 876 F.2d 769 (9th Cir. 1989) (constructive interest in property held by debtor's partners can be avoided); *In re* Crabtree, 871 F.2d 36 (6th Cir. 1989) (deed which failed to meet state law requirements for actual trust creates avoidable constructive trust); *In re* Quality Holstein Leasing, 752 F.2d 1009 (5th Cir. 1985) (trustee's rights superior to those claimed through beneficiary of constructive trust). *But see In re* Gen. Coffee Corp., 828 F.2d 699 (11th Cir. 1987) (constructive trust not avoidable).

445 *But see In re* Hartman Paving, Inc., 745 F.2d 307 (4th Cir. 1984) (deed of trust that would be invalid against bona fide purchaser not avoidable).

446 *See, e.g., In re* Probasco, 839 F.2d 1352 (9th Cir. 1988); McCannon v. Marston, 679 F.2d 13 (3d Cir. 1982); Morris v. Kasparek (*In re* Kasparek), 426 B.R. 332 (B.A.P. 10th Cir. 2010) (bona fide purchaser of one cotenant's interest had no duty to inquire of other cotenants under Kansas law).

447 The principle, adopted in the Code, that if a transfer could be avoided by any creditor it could be avoided by the trustee *in toto*, regardless of how small the actual creditor's claim, is known as the rule of Moore v. Bay, 284 U.S. 4, 52 S. Ct. 3, 76 L. Ed. 133 (1931), the Supreme Court case which first announced it. *See In re* Marlar, 267 F.3d 749 (8th Cir. 2001) (trustee could bring action based on existence of unsecured creditor with right to bring action even if another creditor had unsuccessfully brought fraudulent transfer action in state court).

448 *See, e.g., In re* Craig, 144 F.3d 587 (8th Cir. 1998) (debtor made indirect fraudulent transfer under North Dakota law when he directed that loan funds owed to him be used to pay for residence in wife's name); *In re* Levine, 134 F.3d 1046 (11th Cir. 1998) (transfer of assets into exempt annuities was fraudulent transfer under Florida law). *See also* Nino v. Moyer, 437 B.R. 230, 238 (W.D. Mich. 2009) (when debtor transferred entireties interest to wife, who then quitclaimed it back to debtor, trustee could not avoid first transfer because Uniform Fraudulent Transfers Act did not apply to transfers of property that was exempt from creditors); Sullivan v. Welsh (*In re* Lumbar), 446 B.R. 316 (Bankr. D. Minn. 2011) (transfer of exempt property not avoidable under § 544), *rev'd on other grounds*, 457 B.R. 748 (B.A.P. 8th Cir. 2011) (same principle does not apply to section 548 avoiding power under federal law). *But see In re* Popkin & Stern, 223 F.3d 764 (8th Cir. 2000) (disclaimer of interest in estate was not avoidable under state law so transfer could not be avoided under section 544(b)).

449 Pub. L. No. 105-183, 112 Stat. 517 (1998) (applicable to cases pending on or after June 19, 1998).

450 The "charitable contribution" must meet the definition in section 548(d)(3), as amended by the same Act, and thus must consist of either a financial instrument or cash.

451 Section 544(b) incorporates section 548(a)(2), which incorporates the definition of "qualified religious or charitable entity or organization" in section 548(d)(4), requiring the recipient of the contribution to be an entity described in section 170(c)(1) or 170(c)(2) of the Internal Revenue Code.

452 11 U.S.C. § 544(b)(2).
The law overrules cases such as *In re* Newman, 203 B.R. 468 (D. Kan. 1996) and *In re* Gomes, 219 B.R. 286 (Bankr. D. Or. 1998).

453 *See* § 10.4.2.6.5, *infra*.

454 *In re* Zohdi, 234 B.R. 371 (Bankr. M.D. La. 1999).

455 *But see* § 10.4.2.6, *supra*.

456 *See* McLean v. City of Philadelphia, 891 F.2d 474 (3d Cir. 1989) (city's liens for utility service found avoidable based on failure to properly comply with state lien indexing law); *In re* Janmar, 6 Bankr. Ct. Dec. (LRP) 385, 1 Collier Bankr. Cas. 2d (MB) 1051 (Bankr. N.D. Ga. 1980).

457 *In re* Fed'n of Puerto Rican Organizations, 155 B.R. 44 (E.D.N.Y. 1993).

458 United States v. Dewes, 315 B.R. 834 (N.D. Ind. 2004) (tax lien recorded outside chain of title).

459 Here again the meaning of "voluntary" in section 522(g) is unclear. Would a constructive trust created by the debtor's voluntary acts be

The section 544(b) power will likely be used most by debtors to attempt avoidance through incorporation of state fraudulent transfer laws.[460] In some states this law is based on the Uniform Fraudulent Conveyance Act (UFCA). At least forty-three others and the District of Columbia have adopted the Uniform Fraudulent Transfer Act (UFTA). Still other states have varying case law derived from the old English Statute of 13 Elizabeth.

A possible difficulty in using the UFCA is the question of whether it is applicable at all to involuntary transfers. This issue was resolved in the Uniform Fraudulent Transfer Act, which is clearly applicable to involuntary transfers. However, a specific provision was included in the UFTA to except "a regularly conducted, noncollusive foreclosure sale or execution of a power of sale . . . upon default under a mortgage, deed of trust or security agreement."[461] If avoidance of involuntary transfers is possible, then a wide variety of execution sales and defectively conducted foreclosures could be invalidated by debtors' use of this section. In each case, state law is the determining factor. This issue is further addressed below in the discussion of the section 548 avoiding powers for transfers deemed fraudulent under federal law.

10.4.2.6.3 Statutory liens—§ 545

Under section 545, certain statutory liens may be avoided. These include any lien that first becomes effective upon insolvency or insolvency proceedings of various types, liens which could be defeated by a bona fide purchaser on the date of commencement of the case, liens for rent and liens of distress for rent. Such liens may be avoided even if they have already been enforced by a sale before the filing of the bankruptcy case.[462]

Debtors are likely to use section 545 in states where landlords' liens and distress for rent are common.[463] It can also be used in cases involving mechanics' liens,[464] innkeepers' liens, and other statutory liens, to the extent those liens are subject to the rights of bona fide purchasers under state law.[465] However, it should be noted that statutory liens may lose their character as statutory liens in some states once they are enforced, and thus become immunized to attack.[466] On the other hand, if the lien becomes effective only upon recordation, it may not be a statutory lien at all, but rather a judicial lien,[467] because it does not arise solely by force of a statute.[468]

Among the liens probably not avoidable under this section are tax liens. A 2005 amendment to section 545(2) excluded from the "bona fide purchaser" test a purchaser described in section 6323(a) of the Internal Revenue Code, which provides that unfiled or improperly filed tax liens are not valid against a purchaser or judgment lien creditor. State taxing authorities with similar provisions are also protected. This amendment resolved a prior split in the case law.[469] Another 2005 amendment specifically protects a warehouseman's lien for storage and handling of goods.[470]

---

a voluntary transfer if the debtor did not realize those acts would create a constructive trust?

460 *See, e.g.*, Havee v. Belk, 775 F.2d 1209 (4th Cir. 1985). *Cf.* Evans v. Wolinsky, 347 B.R. 9 (D. Vt. 2006) (no fraudulent transfer under Vermont law when property that was transferred was entireties property not subject to claims of any creditor).

461 Section 3 of the Uniform Act creates a presumption that the value given for a transfer of this type is reasonably equivalent value. It may nevertheless be possible under the UFTA to challenge a foreclosure sale as not regularly conducted or non-collusive. *Cf. In re* Knapper, 407 F.3d 573 (3d Cir. 2005) (section 544(b) could not be used to avoid a foreclosure sale when there was a defect in service of the foreclosure complaint).

462 H.R. Rep. No. 95-595, at 371 (1977).

463 *See, e.g., In re* Wedemeier, 237 F.3d 938 (8th Cir. 2001) (landlord's lien avoided).

464 *See In re* English, 112 B.R. 20 (Bankr. W.D. Ky. 1989) (mechanic's lien avoided when debtor had personal knowledge of intent to file lien but, in capacity of bona fide purchaser for value, could avoid lien which had not yet been perfected at time of filing); *In re* Saberman, 3 B.R. 316 (Bankr. N.D. Ill. 1980) (mechanic's lien avoided by debtor because under state law it would have been invalid against bona fide purchaser).

465 *In re* Nicolescu, 311 B.R. 27 (Bankr. D. Conn. 2004) (Medicaid lien on personal injury proceeds was avoidable under section 545); *In re* U.S. Leather, Inc., 271 B.R. 306 (Bankr. E.D. Wis. 2001) (water and sewer lien not perfected as of petition date). *See In re* Am. W. Airlines, 217 F.3d 1161 (9th Cir. 2000) (unperfected city tax lien was avoidable because it was not enforceable against bona fide purchaser on petition date); *In re* Loretto Winery, Ltd., 898 F.2d 715 (9th Cir. 1990) (trustee could not, as hypothetical bona fide purchaser, avoid statutory California producer's lien on partially processed grapes, because lien was good against bona fide purchasers).

466 *See In re* Mascenik, 6 Bankr. Ct. Dec. (LRP) 763 (D. Colo. 1980) (landlord's lien already enforced by sale could not be avoided).

467 *In re* Barbe, 24 B.R. 739 (Bankr. M.D. Pa. 1982), *limited by* Graffen v. Philadelphia, 984 F.2d 91, 97 (3d Cir. 1992).

468 See 11 U.S.C. § 101(53) defining "statutory lien."

469 *See In re* Berg, 121 F.3d 535 (9th Cir. 1997) (trustee not entitled to bona fide purchaser status and could not avoid tax lien); *In re* Janssen, 213 B.R. 558 (B.A.P. 8th Cir. 1997) (same); *In re* Walter, 45 F.3d 1023 (6th Cir. 1995) (trustee not entitled to protections that Internal Revenue Code § 6323(b)(2) gives to purchaser for full consideration); *In re* Hudgins, 967 F.2d 973 (4th Cir. 1992) (tax lien filed against Michael Hudgins, Inc. avoidable with respect to debtor's non-business assets, even though the corporation had ceased to exist prior to filing of the lien, because notice of lien did not put bona fide purchasers on notice that debtor's personal assets were liened); *In re* Stanford, 826 F.2d 353 (5th Cir. 1987) (state tax lien not avoidable when it was good against bona fide purchaser under state law); *In re* Sierer, 121 B.R. 884 (Bankr. N.D. Fla. 1990) (permitting avoidance of perfected federal tax liens on automobiles, money market account, household goods, stocks, IRA, tools, promissory note and cash, but not as to insurance), *aff'd sub nom.* United States v. Sierer, 139 B.R. 752 (N.D. Fla. 1991).

Several other courts had held that a debtor could not avoid a properly filed tax lien due to the operation of section 522(c)(2)(B), which according to those courts prohibits exemptions from impairing the effect of a tax lien. *In re* Straight, 207 B.R. 217 (B.A.P. 10th Cir. 1997); *In re* Mattis, 93 B.R. 68 (Bankr. E.D. Pa. 1988); *In re* Perry, 90 B.R. 565 (Bankr. S.D. Fla. 1988). *Cf. In re* Suarez, 182 B.R. 916 (Bankr. S.D. Fla. 1995) (section 522(c)(2) not applicable because notice of tax lien was not properly filed).

470 11 U.S.C. § 546(i).

10.4.2.6.4 Preferences—§ 547

10.4.2.6.4.1 In general

By far the most frequently used trustee avoiding power is the power to avoid preferences, codified in 11 U.S.C. § 547. With certain exceptions, set forth in section 547(c) and (i), the trustee may avoid any transfer of property of the debtor:

- To or for the benefit of a creditor;[471]
- For or on account of an antecedent debt owed by the debtor before such transfer was made;[472]
- Made while the debtor was insolvent;[473]
- Made
  (A) on or within ninety days before the date of filing of the petition[474] or
  (B) between ninety days and one year before the date of filing of the petition, if such creditor, at the time of such transfer was an insider;[475] and
- That enables such creditor to receive more than such creditor would receive if
  (A) the case were a case under chapter 7 of the Code;
  (B) the transfer had not been made; and
  (C) such creditor received payment of such debt to the extent provided by the provisions of the Code.[476]

---

[471] The benefit may be indirect, as when a guarantor benefits from the payment of a debt of the debtor which she guaranteed. Because the guarantor would normally have a contingent claim against the debtor for contribution or indemnification in the event the guarantor ultimately paid the debt, the guarantor is a creditor who benefits from the transfer and has therefore received a preference. See In re Robinson Bros. Drilling, 877 F.2d 32 (10th Cir. 1989) (payments to non-insider creditors made at arm's length are preferences subject to one-year limitations period because the payments ultimately benefit insider guarantors); Levit v. Ingersoll Rand Fin. Corp., 874 F.2d 1186 (7th Cir. 1989) (same); In re C-L Cartage Co., 899 F.2d 1490 (6th Cir. 1990) (same). See also In re Wesley Indus., 30 F.3d 1438 (11th Cir. 1994) (transfer of cash collateral that benefited insider within one year before petition could be a preference); § 10.4.2.6.4.1, infra (and cases cited therein).

A criminal restitution payment can be avoided as a preference even though it benefits society as well as the victim-creditor. State Compensation Ins. Fund v. Zamora (In re Silverman), 616 F.3d 1001 (9th Cir. 2010).

[472] The transfer of a security interest in connection with a car loan, for example, is not on account of an antecedent debt. In re McFarland, 131 B.R. 627 (E.D. Tenn. 1990), aff'd, 943 F.2d 52 (6th Cir. 1991).

[473] "Insolvent" is defined in 11 U.S.C. § 101(32) in a way that would include virtually all low-income debtors. Under that definition a debtor is solvent only if his or her assets exclusive of exempt property exceed his or her obligations. In re Babiker, 180 B.R. 458 (Bankr. E.D. Va. 1995). See also In re Taxman Clothing Co., 905 F.2d 166 (7th Cir. 1990) (costs of sale must be deducted in computing debtor's assets); In re Koubourlis, 869 F.2d 1319 (9th Cir. 1989) (creditor must present evidence to rebut presumption of insolvency and cannot simply question debtor's accounting methods); Porter v. Yukon Nat'l Bank, 866 F.2d 355 (10th Cir. 1989) (trustee need not present expert evidence concerning insolvency); In re Xonics Photochemical, Inc., 841 F.2d 198 (7th Cir. 1988) (contingent asset or liability must be reduced to its present or expected value for purposes of determining debtor's insolvency).

Under 11 U.S.C. § 547(f) there is a rebuttable presumption that the debtor was insolvent during the ninety days prior to filing a case. Once the presumption is rebutted, the burden of persuasion may shift back to the debtor or trustee. Clay v. Traders Bank of Kan. City, 708 F.2d 1347 (8th Cir. 1983).

[474] The ninety-day period is calculated by counting backward from the petition filing date. In re Nelson Co., 959 F.2d 1260 (3d Cir. 1992). Conversion from one chapter to another does not start the running of a new preference period. Vogel v. Russell Transfer, Inc., 852 F.2d 797 (4th Cir. 1988). The period is not extended just because the final day for filing falls on a weekend or holiday. In re Greene, 223 F.3d 1064 (9th Cir. 2000); In re Butler, 3 B.R. 182 (Bankr. E.D. Tenn.

1980). See also Decatur Contracting v. Belin, Belin & Naddeo, 898 F.2d 339 (3d Cir. 1990).

The Code provides that a transfer is perfected only when a bona fide purchaser from the debtor of real property or a judicial lien creditor on a simple contract for personal property or fixtures cannot acquire an interest superior to the trustee. 11 U.S.C. § 547(e). Thus, a transfer of a security interest normally occurs only when it has been perfected. In re Nelson Co., 959 F.2d 1260 (3d Cir. 1992) (transfer of judicial lien occurs when judgment is filed and docketed in county where debtor owns property). But a belated perfection of a security interest may be deemed under state law to relate back to the date it was granted. In re Hesser, 984 F.2d 345 (10th Cir. 1993). See also § 10.4.2.6.4.2, infra.

For purposes of this section, a transfer made by check is deemed made when the check is honored. Barnhill v. Johnson, 503 U.S. 393, 112 S. Ct. 1386, 119 L. Ed. 2d 519 (1992).

[475] "Insider" is defined at section 101(31) to include relatives of the debtor. "Relative" is defined at section 101(45). See In re Strickland, 230 B.R. 276 (Bankr. E.D. Va. 1999) (boyfriend of debtor's mother not an insider).

Many of the cases involving insiders arise from payments on debts guaranteed by insiders. See In re Suffola, Inc., 2 F.3d 977 (9th Cir. 1993) (payment to outside creditor on debt guaranteed by insider was a payment for the benefit of the insider); In re Robinson Bros. Drilling, 877 F.2d 32 (10th Cir. 1989) (payments to non-insider creditors may be avoided as preferential going back one year from date of bankruptcy because debtor's insiders obtained release by virtue of the payments); Levit v. Ingersoll Rand Fin. Corp., 874 F.2d 1186 (7th Cir. 1989) (payments to non-insider creditors may be avoided if made during one year insider preference period if they benefited insiders who guaranteed the debts being paid). See also In re Westex Foods, Inc., 950 F.2d 1187 (5th Cir. 1992) (transfers by debtor garnishee to non-insider creditor in satisfaction of judgment against garnishee's president avoided because they benefited president, who was insider); In re C-L Cartage Co., 899 F.2d 1490 (6th Cir. 1990) (payments made within year before filing to bank in satisfaction of obligation to debtor's president and president's mother were avoidable).

The results, but not the reasoning, of many of these cases were overruled by amendments creating 11 U.S.C. §§ 547(i) and 550(c), which prohibit avoidance of a transfer as to a non-insider or recovery of money or property transferred through insider preferences made more than ninety days before the petition from anyone other than the insider creditor who was preferred. However, this amendment does not prevent avoidance or recovery from a non-insider when an insider was preferred during the ninety days before the filing of the petition.

[476] The date on which the bankruptcy petition is filed rather than the date on which the turnover proceeding is filed is probably the correct date for constructing a hypothetical chapter 7 case to determine how much the creditor would receive. In re Tenna Corp., 801 F.2d 819 (6th Cir. 1986).

For the purpose of creating a hypothetical distribution, payments which the debtor has voluntarily agreed to make pursuant to a reaffirmation agreement are not included. In re Finn, 86 B.R. 902

The basic purpose of this section is to promote equality among creditors by invalidating prebankruptcy seizures or transfers of the debtor's property that would give particular creditors more than they would receive in a chapter 7 liquidation. It also serves to deter creditors from engaging in a race to get at the debtor's property before bankruptcy, because they know that if they do obtain the property and perhaps hasten a bankruptcy, they will only have to surrender it to a trustee exercising the power to avoid preferences.[477]

The first issue in preference analysis is, of course, whether property of the debtor has been transferred at all. In some cases the debtor may merely be transferring property held in trust for others.[478] But if a party owing a debt to the debtor, as part of a transaction involving the debtor, pays that debt to a creditor of the debtor at the debtor's request, there has been a transfer of the debtor's property.[479] And if a debtor borrows money from one creditor and chooses to use it to pay another, the debtor has transferred her own property. Thus, several appellate courts have held that credit card balance transfers can be avoided because the debtor exercised dominion over the funds by choosing which creditor to repay.[480]

In addition, all of the elements listed above must be present for a transfer to be considered a preference. Thus, if a validly secured creditor, with a security interest not otherwise avoidable, repossesses property worth less than the amount of the secured debt, no preference exists as that creditor would have had a right to that property or its full value in a liquidation.[481] But if an unsecured or partially secured creditor receives a payment on the debt within ninety days, that payment probably is a preference, as it will presumably be applied to that portion of the debt which is unsecured, and will allow the secured creditor to receive more than the total it would otherwise receive in a liquidation.[482] If property is transferred in exchange for a new debt, rather than an antecedent debt, no preference exists, nor does one exist if the property the creditor receives belongs to someone other than the debtor, such as a co-maker, including money that passes through the debtor's hands but is "earmarked" solely for payment to the creditor.[483] Of course, a

---

(Bankr. E.D. Mich. 1988), *rev'd and remanded on other grounds*, 909 F.2d 903 (6th Cir. 1990).

The fact that the debtor might have been able to exempt the property which was transferred is not a defense to a trustee's preference action. *In re* Noblit, 72 F.3d 757 (9th Cir. 1995). *See also* § 10.4.2.5, *supra*.

477 H.R. Rep. No. 95-595, at 177, 178 (1977).
478 Begier v. Internal Revenue Serv., 496 U.S. 53, 110 S. Ct. 2258, 110 L. Ed. 2d 246 (1990) (excise taxes which are supposed to be held by businesses in trust for the IRS are trust property of the IRS regardless of whether they are held in the debtor's general account; therefore payments of those funds to the IRS cannot be preferential even if made within ninety days of the debtor's bankruptcy); *In re* Reale, 584 F.3d 27 (1st Cir. 2009) (debtor had sufficient control over gift funds that they were considered debtor's property transferred to creditor). *See In re* Unicom Computer Corp., 13 F.3d 321 (9th Cir. 1994) (transfer of funds that were held in constructive trust was not a preference); *In re* Cal. Trade Technical Schools, Inc., 923 F.2d 641 (9th Cir. 1991) (debtor trade school's repayments of federal student assistance program monies effectively became trust funds upon their deposit and thus were not property of the debtor); *In re* Royal Golf Prods. Corp., 908 F.2d 911 (6th Cir. 1990) (payment to creditor by debtor's shareholder on behalf of debtor was a preferential transfer when debtor granted security interest to shareholder in exchange for payment, to the extent of the value of the security interest which depleted the estate); First Fed. of Mich. v. Barrow, 878 F.2d 912 (6th Cir. 1989) (unless creditor can trace funds held by debtor in commingled account, creditor cannot assert that payment was return of funds held in trust); *In re* Wey, 854 F.2d 196 (7th Cir. 1988) (no transfer made when debtor forfeits a down payment made in connection with a real estate contract); *In re* Bullion Reserve of N. Am., 836 F.2d 1214 (9th Cir. 1988) (payments by debtor to investor in "Ponzi" scheme were not a return of money held by debtor in trust; therefore a potentially avoidable transfer did occur).
479 *In re* Interior Wood Prods., 986 F.2d 228 (8th Cir. 1993) (payment to unsecured creditor by purchaser of debtor's assets was a preference); *In re* Food Catering & Hous., Inc., 971 F.2d 396 (9th Cir. 1992) (same). *See also In re* Kemp Pac. Fisheries, 16 F.3d 313 (9th Cir. 1994) (payment by check from debtor's account, which bank honored despite the fact that account was temporarily overdrawn, was a transfer of debtor's property).

480 *In re* Egidi, 571 F.3d 1156 (11th Cir. 2009); *In re* Dilworth, 560 F.3d 562 (6th Cir. 2009); *In re* Marshall, 550 F.3d 1251, 1255 (10th Cir. 2008).
481 *See In re* Edl, 207 B.R. 611 (Bankr. W.D. Wis. 1997) (payment of fees to attorney was not a preference because attorney had equitable lien on divorce proceeds under state law).

However, a security interest does not insulate a payment from being a preference if the security interest is in property owned by an entity other than the debtor, as that security interest would not provide better treatment for the creditor in the distribution of the *debtor's* assets. *In re* Virginia-Carolina Fin. Corp., 954 F.2d 193 (4th Cir. 1992).

482 *In re* Clark Pipe & Supply Co., 893 F.2d 693 (5th Cir. 1990); Porter v. Yukon Nat'l Bank, 866 F.2d 355 (10th Cir. 1989) (payment to undersecured creditor constitutes preference when unsecured claims would not be paid in full in liquidation); Drabkin v. A.I. Credit Corp., 800 F.2d 1153 (D.C. Cir. 1986); *In re* Lewis W. Shurtleff, Inc., 778 F.2d 1416 (9th Cir. 1985); *In re* McCormick, 5 B.R. 726 (Bankr. N.D. Ohio 1980).
483 *In re* Super. Stamp & Coin Co., 223 F.3d 1004 (9th Cir. 2000) (earmarking doctrine applied to prevent avoidance of transfer because transfer was funded by loans specifically designated for payment to transferee); *In re* Heitkamp, 137 F.3d 1087, 1088, 1089 (8th Cir. 1998); *In re* Ward, 230 B.R. 115 (B.A.P. 8th Cir. 1999) (earmarking doctrine protects lien obtained by creditor that refinanced debtor's auto loan because creditor's advance could be used only to pay auto loan). *But see In re* Egidi, 571 F.3d 1156 (11th Cir. 2009) (earmarking doctrine not applicable to credit card balance transfer); *In re* Dilworth, 560 F.3d 562 (6th Cir. 2009) (same); *In re* Marshall, 550 F.3d 1251, 1255 (10th Cir. 2008) (same); *In re* Lee, 530 F.3d 458 (6th Cir. 2008) (earmarking doctrine did not protect mortgage not recorded within specific time allowed by section 547(e)(2)); *In re* Lazarus, 478 F.3d 12 (1st Cir. 2007) (earmarking doctrine could not protect mortgage granted in refinancing transaction that was not promptly recorded); *In re* Bohlen Enters., Ltd., 859 F.2d 561 (8th Cir. 1988) (for earmarking doctrine to apply to funds lent to debtor to pay off an antecedent debt and thereby save payment from preference avoidance, debtor must have no control over the use of the non-debtor transferor's funds); *In re* Hartley, 825 F.2d 1067 (6th Cir. 1987) (debtor's transfer of security interest to third party who paid debtor's antecedent debt was a preference). *Cf. In re* Hurt, 202 B.R. 611 (Bankr. C.D. Ill. 1996) (transfers to credit card grantors made by payments with balance transfer checks issued

transfer outside the specified time periods cannot be a preference; section 547(e) sets forth rules for determining the date a transfer is deemed to have occurred.[484]

10.4.2.6.4.2 Exceptions to preference avoiding power

The major exceptions to the preference avoiding power are listed in section 547(c).[485] The first is for exchanges that are intended to be and are in fact "substantially contemporaneous" exchanges for new value, for example, cash purchases, purchases paid for immediately by check, or security interests securing new value.[486] The Code does not define "substantially contemporaneous."[487] Also excepted are transfers made prior to the debtor's receipt of new value from the creditor, as long as the creditor obtained no other non-avoidable security for the new value.[488]

Similarly, payments on debts incurred in the ordinary course of business or financial affairs of the debtor and transferee are excepted.[489] This exception includes most payments for current

---

by new credit card grantor not protected by earmarking doctrine when funds made available by new creditor were not designated for particular specified creditors).

One court has also held that no preference exists to the extent a creditor is paid more than the amount of its claim. *In re* Barge, 875 F.2d 508 (5th Cir. 1989). Presumably, however, a fraudulent transfer has occurred. *Id. See* § 10.4.2.6.5, *infra*.

484 Wells Fargo Home Mortg., Inc. v. Lindquist, 592 F.3d 838 (8th Cir. 2010) (under § 547(e)(2)(C), unrecorded mortgage deemed recorded immediately before petition); *In re* Hedrick, 524 F.3d 1175 (11th Cir. 2008) (transfer deemed to occur on date of refinancing transaction, rather than date of perfection, by virtue of section 547(e)(2)).

485 The creditor has the burden of establishing that it falls within one of the defenses. *In re* Chase & Sanborn Corp., 904 F.2d 588 (11th Cir. 1990).

486 11 U.S.C. § 547(c)(1). *See In re* Elec. Metal Prods., Inc., 916 F.2d 1502 (10th Cir. 1990) (attorney's promise to continue working on litigation did not constitute new value); *In re* Kumar Bavishi & Assocs., 906 F.2d 942 (3d Cir. 1990) (prepetition payments of preexisting debts owed by debtor partnership to limited partners in exchange for partners personally guaranteeing loan to debtor partnership, which partnership was unable to obtain without guarantees, constituted transfers for new value); *In re* Chase & Sanborn Corp., 904 F.2d 588 (11th Cir. 1990) (corporate debtor's prepetition payments to individual controlling another corporation for which the debtor corporation had guaranteed a debt constituted payments "for or on account of antecedent debt" despite contingent nature of guarantee); *In re* Spada, 903 F.2d 971 (3d Cir. 1990) (when three loans were consolidated into a new loan, a partial preference was granted to the extent that amount received by creditor was in excess of new value surrendered to debtor by creditor); *In re* Nucorp Energy, Inc., 902 F.2d 729 (9th Cir. 1990) (transfer of money from debtor to creditor in exchange for release of lien was not for new value when property subject to lien was valueless at time of transfer); *In re* Meredith Manor, Inc., 902 F.2d 257 (4th Cir. 1990) (advances and repayments pursuant to open credit line resulted in preferences to extent of difference between total preferences and total advances, provided that each advance could only offset transfers from the debtor prior to that particular advance); Lewis v. Diethorn, 893 F.2d 648 (3d Cir. 1990) (payment to settle case and thereby remove *lis pendens* constitutes exchange for new value); *In re* Allen, 888 F.2d 1299 (10th Cir. 1989) (transfer of interest under escrow agreement for money paid by creditor is exchange for new value); E.R. Fegert, Inc. v. Seaboard Sur. Co., 887 F.2d 955 (9th Cir. 1989) (payment to third parties which reduces surety's equitable lien is exchange for new value); *In re* Jet Fla. Sys., Inc., 861 F.2d 1555 (11th Cir. 1988) (restoration of debtor's prior status through forbearance of creditor does not constitute new value for payment); *In re* Bellanca Aircraft Corp., 850 F.2d 1275 (8th Cir. 1988) (payment made by creditor to other creditors of the debtor can constitute new value for debtor's payments); *In re* Pitman, 843 F.2d 235 (6th Cir. 1988) (transfer of mortgage is exchange for new value when it is made pursuant to an executory contract for sale of property and the debtor receives a deed at the time of transfer); *In re* Energy Co-op, Inc., 832 F.2d 997 (7th Cir. 1987) (release of existing liability not "new value"); *In re* Calvert, 227 B.R. 153 (B.A.P. 8th Cir. 1998) (release of security interest obtained when debt was first incurred did not provide new value).

487 *See In re* Hedrick, 524 F.3d 1175 (11th Cir. 2008) (recording of mortgage within eight days was substantially contemporaneous); *In re* JWJ Contracting Co., 371 F.3d 1079 (9th Cir. 2004) (lien release granted when NSF check was given to creditor was not substantially contemporaneous with later cashier's check given to replace NSF check); *In re* Dorholt, Inc., 224 F.3d 871 (8th Cir. 2000) (transfer of security interest can be substantially contemporaneous even if security interest not perfected within time period allowed for relation back under section 547(e)(2)); *In re* Lewellyn & Co. Inc., 929 F.2d 424 (8th Cir. 1991) (new value can be given before or after the transfer; test is whether exchange is "substantially" contemporaneous); *In re* Arnett, 731 F.2d 358 (6th Cir. 1984) (thirty-three days later not substantially contemporaneous); *In re* Standard Food Servs., Inc., 723 F.2d 820 (11th Cir. 1984) (check replacing earlier contemporaneous bounced check not substantially contemporaneous).

The court may look to the intent of the parties in order to determine whether an "exchange" has really taken place. *See In re* Prescott, 805 F.2d 719 (7th Cir. 1986) (bank's taking possession of the debtor's certificate of deposit held not to be an exchange of value when bank simultaneously allowed overdrafts on debtor's other accounts).

Also at issue may be the actual value of the property exchanged, as it bears on the issue of whether a quid pro quo was really intended. But at least one court of appeals has held that a valuation is not required. *In re* George Rodman, Inc., 792 F.2d 125 (10th Cir. 1986).

488 11 U.S.C. § 547(c)(4). *See generally In re* JKJ Chevrolet, Inc., 412 F.3d 545 (4th Cir. 2005) (creditor must show that new value was not repaid or was repaid by an avoidable transfer); S. Technical College, Inc. v. Hood, 89 F.3d 1381 (8th Cir. 1996) (debtor's use of leased properties after payment to lessor constituted new value to extent lender did not have security therefor); *In re* Kroh Bros. Dev. Co., 930 F.2d 648 (8th Cir. 1991) (creditor may be able to assert "new value" defense even though it had received consideration for the new value from a third party); *In re* N.Y. City Shoes, Inc., 880 F.2d 679 (3d Cir. 1989).

To assert this defense, the new value for each transfer must be given after the transfer that the debtor seeks to avoid. *In re* Toyota of Jefferson, Inc., 14 F.3d 1088 (5th Cir. 1994). *See also In re* Tenn. Chem. Co., 112 F.3d 234 (6th Cir. 1997) (date of receipt of check, rather than date check was honored, used to determine timing of new value).

489 11 U.S.C. § 547(c)(2). *See, e.g.*, Kleven v. Household Bank, 334 F.3d 638 (7th Cir. 2003) (payments on tax refund anticipation loans were in ordinary course of business, even if debtors had never had such a loan before); *In re* Jan Weilert, RV, Inc., 315 F.3d 1192 (9th Cir. 2003) ("ordinary business terms" encompasses wide range of practices of similarly situated debtors); Fid. Sav. & Inv. Co. v. New Hope Baptist, 880 F.2d 1172 (10th Cir. 1989) (payments made by

utility services, goods bought with payment due in thirty days, and most charge accounts. Section 547(c)(2) applies equally to long-term and short-term debt.[490] To be within the ordinary course of business, the debt must have been incurred in the ordinary course of the debtor's business and financial affairs and the payments must either (1) be ordinary in relation to other business dealings between creditor and debtor, made according to ordinary business terms, or (2) be ordinary in relation to standards in the relevant industry.[491] Unusually late payments are ordinarily not excepted, however.[492] Payments made pursuant to settlement agreements have been found to be outside the ordinary course of a debtor's business.[493] Nor may a payment following a special or unusual request by a creditor for payment be considered to be within the ordinary course of business.[494] It is not clear whether a major loan of a type incurred only once or a few times in a debtor's lifetime would be considered to be in the ordinary course of the debtor's financial affairs.[495] The "ordinary course" language may also open the door to challenges of fraudulent or unfair transactions in which security interests are taken in the debtor's property, or loans and refinancings prompted by extraordinary factors in the debtor's situation.

Certain liens created within ninety days before filing of the petition are also protected from preference avoidance. These are:

- Security interests that secure new value given by the secured party to enable the debtor to acquire property and used by the debtor for that purpose, if perfected within thirty days after the debtor receives possession of the property;[496]
- Security interests in inventory or receivables, to some extent;[497] and
- Statutory liens that are not avoidable under section 545.[498]

---

lender to redeem investor's savings certificates are within ordinary course of business); *In re* Fulghum Constr. Corp., 872 F.2d 739 (6th Cir. 1989) (repayment of advances to debtor's sole shareholder, though irregular, were consistent with ordinary course of dealing between parties); *In re* Smith-Douglass, Inc., 842 F.2d 729 (4th Cir. 1988) (payment of interest as it comes due is in the ordinary course of business); *In re* Colonial Discount Corp., 807 F.2d 594 (7th Cir. 1987) (debtor's transaction typical of affairs over past twenty years); *In re* Powerine Oil Co., 126 B.R. 790 (B.A.P. 9th Cir. 1991) (payments made outside time for payment specified in the contract are not within the ordinary course of business); *In re* Loretto Winery, Ltd., 107 B.R. 707 (B.A.P. 9th Cir. 1989) (determination of ordinary course requires objective evaluation of similarly situated businesses). *See generally In re* Molded Acoustical Prods., 18 F.3d 217 (3d Cir. 1994) (discussion of "ordinary business terms").

490 Union Bank v. Wolas, 502 U.S. 151, 112 S. Ct. 527, 116 L. Ed. 2d 514 (1991).

491 Prior to the 2005 amendments these requirements all had to be met, as opposed to meeting one of the two alternatives, either of which is sufficient, under the amended 11 U.S.C. § 547(c)(2). *In re* A.W. & Assocs., 136 F.3d 1439 (11th Cir. 1998) (court must consider industry standards to determine whether payment was in ordinary course of business); *In re* Fred Hawes Org., 957 F.2d 239 (6th Cir. 1992).

As with other exceptions in section 547(c), it is the transferee's burden to present evidence supporting the exception, such as evidence of normal industry practices. *See In re* Roblin Indus., 78 F.3d 30 (2d Cir. 1996).

492 *In re* Gateway Pac. Corp., 153 F.3d 915 (8th Cir. 1998); *In re* Xonics Imaging Inc., 837 F.2d 763 (7th Cir. 1988) (late payment of rent after grace period not in ordinary course of business); *In re* Ewald Bros., Inc., 45 B.R. 52 (Bankr. D. Minn. 1984).

Late payments may sometimes be considered within the ordinary course of business if they are consistent with the pattern of prior payments and within the range of ordinary practices of similar firms. *In re* Tolona Pizza Prods. Corp., 3 F.3d 1029 (9th Cir. 1993); *In re* Yurika Foods Corp., 888 F.2d 42 (6th Cir. 1989) (evidence that payments are commonly made late both by particular debtor and by others in the industry supports conclusion that such payments are in ordinary course of business).

493 *In re* Richardson, 94 B.R. 56 (Bankr. E.D. Pa. 1988) (public housing tenants' payment made pursuant to settlement of eviction action found to be an avoidable preference).

494 *See, e.g., In re* Meredith Hoffman Partners, 12 F.3d 1549 (10th Cir. 1993) (escrow arrangement under which creditor received payments was not a normal financing relationship); *In re* J.P. Fyfe, Inc., 891 F.2d 66 (3d Cir. 1989) (payment made pursuant to special arrangement reached after creditor learned of debtor's financial problems not within ordinary course of business); *In re* Seawinds, Ltd., 888 F.2d 640 (9th Cir. 1989) (payments made under creditor pressure not within ordinary course); *In re* Craig Oil Co., 785 F.2d 1563 (11th Cir. 1986) (request "for a show of good faith" when debtor is in difficult financial straits takes a payment out of the ordinary course of business exception).

495 *See In re* Finn, 86 B.R. 902 (Bankr. E.D. Mich. 1988) (long-term loan is not within the debtor's ordinary course of business), *rev'd* 909 F.2d 903 (6th Cir. 1990) (incurring long-term consumer debt may be in ordinary course of debtor's affairs, depending upon the facts of the case). *See also* Union Bank v. Wolas, 502 U.S. 151, 112 S. Ct. 527, 116 L. Ed. 2d 514 (1991) (section 547(c)(2) applies to long-term debt); *In re* Bishop, Baldwin, Rewald, Dillingham & Wong, 819 F.2d 214 (9th Cir. 1987) (payment as part of a Ponzi scheme not made in ordinary course of business).

496 11 U.S.C. § 547(c)(3); Fid. Fin. Servs. Inc. v. Fink, 522 U.S. 211, 118 S. Ct. 651, 139 L. Ed. 2d 571 (1998) (time period in Code takes precedence over longer perfection period in state law).

Absent a state statutory remedy, delay in perfection caused by government bureaucratic delays does not extend the permitted time for perfection. McCarthy v. BMW Bank of N. Am., 509 F.3d 528 (D.C. Cir. 2007).

The time period for perfection was changed from ten days to twenty days by the 1994 amendments to the Code, and changed again from twenty days to thirty days by the 2005 amendments. *See In re* Davis, 734 F.2d 604 (11th Cir. 1984); *In re* Arnett, 731 F.2d 358 (6th Cir. 1984).

Nor can transfers outside the section 547(c)(3) time period be protected under the "contemporaneous exchange exception." *In re* Holder, 892 F.2d 29 (4th Cir. 1989); *In re* Tressler, 771 F.2d 791 (3d Cir. 1985) (agreeing that transfer perfected after time period is not protected by this provision or the "contemporaneous exchange" exception); *In re* Vance, 721 F.2d 259 (9th Cir. 1983). *But see In re* Dorholt, Inc., 224 F.3d 871 (8th Cir. 2000) (transfer of security interest can be substantially contemporaneous even if security interest not perfected within time period allowed for relation back under different Code provision). Similarly, the earmarking doctrine cannot override the specific time period set forth by the Code. *In re* Lee, 530 F.3d 458 (6th Cir. 2008).

497 11 U.S.C. § 547(c)(5).

498 11 U.S.C. § 547(c)(6); *In re* Lionel Corp., 29 F.3d 88 (2d Cir. 1994) (mechanic's lien could not be avoided under section 547).

Under section 547(c)(7), as amended by the 2005 amendments, a preference also may not be avoided if the transfer was a bona fide payment of a debt for a domestic support obligation.[499] The definition of what constitutes a domestic support obligation is a flexible one, which has given rise to much litigation under the exception to discharge provisions of Code section 523(a)(5).[500] It is clear, however, that this exception to the preference avoiding power does not apply to debts that have been assigned to any entity other than a governmental unit, except if it is assigned solely for purposes of collection.[501]

Under section 547(h), as added by the 2005 amendments, a preference may not be avoided if the transfer was part of a debt repayment plan between the debtor and any creditor, if the plan was created by an approved nonprofit credit counseling agency.[502]

Finally, there are minimum dollar limitations on the preference avoiding power. Neither the trustee nor the debtor in a case filed by a consumer debtor may avoid a preference or preferences totaling less than $600 to a single creditor if the debtor is an individual whose debts are primarily consumer debts.[503] This provision, undoubtedly directed at consumer debtor preference actions against loan companies and utilities, reduces the number of preferences avoidable by debtors under 11 U.S.C. § 522(h).[504] It is important to note, however, that it applies only to section 547, and not to any of the other avoiding powers. Thus, for example, debtors may be able to use the lien avoidance provisions under section 522(f) to recover garnished wages still in the hands of their employers.[505] If the debtor retains a property interest in the garnished wages under state law, and the debtor can claim that interest as exempt using a wild card or some other exemption, the judicial lien on the wages resulting from the garnishment procedure may be voided and the funds returned to the debtor.[506]

With respect to other debtors, a preference cannot be avoided if the aggregate value of the property transferred or affected by the transfer is less than $5850.[507]

10.4.2.6.4.3 Debtor's use of preference avoiding power

The debtor's use of the section 547 avoiding powers through section 522(h) can be quite varied. Levies and execution sales by otherwise unsecured creditors,[508] including wage garnishments[509] within ninety days prior to filing of the bankruptcy, are

---

However, the statutory lien must be perfected as of the petition date for this exemption to apply. *In re* Nucorp Energy, Inc., 902 F.2d 729 (9th Cir. 1990).

499 "Domestic support obligation" is defined in 11 U.S.C. § 101(14A). Payments on divorce debts that are not domestic support obligations remain subject to preference avoidance. *In re* Paschall, 408 B.R. 79 (E.D. Va. 2009), aff'd, 388 Fed. Appx. 299 (4th Cir. 2010).

500 See § 15.4.3.5, *infra*. See also Henry J. Sommer & Margaret Dee McGarity, Collier Family Law and the Bankruptcy Code ¶¶ 6.04, 6.05 (1992).

501 11 U.S.C. § 101(14A).

502 See § 7.3.8, *supra*, for a discussion of approved nonprofit credit counseling agencies.

503 11 U.S.C. § 547(c)(8) (formerly section 547(c)(7)). See *In re* Holyfield, 50 B.R. 695 (Bankr. D. Md. 1985).

This provision does not, however, allow a creditor receiving an avoided preference to retain the initial $599.99. *In re* Via, 107 B.R. 91 (Bankr. W.D. Va. 1989); *In re* Vickery, 63 B.R. 222 (Bankr. E.D. Tenn. 1986). It also does not shield particular transfers under $600 if the aggregate of all transfers to a creditor is at least $600. *In re* Hailes, 77 F.3d 873 (5th Cir. 1996); *In re* Clark, 217 B.R. 89 (E.D. Ky. 1995); *In re* Djerf, 188 B.R. 586 (Bankr. D. Minn. 1995); *In re* Alarcon, 186 B.R. 135 (Bankr. D.N.M. 1995).

504 But see § 10.4.2.3.1, *supra*.

505 See § 10.4.2.3, *supra*.

506 *In re* Thomas, 215 B.R. 873 (Bankr. E.D. Mo. 1997); *In re* Young-

blood, 212 B.R. 593 (Bankr. E.D. Ill. 1997); *In re* Garcia, 155 B.R. 173 (N.D. Ill. 1993); *In re* Nunally, 103 B.R. 376 (Bankr. D.R.I. 1989); *In re* Buzzell, 56 B.R. 197 (Bankr. D. Md. 1986).

507 11 U.S.C. § 547(c)(9). See W. States Glass Corp. v. Barris (*In re* Bay Area Glass, Inc.), 454 B.R. 86 (B.A.P. 9th Cir. 2011) (if amount is above threshold, entire transfer is avoidable, not just amount in excess of threshold).

508 Deel Rent-A-Car v. Levine, 721 F.2d 750 (11th Cir. 1983); Johnson v. CACH, L.L.C. (*In re* Johnson), 2010 WL 5296944 (E.D. Mich. Dec. 20, 2010) (avoiding transfer of funds garnished from debtor's state tax refund); *In re* Smith, 382 B.R. 279 (Bankr. D. Md. 2006) (bank account garnishment); *In re* Bova, 272 B.R. 49 (Bankr. D.N.H. 2002) (avoiding attachment of real estate obtained to secure criminal restitution order); *In re* Rhoads, 130 B.R. 565 (Bankr. C.D. Cal. 1991) (recordation of abstract of judgment avoided as preferential); *In re* Hines, 3 B.R. 370 (Bankr. D.S.D. 1980) (execution sale avoided by debtors).

However, a levy may be held to relate back to the date of the writ of execution under state law, at least in the Third and Fifth Circuits. *In re* Latham, 823 F.2d 108 (5th Cir. 1987); *In re* RAMCO Am. Int'l, 754 F.2d 130 (3d Cir. 1985). See also *In re* Lane, 980 F.2d 601 (9th Cir. 1992) (judgment lien related back to date creditor obtained *lis pendens* due to operation of section 547(e)(1), which deems transfer of real estate to have been perfected when a bona fide purchaser could not acquire a superior interest in the property); *In re* Wind Power Sys., Inc., 841 F.2d 288 (9th Cir. 1988) (attachment lien by levy in California relates back to date on which creditor obtained a temporary protective order covering the debtor's assets); *In re* Ware, 99 B.R. 103 (Bankr. M.D. Fla. 1989) (judgment lien).

509 *In re* Wade, 219 B.R. 815 (B.A.P. 8th Cir. 1998) (debtor could avoid garnishment of wages earned within ninety days of petition); *In re* Pierce, 6 B.R. 18 (Bankr. N.D. Ill. 1980). See also Bank of Am. (USA) v. Stine, 252 B.R. 902 (D. Md. 2000) (state statute making exemptions inapplicable to wage garnishment did not preclude avoidance of garnishment as preference and exemption of proceeds), aff'd sub nom. *In re* Stine, 360 F.3d 455 (4th Cir. 2004).

Some courts had held that under particular state laws the garnishment must have been first initiated within the ninety days. *In re* Conner, 733 F.2d 1560 (11th Cir. 1984); *In re* Riddervold, 647 F.2d 342 (2d Cir. 1981). See also *In re* Battery One-Stop Ltd., 36 F.3d 493 (6th Cir. 1994) (transfer occurred under Ohio law when notice of garnishment was served); *In re* Hagen, 922 F.2d 742 (11th Cir. 1991) (when attorney's charging lien was created prior to ninety-day period, transfer of amount of lien during preference period does not constitute avoidable preference).

These cases do not properly recognize the provision in section 547(e)(3) that the transfer is not made until the debtor has acquired rights in the property. See *In re* Morehead, 249 F.3d 445 (6th Cir. 2001) (*Riddervold* and *Coppie* ignore plain meaning of section 547(e)(3)); *In re* James, 257 B.R. 673 (B.A.P. 8th Cir. 2001) (transfers pursuant to garnishment order did not occur until debtor earned wages); *In re* Johnson, 239 B.R. 416 (Bankr. M.D. Ala. 1999) (transfer occurred when debtor acquired interest in wages); *In re* Kaufman, 187 B.R. 167 (Bankr. E.D. La. 1995) (same); *In re*

clearly avoidable. A payment made pursuant to a criminal restitution order can be recovered, even if it was made through a third party, such as a court clerk.[510] Tax refund intercepts made by the Internal Revenue Service on behalf of another entity, such as a state student loan guarantee agency, or another governmental agency can be set aside as preferences if made within the ninety day look-back period. These types of transfers normally meet all of the required tests for preferences and are definitely considered involuntary.[511] Additionally, payments made to and retained by collection agencies can be recovered directly from the agency.[512] The fact that a debt is nondischargeable (other than as a domestic support obligation) should not affect the use of this power.[513] Thus, a debtor may be able to set aside a tax levy,[514] or perhaps other tax payments.[515] Of course, there may be little purpose in doing so if the taxes paid are nondischargeable and will simply have to be paid again.

Repossessions pursuant to valid security interests which could not otherwise be avoided generally do not constitute preferences.[516] However, if the security interest was extracted within the preference period in exchange for forbearance on a preexisting debt,[517] or if new security during that period for a refinancing exceeds the new value given, then the security interest and any enforcement of it would constitute preferences. Also, if property of greater value than the debt has been acquired by the creditor because a sale has not yet been scheduled, because the creditor has chosen to exercise a right of strict foreclosure and keep the property, or because the creditor has acquired the property at a foreclosure sale, then the creditor may be deemed to have received a preference by recovering property of greater value than it would receive in a liquidation.[518]

Security interests in general, though, raise the thorny problems of voluntariness. Security interests are almost voluntary by definition. Section 101(51) defines security interest as a "lien created by agreement." But what of the security interest granted only under threat of dire consequences for example, foreclosure or eviction? Like the payment of utility arrearages under a threat of midwinter cutoff, rent arrearages under threat of eviction, or debt arrearages under threat of imprisonment, such a transfer can quite arguably be considered involuntary and made under duress.[519] Other transfers that might well be considered involuntary include those pursuant to contractual terms that a debtor does not understand.[520] As it is widely accepted that many of the terms used in consumer credit contracts are neither bargained for nor understood by consum-

---

Polce, 168 B.R. 580 (Bankr. N.D. W. Va. 1994) (same); *In re* Larson, 21 B.R. 264 (Bankr. D. Utah 1982); *In re* Cox, 10 B.R. 268 (Bankr. D. Md. 1981).

They were also undermined by the Supreme Court's decision in Barnhill v. Johnson, 503 U.S. 393, 112 S. Ct. 1386, 118 L. Ed. 2d 39 (1992), which held that a transfer by check did not occur until the bank honored the check. *See In re* Freedom Group, 50 F.3d 408 (7th Cir. 1995) (*Barnhill* overruled cases that had held that notice of garnishment of bank account constituted transfer); *In re* Arway, 227 B.R. 216 (Bankr. W.D.N.Y. 1998) (*Riddervold* case overruled by *Barnhill*).

For a sample complaint to avoid transfer of garnished wages, see Form 98, Appx. G.9, *infra*.

510 *In re* Kirk, 38 B.R. 257 (Bankr. D. Kan. 1984).
511 *See In re* Smith, 382 B.R. 279 (Bankr. D. Md. 2006) (debtor's signing of consent to disbursement of funds already attached did not render transfer voluntary).
512 *In re* Mill St., Inc., 96 B.R. 268 (B.A.P. 9th Cir. 1989).
513 *See In re* Chase & Sanborn Corp., 904 F.2d 588 (11th Cir. 1990) (prebankruptcy fraud does not preclude avoiding preferential payments on the resulting debt); *In re* Car Renovators, 946 F.2d 780 (11th Cir. 1991) (nondischargeable restitution payment may be avoided as a preference).
514 *In re* Williams, 153 B.R. 74 (Bankr. S.D. Ala. 1992) (IRS levy on debtor's wages within ninety days before petition avoided as preference), *aff'd*, 156 B.R. 77 (S.D. Ala. 1993); *In re* Ballard, 131 B.R. 97 (Bankr. W.D. Wis.); *In re* RBT Roofing Structures, 42 B.R. 908 (Bankr. D. Nev. 1984), *aff'd*, 887 F.2d 981 (9th Cir. 1989).

However, the actual fixing of a tax lien is not avoidable to the extent that it is a statutory lien not avoidable under 11 U.S.C. § 545. *In re* Biddle, 31 B.R. 449 (Bankr. N.D. Iowa 1983).

Note, however, there are important issues related to sovereign immunity. *See* § 14.3.2.2, *infra*. Establishing a waiver of sovereign immunity is a necessary prerequisite to avoiding a tax levy as a preference.
515 Drabkin v. District of Columbia, 824 F.2d 1102 (D.C. Cir. 1987).
Again the question of voluntariness arises. In view of the criminal penalties for nonpayment, are tax payments voluntary?
516 *See In re* Cannon, 237 F.3d 716 (6th Cir. 2000) (bank's charge backs against debtor's account for deposited checks returned for insufficient funds were based on security interest under Tennessee law).

517 In general it has been held that forbearance from taking an action which could be taken by the creditor, such as eviction or foreclosure, does not constitute new value. *See In re* Air Conditioning of Stuart, 845 F.2d 293 (11th Cir. 1988); *In re* Jet Fla. Sys., Inc., 841 F.2d 1082 (11th Cir. 1988) (landlord's forbearance in terminating lease does not constitute new value); *In re* Duffy, 3 B.R. 263 (Bankr. S.D.N.Y. 1980).
518 *In re* Villarreal, 2009 WL 2601298 (Bankr. S.D. Tex. Aug. 24, 2009) (foreclosure sale avoided); *In re* Andrews, 262 B.R. 299 (Bankr. M.D. Pa. 2001) (foreclosure sale can be avoided if secured claim was substantially less than property value obtained by creditor); *In re* Park N. Partners, Ltd., 85 B.R. 916 (Bankr. N.D. Ga. 1988) (creditor received preference when it purchased property of debtor at foreclosure sale, the value of which exceeded the amount of the debtor's secured obligation to the creditor); *In re* Fountain, 32 B.R. 965 (Bankr. W.D. Mo. 1983) (property purchased at foreclosure sale worth more than secured debt); *In re* Seidel, 27 B.R. 347 (Bankr. E.D. Pa. 1983) (truck returned to creditor worth more than secured debt). *See also In re* Missionary Baptist Found., 796 F.2d 752 (5th Cir. 1986) (question of the value of the transferred property arises which should be determined in the bankruptcy court); *In re* Winters, 119 B.R. 283 (Bankr. M.D. Fla. 1990) (foreclosure sale held to be preference). *But see In re* Ehring, 900 F.2d 184 (9th Cir. 1990) (creditor who purchased debtor's house at prepetition foreclosure sale did not receive more from foreclosure than it would have in a liquidation, even though creditor resold property prepetition for more than amount of outstanding debt).
519 *See In re* Mason, 69 B.R. 876 (Bankr. E.D. Pa. 1987) (payments of rents into escrow pursuant to court order pending appeal held involuntary). *See also* § 10.4.2.5, *supra*.
520 *See In re* Davis, 169 B.R. 285 (E.D.N.Y. 1994) (sale/leaseback agreement in which the debtor executed a deed to avoid a threatened foreclosure found to be involuntary based on misrepresentations made by the transferee).

ers, this provision could result in setting aside wage assignments[521] and other security arrangements.

10.4.2.6.5 Fraudulent transfers—§ 548

Besides the power to avoid transfers fraudulent under state law that is bestowed upon the trustee through section 544, the Code also contains its own fraudulent transfer avoidance power, in section 548.

Under the Code's definition, the trustee may avoid a transfer or obligation if the transfer[522] or obligation was made or incurred within two years before the case was filed and:

(1) The transfer or obligation was made or incurred with actual intent to hinder, delay or defraud[523] any entity to which the debtor was or became indebted, on or after the date that the transfer occurred or obligation was incurred or

(2)(A) The debtor received less than a reasonably equivalent value for the transfer or obligation and

(B)(i) the debtor was insolvent[524] on the date of the transfer or obligation or became insolvent as a result of the transfer or obligation, or

(ii) the debtor was engaged in business or was about to engage in a business or transaction with unreasonably small capital, or

(iii) the debtor intended to incur, or believed that he or she would incur, debts beyond his or her ability to pay.[525]

Occasionally, consumer debtors, or their friends or relatives, may face the trustee's use of this avoiding power to undo gifts debtors have made during the two years preceding bankruptcy.[526] And trustees have also attempted to avoid transfers for gambling losses as transfers made without reasonably equivalent value in exchange.[527]

Because some courts had allowed trustees to set aside religious contributions,[528] Congress amended section 548 to specifically protect most religious or charitable contributions from avoidance by the trustee. The Religious Liberty and Charitable Donation Protection Act of 1998[529] amended the Code to provide that charitable gifts to qualified religious or charitable entities or organizations are protected from avoidance under section 548(a)(1)(B).[530] Such contributions are protected if they did not exceed fifteen percent of the debtor's gross income in the year they were made or, if they were greater than that

---

521 *In re* Peterson, 14 Clearinghouse Rev. 459, Clearinghouse No. 29,153 (Bankr. W.D. Mich. 1980) (wage assignment deemed involuntary due to lack of debtor understanding).

522 A threshold question is whether a transfer of the debtor's property has occurred at all. *See In re* Laughlin, 602 F.3d 417 (5th Cir. 2010) (renouncing interest in estate before petition is not a transfer of property under Louisiana law); *In re* Costas, 555 F.3d 790 (9th Cir. 2009) (disclaimer of inheritance not a fraudulent transfer); *In re* Atchison, 925 F.2d 209 (7th Cir. 1991) (no transfer occurs under state law when debtor disclaims inheritance); MacKenzie v. Badillo (*In re* Meza), 465 B.R. 152 (Bankr. D. Ariz. 2012) (removal of debtor as beneficiary of life insurance not a transfer, because beneficiary of life insurance has no property rights during life of insured under Arizona law); *In re* Kellman, 248 B.R. 430 (Bankr. M.D. Fla. 1999) (adding wife's name as joint owner of bank account was done only as convenience to deal with possible disability of husband, so removal of her name was not transfer of any interest in account to husband). *But see In re* Green, 986 F.2d 145 (6th Cir. 1993) (in unusual situation of debtor who, having a contractual right to receive property under a will, agreed to give up that right, the exercise of a power of appointment to terminate the debtor's rights under a will was found to be a fraudulent transfer); *In re* Stevens, 112 B.R. 175 (Bankr. S.D. Tex. 1989).

523 Although a single "badge of fraud" may spur suspicion of fraudulent intent, confluence of several badges can be conclusive evidence of actual intent to defraud. Max Sugarman Funeral Home Inc. v. A.D.B. Investors, 926 F.2d 1248 (1st Cir. 1991). *See also* Kelly v. Armstrong, 141 F.3d 799 (8th Cir. 1998) (presence of multiple badges of fraud shifts burden of production and persuasion to debtor).

524 It should be remembered that insolvency is defined at 11 U.S.C. § 101(32) as something other than normal balance sheet insolvency. In determining whether a debtor is insolvent, the liability on a contingent debt, such as a guarantee, is computed by multiplying the amount of the debt by the probability that the debtor would have to pay it. Covey v. Commercial Nat'l Bank of Peoria, 960 F.2d 657 (7th Cir. 1992).

525 An additional ground, relating to insider employment contracts in business cases, was added in 2005.

526 *See, e.g., In re* Bledsoe, 569 F.3d 1106 (9th Cir. 2009) (transfer by judgment in regularly conducted dissolution proceeding conclusively presumed to be for reasonably equivalent value); *In re* Erlewine, 349 F.3d 205, 212 (5th Cir. 2003) (same); *In re* Roosevelt, 220 F.3d 1032 (9th Cir. 2000) (trustee permitted to avoid transfer of property pursuant to marital settlement agreement because wife's relinquishment of community property income in debtor's professional education not considered value under section 548); Butler v. Nationsbank, 58 F.3d 1022 (4th Cir. 1995) (trustee permitted to recover payment made by debtor to satisfy her husband's debt); *In re* Trujillo, 215 B.R. 200 (B.A.P. 9th Cir. 1997) (trustee permitted to avoid transfer of vehicle titles to debtors' children, even though vehicles could have been exempted had they not been transferred). *See also* Havoco of Am., Ltd. v. Hill, 197 F.3d 1135 (11th Cir. 1999) (creditor could not challenge as fraudulent, by way of objection to exemptions, transfer of property to entireties; adversary proceeding including wife as defendant was necessary); *In re* Loomer, 198 B.R. 755 (Bankr. D. Neb. 1996) (trustee could not recover alleged fraudulent transfer to pension plan because plan assets were protected from alienation, but trustee could obtain judgment against debtors, as parties benefited by transfer, which would be enforceable against non-ERISA, nonexempt assets). *Compare In re* Fornabio, 187 B.R. 780 (Bankr. S.D. Fla. 1995) (because homestead was completely exempt under Florida law, transfer of homestead to wife was not an attempt to hinder, delay, or defraud creditors) *with* Tavenner v. Smoot, 257 F.3d 401 (4th Cir. 2001) (fact that property was exemptible was not a defense to fraudulent transfer proceeding).

527 *See In re* Chomakos, 69 F.3d 769 (6th Cir. 1995) (denying avoidance because debtors received reasonably equivalent value for their bets).

528 *See, e.g., In re* Newman, 203 B.R. 468 (D. Kan. 1996); *In re* Gomes, 219 B.R. 286 (Bankr. D. Or. 1998).

529 Pub. L. No. 105-183, 112 Stat. 517 (1998).

530 The 1998 Act also redesignated the subsections of section 548, so that section 548(a)(1)(B) is the former section 548(a)(2).

amount, were consistent with past giving practices of the debtor.[531] Under the language of the provision, the fifteen percent limit applies to each transfer individually, even if the aggregate in a single year exceeds fifteen percent.[532] However, some courts have read the language to mean that if the fifteen percent limit is exceeded and there was no past giving no part of the contribution is protected.[533] The Act also defined, for purposes of section 548, as well as amendments to sections 544, 707(b) and 1325(b), the terms "charitable contribution" and "qualified religious or charitable entity or organization." Section 548(d)(3) defines "charitable contribution" as a contribution made by a natural person consisting or cash or a financial instrument, and section 548(d)(4) defines "qualified religious or charitable entity or organization" as an entity described in section 170(c)(1) or 170(c)(2) of the Internal Revenue Code.

The most important of section 548's provisions for consumer debtors is the provision which classifies as fraudulent any transfer that occurred within the two years preceding the petition for less than reasonably equivalent value while the debtor was insolvent. As most consumer debtors are insolvent under the Code's definition in 11 U.S.C. § 101(32), this section allows the debtor to avoid any transfer (as transfer is broadly defined in section 101(54)) within the previous two years[534] which was for less than reasonably equivalent value, as long as the transfer was not voluntary and the debtor did not conceal the property.[535]

A common use of this power by consumer debtors in the past was to avoid transfers such as mortgage foreclosures, tax sales,[536] repossessions or execution sales when the property in question was worth significantly more than the value received for it.[537] Despite seemingly clear language in the statute supporting such use, the Supreme Court held in *BFP v. Resolution Trust Corp.*,[538] that a regularly conducted, non-collusive foreclosure sale could not be avoided under section 548.

The court's holding appears to also preclude use of section 548 in cases in which secured creditors sell property at public auctions pursuant to Article 9 the Uniform Commercial Code, but should leave open the possibility of challenging a private sale or a strict foreclosure pursuant to the provisions of that Article or in a mortgage context.[539] In the *BFP* opinion, the Supreme Court expressly limited its holding to mortgage foreclosure sales of real estate, stating that "the considerations bearing on other foreclosures and forced sales (to satisfy tax liens, for example) may be different."[540] For tax foreclosures which do not involve a formal sale of the property (for example, when the purchaser obtains a lien or a certificate rather than an actual deed), the *BFP* analysis should not be relevant.[541] Typically, the purchaser of a tax lien pays only the amount of delinquent taxes, an amount which bears no relationship to the value of the property. For this reason, there is no

---

531 11 U.S.C. § 548(a)(2).
 Gross income for a sole proprietor is income before deduction of business expenses. *In re* Lewis, 401 B.R. 431, 442 (Bankr. C.D. Cal. 2009).
532 *But see* Universal Church v. Geltzer, 463 F.3d 218 (2d Cir. 2006) (contributions to single transferee must be aggregated for each year).
533 *Compare In re* Jackson, 249 B.R. 373 (Bankr. D.N.J. 2000) ($20,000 contribution fully avoided because it was not consistent with past practices), *with* Wadsworth v. Word of Life Christian Ctr. (*In re* McGough), 467 B.R. 220 (B.A.P. 10th Cir. 2012) (only amount in excess of $15,000 was avoidable).
534 Section 548(d)(1) governs how the time period is calculated. In the context of a judicial sale, one court of appeals has held that the significant transfer occurs on the date of the sale rather than the date on which the transfer is recorded. That court thus found a transfer to be outside of the then one-year statutory period preceding the debtors' bankruptcy. Butler v. Lomas & Nettleton Co., 862 F.2d 1015 (3d Cir. 1988).
 The transfer of property in an Illinois tax foreclosure sale occurs upon the recording of a tax deed by the buyer. Smith v. SIPI, L.L.C. (*In re* Smith), 614 F.3d 654 (7th Cir. 2010).
535 11 U.S.C. § 522(h).
536 At least one appellate court has held that in a proceeding to set aside a tax sale conducted by selling a tax sale certificate, the proceeding must be brought against the taxing authority as well as the tax sale purchaser. *In re* Slack-Horner Foundries, Inc., 971 F.2d 577 (10th Cir. 1992).
537 *See, e.g., In re* Hulm, 738 F.2d 323 (8th Cir. 1984).
538 511 U.S. 531, 114 S. Ct. 1757, 128 L. Ed. 2d 556 (1994).
539 *In re* Sherman, 223 B.R. 555 (B.A.P. 10th Cir. 1998) (*BFP* decision not applicable to tax sale with no competitive bidding); *In re* Williams, 473 B.R. 307 (Bankr. E.D. Wis. 2012) (strict foreclosure on tax lien not protected from avoidance); *In re* Chase, 328 B.R. 675 (Bankr. D. Vt. 2005) (foreclosure under Vermont strict foreclosure statutes does not create presumption of transfer for reasonably equivalent value under *BFP* because statutes provide no judicial oversight of debt to value ratios, no discretionary redemption period, and no right for debtor to move for judicial sale when mortgage does not contain sale provision); *In re* Fitzgerald, 255 B.R. 807 (Bankr. D. Conn. 2000) (*BFP* decision not applicable to strict foreclosure); *In re* Fitzgerald, 237 B.R. 252 (Bankr. D. Conn. 1999) (*BFP* not applicable to foreclosure without public sale); *In re* Wentworth, 221 B.R. 316 (Bankr. D. Conn. 1998) (tax forfeiture proceeding without judicial oversight or competitive bidding not governed by *BFP* decision); *In re* Grady, 202 B.R. 120 (Bankr. N.D. Iowa 1996) (*BFP* not applicable to land contract forfeiture).
 The *BFP* decision does not appear to apply at all to tax lien execution or other process which does not involve an auction. *See, e.g., In re* McKeever, 132 B.R. 996 (Bankr. N.D. Ill. 1991).
540 *BFP*, 114 S. Ct. at 1757 n.3. *But see In re* McGrath, 170 B.R. 78 (Bankr. D.N.J. 1994) (applying *BFP* analysis to tax sales). *See also* § 10.4.2.6.6, *infra*.
541 *See, e.g., In re* Sherman, 223 B.R. 555 (B.A.P. 10th Cir. 1998) (*BFP* does not apply to Wyoming tax sale when statutory procedure does not provide for competitive bidding); *In re* Murphy, 331 B.R. 107 (Bankr. S.D.N.Y. 2005) (because New York tax forfeiture law does not provide for public sale or competitive bidding, there can be no presumption that transfers are for reasonably equivalent value); *In re* Butler, 171 B.R. 321 (Bankr. N.D. Ill. 1994); *In re* McKeever, 132 B.R. 996 (Bankr. N.D. Ill. 1991).
 In Illinois, the property transfer is an administrative act based on prior sale of the *tax lien* and a failure to redeem; there is no property sale to which the *BFP* analysis could apply. *See also* Smith v. SIPI, L.L.C. (*In re* Smith), 614 F.3d 654 (7th Cir. 2010); *In re* Grandoe Country Club Co., Ltd., 252 F.3d 1146 (10th Cir. 2001) (*BFP* analysis applied because tax sale under state law subject to competitive bidding procedure).

logical basis on which to conclude that the tax lien purchase price is a "reasonably equivalent value."

Obviously, the court's ruling also leaves open the possibility of using section 548 to avoid transfers pursuant to foreclosure sales that were not regularly conducted or that were collusive.[542] Additionally, sales may be challenged in most states where the price received is considered "grossly" inadequate.[543] The bankruptcy court, if that is the preferred forum, should have jurisdiction over an action to set aside a sale on state law grounds, because it would be an action to recover property for the estate.[544] Such an action, or an action raising other state law defects in the sale, may be brought directly in the bankruptcy court or by removal of a state court foreclosure proceeding.[545]

Alternatively, in certain states the transfer associated with a foreclosure is not completed until the occurrence of an event which occurs after the sale. If bankruptcy is filed in the period before the sale is complete under state law, there is no transfer to avoid, because the debtor still owns the property.[546] However, it may be a good idea to obtain and record an order to the effect that the sale process is stayed by bankruptcy if the fact of the auction has already been recorded. This recommendation would be especially prudent if the purchaser at sale is a third party.

Other creative uses of section 548 such as to avoid forfeitures under real estate sale agreements,[547] real estate installment sales contracts,[548] pawnbroker agreements[549] including automobile title pawns,[550] or extortionate charges under consumer contracts[551] should also be considered. Use of this avoiding power may be an effective way of remedying home equity scams, in which mortgagors in trouble are tricked into conveying title to their properties to those who say they will help them.[552] Similarly, the grant of a mortgage or other security interest by a cosigner or accommodation party who received no consideration in a transaction may be challenged, because only the value that the debtor received should be considered relevant under section 548. Such transactions may not always be considered involuntary in which case action by the trustee would be required.[553] When the two-year limitation period under section 548 has passed, it may be possible to seek to avoid such transfers pursuant to section 544 under a longer state law limitations period for fraudulent transfers.

A major limitation on the use of section 548 should be noted, however. Under subsection 548(c), if a transfer is avoidable only under section 548, any transferee who takes for value and in good faith is given a lien on the interest transferred or may enforce the obligation incurred to the extent of the value given to the debtor.[554] If the creditor had executed on a previously unsecured debt, this lien might not be avoidable under any of the debtor's other avoiding powers. However, it could presumably be paid in installments in a chapter 13 plan.[555]

Several issues may arise when section 548(c) is invoked. The most important is probably that of good faith, because the subsection can only be invoked by a good-faith transferee. In

---

542 See In re Ryker, 301 B.R. 156 (D.N.J. 2003) (avoiding foreclosure sale, which took place after having been postponed without new advertising advising potential bidders that debtor had in the interim paid seventy-five percent of the debt).

543 See, e.g., In re Schleier, 290 B.R. 45 (Bankr. S.D.N.Y. 2003) (sale invalid under New York law due to shocking inadequacy of sales price); Gumz v. Chickering, 19 Wis. 2d 625, 121 N.W.2d 279 (Wis. 1963). See generally Robert M. Washburn, The Judicial Legislative Response to Price Inadequacy in Mortgage Foreclosure Sales, 53 S. Cal. L. Rev. 843 (1980).

544 For a discussion of bankruptcy court jurisdiction, see § 14.2, infra.

545 See, e.g., In re Graves, 33 F.3d 242 (3d Cir. 1994) (sheriff's sale was voidable because purchaser had notice of unrecorded ownership interest of the debtor); In re Pontes, 310 F. Supp. 2d 447 (D.R.I. 2004) (tax sale invalidated based on due process grounds when state statute failed to require meaningful notice of the right to redeem property after tax sale); In re Edry, 201 B.R. 604 (Bankr. D. Mass. 1996) (foreclosure sale could be avoided under state law when mortgagee did not give amount of notice usually given in such sales and when price fell below state law standards of adequacy).

For a discussion of removal of state court actions, see § 14.4.1, infra.

546 See § 11.6.2.2, infra.

547 See In re McConnell, 934 F.2d 662 (5th Cir. 1991) (forfeiture of $600,000 down payment under real estate sale agreement avoided as fraudulent transfer).

548 In re Grady, 202 B.R. 120 (Bankr. N.D. Iowa 1996) (BFP does not apply to forfeiture of real estate installment sale contract; property interest of $40,000 forfeited to satisfy $16,000 debt under the contract constituted fraudulent transfer).

549 In re Carter, 209 B.R. 732 (Bankr. D. Or. 1997) (forfeiture of right to redeem jewelry from pawnbroker was involuntary transfer avoidable by debtor under section 522(h)).

550 In re Jones, 304 B.R. 462 (Bankr. N.D. Ala. 2003) (debtor in title pawn transaction did not receive reasonably equivalent value); In re Bell, 279 B.R. 890 (Bankr. N.D. Ga. 2002) (pawnbroker preliminarily enjoined from selling car worth over $10,000 that was taken for failure to pay $5300 redemption price on $4000 loan).

551 For example, large check cashing fees or loan broker charges might be challenged as fraudulent transfers. In such cases, a major question will be whether the transfer was voluntary. See In re Wernly, 91 B.R. 702 (Bankr. E.D. Pa. 1988) ($1150 fee paid to check cashing company to cash check was not paid due to fraud or duress so as to make the payment involuntary and therefore avoidable). But see Kendall v. Able Debt Settlement, Inc. (In re Kendall), 440 B.R. 526 (B.A.P. 8th Cir. 2010) (debtor received reasonably equivalent value from debt settlement company, even if service was illegal, at least in absence of evidence that debt settlement was not achievable).

552 See, e.g., In re Davis, 169 B.R. 285 (E.D.N.Y. 1992) (conveyance in sale/leaseback transaction based on misrepresentations of transferee and without understanding of consequences found to be involuntary); In re Feeley, 429 B.R. 56 (Bankr. D. Mass. 2010) (trustee recovered money lost by debtors in foreclosure rescue scam).

553 See § 10.4.2.6, supra.

554 See In re Sherman, 67 F.3d 1348 (8th Cir. 1995) (parents of debtors, who knew about suspicious nature of debtors' transfer of properties to them not entitled to lien as good faith transferees; bank to whom parents gave security interests and that had knowledge of some of the facts was not an immediate transferee from initial transferee that took in good faith and was therefore protected from recovery under section 550(b)); In re Grueneich, 400 B.R. 688 (B.A.P. 8th Cir. 2009) (debtor's parents who were aware of his insolvency did not act in good faith); In re Jones, 304 B.R. 462 (Bankr. N.D. Ala. 2003) (title pawn lender given lien to extent it gave value).

555 See Chapter 11, infra, for a discussion of dealing with secured claims in chapter 13.

many cases the transferee is the creditor or a party closely connected with the creditor. If the transferee knew of the debtor's insolvency, or even had reason to inquire into the financial straits of the debtor, good faith may be found lacking, especially if the value given was grossly inadequate.[556] Other problems may include a determination of how much value was given to the debtor if the amount of the debt was in dispute. Because the lien is measured by value given to the debtor, it seems fairly clear that costs incurred in the process of transfer should not be included in this figure.[557]

An additional 2005 amendment to section 548 makes a transfer to a self-settled trust or similar device within ten years before the filing of the petition avoidable if the transfer was made with the intent to hinder, delay, or defraud creditors.[558] This provision was enacted primarily to deal with state laws in several states that permitted self-settled trusts, in which the grantor is also a beneficiary, to be used to protect assets from the claims of creditors. It would not often be applicable in the case of a consumer debtor, except perhaps an extremely wealthy debtor who had the resources to create such a trust.

10.4.2.6.6 Postpetition transfers—§ 549

In line with the general principle that filing a bankruptcy freezes the debtor's property for administration by the bankruptcy court, section 549 allows the trustee to avoid most postpetition transfers of the debtor's property. Like the other avoiding powers, this power may be exercised by the debtor under Code section 522(h), if the property was not concealed and the transfer was not voluntary. As elsewhere in the Code, "transfer" is broadly defined to mean almost any parting with an interest in property.[559]

There are a number of exceptions to this general rule.[560] One of the most important protects third party transferors of the debtor's property that have no notice of the bankruptcy case.[561] The most typical example is a bank that transfers funds in a debtor's bank account to honor a check drawn by the debtor. However, section 549(a)(2)(A) protects only the party that makes the transfer, and not the transferee.[562] In addition, any transfer authorized by a specific Code provision[563] or by the bankruptcy court is not avoidable.[564]

Besides these exceptions, several others exist. Transfers made by a debtor against whom an involuntary case has been filed are protected, if they arise out of the debtor's normal affairs.[565] However, such transfers may be invalidated to the extent they are intended to satisfy prepetition debts.[566] And there are two exceptions applicable only to real property.[567] A postpetition transfer of such property may not be avoided if it was sold to:

- A good faith purchaser;[568]
- Without knowledge of the bankruptcy;[569]
- For present fair equivalent value;[570]
- Unless a copy or notice of the bankruptcy petition was filed in the county recording office before the transfer was so far perfected that it could not be invalidated by a bona

---

556 Goldman v. Capital City Mortg. Corp. (*In re* Nieves), 648 F.3d 232 (4th Cir. Md. 2011) (willful ignorance of facts negated good faith); *In re* Armstrong, 285 F.3d 1092 (8th Cir. 2002) (casino transferee was not in good faith when it was on notice that debtor was having financial difficulties and might be insolvent); *In re* Carr, 40 B.R. 1007 (Bankr. D. Conn. 1984). *See* 5 Collier on Bankruptcy ¶ 548.09[2] (16th ed.).

557 *In re* Richardson, 23 B.R. 434 (Bankr. D. Utah 1982). *But see In re* Jones, 20 B.R. 988 (Bankr. E.D. Pa. 1982) (including sheriff's costs in lien given to buyer).

558 11 U.S.C. § 548(e).

559 11 U.S.C. § 101(54).

560 If no exception applies, the transfer is avoidable, no matter how harsh the result. *See In re* Rice, 83 B.R. 8 (B.A.P. 9th Cir. 1987) (transferee has no rights in transferred property when it does not come within an exception to section 549).

If an exception does apply, and the transfer is also not avoidable under section 544, the transfer does not violate the automatic stay. 11 U.S.C. § 362(b)(24).

561 11 U.S.C. § 549(a)(2)(A) (incorporating 11 U.S.C. § 542(c)).

562 *In re* Pyatt, 486 F.3d 423 (8th Cir. 2007) (trustee's remedy in such a situation is to seek recovery from payee of check under section 549 and not from debtor); *In re* Meadows, 396 B.R. 485 (B.A.P. 6th Cir. 2008) (postpetition cashing of debtor's check by payday lender did not violate automatic stay but was avoidable under section 549); *In re* Mills, 176 B.R. 924 (D. Kan. 1994) (transferee who received money when bank honored check postpetition received an avoidable transfer); *In re* W & T Enters., Inc., 84 B.R. 838 (Bankr. M.D. Fla. 1988) (bank honoring check payable to itself is liable for postpetition transfer).

563 For example a transfer made within the ordinary course of the debtor's business pursuant to 11 U.S.C. § 363 is not avoidable. *See In re* Dant & Russell, 853 F.2d 700 (9th Cir. 1988).

564 11 U.S.C. § 549(a)(2)(B). *See* Farm Credit Bank of Omaha v. Franzen, 926 F.2d 762 (8th Cir. 1991) (foreclosure sale held following relief from stay is not avoidable under section 549); Vogel v. Russell Transfer, Inc., 852 F.2d 797 (4th Cir. 1988).

A debtor's transfer of exempt property or its proceeds is not avoidable because, once exempted, the property is not property of the estate. *In re* Reed, 184 B.R. 733 (Bankr. W.D. Tex. 1995). *But see* Manion v. Providian Nat'l Bank, 269 B.R. 232 (D. Colo. 2001).

565 11 U.S.C. § 549(a)(2)(A) (incorporating 11 U.S.C. § 303(f)).

566 11 U.S.C. § 549(b). *See generally In re* Texas Research, Inc., 862 F.2d 1161 (5th Cir. 1989).

567 *See In re* Shamblin, 890 F.2d 123 (9th Cir. 1989) (tax sale transfers claim rather than property under Illinois law so exceptions do not apply).

568 *See* Hopkins v. Suntrust Mortg., Inc., 441 B.R. 656 (Bankr. D. Idaho 2010) (lender that refinanced debtors' mortgages and took new mortgage not in good faith because it had notice of bankruptcy); *In re* Taft, 262 B.R. 55 (Bankr. M.D. Pa. 2001) (tax sale purchaser was not in good faith when it had reason to believe debtor had interest in property and was in bankruptcy).

569 *See In re* Allen, 816 F.2d 325 (7th Cir. 1987) (mortgagee/purchaser at foreclosure sale was not good faith purchaser without knowledge of the bankruptcy when mortgagee had been told bankruptcy petition would be filed that day).

570 *See In re* Miller, 454 F.3d 899 (8th Cir. 2006) (fact that sale was conducted in compliance with state law does not preclude argument that fair equivalent value was not paid, but remaining liens on property must be considered); *In re* Shaw, 157 B.R. 151 (B.A.P. 9th Cir. 1993) (price of $36,049 at regularly conducted tax sale was not fair equivalent value of property with a value of $76,000); *In re* Powers, 88 B.R. 294 (Bankr. D. Nev. 1988) (seventy-three percent of value not fair equivalent value).

fide purchaser or judicial sale purchaser.[571]

To the extent that a good faith purchaser meets all of the requirements except present fair equivalent value, that purchaser has a lien to the extent of any present value given.[572] It should be noted, however, that this section speaks only of *present value* given in return for the property. This limitation means that to the extent a purchaser has taken the property in satisfaction of a prior debt, that purchaser is not protected.[573]

It is also important to note that the definition of "purchaser" in section 101 of the Code is "transferee of a voluntary transfer and includes immediate or mediate transferee of such transferee." Thus section 549(c) does not apply at all to involuntary transfers, a fact that seems to have escaped some courts considering such transfers (perhaps because it was never argued by the debtor or trustee). In general, therefore, section 549(c) does not protect involuntary sales carried out in violation of the automatic stay which, like most actions in violation of the stay, are void.[574]

The debtor may use section 549 in conjunction with the automatic stay provisions to invalidate involuntary postpetition transfers.[575] One example of a case in which the stay might need such supplementation is a repossession ordered by a creditor without notice of the bankruptcy. Although the creditor would probably not be held in contempt as it had no notice of the case, the repossession could clearly be reversed. A setoff after the bankruptcy could be similarly undone. And in chapter 13 cases in which the debtor's postpetition income is property of the estate,[576] any deduction by a credit union from wages would be avoidable.[577] To prevent any problems in effecting this last type of avoidance, it is advisable to withdraw, before the bankruptcy, any prior authorization for such deductions that might muddy the issue of voluntariness.

For purposes of section 549, it has been held that a transfer by check occurs when the check is delivered.[578] However, due to Supreme Court precedent to the contrary under section 547,[579] more recent rulings under this section have held that the date of transfer by check occurs on the date it is honored.[580] For this reason, debtors must be careful to assure that any large check written shortly before the bankruptcy petition, such as a check for a mortgage payment, has been honored. Otherwise, there is a danger that the trustee could recover the funds from the payee of the check.[581]

10.4.2.6.7 Setoff—§ 553

The Code gives the trustee the power to avoid some, but not all, setoffs of mutual debts in the ninety days prior to filing of the petition.[582] If a setoff is otherwise permissible under non-bankruptcy law,[583] section 553 provides certain tests which

---

571 11 U.S.C. § 549(c).

The bona fide purchaser test in this section assumes a hypothetical purchaser with no notice of the transfer. *In re* Ward, 837 F.2d 124 (3d Cir. 1988). *See also* United States, *ex rel.* Agric. Stabilization Serv. v. Gerth, 991 F.2d 1428 (8th Cir. 1993) (obligation on prepetition contract was not transformed by debtors assumption of contract into postpetition obligation against which creditor could offset postpetition debt); *In re* Konowitz, 905 F.2d 55 (4th Cir. 1990) (when interest taken by purchaser at prepetition foreclosure sale was not perfected before bankruptcy was filed, sale was subject to avoidance); *In re* Walker, 861 F.2d 597 (9th Cir. 1988) (confirmation of foreclosure sale did not constitute requisite perfection of transfer under California's recording statute).

572 11 U.S.C. § 549(c).

573 *In re* Major, 218 B.R. 501 (Bankr. W.D. Mo. 1998) (credit bid by foreclosing creditor was not present fair equivalent value). *But see In re* T.F. Stone Co., 72 F.3d 466 (5th Cir. 1996) (price obtained at regularly conducted, non-collusive tax sale deemed present fair equivalent value under section 549(c)).

574 *See* 40235 Wash. St. Corp. v. Lusardi, 329 F.3d 1076 (9th Cir. 2003) (section 549(c) not available for transactions that are void because they occurred in violation of automatic stay); *In re* Schwartz, 954 F.2d 569 (9th Cir. 1991) (section 549(c) applies to unauthorized transfers of estate property which are not otherwise prohibited by the Code); *In re* Ford, 296 B.R. 537 (Bankr. N.D. Ga. 2003); *In re* Smith, 224 B.R. 44 (Bankr. E.D. Mich. 1998). *But see In re* Taylor, 884 F.2d 478 (9th Cir. 1989).

575 For discussion of the effect of the automatic stay on the validity of transfers see § 9.6, *supra*. *See also* United States Dep't of Treasury v. Owens, 390 B.R. 808 (W.D. Pa. 2008) (debtor could use section 549 to avoid tax liens imposed by assessments during pendency of bankruptcy case); *In re* Gandara, 257 B.R. 549 (Bankr. D. Mont. 2000) (section 549 could be used to invalidate payment made in exchange for dismissal of criminal bad check case even if payment was not prohibited by automatic stay).

576 11 U.S.C. § 1306(a).
577 *In re* Shepherd, 12 B.R. 151 (E.D. Pa. 1981).
578 Quinn Wholesale, Inc. v. Northen, 873 F.2d 77 (4th Cir. 1989).
579 Barnhill v. Johnson, 503 U.S. 393, 112 S. Ct. 1386, 119 L. Ed. 2d 519 (1992) (transfer by check occurs when check is honored for purposes of preference analysis).
580 *In re* Oakwood Mkts., 203 F.3d 406 (6th Cir. 2000). *See also In re* Mora, 199 F.3d 1024 (9th Cir. 1999) (transfer of cashier's check is on date of delivery, but suggesting that transfer of ordinary check is on date it is honored).
581 *See In re* Pyatt, 486 F.3d 423 (8th Cir. 2007) (trustee's remedy in such a situation is to seek recovery from payee of check under section 549 and not from debtor); *In re* Mora, 199 F.3d 1024 (9th Cir. 1999) (trustee recovered large payment deemed made to mortgage company by check transferring prepetition funds that were deemed transferred after petition was filed). Some trustees have attempted to use section 542 to recover funds paid postpetition on prepetition checks from the debtor. *See* § 9.9.1, *supra*.
582 The automatic stay prevents setoffs after the petition is filed, though the stay may be lifted if certain prerequisites are met and a creditor may "freeze" a debtor's account in anticipation of set off. Citizens Bank of Md. v. Strumpf, 516 U.S. 16, 116 S. Ct. 286, 133 L. Ed. 2d 258 (1995). *See* Ch. 9, *supra*.

Generally, the right to setoff will involve a bank account or other "cash collateral" as defined in 11 U.S.C. § 363(a), which under 11 U.S.C. § 363(c)(2) cannot be used, that is, withdrawn from the bank, without notice and a hearing or consent of the creditor. No setoff probably occurs when the bank has foreclosed a valid security interest in an account. *See* Smith v. Mark Twain Nat'l Bank, 805 F.2d 278 (8th Cir. 1986). *Cf. In re* Knudson, 929 F.2d 1280 (8th Cir. 1991) (security agreement in bank accounts held invalid).

However, when such assets are seized there may be an issue related to the automatic stay.
583 *See In re* Capps, 251 B.R. 73 (Bankr. D. Neb. 2000) (debtor entitled to recover funds setoff by bank because they were Social Security benefits which bank was prohibited from seizing by 42 U.S.C. § 407(a)).

must be met before it can be avoided. At the same time, section 553 preserves the right of setoff after a bankruptcy petition, except as prohibited elsewhere in the Code, such as by the automatic stay.

First, a setoff may be avoided or otherwise invalidated if it is not for a mutual debt. If the debtor owes the debt in a capacity other than that in which a debt is owed to the debtor, no mutuality exists and no setoff is permitted. For example, if the debtor has deposited money in his or her individual account, a setoff of that deposit against the debtor's obligation as a trustee for another person by the bank may be avoided, as it is against the debtor in a different capacity. This principle is frequently applied to set-offs involving debtors' IRA accounts.[584] Similarly, a creditor may not set off a prepetition claim against a postpetition claim, both because of the express wording of section 553(a) and because the debts are not considered to be mutual.[585]

However, it is not always easy to determine whether mutual debts exist.[586] In particular, courts have disagreed about whether debts owed to different agencies of the same government are mutual debts.[587]

Second, a setoff may be avoided if it is exercised to satisfy a claim against the debtor other than an allowable claim. Thus, if defenses to the claim's allowance, including defenses to the claim itself, are successfully asserted, a setoff may be avoided.[588] However, one court of appeals had held that a creditor need not file a proof of claim as a prerequisite to asserting a right of set-off.[589] And a claim may be eligible for setoff even if it has not been reduced to judgment.[590]

Third, if a creditor exercising a setoff acquires its claim from another entity either after the filing of the petition or within ninety days before filing while the debtor was insolvent, the setoff may be avoided.[591]

Fourth, if a creditor exercising a setoff has caused the debtor to increase the amount owed by the creditor to the debtor (for example, by pressuring the debtor to "build up" its bank deposits) while the debtor was insolvent in order to obtain a setoff, the setoff so obtained may be avoided.[592]

Finally, a setoff may be avoided to the extent that it results in the creditor's improving its position over what it was either (1) ninety days prior to the filing of the petition or (2) if no "insufficiency" existed on that date, the first date an insufficiency existed.[593] The Code defines "insufficiency" as the "amount, if any, by which a claim against the debtor exceeds a mutual debt owing to the debtor by the holder of such claim."[594] For example, if the debtor owed $5000 to a bank and ninety days prior to the filing of the case had a deposit balance of $200, there would be an insufficiency on that date of $4800 ($5000 minus $200). If forty days prior to the filing the bank was then owed $3000 and the debtor had a deposit of $2000 there would be an insufficiency on that date of only $1000 ($3000 minus $2000). If the bank then set off against the entire

---

See further discussion later in this subsection.

584 *In re* Mastroeni, 57 B.R. 191 (Bankr. S.D.N.Y. 1986); *In re* Gillett, 55 B.R. 675 (Bankr. S.D. Fla. 1985); *In re* Todd, 37 B.R. 836 (Bankr. W.D. La. 1984) (avoiding setoff of debt against debtor's IRA account). *See also In re* Bevill, Bresler & Schulman Asset Mgmt., 896 F.2d 54 (2d Cir. 1990) (creditor withholding income from government bonds which rightfully belonged to debtor was mere trustee holding debtor's funds and thus owed debtor no debt which could be set off).

585 Cooper Jarrett Inc. v. Cent. Trans., Inc., 726 F.2d 93 (3d Cir. 1984); *In re* Harris, 260 B.R. 753 (Bankr. D. Md. 2001) (credit union could not set off postpetition deposits against prepetition debt or claim that security interest in account extended to those deposits); *In re* Kleather, 208 B.R. 406 (Bankr. S.D. Ohio 1997) (bank could not setoff prepetition debt against postpetition deposits despite fact that debtor had withdrawn prepetition deposits after petition was filed); *In re* Figgers, 121 B.R. 772 (Bankr. S.D. Ohio 1990) (to qualify for setoff, debts must be individual and prepetition); *In re* Princess Baking Corp., 5 B.R. 587 (Bankr. S.D. Cal. 1980). *See also In re* Davidovich, 901 F.2d 1533 (10th Cir. 1990) (chapter 7 debtor's former partner not entitled to offset amounts debtor allegedly owed pursuant to postpetition real estate partnership defaults); *In re* Houston, 463 B.R. 452 (Bankr. E.D. Mich. 2011) (no setoff permitted against joint account when nondebtor had deposited money and was deemed owner of funds under state law); *In re* McDonald, 2010 Bankr. LEXIS 2470 (Bankr. S.D. Ohio Aug. 18, 2010) (where credit union did not freeze account immediately and balance was reduced before freeze, it had right to set off only against lowest postpetition balance, thus ensuring there was no setoff against postpetition deposits). *Cf. In re* United Sciences of Am., Inc., 893 F.2d 720 (5th Cir. 1990) (mutuality created by agreement between bank and debtor depositor pursuant to which bank deposited proceeds of credit card transactions in debtor's account and debtor authorized bank to charge its account for charge backs and other fees); Braniff Airways, Inc. v. Exxon Co. U.S.A., 814 F.2d 1030 (5th Cir. 1987) (mutuality found when debtor had made unused prepayments to creditor holding claim). *But see In re* Bacigalupi, Inc., 60 B.R. 442 (B.A.P. 9th Cir. 1986).

Bacigalupi is distinguishable insofar as it involves a setoff against a state court judgment obtained by the debtor after filing bankruptcy. The setoff essentially allowed the creditor to recoup its counterclaim.

The Internal Revenue Service has sometimes attempted to ignore a lack of mutuality. *See, e.g., In re* Glenn, 198 B.R. 106 (Bankr. E.D. Pa. 1996) (IRS could not offset postpetition refund against prepe-

tition debt). *Glenn* was reversed at 207 B.R. 418 (E.D. Pa. 1997) on the issue of when the debtor acquires the right to a tax refund. *In re* Hammett, 21 B.R. 923 (Bankr. E.D. Pa. 1982) (postpetition setoff not permitted when debtor had postpetition claim for refund and IRS had prepetition claim for taxes). *See also* § 2.5.3, *supra*. See also discussion of Internal Revenue Service actions in § 9.6, *supra*.

586 *See In re* Elcona Homes Corp., 863 F.2d 483 (7th Cir. 1988).

587 *See* United States v. Maxwell, 157 F.3d 1099 (7th Cir. 1998) (federal government a single entity for setoff purposes); *In re* Turner, 84 F.3d 1294 (10th Cir. 1996) (en banc) (United States is a unitary creditor for setoff purposes); Doe v. United States, 58 F.3d 494 (9th Cir. 1995). *But see* Westamerica Bank v. United States, 178 B.R. 493 (N.D. Cal. 1995) (mutuality did not exist for debts involving different agencies).

588 11 U.S.C. § 553(a)(1).

589 *In re* G.S. Omni Corp., 835 F.2d 1317 (10th Cir. 1987).

590 *In re* Bevill, Bresler & Schulman Asset Mgmt., 896 F.2d 54 (2d Cir. 1990).

591 11 U.S.C. § 553(a)(2).

592 11 U.S.C. § 553(a)(3). *See In re* Dutton, 15 B.R. 318 (Bankr. D.N.J. 1981).

593 11 U.S.C. § 553(b)(1).

594 11 U.S.C. § 553(b)(2).

deposit, that setoff could be avoided in its entirety, because on the date of the setoff the bank's insufficiency position had improved to the extent of $3800 ($4800 minus $1000) an amount greater than the amount of the setoff. If, instead of $200, there had been $2500 on deposit ninety days before filing then the improvement in position would have been $1500 and that amount of the $2000 setoff would be avoidable.[595] And if the amount on deposit ninety days before the filing had been $6000 and then, three days before filing the debtor for the first time withdrew $3500, then the first insufficiency would be $1500. A setoff after that date would be avoidable to the extent that the insufficiency on the date of the setoff exceeded $1500.[596]

Arguably, any deposit to a creditor bank is a transfer to the bank which could be avoided as a setoff if it improved the bank's position.[597] However, there was also a significant line of pre-Code cases holding that deposits in the ordinary course of business were not preferences.[598] In any case, this issue rarely arises with respect to the debtor's avoiding powers, as the deposit is normally a voluntary transfer and thus not avoidable under 11 U.S.C. § 522(h).

Also, it is important to note that section 553(b) addresses only setoffs made prior to the filing of the petition. It does not appear that the improvement-in-position test applies at all to setoffs of mutual prepetition claims after filing, once the automatic stay is no longer in effect. Generally, such setoffs by creditors having the right to setoff for mutual debts are permissible, though they may be prohibited by a court in exercise of its discretion.[599] However, several courts have held that no setoff may be had against exempt property.[600] Setoff may also be prohibited when a creditor has expressly waived its setoff rights.[601] Creditors occasionally attempt to use the doctrine of "recoupment" to justify refusal to pay to the debtor or trustee money that they owe the debtor, claiming that it is reduced by money the debtor owed them with respect to the same transaction. This doctrine is quite limited.[602]

The right to setoff can be eliminated by a confirmed plan that does not preserve that right or modifies it.[603] In addition, a creditor waives its right to setoff to the extent that it releases funds held prepetition that were subject to setoff, and cannot setoff against funds acquired from the debtor postpetition to collect a prepetition debt.[604]

---

595 The bank's position would have improved from a deficiency of $2500 ($5000 minus $2500) to a deficiency of $1000 ($3000 minus $2000).

596 For application of these principles in cases in which debtor avoided setoffs, see Riley v. U.S. Dep't of Agric. Rural Dev. (*In re* Riley), 472 B.R. 422 (Bankr. W.D. Ky. 2012) (debtors could avoid setoff of tax refund when federal government improved its position within 90 days before petition); *In re* Goodman, 2012 WL 529574 (Bankr. E.D.N.C. Feb. 17, 2012) (Social Security Administration improved its position when debtor became eligible for large retroactive payment during 90 day period); *In re* Duncan, 10 B.R. 13 (Bankr. D. Tenn. 1980). *See also* Durham v. SMI Indus., Corp., 882 F.2d 881 (4th Cir. 1989) (setoff may be recovered to the extent amount creditor received exceeded amount it paid); *In re* Moreira, 173 B.R. 965 (Bankr. D. Mass. 1994) (debtor could challenge setoff against credit union account to extent she could claim funds in account were exempt); *In re* Stall, 125 B.R. 754 (Bankr. S.D. Ohio 1991) (setoff of tax refund against prepetition student loan obligation did not result in improvement of position); *In re* Fox, 62 B.R. 432 (Bankr. D.R.I. 1986) (avoiding Veterans Administration withholding of benefits to recover money paid out on a mortgage guarantee).

597 See S. Rep. No. 95-989, at 27 (1978) and H.R. Rep. No. 95-595, at (1977), stating the term "transfer" includes a deposit in a bank account. *See also In re* Bohlen Enters., Ltd., 859 F.2d 561 (8th Cir. 1988) (deposit not in ordinary course of business made for purpose of creating right of setoff is avoidable under section 553(a)(3)). *But see* Coral Petroleum, Inc. v. Banque Paribas-London, 797 F.2d 1351 (5th Cir. 1986).

598 *See* Laws v. United Mo. Bank of Kan. City, 98 F.3d 1047 (8th Cir. 1996) (routine advances against uncollected deposits do not create a debt).

599 *See* Ch. 14, *infra*.

600 *In re* Alexander, 245 B.R. 280 (W.D. Ky. 1999) (IRS setoff to collect dischargeable prepetition debt prohibited by § 522(c)); *In re* Jones, 230 B.R. 875 (M.D. Ala. 1999) (same); *In re* Okigbo, 2009 WL 5227844 (Bankr. D. Md. Dec. 29, 2009) (setoff against exempt property not permitted by state law, and credit union's asserted lien not valid under 12 C.F.R. § 226.12); *In re* Kleinsmith, 361 B.R. 504 (Bankr. S.D. Iowa 2006) (no setoff permitted against account containing exempt child support); *In re* Tarbuck, 318 B.R. 78 (Bankr. W.D. Pa. 2004) (debtor could exempt funds otherwise subject to right of setoff if bank had not exercised right prepetition); *In re* Sharp, 286 B.R. 627 (Bankr. E.D. Ky. 2002) (same); *In re* Killen, 249 B.R. 585 (Bankr. D. Conn. 2000) (same); *In re* Miel, 134 B.R. 229 (Bankr. W.D. Mich. 1991) (Internal Revenue Service could not carry out postpetition offset of dischargeable prepetition taxes owed against tax refund claimed as exempt by debtor); *In re* Wilde, 85 B.R. 147 (Bankr. D.N.M. 1988); *In re* Haffner, 12 B.R. 371 (Bankr. M.D. Tenn. 1981). *See also In re* Monteith, 23 B.R. 601 (Bankr. N.D. Ohio 1982) (IRS not allowed to setoff against exempt property to collect dischargeable taxes). *But see* United States v. Luongo, 259 F.3d 323 (5th Cir. 2001) (IRS permitted to setoff prepetition refund against discharged tax debt); *In re* Lares, 188 F.3d 1166 (9th Cir. 1999) (Idaho law permitted prebankruptcy exercise of contractual right of setoff against proceeds of homestead sale); *In re* Gould, 401 B.R. 415 (B.A.P. 9th Cir. 2009) (IRS right to setoff trumps exemption), *aff'd*, 603 F.3d 1100 (9th Cir. 2010); *In re* Madigan, 270 B.R. 749 (B.A.P. 9th Cir. 2001) (long term disability insurer could not recoup from post-discharge claim for disability benefits based on prepetition overpayment because benefits did not arise from same transaction); *In re* Pieri & Boucher, 86 B.R. 208 (B.A.P. 9th Cir. 1988) (landlord allowed to setoff claims against debtors' counterclaims, although debtors' counterclaims were listed as exempt).

601 *In re* Calore Express, 288 F.3d 22 (1st. Cir. 2002) (IRS waived its right of setoff by stating in proof of claim that its claim for prepetition taxes was not subject to setoff; factual question as to whether waiver may have been later rescinded).

602 *See In re* Malinowski, 156 F.3d 131 (2d Cir. 1998) (state unemployment agency could not recoup overpayment arising from one period of unemployment from benefits due for a different period of unemployment); U.S. *ex rel*. Postal Serv. v. Dewey Freight, 31 F.3d 620 (8th Cir. 1994).

603 *In re* Cont'l Airlines, 134 F.3d 536 (3d Cir. 1998); *In re* Ealy, 392 B.R. 408 (Bankr. E.D. Ark. 2008), *appeal dismissed by In re* Ealy, 396 B.R. 20 (B.A.P. 8th Cir. 2008) (plan takes precedence and IRS is therefore unable to exercise its postpetition right of setoff absent a sufficient basis for a postconfirmation lifting of the automatic stay).

604 *In re* Orr, 234 B.R. 249 (Bankr. N.D.N.Y. 1999); *In re* Kleather, 208 B.R. 406 (Bankr. S.D. Ohio 1997).

10.4.2.6.8 Liens securing fines, penalties and forfeitures— § 724(a)

The final type of transfer that is avoidable by the trustee, and sometimes by the debtor, is described in section 724(a), which in turn incorporates section 726(a)(4). Because this avoiding power is contained in chapter 7, it applies only in cases under that chapter, and not in chapter 13 cases.

Basically, this section allows avoidance of liens for penalties, fines, punitive damages, multiple damages, and the like, to the extent the amount secured by that lien does not represent compensation for actual pecuniary loss. Under this section, to the extent a tax lien secures penalties for late payment, for example, it can be avoided.[605] In cases involving judgment liens, this power will add little to the debtor's arsenal beyond the broader power which is available under 11 U.S.C. § 522(f)(1)(A).[606]

However, under some consumer contracts the power may be available to challenge that portion of a lien which represents a penalty, including, for example, late charges and prepayment penalties. In such cases one issue likely to arise for a debtor seeking to use the power is the voluntariness of the transfer. The debtor should argue that the imposition of the penalty represents a separate involuntary transfer from the underlying transaction granting the security interest.[607]

The trustee also has the power under section 724(b) to subordinate certain tax liens to some priority claims. The debtor does not share this power, and the trustee's use of it can create serious problems for the debtor. This provision is discussed in an earlier chapter.[608]

10.4.2.7 Other Limitations on Debtor's Use of Trustee Avoiding Powers

In addition to the overriding limitations on section 522(g) and (h) that the debtor may not avoid any voluntary transfer or transfer when the debtor concealed property,[609] there are a number of other limitations on the debtor's avoiding powers.

Naturally, the avoiding powers are limited by the extent of the debtor's available exemptions. Subsection 522(j) permits exemption of particular property only to the extent that the exemption for that type of property is still available.

More importantly, the avoiding powers are subject to the limitations placed upon the trustee by sections 546 and 550. Section 546 sets a statute of limitations for avoidance actions at the earlier of 1) two years after the entry of the order for relief (normally the date of the petition) or 2) the time the case is closed or dismissed.[610] However, if a trustee is appointed or elected under particular Code sections before the two years has run, there has been no prior trustee, and the case is not closed or dismissed, the time is extended to one year after the trustee is appointed or elected if that is later.[611] The limitations period may be tolled if the debtor or others conceal material facts necessary to discover the avoidable transfer.[612] The limitations period may also be waived.[613]

Section 546 also subordinates the trustee's powers to any applicable law that allows perfection of an interest to relate back to an earlier date,[614] and to certain sellers' rights of reclamation of goods sold.[615]

10.4.2.8 Recovery of Property After Transfer Is Avoided

When a transfer is avoided, section 550 generally allows recovery of the transferred property (or its value in some cases) from both the initial transferee and a subsequent transferee.[616]

---

605 *See, e.g., In re* Davis, 22 B.R. 523 (Bankr. W.D. Pa. 1982) (IRS lien avoided to extent it was penalty). *But see In re* DeMarah, 62 F.3d 1248 (9th Cir. 1995) (debtor could not use section 724(a) to avoid a tax lien due to operation of section 522(c)(2)).

606 *See* § 10.4.2.3, *supra*.

607 *See* §§ 10.4.2.5, 10.4.2.6, *supra*.

608 *See* § 6.3.3, *supra*.

609 *But see* § 10.4.2.5, *supra*.

610 11 U.S.C. § 546(a); Sandoval v. Century Bank (*In re* Sandoval), 470 B.R. 195 (Bankr. D.N.M. 2012) (debtor could not use trustee avoiding power after case closed).

This amendment resolved confusion in the cases concerning how the statute of limitations was to be computed in cases when there initially was no trustee appointed.

611 11 U.S.C. § 546(a).

This last time period is usually relevant in cases commenced under chapter 11 in which a trustee, other than a chapter 7 interim trustee appointed under section 701, is appointed or elected later in the case. *In re* Am. Pad & Paper Co., 478 F.3d 546 (3d Cir. 2007) (plain language not applicable when interim trustee was appointed within two-year period, but permanent trustee elected after two-year period).

612 *See In re* Olsen, 36 F.3d 71 (9th Cir. 1994) (statute could be equitably tolled due to debtors' conduct failing to comply with duty to cooperate with trustee); *In re* Petty, 93 B.R. 208 (B.A.P. 9th Cir. 1988) (trustee allowed to reopen case and proceed with avoidance action when the debtor's interest in property was not properly disclosed).

613 *In re* Pugh, 158 F.3d 530 (11th Cir. 1998).

614 11 U.S.C. § 546(b); *In re* WWG Indus., Inc., 772 F.2d 810 (11th Cir. 1985). *See* Sovereign Bank v. Hepner (*In re* Roser), 613 F.3d 1240 (10th Cir. 2010) (avoiding power was subject to state law allowing postpetition perfection of lien on automobile to relate back if completed within 30 days); *In re* Griggs, 965 F.2d 54 (6th Cir. 1992) (lender could correct absence of notation of its lien on mobile home pursuant to Kentucky law which permitted retroactive perfection of security interests); *In re* Yobe Elec., Inc., 728 F.2d 207 (3d Cir. 1984). *See also* 11 U.S.C. § 362(b)(3).

615 11 U.S.C. § 546(c), (d). *See, e.g., In re* Pester Ref. Co., 964 F.2d 842 (8th Cir. 1992); *In re* Griffin Retreading Co., 795 F.2d 676 (8th Cir. 1986).

616 11 U.S.C. § 550(a). *See In re* Bean, 252 F.3d 113 (2d Cir. 2001) (recovery under section 550 limited to value of debtor's equity interest that was transferred); *In re* Willaert, 944 F.2d 463 (8th Cir. 1991) (proceeds of sale of transferred property can be recovered); *In re* Bremer, 408 B.R. 355 (B.A.P. 10th Cir. 2009) (when preservation of lien is sufficient to avoid transfer, trustee cannot recover value transferred); *In re* Taylor, 599 F.3d 880 (9th Cir. 2010) (bankruptcy court, in its discretion, can award either property or its value). *Cf. In re* Cohen, 300 F.3d 1097 (9th Cir. 2002) (when debtor transferred to her husband a cashier's check made payable to husband's creditor, creditor was only party that could exercise dominion and control and was therefore initial transferee).

In some cases, after an avoidance proceeding, a separate action must be brought under section 550 to recover the property that was transferred.[617] Usually, though, the avoidance proceeding should also seek recovery of property under section 550.

There are several major exceptions to the general right to recover property after a transfer is avoided, however. The debtor may not recover from any transferee subsequent to the initial transferee if that transferee has either (1) taken for value in good faith without knowledge of the voidability of the transfer or (2) taken from a prior transferee who has taken for value in good faith and without knowledge.[618] (In such cases, the only recovery can be the value of the property from the initial transferee.) It is the burden of the transferee to show good faith and lack of knowledge.[619] And, if an initial transferee acted in good faith,[620] the transferee, while returning the property, retains a lien for the cost or increase in value due to any improvements on the property, whichever is less.[621]

However, a trustee should not be permitted to exercise rights greater than those of a lienholder whose lien is avoided. Thus, if a trustee avoids the lien of a creditor on a vehicle, the trustee has no right to recover a money judgment against the creditor holding the lien or to take the vehicle. The trustee has the right to step into the shoes of the creditor through preservation of the transfer.[622]

Generally, a transferee of an avoided transfer from whom property has been recovered is given a claim against the estate under section 502(h). A transferee of an avoided transfer in payment of a claim which would have been nondischargeable may also, in some cases, again be able to assert that claim against the debtor.[623]

Finally, an action to recover property subsequent to the avoidance of a transfer must be commenced within one year after the avoidance, or before the case is closed, whichever comes first.[624]

10.4.2.9 Preservation of Avoided Transfers or Recovered Property

An important but often overlooked addition to the avoiding powers is the right to preserve avoided transfers for the benefit of the debtor. Subsection 522(i)(2) provides that a transfer avoided or property recovered by the debtor or the trustee may be preserved for the benefit of the debtor to the extent that the debtor may exempt that property under section 522(g) or could have avoided the transfer under section 522(f)(1)(B).[625]

The result, in effect, is that the debtor steps into the shoes of the holder of the avoided transfer *vis-a-vis* any other entity with rights junior to that holder, and thereby obtains rights superior to junior lienholders.[626] For example, if two joint debtors have a home worth $10,000 which has an $8000 judicial lien and a $10,000 mortgage junior to the judicial lien, the debtors, if they are able to exempt their $10,000 interest (as they could under the federal exemptions) may avoid the judicial lien under section 522(f)(1).[627] Without preservation of that lien (a trans-

---

A party must have actual dominion or control over funds to qualify as a transferee. *See In re* Hurtado, 342 F.3d 528 (6th Cir. 2003) (when debtors transferred money to individual's bank account, that individual had dominion and control over the funds even though she used them as directed by debtors). Thus a bank receiving funds to be deposited in a bank account is normally not a transferee, because the person owning the account ordinarily controls that money. *In re* First Sec. Mortgage, 33 F.3d 42 (10th Cir. 1994).

617 *See In re* Cowan, 273 B.R. 98 (B.A.P. 6th Cir. 2002) (if avoidance of lien provides trustee with complete relief, no action under section 550 is necessary).

618 11 U.S.C. § 550(b). *See In re* Bressman, 327 F.3d 229 (3d Cir. 2003) (law firms did not know that they were being paid with estate assets for representation in criminal case); *In re* Cohen, 226 B.R. 1 (B.A.P. 9th Cir. 1999) (when debtor gave funds to her husband, who then purchased cashier's check and sent it to creditor, husband was initial transferee).

One court of appeals has held that actual rather than constructive notice must be shown to recover transferred property under section 550. *In re* Columbia Data Prods., Inc., 892 F.2d 26 (4th Cir. 1989); Smith v. Mixon, 788 F.2d 229 (4th Cir. 1986).

That court later elaborated that knowledge of the avoidability of the transaction is knowledge of facts that would lead a reasonable person to believe the transfer was avoidable and good faith requires that the transferee not be willfully ignorant of the facts. Goldman v. Capital City Mortg. Corp. (*In re* Nieves), 648 F.3d 232 (4th Cir. 2011).

619 *In re* Whaley, 229 B.R. 767 (Bankr. D. Minn. 1999) (transferee that did not produce evidence of good faith or lack of knowledge liable for recovery of preference).

620 Willful ignorance does not constitute good faith under section 550. *In re* Harbour, 845 F.2d 1254 (4th Cir. 1988) (transfer recovered from initial transferee who kept herself willfully ignorant of the circumstances of the transaction even though she retained no funds from the transfer for herself). *See also In re* Grueneich, 400 B.R. 688 (B.A.P. 8th Cir. 2009) (debtor's parents who were aware of his insolvency did not act in good faith).

621 11 U.S.C. § 550(e). *See, e.g., In re* Black & White Cattle Co., 783 F.2d 1454 (9th Cir. 1986).

Improvements are defined in this section to include physical changes, repairs, payment of taxes, payments of any debt secured by a lien, and discharge of any lien superior to the rights of the trustee.

622 Rodriguez v. Drive Fin. Servs. L.P. (*In re* Trout), 609 F.3d 1106 (10th Cir. 2010). *See* § 10.4.2.9, *infra*.

623 *In re* Laizure, 548 F.3d 693 (9th Cir. 2008). *But see* Terry v. Std. Ins. Co. (*In re* Terry), 453 B.R. 760 (Bankr. W.D. Mo. 2011) (where disability insurer recouped disability benefits from debtor's lump sum social security payment and then turned funds over to trustee based on alleged preference, it would be inequitable to allow another recoupment from debtor's future benefits, which would force debtor to pay the money back twice).

624 11 U.S.C. § 550(f).

625 *See In re* Bell, 194 B.R. 192 (Bankr. S.D. Ill. 1996) (because debtors' granting of security interest in vehicles was voluntary, when trustee avoided unrecorded security interests the liens were preserved for benefit of the estate and increased the amount of nonexempt property, so that debtors had to pay increased amount to unsecured creditors under section 1325(a)(4) "best interests of creditors" test). *See also In re* Haberman, 516 F.3d 1207, 1212 (10th Cir. 2008) (preservation of lien only pertains to lien rights in property and not contractual rights).

626 However, the preservation of the lien gives no greater rights than those which the original lienholder possessed. *In re* Carvell, 222 B.R. 178 (B.A.P. 1st Cir. 1998).

627 *See* Kors, Inc. v. Howard Bank, 819 F.2d 19 (2d Cir. 1987); *In re* Newcomb, 2010 WL 383838 (Bankr. D. Mass. Jan. 26, 2010) (debtor stepped into shoes of holder of avoided liens and had lien

fer) for their benefit, however, this avoidance would not benefit the debtors, because it would merely move the mortgage up in priority from a position of being secured in the amount of $2000 and unsecured in the amount of $8000 to being fully secured in the amount of $10,000. By allowing the debtors to preserve the avoided judicial lien for their own benefit, the Code keeps the mortgage in its previous position, that is, secured only to the extent of $2000 and unsecured as to the remaining $8000. Needless to say, this power can be of great importance in cases in which there are multiple liens on a particular property.

It is unclear what, if any, affirmative action must be taken to preserve a transfer under section 522(i)(2). Unlike the trustee's power to have transfers preserved under section 551,[628] it appears that the preservation for the debtor may not be automatic, because the language of section 522(i)(2) states that a transfer "may be preserved," and not that it "is preserved." In view of this language, it is advisable to seek preservation affirmatively as part of the relief when a transfer is avoided, in order to eliminate any possible doubts as to this question. Proper recording of any order so obtained will have the practical benefit of preserving the value of the exemption for the debtor if, for example, the property is sold many years after bankruptcy and a title company is distributing the proceeds of sale.

10.4.2.10 Limits on Availability of Debtor's Avoiding Powers As Applied to Liens Predating the Bankruptcy Reform Act

A flood tide of cases challenging the retroactive application of the debtor's powers to avoid pre-Code liens under 11 U.S.C. § 522(f) reached the United States Supreme Court in 1982. In *United States v. Security Industrial Bank*,[629] the Court held, in order to avoid reaching a difficult constitutional question, that Congress' failure to explicitly deal with retroactivity evidenced an intent that the avoiding powers were to apply only prospectively. Thus, it is now settled that nonpossessory, nonpurchase-money security interests which existed prior to enactment of the Bankruptcy Reform Act on November 6, 1978 cannot be avoided under section 522(f)(1)(B).[630] Given the rationale for the court's decision, it is likely that pre-enactment judicial liens are similarly immune from avoidance under section 522(f)(1)(A).[631] However, at least one court of appeals has held that because judicial liens, especially confessed judgments, were avoidable in some instances under the former Bankruptcy Act, pre-Code judicial liens may be avoided notwithstanding *Security Industrial Bank*.[632]

The Supreme Court expressly declined to decide whether its holding would apply to liens created in the gap period between enactment of the Code and its effective date, about one year later. The constitutional objections to avoidance in such cases have not been found substantial by most lower courts considering the issue, because once the statute was passed all creditors were placed on notice of the status of the liens created by contracts after November 6, 1978.[633] Based on this distinction, the major underpinning for the Supreme Court's ruling is not present for these "gap" liens. It may be significant that shortly after the *Security Industrial Bank* decision, the Court denied certiorari in the only court of appeals case that had expressly considered the gap issue, a decision holding that "gap period" liens could be avoided.[634] Since then, three other courts of appeals have also held that such liens are avoidable.[635]

The Supreme Court's decision also left unanswered a number of other questions. Is the lien created by a refinancing of a consumer debt after the effective date of the Code considered to be a post-Code lien? Creditors may argue that they are protected by a clause in their contracts stating that the lien in the original contract secures future indebtedness. This argument should fail because the parties agreed to a new contract after the Code, a contract in which the terms of the prior contract could be modified, and in which the provisions of the Code became implied terms.[636] Given the propensity of some finance companies to keep debtors as continuous customers by repeated refinancings over the years, any contrary holding would allow security interests in household goods to continue for many years.

Even less clear is the question of whether a new judicial lien is created by state law revival procedures, which in many places must be complied with periodically in order to maintain the lien or its priority. The answer to this question is likely to be found in a careful reading of state law.[637]

---

senior to unrecorded mortgage and deed); *In re* Losieniecki, 17 B.R. 136 (Bankr. W.D. Pa. 1981). *But see In re* Simonson, 758 F.2d 103 (3d Cir. 1985) (refusing to apply section 522(i)(2) or avoid liens when total of mortgages exceeded value of property even though intervening judicial liens rendered one mortgage largely unsecured).

The *Simonson* case was overruled by the 11 U.S.C. § 522(f)(2), enacted in 1994. See § 10.4.2.3.1, *supra*.

628 *See In re* Van De Kamp's Dutch Bakeries, 908 F.2d 517 (9th Cir. 1990) (transfer avoided by trustee as fraudulent was automatically preserved for benefit of estate, regardless whether interest could have been avoided by competing creditor in prepetition state court proceeding).

629 459 U.S. 70, 103 S. Ct. 407, 74 L. Ed. 2d 235 (1982).

630 11 U.S.C. § 522(f)(2) was redesignated 11 U.S.C. § 522(f)(1)(A) by the 1994 amendments to the Code.

631 *In re* White, 25 B.R. 339 (B.A.P. 1st Cir. 1982) (retroactive avoidance of judicial liens not permitted).

Also, shortly after the Supreme Court decided *Security Indus. Bank*, the Court vacated and remanded *In re* Ashe, 669 F.2d 105 (3d Cir. 1982), a case which had previously upheld the retroactive avoidance of judicial liens under section 522(f). Commonwealth Nat'l Bank v. Ashe, 459 U.S. 1082, 103 S. Ct. 563, 74 L. Ed. 2d 927 (1982) (mem.).

632 *In re* Ashe, 712 F.2d 864 (3d Cir. 1983).

633 See, for example, *In re* Webber, 674 F.2d 796 (9th Cir. 1982), and cases cited therein.

634 *In re* Webber, 674 F.2d 796 (9th Cir. 1982).

635 *In re* Washburn & Roberts, Inc., 795 F.2d 870 (9th Cir. 1986); *In re* Ashe, 712 F.2d 864 (3d Cir. 1983); *In re* Groves, 707 F.2d 451 (10th Cir. 1983).

636 Marcus Brown Holding Co. v. Feldman, 256 U.S. 170, 41 S. Ct. 465, 65 L. Ed. 877 (1921).

637 *See* First Nat'l Bank & Trust Co. v. Daniel, 701 F.2d 141 (11th Cir. 1983) (consolidation note did not create new lien); *In re* Hickey, 32

Finally, there will be issues as to the retroactivity of the debtor's other avoiding powers, under 11 U.S.C. § 522(h), which incorporate the trustee's powers. At least to the large extent that the trustee's powers are unchanged from prior law, debtors have good arguments that those powers are not barred by *Security Industrial Bank*. In every such case in which the debtor exercises an avoiding power, the creditor's rights are impaired to no greater extent than they could have been before the Code, by the trustee's own exercise of his or her powers.[638]

In any case, the issue of retroactive application has become largely academic due to the passage of time. It has virtually disappeared, and it will reappear only to the extent the law is again changed.[639]

10.5 Protection of Exempt Property After Discharge

Still another important feature of the bankruptcy exemption scheme is the continuing protection given to exempt property after the discharge. Section 522(c) provides that, with a few exceptions, no creditor holding a prebankruptcy claim may ever execute against the property that has been claimed as exempt.

The principal significance of this subsection is that even creditors holding claims that were not discharged may not reach exempt property to execute on their still-valid claims. Thus, if a debt is not discharged because of a false financial statement, because the debt was not listed, because of fraud, or willful and malicious injury, or on a student loan, the debtor may nevertheless be fully protected from execution on that debt if she has no property except the property exempted in the bankruptcy case.[640] The only exceptions to this general rule are debts for nondischargeable domestic support obligations,[641] liens that are not avoided during the bankruptcy, tax liens, and any student loans, scholarships, or grants obtained by fraud.[642]

Some trustees have argued that these exceptions, which were modified only slightly in 2005,[643] allow them to liquidate exempt property to satisfy claims of such creditors. However, the exceptions do not change the fact that the property is exempt, and therefore removed from the bankruptcy estate, and the trustee only has power to liquidate property of the bankruptcy estate.[644] For this reason, many courts have held that a trustee may not liquidate exempt property to satisfy a domestic support obligation.[645]

Section 522(c) serves the obvious purpose of ensuring that the debtor's fresh start is not frustrated by preexisting debts. It gives the exemptions a permanent character, protecting that minimum grubstake afforded by the exemption provisions (either state or federal) from almost every attack arising out of the debtor's prebankruptcy circumstances.

The protections of section 522(c) do give rise to some issues as to how the exemptions will be applied in later executions on nondischarged prebankruptcy debts. Clearly, property acquired after the bankruptcy is not protected, unless the debtor is able to exempt it under one of the provisions allowing exemption of the right to receive certain benefits in the future.[646] But does the exemption apply forever to the items exempted, or only to the extent of the value exempted?[647] In other words, is a debtor's increased equity in a home totally protected because the home was exempted in the bankruptcy? Certainly, such protection would further the purpose of protecting the debtor's basic necessities if the increase was caused simply by inflation. But the result might be different if the increased equity was purchased with after-acquired assets used to make mortgage pay-

---

B.R. 588 (Bankr. S.D. Ohio 1983) (continuation statement not a new lien).

638 *See In re* Ashe, 712 F.2d 864 (3d Cir. 1983).

639 *See In re* Wilson, 90 F.3d 347 (9th Cir. 1996) (1994 change to section 522(f) does not apply retroactively).

640 *See In re* Cunningham, 513 F.3d 318 (1st Cir. 2008) (creditor holding nondischargeable debt could not execute against proceeds of homestead that was exempted in bankruptcy because allowing creditor to pursue proceeds would contravene section 522(c)'s permanent immunization of exempt property from prepetition claims); *In re* Vaughan, 311 B.R. 573 (B.A.P. 10th Cir. 2004) (for this reason debtors could avoid lien for attorney fees incurred in postpetition dischargeability proceeding).

641 "Domestic support obligation" is defined in 11 U.S.C. § 101(14A).

642 11 U.S.C. § 522(c).

However, these exceptions generally do not eliminate state law protections for property that would never have been subject to such claims outside of bankruptcy. *In re* Davis, 170 F.3d 475 (5th Cir. 1999) (en banc). *See also In re* Dishong, 188 B.R. 51 (Bankr. S.D. Fla. 1995) (tax lien preserved by section 522(c)(2) cannot be used to attach property acquired postpetition for payment of discharged taxes); *In re* Monteith, 23 B.R. 601 (Bankr. N.D. Ohio 1982) (IRS not permitted to setoff postpetition tax refund against *dischargeable* prepetition tax debt).

A 2005 amendment altered this result for domestic support obligations, so that a creditor holding such a claim may execute even on property that would, absent the bankruptcy, have been protected from execution. 11 U.S.C. § 522(c)(1). The existence of the exception does not of itself give creditors with excepted claims the right to levy on exempt assets during the bankruptcy case. *In re* Hebermehl, 132 B.R. 651 (Bankr. D. Colo. 1991).

There may also be an exception for liens for nondischarged federal criminal fines. Although 18 U.S.C. § 3613(e) provides that such fines are not discharged and that liens for such fines shall not be voided in bankruptcy, it does not specifically permit the imposition of a lien after bankruptcy on property protected by section 522(c). However, 18 U.S.C. § 3613(a) provides that such fines are enforceable, notwithstanding any other federal law, against all property of the person fined except property listed in that subsection.

643 Section 522(c)(1) was amended by the 2005 Act.

644 11 U.S.C. §§ 363, 704(a)(1).

645 *See, e.g., In re* Hibbard, 2010 Bankr. LEXIS 2467 (Bankr. S.D. Ohio Aug. 18, 2010); *In re* Bozeman, 376 B.R. 813 (Bankr. W.D. Ky. 2007); *In re* Vandeventer, 368 B.R. 50 (Bankr. C.D. Ill. 2007); *In re* Quezada, 368 B.R. 44 (Bankr. S.D. Fla. 2007); *In re* Ruppel, 368 B.R. 42 (Bankr. D. Or. 2007); *In re* Duggan, 2007 WL 2386577 (Bankr. M.D. Fla. Aug. 15, 2007); *In re* Waters, 2007 WL 1834901 (Bankr. M.D. Ala. June 25, 2007); *In re* Covington, 368 B.R. 38 (Bankr. E.D. Cal. 2006). *See also In re* Wolf, 2012 WL 1856973 (Bankr. E.D. Ky. May 22, 2012) (trustee could not use exempt proceeds of debtor's homestead to pay nondischargeable tax claims).

646 *See, e.g.,* 11 U.S.C. § 522(d)(10), (11).

647 *See In re* Farr, 278 B.R. 171 (B.A.P. 9th Cir. 2002) (section 522(c) applies only to extent of value exempted).

ments. Similarly, with more liquid assets, such as bank accounts, difficult problems of tracing may arise in determining whether certain property was exempted in the bankruptcy.[648] A number of courts have held that, for example, even the right of setoff on exempt property is trumped by section 522(c).[649]

In such cases, there are also questions as to the interplay of the bankruptcy exemptions with the state's normal exemptions from execution. If certain property of the debtor is protected from execution by section 522(c), presumably the debtor may then claim other property as exempt under the state's exemption scheme in the execution. Does it make a difference if, in the bankruptcy, the debtor had been claiming property under the state exemption scheme already, rather than the federal bankruptcy exemptions? In order to promote equality of treatment, it should not.

---

[648] *See In re* Farr, 278 B.R. 171 (B.A.P. 9th Cir. 2002) (creditor holding nondischargeable debt could enforce lien acquired postpetition on portion of debtor's equity that exceeded sum of senior liens and debtor's $100,000 California exemption claimed in chapter 7 case).

[649] *See* § 10.4.2.6.7, *supra*.

Chapter 11 Dealing with Secured Creditors

11.1 Introduction

One of the greatest advances for consumers under the Bankruptcy Code came in the powers they were given with respect to secured debts. Under the prior Bankruptcy Act, relatively little could be done to protect consumer debtors from the holders of secured claims. A straight bankruptcy generally did not affect the status of otherwise valid liens or security interests and, as a practical matter, few Chapter XIII plans could get very far with respect to secured claims unless the holders of those claims agreed to the plan or were not affected by it. Now, in contrast, almost every conceivable type of secured claim can be altered in some way through bankruptcy, often to a tremendous degree and with very significant benefits for the debtor.

Some of the ways that the rights of secured creditors can be affected are covered in previous chapters of this treatise, and those discussions are not repeated here. Chapter 9, *supra*, dealt at length with two of these areas: the automatic stay which, among other things, generally prevents lien creation, perfection, and enforcement once the petition is filed;[1] and the turnover provisions, through which the debtor may recover property from a secured party who has obtained possession of it prior to the case.[2] Chapter 10, *supra*, discusses the various powers of the debtor to avoid transfers, including some liens and security interests which impair the debtor's exemptions.[3] Through use of these powers the debtor can often entirely eliminate security interests in personal property, judicial liens, execution sales, garnishments, repossessions, setoffs, and other transfers of property that occurred before the debtor filed the bankruptcy case.

All of these powers discussed in previous chapters can, of course, enormously improve a debtor's position with respect to many secured claims. This Chapter is devoted to several additional ways in which the problems of secured claims may be lessened or removed. These methods may be used either in conjunction with those options already discussed or when those other remedies are not available.

11.2 Determination of the Allowed Secured Claim

11.2.1 The Concept of the Allowed Secured Claim

11.2.1.1 General Principles

Critical to an understanding of most of the provisions dealing with secured claims is a familiarity with a key concept in the Bankruptcy Code—the "allowed secured claim." Although not defined in the definition section of the Code,[4] the term is explained by section 506, which is applicable to cases under all chapters of the Code.[5]

Code section 506(a) provides that every claim filed which is secured by a lien on property, or subject to a setoff, is an allowed secured claim to the extent of the creditor's interest in the estate's interest in such property or in the amount subject to setoff.[6] To the extent that the creditor's interest, or the amount subject to setoff, is less than the total amount of the claim, the claim is an allowed unsecured claim. Put another way, a secured claim cannot be an allowed secured claim in an amount greater than the value of the estate's interest in the collateral. An undersecured claim which is filed and allowed[7] is therefore divided, or "bifurcated," into two parts: (1) an allowed secured

---

1 11 U.S.C. § 362. *See* § 9.4, *supra*.
2 11 U.S.C. §§ 542, 543. *See* § 9.9, *supra*.
3 11 U.S.C. § 522(f)–(h). *See* § 10.4.2, *supra*.
4 The term "claim," however, is defined at 11 U.S.C. § 101(5).
5 11 U.S.C. § 103(a).
   However, as discussed in § 11.6.1, *infra*, with respect to certain claims secured by purchase money security interests in personal property, section 1325(a) specifically makes section 506 inapplicable to section 1325(a)(5).
6 Disputes sometimes arise about whether a particular transaction gave rise to a secured claim, a lease, or some other type of claim. *See* § 11.8 (rent-to-own contracts), § 12.9.1 (land installment sale contracts and motor vehicle leases), *infra*. In order for an allowed secured claim to exist, the estate must have an interest in the property. Unfortunately, several decisions of the Eleventh Circuit Court of Appeals have erroneously held that Florida and Alabama debtors do not have an interest in motor vehicles after repossession. *See* § 9.9.2, *supra*.
   There are also issues when a claim of the Internal Revenue Service is secured by an ERISA plan that is not property of the estate. Most courts have held the IRS's interest is not an allowed secured claim. Internal Revenue Serv. v. Snyder, 343 F.3d 1171 (9th Cir. 2003) (claim secured by ERISA plan not an allowed secured claim); *In re* Wingfield, 284 B.R. 787 (E.D. Va. 2002) (ERISA plan cannot create an allowed secured claim).
7 Filing and allowance of claims are provided for in 11 U.S.C. §§ 501 and 502.

claim in an amount equal to the value of the collateral and (2) an allowed unsecured claim for any excess of the total claim over the value of the collateral.

One simple example of the application of section 506(a) is a debt, not otherwise subject to defenses or setoffs, in the amount of $2000 secured by an automobile worth $500. With respect to that creditor's claim, the debtor could request a determination that the claim be divided into an allowed secured claim of $500 and an allowed unsecured claim of $1500. Similarly, if, during the entire ninety days prior to the filing of the petition, a debtor had a bank account of $500 subject to setoff by a bank to which the debtor owed $2000, the court would determine that the bank had an allowed secured claim of $500 and an allowed unsecured claim of $1500.

The purpose of this concept is quite apparent. In accord with the general bankruptcy scheme, it looks to the actual interests of the parties existing at the time of the bankruptcy to determine their rights. A secured creditor's interest is measured by what it would receive at that time through enforcement of its lien, and that amount, of course, would be the value of the collateral. The Code, therefore, gives that secured creditor a better position than the unsecured creditors in bankruptcy only to that extent, even if the secured creditor's total claim is much greater than the value of the collateral, because in a practical sense the secured creditor can realize only that value due to its secured status. Its rights to property other than the collateral are no greater than those of other creditors. By treating the amount of the claim which is in excess of the value of the collateral as an unsecured claim, the Code prevents the secured creditor from exercising undue power or getting an unfair advantage in the bankruptcy case over the unsecured creditors out of proportion to the true value of its security interest. There is no special exception to these principles for liens held by the government.[8]

11.2.1.2 Limitations on Claim Bifurcation in Chapter 7

Unfortunately, the Supreme Court somewhat limited the application of the allowed secured claim concept in *Dewsnup v. Timm*.[9] There, despite clear statutory language in Code section 506(d) stating that a lien securing a claim that is not an allowed secured claim is void,[10] the Court held that a chapter 7 debtor could not have a lien declared void on the basis of that language, even though the lien did not secure a claim that was an allowed secured claim under section 506(a). Construing the language extremely narrowly, the Court held that it rendered a lien void only if it secured a claim that was disallowed under section 502 of the Code, such as a claim to which a valid defense existed.[11]

Thus, bifurcation of secured claims is generally relevant in chapter 7 only in the context of redemption under Code section 722, which is discussed later in this chapter.[12] However, a few courts have limited *Dewsnup* to its facts and found that a totally unsecured lien does not come within the prohibition on bifurcation for chapter 7.[13] Additionally, an undersecured judicial lien can be avoided in chapter 7 under the formula created by 11 U.S.C. § 522(f)(2) because it impairs the debtor's exemption.[14]

11.2.1.3 Claim Bifurcation Alive and Well in Other Chapters

After *Dewsnup*, some creditors argued that the decision prevented the use of bankruptcy to void undersecured liens in other contexts than the one presented by that case, including chapter 13. Such arguments were not successful for a number of reasons. First, the Supreme Court made clear in *Dewsnup* that it was limiting its holding to when a chapter 7 debtor relied solely on section 506(d) to render a lien void.[15] It therefore did not purport to affect the law in other chapters, such as chapter 12 and chapter 13. Second, the Court found a lack of legislative history indicating that Congress had intended section 506(d) to be used independently in this manner, a use which would have significantly changed the law in liquidation cases.[16] In contrast, there is clear legislative history indicating congressional intent that a chapter 13 debtor, for example, may free property from a lien by paying the lienholding creditor the present value of its

---

8   *See In re* Voelker, 42 F.3d 1050 (7th Cir. 1994) (value of property subject to tax lien determines what debtor must pay to satisfy lien in chapter 13 plan; however, value of property exempt from levy under Internal Revenue Code must be included in determining allowed secured claim); *In re* Crook, 966 F.2d 539 (10th Cir. 1992) (sovereign immunity was not violated by chapter 12 plan stripping down mortgages held by government).

9   502 U.S. 410, 112 S. Ct. 773, 116 L. Ed. 2d 903 (1992).

10 11 U.S.C. § 506(d) so provides, with certain exceptions which were not pertinent in *Dewsnup*.

11 112 S. Ct. at 777, 116 L. Ed. 2d at 911.

    Based on a close reading of *Dewsnup*, an argument remains that a debtor may strip down a non-recourse loan in chapter 7. (A non-recourse loan is one in which the creditor's only option to collect is to foreclose on or repossess the collateral. Note that in some cases, state law may limit the creditor's remedies to recovery of the collateral.) Because, in the typical non-recourse situation, the creditor has no right to maintain an *in personam* action against the debtor, it follows that the creditor could not have an allowable unsecured claim against the estate for the amount by which it is undersecured. *See* 11 U.S.C. § 502(b)(1). Consequently, that creditor's lien is arguably void to the extent of the undersecurity under section 506(d) and *Dewsnup* because that portion of its claim would neither be secured nor allowable pursuant to section 502.

12 *See* § 11.5, *infra*.

13 *See, e.g.*, McNeal v. GMAC Mortg., L.L.C. (*In re* McNeal), 477 Fed. Appx. 562 (11th Cir. 2012) (non-precedential); *In re* Howard, 184 B.R. 644 (Bankr. E.D.N.Y. 1995) (unsecured judgment lien can be stripped off). *See, e.g.*, *In re* Lavelle, 2009 WL 4043089 (Bankr. E.D.N.Y. Nov. 25, 2009). *But see In re* Talbert, 344 F.3d 555 (6th Cir. 2003) (mortgage cannot be stripped off in chapter 7 case); Ryan v. Homecomings Fin. Network, 253 F.3d 778 (4th Cir. 2001) (wholly unsecured mortgage may not be stripped off in chapter 7); *In re* Laskin, 222 B.R. 872 (B.A.P. 9th Cir. 1998); *In re* Armstrong, 2011 WL 768080 (M.D. Fla. Feb. 28, 2011); *In re* Pomilio, 425 B.R. 11 (Bankr. E.D.N.Y. 2010).

14 *See* § 10.4.2.3, *supra*.

15 112 S. Ct. at 778, n.3, 116 L. Ed. 2d at 911, n.3.

16 112 S. Ct. at 779, 116 L. Ed. 2d at 912.

allowed secured claim through a chapter 13 plan.[17] And third, *Dewsnup* did not deal with situations in which section 506 operates in tandem with another Code section. In fact, it recognized the debtor's right to redeem certain property in section 722,[18] which allows redemption by payment to the lienholder of the amount of its allowed secured claim.[19] Similarly, provisions in chapter 12 and 13 provide that a plan shall be confirmed if it provides for a secured creditor to be paid the amount of its allowed secured claim,[20] that (except as provided in the plan) the confirmation of the plan vests all property of the estate in the debtor free and clear of any lien of any creditor provided for in the plan,[21] and that the terms of the confirmed plan are binding upon all creditors.[22]

The Supreme Court explicitly recognized that most liens could be reduced to the value of their collateral ("stripped down") through a chapter 13 plan in *Associates Commercial Corp. v. Rash*.[23] In that case the Court discussed the amount by which a claim secured by a debtor's property could be stripped down in chapter 13.[24] And, as discussed below, since *Dewsnup* was decided, numerous courts of appeals have held that liens on other property, as well as some home mortgage liens, may still be stripped down through a chapter 13 plan.[25]

11.2.2 Procedure for Determining the Allowed Secured Claim

11.2.2.1 Overview of the Process

A dispute concerning the amount of the allowed secured claim usually arises[26] as an objection filed by the debtor after the creditor has filed its claim.[27] The objection, filed under Bankruptcy Rule 3007, may be included in an adversary proceeding if it raises the validity or extent of the creditor's lien.[28] Therefore, any objection which includes a demand for relief of a kind listed in Bankruptcy Rule 7001 must be filed in the form of a complaint in an adversary proceeding.[29] However, if the only issue is the question of valuation, a motion under Bankruptcy Rule 3012 will suffice as a way to bring the matter before the court.[30]

If the secured creditor fails to file a proof of claim, the debtor may file a claim on behalf of the creditor in the amounts the debtor believes to be secured or unsecured.[31] The creditor then may seek to amend the claim filed by the debtor. In either case, the debtor may initiate a proceeding against the creditor, by complaint or (if valuation is the only issue) by motion, seeking a court order determining the amount of the claim.[32]

A complaint objecting to a secured claim can and should raise any and all defenses to the creditor's claim, because the claim may only be allowed to the extent it is enforceable against the debtor.[33] If the debtor (and thus the bankruptcy estate) no longer has the property which the creditor claims as collateral, because it was transferred, stolen or otherwise lost, the creditor does not have an allowed secured claim under the

---

17 *See* 124 Cong. Rec. H11,107 (daily ed. Sept. 28, 1978) (remarks of Rep. Edwards); 124 Cong. Rec. S17,424 (daily ed. Oct. 6, 1978) (remarks of Sen. DeConcini) (secured creditor's lien retained under section 1325(a)(5) only secures the value of the collateral and is satisfied in full by plan payments equal to present value of allowed secured claim); H.R. Rep. No. 95-595, at 124 (1977).
Certain limitations on this right were added by the 2005 amendments.
18 112 S. Ct. at 776, 116 L. Ed. 2d at 909.
19 *See* § 11.5, *infra*.
20 11 U.S.C. §§ 1225(a)(5), 1325(a)(5). *See* §§ 11.6.1, 17.5.4, *infra*.
21 11 U.S.C. § 1227(b), (c); 11 U.S.C. § 1327(b), (c).
22 11 U.S.C. §§ 1227(a), 1327(a). *See* § 12.11, *infra*.
23 520 U.S. 953, 117 S. Ct. 1879, 138 L. Ed. 2d 148 (1997). *See also In re* McClurkin, 31 F.3d 401, 406 (6th Cir. 1994); *In re* Hammond, 27 F.3d 52, 56 (3d Cir. 1994).
24 *See* § 11.2.2.3, *infra*.
25 *See* §§ 11.2.2, 11.6.1.2, *infra*.
26 As discussed below in this subsection, some courts determine the allowed secured claim in chapter 13 cases, without an objection, in the context of confirming the debtor's chapter 13 plan. A dispute may also arise in the litigation of a motion to redeem under section 722.
27 However, the prior filing of a claim is probably not an absolute prerequisite for seeking a determination of the extent to which a claim is secured. Indeed, it is not at all clear that a secured claim even need be filed to be allowed. Nonetheless, the safer practice is probably for the debtor to file a claim on behalf of the creditor. *See* § 11.6.1.3.3.3, *infra*.
28 Fed. R. Bankr. P. 7001.
The objection is a core proceeding under 28 U.S.C. § 157(b)(2)(K). *See generally* § 13.2.4, *infra*.
29 Fed. R. Bankr. P. 3007(b), 7003. *See* Form 82, Appx. G.8, *infra*.
30 *See* Fed. R. Bankr. P. 3012 advisory committee's note; *In re* Kemp, 391 B.R. 262 (Bankr. D.N.J. 2008) (adversary proceeding not required when only issue is valuation). *See also* Ontra, Inc. v. Wolfe, 192 B.R. 679 (W.D. Va. 1996) (separate adversary proceeding to determine value not necessary if value determined as part of proceeding seeking leave to sell property).
31 Fed. R. Bankr. P. 3004.
A claim filed by the debtor on behalf of a creditor must be filed within thirty days after the deadline for the creditor to file its proof of claim.
32 If the debtor is requesting a determination based on a claim filed by the debtor, the best practice may be to file a complaint seeking declaratory judgment that the claim is allowable only in the amounts reflected in the debtor's proof of claim. Even if the debtor does not seek a declaratory judgment setting the amount of the claim, the creditor may be bound by the debtor's claim, especially if the creditor received notice of the claim, failed to object to it or file an amended claim, and accepted payments under a confirmed plan. Lawrence v. Educ. Credit Mgmt. Corp., 251 B.R. 467 (E.D. Va. 2000), *rev'd on other grounds sub nom. In re* Kielisch, 258 F.3d 315 (4th Cir. 2001). *But see In re* Mansaray-Ruffin, 530 F.3d 230 (3d Cir. 2008) (claim filed by debtor and plan provision declaring debt unsecured insufficient to invalidate lien because no adversary proceeding filed as required by rules and due process considerations).
33 11 U.S.C. § 502(b)(1).
It is not totally clear whether, if the creditor's claim is divided into a secured claim and an unsecured claim, the defenses of the debtor can be applied first to the secured claim rather than the unsecured claim. Certainly, a good argument can be made for this when the defense is in some way logically related to the lien in particular, rather than to the debt in general. *See In re* Jablonski, 70 B.R. 381 (Bankr. E.D. Pa. 1987) (Truth in Lending recoupment subtracted from secured portion of claim).

language of section 506.[34] Or, for example, the debtor may object that the claim is not secured at all, because the purported security interest is invalid.[35]

A creditor must attach to its proof of claim evidence of granting and perfection of a claimed security interest to the proof of claim.[36] If it fails to do so an objection may be filed. An objection may also bring out the fact that such evidence does not exist, or does not comply with Uniform Commercial Code requirements that the collateral be adequately described.[37] The agreement may violate the requirement that the debtor's signature be reasonably legible and below the language concerning the claimed security interest.[38] If the security interest language is in small print, or buried in a credit card agreement, or appears only on a sales slip, unnoticed by the consumer, courts may deem it to be an unenforceable adhesion clause not knowingly signed by the debtor.[39] And consumers may sometimes be able to limit the security agreement to fewer items, or totally invalidate it, by challenging creditors' methods of applying payments to particular items purchased and arguing that the proper method is "first-in, first-out."[40] Similarly, a close reading of the agreement may reveal that it does not secure all of the amounts claimed by the creditor.[41] Objections to claims, and in particular to mortgage claims, are discussed in more detail in Chapter 14, *infra*.[42]

Although some courts determine allowed secured claims as part of the plan confirmation process, the safest practice is to file a complaint or motion objecting to a creditor's secured claim, and to have the claim specifically determined in a separate proceeding. Absent such a proceeding, the claim may be presumed valid.[43] If the court does not affirmatively decide that the claim is not allowable for some particular reason, the claim may be allowed as filed, notwithstanding contrary provisions in the debtor's chapter 13 plan.[44] In any case, the

---

34 *In re* Gilsinn, 224 B.R. 710 (Bankr. E.D. Mo. 1997); *In re* Gabor, 155 B.R. 391 (Bankr. N.D. W. Va. 1993).

35 *See In re* Brigance, 234 B.R. 401 (W.D. Tenn. 1999) ("deferred presentment service" holding check which debtor had obligation to redeem within fourteen days was not holder of a secured claim); *In re* Andrade, 2010 WL 5347535 (Bankr. E.D.N.Y. Dec. 21, 2010) (where debtors had obtained funds based on agreement to place lien on personal injury lawsuit proceeds, lien did not attach when case was settled after bankruptcy petition because proceeds were property of bankruptcy estate); *In re* Reese, 194 B.R. 782 (Bankr. D. Md. 1996) (creditor could not claim Uniform Commercial Code security interest in fixtures which had become part of debtor's realty).

36 Fed. R. Bankr. P. 3001(c), (d).

37 *In re* Esteves Ortiz, 295 B.R. 158 (B.A.P. 1st Cir. 2003) (installment sales agreement did not create security interest); *In re* Renshaw, 68 U.C.C. Rep. Serv. 2d 730 (Bankr. M.D.N.C. 2009) (creditor who had given debtor possession of property that was subject of layaway agreement did not have security interest under state law), *aff'd in part, rev'd in part sub nom*, Hancock v. Renshaw, 421 B.R. 738 (M.D.N.C. 2009); *In re* Shirel, 251 B.R. 157 (Bankr. W.D. Okla. 2000) (phrase "all merchandise" in credit card application did not sufficiently describe collateral and therefore did not create security interest in refrigerator by debtor); U.C.C. § 9-203(1)(a). *See* National Consumer Law Center, Repossessions § 3.2 (7th ed. 2010 and Supp.).

38 *In re* Nedeau, 24 B.R. 1 (Bankr. S.D. Fla. 1982).

39 *See In re* Jackson, 9 U.C.C. Rep. Serv. 1142 (W.D. Mo. 1971); *In re* Gibson, 234 B.R. 776 (Bankr. N.D. Cal. 1999) (cross-collateralization buried in small print was not enforceable); National Consumer Law Center, Unfair and Deceptive Acts and Practices §§ 4.4, 5.6.3 (7th ed. 2008 and Supp.). *But see In re* Conte, 206 F.3d 536 (5th Cir. 2000).

40 *See, e.g., In re* Vandeusen, 147 B.R. 9 (Bankr. E.D.N.C. 1992), *aff'd*, 155 B.R. 358 (E.D.N.C. 1993); *In re* Coomer, 8 B.R. 351 (Bankr. E.D. Tenn. 1980). *See also In re* Freeman, 956 F.2d 252 (11th Cir. 1992) (when agreement provided no method of apportioning payments, purchase money character not preserved); Southeast Bank of Ala. v. Borg-Warner Acceptance Corp., 760 F.2d 1240 (11th Cir. 1985).

See also cases cited in § 10.4.2.5, *supra*.

41 *See, e.g., In re* Stendardo, 991 F.2d 1089 (3d Cir. 1993) (mortgage holder was not entitled to recover amounts it paid for taxes and insurance after it had obtained a judgment absent specific authority in mortgage agreement).

42 *See* § 14.4.3, *infra*.

43 11 U.S.C. § 502(a). *See* H.R. Rep. No. 95-595, at 352 (1977).

44 *In re* Mansaray-Ruffin, 530 F.3d 230 (3d Cir. 2008) (plan provision declaring debt unsecured insufficient to invalidate lien because no adversary proceeding filed); Cen-Pen Corp. v. Hanson, 58 F.3d 89 (4th Cir. 1995) (secured claim was not affected by chapter 13 case, notwithstanding provision of confirmed plan stating that lien of creditor was void, because no separate adversary proceeding had been filed to determine rights of creditor); *In re* Simmons, 765 F.2d 547 (5th Cir. 1985) (secured claim allowed as filed when debtor did not object, notwithstanding contrary provisions in confirmed chapter 13 plan); *In re* Anderson, 305 B.R. 861 (B.A.P. 8th Cir. 2004) (chapter 12 case); *In re* Hobdy, 130 B.R. 318 (B.A.P. 9th Cir. 1991). *See also In re* Bateman, 331 F.3d 821 (11th Cir. 2003) (although mortgage creditor's claim for arrearages had to be disallowed to extent it exceeded amount provided for in confirmed plan, the arrearages disallowed would remain owing after the case because plan could not modify mortgage creditor's secured claim); *In re* Tarnow, 749 F.2d 464 (7th Cir. 1984) (when secured claim was not filed timely and determined, a lien remained valid and was not affected by chapter 11 plan). However, some courts permit the plan confirmation proceeding to be the proceeding in which the valuation determination is made and do not require a separate proceeding for that purpose. If adequate notice is given to the creditor that this will occur, nothing in the Code appears to preclude this procedure. *In re* Fili, 257 B.R. 370 (B.A.P. 1st Cir. 2001) (secured claim filed before bar date but after confirmation hearing disallowed when creditor given fair notice that its claim would be disallowed under chapter 13 plan and creditor ignored the confirmation process); *In re* Millspaugh, 302 B.R. 90 (Bankr. D. Idaho 2003) (debtor permitted to strip off wholly unsecured second mortgage through plan confirmation process and Bankruptcy Rule 3012 valuation motion rather than through an adversary proceeding); *In re* Sadala, 294 B.R. 180 (Bankr. M.D. Fla. 2003) (wholly unsecured second mortgage may be stripped off by motion); *In re* Tucker, 35 B.R. 35 (Bankr. M.D. Tenn. 1983); *In re* Russell, 29 B.R. 332 (Bankr. E.D.N.Y. 1983) (both cases holding that a confirmed plan may determine the status of a claim filed by a secured creditor). *See also In re* Calvert, 907 F.2d 1069 (11th Cir. 1990).

In any event, the fact that a plan has been confirmed does not necessarily preclude the debtor from challenging a proof of claim after confirmation. *In re* Enewally, 368 F.3d 1165 (9th Cir. 2004); *In re* Lewis, 875 F.2d 53 (3d Cir. 1989); *In re* Tomasevic, 275 B.R. 103 (Bankr. M.D. Fla. 2001) (debtor could seek reconsideration under section 502(j) of secured claim that was deemed allowed in confirmed plan); *In re* Adams, 264 B.R. 901 (Bankr. N.D. Ill. 2001) (debtor could seek valuation of allowed secured claim after confir-

creditor involved must receive specific notice that a proceeding concerning its lien is taking place.[45] Even in jurisdictions where it is well known that the court will address the validity and extent of secured claims in the plan confirmation process, notice should include service of a copy of the plan detailing the proposed treatment of the claim on any affected creditor.[46] The notice should also include a clear statement that the creditor's allowed secured claim will be determined at confirmation.[47] Moreover, to be safe, if the creditor is an insured depository institution, such notice should probably be made by certified mail addressed to an officer of the institution.[48]

Assuming the matter is not settled, the issue of value will ultimately be tried and determined by the court. As the proof of claim itself is normally prima facie evidence of the claim,[49] creditors will argue that the debtor has the burden of proof on this issue. However, this argument should fail. While the proof of claim is prima facie evidence under section 502(a), once the party objecting to the claim introduces contrary evidence, the claimant must then bear the ultimate burden of proof.[50]

The methods of contesting and proving value in this context will generally be the same as in the context of proceedings for relief from the automatic stay when value is an issue. Therefore, the discussion of that question in Chapter 9 of this treatise may be helpful. Discovery is often useful, to find out whether the creditor has appraised the collateral and to determine how much the creditor has actually realized by foreclosure on other similar security. Requests for admission may be a way of shifting the cost of a successful proof of value to the creditor if it denies that value.[51] Ultimately, the debtor may have to be prepared to prove a value different from that testified to by the creditor's witnesses, which may require retention of an appraiser or other expert. However, creative discovery, requests for admission as to similar sales and use of industry guides,[52] and so forth, or stipulations of undisputed facts, may provide ways to avoid this expense.

An important difference is that, unlike in proceedings for relief from the stay in which the debtor often tries to prove that the value of property is high so that there is equity in it, under section 506 the debtor's goal is to prove that the value of the property is as low as possible. A number of issues arise in this context, generally going to the language in section 506(a) that "value shall be determined in light of the purpose of the valuation and of the proposed disposition or use of such property."[53]

11.2.2.2 Date of Valuation

11.2.2.2.1 In general

The first issue that arises under section 506 is the date as of which value should be determined. Depending upon whether the property is increasing or decreasing in value, it may be in the debtor's interest to argue for an earlier date or a later one, whichever will produce a lower value. Although there is little difference in most cases, the issue can be significant in cases of rapidly depreciating new automobiles, rapidly appreciating real estate, or property which has been damaged since the filing of the case.

11.2.2.2.2 Statutory rules for some personal property

The 2005 amendments answered the valuation date question for some types of property. Section 506(a)(2) provides that the value of personal property generally should be determined as of the date of the petition, but then establishes a different rule for a subset of such property. The value of personal property acquired for personal, family, or household purposes is to be determined based upon what a retail merchant would charge for property of that kind considering its age and condition *at the time value is determined*. Thus, most personal property in consumer bankruptcy cases will be valued as of the date of the valuation proceeding.

---

mation if confirmed plan did not fix value of secured claim); § 12.11, *infra*. *But see In re* Bateman, 331 F.3d 821 (11th Cir. 2003) (objection to claim must be filed prior to confirmation; court did not address how debtor could object when claim filed after confirmation).

If as a result of a decision on an objection a creditor has been overpaid, the trustee or debtor can recover the overpayment from the creditor. *See In re* Sims, 278 B.R. 457 (Bankr. E.D. Tenn. 2002); *In re* Stevens, 187 B.R. 48 (Bankr. S.D. Ga. 1995).

45 *See In re* White, 908 F.2d 691 (11th Cir. 1990) (bankruptcy court could not *sua sponte* disallow creditor's secured claim without specific notice to creditor that claim was to be challenged); *In re* Calvert, 907 F.2d 1069 (11th Cir. 1990) (specific notice must be given to holder of secured claim that court will determine extent to which its claim is secured at confirmation hearing; mere notice that confirmation hearing will be held is not sufficient); *In re* Shook, 278 B.R. 815 (B.A.P. 9th Cir. 2002) (when debtor listed claim as unsecured in schedules and plan did not specifically address creditor's claim, debtor could not seek to have claim deemed secured four-and-a-half years after confirmation). *But see In re* Karbel, 220 B.R. 108 (B.A.P. 10th Cir. 1998) (notice of motion mailed to creditor at address it had given for motions concerning mobile home transactions satisfied due process even though it concerned different type of collateral).

46 *See In re* Pereira, 394 B.R. 501 (Bankr. S.D. Cal. 2008) (debtor must comply with Bankruptcy Rule 7004(b)(3) and (h) in serving a plan with terms that strip off a wholly unsecured junior lien); *In re* Millspaugh, 302 B.R. 90 (Bankr. D. Idaho 2003); *In re* King, 290 B.R. 641 (Bankr. C.D. Ill. 2003) (discussing requisites of notice required).

47 *See In re* Calvert, 907 F.2d 1069 (11th Cir. 1990).
    Absent such notice due process concerns may be implicated.
48 Fed. R. Civ. P. 7004(h).
49 Fed. R. Bankr. P. 3001(f); H.R. Rep. No. 95-595, at 352 (1977); S. Rep. No. 95-989, at 62 (1978).
50 Heritage Highgate, Inc. v. Scagliotti, 679 F.3d 132 (3d Cir. 2012); *In re* Fid. Holding Co., 837 F.2d 696 (5th Cir. 1988); 9 Collier on Bankruptcy ¶ 3001.09 (16th ed.). *See also* § 14.4.3, *infra*.

51 Fed. R. Bankr. P. 7036 (incorporating Fed. R. Civ. P. 36). *See In re* Sweeten, 56 B.R. 675 (Bankr. E.D. Pa. 1986).
52 *See, e.g.,* Appx. G.8, Form 86, *infra*.
53 *See In re* Midway Partners, 995 F.2d 490 (4th Cir. 1993) (valuation determined in automatic stay proceeding not binding in claim allowance proceeding). *See generally* §§ 9.7.3.3.1, 10.3.3, *supra*.

The Code does not set a valuation date for real property. Under the law prior to 2005, some courts, perhaps in the interest of simplicity, had chosen the filing date of the petition as the valuation date in all cases, on the theory that the parties' rights are frozen as of that date in most other respects.[54] In many cases this approach could be to the debtor's advantage, because the value of real estate usually tends to increase over time. However, in times of declining real estate values, the debtor may seek to set a value as of a later date.[55]

If the debtor seeks a later valuation date for real property, there are several arguments the debtor may make. First, in chapter 13 cases, there is language[56] that the creditor is entitled to the "value as of the effective date of the plan." While that phrase could be interpreted merely as stating a present value standard,[57] it has been held that the amount of the claim should be evaluated as of the date of the confirmation hearing.[58] Another, perhaps better, argument is that under section 506(a) the purpose of the valuation is to protect the interest the creditor has at the time of valuation, because that would be all that could be realized were the creditor to obtain the property at that time. The creditor, after all, has an opportunity to force an earlier valuation by filing a motion for relief from the stay. Some language in the legislative history suggests that the valuation under section 506 may well be different than an earlier valuation under section 362, but it is a bit unclear whether that language refers more to the different purposes of the valuations than to the different dates.[59] Using some of these rationales, a number of courts have used the date of the valuation proceeding (which is often the date of the confirmation hearing) as the critical date for valuation, looking to the value of the property as of that date.[60]

Finally, when there is a postpetition claim in a chapter 13 case, the court may choose the date the claim was filed as the valuation date. Some support for this approach is found both in the Code[61] and in the scant case law on the subject.[62] However, the statutory language in section 1305(b) calling for a determination "as of the date such claim arises" could also be read to call for valuation as of the date the postpetition debt was incurred.[63] Alternatively, the legislative history, which refers to the date of allowance,[64] could be interpreted as calling for valuation as of the date of the valuation proceeding.

11.2.2.3 Method of Valuation

11.2.2.3.1 Valuation standard

More controversial has been the issue of which method to use to determine value once a date has been chosen, an issue that has monetary significance in virtually every case. It is not surprising that many courts have addressed this issue.

Perhaps the easiest case is that of property which has been purchased quite recently in relation to the date of valuation. In such cases, courts have often looked simply to the price actually paid by a willing buyer to a willing seller, and adjusted it for any clear changes in the condition of the property.[65]

The more typical situation involves property of changing value that was purchased substantially in advance of the valuation date. The Supreme Court addressed this issue in the context of valuing a motor vehicle for purposes of a chapter 13 cramdown[66] in *Associates Commercial Corp. v. Rash*.[67] The court rejected the lower court's holding that the appropriate valuation would be the creditor's liquidation value and also rejected the creditor's argument that retail value was the correct figure to use. Instead, the court held that the language of section 506(a) dictated that the debtor's cost of replacing the property be used, but made clear that this cost would not include portions of the retail price that reflect costs a debtor would not

---

54 *In re* Vallejo, 2010 WL 520698 (Bankr. N.D. Cal. Feb. 9, 2010); *In re* Dean, 319 B.R. 474 (Bankr. E.D. Va. 2004); *In re* Willis, 6 B.R. 555 (Bankr. N.D. Ill. 1980); *In re* Siegler, 5 B.R. 12 (Bankr. D. Minn. 1980); *In re* Adams, 2 B.R. 313 (Bankr. M.D. Fla. 1980). *See also In re* Stembridge, 394 F.3d 383 (5th Cir. 2004) (pre-2005 case involving personal property); *In re* Young, 390 B.R. 480 (Bankr. D. Me. 2008) (same result after 2005 amendments); *In re* Hanson, 132 B.R. 406 (Bankr. E.D. Mo. 1991).

55 *See In re* Roach, 2010 WL 234959 (Bankr. W.D. Mo. Jan. 15, 2010) (accepting debtor argument to use confirmation hearing date).

56 11 U.S.C. § 1325(a)(5)(B)(ii).

57 *See* § 11.6.1.3, *infra*.

58 *In re* Landry, 462 B.R. 317 (Bankr. D. Mass. 2011); *In re* Bernardes, 267 B.R. 690 (Bankr. D.N.J. 2001) (when purpose of valuation under section 506(a) is plan confirmation, holder of crammed down mortgage not entitled to reconsideration of its claim based on postconfirmation increase in home value); *In re* Kennedy, 177 B.R. 967 (Bankr. S.D. Ala. 1995) (selecting the confirmation date approach, but collecting cases with a variety of holdings); *In re* McLeod, 5 B.R. 520 (Bankr. N.D. Ga. 1980). *See also* Heritage Highgate, Inc. v. Scagliotti, 679 F.3d 132 (3d Cir. 2012) (chapter 11 case); *In re* Moreau, 140 B.R. 943 (N.D.N.Y. 1992) (when property apparently greatly increases in value after valuation but before confirmation of chapter 13 plan, creditor was entitled to revaluation closer to confirmation date); *In re* Crain, 243 B.R. 75 (Bankr. C.D. Cal. 1999) (effective date of plan was ten days after confirmation order if no appeal taken).

59 S. Rep. No. 95-989, at 68 (1978).

60 *In re* Cook, 415 B.R. 529 (Bankr. D. Kan. 2009); *In re* Militante, 2009 WL 779798 (Bankr. N.D. Cal. Feb. 6, 2009); *In re* Weaver, 5 B.R. 522 (Bankr. N.D. Ga. 1980); *In re* Miller, 4 B.R. 392 (Bankr. S.D. Cal. 1980); *In re* Crockett, 3 B.R. 365 (Bankr. N.D. Ill. 1980). *See also In re* Pierce, 5 B.R. 346 (Bankr. D. Neb. 1980) (value to be determined at date of section 722 redemption proceedings rather than date of petition).

61 11 U.S.C. § 1305(b).

62 *In re* Klein, 20 B.R. 493 (Bankr. N.D. Ill. 1982).

63 11 U.S.C. § 1305(b).

64 H.R. Rep. No. 95-595, at 427 (1977); S. Rep. No. 95-989, at 140 (1978).

65 *In re* Two S Corp., 875 F.2d 240 (9th Cir. 1989) (price obtained through commercially reasonable sale by trustee was conclusive proof of value); *In re* Willis, Jr., 6 B.R. 555 (Bankr. N.D. Ill. 1980); *In re* Savloff, 4 B.R. 285 (Bankr. E.D. Pa. 1980).

   However, because a new car depreciates significantly as soon as it leaves the dealer's lot, the price of a new car will rarely be its market value even a day after it was purchased.

66 *See* § 11.6, *infra*.

67 520 U.S. 953, 117 S. Ct. 1879, 138 L. Ed. 2d 148 (1997).

incur to obtain a similar car in a similar condition, such as warranties, inventory storage, and reconditioning.[68] The court left to the bankruptcy courts, as triers of fact, the best way of determining replacement value based on the evidence presented.

The *Rash* replacement value standard has largely been codified for personal property in section 506(a)(2), which states that the value of personal property shall be determined based on replacement value without deduction of costs of sale or marketing. With respect to property acquired for personal, family, or household purposes, the subsection further elaborates that replacement value means the price a retail merchant would charge for property of the same kind considering the age and condition of the property at the time value is determined. Because factors like reconditioning and warranties clearly affect what a retail merchant would charge, it appears that the general standards adopted after *Rash* for determining replacement value in chapter 13 will continue to be used. However, as discussed below, the value used in redemption proceedings may change.[69]

Because section 506(a)(2), as amended in 2005, states that costs of sale shall not be considered in valuing personal property,. there is certainly a new argument that Congress, by negative implication, has permitted such costs to be deducted with respect to real property. However, to reach this conclusion, a court would have to find that Congress intended to overrule preexisting law under *Rash*.

11.2.2.3.2 Valuation of motor vehicles

Valuation issues arise most frequently, as they did in the *Rash* case, with respect to motor vehicles. Based upon *Rash* and section 506(a)(2), debtors should have little trouble in convincing bankruptcy courts that creditors should not receive the retail value listed in various industry price guides, because that value includes items such as warranties and reconditioning, precisely the items the Supreme Court held must be excluded from the value, and items which section 506(a)(2) excludes from value by requiring that the age and condition of the property be considered. As discussed immediately above, the 2005 amendments should not change debtors' rights in this regard.[70]

Since *Rash*, courts have used a variety of different approaches to valuation of vehicles. Some courts have continued to use presumptive formulas, such as beginning at the midpoint between wholesale and retail value.[71] Others have begun with a presumption of retail value even though that choice does not reflect the necessary deductions from retail value discussed in the *Rash* decision.[72] Others have taken evidence in an attempt to follow the Supreme Court's directives, sometimes coming out even below the wholesale value of the vehicle.[73]

Even if a particular method of valuation is used as a starting point by the court or by agreement between the parties, the debtor may offer evidence that the valuation of a particular vehicle should differ from the presumed value.[74] Initial presentation of relevant evidence by the debtor is especially important, as the debtor has the burden of coming forward with evidence to rebut the creditor's proof of claim, even though the ultimate burden remains on the creditor to prove its claim.[75]

The most promising line of argument for debtors is to focus on the Supreme Court's language that "replacement value" means the price a willing buyer in the debtor's trade, business, or situation would pay a willing seller to obtain property of like age and condition.[76] This language, along with the section 506(a)(2) reference to retail merchants, suggests that debtors look at the prices of cars that are marketed to the public in any retail sphere (as opposed to wholesale prices of vehicles marketed to dealers). Good evidence of retail value may be the prices obtained for similar vehicles on auction sites such as eBay, or the asking prices for similar vehicles on Internet used car sales sites. The prices obtained in such sales, which are "as is" and do not include dealers' overhead such as showroom costs and dealer preparation for sale, are typically far below the retail values in industry guides.[77] Naturally, the cost of repairs to bring the car to average working condition should be deducted from the prices advertised.[78] Alternatively, debtors can base their valuations on values obtained in public auction sales of similar vehicles following repossession. The prices realized at auction sales are also well below the retail value listed in industry guides. Such sales, which also do not have the dealer overhead involved, in fact are often touted by repossessing

---

68 *Id.*, 520 U.S. at 964 n.6.
69 *See* § 11.5, *infra*.
70 *See In re* De Anda-Ramirez, 359 B.R. 794 (B.A.P. 10th Cir. 2007); *In re* Mayland, 2006 WL 1476927 (Bankr. M.D.N.C. May 26, 2006) (court applied section 506(a)(2) in redemption context by using same replacement value standard established by *Rash*, consistent with prior practice in district).
71 *See, e.g., In re* Getz, 242 B.R. 916 (B.A.P. 6th Cir. 2000); *In re* Lyles, 226 B.R. 854 (Bankr. W.D. Tenn. 1998); *In re* Williams, 224 B.R. 873 (Bankr. S.D. Ohio 1998); *In re* Franklin, 213 B.R. 781 (Bankr. N.D. Fla. 1997). *See also In re* Renzelman, 227 B.R. 740 (Bankr. W.D. Mo. 1998) (starting point of five percent less than retail value).
72 *In re* Russell, 211 B.R. 12 (Bankr. E.D.N.C. 1997).
73 *In re* McElroy, 210 B.R. 833 (Bankr. D. Or. 1997) (basing decision primarily on testimony of used car dealer).
74 *See In re* Jenkins, 215 B.R. 689 (Bankr. N.D. Tex. 1997) (encouraging the debtor and creditors bar to reach an accommodation for valuations subject to presentation of evidence in order to limit the court's involvement to special cases).
75 *See In re* Gates, 214 B.R. 467 (Bankr. D. Md. 1997) (proof of claim provides prima facie evidence relevant to valuation, subject to a burden on the debtor of coming forward with evidence sufficient to contradict it).
76 *Id.*, at n.2.
77 Some industry guides, such as the Kelly Blue Book (available at www.kbb.com), have a private party valuation for used cars that can be used for this purpose. *See In re* De Anda-Ramirez, 359 B.R. 794 (B.A.P. 10th Cir. 2007) (Kelley Blue Book private party value meets *Rash* standard); *In re* Martinez, 409 B.R. 35 (Bankr. S.D.N.Y. 2009) (Kelley Blue Book private party value reflects meaning of § 506(a)(2), which incorporates *Rash* decision).
78 *In re* Hauser, 405 B.R. 684 (Bankr. S.D. Fla. 2009) (value should be reduced by retail cost of repairs debtor would have to pay, rather than retailer's discounted repair costs).

sellers as a perfect market of willing buyers and sellers in which to conduct a commercially reasonable sale in order to justify their repossession and deficiency collection practices.[79]

In order to prove the replacement value of a debtor's vehicle, the debtor may of course present expert testimony of an auctioneer or similar witness. The debtor is also competent to give a value of the debtor's property,[80] but that value will be credible only to the extent the debtor provides persuasive reasons to justify it. If the debtor has attempted to sell the vehicle, or purchase a similar one, that experience may be a good basis for expressing an opinion on value. The debtor may also base an opinion on review of Internet sites such as eBay, used car sales sites, and industry guides available on the Internet. It may also be possible to obtain proof in the discovery process, through interrogatories requesting information about the price obtained at auction for similar vehicles which the creditor has recently repossessed, and requests for admission that newspaper ads, eBay listings, or Internet sites accurately reflect the asking price for similar vehicles.[81] Similarly, if the vehicle needs repairs, the creditor can be asked to admit that an estimate of necessary repairs is accurate, so that the amount of the estimate can be deducted from the value of a similar vehicle in good condition. If a creditor denies such requests for admission, the cost of proving the truth of the statements can be shifted to the creditor. Moreover, a party responding to a request for admissions may not simply deny its truth without some investigation; thus, a creditor might even be sanctioned if it denied the truth without making reasonable inquiries, such as calling the telephone number listed in a newspaper advertisement.[82]

11.2.2.3.3 Property other than automobiles

With respect to household goods and other personal property without established industry guides to value, the problem of valuation is more difficult. The *Rash* decision's rejection of retail value for automobiles should clearly prevent purchase price, even from a used furniture store, from becoming the standard. Again, the best guideline is probably the price that would be obtained on eBay, at a flea market or an auction, or in the garage sale market populated by individual buyers and sellers. In some areas there may also be people who, as an occupation, conduct yard sales for others and such people would also be good witnesses, as might a dealer or hobbyist who regularly frequents yard sales.[83] The debtor is also competent to give a value of the debtor's property,[84] but that value will be credible only to the extent the debtor provides persuasive reasons to justify it. Thus, a debtor might be instructed to do research on the Internet or go to a large number of sales and observe the prices of items similar to that in question. In many rural areas, auctioneers may be called to testify concerning the value of different items in that market.

In the case of real estate, an appraisal is often necessary. As in other types of proceedings, there may be ways to avoid or minimize the costs involved. For example, if a court accepts an appraiser's testimony that a property is worth an amount denied by an opposing party in a request for admissions, that party can be required to pay the cost of the appraiser.[85] In other cases, the parties may agree to be bound by the appraisal of an appraiser that both trust, thereby avoiding the expense of the appraiser's court appearance. Often, an appraiser will give an estimate of value that the parties can accept (or which can be a basis for negotiation) based on less than a full-blown appraisal report. Other courts may allow, or require, testimony by affidavits. Finally, a request for production of documents or a request for admissions may turn up a useful appraisal in the creditor's files. It is not uncommon for foreclosing lenders to obtain a low appraisal of real estate in anticipation of foreclosure. In doing so, they hope to protect against a later claim that the property was sold at foreclosure for less than reasonable value.

In any case, it is a good idea for attorneys doing a significant number of bankruptcy cases to develop a relationship with at least one appraiser in whom they have confidence. The prospect of continued business from an attorney will make the appraiser much more willing to cooperate in minimizing costs in a particular case.

Again, a method of proof available in all such cases is to have the debtor testify as to the value of the property, especially when the opposing party has no first-hand knowledge of the property or its condition. Generally, under the Federal Rules of Evidence, a witness may testify as to the value of his or her own property.[86] Even if the debtor has no personal knowledge of the value of the property, the debtor may nevertheless testify as to any problems with the condition of the property which decrease its value below that of other similar property. This evidence can be extremely helpful in refuting a creditor's appraisal, which may not be based on an inspection of the home's interior or knowledge of problems in the surrounding area.[87]

A common issue in valuations of real estate is whether liquidation costs should be deducted when the debtor proposes to retain and use the property. This issue is discussed in more detail in the section directly below. It is clear that no additional

---

79 *See* National Consumer Law Center, Repossessions § 10.10.4 (7th ed. 2010 and Supp.).
80 *See* § 11.3.2, *infra*.
81 *See Resolving Valuation Issues After Rash*, 16 NCLC REPORTS Bankruptcy and Foreclosures Ed. 1 (July/Aug. 1997).
   See also Form 86, Appendix G.8, *infra*, for a sample request for admission.
82 Fed. R. Civ. P. 36(a) (incorporated in Fed. R. Bankr. P. 7036).
83 Under Federal Rules of Evidence 701 and 702, an individual may qualify as an expert or be permitted to express an opinion based upon knowledge and experience not possessed by the average person. *See* Fed. R. Evid. 702 advisory committee's note.

84 *See* § 11.3.2, *infra*.
85 *See* § 11.2.2.2, *supra*; Form 113, Appx. G.10, *infra*.
86 Fed. R. Evid. 701. *See* Joe T. Dehmer Distributors, Inc. v. Temple, 826 F.2d 1463 (5th Cir. 1987); Bingham v. Bridges, 613 F.2d 794 (10th Cir. 1980); Kinter v. United States, 156 F.2d 5 (3d Cir. 1946); *In re* Karakas, 2007 WL 1307906 (Bankr. N.D.N.Y. May 3, 2007).
87 *In re* Lewis, 419 B.R. 804 (Bankr. E.D. Mo. 2009) (finding that value was less than creditor's appraisal based on testimony of debtor that property was in need of significant repairs).

amount should be added for an assignment of rents taken as part of the creditor's collateral, because the rental value is already taken into account in determining the property's market value.[88]

11.2.2.3.4 Computation of value

When there are prior liens on property ahead of the lien which is to be valued, the amount of those liens must first be subtracted to determine if there is value over and above the prior liens. If the prior liens equal or exceed the value of the property, then the allowed secured claim of a creditor with a lower priority lien is equal to zero.[89] When making these calculations, debtor's counsel should make certain to account for tax and municipal liens which take first priority position in most jurisdictions by statute. These are frequently forgotten in the process of determining the allowed secured claims of junior creditors. If the debtor is not the sole owner of the property, the value of the debtor's fractional interest after deduction of liens must then be determined.

Under *Rash* the value would not include the costs involved in listing a property for sale with a real estate broker, because the debtor will not receive any services from a broker. Other costs of sale would also have to be examined under the rationale of *Rash*, which will necessitate reevaluation of decisions which had considered whether costs of sale should be deducted in determining value.[90] However, for cases filed after the effective date of the 2005 amendments, the law may be different for real property. As discussed above, section 506(a)(2) provides that personal property must be valued without deducting costs of sale or marketing. There is a strong argument, by negative implication, that Congress intended a different rule to apply to real property.

Valuation issues can also arise when the property that secures a claim, or a portion of that property, is not property of the estate. For example if the debtor is a one-half owner of a property, the allowed secured claim should be determined by comparing the claim only to the debtor's one-half ownership interest, with the full amount of prior liens deducted from the value of that one-half interest.[91] If the property is owned by the entireties or by joint tenants with a right of survivorship, some courts also require calculation of the value of the survivorship interest.[92] If the debt is secured in whole or in part by an ERISA pension plan, or some other property that is not property of the estate, the value of the non-estate property should not be included in the computation of the allowed secured claim.[93]

An additional issue which may arise with respect to certain types of statutory liens, such as federal tax liens, is whether in assigning a value to property subject to a lien, the value of property exempt from levy should be included. (For example, the Internal Revenue Code exempts certain property from levy on tax liens.)[94] Two courts of appeals, reversing lower courts, have held that all property subject to the lien must be included, even though some of it could not be seized by the Internal Revenue Service.[95] There is certainly a good argument that the lower courts were correct, because the purpose of the exemption from levy is defeated if the debtors have to pay the lienholder the value of the property that is exempt from levy. Other courts have read the Internal Revenue Code exemption to exempt property not just from a levy, as the Ninth Circuit held, but also from the tax lien itself.[96]

Finally, in some cases the estate's interest in the property securing a debt may be valueless because the property is gone. The property may have been destroyed, stolen, or lost to the debtor prior to the bankruptcy, or sold by the debtor subject to the lien. If the property is no longer owned by the debtor, the estate's interest in the property has no value. In such a case, the allowed secured claim is zero and the claim is deemed an allowed unsecured claim.[97]

11.3 Creditors' Efforts to Obtain Security After Bankruptcy Commenced

11.3.1 Overview

The first problem often faced by debtors with secured creditors is that of a creditor's attempt in the bankruptcy court to exercise the rights it would otherwise have available to seize or foreclose on the collateral. These attempts may come in a number of forms.

The most common method is the creditor's motion for relief from the automatic stay which is essentially a request for permission from the bankruptcy court to take action against the debtor outside the bankruptcy forum. These proceedings are discussed in detail in Chapter 9, *supra*.[98]

In an attempt to avoid the difficulties it might face in such a proceeding, or to add to the relief it could obtain, the creditor might file several other types of actions.

---

88 *In re* Thompson, 352 F.3d 519 (2d Cir. 2003).
89 *In re* Smith, 92 B.R. 287 (Bankr. S.D. Ohio 1988).
90 *In re* Taffi, 96 F.3d 1190 (9th Cir. 1996) (en banc).
91 *In re* Abruzzo, 249 B.R. 78 (Bankr. E.D. Pa. 2000) (tenancy in common).
92 *See In re* Pletz, 221 F.3d 1114 (9th Cir. 2000); *In re* Murray, 318 B.R. 211 (Bankr. M.D. Fla. 2004) (entireties interest valued using joint actuarial tables); *In re* Basher, 291 B.R. 357 (Bankr. E.D. Pa. 2003) (interest in entireties property should be determined by joint actuarial analysis).
93 Internal Revenue Serv. v. Snyder, 343 F.3d 1171 (9th Cir. 2003) (claim secured by ERISA plan not an allowed secured claim); *In re* Wingfield, 284 B.R. 787 (E.D. Va. 2002) (ERISA plan cannot create an allowed secured claim). *But see In re* Jones, 206 B.R. 614 (Bankr. D.D.C. 1997).
94 26 U.S.C. § 6334.
95 *In re* Voelker, 42 F.3d 1050 (7th Cir. 1994); United States v. Barbier, 896 F.2d 377 (9th Cir. 1990), *rev'g* 84 B.R. 190 (D. Nev. 1989) *and* 77 B.R. 799 (Bankr. D. Nev. 1987).
96 *In re* Ray, 48 B.R. 534 (Bankr. S.D. Ohio 1985).
97 *In re* Gabor, 155 B.R. 391 (Bankr. N.D. W. Va. 1993) (when debtor's wife took automobile that secured loan and debtor did not know her whereabouts or whereabouts of vehicle, estate's interest in automobile had no value).
98 *See* § 9.7, *supra*.

11.3.2 Reclamation of Property

A creditor may occasionally file a Complaint to Reclaim Property, sometimes known as a Complaint in Reclamation. Although the Code does not specifically provide for such a proceeding, it seems fairly clear that the expanded jurisdiction of the bankruptcy court would include jurisdiction over the assertion of any valid rights that the creditor might have, including a right to gain possession of the collateral. However, these rights are clearly limited by specific provisions contained in the Code. Most important among these limitations is the automatic stay against lien enforcement in section 362(a). Unless the creditor meets the requirements for relief from the stay, there would be no point in proceeding to the question of the creditor's right to possession of the property, as the stay prohibits "any act" to enforce a lien.

Other limitations on the creditor's right to possession that could also be raised to defeat many reclamation complaints would include the debtor's powers under the exemption provisions in section 522,[99] the debtor's right to redeem under section 722,[100] the fact that a creditor is bound by a confirmed chapter 13 plan, giving the debtor the right to possession of the property in question,[101] or the fact that the creditor's lien may be found void under section 506(d) because the creditor is wholly or partially undersecured. Finally, a number of bankruptcy courts have held that they simply do not wish to become involved in creditors' attempts to circumvent normal state court proceedings and have abstained from ruling on creditor claims for repossession.[102] For this reason, creditors seeking possession of property usually file motions for relief from the automatic stay.

11.3.3 Abandonment of Property by the Trustee

Another tactic that is occasionally tried is to have the trustee abandon her interest in the property sought by the secured creditor. Under the previous Act, such abandonment left parties with interests in the property free to proceed outside of the bankruptcy court. A trustee may thus be asked by the creditor to voluntarily abandon the collateral, as the trustee may do under section 554(a), or the court may be requested by a creditor to order such abandonment under section 554(b).

It should first be noted that abandonment is proper only in situations in which the property is either burdensome to the estate or of inconsequential value to the estate.[103] As the first of these conditions will rarely exist, creditors will usually attempt to prove the second, arguing that there is no nonexempt equity, or perhaps no equity at all in the property above the value of the liens.

Especially when there is some equity, these arguments should fail. Any equity is property of the estate, even if claimed as exempt, because Congress has made clear that exempt property is part of the bankruptcy estate under the Code.[104] And property may have value to the estate in a non-monetary sense. In a chapter 13 case, it may be necessary to the production of income, or the necessity for the replacement of property may cause difficulties in completing a successful plan. Furthermore, in both chapters 7 and 13, the debtor may claim an interest of nominal value as exempt, making it clear that the interest is a part of the estate.[105]

More importantly, the limitations described above as to reclamation would also apply in cases in which abandonment is sought. Even if property is abandoned by the trustee, the automatic stay would still prevent any act to obtain possession from the debtor through enforcement of a lien or to collect a prepetition claim, unless such relief from the stay has been granted by the court.[106] Although such acts would not violate the provisions of the stay pertaining to property of the estate, they would violate those provisions prohibiting any act to collect a prepetition claim.[107]

Similarly, the abandonment provisions must be read together with other sections of the Code, for example, sections 506, 522, 722, and 1327. To the extent that abandonment runs counter to the purposes of those sections, it should not be allowed, and the property should be considered of value to the estate.[108] In addition, if property has vested in the debtor through confirmation of a chapter 13 plan,[109] the trustee no longer has an interest in the property that can be abandoned.[110]

Procedurally, abandonment cannot happen before the end of the case, except "after notice and a hearing." Because of the specific meaning given to those words by the Code,[111] the debtor must be certain to request a hearing if notice is given of possible abandonment of property and the debtor is concerned about possible creditor actions, otherwise no hearing is likely to be held. In cases in which the trustee does decide to abandon property the court may prohibit that action. While the trustee

---

99 See Chapter 10, *supra*, for further discussion of the debtor's powers under this section.
100 See § 11.5, *infra*.
101 11 U.S.C. § 1327(a). See § 12.11, *infra*.
102 See *In re* Calabria, 5 B.R. 73 (Bankr. D. Conn. 1980) (state court "far more able" to hear mortgage foreclosure claims).
103 11 U.S.C. § 554.
104 H.R. Rep. No. 95-595, at 368 (1977).
   It is unclear how long exempt property remains property of the estate, however. See discussion of this issue in Chapter 10, *supra*.
105 See cases cited in § 10.4.2.1, *supra*.
106 *In re* Motley, 10 B.R. 141 (Bankr. M.D. Ga. 1981); *In re* Cruseturner, 8 B.R. 581 (Bankr. D. Utah 1981). See also *In re* Boback, 273 B.R. 158 (Bankr. E.D. Tenn. 2002) (distinguishing stay relief from abandonment); *In re* Shelton, 273 B.R. 116 (Bankr. W.D. Ky. 2002) (same).
107 11 U.S.C. § 362(a) (1), (5), (6).
108 See *In re* Hawkins, 8 B.R. 637 (Bankr. N.D. Ga. 1981).
109 11 U.S.C. § 1327(b).
   But see cases cited in § 9.4.3, *supra*, which hold that when property of estate vests in the debtor it is no longer protected by provisions pertaining to property of the estate.
110 *In re* Stark, 8 B.R. 233 (Bankr. N.D. Ohio 1981).
111 11 U.S.C. § 102(1).

does have considerable discretion on this subject, it was generally assumed under the prior Act that it was subject to control by the court.[112]

11.3.4 Disposition by the Trustee Under Section 725

Creditors on rare occasions also have sought to make use of section 725 of the Code which allows the trustee to "dispose of" property. Although the legislative history is not very illuminating, it appears that the purpose of this section is merely to supplement the other powers of the trustee when none of them seem applicable, and perhaps to provide a statutory basis for some types of voluntary reclamations when there is no objection by the trustee. (For example, if the estate has some significant interest in the property securing a claim, section 554 could not be used by the trustee.) By its very language, section 725 indicates that it is to be read together with the various other sections which control disposition of property, including sections 362, 506, 522, and 722. As in section 554, there is no indication that the trustee has the power to dispose of any interest of the debtor in property.

Nonetheless, trustees in a few places have attempted to sell homes and other property in chapter 7 cases, even though there is no equity available for unsecured creditors, in order to realize commissions and fees on such sales. These attempts are clearly improper.[113] Often, they may be prevented simply by bringing them to the attention of the United States trustee. If that is not sufficient, an objection to the sale should be filed with the court.

There is one situation, though, in which it is to the debtor's advantage to have the trustee sell property, regardless of whether there are significant proceeds for creditors. If the debtor will not be able to save a property from foreclosure, a sale by a bankruptcy trustee can sometimes avoid significant capital gains tax liability. Normally, when a property is sold at foreclosure, the owner of the property is liable for taxes on any capital gain over the property's basis. If a property is abandoned by the trustee, and later sold at foreclosure, this could mean a substantial tax liability for the debtor. But if the trustee sells the property, the estate incurs the tax liability and the debtor does not. However, unless the property is not the debtor's principal residence or the capital gain is very large, the danger of debtors being saddled with such capital gains liabilities after foreclosure is eliminated by the provisions of the Internal Revenue Code which allow a capital gains tax exemption for the sale of the debtor's principal residence.[114]

In the event that section 725 is used, its effect and operation is similar to that of section 554. The trustee may act only "after notice and a hearing." Any dispute concerning the trustee's proposed action must be resolved by the court.[115] Certainly, if state law procedural or substantive rights may be lost, the debtor should strongly oppose any attempt by the trustee to sell property that does not have significant nonexempt equity that would be available to unsecured creditors.[116] As a practical matter, this section is little used in consumer cases, because it appears to be intended mainly to give flexibility in the disposition of property in a bankruptcy when there are nonexempt assets for the trustee to administer. Few bankruptcies involving consumer debtors involve any significant administration or distribution of assets by the trustee.

11.3.5 Holding of Cash Collateral by Creditors

A final and conceptually different way in which debtors may be deprived of certain property after bankruptcy, should also be mentioned. After filing a bankruptcy case, a debtor may suddenly find that a bank or credit union to which the debtor owes money refuses to allow withdrawals from the debtor's bank or share account. This refusal occurs because the bank or credit union, if it has a right of setoff under section 553,[117] is considered to be a holder of cash collateral.

If, under section 553, the bank retains a right of setoff, it may not exercise that setoff without first obtaining relief from the automatic stay.[118] However, it is not automatically required to turn over the property to the trustee or the debtor under section 542, because section 542(b) creates an exception excusing payment of a debt to the extent that it may be offset against a claim against the debtor. Moreover, section 542 requires turnover only of property the trustee may use, sell or lease or that the debtor may exempt. The trustee may not use, sell, or lease cash collateral without the creditor's consent unless the court, after notice and a hearing, finds that there is adequate protection[119] and approves such use.[120] In addition, the debtor's exemption rights may also be defeated by a right of setoff

---

112 *See* 5 Collier on Bankruptcy ¶ 554.LH[1] (16th ed.).
    Federal Rule of Bankruptcy Procedure 6007(c) makes clear that, when any party objects, the court shall decide upon the propriety of abandonment.
113 *In re* Kusler, 224 B.R. 180 (Bankr. N.D. Okla. 1998) (criticizing trustee for selling encumbered property which would not realize significant dividends for creditors). *See In re* Williamson, 94 B.R. 958 (Bankr. S.D. Ohio 1988); *In re* Landenreau, 74 B.R. 12 (Bankr. W.D. La. 1987); *In re* Lambert Implement Co., 44 B.R. 860 (Bankr. W.D. Ky. 1984). *See also* § 3.5.2, *supra*.

114 26 U.S.C. § 121. *See* National Consumer Law Center, Foreclosures Ch. 16 (4th ed. 2012).
115 6 Collier on Bankruptcy ¶ 725.02 (16th ed.).
116 *See In re* Landenreau, 74 B.R. 12 (Bankr. W.D. La. 1987); *In re* Lambert Implement Co., 12 Bankr. Ct. Dec. (LRP) 651 (Bankr. W.D. Ky. 1984).
117 See Chapter 10, *supra*, for a discussion of section 553.
118 11 U.S.C. § 362(a)(7).
119 For a discussion of the concept of adequate protection, see Chapter 9, *supra*.
120 11 U.S.C. § 363(c)(2).
    It would be difficult to provide adequate protection in such cases, except perhaps through granting of a lien which clearly exceeded the amount of the cash collateral in value.

allowed under section 553, just as they may be by a valid non-avoidable lien.[121]

The Supreme Court has held that the freezing of a debtor's account by a bank with a right of setoff does not violate the automatic stay. In *Citizens Bank of Maryland v. Strumpf*[122] the court held that an "administrative hold" on the debtor's account was not a setoff prohibited by Code section 362(a)(7) because it did not purport to permanently reduce the account.[123] The court also held that the freeze was not an exercise of control over the debtor's property because the bank account was only a promise by the bank to pay the depositor and the bank was merely refusing to perform on its promise.[124]

In any case, it is clear that a bank has no right of setoff based upon a prepetition debt against property acquired postpetition.[125] To the extent the bank did not have a deposit to setoff against its debt at the time of the petition, it is the holder of an unsecured claim.

The problem of a bank account "freeze" and setoff can generally be prevented simply by making sure the debtor has no money in the account as of the date of the bankruptcy petition. If a debtor has not depleted bank accounts prior to bankruptcy, those accounts, or parts of them, may in effect be seized by the bank or credit union creditor. Once this has occurred, assuming that a valid right of setoff exists[126] and unless there are defenses to the underlying claim or adequate protection can be provided, there may be little that can be done to recover the debtor's funds.

11.4 Statement of Intention with Respect to Property Securing Consumer Debts and with Respect to Personal Property Leases

11.4.1 Overview

Section 521(a)(2) requires the debtor in a chapter 7 case to file a statement of certain intentions with respect to property securing debts and with respect to personal property leases. The debtor need not state all of his or her plans on this statement. All that is required is a statement of whether the debtor intends to retain or surrender the collateral, whether it is claimed as exempt, and whether the debtor intends to reaffirm the debt. The Official Form for the Statement of Intentions has been amended to clarify that it was not intended to require the debtor to choose redemption, surrender, or reaffirmation in every case.[127] The debtor may choose other options besides those listed on the form and state them if the debtor so chooses.[128] In many cases, for example, a debtor may choose to simply continue paying an automobile loan without either redeeming or reaffirming the debt, because the creditor consents or because it is permitted by bankruptcy or nonbankruptcy law.[129] With respect to leases of personal property, the debtor must state whether the debtor intends to assume the lease.[130]

The statement of intention must be filed within thirty days of the filing of a chapter 7 petition or on or before the date of the meeting of the creditors, whichever is earlier.[131] The court, within that period, can also extend the deadline.[132] The statement must be served on the trustee and all creditors named in the statement on or before the date it is filed.[133] Thereafter, the debtor may amend it as of right at any time up to the time when performance is to take place under Code section 521(a)(2)(B).[134] The statement is not required in chapter 13 cases, despite some slight ambiguity on the subject.[135]

Section 521(a)(2) also requires that the debtor "shall perform his intention," within thirty days after the first date set for the meeting of creditors or such additional time as the court for cause within that period allows. In most cases this is quite simple; if the debtor stated an intent to retain or exempt property, that has long since been accomplished. If the debtor's intention is to surrender the property, there is no requirement to deliver it or to execute a deed to effectuate the surrender, because the Code provision was not designed to provide a substitute for normal state law proceedings to enforce a creditor's rights to collateral.[136] If the debtor has stated an intention to redeem the property, filing a motion to redeem should be sufficient, since the debtor has no power to do anything more than that until the motion is decided. Proposing a redemption agreement should also be sufficient, at least if it has not been rejected.[137] The provisions can be seen as setting a guideline for when redemption or reaffirmation should be accomplished if

---

121 However, several courts have held that no setoff may be had against exempt property. See § 10.4.2.6.7, supra.
122 516 U.S. 16, 116 S. Ct. 286, 133 L. Ed. 2d 258 (1995).
123 Id., 116 S. Ct. at 289.
    See § 9.4.4, supra, for further discussion of when a bank account freeze is permissible.
124 116 S. Ct. at 290.
125 See § 10.4.2.6.7, supra.
126 Generally, credit card issuers that are depository institutions are not permitted to set off funds of the card holder held on deposit with the card issuer to collect credit card debts. 15 U.S.C. § 1666h(a).
127 Official Bankruptcy Form 8 (reprinted in Appx. D, infra); 1997 Amendment to Official Form 8 Advisory Committee Note.
128 See § 7.3.11, supra; Official Form 8 (reprinted in Appx. D, infra).
129 See In re Parlato, 185 B.R. 413 (Bankr. D. Conn. 1995); § 11.5.4, infra.
130 A chapter 7 debtor may assume a personal property lease pursuant to section 365(p). See Ch. 12, infra.
131 11 U.S.C. § 521(2).
132 11 U.S.C. § 521(2).
133 Fed. R. Bankr. P. 1007(b)(2).
134 Fed. R. Bankr. P. 1009(b).
135 See § 7.3.11, supra; 4 Collier on Bankruptcy ¶ 521.14[2] (16th ed.).
136 In re Pratt, 462 F.3d 14 (1st Cir. 2006) (debtor surrendering property not required to deliver it to creditor); ; In re Theobald, 218 B.R. 133 (B.A.P. 10th Cir. 1998); Main St. Bank v. Hull, 2008 WL 783772 (E.D. Mich. Mar. 20, 2008) (debtor's failure to take action stated in statement of intention does not affect debtor's rights in the property); In re Cornejo, 342 B.R. 834 (Bankr. M.D. Fla. 2005) (debtor had no duty to deliver vehicle that was surrendered or to satisfy other liens on vehicle).
137 In re Molnar, 441 B.R. 108 (Bankr. N.D. Ill. 2010) (debtor met deadline when redemption proposal made before 30 days after § 341 meeting and creditor did not respond).

that is the debtor's intent. But, as the section expressly provides that it does not affect substantive rights,[138] it should not be a bar to redemptions, even if they are not accomplished by the deadline.[139] The thirty-day guideline may even prove helpful to a debtor who has no other way of stopping a foreclosure or repossession, because it may extend the time a debtor may retain possession of property.[140]

Although the chapter 7 trustee is supposed to "ensure that the debtor shall perform" the stated intention,[141] the Code provides no mechanism for the trustee to use. As a practical matter, trustees rarely become involved. Presumably, the trustee could, on request of the secured creditor, bring the matter to the attention of the court for resolution, something the secured creditor could do just as easily on its own.

The statement of intention thus seems designed primarily as a way for secured creditors to obtain notice of what the debtor plans to do, and as a guideline to when redemption and reaffirmation should occur. However, because substantive rights are expressly left unaffected, the debtor may change his or her mind about what is planned and apparently would not have to file a new statement if that happened.[142] Also, there appears to be no sanction provided for failing to carry through on a stated intention.[143] However, it may result in the termination of the automatic stay with respect to certain personal property.[144]

11.4.2 Effect of 2005 Amendments to Section 521(a)(2) and Related Provisions

11.4.2.1 In General

Section 521 was amended in various respects by the 2005 amendments, and a number of related provisions were also enacted. The changes in statutory language arguably did nothing to change the result of earlier cases which held that a debtor could retain property subject to a security interest if the debtor remained current on payments and other contract obligations. Those cases were based on the plain language of the Code, which in all material respects is unchanged. And there was nothing in the legislative history of the new law that indicated that Congress intended to change the result in such cases or to change the basic bankruptcy policies that those courts found supported that result. Indeed, because the provisions are limited to secured debts and leases involving personal property, the 2005 amendments strengthen the argument that a debtor has a right to continue payments on debts secured by real property and retain the property without reaffirming.[145]

However, many courts have held that the new provisions do permit creditors in some cases to obtain relief from the stay[146] and enforce *ipso facto* clauses that create a default upon the filing of a bankruptcy case[147] if such enforcement is otherwise permitted under nonbankruptcy law.

11.4.2.2 No Material Change to the Statutory Language

The decisions holding that a debtor had other options in addition to reaffirmation, redemption, or surrender were based upon a careful analysis of the plain language of the Bankruptcy Code.[148] As the Supreme Court has repeatedly held, the starting point for the court's inquiry should be the statutory language itself, viewed if necessary in the context of other statutory provisions.[149]

---

138 *See also In re* Price, 370 F.3d 362 (3d Cir. 2004); *In re* Peacock, 87 B.R. 657 (Bankr. D. Colo. 1988). *See generally In re* Winters, 69 B.R. 145 (Bankr. D. Or. 1986).

139 Lowry Fed. Credit Union v. West, 882 F.2d 1543 (10th Cir. 1989); *In re* Alvarez, 2012 WL 441257 (Bankr. N.D. Ill. Feb. 10, 2012); *In re* Herrera, 454 B.R. 559 (Bankr. E.D.N.Y. 2011) (redemption not barred even if debtor does not act within time set in § 521(a)(2)); *In re* Rodgers, 273 B.R. 186 (Bankr. C.D. Ill. 2002) (redemption not barred by expiration of former forty-five day time period from statement of intention); 4 Collier on Bankruptcy ¶ 521.14[3] (16th ed.).

140 *See In re* Simpson, 147 B.R. 14 (Bankr. E.D.N.C. 1992) (debtor's counsel was justified in refusing to consent to relief from stay for creditor to complete foreclosure before expiration of forty-five-day period).

141 11 U.S.C. § 704(a)(3).
   Note that this provision refers to section 521(2)(B), not the redesignated section 521(a)(2)(B).

142 *In re* Militante, 2009 WL 779798 (Bankr. N.D. Cal. Feb. 6, 2009) (debtor could redeem under § 722 even though he had not stated that intention). *See In re* Stefano, 134 B.R. 824 (Bankr. W.D. Pa. 1991); *In re* Eagle, 51 B.R. 959 (Bankr. N.D. Ohio 1985).
   However, the rules do provide for amending the statement. Fed. R. Bankr. P. 1009(b).

143 *In re* Rathbun, 275 B.R. 434 (Bankr. D.R.I. 2001) (adopting opinion in *Donnell*); *In re* Donnell, 234 B.R. 567 (Bankr. D.N.H. 1999) (denying injunctive relief to enforce security interest and refusing to deny discharge of debt or dismiss case); *In re* Weir, 173 B.R. 682 (Bankr. E.D. Cal. 1994) (no implied cause of action or other remedy); *In re* Crooks, 148 B.R. 867 (Bankr. N.D. Ill. 1993) (debtor's statement which erroneously stated intention to retain car did not preclude debtor from later surrendering it). *See also In re* French, 185 B.R. 910 (Bankr. M.D. Fla. 1995) (debtor was justified in refusing to sign reaffirmation agreement that added attorney fees to debt); *In re* Williams, 64 B.R. 737 (Bankr. S.D. Ohio 1986); *In re* Eagle, 51 B.R. 959 (Bankr. N.D. Ohio 1985).

144 11 U.S.C. § 362(h). *See* § 11.4.2.3, *infra*.

145 *See In re* Hart, 402 B.R. 78 (Bankr. D. Del. 2009) (reaffirmation agreement not required to retain possession of real property); *In re* Waller, 394 B.R. 111 (Bankr. D.S.C. 2008) ("ride-through" option for debts secured by real property remains available after 2005 amendments); *In re* Wilson, 372 B.R. 816 (Bankr. D.S.C. 2007) (new amendments permitted retain and pay option with respect to real property); *In re* Bennet, 2006 WL 1540842 (Bankr. M.D.N.C. May 26, 2006). *See also* 11 U.S.C. § 524(j); *In re* Caraballo, 386 B.R. 398 (Bankr. D. Conn. 2008).

146 11 U.S.C. § 362(h). *See* § 11.4.2.3, *infra*.

147 11 U.S.C. § 521(d). *See* § 11.4.2.5, *infra*.

148 *See, e.g., In re* Price, 370 F.3d 362, 378–379 (3d Cir. 2004).

149 Lamie v. United States Tr., 540 U.S. 526, 534, 124 S. Ct. 1023, 1030, 157 L. Ed. 2d 1024 (2004). *See also* Toibb v. Radloff, 501 U.S. 157, 160, 111 S. Ct. 2197, 2199, 115 L. Ed. 2d 145 (1991); United States v. Ron Pair Enters., Inc., 489 U.S. 235, 241–242, 109 S. Ct. 1026, 1030–1031, 103 L. Ed. 2d 290 (1989).
   When the "statute's language is plain, the sole function of the court, at least where the disposition required by the text is not absurd, is to enforce it according to its terms." Hartford Underwriters Ins. Co. v. Union Planters Bank, 530 U.S. 1, 6, 120 S. Ct. 1942,

Courts construing the amended provisions should similarly be guided by the plain language of the Code, as well as by pre-amendment cases interpreting any unchanged language. While there is a perception among some that the creditor lobby that supported the new law intended to abolish the retain and pay option, such a change in result is supported by neither the text of the statute nor its legislative history.

In particular, courts that had found this "fourth option" to exist focused on section 521(2)(C) (now section 521(a)(2)(C)), which provided that "nothing in subparagraphs (A) or (B) of this paragraph shall alter the debtor's or the trustee's rights with regard to such property under this title."[150] They noted that the Code provides several options for dealing with secured property in addition to those that were listed in section 521(2)(A). Therefore, in light of the savings clause preserving the debtor's and the trustee's rights in the property under the Code, the options listed in section 521(a)(2)(A) were not the only available options contemplated by the statute.

The trustee may have the right to avoid the secured creditor's lien using the trustee avoidance powers in the Code.[151] Similarly, the debtor may have the right to avoid the lien under section 522(f) or 522(h). If a lien is avoided, certainly there is no requirement that the debt be reaffirmed. Such a requirement would be contrary to the purpose of lien avoidance, which is to permit the trustee or debtor to retain property unencumbered by a lien. The debtor also has the right to convert a case to chapter 13, at which point the debtor has a variety of rights with respect to secured creditors. Requiring a debtor to redeem, reaffirm, or surrender within the time specified in section 521(a)(2)(B) would prejudice the debtor's right to convert to chapter 13 after that time expired and then utilize the provisions of chapter 13 to modify, or cure a default on, a secured claim.

The existence of such rights under the Code, clearly preserved by the specific language of the savings clause, is inconsistent with a flat requirement that a debtor redeem, reaffirm, or surrender the property within the time frame specified in section 521(a)(2)(B). For this reason, a number of appellate courts held that the pre-2005 wording of the subsection did not restrict debtors from retaining their automobiles while staying current on their loan payments.[152]

The plain language which many courts found supported the availability of a retention option before the 2005 amendments has not been changed in any material respect. The only changes in the language of the section, now section 521(a)(2), were 1) the limitation of the section to consumer debts was eliminated, 2) the time for performance was changed to thirty days after the first date set for the meeting of creditors and 3) an exception was made to the savings clause, insofar as new section 362(h) alters the debtor's or trustee's rights. As discussed below, this exception does not affect the substantive bankruptcy rights that are preserved by the savings clause. In light of the reliance on the savings clause in section 521(a)(2)(C) by numerous courts that found a right to retain and pay, if Congress had meant to eliminate that right it would have eliminated or much more dramatically changed the savings clause.

Similarly, the language of Official Form 8, the statement of intention form, allows the debtor to choose from the same options as were available on the form prior to the amendments and does not require a debtor to specify that the debtor will redeem or reaffirm the debt if property is retained.[153] If the debtor does not intend to redeem or reaffirm the debt, the form permits the debtor to list other retention options.

However, despite the lack of material change in the statutory language of section 521(a)(2) or the official form, some courts have held that the 2005 amendments eliminated the "fourth option" with respect to debts secured by personal property because of the newly enacted sections 362(h), 521(a)(6), and 521(d), discussed below.[154]

11.4.2.3 Section 362(h)

The 2005 amendments created an exception to the savings clause for section 362(h). Section 362(h) terminates the automatic stay with respect to the property if the debtor fails to both 1) timely file a statement of intention or to indicate an intent to redeem, surrender, or retain the property and enter into a reaffirmation agreement *and* 2) take timely action carrying out the stated intention, or the intention stated in an amended statement, unless the debtor states an intention to reaffirm and the creditor refuses to reaffirm on the original terms.[155] Because the debtor must take both actions, failure to file the statement in a timely manner has been deemed sufficient to provide relief from the stay.

However, even if the debtor does not reaffirm, the section's termination of the automatic stay as to such property only permits a creditor to do what it is otherwise permitted to do.[156] It does not answer the question of what actions the creditor is

---

147 L. Ed. 2d 1 (2000) (internal quotations omitted).
150 *See, e.g., In re* Price, 370 F.3d 362 (3d Cir. 2004); *In re* Parker, 139 F.3d 668 (9th Cir. 1998); *In re* Belanger, 962 F.2d 345, 348 (4th Cir. 1992); Lowry Fed. Credit Union v. West, 882 F.2d 1543 (10th Cir. 1989).
151 *See* § 10.4.2.6, *supra*.
152 *See In re* Price, 370 F.3d 362 (3d Cir. 2004); *In re* Parker, 139 F.3d 668 (9th Cir. 1998); *In re* Belanger, 962 F.2d 345, 348 (4th Cir. 1992); Lowry Fed. Credit Union v. West, 882 F.2d 1543 (10th Cir. 1989).
153 The form now also requires a statement of intention with respect to personal property leases. *See* Appx. D, *infra*.
154 *See, e.g., In re* Jones, 591 F.3d 308 (4th Cir. 2010); *In re* Dumont, 581 F.3d 1104 (9th Cir. 2009).
155 *In re* DeSalvo, 2009 WL 5322428 (Bankr. S.D. Ga. Nov. 13, 2009) (filing redemption motion was taking action); *In re* Hinson, 352 B.R. 48 (Bankr. E.D.N.C. 2006) (stay did not terminate when debtor offered to reaffirm on original terms and creditor insisted on including attorney fees in reaffirmation). *Cf. In re* Parker, 363 B.R. 621 (Bankr. M.D. Fla. 2007) (merely negotiating with redemption financer, without notifying secured creditor or continuing payments, was not "taking action").
156 *See In re* Steinhaus, 349 B.R. 694 (Bankr. D. Idaho 2006) (creditor not entitled to order directing that debtor turn over vehicle; rather, creditor left only with state law rights); *In re* Rowe, 342 B.R. 341 (Bankr. D. Kan. 2006).

permitted to take under bankruptcy or nonbankruptcy law. For example, a secured creditor clearly is not permitted to repossess property if its lien has been avoided by the debtor or trustee. Similarly, if a case is converted to chapter 13, the creditor may not prevent the debtor from using the rights conferred by that chapter to deal with the secured debt. These same rights, not mentioned in section 521(a)(2) but clearly available to debtors and trustees, continue to exist under the Code as amended by the 2005 Act, with no material changes. There has been no suggestion that Congress intended to eliminate these rights; thus, a creditor still may not repossess property if that frustrates a debtor's rights. The fact that the stay is terminated slightly earlier than it would ordinarily have been terminated at the end of the case under prior law does not change the debtor's other rights.

Section 362(h) is, rather, merely a codification of court decisions that had held, prior to the 2005 amendments, that a court could not compel a debtor to redeem, reaffirm, or surrender, and that the only remedy for noncompliance with section 521(2) was relief from the stay for the creditor to exercise whatever rights it had.[157] If, for example, neither the debtor nor the trustee sought lien avoidance or other exercise of bankruptcy rights, relief from the stay under section 362(h) could permit repossession. This is a slight change from pre-2005 law, under which the creditor would have had to seek a court order granting relief from the stay in such circumstances. In accord with this change, courts have held that a debtor who does not timely take the steps specified in section 362(h) loses protection from the stay.[158]

In any event, if the stay terminates under section 362(h), a creditor is not entitled to request a "comfort order" confirming the stay is no longer in effect. Section 362(j), which provides for such confirming orders, applies only to termination of the stay under section 362(c).[159]

Importantly, section 362(h) has no applicability if the debtor has timely stated an intention to reaffirm or redeem and then timely entered into a reaffirmation agreement, even if that agreement is later disapproved by the court.[160] Courts have held that in such circumstances the debtor has complied with every Code requirement and has a right to retain the property if payments are kept current.[161]

11.4.2.4 Section 521(a)(6)

11.4.2.4.1 Overview

Another related provision enacted in 2005 is section 521(a)(6). Like section 362(h), this provision does not apply if the debtor timely redeems or enters into a reaffirmation agreement, even if the reaffirmation is disapproved by the court.[162] This provision offers greater relief to a creditor, but under much more limited circumstances. Section 521(a)(6) at first glance seems similar to section 362(h), but there are important differences. First, the creditor must have an "allowed claim." Second, that allowed claim must be for the "purchase price" of the personal property securing the claim. If the creditor does not meet *both* conditions, it may not avail itself of the greater rights afforded in section 521(a)(6).

In addition, the time period stated in section 521(a)(6) for action by the debtor is forty-five days after the meeting of creditors. Although not stated, this presumably means forty-five days after the date the meeting is concluded, or else Congress would have used the same language as in section 521(a)(2)(B), which refers to the first date set for the meeting. Probably the difference in time period is to permit more time to complete a redemption or reaffirmation, as well as to give time for the exercise of lien avoidance and other bankruptcy rights, before the somewhat more serious consequences of section 521(a)(6) apply.

11.4.2.4.2 Requirement of allowed claim

Section 521(a)(6) is limited to creditors with an allowed claim. The term "allowed claim," although not defined in the Bankruptcy Code, is generally recognized, frequently used, and well understood. To be an allowed claim, a proof of claim must be filed.[163] While creditors rarely filed proofs of claim in chapter 7 no asset cases before the 2005 amendments, requiring the filing of documentation supporting the claim would seem an appropriate prerequisite before section 521(a)(6) may take effect.[164] And there are other likely reasons why Congress used

---

157 See, e.g., In re Silvestri, 294 B.R. 421 (Bankr. D.R.I. 2003); In re Donnell, 234 B.R. 567 (Bankr. D.N.H. 1999).
158 See, e.g., In re Jones, 591 F.3d 308 (4th Cir. 2010); In re Dumont, 581 F.3d 1104 (9th Cir. 2009).
159 In re Hill, 364 B.R. 826 (Bankr. M.D. Fla. 2007); In re Grossi, 365 B.R. 608 (Bankr. E.D. Va. 2007); In re Conley, 358 B.R. 337 (Bankr. N.D. Ohio 2006); In re Dienberg, 348 B.R. 482 (Bankr. N.D. Ind. 2006).
160 In re Chim, 381 B.R. 191 (Bankr. D. Md. 2008); In re Moustafi, 371 B.R. 434 (Bankr. D. Ariz. 2007); In re Husain, 364 B.R. 211 (Bankr. E.D. Va. 2007); In re Blakely, 363 B.R. 225 (Bankr. D. Utah 2007); In re Bower, 2007 WL 2163472 (Bankr. D. Or. July 26, 2007); In re Quintero, 2006 WL 1351623 (Bankr. N.D. Cal. May 17, 2006) (automatic stay does not terminate under section 362(h) if debtor enters into reaffirmation agreement that court later disapproves because creditor failed to provide required reaffirmation disclosures under section 524(k)).
161 See, e.g., In re Baker, 400 B.R. 136 (D. Del. 2009); Coastal Fed. Credit Union v. Hardiman, 398 B.R. 161 (E.D.N.C. 2008); In re Waller, 394 B.R. 111 (Bankr. D.S.C. 2008); In re Moustafi, 371 B.R. 434 (Bankr. D. Ariz. 2007). See, e.g., In re Perez, 2010 WL 2737187 (Bankr. D.N.M. July 12, 2010).
162 In re Baker, 390 B.R. 524 (Bankr. D. Del. 2008), aff'd, 400 B.R. 136 (D. Del. 2009); In re Quintero, 2006 WL 1351623 (Bankr. N.D. Cal. May 17, 2006) (section 521(a)(6) does not require reaffirmation agreement to be approved).
163 See § 11.2.2, supra.
164 Coastal Fed. Credit Union v. Hardiman, 398 B.R. 161 (E.D.N.C. 2008); In re Moustafi, 371 B.R. 434 (Bankr. D. Ariz. 2007) (section 521(a)(6) inapplicable when creditor failed to file proof of claim); In re Donald, 343 B.R. 524, 536 (Bankr. E.D.N.C. 2006) ("At a minimum, the filing of a proof of claim would establish the amount of the claim and would provide the documentation that supports the

the term "allowed claim" in section 521(a)(6). For a claim to be allowed, not only must it be filed under section 502, but also any objection to the claim must be resolved.[165] Without the inclusion of the word "allowed," not only would there be no documentation of the claim in the bankruptcy court, but also the debtor would have no opportunity to contest the claim. The inclusion of the word "allowed" thus ensures that a creditor cannot take advantage of section 521(a)(6) unless its claim is either undisputed or has been upheld by the bankruptcy court.[166] Similarly, a claim would not be an allowed secured claim if the debtor or trustee could exercise avoiding powers to eliminate the creditor's lien.[167]

11.4.2.4.3 Requirement of claim for the purchase price

Another significant difference between section 362(h) and section 521(a)(6) is that the creditor's claim must be "for the purchase price" of personal property. Section 362(h) does not contain the language that the claim must be for the purchase price. Based on the plain language, this requirement should mean that the creditor must have a claim for the full purchase price, which is different than a "purchase-money security interest."[168] However, other courts have interpreted this provision to mean simply that the creditor has a purchase money security interest.[169]

Again, there are reasons that Congress would have wanted to use this language to limit the applicability of section 521(a)(6), which gives the creditor greater rights. One of the abuses claimed by creditors in their lobbying for the 2005 amendments was the purchase of a vehicle or other personal property right before bankruptcy, followed by the use of bankruptcy to reduce the secured creditor's rights.[170] In chapter 13 cases, Congress enacted a paragraph at the end of section 1325(a) that modifies debtors' rights with respect to recently purchased property. Section 521(a)(6) is a similar limitation that applies in chapter 7 cases to such a situation.

11.4.2.4.4 Rights of creditors and debtors when section 521(a)(6) applies

If the creditor has satisfied both conditions discussed above, however they are interpreted by the court, section 521(a)(6) changes the rights of creditors and debtors. First, section 521(a)(6) provides that an individual debtor shall "not retain possession" of the property if the debtor does not redeem or reaffirm within the stated time period.[171] Second, the "creditor may take whatever action" as to the property as permitted by *"applicable nonbankruptcy law."*

This language means that the debtor, when section 521(a)(6) applies, loses the bankruptcy right to possession if the debtor does not redeem or reaffirm within the stated time. It also, unlike section 362(h), permits the creditor to take whatever action is permitted under nonbankruptcy law, presumably regardless of bankruptcy rights that have not yet been exercised.[172] This distinction further supports the conclusion, discussed above, that section 362(h) does not afford relief that is so broad; otherwise, Congress would not have used the additional language it inserted in section 521(a)(6) to specify that the creditor could take any action permitted by nonbankruptcy law.

However, the language of section 521(a)(6) also qualifies the creditor's rights. First, it makes clear once again that the creditor's remedy is simply relief from the automatic stay, reinforcing the pre-amendment case law that the debtor cannot be compelled by the bankruptcy court to surrender the property. Second, the creditor may only take actions permitted by nonbankruptcy law. In other words, the debtor is only surrendering the property in the sense that the debtor is not asserting bankruptcy rights that have not already been asserted. Debtors are specifically permitted to retain all rights afforded to them by nonbankruptcy law. In many states, such nonbankruptcy rights may still prevent the creditor from repossessing the property if the debtor is current in payments.[173]

It is unlikely that Congress in enacting such different language in section 521(a)(6) than in section 362(h) could have meant the two provisions to cover the same transactions or to mean the same thing. The greater rights available to a creditor that meets the narrower criteria of section 521(a)(6) are not available unless the prerequisites for the application of that provision are met.

---

creditor's invocation of an ipso facto clause. Without a proof of claim, a debtor who is current with payments to the creditor stands to lose valuable and necessary property without anything being filed with the bankruptcy court.").

165 11 U.S.C. § 502(a) (claim allowed unless a party in interest objects).
166 Section 362(h) permits only a dispute about the original terms of the agreement if the debtor has offered to reaffirm.
167 Another bankruptcy court, in *In re* Rowe, 342 B.R. 341 (Bankr. D. Kan. 2006), decided to simply ignore the word "allowed" because of its view that Congress could not have really meant to enact it. The *Rowe* court erred in ignoring the plain language of the statute, especially because of the contrast between the language of sections 521(a)(6) and 362(h). When Congress has enacted two different provisions on a similar topic at the same time, it must be assumed that Congress acted knowingly in creating differences in language between the two provisions.
168 *See* Coastal Fed. Credit Union v. Hardiman, 398 B.R. 161 (E.D.N.C. 2008); *In re* Donald, 343 B.R. 524, 537 (Bankr. E.D.N.C. 2006) ("Clearly, if Congress intended in § 521(a)(6) for a 'claim for the purchase price' to mean something less than the full purchase price, it would have said so as it did in § 522(f)(1)(B), § 524(k)(3)(G), § 1325(a)(4) and § 1326(a)(4).").
169 *See, e.g., In re* Dumont, 383 B.R. 481 (B.A.P. 9th Cir. 2008), *aff'd*, 581 F.3d 1104 (9th Cir. 2009).
170 *See* § 11.6.1.4, *infra*.

171 Section 521(a)(6) also provides that the property shall no longer be property of the estate. Filing a motion to redeem within the forty-five-day period is a sufficient act to satisfy section 521(a)(6). *In re* DeSalvo, 2009 WL 5322428 (Bankr. S.D. Ga. Nov. 13, 2009).
172 *See, e.g., In re* Jones, 591 F.3d 308 (4th Cir. 2010); *In re* Dumont, 581 F.3d 1104 (9th Cir. 2009). An exception in the provision allows a trustee to preserve property that is valuable to the estate, subject to certain conditions.
173 *See* National Consumer Law Center, Repossessions Ch. 4 (7th ed. 2010 and Supp.).

And, again, it is important to remember that section 521(a)(6) should not apply if the debtor has timely entered into a reaffirmation agreement and the court does not approve that agreement.[174]

11.4.2.5 Section 521(d)

Section 521(d) provides that if a debtor fails to take timely action as specified in section 521(a)(6) or section 362(h)(1) and (2), with respect to property as to which a creditor holds a security interest not otherwise avoidable under sections 522(f), 544, 545, 547, 548, or 549, nothing in title 11 shall limit the operation of an *ipso facto* clause in the credit agreement that makes bankruptcy or insolvency a default under the agreement. It contains similar language with respect to leases of personal property.

By its terms, section 521(d) is triggered by a failure to take the action specified in section 521(a)(6) or paragraphs (1) and (2) of section 362(h), provided that a variety of listed bankruptcy provisions are not applicable. Thus, it does not become operable if the debtor timely redeems or enters into a reaffirmation agreement, even if that agreement is later disapproved by the court.[175] As discussed above, when section 521(d) applies, a creditor is given the right to pursue remedies permitted under nonbankruptcy law (the only law to which an *ipso facto* clause is relevant) only if the requirements of section 521(a)(6) are met. If the creditor otherwise had an unrestricted right to proceed under any applicable nonbankruptcy law, either pursuant to section 362(h) or otherwise, there would be no need to specifically mention nonbankruptcy law in section 521(a)(6). Indeed, there would be no need for section 521(a)(6) at all.

Section 521(d) does not compel a debtor to redeem, reaffirm, or surrender in bankruptcy. Like section 521(a)(2), it does not create substantive rights in bankruptcy and does not prescribe what a debtor must do. It affects only nonbankruptcy rights, when those rights are relevant.

In any event, in some situations a default under an *ipso facto* clause would be waived by the creditor's acceptance of postpetition payments from the debtor, or estoppel would bar claiming a default because of a creditor's postpetition conduct.[176] Alternatively, accepting payments and then repossessing could be considered a lack of the good faith required under the Uniform Commercial Code or it could be seen as an unfair trade practice.[177]

11.4.2.6 Legislative History of the 2005 Amendments

Some of the courts that found a debtor had the right to retain collateral while making current payments noted that the legislative history supported their conclusions. In particular, they noted that nowhere in the legislative history of the original statement of intention provisions did Congress state that debtors had only the options of reaffirmation, redemption, or surrender.[178]

Similarly, there is no indication in the legislative history of the 2005 amendments that those amendments were intended to eliminate ride-through. Again, had this been the intent, it is difficult to believe it would not have been stated. The House Report states only "[t]he bill terminates the automatic stay with respect to personal property if the debtor does not timely reaffirm the underlying obligation or redeem the property."[179]

The passage never mentions ride-through, or the fourth option, or making reaffirmation, redemption, or surrender the debtor's only options. Again, one can only assume that such a major change would have been explicitly mentioned somewhere in the legislative history. The amendments do, as the report states, terminate the automatic stay in the circumstances described. But that fact would not have changed the result in cases that found that debtors have an option to retain their property while continuing to make current payments. The lack of such legislative history is a strong indication that the option has not been eliminated. However, some courts have held that section 362(h) and 521(d) eliminate the fourth option in some cases involving debts secured by personal property.[180]

11.4.2.7 Bankruptcy Policies Supporting the Retain and Pay Option

As discussed above, courts of appeals that held debtors have the "retain and pay" option found their decisions were supported by longstanding bankruptcy policies. These courts discussed the fact that elimination of ride-through would undermine the fresh start policy of the Code, and that reaffirmation was viewed as a classic evil in bankruptcy law, "dealt with in the Code so as not to exalt it or enable it, but, rather, so as to regulate it and scrutinize it, in light of its misuse."[181] They also

---

174 Coastal Fed. Credit Union v. Hardiman, 398 B.R. 161 (E.D.N.C. 2008); *In re* Waller, 394 B.R. 111 (Bankr. D.S.C. 2008); *In re* Baker, 390 B.R. 524 (Bankr. D. Del. 2008), *aff'd*, 400 B.R. 136 (D. Del. 2009); *In re* Moustafi, 371 B.R. 434 (Bankr. D. Ariz. 2007); *In re* Quintero, 2006 WL 1351623 (Bankr. N.D. Cal. May 17, 2006) (section 521(a)(6) does not require reaffirmation agreement to be approved).

175 *In re* Bower, 2007 WL 2163472 (Bankr. D. Or. July 26, 2007); *In re* Moustafi, 371 B.R. 434 (Bankr. D. Ariz. 2007); *In re* Husain, 364 B.R. 211 (Bankr. E.D. Va. 2007).

176 *See, e.g.*, Westinghouse Credit Corp. v. Shelton, 645 F.2d 869 (10th Cir. 1981); Skeels v. Universal CIT Credit Corp., 222 F. Supp. 696, 698 (W.D. Pa. 1963); Mercedes-Benz Credit Corp. v. Morgan, 312 Ark. 225 (Ark. 1993); Farmers State Bank v. Farmland Foods, Inc., 225 Neb. 1 (1987). *See also* National Consumer Law Center, Repossessions Ch. 4 (7th ed. 2010 and Supp.).

177 *See* Entriken v. Motor Coach Fed. Credit Union, 256 Mont. 85 (1992) (right to repossess for failure to maintain insurance waived by later conduct and repossession was unfair trade practice). *See also* National Consumer Law Center, Repossessions Ch. 4 (7th ed. 2010 and Supp.).

178 *See, e.g., In re* Price, 370 F.3d 362, 375 (3d Cir. 2004).

179 H.R. Rep. No. 109-31, at 17 (2005) (available on this treatise's companion website).

180 *See, e.g., In re* Jones, 591 F.3d 308 (4th Cir. 2010); *In re* Dumont, 581 F.3d 1104 (9th Cir. 2009).

181 *See, e.g., In re* Price, 370 F.3d 362, 378 (3d Cir. 2004).

noted the problems that would arise if creditors could dictate onerous reaffirmation terms using the threat of repossession if those terms were not accepted.[182]

These bankruptcy policies have not changed. The Code is still intended to provide a fresh start for honest debtors and the legislative history is replete with statements to that effect. Similarly, reaffirmation remains a disfavored procedure. The 2005 amendments, in fact, enacted significant new provisions that prescribe further requirements for reaffirmation agreements and require more court scrutiny in many cases.[183] Thus, the policies that supported those earlier decisions continue to support interpreting the Code to allow a "retain and pay" option.

11.4.2.8 Practice Tips

Many car lenders understand that economically they are far better off if the debtor continues to make payments, even without reaffirmation, than they are if they repossess the debtor's vehicle, which is often worth far less than the amount of those payments. If they cannot scare the debtor into reaffirming, they simply accept the continued payments. Often, a creditor will let this policy be known.

In other cases, state law may prohibit a creditor from repossessing if payments are current, and in that situation there is no reason to reaffirm the debt, thereby waiving its discharge, if the debtor is not behind in payments.

If neither of these situations exists, the debtor cannot obtain a better deal by redeeming the car,[184] and the debtor is not willing to take the risk that the car will be repossessed, then the best course of action may be for the debtor to enter into a reaffirmation agreement that is not negotiated by the debtor's attorney. Such an agreement must be approved by the court. There is a presumption that it is an undue hardship, and should not be approved, if the debtor's budget does not accommodate the payments.[185] In many such cases the court will not approve the agreement and then, the debtor having executed a reaffirmation agreement (albeit one that was not approved), the debtor will have the right to continue to retain the car as long as payments are current without reaffirming the debt.

11.5 Right of Redemption in Chapter 7 Cases

11.5.1 Purpose

One of the new provisions in the Bankruptcy Code when it was enacted in 1978 was section 722, which provides for a limited right of redemption in chapter 7 cases. In essence, it provides that for certain secured consumer debts the security interest may be eliminated upon payment to the creditor of the value of its collateral, that is, the amount of its allowed secured claim.

The purpose of this section, like that of section 506, is to prevent secured creditors from getting an unfair advantage out of proportion to the value of their security. Section 722, however, is aimed solely at preventing an unfair advantage over the debtor, rather than over the other creditors. Under prior law, a secured creditor had the right to demand full payment or to obtain a reaffirmation of a secured debt after bankruptcy, and to repossess or otherwise recover the collateral if such payment or reaffirmation did not occur. This often allowed the creditor to collect far more than the market value of the collateral due to the fact that the debtor could not easily replace the property securing the debt. Congress felt it was unfair for a creditor holding a security interest in some necessity like a refrigerator to demand payment of a debt of several hundred dollars when the collateral was worth only $50 on the market, simply because the item was irreplaceable for an indigent debtor who could not afford to purchase a new one.[186]

11.5.2 Limitations on the Right to Redeem

Section 722 provides a simple procedure, within the chapter 7 case, for the debtor to remove a creditor's lien by paying the creditor the real value of the property. There are several limitations on that right, however. It is available only to individual debtors, and only with respect to certain property and certain debts. Specifically, it can only be used in cases of dischargeable consumer debts[187] secured by tangible personal property[188] which has been either exempted by the debtor or abandoned by the trustee. It is not available with respect to real estate or intangible liquid assets. And it is doubtful that redemption can occur without creditor agreement after a case is closed (unless, perhaps, the case is reopened), though it can occur after the discharge has been entered.[189]

Although the operation of section 722 is normally quite straightforward, questions occasionally arise as to whether a debt incurred by the owner of a small business is a consumer debt, especially if combined with other debts later incurred for business purposes.[190] Numerous cases have discussed the meaning of the term "consumer debt," which appears several places in the Bankruptcy Code.[191]

---

182 Id.
183 See 11 U.S.C. § 524(k), (m). See also Ch. 15, infra.
184 See § 11.5, infra.
185 See § 15.5.2, infra, for discussion of reaffirmation requirements.
186 H.R. Rep. No. 95-595, at 127, 128 (1977).
187 "Consumer debt" is defined in 11 U.S.C. § 101(8).
188 The term "tangible personal property" has been interpreted broadly for this purpose. In re Walker, 173 B.R. 512 (Bankr. M.D.N.C. 1994) (a fixture such as vinyl siding could still be tangible personal property that was redeemable under section 722 in some cases).
189 In re Hawkins, 136 B.R. 649 (Bankr. W.D. Va. 1991).
190 See In re Runski, 102 F.3d 744 (4th Cir. 1996) (office equipment used for business purposes could not be redeemed because it was not intended primarily for personal, family, or household use); In re Boitnott, 4 B.R. 122 (Bankr. W.D. Va. 1980) (auto loan for vehicle used by family later consolidated with business loan held to be consumer debt).
191 See, for example, 11 U.S.C. § 707(b), discussed in Chapter 13, infra, and 11 U.S.C. § 1301, discussed in Chapter 9, supra.

Dealing with Secured Creditors § 11.5.4

There may also be questions concerning whether property has been or can be claimed as exempt, because unless the property is exempted or abandoned, section 722 cannot be utilized. Generally, these questions are dealt with in those sections of this treatise concerning exemptions[192] and abandonment.[193] In redemption cases, the questions usually arise when the debtor has no equity in the property and the creditor asserts that, therefore, it cannot be claimed as exempt. As discussed in Chapter 10, *supra*, so long as the debtor has any legal interest in property, that property may be claimed as exempt.[194] In any case, if the debtor does not have any equity, it should not be difficult to have the estate's interest abandoned by the trustee under section 554 of the Code.

It is clear that once any interest in the property is exempted, the entire property may be redeemed.[195] This is necessarily true because the debtor never has a right to exempt that property interest which is subject to the lien; the debtor may only exempt his or her own residual interest in the property. If the right to redeem were limited to the interest exempted, it could never reach any interest subject to a lien. Nor is the right of redemption limited to the dollar values of the exemption. If the debtor exempts some interest, then the remaining interest subject to the lien may be dealt with under section 722.[196] (However, if the debtor has nonexempt equity in the property, section 722 will not affect the estate's rights to the equity.)[197]

11.5.3 Redemption by Payment in Installments

A final issue is whether section 722 gives the debtor the right to pay the amount of the allowed secured claim in installments. Even before section 722 was amended to require payment in full at the time of redemption, most courts had found that, because section 524 provides for reaffirmation *agreements*, both parties must concur in any arrangement for installment payments under section 722.[198] These courts generally held that unless the creditor agrees otherwise, the debtor must redeem through cash payment of the redemption amount, and that neither the debtor nor the court can impose an installment arrangement upon the creditor.[199]

This requirement may present a problem to the debtor who cannot afford to pay the entire allowed secured claim in cash and is unwilling or unable to negotiate a reaffirmation agreement. Two possible solutions are treatment of the debt under chapter 13 or simply continuing the payments on the entire debt without reaffirming. (The latter solution would not permit the reduction of the debt to the value of the collateral.) Both of these options are discussed in this chapter.

There may also be another way of overcoming the language in section 722 prohibiting redemption in installments when the creditor does not consent. Section 521(a)(2)(B), gives the court the authority to grant additional time for the debtor to perform an intended redemption. Thus, a debtor should have a clear right under that section to request additional time to redeem, during which the debtor could save the money necessary.[200] None of the decisions which barred redemption in installments held that a court could not grant such a request under section 521(a)(2)(B).

Still another option for a debtor who cannot afford to redeem in a lump sum is to obtain financing of the lump sum. If the vehicle is worth significantly less than the amount due on the existing car loan, or if the debtor is delinquent on the loan, financing a redemption may be the most advantageous alternative. Financing a redemption may cost less to the debtor than the alternatives of continuing to pay the original loan, obtaining another vehicle with a high-interest loan (if credit is available), or filing a chapter 13 case, which could require payments to other creditors as well as additional fees and costs.[201]

11.5.4 Secured Creditors Who Refuse to Agree to Continued Installment Payments

The secured creditor who refuses installment payments may also present a problem to the chapter 7 debtor who is current on payments for a secured debt such as an automobile loan or a mortgage. Secured creditors whom the debtor does not propose to affect in the bankruptcy will often simply continue to accept payments and not attempt to enforce their security interests as long as payments are current. Occasionally, however, a creditor will try to foreclose on the basis of a contract clause that makes the bankruptcy itself a default on the obligation (an "*ipso facto* clause").

As discussed above, Congress has now stated in section 521(d) limited circumstances in which an *ipso facto* clause may operate.[202] The limitation of section 521(d) to personal property security interests creates a strong argument that an *ipso facto*

---

192 See Ch. 10, *supra*.
193 See § 3.5, *supra*.
194 Once the property has been listed as exempt and the deadline for objecting to exemptions has run, the creditor will be barred from raising any issue about the validity of the exemption. 11 U.S.C. § 522(*l*); Fed. R. Bankr. P. 4003(b). *See* Taylor v. Freeland & Kronz, 503 U.S. 638, 112 S. Ct. 1644, 118 L. Ed. 2d 280 (1992).
195 6 Collier on Bankruptcy ¶ 722.04 (16th ed.).
196 *Id.*
197 Indeed, there is some question whether the right of redemption exists when there is some nonexempt equity. *See* Bare, *The Bankruptcy Reform Act of 1978*, 47 Tenn. L. Rev. 567, 568 (1980) (suggesting that there is not a right of redemption in such cases).
198 *In re* Bell, 700 F.2d 1053 (6th Cir. 1983); *In re* Polk, 76 B.R. 148 (B.A.P. 9th Cir. 1987); *In re* Harp, 76 B.R. 185 (Bankr. N.D. Fla. 1987); *In re* Cruseturner, 8 B.R. 581 (Bankr. D. Utah 1981); *In re* Zimmerman, 4 B.R. 739 (Bankr. S.D. Cal. 1980); *In re* Miller, 4 B.R. 305 (Bankr. E.D. Mich. 1980); *In re* Stewart, 3 B.R. 24 (Bankr. N.D. Ohio 1980). *See also In re* Vinson, 5 B.R. 32 (Bankr. N.D. Ga. 1980) (debtor may not unilaterally reaffirm home mortgage).

199 In many cases, of course, the debtor may wish to avoid a reaffirmation agreement. For the considerations involved, see Chapter 8, *supra*, and Chapter 15, *infra*.
200 *See* 6 Collier on Bankruptcy ¶ 722.05[2] (16th ed.).
201 Potential sources of redemption financing, albeit at high interest rates, are 722 Redemption Funding at (888) 278-6121 and Redemption Financial Services at (877) 265-8844.
202 *See* § 11.4.2.5, *supra*.

clause in a mortgage can never be enforced. In addition it may be argued that in this context enforcement of such a contract clause is unconscionable or not in good faith under the Uniform Commercial Code or other law, such as the legal doctrine that deems acceptance of payments a waiver of the default.[203]

If such arguments are not effective, the debtor can usually obtain relief by converting the case to a chapter 13, if the case is still pending, or by commencing a new chapter 13 case after the chapter 7 case is closed. Once the debtor is in chapter 13, there are effective restraints on the secured creditor, as discussed later in this chapter.

Indeed, the threat of conversion to chapter 13, in which the creditor can be forced to accept installments and possibly reduced payments as well, or of other litigation, is usually sufficient to force a creditor to accept a redemption in which the allowed secured claim is reaffirmed and paid in installments. The threat may be so effective that the creditor may even agree to an arrangement more advantageous to the debtor—that the creditor will not enforce its security interest as long as certain payments on an amount reduced to the value of the collateral are made—without the debtor reaffirming the debt.[204] Nothing in the Code precludes such an arrangement, which has the significant advantage of eliminating any possible liability of the debtor for a later deficiency judgment based upon a reaffirmed debt in states where deficiency judgments are permitted.

However, if the debtor cannot convert to chapter 13, or file a chapter 13 case, and the debtor is in danger of repossession after bankruptcy if personal liability is not reaffirmed, the debtor with a secured car loan may have few practical alternatives to agreeing to reaffirm the debt or purchasing another used car. Sometimes, especially if the debtor's loan is already at a high interest rate, the most advantageous option is to retain the car for several months during the chapter 7 case, not making payments while attempting to negotiate a favorable redemption or reaffirmation and, if that fails, to buy another used vehicle at a similarly high interest rate. It may even be possible to have friends or family of the debtor go to the auction of the debtor's vehicle and purchase it for the low price at which such cars are typically sold. If the debtor insists on reaffirmation, the attorney must consider whether he or she can sign the certification that must accompany the reaffirmation.[205] In such cases, the debtor's counsel should at a minimum resist a reaffirmation for more than the current value of the collateral and should not agree to any additional charges, such as attorney fees, being added to the debt. Finally, as discussed above,[206] the debtor may execute a reaffirmation that is not negotiated by the attorney and, if that reaffirmation is not approved by the court,

the debtor will have the right to continue to retain the property as long as payments are current.

An alternative approach, especially effective for appliances and items of personal property with relatively little value, is to ignore the security interest entirely and wait to see if the creditor takes postbankruptcy action to repossess. Many creditors take no such action because repossession and resale is not economical. Moreover, debtors can be advised not to allow repossessing agents into their homes. The creditor cannot breach the peace in order to repossess. Usually, creditors who cannot achieve repossession of collateral simply give up, rather than incur the expense necessary to pursue *in rem* actions, like replevin, that are required in most states to force the debtor to surrender personal property.[207]

11.5.5 Uses in Practice

The right to redeem is used most often to reduce the amount payable on purchase money or possessory security interests in high value[208] household goods such as appliances, and on both purchase-money and non-purchase money (or possessory) security interests in motor vehicles. The former, unlike non-possessory non-purchase money security interests in household goods and certain other items, are not avoidable under section 522.[209] Similarly, security interests in motor vehicles are not normally avoidable unless they are non-purchase money and non-possessory and the vehicle is a tool of the trade of the debtor or a dependent.[210]

When redemption for a cash payment is possible, it provides a simple procedure by which the debtor may eliminate the security interest as well as the debt (which is discharged) once and for all. In some cases, when the property has no resale value or is subject to more than one lien, a secured creditor's interest may be totally eliminated under section 722 if the liens ahead of that creditor are greater than the value of the property.[211]

---

203 See U.C.C. §§ 1-203, 1-208, 2-302. See also In re Rose, 21 B.R. 272 (Bankr. D.N.J. 1982) (creditor's acceptance of payments after bankruptcy waived any contractual right to accelerate debt upon debtor's bankruptcy).
204 See Form 79, Appendix G.8, *infra*, for a sample of such an agreement.
205 See § 15.5.2.7, *infra*.
206 See § 11.4.2.8, *supra*.

207 A variety of approaches to dealing with repossession of property are discussed in detail in National Consumer Law Center, Repossessions (7th ed. 2010 and Supp.).
208 As discussed in § 11.5.4, *supra*, creditors rarely bother to attempt repossession of lower value items, so redemption is not necessary as a practical matter.
209 For a discussion of these rights, see Chapter 10, *supra*.
210 See § 10.4, *supra*.
211 *In re* Groth, 269 B.R. 766 (Bankr. S.D. Ohio 2001) (creditor who refused to accept surrender of boat required to allow debtor to redeem for one dollar); *In re* Williams, 228 B.R. 910 (Bankr. N.D. Ill. 1999) (redemption allowed for the amount required to obtain release of the lien); *In re* Altenberg, 6 Bankr. Ct. Dec. (LRP) 331, 1 Collier Bankr. Cas. 2d (MB) 807, (Bankr. S.D. Fla. 1980) (redemption allowed by payment of filing fee for notice of lien discharge to creditor whose lien was subordinate to lien which exceeded value of debtor's automobile). *See also In re* Pratt, 462 F.3d 14 (1st Cir. 2006) (while creditor had no duty to repossess surrendered vehicle subject to lien, refusal to provide title that would allow debtors to dispose of car violated discharge injunction).

The only factual issue that is likely to arise is the value of the property. The discussions of valuation elsewhere in this book have some relevance to redemption.[212] As in cases involving the automatic stay or exemptions, the date of valuation may be critical. Because the type of property subject to redemption usually depreciates in value over time, it is normally to the debtor's advantage to have the valuation date be the date of redemption rather than the date the bankruptcy petition was filed. As discussed above, for property used for personal, family, or household purposes, the language of section 506(a)(2) clearly requires valuation to be based on the property's age and condition at the time value is determined.[213]

Section 722 may be used without resort to the court in the first instance. When the parties agree to value and terms, redemption is accomplished simply by paying the creditor.[214] Of course, when there is no agreement, the court's intervention is necessary, sought either by a motion to redeem,[215] or perhaps a complaint for declaratory judgment to determine that an amount tendered is, in fact, the amount of the allowed secured claim. The debtor need not wait until the time for dischargeability complaints has expired to file such a proceeding,[216] and normally should act earlier, in order to act within the time set forth in section 521(a)(2)(B).[217]

Some retailers have responded to court hostility to their overly aggressive reaffirmation tactics[218] by instead insisting that consumers redeem personal property that is subject to a security interest through installment payments. As the personal property involved would have little or no value if it were repossessed, the redemption may be an unwise and expensive means for a debtor to retain the property. Creditors that encourage debtors to make this unwise choice may seek to use the redemption process to avoid the procedural requirements and court oversight necessary to obtain a valid reaffirmation.[219] Several courts have asserted authority to review and reject redemption agreements that are unfair to a debtor.[220] And it should be remembered that in many cases the value of the property may be so low that it is very unlikely that the creditor would repossess it even if there is no redemption.

11.6 Using Chapter 13 to Deal with Secured Creditors

11.6.1 Modification of Secured Creditors' Rights in Claims Not Secured Only by Real Estate That Is the Debtor's Principal Residence

11.6.1.1 In General

Perhaps the greatest powers to affect the rights of secured creditors are found in the provisions of chapter 13. Bankruptcy Code section 1322 provides that the debtor's plan may modify the rights of holders of most secured claims, other than some claims secured only by a security interest in real property that is the debtor's principal residence. In addition, section 1322(b)(3) and (b)(5) provide that as to any claim, including a claim secured only by the debtor's principal residence, the plan may provide for the curing of a default over a reasonable period of time.

Most of the flexibility given to the debtor in chapter 13 comes from the broad right to modify the rights of secured creditors.[221] In bankruptcy parlance, this right to limit the enforceability or change the terms of a creditor's contract over the creditor's objection is called a "cramdown."

The Code does not define the term "modify" which appears in section 1322(b)(2), so that presumably it may be given its broadest possible meaning, in other words, that any term of the contract is subject to change. Thus, except as limited by other Code provisions,[222] the debtor might propose to pay a lower total amount than originally agreed, to lower the amount of payments, to pay the claim over a longer period of time, to defer payments until after other debts are paid, to eliminate various oppressive terms, or even to eliminate totally the creditor's lien. When the interest of a tenant by the entirety extends to the whole of the property under state law, one co-tenant filing a chapter 13 case may strip off a lien without the participation of the other co-tenant.[223]

---

212 See §§ 9.7.3.3.1, 11.2.2.3.3, *supra*.

213 See § 11.2.2.2, *supra*.

214 Arruda v. Sears Roebuck & Co., 273 B.R. 332 (D.R.I. 2002), *aff'd*, 310 F.3d 13 (1st Cir. 2002). *But see In re* White, 231 B.R. 551 (Bankr. D. Vt. 1999) (court approval of redemption agreements required by local rule); *In re* Spivey, 230 B.R. 484 (Bankr. E.D.N.Y. 1999) (redemption agreement must be presented to court by motion for approval under Fed. R. Bankr. P. 6008), *rev'd*, 265 B.R. 357 (E.D.N.Y. 2001); *In re* Lopez, 224 B.R. 439 (Bankr. C.D. Cal. 1998) (same).

215 Fed. R. Bankr. P. 6008.
  See Form 75, Appendix G.8, *infra*, for a sample of such a motion.

216 *In re* Jewell, 232 B.R. 904 (Bankr. E.D. Tex. 1999).

217 If the debtor wishes to redeem property under § 722 after the bankruptcy case has been closed, and the debtor is unable to reach an agreement with the creditor on value or the terms of redemption, the debtor may request that the bankruptcy court reopen the case and resolve a motion to redeem. *See* Arruda v. Sears Roebuck & Co., 310 F.3d 13 (1st Cir. 2002).

218 *See* § 15.5.2.5, *infra*.

219 11 U.S.C. § 524(c), (d).

220 Fed. R. Bankr. P. 6008; *In re* White, 231 B.R. 551 (Bankr. D. Vt. 1999) (upholding general order that required filing of redemption agreements); *In re* Lopez, 224 B.R. 439 (Bankr. C.D. Cal. 1998). *But see In re* Spivey, 265 B.R. 357 (E.D.N.Y. 2001).

221 For purposes of the provisions of chapter 13, and depending upon state law, many courts have held land installment sale contracts to be secured debts, because they serve the same function as mortgages. *See* § 12.9.1, *infra*.

222 *See* §§ 11.6.1.2–11.6.1.3, *infra*.

223 Strausbough v. Co-op Servs. Credit Union, 426 B.R. 243 (Bankr. E.D. Mich. 2010). *But see In re* Pierre, 468 B.R. 419 (Bankr. M.D. Fla. 2012); *In re* Hunter, 284 B.R. 806 (Bankr. E.D. Va. 2002).

11.6.1.2 Limitations on Modifying Certain Debts Secured Only by Real Estate That Is Debtor's Principal Residence

11.6.1.2.1 In general

The debtor's rights to modify are subject to several major limitations. First, except to the extent of curing a default over a reasonable period of time, the right to modify does not extend to certain debts secured only by a security interest in real property that is the debtor's principal residence.[224] If a debt falls within this exception, set forth in Code section 1322(b)(2), and the debt is not subject to one of several exceptions to the exception discussed below, the plan may not alter the interest rate, payment amount or other terms of the mortgage.

In *Nobelman v. American Savings Bank*,[225] the Supreme Court interpreted section 1322(b)(2) and held that creditors whose claims are not subject to modification are also protected from having their liens stripped down to the value of the collateral pursuant to Code section 506. The Court held that even if a plan modified only the unsecured portion of a protected claim, the plan would still contravene section 1322(b)(2), because it would modify the rights of a creditor holding an allowed secured claim secured solely by real estate that is the debtor's principal residence.[226]

11.6.1.2.2 Security interests in the debtor's residence that are not protected by section 1322(b)(2)

11.6.1.2.2.1 Overview

The limitation in section 1322(b)(2), while important, is not as broad as it first appears. In addition to the general exception to the anti-modification provision for curing defaults on long-term debts discussed later in this chapter, there are a number of other exceptions based on the type of security interest involved, such as the following:

- The security interest of the creditor is not secured by any portion of the debtor's principal residence (for example, a wholly unsecured junior mortgage);
- The final payment on the mortgage debt will come due during the course of a chapter 13 plan (for example, short-term and balloon payment mortgages);
- The claim is not secured only by the debtor's principal residence because the creditor has taken additional security (for example, appliances or other personal property located in the residence);
- The claim is not secured only by real property that is the debtor's principal residence because the collateral serves as both the debtor's residence and as income producing property (in other words, a multi-family property);
- The collateral is not considered real property under state law (for example, a mobile home).

11.6.1.2.2.2 Strip off of wholly unsecured junior mortgages

Many courts have held that the *Nobelman* holding does not apply in cases in which a junior mortgage is totally undersecured due to the fact that senior liens equal or exceed the value of the property. In *Nobelman* the Supreme Court rested its holding on the fact that the creditor, after bifurcation of its claim under section 506(a), had a secured claim as well as an unsecured claim, and therefore was a "holder of a secured claim."[227] When the creditor, after bifurcation, holds only an unsecured claim, it is not a "holder of secured claim" and does not come within the ambit of section 1322(b)(2). This interplay between section 506(a) and section 1322(b)(2) has led most courts to conclude that a wholly unsecured junior mortgage may be "stripped off" in a chapter 13 case, so that the mortgage debt may be treated as an unsecured claim under the debtor's plan.[228] In determining whether a junior lien creditor holds only

---

224 The determination of whether a property is the debtor's principal residence is made as of the date of the bankruptcy filing. *In re* Wetherbee, 164 B.R. 212 (Bankr. D.N.H. 1994) (debtor who no longer resided at property could modify mortgage on that property). *See also In re* Johnson, 269 B.R. 246 (Bankr. M.D. Ala. 2001) (creditor with mortgage on real estate where mobile home was situated but not on mobile home did not have lien on debtor's principal residence).

225 508 U.S. 324, 113 S. Ct. 2106, 124 L. Ed. 2d 228 (1993).

226 508 U.S. at 331, 332.

This portion of the court's reasoning leads to an argument that if the mortgage holder has no basis for an unsecured claim, that is, if it has no rights other than to foreclose on the collateral, then those rights are not modified by stripdown. For example, when a debtor files a chapter 7 case followed by a chapter 13 case, the personal liability is extinguished by the chapter 7 discharge so that no modification occurs when only the secured portion of the debt is paid in chapter 13. This argument was rejected in *In re* Kirchner, 216 B.R. 417 (Bankr. W.D. Wis. 1997). A similar issue may arise in connection with a non-recourse loan.

227 In deciding that the creditor in *Nobelman* was the holder of a secured claim, the Court held that "[p]etitioners were correct in looking to § 506(a) . . . to determine the status of the bank's secured claim. . . . But even if we accept petitioners' valuation, the bank is still the 'holder' of a 'secured claim,' because petitioners' home retains $23,500 of value as collateral." Nobelman v. Am. Sav. Bank, 508 U.S. 324, 113 S. Ct. 2106, 2110, 124 L. Ed. 2d 228 (1993).

228 *In re* Zimmer, 313 F.3d 1220 (9th Cir. 2003); *In re* Lane, 280 F.3d 663 (6th Cir. 2002); *In re* Pond, 252 F.3d 122 (2d Cir. 2001); *In re* Dickerson, 222 F.3d 924 (11th Cir. 2000); *In re* Tanner, 217 F.3d 1357 (11th Cir. 2000); *In re* Bartee, 212 F.3d 277 (5th Cir. 2000); *In re* McDonald, 205 F.3d 606 (3d Cir. 2000); *In re* Griffey, 335 B.R. 166 (B.A.P. 10th Cir. 2005); *In re* Mann, 249 B.R. 831 (B.A.P. 1st Cir. 2000); Johnson v. Asset Mgmt. Group, L.L.C., 226 B.R. 364 (D. Md. 1998); Wright v. Commercial Credit Corp., 178 B.R. 703 (E.D. Va. 1995); *In re* Woodhouse, 172 B.R. 1 (Bankr. D.R.I. 1994); *In re* Kidd, 161 B.R. 769 (Bankr. E.D.N.C. 1993); *In re* Lee, 161 B.R. 271 (Bankr. W.D. Okla. 1993). *See also In re* Gonzales, 2010 WL 1571172 (Bankr. S.D. Fla. Apr. 20, 2010) (lien securing condominium association fees was not subject to anti-modification provisions of § 1332(b)(2) and could be stripped off except for portion based on Florida statute that was part of first mortgagee's secured claim); *In re* Mooney, 301 B.R. 627 (Bankr. W.D.N.Y. 2003) (subsidy recapture amount on U.S. Dep't of Agriculture subsidized first mortgage counted for purposes of determining

an unsecured claim, the amount owed on all senior liens,[229] including statutory liens for outstanding property taxes, should be considered.[230] When the interest of a tenant by the entirety extends to the whole of the property under state law, one co-tenant filing a chapter 13 case may strip off a lien without the participation of the other co-tenant.[231]

Although a few courts have held otherwise, a chapter 13 debtor should be able to strip off a totally unsecured lien even if the debtor is not eligible for a discharge in the case.[232] The eligibility for a discharge affects only personal liability, not liens on property. Moreover, the section 1325(a)(5)(B)(i) requirement of a discharge or full payment does not prevent stripping the lien, because that provision applies only to allowed secured claims, and a wholly unsecured claim is not an allowed secured claim.[233] Similarly, the courts that have relied upon *In re Dewsnup* in denying such lien avoidance[234] have ignored the fact that *Nobelman* was decided after *Dewsnup* and, unlike *Dewsnup,* was specifically applicable to chapter 13 cases.

11.6.1.2.2.3 Short-term and balloon payment mortgages

In a 1994 Code amendment Congress cut back significantly on the limitations on modification, and hence the *Nobelman* holding. Section 1322(c)(2) provides that *notwithstanding section 1322(b)(2)*, in a case in which the last payment on the original payment schedule for a claim secured only by a mortgage on the debtor's principal residence is due before the due date of the final plan payment, the plan may modify the creditor's rights pursuant to Code section 1325(a)(5). That section, as discussed below,[235] generally permits a debtor to pay only the allowed secured claim of a creditor, to modify payment terms and interest rates, and to treat the unsecured portion of an undersecured claim as an unsecured claim in the chapter 13 plan. Thus, debtors are permitted to modify many short term mortgages, mortgages on which the debtor's payments are nearly complete, and mortgages with balloon payments falling due before the end of the chapter 13 plan.[236] It is not surprising that Congress carved out these types of mortgages from those which could not be modified. Short-term mortgages and those with balloon payments are not usually purchase money mortgages, which section 1322(b)(2) was primarily drafted to protect. They are also more likely to carry high interest rates and other unfair terms, a fact Congress recognized in passing the Home Ownership and Equity Protection Act of 1994 (HOEPA)[237] at roughly the same time as the 1994 bankruptcy amendments. It is also not surprising that Congress would permit more flexibility for debtors who have nearly reached the end of their payments on long-term mortgages, as those debtors are typically long-time home owners, often elderly and often with a large amount of equity in their homes that could be lost in foreclosure.[238]

---

whether second mortgage was wholly unsecured); 8 Collier on Bankruptcy ¶ 1322.06[1][a] (16th ed.). *But see In re* Barnes, 207 B.R. 588 (Bankr. N.D. Ill. 1997); *In re* Neverla, 194 B.R. 547 (Bankr. W.D.N.Y. 1996).

229 The senior lien amount should include all amounts the debtor is contractually obligated to pay to satisfy the secured claim. This total may include, for example, a prepayment penalty obligation on a senior mortgage. *See In re* Barrett, 370 B.R. 1 (Bankr. D. Me. 2007) (five percent prepayment penalty counted in amount of mortgage claim for purposes of section 522(f) judicial lien avoidance).

230 Statutory liens for outstanding property taxes, water and sewer charges usually have priority over junior mortgages on the property. In some states, these liens do not arise or become perfected until the tax or other obligation remains unpaid for a specified time period.

231 Strausbough v. Co-op Servs. Credit Union, 426 B.R. 243 (Bankr. E.D. Mich. 2010). *But see In re* Pierre, 468 B.R. 419 (Bankr. M.D. Fla. 2012); *In re* Hunter, 284 B.R. 806 (Bankr. E.D. Va. 2002).

232 *In re* Fisette, 455 B.R. 177 (B.A.P. 8th Cir. 2011); Zeman v. Waterman (*In re* Waterman), 469 B.R. 334 (D. Colo. 2012); *In re* Fair, 450 B.R. 853 (E.D. Wis. 2011); Carroll v. Key Bank, 2011 WL 6338912 (D. Utah Dec. 19, 2011); Hart v. San Diego Credit Union, 449 B.R. 783 (S.D. Cal. 2010); *In re* Miller, 462 B.R. 421 (Bankr. E.D.N.Y. 2011); *In re* Okosisi, 451 B.R. 90 (Bankr. D. Nev. 2011) (noting that unsecured portion of claim must be treated as unsecured claim in bankruptcy case); *In re* Davis, 447 B.R. 738 (Bankr. D. Md. 2011), *aff'd,* 2012 WL 439701 (D. Md. Jan. 12, 2012); *In re* Hill, 440 B.R. 176 (Bankr. S.D. Cal. 2010). *But see In re* Victorio, 454 B.R. 759 (Bankr. S.D. Cal. 2011), *aff'd,* 2012 WL 628310 (S.D. Cal. Feb. 24, 2012); *In re* Gerardin, 447 B.R. 342 (Bankr. S.D. Fla. 2011).

233 Frazier v. Real Time Resolutions, Inc., 469 B.R. 889 (E.D. Cal. 2012); *In re* Fair, 450 B.R. 853 (E.D. Wis. 2011); *In re* Hill, 440 B.R. 176 (Bankr. S.D. Cal. 2010); *In re* Tran, 431 B.R. 230 (Bankr. N.D. Cal. 2010), *aff'd,* 814 F. Supp. 2d 946 (N.D. Cal. 2011).

234 *In re* Gerardin, 447 B.R. 342 (Bankr. S.D. Fla. 2011).

---

235 *See* § 11.6.1.3, *infra.*

236 *In re* Paschen, 296 F.3d 1203 (11th Cir. 2002) (statutory exception to Code's anti-modification provision permits debtors to bifurcate and cram down undersecured, short-term home mortgages); *In re* Eubanks, 219 B.R. 468 (B.A.P. 6th Cir. 1998) (short term mortgage modifiable); *In re* Brannon, 2010 WL 1657642 (Bankr. M.D. Ala. Apr. 21, 2010) (debtor could modify mortgage that fully matured before petition date regardless of fact that junior nonmodifiable mortgages existed); *In re* Brown, 428 B.R. 672 (Bankr. D.S.C. 2010) (debtor who inherited from mother property subject to reverse mortgage which had been accelerated prepetition may pay mortgage debt over 60-month plan); *In re* Mattson, 210 B.R. 157 (Bankr. D. Minn. 1997) (section 1322(b)(2) protections did not apply to loans maturing before end of plan); *In re* Young, 199 B.R. 643 (Bankr. E.D. Tenn. 1996) (debtors could strip down mortgage if last payment was due before final scheduled plan payment); *In re* Sarkese, 189 B.R. 531 (Bankr. M.D. Fla. 1995) (debtors could pay off mortgage which had ballooned prior to bankruptcy using the cramdown provisions of section 1325(a)(5)); *In re* Lobue, 189 B.R. 216 (Bankr. S.D. Fla. 1995) (debtor could pay matured mortgage through plan). *See also In re* Nepil, 206 B.R. 72 (Bankr. D.N.J. 1997) (loan on which creditor had obtained foreclosure judgment could be treated as loan on which final payment due before end of plan). *But see In re* Witt, 113 F.3d 508 (4th Cir. 1997) (stripdown not permitted under section 1322(c)(2), because it provides for modification of payments and not claims).

The *Witt* court misreads section 1322(c)(2) because the statute plainly refers to "claims as modified."

237 Pub. L. No. 103-325, tit. I, subtit. B, 108 Stat. 2160 (1994) (codified largely at 15 U.S.C. § 1639).

For a discussion of HOEPA, see National Consumer Law Center, Truth in Lending § 9.1 (8th ed. 2012).

238 *See* 8 Collier on Bankruptcy ¶ 1322.17 (16th ed.).

11.6.1.2.2.4 Mortgages with additional security

The limitation on modification in section 1322(b)(2) also does not apply if the creditor has other security besides the mortgage.[239] Many claims secured by real estate are also secured by household goods,[240] or at least the possible refund of proceeds from credit insurance.[241] Even in first mortgages, there are sometimes clauses giving creditors security interests in appliances or other property.[242] In other cases, the lender has also taken a security interest in other real estate, such as rental units owned by the debtor or farmland.[243] And many banks have, either by law or by way of a deposit agreement, the right of setoff against a debtor's bank account.[244] A creditor is not permitted to release security interests in such other property in order to gain protection from the limitation in section 1322(b)(2).[245] Moreover, it is irrelevant whether a debtor retains the other property securing the debt after the petition is filed; the key issue is whether such other collateral existed on the date the petition was filed.[246] Indeed, there is no requirement that the additional security for the debt be property that belongs to the debtor.[247]

In deciding whether the agreement provides for security in other collateral, courts have often considered whether the additional collateral provides something more to the creditor than might already exist as a component of its security interest in the real property.[248] However, the plain language of section 1322(b)(2) suggests that the protection against modification should not apply if any additional collateral is provided for in the security agreement, regardless of the value it provides independent of the debtor's principal residence, and it should not matter that the security interest is contained in "boilerplate" language commonly found in mortgage documents.[249] In some cases, the issue may turn on questions of state property law as to whether the collateral is an inherent component of the real property, or treated separately.

The 2005 amendments somewhat limited what might be considered as additional collateral, by defining "debtor's principal residence" to include "incidental property," which is separately defined.[250] "Incidental property" is defined as "property commonly conveyed with a principal residence in the area where the property is located, all easements, rights, appurtenances, fixtures, rents, royalties, mineral rights, oil or gas rights, profits, water rights, escrow funds, or insurance proceeds," as well as all replacements or additions. Prior to 2005, courts had found many of these items insufficient to create additional collateral for purposes of section 1322(b)(2).

On the other hand, the specificity in the new definition of incidental property clarifies that security interests in types of property not enumerated, such as other real estate, appliances, furniture, bank accounts, credit insurance refunds, motor vehicles, claim proceeds other than from insurance or property of entities other than the debtor, are sufficient to deny the protection against modification. Indeed, an additional security interest in any type of property not commonly conveyed with a principal residence in the area where the property is located should have that effect. In addition, to the extent that incidental property is not real property, the inclusion of incidental property, such as an escrow account,[251] as collateral does not change the

---

239 *See* Scarborough v. Chase Manhattan Mortg. Corp. (*In re* Scarborough), 461 F.3d 406 (3d Cir. 2006); Lomas Mortgage v. Louis, 82 F.3d 1 (1st Cir. 1996); *In re* Hammond, 27 F.3d 52 (3d Cir. 1994); *In re* Graham, 144 B.R. 80 (Bankr. N.D. Ind. 1992) (when bank extended mortgages on real estate other than debtors' residence which contained clause stating the mortgages also secured existing indebtedness to the bank, original mortgage debt on residence became a debt secured by liens on the nonresidential properties). *See also In re* Zaldivar, 441 B.R. 389 (Bankr. S.D. Fla. 2011) (predominant purpose of duplex purchase was not to provide debtor's residence).

240 As the Supreme Court's decision in *Nobelman* relied on the "plain meaning" of the statute, most courts have concluded that it has no bearing on situations in which the creditor is secured by property other than the debtor's principal residence. *In re* Hammond, 27 F.3d 52 (3d Cir. 1994); *In re* Bouvier, 150 B.R. 24 (Bankr. D.R.I. 1993).

The *Hammond* case was cited favorably as representing current law by the legislative history to the 1994 amendments to the Code. 140 Cong. Rec. H10,764 (daily ed. Oct. 4, 1994).

241 Transouth Fin. Corp. v. Hill, 106 B.R. 145 (W.D. Tenn. 1989); *In re* Pedigo, 283 B.R. 493 (Bankr. E.D. Tenn. 2002); *In re* Selman, 120 B.R. 576 (Bankr. D.N.M. 1990); *In re* Stiles, 74 B.R. 208 (Bankr. N.D. Ala. 1987). *But see In re* Washington, 967 F.2d 173 (5th Cir. 1992) (mere fact that debtor obtained credit life and disability insurance was not additional security, at least in case in which insurance was voluntary and could be canceled by the debtors, and there was no language pledging the policy as security for the loan or assigning its proceeds to the creditor).

242 Wilson v. Commonwealth Mortgage Corp., 895 F.2d 123, 128–129 (3d Cir. 1990) (appliances and furniture); *In re* Jablonski, 70 B.R. 381 (Bankr. E.D. Pa. 1987) (security interest covered appliances and also rents, issues, and profits), *aff'd on other grounds*, 88 B.R. 652 (E.D. Pa. 1988). *See also In re* Thomas, 344 B.R. 386 (Bankr. W.D. Pa. 2006) (additional security in "Miscellaneous Proceeds," which included any compensation, settlement, award of damages, or proceeds, other than hazard insurance proceeds, paid by a third party).

243 *See* § 11.6.1.2.2.4, *infra*.

244 *In re* Libby, 200 B.R. 562 (Bankr. D.N.J. 1996) (security interest in all money, securities, and property in bank's possession, even if no such property was held by bank, constituted additional security); *In re* Crystian, 197 B.R. 803 (Bankr. W.D. Pa. 1996) (escrow funds and right to set off against checking account constituted additional security).

245 *In re* Johns, 37 F.3d 1021, 1025 (3d Cir. 1994) (merger of mortgage into foreclosure judgment does not eliminate security); *In re* Baksa, 5 B.R. 184 (Bankr. N.D. Ohio 1980).

246 *In re* Groff, 131 B.R. 703 (Bankr. E.D. Wis. 1991) (debtor could surrender some of the property securing the debt other than the real estate after the petition was filed and still be permitted to modify claim secured by principal residence). *See also In re* Scarborough, 461 F.3d 406 (3d Cir. 2006) (relevant date is date of mortgage); United States Dep't of Agric. v. Jackson, 2005 WL 1563529 (M.D. Ga. July 1, 2005) (relevant date is date of loan agreement).

247 *In re* Bouvier, 160 B.R. 24 (Bankr. D.R.I. 1993).

248 *In re* Ferandos, 402 F.3d 147 (3d Cir. 2005) (security interest in rents did not constitute interest in additional collateral under New Jersey law); *In re* French, 174 B.R. 1 (Bankr. D. Mass. 1994).

249 *In re* Hammond, 27 F.3d 52 (3d Cir. 1994).

250 11 U.S.C. § 101(13A), (27B).

251 A number of courts, prior to 2005, found escrow accounts to be additional security. *See In re* Donadio, 269 B.R. 336 (Bankr. M.D. Pa. 2001); *In re* Stewart, 263 B.R. 728 (Bankr. W.D. Pa. 2001)

fact that the debt is not secured solely by real property that is the debtor's principal residence; it is secured by real and personal property.[252]

11.6.1.2.2.5 Mortgages on multi-family residences

Similar to the consideration of additional security, a mortgage claim is not entitled to the anti-modification protection if the collateral is not solely the debtor's principal residence. The use of the word "is" in the phrase "real property that is the debtor's principal residence" makes clear that the "real property" can only be the "debtor's principal residence." If the security is not only the debtor's principal residence, such as when the collateral is a multi-unit property, then modification is permitted.[253] This construction of the statutory language is consistent with Congress' use of the word "residence" rather than "dwelling."[254] However, courts have disagreed about the relevant date for determining whether the property is the debtor's principal residence.[255]

11.6.1.2.2.6 Liens that are not security interests in real property

Finally, the limitation by its terms applies only when the claim is secured solely by a "security interest" in real property that is the debtor's residence. A security interest, as defined by the Code, must be a lien created by agreement,[256] and the limitation is thus not applicable when the claim is secured by a judicial lien or a statutory lien.[257] Nor does the limitation apply to property that is the debtor's principal residence if it is not real property, as in the case of a mobile home that is not considered to be realty under state law.[258]

(even though collateral not in hands of mortgage holder on petition date).

252 *In re* Bradsher, 427 B.R. 386 (Bankr. M.D.N.C. 2010) ("incidental property" definition added by 2005 Act did not protect mortgage from modification because security interest taken in escrow account is treated as personal property under N.C. law).

The fact that the collateral must be real property remains well-established, as demonstrated by cases holding that the limit on cramdown does not apply to mobile homes that are not real property. See § 11.6.1.2.2.5, *infra*.

253 *In re* Scarborough, 461 F.3d 406 (3d Cir. 2006) (based on plain language of section 1322(b)(2), namely use of the word "is" in the phrase "real property that is the debtor's principal residence," court held that anti-modification protection does not apply to claim secured by both debtor's principal residence and other rental property that is not debtor's principal residence); Lomas Mortgage v. Louis, 82 F.3d 1 (1st Cir. 1996) (holder of mortgage on three unit building that included the debtor's residence not protected by 11 U.S.C. § 1322(b)(2)); *In re* Maddaloni, 225 B.R. 277 (D. Conn. 1998) (debtor occupied one unit of multifamily building); *In re* Zaldivar, 441 B.R. 389 (Bankr. S.D. Fla. 2011); *In re* Del Valle, 186 B.R. 347 (Bankr. D. Conn. 1995); *In re* McVay, 150 B.R. 254 (Bankr. D. Or. 1993) (creditor holding security interest in property that was used by debtors as a "bed and breakfast" was not secured solely by debtor's principal residence); *In re* Foster, 61 B.R. 492 (Bankr. N.D. Ind. 1986) (security interest also covered farm on which residence was located); *In re* Leazier, 55 B.R. 870 (Bankr. N.D. Ind. 1985) (creditor held security interest in debtor's farm as well as residence). See *In re* Ramirez, 62 B.R. 668 (Bankr. S.D. Cal. 1986) (units at property were also used to generate rental income). See also *In re* LaFata, 483 F.3d 13 (1st Cir. 2007) (anti-modification provisions of section 1322(b)(2) do not apply if the debtor's principal residence only encroaches on the mortgaged property).

The *Ramirez* case was cited favorably as representing current law by the legislative history to the 1994 amendments to the Code. H.R. Rep. No. 103-835, at 46 n.13 (1994), *reprinted in* 1994 U.S.C.C.A.N. 3340. But see *In re* Marenaro, 217 B.R. 358 (B.A.P. 1st Cir. 1998) (fact that debtor's property was designated as three separate lots did not mean debt was secured by property other than residence when property had never been divided for other use).

254 If Congress intended to include multi-family residential properties, it could have used terms other than "principal residence," as it has in other statutes. For example, the Truth in Lending Act permits consumers to rescind certain mortgages on property used as a "principal dwelling." 15 U.S.C. § 1635(b)(2). In that context, Congress defined "dwelling" to encompass "a residential structure or mobile home which contains one to four family housing units." 15 U.S.C. § 1602(v). Congress neither used the term "dwelling" nor created a similarly defined term encompassing one to four family residences in identifying claims eligible for protection from modification in section 1322(b)(2). See *In re* Adebanjo, 165 B.R. 98, 104 (Bankr. D. Conn. 1994) (Congress has repeatedly used the term "dwelling" in other statutes and defined that term to include one to four family residences).

255 *Compare In re* Scarborough, 461 F.3d 406 (3d Cir. 2006), *and In re* Moore, 441 B.R. 732 (Bankr. N.D.N.Y. 2010) (both holding date of mortgage transaction is relevant time period for determining if mortgage is subject to anti-modification provision), *with* Benafel v. One West Bank (*In re* Benafel), 461 B.R. 581 (B.A.P. 9th Cir. 2011) (principal residence should be determined as of petition date), *and* Onewest Bank v. Bocobo (*In re* Bocobo), 2011 U.S. Dist. LEXIS 74509 (D. Nev. July 8, 2011) (date can vary depending on equities of case).

256 11 U.S.C. § 101(51). See also 11 U.S.C. § 101(53).

257 Salta Group, Inc. v. McKinney, 380 B.R. 515 (C.D. Ill. 2008) (debtor could pay off tax sale redemption amount through chapter 13 plan); Williams v. Montclair Prop. Owner Ass'n (*In re* Cook), 2010 WL 4687953, n.2 (Bankr. E.D. Va. Nov. 10, 2010) (exception not applicable to lien for homeowner association assessments); *In re* Hammond, 420 B.R. 633 (Bankr. W.D. Pa. 2009) (debtor could pay off tax lien purchased by third party and modify claim under section 1325(a)(5)); *In re* Bates, 270 B.R. 455 (Bankr. N.D. Ill. 2001) (claim of tax sale purchaser for redemption amount can be paid under plan and treated like any other secured claim); *In re* McDonough, 166 B.R. 9 (Bankr. D. Mass. 1994); *In re* Cullen, 150 B.R. 1 (Bankr. D. Me. 1993); *In re* Seel, 22 B.R. 692 (Bankr. D. Kan. 1982) (limitation of 11 U.S.C. § 1322(b)(2) not applicable to mechanic's lien). See *In re* Starks, 73 UCC Rep. Serv. 2d 471 (Bankr. E.D. Ky. 2011); *In re* Melara, 441 B.R. 749 (Bankr. M.D.N.C. 2011). See also *In re* Prevo, 393 B.R. 464 (Bankr. S.D. Tex. 2008) (entity that acquired tax lien when it paid debtor's tax claim and then had debtor sign note and deed of trust was not protected from modification because debt was secured by tax lien as well as deed of trust).

These terms are mutually exclusive. H.R. Rep. No. 95-595, at 312 (1977); S. Rep. No. 95-989, at 25 (1978). But see *In re* Perry, 235 B.R. 603 (S.D. Tex. 1999) (assessment lien of home owners' association was a lien created by agreement and therefore a "security interest" and not modifiable).

258 *In re* Thompson, 217 B.R. 375 (B.A.P. 2d Cir. 1998) (mobile home is personalty under New York law); *In re* Plaster, 101 B.R. 696 (Bankr. E.D. Okla. 1989). See also *In re* Johnson, 269 B.R. 246 (Bankr. M.D. Ala. 2001) (creditor with mortgage on real estate where mobile home was situated, but not on mobile home, did not

§ 11.6.1.2.3 Consumer Bankruptcy Law and Practice

The definition of "debtor's principal residence" added by the 2005 amendments[259] does not change this result because no change was made to the language in section 1322(b)(2) requiring that a security interest in real property be involved. The definition of "debtor's principal residence" is "a residential structure, without regard to whether that structure is attached to real property" and "includes a mobile or manufactured home." However, while a mobile home may be a debtor's principal residence under the new definition, if it is personal property under applicable nonbankruptcy law, then a debt secured by the mobile home is not secured "only by a security interest in real property" that is the debtor's principal residence.[260] Only if a mobile home or cooperative is real property under applicable nonbankruptcy law would the limitations on modification apply.[261]

11.6.1.2.3 Right to cure defaults is not impaired by section 1322(b)(2)

The limitation of section 1322(b)(2) does not apply to the debtor's right to waive or cure a default on any secured claim, either under section 1322(b)(3) (for claims maturing before the end of the plan) or section 1322(b)(5) (for claims maturing after the end of the plan). Courts have held that when the plan otherwise conforms to section 1325(a) or section 1322(b)(5),[262] a plan may cure or waive a default even on a claim secured only by real property that is the debtor's principal residence, because a cure is not a "modification."[263] Using this reasoning, courts have held that chapter 13 plans proposing to pay such claims in full may effectuate a cure under section 1322(b)(3) that is not a modification prohibited by section 1322(b)(2).[264] This interpretation was confirmed by the 1994 amendments to the Code. Section 1322(c)(1) refers to cures of defaults with respect to liens on a debtor's principal residence pursuant to 1322(b)(3) or (5), and states that the plan may propose such cures notwithstanding section 1322(b)(2).

In addition, section 1322(b)(3) may provide other tools for the debtor. As section 1322(b)(3) also refers to waiving a default, a debtor may be able to eliminate the effects of a due on sale clause that is asserted by a creditor as grounds for foreclosure.[265]

11.6.1.3 Provisions Dealing with Allowed Secured Claims Provided for by the Plan

11.6.1.3.1 Overview

In addition to section 1322(b)(2) and adequate protection, a third important factor in determining whether the court will approve the modification of a secured creditor's rights is compliance with section 1325(a)(5). Section 1325(a) provides that the court shall approve a plan if certain standards[266] are met. One of these is that of section 1325(a)(5), which states that as to each allowed secured claim provided for by the plan one of the following conditions should be met:

(A) The holder of the claim has accepted the plan; or

(B) (i) The plan provides that the holder of the claim retain the lien securing such claim until the earlier of payment of the underlying debt or chapter 13 discharge, with the lien retained to extent recognized under nonbankruptcy law if case is dismissed or converted;[267] (ii) the value, as of the effective date of the plan, of property to be distributed under the plan on account of such claim is not less than the allowed amount of such claim; and (iii) property distributed to the secured creditor be in equal monthly payments sufficient, if the property is personal property, to provide adequate protection; or

(C) The debtor surrenders the property securing such claim to such holder.

As discussed below, language added in 2005 at the end of section 1325(a) dictates that different rules apply, to some extent, for certain claims secured by purchase money security interests in recently purchased personal property.[268]

11.6.1.3.2 Creditor acceptance of plan or debtor's surrender of collateral

The first and third of these options are fairly simple. If the creditor consents to modification of its rights, by negotiated

---

have lien on debtor's principal residence); *In re* Thurston, 73 B.R. 138 (Bankr. N.D. Tex. 1987) (security interest in mobile home, without more, may not involve "real property" within meaning of section 1322(b)(2)). *Cf. In re* Cluxton, 327 B.R. 612 (B.A.P. 6th Cir. 2005) (mobile home was realty under Ohio law based on facts of case); *In re* Carter, 116 B.R. 156 (Bankr. W.D. Mo. 1990).

259 11 U.S.C. § 101(13A).
260 11 U.S.C. § 1322(b)(2).
261 *See In re* Reinhardt, 563 F.3d 558 (6th Cir. 2009); *In re* Ennis, 558 F.3d 343 (4th Cir. 2009); *In re* Coleman, 392 B.R. 767 (B.A.P. 8th Cir. 2008); *In re* Davis, 386 B.R. 182 (B.A.P. 6th Cir. 2008); Green Tree Servicing, L.L.C. v. Harrison, 2009 WL 82565 (W.D. La. Jan. 12, 2009); *In re* Shepherd, 381 B.R. 675 (E.D. Tenn. 2008); Moss v. Greentree-Ala., L.L.C., 378 B.R. 655 (S.D. Ala. 2007); *In re* Jordan, 403 B.R. 339 (Bankr. W.D. Pa. 2009); *In re* Oliveira, 378 B.R. 789 (Bankr. E.D. Tex. 2007). *But see In re* Lunger, 370 B.R. 649 (Bankr. M.D. Pa. 2007).
262 *See* §§ 11.6.1.3, 11.6.2, Ch. 12, *infra*.
263 *In re* Litton, 330 F.3d 636 (4th Cir. 2003); *In re* Clark, 738 F.2d 869 (7th Cir. 1984); Grubbs v. Houston First Am. Sav. Ass'n, 730 F.2d 236 (5th Cir. 1984) (en banc); *In re* Taddeo, 685 F.2d 24 (2d Cir. 1982). *See also* 8 Collier on Bankruptcy ¶ 1322.07[2] (16th ed.).
264 *In re* Spader, 66 B.R. 618 (W.D. Mo. 1986); *In re* Larkins, 50 B.R. 984 (W.D. Ky. 1985); *In re* Williams, 109 B.R. 36 (Bankr. E.D.N.Y. 1989); *In re* Klein, 106 B.R. 396 (Bankr. E.D. Pa. 1989); *In re* Bolden, 101 B.R. 582 (Bankr. E.D. Mo. 1989). *But see* First Nat'l Fid. Corp. v. Perry, 945 F.2d 61 (3d Cir. 1991); *In re* Seidel, 752 F.2d 1382 (9th Cir. 1985).

265 *See In re* Garcia, 276 B.R. 627 (Bankr. D. Ariz. 2002) (due-on-sale clause violation could be cured under section 1322(b)(3)); 8 Collier on Bankruptcy ¶ 1322.07[2] (16th ed.). *See generally Enforceability of Due On Sale Clauses*, 12 NCLC REPORTS Bankruptcy and Foreclosures Ed. 20 (Mar./Apr. 1995) (discussion of federal limitations on due on sale clauses as grounds for foreclosure).
266 *See* Ch. 12, *infra*, for general discussion of confirmation standards.
267 Absent such a provision the lien is eliminated upon confirmation. 11 U.S.C. § 1327(c).
268 *See* § 11.6.1.5, *infra*.

settlement or otherwise, there is no reason for the court to be concerned. A number of courts have held that a secured creditor who does not object to a plan may be deemed to have accepted it.[269] And if the debtor surrenders the collateral to the creditor, that creditor, in effect, is no longer a secured creditor, but only an unsecured creditor with respect to whatever debt remains after the creditor liquidates the collateral.[270] The debtor need not deliver the collateral in order to surrender it.[271] The debtor also does not need to secure the creditor's consent to exercise the option to surrender the property securing the debt.[272]

Occasionally it may be to the debtor's advantage to file a plan choosing the surrender option for personal property of limited value, such as household appliances, if the debtor is confident the creditor will not exercise its rights to take possession of the property. The creditor can then be treated in the plan as holding an unsecured claim.[273]

11.6.1.3.3 Payment of allowed secured claim through plan when creditor does not accept plan

11.6.1.3.3.1 Lien retention and present value of payments—the chapter 13 cramdown

The most complicated provision is the second, which deals with retention of the property when the creditor does not consent to the plan. To meet this standard, the plan must specifically provide that the creditor retains a lien, that is, that the creditor will continue to have priority rights to the property subject to the lien.[274] However, some of the rights usually associated with the lien are necessarily limited by chapter 13, such as the right to repossess. The main purpose of the lien retention is to preserve the creditor's rights in the property if the plan ends in failure before the creditor receives the amount to which it is entitled on its allowed secured claim.[275]

For this reason, to be entitled to confirmation the plan must provide that the lien is retained until either the full underlying debt is paid or the debtor receives a discharge.[276] Once the full debt has been paid the lien may be eliminated, and the plan may so provide. In such circumstances, it should be possible to have the lien satisfied even before the plan is completed. Occasionally the debtor will be able to immediately pay the amount of the claim, either in cash or by transferring property, thereby giving the creditor present value. In some cases, a portion of the collateral may be divided from the remainder and transferred to the creditor to pay the claim.[277]

The requirement that liens be retained until full payment or discharge, added by the 2005 amendments, is apparently an attempt to overrule cases under the prior language that required elimination of the creditor's lien when the allowed secured claim had been paid.[278] It is unclear what happens when the creditor holds a nonrecourse claim, with respect to which there is no personal liability. In such a case, there are strong arguments that the only claim is an *in rem* claim, that is, the allowed secured claim, that there is no other "underlying debt," and that the lien must be satisfied once the allowed secured claim is paid.[279]

---

269 *In re* Andrews, 49 F.3d 1404, 1409 (9th Cir. 1995); *In re* Szostek, 886 F.2d 1405 (3d Cir. 1989); *In re* Ruti-Sweetwater, Inc., 836 F.2d 1263 (10th Cir. 1988) (chapter 11 case); *In re* Castleberry, 437 B.R. 705 (Bankr. M.D. Ga. 2010); *In re* Davis, 411 B.R. 225 (Bankr. D. Md. 2008) (denying trustee's objection to plan because creditor had not objected to plan's not providing present value interest, meaning creditor had accepted plan and plan complied with section 1325(a)(5)); *In re* Brown, 108 B.R. 738 (Bankr. C.D. Cal. 1989).

270 The debtor may also choose to surrender only part of the collateral securing the debt, thereby reducing the allowed secured claim that must be paid. United States v. White, 340 B.R. 761, 766 (E.D.N.C. 2006) (debtor may bifurcate secured claim through partial surrender and propose more than one option under section 1325(a)(5)), *aff'd on other grounds*, 487 F.3d 199 (4th Cir. 2007) (because Internal Revenue Service could obtain the property only by way of adversarial litigation, the debtors were not relinquishing all of their legal rights to the property, including the rights to possess and use it, and therefore debtors did not "surrender" property under section 1325(a)(5)(C)); *In re* McCommons, 288 B.R. 594 (Bankr. M.D. Ga. 2002) (debtor could surrender some items of collateral and keep others); *In re* Groff, 131 B.R. 703 (Bankr. E.D. Wis. 1991) (debtor could surrender collateral other than residence plus thirty acres and pay only the value of remaining collateral). *But see In re* Williams, 168 F.3d 845 (5th Cir. 1999) (debtor had to either transfer entire property or pay claim).

As discussed in § 11.6.1.5, *infra*, this rule may not apply to certain purchase money security interests described in the paragraph at the end of section 1325(a).

271 *In re* Anderson, 316 B.R. 321 (Bankr. W.D. Ark. 2004).

272 *In re* White, 282 B.R. 418 (Bankr. N.D. Ohio 2002); *In re* Harris, 244 B.R. 557 (Bankr. D. Conn. 2000).

273 However, this strategy may have a negative effect on the calculation of the debtor's disposable income, because some courts refuse to deduct payments on secured debts in that calculation if the debtor intends to surrender the property. See § 13.4.5.3.2, *infra*.

274 *See In re* Hanna, 912 F.2d 945 (8th Cir. 1990) (similar provision in chapter 12 case meant that creditor had to retain lien in herd of livestock, including offspring, rather than particular animals, and that herd had to be maintained at level to ensure lender was adequately protected). *But see In re* Pence, 905 F.2d 1107 (7th Cir. 1990) (when secured creditor failed to object to chapter 13 plan provision substituting collateral, creditor was bound by confirmed plan).

275 Section 1325(a)(5)(B)(i) does not require that a chapter 13 plan protect the lien holder from a diminution in value of the lien while the claim is being paid under the plan. *In re* Harris, 304 B.R. 751 (Bankr. E.D. Mich. 2004) (plan need not provide that automobile lender receive payments after confirmation in amount necessary to cover collateral's monthly depreciation).

276 11 U.S.C. § 1325(a)(5)(B)(i)(I).

277 *In re* Kerwin, 996 F.2d 552 (2d Cir. 1993) (chapter 12 debtor could pay secured claim by transferring to holder portion of collateral equal to amount of claim). *But see In re* Williams, 168 F.3d 845 (5th Cir. 1999) (debtor had to either transfer entire property or pay claim).

278 *See, e.g., In re* Campbell, 180 B.R. 686 (M.D. Fla. 1995); *In re* Lee, 162 B.R. 217 (D. Minn. 1993).

279 *But see In re* Picht, 428 B.R. 885 (B.A.P. 10th Cir. 2010) (debtor who did not receive discharge could not obtain lien release until satisfying other prong of § 1325(a)(5)(B)(i)(I) by paying debt determined under nonbankruptcy law).

However, a debtor still may be able to take advantage of the reduced payments resulting from loan modification during the term of a chapter 13 plan, even if the debt will not be discharged. *In re* Casey, 428 B.R. 519 (Bankr. S.D. Cal. 2010).

The practical impact of this provision on debtors who are not eligible to receive a discharge due to a prior discharge[280] is that they can temporarily modify the allowed secured claim during the chapter 13 case, but ultimately may be required to pay the full amount of the claim at contract interest rates.[281] For debtors who cannot complete a plan but who have completely paid an allowed secured claim, it makes more attractive the options of a hardship discharge or a modification that allows plan completion, so that a discharge is entered and the lien can be eliminated.[282] It is important to note that the fact that a lien is retained to the extent recognized by applicable nonbankruptcy law if the case is converted does not affect the amount that may be necessary to redeem the property in a chapter 7 case. That amount is determined by sections 722 and 506(a)(2) of the Code.[283]

To meet the standard of section 1325(a)(5), the plan must also provide that the present value of the payments to be made to the creditor under the plan equals the amount of the allowed secured claim.[284] This means that, if payments are to be made over time, the creditor must receive interest on the amount of the allowed secured claim so that the amount it ultimately receives is equivalent economically to what it would have received if the allowed secured claim had been immediately paid in cash. This standard is discussed further below.[285]

11.6.1.3.3.2 Payments in equal monthly amounts and provision of adequate protection

Section 1325(a)(5)(B)(iii), enacted in 2005, adds two additional standards. First, if property is to be distributed in periodic payments, the payments must be in equal monthly amounts. It is important to note that this provision refers to the distributions to the holder of the allowed secured claim and not to the debtor's plan payments to the trustee. As long as the plan provides that the trustee's distributions to the holder of the allowed secured claim be made in equal monthly amounts, the debtor's plan payments need not be.[286]

It is unlikely that the equal-monthly-payments requirement applies to the cure of a mortgage default under section 1322(b)(5). Although the Supreme Court had found that 1325(a)(5) applies to an "arrearage claim" in *Rake v. Wade*,[287] Congress overruled the result in that case by enacting section 1322(e). Therefore, section 1325(a)(5) is not applicable to the curing of defaults on long-term debts.[288] Similarly, by the plain terms of section 1325(a)(5), it is not applicable if the creditor accepts the plan, and acceptance may be inferred from a lack of an objection.[289]

There also is no requirement that the equal monthly amounts extend throughout the plan. A debtor may, for example, provide for equal monthly amounts to be distributed to a particular secured creditor for the first twenty-four months of a thirty-six-month plan or, if the requirement of providing adequate protection is met, the last twenty-four months of a thirty-six-month plan.[290] Indeed, there has been relatively little litigation about this requirement because most secured creditors would prefer to be paid larger payments near the beginning of the plan than smaller payments throughout the plan. This provision does not apply when a debtor makes a lump sum payment to the trustee, because it only applies when the plan provides for periodic payments.

The requirement of adequate protection in section 1325(a)(5)(B)(iii)(II) simply codifies once more the right of the holder of an allowed secured claim to receive payments during the plan that are sufficient to provide adequate protection of the creditor's interest in the property, as was already provided by sections 362 and 363 of the Code.[291] For the period prior to plan confirmation, section 1326(a)(1)(C) of the Code similarly provides for payments sufficient to provide adequate protection to creditors holding claims secured by personal property, to be made directly to the creditor unless the court orders otherwise.[292]

Interestingly, these adequate protection provisions added in 2005 apply only to personal property.[293] To the extent that section 1326(a) limits the right to adequate protection to creditors with allowed claims and specifies how it is to be provided, it may affect a creditor's right to demand it. However, it seems

---

280 11 U.S.C. § 1328(f). See § 12.10.1, *infra*.
281 *In re* Lilly, 378 B.R. 232 (Bankr. C.D. Ill. 2007).
282 See § 8.7, *supra*.
283 See § 11.5, *supra*.
284 For purposes of this requirement, the Supreme Court has held that the arrearages on a mortgage being cured under a chapter 13 plan are an allowed secured claim. Rake v. Wade, 508 U.S. 464, 473, 113 S. Ct. 2187, 2192, 2193, 124 L. Ed. 2d 424, 434 (1993).
  Congress subsequently overruled this decision for most mortgages by enacting section 1322(e). See § 11.6.2.7, *infra*.
285 See § 11.6.1.3.3.6, *infra*, for discussion of present value interest.
286 On the other hand, at least one court has held that the payments that must be equal are the debtor's payments to the trustee, and that therefore devoting some of those payments to attorney fees and then increasing the payment to a secured creditor does not violate the requirement. *In re* Erwin, 376 B.R. 897 (Bankr. C.D. Ill. 2007).
287 508 U.S. 464, 113 S. Ct. 2187, 124 L. Ed. 2d 424 (1993).
288 *In re* Davis, 343 B.R. 326 (Bankr. M.D. Fla. 2006).
  However, section 1325(a)(5) is applicable to the payment of a home-secured claim pursuant to section 1322(c) and, as a result, debtors may need to comply with the equal-monthly-payment requirement if the claim is paid under that section. See *In re* Lemieux, 347 B.R. 460 (Bankr. D. Mass. 2006).
289 *In re* Tonioli, 359 B.R. 814 (Bankr. D. Utah 2007); *In re* Schultz, 363 B.R. 902 (Bankr. E.D. Wis. Jan. 12, 2007). See § 11.6.1.3.2, *supra*.
290 *In re* Brennan, 455 B.R. 237 (Bankr. M.D. Fla. 2009); *In re* Hernandez, 2009 WL 1024621 (Bankr. N.D. Ill. Apr. 14, 2009). See *In re* Marks, 394 B.R. 198 (Bankr. N.D. Ill. 2008); *In re* Hill, 397 B.R. 259 (Bankr. M.D.N.C. 2007); *In re* DeSardi, 340 B.R. 790 (Bankr. S.D. Tex. 2006).
291 See *In re* Hernandez, 2009 WL 1024621 (Bankr. N.D. Ill. Apr. 14, 2009) (plan providing adequate protection did not have to eliminate all possibility that adequate protection could become inadequate in the future).
292 See Ch. 12, *infra*.
293 A debtor who is retaining personal property subject to a lease or securing a purchase money claim in a chapter 13 case is also required, within sixty days after the petition, to provide the lessor or creditor reasonable evidence of the maintenance of any required insurance coverage. 11 U.S.C. § 1326(a)(4). See § 8.3.13, *supra*.

pretty clear that otherwise, at least until a plan is confirmed, a creditor may request relief from the automatic stay if adequate protection has not been provided.[294]

Decisions under prior law held that a creditor may not, after confirmation, seek relief from the stay based on a lack of adequate protection because the issue of adequate protection should have been raised before confirmation, and confirmation of the plan is res judicata on the issue of adequate protection.[295] The fact that provision of adequate protection has now been explicitly included in the standards for plan confirmation further buttresses those cases. It also seems clear that preconfirmation adequate protection payments made under section 1326(a)(1)(C) should be credited toward the amount the debtor must pay under the plan.[296]

11.6.1.3.3.3 Filing of the secured claim

Preliminarily, if the debtor seeks to deal with a secured claim through the plan, there must first be an allowed secured claim. If the creditor does not file a claim, the debtor may have to do so on the creditor's behalf.[297] The Bankruptcy Rules provide that this may be done by the debtor at any time within thirty days after the deadline for the creditor to file its proof of claim.[298] It was held by some courts, under the prior bankruptcy rules, that if a secured claim was not filed and determined, it passed through the bankruptcy unaffected,[299] and could not receive greater distributions than unsecured claims.[300] Although the current rules seem to permit distribution to an allowed secured claim pursuant to a plan without regard to whether the claim was filed, it is still safest to make sure a secured claim is filed if it is to be provided for in the plan.

For this reason, it is generally a good idea to check the claims docket for the case shortly after the meeting of creditors. If a secured creditor whom the debtor proposes to pay in the plan has not filed a proof of claim, one should be filed on behalf of that creditor within the deadline in an amount consistent with the debtor's schedules and plan.[301] If the deadline for filing a claim on behalf of a creditor has passed, the court may permit a late proof of claim pursuant to Federal Rule of Bankruptcy Procedure 9006(b)(1).

11.6.1.3.3.4 Plan need not provide for all secured claims

On the other hand, in some cases the debtor may not wish to provide for a secured claim in the plan. Section 1325(a)(5) does not require the plan to provide for all secured claims; it merely sets forth standards to be met if the plan does provide for an allowed secured claim.[302] In such cases, the debtor may argue that the secured creditor will be bound by the plan in any case under section 1327(a) and unable to foreclose until after the plan is completed.[303] This course of action involves some risk, however, at least until the courts conclusively hold that section 1327(a) overrides the provisions under which the creditor could seek relief from the automatic stay.[304]

The debtor may decide not to provide for a secured creditor in the plan because the debtor is unable or unwilling to pay that creditor through the plan. For example, the debtor may owe a large mortgage to a relative who is not likely to foreclose. Or the debtor may be current on an automobile loan and may wish

---

294 See Chapter 9, *supra*, for a further discussion of adequate protection.
295 *In re* Evans, 30 B.R. 530 (B.A.P. 9th Cir. 1983); *In re* Guilbeau, 74 B.R. 13, 14 (Bankr. W.D. La. 1987); *In re* Lewis, 8 B.R. 132 (Bankr. D. Idaho 1981); *In re* Brock, 6 B.R. 105 (Bankr. N.D. Ill. 1980). *See also In re* Carvalho, 335 F.3d 45 (1st Cir. 2003) (relief from stay based upon postpetition default did not nullify confirmed plan provisions bifurcating claim); *In re* Humphrey, 309 B.R. 777 (Bankr. W.D. Mo. 2004) (creditor not entitled to relief from stay because lack of adequate protection stemmed solely from creditor's failure to file proof of claim). *But see In re* Andrews, 49 F.3d 1404 (9th Cir. 1995) (suggesting that plan's failure to provide adequate protection would justify objection to confirmation under 11 U.S.C. § 1325(a)(1)); *In re* Simmons, 765 F.2d 547 (5th Cir. 1985) (confirmed plan does not eliminate creditor's lien when no objection to the claim was filed or determined but plan called for claim to be treated as unsecured).
296 *In re* Brown, 348 B.R. 583 (Bankr. N.D. Ga. 2006).
297 Most courts and chapter 13 trustees expect a debtor to file a claim for the creditor if that claim is to be paid by the plan. And it seems clear that if no claim is filed and the chapter 13 plan does not provide for the secured creditor, the creditor's lien is not impaired by the bankruptcy. *In re* Thomas, 883 F.2d 991 (11th Cir. 1989). *See also* § 11.6.1.3.3.4, *infra*; § 12.11, *infra*.
298 Fed. R. Bankr. P. 3002(c), 3004.
  Rule 3004 does not appear to allow a creditor to file a superseding claim to a claim filed by the debtor or trustee because it only allows a claim filed pursuant to Rule 3002 or 3003(c). *See also In re* Hill, 286 B.R. 612 (Bankr. E.D. Pa. 2002) (discussing case law); Fed. R. Bankr. P. 3004 advisory committee's note.
  The creditor may seek to amend a claim filed by the debtor, however.
299 *In re* Honaker, 4 B.R. 415 (Bankr. E.D. Mich. 1980); *In re* Robertson, 4 B.R. 213 (Bankr. D. Colo. 1980).
300 11 U.S.C. § 1322(a)(3) does not allow unfair classification of similar claims. *See* Ch. 12, *infra*. *See also In re* Price, 1 Collier Bankr. Cas. 2d (MB) 221, Bankr. L. Rep. (CCH) ¶ 67,287 (Bankr. N.D. Cal. 1979) (confirming plan but not allowing favored treatment to secured claim).
301 *See* Form 72, Appx. G.8, *infra*.
302 There is no requirement that a chapter 13 plan provide for all secured claims. *See also In re* Bisch, 159 B.R. 546 (B.A.P. 9th Cir. 1993) (tax lien which was not provided for in plan remained enforceable after bankruptcy). *See generally In re* Evans, 66 B.R. 506 (Bankr. E.D. Pa. 1986), *aff'd*, 77 B.R. 457 (E.D. Pa. 1987).
303 *See In re* Rebuelta, 27 B.R. 137 (Bankr. N.D. Ga. 1983); *In re* Willey, 24 B.R. 369 (Bankr. E.D. Mich. 1982).
304 *In re* Penrod, 50 F.3d 459 (7th Cir. 1995) (default rule in chapter 11, based on language of section 1141(c), is that if confirmed plan provides for creditor but is silent about whether creditor retains its lien, that lien is automatically extinguished).
  The *Penrod* rationale should apply equally in chapter 13 under section 1327(c). *See In re* Pettit, 18 B.R. 832 (Bankr. S.D. Ohio 1982) (if secured claim not timely filed, operation of 11 U.S.C. § 1327(c) results in holder of secured claim losing the security). *But see In re* Hines, 20 B.R. 44 (Bankr. S.D. Ohio 1982) (secured claim holder may be entitled to full payment or surrender of collateral when plan does not provide full payment). *See also In re* Tarnow, 749 F.2d 464 (7th Cir. 1984) (claim that was disallowed only because it was filed late remains enforceable against debtor); *In re* Junes, 99 B.R. 978 (B.A.P. 9th Cir. 1989) (when federal tax lien was not provided for in chapter 13 plan it survived bankruptcy case unimpaired); § 11.6.1.3.3.2, *infra*.

to continue payments outside the plan to avoid the trustee's charges.[305] Or the debtor may believe that the creditor will never seek to enforce its lien.[306] Nothing in the Code requires that all secured claims be provided for in a chapter 13 plan. However, if the plan does not provide for the claim, the debtor's personal liability on that claim will not be discharged.[307]

11.6.1.3.3.5 Determination of allowed secured claim

Assuming that a secured claim is filed, it will be allowed in the amount requested unless an objection is raised.[308] If an objection is raised, the claim must then be determined and allowed. In some cases, especially when a mortgage has been assigned and securitized, there may be an initial issue of whether the entity filing the claim is even the proper party.[309] However, if the debtor seeks to deal with a mortgage in the plan, there ultimately must be some determination of the amount of the mortgage claim.

As discussed earlier in this chapter, if such a determination is sought, section 506(a) generally provides that the allowed secured claim cannot be greater than the value of the collateral.[310] As discussed below, this principle does not necessarily apply to claims secured by purchase money security interests in recently purchased personal property.[311] An allowed secured claim may also be reduced to the extent that it is subject to defenses that the debtor may raise as objections to the claim. However, if the value of the collateral is greater than the amount claimed, section 506(b) provides that the allowed secured claim generally can include interest earned to the date of confirmation, plus any reasonable fees, costs, and charges under the original agreement or the state statute under which the claim arose.[312]

permitted as part of oversecured creditor's allowed secured claim); *In re* Hitch, 2009 WL 1542791 (Bankr. C.D. Ill. May 29, 2009) (section 506(b) bars creditor from adding postpetition costs of liquidating collateral to unsecured deficiency claim). *See also In re* Porcheddu, 338 B.R. 729 (Bankr. S.D. Tex. 2006) (creditor's attorney sanctioned for submitting fee statements falsely claiming they were based on contemporaneous time records); *In re* Nair, 320 B.R. 119 (Bankr. S.D. Tex. 2004), *aff'd*, 202 Fed. Appx. 765 (5th Cir. 2006) (creditor's attorney sanctioned for submitting agreed order that would require payment of attorney fees on undersecured claim); *In re* Biazo, 314 B.R. 451 (Bankr. D. Kan. 2004) (fees for stay relief motion not allowed when not requested in motion, creditor had no allowed secured claim because it had failed to file proof of claim, and creditor had not shown it was oversecured).

The language adding fees authorized by statute was added by a 2005 amendment. It is doubtful that this language would provide for postpetition judgment interest unless the claim underlying the judgment arose from a statute rather than a contract. *Cf. In re* Stendardo, 991 F.2d 1089 (3d Cir. 1993) (mortgage holder was not entitled to interest or fees after mortgage merged into judgment absent specific language in mortgage).

This section is somewhat ambiguous as to whether interest must be allowed as part of the claim at the contract rate in every case. Some courts have held it need not be. *In re* Marx, 11 B.R. 819 (Bankr. S.D. Ohio 1981); *In re* Minguey, 10 B.R. 806 (Bankr. W.D. Wis. 1981). *See also In re* Kalian, 178 B.R. 308 (Bankr. D.R.I. 1995) (creditor not permitted to add interest at "default rate" that was higher than contractual pre-default rate).

In United States v. Ron Pair Enters., Inc., 489 U.S. 235, 109 S. Ct. 1026, 103 L. Ed. 2d 290 (1989), the Supreme Court held that the plain language of 11 U.S.C. § 506(b) authorized the inclusion of postpetition interest in oversecured claims on nonconsensual liens (in that case a tax lien) as well as on liens created by agreement. In any case, however, if the interest is pursuant to an agreement, the creditor may not claim a rate higher than the agreement provides, even if it loses "opportunity costs." *In re* Anderson, 833 F.2d 834 (9th Cir. 1987).

Interest payable to an oversecured creditor may also, in proper circumstances, be reduced on equitable grounds. *In re* Lapiana, 909 F.2d 221 (7th Cir. 1990). Several courts of appeals have held that this section allows attorney fees provided by an agreement even when prohibited by state law. *In re* Schriock Const. Co., 104 F.3d 200 (8th Cir. 1997); *In re* 286 Ltd., 789 F.2d 674 (9th Cir. 1986); Unsecured Creditors' Comm. v. Walter E. Heller, 768 F.2d 580 (4th Cir. 1985). Such decisions have been criticized for, *inter alia*, ignoring section 502(b)(1) which separately disallows claims that are unenforceable against the debtor under applicable law. *See* Commentary, 8 Attorney's Fees Awards Reporter, No. 5, p. 19 (1985).

In general, courts have strictly construed contractual provisions providing for fees and costs, and have disallowed unreasonable fees. *See, e.g., In re* Sublett, 895 F.2d 1381 (11th Cir. 1990) (denying interest on attorney fees not authorized by agreement); First Brandon Nat'l Bank v. Kerwin-White, 109 B.R. 626 (D. Vt. 1990) (provision in agreement providing attorney fees for taking possession of collateral after default did not apply to taking possession through bankruptcy proceedings); *In re* Tucker, 391 B.R. 404 (Bankr. S.D. Tex. 2008) (terms of note permitted fees only if note had been accelerated); *In re* Clark, 299 B.R. 694 (Bankr. S.D. Ga. 2003) (fees not permitted by state law due to failure to give required notice were not allowable); *In re* Hatala, 295 B.R. 62 (Bankr. D.N.J. 2003) (language of mortgage permitted fees only for foreclosure proceeding, not subsequent fees); *In re* Shaffer, 287 B.R. 898 (Bankr. S.D. Ohio 2002) (creditor not entitled to attorney fees for stay motion because such fees not authorized by statute nor enforceable under the contract). *See also* § 11.6.2.7.1, *infra*.

---

305 *See In re* Delauder, 189 B.R. 639 (Bankr. E.D. Va. 1995) (permitting direct payment of auto loan pursuant to provisions for curing long term debt under section 1322(b)(5); court did not discuss, probably because debtor did not argue, the fact that section 1325(a)(5) does not require plan to provide for all secured debts).

306 Most holders of security interests in low-value personal property never seek to enforce them. In many cases, the debtor's attorney will know from experience that there is no danger of repossession. In other cases, holders of municipal or tax liens may be known to rarely foreclose on them or may be willing to arrange payments over much longer periods than five years. Similarly, in some cases, there may be little fear that a family member intends to enforce a mortgage or other lien.

307 11 U.S.C. § 1328(a), (b).

308 *See* § 11.2, *supra*.

309 *See, e.g., In re* Wells, 407 B.R. 873 (Bankr. N.D. Ohio 2009) (proof of claim filed did not show standing to file claim). *See also* § 14.4.3, *infra*.

310 *See* § 11.2.1, *supra*.

The Supreme Court's *Nobelman* decision, affecting some home mortgages, does not affect the ability of the debtor to strip down other liens in chapter 13.

311 *See* § 11.6.1.4, *infra*.

312 11 U.S.C. § 506(b); *In re* Auto Specialties, 18 F.3d 358 (6th Cir. 1994) (oversecured creditor entitled to add to its claim reasonable attorney fees provided for in loan agreement); Mack Fin. Corp. v. Ireson, 789 F.2d 1083 (4th Cir. 1986) (reasonable late charges

In determining what fees are reasonable and thus may be allowed as part of the allowed secured claim, the issue is a question of federal law and the bankruptcy court need not award as much as the contract or state law might allow,[313] though section 506(b) appears to preclude an award greater than that provided in the contract.[314] Several courts have held that if the debt has been reduced to judgment, the applicable interest rate is no longer the contract rate, but rather the judgment interest rate.[315]

Some creditors also add to their claims, or otherwise attempt to charge, a variety of other amounts, such as bankruptcy monitoring fees,[316] duplicative escrow charges,[317] and duplicative interest charges.[318] It is critical to carefully examine and recompute claims filed by secured creditors to insure that the claims are correct, and to object if they are excessive. Once an objection is filed, a secured claim holder has the burden of producing evidence of the reasonableness of its fees and charges.[319] A detailed discussion of objecting to such overcharges is provided elsewhere in this treatise.[320]

11.6.1.3.3.6 Trustee's fee and present value interest

Once the allowed secured claim has been determined, it is then necessary to compute what payments will equal the present value of that claim. In order to do this it is also necessary to know the amount of the trustee's fees and expenses, if the claim is to be paid through the plan,[321] and also the interest rate to be applied.

The former can easily be learned from the trustee, but the latter had, until recently, been a matter of considerable dispute.[322] Creditors, naturally, argued for high interest rates, usually the contract rates, while debtors attempted to secure lower rates, such as the legal rate of interest provided by state law. The Supreme Court largely resolved this dispute in *Till v. SCS Credit Corp*.[323] The Court held that a formula method is to be used, with the prime rate of interest[324] as the starting point, adjusted by a factor for risk.[325] Although not setting any amount for the risk factor, the Court cited cases adding one to

---

If the secured claim does not arise from an agreement, no postpetition fees, charges or penalties may be added, because section 506(b) allows only those provided for under the agreement under which the claim arose. *In re* Gledhill, 164 F.3d 1338 (10th Cir. 1999) (*Ron Pair* allows postpetition interest to nonconsensual secured creditors but not attorney fees); *In re* Brentwood Outpatient, Ltd., 43 F.3d 256 (6th Cir. 1994); *In re* Pointer, 952 F.2d 82 (5th Cir. 1992) (only creditors who have voluntary secured claims created by agreement may recover postpetition penalties, fees, and costs).

313 *In re* Welzel, 275 F.3d 1308 (11th Cir. 2001) (en banc) (bankruptcy court must independently determine reasonableness of fees as a matter of federal law because section 506(b) preempts state law); *In re* Hudson Shipbuilders, Inc., 794 F.2d 1051 (5th Cir. 1986); *In re* 268 Ltd., 789 F.2d 674 (9th Cir. 1986); *In re* Wasson, 402 B.R. 561 (Bankr. W.D.N.Y. 2008) (flat fee disallowed absent documentation of time spent on case); *In re* Sacko, 394 B.R. 90 (Bankr. E.D. Pa. 2008) (attorney fees higher than reasonable amounts); *In re* Hight, 393 B.R. 484 (Bankr. S.D. Tex. 2008) (flat fees, including foreclosure fee for foreclosure that was not completed, not proven to be reasonable); *In re* Valdez, 324 B.R. 296 (Bankr. S.D. Tex. 2005) (fees denied for stay relief motion that was imprudent). *See also In re* Hoopai, 581 F.3d 1090 (9th Cir. 2009) (§ 506(b) displaces state law with respect to preconfirmation fees but state law governs postconfirmation fees).

However, for chapter 13 cure plans involving agreements entered into after October 22, 1994, some courts have held that section 1322(e) trumps section 506(b) and requires that allowance of fees in an arrearage claim be determined under applicable nonbankruptcy law and the underlying agreement. *See* Deutsche Bank Nat'l Trust Co. v. Tucker, 621 F.3d 460 (6th Cir. 2010) (undersecured mortgage claim holder entitled to fees and costs in arrearage claim).

314 *In re* Laymon, 958 F.2d 72 (5th Cir. 1992) (section 506(b) interest calculated at contract rate in case in which no judgment existed; whether to use higher contract "default rate" depended upon the equities involved); *In re* Johnson-Allen, 67 B.R. 968 (Bankr. E.D. Pa. 1986). *See also* § 11.6.2.7.1, *infra*.

315 *See, e.g., In re* Presque Isle Apartments, Ltd. P'ship, 118 B.R. 331 (Bankr. W.D. Pa. 1990); *In re* Lehal Realty Assocs., 112 B.R. 588 (Bankr. S.D.N.Y. 1990); *In re* Herbert, 86 B.R. 433 (Bankr. E.D. Pa. 1988). *See also In re* Guarnieri, 308 B.R. 122 (D. Conn. 2004) (after acceleration and judgment no late charges could accrue as no separate payments were due).

316 *See, e.g., In re* Prevo, 394 B.R. 847 (Bankr. S.D. Tex. 2008) (broker price opinion fees, late charges, and foreclosure fees not allowed when they were not documented); *In re* Stewart, 391 B.R. 327 (Bankr. E.D. La. 2008) (drive-by inspection fees and fees for broker price opinions were not reasonable); *In re* Stark, 242 B.R. 866 (Bankr. W.D.N.C. 1999) (mortgage company violated automatic stay by adding monitoring fees to debtors' monthly statements).

317 Such escrow charges are included in arrears that a creditor claims are due and then added again to the claim as an "escrow deficit."

318 *In re* Wines, 239 B.R. 703 (Bankr. D.N.J. 1999). *See also* § 14.4.3.4, *infra*.

Many creditors add "interest on arrears" to their claims, even though the trustee computes and adds interest to the claim filed by the creditor.

319 *In re* Atwood, 293 B.R. 227 (B.A.P. 9th Cir. 2003) (unsworn memorandum of counsel that did not include fee agreement or disclose its terms, and did not state what tasks were performed in the case, deprived claim of Rule 3001(f) presumption of validity); *In re* Coates, 292 B.R. 894 (Bankr. C.D. Ill. 2003) (once objection to claim is filed, party asserting claim must place into evidence terms of the fee contract with the attorney, time records, a copy of any judgment including fees, and receipts or invoices for expenses).

320 *See* § 14.4.3.4, *infra*.

321 For a discussion of paying "inside" or "outside" the plan, see Chapter 12, *infra*.

322 A creditor waives the right to dispute the interest rate if creditor fails to assert its arguments prior to or at the confirmation hearing. *In re* Szostek, 886 F.2d 1405 (3d Cir. 1989); *In re* Blair, 21 B.R. 316 (Bankr. S.D. Cal. 1982).

323 541 U.S. 465, 124 S. Ct. 1951, 158 L. Ed. 2d 787 (2004).

Although the plurality decision represented the views of only four justices, Justice Thomas concurred in the judgment of the court, and the plurality opinion has been treated as binding authority. *See, e.g., In re* Am. Homepatient, Inc., 420 F.3d 559 (6th Cir. 2005).

324 The prime rate of interest may be found on the Internet at: http://federalreserve.gov/releases/h15/data.htm#top.

325 To the extent that application of *Till* does not produce a lower rate, debtors who are on active duty in the armed forces may obtain plan confirmation of a present value interest rate of six percent pursuant to the Servicemembers Civil Relief Act. 50 U.S.C. app. § 527(c). *See In re* Watson, 292 B.R. 441 (Bankr. S.D. Ga. 2003) (plan modified to reduce interest rate from twelve percent to six percent while debtor on active duty).

three percent to the interest rate. The amount added for risk should not be large and may be close to zero. If the creditor is significantly oversecured, the equity cushion will provide protection against risk.[326] In other cases, assuming that risks of loss by fire or other damage are covered by insurance, as they typically are, the only real risk the creditor usually faces under a bankruptcy plan is the risk of a little delay in payments. If the debtor falls more than a little behind in payments, the chapter 13 plan will normally fail. In that event, the plan will be inoperative and the contract terms will be restored, including the interest rates and late charge provisions set forth therein, which would typically compensate the creditor for any delay.

The Supreme Court held that an objecting creditor has the burden of going forward with evidence that the interest rate proposed by the debtor is inadequate.[327] It has been held that the chapter 13 trustee, as representative of the unsecured creditors, does not have standing to object to the alleged inadequacy of provisions dealing with secured creditors in the plan.[328]

Once the necessary figures are known, it is possible to compute what payments, over what period of time, will be sufficient to pay the allowed secured claim, plus the necessary interest, plus the trustee's fees. This computation can be done most easily by first applying the annual percentage rate to the allowed secured claim for the number of payments and the time period desired.[329] After these payments are calculated, the trustee's percentage fee may simply be added to each payment.[330]

11.6.1.3.3.7 Plans not complying with section 1325(a)(5) may be confirmed

A final question which arises as to section 1325(a)(5) is whether the court may, over a creditor's objection, approve a plan providing for a secured claim which does not pay the amount set forth in 1325(a)(5)(B). Although most courts seem to have assumed that payment of at least that amount is mandatory, the language of the section indicates otherwise. Unlike section 1322(a) which states that the plan must meet certain requirements, section 1325(a) states that the court shall confirm the plan if it meets certain standards and is silent as to plans which do not meet those standards. It does not state that such plans shall not be confirmed. Nor does it state, as does section 1129(a), that the court shall confirm the plan *only if* certain "requirements" are met. Given Congress' placement of the mandatory provisions for chapter 13 plans in section 1322(a), the better reading of the two sections together is that courts have discretion to confirm any plan that complies with section

---

The same protections are available to dependents of servicemembers. 50 U.S.C. app. § 511(4).

A statutory exception to the *Till* doctrine was enacted in 2005 with respect to tax claims, for which present value interest is to be the statutory rate of interest. 11 U.S.C. § 511. It is unclear whether this provision applies to purchasers of tax obligations. *Compare In re* Princeton Office Park, L.P., 423 B.R. 795 (Bankr. D.N.J. 2010) (holder of N.J. tax sale certificate did not hold tax claim under § 511), *and In re* Sheffield, 390 B.R. 302 (Bankr. S.D. Tex. 2008) (promissory note obligation to creditor that had paid debtor's tax claim was not a tax claim entitled to statutory interest), *with* Tax Ease Funding, L.P. v. Kizzee-Jordan, 2009 WL 3186727 (S.D. Tex. Sept. 28, 2009) (creditor that paid debtor's tax claim and was assignee of claim could collect same rate of interest as taxing authority). It has also been held that a penalty rate is not "interest" under section 511, and need not be paid as part of the present value rate. *In re* Gift, 469 B.R. 800 (Bankr. M.D. Tenn. 2012).

326 *In re* Cachu, 321 B.R. 716 (Bankr. E.D. Cal. 2005) (nominal 0.5% adjustment because creditor had substantial equity cushion). An oversecured creditor is not entitled to receive its contract rate of interest after confirmation simply because it is oversecured. First United Sec. Bank v. Garner (*In re* Garner), 663 F.3d 1218 (11th Cir. 2011).

327 124 S. Ct. at 1961. *See In re* Trejos, 352 B.R. 249 (Bankr. D. Nev. 2006) (evidentiary burden falls squarely on creditor to establish need for a higher interest rate than one proposed by debtor; rate 0.5% above prime rate approved), *aff'd on other grounds*, 374 B.R. 210 (B.A.P. 9th Cir. 2007).

328 *In re* Brown, 108 B.R. 740 (Bankr. C.D. Cal. 1989). *See also In re* Overbaugh, 559 F.3d 125 (2d Cir. 2009) (trustee could object to debtor's attempt to reclassify secured claim as unsecured); *In re* Andrews, 49 F.3d 1404 (9th Cir. 1995) (trustee may not raise issues under section 1325(a)(5), but may raise issue of adequate protection of secured creditor under section 1325(a)(1)).

329 It is important to note that the rate must be applied to a declining balance. Thus, a ten percent rate on $100 to be paid over three years does *not* yield $30 interest. Tables setting out the necessary payments in amortizations providing equal payments throughout the plan are readily available in many places, such as the Appendix to Regulation Z under the Truth in Lending Act, which can be obtained from the Federal Reserve Board. There are also spreadsheet programs and inexpensive pocket calculators available which are programmed to do such calculations. However, there is no requirement that all plan payments be equal. The plan may provide for graduated payments, increasing over time as the debtor's situation is anticipated to improve, provided that the plan is feasible and that the trustee's distributions to the holder of the allowed secured claim will be made in equal monthly amounts. See § 11.6.1.3.3.2, *supra*.

Negative amortization is not per se impermissible. *See* Great W. Bank v. Sierra Woods Group, 953 F.2d 1174 (9th Cir. 1992) (chapter 11 case).

330 To compute the trustee's fee precisely, the debtor must determine what total payment will provide for both the fee and the desired payment to creditors. In jurisdictions where trustees are permitted to compute the fee as a percentage of the total payment, and not of the payment to creditors, one cannot simply add ten percent to the payments to creditors to determine the necessary fee. *In re* BDT Farms, 21 F.3d 1019 (10th Cir. 1994) (court deferred to United States trustee's interpretation that trustee entitled to collect percentage fee on all monies received, including monies used to pay trustee's fees).

For example, if the payment to creditors is $9.00/month, the trustee's fee, at ten percent, would be $1.00 or ten percent of the total payment of $10.00 ($9.00 to creditors and $1.00 to trustee), rather than $.90. In districts where such trustees administer cases, for a ten percent fee the payment to creditors must be multiplied by 1.1111 to obtain the correct total payment. (This multiple is determined using the formula $10 + X = 10X$.) However, other trustees do compute the fee based on a percentage of the amounts paid to creditors rather than a percentage of the total amount paid to the trustee. *See In re* Wallace, 167 B.R. 531 (Bankr. E.D. Mo. 1994), *aff'd sub nom.* Pelofsky v. Wallace, 102 F.3d 350 (8th Cir. 1996) (chapter 12 trustee could calculate percentage fee only based upon payments disbursed to creditors); *In re* Edge, 122 B.R. 219 (Bankr. D. Vt. 1990).

1322(a) and must confirm a plan that complies with both sections 1322(a) and 1325(a).[331] In any case, it seems clear that if a creditor or trustee does not raise an objection under section 1325, the plan may be confirmed notwithstanding the fact that it does not meet all of the standards in that section. Most courts have interpreted a failure to object as the secured creditor's acceptance of the plan, which is an alternative to the requirement that present value interest be provided.[332]

It should also be remembered that the standards of section 1325(a)(5) apply only to those secured claims *provided for* by the plan.[333] In some cases a debtor may be unwilling or unable to make the payments a court might require under that section to one or more particular secured claims. In such cases it is perfectly permissible to state that the plan does not provide for those claims.[334] Although this may mean that the holders of these claims are entitled to relief from the stay and will have to be dealt with outside of bankruptcy, that outcome may be preferable to trying to pay the allowed secured claims in the bankruptcy, particularly if the filing of the chapter 13 case stemmed from other problems.

11.6.1.4 Different Rules for Secured Claims Described in Paragraph at End of Section 1325(a)

The 2005 amendments added language at the end of section 1325(a) that removes certain claims from the protections of section 1325(a)(5). This new language, sometimes called the "hanging paragraph" because it is not numbered, states that for purposes of section 1325(a)(5), section 506 of the Code shall not apply to certain claims. The language appears to provide that those claims, therefore, cannot be determined to be allowed secured claims under section 506(a) and are not within the ambit of section 1325(a)(5). However, notwithstanding the statutory language, courts have held that the inapplicability of section 506 simply means that a creditor's claim may not be bifurcated into an allowed secured claim and an allowed unsecured claim.[335]

Arguably this exclusion means that claims covered by this new language may still be modified under section 1322(b)(2) of the Code,[336] which allows modification of the rights of holders of secured claims, with certain exceptions, but the restrictions on modification that apply to allowed secured claims under section 1325(a)(5) do not apply. A debtor would presumably be bound only by the dictates of good faith and the other provisions of the Code in determining how such claims may be modified. However, as discussed below, most courts have not taken this approach and have instead seen the new language as a restriction on the right to reduce the amount of the allowed secured claim to the value of the creditor's interest in the collateral.

The claims encompassed by this language at the end of section 1325(a) are two types of purchase money security interests. The first type is a purchase money security interest for a debt incurred within 910 days[337] preceding the filing of the petition, if the collateral for that debt "consists of" a motor vehicle, as defined in section 30102 of title 49 of the United States Code, which was acquired for the personal use of the debtor. This language would not include a mobile home, because mobile homes do not fit within the definition found in 49 U.S.C. § 30102.[338] It also does not include a vehicle purchased for business use or for the use of someone other than the debtor, such as a spouse or child of the debtor.[339] The language "the

---

331 *In re* Chappell, 984 F.2d 775 (7th Cir. 1993) (secured creditor required to satisfy mortgage after being paid full amount of claim filed but no postpetition interest, pursuant to confirmed chapter 13 plan to which creditor did not object, that provided for payment of amount in proof of claim to satisfy claim); *In re* Szostek, 886 F.2d 1405 (3d Cir. 1989); *In re* Wampler, 345 B.R. 730 (Bankr. D. Kan. 2006) (court has discretion to confirm chapter 13 plan over creditor's objection even if section 1325 requires postpetition interest be paid on creditor's claim as plan filed in good faith and otherwise satisfies section 1322(a)); *In re* Brady, 86 B.R. 166 (Bankr. D. Minn. 1988). *Cf. In re* Escobedo, 28 F.3d 34 (7th Cir. 1994) (provisions of section 1322(a), unlike those of section 1325(a), are mandatory). *But see* Shaw v. Aurgroup Fin. Credit Union, 552 F.3d 447 (6th Cir. 2009) (section 1325(a) provisions are mandatory; distinguishing *Szostek* as case in which there was no objection by secured creditor); *In re* Jones, 530 F.3d 1284 (10th Cir. 2008) (conditions set forth in section 1325(a) are required for confirmation if creditor or trustee objects to plan); *In re* Barnes, 32 F.3d 405 (9th Cir. 1994) (provisions of section 1325(a)(5) are mandatory, and plan not paying present value of allowed secured claim could not be confirmed over creditor's objection).

332 *See* § 11.6.1.3, *supra*.

333 *See* § 11.6.1.3.3.4, *supra*.

334 *In re* Evans, 66 B.R. 506 (Bankr. E.D. Pa. 1986), *aff'd*, 77 B.R. 457 (E.D. Pa. 1987); 8 Collier on Bankruptcy ¶ 1325.06[1][b] (16th ed.).

335 *See In re* Dean, 537 F.3d 1315 (11th Cir. 2008); *In re* Ballard, 526 F.3d 634 (10th Cir. 2008).

336 *In re* Johnson, 337 B.R. 269 (Bankr. M.D.N.C. 2006) (plan may modify term and interest rate under section 1322(b)(2) on "910 vehicle" loan).

337 A case is not filed in bad faith merely because it is filed after the 910-day period has run and an earlier dismissed case was filed when the 910-day period still applied. *In re* Murphy, 375 B.R. 919 (Bankr. M.D. Ga. 2007).

 The 910-day period is not tolled during the pendency of a prior bankruptcy case. Hingiss v. MMCC Fin. Corp., 463 B.R. 877 (E.D. Wis. June 20, 2011); *In re* Williams, 2009 Bankr. LEXIS 3365 (Bankr. D.S.C. Oct. 28, 2009); *In re* Maas, 416 B.R. 767 (Bankr. D. Kan. 2009).

338 Under 49 U.S.C. § 30102(a)(6), " 'motor vehicle' means a vehicle driven or drawn by mechanical power and manufactured primarily for use on public streets, roads, and highways, but does not include a vehicle operated only on a rail line." *See In re* Green, 360 B.R. 34 (Bankr. N.D.N.Y. 2007) (travel trailer not a motor vehicle as defined in provision).

339 *In re* Strange, 424 B.R. 584 (Bankr. M.D. Ga. 2010) (vehicle purchased for primary use of debtor's husband and only incidental use by debtor not subject to provision); *In re* Medina, 362 B.R. 799 (Bankr. S.D. Tex. 2007) (vehicle that enabled debtor to travel to work was not acquired for personal use); Toyota Motor Credit Corp. v. Johnson, 2007 WL 2702193 (W.D. La. Sept. 11, 2007) (vehicle purchased for both work and personal use); *In re* Lewis, 347 B.R. 769 (Bankr. D. Kan. 2006) (vehicle purchased for use of debtor's adult daughter not within scope of provision); *In re* Jackson, 338 B.R. 923 (Bankr. M.D. Ga. 2006) (vehicle purchased by debtor for personal use of his non-debtor spouse).

collateral consists" suggests that if there is any other collateral for the debt, the paragraph is inapplicable. In addition, the term "purchase money security interest," in many jurisdictions, would not include such obligations or transactions in which the collateral secures a debt other than its own price.[340] Thus, in the common situation in which a debtor trades in a vehicle that is worth less than the amount owed on the loan secured by the vehicle and must finance the difference as part of the purchase of a new vehicle, the creditor does not have a purchase money security interest securing the full amount of its claim.[341] If this is the case, some courts have held that the creditor's claim does not fall within the purview of the added language that requires the entire debt to be purchase money.[342] Other courts have looked to state law to determine whether the disqualification applies to the entire transaction under what is called the "transformation rule"[343] or only to the portion that is not purchase money—that is, the trade-in vehicle's negative equity—under the "dual status rule."[344] In any event, it seems clear that a refinancing or consolidation of the loan destroys its purchase money status.[345]

The second type of claim encompassed by this new language is a purchase money security interest for a debt incurred within one year preceding the filing of the petition, if the collateral consists of any other thing of value.[346] Because the singular includes the plural in the Bankruptcy Code, this provision would include collateral that consists of multiple things of value as well.[347] Courts have disagreed about whether "any other thing of value" can include a motor vehicle not acquired for the personal use of the debtor.[348] Although this language could potentially include a purchase money mortgage on real property, such claims are often not subject to modification because of the limitations in section 1322(b)(2). In any event, the new language does not limit the debtor's right to cure a default on a purchase money mortgage under section 1322(b)(3) and section 1322(b)(5), or to modify a mortgage under section 1322(b)(2) (to the extent that the limitation in that subsection for home secured loans is not applicable).[349]

Most courts have held that the language added at the end of section 1325(a) was intended to prohibit the use of section 506(a) to bifurcate a secured claim into an allowed secured claim and an allowed unsecured claim as part of the cramdown permitted by section 1325(a)(5)(B). However, because the language instead renders section 506(a) inoperable as to certain creditors (that is, it classifies those creditors as no longer holders of allowed secured claims),[350] it does not clearly carry out such an intent, if that indeed was the intent. In fact, earlier versions of the 2005 bankruptcy legislation had contained language which eliminated only the section 506(a) bifurcation of certain claims into secured and unsecured claims based on the value of the property, but did not eliminate their status as allowed secured claims.[351] However that language was not retained. Courts are required to implement the language of the statute and not what they think Congress might have intended instead.[352]

Even if a court does interpret the added language as prohibiting confirmation of a plan that does not pay the full claim of a creditor holding a claim described at the end of section 1325(a), the debtor may propose a plan that pays the creditor only the value of the collateral as a secured claim, offering surrender of the property as an alternative. Many creditors will accept such a plan because they prefer payment of the collateral's value with present value interest to return of the collateral. If the collateral is surrendered in satisfaction of a claim within the ambit of the language at the end of section 1325(a), some courts have held that the creditor may not be paid any

---

340 *In re* Honcoop, 377 B.R. 719 (Bankr. M.D. Fla. 2007) (security interest was not purchase money to extent it secured debt for gap insurance covering damage to vehicle that exceeded value of collateral); *In re* Hayes, 376 B.R. 655 (Bankr. M.D. Tenn. 2007) (cramdown not precluded to extent negative equity and gap insurance were financed); *In re* Horn, 338 B.R. 110 (Bankr. M.D. Ala. 2006) (automobile loan that had been refinanced on four separate occasions, each with new cash advances, was not purchase-money obligation under Alabama law and therefore not covered by 910-day provision). *See also* § 10.4.2.4, *supra*.

341 *In re* Penrod, 392 B.R. 835 (B.A.P. 9th Cir. 2008), *aff'd*, 611 F.3d 1158 (9th Cir. 2010); *In re* Acaya, 369 B.R. 564 (Bankr. N.D. Cal. 2007). *But see* Howard v. AmeriCredit Fin. Servs., 597 F.3d 852 (7th Cir. 2010); *In re* Dale, 582 F.3d 568 (5th Cir. 2009); *In re* Mierkowski, 580 F.3d 740 (8th Cir. 2009); *In re* Ford, 574 F.3d 1279 (10th Cir. 2009); *In re* Price, 562 F.3d 618 (4th Cir. 2009); *In re* Graupner, 537 F.3d 1295 (11th Cir. 2008); *In re* Peaslee, 13 N.Y.3d 75, 913 N.E.2d 387, 885 N.Y.S.2d 1 (2009).

342 *In re* Mitchell, 379 B.R. 131 (Bankr. M.D. Tenn. 2007).

343 *In re* Blakeslee, 377 B.R. 724 (Bankr. M.D. Fla. 2007). *See* National Consumer Law Center, Repossessions (7th ed. 2010 and Supp.).

344 *In re* Penrod, 392 B.R. 835 (B.A.P. 9th Cir. 2008); *In re* Crawford, 397 B.R. 461 (Bankr. E.D. Wis. 2008); *In re* Busby, 393 B.R. 443 (Bankr. S.D. Miss. 2008); *In re* Munzberg, 388 B.R. 529 (Bankr. D. Vt. 2008); *In re* Mancini, 390 B.R. 796 (Bankr. M.D. Pa. 2008); *In re* Weiser, 381 B.R. 263 (Bankr. W.D. Mo. 2007). *See also In re* White, 352 B.R. 633 (Bankr. E.D. La. 2006) (no purchase money security interest for amounts used to purchase insurance and extended warranty).

345 *In re* Cunningham, 2012 WL 1604686 (Bankr. W.D.N.C. May 8, 2012); *In re* Naumann, 2010 WL 2293477 (Bankr. S.D. Ill. June 8, 2010); *In re* Allen, 2010 WL 1439691 (Bankr. M.D. Tenn. Apr. 9, 2010).

346 *In re* Quevedo, 345 B.R. 238 (Bankr. S.D. Cal. 2006) (creditor must hold purchase money security interest to be protected); *In re* Curtis, 345 B.R. 756 (Bankr. D. Utah 2006) (same).

347 *See* 11 U.S.C. § 102(7).

348 *Compare In re* Cabell, 2011 WL 6018277 (Bankr. N.D. Ind. June 10, 2011) (motor vehicle acquired for business purposes not other thing of value), *In re* Ford, 2008 WL 1925153 (Bankr. E.D. Wis. Apr. 29, 2008) (other thing of value did not include motor vehicles), *and In re* Horton, 398 B.R. 73 (Bankr. S.D. Fla. 2008) (same), *with In re* Littlefield, 387 B.R. 1 (Bankr. D. Me. 2008) (other thing of value could be motor vehicle).

349 *See* § 11.6.1.2, *infra*.

350 *But see In re* Dean, 537 F.3d 1315 (11th Cir. 2008); Citifinancial Auto v. Hernandez-Simpson, 369 B.R. 36 (D. Kan. 2007).

351 *See, e.g.*, H.R. 833, 106th Cong. § 122 (1999).

352 Among the many issues created by this new provision, an oversecured creditor who is not the holder of an allowed secured claim by operation of this language is not entitled to preconfirmation interest and reasonable attorney fees based on section 506(b).

unsecured deficiency claim.[353] As many of these courts have noted, if a creditor covered by this language is deemed to have an allowed secured claim in the full amount of its claim, the language makes no distinction between the different subparagraphs of section 1325(a)(5), and the creditor must be deemed to have an allowed secured claim in that amount for each of those subparagraphs.

To the extent that present value interest must be paid under section 1325(a)(5), courts have uniformly held that the "hanging paragraph" at the end of section 1325(a) does not affect the present value requirement and have applied the standards set out in *Till v. SCS Credit Corp.*[354] Thus a creditor may have less incentive to demand full payment of its claim. If the contract rate is less than the applicable *Till* rate and a creditor covered by the added language is deemed to have an allowed secured claim in the full amount of its claim, it may be advantageous for the debtor to provide for the curing of any default on the claim and maintenance of payments at the contract rate under section 1322(b)(5) rather than payment of claim under section 1325(a)(5)(B)(ii).

11.6.1.5 Voluntary Loan Modifications in Conjunction with Bankruptcy

The enormous foreclosure crisis that began in 2007 has given rise to a number of voluntary loan modification programs, including the Treasury Department's Home Affordable Modification Program (HAMP).[355] Directives issued by Treasury now prohibit mortgage servicers participating in HAMP from discriminating against homeowners in bankruptcy,[356] as well as against those who previously discharged the personal liability on their mortgage loans.[357] A debtor in an active bankruptcy case must be considered for HAMP if a request is made to the servicer, and a debtor who was given a trial modification before filing bankruptcy may not be denied a permanent modification on the basis of the bankruptcy filing.[358] The Treasury guidelines also provide that if a debtor in an active chapter 13 case is in a trial modification and makes postpetition payments in the amount required by the trial plan, the servicer may not object to confirmation, move for stay relief, or move for dismissal of the bankruptcy case on the grounds that the debtor did not pay the non-modified mortgage payments.[359]

Debtors who file chapter 13 cases may now seek HAMP modifications that can be combined with relief from other debts in chapter 13 to give debtors the best chance to save their homes and get a fresh start.[360] Chapter 13 relief from other debts, especially junior mortgages that can sometimes be treated as unsecured debts[361] or modified because they are otherwise not subject to section 1322(b)(2),[362] will make it far more likely that a debtor can keep up with the payments on the modified mortgage. Debtors who have fallen behind on payments under a loan modification agreement may also seek to cure that default in a chapter 13 case.[363]

In addition, some bankruptcy courts have instituted mediation programs that bring mortgage servicers to the table in an attempt to ensure that loan modifications are fairly considered.[364] Typically, these programs require the representative of

---

353 However, most appellate courts have held that a creditor retains an unsecured deficiency claim if the debtor surrenders the property. AmeriCredit Fin. Servs. v. Tompkins, 604 F.3d 753 (2d Cir. 2010); *In re* Barrett, 543 F.3d 1239 (11th Cir. 2008); Tidewater Fin. Co. v. Kenney, 531 F.3d 312 (4th Cir. 2008); *In re* Ballard, 526 F.3d 634 (10th Cir. 2008); *In re* Long, 519 F.3d 288 (6th Cir. 2008); Capital One Auto Fin. v. Osborn, 515 F.3d 817 (8th Cir. 2008); *In re* Wright, 492 F.3d 829 (7th Cir. 2007); *In re* Rodriguez, 375 B.R. 535 (B.A.P. 9th Cir. 2007).

354 Drive Fin. Servs., Ltd. P'ship v. Jordan, 521 F.3d 343 (5th Cir. 2008); *In re* Morris, 370 B.R. 796 (E.D. Wis. 2007); *In re* Brown, 339 B.R. 818 (Bankr. S.D. Ga. 2006); *In re* Wright, 338 B.R. 917 (Bankr. M.D. Ala. 2006); *In re* Johnson, 337 B.R. 269 (Bankr. M.D.N.C. 2006). See § 11.6.1.3.3.6, *supra*.

355 These programs are discussed in detail in National Consumer Law Center, Foreclosures Ch. 2 (4th ed. 2012).

356 *See* Making Home Affordable Handbook for Servicers of Non-GSE Mortgages (version 3.3) Chapter II, § 1.2, *available at* www.hmpadmin.com/portal/programs/hamp/servicer.html.

Although servicers are not required to solicit debtors for HAMP, they must work with the debtor or the debtor's counsel to obtain court or trustee approval of the modification in keeping with local court rules and procedures. This includes extending the trial period plan as necessary to accommodate delays in obtaining court approval or receiving trial period payments from the trustee. Making Home Affordable Handbook for Servicers of Non-GSE Mortgages (version 3.3) Chapter II, § 8.5.

357 *See* Making Home Affordable Handbook for Servicers of Non-GSE Mortgages (version 3.3) Chapter II, §§ 1.2, 10.1; Fannie Mae Announcement 08-03 (Dec. 12, 2008) (same); Dep't of Hous. & Urban Dev. Mortgagee Letter 2008-32 (Oct. 17, 2008).

For borrowers who obtained a prior chapter 7 discharge, the HAMP Modification Agreement will be amended to insert the following language in section 1: "I was discharged in Chapter 7 bankruptcy proceeding subsequent to the execution of the Loan Documents. Based on this representation, Lender agrees that I will not have personal liability on the debt pursuant to this Agreement." Making Home Affordable Handbook for Servicers of Non-GSE Mortgages (version 3.3) Chapter II, §§ 1.2, 10.1. *See also In re* Bellano, 2011 WL 3563012 (Bankr. E.D. Pa. Aug. 11, 2011) (refusing to reopen bankruptcy to file reaffirmation involving HAMP modification based in part on HAMP directive); *In re* Tincher, 2011 WL 2650569, at *3 (Bankr. D.S.C. July 5, 2011) ("This directive makes clear that debtors who file bankruptcy were intended to be eligible for HAMP post-bankruptcy, without being required to reaffirm their mortgage debt.").

358 Making Home Affordable Handbook for Servicers of Non-GSE Mortgages (version 3.3) Chapter II, §§ 1.2, 8.5.

359 *Id.* at § 8.6.

360 *See In re* Wilcox, 438 B.R. 428 (Bankr. D. Colo. 2010) (plan could incorporate modification to which lender consented despite § 1322(b)(2)).

361 *See* § 11.6.1.2.2.2, *supra*.

362 *See* §§ 11.6.1.2.2.3–11.6.1.2.2.6, *supra*.

363 *In re* Weatherell, 2010 WL 3938225 (Bankr. D. Vt. Sept. 29, 2010).

364 Programs have been adopted in the Southern District of New York, Eastern District of New York, District of Rhode Island, District of New Jersey, Middle District of Florida, Eastern District of Wisconsin, and Northern District of Indiana. Copies of the guidelines, orders, and forms for these programs can be obtained at NCLC's Bankruptcy Mortgage Project website, at www.bankruptcymortgage

the servicer to have authority to agree to a modification and, in most cases, the court will not act on any request for relief from the automatic stay or objection to plan modification unless the servicer has made reasonable efforts to achieve a loan modification. Obviously, bankruptcy judges vary in how much pressure they are willing to apply to achieve agreements. Alternatively, if debtors are denied a modification to which they believe they are entitled, or the mortgage creditor wrongly contends that an enforceable agreement has not been consummated, they may litigate these issues in the bankruptcy court.[365]

Courts vary in how loss mitigation is incorporated into chapter 13 plans. Some will undoubtedly defer confirmation until an agreement is reached, while others will confirm a plan based on trial plan payments, subject to modification of the plan, if necessary, once there is a permanent modification.[366] Although the loan modification itself should not require court approval, a plan modification to incorporate it does require the normal motion to modify the plan.[367]

A debtor may also combine a loan modification with chapter 7 relief to better enable the debtor to concentrate resources on the modified mortgage. In some cases, a bankruptcy court may assist chapter 7 debtors in obtaining fair consideration of a modification request. The court-adopted mediation programs often apply to chapter 7 debtors as well as those in chapter 13. And, in at least one case, a court has delayed the discharge, maintaining the automatic stay, until the lender decided whether to grant a modification.[368]

11.6.2 Right to Cure Defaults on Long-Term Debts Including Mortgages on Debtor's Residence

11.6.2.1 Overview

There are certain claims that the debtor cannot pay within the time period of the proposed plan, which can never exceed five years,[369] simply because they are large long-term obligations that have many years of payments remaining before they are due to be fully satisfied. Section 1322(b)(5) allows the debtor to cure a default on such an obligation within a reasonable period of time without having to pay the entire debt balance within the time period of the plan. The normal method of accomplishing cure is for the debtor to pay the mortgage arrearages[370] "through the plan" over a period of three to five years, and to maintain current payments to the lender, which may be paid directly or through the trustee as a conduit.[371] This provision can be utilized to cure both prepetition and postpetition defaults.[372] It should also be possible to cure a default on a mortgage loan modification agreement.[373]

---

project.org/. Such mediation programs are within the inherent power of the court to manage its cases under § 105. *In re* Sosa, 443 B.R. 263 (Bankr. D.R.I. 2011).

365 *See, e.g., In re* Mitchell, 2012 WL 2974781 (Bankr. D. Mass. July 20, 2012) (granting creditor's summary judgment motion but giving debtor option to amend the complaint to allow claim that trial period plan was a separate enforceable contract); *In re* Hinson, 2012 WL 1354807 (Bankr. E.D.N.C. Apr. 17, 2012) (finding that a HAMP violation could create the basis for an unfair and deceptive act claim under state law even though it is widely accepted that there is no private cause of action under HAMP); Ossman v. CitiMortgage, Inc. (*In re* Ossman), 2012 WL 315485 (Bankr. C.D. Cal. Jan. 31, 2012) (denying motion to dismiss); Cruz v. Hacienda Assocs., L.L.C. (*In re* Cruz), 446 B.R. 1 (Bankr. D. Mass. 2011) (enjoining foreclosure while HAMP application pending); *In re* Pico, 2011 WL 3501009 (Bankr. S.D. Cal. Aug. 9, 2011) (finding that debtor and servicer intended that HAMP Loan Modification Agreement be binding once debtor signed, notarized, and returned it to servicer); *In re* De La Fuente, 430 B.R. 764 (Bankr. S.D. Tex. 2010) (postdischarge contempt sanctions imposed on mortgage creditor for failing to comply with agreed judgment upon completion of debtor's mortgage cure plan); *In re* Dumbuya, 428 B.R. 410 (Bankr. N.D. Ohio 2009) (mortgage modification enforceable even without creditor signature; creditor not permitted to disavow agreement on equitable grounds and because modification terms were incorporated into binding plan confirmation order).

Enforcement of debtors' entitlement to loan modifications is discussed in National Consumer Law Center, Foreclosures § 7.4.5 (4th ed. 2012).

366 Making Home Affordable Handbook for Servicers of Non-GSE Mortgages (version 3.3) Chapter II, § 8.6. *See also In re* Arizmendi, 2011 WL 2182364 (Bankr. S.D. Cal. May 26, 2011) (finding that trial plan payments provided sufficient adequate protection even though contract interest not being paid).

367 *In re* Wofford, 449 B.R. 362 (Bankr. W.D. Wis. 2011) (no need for court approval of modification that did not involve the extension of new credit or the transfer of an interest in the debtor's property, but plan modification requires court approval). *See* Motion to Modify Plan to Permit Mortgage Loan Modification, Form 153.1, *reprinted at* Appx G.13, *infra*; Motion for Approval of Mortgage Loan Modification, Form 153.2, *reprinted at* Appx G.13, *infra*; Order Approving Mortgage Loan Modification, Form 153.3, *reprinted at* Appx G.13, *infra*.

368 *In re* Roderick, 425 B.R. 556 (Bankr. E.D. Cal. 2010). *See also In re* Gordy, 2009 WL 2924683 (Bankr. D. Md. Sept. 8, 2009) (debtor and lender agreed to loan modification and dismissal of chapter 13 case after discharge of most debts in earlier chapter 7 case).

369 11 U.S.C. § 1322(c).

370 In computing the arrearages, mortgage lenders must include the escrow portion of the payments that are delinquent. They cannot adjust the postpetition current payments to include the delinquent escrow. *In re* Rodriguez, 629 F.3d 136 (3d Cir. 2010); Campbell v. Countrywide Home Loans, Inc. (*In re* Campbell), 545 F.3d 348 (5th Cir. 2008); *In re* Beaudet, 455 B.R. 671 (Bankr. M.D. Tenn. 2011).

371 *See* § 11.6.2.6, *infra*.

372 *In re* Mendoza, 111 F.3d 1264 (5th Cir. 1997) (debtor could modify plan to cure postconfirmation default); *In re* Hoggle, 12 F.3d 1008 (11th Cir. 1994) (debtor could modify plan to cure postconfirmation default); *In re* McCollum, 76 B.R. 797 (Bankr. D. Or. 1987); *In re* Simpkins, 16 B.R. 956 (Bankr. E.D. Tenn. 1982). *See also In re* Carvalho, 335 F.3d 45 (1st Cir. 2003) (lifting of stay did not preclude debtors from seeking to cure postpetition default and obtain bifurcation of creditor's claim when creditor did not initiate foreclosure proceedings after stay lifted and debtors continued to make plan payments); 8 Collier on Bankruptcy ¶ 1322.09[2] (16th ed.).

373 *See In re* Ward, 392 B.R. 788 (Bankr. W.D. Mo. 2008) (debtor entitled to cure loan as modified by forbearance agreement; agreement terms purporting to nullify modification if bankruptcy was filed were invalid); *In re* Epps, 110 B.R. 691 (E.D. Pa. 1990) (debtor did not lose the benefit of Dep't of Housing and Urban Development forbearance agreement when prebankruptcy default on agree-

While section 1322(b)(3) may be used to cure defaults on short-term debts secured only by a security interest in the debtor's principal residence,[374] and such debts may be modified pursuant to sections 1322(c)(2) and 1325(a)(5), section 1322(b)(5) may in some cases be the only feasible remedy available with respect to defaults on long-term home mortgages. In addition, courts have generally ruled that land installment sales contracts are secured debts,[375] so that they too should be subject to the cure provisions of section 1322(b)(5), as well as the other provisions for dealing with secured claims.

11.6.2.2 Cure of Mortgages After Acceleration or Foreclosure Judgment

Although a few early cases held otherwise, it is now well established that defaults on long-term debts such as mortgages may be cured under this section even if there has already been an acceleration or judgment which caused the entire balance to become due.[376] Indeed, at least one state court has held that, because a confirmed plan deaccelerating a mortgage debt is binding on a creditor, if that creditor later gets relief from the automatic stay the creditor must begin its foreclosure anew by reaccelerating the debt.[377]

In 1994, Congress codified those cases permitting cure after acceleration and judgment, by enacting section 1322(c)(1). That subsection provides that a default with respect to a lien on the debtor's principal residence may be cured under paragraph 1322(b)(3) or (b)(5) until such residence is sold at a foreclosure sale conducted in accordance with applicable nonbankruptcy law.

This statutory language suggests that a cure may be effectuated under chapter 13 as long as the sale has not been completed under state law as of the time of the bankruptcy petition. Thus, if any step in the sale remains to be taken, such as an order confirming the sale or delivery of a deed, the debt giving rise to the foreclosure may be cured pursuant to section 1322(b)(3) or (b)(5).[378] And if the sale is not validly conducted pursuant to applicable nonbankruptcy law, the debtor retains the right to cure.[379]

---

ment was cured under chapter 13 plan).

374 See § 11.6.1.2, *supra*.

375 *In re* Johnson, 75 B.R. 927 (Bankr. N.D. Ohio 1987); *In re* Leazier, 55 B.R. 870 (Bankr. N.D. Ind. 1985); *In re* Britton, 43 B.R. 605 (Bankr. E.D. Mich. 1984); *In re* Love, 38 B.R. 771 (Bankr. D. Mass. 1983); *In re* Booth, 19 B.R. 53 (Bankr. D. Utah 1982). See *In re* Frazer, 377 B.R. 621 (B.A.P. 9th Cir. 2007) (although it was not the equivalent of a mortgage under Montana law, land sale contract could be cured as long term debt under section 1322(b)(5)). *See also* § 12.9.1, *infra*. *But see* Brown v. First Nat'l Bank in Lenox, 844 F.2d 580 (8th Cir. 1988); Shaw v. Dawson, 48 B.R. 857 (D.N.M. 1985). The treatment of such contracts as similar to mortgages under state law will often be determinative in deciding that they are to be treated like secured debts. If land installment sale contracts are held to be executory contracts, defaults on such contracts may still be cured. There would then be an issue whether such debts could be cured as long-term debts under section 1325(b)(5) or whether they must be cured "promptly" under section 365(b)(1)(A).

376 *In re* Thompson, 894 F.2d 1227 (10th Cir. 1990); *In re* Metz, 820 F.2d 1495 (9th Cir. 1987); *In re* Terry, 780 F.2d 894 (11th Cir. 1986); *In re* Clark, 738 F.2d 869 (7th Cir. 1984); Grubbs v. Houston First Am. Sav. Ass'n, 730 F.2d 236 (5th Cir. 1984) (en banc); *In re* Taddeo, 685 F.2d 24 (2d Cir. 1982) (to deprive debtors of the right to cure after an acceleration would undermine the purpose of the cure provisions). *See also In re* Glenn, 760 F.2d 1428 (6th Cir. 1985); *In re* Nelson, 59 B.R. 417 (B.A.P. 9th Cir. 1985). *But see In re* Roach, 824 F.2d 1370 (3d Cir. 1987) (under New Jersey law, debtor's right to cure home mortgage default expired when mortgagee obtained foreclosure judgment).

377 Fed. Nat'l Mortgage Ass'n v. Miller, 123 Misc. 2d 431, 473 N.Y.S.2d 743 (Sup. Ct. 1984).

378 *In re* Jenkins, 422 B.R. 175, 181 (Bankr. E.D. Ark. 2010) (use of the word "sold," which is the past tense of "sell," implies the requirement that the foreclosure process, not just the sale, has been concluded). *See In re* Gomez, 388 B.R. 279 (Bankr. S.D. Tex. 2008) (legal title never passed to purchaser at foreclosure sale under Texas law because substitute trustee's deed was not prepared or delivered before debtors' bankruptcy filing); *In re* Love, 353 B.R. 216 (Bankr. W.D. Tenn. 2006) (Tennessee non-judicial foreclosure not complete until trustee's deed signed); *In re* Wescott, 309 B.R. 308 (Bankr. E.D. Wis. 2004) (sale not complete until court order of confirmation); *In re* Pellegrino, 284 B.R. 326 (Bankr. D. Conn. 2002) (same result under Connecticut law); *In re* Dow, 250 B.R. 6 (Bankr. D. Mass. 2000) (under Massachusetts law, sale is not final until purchaser at foreclosure sale executes memorandum of sale); *In re* Faulkner, 240 B.R. 67 (Bankr. W.D. Okla. 1999) (Oklahoma foreclosure not completed until auction confirmed by court); *In re* Beeman, 235 B.R. 519 (Bankr. D.N.H. 1999) (New Hampshire foreclosure not completed until deed recorded); *In re* Tomlin, 228 B.R. 916 (Bankr. E.D. Ark. 1999) (Arkansas foreclosure not final until deed recorded); *In re* Donahue, 231 B.R. 865 (Bankr. D. Vt. 1998) (Vermont judicial foreclosure not complete until court order of confirmation filed in land records); *In re* Rambo, 199 B.R. 747 (Bankr. W.D. Okla. 1996) (sale not complete until court enters order confirming sale); *In re* Barham, 193 B.R. 229 (Bankr. E.D.N.C. 1996) (debtor may cure if foreclosure sale has not been completed by expiration of period for upset bid); *In re* Jaar, 186 B.R. 148 (Bankr. M.D. Fla. 1995) (foreclosure sale not completed until certificate of sale filed with clerk of court). *See also In re* Brown, 249 B.R. 193 (Bankr. N.D. Ill. 2000) (buyer under real estate installment sales agreement still had right to cure after seller declared forfeiture because buyer had right to cure and reinstate contract under state law). *But see In re* Connors, 497 F.3d 314 (3d Cir. 2007) (debtor no longer had right to cure under New Jersey law after hammer fell at foreclosure sale); *In re* Cain, 423 F.3d 617 (6th Cir. 2005) (foreclosure sale is auction and right to cure terminates on sale date under Michigan law); Colon v. Option One Mortgage Corp., 319 F.3d 912 (7th Cir. 2003) (right to cure under Illinois law is cut off upon completion of sale if time for redemption has run and does not continue until order confirming sale); *In re* Canney, 284 F.3d 362 (2d Cir. 2002); *In re* Smith, 85 F.3d 1555 (11th Cir. 1996) (dicta that right to cure does not exist during statutory redemption period); *In re* Froehle, 286 B.R. 94 (B.A.P. 8th Cir. 2002) (redemption period following tax sale under Iowa law not tolled beyond sixty-day period provided for in section 108(b), and debtor may not use cure provisions under chapter 13 to redeem property); *In re* Bebensee-Wong, 248 B.R. 820 (B.A.P. 9th Cir. 2000) (relief from stay granted to foreclosure sale purchaser was not abuse of discretion because under California law recording of trustee's deed related back to date of sale, which occurred before bankruptcy); *In re* McCarn, 218 B.R. 154 (B.A.P. 10th Cir. 1998) (property was "sold" on date of foreclosure sale under Wyoming law); *In re* Ferrell, 179 B.R. 530 (W.D. Tenn. 1994).

11.6.2.3 Cure of Mortgages That Mature Before the Bankruptcy Case or Before the End of the Plan

Section 1322(c) also makes clear that the time period for cure under section 1322(b)(3) may extend beyond the last scheduled payment date on the mortgage, as many courts had held,[380] and overrules the result of those courts that had held otherwise.[381] Notwithstanding the limitations of section 1322(b)(5), section 1322(c)(1) clearly permits cure of home mortgages under section 1322(b)(3) as well as under section 1322(b)(5), and section 1322(c)(2) permits modification of mortgages that mature before the end of the plan. Therefore, a debtor may cure a mortgage that has a balloon payment that has already fallen due, or that will fall due during the plan, by paying the balance over the course of a chapter 13 plan.[382]

Prior to the 1994 amendments, several courts of appeals held, for different reasons, that there was no right to cure a default once a foreclosure sale had taken place,[383] though by the operation of Code section 108 there was a sixty day tolling of any right to redeem.[384] Other courts have held that the right to cure may exist until the expiration of state law rights of redemption.[385] As discussed above, the language of section 1322(c)(1), enacted after these decisions, suggests that a cure can occur at least until every step of a foreclosure sale is completed and perhaps until all state law cure rights no longer exist.[386] Additionally, in the limited situations in which a foreclosure can be set aside pursuant to state law, the right to cure may be reinstated.[387]

11.6.2.4 Cure Permitted Even If Debtor Has No Personal Liability

A cure may also be effected under section 1322(b)(5) despite the fact that the debtor has no personal liability on the underlying obligation due to its discharge in a prior bankruptcy, as the creditor continues to have a claim, and a "claim against the debtor" is defined to include a claim against property of the debtor.[388] Similarly, a debtor who has taken over payments on

---

The legislative history also suggests that the 1994 amendment was not intended to override decisions setting a later cutoff of the right to cure, stating that "if the state provides the debtor more extensive 'cure' rights (through, for example, some later redemption period), the debtor would continue to enjoy such rights in bankruptcy." H.R. Rep. No. 103-835, at 52 (1994), reprinted in 1994 U.S.C.C.A.N. 3340. Thus, the provision should be viewed as permissive, rather than restrictive; it does not state that no cure may occur after the property is sold if that is otherwise permitted by state law. Indeed, an earlier version of the bill, S.540, § 301, 103d Cong. (1994), would have permitted cure in any case in which the debtor retained "any legal or equitable interest, including a right of redemption." Different rules may apply to the ability to pay redemption amounts in tax sale situations. See, e.g., Salta Group, Inc. v. McKinney, 380 B.R. 515 (C.D. Ill. 2008) (debtor could pay off redemption amount through chapter 13 plan); In re Kasco, 378 B.R. 207 (Bankr. N.D. Ill. 2007) (stay relief denied because debtor had right to pay off tax sale redemption amount through plan).

379 In re Schwartz, 366 B.R. 265 (Bankr. D. Mass. 2007) (sale not valid because assignment of mortgage to party that conducted sale did not occur until after sale). See In re Cooper, 317 B.R. 500 (Bankr. E.D. Tenn. 2004) (errors in advertisements rendered sale invalid).

380 Grubbs v. Houston First Am. Sav. Ass'n, 730 F.2d 236 (5th Cir. 1984); In re Spader, 66 B.R. 618 (W.D. Mo. 1986) (residential mortgage maturing prepetition could be cured in chapter 13); In re Larkins, 50 B.R. 984 (W.D. Ky. 1985); In re Dochniak, 95 B.R. 100 (Bankr. W.D. Ky. 1988); In re McSorley, 24 B.R. 795 (Bankr. D.N.J. 1982); In re Simpkins, 16 B.R. 956 (Bankr. E.D. Tenn. 1982). See § 11.6.1.2.3, supra.

381 In re Harlan, 783 F.2d 839 (9th Cir. 1986); In re Seidel, 752 F.2d 1382 (9th Cir. 1985); In re Fontaine, 27 B.R. 614 (B.A.P. 9th Cir. 1982) (chapter 13 debtor may not cure prepetition balloon payment default). Cf. In re Clark, 738 F.2d 869, 874 (7th Cir. 1984) (suggesting that section 1322(b)(5) cure cannot extend beyond last payment date).

382 See § 11.6.1.2.2.2, supra; In re Paschen, 296 F.3d 1203 (11th Cir. 2002); In re Eubanks, 219 B.R. 468 (B.A.P. 6th Cir. 1998); In re Chang, 185 B.R. 50 (Bankr. N.D. Ill. 1995). See also In re Jefferson, 263 B.R. 231 (Bankr. N.D. Ill. 2001) (section 1322(c)(1) permitted cure of lien obtained by condominium association on debtor's home if lien had not yet been foreclosed upon).

383 Justice v. Valley Nat'l Bank, 849 F.2d 1078 (8th Cir. 1988); In re Roach, 824 F.2d 1370 (3d Cir. 1987) (conclusion rests on New Jersey law); In re Glenn, 760 F.2d 1428 (6th Cir. 1985) (conclusion appears to be based on federal law). See also In re Tynan, 773 F.2d 177 (7th Cir. 1985).

384 See § 9.4.3, supra; In re Tynan, 773 F.2d 177 (7th Cir. 1985).

385 See In re Chambers, 27 B.R. 687 (Bankr. S.D. Fla. 1983). See also In re Thompson, 894 F.2d 1227, 1230 n.6 (10th Cir. 1990) (suggesting that cure may be possible after foreclosure sale if no third-party purchaser present); 8 Collier on Bankruptcy ¶ 1322.09[6] (16th ed.). But see In re Smith, 85 F.3d 1555 (11th Cir. 1996) (state law right to redeem cannot be exercised by curing the arrears in installments in bankruptcy; unclear whether entire balance due could be paid in installments).

386 In re Grassie, 293 B.R. 829 (Bankr. D. Mass. 2003) (debtor retains equity of redemption when bankruptcy petition was filed minutes after foreclosure sale and after memorandum of sale signed by purchaser but before memorandum signed by auctioneer); In re Benson, 293 B.R. 234 (Bankr. D. Ariz. 2003) (trustee's sale is not complete under Arizona law until the bid price is paid; sale invalidated as debtor filed bankruptcy after fall of auctioneer's hammer but before high bidder paid bid price); In re Brown, 282 B.R. 880 (Bankr. E.D. Ark. 2002) (judicial foreclosure not complete under Arkansas law until sale is confirmed by court; bankruptcy filed after sale but one day before sale confirmed). See § 11.6.2.2, supra. See also In re Schleier, 290 B.R. 45 (Bankr. S.D.N.Y. 2003) (clerk's time-stamp on bankruptcy petition created mere rebuttable presumption which debtor rebutted with evidence that petition was in possession of clerk and actually filed minutes before the completion of the sale). But see In re Connors, 497 F.3d 314 (3d Cir. 2007) (debtor no longer had right to cure under New Jersey law after hammer fell at foreclosure sale); Colon v. Option One Mortgage Corp., 319 F.3d 912 (7th Cir. 2003) (right to cure under Illinois law is cut off upon completion of sale if time for redemption has run and does not continue until order confirming sale); In re Canney, 284 F.3d 363 (2d Cir. 2002) (under Vermont strict foreclosure law, automatic stay does not permit debtor to redeem property after end of redemption period, except as extended for sixty days by 11 U.S.C. § 108(b); court did not consider application of section 1322(c)(1)); In re Tucker, 290 B.R. 134 (Bankr. E.D. Mo. 2003) (deed of trust foreclosure sale complete under Missouri law even though bankruptcy filed before trustee's deed recorded).

387 See § 10.4.2.6.5, supra.

388 11 U.S.C. § 102(2); Johnson v. Home State Bank, 501 U.S. 78, 111

a mortgage when a property has been transferred to him or her may cure despite the absence of personal liability on the original obligation.[389]

11.6.2.5 Length of Time Permitted for Cure

The Code does not define what period of time is "reasonable" for the purpose of section 1322(b)(5). Necessarily, this depends to some extent on the facts and circumstances of each case.[390] It is not safe to assume that cure over the entire length of the plan will be found reasonable,[391] although in many cases that long a time period is allowed.[392] Many bankruptcy courts routinely permit three to five years to cure a mortgage default, if necessary.

It may also be possible to obtain a longer period of time to cure by arguing that the time for a plan to run does not begin until confirmation of the plan. At least one court of appeals has held that the plan can run for sixty months from that date.[393] In any case, the amount of time a prior bankruptcy case was pending is not counted toward the sixty-month maximum for plan duration.[394]

11.6.2.6 Method of Maintaining Current Payments on Debts Being Cured

Most courts permit current payments on long-term obligations that are being cured to be paid directly by the debtor, sometimes referred to as payments "outside the plan."[395] And, as the payments on long-term obligations are often higher than on any others, it is a common practice to have the debtor disburse them to avoid adding the substantial cost of the trustee's percentage fees and expenses (up to ten percent).[396]

However, some trustees and practitioners prefer payment of current mortgage payments through the chapter 13 trustee. This method has the advantage of making payment more likely if the debtor's payments to the trustee are made by wage deductions. It also provides a better method of keeping track of payments made, through the trustee's records, which avoids the necessity of trying to reconstruct a debtor's fragmentary records or canceled checks or money order receipts if a dispute later arises. Often, trustees who funnel current mortgage payments through their offices are able to greatly reduce their percentage fees because much more money is flowing through their systems. However, a trustee does not have the right to insist that current mortgage payments be made through the trustee in all cases.[397]

11.6.2.7 Amount Necessary to Effectuate Cure

11.6.2.7.1 Attorney fees and costs

Another question arising under section 1322(b)(5) is the extent to which creditors may collect attorney fees and costs as

---

S. Ct. 2150, 115 L. Ed. 2d 66 (1991).

389 *In re* Curinton, 300 B.R. 78 (Bankr. M.D. Fla. 2003) (debtor could cure mortgage on home that was transferred to him from his business even though mortgage remained in corporation's name); *In re* Rosa, 261 B.R. 136 (Bankr. D.N.J. 2001) (debtor could cure default on mortgage on her property even though mortgage was in name of her spouse); *In re* Trapp, 260 B.R. 267 (Bankr. D.S.C. 2001) (debtor could cure mortgage with due on sale clause on property she had purchased from mortgagors); *In re* Rutledge, 208 B.R. 624 (Bankr. E.D.N.Y. 1997); *In re* Wilcox, 209 B.R. 181 (Bankr. E.D.N.Y. 1996) (debtor could pay off mortgage on inherited home even though under "reverse mortgage" provisions mortgage came due when debtor's father died); *In re* Everhart, 87 B.R. 35 (Bankr. N.D. Ohio 1988). *See also In re* Garcia, 276 B.R. 627 (Bankr. D. Ariz. 2002) (due-on-sale clause violation did not prevent debtor who had become owner of property from curing).

390 *In re* Steinacher, 283 B.R. 768 (B.A.P. 9th Cir. 2002) (invalidating local rule that required short cure period for any debtor who had previous chapter 13 case pending within six months before current case).

391 *In re* Coleman, 5 B.R. 812 (Bankr. W.D. Ky. 1980) (reasonable time not synonymous with three-year duration of typical plan).

392 *In re* Hence, 255 Fed. Appx. 28 (5th Cir. 2007) (payments in fifteenth through fifty-seventh month of plan provided cure in reasonable time); *In re* Capps, 836 F.2d 773 (3d Cir. 1987) (sixty months); *In re* King, 23 B.R. 779 (B.A.P. 9th Cir. 1982) (cure over duration of plan not unreasonable); Philadelphia Sav. Fund Soc'y v. Stewart, 16 B.R. 460 (E.D. Pa. 1981) (three years, four months); *In re* Chavez, 117 B.R. 730 (Bankr. S.D. Fla. 1990) (three years); *In re* Harmon, 72 B.R. 458 (Bankr. E.D. Pa. 1987) (cure during period of five years not unreasonable); *In re* Johnson, 6 B.R. 34 (Bankr. N.D. Ill. 1980) (three years).

393 West v. Costen, 826 F.2d 1376 (4th Cir. 1987); *In re* Serna, 193 B.R. 537 (Bankr. D. Ariz. 1996) (sixty months run from due date of first payment after confirmation of plan). *See also* PNC Mortgage Co. v. Dicks, 199 B.R. 674 (N.D. Ind. 1996) (arrearages could be cured over remaining twenty-five year term of mortgage); *In re* Black, 78 B.R. 840 (Bankr. S.D. Ohio 1987) (no dismissal when payments extend over sixty-six months, if plan complied with duration requirements of the Code at the time of confirmation).

394 *In re* Martin, 156 B.R. 47 (B.A.P. 9th Cir. 1993).

395 Payments outside the plan are not made through the trustee. *See* Ch. 12, *infra*.

396 *In re* Lopez, 372 B.R. 40 (B.A.P. 9th Cir. 2006) (overruling trustee's objection to debtor acting as disbursement agent on current payments), *aff'd*, 550 F.3d 1202 (9th Cir. 2008); *In re* Land, 96 B.R. 310 (D. Colo. 1988); *In re* Vigil, 344 B.R. 624 (Bankr. D.N.M. 2006) (there is no general rule that all payments must be made through trustee, and debtor need not demonstrate special circumstances to make current payments directly); *In re* Clay, 339 B.R. 784 (Bankr. D. Utah 2006); *In re* Burkhart, 94 B.R. 724 (Bankr. N.D. Fla. 1988); *In re* Erickson P'ship, 77 B.R. 738 (Bankr. D.S.D. 1987), *aff'd*, 83 B.R. 725 (D.S.D. 1988). *But see In re* Foster, 670 F.2d 478 (5th Cir. 1982) (trustee's commission must be paid on payments outside the plan); *In re* Giesbrecht, 429 B.R. 682 (B.A.P. 9th Cir. 2010) (debtors do not have absolute right to pay current mortgage payments directly).

The *Erickson Partnership* decision noted a change in statutory language which may overrule the *Foster* result. *See* 8 Collier on Bankruptcy ¶ 1302.05[1][c] (16th ed.).

397 *In re* Lopez, 372 B.R. 40 (B.A.P. 9th Cir. 2007) (2005 amendments did not eliminate debtor's right to make current payments directly to mortgagee), *aff'd*, 550 F.3d 1202 (9th Cir. 2008); *In re* Vigil, 344 B.R. 624 (Bankr. D.N.M. 2006); *In re* Clay, 339 B.R. 784 (Bankr. D. Utah 2006).

part of the amount needed to cure.[398] The answer usually turns upon the precise language of the contract and state law. Section 506(b) of the Code, applicable to determining the amount payable to the holder of an oversecured claim, provides for collection of such charges only if provided for in the parties' agreement.[399] For agreements entered into after October 22, 1994, section 1322(e) similarly requires that the creditor's right to collect attorney fees and costs must be provided for in the underlying agreement.[400] Agreements departing from the standard "American rule" that each party must bear its own fees are to be strictly construed, especially when drafted by the creditor trying to collect fees.[401] In addition, many state statutes place significant limitations on fee arrangements[402] or prohibit them entirely.[403] Such state laws are usually read into any contract to which they are applicable as implied terms.

In any case, fees should be allowed in a cure situation only to the extent that they are reasonable and necessary.[404] When a creditor's litigation is unsuccessful or unnecessary, it should not be rewarded by the assessment of attorney fees against the debtor.[405] Similarly, if the creditor does not provide adequate records to establish that its attorney fees are fair and reasonable, the fees should be denied.[406] The filing of a claim does not require an attorney, and thus no attorney fees may be charged for that task.[407] Some courts have held that the inclusion in a

---

398 For a discussion of overcharges on mortgage claims in chapter 13 cases, see § 14.4.3.4, *infra*.

399 *See* § 11.6.1.3.3.5, *supra*.

400 *See* Deutsche Bank Nat'l Trust Co. v. Tucker, 621 F.3d 460 (6th Cir. 2010) (undersecured mortgage claim holder entitled to fees and costs in arrearage claim as § 1322(e) controls amount necessary to cure defaults in chapter 13 cases). *See also In re* Covemaker, 2011 WL 2020856 (Bankr. C.D. Ill. May 23, 2011) (attorney fees held unreasonable under § 1322(e)); *In re* Plant, 288 B.R. 635 (Bankr. D. Mass. 2003) (section 1322(e) rather than section 506(b) determines creditor's entitlement to prepetition fees in chapter 13 cure situation).

401 *In re* Hatcher, 208 B.R. 959 (B.A.P. 10th Cir. 1997) (creditor had no right, under section 506(b) or otherwise, to postpetition attorney fees in addition to fees provided for in mortgage contract); Wells Fargo Bank v. Collins, 2010 WL 3303663 (S.D. Tex. Aug. 19, 2010) (creditor could not charge for preparing proof of claim because it did not come within deed of trust provision permitting fees for actions "reasonable or appropriate to protect Lender's interest in the Property *and* rights under this Security Instrument"), *aff'd*, 437 Fed. Appx. 314 (5th Cir. 2011); *In re* Baron, 2011 WL 1403035 (Bankr. N.D. Cal. Apr. 12, 2011) (disallowing fees because creditor failed to provide notice to debtor before paying attorney fees as required by deed of trust); *In re* Hatala, 295 B.R. 62 (Bankr. D.N.J. 2003) (mortgage provided for fees only in foreclosure and not for fees incurred after foreclosure judgment); *In re* Romano, 174 B.R. 342 (Bankr. M.D. Fla. 1994) (interpreting ambiguous attorney fee provision in note against drafter); *In re* Kennedy Mortgage Co., 23 B.R. 466 (Bankr. D.N.J. 1982) (instrument did not allow fees when collection was by way of setoff); *In re* Roberts, 20 B.R. 914 (Bankr. E.D.N.Y. 1981) (participation in chapter 13 proceedings was not included in the attorney fees provision of the mortgage). *See also In re* United Nesco Container Corp., 68 B.R. 970 (Bankr. E.D. Pa. 1987) (equipment lease providing for attorney fees in the event of repossession would not be interpreted broadly so as to include attorney fees incurred by lessor in pursuing claim in bankruptcy court). *But see In re* Velazquez, 660 F.3d 893 (5th Cir. 2011) (rejecting interpretation of uniform deed of trust taken in *Collins* and construing "and" to mean "either or both" thereby permitting recovery of attorney fees for preparing proof of claim).

402 *In re* Obie, 2009 WL 4113587 (Bankr. M.D.N.C. Nov. 24, 2009) (disallowing fees because notice required by state law was not sent); *In re* Wilder, 22 B.R. 294 (Bankr. M.D. Ga. 1982) (statutory attorney fees could not be collected for work that could have been performed by non-lawyers). *See also* § 11.6.1.3.3.5, *supra*.

403 *In re* Lake, 245 B.R. 282 (Bankr. N.D. Ohio 2000) (boilerplate fee provisions in a mortgage were not product of free and understanding negotiation and therefore were unenforceable under Ohio law); *In re* Bertsch, 17 B.R. 284 (Bankr. N.D. Ohio 1982) (assessment of bank's attorney fees against debtor disallowed as contrary to Ohio public policy).

404 *In re* McMullen, 273 B.R. 558 (Bankr. C.D. Ill. 2001) (flat fee covering attorney fees for entire foreclosure proceeding found excessive when not pro-rated to cover only services actually performed prior to bankruptcy filing); *In re* A.J. Lane & Co., 113 B.R. 821 (Bankr. D. Mass. 1990) (prepayment charge disallowed because it was unreasonable); *In re* Bailey, 23 B.R. 222 (Bankr. E.D. Pa. 1982) (attorney fees and costs denied for unsuccessful proceeding for relief from automatic stay).

One bankruptcy court has held that it must make its own independent determination of whether fees are reasonable for the purposes of the Code, even if they have already been reduced to judgment by a creditor. *In re* Harper, 146 B.R. 438 (Bankr. N.D. Ind. 1992). *See also In re* Welzel, 275 F.3d 1308 (11th Cir. 2001) (en banc) (bankruptcy court must independently determine reasonableness of fees as a matter of federal law because section 506(b) preempts state law).

405 *In re* Crowley, 293 B.R. 628 (Bankr. D. Vt. 2003) (excessive time spent by creditor attorney in drafting default letters, a modification agreement, and for pursuing new legal theory in stay relief proceeding found to be unnecessary and not recoverable under note).

406 *In re* Hight, 393 B.R. 484 (Bankr. S.D. Tex. 2008) (disallowing creditor's prepetition attorney fees for preparation of foreclosure when creditor failed to provide evidence showing what work was done, who did the work, their hourly rate, and time spent); *In re* Porcheddu, 338 B.R. 729 (Bankr. S.D. Tex. 2006) (foreclosure law firm sanctioned for filing false fee applications and misrepresenting that fee statements were based on contemporaneous time records); *In re* Harmon, 72 B.R. 458 (Bankr. E.D. Pa. 1987).

The creditor and its counsel have the burden of proving that the fees requested are reasonable. *In re* Coates, 292 B.R. 894 (Bankr. C.D. Ill. 2003) (claim of mortgage servicer for attorney fees, foreclosure expenses, and other charges denied as servicer failed to produce evidence that would satisfy its burden of proving reasonableness); *In re* Staggie, 255 B.R. 48 (Bankr. D. Idaho 2000) (burden of proof not satisfied because counsel's billing summary failed to provide detailed breakdown of time entries).

407 *In re* Thompson, 2010 WL 346391 (Bankr. D.R.I. Jan. 28, 2010) (no attorney fees permitted for "garden variety" mortgage proof of claim in consumer case). *See In re* E. Side Investors, 702 F.2d 214 (11th Cir. 1983); *In re* Wasson, 402 B.R. 561 (Bankr. W.D.N.Y. 2008) (no fees permitted for routine proof of claim); *In re* Madison, 337 B.R. 99 (Bankr. N.D. Miss. 2006) (disallowing attorney fees for preparation of proof of claim, which is ministerial in nature, but allowing $150 fee for other services performed by law firm in facilitating filing of accurate proof of claim by mortgage servicer); *In re* Marks, 2005 WL 4799326 (Bankr. W.D. La. Nov. 30, 2005); *In re* Noletto, 280 B.R. 868 (Bankr. S.D. Ala. 2001); *In re* Allen, 215 B.R. 503 (Bankr. N.D. Tex. 1997) (preparation of claim is ministerial act for which no attorney fees should be charged to debtor); *In re* Thomas, 186 B.R. 470 (Bankr. W.D. Mo. 1995) (lender that filed proof of claim without attorney assistance not

proof of claim of any attorney fee incurred in connection with the bankruptcy case is improper unless the fee has been sought and approved under Federal Rule of Bankruptcy Procedure 2016, because the fee would be paid from property of the bankruptcy estate.[408] Other courts have held that a creditor may include an attorney fee demand in a proof of claim without filing an application under Rule 2016 if the claim is sufficiently detailed and provides adequate notice to the debtor.[409]

11.6.2.7.2 Interest on arrears

Another important question is how interest is to be computed when a long-term obligation is cured under section 1322(b)(5). Unfortunately, the Supreme Court, in *Rake v. Wade*,[410] rejected the holdings of most lower courts and held that a creditor may demand that interest be paid on arrears being cured through a chapter 13 plan. The Court reached this result by holding that the arrearages constitute a separate "allowed secured claim,"[411] notwithstanding that the definition of allowed secured claim in the Code encompasses the creditor's entire claim and does not carve out a special category of claims that would include only arrears.[412]

The Court held that interest on the arrears for the period preceding plan confirmation could be required with respect to an oversecured mortgage because section 506(b) of the Code permits creditors to demand preconfirmation interest on any oversecured claim.[413] For the period after confirmation the Court found section 1325(a)(5) applicable to the "arrearage claim," and thus held that a creditor could demand present value interest[414] on the arrears as a condition of plan confirmation. However, because there is only a right to postconfirmation interest to the extent that the arrears constitute an allowed secured claim, a creditor who is undersecured may not demand postconfirmation interest to the extent it is not fully secured.[415]

In 1994, Congress overruled the result of *Rake v. Wade* by enacting a new section 1322(e) of the Code, which provides that in a cure of a default through a chapter 13 plan the interest or other charges that need be paid must be determined in accordance with the underlying contract and applicable state law.[416] The subsection makes clear that it is an exception to both section 506(b) and section 1325(a)(5), thus covering both bases for the *Rake* holding, and the legislative history leaves no doubt of Congress' intent to overrule that case.[417] Unfortunately, unlike any other provision of the 1994 amendments, section 1322(e) is only effective with respect to agreements entered into after the enactment date of the amendments, October 22, 1994.[418] Thus, mortgages made before that date are still governed by the *Rake* holding.

---

entitled to attorney fees); *In re* Trombley, 31 B.R. 386 (Bankr. D. Vt. 1983); *In re* Banks, 31 B.R. 173 (Bankr. N.D. Ala. 1982). *But see In re* Conde-Dedonato, 391 B.R. 247 (Bankr. E.D.N.Y. 2008) (permitting creditor to recover $200 plan review fee and $150 proof of claim fee); *In re* Moye, 385 B.R. 885 (Bankr. S.D. Tex. 2008) (allowing $200 fee for preparation of proof of claim).

See also § 14.4.3.4, *infra*, for discussion of other "costs" which mortgage creditors attempt to collect.

408 *In re* Patterson, 444 B.R. 564 (Bankr. E.D. Wis. 2011); *In re* Moffitt, 408 B.R. 249 (Bankr. E.D. Ark. 2009) (Rule 2016 application required when fees to be paid by estate); *In re* Padilla, 379 B.R. 643 (Bankr. S.D. Tex. 2007); *In re* Tate, 253 B.R. 653 (Bankr. W.D.N.C. 2000). *See also In re* Plant, 288 B.R. 635 (Bankr. D. Mass. 2003) (Rule 2016 application required if creditor's claim for fees contested by debtor); Powe v. Chrysler Fin. Corp., 281 B.R. 336 (Bankr. S.D. Ala. 2001) (private right of action under section 105 exists to enforce secured creditor's duty to adequately disclose attorney fees sought from debtors; nationwide class of debtors certified challenging creditor's disclosure); *In re* Noletto, 281 B.R. 36 (Bankr. S.D. Ala. 2000) (fees that are not properly claimed or disclosed with specificity, or omitted from an arrearage claim to be paid under debtor's plan, are per se unreasonable); *In re* Gifford, 256 B.R. 661 (Bankr. D. Conn. 2000) (court noted that in future cases it would follow *Tate* and require oversecured creditors to seek approval of fees under Rule 2016). *But see* Telfair v. First Union Mortgage Corp., 216 F.3d 1333 (11th Cir. 2000) (when mortgage company assessed fees on payments made directly to mortgage company outside the plan, and property of the estate had revested in the debtor at confirmation, Rule 2016 was not applicable).

409 *In re* Powe, 281 B.R. 336 (Bankr. S.D. Ala. 2001). *See also In re* Atwood, 293 B.R. 227 (B.A.P. 9th Cir. 2003) (proof of claim lacking specific detail fails to meet creditor's evidentiary burden on reasonableness of fees).

410 508 U.S. 464, 113 S. Ct. 2187, 124 L. Ed. 2d 424 (1993).
411 113 S. Ct. at 2192, 2193.
412 *See* 11 U.S.C. § 506(a).

413 113 S. Ct. at 2191, 2192.

Hence, creditors who are not oversecured cannot demand preconfirmation interest.

414 113 S. Ct. at 2192, 2193. *See also In re* Cabrera, 99 F.3d 684 (5th Cir. 1996) (present value interest in cure had to be paid at rate provided in note).

415 *In re* Johnson, 203 B.R. 775 (Bankr. M.D. Fla. 1996); *In re* Arvelo, 176 B.R. 349 (Bankr. N.J. 1995).

416 *In re* Young, 310 B.R. 127 (Bankr. E.D. Wis. 2003) (note provision that interest due until paid in full not sufficient to require interest on arrearage under section 1322(e)); *In re* Bumgarner, 225 B.R. 327 (Bankr. D.S.C. 1998) (interest on arrears must be authorized both by contract and state law, and was not authorized by contract language permitting ongoing interest on principal). *See also In re* Trabal, 254 B.R. 99 (D.N.J. 2000) (interest on arrears required because mortgage "significantly more specific" than in *Bumgarner* by providing for payment of "all other sums, with interest"; no specific reference to bankruptcy arrears required); *In re* Koster, 294 B.R. 737 (Bankr. E.D. Mo. 2003) (note language required payment of interest on portion of arrearage attributable to principal and attorney fee advances but not late charges and "additional charges").

417 H.R. Rep. No. 103-835, at 55 (1994), *reprinted in* 1994 U.S.C.C.A.N. 3340.

418 Pub. L. No. 103-394, § 702(b)(2)(D), 108 Stat. 4106 (1994).

The legislative history provides that for this purpose a refinancing is considered a new agreement. H.R. Rep. No. 103-835, at 55 (1994), *reprinted in* 1994 U.S.C.C.A.N. 3340. *See In re* Harding, 274 B.R. 173 (Bankr. D. Md. 2002) (modification agreement entered into after October 22, 1994, that modified terms of 1986 mortgage was refinancing and governed by section 1322(e)).

11.6.2.8 Effect of Cure

11.6.2.8.1 Overview

The effect of a cure under section 1322(b)(5) is to nullify all consequences of the default.[419] Thus, in the case of a long-term mortgage, the debtor would normally be returned to the original amortization schedule once the default has been cured. Unfortunately, holders of long-term mortgages do not always comply with this principle, and debtors' attorneys may have to bring proceedings at the end of a chapter 13 plan to ensure that the cure is fully effectuated and not subverted by a mortgage holder's contrary bookkeeping practices.[420] Errors in crediting payments can often be remedied under 11 U.S.C. § 524(i).[421] The court should reopen a case to effectuate such a remedy.[422] Otherwise, the cure provisions would be rendered almost meaningless.[423] The chances for success in such proceedings is enhanced if the chapter 13 plan specifically provided how payments are to be applied and further provided that once the mortgage is cured under the plan the debtor will be treated as if the default never existed and returned to the original amortization schedule.[424] Indeed, the absence of such specific language may make it more difficult to enforce the debtor's rights.[425]

The cure provisions, then, are particularly useful in a case in which the debtor is behind on a mortgage and the creditor refuses to allow the debtor to bring the payments up to date

---

[419] *See In re* Southeast Co., 868 F.2d 335 (9th Cir. 1989) (chapter 11 cure); *In re* Jones, 366 B.R. 584 (Bankr. E.D. La. 2007) (confirmation of plan providing for cure "recalibrates" amounts due as of petition date), *aff'd in part, rev'd in part*, 391 B.R. 577 (E.D. La. 2008). *See also In re* Ward, 392 B.R. 788 (Bankr. W.D. Mo. 2008) (debtor entitled to cure loan as modified by forbearance agreement); *In re* Epps, 110 B.R. 691 (E.D. Pa. 1990) (debtor did not lose the benefit of Dep't of Housing and Urban Development forbearance agreement when prebankruptcy default on agreement was cured under chapter 13 plan).

The House Report to the Bankruptcy Reform Act of 1994 reaffirms that this is the intent of Congress. "It is the Committee's intention that a cure pursuant to a plan should operate to put the debtor in the same position as if the default had never occurred." H.R. Rep. No. 103-835, at 55 (1994), *reprinted in* 1994 U.S.C.C.A.N. 3340.

[420] *See, e.g.*, Chase Manhattan Mortgage Corp. v. Padgett, 268 B.R. 309 (S.D. Fla. 2001) (mortgagee waived its rights to charge debtor for postpetition escrow advances because it never notified debtors that they should increase monthly payments); *In re* Johnson, 384 B.R. 763 (Bankr. E.D. Mich. 2008) (same); *In re* Dominique, 368 B.R. 913 (Bankr. S.D. Fla. 2007) (same); *In re* Rizzo-Cheverier, 364 B.R. 532 (Bankr. S.D.N.Y. 2007) (mortgage creditor's attempt to collect late fees, unspecified "corporate advances," and other amounts resulting from its misapplication of plan payments violated discharge injunction); *In re* Riser, 289 B.R. 201 (Bankr. M.D. Fla. 2003) (mortgage company not entitled to payments for any charges incurred before or during bankruptcy that were not provided for in confirmed plan); *In re* Chess, 268 B.R. 150 (Bankr. W.D. Tenn. 2001) (mortgage company that did not notify debtor of escrow increases or respond to trustee's customary motion to deem mortgage current at end of plan could not assert debtor was in arrears at end of plan); *In re* Wines, 239 B.R. 703 (Bankr. D.N.J. 1999) (debtor overcharged interest based on creditor misapplying payments received outside the plan to prepetition arrears); *In re* McCormack, 203 B.R. 521 (Bankr. D.N.H. 1996) (mortgagee bank held liable for $10,000 punitive damages when it did not adjust its computer records to reflect effect of plan confirmation and sent debtor demand letter expressing intent to collect fees that were not due under plan); *In re* Ronemus, 201 B.R. 458 (Bankr. N.D. Tex. 1996) (creditor assessed $10,000, plus $3000 attorney and accountants' fees after discharge due to mortgagee charging late charges on current payments made during bankruptcy and for charging filing fee, attorney fees and expenses to debtor's escrow account without permission of court); *In re* Rathe, 114 B.R. 253 (Bankr. D. Idaho 1990); *In re* Ward, 73 B.R. 119 (Bankr. N.D. Ga. 1987) (late charges may not be added to current payments made pursuant to plan unless those payments are not made on time). *See also In re* Garvida, 347 B.R. 697 (B.A.P. 9th Cir. 2006) (creditor's claim of amount due at refinancing reduced due to creditor's failure to produce evidence to rebut debtor's evidence of correct balance); *In re* Murdock, 337 B.R. 308 (Bankr. N.D. Ohio 2005) (creditor could not claim amounts were due in excess of those paid under plan when creditor could not explain its own accounting statements); *In re* Harris, 297 B.R. 61 (Bankr. N.D. Miss. 2003) (prohibiting mortgage lender from charging late fees based on delay by trustee in disbursing ongoing mortgage payments does not violate anti-modification restrictions in section 1322(b)(2)), *aff'd*, 312 B.R. 591 (N.D. Miss. 2004). *But see In re* Joubert, 411 F.3d 452 (3d Cir. 2005) (no cause of action for improper charges under section 105; remedy is contempt proceeding in bankruptcy court); Mann v. Chase Manhattan Mortgage Corp., 316 F.3d 1 (1st Cir. 2003) (mortgage company adding charges to debtor's account in its internal bookkeeping, absent any overt attempt to collect the fees, did not violate automatic stay).

Servicers often violate RESPA's escrow requirements in the course of chapter 13 cases. *See, e.g., In re* Payne, 387 B.R. 614 (Bankr. D. Kan. 2008); *In re* Johnson, 384 B.R. 763 (Bankr. E.D. Mich. 2008). *See generally* 12 U.S.C. § 2609; Reg. X, 24 C.F.R. § 3500.17; National Consumer Law Center, Foreclosures § 9.3.2 (4th ed. 2012).

Challenges to mortgage overcharges are discussed further in § 14.4.3.4.1, *infra*.

[421] *See* § 14.4.3.4.8, *infra*.

[422] *See* § 15.5.5.7, *infra*.

[423] *In re* Janssen, 396 B.R. 624 (Bankr. E.D. Pa. 2008); *In re* McDonald, 336 B.R. 380 (Bankr. N.D. Ill. 2006); *In re* Venuto, 343 B.R. 120 (Bankr. E.D. Pa. 2006).

[424] *See, e.g.*, Home Funds Direct v. Monroy (*In re* Monroy), 650 F.3d 1300 (9th Cir. 2011) (plan provisions requiring monthly statements or coupon books, as well as notice of payment changes and fees, did not modify rights of mortgage holders); *In re* Wright, 461 B.R. 757 (Bankr. N.D. Iowa 2011) (mortgagee sanctioned for failing to give notices of payment changes required by plan); *In re* Ramsey, 421 B.R. 431 (Bankr. M.D. Tenn. 2009) (plan requiring application of payments on pre-confirmation arrearages only to such arrearages and providing notice of any interest rate change, payment change, or escrow advance to debtors, debtors' attorney, and the chapter 13 trustee, did not violate § 1322(b)(2)); *In re* Winston, 316 B.R. 32 (Bankr. N.D.N.Y. 2009) (upholding provisions requiring mortgage deemed cured for accounting purposes, application of current mortgage payments to month in which they are received *In re* Emery, 387 B.R. 721 (Bankr. E.D. Ky. 2008) (plan provision requiring debtor's monthly mortgage payments to be deemed current did not constitute impermissible modification); *In re* Watson, 384 B.R. 697 (Bankr. D. Del. 2008) (provisions relating to postpetition charges did not modify mortgagees' rights under section 1322(b)(2)); Form 18, Appx. G.3, *infra. See also* §§ 11.6.2.8.1, 14.4.3.4.8, *infra*.

[425] *See In re* Nosek, 544 F.3d 34 (1st Cir. 2008) (plan terms not sufficiently specific to permit sanctions for misapplication of payments).

gradually. In essence, they provide a method of forcing the creditor to be reasonable, by giving the debtor a right to cure over a reasonable time, at least when the creditor has adequate protection and cannot obtain relief from the automatic stay.[426]

11.6.2.8.2 Use of Rule 3002.1 to ensure cure is effectuated

11.6.2.8.2.1 Application of Rule 3002.1

The Federal Rules of Bankruptcy Procedure, adopted in 2011, provide a procedure for resolving the widespread problems in mortgage cure plans caused by inaccurate proofs of claim and creditor postpetition fees and accounting practices. Bankruptcy Rule 3002.1 compels disclosure of mortgage payment changes and postpetition fees and expenses. It also establishes a procedure for resolving payment disputes and determining whether the debtor has fully cured a mortgage default.

Another rule amendment made in 2011 requires disclosure of prepetition default fees and arrearage amounts on the initial proof of claim filed by the mortgage creditor. Rule 3001(c)(2)(C) requires the mortgage creditor to attach to its proof of claim the Mortgage Proof of Claim Attachment form.[427] The form instructs the creditor to disclose and itemize the components of the prepetition mortgage arrearage. If the mortgage account includes an escrow account, the mortgage creditor must also attach to the proof of claim an escrow account statement prepared as of the petition date in a form consistent with applicable nonbankruptcy law.[428]

Rules 3001(c)(2)(C) and 3002.1 apply to claims that are (1) secured by the debtor's principal residence and (2) provided for under section 1322(b)(5) in the debtor's plan.[429] If the plan does not provide for the curing of a mortgage default, for example because the mortgage is current or the case is filed to deal with a nonmortgage problem, or if the plan does not provide for the maintenance of postpetition mortgage payments, the creditor is not required to comply with Rule 3002.1.[430] However, some courts may require that the payment change and fee notices be sent regardless of the plan treatment in order for interested parties to have information needed to provide for the creditor's claim.[431] The rule requirements should continue to apply even after stay relief has been granted to the mortgage creditor, at least until the mortgage has been foreclosed, the plan is modified to provide for treatment of the claim other than under section 1322(b)(5), or the claim is withdrawn.[432] Compliance with the rules is mandatory, and the court lacks discretion to extend the time deadlines or excuse performance.[433]

One court has erroneously held that Rule 3002.1 does not apply if the debtor is the disbursing agent for the postpetition maintenance payments under the plan.[434] Nothing in the rule suggests that it applies only in districts where the trustee disburses the postpetition mortgage payments. In fact, the Committee Note to Rule 3002.1 explicitly states that the rule applies "whether the trustee or the debtor is the disbursing agent for the postpetition mortgage payments."[435]

11.6.2.8.2.2 Notice of payment change—Rule 3002.1(b)

Rule 3002.1(b) requires the creditor to "file and serve on the debtor, debtor's counsel, and the trustee a notice of any change in the payment amount, including any change that results from an interest rate or escrow account adjustment, no later than 21 days before a payment in the new amount is due." Notice must be given on Official Form 10 (Supplement 1), the Notice of Mortgage Payment Change.[436] The form shall be filed as a supplement to the creditor's proof of claim and is not entitled to presumptive validity under Rule 3001(f).[437] The Supplement 1 form requires the creditor to state the basis for the changed payment amount, the current and new payment amounts, and the date when the change will take effect.

The two most common payment changes on mortgage accounts result from interest rate and escrow account adjustments. These changes are subject to disclosure requirements under the Truth in Lending Act for adjustable rates and the Real Estate Settlement Procedures Act for escrow accounts. The mortgage creditor is required to attach to the Supplement 1 form an escrow account statement or interest rate change notice in a form consistent with applicable nonbankruptcy law (TILA and RESPA). Thus, the form operates essentially as a cover sheet by providing limited information and relying upon the more extensive disclosures given under these other laws as an attachment. Because mortgage servicers routinely provide these notices to borrowers outside bankruptcy without the assistance

---

426 See Chapter 9, *supra*, for a discussion of relief from the automatic stay.

427 Fed. R. Bankr. P. 3001(c)(2)(C); Official Form 10 (Attachment A), *reprinted in* Appx. D, *infra*.

428 Fed. R. Bankr. P. 3001(c)(2)(C). For a discussion of the requirements for escrow account statements under Real Estate Settlement Procedures Act, see National Consumer Law Center, Foreclosures § 9.3.3 (4th ed. 2012).

429 Fed. R. Bankr. P. 3002.1(a).

430 *In re* Wallett, 2012 WL 4062657 (Bankr. D. Vt. Sept. 14, 2012) (notices of postpetition fees were not required because the mortgage was not on the debtors' primary residence and the mortgage claim was not treated under § 1322(b)(5)); *In re* Garduno, 2012 WL 2402789 (Bankr. S.D. Fla. June 26, 2012) (Rule 3002.1 did not apply because the debtors' plan stated that mortgage creditor would receive $0.00 and claim was not provided for under § 1322(b)(5)).

431 *In re* Kraska, 2012 WL 1267993 (Bankr. N.D. Ohio Apr. 13, 2012) (requiring compliance with Rule 3002.1 even though the debtor's plan provided for surrender of the property, based on the view that postpetition payment change and fee notices will assist the parties in reviewing and challenging any deficiency claim that may be filed by the creditor), *motion granted and opinion stricken* (Sept. 19, 2012).

432 *In re* Thongta, 2012 WL 5050669 (Bankr. E.D. Wis. Oct. 18, 2012) (trustee was not required to file a Notice of Final Cure Payment under Rule 3002.1(f) because creditor withdrew its claim after stay relief was granted).

433 *In re* Adkins, 477 B.R. 71 (Bankr. N.D. Ohio 2012) (finding no exception to the payment change notice requirement for HELOCs or authority to excuse compliance).

434 *In re* Merino, 2012 WL 2891112 (Bankr. M.D. Fla. July 16, 2012).

435 *See* Appx. B.3, *infra*.

436 Fed. R. Bankr. P. 3002.1(d). Official Form 10 (Supplement 1) is reprinted in Appx. D, *infra*.

437 Fed. R. Bankr. P. 3002.1(d).

of counsel, debtors should not be charged attorney fees for the servicer's preparation and filing of the Rule 3002.1(b) notices.[438]

The form can accommodate payment changes for reasons other than interest rate or escrow adjustments. For example, the debtor and creditor may enter into a loan modification while the chapter 13 case is pending. If the loan modification results in a payment change, the creditor should file and serve Supplement 1, noting the change in Part 3 of the form and attaching a copy of the loan modification agreement to the form.[439]

11.6.2.8.2.3 Notice of postpetition fees—Rule 3002.1(c)

Rule 3002.1(c) requires the creditor to give notice of any postpetition fees or charges assessed against the debtor's account within 180 days of when they are incurred. The notice must be given on Official Form 10 as Supplement 2, the Notice of Postpetition Mortgage Fees, Expenses, and Charges.[440] Like the payment change notice, the postpetition fee notice should be filed as a supplement to the creditor's proof of claim and is not entitled to presumptive validity under Rule 3001(f).[441]

In the event that multiple Supplement 2 forms are filed during a chapter 13 case, creditors are instructed on the form to list a particular fee only once, as the form does not request a cumulative or running account of the fees. Additionally, amounts for taxes and insurance disbursed under an escrow account and fees that have been previously itemized and approved by the court, as in a stay relief consent order for example, would not be listed on the form.[442] The instruction in Part 1 of the form makes this clear by stating: "Do not include any escrow account disbursements or any amounts previously itemized in a notice filed in this case or ruled on by the bankruptcy court."

Not all fees incurred on the debtor's mortgage account are subject to the rule. Only those fees which are incurred in connection with the claim and which the creditor contends are recoverable against the debtor or the debtor's principal residence must be noticed.[443] Thus, the creditor might incur an attorney fee on the account, but determine that it is not recoverable against the debtor or the debtor's property. In that case, the creditor should not list the fee on the Supplement 2 form. The creditor's decision to treat the fee as non-recoverable (and therefore not noticed during the 180-day period) should also mean that the creditor is precluded from seeking collection of the fee from the debtor after the 180-day notice period has passed.[444]

As for the timing of the disclosure, it is based on the time when the fee is incurred, not when it is determined to be recoverable. Thus, the notice must be served within 180 days after the date on which a fee is incurred.

11.6.2.8.2.4 Fee dispute procedure—Rule 3002.1(e)

The debtor has one year from the date of the notice to object to the propriety of any postpetition fee or charge.[445] The time periods were set so that if there were multiple notices over a period of months, the debtor could more efficiently respond to them with a single objection, rather than multiple proceedings. At the same time, they permit a determination regarding the propriety of the charges before they accumulate to an amount the debtor may be unable to pay. If an objection is filed, the court shall determine whether the fees and charges are required by the mortgage agreement and applicable nonbankruptcy law to cure a default or maintain payments under section 1322(b)(5). This procedure should be helpful to debtors in jurisdictions where courts have previously refused to address disputes involving postpetition fees, particularly in cases in which the debtor is the disbursing agent for ongoing payments.[446]

11.6.2.8.2.5 Notice of final cure payment—Rule 3002.1(f) and Rule 3002.1(h)

Rule 3002.1(f) provides that "[w]ithin 30 days after the debtor completes all payments under the plan, the trustee shall file and serve on the holder of the claim, the debtor, and debtor's counsel a notice stating that the debtor has paid in full the amount required to cure any default on the claim." The notice must also inform the creditor of its obligation to file a response to the notice. If the trustee does not send this notice, the debtor may do so.[447] The creditor is then given thirty days to respond to the notice by filing a statement indicating (1) whether it agrees that the debtor has fully cured the default on the claim, and (2) whether the debtor is current on all postpetition payments consistent with the "maintenance of payments" requirement in section 1322(b)(5). If the creditor states that postpetition amounts are owed, it must itemize any amounts it claims are due and unpaid as of the date of the statement.[448] The response statement should be filed as a supplement to the creditor's claim and is not entitled to presumptive validity under Rule 3001(f).[449]

---

438 *In re* Adams, 2012 WL 1570054 (Bankr. E.D.N.C. May 3, 2012) (disallowing $50 charge for filing a Notice of Mortgage Payment Change).

439 Some bankruptcy courts require, in a chapter 13 case, that the court approve a loan modification agreement before it can take effect.

440 Fed. R. Bankr. P. 3002.1(d). Official Form 10 (Supplement 2) is reprinted in Appx. D, *infra*.

441 Fed. R. Bankr. P. 3002.1(d).

442 *In re* Sheppard, 2012 WL 1344112 (Bankr. E.D. Va. Apr. 18, 2012) (granting trustee's motion under Rule 3002.1(e) to disapprove as duplicative an $800 attorney fee that had already been approved by the court as part of a stay relief consent order).

443 Fed. R. Bankr. P. 3002.1(c).

444 *See* § 11.6.2.8.2.6, *infra*.

445 Fed. R. Bankr. P. 3002.1(e). *See* sample motion, Form 145.1, Appx. G.12, *infra*.

446 *See, e.g.,* Telfair v. First Union Mortgage Corp., 216 F.3d 1333 (11th Cir. 2000). *See also* § 14.4.3.4.5, *infra*.

447 The notice must inform the creditor of its obligation to file a response to the notice. *See* sample notice, Form 145.2, Appx. G.12, *infra*.

448 Fed. R. Bankr. P. 3002.1(g).

449 *See In re* Sheppard, 2012 WL 1344112 (Bankr. E.D. Va. Apr. 18, 2012) (finding that documents filed as claim supplements under the

The trustee or the debtor may then, within twenty-one days, file a motion for the court to resolve the issue and to obtain an order declaring that the debtor has cured the default and paid all required postpetition amounts.[450] It is advisable for the debtor to file this motion if the mortgage holder has failed to respond to the Notice of Final Cure Payment, so as to obtain an order that the mortgage has been fully cured and is current.

It is important to note that the triggering event for the cure notice is plan completion, even though the mortgage default may have been cured months or years earlier depending upon how the chapter 13 plan distributions were made by the trustee. Thus, the debtor's attorney should carefully review the creditor's statement to ensure that fees or amounts are not claimed as due for the first time in the response statement. A request for sanctions should be sought in a motion filed under Rule 3002.1(h) for any fees or amounts that should have been previously disclosed in a timely manner under Rules 3002.1(b) and 3002.1(c).[451]

Creditors should not be permitted to charge attorney fees for the documents they are required to file under Rule 3002.1. The rule simply provides a procedure for giving notice of payment changes and charges that a creditor already had an obligation to give to the debtor.[452] And such notices, or responses to notices that debtor has cured, are administrative in nature, and do not require an attorney to make the computations required.[453]

11.6.2.8.2.6 Sanctions for noncompliance—Rules 3001(c)(2)(D) and 3002.1(i)

The enforcement mechanism for the rules is provided by Rule 3001(c)(2)(D) and Rule 3002.1(i). If a creditor fails to comply with the requirement for notice of prepetition arrearage amounts and postpetition payment changes or fees, or if it fails to contest the complete cure of the delinquency, the court may preclude it from offering any evidence that would have been in the notices, i.e., the amounts of the payment changes, fees, or other amounts allegedly due but unpaid at the end of the case.[454] The court may also award attorney fees and other expenses to the debtor for the additional proceedings necessary to resolve the issue.[455]

A potential concern is that the evidence preclusion sanction applies only in proceedings in the bankruptcy court. Thus, if a creditor claims after the bankruptcy that the mortgage remains in default, or asserts for the first time in a state foreclosure proceeding that fees that were incurred during the bankruptcy have not been paid, the debtor may need to file a motion to reopen the bankruptcy case and seek sanctions under Rule 3002.1(i). This return to bankruptcy court is supported by the Committee Note to the rule.[456] The debtor should normally be able to collect attorney fees for the extra work involved as part of the sanction imposed by the court.

Another possible response to a threatened postbankruptcy foreclosure would be for the debtor to argue in the state court foreclosure proceeding that the creditor is judicially estopped from asserting that the account is in default based on fees that should have been disclosed in the bankruptcy case. Judicial estoppel is an equitable doctrine under which a party is precluded from asserting a claim in a legal proceeding that is inconsistent with a claim made in a previous proceeding.[457] The doctrine is particularly appropriate in cases in which a party was aware in the earlier proceeding of the factual basis for a claim they are pursuing in the later proceeding and there was a duty to disclose information related to the claim in the earlier proceeding.[458] This would apply to mortgage creditors who are obligated to disclose fees under Rule 3002.1(c).

11.6.2.8.2.7 Rule 3002.1 and the attorneys general settlement with major servicers

The settlement agreement between the state attorneys general and the five leading mortgage servicers, finalized in April 2012, contains terms that mandate compliance by the servicers with Bankruptcy Rules 3001 and 3002.1. The applicable servicing requirements became effective on October 2, 2012. The affected servicers are Bank of America, JP Morgan Chase, Wells Fargo, Citibank, and Ally/GMAC.[459]

With respect to proofs of claim, the five servicers must ensure that any factual assertions made on the claim form or in any attachments to the claim are accurate, complete, and supported by competent and reliable evidence.[460] If the servicer has filed a proof of claim in a case pending before the settlement that contains materially inaccurate information, the servicer must not rely upon the claim and must file an amended claim, at the servicer's expense, within thirty days of acquiring knowledge of the inaccuracy.[461] The servicers are prohibited from collecting any attorney fees or other charges for the

---

rules should not be treated as a claim or a demand for payment).
450 Fed. R. Bankr. P. 3002.1(h). *See* sample motion, Form 146, Appx. G.12, *infra*.
451 *See* Fed. R. Bankr. P. 3002.1(i); § 11.6.2.8.2.6, *infra*.
452 *In re* White, 2012 Bankr. LEXIS 1884 (Bankr. E.D.N.C. Apr. 30, 2012).
453 *In re* Hunt, 2012 Bankr. LEXIS 2981 (Bankr. M.D.N.C. June 26, 2012); *In re* Adams, 2012 WL 1570054 (Bankr. E.D.N.C. May 3, 2012); *In re* Carr, 468 B.R. 806 (Bankr. E.D. Va. 2012) (response statement under Rule 3002.1(g) is not a pleading and its preparation does not involve the practice of law).
454 Fed. R. Bankr. P. 3001(c)(2)(D)(i) and 3002.1(i)(1).
455 Fed. R. Bankr. P. 3001(c)(2)(D)(ii) and 3002.1(i)(2).
456 The Committee Note to Rule 3002.1(i) states: "If, after the chapter 13 debtor has completed payments under the plan and the case has been closed, the holder of a claim secured by the debtor's principal residence seeks to recover amounts that should have been but were not disclosed under this rule, the debtor may move to have the case reopened in order to seek sanctions against the holder of the claim under subdivision (i)."
457 *See* § 14.3.2.6.3, *infra*.
458 *See, e.g.,* Lewis v. Weyerhaeuser Co., 141 Fed. Appx. 420 (6th Cir. 2005); Barger v. City of Cartersville, 348 F.3d 1289 (11th Cir. 2003); Hamilton v. State Farm Fire & Cas. Co., 270 F.3d 778 (9th Cir. 2001); *In re* Coastal Plains, Inc., 179 F.3d 197 (5th Cir. 1999).
459 The full text of each agreement is available at www.nationalmortgagesettlement.com.
460 Settlement Term Sheet, Exhibit A (Servicing Standards), § I.A.1.
461 *Id.* at § I.A.15.

preparation or submission of a proof of claim or motion for relief that is later withdrawn or denied as a result of a "substantial misstatement" as to the amount due.[462]

The five servicers are required to attach to the proof of claim the original or duplicate of the note, including all indorsements, a copy of any mortgage or deed of trust (including, if applicable, evidence of recordation in the applicable land records) and copies of any assignments of the mortgage or deed of trust required to demonstrate the right to enforce the borrower's note under applicable state law.[463] If the note has been lost or destroyed, a lost note affidavit shall be submitted. The servicer must include a statement in the claim setting forth the basis for asserting that the applicable party has the right to foreclose. Finally, the servicer must attach Official Form 10 (Attachment A) as required by Rule 3001(c)(2)(C) and comply with all other requirements in Rule 3001 for preparing the proof of claim.[464]

The settlement also provides that the five servicers must comply with the notice requirements under Rule 3002.1(b) (notice of payment changes), Rule 3002.1(c) (notice of postpetition fees or charges), and Rule 3002.1(g) (response to notice of final cure payment).[465] Importantly, the settlement imposes a sanction for noncompliance separate from that available under Rule 3002.1(i). If the servicer fails to provide a payment change notice as required by Rule 3002.1(b), the servicer shall waive and not collect any late charge or other fees imposed solely as a result of the borrower's failure to timely make the changed payment.[466] If the servicer fails to timely provide notice of fees, expenses, or charges as required by 3002.1(c) and Rule 3002.1(g), they are deemed waived and may not be collected from the borrower.[467] However, there is an exception for "independent charges," which are fees paid by the servicer that are either specifically authorized by the borrower or have been advanced by the servicer for taxes, homeowners association fees, liens, or insurance.

The settlement also addresses payment application issues in chapter 13 cases.[468] The servicers must ensure that there is prompt and proper application of payments made on prepetition arrearage and postpetition payment amounts.[469] The debtor is to be treated as being current so long as the debtor is making payments in accordance with the confirmed plan and any later effective payment change notices. Upon dismissal of the debtor's bankruptcy case, the granting of a servicer's stay relief motion, or entry of a discharge, the servicer is required to update and reconcile its records to reflect payments made during the case, and the waiver of any fee, expense, or charge as required under provisions of the settlement.

The terms of the attorney generals' settlement, including the servicing guidelines, are not directly enforceable by borrowers. The terms are part of a consent decree approved by the United States District Court for the District of Columbia. The attorneys general have created an enforcement mechanism whereby they can bring the matter back before the court for the imposition of sanctions and further enforcement if they can show a record of non-compliance by the servicers. Violation of the standards should support homeowners' claims that non-complying servicers are violating a clear industry standard, thus implicating UDAP laws and requirements that parties implement the terms of their contracts under a standard of good faith and fair dealing.[470] Similarly, bankruptcy courts may apply equitable principles in granting claim objections or denying stay relief when servicers have flaunted these standards. The failure to comply with the guidelines can also provide additional support for a request for sanctions under Rule 3001(c) and Rule 3002.1(i).

11.7 Use of Section 506 to Reduce Liens That Are Not Paid Under Section 1325(a)(5)

The allowed secured claim concept is effectuated by section 506(a) and 506(d) of the Code. Section 506(a) bifurcates the claim into its secured and unsecured portion and section 506(d) provides that "[t]o the extent that a lien secures a claim that is not an allowed secured claim [as determined under section 506(a)] *such lien is void* unless" such a claim was disallowed only because it was for an unmatured domestic support obligation or such claim was not an allowed claim only because no entity filed a proof of claim.[471]

In *Dewsnup v. Timm*,[472] the Supreme Court held that section 506(d) could not be used independently of section 722 to void a lien in a chapter 7 case. Despite the clear statutory language of section 506(d), noted by the dissent, providing that a lien is void to the extent it does not secure an allowed secured claim, the Court based its decision on the fact that Congress had given no indication in the legislative history that it intended the section to act as an independent avoiding power in chapter 7

---

462 *Id.* at § VI.D.1. A related provision in § VI.D.2 provides that the servicers shall not collect late fees due to delays in receiving the debtor's full payments, including trial period or permanent modification payments as well as post-petition conduit payments, that the debtor has timely made to a chapter 13 trustee.
463 Settlement Term Sheet, Exhibit A (Servicing Standards), § I.D.1.
464 *See* § 11.6.2.8.2.1, *supra*.
465 *Id.* at § III.B.1.
466 *Id.* at § III.B.1.e.
467 *Id.* at § III.B.1.c; § III.B.1.d.
468 *See* § 11.6.2.8.1, *supra*; § 14.4.3.4.8, *infra*.
469 Settlement Term Sheet, Exhibit A (Servicing Standards), § I.B.11.

470 *See, e.g.,* Wigod v. Wells Fargo Bank, 673 F.3d 547 (7th Cir. 2012) (private enforcement of HAMP guidelines); *In re* Hinson, 2012 WL 1354807 (Bankr. E.D.N.C. Apr. 17, 2012) (finding that a HAMP violation could create the basis for an unfair and deceptive act claim under state law even though it is widely accepted that there is no private cause of action under HAMP).
471 (Emphasis added.) *But see* Dewsnup v. Timm, 502 U.S. 410, 112 S. Ct. 773, 116 L. Ed. 2d 903 (1992) (section 506(d) does not operate to void lien on unsecured portion of claim in chapter 7 case); *In re* Tarnow, 749 F.2d 464 (7th Cir. 1984) (lien not void when claim disallowed only because it was not timely filed). *See also* § 11.6.1.3.3.3, *supra*.
472 502 U.S. 410, 112 S. Ct. 773, 116 L. Ed. 2d 903 (1992).

cases. However, the courts have not extended this ruling to chapter 13 cases.[473]

As discussed above,[474] when an allowed secured claim is provided for in a chapter 13 plan and the holder of the claim is paid the full present value of the allowed secured claim under section 1325(a)(5), the lien is satisfied once the discharge is entered and any remaining claim is only an unsecured claim, as fully dischargeable by the chapter 13 discharge as it would have been if no lien had existed. The only exception to this general rule would be a claim at least partially secured solely by the debtor's principal residence, if under section 1322(b)(2) that claim could not be bifurcated.[475] In fact, if no claim is filed by an undersecured creditor for the portion of the claim found to be unsecured, the creditor is not entitled to any distributions on that part of the claim.[476]

Except with respect to claims described at the end of section 1325(a), section 506 also should be available to provide a vehicle for reducing or eliminating a lien in a chapter 13 case in which the allowed secured claim is not fully paid through the chapter 13 plan, unless the holder of the claim is protected from modification by Code section 1322(b)(2). Whenever the debtor or some other party requests a determination of the value of an undersecured claim under section 506(a), or successfully objects to a secured claim on any basis, section 506(a) renders the creditor's claim an allowed unsecured claim to the extent that it exceeds the amount of the allowed secured claim as determined by the court. A chapter 13 plan may provide for treatment of the unsecured portion of the claim in the same manner as it provides for other unsecured claim holders, including a discharge of the unsecured portion of the claim, because the Code permits any plan provision not inconsistent with other provisions of the statute.[477] The plan can similarly provide that the lien is void to the extent it exceeds the allowed secured claim of the creditor because section 1325(a)(5)(B), providing for allowed secured claims, only requires that the holder of the claim retain the lien securing the allowed secured claim, and not the allowed unsecured portion of the claim.[478] Thus, at the end of the case, the personal liability on the claim will be fully discharged and the lien will be reduced to the amount of the allowed secured claim, minus any principal payments made during the case.[479]

The ultimate ramifications of such lien avoidance have not been addressed by many courts. For example, if $5000 of a $15,000 lien is avoided, how are the monthly payments restructured? Are the next $5000 in payments due deemed paid, or is the final $5000 in payments excused? Generally, the reported decisions have resolved these issues by holding that a debtor who cures a mortgage default in chapter 13, but has a remaining balance on a stripped down lien, may not alter the monthly payment or interest rate, with the result being that the term of the loan is shortened.[480] And one court has held that when a secured claim is bifurcated under section 506, any recoupment under the Truth in Lending Act or any payment on the arrears is applied to the allowed secured claim rather than to the allowed unsecured claim.[481]

11.8 Rent-to-Own Transactions in Bankruptcy

A comprehensive discussion of the myriad consumer issues arising in rent-to-own transactions is provided elsewhere in this series,[482] and is beyond the scope of this treatise. For several

---

473 See § 11.2.1, supra.
474 See § 11.6.1.3, supra.
475 See § 11.6.1.2, supra.
　　If a mortgage on a debtor's principal residence is not even partially secured, because the entire equity is encumbered by prior liens, *Nobelman* leaves open the argument that the mortgage may still be modified. In deciding that the creditor in that case was the holder of a secured claim, the Court held that "[p]etitioners were correct in looking to § 506(a) . . . to determine the status of the bank's secured claim. . . . But even if we accept petitioners' valuation, the bank is still the 'holder' of a 'secured claim,' because petitioners' home retains $23,500 of value as collateral." Nobelman v. Am. Sav. Bank, 508 U.S. 324, 113 S. Ct. 2106, 2110, 124 L. Ed. 2d 228 (1993).
　　Thus, had the home been of no value to the creditors as collateral, the court would presumably have found that the bank was not the holder of a secured claim entitled to have its rights protected by section 1322(b)(2). A variety of courts have adopted this reasoning. See § 11.6.1.2.2, supra.
476 *In re* Burrell, 85 B.R. 799 (Bankr. N.D. Ill. 1988).
477 11 U.S.C. § 1325(b)(10).

478 *In re* Hart, 923 F.2d 1410 (10th Cir. 1991); Wilson v. Commonwealth Mortgage Corp., 895 F.2d 123 (3d Cir. 1990); *In re* Hougland, 886 F.2d 1182 (9th Cir. 1989).
479 See Monk v. LSI Title Co. of Or., L.L.C. (*In re* Monk), 2011 WL 212831 (Bankr. D. Or. Jan. 21, 2011) (when chapter 13 trustee's objection to creditor's mortgage claim, based on lack of documentation of security interest and perfection, led to disallowance of claim, lien was void and could not be enforced by creditor after bankruptcy).
480 *In re* Bellamy, 962 F.2d 176 (2d Cir. 1992); *In re* Gilbert, 472 B.R. 126 (Bankr. S.D. Fla. Feb. 27, 2012) (discussing how payments are applied in cure/stripdown scenario); *In re* Elibo, 447 B.R. 359 (Bankr. S.D. Fla. 2011) (debtor could not lower interest rate on reduced mortgage, but could cure within plan period and then make payments until reduced principal was paid); *In re* Murphy, 175 B.R. 134 (Bankr. D. Mass. 1994) (after bifurcation, debtor cannot amortize allowed secured claim over balance of the term of the mortgage); *In re* Brown, 175 B.R. 129 (Bankr. D. Mass. 1994) (arrearage portion of allowed claim cannot be assigned to the unsecured claim and discharged after bifurcation); *In re* Session, 128 B.R. 147 (Bankr. E.D. Tex. 1991); *In re* Franklin, 126 B.R. 702 (Bankr. N.D. Miss. 1991); *In re* Hayes, 111 B.R. 924 (Bankr. D. Or. 1990). See also Pierrotti v. Internal Rev. Serv. (*In re* Pierrotti), 645 F.3d 277 (5th Cir. 2011) (because tax debt was not long term debt curable under § 1322(b)(5), debtors could not utilize cure provisions to extend debt beyond plan period); Sapos v. Provident Inst. of Sav., 967 F.2d 918 (3d Cir. 1992); Fed. Nat'l Mortgage Ass'n v. Ferreira, 223 B.R. 258 (D.R.I. 1998) (debtor may cure with respect to secured portion of bifurcated claim). But see *In re* Enewally, 368 F.3d 1165 (9th Cir. 2004) (debtor must pay secured portion of allowed claim within term of plan).
481 *In re* Jablonski, 70 B.R. 381 (Bankr. E.D. Pa. 1987).
482 The following volumes of the National Consumer Law Center's *Consumer Credit and Sales Legal Practice Series* cover rent-to-own

reasons, bankruptcy court may be an excellent forum for consumer advocates who seek a remedy for the abuses of the rent-to-own industry.

Most importantly, the automatic stay provides probably the fastest and surest way to prevent continued harassment of delinquent debtors by rent-to-own companies.[483] Because rent-to-own property in the debtor's possession becomes property of the estate upon filing of a bankruptcy case, the automatic stay immediately enjoins continued efforts by a rent-to-own creditor to collect delinquent payments or to recover property. If a rent-to-own creditor continues to seek payment or repossession, it will be liable pursuant to 11 U.S.C. § 362(k) for its violations of the stay.[484] Especially in view of some of the industry's traditional collection practices, the full range of section 362(k) remedies, including punitive damages, may be appropriate.[485]

Numerous potential issues arise in addressing how rent-to-own contracts should be treated in bankruptcy. The dealer will argue that the contract is a lease agreement representing an executory contract, and that the debtor's options are limited to assuming or rejecting the contract pursuant to 11 U.S.C. § 365.[486] The debtor should argue instead that the contract creates a secured debt, giving rise to the full panoply of remedies discussed in this chapter. In fact there is ample precedent for treating installment sale contracts for real property[487] and leases with purchase options[488] as security agreements. Many cases that have addressed the property interests created by rent-to-own contracts support the view that they should be treated as credit sales in bankruptcy cases.[489] However, although state law treatment of the transaction is not determinative, practitioners should check the current status of state law as many states have adopted industry sponsored legislation that exempts such contracts from Uniform Commercial Code Article 9, state retail installment sales acts, or other state credit legislation.[490] Treatment of the contract as a security agreement gives rise to rights such as the debtor's right to redeem,[491] the right to modify the creditor's rights or to cure any default,[492] and the right to limit the creditor's secured claim to the value of the collateral.[493]

Whether the contract is treated as executory, as a security agreement, or otherwise, the debtor should not forego the opportunity to litigate the amount of the rent-to-own company's proof of claim, if any, and to lodge such claims or counterclaims as the debtor may possess.[494] Such claims may include usury, unfair trade practices, Uniform Commercial Code claims, debt collection claims, and truth-in-lending or consumer leasing claims. Often the bankruptcy court will be the most sympathetic forum for debtors who seek to address these creditor abuses.

11.9 Automobile Title Pawn Transactions in Bankruptcy

Another fast-growing business preying on low income families is "title pawn" lending. The typical title pawn contract is a loan of a small amount of money, accompanied by a "pawn"

---

issues: Unfair and Deceptive Acts and Practices § 8.8 (7th ed. 2008 and Supp.); The Cost of Credit: Regulation, Preemption, and Industry Abuses § 7.5.3 (4th ed. 2009). *See also* National Consumer Law Center, Foreclosures Ch. 13 (4th ed. 2012); Truth in Lending § 2.4.2 (8th ed. 2012).

483 11 U.S.C. § 362.
See Chapter 9, *supra*, for a discussion of the automatic stay.

484 *See* § 9.6, *supra*.
One bankruptcy case has addressed these issues in the context of a rent-to-own transaction. Mercer v. D.E.F., Inc., 48 B.R. 562 (Bankr. D. Minn. 1985).

485 Mercer v. D.E.F., Inc., 48 B.R. 562 (Bankr. D. Minn. 1985) ($6500 actual and punitive damages plus attorney fees and costs).

486 *See* § 12.9, *infra*.

487 *In re* Johnson, 75 B.R. 927 (Bankr. N.D. Ohio 1987); *In re* Leazier, 55 B.R. 870 (Bankr. N.D. Ind. 1985); *In re* Britton, 43 B.R. 605 (Bankr. E.D. Mich. 1984); *In re* Booth, 19 B.R. 53 (Bankr. D. Utah 1982).

488 *See* Auto. Leasing Specialists, L.L.C. v. Little, 392 B.R. 222 (W.D. La. 2008) (economic reality was that lease with option to buy for nominal amount was secured debt); *In re* Crummie, 194 B.R. 230 (Bankr. N.D. Cal. 1996) (GM "SmartBuy" contract deemed credit sale, not lease); *In re* Lewis, 185 B.R. 66 (Bankr. N.D. Cal. 1995) (General Motors "SmartBuy" contract deemed credit sale and not lease); *In re* Coors of Cumberland, Inc., 19 B.R. 313 (Bankr. M.D. Tenn. 1982). *See also In re* Celeryvale Transp., Inc., 822 F.2d 16 (6th Cir. 1987); Fogie v. Rent-A-Center, Inc., 867 F. Supp. 1398 (D. Minn. 1993) (rent-to-own contract was consumer credit sale under Minnesota law), *aff'd sub nom.*, Fogie v. Thorn Americas, 95 F.3d 645 (8th Cir. 1996). *But see In re* Powers, 983 F.2d 88 (7th Cir. 1993); *In re* Mahoney, 153 B.R. 174 (E.D. Mich. 1992); *In re* Charles, 278 B.R. 216 (Bankr. D. Kansas 2002) (while court might have reached different result under former U.C.C., agreement was clearly a lease under revised U.C.C. § 1-207(37)).

489 *See* S.C. Rentals v. Arthur, 187 B.R. 502 (D.S.C. 1995); *In re* Smith, 262 B.R. 365 (Bankr. E.D. Va. 2000); *In re* Burton, 128 B.R. 807 (Bankr. N.D. Ala.), *aff'd*, 128 B.R. 820 (N.D. Ala. 1989); *In re* Aguilar, 101 B.R. 481 (Bankr. W.D. Tex. 1989); *In re* Rose, 94 B.R. 103 (Bankr. S.D. Ohio 1988); *In re* Fogelsong, 88 B.R. 194 (Bankr. C.D. Ill. 1988); *In re* Brown, 82 B.R. 68 (Bankr. W.D. Ark. 1987); *In re* Puckett, 60 B.R. 223 (Bankr. M.D. Tenn. 1986); Sight & Sound of Ohio, Inc. v. Wright, 36 B.R. 885 (Bankr. S.D. Ohio 1983); Murphy v. McNamara, 36 Conn. Supp. 183, 416 A.2d 170, 28 U.C.C. Rep. Serv. 911 (Super. Ct. 1979); Broad v. Curtis Mathes Sales, Co., Clearinghouse No. 36,376 (Me. Super. Ct. Feb. 7, 1984). *See also* 6 Collier on Bankruptcy ¶ 722.03 (16th ed.). *But see In re* Glenn, 102 B.R. 153 (Bankr. E.D. Ark. 1989); *In re* Harris, 102 B.R. 128 (Bankr. S.D. Ohio 1989) (relying on special state lease-purchase statute); *In re* Huffman, 63 B.R. 737 (Bankr. N.D. Ga. 1986) (RTO contract lease not security agreement because it was terminable); *In re* Martin, 64 B.R. 1 (Bankr. S.D. Ga. 1984) (seventy-seven payment freezer contract lease not security agreement because it was terminable). *See generally* National Consumer Law Center, Unfair and Deceptive Acts and Practices § 8.8 (7th ed. 2008 and Supp.); National Consumer Law Center, Repossessions § 14.3 (7th ed. 2010 and Supp.).

490 National Consumer Law Center, Repossessions § 14.3 (7th ed. 2010 and Supp.).

491 11 U.S.C. § 722. *See* § 11.5, *supra*.

492 *See* § 11.6, *supra*.
Given the unfairness of most rent-to-own contracts to the consumer, cure of a default may not be in the debtor's best interests.

493 11 U.S.C. § 506. *See* § 11.7, *supra*.

494 *See* Ch. 14, *infra*.

of the automobile title to the lender and sometimes a lease-back of the car to the borrower. The effective interest rates in such transactions are often several hundred percent or more.[495]

Courts have treated such transactions as disguised non-possessory security interests. Thus, the normal rights of cramdown in chapter 13 apply.[496] Chapter 13 thus provides a method of reducing the exorbitant finance charges, and often the amount of the secured claim owed to such lenders. Similarly, the right of redemption under section 722[497] may allow a debtor to eliminate the lien of such a lender by paying the value of the lender's allowed secured claim in cash. If the vehicle is used as a tool of the debtor's trade and therefore may be claimed as exempt, the lien may be totally avoided under section 522(f).[498]

Even if possession of the property has been lost prior to bankruptcy, it may be possible to regain the vehicle. In most cases, a section 542 turnover would be required if the creditor still has possession.[499] In some cases, the taking of possession or other acts to improve the creditor's position may also constitute an avoidable preference.[500]

---

495 *See* National Consumer Law Center, The Cost of Credit: Regulation, Preemption, and Industry Abuses § 7.5.2.3 (4th ed. 2009).

496 *In re* Schwalb, 347 B.R. 726 (Bankr. D. Nev. 2006) (also finding creditor liable for damages based on violations of U.C.C. in enforcing lien); *In re* Burnsed, 224 B.R. 496 (Bankr. M.D. Fla. 1998).

497 *See* § 11.5, *supra*.

498 *See* § 10.4.2.4, *supra*.

499 *See* § 9.9, *supra*. *See also In re* Johnson, 289 B.R. 251 (Bankr. M.D. Ga. 2002) (automobile repossessed and not redeemed by debtor during grace period was subject to turnover because contract violated statutory requirements for auto title pawn loan).

  Even if the court determines that the debtor no longer has a property interest in the automobile based on the prepetition expiration of the period for redeeming pawned property, the debtor may still be able to obtain turnover by setting aside the repossession of the automobile as a fraudulent transfer under section 548. *See In re* Bell, 279 B.R. 890 (Bankr. N.D. Ga. 2002); § 10.4.2.6.5, *supra*.

500 *In re* Mattheiss, 214 B.R. 20 (Bankr. N.D. Ala. 1997). *See* § 10.4.2.6.4, *supra*.

Chapter 12 Issues Arising in Chapter 13 Cases

12.1 Introduction

No part of the Bankruptcy Code caused more controversy or confusion in its early days than the greatly revised chapter 13. In drafting that chapter, Congress made an explicit effort to encourage greater use of its provisions, which had been rarely employed in most parts of the country under the prior Bankruptcy Act. Even where it had been used, practices under the old Chapter XIII varied widely among judicial districts, with substantial deviations from the strict terms of the Act.

Chapter 13, as enacted in 1978, contained many different provisions designed to make it more attractive to debtors, for the first time providing consumers with the flexibility to rearrange their affairs in plans that parallel the types of plans that corporations have long been able to devise. There were only a few basic requirements that chapter 13 plans were required to meet in order to provide some protections to creditors. Beyond these requirements, the debtor had enormous freedom to create a plan that best suits her circumstances.

Unfortunately, because chapter 13 was so new and so different, creditors and some judges initially resisted its liberality. Because little relevant case law existed under the old Act and because the legislative history was relatively scant, widely divergent opinions arose concerning the use of chapter 13. Some judges tried to apply concepts developed under prior law and failed to take into account adequately the congressional intent to liberalize the law. This judicial hostility to the new powers given to debtors, combined with some unfortunate "hard cases" of the type which made bad law, led to a rash of decisions which imposed new judge-made limitations found nowhere in the statute. Of course, there were also many decisions applying the statute more faithfully, but the result was a tremendous disparity in the extent to which chapter 13 was a viable vehicle for debtors in different judicial districts.

As experience under chapter 13 grew and cases reached the appellate courts, most of these problems disappeared. Further clarification came from Congress in 1984 and 1994, when new amendments addressed some of the most litigated issues. Hence, there was a large body of law to turn to in interpreting chapter 13, and both knowledge and use of its liberal provisions increased considerably. However, even today there remain significant variations in local custom with respect to the types of plans that courts and trustees feel are appropriate.

Unfortunately, the 2005 amendments to the Bankruptcy Code substantially altered chapter 13 in a number of ways, most of which limited the advantages that were originally designed to encourage chapter 13 cases. Among the changes were significant curtailment of the broader chapter 13 "superdischarge,"[1] limits on obtaining a discharge after a prior bankruptcy discharge,[2] burdensome new paperwork and payment requirements,[3] limits on the ability to modify secured debts,[4] less favorable treatment for many debtors who unsuccessfully attempt chapter 13 and then dismiss and re-file[5] or convert to chapter 7,[6] requirements that additional debts newly classified as priority debts be paid in full in most cases,[7] the credit counseling and credit education requirements,[8] impediments to curing a default on a residential lease,[9] and cumbersome, sometimes inflexible new standards for payments to unsecured creditors that will also require longer plans in some cases.[10] Not surprisingly, courts have varied greatly in their application of these provisions and it will again take years before appellate case law brings some degree of uniformity. Although the 2005 amendments were supposedly intended to increase the use of chapter 13, they have, if anything caused a decrease in the percentage of bankruptcy cases that are filed under chapter 13.

12.2 Eligibility for Chapter 13

12.2.1 Introduction

A threshold issue, which has occasionally been troublesome, concerns eligibility to file a chapter 13 case. In addition to section 109(a) and the section 109(h) credit counseling requirement, which are applicable to cases under all chapters filed by individual debtors, the key chapter 13 eligibility provision is section 109(e) of the Code. That section provides that to be a chapter 13 debtor, the debtor must:

- Be an individual with regular income or an individual with regular income and that individual's spouse;
- Owe non-contingent, liquidated unsecured debts of less than $360,475 on the date of filing; and

---

1 11 U.S.C. § 1328(a). See § 15.4.1, infra.
2 11 U.S.C. § 1328(f). See § 12.10.1, infra.
3 See, e.g., 11 U.S.C. §§ 521, 1308, 1326(a). See also Chs. 7, 8, supra.
4 11 U.S.C. § 1325(a). See Ch. 11, supra.
5 11 U.S.C. § 362(c)(3),(4). See Ch. 9, supra.
6 11 U.S.C. § 348(f). See §§ 8.7.5.4, supra, 13.7.2, infra.
7 11 U.S.C. §§ 507(a), 1322(a)(2), (4). See § 12.3.6.1, infra.
8 11 U.S.C. §§ 109(h), 1328(g). See Chs. 7, 8, supra.
9 11 U.S.C. § 362(b)(22). See Ch. 9, supra.
10 11 U.S.C. § 1325(b). See § 12.3.4, infra.

- Owe non-contingent, liquidated, secured debts of less than $1,081,400 on that date.

In accordance with section 104, these amounts are adjusted periodically for inflation. They were last adjusted on April 1, 2010 and will be adjusted every three years thereafter, so the next adjustment is due on April 1, 2013.

In consumer cases, issues may arise as to any of these requirements, which could preclude the filing of a chapter 13 case.

12.2.2 Individuals with Regular Income

Probably the most common issue for low-income debtors is whether the debtor is an "individual with regular income." This phrase is defined in section 101(30) as an "individual whose income is sufficiently stable and regular to enable such individual to make payments under a plan under chapter 13." The legislative history makes clear that the intent of the statute is to include others besides wage earners, and to expand eligibility to recipients of public benefits such as welfare and Social Security, small business proprietors, and those supported by other income such as alimony or pensions.[11]

It is somewhat unclear, however, whether a spouse who is not separated or divorced is eligible to file without the other spouse filing jointly, if only the non-filing spouse brings income into the family. Quite arguably, a non-working spouse who receives a regular amount of income for expenses from the income-earning spouse may file alone. Indeed, a schedule of regular payments from the non-filing spouse to the trustee could even be ordered by the court as part of the plan under section 1325(c). Similarly, payments from other friends or relatives may sometimes satisfy the regular income requirement, as long as there is a reasonable assurance that the payments will continue.[12] If a hearing on this issue is held, proof in the form of testimony from the friend or relative and, if possible, documentary evidence concerning the regularity of prior financial support should be produced.

Regardless of its source, the amount of the debtor's income must be sufficient to fund payments under a plan. Presumably, this requirement means that the income must be sufficient for a plan proposed by the debtor that complies with the Code.

The case law concerning who is an individual with regular income has been relatively scarce. Some creditors have argued that a husband and wife who operate a business should be considered partners, and thus not eligible for chapter 13.[13] The resolution of that challenge turned simply upon a finding that the requisites for establishing a partnership under state law had not been met.[14] However, even if an individual is a member of a partnership or a husband and wife are considered partners, the individuals who are partners should not be precluded from filing under chapter 13. Although a partnership cannot file a chapter 13 case, an individual who happens to be a partner is clearly eligible, provided that the other eligibility requirements are met.[15] In such a case, the partnership's assets would not become property of the bankruptcy estate, but the individual's interest in the partnership itself would become property of the estate.[16] Similarly, the individual's liability for partnership debts would be considered a debt in the case, which could affect eligibility for chapter 13 under the debt limitations[17] unless such liability were considered to be contingent.

More often, courts are concerned about whether asserted regular income really exists. One debtor who provided the court with no factual evidence that he was earning regular income as a cabinetmaker sufficient to make the payments proposed was found ineligible to file a chapter 13 case.[18] Similarly, when a debtor with no past income merely anticipates future income, the case may be dismissed or converted to chapter 7, unless there is clear evidence that the income will be forthcoming.[19] Even when it appears on paper that the debtor's income is sufficient, the court may deem evidence of inability to make similar payments proposed under a previous plan to cast doubt on the debtor's stated budget.[20] And when the debtor's statement does not show income sufficient to make the necessary level of payments, it is likely that the court will find the debtor ineligible for chapter 13.[21] On the other hand, the income need not be absolutely assured; a farmer whose income is dependent on good weather and fair prices for crops should not be denied access to chapter 13 merely because his future income is somewhat speculative.[22] In many cases, these issues are re-

---

11 H.R. Rep. No. 95-595, at 13, 312 (1977). *See In re* Hammonds, 729 F.2d 1391 (11th Cir. 1984) (AFDC payments may be used to fund chapter 13 plan). *See also In re* Lapin, 302 B.R. 184 (Bankr. S.D. Tex. 2003) (withdrawals from individual retirement account could constitute portion of regular income needed for plan); *In re* Cole, 3 B.R. 346 (Bankr. S.D. W. Va. 1980).

12 *In re* Antoine, 208 B.R. 17 (Bankr. E.D.N.Y. 1997) (unemployed carpenter was individual with regular income because wife made oral commitment to devote her salary to plan); *In re* Varian, 91 B.R. 653 (Bankr. D. Conn. 1988) (commitment of non-filing spouse to make payments to trustee was sufficient to provide regular income); *In re* Campbell, 38 B.R. 193 (Bankr. E.D.N.Y. 1984) (contributions of relatives who had substantial interest in plan's success could constitute income needed for plan). *But see In re* Fischel, 103 B.R. 44 (Bankr. N.D.N.Y. 1989) (non-debtor's commitment to make payments was too tenuous when debtor and non-debtor were not related and there was no record regarding stability of shared living arrangement).

13 *In re* Ward, 6 B.R. 93 (Bankr. M.D. Fla. 1980).

14 *Id.*

15 *See* 8 Collier on Bankruptcy ¶ 1304.01[3] (16th ed.). *See also* Biery, *Debt Adjustment under Chapter 13 of the Bankruptcy Reform Act of 1978*, 11 St. Mary's L.J. 473, 477 (1979); H.R. Rep. No. 95-595, at 320 (1977).

16 *See* 8 Collier on Bankruptcy ¶ 1304.01[3] (16th ed.).

17 *See* § 12.2.3, *infra*.

18 *In re* Wilhelm, 6 B.R. 905 (Bankr. E.D.N.Y. 1980). *See also In re* Spurlin, 350 B.R. 716 (Bankr. W.D. La. 2006) (unemployed debtor with no broker's license could rely on anticipated broker commissions to satisfy regular income requirement).

19 *In re* Mozer, 1 B.R. 350 (Bankr. D. Colo. 1979).

20 *In re* Burns, 6 B.R. 286 (Bankr. D. Colo. 1980) (holding alternatively that plan of such individuals not offered in good faith).

21 *In re* Terry, 630 F.2d 634 (8th Cir. 1980).

22 *In re* Fiegi, 61 B.R. 994 (Bankr. D. Or. 1986) (proceeds projected

solved in the context of a determination about the feasibility of the plan rather than about whether the debtor has regular income.[23]

In view of these issues, a prudent approach would be to begin regularly setting aside an amount equal to the plan payments as soon as the case is filed, if not earlier. Under the Code, plan payments to the trustee must begin within thirty days after the order for relief, normally the date of the filing of the petition,[24] usually before the meeting of creditors and confirmation of the plan, unless the court orders otherwise.[25] If such payments are regularly made or set aside, there can then be little doubt as to the debtor's ability to perform under the plan. Conversely, the failure to make preconfirmation payments often leads to dismissal of the case, unless the debtor provides a valid explanation or can modify the plan to abate or lower the payments.

12.2.3 Debt Limitations

12.2.3.1 Determining Whether Debts Are Secured or Unsecured

Issues may also arise concerning the dollar-amount limitations on claims against debtors who file chapter 13 cases, limitations designed to exclude large businesses from evading the requirements of chapter 11.[26]

For these limits to be met, in some cases, it may be critical whether an undersecured debt is considered a secured or an unsecured debt. Depending upon the facts of a particular case, the debtor may wish to argue that the entire amount of a secured debt should be considered against the $1,081,400 limit on secured debts, or that only the amount of the allowed secured claim (equal to the value of the collateral)[27] should be measured against that limit, with the unsecured portion of the claim secured against the $360,475 limit on unsecured debts.

One early case considering this question illustrates the problem. *In re Ballard*[28] involved debtors who owed secured creditors over $350,000 (the limit on secured debts at the time), but whose property securing that debt was worth less than $350,000. The creditor asserted that the debtors were ineligible for chapter 13 because their secured debts were too high. It argued that claims are not filed or determined in a case until after the initial stages when the debtor's eligibility is decided, and that therefore the value of the collateral could not be looked to because the court would have to rely on the debtor's valuation in the schedules. (The creditor cited no reason why that valuation could not be challenged.)

The court rejected these arguments. It looked first to statements in the legislative history which referred to the $350,000 limit as a limit on "secured claims,"[29] and also to the statutory definition of "debt"[30] which incorporates the definition of "claim."[31] The court also found that because a debtor could almost always create a security interest, practically at will, it would undermine the intent of the congressional limitations to allow the debtor to convert unsecured claims to secured claims in order to qualify for chapter 13. *Ballard* was later followed by all of the courts of appeals that have decided the issue to date.[32] Indeed, one court of appeals has gone so far as to hold that a debt secured by a lien that can be avoided by the debtor under section 522(f) should be considered an unsecured debt for eligibility purposes.[33]

Although the holding in *Ballard* and the cases which have followed it may often be helpful to consumer debtors with similar fact situations, at least as many debtors will have the opposite problem, in view of the lower limit on unsecured debts for chapter 13 eligibility.[34] These debtors will want to argue that Congress meant a distinction by using that word "debt" rather than "claim" in section 109(e), and that the *Ballard* court's reading of the definitions was superficial. The definition of "debt" as a "liability on a claim" could just as easily mean the total liability on a claim, whether secured or unsecured, before that claim is divided into its secured and unsecured parts under section 506(a). This result, too, has some support in the case law.[35]

Courts have similarly disagreed regarding whether a debt that is secured by property of someone other than the debtor should be considered a secured debt for purposes of section 109(e). It has been held that such debts should be considered secured debts as contemplated by that section,[36] and it has also

---

from annual harvests sufficiently regular income to make annual payments proposed in farmer's plan); *In re* Hines, 7 B.R. 415 (Bankr. D.S.D. 1980).

23 See § 12.5, *infra*.
24 The petition constitutes the order for relief. 11 U.S.C. § 301(b). If a case is converted, the conversion is the order for relief. 11 U.S.C. § 348(a).
25 11 U.S.C. § 1326(a)(1).
26 H.R. Rep. No. 95-595, at 119 (1977).
27 11 U.S.C. § 506(a). *See* Ch. 11, *supra*.
28 4 B.R. 271 (Bankr. E.D. Va. 1980).

29 124 Cong. Rec. H11,089 (daily ed. Sept. 24, 1978) (remarks of Rep. Edwards); 124 Cong. Rec. S17,406 (daily ed. Oct. 6, 1978) (remarks of Sen. DeConcini), *reprinted in* 1978 U.S.C.C.A.N. 6441, 6509.
30 11 U.S.C. § 101(12) defines "debt" as "liability on a claim."
31 11 U.S.C. § 101(5) defines "claim" as including a "right to payment, whether or not such right is . . . secured, or unsecured."
32 *In re* Ficken, 2 F.3d 299 (8th Cir. 1993); *In re* Balbus, 933 F.2d 246 (4th Cir. 1991); Miller v. United States *ex rel.* Farmers Home Admin., 907 F.2d 80 (8th Cir. 1990); *In re* Day, 747 F.2d 405 (7th Cir. 1984). *See also* Cavaliere v. Sapir, 208 B.R. 784 (D. Conn. 1997) (only secured portion of mortgage claims counted in determining chapter 13 eligibility when debtor had previously discharged personal liability in chapter 7); *In re* Jerome, 112 B.R. 563 (Bankr. S.D.N.Y. 1990).

The court in *Balbus* rejected a creditor's argument that the hypothetical costs of liquidating the debtor's property should be deducted in determining the amounts of the secured and unsecured claims for this purpose.

33 *In re* Scovis, 249 F.3d 975 (9th Cir. 2001). *See also In re* Werts, 410 B.R. 677 (Bankr. D. Kan. 2009) (applying same rationale to lien being stripped off under section 506(a)).
34 *See, e.g., In re* Day, 747 F.2d 405 (7th Cir. 1984); *In re* Bobroff, 32 B.R. 933 (Bankr. E.D. Pa. 1983).
35 *In re* Holland, 293 B.R. 425 (Bankr. N.D. Ohio 2002); *In re* Morton, 43 B.R. 215 (Bankr. E.D.N.Y. 1984).
36 Branch Banking & Trust Co. v. Russell, 188 B.R. 542 (E.D.N.C.

been held that, because they are not secured by the debtor's property, they should be considered unsecured debts.[37]

As the value of real estate has drastically declined from high levels in some parts of the country, the bifurcation of secured debts into their secured and unsecured portions has threatened to make increasing numbers of debtors ineligible for chapter 13 based on the high amounts of mortgage debt that would be deemed unsecured.[38] Courts have accepted at least two different arguments that such bifurcation should not occur in some cases. First, courts have noted that mortgages secured only by real estate that is the debtor's principal residence generally cannot be bifurcated in chapter 13.[39] For such nonmodifiable mortgages, some courts have accepted the argument that it makes no sense to bifurcate them for purposes of a section 109(g) determination of chapter 13 eligibility.[40] Second, if a mortgage is nonrecourse, meaning that the creditor can look only to the property and there can be no deficiency judgment after a foreclosure, some courts have found that no unsecured debt can result.[41]

12.2.3.2 Determining Whether Debts Are Liquidated and Non-Contingent

Further problems may arise in determining whether debts are liquidated or non-contingent and therefore countable toward the debt limitations. Neither term is defined in the Code, and thus state law concepts may come into play. As to these questions, all debtors filing chapter 13 cases will have a common interest—to classify the maximum number of debts as non-liquidated or contingent.

Regarding whether a debt is liquidated, the clearest cases are at the extremes. A note as to which a judgment has been entered and to which there are no defenses is perhaps the paradigm of a liquidated debt.[42] A tort claim for personal injuries and pain and suffering, which has not been adjudicated, is clearly unliquidated. Between the extremes, however, there is more doubt. If a debtor can assert any defense to a debt that is not foreclosed by res judicata or otherwise, it should be argued that the debt is not liquidated. Many of the definitions of "liquidated" suggest that when the amount owing is neither agreed upon nor fixed by operation of law the debt is not liquidated.[43] And even if the defenses go to only a part of the amount due, these definitions indicate that the debt as a whole should be considered unliquidated because its precise amount is not settled.[44] However, this test does not require that to be liquidated the debt must be *both* agreed upon and fixed by operation of law, so some courts have held that if the amount claimed is readily ascertainable, it is liquidated even if the debtor disputes liability.[45]

1995); *In re* White, 148 B.R. 283 (Bankr. N.D. Ohio 1992); *In re* Gorman, 58 B.R. 372 (Bankr. E.D.N.Y. 1986). *See also In re* Lindsey, Stephenson & Lindsey, 995 F.2d 626 (5th Cir. 1993).

37 *In re* Lower, 311 B.R. 888 (Bankr. D. Colo. 2004) (debt considered secured only to the extent of the estate's interest in collateral); *In re* Tomlinson, 116 B.R. 80 (Bankr. E.D. Mich. 1990).

38 *See, e.g., In re* Werts, 410 B.R. 677 (Bankr. D. Kan. 2009).

39 11 U.S.C. § 1322(b)(2). *See* § 11.11.6.1.2, *supra*.

40 *In re* Tolentino, 2010 WL 1462772 (Bankr. N.D. Cal. Apr. 12, 2010); *In re* Munoz, 428 B.R. 516 (Bankr. S.D. Cal. 2010); *In re* Smith, 419 B.R. 826 (Bankr. C.D. Cal. 2009). *But see In re* Werts, 410 B.R. 677 (Bankr. D. Kan. 2009). However, if the debtor's plan proposes to strip off a wholly unsecured claim based on one of the accepted exceptions to the anti-modification provision in section 1322(b)(2), the court may treat the claim as unsecured. *See In re* Lantzy, 2010 WL 6259984 (B.A.P. 9th Cir. Dec. 7, 2010); *In re* Smith, 435 B.R. 637 (B.A.P. 9th Cir. 2010); *In re* Bernick, 440 B.R. 449 (Bankr. E.D. Va. 2010).

41 Cavaliere v. Sapir, 208 B.R. 784 (D. Conn. 1997) (unsecured portion of mortgage claims discharged in prior chapter 7 bankruptcy not considered secured or unsecured debts for chapter 13 debt limitations); *In re* Shenas, 2011 WL 3236182 (Bankr. N.D. Cal. July 28, 2011) (discharged personal liability on mortgage debt not considered in unsecured debt calculation); *In re* Tolentino, 2010 WL 1462772 (Bankr. N.D. Cal. Apr. 12, 2010). *But see In re* DiClemente, 2012 WL 3314840 (D.N.J. Aug 13, 2012) (in rem claims of mortgage creditors following discharge of debtor's personal liability on mortgages in prior chapter 7 treated as unsecured debts for purposes of section 109(e)).

42 *See In re* Vaughan, 36 B.R. 935 (N.D. Ala. 1984) (readily calculable contract debt was liquidated). *See also In re* Papatones, 143 F.3d 623 (1st Cir. 1998) (debt which had been adjudicated by court but not yet reduced to a docketed judgment was liquidated); *In re* Hammers, 988 F.2d 32 (5th Cir. 1993) (bankruptcy court could not look behind judgment to determine that part of claim was not allowable when claim had already been adjudicated by another tribunal).

43 *In re* Horne, 277 B.R. 320 (Bankr. E.D. Tex. 2002) (debt was unliquidated when court had discretion in determining amount of damages). *See* Black's Law Dictionary 1079, 1080 (6th ed. 1990). *See also In re* Hull, 251 B.R. 726 (B.A.P. 9th Cir. 2000) (claim not liquidated because trial on the merits would have been necessary to liquidate claim); *In re* Verdunn, 160 B.R. 682 (Bankr. M.D. Fla. 1993), *aff'd*, 187 B.R. 996 (M.D. Fla. 1995) (alleged tax fraud claim was unliquidated because tax liabilities could not be readily determined from documents presented), *rev'd*, 89 F.3d 799 (11th Cir. 1996); *In re* Harbaugh, 153 B.R. 54 (Bankr. D. Idaho 1993) (tax claim was liquidated only to extent it was undisputed or capable of being easily determined without evidentiary hearing); *In re* Robertson, 143 B.R. 76 (Bankr. N.D. Tex. 1992) (IRS claim for almost $900,000 was contingent and unliquidated because IRS had not yet proved tax law violations, which debtor disputed); *In re* Lambert, 43 B.R. 913 (Bankr. D. Utah 1984) (debt subject to bona fide dispute not counted); *In re* King, 9 B.R. 376 (Bankr. D. Or. 1981).

44 *But see In re* Quintana, 915 F.2d 513 (9th Cir. 1990) (existence of a counterclaim does not reduce amount of claim for purposes of measuring amount of debt for eligibility under chapter 12).

45 Mazzeo v. United States, 131 F.3d 295 (2d Cir. 1997); United States v. Verdunn, 89 F.3d 799 (11th Cir. 1996) (federal income tax liabilities and penalties were liquidated because they were easily ascertainable through application of fixed legal standards); *In re* Knight, 55 F.3d 231 (7th Cir. 1995) (fact that debt is disputed does not make it unliquidated if amount claimed is easily ascertainable); *In re* Wenberg, 902 F.2d 768 (9th Cir. 1990) (when creditor's damages were unliquidated, but award of attorney fees to creditor was "readily ascertainable" and therefore liquidated, attorney fees award was included in computation of debts), *aff'g* 94 B.R. 631 (B.A.P. 9th Cir. 1988); *In re* De Jounghe, 334 B.R. 760 (B.A.P. 1st Cir. 2005) (neither fact that debt was disputed nor possibly avoidable on a preference theory rendered debt unliquidated); *In re* Crescenzi, 69 B.R. 64 (S.D.N.Y. 1986); *In re* Arcella-Coffman, 318 B.R. 463 (Bankr. N.D. Ind. 2004) (claim is liquidated when judgment or discretion not required to establish amount). *But see In re*

The question of contingency is somewhat more complicated. Generally, a contingent debt is one which is dependent upon some future event that may never occur.[46] An example is an agreement to pay a debt if (and only if) another person does not do so.[47] Cosigners on debts may be in this position depending on the terms of the contract and state law. The exact status of a debt must always be determined by both the applicable law and the facts. There may be a dispute regarding whether the condition upon which the debt is contingent has occurred, which may in turn depend upon whether there were valid defenses that justified nonpayment by a principal debtor. Alternatively, the court may find that, due to known facts, the outcome of another proceeding need not be awaited for it to decide that the condition has occurred.[48] It may also find that, as a matter of state law, the creditors need not pursue other assets or co-obligors before looking to the debtor for payment.[49]

12.2.3.3 Procedure for Determining Eligibility

The courts have also differed concerning whether a hearing is necessary to determine the amount of non-contingent liquidated claims. While some courts have held that such a hearing may be appropriate,[50] the Sixth and Seventh Circuits have held that the court should normally rely solely upon the representations in the debtor's chapter 13 filings, provided that the representations are made in good faith.[51] The Sixth Circuit found that the dollar limits of section 109(e) are analogous to the amount in controversy jurisdictional requirement in federal diversity cases. Noting that section 109(e) states nothing about computing eligibility after a hearing on disputed claims, and that the Code contemplates that a chapter 13 case will move expeditiously to confirmation, the Sixth Circuit concluded that a hearing on threshold eligibility issues would defeat the Code's objectives.[52]

As in the diversity situation, the Sixth Circuit held that having a hearing on the merits of the claim at the outset of the case is unnecessary and that the case should not be dismissed unless it appears to a legal certainty that the debtor is not eligible.[53] If, based upon good faith statements in the debtor's schedules, it appears that the debtor meets the requirements of section 109(e) when the case is commenced, the case may proceed as a chapter 13, even if subsequent determinations prove that this initial determination was incorrect, because eligibility is determined as of the date the petition is filed.[54] In a similar vein, other courts have held that eligibility provisions contained in section 109 are not jurisdictional.[55] Obviously, this protects judgments and orders entered in a bankruptcy case from collateral attack on the basis of the provisions of section 109.[56]

12.2.3.4 Strategies for Avoiding Eligibility Problems

For the debtor, it is essential to avoid eligibility issues when possible. This may sometimes be accomplished simply by filing separate cases for a husband and wife rather than filing a joint petition. Because the debt limitation amounts would then apply separately to the debts of each, rather than to their combined debts as in a joint case,[57] the total amount of combined debt

---

Ho, 274 B.R. 867 (B.A.P. 9th Cir. 2002) (substantial dispute about liability, requiring contested evidentiary hearing, can make debt unliquidated); United States v. May, 211 B.R. 991 (M.D. Fla. 1997) (debt found to be unliquidated because it could not be readily determined until Tax Court litigation was resolved).

46 Black's Law Dictionary 392 (6th ed. 1990). *See In re* Knight, 55 F.3d 231 (7th Cir. 1995) (debt is non-contingent if events giving rise to liability occurred before bankruptcy case was filed); *In re* Fostvedt, 823 F.2d 305 (9th Cir. 1987).

47 *But see In re* Marchetto, 24 B.R. 967 (B.A.P. 1st Cir. 1982) (Massachusetts co-maker who signs as accommodation party is liable as a maker and bound without prior recourse to the principal); Glaubitz v. Grossman, 2011 WL 147931 (E.D. Wis. Jan. 18, 2011) (guaranty treated as a contingent liability).

48 *See In re* Prince, 5 B.R. 432 (Bankr. W.D.N.Y. 1980) (court need not await outcome of chapter 7 proceeding concerning debtors' business to determine amount they would owe on loans they guaranteed when it was clear that over $100,000 in unsecured claims would not be paid in chapter 7 case).

49 *In re* Fostvedt, 823 F.2d 305 (9th Cir. 1987) (debtor was jointly and severally liable); *In re* Glaubitz, 436 B.R. 99, 106 (Bankr. E.D. Wis. 2010) (contract did not require creditor to exhaust remedies against principal or its property); *In re* Kaufman, 93 B.R. 319 (Bankr. S.D.N.Y. 1988) (liability of an agent for an undisclosed principal was unconditional under state law). *See In re* Kelsey, 6 B.R. 114 (Bankr. S.D. Tex. 1980) (creditors of partnership need not first pursue partnership assets before looking to assets of a partner).

50 *See, e.g., In re* Sylvester, 19 B.R. 671 (B.A.P. 9th Cir. 1982).

51 *In re* Lybrook, 951 F.2d 136 (7th Cir. 1991); *In re* Pearson, 773 F.2d 751 (6th Cir. 1985).

52 *In re* Pearson, 773 F.2d 751, 756, 757 (6th Cir. 1985). *But see* Lucoski v. Internal Revenue Serv., 126 B.R. 332 (S.D. Ind. 1991) (court may look beyond the schedules if it determines, within reasonable period of time, that debts exceed statutory limits).

53 *Pearson*, 773 F.2d at 757.

54 *Id.*, at 758. *See also In re* Slack, 187 F.3d 1070 (9th Cir. 1999) (eligibility determined as of date of petition; postpetition state court judgment did not affect eligibility); *In re* Ridgon, 94 B.R. 602 (Bankr. W.D. Mo. 1988) (court looked beyond debtors' schedules to find debtors ineligible only because schedules were filed in bad faith).

Similarly, if a debt is contingent or unliquidated at the time of a chapter 7 petition, but becomes liquidated before a debtor converts a case to chapter 13, the debt must nonetheless be considered contingent or unliquidated, because the relevant date for determining its status is the date of the original bankruptcy petition. *In re* Bush, 120 B.R. 403 (Bankr. E.D. Tex. 1990).

Even when debtors may have misrepresented their eligibility, if a creditor fails to raise the issue in a timely fashion and instead waits until after confirmation of a plan, a motion to dismiss will be denied because eligibility is not jurisdictional. *In re* Jones, 134 B.R. 274 (N.D. Ill. 1991).

55 Rudd v. Laughlin, 866 F.2d 1040 (8th Cir. 1989) (fact that debtors were ineligible for chapter 13 did not deprive bankruptcy court of jurisdiction necessary to enter valid order converting case to chapter 7); *In re* Jarvis, 78 B.R. 288 (Bankr. D. Or. 1987). *See also In re* Republic Trust & Sav. Co., 59 B.R. 606 (Bankr. N.D. Okla. 1986) (eligibility challenged in chapter 11).

56 *In re* Jarvis, 78 B.R. 288 (Bankr. D. Or. 1987).

57 Although the language of 11 U.S.C. § 109(e) appears to consider the combined debts of both joint filers, some courts have held other-

permitted can be increased to the extent that the debts owed are not joint obligations.

In other cases, if one spouse owes a large debt which exceeds the eligibility limits and the other does not, the goals of the bankruptcy often may be accomplished by filing a chapter 13 petition for only the spouse not owing the large debt. In such a case, the codebtor stay would protect the non-filing spouse with respect to most joint debts[58] and the incomes of both spouses could be used to cure or satisfy the claims of secured creditors or other creditors.

If a large tort judgment is imminent, a chapter 13 petition may be filed before it is entered, even if a bankruptcy is not then contemplated, to preserve the option if it later becomes necessary. And debtors should be wary of agreeing to settlements or judgments that could push their liquidated debt totals near the limit. Because the key date is the date the petition is filed, other actions, such as settlements of disputed amounts that alter the debtor's debt amounts or the character of the debts as secured or unsecured, may still be taken after the bankruptcy case is filed without affecting the debtor's eligibility for chapter 13.[59]

Occasionally, a debtor with unsecured debts above the limit may have to file a chapter 7 case to deal with some of his or her debts, in the hope that the chapter 7 case will be sufficient. If it is not, the debtor may then be eligible to file a chapter 13 case because the unsecured debts have been discharged in the prior chapter 7 case.[60] However, because eligibility is determined as of the date of the petition, a debtor may not convert a chapter 7 case to chapter 13 based upon the discharge in the chapter 7 case of unsecured debts above the eligibility level.[61] If a chapter 13 case follows closely after a chapter 7 case in such circumstances, the debtor will not be eligible for a chapter 13 discharge[62] and there may also be an issue regarding whether the two filings constitute a bad faith subterfuge to avoid the chapter 13 dollar limitations.

Finally, the limitation on secured debts may be good reason to give a low or high estimate of the value of collateral, in case the court looks to that measure.[63] Like all of the decisions to be made, however, these strategies must be determined in the context of the entire case, which might for other reasons dictate settling a claim or giving a different estimate of the value of collateral for purposes of allowed secured claim valuation or in order to maintain the automatic stay.[64]

12.3 What Amount Must Be Paid to Unsecured Creditors?

12.3.1 Overview

No single question under the Code stirred more debate in the statute's early years than the issue of how much the debtor must pay to unsecured creditors in a chapter 13 plan. Hundreds of courts debated the question, coming to a fairly consistent, if vague, result. That result was codified by the enactment of section 1325(b) in 1984, and the legal issue receded, except in occasional cases.

The 2005 amendments made significant changes to section 1325(b) that will revive this issue as a matter of controversy. In addition, several other Code sections are implicated in determining payments to unsecured creditors.

12.3.2 The Best Interests of Creditors Test

One standard delineating how much unsecured creditors are to receive in a chapter 13 case is known as the "best interests of creditors" test. The Code provides that, if all other requirements are met, the court "*shall* confirm a plan if . . . the value, as of the effective date of the plan, of property to be paid under the plan on account of each allowed unsecured claim is not less than the amount would be paid on the claim [in a chapter 7 case]."[65] This test was inserted into the Code to ensure that general unsecured creditors would not be harmed by a debtor's choice of chapter 13 over chapter 7. By giving such creditors payments with a present value equivalent to the value of the property that would be distributed to them in chapter 7, that is, including interest to compensate for delay in their receipt,[66] the Code gives them as much as they would have received in a chapter 7 liquidation.

Because the court must compare the chapter 13 distributions to the outcome of a chapter 7 case, the appropriate date for valuing the nonexempt property that would be distributed to creditors is the filing date of the chapter 13 petition, because the

---

wise. *See In re* Hannon, 455 B.R. 814 (Bankr. S.D. Fla. 2011); *In re* Bosco, 2010 WL 4668595 (Bankr. E.D.N.C. Nov. 9, 2010); *In re* Werts, 410 B.R. 677 (Bankr. D. Kan. 2009) (debts not combined for eligibility test in joint case).

58 See § 9.4.5, *supra*, for discussion of the chapter 13 codebtor stay.
59 *See In re* Dally, 110 B.R. 630 (Bankr. D. Conn. 1990) (mortgage debts could not be excluded from total of secured debts based upon debtor's attempted Truth in Lending rescission of those debts after the bankruptcy petition was filed).
60 *See In re* Shenas, 2011 WL 3236182 (Bankr. N.D. Cal. July 28, 2011) (discharged personal liability on mortgage debt not considered in unsecured debt calculation); Cavaliere v. Sapir, 208 B.R. 784 (D. Conn. 1997) (only secured portion of mortgage claims counted in determining chapter 13 eligibility when debtor had previously discharged personal liability in chapter 7); § 12.10, *infra* (a discussion of chapter 13 cases after prior bankruptcies).
61 *In re* Stern, 266 B.R. 322 (Bankr. D. Md. 2001).
62 11 U.S.C. § 1328(f).
63 If the value of collateral test is used, however, it is not clear that the collateral would have to be only that belonging to the debtor. *See* § 12.2.3.1, *supra*.

64 See Chapter 9, *supra*, for a discussion of valuing collateral in the context of the stay. See Chapter 11, *supra*, for discussion of allowed secured claim valuation.
65 11 U.S.C. § 1325(a)(4) (emphasis added).
66 *But see In re* Smith, 431 B.R. 607 (Bankr. E.D.N.C. 2010) (*Till* rate used for secured creditors inapplicable; federal judgment rate of interest should be used).

For a discussion of present value and possible interest rates, see Chapter 11, *supra*. As to the latter, however, the court should also take into account the delay which occurs before creditors receive dividends in a chapter 7 case.

filing date is the date of valuation in a chapter 7 case.[67] Property acquired after the petition is filed, and postpetition appreciation in property values, generally should not be included in the determination of what creditors would receive for purposes of the best interests of creditors test.[68] And the best interests test cannot be used as a method of arguing that property is not exempt when no timely objection to exemptions has been filed.[69] However, the best interests calculation must take into account the net amount, after trustee and attorney fees, that a chapter 7 trustee would be likely to recover in avoiding powers proceedings.[70]

Moreover, the court must take into account the costs of sale that would be incurred by a chapter 7 trustee,[71] which could include a capital gains tax on any increase in value of property since the debtor acquired it.[72] These costs would also include mortgage payments and other carrying costs from the date of the petition to the date of sale.

In some cases, the best interests test may require different unsecured creditors to receive different percentage recoveries. For example, if there is community property or entireties property involved, the Code's distribution rules give different rights to creditors depending upon whether they have joint or community claims.[73] The amount of nonexempt assets may be such that only priority creditors would receive distributions in a chapter 7 case. While questions might arise as to which claims to consider in determining whether this test is met,[74] there is no doubt that, unless the proposed plan meets the standard, a creditor may challenge it and the court need not confirm it.[75]

---

67 *In re* Nielsen, 86 B.R. 177 (Bankr. E.D. Mo. 1988).

68 *In re* Treinen, 2006 WL 2136055 (Bankr. N.D. Ill. July 7, 2006) (additional postpetition income could be used to decrease length of plan, but could not be used to increase base amount available to unsecured creditors); *In re* Sanchez, 270 B.R. 322 (Bankr. D.N.H. 2001) (cause of action that arose after filing of bankruptcy petition not considered in best interests test). *See In re* Richardson, 283 B.R. 783 (Bankr. D. Kan. 2002) (insurance proceeds received postconfirmation are property of the debtor under section 1327(b) and may be used to pay off plan early); 8 Collier on Bankruptcy ¶ 1325.05[2][a] (16th ed.). *See also In re* Batten, 351 B.R. 256 (Bankr. S.D. Ga. 2006) (tort claim based on postpetition events did not have to be disclosed, even if case later converted to chapter 7); *In re* Britton, 288 B.R. 170 (Bankr. N.D.N.Y. 2002) (plan failed to satisfy "best interest of creditors" test as it did not provide for debtors' right to receive postpetition payments under annuity, which was property of the debtor's estate because annuity had been established prepetition in settlement of personal injury claim).

In rare cases, the debtor may acquire property after the petition that would be property of a chapter 7 estate due to section 541(a)(5) which brings into the estate marital settlements, life insurance proceeds, and inheritances acquired within 180 days of the petition. This property probably would be considered in the best interests test, at least if it were acquired prior to confirmation of the plan.

69 *In re* Tyson, 359 B.R. 239 (Bankr. E.D. Ark. 2007).

70 *In re* Loeffler, 2011 WL 6736066 (Bankr. D. Colo. Dec. 21, 2011) (although debtor did not have to pay funds equivalent to what a trustee could recover in fraudulent transfer proceeding, plan required to provide that, if chapter 13 trustee brought such a proceeding, any recovery would be distributed to unsecured creditors); *In re* Johnson, 446 B.R. 921 (Bankr. W.D. Wis. 2011) (test required likely proceeds of preference proceedings to be included).

71 *In re* Locklear, 386 B.R. 911 (Bankr. S.D. Ga. 2007) (permitting deduction of hypothetical costs of sale and trustee commission; *In re* Delbrugge, 347 B.R. 536 (Bankr. N.D. W. Va. 2006); *In re* Dixon, 140 B.R. 945 (Bankr. W.D.N.Y. 1992) (ten percent cost of sale of real estate could be deducted from market value); *In re* Rivera, 116 B.R. 17, 18 (Bankr. D. P.R. 1990); *In re* Hieb, 88 B.R. 1019 (Bankr. D.S.D. 1988); *In re* Barth, 83 B.R. 204 (Bankr. D. Conn. 1983); 8 Collier on Bankruptcy ¶ 1325.05[2][d] (16th ed.). *See also In re* Hardy, 755 F.2d 75, 77, 78 (6th Cir. 1985) (implicitly accepting administrative costs of liquidation as part of hypothetical liquidation analysis).

A few districts have adopted informal rules allowing a certain percentage to be used as an estimate for costs of liquidation. *See also In re* Taunton, 306 B.R. 1 (M.D. Ala. 2004) (valuation of debtors' interest in property being sold to their son under a lease-purchase agreement had to take into account the value of son's interest under the contract).

In chapter 7 estates with small amounts of assets, the trustee fees and costs under section 326 often consume most of the assets.

72 *In re* Young, 153 B.R. 886 (Bankr. D. Neb. 1993); *In re* Dixon, 140 B.R. 945 (Bankr. W.D.N.Y. 1992); *In re* Card, 114 B.R. 226 (Bankr. N.D. Cal. 1990) (because the estate is assessed with a capital gains tax if it sells the property, the result is that when property has appreciated, but most of its value can be exempted, the debtor gains a "super homestead" exemption). *See* 26 U.S.C. § 1398 (taxation of a chapter 7 estate). *See also In re* Barden, 105 F.3d 821 (2d Cir. 1997) (trustee not permitted to use debtor's one time capital gains tax exclusion or stepped-up basis that was available to debtor for sale of debtor's principal residence); *In re* Winch, 226 B.R. 591 (Bankr. S.D. Ohio 1998) (trustee could not use debtor's capital gains exclusion even though it is no longer a one-time exclusion, because it was meant to make funds available for taxpayers' future living expenses). *But see In re* Popa, 238 B.R. 395 (N.D. Ill. 1999) (trustee can take debtor's capital gains exclusion for personal residence, which is no longer a one-time exclusion but may be claimed every two years); *In re* Kerr, 237 B.R. 488 (W.D. Wash. 1999) (same).

73 11 U.S.C. § 726(c). *See In re* Raynard, 354 B.R. 834 (B.A.P. 9th Cir. 2006) (plan paying 100% to joint creditors who could reach entireties property and smaller amount to other creditors did not unfairly discriminate); *In re* Chandler, 148 B.R. 13 (Bankr. E.D.N.C. 1992) (because section 522(b)(2)(B) permits exemption of entireties property from creditors not holding claims against both spouses, plan paying one-hundred percent to joint claims and 9.6% to non-joint claims satisfied best interests test).

74 *See In re* Weiss, 4 B.R. 327 (Bankr. S.D.N.Y. 1980) (court should look only to claims filed as of section 341 meeting in applying test).

75 *In re* Hardy, 755 F.2d 75 (6th Cir. 1985) (confirmation denied when unsecured creditors who would have received one-hundred percent payment in chapter 7 case were not provided interest in addition to one-hundred percent payment in chapter 13 plan); *In re* Beguelin, 220 B.R. 94 (B.A.P. 9th Cir. 1998) (unsecured creditor entitled to interest on claim when it would have received interest in chapter 7 liquidation). *See also In re* Williams, 3 B.R. 728 (Bankr. N.D. Ill. 1980).

However, unless the present value of payments which an unsecured creditor, whether priority or non-priority, will receive is less than the amount it would receive in a liquidation case under chapter 7, there is no requirement that "present value payments," that is, interest, be paid over and above the creditor's claim. *In re* Young, 61 B.R. 150 (Bankr. S.D. Ind. 1986).

12.3.3 Use of the Good Faith Test Prior to the Enactment of the Section 1325(b) Disposable Income Test

When the Code first went into effect, many courts were dissatisfied that the best interests of creditors test looked only to the debtor's assets and not to income. Faced with plans proposing little or no payment to unsecured creditors from debtors who clearly had sufficient income to make substantial payments, they devised a wide variety of standards for confirming plans, under the general standard of section 1325(a)(3) that the plan be proposed in good faith. These standards often required "substantial" or "meaningful" payments to creditors holding unsecured claims; in one court, no plan proposing less than seventy-percent payment of such claims was approved.[76]

At the other end of the spectrum, many courts refused to view the good faith test as having any relevance to the amount paid to unsecured creditors. These courts, and most commentators,[77] looked to the more specific language of section 1325(a)(4) as being dispositive of what unsecured creditors must be paid. They pointed out that, although references in the legislative history of the Code mentioned Congressional intent to encourage or enable debtors to make substantial payments to unsecured creditors, there was no indication whatsoever that this was to be required.

The cases refusing to apply the good faith test to the amount paid under the plan also relied on a somewhat more substantial body of case law interpreting the term "good faith" under the prior Bankruptcy Act. These cases[78] pointed to a line of opinions under several chapters of that Act, holding "good faith" to have a narrower meaning.[79] Those opinions did not permit the "good faith" test to preclude taking advantage of the plain provisions of a statute. Rather, they held that good faith means honesty in fact, and the absence of extraordinary circumstances such as fraud, malfeasance or concealment of assets.[80] It appears to be conceded by all parties that this is the meaning of "good faith" in chapter 11 proceedings, and that mere "selfishness" or acting in one's own enlightened self-interest does not constitute bad faith.[81]

In addition, some of the courts that totally rejected use of the good faith test as a quantitative measure of payments of unsecured claims looked to the practical consequences. Perhaps most importantly for low-income debtors, requiring meaningful or substantial payments threatened to become a barrier to the other benefits of chapter 13, such as the right to cure defaults or the right to "cram down"[82] as to secured creditors.[83] Low-income debtors could have been found, generally, to be too poor to be filing in good faith.

In view of these conditions, some courts found that, at least if the chapter 13 plan served any special rehabilitative purpose, meaningful payments to unsecured creditors should not be required of debtors who are unable to make them.[84] In a similar vein, other courts found that when no payments were to be made to any creditors, the case was merely a disguised liquidation, and there was no reason to allow it to proceed under chapter 13.[85] Some of these courts dismissed or converted such cases on jurisdictional grounds.[86] Presumably, most of these courts would have agreed that when the debtor makes some legitimate use of chapter 13, such as saving a home from foreclosure or providing for other payments to secured creditors, a chapter 13 case is permissible even if the debtor proposes no payments to unsecured creditors.

The courts, however, differed on what was a legitimate use and what was an abuse of chapter 13. A good number held that it was an abuse of chapter 13 to obtain a discharge of debts not dischargeable under chapter 7 without substantial payment of such debts.[87] A roughly equal number, though, held that such

---

76 *See generally* Conrad K. Cyr, *The Chapter 13 "Good Faith" Tempest: An Analysis And Proposal For Change*, 55 Am. Bankr. L. J. 271 (1981).

77 *See, e.g.*, Biery, *Debt Adjustment under Chapter 13 of the Bankruptcy Reform Act of 1978*, 11 St. Mary's L.J. 473, 489 (1979); Kaplan, *Chapter 13 of the Bankruptcy Reform Act of 1978: An Attractive Alternative*, 28 DePaul L. Rev. 1045, 1051 (1979); Joe Lee, *Chapter 13 nee Chapter XIII*, 53 Am. Bankr. L.J. 303, 319 (1979); Merrick, *Chapter 13 of the Bankruptcy Reform Act of 1978*, 56 Denv. L.J. 585, 615 (1979).

78 *See, e.g.*, *In re* Harland, 3 B.R. 597 (Bankr. D. Neb. 1980); *In re* Cloutier, 3 B.R. 584 (Bankr. D. Colo. 1980).

79 *See, e.g.*, Sumida v. Yumen, 409 F.2d 654 (9th Cir. 1969); Gonzalez Hernandez v. Borgas, 343 F.2d 802 (1st Cir. 1965); *In re* Pine Hill Collieries Co., 46 F. Supp. 669 (Bankr. E.D. Pa. 1942). *See also* Neustadter, *Consumer Insolvency Counseling for California in the 1980s*, 19 Santa Clara L. Rev. 817, 910 n.345 (1979).

80 *In re* Wiggles, 7 B.R. 373 (Bankr. N.D. Ga. 1980); *In re* Thacker, 6 B.R. 861 (Bankr. W.D. Va. 1980); *In re* Cloutier, 3 B.R. 584 (Bankr. D. Colo. 1980); *In re* Keckler, 3 B.R. 155 (Bankr. N.D. Ohio 1980).

Several courts have applied this meaning of good faith to refuse confirmation of plans which smacked of fraud. *See, e.g.*, *In re* Lockwood, 5 B.R. 294 (Bankr. S.D. Fla. 1980); *In re* Tanke, 4 B.R. 339 (Bankr. D. Colo. 1980); *In re* Ballard, 4 B.R. 271 (Bankr. E.D. Va. 1980).

81 Kane v. John-Manville Corp., 843 F.2d 636, 649 (2d Cir. 1988); *In re* Sun Country Dev., Inc., 764 F.2d 406 (5th Cir. 1985). See 7 Collier on Bankruptcy ¶ 1129.02[3] (16th ed.) (discussing the meaning of "good faith" in 11 U.S.C. § 1129(a)(3), the provision which parallels the chapter 13 good-faith test).

82 See Chapter 11, *supra*, for a discussion of these rights.

83 *See In re* Roy, 5 B.R. 611 (Bankr. M.D. Ala. 1980); *In re* Moss, 5 B.R. 123 (Bankr. M.D. Tenn. 1980); *In re* Cloutier, 3 B.R. 584 (Bankr. D. Colo. 1980).

84 *In re* Stollenwerck, 8 B.R. 297 (M.D. Ala. 1981); *In re* Zellmer, 6 B.R. 497 (Bankr. N.D. Ill. 1980); *In re* Johnson, 6 B.R. 34 (Bankr. N.D. Ill. 1980); *In re* Roy, 5 B.R. 611 (Bankr. M.D. Ala. 1980); *In re* Bellgraph, 4 B.R. 421 (Bankr. W.D.N.Y. 1980).

85 *See, e.g.*, *In re* Terry, 630 F.2d 634 (8th Cir. 1980) (plan with no payments to any creditor cannot be confirmed, and debtor unable to make any payments is ineligible under 11 U.S.C. § 109(e), but there are no minimum percentages necessary); *In re* Wiggles, 7 B.R. 373 (Bankr. N.D. Ga. 1980). *See also In re* Seman, 4 B.R. 568 (Bankr. S.D.N.Y. 1980). *But see In re* Hardy, 56 B.R. 95 (Bankr. N.D. Ala. 1985) (plan could be confirmed despite fact that no creditor would receive any payment due to the fact that no creditor had filed a claim).

86 *In re* Wiggles, 7 B.R. 373 (Bankr. N.D. Ga. 1980).

87 *See, e.g.*, *In re* Brown, 7 B.R. 529 (Bankr. S.D.N.Y. 1980); *In re* DeSimone, 6 B.R. 89 (Bankr. S.D.N.Y. 1980); *In re* Bloom, 3 B.R.

use of the broader discharge was contemplated by Congress and was not, in itself, an abuse constituting bad faith.[88] These latter cases were, and continue to be, the better reasoned insofar as they effectuate the differences in the discharge available under chapter 7 and chapter 13 as enacted by Congress.[89] Generally, the appellate courts held that the fact that the plan will discharge debts not dischargeable in a chapter 7 case can only be considered as a bar to confirmation if it is combined with other factors showing abuse in the court's consideration of all of the circumstances.[90] The same rationale applies to the dischargeability of debts in chapter 13 which have been specifically held nondischargeable in a prior chapter 7 case.[91]

One thing nearly all courts have agreed on is that a creditor that holds an unsecured claim that is not dischargeable in chapter 7 may not argue that, because its claim will be discharged in chapter 13, it will receive less than it would receive in a chapter 7 liquidation. The cases pointed to the plain language of section 1325(a)(4), which considers the amount the creditor "would be paid" in the chapter 7 case, and not whether the creditor would still have the right to pursue a nondischargeable claim after the case.[92]

Finally, a substantial number of courts held that whether unsecured creditors receive meaningful payments is a component of the good faith test, but that the court must consider all of the facts and circumstances of each case to determine if chapter 13 has been abused.[93] The circumstances that various courts listed as relevant included the following:

- Whether the percentage paid to unsecured creditors is "meaningful";[94]
- The ability of the debtor to pay;
- Whether the debtor is making his or her best effort;[95]
- Whether the debtor is making an "honest and sincere effort";
- The present and potential earnings of the debtor;
- Whether the payments meet a "rule of thumb" requirement of ten percent of take home pay;[96]
- The length of the proposed plan;[97]
- Whether the debtor has been in bankruptcy before, especially if the six-year bar to a chapter 7 case is applicable;
- Whether the debtor is attempting to obtain a discharge of debts not dischargeable under chapter 7;
- The amount and type of debt involved;
- The extent to which secured claims are involved;
- The relation of attorney fees and administrative costs to the amount paid to unsecured creditors;
- Whether the debtor has created preferences or preferred classes of creditors;
- The availability of property that could be liquidated; and
- Whether the case is a disguised chapter 7 case.

Thus, consideration of all the circumstances, which apparently appealed to many bankruptcy courts as a compromise between the extreme positions on this question, meant different things to different judges. A decision to weigh all of the circumstances did not yield a clear and discernible standard by which the debtor could predict whether a plan would be approved or whether a chapter 13 case would be worthwhile. Moreover, it burdened the courts with innumerable subjective questions which, to be dealt with fairly, would take a great deal of time and expense to decide.

Ultimately, most of the courts of appeals addressed the good faith issue. The District of Columbia Circuit Court of Appeals held that the good faith standard is not aimed at the level of repayment to unsecured creditors at all and is directed only at honesty of intention.[98] The other circuit courts settled on a fairly liberal version of the "all of the circumstances" compromise, the percentage of payment on unsecured claims is one factor to examine, but it is never the only factor.[99] All of these

---

467 (Bankr. C.D. Cal. 1980); *In re* Cole, 3 B.R. 346 (Bankr. S.D. W. Va. 1980).

88 *In re* Street, 55 B.R. 763 (B.A.P. 9th Cir. 1985). *See, e.g., In re* Easley, 72 B.R. 948 (Bankr. M.D. Tenn. 1987); *In re* Thorson, 6 B.R. 678 (Bankr. D.S.D. 1980); *In re* McBride, 4 B.R. 389 (Bankr. M.D. Ala. 1980); *In re* Bonder, 3 B.R. 623 (Bankr. E.D.N.Y. 1980); *In re* Peoro, Bankr. L. Rep. (CCH) ¶ 67,413 (Bankr. N.D. Cal. 1980); *In re* Keckler, 3 B.R. 155 (Bankr. N.D. Ohio 1980). *See also* Neufeld v. Freeman, 794 F.2d 149 (4th Cir. 1986).

89 *See* § 15.4.1, *infra*; *In re* Chaffin, 816 F.2d 1070 (5th Cir. 1987), *modified*, 836 F.2d 215 (5th Cir. 1988). *Compare* 11 U.S.C. § 1328(a) *with* 11 U.S.C. § 523(a).

90 *In re* Chaffin, 816 F.2d 1070 (5th Cir. 1987), *modified*, 836 F.2d 215 (5th Cir. 1988); Educ. Assistance Corp. v. Zellner, 827 F.2d 1222 (8th Cir. 1987); *In re* Rimgale, 669 F.2d 426 (7th Cir. 1982). *See also In re* Rasmussen, 888 F.2d 703 (10th Cir. 1989) (when debtor who originally had debts in excess of chapter 13 debt limits had discharged all debts, except one debt held nondischargeable in chapter 7 case, and two weeks later filed chapter 13 case proposing to pay 1.5% of debt not discharged in chapter 7, which was only debt listed in chapter 13 statement, plan was not filed in good faith and was manipulation of the bankruptcy process).

91 *In re* Chaffin, 816 F.2d 1070 (5th Cir. 1987), *modified*, 836 F.2d 215 (5th Cir. 1988).

92 *See, e.g., In re* Klein, 57 B.R. 818 (B.A.P. 9th Cir. 1985).

93 *See In re* Polak, 9 B.R. 502 (W.D. Mich. 1981); *In re* Melroy, 7 B.R. 513 (E.D. Cal. 1980); *In re* Burrell, 6 B.R. 360 (N.D. Cal. 1980); *In re* Iacovoni, 2 B.R. 256 (Bankr. D. Utah 1980).

94 A few of the courts would have gone no further in their analysis of "all the circumstances" if this percentage were not also "substantial," regardless of the other circumstances. *See, e.g., In re* Iacovoni, 2 B.R. 256 (Bankr. D. Utah 1980). These holdings are squarely contrary to the 1984 amendments instituting an "ability-to-pay" test, discussed in § 12.3.4, *infra*.

95 This test seems at variance with the language of the statute which clearly distinguishes "good faith" and "best effort" as two different standards. *See* 11 U.S.C. § 727(a)(9).

96 *See In re* Curtis, 2 B.R. 43 (Bankr. W.D. Mo. 1979).
This test also is contrary to the new ability-to-pay test if debtors cannot afford ten percent dividends. *See* § 12.3.4, *infra*.

97 *Compare In re* Henry, 4 B.R. 220 (Bankr. M.D. Tenn. 1980) (four-month plan denied confirmation) *with In re* Poff, 7 B.R. 15 (Bankr. S.D. Ohio 1980) (denying confirmation to five year plan as too long unless at least seventy percent of unsecured claims paid).

98 Barnes v. Whelan, 689 F.2d 193 (D.C. Cir. 1982).

99 *In re* Smith, 286 F.3d 461 (7th Cir. 2002) (the fact that debts not dischargeable in chapter 7 and debtor could pay only ten percent of debt through plan not sufficient to find lack of good faith); *In re* Hines, 723 F.2d 333 (3d Cir. 1983); Flygare v. Boulder, 709 F.2d

§ 12.3.4   *Consumer Bankruptcy Law and Practice*

decisions left open the possibility of plans providing zero or nominal payment plans to unsecured creditors in cases in which they are necessary and appropriate to achieve debtors' goals. Although the issue of repayment to unsecured creditors eventually ceased to be a major factor in courts' determinations of good faith, other factors discussed in these decisions continue to be considered in courts' good faith analyses.[100] Since the enactment of the 2005 amendments to section 1325(b) as discussed below, some chapter 13 trustees and unsecured creditors have attempted to resurrect the argument that good faith requires debtors to pay more than is required by the disposable income test. The vast majority of courts have rejected these renewed attempts to reframe disposable income objections as good faith objections.[101]

12.3.4 The Ability to Pay (Disposable Income) Test

12.3.4.1 Introduction

Some of the issues that so troubled the courts that interpreted the good faith test under the original 1978 Act were resolved by the 1984 amendments to the Bankruptcy Code. In a new section 1325(b), courts were given express instructions regarding whether and how to take into account the debtor's income. At the same time, by adding a new subsection separate and apart from the good faith standard, Congress made clear its intent that the good faith test revert to its more traditional meaning, which did not concern the size of the debtor's payments.[102]

Section 1325(b) was amended in 2005 to decrease the discretion of the court in determining disposable income. The amended provisions are more specific regarding income and expenses that may be considered by the court and, for higher income debtors, they import the chapter 7 means test formula to determine a debtor's expenses and may require a plan of greater length.[103] These new rules have given rise to a substantial amount of case law and will undoubtedly be the subject of varying interpretations for years to come.

Section 1325(b) provides that if (and only if)[104] an unsecured creditor or the chapter 13 trustee objects to confirmation of the plan, the court must determine whether the plan either 1) pays the objecting creditor in full or 2) commits to payment of unsecured creditors all of the debtor's "disposable income" for the "applicable commitment period," which is defined in section 1325(a)(4).

"Disposable income" in turn is defined as that portion of the "current monthly income" received by the debtor (other than child support payments, foster care payments, or reasonably necessary disability payments for a dependent child) that is not reasonably necessary for the maintenance or support of the debtor or dependents of the debtor.[105] If a debtor is engaged in business, "disposable income" also excludes funds necessary for the continuation, preservation, and operation of the business.[106] However, although the test requires payment into the plan of the amount of disposable income for the "applicable commitment period," that amount may be paid over a longer period of time (but not in excess of five years), if the debtor chooses to do so, for example, in order to continue otherwise impermissible expenses or to live without the strictures of such a tight budget.[107]

Section 1325(b) makes clear that a debtor need not have enough income to make substantial payments or, indeed, any payments to unsecured creditors. If a debtor has no disposable

---

1344 (10th Cir. 1983); *In re* Kitchens, 702 F.2d 885 (11th Cir. 1983); *In re* Estus, 695 F.2d 311 (8th Cir. 1982); Deans v. O'Donnell, 692 F.2d 968 (4th Cir. 1982); *In re* Goeb, 675 F.2d 1386 (9th Cir. 1982) (one percent plan confirmable unless evidence of bad faith); *In re* Rimgale, 669 F.2d 426 (7th Cir. 1982).

100 *See* § 12.3.5, *infra*.

101 *In re* Richall, 470 B.R. 245 (Bankr. D.N.H. 2012) (debtors had not filed plan or case in bad faith just because they were paying creditors in full through lower monthly payments than those that trustee argued they could afford); *In re* Sweet, 428 B.R. 917 (Bankr. M.D. Ga. 2010) (rejecting trustee argument that debtors should surrender home to reduce housing costs and pay more to creditors); *In re* Austin, 372 B.R. 668 (Bankr. D. Vt. 2007); *In re* Farrar-Johnson, 353 B.R. 224 (Bankr. N.D. Ill. 2006); *In re* Barr, 341 B.R. 181 (Bankr. M.D.N.C. 2006). *See also* § 12.3.4.4, *infra*. *But see In re* McGillis 370 B.R. 720 (Bankr. W.D. Mich. 2007) (denying confirmation of debtor's plan which satisfied mechanical disposable income test of section 1325(b), but did not satisfy good faith requirement as Schedules I and J demonstrated debtor had greater ability to pay).

102 *In re* Keach, 243 B.R. 851 (B.A.P. 1st Cir. 2000) (1984 disposable income amendment makes clear that meaning of good faith is simple honesty of purpose); *In re* Red, 60 B.R. 113 (Bankr. E.D. Tenn. 1986); 8 Collier On Bankruptcy ¶ 1325.04[1] (16th ed.). *But see* Neufeld v. Freeman, 794 F.2d 149 (4th Cir. 1986) (looking to some of the factors it had listed prior to 1984 amendments, though not to percentage of payments to unsecured creditors). It is not clear whether the court in *Neufeld* considered the effect of the 1984 amendments.

103 *See* § 12.3.4.4.6, *supra*.

104 D'Elia v. Waage (*In re* D'Elia), 2011 WL 1326819 (M.D. Fla. Apr. 6, 2011) (improper to deny confirmation when there was no objection, rejecting trustee's claim that he had "standing objection" based on negative recommendation); *In re* Benson, 352 B.R. 740 (Bankr. E.D.N.C. 2006) (when trustee agreed to plan, court could not consider disposable income test in absence of a creditor objection).

105 11 U.S.C. § 1325(b)(2). *See also In re* Gray, 2009 WL 2475017 (Bankr. N.D. W. Va. Aug. 11, 2009) (living companion of 20 years found to be dependent in chapter 11 case).

"Dependent" may include a debtor's aging parent, even if the debtor provides less than half the parent's support. *In re* Tracey, 66 B.R. 63 (Bankr. D. Md. 1986). *See also In re* Bauer, 309 B.R. 47 (Bankr. D. Idaho 2004) (mother in a different state found a dependent based on debtor's ten years of providing assistance, the amount of such assistance, the use to which it was put, the mother's financial needs and lack of income, and the lack of other sibling support, even though mother not claimed as tax dependent).

106 11 U.S.C. § 1325(b)(2)(B).

107 *In re* Mendoza, 274 B.R. 522 (Bankr. D. Ariz. 2002) (debtors could continue retirement contributions because plan extending more than thirty-six months paid unsecured creditors amount equal to debtors' disposable income for thirty-six months); *In re* Elrod, 270 B.R. 258 (Bankr. E.D. Tenn. 2001).

income as computed under section 1325(b), then a plan may be confirmed without payments to unsecured creditors if the other requirements of chapter 13 are met.[108] The legislative history of the original section 1325(b)[109] expressly states that the so-called zero payment plan is permissible in certain circumstances,[110] and nothing in the legislative history of the 2005 amendments suggests otherwise.

Overall, the ability-to-pay test has largely laid to rest problems which had made chapter 13 virtually unavailable to low-income debtors in some districts. It should now be clear that, if the other specific requirements of chapter 13 are met, no debtor is too poor to file a chapter 13 case simply because the debtor cannot afford to pay general unsecured creditors. However, notwithstanding the clear dictates of the statute, some trustees and judges still attempt to enforce informal rules requiring minimum payments to unsecured creditors.

12.3.4.2 Procedure for Objections Based upon Section 1325(b)

The procedure for objections to confirmation of a plan under section 1325(b) is the same as that for other objections to confirmation and is thus governed by Federal Rule of Bankruptcy Procedure 3015(g). That rule requires that objections be filed with the court and served on the debtor and the trustee. They must be timely filed, within a time fixed by the court.[111] Normally, the objections will be based upon the debtor's Statement of Current Monthly Income and Calculation of Applicable Commitment Period and Disposable Income,[112] and often the debtor's schedules of current income and expenditures. It therefore behooves the debtor to complete those portions of the forms carefully, with both the ability-to-pay and feasibility tests[113] in mind. Because only the trustee or the holder of an allowed unsecured claim may file an objection, a creditor who has not filed a claim does not have standing to object to confirmation.[114]

Once an objection is filed, the creditor will have at least an initial burden of production.[115] Assuming that burden is met, the debtor may defeat the objection by proving one of two things. First, the debtor may show that an objecting creditor will be paid in full. Alternatively, the plan can be confirmed if the debtor is committing to unsecured creditors all of his or her "disposable income" for the applicable commitment period.

12.3.4.3 Full Payment Test

Obviously, the full payment test is met if all unsecured claims are to be paid in full. It may also be met if the objecting claimant can be separately classified and paid in full, even if other creditors will not receive full payment.[116] Occasionally, it may be worthwhile to amend the plan to add such classification to satisfy the troublesome creditor, especially if the debtor anticipates difficulty in meeting the alternative disposable income standard. However, if the trustee objects to confirmation, the "full payment" test will likely require that all allowed unsecured claims be paid in full. Even then, though, it is likely that only full payment of the original claim is necessary, and not the payment of additional interest to give the creditor the present value of its money.[117] And, if the plan provides for full payment, the debtors may make such payment in monthly installments lower than those otherwise dictated by the disposable income test for debtors who are not making full payment.[118]

12.3.4.4 Disposable Income Test

12.3.4.4.1 Use of "current monthly income"

If an objection under section 1325(b) is filed and the full payment standard cannot be met, the court must then determine whether the debtor has committed to unsecured creditors all of her "projected disposable income" for the applicable commitment period.

One major change in the disposable income test enacted by the 2005 amendments is the use of "current monthly income" as the basis for determining disposable income. For all debtors, disposable income is based on "current monthly income," which is defined in section 101 of the Code as the average of the last six months income received from all sources by the

---

108 *In re* Guzman, 345 B.R. 640 (Bankr. E.D. Wis. 2006) (overruling trustee's objection to plan when debtor's Official Form 22C showed no projected disposable income available for unsecured creditors); *In re* Alexander, 344 B.R. 742 (Bankr. E.D.N.C. 2006) (confirming zero percent plans when debtors had no disposable income based on formula in section 1325(b)).

109 The ability-to-pay test was adopted from a proposal made by the National Bankruptcy Conference. *See Oversight Hearings on Personal Bankruptcy Before the Subcomm. on Monopolies and Commercial Law of the House Comm. on the Judiciary*, 97th Cong. 181–223 (1981–1982).

110 *Id.*, at 223.

111 *In re* Gaona, 290 B.R. 381 (Bankr. S.D. Cal. 2003) (objections untimely under local rule); *In re* Harris, 275 B.R. 850 (Bankr. S.D. Ohio 2002) (objections filed after deadline established in clerk's notice were untimely); *In re* Carbone, 254 B.R. 1 (Bankr. D. Mass. 2000) (objection untimely when filed after deadline set by local rule).

112 Official Form 22C (reprinted in Appx. D, *infra*).

113 *See* § 12.5, *infra*.

114 *In re* Sheppard, 173 B.R. 799 (Bankr. N.D. Ga. 1994); *In re* Stewart, 46 B.R. 73 (Bankr. D. Or. 1985).

A creditor who has not filed a proof of claim may however still have standing to object to a debtor's plan on grounds other than sufficiency of distribution under section 1325(b). *In re* Jensen, 369 B.R. 210 (Bankr. E.D. Pa. 2007).

115 Educ. Assistance Corp. v. Zellner, 827 F.2d 1222 (8th Cir. 1987); *In re* Fries, 68 B.R. 676 (Bankr. E.D. Pa. 1986).

116 *See* § 12.4, *infra*, for a discussion of permissible classifications of claims.

117 *In re* Stewart-Harrel, 443 B.R. 219 (Bankr. N.D. Ga. 2011); *In re* Eaton, 130 B.R. 74 (Bankr. S.D. Iowa 1991). *See* 8 Collier on Bankruptcy ¶ 1325.11[3] (16th ed.).

118 *In re* Johnson, 2011 WL 1671536 (Bankr. N.D. Iowa May 3, 2011); *In re* Stewart-Harrel, 443 B.R. 219 (Bankr. N.D. Ga. 2011). *But see In re* Moffet, 455 B.R. 718 (Bankr. N.D. Iowa 2011) (promise of full payment cannot rely on speculative sources of funds).

debtor (or, in a joint case, by the debtor and the debtor's spouse), derived during that period,[119] with certain adjustments.[120] An alternative period for determining current monthly income, discussed below, may be established by the court if the debtor has not filed schedule I.[121]

Current monthly income is defined to exclude benefits received under the Social Security Act and certain other payments.[122] The definition also makes clear that the income of other household members, including a non-debtor spouse, can only be considered to the extent that it is regularly contributed to household expenses of the debtor or the debtor's dependents.[123]

After the debtor's current monthly income is calculated, section 1325(b) allows debtors to subtract certain specified exclusions[124] and reasonably necessary expenses.[125] The result is then projected in accordance with the "applicable commitment period" to determine the amount of disposable income that must be paid to unsecured creditors.[126]

The perceived incongruity between the use of historical income figures in the definition of current monthly income and the use of the term "projected disposable income" in section 1325(b)(1)(B) has troubled several courts.[127] Contrary to the plain language of the statute, which merely requires courts to project historical figures,[128] these courts have held that "projected disposable income" must take into account the debtor's anticipated future income and, in some cases, future expenses.[129] A few of these courts have erroneously used the word "projected" as an excuse to calculate the debtor's disposable income as simply the difference between Schedule I income and Schedule J expenses. However, many courts recognize that this approach not only fails to account for secured debts that must be paid through the plan (because Schedule I and J do not permit deduction for items such as mortgage arrearages), it also reads out of the statute the exclusions from current monthly income and disposable income that Congress enacted.

Most of the courts that believe the word "projected" dictates some adjustment have decided to disregard the debtor's prior income or expenses if circumstances have changed in a way that is likely to be long-lasting. Because the term "disposable income" is included within "projected disposable income," they have still generally applied the same methodology in determining projected disposable income, using the exclusions and formulas that would otherwise be used, but based on the debtor's expected circumstances going forward. Such decisions acknowledge that the provisions defining disposable income would otherwise be rendered meaningless. A number of courts have adopted the approach of adjusting the debtor's income to take into account circumstances at the time of confirmation, while retaining the statutory exclusions from income and, if applicable, the means test formula for calculating expenses.[130]

---

119 Income derived from an earlier period, such as commissions or other funds based on earlier earnings, is not included. Debtors in a joint case cannot do the means test calculations separately, even if they have separate households. Harman v. Fink (*In re* Harman), 435 B.R. 596 (B.A.P. 8th Cir. 2010).

This rule may dictate filing separate cases for such debtors.

120 See § 13.4.3.2, *infra*.

121 11 U.S. § 101(10A)(A)(ii). See also § 13.4.3.2.1, *infra*.

122 11 U.S.C. § 101(10)(B). *See In re* Ragos, 2012 WL 5292949 (5th Cir. Oct 29, 2012); *In re* Cranmer, 2012 WL 5235365 (10th Cir. Oct 24, 2012); Baud v. Carroll, 634 F.3d 327 (6th Cir. 2011); *In re* Welsh, 465 B.R. 843 (B.A.P. 9th Cir. 2012) (same); Fink v. Thompson (*In re* Thompson), 439 B.R. 140 (B.A.P. 8th Cir. 2010) (debtors not required to devote Social Security income to plan; considering it lack of good faith would render definition of current monthly income meaningless); *In re* Bartelini, 434 B.R. 285 (Bankr. N.D.N.Y. 2010) (debtor could not be required to devote Social Security income to plan); *In re* Wilson, 397 B.R. 299 (Bankr. M.D.N.C. 2008) (Social Security income of non-filing spouse not included in calculation of debtor's projected disposable income); *In re* Barfknecht, 378 B.R. 154 (Bankr. W.D. Tex. 2007) (rejecting trustee's objection to confirmation on basis that plan lacked good faith due to exclusion of Social Security benefits from projected disposable income); *In re* Upton, 363 B.R. 528 (Bankr. S.D. Ohio 2007) (benefits received under the Social Security Act not considered in determining projected disposable income). *See also* § 13.4.3.2.7, *infra*.

123 11 U.S.C. § 101(10)(B). *See In re* Vollen, 426 B.R. 359 (Bankr. D. Kan. 2010) (amounts withheld from nondebtor spouse's pay for taxes, repayment of pension loan, and contributions to retirement plan were not regularly contributed for household expenses); *In re* Clemons, 2009 WL 1733867 (Bankr. C.D. Ill. June 16, 2009) (amounts paid by nondebtor spouse, who was not dependent of debtor, for mortgage and car payments on property titled only in her name were not paid for household expenses of debtor and dependents); *In re* Quarterman, 342 B.R. 647 (Bankr. M.D. Fla. 2006) (objecting trustee failed to meet burden of showing that debtor's spouse contributed amount sufficient to require increase in debtor's proposed plan payments).

See Chapter 13, *infra*, for further discussion of current monthly income.

124 See § 12.3.4.4.3, *supra*.

125 See § 12.3.4.4.5, *supra*.

126 *In re* Kagenveama, 541 F.3d 868 (9th Cir. 2008); *In re* Girodes, 350 B.R. 31 (Bankr. M.D.N.C. 2006) (disposable income and projected disposable income are one and the same and defined by section 1325(b)(2)); *In re* Rotunda, 349 B.R. 324 (Bankr. N.D.N.Y. 2006); *In re* Guzman, 345 B.R. 640 (Bankr. E.D. Wis. 2006) (overruling trustee's objection to plan when debtor's Official Form 22C showed no projected disposable income available for unsecured creditors); *In re* Alexander, 344 B.R. 742 (Bankr. E.D.N.C. 2006) (confirming zero percent plans when debtors had no disposable income based on formula in section 1325(b)); *In re* Barr, 341 B.R. 181 (Bankr. M.D.N.C. 2006).

127 *In re* Kibbe, 361 B.R. 302, 314 (B.A.P. 1st Cir. 2007) (projected disposable income had to be based on debtor's anticipated income over term of plan). *See also In re* LaSota, 351 B.R. 56 (Bankr. W.D.N.Y. 2006); *In re* Dew, 344 B.R. 655 (Bankr. N.D. Ala. 2006).

128 *In re* Kagenveama, 541 F.3d 868 (9th Cir. 2008); *In re* Musselman, 394 B.R. 801 (E.D.N.C. 2008).

129 *In re* Nowlin, 576 F.3d 258 (5th Cir. 2009) (court may adjust based on evidence of present or reasonably certain future events that will substantially change the debtor's financial situation); McCarty v. Lasowski (*In re* Lasowski), 575 F.3d 815 (8th Cir. 2009) (taking into account end of loan repayment shortly after plan commenced); *In re* Lanning, 545 F.3d 1269 (10th Cir. 2008) (court properly adjusted for decline in debtor's income), *cert. granted*, 2009 WL 273221 (U.S. Nov. 2, 2009), *aff'd*, 130 S. Ct. 2464 (2010); *In re* Frederickson, 545 F.3d 652 (8th Cir. 2008).

130 *See, e.g., In re* Teixeira, 358 B.R. 484 (Bankr. D.N.H. 2006) (citing other cases).

Some courts have also held that when there has been a permanent change in the debtor's expenses, for example due to the surrender of property that is collateral for a secured debt, that change should also be taken into account.[131]

The Supreme Court resolved this issue in *Hamilton v. Lanning*.[132] The Court held that the word "projected" gave the bankruptcy court the flexibility to adjust the debtor's current monthly income to take into account changes in the debtor's income that are known or virtually certain at the time of confirmation. The Court found that the ordinary meaning of the term "projected" encompassed more than simply multiplying the debtor's current monthly income by the number of months in the applicable commitment period and had a meaning that could take into account known or virtually certain changes in income.

However, the Court made clear that such adjustments to the statutory formula for computing disposable income should be made "only in unusual cases" in which there is known or virtually certain information about changes in the components in the formula that are based on actual income.[133] There is no suggestion in the decision that a bankruptcy court can rely on the term "projected" to otherwise deviate from the formula by, for example, including income that the definition of current monthly income excludes, such as social security benefits, or altering expense allowances permitted by the statute.[134]

In the wake of *Lanning*, courts will no doubt adopt a variety of approaches to the issue of how much discretion they have. It seems clear that debtors who have reductions in their income will be able to argue that their payments should be lower than if they were computed based on the definition of current monthly income in Code section 101. Trustees will undoubtedly argue that when income has increased the payments should be higher.[135]

Although the facts of *Lanning* concerned only a change in the debtor's income, the final paragraph of the decision states that the court can also take into account known or virtually certain changes in expenses. As with changes in income, only expense allowances based on the debtor's actual expenses should be subject to adjustment. Expense allowances that are based on amounts specified in the National and Local IRS Standards should control even if they differ from the expense amounts the debtor has listed on Schedule J, since differences between these amounts are not based on a change.

If the debtor's income has decreased at the time the petition is filed, and is unlikely to change, another alternative is to seek permission to delay the filing of Schedule I. The definition of "current monthly income" permits the normal six-month prepetition calculation period to be disregarded if the debtor does not file the schedule of current income required by section 521(a)(2)(B)(ii) (Schedule I) and the court determines current income as of a different date.[136] Thus several courts have permitted debtors who have not filed Schedule I to use a later date for the calculation of current monthly income that takes into account the decrease in income.[137]

In any event, a trustee should not file an objection under section 1325(b) if the debtor is paying all disposable income based on the debtor's income at the time of the petition. Trustees have no legitimate interest in objecting to plans when debtors are paying all that they can truly afford. Thus, unless an unsecured creditor objects, a reasonable plan based on the debtor's true income may be confirmed, because section 1325(b), by its own terms, comes into play only if an objection is filed. Even unsecured creditors are not likely to object. Unsecured creditors rarely have an interest in forcing debtors into chapter 7, which would be the usual result of an objection, especially if debtors are below median income and therefore not subject to the new means test.[138]

12.3.4.4.2 Exclusions from disposable income

12.3.4.4.2.1 Overview

The 2005 amendments also created exclusions from disposable income. As discussed above, there are exclusions in the definition of current monthly income for benefits under the Social Security Act and certain other payments. The definition also makes clear that the income of other household members, including a non-debtor spouse, can be considered only to the extent that it is regularly contributed to household expenses of the debtor or a dependent of the debtor.[139] There are additional exclusions from current monthly income, discussed below, that are applicable only in chapter 13 cases.

---

131 *In re* Turner, 574 F.3d 349 (7th Cir. 2009) (debtor could not deduct secured debt payments on property to be surrendered); *In re* Thomas, 395 B.R. 914 (B.A.P. 6th Cir. 2008) (same).

Other courts permit deduction of amounts that are contractually due on secured debts, even if the property is to be surrendered. *See, e.g., In re* Roberts, 2008 WL 5979832 (D. Nev. Sept. 4, 2008); *In re* Willette, 395 B.R. 308, 327–328 (Bankr. D. Vt. 2008); *In re* Oliver, 2006 WL 2086691, at *3 (Bankr. D. Or. June 29, 2006). They also permit deduction of such amounts regardless of whether the lien will be reduced or eliminated in chapter 13. *In re* Marshall, 407 B.R. 1 (Bankr. D. Mass. 2009).

132 Hamilton v. Lanning, 130 S. Ct. 2464 (2010).
133 Hamilton v. Lanning, 130 S. Ct. 2464, 2475 (2010).
134 *See In re* Ragos, 2012 WL 5292949 (5th Cir. 2012) (*Lanning* does not undermine analysis that social security benefits must be excluded from projected disposable income); *In re* Cranmer, 2012 WL 5235365 (10th Cir. Oct 24, 2012) (bankruptcy court incorrectly applied *Lanning* and erroneously concluded that social security benefits should be included in projected disposable income).
135 *See, e.g., In re* Darrohn, 615 F.3d 470 (6th Cir. 2010) (bankruptcy court failed to consider debtor's change in income and erroneously relied upon current monthly income calculation, which included ninety-day period of debtor's unemployment).

136 11 U.S.C. § 101(10a)(A)(ii).
137 *In re* Dunford, 408 B.R. 489 (Bankr. N.D. Ill. 2009); *In re* Hoff, 402 B.R. 683 (Bankr. E.D.N.C. 2009); *In re* Montgomery, 2008 WL 597180, at *2 (Bankr. M.D.N.C. Mar. 4, 2008).
138 See Chapter 13, *infra*, for discussion of the chapter 7 means test.
139 11 U.S.C. § 101(10A).

12.3.4.4.2.2 Child support, foster care, and similar payments

The definition of disposable income excludes child support payments, foster care payments, or disability payments received for a dependent child to the extent reasonably necessary to be expended for the child.[140] If courts exclude these payments, which may well go to expenses for the debtor's dependents, the debtor's income will be reduced. But courts might exclude expenses for the child to the extent they are covered by these payments. If so, the provision would be rendered almost meaningless. Its main remaining effect would occur only if the payments exceed the child's pro-rata share of family expenses. Then the result would be that payments meant for the child would not be diverted to pay debts or imputed to the expenses of other household members. And courts could not exclude the expenses of the child if the debtor's current monthly income is over the median income, because expenses would be determined under the rigid means test formula, based on household size, as discussed below.[141]

12.3.4.4.2.3 Payments on domestic support obligations

Payments made on domestic support obligations by the debtor that are first payable after the petition is filed are excluded from the definition of disposable income.[142] This amendment simply gives effective priority to current support payments, which were ordinarily deducted from the debtor's budget under pre-2005 law.

12.3.4.4.2.4 Repayments of pension loans and pension contributions

Another important exclusion from disposable income consists of funds used for repayments of pension loans. New section 1322(f) provides that amounts required to repay loans described in section 362(b)(19), which are generally loans from qualified pension plans,[143] shall not constitute disposable income under section 1325(b).[144] This amendment reverses the holdings of most courts prior to the 2005 amendments.[145] It is consistent with the increased protections given by the 2005 Act to retirement savings[146] and the fact that continued collection of such loans (usually through wage withholding) is permitted by section 362(b)(19).[147] It also may be a recognition that debtors have often incurred such loans in attempts to pay other debts, so that repayment of the loans is really repaying an obligation incurred to pay other creditors. Although not all courts agree, the full amount of the monthly loan payment should be deducted in the means test even if the loan will be paid off before the end of the plan.[148] The debtor has no power to reduce the monthly payment on the loan during the chapter 13 case, as could be done with a car loan, so the debtor cannot prorate the loan payments over the plan.

Certain pension or benefit contributions withheld from the debtor's wages by an employer, or received by the debtor from an employer, are also not disposable income for purposes of section 1325(b).[149] There is no requirement that the debtor show these contributions to be reasonable or necessary.[150] Section 541(b)(7), which so provides, does not distinguish between voluntary and involuntary contributions, so it appears to encompass both.[151] The contribution must be to either an Employee Retirement Income Security Act (ERISA) plan, an employee benefit plan which is a governmental plan under section 414(d) of Internal Revenue Code (IRC), a deferred compensation plan under section 457 of the IRC, or a tax-deferred annuity under section 403(b) of the IRC.[152]

12.3.4.4.3 Use of means test expense calculations for debtors with incomes above median income

Perhaps the most dramatic change in the disposable income test is the use of the section 707(b) means test expense calculations for some debtors. New section 1325(b)(3) provides that for debtors whose current monthly income is above the state

---

140 11 U.S.C. § 1325(b)(2).
141 See § 12.3.4.4.3, infra.
142 11 U.S.C. § 1325(b)(2)(A)(i).
143 See Ch. 9, supra.
144 In re Roth, 2010 WL 2485951 (Bankr. D.N.J. June 14, 2010); In re Glisson, 430 B.R. 920 (Bankr. S.D. Ga. 2009); In re Puetz, 370 B.R. 386 (Bankr. D. Kan. 2007); In re Njuguna, 357 B.R. 689 (Bankr. D.N.H. 2006) (funds used for pension loan payments not disposable income); In re Johnson, 346 B.R. 256 (Bankr. S.D. Ga. 2006) (same).
145 See, e.g., Hebbring v. United States Tr., 463 F.3d 902 (9th Cir. 2006) (contributions considered on case-by-case basis under pre-2005 law); In re Anes, 195 F.3d 177 (3d Cir. 1999).
146 See, e.g., 11 U.S.C. § 522(b)(3)(C), 522(d)(12); § 8.3, infra. See also H.R. Rep. No. 109-31, at 63–64 (2005) (available on this treatise's companion website).
147 See Ch. 9, supra.
148 In re Roberts, 2008 WL 4279549 (Bankr. E.D. Pa. Sept. 17, 2008); In re Haley, 354 B.R. 340 (Bankr. D.N.H. 2006); In re Wiggs, 2006 WL 2246432 (Bankr. N.D. Ill. Aug. 4, 2006). See also In re Egan, 458 B.R. 836 (Bankr. E.D. Pa. 2011) (debtors permitted to increase plan contributions once loan payments completed). But see Burden v. Seafort (In re Seafort), 669 F.3d 662 (6th Cir. 2012) (income made available by completion of loan payments must be paid into plan); In re Nowlin, 576 F.3d 258 (5th Cir. 2009) (court can require increased plan payments when loan repaid); In re Lasowski, 575 F.3d 815 (8th Cir. 2009) (only actual amount of payments to be made over plan period can be deducted).
149 11 U.S.C. § 541(b)(7); In re Roth, 2010 WL 2485951 (Bankr. D.N.J. June 14, 2010); In re Glisson, 430 B.R. 920 (Bankr. S.D. Ga. 2009); In re Gibson, 2009 WL 2868445 (Bankr. D. Idaho Aug. 31, 2009) (contributions could be deducted even though debtor had not made any contributions in six months prior to petition); In re Njuguna, 358 B.R. 849 (Bankr. D.N.H. 2007) (funds used for contributions to pension plan not disposable income); In re Johnson, 346 B.R. 256 (Bankr. S.D. Ga. 2006) (same). But see Burden v. Seafort (In re Seafort), 669 F.3d 662 (6th Cir. 2012) (debtors who were not making contributions at beginning of case could deduct contributions begun later, even if the payments resulted from the fact that repayment of a pension loan had been completed); § 12.3.4.4.1, note 123, supra.
150 In re Devilliers, 358 B.R. 849 (Bankr. E.D. La. 2007).
151 In re Devilliers, 358 B.R. 849 (Bankr. E.D. La. 2007).
152 11 U.S.C. § 541(b)(7)(A), (B).

median income for the applicable family size, reasonably necessary expenses are to be calculated using the means test formula found in section 707(b)(2)(A) and (B) in order to determine payments to unsecured creditors. Because this provision is based on the backward-looking current monthly income standard rather than actual income, it may apply to debtors with actual income well below the state median income at the time they file the bankruptcy petition and throughout the plan. The trustee is not compelled to object to a plan that does not meet this standard, and a trustee should not object to a plan, or a later modification of a plan, if it pays all the debtor can truly afford.[153]

At the same time, this provision permits debtors to deduct amounts allowed by the means test, even if they seem excessive to a trustee or creditor[154] and even if they exceed the debtor's actual expenses.[155] Generally, the analysis under the means test should be the same as in chapter 7, which is discussed elsewhere in this treatise.[156] The Supreme Court has held that these expenses do not include the automobile ownership allowance if the debtor has no current car loan or lease payment at the time of the petition.[157] However, the court also strongly implied that if there was even a single payment due, the allowance should be permitted, with any later change in the debtor's circumstances dealt with by plan modification.[158] Secured debt payments are deductible, no matter how high,[159] and perhaps even if the debtor plans to surrender the collateral.[160] Because the payments for secured debts are prorated over five years by the means test, and because the debtor's other expenses may have increased by the time secured debts are paid off, courts have usually rejected trustees' arguments that plan payments should be stepped up when the secured debt payments are completed, suggesting that future ability to pay is better dealt with through a motion to modify the plan, if appropriate.[161] Moreover, secured debt payments due under the contract are deductible in the full scheduled amount even if the debtor will have to pay less in a chapter 13 plan because the debt can be crammed down under section 1325(a)(5) of the Code.[162] As a result, this calculation gives the debtor a cushion equal to the difference between the amount owing on a secured debt (or the Internal Revenue Service's National Standard, if higher)[163] and the amount payable on the debt in the chapter 13 case. It may also provide some leeway from the strictures of the Internal Revenue Service standards for other expenses. Other expenses that were sometimes not allowed under the law prior to the 2005 amendments, such as a limited amount for private school education, are also permitted.[164]

If the means test calculation is performed correctly, using the debtor's actual expected tax liabilities as expenses rather than the amounts withheld from the debtor's pay, any tax refund that the debtor expects to receive will have been taken into account as part of that calculation. In such cases, courts should reject trustees' attempts to force debtors to turn over their tax refunds as part of their plan payments.[165]

In addition, the provisions of the means test permitting the court to adjust expenses for special circumstances are among those incorporated under this provision, so if there are other expenses for which there is no reasonable alternative, the court can take those facts into account.[166] Ultimately, the special

---

153 See § 12.3.4.4, *supra*.
154 *In re* Farrar-Johnson, 353 B.R. 224 (Bankr. N.D. Ill. 2006) (Schedule J expenses for above median income debtor irrelevant to determination of disposable income; means test expenses controlling).
155 *In re* Morgan, 374 B.R. 353 (Bankr. S.D. Fla. 2007) (expenses determined under IRS standards even if they exceed amounts on Schedule J); *In re* Naslund, 359 B.R. 781 (Bankr. D. Mont. 2006); *In re* Farrar-Johnson, 353 B.R. 224 (Bankr. N.D. Ill. 2006); *In re* Guzman, 345 B.R. 640 (Bankr. E.D. Wis. 2006).
156 See § 13.4.5, *infra*.
157 Ransom v. FIA Card Servs., 131 S. Ct. 716, 178 L. Ed. 2d 603 (2011). *See In re* Scott, 457 B.R. 740 (Bankr. S.D. Ill. 2011) (debtor could claim full ownership allowance even though actual expenses were less); *In re* O'Neill Miranda, 449 B.R. 182 (Bankr. D. P.R. 2011) (same).
158 Ransom v. FIA Card Servs., 131 S. Ct. 716, 729, 178 L. Ed. 2d 603, 616–17 (2011).
159 11 U.S.C. § 707(b)(2)(A)(iii); *In re* Hylton, 374 B.R. 579 (Bankr. W.D. Va. 2007) (future secured debt payments deductible without regard to amount or whether the property is reasonable or necessary); *In re* Austin, 372 B.R. 668 (Bankr. D. Vt. 2007); *In re* Barrett, 371 B.R. 860 (Bankr. S.D. Ill. 2007) (plain language of statute permitted single debtor to deduct payments for two cars). See § 2.3.3.2, *supra*.
  Some secured debt payments, such as payments on arrears, may be deducted if necessary in a chapter 13 case to maintain the debtor's possession of the debtor's primary residence, motor vehicle, or other property necessary for the support of the debtor or the debtor's dependents. See 11 U.S.C. § 707(b)(2)(A)(iii)(II).
160 *In re* Burmeister, 378 B.R. 227 (Bankr. N.D. Ill. 2007) (means test calculated based upon amounts contractually due on petition date). *But see* Morris v. Quigley (*In re* Quigley), 673 F.3d 269 (4th Cir. 2012) (surrender is a known or virtually certain change that can be taken into account under *Lanning* decision); *In re* Darrohn, 615 F.3d 470 (6th Cir. 2010); *In re* Turner, 574 F.3d 349 (7th Cir. 2009); Zeman v. Liehr (*In re* Liehr), 439 B.R. 179 (B.A.P. 10th Cir. 2010); *In re* Smith, 418 B.R. 359 (B.A.P. 9th Cir. 2009).
161 *In re* Willette, 395 B.R. 308, 327–328 (Bankr. D. Vt. 2008); *In re* McLain, 378 B.R. 39 (Bankr. N.D.N.Y. 2007); *In re* Charles, 375 B.R. 338 (Bankr. E.D. Tex. 2007). *But see In re* Turner, 574 F.3d 349 (7th Cir. 2009) (debtor could not deduct secured debt payments on property to be surrendered); *In re* Thomas, 395 B.R. 914 (B.A.P. 6th Cir. 2008) (same).
162 *In re* Roberts, 2008 WL 5979832 (D. Nev. Sept. 4, 2008); *In re* Marshall, 407 B.R. 1 (Bankr. D. Mass. 2009); *In re* Oliver, 2006 WL 2086691 (Bankr. D. Or. June 29, 2006) (chapter 13 debtor may deduct average payments on debts secured by collateral when debtors have moved to avoid liens on the collateral). *But see In re* Martinez, 418 B.R. 347 (B.A.P. 9th Cir. 2009) (debtors could not deduct payments on secured debts when liens would be stripped off); *In re* Grant, 423 B.R. 320 (Bankr. S.D. Cal. Jan. 26, 2010) (same).
163 See Chapter 13, *infra*, for discussion of means test calculations.
164 See Ch. 13, *infra*.
165 *In re* Robenhorst, 2011 WL 5877081 (E.D. Wis. Nov. 23, 2011); *In re* Grunauer, 2010 WL 2425945 (Bankr. E.D. Va. 2010).
166 11 U.S.C. § 707(b)(2)(B)(i). *See In re* Crabtree, 2007 WL 3024030 (Bankr. D. Mont. Oct. 12, 2007) (increased expenses for codebtors maintaining separate households constituted special circumstances); Ch. 13, *infra*.

circumstances test is not very different than the reasonably necessary test used prior to the 2005 amendments.[167]

12.3.4.4.4 Administrative expenses

As a result of poor drafting, it is not crystal clear how administrative expenses are to be paid in a chapter 13 case. There has been some concern that the provisions incorporated from section 707(b) would limit the debtor's administrative expenses to the ten percent cap found in those provisions.[168] Such a limit would render almost every chapter 13 case impossible, because the expenses necessary to administer the case almost always exceed ten percent. Trustees will presumably not file such objections if their effect would be to put themselves out of business. Indeed, if the administrative expenses were limited to ten percent, trustees would share those funds pro rata with other administrative claimants and could not recover their full percentage payment.[169]

However, unlike in the section 707(b) means test (in which the ten percent cap applies to hypothetical administrative expenses), the administrative expenses in chapter 13 are real priority claims that should be counted as such. Therefore, in calculating disposable income, a debtor should deduct as priority claims all administrative expenses not already accounted for in the means test calculation.[170]

Alternatively, if an objection is filed, courts should recognize that an administrative expense is an unsecured claim and section 1325(b) requires disposable income remaining after the means test deductions to be paid to "unsecured creditors," not just non-priority creditors.[171] Creditor is defined as an entity holding a prepetition claim.[172] Normally, the debtor's attorney seeking payment of fees is seeking payment of primarily prepetition fees and is therefore a "creditor." In addition, interpreting section 1325(b) to preclude payment of administrative expenses would place it in direct conflict with section 1326(b), which requires payment of "any unpaid claim" under section 507(a)(2), which provides for administrative claim priority. In light of all these issues, courts have eschewed a reading of the statute that precludes payment of the expenses necessary to administer the case.

The same reasoning should apply for debtors with income below the state median income. Just as priority debts are deducted in determining disposable income for above median income debtors, so too should they be deducted for below median income debtors. Alternatively, it can be argued that payments to "unsecured creditors" under section 1325(b) can include payments of administrative expenses to the debtor's attorney who is a creditor.[173] If a creditor raises an objection, the trustee could argue that other provisions such as section 1326 and 28 U.S.C. § 586 provide for payment of trustee's fees, and section 1325(b) should not be read in a way that would contradict those sections. And debtors with incomes either above or below state median income may also argue that because administrative expenses are reasonable and necessary legal expenses, the administrative claims should be allowed in chapter 13 as other necessary expenses under the Internal Revenue Service standards.[174]

12.3.4.4.5 Calculation of expenses for debtors below median income

Because of poor drafting it is not totally clear how secured creditors are to be paid by debtors whose incomes fall below state median income. Section 1325(b)(1)(B) uses language that was found in the subsection prior to the 2005 amendments to describe how much is to be paid into the plan for all creditors, but now states that this amount is to be paid to "unsecured creditors." This phrasing created a possible interpretation that debtors below median income cannot pay any money to secured creditors. In light of the fact that section 1325(b)(3) now considers payments to secured creditors a part of the "amounts reasonably necessary to be expended" for support of the debtor and dependents with respect to debtors over median income, the better interpretation is to read the requirements for debtors below median income the same way, allowing necessary secured debt payments to be considered as reasonably necessary expenses. Some courts have implicitly done so in applying the pre-2005 version of section 1325(b)(1)(B), disallowing large secured debt payments made by debtors on items such as luxury automobiles as expenses that are not reasonably necessary.[175] Again, trustees have not raised such objections, as it would eliminate most of their cases. It is also absurd to think that the 2005 Act somehow makes one of the most fundamental and often used provisions of the Code, the right to cure a mortgage default under section 1325(b)(5), available only to debtors whose income falls above median income.

Because changes in income or expenses can rarely be foreseen, the court normally looks to the debtor's current financial situation to decide this issue. Although the legislative history

---

167 See § 12.3.3.4.6, infra.
168 See 11 U.S.C. § 707(b)(2)(A)(ii)(III); § 2.3.3.7, supra.
169 See 11 U.S.C. § 1326(b).
170 In re Sharp, 415 B.R. 803 (Bankr. D. Colo. 2009).
171 In re Puetz, 370 B.R. 386 (Bankr. D. Kan. 2007).
    The Official Forms appear to take this position. See Official Forms 22A–22C advisory committee's note (reprinted in Appx. D, infra).
    The confusion is compounded because section 707(b)(2)(A)(iv) allows the deduction of priority claims in the means test calculation, in addition to the chapter 13 administrative expenses of up to ten percent allowed by section 707(b)(2)(A)(ii)(III). Then, section 1325(b) requires the disposable income remaining after the calculation to be paid to unsecured creditors generally, presumably including priority claims. It is doubtful that any court would allow the double-counting, or even triple-counting, of administrative expenses that this language suggests. But see In re Renteria, 420 B.R. 526 (S.D. Cal. 2009) (term construed to mean general unsecured creditors to avoid double-counting); In re Wilbur, 344 B.R. 650 (Bankr. D. Utah 2006) (term "unsecured creditors" in section 1325(b) construed to refer only to general unsecured creditors).
172 See 11 U.S.C. § 101(10).
173 See In re Echeman, 378 B.R. 177 (Bankr. S.D. Ohio 2007).
174 See 11 U.S.C. § 707(b)(2)(A)(ii)(I); Ch. 13, infra.
175 See, e.g., In re Rogers, 65 B.R. 1018 (Bankr. E.D. Mich. 1986).

contains little indication as to what expenses may be considered reasonably necessary and therefore properly deductible from a below median income debtor's income, a different amendment passed in 1984 does offer some guidance. Section 523(a)(2)(C) defines "luxury goods or services" as those which are *not* reasonably required for the support of the debtor or the debtor's dependents. A necessary corollary to that definition is the principle that all other expenses are reasonably required for such support.[176]

This definition therefore strongly supports the argument that the court's inquiry for below median income debtors' expenses should be limited to determining whether debtors have included expenses for luxuries in their budgets, rather than whether they conform to some predetermined level of expenses.[177] Courts cannot reasonably or fairly make decisions beyond that regarding what expenses are more necessary or truly necessary. Different debtors will have widely varying expenses for housing and transportation, depending on their age, mobility, and place of residence, yet all but luxury-style residences should be considered necessary. Similarly, some debtors will feel that parochial school or other items are absolutely required.[178] The courts can realistically go no further than deciding whether clearly unnecessary luxuries are included in the budget, and they should not attempt to do so. And, if a debtor's total expenses are average or less than average, it is doubtful that the court should even look at the expenses individually, because such debtors could only afford luxuries by making sacrifices in other parts of their budgets. Certainly a court should not question expenses that total less than those permitted for higher income debtors under section 1325(b)(3).

The cases under section 1325(b) prior to 2005 generally followed these principles. It was held that the debtor need not commit to the plan every last dollar that is not necessary for expenses and may preserve a small cushion to guard against life's unexpected events.[179] The debtor should not be required to borrow or withdraw money from a retirement plan to fund a chapter 13 plan.[180] Nor should the debtor be expected to commit income that may never be received because its receipt is uncertain or speculative.[181] On the other hand, courts have denied confirmation to debtors paying substantial private school tuitions[182] and making payments on an expensive sports car.[183] Moreover, the mere fact that income, such as veterans benefits, may be exempt or not subject to alienation does not mean that the income is not considered in applying the disposable income test,[184] unless it is specifically excluded by the statute, as are benefits under the Social Security Act, for example.

Generally, section 1325(b) continues to follow case law holding that if only one spouse files a chapter 13 case, the other spouse's income is not considered fully available for chapter 13 payments.[185] As under prior law, the definition of current monthly income includes the non-filing spouse's income only to the extent it is used for the debtor's household expenses, and thereby reduces the amount the debtor needs to pay.[186] Therefore, depending on the household's income and expenses, there may or may not be an advantage with respect to disposable income in filing for only one spouse.

---

176 *See In re* Jones, 55 B.R. 462 (Bankr. D. Minn. 1985).

177 *See, e.g.*, Dow Chem. Emples. Credit Union v. Collins, 2011 WL 2746210 (E.D. Mich. July 14, 2011) (affirming confirmation of plan where debtor budgeted $300/month for cigarettes and $300 for family recreation); *In re* Gonzales, 297 B.R. 143 (Bankr. D.N.M. 2003) (food budget of $700/month for father, mother, and two teenage children not unreasonable under circumstances, nor was support of adult child in household).

178 *See In re* Burgos, 248 B.R. 446 (Bankr. M.D. Fla. 2000) (private school tuition allowed as reasonable expense based on debtors' sincere religious beliefs).

179 *In re* Greer, 60 B.R. 547 (Bankr. C.D. Cal. 1986); *In re* Otero, 48 B.R. 704 (Bankr. E.D. Va. 1985). *See also In re* Smith, 207 B.R. 888 (B.A.P. 9th Cir. 1996) (necessity of life insurance premiums must be considered on case-by-case basis); *In re* Woodman, 2003 WL 23709465 (D. Me. Sept. 19, 2003) (tobacco expenses allowed), *aff'd*, 379 F.3d 1 (1st Cir. 2004).

180 *In re* Solomon, 67 F.3d 1128 (4th Cir. 1995); *In re* Short, 176 B.R. 886 (Bankr. S.D. Ind. 1995); *In re* Stones, 157 B.R. 669 (Bankr. S.D. Cal. 1993). *See also In re* Smith, 222 B.R. 846 (Bankr. N.D. Ind. 1998) (debtor not required to take cash distribution from profit sharing plan when that would have caused her to incur significant taxes and penalties).

181 *In re* Killough, 900 F.2d 61 (5th Cir. 1990) (affirming confirmation of plan without requiring debtor to include projected overtime in calculating budget).

182 *In re* Watson, 403 F.3d 1 (1st Cir. 2005) (parochial school tuition not reasonably necessary and its disallowance did not violate Religious Freedom Restoration Act, 42 U.S.C. §§ 2000bb-1 to 2000bb-4); *In re* Lynch, 299 B.R. 776 (W.D.N.C. 2003) ($567 per month for Catholic school tuition not reasonable when debtors argued need for school that was "more advanced" and did not teach evolution); Univest-Coppell Vill., Ltd. v. Nelson, 204 B.R. 497 (E.D. Tex. 1996); *In re* Jones, 55 B.R. 462 (Bankr. D. Minn. 1985). *But see In re* Cleary, 357 B.R. 369 (Bankr. D.S.C. 2006) ($1513 monthly tuition expense for seven children permitted when debtor and his wife had strongly held religious convictions, debtor's wife would not work outside the home except to provide additional income to pay for private school tuition, and family sacrificed other basic expenses to fund private school); *In re* Webb, 262 B.R. 685 (Bankr. E.D. Tex. 2001) (private school tuition was necessary for child with learning and emotional problems).

183 *In re* Rogers, 65 B.R. 1018 (Bankr. E.D. Mich. 1986). *See also In re* Hedges, 68 B.R. 18 (Bankr. E.D. Va. 1986) (plan including continued payment for recreational boat denied confirmation).

184 *In re* Freeman, 86 F.3d 478 (6th Cir. 1996) (exempt status of tax refund under state law irrelevant to disposable income test); *In re* Hagel, 184 B.R. 793 (B.A.P. 9th Cir. 1995); *In re* Waters, 384 B.R. 432 (N.D. W. Va. 2008) (veterans benefits included in calculating disposable income); *In re* Sohn, 300 B.R. 332 (Bankr. D. Minn. 2003) (projected exempt tax refunds under Earned Income Tax Credit program must be included in calculating disposable income).

185 *See In re* Bottelberghe, 253 B.R. 256 (Bankr. D. Minn. 2000). *But see In re* Hull, 251 B.R. 726 (B.A.P. 9th Cir. 2000) (under Washington state's community property laws, each spouse had vested interest in income of other spouse).

186 *See In re* Nahat, 278 B.R. 108 (Bankr. N.D. Tex. 2002) (income of non-debtor spouse considered in debtor's case after deduction of payments on non-debtor's own credit cards; non-debtor spouse was not required to devote her income to paying husband's debts to detriment of her own creditors).

The disposable income test also does not require the debtor to commit exempt assets, as opposed to income, to the plan.[187] However there may sometimes be disputes about whether certain funds, such as an income stream from an annuity or individual retirement account, constitute assets or income.[188]

The issue of tax refunds received during the plan is also complicated. If debtors have reported their income on Schedule I as being reduced by withholding taxes that are, in fact, more than necessary, resulting in a tax refund, most courts require that some or all of that refund be counted as additional income. In some courts, debtors' plans are expected to commit all or a part of future tax refunds to the plan, at least absent a showing of some necessary expenses for which those refunds will be used.[189]

Because some courts had restricted debtors' tithing or other church contributions in applying the disposable income standard,[190] Congress amended the Code in 1998 to make clear that such contributions are permissible and need not be curtailed in order to pay more to creditors. The Religious Liberty and Charitable Donation Protection Act of 1998[191] amended section 1325(b) to provide that charitable contributions[192] to qualified religious or charitable entities or organizations,[193] in an amount not exceeding fifteen percent of the debtor's gross income in any year, are permissible expenses for a chapter 13 debtor under the ability to pay test. No similar change was made for chapter 12 debtors, however. The amendment does not require that the permissible contributions be made to a religious organization, perhaps because Congress feared constitutional church-state problems. Nor does it apply only if the debtor had made such contributions in the past.[194] Thus, a chapter 13 debtor may choose to pay up to fifteen percent of his or her income to charity rather than to creditors over the course of a chapter 13 plan.

Some judicial hostility to the provision was apparent in some of the first cases decided on charitable contributions in chapter 13 since the amendment was passed. A few courts have concluded that a contribution must be "reasonably necessary to be expended for the maintenance or support of the debtor" or the debtor's dependents.[195] Though this reading might be possible based on the ambiguous structure of the new provision, it clearly eviscerates the statutory language and ignores congressional intent.[196] The problem in holding that only "reasonably necessary" contributions can be made is illustrated by the difficulty in articulating standards to evaluate the size and type of contributions which are to be considered reasonably necessary for the maintenance and support of the debtor or the debtor's dependents.[197] However, it is doubtful that most trustees or courts will seek to flout the obvious Congressional intent to permit such gifts.

12.3.4.4.6 Applicable commitment period and plan length

Another very significant change in the disposable income test is the number of months' worth of disposable income which must be committed if an objection is raised. New section 1325(b)(4) sets an "applicable commitment period" for section 1325(b) objections. The applicable commitment period is three years if the current monthly income of the "debtor and the debtor's spouse combined" is below the applicable state median income, but is five years if the current monthly income of the debtor and the debtor's spouse combined is above the applicable state median income for the size of the debtor's household.[198] Of course, the applicable commitment period, and indeed the computation of disposable income, has no

---

187 *In re* Graham, 258 B.R. 286 (Bankr. M.D. Fla. 2001) (proceeds of personal injury settlement based on cause of action that was an exempted asset were not income); *In re* Kerr, 199 B.R. 370 (Bankr. N.D. Ill. 1996) (proceeds from sale of exempt homestead need not be committed to plan). *See also In re* Baker, 194 B.R. 881 (Bankr. S.D. Cal. 1996) (exempt life insurance proceeds not disposable income, but interest on proceeds would be disposable income). *But see* Barbosa v. Solomon, 235 F.3d 31 (1st Cir. 2000) (proceeds from sale of home, on which mortgage had been stripped off due to lack of equity prior to confirmation, required to be paid to creditors in modified plan when home sold for twice the value used for stripping of liens).

188 *See In re* Mobley, 2011 WL 6812551 (Bankr. E.D. Mich. Dec. 1, 2011) (fully exempted personal injury award received prepetition was an asset and not income); *In re* Diaz, 459 B.R. 86 (Bankr. C.D. Cal. 2011) (tax refund derived from prepetition earnings was not income, but rather a prepetition asset).

189 *But see In re* Grier, 464 B.R. 839 (Bankr. N.D. Iowa 2011) (under *Lanning* decision, only known or virtually certain tax refunds can be considered).

190 *See, e.g., In re* Sturgeon, 51 B.R. 82 (Bankr. S.D. Ind. 1985).

191 Pub. L. No. 105-183, 112 Stat. 517 (1998).

A 2006 amendment clarified that this provision also applies to debtors whose expenses are determined under section 1325(b)(3). Pub. L. No. 109-439, 120 Stat. 3285 (2006).

192 The "charitable contribution" must meet the definition in section 548(d)(3), as amended by the same Act, and thus must consist of either a financial instrument or cash.

193 Section 1325(b) incorporates the definition of "qualified religious or charitable entity or organization" in section 548(d)(4), which in turn requires the recipient of the contribution to be an entity described in sections 170(c)(1) or 170(c)(2) of the Internal Revenue Code.

194 Compare 11 U.S.C. § 548(a)(2)(B) with 11 U.S.C. § 707(b), both of which appear to, in some cases, take past contributions into consideration. *See also In re* Gamble, 2011 Bankr. LEXIS 2757 (Bankr. M.D.N.C. June 14, 2011) (debtors permitted to increase contributions after bankruptcy petition filed because they remained below 15% cap).

195 *See, e.g., In re* Buxton, 228 B.R. 606 (Bankr. W.D. La. 1999).

196 *In re* Cavanagh, 250 B.R. 107 (B.A.P. 9th Cir. 2000) (Congress intended that contributions within limit be deemed reasonable and necessary); *In re* Kirschner, 259 B.R. 416 (Bankr. M.D. Fla. 2001) (court follows *Cavanagh* though requires debtors to provide ongoing documentation that contributions actually made during life of plan).

197 In *In re* Buxton, 228 B.R. 606 (Bankr. W.D. La. 1999) the court seems to require that reasonableness be demonstrated by limited contributions made from otherwise discretionary income. This limitation swallows the rule.

198 Household size should be determined in the same manner as for the chapter 7 means test, discussed in § 13.4.3.3, *infra. See In re* Smith, 396 B.R. 214 (Bankr. W.D. Mich. 2008) (to determine applicable commitment period, household includes all persons residing in housing unit, whether or not they are related to the debtor).

relevance if the debtor's plan proposes to pay unsecured creditors in full.[199]

One immediate issue in interpreting this provision is that a non-debtor spouse does not have any current monthly income, because "current monthly income" is defined as income received by the debtor (or in a joint case by the debtor and the debtor's spouse).[200] Thus, by definition, income of a non-debtor spouse that is not paid toward the debtor's expenses does not constitute current monthly income.[201] This statutory language should be given effect because Congress must be assumed to know that its definitions will be used, and the definition itself makes clear the limited circumstances in which a spouse's income is current monthly income. The provision would still serve an important purpose under this interpretation, preventing two spouses from avoiding the five-year commitment period by filing separate cases, because in that situation the debtor's spouse, being a bankruptcy debtor also, would have current monthly income.[202]

A contrary interpretation would mean that the income of a separated spouse would be included, even if that spouse contributed nothing to the household.[203] The debtor may not even know what a separated spouse's income is, so it may be hard to base an objection on it. In addition, the household size of the debtor for calculating the median income level would not be increased to take into account the members of the non-debtor spouse's household. For these reasons, including a separated spouse's total income makes no policy sense. Presumably, trustees will not invoke section 1325(b) to demand a five-year commitment period based on income that in reality is unavailable to the debtor.

Because current monthly income does not change during the case—it remains the average income for the six months before the petition was filed[204]—the debtor cannot be forced to change the commitment period if the debtor's income later increases from below median income to above median income.[205]

If the current monthly income of the debtor and the debtor's spouse is above the state median income, the applicable commitment period is five years.[206] This requirement could discourage some debtors who might otherwise have filed under chapter 13. It will also make plans more likely to fail, because there will be sixty-six percent more time for an unexpected drop in income or an emergency expense to occur. The trustee is not compelled to demand a five-year plan from the debtor, however. This five-year requirement is only applicable when an objection to confirmation is filed.[207]

It is important to note that the changes to section 1325(b) do not necessarily dictate the length of the plan itself. Rather, the amendments simply require the debtor to commit all of the debtor's projected disposable income for a three or five-year period. Section 1322(d), which controls the length of the plan, was amended by the 2005 Act to say only that a plan for a debtor above median cannot be *longer* than five years.[208] Thus, although the test requires payment into the plan of the amount of disposable income that a debtor whose income is above the median income is projected to have over the five-year postpetition period, that amount may be paid over a shorter period of time if the debtor chooses to do so.[209] Nonetheless, in most cases, the better strategy for the debtor will probably be to propose a five-year plan in this situation and then, if the debtor desires, simply complete plan payments before the five years elapses.[210] Of course, if the debtor's disposable income is zero, then either commitment period is met regardless of the plan length because the plan will always be committing thirty-six or sixty times the debtor's disposable income, which in either case totals zero.[211]

Another limitation on the five-year commitment period requirement is that it does not appear to apply to the modification of plans. Section 1329 was amended only to say that a modified plan cannot be *longer* than the applicable commitment period unless the court approves, with a five-year maximum. Although

---

199 *See In re* Ross, 375 B.R. 437 (Bankr. N.D. Ill. 2007) (plan need not propose payment of interest on unsecured claims), *amended on reconsideration*, 377 B.R. 599 (Bankr. N.D. Ill. 2007); *In re* Jones, 374 B.R. 469 (Bankr. D.N.H. 2007) (same); § 12.3.4.3, *supra*.

200 11 U.S.C. § 101(10)(B). *See* Ch. 13, *infra*.

201 *In re* Vollen, 426 B.R. 359 (Bankr. D. Kan. 2010); *In re* Stansell, 395 B.R. 457 (Bankr. D. Idaho 2008); *In re* Grubbs, 2007 WL 4418146 (Bankr. E.D. Va. Dec. 14, 2007).

202 Official Form 22C, line 13, permits a debtor to take the position that a non-debtor spouse's income is not included to the extent it is not contributed to household expenses, as would be the case with most separated debtors.

203 In contrast with section 1325(b)(4), the safe harbor median income test has a provision permitting the income of a separated spouse to be disregarded. *See* 11 U.S.C. § 707(b)(7)(B); Ch. 13, *infra*.

204 11 U.S.C. § 101(10)(A). *See* Ch. 13, *infra*.

205 *In re* Beasley, 342 B.R. 280 (Bankr. C.D. Ill. 2006) (debtor only required to file three-year plan even though significant portion of six-month period used to determine current monthly income included summer months for which debtor's wife, a schoolteacher, received no income).

206 11 U.S.C. § 1325(b)(4).

207 *See In re* Moore, 367 B.R. 721 (Bankr. D. Kan. 2007) (five-year commitment period applied even though debtors' income had recently dropped below median income level, but trustee has discretion not to object to shorter period).

208 11 U.S.C. § 1322(d)(1).

209 *In re* Kagenveama, 541 F.3d 868 (9th Cir. 2008); *In re* Musselman, 394 B.R. 801 (E.D.N.C. 2008); *In re* Henderson, 455 B.R. 203 (Bankr. D. Idaho 2011) (*Kagenveama* still good law in 9th Circuit); *In re* Swan, 368 B.R. 12 (Bankr. N.D. Cal. 2007); *In re* Fuger, 347 B.R. 94 (Bankr. D. Utah 2006). *But see* Baud v. Carroll, 634 F.3d 327 (6th Cir. 2011) (five year period is temporal requirement); Whaley v. Tennyson (*In re* Tennyson), 611 F.3d 873 (11th Cir. 2010); *In re* Frederickson, 545 F.3d 652 (8th Cir. 2008); Pellegrino v. Boyajian (*In re* Pellegrino), 423 B.R. 586 (B.A.P. 1st Cir. 2010) (one month plan did not satisfy 36 month commitment period); *In re* Girodes, 350 B.R. 31 (Bankr. M.D.N.C. 2006).

210 *See In re* Smith, 449 B.R. 817 (Bankr. M.D. Fla. 2011) (debtor could pay off plan early if no creditors objected). Once plan payments are completed, no party can move for modification of the plan. However, even this strategy may attract opposition from a trustee, so it is usually preferable simply to make payments over the five year period.

211 *In re* Kagenveama, 541 F.3d 868 (9th Cir. 2008); *In re* Brady, 361 B.R. 765 (Bankr. D.N.J. 2007); *In re* Fuger, 347 B.R. 94 (Bankr. D. Utah 2006); *In re* Alexander, 344 B.R. 742 (Bankr. E.D.N.C. 2006).

there had been some dispute under current law as to whether section 1325(b) applies to modifications, this specific reference seems to make clear that this part of section 1325(b), at least, does not apply. Courts have therefore ruled that a debtor is not bound by the original commitment period when a modification is sought.[212] Without a modification the only resolution for a debtor's inability to complete a plan, even after three years, would be conversion, dismissal, or a hardship discharge.

12.3.4.5 Postconfirmation Modification of Plan Based Upon Change in Circumstances

Finally, the Code provides a mechanism to deal with unanticipated changes in the debtor's income or expenses. Section 1329(a) permits a debtor, unsecured creditor, or trustee to seek modification of the plan, raising or lowering payments. Sections 1322(a), 1322(b), 1323(c), and 1325(a) apply to any request to modify the plan.[213] Notice of the request for modification must be served on all creditors.[214] Thus, when there has been a substantial and unanticipated change for the better in the debtor's financial condition after confirmation, the trustee or an unsecured creditor may move for a modification that increases the debtor's payments.[215] As a practical matter, however, this section is utilized primarily by debtors seeking to lower payments because of lower income or higher expenses, because the trustee and creditors will usually have no knowledge of changes in the debtor's situation.[216]

Although section 1329(a) does not by its terms limit creditors' motions to cases in which there has been a change in income or expenses, any motions filed on other grounds, which could have been raised earlier, should be barred by the res judicata effect of the confirmation order.[217] Also, if the debtor is able to complete payments under the original plan before a motion to modify is filed, the court is precluded from modifying the plan, because Code section 1329(a) permits modification only "before completion of payments under [the confirmed] plan."[218]

---

212 See § 12.3.4.5, infra.

213 See In re Auernheimer, 437 B.R. 405 (Bankr. D. Kan. 2010) (best interests test of § 1325(a)(4) can be determined based on facts known at time of modification about lower value of property).

214 Fed. R. Bankr. P. 2002(a)(5), 3015(g); In re Arnold, 2010 WL 3810862 (Bankr. N.D.N.Y. Sept. 27, 2010).

215 In re Murphy, 474 F.3d 143 (4th Cir. 2007) (refinancing that exchanged debt for cash by debtors with reduced income not a substantial change, but sale of property for amount in excess of what could be anticipated at confirmation was a substantial change); In re Brown, 332 B.R. 562 (Bankr. N.D. Ill. 2005) (refinancing not a plan modification and proceeds not required to be paid into plan because debtor's balance sheet not changed by exchange of debt for cash and creditors would be paid more quickly than under original plan). See In re Arnold, 869 F.2d 240 (4th Cir. 1989) (debtor's income rose from $80,000 per year to $200,000 per year); In re Powers, 202 B.R. 618 (B.A.P. 9th Cir. 1996) (five hundred dollars increase in debtor's income justified plan modification, even after taking into account debtor's increased expenses); In re Fitak, 121 B.R. 224 (S.D. Ohio 1990) (sale of debtors' property 57 months after confirmation for $20,000 more than value estimated at time of confirmation was not an unanticipated change of circumstances justifying modification motion of creditor because property would have been expected to appreciate over time); In re Flennory, 280 B.R. 896 (Bankr. S.D. Ala. 2001) (receipt of tax refund was not change of circumstances that could not have been anticipated and did not justify modification).

However, some courts have held that under a literal reading of section 1329, the ability to pay test of section 1325(b) is not applicable to postconfirmation modifications. In re Forbes, 215 B.R. 183 (B.A.P. 8th Cir. 1997); In re Anderson, 153 B.R. 527 (Bankr. M.D. Tenn. 1993).

Moreover, if no objection to plan confirmation was made by a creditor on the basis of ability to pay, the issue may not later be raised for the first time by a motion to modify the plan, at least with respect to any income which might have been anticipated at the time of confirmation. In re Grissom, 137 B.R. 689 (Bankr. W.D. Tenn. 1992).

216 In re Kapp, 315 B.R. 87 (Bankr. W.D. Mo. 2004) (temporary suspension of payments based on unanticipated expenses and change in income).

See § 8.7.4, supra, for further discussion of plan modification. Some trustees do require annual reports of debtors' income and expenses. See Petro v. Mishler, 276 F.3d 375 (7th Cir. 2002). 11 U.S.C. § 521(f) permits trustees and creditors to request postpetition tax returns and annual statements of income and expenses. The right to request tax returns is greatly limited by privacy guidelines established by the Director of the Administrative Office of the United States Courts. See Ch. 8, supra.

217 In re Kirkland, 2010 WL 2013451 (Bankr. S.D. Ill. May 20, 2010) (creditor could not object to modification based on issue that could have been raised at confirmation); In re Storey, 392 B.R. 266 (B.A.P. 6th 2008); In re Klus, 173 B.R. 51 (Bankr. D. Conn. 1994); In re Bonanno, 78 B.R. 52 (Bankr. E.D. Pa. 1987); 8 Collier on Bankruptcy ¶ 1329.02 (16th ed.). See also Johnson v. Fink (In re Johnson), 458 B.R. 745 (B.A.P. 8th Cir. 2011) (debtors could not modify plan in ways not necessitated by reduction in income because of binding effect of plan). But see In re Meza, 467 B.R. 874 (5th Cir. 2006) (no substantial change of circumstances required); Barbosa v. Solomon, 235 F.3d 31 (1st Cir. 2000) (plan may be modified without showing change of circumstances); In re Witkowski, 16 F.3d 739 (7th Cir. 1994) (changed circumstances not a prerequisite for trustee's motion to modify plan after confirmation); In re Brown, 219 B.R. 191 (B.A.P. 6th Cir. 1998) (no substantial change of circumstances need be shown); In re Than, 215 B.R. 430 (B.A.P. 9th Cir. 1997) (no substantial and unanticipated changed circumstances required for trustee's motion to modify plan).

For a discussion of the binding effect of a confirmed plan, see § 12.11, infra.

218 In re Profit, 283 B.R. 567 (B.A.P. 9th Cir. 2002); Bayshore Nat'l Bank v. Smith, 252 B.R. 107 (E.D. Tex. 2000), aff'd, 252 F.3d 1357 (5th Cir. Tex. 2001) (table); In re Casper, 154 B.R. 243 (N.D. Ill. 1993); In re McCarthy, 391 B.R. 372 (Bankr. N.D. Tex. 2008); In re Forte, 341 B.R. 859 (Bankr. N.D. Ill. 2005); In re Pancurak, 316 B.R. 173 (Bankr. W.D. Pa. 2004); In re Richardson, 283 B.R. 783 (Bankr. D. Kan. 2002); In re Jordan, 161 B.R. 670 (Bankr. D. Minn. 1993); In re Moss, 91 B.R. 563 (Bankr. C.D. Cal. 1988); 8 Collier on Bankruptcy ¶ 1329.08 (16th ed.). See also In re Smith, 449 B.R. 817 (Bankr. M.D. Fla. June 6, 2011) (debtors permitted to pay off plan early over trustee's objection in absence of any creditor objection); In re Celeste, 310 B.R. 286 (Bankr. D. Md. 2004) (debtor entitled to discharge once debtor's checks completing payments are honored, even if trustee has not completed distributions). Cf. In re Meza, 467 F.3d 874 (5th Cir. 2006) (plan may be modified if motion is filed before completion of payments, even if payments completed before motion is heard).

A few courts have tried to take into account possible increases in debtors' incomes in advance by requiring that plan payments increase by the same percentage as the debtor's income, or by some percentage of any additional income that the debtor receives.[219] These cases are misguided for several reasons. First, the legislative history gives no indication that such automatic increases were contemplated; the mechanism discussed in the proposal that led to the 1984 amendments was the motion to modify the plan.[220] Second, such automatic increases would create monitoring and verification problems, making it difficult for the court or the trustee to know when, or if, the debtor had completed payments under the plan. Finally, any automatic increase provision could not take into account inflation or other expenses which could decrease the debtor's *real* disposable income. A three percent salary increase in a period when the cost of living increases by six percent is a decrease in real income that leaves the debtor less able to afford plan payments. It is for precisely such reasons that the only proper method for increasing plan payments is a case by case approach through motions to amend chapter 13 plans.[221]

As the Ninth Circuit Court of Appeals held in *In re Anderson*,[222] a debtor should not be required to pledge increased plan payments based upon later increases in income in order to obtain confirmation. The procedure of the bankruptcy court in that case, permitting the trustee to determine that plan payments should be increased without a motion to modify the plan, was disapproved as contrary to the statutory scheme which contemplates a modification motion as the appropriate vehicle to change plan payments.[223] Similarly, it is not proper to condition plan confirmation on the debtor submitting future periodic reports of income with current pay stubs.[224]

One specific type of modification that Congress has explicitly permitted is a modification to enable the debtor to purchase health insurance, presumably in recognition of the fact that such insurance is important to the health of debtors and their families as well as the stability of their budgets. The debtor may move to modify the plan to reduce the plan payments in order to purchase health insurance for the debtor and any dependent who does not have health insurance.[225] The debtor must demonstrate that the expense is reasonable and necessary and not more than necessary to maintain a previously lapsed policy if the debtor had one. Upon request of a party in interest the debtor must provide proof that health insurance was purchased.

It is not at all clear that section 1325(b) applies to modifications under section 1329. Section 1325(b) is not mentioned in section 1329(b)(1), which requires modifications to comply with other provisions of section 1325, leading some courts to find section 1325(b) inapplicable to modifications.[226] The fact that a reference to section 1325(b) was added to section 1329 in 2005, but only for use in determining the maximum length of a modified plan, further suggests that section 1325(b) is not otherwise applicable.[227] If that is the case, then courts may have more discretion in approving modified plans, which could help or harm a debtor in a particular case. If courts have such discretion, a significant change of circumstances should be needed to modify a plan that complies with section 1325(b). Otherwise, courts could simply modify a plan at any time in a manner that ignores section 1325(b) and thereby render it almost meaningless.[228]

12.3.5 Use of the Good Faith Test After the 1984 Amendments

Although use of the good faith test of 11 U.S.C. § 1325(a)(3) to challenge a plan based solely upon the amount of a debtor's payment to unsecured creditors[229] has largely been put to rest by the "ability to pay" (disposable income) test,[230] creditors have continued to invoke section 1325(a)(3) to challenge other perceived debtor abuses. Some courts have read the disposable income test as simply eliminating certain issues—those going to whether minimal payments to unsecured creditors evidence bad faith—from the "all of the circumstances" examination of good faith.[231] However, even when courts continue to evaluate the totality of the circumstances,[232] it should be argued that the

---

219 *See, e.g., In re* Akin, 54 B.R. 700 (Bankr. D. Neb. 1985); *In re* Krull, 54 B.R. 375 (Bankr. D. Colo. 1985).

220 *Oversight Hearings on Personal Bankruptcy Before the Subcomm. on Monopolies and Commerce of the House Comm. on the Judiciary*, 97th Cong. 215, 221 (1981–1982).

221 8 Collier on Bankruptcy ¶ 1325.11[4][b] (16th ed.).

222 21 F.3d 355 (9th Cir. 1994).

223 *But see In re* Broken Bow Ranch, 33 F.3d 1005 (8th Cir. 1994) (when confirmed chapter 12 plan did provide for general obligation to pay all disposable income at the end of three years to unsecured creditors, rather than specific amounts, debtors could be required to pay amounts that court determined were not necessary for support of debtor or dependents or operation of farm in order to obtain discharge, even though debtor would have to borrow to finance future operations).

224 Petro v. Mishler, 276 F.3d 375 (7th Cir. 2002).

225 11 U.S.C. § 1329(a)(4).

226 *See, e.g., In re* Sunahara, 326 B.R. 768 (B.A.P. 9th Cir. 2005); King v. Robenhorst (*In re* Robenhorst), 2011 WL 5877081 (E.D. Wis. Nov. 22, 2011); *In re* Tibbs, 478 B.R. 458 (Bankr. S.D. Fla. 2012); *In re* Davis, 439 B.R. 863 (Bankr. N.D. Ill. 2010); *In re* Walker, 2010 WL 4259274 (Bankr. C.D. Ill. Oct. 21, 2010).

227 *See In re* McCully, 398 B.R. 590 (Bankr. N.D. Ohio 2008) (debtors not bound by original applicable commitment period when income fell); *In re* Ewers, 366 B.R. 139 (Bankr. D. Nev. 2007) (because section 1325(b) does not apply to modification, debtor could modify to reduce term of plan to less than five-year commitment period when income dropped); *In re* Robert, 366 B.R. 27 (Bankr. W.D. Ark. 2007) (debtor could modify plan to pay less than amount originally determined under section 1325(b) when income dropped; section 1325(b) does not apply to modification).

228 *See In re* York, 415 B.R. 377 (Bankr. W.D. Wis. 2009) (modification cannot be used to change results of § 1325(b) formula when there has been no change in circumstances).

229 *See* § 12.3.3, *supra*.

230 *See* § 12.3.4, *supra*.

231 *In re* Smith, 848 F.2d 813 (7th Cir. 1988); Educ. Assistance Corp. v. Zellner, 827 F.2d 1222 (8th Cir. 1987); *In re* Smith, 100 B.R. 436 (S.D. Ind. 1989).
 See § 12.3.3, *supra*, for discussion of earlier cases on good faith.

232 *See In re* Young, 237 F.3d 1168 (10th Cir. 2001) (plan could be in

inquiry into good faith should be limited to such issues as the debtor's honesty in completing the schedules and intention to effectuate a chapter 13 plan as proposed.[233] Nonetheless, some courts continue to impose limitations that are based on subjective judgments about the appropriate purposes for which a debtor may use chapter 13, and which take into account the amount of the payments proposed.[234]

Some chapter 13 trustees have attempted to utilize the good faith test in cases filed under the 2005 Act to argue that debtors who allegedly can make greater payments than those required by the formula in section 1325(b) have not proposed their plans in good faith. Now that section 1325(b) has been amended to be even more specific about how the debtor's disposable income should be calculated, these arguments are weaker than ever. In reality, these arguments usually seek to overturn specific policy judgments made by Congress that certain income (for example, Social Security benefits) should not be counted, or that debtors should be afforded the right to living expenses commensurate with those permitted under the section 707(b)(2) means test formula. Courts should reject such arguments which are based primarily on a desire to ignore changes in the law and do things the way they were always done in the past.[235]

The 2005 amendments also added a new confirmation standard based upon whether the bankruptcy petition was filed in good faith.[236] Because many courts had held that a chapter 13 case could be dismissed if the petition was not filed in good faith, this does not represent a major change in the law.[237] However, it does suggest that the remedy for lack of good faith in filing the petition may be denial of plan confirmation, rather than dismissal.

The 2005 amendments also added a good faith test for maintaining or obtaining automatic stay protections in certain cases of repeat filings.[238] However, that good faith test differs in its focus from the test under section 1325(a)(4) and a finding that the debtor has not met that test should not necessarily preclude a finding of good faith for plan confirmation.[239]

12.3.6 Payments to Unsecured Priority Creditors

12.3.6.1 Priority Claims

One group of unsecured claims must normally be paid in full through the chapter 13 plan. Section 1322(a)(2) of the Code requires that the plan provide for payment in full of all claims entitled to priority under Code section 507(a), unless the holder of the claim agrees otherwise.

A priority creditor who fails to object to a plan proposing less than full payment may be deemed to have agreed to it.[240] In any case, if such a plan is confirmed, the creditor is bound by it.[241]

---

good faith despite debtor's conversion from chapter 7 in order to deal with nondischargeable punitive damages award); *In re* Gier, 986 F.2d 1326 (10th Cir. 1993) (bankruptcy court did not err in denying confirmation after finding that there were discrepancies in debtor's testimony about available income, debtor was motivated by desire not to pay creditors rather than inability to pay them, chapter 13 case was filed before chapter 7 case was concluded and plan proposed to discharge debt that was nondischargeable in chapter 7 case); *In re* LeMaire, 898 F.2d 1346 (8th Cir. 1990) (en banc); *In re* Okoreeh-Baah, 836 F.2d 1030 (6th Cir. 1988); *In re* Chaffin, 816 F.2d 1070 (5th Cir. 1987), *modified*, 836 F.2d 215 (5th Cir. 1988); Neufeld v. Freeman, 794 F.2d 149 (4th Cir. 1986).

233 Educ. Assistance Corp. v. Zellner, 827 F.2d 1222 (8th Cir. 1987); *In re* Keach, 243 B.R. 851 (B.A.P. 1st Cir. 2000); *In re* Mims, 2011 WL 1749809 (Bankr. S.D. Miss. May 6, 2011) (unintentional errors in schedules did not rise to bad faith); *In re* Gathright, 67 B.R. 384 (Bankr. E.D. Pa. 1986); *In re* Red, 60 B.R. 113 (Bankr. E.D. Tenn. 1986). *See also In re* Doersam, 849 F.2d 237 (6th Cir. 1988) (questionable listing of expenses combined with bulk of debts being student loans yielded finding that plan not proposed in good faith); 8 Collier on Bankruptcy ¶ 1325.04[1] (16th ed.).

234 *See, e.g.*, Noreen v. Slattengren, 974 F.2d 75 (8th Cir. 1992) (finding lack of good faith in plan of debtor who sought to eliminate liability for child sexual abuse with minimal payments); *In re* LeMaire, 898 F.2d 1346 (8th Cir. 1990) (en banc) (good faith found lacking in large part due to heinous nature of debtor's prepetition acts); *In re* Gilmore, 217 B.R. 228 (Bankr. S.D. Ohio 1998) (debtor's prepetition conduct in stopping payment on payday loan checks not evidence of bad faith); *In re* Hawes, 73 B.R. 584 (Bankr. W.D. Wis. 1987) (use of chapter 13 in part to block employer's efforts to enforce a covenant not to compete constitutes bad faith). *See also In re* Tucker, 989 F.2d 328 (9th Cir. 1993) (bankruptcy court failed to make sufficient factual findings about whether debtor had acted equitably). *Cf. In re* Robinson, 987 F.2d 665 (10th Cir. 1993) (creditor who failed to argue in bankruptcy court that debt for improper sexual activities by pastoral counselor would have been nondischargeable as willful and malicious injury could not obtain reversal of confirmation order based on that argument).

235 *See In re* Ragos, 2012 WL 5292949 (5th Cir. Oct 29, 2012); *In re* Cranmer, 2012 WL 5235365 (10th Cir. Oct 24, 2012); *In re* Mancl, 381 B.R. 537 (W.D. Wis. 2008); *In re* Sweet, 428 B.R. 917 (Bankr. M.D. Ga. Apr. 30, 2010) (rejecting trustee argument that debtors should surrender home to reduce housing costs and pay more to creditors); *In re* Rotunda, 349 B.R. 324 (Bankr. N.D.N.Y. 2006); *In re* Barr, 341 B.R. 181 (Bankr. M.D.N.C. 2006).

236 11 U.S.C. § 1325(a)(7). *See In re* Tomer, 2009 WL 2029798 (W.D. Va. July 2, 2009) (discussing different analysis for good faith filing of petition).

237 See Chapter 13, *infra*, for discussion of dismissal of cases.

238 *See* § 9.3.3, *supra*.

239 *In re* Tomasini, 339 B.R. 773 (Bankr. D. Utah 2006).

240 *See In re* Lindgren, 85 B.R. 447 (Bankr. N.D. Ohio 1988); *In re* Hebert, 61 B.R. 44 (Bankr. W.D. La. 1986). *See also In re* Teligent, Inc., 282 B.R. 765 (Bankr. S.D.N.Y. 2002) (chapter 11 case interpreting similar language). *But see* Kennedy v. Kennedy (*In re* Kennedy), 2011 WL 1322297 (Bankr. S.D. Ga. Mar. 25, 2011) (debtor could not bind claimant who had filed priority claim to treatment as nonpriority claim through provisions of confirmed plan; objection to claim necessary); *In re* Northrup, 141 B.R. 171 (N.D. Iowa 1991).

241 *In re* Riley, 204 B.R. 28 (Bankr. E.D. Ark. 1996) (tax debt was provided for by debtor's chapter 13 plan and thus discharged, even though modified plan omitted debt, when taxing authority had knowledge of case, participated in process and filed other proofs of claim). *See* § 12.11, *infra*. *But see In re* Hairopoulos, 118 F.3d 1240 (8th Cir. 1997) (tax claim was not provided for when Internal Revenue Service did not receive proper notice of conversion to chapter 13 and other significant dates); *In re* Escobedo, 28 F.3d 34 (7th Cir. 1994) (confirmation of plan that did not pay priority claims in full was "nugatory" and case could be dismissed even though

The only exception to this general rule is contained in section 1322(a)(4), which provides that, although support owed to the government is now a priority debt, it need not be paid in full if the debtor proposes a five-year plan committing all the debtor's disposable income and the debtor cannot pay the support obligation in full.[242] This provision is intended to prevent large government support debts from making a mortgage cure and other chapter 13 remedies unavailable. Unpaid support will, of course, not be discharged, as is true under existing law.[243] The fact that support owed to the government is now a priority debt should make clear that it can be separately classified and paid before general unsecured debts.[244]

The most common types of priority claims in chapter 13 cases are claims for administrative expenses,[245] such as the debtor's attorney fees[246] or the trustee's fees,[247] and tax claims.[248] In some cases, debtors may owe debts in the nature of alimony, maintenance, or support that are domestic support obligations as defined in section 101 and therefore priority claims.[249] Debtors who have been in business may also owe priority debts for wages or consumer deposits.[250] While attorney fees and trustee's fees are to be expected in most chapter 13 cases, the requirement that other priority claims be paid in full may be difficult for some debtors to meet.

It should be noted, however, that section 1322(a)(2) does not require that priority creditors receive the present value of their claims, that is, the claims plus interest, over the course of the plan, as does the best interests of creditors test.[251] Nor does it require that priority claims be paid before other claims. The only exception to this general rule is contained in section 1326(b), which provides that administrative claims, such as trustee fees and attorney fees, should be paid before other claims.[252] In some cases, a debtor may want to provide for payment of large priority claims only after the secured claims are paid in full. If the plan so provides and the debtor is then for some reason unable to complete the plan, there is a better chance that the secured claims will have been satisfactorily dealt with by the time the plan fails, in which case the debtor may seek a hardship discharge[253] or choose to convert the case to chapter 7.[254] If the debtor chooses either of these alternatives, priority claims need not be paid in the bankruptcy case, although the unpaid priority taxes and domestic support obligation debts will not be discharged.[255] Because interest on such debts is also nondischargeable, the debtor may seek to pay interest on them during the chapter 13 case. However, section 1322(b)(10) permits such payments only if the plan proposes to pay all other allowed claims in full.

Generally, a debtor should provide for payment of priority claims, especially those that are nondischargeable, before general unsecured claims are paid. Then, if the plan fails before it can be completed, there will be a greater chance that priority claims have been paid in full or almost paid in full, which could keep open the option of modifying the plan, because any modified plan must also provide for full payment of priority claims.[256] Alternatively, if the debtor seeks a hardship discharge or converts to chapter 7, taxes or domestic support obligations that would not have been discharged will no longer be owed to the extent they have already been paid in the chapter 13 plan.

---

there was no appeal of confirmation order and debtor had completed plan payments).

242 *In re* Penaran, 424 B.R. 868 (Bankr. D. Kan. 2010) (claim treated as support owed to governmental unit when proof of claim was ambiguous with respect to obligee). *See In re* Williams, 387 B.R. 211 (Bankr. N.D. Ill. 2008) (provision did not apply to priority claim filed by state when claim was filed on behalf of custodial parent and was not owed to the state itself).

243 11 U.S.C. § 523(a)(5). *See* § 15.4.3.5, *infra*.

244 *See* § 12.4.3, *infra*.

245 A capital gain from a postpetition sale of property is not an administrative expense nor a priority claim because the chapter 13 estate is not a separate entity. Hall v. United States, 132 S. Ct. 1882, 182 L. Ed. 2d 840 (2012) (chapter 12 case). Therefore, if a debtor plans to sell property during the case, the plan should provide that such taxes are to be paid from the proceeds of the sale, or the debtor's budget should provide for payment of them outside the plan.

246 *See* § 16.4.1, *infra*, for a discussion of payment of attorney fees through a chapter 13 plan.

247 *See* § 7.3.12, *supra*, for discussion of the chapter 13 trustee's fees. Chapter 7 trustees sometimes seek priority treatment for their fees in cases converted from chapter 7, but some courts have held that they are limited to a percentage of chapter 7 disbursements, if any, by 11 U.S.C. § 326. *See In re* Murphy, 272 B.R. 483 (Bankr. D. Colo. 2002) (see also cases cited therein).

248 Not all tax claims are entitled to priority. *See* § 3.5, *supra*. However, a debtor may treat as a priority prepetition claim a tax that is not yet due, if it is for a tax year that ended before the petition date. Mich. Dep't of Treasury v. Hight (*In re* Hight), 670 F.3d 699 (6th Cir. 2012).

249 11 U.S.C. § 507(a)(1).

It should be noted that such claims are not entitled to priority if they are not actually in the nature of alimony, maintenance, or support, or if they have been assigned to an entity other than a governmental unit. 11 U.S.C. § 507(a)(1). *See, e.g., In re* Poole, 383 B.R. 308 (Bankr. D.S.C. 2007) (denying objection to confirmation by debtor's ex-wife because her claims were not in nature of support and therefore not priority claims).

See § 15.4.3.5.3, *infra*, discussing the definition of domestic support obligation. Also, claims for unmatured domestic support obligations are not allowable. 11 U.S.C. § 502(b)(5).

250 *See* § 3.5, *supra*, for discussion of the various types of priority debts.

251 *In re* Hageman, 108 B.R. 1016 (Bankr. N.D. Ind. 1989); *In re* Hieb, 88 B.R. 1019 (Bankr. D.S.D. 1988). *See* § 12.3.1, *supra. Cf.* 11 U.S.C. § 1325(b)(4).

Of course, if the priority claim would have been paid in full in a chapter 7 case, such present value interest would be required under the best interests of creditors test itself.

252 *See In re* Sanders, 347 B.R. 776 (N.D. Ala. 2006) (there is no requirement that domestic support obligations be paid before administrative expenses). *See also* § 16.4, *infra* (discussion of paying attorney fees through a chapter 13 plan).

253 11 U.S.C. § 1325(b). *See* § 8.7.5, *supra*.

254 11 U.S.C. § 1307(a). *See* § 8.7.5, *supra*.

255 11 U.S.C. § 523(a)(1), (5), (15). *See* §§ 15.4.3.1, 15.4.3.5, 15.4.3.13, *infra*.

256 *See* § 8.7.5, *supra*.

It is quite clear that a priority creditor need not be paid if it fails to file a claim.[257] Occasionally, taxing authorities will fail to file claims for priority taxes; in such cases, provided the taxes were properly scheduled and the taxing authority had notice of the case, the taxes may be discharged when the plan is completed if they are not nondischargeable under section 1328(a), just as any other unsecured claim would be.[258] A similar analysis applies when a taxing authority fails to file a claim for the full amount that it later claims is owed. Generally, if the omitted amounts derive from a different year or a different transaction, courts will not allow them to be added to the taxing authority's proof of claim by amendment after the claims bar date has passed.[259]

However, if a priority domestic support obligation claim is not filed, or a claim for a priority tax that is nondischargeable under section 1328(a), the debt will not be discharged at the end of the case. Therefore, it is usually in the debtor's interest to file a claim for such a priority tax or support creditor, if the debtor can afford to pay the claim in the plan, to assure that the creditor is paid ahead of non-priority unsecured creditors.[260] Alternatively, if the claim is to be paid by the debtor directly to the creditor outside the plan, the debtor should ensure that his or her budget is adjusted to take into account such payments.

Some creditors, in an effort to receive payments which exceed the amount to which they are legitimately entitled, will file priority claims even when they have no right to priority treatment under the Code. For example, some utility companies commonly assert an inappropriate priority for prepetition utility debts. Similarly, some secured creditors assert priority status even though priority claims, by definition, must be unsecured.[261] When bogus priorities are asserted, an objection to the claim is required, perhaps with a request for sanctions under Federal Rule of Bankruptcy Procedure 9011 if the claimed priority is frivolous.[262]

12.3.6.2 Required Filing of Tax Returns

Responding to complaints from government agencies that they could not compute tax claims in chapter 13 cases without returns filed by the debtors, Congress enacted section 1308 and two accompanying provisions that require chapter 13 debtors to file prepetition tax returns with the appropriate taxing authorities. By the day before the first scheduled section 341 meeting, the debtor must file all tax returns that the debtor was required to file for all taxable periods ending in the four years before the petition.[263]

If the debtor was not required to file a return for a particular year no return need be filed, although under local practice the debtor may need to file, or send to the trustee, a document stating that fact. Presumably this provision includes only returns that were not already filed, although it does not explicitly say so and, again, the debtor may have to provide documentation or a declaration indicating that the returns were filed.

If returns are not provided by this deadline, the trustee may hold the section 341 meeting open for a period of up to 120 days or, for a return that was not past due on the petition date, until the latest automatic extension date.[264] The debtor may also move for an extension of time to file returns beyond the time established by the trustee, but not more than thirty days after the trustee's deadline or, if a return was not past due on the petition date, beyond the latest automatic extension date. The debtor must demonstrate that the failure to file returns as required by this section is for reasons beyond the debtor's control, and the court's order must be entered before the "tolling of any applicable filing period."[265] Although the meaning of this "tolling" language is not entirely clear, debtors should be sure to file an early motion for an extension of time when returns cannot be filed by the date of the creditors meeting unless it is certain the trustee will hold the meeting open. Some courts have held that even if a debtor's return for a prior year is not yet due under tax law, the failure to file it before the creditors meeting or obtain an extension from the court mandates the granting of a motion to dismiss if the trustee does not hold open the creditors meeting.[266]

Section 1307(e) of the Bankruptcy Code provides a new, seemingly mandatory, ground for dismissal or conversion of a chapter 13 case if the debtor does not file the tax returns required by section 1308. In addition, section 1325(a)(9) creates a new standard for plan confirmation that will prevent confirmation if the debtor has not filed the returns required by section 1308. Together, these provisions will make it virtually impossible for a debtor to obtain plan confirmation and complete a chapter 13 case without filing all returns that are required for the four years in question.

As a practical matter chapter 13 debtors will often have to expend funds to have tax returns prepared in order to qualify for chapter 13 relief, even if they do not owe any taxes, further increasing the cost of bankruptcy. If the returns are prepared after the petition is filed, such funds should be either an administrative expense (if prepared by the debtor's attorney) or an "other necessary expense" to be deducted in the disposable

---

257 Priority administrative expenses are exceptions to this rule. An entity seeking allowance of an administrative expense files a "request," which is not governed by the claims deadline but must normally be timely. 11 U.S.C. § 503(a).

258 *In re* Tomlan, 907 F.2d 114 (9th Cir. 1990); *In re* Richard, 50 B.R. 339 (E.D. Tenn. 1985); *In re* Rothman, 76 B.R. 38 (Bankr. E.D.N.Y. 1987). *See also* § 15.4.1, *infra*.

It is also now clear, under section 502(b)(9), that late filed claims must be disallowed. However, the debtor probably has to object to such claims to ensure that they will be disallowed.

259 *See* § 14.4.3, *infra*.

260 See § 8.4, *supra*, for a discussion of claims filed by the debtor.

261 11 U.S.C. § 507.

262 See § 14.4.3, *infra*, for a discussion of objections to claims. Federal Rule of Bankruptcy Procedure 9011 requires twenty-one days prior notice of any request by a party for sanctions under that rule.

---

263 11 U.S.C. § 1308(a).
264 11 U.S.C. § 1308(b)(1).
265 11 U.S.C. § 1308(b)(2).
266 *See, e.g., In re* Cushing, 401 B.R. 528 (B.A.P. 1st Cir. 2009).

income test[267]—so the expenses will often reduce payments to unsecured creditors.

Once the returns are filed, the taxing authority is given a new deadline to file a proof of claim, which may extend beyond the normal deadline. Section 502(b)(9) states that a tax claim shall be timely if it is filed on or before sixty days after the relevant tax return filed under section 1308. Although this statutory provision is not crystal clear, the Bankruptcy Rules provide that the deadline for a tax claim can only be extended, not shortened, if a return is filed under section 1308.[268]

12.3.6.3 Postpetition Domestic Support Obligation Payments

The 2005 amendments added several provisions which also make clear that a chapter 13 debtor must continue to make payments on domestic support obligations that first become due after the petition is filed. Section 1307(a)(11) provides that a case may be dismissed or converted if the debtor becomes delinquent in such payments. Under section 1325(a)(8) a plan is not entitled to confirmation unless the debtor has remained current in postpetition domestic support payments. And under section 1328(a)(1), to receive a full-compliance chapter 13 discharge after completing plan payments a debtor must certify that all postpetition domestic support obligation payments have been made.

12.4 Classification of Claims

12.4.1 In General

One of the powers that chapter 13 gives to debtors is the right to designate classes of claims.[269] In essence, this is the right to treat some claims better than others in the chapter 13 plan. However, this right is subject to an important limitation. The plan may not "discriminate unfairly" against any class of claims.[270] Generally, this means that if certain claims are placed in a separate class for preferred treatment, some distinguishing characteristic of those claims must justify that preferred treatment, making it "fair."[271] Otherwise, one of the cardinal principles of bankruptcy, equality among creditors, would be undermined. Thus, for example, a plan providing greater payments to creditors who would receive more in a chapter 7 case because of their rights against entireties property is not unfair discrimination.[272]

Unfortunately, chapter 13 gives little indication of what should be considered to be fair. It does make clear, because it allows classes of unsecured claims, that all unsecured claims need not be in the same class. Section 1322(b)(1) also refers to section 1122, which provides for classification of claims in chapter 11 cases. That section, in turn, provides a little more guidance. A claim may be placed in a class only if it is "substantially similar" to other claims in the class,[273] and a separate class of small unsecured claims may be created for administrative convenience.[274] The legislative history of this section further states that it is meant to codify preexisting case law.[275]

Although helpful, none of these guidelines fully prepared bankruptcy courts for all of the types of classifications that consumers would propose in chapter 13 cases. Some classifications have posed few problems; it is clear that secured claimants and priority claimants have greater rights in bankruptcy than unsecured claimants. Separate classifications of such claims merely carry forward the policies evident in the Code.[276] And, if the debtor wishes, there is no doubt that such claims may even be divided into separate classes for different treatment in order of their priority or lien status.[277]

Although fairness depends on the order of payment as well as the amount, it is not considered unfair to pay creditors with a lower priority before paying those with a higher status; section 1322(a)(2) requires only that all priority claims be paid in full, except as provided in section 1322(a)(4). Section 1322(b)(4) expressly permits payments on any unsecured claim to be made concurrently with payments on any secured claim or any other unsecured claim.[278] A few courts have required payment of the debtor's attorney fees concurrently with unsecured debts, despite their priority status, to assure that the debtor's attorney maintains an interest in the case.[279] Other courts have permitted payment of attorney fees prior to other claims, recognizing that

---

267 See § 12.3.3.4.6, supra; Ch. 13, infra.
268 Fed. R. Bankr. P. 3002(c)(1).
269 11 U.S.C. § 1322(b)(1).
270 11 U.S.C. § 1322(b)(1).
271 See In re Furlow, 70 B.R. 973 (Bankr. E.D. Pa. 1987).
272 In re Raynard, 354 B.R. 834 (B.A.P. 9th Cir. 2006) (plan paying 100% to joint creditors who could reach entireties property and smaller amount to other creditors did not unfairly discriminate). See also § 12.3.2, supra.

273 11 U.S.C. § 1122(a).
274 11 U.S.C. § 1122(b).
  The debtor might wish to pay off a large number of small claims first in order to satisfy most of his or her creditors quickly, especially if future business with those claimants is contemplated. See also In re Terry, 78 B.R. 171 (Bankr. E.D. Tenn. 1987) (first $1000 and ten percent of remaining balance to be paid on unsecured claims); In re Ratledge, 31 B.R. 897 (Bankr. E.D. Tenn. 1983) (plan confirmed that proposed payment of first $500 and ten percent of remaining balance to all unsecured creditors).
275 S. Rep. No. 95-989, at 118 (1978); H.R. Rep. No. 95-595, at 406 (1977).
276 In re Stewart, 290 B.R. 302 (Bankr. E.D. Mich. 2003) (each secured claim may be separately classified, and secured claims need not be paid concurrently). See 7 Collier on Bankruptcy ¶ 1122.03[3] [c] (16th ed.).
277 See 7 Collier on Bankruptcy ¶ 1122.03[3][b], [c] (16th ed.).
278 The Supreme Court has held that, as to tax payments, a chapter 11 debtor may allocate payments to a particular tax liability if the allocation furthers the debtor's reorganization, despite the claims of the Internal Revenue Service that it had the right to allocate the payments due to their involuntary nature. United States v. Energy Res., Inc., 495 U.S. 545, 110 S. Ct. 2139, 109 L. Ed. 2d 580 (1990). See § 12.4.3, infra. The language of section 1322(b)(4) and the fact that a chapter 13 plan is, in all cases, completely voluntary in nature should militate for a similar result in chapter 13.
279 See § 16.4.1, infra.

this is specifically dictated by section 1326(a)(2).[280] For the same reason domestic support obligations need not be paid before attorney fees.[281] Section 1322(b)(5) also permits unsecured claims with a final payment due after the conclusion of the plan to be dealt with in a different manner, through maintenance of payments and curing of defaults.[282] And section 1322(b)(10) permits payment of interest on nondischargeable claims, provided that the plan proposes to pay all allowed unsecured claims in full.

12.4.2 Claims with Cosigners

The most commonly proposed classification confronted by the courts has been that providing for favored treatment (usually one-hundred percent payment) to creditors who have obtained cosigners on their claims. Because in consumer cases these cosigners are almost always the debtor's close friends or relatives, it is not surprising that debtors have wanted to place a higher priority on payment of these debts to avoid the bad feelings or embarrassment that could be engendered if the creditor sought payment from their cosigners. Debtors in such cases have argued that, for them, there was a substantial difference between these and other unsecured claims.

Although the courts had not been particularly sympathetic to these arguments,[283] Congress apparently did agree with them. The 1984 amendments to the Code specifically permit separate classification of claims with cosigners.[284] The legislative history recognized that practical differences exist between cosigned claims and other claims, and that those differences cause debtors to pay creditors voluntarily outside the plan if classification is not permitted, thereby jeopardizing their ability to make plan payments.[285] These practical differences were found to justify separate classification.[286] Under the language of the amended section 1322(b)(1), debtors are permitted to separately classify and treat differently cosigned debt without showing that such treatment is fair.[287] Presumably, as some courts have held that creditors may proceed against cosigners in chapter 13 unless the plan proposes to pay the claim in full including interest,[288] separate classification of such claims can also be utilized to pay interest on them when no other creditors receive interest under the plan.[289] With no basis in the plain language of the Code, a few courts have held that separate classification of cosigned debts may not be used to pay a lower percentage of those claims than other unsecured claims—even when the cosigner is up to date on payments.[290] Others have permitted some discrimination in favor of cosigned claims but not discrimination they believe is disproportionate.[291] These cases are wrongly decided and may frustrate a debtor's plan. Additionally, unnecessary double payments may be made.[292]

12.4.3 Other Classifications

Debtors in chapter 13 cases have also proposed a number of other types of classifications. Several have classified separately debts that would likely be nondischargeable in a chapter 7 case or in both chapters 7 and 13. Although not all such claims are given priority in liquidation, such classifications have been allowed by some courts.

For example, plans proposing favored treatment of child support arrearages were approved based on the nondischargeability of such debts and the different enforcement mechanisms available, for example, contempt of court.[293] In *In re Leser*[294] the Eighth Circuit Court of Appeals held that the strong public policy in favor of obtaining funds for child support claims, including those assigned to governmental units, dictated that they could be separately classified and paid more than other unsecured claims. Of course, now that Congress has made all domestic support obligation debts priority claims, including those assigned to governmental units,[295] there can be no doubt

---

280 *See, e.g., In re* Tenney, 63 B.R. 110 (Bankr. W.D. Okla. 1986).
281 *In re* Sanders, 341 B.R. 47 (Bankr. N.D. Ala. 2006), *aff'd*, 347 B.R. 776 (N.D. Ala. 2006).
282 *See* Joe Lee, *Chapter 13 nee Chapter XIII*, 53 Am. Bankr. L. J. 303, 313 (1979).
283 *See, e.g.*, Barnes v. Whelan, 689 F.2d 193 (D.C. Cir. 1982) (plan proposing one-hundred percent payment to cosigned debts and one percent to other debts discriminated unfairly; court left open possibility that complete equality of treatment might not be necessary, depending on the individual debtor's circumstances); *In re* Wade, 4 B.R. 98 (Bankr. M.D. Tenn. 1980); *In re* Iacovoni, 2 B.R. 256 (Bankr. D. Utah 1980).
284 11 U.S.C. § 1322(b)(1).
285 S. Rep. No. 98-65, at 17 (1983). *See also In re* Ross, 161 B.R. 36 (Bankr. C.D. Ill. 1993) (permitting separate classification of debt guaranteed by debtor's employer, who allegedly would have discharged debtor if debt was not paid).
286 S. Rep. No. 98-65, at 17 (1983).
 Despite the 1994 amendments, several courts have held that separate classification of codebtor claims is subject to the unfair discrimination test. *See, e.g., In re* Applegarth, 221 B.R. 914 (Bankr. M.D. Fla. 1998); *In re* Thompson, 191 B.R. 967, 971 (Bankr. S.D. Ga. 1996) (discrimination in favor of creditors with cosigners was intended to be "per se" fair discrimination). *See also In re* Renteria, 470 B.R. 838 (B.A.P. 9th Cir. 2012) (without deciding whether unfair discrimination rule should apply, court held that plan confir-

mation cannot be denied solely because the plan treats a codebtor consumer claim more favorably than all other unsecured claims); *In re* Hill, 268 B.R. 548 (B.A.P. 9th Cir. 2001) (debts incurred through debtor's use of mother's credit cards did not give rise to debtor's joint liability to card grantor, so codebtor clause in section 1322(b)(1) did not apply, and debt was not eligible for separate classification).
287 *In re* Dornon, 103 B.R. 61 (Bankr. N.D.N.Y. 1989).
288 *See* § 9.4.5, *supra*.
289 Southeastern Bank v. Brown, 266 B.R. 900 (S.D. Ga. 2001); *In re* Monroe, 281 B.R. 398 (Bankr. N.D. Ga. 2002); *In re* Austin, 110 B.R. 430 (Bankr. E.D. Mo. 1990).
290 *See, e.g., In re* Markham, 224 B.R. 599 (Bankr. W.D. Ky. 1998).
291 *In re* Chacon, 202 F.3d 725 (5th Cir. 1999).
292 As a practical matter, creditors are unlikely to object to a plan as long as payments are being made by the codebtor.
293 *In re* Haag, 3 B.R. 649 (Bankr. D. Or. 1980); *In re* Curtis, 2 B.R. 43 (Bankr. W.D. Mo. 1979).
294 939 F.2d 669 (8th Cir. 1991). *See also* Henry J. Sommer & Margaret Dee McGarity, Collier Family Law and the Bankruptcy Code ¶ 8.07 (1992).
295 11 U.S.C. § 507(a)(1).

about the propriety of giving those debts more favored treatment. For the same reason priority debts resulting from driving while under the influence of alcohol or drugs may be separately classified.[296]

Similarly, separate classification of student loan debts has been allowed by some courts.[297] Some of the same arguments applicable to child support debts also apply in the student loan context. As in the case of child support, the exception to the chapter 13 discharge for student loans is not one based on the fault of the debtor, or intended to punish the debtor. It was passed as part of a budget act as a way of providing revenues to the government.[298] Congressional action making the debt nondischargeable is, in itself, evidence that payment of student loan debts has special social importance. Therefore, it is entirely in keeping with these purposes to allow separate classification and greater payments which will increase the amount the government collects on such debts. Indeed, absent such classification, many debtors would be forced to default on student loans they had kept current. At least one court has also pointed out that separate classification has another reasonable basis because, absent payment of a student loan, a debtor is often ineligible to obtain other financial assistance or to return to school.[299] In some states, failure to pay a student loan may even cause the loss of a professional license.[300] For some courts, it has been a sufficient basis for classification that the debt is nondischargeable in chapter 13 and the debtor, therefore, has a significant interest in paying as much of it as possible.[301]

When such classifications have been rejected, it has often been, at least in part, due to a lack of proof that the claims would indeed be nondischargeable.[302] In any case, debtor should be able to cure and maintain payments on a long-term student loan pursuant to section 1322(b)(5), even if that means that the student loan creditor receives more than other unsecured creditors.[303] This may achieve the same practical result as separate classification, even in jurisdictions where separate classification is not otherwise allowed.

Likewise, when the Code provides special treatment for particular contracts, such as executory contracts and unexpired leases, that treatment can be carried out through classification. As discussed below,[304] to assume an executory contract or unexpired lease the debtor must promptly cure a default. The debtor may effectuate that cure by paying the arrears on the contract, even if those arrears might otherwise be an unsecured claim, prior to other claims.[305]

---

296 11 U.S.C. § 507(a)(10).
297 *In re* King, 460 B.R. 708 (Bankr. N.D. Tex. 2011) (discrimination not unfair when plan proposed to pay all projected disposable income to general unsecured creditors); *In re* Mason, 456 B.R. 245 (Bankr. N.D. W.Va. 2011) (approving plan providing for 72% distribution on debtor's student loan debts as compared to only 8% distribution to other unsecured creditors); *In re* Abaunza, 452 B.R. 866 (Bankr. S.D. Fla. 2011) (discrimination not unfair, even though distribution to general unsecured creditors was 0.86%); *In re* Truss, 404 B.R. 329 (Bankr. E.D. Wis. 2009); *In re* Orawsky, 387 B.R. 128 (Bankr. E.D. Pa. 2008) (proposed discrimination in favor of student loan creditor not unfair when debtor was, in addition, committing all projected disposable income to unsecured creditors); *In re* Tucker, 159 B.R. 325 (Bankr. D. Mont. 1993); *In re* Foreman, 136 B.R. 532 (Bankr. S.D. Iowa 1992); *In re* Boggan, 125 B.R. 533 (Bankr. N.D. Ill. 1991); *In re* Freshley, 69 B.R. 96 (Bankr. N.D. Ga. 1987). See also *In re* Knight, 370 B.R. 429 (Bankr. N.D. Ga. 2007) (nondischargeable student loan obligations may be treated by above-median debtor as additional expenses for "special circumstances" thereby reducing disposable income available to other unsecured creditors). But see *In re* Groves, 39 F.3d 212 (8th Cir. 1994) (plan could not discriminate in favor of student loans solely due to their nondischargeability); *In re* Bentley, 266 B.R.229 (B.A.P. 1st Cir. 2001) (plan paying student loan in full and only three percent on other claims was unfairly discriminatory); *In re* Sperna, 173 B.R. 654 (B.A.P. 9th Cir. 1994); *In re* Willis, 197 B.R. 912 (N.D. Okla. 1996); McCullough v. Brown, 162 B.R. 506 (N.D. Ill. 1994); *In re* Scheiber, 129 B.R. 604 (Bankr. D. Minn. 1991); *In re* Furlow, 70 B.R. 973 (Bankr. E.D. Pa. 1987) (separate classification of student loan debt not allowed without further explanation of reasons).
298 Omnibus Budget Reconciliation Act of 1990, Pub. L. No. 101-508, 104 Stat. 1388.
  A similar argument could be made with respect to criminal restitution debts and non-priority drunk driving debts that are nondischargeable in chapter 13, in that they were made nondischargeable by amendments designed to give greater amounts of money to victims. Criminal Victims Protection Act of 1990, Pub. L. No. 101-581, 104 Stat. 2865. See *In re* Etheridge, 297 B.R. 810 (Bankr. M.D. Ala. 2003) (debtor permitted to separately classify bad check debt that was subject of criminal proceedings).
299 *In re* Freshley, 69 B.R. 96 (Bankr. N.D. Ga. 1987) (separate classification of student loan debt allowed so debtor could return to school).
300 *In re* Kalfayan, 415 B.R. 907 (Bankr. S.D. Fla. 2009) (permitting preferred treatment because loss of optometry license would jeopardize entire plan).
301 *In re* Boggan, 125 B.R. 533 (Bankr. N.D. Ill. 1991). See also 8 Collier on Bankruptcy ¶ 1322.05[2] (16th ed.). But see *In re* Groves, 39 F.3d 212 (8th Cir. 1994) (plan could not discriminate in favor of student loans solely due to their nondischargeability); *In re* Sperna, 173 B.R. 654 (B.A.P. 9th Cir. 1994) (same); *In re* Willis, 197 B.R. 912 (N.D. Okla. 1996); McCullough v. Brown, 162 B.R. 506 (N.D. Ill. 1994); *In re* Scheiber, 129 B.R. 604 (Bankr. D. Minn. 1991); *In re* Furlow, 70 B.R. 973 (Bankr. E.D. Pa. 1987) (separate classification of student loan debt not allowed without further explanation of reasons).
302 See *In re* Gay, 3 B.R. 336 (D. Colo. 1980); *In re* Fonnest, 5 Bankr. Ct. Dec. (LRP) 1236, 1 Collier Bankr. Cas. 2d (MB) 383 (N.D. Cal. 1980).
303 *In re* Johnson, 446 B.R. 921 (Bankr. E.D. Wis. 2011); *In re* Potgieter, 436 B.R. 739 (Bankr. M.D. Fla. 2010); *In re* Kalfayan, 415 B.R. 907 (Bankr. S.D. Fla. 2009); *In re* Machado, 378 B.R. 14 (Bankr. D. Mass. 2007); *In re* Knight, 370 B.R. 429 (Bankr. N.D. Ga. 2007) (student loan payments could qualify as special circumstances justifying deduction from disposable income for above median income debtor); *In re* Webb, 370 B.R. 418 (Bankr. N.D. Ga. 2007); *In re* Sullivan, 195 B.R. 649 (Bankr. W.D. Tex. 1996); *In re* Cox, 186 B.R. 744 (Bankr. N.D. Fla. 1995); *In re* Benner, 156 B.R. 631 (Bankr. D. Minn. 1993). See also *In re* Boscaccy, 442 B.R. 501 (Bankr. N.D. Miss. 2010) (cure and maintenance of payments permitted in most circumstances). But see *In re* Labib-Kiyarash, 271 B.R. 189 (B.A.P. 9th Cir. 2001) (different treatment of long-term debt under section 1322(b)(5) still subject to scrutiny for unfair discrimination); *In re* Coonce, 213 B.R. 344 (Bankr. S.D. Ill. 1997).
304 See § 12.9.2, *infra*.
305 *In re* Davis, 209 B.R. 893 (Bankr. N.D. Ill. 1997).
  Assumption of the executory contract or lease renders the amount necessary to cure a priority administrative expense, which clearly can be separately classified. *In re* Klein Sleep Prods., Inc., 78 F.3d 18 (2d Cir. 1996). See 4 Collier on Bankruptcy ¶ 503.06[6][b] (16th ed.).

Other proposals have involved preferred treatment to creditors with a special relationship to the debtor or with claims of a special nature. Courts have sometimes approved more favored treatment for doctors, landlords, trade creditors necessary for continued operation of a business, attorneys, and even banks from which future credit is needed.[306] If the debtor must discriminate among creditors to maintain the income necessary for the plan, such discrimination is likely to be allowed.[307] Such decisions have been justified by the fact that these debts were more likely to be paid in the nonbankruptcy world and that the plan or even the debtor's well-being might be endangered without payment to such creditors, for example, if the only doctor in town refused treatment because of a discharged debt.[308] The sparse legislative history on the subject also seems to support a broad view of the debtor's right to classify claims,[309] as does the justification given by Congress for separate classification of cosigned debts.[310] However, some courts decide these issues differently.[311]

Classification may also be used to designate which portion of a claim for federal taxes a debtor wishes to pay. Generally, the debtor will wish to classify tax claims to make sure that priority, nondischargeable, and secured tax claims are paid prior to dischargeable unsecured tax claims. The Supreme Court has specifically held that a chapter 11 debtor may so designate the payments under its plan when plan payments are voluntary,[312] so a chapter 13 debtor whose payments are, if anything, more voluntary than those of a chapter 11 debtor, should certainly be able to designate which tax years are being provided for in the plan. Occasionally, a debtor may also wish to separately classify prepetition tax penalty claims and seek to have them equitably subordinated to other unsecured claims if, for example, the debtor would prefer to see the general unsecured creditors get paid rather than the taxing authorities. Most courts have held that, at least in some cases, tax penalty claims can be equitably subordinated.[313] Similarly, if debtors want more of their distributions paid to medical providers, family member creditors, or local merchants, they may subordinate other penalty claims, such as credit card late charges, that are subordinated in chapter 7 under section 726(a)(4).[314]

Finally, some courts have gone behind the classifications of debts explicitly stated in plans to find different treatment which has been implicitly granted to certain unsecured claims. Such differing treatment has usually occurred when debts are partially secured. In such cases, the partially secured debt should be divided into a secured claim and an unsecured claim.[315] Thus, full payment of the partially secured claim would mean full payment of the unsecured portion as well as the secured portion. When this has been proposed and when other unsecured creditors were not to be paid in full, confirmation of the plan has been denied.[316] However, courts are unlikely to explore this issue unless it is raised by a party in interest.

12.4.4 Payments Directly to Creditors

Another type of provision that may be a classification is the designation of certain claims to be paid "outside the plan." What this means is that the debtor will make payments on these claims directly to the creditor, instead of through the trustee. Such provisions may offer a number of advantages. They usually save the debtor from paying the trustee's fees and costs of up to ten percent on such debts, a factor that may be important in cases in which the payments on one debt, such as a home mortgage, are particularly large. For this reason, trustees have sometimes objected to payments outside the plan. Generally, courts have dismissed these objections.[317] Payments

---

306 *In re* Hill, 4 B.R. 694 (Bankr. D. Kan. 1980) (physicians, dentists, lawyers); *In re* Kovich, 4 B.R. 403 (Bankr. W.D. Mich. 1980) (landlord); *In re* Sutherland, 3 B.R. 420 (Bankr. W.D. Ark. 1980) (trade creditors, medical debts, banks). *See also* Connors, *Bankruptcy Reform: Relief for Individuals with Regular Income*, 13 U. Rich. L. Rev. 219, 237 (1978).

Similar issues arise in chapter 11 cases, in which courts often allow full payment of creditors essential to the debtor's business through "first day orders" under the "critical vendor doctrine."

307 *See In re* Gallipo, 282 B.R. 917 (Bankr. E.D. Wash. 2002) (debtor allowed to separately classify and pay traffic fines because nonpayment would have jeopardized her ability to get to work).

308 For a discussion of the principles applied in such cases, see Charles F. Vihon, *Classification of Unsecured Claims; Squaring a Circle?*, 55 Am. Bankr. L. J. 143 (1980).

309 *See Bankruptcy Act Revision: Hearings on H.R. 31 and H.R. 32 Before the Subcomm. on Civil and Constitutional Rights of the House Comm. on the Judiciary*, 94th Cong. 1425, 1426 (1976) (statement of Claude L. Rice).

310 *See* § 12.4.2, *supra*.

311 *See, e.g., In re* Jones, 138 B.R. 536 (Bankr. S.D. Ohio 1991) (debtor could not give favored treatment to loan from his retirement fund); *In re* Harris, 62 B.R. 391 (Bankr. E.D. Mich. 1986) (denying confirmation to plan providing greater payment to consumer creditors than to business creditors).

312 United States v. Energy Res., Inc., 495 U.S. 545, 110 S. Ct. 2139, 109 L. Ed. 2d 580 (1990).

313 Burden v. United States, 917 F.2d 115 (3d Cir. 1990); *In re* Virtual Network Servs. Corp., 902 F.2d 1246 (7th Cir. 1990); Schultz Broadway Inn v. United States, 912 F.2d 230 (8th Cir. 1990). *But see* United States v. Noland, 517 U.S. 535, 116 S. Ct. 1524, 134 L. Ed. 2d 748 (1996) (tax penalties that are postpetition administrative expenses cannot be subordinated).

314 If a creditor fails to break out such penalty charges in a proof of claim, an objection to the claim may be filed. See § 14.4.3.5, infra.

315 11 U.S.C. § 506(a). *See* Ch. 11, *supra*.

316 *In re* Cooper, 3 B.R. 246 (Bankr. S.D. Cal. 1980); *In re* Tatum, 1 B.R. 445 (Bankr. S.D. Ohio 1979); *In re* Bevins, 1 B.R. 442 (Bankr. S.D. Ohio 1979). *But see In re* Delauder, 189 B.R. 639 (Bankr. E.D. Va. 1995) (permitting direct payment of auto loan pursuant to provisions for curing long term debt under section 1322(b)(5) even though creditor was undersecured). *Cf. In re* Dingley, 189 B.R. 264 (Bankr. N.D.N.Y. 1995) (plan which proposes to pay a present value interest rate to a secured creditor under section 1325(a)(5) which exceeds the minimum required to confirm the plan found to inequitably reduce the dividend to unsecured creditors thus warranting denial of confirmation).

317 *In re* Lopez, 550 F.3d 1202 (9th Cir. 2008); *In re* Aberegg, 961 F.2d 1307 (7th Cir. 1992); *In re* Vigil, 344 B.R. 624 (Bankr. D.N.M. 2006) (nothing in 2005 amendments changed debtor's ability to make direct payments to creditors); *In re* Clay, 339 B.R. 784 (Bankr. D. Utah 2006); *In re* Grear, 163 B.R. 524 (Bankr. S.D. Ill. 1994) (proceeds of collateral could be paid directly to secured creditor

outside the plan may also avoid the delays sometimes encountered when payments are made through the trustee. In any case, to the extent that the plan provides a creditor with a greater benefit from having payments made outside the plan, that designation may constitute a classification subject to the unfair discrimination test.[318]

On the other hand, some trustees and practitioners prefer payment of the current mortgage payments through the trustee. Payments through the trustee may be more likely to be made, especially if they are made through a wage-deduction order. Moreover, the trustee is able to easily provide an accounting of the payments, eliminating most disputes about whether payments have been made and obviating the need to reconcile the debtor's often fragmentary records of canceled checks and money order receipts. Although such payments are subject to the trustee's fee, in districts where current mortgage payments are routinely made through the trustee, the percentage fee is often at a much lower rate because the trustee's receipts are far higher.

12.4.5 Payments to Former Chapter 7 Trustees

A chapter 7 trustee may be allowed compensation due to a previous dismissal or conversion of a case under section 707(b). If the court allows such compensation, the Code limits how much of it can be paid before the payment of general unsecured claims. It is to be paid in monthly payments prorated over the entire "remaining" term of the chapter 13 plan.[319] Monthly payments cannot exceed the greater of $25 per month or five percent of the total to be paid to unsecured non-priority creditors, divided by the number of months in the plan.[320] In most cases, this limitation means that the payment amount under this provision will be no more than $25 per month (or $1500 over a five-year plan), because most chapter 13 plans do not pay more than $500 per month to unsecured non-priority creditors.

In light of the fact that section 1326(b)(3) mentions payments to a former chapter 7 trustee only when the case has been converted after a motion under section 707(b), it may be difficult for such trustees to argue for compensation from the estate in other cases.[321]

12.4.6 Practical Considerations

It is generally in the debtor's interest to classify some claims. Large secured claims may be paid directly to the creditors to avoid considerable trustee expenses. Also it is usually advantageous to pay other secured claims, when liens cannot be avoided and the claims are not dischargeable in chapter 13 or chapter 7, especially those that are priority claims, before general unsecured claims. If that is done, then after the chapter 13 case, or if later circumstances force a conversion to chapter 7 or dismissal, the debtor may have paid off, or at least reduced, those claims which would be most troublesome in chapter 7 or outside of bankruptcy. In addition, the debtor usually wants to provide for early payment of dischargeable priority claims at least before other unsecured claims. Once these are paid, if circumstances change, the debtor may choose to modify the plan to terminate earlier, assuming that the other mandatory requirements of chapter 13 have also been met by then. If priority claims have not yet been paid in full, such modification is not available; the options may be limited to a hardship discharge, conversion to chapter 7, or dismissal.[322]

In view of the courts' general hostility to special treatment for certain unsecured debts, the debtor may not be able to provide for such treatment in the plan. However, other alternatives that accomplish a similar result may be available. The debtor may be able to propose a plan that gives a low percentage payment to all unsecured creditors, and then make *voluntary* payments outside the plan to the preferred creditors. Because the plan would not provide for these payments, however, the debtor would not be bound to make them under section 1327(a). Nor could the debtor formally promise the creditor that the payments would be made without running afoul of the reaffirmation provisions in section 524.[323] A creditor who receives continued voluntary payments is not likely to deny services on the basis of a bankruptcy. Thus, as long as the

---

without payment of trustee's fee). *See In re* Bettger, 105 B.R. 607 (Bankr. D. Or. 1989) (proceeds of sale of real estate could be paid directly to creditors). *See also In re* Beard, 45 F.3d 113 (6th Cir. 1995) (no fee payable on direct payments to creditors under chapter 12 plan); *In re* Wagner, 36 F.3d 723 (8th Cir. 1994) (same); 8 Collier on Bankruptcy ¶ 1302.05[1][c] (16th ed.). *But see In re* Fulkrod, 973 F.2d 801 (9th Cir. 1992) (chapter 12 debtor may not avoid trustee commission by making payments directly to impaired creditors); *In re* Foster, 670 F.2d 478 (5th Cir. 1982) (payments may be made outside the plan in some cases, but they are still subject to trustee's percentage fee; courts should consider lowering percentage to reflect trustee's lesser responsibilities in such circumstances); *In re* Giesbrecht, 429 B.R. 682 (B.A.P. 9th Cir. 2010) (debtors have no absolute right to make direct payments, and court has discretion to require payments to be made through trustee); Perez v. Peake, 373 B.R. 468 (S.D. Tex. 2007) (upholding local rule requiring postpetition mortgage payments to be made through trustee).

The argument that no trustee fee is required on payments made directly to creditors was strengthened by the 1986 amendments, replacing language in section 1302(e)(2) that the fee be collected from "all payments under plans" with language in 28 U.S.C. § 586(e)(2) that the fee shall be collected from all payments received by the trustee, so that the cases prohibiting direct payment may no longer be good law. A number of courts, including at least one court in the Fifth Circuit, have found that the 1986 amendments overrule *Foster* and provide authority for permitting payments directly to a creditor without deduction of the trustee's commission on those payments. *In re* Donald, 170 B.R. 579 (Bankr. S.D. Miss. 1994); *In re* Burkhart, 94 B.R. 724 (Bankr. N.D. Fla. 1988); *In re* Wright, 82 B.R. 422 (Bankr. W.D. Va. 1988).

318 *In re* Haag, 3 B.R. 649 (Bankr. D. Or. 1980); *In re* Iacovoni, 2 B.R. 256 (Bankr. D. Utah 1980).

319 11 U.S.C. § 1326(b)(3).
320 11 U.S.C. § 1326(b)(3)(B).
321 *See In re* Silvus, 329 B.R. 193 (Bankr. E.D. Va. 2005) (denying former chapter 7 trustee compensation in case converted to chapter 13 and discussing conflicting pre-2005 case law).
322 See § 8.7.5, *supra*, for a discussion of these options.
323 See § 15.5.2, *infra*, for a discussion of reaffirmation.

payments are not provided for in the plan or binding upon the debtor, and the plan otherwise complies with chapter 13 (large voluntary payments might not be possible due to the ability-to-pay test[324] if an objection is raised on that basis), there should be no impediment to giving preferred treatment voluntarily to particular creditors outside the plan.[325]

12.5 Feasibility of the Plan

In drafting a plan, a consumer debtor's counsel must also be aware of section 1325(a)(6). This subsection requires that "the debtor will be able to make all payments under the plan and to comply with the plan." If the plan does not meet this standard, sometimes called the "feasibility" test, confirmation may be denied.

Thus, the schedules' property and budget figures must show sufficient income or other financial resources to enable the debtor to make the payments proposed. If the debtor does not present such evidence as is necessary to convince the court that payments can be made, the plan may be found not feasible.[326] Similarly, if the plan calls for a very large lump sum payment at the end of the plan, with no reasonable explanation of how the debtor will fund it, the plan will be found not to meet the feasibility test.[327] The court may consider whether necessaries such as potential medical expenses and clothing have been provided for,[328] and whether there is sufficient "cushion" or "play" in the budget to cover unexpected expenses and inflation.[329] Finally, it may simply find the expense estimates to be unreasonably low.[330]

In view of the possibility of such scrutiny, it is important to note on the schedules of income and expenditures such facts as coverage of all medical expenses by medical assistance, receipt of food stamps and emergency fuel grants, and any other non-cash variations from a normal budget. Even with these, a "cushion" for unexpected expenses is virtually unheard of for low-income people. The best way of showing ability to make payments is to begin making the monthly payments before the confirmation hearing, as section 1326(a) requires. If a debtor has demonstrated an ability to pay the monthly amounts provided in the plan, then few courts will deny a debtor the opportunity to at least try to comply with the plan.[331]

All of these considerations dictate careful construction of a reasonable budget which, if possible, allows a small cushion over and above the required plan payments. As the court may also look to ability to pay if an objection is filed under section 1325(b), however, this cushion should not be overly large, lest the court decide the debtor could pay more into the plan. Ultimately, the debtor must steer a course between the Scylla and Charybdis of feasibility and ability to pay to create the optimum chance of confirmation. The feasibility ceiling on payments may not be far above the ability-to-pay floor.

12.6 Other Plan Provisions

12.6.1 Payment of Debtor's Income Directly to Trustee

Section 1325(c) provides that, after confirmation,[332] the court may order any entity from whom the debtor receives income to pay all or part of that income directly to the trustee. Such an order, known as a "wage order," is often sought by attorneys representing debtors (with their clients' concurrence) to ensure that they receive their own fees, which are priority administrative expenses, and to maximize the chance that payments will be made. The court may sometimes view an application for a wage order as a sign of the debtor's seriousness, and thus it may help obtain confirmation. Indeed, in some courts they are almost a requirement.

Most courts require a separate application or motion to be filed in order to obtain a wage order.[333] Because it is a court order, the court can enforce compliance with the wage order by a recalcitrant employer, if necessary.[334]

Such orders may offer less attraction in legal services cases, because they reduce the debtor's flexibility in budgeting and possibly deviating slightly from the established payment sched-

---

324 See § 12.3.4, *supra*.
325 See *In re* Iacovoni, 2 B.R. 256 (Bankr. D. Utah 1980).
326 *In re* Epps, 6 Bankr. Ct. Dec. (LRP) 379, 2 Collier Bankr. Cas. 2d (MB) 97 (Bankr. S.D.N.Y. 1980); *In re* Nance, 4 B.R. 50 (Bankr. W.D. Mo. 1980).
327 *In re* Fantasia, 211 B.R. 420 (B.A.P. 1st Cir. 1997) (plan not feasible when debtors offered no evidence to show they could carry out intent of making large balloon payment by refinancing a parcel of property); *In re* Gavia, 24 B.R. 573 (B.A.P. 9th Cir. 1982) (plan based upon sale of residence, which was not likely, denied confirmation); *In re* Seem, 92 B.R. 134 (Bankr. E.D. Pa. 1988) (plan to sell real estate at end of plan period was too speculative to meet test); *In re* Schenck, 67 B.R. 137 (Bankr. D. Mont. 1986).

However, a balloon payment at the end of a plan is not always found infeasible. See *In re* Gregory, 143 B.R. 424 (Bankr. E.D. Tex. 1992) (plan with large balloon payment at end based on proposed sale of debtors' home was not too speculative); *In re* Groff, 131 B.R. 703 (Bankr. E.D. Wis. 1991) (balloon payment on mortgage at end of plan permitted).

328 *In re* Washington, 6 B.R. 226 (Bankr. E.D. Va. 1980); *In re* Hockaday, 3 B.R. 254 (Bankr. S.D. Cal. 1980).
329 *In re* Lilley, 29 B.R. 442 (B.A.P. 1st Cir. 1983); *In re* Washington, 6 B.R. 226 (Bankr. E.D. Va. 1980) ($44.93/mo. cushion insufficient); *In re* Coleman, 5 B.R. 812 (Bankr. W.D. Ky. 1980) ($4.00/mo. cushion insufficient); *In re* Hockaday, 3 B.R. 254 (Bankr. S.D. Cal. 1980) ($10.00/mo. cushion insufficient); *In re* Howard, 3 B.R. 75 (Bankr. S.D. Cal. 1980).
330 *In re* Lucas, 3 B.R. 252 (Bankr. S.D. Cal. 1980).

331 See *In re* Ryals, 5 B.R. 522 (Bankr. E.D. Tenn. 1980) (court reluctant to judge what sacrifices a debtor can make).
332 Despite the language of section 1325(c), most courts enter such orders before confirmation. See *In re* Torres, 191 B.R. 735 (Bankr. N.D. Ill. 1996) (court has authority under section 105(a) to enter preconfirmation wage order).
333 See Forms 20, 21, Appx. G.3, *infra*.
334 *In re* Worrell, 113 B.R. 236 (Bankr. E.D. Va. 1990). See Nowlin v. RNR, L.L.C., 2009 WL 2872916 (Bankr. M.D. Tenn. Aug. 27, 2009) (sanctioning employer for repeated noncompliance with orders regarding wage withholding).

ule if necessary. Still, they should be explained and offered as an option to clients who have doubts as to their self-discipline in making payments.

Clients should also know that there is a possibility that the court will enter a wage order regardless of their wishes.[335] In some courts this possibility is more remote than others. Some trustees now routinely request wage orders by motion for all employed debtors. When a debtor does not want a wage order entered, (for example, if the debtor does not wish an employer to know about the bankruptcy) opposition to a wage order should be made known to the trustee or the court. This may require a response opposing the trustee's motion.

One issue which arose with respect to subsection 1325(c) is whether it overrides the non-assignability provisions of the Social Security Act and of other federal laws which prohibit assignment or attachment of benefits. Looking to legislative history, which clearly contemplates the filing of chapter 13 cases by recipients of such benefits,[336] courts generally found the Bankruptcy Code to repeal the earlier statutes implicitly to the extent of allowing such orders (despite the objection of the Social Security Administration).[337] However, Congress then amended the Social Security Act to state that such repeal by implication was not intended.[338] Since that amendment, courts have become more reluctant to find that Congress intended to repeal by implication the anti-assignment provisions of federal benefits statutes.[339] Courts have also refused to enter payment orders against retirement plans that are not property of the estate.[340] However, other benefits, including assignable public assistance payments, can be subject to such an order.[341]

Another issue that has occasionally arisen is the practice of a few employers to charge the debtor a fee for complying with the wage order.[342] Such a fee may be challenged as discrimination based upon bankruptcy that violates section 525,[343] especially if it is not charged in other similar situations, such as attachments for child support, or as a violation of the automatic stay to the extent it is a taking of property of the estate. Perhaps, the best way to prevent assessment of a fee is to include language in the form of wage order submitted to the court that prohibits the employer from charging the debtor a fee for complying with the order.

Of course, with respect to any wage order, it is important to remember that the debtor may dismiss a chapter 13 case at any time as a matter of right if the case has not been converted from another chapter.[344] Therefore, the debtor always retains the right to end the assignment of benefits or of any other income almost instantly.

12.6.2 Payment of Interest and Penalties

Normally, postpetition interest, late fees, and other charges are not considered to be part of a creditor's claim.[345] Carried over from case law under the prior Act[346] is the principle that such charges are in the nature of penalties that will not be enforced by the bankruptcy court, a court of equity. Not even priority claims, such as unsecured debts for taxes, are entitled to interest,[347] which can be a significant advantage of chapter

---

335 *See In re* Berry, 5 B.R. 515 (Bankr. S.D. Ohio 1980).

336 S. Rep. No. 95-989, at 24 (1978); H.R. Rep. No. 95-595, at 312 (1977). *See In re* Hammonds, 729 F.2d 1391 (11th Cir. 1984) (Aid to Families with Dependent Children benefits); Regan v. Ross, 691 F.2d 81 (2d Cir. 1982) (state employee pension benefits subjected to income deduction order despite state law's anti-assignment provisions and despite provisions of Internal Revenue Code and Treasury regulations); *In re* Simmons, 94 B.R. 74 (W.D. Pa. 1988) (state teachers retirement fund subjected to deduction order despite state statute prohibiting assignment of rights to benefits); *In re* Cochran, 141 B.R. 270 (Bankr. M.D. Ga. 1992) (Code modified Anti-Assignment Act to allow assignment of debtor's tax refunds to United States trustee through income deduction order); *In re* Sampson, 95 B.R. 66 (Bankr. W.D. Mich. 1988) (payroll order could be entered in case of enlisted serviceman despite federal statute prohibiting assignment of pay); *In re* Wood, 23 B.R. 552 (Bankr. E.D. Tenn. 1982) (pension benefits subject to order to pay directly to trustee despite Employee Retirement Income Security Act); *In re* Williams, 20 B.R. 154 (Bankr. E.D. Ark. 1982) (seaman's wages).

Those cases which dealt with funds held in ERISA plans are probably no longer good law in light of the Supreme Court's decision in Patterson v. Shumate, 504 U.S. 753, 112 S. Ct. 2242, 119 L. Ed. 2d 519 (1992), which held that the anti-alienation provisions in such plans prevent them from becoming property of the bankruptcy estate.

337 United States v. Devall, 704 F.2d 1513 (11th Cir. 1983); Michigan Employment Sec. Comm'n v. Jenkins, 64 B.R. 195 (W.D. Mich. 1986).

338 Pub. L. No. 98-21, § 336, 97 Stat. 65 (1983). *See In re* Buren, 725 F.2d 1080 (6th Cir. 1984); H.R. Rep. No. 98-25, at 82 (1983).

339 *In re* Roach, 94 B.R. 440 (W.D. Mich. 1988) (veterans' benefits not subject to order that payments be made directly to trustee).

340 *See* McLean v. Cent. States Pension Funds, 762 F.2d 1204 (4th Cir. 1985); *In re* Watkins, 95 B.R. 483 (W.D. Mich. 1988) (debtor's interest in pension plan could not be subject to payment order); *In re* Snipe, 276 B.R. 723 (Bankr. D.D.C. 2002).

341 *But see In re* Knapp, 294 B.R. 334 (W.D. Wash. 2003) (order to Internal Revenue Service to pay tax refunds to trustee violated sovereign immunity).

342 *See, e.g.,* United States v. Santoro, 208 B.R. 645 (E.D. Va. 1997) (administrative fee charged by U.S. Postal Service was improper because section 1325(c) payroll deduction was not a garnishment on which fee could be charged pursuant to 5 U.S.C. § 5520(a)); *In re* Hudson, 216 B.R. 244 (Bankr. W.D. Tenn. 1997) (payments to chapter 13 trustee not a garnishment), *aff'd,* 230 B.R. 542 (W.D. Tenn. 1999). *But see In re* Heath, 115 F.3d 521 (7th Cir. 1997) (bankruptcy court did not have jurisdiction to consider challenge to $50 fee charged by U.S. Postal Service for complying with wage order).

343 *See* § 15.5.4, *infra.*

344 11 U.S.C. § 1307(b). *See* § 13.2, *infra.*

345 11 U.S.C. § 502(b)(2).

346 *See, e.g., In re* Jones, 2 B.R. 150 (Bankr. M.D. Tenn. 1980) (and cases cited therein). *See also In re* Clayborn, 11 B.R. 117 (Bankr. E.D. Tenn. 1981) (attorney fees for filing a claim could not be included in unsecured claim).

347 *In re* Hieb, 88 B.R. 1019 (Bankr. D.S.D. 1988); *In re* Young, 61 B.R. 150 (Bankr. S.D. Ind. 1986); *In re* Christian, 25 B.R. 438 (Bankr. D.N.M. 1982). *See also In re* Kingsley, 86 B.R. 17 (Bankr. D. Conn. 1988) (postpetition tax claim which was a priority administrative expense could be paid without addition of interest).

13 for a debtor who has large tax debts that are priority claims but are dischargeable.

Under the Bankruptcy Code a few exceptions to this general rule exist. As discussed earlier in this chapter,[348] a debtor may have to pay interest to meet the "best interests of creditors" test if the debtor has a substantial amount of nonexempt property. In addition, section 1325(a)(5) may require payment of interest to give secured creditors the present value of their allowed secured claims,[349] and section 1322(b)(5) may require some payment of interest to cure a default on a long-term debt.[350] Moreover, if a debt is nondischargeable in chapter 13 and postpetition interest on that debt must be paid, then the debtor may choose to propose that such interest be paid either in the plan or by direct payments to the creditor.[351]

Thus, in drafting a plan one must be aware of the several possibilities as to interest rates. Particular claims may be entitled to no interest (such as most unsecured claims), to interest at a rate necessary to meet a present value test,[352] or possibly to interest at a contract or statutory rate.[353]

12.6.3 Length of Plan

Although it contains provisions that set maximum limits on the length of plans, chapter 13 contains no minimum time period.[354] A plan may not exceed three years in length, unless 1) the current monthly income of the debtor and the debtor's spouse combined exceeds the applicable state median income or 2) the court specifically finds that there is good cause for a longer plan. In either case a plan of up to five years may be approved.[355] The procedure for obtaining court approval, when it is required, is not set forth specifically in the Federal Rules of Bankruptcy Procedure. Some courts require that a separate application and order be filed, although it may be possible to incorporate the approval into the plan confirmation process.[356]

Good cause for a longer plan may be that the debtor needs the additional time to meet the tests of sections 1325(a)(4) or 1325(a)(5), by paying the present value of nonexempt property or the collateral securing a debt.[357] It may also be that four or five years is the minimum reasonable time in which a debtor can cure a default under section 1322(b)(5) on a long-term debt.[358] However, the debtor's desire to pay more to unsecured creditors may not be sufficient cause,[359] especially because a debtor can continue to pay creditors voluntarily after the end of the plan, if the debtor chooses, without being bound to do so.

It is clear that plans that last less than three years may be confirmed as of right, as long as they comply with the other tests of chapter 13, including the ability-to-pay (disposable income) test.[360] A plan may last only eighteen months,[361] or it may consist of only one payment, liquidating property designated by the debtor, if unsecured creditors are paid in full or if no party objects.

12.6.4 Adjustments in Trustee's Charges

A possible alternative to making large payments outside the plan is to request an adjustment in the percentage charged by

---

348 See § 12.3.2, supra.
349 See § 11.6.1.3, supra.
 Oversecured creditors may also claim postpetition interest to the date of confirmation under section 506(b).
350 See § 11.6.2, supra.
351 11 U.S.C. § 1322(b)(10) clearly permits such a provision if the debtor's plan provides for payment of other unsecured debts in full. Otherwise, the permissibility of such a provision may hinge on whether that debt may be separately classified and treated differently in the relevant jurisdiction. See § 12.4.3, supra.
352 See § 11.2.2.2.1, supra, for a discussion of present value under 11 U.S.C. §§ 1325(a)(4) and 1325(a)(5). An oversecured creditor may also be entitled to interest pursuant to 11 U.S.C. § 506(b). See § 11.6.1.3.3.5, supra. However, it should never be the case that present value interest and interest under section 506(b) are awarded for the same time period.
353 See 11 U.S.C. § 511, which provides that tax claims are entitled to interest at the rate set by the relevant tax law.
354 Notwithstanding this fact, many trustees argue the applicable commitment period under section 1325(b)(4) is a minimum plan period. See § 12.3.4.4.6, supra.
355 11 U.S.C. § 1322(d).
 It should be noted that although the plan must call for payments to be made within a period not to exceed five years, the five-year limitation may run from the date the first payment under the plan becomes due following confirmation, rather than from the date of bankruptcy filing. See West v. Costen, 826 F.2d 1376 (4th Cir. 1987); In re Endicott, 157 B.R. 255 (W.D. Va. 1993); In re Serna, 193 B.R. 537 (Bankr. D. Ariz. 1996) (sixty months runs from due date of first payment after confirmation of plan). But see In re Musselman, 341 B.R. 652 (Bankr. N.D. Ind. 2005) (sixty months runs from due date of debtor's first payment under plan, which is thirty days after petition filed).
 A court may allow a debtor who has become a few months delinquent in a five-year plan to complete the plan. See In re Henry, 368 B.R. 696 (N.D. Ill. 2007) (fact that debtor needed longer than sixty months to complete sixty-month plan is not cause for dismissal); In re Aubain, 296 B.R. 624 (Bankr. E.D.N.Y. 2003) (reinstating dismissed case so debtor could complete plan after expiration of sixty months); In re Brown, 296 B.R. 20 (Bankr. N.D. Cal. 2003) (refusing to dismiss case when debtor needed some extra time beyond sixty months to complete plan); In re Harter, 279 B.R. 284 (Bankr. S.D. Cal. 2002) (debtor could complete plan within reasonable time after five-year plan's scheduled completion date); In re Black, 78 B.R. 840 (Bankr. S.D. Ohio 1987) (Bankruptcy Code contains no provision for dismissing a chapter 13 case because payments extend over sixty-six months, if the plan complied with the duration limitations of the Code at the time of confirmation); In re Eves, 67 B.R. 964 (Bankr. N.D. Ohio 1986) (modification which could have been effective before five years following first payment after plan confirmation was timely, even though proposed modification was filed more than five years after first plan payment was made).
356 See Form 17, Appendix G.3, infra, a plan which contains a paragraph that confirmation shall be deemed a finding that good cause exists for a five-year plan.
357 See § 11.2.2.2.1, supra, for discussion of these tests.
358 In re Masterson, 147 B.R. 295 (Bankr. D.N.H. 1992); In re Fries, 68 B.R. 676 (Bankr. E.D. Pa. 1986).
 See § 11.6.2, supra, for a discussion of curing such defaults.
359 In re Festa, 65 B.R. 85 (Bankr. S.D. Ohio 1986).
360 See § 12.3.3, supra.
361 In re Markman, 5 B.R. 196 (Bankr. E.D.N.Y. 1980).

the trustee for expenses and compensation. The justification for this would be that with respect to such large payments, the commission would be unduly large in proportion to the expense and work involved.

At least one court has adopted this principle and limited the percentage commission to only part of the debtor's monthly payments. However, in that case,[362] the payments were $6000 per month, far higher than those likely in the typical consumer bankruptcy. The court's limitation provided that the nine percent commission could be charged against only the first $600 paid per month. Similarly, another bankruptcy court has held that it had discretion to adjust fees despite the fact that the trustee was serving in a district subject to the United States Trustee program.[363] However, in most cases, payments outside the plan have proved to be an easier way to deal with the problem of large trustee fees.

Another possible adjustment which may be requested is a reduction in the normal minimum fee of five dollars per month set forth in section 330(c). This fee must be paid unless the court orders otherwise, and such an order is appropriate in cases in which low-income debtors can only afford very modest plan payments.[364] It should be considered proper to include a provision adjusting the minimum payment in a chapter 13 plan; if so, the order of confirmation would constitute the order required by section 330(c) for an exception to the usual minimum fee.[365]

12.6.5 Liquidation of Property in Chapter 13

Occasionally, nonbankruptcy law may prevent a debtor from selling property to realize exempt equity or to pay creditors. This may occur, for example, if only one of two cotenants by the entirety wishes to sell property that can be conveyed only by both spouses under state law. Or it may be that a sale of real estate is impossible to complete in time to prevent an imminent foreclosure.

In such cases, a chapter 13 plan that provides for the liquidation of property is often a solution. Filing the petition will stay all proceedings against the property, allowing time for a sale.[366] The plan[367] may then provide for the method of sale and the distribution of the proceeds, as well as the trustee's use of the power to partition entireties property under 11 U.S.C. § 363(h), if necessary.[368]

When liens on the property can be avoided to create exempt equity, it is advisable to do so before the sale is completed.[369] In some cases use of the bankruptcy process will thereby help a debtor preserve an exemption which is unavailable under state law because an execution sale is a prerequisite to claiming the exemption.

If sale of real property is contemplated, it is advisable to obtain a specific order authorizing the sale free and clear of liens, in order to satisfy any title insurance company doubts. The order requested should specify the distribution of the proceeds, and set the compensation of any real estate broker. This can generally be accomplished by a motion seeking such an order, naming all lienholders and other affected parties as respondents.[370]

Under 11 U.S.C. § 1322(b)(8) it is clear that property may be liquidated in a chapter 13 plan.[371] It is less clear whether such a provision obviates the necessity to submit some income to the trustee as required by 11 U.S.C. § 1322(a)(1).[372] To be safe, the plan should provide for at least minimal payments in addition to the liquidation of property.[373] Even when a mortgage will be cured and satisfied by the sale of property, the court may still

---

362 *In re* Eaton, 1 B.R. 433 (Bankr. M.D.N.C. 1979).
363 *In re* Melita, 91 B.R. 358 (Bankr. E.D. Pa. 1988). *But see In re* Schollett, 980 F.2d 639 (10th Cir. 1992) (court had no authority to adjust standing trustee's fees in U.S. trustee district); *In re* Savage, 67 B.R. 700 (D.R.I. 1986).
364 8 Collier on Bankruptcy ¶ 1302.05 (16th ed.).
365 *Id.*
366 See Chapter 9, *supra*, for discussion of the automatic stay.
367 For an example of such a plan, see Form 22, Appx. G.3, *infra*.
368 The trustee is permitted, with limited exceptions, to partition entirety or joint property that a single cotenant may not partition under state law. 11 U.S.C. § 363(h); *In re* Mastel, 2010 WL 234971 (Bankr. D. Mont. Jan. 15, 2010) (debtors could seek partition of property and sale pursuant to chapter 13 plan). *See In re* Belyea, 253 B.R. 312 (Bankr. D.N.H. 1999) (debtor could partition jointly held property under section 363(h) as part of chapter 13 plan confirmation process); § 2.5, *supra*. *But see In re* Wrublik, 312 B.R. 284 (Bankr. D. Md. 2004) (debtor does not have trustee's power to seek a sale under section 363(h)).

Under section 363(h), the appropriate inquiry is whether the benefit to the estate accruing from sale of the property would outweigh the detriment to the co-owner occurring due to partition. Courts may apply a variety of factors in making such a determination. *Compare In re* Ray, 73 B.R. 544 (Bankr. M.D. Ga. 1987) (partition refused) *with In re* Vassilowitch, 72 B.R. 803 (Bankr. D. Mass. 1987) (partition authorized). *See generally* Henry J. Sommer & Margaret Dee McGarity, Collier Family Law and the Bankruptcy Code ¶ 2.06[3] (1992).
369 *See* § 10.4, *supra*.
370 *See* Form 72, Appx. G.8, *infra*.

If the court has not approved the broker's fee in advance, it may not permit the payment of the fee from estate assets pursuant to section 330(a). In some districts, it may be necessary to obtain an order appointing the broker as a professional person in the case pursuant to section 327(a). *See In re* Haley, 950 F.2d 588 (9th Cir. 1991) (refusing commission to broker who had not been given approval to act as broker for debtor's property in chapter 11 case).

Probably a chapter 13 debtor who retains a broker is not subject to the provisions governing employment of professionals by the trustee. However, some courts may feel otherwise if estate assets are to be used to pay the broker.
371 *But see In re* Anderson, 18 B.R. 763 (Bankr. S.D. Ohio 1982) (plan not feasible when its success contingent on sale of realty in adverse market), *aff'd*, 28 B.R. 268 (S.D. Ohio 1982).
372 *Compare In re* Smith, 51 B.R. 273 (Bankr. D.D.C. 1984) (motion to dismiss denied when already confirmed plan funded solely from sale of property) *with In re* Anderson, 21 B.R. 443 (Bankr. N.D. Ga. 1981) (liquidation of residence of unemployed debtor did not provide regular income necessary for chapter 13 eligibility).
373 Such payments could also be required to meet the ability to pay test under 11 U.S.C. § 1325(b), the best interests of creditors test under 11 U.S.C. § 1325(a)(4), or to pay priority claims in full as required by 11 U.S.C. § 1322(a)(2). *See* §§ 12.3.2, 12.3.4, 12.3.6.1, *supra*.

require maintenance of current payments until the sale takes place unless there is adequate protection in the form of equity in the property.[374] In any case, the sale of property through a chapter 13 plan is often a useful device, especially if an impending foreclosure threatens the loss of a large amount of equity built up over years of ownership.

12.6.6 Refinancing a Property During a Chapter 13 Case

In times of low mortgage interest rates, even a bankruptcy debtor may be able to refinance her mortgage at a lower rate than the existing mortgage. In past years of loose credit, if a debtor could show a good payment history in a chapter 13 plan of at least a year's duration, the debtor could qualify for a mortgage refinancing at relatively reasonable rates. Such a refinancing may be preferable to continuing to make payments under the chapter 13 plan, especially if the refinancing would lower the debtor's monthly payments. For debtors who anticipate having trouble keeping up with payments, it may be the only way to salvage the benefits of chapter 13.

It is generally preferable to refinance a mortgage as part of a plan or a modified plan, rather than to dismiss the chapter 13 case before refinancing and lose the discharge of debts, lien avoidance rights, and other rights under chapter 13.[375] If a plan has already been in effect for longer than the applicable commitment period, there should be little opposition to a modification that allows the debtor to pay off the remaining plan payments through a refinancing.[376] If the plan has been in effect for less than that period, a trustee or unsecured creditor may oppose such a modification on the grounds that the debtor should continue monthly payments for the remainder of the thirty-six months. A debtor should be able to make a good argument against such opposition, because by refinancing the remaining payments, which had been based on the debtor's ability to pay, the debtor is still making those payments. In essence, the debtor is simply taking on a mortgage to borrow the money for those payments, and will be paying that money back to the new lender. Requiring additional plan payments would make the debtor pay the money twice.

A trustee or creditor may also argue that cash proceeds from the refinancing constitute disposable income. This argument should fail, because these proceeds are simply the proceeds of exempt property or its appreciation, which the debtor is entitled to keep, at least if the debtor's equity was originally fully exempt.[377] Moreover, there are strong arguments that section 1325(b) is not applicable to plan modifications.[378]

Plan provisions for refinancing a mortgage should give some thought to the mechanics of the process. To avoid problems arising at the last minute from an excessive payoff demand on an existing mortgage, the plan may provide for the debtor to pay such a demand at the closing of the new loan, with continued jurisdiction in bankruptcy court to resolve the dispute thereafter.[379] If possible, the plan should also provide that remaining mortgage arrears be paid at the closing of the new loan, rather than through the trustee, so that the prior mortgage can be completely paid off at closing; absent a complete pay off the existing mortgage holder may balk at providing a mortgage satisfaction, without which the new lender may not be willing to close the new loan. Such a provision would also avoid the trustee's percentage fee on the remaining arrearage claim, which is one reason why a trustee might oppose it.

12.7 Do the Section 1325(a) Standards Set Mandatory Requirements?

One question which the courts have begun to confront is whether the bankruptcy court has discretion to confirm a plan that does not meet all of the tests of section 1325(a). It is clear that if these tests are met, as well as the other requirements of chapter 13, the plan must be confirmed.[380] But what of the case in which they are not?

Most courts and commentators in the first years of practice under the Code, especially those cited earlier in this chapter who found good faith to be mandatory, appear to have assumed that all of the section 1325(a) tests must be met before a plan

---

374 In re Gavia, 24 B.R. 573 (B.A.P. 9th Cir. 1982). Cf. In re Vanasen, 81 B.R. 59 (D. Or. 1987) (allowing debtors reasonable time to sell property did not violate prohibition against modification of mortgage claims in § 1322(b)(2)); In re McCann, 27 B.R. 678 (Bankr. S.D. Ohio 1982) (such payments unnecessary when mortgage had been accelerated).

Equity in the property protects the creditor from loss on its claim due to delay in the event that the expected sale falls through. See § 9.7.3.2.2, supra.

375 However, if the case is dismissed, the debtor should be able to retain all of the proceeds from the refinancing in the hands of the trustee. In re Tran, 309 B.R. 330 (B.A.P. 9th Cir. 2004), aff'd, 177 Fed. Appx. 754 (9th Cir. 2006).

376 An example of a plan including such provisions is included in Form 153, Appx. G.13, infra. See also In re McCollum, 363 B.R. 789 (E.D. La. 2007) (debtor permitted to sell house and apply nonexempt proceeds to pay off plan). But see In re Magallanes, 2010 Bankr. LEXIS 1387 (Bankr. N.D. Ind. May 13, 2010) (60-month maximum runs from first preconfirmation plan payment date).

377 See also In re McCollum, 363 B.R. 789 (E.D. La. 2007) (proceeds of home sale not disposable income).

378 King v. Robenhorst (In re Robenhorst), 2011 WL 5877081 (E.D. Wis. Nov. 22, 2011); In re Sunahara, 326 B.R. 768 (B.A.P. 9th Cir. 2005); In re Braune, 385 B.R. 167 (Bankr. N.D. Tex. 2008) (section 1325(b) applicable only if trustee or creditor files objection to confirmation and not when trustee proposes plan modification; trustee had opportunity to object at confirmation to debtor receiving proceeds of lawsuit that had been disclosed before confirmation). But see Barbosa v. Solomon, 235 F.3d 31 (1st Cir. 2000) (proceeds from sale of home, on which mortgage had been stripped off due to lack of equity prior to confirmation, required to be paid to creditors in modified plan when home sold for twice the value used for stripping of liens).

379 See In re Garvida, 347 B.R. 697 (B.A.P. 9th Cir. 2006) (discussing procedure and burden of proof in such disputes).

380 Petro v. Mishler, 276 F.3d 375 (7th Cir. 2002) (plan must be confirmed if standards of section 1325(a) met and court may not set additional requirements).

can be confirmed. More recently, however, courts have recognized that they have discretion to confirm a plan without all of these standards being met.

The language of chapter 13 indicates that Congress did intend these tests to be discretionary rather than mandatory. Unlike section 1322(a), section 1325(a) does not state that "the plan shall" have certain provisions. It states only that if those tests are met then confirmation is mandatory. Unlike section 1325(b), section 1325(a) does not state that a court "may not approve the plan" if certain tests are not met. And unlike section 1129 of the Code governing chapter 11 plans, section 1325 does not state that a plan shall be confirmed "only if" the listed standards are met. In view of the obvious difference in the language of these closely related sections, it seems clear that Congress did intend a distinction between the tests of section 1322(a) and those of section 1325(a).

Such a distinction makes sense in view of the policies of chapter 13. Giving discretion to the court to approve plans of debtors who cannot meet the "best interests of creditors" test, for example, or who cannot pay the full amount of an allowed secured claim over the course of the plan, enhances the flexibility of chapter 13. The court still has the discretion to prevent abuses; if creditors do not object to the plan, it is difficult to see why the court should deny confirmation. And, in line with the broad rehabilitative policy of chapter 13, there seems little reason to exclude automatically from relief debtors doing their best under such circumstances.

The positions discussed above have been adopted by several courts, including the Third Circuit Court of Appeals. In *In re Szostek*,[381] that court agreed that the standards set forth in section 1325(a) are not mandatory and that a plan can be confirmed that does not meet those standards.[382] In the *Szostek* case, the plan did not provide present value interest to a secured creditor, but the plan was confirmed after the creditor failed to object to confirmation. Alternatively, the court held that the failure to object to confirmation could be deemed to be acceptance of the plan under section 1325(a)(5)(A).[383] However, the Sixth Circuit Court of Appeals has held, in a case in which there was an objection to confirmation, that the section 1325(a) standards are mandatory.[384]

Given this interpretation of section 1325(a), there are a number of other possible plan provisions that may become advantageous to the debtor. As to allowed secured claims, it might be possible to pay only a portion of the claim over the course of the plan and the rest after the bankruptcy, with the holder of the claim retaining its lien. Or the plan may provide that the property becomes vested in the debtor without lien retention by the claim holder, giving some other protection in lieu of the lien.[385] Finally, the plan could provide for payment of less than the amount required by the "best interests of creditors" test, perhaps by paying, over time, only the total amount that would be paid in a liquidation, without the additional interest necessary for the "present value" calculation which the test would require.

In most cases, probably little would be lost by proposing some of these provisions, if appropriate. It seems clear that if no objection is raised to such a provision and the plan is confirmed, the provision will be binding on all creditors, even if it is later found contrary to chapter 13, by virtue of the res judicata effect of plan confirmation.[386] If an objection is filed and confirmation is denied, a debtor is normally given the opportunity to modify the plan to meet the objection which has barred confirmation. However, recent Supreme Court dictum[387] casts some doubt on whether bankruptcy courts would permit such a strategy, and the attitude of the local courts must be taken into account.

12.8 Use and Possession of Property of the Estate and Adequate Protection

12.8.1 Continuing Use of Property

One of the principal advantages of chapter 13 is that the debtor has the right to possession of all property of the estate, whether exempt[388] or nonexempt. Section 1306 specifically provides that "the debtor shall remain in possession of all property of the estate." Although this language speaks only of "remaining" in possession, it seems clear that the section also applies to property the estate acquires after commencement of the case, pursuant to sections 542 and 543[389] or the various avoiding powers. The entire thrust of this section and section 1303 is to transfer to the debtor virtually all of the powers and

---

381 886 F.2d 1405 (3d Cir. 1989).
382 *See also In re* Escobedo, 28 F.3d 34 (7th Cir. 1994) (distinguishing section 1322(a), which does set mandatory requirements); *In re* Brady, 86 B.R. 166 (Bankr. D. Minn. 1988). *But see In re* Jones, 530 F.3d 1284 (10th Cir. 2008) (conditions set forth in section 1325(a) are required for confirmation if creditor or trustee objects to plan); *In re* Barnes, 32 F.3d 405 (9th Cir. 1994) (provisions of section 1325(a)(5) are mandatory, and plan not paying present value of allowed secured claim could not be confirmed over creditor's objection).
383 *In re* Szostek, 886 F.2d 1405, 1413 (3d Cir. 1989); *In re* Ruti-Sweetwater, Inc., 836 F.2d 1263 (10th Cir. 1988) (chapter 11 case); *In re* Brown, 108 B.R. 738 (Bankr. C.D. Cal. 1989). *See also In re* Escobedo, 28 F.3d 34 (7th Cir. 1994) (distinguishing section 1322(a), which does set mandatory requirements).
384 Shaw v. Aurgroup Fin. Credit Union, 552 F.3d 447 (6th Cir. 2009).

385 *In re* Pence, 905 F.2d 1107 (7th Cir. 1990).
386 11 U.S.C. § 1327(a); *In re* Szostek, 886 F.2d 1405 (3d Cir. 1989). *See* § 12.11, *infra*; 8 Collier on Bankruptcy ¶ 1327.02[1] (16th ed.). *But see In re* Escobedo, 28 F.3d 34 (7th Cir. 1994) (confirmation of plan that did not satisfy mandatory requirements of section 1322(a) was a nullity).
Since *Escobedo*, a court in the Seventh Circuit has held that confirmation of a plan that did not satisfy section 1322(a) could not be attacked after the debtor received a discharge. *In re* Puckett, 193 B.R. 842 (Bankr. N.D. Ill. 1996).
387 United Student Aid Funds, Inc. v. Espinosa, 130 S. Ct. 1367, 1381, 176 L. Ed. 2d 158, 174 (2010) (misstating the language of § 1325(a) and stating that bankruptcy courts should review plans for compliance with § 1325(a)).
388 For a discussion of rights to possess exempt property in chapter 7 cases, see § 10.1.2, *supra*.
389 For discussion of sections 542 and 543 see § 9.9, *supra*.

rights that the trustee would otherwise have with respect to property of the estate.[390]

For the same reason, debtors are free to use, sell, or lease property of the estate in the same manner as they ordinarily did prior to the case. Although a slight problem of drafting makes this less than crystal clear in the Code,[391] it has been universally assumed that this was the intent of the Congress.[392] There would, after all, be little point in the debtor retaining possession of property if it could not be used. And section 363(e), which is incorporated into chapter 13 by section 1303, only provides for prohibiting or conditioning such use, sale, or lease of property when an entity having an interest in the property does not have adequate protection. Moreover, notice and a hearing are only required under section 363(b), also incorporated into chapter 13, when use, sale, or leasing not in the ordinary course of business is proposed. Finally, to require a hearing before each debtor could use his or her property would impose a monumental and needless burden on the court, and that was obviously not intended by Congress.

12.8.2 Adequate Protection

12.8.2.1 Overview

As mentioned above, parties with interests in property have a right to adequate protection if the property is used, as provided under section 363(e). "On request," the court may prohibit or condition the use of a home or a car, for example, by requiring fire or collision insurance to protect a secured party against damage resulting from use. Such issues are normally decided at a hearing, which might well occur in conjunction with a hearing on a party's request for relief from the automatic stay, relief to which it might also be entitled if adequate protection is not furnished.[393] In any case, the issues are similar to those in a hearing on relief from the stay, and the debtor must assume the trustee's burden of proof on the issue of adequate protection under section 363(e).

12.8.2.2 Adequate Protection Payments

12.8.2.2.1 When payments required

With respect to allowed claims secured by purchase money security interests in personal property, as well as personal property leases, the Code sets forth special requirements for adequate protection. Section 1326(a)(1)(C) requires a chapter 13 debtor to make adequate protection payments directly to a creditor holding an allowed claim secured by personal property to the extent it is "attributable to the purchase of such property by the debtor for that portion of the obligation that becomes due after the order for relief."

These payments are to commence within thirty days after the filing of the plan or the order for relief, whichever is earlier.[394] Plan payments are to be reduced by the amount of the adequate protection payments and the trustee is to be provided evidence of payments made, including the amounts and dates of the payments.[395] This new requirement promises bookkeeping headaches for the debtor, debtor's attorney, and chapter 13 trustee, who must keep track of this separate set of payments and integrate the amounts with the plan's payment requirements.

Adequate protection payments under section 1326(a)(1)(C) need only be provided for the portion of the claim that becomes due after the order for relief.[396] This limitation should mean that no adequate protection payments need to be provided for any arrears portion of a claim. If payments have been accelerated, it is possible that no portion of the claim becomes due after the order for relief.[397] In addition, adequate protection payments need be made only to the extent an obligation is for purchase money and the property was purchased by the debtor.[398] If the property was originally titled in the name of another, such as a

---

390 Smith v. Rockett, 522 F.3d 1080 (10th Cir. 2008); Crosby v. Monroe County, 394 F.3d 1328 (11th Cir. 2004); Cable v. Ivy Tech State College, 200 F.3d 467 (7th Cir. 1999) (after conversion to chapter 13, chapter 7 trustee automatically dropped from discrimination case and debtor became real party in interest with standing to prosecute case on behalf of bankruptcy estate); Murray v. Bd. of Educ., 248 B.R. 484 (S.D.N.Y. 2000) (chapter 13 debtor had standing to bring Title VII action even though she inadvertently omitted it from schedules); *In re* Bowker, 245 B.R. 192 (Bankr. D. N.J. 2000) (chapter 13 debtor, not the trustee, has standing to retain special counsel to prosecute personal injury litigation that is property of the estate); *In re* James, 210 B.R. 276 (Bankr. S.D. Miss. 1997) (chapter 13 debtor has right to control whether a prepetition lawsuit should be settled). See 8 Collier on Bankruptcy ¶ 1303.01 (16th ed.).

391 None of the sections incorporated into chapter 13 by section 1303 specifically grants the non-business debtor the right to use property of the estate in the ordinary course of business as does section 363(c)(1) for business debtors incorporated by section 1304. Presumably this is only because non-business debtors could not use, sell or lease property in the course of a business.

392 *In re* LaFlamme, 397 B.R. 194 (Bankr. D.N.H. 2008). *See* 8 Collier on Bankruptcy ¶ 1303.01 (16th ed.). *But see* Fatsis v. Braunstein (*In re* Fatsis), 405 B.R. 1 (B.A.P. 1st Cir. 2009) (non-business debtor could not sell large amount of stock without court permission when confirmation order prohibited such sale).

"The chapter 13 debtor is vested with the identical rights and powers conferred upon a liquidation trustee under section 363, relating to the use, sale, and lease of property of the estate." *Id.* (citing identical language in S. Rep. No. 95-989, at 140 (1978)).

393 See Chapter 9, *supra*, for discussion of adequate protection and relief from the automatic stay. However, adequate protection rights may be lost by a party if they are not protected in a confirmed plan to which that party does not object. *In re* Minzler, 158 B.R. 720 (Bankr. S.D. Ohio 1993) (creditor could not prevail on motion for relief from stay due to lack of adequate protection on leases allegedly misclassified as secured claims because creditor was bound by confirmed plan to which it had not objected).

394 11 U.S.C. § 1326(a)(1).
395 11 U.S.C. § 1326(a)(1)(C).
396 11 U.S.C. § 1326(a)(1)(C).
397 *In re* Smith, 355 B.R. 519 (Bankr. D. Md. 2006) (no adequate protection payments necessary under section 1326(a)(1)(C) because creditor had accelerated debt and obtained judgment, and debtor did not propose to de-accelerate debt).
398 11 U.S.C. § 1326(a)(1)(C).

non-debtor spouse, it probably was not purchased by the debtor. And adequate protection payments need only be paid on an allowed claim. Under section 502(a) of the Code, a claim is deemed allowed when a proof of claim is filed, but only if no objection to the proof of claim is made, so adequate protection payments should not be due until the creditor files a proof of claim to which no objection is filed.

The adequate protection provision was obviously designed primarily for car lenders. As a practical matter, although it technically applies to appliance and furniture creditors, it is unlikely they will do much to enforce these provisions because any adequate protection payments they would receive would be minimal, and these creditors generally do not want the property back if they can collect anything on secured claims.

12.8.2.2.2 Determining the amount and timing of payments

The amount of the adequate protection payments presumably will initially be set by the debtor and be based on the rate of the collateral's depreciation. The rate of depreciation can be calculated for a vehicle by looking at the change in industry guide values over the previous few months.[399] However, if the claim is substantially over secured, and will remain over secured, there should be no need for adequate protection payments, or they should be nominal.[400] In addition, the amount of the payments can be modified by order of the court "pending confirmation of a plan,"[401] which suggests that the plan will govern thereafter.

The court may "modify, increase, or reduce" the payments required upon notice and a hearing.[402] Some courts or trustees have used this section to adopt local rules or general orders that route payments through the trustee in order to ease the bookkeeping nightmare the payments would otherwise create if they were made directly by the debtor to the secured creditor.[403] For ease of calculation, some courts have set a presumptive monthly adequate protection amount of one percent of the balance of the debt or of the value of the vehicle.

There is no requirement that the adequate protection payments be made at any particular time interval. For ease of administration when payments are not routed through the trustee, the debtor's attorney may wish to make one payment, directly to the creditor through the attorney's office, to facilitate bookkeeping and provide evidence to the trustee. There would appear to be no disadvantage to doing so when such a payment for the preconfirmation period is less than a full plan payment (as will usually be the case), as the amount paid will be deducted from the plan payments due.[404]

The statute does not specifically state whether adequate protection payments end as of plan confirmation. There is nothing in the provision that gives an ending date. However the plan is required by language added to section 1325(a)(5) to provide that payments on allowed secured claims under the plan be sufficient to provide adequate protection, and the plan can certainly provide that adequate protection shall be provided by the postconfirmation plan payments.

12.8.2.2.3 Remedy for failure to make payments

The remedy for failure to make adequate protection payments is likely to be relief from the automatic stay, the same remedy existing under prior law for failure to provide adequate protection. The main difference is that prior law in effect placed the burden on the creditor to demand adequate protection, usually by filing a motion. But a creditor will still have to file a motion for relief from the stay if adequate protection payments have not been provided, and the court may well allow a debtor to cure such a default in payments. Theoretically failure to make payments required by section 1326 could be grounds for dismissal, but a creditor will usually prefer stay relief and the trustee will have no reason to seek dismissal of an otherwise viable plan.

12.8.3 Payments to Personal Property Lessors

Debtors are required to make scheduled lease payments to personal property lessors for the portion of the obligation that becomes due after the order for relief.[405] The debtor must deduct such payments from the plan payments to the trustee and provide evidence of the lease payments to the trustee, including dates and amounts.[406] Although this provision was undoubtedly meant to protect automobile lessors, it applies to all personal property leases. Such leases are not common for other types of property, but this provision could bring to a head disputes about whether rent-to-own contracts are leases.[407]

Generally, chapter 13 debtors make current automobile lease payments to lessors if they assume the lease under section 1322(b)(7) of the Code. A chapter 13 debtor who does not wish to assume the lease does not make payments. Section 1326(a)(1)(B) should not be read to require lease payments from a debtor who does not wish to assume the lease. In such a situation, the lessor can seek relief from the automatic stay, if the stay with respect to the particular property has not termi-

---

399 *In re* Robson, 369 B.R. 377 (Bankr. N.D. Ill. 2007) (using depreciation according to industry price guide for month following petition filing). *See also In re* Dowell, 2008 WL 4975881 (Bankr. D. Ariz. Nov. 19, 2008) (adequate protection payments based on actual value of vehicle, even if vehicle was purchased within 910 days before petition).
400 *See* § 9.7.3.2.2, *supra*.
401 11 U.S.C. § 1326(a)(3).
402 11 U.S.C. § 1326(a)(3).
403 *See In re* Jones, 2007 WL 2609790 (N.D.N.Y. Sept. 4, 2007) (upholding bankruptcy court standing order to permit adequate protection payments through trustee), *vacated as moot*, 2008 WL 5063809 (2d Cir. Nov. 25, 2008); *In re* Brown, 348 B.R. 583 (Bankr. N.D. Ga. 2006) (court had power under section 1326(a)(1) to permit payments through trustee).

404 Section 1326(a)(1)(C) provides that the plan payments are to be reduced by the amount of the adequate protection payments.
405 11 U.S.C. § 1326(a)(1)(B).
406 11 U.S.C. § 1326(a)(1)(B).
407 *See* § 11.8, *supra*.

nated.[408] There is no indication the provision was intended to affect the right to assume or reject a lease.[409]

12.8.4 Proof of Insurance

Under section 1326(a)(4), a debtor who is retaining personal property subject to a lease or which secures a purchase money claim is required to provide the lessor or creditor reasonable evidence of the maintenance of any required insurance coverage. Normally, such creditors or lessors already know if insurance lapses, as they are named as loss payees in the policy. Only when insurance has lapsed will such evidence be important to creditors or lessors. If insurance is in force, the creditor is not likely to move for relief from the stay because the debtor has not notified the creditor of facts it already knows.

The debtor is required to continue to provide evidence of coverage "for as long as the debtor retains possession of the property."[410] This provision does not specify how often such evidence should be provided. Should it be annually, monthly, hourly? Creditors and lessors will not really be concerned, because they will be notified if insurance lapses.

12.8.5 Vesting of Property Upon Confirmation

Once a chapter 13 plan is confirmed, property of the estate vests in the debtor unless the plan or order confirming the plan provides otherwise.[411] Some courts have held that this causes the property to lose the protection of the provisions of the automatic stay which protect property of the estate.[412] However, other courts have adopted the better view that the property continues to retain the character of property of the estate, albeit vested in the debtor, after confirmation.[413] To avoid problems in this regard, it is often advisable to provide in a chapter 13 plan that property of the estate does not vest in the debtor until the closing of the case.[414]

---

408 See Ch. 9, supra. See also 11 U.S.C. § 365(p)(1); § 12.9, infra.
409 The title of the provision of the 2005 Act which amended section 1326 is "Adequate Protection of Lessors and Purchase Money Secured Creditors." See Pub. L. No. 109-8, § 309(c), 119 Stat. 23 (2005).
410 11 U.S.C. § 1326(a)(4).
411 11 U.S.C. § 1327(b); In re Chaparro Martinez, 293 B.R. 387 (Bankr. N.D. Tex. 2003) (after confirmation exempt personal injury cause of action vested in debtor and debtor did not need court approval to settle case or pay their attorney from proceeds). See 8 Collier on Bankruptcy ¶¶ 1327.03, 1327.04 (16th ed.). But see In re Waldron, 536 F.3d 123 (11th Cir. 2008) (personal injury cause of action that debtor acquired after confirmation did not revest in debtor at confirmation and was property of estate; debtor had no duty to automatically amend schedules to list it, but court could require that).
412 In re Fisher, 203 B.R. 958 (N.D. Ill. 1997), rev'g 198 B.R. 721 (Bankr. N.D. Ill. 1996). See §§ 9.3.1, 9.4.3, supra.
413 Sec. Nat'l Bank of Marshalltown, Iowa v. Neiman, 1 F.3d 687 (8th Cir. 1993); In re Kolenda, 212 B.R. 851 (W.D. Mich. 1997).
414 Patterson v. Homecomings Fin., L.L.C., 425 B.R. 499 (E.D. Wis. 2010) (overcharges in refinancing during chapter 13 case were

12.9 Unexpired Leases and Executory Contracts

12.9.1 Definition of Executory Contract

Another important feature of chapter 13 is found in section 1322(b)(7). This section provides that the debtor has the power to assume or reject any executory contract or unexpired lease. Prior to 2005 this power could be exercised in a chapter 7 case only by the trustee.[415] Indeed, a default or anticipated difficulties with respect to an executory contract or lease may be a prime reason for choosing to file under chapter 13.[416]

---

property of estate because confirmation order provided that home against which overcharges were assessed remained estate property); In re Clark, 207 B.R. 559 (Bankr. S.D. Ohio 1997) (Internal Revenue Service violated automatic stay by levying on postpetition wages, which under plan provision were property of the estate).
See sample chapter 13 plans, Forms 18 and 24, Appendix G.3, infra.
415 11 U.S.C. § 365(d). In chapter 7, an executory contract or unexpired lease is automatically deemed rejected by the trustee unless the trustee assumes it within sixty days after the case is commenced. Once assumption or rejection by the trustee occurs in a chapter 7 case, the consequences are basically the same as in a chapter 13 case. Assumption by the debtor in a chapter 7 case is discussed in § 12.9.5, infra.
416 Although all real property leases of a debtor are usually deemed rejected by operation of law in chapter 7 cases, this usually has little practical effect. Most lessors are unaware that the bankruptcy has any effect on a lease when payments are current and, because they usually have no special desire to evict a rent-paying tenant, they continue to treat the lease as still in effect. However, a landlord may attempt to evict a tenant based upon the trustee's deemed rejection. In such cases, the debtor should be able to successfully argue that the trustee's rejection did not involve the debtor's interest except insofar as the trustee, by rejection, abandoned the leasehold interest back to the debtor. Rejection is not equivalent to the termination of a lease. In re Ranch House of Orange-Brevard, Inc., 773 F.2d 1166 (11th Cir. 1985); In re T.F.P. Res., Inc., 56 B.R. 112 (Bankr. S.D.N.Y. 1985); In re Storage Tech. Corp., 53 B.R. 471 (Bankr. D. Colo. 1985) (rejection is a breach of lease that may be waived, not a termination of lease).
Several courts have adopted this interpretation to avoid a harsh result after an automatic chapter 7 rejection. In re Reed, 94 B.R. 48 (E.D. Pa. 1988) (rejection results in abandonment of lease to debtor); In re Rodall, 165 B.R. 506 (Bankr. M.D. Fla. 1994) (same). See also In re Austin Dev. Co., 19 F.3d 1077 (5th Cir. 1994) (rejection of lease does not terminate lease with respect to parties that have not rejected it nor affect their rights); In re Szymecki, 87 B.R. 14 (W.D. Pa. 1988) (automatically rejected public housing lease is abandoned to debtor); In re Knight, 8 B.R. 925 (Bankr. D. Md. 1981); Dime Sav. Bank of N.Y. v. Pesce, 217 A.D. 299, 636 N.Y.S.2d 747 (1995).
And the 1984 amendments to the Code support this interpretation. While they require a non-residential tenant to vacate a property if a lease is not assumed, 11 U.S.C. § 365(d)(4), they contain no such requirement for a residential tenant. In addition, if a landlord accepts rental payments after the expiration of the sixty-day period, the debtor may argue that any rejection of the lease has been waived. Another alternative might be for the debtor to convert to chapter 13 or begin a new chapter 13 case to assume the lease. See In re Sims, 213 B.R. 641 (Bankr. W.D. Pa. 1997) (chapter 13 debtor could assume lease that had been automatically rejected in prior chapter 7 case, because lease continued to exist after rejection).

The Code does not define exactly what it means by the term "executory contract," and whether a particular contract is executory is sometimes an important question. Generally speaking, an executory contract is one "on which performance remains due to some extent on both sides."[417] Perhaps the prototype of such a contract is the unexpired lease, which is of course specifically included.

A more specific definition adopted by some courts classifies a contract as executory if "the obligations of both parties are so far unperformed that the failure of either party to complete performance would constitute a material breach and thus excuse the performance of the other."[418] However, other definitions have looked mainly to whether the debtor has an obligation other than one to pay money for property and services already received before the bankruptcy. If so, the contract is executory.[419]

Under any of these definitions, there are several types of executory contracts into which consumer debtors routinely enter. They include purchase and sale agreements for real estate,[420] options for the sale of real estate or other property,[421] most automobile leases,[422] layaway contracts,[423] contingent fee contracts with attorneys,[424] insurance contracts,[425] personal services contracts,[426] installment payment contracts for cemetery plots, book clubs, magazine subscriptions, health clubs, appliance or motor vehicle service contracts that are paid for in installments, and (if they are not considered credit sales) rent-to-own contracts.[427]

The Seventh Circuit Court of Appeals has held that an employee's agreement to participate in an Employee Stock Ownership Plan (ESOP) is not an executory contract which could be rejected to avoid the wage reduction involved while at the same time maintaining the employment that was a part of the contract.[428] And, there is considerable dispute regarding whether a covenant not to compete may be rejected as an executory contract.[429] The Third Circuit Court of Appeals has held that a personal services contract, which could contain such a covenant, may be rejected.[430] And one court has held that a postnuptial agreement is an executory contract, at least if the parties are not yet divorced.[431]

In a rare case, a chapter 7 trustee may seek to assume a residential lease with significant value. *See In re* Toledano, 299 B.R. 284 (Bankr. S.D.N.Y. 2003) (trustee permitted to assume and assign, for $150,000, debtor's rights in rent stabilized lease for Manhattan luxury apartment).

417 H.R. Rep. No. 95-595, at 347 (1977). *See, e.g., In re* Streets & Beard Farm P'ship, 882 F.2d 233 (7th Cir. 1989) (defining executory contract for purposes of bankruptcy).

418 *In re* Texscan Corp., 976 F.2d 1269 (9th Cir. 1992) (insurance contract was not executory when failure of debtor to pay premiums would not relieve insurer of obligation to perform); *In re* Streets & Beard Farm P'ship, 882 F.2d 233 (7th Cir. 1989) (assumption or rejection of executory contract intended to apply to contracts in which significant unperformed obligations remain on both sides); *In re* Wegner, 839 F.2d 533, 536 (9th Cir. 1988); Jensen v. Cont'l Corp., 591 F.2d 477 (8th Cir. 1979); *In re* Columbia Gas Sys., Inc., 146 B.R. 106 (D. Del. 1992) (class action consent decree was not executory contract because failure of either to complete performance of obligations would not excuse performance of the other), *aff'd*, 50 F.3d 233 (3d Cir. 1995), Vern Countryman, *Executory Contracts in Bankruptcy*, 57 Minn. L. Rev. 439, 460 (1973).

For one criticism of this definition see Mitchell R. Julis, *Classifying Rights and Interests Under the Bankruptcy Code*, 55 Am. Bankr. L.J. 233, 252–259 (1981).

419 *See* Shanker, *The Treatment of Executory Contracts and Leases in the 1978 Bankruptcy Code*, 25 Prac. Law. (No. 7) 11, 26 (1979).

420 Such contracts remain executory and may be rejected even after one party has tendered performance. *In re* Alexander, 670 F.2d 885 (9th Cir. 1982). *See also In re* Hammons, 2010 WL 3447689 (Bankr. W.D. Tex. Aug. 30, 2010) (sellers could reject purchase and sale agreement; buyers had no right to remain in possession because they had not made payments that were due). But courts may refuse to allow rejection of a purchase and sale agreement if they find that this was the sole purpose of the bankruptcy filing. *In re* Waldron, 785 F.2d 936 (11th Cir. 1986); *In re* Chinichian, 784 F.2d 1440 (9th Cir. 1986). *But see In re* W & L Assocs., Inc., 71 B.R. 962 (Bankr. E.D. Pa. 1987).

421 *In re* Robert L. Helms Constr. & Dev. Co., 139 F.3d 702 (9th Cir. 1998) (en banc); *In re* Hardie, 100 B.R. 284 (Bankr. E.D.N.C. 1989).

422 *In re* Wallace, 122 B.R. 222 (Bankr. D.N.J. 1990).

It is often difficult to tell whether an automobile transaction is a sale or a lease. It is usually to the debtor's advantage if the transaction is deemed a credit sale. *See In re* Mandrell, 246 B.R. 528 (Bankr. D.S.C. 1999) (applying "economic test" of whether debtor acquired substantial equity in vehicle, determining that transaction was not a lease); *In re* Crummie, 194 B.R. 230 (Bankr. N.D. Cal. 1996) (General Motors "SmartBuy" contract deemed credit sale, not lease); *In re* Lewis, 185 B.R. 66 (Bankr. N.D. Cal. 1995) (General Motors "SmartBuy" contract was a credit sale, not a lease).

For a discussion of the distinctions between automobile leases and credit sales for purposes of coverage of the Truth in Lending Act and the Consumer Leasing Act, see National Consumer Law Center, Truth in Lending § 10.2.3 (8th ed. 2012).

423 *In re* Davies, 27 B.R. 898 (Bankr. E.D.N.Y. 1983).

424 *In re* Aesthetic Specialties, Inc., 37 B.R. 679 (B.A.P. 9th Cir. 1984); *In re* Ashley, 41 B.R. 67 (Bankr. E.D. Mich. 1984).

425 *In re* Garnas, 38 B.R. 221 (Bankr. D.N.D. 1984).

426 *In re* Allain, 59 B.R. 107 (Bankr. W.D. La. 1986) (non-competition clause as well as remainder of dentist's contract for joint practice was rejected). *See also* Turner v. Avery, 947 F.2d 772 (5th Cir. 1991) (chapter 7 trustee could not assume debtor attorney contingent fee contracts with clients because under section 365(c)(1)(A) the trustee may not assume contract if other party has right to decline performance from substitute for original contracting party under state law; however, trustee was entitled to fees earned prior to filing of bankruptcy petition as property of the estate). *But see In re* Carrere, 64 B.R. 156 (Bankr. C.D. Cal. 1986) (television actress did not have right to reject personal services contract in chapter 11 case).

427 *See* § 11.8, *supra*.

428 *In re* Crippin, 877 F.2d 594 (7th Cir. 1989).

429 *Compare In re* Register, 95 B.R. 73 (Bankr. M.D. Tenn. 1989), *aff'd*, 100 B.R. 360 (M.D. Tenn. 1989), *and In re* Allain, 59 B.R. 107 (Bankr. W.D. La. 1986) (non-competition clause as well as remainder of dentist's contract for joint practice was rejected), *with In re* Don & Lin Trucking Co., 110 B.R. 562 (Bankr. N.D. Ala. 1990).

430 *In re* Taylor, 913 F.2d 102 (3d Cir. 1990). *But see In re* Udell, 18 F.3d 403 (7th Cir. 1994) (granting relief from the automatic stay to enforce injunction obtained under covenant not to compete because equitable claim for injunction, which could be obtained under state law in addition to damages, was not a "claim" as defined in 11 U.S.C. § 101(5)(B)).

431 *In re* Lawson, 146 B.R. 663 (Bankr. E.D. Va. 1992).

Another type of contract that might present problems under this section is the land installment sales agreement, in which a debtor pays for property in installments, receiving a deed only when most or all of the payments have been made to the seller. A number of courts have held such arrangements to be executory contracts, and have required debtors wishing to maintain them to cure defaults promptly.[432] However, whether this must always be so may depend on the nature of the agreement and the applicable state law. In some places, retention of the deed may be functionally equivalent to taking a security interest,[433] placing the transaction within the ambit of secured claims covered by sections 1322(b)(2), (b)(5) and 1325(a)(5) rather than section 365. Such a situation would be more analogous to a creditor holding the title to an automobile as security, an arrangement which seems clearly outside the scope of the executory contract provisions.[434]

12.9.2 Assumption of a Lease or Executory Contract in Chapter 13

In many cases, a debtor will have much to gain from assumption of an executory contract or unexpired lease. For example, if moving would cause a hardship, or if a residential lease has favorable terms, it is usually advantageous to keep it in effect. This may be particularly true in a rent control jurisdiction[435] or in public housing, as the debtor's occupancy may not otherwise be terminable even at the end of the lease term. (Staying beyond the term otherwise allowable may also be possible due to the operation of the automatic stay during the course of the plan.)[436]

The approval of the court is required for the debtor to assume an executory contract or lease.[437] The debtor must be willing to assume the burdens as well as the benefits of the contract; a debtor may not assume only its favorable aspects.[438] Once a lease is assumed, the rent due becomes a priority administrative expense, even if the debtor later decides to reject the lease.[439] Therefore, there should be no problem in separately classifying any prepetition rent due and paying it before other debts.[440]

To assume a lease or executory contract, the debtor must be willing and able to cure any default promptly or must provide adequate assurance that the default will be promptly cured.[441] If there has been a default, the debtor must also compensate the

---

432 *In re* Terrell, 892 F.2d 469 (6th Cir. 1989); *In re* Streets & Beard Farm P'ship, 882 F.2d 233 (7th Cir. 1989); *In re* Speck, 798 F.2d 279 (8th Cir. 1986); *In re* Rose, 7 B.R. 911 (Bankr. S.D. Tex. 1981); *In re* Vertich, 5 B.R. 684 (Bankr. D.S.D. 1980).

433 *In re* Kane, 248 B.R. 216 (B.A.P. 1st Cir. 2000) (installment land sales contract not an executory contract), *aff'd*, 254 F.3d 325 (1st Cir. 2001); *In re* Rehbein, 60 B.R. 436 (B.A.P. 9th Cir. 1986). See *In re* Climer, 10 B.R. 872 (W.D. Tenn. 1977); *In re* Johnson, 75 B.R. 927 (Bankr. N.D. Ohio 1987); *In re* Adolphson, 38 B.R. 776 (Bankr. D. Minn.), *aff'd*, 38 B.R. 780 (D. Minn. 1983); *In re* Cox, 28 B.R. 588 (Bankr. D. Idaho 1983); *In re* Booth, 19 B.R. 53 (Bankr. D. Utah 1982).

434 Heartline Farms, Inc. v. Daly, 934 F.2d 985 (8th Cir. 1991); *In re* Rojas, 10 B.R. 353 (B.A.P. 9th Cir. 1981).

435 *See In re* Yasin, 179 B.R. 43 (Bankr. S.D.N.Y. 1995) (rent stabilized lease could be assumed by chapter 13 debtor, preserving right of renewal; even if lease is rejected it may be possible for tenant to renew lease).

436 See discussion of leases in Chapter 9, *supra*. For an example of a plan assuming a lease, see Form 24, Appendix G.3, *infra*.

437 *In re* Harris Mgmt. Co., 791 F.2d 1412 (9th Cir. 1986); *In re* Whitcomb & Keller Mortgage Co., 715 F.2d 375 (7th Cir. 1983).
Although a formal motion under Federal Rule of Bankruptcy Procedure 6006 to assume an executory contract may be better practice, it has been held that confirmation of a chapter 13 plan containing a provision for assumption of a lease constitutes court approval as required by 11 U.S.C. § 365(a). Dep't of Air Force v. Carolina Parachute Corp., 907 F.2d 1469 (4th Cir. 1990) (chapter 11 case); *In re* Hall, 202 B.R. 929 (Bankr. W.D. Tenn. 1996); *In re* Flugel, 197 B.R. 92 (Bankr. S.D. Cal. 1996); *In re* Aneiro, 72 B.R. 424 (Bankr. S.D. Cal. 1987). *But see* Sea Harvest Corp. v. Riviera Land Co., 868 F.2d 1077 (9th Cir. 1989) (nonresidential real property lease deemed rejected in chapter 11 case when not assumed by motion within applicable time limits).
The *Sea Harvest* case may not be relevant to residential leases and executory contracts not involving real property, because there are normally no time limits for assumption, except when the court has set one pursuant to 11 U.S.C. § 365(d)(2). Federal Rule of Bankruptcy Procedure 6006 specifically applies to proceedings to assume *other than as part of a plan*.

438 Dep't of Air Force v. Carolina Parachute Corp., 907 F.2d 1469 (4th Cir. 1990). *See also In re* Pittman, 289 B.R. 448 (Bankr. M.D. Fla. 2003) (chapter 13 plan may not modify term in auto lease requiring lump sum payment of purchase option).

439 *In re* Klein Sleep Prods., Inc., 78 F.3d 18 (2d Cir. 1996); *In re* Juvennelliano, 464 B.R. 651 (Bankr. D. Del. 2011) (balance due on assumed car lease after default and repossession was administrative expense, but attorney fees added by creditor were not because they provided no benefit to estate); *In re* Michalek, 393 B.R. 642 (Bankr. E.D. Wis. 2008) (lease payments were administrative expenses after repossession even though they had been paid directly to creditor); *In re* Masek, 301 B.R. 336 (Bankr. D. Neb. 2003) (because debtors had assumed automobile lease, balance of amount due on lease was administrative expense even though car had been repossessed); *In re* Wright, 256 B.R. 858 (Bankr. W.D.N.C. 2001) (rejection damages were priority claim when debtor first assumed lease under confirmed chapter 13 plan and later modified plan to reject lease). *Cf. In re* Parmenter, 527 F.3d 606 (6th Cir. 2008) (even though debtor assumed lease, payments were not administrative expense because they were not included in list of administrative expenses in confirmed plan; modification of plan to pay more to car lessor was not permissible modification); *In re* Allen, 362 B.R. 866 (Bankr. N.D. Ohio 2007) (plan language calling for debtor to cure and maintain payments did not constitute assumption giving rise to administrative expense; *In re* Badgley, 308 B.R. 293 (Bankr. E.D. Mich. 2004) (automobile lessor not entitled to administrative claim for postpetition lease payments once debtors amended plan prior to confirmation to provide for lease rejection, even though debtors' initial plan provided for lease assumption); *In re* Scott, 209 B.R. 777 (Bankr. S.D. Ga. 1997) (when no plan had been confirmed and court had not otherwise approved lease assumption, postpetition rent was not administrative expense).

440 *In re* Davis, 209 B.R. 893 (Bankr. N.D. Ill. 1997).

441 11 U.S.C. § 365(b)(1).
However, a debtor need not pay a lease penalty for failure to perform non-monetary obligations under the lease in order to cure. 11 U.S.C. § 365(b)(2)(D). *See In re* Parker, 269 B.R. 522 (D. Vt. 2001) (cure requires payment only of amounts for which debtor, liable under nonbankruptcy law and in particular case, did not include attorney fees or repair and utility charges).

other party for any actual pecuniary loss resulting from the default, as well as provide adequate assurance of future performance under the contract or lease.[442] Such assurance is not required if no default exists.[443] It also may not be necessary if the default is a non-monetary default, especially if it is not curable after the bankruptcy case is filed.[444]

These requirements raise other issues. How promptly must the default be cured?[445] What is meant by adequate assurance?[446] "Promptness" will no doubt depend upon all of the circumstances of the individual case, including the amount in default, term of the contract or lease, and relative needs of the contracting parties. The phrase "adequate assurance" was adopted by the Commission on Bankruptcy Laws from the Uniform Commercial Code, section 2-609. According to the comment to that section and case law thereunder this might consist of a cosigner, or a deposit, or even a simple showing of cash flow or credit sufficient to perform under the contract.[447]

There may also be a dispute regarding whether, in fact, a default exists on the part of the debtor.[448] If it does not, no cure or adequate assurance is required by section 365(b). Naturally, such issues, whether relating to claims on consumer contracts or rights under implied warranties of habitability in residential leases, may be litigated in the bankruptcy court. However, disputes about the contract's validity or breach of the contract need not be resolved in determining whether the contract may be assumed, and may instead be resolved after the assumption.[449] Once the contract has been assumed, the rights of the parties may be determined under the law that would ordinarily be applicable, absent contrary provisions in the Bankruptcy Code.[450]

Finally, the non-debtor party to the lease or contract may argue that it cannot be assumed because it was validly terminated prior to the bankruptcy.[451] This issue is particularly likely to arise in a case when the bankruptcy petition has been filed on the eve of an eviction. A number of courts and authorities have held that this argument is correct, finding that there is no contract or lease to assume.[452]

The debtor seeking to assume has a number of strong counterarguments available, however. There may be questions as to whether the contract was validly terminated under state law,[453] or whether the debtor has a right to cure the default still available.[454] Section 108(b) of the Code may have extended such a cure period automatically to sixty days after the case was filed,[455] or the court may hold that the debtor has the right to cure under section 1322(b)(3).[456] At least one court has held that the effect on the automatic stay is to "erase" a judgment for possession which would otherwise terminate a lease, returning the lease to viability.[457]

The debtor may also be able to argue that the contract was ended due to a nonpayment resulting from the debtor's insolvency. If the contract was ended pursuant to provisions of applicable law which allowed termination because of nonpayment, and that nonpayment was caused by the insolvency or financial condition of the debtor, it may be argued that the

---

442 11 U.S.C. § 365(b)(1).
443 *In re* Perretta, 7 B.R. 103 (Bankr. N.D. Ill. 1980).
444 11 U.S.C. § 365(b)(2)(D). *See In re* Bankvest Capital Corp., 360 F.3d 291 (1st Cir.) (chapter 11 debtor not required to cure nonmonetary defaults in order to assume contract).

   However, the 2005 amendments to this provision appear to require cure of most nonmonetary defaults. *In re* Empire Equities Capital Corp., 405 B.R. 687 (Bankr. S.D.N.Y. 2009).
445 *See In re* Coffman, 393 B.R. 829 (Bankr. S.D. Ohio 2008) (cure required by end of remaining three years of auto lease term); *In re* Reed, 226 B.R. 1 (Bankr. W.D. Ky. 1998) (under circumstances of case, cure within six months was required on car lease); *In re* Yokley, 99 B.R. 394 (Bankr. M.D. Tenn. 1989) (two years too long under circumstances of case); *In re* Coors of N. Miss., 27 B.R. 918 (Bankr. N.D. Miss. 1983) (three years may be prompt depending upon circumstances).
446 These issues may be particularly troubling in cases of non-monetary defaults. *See, e.g., In re* Yardley, 77 B.R. 643 (Bankr. M.D. Tenn. 1987) (default arising from tenant debtor's altercation with a security guard at his apartment complex).
447 *See* Don Fogel, *Executory Contracts and Unexpired Leases in the Bankruptcy Code*, 64 Minn. L. Rev. 341, 356–358 (1980).
448 *See, e.g., In re* Perretta, 7 B.R. 103 (Bankr. N.D. Ill. 1980) (lessor has waived right to prompt payment by accepting late payments, so late payment not a default).
449 *In re* Orion Pictures Corp., 4 F.3d 1095 (2d Cir. 1993); *In re* Coffman, 393 B.R. 829 (Bankr. S.D. Ohio 2008) (adequate assurance provided by plan payments through trustee).
450 Wainer v. A.J. Equities, 984 F.2d 679 (5th Cir. 1993).
451 The automatic stay prevents the non-debtor party to a contract from acting to terminate the contract postpetition. *See In re* Computer Communications, Inc., 824 F.2d 725 (9th Cir. 1987).
452 *See, e.g.*, Robinson v. Chicago Hous. Auth., 54 F.3d 316 (7th Cir. 1995); *In re* Hospitality Assocs., 6 B.R. 778 (Bankr. D. Or. 1980).
453 *See, e.g., In re* Dash, 267 B.R. 915 (Bankr. D.N.J. 2001) (lease had not been terminated when lessor had repossessed vehicle but had not notified debtor that lease was terminated); *In re* Gant, 202 B.R. 952 (Bankr. N.D. Ill. 1996) (lease not terminated because landlord's acceptance of rent check waived right to forfeiture of lease); *In re* Bronx-Westchester Mack Corp., 4 B.R. 730 (Bankr. S.D.N.Y. 1980).
454 *In re* Stolz, 197 F.3d 625 (2d Cir. 1999) (lease may be assumed even after judgment in state court eviction action based on tenant's possessory interest and unexpired right to cure under state law); Robinson v. Chicago Hous. Auth., 54 F.3d 316 (7th Cir. 1995) (tenant has right to assume terminated lease as long as tenant has any way to revive lease under state law); *In re* Windmill Farms, Inc., 841 F.2d 1467 (9th Cir. 1988) (lease may be assumed, even if it has been terminated, if state law gives lessee a right to prevent forfeiture); Moody v. Amoco Oil Co., 734 F.2d 1200 (7th Cir. 1984); Ross v. Metro. Dade County, 142 B.R. 1013 (S.D. Fla. 1992) (debtor could assume public housing lease because state anti-forfeiture doctrine gave right to prevent eviction through cure of default), *aff'd*, 987 F.2d 774 (11th Cir. 1993); *In re* Mims, 195 B.R. 472 (Bankr. W.D. Okla. 1996) (execution of writ of assistance is step in eviction process that terminates Oklahoma debtor's right to assume lease); *In re* Shannon, 54 B.R. 219 (Bankr. M.D. Tenn. 1985); *In re* Easthampton Sand & Gravel Co., 25 B.R. 193 (Bankr. E.D.N.Y. 1982). *See also In re* Di Giorgio, 200 B.R. 664 (C.D. Cal. 1996) (California statute permitting eviction after filing of bankruptcy found invalid), *vacated as moot*, 134 F.3d 971 (9th Cir. 1998).
455 *But see* Moody v. Amoco Oil Co., 734 F.2d 1200 (7th Cir. 1984).
456 Most of the cases considering section 365 have been under chapter 11, which has no comparable provision.
457 *In re* Mulkey of Mo., Inc., 5 B.R. 15 (Bankr. W.D. Mo. 1980) (denying relief from the stay because adequate protection provided and property necessary for reorganization).

§ 12.9.3   Consumer Bankruptcy Law and Practice

contract was, in fact, conditioned upon the insolvency or financial condition of the debtor. If it is, the termination is invalid under 11 U.S.C. § 365(e).[458]

In addition, section 365(c)(3) specifically prohibits assumption of a terminated lease only if the lease is for nonresidential real property. By implication, a residential lease may be assumed despite its prior termination. Similarly, although section 362(b)(10) provides an exception to the automatic stay as to nonresidential property under a lease which has expired before the case, there is no such exception for residential real property.[459] These distinctions were obviously not accidental. Congress intended to provide protection to consumer debtors against evictions when those evictions are based simply on tenants' prepetition lease defaults or on tenants' bankruptcy filings.

In any event, though, if a landlord has obtained a judgment for possession prior to the petition and is seeking to pursue an eviction, the debtor's options may be limited by the exception to the automatic stay provided in section 362(b)(22). The debtor is only entitled to the automatic stay's protection under section 362(a)(3) if the debtor has a right to cure and deposits a month's rent payment with the petition. Thereafter, the protection of section 362(a)(3) can be maintained beyond thirty days from the petition only if the default is completely cured by that time. This provision is discussed elsewhere in this treatise at greater length.[460] In any case, if the debtor has not been evicted prior to confirmation of a plan providing for assumption of the lease, the binding effect of the plan should preclude the landlord from evicting the debtor, except with leave of the bankruptcy court upon a plan default.[461]

12.9.3 Rejection of Leases or Executory Contracts

12.9.3.1 Overview

Problems are less likely to arise when the debtor chooses to reject an executory contract. This choice may be advantageous in a variety of situations, as many of the types of executory contracts listed above are unfair and burdensome to consumers. As discussed above,[462] it may also be possible to reject contracts imposing restrictions on the debtor, such as a covenant not to compete with a former employer or business in which the debtor was involved. Like assumption, rejection can be accomplished by a provision in a confirmed chapter 13 plan or by a separate motion.[463]

The effect of rejection is to give the other contracting party a damage claim.[464] The rejection is deemed a breach of the contract as of the time immediately prior to the filing of the bankruptcy petition.[465] As with any claim, the debtor may object to the amount claimed.[466] If the contract is secured, however, and is to be provided for in the plan, the plan may have to provide for the claim to be paid consistent with the chapter 13 standards for secured claims in order to obtain confirmation.[467]

12.9.3.2 Residential Leases

The rejection of a residential lease in chapter 13 is advantageous to a debtor mainly when the debtor plans to move or has vacated the premises prior to the end of the lease term. The unpaid rent from the period prior to the bankruptcy usually becomes a general unsecured claim,[468] which is often paid little or nothing during the case. And the lessor's potential claim for lost rents is limited to one year's rent or fifteen percent of the rent due for the remaining term of the lease, whichever is more.[469]

---

458 *See In re* Computer Communications, Inc., 824 F.2d 725 (9th Cir. 1987). *See also* Shanker, *The Treatment of Executory Contracts and Leases in the 1978 Bankruptcy Code*, 25 Prac. Law. (No. 7) 11, 17, 18. (1979).

459 *In re* Reinhardt, 209 B.R. 183 (Bankr. S.D.N.Y. 1997) (debtor's possessory interest in residential lease protected by automatic stay as section 362(b)(10) exception does not apply).

460 *See* Ch. 9, *supra*.

461 *See* § 12.11, *infra*.

462 *See* § 12.9.1, *supra*.

463 *In re* Milstead, 197 B.R. 33 (Bankr. E.D. Va. 1996) (rejection occurred upon confirmation of chapter 13 plan providing for rejection).

464 11 U.S.C. § 502(g).

This result applies even if the non-debtor party to the contract might have had a right to specific performance in a nonbankruptcy forum, provided that right is a claim under the definition in section 101(5)(B). *See In re* Aslan, 65 B.R. 826 (Bankr. C.D. Cal. 1986).

Also, the parties to the lease or contract are not relieved of other duties which are imposed upon them by law, such as statutes or regulations governing landlord-tenant relations. Saravia v. 1736 18th Street, N.W. Ltd. P'ship, 844 F.2d 823 (D.C. Cir. 1988).

As rejection constitutes a breach by the estate, the consequences of the breach depend on state law. *See* Bargain Mart v. Lipkis, 212 Conn. 120, 561 A.2d 1365 (1989).

465 *In re* Miller, 282 F.3d 874 (6th Cir. 2002) (claim for damages based upon rejected lot lease was discharged even though vacant mobile home remained on lot after petition was filed); *In re* Aslan, 909 F.2d 367 (9th Cir. 1990); *In re* Badgley, 308 B.R. 293 (Bankr. E.D. Mich. 2004) (claim arising from rejection was not administrative claim, even though debtor's original, unconfirmed plan, had provided for assumption of lease); *In re* Beck, 272 B.R. 112 (Bankr. E.D. Pa. 2002) (claim for excess mileage under rejected automobile lease was prepetition claim even if it arose postpetition and debtor had continued to make lease payments postpetition). *Cf. In re* Werbinski, 271 B.R. 514 (Bankr. E.D. Mich. 2001) (landlord could collect post-rejection rent when debtors remained on premises after rejection).

466 *See* § 14.4.3, *infra*, for a discussion of objections to claims.

467 *See* Ch. 11, *supra*. *See generally* Leasing Serv. Corp. v. First Tenn. Bank, 826 F.2d 434 (6th Cir. 1987) (rejection of contract does not affect creditor's secured status).

468 *See In re* Whitcomb & Keller Mortgage Co., 715 F.2d 375 (7th Cir. 1983).

The claim would become a secured claim, however, to the extent there was a security deposit or other security interest.

469 11 U.S.C. § 502(b)(6). *See In re* Highland Superstores, Inc., 154 F.3d 573 (6th Cir. 1998) (cap is to be applied only after any applicable damages are computed under lease and state law); *In re* Tittle, 346 B.R. 684 (Bankr. E.D. Va. 2006) (cap also applies to any lien securing the claim).

However, payment for the period after the case is filed is treated somewhat differently. During the time between filing of the case and the debtor's rejection (and also after rejection, if the debtor stays on), the lessor may be entitled to receive from the estate the reasonable rental value of the property, often known as "use and occupancy payments."[470] However the right to such payments is questionable in a consumer case, as opposed to a business case, if the property was not used for income producing purposes.[471] The rent agreed upon previously is usually deemed to be the fair value,[472] but the court may be persuaded to set the value at a higher or lower level.[473] If the rent provided for in the lease is greater than the fair value of the premises, it may thus be to the debtor's advantage to reject the lease (or simply not assume it) but remain in occupancy paying rent, if the lessor agrees[474] or the court allows the automatic stay to remain in effect.[475] In any case, once requested and allowed by the court, the use and occupancy expense will probably be considered an administrative expense, as a cost and expense of preserving the estate under 11 U.S.C. § 503(b)(1)(A).[476] Thus, in a chapter 13 case, it must be paid in full if filed as a priority claim, unless the case is dismissed, converted, or ended by a hardship discharge.[477]

In a both chapter 13 and chapter 7, because the claim for damages arising from rejection of the lease, including damages relating to postpetition use, is considered a prepetition claim under section 502(g), that claim is normally dischargeable.[478] Therefore, if the debtor does not wish to continue payments to maintain possession of the property, the lessor cannot sue the debtor after a bankruptcy case for damages arising from postpetition use of the property.[479]

12.9.3.3 Credit Insurance

Another common type of contract that could be considered executory is the purchase of credit insurance which accompanies many consumer loans.[480] More often than not, credit insurance is a very bad bargain for the consumer.[481] Rejection of the contract and termination of its benefits results in very little loss of real protection.

If a debtor attempts to reject such a contract in order to obtain a refund for the remaining term, the creditor or insurance company can be expected to argue that the insurance was paid in full by the debtor at the outset of the loan with part of the amount financed. However, the debtor can show in most contracts that nonpayment of the loan will excuse the insurer from its obligation to perform; thus, each party still has obligations which, if breached, excuse performance by the other making the contract executory under even the stricter definition discussed above. Moreover, the debtor can also point to the fact that such contracts typically provide for a refund for the remaining term if the loan is prepaid or, often, in the case of a default, making them more like installment contracts for which insurance is paid over a period of time. In fact, it is not uncommon for the creditor to make the actual payments on the debtor's behalf to the insurance company on an installment basis.

Creditors often take a security interest in the refund on credit insurance. If such a security interest is taken and is valid, there is little to be gained by rejecting the credit insurance on an otherwise unsecured debt which will not be paid in full under the plan. However, rejection of the insurance contract on a secured debt which must be paid in full under the plan could produce a refund of many hundreds, or even thousands, of dollars. This refund, even if held by the creditor as security, will ultimately go towards reducing the total amount payable.[482]

---

470 Farber v. Wards Co., 825 F.2d 684 (2d Cir. 1987). *Cf. In re* Freeman, 297 B.R. 41 (Bankr. E.D. Va. 2003) (administrative expense denied when lessor had sought relief from stay to evict debtor and debtor had not opposed motion or argued property was necessary to case); 3 Collier on Bankruptcy ¶ 365.04[3] (16th ed.).

471 *In re* Perry, 369 B.R. 402 (Bankr. E.D. Wis. 2007) (denying administrative expense when debtor vacated premises after petition was filed and never sought to assume lease).

472 Farber v. Wards Co., 825 F.2d 684 (2d Cir. 1987).

473 Zagata Fabricators v. Super. Air Prods., 893 F.2d 624 (3d Cir. 1990); *In re* Dant & Russell, Inc., 853 F.2d 700 (9th Cir. 1988).

474 Farber v. Wards Co., 825 F.2d 684 (2d Cir. 1987).

475 Zagata Fabricators v. Super. Air Prods., 893 F.2d 624 (3d Cir. 1990); *In re* Thompson, 788 F.2d 560 (9th Cir. 1986) (when debtors only use part of leased premises, they must pay administrative expense only for use and occupancy of that portion). *See In re* Schnabel, 612 F.2d 315, 317 (7th Cir. 1980).

However, some courts hold that when a lease is never assumed or rejected during a chapter 11 bankruptcy case, and presumably also a chapter 13 case, the lease "rides through" and is not affected by the case. *In re* Whitcomb & Keller Mortgage Co., 715 F.2d 375 (7th Cir. 1983); *In re* Cochise College Park, Inc., 703 F.2d 1339 (9th Cir. 1983); *In re* Werbinski, 271 B.R. 514 (Bankr. E.D. Mich. 2001) (landlord could collect post-rejection rent when debtors remained in premises after rejection); 3 Collier on Bankruptcy ¶ 365.03[6] (16th ed.).

The fact that section 365(p)(1) and (3) specifically provide that a personal property lease is rejected if not assumed, without similarly providing for real property leases, strengthens the argument that ride-through applies to the latter.

476 4 Collier on Bankruptcy ¶ 503.03 (16th ed.). *See also* Zagata Fabricators v. Super. Air Prods., 893 F.2d 624 (3d Cir. 1990); *In re* Standard Furniture Co., 3 B.R. 527 (Bankr. S.D. Cal. 1980).

477 11 U.S.C. § 1322(a)(2).

478 Chateau Communities v. Miller, 252 B.R. 121 (E.D. Mich. 2000) (creditor violated automatic stay and discharge injunction by seeking money judgment for postpetition rent), *aff'd on other grounds*, 282 F.3d 874 (6th Cir. 2002).

The fact that a lease may have by its terms automatically renewed for a new term does not convert it into a postpetition obligation. *See In re* Country Club Estates, 227 B.R. 565 (Bankr. S.D. Fla. 1998) (contract which was automatically renewed was still subject to assumption or rejection).

479 *In re* Maupin, 165 B.R. 864 (Bankr. M.D. Tenn. 1994).

480 *See In re* Garnas, 38 B.R. 221 (Bankr. D.N.D. 1984) (insurance contract considered executory).

481 The credit insurance industry is not very well regulated. Consumers typically have a poor understanding of the nature of these policies and of their very limited benefits. *See generally* National Consumer Law Center, Consumer Credit Regulation, ch. 6 (2012).

482 *See In re* Waiwada, 248 B.R. 258 (Bankr. M.D. Pa. 2000) (contract provided that debtor could cancel life and disability insurance, but

When a creditor receives a credit insurance refund, counsel should ensure that an amended claim is filed to reflect the amount of the refund.

12.9.4 Procedure and Tactics

In a chapter 13 case, the debtor is not normally required to choose assumption or rejection until the time of confirmation of the plan.[483] However, the other party may force an earlier election by requesting the court to set a specified earlier date by which the choice must be made.[484] Additionally, although courts are split on this point, a lessor might seek relief from the stay prior to a decision on assumption or rejection, arguing that its interest in the property is not adequately protected.[485] Few real estate lessors in consumer cases take advantage of either method of forcing an election.

Normally, it is to the debtor's advantage to wait until the last possible moment before choosing assumption or rejection, at least with leases. By waiting, the debtor can keep all options open and also postpone the time by which defaults must be promptly cured as part of an assumption. The non-debtor party to the executory contract or lease is bound to honor the contract until it is rejected.[486] During the period before assumption, however, the debtor will normally have to make current payments under section 1326(a) with respect to personal property leases,[487] and may have to cure a default to maintain the automatic stay of section 362(a)(3) with respect to a residential lease.[488]

As discussed earlier, to the extent residential lease payments are not made during this interim period, the debtor-lessee also builds up a debt for use and occupancy, usually at the agreed rate of rental payments. Current payments of rent after the bankruptcy is filed satisfy the debtor's only obligation to the lessor at this time, and usually keep the lessor satisfied to let the proceedings run their course (especially if the lessor is told that back rent payments will eventually be paid under the chapter 13 plan). A lessor who is satisfied with such an arrangement is unlikely to seek counsel to exercise the right to seek adequate protection[489] or to force an early election of assumption or rejection.

After weighing the factors involved, the debtor usually should assume or reject the lease by the time of confirmation.[490] If this is done, the consequences described above will transpire. If the debtor has leased personal property and the lease is not assumed in the confirmed plan, it is deemed rejected and the automatic stay and codebtor stay are terminated as to the property.[491] With respect to other leases, including real estate leases, it is somewhat less clear what will happen. Usually, the automatic stay is still in effect, but the debtor's failure to assume the lease when given the opportunity might be considered cause for relief from the stay under section 362(d).[492] On the other hand, especially if a lease contains burdensome clauses the debtor does not wish to assume, the debtor can argue that the stay should be continued, regardless of the failure to assume (or, for that matter, the conclusion of the lease term), as long as the lessor has adequate protection and continued occupancy is necessary for rehabilitation.[493]

It should be remembered, though, that because use and occupancy claims do have priority, the postpetition rental payments often will have to be paid in a chapter 13 case at some point.[494] However, if the case is converted to chapter 7 or found appropriate for a hardship discharge, such postpetition claims would normally be discharged just as most other unsecured priority claims are discharged in such cases.[495]

Consequently, even if a lease is not assumed, it is not clear that the debtor must therefore vacate the premises.[496] She simply may no longer have that leasehold interest. Also, if there is otherwise an entitlement to remain, as in public housing situations, an eviction may still be prohibited, especially when it would violate the section 525 prohibition on discrimination based solely on the discharged debt for back rent.[497]

---

creditor permitted to retain refund and apply to balance of debt).

483 11 U.S.C. § 365(d)(2).
484 11 U.S.C. § 365(d)(2).
485 *Compare In re* Sweetwater, 40 B.R. 733 (Bankr. D. Utah 1984) (relief from stay not available to lessor prior to assumption or rejection) *with In re* DeSantis, 66 B.R. 998 (Bankr. E.D. Pa. 1986) (contra).
486 *In re* Pub. Serv. Co. of N.H., 884 F.2d 11 (1st Cir. 1989).
487 *See* § 12.9.2, *supra*.
488 *See* Ch. 9, *supra*.
489 See discussion of adequate protection in Chapter 9, *supra*.
490 It is unclear whether a chapter 13 plan can be modified after confirmation to assume or reject a lease. While section 365(d)(2) states that the election must be made before confirmation, section 1322(b)(7) allows a plan (and thus perhaps a modified plan) to provide for assumption or rejection of any lease or executory contract not previously rejected.
491 11 U.S.C. § 365(p)(3).
492 See discussion of relief from the stay in Chapter 9, *supra*.
493 See discussion of relief from the stay with respect to leases in Chapter 9, *supra*. However, some courts have held that when a lease is neither assumed nor rejected, it rides through the bankruptcy case unaffected. *See* § 12.9.3.2, *supra*. Therefore, failing to assume the lease may not relieve the debtor of burdensome lease terms, though if the debtor later leaves the property any liability for rent under the lease would probably be deemed discharged.
494 Postpetition rental expenses for property used by the debtor are usually considered administrative expenses under 11 U.S.C. § 507(a)(1) and are therefore priority claims required to be paid under 11 U.S.C. § 1322(a)(2), at least if the creditor files a claim. *See* § 12.3.6.1, *supra*. *But see In re* Badgley, 308 B.R. 293 (Bankr. E.D. Mich. 2004) (claim arising from rejection was not administrative claim, even though debtor's original, unconfirmed plan, had provided for assumption of lease).
495 A postpetition claim for rent due may usually be filed by a lessor under 11 U.S.C. § 365(g)(1), or perhaps 11 U.S.C. § 1305. While the discharge of postpetition rent may seem a harsh result for the lessor, it should be remembered that the lessor can protect itself against such a loss by demanding adequate protection in the form of a new security deposit, a cosigner, or other device. *See* § 12.9.3.2, *supra*.
496 *See In re* Adams, 65 B.R. 646 (Bankr. E.D. Pa. 1986) (rejection of lease does not automatically grant landlord relief from automatic stay or relieve landlord of necessity of resorting to state court eviction proceedings).
497 11 U.S.C. § 525(a). *See* § 15.5.5.3, *infra*.

The method for actually assuming or rejecting a lease or executory contract is not spelled out in the Code. As Code section 1322(b)(7) permits a plan to provide for assumption or rejection, it is presumably sufficient to simply include a provision in the chapter 13 plan to carry out the debtor's intent.[498] However, in a case under chapter 11, which has similar provisions, one court of appeals has held that a separate motion under Federal Rule of Bankruptcy Procedure 6006 is necessary.[499] But that rule, by its own terms, provides that a motion is necessary to assume a lease or executory contract *other than as part of a plan*.

12.9.5 Assumption or Rejection of Personal Property Leases by Chapter 7 Debtor

12.9.5.1 2005 Amendments

Although assumption of leases was historically only a concern of the debtor in chapter 13 cases, the 2005 amendments added provisions permitting a debtor to assume a lease of personal property. Also added were provisions terminating the automatic stay with respect to leased personal property in certain circumstances.

12.9.5.2 Effect of Lease Rejection in Chapter 7

Section 365(d)(1) provides that if the trustee does not assume or reject an unexpired lease of personal property within sixty days after the filing of the petition, or such longer time as the court orders, the lease is deemed rejected. Under the Code as it existed prior to the 2005 Act, if the lease was rejected and the lessor of personal property wanted to take action against the property before the case was closed, the lessor was required to seek relief from the stay. New section 365(p)(1) provides that the leased property is no longer property of the estate and the stay under section 362(a) is automatically terminated once an unexpired lease is rejected or not timely assumed by the trustee.

In addition, section 362(h) provides that, in certain circumstances, if a chapter 7 debtor does not file a timely statement under section 521(a)(2) indicating an intent to assume a lease of personal property and take timely action pursuant to that statement, the automatic stay is terminated with respect to the property and the property is no longer property of the estate.[500]

12.9.5.3 Lease Assumption by the Debtor in a Chapter 7 Case

Prior to the 2005 amendments, the power to assume or reject an unexpired lease was given only to the trustee in chapter 7 cases.[501] Under the 2005 Act, the debtor is given the right to assume a lease of personal property in a chapter 7 case.[502] Under section 365(p)(2) of the Code the debtor may notify the lessor in writing that the debtor desires to assume the lease.[503] Upon being notified the lessor may, at its option, notify the debtor that it is willing to have the lease assumed, and the lessor may condition the assumption on a cure of any default under the terms set by the contract.

Within thirty days after the section 365(p)(2)(A) notice is provided, the debtor may notify the lessor in writing that the lease is assumed.[504] Although the provisions give the lessor the right to condition the assumption on cure of an outstanding default, as is the case when the trustee chooses to make an assumption, there is no provision permitting a lessor to prohibit an assumption. No court approval is required for such assumption of a lease.[505]

Section 365(p)(2)(B) provides that if the debtor gives notice that the lease is assumed, liability under the lease is assumed by the debtor, and not by the estate. It is not clear what this provision means because the 2005 amendments do not provide any exception to the discharge injunction under section 524 for collection efforts on an assumed lease.[506] Therefore, assump-

---

498 *In re* Hall, 202 B.R. 929 (Bankr. W.D. Tenn. 1996); *In re* Flugel, 197 B.R. 92 (Bankr. S.D. Cal. 1996). See § 12.9.2, *supra*.
499 Sea Harvest Corp. v. Riviera Land Co., 868 F.2d 1077 (9th Cir. 1989).
  It should be noted, however, that this case involved preconfirmation assumption of a lease, which is often necessary in chapter 11, due to the deadline for assuming leases of nonresidential real property in 11 U.S.C. § 365(d)(4). In most chapter 13 cases, the leases involved will be of residential real property and therefore not subject to this deadline. In cases in which assumption cannot occur pursuant to a plan because it must occur earlier, it is clear that merely filing an election to assume, rather than a motion the lessor may oppose, is not sufficient. *In re* Burger Boys, 94 F.3d 755, 763 (2d Cir. 1996). See § 12.9.2, *supra*.
500 See Chapter 11, *supra*, for further discussion of the statement of intention.
501 This power is given to debtors in chapter 13 cases. 11 U.S.C. § 1322(b)(7). *See also* § 12.9.1, *supra*.
502 Although not stated in section 365(p)(2), the negotiation of a lease assumption by the debtor and lessor presumably would occur only if the trustee decides not to assume the lease. Section 362(h)(1)(A) notes that the debtor may indicate on the statement of intention that the debtor shall assume an unexpired lease under section 365(p) "if the trustee does not do so."
503 This decision may also be stated as the debtor's intention on the Statement of Intention (Official Form 8), which was amended by adding a section covering unexpired leases and an option labeled "lease will be assumed pursuant to 11 U.S.C. 362(h)(1)(A)." Although the advisory committee notes indicate that the form change was made to "conform to § 521(a)(6)," no mention of lease assumption is made in section 521(a)(6). Official Form 8 is reprinted in Appx. D, *infra*.
504 Section 365(p)(2)(B) does not specify which of the two notices in section 365(p)(2)(A) it is referring to in setting this time limit. However it probably makes little difference. If the creditor has not given its optional notice stating conditions for cure, the only relevant notice is the debtor's notice; if the creditor does give the notice of conditions for cure the time may run from that later notice, giving the debtor more time to meet those conditions.
505 *In re* Farley, 451 B.R. 235 (Bankr. E.D.N.Y. 2011); *In re* Gaylor, 379 B.R. 413 (Bankr. D. Conn. 2007) (motion for court approval of stipulation was unnecessary).
506 Section 365(p)(2)(C) states that the stay under section 362 and the injunction under section 524(a)(2) are not violated by notification of

tion of a lease would not reinstate the debtor's personal liability on the lease unless the debtor also reaffirmed the debt, which section 365(p)(2) does not require and which requires completion of the elaborate procedures of section 524.[507]

12.10 Chapter 13 Cases After Prior Bankruptcies

12.10.1 Availability of a Discharge

One important distinction between chapter 13 and chapter 7 is the debtor's right to file a chapter 13 case that will result in a discharge within eight years of a prior chapter 7 case that resulted in a discharge. This right exists because sections 727(a)(8) and (9), barring a chapter 7 discharge within eight years after any chapter 7 case resulting in a discharge and six years after many chapter 13 cases in which a discharge was granted, are clearly inapplicable to chapter 13.

Instead, the right to a chapter 13 discharge after a prior discharge is governed by section 1328(f). Before 2005 there was no bar on the ability of the debtor to obtain a chapter 13 discharge after a prior discharge. There is still no restriction on the *filing*[508] of a chapter 13 case after a prior discharge, but the 2005 amendments imposed a time limit on obtaining a chapter 13 *discharge* in a case filed after a prior discharge. A discharge cannot be entered in a chapter 13 case if the debtor received a discharge in a prior chapter 7, 11, or 12 case that was filed within four years before the date of the chapter 13 order for relief.[509]

In addition, under the 2005 Act, a discharge cannot be entered in a chapter 13 case if the debtor received a discharge in a prior chapter 13 case that was filed within two years before the date of the chapter 13 order for relief.[510] As a discharge in most chapter 13 cases will not enter until at least three years after the case is filed, this means that a prior chapter 13 case will almost never be a bar to a second chapter 13 discharge.

Some have suggested that this interpretation cannot be correct because the provision would almost never be applicable. However, the plain meaning of the statutory language compels this result. In addition, the alternative interpretation advanced—that the time periods run from the prior discharge—would make no sense in terms of policy. Because a chapter 7 discharge is usually entered a few months after the filing of the petition, that interpretation would allow a chapter 13 discharge to be entered in less time after the filing of a prior chapter 7 case than after the filing of a prior chapter 13 case. In a case in which the debtor completed a five-year chapter 13 plan, it would also mean that the debtor could file a chapter 7 case and receive a discharge, but not file a chapter 13 case and receive a discharge,[511] if the new case was filed one year and one day after the prior discharge. The legislative history also supports the interpretation that the two years runs from the date the earlier chapter 13 case is filed.[512]

12.10.2 Determining Whether a Prior Discharge Was Under Chapter 7 or Chapter 13

Because the time periods restricting a subsequent discharge differ depending on whether the prior discharge was under chapter 7 or under chapter 13, it is important to be able to distinguish between the two. The language of section 1328(f), taken literally, seems to look to the chapter under which the case was originally "filed," rather than the chapter under which the discharge was granted. Thus, if a case was originally filed under chapter 13 and then converted to chapter 7, a debtor can argue that the two-year limit should apply.[513]

For example, a debtor in a failing chapter 13 case might convert the case to chapter 7 and obtain a discharge, and then need to file a new chapter 13 case less than four years after the original chapter 13 case was filed. Under section 1328(f)(1), the debtor cannot receive a chapter 13 discharge after receiving a discharge in a chapter 7 case that was filed within four years before the date of the chapter 13 order for relief. In this situation the debtor may argue that the new chapter 13 case can result in discharge because the prior discharge was received in a case filed under chapter 13. However, not all courts will accept this argument.[514]

---

the debtor and negotiation of cure under the subsection, but these limited exceptions do not extend to actions to enforce the assumed lease as a personal liability of the debtor.

507 Thompson v. Credit Union Fin. Group, 453 B.R. 823 (W.D. Mich. 2011); *In re* Eader, 426 B.R. 164 (Bankr. D. Md. 2010); *In re* Crawford, 2010 WL 2103580 (Bankr. M.D.N.C. May 19, 2010).
See Chapter 15, *infra*, for discussion of reaffirmation requirements.

508 *See In re* Bateman, 515 F.3d 272 (4th Cir. 2008) (inability to obtain discharge did not make debtor ineligible for chapter 13 relief); *In re* Gagne, 394 B.R. 219 (B.A.P. 1st Cir. 2008). *See also* Carroll v. Sanders (*In re* Sanders), 551 F.3d 397 (6th Cir. 2008) (time period after prior chapter 7 case measured from date of filing of chapter 7 case, not date of discharge).

509 11 U.S.C. § 1328(f)(1); *In re* Dyer, 2007 WL 2915530 (Bankr. E.D. Tenn. Oct. 3, 2007) (time is counted from filing date of prior case to filing date of new case); *In re* Ratzlaff, 349 B.R. 443 (Bankr. D.S.C. 2006); *In re* West, 352 B.R. 482 (Bankr. E.D. Ark. 2006) (same); *In re* Knighton, 355 B.R. 922 (Bankr. M.D. Ga. 2006) (same).

510 11 U.S.C. § 1328(f)(2). *See In re* Bateman, 515 F.3d 272 (4th Cir. 2008) (two-year period ran from filing date of previous case to filing of current case); *In re* Gagne, 394 B.R. 219 (B.A.P. 1st Cir. 2008).

511 *See* 11 U.S.C. § 727(a)(9).

512 H.R. Rep. No. 109-31, at 76 (2005) ("[Section 1328(f)] prohibits the issuance of a discharge in a subsequent chapter 13 case if the debtor received a discharge in a chapter 13 case filed during the two-year period preceding the date of the filing of the subsequent chapter 13 case.").

513 *In re* Hamilton, 383 B.R. 460 (Bankr. W.D. Ark. 2008). *But see In re* Dalton, 2010 WL 55499 (Bankr. M.D.N.C. Jan. 7, 2010); *In re* Grice, 373 B.R. 886 (Bankr. E.D. Wis. 2007) (converted case deemed filed under chapter to which it was converted, but filed at time original petition was filed).

514 *See, e.g., In re* Ybarra, 359 B.R. 702 (Bankr. S.D. Ill. 2007) (time

12.10.3 Repeat Filing Still Permissible Even If Discharge Unavailable

It is important to recognize that it is still possible for a debtor to file a case even if a discharge cannot be granted. The ability to obtain a discharge is not an eligibility requirement for chapter 13.[515] There are a number of circumstances in which a bankruptcy filing can be useful to a debtor even though a discharge cannot be granted. For example, a debtor may file a chapter 13 bankruptcy case to cure a mortgage default or other default. Subject to various limitations, the automatic stay can stop collection activity, foreclosure, or repossession, and may make a bankruptcy case valuable even without a discharge being available.[516] A chapter 7 or chapter 13 case can be used to protect exempt property from creditors, often more property than would be permitted in a state law execution, based on the application of section 522(c), which applies regardless of whether a discharge is granted.[517]

There is no indication in the 2005 amendments that the filing of a case in which no discharge can be granted tolls the time periods between discharges. Thus, for example, consider a debtor who obtained a discharge in a chapter 7 case, then filed a chapter 13 case too soon after the chapter 7 case to qualify for a discharge. The debtor should still be eligible for another chapter 7 discharge eight years after the filing of the first chapter 7 case. Nothing in the amended Bankruptcy Code indicates that the filing of the intervening chapter 13 case, in which no discharge was granted, should have any effect on the running of the eight-year period.

Nevertheless, the hostility of some courts to what they perceive as abuse of chapter 13 has carried over to cases filed shortly after prior bankruptcies. Despite the statute's clear authorization, at least one court has denied confirmation of a plan that proposed full payment of those debts that had not been discharged in an earlier chapter 7 case. The court found that the chapter 7 case and the subsequent chapter 13 case combined to effectuate a plan which resulted in no payment to general unsecured creditors. By that court's definition, such a plan failed the "good faith" test discussed earlier in this chapter.[518]

However, most courts have found nothing improper in the filing of a chapter 13 case after an earlier chapter 7 filing, at least when the combination is not a disguised liquidation.[519] At most, the earlier case should be considered in the determination of whether the later chapter 13 case is filed in good faith.[520] In *Johnson v. Home State Bank*,[521] the Supreme Court made clear that it is possible to file a chapter 13 case after a prior chapter 7 case. The court held that there was no per se bar to such a filing and that any allegations of abuse must be proved in connection with an objection to confirmation under the good faith standard. Similarly, there is no prohibition against one spouse filing a bankruptcy case if the other spouse has filed a prior case, even a case that remains pending.[522]

The filing of a chapter 13 case during a still-pending chapter 7 case, on the other hand, sometimes is not permitted.[523] But when the debtor has already received a discharge in a prior chapter 7 case, the fact that the case has not been administratively closed should not affect the debtor's right to file a subsequent chapter 13 case.[524] And it has also been held that filing a new chapter 13 petition while a previously filed inactive chapter 13 is still pending is not absolutely barred, though it may be indicative of bad faith.[525]

A number of advantages to the debtor spring from the right to file a chapter 13 case after a chapter 7 case. The most obvious is the possibility of refuge from creditors and a fresh start in bankruptcy when a chapter 7 discharge is not available. Because a case initially filed as a chapter 13 case may be dismissed as a matter of right at any time by the debtor,[526] it could serve as a kind of holding action for a year or two until the applicable time bar to a discharge following a prior bankruptcy expired. If the plan were then dismissed before completion, a

---

period for chapter 7 case applied in case converted from chapter 13 to chapter 7).

515 *In re* Bateman, 515 F.3d 272 (4th Cir. 2008) (inability to obtain discharge did not make debtor ineligible for chapter 13 relief); *In re* McGhee, 342 B.R. 256 (Bankr. W.D. Ky. 2006); *In re* Lewis, 339 B.R. 814 (Bankr. S.D. Ga. 2006).

516 See also Chapter 9, *supra*, for a discussion of limitations on the automatic stay imposed by the 2005 amendments.

517 See § 10.5, *supra*.

518 *In re* Diego, 6 B.R. 468 (Bankr. N.D. Cal. 1980).

519 *In re* Baker, 736 F.2d 481 (8th Cir. 1984); *In re* Gayton, 61 B.R. 612 (B.A.P. 9th Cir. 1986); *In re* Tauscher, 26 B.R. 99 (Bankr. E.D. Wis. 1982).

520 *In re* Taylor, 884 F.2d 478 (9th Cir. 1989); *In re* Metz, 820 F.2d 1495 (9th Cir. 1987); *In re* Ponteri, 31 B.R. 859 (Bankr. D.N.J. 1983). See *In re* Rasmussen, 888 F.2d 703 (10th Cir. 1989) (when debtor who originally had debts in excess of chapter 13 debt limits had discharged all debts, except one debt held nondischargeable in chapter 7 case, and two weeks later filed chapter 13 case proposing to pay 1.5% of debt not discharged in chapter 7, which was only debt listed in chapter 13 statement, plan was not filed in good faith and was manipulation of the bankruptcy process). *See also In re* Chisum, 68 B.R. 471 (B.A.P. 9th Cir. 1986) (filing of four successive bankruptcies not an abuse in circumstances of particular case), *aff'd*, 847 F.2d 597 (9th Cir. 1988).

521 501 U.S. 78, 111 S. Ct. 2150, 115 L. Ed. 2d 66 (1991).

522 *In re* Nahat, 315 B.R. 368 (Bankr. N.D. Tex. 2004).

523 *In re* Cowen, 29 B.R. 888 (Bankr. S.D. Ohio 1983). *See also In re* Sanchez-Dobazo, 343 B.R. 742 (Bankr. S.D. Fla. 2006) (no per se rule against filing chapter 13 case while chapter 7 case pending, even before chapter 7 discharge).

524 *In re* Saylors, 869 F.2d 1434 (11th Cir. 1989); *In re* Keach, 243 B.R. 851 (B.A.P. 1st Cir. 2000); *In re* Ragsdale, 315 B.R. 691 (Bankr. E.D. Mich. 2004). *See also In re* Strause, 97 B.R. 22 (Bankr. S.D. Cal. 1989) (filing of chapter 13 case not barred by pending chapter 7 case when debtor's discharge would have been granted but for court's administrative delays). *But see In re* Sidebottom, 430 F.3d 893 (7th Cir. 2005) (debtor could not file chapter 13 case to deal with debts that were still the subject of ongoing proceedings in prior chapter 7 case).

525 *In re* Whitmore, 225 B.R. 199 (Bankr. D. Idaho 1998) (fact that debtor's prior chapter 13 case was still pending for a few days after new chapter 13 case was filed was not in itself cause for dismissal of new case); *In re* Cormier, 147 B.R. 285 (Bankr. D. Me. 1992).

526 11 U.S.C. § 1307(b).

chapter 7 case would not be barred because section 727(a)(9) bars chapter 7 cases only after chapter 13 cases that have resulted in a discharge.[527]

Another possibility is that of successive chapter 13 cases, with one commenced, if necessary, immediately after discharge or dismissal of a previous case.[528] This could be particularly useful if new and unanticipated debts, such as a tort judgment or medical bills, arise after the first chapter 13 case is underway,[529] if debts not discharged in the first chapter 13 case continue to cause insurmountable problems for the debtor, or if problems develop in the first case. The first case may then be dismissed as a matter of right and a new chapter 13 (or chapter 7) case could be commenced. This strategy could also provide a way to reduce the payments necessary to meet the "best interests of creditors" test,[530] if the amount of nonexempt property owned by the debtor was substantially reduced between the filing of the first case and the second case. However, if a request for relief from the stay was filed in the first case, no new case may be commenced for 180 days after the voluntary dismissal of the first case.[531] In addition, section 362(c)(3) or (4) might limit the availability of the automatic stay in the new case absent a court order.[532]

In considering these possible courses of action, practitioners should be aware that an unsympathetic court may find them to be not in good faith and may deny confirmation of the plan in the later chapter 13 case.[533] Especially if it appears that the debtor has willfully incurred many new debts with the specific intent of filing a new chapter 13 case to discharge them, a court may be quite receptive to creditor arguments that the successive petitions are part of a fraudulent scheme and that confirmation should be denied. In such cases, debtors may run a significant risk not only of dismissal, but also of an involuntary conversion to chapter 7. Obviously, it is not good practice to subject debtors to such risks when they can be avoided, and debtors should be discouraged from such behavior which places not only their own cases, but also the credibility of liberal bankruptcy laws, in jeopardy.

12.11 Confirmation of Plan Binds Debtor and All Creditors

The confirmation order is binding upon the debtor and all creditors.[534] Once the appeal period has passed, it is res judicata as to all issues which could have been raised in opposition to confirmation.[535] After confirmation, no creditor may take ac-

---

527 It is doubtful whether a chapter 13 case filed within six years after a prior bankruptcy could be converted to a chapter 7 case after the six-year period expired because the filing date of the chapter 13 case would likely be deemed the filing date of the converted chapter 7 case, thus barring a chapter 7 discharge. In view of this likelihood, dismissal of the chapter 13 case and the filing of a new chapter 7 case seems a safer course than conversion after the six years have run.

528 See In re Smith, 43 B.R. 319 (Bankr. E.D.N.C. 1984) (plan confirmed, with conditions, even though there had been three prior unsuccessful chapter 13 cases). But see 11 U.S.C. § 109(g), placing certain limitations on successive filings, discussed in Chapters 3 and 9, supra.

529 See also § 8.7.3, supra, concerning postpetition claims in chapter 13.

530 See § 12.3.2, supra.

531 11 U.S.C. § 109(g).
    See discussion of this 1984 amendment in Chapters 3 and 9, supra.

532 See Ch. 9, supra.

533 See In re Eisen, 14 F.3d 469 (9th Cir. 1994) (debtor's chapter 13 case dismissed as in bad faith when debtor had had several prior bankruptcy cases, one of which had been dismissed as in bad faith, and had made misrepresentations to court about prior cases and other facts).
    Section 707(b)(3) also permits a chapter 7 case to be dismissed if filed in bad faith. See Ch. 13, infra.

534 11 U.S.C. § 1327(a). The binding effect of a confirmed plan extends to all those in privity with the debtor or a creditor. Sanders Confectionery Prods. v. Heller Fin., 973 F.2d 474 (6th Cir. 1992) (chapter 11 plan was binding on parent corporation of creditor and creditor's law firm, but not shareholder of a creditor). It applies to related proceedings, both core and non-core, which could have been brought. Id.
    However, a confirmed plan that is ambiguous may be construed against its drafter, the debtor. See In re Roberts, 279 F.3d 91 (1st Cir. 2002) (plan which provided that debtor would pay fixed amount to trustee but also provided specified percentage return to unsecured creditors required debtor to pay larger of the two amounts). See also In re Taumoepeau, 523 F.3d 1213, 1218 (10th Cir. 2008) (plan that did not provide for postpetition arrears dealt with in preconfirmation stipulation did not supersede stipulation).

535 United Student Aid Funds, Inc. v. Espinosa, 130 S. Ct. 1367 (2010); Travelers Indem. Co. v. Bailey, 129 S. Ct. 2195, 174 L. Ed. 2d 99 (2009) (parties to bankruptcy case or those in privity with them could not argue court's lack of jurisdiction in challenging final chapter 11 confirmation order); Corbett v. MacDonald Moving Servs., Inc., 124 F.3d 82 (2d Cir. 1997) (lack of subject matter jurisdiction over particular issue dealt with by chapter 11 plan could not be raised after passage of time to appeal confirmation order); In re Ivory, 70 F.3d 73 (9th Cir. 1995) (even if order confirming plan erroneously gave debtor right to redeem property after expiration of redemption period, creditor could not collaterally attack unappealed confirmation order); In re Pence, 905 F.2d 1107 (7th Cir. 1990); In re Szostek, 886 F.2d 1405 (3d Cir. 1989); In re Burrell, 346 B.R. 561 (B.A.P. 1st Cir. 2006) (failure of town to object to plan that would not pay postpetition interest on property taxes precluded later attempt to collect); In re San Miguel Sandoval, 327 B.R. 493 (B.A.P. 1st Cir. 2005) (creditor could not challenge eligibility after confirmation); In re Wellman, 322 B.R. 298 (B.A.P. 6th Cir. 2004) (creditor motion for relief from stay on issues that could have been raised at confirmation was precluded by plan confirmation); Lamarche v. Miles, 416 B.R. 53 (E.D.N.Y. 2009) (lessor could not seek relief from stay with respect to lease because such relief was inconsistent with confirmed plan); United States v. Edmonston, 99 B.R. 995 (E.D. Cal. 1989) (creditor could not contest debtor's eligibility for chapter 13 after confirmation); In re Worland, 2009 WL 1707512 (Bankr. S.D. Ind. June 16, 2009) (child support agency's wage garnishment and tax intercept, while not barred by automatic stay, were inconsistent with confirmed plan and therefore improper); In re Ober, 390 B.R. 60 (Bankr. W.D.N.Y. 2008) (automatic dismissal for alleged failure to file payment advices precluded by plan confirmation, even after case converted to chapter 7); In re Greene, 359 B.R. 262 (Bankr. D. Ariz. 2007) (confirmation precluded trustee from proceeding on "conditional objections" to exemptions); In re Sullivan, 321 B.R. 306 (Bankr. M.D. Fla. 2005)

tions that are inconsistent with the plan.[536] Thus, a creditor may not seek relief from the stay if the debtor is complying with the plan.[537] And no creditor or trustee may later challenge the plan by arguing that it did not comply with some provision of chapter 13, such as the good faith requirement.[538] Similarly, the trustee is bound by the confirmed plan and is responsible for rectifying any erroneous distributions.[539]

Even if a creditor has not been provided all that it is entitled to receive under the statute, such as present value interest for a secured creditor,[540] the creditor that does not timely assert those rights will lose them,[541] just as parties in other proceedings may lose rights by default. For example, a plan provision finding

---

(preconfirmation stay relief order not valid to extent it conflicted with confirmed plan); *In re* Bilal, 296 B.R. 828 (Bankr. D. Kan. 2003) (creditor bound by confirmed plan provision that rescinded mortgage under Truth in Lending act and declared creditor's lien void); *In re* Durham, 260 B.R. 383 (Bankr. D.S.C. 2001) (creditor who claimed to be lessor was bound by plan's provision treating it as secured creditor); *In re* Minzler, 158 B.R. 720 (Bankr. S.D. Ohio 1993) (creditor could not prevail on motion for relief from stay due to lack of adequate protection on leases allegedly misclassified as secured claims because creditor was bound by confirmed plan to which it had not objected); 8 Collier on Bankruptcy ¶ 1327.02[1] (16th ed.). *Cf. In re* Miller, 16 F.3d 240 (8th Cir. 1994) (motion to set aside confirmation of chapter 12 plan filed within ten days of confirmation order treated as timely motion for new trial under Fed. R. Bankr. P. 9023).

536 *In re* Carvalho, 335 F.3d 45 (1st Cir. 2003) (plan terms regarding amounts due remained binding on creditor even though creditor had obtained relief from stay); *In re* Talbot, 124 F.3d 1201 (10th Cir. 1997) (IRS not permitted to demand full payment of its lien when debtors sold home because lien was to have been paid through chapter 13 plan). *But see In re* McGrahan, 459 B.R. 869 (B.A.P. 1st Cir. 2011) (confirmed plan was not specific enough in stating that state support agency could not intercept tax refunds to collect support to be binding on agency).

537 *In re* Diviney, 225 B.R. 762 (B.A.P. 10th Cir. 1998) (unless expressly preserved by confirmed plan or order confirming plan, terms of preconfirmation agreement regarding automatic stay did not survive confirmation); *In re* Hileman, 451 B.R. 522 (Bankr. C.D. Cal. 2011) (pre-confirmation termination of the stay by 11 U.S.C.S. § 362(c)(3) does not divest the debtor of the ability to bind creditors under a confirmed plan); *In re* Garrett, 185 B.R. 620 (Bankr. N.D. Ala. 1995) (preconfirmation order granting relief from automatic stay was superseded by provisions of confirmed plan; after confirmation binding effect of plan precludes relief from stay based upon events which occurred before confirmation). *See also In re* Allen, 300 F.3d 1055 (9th Cir. 2002) (confirmed chapter 11 plan that did not incorporate terms of prior stay relief order and stipulation was nonetheless binding on creditor).

538 *In re* Gregory, 705 F.2d 1118 (9th Cir. 1983); *In re* Storey, 392 B.R. 266, 268 (B.A.P. 6th Cir. 2008) (plan could not be modified to correct trustee's error in calculating plan length); *In re* Bailey, 425 B.R. 825 (Bankr. D. Minn. 2010) (denying on res judicata grounds trustee's motion to extend plan term from 36 to 60 months, which trustee argued was statutorily mandated); *In re* Stansbury, 403 B.R. 741 (Bankr. M.D. Fla. 2009) (disallowing creditor's deficiency claim because confirmed plan provided that collateral would be surrendered in full satisfaction of debt).

The debtor may modify the plan, however, if the modification meets the requirements of section 1329, even without a showing of cause. *In re* Jourdan, 108 B.R. 1020 (Bankr. N.D. Iowa 1989); *In re* Mosely, 74 B.R. 791 (Bankr. C.D. Cal. 1987). *See also In re* Penrod, 50 F.3d 459 (7th Cir. 1995) (confirmed chapter 11 plan which did not specifically preserve creditor's lien extinguished lien of creditor that had participated in reorganization, even if creditor could have successfully objected to plan). *But see In re* Escobedo, 28 F.3d 34 (7th Cir. 1994) (distinguishing mandatory requirements of section 1322(a); trustee could obtain dismissal of a plan not complying with section 1322(a) even after an unappealed confirmation order).

539 *In re* Brent, 2009 WL 1884745 (Bankr. N.D. Ill. June 29, 2009) (trustee could recover overpayments on support debts from creditors); *In re* Wilson, 274 B.R. 4 (Bankr. D.D.C. 2001) (when trustee—who began distributions after confirmation but before governmental claims bar date—made distributions to unsecured creditors of funds that should have gone to larger-than-expected governmental claims, trustee was required to recover erroneous distributions or reimburse estate. *See also In re* Jafary, 333 B.R. 680 (Bankr. S.D.N.Y. 2005) (trustee could not distribute to creditors a refund received after debtor completed payments from secured creditor who had received duplicate payments from debtor).

540 First Nat'l Bank v. Allen, 118 F.3d 1289 (8th Cir. 1997) (failure to object to chapter 12 plan which provided for banks' secured claims, but not their unsecured claims constitutes waiver of the unsecured claims); *In re* Chappell, 984 F.2d 775 (7th Cir. 1993) (lien was eliminated and debt discharged upon full payment of creditor's claim for principal, without interest, pursuant to confirmed chapter 13 plan not providing for interest, to which creditor had not objected); *In re* Szostek, 886 F.2d 1405 (3d Cir. 1989); *In re* Echevarria, 212 B.R. 185 (B.A.P. 1st Cir. 1997) (creditor who failed to object to failure of plan to provide interest on secured claim was bound by plan and could not collect that interest after plan was completed); Malec v. Cook County Clerk (*In re* Malec), 442 B.R. 130 (Bankr. N.D. Ill. 2011) (county violated discharge injunction by assessing penalties and interest that was paid off in full without interest pursuant to terms of confirmed plan). *See* § 11.6.1.3, *supra*. *See also In re* Harrison, 987 F.2d 677 (10th Cir. 1993) (creditor was estopped from arguing that its claim was partially unsecured when plan surrendered property to satisfy proof of claim filed by creditor that stated claim was fully secured; burden was on creditor to amend proof of claim or seek valuation of collateral prior to confirmation); *In re* Pence, 905 F.2d 1107 (7th Cir. 1990) (creditor could not object to substitution of collateral violating lien retention standard of § 1325(a)(5) in confirmed plan). *But see In re* Boyd, 11 F.3d 59 (5th Cir. 1994) (debtor's plan did not revest in debtor property that was never in estate to begin with because it had been conveyed through a foreclosure sale completed thirty-three months before bankruptcy; therefore creditor was not precluded by confirmation of plan from obtaining relief from the automatic stay).

541 Burnett v. Burnett (*In re* Burnett), 646 F.3d 575 (8th Cir. 2011) (spousal support creditor bound by terms of plan that specifically barred her from seeking interest on spousal support after chapter 13 case); *In re* Harvey, 213 F.3d 318 (7th Cir. 2000) (creditor waived any argument about plan provision voiding its lien upon payment of allowed secured claim by not objecting to confirmation); *In re* Herbert, 61 B.R. 44 (Bankr. W.D. La. 1986); *In re* Webb, 932 F.2d 155 (2d Cir. 1991) (creditor could not raise issue of property valuation in objecting to chapter 12 plan modification because creditor had not objected to valuation accepted by court at time of confirmation and creditor was bound by that valuation); *In re* Woods, 130 B.R. 204 (W.D. Va. 1990) (creditor could not argue that bankruptcy court had lacked jurisdiction to enter confirmation order when it did not raise the issue at time of confirmation). *Cf. In re* Booth, 289 B.R. 665 (N.D. Ill. 2003) (plan provision providing for release of creditor's lien prior to completion of plan upon payment of secured portion of claim, although binding on creditor, was trumped by section 349(b)(1) upon dismissal of chapter 13, so lien revested in creditor for unpaid portion of full claim).

that a student loan was dischargeable under the undue hardship provision of section 523(a)(8) was binding on the loan guarantee agency once the plan had been confirmed.[542] As noncompliance with any provision of chapter 13 or other applicable provisions of the Bankruptcy Code may be raised as an objection to confirmation under Code section 1325(a)(1), a creditor has few if any ways to challenge a confirmed plan other than under the very narrow grounds provided for seeking revocation of confirmation.[543]

However, even a provision of a confirmed plan may not be sufficient to invalidate a claim properly filed by a creditor. Some courts have held that the only method contemplated for challenging a filed proof of claim is the process of objecting to the claim.[544] Other courts have allowed the provisions of a confirmed plan to govern over an inconsistent claim.[545] Still others have treated the issue as one of whether the creditor has received constitutionally sufficient notice that its property rights are in jeopardy, suggesting that if sufficient notice is given, a creditor may have its lien reduced by confirmation of a plan.[546]

---

542 Espinosa v. United Student Aid Funds, Inc., 553 F.3d 1193 (9th Cir. 2008), *cert. granted*, 2009 WL 646192 (U.S. June 15, 2009), *aff'd sub nom.* United Student Aid Funds, Inc. v. Espinosa, 130 S. Ct. 1367 (2010).

　Note however that, upon objection, confirmation of a plan containing such a provision has been denied. *In re* Mammel, 221 B.R. 238 (Bankr. D. Iowa 1998). *See also In re* Pardee, 193 F.3d 1083 (9th Cir. 1999) (interest on student loan discharged pursuant to a provision of a confirmed plan).

543 11 U.S.C. § 1330 allows revocation of confirmation to be sought only within 180 days of the confirmation order and only if the confirmation order was procured by fraud. It may be sought only by a creditor provided for in the plan. *In re* Fesq, 153 F.3d 113 (3d Cir. 1998) (confirmation may not be vacated under Federal Rule of Bankruptcy Procedure 9024; revocation based upon fraud is only remedy); *In re* Valenti, 310 B.R. 138 (B.A.P. 9th Cir. 2004) (creditor could not evade 180-day deadline by seeking relief under Federal Rule of Bankruptcy Procedure 9024); *In re* Garvin, 457 B.R. 121 (Bankr. N.D. Fla. 2011) (creditor could not seek relief from plan modification it had not opposed through use of Rule 9024 when no grounds for revocation of confirmation existed); *In re* Kelly, 358 B.R. 443 (Bankr. M.D. Fla. 2006) (trustee could not evade requirements for revocation of confirmation by moving to reopen case so that he could file a motion to convert case to chapter 7); *In re* Robinson, 293 B.R. 59 (Bankr. D. Or. 2002) (Federal Rule of Bankruptcy Procedure 9024 cannot be used to revoke confirmation); *In re* Slack, 280 B.R. 604 (Bankr. D.N.J. 2002) (bad faith not sufficient grounds for revocation of confirmation); *In re* Randolph, 273 B.R. 914 (Bankr. M.D. Fla. 2002) (revocation denied even though debtor made materially false statement because creditor did not prove intent to obtain confirmation by fraud).

　Revocation may not be sought if the alleged fraud was known in time to object to confirmation. *In re* Ritacco, 210 B.R. 595 (Bankr. D. Or. 1997); *In re* Hicks, 79 B.R. 45 (Bankr. N.D. Ala. 1987). *See also In re* Nikoloutsos, 199 F.3d 233 (5th Cir. 1999) (revoking confirmation based on debtor's failure to schedule judgment for $863,440 that had been entered against him); Young v. Internal Revenue Serv., 132 B.R. 395 (S.D. Ind. 1990) (reversing bankruptcy court's decision which had reconsidered plan confirmation on motion of IRS, which alleged it had been improperly treated).

544 *In re* Simmons, 765 F.2d 547 (5th Cir. 1985); *In re* Franklin, 448 B.R. 744 (Bankr. M.D. La. 2011) (*Simmons* was overruled by Supreme Court *Espinosa* decision).

　The Fifth Circuit elaborated on the *Simmons* case in *In re* Howard, 972 F.2d 639 (5th Cir. 1992). There the court held that it is simply necessary to file an objection to a secured claim before the confirmation hearing to put the creditor on notice that its lien is at risk if it does not participate in confirmation proceedings. Thereafter, a confirmed plan may modify the lien of a creditor who has filed a secured claim. *See also In re* Bateman, 331 F.3d 821 (11th Cir. 2003) (although mortgage creditor's claim for arrearages had to be disallowed to extent it exceeded amount provided for in confirmed plan, the arrearages disallowed would remain owing after the case because plan could not modify mortgage creditor's secured claim); Cen-Pen Corp. v. Hanson, 58 F.3d 89 (4th Cir. 1995) (adversary proceeding is required to challenge validity of lien); § 11.2.2, *supra*.

　The fact that a plan has been confirmed, however, does not necessarily preclude the debtor from challenging a proof of claim after confirmation. *In re* Lewis, 875 F.2d 53 (3d Cir. 1989). *Cf. In re* Layo, 460 F.3d 289 (2d Cir. 2006) (trustee and debtor could not challenge mortgage lien as invalid after confirmation of plan that specifically recognized lien as a valid first mortgage); Hope v. Acorn Fin., Inc., 2012 WL 74874 (M.D. Ga. Jan. 10, 2012) (trustee could not avoid creditor's lien after confirmation when claim had been classified as secured claim and trustee had been aware of avoidability before confirmation).

545 *In re* Fili, 257 B.R. 370 (B.A.P. 1st Cir. 2001) (plan which provided for discharge and no distribution to secured creditor prevailed over timely-filed claim); *In re* McGee, 414 B.R. 132 (E.D. Mich. 2009) (confirmed plan provision classifying city's claim as unsecured was binding even though city had filed secured claim); *In re* Ayre, 360 B.R. 880 (C.D. Ill. 2007) (amount of disputed unsecured priority tax claim could be determined by terms of a confirmed plan); *In re* Simmons, 379 B.R. 143 (Bankr. N.D. Ill. 2007) (mortgagee could not seek increase in cure payments in confirmed plan over the amount set forth in its proof of claim and confirmed plan); *In re* Grammar, 310 B.R. 423 (Bankr. E.D. Ark. 2004) (plan governed even though creditor's claim was secured solely by real estate that was debtor's principal residence); *In re* Ramey, 301 B.R. 534 (Bankr. E.D. Ark. 2003) (plan provision with sufficient notice given is binding); *In re* Dickey, 293 B.R. 360 (Bankr. M.D. Pa. 2003) (same); *In re* Hudson, 260 B.R. 421 (Bankr. W.D. Mich. 2001) (confirmation can establish binding decision on amount of allowed secured claim and interest rate, but unsecured claim is normally established through claims allowance process); *In re* Jones, 271 B.R. 397 (Bankr. S.D. Ala. 2000) (confirmation order prevailed over timely claim filed after confirmation); *In re* Harnish, 224 B.R. 91 (Bankr. N.D. Iowa 1998) (when creditor was listed as unsecured in debtor's schedules and treated as unsecured in confirmed plan, plan did not preserve any lien creditor might have had; creditor had duty to monitor confirmation of plan); *In re* Wolf, 162 B.R. 98 (Bankr. D.N.J. 1993); *In re* Tucker, 35 B.R. 35 (Bankr. M.D. Tenn. 1983); *In re* Russell, 29 B.R. 332 (Bankr. E.D.N.Y. 1983).

546 *In re* Mansaray-Ruffin, 530 F.3d 230 (3d Cir. 2008) (plan provision insufficient to invalidate lien when no adversary proceeding filed as required by rules and due process considerations); *In re* Brawders, 503 F.3d 856 (9th Cir. 2007); *In re* Linkous, 990 F.2d 160 (4th Cir. 1993) (notice of confirmation hearing was not adequate to permit reduction of liens when it failed to state that court would consider valuation of security interests at confirmation hearing); *In re* King, 290 B.R. 641 (Bankr. C.D. Ill. 2003) (wholly unsecured lien may be stripped off as part of confirmation process because plan provision provided adequate notice to creditor). *See also In re* Shook, 278 B.R. 815 (B.A.P. 9th Cir. 2002) (when debtor listed claim as unsecured in schedules and plan did not specifically address creditor's claim, debtor could not seek to have claim deemed unsecured four-and-a-half years after confirmation). *See generally* 8 Collier on Bankruptcy ¶ 1327.02[2] (16th ed.).

The binding effect of confirmation can be important in requiring creditors to abide by the terms of the plan even after it has been concluded.[547] If a plan provides that certain payments under the plan will cure a mortgage default, thereby bringing the debtor current on the mortgage, a mortgage lender may not add extra charges or prepetition claims to the ongoing mortgage payments either during the plan or after it has been completed,[548] as some attempt to do. The debtor must be treated as if the default had not occurred and she is current on payments.[549] Practitioners representing debtors who have cured mortgages should advise their clients to be alert to any charges added to their payments that may be related to the earlier default. If such charges are imposed, it may be necessary to enforce the terms of the confirmation order, reopening the chapter 13 case if it has already been completed. Such charges also violate the discharge injunction[550] and in many states additional damages and attorney fees may be available because imposition of illegal charges violates state usury or unfair trade practice laws.[551]

Although the binding effect of a confirmed plan often works in a debtor's favor, some courts have allowed creditors to use it as an argument against a debtor. For example, debtors have been prevented from claiming an exemption in the proceeds of the sale of their home when such an exemption precluded them from paying creditors the amount provided in their plan.[552] It has also been held, erroneously, that confirmation fixes the amount of a claim filed prior to confirmation to which no objection has been made, and the debtor may not later argue that the claim was overstated.[553]

---

547 Taylor v. Chase Home Fin., L.L.C. (*In re* Taylor), 2012 WL 1808858 (Bankr. S.D. Ind. May 17, 2012).

548 *In re* Rizzo-Cheverier, 364 B.R. 532 (Bankr. S.D.N.Y. 2007); *In re* Cleveland, 349 B.R. 522 (Bankr. E.D. Tenn. 2006); *In re* Riser, 289 B.R. 201 (Bankr. M.D. Fla. 2003) (mortgage company not entitled to payments for any charges incurred before or during bankruptcy that were not provided for in confirmed plan); *In re* Rathe, 114 B.R. 253 (Bankr. D. Idaho 1990); *In re* Brown, 121 B.R. 768 (Bankr. S.D. Ohio 1990) (mortgagee must treat debtor as current even when it claimed to have incorrectly computed its proof of claim).

549 Wells Fargo Home Mortg., Inc. v. Borkowski (*In re* Borkowski), 446 B.R. 220 (Bankr. W.D. Pa. 2011) (mortgage lender who did not seek to assert postpetition plan payment during plan as permitted under local procedures and did not object to motion to find plan completed was bound by terms of plan providing mortgage was cured); *In re* Rathe, 114 B.R. 253 (Bankr. D. Idaho 1990). *See In re* Wines, 239 B.R. 703 (Bankr. D.N.J. 1999) (reconciling payments made with proof of claim and cure of default).

This issue may be ameliorated by the promulgation of Fed. R. Bankr. P. 3002.1. *See* § 11.6.2.8.1, *supra*.

See also § 11.6.2.8, *supra*, and § 14.4.3.4.4, *infra*, for further discussion of mortgage overcharges.

550 11 U.S.C. § 524(a)(2), (i). *See* § 15.5.5.7, *infra*. *See also In re* Turner, 221 B.R. 920 (Bankr. M.D. Fla. 1998) (attorney fees and costs awarded for contempt based on accounting on secured debt inconsistent with completion of confirmed chapter 11 plan); *In re* Ronemus, 201 B.R. 458 (Bankr. N.D. Tex. 1996) (creditor assessed $10,000, plus $3000 attorney and accountants' fees after discharge due to mortgagee charging late charges on current payments made during bankruptcy and for charging filing fee, attorney fees and expenses to debtor's escrow account without permission of court).

551 *See generally* National Consumer Law Center, Consumer Credit Regulation Ch. 7 (2012); National Consumer Law Center, Unfair and Deceptive Acts and Practices (7th ed. 2008 and Supp.).

552 *In re* Wolfberg, 255 B.R. 879 (B.A.P. 9th Cir. 2000). *Cf. In re* Summerville, 361 B.R. 133 (B.A.P. 9th Cir. 2007) (plan providing only that debt would be cured with current payments outside the plan did not preclude debtor from later raising defenses in state court).

553 Adair v. Sherman, 230 F.3d 890 (7th Cir. 2000) (debtor precluded from bringing action under Fair Debt Collection Practices Act alleging that proof of claim filed by creditor was excessive). *Cf. In re* Lewis, 875 F.2d 53 (3d Cir. 1989) (confirmation does not necessarily preclude challenge to proof of claim); *In re* Fryer, 172 B.R. 1020 (Bankr. S.D. Ga. 1994) (confirmation did not bar Truth in Lending objection to claim, because objection did not implicate validity of any plan provision).

Chapter 13   Dismissal or Conversion of a Bankruptcy Case

13.1 Introduction

For most consumer debtors, the decision to file bankruptcy and the selection of which chapter to utilize comes after careful thought and consideration of the advantages and disadvantages of that choice. However, in certain emergency situations, such as a pending foreclosure, the decision may be made in haste. Due to a variety of factors, either unknown at the time of filing or arising after the filing, the debtor may wish to voluntarily dismiss the bankruptcy case or to convert it to another chapter. This Chapter discusses the conditions when that may be possible and the effects of case dismissal and conversion.

Involuntary dismissal or conversion, in either a chapter 7 or a chapter 13 case, may also occur for a number of reasons, such as the failure to pay filing fees, the failure to file the required documents, the failure to appear at the meeting of creditors or court hearings, or the failure to make required plan payments. The Bankruptcy Code also permits a bankruptcy court, after notice and a hearing, to dismiss a chapter 7 case filed by a debtor with primarily consumer debts or, with the debtor's consent, to convert the case to chapter 13, if the court finds that granting relief under chapter 7 would be an abuse of its provisions. Means testing to determine whether a presumption of abuse exists applies to those debtors whose current monthly income is above the state median income. This Chapter also discusses when a bankruptcy case may be involuntarily dismissed or converted based on the abuse provisions or for other reasons.

13.2 Voluntary Dismissal of Bankruptcy Cases

Occasionally, a debtor may wish to extricate himself or herself from a bankruptcy that was voluntarily commenced. In chapter 13, the answer to this question is simple. Under section 1307(b) of the Code, the debtor may obtain a dismissal upon request in any chapter 13 case that has not been converted from another chapter.[1] Even when creditors oppose dismissal or seek to convert the case, the debtor's election to dismiss should be honored.[2] However, if a case has been converted to chapter 13 from chapter 7, section 1307(c) provides that the case can be dismissed on the debtor's motion only if dismissal is in the best interests of the creditors and the estate.[3]

Chapter 7 cases present a somewhat more complicated picture. The court may dismiss a case only after notice and a hearing,[4] and only for cause.[5] What constitutes cause for dismissal has been a matter of some dispute and is usually left to the discretion of the court.[6] A number of courts have held that cause does not exist in cases in which the debtor sought only to re-file a petition after paying a favored creditor or to include debts incurred after the first petition was filed.[7] Similarly,

---

[1] However, the bankruptcy court may retain jurisdiction to decide adversary proceedings pending at the time of the dismissal. *In re* Pocklington, 21 B.R. 199 (Bankr. S.D. Cal. 1982). *See In re* Nash, 765 F.2d 1410 (9th Cir. 1985). *See also* § 14.2.4.3, *supra*.

[2] *In re* Barbieri, 199 F.3d 616 (2d Cir. 1999) (court must dismiss and could not convert case to chapter 7 when debtor had moved to dismiss); Procel v. United States Trustee (*In re* Procel), 467 B.R. 297 (S.D.N.Y. 2012) (*Barbieri* remains good law after *Maramma* decision); *In re* Dulaney, 285 B.R. 10 (D. Colo. 2002); Clearstory & Co. v. Blevins, 225 B.R. 591 (D. Md. 1998); *In re* Eddis, 37 B.R. 217 (E.D. Pa. 1984); *In re* Gillion, 36 B.R. 901 (E.D. Ark. 1984); *In re* Williams, 435 B.R. 552 (Bankr. N.D. Ill. 2010) (no bad faith exception to right to dismiss chapter 13 case); *In re* Hamlin, 2010 WL 749809 (Bankr. E.D.N.C. Mar. 1, 2010); *In re* Neiman, 257 B.R. 105 (Bankr. S.D. Fla. 2001) (court follows *Barbieri*); *In re* Rebeor, 89 B.R. 314 (Bankr. N.D.N.Y. 1988); *In re* Benedicktsson, 34 B.R. 349 (Bankr. W.D. Wash. 1983); 8 Collier on Bankruptcy ¶ 1307.03[1] (16th ed.). *See also In re* Cotton, 992 F.2d 311 (11th Cir. 1993) (bankruptcy court could not stay dismissal requested by chapter 12 debtor until after settlement with a major creditor had been confirmed); *In re* Beatty, 162 B.R. 853 (B.A.P. 9th Cir. 1994) (debtor had right to voluntarily dismiss chapter 13 case up until filing, signing, or entry of conversion order); *In re* Fernandes, 346 B.R. 521 (Bankr. D. Nev. 2006) (one of two joint chapter 13 debtors could dismiss his case even if other chose not to dismiss her case). *But see In re* Jacobsen, 609 F.3d 647 (5th Cir. 2010) (no absolute right to dismiss chapter 13 case); *In re* Rosson, 545 F.3d 764 (9th Cir. 2008) (no absolute right to dismiss chapter 13 case); *In re* Molitor, 76 F.3d 218 (8th Cir. 1996) (debtor who did not deny filing multiple bankruptcy cases in bad faith could not respond to conversion motion by dismissing chapter 13 case voluntarily).

[3] *In re* Sobczak, 369 B.R. 512 (B.A.P. 9th Cir. 2007).

[4] See 11 U.S.C. § 102 for the meaning of "after notice and a hearing."

[5] 11 U.S.C. § 707(a); *In re* Cohara, 324 B.R. 24 (B.A.P. 6th Cir. 2005) (even if debtor needed nonexempt annuity payments to pay medical expenses, that was not cause when creditors would be prejudiced by dismissal); *In re* Bartee, 317 B.R. 362 (B.A.P. 9th Cir. 2004) (debtors had not shown cause when they offered no assurance that they had binding agreement to sell business and provided no assurance that they would use proceeds to pay creditors).

[6] *In re* Hickman, 384 B.R. 832 (B.A.P. 9th Cir. 2008).

[7] *In re* Leach, 130 B.R. 855 (B.A.P. 9th Cir. 1991) (court has discretion to deny motion to dismiss chapter 7 case when debtor intended to re-file later when tax liabilities would be dischargeable); *In re* Underwood, 7 B.R. 936 (Bankr. S.D. W. Va. 1980), *aff'd*, 24 B.R. 570 (S.D. W. Va. 1982); *In re* Reynolds, 4 B.R. 703 (Bankr. D.

debtors who seek to dismiss in order to avoid liquidation of nonexempt property are often unsuccessful.[8] Some courts have required the consent of all creditors for a dismissal to be obtained,[9] although such a blanket rule seems too broad in light of section 707.[10]

Most courts are more liberal, allowing dismissal in any case in which no creditor objects after notice.[11] At least one court has held that cause need not be shown in such cases.[12] These courts have generally conditioned dismissal on payment to the trustee of any expenses incurred,[13] and at least a few have held that the trustee has no standing to object to dismissal if such expenses are paid,[14] though others have held otherwise.[15] As a practical matter there is rarely an objection in no-asset cases.

Yet another possibility for obtaining dismissal of a case was created by enactment of the automatic dismissal provisions of section 521(i).[16] However, courts have not always permitted debtors to use their own procedural defaults to obtain dismissal of their cases.[17]

Another issue that may arise is what happens in a chapter 13 case, which could have been dismissed as of right under section 1307(b), after it is converted to chapter 7. The right to dismiss the case is lost upon such a conversion.[18] Thus, before a conversion to chapter 7, it behooves a debtor to consider carefully whether a liquidation bankruptcy is clearly desired. If it is not, or if the debtor is uncertain, it is critical to dismiss the chapter 13 case before an involuntary conversion takes place, so that no dispute about the right to dismiss can arise.[19] The debtor in such a case will then retain the right to file a later chapter 7 case if that is desired, subject to the limitations of 11 U.S.C. § 109(g) if the dismissal follows a request for relief from the automatic stay,[20] and of 11 U.S.C. § 362(c) if the case is filed within one year after the dismissal.[21]

13.3 Typical Causes and Effects of Involuntary Dismissal or Conversion to Chapter 7

13.3.1 Reasons for Dismissal or Conversion

Involuntary dismissal or conversion, in either a chapter 7 or chapter 13 case, may occur for a number of reasons, some of which are listed in sections 707 and 1307(c).[22] Probably the most common causes are failure to pay the filing fees[23] or chapter 13 payments, failure to file appropriate papers, such as the bankruptcy schedules or chapter 13 plan, and failure to appear at a creditors meeting.[24] Often a prelude to such a

---

Me. 1980); *In re* Blackman, 3 B.R. 167 (Bankr. S.D. Ohio 1980). *But see In re* McDaniel, 363 B.R. 239 (M.D. Fla. 2007) (debtor permitted to dismiss case and re-file later, when tax debts became dischargeable, because attorney gave her incorrect advice).

8 *See In re* Maixner, 288 B.R. 815 (B.A.P. 8th Cir. 2003) (desire to save equity to detriment of creditors not cause for dismissal); *In re* Parker, 351 B.R. 790 (Bankr. N.D. Ga. 2006) (debtor could not argue for dismissal based upon fact that he had received credit counseling briefing from non-approved agency after he had averred compliance with counseling requirement). *But see In re* Hull, 339 B.R. 304 (Bankr. E.D.N.Y. 2006) (creditors not prejudiced when *pro se* debtor, upon learning she might lose personal injury claim, promptly sought dismissal to work out payments with creditors and move out of district for her personal safety; debtor had not abused system, and there would be delay in trustee liquidating claim, amount of which was unknown); *In re* Aupperle, 352 B.R. 43 (Bankr. D.N.J. 2005) (debtor who feared loss of home could dismiss when no creditor objected and no indication of bad faith).

9 *In re* Halverson, 6 Bankr. Ct. Dec. (LRP) 241, 1 Collier Bankr. Cas. 2d (MB) 906 (Bankr. W.D. Wis. 1980).

10 *See* Smith v. Geltzer, 507 F.3d 64 (2d Cir. 2007) (discussing factors relevant to voluntary dismissal of debtor who proposed to use nonexempt asset to pay creditors); *In re* Simmons, 200 F.3d 738 (11th Cir. 2000) (affirming denial of debtor's motion to dismiss in light of debtor's past abuse of bankruptcy system); *In re* Hickman, 384 B.R. 832 (B.A.P. 9th Cir. 2008) (fact that some creditors and trustee opposed dismissal as prejudicial to creditors supported finding that denial of dismissal not an abuse of discretion); *In re* Turpen, 244 B.R. 431 (B.A.P. 8th Cir. 2000) (debtor did not have right to dismiss case in which creditors would be fully paid when creditors objected that debtor might not pay if case dismissed); *In re* McDaniel, 363 B.R. 239 (Bankr. M.D. Fla. 2007) (debtor permitted to dismiss when prior counsel had miscalculated tax dischargeability time periods and Internal Revenue Service would have ample time to collect before debtor could re-file and discharge taxes).

11 *In re* Gallman, 6 B.R. 1 (Bankr. N.D. Ga. 1980); *In re* Richards, 4 B.R. 85 (Bankr. M.D. Fla. 1980).

12 *In re* Wirick, 3 B.R. 539 (Bankr. E.D. Va. 1980).

13 *In re* Waldman, 5 B.R. 401 (Bankr. S.D.N.Y. 1980).

14 *In re* Wolfe, 12 B.R. 686 (Bankr. S.D. Ohio 1981); *In re* Jackson, 7 B.R. 616 (Bankr. E.D. Tenn. 1980).

15 *See, e.g.*, Penick v. Tice, 732 F.2d 1211 (4th Cir. 1984) (trustee has standing to object on behalf of unsecured creditors).

16 *See* § 13.3.2, *infra*.

17 *In re* Warren, 568 F.3d 1113 (9th Cir. 2009); Segarra-Miranda v. Acosta-Rivera (*In re* Acosta-Rivera), 557 F.3d 8, 9 (1st Cir. 2009) (court has power to order that filing of documents was not required).

18 11 U.S.C. § 1307(b).

19 *See In re* Hearn, 18 B.R. 605 (Bankr. D. Neb. 1982) (debtor's motion to dismiss chapter 13 case prevailed over contemporaneously filed and well-founded motion to convert to chapter 7). *But see In re* Graven, 936 F.2d 378 (8th Cir. 1991) (chapter 12 case converted to chapter 7 based on fraudulent concealment of assets despite debtor's prior request to voluntarily dismiss).

20 *See* §§ 3.2.1, 9.7.3.2.1, *supra*.

21 *See* § 9.3.3, *supra*.

22 The list of reasons for dismissal is not exclusive. *In re* Gonic Realty Trust, 909 F.2d 624 (1st Cir. 1990) (bankruptcy court not limited to statutorily enumerated grounds for finding "cause" to dismiss or convert chapter 11 case).

23 This fact suggests one method of obtaining a dismissal in a chapter 7 case in which all of the filing fees have not yet been paid, though a dismissal is not always certain to occur in such cases. *But see In re* Howard, 333 B.R. 826 (Bankr. W.D. Va. 2005) (nonpayment of filing fees in earlier case was not cause for dismissal of later case).

24 The 1986 amendments to the Bankruptcy Code contemplate that the United States trustee will be responsible for prosecuting many motions under sections 707 and 1307(c) including all motions under sections 707(a)(3) and 1307(c)(9) and (10). *See In re* Aiello, 428 B.R. 296 (Bankr. E.D.N.Y. 2010) (only United States trustee may bring dismissal motion on these grounds).

dismissal is a court order setting a deadline for the debtor's performance.[25] However, when some reasonable excuse for delay or nonpayment is raised, a motion to dismiss on such grounds is normally denied.[26] When such motions are considered, the debtor's prepetition conduct is irrelevant.[27] Further, it is clear that such dismissals are discretionary rather than mandatory.[28] The rules require that a debtor be given notice and a hearing prior to a dismissal[29] so that the debtor may argue that there is no basis for dismissal or that the court should exercise its discretion to order some other remedy.[30] Except perhaps in egregious cases of repeated bankruptcies in which the debtor does not follow through, dismissals in such cases usually are without prejudice,[31] subject to the limitations of sections 109(g)[32] and 362(c)(3) or (4) of the Code.[33] But in a chapter 13 case there is always a possibility that the court might instead convert the case to chapter 7, under section 1307(c), rather than dismiss it.[34]

Additional grounds for dismissal or conversion added at the behest of taxing authorities in 2005 turn on whether the debtor has filed tax returns with the applicable taxing authorities. If a chapter 13 debtor fails to file tax returns as required by section 1308, section 1307(e) has been held to require dismissal or conversion of the case.[35] This requirement may include returns for the tax year preceding the year the bankruptcy case was filed, even if they are not yet due under the applicable tax laws, if the debtor does not obtain the extension of time permitted under section 1308.[36] And section 521(j)(1) permits a taxing authority to request dismissal if the debtor does not file postpetition returns on time. If the debtor fails, within ninety days after the request, to file the return or obtain an extension of time to file it, section 521(j)(2) provides for dismissal or conversion of the case. However these provisions, which primarily affect chapter 13 cases, do not require actual payment of the taxes in order to avoid dismissal or conversion.[37]

Dismissal or conversion may also occur if the debtor fails to obtain confirmation of a plan, usually when the court has found that the confirmation standards cannot be met.[38] The substan-

---

Although some courts have local rules or procedures providing for "automatic" dismissal if papers are not timely filed, such rules and procedures do not comply with Federal Rule of Bankruptcy Procedure 1017(d), which generally requires a contested matter for dismissal of a case. *See In re* Muessel, 292 B.R. 712 (B.A.P. 1st Cir. 2003) (*sua sponte* dismissal case on alternate grounds without notice or a meaningful opportunity for the debtor to be heard on those grounds violated the debtor's fundamental rights to procedural due process and the express requirements of the Bankruptcy Code); *In re* Davis, 275 B.R. 864 (B.A.P. 8th Cir. 2002) (bankruptcy court did not abuse its discretion in dismissing case of incarcerated debtor who made no attempt to make arrangements to conduct creditors meeting by means other than personal appearance); *In re* Dinova, 212 B.R. 437 (B.A.P. 2d Cir. 1997) (case could not be dismissed on *ex parte* order due to debtor's failure to appear at creditors' meeting even though notice of meeting warned that such dismissal would be sought, because notice and hearing not provided as required); *In re* Krueger, 88 B.R. 238 (B.A.P. 9th Cir. 1988) (dismissal of chapter 13 case without notice and hearing violates due process); *In re* Bucurescu, 282 B.R. 124 (S.D.N.Y. 2002) (reversing dismissal based upon the earlier order, without notice and a hearing regarding compliance with order); *In re* Gen. Order Governing Dismissal of Cases, 210 B.R. 941 (Bankr. M.D. Pa. 1997) (statute requires motion by United States trustee for dismissal based upon failure to file required papers). *But see In re* Tennant, 318 B.R. 860 (B.A.P. 9th Cir. 2004) (no violation of due process when debtor's case dismissed after failing to file missing statement of affairs within time set by court's warning notice). *Cf. In re* Lanehart, 2008 WL 4200776 (Bankr. W.D. Tex. Sept. 8, 2008) (failure to attend status conference with chapter 13 trustee that was scheduled without debtor's agreement was not cause for dismissal).

It remains to be seen how courts will handle "automatic dismissal" under section 521(i), enacted in 2005 and discussed below. *See* § 13.3.2, *infra*.

25 *See* Howard v. Lexington Investments, Inc., 284 F.3d 320 (1st Cir. 2002) (failure to file past due tax returns by deadline set by court). *Cf.* Dep't of Treasury v. Galarza Pagan, 279 B.R. 43 (D. P.R. 2002) (refusal to dismiss for failure to file tax returns after confirmation of chapter 13 plans not an abuse of discretion).

26 *See, e.g., In re* Henry, 368 B.R. 696 (N.D. Ill. 2007) (court not required to dismiss chapter 13 case simply because debtors payments would not be completed within sixty-month plan period); *In re* Duffus, 339 B.R. 746 (Bankr. D. Or. 2006) (trustee should have used "prosecutorial discretion" to decline bringing dismissal motion when tax returns provided three days late); *In re* Faaland, 37 B.R. 407 (Bankr. D.N.D. 1984). *See also In re* Malewicz, 457 B.R. 1 (Bankr. E.D.N.Y. 2010) (denying trustee's motion to dismiss because nondebtor husband did not turn over his share of tax refund as demanded by trustee). *But see In re* McDonald, 118 F.3d 568 (7th Cir. 1997) (dismissal of case for failure to make first plan payment on time was not abuse of discretion).

27 *In re* Lilley, 91 F.3d 491 (3d Cir. 1996).

28 *In re* Green, 64 B.R. 530 (B.A.P. 9th Cir. 1986); *In re* Smith, 85 B.R. 729 (E.D. Va. 1988).

29 Fed. R. Bankr. P. 1017.

30 *See In re* Wilson, 284 B.R. 109 (B.A.P. 8th Cir. 2002) (abuse of discretion to dismiss for improper venue without notice and opportunity for hearing); *In re* Rose, 422 B.R. 896 (Bankr. S.D. Ohio 2010) (declining to dismiss case when petition was filed with electronic signatures before paper copy was signed because debtors promptly rectified the problem).

31 11 U.S.C. § 349(a). *Cf. In re* Hall, Bayoutree Assocs. Ltd., 939 F.2d 802 (9th Cir. 1991) (dismissal for improper venue must be without prejudice).

Even a dismissal with prejudice does not preclude re-filing of a later case when there are changed circumstances. *In re* Smith, 133 B.R. 467 (Bankr. N.D. Ind. 1991). However, it may preclude the discharge of debts that existed at the time of the earlier case. Colonial Auto Ctr. v. Tomlin, 105 F.3d 933 (4th Cir. 1997); Ellsworth v. Lifescape Med. Assocs., P.C. (*In re* Ellsworth), 455 B.R. 904 (B.A.P. 9th Cir. 2011). *See* 3 Collier on Bankruptcy ¶ 349.02 (16th ed.).

32 *See* §§ 3.2.1, 9.7.3.2.1, *supra*.

33 The automatic stay in a new case could be limited by section 362(c)(3) or (4). *See* Ch. 9, *supra*.

34 *See, e.g., In re* Elkin, 5 B.R. 21 (Bankr. S.D. Cal. 1980).

35 *In re* Cushing, 401 B.R. 528 (B.A.P. 1st Cir. 2009).

36 *Id.*; *In re* Broussard, 2009 WL 1531817 (Bankr. W.D. La. May 29, 2009). *See* § 8.3.14, *supra*.

37 *See In re* Maxfield, 2009 WL 2105953 (Bankr. N.D. Ind. Feb. 19, 2009) (pre-2005 case holding that failure to pay taxes not per se cause for dismissal).

38 *See, e.g., In re* Madden, 1 Collier Bankr. Cas. 2d (MB) 1093 (Bankr. S.D. Ohio 1980); *In re* Fredrickson, 5 B.R. 199 (Bankr. M.D. Fla. 1980); *In re* Cadogan, 4 B.R. 598 (Bankr. W.D. La. 1980).

The fact that a debtor's payments are somewhat late and therefore extend beyond the five years prescribed by a plan, however, is not

tive questions arising in such cases are discussed elsewhere in this treatise.[39] Dismissal or conversion for this reason generally occurs only when the debtor does not request the opportunity to present an amended plan satisfactory to the court.[40] Absent an amended plan, the debtor is in the same position as if no plan had been filed, a position from which the case cannot proceed, at least under chapter 13.

Occasionally, a creditor in a consumer case will move for dismissal under sections 305(a), 707(a), or 1307(c). The most common ground for such a motion is bad faith, and some courts have ruled that a chapter 13 petition can be dismissed if it was filed in bad faith.[41] However, the 2005 amendments made filing a petition that was not filed in good faith a grounds for denial of confirmation, suggesting that is the proper remedy.[42] Some creditors seek to circumvent the limitations of section 707(b) prohibiting motions against debtors with below-median income or primarily nonconsumer debts, by moving to have chapter 7 cases dismissed under section 707(a) on the ground that they were filed in bad faith. However ability to pay debts, by itself, should not be sufficient for a finding of bad faith in light of the specific provisions addressing ability to pay in section 707(b).[43]

Such motions should be denied as contrary to the limitation on creditors' motions under section 707(b), which was intended to prevent improper use of claims of abuse by creditors.[44] In fact, as discussed below, the 2005 amendments specifically make the filing of a chapter 7 petition in bad faith grounds for dismissal under section 707(b), but dismissal can be sought by a creditor thereunder only if the debtor is not protected by the median income safe harbor of section 707(b)(6) and the motion is filed before the filing deadline set in Bankruptcy Rule 1017(e)(1).[45] Additionally, a motion to dismiss under either section 707(a) or 1307(c) must be denied for lack of standing if the moving creditor's claim has been or could be disallowed.[46]

Generally death of the debtor is not, in itself, grounds for dismissal. Bankruptcy Rule 1016 provides that the death of a chapter 7 debtor does not abate the case.[47] Thus the debtor's estate can receive the benefits of the bankruptcy. In chapter 13, the rule permits the case to be continued if further administration is possible and in the best interests of the parties. Often continuation is not possible because the chapter 13 case relies on the deceased debtor's income. However there are sometimes family members, or the administrator of the debtor's estate, that are in a position to carry the case to its conclusion.[48]

---

cause for dismissal. *In re* Black, 78 B.R. 840 (Bankr. S.D. Ohio 1987); § 12.6.5, *supra*.

39 See Chapter 12, *supra*, for a discussion of confirmation standards.

40 DeVito v. Pees (*In re* DeVito), 464 B.R. 61 (table), 2010 WL 4269384 (B.A.P. 6th Cir. Oct. 14, 2010) (unpublished) (although debtors had unreasonably delayed case, dismissal under § 1307(c)(1) also required showing of prejudice to creditors and no such showing was made); *In re* Nelson, 343 B.R. 671 (B.A.P. 9th Cir. 2006) (debtor should have been given opportunity to submit amended plan after confirmation was denied); *In re* Minkes, 237 B.R. 476 (B.A.P. 8th Cir. 1999) (case should not have been dismissed based on original plan not being confirmable without giving debtor opportunity to argue plan not deficient or to propose modified plan).

41 *In re* Alt, 305 F.3d 413 (6th Cir. 2002) (bad faith dismissal of chapter 13 case for knowingly omitting from schedules tax debts that rendered debtor ineligible for relief); *In re* Leavitt, 171 F.3d 1219 (9th Cir. 1999) (bad faith can be cause to dismiss chapter 13 case with prejudice); *In re* Lilley, 91 F.3d 491 (3d Cir. 1996) (lack of good faith can be cause for dismissal of chapter 13 case); *In re* Barrett, 964 F.2d 588 (6th Cir. 1992) (debtor's second chapter 13 filing, when he had insufficient income to support plan, was in bad faith but third chapter 13 case, filed after circumstances had changed, was not in bad faith); *In re* Love, 957 F.2d 1350 (7th Cir. 1992) (case dismissed when chapter 13 debtor, who had willfully refused to pay prepetition income taxes as tax protestor, failed to list all of his income and assets and filed case only when IRS began to garnish his wages). *See also In re* Pennino, 299 B.R. 536 (B.A.P. 8th Cir. 2003) (abstention from debtor's sixth bankruptcy case, filed to delay creditor while RICO claims litigated elsewhere, not abuse of discretion); *In re* Cabral, 285 B.R. 563 (B.A.P. 1st Cir. 2002) (bad faith was grounds for reconverting case back to chapter 7). *But see In re* Eastman, 188 B.R. 621 (B.A.P. 9th Cir. 1995) (dismissal under section 305(a) improper unless it benefited debtor as well as creditors).

42 11 U.S.C. § 1325(a)(7). *See* § 12.3.5, *supra*. *See also In re* Curtis, 2010 WL 1444851 (Bankr. S.D. Ill. Apr. 9, 2010) (confirmation of plan precluded argument that petition should be dismissed because not filed in good faith).

43 *In re* Perlin, 497 F.3d 364 (3d Cir. 2007).

44 *In re* Padilla, 222 F.3d 1184 (9th Cir. 2000) (bad faith not cause to dismiss chapter 7 case); *In re* Bridges, 135 B.R. 36 (Bankr. E.D. Ky. 1991) (denying creditor's motion to dismiss under section 707(a) for "cause" because ability to repay debts is not "cause" for dismissal under that section and creditor was attempting to circumvent prohibition of creditors filing motion to dismiss for substantial abuse). *See also In re* Huckfeldt, 39 F.3d 829 (8th Cir. 1994) (court's inquiry under section 707(a) is not into "bad faith" but rather whether cause exists for dismissal); McDow v. Smith, 295 B.R. 69 (E.D. Va. 2003) (ability to pay, by itself, not bad faith warranting dismissal); *In re* Etcheverry, 242 B.R. 503 (D. Colo. 1999) (bad faith not a grounds for dismissal under section 707(a)); *In re* Ryan, 267 B.R. 635 (Bankr. N.D. Iowa 2001) (denying motion to convert case to chapter 11 as attempt to circumvent prohibition of creditor substantial abuse motions); *In re* Khan, 172 B.R. 613 (Bankr. D. Minn. 1994) (question of whether debtor could pay debts was irrelevant to dismissal under section 707(a)). *But see In re* Tamecki, 229 F.3d 205 (3d Cir. 2000) (dismissing chapter 7 case for bad faith on motion of trustee); *In re* Zick, 931 F.2d 1124 (6th Cir. 1991) (creditor's motion to dismiss chapter 7 case for "bad faith" allowed). *See also* § 13.4, *infra*.

45 *In re* Adolph, 441 B.R. 909 (Bankr. N.D. Ill. 2011) (bad faith was not grounds for dismissal under § 707(a) and creditor failed to meet filing deadline).

46 *In re* Abijoe Realty Corp., 943 F.2d 121 (1st Cir. 1991). *But see In re* Torres Martinez, 397 B.R. 158 (B.A.P. 1st Cir. 2008) (creditor may move for dismissal even if claim was disallowed).

47 See § 3.2.1.1, *supra*.

48 *In re* Lewis, 2011 Bankr. LEXIS 1765 (Bankr. E.D.N.C. May 12, 2011) (debtor's family would provide funds by paying rent to executor); *In re* Rose, 422 B.R. 896 (Bankr. S.D. Ohio 2010) (deceased debtor's spouse, who was also personal administrator, could appear for debtor at creditors meeting); *In re* Perkins, 381 B.R. 530 (Bankr. S.D. Ill. 2007) (denying motion to dismiss deceased debtor's chapter 13 case).

13.3.2 "Automatic" Dismissal Under Section 521(i)

The 2005 amendments added a new provision concerning dismissal of a case. Failure to provide documents required by section 521(a)(1) of the Code, but not other documents, may lead to dismissal. Under section 521(i)(1), a case is to be "automatically dismissed" if the debtor does not file the information required by section 521(a)(1) within forty-five days after filing the petition. However, section 521(i)(2) provides that in such circumstances the case is to be dismissed on request of a party of interest within seven days of the request. This reference to court action on request of a party indicates that some court order is necessary for the dismissal to be effective.[49] It also permits the trustee to have discretion concerning whether to move for dismissal.[50] Any other rule would leave great uncertainty about whether a case is validly pending. Additionally, it is not always easy to determine whether the debtor has filed all of the necessary information.[51] The requirement of a court order is also supported by the legislative history, because an earlier version of the bill had provided for automatic dismissal "without need for any order of court."[52]

If the debtor, within the forty-five days after filing the petition, requests additional time, the court may allow up to forty-five additional days for the debtor to file the required documents.[53] The 2005 Act does not address the issue of how the court will deal with a request entered shortly before the forty-fifth day that has not been acted upon before "automatic dismissal" or a request for dismissal by a party. Hopefully the court will determine whether a request for extension has been filed and rule upon it before dismissing a case.

One important issue is whether the new section 521(i)(1) overrides the right of the United States trustee to move for dismissal at an earlier time. The provision states that it applies notwithstanding section 707(a) of the Code. It certainly should override local court practices that automatically dismiss a case at an earlier time for not filing required documents.

If the trustee requests, the court may decline to dismiss the case if the debtor attempted in good faith to file the payment advices required by section 521(a)(1)(B)(iv) and the best interests of creditors are served by administration of the estate.[54] Presumably, because almost all of the documents required by section 521(a)(1) must be provided only if the court does not order otherwise, the debtor could avoid dismissal if the court entered an order that the missing documents were not required.[55] And, even if a case is dismissed, the court may reopen the case and reinstate it upon application of the debtor.[56]

As a practical matter, most courts send the debtor a "deficiency notice" if they believe required papers have not been filed, and often schedule hearings for the debtor to show cause why the case should not be dismissed well before the forty-five day period has run. By doing so, they put the debtor on notice of a potential problem and give the debtor an opportunity to file the missing papers, show that they have already been filed, request an order that the debtor need not file the documents, or explain why they are not required. The failure to grant such an opportunity to contest dismissal would raise serious due process issues.[57]

Interestingly, section 521(i) has been used affirmatively by some debtors to try to obtain voluntary dismissal of their cases.

---

49 CFCU Cmty. Credit Union v. Swimelar, 2008 WL 189929 (N.D.N.Y. Jan. 18, 2008) (dismissal under section 521(i) requires a court order, either on motion of a party or, if *sua sponte*, subject to motion for reconsideration; otherwise due process rights would be violated); *In re* Luders, 356 B.R. 671 (Bankr. W.D. Va. 2006); *In re* Parker, 351 B.R. 790 (Bankr. N.D. Ga. 2006) (if case is already "automatically dismissed," then section 521(i)(2) would be surplusage); *In re* Jackson, 348 B.R. 487 (Bankr. S.D. Iowa 2006). *See also In re* Ober, 390 B.R. 60 (Bankr. W.D.N.Y. 2008) (chapter 13 plan confirmation precluded dismissal for failure to comply with section 521); *In re* Riddle, 344 B.R. 702 (Bankr. S.D. Fla. 2006) (debtors complied with information production requirements). *But see In re* Fawson, 338 B.R. 505 (Bankr. D. Utah 2006).

50 *In re* Gilbert, 403 B.R. 297 (Bankr. W.D.N.Y. 2009).

51 *See* Cmty. Bank v. Riffle, 617 F.3d 171 (2d Cir. 2010) (where debtor had provided most payment advices for 60 days before petition, along with year to date information as of petition date and report from employer showing gross earnings for each pay period, debtors had provided "other evidence" sufficient to replace missing payment advices, even though that evidence did not show all withholdings for each pay period); *In re* Miller, 383 B.R. 767 (B.A.P. 10th Cir. 2008) (filing of most payment advices and chart showing how information on missing advices could be extrapolated from those filed was sufficient to meet requirements of section 521(a)); *In re* Richardson, 406 B.R. 586 (Bankr. W.D.N.Y. 2009) (use of "information" rather than "documents" in section 521(i) means that case need not be dismissed if some required payment advices are not filed); *In re* Wojda, 371 B.R. 656 (Bankr. W.D.N.Y. 2007) (although debtor had not filed all payment advices received in sixty-day period, debtor's payment advices provided "other evidence of payment" and "information required"). *See also In re* Herrera, 398 B.R. 490 (Bankr. S.D. Fla. 2008) (section 521(i) not the proper vehicle for alleging debtor omitted information from papers that were filed).

52 H.R. 3150, 105th Congress § 407 (1998).

53 11 U.S.C. § 521(a)(i)(3).
   For a sample motion for additional time to comply with requirements under section 521(a)(1), see Form 11, Appx. G.3, *infra*.

54 11 U.S.C. § 521(i)(4).

55 *In re* Warren, 568 F.3d 1113 (9th Cir. 2009); Segarra-Miranda v. Acosta-Rivera (*In re* Acosta-Rivera), 557 F.3d 8, 9 (1st Cir. 2009) (court can order that documents not required after forty-five-day period has expired); *In re* Parker, 351 B.R. 790 (Bankr. N.D. Ga. 2006); *In re* Jackson, 348 B.R. 487 (Bankr. S.D. Iowa 2006) (court may "order otherwise" even after forty-five-day period has expired).

56 *In re* Ferro, 2009 WL 4602042 (Bankr. S.D. Tex. Dec. 3, 2009) (dismissal vacated because debtor had received no payment advice and therefore was not required to file any, even though debtor had failed to comply with earlier court order to provide explanation); *In re* Weinraub, 351 B.R. 779 (Bankr. S.D. Fla. 2006) (case reinstated under Fed. R. Bankr. P. 9024). *See In re* Satinoff, 2006 Bankr. LEXIS 745 (Bankr. S.D. Fla. May 3, 2006) (reinstating case dismissed under section 521(e)(2) for failure to timely provide tax return to trustee).

57 CFCU Cmty. Credit Union v. Swimelar, 2008 WL 189929 (N.D.N.Y. Jan. 18, 2008).
   See discussion of due process issues in § 13.3.1, *supra*.

If a debtor has clearly not filed the required information a court might feel constrained to dismiss the case—although it might, alternatively, find it has the power to order that the information is not required.[58]

13.4 Involuntary Dismissal for Abuse of the Provisions of Chapter 7

13.4.1 In General

Section 707(b) permits a bankruptcy court to dismiss a chapter 7 case, after notice and a hearing, if the court finds that granting relief under chapter 7 would be an abuse of its provisions. Because the section applies only to cases "filed" under chapter 7, it is arguably inapplicable to a case originally filed under chapter 13 and later converted to chapter 7.[59]

Section 707(b) applies only to debtors whose debts are primarily consumer debts. A means test, added by section 707(b)(2) of the Code, determines whether there is a presumption of abuse based on the debtor's ability to repay creditors. Importantly, this test does not apply to debtors whose income is below certain standards.

It is also important to note that section 707(b) does not require the court to dismiss a chapter 7 case if the presumption of abuse is not rebutted, or if abuse is otherwise found. The provision states that the court "may" dismiss the case. There may be reasons that dismissal is not appropriate, such as significant assets being available to creditors or the fact that the debtor would not be required to pay creditors in a chapter 13 case.[60]

13.4.2 Section 707(b) Applicable Only to Debtors with Primarily Consumer Debts

Section 707(b) applies only to debtors whose debts are primarily consumer debts.[61] The Bankruptcy Code defines "consumer debt" as "debt incurred by an individual primarily for a personal, family, or household purpose."[62] Thus, for debtors who have incurred most of their debts in business, through investment losses,[63] or through tort liability,[64] section 707(b) should not be a problem. Courts generally use a profit motive test when analyzing whether a debt is a consumer debt. If the debt was incurred with an eye toward profit, such as some student loans, especially for graduate schools, it should be classified as a business debt and not as a consumer debt.[65] This classification of debt based on a profit-making purpose should not change even if a portion of the debt is used for a consumer purpose.[66] Moreover, the profit motive test is not applied exclusively for determining consumer debt.[67] For example, a few courts have held that debts secured by real estate are not consumer debts[68] and, in this and other contexts, courts have

---

58 *See, e.g.,* Simon v. Amir (*In re* Amir), 436 B.R. 1 (B.A.P. 6th Cir. 2010) (bankruptcy courts have the authority to waive § 521(a)(1)'s filing requirements if enforcing those requirements would create an abuse of the bankruptcy process).

59 *See In re* Dudley, 405 B.R. 790 (Bankr. W.D. Va. 2009); *In re* Fox, 370 B.R. 639 (Bankr. D.N.J. 2007). *But see In re* Chapman, 447 B.R. 250 (B.A.P. 8th Cir. 2011); *In re* Kellett, 379 B.R. 332 (Bankr. D. Or. 2007) (section 707(b) applied to converted case but debtors not required to file a new means test form because same information was contained in Official Form 22C filed before conversion).

60 *In re* Jenkins, 2012 WL 2564901 (Bankr. W.D.N.C. July 2, 2012) (debtor no longer had income that caused means test failure); *In re* Siler, 426 B.R. 167 (Bankr. W.D.N.C. 2010) (although retirement plan contributions and loan repayment did not constitute special circumstances, they would be deductible in chapter 13, so creditors would receive nothing in chapter 13 and there was no reason to dismiss case even though presumption of abuse existed); *In re* Mravik, 399 B.R. 202 (Bankr. E.D. Wis. 2008) (debtor would not be required to pay creditors in chapter 13 because pension plan contributions would be permitted expenses and conversion would be meaningless); *In re* Skvorecz, 369 B.R. 638 (Bankr. D. Colo. 2007) (debtor would not be required to pay unsecured creditors in chapter 13 case, so dismissal would lead to absurd result).

61 *See In re* Bannish, 311 B.R. 547 (C.D. Cal. 2004) (different treatment of consumer debtors did not violate equal protection rights).

62 *See* 11 U.S.C. § 101(8).

63 *In re* Stewart, 175 F.3d 796 (10th Cir. 1999) (alimony debts, loan from father-in-law and some student loans used for living expenses were consumer debts); *In re* Burns, 894 F.2d 361, 363 (10th Cir. 1990) (loans used to obtain money to invest in stock market did not constitute consumer debt); *In re* Evans, 334 B.R. 148 (Bankr. D. Md. 2004) (debt owed on loans for printing business are not consumer debts); *In re* Marshalek, 158 B.R. 704 (Bankr. N.D. Ohio 1993) (debt arising from motor vehicle accident was not consumer debt); *In re* Goulding, 79 B.R. 874 (Bankr. W.D. Mo. 1987) (startup business expenses debts were not consumer debts); *In re* Campbell, 63 B.R. 702 (Bankr. W.D. Mo. 1986) (principal liability of debtor was business debt); *In re* Almendinger, 56 B.R. 97 (Bankr. N.D. Ohio 1985). *But see In re* Berndt, 127 B.R. 222 (Bankr. D.N.D. 1991) (unsecured credit card debt used to invest in stock market is a consumer debt).

64 *In re* Marshalek, 158 B.R. 704 (Bankr N.D. Ohio 1993); *In re* White, 49 B.R. 869 (Bankr. W.D.N.C. 1985). *See also In re* Thongta, 401 B.R. 363 (Bankr. E.D. Wis. 2009) (debt arising out of auto accident was not "consumer debt" for purposes of codebtor stay); *In re* Melcher, 322 B.R. 1 (Bankr. D.D.C. 2005) (determination of consumer debt status under § 523(d)).

65 *See In re* Booth, 858 F.2d 1051 (5th Cir. 1988) (test for whether a debt is a business obligation is whether debt was incurred with an eye toward profit); *In re* Rucker, 454 B.R. 554 (Bankr. M.D. Ga. 2011) (whether student loan is consumer debt must be examined on case by case basis).

66 *See In re* Strausbaugh, 376 B.R. 631 (Bankr. S.D. Ohio 2007) (fact that portion of debt was related to home improvements and payment of certain personal expenses did not render the debt a consumer debt).

67 *See also In re* Westberry, 215 F.3d 589, 593 (6th Cir. 2000) (profit motive analysis does not prohibit other debts from being considered outside of consumer debt category; federal income tax debt not considered "consumer debt" for purposes of codebtor stay).

68 *See, e.g., In re* Restea, 76 B.R. 728 (Bankr. D.S.D. 1987). *But see In re* Price, 353 F.3d 1135, 1139 (9th Cir. 2004); *In re* Kelly, 841 F.2d 908 (9th Cir. 1988); *In re* Lapke, 428 B.R. 839 (B.A.P. 8th Cir.

held that tax debts are not consumer debts.[69]

The Code does not define the term "primarily" as used in section 707(b)(1). Most courts have found that "primarily" means more than half of the total amount of debt owed.[70] Yet some courts consider both the percentage of consumer debt as well as the number of consumer debts in deciding whether the debts are primarily consumer debts.[71]

Debtors whose debts are not primarily consumer debts need only check the appropriate box in Part I on Official Form 22A and sign the verification; they do not need to complete the remainder of the form.[72]

13.4.3 Limits on Section 707(b) Motions for Debtors with Incomes Below State's Median Income

13.4.3.1 Overview

Means testing to determine if a presumption of abuse exists under section 707(b) applies only to those debtors whose current monthly income is above the state median income. Section 707(b)(7) provides that a motion seeking to apply the means test under section 707(b)(2) may not be brought if the debtor's current monthly income multiplied by twelve is equal to or less than the highest median income figure for the debtor's state as reported by the Census Bureau.[73] As stated in the 2005 Act's legislative history: "The Act's second safe harbor only pertains to a motion under section 707(b)(2), that is, a motion to dismiss based on a debtor's ability to repay. It does not allow a judge, United States trustee, bankruptcy administrator or party in interest to file such motion if the income of the debtor (including a veteran, as that term is defined in 38 U.S.C. § 101) and the debtor's spouse is less than certain monetary thresholds."[74]

This safe harbor should mean that an abuse motion based solely on *ability to repay* cannot be brought against a debtor whose income is below the threshold, either under the means test in section 707(b)(2) or the general abuse provision found in section 707(b)(1) and (b)(3). Otherwise, an entity pursuing such a motion under section 707(b)(1) would essentially be advancing a means test different than the bright line test set out by Congress precisely because it did not want vague and undefined determinations of ability to repay. Consequently, the bright line test set forth by Congress will protect some debtors who might have been subject to section 707(b) motions under prior law.

In addition, no section 707(b) abuse motion may be brought against a debtor on other grounds, other than by a judge, United States trustee, or bankruptcy administrator, if the current monthly income of the debtor, or in a joint case of the debtor and the debtor's spouse, is below the state median income.[75] This provision is consistent with prior law, which explicitly stated that section 707(b) motions could be granted on the court's own motion or on the motion of the United States trustee. For debtors with current monthly incomes above the state median income, section 707(b) now permits creditors and other parties in interest, including panel trustees, to file dismissal motions under the general abuse provisions of section 707(b)(1) and under the means test of section 707(b)(2).[76]

2010) (mortgage was consumer debt, even if debtor did not sign note or deed of trust, because it was a claim against debtor's property and funds obtained were used for personal, family, or household purposes); *In re* Cox, 315 B.R. 850 (B.A.P. 8th Cir. 2004); *In re* Davis, 378 B.R. 539 (Bankr. N.D. Ohio 2007) (debtor's mortgage debt does not qualify as business debt because debtor was not regularly employed in fixing up homes and selling them for a profit); *In re* Johnson, 318 B.R. 907, 914 (Bankr. N.D. Ga. 2005); *In re* Dickerson, 193 B.R. 67, 70 (Bankr. M.D. Fla. 1996).

69 *See, e.g., In re* Westberry, 215 F.3d 589 (6th Cir. 2000) (federal income tax debt not considered "consumer debt" for purposes of codebtor stay); *In re* Brashers, 216 B.R. 59 (Bankr. N.D. Okla. 1998); *In re* Conover, 1998 WL 34066145 (Bankr. S.D. Ga. Jan. 20, 1998); *In re* Stovall, 209 B.R. 849 (Bankr. D. Va. 1997) (personal property taxes are not consumer debts); *In re* Dye, 190 B.R. 566 (Bankr. N.D. Ill. 1995); *In re* Greene, 157 B.R. 496 (Bankr. D. Ga. 1993).

See § 9.4.5, *supra* (discussing codebtor stay applicability to consumer debts).

70 *See, e.g., In re* Stewart, 175 F.3d 796 (10th Cir. 1999); *In re* Kelly, 841 F.2d 908 (9th Cir. 1988); *In re* Booth, 858 F.2d 1051 (5th Cir. 1988) (court looked to dollar amounts of debts rather than number of creditors to decide if debts primarily consumer debts); *In re* Baird, 456 B.R. 112 (Bankr. M.D. Fla. 2010); *In re* Victoria, 389 B.R. 250 (Bankr. M.D. Ala. 2008); *In re* Lapke, 2008 WL 355575 (Bankr. D. Neb. Jan. 23, 2008) (debtor's debts are primarily consumer debts if more than half of dollar amount owed is on consumer debts); *In re* Beacher, 358 B.R. 917 (Bankr. S.D. Tex. 2007) (determination based on amount of debts, not number of debts); *In re* Hoffner, 2007 WL 4868310 (Bankr. D.N.D. Nov. 21, 2007); *In re* Restea, 76 B.R. 728 (Bankr. D.S.D. 1987) (debts not primarily consumer debts when fifty-three percent of debts were consumer debts); *In re* Bell, 65 B.R. 575 (Bankr. E.D. Mich. 1986) (applying numerical test in comparing amount of consumer debts (thirty-one percent) to amount of business debts). *See also In re* Mohr, 436 B.R. 504 (S.D. Ohio 2010) (for purposes of calculating amount of nonconsumer debt, long-term lease obligations are not reduced to amount allowable under section 502(b)(6)), *aff'd* U.S. Trustee v. Mohr, 436 B.R. 504 (S.D. Ohio 2010); Watson v. Stonewall Jackson Mem'l Hosp. Co. (*In re* Watson), 2010 WL 4496837 (Bankr. N.D. W. Va. Nov. 1, 2010) (creditor sanctioned for filing nonconsumer claim in amount less than it was owed so that debtor would have primarily consumer debts).

71 *See, e.g., In re* Sudderth, 2007 WL 119141 (Bankr. M.D.N.C. Jan. 9, 2007) (reviewing the ratio of the dollar amount of consumer debt to non-consumer debt and finding it to be controlling, but also considering the number of business and non-business debts).

72 *See* Official Form 22A (reprinted in Appx. D, *infra*).

73 The use of different states' median incomes has been found not to violate the Constitution's Bankruptcy Clause, which empowers Congress to enact uniform bankruptcy laws. Schultz v. United States, 529 F.3d 343 (6th Cir. 2008).

74 H.R. Rep. No. 109-31, at 51 (2005) (available on this treatise's companion website). *See also* § 13.4.7.1, *infra*.

75 11 U.S.C. § 707(b)(6).

76 11 U.S.C. § 707(b)(1), (6), (7).

13.4.3.2 Determining the Debtor's Current Monthly Income

13.4.3.2.1 A six-month average normally used

"Current monthly income" is defined in section 101 of the Bankruptcy Code as the average of the last six months' income received from all sources by the debtor (or, in a joint case, by the debtor and the debtor's spouse), derived during the six-month period,[77] with certain adjustments.[78] As a result, the debtor's actual income at the time the petition is filed may be significantly below or above current monthly income, which is a six-month average.

The six-month period is defined as the six months ending on the last day of the month before the petition is filed or, if the debtor does not file Schedule I, the date the court determines current income. Thus the timing of filing the petition may determine whether a particular month puts the debtor over or under the median income safe harbor, or the amount that would create a presumption of abuse under the means test, or some other consequence. If a debtor's income has recently increased, the debtor may want to file quickly. If a debtor's income has decreased, waiting a few months may be preferable if no emergency requires an immediate filing.

Alternatively, the debtor may be able to defer the filing of Schedule I, which would result in a later six-month period being used.[79] Some courts have allowed debtors to defer the filing of this schedule so that current monthly income will more accurately reflect the debtor's actual income.[80] Because the debtor controls whether Schedule I is filed, the trustee or creditors will generally be unable to request the use of an alternative measuring period.[81] Debtors seeking to use an alternative time period for calculating current monthly income should file a motion to that effect along with a motion to excuse the filing of Schedule I within the time required by section 521(a)(1) and Bankruptcy Rule 1007(c).

All individual debtors in chapter 7, all individual debtors in chapter 11, and all chapter 13 debtors are required to prepare and file a Statement of Current Monthly Income, which is included in the rules and forms adopted in order to implement the 2005 amendments.[82] In Part II of the Statement, the debtor lists the income information used in calculating current monthly income for the section 707(b)(7) safe harbor. If this current monthly income amount is below the applicable state median income, as reflected in Part III of the Statement, the debtor checks the box on the top of the form stating that "the presumption does not arise" and is not required to fill out the remaining means test calculations in Parts IV through VI of the form.

13.4.3.2.2 Payments toward household expenses of debtor or dependents on a regular basis

Included in current monthly income is any amount *paid* by any entity *toward the household expenses* of the debtor or the debtor's dependents *on a regular basis*.[83] Amounts not used for such a purpose or not received on a regular basis are not included. For example, the definition would exclude child support received on a sporadic basis.[84] Similarly, expenses paid for a dependent not in the household should not be considered a payment toward household expenses.

13.4.3.2.3 Treatment of spouse's income

If a joint case is filed, current monthly income includes all income received by the debtor and the debtor's spouse. If a married debtor files alone and the debtor's non-debtor spouse is not a dependent, income received by the non-debtor spouse (or from some other entity) that is not used for the household expenses of the debtor and the debtor's dependents is not included in current monthly income for purposes of the means test under section 707(b)(2).[85] Certainly, those portions of the non-debtor spouse's income devoted to payment of the spouse's debts, insurance, transportation expenses, personal items, cloth-

---

77 The language requiring that the income be derived during the six-month period should prevent the inclusion of income earned earlier, such as commissions and, to the extent not already counted as part of the debtor's gross income, tax refunds. See In re Meade, 420 B.R. 291 (Bankr. W.D. Va. 2009) (counting only half of debtor's annual bonus because the remainder was not derived in six months prior to petition). See also In re Arnoux, 442 B.R. 769 (Bankr. E.D. Wash. 2010) (income "derived" from debtor's work during the six months before filing but not received during that period is not "current monthly income"); In re Beasley, 342 B.R. 280 (Bankr. C.D. Ill. 2006) (in determining current monthly income in a chapter 13 case court rejected trustee's argument that non-debtor spouse's income as school teacher should be annualized when she received less or no income in several summer months during the prepetition six-month period, as court required to strictly apply definition).

78 11 U.S.C. § 101(10A).
   Under this definition, income must be both "received" and "derived" during the six-month period. In re Arnoux, 442 B.R. 769 (Bankr. E.D. Wash. 2010) (income must be both derived and received during 6-month period, so pay received after petition for work done before petition is not counted). See § 13.4.3.2.7, infra (discussing excluded income).

79 11 U.S.C. § 101(10A)(ii).

80 In re Dunford, 408 B.R. 489 (Bankr. N.D. Ill. 2009); In re Hoff, 402 B.R. 683 (Bankr. E.D.N.C. 2009); In re Montgomery, 2008 WL 597180, at *2 (Bankr. M.D.N.C. Mar. 4, 2008).

81 See In re Crink, 2008 WL 2944652 (Bankr. M.D.N.C. July 31,

2008). However, in chapter 13 cases, the court may take into account known or virtually certain changes in the debtor's income. See § 12.3.4.4.1, supra.

82 See Official Forms 22A–22C (reprinted in Appx. D, infra). If a chapter 7 debtor is exempted from the means test because the debtor's debts are not primarily consumer debts, or under the exemption for recent members of the military, the debtor need only check the applicable box on this form and need not complete the remainder of the form.

83 11 U.S.C. § 101(10A), (B).

84 Although current monthly income is used to determine disposable income in chapter 13 cases based on the amendments made to section 1325, child support payments are excluded from disposable income. See Ch. 12, supra.

85 11 U.S.C. § 101(10A), (B).

ing, and recreation should not be included.[86] In addition, to the extent the non-debtor spouse pays her own portion of housing, food and other expenses, such amounts should not be included if that spouse is not a dependent of the debtor. To include more of a non-debtor spouse's income as available to the debtor's creditors would be the equivalent of imposing an involuntary bankruptcy on the spouse, to the detriment not only of the non-debtor spouse, but also the creditors of that spouse, who might not be paid due to diversion of the income to the debtor's creditors.[87] This exclusion may dictate consideration of whether or not to file a joint case, or perhaps two separate cases. The burden is on the party moving for dismissal to prove that the debtor has not included amounts paid by others for household expenses of the debtor or the debtor's dependents; it will not be presumed that people living together pool their incomes to pay household expenses.[88]

For purposes of the safe harbor from the means test the Advisory Committee on Bankruptcy Rules adopted a different position in regard to a non-debtor spouse's income, apparently based on the language in section 707(b)(7)(B). If a married debtor files separately the new form Statement of Current Monthly Income and Means Test Calculation provides that the non-debtor spouse's income is considered for purposes of the safe harbor test under section 707(b)(7).[89] This provision ignores the fact that the definition of current monthly income clearly provides that one must be a bankruptcy debtor to have current monthly income.[90] In any case, there is no dispute that the income of a separated spouse is not counted in a case filed by only one spouse if the spouses are not living separately to evade the means test and the debtor files a sworn statement to that effect, and the debtor discloses payments from the non-debtor spouse that are included in current monthly income.[91]

13.4.3.2.4 Treatment of business income

The definition of current monthly income appears to include the debtor's gross business income, rather than net income, especially because, in chapter 13, section 1325(b) explicitly provides for business expenses to be deducted from the debtor's current monthly income.[92] However, the forms adopted by the Judicial Conference count only net business income and net rental income toward current monthly income.[93] The primary difference between the two methods in chapter 7 cases is that the deduction of business expenses in calculating current monthly income, instead of as a deduction later in the means test,[94] will bring the current monthly income of some debtors below the safe harbor amounts and relieve them from being subject to the means test.

13.4.3.2.5 Treatment of capital gains and losses

It is unclear whether income from capital gains is included in current monthly income and whether capital losses may be deducted from that income. The issue may turn on whether the income is received on a regular basis. If capital gains income is considered, the debtor may want to plan for sales of assets accordingly. In any event, it would seem that only increases in value that occurred during the six-month period could be included. Capital gains are not included as income under the definitions used in computing the Census Bureau's median income figures, to which the debtor's income is compared, strongly suggesting that they should not be considered income for the means test.[95]

13.4.3.2.6 Withdrawals from an IRA or pension plan

There may also be questions about how to treat one-time withdrawals from an individual retirement account (IRA) or

---

86 See In re Gregory, 2011 WL 5902884 (Bankr. E.D.N.C. Aug. 17, 2011) (payments made by nonfiling spouse to maintain and improve former residence were not for household expenses of debtor or dependents, even if they might benefit debtor if former residence was later sold); Sturm v. United States Tr., 455 B.R. 130 (N.D. Ohio 2011) (payments made by nondebtor spouse on mortgage for house in which he and debtor resided were not part of debtor's current monthly income, but because debtor had no housing expense, she could not deduct IRS housing ownership allowance); In re Clemons, 2009 WL 1733867 (Bankr. C.D. Ill. June 16, 2009) (payments made by nondebtor spouse for mortgage on house titled in his name were not paid for household expenses of debtor because they were not expenses actually incurred by debtor); In re Shahan, 367 B.R. 732 (Bankr. D. Kan. 2007) (non-debtor spouse's car and house payments, on property that was not property of estate, were not included in current monthly income, nor were her recreation and miscellaneous personal payments); In re Travis, 353 B.R. 520 (Bankr. E.D. Mich. 2006) (clothing and personal items could be included in "marital adjustment" but food and utilities could not).
87 See In re Welch, 347 B.R. 247 (Bankr. W.D. Mich. 2006) (decided under former section 707(b)).
88 In re Roll, 400 B.R. 674, 677 (Bankr. W.D. Wis. 2008).
89 See Official Form 22A (reprinted in Appx. D, infra).
90 See In re Stansell, 395 B.R. 457 (Bankr. D. Idaho 2008) (interpreting similar language in section 1325(b)(4)); In re Grubbs, 2007 WL 4418146 (Bankr. E.D. Va. Dec. 14, 2007) (interpreting similar language in section 1325(b)(4)). The proponents of the form argue that it is justified by the language "current monthly income of the debtor . . . and the debtor's spouse combined" in section 707(b)(7). However, this language does not alter the definition of current monthly income, which only a debtor can have. Most likely this language was included to prevent evasion of the means test by two spouses filing separate petitions, in which case, both spouses are debtors with current monthly income that can be counted. In any event, the only consequence of it being included for purposes of section 707(b)(7) is that the debtor may be required to complete the entire means test form. In doing so, the debtor deducts a spouse's income to the extent it is not regularly paid toward household expenses.
91 11 U.S.C. § 707(b)(7)(B). See Line 2b, Official Form 22A (reprinted in Appx. D, infra).
92 See In re Wiegand, 386 B.R. 238 (B.A.P. 9th Cir. 2008); In re Sharp, 394 B.R. 207 (Bankr. C.D. Ill. 2008).
93 See Official Form 22A (reprinted in Appx. D, infra). See also In re Roman, 2011 WL 5593143 (Bankr. D. P.R. Nov. 16, 2011) (looking at gross rather than net income would present a distorted picture).
94 Expenses necessary to produce income should be deductible as "other necessary expenses" under the Internal Revenue Service expense standards.
95 See definitions at www.census.gov/acs/www/Downloads/2004/usedata/Subject_Definitions.pdf.

pension plan. Although these withdrawals may well be taxable income, the definition of current monthly income specifically provides that tax treatment is not determinative.[96] Such withdrawals, for purposes of determining a debtor's ability to pay, are much more akin to withdrawals from a bank account, and the IRA or pension should be considered as an asset rather than a source of income.[97] This conclusion is bolstered by the great lengths to which Congress went in the 2005 Act to protect retirement savings.[98] Obviously, to the extent such withdrawals could not continue because an account was depleted or needed for retirement, a debtor could also argue that even if they were counted as income, special circumstances should rebut the presumption that such income would be available to fund a chapter 13 plan.

13.4.3.2.7 *Explicit statutory exemptions from current monthly income*

Excluded from current monthly income are benefits received under the Social Security Act, and payments made to victims of war crimes, crimes against humanity, and international terrorism on account of such status.[99] This provision will bring many elderly and disabled debtors below the median income thresholds. It would exclude from a debtor's current monthly income benefits paid to a child. On the other hand, private disability benefits and Veterans' Administration (VA) disability benefits are not excluded by this provision.[100] However, at least one court has held that language in the federal statute creating railroad retirement benefits, similar to the protection of Social Security benefits in the Social Security Act, can also be a basis for excluding those benefits from the calculation of current monthly income.[101]

The 2005 Act does not just exclude Social Security payments, but any benefits paid under the Social Security Act. Such benefits include Supplemental Security Income (SSI) for the elderly and disabled,[102] unemployment compensation,[103] public assistance under the Temporary Assistance for Needy Families (TANF) program,[104] and funds received through programs administered under block grants made to the states to provide social services.[105] However, the Advisory Committee on Bankruptcy Rules could not agree whether unemployment compensation is a "benefit received under the Social Security Act," and consequently the new form Statement of Current Monthly Income and Means Test Calculation (Official Form 22A) takes no position on whether it should be excluded from current monthly income.[106] Instead, the form provides an alternative in which the debtor can list unemployment compensation as countable income or list it separately and not countable if the debtor "contends" it is a benefit under the Social Security Act.[107]

13.4.3.2.8 *Other possible types of income*

Issues can also arise regarding other possible types of income. In general it makes sense to look to the Census Bureau's definition of income in considering these questions, because the median income figures used in the means test are based on those definitions. The Census Bureau excludes from income (in

---

96 11 U.S.C. § 101(10A)(A); *In re* Wayman, 351 B.R. 808 (Bankr. E.D. Tex. 2006).

See also the Census Bureau's definition of income, which does not include non-regular IRA withdrawals as income.

97 Zahn v. Fink (*In re* Zahn), 391 B.R. 840 (B.A.P. 8th Cir. 2008); *In re* Cram, 414 B.R. 674 (Bankr. D. Idaho 2009); *In re* Mendelson, 412 B.R. 75 (Bankr. E.D.N.Y. 2009); Simon v. Zittel, 2008 WL 750346 (Bankr. S.D. Ill. Mar. 19, 2008); *In re* Wayman, 351 B.R. 808 (Bankr. E.D. Tex. 2006).

98 See 11 U.S.C. § 522(c)(3), (d)(12), discussed in Chapter 10, *supra*; 11 U.S.C. § 362(b)(19), discussed in Chapter 9, *supra*; and 11 U.S.C. §§ 541(b)(7) and 1322(f), discussed in Chapter 12, *supra*.

99 11 U.S.C. § 101(10A)(B). *See In re* Ragos, 2012 WL 5292949 (5th Cir. Oct 29, 2012) (also holding that excluding such income was not bad faith); *In re* Cranmer, 2012 WL 5235365 (10th Cir. Oct 24, 2012) (also holding that excluding such income was not bad faith); *In re* Welsh, 465 B.R. 843 (9th Cir. B.A.P. 2012) (also holding that excluding such income was not bad faith); Vandenbosch v. Waage (*In re* Vandenbosch), 459 B.R. 140 (M.D. Fla. 2011) (same); Fink v. Thompson (*In re* Thompson), 439 B.R. 140 (B.A.P. 8th Cir. 2010); *In re* Kibbe, 361 B.R. 302, 314 (B.A.P. 1st Cir. 2007) (benefits under Social Security Act must be excluded even if court makes other adjustments to determine chapter 13 projected disposable income).

It is less clear whether amounts paid by others for the debtor's household expenses are excluded if those amounts are derived from Social Security benefits. *See In re* Olguin, 429 B.R. 346 (Bankr. D. Colo. 2010) (funds lost character of Social Security benefits when they were transferred to debtors by original recipients).

100 Blausey v. United States Tr., 552 F.3d 1124 (9th Cir. 2009) (private disability benefits); *In re* Hedge, 394 B.R. 463 (Bankr. S.D. Ind. 2008) (VA benefits); *In re* Waters, 384 B.R. 432 (Bankr. N.D. W. Va. 2008) (VA benefits).

101 *In re* Scholz, 427 B.R. 864 (Bankr. E.D. Cal. 2010), *vacated and remanded by* Meyer v. Scholz (*In re* Scholz), 447 B.R. 887, 895 (B.A.P. 9th Cir. 2011) (benefits were excluded for a different reason—the anti-anticipation clause of 45 U.S.C. § 231m(a)).

102 Subchapter XVI of the Social Security Act, 42 U.S.C. §§ 1381–1383f.

103 Subchapters III, XII, XIII, and XV of the Social Security Act, 42 U.S.C. §§ 501–504, 1321–1324; *In re* Munger, 370 B.R. 21 (Bankr. D. Mass. 2007); *In re* Sorrell, 359 B.R. 167 (Bankr. S.D. Ohio 2007). *But see In re* Washington, 438 B.R. 348 (M.D. Ala. 2010).

Significantly, unemployment compensation was specifically mentioned when the amendment excluding benefits under the Social Security Act was added to the legislation. *See* 145 Cong Rec. H2770 (daily ed. May 5, 1999) (statement of Rep. Conyers).

104 Subchapter IV of the Social Security Act, 42 U.S.C. §§ 601–687.

105 Subchapter XX of the Social Security Act, 42 U.S.C. §§ 1397–1397f.

106 The inability of the Advisory Committee to reach agreement that unemployment compensation should be excluded is surprising given the 2005 Act's legislative history. The amendment which removed Social Security Act benefits from current monthly income was introduced by Rep. John Conyers to an earlier version of the bankruptcy legislation, H.R. 833, on May 5, 2005, the same day the House approved H.R. 833. *See* 145 Cong. Rec. H2702 (daily ed. May 5, 2005). Unemployment compensation was specifically referred to in Rep. Conyers' remarks as the kind of income the amendment would remove from current monthly income.

107 *See* Official Form 22A advisory committee's note (reprinted in Appx. D, *infra*); Official Form 22A (reprinted in Appx. D, *infra*).

addition to capital gains and retirement account withdrawals): money received from the sale of an asset (unless the debtor is in the business of selling such assets); food stamps; public housing subsidies; medical care; employer contributions to benefits; money borrowed; exchange of money between relatives in a household; gifts and lump-sum inheritances; and insurance payments and other lump sum receipts.[108]

13.4.3.3 Determining Whether Current Monthly Income Is Above State's Median Family Income

In order to determine whether the debtor's current monthly income is above the state's median family income the debtor's current monthly income (multiplied by twelve) is compared with the applicable state's median family income. "Median family income" is defined in section 101 of the Bankruptcy Code as the median family income calculated and reported by the Bureau of the Census in the then most recent year.[109] If no Census Bureau figure exists for a particular family size for the current year, then the most recent census figure is to be adjusted to reflect the change in the Consumer Price Index during the most recent year. Each August the Census Bureau publishes figures for families of two, three and four, as well as for one earner families, for the preceding year. The applicable state median income figures are available on the website of the Executive Office of the United States Trustee.[110]

The median income test looks at the median income for the "applicable" state. It is not clear whether the applicable state is the debtor's state of residence or the debtor's state of domicile, if the two are different.[111] Military (or other) debtors temporarily stationed in a low median income state could be disadvantaged if the state of residence is used. Most likely the tendency of those administering the means test will be to look first to the median income of the state in which the case is filed, but there may be strong arguments in particular cases for using the median income for a different state.

To determine the appropriate median family income for the safe harbor provisions found in section 707(b)(6) and (b)(7), these subsections specify that the *household* size of the debtor is to be used, which may include non-related individuals living in the household. The debtor's household size and figures are then compared to the Census figures for a *family* size of the same number, with certain exceptions. Household size appears to be determined as of the date of the filing of the petition.[112]

For debtors in a one-person household, the Census figures for a "1 earner" family are to be used.[113] If the Census figures for state median income for two, three, or four person families are lower than the Census figures for the median income for a smaller family, the figure for the smaller household is to be used. (In some states the median income for a family of three is higher than that for a family of four.)

In households larger than four members, $625 per month is added to the median income figure for a family of four for each additional family member.[114] This procedure permits a higher income to be utilized, even though in many states larger families have lower median incomes. This $625 per month figure will be periodically adjusted for inflation under section 104 of the Code.

There can sometimes be disputes about who should be counted as a member of the debtor's household for this purpose. For example, a debtor may support a child who is a college student away at school for a good part of the year. Or the debtor may have joint custody of a child who lives part of the time with the other parent. If the debtor pays substantial expenses for a child in such situations, such a child should be counted as a household member to carry out the purpose of using an appropriate median income amount.

Unrelated household members present different problems. The Census Bureau defines "household" as including "all the people who occupy a housing unit as their usual place of residence."[115] Although there is also a definition of "family household" that is limited to individuals related by birth, marriage, or adoption, the Code does not use the term "family household" or "family" in determining which median family income to use. It uses the term "household" and it makes sense to use the census definition of the term "household" when determining which census figures to use.

The United States Trustee Program has at times taken the position that an individual cannot be counted as a household member unless the individual was a dependent of the debtor for tax purposes. Not only does this argument ignore the census (and common sense) definition of household, but it also is

---

108 See definitions at www.census.gov/acs/www/Downloads/2007/usedata/Subject_Definitions.pdf. *See also In re* Breeding, 366 B.R. 21 (Bankr. E.D. Ark. 2007) (redemption of certificates of deposit did not produce income).
109 11 U.S.C. § 101(39A).
110 The median income figures are available at www.usdoj.gov/ust/bapcpa/meanstesting.htm. The median income figures are also reprinted in Appx. I.1, *infra*.
111 *Compare In re* McUne, 358 B.R. 397, 399 (Bankr. D. Or. 2006) (referring to "household size in his domiciliary state") *with In re* Naslund, 359 B.R. 781, 785 (Bankr. D. Mont. 2006) (referring to "applicable median family income as determined by the debtor's place of residence and household size").

112 *See In re* Hernandez, 2012 WL 1067692 (Bankr. D. Wyo. Mar. 23, 2012) (for purpose of determining chapter 13 applicable commitment period, debtor could count as household members new wife and dependent children resulting from marriage after petition and before confirmation date).
113 11 U.S.C. § 707(b)(6), (7).
  The 2005 Act uses the phrase "1 earner" because the decennial census reports median family income in a data set that covers only two-person and larger families (for example: PCT118. Median Family Income In 1999 (Dollars) By Family Size). The Act therefore had to reference another Census Bureau data set that tracks median incomes for workers (for example: PCT115. Median Family Income In 1999 (Dollars) By Number Of Workers In Family In 1999).
114 11 U.S.C. § 707(b)(6), (7).
115 See the Census Bureau's website at http://factfinder.census.gov/home/en/epss/glossary_h.html#household.

§ 13.4.4   Consumer Bankruptcy Law and Practice

contrary to the legislative history of the means test. An earlier version of the bill provided that: "(9) For the purposes of this subsection, a family or household shall consist of the debtor, the debtor's spouse, and the debtor's dependents, but not a legally separated spouse unless the spouse files a joint case with the debtor."[116] This language was omitted from later versions of the bill, indicating that Congress rejected the determination of household size based on dependent status. In many cases such an interpretation would produce nonsensical results, such as when a debtor who is a divorced parent has agreed to allow her former spouse to claim their children as dependents, even though the children reside with the debtor parent and she provides most of their support. Under this United States trustee argument, such a parent living with her four children would be considered a single person household. In any event, the Internal Revenue Code's definition of dependent is not limited to blood relatives.[117] And courts have given a broad definition to the term "dependent" for purposes of section 1325(b), going beyond the Internal Revenue Code's provisions.[118]

Many courts have taken the "heads on beds" approach and included all people living in the residence as household members.[119] Others have taken the "economic unit" approach, counting all individuals who share expenses.[120]

13.4.4 Safe Harbor for Disabled Veterans, Reservists, and National Guard Members

The 2005 amendments create a separate safe harbor from the means test for debtors who are disabled veterans (as defined in 38 U.S.C. § 3741(1)), if their "indebtedness occurred primarily" during a period when they were on active duty or "performing a homeland defense activity."[121] The Act further provides that such debtors are not required to file a statement concerning the means test calculations. If a chapter 7 debtor meets the statutory qualifications for a disabled veteran, only Part I of the Statement of Current Monthly Income and Means Test Calculation need be completed.[122]

Section 707(b) was amended in 2008 to add a new subsection 707(b)(2)(D)(ii), which exempts from means testing debtors who are members of the military reserves or National Guard for the period when they are on active duty[123] or performing homeland defense activities,[124] and for 540 days thereafter.[125] If a chapter 7 debtor meets the statutory qualifications, only Part I of the Statement of Current Monthly Income and Means Test Calculation need be completed.[126] The amendment is effective for cases filed during the seven-year period beginning on October 20, 2008.

At least one court, however, has held it can still consider the ability of a debtor protected by these provisions to pay debts based on income and expenses under section 707(b)(3).[127] Decisions of this type eviscerate the protections that were intended, rendering them close to meaningless, even for the few debtors to which they actually apply.

13.4.5 The Means Test Formula

13.4.5.1 Introduction

If the debtor is not protected by the disabled veteran, reservists, National Guard, or median income safe harbors and has primarily consumer debts, a means test formula is then applied to determine whether a presumption of abuse exists. In general terms, the means test formula begins with the debtor's current monthly income, and deducts from that income certain allowed expenses to come up with a monthly amount presumed to be available to general unsecured creditors. If the debtor's income exceeds expenses by a certain amount (in relation to the amount of unsecured debt), then there is a presumption of abuse. The

---

116 H.R. 833, 106th Cong. § 102 (1999) as reported in House (language would have been codified as section 707(b)(2)(A)(v)). In addition, another section of the 2005 Act specifically referred to "persons claimed as dependents for purposes of the Internal Revenue Code," also demonstrating that if Congress had wanted to limit households to include only those who were tax dependents, it knew how to do so. Pub. L. No. 109-8, § 1308, 119 Stat. 23 (2005) (available on the companion website to this treatise).

117 Qualifying relative includes "[a]n individual . . . who, for the taxable year of the taxpayer, has the same principal place of abode as the taxpayer and is a member of the taxpayer's household." 26 U.S.C. § 152(d)(2)(H).

118 See, e.g., In re Gray, 2009 WL 2475017 (Bankr. N.D. W. Va. Aug. 11, 2009) (twenty-year living companion was dependent); In re Smith, 269 B.R. 686, 689–690 (Bankr. W.D. Mo. 2001) (allowing expenses of twenty-year-old daughter living at home and attending college); In re Wegner, 91 B.R. 854, 859 (Bankr. D. Minn. 1988) (allowing expenses for adult children and grandchildren); In re Tracey, 66 B.R. 63 (Bankr. D. Md. 1986) (dependent can include aging parent for whom debtor provides less than fifty percent of support).

119 See In re Epperson, 409 B.R. 503, 507 (Bankr. D. Ariz. 2009); In re Ellringer, 370 B.R. 905 (Bankr. D. Minn. 2007) (Census Bureau's definition of household used to determine that unrelated adult was member of debtor's household; however, the non-debtor's income was included in current monthly income only to extent paid for expenses of debtor and debtor's dependents).

120 See also Johnson v. Zimmer, 686 F.3d 224 (4th Cir. 2012) (children with debtor part time considered as fractional household members); In re De Bruyn Kops, 2012 WL 438623 (Bankr. D. Idaho Feb. 9, 2012) (children with debtor part time who were his financial dependents counted as household members); In re Robinson, 449 B.R. 473 (Bankr. E.D. Va. 2011) (debtor who had shared custody of four children, four days a week considered to have household size of three); In re Jewel, 365 B.R. 796 (Bankr. S.D. Ohio 2007) (debtors' adult daughter and her three minor children included within household even though not listed as dependents on debtors' most recent tax return).

121 11 U.S.C. § 707(b)(2)(D).
122 See Official Form 22A (reprinted in Appx. D, infra).
123 The call to active duty, which is defined in 10 U.S.C. § 101(d)(1), must have occurred after September 11, 2001, and be for a period of at least ninety days.
124 The homeland defense activity, which is defined in 32 U.S.C. § 901(1), must be for a period of at least ninety days.
125 See Pub. L. No. 110-438, 122 Stat. 5000 (2008) (redesignating portions of section 707(b)(2)(D) and adding section 707(b)(2)(D)(ii)), as amended by Pub. L. No. 112-64 (2011).
126 See Official Form 22A (reprinted in Appx. D, infra).
127 In re Green, 431 B.R. 187 (Bankr. S.D. Ohio 2010).

means test formula is complex, and will be detailed in this section.

Section 707(b)(2)(A) provides a list of the debtor's monthly expenses that are permitted to be deducted for purposes of the abuse analysis. For some items the amounts are determined based on the three categories of allowed expenses provided for in the Internal Revenue Service's collection guidelines: national standards, local standards, and other necessary expenses.[128] Other items may be an allowed expense based on the debtor's actual expenditures if they fall within one of the categories specifically referenced in the statute.

13.4.5.2 Deduction of IRS Expense Allowances

13.4.5.2.1 General

The debtor is allowed to deduct from current monthly income expenses allowed by the Internal Revenue Service (IRS) in its financial standards used in collecting taxes. These expenses are allowed for the debtor and the debtor's dependents, and for the debtor's spouse in a joint case. Expenses for a dependent are allowed even if the dependent is not in the same household. As discussed above, the term "dependent" should be defined broadly. The Internal Revenue Code's definition of dependent is not limited to blood relatives.[129] And, in the past, courts have given a broad definition to the term "dependent" for purposes of section 1325(b), going beyond the Internal Revenue Code's provisions.[130] The allowance for certain expenses of a spouse only in a joint case, if the spouse is not a dependent, may provide an incentive to file a joint case. Note that the non-allowance of some expenses for a spouse who does not file a joint case does not mesh with the inclusion of the spouse's circumstances in other provisions.

With some exceptions, the debtor is allowed to deduct the amounts specified in the IRS national and local standards, even if the debtor actually spends less. The debtor may spend more for one category and less for another, but the amounts listed for the category in the national and local standards are used. For expenses under the categories listed in the IRS's other necessary expenses, however, the debtor may only deduct actual expense amounts.

The debtor may not deduct any payments for debts as part of the deductions determined by the Internal Revenue standards. Such payments are, however, deducted if they are for priority or secured debts, so this provision appears mainly designed to avoid double counting.[131] Although IRS standards allow debtors to deduct some unsecured debts, this provision overrides those standards, and unsecured debts are deductible only as allowed by other provisions (for example, as priority debts). In addition, the debtor generally cannot deduct amounts for debts that are non-priority but nondischargeable, unless the court finds such a deduction to be justified as a special circumstance under section 707(b)(2)(B).

13.4.5.2.2 IRS national standards for food, clothing, housekeeping supplies, personal care, and miscellaneous expenses

The IRS national standards provide for the debtor's allowed living expenses in five categories: food, clothing and services, housekeeping supplies, personal care products and services, and miscellaneous items.[132] The amounts listed in the national standards for these categories apply to debtors in every state.

The debtor is allowed an upward adjustment of five percent in the allowable food and clothing expenses if such an adjustment can be demonstrated to be reasonably necessary.[133] Certainly this standard should be possible to satisfy in urban or rural areas where food prices are higher. It should also be demonstrable when debtors have skimped on food or clothing due to their financial problems. Nevertheless, the amounts involved are not large, so the adjustment will be significant only for debtors very close to the presumption cut-off.

To claim the five percent adjustment in food and clothing expenses, the debtor may list the additional expense amount on a designated line item in Part V of the Statement of Current Monthly Income and Means Test Calculation.[134] The form indicates that the debtor must provide the trustee with documentation demonstrating that the additional amount claimed is reasonable and necessary, and the Rules state that this documentation should be brought to the meeting of creditors.[135]

---

128 The Internal Revenue Service (IRS) developed these standards as guidelines for its own debt collectors, subject to individual collector's exercise of discretion and consideration of exceptions. The IRS Financial Analysis Handbook provides an overview of the collection standards and is reprinted in Appx. I.2.1, *infra*. However, as discussed below, the standards are not necessarily applied as dictated by the IRS financial analysis procedures. Section 103 of the 2005 Act suggests as the "sense of Congress" that the IRS has authority to alter the standards to "accommodate their use under section 707(b)." Pub. L. No. 109-8, § 103, 119 Stat. 23 (2005).

129 Qualifying relative includes "[a]n individual . . . who, for the taxable year of the taxpayer, has the same principal place of abode as the taxpayer and is a member of the taxpayer's household." 26 U.S.C. § 152(d)(2)(H).

130 *See , e.g., In re* Gray, 2009 WL 2475017 (Bankr. N.D. W. Va. Aug. 11, 2009) (live-in companion of many years considered dependent); *In re* Tracey, 66 B.R. 63 (Bankr. D. Md. 1986) (dependent can include aging parent for whom debtor provides less than fifty percent of support).

131 Section 707(b)(2)(A)(ii)(I) provides that: "Notwithstanding any other provision of this clause, the monthly expenses of the debtor shall not include any payments for debts." However, payments on secured and priority debts are allowed expenses pursuant to provisions of other clauses of section 707(b)(2)(A). *See* §§ 13.4.5.3.2, 13.4.5.3.3, *infra*.

132 11 U.S.C. § 707(b)(2)(A)(ii)(I).
The IRS national standards are reprinted in Appx. I.2.2, *infra*.

133 11 U.S.C. § 707(b)(2)(A)(ii)(I). *See In re* Davis, 2011 WL 5884015 (Bankr. N.D. Tex. Nov. 22, 2011) (obligatory business lunches were reasonably necessary).

134 *See* Official Form 22A (reprinted in Appx. D, *infra*).

135 Fed. R. Bankr. P. 4002(b)(2)(C).

13.4.5.2.3 IRS national standard for out-of-pocket health care expenses

The IRS national standards provide an allowance for out-of-pocket health care expenses.[136] Based on the updated 2012 figures, each debtor in the household under age 65 is permitted a health care allowance of $60, and each debtor over age 65 is permitted an allowance of $144. These allowances are permitted even if actual expenses are less.[137] If the debtor has health care expenses in excess of this standard allowance, these additional expenses may be claimed as an "other necessary expense."[138] The out-of-pocket health care standard amount is allowed in addition to the amount debtors pay for health insurance, which may be claimed as a separate allowed expense.[139]

13.4.5.2.4 IRS local standards for transportation expenses

The debtor may also claim transportation expenses under the regional IRS local standards for transportation, which differentiate between ownership costs, operating costs, and public transportation costs.[140] The ownership costs expense is provided as a national standard that is the same no matter where the debtor resides. Based on the updated 2012 figures, the debtor is permitted an ownership expense of $517 for one car and $1034 for two cars. More current figures may be available on the United States Trustee Program website.[141] These numbers represent the total amount that is to be deducted for a true lease of a vehicle, regardless of whether lease payments are higher or lower.

The operating costs section of the IRS transportation standards are provided by Census Bureau region and metropolitan statistical area (MSA). A table provided by the IRS lists the states that are included within each Census Bureau region.[142] If the debtor lives within an MSA (MSAs are defined by county and city), the MSA standard is applicable. If the debtor does not reside in an MSA, the regional standard is used. A dollar amount is provided based on whether the debtor has one car or two cars. For example, if the debtor lives in the Midwest region and does not live in an MSA such as Chicago or Cleveland, the debtor would be allowed (based on 2012 figures): $212 for operating costs if one car is owned, and $424 if two cars are owned. If the debtor lives in the Chicago MSA, the allowances are $262 for operating costs for one car, and $524 for two cars. In addition, if the vehicle is over six years old or has mileage of over 75,000 miles an additional $200 per month of operating expenses may be claimed.[143]

The public transportation expense is set as a national standard that is the same no matter where the debtor resides. Based on the updated 2012 figures, the debtor is permitted a public transportation expense of $182. If the debtor has a car and also uses public transportation, the debtor may claim the public transportation expense in addition to the ownership and operating allowances.

As discussed in § 13.4.5.3.2, *infra*, a separate expense deduction is permitted for payments on secured debts. There was originally some doubt about whether a debtor may deduct the IRS ownership allowance if the debtor's remaining car payments divided by sixty are less than the ownership allowance. It is now generally accepted, as reflected in the Official Forms for the means test,[144] that the full IRS ownership allowance may be claimed, because the operative language in the means test merely states that the debtor may deduct the transportation allowance "specified" but the monthly expenses shall not include any payments for debts.[145] This language has generally been interpreted as meaning that the car payments should not be double counted, that is, they should not be added to the transportation expense allowance. If the car payments exceed the allowance, the means test and Official Form 22A (and Official Form 22C in chapter 13 cases) allow the excess to be deducted as secured debt payments.[146]

However, the Supreme Court has ruled, in *Ransom v. FIA Card Services*,[147] that a debtor may not claim the Internal Revenue Service ownership allowance for a vehicle if there are no remaining loan or lease payments due on the date of the petition. The court held that in such cases the allowance is not applicable. Obviously, this decision raises questions of timing and strategy, especially because the court held that if even one

---

136 The health care allowance was added to the IRS Collection Financial Standards on October 1, 2007, and was recognized by the United States Trustee Program as effective for bankruptcy purposes on January 1, 2008.
137 *In re* Melancon, 400 B.R. 521 (Bankr. M.D. La. 2009).
138 *See* § 13.4.5.2.6, *infra*.
139 *See* § 13.4.5.3.4, *infra*.
140 11 U.S.C. § 707(b)(2)(A)(ii)(I).
   The IRS allowable living expenses for transportation are reprinted in Appx. I.2.4, *infra*. On October 1, 2007, the IRS made substantial changes to its Collection Financial Standards, which were recognized by the United States Trustee Program as effective for bankruptcy purposes on January 1, 2008. The IRS removed the public transportation allowance from the vehicle operating expense and there is now a separate public transportation expense amount. The ownership and operating cost allowances for a second vehicle are now the same as the allowances for the first vehicle.
141 The website is located at www.usdoj.gov/ust/eo/bapcpa/meanstesting.htm.
142 The table is reprinted in Appx. I.2.4, *infra*. More current figures may be available on the United States Trustee Program's website, www.usdoj.gov/ust/eo/bapcpa/meanstesting.htm.

143 *In re* Baker, 2011 WL 576851 (Bankr. D. Mont. Feb. 9, 2011); *In re* Byrn, 410 B.R. 642 (Bankr. D. Mont. 2008); *In re* Brown, 376 B.R. 601 (Bankr. S. D. Tex. 2007); *In re* Howell, 366 B.R. 153 (Bankr. D. Kan. 2007); *In re* Carlin, 348 B.R. 795 (Bankr. D. Ore. 2006); *In re* Barraza, 346 B.R. 724 (Bankr. N.D. Tex. 2006); *In re* Oliver, 350 B.R. 294 (Bankr. W.D. Tex. 2006); Internal Revenue Serv., Internal Revenue Manual, Financial Analysis Handbook § 5.8.5.20.3. *But see In re* Sisler, 464 B.R. 705 (Bankr. W.D. Va. 2012); *In re* Schultz, 463 B.R. 492 (Bankr. W.D. Mo. 2011); *In re* Hargis, 451 B.R. 174 (Bankr. D. Utah 2011) ($200 may be claimed for older car only if there is evidence that additional expenses actually exist); *In re* Van Dyke, 450 B.R. 836 (Bankr. C.D. Ill. 2011) (same).
144 Official Forms 22A, 22C (reprinted in Appx. D, *infra*).
145 *See* 11 U.S.C. § 707(b)(2)(A)(ii)(I).
146 *See* Lines 23, 24, Official form 22A (reprinted in Appx. D, *infra*).
147 131 S. Ct. 716, 178 L. Ed. 2d 603 (2011).

payment remains due on a vehicle loan or lease, whether on a purchase money loan or a later loan secured by the vehicle, the allowance may be claimed.[148]

Courts have generally permitted debtors to take deductions for the number of cars that they own, even if this number exceeds two or exceeds the number of drivers in the household.[149]

13.4.5.2.5 IRS local standards for housing and utilities

The debtor may take as an expense deduction a housing allowance under the IRS local standards.[150] Debtors should not be penalized for spending less than the housing allowance permits, and most courts have so held.[151] Housing allowances are specified for each county, dependent on family size, and on the Official Form are broken into separate housing and utilities allowances for "non-mortgage expenses" and for mortgage or rent payments. Although the IRS does not break the housing allowance into these components, and therefore it is not clear that the statute authorizes such division of housing expenses, the division is not normally detrimental to the debtor and the amounts intended by the United States Trustee Program to be used are found on its website.[152]

Mortgage payments that are separately deducted as payments on secured debt are treated much like car loan payments. They should be deducted from the mortgage allowance, which avoids them being double counted.[153]

If utility payments cause the debtor's "operating expenses" to exceed the "non-mortgage" component of the housing allowance, they are covered by a separate provision that allows an additional deduction for documented, reasonable, and necessary "home energy costs" in excess of the IRS standard.[154]

Major home repairs in excess of the housing allowance could be considered an "other necessary" expense, as set out in § 13.4.5.2.6, *infra*. It would be hard to argue that major required plumbing or roof repairs are not necessary for the welfare of a debtor's family. Even if they could not be deducted as "other necessary expenses," they would constitute special circumstances that could rebut a presumption of abuse, as discussed below.[155]

13.4.5.2.6 Other necessary expenses allowed under IRS standards

Although most of the IRS collection standards do not consider a debtor's actual expenses, the debtor may deduct actual expense amounts for the categories specified by the IRS as "other necessary expenses."[156] It is unclear whether the expenses in these categories must meet the IRS qualification that they be necessary to health and welfare or the production of income. It is also unclear whether the expenses should be averaged over the prior six months or whether the current amounts should be stated.[157]

According to the legislative history, the IRS list of other necessary expenses is to be considered *nonexclusive*.[158] Therefore, the court should have discretion to determine whether other expenses necessary to a family's health and welfare or to the production of income may be deducted. However, the Official Forms erroneously take the position that only expenses for the specific categories itemized in the Internal Revenue Manual can be deducted, apparently concluding that the reference in the Manual to expenses necessary for the health and welfare of the debtor's family or for production of income is not a "category" of expenses.[159] Limiting "other necessary expenses" to those on the form would preclude debtors from deducting necessary expenses such as an alarm system in a high-crime neighborhood, household help for the infirm, and uniforms or work tools for employees. In any event, even if the court decides the debtor cannot claim other necessary expenses categories not listed in the form, such expenses necessary for

---

148 *Id.*, 131 S. Ct. at 29, 178 L. Ed. 2d at 617. *See also In re* Scott, 457 B.R. 740 (Bankr. S.D. Ill. 2011) (debtor could claim full ownership allowance even though actual expenses were less); *In re* O'Neill Miranda, 449 B.R. 182 (Bankr. D. P.R. 2011) (same).

149 *In re* Joest, 450 B.R. 381 (Bankr. N.D.N.Y. 2011) (two vehicles for single debtor); *In re* Cole, 427 B.R. 467 (Bankr. C.D. Ill. 2010) (same); *In re* Stallings, 2009 WL 1241263 (Bankr. E.D.N.C. May 4, 2009) (four vehicles for four drivers); *In re* Styles, 397 B.R. 771 (Bankr. W.D. Va. 2008) (two vehicles for single debtor); *In re* Comstock, 389 B.R. 888 (Bankr. N.D. Cal. 2008) (two vehicles for single debtor).

150 11 U.S.C. § 707(b)(2)(A)(ii)(I).
   The IRS local standards for housing and utilities are available at www.irs.gov/businesses/small/article/0,,id=104696,00.html (then search by state).

151 *See In re* Reinstein, 393 B.R. 838 (Bankr. E.D. Wis. 2008) (debtor deducted allowed amount of $712 instead of actual rent payment of $640); *In re* Swan, 368 B.R. 12 (Bankr. N.D. Cal. 2007) (debtor claimed expense of $1644 but only paid $800); *In re* Naslund, 359 B.R. 781 (Bankr. D. Mont. 2006) (debtors claimed the standard allowance of $772 per month, even though they only actually paid $545 per month).

152 Located at www.usdoj.gov/ust/eo/bapcpa/meanstesting.htm.

153 *See* § 13.4.5.3.2, *infra*, for a more complete discussion of the treatment of secured debts.

154 11 U.S.C. § 707(b)(2)(A)(ii)(V).
   The phrase "home energy costs" is not defined. The IRS Financial Analysis Handbook describes "utilities" as including "gas, electricity, water, fuel, oil, bottled gas, trash and garbage collection, wood and other fuels, septic cleaning, and telephone." Internal Revenue Service, Internal Revenue Manual, Financial Analysis Handbook § 5.15.1.9(1)(A).

155 *See* § 13.4.6.2, *infra*.

156 11 U.S.C. § 707(b)(2)(A)(ii)(I).
   A description of the other necessary expenses is contained in section 5.15.1.10 of the IRS Financial Analysis Handbook, which is reprinted in Appx. I.2.1, *infra*.

157 *See In re* Thelen, 431 B.R. 601 (Bankr. E.D.N.C. 2010) (it was appropriate to average childcare expenses over prior six months when debtor's income had dropped due to loss of work and child care expenses had also dropped).

158 H.R. Rep. No. 109-31, at 14 n.66 (2005) (available on this treatise's companion website).

159 Part VII of Official Form 22A does permit the debtor to list other necessary expenses not otherwise stated on the form, but these expenses are not deducted from current monthly income in determining whether a presumption of abuse arises.

family's health and welfare or production of income could be considered to be special circumstances.[160]

The IRS list of other necessary expenses includes:

- Child care;
- Court ordered payments, including alimony, support, and other court-ordered payments (like restitution);
- Expenses for the care of elderly, invalid, or handicapped individuals;
- Education required for employment or for special needs children if suitable education is not available from public schools;
- Necessary medical and dental expenses;[161]
- Involuntary deductions from wages, including union dues, uniforms, 401(k) plan loan repayments,[162] and so forth;
- Term life insurance premiums;
- Taxes, including withholding taxes;[163]
- Optional telephone services, such as special long distance, pager, call waiting, and extraordinary cell phone expenses;[164] and
- Internet service.[165]

13.4.5.3 Other Expenses That May Be Deducted

13.4.5.3.1 In general

In addition to expenses covered under the IRS guidelines, section 707(b) provides a list of expense items that may be deducted from the debtor's current monthly income in a range of categories, such as health insurance costs, expenses to maintain safety from domestic violence, certain expenses to care for others, costs necessary in a chapter 13 case, certain educational expenses, and charitable contributions.[166] Some of these items are deductible under the IRS standards and presumably should not be double counted.

13.4.5.3.2 Deduction for secured debts

The debtor may deduct the average monthly payments made on secured debts.[167] This amount is determined by taking the sum of (1) the total of all amounts "scheduled as contractually due" to secured creditors in each month of the sixty months following the date of the petition, and (2) any additional payments to secured creditors that would need to be paid under a chapter 13 plan as described below.[168] This total is then divided by sixty to determine the monthly amount.

This provision clearly includes all regular mortgage and car loan payments regardless of how much they are, including any escrow payments. Indeed, the Official Forms direct that taxes and insurance required by a mortgage should be deducted even if not paid into escrow. It also includes all payments to creditors secured by personal property, such as appliances, even if the appliance is worth little and its purchase price is a small portion of the debt. And there is no exception for payments contractually due to creditors holding liens that might be avoidable or on property the debtor may intend to surrender.[169]

---

160 See § 13.4.6.2, infra. See also In re Thompson, 350 B.R. 770 (Bankr. N.D. Ohio 2006) (fact that debtor could only end 401(k) plan loan repayments by ending employment constituted special circumstances rebutting presumption of abuse), rev'd on other grounds sub nom. Eisen v. Thompson, 370 B.R. 762 (N.D. Ohio June 29, 2007) (erroneously holding 401(k) loan was not a secured debt).

161 See DeHart v. Gregory (In re Gregory), 452 B.R. 895 (Bankr. M.D. Pa. 2011) (expenses permitted for 15-year-old daughter's horseback riding, dance, and piano lessons recommended by psychologist to help with her major depression).

162 Most such loan repayments are involuntary and the debtor has no option to discontinue them. The creditor is also not stayed from collecting them, 11 U.S.C. § 362(b)(19), and they are not considered disposable income in chapter 13. 11 U.S.C. § 1322(f). Because section 1322(f) prohibits the modification of the terms of a pension loan, one court has held, in applying section 707(b)(2) in a chapter 13 case, that the debtor is entitled to deduct the actual monthly payment amount on the 401(k) loan, not an amount based on the loan balance divided by the length of the plan. See In re Wiggs, 2006 WL 2246432 (Bankr. N.D. Ill. Aug. 4, 2006). But see In re Egebjerg, 574 F.3d 1045 (9th Cir. 2009) (payments were not involuntary because debtor could opt to treat them as an early withdrawal; payments also not necessary to debtor's health and welfare).

163 The debtor is entitled to make a reasonable and good faith estimate of tax liability. However, excess withholding may not be considered reasonable and necessary. See In re Stimac, 366 B.R. 889 (Bankr. E.D. Wis. 2007) (rebuttable presumption that taxes actually paid, as evidenced by most recent tax return, divided by twelve is proper amount to be deducted); In re Raybon, 364 B.R. 587 (Bankr. D.S.C. 2007) (good faith estimate permitted); Baxter v. Johnson, 346 B.R. 256 (Bankr. S.D. Ga. 2006) (excess withholdings are not actual, reasonable and necessary).

Including actual tax liabilities as expenses, and not excess withholdings that will result in a refund, also will avoid the problem of chapter 13 trustees demanding tax refunds as "disposable income," since the amounts resulting in the refunds would already have been included in the disposable income figure that determines the debtor's plan payments. This will avoid the issue of what happens when a chapter 13 trustee demands a refund that the debtor has already spent.

164 Although basic cell phone expenses are now included in the local standards housing allowances, extraordinary expenses over and above those allowed as part of the housing allowance may be necessary. See In re Petro, 381 B.R. 233 (Bankr. M.D. Tenn. 2007) ($350 monthly cell phone expense found necessary when debtor worked far from her four children's schools), rev'd on other grounds, 395 B.R. 369 (B.A.P. 6th Cir. 2008). In addition, the costs of additional telephones and cell phones, and related services, are deductible as other necessary expenses if they are used for the production of income.

165 Effective on October 3, 2011, the IRS revised the "Local Standards: Housing and Utilities" category to include internet service in the allowance. Thus, only Internet service that is used for the production of income may now be treated as another necessary expense item.

166 11 U.S.C. § 707(b)(2)(A)(ii).

167 11 U.S.C. § 707(b)(2)(A)(iii).

This section does not provide an allowance for payments on a car lease, so a deduction for lease payments should be taken as an Ownership Costs expense under the IRS transportation standard.

168 In re Carlton, 370 B.R. 188 (Bankr. C.D. Ill. 2007) (debtors could deduct payments for three vehicles).

169 In re Rudler, 576 F.3d 37 (1st Cir. 2009); McDow v. Harvey, 2010 WL 537872 (W.D. Va. Feb. 12, 2010); Fokkena v. Hartwick, 373

An issue that may arise is what the phrase "scheduled as contractually due" refers to when there is a minimum required payment, as on a credit card. When minimum payments include a high interest rate, they may add up to more than the amount of the debt. Similarly, when the total debt is contractually due immediately, as with a tax lien or other liens, can the debtor add the applicable interest over sixty months?[170]

The deduction for secured debts can be taken in addition to the IRS standard deductions, as long as double counting is avoided.[171] And a debtor may take as a deduction necessary secured debt payments on a home, even if the total exceeds the IRS housing mortgage payment allowance. In effect the debtor is permitted a deduction of the larger of the secured debt payments or the mortgage allowance.

The result should be same for cars. The IRS transportation ownership allowance may exceed any remaining secured debt payments. In that case the larger of the two amounts should be allowed.

The debtor also may deduct any other payments to secured creditors that would be necessary in a chapter 13 case to maintain the debtor's possession of the debtor's primary residence, motor vehicle, or other property necessary for the support of the debtor or the debtor's dependents.[172] Again, the monthly amount is derived by taking all necessary payments over the next sixty months, and then dividing by sixty. Such payments would include:

- Any arrears, including charges and attorney fees, owed on mortgages;
- Arrears on car loans, plus fees;
- Amounts on cross-collateralized debts, for example, to credit unions;
- Any additional arrears on secured purchases of appliances or other property;
- Arrearage payments on other liens on such property; and
- Any other amounts that would have to be paid to the secured creditors during the chapter 13 case.

Issues may arise whether condominium or home owner association fees can be deducted under this provision. Although payment of such fees is normally required by a mortgage, they are not paid to or through the mortgagee. However, the mortgage may provide that the mortgagee can advance such fees if they are unpaid, with the advance secured by the mortgage.[173] In most states nonpayment of the fees also gives rise to a lien, so they could be considered payments to a secured creditor. Alternatively, they should qualify as expenses required by special circumstances if they cannot be accommodated by the housing expense allowance.

Most courts have held, erroneously, that loans from the debtor's pension plan are not secured debts.[174] However, some courts have declined to dismiss a case when the presumption of abuse arises solely due to pension loan repayments, or under the section 707(b)(3) totality of circumstances test, because such payments are excluded from disposable income in chapter 13 by section 1322(f).[175]

13.4.5.3.3 Deduction for priority debts

The debtor may deduct as an allowed monthly expense payments on priority debts, calculated by finding the total amount of debts entitled to priority, and then dividing by sixty.[176] Such debts include priority taxes, domestic support obligations (including support debts assigned to a governmental unit), and priority drunk driving debts.

There may be issues in determining whether domestic relations debts are in the nature of alimony and support and therefore priority, and also whether they are nondischargeable. Debtors may be estopped from claiming the debts are dischargeable if they claim the debts are in nature of support for purposes of the means test. However, because property settlement debts, including debts from hold harmless agreements, are no longer dischargeable in chapter 7, the debtor may have no great interest in claiming that such debts are not support.[177] In any event, even if the debt is a property settlement, if it is part of a court ordered payment, it may be deductible as an "other necessary expense."[178]

Domestic support obligations are deductible as priority debts even if they pay for expenses that might not otherwise be

---

B.R. 645 (D. Minn. 2007); *In re* Randle, 2007 WL 2668727 (N.D. Ill. July 20, 2007) (debtor could deduct payments on property she intended to surrender); In re Vecera, 430 B.R. 840 (Bankr. S.D. Ind. 2010); *In re* Labruno, 2009 Bankr. LEXIS 2007 (Bankr. M.D. Fla. Apr. 24, 2009); *In re* Foster, 2009 WL 395391 (Bankr. S.D. Fla. Feb. 11, 2009); *In re* Zak, 361 B.R. 481 (Bankr. N.D. Ohio 2007) (payments remained contractually due even though mortgage holder had obtained relief from stay to foreclose); *In re* Hartwick, 359 B.R. 16 (Bankr. D.N.H. 2007). *Cf. In re* Barger, 2010 WL 1904771 (Bankr. M.D.N.C. May 7, 2010) (in motion under § 707(b)(3), court would not penalize debtor who had surrendered car prepetition, because she would need to replace it). *But see In re* Turner, 574 F.3d 349 (7th Cir. 2009) (deduction not permitted when projecting disposable income under section 1325(b) because it is known that debtor will not incur expense).

170 *See In re* Willette, 395 B.R. 308, 329 (Bankr. D. Vt. 2008) (permitting deduction of regular payments on home subject to foreclosure, but not total accelerated balance).

171 Official Form 22A avoids double counting by deducting the secured debt payments from the mortgage expense allowance.

172 11 U.S.C. § 707(b)(2)(A)(iii)(II).

173 *See In re* Bermann, 399 B.R. 213 (Bankr. E.D. Wis. 2009) (permitting deduction).

174 See *In re* Egebjerg, 574 F.3d 1045 (9th Cir. 2009) and cases cited therein. The cases relied upon in *In re Egebjerg* are of questionable validity. *See* § 15.5.1.1, *infra*.

175 *In re* Childers, 2009 WL 1442013 (Bankr. D. Neb. May 20, 2009); *In re* Mravik, 399 B.R. 202 (Bankr. E.D. Wis. 2008) (debtor would not be required to pay creditors in chapter 13 because pension plan contributions would be permitted expenses and conversion would be meaningless); *In re* Latone, 2008 WL 5049460 (Bankr. D. Ariz. Oct. 23, 2008); *In re* Skvorecz, 369 B.R. 638 (Bankr. D. Colo. 2007) (debtor would not be required to pay unsecured creditors in chapter 13 case, so dismissal would lead to absurd result).

176 11 U.S.C. § 707(b)(2)(A)(iv).

177 See Chapter 15, *infra*, for a discussion of the family law dischargeability changes.

178 *See* § 13.4.5.2.6, *supra*.

deductible. For example, payments for private school tuition, college tuition, or other expenses for dependents or nondependents, may be priority domestic support obligations.[179]

Similarly, debtors now have an incentive to have many tax debts treated as priority debts. If they have unfiled returns that would make the debts for those tax years nondischargeable in both chapter 7 and chapter 13, it is in their interest to file a bankruptcy petition while the debts are priority debts, both to increase deductions under the means test and, in chapter 13, to separately classify them. These considerations also suggest that attorneys may want to give different advice about what debts a debtor should prioritize for payment before bankruptcy.

13.4.5.3.4 Deduction for health insurance

The debtor may deduct reasonably necessary expenses for health insurance, disability insurance, and a health savings account for the debtor, the debtor's dependents, and the debtor's spouse.[180] For debtors who do not have such insurance, obtaining it before a bankruptcy case is filed can be an important step toward financial stability. In addition, it is a significant expense that can be deducted under the means test.

13.4.5.3.5 Deduction for expenses to maintain safety from domestic violence

The debtor may also deduct reasonably necessary expenses to maintain the safety of the debtor and the family of the debtor from domestic violence, as identified under section 309 of the Family Violence Prevention and Services Act or other applicable federal law.[181] The debtor's use of this deduction must be kept confidential by the court, but it is unclear how this confidentiality provision will be implemented. As the court is to keep these expenses confidential, will the trustee, for example, be permitted to review them?

13.4.5.3.6 Deduction for support of elderly and disabled family members

Other expenses that may be deducted include the "continuation of" actual, reasonable, and necessary expenses for the care and support of an elderly, chronically ill, or disabled household member or an immediate family member (parent, grandparent, sibling, child, grandchild, other dependent, or spouse in a joint case if not a dependent).[182] This deduction is broader than the similar IRS Other Necessary Expense category, as it is not limited to dependents.[183] It also includes not simply care, but support, which may not be included in the IRS category.

Because of the way this provision is worded, there is a strong argument that support for an immediate family member may be deducted even if that person is not elderly or disabled. Such a reading would permit deduction of child support payments that are not ordered by a court or payments for support of adult children who are not in the debtor's household.

13.4.5.3.7 Deduction for administrative expenses

If a debtor is eligible to file chapter 13, the debtor may deduct administrative expenses that would be incurred in a chapter 13 case in the district where the debtor resides, subject to a cap on such expenses of ten percent of projected plan payments.[184] This amount should include payments for attorney fees to debtor's counsel. If the debtor is not eligible to file a chapter 13 case, the debtor can argue that chapter 11 administrative expenses should be deducted as a special circumstance.

The ability to deduct chapter 13 administrative expenses requires the debtor's counsel to construct a hypothetical chapter 13 plan, including calculation of amounts that would be paid to secured and priority creditors and amounts that would be required to be paid unsecured creditors under the section 1325(b) application of the means test standards, in order to calculate a monthly plan payment. If current monthly mortgage payments are to be paid through the plan, as they are in some districts, they should be included in the calculation.

The Executive Office of the United States Trustee is required to publish schedules of administrative expense percentages to be used in calculating the deduction for each district, and has published such percentage figures for each district.[185] However, it is obvious that, despite the clear definition of administrative expenses in the Bankruptcy Code, the percentages published do not include any administrative expenses other than the chapter 13 trustee's percentage fee. Thus, if the published figures cause a presumption of abuse to arise because all administrative expenses (up to the 10% cap) are not counted, the debtor should be able to challenge those figures as clearly contrary to the statute.

13.4.5.3.8 Deduction for education expenses

The debtor may deduct actual public or private school educational expenses of up to $1775 per each child under eighteen years of age.[186] The debtor must provide documentation of such expenses and a detailed explanation of why such expenses are reasonable and necessary, and why such expenses are not already accounted for in the IRS national standards, local standards, or other necessary expenses. There is no explicit

---

179 *In re* Maiorino, 435 B.R. 806 (Bankr. D. Mass. 2010) (college tuition and related expenses, including student loan payments, for two children were required by state court order).
180 11 U.S.C. § 707(b)(2)(A)(ii)(I).
181 11 U.S.C. § 707(b)(2)(A)(ii)(I).
182 11 U.S.C. § 707(b)(2)(A)(ii)(II). *See In re* Barbutes, 436 B.R. 519 (Bankr. M.D. Tenn. 2010) (pool upkeep necessary for debtor wife's health problems and because failure to maintain pool would damage property).
183 *See In re* Clingman, 400 B.R. 555 (Bankr. S.D. Tex. 2009) (mortgage payments for home occupied by debtor's parents, with no showing they were dependents).
184 11 U.S.C. § 707(b)(2)(A)(ii)(III).
185 These percentages are listed on the United States Trustee Program's website at www.usdoj.gov/ust/eo/bapcpa/mt/ch13_exp_mult.htm.
186 11 U.S.C. § 707(b)(2)(A)(ii)(IV).

provision for a determination of whether the expenses are reasonable and necessary after the debtor supplies documentation stating they are.

This $1775 allowance is insufficient for virtually all parochial or private schools, and does not cover high school students over eighteen. To seek a deduction for a higher amount the debtor may be able to argue special circumstances, for example, that pulling children out of school in the middle of the year is very disruptive. In any event, the deduction can be used for other expenses such as school supplies, uniforms, and expenses for school sports or trips.

13.4.5.3.9 Deduction for charitable contributions

Finally, section 707(b)(1) provides, as under current law, that the debtor may continue to make charitable and religious contributions.[187]

13.4.6 Application of the Means Test Formula

13.4.6.1 Presumption of Abuse

A presumption of abuse arises under the means test if the debtor's current monthly income after all monthly allowed expenses are deducted, multiplied by 60, is the lesser of $11,725 or 25% of non-priority unsecured debt, as long as that 25% is at least $7025.[188] For debtors with $46,900 or more in general unsecured debt, a presumption of abuse arises if the amount is $11,725 ($195.42 per month) or more. For debtors with less than $28,100 in general unsecured debt, a presumption of abuse arises if the amount is $7025 ($117.09 per month) or more. For debtors with between $28,100 and $46,900 in general unsecured debt, the presumption of abuse arises if the amount is 25% or more of the unsecured debt.

To determine the amount of non-priority unsecured debt, presumably, the court will look to the amount listed on the debtor's schedules. Probably the unsecured portion of an undersecured claim should be counted for this purpose, as it usually is under section 109(e) of the Bankruptcy Code. Because the terms non-contingent and unliquidated, present in section 109(e), are not present in section 707(b)(2)(A)(i), contingent and unliquidated debts should also be estimated and included.

13.4.6.2 Rebutting the Presumption of Abuse

To rebut the presumption of abuse if a motion to dismiss or convert is filed, section 707(b)(2)(B)(i) states that the debtor must demonstrate that "special circumstances" exist which would cause the debtor to fall below the presumed abuse tolerances set by the means test formula. The special circumstances must "justify additional expenses or adjustments of current monthly income for which there is no reasonable alternative."[189] This standard is essentially a reasonableness test and significant discretion is vested in the court.

The debtor has a strong motivation to show special circumstances, because debtors who lose means test motions are unlikely to be able to convert to chapter 13. Such debtors would be subjected to most of the same living expense standards as apply in chapter 7.[190] As they were not able to meet those living expense standards prior to filing a chapter 7 bankruptcy, they usually would not be able to meet them for the duration of a chapter 13 case.

Special circumstances must dictate an adjustment in income or expenses that changes the result of the means test formula sufficiently to eliminate the presumption of abuse. Examples that are given in the statute are a serious medical condition or a call to active duty in the armed forces. As mentioned in § 13.4.4, *supra*, there is also a complete safe harbor from the means test for disabled veterans whose debts were incurred primarily during active duty or homeland defense.

With respect to income, the most obvious special circumstance would be a reduction in income from the "current monthly income" figure based on income that the debtor is no longer actually receiving as of the petition date. A special circumstance with respect to expenses could be that the projected moving expenses and disruption to the debtor's children that would arise from a move to a lower-rent apartment would justify a higher rent than the IRS standards allow. There are many other possibilities, such as high commuting costs,[191] increased price of gas,[192] security costs in dangerous neighborhoods, cost of infant formula and diapers, and additional expenses due to the postpetition birth of child.[193] For example, married debtors who are separated may add expenses for a second residence,[194] as may a debtor who has to maintain a separate residence in another city for employment reasons.[195] Extra housing expenses necessitated by a special needs child may be special circumstances.[196] Extra automobile costs necessitated by high business mileage can be special circumstances,[197] as can support payments not counted in the means test.[198]

---

187 The contributions must meet the definition of "charitable contribution" under section 548(d)(3) to a qualified religious or charitable entity or organization, as defined in section 548(d)(4). *See In re Bender*, 373 B.R. 25 (Bankr. E.D. Mich. 2007).

188 11 U.S.C. § 707(b)(2)(A)(i).

189 11 U.S.C. § 707(b)(2)(B)(i).

190 However, there are some significant differences when the means test is applied in chapter 13. *See* Ch. 12, *supra*.

191 *In re Batzkiel*, 349 B.R. 581 (Bankr. N.D. Iowa 2006).

192 According to Sen. Grassley, the bill's lead sponsor, "if the costs of gas have increased significantly over the costs of gas used by the Internal Revenue Service, the excess costs of gasoline over the IRS standard should and would be allowed under the special circumstances provision." 147 Cong. Rec. S2363 (daily ed. Mar. 15, 2001) (remarks of Sen. Grassley on predecessor bill with identical special circumstances language).

193 *In re Martin*, 371 B.R. 347 (Bankr. C.D. Ill. 2007).

194 *In re Crego*, 387 B.R. 225 (Bankr. E.D. Wis. 2008).

195 *In re Graham*, 363 B.R. 844 (Bankr. S.D. Ohio 2007).

196 *In re Scarafiotti*, 375 B.R. 618 (Bankr. D. Colo. 2007).

197 *In re Turner*, 376 B.R. 370 (Bankr. D.N.H. 2007).

198 *In re Littman*, 370 B.R. 820 (Bankr. D. Idaho 2007).

Expenses that are unique to the debtor's housing situation, such as the necessity of maintaining a swimming pool in a safe condition, may qualify.[199] The necessity of repaying a 401(k) loan has been found by some courts to be special circumstances, though others have disagreed.[200] And several courts have held that the need to make continued student loan payments can constitute special circumstances.[201]

The debtor must provide an itemization of expenses, "documentation" for the expense or adjustment to income, and a detailed explanation of why it is "necessary and reasonable," including a sworn statement as to accuracy.[202] It may be difficult to provide documentation for some expenses, especially cash expenses, such as gas for debtors who can no longer use credit cards. Debtors may have to keep records or the attorney may need to obtain a letter from the provider of a service or from some other source.

It is unclear where and when the documentation will be submitted. Bankruptcy Rule 4002(b)(2)(C) provides that it should be presented at the section 341(a) meeting of creditors. This timing would allow the United States trustee to review the information prior to the deadline for a statement of whether the trustee believes the case is abusive.[203] United States trustees will not be interested in bringing section 707(b) motions they are likely to lose. Section 707(b)(2)(B)(i) states that the debtor must demonstrate that the special circumstances exist in a proceeding under section 707(b). Consequently, if a motion to dismiss or convert is brought, documentation would also be submitted in that proceeding.

13.4.6.3 Discretionary Dismissal

Section 707(b) states that the court "may" dismiss a case if it finds that the granting of relief would be an abuse. The discretionary language of section 707(b) means that a case will not necessarily be dismissed even for a debtor who has triggered the presumption of abuse and has not rebutted that presumption through special circumstances. For example, one court refused to dismiss a debtor's chapter 7 case when conversion to chapter 13 would not result in any payments to creditors.[204]

13.4.7 Other Changes in the Abuse Standard Under Section 707(b)

13.4.7.1 No Challenges Based on Ability to Pay for Debtors with Incomes Below Median Income

With the new specific means testing provisions, debtors should not be subjected to section 707(b) motions based on ability to pay, if their incomes fall below the median income threshold. There are numerous statements in the legislative history that means testing applies only for debtors with incomes above the median income.[205] Congress has now set specific guidelines for who should be determined able to pay debts. This bright line test was intended not only to catch abusers, but also to protect other debtors.[206] Provisions enacted to protect debt-

---

199 *See In re* Davis, 2011 Bankr. LEXIS 4493 (Bankr. N.D. Tex. Nov. 22, 2011) (permitting expenses for pool maintenance, septic tank maintenance, yard maintenance, and trash disposal that were not typical in county to which local housing standard was applicable, where requiring debtors to move could require greater expenditures).

200 *In re* Cribbs, 387 B.R. 324 (Bankr. S.D. Ga. 2008) (special circumstances found when loan was used in attempt to avoid bankruptcy by repaying creditors); *In re* Lenton, 358 B.R. 651 (Bankr. E.D. Pa. 2006). *But see In re* Egebjerg, 574 F.3d 1045 (9th Cir. 2009) (pension loans were not unusual or special).

201 *In re* Sanders, 454 B.R. 855 (Bankr. M.D. Ala. 2011) (loans for child guaranteed by debtors); *In re* Martin, 371 B.R. 347 (Bankr. C.D. Ill. 2007); *In re* Knight, 370 B.R. 429 (Bankr. N.D. Ga. 2007); *In re* Delbecq, 368 B.R. 754 (Bankr. S.D. Ind. 2007); *In re* Haman, 366 B.R. 307 (Bankr. D. Del. 2007); *In re* Templeton, 365 B.R. 213 (Bankr. W.D. Okla. 2007). *See also In re* Pageau, 383 B.R. 221 (Bankr. D.N.H. 2008) (although special circumstances not found, court noted that there may have been different result if loans were incurred for training or education following an injury, disability, or employer plant closing). *But see In re* Siler, 426 B.R. 167 (Bankr. W.D.N.C. 2010); *In re* Carrillo, 421 B.R. 540, 545 (Bankr. D. Ariz. 2009).

202 11 U.S.C. § 707(b)(2)(B)(ii).

203 For an example of a statement of special circumstances that may be submitted to a United States trustee prior to a proceeding, see Form 15, Appx. G.3, *infra*.

204 *See In re* Jenkins, 2012 WL 2564901 (Bankr. W.D.N.C. July 2, 2012) (debtor no longer had income that caused means test failure); *In re* Siler, 426 B.R. 167 (Bankr. W.D.N.C. 2010) (although retirement plan contributions and loan repayment did not constitute special circumstances, they would be deductible in chapter 13, so creditors would receive nothing in chapter 13 and there was no reason to dismiss case even though presumption of abuse existed); *In re* Mravik, 399 B.R. 202 (Bankr. E.D. Wis. 2008) (debtor would not be required to pay creditors in chapter 13 because pension plan contributions would be permitted expenses and conversion would be meaningless); *In re* Skvorecz, 369 B.R. 638 (Bankr. D. Colo. 2007) (debtor would not be required to pay unsecured creditors in chapter 13 case, so dismissal would lead to absurd result). *But see In re* Haman, 366 B.R. 307 (Bankr. D. Del. 2007) (court must dismiss case in which there is a presumption of abuse unless special circumstances exist).

205 *See, e.g.*, H.R. Rep. No. 109-31, at 51 (2005) (available on this treatise's companion website).

206 The legislative history supports this conclusion. "We know that 80 percent of the people who file for bankruptcy make below median income. That means under the provisions of this bill, no fundamental changes will occur. They cannot be made to go into a chapter 13 unless they choose to do so." 151 Cong. Rec. S2054 (daily ed. Mar. 4, 2005) (statement of Sen. Sessions). "Any debtor who earns less than their State's median income and that includes about 80 percent of the debtors in question will remain in chapter 7." 151 Cong. Rec. S2113 (daily ed. Mar. 7, 2005) (statement of Sen. McConnell). "This bill clearly provides that people of limited income can still file under chapter 7 and get that fresh start.... There is a specific safe harbor built in for these individuals, so their debts can be wiped away, as is done right now." 151 Cong. Rec. S1856 (daily ed. Mar. 1, 2005) (statement of Sen. Grassley).

ors cannot be disregarded by a creditor or trustee in bringing an abuse motion, essentially by asserting some alternative means test other than that enacted by Congress. Even under prior law, section 707(b) motions based on ability to pay were almost always filed against higher-income debtors.

The United States Trustee Program has taken the position that ability to pay can be a basis for dismissal under the "totality of the circumstances" and "bad faith" provisions of section 707(b)(3), even if the debtor's current monthly income is below the applicable median income. As discussed below, such a use of the discretionary abuse provisions would eviscerate the bright line protections for lower-income debtors that Congress enacted.

13.4.7.2 Substantial Abuse Standard Changed to Abuse Standard

A case may now be dismissed under section 707(b) of the Code for "abuse," rather than for "substantial abuse."[207] This change is not likely to affect the result of section 707(b) motions, because few courts placed much weight on the requirement that the abuse be "substantial." The term "abuse" denotes conduct sufficiently deplorable that a court would not accept it; no court had held under prior law that a debtor's petition was an abuse but could nonetheless be permitted because it was not a substantial abuse.

13.4.7.3 Elimination of Explicit Presumption Favoring the Debtor

The 2005 amendments also eliminated the language in former section 707(b) that established a presumption in favor of granting a discharge to the debtor.[208] Congress had intended this presumption to limit the use of section 707(b) challenges only to egregious cases, but courts had largely ignored this presumption. It is not clear what the elimination of the language does, except in cases in which a presumption of abuse under the means test arises. The moving party will still have the burden of proof.

Even when a presumption of abuse arises under the means test, it is not clear what the elimination of the presumption in favor of discharge will have on the parties' evidentiary burdens. Does it just eliminate the burden of going forward on the motion? Once the presumption is overcome, is the bubble burst and does the burden of proof shift back to the moving party?

13.4.7.4 Dismissal for Bad Faith or Based on a Totality of Circumstances Showing Abuse

If the presumption of abuse is rebutted or does not arise, a court may still dismiss the case if the petition was filed in bad faith, or "the totality of the circumstances of the debtor's financial situation demonstrates abuse."[209] This provision does not change the law in most circuits, where a bad faith filing was grounds for dismissal under section 707(a). A bad faith finding was the equivalent to finding the case was an "abuse," normally based on an examination of the totality of the underlying circumstances.[210]

By placing the bad faith dismissal provision in section 707(b), Congress eliminated the possibility of a party or trustee moving for dismissal based on bad faith or the totality of circumstances if the debtor's income is under the median income threshold.[211]

The United States Trustee Program has argued that a debtor's filing may be abusive under the totality of the circumstances test based solely upon the debtor's ability to pay debts. This argument is erroneous, because to accept it would be to allow courts to implement a means test different than the objective test carefully crafted by Congress—crafted precisely because Congress did not wish courts to have so much discretion with respect to this issue.[212] Even under the law before the 2005 amendments, ability to pay, by itself, did not necessitate a finding of bad faith warranting dismissal under section 707(a).[213]

With the creation of the means test, Congress has effectively withdrawn consideration of the debtor's ability to pay from the more subjective and inherently vague inquiries under section 707(b)(3). The effect of the means test in eliminating the debtor's ability to pay as a factor from consideration under the "bad faith" test and the "totality of the circumstances" test of section 707(b)(3) is analogous to the effect the disposable income test of section 1325(b) had on the good faith test of section 1325(a)(3). Prior to the enactment of the disposable income test, some courts interpreted good faith to require "meaningful" payments to unsecured creditors; other courts took the opposite approach, interpreting the good faith requirement to refer to honesty and not to a debtor's substantive obligation with regard to level of payment. Some courts took a compromise position in which they looked to the "facts and circumstances" of each case and considered a number of factors, including a debtor's honesty and the levels of payments.[214] In 1984, Congress added the disposable income test,

---

207 11 U.S.C. § 707(b)(1).
208 Prior to the 2005 amendments section 707(b) contained the statement: "There shall be a presumption in favor of granting the relief requested by the debtor." Former 11 U.S.C. § 707(b).
209 11 U.S.C. § 707(b)(3).
210 See, e.g., In re Green, 934 F.2d 568 (4th Cir. 1991).
211 11 U.S.C. § 707(b)(6). See § 2.2.1, supra. See also In re Adolph, 441 B.R. 909 (Bankr. N.D. Ill. 2011) (bad faith was not grounds for dismissal under § 707(a) and creditor failed to meet filing deadline for § 707(b) motion).
212 In re Lavin, 424 B.R. 558 (Bankr. M.D. Fla. 2010) (ability to pay from postpetition income not sufficient to show abuse absent any other bad faith or bad conduct); In re Walker, 381 B.R. 620 (Bankr. M.D. Pa. 2008) (enactment of means test meant that income and expenses not a basis for dismissing case of debtor who passed means test); In re Nockerts, 357 B.R. 497 (Bankr. E.D. Wis. 2006) (totality of circumstances test must involve more than ability to pay). See also In re Baldino, 369 B.R. 858 (Bankr. M.D. Pa. 2007) (section 707(b)(3) cannot be used to allow consideration of non-filing spouse's income that was expressly excluded by Congress from means test calculation).
213 In re Perlin, 497 F.3d 364 (3d Cir. 2007).
214 See § 12.3.3, supra; 8 Collier on Bankruptcy ¶ 1325.LH (16th ed.).

which effectively replaced the use of the good faith test as the means for determining the adequate level of payments to creditors. As a result, most courts treat the disposable income test as eliminating the issue of adequate level of payments to creditors from the "facts and circumstances" of the case in applying the good faith test.[215] Most courts still consider other factors under the "facts and circumstances" of the good faith test, but rely on the disposable income test as the vehicle for determining the adequate level of payments to creditors.

The legislative history supports the conclusion that the means test is the way Congress chose to provide a uniform measure of ability to pay. Senator Hatch, a prime sponsor of the bill stated:

> All [the means test] does is identify those who can repay at least some of their debts. It makes certain they enter into a chapter 13 reorganization and repayment plan rather than let them simply walk away from their obligations, no matter how steep or outrageous.... The means test contained in the bill will provide a uniform standard to bankruptcy judges to evaluate the ability of bankruptcy filers to repay debts.[216]

Senator Grassley, another prime sponsor, emphasized that the means test is the mechanism to objectively determine a debtor's ability to pay by stating that "there is a simple process called a means test, where one puts down all of their income and assets and what they owe and through that makes a determination of whether they have the ability to repay some of their debt."[217] Comments by Representative Goodlatte also confirm that Congress intended a bright-line test to determine abuse based on a debtor's ability to pay. He stated that:

> The means test applies clear and well-defined standards to determine whether a debtor has the financial capability to pay his or her debts. The application of such objective standard will help ensure that the fresh start provisions of Chapter VII will be granted to those who need them, while debtors that can afford to repay some of their debts are steered toward filing chapter 13 bankruptcies.[218]

Consideration of a debtor's ability to pay under a section 707(b)(3) inquiry would not only be duplicative and unnecessary, it would once again create a subjective and variable test that would render the amendments to section 707(b) meaningless. It would be contrary to the Congressional record, not to mention illogical, to find that Congress developed such an elaborate, objective test intending that courts should effectively ignore its mandate and return to the nebulous inquiries of the past. In essence, to determine that a debtor has the ability to pay debts even though the means test concludes otherwise would be to invent a new means test, different from the uniform standard enacted by Congress after great deliberation and effort to ensure that it appropriately balanced all of the interests involved.

Ignoring the means test result would also result in contravening policy choices carefully made by Congress as to factors that should be considered in determining a debtor's ability to pay. For example, Congress specifically excluded Social Security benefits from current monthly income; a choice that is consistent with other amendments that protect retirement benefits at the expense of creditors. By comparing the *total* of allowed expenses to the debtor's current monthly income, Congress clearly intended that a debtor might spend more than the allowance for one category (for example, rent) and less for another (for example, food). Courts should not undermine this policy by considering additional income available when the debtor's expenses for a particular item are less than the means test allows.[219] Similarly, by permitting debtors to deduct the amounts specified in the IRS guidelines rather than limiting debtors to actual expenses, Congress has chosen not to penalize debtors who attempt to save money by spending less than the IRS allowances. And courts should not undermine the legislative compromises made between secured and unsecured creditors by ruling that secured debts are too high and a debtor should not be paying all secured debts.[220] By asking courts to determine whether a debtor's ability to pay constitutes an abuse through methods other than the means test, the United States Trustee Program is attempting to circumvent the policy decisions made by Congress. Neither the United States trustee nor the courts should second-guess Congress' choices. Moreover, it is not the function of the United States trustee to favor unse-

---

See also Flygare v. Boulden, 709 F.2d 1344, 1347–1348 (10th Cir. 1983); *In re Estus*, 695 F.2d 311, 316–317 (8th Cir. 1982).

215 *See* § 12.3.3, *supra*; 8 Collier on Bankruptcy ¶ 1325.04[1] (16th ed.). *See also In re Smith*, 848 F.2d 813 (7th Cir. 1988); *Educ. Assistance Corp. v. Zellner*, 827 F.2d 1222 (8th Cir. 1987).

216 151 Cong. Rec. S1842–S1843 (daily ed. Mar. 1, 2005) (statement of Sen. Hatch).

217 151 Cong. Rec. S2327 (daily ed. Mar. 9, 2005) (statement of Sen. Grassley). *See also* 151 Cong. Rec. S1856 (daily ed. Mar. 1, 2005) (statement of Sen. Grassley) ("This bill clearly provides that people of limited income can still file under chapter 7 and get that fresh start.... There is a specific safe harbor built in for these individuals, so their debts can be wiped away, as is done right now.").

218 151 Cong. Rec. H2053 (daily ed. Apr. 14, 2005) (statement of Rep. Goodlatte).

219 See cases cited in § 13.4.3.2.7, *supra*, holding that failure to devote Social Security benefits to payment of creditors is not bad faith.

220 *Moutousis v. United States (In re Moutousis)*, 418 B.R. 703 (E.D. Mich. 2009) (same); *In re Lorenca*, 422 B.R. 665 (Bankr. N.D. Ill. 2010) (denying dismissal motion that was based on allegedly excessive mortgage payments of debtors); *In re Rudmose*, 2010 WL 4882059 (Bankr. N.D. Ga. Nov. 8, 2010) (same; dismissal not warranted just because house debtors reasonably bought ten years earlier was now too big and expensive for them); *In re Dumas*, 419 B.R. 704 (Bankr. E.D. Tex. 2009) (same); *In re Jensen*, 407 B.R. 378, 391 (Bankr. C.D. Cal. 2008) (debtors should not be required to default on secured debts; debtors also did not need to reaffirm secured debts to deduct them, even though United States trustee suspected they would abandon collateral after bankruptcy); *In re Johnson*, 399 B.R. 72 (Bankr. S.D. Cal. 2008). *See also In re Wick*, 421 B.R. 206 (Bankr. D. Md. 2010) (denying objections to confirmation that were based on debtor's allegedly excessive mortgage payments). *But see Calhoun v. United States Tr.*, 650 F.3d 338 (4th Cir. 2011) (affirming finding of abuse based on debtors' extravagant and excessive expenses, without consideration of Social Security income).

cured creditors over secured creditors by forcing a debtor to default on secured debts in order to pay unsecured debts. Rather the goal of the court and the Unites States trustees should be simply to apply the law as Congress wrote it.

13.4.7.5 Dismissal for an Abusive Rejection of an Executory Contract

Section 707(b)(3) adds a new provision providing for dismissal based on a rejection of an executory personal services contract. Dismissal based on these grounds was a compromise reached by Congress on an issue related to music recording contracts rejected by debtors. A case may be abusive if a contract is rejected for reasons other than the financial need of the debtor. This provision only applies in chapter 7, because section 103(a) of the Code limits the applicability of provisions in chapter 7 to chapter 7 cases.

13.4.8 Procedures for Means Testing Under Section 707(b)

The bankruptcy clerk must provide written notice to creditors within ten days after the filing of the petition when the case is presumed to be abusive.[221] This notice is based on the Statement of Current Monthly Income and Means Test Calculation, which requires the debtor to indicate whether a presumption of abuse arises.[222] This statement may be amended if an initial calculation proves to be incorrect. If the debtor does not file the statement within ten days of the petition, the clerk must instead notify creditors that the debtor has not filed the statement and that further notice will be given if the debtor later files a statement indicating a presumption of abuse.[223] The applicable notice is given as part of the notice of the meeting of creditors.[224]

Section 704(b)(1) of the Code establishes time frames for the United States trustee or bankruptcy administrator to take certain actions relating to the means test. They must review all materials filed by debtors, and within ten days after the meeting of creditors file a statement as to whether a presumption of abuse arises. Presumably the ten days runs from the conclusion of the creditors meeting.[225] However, there is certainly an argument, based on the statutory reference to the "first meeting of creditors" that the time runs from the first date set for the meeting, and that failure to file a statement of presumed abuse precludes a later motion to dismiss based on the means test presumption.[226] And, when there is no dispute about the deadline, several courts have held that the United States trustee may not file a motion based on the presumption of abuse if the statement is not timely filed.[227] In some instances the United States trustee has filed a statement within the ten-day period indicating that it has not yet determined whether the presumption of abuse arises. Several courts have held that this statement of "no determination" is insufficient to satisfy the United States trustee's obligation under section 704(b)(1)(A).[228]

Within seven days of the filing of the statement under section 704(b)(1)(A), the bankruptcy court must provide a copy of the statement to all creditors.[229] It would appear that the court can provide the statement electronically to the extent possible. Within thirty days after the filing of the statement by the United States trustee or bankruptcy administrator that a presumption of abuse arises, they must either file a motion to dismiss or convert under section 707(b) or file a new statement setting forth the reasons why such a motion is not appropriate. Creditors are no longer prohibited from communicating with the United States trustee or bankruptcy administrator about section 707(b) motions or providing information to the court (except through improper *ex parte* contacts).[230] The debtor's counsel may also wish to communicate with the United States trustee or Bankruptcy Administrator to explain why a motion to dismiss is inappropriate based on special circumstances or a different interpretation of the means test.

Rule 1017(e) requires that notice of a motion to dismiss on the basis of abuse include all matters to be submitted to or considered by the court at the hearing. Bankruptcy Rule 1007(e)(1) requires the motion to state with particularity the circumstances alleged to constitute abuse. Because the Code and the Rules require a hearing prior to dismissal, debtor's counsel has an opportunity to present evidence and arguments to overcome evidence presented to show substantial abuse.[231] A motion

---

221 11 U.S.C. § 342(d).
  "Written notice" as provided under this section probably would encompass electronic notice.
222 *See* Official Form 22A (reprinted in Appx. D, *infra*).
223 Fed. R. Bankr. P. 5008.
224 Official Forms 9A, 9C, reprinted in Appx. D, *infra*.
225 *In re* Reed, 422 B.R. 214 (C.D. Cal. 2009). *See In re* Molitor, 395 B.R. 197 (Bankr. S.D. Ga. 2008).
226 *See In re* Clark, 393 B.R. 578 (Bankr. E.D. Tenn. 2008); *In re* Close, 384 B.R. 856 (D. Kan. 2008).

227 *In re* Draisey, 395 B.R. 79 (B.A.P. 8th Cir. 2008) (deadline precludes motion based on presumption, but not motion under section 707(b)(3)); *In re* Reed, 422 B.R. 214 (C.D. Cal. 2009); *In re* Wise, 453 B.R. 220 (Bankr. D. Vt. 2011); *In re* Perrotta, 378 B.R. 434 (Bankr. D.N.H. 2007); *In re* Robertson, 370 B.R. 804 (Bankr. D. Minn. 2007). *See also In re* Byrne, 376 B.R. 700 (Bankr. W.D. Ark. 2007) (although section 704(b)(1) statement is prerequisite to motion based on presumption of abuse, it is not required for motion under section 707(b)(3) when presumption does not arise or is rebutted).
228 *See, e.g., In re* Robertson, 370 B.R. 804 (Bankr. D. Minn. 2007). *See, e.g., In re* Reed, 422 B.R. 214 (C.D. Cal. 2009).
229 11 U.S.C. § 704(b)(1)(B).
230 Section 102(e) of the 2005 Act states: "Nothing in this title shall limit the ability of a creditor to provide information to a judge (except for information communicated *ex parte*, unless otherwise permitted by applicable law), United States trustee (or bankruptcy administrator, if any), or trustee." Pub. L. No. 109-8, § 102(e), 119 Stat. 23 (2005). However it does not appear that this language amends any section of the Code or that it will be codified as a Code provision.
231 Fed. R. Bankr. P. 1017(e). *See, e.g., In re* Strong, 84 B.R. 541 (Bankr. N.D. Ind. 1988) (procedure required before *sua sponte* dismissal includes notice to debtor of court's concerns and opportunity for debtor and/or counsel to explain); *In re* Gaukler, 63 B.R. 224 (Bankr. D.N.D. 1986) (court would not impose its own values

under section 707(b) must be made within sixty days following the first date set for the meeting of creditors and cannot be entertained once a discharge is entered.[232] Additionally, failure to properly provide notice or to hold the requisite hearing would certainly be grounds for challenging dismissal pursuant to section 707(b).[233] Although the question is not free from doubt, the legislative history suggests that review in an appeal should be under an error of law, rather than an abuse of discretion, standard.[234]

It is safe to say that a dismissal under section 707(b) is without prejudice.[235] If the debtor's circumstances change, she is free to file again at any time, although there may be limitations to the automatic stay available if the case is filed within one year after the dismissal.[236] The debtor also, of course, may choose to convert the case to chapter 13 to avoid dismissal.[237]

13.5 Chapter 7 Involuntary Dismissal Based on Certain Crimes

Section 707(c) of the Code provides that a voluntary chapter 7 case may be dismissed on the motion of a victim of a "crime of violence"[238] or a "drug trafficking crime."[239] Section 707(c)(2) makes clear that a conviction is required. Dismissal must also be in the "best interest of the victim." However the court may not dismiss a case under this section if the debtor establishes by a preponderance of the evidence that the filing is necessary to satisfy a claim for a domestic support obligation.

This provision is rarely invoked. A victim of a crime of violence would usually be better off bringing a nondischargeability action under section 523(a)(6), because other debts would be discharged and the debtor would be in a better position to satisfy the debt owed to the victim post-discharge.[240] Moreover, most drug trafficking crimes probably do not have identifiable victims.

13.6 Effect of Dismissal

A dismissal generally places the debtor and the creditors back in the situation they were in before the case began. Unless the court orders otherwise, a dismissal vacates most bankruptcy orders and returns the parties as much as possible to the status quo prior to the filing of the petition.[241] A chapter 13 trustee should return to the debtor any funds that she is still holding, except for administrative expenses allowed by the court and adequate protection payments ordered by the court under section 1326(a)(3).[242] In some cases, dismissal may be the best option for a debtor who cannot complete a chapter 13 plan, leaving the debtor to deal with creditors as if no bankruptcy had occurred. Obviously, to the extent that creditors have been paid before the case is dismissed, the debtor is entitled to the benefit of these payments. Some debts may have been completely paid, or partially paid to an extent sufficient for the debtor to work out an agreement directly with the creditors on the remaining balances due.

Once the case is dismissed, the debtor has the option to file again under either chapter 13 or chapter 7. However, if this option is in the debtor's interest, care should be taken to ensure that the anticipated subsequent case will not be barred by section 109(g),[243] and the possible limitations on the automatic stay under section 362(c)(3) or (4) must also be considered.[244]

It should be noted that both the right to dismiss and the right to convert may be lost if the debtor does not exercise them in a timely manner. Once the case is converted to a chapter 7 case, perhaps on request of creditors, the chapter 13 right to dismiss

---

after proof that debtor's expenses actually included disproportionate religious contributions); *In re* Hamze, 57 B.R. 37 (Bankr. E.D. Mich. 1985) (debtor's disproportionate consumer debt for trip to Lebanon was reasonable in light of explanation that his family's home had been hit by gun shells).

232 Fed. R. Bankr. P. 1017(e); *In re* Cronk, 124 B.R. 759 (Bankr. N.D. Ill. 1990).

The United States trustee may, within the sixty-day period, request an extension of the deadline for cause. *See In re* Bomarito, 448 B.R. 242 (Bankr. E.D. Cal. 2011) (U.S. trustee motion for extension denied where no cause existed, in that U.S. trustee had taken no action before extension motion was filed, case was not complex, and debtors had not been uncooperative).

233 *See, e.g.*, Cent. Bank of Wooday-Hewitt v. Spark, 61 B.R. 285 (W.D. Tex. 1986).

234 S. Rep. No. 98-65, at 53, 54 (1983). *But see In re* Behlke, 358 F.3d 429 (6th Cir. 2004) (applying abuse of discretion standard).

The standard may be different depending on whether the appeal concerns application of the means test rules or the more discretionary "all of the circumstances" bad faith standard.

235 11 U.S.C. § 349(a).

236 11 U.S.C. § 362(c)(3),(4). *See* Ch. 9, *supra*.

The stay limitations of section 362(c)(3) and (4), however, do not apply if the prior case was dismissed under section 707(b) and the new case is not filed under chapter 7. *See* §§ 9.3.3.2, 9.3.3.3, *supra*.

237 11 U.S.C. § 707(b)(1).

238 The term "crime of violence" has the meaning given such term in 18 U.S.C. § 16.

239 The term "drug trafficking crime" has the meaning given such term in 18 U.S.C. § 924(c)(2).

240 This supposition may not be true, however, if federal exemptions are claimed by the debtor, as more property might thereby be protected from execution than under state law.

241 11 U.S.C. § 349(b).

242 11 U.S.C. § 1326(a)(2); *In re* Nash, 765 F.2d 1410 (9th Cir. 1985); *In re* Majkowski, 2011 WL 2652386 (Bankr. N.D. W. Va. July 6, 2011); *In re* Sexton, 397 B.R. 375 (Bankr. M.D. Tenn. 2008) (trustee required to return funds to debtor even though federal agency attempted to levy on them); *In re* Hampton, 383 B.R. 560 (Bankr. S.D. Ga. 2008) (court deducted attorney fees allowed as administrative expenses and adequate protection payments from amount returned to debtor). *But see In re* Steenstra, 307 B.R. 732 (B.A.P. 1st Cir. 2004) (creditor could levy on funds in trustee's hands to which debtor is entitled upon dismissal); *In re* Witte, 279 B.R. 585 (Bankr. E.D. Cal. 2002) (when debtor's house had been sold pursuant to court order prior to dismissal, proceeds held by trustee were not plan proceeds that had to be returned to debtor; instead had to be turned over to holders of liens on house).

243 *See* §§ 3.2.1, 9.7.3.1.5, *supra*, for a discussion of 11 U.S.C. § 109(g) and other issues connected with serial bankruptcy filings. Additionally it should be noted that, unless there is some change in circumstances, a subsequent chapter 13 case may be alleged to be filed in bad faith. *See generally* § 12.3.3, *supra*.

244 *See* Chapter 9, *supra*, for discussion of section 362(c)(3) and (4).

the case ceases to exist. Similarly, once a case is dismissed over the debtor's objection, no further right to convert exists. Thus it is important to exercise these rights before an involuntary conversion or dismissal occurs. Although a new chapter 7 petition can usually be filed after a chapter 13 case is dismissed,[245] it would entail needless effort and a new filing fee. The consequences of an involuntary conversion can be worse; conversion may mean the loss of nonexempt property that is critical to the debtor's affairs.

13.7 Conversion of a Bankruptcy Case

13.7.1 Conversion from Chapter 7 to Chapter 13

Another way of initiating chapter 13 relief is through conversion from a chapter 7 case. Any debtor who has begun a chapter 7 case may convert it to a chapter 13 case at any time during the case provided the debtor is eligible for relief under chapter 13.[246]

The Supreme Court has held that the right of a debtor to convert from chapter 7 to chapter 13 is not absolute and can be denied for bad faith.[247] The Court held that, in the rare situation in which a case would be subject to immediate dismissal or conversion back to chapter 7 under section 1307(a) for bad faith, a bankruptcy court may deny a conversion to chapter 13, essentially because the debtor is not eligible for chapter 13.[248]

A court determination that debts are nondischargeable in chapter 7 does not preclude conversion and, in fact, conversion may be the best strategy in such a situation given the somewhat broader discharge available in chapter 13.[249]

A debtor may convert a case from chapter 7 to chapter 13 as of right only if the case was commenced as a chapter 7 case; if the case had previously been converted to chapter 7, a second (or third) conversion may occur only with the court's permission.[250] A few courts have held that a debtor who has already once converted a case from another chapter to chapter 7 may not be permitted to convert it to chapter 13 thereafter, even at the discretion of the court.[251] This reading of Code section 706 is at odds with normal rules of statutory construction. Section 706(a) of the Code provides that *the debtor* may convert a case to another chapter as a matter of right if the case has not been previously converted. Section 706(c) states that *the court* may not convert a case to chapter 13 unless the debtor so requests. Because the debtor has an almost absolute right to convert the case when the case has not been previously converted, section 706(c) would make no sense unless there were other situations when the court could convert the case to chapter 13 in addition to those in which the debtor could convert the case. Such situations, obviously, would be those in which the debtor requested conversion after there had been a prior conversion, as the court is not permitted to convert the case to chapter 13 except at the request of the debtor.[252] In any event, limitations in section 706 do not apply when the case is converted under section 707(b).[253]

13.7.2 Conversion from Chapter 13 to Chapter 7

The debtor has an absolute right to convert a chapter 13 case to chapter 7,[254] without any showing of hardship, and in many respects such a conversion provides the same relief as the chapter 13 hardship discharge.[255] If only one of two joint debtors wishes to convert to chapter 7, the case can be converted for that debtor and can continue under chapter 13 for the

---

245 A new petition is expressly barred after an involuntary dismissal only if the debtor willfully disobeyed court orders or willfully failed to appear to prosecute the case, and then only for 180 days. 11 U.S.C. § 109(g). See § 3.2.1, *supra*.
However the automatic stay in a new case could be limited by section 362(c)(3) or (4).
246 11 U.S.C. § 706(a).
247 Marrama v. Citizens Bank of Mass., 549 U.S. 365, 127 S. Ct. 1105, 166 L. Ed. 2d 956 (2007).
248 *In re* Tufano, 2011 WL 1473384 (Bankr. M.D. Pa. Apr. 19, 2011) (conversion permitted because debtors' false representations in statement of affairs were result of bad advice from former counsel and debtors had shown good faith in rectifying them).
249 *Compare* 11 U.S.C. § 727 *with* 11 U.S.C. § 1328. See Ch. 15, *infra*.
One court has held that a case may be converted for this reason even after the debtor's chapter 7 discharge is granted. *In re* Caldwell, 67 B.R. 296 (Bankr. E.D. Tenn. 1986). See also *In re* Starling, 359 B.R. 901 (Bankr. N.D. Ill. 2007) (case could be converted after discharge if court granted debtors relief from discharge order prior to conversion). After discharge, however, it may be less problematic to simply re-file under chapter 13, because such filing is not barred by any provision of the Code. See § 12.10, *supra*.

250 11 U.S.C. § 706(a), (b). See *In re* Masterson, 141 B.R. 84 (Bankr. E.D. Pa. 1992); *In re* Walker, 77 B.R. 803 (Bankr. D. Nev. 1987) (section 706(a) constitutes an absolute ban on reconversion); *In re* Hollar, 70 B.R. 337 (Bankr. E.D. Tenn. 1987).
251 *See, e.g., In re* Carter, 84 B.R. 744 (D. Kan. 1988); *In re* Hanna, 100 B.R. 591 (Bankr. M.D. Fla. 1989).
252 In jurisdictions in which reconversion is problematic, filing a new case under chapter 13 after completion of the chapter 7 case is nevertheless possible, because such re-filing is permitted under the Code. See § 12.10, *supra*. This strategy would not work, of course, if the need to reconvert is based on a creditor action, such as foreclosure, which will be completed before the new case can be filed. The debtor also would not be eligible for a chapter 13 discharge but would presumably not need one, because most debts would have been discharged in the chapter 7 case.
253 Advanced Control Solutions, Inc. v. Justice, 639 F.3d 838 (8th Cir. 2011).
254 11 U.S.C. § 1307(a); *In re* Taylor, 472 B.R. 570 (C.D. Cal. 2012); *In re* Majkowski, 2011 WL 2652386 (Bankr. N.D. W. Va. July 6, 2011) (right to convert under § 1307(a) is absolute; bankruptcy court erred in dismissing chapter 13 for lack of payments after conversion had occurred); Nady v. Defrantz (*In re* Defrantz), 454 B.R. 108 (B.A.P. 9th Cir. 2011) (no bad faith exception to right to convert). *But see In re* Spiser, 232 B.R. 669 (Bankr. N.D. Tex. 1999) (case could not be converted after both debtors had died).
The Bankruptcy Rules provide that the debtor need only file a notice of conversion and that no court order is necessary to effect the conversion. Fed. R. Bankr. P. 1017(d).
255 The hardship discharge is discussed in § 8.7.5.3, *supra*.

debtor who does not wish to convert.[256] A new set of schedules generally need not be filed; however, a statement of intention must be submitted within thirty days after the order of conversion is entered or before the first date set for the meeting of creditors, whichever is earlier.[257] A chapter 7 means test calculation form may also be required after conversion.[258]

The debtor must also file a supplemental schedule of debts arising since the chapter 13 case was initially filed.[259] These will be treated as if they arose prior to the commencement of the case.[260] Thus, when applicable, the automatic stay prevents creditor action on these debts, and they may be discharged.[261] After the conversion, the debtor's nonexempt property, if any, is liquidated, and the debtor receives a chapter 7 discharge.

Prior to the 1994 amendments to the Code, some courts had held that the property of the estate in a converted case included all property acquired after the petition was filed and before the conversion.[262] However, it is now clear that property acquired postpetition may be included in the chapter 7 estate only if the case is converted in bad faith.[263] And section 348(f)(2), the provision creating this bad faith exception, applies only if the debtor converts the case, and not when conversion is sought by another party.[264] In addition, for exemption purposes, any postpetition increase in the value of property acquired prepetition should not be included in the estate after conversion.[265] Even in the rare cases in which postpetition property is found to be property of the estate because of bad faith, the debtor should be entitled to exempt postpetition earnings held by the trustee and other property acquired after the chapter 13 case was filed, at least to the extent of applicable exemptions.[266] If there is nonexempt property in the estate, it is liquidated regardless of what the unsecured creditors have already received under the plan (at least to the extent necessary to pay all creditors in full).[267] Therefore, in cases in which the debtor has nonexempt assets and can meet the requirements, a hardship discharge is often preferable to conversion. Similarly, a hardship discharge or dismissal may be better for the debtor if there are grounds for denial of a chapter 7 discharge.[268]

On the other hand, an advantage of conversion is that it allows postpetition debts arising before conversion to be treated as if they arose prepetition.[269] These debts may thus be discharged if they are dischargeable in chapter 7.[270] This rule may make conversion an attractive option if the debtor has significant unsecured postpetition debts.

Conversion of the case does not create a new automatic stay when relief from the stay has been previously granted.[271] It may sometimes be possible, however, to move to have a stay reimposed if the debtor can ensure that the creditor's rights will be protected.[272]

The debtor may wish to convert if the reasons for the initial choice of chapter 13 no longer apply. For example, the debtor may have chosen chapter 13 to protect property, such as an

---

256 *In re* Seligman, 417 B.R. 171 (Bankr. E.D.N.Y. 2009).

257 Fed. R. Bankr. P. 1019(1). *See* Official Form 8 (reprinted in Appx. D, *infra*).

Additional (postpetition) debts to existing creditors, such as utilities, should be listed to ensure that they are discharged.

258 Official Form 22A (reprinted in Appx. D, *infra*). *See In re* Kellett, 379 B.R. 332 (Bankr. D. Or. 2007) (new Official Form 22 required, may be waived upon motion); *In re* Fox, 370 B.R. 639 (Bankr. D.N.J. 2007) (new Official Form 22 not required after conversion); *In re* Edwards, 367 B.R. 921 (Bankr. S.D. Ga. 2007) (new Official Form 22 not required for below-median-income debtors because information would be unchanged from original Form 22C). *See also In re* Dudley, 405 B.R. 790 (Bankr. W.D. Va. 2009) (§ 707(b) does not apply in case converted from chapter 13 to chapter 7); § 13.4.1, *supra*.

259 Fed. R. Bankr. P. 1019(5).

260 11 U.S.C. § 348(d); *In re* Fickling, 361 F.3d 172 (2d Cir. 2004); *In re* Deiter, 33 B.R. 547 (Bankr. W.D. Wis. 1983).

261 It is not uncommon, for example, for postpetition utility arrearages to be discharged following conversion from chapter 13 to chapter 7.

262 11 U.S.C. § 1306(a); *In re* Calder, 973 F.2d 862 (10th Cir. 1992); *In re* Lybrook, 951 F.2d 136 (7th Cir. 1991); Resendez v. Lindquist, 691 F.2d 397 (8th Cir. 1982); *In re* Winchester, 46 B.R. 492 (B.A.P. 9th Cir. 1984. *Cf. In re* Young, 66 F.3d 376 (1st Cir. 1995) (1994 amendments show congressional intent that property be determined as of date chapter 13 case was commenced); *In re* Williamson, 804 F.2d 1355 (5th Cir. 1986) (homestead exemption eligibility determined as of date of first bankruptcy filing); Koch v. Myrvold, 784 F.2d 862 (8th Cir. 1986) (property inherited after 180 days from filing of chapter 11 case not property of estate when case converted to chapter 7); *In re* Bobroff, 766 F.2d 797 (3d Cir. 1985) (property acquired during chapter 13 case would not become property of estate after conversion to chapter 7).

263 11 U.S.C. § 348(f)(2). *See In re* Bejarano, 302 B.R. 559 (Bankr. N.D. Ohio 2003) (no bad faith in converting case after acquisition of tax refunds and personal injury claims); *In re* Wiczek-Spalding, 223 B.R. 538 (Bankr. D. Minn. 1998) (taking advantage of Code protections is not bad faith on part of debtor who converted to chapter 7 to exclude employee severance pay from property of estate).

264 *In re* Bostick, 400 B.R. 348, 359 (Bankr. D. Conn. 2009).

265 Taylor v. Burns, 344 B.R. 523 (W.D. Ky. 2004) (tax refunds derived from postpetition wages were not property of estate in chapter 7 case after conversion from chapter 13); *In re* Slack, 290 B.R. 282 (Bankr. D.N.J. 2003), *aff'd*, 112 Fed. Appx. 868 (3d Cir. 2004); *In re* Page, 250 B.R. 465 (Bankr. D.N.H. 2000); *In re* Horton, 130 B.R. 326 (Bankr. D. Colo. 1991). *See also* Warren v. Peterson, 298 B.R. 322 (N.D. Ill. 2003) (property was implicitly valued by confirmation order at value listed on schedules and that valuation applies if case converted to chapter 7).

For purposes of determining an allowed secured claim, any valuations of property made in the chapter 13 case do not apply in a case converted to chapter 7. 11 U.S.C. § 348(f)(1)(B).

266 Arkison v. Plata, 958 F.2d 918 (9th Cir. 1992); *In re* Brown, 118 B.R. 1008 (Bankr. E.D. Mo. 1990). *But see* Resendez v. Lindquist, 691 F.2d 397 (8th Cir. 1982).

267 *See In re* John, 352 B.R. 895 (Bankr. N.D. Fla. 2006).

268 *See* Standiferd v. United States (*In re* Standiferd), 641 F.3d 1209 (10th Cir. 2011) (discharge may be denied for preconversion order of court).

269 11 U.S.C. § 348(d); *In re* Deiter, 33 B.R. 547 (Bankr. W.D. Wis. 1983).

270 *See* Ch. 15, *infra*.

271 *See generally In re* State Airlines, 873 F.2d 264 (11th Cir. 1989) (conversion from chapter 11 to chapter 7 does not trigger new stay).

272 A stay may be available under 11 U.S.C. § 105 particularly as to property that might be liquidated for the benefit of unsecured creditors. This stay may allow a debtor facing foreclosure to obtain the benefit of an applicable homestead exemption in the liquidation process.

automobile, from repossession.[273] If that property is later destroyed or is no longer of value to the debtor, chapter 13 may no longer be necessary.

Conversion may also be advantageous when the debtor is unable to complete her plan and is ineligible for a hardship discharge, yet wishes to obtain a discharge of unsecured debts or to preserve the effect of lien avoidance or other orders obtained under chapter 13. If a case is voluntarily or involuntarily dismissed, rather than converted, liens avoided in the bankruptcy are reinstated.[274]

Conversion to chapter 7 can also be ordered against the debtor's will upon request of a party in interest, such as a creditor. The court may order conversion only "for cause," such as unreasonable delay to the prejudice of creditors, failure to file a timely plan, failure to commence plan payments, denial of confirmation along with denial of time to file a modified plan, a material default by the debtor in performance of a plan, revocation of confirmation, or termination of a plan according to its own terms.[275] However, if the debtor is a farmer, the Code provides that the court may not convert the case to chapter 7 unless the debtor so requests.[276] There are also some situations in which, because of the scope of relief available in chapter 11 or 12, conversion to those chapters may be an alternative to remaining in chapter 13.[277]

13.7.3 Effect of Conversion

Section 348(f) of the Code provides that property of the estate in a case converted to chapter 7 from chapter 13 does not include property acquired after the original petition was filed.[278] The only exception to this rule is when the case is converted in "bad faith," in which case the court can order that property acquired during the chapter 13 case becomes property of the chapter 7 estate.[279] There is little guidance regarding what a bad faith conversion might be.[280] Presumably, a conversion could be found to be in bad faith if the debtor never really intended to proceed under chapter 13. Courts should not find bad faith in cases in which the debtor is unable to complete a plan due to financial hardship, even if the debtor has acquired significant property interests since the original filing.

However, if the debtor had significant nonexempt property at the outset of the chapter 13 case, that property is considered property of the estate to the extent the debtor retains it at the time of conversion.[281] The trustee is entitled to liquidate property only if there is still nonexempt equity in the property at the time of the conversion.[282] Such property can be liquidated by a chapter 7 trustee if the case is converted, even if the debtor has made some payments to unsecured creditors.[283] In this situation a chapter 13 hardship discharge, if available, is usually a better alternative, and even dismissal may be preferable to conversion.[284]

The 2005 amendments to section 348(f) muddied the law regarding treatment of secured claims in converted cases. For cases filed before October 17, 2005, section 348(f)(1)(B) provided that any valuations of property and of allowed secured claims made in a chapter 13 case were binding in the converted case and that allowed secured claims were reduced by the amounts paid under the chapter 13 plan. The 2005 amendments altered section 348(f)(1)(B) by providing that such valuations apply only in a case converted to chapter 11 or 12, but not in a case converted to chapter 7.

The 2005 amendments also added new section 348(f)(1)(C), which applies to cases converted from chapter 13 to chapter 7. This subsection provides that, with respect to cases converted

---

273 See generally Chapter 11, *supra*, for a discussion of the use of chapter 13 in dealing with secured creditors.
274 11 U.S.C. § 349. See In re Sadler, 935 F.2d 918 (7th Cir. 1991).
275 11 U.S.C. § 1307(c).
276 11 U.S.C. § 1307(f).
This provision is in accord with the general bar against involuntary bankruptcies involving farmers. *See* 11 U.S.C. § 303(a).
277 11 U.S.C. § 1307(d).
For example, when the chapter 13 debt limits make dismissal unexpectedly likely under 11 U.S.C. § 109(e), conversion to chapter 11 remains possible. Rudd v. Laughlin, 866 F.2d 1040 (8th Cir. 1989); *In re* Wenberg, 94 B.R. 631 (B.A.P. 9th Cir. 1988), *aff'd*, 902 F.2d 768 (9th Cir. 1990). *See* § 6.3.4, *supra*, (brief discussion of chapter 11); Ch. 17, *infra* (brief discussion of chapter 12).
278 11 U.S.C. § 348(f)(1)(A); *In re* Stamm, 222 F.3d 216 (5th Cir. 2000) (wages of debtor in hands of chapter 13 trustee at time of conversion not property of chapter 7 estate and must be returned to debtor); DeHart v. Michael, 446 B.R. 665 (M.D. Pa. 2011) (undistributed funds held by chapter 13 trustee at time of conversion must be returned to debtor; Taylor v. Burns, 344 B.R. 523 (W.D. Ky. 2004) (tax refunds based upon postpetition wages not property of estate after conversion); *In re* Burt, 2009 WL 2386102 (Bankr. N.D. Ala. July 31, 2009) (equity created by mortgage payments during chapter 13 case did not inure to benefit of chapter 7 estate after conversion); *In re* Niles, 342 B.R. 72 (Bankr. D. Ariz. 2006) (postpetition appreciation over valuation that was implicitly accepted by plan confirmation was not property of chapter 7 estate after conversion).

279 11 U.S.C. § 348(f)(2).
280 *See In re* Bejarano, 302 B.R. 559 (Bankr. N.D. Ohio 2003) (using conversion provisions to protect assets acquired after petition but before conversion not bad faith); *In re* Wiczek-Spalding, 223 B.R. 538 (Bankr. D. Minn. 1998) (taking advantage of Code provisions is not bad faith on part of debtor who converted to chapter 7 to exclude employee severance pay from property of estate).
281 *Cf.* Warfield v. Salazar (*In re* Salazar), 465 B.R. 875 (B.A.P. 9th Cir. 2012) (tax refund to which debtors were entitled on date of chapter 13 petition was not property estate after conversion because it had been spent); *In re* Krick, 373 B.R. 593 (Bankr. N.D. Ind. 2007) (because debtor had conveyed property after confirmation and before conversion, it was not property of chapter 7 estate after conversion).
282 *In re* Lang, 437 B.R. 70 (Bankr. W.D.N.Y. 2010) (property is to be valued as of conversion date, even if value has decreased since petition).
283 *See In re* John, 352 B.R. 895 (Bankr. N.D. Fla. 2006). *But see In re* Grein, 435 B.R. 695 (Bankr. D. Colo. 2010) (in case converted from chapter 7 to chapter 13 and then reconverted, chapter trustee could not liquidate nonexempt assets because unsecured creditors had already received more than they would have received in chapter 7 filed on petition date).
284 The hardship discharge is discussed in § 8.7.5.3, *supra*.

from chapter 13, the claim of any creditor holding security[285] shall continue to be secured by that security unless the full amount of such claim determined under applicable nonbankruptcy law has been paid as of the date of conversion, notwithstanding any valuation or determination of the amount of the allowed secured claim made for purposes of the case under chapter 13.[286]

This language raises a number of questions. The language does not conflict with the first portion of section 348(f)(1)(B), as it contains no dictate concerning the valuation of property. However, for cases converted to chapter 7, this change means that the valuation of property must be determined by reference to some other source of law, because section 348(f)(1)(B) is made explicitly inapplicable to cases converted to chapter 7. This change may be advantageous to debtors who have converted to chapter 7 because, at least with respect to personal property, the property's value is likely to have gone down during the pendency of the chapter 13 case. For these debtors the valuation of the property should be determined under section 506(a)(2) of the Code, which provides that, with respect to personal property acquired for personal, family, or household purposes, replacement value shall be determined "*considering the age and condition of the property at the time value is determined.*"[287] This provision would apply to a redemption proceeding under section 722 of the Code in the converted case, which could occur several years after the chapter 13 valuation and after significant depreciation of the property has occurred.[288] In any event, if the debtor has paid off the allowed secured claim on personal property, such as a vehicle, the full benefit of having paid off that claim may be lost in a conversion because the debtor may still have to make additional payments to retain the property. In such situations a hardship discharge, if available, offers the advantage of allowing the debtor to retain the collateral without making further payments.

In the determination of exemptions, creditors cannot benefit from an increase in the debtor's equity because value is defined in section 522(a)(2) as value on the date of the petition,[289] but the debtor may be precluded from lowering the value for exemption purposes if the property has depreciated. To the extent that these rules would work a significant hardship on the debtor, it may be wise to consider dismissal of the chapter 13 case and the filing of a new chapter 7 petition instead of conversion, subject to the limits on re-filing of section 109(g)[290] and the possible automatic stay limitations of section 362(c)(3) or (4).[291]

In any case, postpetition debts are included in the ultimate chapter 7 discharge,[292] which could be a major advantage if the debtor has incurred significant new debts after filing. A postpetition debt would be included in a chapter 13 hardship discharge only if the creditor had filed a postpetition claim, the trustee's approval had been obtained, and it had been incorporated into the plan.[293]

On the other hand, although priority claims would be discharged to the extent allowed in chapter 7, secured claims and claims that are nondischargeable in chapter 7 would remain to be dealt with after discharge. And if objections to a discharge are possible under 11 U.S.C. § 727, conversion to chapter 7 may not be advantageous to the debtor.[294]

If the debtor cannot obtain approval of a modified plan, is ineligible for a hardship discharge, and yet still wishes to obtain some bankruptcy relief, conversion may be the only option. Because voluntary or involuntary dismissal reinstates not only all prepetition debts but also all avoided liens,[295] conversion may be necessary in such cases to retain the benefit of successful litigation under chapter 13.[296]

---

285 The term "security" is defined in section 101 to mean paper securities, such as stocks and bonds, so it is unclear to what debts this language even applies.
286 11 U.S.C. § 348(f)(1)(C)(i).
287 11 U.S.C. § 506(a)(2) (emphasis added).
288 See § 5.4.2, supra.
289 See *In re* Slack, 290 B.R. 282 (Bankr. D.N.J. 2003), *aff'd*, 112 Fed. Appx. 868 (3d Cir. 2004); *In re* Page, 250 B.R. 465 (Bankr. D.N.H. 2000). *See also* § 4.7.4, supra.
290 *See* § 9.7.3.1.5, *supra*.
291 See Chapter 9, *supra*, for discussion of section 362(c)(3).
292 11 U.S.C. § 348(d).
    Moreover, 11 U.S.C. § 348(a) provides that the conversion date would be the date of the order for relief. Because 11 U.S.C. § 348(b) applies 11 U.S.C. § 727(b) to that date, all debts arising before the conversion date are discharged. *See In re* Fickling, 361 F.3d 172 (2d Cir. 2004) (conversion from chapter 11; no exception for administrative expenses); *In re* Deiter, 33 B.R. 547 (Bankr. W.D. Wis. 1983). *See also In re* Winchester, 46 B.R. 492 (B.A.P. 9th Cir. 1984).
293 11 U.S.C. § 1328(c), (d). *See* § 8.7.2, *supra*.
294 United States Tr. v. Skinner (*In re* Skinner), 2010 WL 3469993 (Bankr. S.D. Miss. Sept. 1, 2010) (§ 727(a)(8) eight year bar to discharge after prior chapter 7 case resulting in discharge ran from date of original chapter 13 petition, not date of conversion).
295 11 U.S.C. § 349.
296 *See In re* Hargis, 103 B.R. 912 (Bankr. E.D. Tenn. 1989) (effect of lien avoidance won in chapter 13 preserved after conversion to chapter 7).

Chapter 14   Litigating in the Bankruptcy Court

14.1 Introduction

Under the Bankruptcy Act of 1898, consumer bankruptcy cases were almost uniformly handled in a routine manner by all parties involved, more as matters of administrative processing than as proceedings involving legal issues to be litigated. Few contested disputes arose in such cases, and most of those that did arise were resolved not in the bankruptcy courts, but rather in state courts, because of the limited jurisdiction of the bankruptcy referees under the Act. Virtually the only litigated matters that involved consumer debtors were complaints objecting to the discharge of particular debts, and even those cases had been forced into bankruptcy courts only by relatively recent amendments to the Act of 1898.

All of this has changed radically under the Bankruptcy Code. Not only does the Code make the basic bankruptcy case a much more attractive alternative for consumer debtors, but also other provisions in the Bankruptcy Reform Act have brought about a major expansion of many different kinds of consumer litigation in the bankruptcy courts.

Central to this change was the greatly expanded jurisdiction of the bankruptcy courts under the 1978 Act.[1] In the years since the Code was enacted, these courts have heard numerous and varied claims of types never before brought before them, including damage claims for injury to property[2] or for unfair trade practices,[3] Truth in Lending actions,[4] actions to rescind contracts,[5] and class actions under the Civil Rights Acts for enforcement of rights provided by federal welfare programs.[6]

Generally, the bankruptcy courts were quick to recognize and exercise their increased jurisdiction in these cases, although a few resisted.[7] Only when no significant relation existed between the cause of action and the bankruptcy's purpose or success was jurisdiction found to be lacking.[8]

Then, in 1982, new and major uncertainties arose, with the Supreme Court's decision in *Northern Pipeline Construction Co. v. Marathon Pipe Line Co.*,[9] which declared the entire bankruptcy jurisdictional scheme to be unconstitutional. For almost two years after that decision, the bankruptcy system operated under makeshift emergency jurisdictional rules which were themselves of questionable constitutionality.[10] Finally, on July 10, 1984, a new jurisdictional structure was enacted as part of the Bankruptcy Amendments and Federal Judgeship Act of 1984.[11] As discussed below, that scheme creates a host of different issues, not the least of which is the constitutionality of some of its own provisions under the *Northern Pipeline* case. This chapter considers how best to utilize the jurisdiction of the bankruptcy forum and some of the issues most likely to arise in bankruptcy litigation, including particularly the litigation of issues under nonbankruptcy law.

14.2 Bankruptcy Court Jurisdiction Under the 1984 Amendments

14.2.1 A Brief History[12]

In 1978, when Congress passed the Bankruptcy Reform Act, bankruptcy jurisdiction was identified as a primary area in need of reform. For the previous eighty years, under the Bankruptcy Act of 1898, few topics had been the subject of more litigation. The system that existed was one of piecemeal jurisdiction, and

---

1 See § 14.2, *infra*.
2 *See, e.g., In re* Thompson, 3 B.R. 312 (Bankr. D.S.D. 1980).
3 *See, e.g., In re* Fleet, 95 B.R. 319 (E.D. Pa. 1989) (mortgage counselors who referred clients to bankruptcy attorney committed unfair trade practices); *In re* Gibbs, 9 B.R. 758 (Bankr. D. Conn. 1981), *aff'd*, 76 B.R. 257 (D. Conn. 1983).
4 *See, e.g., In re* Claypool, 2 Collier Bankr. Cas. 2d (MB) 64 (Bankr. M.D. Fla. 1980).
5 *See, e.g., In re* Griffith, 6 B.R. 753 (Bankr. D.N.M. 1980).
6 *See, e.g.,* Morris v. Philadelphia Elec. Co., 45 B.R. 350 (E.D. Pa. 1984); *In re* Maya, 8 B.R. 202 (Bankr. E.D. Pa. 1981).
7 *See, e.g.,* Marshall v. Marshall, 547 U.S. 293, 126 S. Ct. 1735, 164 L. Ed. 2d 480 (2006) (debtor's claim that creditor tortiously interfered with a gift from her deceased husband was well within bankruptcy court's jurisdiction and not barred by a "probate exception," if such an exception exists); *In re* Universal Profile, 6 B.R. 194 (Bankr. N.D. Ga. 1980) (creating a "domestic relations exception" to the general grant of jurisdiction to avoid becoming involved in a marital dispute affecting property of the estate over which the court appeared to have exclusive jurisdiction). The *Marshall* case returned to the Supreme Court in 2011 as *Stern v. Marshall*, 131 S. Ct. 2594, 180 L. Ed. 2d 475 (2011), in which the court held that, although bankruptcy jurisdiction existed, the bankruptcy court could not enter a final judgment. *See* § 14.2.1, *infra*.
8 *See In re* Turner, 724 F.2d 338 (2d Cir. 1983) (conversion action brought by debtor would have no impact on bankruptcy and was therefore not related to bankruptcy case).
9 458 U.S. 50, 102 S. Ct. 2858, 73 L. Ed 2d 598 (1982).
10 *See* Vern Countryman, *Emergency Rule Compounds Emergency*, 57 Am. Bankr. L. J. 1 (1983). *See also* § 14.2.1, *infra*.
11 Pub. L. No. 98-353, 98 Stat. 333 (1984).
12 For a more detailed recounting of how bankruptcy jurisdiction arrived at its present state, see Vern Countryman, *Scrambling to Define Bankruptcy Jurisdiction: The Chief Justice, the Judicial Conference, and the Legislative Process*, 22 Harv. J. on Legis. 1 (1985).

in larger corporate cases simultaneous litigation concerning the same bankruptcy debtor was often conducted in numerous courts. The bankruptcy courts had only limited powers, most of them tied to jurisdiction over the debtor's property. Beyond those powers, matters could be tried in the bankruptcy court only with the consent, express or implied, of the parties. Uncertainty as to jurisdiction continued to cause litigation and expense in many cases.

The 1978 Act sought to remedy all of these ills by creating a single court, the new bankruptcy court, with jurisdiction over all matters related in any way to the bankruptcy.[13] But when Congress refused to make that court a full-fledged federal court as defined by Article III of the Constitution, it sowed the seeds of new uncertainties. These reached fruition in the *Northern Pipeline* case,[14] when the new structure was rejected in its entirety by the Supreme Court.

For the next two years, the bankruptcy courts operated without any clear statutory authority, under an emergency rule giving them jurisdiction delegated from the district court. This rule created a new distinction between proceedings that were integral to the bankruptcy process and those that were only "related" to it, the latter being the type of case which the Supreme Court had found clearly beyond the power of a non-Article III judge. All cases and proceedings were referred initially to bankruptcy judges under the rule, but district courts retained the authority to review all bankruptcy court actions de novo. And in "related proceedings," unless the parties agreed otherwise, a bankruptcy judge was empowered only to enter a proposed order or judgment to be reviewed in every case by the district court. The rule contained a non-exhaustive list of proceedings that would not be considered "related." Finally, it expressly prohibited bankruptcy judges from conducting certain types of proceedings, including appeals from other bankruptcy courts and jury trials.

The emergency rule was immediately challenged in numerous courts on the grounds that it did not comply with the Supreme Court's decision in *Northern Pipeline*. Every court of appeals to consider the issue upheld the rule, however, and the Supreme Court declined to resolve the issue conclusively by denying certiorari whenever it was sought.[15] Ultimately, because no court of appeals had found it invalid and because it appeared to work reasonably well, the emergency rule formed the basis of the jurisdictional scheme enacted in 1984.[16]

Thus, on July 10, 1984 yet another bankruptcy court jurisdictional scheme came into being.[17] This system was further embellished with several amendments affecting jurisdictional issues in the Bankruptcy Reform Act of 1994,[18] and by minor changes made by the 2005 bankruptcy amendments.[19] Because Congress again declined to give bankruptcy judges Article III status, but still attempted to keep most "related issues" in the bankruptcy system, mechanisms were once more necessary to prevent bankruptcy courts from deciding issues that the Supreme Court had reserved for Article III courts. And as no precise definition of how those issues could be identified has been given by the Supreme Court, there continues to be some doubt over whether the current structure is constitutional.[20]

For over twenty years, there were no definitive Supreme Court decisions. However, the Supreme Court decision in *Granfinanciera, S.A. v. Nordberg*[21] contained a number of hints that at least part of this new jurisdictional scheme could be found unconstitutional, because it vests in the bankruptcy court powers that may only be exercised by district courts.

The potential for part of the 1984 jurisdictional scheme to be found unconstitutional was realized with the Supreme Court's decision in *Stern v. Marshall*.[22] The Court found that although Congress had intended to give the bankruptcy court the power to render final judgments in all counterclaims filed against creditors that had filed claims in a bankruptcy case by designating such proceedings as core proceedings, that delegation of power to non-Article III judges was unconstitutional. *Stern* involved a state law counterclaim against a creditor for tortious interference with an expected inheritance. The Court held that such a state common law claim, designed to augment the

---

13 *See* H.R. Rep. No. 95-595, at 220–230 (1977).

14 N. Pipeline Constr. Co. v. Marathon Pipe Line Co., 458 U.S. 50, 102 S. Ct. 2858, 73 L. Ed. 2d 598 (1982).

15 *See, e.g., In re* Stewart, 741 F.2d 127 (7th Cir. 1984); *In re* Kaiser, 722 F.2d 1574 (2d Cir. 1983); White Motor Corp. v. Citibank, 704 F.2d 254 (6th Cir. 1983); *In re* Hansen, 702 F.2d 728 (8th Cir. 1983); *In re* Braniff Airways, Inc., 700 F.2d 214 (5th Cir. 1983). *See also In re* Comm. of Unsecured Creditors of F.S. Communications Corp., 760 F.2d 1194 (11th Cir. 1985).

16 *See* 130 Cong. Rec. E1107–E1110 (daily ed. Mar. 20, 1984) (remarks of Rep. Kastenmaier); 130 Cong. Rec. H1847–H1849 (daily ed. Mar. 21, 1984) (remarks of Rep. Kindness).

The legislative history of the 1984 amendments on jurisdiction consists primarily of the floor debates that occurred on March 21, 1984 in the House of Representatives, and June 19, 1984 in the Senate (130 Cong. Rec. S7617–S7625), as well as the Conference Report of June 29, 1984 (130 Cong. Rec. S8887–S8900).

17 A drafting error in the 1984 amendments accidentally re-enacted, in section 121(a) of Pub. L. No. 98-353, 98 Stat. 333 (1984), the 1978 court system provisions that had been repealed eight sections earlier in section 113 of the same law. Courts have thus far agreed that section 121(a) was a mistake and ignored it. *See, e.g.*, Precon, Inc. v. JRS Realty Trust, 47 B.R. 432 (D. Me. 1985); *In re* Long, 43 B.R. 692 (Bankr. N.D. Ohio 1984).

18 Pub. L. No. 103-394, 108 Stat. 4106 (1994) (amending 28 U.S.C. §§ 157, 1334, 158, 2075).

19 Pub. L. No. 109-8, 119 Stat. 23 (2005) (amending 28 U.S.C. §§ 152, 157, 158, 1334, 1409, 1410, 2075).

20 *See, e.g., In re* Mankin, 823 F.2d 1296 (9th Cir. 1987) (bankruptcy court jurisdiction over trustee's use of state fraudulent conveyance statute held constitutional).

There was also litigation concerning whether the "retroactive" reinstatement of sitting bankruptcy judges by Congress, after their statutory authority expired on June, 1984, was constitutional. Those constitutional challenges failed. *In re* Benny, 812 F.2d 1133 (9th Cir. 1987); *In re* Koerner, 800 F.2d 1358 (5th Cir. 1986) (retroactive extension of term of office for bankruptcy judges does not violate appointments clause of the Constitution); *In re* Lombard-Wall Inc., 48 B.R. 986 (S.D.N.Y. 1985). *See also In re* Moens, 800 F.2d 173 (7th Cir. 1986) (challenge to constitutionality of BAFJA rendered moot when bankruptcy judge sitting pursuant to the Act resigns).

21 492 U.S. 33, 109 S. Ct. 2782, 106 L. Ed. 2d 26 (1989); § 14.2.7, *infra*.

22 131 S. Ct. 2594, 180 L. Ed. 2d 475 (2011).

bankruptcy estate and unlike a preference claim based on federal bankruptcy law, was not so much a part of the bankruptcy case that it could be decided by an Article I court under the public rights doctrine, even though some of the factual issues overlapped with the creditor's claim in the bankruptcy case. Because the Court did not draw a precise line distinguishing what types of counterclaims remain subject to a final decision by the bankruptcy court, there will be litigation regarding that issue for years to come.

However, it is important to note that the Court did not find the counterclaim to be beyond the bankruptcy jurisdiction conferred on district courts by section 1334 of title 28. Therefore, it should be possible for the courts to establish a system, similar to that used in non-core proceedings, in which the bankruptcy court submits proposed findings of fact and conclusions of law to the district court for review and entry of final judgment.[23] Some districts have adopted local rules adopting those procedures for proceedings where the bankruptcy court cannot enter a final judgment. It is also likely that, as with non-core proceedings, the parties will remain free to consent to the entry of final judgment by the bankruptcy court.

14.2.2 Initial Referral of Bankruptcy Matters to the Bankruptcy Courts

The 1984 amendments are structured on the premise that the power to decide all cases and proceedings involving bankruptcy ultimately resides in the federal district court. The statute confers this power in 28 U.S.C. § 1334, which gives the district court original and exclusive jurisdiction over all cases under title 11 (the Bankruptcy Code);[24] original but not exclusive jurisdiction over proceedings arising under title 11 or arising in or related to cases under title 11;[25] and exclusive jurisdiction over all property of the bankruptcy estate.[26] This section thus gives the district court essentially the same broad initial jurisdiction which was conferred upon the bankruptcy courts by the Bankruptcy Reform Act of 1978.

The breadth of the statutory grant of jurisdiction is vast but not unlimited. A number of courts have adopted the test set forth by the Third Circuit Court of Appeals for determining whether a proceeding is at least "related to" a bankruptcy case—whether the outcome of the proceeding could conceivably have any effect on the administration of the bankruptcy case.[27] However, the Supreme Court has declined to precisely define "related to" in the context of bankruptcy jurisdiction.[28]

Under the current scheme, virtually all bankruptcy matters are immediately referred by the district court to the bankruptcy court, which is now a "unit" of the district court.[29] A bankruptcy judge is thus analogous in some ways to a magistrate judge. This referral to the bankruptcy court occurs pursuant to section 157 of title 28, which sets forth the fairly complicated division of responsibilities between the bankruptcy court and district court. The amendments give the district court discretion to refer any or all bankruptcy cases or proceedings, including those only related to the bankruptcy, to the bankruptcy judges for the district.[30] The district court also has discretion to refer actions which are related to the bankruptcy and which are pending in the district court at the time the bankruptcy is filed.[31] As a practical matter, district courts immediately refer all such cases and proceedings to their bankruptcy courts (generally by blanket order of referral), and in virtually every district there remains a separate bankruptcy court clerk's office to process all bankruptcy filings.[32] Indeed, when a blanket order of referral has been promulgated, actions relating to a bankruptcy case may not be filed with the district court and must be filed with the bankruptcy court.[33] Thus, in almost all cases, bankruptcy papers continued to be filed initially with the clerk of the bankruptcy court.

Once a matter is begun in the bankruptcy court, though, there is no assurance that it will stay there. Nor is there a single uniform way that it will be treated if it does remain. The new jurisdictional scheme deploys a variety of procedural mechanisms for the transfer or ultimate resolution of different types of proceedings. These mechanisms are discussed below.

---

23 See Rosenberg v. Harvey A. Bookstein, 479 B.R. 584 (D. Nev. 2012) (fraudulent conveyance claims must be decided by an Article III court but matter may be referred to bankruptcy judge to issue proposed findings of fact and conclusions of law); Blixseth v. Brown, 470 B.R. 562 (D. Mont. 2012) (bankruptcy courts have power to enter proposed findings of fact and conclusions of law in Stern-type proceedings).

24 28 U.S.C. § 1334(a).

25 28 U.S.C. § 1334(b).

26 28 U.S.C. § 1334(e)(1).

27 Pacor v. Higgins, 743 F.2d 984 (3d Cir. 1984). See also In re Time Constr., Inc., 43 F.3d 1041 (6th Cir. 1995) (bankruptcy court has jurisdiction over proceeding if outcome could alter debtor's rights, options or freedom of action).

This jurisdiction continues for many purposes even after a case is dismissed or closed. In re Aheong, 276 B.R. 233 (B.A.P. 9th Cir. 2002). See In re McAlpin, 278 F.3d 866 (8th Cir. 2002) (objection to claim filed after chapter 13 case had been completed and closed was not within bankruptcy court's jurisdiction because it could have no effect on bankruptcy case).

28 See Celotex Corp. v. Edwards, 514 U.S. 300, 308 n.6, 115 S. Ct. 1493, 131 L. Ed. 2d 403 (1995).

29 28 U.S.C. § 151.

30 28 U.S.C. § 157(a).

One court of appeals has held that it is also permissible for a district court to refer a core bankruptcy proceeding to a magistrate upon the parties' consent, but that the practice should be limited to situations in which there is a compelling need to do so. In re Nix, 864 F.2d 1209 (5th Cir. 1989). See also In re San Vicente Med. Partners Ltd., 865 F.2d 1128 (9th Cir. 1989) (consent to trial of bankruptcy matter before magistrate must be knowing and explicit).

31 See Philippe v. Shape, Inc., 103 B.R. 355 (D. Me. 1989).

One court has held that a motion for directed referral is the appropriate means to request that such a case be referred. Thomas Steel Corp. v. Bethlehem Rebar Indus., 101 B.R. 16 (Bankr. N.D. Ill. 1989).

32 28 U.S.C. § 156(b).

The remaining districts have a deputy clerk for bankruptcy, often in a separate office.

33 Vreugdenhil v. Hoekstra, 773 F.2d 213 (8th Cir. 1985); Cent. Nat'l Bank v. Kwak, 49 B.R. 337 (N.D. Ohio 1985).

14.2.3 The Bankruptcy Case

The bankruptcy case, that is the case under title 11 initiated by the filing of a petition under chapters 7, 9, 11, 12, 13, or 15 of that title, continues to be within the province of the bankruptcy court for entry of the orders that are essential for bankruptcy relief.[34] The bankruptcy court may enter as final orders: the order for relief under each chapter;[35] orders distributing property of the estate and setting aside exemptions; discharge orders; and other similar orders in the main bankruptcy case. As with every type of matter referred to the bankruptcy court, however, the district court may withdraw the entire bankruptcy case or part of it from the bankruptcy court.[36]

14.2.4 Types of Proceedings

14.2.4.1 Adversary Proceedings, Contested Matters, and Applications

Generally, a "proceeding" is a litigated controversy in connection with the bankruptcy case, either a contested matter governed by Bankruptcy Rule 9014 or an adversary proceeding under Bankruptcy Rules 7001–7087. An "adversary proceeding" is essentially a lawsuit within the bankruptcy case and the rules governing such proceedings closely parallel the Federal Rules of Civil Procedure, requiring the proceeding to be commenced by a complaint, providing federal civil discovery procedure and the like.[37] Bankruptcy Rule 7001 specifies those types of proceedings that must be brought as adversary proceedings.[38]

Most other proceedings are "contested matters," essentially treated as motions within the main bankruptcy case. Bankruptcy Rule 9014, which governs contested matters, specifies that some but not all of the adversary proceeding rules ordinarily apply to such proceedings.[39] A few types of matters, usually very routine and uncontested, are designated as "applications," for example, an application to pay the filing fee in installments.[40]

14.2.4.2 Core and Non-Core Proceedings

Many of the bankruptcy procedural mechanisms revolve around the distinction between "core" and "non-core" proceedings. The statute provides that a bankruptcy judge may hear and enter final judgments and orders in any core proceeding, as defined by section 157(b)(2) of title 28.[41] In delineating core proceedings, Congress attempted to identify proceedings within a bankruptcy case or arising under the Bankruptcy Code which did not fall into the category of "related" cases which the Supreme Court, in *Northern Pipeline*, prohibited a bankruptcy judge from deciding. Core proceedings include, "but are not limited to":[42]

(A) Matters concerning the administration of the estate;
(B) Allowance or disallowance of claims against the estate or exemptions from property of the estate, and estimation of claims of interest for the purposes of confirming a plan under chapter 11 or 13 of title 11 but not the liquidation or estimation of contingent or unliquidated personal injury tort or wrongful death claims against the estate for purposes of distribution in a case under title 11;[43]
(C) Counterclaims by the estate against persons filing claims against the estate;[44]
(D) Orders in respect to obtaining credit;
(E) Orders to turn over property of the estate;
(F) Proceedings to determine, avoid, or recover preferences;
(G) Motions to terminate, annul or modify the automatic stay;
(H) Proceedings to determine, avoid, or recover fraudulent conveyances;
(I) Determinations as to the dischargeability of particular debts;[45]

---

34 28 U.S.C. § 157(b)(1).
35 *See* 11 U.S.C. §§ 301, 303(h).
36 *See* § 14.2.5, *infra*.
37 Fed. R. Bankr. P. 7001–7087. *See In re* Adair, 965 F.2d 777 (9th Cir. 1992) (procedure of taking direct testimony by written declaration complied with Federal Rules of Evidence and Federal Rules of Civil Procedure incorporated in Bankruptcy Rules).
38 At least one court of appeals has held that the requisites of an adversary proceeding can be waived by the parties. *In re* Vill. Mobile Homes, Inc., 947 F.2d 1282 (5th Cir. 1991).
39 Federal Rule of Bankruptcy Procedure 9014 also provides that the court may order that additional adversary proceeding rules shall be applicable in a particular proceeding, or that some of the rules specified in Rule 9014 shall not be applicable.
40 Some types of applications, such as an application for attorney fees under Federal Rule of Bankruptcy Procedure 2016(a), may be contested. The designation of such proceedings as applications is probably just a custom carried over from prior rules.

41 However, the bankruptcy court need not enter a final judgment. Teton Exploration Drilling, Inc. v. Bokum Res. Corp., 818 F.2d 1521 (10th Cir. 1987) (when bankruptcy court erroneously treated matter as non-core, district court's adoption of bankruptcy court's opinion constituted valid judgment).
42 28 U.S.C. § 157(b)(2).
    Proceedings not specifically listed may be core proceedings if they concern fundamental functions of the bankruptcy court, such as determining the nature and extent of the estate. *In re* Goodman, 991 F.2d 613 (9th Cir. 1993) (proceeding brought by debtor-subtenant to enjoin unlawful detainer against tenant was core proceeding).
43 *See, e.g., In re* Manville Forest Prods. Corp., 896 F.2d 1384 (2d Cir. 1990); *In re* Meyertech Corp., 831 F.2d 410 (3d Cir. 1987) (creditor's breach of warranty action was a core proceeding seeking allowance of claim).
44 Although a counterclaim based on a state law cause of action is properly designated as a core proceeding under section 157(b)(2)(C), the bankruptcy court may not have jurisdiction to render a final judgment in such a proceeding if the counterclaim is not resolved as part of the process of determining the creditor's proof of claim. The bankruptcy court in that situation would need to submit proposed findings of fact and conclusions of law to the district court for review and entry of final judgment. *See* Stern v. Marshall, 131 S. Ct. 2594, 180 L. Ed. 2d 475 (2011); § 14.2.1, *supra*. *See also* Ortiz v. Aurora Health Care, Inc., 665 F.3d 906 (7th Cir. 2011) (bankruptcy court did not have power to enter final judgment on state law claim based on medical providers including improper information in proofs of claim).
45 *See* Sasson v. Sokoloff (*In re* Sasson), 424 F.3d 864 (9th Cir. 2005)

(J) Objections to discharges;
(K) Determinations of the validity, extent, or priority of liens;
(L) Confirmations of plans;
(M) Orders approving the use or lease of property, including the use of cash collateral;
(N) Orders approving the sale of property other than property resulting from claims brought by the estate against persons who have not filed claims against the estate;
(O) Other proceedings affecting the liquidation of the assets of the estate or the adjustment of the debtor-creditor or the equity security holder relationship, except personal injury tort or wrongful death claims;[46] and
(P) Recognition of foreign proceedings and other matters under chapter 15 of title 11.

This list is similar to the list of proceedings defined as not "related" under the emergency rule in effect from 1982 to 1984. Nevertheless, there are differences between the two lists, so that even courts that approved the emergency rule may not necessarily agree that every item on the list created by the 1984 Amendments may be delegated to a non-Article III court. And, of course, the Supreme Court never approved even the list set out in the emergency rule. Therefore, constitutional issues remain, as in *Stern v. Marshall*, particularly with respect to proceedings found to be included in category (O).[47]

If the bankruptcy court does not have core jurisdiction to decide a proceeding, then the proceeding falls into one of two other jurisdictional pigeonholes. In some cases, there is no jurisdiction for the court to decide the issue at all. In others, the issue is related to the bankruptcy case so that the court may exercise "non-core" jurisdiction, but may only recommend findings of fact and conclusions of law to the district court unless the parties consent to entry of a final judgment by the bankruptcy court. These issues are discussed in the two following subsections as is the procedure by which the court determines the extent of its jurisdiction.

14.2.4.3 Court's Determination of Jurisdictional Questions

The first question that must be answered in determining jurisdiction over a proceeding is whether there is any federal bankruptcy jurisdiction over the matter at all.[48] Some proceedings may be so remote from the bankruptcy that they will have no impact on the bankruptcy case and cannot be considered even to be related to it.[49] In such instances, the bankruptcy court may never hear the proceeding, and a district court may hear it only if there is some nonbankruptcy basis for federal jurisdiction.

However, even in such cases, there may be bankruptcy jurisdiction over the property involved.[50] And when there is

---

(bankruptcy court may enter money judgment in dischargeability proceeding).

46 Because the question of a discharge is a core matter, the question whether someone violated the discharge injunction must also be a core matter. *In re* Schatz, 122 B.R. 327 (N.D. Ill. 1990); Burns v. LTD Acquisitions, L.L.C. (*In re* Burns), 2010 WL 642312 (Bankr. S.D. Tex. Feb. 18, 2010) (also holding that state law unfair debt collection claims based on same facts are either core or related proceedings).

47 *See, e.g.,* Briden v. Foley, 776 F.2d 379 (1st Cir. 1985) (core bankruptcy proceeding with respect to a public right may constitutionally be decided by an Article I court). *See also* § 14.2.1, *supra*.

48 Of course, constitutional limitations on the power of federal courts to resolve cases, such as the requirement of a "case or controversy" also may apply to preclude bankruptcy court decision-making. *In re* Kilen, 129 B.R. 538 (Bankr. N.D. Ill. 1991).

49 *See, e.g., In re* Boone, 52 F.3d 958 (11th Cir. 1995) (chapter 7 debtor's suit based upon postpetition cause of action would have no impact on bankruptcy case); Specialty Mills v. Citizens State Bank, 51 F.3d 770 (8th Cir. 1995) (damage action by debtor's lessee against a creditor based upon motion filed in bankruptcy case would not affect bankruptcy case); *In re* Gallucci, 931 F.2d 738 (11th Cir. 1991) (trustee's action to recover property which would not belong to bankruptcy estate is not related to bankruptcy case); *In re* Lemco Gypsum, Inc., 910 F.2d 784 (11th Cir. 1990) (dispute between debtor's landlord and purchaser of debtor's assets was non-related because it did not affect other creditors and could not have effect on debtor's estate); *In re* Bobroff, 766 F.2d 797 (3d Cir. 1985) (postpetition tort claim of debtor not within bankruptcy jurisdiction); Pacor, Inc. v. Higgins, 743 F.2d 984 (3d Cir. 1984) (determination of products liability action between original plaintiff and defendant, when debtor was third party defendant, would not affect bankruptcy estate because it would not determine any rights of the debtor). *See also In re* Resorts Int'l, 372 F.3d 154 (3d Cir. 2004) (jurisdiction cannot be created by a confirmed plan when it does not otherwise exist); *In re* Gardner, 913 F.2d 515 (10th Cir. 1990) (when debtor had no interest in property following divorce order awarding property to debtor's ex-spouse, bankruptcy court lacked jurisdiction to determine whether ex-spouse's interests in property were superior to those of government); Home Ins. Co. v. Cooper & Cooper Ltd., 889 F.2d 746 (7th Cir. 1989) (district court must determine whether action is related to bankruptcy before circuit court can address merits of appeal); *In re* Hall's Motor Trans., 889 F.2d 520 (3d Cir. 1989) (bankruptcy court lacks jurisdiction to entertain action by purchaser of property from bankruptcy estate to enjoin enforcement of local zoning ordinance); *In re* Am. Hardwoods, Inc., 885 F.2d 621 (9th Cir. 1989) (bankruptcy court lacks jurisdiction to permanently enjoin creditor from enforcing state court judgment against non-debtor guarantors); Nat'l City Bank v. Coopers & Lybrand, 802 F.2d 990 (8th Cir. 1986) (action alleging accountant malpractice did not arise under or relate to bankruptcy proceeding).

Similarly, in some cases in which the debtor seeks to protect a non-debtor third party from liability at the hands of a creditor, the court may not have power to enter an injunction. *Cf.* United States v. Huckabee Auto Co., 783 F.2d 1546 (11th Cir. 1986) (bankruptcy court lacks jurisdiction to enjoin IRS from imposing tax liability on non-debtor third party even to the extent that such liability would affect debtor's ability to reorganize).

50 *See In re* Moody, 837 F.2d 724 (6th Cir. 1987) (district court had jurisdiction to make order affecting debtor's postpetition property in favor of bankruptcy trustee); *In re* Teel, 34 B.R. 762 (B.A.P. 9th Cir. 1983) (bankruptcy court retained exclusive jurisdiction over community property despite marital dissolution action in state court). *But see In re* McClellan, 99 F.3d 1420 (7th Cir. 1996) (bankruptcy court had no jurisdiction to make orders concerning ERISA plan that was excluded from bankruptcy estate); *In re* Edwards, 962 F.2d 641 (7th Cir. 1992) (bankruptcy court had no jurisdiction over lien priority dispute and purchaser of property after property had been sold free and clear of liens); *In re* Fietz, 852 F.2d 455 (9th Cir. 1988) (after confirmation of chapter 13 plan, if recovery of property of the estate can no longer affect the bankruptcy case and property of

some effect on the bankruptcy estate or the administration of the case, the matter at least is a non-core, related proceeding.[51] Generally, each claim included in a proceeding must be analyzed separately because some claims may be related while others are not.[52]

Occasionally, a court may rule that it lacks jurisdiction over an issue in a bankruptcy proceeding, because of a prior binding ruling on that issue in state court. The application of the "*Rooker-Feldman*"[53] doctrine deprives a federal court of jurisdiction when its ruling on an issue effectively would require overturning a prior decision of the state court.[54] The doctrine exists independently of claim and issue preclusion.

Thus, whenever possible, the debtor should avoid a state court decision on an issue which might later be resolved in a bankruptcy proceeding. This can sometimes be accomplished by removal[55] or the filing of an independent bankruptcy court proceeding. If a state court decision is unavoidable, a debtor may seek to establish, based on the record, that the issues are different in the bankruptcy proceeding than they were in the state court.[56] Alternatively, state court appeals or motions for reconsideration or for relief from judgment are not precluded unless the automatic stay applies to the action.[57]

If there is some basis for bankruptcy jurisdiction, the proceeding must be either a core proceeding or a non-core proceeding. In an adversary proceeding, the complaint, and also any counterclaim, cross-claim or third party complaint, must

---

51 *See, e.g.*, Baker v. Simpson, 613 F.3d 346 (2d Cir. 2010) (claim of professional malpractice by court-appointed counsel within a bankruptcy case arises in a case under title 11); *In re* Time Constr., Inc., 43 F.3d 1041 (6th Cir. 1995) (bankruptcy court has jurisdiction over proceeding if outcome could alter debtor's rights, options or freedom of action); Abramowitz v. Palmer, 999 F.2d 1274 (8th Cir. 1993) (action to impose constructive trust on non-debtor spouse's interest in home was related to bankruptcy case because home was purchased with fraudulently obtained funds and court needed to determine rights of spouse to fully and fairly resolve rights of debtor); *In re* Marcus Hook Dev. Park, Inc., 943 F.2d 261 (3d Cir. 1991) (test is whether proceeding could "conceivably" have any effect on the estate being administered in bankruptcy); Robinson v. Mich. Consol. Gas Co., 918 F.2d 579 (6th Cir. 1990) (action brought by debtor's tenants against trustee and utility for wrongful discontinuation of utility service was related proceeding because recovery was sought from estate); Diamond Mortgage Corp. of Ill. v. Sugar, 913 F.2d 1233 (7th Cir. 1990) (corporate debtor's malpractice action against former attorneys was related to corporation's bankruptcy case because resolution might impact on assets available for distribution); Kaohani Ohana, Ltd. v. Sutherland, 873 F.2d 1302 (9th Cir. 1989) (bankruptcy jurisdiction exists whenever litigation may alter potential obligations arising out of claims pending against the estate); *In re* Contractors Equip. Supply Co., 861 F.2d 241 (9th Cir. 1988) (bankruptcy court had jurisdiction over suit between non-debtor third party and secured creditor because non-debtor was seeking to recover property in which debtor retained an interest); *In re* Majestic Energy Corp., 835 F.2d 87 (5th Cir. 1988) (bankruptcy court could determine effect of agreement related to debtor's stock after plan confirmation because issues presented were related to the debtor's bankruptcy case and parties had consented to bankruptcy court determination); *In re* Wood, 825 F.2d 90 (5th Cir. 1987) (case involved possible liability of estate for wrongful appropriation of assets); *In re* Xonics, Inc., 813 F.2d 127 (7th Cir. 1987) (payment to debtor's other creditors would depend on competing claims to pool of money); *In re* Dogpatch, U.S.A., Inc., 810 F.2d 782 (8th Cir. 1987) (outcome of proceeding would have effect on estate and possibly impose liability on the debtor); *In re* S. Indus. Banking Corp., 809 F.2d 329 (6th Cir. 1987) (cause of action arose because of bankruptcy proceeding and was based on bankruptcy law and debt alleged as setoff was owed by debtor).

The bankruptcy court has the concurrent jurisdiction to determine a debtor's tax liability under 11 U.S.C. § 505(a), even if the parties have been granted relief from the stay to pursue litigation over the same issue in the United States Tax Court. United States v. Wilson, 974 F.2d 514 (4th Cir. 1992).

However, the bankruptcy court may not determine tax liability if that liability has already been adjudicated by the Tax Court. *In re* Bunyan, 354 F.3d 1149 (9th Cir. 2004) (bankruptcy court lacked jurisdiction to consider issues previously decided by final orders of tax court); *In re* Teal, 16 F.3d 619 (5th Cir. 1994). *See also In re* Cody, Inc., 338 F.3d 89 (bankruptcy court lacked jurisdiction over issues of debtor's tax-exempt status that had already been decided in nonbankruptcy proceedings).

52 *See, e.g., In re* Reed, 94 B.R. 48 (E.D. Pa. 1988) (bankruptcy court could decide chapter 7 debtor's claims related to a postpetition fire insofar as fire damaged personal property of her estate, but could not determine whether landlord had properly fulfilled obligations as

to leasehold interest acquired postpetition which was not property of the debtor's estate).

53 *See* D.C. Ct. of Appeals v. Feldman, 460 U.S. 462, 103 S. Ct. 1303, 75 L. Ed. 2d 206 (1983) (federal courts lack jurisdiction to consider issues which are "inextricably intertwined" with a state court's decision); Rooker v. Fid. Trust Co., 263 U.S. 413, 44 S. Ct. 149, 68 L. Ed. 362 (1923). *See also* Lance v. Dennis, 126 S. Ct. 1198, 1201, 163 L. Ed. 2d 1059 (2006) (doctrine is narrow and limited to cases "brought by state court losers complaining of injuries caused by state-court judgments rendered before the district court proceedings commenced and inviting district court review of those judgments") *citing* Exxon Mobil Corp. v. Saudi Basic Indus. Corp., 544 U.S. 280, 125 S. Ct. 1517, 161 L. Ed. 2d 454 (2005).

54 *See, e.g., In re* Knapper, 407 F.3d 573 (3d Cir. 2005) (doctrine deprived bankruptcy court of jurisdiction over adversary proceeding brought by chapter 13 debtor seeking to set aside foreclosure and sheriff's sale of her property because debtor's federal due process claim was "inextricably intertwined" with the final state court foreclosure judgment); *In re* Abboud, 237 B.R. 777 (B.A.P. 10th Cir. 1999) (bankruptcy court would not decide objection to proof of claim when sole basis of objection had been raised in state court proceeding and rejected by state court); *In re* Ferren, 227 B.R. 279 (B.A.P. 8th Cir. 1998) (court lacked jurisdiction to resolve adversary proceeding seeking turnover of funds that had been disbursed pursuant to decision of state court to creditors whose claims had arguably been discharged), *aff'd*, 203 F.3d 559 (8th Cir. 2000). *Compare In re* Gruntz, 202 F.3d 1074 (9th Cir. 2000) (en banc) (state court ruling on applicability of automatic stay was subject to bankruptcy court's ultimate authority to determine scope of stay, so *Rooker-Feldman* doctrine does not apply), *with In re* Pope, 209 B.R. 1004 (Bankr. D. Kan. 1997) (review of state court determination that litigant's actions did not violate stay is barred by *Rooker-Feldman*).

55 *See* § 14.4.1, *infra*.

56 *See, e.g., In re* Weinraub, 361 B.R. 586, 594 (Bankr. S.D. Fla. 2007) (debtor's TILA claims brought in adversary proceeding challenging transfer of home as part of foreclosure rescue scheme were not "inextricably intertwined" with state court default in eviction proceeding).

57 *See* § 9.4.2, *supra*.

contain a statement of whether the action is core or non-core.[58] The determination of whether a proceeding is a core proceeding is to be made initially by the bankruptcy court, on its own motion or on motion of a party.[59] But if no motion has been made by a party, and the parties have not explicitly disagreed on the issue, there is probably no necessity for a formal determination at the outset of every proceeding. The mere fact that a proceeding involves an issue of state law does not make it a non-core proceeding.[60] Many of the proceedings listed as core proceedings involve issues of state law, and bankruptcy courts have always considered state law issues in some contexts.

The issue of whether a proceeding is core or non-core may not always be clear. It is probably correct to assume that any proceeding asserting a right created by the Bankruptcy Code, or which could only arise in bankruptcy, is a core proceeding.[61] If the proceeding is based upon state or federal nonbankruptcy law, however, it must be examined further. Generally, if it is brought as a counterclaim or otherwise against a creditor of the debtor, the proceeding is considered a core proceeding.[62] If the proceeding is brought against a non-creditor third party, it usually is not a core proceeding.[63] If the proceeding is brought against the debtor by a person who is not a prepetition creditor, the proceeding may or may not fit into any of the categories of core proceedings. In some cases, the determination may involve a claim-by-claim analysis, with some claims being core and some non-core.[64]

Even in cases in which jurisdiction is found, an additional issue which occasionally arises is the bankruptcy court's power to enter certain types of equitable relief requested by a party. Code section 105 generally gives the bankruptcy court power to issue orders, process and judgments "necessary or appropriate" to carry out the provisions of the Bankruptcy Code.[65] Section 105 is not, however, a substantive grant of jurisdiction.[66] It also does not give the bankruptcy court unlimited power to create substantive rights or to issue equitable relief contrary to the Bankruptcy Code or applicable law.[67]

---

58 Fed. R. Bankr. P. 7008(a).
59 28 U.S.C. § 157(b)(3).
60 28 U.S.C. § 157(b)(3). *See In re* Manville Forest Prods. Corp., 896 F.2d 1384 (2d Cir. 1990); *In re* Wood, 825 F.2d 90 (5th Cir. 1987); *In re* Martinez, 2007 WL 1174186 (Bankr. S.D. Tex. Apr. 19, 2007) (rejecting argument that objection to creditor's claim based solely on Truth in Lending Act and state law is non-core proceeding). *See also* § 14.2.4.2, *supra*.
61 *In re* Harbour, 840 F.2d 1165 (4th Cir. 1988); *In re* Wood, 825 F.2d 90 (5th Cir. 1987). *See In re* McLaren, 990 F.2d 850 (bankruptcy court could determine dischargeability of a debt as a core proceeding, and the validity of the debt was also a core issue), *superseding* 983 F.2d 56 (6th Cir. 1993). *See also* Moody v. Amoco Oil, 734 F.2d 1200 (7th Cir. 1984) (proceeding to assume contract under section 365 not a "related" case under emergency rule); *In re* Goldrich, 45 B.R. 514 (Bankr. E.D.N.Y. 1984) (action to enforce nondiscrimination provisions of 11 U.S.C. § 525 a core proceeding), *rev'd on other grounds*, 771 F.2d 28 (2d Cir. 1985). *But see* Granfinanciera, S.A. v. Nordberg, 492 U.S. 33, 109 S. Ct. 2782, 106 L. Ed. 2d 26 (1989).
62 28 U.S.C. § 157(b)(2)(C), (O); *In re* Baudoin, 981 F.2d 736 (5th Cir. 1993) (debtor's lender liability suit against creditor was core proceeding). *But see* Stern v. Marshall, 131 S. Ct. 2594, 180 L. Ed. 2d 475 (2011) (even though state common law counterclaim against creditor that filed proof of claim was core, bankruptcy court did not have jurisdiction to enter final judgment on counterclaim); *In re* Brickell Inv. Corp., 922 F.2d 696 (11th Cir. 1991) (application for attorney fees against IRS is non-core proceeding even though request stems from core proceeding, but could be a related proceeding because bankruptcy court is not a "court of the United States" as specified in 26 U.S.C. § 7430); *In re* Castlerock Properties, 781 F.2d 159 (9th Cir. 1986).
    In addition, personal injury tort or wrongful death claims are expressly made non-core proceedings. *See* § 14.2.6, *infra*.
63 *See, e.g., In re* Cinematronics, Inc., 916 F.2d 1444 (9th Cir. 1990) (state law claims against corporate debtor's principal shareholder/president for his postpetition conduct were non-core when claims would not directly affect estate or confirmation of plan); Howell Hydrocarbons, Inc. v. Adams, 897 F.2d 183 (5th Cir. 1990) (RICO claims brought by seller of jet fuel against shareholders, officers, directors and managing agent of debtor buyer's parent corporation were non-core, non-related proceedings); Rosen-Novak Auto Co. v. Honz, 783 F.2d 739 (8th Cir. 1986) (action against debtor's insurer); *In re* Vinci, 108 B.R. 439 (Bankr. S.D.N.Y. 1989) (debtor's civil rights claim against non-creditor is a non-core related proceeding). *But see In re* Cassidy Land & Cattle Co., 836 F.2d 1130 (8th Cir. 1988) (debtor's action to foreclose on mortgage which constituted sole asset of bankruptcy estate is core proceeding in the nature of a turnover action); *In re* Arnold Print Works, 815 F.2d 165 (1st Cir. 1987) (debtor in possession's action to collect on contract made after bankruptcy as part of estate administration was core proceeding). *See also In re* Orion Pictures, 4 F.3d 1095 (2d Cir. 1993) (contract suit against party to executory contract that debtor wished to assume was non-core proceeding).
64 Halper v. Halper, 164 F.3d 830 (3d Cir. 1999).
65 *See* Marrama v. Citizens Bank of Mass., 549 U.S. 365, 127 S. Ct. 1105, 166 L. Ed. 2d 956 (2007); *In re* Hardy, 97 F.3d 1384 (11th Cir. 1996); Browning v. Navarro, 887 F.2d 553 (5th Cir. 1989) (section 105 is an authorization under the anti-injunction act, 28 U.S.C. § 2283, giving the bankruptcy court power to vacate a fraudulent state court judgment held against the estate); *In re* Matthys, 2010 WL 2176086 (Bankr. S.D. Ind. May 26, 2010) (§ 105 available to remedy creditor's violation of Fed. Rule of Bankr. P. 9037 by failing to redact Social Security numbers); *In re* Galloway, 2010 WL 364336 (Bankr. N.D. Miss. Jan. 29, 2010) (court has power to order sanctions under § 105 for mortgage overcharges); *In re* Batiste, 2009 WL 2849077 (Bankr. E.D. La. July 14, 2009) (ordering sanctions under § 105 against mortgage servicer that was repeat offender, even after servicer settled with debtor). *See also* 2 Collier on Bankruptcy ¶ 105.01[2] (16th ed.).
66 *See* Official Comm. of Equity Holders v. Mabey, 832 F.2d 299 (4th Cir. 1987); *In re* Sequoia Auto Brokers Ltd., 827 F.2d 1281 (9th Cir. 1987) (section 105 is not a substantive grant of authority empowering bankruptcy judges to enter contempt orders).
67 Norwest Bank Worthington v. Ahlers, 485 U.S. 197, 108 S. Ct. 963, 99 L. Ed. 2d 169 (1988) ("Whatever equitable powers remain in the bankruptcy courts must and can only be exercised within the confines of the Bankruptcy Code."). *See also In re* Ionosphere Clubs, Inc., 922 F.2d 984 (2d Cir. 1990) (powers under section 105 cannot be exercised in derogation of other sections of the Code); *In re* Weissman, 126 B.R. 889 (Bankr. N.D. Ill. 1991) (bankruptcy judge has no power to alter priorities contained in the Code); *In re* Gerst, 106 B.R. 429 (Bankr. E.D. Pa. 1989) (bankruptcy court has power to issue injunction requiring that debtor's landlord repair conditions which constitute serious risk to health and safety of residents). *Compare In re* Am. Hardwoods, Inc., 885 F.2d 621 (9th Cir. 1989) (section 105 does not give the bankruptcy court power to

A few courts have used this principle to improperly limit the authority of bankruptcy courts to address creditor violations of the bankruptcy law. In some cases, courts have denied remedies under section 105 to parties seeking relief from creditor fraud or egregious violations of the discharge injunction on the basis that no private right of action exists under section 105.[68] These courts ignore the importance of the statutory power to issue orders, process and judgments necessary and appropriate to carry out the provisions of the Bankruptcy Code.[69] Clearly, in order to seek the court's use of that authority, a party in interest must bring the problem to the attention of the court, by complaint or otherwise, seeking to have the provisions of the Code effectuated—whether by restitution or some other equitable remedy.

One further issue which may arise involves the scope of the bankruptcy court's jurisdiction over a case after it has been closed or dismissed. Many matters "arising under" or "related to" a bankruptcy proceeding may be brought before the court after a case has ended, even if the case is not formally reopened.[70] Nothing in the Bankruptcy Code or title 28 of the United States Code precludes a bankruptcy court from exercising jurisdiction over such matters.

As a practical matter, all of the proceedings in a routine consumer bankruptcy case are normally considered core proceedings, so these jurisdictional provisions have no significant effect on them. Such proceedings will generally continue to be heard in the bankruptcy court, subject to appeal to higher courts. Other proceedings, though, including many of the types of actions discussed later in this Chapter, do raise issues as to where they should be heard. And the distinction between core proceedings and non-core proceedings is only the first step in resolving those issues under the bankruptcy jurisdictional scheme. Even if a proceeding is found to be a core proceeding, there is no assurance that the bankruptcy court will decide the matter or enter proposed findings of fact and conclusions of law, or that the proceeding will remain in the bankruptcy court.

14.2.4.4 Procedure in Non-Core Proceedings

If a proceeding is determined to be a non-core proceeding, it is still normally initiated in the bankruptcy court pursuant to the district court's referral. The proceeding may be heard by the bankruptcy court and that court may make interlocutory orders.[71] However, the bankruptcy judge may not enter a final judgment or order, unless all parties consent.[72] A party's consent is to be set forth in the pleadings.[73] However, consent may also be implied by a party's actions.[74] If such consent is not

---

permanently enjoin creditors from enforcing a judgment against non-debtor guarantors of a corporate debtor) *with In re* A.H. Robins Co., 880 F.2d 694 (4th Cir. 1989) (section 105 permits court to enjoin suit against non-debtor corporate officers and directors in order to effectuate debtor's confirmed plan).

68 *See, e.g.,* Cox v. Zale Del., Inc., 239 F.3d 910 (7th Cir. 2001); Pertuso v. Ford Motor Cr. Co., 233 F.3d 417 (6th Cir. 2000); Holloway v. Household Auto. Fin. Corp., 227 B.R. 501 (N.D. Ill. 1998) (no private right of action under section 105 to address creditors fraudulently filed or inflated proofs of claim); *In re* Wiley, 224 B.R. 58 (Bankr. N.D. Ill. 1998) (no private right of action to enforce discharge injunction), *vacated and modified on other grounds,* 237 B.R. 677 (Bankr. N.D. Ill. 1999). *But see* Malone v. Norwest Fin. Cal., Inc., 245 B.R. 389 (E.D. Cal. 2000) (section 105 creates right of action to enforce discharge injunction in action involving unfiled reaffirmation agreements).

69 Bessette v. Avco Fin. Servs., Inc., 230 F.3d 439 (1st Cir. 2000) (section 524 may be enforced through section 105); *In re* Harris, 312 B.R. 591 (N.D. Miss. 2004) (section 105 may be used to grant relief to debtors for mortgage creditor's charging of late fees in violation of section 1322(b)(5)); *In re* Padilla, 379 B.R. 643 (Bankr. S.D. Tex. 2007) (court has authority under section 105 to order disgorgement of fees charged to debtors in violation of confirmed plan and without proper Rule 2016 application); *In re* Sanchez, 372 B.R. 289 (Bankr. S.D. Tex. 2007) (section 506 and Bankruptcy Rule 2016 may be enforced under section 105 in case involving mortgage creditor's failure to disclose postconfirmation fees charged to debtor). *See also* § 15.5.5.7, *infra.*

70 *See, e.g., In re* Statistical Tabulating Corp., 60 F.3d 1286 (7th Cir. 1995) (bankruptcy court could reopen dismissed bankruptcy case to decide remand of appeal which was not mooted by dismissal); *In re* Universal Farming Indus., 873 F.2d 1334 (9th Cir. 1989) (appeal of case determining priority of interests in debtor's property not mooted by dismissal of underlying bankruptcy); *In re* Franklin, 802 F.2d 324 (9th Cir. 1986) (bankruptcy court could construe its order in a prior bankruptcy case which had not been reopened). *See also In re* Porges, 44 F.3d 159 (2d Cir. 1995) (bankruptcy court could retain jurisdiction over adversary proceeding after underlying bankruptcy case was dismissed); *In re* Carreher, 971 F.2d 327 (9th Cir. 1992) (bankruptcy court could retain jurisdiction over related fraud claims of the debtor after dismissing debtor's bankruptcy case); *In re* Morris, 950 F.2d 1531 (11th Cir. 1992) (bankruptcy court could retain jurisdiction over adversary proceeding after main chapter 11 case was dismissed); *In re* Smith, 866 F.2d 576 (3d Cir. 1989) (bankruptcy court could retain jurisdiction over adversary proceeding after bankruptcy case closed to complete litigation of related claims).

Of course, certain matters may be mooted by the dismissal or close of the case. *See In re* Petty, 848 F.2d 654 (5th Cir. 1988) (court's jurisdiction over motion to have lease deemed rejected ends upon dismissal of case). *But see* Chapman v. Currie Motors, 65 F.3d 78 (7th Cir. 1995) (district court could relinquish jurisdiction over proceeding based upon state law after bankruptcy case dismissed); *In re* Querner, 7 F.3d 1199 (5th Cir. 1993) (bankruptcy court should not have retained jurisdiction over probate matter after bankruptcy case closed when bankruptcy judge had not become deeply involved in matter, had no special knowledge about probate and had no reason to believe outcome could affect bankruptcy estate).

71 *In re* Kennedy, 48 B.R. 621 (Bankr. D. Ariz. 1985).

72 28 U.S.C. § 157(c)(1), (2); *In re* Pioneer Inv. Servs. Co., 946 F.2d 445 (6th Cir. 1991).

73 Fed. R. Bankr. P. 7008(a).

74 *In re* Tex. Gen. Petroleum Corp., 52 F.3d 1330 (5th Cir. 1995) (party that does not object to bankruptcy court's assumption of core jurisdiction consents to entry of final judgment by bankruptcy court); *In re* Johnson, 960 F.2d 396 (4th Cir. 1992) (by allowing bankruptcy judge to enter dispositive order parties impliedly consented to core jurisdiction); *In re* G.S.F. Corp., 938 F.2d 1467 (1st Cir. 1991) (consent implied by parties' filing settlement agreement for final approval by bankruptcy court); *In re* Men's Sportswear, Inc., 834 F.2d 1134 (2d Cir. 1987) (failure to object to bankruptcy court's assumption of core jurisdiction may constitute implied consent); *In re* Daniels-Head & Assocs., 819 F.2d 914 (9th Cir. 1987). *But see* Fed. R. Bankr. P. 7008 advisory committee's note to 1987 amendment. *See also In re* BNI Telecomms., 246 B.R. 845 (B.A.P.

obtained, the bankruptcy court may only submit proposed findings of fact and conclusions of law to the district court.[75]

If (and only if) a party timely objects[76] to any of the proposed findings and conclusions, the district court must conduct a de novo review of the pertinent portions of proceedings.[77] Arguably, if no party objects, the district court must accept the proposed findings and conclusions of the bankruptcy court.[78] The failure to file objections to recommended findings of fact and conclusions of law has been held to constitute a waiver of any right to appeal a district court's order adopting such recommendations.[79]

14.2.5 Withdrawal to the District Court

14.2.5.1 In General

Regardless of whether a matter is or is not a core proceeding, it may still come to be heard initially in the district court. The bankruptcy jurisdictional provisions provide that after the initial referral to the bankruptcy court a bankruptcy proceeding, or even the bankruptcy case itself in whole or in part, may be withdrawn back to the district court.[80] Withdrawal is discretionary in some cases and mandatory in others. Such withdrawal may be upon "timely" motion of a party or on the court's own motion.[81]

Because the withdrawal decision appears to be one that can be made only by the district court, any motion for withdrawal must be addressed to that court.[82] However, the 1987 Advisory Committee Note to Federal Rule of Bankruptcy Procedure 5011 indicates that the motion should be filed with the bankruptcy clerk.

Rule 5011 does not appear to clarify time limits for filing a motion for withdrawal.[83] It should be remembered, however, that a motion for withdrawal, whenever filed, does not operate as a stay of the proceeding in the bankruptcy court. If a stay pending determination of a motion for withdrawal is desired, a motion for a stay should be presented in the first instance to the bankruptcy judge.[84]

14.2.5.2 Mandatory Withdrawal

In certain classes of cases or proceedings, including core proceedings, if a party timely[85] moves for withdrawal to the district court, that motion must be granted. Such mandatory withdrawal upon motion must occur whenever the resolution of a proceeding "requires consideration of both title 11 and other laws of the United States regulating organizations or activities affecting interstate commerce."[86] Although the general purpose of this section is clear—to prevent bankruptcy courts from deciding, over the objections of a party, substantial questions under statutes such as the antitrust and securities laws—the precise scope of the section is not.

What is meant by "consideration of both title 11 and other laws?" Does the section apply to matters considering federal laws regulating interstate commerce but not title 11? It may not. Some courts have held that both bankruptcy law and other federal law issues must coexist for mandatory withdrawal to be proper.[87]

---

75 28 U.S.C. § 157(c)(1); Fed. R. Bankr. P. 9033.
76 Pursuant to Federal Rule of Bankruptcy Procedure 9033(b) objections must be filed within fourteen days after service of the proposed findings of fact and conclusions of law. Service of objections then triggers a fourteen-day period for a response by any other party. Further, pursuant to Rule 9033(c), upon request made prior to expiration of the fourteen-day period for objections, the bankruptcy judge is empowered to extend the time allowed for filing objections for up to twenty-one days.
77 28 U.S.C. § 157(c)(1); Fed. R. Bankr. P. 9033.
    When it was shown that the district court conducted no hearing and did not consider the actual testimony in bankruptcy court, no de novo review occurred. In re Castro, 919 F.2d 107 (9th Cir. 1990).
    A party claiming that the district court had not conducted a de novo review has the burden of proof. The fact that the record remained with the clerk of the bankruptcy court is not sufficient to show that a de novo review has not been conducted by the district court. In re Dillon Constr. Co., 922 F.2d 495 (8th Cir. 1991).
78 There is no provision in Federal Rule of Bankruptcy Procedure 9033 for review absent a timely objection.
79 In re Nantahala Vill., Inc., 976 F.2d 876 (4th Cir. 1992).
80 28 U.S.C. § 157(d).
81 28 U.S.C. § 157(d). See Anderson v. Fed. Deposit Ins. Corp., 918 F.2d 1139 (4th Cir. 1990) (district court's retention of jurisdiction after plaintiff filed bankruptcy and trustee was substituted as plaintiff effectively withdrew matter from bankruptcy court).
    When a district court withdraws the reference after the bankruptcy court has rendered a decision, the district court may exercise its original jurisdiction to reshape relief. In re Moody, 899 F.2d 383 (5th Cir. 1990).

82 Fed. R. Bankr. P. 5011(a); In re Porter, 295 B.R. 529 (Bankr. E.D. Pa. 2003) (bankruptcy court has no authority to send case back to district court, because only district court may withdraw reference).
83 See In re IQ Telecomms., Inc., 70 B.R. 742 (N.D. Ill. 1987) (motion before answer was due was timely, but motion made over one year after proceeding began was not timely).
84 Fed. R. Bankr. P. 5011(c); In re Morse Elec. Co, Inc., 47 B.R. 234 (Bankr. N.D. Ind. 1985). See also In re Roppolo, 111 B.R. 113 (Bankr. W.D. La. 1990) (request for stay of fraudulent conveyance proceedings pending resolution of motion for withdrawal denied).
85 There are currently no rules to determine timeliness under this section. However, a motion for withdrawal of reference presumably must be filed prior to dismissal or discharge. In re Mandalay Shores Coop. Hous. Ass'n, Inc., 58 B.R. 586 (N.D. Ill. 1986).
    One court has held that a motion for withdrawal more than six months after the grounds for the motion were discovered is untimely. Laine v. Gross, 128 B.R. 588 (D. Me. 1991). That court was concerned that withdrawal was not sought until after a motion to dismiss had been resolved by the bankruptcy court.
86 28 U.S.C. § 157(d).
87 In re Anthony Tammaro, Inc., 56 B.R. 999 (D.N.J. 1986); In re Maislin Indus., 50 B.R. 943 (Bankr. E.D. Mich. 1985). See also In re Auto Specialties Mfg. Co., 134 B.R. 227 (W.D. Mich. 1990) (filing of RICO claim did not require withdrawal unless there was showing that claim was facially valid, that it presented questions of first impression, or that case required construction of both the Bankruptcy Code and the RICO statute); In re Chateaugey Corp., 109 B.R. 613 (S.D.N.Y. 1990) (although underlying case involved

How much "consideration" is necessary for the section to apply? Presumably, there would have to be more than mere consideration of a federal commerce statute by way of analogy. The legislative history suggests that the interstate commerce statute must be material to the resolution of the proceeding.[88] Some courts have suggested that there must be a need for "substantial and material" consideration of such a statute for withdrawal to be required.[89] The Seventh Circuit has stated that consideration means the interpretation, as opposed to the mere application of the nonbankruptcy statute, or the resolution of significant open issues of law.[90] Another court has stated that withdrawal is mandatory when the bankruptcy issues are secondary to the nonbankruptcy federal issues.[91]

Mandatory withdrawal may be a very real possibility in some consumer bankruptcy proceedings. For example, debtors may raise a variety of federal consumer protection laws by way of objections to claims or otherwise. In such cases, either party may move for, and possibly obtain, withdrawal of the proceeding to the district court.[92] Naturally, whether the debtor will wish to make a motion for withdrawal will depend on a variety of factors, including the judges involved, the likelihood of delay, and other aspects of the case. The debtor may wish to argue that individual consumer protection cases are not what Congress had in mind when it described laws regulating interstate commerce. However, a motion for withdrawal is certainly an option which must be considered whenever it is available.

14.2.5.3 Discretionary Withdrawal

The district court may also withdraw any case or proceeding at its discretion, either upon motion of a party or upon its own motion. The standards for discretionary withdrawal are far from clear, although the statute requires "cause."[93] Certainly, withdrawal makes sense when there is already related litigation in the district court.[94] Withdrawal may also be appropriate when the parties or the court believe that a case will have wide-ranging consequences and is likely to be reviewed de novo by the district court in any event. But when core issues predominate and the objectives of the Bankruptcy Code will potentially be impaired, a district court should generally deny a motion to withdraw the reference and permit the bankruptcy court to retain jurisdiction.[95] And, absent exceptional circumstances, it does not seem appropriate for a district court to withdraw the reference of a case or proceeding after receiving an appeal of a final order of the bankruptcy court, because such a withdrawal would frustrate the normal process of the appeal.[96]

---

both bankruptcy and other federal law, when party sought injunction of that case, withdrawal was properly denied because court did not need to consider other federal law).

88 130 Cong. Rec. S6081 (daily ed. June 19, 1984) (remarks of Sen. DeConcini). *See, e.g.*, Dow Jones/Group W Television Co. v. NBC, Inc., 127 B.R. 3 (S.D.N.Y. 1991) (withdrawal denied when bankruptcy court had merely to apply settled principles of federal antitrust law to the proceeding).

89 *In re* Ionosphere Clubs, Inc., 922 F.2d 984 (2d Cir. 1990); *In re* Adelpi Inst., Inc., 112 B.R. 534 (S.D.N.Y. 1990) (requirement that matter require substantial and material consideration of other federal law excludes from mandatory withdrawal cases which involve only application of other federal law to particular set of facts); *In re* Carolina Produce Distributors, Inc., 110 B.R. 207 (W.D.N.C. 1990) (adversary proceeding under Perishable Agricultural Commodities Act did not involve substantial material question of both bankruptcy law and other federal law required only application of the other federal law to the facts and consideration of state law); *In re* Amfesco Indus., Inc., 81 B.R. 777 (E.D.N.Y. 1988) (question presented did not require substantial and material consideration of the copyright laws); *In re* White Motor Corp., 42 B.R. 693 (N.D. Ohio 1984). *See also In re* Baker, 86 B.R. 234 (D. Colo. 1988) (withdrawal required when question as to dischargeability of debt required "substantial consideration" of 42 U.S.C. § 1983 and Bankruptcy Code dischargeability provisions).

90 *In re* Vicars Ins. Agency, Inc., 96 F.3d 949 (7th Cir. 1996). *See also* Rodriguez v. Countrywide Home Loans, Inc., 421 B.R. 341 (S.D. Tex. 2009) (having to apply settled RESPA law to determine mortgage overcharges did not require withdrawal).

91 Wooten v. Dep't of Interior, 52 B.R. 74 (W.D. La. 1985). *See* Alfonseca-Baez v. Doral Fin. Corp., 376 B.R. 70 (D. P.R. 2007) (creditor's motion for withdrawal denied when primary issue was whether proof of claim was proper).

92 Newell v. Wells Fargo Bank (*In re* Newell), 2010 WL 5396018 (N.D. Cal. Dec. 23, 2010) (mandatory withdrawal of proceeding alleging violation of Home Affordable Modification Program by lender where no party argued to contrary). *But see* Prince v. Countrywide Home Loans, Inc., 2008 WL 4572545 (M.D. Tenn. Oct. 8, 2008) (mandatory withdrawal denied because debtor's RESPA and FDCPA claims involved same facts as bankruptcy and state law claims, and did not require substantial and material consideration of federal statutes).

93 28 U.S.C. § 157(d); *In re* Parklane/Atlanta Joint Venture, 927 F.2d 532 (11th Cir. 1991) ("cause" is not an "empty requirement," but may be satisfied in a situation in which bankruptcy court disposition of case might be unappealable); *In re* Wilson, 2012 WL 3043170 (E.D. La. July 25, 2012) (fact that bankruptcy court could not order criminal contempt sanctions that were deemed appropriate was cause); Halvajian v. Bank of N.Y., 191 B.R. 56 (D.N.J. 1995) (fact that bankruptcy court lacked supplemental jurisdiction under 28 U.S.C. § 1367 to hear third party state law indemnification claim that defendant wished to raise not cause for withdrawal, because claim could be raised in separate action). *See also In re* Canter, 299 F.3d 1150 (9th Cir. 2002) (granting mandamus to review withdrawal of reference that was inappropriate because bankruptcy court was already familiar with case and had already entered order and because withdrawal created inefficiency and disrupted bankruptcy administration).

However, the district court will almost certainly refuse to exercise its discretion to withdraw a core matter, especially when the basis for core jurisdiction is the creditor's presumably voluntary filing of a proof of claim. *See* Bedford Computer Corp. v. Ginn Publ'g, Inc., 63 B.R. 79 (D.N.H. 1986).

It would also likely be inappropriate for a district court to withdraw the reference *nunc pro tunc* in order to validate its own order entered in violation of the stay. *Cf.* Mission Indians v. Am. Mgmt. & Amusement, 840 F.2d 1394 (9th Cir. 1987) (reference withdrawn *nunc pro tunc* in conjunction with an order entered after order partially lifting stay).

94 *See* Carlton v. BAWW, Inc., 751 F.2d 781 (5th Cir. 1985). *Cf.* Mar. Elec. Co. v. United Jersey Bank, 959 F.2d 1194 (3d Cir. 1991) (district court other than one in jurisdiction where bankruptcy case is filed may retain and exercise "related to" jurisdiction over case involving debtor which is already pending).

95 Rodriguez v. Countrywide Home Loans, Inc., 421 B.R. 341 (S.D. Tex. 2009).

96 *In re* Hall, Bayoutree Assocs. Ltd., 939 F.2d 802 (9th Cir. 1991)

14.2.6 Personal Injury and Wrongful Death Claims

A special exception to the broad categories of core proceedings was created by Congress for all personal injury tort and wrongful death claims against the debtor or the estate.[97] The 1984 amendments, in a provision probably designed to curb manufacturers seeking refuge in bankruptcy from asbestos and other product liability claims, require all such claims to be tried either in the district court in which the bankruptcy case is pending or the district court where the claim arose, as determined by the district court in which the bankruptcy is pending.[98]

Although the language of section 157(b)(5) is vague, it was probably not intended to include personal injury and wrongful death claims held by the debtor against a third party. Such claims are usually considered non-core proceedings, which can be heard in the bankruptcy court but not finally determined by that court without the consent of the parties.[99] There may also be disputes as to what types of claims qualify as personal injury claims.[100]

This provision also was not meant to preclude bankruptcy courts from determining issues related to the dischargeability of claims against the debtor involving personal injury or wrongful death.[101] However, bankruptcy courts may be unwilling to exercise their discretion to liquidate those claims if they have not been liquidated elsewhere.[102]

Section 157(b)(5) requires personal injury tort and wrongful death claims to be tried in the district court. The section does not explicitly require that pre-trial proceedings be in the district court, and this omission presumably was deliberate, to leave open the possibility of pre-trial proceedings before a bankruptcy judge.[103]

Section 157(b)(2)(B) excludes from the core proceedings list "liquidation or estimation" of personal injury tort or wrongful death claims for purposes of distribution. The section thus does not appear to preclude estimation of these claims for purposes of deciding whether a plan may be confirmed.[104] It also does not preclude discretionary abstention which would allow such claims to be tried in state courts.

14.2.7 Jury Trials in the Bankruptcy Court

Unlike the temporary emergency rule governing bankruptcy jurisdiction from 1982 to 1984, the current jurisdictional statutes contain no prohibition of jury trials conducted by the bankruptcy court. The 1984 amendments specifically preserve the right to a jury trial with regard to personal injury and wrongful death claims.[105] However, that trial may not take place before a bankruptcy judge.[106] It is doubtful that this provision was intended to affect other rights to jury trials that previously existed.[107]

Other questions about jury trial rights in bankruptcy survived the 1984 amendments. Most importantly, these included the degree to which traditional jury trial rights are affected by the Code and the post-*Marathon* jurisdictional scheme and whether jury trials may be conducted by bankruptcy judges.

The first question was addressed by the Supreme Court in *Granfinanciera, S.A. v. Nordberg*.[108] The Court held that under the Seventh Amendment, a defendant in a preference or fraudulent conveyance action who has not filed a claim against the estate retains the right to trial by jury. The Court applied a traditional Seventh Amendment analysis and determined that a preference or fraudulent conveyance action is, by tradition, an action at law as to which jury trial rights are constitutionally preserved.[109] Presumably, in the future, a similar analysis will

---

(district court's decision to reach issue not raised on appeal cannot constitute a de facto withdrawal of the reference); *In re* Pruitt, 910 F.2d 1160 (3d Cir. 1990) (writ of *mandamus* issued directing district court to consider appeal from bankruptcy court order dismissing case, rather than withdraw reference after the dismissal). *See In re* Powelson, 878 F.2d 976 (7th Cir. 1989) (writ of mandamus issued directing district court to determine appeal of confirmation order rather than withdraw reference and substitute alternative non-appealable "interim" plan).

97 28 U.S.C. § 157(b)(2)(B), (O).
98 28 U.S.C. § 157(b)(5).
99 28 U.S.C. § 157(c). *See In re* Vinci, 108 B.R. 439 (Bankr. S.D.N.Y. 1989) (civil rights claim by debtor against non-creditor governmental entities is a non-core, related proceeding).
100 *See, e.g.,* Moore v. Idealease of Wilmington, 358 B.R. 248 (E.D.N.C. 2006) (civil rights claims were personal injury claim); *In re* Grimes, 388 B.R. 195 (Bankr. N.D. W. Va. 2008) (claim for negligent financial advice not a personal injury claim); *In re* Sheehan Mem'l Hosp., 377 B.R. 63 (Bankr. W.D.N.Y. 2007) (employment discrimination claim not a personal injury tort); *In re* Littles, 75 B.R. 240 (Bankr. E.D. Pa. 1987) (claim under Fair Debt Collection Practices Act was not personal injury claim under section 157(b)(5)), *conclusions adopted,* Littles v. Lieberman, 90 B.R. 669 (E.D. Pa. 1988). *See* Elkes Dev., L.L.C. v. Arnold (*In re* Arnold), 407 B.R. 849 (Bankr. M.D.N.C. 2009) (libel and slander claims were personal injury tort claims). *See also In re* Gary Brew Enters., Ltd., 198 B.R. 616 (Bankr. S.D. Cal 1996) (employment discrimination claim was in nature of personal injury tort); *In re* Vinci, 108 B.R. 439 (Bankr. S.D.N.Y. 1989) (civil rights claim which did not involve bodily injury is not a claim for personal injury).
101 *See* 11 U.S.C. § 523(a)(6); 28 U.S.C. § 157(b)(2)(I). *See also* § 15.4.3.6, *infra*.
102 *Cf. In re* Saunders, 103 B.R. 299 (Bankr. N.D. Fla. 1988) (bank-

ruptcy court can exercise discretion to have potentially nondischargeable debt liquidated in forum where parties had been litigating for two years prior to bankruptcy).
103 *In re* Chateaugay Corp., 111 B.R. 67 (Bankr. S.D.N.Y. 1990) (bankruptcy court could make initial determination regarding proper parties and statutory defenses). *But see* Pettibone Corp. v. Easley, 935 F.2d 120 (7th Cir. 1991) (bankruptcy judge cannot hear any part of a personal injury case).
104 1 Collier on Bankruptcy ¶ 3.06[1] (16th ed.).
105 28 U.S.C. § 1411.
106 28 U.S.C. § 157(b)(5).
107 *See* 1 Collier on Bankruptcy ¶ 3.08[1] (16th ed.). *See also In re* Graham, 747 F.2d 1383 (11th Cir. 1984) (interpreting prior statutory language that jury rights "provided by any statute" not affected by Bankruptcy Reform Act).
108 492 U.S. 33, 109 S. Ct. 2782, 106 L. Ed. 2d 26 (1989).
109 *But see In re* Tex. Gen. Petroleum Corp., 52 F.3d 1330 (5th Cir. 1995) (no jury trial existed in fraudulent transfer proceeding when only issue in proceeding was legal issue of standing).

have to take place when jury trials are demanded, on an issue by issue basis.[110] Courts have held, for example, that there is no constitutional right to a jury trial in a dischargeability action.[111] Similarly, because a turnover action under section 542 is essentially equitable, seeking to obtain property of the estate over which the bankruptcy court has *in rem* jurisdiction, a defendant allegedly holding estate property has no right to a jury trial, even if that property is cash.[112]

When the defendant files a claim against the estate, that party's right to a jury trial is waived.[113] In addition, other limitations on the availability of a jury trial, such as the necessity for a timely jury demand, continue to apply and jury trials may be denied for failure to comply with procedural requirements.[114]

The fact that a proceeding is "core" under the jurisdictional scheme established by the 1984 amendments will not be dispositive in determining whether a jury trial right attaches.[115]

Additionally, one court has held that a debtor may retain and assert certain jury trial rights following a bankruptcy petition.[116]

The *Granfinanciera* decision explicitly leaves open the other significant issue regarding jury trials in bankruptcy, that is, whether bankruptcy judges may conduct them. It has always been fairly clear that in non-core matters it would be uneconomic and inefficient to hold jury trials in bankruptcy courts unless the parties consented to entry of final judgment by the bankruptcy judge, because the parties would have a right to a trial de novo in district court.[117] However, after *Granfinanciera*, some core matters clearly carry jury trial rights and significant questions may arise as to whether they may be tried in bankruptcy court. That issue turns in part on whether the Seventh Amendment mandates a jury trial in front of an Article III judge.[118]

To the extent that there was also an issue concerning the bankruptcy court's statutory authority to conduct a jury trial, the situation was clarified by the Bankruptcy Reform Act of 1994.[119] That Act added 28 U.S.C. § 157(e), which provides that if there is a right to a jury trial in a proceeding a bankruptcy judge may hear, the bankruptcy judge may conduct the jury trial if spe-

---

110 *See generally In re* M & L Bus. Mach. Co., 59 F.3d 1078 (10th Cir. 1995) (no jury trial right in trustee's action under section 549, which was equitable in nature); *In re* O.P.M. Leasing Servs., Inc., 48 B.R. 824 (S.D.N.Y. 1985); Macon Prestressed Concrete Co. v. Duke, 46 B.R. 727 (M.D. Ga. 1985).

111 *In re* McLaren, 3 F.3d 958 (6th Cir. 1993) (debtor has no right to jury trial in dischargeability proceeding); *In re* Hallahan, 936 F.2d 1496 (7th Cir. 1991) (debtor has no right to jury trial in dischargeability proceeding); *In re* Hooper, 112 B.R. 1009 (B.A.P. 9th Cir. 1990) (creditor has no right to jury trial in dischargeability proceeding).

112 Braunstein v. McCabe, 571 F.3d 108 (1st Cir. 2009).

113 Langenkamp v. Culp, 498 U.S. 42, 111 S. Ct. 330, 112 L. Ed. 2d 343 (1990). *See also* Billing v. Ravin, Greenberg & Zackin, 22 F.3d 1242 (3d Cir. 1994) (no right of jury trial for malpractice claim asserted as a defense to a proof of claim); *In re* EXDS, 301 B.R. 436 (Bankr. D. Del. 2003) (creditor could not vitiate waiver of jury trial right by withdrawing claim after it was filed). *But see* Smith v. Dowden, 47 F.3d 940 (8th Cir. 1995) (withdrawal of claim before fraudulent transfer proceeding was commenced rendered claim a nullity, so jury trial was not waived).

114 *See In re* Latimer, 918 F.2d 136 (10th Cir. 1990) (oral request for jury trial not sufficient; even if it had been, failure to combine jury request with request for transfer to district court resulted in waiver of right to jury trial); *In re* Wynn, 889 F.2d 644 (5th Cir. 1989) (party who participated in determination of proceeding without reminding court of his jury trial request waived his jury trial rights); *In re* Sand Hills Beef Corp., 199 B.R. 740 (D. Colo. 1996) (failure to request transfer to district court when jury trial was requested resulted in waiver of right to jury trial); *In re* Blackwell *ex rel.* Estate of I.G. Servs., 279 B.R. 818 (Bankr. W.D. Tex 2002) (party that demanded jury trial waived right to jury by failing to move to withdraw reference, because bankruptcy court could not unilaterally transfer proceeding to district court). *Cf. In re* Corey, 892 F.2d 829 (9th Cir. 1989) (entity controlled by parties who had filed claims against the estate deemed to have filed a claim and therefore ineligible for jury trial).

115 The fairly substantial body of case law which concluded that there are no jury trial rights in core proceedings or in proceedings arising under a specific statutory provision of the Bankruptcy Code has been overruled. *See, e.g.*, Beard v. Braunstein, 914 F.2d 434 (3d Cir. 1990) (party's right to jury trial of claims raised in bankruptcy proceeding does not depend on whether proceeding is designated core or non-core); *In re* Harbour, 840 F.2d 1165 (4th Cir. 1988).

116 *In re* Jensen, 946 F.2d 369 (5th Cir. 1991) (when state court case is removed to bankruptcy court by a creditor, debtor retains jury trial rights notwithstanding voluntary decision to file bankruptcy). *See also* Germain v. Conn. Nat'l Bank, 988 F.2d 1323 (2d Cir. 1993) (filing of bankruptcy case did not waive any right chapter 7 trustee might have to a jury trial).

117 *See, e.g., In re* Orion Pictures, 4 F.3d 1095 (2d Cir. 1993) (bankruptcy court could not constitutionally conduct jury trial in non-core proceeding); *In re* Cinematronics, Inc., 916 F.2d 1444 (9th Cir. 1990) (withdrawal of reference repaired when non-core defendant demands jury trial to which it is entitled and parties do not consent to final judgment by bankruptcy court); Beard v. Braunstein, 914 F.2d 434 (3d Cir. 1990); *In re* Am. Cmty. Servs., Inc., 86 B.R. 681 (D. Utah 1988); Macon Prestressed Concrete Co. v. Duke, 46 B.R. 727 (M.D. Ga. 1985); *In re* Morse Elec. Co., 47 B.R. 234 (Bankr. N.D. Ind. 1985). *But see In re* Hardesty, 190 B.R. 653 (D. Kan. 1995) (when jury trial demanded in non-core proceeding, withdrawal of reference not necessary until case is ready for trial).

118 *Compare In re* Clay, 35 F.3d 190 (5th Cir. 1994) (bankruptcy judge had no constitutional or statutory authority to conduct jury trial absent consent of the parties, even in core proceedings); *In re* Stansbury Poplar Place, Inc., 13 F.3d 122 (4th Cir. 1993) (bankruptcy judge has no statutory authority to conduct jury trial); *In re* Grabill Corp., 967 F.2d 1152 (7th Cir. 1992) (bankruptcy judge not authorized to conduct jury trial); *In re* Baker & Getty Fin. Servs., Inc., 954 F.2d 1169 (6th Cir. 1992) (bankruptcy judge not authorized to conduct jury trial) *and In re* United Mo. Bank of Kansas City, 901 F.2d 1449 (8th Cir. 1990) (bankruptcy judge lacks authority to conduct jury trial in preference action) *with In re* Ben Cooper, Inc., 896 F.2d 1394 (2d Cir. 1990), *reinstated after remand*, 924 F.2d 36 (2d Cir. 1991); *In re* Jackson, 118 B.R. 243 (E.D. Pa. 1990) (bankruptcy judge has authority to conduct jury trials in core proceedings) *and In re* Kroh Bros. Dev. Co., 108 B.R. 228 (W.D. Mo. 1989) (bankruptcy judge has authority to conduct jury trials in core matters).

All cases cited above in this note were decided under the law as it existed prior to the 1994 amendment adding 28 U.S.C. § 157(e) discussed below.

119 Pub. L. No. 103-394, 108 Stat. 4106 (1994).

cially designated by the district court to do so and with the express consent of all parties. The statute does not make clear whether the special designation is to be made once for all cases before a particular bankruptcy judge or on a case-by-case basis. At least some district courts have made blanket special designations for their bankruptcy judges.

The procedure for requesting a jury trial is set forth in Federal Rule of Bankruptcy Procedure 9015. The rule incorporates Federal Rules of Civil Procedure 38, 39, 47–51 and 81(c), making them applicable in bankruptcy cases, except that the demand for a jury trial must be filed in accordance with Bankruptcy Rule 5005. Separate consents or a joint consent to a jury trial must be filed no later than the deadline for such consents under local rules.[120]

In any event, even when a party has properly asserted its right to a jury trial, the bankruptcy court may continue to conduct pre-trial proceedings and may rule on dispositive pre-trial motions.[121]

14.2.8 Contempt Powers of the Bankruptcy Courts

The 1984 amendments also cast doubt upon the power of bankruptcy courts to enter contempt orders. A few courts have held that bankruptcy judges do not have the contempt power because they are not Article III judges.[122] But most have found that civil contempt proceedings, at least when the proceedings involve bankruptcy stays such as the section 362 automatic stay, are core proceedings in which the bankruptcy court may enter final orders.[123] Even those courts, however, have expressed doubt about the power to enter a criminal contempt order.[124] Because most courts have held that bankruptcy courts do have contempt powers,[125] Federal Rule of Bankruptcy Procedure 9020 was amended to eliminate the special procedures that had been adopted when the contempt power was in doubt, and to provide that a motion for an order of civil contempt is to be litigated as a contested matter under Rule 9014.[126]

14.3 Advantages of the Bankruptcy Court As a Forum

14.3.1 Possibilities of a Fairer Result for the Consumer Client

Depending on the circumstances, the bankruptcy court may be a preferable forum for the litigation of many types of cases that involve consumer debtors. When the debtor is in bankruptcy and has a choice of forums, a number of factors should be considered. But even if a client is not in bankruptcy, the litigation advantages offered by the federal bankruptcy forum may be so great that they justify filing a bankruptcy petition even if it otherwise might not be needed.

In many districts, the bankruptcy judges and federal judges may be a good deal more sympathetic to the consumer's case than judges in other local courts. Not only do bankruptcy judges regularly see the problems of debtors in trouble, but also they are generally more aware of the unfair creditor practices that often take place. Many bankruptcy judges are pleased to be presented with novel and creative cases that provide both a change of pace from routine bankruptcy matters and a means for ruling on unfair practices.

In addition, most bankruptcy judges are far more knowledgeable in commercial law, and often in consumer law, than the average state judge, because the cases they see usually involve such issues. To the extent that some bankruptcy judges are not yet familiar with consumer law, the concentration of a significant number of consumer cases in their courts will soon enhance their expertise. In addition, both bankruptcy and federal appellate judges may be more disposed, because of lower case

---

120 Fed. R. Bankr. P. 9015(b).
121 *In re* Healthcentral.com, 504 F.3d 775 (9th Cir. 2007); Jobin v. Kloepfer (*In re* M & L Bus. Mach. Co.), 159 B.R. 932, 934–935 (D. Colo. 1993); Stein v. Miller, 158 B.R. 876, 879–880 (S.D. Fla. 1993).
122 *See, e.g., In re* Sequoia Auto Brokers Ltd., 827 F.2d 1281 (9th Cir. 1987); *In re* Indus. Tool Distrib., Inc., 55 B.R. 746 (N.D. Ga. 1985); *In re* Omega Equip. Corp., 51 B.R. 569 (D.D.C. 1985).
123 *See, e.g., In re* Terrebonne Fuel & Lube, Inc., 108 F.3d 609 (5th Cir. 1997); *In re* Power Recovery Sys., Inc., 950 F.2d 798 (1st Cir. 1991) (bankruptcy courts have contempt powers provided that proper notice of procedures is given); *In re* Castro, 919 F.2d 107 (9th Cir. 1990) (bankruptcy court has civil contempt power to enforce discharge order in core proceeding); *In re* Schafer, 146 B.R. 477 (D. Kan. 1992) (bankruptcy court had power to find party in contempt for violating discharge injunction); *In re* DePew, 55 B.R. 106 (Bankr. E.D. Tenn. 1985). *See also* United States v. Revie, 834 F.2d 1198 (5th Cir. 1987) (district court can hold party in criminal contempt for failing to appear at hearing in bankruptcy court to show cause why he had not obeyed bankruptcy court order; bankruptcy court had jurisdiction at least to determine if its order was being obeyed).
124 *See* United States v. Guariglia, 962 F.2d 160 (2d Cir. 1992) (district court had authority to punish criminal contempt of bankruptcy court's order in first instance); *In re* Hipp, Inc., 895 F.2d 1503 (5th Cir. 1990) (bankruptcy court without power to preside over criminal contempt proceedings except perhaps those involving contempt committed in or near its presence). *See also In re* Dyer, 322 F.3d 1178 (9th Cir. 2003) (no authority under section 105(a) to award criminal contempt sanctions); *In re* Magwood, 785 F.2d 1077 (D.C. Cir. 1986); *In re* Ho, 2012 WL 405092 (E.D. La. Feb. 8, 2012) (contempt order that was intended to punish was criminal in nature and beyond bankruptcy court's jurisdiction); *In re* Armstrong, 304 B.R. 432 (B.A.P. 10th Cir. 2004) (contempt order imposing fines for violations of litigation injunction was in nature of criminal contempt, which bankruptcy court did not have jurisdiction to impose); *In re* Lickman, 288 B.R. 291 (Bankr. M.D. Fla. 2003) (referring contempt matter to district court because bankruptcy court may not enter punitive or criminal contempt orders); *In re* Crabtree, 47 B.R. 150 (Bankr. E.D. Tenn. 1985). *But see In re* Ragar, 3 F.3d 1174 (8th Cir. 1993) (bankruptcy court order finding attorney in criminal contempt and giving ten days for attorney to request de novo hearing in district court was valid).
125 *See, e.g., In re* Terrebone Fuel & Lube, Inc., 108 F.3d 609 (5th Cir. 1997); *In re* Rainbow Magazine, Inc., 77 F.3d 278 (9th Cir. 1996).
126 *See* Fed. R. Bankr. P. 9020 advisory committee's note (2001).

loads and the greater availability of law clerk assistance, to consider carefully bona fide legal arguments on behalf of debtors.

Litigation in the bankruptcy case may provide a method of avoiding a forum in which the debtor has little chance of prevailing. In a rural area, it may be the only way to avoid a hostile state judge who hears every case filed in that particular locality. It may also provide a means to avoid courts that have become high-volume mills (usually for the benefit of debtors' adversaries) for eviction, foreclosure, and collection cases.

The bankruptcy system also offers better discovery than many state courts, because it is governed by the Federal Rules of Bankruptcy Procedure, which basically incorporate the liberal federal discovery rules. In busy metropolitan areas, litigation in bankruptcy court and federal court usually proceeds more quickly and expeditiously than in state courts serving the same jurisdiction.

14.3.2 Avoidance of Substantive or Procedural Difficulties

14.3.2.1 *In Personam* Jurisdiction, Venue and Service Requirements

In specific cases, a bankruptcy proceeding may offer a way around a difficult procedural problem which could prove fatal in any other forum. Certain provisions governing bankruptcy litigation make it a useful way to avoid such problems.

One extremely helpful provision allows nationwide service of process in most bankruptcy proceedings. Generally, any case within the district court's bankruptcy jurisdiction that involves the debtor, that is, relating in any way to the bankruptcy or the debtor's property,[127] may be filed in the bankruptcy court in which the bankruptcy case has been filed, regardless of whether the state or federal courts in that state would otherwise have had "long-arm jurisdiction" over the defendant.[128] There is no "minimum contacts" test which must be met before an out-of-state defendant can be sued in the forum district's bankruptcy court,[129] and so, in some cases, the bankruptcy court may be the only place other than a defendant's home state where litigation can be commenced against a particular party.

The major exception to this general venue provision applies to trustees who commence cases either to recover less than $1175 or, if against a non-insider,[130] less than $11,725, or for consumer debts (that is, against a consumer), less than $17,575, in a district other than that where the defendant resides.[131] It is not clear whether the exceptions apply to proceedings brought under the trustee's avoiding powers.[132] In any event, because the exceptions apply only to the trustee, they seem unlikely to affect litigation initiated by debtors.

Another exception to the general venue rules can occur under 28 U.S.C. § 1412. That section provides that even if venue is proper in the district where suit has been brought, the litigation may be transferred to any other district in the interest of justice and for the convenience of the parties.[133] Because consumer debtors rarely have the resources to litigate in distant forums, it will be a rare case in which an out-of-state defendant successfully invokes this provision to transfer a case commenced by a consumer client.

Moreover, service of process generally can be made by first class mail.[134] An exception to the general right to serve by first class mail was created by the Bankruptcy Reform Act of 1994,[135] which amended Federal Rule of Bankruptcy Procedure 7004 to provide that service of process on an insured depository institution in a contested matter or adversary proceeding must be made by certified mail to an officer of the institution unless certain requirements have been met.[136]

Section 342(c) of the Code states that all notices required to be given by the debtor to a creditor must contain the debtor's name, address, and last four digits of the debtor's taxpayer identification (Social Security) number.[137] It may not always be

---

127 28 U.S.C. § 1334(b), (e).
128 28 U.S.C. § 1409(a).
129 *In re* Fed. Fountain, Inc., 165 F.3d 600 (8th Cir. 1999) (en banc) (nationwide service is constitutional); *In re* Hogue, 736 F.2d 989 (4th Cir. 1984) (finding nationwide service of process constitutional); *In re* G. Weeks Sec., Inc., 3 B.R. 215 (Bankr. W.D. Tenn. 1980).
130 "Insider" is defined in 11 U.S.C. § 101(31).
131 28 U.S.C. § 1409(b).
    There are several other exceptions relating to debtors in business.

See 28 U.S.C. § 1409(c), (d), (e); *In re* Little Lake Indus., Inc., 158 B.R. 478 (B.A.P. 9th Cir. 1993) (debtor in possession could bring preference action for less than $1000 only in defendant's home district).
132 *See* Redmond v. Gulf City Body & Trailer Works, Inc. (*In re* Sunbridge Capital, Inc.), 454 B.R. 166 (Bankr. D. Kan. 2011) (collecting cases).
133 *See In re* Good Hope Refineries, Inc., 4 B.R. 290 (Bankr. D. Mass. 1980). *Cf.* Mar. Elec. Co. v. United Jersey Bank, 959 F.2d 1194 (3d Cir. 1991) (district court other than one in jurisdiction where bankruptcy case is filed may retain and exercise "related to" jurisdiction over case involving debtor which is already pending).
    Presumably the debtor can remove a case like *Maritime Electric* to the district where the bankruptcy is pending or move to have the case referred there. *See* § 14.4.1, *infra*.
134 Fed. R. Bankr. P. 7004(b). *See In re* Park Nursing Ctr., Inc., 766 F.2d 261 (6th Cir. 1985) (service by mail is constitutional). *But see In re* Frazier, 394 B.R. 399 (Bankr. E.D. Va. 2008) (when service was made only by certified mail and defendant never claimed mail, certainty that defendant had not received complaint resulted in finding that valid service had not occurred; problem could be avoided by serving both by regular mail and certified mail).
135 Pub. L. No. 103-394, 108 Stat. 4106 (1994).
136 Fed. R. Bankr. P. 7004(h).
    Process may be served by first class mail if (1) the institution has appeared by its attorney, (2) the court so orders after service of an application for such an order by certified mail on the institution, or (3) the institution agrees to waive service by certified mail and designates an officer to receive service. *See In re* Hamlett, 322 F.3d 342 (4th Cir. 2003) (default judgment vacated because service made on registered agent rather than officer of institution). Information about whether a particular entity is an insured depository institution may be obtained on the Federal Deposit Insurance Corporation's website at http://www2.fdic.gov/structur/search/findoneinst.asp.
137 11 U.S.C. § 342(c). *See* H.R. Rep. No. 103-835, at 51 (1994),

clear what constitutes a notice under this provision. For example, is a motion a notice? It is probably simplest to routinely include the required information on any correspondence giving official notice to creditors.[138]

Section 342(c)(2) also requires a "notice required by this title" to be sent to a particular address if such an address was provided by a creditor before bankruptcy. Very few notices are required by title 11 itself, as opposed to the Federal Rules of Bankruptcy Procedure, and the only consequence of incorrect notice appears to be protection for the creditor from certain monetary penalties in some cases.[139] It is also unclear whether the section 342 rules for notice addresses override the service requirements of Bankruptcy Rule 7004. However, when possible, it is advisable, in addition to using the address dictated by the rules, to send a copy of any notice required by title 11 to the address dictated by section 342(c), unless the creditor has notified the debtor under section 342(e) that a different address should be used.

14.3.2.2 Sovereign Immunity

In some cases, sovereign immunity poses a complete bar to recovery of a particular claim in state or federal court. For certain purposes, the Bankruptcy Code provides a means to overcome this bar.

Especially as amended by the Bankruptcy Reform Act of 1994,[140] section 106 of the Code contains a broad abrogation of sovereign immunity with respect to governmental units.[141] Sovereign immunity is expressly abrogated with respect to a wide range of statutory provisions listed in section 106(a). Included among these are virtually all of the provisions which normally would give rise to claims against the government in bankruptcy.

A notable exception to the list is section 541 of the Code. The legislative history states that the amendment was not intended to permit a debtor to sue the government on a prebankruptcy cause of action when suit would otherwise have been barred by sovereign immunity.[142] But section 542 is included in the list, and section 542(h) permits a debtor to recover "a debt that is property of the estate and that is matured, payable on demand, or payable on order" except to the extent it may be offset under section 553.

The legislative history[143] states clearly that the amendment was intended to abrogate both federal sovereign immunity and state 11th Amendment immunity, overruling *Hoffman v. Connecticut Department of Income Maintenance*[144] and *United States v. Nordic Village Inc.*[145] In consumer cases, this history should remove any doubts about federal governmental monetary liability and the immunity of other entities that are not states,[146] not only for transfer avoidance, but also for stay and discharge violations, as well as sanctions under Federal Rule of Bankruptcy Procedure 9011.[147]

However, the ability of Congress to abrogate the states' Eleventh Amendment immunity may be somewhat limited by the Supreme Court's decision in *Seminole Tribe of Florida v. Florida*.[148] The reach of *Seminole Tribe* was greatly diminished by the Court's later decision in *Central Virginia Community College v. Katz*,[149] which appears to permit most, and perhaps all, bankruptcy proceedings to be brought against state governments based upon the Bankruptcy Clause of the Constitution. Indeed, in that case the Court found that the abrogation of sovereign immunity in section 106 was unnecessary.[150] However the precise contours of the right to sue a state government have yet to be developed by the courts.[151]

This problem may be avoided occasionally if it is possible to argue that the entity being sued is not a state or an arm of a state.[152] In some cases involving state action in which the state has not filed a proof of claim or otherwise waived its immunity,[153] debtors may be barred from suing for damages in the

---

reprinted in 1994 U.S.C.C.A.N. 3340.
138 See Official Form 16A (reprinted in Appx. D, *infra*).
139 11 U.S.C. § 342(g)(2). *See* Ch. 9, *supra*.
140 Pub. L. No. 103-394, 108 Stat. 4106 (1994).
  Unlike most parts of the 1994 amendments, the amendments to section 106 were effective with respect to cases pending on the enactment date of October 22, 1994, even if they were on appeal. Pub. L. No. 103-394, § 702, 108 Stat. 4106 (1994); *In re* Price, 42 F.3d 1068 (7th Cir. 1994).
141 "Governmental unit" is defined in 11 U.S.C. § 101(27). The definition excludes a United States trustee, but only when acting as a trustee. Nonetheless, one court has erroneously held that there is no waiver at all with respect to the United States trustee. Balser v. Dep't of Justice, 327 F.3d 903 (9th Cir. 2003).
142 140 Cong. Rec. H10,766 (Oct. 4, 1994) (remarks of Rep. Brooks).
143 *Id.*
144 492 U.S. 96, 109 S. Ct. 2818, 106 L. Ed. 2d 76 (1989).
145 503 U.S. 30, 112 S. Ct. 1011, 117 L. Ed. 2d 181 (1992).
146 *See* Krystal Energy Co. v. Navajo Nation, 357 F.3d 1055 (9th Cir. 2004) (Indian tribe's immunity abrogated by § 106(a)). *But see* Bucher v. Dakota Fin. Corp. (*In re* Whitaker), 474 B.R. 687 (B.A.P. 8th Cir. 2012) (section 106 does not mention Indian tribes); *In re* Mayes, 294 B.R. 145 (B.A.P. 10th Cir. 2003) (when debtor did not raise section 106 argument, tribe's common law immunity precluded lien avoidance motion).
147 Hanna Oil Co. v. Internal Revenue Serv., 198 B.R. 672 (W.D. Va. 1996). *But see In re* Rivera Torres, 432 F.3d 20 (1st Cir. 2005) (section 106(a) did not waive federal government's immunity from emotional distress damages).
148 517 U.S. 44, 116 S. Ct. 1114, 134 L. Ed. 2d 252 (1996).
149 546 U.S. 356, 126 S. Ct. 990, 163 L. Ed. 2d 945 (2006).
150 *Id.*, 546 U.S. at 362. *See* Florida Dep't of Revenue v. Omine (*In re* Omine), 485 F.3d 1305 (11th Cir. 2007) (actions to force a state creditor to honor the automatic stay are permitted as proceedings necessary to effectuate the *in rem* jurisdiction of the bankruptcy court).
151 *See* Fla. Dep't of Revenue v. Diaz (*In re* Diaz), 647 F.3d 1073 (11th Cir. 2011) (sovereign immunity abrogated as to discharge violation claim, but not stay violation claim, because proceeding was brought long after stay was necessary to protect *in rem* bankruptcy jurisdiction).
152 *In re* Lees, 264 B.R. 884 (W.D. Tenn. 2001) (student loan agency was not arm of state entitled to immunity).
153 Generally, a party that files a proof of claim is deemed to submit to the bankruptcy court's jurisdiction, at least as to a claim arising out of the same transaction that created the government's claim. Arecibo Cmty. Health Care, Inc. v. Puerto Rico, 270 F.3d 17 (1st Cir. 2001); *In re* Rose, 187 F.3d 926 (8th Cir. 1999) (state waived Eleventh

§ 14.3.2.2   Consumer Bankruptcy Law and Practice

bankruptcy court, and may still have to resort to devices used in other areas of the law, such as suits against state officers for injunctive relief. The *Ex parte Young* doctrine holds that an action brought against state officials in their individual capacities seeking prospective declaratory and injunctive relief for continuing violations of federal law is not barred by the Eleventh Amendment.[154] For example, a suit seeking a declaration that a particular action violates the automatic stay that may not be brought against the state normally could be brought for injunctive and declaratory relief against the state officer heading the relevant state agency.[155] The discharge itself is an injunction, which can be[156] enforced against a state officer,[157] as may the automatic stay, the discrimination protections,[158] the turnover requirements (except if seeking a money judgment)[159] and a confirmed plan.[160]

To whatever extent a suit for damages against the state caused by violations of federal bankruptcy law may not be brought, it may not be brought even in the state courts, unless the state has waived its sovereign immunity. In another recent decision the Supreme Court has held that such a suit would offend the structure of the Constitution, which preserved state sovereignty.[161]

However, the Supreme Court has clearly held that because bankruptcy is an *in rem* proceeding, affecting the debtor's property, the bankruptcy case itself is not a suit against the state and the discharge of a debt to the state is not barred by the Eleventh Amendment.[162] The court's jurisdiction over the dischargeability of debt, just like its jurisdiction to confirm a plan of reorganization, derives not from jurisdiction over the state or other creditors, but rather from jurisdiction over debtors and their estates.[163] Similarly, court proceedings about the debtor's property, such as proceedings to avoid liens on the property or to compel turnover of preferential transfers, are not suits against the state that implicate a state's sovereign immunity because they are ancillary to a bankruptcy court's *in rem* jurisdiction.[164]

As a limitation on the broad abrogation of sovereign immunity in section 106(a), the state and federal government extracted provisions limiting punitive damages and attorney fees awards. Section 106(a)(3) prohibits an award of punitive damages and limits attorney fee awards. However, this section should not be read to prohibit all monetary sanctions that are not compensatory damages.[165] "Punitive damages" should be given its normal meaning, limited to cases in which that term has traditionally been used to describe a monetary award (as opposed to "sanctions" under Federal Rules of Bankruptcy Procedure 7037 or 9011). Attorney fees and costs are limited to

---

Amendment with respect to claims for which it filed proofs of claim); *In re* Jackson, 184 F.3d 1046 (9th Cir. 1999) (state waived Eleventh Amendment with respect to tax claims by filing proof of claim); *In re* Burke, 146 F.3d 1313 (11th Cir. 1998) (state waived Eleventh Amendment by filing proofs of claim in debtors' cases); *In re* Straight, 143 F.3d 1387 (10th Cir. 1998); *In re* Rose, 227 B.R. 518 (W.D. Mo. 1997) (state waived Eleventh Amendment protection from being sued to determine dischargeability of student loan by filing claim for student loan debt); *In re* Bliemeister, 251 B.R. 383 (Bankr. D. Ariz. 2000) (state waived sovereign immunity by seeking summary judgment in adversary proceeding involving dischargeability of state's claim), *aff'd*, 296 F.3d 858 (9th Cir. 2002); *In re* Huffine, 246 B.R. 405 (Bankr. E.D. Wash. 2000) (state waived sovereign immunity by signing student loan participation agreement); *In re* Lazar, 200 B.R. 358 (Bankr. C.D. Cal. 1996); *In re* Burke, 200 B.R. 282 (Bankr. S.D. Ga. 1996). *See also In re* Innes, 184 F.3d 1275 (10th Cir. 1999) (state consented to litigation in federal court by signing participation agreement with U.S. Department of Education agreeing to oppose dischargeability complaints); *In re* Platter, 140 F.3d 676 (7th Cir. 1998) (state waived Eleventh Amendment immunity by filing dischargeability complaint); *In re* White, 139 F.3d 1268 (9th Cir. 1998) (sovereign immunity waived by participation in case through objection to plan confirmation and voting against plans); *In re* Barrett Ref. Corp., 221 B.R. 795 (Bankr. W.D. Okla. 1998) (state could not undo waiver by withdrawing proof of claim).

Cases concerning whether all agencies of a state or federal government are deemed a single entity for setoff purposes will be relevant. See cases cited below in this subsection. *But see* Magnolia Venture Capital Corp. v. Prudential Sec., Inc., 151 F.3d 439 (5th Cir. 1998) (venue provision in pledge agreement not sufficient to waive Eleventh Amendment immunity because official signing it was not shown to have authority to waive immunity); *In re* Creative Goldsmiths of Wash., 119 F.3d 1140 (4th Cir. 1997) (Eleventh Amendment immunity not waived by filing unrelated claim). *See also* 11 U.S.C. § 106(b).

154 *See* Coeur d'Alene Tribe of Idaho, 531 U.S. 261, 269, 117 S. Ct. 2028, 138 L. Ed. 2d 438 (1997); Green v. Mansour, 474 U.S. 64, 106 S. Ct. 423, 88 L. Ed. 2d 371 (1985); *Ex parte* Young, 209 U.S. 123, 28 S. Ct. 441, 52 L. Ed. 2d 714 (1908); *In re* LTV Steel Co., 264 B.R. 455 (Bankr. N.D. Ohio 2001) (action to enforce automatic stay could be brought against state officials under *Ex parte Young* doctrine).

155 *In re* Ellett, 243 B.R. 741 (B.A.P. 9th Cir. 1999) (suit against state tax official to enjoin collection of taxes discharged in chapter 13 may proceed under *Ex parte Young* doctrine), *aff'd sub nom.* Ellett v. Goldberg, 254 F.3d 1135 (9th Cir. 2001); *In re* DeAngelis, 239 B.R. 426 (Bankr. D. Mass. 1999).

156 *In re* Rainwater, 233 B.R. 126 (Bankr. N.D. Ala. 1999).

157 *In re* Lapin, 226 B.R. 637 (B.A.P. 9th Cir. 1998).

158 *In re* Kidd, 227 B.R. 161 (Bankr. E.D. Ark. 1998).

159 *In re* Zywiczynski, 210 B.R. 924 (Bankr. W.D.N.Y. 1997).

160 Maryland v. Antonelli Creditors' Liquidating Trust, 123 F.3d 777 (4th Cir. 1997).

161 Alden v. Maine, 527 U.S. 706, 119 S. Ct. 2240, 144 L. Ed. 2d 636 (1999).

162 Tenn. Student Assistance Corp. v. Hood, 541 U.S. 440, 124 S. Ct. 1905, 158 L. Ed. 2d 764 (2004).

163 *Id.*

164 Cent. Va. Cmty. College v. Katz, 126 S. Ct. 990, 163 L. Ed. 2d 945 (2006). *See also In re* Slayton, 409 B.R. 897 (Bankr. N.D. Ill. 2009) (permitting suit for damages against state for alleged violations of §§ 524 and 525).

165 Section 106(a) provides that a bankruptcy court may issue an order or judgment awarding a "money recovery" against a governmental unit, which should include a recovery of emotional distress damages and other actual damages. However, one court of appeals has held that section 106(a) does not waive immunity from an award of emotional distress damages as a contempt sanction for violation of the discharge injunction. *In re* Rivera Torres, 432 F.3d 20 (1st Cir. 2005). *But see In re* Griffin, 415 B.R. 64 (Bankr. N.D.N.Y. 2009) (section 106(a) provides for abrogation of sovereign immunity for award of actual damages, including damages for emotional distress).

those consistent with 28 U.S.C. § 2412(d)(2)(A) (the Equal Access to Justice Act).[166]

It is also unclear whether section 106(a)(3) is simply an exception to the abrogation of sovereign immunity, or whether it goes beyond that. Some governmental units, such as municipalities, never had sovereign immunity.[167] In other situations, such as actions for contempt, sovereign immunity is generally not implicated.[168] The structure of the new section 106 suggests that the punitive damages language in section 106(a)(3) is designed to modify and limit the general abrogation language in section 106(a), and not to create new restrictions on litigation against entities or on claims that never were barred by immunity. Similar issues exist with respect to application of the attorney fee limitations in section 106(a)(3).[169]

The sovereign immunity provisions were also clarified with respect to counterclaims against the government. Under section 106(b) (formerly section 106(a)), such a counterclaim may be asserted only if the governmental unit has actually filed a proof of claim in the bankruptcy case.[170] This reverses the result reached by some courts, which had held that a counterclaim could be asserted if the government had taken an action that could be deemed an "informal proof of claim."[171] As under prior law, the counterclaim must be a compulsory counterclaim to the government's claim, arising out of the same transaction or occurrence to come within this section.[172]

A debtor or trustee may also offset against a claim or interest of a governmental unit any claim against the governmental unit that is property of the estate.[173] However, in some cases courts will have to define whether different agencies of the same government are the same governmental unit for purposes of this section.[174]

Because it is still possible that some actions may not be brought directly against a state that has not waived its immunity,[175] proceedings seeking injunctive or declaratory relief should also be brought under the *Ex parte Young* doctrine.[176] Because civil contempt damages and attorney fees are considered prospective relief, they may be awarded against a state officer notwithstanding the state's Eleventh Amendment immunity.[177] Additionally, nonbankruptcy limitations on and waivers of sovereign immunity remain applicable in bankruptcy.[178]

---

166 This incorporates limits on the amount of fees, but not other substantive limitations of the EAJA. *See generally* §§ 16.5, 16.5.4, *infra*.

167 *See, e.g.*, Owen v. City of Independence, 445 U.S. 622, 100 S. Ct. 1398, 63 L. Ed. 2d 673 (1980); Mancuso v. New York State Thruway Auth., 86 F.3d 289 (2d Cir. 1996); Christy v. Pennsylvania Turnpike Comm'n, 54 F.3d 1140 (3d Cir. 1995); Metcalf & Eddy v. Puerto Rico Aqueduct & Sewer Auth., 991 F.2d 935 (1st Cir. 1993); *In re* Durant, 239 B.R. 859 (Bankr. N.D.N.Y. 1999) (county social services department was not an arm of the state entitled to immunity).

168 Because of the potential attorney fee limitation under section 106, it may make sense when sovereign immunity is implicated to continue to include a contempt claim when that claim is available.

169 *See* § 16.5, *infra*.

170 *See* Aer-Aerotron v. Texas Dep't of Transp., 104 F.3d 677 (4th Cir. 1997) (postpetition letters to debtor demanding payment did not constitute proof of claim for purposes of this section); Carrington Gardens Assocs. v. United States, 258 B.R. 622 (E.D. Va. 2001) (government waived sovereign immunity by filing proof of claim even though debtor's claim was not strictly a counterclaim when proof of claim was filed after adversary complaint was brought against agency), *aff'd*, 49 Fed. Appx. 427 (4th Cir. 2002) (table); *In re* Gibson, 176 B.R. 910 (Bankr. D. Or. 1994) (federal government considered one governmental unit, so proof of claim waived sovereign immunity for all agencies under predecessor to this provision). *See also* Lapides v. Bd. of Regents, 535 U.S. 613, 122 S. Ct. 1640, 152 L. Ed. 2d 806 (2002) (by removing action to federal court, a state waives Eleventh Amendment immunity, relying on Gardner v. N.J., 329 U.S. 565, 574, 67 S. Ct. 467, 91 L. Ed. 504 (1947), which held that filing a proof of claim waives a state's immunity); *In re* Stanley, 273 B.R. 907 (Bankr. N.D. Fla. 2002) (having waived immunity by filing proofs of claim, state could not reinstate immunity by withdrawing them).

171 *See, e.g.*, Sullivan v. Town & Country Nursing Home Servs., Inc., 963 F.2d 1146 (9th Cir. 1992).

172 *In re* Supreme Beef Processors, Inc., 391 F.3d 629 (5th Cir. 2004) (claims did not arise out of same transaction or occurrence and could not be asserted under section 106(b), but could be set off against government claim under section 106(c)), *later decision at* 468 F.3d 248 (5th Cir. 2006) (disallowing setoff under section 106(c)). *See* Lazar v. California, 237 F.3d 967 (9th Cir. 2001) (state's proof of claim arose out of same transaction or occurrence as mandamus action against state seeking payment of claims from Underground Storage Tank Cleanup Trust); *In re* Price, 42 F.3d 1068 (7th Cir. 1994) (violation of automatic stay arose out of same transaction as government's tax claim); *In re* Graham, 981 F.2d 1135 (10th Cir. 1992) (section 106(a) requires claims against government to be compulsory counterclaims for sovereign immunity waiver under that subsection); *In re* Rebel Coal Co., 944 F.2d 320 (6th Cir. 1991) (preference claim arising from garnishment for fines did not arise from same transaction or occurrence as government's claim for remaining fines, so sovereign immunity not waived under section 106(a)). *Cf.* United States v. Pullman Constr. Indus., Inc., 153 B.R. 539 (N.D. Ill. 1993) (preference action against Internal Revenue Service was compulsory counterclaim to government's claim for taxes).

173 11 U.S.C. § 106(c).

174 *See In re* Charter Oak Assocs., 361 F.3d 760 (2d Cir. 2004) (proof of claim filed by state tax agency waived immunity for claim against state social services agency); *In re* Hal, Inc., 122 F.3d 851 (9th Cir. 1997) (federal government is unitary creditor for purposes of setoff rights); *In re* Turner, 84 F.3d 1294 (10th Cir. 1996) (en banc) (federal government is unitary creditor for bankruptcy purposes so debt owed to one agency may be set off against claim of another); Doe v. United States, 58 F.3d 494 (9th Cir. 1995) (all agencies of United States are a single governmental unit); § 10.4.2.6.7, *supra*.

175 Murphy v. Michigan Guar. Agency, 271 F.3d 629 (5th Cir. 2001); *In re* Mitchell, 209 F.3d 1111 (9th Cir. 2000).

176 *See Ex parte* Young, 209 U.S. 123, 28 S. Ct. 441, 52 L. Ed. 714 (1908).

177 *In re* Colon, 114 B.R. 890 (Bankr. E.D. Pa. 1990). *See also In re* Bryant, 116 B.R. 272 (Bankr. D. Kan. 1990) (IRS had no defense of sovereign immunity when it violated discharge injunction), *aff'd*, 1991 WL 204911 (D. Kan. Sept. 9, 1991); *In re* Adams, 115 B.R. 59 (Bankr. D.N.J. 1990) (wage order entered against debtor employed by Navy did not violate sovereign immunity because order provided injunctive, not monetary, relief). *But see In re* Gustafson, 934 F.2d 216 (9th Cir. 1991) (state immune from money damages for violations of the stay without express consideration of potential contempt remedies).

178 *See In re* Epps, 110 B.R. 691 (E.D. Pa. 1990) (debtor's action against Dep't of Housing and Urban Development for equitable relief was not barred by sovereign immunity because it was per-

One other way of dealing with federal sovereign immunity problems may be available under the Tucker Act[179] and the "Little Tucker Act."[180] The latter statute permits non-tort suits for money damages arising under federal law to be brought against the federal government in district court if the amount sought is less than $10,000.[181] Thus, a debtor or trustee should be able to file such a proceeding arising under the Bankruptcy Code, or the Constitution or any other federal statute, in the district court. Probably, if the proceeding arises under the Code, it would automatically be referred to the bankruptcy court under the general order of reference applicable in that district court.[182]

14.3.2.3 Overcoming Barriers to Federal Court Access

The district court's broad bankruptcy jurisdiction may also be helpful in cases in which a federal court is otherwise likely to abstain or refuse to hear a case under the doctrines announced in the *Pullman*[183] or *Younger*[184] cases and their progeny. The explicit provision by Congress of bankruptcy jurisdiction for proceedings related to the bankruptcy case may be sufficient to overcome these obstacles to federal court access which have been created by the Supreme Court. Thus, if a decision of an unclear state law question is clearly important to the debtor's successful bankruptcy, the nexus with the ongoing bankruptcy case may justify a federal court deciding a question from which it would have otherwise abstained under the *Pullman* doctrine.

Of course, to the extent either of these doctrines are seen as reflecting constitutional limitations on federal court jurisdiction, Congress has no power to infringe upon them. And there is also a strong likelihood that the federal courts will interpret their power to abstain "in the interest of justice," or "comity," or "respect for state law,"[185] and the mandatory abstention provisions in the bankruptcy jurisdictional scheme[186] to incorporate the *Pullman* and *Younger* doctrines.[187] It should be noted, however, that abstention is usually not appropriate in cases involving property of the debtor, over which the district court has exclusive jurisdiction.[188]

Finally, the bankruptcy court may be a better place to litigate disputes with the Internal Revenue Service or other taxing agencies. Section 505(a) of the Code permits the bankruptcy court to determine the amount or legality of any tax, any fine or penalty relating to a tax, or any addition to a tax, whether or not it has been assessed, paid, or contested before the bankruptcy case.[189] For example, a bankruptcy court may determine whether a debtor is entitled to relief from tax liability under the "innocent spouse" provisions of the Internal Revenue Code.[190] The only exceptions to this rule are that (1) the court may not determine the amount or legality of such claims if it has been previously contested and adjudicated by a judicial or administrative tribunal of competent jurisdiction,[191] (2) the court cannot determine a trustee's request for a refund before 120 days from the date the trustee requests the refund or, if earlier, the date the refund request is ruled upon by the governmental unit from which it requested,[192] and (3) an *ad valorem* property tax may not be contested if the deadline for contesting it has expired.[193] However, the bankruptcy court is not likely to determine a tax liability if it is clearly nondischargeable and will not be paid in the bankruptcy case.

---

mitted under Administrative Procedure Act).

179 28 U.S.C. § 1491. *See generally* Dennis M. Garvis & Frank W. Koger, *If at First You Don't Succeed . . . ; An Alternative Remedy After Nordic Village*, 66 Am. Bankr. L.J. 423 (1992).

180 28 U.S.C. § 1346(a) (2).

181 28 U.S.C. § 1346(a) (2).

Claims over $10,000 must be brought in the United States Claims Court. 28 U.S.C. § 1491. *But see* Bowen v. Massachusetts, 487 U.S. 879, 906 n.42, 108 S. Ct. 2722, 2738 n.42, 101 L. Ed. 2d 749, 771 (1988) (legislation upon which claim is based must be such that it can fairly be interpreted as mandating compensation by the federal government for damage sustained); Sheehan v. United States, 2012 WL 1637967 (N.D. W. Va. May 8, 2012) (no jurisdiction unless there is an express provision for payment from funds appropriated by Congress).

182 *See* Dennis M. Garvis & Frank W. Koger, *If at First You Don't Succeed . . . ; An Alternative Remedy After Nordic Village*, 66 Am. Bankr. L.J. 423, 434 (1992).

However, if the debtor is seeking damages against the IRS for violations of the automatic stay or discharge injunction, the debtor may file the action directly in the bankruptcy court. *See* 26 U.S.C. § 7433(e).

183 R.R. Comm'n of Texas v. Pullman Co., 312 U.S. 496, 61 S. Ct. 643, 85 L. Ed. 971 (1941). *See generally* James W. Moore et al., *Moore's Federal Practice and Procedure* ¶ 0203 (2d ed.).

184 Younger v. Harris, 401 U.S. 37, 91 S. Ct. 746, 27 L. Ed. 2d 669 (1971). *See generally* Charles A. Wright et al., *Federal Practice and Procedure: Jurisdiction* § 4251 *et seq.* (2d ed. 1988).

185 28 U.S.C. § 1334(c). *See* § 14.5, *infra*.

186 28 U.S.C. § 1334(c).

187 *See In re* Davis, 691 F.2d 176 (3d Cir. 1982) (injunction prohibiting bad check prosecution improper under *Younger* doctrine).

188 28 U.S.C. § 1334(e)(1). *See also* H.R. Rep. No. 95-595, at 466 (1977) (stating that abstention in such cases would not be "in the interest of justice").

189 Courts have generally found that the Tax Injunction Act, 28 U.S.C. § 1341, does not deprive bankruptcy courts of jurisdiction when the more specific grant of authority under section 505 applies. *See, e.g.,* Ellett v. Goldberg, 254 F.3d 1135 (9th Cir. 2001); *In re* Stoecker, 179 F.3d 546 (7th Cir. 1999); City Vending of Muskogee, Inc. v. Oklahoma Tax Comm'n, 898 F.2d 122 (10th Cir. 1990); Carrollton-Farmers Branch v. Johnson & Cravens, 858 F.2d 1010 (5th Cir. 1988), *modified*, 867 F.2d 1517 (5th Cir.), *vacated on other grounds*, 889 F.2d 571 (5th Cir. 1989); Adams v. Indiana, 795 F.2d 27, 30 (7th Cir. 1986); *In re* Pontes, 310 F. Supp. 2d 447 (D.R.I. 2004).

190 26 U.S.C. § 6015(b), (c). *See In re* Hinckley, 256 B.R. 814 (Bankr. M.D. Fla. 2000) (debtor granted relief from liability). *But see In re* French, 255 B.R. 1 (Bankr. N.D. Ohio 2000) (only the agency could determine whether individual was "innocent spouse").

191 11 U.S.C. § 505(a)(2)(A). *See In re* Baker, 74 F.3d 906 (9th Cir. 1996). *See also* § 14.2.4.3, *supra*.

192 11 U.S.C. § 505(a)(2)(B).

193 11 U.S.C. § 505(a)(2)(C).

14.3.2.4 Recoupment Claims in Bankruptcy After Expiration of Limitations Periods

Bankruptcy court can also be an important forum for raising consumer claims against creditors after the statute of limitations on those claims has run.[194] In *In re Coxson*,[195] for example, the Fifth Circuit concluded that a Truth in Lending Act claim could be raised defensively by way of an adversary proceeding objecting to a proof of claim in a chapter 13 case—even though the limitations period had passed.[196]

When a creditor seeks to collect on a debt, many states and federal common law allow offset of claims that the debtor may have emerging from the same set of operative facts that gave rise to the debt—even if the limitations period has run.[197] In most states and under federal law, this process is known as recoupment. In some states there is a statutory basis for recoupment, while in others recoupment has developed as a common law remedy.

Recoupment can similarly be used to raise otherwise untimely usury,[198] fraud, unfair trade practice,[199] warranty,[200] and other damage claims emerging from the facts giving rise to the formation of the loan contract.

Recoupment has been permitted in the bankruptcy process by objection to a creditor's proof of claim.[201] The creditor's claim is an action to collect the debt and the objection to the claim is effectively defensive. The underlying rationale is the same as with any recoupment; parties should not be required to pay sums to which they have an underlying defense. If anything, the principle should be stronger in bankruptcy, because a defense to one creditor's claim is likely to lead to greater recovery for other creditors.

When recoupment is expected to be raised in bankruptcy, it is a good idea to mark the creditor's claim in the schedules as "disputed." Additionally, careful practice may require listing the availability of a recoupment claim as an asset and exempting it at a nominal valuation if an exemption is available.

An occasional problem arises when a secured creditor does not file a proof of claim against which recoupment may be asserted. Because the liens associated with secured claims survive a discharge, these creditors retain their right to enforce a lien following bankruptcy. The best strategy in such cases is to file a proof of claim on behalf of that creditor pursuant to Federal Rule of Bankruptcy Procedure 3004.[202] That claim can expressly deduct the recoupment claim. Filing and serving such a claim will put the creditor in the difficult position of having to choose between filing an amended claim and thereby setting up the opportunity for an adversary proceeding seeking recoupment, or ignoring the claim and accepting the potential res judicata consequences of having the claim resolved in the bankruptcy process.

14.3.2.5 Avoiding Mandatory Arbitration Agreements

Mandatory arbitration clauses are now prevalent in consumer contracts of all kinds. These clauses force consumers to submit their claims to an arbitrator who issues a final, binding ruling on the merits, with virtually no opportunity for judicial review. Bankruptcy court can be a favorable forum for avoiding arbitration clauses so that consumer claims may be litigated in court.

The Federal Arbitration Act requires that when a valid and enforceable arbitration agreement exists, courts must halt their

---

194 Recoupment is more likely to be important in addressing secured and priority claims. Recoupment is also available against unsecured claims, but as many such claims are paid at less than their full amount the importance of recoupment for unsecured claims is diminished.

195 43 F.3d 189 (5th Cir. 1995).

196 *See Supreme Court Bars Most Rescission By Recoupment*, 16 NCLC REPORTS *Bankruptcy and Foreclosures Ed.* 17 (Mar./Apr. 1998). *Cf.* Beach v. Ocwen Fed. Sav. Bank, 523 U.S. 410, 118 S. Ct. 1408, 140 L. Ed. 2d 566 (1998) (rescission by recoupment not allowed except when consistent with state law in the context of a foreclosure case).

197 A Supreme Court citation for this principle is *Bull v. United States*, 295 U.S. 247, 262, 55 S. Ct. 695, 79 L. Ed. 1421 (1935), in which the Court said: "[R]ecoupment is in the nature of a defense arising out of some feature of the transaction upon which the plaintiff's action is grounded. Such a defense is never barred by the statute of limitations so long as the main action itself is timely." *See also In re* Monongehela Rye Liquors, 141 F.2d 864 (3d Cir. 1944).

198 *See, e.g.,* National Consumer Law Center, National Consumer Law Center, Consumer Credit Regulation § 7.7.5 (2012); National Consumer Law Center, Unfair and Deceptive Acts and Practices § 12.2.5 (8th ed. 2012).

199 National Consumer Law Center, Unfair and Deceptive Acts and Practices § 12.3.5 (7th ed. 2008 and Supp.).

200 National Consumer Law Center, Consumer Warranty Law § 7.6.9 (4th ed. 2010 and Supp.).

201 *See, e.g.,* Davis v. Wells Fargo Fin. Alabama Inc., 2012 WL 447668 (Bankr. N.D. Ala. Feb. 6, 2012) (debtor is entitled to attorney fees if Truth in Lending Act claim is successful even if claim is asserted defensively in an action for recoupment); *In re* Beach, 447 B.R. 313 (Bankr. D. Idaho 2011) (Truth in Lending Act's one-year statute of limitations period did not apply to debtors' recoupment claims asserted in state court foreclosure action that was removed to bankruptcy court); *In re* Wentz, 393 B.R. 545 (Bankr. S.D. Ohio 2008) (debtor's claims under Truth in Lending Act and Real Estate Settlement Procedures Act, and related claims for attorney fees and costs, allowed by recoupment to reduce creditor's claim); *In re* Thompson, 350 B.R. 842 (Bankr. E.D. Wis. 2006) (damages for violations of Real Estate Settlement Procedures Act awarded by way of recoupment to reduce mortgage creditor's proof of claim); *In re* Harvey, 2003 WL 21460063 (Bankr. E.D. Pa. June 9, 2003) (time-barred recoupment claim under Real Estate Settlement Procedures Act may be brought in response to mortgage lender's proof of claim); *In re* Maxwell, 281 B.R. 101 (Bankr. D. Mass. 2002) (debtor allowed to assert by way of recoupment time-barred claim under the Fair Debt Collection Practices Act against mortgage servicer); *In re* McNinch, 250 B.R. 848 (Bankr. W.D. Pa. 2000) (one-year statute of limitations for Truth In Lending Act damages claim did not apply to claim asserted by recoupment in response to creditor's proof of claim), *aff'd sub nom.* McNinch v. Harris Trust Sav. Bank, 281 F.3d 222 (3d Cir. 2001) (table); *In re* Jones, 122 B.R. 246 (W.D. Pa. 1990); *In re* Werts, 48 B.R. 980 (E.D. Pa. 1985); *In re* Bishop, 79 B.R. 94 (Bankr. D.D.C. 1987).

202 That rule sets a deadline for filing of thirty days after expiration of the bar date applicable to the claim. *See* § 14.4.3.3, *infra*.

proceedings while an arbitrator determines the rights of the parties to the arbitration agreement and adjudicates the dispute in controversy.[203] This strong federal presumption that valid arbitration agreements should be enforced is often in direct conflict with the goal of bankruptcy jurisdiction to have one centralized forum for the prompt resolution of disputes affecting the bankruptcy estate.[204] This conflict between the Bankruptcy Code and the Federal Arbitration Act has led most courts to hold that, at least as to core proceedings, a bankruptcy judge may refuse to enforce an arbitration agreement and may stay any pending arbitration proceedings.[205]

In exercising discretion whether to enforce an arbitration agreement, bankruptcy courts generally consider the degree to which (1) the nature and extent of the litigation and evidence would make the judicial forum preferable to arbitration, (2) the extent to which special expertise is necessary to resolve the dispute, and (3) the extent to which the bankruptcy court may more efficiently and economically resolve the dispute without depleting estate assets.[206] Another factor given considerable weight is that bankruptcy courts can more appropriately consider the interests of creditors who are not a party to the arbitration agreement and who would likely be precluded from participating in the arbitration forum.[207]

These considerations generally favor resolution in the bankruptcy forum of claims and defenses raised as objections to a creditor's proof of claim, particularly when prompt adjudication of the claim is necessary to the plan confirmation process.[208] Similarly, the terms of a confirmed plan which provides for resolution of disputes other than through arbitration are normally binding on the parties.[209] In addition, an arbitration clause should not prevent a bankruptcy court from resolving creditor abuses involving the bankruptcy process itself, such as violations of the automatic stay and discharge injunction, as these proceedings are core proceedings involving the bankruptcy court's inherent power to enforce its own orders.[210] And

---

203 9 U.S.C. § 3.
 For a more detailed discussion of arbitration, see National Consumer Law Center, Consumer Arbitration Agreements (6th ed. 2011 and Supp.). *See also In re* Lucas, 312 B.R. 407 (Bankr. D. Nev. 2004) (arbitration agreement was unenforceable contract of adhesion).

204 Zimmerman v. Cont'l Airlines, Inc., 712 F.2d 55 (3d Cir. 1983); *In re* Hemphill Bus Sales, Inc., 259 B.R. 865 (Bankr. E.D. Tex. 2001); *In re* Knepp, 229 B.R. 821 (Bankr. N.D. Ala. 1999).

205 *In re* White Mountain Mining Co., 403 F.3d 164 (4th Cir. 2005); *In re* Gandy, 299 F.3d 489 (5th Cir. 2002); *In re* United States Lines, Inc., 197 F.3d 631 (2d Cir. 1999); Selcke v. New England Ins. Co., 995 F.2d 688 (7th Cir. 1993); *In re* Brown, 354 B.R. 591 (D.R.I. 2006); *In re* Spectrum Info. Techs., Inc., 183 B.R. 360 (Bankr. E.D.N.Y. 1995); *In re* Sacred Heart Hosp., 181 B.R. 195 (Bankr. E.D. Pa. 1995). *See* Mette H. Kurth, *An Unstoppable Mandate and an Immovable Policy: The Arbitration Act and the Bankruptcy Code Collide*, 43 UCLA L. Rev. 999 (1996).
 If the dispute does not involve a core proceeding and arbitration will not undermine the administration of the estate, courts are more likely to enforce the arbitration clause. *In re* Elec. Machinery Enters., Inc., 479 F.3d 791 (11th Cir. 2007); *In re* Crysen/Montenay Energy Co., 226 F.3d 160 (2d Cir. 2000); *In re* Nat'l Gypsum Co., 118 F.3d 1056 (5th Cir. 1997); Hays & Co. v. Merrill Lynch, Pierce, Fenner & Smith, Inc., 885 F.2d 1149 (3d Cir. 1989).

206 *In re* Hemphill Bus Sales, Inc., 259 B.R. 865 (Bankr. E.D. Tex. 2001); *In re* Slipped Disc Inc., 245 B.R. 342 (Bankr. N.D. Iowa 2000); *In re* Trident Shipworks, Inc., 243 B.R. 130 (Bankr. M.D. Fla. 1999); *In re* Edgerton, 98 B.R. 392 (Bankr. N.D. Ill. 1989).

207 *In re* First Alliance Mortgage Co., 280 B.R. 246 (C.D. Cal. 2002) (arbitration of class TILA and UDAP claims against debtor mortgage lender would deplete estate assets and negatively impact creditors); *In re* United Companies Fin. Corp., Inc., 277 B.R. 596 (Bankr. D. Del. 2002) (arbitration agreement exclusion for bankruptcy proceedings interpreted as applying not just when borrower files bankruptcy but also when lender as debtor files bankruptcy); *In re* Hemphill Bus Sales, Inc., 259 B.R. 865 (Bankr. E.D. Tex. 2001). *See also In re* Bethlehem Steel Corp., 390 B.R. 784 (Bankr. S.D.N.Y. 2008) (claims belonging exclusively to trustee or debtor in possession who were not parties to the arbitration agreement, such as statutory avoidance claims, are not subject to arbitration).

208 *See In re* Brown, 354 B.R. 591 (D.R.I. 2006) (affirming bankruptcy court's exercise of discretion to deny arbitration of core proceeding involving TILA rescission claim); Yarbrough v. Green Tree Servicing L.L.C. (*In re* Yarbrough), 2010 WL 3885046 (Bankr. M.D. Ala. Sept. 29, 2010) (strong policy interest exists in keeping adjudication of claim objection in one central forum). *But see In re* Dixon, 428 B.R. 911 (Bankr. N.D. Ga. 2010); *In re* Paul, 399 B.R. 81 (Bankr. D. Mass. 2008) (claim objection is a proceeding derived exclusively from the Code and should be decided by the bankruptcy court, even when basis for objection involves a prepetition breach of contract claim); *In re* Hicks, 285 B.R. 317 (Bankr. W.D. Okla. 2002) (potential costs of arbitration would adversely affect debtor and creditors); *In re* Laroque, 283 B.R. 640 (Bankr. D.R.I. 2002) (denying enforcement of arbitration clause to decide Truth in Lending rescission issues); *In re* Serv. Marine Indus., Inc., 2000 WL 1673061 (E.D. La. Nov. 3, 2000) (staying the bankruptcy proceeding to allow a creditor to arbitrate an objection to its claim would prejudice the rights of all other creditors and delay the administration of the debtor's bankruptcy). *But see* MBNA Am. Bank v. Hill, 436 F.3d 104 (2d Cir. 2006); *In re* Mintze, 434 F.3d 222 (3d Cir. 2006).

209 Ernst & Young L.L.P v. Baker O'Neal Holdings, 304 F.3d 753 (7th Cir. 2002) (chapter 11 case). *See also* § 12.11, *supra*.

210 Jernstad v. Green Tree Servicing, Inc., 2012 U.S. Dist. LEXIS 108988 (N.D. Ill. Aug. 2, 2012) (arbitration clause no longer operable after debt was discharged); Hooks v. Acceptance Loan Co., 2011 WL 2746238 (M.D. Ala. July 14, 2011) (arbitration of contempt proceeding based on alleged violation of bankruptcy discharge order would inherently conflict with the Bankruptcy Code and undermine bankruptcy court's authority to enforce its orders); *In re* Rushing, 443 B.R. 85 (Bankr. E.D. Tex. 2010) (bankruptcy court is the "best-equipped forum" to evaluate stay violations and to ensure that protections provided by the automatic stay are "safeguarded in a centralized forum"); Zimmerli v. Ocwen Loan Servicing, L.L.C., 432 B.R. 238 (Bankr. N.D. Tex. 2010) (denying enforcement of arbitration agreement in action alleging automatic stay violation and contempt of court order by mortgage servicer for seeking payment of amounts paid under completed chapter 13 plan); *In re* Payton Constr. Corp., 399 B.R. 352 (Bankr. D. Mass. 2009) (arbitration of turnover demand and administrative expense claim conflicts with grant of exclusive jurisdiction to bankruptcy court over estate); *In re* Paul, 399 B.R. 81 (Bankr. D. Mass. 2008) (avoidance, fraudulent transfer, and equitable subordination claims are statutory causes of action arising exclusively under Bankruptcy Code); *In re* Martin, 387 B.R. 307 (Bankr. S.D. Ga. 2007) (arbitration clause not applicable to claim under section 544, which existed only because bankruptcy was filed); *In re* Friedman's, Inc., 372 B.R. 530 (Bankr. S.D. Ga. 2007) (rejecting demand for arbi-

a party may waive any right it has to compel arbitration by participating in the bankruptcy proceeding prior to invoking the arbitration clause.[211]

14.3.2.6 Avoiding Standing and Judicial Estoppel Problems

14.3.2.6.1 In general

Legal claims against third parties are property of the debtor that is frequently overlooked in bankruptcy cases. Failure to identify and list these claims on the bankruptcy schedules can have significant consequences. The debtor may be deprived of standing to pursue an omitted claim either during or after the bankruptcy, or the debtor may be judicially estopped from pursuing the claim after the bankruptcy case is closed. Debtors can avoid these problems by carefully listing all potential claims and asserting available exemptions.[212]

14.3.2.6.2 Standing

The commencement of a bankruptcy case creates a bankruptcy estate that consists of all the debtor's property, which includes potential causes of action.[213] Such claims remain property of the estate unless exempted by the debtor, administered by the trustee, or abandoned by the trustee.[214] In a chapter 7 case prepetition claims not exempted by the debtor may be administered and liquidated by the trustee.[215] When administering prepetition causes of action the trustee may be substituted as the plaintiff in a pending action, may bring an action not yet filed, or may sell the claims if they are transferable.[216] Alternatively, property may be abandoned by the trustee in one of two ways: (1) if, on request by the trustee or party in interest and after notice and hearing, the court finds that the property is "burdensome" or of "inconsequential value and benefit to the estate"; or (2) by the closing of the case.[217] Because undisclosed claims generally are not exempted, administered, or abandoned, they remain property of the estate.[218] As the representative of the estate, only the trustee, not the debtor, will have standing to pursue unscheduled claims after the bankruptcy case is closed.[219]

Debtors may also face standing problems if they seek to bring an adversary proceeding in the bankruptcy court or an action in another court based on a nonexempt, prepetition claim while the chapter 7 case is pending.[220] To avoid this standing issue the debtor should request that the trustee become a co-plaintiff[221] or request that the trustee formally abandon the claim.

In a chapter 13 case the debtor normally has the right to fully control any litigation because the debtor remains in possession of all property of the estate.[222] Therefore most courts have held that a chapter 13 debtor has standing to pursue a prepetition claim.[223]

---

tration of trustee's action to remedy stay violation); *In re* Merrill, 343 B.R. 1 (Bankr. D. Me. 2006) (court exercised discretion to deny motion to compel arbitration of stay violation claim); *In re* Cavanaugh, 271 B.R. 414 (Bankr. D. Mass. 2001) (arbitration clause did not apply to dispute concerning violation of automatic stay because it did not involve contractual rights); *See In re* Grant, 281 B.R. 721 (Bankr. S.D. Ala. 2000). *See also In re* Startec Global Communications Corp., 300 B.R. 244 (D. Md. 2003) (arbitration clause referring to claims arising out of or connected with agreement did not encompass alleged violations of court orders but, even if it did, bankruptcy court did not abuse discretion in refusing to enforce clause), *stay granted*, 303 B.R. 605 (D. Md. 2004).

211 MC Asset Recovery L.L.C. v. Castex Energy, Inc. (*In re* Mirant Corp.), 613 F.3d 584 (5th Cir. 2010) (party seeking to invoke arbitration clause had not raised arbitration issue until after partial denial of its third motion to dismiss); Lewallen v. Green Tree Servicing, L.L.C., 487 F.3d 1085 (8th Cir. 2007) (creditor waived arbitration clause by filing a claim and litigating in bankruptcy court for many months before seeking arbitration).

212 For a detailed discussion of listing and asserting exemptions in contingent and unliquidated claims, see Chapter 7, *supra*.

213 11 U.S.C. § 541(a)(1). *See* § 2.5, *supra*.

214 11 U.S.C. § 554(d).

215 11 U.S.C. § 704(a)(1).

216 Section 323 of the Code provides that the trustee is the legal "representative of the estate" and is the proper party in interest "to sue and be sued." *See In re* Engelbrecht, 368 B.R. 898 (Bankr. M.D. Fla. 2007) (substitution of trustee for debtor in prepetition state court auto accident action related back to debtor's original filing of the action).

217 11 U.S.C. § 554. *See* Barletta v. Tedeschi, 121 B.R. 669 (N.D.N.Y. 1990) (denying debt collector's motion to dismiss Fair Debt Collection Practices Act claim based upon consumer's lack of standing when bankruptcy trustee acknowledged his intention to abandon the consumer's claim but never formally did so); Form 108, Appx. G.10, *infra* (sample motion for abandonment).

218 11 U.S.C. § 554(d).

However, the debtor's failure to schedule a cause of action should not preclude the trustee from pursuing the action. *See* Reed v. City of Arlington, 650 F.3d 571 (5th Cir. 2011) (en banc); Parker v. Wendy's Int'l, Inc., 365 F.3d 1268 (11th Cir. 2004). *See also* Wood v. Household Fin. Corp., 341 B.R. 770 (W.D. Wash. 2006) (chapter 7 trustee not barred on judicial estoppel grounds from prosecuting prepetition cause of action that debtors failed to disclose on schedules and trustee only learned about after case was closed).

219 *See, e.g.*, Biesek v. Soo Line R. Co., 440 F.3d 410 (7th Cir. 2006) (trustee, not debtor, is real party in interest to prosecute undisclosed prepetition claim); *In re* Riazuddin, 363 B.R. 177 (B.A.P. 10th Cir. 2007); *In re* Tennyson, 313 B.R. 402 (Bankr. W.D. Ky. 2004) (trustee, not debtor, is party with standing to pursue unscheduled rescission claim against mortgage lender); *In re* Davis, 158 B.R. 1000 (Bankr. N.D. Ind. 1993). *See also* Barger v. City of Cartersville, 348 F.3d 1289 (11th Cir. 2003) (trustee is real party in interest and should replace debtor going forward even though lower court never directed trustee to substitute for debtor).

220 *In re* Hopkins, 346 B.R. 294 (Bankr. E.D.N.Y. 2006) (during pendency of chapter 7 case, only trustee, not debtor, had standing to bring adverse possession action); *In re* Darrah, 337 B.R. 313 (Bankr. N.D. Ohio 2005) (chapter 7 debtor lacked standing to pursue prepetition cause of action under the Real Estate Settlement Procedures Act).

221 *See* Fed. R. Bankr. P. 7017 (permitting joinder, or substitution, of the real party in interest).

222 11 U.S.C. §§ 1303, 1306(b).

223 Crosby v. Monroe County, 394 F.3d 1328 (11th Cir. 2004); Cable v. Ivy Tech State College, 200 F.3d 467 (7th Cir. 1999) (after conversion to chapter 13, chapter 7 trustee automatically dropped out of discrimination case and debtor became real party in interest with

14.3.2.6.3 Judicial estoppel

In addition to standing problems, debtors may be judicially estopped from pursuing unscheduled claims after bankruptcy. Judicial estoppel is an equitable doctrine under which a party is precluded from asserting a claim in a legal proceeding that is inconsistent with a claim made in a previous proceeding.[224] While there is no bright line test to determine when the doctrine may be invoked, courts generally consider (1) whether the party's later position was clearly inconsistent with its earlier position, (2) whether the party has succeeded in persuading the court to accept the earlier position, so that later judicial acceptance would suggest that the first or second court was deliberately mislead, and (3) whether the party seeking to assert an inconsistent position would derive an unfair advantage or impose an unfair detriment on the opposing party.[225]

Many courts have held that the harsh consequences of applying judicial estoppel are not appropriate in cases of mistake or inadvertence.[226] A debtor's failure to disclose a cause of action might be deemed inadvertent if the debtor was unaware of the unlisted claim when the schedules were prepared and lacked knowledge of the factual or legal basis for the claim, or if there was no motive for concealment.[227] Application of judicial estoppel has also been found inappropriate when a debtor's failure to disclose a claim occurred without bad faith.[228] Although one Circuit Court had initially suggested that a debtor's intent to manipulate the court system could be implied simply by the debtor's failure to disclose the claim on the schedules, a more recent decision from that court makes clear that a finding of specific intent is required.[229]

Courts are more likely to refuse to apply judicial estoppel when a debtor does not actively conceal the asset and instead takes timely affirmative action to fully inform the court and the trustee of the asset's existence.[230] By contrast, courts have typically applied the doctrine in cases in which the debtor had been actively pursuing the unscheduled claim in another court or was aware of the factual basis for the claim at the time of the

---

standing to prosecute case on behalf of the bankruptcy estate); Looney v. Hyundai Motor Mfg. Ala., L.L.C., 330 F. Supp. 2d 1289 (M.D. Ala. 2004) (chapter 13 debtor had standing to litigate employment discrimination action which was property of bankruptcy estate); Beasley v. Personal Fin. Corp., 279 B.R. 523 (S.D. Miss. 2002); Donato v. Metro. Life Ins. Co., 230 B.R. 418 (N.D. Cal. 1999) (debtor had concurrent standing with chapter 13 trustee to litigate prepetition causes of action against former employer); In re Mosley, 260 B.R. 590 (Bankr. S.D. Ga. 2000); In re James, 210 B.R. 276 (Bankr. S.D. Miss. 1997); In re Wirmel, 134 B.R. 258 (Bankr. S.D. Ohio 1991).

224 New Hampshire v. Maine, 532 U.S. 742, 750–751, 121 S. Ct. 1808, 149 L. Ed. 2d 968 (2001) ("the circumstances under which judicial estoppel may appropriately be invoked are probably not reducible to any general formulation of principle"). See also 18 Moore's Federal Practice § 134.30, at 134-62 (3d ed. 2000) ("The doctrine of judicial estoppel prevents a party from asserting a claim in a legal proceeding that is inconsistent with a claim taken by that party in a previous proceeding.").

225 New Hampshire v. Maine, 532 U.S. 742, 750–751, 121 S. Ct. 1808, 149 L. Ed. 2d 968 (2001). See also Kane v. Nat'l Union Fire Ins. Co., 535 F.3d 380 (5th Cir. 2008) (no judicial estoppel because debtors would not be likely to benefit from trustee liquidating undisclosed claim); Stallings v. Hussmann Corp., 447 F.3d 1041 (8th Cir. 2006) (no judicial estoppel because debtor gained no advantage from a bankruptcy case that was dismissed and claim arose after petition was filed); In re Riazuddin, 363 B.R. 177 (B.A.P. 10th Cir. 2007) (failure to list asset did not benefit debtor because if case was reopened, as debtor requested, asset would be administered as if it had been disclosed); Kurchack v. Life Ins. Co., 725 F. Supp. 2d 855 (D. Ariz. 2010) (debtor derived no benefit by failing to list disability benefits claim on schedules, since claim would have been exempt); Best v. Kroger Co., 339 B.R. 180 (W.D. Tenn. 2006) (debtor derived no benefit from nondisclosure because debtor completed 100% chapter 13 plan); Hoffman v. Truck Driving Academy, Inc., 777 So. 2d 151 (Ala. Civ. App. 2000) (no judicial estoppel when creditor failed to show it was prejudiced by debtor's failure to disclose claims in bankruptcy); IBF Participating Income Fund v. Dillard-Winecoff L.L.C., 275 Ga. 765, 573 S.E.2d 58 (2002) (fact that claim was not scheduled produced no advantage for debtor because bankruptcy case was ultimately dismissed); Johnson v. Si-Cor, 107 Wash. App. 902, 28 P.3d 832 (2001) (no evidence that failure to disclose claim benefited debtor).

226 Browning v. Levy, 283 F.3d 761 (6th Cir. 2002); Aziz v. Dollar Tree Stores, Inc., 2005 WL 2290593 (E.D. Tenn. Sept. 20, 2005).

227 Ajaka v. Brooksamerica Mortgage Corp., 453 F.3d 1339 (11th Cir. 2006) (remand required to determine if debtor had intent to manipulate judicial system by failing to disclose claims), appeal after remand, 278 Fed. Appx. 916 (11th Cir. 2008) (lower court's finding that debtor so intended affirmed); Browning v. Levy, 283 F.3d 761 (6th Cir. 2002); In re Baldwin, 307 B.R. 251 (M.D. Ala. 2004) (judicial estoppel did not apply because debtor was not aware of lender liability claim when bankruptcy filed, and later promptly amended schedules). But see Love v. Tyson Foods, Inc., 677 F.3d 258 (5th Cir. 2012) (judicial estoppel applied because debtor did not argue inadvertence).

228 Eubanks v. CBSK Fin. Group, Inc., 385 F.3d 894 (6th Cir. 2004); In re Riazuddin, 363 B.R. 177 (B.A.P. 10th Cir. 2007) (refusal to reopen case erroneous because debtor's intent not considered); Dawson v. J.G. Wentworth & Co., 946 F. Supp. 394 (E.D. Pa. 1996) (summary judgment precluded because question of material fact existed as to whether debtor, who later amended schedules to include claim, acted in good or bad faith in omitting claims from original schedules).

229 Ajaka v. BrooksAmerica Mortgage, 453 F.3d 1339 (11th Cir. 2006) (reversing summary judgment for defendant and finding questions of material facts existed as to whether debtor had motivation and intent to manipulate the judicial system).

230 In re Kane, 628 F.3d 631 (3d Cir. 2010) (former debtor sufficiently disclosed her equitable distribution claim in her bankruptcy case); Snowden v. Fred's Stores of Tenn., Inc., 419 F. Supp. 2d 1367 (M.D. Ala. 2006) (debtor not judicially estopped when she became aware of potential cause of action postpetition and amended schedules four months later); Moore v. Cycon, 2006 WL 2375477 (W.D. Mich. Aug. 16, 2006) (debtor who informed court and trustee of potential claims and later amended her schedules not judicially estopped from bringing Truth in Lending Act and Home Ownership Equity Protection Act claims); Johnson v. PS Ill. Trust, 2006 WL 1030192 (N.D. Ill. Apr. 19, 2006) (judicial estoppel not applicable when debtor disclosed lawsuit prior to confirmation); In re Baldwin, 307 B.R. 251 (M.D. Ala. 2004) (judicial estoppel did not apply because debtor was not aware of lender liability claim when bankruptcy filed, and later promptly amended schedules); Elliott v. ITT Corp., 150 B.R. 36 (N.D. Ill. 1992).

bankruptcy filing.[231] Reliance on counsel in omitting potential causes of action has generally been insufficient to overcome the application of the judicial estoppel doctrine.[232]

Judicial estoppel has also been applied in cases in which debtors have amended their initial schedules but failed to include postpetition claims that were part of the bankruptcy estate.[233] At least one court has also applied the doctrine to limit any benefit to a chapter 13 debtor, when the debtor failed to disclose a claim she learned of prior to confirmation.[234] However the doctrine generally will not bar a debtor from pursuing unscheduled claims that seek injunctive relief.[235]

The consequences of failing to schedule a claim can be mitigated sometimes, if the debtor has not acted in bad faith, by reopening the bankruptcy case and amending the debtor's schedules.[236]

14.4 Bringing a Matter Before the Bankruptcy Forum

14.4.1 Removal

14.4.1.1 In General

A dispute may be brought into the bankruptcy system in a number of ways. Depending upon the nature of the dispute and the tactics of the parties, most litigation takes place through either adversary proceedings or contested matters within the bankruptcy case.[237]

The most dramatic method of bringing a matter into bankruptcy court is through the removal of an action already pending in another court. Under 28 U.S.C. § 1452 nearly all actions over which the district court would have bankruptcy jurisdiction may be removed to the district court in the jurisdiction where the removed action is pending.[238] However, if the debtor's bankruptcy case is pending in a different court, removed

---

231 *See* Reed v. City of Arlington, 620 F.3d 477 (5th Cir. 2010); Lewis v. Weyerhaeuser Co., 141 Fed. Appx. 420 (6th Cir. 2005) (applying judicial estoppel when debtor knew of potential employment discrimination claim prior to bankruptcy filing, had motive to conceal it, and did not disclose it on bankruptcy schedules); Barger v. City of Cartersville, 348 F.3d 1289 (11th Cir. 2003) (applying doctrine to prevent plaintiff from seeking money damages in employment discrimination case filed prepetition that she failed to list on bankruptcy schedules); Hamilton v. State Farm Fire & Cas. Co., 270 F.3d 778 (9th Cir. 2001) (debtor judicially estopped from bringing insurance claims when debtor listed insurance losses as liabilities, but did not list claim against insurer as asset on bankruptcy schedules); *In re* Coastal Plains, Inc., 179 F.3d 197 (5th Cir. 1999) (debtor's knowledge of enough information to suggest that it may have a possible cause of action coupled with failure to schedule claim sufficient to support application of judicial estoppel doctrine); *In re* Johnson, 345 B.R. 816 (Bankr. W.D. Mich. 2006) (debtor who had filed and was actively pursuing wrongful discharge claim in federal court, yet failed to disclose the claim in her subsequent bankruptcy proceeding, judicially estopped from pursuing claim).

232 Cannon-Stokes v. Potter, 453 F.3d 446 (7th Cir. 2006). *See* Lewis v. Weyerhaeuser Co., 141 Fed. Appx. 420 (6th Cir. 2005) (debtor bound by actions of counsel, taken with her consent, in deciding not to disclose cause of action); Barger v. City of Cartersville, 348 F.3d 1289 (11th Cir. 2003).

233 *See* Burnes v. Pemco Aeroplex Inc., 291 F.3d 1282 (11th Cir. 2002) (plaintiff filed for chapter 13 bankruptcy, filed a charge of discrimination with the Equal Employment Opportunity Commission, filed an employment discrimination lawsuit, converted to chapter 7, amended schedules, and still failed to disclose cause of action). However, most claims that arise postpetition are not assets of the estate and judicial estoppel does not apply to them. *In re* Wakefield, 312 B.R. 333 (Bankr. N.D. Tex. 2004).

234 Autos, Inc. v. Gowin, 330 B.R. 788 (D. Kan. 2005) (order dismissing cause of action not appropriate remedy). *But see* Byrd v. Wyeth, Inc., __ F. Supp. 2d __, 2012 WL 516077 (S.D. Miss. Feb. 15, 2012) (issue of whether postconfirmation claim in chapter 13 case belonged to estate was sufficiently murky that it would be inequitable to apply judicial estoppel because of nondisclosure); *In re* Smith, 293 B.R. 786 (Bankr. D. Kan. 2003) (in chapter 7 case postpetition claim not property of the estate when debtor did not have symptoms of injury from weight reduction drug until after the bankruptcy was filed); *In re* Carter, 258 B.R. 526 (Bankr. S.D. Ga. 2001) (chapter 13 debtors' failure to list tort claim that arose postconfirmation and was not necessary for the maintenance of the plan did not judicially estop debtors from pursuing claim); Chicon v. Carter, 258 Ga. App. 164, 526 S.E.2d 413 (2002) (tort claim that arose after confirmation of plan not part of bankruptcy estate and debtors obtained no unfair advantage by not disclosing it).

235 Barger v. City of Cartersville, 348 F.3d 1289, 1297 (11th Cir. 2003) (debtor's injunctive relief claim for reinstatement "would have added nothing of value to the bankruptcy estate even if she properly disclosed it").

236 *See* Tucker v. Closure Sys. Int'l, 2011 WL 4479112 (S.D. Ind. Sept. 27, 2011) (no judicial estoppel where debtor amended schedules during bankruptcy case); *In re* Riazuddin, 363 B.R. 177 (B.A.P. 10th Cir. 2007); *In re* Lopez, 283 B.R. 22 (B.A.P. 9th Cir. 2002) (debtor should have been permitted to reopen and amend to schedule cause of action because, even if claim had been intentionally concealed, asset could be administered to benefit creditors); *In re* Rochester, 308 B.R. 596 (Bankr. N.D. Ga. 2004) (debtor allowed to reopen bankruptcy case to add products liability claim as debtor's failure to list claim in original schedules was not intentional or in bad faith). *See also In re* Goswami, 304 B.R. 386 (B.A.P. 9th Cir. 2003) (debtors permitted to reopen bankruptcy five years after case closed so as to amend their schedules and claim property as exempt, in order to avoid a judicial lien on the property).

237 *See* §§ 1.4.2, 14.2.4, *supra*.

238 *See, e.g., In re* Mem'l Estates, 950 F.2d 1364 (7th Cir. 1991) (mortgage foreclosure case properly removed to bankruptcy court when property was debtor's principal asset and foreclosure would have affected debtor's estate); Gandy v. Peoples Bank and Trust Co., 224 B.R. 340 (S.D. Miss. 1998) (state law action would have effect on bankruptcy estate and therefore was related to bankruptcy case); *In re* Blaylock, 394 B.R. 359 (Bankr. E.D. Pa. 2008) (city tax sale petition successfully removed by debtor based on "related to" jurisdiction despite failure of debtor to file notice of removal in state court).

Exceptions are tax court cases and civil actions by governmental units to enforce police or regulatory powers. A proceeding also may not be removed from an agency such as the National Labor Relations Board. *In re* Adams Delivery Serv., 24 B.R. 589 (B.A.P. 9th Cir. 1982).

Presumably, the court's jurisdiction must be over the claim of the plaintiff in the case; as under other federal removal statutes, an anticipated federal defense to the claim, even if pleaded in the complaint, would not be sufficient. *See* Rivet v. Regions Bank of La., 522 U.S. 470, 118 S. Ct. 921, 139 L. Ed. 2d 912 (1998).

cases may presumably then be consolidated or otherwise transferred to that court.[239] Many courts skip this step and permit removal directly to the bankruptcy court.[240] Removed cases are then referred, like other bankruptcy matters, to the bankruptcy court.[241] The power to remove an action may be exercised by either plaintiff or defendant at any stage of the proceedings in the case that is removed, provided the deadlines of the Federal Rules of Bankruptcy Procedure are met.[242]

One question which may arise is how to handle cases involving the debtor or estate property which were pending in the district court at the time bankruptcy was filed. Because removal is made to district court, it does not make sense to remove such an action unless it is pending in a district court different from that of the bankruptcy.[243] However, it may be appropriate to ask the district court to refer such matters to the bankruptcy court if they are related to the bankruptcy.[244]

The removal of an action is often both a surprise and a problem for an opposing party that is unfamiliar with the bankruptcy system. It may also be an excellent way to permanently alter the course of state court litigation that has been going unfavorably. Once the action is removed, federal procedural law (which may be more favorable to the debtor's case) will govern.[245] Substantive rights, such as the right of a party to a jury trial, should be unaffected.[246]

14.4.1.2 Procedure for Removal

The procedure for removal is governed by Federal Rule of Bankruptcy Procedure 9027, which requires that a notice of removal be filed with the clerk of the bankruptcy court for the district in which the action to be removed is pending. The notice must contain a short and plain statement of the facts which entitle the party filing the notice to removal, and a statement of whether the removed action is core or non-core. If it is non-core, there must also be a declaration of whether or not the party filing the notice consents to entry of final orders by the bankruptcy judge.[247] The notice must also be accompanied by a copy of all process and pleadings in the removed case.[248] A copy of the notice of removal must be served on all other parties to the removed action, and a copy of the notice must be filed with the court where the action was previously pending.[249]

It is critical, however, to be aware of the time limits within which removal is allowed. For cases pending when the bankruptcy case was commenced, Federal Rule of Bankruptcy Procedure 9027(a)(2) requires a notice of removal to be filed within ninety days after the order for relief (or thirty days after entry of an order terminating an automatic stay of the action to be removed, if later).[250] For cases initiated after the bankruptcy case is commenced, the deadline for removal is thirty days after the initial service of process.[251] Most courts have held that these time limits are mandatory and may not be waived.[252] However, the time may be extended pursuant to Federal Rule of Bankruptcy Procedure 9006(b), upon motion to the court to which the action is to be removed.[253]

14.4.1.3 Procedure After Removal

Upon removal, other parties to the case who have filed pleadings in the removed case are required to file a statement admitting or denying the allegation in the removal notice concerning the court's core or non-core jurisdiction.[254] That

---

239 See, e.g., In re Nat'l Developers, Inc., 803 F.2d 616 (11th Cir. 1986).
240 See In re Coastal Plains, Inc., 338 B.R. 703 (N.D. Tex. 2006) (citing cases).
241 See § 14.2.2, supra.
242 See, e.g., In re Massey, 3 B.R. 110 (Bankr. D. Colo. 1980) (removal after jury verdict had been set aside by judge).
243 One court has held that any district court can exercise jurisdiction over a case related to a bankruptcy pending in another jurisdiction. Mar. Elec. Co. v. United Jersey Bank, 959 F.2d 1194 (3d Cir. 1991). That court suggests that a motion for change of venue under 28 U.S.C. § 1412 is necessary to have the case heard where the bankruptcy is pending. It is not clear whether the court would consider the removal option improper in these circumstances.
244 See generally Philippe v. Shape, Inc., 103 B.R. 355 (D. Me. 1989) (case pending in district court which is related to bankruptcy case would be referred to bankruptcy court); In re Shelbyville Mixing Ctr., Inc., 288 B.R. 765 (Bankr. E.D. Ky. 2002) (case cannot be removed from district court to bankruptcy court); Thomas Steel Corp. v. Bethlehem Rebar Indus., 101 B.R. 16 (Bankr. N.D. Ill. 1989) (case cannot be removed from district court to bankruptcy court; however, district court can entertain a motion for directed referral).
245 In re Miller, 90 B.R. 762 (Bankr. E.D. Pa. 1988); In re Vic Snyder, Inc., 22 B.R. 332 (Bankr. E.D. Pa. 1982) (Federal Rule of Civil Procedure 60, made applicable through then-applicable R. Bankr. P. 914, governed relief from judgment in removed action). See Fed. R. Bankr. P. 9027(g) (procedure after removal is governed by rules for adversary proceedings).
246 See, e.g., In re Jensen, 946 F.2d 369 (5th Cir. 1991) (after removal of a state court action by a creditor, debtor retained the right to a jury trial). See generally § 14.2.7, supra.
247 Fed. R. Bankr. P. 9027(a)(1).
248 Fed. R. Bankr. P. 9027(a)(1). See annotated forms in Appendix G.12, infra.

Although Rule 9027 requires filing of removal notices with the clerk "for the district," it appears that when a bankruptcy clerk has been appointed, filing with the bankruptcy court as a unit of the district court is contemplated. See In re Hendersonville Condo. Homes, 84 B.R. 510 (M.D. Tenn. 1988).

When the record in the removed case is unavailable for reasons beyond the control of the removing party, the court is empowered to allow the record to be supplied by affidavit or otherwise. Fed. R. Bankr. P. 9027(h).
249 Fed. R. Bankr. P. 9027(b), (c).

These notices must be given or filed "promptly" pursuant to Rule 9027, but the consequences of delay or failure to comply are unclear.
250 If process has not yet been served in such a case, it may be served in accordance with Federal Rule of Bankruptcy Procedure 7004(f). See § 14.3.2.1, supra.
251 Fed. R. Bankr. P. 9027(a)(3); Creasy v. Coleman Furniture Corp., 763 F.2d 656 (4th Cir. 1985). See In re Eagle Bend Dev., 61 B.R. 451 (Bankr. W.D. La. 1986) (failure to serve process may extend the deadline).
252 In re McCallum, 7 B.R. 76 (Bankr. C.D. Cal. 1980).
253 Caperton v. A.T. Massey Coal Co., 251 B.R. 322 (S.D. W. Va. 2000).
254 Fed. R. Bankr. P. 9027(e)(3).

statement must also state, if the party alleges the action is non-core, whether the party consents to entry of final judgment by the bankruptcy court.[255] It must be filed within fourteen days of the notice of removal and be mailed to every other party.[256]

After a case has been removed, the parties may not proceed further in the court from which it was removed unless the case is later remanded to that court.[257] The bankruptcy court may issue any necessary orders and process to bring all proper parties before the court. The judge may also order the removing party to file some or all of the record in the removed case.[258] A removed action is treated as an adversary proceeding in the bankruptcy court.[259] Pleading again is not necessary unless the court so orders.[260]

14.4.1.4 Remand of Removed Actions

Once a case has been removed, any of the other parties to the case can seek to have the case remanded. Under 28 U.S.C. § 1452(b), the court to which a claim or cause of action is removed may remand the claim or cause of action "on any equitable grounds." Federal Rule of Bankruptcy Procedure 9027(d) provides that a motion for remand must be brought and heard as a contested matter pursuant to the Rule 9014.[261] If a timely motion to remand is not filed, the bankruptcy court may hear the matter even if the removal was improper, assuming the court has jurisdiction.[262] When the matter is core, presumably the bankruptcy judge is empowered to enter a final order remanding the case.[263] If non-core, a recommendation governed by Rule 9033 is probably appropriate unless all parties consent to final disposition by the bankruptcy court.[264]

Once entered, an order remanding a claim is not reviewable by the court of appeals by appeal or otherwise.[265] An order refusing to remand a claim removed pursuant to 28 U.S.C. § 1452 is also not reviewable by a court of appeals.[266] However, these limitations should not prevent appeals to the district court, under 28 U.S.C. § 158(a), of final bankruptcy court orders requiring or denying remand.[267]

Generally, the decision with respect to remand is based upon the same type of considerations applicable to decisions on whether to abstain.[268] These considerations include the convenience of the parties, comity with state courts, judicial economy, and the likelihood of delay.[269] Of course, a case should also be remanded if bankruptcy jurisdiction does not exist.[270]

Another issue which frequently arises in the context of a motion for remand is whether an entire action may be removed to the bankruptcy forum when many of the claims or parties have no relation to the bankruptcy case. It is generally agreed that the presence of such claims and parties does not destroy bankruptcy jurisdiction over the entire case.[271] However, many

---

255 Fed. R. Bankr. P. 9027(e)(3). *But see* Allied Signal Recovery Trust v. Allied Signal, Inc., 298 F.3d 263 (3d Cir. 2002) (order permitting remand of case to state court in state other than that from which it had been removed was reviewable by mandamus).
256 Fed. R. Bankr. P. 9027(e)(3).
257 Fed. R. Bankr. P. 9027(c).
258 Fed. R. Bankr. P. 9027(e)(2).
259 Fed. R. Bankr. P. 9027(g).
260 *Id.*
261 *See generally* § 1.4.2, *supra*.
   It is not clear whether 28 U.S.C. § 1447 applies to cases removed under section 1452. *See* Fed. R. Bankr. P. 9027 advisory committee's note (rule conforms substantially to 28 U.S.C. §§ 1446–1450). If it does, it requires a remand motion made on any basis other than lack of jurisdiction to be filed within thirty days after the notice of removal. *In re* Gold Messenger, Inc., 221 B.R. 259 (D. Colo. 1998). *But see In re* Ciclon Negro, Inc., 260 B.R. 832 (Bankr. S.D. Tex. 2001) (thirty-day limit does not apply).
262 Orange County Water Dist. v. Unocal Corp., 584 F.3d 43 (2d Cir. 2009).
263 *In re* Borelli, 132 B.R. 648 (N.D. Cal. 1991).
264 *See* 28 U.S.C. § 157(c)(1).
265 28 U.S.C. § 1452(b); Things Remembered v. Petrarca, 516 U.S. 124, 116 S. Ct. 494, 133 L. Ed. 2d 461 (1995) (court of appeals may not review order remanding case based upon defect in procedure or lack of jurisdiction regardless of whether removal was pursuant to 28 U.S.C. § 1452(a) or 28 U.S.C. § 1441(a)); Good v. Voest-Alpine Indus., Inc., 398 F.3d 918 (7th Cir. 2005). *See also In re* Robertson, 258 B.R. 470 (M.D. Ala. 2001) (although court of appeals could not hear appeal of decision remanding case, district court had jurisdiction over such an appeal).
266 28 U.S.C. § 1452(b); *In re* Cathedral of Incarnation, 90 F.3d 28 (2d Cir. 1996). *See also In re* Seven Fields Dev. Corp., 505 F.3d 237 (3d Cir. 2007) (statute did not preclude review of decision not to remand if decision was based on jurisdiction rather than on equitable grounds); *In re* Bissonet Investments L.L.C., 320 F.3d 520 (5th Cir. 2003) (court of appeals could review decision not to remand that was based on jurisdiction rather than equitable grounds); *In re* Celotex Corp., 124 F.3d 619 (4th Cir. 1997) (court of appeals could review denial of remand to extent motion for remand was based on district court's alleged lack of jurisdiction); *In re* U.S. Brass Corp. 110 F.3d 1261 (7th Cir. 1997) (discussing possible exceptions to rule).
267 *See In re* Robertson, 258 B.R. 470 (M.D. Ala. 2001); *In re* Borelli, 132 B.R. 648 (N.D. Cal. 1991); Fed. R. Bankr. P. 9027 advisory committee's note to 1991 amendments. *See also In re* Goerg, 930 F.2d 1563 (11th Cir. 1991) (right of review by Article III court is constitutionally required).
268 *See* § 13.5, *infra*. *See also* Reed v. Miss. Farm Bureau Mut. Ins. Co., 299 B.R. 804 (S.D. Miss. 2003) (remand required when mandatory abstention appropriate); *In re* Revco D.S., Inc., 99 B.R. 768 (N.D. Ohio 1989) (grounds for mandatory abstention require remand of removed action).
269 *See* Browning v. Navarro, 743 F.2d 1069 (5th Cir. 1984); Allen v. J.K. Harris & Co., 331 B.R. 634 (E.D. Pa. 2005) (remand appropriate when an action involves many non-debtor class members and primarily state law issues); *In re* Roper, 203 B.R. 326 (Bankr. N.D. Ala. 1996) (remanding to state court actions brought by debtors against creditors for unfair practices).
270 *In re* Harris, 306 B.R. 357 (M.D. Ala. 2004) (no bankruptcy jurisdiction over state law claims when debtors' chapter 13 cases had already been dismissed or completed).
271 *See In re* Wood, 825 F.2d 90 (5th Cir. 1987) (non-debtor third party properly joined in core proceeding); *In re* Salem Mortgage Co., 783 F.2d 626, 634 (6th Cir. 1986); *In re* Red Ash Coal & Coke Corp., 83 B.R. 399 (W.D. Va. 1988) (bankruptcy court has non-core jurisdiction over removed actions including claims against non-debtor guarantors of debtor's notes); *In re* Auburn Med. Realty, 19 B.R. 113 (B.A.P. 1st Cir. 1982); *In re* Griffith, 6 B.R. 753 (Bankr. D.N.M. 1980); *In re* Greco, 3 B.R. 18 (Bankr. D. Haw. 1979); Kennedy, *The Bankruptcy Court Under the New Bankruptcy Law:*

of the same courts holding that jurisdiction exists in such cases have proceeded to remand all or parts of these cases.[272]

14.4.2 Litigation of Other Claims Commenced by the Debtor

Even if the time limit for removal has expired or the debtor has decided not to remove an action in state court (continuation of any action against the debtor usually being stayed under 11 U.S.C. § 362(a)),[273] a dispute already pending elsewhere may still be brought into bankruptcy court. It is well-established that the pendency of an action in one court does not bar a subsequent action in another for the same or similar relief.[274] The failure to remove the first lawsuit to the bankruptcy forum does not change this rule.[275]

The debtor may commence an adversary proceeding for damages, equitable, or declaratory relief to bring such a case before the bankruptcy forum. Often, such an adversary action may be framed as an objection to proof of claim. In such cases, a debtor may be able to address issues and present claims against a creditor holding a valid judgment, especially if it is a judgment by default.[276] By becoming the plaintiff, the debtor is often able to frame the litigation in the most advantageous way. The debtor may bring virtually any type of action based upon prepetition claims,[277] and some postpetition claims, into the federal bankruptcy system (subject, of course, to abstention when the court deems appropriate).[278]

The debtor should list on the bankruptcy schedules and claim as exempt, if possible, any claims that the debtor plans to assert, also noting that the debts to the creditors involved are disputed. However, if claims are not discovered until later, the failure to schedule them initially is not fatal, because schedules may be amended,[279] and because there is rarely any prejudice to the creditor if schedules are amended during the case.[280] If a claim cannot be claimed as fully exempt, a chapter 7 debtor may suggest that the trustee become co-plaintiff. If the trustee is unwilling to bear this expense, the debtor may then be able to request that the trustee abandon the claim.[281] In chapter 13, the debtor normally has the right to fully control any litigation, because the debtor remains in possession of all property of the estate.[282]

Its Structure, Jurisdiction, Venue and Procedure, 11 St. Mary's L.J. 251, 286–289 (1979).

Indeed, a case may be related to the bankruptcy case even if the debtor is not a party. *In re* Me. Marine Corp., 20 B.R. 426 (Bankr. D. Me. 1982).

272 *In re* Bellucci, 9 B.R. 887 (Bankr. D. Mass. 1981); *In re* Griffith, 6 B.R. 753 (Bankr. D.N.M. 1980); *In re* Greco, 3 B.R. 18 (Bankr. D. Haw. 1979). *See also In re* Haw. Mini Storage Sys., Inc., 4 B.R. 489 (Bankr. D. Haw. 1980).

273 See Chapter 9, *supra*, for discussion of the automatic stay.

274 *In re* N. Pipeline Constr. Co., 6 B.R. 928 (Bankr. D. Minn. 1980), *rev'd on other grounds sub nom.* N. Pipeline Constr. Co. v. Marathon Pipe Line Co., 458 U.S. 50 (1982).

275 *Id.*

276 Unless a state has a compulsory counterclaim rule, counterclaims, including recoupment under the Truth in Lending Act, are not barred by a judgment on the creditor's claim and may be raised in a later proceeding. *See* Restatement (Second) of Judgments § 22 (1982). *See also In re* Hamlett, 63 B.R. 492 (Bankr. M.D. Fla. 1986). *But see In re* Trans State Outdoor Adver. Co., 140 F.3d 618 (5th Cir. 1998) (bankruptcy court could not redetermine tax liability that had been adjudicated in an administrative hearing); Kelleran v. Andrijevic, 825 F.2d 692 (9th Cir. 1987) (bankruptcy court could not disregard state court judgment of liability); § 14.4.3.3, *infra*.

277 *See, e.g., In re* Dobrowsky, 735 F.2d 90 (3d Cir. 1984) (insurance claim of the debtor); *In re* Russell, 181 B.R. 616 (M.D. Ala. 1995) (action brought for unfair sales practices); *In re* Carter, 177 B.R. 951 (N.D. Okla.) (rescinding mortgage based upon economic duress), *aff'd*, 45 F.3d 439 (10th Cir. 1994); *In re* Daniel, 137 B.R. 884 (D.S.C. 1992) (debtor and trustee awarded damages for wrongful repossession of mobile home); *In re* Fleet, 95 B.R. 319 (E.D. Pa. 1989) (class action seeking unfair trade practice damages for consumers injured by business whose services consisted solely of providing referrals to bankruptcy attorney); Hinson v. Countrywide Home Loans, Inc. (*In re* Hinson), __ B.R. __, 2012 WL 1354807 (Bankr. E.D.N.C. Apr. 17, 2012) (state law claims based on lender's malfeasance with respect to mortgage modification program); *In re* Arsenault, 184 B.R. 864 (Bankr. D.N.H. 1995) (denying interest to mortgagee that imposed excessive charges); *In re* Madison, 42 B.R. 302 (Bankr. E.D. Pa. 1984) (suit seeking judicial review of decision by HUD to deny assignment program benefits to debtor), *aff'd*, 60 B.R. 837 (E.D. Pa. 1986).

278 *See* § 14.3.2.3, *supra*; § 14.5, *infra*.

279 *See* § 8.3.2, *supra*.

280 *See* Ryan Operations, Gen. P'ship v. Santiam-Midwest Lumber Co., 81 F.3d 355 (3d Cir. 1996) (suit on claim not listed in bankruptcy schedules not barred by judicial estoppel, as debtor had not attempted to play fast and loose with rules and failure to list claim had no impact on bankruptcy case); Donato v. Metro. Life Ins. Co., 230 B.R. 418 (N.D. Cal. 1999) (failure to disclose lawsuit as an asset on schedules did not judicially estop debtor from pursuing it); Elliott v. ITT Corp., 150 B.R. 36 (N.D. Ill. 1992) (failure to initially schedule debt as disputed or note cause of action and failure to deal with it in prior chapter 13 cases which had been dismissed did not estop debtors from raising consumer protection claims against creditor after those claims were discovered). *Cf.* Payless Wholesale Distribs. v. Alberto Culver Inc., 989 F.2d 570 (1st Cir. 1993) (intentional failure to list claims in bankruptcy warrants dismissal of later filed action based on those claims).

281 *See* § 8.3.11, *supra*.

282 11 U.S.C. § 1306(b); Crosby v. Monroe County, 394 F.3d 1328 (11th Cir. 2004); Cable v. Ivy Tech State College, 200 F.3d 467 (7th Cir. 1999) (chapter 13 debtor can bring claim in own name); Olick v. Parker & Parsley Petroleum Co., 145 F.3d 513 (2d Cir. 1998) (chapter 13 debtor has standing to litigate causes of action); Looney v. Hyundai Motor Mfg. Ala., L.L.C., 330 F. Supp. 2d 1289 (M.D. Ala. 2004) (chapter 13 debtor has standing to pursue employment discrimination action); Donato v. Metro. Life Ins. Co., 230 B.R. 418 (N.D. Cal. 1999) (chapter 13 debtor had standing to litigate prepetition causes of action); Case v. Wells Fargo Bank, 359 B.R. 709 (Bankr. E.D. Wis. 2006) (debtors have standing to seek recovery from mortgage creditors of alleged overpayments of interest), *aff'd in part, rev'd in part on other grounds*, 369 B.R. 395 (E.D. Wis. 2007); *In re* Wirmel, 134 B.R. 258 (Bankr. S.D. Ohio 1991) (conversion from chapter 7 to chapter 13 removed civil rights cause of action from trustee's control).

14.4.3 Objections to Claims

14.4.3.1 Overview

Another way of raising issues in the bankruptcy court is by objecting to claims filed by creditors. There are many grounds for objections that might be filed. In a chapter 13 case, for example, debtors may object to claims that they do not want to pay if those claims have not been timely filed,[283] or if they do not otherwise conform to the rules.[284] Section 502 of the Code also permits objections to claims on various other grounds, such as the inclusion of unmatured interest, which may be part of the "balance" on a loan in which interest is precomputed.[285] However, the Supreme Court has rejected at least some arguments that an unsecured claim for postpetition attorney fees based on a contractual attorney fees clause cannot be allowed.[286]

Even in a chapter 7 case, there may be a need to object to a claim. Under an erroneous Ninth Circuit decision,[287] a failure to object to a claim can give the claim res judicata effect, regardless of the fact that the claim is never served on the debtor and the fact that the case is a no-asset chapter 7 case in which objecting to the claim serves no purpose in the bankruptcy.

The rules do not set a time limit for objections to claims. However, in chapter 13 cases some courts have set deadlines by local rule, or issue an "order on claims" soon after the deadline for filing claims has passed, and will not consider objections filed after that order. It is not clear that such deadlines are valid, especially if the resolution of the objection is not necessary to the chapter 13 plan confirmation process, as the Federal Rules of Bankruptcy Procedure do not set a deadline.[288] Although Bankruptcy Rule 3001(f) provides that a properly filed proof of claim is prima facie evidence of the validity and amount of the claim, some courts hold that there need not be a hearing to disallow the claim if the claimant has been given notice and an opportunity for a hearing.[289]

14.4.3.2 Claims Filed After Bar Date for Claims

A creditor's failure to file a timely proof of claim is often a convenient basis to strike a claim which the debtor does not want to pay at all. The time limit for filing claims in cases under chapters 7, 12, and 13 in most instances is ninety days from the first date set for the meeting of creditors.[290] Claims by govern-

---

283 See § 14.4.3.2, *infra*.
284 *In re* Milton, 1990 WL 122048 (Bankr. S.D. Cal. Apr. 17, 1990) (IRS' claim disallowed because it did not state type of tax, tax period or amount and was therefore insufficient under Fed. R. Bankr. P. 3001). *See also* Greer v. O'Dell, 305 F.3d 1297 (11th Cir. 2002) (servicing agent could be real party in interest with standing to file a proof of claim); *In re* Sims, 278 B.R. 457 (Bankr. E.D. Tenn. 2002) (chapter 13 debtor has standing to object to claims and recover overpayments on inflated claims even if the base plan that confirmed in which amount debtor pays into plan will not change); *In re* Chain, 255 B.R. 278 (Bankr. D. Conn. 2000) (failure to attach any documentation to claim resulted in creditor being denied normal presumption that claim was valid).
   However, in most cases, defects in form will not cause disallowance of the claim without an opportunity for the creditor to cure the defect. *In re* Stoecker, 5 F.3d 1022 (7th Cir. 1993) (court could not disallow claim lacking required attachment of writing on which it was based without first granting leave to amend).
285 11 U.S.C. § 502(b)(2). *But see In re* Kielisch, 258 F.3d 315 (4th Cir. 2001) (non-allowability of unmatured interest on nondischargeable student loan did not mean that postpetition interest on loan was not nondischargeable).
286 Travelers Cas. & Sur. Co. of Am. v. Pac. Gas & Elec., 549 U.S. 443, 127 S. Ct. 1199, 1204, 167 L. Ed. 2d 178 (2007). However, the Supreme Court's ruling was limited to a single argument against such fees and other arguments exist. *See In re* Seda France, Inc., 2011 WL 3022563 (Bankr. W.D. Tex. July 22, 2011) (disallowing postpetition attorney fees on unsecured claims because on contrasting language in § 506(b)).
287 Siegel v. Fed. Home Loan Mortgage Corp., 143 F.3d 525 (9th Cir. 1998). *See also* EDP Med. Computer Sys., Inc. v. United States, 480 F.3d 621 (2d Cir. 2007) (failure to object to proof of claim in asset case made claim allowance res judicata, especially because claim was allowed by specific court order). *Cf.* County Fuel Co. v. Equitable Bank Corp., 832 F.2d 290 (4th Cir. 1987) (statement in dicta that it is 'doubtful' that a creditor's proof of claim, to which the debtor had not objected, barred the debtor's subsequent suit against the creditor).

288 *In re* Morton, 298 B.R. 301 (B.A.P. 6th Cir. 2003); *In re* Herrera v. JP Morgan Chase Bank, 369 B.R. 395 (E.D. Wis. 2007) (when court had not set deadline for objections to claim, there was no deadline; trustee had no power to issue notice setting a deadline); *In re* Stukes, 357 B.R. 879 (Bankr. M.D. Fla. 2006) (objection that could not have been fully litigated before confirmation hearing not precluded by confirmation); Hildebrand v. Hays Imports, Inc. (*In re* Johnson), 279 B.R. 218, 224 (Bankr. M.D. Tenn. 2002); *In re* Fryer, 172 B.R. 1020 (Bankr. S.D. Ga. 1994) (TILA objection to creditor's claim was not barred by res judicata effect of confirmed plan, as objection did not implicate validity of any plan provision). *See also* Internal Revenue Serv. v. Kolstad (*In re* Kolstad), 928 F.2d 171, 174 (8th Cir. 1991) ("There is no bar date or deadline for filing objections."); *In re* Barton, 249 B.R. 561, 566 (Bankr. E.D. Wash. 2000) ("If Congress had intended objections to claims to be filed prior to Chapter 13 plan confirmation, it would have been a simple matter to write such a deadline into the statute."). *But see In re* Bateman, 331 F.3d 821 (11th Cir. 2003) (although section 502(a) does not provide time limit to file an objection, it must be filed prior to plan confirmation).
289 *In re* Pierce, 435 F.3d 891 (8th Cir. 2006).
290 Fed. R. Bankr. P. 3002(c).
   Prior to the 1994 amendments to the Code, the rule's dictate that late-filed claims cannot be allowed had been found by some courts to be inconsistent with the Code. *See, e.g., In re* Hausladen, 146 B.R. 557 (Bankr. D. Minn. 1992). Most courts rejected this approach, however, and had found the rule to be valid. *See, e.g., In re* Johnson, 156 B.R. 557 (Bankr. N.D. Ill. 1993); *In re* Zimmerman, 156 B.R. 192 (Bankr. W.D. Mich. 1993). *See also* Jones v. Arross, 9 F.3d 79 (10th Cir. 1993) (late filed claim in chapter 12 case disallowed, citing *Zimmerman*). And even the courts permitting late-filed claims had found that a chapter 13 plan may treat late-filed claims differently than those which were filed on time. *See In re* Hausladen, 146 B.R. 557 (Bankr. D. Minn. 1992). Thus plan provisions separately classifying late claims and providing for little or no dividends to be paid to them should be considered.
   This issue was largely mooted by the 1994 amendments to the Code, which added 11 U.S.C. § 502(b)(9), specifically providing that late filed claims are, upon objection, to be disallowed. This amendment does create the necessity of objecting to such claims.

mental units may be filed until 180 days after the order for relief.[291] (The order for relief is normally the date the petition is filed.) The deadline may be extended further for a tax claim in some cases if the debtor files a tax return to comply with section 1308 and the 180-day deadline expires less than sixty days after the return is filed.[292]

If a claim is not filed on time and an objection to the claim is filed, the claim should be disallowed.[293] However, the court may sometimes find that some other filing by the creditor with the court served as a timely informal proof of claim.[294] The situations in which a court may extend the time for filing a claim in a chapter 7, 12, or 13 case are few and they are delimited in the applicable rule.[295] In contrast, the time limits vary on a case-by-case basis in chapter 11 and extensions are available when the failure to act was based on excusable neglect.[296]

---

[291] 11 U.S.C. § 502(b)(9).

Based upon the wording of this section, an argument can be made that late-filed priority claims are allowed only in chapter 7 cases, because tardy filings are not permitted by the Federal Rules of Bankruptcy Procedure and are authorized only as described in section 726(a) which, under 11 U.S.C. § 103(b), applies only in chapter 7 cases.

[292] 11 U.S.C. § 502(b)(9); Fed. R. Bankr. P. 3002(c)(1).

[293] Fed. R. Bankr. P. 3002(c); *In re* Greenig, 152 F.3d 631 (7th Cir. 1998) (court does not have equitable powers to allow late claim in chapter 12); *In re* Aboody, 223 B.R. 36 (B.A.P. 1st Cir. 1998) (late claim not permissible in chapter 13 even if there was "excusable neglect"). *See also In re* MarchFIRST, Inc., 573 F.3d 414 (7th Cir. 2009) (proof of claim submitted by fax disallowed because fax was not a permissible method of filing proof of claim); *In re* Davis, 430 B.R. 62 (Bankr. W.D.N.Y. 2010) (although a tardy claim filed by a creditor was eligible for distribution after timely filed claims, there was no similar provision allowing distributions when tardy claim was filed by trustee); *In re* Dennis, 230 B.R. 244 (Bankr. D.N.J. 1999) (creditor whose late claim was disallowed had no standing to object to plan's treatment of part of claim which had been disallowed).

If no objection to the claim is filed the claim may well be allowed. By making untimeliness an objection to be raised under section 502(b), Congress may have implicitly provided that if no objection is filed the claim is allowed pursuant to section 502(a). *In re* Jensen, 232 B.R. 118 (Bankr. N.D. Ind. 1999). Thus, if a debtor wants to make sure a claim will be paid and that claim has not been filed by the deadline for claims, the debtor should not object to a late claim, or should file a late claim for the creditor and ask the trustee to cooperate by not objecting to it. *See In re* Miranda, 269 B.R. 737 (Bankr. S.D. Tex. 2001) (if plan provides for payment of all unsecured claims and does not exclude unknown or late-filed claims, late-filed claim to which no objection is made should be paid under plan).

[294] *In re* Holm, 931 F.2d 620 (9th Cir. 1991) (creditor's chapter 11 disclosure statement treated as informal claim); *In re* Charter Co., 876 F.2d 861 (11th Cir. 1989) (motion for relief from stay which clearly sets out nature of claim can constitute informal proof of claim); *In re* Haugen Constr. Servs., Inc., 876 F.2d 681 (8th Cir. 1989) (creditor's letter to United States trustee explicitly stating nature and amount of claim constitutes amendable informal proof of claim); *In re* Anderson-Walker Indus., Inc., 798 F.2d 1285 (9th Cir. 1986) (informal proof of claim must explicitly state nature and amount of claim and must evidence intent to hold debtor liable); *In re* Sambo's Restaurant's Inc., 754 F.2d 811 (9th Cir. 1985) (requisites of an informal proof of claim); Wilkens v. Simon Bros. Inc., 731 F.2d 462 (7th Cir. 1984). *See also In re* Unioil, 962 F.2d 988 (10th Cir. 1992) (permitting amendment of claim to state that it was filed by creditor as trustee for another, rather than in his individual capacity, when content of proof of claim was not changed); *In re* Kolstad, 101 B.R. 492 (Bankr. S.D. Tex. 1989) (creditor can amend proof of claim filed by debtor on its behalf even though it did not file a timely proof of claim), *aff'd*, 928 F.2d 171 (5th Cir. 1991). *But see In re* Reliance Equities, 966 F.2d 1338 (10th Cir. 1992) (trustee's awareness that claim existed did not constitute an informal proof of claim that could be amended after bar date for claims); *In re* A.H. Robins Co., 862 F.2d 1092 (4th Cir. 1988) (bare statement of intention to make a claim insufficient as informal proof); *In re* Edwards, 2010 WL 3807161 (Bankr. M.D. Ala. Sept. 23, 2010) (proof of claim mailed to chapter 13 trustee was not timely filed with clerk); *In re* Minbatiwalla, 424 B.R. 104 (Bankr. S.D.N.Y. 2010) (documents filed by entity whose lien had been avoided did not constitute informal proof of claim).

[295] Fed. R. Bankr. P. 3002(c), 9006(b)(3). *See In re* Coastal Alaska Lines, 920 F.2d 1428 (9th Cir. 1990) (bankruptcy court had no discretion to enlarge time for filing claim in chapter 7 case; unscheduled creditor with knowledge of the bankruptcy who failed to file timely claim was not entitled to participate in distribution of assets with other timely filed claims); *In re* Mozingo, 2009 WL 703206 (Bankr. E.D.N.C. Mar. 10, 2009) (assignee of claim that did not receive notice of case not entitled to waiver of deadline because it had business practice of not notifying debtors when assignments made to it); *In re* Shelton, 116 B.R. 453 (Bankr. D. Md. 1990) (trustee's objection to untimely unsecured claim sustained even though no prejudice would result). *See also In re* Gardenhire, 209 F.3d 1145 (9th Cir. 2000) (time period for filing claims did not stop running during time case was erroneously dismissed before case was reinstated); *In re* Johnson, 901 F.2d 513 (6th Cir. 1990) (IRS failed to timely file claim, in case converted to chapter 7, for administrative expenses incurred in superseded chapter 11 case); *In re* Stuart, 31 B.R. 18 (Bankr. D. Conn. 1983) (student loan creditor precluded from amending timely filed claim against wife in joint case to add claim against husband).

However, a late-filed claim may be paid in some circumstances in a chapter 7 case. A tardily filed nonpriority unsecured claim can be paid under section 726(a)(3) if funds remain after full payment of timely-filed claims and certain claims of creditors without notice.

Significant errors in the notice of the bar date though may provide cause for allowing a late claim. *Compare In re* Herd, 840 F.2d 757 (10th Cir. 1988) (listing of incorrect bar date in chapter 11 case makes notice insufficient) *and In re* Johnson, 95 B.R. 197 (Bankr. D. Colo. 1989) (notice sent to "IRS-Ogden, Utah" in chapter 13 case is insufficient and merited allowance of untimely proof of claim) *with In re* Robintech, Inc., 863 F.2d 393 (5th Cir. 1988) (incorrect address on notice does not excuse creditor's late filing absent proof that late receipt caused late filing).

Another issue related to timeliness of proofs of claim involves the treatment of creditors who did not receive notice of the bar date. Some courts may allow them additional time to file a proof of claim. *See, e.g., In re* Yoder, 758 F.2d 1114 (6th Cir. 1985); *In re* Harris, 447 B.R. 254 (Bankr. W.D. Ark. 2011) (creditor who did not receive notice allowed to file late claim in chapter 13 case).

In other cases, debts owed to creditors without timely notice of the bar date may not be discharged. *See In re* Spring Valley Farms, Inc., 863 F.2d 832 (11th Cir. 1989). *See generally* 11 U.S.C. § 523(a)(3); § 15.4.3.3, *infra*. There is, however, a presumption of receipt of any notices mailed by the court.

[296] Fed. R. Bankr. P. 3003(c)(3), 9006(b)(1).

The Supreme Court has defined excusable neglect fairly liberally, to include inadvertence, mistake, or carelessness, in the context of

An objection to late filed claims may be particularly valuable with respect to tax creditors claiming priority in chapter 13, at least if the tax is dischargeable,[297] because otherwise those claims must be paid in full.[298] For this reason, and because the Internal Revenue Service (IRS) sometimes seems to have difficulty responding to bankruptcy filings,[299] much of the litigation on the timeliness of claims involves tax claims in chapter 13.[300] In cases in which the IRS has attempted to correct its errors by amending a claim it did file on time, courts usually have precluded the IRS from amending the claim for one tax year to include claims for other types of taxes or for the same taxes due in other years.[301]

Amendments to other sorts of claims are similarly disfavored, especially when they change the fundamental nature of the claim.[302]

14.4.3.3 Claims Not Enforceable Against the Debtor

The Code provides that no claim may be allowed to the extent that it is unenforceable against the debtor.[303] This means that the debtor may assert in an objection to a claim any defenses or setoffs the debtor may have with respect to that claim. The objection is then resolved in the bankruptcy forum,[304] which is usually, but not always, the bankruptcy court.[305] If the objection relates to matters such as the extent or validity of a lien, or if it includes a demand for relief of the kinds listed in Bankruptcy Rule 7001, it must be filed by way of complaint.[306] Otherwise, the objection initiates a contested matter.[307] Although a properly filed proof of claim is considered prima facie valid, once some evidence is produced in support of

---

filing a late claim in a chapter 11 case. Pioneer Inv. Servs. Co. v. Brunswick Assocs., 507 U.S. 380, 113 S. Ct. 1489, 123 L. Ed. 2d 74 (1993). *See* Maressa v. A.H. Robins Co., 839 F.2d 220 (4th Cir. 1988); *In re* Int'l Horizons, Inc., 751 F.2d 1213 (11th Cir. 1985); *In re* Pigott, 674 F.2d 1011 (3d Cir. 1982). *See also In re* Pioneer Inv. Servs. Co., 943 F.2d 673 (6th Cir. 1991) (late claims allowable in chapter 11 based on excusable neglect standard), *aff'd*, 507 U.S. 380 (1993); Chrysler Motors Corp. v. Schneiderman, 940 F.2d 911 (3d Cir. 1991) (loss of claim filed by regular mail in chapter 11 case does not permit second claim to be filed late based on excusable neglect); *In re* Vertientes Ltd., 845 F.2d 37 (3d Cir. 1988) (listing creditor's claim on schedules in chapter 11 as uncontested does not estop debtor from objecting to late filed proof of claim).

297 If the tax claim is nondischargeable the debtor may prefer that it be paid, because if it is a priority claim it can be paid before general unsecured creditors whose claims are usually discharged regardless of what they are paid in the chapter 13 case.

298 *See* § 12.3.6.1, *supra*.

299 The IRS, like other government units, now has a special extended deadline for filing claims. Under 11 U.S.C. 502(b)(9), claims of government units may be filed until the later of 180 days after the order for relief or the claims bar date provided under Federal Rules of Bankruptcy Procedure 3002 or 3003. If a tax return is filed under section 1308, the time may be further extended under section 502(b)(9) and Bankruptcy Rule 3002(c)(1).

300 *See In re* Osborne, 76 F.3d 306 (9th Cir. 1996) (IRS claim for payroll taxes disallowed as untimely and could be discharged in chapter 13 case); *In re* Chavis, 47 F.3d 818 (6th Cir. 1995) (untimely proof of IRS claim in chapter 13 case disallowed); *In re* Ripley, 926 F.2d 440 (5th Cir. 1991) (objection to late filed claim of IRS denied because taxes were not due prepetition); *In re* Carr, 134 B.R. 370 (Bankr. D. Neb. 1991) (IRS not permitted to amend claim after confirmation of plan and after court enters order allowing claims); *In re* Garner, 113 B.R. 352 (Bankr. N.D. Ohio 1990) (IRS barred from amending claim thirteen months after confirmation to change claim from unsecured to priority status).

301 United States v. Roberson, 188 B.R. 364 (D. Md. 1995) (IRS precluded from amending existing claim after bar date when supplemental claims involved tax debt for different tax year); *In re* Baker, 129 B.R. 607 (E.D. Mo. 1991) (same); United States v. Owens, 84 B.R. 361 (E.D. Pa. 1988) (IRS cannot amend existing timely filed proof of claim after bar date to include delinquencies for additional tax years). *See also In re* Alliance Operating Corp., 60 F.3d 1174 (5th Cir. 1995) (amendment changing claim from general unsecured claim to priority claim not permitted after deadline for claims had passed); *In re* Taylor, 280 B.R. 711 (Bankr. S.D. Ala. 2001) (creditor could not amend claim long after bar date to change it from unsecured to secured). *But see In re* Tanaka Bros. Farms, Inc., 36 F.3d 996 (10th Cir. 1994) (IRS could amend timely estimated claim to conform to debtor's recently filed tax returns); *In re* Hemingway Transp., Inc., 954 F.2d 1 (1st Cir. 1992); *In re* Unroe, 937 F.2d 346

(7th Cir. 1991) (bankruptcy court has discretion to treat IRS claim for one tax year as notice of intent to collect for a different tax year).

302 *See, e.g., In re* George, 426 B.R. 895 (Bankr. M.D. Fla. 2010) (refusing to permit amendment changing second mortgage holder's claim from secured to unsecured when it would greatly disrupt chapter 13 plan).

303 11 U.S.C. § 502(b)(1); *In re* Hardison, 2011 WL 576066 (Bankr. M.D. Tenn. Feb. 9, 2011) (statute of limitations barred claim).

In determining enforceability, federal common law choice of law rules apply. *See In re* Miller, 292 B.R. 409 (B.A.P. 9th Cir. 2003) (because choice of law rules dictated following Nevada rather than California law, claim for gambling debt allowed).

304 *See, e.g., In re* Venture Mortgage Fund, Ltd. P'ship, 282 F.3d 185 (2d Cir. 2002) (claims based on usurious loans disallowed); *In re* Guardian Trust Co., 260 B.R. 404 (S.D. Miss. 2000) (neither debtor nor trustee need file administrative request for tax refund or comply with IRS statute of limitations to assert refund claim by way of offset to IRS claim); *In re* Goldberg, 297 B.R. 465 (Bankr. W.D.N.C. 2003) (sustaining objection to student loan claim when school closed one week after debtor enrolled and rejecting argument that debtor had to exhaust administrative remedies); *In re* Dooley, 41 B.R. 31 (Bankr. N.D. Ga. 1984) (successful objection to inadequately documented claim for attorney fees); *In re* Hamby, 19 B.R. 776 (Bankr. N.D. Ala. 1982) (Uniform Commercial Code repossession violations asserted as objections to claim for deficiency).

305 See discussion of discretionary and mandatory withdrawal to district court in § 14.2.5, *supra*. *See also In re* Ferris, 764 F.2d 1475 (11th Cir. 1985) (debtor's counterclaim raising state consumer law violations is a core proceeding).

306 Fed. R. Bankr. P. 3007(b); *In re* Hardaway, 421 B.R. 226 (Bankr. N.D. Miss. 2010) (adversary appropriate when objection combined with other claims that required adversary proceeding).

307 Federal Rule of Bankruptcy Procedure 9014 governs such proceedings. Because contested matters are governed by Federal Rule of Bankruptcy Procedure 7041, once an answer to the objection has been filed, there is no right of the objecting party to withdraw the objection without the creditor's consent. *In re* Fairchild, 969 F.2d 866 (10th Cir. 1992).

Also, a debtor or trustee should be careful to serve an objection to the claim of the federal government on all parties required to receive service under Bankruptcy Rule 7004, including the attorney general and United States attorney, and to comply with Bankruptcy Rule 2002(g) requiring service at the address listed in the proof of claim. *See In re* Miller, 16 F.3d 240 (8th Cir. 1994).

an objection, the burden of proof is on the creditor to substantiate its claim.[308] However, with respect to tax claims, the Supreme Court has held that the burden of proof outside of bankruptcy carries over to bankruptcy proceedings.[309]

In some cases a creditor will file a claim which it knows or should have known is baseless in whole or part. That conduct should be subject to sanctions under Federal Rule of Bankruptcy Procedure 9011,[310] and very likely as an unfair or deceptive practice as well.[311] Damages and attorney fees should be available under these theories.

The debtor may wish to object to a claim which has been the subject of prior litigation. However, when judgment has been entered by a nonbankruptcy court on a claim, normal rules of res judicata and collateral estoppel apply.[312]

In some cases, creditors (and particularly secured creditors) do not file claims to which objections can be filed.[313] In such cases, especially if the debtor seeks a determination of the amount due on the claim, the debtor may file a claim for the amount the debtor believes is due on behalf of the creditor to bring the matter before the court.[314] Under the Rules, this may be done if the creditor does not file a claim before the claims deadline expires.[315] Although superseding claims may not be filed by a creditor after the bar date, a few courts have allowed creditors to amend the debtor's claim even after the bar date has passed.[316] If such an amended claim is filed, the debtor may then file whatever objections are appropriate. If no amended claim is filed, the claim filed by the debtor, if allowed by the court, should determine the rights of the parties thereafter.[317] Another approach, which may be preferable if there is a dispute about whether a valid lien exists, is to seek a declaratory judgment that the debtor's proof of claim on behalf of the creditor is valid and binding.[318]

14.4.3.4 Objecting to Claims Filed by Mortgage Creditors and Challenging Servicing Abuses

14.4.3.4.1 In general

Because the debtor's main objective in many chapter 13 bankruptcy cases is to cure and reinstate a mortgage, minimizing the cost of reinstatement requires careful review of the creditor's proof of claim to prevent overcharges. This should include review of the Mortgage Proof of Claim Attachment filed with the mortgage creditor's proof of claim, which requires disclosure of the components of the prepetition arrearage.[319] Some servicers consistently inflate their claims by miscalculation, misunderstanding the loan contract, or deliberate addition of unauthorized fees.[320] Raising these objections can make an apparently unworkable chapter 13 plan feasible or can

---

308 *In re* Fid. Holding Co., Ltd., 837 F.2d 696 (5th Cir. 1988); *In re* Tesmetges, 87 B.R. 263 (Bankr. S.D.N.Y. 1988). *See also In re* Circle J Dairy, Inc., 112 B.R. 297 (W.D. Ark. 1989) (when claim itself calls into question its amount, it cannot be given prima facie validity); *In re* Koch, 83 B.R. 898 (Bankr. E.D. Pa. 1988) (general standard of proof is a preponderance of the evidence).

309 Raleigh v. Illinois Dep't of Revenue, 530 U.S. 15, 120 S. Ct. 1951, 147 L. Ed. 2d 13 (2000).

310 The rule now covers pleadings filed by unrepresented creditors and debtors as well as attorneys. A related issue is whether the party listed as creditor or agent for the creditor on the proof of claim has standing to file the claim. This issue is discussed in § 14.4.3.4.7, *infra*.

311 Helpful pleadings on this issue are published in *Suit Against Taxing Agency for Filing Baseless Chapter 13 Proofs of Claim*, National Consumer Law Center, Consumer Law Pleadings No. 3, § 7.2 (Index Guide with Companion Website).
   But see Holloway v. Household Auto. Fin. Corp., 227 B.R. 501 (N.D. Ill. 1998) (UDAP remedies are preempted by Bankruptcy Code consumer protections). *Holloway* is wrongly decided. *See generally* National Consumer Law Center, Unfair and Deceptive Acts and Practices § 6.10.7 (7th ed. 2008 and Supp.).

312 *In re* Baker, 74 F.3d 906 (9th Cir. 1996) (res judicata effect of prior final judgment of Tax Court precluded debtor from relitigating tax liability through objection to claim); *In re* Laing, 945 F.2d 354 (10th Cir. 1991) (state court judgment on note must be given preclusive effect upon objections to proof of claim). *See In re* Brady, Tex. Mun. Gas Corp., 936 F.2d 212 (5th Cir. 1991) (state court determination concerning creditor's rights against debtor's successor in interest is entitled to full faith and credit even if erroneous). *Cf. In re* Mantz, 343 F.3d 1207 (9th Cir. 2003) (bankruptcy court could consider objection to state tax claim because there had been no final adjudication of tax liability prior to the bankruptcy).

313 It should be noted that no notice to the debtor of filing of a claim is required by the current rules. The only way to be certain as to whether a claim has been filed is to check the bankruptcy court file.

314 11 U.S.C. § 501(c).

315 Fed. R. Bankr. P. 3004.
   The debtor has until thirty days after the claims bar date to file a proof of claim on behalf of a creditor. *Id*. This time may be extended if the debtor's failure to file timely is based on excusable neglect. Fed. R. Bankr. P. 9006(b); *In re* Davis, 936 F.2d 771 (4th Cir. 1991).

316 Fed. R. Bankr. P. 3004; *In re* Kolstad, 928 F.2d 171 (5th Cir. 1991) (court has discretion to allow IRS to amend debtor's proof of claim after the bar date); *In re* Bishop, 122 B.R. 96 (Bankr. E.D. Mo. 1990) (claim of IRS filed after debtor filed claim for IRS was effective as an amended claim, even though filed after claims bar date).

317 *See also In re* Borne Chem. Co., 691 F.2d 134 (3d Cir. 1982) (court may estimate value of claims in bankruptcy proceeding for purposes of bankruptcy case).

318 *See In re* Kilen, 129 B.R. 538 (Bankr. N.D. Ill. 1991) (debtor can object to the proof of claim it files on behalf of a creditor).
   If no such action is filed, when the debtor files an unsecured claim on behalf of a creditor which believes it is secured, that creditor may argue later that its lien passed through the case unaffected. In a chapter 13 case, that argument should fail, because the creditor is bound by a chapter 13 plan of which it had notice. *See* § 12.11, *supra*. But the cautious approach is probably to seek a clear determination from the court at the time of the bankruptcy case.

319 Fed. R. Bankr. P. 3001(c)(2); § 11.6.2.8.1, *supra*; Official Form 10 (Attachment A), *reprinted in* Appx. D, *infra*. If the mortgage account includes an escrow account, the mortgage creditor must attach to the proof of claim an escrow account statement prepared as of the petition date in a form consistent with applicable nonbankruptcy law. For a discussion of the requirements for escrow account statements under the RESPA, see National Consumer Law Center, Foreclosures § 9.3.3 (4th ed. 2012).

320 *See, e.g., In re* Bateman, 435 B.R. 600 (Bankr. E.D. Ark. 2010) (claim reduced based on creditor's miscalculation of prepetition late charges and misapplication of prepetition and postpetition payments; attorney fees awarded to debtor for successful claim objection).

provide much more breathing room for a family struggling to afford large plan payments.

Other problems relate to the way servicers apply payments in chapter 13 cases. The effect of a cure in a chapter 13 case is to nullify all consequences of the prebankruptcy default.[321] Once the debtor's chapter 13 plan is confirmed in a case involving a long-term mortgage, the debtor's ongoing regular mortgage payments should be applied from the petition date based on the mortgage contract terms and original loan amortization as if no default exists.[322] All prepetition arrearages are paid separately under the plan as a part of the mortgage servicer's allowed claim.[323]

Ignoring the effect of plan confirmation, mortgage creditors routinely treat timely postpetition payments as if they were late. They do so because of the industry practice outside of bankruptcy of crediting payments received to the oldest outstanding installment due, and the failure of the servicing industry to develop an automated system to deal with the bifurcated payment application requirements in chapter 13 cases. Servicers often attempt to manually override their automated systems, but this cannot realistically be done without error for the three to five year duration of the plan.

These problems cause additional costs to be imposed on consumer debtors in the form of unauthorized fees. As payments are deemed late or insufficient, the automated servicer systems treat payments as unapplied and divert them to suspense accounts, impose late fees and additional interest charges, and order property inspections and other default related services.[324] In addition, debtors are often not notified of interest rate adjustments on adjustable rate mortgages or payment changes on escrow accounts, leaving debtors who successfully complete their chapter 13 plans with bills for thousands of dollars of previously undisclosed improper fees when they emerge from bankruptcy.[325]

When an overcharge appears deliberate, or in situations involving inadvertent overcharges which the servicer fails to correct after due notice, debtor's attorneys should consider seeking relief (and attorney fees) under a variety of legal theories, including claims under unfair trade practice and debt collection protection statutes, the Real Estate Settlement Procedures Act,[326] and in egregious cases, sanctions under Rule 9011.[327] For cases involving interest overcharges, usury claims may also be available.[328] Payment application problems may be remedied through stay violation proceedings under section 362(k),[329] and contempt proceedings for violation of the confirmation order and discharge injunction, with sanctions im-

---

321 See § 11.6.2.8, supra. See also House Report to the Bankruptcy Reform Act of 1994, H.R. Rep. No. 103-835, at 55 (1994), reprinted in 1994 U.S.C.C.A.N. 3340 ("It is the Committee's intention that a cure pursuant to a plan should operate to put the debtor in the same position as if the default had never occurred.").

322 See § 11.6.2.8, supra; In re Boday, 397 B.R. 846 (Bankr. N.D. Ohio 2008); In re Wines, 239 B.R. 703 (Bankr. D.N.J. 1999); In re Rathe, 114 B.R. 253 (Bankr. D. Idaho 1990).

323 Rake v. Wade, 508 U.S. 464, 473, 113 S. Ct. 2187, 124 L. Ed. 2d 424 (1993) (as authorized by section 1322(b)(5), mortgage creditor's claim is effectively "split . . . into two separate claims—the underlying debt and the arrearages"); In re Hudak, 2008 WL 4850196 (Bankr. D. Colo. Oct. 24, 2008) (Bankruptcy Code, not language of deed of trust, determines how ongoing payments will be applied while debtor cures default in chapter 13).

324 See, e.g., Wells Fargo Bank v. Jones, 391 B.R. 577 (E.D. La. 2008) (mortgage creditor collected at closing on court-approved refinancing additional $24,450 in illegal postpetition fees and interest charges imposed during chapter 13 case), aff'd following remand, In re Jones, 2012 WL 1155715 (Bankr. E.D. La. Apr. 5, 2012) (sanctioning servicer more than $3 million for its "highly reprehensible" actions including routine misapplication of payments and overcharging accounts).

325 See, e.g., In re Dominique, 368 B.R. 913 (Bankr. S.D. Fla. 2007) (servicer failed to provide escrow statements during chapter 13 plan and just before plan completion provided debtors with an escrow account review indicating a $6397 escrow deficiency); In re Rizzo-Cheverier, 364 B.R. 532 (Bankr. S.D.N.Y. 2007) (servicer allowed deficiency in escrow account to accrue and then, without notice to debtor, applied trustee plan payments intended for prepetition arrears to postpetition escrow deficiency). See § 14.4.3.4.2, infra.

This problem led to the promulgation of new Federal Rule of Bankruptcy Procedure 3002.1 requiring prompt disclosure of all fees incurred and payment changes during a chapter 13 case. See § 11.6.2.8.1, supra. Payment changes are to be reported on Official Form 10 (Supplement 1), reprinted in Appx. D, infra.

326 See Chase Manhattan Mortgage Corp. v. Padgett, 268 B.R. 309 (S.D. Fla. 2001) (because the lender had failed to provide annual notice of escrow deficiencies as required by both the Real Estate Settlement Procedures Act, its accompanying regulations, and Florida law, it had waived postpetition escrow increases); In re Johnson, 384 B.R. 763 (Bankr. E.D. Mich. 2008); In re Dominique, 368 B.R. 913 (Bankr. S.D. Fla. 2007). See also In re Wright, 461 B.R. 757 (Bankr. N.D. Iowa 2011) (awarding actual damages of $10,000, punitive damages of $40,000, and attorney fees for servicer's violation of plan terms in failing to notify trustee, debtor, or debtor's counsel of changes in mortgage payments); In re Foreman, 2010 WL 2696630 (Bankr. M.D.N.C. July 7, 2010) (creditor waived its right to collect postpetition arrears because it did not comply with plan that required notice of change in monthly payment and instead permitted a $12,000 arrearage to accrue); In re Armstrong, 394 B.R. 794 (Bankr. W.D. Pa. 2008) (mortgage creditor waived right to collect additional interest and other payment amount increases because it failed to provide notice of payment change under adjustable rate mortgage). See generally National Consumer Law Center, Foreclosures Ch. 7–9 (4th ed. 2012).

327 See In re Nosek, 406 B.R. 434 (D. Mass. 2009) (sanctions imposed when mortgage servicer company represented it owned mortgage and never advised court of transfer of servicing rights), aff'd in pertinent part, Ameriquest Mortgage Co. v. Nosek, 609 F.3d 6 (1st Cir. 2010).

328 National Consumer Law Center, Consumer Credit Regulation Ch. 7 (2012).

329 In re Rodriguez, 629 F.3d 136 (3d Cir. 2010); In re Mattox, 2011 WL 3626762 (Bankr. E.D. Ky. 2011) (holding that misapplication of payments may constitute a violation of the automatic stay); In re Myles, 395 B.R. 599 (Bankr. M.D. La. 2008) (debtor may assert claims for breach of contract and stay violation against creditor who improperly treated postpetition payments as if loan in default); In re Payne, 387 B.R. 614 (Bankr. D. Kan. 2008) (servicer who improperly created a postpetition escrow arrearage by applying debtors' payments to prepetition debt rather than to the currently due monthly installments violated section 362(a)(6)); In re Sanchez, 372 B.R. 289 (Bankr. S.D. Tex. 2007) (mortgage creditor's application of mortgage payments it received from the trustee to postpetition attorney fees, costs, and property inspection fees, without advising

posed based on the court's authority under Code sections 105 and 524(i).[330] Abusive practices which impact a large group of debtors may be amenable to class action treatment.[331]

If a creditor fails to comply with the requirement under Rule 3002.1 for notice of postpetition payment changes or fees, or if it fails to contest the complete cure of the delinquency, the court may preclude it from offering any evidence that would have been in the notices, i.e., the amounts of the payment changes, fees, or other amounts allegedly due but unpaid at the end of the case.[332] The court may also award attorney fees and other expenses to the debtor for the additional proceedings necessary to resolve the issue.[333]

Informal discovery on the elements of a creditor's claim can be obtained under the Real Estate Settlement Procedures Act with potential sanctions for failure to provide timely information. If a borrower sends a "qualified written request" asserting the account is in error or asking a question about the account, a mortgage servicer must within sixty business days conduct an investigation if an error is alleged; provide the requested information; make any necessary corrections to the account; and inform the consumer of the actions taken.[334] Once an objection to claim or other action is filed, full discovery under the Federal Rules of Bankruptcy Procedure becomes available.[335] As the claim objection would raise issues about the extent of a lien and goes beyond issues of property valuation, it must be pursued as an adversary proceeding.[336]

14.4.3.4.2 Escrow overcharges

One of the most common problems found in reviewing mortgage claims is abuse in the collection of escrow arrears.[337] Often, this occurs because servicers fail to consider the effect of a chapter 13 cure plan and use the total amount of escrow arrears in reevaluating the borrower's escrow account after the chapter 13 case is filed. This review of the escrow account is then used as the basis for calculating the debtor's new postpetition escrow payment going forward. However in most cases prepetition escrow payment arrears have already been included in the bankruptcy proof of claim and are being paid through the chapter 13 plan. Because those arrears are being paid under the plan, this practice can lead to double or sometimes triple payment (when the escrow arrears are already double counted in the proof of claim).[338]

Mortgage servicers are required under the Real Estate Settlement Procedures Act to reevaluate each borrower's escrow account on an annual basis.[339] When a chapter 13 case is filed to cure a mortgage default, the servicer should conduct an escrow account analysis to determine the debtor's new escrow payment before the first postpetition payment is due.[340] Rule 3001(c)(2) requires the mortgage creditor to attach to its proof of claim an escrow account statement prepared as of the petition date in a form consistent with applicable nonbankruptcy law, and to disclose the amount of the prepetition escrow account arrearage on the Mortgage Proof of Claim Attach-

---

the debtor, violated the stay); *In re* McCormack, 203 B.R. 521 (Bankr. D.N.H. 1996).

330 *In re* Galloway, 2010 WL 364336 (Bankr. N.D. Miss. Jan. 29, 2010) (court has power to order sanctions under § 105 for mortgage overcharges); *In re* Batiste, 2009 WL 2849077 (Bankr. E.D. La. July 14, 2009) (ordering sanctions under § 105 against mortgage servicer that was repeat offender, even after servicer settled with debtor); *In re* Boday, 397 B.R. 846 (Bankr. N.D. Ohio 2008) (creditor violated plan confirmation order and discharge order by failing to apply portions of debtor's ongoing postpetition payments to reduce principal balance as if loan were not in default); *In re* Rodriguez, 396 B.R. 436 (Bankr. S. D. Tex. 2008) (court has inherent contempt power and authority under § 105 to remedy servicers' errors in applying payments contrary to plan terms). See § 14.4.3.4.8, *infra*.

331 *See In re* Rodriguez, 695 F.3d 360 (5th Cir. 2012) (class action brought to recover fees that were not disclosed during bankruptcy case); § 14.7, *infra*.

332 Fed. R. Bankr. P. 3002.1(i)(1). *See* § 11.6.2.8.1, *supra*.

333 Fed. R. Bankr. P. 3002.1(i)(2).

334 12 U.S.C. § 2605(e)(1)(B)(2); 24 C.F.R. § 3500.21(e)(3). *See* National Consumer Law Center, Foreclosures §§ 9.2.2.5, 9.2.2.6 (4th ed. 2012).

For a sample "qualified written request," see Form 87, Appx. G.8, *infra*. The appropriate address for the qualified written request can usually be obtained from the website of the servicer or may be obtained by calling the servicer. Some mortgage holders and servicers claim that RESPA is not applicable when the borrower is in bankruptcy. There is no basis for this argument. *See* Conley v. Cent. Mortgage Co., 2009 WL 2498022 (E.D. Mich. Aug. 11, 2009); Chase Manhattan Mortgage Corp. v. Padgett, 268 B.R. 309 (S.D. Fla. 2001); *In re* Moffitt, 390 B.R. 368 (Bankr. E.D. Ark. 2008); *In re* Payne, 387 B.R. 614 (Bankr. D. Kan. 2008); *In re* Johnson, 384 B.R. 763 (Bankr. E.D. Mich. 2008); *In re* Laskowski, 384 B.R. 518 (Bankr. N.D. Ind. 2008); *In re* Figard, 382 B.R. 695 (Bankr. W.D. Pa. 2008); *In re* Padilla, 379 B.R. 643 (Bankr. S.D. Tex. 2007); *In re* Sánchez-Rodríguez, 377 B.R. 1 (Bankr. D. P.R. 2007); *In re* Holland, 374 B.R. 409 (Bankr. D. Mass. 2007). *See also* National Consumer Law Center, Foreclosures § 9.2.6.1 (4th ed. 2012).

335 Federal Rules of Bankruptcy Procedure 7026–7037 as made applicable to contested matters by Federal Rule of Bankruptcy Procedure 9014.

336 Fed. R. Bankr. P. 3007(b), 7001. *See* § 14.2.4.1, *supra*.

337 Many first mortgage claims include required escrow payments for taxes and insurance. (In some states, consumer escrows associated with mortgage claims are called "impound accounts.") In situations in which modification of mortgage terms is allowed, it may be possible to cancel the escrow account in order to pay the holder only principal and interest. In that event, the debtor would usually have to pay taxes and insurance separately. *See generally* § 11.6.1, *supra*.

338 *See In re* Newcomer, 438 B.R. 527 (Bankr. D. Md. 2010) (by improperly collecting prepetition escrow deficiency from postpetition payments, servicer collected same amount twice); *In re* Pitts, 354 B.R. 58 (Bankr. E.D. Pa. 2006) (incongruity of proof of claim that seemed to claim taxes as a separate item as well as escrow deficiency satisfied debtor's burden of challenging validity of claim and mortgage company failed to meet burden of presenting evidence justifying taxes claimed).

339 *See* 12 U.S.C. § 2609(c); National Consumer Law Center, Foreclosures § 9.3.2 (4th ed. 2012). *See also In re* Laskowski, 384 B.R. 518 (Bankr. N.D. Ind. 2008) (bankruptcy exemption in Regulation X relating to escrow statement does not relieve servicer of duty to conduct annual escrow analysis).

340 Chapter 13 plan payments generally begin no later than thirty days after the case is filed. *See* 11 U.S.C. § 1326(a).

ment.[341] The Real Estate Settlement Procedures Act permits the servicer to conduct such an analysis in this situation before the end of debtor's normal escrow account year.[342] In order to give effect to the cure plan, the servicer must treat all unpaid prepetition escrow payments as if they have been paid when conducting this analysis. These unpaid prepetition escrow payments are part of mortgage holder's arrearage claim to be paid under the plan and such charges may not be collected in postpetition escrow payments.[343] Thus, prepetition escrow account shortages and deficiencies, often representing amounts disbursed by the servicer for taxes, insurance, and other escrow items when there were insufficient funds in the debtor's escrow account, are largely paid as part of the mortgage holder's arrearage claim during the longer cure period under the plan rather than in the shorter one-year period following the case filing as part of debtor's escrow portion of the postpetition mortgage maintenance payments. If done correctly, in most cases this procedure will produce a lower monthly escrow payment to be included as part of the debtor's total postpetition maintenance payments.

Escrow overcharges may also arise because fees and charges associated with foreclosure are broken out as separate elements of the arrears. At the same time, the servicer may have also included those fees and charges in the borrower's escrow account when they were paid out.[344] Based on miscommunication, ignorance, or inattention, these fees are then double counted in the proof of claim: once as "foreclosure costs" and again as a portion of the amount denominated as "payment arrears."

Proofs of claim should be reviewed for these problems. When the line item for escrow arrears appears to be out of line, (for example, if it is more than the amount of the monthly payment for taxes and insurance multiplied by the number of months the debtor is in arrears), then more information should be requested, by discovery if necessary.[345] At the same time, debtors should be told to be on the alert for unusual changes in their monthly payment amounts while the chapter 13 case is pending. Of equal concern, debtors should be told to notify their attorney if the servicer fails to provide annual escrow statements and payment change notices during the chapter 13 case.

14.4.3.4.3 Interest overcharges

Several problems related to interest charges can arise as well. A common problem arises when servicers itemize or otherwise include in the proof of claim interest on arrears[346] claims which will accrue postpetition under the plan. In jurisdictions where the trustee automatically calculates and pays that interest, some debtors end up paying double.

In order to prevent this problem, the Code requires that claims for unmatured interest be disallowed.[347] An objection to claim may be necessary. Although many trustees are conscientious about not double paying interest, debtor's counsel cannot rely on the trustee to catch this error.

Another interest charge abuse which has been reported is a secured proof of claim for the entire amount of precomputed interest (for a loan on which the balance is calculated to include precomputed interest for the entire term of the loan under state law). That practice, which includes in the balance interest not yet earned, can undermine plans which propose to modify the secured claim and pay it on an amortization schedule different from that contained in the contract, and it can distort the amount of interest on arrears to which that creditor is entitled.

Even if the credit contract allows precomputed interest, the filing of a claim including such interest should be challenged in bankruptcy as inconsistent with 11 U.S.C. § 1325(a)(5) and 11 U.S.C. § 502(b)(2). At a minimum, the debtor is entitled to have appropriate interest rebates calculated. (In some transactions creditors may argue that these calculations must be made under the very unfair Rule of 78's, but depending upon the contract and state or federal law these arguments can often be defeated, as the Rule of 78's may be abrogated by statute or applicable only in the event of prepayment or other specified event.)[348] If interest on arrears is permitted, the debtor and the

---

341 Fed. R. Bankr. P. 3001(c)(2); Official Form 10 (Attachment A), *reprinted in* Appx. D, *infra*.
342 RESPA's implementing regulation, Regulation X, provides that in certain situations the servicer need not wait until the end of the twelve-month escrow computation year to perform an escrow analysis. If the analysis is done before the end of the twelve-month computation year, the servicer is required to send the borrower a "short year statement" which will change one escrow account computation year to another, and establish the beginning date of the new computation year. *See* Reg. X, 24 C.F.R. § 3500.17(i)(4).
343 *In re* Rodriguez, 629 F.3d 136 (3d Cir. 2010); Campbell v. Countrywide Home Loans, Inc., 545 F.3d 348 (5th Cir. 2008); *In re* Beaudet, 455 B.R. 671 (Bankr. M.D. Tenn. 2011).
344 Fees paid to third-party vendors who provide foreclosure services are often referred to as "corporate advances." Although these advances are not typically treated as an escrow item, servicers occasionally disburse funds from the borrower's escrow account to pay for these foreclosure expenses.
345 The portion of the prepetition escrow account arrearage attributable to the monthly payments in arrears should be listed on the Mortgage Proof of Claim Attachment in Part 3, Item 2, under "Amount of installment payments due." Any other amount representing a prepetition "escrow shortage or deficiency" that is not already included in the installment payments due as listed in Part 3 should be listed in the form's Part 2, Item 13. *See* Official Form 10 (Attachment A), *reprinted in* Appx. D, *infra*.
346 This interest is required to be paid based on Rake v. Wade, 508 U.S. 464, 113 S. Ct. 2187, 124 L. Ed. 2d 424 (1993). The requirement of payment of interest on arrears is not applicable to secured claims related to mortgages which were consummated after October 22, 1994 unless the parties' agreement requires that payment. 11 U.S.C. § 1322(e). *See* § 11.6.2.7.2, *supra*.
347 11 U.S.C. § 502(b)(2).
348 *In re* McMurray, 218 B.R. 867 (Bankr. E.D. Tenn. 1998) (Rule of 78's was only authorized, and was not required, when debtor prepaid loan).
  See NCLC's *Consumer Credit Regulation* § 5.8.6.3 (2012) for a discussion of the rule and the limited situations in which it continues to be legal.

trustee will also need to carefully calculate the appropriate interest on arrears payment so that only the arrears generate interest.

14.4.3.4.4 Late charge abuses and other mistakes in crediting payments

Despite a chapter 13 plan to cure arrears, some creditors continue to treat timely payments received postpetition as if they were late. This occurs based on the industry practice of crediting payments received to the oldest outstanding installment. Although this practice may be appropriate if there is no bankruptcy pending, it is not appropriate in situations in which the prepetition arrears are being paid according to a proof of claim (which may already include late charges for those payments) and the debtor's chapter 13 plan.

Hidden late charges are only one of several pervasive problems with incorrect crediting of payments made to cure a default under a chapter 13 plan.[349] These problems may not be easily detectable without reviewing loan payment records.[350] At a minimum, when a debtor has cured a default, payment records should be reviewed at the close of the case to make sure that they reflect the cure. Debtors should be encouraged to alert attorneys, even after bankruptcy is completed, if they receive communications regarding their mortgage that they do not understand. It is extremely common for illegal charges to be added to a mortgage after a bankruptcy is complete; sometimes they are discovered for the first time only when the debtor receives a pay-off statement.[351] Careful drafting of the debtor's plan to specifically direct how payments are be applied, as discussed below, can provide a basis for challenging improper fees during and after the bankruptcy case.

14.4.3.4.5 Bankruptcy monitoring fees and other bankruptcy fees

Many mortgage holders and servicers charge borrowers who file bankruptcy a fee for monitoring the bankruptcy case, even in chapter 7 cases in which the borrower is current on monthly mortgage payments and plans to continue to make monthly payments as they come due. These "monitoring" fees may be $250 or more and are automatically assessed to the borrower's account as soon as the bankruptcy is filed. They may include fees for periodic inspections of the property or broker price opinions. Lenders generally assert that these fees are authorized by language in their loan notes that obligates the borrower to pay any costs incurred in defending its security interest.

Holders and servicers often claim a right to fees for filing a proof of claim. Proof of claim fees may be charged alone or combined with "monitoring" fees, and are generally in the range of $150 to $400.[352] Additional fees may be charged for pursuing motions for relief from stay, objections to confirmation, or for responding to a debtor's objection to claim.[353]

There are several possible bases on which creditors' bankruptcy servicing fees can be challenged. However, the first problem in some cases is discovering that they exist, because the fees are sometimes charged to the debtor's escrow account or to a suspense account, and collected going forward by adjustment to future payments rather than as elements of a proof of claim.[354] More often, these fees are assessed to the debtor's account but never disclosed until after a stay relief motion is filed or the bankruptcy case is concluded. A qualified written request under the Real Estate Settlement Procedure Act may be sent requesting that the servicer disclose whether any monitoring or other fees have been charged.[355]

Typically, the contract clause on which the holder relies is a general provision which does not expressly authorize the imposition of "bankruptcy monitoring fees" or "proof of claim fees," but which applies more generally to attorney fees and other costs of defending the mortgage in a court action.[356] For example, one large loan servicing company that routinely imposes these fees relies upon the following provision contained in its standard mortgage:

> (9) Litigation. Borrower shall defend this mortgage in any action purporting to affect such property whether or not it affects the lien hereof, or purporting to affect the lien hereof or purporting to affect the rights or powers of Lender, and shall file and prosecute all necessary claims and actions to prevent or recover for any damage to or destruction of such property; and Lender is hereby authorized, without obligation to do so, to prosecute and defend any such action, whether

---

349 *Debtors Force Mortgage Servicer to Remedy Chapter 13 Violations*, 12 NCLC REPORTS *Bankruptcy and Foreclosures Ed.* 43 (Mar./Apr. 1994). *See also In re* Hannon, 421 B.R. 728 (Bankr. M.D. Pa. 2009) (mortgage creditor had duty to amend proof of claim to reflect refund of sheriff's sale deposit to creditor).

350 *See* Jones v. Wells Fargo Home Mortg., Inc. (*In re* Jones), 2012 WL 1155715 (Bankr. E.D. La. Apr. 5, 2012) (misapplication of plan payments to undisclosed charges contrary to both plan and mortgage terms); *In re* Boday, 397 B.R. 846 (Bankr. N.D. Ohio 2008) (after reviewing payment records showing that plan payments had been misapplied, court ordered mortgage creditor to adjust its records to reflect amount owed based on original amortization schedule); *In re* Wines, 239 B.R. 703 (Bankr. D.N.J. 1999) (example of case reconciling payments made and proof of claim).

351 *See, e.g.*, Wells Fargo Bank v. Jones, 391 B.R. 577 (E.D. La. 2008) (mortgage creditor collected additional $24,450 in illegal postpetition fees and interest charges at closing on court-approved refinancing).

352 *In re* Collins, 2009 WL 1607737 (Bankr. S.D. Tex. June 8, 2009) ($250 fee charged for initial set-up work including both internal administrative tasks and filing of initial proof of claim), *aff'd*, Wells Fargo Bank v. Collins, 437 Fed. Appx. 314 (5th Cir. 2011).

353 *See* § 11.6.2.7.1, *supra*.

354 Clients should be alerted to report any correspondence reflecting significant escrow payment changes to determine whether this problem has arisen.

355 *See* § 14.4.3.4.1, *supra*; Form 87, Appx. G.8, *infra*.

356 It is clear that bankruptcy monitoring fees can never be allowed without contractual authorization for charging those fees. *See In re* Hatcher, 208 B.R. 959 (B.A.P. 10th Cir. 1997) (no postpetition attorney fees allowed absent mortgage provision authorizing fees); *In re* LaRoche, 115 B.R. 93 (Bankr. N.D. Ohio 1990).

brought by or against Borrower or Lender, or with or without suit, to exercise or enforce any other right, remedy, or power available or conferred hereunder, whether or not judgment be entered in any action or proceeding; and Lender may appear or intervene in any action or proceeding, and retain counsel therein, and take such action therein, as either may be deemed necessary or advisable, and may settle, compromise or pay the same or any other claims and, in so doing, may expend and advance such sums of money as either may deem necessary. Whether or not Borrower so appears or defends, Borrower on demand shall pay all costs and expenses, including but not limited to reasonable attorney fees of Lender including costs of evidence of title, in any such action or proceeding in which Lender may appear by virtue of being made a party defendant or otherwise, and irrespective of whether the interest of Lender in such property or their respective powers hereunder may be affected by such action. . . .

In addition to being an unbargained-for term which is imposed in the boilerplate, this language, upon close reading, does not appear to authorize a bankruptcy monitoring fee. The provision appears to apply only when the borrower or lender defends the mortgage in a case which purports to affect the property, the lien, or the lender's powers or rights, or in actions to enforce the lender's rights, or in actions to recover for damage to or destruction of the property. A borrower's chapter 13 bankruptcy, because of the anti-modification provision in section 1322(b)(2), does not affect the property or the lien and is not an action to enforce the holder's rights.[357]

According to the quoted paragraph, whether or not the borrower defends the action, the borrower is required to pay all of the lender's costs and expenses of any such action *in which the lender appears*, including reasonable attorney fees. Monitoring to determine whether an appearance is necessary is not covered.

Some mortgages contain provisions for recovery of fees which refer to bankruptcy proceedings. For example, a common mortgage and deed of trust provision states that if "there is a legal proceeding that may significantly affect Lender's rights in the property (such as a proceeding in bankruptcy, . . .), then Lender may do and pay whatever is reasonable or appropriate to protect the value of the Property and Lender's rights in the Property. . . ." Because this language refers to "a proceeding *in* bankruptcy," it may be construed as applying only when an adversary proceeding within the bankruptcy case is filed against the holder rather than the filing of a bankruptcy case itself, and therefore would not generally permit recovery of monitoring and proof of claim fees.

Often mortgage provisions relating to recovery of fees such as those quoted here are ambiguous. It is a basic principle of contract law that any ambiguity in a contract is construed against the drafter, in this case the lender.[358] Equally importantly, courts have strictly construed contractual provisions providing for fees and costs.[359]

Of course, the analysis of any particular case will depend on the language of the loan contract at issue. As the language quoted here illustrates, advocates should review the language of the contract closely to determine whether it actually says what the lender claims that it says, and whether it is ambiguous.[360] State law may also limit the fees that can be collected.[361]

If a holder or servicer attempts to collect a bankruptcy fee from property of the estate while the automatic stay is in effect by adding the fee to the debtor's account, it has violated Code section 362(a)(3). Section 362(a)(3) prohibits "any act to obtain possession of property of the estate or of property from the estate or to exercise control over property of the estate" while the stay is in effect. In a chapter 13 case, all property the debtor acquires during the entire time the case is pending is property of the estate pursuant to section 1306(a). By seeking payment of this fee directly from the debtor, the holder violates the stay.[362] Likewise, collection of the fee if it is not provided for

---

357 *In re* Thomas, 186 B.R. 470 (Bankr. W.D. Mo. 1995).
   Even if there is a default, and a case is brought under chapter 13, the bankruptcy arguably does not affect the holder's rights, if the Code protects the holder's claim from being modified under 11 U.S.C. § 1322(b)(2). *In re* Romano, 174 B.R. 342 (Bankr. M.D. Fla. 1994).

358 *In re* Stark, 242 B.R. 866 (Bankr. W.D.N.C. 1999) (bankruptcy monitoring fees disallowed as ambiguous mortgage contract construed against lender); *In re* Williams, 1998 WL 372656 (Bankr. N.D. Ohio June 10, 1998) (ambiguous contract term inadequate basis to support creditor's request for fees for motion for relief from stay).

359 *See, e.g., In re* Sublett 895 F.2d 1381 (11th Cir. 1990); First Brandon Nat'l Bank v. Kerwin-White, 109 B.R. 626 (D. Vt. 1990); *In re* Baron, 2011 WL 1403035 (Bankr. N.D. Cal. Apr. 12, 2011) (disallowing fees because creditor failed to provide notice to debtor before paying attorney fees as required by deed of trust). *See also In re* Romano, 174 B.R. 342 (Bankr. M.D. Fla. 1994) (interpreting loan note's ambiguous attorney fee provision against the lender/drafter). *Cf. In re* Majchrowski, 6 F. Supp. 2d 946 (N.D. Ill. 1998) (standard form mortgage provision allows lender to charge a fee for filing proof of claim and is not ambiguous so as to require construction against the drafter).

360 *See In re* Hatala, 295 B.R. 62 (Bankr. D.N.J. 2003) (mortgage provided for fees only in foreclosure and not for fees incurred after foreclosure judgment; fees limited to those permitted by state rules); *In re* Woodham, 174 B.R. 346 (Bankr. M.D. Fla. 1994) (analysis of provision which does not specifically provide for attorney fees in bankruptcy).

361 *In re* Ransom, 361 B.R. 895 (Bankr. D. Mont. 2007) (Montana law limited fees to lesser of one percent of amount due or $1000). *See* § 11.6.2.7.1, *supra*.

362 Wells Fargo Bank v. Jones, 391 B.R. 577 (E.D. La. 2008) (mortgage creditor's assessment and collection of undisclosed and improper postpetition inspection fees and other charges violated automatic stay); *In re* Stark, 242 B.R. 866 (W.D.N.C. 1999) (sanctions imposed for violating stay by attempting to collect inspection and monitoring fees); *In re* Patterson, 444 B.R. 564 (Bankr. E.D. Wis. 2011) (refusing to dismiss complaint alleging stay violation based on creditor's collection of undisclosed $350 proof of claim fee); *In re* Payne, 387 B.R. 614 (Bankr. D. Kan. 2008) (unlawful servicer conduct, including assessing undisclosed postpetition fees, may be pursued as automatic stay violation); *In re* Sanchez, 372 B.R. 289, 311 (Bankr. S.D. Tex. 2007) (assessing postpetition attorney fees,

by the plan would bring into play the debtor's remedies under section 524(i), as discussed below.[363] Some courts have held that a creditor must file an application under Bankruptcy Rule 2016 before assessing any fee that could be collected from property of the estate.[364] Others have adopted local rules requiring the mortgage holder to give notice to the debtor, debtor's counsel, and trustee of any postpetition fees or changes in the debtor's payments during the plan, and have held that if such notice is not given the increased amounts are waived.[365]

In addition, it is an unfair and deceptive practice to state that a fee is authorized by the contract when it is not.[366] It is also unfair and deceptive to impose a fee that is not authorized.[367]

Relying on confusing, ambiguous, or misleading contract clauses (which the above-quoted clause certainly is) may also be a unfair or deceptive act or practice (UDAP) violation.[368]

There may also be questions about whether the monitoring or proof of claim fee represents a charge for the provision of legal services. If all the attorney for the holder is doing is "monitoring" the bankruptcy, that is, receiving court notices, reading them, keeping them, and so forth, or preparing a proof of claim, then these activities may not constitute the practice of law and should not be compensable as an attorney fee.[369] These routine administrative services are generally not compensable under any reading of typical mortgage provisions.[370] Moreover, while proof of claim preparation in many cases has been outsourced to large national firms that purport to be law firms, the actual

---

costs, and property inspection fees without court approval violated section 362(a)(3)); *In re* Banks, 31 B.R. 173 (Bankr. N.D. Ala. 1982). *But see* Jacks v. Wells Fargo Bank (*In re* Jacks), 642 F.3d 1323 (11th Cir. 2011) (lender did not violate § 362, § 506(b), or Rule 2016 when it assessed additional fees but did not try to collect them during chapter 13 case); Mann v. Chase Manhattan Mortgage Corp., 316 F.3d 1 (1st Cir. 2003) (mortgage company did not violate automatic stay by adding fees to debtor's account if it never attempted to collect those fees from debtor; court glossed over fact that addition of fees increased lien on debtor's property). The *Jacks* and *Mann* decisions will be of little relevance after the effective date of Fed. R. Bankr. P. 3002.1.

In order to avoid unknown charges being assessed against a debtor's mortgage account, it may be advisable to file a motion at the end of a chapter 13 case seeking an order that the mortgage default has been cured and the mortgage is current. Some courts have enacted local rules making such a procedure routine. *See, e.g., In re* Eddins, 2008 WL 4905477 (Bankr. N.D. Miss. Oct. 20, 2008). An example of such a motion can be found in Form 146, Appendix G.12, *infra*. In addition, if the creditor files a statement in response to the trustee's notice of final cure payment under Rule 3002.1(f) indicating that postpetition amounts are owed, the debtor may, within twenty-one days, file a motion for the court to resolve the issue and to obtain an order declaring that the debtor has cured the default and paid all required postpetition amounts. Fed. R. Bankr. P. 3002.1(h). *See* § 11.6.2.8.1, *supra*. A sample motion can be found in Form 146, Appx. G.12, *infra*.

If the debtor does not discover improper charges until after they have been paid, the debtor should still be able to challenge the fees. *See In re* Staggie, 255 B.R. 48 (Bankr. N.D. Idaho 2000) (bankruptcy court has authority under section 506 to review attorney fees of secured creditor even if the collateral has been sold and the fees paid by debtor). In an opinion that was wrongly decided, and may be avoided by counsel through careful drafting of the chapter 13 plan, the Eleventh Circuit rejected a debtor's challenge to a mortgage lender's collection of attorney fees and expenses from mortgage payments made outside the plan because it held that such payments were not property of the estate protected by the automatic stay after confirmation. Telfair v. First Union Mortgage Corp., 216 F.3d 1333 (11th Cir. 2000).

363 *See* § 14.4.3.4.4, *supra*.

364 *See, e.g., In re* Moffitt, 408 B.R. 249, 259 (Bankr. E.D. Ark. 2009); *In re* Padilla, 379 B.R. 643 (Bankr. S.D. Tex. 2007). *See, e.g., In re* Hines, 2009 WL 1726371 (Bankr. N.D. Miss. June 18, 2009).

365 Armstrong v. Lasalle Bank, 394 B.R. 794 (Bankr. W.D. Pa. 2008).

366 *See generally* National Consumer Law Center, Unfair and Deceptive Acts and Practices § 5.6.4.2 (7th ed. 2008 and Supp.).

367 *But see* Simmons v. Roundup Funding, L.L.C., 622 F.3d 93 (2d Cir. 2010) (Fair Debt Collection Practices Act remedies not available for abusive actions in filing a proof of claim because bankruptcy system had its own remedies); *In re* McMillen, 440 B.R. 907 (Bankr. N.D. Ga. 2010) (same). *See generally* National Consumer Law Center, Unfair and Deceptive Acts and Practices § 6.10.7 (7th ed. 2008 and Supp.).

368 *See* Michaels v. Amway Corp., 206 Mich. App. 644, 522 N.W.2d 703 (1994).

369 *In re* Thomas, 186 B.R. 470 (Bankr. W.D. Mo. 1995) (lender that filed proof of claim without attorney assistance not entitled to attorney fee). *See* State Unauthorized Practice of Law Comm. v. Paul Mason, 46 F.3d 469 (5th Cir. 1995).

In disallowing a proof of claim fee, one court described the work as follows: "The information contained in a proof of claim generally comes from a creditor's file and is not legal in nature to the extent attorney involvement is required. The process generally requires filling in blanks on the form and attaching documentation." *See In re* Marks, 2005 WL 4799326, at *2–*3 (Bankr. W.D. La. Nov. 30, 2005).

370 *See In re* Madison, 337 B.R. 99, 105 (Bankr. N.D. Miss. 2006) (no attorney fee should be allowed for preparation of proof of claim or for "additional legal services such as file setup, attorney review of loan documents, or attorney review of bankruptcy plan as those services are unnecessary for preparation and filing of a proof of claim, which is basically a mathematical computation"); *In re* Allen, 215 B.R. 503 (Bankr. N.D. Tex. 1997); *In re* Banks, 31 B.R. 173 (Bankr. N.D. Ala. 1982); *In re* Cipriano, 8 B.R. 697 (Bankr. D.R.I. 1981). *See also In re* Porter, 399 B.R. 113 (Bankr. D.N.H. 2008) (no special legal knowledge required for routine reviews of debtors' schedules and financial qualifications to determine whether reaffirmation agreements were appropriate; denying claim for attorney fees related to this work). *But see In re* Majchrowski, 6 F. Supp. 2d 946 (N.D. Ill. 1998) (standard form mortgage provision allows lender to charge a fee for filing proof of claim and for property inspections associated with foreclosure).

The latter court appears to have been hostile to pursuit of these claims in this case as a RICO class action. Incredibly, the court states that the contract authorizes fees even if they are not "reasonable, economical or fair to the borrower." *Id.* at 965.

Courts have not permitted mortgage creditors to charge attorney fees for the notices they are required to file under Rule 3002.1, because such notices are administrative in nature and do not require an attorney to make the computations required. *In re* Hunt, 2012 Bankr. LEXIS 2981 (Bankr. M.D.N.C. June 26, 2012); *In re* Adams, 2012 WL 1570054 (Bankr. E.D.N.C. May 3, 2012) (disallowing $50 charge for filing a Notice of Mortgage Payment Change); *In re* Carr, 468 B.R. 806 (Bankr. E.D. Va. 2012) (response statement under Rule 3002.1(g) is not a pleading and its preparation does not involve the practice of law). *See also* § 11.6.2.8.2, *supra*.

work is often not performed by paralegals or other legal professionals, and it may not be done under the supervision of an attorney.[371]

Several holders and servicers charge a flat rate monitoring or proof of claim fee to all borrowers in bankruptcy. This uniform charge is obviously not based on actual costs or expenses in "monitoring" the borrower's bankruptcy. Instead, it is an attempt to spread costs among all borrowers who file bankruptcy. Contract provisions providing for attorney fees are only enforceable "to the extent that it is shown that the creditor has been damaged by having to pay, or assume the payment of attorney fees or other collection expenses."[372] These provisions often allow the holder or servicer to recover only fees and costs that have been actually "disbursed" to a third party to protect the collateral or the holder's rights.[373] Similarly, if a holder or servicer is charging for other costs based on a contract provision, it should be required to justify the costs and show that they were actually incurred.[374]

In addition to being actually incurred by the holder, the fee must be reasonable and it must be properly documented. If the holder or servicer cannot document the basis for a charge after a debtor's good faith request for it to do so through the formal claim objection process, discovery, or other informal means, the court should disallow the charge.[375] If the fee is for services that are unnecessary or inappropriate, then it is not reasonable.[376] In most circumstances it is not necessary for the holder to do anything to protect its interest in a bankruptcy case.[377] A holder can adequately monitor a case simply by making sure that it continues to receive payments (which is what the lender does in any event). The Bankruptcy Code and Rules expressly provide for notice to a creditor if any action is taken which affects its mortgage.[378] A holder can rely on receiving those notices without any affirmative action to monitor the case.

The fee also may be unreasonable if it exceeds the cost of the services performed.[379] Unreasonable or excessive charges may also violate the requirement of good faith and fair dealing implied in any contractual relationship.[380]

14.4.3.4.6 Undisclosed fees and payment changes

In curing a default under section 1322(b)(5), the debtor makes payments under the plan on the prepetition arrearage and

---

371 *In re* Taylor, 407 B.R. 618 (Bankr. E.D. Pa. 2009) (proofs of claim filed by national firm were prepared by clerks who are not legally trained and are not paralegals, and attorney for firm reviews only a random sample of ten percent of filed claims), *aff'd in part, rev'd in part,* 655 F.3d 274 (3d Cir. 2011).

372 *In re* Banks, 31 B.R. 173, 178 (Bankr. N.D. Ala. 1982) (citing Annotation, 17 A.L.R.2d 288 § 8, at 298 (1951)).

373 *In re* Rangel, 408 B.R. 650, n.11 (Bankr. S.D. Tex. 2009) (proof of claim fee disallowed because servicer did not produce any evidence that fee was actually disbursed to law firm and fee application merely stated that it had been invoiced), *rev'd on other grounds, In re* Velazquez, 660 F.3d 893 (5th Cir. 2011).

374 *See* Korea First Bank v. Lee, 14 F. Supp. 2d 530 (S.D.N.Y. 1998) (lender can collect no more than it agreed to pay its counsel).

375 *In re* Prevo, 394 B.R. 847 (Bankr. S.D. Tex. 2008) (foreclosure fees, broker's price opinion fees, and late charges disallowed because the lender failed to submit documentation and comply with basic requirements of Official Form 10 and Fed. R. Bankr. P. 3001, such as invoices detailing who performed what services and for how long, supporting the reasonableness of the fees); *In re* Sacko, 394 B.R. 90 (Bankr. E.D. Pa. 2008) (disallowing servicer's charges for property inspections, property preservation costs, and escrow advances, and limiting assessment of sheriff's sale costs and attorney fees due to servicer's failure to meet burden of production in documenting need for the charges); *In re* Williams, 1998 WL 372656 (Bankr. N.D. Ohio June 10, 1998) (bank failed to meet burden of proving its fees are reasonable, by failing to provide adequate documentation). *Cf. In re* Maywood, Inc., 210 B.R. 91 (Bankr. N.D. Tex. 1997) (fees disallowed for lender's bankruptcy monitor in chapter 11 case when the monitor spent the bulk of his time playing games on his laptop computer, reading the newspaper, and practicing his putting).

If fees or expenses are to be collected from property of the estate, they should be itemized and requested in an application filed pursuant to Federal Rule of Bankruptcy Procedure 2016.

376 *See* Wells Fargo Bank v. Jones, 391 B.R. 577 (E.D. La. 2008) (mortgage creditor failed to show that monthly property inspections during chapter 13 case were necessary and reasonable); *In re* Stewart, 391 B.R. 327 (Bankr. E.D. La. 2008) (multiple broker's price opinions, property inspection, and other fees found unreasonable); *In re* Good, 207 B.R. 686 (Bankr. D. Idaho 1997) (assessing reasonableness of fees charged by mortgage lender). *See also In re* Dalessio, 74 B.R. 721 (B.A.P. 9th Cir. 1987); *In re* Jones, 366 B.R. 584 (Bankr. E.D. La. 2007); *In re* Jemps, Inc., 330 B.R. 258 (Bankr. D. Wyo. 2005) (attorney "thoroughness to the point of overzealousness" not compensable, even if creditor approves, particularly if creditor is oversecured and services not needed to protect its interest).

377 *In re* Stewart, 391 B.R. 327 (Bankr. E.D. La. 2008) (finding no reasonable basis for assessing multiple drive-by inspection charges and paying for broker's price opinion when borrower was current in long-term chapter 13 case and servicer was regularly in contact with borrower); *In re* Payne, 387 B.R. 614 (Bankr. D. Kan. 2008) (rejecting servicer's attempt to charge debtor for twenty-three drive-by inspections made during period when debtor was in open and clear occupancy of home and in constant contact with servicer).

In re Stewart was reversed to the extent it entered injunctive relief. Wells Fargo Bank v. Stewart (*In re* Stewart), 647 F.3d 553 (5th Cir. 2011).

378 Fed. R. Bankr. P. 3015, 7004, 9014.

379 *See generally* Franks v. Associated Air Cu. Inc., 663 F.2d 583 (5th Cir. 1982) (gross overcharges violate UDAP); *In re* Staggie, 255 B.R. 48 (Bankr. D. Idaho 2000) (excessive attorney fees sought under section 506(b) disallowed as not reasonable); Russell v. Fid. Consumer Discount Co., 72 B.R. 855 (Bankr. E.D. Pa. 1987) (grossly excessive fee was unconscionable).

380 Burnham v. Mark IV Homes, Inc., 387 Mass. 575, 441 N.E.2d 1027, 1031 (1982). *See* Unif. Commercial Code § 1-203.

Some state debt collection statutes or regulations apply to creditors as well as debt collectors. *See* National Consumer Law Center, Collection Actions Ch. 11 (2d ed. 2011 and Supp.). The federal Fair Debt Collection Practices Act (FDCPA) applies only to third party collectors. However, the FDCPA does apply if the debt was acquired by the debt collector or mortgage lender (or servicer) at a time when the debt was in default. *See* National Consumer Law Center, Fair Debt Collection (7th ed. 2010 and Supp.). Most debt collection statutes and regulations prohibit the collection of any amount not authorized by contract or applicable law. *See, e.g.,* Martinez v. Albuquerque Collection Servs., 867 F. Supp. 1495 (D.N.M. 1994) (collection agency violated FDCPA by collecting inflated charges for attorney fees).

provides for the "maintenance of payments while the case is pending." For a cure plan to be successful there must be full disclosure of all postpetition "maintenance" payments.[381] Unfortunately, it has become common for mortgage creditors to add fees and charges to mortgage accounts without notice to the borrower, trustee, or bankruptcy court while the bankruptcy case is pending, without disclosing the fees in a proof of claim or amended claim, and without seeking court approval. Some creditors secretly maintain these charges on the debtor's account while the bankruptcy is pending and wait to collect the fees once the bankruptcy case is closed or when the loan is paid off or refinanced. In some cases, postpetition fees assessed prior to plan confirmation are included in the arrearage amount on the proof of claim but are not separately listed or itemized. Some servicers refuse to provide normal escrow account statements and payment change notices to debtors in bankruptcy, depriving these debtors of the opportunity to pay the amounts due during the chapter 13 case and subjecting them to later collection efforts.[382]

As a result of these practices, debtors who complete their plans often emerge from a chapter 13 case only to have the servicer begin foreclosure anew based on claims of unpaid fees for such items as attorney fees, property inspections, broker price opinions, and other charges allegedly incurred during the chapter 13 case. The fundamental unfairness of these practices has led a number of courts to find that mortgage holders and servicers who fail to disclose fees, payment increases, and account deficiencies waive their right to collect these amounts.[383]

Collection of undisclosed fees may also result in a violation by the mortgage creditor of the automatic stay or discharge injunction.[384] The prevalence of these problems led to the promulgation of new Federal Rule of Bankruptcy Procedure 3002.1 requiring prompt disclosure of all fees incurred and payment changes during a chapter 13 case. That rule, which should reduce or eliminate such problems, is discussed earlier in this treatise.[385]

14.4.3.4.7 Standing challenges to proofs of claim based on securitized mortgage debt

As securitization of mortgages has become widespread, it has become increasingly difficult for mortgage servicers to provide documentation of their standing to assert the rights of mortgage holders. Original documents are lost in the securitization chain and cannot be produced or, when they are located, they are frequently missing the endorsements or assignments necessary to prove their transfers in the chain. Courts have ruled that, without documentary proof that an entity is in fact the party entitled to enforce a mortgage, that entity cannot file a proof of claim (or seek relief from the automatic stay.)[386] Lenders' use of the Mortgage Electronic Registration System (MERS) as the named mortgagee in order to avoid normal recording procedures for transfers of mortgages has also led to an inability to enforce loans when proceedings are brought in the name of MERS.[387]

---

381 *In re* Sanchez, 372 B.R. 289, 297 (Bankr. S.D. Tex. 2007) ("in order for the bankruptcy system to function—every entity involved in a bankruptcy proceeding must fully disclose all relevant facts"); *In re* Jones, 366 B.R. 584, 602–603 (Bankr. E.D. La. 2007) ("Bankruptcy courts cannot function if secured lenders are allowed to assess postpetition fees without disclosure and then divert estate funds to their satisfaction without court approval."), *aff'd in part, rev'd in part*, 391 B.R. 577 (E.D. La. 2008).

382 *See, e.g., In re* Dominique, 368 B.R. 913 (Bankr. S.D. Fla. 2007) (servicer failed to provide escrow statements during chapter 13 plan and just before plan completion provided debtors with an escrow account review indicating a $6397 escrow deficiency); *In re* Rizzo-Cheverier, 364 B.R. 532 (Bankr. S.D.N.Y. 2007) (servicer allowed deficiency in escrow account to accrue and then, without notice to debtor, applied trustee plan payments intended for prepetition arrears to postpetition escrow deficiency).

383 PNC Bank v. Black, 2010 WL 5418898 (S.D. Ind. Dec. 23, 2010) (affirming bankruptcy court order deeming mortgage current and prohibiting mortgage creditor from collecting $23,232.63 in undisclosed postpetition escrow advances); *In re* Foreman, 2010 WL 2696630 (M.D.N.C. July 7, 2010) (creditor waived its right to collect postpetition arrears because it did not comply with plan that required notice of change in monthly payment and instead permitted a $12,000 arrearage to accrue); Craig-Likely v. Wells Fargo Home Mortgage, 2007 WL 5185289 (E.D. Mich. Mar. 2, 2007); Chase Manhattan Mortgage Corp. v. Padgett, 268 B.R. 309 (S.D. Fla. 2001) (servicer waived right to collect escrow account deficiency because it failed to notify borrowers of deficiencies as required by RESPA); *In re* Wright, 461 B.R. 757 (Bankr. N.D. Iowa 2011) (awarding actual damages of $10,000, punitive damages of $40,000, and attorney fees for servicer's failure to notify trustee, debtor, or debtor's counsel of changes in mortgage payments as required by confirmed plan); *In re* Armstrong, 394 B.R. 794, 798–799 (Bankr. W.D. Pa. 2008) (servicer waived right to increased mortgage payments by failing to give notice of payment changes on an adjustable rate mortgage in violation of local rule); *In re* Payne, 387 B.R. 614, 637 (Bankr. D. Kan. 2008) ("When a lender silently accepts payments for over three years without notifying the borrower the payments are insufficient, when the borrower believes his taxes and insurance are being paid by his monthly payments to his lender, and when the borrower has no reason to know the lender is advancing taxes and insurance and thereby increasing borrower's indebtedness, the lender waives his right to recover the advances from the borrower."); *In re* Johnson, 384 B.R. 763 (Bankr. E.D. Mich. 2008) (even though debtor's chapter 13 case was dismissed, court found that creditor waived its right to recover arrearage for taxes and insurance by failing over five-year period to comply with RESPA and local rule requiring disclosure of payment increases); *In re* Dominique, 368 B.R. 913, 921 (Bankr. S.D. Fla. 2007) (creditor who failed to perform annual escrow analysis and give annual notice of any escrow deficiency waived its right to recover deficiency).

384 *In re* Ellzey, 2010 WL 3924011 (E.D. La. Sep 29, 2010) (mortgage creditor willfully violated stay and discharge order by reinstituting foreclosure proceeding after chapter 13 discharge entered and attempting to collect prepetition arrearage amounts).

385 *See* § 11.6.2.8.1, *supra*.

386 *See, e.g., In re* Wells, 407 B.R. 873 (Bankr. N.D. Ohio 2009) (proof of claim was not prima facie valid when note underlying mortgage was never negotiated to entity filing proof of claim).

387 *In re* Hawkins, 2009 Bankr. LEXIS 877 (Bankr. D. Nev. Mar. 31, 2009).

For a detailed discussion of MERS, see National Consumer Law Center, Foreclosures § 5.9 (4th ed. 2012).

Claimants who file proofs of claim arising out of securitized mortgage debt can face challenges based on standing. In sustaining these challenges courts apply standing principles in much same way they do when they deny motions for relief from the stay for lack of standing.[388] Once a proof of claim loses the presumption of validity due to a failure to comply with the documentation requirements of Bankruptcy Rule 3001(c) and (d), the claimant bears the burden of proof to show it is the holder of the claim or otherwise has standing to enforce the claim.[389] The claimant must prove that it was either the creditor to whom the debt was owed (the current holder of the note) or was an authorized representative of the current note holder when it filed the proof of claim. As has occurred in the stay relief context, courts may find that a mortgage servicer's witnesses who lack firsthand knowledge of a transaction's history are unable to present competent evidence to meet the claimant's burden of proof on standing.[390] Furthermore, because standing goes to the court's subject matter jurisdiction, creditors cannot argue that statements in the debtor's schedules or plan acknowledging the party as the holder waive later standing objections.[391]

Defects leading to disallowance of proofs of claim on standing grounds include failure to produce evidence of proper assignments of the note from the original lender to the current claimant and failure to show possession of the note at the time the proof of claim was filed.[392] Loan servicers who have authority to do so from a current note holder may file a proof of claim.[393] However state laws often require a power of attorney to authorize these actions by an agent.[394] Several courts have denied proofs of claim when limited powers of attorney either did not expressly authorize a party to assign or transfer a note, or did not authorize the claimant to file a proof of claim on behalf of the note holder.[395] Bankruptcy Rule 9011 obligates those filing claims to investigate the facts before filing a claim asserting ownership of an obligation. Courts have imposed or threatened to impose sanctions against counsel and creditors who file proofs of claim without reasonable prior investigation.[396]

14.4.3.4.8 Responding to mortgage servicer abuses by making use of section 524(i)

Problems with inflated proofs of claims and misapplication of plan payments such as those discussed above can be remedied as violations of the discharge injunction, violation of the debtor's order of confirmation through contempt proceedings, breach of an implied covenant of duty of good faith and fair

---

388 *See, e.g., In re* Wells, 407 B.R. 873, 878 (Bankr. N.D. Ohio 2009) (standing requirements a creditor must meet to file a proof of claim and to seek relief from stay are the same). *See generally* § 9.7.3.1.1, *supra* (discussing objections to movant's standing to file motion for relief from stay).

389 For a discussion of the presumption of validity provided under Bankruptcy Rule 3001(f) to a properly filed claim, see § 14.4.3.5, *infra*.

390 *In re* Parrish, 326 B.R. 708 (Bankr. N.D. Ohio 2005) (objection to proof of claim sustained when claimant failed to produce competent evidence it was current holder of note or authorized agent of holder). *See also In re* Vargas, 369 B.R. 511 (Bankr. C.D. Cal. 2008) (evidence from a written declaration and from clerical witness not admissible to establish purported mortgage holder's standing to file motion for relief from stay).

391 *In re* Newcare Health Corp., 244 B.R. 167 (B.A.P. 1st Cir. 2000).

392 Musselman v. Deutsche Bank Trust Co. (*In re* Balderrama), 451 B.R. 185 (Bankr. M.D. Fla. 2011) (proof of a validly endorsed note was required by Florida law); Kemp v. Countrywide Home Loans, Inc. (*In re* Kemp), 440 B.R. 624 (Bankr. D.N.J. 2010) (bank could not enforce note when it did not have possession of note or endorsement to bank); *In re* Minbatiwalla, 424 B.R. 104 (Bankr. S.D.N.Y. 2010) (entity that filed proof of mortgage claim failed to respond to debtor's request for documentation, so claim disallowed even though debtor had listed it in schedules); *In re* Wells, 407 B.R. 873 (Bankr. N.D. Ohio 2009) (evidence failed to show claimant possessed note when claimant filed proof of claim); *In re* Gilbreath, 395 B.R. 356 (Bankr. S.D. Tex. 2008) (claimant lacked standing to file proof of claim because claimant failed to file documents showing it was present holder of note); *In re* Hayes, 393 B.R. 259 (Bankr. D. Mass. 2008) (trustee for investment trust failed to provide evidence that debtor's mortgage was included in trust; no evidence of servicing agreement authorizing servicer to file proof of clam for an identified mortgage holder); *In re* Parrish, 326 B.R. 708 (Bankr.

N.D. Ohio 2005) (claimant failed to show it held note or was authorized agent for current holder). *See also* Cogswell v. CitiFinancial Mortg. Co., 624 F.3d 395 (7th Cir. 2010) (possession of note required in order to foreclose under Illinois law); *In re* Burrow, 2011 WL 1103354 (Bankr. E.D. Ark. Mar. 22, 2011) (disallowing foreclosure fees for foreclosure proceedings carried out before note had been assigned, and disallowing fees for the assignment and other exorbitant fees).

393 Greer v. O'Dell, 305 F.3d 1297 (11th Cir. 2002) (because authorized servicing agent for creditor had pecuniary interest in claim process, it had standing to file proof of claim); Wells Fargo Bank v. Guevara, 2010 WL 5824040 (N.D. Tex. Aug. 18, 2010) (servicer did not have standing when it failed to show servicing agreement with current note holder); *In re* Conde-Dedonato, 391 B.R. 247 (Bankr. E.D.N.Y. 2008) (because mortgage servicer had pecuniary interest in claim process, it had standing to file proof of claim); *In re* Viencek, 273 B.R. 354 (Bankr. N.D.N.Y. 2002) (mortgage servicer with financial interest in collection of debt met standing requirements to file proof of claim).

394 The official form for a Proof of Claim, Official Form 10, instructs the person who is filing and signing the claim to attach a copy of a power of attorney, if any.

395 *In re* Wells, 407 B.R. 873 (Bankr. N.D. Ohio 2009) (limited power of attorney did not authorize servicer to file proof of claim); *In re* Hayes, 393 B.R. 259 (Bankr. D. Mass. 2008) (limited power of attorney did not authorize assignment in chain to current claimant).

396 See *In re* Taylor, 655 F.3d 274 (3d Cir. 2011) (misleading statements in proof of claim and in motion for relief from stay would support sanctions); *In re* Obasi, 2011 WL 6336153 (Bankr. S.D.N.Y. Dec. 19, 2011) (practice of submitting POCs without review by the attorney whose electronic signature was affixed thereto clearly violated Rule 9011); *In re* Nosek, 406 B.R. 434 (D. Mass. 2009) (sanctioning servicer and law firm for misrepresenting status of holder of note, including filing erroneous proof of claim, during protracted litigation); *In re* Lee, 408 B.R. 893 (Bankr. C.D. Cal. 2009) (Rule 9011 sanctions imposed for failure to disclose transfer of ownership of note, failure to join true owner in motion for relief from stay, and submission of copy of note that was not true and correct copy of the original); *In re* Hayes, 393 B.R. 259, 269 (Bankr. D. Mass. 2008) (threatening Rule 9011 sanctions for future misrepresentations of claimants' status as holders of notes).

dealing, and as unfair trade practices.[397] Attorney fees should be available in each case.

In addition, under section 524(i), a creditor's willful failure to credit payments received under a confirmed plan in accordance with the plan constitutes a violation of the injunction of section 524(a).[398] Although section 524(a) previously was limited to violations of the discharge order, section 524(i) is not limited to acts occurring after discharge. A section 524(i) enforcement proceeding will in most instances involve actions taken by a creditor before the discharge is entered.

The section does not apply, however, if confirmation of the plan has been revoked, the plan is in default, or the creditor has not received the plan payments as required by the plan. The provision is also limited to cases in which the failure to credit payments has caused material injury to the debtor.

Presumably this provision was added in response to decisions in which courts questioned whether they had the ability to remedy a creditor's failure to credit payments properly. For example, it provides a remedy that the Court of Appeals for the Eleventh Circuit found missing in *Telfair v. First Union Mortgage Corp.*,[399] when a chapter 13 debtor challenged a creditor's application of plan payments to charges not contemplated by the plan. The amended statute also makes clear that a failure to properly credit plan payments that results in a postdischarge assertion that the debtor is in default is not simply a matter for state courts to resolve, but rather a critical issue that must be resolved by the bankruptcy court to ensure that the provisions and purposes of a plan are effectuated.

The willfulness requirement of section 524(i) should not be a significant obstacle for debtors. As in section 362(k)(1), willfulness should be interpreted to mean simply that the creditor intended to commit the act, that is, credit the payment in the manner it did; the debtor should not need to prove that the creditor intended to violate the Code or the plan provisions.[400] Absent a creditor's proof that the improper crediting was a mistake in conflict with the creditor's normal procedures, the creditor should be presumed to have intended its acts.

The material injury requirement will be met in virtually every case involving a secured creditor. The failure to properly credit payments will almost always result in a higher pay off balance for the debtor and therefore a larger lien on the debtor's property than if the payments were credited properly. A creditor that has collected the payments made by the debtor under the plan and credited them in a manner leading to a higher balance remaining on a debt has caused a material injury to the debtor. Similarly, a creditor who has reported negative information on the debtor's credit report about nonpayment or collection efforts with respect to fees resulting from the improper crediting of payments has caused a material injury to the debtor.

A common example of such an injury is the assessment of postpetition charges to the debtor that are not in accordance with the terms of the confirmed plan. If a creditor could subvert the terms of a plan simply by adding such charges, the cure of a default under the plan would be meaningless. As with other provisions of the injunction under section 524(a), a court can hold a creditor in contempt for violating section 524(i).[401]

In an action seeking to establish a violation of section 524(i), the debtor must prove that the creditor failed to credit payments "in the manner required by the plan." Thus, to invoke the protections of section 524(i), the debtor's chapter 13 plan should contain precise language directing how payments are to be applied.[402] If the court's local rules contain provisions which sufficiently direct how payments are to be applied by mortgage creditors, the debtor may wish to incorporate these local rule provisions into the plan by reference.[403]

Several courts have provided guidance on the types of plan provisions implementing section 524(i) which may be approved.[404] A plan term may require that upon entry of the

---

397 See § 12.11, *supra*.

See *Suit Against Mortgage Servicer for Disregarding Chapter 13 Plan Payments*, National Consumer Law Center, Consumer Law Pleadings No. 3, § 7.1 (Index Guide with Companion Website) for a helpful sample complaint on this issue. See also *In re* Harris, 312 B.R. 591 (N.D. Miss. 2004) (section 105(a) may be used to enforce Bankruptcy Code provisions that prohibit mortgage lender from charging late fees based on delay by trustee in disbursing postpetition mortgage payments); *In re* Nibbelink, 403 B.R. 113 (Bankr. M.D. Fla. 2009) (punitive damages for postdischarge attempts to collect fees not permitted by chapter 13 plan); *In re* Sanchez, 372 B.R. 289 (Bankr. S.D. Tex. 2007) (section 105(a) gave court power to sanction creditor's charging of undisclosed and improper fees); *In re* Rizzo-Cheverier, 364 B.R. 532 (Bankr. S.D.N.Y. 2007) (treating debtor as being in default after she had cured under her plan violated the discharge injunction); *In re* Turner, 221 B.R. 920 (Bankr. M.D. Fla. 1998) (attorney fees and costs awarded for contempt based on accounting on secured debt inconsistent with completion of confirmed chapter 11 plan); *In re* McCormack, 203 B.R. 521 (Bankr. D.N.H. 1996) (mortgagee bank held liable for $10,000 punitive damages when it did not adjust its computer records to reflect effect of plan confirmation and sent debtor demand letter expressing intent to collect fees that were not due under plan). *But see In re* Joubert, 411 F.3d 452 (3d Cir. 2005) (section 105 does not provide cause of action for violations of section 506(b)).

398 To facilitate proof of a section 524(i) violation, the debtor's plan should clearly specify how creditor payments are to be applied. Sample plan language is provided in Form 18, Appx. G.3, *infra*. See also *Challenging Mortgage Servicer "Junk" Fees and Plan Payment Misapplication: Making Use of New Section 524(i)*, 25 NCLC REPORTS Bankruptcy and Foreclosures Ed. 11 (Nov./Dec. 2006).

399 216 F.3d 1333 (11th Cir. 2000).

400 See § 9.6, *supra*.
401 See § 15.5.1.4, *infra*.
402 See *In re* Nosek, 544 F.3d 34 (1st Cir. 2008) (reversing award of sanctions against mortgage servicer because debtor's plan failed to specify how payments were to be applied).

An example of a plan provision addressing mortgage claims can be found in Form 18, Appx. G.3, *infra*. See also *Challenging Mortgage Servicer "Junk" Fees and Plan Payment Misapplication: Making Use of New Section 524(i)*, 25 NCLC REPORTS Bankruptcy and Foreclosures Ed. 11 (Nov./Dec. 2006); *Making Use of Section 524(i) Revisited*, 26 NCLC REPORTS Bankruptcy and Foreclosures Ed. 16 (Jan./Feb. 2008).

403 *In re* Anderson, 382 B.R. 496 (Bankr. D. Or. 2008) (certain plan provisions were "surplusage" because addressed by either contract between the parties or by local rules).

404 *See, e.g., In re* Emery, 387 B.R. 721 (Bankr. E.D. Ky. 2008) (proposed special mortgage provision does not violate section

confirmation order, the debtor's mortgage account is to be deemed current for purposes of the application of ongoing postpetition payments.[405] Courts have uniformly approved plan provisions which require the mortgage holder or servicer to make appropriate adjustments to the ongoing maintenance payments based on the note and security agreement and applicable nonbankruptcy law, including payment changes based on escrow account analysis and interest rate provisions in an adjustable rate mortgage, and to notify the debtor, debtor's attorney, and trustee of such payment changes.[406] A plan term may require a servicer to give notice to the debtor (and the trustee) before it attempts to impose fees and charges that may affect the debtor's postpetition payments.[407] Local court rules can establish a similar requirement.[408] A plan term or local rule should establish a procedure for resolving disputes over these charges and provide that servicers' claims for postpetition fees will be disallowed if the servicer fails to comply with the notice requirement.[409]

In order to avoid unknown charges being assessed against a debtor's mortgage account after the debtor cures the default and the chapter 13 case is closed, it is advisable to file a motion at the end of a chapter 13 case seeking an order that the mortgage default has been cured and the mortgage is current.[410]

14.4.3.5 Objecting to Claims Filed by Debt Buyers

Federal Rule of Bankruptcy Procedure 3001 requires that when a claim is based on a writing, an original or duplicate of the writing must be filed with the proof of claim.[411] Rule 3001(a) states that the proof of claim "shall conform substantially to the appropriate Official Form" and the instructions contained on the claim form (Official Form 10) state that the claimant must attach supporting documents.[412] If the total amount claimed includes interest or other charges, Rule 3001(c)(2)(A) also requires an itemized statement of all interest or additional charges be filed with the claim. An unsubstantiated claim is facially defective and not entitled to the presumption of validity.[413] Without this presumption, a facially defective claim provides evidence to "dispute its own validity" and shall be disallowed upon a general objection unless the creditor introduces evidence that proves the claim.[414] And, of course, the

---

1322(b)(2)); *In re* Watson, 384 B.R. 697 (Bankr. D. Del. 2008); *In re* Aldrich, 2008 WL 4185989 (Bankr. N.D. Iowa Sept. 4, 2008) (discussing plan provisions that would be presumptively acceptable in future plans); *In re* Andrews, 2007 WL 2793401 (Bankr. D. Kan. Sept. 26, 2007); *In re* Collins, 2007 WL 2116416 (Bankr. E.D. Tenn. July 19, 2007) (plan provisions imposing procedural notice requirements on mortgage creditor do not violate section 1322(b)(2)). *See, e.g., In re* Herrera, 422 B.R. 698 (B.A.P. 9th Cir. 2010) (proposed plans incorporating provisions approved by the district's bankruptcy judges that imposed reporting and other requirements on mortgage creditors do not conflict with RESPA or violate § 1322(b)(2)), *aff'd sub nom. In re* Monroy, 650 F.3d 1300 (9th Cir. 2011). *See also In re* Jones, 2007 WL 2480494 (Bankr. E.D. La. Aug. 29, 2007) (describing procedures related to payment application and notification of fees mortgage servicer would need to implement to avoid imposition of sanctions), *remanded*, Wells Fargo Bank v. Jones, 391 B.R. 577 (E.D. La. 2008).

405 *In re* Booth, 399 B.R. 316 (Bankr. E.D. Ark. 2009); *In re* Ramsey, 421 B.R. 431 (Bankr. M.D. Tenn. 2009); *In re* Emery, 387 B.R. 721 (Bankr. E.D. Ky. 2008); *In re* Patton, 2008 WL 5130096 (Bankr. E.D. Wis. Nov. 19, 2008); *In re* Andrews, 2007 WL 2793401 (Bankr. D. Kan. Sept. 26, 2007); *In re* Collins, 2007 WL 2116416 (Bankr. E.D. Tenn. July 19, 2007). *But see In re* Segura, 2009 WL 416847 (Bankr. D. Colo. Jan. 9, 2009) (refusing to approve plan term deeming payments current upon confirmation).

Some courts have approved similar provisions only if qualifying language is added which specifies that the "deeming current" is contingent upon successful completion of the plan. *See, e.g., In re* Nelson, 408 B.R. 394 (Bankr. D. Colo. 2009); *In re* Winston, 416 B.R. 32 (Bankr. N.D.N.Y. 2009); *In re* Hudak, 2008 WL 4850196 (Bankr. D. Colo. Oct. 24, 2008).

406 *See, e.g., In re* Segura, 2009 WL 416847 (Bankr. D. Colo. Jan. 9, 2009); *In re* Emery, 387 B.R. 721 (Bankr. E.D. Ky. 2008); *In re* Watson, 384 B.R. 697 (Bankr. D. Del. 2008); *In re* Anderson, 382 B.R. 496 (Bankr. D. Or. 2008); *In re* Patton, 2008 WL 5130096 (Bankr. E.D. Wis. Nov. 19, 2008); *In re* Hudak, 2008 WL 4850196 (Bankr. D. Colo. Oct. 24, 2008); *In re* Aldrich, 2008 WL 4185989 (Bankr. N.D. Iowa Sept. 4, 2008). *See also In re* Booth, 399 B.R. 316 (Bankr. E.D. Ark. 2009) (provision requiring payment change notice approved but only as to debtor, not trustee and debtor's counsel).

This type of plan provision requires mortgage creditors to service the loan in the customary manner as they would for home owners outside of bankruptcy. Based on the Real Estate Settlement Procedures Act, that would mean performing an annual escrow analysis and notifying borrowers of any changes in escrow deposits and balances at least once per year within thirty days after performing the analysis. 12 U.S.C. § 2609. Based on the Truth in Lending Act, for adjustable rate mortgages that would require notification of payment amount changes at least twenty-five days before the due date for the new payment amount. 12 C.F.R. § 226.20(c).

407 *In re* Segura, 2009 WL 416847 (Bankr. D. Colo. Jan. 9, 2009); *In re* Watson, 384 B.R. 697 (Bankr. D. Del. 2008); *In re* Patton, 2008 WL 5130096 (Bankr. E.D. Wis. Nov. 19, 2008); *In re* Aldrich, 2008 WL 4185989 (Bankr. N.D. Iowa Sept. 4, 2008) (finding plan term requiring annual notice and also notice ninety days before final payment to be "presumptively acceptable" to the court).

408 *See, e.g., In re* Armstrong, 394 B.R. 794 (Bankr. W.D. Pa. 2008); *In re* Payne, 387 B.R. 614 (Bankr. D. Kan. 2008).

409 *In re* Watson, 384 B.R. 697 (Bankr. D. Del. 2008) (plan provision providing for notice of mortgage fees and charges and procedure for handling disputes approved); *In re* Aldrich, 2008 WL 4185989 (Bankr. N.D. Iowa Sept. 4, 2008) (plan provision providing for waiver of any undisclosed fees would be "presumptively acceptable" to the court).

410 *See In re* Passavant, 444 B.R. 378 (Bankr. S.D. Ohio 2010) (debtors did not need to file adversary proceeding in order to seek order deeming their mortgage obligation current). Federal Rule of Bankruptcy Procedure 3002.1(h) provides for such a motion. An example of such a motion can be found in Form 146, Appendix G.12, *infra*.

411 Fed. R. Bankr. P. 3001(c).

If the writing has been lost or destroyed, a statement describing the loss or destruction must be filed.

412 *See* Official Form 10 ("Attach redacted copies of any documents that show the debt exists and a lien secures the debt.") (reprinted in Appx. D, *infra*).

413 *See In re* Consol. Pioneer Mortgage, 178 B.R. 222 (B.A.P. 9th Cir. 1995); *In re* Chain, 255 B.R. 278 (Bankr. D. Conn. 2000); *In re* Lindell Drop Forge Co., 111 B.R. 137 (Bankr. W.D. Mich. 1990).

414 *In re* Kirkland, 572 F.3d 838, 841 (10th Cir. 2009) (claim disallowed because creditor failed to provide any documentation in proof of claim or to meet burden of proof at trial; fact that debtor had

prima facie presumption of validity can be rebutted by evidence provided by the debtor, such as the debtor's lack of past dealings with the creditor.[415]

An exception to the general rule requiring a proof of claim to be accompanied by the writing on which it is based excuses holders of claims based on open end or revolving consumer credit agreements not secured by a security interest in the debtor's real estate. In such cases, Rule 3001(c)(3) instead requires the proof of claim to be accompanied by a statement of (i) the name of the entity from whom the creditor purchased the account; (ii) the name of the entity to whom the debt was owed at the time of an account holder's last transaction on the account; (iii) the date of an account holder's last transaction; (iv) the date of the last payment on the account; and (v) the date on which the account was charged to profit and loss. Further, on written request of a party in interest, the holder of such a claim must provide the writing on which the claim is based within thirty days.[416] Failure to comply with these requirements should deprive the claim of prima facie validity.[417] If there is an objection to the claim, the court should be asked to exclude from evidence documents not provided in accordance with the rule and award attorney fees and expenses to the debtor under Rule 3001(b)(2)(D). With the increasing prevalence of debt buyers who buy millions of dollars of unsecured consumer credit claims for pennies on the dollar, and who often do not even possess the writings upon which the claims are based, debtors have sometimes successfully objected to proofs of claims that do not comply with the documentation requirements. Proofs of claim are filed in this manner without any actual review of loan documents or account statements. In addition, debt buyers often fail to check the box in paragraph 4 on Official Form 10 that confirms that the total amount claimed includes interest or other charges, even though they are undeniably seeking interest and other charges, and often admit this fact by adding language in another section of the claim form: "Claim may include contractual interest and/or late charges." They sometimes also fail to check the most commonly used boxes in paragraph 1 on Official Form 10 for "money loaned," "service performed," or "goods sold," and instead check the "other" box, inserting the description "credit card debt." Some have gone so far as to alter the instructions in paragraph 8 on Official Form 10 under "Supporting Documents" by eliminating the mandatory attachment requirement and adding a self-serving statement that copies of account statements are available upon request.[418]

Courts have found that the purpose of Rule 3001 is subverted by such claims, as the parties charged with policing the claims process are denied necessary information,[419] and that affording prima facie validity to such claims can only "lead to abuses of the claim system."[420] Strict compliance with Rule 3001 is necessary to ensure that an appropriate "sifting process" occurs in the evaluation of claims, otherwise "unmeritorious or excessive claims might dilute the participation of the legitimate claimants."[421] In fact, objections to debt buyers' unsubstantiated claims are often answered with amended claims seeking lower amounts in which questionable fees are removed. In other cases it has been found that the original claims included postpetition interest or were barred by a statute of limitations.[422]

Another purpose of Rule 3001 is to distinguish among claims that are treated differently in bankruptcy. In chapter 7, for example, claims for penalties such as late charges and overlimit fees have a lower priority in distribution.[423] If the proof of

---

scheduled claim was not evidence that could be used against trustee's objection); *In re* Tran, 369 B.R. 312 (S.D. Tex. 2007) (upon objection to an improperly documented proof of claim not entitled to prima facie validity, claimant has burden of production); *In re* Circle J Dairy, Inc., 112 B.R. 297, 300 (W.D. Ark 1989); *In re* Gilbreath, 395 B.R. 356 (Bankr. S.D. Tex. 2008) (claims disallowed when creditor provided documentation only after objections filed, and in connection with "eleventh hour amendments" which court refused to approve); *In re* Porter, 374 B.R. 471 (Bankr. D. Conn. 2007) (claims disallowed when not documented because creditors did not respond to debtor's request for documentation); *In re* Taylor, 363 B.R. 303 (Bankr. M.D. Fla. 2007) (claim disallowed when creditor failed to offer documents to supplement undocumented claim). *See also In re* Wingerter, 376 B.R. 221 (Bankr. N.D. Ohio 2007) (Bankruptcy Rule 9011 requires a claim purchaser, before filing a proof of claim with a bankruptcy court, to obtain originating documents or, when such documents are not available, a clear understanding of the nature of the original dealings that support the assertion of a claim against the particular debtor), *appeal dismissed as moot*, 394 B.R. 859 (B.A.P. 6th Cir. 2008), *further decision at In re* Wingerter, 594 F.3d 931 (6th Cir. 2010) (reversing sanctions imposed on debt buyer). *But see In re* Heath, 331 B.R. 424 (B.A.P. 9th Cir. 2005) (even if claim does not have prima facie validity under Fed. R. Bankr. P. 3001(f), it remains objector's burden to come forward with evidence to support disallowance); *In re* Dove-Nation, 318 B.R. 147 (B.A.P. 8th Cir. 2004) (same result as *Heath*, but recognizing that if objector meets burden of coming forward with evidence, burden of proof is on claimant); *In re* Burnett, 306 B.R. 313 (B.A.P. 9th Cir. 2004) (assignee of claim did not have to disclose amount it paid for claim), *aff'd*, 435 F.3d 971 (9th Cir. 2006).

415 *See In re* Walker, 2012 WL 1804764 (Bankr. S.D. Tex. May 17, 2012) (once prima facie validity rebutted by debtor's affidavit that he never dealt with claimant, claimant had burden of proof); *In re* Braughton, 2011 WL 2945828 (Bankr. S.D. Tex. July 21, 2011) (utility's claim disallowed based on debtor's testimony that he had not had service from that utility).

416 Fed. R. Bankr. P. 3001(c)(3)(B).

417 2012 Advisory Committee Note to Rule 3001.

418 *See In re* Hughes, 313 B.R. 205 (Bankr. E.D. Mich. 2004).

419 *In re* Trail Ends Lodge, Inc., 51 B.R. 209 (D. Vt. 1985).

420 *In re* Circle J Dairy, Inc., 112 B.R. 297, 301 (W.D. Ark 1989). *See also In re* Lytell, 2012 WL 253111 (E.D. La. Jan. 26, 2012) (no prima facie validity for claim not complying with Rule 3001(c)).

421 Gardner v. New Jersey, 329 U.S. 565, 67 S. Ct. 467, 91 L. Ed. 504 (1947).

422 *See, e.g., In re* Hess, 404 B.R. 747 (Bankr. S.D.N.Y. 2009) (admonishing debtors' counsel and trustees to review claims to ensure time-barred claims are not allowed); *In re* Andrews, 394 B.R. 384 (Bankr. E.D.N.C. 2008) (four claims withdrawn after objections filed based on statute of limitations). *See also In re* Rogers, 391 B.R. 317 (Bankr. M.D. La. 2008) (Fair Debt Collection Practices Act and Fed. R. Bankr. P. 9011 may be used as remedies when creditor files a claim on which statute of limitations has run).

423 11 U.S.C. § 726(a)(4).

claim does not break out these charges, a court may find that the entire claim must be given this lower priority.[424] A chapter 13 plan may classify such penalty claims and provide for later payment or no payment on them, in which case an objection to a proof of claim would be in order if it does not specify the portion of the claim that is for penalty charges.

Claims have also been disallowed because they were filed by entities that could not prove they owned the debts. As securitization of consumer debts has become widespread, it has become increasingly difficult for claimants and purchasers of credit accounts to provide documentation of their standing to assert rights as the holder of a claim.[425] Many of the same standing problems which confront mortgage holders and servicers in filing proofs of claim and seeking relief from the automatic stay, which are discussed elsewhere in this treatise,[426] are also present when debt collectors and buyers file claims on credit card and other unsecured accounts. Because consumer claims are often transferred through bulk sales involving blanket assignments of numerous claims, they may be withdrawn or disallowed when the debt buyer is unable to prove ownership by establishing a chain of tile linking the debtor's original debt to the claimant.[427]

Some courts have held that if a claim is assigned, the assignment is a writing upon which the claim is based, and therefore should be attached to the claimant's proof of claim.[428] In most cases involving purchased credit card debt, the assignment is the document which establishes the claimant's legal entitlement to the claim and its right to payment from the debtor to the exclusion of the original creditor named in the card agreement and all prior transferees. Without the assignment, there is no written agreement obligating the debtor to pay the debt buyer. If a claim is listed on the debtor's schedules as owing to another creditor, some evidence establishing the claimant's ownership of the claim and right to payment on the debt should be provided before a claim is afforded prima facie validity.[429]

The debt buyers sometimes contend that credit card issuers and debt buyers do not have to provide documentation if they pursue claims under an "open-account" theory, ignoring the fact that open account claims are typically "founded upon contract" and require proof of the "necessary elements of a contract action."[430] More important, the *theory* upon which a creditor asserts a claim does not determine the need for compliance with Rule 3001's requirements. Rule 3001 does not state that writings must be provided only if the creditor's claim is based on a particular theory, nor does it provide an exception for "open-accounts" or any other theory of liability. Such an exception would of course swallow the rule as just about any claimant could demand presumptive validity of claims filed without documentation simply by stating when challenged that the claim is based on a quasi-contract, *quantum meruit*, or unjust enrichment theory. The plain language of Rule 3001 requires that if the claim is based on a writing, it must be filed with the proof of claim or timely provided upon request.

And there can be no question that a writing provides the contractual basis for credit card debt.[431] In fact, the typical card member agreement is the controlling document that carefully delineates the rights and responsibilities between the card issuer and borrower. It specifies that use of the card is an affirmance

---

424 *In re* Plourde, 418 B.R. 495 (B.A.P. 1st Cir. 2009).

425 Section 501(a) and Bankruptcy Rule 3001(b) make clear that only a creditor (or indenture trustee) and the creditor's authorized agent may execute and file a proof of claim. To be a creditor, an entity must have a claim, which means a right to payment. 11 U.S.C. § 101(5), (10). In the case of a consumer loan transaction, if a proof of claim is not filed by an entity to whom the original obligation was payable, typically the claimant will be a transferee who asserts a right to payment derived from the debtor's original creditor.

426 See §§ 9.7.3.1.1, 14.4.3.4.7, *supra*.

427 *See In re* Melillo, 392 B.R. 1, 6 (B.A.P. 1st Cir. 2008) (disallowing claim of alleged assignee that provided no proof of ownership; proof of claim is not prima facie evidence of ownership of claim); Pursley v. eCAST Settlement Corp. (*In re* Pursley), 451 B.R. 213 (Bankr. M.D. Ga. 2011) (no documentation that eCAST was assignee of claim); *In re* O'Brien, 440 B.R. 654 (Bankr. E.D. Pa. 2010) (no documentation of assignment included with proof of claim); *In re* Gilbreath, 409 B.R. 84, 121 (Bankr. S.D. Tex. 2009) (listing numerous deficiencies in "proof" of ownership submitted by debt buyer); *In re* Stauder, 396 B.R. 609, 612 (Bankr. M.D. Pa. 2008) (claims disallowed when alleged assignee provided no evidence of assignment other than hearsay affidavit and did not produce actual assignment; but another claim scheduled by debtor as owed to assignee was allowed based on debtor's admission); *In re* Povey, 2008 WL 1376271 (Bankr. E.D. Okla. Apr. 9, 2008); *In re* Leverett, 378 B.R. 793 (Bankr. E.D. Tex. 2007); *In re* Wingerter, 376 B.R. 221 (Bankr. N.D. Ohio 2007) (claimant attempted to withdraw claim after admitting it lacked documentation sufficient to establish it was creditor of debtor), *appeal dismissed as moot*, 394 B.R. 859 (B.A.P. 6th Cir. 2008). *See also In re* Kincaid, 388 B.R. 610 (Bankr. E.D. Pa. 2008) (although claims were not afforded prima facie validity because claimant failed to establish proper assignment, they were allowed based on admissions contained in debtor's schedules); *In re* Armstrong, 320 B.R. 97 (Bankr. N.D. Tex. 2005) (failure to attach transfer documents to claim results in loss of prima facie validity).

428 *In re* White, 2008 WL 269897 (Bankr. N.D. Tex. Jan. 29, 2008); *In re* Armstrong, 320 B.R. 97 (Bankr. N.D. Tex. 2005); *In re* Hughes, 313 B.R. 205 (Bankr. E.D. Mich. 2004).

429 *In re* Gilbreath, 395 B.R. 356 (Bankr. S.D. Tex. 2008); *In re* Kincaid, 388 B.R. 610 (Bankr. E.D. Pa. 2008); *In re* Povey, 2008 WL 1376271 (Bankr. E.D. Okla. Apr. 9, 2008); *In re* Leverett, 378 B.R. 793 (Bankr. E.D. Tex. 2007). *See also In re* Foy, 469 B.R. 209 (Bankr. E.D. Pa. 2012) (when debt had been reduced to judgment, debt was replaced by judgment and claimant was required to show assignment of judgment).

Information listed by the debtor on Schedule F that is consistent with the claim, such as an account number and balance, "merely support[s] the existence of the claim and the balance due," but does "not establish ownership." *See In re* Melillo, 392 B.R. 1, 6 (B.A.P. 1st Cir. 2008).

430 Asset Acceptance Corp. v. Proctor, 156 Ohio App. 3d 60, 804 N.E.2d 975 (2004).

In addition, the plaintiff must "prove that the contract involves a transaction that usually forms the subject of a book account." *Id. See also* 1 Am. Jur. 2d *Accounts and Accounting* § 8 (2006).

431 *In re* Tran, 369 B.R. 312 (S.D. Tex. 2007). *See In re* Hughes, 313 B.R. 205 (Bankr. E.D. Mich. 2004); *In re* Henry, 311 B.R. 813 (Bankr. W.D. Wash. 2004).

of the contract terms contained in the written card member agreement (and its periodic amendments). Creditors in most jurisdictions are not permitted to make such an election. An action on an "open-account" may be based on an express or implied contract, but if an enforceable express contract exists between the parties on the relevant subject matter, the creditor cannot recover under an implied contract.[432] Such a ruling is quite appropriate as an implied-in-law contract is a legal fiction that should not be imposed by a court to subvert the express intent of the parties. Moreover, absent the written agreement, credit card lenders have no legal claim to the substantial interest charges, late fees, bad check charges, over-the-limit fees and other costs included in virtually all credit card claims.[433] In addition, prejudgment interest and costs may not be recovered in many jurisdictions on claims based on *quantum meruit* and implied contract, absent a specific statutory entitlement, because of the unliquidated nature of such claims.[434] Thus, a claim that includes interest filed by a credit card claimant who has disavowed the card member agreement is self-contradictory and should be disallowed.

Some debt buyers have also argued that debtors should not be permitted to object to claims when they have listed the amount allegedly owing on their schedules and not noted it as disputed and some courts have expressed disapproval of objections in which there is no "legitimate" dispute. However, the schedules are not filed for the purposes of claim allowance except in chapter 11 cases.[435] Typically, when debtors complete their schedules they have no way of computing the amounts due under complex credit card contracts and just list the amount stated on a recent statement. Nonetheless, to avoid such problems and to make clear there is a legitimate dispute about the debt, debtors should mark debts as disputed in the schedules if an objection is anticipated (because they have no way of verifying the amounts claimed on monthly statements) and then contest the amount claimed in the objection to claim. It has not been uncommon for creditors facing such objections to admit that the claim is inflated or barred by a statute of limitations, or that they have no idea how the claim amount was calculated. In addition, debtors usually have no way of being sure whether a claim has been validly assigned, and therefore may legitimately dispute a debt on the schedules and object that they have never heard of the debt buyers filing claims in their cases, thus requiring the debt buyers to prove with competent evidence that the claims have in fact been assigned to them and are owing to them.[436]

14.4.3.6 Objecting Based Upon Prepetition Settlement Attempts—Section 502(k)

The 2005 amendments included a provision that permits the debtor to seek a reduction in an unsecured creditor's claim if the creditor unreasonably refused to negotiate, prior to the filing of the bankruptcy, a "reasonable alternative repayment schedule."[437] The debtor must attempt to negotiate the repayment plan through an approved nonprofit budgeting and credit counseling agency.[438] If the creditor unreasonably refuses to negotiate such a plan, a debtor who later files bankruptcy may bring a motion or objection to the claim, requesting that the court reduce the creditor's claim by no more than twenty percent of the claim amount.[439]

For this provision to apply the debtor's repayment offer must be made at least sixty days before the petition is filed[440] and it must provide for payment of at least sixty percent of the amount of the outstanding debt, over a period not to exceed the debt's repayment period.[441] In addition, "no part of the debt under the alternative repayment schedule [can be] nondischargeable."[442] It is unclear what this last requirement means, but probably it should be interpreted to mean that the provision does not apply if the original debt was nondischargeable in the chapter chosen by the debtor. The debtor has the burden of proving that the creditor unreasonably refused to consider the debtor's proposal and that the proposal was made at least sixty days before the petition was filed.[443]

While this provision is not likely to be used in many cases, debtors considering the filing of a chapter 13 case in which a 100% chapter 13 plan must be proposed based on the best interests of creditors test or for some other reason might attempt to offer a prepetition settlement so they can invoke this provision. If a nonprofit budget and credit counseling agency refuses to make such a proposal to a creditor, then that agency should be reported to the United States trustee for attempting to frustrate the provisions of the Code.

---

432 17A Am Jur. 2d *Contracts* § 13. *See, e.g.,* Clark-Fitzpatrick v. Long Island, 516 N.E.2d 190 (N.Y. 1987).

433 In *In re* Blair, Civ. No. 02-1140 (Bankr. W.D.N.C. filed Feb. 10, 2004), the court ordered that a credit card issuer may no longer file proofs of claim without itemization. As findings of fact in the Order, claims filed in eighteen separate debtor cases are broken down as between principal and interest and fees. In most all of the claims, interest and fees comprise more than half of the total claim. For example, in Case No. 03-20018, the creditor filed a claim in the amount of $943.58, of which $199.63 is listed as principal and $743.95 is listed as interest and fees. In Case No. 03-100157, a claim of $1011.97 is comprised of $273.33 in principal and $738.64 in interest and fees.

434 22 Am. Jur. 2d *Damages* § 468 (2006). *See, e.g.,* Farmah v. Farmah, 348 N.C. 586, 500 S.E.2d 662 (1998).

435 *See* 11 U.S.C. § 1111(a) (not applicable in other chapters).

436 *See In re* Tran, 369 B.R. 312 (S.D. Tex. 2007) (absent proof of validity and amount of debt, debtor's objection that she owed nothing to assignee upheld).

437 11 U.S.C. § 502(k).

438 *See* § 7.3.5, *supra.*

439 For a sample objection to claim seeking reduction of claim amount pursuant to section 502(k), see Form 20, Appx. G.3, *infra.*

440 *See In re* Hayes, 385 B.R. 644 (Bankr. N.D. Ohio 2007) (affidavit that offer was made "on or about" particular date did not prove that sixty-day requirement was met because it was not sufficiently specific).

441 11 U.S.C. § 502(k)(1)(B).

442 11 U.S.C. § 502(k)(1)(C).

443 11 U.S.C. § 502(k)(2).

14.4.3.7 Reconsideration of Claims

Both 11 U.S.C. § 502(j) and Federal Rule of Bankruptcy Procedure 3008 provide for the reconsideration of previously allowed claims.[444] A motion for reconsideration may be appropriate in a number of circumstances.[445] One situation which arises not infrequently is that of a debtor who cannot maintain the chapter 13 plan payments necessary to keep a motor vehicle. In such a case, the vehicle may be liquidated by the creditor after either a voluntary surrender by the debtor or a repossession. The liquidation results not only in a reduction in the creditor's claim but the creditor becoming unsecured with respect to any deficiency claim. Courts have found such circumstances to be appropriate bases for reconsideration of the creditor's claim to reflect the payment by liquidation and new status as unsecured, often leading to a modification of the chapter 13 plan reducing payments to that creditor.[446]

14.4.4 An Example: Truth in Lending Claims of the Debtor

One common type of claim the debtor might want to bring using these procedures would be an action under the Truth in Lending Act.[447] Such an action could be removed to the bankruptcy court or brought initially in bankruptcy court by a complaint against the creditor, with the cause of action and any proceeds thereof claimed as exempt property (assuming the debtor has exemptions available to cover the amount of property).[448] If the cause of action cannot be claimed as exempt, it is usually not difficult to persuade a trustee to abandon it, as few trustees are interested in such claims, and that step should be taken.[449]

A number of courts have held that the recovery in such an action must be paid in cash to the debtor/plaintiff and cannot be set off against a debt discharged in the bankruptcy.[450] And when a creditor's claim is fully secured by a non-voidable lien, a successful Truth in Lending claim will at least reduce the amount which must be paid and reward the debtor's counsel with attorney fees.[451] Furthermore, a successful Truth in Lending rescission suit may void the creditor's lien entirely and leave the creditor with an unsecured claim.[452] Finally, special

---

444 Pursuant to Rule 2002(g), a motion for reconsideration should ordinarily be served on the claimant at the address listed on the proof of claim. *See In re* Barker, 306 B.R. 339 (Bankr. E.D. Cal. 2004) (notice of reconsideration served on original creditor listed on claim proper because debt buyer assignee failed to update court filing by submitting Rule 3001(e)(1) transfer statement).

If the claimant is an insured depository institution, service should also be made by certified mail upon an officer of the institution unless certain requirements have been met. *See* Fed. R. Bankr. P. 7004(h); § 14.3.2.1, *supra*.

445 The debtor may seek reconsideration of a claim even after it has been paid if sufficient cause exists. *In re* Barker, 306 B.R. 339 (Bankr. E.D. Cal. 2004) (court granted request for reconsideration of claim made by executrix as debtor was in final stages of illness at time claim allowed and paid).

446 *See In re* Zieder, 263 B.R. 114 (Bankr. D. Ariz. 2001). *See also* § 8.7.4, *supra*.

447 15 U.S.C. §§ 1601–1677. *See generally* National Consumer Law Center, Truth in Lending (7th ed. 2010 and Supp.).

The trustee in a chapter 13 case could also bring a Truth in Lending action on the debtor's behalf. *In re* Weaver, 632 F.2d 461 (5th Cir. 1980).

In cases in which the trustee or a debtor-in-possession brings the action, the statute of limitations, if it had not expired as of the filing of the petition, would be extended until two years after the bankruptcy filing. 11 U.S.C. § 108(a). *See* Cunningham v. Healthco, 824 F.2d 1448 (5th Cir. 1987). *See also* Thomas v. GMAC Residential Funding Corp., 309 B.R. 453 (D. Md. 2004) (section 108(b) extends right of rescission under Truth in Lending Act by sixty days after filing of bankruptcy petition).

448 *See, e.g., In re* Polis, 217 F.3d 899 (7th Cir. 2000) (TILA claim could be valued for exemption purposes based on fair market value, discounted for contingency, on date of bankruptcy petition); Christy v. Heights Fin. Corp., 101 B.R. 542 (C.D. Ill. 1987) (debtor had standing to assert Truth in Lending claim that had been exempted); *In re* Abele, 77 B.R. 460 (E.D. Pa. 1987) (four transactions rescinded under Truth in Lending Act), *aff'd*, 845 F.2d 1009 (3d Cir. 1988); *In re* Ball, 201 B.R. 204 (Bankr. N.D. Ill. 1996) (value of debtor's interest in TILA claim comes into estate, but not enhancement of that value obtained by service as class representative); *In re* Marshall, 121 B.R. 814 (Bankr. C.D. Ill. 1990) (debtor's Truth in Lending claim not compulsory counterclaim which had to be raised prior to confirmation of chapter 13 plan, and in any case failure to assert such a counterclaim would not bar later adversary proceeding against bank as it was exemptible property of the debtor), *aff'd*, 132 B.R. 904 (C.D. Ill. 1991); *In re* Piercy, 18 B.R. 1004 (Bankr. W.D. Ky. 1982) (Truth in Lending rescission enforced by bankruptcy court). *See also In re* Mansaray-Ruffin, 530 F.3d 230 (3d Cir. 2008) (confirmed plan could not determine TILA rescission claim; adversary proceeding necessary); *In re* Scrimpsher, 17 B.R. 999 (Bankr. N.D.N.Y. 1982) (debt collection violations raised as counterclaim to dischargeability complaint).

449 *See* Bryson v. Bank of N.Y., 584 F. Supp. 1306 (S.D.N.Y. 1984) (abandonment necessary prior to debtor's Truth in Lending action); Cole v. Pulley, 468 N.E.2d 652 (Mass. App. Ct. 1984) (debtor who filed bankruptcy could not bring actions that were not abandoned by the trustee. *See also* Barletta v. Tedeschi, 121 B.R. 669 (N.D.N.Y. 1990) (closing of case effected abandonment by trustee of debtor's action under Fair Debt Collection Practices Act); § 14.3.2.6, *supra*.

For a discussion of abandonment of property by the trustee, see § 11.3.3, *supra*.

450 *See, e.g.,* Griggs v. Provident Consumer Discount Co., 680 F.2d 927 (3d Cir.), *rev'd on other grounds*, 459 U.S. 56 (1982); *In re* Riggs, 623 F.2d 68 (9th Cir. 1980); Newton v. Beneficial Fin. Co., 558 F.2d 731 (5th Cir. 1977) (Truth in Lending damages are meant to penalize the creditor and thus should always be assessed); *In re* Hill, 2 Collier Bankr. Cas. 2d (MB) 84 (M.D. Fla. 1980). *But see* Binick v. Avco Fin. Servs. of Neb., Inc., 435 F. Supp. 359 (D. Neb. 1977).

It should be noted that some of these cases were under the prior Act, which had wording slightly different from the new setoff provision, 11 U.S.C. § 553. Also *In re* Riggs, 623 F.2d 68 (9th Cir. 1980), and other cases cited therein set forth a test of discretion under which a setoff could sometimes be allowed. *See also In re* Johnson, 13 B.R. 185 (Bankr. M.D. Tenn. 1981) (section 553 does not permit setoff against claim abandoned to debtor; section 553 applies only to setoffs against the bankruptcy estate).

451 15 U.S.C. § 1640(a). *See In re* McCausland, 63 B.R. 665 (Bankr. E.D. Pa. 1986). *See also In re* Thompson, 350 B.R. 842 (Bankr. E.D. Wis. 2006) (permitting recoupment and awarding attorney fees for RESPA violations).

452 *See* Cromwell v. Countrywide Home Loans, Inc., 2012 WL 4127910 (D. Mass. Sept. 20, 2012); *In re* Bell, 309 B.R. 139 (Bankr. E.D. Pa.

Truth-in-Lending protections apply to more recent high-rate home equity loans.[453]

In many cases, however, an action against the creditor for damages may not be possible because of the passage of the one-year statute of limitations applicable to affirmative Truth in Lending actions.[454] And, although the courts of many states have held that Truth in Lending claims may still be asserted defensively in state courts by way of recoupment after the passage of one year, there is a substantial split in authority on that question.[455] Courts in a number of states do not allow a debtor to offset damages arising out of Truth in Lending violations against a creditor's claim for the balance due in a consumer credit transaction.

The availability of objections to claims in bankruptcy court may alleviate this problem in those states that do not allow recoupment.[456] It is clear that recoupment is a matter of procedure, to be determined in the federal courts on the basis of federal law. It is also generally agreed that federal law does permit recoupment,[457] and therefore state decisions barring recoupment should not be applicable in bankruptcy court to objections to claims raising Truth in Lending recoupment. Moreover, under the Truth in Lending Simplification Act, recoupment is specifically permitted unless the applicable procedural law provides otherwise.[458] As the applicable procedural law in bankruptcy court is federal law, there should be little doubt as to the propriety of recoupment to reduce or eliminate creditors' claims. Thus, debtors in states barring recoupment should still be able to make use of that valuable doctrine if they can bring their litigation into the bankruptcy court and their attorneys can collect statutory attorney fees for their efforts.[459] However, the Supreme Court has greatly limited the rights of consumers to invoke the Truth in Lending rescission remedy by way of recoupment after the normal three year period has run.[460]

2004) (debtor permitted to pay tender obligation, as determined by court after setoff of damages awarded to debtor, over life of chapter 13 plan), *as amended upon reconsideration*, 314 B.R. 54 (Bankr. E.D. Pa. 2004); *In re* Bilal, 296 B.R. 828 (Bankr. D. Kan. 2003) (debtors effectuated rescission and voiding of mortgage through provisions of confirmed plan); *In re* Williams, 291 B.R. 636 (Bankr. E.D. Pa. 2003) (court treated consumer's tender obligation as unsecured and did not make rescission conditional upon tender but required debtor to classify tender claim separately and pay it in full over life of chapter 13 plan); *In re* Rodrigues, 278 B.R. 683 (Bankr. D.R.I. 2002). *But see* Quenzer v. Advanta Mortgage Corp. USA, 288 B.R. 884 (D. Kan. 2003) (court has discretion to require repayment of principal as condition of voiding lien); Ray v. Citifinancial Inc., 228 F. Supp. 2d 664 (D. Md. 2002) (bankruptcy court may condition TIL rescission upon tender but also has discretion to reduce or eliminate creditor's lien without requiring tender based on equitable considerations).

For a more detailed discussion of TILA tender requirements in bankruptcy, see National Consumer Law Center, Truth in Lending § 6.8.4 (7th ed. 2010 and Supp.).

453 15 U.S.C. § 1639 (Home Ownership and Equity Protection Act). *See* National Consumer Law Center, Truth in Lending Ch. 9 (7th ed. 2010 and Supp.).

If the debtor intends to file an adversary proceeding in a chapter 13 that seeks rescission under TILA, the debtor's schedules and plan should treat the creditor's claim in a manner that is consistent with rescission, and it is advisable that the debtor file the complaint prior to confirmation. An example of a chapter 13 plan providing for TIL rescission can be found in Form 23, Appx. G.3, *infra*.

454 15 U.S.C. § 1640(e).

Note, however, that if the limitations period has not expired prepetition, the period may be tolled or extended by operation of 11 U.S.C. § 108(a). That provision, however, generally only applies when the claim is ultimately brought by the trustee on behalf of the estate. *But see In re* Gaskins, 98 B.R. 328 (Bankr. E.D. Tenn. 1989) (section 108(a) applies to claim brought on behalf of estate by chapter 13 debtor).

455 *Compare* Household Consumer Discount Co. v. Vespaziani, 490 Pa. 209, 415 A.2d 689 (1980) *with* Hewlett v. John Blue Employees Fed. Credit Union, 344 So. 2d 505 (Ala. Civ. App. 1976).

Amendments to the law may have undercut some of the cases prohibiting recoupment after the limitations period has run. National Consumer Law Center, Truth in Lending § 7.2.5 (7th ed. 2010 and Supp.).

456 *See, e.g., In re* Jones, 122 B.R. 246 (W.D. Pa. 1990); Werts v. Fed. Nat'l Mortgage Ass'n, 48 B.R. 980 (E.D. Pa. 1985) (filing proof of claim was "action to collect the debt" allowing debtor to file recoupment claim under 15 U.S.C. § 1640(e)); *In re* Wentz, 393 B.R. 545 (Bankr. S.D. Ohio 2008) (debtor's claims under TILA and the Real Estate Settlement Procedures Act, and related claims for attorney fees and costs, allowed by recoupment to reduce creditor's claim); *In re* Hanna, 31 B.R. 424 (Bankr. E.D. Pa. 1983) (debtor allowed to raise Truth in Lending recoupment claim beyond one year statute of limitations because state courts permitted it under doctrine of federal common law); *In re* Galea'i, 31 B.R. 629 (Bankr. D. Haw. 1981). *See also* Beach v. Bank of Am. (*In re* Beach), 447 B.R. 313 (Bankr. D. Idaho 2011) (TILA claim could be asserted by recoupment against creditor proceeding with nonjudicial foreclosure); Westbrooks v. FNB United Corp. (*In re* Westbrooks), 440 B.R. 677 (Bankr. M.D.N.C. 2010) (Equal Credit Opportunity Act claim may be raised by recoupment after statute of limitations has run); *In re* Maxwell, 281 B.R. 101 (Bankr. D. Mass. 2002) (debtor allowed to assert by way of recoupment time-barred claims under the Fair Debt Collection Practices Act against mortgage servicer); *In re* McNinch, 250 B.R. 848 (Bankr. W.D. Pa. 2000) (one-year statute of limitations for Truth In Lending damages claim did not apply to claim asserted by recoupment in response to creditor's proof of claim), *aff'd sub nom.* McNinch v. Harris Trust Sav. Bank, 281 F.3d 222 (3d Cir. 2001); *In re* Remington, 19 B.R. 718 (Bankr. D. Colo. 1982) (debtor allowed to raise claim under Equal Credit Opportunity Act as objection to claim despite fact that two year statute of limitations under that Act had expired); National Consumer Law Center, Truth in Lending § 7.2.5 (7th ed. 2010 and Supp.).

457 Bull v. United States, 295 U.S. 247, 55 S. Ct. 695, 79 L. Ed. 1421 (1937); *In re* Coxson, 43 F.3d 189 (5th Cir. 1995) (applying federal law to permit bankruptcy debtor to assert TILA recoupment against creditor's claim); Pa. R.R. Co. v. Miller, 124 F.2d 160 (5th Cir. 1942).

458 15 U.S.C. § 1640(e).

459 Statutory attorney fees have regularly been awarded after successful recoupment claims. *In re* DiCianno, 58 B.R. 810 (Bankr. E.D. Pa. 1986); United Mission Bank v. Robinson, 7 Kan. App. 2d 120, 638 P.2d 372 (1981); Olinde Hardware & Supply Co. v. London, 387 So. 2d 1246 (La. Ct. App. 1981); Ford v. Defenbaugh, 403 So. 2d 863 (Miss. 1981); Allied Fin. v. Garza, 626 S.W.2d 120 (Tex. App. 1981); National Consumer Law Center, Truth in Lending § 8.9.2.2 (7th ed. 2010 and Supp.).

460 *See* Beach v. Ocwen Fed. Sav. Bank, 523 U.S. 410, 118 S. Ct. 1408, 140 L. Ed 2d 566 (1998) (limiting Truth in Lending right of

14.4.5 Habeas Corpus

Another power of the federal courts, which might prove useful on occasion, is the power to issue writs of habeas corpus. The Bankruptcy Reform Act of 1978 had expressly granted the power to issue these writs to the bankruptcy courts, but this provision was not retained by the 1984 amendments. Prior to 1978, the Rules of Bankruptcy Procedure had provided that a bankruptcy judge could issue a writ for certain purposes.[461] Thus far a new bankruptcy rule has not been promulgated to fill the statutory gap. In the absence of a new rule, any writ of habeas corpus may have to be issued by the district court.[462]

Such a writ could be issued for a number of purposes. Most important of these is to obtain release of a debtor imprisoned on process in a civil action issued for collection of a debt which is either dischargeable or provided for in the debtor's plan. The most likely cases for use of a writ of habeas corpus by consumer clients are those in which a debtor is imprisoned for failure to comply with family support orders issued by a state court. It is an unfortunate fact that, all too often, indigents are jailed for not paying support obligations they are unable to meet.

Often these obligations are owed to a state or local welfare department, which is assigned the right to collect them because the debtor's family has received public assistance. While these obligations may not be discharged in a chapter 7 case,[463] they may be paid through a chapter 13 plan, under the protection of the bankruptcy court.[464]

A less frequent use of the writ of habeas corpus is to free those debtors imprisoned through the use of supplementary process and contempt orders which are still available in several states as collection remedies.[465] Similarly, the issue may arise in the context of imprisonment for failure to make payment of court-ordered restitution.[466] Debtors jailed in these proceedings, essentially for not paying their debts, may be able to gain their freedom through the bankruptcy court.[467]

14.5 Abstention

14.5.1 In General

In addition to jurisdiction over a broad array of cases, 28 U.S.C. § 1334 also confers the power to decline to exercise that jurisdiction. The court is allowed to abstain, under 28 U.S.C. § 1334(c), from hearing proceedings arising under title 11 (the Bankruptcy Code) or arising in or related to cases under title 11, "in the interest of justice, or in the interest of comity with State courts or respect for State law." Moreover, in certain circumstances it is required to abstain upon timely motion of a party.

Rule 5011(b) provides that a request for abstention should be made by motion pursuant to Federal Rule of Bankruptcy Procedure 9014.[468] In core proceedings the bankruptcy court can make a final decision on such a motion.[469] That decision is then appealable to the district court, but no higher unless the appeal challenges a determination that mandatory abstention is not required.[470] In non-core matters, the bankruptcy court can make a recommendation subject to review by the district court pursuant to Federal Rule of Bankruptcy Procedure 9033. No appeal of the district court decision is allowed, unless the decision decides that the mandatory abstention provisions are not applicable.[471]

14.5.2 Mandatory Abstention

As the result of strong pressure from states' rights advocates in the United States Senate, the 1984 bankruptcy amendments introduced another new concept into the bankruptcy jurisdictional scheme—that abstention is mandatory if certain require-

---

rescission by recoupment to situations in which it is permitted after foreclosure by state law). *But see In re* Fidler, 210 B.R. 411 (Bankr. D. Mass. 1997), *reaffirmed on motion to vacate,* 226 B.R. 734 (Bankr. D. Mass. 1998) (Massachusetts law permitted rescission after three-year period permitted by Truth in Lending Act). *See also* National Consumer Law Center, Truth in Lending § 6.3.3 (7th ed. 2010 and Supp.).

461 Former R. Bankr. P. 913.
462 *See* Bryan v. Rainwater (*In re* Rainwater), 254 B.R. 273, 276 (N.D. Ala. 2000) (bankruptcy court does not have authority to issue writ of habeas corpus); *In re* Cornelious, 214 B.R. 588 (Bankr. E.D. Ark. 1997) (bankruptcy court did not have jurisdiction to issue writ of habeas corpus).

In one case the debtor successfully brought an adversary proceeding seeking release from state custody without seeking a writ of habeas corpus. The district court affirmed the bankruptcy court's order releasing the debtor. *In re* Hucke, 128 B.R. 675 (D. Or. 1991). Although the court of appeals reversed, Hucke v. Oregon, 992 F.2d 950 (9th Cir. 1993), the reversal was based on grounds other than whether a bankruptcy court could order a debtor's release.

Of course, habeas relief may also be available through state court procedures. Marrow v. Williams, 25 Clearinghouse Rev. 717 (Okla. 1991) (habeas corpus relief granted to debtor held under state court contempt order requiring payment of divorce debt).
463 11 U.S.C. § 523(a)(5), *as amended by* Pub. L. No. 97-35, § 2335, 95 Stat. 357 (1981).

See § 15.4, *infra,* for a further discussion of exceptions to discharge.
464 *See generally* § 12.4, *supra*; Henry J. Sommer & Margaret Dee McGarity, Collier Family Law and the Bankruptcy Code Ch. 8 (1992).

465 *See, e.g.,* Juidice v. Vail, 430 U.S. 327, 97 S. Ct. 1211, 51 L. Ed. 2d 376 (1977) (imprisonment on contempt arising out of consumer debt-related proceedings).
466 *But see In re* Gruntz, 202 F.3d 1074 (9th Cir. 2000) (en banc) (denying release of debtor imprisoned for criminal nonsupport).
467 *But see In re* Bona, 110 B.R. 1012 (Bankr. S.D.N.Y. 1990) (court would not release debtor from prison absent showing that debt on which imprisonment had been obtained was dischargeable), *aff'd,* 124 B.R. 11 (S.D.N.Y. 1991).
468 Note also that a motion for abstention does not act as a stay of the proceedings in the case, so that if a stay is desired a motion for a stay should be presented to the bankruptcy court pursuant to Federal Rule of Bankruptcy Procedure 5011(c).
469 Navon v. Mariculture Prods. Ltd., 395 B.R. 818, 823 (D. Conn. 2008).
470 28 U.S.C. § 1334(d).
471 28 U.S.C. § 1334(d); United States v. Paolo (*In re* Paolo), 619 F.3d 100 (1st Cir. 2010).

§ 14.5.2   *Consumer Bankruptcy Law and Practice*

ments are met.[472] These requirements, set forth in 28 U.S.C. § 1334(c)(2), are:

- A timely motion filed by a party;[473]
- In a proceeding based upon a state law claim or cause of action;
- That is a related proceeding and not one arising under title 11 or in a case under title 11;
- Where the claim or cause of action could not have been commenced in a federal court absent section 1334's jurisdiction; and
- An action is commenced and can be timely adjudicated in a state court of appropriate jurisdiction.

The section further provides that it is not intended in any way to limit the applicability of the section 362 automatic stay as it applies to property of the bankruptcy estate. Thus, a decision that mandatory abstention is warranted is not cause for granting relief from the automatic stay.[474]

It is important to note at the outset those proceedings to which mandatory abstention does not apply. Mandatory abstention does not apply to any core proceeding,[475] and is also inapplicable to any proceeding on personal injury tort or wrongful death claims.[476]

Other questions concerning the reach of the mandatory abstention provision do not have clear answers. There is currently no rule to determine when an abstention motion is timely. Until such a rule is promulgated, courts will no doubt use normal standards of reasonableness to decide whether an abstention motion has been filed too late.

Similarly, it may not always be readily apparent when a proceeding is "based upon a state law or cause of action." What happens when a proceeding raises both state and federal claims? Is it bifurcated or is abstention mandatory as to the entire proceeding? Nor is it easy to determine whether a state court proceeding will be "timely adjudicated," either in terms of what would be "timely" or in terms of predicting the timing of state court proceedings.[477] Courts have generally held that the burden of proving a state court action would be timely adjudicated rests with the party moving for abstention.[478]

Finally, must an action already have been commenced in state court for the section to apply? It has been suggested that this section would permit the district court to conditionally abstain, with the requirement that a state court proceeding be commenced within a short period of time.[479] But courts generally seem to require that the state court action already be commenced for mandatory abstention to be proper.[480]

In any event, the court's decision to abstain under this section is not reviewable by the court of appeals, by appeal or otherwise.[481] This principle probably does not preclude review on the basis that the court did not have jurisdiction in the first instance.[482] By its terms, section 1334(d) does not preclude district court review of a decision to abstain.[483] A decision not to abstain is also not appealable beyond the district court, unless the decision denies a motion for mandatory abstention.

It seems clear that the mandatory abstention provisions were designed primarily to deal with claims of the sort involved in the *Northern Pipeline* case, that is, state law claims of the

---

472   *See, e.g.*, Stoe v. Flaherty, 436 F.3d 209 (3d Cir. 2006) (mandatory abstention provisions apply to removed cases); Reed v. Miss. Farm Bureau Mut. Ins. Co., 299 B.R. 804 (S.D. Miss. 2003) (remand required when mandatory abstention appropriate); Luevano v. Dow Corning Corp., 183 B.R. 751 (W.D. Tex. 1995) (product liability action against debtor's codefendant was subject to mandatory abstention); Borintex Mfg. Corp. v. Banco Governmental de Fomenta Para Puerto Rico, 102 B.R. 8 (Bankr. D. P.R. 1989) (grounds for mandatory abstention found after action removed from state court).

473   *See In re* AHT Corp., 265 B.R. 379 (Bankr. S.D.N.Y. 2001) (motion filed two-and-a-half months after complaint and only after denial of motion to dismiss was not timely).

474   *In re* Conejo Enters., 96 F.3d 346 (9th Cir. 1996).

475   28 U.S.C. § 1334(c); *In re* S.G. Phillips Constructors, Inc., 45 F.3d 702 (2d Cir. 1995) (mandatory abstention inapplicable with respect to determination of proof of claim filed by creditor); *In re* Ben Cooper, Inc., 924 F.2d 36 (2d Cir. 1991); Wolfe v. Greentree Mortgage Corp., 2010 WL 391629 (N.D. W. Va. Jan. 26, 2010) (action seeking invalidation of lien was core proceeding, so mandatory abstention not applicable).

476   28 U.S.C. § 157(b)(4).

477   *See* Parmalat Capital Fin. Ltd. v. Bank of Am., Corp., 671 F.3d 261 (2d Cir. 2012) (fact that state court proceeding would take only months longer not enough to defeat abstention; timely adjudication did not require faster adjudication than in bankruptcy court).

478   *See, e.g.*, Stoe v. Flaherty, 436 F.3d 209, 219 n.5 (3d Cir. 2006). *But see* Parmalat Capital Fin. Ltd. v. Bank of Am. Corp., 639 F.3d 572 (2d Cir. 2011); XL Sports, Ltd. v. Lawler, 49 Fed. Appx. 13, 20 (6th Cir. 2002).

479   *See, e.g.*, Taggart, *The New Bankruptcy Court System*, 30 Prac. Law. 11, 18 (Dec. 1984).

480   *See, e.g.*, McDaniel v. ABN Amro Mortgage Group, 364 B.R. 644 (S.D. Ohio 2007) (mandatory abstention provision did not apply to debtor's Truth in Lending Act and Home Ownership Equity Protection Act adversary claims because no proceeding has been commenced in a state forum); *In re* Container Transp., Inc., 86 B.R. 804 (E.D. Pa. 1988); Ram Constr. Co. v. Port Auth. of Allegheny County, 49 B.R. 363 (W.D. Pa. 1985); *In re* Excelite Corp., 49 B.R. 923 (Bankr. N.D. Ga. 1985).

481   28 U.S.C. § 1334(d). *See also In re* Potts, 724 F.2d 47 (6th Cir. 1984).

Notwithstanding section 1334(c)(2), a final bankruptcy court order and abstention is reviewable by the district court on appeal pursuant to 28 U.S.C. § 158(a). *See In re* Goerg, 930 F.2d 1563 (11th Cir. 1991) (right of appeal to Article III court of abstention decision under 11 U.S.C. § 305 is constitutionally required).

482   *See* Kennedy, *The Bankruptcy Court Under the New Bankruptcy Law: Its Structure, Jurisdiction, Venue, and Procedure*, 11 St. Mary's L. J. 251, 288–289 (1979). *See also* Pacor, Inc. v. Higgins, 743 F.2d 984 (3d Cir. 1984) (issue of jurisdiction is reviewable even in connection with decision on remand); *In re* Adams Delivery Serv., 24 B.R. 589 (B.A.P. 9th Cir. 1982) (decision to assume jurisdiction of removed proceeding could be reviewed if challenge was aimed at the bankruptcy court's jurisdiction). *But see* Things Remembered v. Petrarca, 516 U.S. 124, 116, S. Ct. 494, 133 L. Ed. 2d 461 (1995) (court of appeals may not review order remanding case based upon defect in procedure or lack of jurisdiction regardless of whether removal was pursuant to 28 U.S.C. § 1452(a) or 28 U.S.C. § 1441(a)).

483   *See* Fed. R. Bankr. P. 5011 advisory committee's note to 1991 amendment.

debtor against non-creditors. These claims arise only occasionally in consumer bankruptcy cases.

14.5.3 Discretionary Abstention

The 1984 amendments preserved the power of the bankruptcy forum to abstain from other proceedings as well. The statute added to the previous language, which allowed abstention "in the interest of justice," language permitting abstention "in the interest of comity with State courts or respect for State law."[484] As these were considerations already taken into account by most courts, it is unclear whether this additional emphasis changed the results in many cases.

The standards to be applied in the use of this discretion are not clear from the statute. The legislative history of the 1978 Act suggested that there may be cases in which it is more appropriate for a state court to hear a particular matter of state law,[485] usually when there is an unsettled question of state law, or a case such as a divorce or child custody matter, which is only tangentially related to the bankruptcy. One possibility in divorce cases is to have the state court decide the marital interests, but to retain jurisdiction over the property for all other purposes.[486]

Courts have also considered whether a duplication of efforts will occur. If certain issues are likely to be litigated in the bankruptcy forum in any case, such as in the allowance of a claim, there is a tendency to retain jurisdiction over those issues for all purposes.[487] This is especially true if the estate cannot be administered without resolution of the dispute[488] or if requiring litigation in courts other than the bankruptcy forum would impose a hardship on the debtor.[489] In some cases, the bankruptcy court may abstain with respect to certain issues, and reserve other issues for its own decision.[490]

Considerations of timing and convenience may also be determinative. If the court feels it is capable of expeditiously resolving a matter, it usually retains the case.[491] Similarly, the court may look to whether it customarily handles the type of question involved, and decline to hear the case if it does not.[492] When issues have been raised after having been fully litigated in a state court action, the court generally defers to the state appeals process, not only to avoid litigation of the same claim, but also as a matter of comity within the federal system.[493] However, when a proceeding concerns property of the estate, over which the district court has exclusive jurisdiction, the bankruptcy forum is normally more appropriate for the litigation of that proceeding.[494]

Obviously, it is important to frame bankruptcy litigation, whether commenced by removal or as an original proceeding, with these considerations in mind. To the extent the case can be framed as one bound up with the bankruptcy's administration and involving matters the bankruptcy forum can expeditiously handle, the chances of staying in the bankruptcy system are improved.[495]

14.6 *In Forma Pauperis*—Filing Fee Waivers in Bankruptcy Cases and Proceedings

14.6.1 General Principles

The possibilities for extensive litigation in connection with bankruptcy cases raise a familiar problem for low-income clients—how to deal with filing fees they cannot afford.[496] Fortunately, under the present fee schedule set by the Administrative Office of the United States Courts, there is no filing fee required for adversary complaints filed by debtors.[497] Unfortunately, there are substantial fees or bonds involved for other proceedings, for example, adversary proceedings commenced by non-debtor parties and appeals.[498]

---

484 28 U.S.C. § 1334(c)(1).
485 H.R. Rep. No. 95-595, at 446 (1977).
486 *See In re* White, 851 F.2d 170 (6th Cir. 1988). *See generally* Henry J. Sommer & Margaret Dee McGarity, Collier Family Law and the Bankruptcy Code Ch. 5 (1992).
487 *In re* Lucasa Int'l, Ltd., 6 B.R. 717 (Bankr. S.D.N.Y. 1980); *In re* Bros. Coal Co., 6 B.R. 567 (Bankr. W.D. Va. 1980). *Cf. In re* Collins & Aikman Corp., 2009 WL 1469630 (E.D. Mich. May 26, 2009) (abstention in case in which debtor was defendant appropriate when case would have to be tried in state court against non-debtor defendants in any event and state court litigation was far advanced).
488 *In re* Lucasa Int'l, Ltd., 6 B.R. 717 (Bankr. S.D.N.Y. 1980).
489 *In re* N. Pipeline Constr. Co., 6 B.R. 928 (Bankr. D. Minn. 1980), *rev'd on other grounds sub nom.* N. Pipeline Constr. Co. v. Marathon Pipe Line Co., 458 U.S. 50, 102 S. Ct. 2858, 73 L. Ed. 2d 598 (1982).
490 *See, e.g., In re* Al Copeland Enters., Inc., 153 F.3d 268 (5th Cir. 1998).
491 *In re* Lucasa Int'l, Ltd., 6 B.R. 717 (Bankr. S.D.N.Y. 1980); *In re* Project Oneco, 3 B.R. 284 (Bankr. D. Colo. 1980).
492 *Compare In re* Cole Assocs. Inc., 7 B.R. 154 (Bankr. D. Utah 1980) (bankruptcy court routinely hears questions under Uniform Commercial Code), *with* Carver v. Carver, 954 F.2d 1573 (11th Cir. 1992) (state court better able to resolve dispute about debtor's divorce decree obligations).
493 *In re* Moore, 5 B.R. 67 (Bankr. N.D. Tex. 1980); *In re* Tidwell, 4 B.R. 100 (Bankr. N.D. Tex. 1980).
   See also § 14.2.4.3, *supra*, discussing the *Rooker-Feldman* doctrine.
494 McDaniel v. ABN Amro Mortgage Group, 364 B.R. 644 (S.D. Ohio 2007) (bankruptcy court abused its discretion in permissively abstaining from hearing Truth in Lending Act and Home Ownership Equity Protection Act adversary claims); *In re* S.E. Hornsby & Sons Sand & Gravel Co., 45 B.R. 988 (Bankr. M.D. La. 1985).
495 *In re* Janssen, 396 B.R. 624 (Bankr. E.D. Pa. Nov. 7, 2008) (in granting debtor's motion to reopen chapter 13 case for purpose of determining whether debtor had cured his prepetition mortgage default, court refused to abstain despite pending state court foreclosure case, in part due to court's interest in protecting integrity of bankruptcy system).
496 For a more extensive discussion of filing fee waivers in bankruptcy, see Henry J. Sommer, *In Forma Pauperis in Bankruptcy: The Time Has Long Since Come*, 2 Am. Bankr. Inst. L. Rev. 93 (1994).
497 The fee schedule is reproduced in Appx. C.3, *infra*.
498 However, there is no fee for a child support creditor to file either a motion for relief from the stay or an adversary complaint. *See*

§ 14.6.2   Consumer Bankruptcy Law and Practice

An analysis of the question of *in forma pauperis* filings in bankruptcy court must begin with the fact that, except as provided by statute, a debtor's bankruptcy petition may not be filed without the filing fee. The Supreme Court ruled in *United States v. Kras*,[499] that due process does not require a right to waiver of the basic bankruptcy filing fee for indigents. Congress, when it enacted the Code in 1978, declined to grant such a right statutorily, although it did continue the previous statutory provisions allowing for payment of the fee in installments.[500]

In one of the few positive changes made by the 2005 amendments to the Code, Congress expressly authorized fee waivers for indigents, with the exception of statutory filing fees for bankruptcy petitions filed under chapters other than chapter 7.[501] This change generally codifies case law with respect to fees other than fees for the bankruptcy petition itself. Most reported cases, and several which had not been reported, had accepted the basic principle that bankruptcy proceedings, other than the actual bankruptcy petition, are subject to 28 U.S.C. 1915(a)[502] and may be instituted *in forma pauperis*.[503] They had also permitted debtors to waive the miscellaneous fees that are now required by the Judicial Conference's Bankruptcy Court Miscellaneous Fee Schedule upon the initial filing of a case.[504] Courts had also permitted the costs of appeal to be waived upon a showing of indigence unless the appeal is considered frivolous.[505]

14.6.2 Statutory Authority of Bankruptcy Courts to Waive Fees

14.6.2.1 Chapter 7 Filing Fee

In an important positive change from prior law,[506] and in a step that, for some debtors, should help blunt the effect of several chapter 7 filing fee increases, section 1930(f) of title 28, United States Code permits the waiver of chapter 7 filing fees for debtors with incomes less than 150% of the applicable official poverty line based on family size.[507] In addition to the income test the debtor must be unable to pay the filing fee in installments.

The rules adopted by the Judicial Conference implement the fee waiver provision by adding Bankruptcy Rule 1006(c).[508] The rule provides that a voluntary chapter 7 petition shall be

---

Judicial Conference of the United States, Bankruptcy Court Miscellaneous Fee Schedule ¶¶ 6, 20 (reprinted in Appx. C.2, *infra*). A child support creditor or a representative of that creditor must file Form B281 in order to qualify for the exemption. A copy of that form may be found in Appx. E.11, *infra*.

499 409 U.S. 434, 93 S. Ct. 631, 34 L. Ed. 2d 626 (1973).
500 28 U.S.C. § 1930(a).

See Chapter 7, *supra*, for a discussion of the procedure for applications to pay filing fees in installments. *But see In re* Reed, 4 B.R. 486 (Bankr. M.D. Tenn. 1980) (filing fees other than initial petition filing fee may not be paid in installments; the debtor did not request waiver of the filing fee in this case, nor was that possibility discussed).

501 28 U.S.C. § 1930(f)(1).
502 The current version of 28 U.S.C. § 1915(a)(1), amended by the Prison Litigation Reform Act of 1996, refers to "assets such prisoner possesses." Courts agree that this phrase is a typographical error and that the word "prisoner" should be "person." *See* Martinez v. Kristi Kleaners, 364 F.3d 1305 (11th Cir. 2004) (acknowledging that individuals not incarcerated may proceed *in forma pauperis*); Haynes v. Scott, 116 F.3d 137 (5th Cir. 1997) (concluding that section 1915(a)(1) applies both to prisoners and non-prisoners); Floyd v. U.S. Postal Serv., 105 F.3d 274, 275 (6th Cir. 1997) (superseded on other grounds) (term "prisoner possesses" was erroneously substituted for "person possesses"); Leonard v. Lacy, 88 F.3d 181, 183 (2d Cir. 1996) (indicating that "prisoner possesses" is an error by use of "[sic]").
503 *In re* Fitzgerald, 192 B.R. 861 (Bankr. E.D. Va. 1996); *In re* Lindsey, 178 B.R. 895 (Bankr. N.D. Ga. 1995); *In re* Brooks, 175 B.R. 409 (Bankr. S.D. Ala. 1994); *In re* McGinnis, 155 B.R. 294 (Bankr. D.N.H. 1993); *In re* Melendez, 153 B.R. 386 (Bankr. D. Conn. 1993); *In re* Sarah Allen Home, Inc., 4 B.R. 724 (Bankr. E.D. Pa. 1980); *In re* Palestino, 4 B.R. 721 (Bankr. M.D. Fla. 1980); *In re* Weakland, 4 B.R. 114 (Bankr. D. Del. 1980). *See In re* Ravida, 296 B.R. 278 (B.A.P. 1st Cir. 2003) (court had power to waive appeal fees but declined to do so because appeal was frivolous); *In re* Broady, 96 B.R. 221 (Bankr. W.D. Mo. 1988) (frivolous appeal cannot be prosecuted *in forma pauperis*); *In re* Shumate, 91 B.R. 23 (Bankr. W.D. Va. 1988) (although *in forma pauperis* is permissible, debtor living extravagant lifestyle not permitted to appeal *in forma pauperis*); *In re* Moore, 86 B.R. 249 (Bankr. W.D. Okla. 1988) (*in*

forma pauperis permitted, but bankruptcy court without authority to order transcription of record *in forma pauperis*). *See also* DeLeon v. Gurda Farms, Inc., 10 B.R. 479 (S.D.N.Y. 1980) (appeal to district court under prior Act allowed without fees pursuant to 28 U.S.C. § 1915(a)).

504 *In re* Stansbury, 226 B.R. 360 (Bankr. E.D. Pa. 1998) (waiving $45 in miscellaneous fees due upon filing).

The Fee Schedule requires a $46 noticing fee in every chapter 7 and chapter 13 case and a $15 fee for trustee compensation in every chapter 7 case. Judicial Conference of the United States, Bankruptcy Court Miscellaneous Fee Schedule ¶¶ 8, 9 (reprinted in Appx. C.3, *infra*). A form application for waiver of such fees is found at Form 17, Appendix G.3, *infra*.

505 28 U.S.C. § 1915(a); Flores v. Salven (*In re* DDJ, L.L.C.), 2011 U.S. Dist. LEXIS 120356 (E.D. Cal. Oct. 17, 2011); *In re* Heghmann, 324 B.R. 415 (B.A.P. 1st Cir. 2005). *See* 28 U.S.C. § 1915(a) (3), (e)(2) (frivolous appeal may not proceed *in forma pauperis*). *See also In re* Perry, 223 B.R. 167 (B.A.P. 8th Cir. 1998) (appeal of dismissal of seventh in a string of chapter 13 cases taken in bad faith and *in forma pauperis* status denied).

506 *See* former 28 U.S.C. § 1930(a) (codifying United States v. Kras, 409 U.S. 434, 93 S. Ct. 631, 34 L. Ed. 2d 626 (1973)).

507 The poverty line figures used are those provided by the Office of Management and Budget, and revised annually in accordance with section 673(2) of the Omnibus Budget Reconciliation Act of 1981. The current poverty figures can be found at www.census.gov/hhes/poverty/threshld/thresh00.html.

For purposes of comparing the debtor's income to 150% of the poverty level, the Judicial Conference Guidelines dictate using the debtor's income as stated on Line 16 of Schedule I, net of payroll deductions. *See In re* Donahue, 410 B.R. 751 (Bankr. N.D. Ga. 2009); Appx. H.6, § II.A.3, *infra*. *See also In re* Frye, 440 B.R. 685 (Bankr. W.D. Va. 2010) (determining family size under IRS definition of dependent and finding 19-year-old daughters who were students counted as members of family).

508 *See* Appx. B, *infra*.

accepted for filing if accompanied by a debtor's application requesting a fee waiver using Official Form 3B.[509]

For determination of income eligibility, Official Form 3B requests that the debtor state the income that is or will be listed on Line 16 of Schedule I for "Total Combined Monthly Income." A non-filing spouse's income must be included unless the spouses are separated. In addition the monthly net income of any dependents of the debtor, if they are part of the debtor's stated family size, must be included. Non-cash governmental assistance, such as food stamps or housing subsidies, is not to be included as income.[510]

In determining whether the debtor has the ability to pay the filing fee in installments, the Interim Procedures adopted by the Judicial Conference instruct the court to consider the "totality of the circumstances" based on the information concerning the debtor's expenses and assets stated on Official Form 3B.[511] If Schedules A, B, and J are submitted with the petition and attached to Official Form 3B, designated portions of Form 3B requesting duplicative information about income and assets need not be completed.

One issue that has arisen with respect to consideration of all of the debtor's circumstances is whether a debtor qualifies for a fee waiver if the debtor is expecting a tax refund shortly after the bankruptcy petition is filed. If the debtor is in this situation, the application for a waiver should carefully explain why the refund would not be available to pay the filing fee, for example, because it is needed for essential expenses like emergency home repairs, medical expenses, or other necessities. If the debtor is unable to provide such an explanation, it may be better to delay the bankruptcy petition until the refund has been spent, if possible, and document that the refund was spent reasonably.

If a case is converted from chapter 13 to chapter 7, the debtor may seek a waiver of any unpaid balance of the filing fee.[512] If the chapter 7 filing fee has been waived and the debtor later converts to a case under chapter 13, the debtor must then pay the chapter 13 filing fee.[513] The order granting conversion should set a reasonable period of time for the debtor to pay the fee in full or in installments.[514]

The new fee waiver provision does not rule out the possibility that a court could grant a waiver if the attorney representing the debtor is being paid.[515] In fact, some fee waivers were granted in cases in which attorneys had been paid, often on a reduced fee basis, during the three-year fee waiver pilot program that was conducted prior to the enactment of the 2005 Act.[516] Part D of the Application for Waiver (Official Form 3B) requests that the debtor list all payments that have been made or promised to an attorney or petition preparer.[517]

14.6.2.2 Other Filing Fees

The amendments also clarified that bankruptcy courts can waive other filing fees for indigent debtors and creditors. The courts are given specific authority to waive other fees for debtors who qualify for the waiver of the chapter 7 petition filing fee.[518] In addition, the statute makes clear that the courts may waive filing fees imposed under any part of 28 U.S.C. § 1930 for other debtors and creditors, in accordance with Judicial Conference policy. No such policy has been adopted with respect to such fees, so courts will presumably continue to waive fees for indigents as they had generally been doing prior to the amendments. Moreover, certain fees faced by indigents are not imposed under section 1930, and for those fees debtors

---

509 A copy of Official Form 3B is reprinted in Appendix D, *infra*.

510 *See* Judicial Conference of the United States, Interim Procedures Regarding the Chapter 7 Fee Waiver Provisions (available in Appx. H.6, *infra*, and on this treatise's companion website). *See also In re* Stabell, 2011 WL 611852 (Bankr. S.D. Ga. Feb. 10, 2011) (food stamps deducted in determining whether debtors below 150% of poverty level); *In re* Nuttall, 334 B.R. 921 (Bankr. W.D. Mo. 2005) ($450 in food stamps deducted from monthly income stated on Schedule I).

511 Judicial Conference of the United States, Interim Procedures Regarding the Chapter 7 Fee Waiver Provisions (available in Appx. H.6, *infra*, and on this treatise's companion website). *See In re* Van Luvender, 2008 WL 4716951 (Bankr. S.D. Fla. Oct. 22, 2008) (it would be impractical and inequitable to require debtor to borrow against or sell exempt vehicle to pay filing fees); *In re* Machia, 360 B.R. 416 (Bankr. D. Vt. 2007) (anticipated receipt of tax refund did not deprive debtor of eligibility for fee waiver); *In re* Nuttall, 334 B.R. 921 (Bankr. W.D. Mo. 2005) (after comparing debtors' expenses with IRS national and local standards used for the means test, court found expenses were reasonable and that debtors had no ability to pay filing fee in installments). *See also In re* Young, 2010 WL 5476750 (Bankr. S.D. Ga. Dec. 10, 2010) (fact that debtor had $2000 in bank account and had paid attorney $1231 showed she could pay filing fee); *In re* Davis, 372 B.R. 282 (Bankr. W.D. Va. 2007) (although debtor had no excess income to pay filing fee, fact that she had deposited $299 in escrow with the legal aid program representing her in the event court denied the fee waiver showed that she had available assets to pay filing fee).

512 *See* Judicial Conference of the United States, Interim Procedures Regarding the Chapter 7 Fee Waiver Provisions (available in Appx. H.6, *infra*, and on this treatise's companion website).

513 *Id.*

514 *Id.*

515 *Id. See In re* Stickney, 370 B.R. 31 (Bankr. D.N.H. 2007) (one time assistance received from relative to help debtor with payment of attorney fees did not prevent fee waiver); *In re* Johnson, 2006 WL 2883143 (Bankr. M.D. Tenn. Oct. 4, 2006) (waiver granted for debtor who paid $600 to bankruptcy attorney).

516 *See, e.g., In re* Shannon, 180 B.R. 189 (Bankr. W.D. Tenn. 1995) (debtor who paid $100 to attorney not disqualified from receiving fee waiver); *In re* Koren, 176 B.R. 740 (Bankr. E.D. Pa. 1995) (prior payment to attorney not absolute bar to obtaining *in forma pauperis* relief in the pilot program).

In 1993, Congress authorized a three-year pilot program in six judicial districts in which fee waivers were allowed, and also directed the Judicial Conference to conduct a study on the pilot program. *See* Pub. L. No. 103-121, § 111, 107 Stat. 1153 (1993). In 1998, the Federal Judicial Center submitted a comprehensive report in which it found that a relatively small number of debtors sought fee waivers (under five percent) and most of the waivers were granted. The report also found that there were no increases in abusive filings and the cost to the system was modest. A copy of the report, Implementing and Evaluating the Chapter 7 Filing Fee Waiver Program, is available at www.fjc.gov/public/pdf.nsf/lookup/IFPRepor.pdf/$file/IFPRepor.pdf.

517 *See* Official Form 3B (reprinted in Appx. D, *infra*).

518 28 U.S.C. § 1930(f)(2).

would appear to be relegated back to section 1915 of title 28, the general in forma pauperis statute.[519] Additionally, important due process arguments are still available concerning many fees, particularly for indigent creditors.[520]

14.7 Class Actions in Bankruptcy Court

Among the Federal Rules of Civil Procedure incorporated by reference into the Federal Rules of Bankruptcy Procedure is Rule 23, which governs proceedings brought on behalf of or against a class.[521] Thus, there can be little doubt that it is possible and proper to bring class actions in appropriate adversary proceedings.[522] For example, one court has allowed a class dischargeability proceeding on behalf of students who had enrolled in a chapter 11 debtor's fraudulent business schools.[523] Because Federal Rule of Bankruptcy Procedure 9014 permits a court to make the class action rule applicable to contested matters as well, it is even possible that there could be contested matters brought by or against a class.

However, the bankruptcy system has grappled with questions concerning which types of proceedings may properly be heard on a class basis. Perhaps the easiest type of case to allow would be one brought on behalf of a class of debtors, all of whom had filed bankruptcy cases, to enforce some right against another party.[524] Such a case would not involve any particularly difficult questions of jurisdiction because all of the class members would have already submitted to the jurisdiction of the bankruptcy forum. However, some courts have questioned whether jurisdiction exists to certify a nationwide class action involving debtors from other districts if the cause of action seeks damages that would be estate property.[525]

Similarly, it seems appropriate to have a class action or class proof of claim for a determination of common claims arising out of the same transaction or similar transactions.[526] A class

---

519 See Stephen v. Fukushima (*In re* Stephen), 2011 Bankr. LEXIS 2100 (B.A.P. 9th Cir. June 1, 2011) (bankruptcy appellate panel could not waive appeal fees under 28 U.S.C. § 1915 because Ninth Circuit had held bankruptcy court was not a "court of the United States"; it is not clear from the opinion whether the debtor sought a fee waiver under § 1930(f), which applies to fees for appeals from bankruptcy courts imposed under § 1930(b)).

520 See, e.g., *In re* Lassina, 261 B.R. 614 (Bankr. E.D. Pa. 2001); *In re* Sarah Allen Home Inc., 4 B.R. 724 (Bankr. E.D. Pa. 1980).

521 Fed. R. Bankr. P. 7023.
  However, Federal Rule of Civil Procedure 23(f), which permits an interlocutory appeal of class certification by a district court to the court of appeals, is not incorporated insofar as it would allow a party to bypass an appeal to a district court or bankruptcy appellate panel. Chrysler Fin. Corp. v. Powe, 312 F.3d 1241 (11th Cir. 2002).

522 Begley v. Philadelphia Elec. Co., 30 B.R. 469 (E.D. Pa. 1983), *aff'd*, 760 F.2d 46 (3d Cir. 1985); *In re* Fleet, 53 B.R. 833 (Bankr. E.D. Pa. 1985) (class action based on state law could be brought when cause of action was estate property, and debtors' cause of action alleged abuse of bankruptcy system). *See also In re* Salem Mortgage Co., 783 F.2d 626 (6th Cir. 1986) (bankruptcy court has power to enter consent order in consumer class action against debtor mortgage company under the Michigan Consumer Protection Act).

523 *In re* Livaditis, 132 B.R. 897 (Bankr. N.D. Ill. 1991). *But see In re* Hanson, 104 B.R. 261 (Bankr. N.D. Cal. 1989) (class dischargeability proceeding not allowed).

524 *In re* Rodriguez, 695 F.3d 360 (5th Cir. 2012) (affirming bankruptcy court's grant of class certification for plaintiffs' injunctive relief claim based on mortgage overcharges); Wilborn v. Wells Fargo Bank (*In re* Wilborn), 609 F.3d 748 (5th Cir. 2010) (no requirement that all debtor class members have cases before judge hearing class action, but class issues failed superiority and predominance tests); Patterson v. Homecomings Fin. L.L.C., 425 B.R. 499 (E.D. Wis. 2010) (class action in district court challenging mortgage overcharges to bankruptcy debtors). *See, e.g.*, Bessette v. Avco Fin. Servs., Inc., 230 F.3d 439 (1st Cir. 2000) (bankruptcy or district court may certify class action seeking enforcement of discharge injunction because statutory injunction under section 524 is uniform in every bankruptcy case); Bank United v. Manley, 273 B.R. 229 (N.D. Ala. 2001) (affirming certification of nationwide class of debtors challenging mortgage overcharges); *In re* Cano, 410 B.R. 506 (Bankr. S.D. Tex. 2009) (bankruptcy court has subject matter jurisdiction over nationwide class action alleging that mortgage creditor's postdischarge attempts to collect undisclosed fees incurred during class members' chapter 13 cases violate plan confirmation orders); *In re* Montano, 398 B.R. 47 (Bankr. D.N.M. 2008) (class certified for discharge violations based upon failure to correctly report discharge of debts on credit reports); *In re* Sims, 278 B.R. 457 (Bankr. E.D. Tenn. 2002) (bankruptcy court has jurisdiction to certify nationwide class of trustees and debtors challenging claims of credit card company that included unmatured interest); *In re* Tate, 253 B.R. 653 (Bankr. W.D.N.C. 2000) (class action challenging fees improperly included by mortgage company in proofs of claim); *In re* Noletto, 244 B.R. 845 (Bankr. S.D. Ala. 2000) (nationwide class of bankruptcy debtors is permitted); *In re* Coggin, 155 B.R. 934 (Bankr. E.D.N.C. 1993) (class action against creditor seeking to have liens declared void, with enforcement enjoined and damages, due to noncompliance with state law accounting method); *In re* Watts, 76 B.R. 390 (Bankr. E.D. Pa. 1987) (class action on behalf of bankruptcy debtors challenging discrimination against debtors in mortgage assistance program), *rev'd on other grounds*, 876 F.2d 1090 (3d Cir. 1989). *See also* Malone v. Norwest Fin. Cal., Inc., 245 B.R. 389 (N.D. Cal. 2000) (finding private right of action under section 524 in class action for reaffirmation abuses); Conley v. Sears, Roebuck & Co., 222 B.R. 181 (D. Mass. 1998); *In re* Harris, 280 B.R. 876 (Bankr. S.D. Ala. 2001) (in case challenging attorney fees improperly posted to debtors' mortgage accounts, class certification under Rule 7023(b)(2) was appropriate because most fees had not yet been collected or only partially paid by debtors, and declaratory and injunctive relief removing fees from accounts and providing restitution for those paid was predominant form of relief); *In re* Mosley, 260 B.R. 590 (Bankr. S.D. Ga. 2000) (putative class action challenging $50 fee by employer for processing chapter 13 wage order not mooted by refund of $50 to chapter 13 trustee). *But see* Dechert v. Cadle Co., 333 F.3d 801 (7th Cir. 2003) (bankruptcy trustee ordinarily not an appropriate class representative).

525 *See In re* Singleton, 284 B.R. 322 (D.R.I. 2002) (reversing bankruptcy court ruling that it had jurisdiction to certify nationwide class action); Bessette v. Avco Fin. Servs., Inc., 279 B.R. 442 (D.R.I. 2002) (bankruptcy court and district court lack jurisdiction over discharges issued by bankruptcy courts in other districts); *In re* Williams, 244 B.R. 858 (S.D. Ga. 2000) (class action permitted if limited to debtors in judicial district where case filed). *See also* Beck v. Gold Key Lease, Inc., 283 B.R. 163 (Bankr. E.D. Pa. 2002) (finding jurisdiction to certify class limited to district in which discharges issued). *Cf. In re* Rojas, 2009 WL 2496807 (Bankr. S.D. Tex. Aug. 12, 2009) (nationwide class of debtors permissible).

526 *In re* Charter Co., 876 F.2d 861 (11th Cir. 1989) (class proof of claim allowable in bankruptcy); *In re* Am. Reserve Corp., 840 F.2d

proof of claim, however, probably requires a separate motion to certify the class under the relevant rules, although such a motion may not be necessary if no objection to the claim is filed.[527]

More difficult would be cases in which most class members were not debtors in bankruptcy. For example, if a Truth in Lending class action were brought in connection with a bankruptcy by the debtor who had filed the bankruptcy case, the creditor-defendant might well argue that it would be inappropriate for a bankruptcy court to consider a matter only tangentially related to the bankruptcy case, and that therefore the court has no jurisdiction.[528] The 1984 jurisdictional amendments may lessen this problem as to matters, such as Truth in Lending actions, which could have been brought in federal court regardless of the bankruptcy, but they will probably heighten the concern over state law causes of action brought into the federal system.

Once jurisdiction is established, it seems fairly clear that parties not directly involved in the bankruptcy may become involved in some bankruptcy proceedings.[529] As the Federal Rules of Bankruptcy Procedure contemplate class actions, there is no reason why the same principles would not allow non-debtor class members to be involved in a bankruptcy proceeding. Indeed, the bankruptcy forum may provide a particularly appropriate forum for such actions because of its expertise in commercial and consumer law.

14.8 Involuntary Bankruptcy Cases

Involuntary bankruptcy cases against consumers, in which creditors force the liquidation of debtors' nonexempt assets, were extremely rare under the prior Bankruptcy Act. Although the requirements for commencing an involuntary bankruptcy have been relaxed somewhat under the Code,[530] such cases continue to be very uncommon.

Creditors are not eager to file involuntary consumer cases for a number of reasons. First, the prerequisites are not easy to meet. A single creditor may file an involuntary case only if the debtor has fewer than twelve unsecured creditors and only if the creditor holds a non-contingent, undisputed, unsecured claim of at least $14,425.[531] If the debtor has twelve or more creditors that hold claims which are totally or partially unsecured, three of them, with non-contingent undisputed claims aggregating at least $14,425, must join in the petition.[532] The fact that claims

---

487 (7th Cir. 1988); *In re* First Alliance Mortgage Co., 269 B.R. 428 (C.D. Cal. 2001) (class certification granted based on borrowers' class proof of claim for TILA and UDAP claims against debtor-lender); *In re* Birting Fisheries, Inc., 178 B.R. 849 (W.D. Wash. 1995) (class proof of claim permitted for employee wage claims), *aff'd*, 92 F.3d 939 (9th Cir. 1996); *In re* Chateaugay Corp., 104 B.R. 626 (S.D.N.Y. 1989) (class proof of claim permissible for creditors who did not file individual proofs); *In re* Commonpoint Mortgage Co., 283 B.R. 469 (Bankr. W.D. Mich. 2002) (borrowers' class proof of claim certified alleging UDAP and other state law claims against originating lender); *In re* United Companies Fin. Corp., Inc., 276 B.R. 368 (Bankr. D. Del. 2002) (certification of class proof of claim based on debtor's failure to comply with state loan broker law avoids burden of conducting 291 separate claim hearings); *In re* Sheffield, 281 B.R. 24 (Bankr. S.D. Ala. 2000) (certification granted of nationwide class of debtors challenging creditor's failure to adequately disclose attorney fees in proofs of claim, but not on issue of reasonableness of fees); *In re* Retirement Builders, Inc., 96 B.R. 390 (Bankr. S.D. Fla. 1988) (class proof of claim authorized for 2000 claimants in state court class action). *See also In re* Sims, 278 B.R. 457 (Bankr. E.D. Tenn. 2002) (trustee has standing to pursue class objection to claims on behalf of nationwide class of chapter 13 trustees). *But see In re* Standard Metals, 817 F.2d 625 (10th Cir.), *vacated on reh'g and decided on other grounds*, 839 F.2d 1383 (1987) (claims must be considered individually); *In re* Woodmoor Corp., 4 B.R. 186 (Bankr. D. Colo. 1980) (claims must be considered individually).

527 *See* Gentry v. Siegel, 668 F.3d 83 (4th Cir. 2012) (class proofs of claim serve their function only on a conditional basis; if the approves class representation, approval will function retroactively to legitimize class proof of claim, but if court rejects such representation, putative class members must file individual proofs of claim); Reid v. White Motor Corp., 886 F.2d 1462 (6th Cir. 1989) (bankruptcy rules permit filing of class proofs of claim, however, claim may be denied for failure to follow procedural requirements of Federal Rule of Civil Procedure 23 as made applicable by Federal Rule of Bankruptcy Procedure 7023); *In re* Charter Co., 876 F.2d 861 (11th Cir. 1989) (no motion for class certification is required unless an objection to class proof of claim is filed); *In re* Mortgage & Realty Trust, 125 B.R. 575 (Bankr. C.D. Cal. 1991) (proper in chapter 11 case to wait for deadline for objection to claim to run before filing motion to certify class).
Better practice would probably be to file a motion for class certification at or near the time of filing the proof of claim.

528 28 U.S.C. § 1334(b). *See In re* Porter, 295 B.R. 529 (Bankr. E.D. Pa. 2003) (bankruptcy court jurisdiction does not extend over TILA claims of putative class comprised mostly of non-debtors); *In re* Smith, 95 B.R. 286 (Bankr. S.D.N.Y. 1988) (no jurisdiction over individual or class claims arising from IRS tax refund intercept).
However it could be argued that the cause of action is property of the estate, and that therefore the court has exclusive jurisdiction over the *debtor's* claim. 28 U.S.C. § 1334(e)(1).

529 *See generally* § 14.4.1.4, *supra*.

530 *See* Donnelly, *The New (Proposed?) Bankruptcy Act: The Development of Its Structural Provisions and Their Impact on the Interests of Consumer Debtors*, 18 Santa Clara L. Rev. 291 (1978).

531 11 U.S.C. § 303(b)(2).
This amount is adjusted every three years pursuant to 11 U.S.C. § 104.
In calculating whether there are more than twelve unsecured creditors for the purpose of determining whether a case may be filed by a single creditor, even relatively small claims must be counted. *See In re* Runyan, 832 F.2d 58 (5th Cir. 1987) (unsecured claim of $600 not considered *de minimis*, even assuming *de minimis* claims could be excluded). *Compare In re* Blaine Richards & Co., 10 B.R. 424 (Bankr. E.D.N.Y. 1981) (creditors with small current trade account claims excluded) *with In re* 7H Land & Cattle Co., 6 B.R. 29 (Bankr. D. Nev. 1980) (single creditor must make showing of special circumstances, such as fraud, to be successful petitioner).
Creditors also are not permitted to disregard the separate existence of a corporation by asserting that debts of the corporation are debts that can be counted as debts of its principal (absent grounds to pierce the corporate veil). *In re* Sims, 994 F.2d 210 (5th Cir. 1993).

532 11 U.S.C. § 303(b)(1).
One court of appeals has held that only some of the petitioning creditors must be fully or partially unsecured. Paradise Hotel Corp. v. Bank of Nova Scotia, 842 F.2d 47 (3d Cir. 1988).

subject to bona fide dispute may not be included was made clear by specific language added in the 1984 amendments,[533] and the 2005 amendments further clarified that a claim is considered disputed if there is a dispute about either liability or amount.[534] Moreover, an involuntary bankruptcy may never be filed against a farmer.[535] It also appears that an involuntary petition cannot be filed against a husband and wife jointly.[536]

Second, creditors are reluctant to force consumers into bankruptcy because of all the advantages (discussed throughout this treatise) that consumers can obtain under the Bankruptcy Code. Thus, trying to use bankruptcy to collect a claim could backfire on the creditor; at best, it only allows the creditor to share the debtor's assets with all other creditors. These assets in many states do not include property that is exempt under the federal bankruptcy exemptions, leaving less for creditors than would be available under state law execution procedures. On the other hand, it may be that the limitations on state homestead exemptions in bankruptcy[537] enacted in 2005 could change this calculus in cases in which a creditor cannot reach a debtor's valuable homestead under applicable nonbankruptcy law.

Third, bringing an involuntary bankruptcy can be very risky for a petitioning creditor. If the petition is not successful (and the court may dismiss[538] it or abstain[539] from hearing it in some cases), the court is authorized to award to the debtor not only attorney fees and costs, but also compensatory and punitive damages.[540]

In those rare instances in which a consumer is faced with an involuntary bankruptcy petition, the first decision which must be made is whether to contest the case. In some instances, particularly if a creditor has acted without much knowledge of the bankruptcy laws, debtors may be better off going through with the bankruptcy and taking advantage of the numerous protections available to them.[541] In such cases, the debtor would not contest the petition, but might wish to exercise the absolute right to convert the liquidation case to a chapter 13 case.[542]

A debtor who wishes to contest an involuntary petition must file a responsive pleading;[543] otherwise, the petition may be granted by default.[544] It may be possible to raise a number of defenses. If the petition has been filed by only one creditor, the debtor may show that more than twelve creditors holding unsecured claims exist and that therefore one petitioning creditor is not sufficient.[545] Most consumers have more than twelve creditors, counting utilities, friends, and so forth. However, if the petition is denied on this basis, the court may allow other creditors to intervene to make up the requisite number.[546] When a creditor knows that more than twelve creditors exist, but nonetheless files as a single petitioning creditor, the petition may

---

533 11 U.S.C. § 303(b). See In re Reid, 773 F.2d 945 (7th Cir. 1985).
534 11 U.S.C. § 303(b)(1).
535 11 U.S.C. § 303(a). But see In re Marlar, 432 F.3d 813 (8th Cir. 2005) (prohibition of involuntary case against a farmer is not jurisdictional and can be waived if not timely raised as a defense).

"Farmer" is defined at 11 U.S.C. § 101(20). In determining whether a debtor meets this definition, it has been held that income from the sale of farm machinery to scale back farming was income from a "farming operation," but that land rental income was not. *In re* Armstrong, 812 F.2d 1024 (7th Cir. 1987). It has also been held that an individual retirement account (IRA) distribution was not income from farming despite the fact that IRA contributions came from earlier farm income. *In re* Wagner, 808 F.2d 542 (7th Cir. 1987).

536 *In re* Benny, 842 F.2d 1147 (9th Cir. 1988) (married couple not a "person," only voluntary joint petitions authorized by Code); *In re* Jones, 112 B.R. 770 (Bankr. E.D. Va. 1990); *In re* Calloway, 70 B.R. 175 (Bankr. N.D. Ind. 1986) (joint involuntary petition is improper).
537 See Chapter 10, *supra*, for discussion of homestead exemption limitations.
538 11 U.S.C. § 707(a).
539 11 U.S.C. § 305(a).
540 11 U.S.C. § 303(i). See Orange Blossom L.P. v. S. Cal. Sunbelt Developers, Inc. (*In re* S. Cal. Sunbelt Developers, Inc.), 608 F.3d 456 (9th Cir. 2010) (awarding costs, fees, and punitive damages against petitioning creditors and holding individuals who controlled creditors jointly liable for costs and fees for obtaining dismissal of the petition); *In re* Miles, 430 F.3d 1083 (9th Cir. 2005) (damages provision preempts state law claims and does not give standing to debtor's wife); Higgins v. Vortex Fishing Sys., Inc., 379 F.3d 701 (9th Cir. 2004) (fees and costs based on totality of circumstances test and cannot include fees for appeal, which must be awarded by appellate court); *In re* Reid, 854 F.2d 156 (7th Cir. 1988). *See also In re* Am. President Lines, Ltd., 804 F.2d 1307 (D.C. Cir. 1986)

(sanctions awarded against creditor for frivolous appeal of dismissal of involuntary bankruptcy).
541 Even if the case is not contested, the debtor may retain its right to challenge the bad faith of the creditors which filed the involuntary petition. See Paradise Hotel Corp. v. Bank of Nova Scotia, 842 F.2d 47 (3d Cir. 1988).
542 11 U.S.C. § 706.

Section 303 does not provide for involuntary chapter 13 cases, but nothing prevents an involuntary debtor who prefers that chapter from converting. *See also In re* Graham, 21 B.R. 235 (Bankr. N.D. Iowa 1982) (individual debtor could not be involuntarily forced into chapter 11 reorganization).

Conversion cures any jurisdictional defects in the original involuntary petition. *In re* Benny, 842 F.2d 1147 (9th Cir. 1988).
543 Fed. R. Bankr. P. 1011(b).
544 See *In re* Nina Merch. Corp., 5 B.R. 743 (Bankr. S.D.N.Y. 1980). *See also In re* Mason, 709 F.2d 1313 (9th Cir. 1983) (defense not raised in answer is waived).
545 This defense must be timely raised by the debtor, because it probably does not go to the jurisdiction of the court. *See In re* Earl's Tire Serv., 6 B.R. 1019 (Bankr. D. Del. 1980).

It is also unclear whether every small debt of the debtor must be counted. *See also* King v. Fid. Nat'l Bank of Baton Rouge, 712 F.2d 188 (5th Cir. 1983) (involuntary petition dismissed as to one of two respondent spouses when that spouse not subject to claims of petitioning creditors). *Compare In re* Blaine Richards & Co., 10 B.R. 424 (Bankr. E.D.N.Y. 1981) (creditors with small current trade account claims excluded) *with In re* 7H Land & Cattle Co., 6 B.R. 29 (Bankr. D. Nev. 1980) (single creditor must make showing of special circumstances, such as fraud, to be successful petitioner).
546 11 U.S.C. § 303(c).

However the court may set an earlier deadline for creditors to join the petition. *In re* DSC, Ltd., 486 F.3d 940 (6th Cir. 2007).

Holders of small recurring claims are included in counting the debtor's creditors. *In re* Rassi, 701 F.2d 627 (7th Cir. 1983). *See also In re* Runyan, 832 F.2d 58 (5th Cir. 1987) (even if *de minimis* claims could be excluded, $600 and $800 claims were not *de minimis*); *In re* Nazarian, 5 B.R. 279 (Bankr. D. Md. 1980); *In re* Kreidler Imp. Corp., 4 B.R. 256 (Bankr. D. Md. 1980); *In re* Trans-High Corp., 3 B.R. 1 (Bankr. S.D.N.Y. 1980).

be dismissed as filed in bad faith.[547] Compensatory and punitive damage claims would then be available against that creditor.[548]

The debtor might also challenge the petition on the grounds that some of the creditors hold contingent claims or claims subject to a bona fide dispute that do not qualify them to file as petitioners.[549] Certain claims, such as unliquidated tort claims and claims against guarantors of notes upon which there has been no default, are pretty clearly disputed, or contingent because they depend upon the occurrence of future events. But claims which are simply unmatured probably are not contingent.[550] In addition, it has been held that if the debtor has a "bona fide" defense, counterclaim or setoff, that fact may serve to extinguish the right of the creditor to join an involuntary petition.[551] Moreover, case law under the prior Act, holding that a creditor who has received a preference may not join in the petition, probably remains valid under the Code.[552]

The debtor may also contest the basic allegation of the petition, which the creditors have the burden of proving—that the debtor is generally not paying debts as they come due. This is known as the "equity test" of insolvency. Its meaning is not entirely clear, because it is a new concept in American bankruptcy law. It has generally been the rule that even if a debtor is insolvent under a balance sheet test (having liabilities greater than assets) that debtor may still be found to be paying debts as they come due.[553] Moreover, the failure to pay one or only a small percentage of creditors is not considered to be a "general" failure to pay debts as they come due.[554] However, when only a single creditor is not being paid, involuntary bankruptcy has been granted under the following circumstances:

- The creditor is the only creditor of the debtor;
- The creditor is a significant creditor and special circumstances such as fraudulent conduct exist; or
- The debtor admits inability to pay other creditors.[555]

Decisions under the Code have tended to adopt these principles.[556] In determining whether debts are being paid as they come due, the debtor's defenses to the claims can be very important. If the debtor succeeds in such defenses, then the debt has not come due and need not have been paid.[557] Finally, courts have held that making partial payments to all creditors is not paying those debts as they come due[558] although the result might be different if the creditors had agreed to partial payments, because then only those partial payments would be due.

However, although an individual must be eligible to be a debtor under section 109 to be the subject of an involuntary petition, courts have not been receptive to the argument that an involuntary petition cannot be filed against an individual who has not obtained a credit counseling briefing under section 109(h). Case law to date has noted that such an interpretation would preclude all involuntary cases against individuals, and have focused on the language in section 109(h)(1) referring to "the filing of the petition by such individual" to hold that the counseling requirement does not apply to a petition filed against an individual.[559]

Of course, in defending against an involuntary bankruptcy, the debtor's attorney should aggressively use the weapons the Code provides. By counterclaims, debtors should quickly let petitioning creditors know that they will seek attorney fees and damages under Code section 303(i). Such damages presumably can include compensation for the anxiety and the loss of reputation or credit standing that the debtor will probably suffer as a result of the petition being filed. Discovery should then be

---

547 Basin Elec. Power Coop. v. Midwest Processing Co., 769 F.2d 483 (8th Cir. 1985).

548 11 U.S.C. § 303(i).

549 A claim is subject to bona fide dispute if there is an objective basis for either a legal or factual dispute regarding the alleged debt. *In re* Byrd, 357 F.3d 433 (4th Cir. 2004) (debt reduced to judgment may be subject to bona fide dispute if appeal pending or possible on legitimate issue); *In re* BDC 56 L.L.C., 330 F.3d 111 (2d Cir. 2003) (creditor has burden of making prima facie case of no bona fide dispute); *In re* Vortex Finishing Sys., Inc., 262 F.3d 985 (9th Cir. 2001) (bona fide dispute may be legal or factual dispute about whether money is owed), *amended by* 277 F.3d 1057 (9th Cir. 2002); *In re* Rimell, 946 F.2d 1363 (8th Cir. 1991) (debtor has ultimate burden to establish facts demonstrating bona fide dispute and court may conduct some analysis of legal issues to determine whether dispute is bona fide); *In re* Busick, 831 F.2d 745 (7th Cir. 1987). *See also* B.D.W. Assocs., Inc. v. Busy Beaver Bldg. Ctrs. Inc., 865 F.2d 65 (3d Cir. 1989); Bartmann v. Maverick Tube Corp., 853 F.2d 1540 (10th Cir. 1988).

Under the 2005 amendments to section 303(h), the bona fide dispute may be with respect to either liability or the amount of the debt.

Note though that if one or more creditors are disqualified, it may be possible for others to join to remedy the deficiency. 11 U.S.C. § 303(c). *See In re* Rimell, 946 F.2d 1363 (8th Cir. 1991).

550 *See In re* All Media Properties, Inc., 5 B.R. 126 (Bankr. S.D. Tex. 1980), *aff'd*, 646 F.2d 193 (5th Cir. 1981).

551 *See In re* BDC 56 L.L.C., 330 F.3d 111 (2d Cir. 2003) (related counterclaims may be considered); *In re* Kreidler Imp. Corp., 4 B.R. 256 (Bankr. D. Md. 1980). *But see In re* Seko Inv., Inc., 156 F.3d 1005 (9th Cir. 1998) (existence of counterclaim does not render claim subject to bona fide dispute when there is no dispute about creditor's claim against debtor).

552 *In re* Kreidler Imp. Corp., 4 B.R. 256 (Bankr. D. Md. 1980).

553 *In re* Cent. Hobron Assocs., 41 B.R. 444 (D. Haw. 1984).

554 *In re* Nordbrock, 772 F.2d 397 (8th Cir. 1985); *In re* Dill, 731 F.2d 629 (9th Cir. 1984). *See In re* Concrete Pumping Serv., Inc., 943 F.2d 627 (6th Cir. 1991) (debtor not paying debts as they come due when in default on its only debt). *See also* John Honsberger, *Failure to Pay One's Debts Generally as They Become Due: The Experience of France and Canada*, 54 Am. Bankr. L.J. 153, 156 (1980). *But see In re* Hill, 8 B.R. 779 (Bankr. D. Minn. 1981) (petition granted when three largest creditors not being paid).

555 John Honsberger, *Failure to Pay One's Debts Generally as They Become Due: The Experience of France and Canada*, 54 Am. Bankr. L.J. 153 at 158 (1980).

556 *In re* 7-H Land & Cattle Co., 6 B.R. 29 (Bankr. D. Nev. 1980); *In re* Hill, 5 B.R. 79 (Bankr. D. Minn. 1980); *In re* J. V. Knitting Servs., 4 B.R. 597 (Bankr. S.D. Fla. 1980).

557 *In re* All Media Properties, Inc., 5 B.R. 126 (Bankr. S.D. Tex. 1980), *aff'd*, 646 F.2d 193 (5th Cir. 1981); *In re* Kreidler Imp. Corp., 4 B.R. 256 (Bankr. D. Md. 1980).

558 *In re* Duty Free Shops Corp., 6 B.R. 38 (Bankr. S.D. Fla. 1980). *See also In re* Bishop, Baldwin, Rewald, Dillingham & Wong, 779 F.2d 471 (9th Cir. 1986).

559 *In re* Allen, 378 B.R. 151 (Bankr. N.D. Tex. 2007).

available to inquire into issues such as the petitioning creditors' bad faith in filing, and perhaps their assets, which are relevant to awards of punitive damages. And, because involuntary cases against consumers are almost never filed, the court may be sympathetic to a claim for punitive damages when such a drastic remedy is wrongfully invoked. If such damages are sought and awarded in those cases that are filed, involuntary consumer bankruptcies will continue to be rare.

The 2005 amendments to the Code also added protections for debtors who are the subject of frivolous involuntary petitions that, notwithstanding dismissal of the petitions, impaired debtors' credit histories.[560] Under section 303(*l*), after a petition is dismissed, the court may enter an order that prohibits the reporting of the petition by consumer reporting agencies.[561] If the petition contains false, fictitious, or fraudulent statements, the debtor may also obtain an order sealing the records of the case[562] and, ultimately, an order expunging them.[563]

14.9 Bankruptcy Appeals

14.9.1 Appeals from the Bankruptcy Court

The 1984 amendments to title 28 altered not only the jurisdictional scheme applicable to initial bankruptcy proceedings but also the avenues available for appeals. While these avenues may vary depending upon the judicial district or circuit where a proceeding is litigated, they generally closely resemble the appellate mechanisms which existed prior to 1979.

The usual forum for appeals from decisions of a bankruptcy court is the district court.[564] (While objections to proposed findings of fact and conclusions of law under 28 U.S.C. § 157(c)(1) are also decided by the district court, different rules apply to them.)[565]

However, the other innovation of the 1978 Act, the bankruptcy appellate panel, has been retained to a limited degree. An appeal that would otherwise go to the district court may be heard by an appellate panel of three bankruptcy judges[566] if all of the following conditions are met:

- The judicial council of the circuit has established a bankruptcy appellate panel;[567]
- The district judges for the district, by majority vote, authorize referral of appeals from that district to the appellate panel;[568] and
- All parties consent.[569]

Most courts have held that decisions of a bankruptcy appellate panel, like decisions of one district judge in a multi-judge district, are not binding on bankruptcy courts in the same circuit.[570]

The Bankruptcy Reform Act of 1994,[571] contained several amendments designed to encourage, but not require the use of bankruptcy appellate panels, referred to in that Act as a judicial circuit's "bankruptcy appellate panel service."[572] Under the amendments, each circuit was required to set up a bankruptcy appellate panel service (BAPS) unless 1) there were insufficient judicial resources available (for example, not enough bankruptcy judges volunteer or perhaps because of the expense of a BAPS) *or* 2) establishment "would result in undue delay or increased cost to parties" in bankruptcy cases.[573] The legislation resulted in appellate panels being established in about half of the circuits.[574]

As the district judges in a district must still authorize referral of appeals to a BAPS, each district court can veto the use of appellate panels for appeals arising in its district, and some districts have done so. A majority of district judges in a circuit may seek to dissolve a BAPS after at least one year of implementation, or the circuit may reconsider on its own motion after three years. A BAPS judge may not hear an appeal from her own district.[575]

Under current 28 U.S.C. § 158(c), if a bankruptcy appellate panel may hear an appeal, the parties must consent to the panel hearing it. The appellant can elect to go to district court instead.

---

560 A number of such petitions had been filed against judges and other prominent people by disgruntled litigants and other assorted fringe elements.
561 11 U.S.C. § 303(*l*)(2).
562 11 U.S.C. § 303(*l*)(1).
563 11 U.S.C. § 303(*l*)(3).
564 28 U.S.C. § 158(a).
   The district court may not refer a bankruptcy appeal to a magistrate. Va. Beach Fed. Sav. & Loan Ass'n v. Wood, 901 F.2d 849 (10th Cir. 1990) (magistrates not permitted to enter final decisions in bankruptcy appeals); Minerex Erodel, Inc. v. Sina, Inc., 838 F.2d 781 (5th Cir. 1988); *In re* Elcona Homes Corp., 810 F.2d 136 (7th Cir. 1987). *But see* Hall v. Vance, 887 F.2d 1041 (10th Cir. 1989) (bankruptcy appeal may be referred to magistrate for advisory hearing as long as district court reserves to itself the power to make a final decision).
565 Fed. R. Bankr. P. 9033. See § 14.2.5.1, *supra*.
566 A single judge of the appellate panel may not determine the appeal alone. *In re* Caiati, 842 F.2d 1135 (9th Cir. 1988).

567 28 U.S.C. § 158(b)(1).
   Some but not all circuits have appellate panels. The First Circuit panel hears appeals from all districts in the circuit. The Sixth Circuit appellate panel hears appeals arising only in the Northern and Southern Districts of Ohio. The Eighth Circuit panel hears appeals arising anywhere in the circuit except the districts of North Dakota and South Dakota. The Ninth Circuit panel hears appeals from all districts. The Tenth Circuit's panel hears appeals arising throughout the circuit except for those arising in the District of Colorado.
568 28 U.S.C. § 158(b)(2).
569 28 U.S.C. § 158(b)(1).
570 *In re* Carrozzella & Richardson, 255 B.R. 267 (Bankr. D. Conn. 2000).
571 Pub. L. No. 103-394, 108 Stat. 4106 (1994).
572 28 U.S.C. § 158(b)(1).
573 28 U.S.C. § 158(b)(1).
574 The First Circuit panel hears appeals from all districts in the circuit. The Sixth Circuit appellate panel hears appeals arising only in the Northern and Southern Districts of Ohio. The Eighth Circuit panel hears appeals arising anywhere in the circuit except the districts of North Dakota and South Dakota. The Ninth Circuit panel hears appeals from all districts. The Tenth Circuit's panel hears appeals arising throughout the circuit except for those arising in the District of Colorado.
575 28 U.S.C. § 158 (b)(5).

However, this election must be made in a separate written statement filed at the time of filing the appeal.[576] The appellee may elect to go to district court up to thirty days after *service* of the notice of appeal.[577] If neither party affirmatively elects to go to district court, the parties are deemed to have consented to a bankruptcy appellate panel hearing the appeal.

An appeal from the bankruptcy court may be taken with respect to any final order. It may also be taken, either to the district court or if appropriate an appellate panel, from an interlocutory order, if leave of the district court or the appellate panel is granted.[578] However, it takes exceptional circumstances to justify an interlocutory appeal,[579] especially given the right to move for withdrawal of a proceeding to the district court prior to the bankruptcy court's decision.[580] It is clear that unlike the district court, the bankruptcy court does not have the power to certify an interlocutory order for immediate appeal.[581] And once an appeal is taken to district court, the district court may not function as a trial level bankruptcy court and presumably may not withdraw the reference.[582]

Thus far, the only court of appeals to rule on the matter has found the bankruptcy appellate panels to be constitutional. Because the decision of the appellate panel is reviewed de novo in any further appeal to the court of appeals, the Ninth Circuit discerned no constitutional infirmity in a panel deciding appeals initially as an adjunct to the court of appeals.[583]

14.9.2 Direct Appeal from Bankruptcy Court to Court of Appeals

Section 158(d)(2) of title 28 permits direct appeals from the bankruptcy court to the court of appeals in certain limited circumstances, but only if authorized by the court of appeals after the filing of a petition for such an appeal. A direct appeal may be requested at any time after the notice of appeal is filed if either the court (which may be the bankruptcy court, the district court, or the bankruptcy appellate panel)[584] or all of the parties to the appeal acting jointly certify that:

- The judgment, order, or decree involves a question as to which there is no controlling circuit or Supreme Court authority or a matter of public importance; or
- The judgment, order, or decree involves a question of law requiring resolution of conflicting decisions; or
- An immediate appeal may materially advance the progress of the case or proceeding in which the appeal is taken.[585]

The court must make such a certification if it receives a request for it made by a majority of the appellants and a majority of the appellees, and may make such a certification if it determines it is true, either on its own motion or upon the request of a party filed within sixty days of entry of the judgment, order, or decree.[586]

---

576 28 U.S.C. § 158(c)(1)(A); Fed. R. Bankr. P. 8001(e); Official Form 17 (reprinted in Appx. D, *infra*). *See In re* Hupp, 383 B.R. 476 (B.A.P. 9th Cir. 2008) (document that also sought direct appeal by court of appeals was not a separate document meeting requirement of Bankruptcy Rule 8001(e)).

For a sample election form, see Form 108, Appx. G.10, *infra*. *See In re* Ioane, 227 B.R. 181 (B.A.P. 9th Cir. 1998) (statement of election filed after notice of appeal not timely even though notice of appeal was premature and was not deemed filed until date of judgment, which was after statement of election); *In re* Sullivan Jewelry, Inc., 218 B.R. 439 (B.A.P. 8th Cir. 1998) (statement in notice of appeal that appeal was to district court did not satisfy requirement of separate written statement); *In re* County of Orange, 183 B.R. 593 (B.A.P. 9th Cir. 1995). *See also In re* Brown, 273 B.R. 194 (B.A.P. 8th Cir. 2002) (appellate panel did not have jurisdiction over debtor's appeal when creditor had elected to have its closely interwoven appeal from same order heard by district court).

577 28 U.S.C. § 158(c)(1)(B). *See In re* Snell, 237 B.R. 636 (B.A.P. 6th Cir. 1999) (cross-appellants had to file statement with their cross-appeal, so statement filed one day thereafter was not effective, nor was statement in notice of cross-appeal, because it was not a separate statement); *In re* King, 235 B.R. 658 (B.A.P. 10th Cir. 1999) (time runs from date of service of notice of appeal by court); *In re* Mackey, 232 B.R. 784 (B.A.P. 9th Cir. 1999) (thirty-day period extended by three days under Fed. R. Bankr. P. 9006(e) when notice of appeal served by mail).

578 No certification by the bankruptcy court is required. *In re* Bertoli, 812 F.2d 136 (3d Cir. 1987).

579 *In re* Wood & Locker, Inc., 868 F.2d 139 (5th Cir. 1989); *In re* Nat'l Shoes, 20 B.R. 672 (B.A.P. 1st Cir. 1982); Patrick v. Dell Fin. Servs., 366 B.R. 378 (M.D. Pa. 2007) (interlocutory appeal should be allowed only if: (1) a controlling question of law is involved; (2) the question is one on which there is a substantial ground for difference of opinion; and (3) an immediate appeal would materially advance the ultimate termination of the litigation); *In re* Hooker Investments, Inc., 122 B.R. 659 (S.D.N.Y. 1991) (interlocutory appeal permitted from order setting bar date for proofs of claim). *See also In re* Chateaugay Corp., 876 F.2d 8 (2d Cir. 1989) (court of appeals has jurisdiction to review a district court decision that a particular order is interlocutory; presumably a reversal would mandate remand to district court for full consideration of the appeal); *In re* Johns-Manville Corp., 42 B.R. 651 (S.D.N.Y. 1984).

580 28 U.S.C. § 157(d).

581 Commerce Bank v. Mountain View Vill., Inc., 5 F.3d 34 (3d Cir. 1993).

582 *In re* Powelson, 878 F.2d 976 (7th Cir. 1989) (writ of mandamus issued directing district court to determine appeal of confirmation order rather than withdraw reference and substitute alternative non-appealable "interim" plan). *See* Dallas v. S.A.G., Inc., 836 F.2d 1307 (11th Cir. 1988) (district court may not open default judgment on appeal when the issue had not been raised before the bankruptcy court); *In re* Davis, 169 B.R. 285 (E.D.N.Y. 1994) (district court deciding appeal could not consider new evidence not presented in bankruptcy court).

583 *In re* Burley, 738 F.2d 981 (9th Cir. 1984). *See also In re* Salter, 279 B.R. 278 (B.A.P. 9th Cir. 2002) (bankruptcy appellate panel was court "established by Act of Congress" and had authority under All Writs Act to issue writ of mandamus). *But see In re* Dartmouth Hous. Nursing Home, Inc., 30 B.R. 56 (B.A.P. 1st Cir. 1983), *aff'd on other grounds*, 726 F.2d 26 (1st Cir. 1984).

584 The court that is required to certify the appeal, under Federal Rule of Bankruptcy Procedure 8001(f)(2), is the court where the case is pending. That court is the bankruptcy court until the record on appeal has been filed with the district court or appellate panel. *In re* Frye, 389 B.R. 87 (B.A.P. 9th Cir. 2008).

585 28 U.S.C. § 158(d)(2)(A).

586 28 U.S.C. § 158(d)(2)(B).

Bankruptcy Rule 8001(f) provides procedures to be followed and directs that a certification of appeal shall be filed using Official Form 24.[587]

Courts of appeal have shown varying degrees of receptivity to direct appeals. While some requests for direct appeal have been granted, one court of appeals denying a direct appeal opined that it would most likely be granted when there is uncertainty in the bankruptcy court or when the bankruptcy court's decision was either manifestly correct or incorrect, and would be less likely to be granted when issues would benefit from percolation through the normal appeal process.[588]

14.9.3 Appeals from the District Court or Appellate Panel

Appeals from the district courts, whether in their trial or appellate capacities and from bankruptcy appellate panels in all matters decided by them, are heard in the courts of appeals.[589] Final decisions, judgments, orders and decrees may be appealed from the district court acting in its appellate capacity or from an appellate panel.[590] It is now clear that district court decisions on appeals of interlocutory bankruptcy orders are also appealable to the court of appeals.[591]

Presumably, the normal federal appellate jurisdictional statutes[592] and rules apply to appeals from the district court when it acts as a trial court or decides cases in which it has received recommended findings from the bankruptcy court.[593] Similarly, the appeals court retains its authority to issue *mandamus* and to exercise its supervisory authority over lower courts in bankruptcy matters originating either in bankruptcy or district court.[594] In at least one case, this supervisory authority was exercised to treat an appeal from an order found to be interlocutory as a request for a writ of *mandamus* and thereby to hear the appeal on its merits.[595]

---

587 *See* Appx. D, *supra.*
588 Weber v. United States Tr., 484 F.3d 154 (2d Cir. 2007). *See also In re* Davis, 512 F.3d 856 (6th Cir. 2008) (direct appeal denied when it would not advance litigation and extent of conflict unclear).
589 28 U.S.C. § 158(d).
  Exceptions are a district court's review of a bankruptcy court order either granting or denying a motion to dismiss or suspend proceedings, 11 U.S.C. § 305(a),(c), and certain decisions to abstain, 28 U.S.C. § 1334(d), or remand, 28 U.S.C. § 1441(e)(5), 1452(b), which may not be reviewed by a court of appeals. *See In re* Axona Int'l Credit & Commerce Ltd., 924 F.2d 31 (2d Cir. 1991).
590 28 U.S.C. § 158(d). *See In re* Kujawa, 323 F.3d 628 (8th Cir. 2003) (bankruptcy appellate panel decision dismissing appeal because order appealed was not a final order was itself a final order that could be appealed); *In re* Johns-Manville Corp., 920 F.2d 121 (2d Cir. 1990) (court of appeals determines first whether bankruptcy court order final and, second, whether district court's disposition rendered matter non-appealable); *In re* Frederick Petroleum Corp., 912 F.2d 850 (6th Cir. 1990) (court of appeals had no jurisdiction unless district court certified that its partial disposition was final under Rule 54(b)).
  However, in some cases the collateral order doctrine may be invoked to allow appeals of non-final orders. To come within the collateral order doctrine a district court order must conclusively determine a disputed question, resolving an important issue that is completely severed from the merits of the action and effectively unreviewable on appeal from final judgment. *See In re* Looney, 823 F.2d 788 (4th Cir. 1987) (order continuing automatic stay entered without hearing).
  Several courts of appeal have held that constitutional issues related to the Bankruptcy Code do not present reviewable collateral orders when decided by the district court. *In re* Koerner, 800 F.2d 1358 (5th Cir. 1986); *In re* Moens, 800 F.2d 173 (7th Cir. 1986); *In re* Benny, 791 F.2d 712 (9th Cir. 1986). *But see In re* Parklane/ Atlanta Joint Venture, 927 F.2d 532 (11th Cir. 1991) (appeal of interlocutory order withdrawing reference allowed under collateral order doctrine when constitutional issues were asserted as grounds for order).
591 28 U.S.C. § 1292(b); Conn. Nat'l Bank v. Germain, 503 U.S. 249, 112 S. Ct. 1146, 117 L. Ed. 2d 391 (1992).
  However, the district court must clearly indicate its intent to certify the decision for appeal. Askanase v. Livingwell, Inc., 981 F.2d 807 (2d Cir. 1993) (district court's characterization of order as "appealable" without any reference to Fed. R. Civ. P. 54(b) was not sufficient). *But see In re* Watman, 304 B.R. 553 (B.A.P. 1st Cir. 2004) (section 1292(b) does not apply to decisions of a bankruptcy appellate panel reviewing a bankruptcy court decision).
592 28 U.S.C. §§ 1291, 1292. *See In re* Am. Safety Indem. Co., 502 F.3d 70 (2d Cir. 2007) (court had no jurisdiction over appeal filed more than thirty days after judgment, even though district court made a technical correction to judgment less than thirty days before notice of appeal filed).
593 *See* Fed. R. App. P. 6(a); Metro Transp. Co. v. N. Star Reinsurance Co., 912 F.2d 672 (3d Cir. 1990) (when an issue was decided solely by the district court and not as a result of appeal from bankruptcy court, court of appeals would review based on general appellate jurisdictional statutes); *In re* Bishop, Baldwin, Rewald, Dillingham & Wong, 856 F.2d 78 (9th Cir. 1988); *In re* Haw. Corp., 796 F.2d 1139 (9th Cir. 1986); *In re* Manoa Fin. Co., 781 F.2d 1370 (9th Cir. 1986); *In re* Amatex Corp., 755 F.2d 1034 (3d Cir. 1985). *See also In re* Topco, 894 F.2d 727 (5th Cir. 1990) (when district court sits as trial court on bankruptcy matter, thirty-day time limit on appeals governs an appeal to court of appeals, under both 28 U.S.C. § 158(d) and § 1291; Browning v. Navarro, 887 F.2d 553 (5th Cir. 1989) (compliance with time limits in appellate rules required on appeal from interlocutory order of district court sitting as bankruptcy court); *In re* Apex Oil Co., 884 F.2d 343 (8th Cir. 1989) (district court has no jurisdiction over appeal from bankruptcy court order signed by a district judge); *In re* Barrier, 776 F.2d 1298 (5th Cir. 1985) (mandamus jurisdiction); *In re* Orbitec Corp., 520 F.2d 358 (2d Cir. 1975) (party seeking extension of time to file appeal under Fed. R. App. P. 4(a)(5) should file a protective appeal within extension period sought, as neither lower court nor appellate court has power under that rule to permit filing of appeal more than thirty days after original deadline).
594 *See In re* Furlong, 885 F.2d 815 (11th Cir. 1989) (exceptional circumstances justify appeals court in exercising supervisory authority to set aside bankruptcy court judgment when non-participating parties may not have received proper notice); *In re* Powelson, 878 F.2d 976 (7th Cir. 1989) (writ of *mandamus* issued directing district court to determine bankruptcy appeal rather than withdraw reference). *See also In re* Pruitt, 910 F.2d 1160 (3d Cir. 1990) (order withdrawing reference non-appealable, but *mandamus* would issue when district court improperly withdrew reference after bankruptcy court had already dismissed case); *In re* Durability, Inc., 893 F.2d 264 (10th Cir. 1990) (court may retain jurisdiction over appeal of non-final order to allow parties an opportunity to obtain resolution of the remaining issues in bankruptcy court and thus render order final).
595 *In re* Hooker Inv., Inc., 937 F.2d 833 (2d Cir. 1991) (dismissing

14.9.4 What Is a Final Order?

No issue has been more frequently litigated in bankruptcy appeals than the initial jurisdictional issue of whether a final order exists from which an appeal may be taken to the court of appeals, or to a district court or appellate panel without leave of court. There is no statutory provision explaining what is or is not a final order, judgment, or decree, but a wealth of case law does exist. A final order is "one which ends the litigation . . . and leaves nothing for the court to do but execute the judgment."[596]

Generally, the courts of appeal agree that orders granting or denying injunctions, including orders granting or denying relief from the automatic stay, and orders conferring rights in specific property are appealable.[597] Similarly, a district court order reversing a final order of the bankruptcy court is appealable, unless further factual development is necessary.[598] The circuit courts have also considered as final orders an order to produce allegedly privileged materials,[599] a district court's reversal of an order denying a right to intervene in a proceeding[600] or an order dismissing a dischargeability proceeding,[601] an order confirming a debtor's plan,[602] an order for relief in an involuntary case,[603] an order dismissing an involuntary bankruptcy petition,[604] an order granting priority status,[605] an order avoiding a transfer,[606] an order granting or dismissing a complaint seeking a determination as to ownership of property,[607] an order disallowing an exemption,[608] an order fixing the amount of a creditor's claims,[609] an order granting a default judgment against debtor as a discovery sanction on a complaint to deny discharge,[610] a civil contempt order,[611] and an order of a district court erroneously concluding that it has no jurisdiction to review a final order of a bankruptcy court.[612] Other orders which have been held final include an order fixing venue for product liability cases,[613] an order confirming a judicial sale of property of the estate,[614] an order regarding obligations upon

---

appeal and denying implied request for *mandamus*).

596 Catlin v. United States, 324 U.S. 229, 233, 65 S. Ct. 631, 89 L. Ed. 911 (1945). *See In re* Brown, 484 F.3d 1116 (9th Cir. 2007) (minute entry stating that motion for summary judgment was granted, and taking under advisement a related motion for sanctions, was not final order); *In re* Boca Arena, 184 F.3d 1285 (11th Cir. 1999) (order that does not dispose of all claims of all parties not a final order); *In re* Cont'l Airlines, Inc., 932 F.2d 282 (3d Cir. 1991) (various factors applicable to determination of whether a bankruptcy order is final include impact of issue on assets of bankruptcy estate, whether fact-finding is complete, preclusive effect of decision on merits and judicial economy).

597 *See, e.g.*, FRG, Inc. v. Manley, 919 F.2d 850 (3d Cir. 1990) (order equivalent to denial of motion for relief from stay); *In re* Sonnax Indus., Inc., 907 F.2d 1280 (2d Cir. 1990) (denial of motion for relief from stay); *In re* Apex Oil Co., 884 F.2d 343 (8th Cir. 1989) (denial of motion to lift stay); *In re* W. Elecs., Inc., 852 F.2d 79 (3d Cir. 1988) (denial of motion to lift stay); *In re* La. World Exposition, Inc., 832 F.2d 1391 (5th Cir. 1987) (denial of injunction); Turshen v. Chapman, 823 F.2d 836 (4th Cir. 1987); *In re* Moody, 817 F.2d 365 (5th Cir. 1987) (turnover order); *In re* Sun Valley Foods Co., 801 F.2d 186 (6th Cir. 1986); *In re* Boomgarden, 780 F.2d 657 (7th Cir. 1985); *In re* Kemble, 776 F.2d 802 (9th Cir. 1985); *In re* Feit & Drexler, 760 F.2d 406 (2d Cir. 1985); *In re* Leimer, 724 F.2d 744 (8th Cir. 1984); *In re* Comer, 716 F.2d 168 (3d Cir. 1983); *In re* Maiorino, 691 F.2d 89 (2d Cir. 1982). *See also In re* Fugazy Express, 982 F.2d 769 (2d Cir. 1992) (parties could not agree to act in derogation of the stay and then argue that bankruptcy court order disapproving those actions was a denial of relief from the stay); *In re* Lomas Fin. Corp., 932 F.2d 147 (2d Cir. 1991) (when ambiguity exists on request for injunctive relief, appellate court can direct parties to seek supplemental statement before deciding whether order is final). *But see In re* Henriquez, 261 B.R. 67 (B.A.P. 1st Cir. 2001) (order denying relief from stay not always a final order). *Cf. In re* Regency Wood Apartments, Ltd., 686 F.2d 899 (11th Cir. 1982) (district court's reversal of order denying relief from automatic stay not appealable when district court simply directed further proceedings).

598 *In re* Gardner, 810 F.2d 87 (6th Cir. 1987); *In re* Stanton, 766 F.2d 1283 (9th Cir. 1985); *In re* Marin Motor Oil, Inc., 689 F.2d 445 (3d Cir. 1982); *In re* Cross, 666 F.2d 873 (5th Cir. 1982).

599 *In re* Int'l Horizons, Inc., 689 F.2d 996 (11th Cir. 1982).

600 *In re* Benny, 791 F.2d 712 (9th Cir. 1986); *In re* Marin Motor Oil, Inc., 689 F.2d 445 (3d Cir. 1982).

601 *In re* Dominguez, 51 F.3d 1502 (9th Cir. 1995).

602 *See In re* Maiorino, 691 F.2d 89 (2d Cir. 1982). *But see In re* McKinney, 610 F.3d 399 (7th Cir. 2010) (order denying objection to confirmation was not final when bankruptcy court had not yet decided on interest rate and other issues regarding creditor's claim under confirmed plan).

603 *In re* McGinnis, 296 F.3d 730 (8th Cir. 2002); *In re* Mason, 709 F.2d 1313 (9th Cir. 1983).

604 *In re* Sweet Transfer & Storage, Inc., 896 F.2d 1189 (9th Cir. 1990).

605 *In re* Olson, 730 F.2d 1109 (8th Cir. 1984); *In re* Saco Local Dev. Corp., 711 F.2d 441 (1st Cir. 1983).

606 *In re* Allen, 816 F.2d 325 (7th Cir. 1987); *In re* Sandy Ridge Oil Co., 807 F.2d 1332 (7th Cir. 1987).

607 Commerce Bank v. Mountain View Vill., Inc., 5 F.3d 34 (3d Cir. 1993) (order determining that rents were not property of the estate); *In re* Ellsworth, 722 F.2d 1448 (9th Cir. 1984); *In re* Bestmann, 720 F.2d 484 (8th Cir. 1983). *But see In re* Morrell, 880 F.2d 855 (5th Cir. 1989) (order determining ownership of property not final when related damage claim remains unresolved).

608 *In re* England, 975 F.2d 1168 (10th Cir. 1992); *In re* Slimick, 928 F.2d 304 (9th Cir. 1990); *In re* Barker, 768 F.2d 191 (7th Cir. 1985); *In re* White, 727 F.2d 884 (9th Cir. 1984); *In re* Woods, 288 B.R. 220 (B.A.P. 8th Cir. 2003). *But see In re* Wisz, 778 F.2d 762 (11th Cir. 1985).

609 *In re* Perry, 391 F.3d 282 (1st Cir. 2004) (order overruling objection to claim is appealable); *In re* Stoecker, 5 F.3d 1022 (7th Cir. 1993) (order establishing that creditor had secured claim in certain amount); *In re* Moody, 849 F.2d 902 (5th Cir. 1988); *In re* Colley, 814 F.2d 1008 (5th Cir. 1987); *In re* Morse Elec. Co., 805 F.2d 262 (7th Cir. 1986). *See also In re* Unroe, 937 F.2d 346 (7th Cir. 1991) (order denying objection to claim is final even though debtor's contempt proceeding against same creditor remained pending); Walsh Trucking v. Ins. Co. of N. Am., 838 F.2d 698 (3d Cir. 1988) (order expunging creditor's claim is final order).

610 *In re* Golant, 239 F.3d 931 (7th Cir. 2001).

611 *In re* United States Abatement Corp., 39 F.3d 563 (5th Cir. 1984) (civil contempt order not "final" for purposes of appeal unless two actions occur: (1) a finding of contempt is issued; and (2) an appropriate sanction is imposed).

612 *In re* Bestmann, 720 F.2d 484 (8th Cir. 1983).

613 A.H. Robins Co. v. Piccinin, 788 F.2d 994 (4th Cir. 1986).

614 *In re* Met-L-Wood Corp., 861 F.2d 1012 (7th Cir. 1988). *See also In re* Fin. News Network, Inc., 931 F.2d 217 (2d Cir. 1991) (district court's order remanding to bankruptcy court for consideration of

rejection of a lease,[615] an order holding that a debtor could not designate how payments to the Internal Revenue Service should be credited,[616] an order determining that a lease had not been properly terminated,[617] a decision to abstain from hearing personal injury claims against the debtor,[618] and an order denying a motion to dismiss for bad faith.[619]

There is an apparent split in authority over whether the refusal to confirm a plan, when the case is not dismissed, is appealable.[620] Similar issues would be raised with respect to denial of a motion to modify a plan.[621]

An order denying a trustee's motion to convert a case from chapter 13 to chapter 7 has been held non-appealable,[622] as has a district court decision reversing a summary judgment order in favor of a creditor defendant in a preference action,[623] an order denying summary judgment,[624] an order holding a landlord to be adequately protected,[625] orders remanding cases for further consideration, unless the remand is for the bankruptcy court to perform purely ministerial tasks,[626] an order withdrawing a case to district court and changing venue,[627] an order refusing to withdraw the reference,[628] an order setting a trial date,[629] an order denying approval of a settlement agreement,[630] an order dismissing one count of a counterclaim,[631] an order dismissing

---

competing disqualified bid is not a final order).

615 *In re* Vause, 886 F.2d 794 (6th Cir. 1989) (court may hear appeal by landlord regarding future damages due for rejection of lease even though debtor's prepetition obligation on lease was not yet fixed); Saravia v. 1736 18th St., N.W. Ltd. P'ship, 844 F.2d 823 (D.C. Cir. 1988) (order relieved debtor of obligation to comply with local housing code).

616 *In re* Technical Knockout Graphics, Inc., 833 F.2d 797 (9th Cir. 1987).

617 *In re* Mkt. Square Inn, Inc., 978 F.2d 116 (3d Cir. 1992).

618 *In re* Pan Am. Corp., 950 F.2d 839 (2d Cir. 1991).

619 Brown v. First Jersey Nat'l Bank, 916 F.2d 120 (3d Cir. 1990). *But see In re* Rega Properties, Ltd., 894 F.2d 1136 (9th Cir. 1990) (order denying motion to dismiss petition as filed in bad faith was not final order). But see also cases cited below finding orders denying motions to dismiss non-appealable.

620 *Compare* Lewis v. Farmers Home Admin., 992 F.2d 767 (8th Cir. 1993) (order denying confirmation of chapter 13 plan and setting forth elements of acceptable plan was not final); *In re* Simons, 908 F.2d 643 (10th Cir. 1990) (denial of confirmation without dismissal of underlying case was not final and appealable); Travelers v. KCC-Leawood Corporate Manor I, 908 F.2d 343 (8th Cir. 1990) (district court order finding that bankruptcy court had implicitly denied confirmation and remanding case to bankruptcy court was not final appealable order) *and In re* Maiorino, 691 F.2d 89 (2d Cir. 1982) (refusal to confirm is interlocutory order) *with In re* Foster, 670 F.2d 478 (5th Cir. 1982) (appeal of refusal to confirm plan heard by court of appeals).

621 *See In re* Vincent, 301 B.R. 734 (B.A.P. 8th Cir. 2003) (order denying modification motion not final order).

622 *In re* Kutner, 656 F.2d 1107, 1112 (5th Cir. 1981); *In re* Hayes Bankruptcy, 220 B.R. 57 (N.D. Iowa 1998).

623 *In re* Emerald Oil Co., 694 F.2d 88 (5th Cir. 1982).

624 City of New York v. Exxon Corp., 932 F.2d 1020 (2d Cir. 1991) (order granting partial summary judgment not appealable); *In re* Durability, Inc., 893 F.2d 264 (10th Cir. 1990) (order granting only partial summary judgment); *In re* Smith, 735 F.2d 459 (11th Cir. 1984).

625 *In re* Alchar Hardware, 730 F.2d 1386 (11th Cir. 1984).

626 *In re* Holland, 539 F.3d 563 (7th Cir. 2008) (district court order ruling that Florida exemption law applied was not final because debtor's exemptions remained to be decided on remand); *In re* St. Charles Preservation Investors, Ltd., 916 F.2d 727 (D.C. Cir. 1990) (order remanding case to bankruptcy court to determine rights and priorities of creditors was not final and appealable); Capital Credit Plan of Tenn., Inc. v. Shaffer, 912 F.2d 749 (4th Cir. 1990) (district court order affirming bankruptcy court order confirming plan and remanding two issues to bankruptcy court for resolution was not final decision); *In re* Bucyrus Grain Co., 905 F.2d 1362 (10th Cir. 1990) (district court's reversal of bankruptcy court's grant of relief from stay and remand for determination of amount of creditor's claim required significant further proceedings and was not final); *In re* M.S.V., Inc., 892 F.2d 5 (1st Cir. 1989); *In re* Schneider, 873 F.2d 1155 (8th Cir. 1989) (remand for bankruptcy court to determine proper interest rate not appealable); *In re* Dixie Broad., Inc., 871 F.2d 1023 (11th Cir. 1989) (remand for bankruptcy court to determine whether bankruptcy was brought in bad faith not appealable final order); *In re* Gould & Eberhart Gear Mach. Corp., 852 F.2d 26 (1st Cir. 1988); *In re* Miscott Corp., 848 F.2d 1190 (11th Cir. 1988) (remand for further factual development in regard to award of attorney fees); Bowers v. Conn. Nat'l Bank, 847 F.2d 1019 (2d Cir. 1988); *In re* Briglevich, 847 F.2d 759 (11th Cir. 1988); *In re* Vekco, 792 F.2d 744 (8th Cir. 1986) (but order requiring remand could be final order if only ministerial tasks remain to be performed in the bankruptcy case); *In re* County Mgmt., Inc., 788 F.2d 311 (5th Cir. 1986); *In re* Commercial Contractors, Inc., 771 F.2d 1373 (10th Cir. 1985); *In re* Stanton, 766 F.2d 1283 (9th Cir. 1985); *In re* Fox, 762 F.2d 54 (7th Cir. 1985); *In re* Goldblatt Bros., Inc., 758 F.2d 1248 (7th Cir. 1985); *In re* Riggsby, 745 F.2d 1153 (7th Cir. 1984); *In re* Martinez, 721 F.2d 262 (9th Cir. 1983); *In re* Bassak, 705 F.2d 234 (7th Cir. 1983); *In re* Hansen, 702 F.2d 728 (8th Cir. 1983) (order remanding for de novo trial); *In re* Glover, 697 F.2d 907 (10th Cir. 1983) (order remanding for further consideration of priority issue); *In re* Compton Corp., 889 F.2d 1104 (Temp. Emer. Ct. App. 1989) (order reversing judgment subordinating creditor's claim not final, because bankruptcy court had to determine amount of claim on remand). *See also In re* Harrington, 992 F.2d 3 (1st Cir. 1993) (order remanding case to permit bankruptcy court to docket notice of appeal); *In re* Grey, 902 F.2d 1479 (10th Cir. 1990) (court of appeals had jurisdiction to consider issues raised by debtor even though debtor did not appeal as to those issues until after district court's post-remand order); *In re* Brown, 803 F.2d 120 (3d Cir. 1986) (district court order finding creditor in violation of the automatic stay, but remanding for determination of damages held non-final). *But see In re* Dominguez, 51 F.3d 1502 (9th Cir. 1995) (permitting appeal of order reversing dismissal of a dischargeability proceeding).

627 Good v. Voest-Alpine Industries, Inc., 398 F.3d 918 (7th Cir. 2005) (order withdrawing reference not appealable); *In re* Pruitt, 910 F.2d 1160 (3d Cir. 1990) (order withdrawing reference non-appealable, but *mandamus* would issue when district court improperly withdrew reference after bankruptcy court had already dismissed case); *In re* Dalton, 733 F.2d 710 (10th Cir. 1984). *See also In re* U.S. Lines, 216 F.3d 228 (2d Cir. 2000) (determination concerning venue for claims against debtor not final order); *In re* King Mem'l Hosp., 767 F.2d 1508 (11th Cir. 1985) (order withdrawing reference of adversary proceeding). *But see In re* Parklane/Atlanta Joint Venture, 927 F.2d 532 (11th Cir. 1991) (order withdrawing reference in particular case was appealable under collateral order exception to final judgment rule).

628 *In re* The Kissel Co., 105 F.3d 1324 (9th Cir. 1997); Allegheny Int'l v. Allegheny Ludlum Steel Corp., 920 F.2d 1127 (3d Cir. 1990); *In re* Lieb, 915 F.2d 180 (5th Cir. 1990); *In re* Mem'l Estates, 837 F.2d 762 (7th Cir. 1988); *In re* Chateaugay Corp., 826 F.2d 1177 (3d Cir. 1987). *See* § 14.9.3, *supra*.

629 Gold v. Johns-Manville, 723 F.2d 1068 (3d Cir. 1983).

630 *In re* Tidewater Group, Inc., 734 F.2d 794 (11th Cir. 1984).

631 *In re* King City Transit Mix, Inc., 738 F.2d 1065 (9th Cir. 1984). *See*

Litigating in the Bankruptcy Court § 14.9.5

less than all claims,[632] an order denying a motion to dismiss,[633] and an order denying a stay of state court proceedings to a bankruptcy debtor's codefendant.[634] Other orders which have been held non-final include interlocutory sanctions orders,[635] a refusal to permit rejection of a labor contract,[636] an order granting a jury trial in the bankruptcy court,[637] an order denying a jury trial,[638] an order denying motions to compel trustee performance,[639] an order dismissing a claim for punitive damages,[640] an order permitting a prejudgment attachment and the equivalent of a *lis pendens*,[641] an order rejecting an assertion of sovereign immunity,[642] an order granting a stay pending appeal,[643] an order granting an extension of time to file a proof of claim,[644] a discovery order,[645] and an order extending time for filing complaints objecting to chapter 7 discharge.[646]

14.9.5 Procedure on Appeals

Procedure on appeals from the district court and from the appellate panels is governed by the Federal Rules of Appellate Procedure.[647] For example, an appeal to a court of appeals may be dismissed as to parties who are not named in the notice of appeal.[648] The appellate rules incorporate Federal Rule of Bankruptcy Procedure 8015, however, which applies to motions for rehearing of district court or appellate panel decisions. Such motions must be timely filed pursuant to Federal Rule of Bankruptcy Procedure 9006(a).[649]

The procedure on appeals from the bankruptcy court to the district court or bankruptcy appellate panel is governed primarily by the Federal Rules of Bankruptcy Procedure.[650] The statute specifically states that appeals must be taken in the fourteen-day time period provided by Federal Rule of Bankruptcy Procedure 8002.[651] This fourteen-day deadline is jurisdictional[652] and cannot be waived, though it may be extended by the bankruptcy court for up to twenty-one days.[653] If a party

---

also *In re* White Beaty View, Inc., 841 F.2d 524 (3d Cir. 1988) (summary judgment against one defendant not a final order when claims against other defendant, counterclaims and crossclaim remain to be decided).

632 *In re* Tri-Valley Distrib., 533 F.3d 1209 (10th Cir. 2008).
633 *In re* Vlasek, 325 F.3d 955 (7th Cir. 2003); *In re* Allen, 896 F.2d 416 (9th Cir. 1990) (denial of motion to dismiss involuntary case); *In re* Phillips, 844 F.2d 230 (5th Cir. 1988); *In re* Greene County Hosp., 835 F.2d 589 (5th Cir. 1988); *In re* Empresas Noroeste Inc., 806 F.2d 315 (1st Cir. 1986); *In re* Benny, 791 F.2d 712 (9th Cir. 1986); John E. Burns Drilling v. Cent. Bank of Denver, 739 F.2d 1489 (10th Cir. 1984). *See also In re* Bowman, 821 F.2d 245 (5th Cir. 1987) (order reversing dismissal of case); *In re* Andy Frain Servs., Inc., 798 F.2d 1113 (7th Cir. 1986) (order refusing to dismiss a chapter 11 case held non-appealable); *In re* 405 N. Bedford Dr. Corp., 778 F.2d 1374 (9th Cir. 1985). *But see* McDow v. Dudley, 662 F.3d 284 (4th Cir. 2011) (denial of § 707(b) motion to dismiss was final order); *In re* Ross-Tousey, 549 F.3d 1148, 1153 (7th Cir. 2008) (denial of motion to dismiss chapter 7 case was final order); *In re* Geberegeorgis, 310 B.R. 61 (B.A.P. 6th Cir. 2004) (permitting appeal of order vacating dismissal of case).
634 Evilsizor v. Eagle-Picher Indus., Inc., 725 F.2d 97 (10th Cir. 1984); Lynch v. Johns-Manville Sales Corp., 701 F.2d 43, 44 (6th Cir. 1983). *See also In re* Hester, 899 F.2d 361 (5th Cir. 1990) (district court order denying stay pending appeal of bankruptcy court order was not final).
635 Klestadt & Winters, L.L.P. v. Cangelosi, 672 F.3d 809 (9th Cir. 2012) (sanctions order not final when not completely separable from merits of case); *In re* Watson, 884 F.2d 879 (5th Cir. 1989) (sanctions order is interlocutory pending final judgment); *In re* Jeanette Corp., 832 F.2d 43 (3d Cir. 1987). *See also In re* Behrens, 900 F.2d 97 (7th Cir. 1990) (order finding violation of discharge injunction not final when bankruptcy court never set amount of damages or fees for which it found creditor liable).
636 *In re* Landmark Hotel & Casino, 872 F.2d 857 (9th Cir. 1989).
637 *In re* Bowers-Siemon Chemicals Co., 123 B.R. 821 (N.D. Ill. 1991).
638 *In re* Popkin & Stern, 105 F.3d 1248 (8th Cir. 1997).
639 Algeran Inc. v. Advance Ross Corp., 759 F.2d 1421 (9th Cir. 1985).
640 *In re* Russell, 957 F.2d 534 (8th Cir. 1992).
641 *In re* Unanue Casal, 998 F.2d 28 (1st Cir. 1993).
642 Pullman Constr. Indus., Inc. v. United States, 23 F.3d 1166 (7th Cir. 1994).
643 *In re* Trans World Airlines, 18 F.3d 208 (3d Cir. 1994).
644 *In re* New Life Health Ctr. Co., 102 F.3d 428 (9th Cir. 1996).
645 *In re* Kujawa, 323 F.3d 628 (8th Cir. 2003).
646 *In re* Aucoin, 35 F.3d 167 (5th Cir. 1994); *In re* Gaines, 932 F.2d 729 (8th Cir. 1991).

647 Federal Rule of Appellate Procedure 6 was amended effective December 1, 1989. The rule as amended controls appeals from final decisions of both district courts and bankruptcy appellate panels. Also amended to encompass bankruptcy appeals were Federal Rules of Appellate Procedure 1 and 2. A new Form 5 was added for bankruptcy appeals. *See In re* Worcester, 811 F.2d 1224 (9th Cir. 1987).
648 Fed. R. App. P. 3(c); *In re* Unioil, 948 F.2d 678 (10th Cir. 1991); Barnett v. Stern, 909 F.2d 973 (7th Cir. 1990) (failure to name all parties in notice of appeal, even if included in caption, violates Federal Rule of Appellate Procedure 3(c) and deprives appellate court of jurisdiction over those parties not named).
649 *In re* Eichelberger, 943 F.2d 536 (5th Cir. 1991). *See* Fed. R. App. P. 6(b)(2)(i).
650 As discussed in § 14.9.3, *supra*, procedure on direct appeals from the bankruptcy court to the court of appeals is governed by section 1233 of the 2005 Act, Pub. L. No. 109-08, 119 Stat. 23 (2005), and by Bankruptcy Rule 8001(f).
651 28 U.S.C. § 158(c)(2). *See In re* Burns, 322 F.3d 421 (6th Cir. 2003) (failure to file timely notice of appeal of order cannot be remedied by amending notice of appeal of another order); *In re* Arrowhead Estates Dev. Co., 42 F.3d 1306 (9th Cir. 1994) (notice of appeal filed after the bankruptcy court's oral announcement of decision but before its entry is effective).
652 *In re* Caterbone, 640 F.3d 108 (3d Cir. 2011) (court of appeals had no jurisdiction to hear appeal when district court dismissed appeal based on lack of timely appeal); *In re* Mouradnick, 13 F.3d 326 (9th Cir. 1994) (untimely appeal dismissed for lack of jurisdiction); *In re* Souza, 795 F.2d 855 (9th Cir. 1986) (former ten-day limit to be strictly construed); *In re* Abdallah, 778 F.2d 75 (1st Cir. 1985); *In re* Universal Minerals, 755 F.2d 309 (3d Cir. 1985). *See In re* LBL Sports Ctr., Inc., 684 F.2d 410 (6th Cir. 1982); *In re* Robinson, 640 F.2d 737 (5th Cir. 1981); *In re* Ramsey, 612 F.2d 1220 (9th Cir. 1980). *But see* Fadayro v. Ameriquest Mortgage Co., 371 F.3d 920 (7th Cir. 2004) (fact that timely filed notice of appeal was incorrectly completed did not deprive court of jurisdiction).

As with nonbankruptcy appeals, the time for appeal begins to run from the date the order is entered on the docket. *See* Reid v. White Motor Corp., 886 F.2d 1462 (6th Cir. 1989) (when order is entered on wrong docket, time for appeal does not begin to run until the mistake is corrected).
653 Fed. R. Bankr. P. 8002(c). *See* Moore v. Hogan, 851 F.2d 1125 (8th Cir. 1988) (request for extension on twenty-first day after time for

files a motion under Federal Rule of Bankruptcy Procedure 9023 or 9024 within fourteen days after entry of the judgment, the appeal period is fourteen days from the disposition of that motion.[654] Although the appeal period in bankruptcy was extended from ten days to fourteen days based on the time-computation changes made to the Bankruptcy Rules in 2009, it is still a short period and a decision on whether to appeal must be made relatively quickly.[655] A cross-appeal by any other party must be filed within fourteen days of when a notice of appeal is filed.[656]

Within fourteen days after filing the notice of appeal, the appellant must file with the clerk of the bankruptcy court, and serve on the appellee, a designation of items to be included in the record on appeal and a statement of issues to be presented.[657] If these materials are not timely filed, the appeal may be dismissed.[658] Within fourteen days after the appellant's statement is served, the appellee may file and serve a designation of additional items to be included in the record and a counterstatement of issues.[659] The party designating any item to be included in the record must provide the clerk with a copy of that item; otherwise the clerk prepares a copy at that party's expense.[660]

Other Bankruptcy Rules governing appeals[661] pertain to other aspects of the process, including the deadlines for filing briefs, set by Federal Rule of Bankruptcy Procedure 8009(a), and other matters.[662] The deadline for the appellant's brief is fourteen days after the appeal is docketed in the district court.[663] The appellee's brief, which should also include argument pertinent to any cross-appeal, is due fourteen days after service of the appellant's brief. The appellant may file a reply brief within fourteen days after the appellee's brief and, if there is a cross appeal, the appellee may file a reply brief with respect to the cross appeal within fourteen days after the appellant's reply brief is served. However, the language in 28 U.S.C. § 158(c) stating that appeals from bankruptcy courts are to be "taken in the same manner as appeals in civil proceedings generally taken to the courts of appeals from the district courts" could be interpreted otherwise.

Because an appeal does not operate as a stay of the bankruptcy court order that is being appealed, debtor's counsel should carefully consider the need for a motion for a stay at the time of any appeal, especially if there is any potential that the debtor's property may be sold; there is a strong mootness doctrine in bankruptcy appeals.[664] A motion for a stay pending

---

appeal had run is untimely); *In re* Bradshaw, 283 B.R. 814 (B.A.P. 1st Cir. 2002) (motion for extension faxed to clerk's office after business hours was untimely); *In re* Betacom of Phoenix, Inc., 250 B.R. 376 (B.A.P. 9th Cir. 2000) (party seeking extension of time need not prove "special circumstances").

However, if the appeal is filed by a prisoner it is deemed filed when it is deposited with prison authorities, addressed to clerk of court with postage paid. *In re* Flanagan, 999 F.2d 753 (3d Cir. 1993).

654 Fed. R. Bankr. P. 8002(b); *In re* Watson, 41 F.3d 493 (9th Cir. 1994).

Subsequent motions for reconsideration, though served within fourteen days of the order denying the initial motion for reconsideration but more than fourteen days after the original judgment, do not toll the appeal time on the original judgment. *See In re* Columba, 257 B.R. 368 (B.A.P. 1st Cir. 2001).

655 *See* Fed. R. Bankr. P. 9006(a).
656 Fed. R. Bankr. P. 8002(a).
657 Fed. R. Bankr. P. 8006.
658 *In re* Lynch, 430 F.3d 600 (2d Cir. 2005) (dismissal of appeal for failure to file designation of record and statement of issues not an abuse of discretion); *In re* CPDC, Inc. 221 F.3d 693 (5th Cir. 2000) (untimely filing of statement of issues and incomplete designation of record did not warrant dismissal of appeal when there was no evidence of prejudice to any party); *In re* M.A. Baheth Constr. Co., 118 F.3d 1082 (5th Cir. 1997); *In re* Bulic, 997 F.2d 299 (7th Cir. 1993) (appeal was properly dismissed when debtors failed to file statement of issues or designation of record within former ten day period as required by rules and bankruptcy was a bad faith delaying tactic); *In re* Serra Builders, 970 F.2d 1309 (4th Cir. 1992) (appeal could be dismissed when debtor filed designation of the record for appeal fifteen days late); *In re* Fitzsimmons, 920 F.2d 1468 (9th Cir. 1990) (appeal dismissed due to appellant's bad faith conduct in failing to perfect appeal by delaying in designation and preparation of record); *In re* Champion, 895 F.2d 490 (8th Cir. 1990) (it was not abuse of discretion to dismiss appeal when appellant failed to file a designation of items to be included in record and issues to be presented on appeal required by Bankruptcy Rule 8006). *But see In re* SPR Corp., 45 F.3d 70 (4th Cir. 1995) (court should consider issues of bad faith or negligence, explanation for delay, prejudice to other parties, impact of sanction, and other alternative sanctions before dismissing appeal for untimely filing of statement of issues).

659 Fed. R. Bankr. P. 8006.

660 Fed. R. Bankr. P. 8006.
661 Fed. R. Bankr. P. 8001–8019.
662 *In re* Morrissey, 349 F.3d 1187 (9th Cir. 2003) (affirmance due to appellant's egregious violations of rules not an abuse of discretion); Telesphere Communications v. 900 Unlimited, Inc., 177 F.3d 612 (7th Cir. 1999) (no abuse of discretion in dismissal of appeal for failure to file timely brief); Greco v. Stubenberg, 859 F.2d 1401 (9th Cir. 1988) (appeal dismissed for failure to comply with district court deadlines for procuring relevant transcripts); *In re* Tampa Chain Co., 835 F.2d 54 (2d Cir. 1987) (appeal dismissed for failure to file brief for seven months); *In re* Beverly Mfg. Corp., 778 F.2d 666 (11th Cir. 1985) (improper to dismiss for failure to file brief when failure was caused by delay in processing record); *In re* Thompson, 140 B.R. 979 (N.D. Ill. 1992) (appeal dismissed for negligent failure to designate record and issues on appeal), *aff'd*, 4 F.3d 997 (7th Cir. 1993) (table). *See In re* Scheri, 51 F.3d 71 (7th Cir. 1995) (remanding decision to dismiss appeal for failure to file timely brief so district court could explain basis for determination that dismissal was appropriate sanction); *In re* Hill, 775 F.2d 1385 (9th Cir. 1985) (dismissal of appeal for late filing of brief was abuse of discretion absent consideration of lesser sanctions); *In re* Braniff Airways, Inc., 774 F.2d 1303 (5th Cir. 1985) (appeal dismissed when appellant's brief was long overdue). *See also* Nielsen v. Price, 17 F.3d 1276 (10th Cir. 1994) (debtors' duty to designate record and file brief was not stayed by their second bankruptcy filing after the appeal was filed).

However, it is important to note that the fourteen-day period for filing a brief after an appeal has been docketed with the district court does not begin to run until the clerk gives notice that the appeal has been docketed. Jewelcor, Inc. v. Asia Commercial Co., 11 F.3d 394 (3d Cir. 1993).

663 Fed. R. Bankr. P. 8009(a). *But see In re* Enron Corp., 475 F.3d 131 (2d Cir. 2007) (period for filing brief does not begin to run until notice of docketing is sent to parties).

664 *See* 11 U.S.C. § 363(m); *In re* Sullivan Cent. Plaza, I, Ltd., 914 F.2d

appeal must be presented in the first instance to the trial court.[665]

On most other procedural points, bankruptcy appeals are not significantly different from appeals from any other nonbankruptcy federal order or judgment. The same basic jurisprudential principles apply. For example, new issues generally may not be raised for the first time on appeal from a bankruptcy determination.[666] The appellate court has discretion to take judicial notice of bankruptcy records in the underlying case.[667] Appeals may be dismissed when the party appealing lacks standing to appeal.[668] Claims may be considered abandoned on appeal when they are not briefed.[669]

Under either set of rules, findings of fact by the bankruptcy court are reviewable under a "clearly erroneous" standard.[670] The adoption of this standard, which precludes full review of the case by an Article III court, is a departure from the temporary emergency rule adopted in response to the *Northern Pipeline* case and could not constitutionally apply to a proceeding where the bankruptcy court did not have the power to enter a final judgment.[671]

---

731 (5th Cir. 1990) (when creditor was granted relief from stay and foreclosed on property in question, appeal was moot even if no grounds had existed for original relief from stay); *In re* Mann, 907 F.2d 923 (9th Cir. 1990) (debtor's failure to obtain stay of foreclosure sale pending appeal rendered moot appeal of bankruptcy court's ruling on foreclosure action); *In re* Holywell Corp., 901 F.2d 931 (11th Cir. 1990) (when plan was substantially consummated after debtors failed to post appeal bond, appeal of bankruptcy court decision determining amount of creditor's lien was moot); *In re* Crystal Oil Co., 854 F.2d 79 (5th Cir. 1988) (appeal from confirmation order moot without stay when parties made commitments in reliance on plan); *In re* Onouli-Kona Land Co., 846 F.2d 1170 (9th Cir. 1988); Cent. States, Southeast & Southeast Areas Pension Fund v. Cent. Trans., Inc., 841 F.2d 92 (4th Cir. 1988) (appeal of confirmation order moot because plan was substantially consummated and beyond point of being undone); Miami Ctr. Ltd. P'ship v. Bank of N.Y., 838 F.2d 1547 (11th Cir. 1988) (appeal from confirmation order moot without stay); *In re* Van Ipreen, 819 F.2d 189 (8th Cir. 1987) (sale of collateral rendered appeal moot); *In re* Lashley, 825 F.2d 362 (11th Cir. 1987) (foreclosure sale rendered appeal moot); *In re* Matos, 790 F.2d 864 (11th Cir. 1986); *In re* Ahmed, 420 B.R. 518 (Bankr. C.D. Cal. 2009) (refusing to set aside or vacate chapter 13 discharge entered while appeal from confirmation order was pending because creditor had not obtained stay pending appeal). *But see In re* Seidler, 44 F.3d 945 (11th Cir. 1995) (confirmation of chapter 13 plan did not render moot mortgage holder's appeal of order removing mortgage lien from property); *In re* Met-L-Wood Corp., 861 F.2d 1012 (7th Cir. 1988) (fraud is grounds for setting aside judicial sale even though no stay was sought); *In re* Valley Ranches Inc., 823 F.2d 1373 (9th Cir. 1987) (appeal not moot though property had been sold).

665 Fed. R. Bankr. P. 8005; *In re* Ho, 265 B.R. 603 (B.A.P. 9th Cir. 2001).

666 *In re* E.R. Fegert, Inc., 887 F.2d 955 (9th Cir. 1989).

667 *Id.*

668 Holmes v. Silver Wings Aviation, Inc., 881 F.2d 939 (10th Cir. 1989) (debtors may not appeal attorney fee award which will not affect the total amount paid out under their plan).

669 *In re* Brown Family Farms, Inc., 872 F.2d 139 (6th Cir. 1989).

670 Fed. R. Civ. P. 52(a); Fed. R. Bankr. P. 8013. *See, e.g., In re* Branding Iron Motel, Inc., 798 F.2d 396 (10th Cir. 1986); *In re* Pearson Bros. Co., 787 F.2d 1157 (7th Cir. 1986) (discussing the strict standard for reversal of factual determinations of the bankruptcy court embodied by the "clearly erroneous" test); *In re* X-Cel, Inc., 776 F.2d 130 (7th Cir. 1985). *See also In re* Cornelison, 901 F.2d 1073 (11th Cir. 1990) (when confirmation order merely reproduced language of Bankruptcy Code and did not contain findings of fact, remand was required because no findings could be reviewed); *In re* Revco D. S. Inc., 901 F.2d 1359 (6th Cir. 1990) (remand required for factual finding on "good faith" issue).

671 *See* § 14.2.1, *supra* (discussion of limits on bankruptcy court power).

Chapter 15   The Discharge: Protecting It and Using It

15.1 Introduction

Ultimately, the principal goal of most bankruptcies is the discharge, which frees the debtor from personal liability on almost all debts. It is this clean slate that normally gives debtors the fresh start that bankruptcy is meant to provide. The Bankruptcy Code expanded the protections of the discharge in an effort to help debtors further and to prevent creditors and others from vitiating its benefits.

However, the discharge and its fruits are not quite absolute, nor are they automatic in every bankruptcy case. Under certain limited circumstances the court may deny a discharge, or the discharge may be inapplicable to some debts. Even after it is granted, in rare instances, the discharge may be revoked. Fortunately, many of these occasional pitfalls and roadblocks can be avoided in a well-handled bankruptcy case.

As discussed earlier in this treatise,[1] the procedure for obtaining a discharge is normally quite simple. In a chapter 7 case, a discharge order is usually entered a little over sixty days after the first date set for the meeting of creditors, assuming that the debtor has filed a certificate evidencing completion of the required personal financial management course[2] and that no objection to discharge has been filed by that time.[3] In a chapter 13 case, the discharge is granted after the debtor completes payments under a confirmed plan or upon the court granting a motion by the debtor for a hardship discharge, provided that the debtor has also filed a certificate of completion of the required personal financial management course.[4] In both chapters, the court may choose to hold a discharge hearing, but is not required to do so unless the debtor chooses to reaffirm a debt and the debtor was not represented by an attorney in negotiating the reaffirmation agreement.[5]

This Chapter covers two aspects of the discharge—the difficulties that can arise in obtaining it and the benefits it can provide for consumer clients.

15.2 Objections to Discharge in Chapter 7 Cases

15.2.1 How They Arise

In a chapter 7 case, but not in a chapter 13 case,[6] a serious obstacle may arise from an objection to the discharge. Such objections, which are quite rare, may be raised in a complaint,[7] filed by the United States trustee, the trustee or a creditor.[8] The

---

1 See § 8.8, *supra*.
2 See Chapter 8, *supra*, for discussion of the financial education requirement and possible waiver of the requirement.
3 See Fed. R. Bankr. P. 4004(c).

    Rule 4004(c) also lists several other exceptions to this general rule, such as the filing of a motion under section 707(b) or a request for an extension of time to object to discharge or file such a motion. The discharge may also be delayed under section 522(q) if the debtor is subject to a proceeding that could impact that provision. See § 10.2.3.4.5.6, *supra*.

4 See 11 U.S.C. § 1328; *In re* McCarthy, 391 B.R. 372 (Bankr. N.D. Tex. 2008) (at least when completion of payments was foreseeable result of debtor's sale of property, trustee could not oppose discharge); *In re* Estrad, 322 B.R. 149 (Bankr. E.D. Cal. 2005) (discharge should not be delayed until trustee files final report and account); *In re* Celeste, 310 B.R. 286 (Bankr. D. Md. 2004) (completion of payments accomplished at time when debtor completes payments to trustee, and not when trustee has completed disbursements). If the debtor is subject to an order to pay a domestic support obligation, the debtor must also file a certification that payments have been made under that order. See § 12.3.6.3, *supra*. In some districts, a certification regarding this issue is required of all debtors. The discharge may also be delayed under section 522(q) if the debtor is subject to a proceeding that could impact that provision. See § 10.2.3.4.5.6, *supra*.

5 See 11 U.S.C. § 524(d).
6 The grounds for denial of discharge listed in section 727 only apply in chapter 7 cases. 11 U.S.C. § 103(b). This may be a good reason to start a case under chapter 13 in some instances, or convert to chapter 13 if problems arise. This is not to say, however, that a chapter 13 discharge could not be opposed on the grounds that the plan had not been completed or that a hardship discharge was not warranted. Creditors may also argue, under section 1328(f), that a debtor is not entitled to discharge because of a prior discharge. And, of course, creditors may object earlier to confirmation of the plan. See Ch. 12, *supra*.
7 Fed. R. Bankr. P. 7001. See *In re* Markus, 313 F.3d 1146 (9th Cir. 2002) (*pro se* motion objecting to discharge filed within time limits did not constitute complaint because it did not meet pleading requirements).
8 11 U.S.C. § 727(c)(1).

    A party whose claim has been disallowed is not a creditor entitled to object to discharge. *In re* Vahlsing, 829 F.2d 565 (5th Cir. 1987). See also *In re* Klinger, 301 B.R. 519 (Bankr. N.D. Ill. 2003) (creditor whose claim had already been found nondischargeable had no standing to seek revocation of discharge).

    Similarly, a bankruptcy court may not deny a chapter 7 discharge to the joint debtor spouse of a debtor under section 727(a)(2)(A), regardless of the joint debtor's intent, in the absence of consolidation, when the complaining party is not a creditor of the joint debtor. Warchol v. Barry (*In re* Barry), 451 B.R. 654, 661 (B.A.P. 1st Cir. 2011). And one court has held that a party that purchases a claim from a creditor is not itself a creditor entitled to object to discharge.

451

complaint must be filed within sixty days of the first date set for the meeting of creditors,[9] unless the court, for cause and based upon a motion filed before that time expires, extends the deadline.[10] If a party learns of facts that would be a basis for revocation of discharge before the discharge is actually entered, but after the deadline for objections to discharge, that party may file a prompt motion to extend the time for an objection to discharge under Rule 4004(b)(2). This is the only exception to the normal deadline for such motions under Rule 4004(b)(1). Some courts have found that the deadline can be subject to extension even if an extension is not sought as required by the rules.[11] In view of the wording of section 727(a) of the Code, it may be possible for the court, *sua sponte*, to deny a discharge, if it knows of facts which would bar the debtor from that relief.[12] However, this almost never happens, because such an active partisanship of the court in a case is out of keeping with its role under the Code as a neutral arbiter of disputes brought before it rather than a participant. While the rules are clear that the objector to a discharge has the burden of proof,[13] how would that burden be carried if the court itself raised the objection?

If a discharge is denied in a chapter 7 case, the effect is quite serious. The debtor loses any nonexempt property to creditors, and creditors that are not paid in full may still pursue the debtor after the bankruptcy for the remaining amounts due. Although property claimed as exempt by the debtor cannot be taken to satisfy these creditors[14] (which might well protect all of the debtor's property), any property acquired after the bankruptcy could be subjected to process.[15]

Some courts have stated that objections to discharge, particularly those involving fraud, must be proved by "clear and convincing" evidence,[16] but those holdings have been called into question by the Supreme Court's decision in *Grogan v. Garner*.[17] At a minimum, the reasons for denying a discharge must be real and substantial and not merely technical and conjectural.[18] And, since *Grogan*, it has been held that the provisions on objections to discharge should be construed liberally in favor of the debtor.[19] Although proof of actual intent to defraud is necessary to prove most objections to discharge, courts have generally held that such proof may be made by circumstantial evidence.[20]

Once an objection to discharge has been filed, it may not be voluntarily dismissed by the objecting party, except after notice to the trustee, United States trustee, and other persons as the court directs, and it may be dismissed only on order of the court containing such terms and conditions as the court deems proper.[21] This rule is to ensure that a creditor does not bring an objection to discharge to coerce a settlement with the debtor

---

In re Beugen, 99 B.R. 961 (B.A.P. 9th Cir. 1989), *aff'd*, 930 F.2d 26 (9th Cir. 1991) (table).

9 Fed. R. Bankr. P. 4004(a). *But see* Tiffany & O'Shea, L.L.C. v. Schrag (*In re* Schrag), 464 B.R. 909 (D. Or. 2011) (allowing complaint filed eighty-three minutes late because of alleged technical problems with court's electronic filing system).

The time limits may be waived, however, if the debtor fails to assert untimeliness as a defense. Kontrick v. Ryan, 540 U.S. 443, 124 S. Ct. 906, 157 L. Ed. 2d 867 (2004). Also, an amendment filed after the deadline may relate back to the original timely filed complaint in some cases if the amendment is closely connected to the allegations of the original complaint. Disch v. Rasmussan, 417 F.3d 769 (7th Cir. 2005) (permitting addition of section 727 count to section 523 complaint and permitting revocation of discharge under Fed. R. Bankr. P. 9024); *In re* Gunn, 111 B.R. 291 (B.A.P. 9th Cir. 1990). *Cf. In re* Riggert, 399 B.R. 453 (Bankr. N.D. Tex. 2009) (amendment that added new grounds for objection was not timely under rules).

At least one appellate court has held that the time limits begin anew if the case is converted from chapter 11 to chapter 7. *In re* Jones, 966 F.2d 169 (5th Cir. 1992). Another has held that expiration of the deadline did not prevent the court from reconsidering its earlier denial of a timely motion for extension of the deadline. Farouki v. Emirates Bank Int'l, Ltd., 14 F.3d 244 (4th Cir. 1994). The time period does not start anew if a case is dismissed after it has run and then the case is reinstated. *In re* Avalos, 361 B.R. 129 (Bankr. S.D. Tex. 2007).

10 Fed. R. Bankr. P. 4004 (a), (b). *See* Frati v. Gennaco, 2011 WL 241973 (D. Mass. Jan. 24, 2011) (extension obtained by trustee did not apply to other parties). *But see In re* Dominguez, 51 F.3d 1502 (9th Cir. 1995) (creditor's memorandum raising issues relating to discharge was sufficient to place chapter 11 debtor on notice of objection, so that later complaint related back to discharge memorandum); *In re* Moss, 266 B.R. 408 (B.A.P. 8th Cir. 2001) (untimely complaint would be allowed because trustee relied on court order, later set aside, extending time to file discharge objections).

11 *See In re* Moss, 289 F.3d 540 (8th Cir. 2002) (untimely complaint accepted because untimeliness was caused by court's error).

12 11 U.S.C. § 727(c) states that only the trustee or a creditor may object, with the court seemingly limited to acting on request of a party. However, the court may not deny a discharge based on the court's general power under section 105 when the specific grounds listed in section 727 have not been determined. *In re* Yadidi, 274 B.R. 843 (B.A.P. 9th Cir. 2002).

13 Fed. R. Bankr. P. 4005. *But cf. In re* Freedman, 693 F.2d 50 (8th Cir. 1982) (once creditor raises reasonable grounds to support a finding that the debtor committed proscribed acts, debtor has burden of proving that he or she did not do so or did not have requisite intent).

14 11 U.S.C. § 522(c).

Of course, the exemptions would not defeat valid non-avoidable liens, or protect property from execution to collect domestic support obligations. *See* § 10.5, *supra*.

15 That property, though, could conceivably be protected under state exemption laws.

16 *See, e.g., In re* Mayo, 94 B.R. 315 (Bankr. D. Vt. 1988); *In re* Garcia, 88 B.R. 695 (Bankr. E.D. Pa. 1988). *But see, e.g., In re* Riso, 74 B.R. 750 (Bankr. D.N.H. 1987) (preponderance of the evidence).

17 498 U.S. 279, 111 S. Ct. 654, 112 L. Ed. 2d 755 (1991) (preponderance of the evidence standard applies to exception to dischargeability under 11 U.S.C. § 523(a)).

Following *Grogan*, it may still be possible to argue that the clear and convincing standard should apply under section 727, because the consequences of denial of discharge are more severe than those of making a single debt nondischargeable. *But see In re* Scott, 172 F.3d 959 (7th Cir. 1999) (proof by preponderance of evidence); *In re* Adams, 31 F.3d 389 (6th Cir. 1994) (same); Farouki v. Emirates Bank Int'l, Ltd., 14 F.3d 244 (4th Cir. 1994) (same); *In re* Serafini, 938 F.2d 1156 (10th Cir. 1991) (extending preponderance standard to section 727 based on *Grogan*).

18 *In re* Burgess, 955 F.2d 134 (1st Cir. 1992).

19 Rosen v. Bezner, 996 F.2d 1527 (3d Cir. 1993).

20 *See, e.g., In re* Chastant, 873 F.2d 89 (5th Cir. 1989); *In re* Sklarin, 69 B.R. 949 (Bankr. S.D. Fla. 1987).

21 Fed. R. Bankr. P. 7041.

that only benefits that creditor, and likewise that a debtor, who may lose the discharge of all debts, does not attempt to "buy off" the objecting creditor to preserve that discharge.[22] However, the rule does not absolutely preclude approval of settlements of complaints objecting to discharge, especially if the proceeds of the settlement are paid to the bankruptcy estate.[23]

15.2.2 Grounds for Objecting to Discharge

15.2.2.1 Debtor Is Not an Individual—11 U.S.C. § 727(a)(1)

Of the grounds for denial of discharge that are listed in 11 U.S.C. § 727(a), the first is never applicable in consumer cases. This provision, which prohibits a discharge if the debtor is not an individual, is meant simply to deny a discharge to corporations or partnerships.[24] (The prohibition on non-individuals does not apply to the estate of a deceased debtor, which is entitled to the benefits of the debtor's discharge.)[25] The remaining grounds are discussed below in the order in which they appear in the statute.

15.2.2.2 Intentional Concealment, Transfer or Destruction of Property—11 U.S.C. § 727(a)(2)

Probably the most common objection to discharge is that the debtor has intentionally transferred[26] or concealed assets[27] in order to prevent creditors from obtaining access to them in bankruptcy.[28] This blatant type of fraudulent conduct strikes at the very heart of the bankruptcy law, defeating its purpose of distributing nonexempt property to creditors.

Several limitations to this bar to discharge are present both explicitly and implicitly in the statute. First, the debtor must have committed the act with actual intent to hinder, delay, or defraud a creditor or officer of the estate. Thus, the standard for objection is stricter than that contained in many types of fraudulent transfer provisions under which a constructive intent can be presumed on the basis of the debtor's financial condition. Without this very specific intent, a discharge will not be denied.[29]

Many of the recent cases under this provision have examined the debtor's prebankruptcy conversion of nonexempt assets into assets that are exempt in bankruptcy. Several of the decisions turn on whether the exemption planning was done with intent to defraud creditors.[30] Given that the debtor has control over the

---

22 *See In re* Chalasani, 92 F.3d 1300 (2d Cir. 1996); *In re* Perez, 411 B.R. 386 (D. Colo. May 20, 2009) (when United States trustee sought to dismiss his discharge objection because, after extensive investigation, he found it meritless, and debtor gave no consideration, discharge should be granted); *In re* Kallstrom, 298 B.R. 753 (B.A.P. 10th Cir. 2003) (affirming refusal to approve settlement in which benefits of settlement went only to objecting creditor); *In re* Traxler, 277 B.R. 699 (Bankr. E.D. Tex. 2002) (refusing to approve settlement that would have made debts to certain creditors nondischargeable because it produced no benefit to estate or to other general creditors); *In re* Stout, 262 B.R. 862 (Bankr. D. Colo. 2001) (refusing to approve settlement in which debtor paid money to objecting creditor). *See also In re* Diamond, 346 F.3d 224 (1st Cir. 2003) (creditor's threat to seek revocation of debtor's real estate license made during settlement negotiations of section 727 action could be sufficiently coercive as to violate automatic stay).
23 *See In re* Maynard, 269 B.R. 535 (D. Vt. 2001).
24 S. Rep. No. 95-989, at 98 (1978).
25 H.R. Rep. No. 95-595, at 368 (1977). *See* Fed. R. Bankr. P. 1016.
26 "Transfer" is very broadly defined in 11 U.S.C. § 101(54).
27 The "transfer" must be of the debtor's own property. *In re* Thurman, 901 F.2d 839 (10th Cir. 1990).
28 *See, e.g., In re* Adams, 31 F.3d 389 (6th Cir. 1994) (debtors used and made unauthorized postpetition transfers of accounts receivable which were cash collateral); *In re* Perez, 954 F.2d 1026 (5th Cir. 1992) (debtor transferred fifty percent of tax refund attributable to his business to his wife); *In re* Kaiser, 722 F.2d 1574 (2d Cir. 1983); *In re* Swegan, 383 B.R. 646 (B.A.P. 6th Cir. 2008) ("concealment" as ground to deny discharge may include debtor's false statements at prebankruptcy debtor's examination regarding non-receipt of insurance proceeds, but proof of fraudulent intent required before denial of discharge may be ordered).
29 *See, e.g., In re* Pratt, 411 F.3d 561 (5th Cir. 2005) (no fraudulent intent because debtor had drug problems); *In re* Dennis, 330 F.3d 696 (5th Cir. 2003) (minimal amounts of transfers to minor child showed no intent); *In re* Miller, 39 F.3d 301 (11th Cir. 1994) (motivation for transfer was not fraudulent when debtors were trying to keep business alive and satisfy their largest creditor, who was transferee); Rosen v. Bezner, 996 F.2d 1527 (3d Cir. 1993) (remand for further findings on intent); *In re* Moreno, 892 F.2d 417 (5th Cir. 1990); *In re* Shults, 28 B.R. 395 (B.A.P. 9th Cir. 1983); *In re* Boyer, 384 B.R. 44 (D. Conn. 2008) (creditor failed to show that debtor had intent to defraud when making property transfers and omitting certain property items from schedules), *aff'd*, 328 Fed. Appx. 711 (2d Cir. 2009); *In re* Johnson, 80 B.R. 953 (Bankr. D. Minn. 1987) (debtor's intent to prevent creditors from "depriving him of wealth" not fraudulent), *aff'd*, 880 F.2d 78 (8th Cir. 1989); *In re* Dee, 6 B.R. 784 (Bankr. W.D. Pa. 1980) (debtor did not know she was signing a deed when she signed papers at husband's request); *In re* Davis, 3 B.R. 525 (Bankr. D. Md. 1980) (debtor acted solely on advice of counsel); *In re* Viola, 3 B.R. 219 (Bankr. M.D. Fla. 1980) (debtor's purchase of truck in mother's name was result of request by dealership's finance manager); *In re* Vail, 1 B.R. 132 (Bankr. E.D. Pa. 1979) (debtors' transfer of property to children had been planned for fifteen years and was accomplished when debtors were in good financial condition). *See also In re* Swift, 3 F.3d 929 (5th Cir. 1993) (trial court's findings on intent upheld unless clearly erroneous); McCormick v. Sec. State Bank, 822 F.2d 806 (8th Cir. 1987) (debtor concealed assets from creditor prior to bankruptcy and purchased a house in name of himself and his wife in clandestine manner).
30 *See, e.g., In re* Bowyer, 932 F.2d 1100 (5th Cir. 1991) (using savings to pay down mortgage was without requisite intent to defraud creditors); *In re* Johnson, 880 F.2d 78 (8th Cir. 1989) (conversion of property to make use of homestead exemption does not in itself establish fraud absent proof of actual intent to defraud; *In re* Smiley, 864 F.2d 562 (7th Cir. 1989) (conversion of nonexempt assets to exempt assets not in itself fraudulent, absent specific intent to hinder or delay creditors shown by concealment or misrepresentation); Ford v. Poston, 773 F.2d 52 (4th Cir. 1985) (conversion of nonexempt property to exempt property is normally permissible, but a court may find extrinsic elements of fraud); *In re* Carey, 112 B.R. 401 (W.D. Okla. 1989) (debtor's prepetition conduct in converting, over twenty-one-month period, nonexempt assets into cash which was used to pay mortgage on exempt homestead did not warrant denial of discharge), *aff'd*, 938 F.2d 1073 (10th Cir. 1991); *In re*

timing of a voluntary bankruptcy, it would appear to be unfair to require that the debtor maintain nonexempt assets to satisfy creditors' claims in bankruptcy when the debtor could protect those assets under state or federal law by making them exempt before the case is filed.[31] The courts have taken a fairly subjective approach to this issue, depending on the amount of money shielded from creditors, with a good deal of discretion afforded to the trial court.[32]

Exemption planning obviously must be distinguished from the transfer of assets completely out of the debtor's name for little or no consideration, particularly if the debtor has some access to or full use of those assets. The courts have denied a discharge when there has been an obvious dissipation of assets in contemplation of bankruptcy[33] or a suspicious transfer to relatives for little or no consideration.[34] They have even denied a discharge when money was "transferred" from a debtor's bank account to the debtor, when it was shown that the transfer was an attempt to avoid attachment of the account and thus hinder creditors.[35] However, if the debtor has recovered substantially all of the property transferred before the bankruptcy is filed and truthfully discloses the transfers, the debtor should not be denied a discharge under this subsection.[36]

Additionally, the challenged action must have taken place within one year prior to the bankruptcy or sometime after the bankruptcy was filed.[37] And it must have involved property that would have been available to creditors. If the debtor had no equity in the property, the bar to discharge is usually not considered applicable.[38] The same result would probably be reached with respect to property that the debtor could claim as exempt.[39]

15.2.2.3 Unjustified Failure to Keep Books or Records As to Finances—11 U.S.C. § 727(a)(3)

The Code provides for denial of discharge if the debtor has "concealed, destroyed, mutilated, falsified, or failed to keep or preserve any recorded information" concerning his or her finances, but only if such act or failure to act was not justified under the circumstances.[40] The exception to the general rule, which excuses the failure to keep records if it was "justified," has prevented the application of this subsection in most consumer cases.

Most consumers, of course, do not keep books and records in the conventional sense. What they have, at most, is a collection of receipts, bills, canceled checks, loan documents, and payment books. Certainly, a consumer debtor who has any of these documents may honestly say that books or records have been kept. The section should only come into play if the consumer's records are so deficient that the court and the parties cannot ascertain an accurate picture of the debtor's financial affairs.[41] And, as this provision is really directed at independent busi-

---

Crater, 286 B.R. 756 (Bankr. D. Ariz. 2002) (timing of debtors' transfer of property and use of sale proceeds to pay down mortgage did not prove fraudulent intent).

31 For a further discussion of exemption planning see § 6.5.2.2 and § 10.4.1, *supra*.

32 *See* Frank W. Koger & Sheryl A. Reynolds, *Is Prefiling Engineering Prudent Planning or Section 727 Fraud? (Or, When Does a Pig Become a Hog?)*, 93 Comm. L. J. 465 (1988).

33 *In re* Marcus, 45 B.R. 338 (S.D.N.Y. 1984) (debtor sold property for far less than it was worth); *In re* Kegley, Bankr. L. Rep. (CCH) ¶ 67,397 (Bankr. W.D. Wash. 1980) (debtors used funds for pleasure trip after conferring with attorneys regarding bankruptcy).

34 Cohen v. Bucci, 905 F.2d 1111 (7th Cir. 1990) (denial of discharge when debtor had transferred assets to wife and son); *In re* Chastant, 873 F.2d 89 (5th Cir. 1989) (trust gratuitously created for children suggests fraudulent motive); *In re* Olivier, 819 F.2d 550 (5th Cir. 1987) (debtors concealed beneficial interest they retained in home they transferred to parent immediately after automobile accident seven years earlier); Ford v. Poston, 773 F.2d 52 (4th Cir. 1985) (debtor transferred real estate to himself and his wife and extrinsic evidence indicated fraudulent purpose). *See also In re* Aubrey, 111 B.R. 268 (B.A.P. 9th Cir. 1990) (transfer of security interest in assets to third party without credible evidence substantiating debt to third party warranted denial of discharge).

35 *In re* Bernard, 96 F.3d 1279 (9th Cir. 1996) (relying on broad definition of "transfer" to include deposits and withdrawals from bank account).

36 *In re* Adeeb, 787 F.2d 1339 (9th Cir. 1986). *But see* Vill. of San Jose v. McWilliams, 284 F.3d 785 (7th Cir. 2002) (debtors cannot shield themselves from creditor's objection to discharge based on section 727(a) by attempting to remedy the fraud, disclosing the transfers and reconveying the property); *In re* Bajgar, 104 F.3d 495 (1st Cir. 1997) (postpetition reconveyance of property back to debtor did not cure prepetition conveyance found to have been fraudulent); *In re* Davis, 911 F.2d 560 (11th Cir. 1990) (discharge denied when debtor transferred interest in marital home to wife within one year of filing petition even though he retransferred property to himself day before bankruptcy was filed).

37 11 U.S.C. § 727(a)(2)(A). *See In re* Roosevelt, 87 F.3d 311 (9th Cir.), *as amended by* 98 F.3d 1169 (1996) (marital agreement transferring debtor's community property interest was effective upon signing and therefore beyond one year limit); *In re* Basso, 397 B.R. 556 (B.A.P. 1st Cir. 2008) (concealment did not continue when debtor announced his interest by filing homestead declaration). *But see In re* Keeney, 227 F.3d 679 (6th Cir. 2000) (one-year period met by continuing concealment doctrine, because concealment of debtor's secret interest in property continued within year before bankruptcy); *In re* Lawson, 122 F.3d 1237 (9th Cir. 1997) (objection based on deed of trust transferred over one year before petition allowed under continuing concealment doctrine); Rosen v. Bezner, 996 F.2d 1527 (3d Cir. 1993) (continuing concealment could bring transfer that was more than one year prior to petition within scope of section); *In re* Olivier, 819 F.2d 550 (5th Cir. 1987) (same); *In re* Kauffman, 675 F.2d 127 (7th Cir. 1981) (finding continuing concealment of assets more than one year after formal transfer of property when debtor continued to use property as his own).

38 *See, e.g., In re* Harris, 6 B.R. 529 (Bankr. M.D. Tenn. 1980) (see also cases cited therein).

39 *See, e.g., In re* Lippow, 92 F.2d 619 (7th Cir. 1937) (decided under similar language in prior Act).

40 11 U.S.C. § 727(a)(3). *See In re* Cacioli, 463 F.3d 229 (2d Cir. 2006) (debtor justified in relying on his business partner to maintain partnership records); *In re* Cox, 41 F.3d 1294 (9th Cir. 1994) (debtor wife's reliance on husband to keep records was justified under all the circumstances). *See also* Meridian Bank v. Alten, 958 F.2d 1226 (3d Cir. 1992) (debtor has burden of establishing adequate justification).

41 *In re* French, 499 F.3d 345 (4th Cir. 2007).

nesses,[42] and perhaps gamblers,[43] even a total lack of records has been excused in the cases of wage-earners and other low-income people.[44] Because this subsection is basically unchanged from the prior Act (except for wording), case law interpreting that Act should still be applicable. As long as the debtor did not have any particular reason to anticipate the need for records and there are other ways to ascertain the debtor's financial affairs, this provision should present few problems in consumer cases.

15.2.2.4 Dishonesty in Connection with the Bankruptcy Case—11 U.S.C. § 727(a)(4)

Not surprisingly, debtors who attempt to perpetrate a fraud upon the bankruptcy court are not treated kindly by the Code. Those who make a false oath (commit perjury), present false claims, give or take bribes, or withhold records are denied a discharge.[45] This provision clearly extends to the bankruptcy statements and schedules, which are submitted under oath.

However, like many of the other bars to discharge, the false oath objection is limited by its terms and by case law to the more serious types of cases. The false oath must be in regard to a matter that is material to the proceedings and that could have a real effect on creditors and the estate.[46] The false oath must be intentional; false answers resulting from carelessness or ignorance do not bar a debtor's discharge.[47] And the false oath must be in connection with the administration of the case itself;

---

[42] See, e.g., Union Planters Bank v. Connors, 283 F.3d 896 (7th Cir. 2002) (debtors who were sophisticated in business and owned and invested in several enterprises denied discharge for failing to account for large financial transactions); In re Juzwiak, 89 F.3d 424 (7th Cir. 1996) (owner of trucking business did not keep records that allowed meaningful reconstruction of debtor's transactions); Meridian Bank v. Alten, 958 F.2d 1226 (3d Cir. 1992) (debtor a sophisticated business person held to a high level of accountability in record keeping; neither small legal practice nor fear of execution by creditors constitutes adequate justification for failure to keep adequate records); In re Resnick, 4 B.R. 602 (Bankr. S.D. Fla. 1980) (debtor having no records explaining "loss" of half a million dollars denied discharge).

[43] See In re Dolin, 799 F.2d 251 (6th Cir. 1986) (debtor's chemical dependency and compulsive gambling did not excuse failure to keep records). But see In re Sauntry, 390 B.R. 848 (Bankr. E.D. Tex. 2008) (debtors adequately explained lack of detailed financial records as due to husband's practice of concealing his gambling winnings and losses from wife).

[44] See, e.g., In re Humphries, 469 F.2d 643 (5th Cir. 1972); Morris Plan Indus. Bank v. Henderson, 131 F.2d 975 (2d Cir. 1942).

A debtor who customarily and regularly disposes of canceled checks or the like should not be denied a discharge. In re Buda, 373 B.R. 189 (Bankr. S.D. Fla. 2007) (debtor who had been victim of theft by former boyfriend adequately explained how personal circumstances limited her ability to keep more complete financial records and documents showing use of proceeds of sale of her home); In re Zaidan, 86 B.R. 296 (Bankr. S.D. Fla. 1988). See also In re Cox, 41 F.3d 1294 (9th Cir. 1994) (factors to be considered in deciding if failure to keep records is justified by reliance on spouse are debtor's intelligence and education, debtor's experience in business, extent of debtor's involvement in businesses with respect to which debts arose, debtor's reliance on spouse to keep records, including what debtor saw or was told, nature of marital relationship, and any recordkeeping or inquiry duties debtor had under state law).

[45] 11 U.S.C. § 727(a)(4). See, e.g., In re Keeney, 227 F.3d 679 (6th Cir. 2000) (failure to schedule as asset debtor's secret interest in property purportedly transferred prior to bankruptcy); Farouki v. Emirates Bank Int'l, Ltd., 14 F.3d 244 (4th Cir. 1994) (debtor falsely denied ownership interest in family-owned business); In re Calder, 907 F.2d 953 (10th Cir. 1990) (failure to disclose substantial assets in schedules warranted denial of discharge); Williamson v. Fireman's Fund Ins., 828 F.2d 249 (4th Cir. 1987) (false oaths concealed pattern of gratuitous transfers); In re Tully, 818 F.2d 106 (1st Cir. 1987) (failing to list assets); In re Guadarrama, 284 B.R. 463 (C.D. Cal. 2002) (knowing use of false Social Security number).

The fact that a debtor's bankruptcy discharge may be denied for filing false certifications does not preclude other sanctions that are appropriate, for example, under Federal Rule of Bankruptcy Procedure 9011, if the debtor files false certifications in an adversary proceeding. In re Gioioso, 979 F.2d 956 (3d Cir. 1992).

[46] Compare In re Beaubouef, 966 F.2d 174 (5th Cir. 1992) (failure to disclose interest in corporation with intent to deceive warranted denial of discharge); Swicegood v. Ginn, 924 F.2d 230 (11th Cir. 1991) (omission from schedules of watch and set of silverware worth $1400 was material even though debts to be discharged totaled $861,778.19); In re Olson, 916 F.2d 481 (8th Cir. 1990) (debtor's failure to list interest in dinner theater of questionable value and nominally owned by wife was material misrepresentation); In re Chalik, 748 F.2d 616 (11th Cir. 1984) (debtor omitted any reference in statement of affairs to 12 corporations with assets of $2.1 million in which he had been involved); In re Harris, 385 B.R. 802 (B.A.P. 1st Cir. 2008) (denial of discharge on "false oath" ground not clearly erroneous when debtor admitted she deliberately omitted credit card debts from her schedules because she feared further harm to her credit); In re Khalil, 379 B.R. 163 (B.A.P. 9th Cir. 2007) (deliberate omission of debt owed to relatives of debtors constituted "false oath" as grounds to deny discharge) and In re Bell, Jr., 8 B.R. 110 (Bankr. E.D. Va. 1980) (debtor's denial of later-admitted transfer of assets barred discharge) with In re Agnew, 818 F.2d 1284 (7th Cir. 1987) (failure to disclose property not subject to claims of creditors did not bar discharge) and In re Fischer, 4 B.R. 517 (Bankr. S.D. Fla. 1980) (debtor's false statement that he was unemployed would not have affected bankruptcy, so discharge not barred). But see Mertz v. Rott, 955 F.2d 596 (8th Cir. 1992) (failure to disclose anticipated estate tax refund, on three separate occasions, justified denial of discharge even though refund was found by lower court to be exempt).

[47] In re Pratt, 411 F.3d 561 (5th Cir. 2005) (no fraudulent intent because debtor had drug problems and some nondisclosures resulted from debtor's ignorance); In re Brown, 108 F.3d 1290 (10th Cir. 1997) (no inference of fraudulent intent when debtor promptly brings mistake to trustee's or court's attention); In re Espino, 806 F.2d 1001 (11th Cir. 1986) (failure to list contingent obligation did not bar discharge when no intent to defraud creditors). See also In re Varrasso, 37 F.3d 760 (7th Cir. 1994) (circumstantial evidence of intent would rarely be sufficient to grant summary judgment denying discharge); 6 Collier on Bankruptcy ¶ 727.04 (16th ed.). Cf. In re Sholdra, 249 F.3d 380 (5th Cir. 2001) (doctor who knew he was submitting false information under oath could not blame his attorney's paralegal or his wife who allegedly managed his business). But see In re Retz, 606 F.3d 1189 (9th Cir. 2010) (debtor had duty to read schedules and statements and could not avoid denial of discharge by saying he signed them in blank on advice of attorney, who in fact denied giving such advice).

It may be the debtor's burden to show lack of intent once there is proof of a false oath as to a material fact. See In re Tully, 818 F.2d 106 (1st Cir. 1987).

fraudulent conduct in connection with a particular debt can be grounds only for an exception to the discharge of that debt.[48]

Finally, a finding that one debtor in a joint case made a false oath does not necessarily bar the other debtor from receiving a discharge.[49] If the joint debtor had no interest in property omitted from the schedules or no knowledge of the facts which were falsely stated, that debtor remains entitled to a discharge.[50]

15.2.2.5 Failure to Explain Loss or Deficiency of Assets—11 U.S.C. § 727(a)(5)

This provision barring discharge is often grouped with the previous two relating to the debtor's honesty with regard to the bankruptcy case. Once a creditor carries its burden of establishing that assets have been lost or dissipated, this section places the burden on the debtor to explain the loss or dissipation.[51] Courts interpreting this section have been concerned primarily with debtors who previously had large amounts of property or money, a situation which, unfortunately, few consumer clients have ever experienced. In most consumer cases, the obvious use of any diminishing assets was for basic living expenses. Even if this were not the case, this subsection is not intended as a vehicle through which the court may pass judgment on the wisdom of the debtor's expenditures.[52] And the failure of a spouse who took no part in her husband's business to explain a loss of assets will not bar her discharge simply because she filed a joint petition with him.[53]

15.2.2.6 Refusal to Obey Court Orders or to Testify—11 U.S.C. § 727(a)(6)

If the debtor refuses to comply with direct court orders, a discharge may be denied.[54] This unusual situation arises most often when a debtor has been ordered to turn over property which he or she expected to keep in the bankruptcy and that the debtor may no longer even possess. For example, debtors who are poorly advised sometimes spend tax refunds that they receive after filing their cases. When those refunds are not exempt, they constitute property of the estate that the court orders turned over to the trustee. If the debtor is unable to deliver the amount of the refund within a reasonable time, the discharge may be denied.[55] However, not every failure to comply with a court order warrants a denial of discharge.[56]

Debtors who refuse to testify may also be denied a discharge. However, if a debtor properly invokes the privilege against self-incrimination, discharge cannot be denied unless immunity has been offered with respect to the matter concerning which the privilege was invoked.[57] Presumably, debtors also will not be ordered to answer questions when other privileges are properly invoked.

15.2.2.7 Commission of Prohibited Acts in Connection with Another Bankruptcy Case Concerning an Insider—11 U.S.C. § 727(a)(7)

Debtors who have committed any of the fraudulent acts listed in the previous sections, 11 U.S.C. § 727(a)(2) to (a)(6), within one year before filing their cases, or after filing their cases, are barred from discharge if the act was committed in connection with another case concerning an "insider." The

---

48 See § 15.4.3.2, infra.
49 See, e.g., In re Montgomery, 86 B.R. 948 (Bankr. N.D. Ind. 1988).
50 In re Carp, 340 F.3d 15 (1st Cir. 2003) (wife not automatically an agent of husband or responsible for husband's failure to disclose property; her knowledge and fraudulent intent must be proved).
51 In re D'Agnese, 86 F.3d 732 (7th Cir. 1996) (debtor's vague and uncorroborated explanation of what happened to jewelry, crystal and silver worth over $300,000 was inadequate); In re Hawley, 51 F.3d 246 (11th Cir. 1995) (debtor with no documentation and vague explanations failed to explain satisfactorily loss of $13 million in assets); In re Hughes, 873 F.2d 262 (11th Cir. 1989) (case remanded to allow debtor an opportunity to explain loss of assets); In re Chalik, 748 F.2d 616 (11th Cir. 1984); In re Martin, 698 F.2d 883 (7th Cir. 1983) (although creditor had ultimate burden of proof in proceeding, once evidence of loss or deficiency of assets is presented, debtor has burden of going forward with evidence to explain loss; debtor also could be denied discharge for concealment of such assets when no explanation provided); In re Sklarin, 69 B.R. 949 (Bankr. S.D. Fla. 1987) (loss of corporate assets which the debtor controlled as alter ego).
52 In re Lindemann, 375 B.R. 450 (Bankr. N.D. Ill. 2007) (debtor who had no accounting background adequately documented how she spent $25,000 borrowed from creditor; generally discussing standards and burden of proof related to financial recordkeeping challenges); In re Nye, 64 B.R. 759 (Bankr. E.D.N.C. 1986) (requirement of satisfactory explanation required only that debtor explain loss and not that explanation be meritorious).

However, the court may require an explanation showing good faith and businesslike conduct. See 6 Collier on Bankruptcy ¶ 727.08 (16th ed.). See also In re Dolin, 799 F.2d 251 (6th Cir. 1986) (debtor's drug addiction and compulsive gambling were not satisfactory explanations for deficiency of assets).
53 In re Suttles, 819 F.2d 764 (7th Cir. 1987); In re MacPherson, 101 B.R. 324 (Bankr. M.D. Fla. 1989), aff'd, 129 B.R. 259 (M.D. Fla. 1991).
54 11 U.S.C. § 727(a)(6). See, e.g., In re Jones, 966 F.2d 169 (5th Cir. 1992) (debtors disobeyed order of court by assigning interest in insurance proceeds). See also Standiferd v. United States (In re Standiferd), 641 F.3d 1209 (10th Cir. 2011) (failure to abide by chapter 13 confirmation order prior to conversion to chapter 7 precluded discharge).
55 In re Kages, 381 B.R. 550 (B.A.P. 8th Cir. 2008) (debtor's discharge revoked for failing to turn over tax refund after being advised orally and in writing to turn over refund, even if refund was received after discharge).
56 In re Burgess, 955 F.2d 134 (1st Cir. 1992) (failure to file statements and schedules by date set by court did not warrant denial of discharge when there was no evidence of harm to creditors or contumacy); In re Green, 335 B.R. 181 (Bankr. D. Utah 2005) (pro se debtor who was unaware of order to turn over tax refund and had spent the money did not willfully violate order).
57 11 U.S.C. § 727(a)(6)(B). See In re Martin-Trigona, 732 F.2d 170 (2d Cir. 1984) (use and derivative use immunity are constitutionally coextensive with Fifth Amendment privilege in a bankruptcy hearing; discharge may constitutionally be denied for failure to testify after grant of immunity); In re J.M.V., Inc., 90 B.R. 737 (Bankr. E.D. Pa. 1988) (debtor not required to answer questions from bankruptcy trustee that could form link in chain of evidence to prosecute him; however answers may be compelled if court determines connections between debtor's answers and crimes in question are insufficient to carry burden necessary to sustain privilege).

Code defines "insider" to include relatives and partners, as well as partnerships and corporations of which the debtor is a director, officer, or person in control.[58]

Although this section is undoubtedly directed principally at debtors who have been involved in bankrupt corporations and partnerships,[59] it could also be applied to occasional consumer cases. These would most likely involve a husband and wife or other related persons who committed the specified fraudulent acts.[60]

15.2.2.8 Prior Discharge in Chapter 7, Chapter 11, or Their Predecessors—11 U.S.C. § 727(a)(8)

This subsection contains an eight-year bar against successive bankruptcy discharges for debtors who have received prior discharges under chapter 7 or chapter 11. It is important to note, first of all, that it applies only to prior cases in which a discharge was granted. If a prior bankruptcy case was terminated without a discharge, by a dismissal for example, this objection to discharge may not be raised. (However, in the rare case of dismissal with prejudice, debts listed in the prior case may not be discharged.)[61] Moreover, this subsection does not bar discharge following prior discharges under chapter 13; those cases are dealt with by a different provision.[62] And, as with all of the provisions of section 727(a), this section has no applicability in cases in which the debtor seeks a chapter 13 discharge.[63] Unlike other provisions of the Code that take into account a prior bankruptcy filing that did not result in a discharge,[64] subsections 727(a)(8) and (9) do not consider cases in which a discharge was not granted, and there is no equitable tolling of the time periods in those provisions.[65] Lastly, it should be noted that the eight-year period runs from the date the earlier bankruptcy case was commenced, not from the date of the discharge.[66]

15.2.2.9 Prior Discharge Under Chapter 13—11 U.S.C. § 727(a)(9)

The Code also bars a chapter 7 discharge in many cases when a debtor has received a discharge under chapter 13 or its predecessor within the previous six years.[67] Again, this subsection applies only if the earlier case proceeded to a discharge.

A significant exception to this general rule allows a chapter 7 discharge when the previous case completely, or in large part, paid unsecured debts. Thus, if one-hundred percent of the allowed unsecured claims in the previous case were paid, this subsection is not applicable. Similarly, if the actual payments under the previous chapter 13 plan comprised at least seventy percent of the allowed unsecured claims in that case,[68] and the court finds that the plan was proposed by the debtor in good faith and was the debtor's "best effort," a subsequent chapter 7 discharge within six years is not barred. The drafters of the Code anticipated that a debtor could receive this "best effort" determination when the original chapter 13 plan was confirmed.[69]

15.2.2.10 Written Waiver of Discharge—11 U.S.C. § 727(a)(10)

Finally, the court may deny a discharge based upon a court-approved written waiver of discharge executed after the order for relief.[70] Obviously, this section has no applicability to the purported waivers of bankruptcy rights that creditors obtain in granting loans. Given the strict standards set forth for the reaffirmation of even a single debt, discussed later in this chapter, few waivers of discharge are approved.[71]

Probably, the court will approve a waiver of discharge only when it seems likely that no discharge could be granted any-

---

58 11 U.S.C. § 101(31).
59 *See, e.g., In re* Watman, 301 F.3d 3 (1st Cir. 2002) (dental practice was "insider" of debtor); *In re* Krehl, 86 F.3d 737 (7th Cir. 1996) (debtor destroyed records of corporation of which he had previously been president).
60 *See, e.g., In re* Mart, 90 B.R. 547 (Bankr. S.D. Fla. 1988).
61 *See* 3 Collier on Bankruptcy ¶ 349.02[2] (16th ed.).
62 See § 15.2.2.9, *infra*, for a discussion of the circumstances in which a chapter 7 discharge is barred following a discharge in chapter 13.
63 *See* Johnson v. Home State Bank, 501 U.S. 78, 111 S. Ct. 2150, 115 L. Ed. 2d 66 (1991).
    See 11 U.S.C. § 1328(f) and § 12.10.1, *supra*, for discussion of chapter 13 discharges after prior discharges.
64 *See, e.g.,* 11 U.S.C. §§ 109(g), 507(a)(8)(ii)(II).
65 Tidewater Fin. Co. v. Williams, 498 F.3d 249 (4th Cir. 2007).
66 *See* United States Tr. v. Skinner (*In re* Skinner), 2010 WL 3469993 (Bankr. S.D. Miss. Sept. 1, 2010) (when later case was filed under chapter 13 and then converted, original petition date of later case controls); *In re* Canganelli, 132 B.R. 369 (Bankr. N.D. Ind. 1991) (when prior case was filed under chapter 13 and converted to chapter 7, original filing date controls).
    When a case has been converted from another chapter to chapter 7, the relevant date is the date the original bankruptcy petition was filed, not the conversion date. *In re* Burrell, 148 B.R. 820 (Bankr. E.D. Va. 1992).
67 11 U.S.C. § 727(a)(9).
68 *See In re* Griffin, 352 B.R. 475 (B.A.P. 8th Cir. 2006) (reversing bankruptcy court's denial of discharge; total amount of payments under the plan, not the amount of payments to unsecured creditors, must equal at least seventy percent of the allowed unsecured claims).
69 124 Cong. Rec. S17,415 (daily ed. Oct. 6, 1978) (remarks of Sen. DeConcini); 8 Collier on Bankruptcy ¶ 1328.07[3] (16th ed.).
    For this reason, some attorneys include a provision in their form chapter 13 plans that confirmation will constitute a finding that the plan is the debtor's "best effort" within the meaning of section 727(a)(9). For an example of such a provision, see Form 28, Appendix G.3, *infra*.
70 11 U.S.C. § 727(a)(10).
    In a voluntary case, the order for relief occurs as of the filing of the petition. 11 U.S.C. § 301.
71 *See In re* Asbury, 408 B.R. 817 (Bankr. W.D. Mo. 2009) (waiver rejected when court not convinced that debtor had demonstrated that a written waiver of discharge was in his best interest or that he clearly understood its legal consequences), *aff'd*, 423 B.R. 525 (B.A.P. 8th Cir. 2010) (court could also consider effect on creditors who would have to pursue additional litigation in denying debtor's waiver of discharge); *In re* Martin, 211 B.R. 23 (Bankr. E.D. Ark. 1997) (waiver not approved because debtor did not understand its legal effect).

way. Thus, it may be a method of settling a complaint objecting to discharge that would prevent the disclosure of damaging or embarrassing facts about the debtor. Even in such cases, a debtor may be able to obtain a better settlement, excepting only debts to particular creditors from the discharge or compromising the amounts owed in consideration of the settlement.

15.2.2.11 Failure to Complete Course in Personal Financial Management—11 U.S.C. § 727(a)(11)

As discussed in an earlier chapter, all individual debtors in chapter 7 and chapter 13 cases, with very limited exceptions, must complete a personal financial management course offered by an approved provider as a prerequisite for receiving a discharge.[72] Section 727(a)(11) contains this requirement, although it is unlikely an objection to discharge will be the procedure for implementing it. Bankruptcy Rule 1007(c) sets the deadline for filing a certificate in a chapter 7 case at sixty days after the first date set for the meeting of creditors. This deadline may be extended by the court under Rule 9006(b), but if the debtor fails to comply with the financial education requirement, the court will close the case without a discharge.[73]

However, unlike most of the bars to discharge contained in section 727, this one may in some cases be cured. Courts normally permit the debtor to reopen the case after the education requirement has been met in order to receive a discharge.[74] Nonetheless, because this is a matter of judicial discretion, every effort should be made to ensure the debtor completes the course in a timely fashion or obtains an extension of time, to avoid the possibility that the court may not agree to reopen a closed case. Moreover, pursuant to the policy of the Judicial Conference, the debtor must pay a new filing fee to reopen the case for this purpose,[75] which should provide a strong incentive for debtors to complete the course in a timely manner.

15.2.2.12 Delay of Discharge to Determine Homestead Exemption Rights—11 U.S.C. § 727(a)(12)

As discussed in an earlier chapter,[76] section 727(a)(12) provides a mechanism for the court to delay a discharge if there is uncertainty about whether the homestead limitation of section 522(q) applies. Such uncertainty would usually arise because of litigation or a criminal prosecution that has not been completed at the time the discharge order would ordinarily be entered. If that is the case, the creditor, or perhaps another party such as the trustee, may file a motion to delay the dischar30ge. Bankruptcy Rule 4004(c)(I) provides that the discharge is not to be entered if such a motion is pending. If the motion is granted, presumably the debtor would need to file a later motion to obtain the discharge once it becomes clear whether section 522(q)(1) applies.

15.3 Revocation of Discharge—11 U.S.C. § 727(d)

Even more rare than an objection to the debtor's discharge is a complaint seeking revocation of the discharge. Such a complaint must be filed within relatively short time limits and must allege the existence of one of the limited sets of circumstances that allow revocation.

Specifically, the discharge may be revoked only:[77]

- If the discharge was obtained through fraud of the debtor, of which the requesting party was unaware until after the discharge;
- If the debtor committed an act described in section 727(d)(2), that is, knowingly and fraudulently failed to report the acquisition of property that would be property of the estate or failed to deliver or surrender such property to the trustee;[78]
- If the debtor committed an act described in section 727(a)(6), that is, failed to obey an order of the court;[79] or
- If the debtor has failed to satisfactorily explain either a material misstatement or a failure to make necessary docu-

---

72 See § 8.3.3, supra.
73 Fed. R. Bankr. P. 4004 advisory committee's note (2008).
74 See Form 160, Appx. G.12, infra.
75 Bankruptcy Court Miscellaneous Fee Schedule, item 11 (reprinted in Appx. C.3, infra).
76 See Ch. 10, supra.

77 The provisions permitting revocation of a bankruptcy discharge found in the Bankruptcy Code are exclusive and may not be supplemented by other factors which might in other contexts warrant relief from a judgment. See In re Zimmerman, 869 F.2d 1126 (8th Cir. 1989); In re Rodwell, 280 B.R. 100 (Bankr. D.N.J. 2002) (debtors' failure to respond to trustee's request for information was not within enumerated grounds for revocation of discharge). See also In re Markovich, 207 B.R. 909 (B.A.P. 9th Cir. 1997) (debtor not permitted to seek revocation of discharge to convert to chapter 13 after creditor obtained judgment that its debt was nondischargeable); In re Wyciskalla, 156 B.R. 579 (Bankr. S.D. Ill. 1993) (debtor had no right to seek revocation of his own discharge because he had reconsidered advisability of his original filing); In re Jones, 111 B.R. 674 (Bankr. E.D. Tenn. 1990) (chapter 7 debtor, who had obtained discharge, would not be allowed to convert case to chapter 13 and obtain revocation of chapter 7 discharge). But see In re Cisneros, 994 F.2d 1462 (9th Cir. 1993) (despite limitations in section 727(d), court could enter order vacating discharge on grounds set forth in Fed. R. Bankr. P. 9024).
78 See, e.g., In re Yonikus, 974 F.2d 901 (7th Cir. 1992) (debtor's failure to report prepetition personal injury claim warranted revocation of discharge even if it could be claimed as exempt). See also In re Putnam, 85 B.R. 881 (Bankr. M.D. Fla. 1988) (refusal to revoke discharge when debtor did not report an asset which he honestly believed had no value to the estate).
When debtors are not clearly put on notice that a turnover of the property is demanded there may not be the knowing and fraudulent intent required by this subsection. In re Schwartz, 64 B.R. 285 (Bankr. D.N.H. 1986).
79 See, e.g., In re Jordan, 521 F.3d 430 (4th Cir. 2008) (debtor did not willfully disobey court order prohibiting transfers of property without court approval when, as layperson, she did not understand that refinancing her home was a transfer of property); In re Levine, 50 B.R. 587 (Bankr. S.D. Fla. 1985) (debtor failed to obey order to surrender income tax refund check).

ments or things available in an audit conducted under the auspices of the United States trustee or bankruptcy administrator.[80]

To obtain revocation of a discharge for fraud it is not sufficient to show that the debtor's fraud rendered a particular debt nondischargeable; the plaintiff must show that the bankruptcy discharge itself would not have been granted but for the fraud.[81] The plaintiff must also allege fraud with particularity, including the time, place and contents of any false representation, as well as its consequences.[82] In addition, the party requesting revocation of discharge must not have learned of the fraud before the discharge was entered.[83] If a party learns of facts that would be a basis for revocation of discharge before the discharge is actually entered, but after the deadline for objections to discharge, that party may file a prompt motion to extend the time for an objection to discharge under Rule 4004(b)(2).[84] This is the only exception to the normal deadline for such motions under Rule 4004(b)(1).

It is also important to note that the revocation of discharge provision concerning audits turns not on whether the debtor made a misstatement or failed to make documents or things available, but rather on whether the debtor "satisfactorily" explained the misstatement or failure. Courts should not expect that consumer debtors will necessarily have all the documents auditors request because, as discussed above, many consumer debtors do not keep extensive documentation of their financial affairs.[85] There may also be some debate regarding what it means to make records available. It should be sufficient for debtors to sign a release allowing an auditor to request records of financial accounts, rather than having to obtain those records themselves.

A complaint raising any of these allegations must be filed within one year of the discharge unless the case is closed after the one year has passed, in which case the second and third grounds set forth above may be raised until the date the case is closed.[86] A closed bankruptcy case must also be reopened for such a complaint to be filed, but the failure of a plaintiff to move to reopen may not be sufficient grounds to defeat the complaint.[87]

Although section 727 does not apply to chapter 13 cases, a creditor or trustee may also move to revoke a chapter 13 discharge within one year of when it was granted if the discharge was obtained by fraud and that fraud was not known by the requesting party until after the discharge was granted.[88] Some courts have also relied on Federal Rule of Bankruptcy Procedure 9024, the equivalent of Federal Rule of Civil Procedure 60, to vacate a discharge when there has been an error in the trustee's handling of the case.[89] It is not clear why, if a trustee has erred to the detriment of a creditor, it would not be more appropriate for the creditor to be compensated by the trustee.

15.4 Exceptions to Discharge

15.4.1 Differences Between Chapter 7 and Chapter 13[90]

Somewhat less serious than an objection to discharge that could prevent a debtor from receiving any discharge at all is the

---

80 11 U.S.C. § 727(d).
    See Chapter 8, *supra*, for discussion of audits.
81 *In re* Nielsen, 383 F.3d 922 (9th Cir. 2004) (although debtor failed to list creditor on mailing matrix, discharge would have been granted and creditor would not have received any distribution in no-asset case in any event); *In re* Edmonds, 924 F.2d 176 (10th Cir. 1991). *See also In re* Donald, 240 B.R. 141 (B.A.P. 1st Cir. 1999) (less than full disclosure of nature of lawsuit against debtor did not rise to level of fraud).
82 *In re* Edmonds, 924 F.2d 176 (10th Cir. 1991).
83 Mid-Tech Consulting v. Swendra, 938 F.2d 885 (8th Cir. 1991) (creditor knew of omission from schedules before discharge was entered and failed to timely investigate it); *In re* Vereen, 219 B.R. 691 (Bankr. D.S.C. 1997) (complaint dismissed because trustee did not exercise due diligence in investigating possible fraud before discharge); *In re* Kaliana, 202 B.R. 600 (Bankr. N.D. Ill. 1996) (because bank had constructive notice of debtor's hidden bank account, through information in its own files, discharge would not be revoked despite debtor's failure to disclose account). *But see* Disch v. Rasmussan, 417 F.3d 769 (7th Cir. 2005) (permitting addition of section 727 count to section 523 complaint and permitting revocation of discharge under Fed. R. Bankr. P. 9024).
84 *See In re* Moseley, 470 B.R. 223 (Bankr. M.D. Fla. 2012) (extending deadline, but denying extension of deadline for dischargeability complaint because there was no equivalent exception).
85 *See* § 15.2.2.3, *supra*.

86 11 U.S.C. § 727(e).
    The one-year period is not tolled by a debtor's fraudulent concealment of assets. *In re* Smith, 379 B.R. 315 (Bankr. N.D. Ill. 2007) (time limit for filing complaint to revoke discharge strictly applied against creditors who had prior knowledge of debtors' alleged fraud in omitting them from list of scheduled creditors); *In re* Dolliver, 255 B.R. 251 (Bankr. D. Me. 2000); *In re* Frank, 146 B.R. 851 (Bankr. N.D. Okla. 1992). *See also In re* Fellheimer, 443 B.R. 355 (Bankr. E.D. Pa. 2010) (one year period not subject to equitable tolling and could not be waived based on equitable or promissory estoppel); *In re* Bevis, 242 B.R. 805 (Bankr. D.N.H. 1999) (deadline of one year after case closing not extended even if debtor failed to list assets which, therefore, were not administered); *In re* Phillips, 233 B.R. 712 (Bankr. W.D. Tex. 1999) (one-year period not subject to equitable tolling); *In re* Blanchard, 241 B.R. 461 (Bankr. S.D. Cal. 1999) (same).
87 *In re* Leach, 194 B.R. 812 (E.D. Mich. 1996) (reopening necessary, but decision of the bankruptcy court to allow adversary proceeding to go forward deemed tantamount to reopening).
88 11 U.S.C. § 1328(e).
89 *See In re* Midkiff, 342 F.3d 1194 (10th Cir. 2003) (discharge temporarily vacated so trustee could collect debtor's tax refund and distribute it to creditors in accordance with plan); *In re* Cisneros, 994 F.2d 1462 (9th Cir. 1993); *In re* Midkiff, 271 B.R. 383 (B.A.P. 10th Cir. 2002); *In re* Avery, 272 B.R. 718 (Bankr. E.D. Cal. 2002).
90 Note that the exceptions to discharge found in section 523(a) are applicable in chapter 11 cases filed by individuals. 11 U.S.C. § 1141(d)(2). However, none of these exceptions applies when a reorganized corporate debtor receives a chapter 11 discharge. 11 U.S.C. § 1141(d)(1). Because corporations cannot obtain a discharge under chapter 7 because of 11 U.S.C. § 727(a)(1), it is

problem of a particular debt that is not covered by the discharge a debtor does receive. When the debtor receives a discharge that is not applicable to all debts, those debts that are excepted from discharge can seriously undermine the benefits a bankruptcy would otherwise provide. The general rule is that a prepetition debt is discharged unless a specific exception to the discharge provides otherwise.[91]

One of the important features of chapter 13 is the inapplicability of some of the chapter 7 provisions that exclude certain types of debts from the effect of the discharge. If a debtor earns a chapter 13 discharge by completing a confirmed plan,[92] most debts provided for in the plan are discharged. The exceptions to that discharge are: unfiled or late filed taxes as provided under section 523(a)(1)(B); fraudulently filed taxes as provided under section 523(a)(1)(C); withheld taxes described in section 507(a)(8)(C); debts incurred through fraud or false pretenses that are nondischargeable under 11 U.S.C. § 523(a)(2) or (a)(4) (provided the court finds the debt nondischargeable upon a timely complaint filed by the creditor); debts not listed on the schedules that are nondischargeable under 11 U.S.C. § 523(a)(3); domestic support obligations that are nondischargeable under 11 U.S.C. § 523(a)(5); debts for educational loans and grants that are nondischargeable under 11 U.S.C. § 523(a)(8); debts for drunk driving debts that are nondischargeable under 11 U.S.C. § 523(a)(9); certain criminal fines and restitution debts, discussed below;[93] restitution or damages awarded in a civil action for willful or malicious injury by the debtor that caused personal injury or death;[94] and long-term debts provided for under the section 1322(b)(5) cure provisions, which have a final payment that is due after the last payment of the plan is due.[95]

Before it was significantly curtailed by the 2005 amendments, this enhanced discharge for debtors completing a chapter 13 plan was often referred to as the chapter 13 "superdischarge." Although it is still somewhat broader than the chapter 7 discharge, it probably no longer warrants that nickname.

However, this discharge cannot be granted unless all claims given priority under 11 U.S.C. § 507, such as alimony, maintenance, or support arrearages and many taxes, are also paid in full, because a plan must with limited exceptions provide for full payment of such debts.[96] Thus, as a practical matter, priority tax debts too are not dischargeable through a normal chapter 13 discharge.

Some of the other debts that are excepted from discharge in a chapter 7 case and are discussed below are included in the normal chapter 13 discharge. This difference, as discussed elsewhere in this treatise,[97] can be an important factor in the choice of chapter 13 rather than chapter 7 in some cases, or in a decision to convert from chapter 7 to chapter 13. In view of the inapplicability of some of the exceptions to discharge in chapter 13, courts have ruled that there is no purpose to complaints challenging dischargeability on those inapplicable grounds in chapter 13 cases and have dismissed such complaints.[98] However, some courts have taken the presence of debts that are allegedly nondischargeable under chapter 7 into consideration in ruling upon whether the plan has been filed in good faith.[99]

This difference between chapter 7 and chapter 13 does not exist if the debtor obtains a chapter 13 hardship discharge under section 1328(b). In such cases, the exceptions to discharge are

---

unnecessary to seek to have corporate debts found nondischargeable under that chapter. *See* § 18.5.4.2, *infra*; Garrie v. James L. Gray, Inc., 912 F.2d 808 (5th Cir. 1990) (corporation can only receive a discharge if it reorganizes under chapter 11; 11 U.S.C. § 1141(d)).

91 *But see In re* Laizure, 548 F.3d 693 (9th Cir. 2008) (when debtor's repayment of an embezzlement debt was avoided as a preference, compensating claim resulting from section 502(h) revived nondischargeability of prior debt).

92 *See* Bayshore Nat'l Bank v. Smith, 252 B.R. 107 (E.D. Tex. 2000) (once payments are complete, even if they are completed early, the debtor is entitled to discharge), *aff'd*, 252 F.3d 1357 (5th Cir. 2001) (table); *In re* Westenberg, 365 B.R. 895 (Bankr. E.D. Wis. 2007) (debtor entitled to discharge when all payments called for in plan had been made even though two secured creditors were not fully paid; secured creditors were aware of plan provisions that extended their payments beyond plan period and allowed them to retain liens so all parties were bound by confirmed plan). *See also* § 12.3.4.5, *supra* (once payments are complete no party may move to modify plan).

93 *See* § 15.4.3.7, *infra*.
94 *See* § 15.4.3.6, *infra*.
95 11 U.S.C. § 1328(a)(1).

96 11 U.S.C. § 1322(a)(2), (4).
   Section 1322(a)(4) creates a limited exception for domestic support obligations owed to governmental units in certain circumstances, although those debts remain nondischargeable. *See* § 12.3.6.1, *supra*. And a priority claim holder may consent to less than full payment. However, a priority claim need not be paid if no claim is filed, and such a claim can then be discharged, if it is otherwise dischargeable. *See In re* Joye, 578 F.3d 1070 (9th Cir. 2009) (taxes incurred before petition date were claims that were dischargeable even if they were not payable until after petition date); *In re* Tomlan, 102 B.R. 790 (E.D. Wash. 1989) (IRS failure to file timely claim deprives it of priority status so that its claim was discharged without full payment under chapter 13 plan), *aff'd*, 907 F.2d 114 (9th Cir. 1990); *In re* Richards, 50 B.R. 339 (E.D. Tenn. 1985); *In re* Riley, 204 B.R. 28 (Bankr. E.D. Ark. 1996) (when debtor's original plan provided for payment of priority tax claim and creditor did not object to modification of plan which omitted payment of tax claim, claim was discharged at conclusion of modified plan); *In re* Goodwin, 58 B.R. 75 (Bankr. D. Me. 1986) (priority tax claim discharged when debtor's plan would have paid claim but timely proof of claim not filed). *See also In re* Hageman, 108 B.R. 1016 (Bankr. N.D. Iowa 1989) (IRS not entitled to be paid postpetition interest on priority claims); *In re* Vlavianos, 71 B.R. 789 (Bankr. W.D. Va. 1986) (court denied IRS motion to amend claim upward at end of case; amounts not in claim were discharged); § 15.4.3.1.2, *infra*.

97 *See* § 6.3, *supra*, for a discussion of the choice between chapter 7 and chapter 13.

98 *In re* Lewis, 5 B.R. 575 (Bankr. N.D. Ga. 1980). *See also In re* Dole, 7 B.R. 986 (Bankr. D. Idaho 1981) (debt discharged in chapter 13 even after revocation of earlier discharge under Bankruptcy Act).
   This principle is so clear that an improper dischargeability complaint in chapter 13 might be appropriate grounds for sanctions under 11 U.S.C. § 523(d) or Federal Rule of Bankruptcy Procedure 9011. Section 523(d) is applicable even to cases to which section 523(a)(2) exceptions to discharge are not.

99 *See* § 12.3.3, *supra*, for discussion of the "good faith" question.

the same as in chapter 7.[100] (The debtor is also excused from the requirement, not present in chapter 7, that all priority debts, with limited exceptions, be paid.)

15.4.2 How Exceptions to Discharge Are Raised

The Bankruptcy Code makes an important distinction between two categories of exceptions to discharge. The first category consists of debts that are excepted from the discharge regardless of whether the issue is raised during the bankruptcy case. The exceptions falling into this category, each of which is discussed below, are those covered by subsections (a)(1), (a)(3), (a)(5), and (a)(7) to (a)(19) of section 523, as well as subsections (a)(1), (a)(3), and (a)(4) of section 1328. These subsections include exceptions for taxes, debts not listed by the debtor, domestic support obligations, certain fines, penalties, and restitution debts, student loans, certain debts incurred through drunk driving, debts when a discharge was denied or waived in a prior bankruptcy, debts incurred to pay nondischargeable federal taxes, marital property settlement debts, debts for certain condominium or cooperative assessments, court costs owed by prisoners and certain support debts owed to governmental units and, in chapter 13, certain debts for willful or malicious acts causing personal injury or death. Creditors that hold claims covered by these exceptions are free to assert them against the debtor after the bankruptcy, without the permission of the bankruptcy court.[101]

The second category of exceptions consists of debts that are excluded from the discharge only if their nondischargeability is raised and determined during the bankruptcy case. The debts that fall into this category are those specified in subsections (a)(2), (a)(4), and (a)(6) of section 523.[102] These subsections deal with debts incurred by fraud, false pretenses, or false financial statements, debts for fraud on the part of fiduciaries, and, in a chapter 7, 11, or 12 case, debts for willful and malicious injuries.[103] The rules require that a creditor raise these nondischargeability issues by filing an adversary proceeding.[104] Although the bankruptcy court probably has jurisdiction to also enter a money judgment in such a proceeding,[105] it usually will not do so.

The deadline for commencing such a proceeding in all chapters is sixty days after the first date set for the section 341 meeting of creditors.[106] The fact that the meeting of creditors is postponed has no effect on the deadline set under Rule 4007(c), which runs from the first date set for the meeting. Some courts had held that this deadline is jurisdictional and could not be waived by a failure to object to an untimely complaint.[107] However, the Supreme Court has held that a similar deadline in Rule 4004(a) is not jurisdictional and that the debtor may waive the right to object to an untimely complaint if the debtor fails to assert untimeliness as a defense.[108]

The court gives at least thirty days' notice of this deadline, normally combined with the notice of the meeting of credi-

---

100 11 U.S.C. § 1328(b).
  The hardship discharge also does not include long-term debts which were to be cured under the debtor's plan. 11 U.S.C. § 1328(b).
101 However, property claimed as exempt in the bankruptcy may not be reached by such creditors, except those who hold claims for taxes, domestic support obligations, or a student loan or scholarship obtained by fraud. 11 U.S.C. § 522(c).
102 11 U.S.C. § 523(c).
  This provision contains an exception applicable only to agencies regulating federal depository institutions. A debt under section (a)(2), (a)(4), (a)(6), or (a)(11) may be found nondischargeable outside the normal time limits when owed in some circumstances to a "Federal depository institution regulatory agency" which does not have the ability to "reasonably comply" with the requirement of a timely filed complaint to determine dischargeability. 11 U.S.C. § 523(c)(2). When there is no ability to "reasonably comply," it is unclear what alternative time limit will apply. See generally § 15.4.3.11, infra.
103 As the bankruptcy court has exclusive jurisdiction to determine the dischargeability of these debts, a settlement containing a waiver of dischargeability of such debts entered by a nonbankruptcy court is unenforceable. Whitehouse v. La Roche, 277 F.3d 568 (1st. Cir. 2002).
104 Fed. R. Bankr. P. 7001.
  This means that the adversary rules, Federal Rules of Bankruptcy Procedure 7001–7087, are applicable. If, for example, the summons and complaint are not served within 120 days as required by Federal Rule of Civil Procedure 4(j) (made applicable by Federal Rule of Bankruptcy Procedure 7004(a)) and no good cause is shown the complaint must be dismissed. In re Kirkland, 86 F.3d 172 (10th Cir. 1996) (when creditor filed timely dischargeability complaint but failed to make timely service of complaint, complaint was dismissed); In re Love, 242 B.R. 169 (E.D. Tenn. 1999); In re Heinz, 131 B.R. 38 (Bankr. D. Md. 1991).
  If the normal requirements for a class action are met, a class action dischargeability complaint may be filed pursuant to Federal Rule of Bankruptcy Procedure 7023. See In re Duck, 122 B.R. 403 (Bankr. N.D. Cal. 1990); § 14.7, supra.
105 Sasson v. Sokoloff, 424 F.3d 864 (9th Cir. 2005).
106 Fed. R. Bankr. P. 4007(c). In chapter 13 cases filed before the effective date of the 2005 amendments in which the debtor seeks a hardship discharge, a different deadline is set by the court pursuant to Federal Rule of Bankruptcy Procedure 4007(d). This rule continues to apply to debts that are alleged to be nondischargeable under section 523(a)(6), because such debts are dischargeable in chapter 13 unless the debtor receives a hardship discharge. See In re Liescheidt, 404 B.R. 499 (Bankr. C.D. Ill. 2009) (complaint under section 523(a)(2) and (4) filed after the bar date was untimely, and claims under section 523(a)(6) were premature because the debtor had not sought a hardship discharge. The deadlines under Rule 4007 are extended, under Bankruptcy Rule 9006(a), to the next workday following a Saturday, Sunday, or holiday. In re Burns, 102 B.R. 750 (B.A.P. 9th Cir. 1989). The deadline supplants state statutes of limitations for fraud cases, at least with respect to whether a dischargeability complaint may be brought. In re McKendry, 40 F.3d 331 (10th Cir. 1994).
  This deadline does not apply in some cases in which a federal depository institutions regulatory agency seeks to recover a debt from an "institution-affiliated party" as defined by 11 U.S.C. § 101. 11 U.S.C. § 523(c)(2). See also In re Wlaschin, 260 B.R. 306 (Bankr. M.D. Fla. 2000) (deadline extended pursuant to Soldiers' and Sailors' Relief Act).
107 In re Kirsch, 65 B.R. 297 (Bankr. N.D. Ill. 1986).
108 Kontrick v. Ryan, 540 U.S. 443, 124 S. Ct. 906, 157 L. Ed. 2d 867 (2004).

§ 15.4.2   Consumer Bankruptcy Law and Practice

tors.[109] The deadline may be extended upon motion for cause only if such a motion is filed before the deadline passes.[110] Only a creditor, and not the trustee, is a party in interest entitled to request an extension of the deadline.[111] Such a request must set forth a specific and satisfactory explanation why the creditor is unable to file a timely complaint,[112] and when additional time is granted, it applies only to the creditor who requested it.[113] The debtor should be given the opportunity to respond to the motion.[114] The court has no discretion to extend the time limit once the deadline has passed.[115]

The complaint must be properly filed by the deadline.[116] Mere mailing by the deadline is not sufficient.[117] Nor, perhaps, is filing without paying the necessary filing fee sufficient.[118]

If the creditor does file a dischargeability complaint, the debtor must respond or a default judgment may be entered, though the court retains its usual discretion to vacate a default judgment on motion.[119]

If a creditor does not file a complaint alleging nondischargeability of its claim before the deadline, or any extension, and the claim is within the categories of exceptions to which the deadline applies under section 523(c), then the claim is permanently discharged when the discharge order is entered. The debtor may then raise the deadline as a complete defense to any later dischargeability action. Even if the creditor did not receive proper notice of the deadline, it is strictly applied by the courts if the creditor had timely notice of the bankruptcy case.[120] The creditor's filing of a motion for relief from the stay or other

---

109 See Official Form 9 (reprinted in Appx. D, infra).
110 Fed. R. Bankr. P. 4007(c); In re Nordin, 299 B.R. 915 (B.A.P. 8th Cir. 2003) (court has no authority to grant motion to extend time if filed after deadline). See In re Lewis, 224 B.R. 619 (Bankr. S.D. Ohio 1997) (creditor's claim that more time was needed to pursue settlement negotiations not sufficient cause when debtor's counsel stated no discussion had occurred since the meeting of creditors).
111 In re Farmer, 786 F.2d 618 (4th Cir. 1986); In re Owen-Moore, 435 B.R. 685 (Bankr. S.D. Cal. 2010). But see In re Brady, 101 F.3d 1165 (6th Cir. 1996) (trustee had standing to seek extension of dischargeability complaint deadline on behalf of creditors).
112 See In re Englander, 79 B.R. 897 (B.A.P. 9th Cir. 1988) (complaint which failed to allege specific grounds for nondischargeability permitted when cured by amended complaint after bar date; but plaintiff's attorney sanctioned); In re Sirmans, 2009 WL 1456813 (E.D. Cal. May 21, 2009) (difficulty in state court in obtaining discovery from the debtor did not justify appellant's failure to pursue any discovery whatsoever in the bankruptcy case or to file a complaint based upon information appellant already had); In re Littell, 58 B.R. 937 (Bankr. S.D. Tex. 1986); In re Marino, 195 B.R. 886 (Bankr. N.D. Ill. 1996) (grounds for extension not shown when creditor's attorney had notice of case two months before deadline).
113 In re Ichinose, 946 F.2d 1169 (5th Cir. 1991) (order extending time as to one creditor is not implicit extension of deadline as to other creditors). But see In re Demos, 57 F.3d 1037 (creditor could rely on extension of deadline granted to trustee when extension order erroneously purported to grant extension for all creditors).
114 Pa. Lawyers Fund v. Moore (In re Moore), 442 B.R. 405 (Bankr. W.D. Pa. 2011).
115 In re Hill, 811 F.2d 484 (9th Cir. 1987); Lure Launchers, L.L.C. v. Spino, 306 B.R., 718 (B.A.P. 10th Cir. 2004) (court cannot grant extension when motion filed after deadline); In re Brown, 102 B.R. 187 (B.A.P. 9th Cir. 1989) (court has no discretion to extend the deadline even for extraordinary circumstances such as natural disasters); In re Miller, 188 B.R. 1021 (Bankr. S.D. Fla. 1995) (motion filed one day after deadline was not timely even though it was served on debtor on deadline date); In re Beam, 73 B.R. 434 (Bankr. S.D. Ohio 1987) (court cannot extend deadline even though an objection was timely, but erroneously, filed in an unrelated case). See also In re Kirkland, 86 F.3d 172 (10th Cir. 1996) (when creditor filed timely dischargeability complaint but failed to make timely service of complaint, complaint was dismissed); In re Langston, 319 B.R. 667 (D. Utah 2005) (affirming dismissal of complaint for failure to timely serve process). But see Kontrick v. Ryan, 124 S. Ct. 906, 157 L. Ed. 2d 867 (2004) (deadline is not jurisdictional and debtor may waive right to object to untimely complaint by failing to object to Judge's order extending deadline); In re Maughan, 340 F.3d 337 (6th Cir. 2003) (wrongly holding that deadline may be equitably tolled based on debtor's behavior); In re Roberts, 331 B.R. 876 (B.A.P. 9th Cir. 2005) (debtor waived argument that complaint was not served by failing to assert it in motion to dismiss or answer), aff'd, 241 Fed. Appx. 420 (9th Cir. 2007); In re Albert, 113 B.R. 617 (B.A.P. 9th Cir. 1990) (court may extend deadline pursuant to request made after expiration of original deadline but before expiration of extended deadline).
116 See In re Gomez, 2011 WL 477857 (Bankr. D. Mass. Feb. 4, 2011) (Rule 9011 sanctions against creditor attorney who refused to withdraw clearly late complaint); Rescuecom Corp. v. Khafaga (In re Khafaga), 431 B.R. 329 (Bankr. E.D.N.Y. 2010) (amended complaint raising new operative facts did not relate back to timely filed complaint); In re Ryan, 408 B.R. 143 (Bankr. N.D. Ill. 2009) (dismissal of earlier timely complaint without prejudice did not permit later untimely complaint).
117 See In re Strickland, 50 B.R. 16 (Bankr. M.D. Ala. 1985). But see In re Coggin, 30 F.3d 1443 (11th Cir. 1994) (disagreeing with cases holding that motion for extension of deadline must be filed and also served by deadline); In re Toler, 999 F.2d 140 (6th Cir. 1993) (complaint filed before deadline was timely despite the fact that it was not accompanied by summons as required by local rules).
118 See In re Rutherford, 427 B.R. 656 (Bankr. S.D. Ohio 2010); In re Smolen, 48 B.R. 633 (Bankr. N.D. Ill. 1985).
119 See In re Emmerling, 223 B.R. 860 (B.A.P. 2d Cir. 1997); In re Lee, 186 B.R. 695 (B.A.P. 9th Cir. 1995).
120 In re Williamson, 15 F.3d 1037 (11th Cir. 1994) (creditor did not need to receive specific notice of deadline if it had timely notice of case); In re Gordon, 988 F.2d 1000 (9th Cir. 1993) (creditors not entitled to equitable relief from deadline when they had notice fifty-seven days before time period expired); In re Green, 876 F.2d 854 (10th Cir. 1989) (actual notice of the bankruptcy filing is sufficient); In re Price, 871 F.2d 97 (9th Cir. 1989) (knowledge of the bankruptcy is sufficient); In re Alton, 837 F.2d 457 (11th Cir. 1988); Neely v. Marchison, 815 F.2d 345 (5th Cir. 1987); In re Bucknum, 105 B.R. 25 (B.A.P. 9th Cir. 1989), aff'd, 951 F.2d 204 (9th Cir. 1991); In re Ricketts, 80 B.R. 495 (B.A.P. 9th Cir. 1987); In re Walker, 103 B.R. 281 (D. Utah 1989). But see In re Isaacman, 26 F.3d 629 (6th Cir. 1994) (creditor could file late dischargeability complaint that was within time period stated in erroneous notice from court reasonably relied upon by creditor); In re Anwiler, 958 F.2d 925 (9th Cir. 1992) (creditor could file late dischargeability complaint that was within time period stated in erroneous notice from court reasonably relied upon by creditor); In re Reichmeier, 130 B.R. 539 (Bankr. W.D. Mo. 1991) (creditor entitled to rely on mistaken notice of deadline, when notice was one day off); In re Eliscu, 85 B.R. 480 (Bankr. N.D. Ill. 1988) (creditor with no notice of the case at all not subject to the deadline).

Normally, a certificate of mailing in the bankruptcy court file listing a creditor creates a presumption that the creditor received notice of the case. In re Bucknum, 951 F.2d 204 (9th Cir. 1991)

pleading is not sufficient to put the debtor on notice of issues concerning dischargeability; therefore, the subsequent filing of a dischargeability complaint does not relate back to the date such document was filed.[121] Similarly, once the deadline has run, a creditor may not amend an existing complaint to raise an entirely new ground for nondischargeability.[122] Upon conversion to chapter 7, however, a new period arises for filing complaints.[123]

The rules permit the debtor or any creditor to file a complaint to determine dischargeability of a debt.[124] For the types of discharge exceptions that a creditor need not raise during the bankruptcy case, the debtor may file an adversary proceeding in order to have dischargeability issues resolved during the bankruptcy case.[125] The debtor may prefer to litigate dischargeability questions in the bankruptcy court, which is often a more sympathetic and knowledgeable forum than the one that might be chosen later by the creditor. (The debtor may also remove a later case brought by the creditor to the bankruptcy forum.)[126] An action may be brought by the debtor seeking a declaratory judgment that a particular debt is dischargeable and an injunction against it being collected. Such a complaint would not be governed by the deadline discussed above, which is applicable only to those dischargeability complaints that must be filed in the bankruptcy court under section 523(c).[127] The Eleventh Amendment is not a bar to a complaint seeking a determination of dischargeability even if a state agency is named as the defendant.[128]

For some situations in which discharge under the Code is ambiguous, such as certain tax debts to which a time period applies, it is a good idea to clarify with the creditor whether or not it thinks the debt is dischargeable so that problems do not rise after the close of the case. Otherwise the creditor may concede that the debt is dischargeable, but fail to take necessary action to modify its records. An exchange of letters, a stipulation, or a consent order is a useful tool to create a record that will resolve future questions.

Another possibility is to defer the question of dischargeability and to have it resolved later if collection activity is commenced. The discharge can then be interposed as a defense to repayment in the nonbankruptcy forum (or the bankruptcy case can be reopened to address the issue). One advantage of this strategy is that it avoids unnecessary litigation when the creditor is unlikely to commence future collection activities. On the other hand, failure to resolve questions about dischargeability during the bankruptcy creates uncertainty about the scope of the discharge that can seriously undermine the effectiveness of the debtor's fresh start. Once a nonbankruptcy court has ruled on dischargeability the bankruptcy court may not alter that ruling.[129]

15.4.3 Which Debts Are Excepted from Discharge?

15.4.3.1 Taxes—11 U.S.C. §§ 523(a)(1), 1328(a)(2)

15.4.3.1.1 Taxes that cannot be discharged

Taxes are the debts that are most frequently nondischargeable in bankruptcy cases. However, it is important to realize

---

(creditors did not overcome presumption merely by stating they did not receive notice).

121 *In re* Goscicki, 207 B.R. 893 (B.A.P. 9th Cir. 1997) (neither adversary cover sheet nor notice to bankruptcy court of potentially nondischargeable claims was substitute for adversary proceeding necessary to challenge dischargeability of debt); *In re* Kennerley, 995 F.2d 145 (9th Cir. 1993) (motion for relief could not be considered equivalent of dischargeability complaint or motion to extend time for filing dischargeability complaint); *In re* McGuirt, 879 F.2d 182 (5th Cir. 1989) (objection to dischargeability does not relate back to date of filing motion for relief); *In re* Harrison, 71 B.R. 457 (Bankr. D. Minn. 1987) (objection to discharge cannot be amended to present grounds for exception to discharge after the deadline has passed). *See In re* Markus, 313 F.3d 1146 (9th Cir. 2002) (*pro se* motion objecting to discharge filed within time limits did not constitute complaint because it did not meet pleading requirements).

122 *In re* Bercier, 934 F.2d 689 (5th Cir. 1991); *In re* Young, 428 B.R. 804 (Bankr. N.D. Ind. 2010). *See also In re* Dollar, 257 B.R. 364 (Bankr. S.D. Ga. 2001) (creditor may not amend complaint objecting to discharge to substitute nondischargeability claim); § 15.4.3.3, *infra*.

123 Fed. R. Bankr. P. 1019(2). *See In re* Marino, 181 F.3d 1142 (9th Cir. 1999) (dismissal of complaint for late filing in chapter 11 did not bar new complaint after case converted to chapter 7); *In re* Goralnick, 81 B.R. 570 (B.A.P. 9th Cir. 1987); Marquette Nat'l Bank v. Richards, 780 F.2d 24 (8th Cir. 1985) (conversion from chapter 11 to chapter 7).

But if a case is converted from chapter 7 to another chapter and then reconverted to chapter 7, no new time period arises. Fed. R. Bankr. P. 1019(2). *See In re* DiPalma, 94 B.R. 546 (Bankr. N.D. Ill. 1988).

124 Fed. R. Bankr. P. 4007(a). *But see In re* Hamada, 291 F.3d 645 (9th Cir. 2002) (bank that had issued letter of credit as part of collateral for *supersedeas* bond in appeal of judgment for original creditor who had obtained nondischargeability judgment, and which debtor agreed to indemnify, was not subrogated to rights of original creditor under 11 U.S.C. § 509 because debtor's obligation to bank was purely contractual); *In re* Edmond, 934 F.2d 1304 (4th Cir. 1991) (state consumer protection act gives state's consumer protection agency *parens patriae* standing to bring nondischargeability action on behalf of group of injured consumers).

A creditor must have an enforceable claim to file a dischargeability complaint. Westbrook v. Westbrook (*In re* Westbrook), 2010 WL 2080036 (Bankr. D.N.H. May 19, 2010) (proceeding could not be brought based on claim barred by statute of limitations).

125 *But cf. In re* Case, 937 F.2d 1014 (5th Cir. 1991) (bankruptcy court may not *sua sponte* address dischargeability of a debt; that is, to declare a debt for attorney fees in connection with an adversary proceeding nondischargeable).

126 See § 14.4.1, *supra*, for discussion of removing matters within the federal courts' bankruptcy jurisdiction.

127 Federal Rule of Bankruptcy Procedure 4007(b) permits such a complaint to be filed at any time.

128 Tennessee Student Assistance Corp. v. Hood, 541 U.S. 440, 124 S. Ct. 1905, 158 L. Ed. 2d 764 (2004).

129 *In re* Goetzman, 91 F.3d 1173 (9th Cir. 1996) (*Rooker-Feldman* doctrine prevents relitigation of questions related to discharge resolved by state court foreclosure judgment against debtors). *See also* § 15.4.4, *infra*.

that not all taxes are nondischargeable.[130] A rather complicated series of cross-references within the Code[131] can be followed to the conclusion that, basically,[132] only the types of taxes listed below are not discharged in consumer chapter 7 or chapter 12 cases:

- Any tax for which a return, or equivalent report or notice, if required, was not filed,[133] for which a fraudulent return, report, or notice was filed,[134] or which the debtor willfully attempted to evade;[135]
- Any tax with respect to which a late return was filed within two years before the date of filing of the bankruptcy;[136]
- Taxes on income or gross receipts
  (a) for which a return, if required, was last due within three years of the filing of the bankruptcy, or
  (b) assessed within 240 days before filing of the bankruptcy,[137] or

---

130 Even if a tax is discharged, liens based on the underlying debt may remain legally enforceable *in rem* claims. *In re* Isom, 901 F.2d 744 (9th Cir. 1990).

131 11 U.S.C. § 523(a)(1) refers to 11 U.S.C. § 507(a)(3) and § 507(a)(8), the former of which refers in turn to 11 U.S.C. § 502(f).

132 Not included in the list are some "gap" tax claims arising in involuntary cases, which are provided for in 11 U.S.C. § 502(f). There are special provisions dealing with cases in which there has been an offer of compromise (11 U.S.C. § 507(a)(8)(A)(ii)), taxes to be withheld by employers or paid by employers on priority wages (11 U.S.C. § 507(a)(8)(C), (D)), and certain unpaid customs duties (11 U.S.C. § 507(a)(8)(F)). Also not included are sales taxes which are to be collected by some business debtors. *See In re* Shank, 792 F.2d 829 (9th Cir. 1986).

133 A California statute that required the debtor to notify the state taxing authority that the IRS had assessed a deficiency did not require the filing of a new state tax return for purposes of this section. *In re* Jackson, 184 F.3d 1046 (9th Cir. 1999).

The language added to section 523(a)(1) concerning a report or notice may have been an attempt to overrule this result. However it is not clear that the new language accomplishes this result. The *Jackson* decision was based not only on the holding that a "return" did not mean a "report," but also on the principle that once a debtor has filed a return for a particular year that person has satisfied the requirement of filing a return. The court quoted an earlier decision: "Once a debtor has filed 'a return' for a tax which is 'required' to be so reported that provision [section 523(a)(1)(B)(i)] has been met.... Once a requirement has been satisfied, it does not become 'unsatisfied' because some new requirement has been superadded." *In re* Dyer, 158 B.R. 904, 906 (Bankr. W.D.N.Y. 1993). *But see* Maryland v. Ciotti, 638 F.3d 276 (4th Cir. 2011) (debtor's failure to file report with state tax authorities after federal taxes were adjusted rendered state taxes nondischargeable).

134 *See In re* Dorminy, 301 B.R. 599 (Bankr. M.D. Fla. 2003) (pre-bankruptcy stipulated decision by tax court that debtor liable for fraud penalty did not prevent debtor from litigating fraud issue for purposes of dischargeability).

135 11 U.S.C. § 523(a)(1)(B)(i), (C); Cassidy v. Comm'r, 814 F.2d 477 (7th Cir. 1987).

The courts have disagreed on what constitutes "evasion" of taxes. *See* United States v. Coney, 689 F.3d 365 (5th Cir. 2012) (debtors may evade collection even if they have filed returns and not evaded assessment); United States v. Storey, 640 F.3d 739 (6th Cir. 2011) (simply failing to pay is not evasion; no evasion where debtor did not live lavishly or devote money to philanthropy or recreation instead of paying taxes); United States v. Mitchell (*In re* Mitchell), 633 F.3d 1319 (11th Cir. 2011) (purchasing house in wife's name, closing bank account, and transferring earnings to corporation to protect them from levy constituted evasion); *In re* Jacobs, 490 F.3d 913 (11th Cir. 2007) (placing assets in name of wife to avoid attachment of tax lien is evasion); *In re* Gardner, 360 F.3d 551 (6th Cir. 2004) (placing assets in nominee accounts and failing to pay taxes when debtor had ability to do so was evasion); *In re* Fretz, 244 F.3d 1323 (11th Cir. 2001) (alcoholic doctor who knew he should file returns and had means to pay taxes evaded taxes); *In re* Griffith, 206 F.3d 1389 (11th Cir. 2000) (en banc) (exception applies when the debtor engaged in affirmative acts seeking to evade or defeat collection of taxes); *In re* Tudisco, 183 F.3d 133 (2d Cir. 1999) (false affidavit to employer and debtor's knowledge that he had to file returns and pay taxes established mens rea required by this exception); *In re* Fegely, 118 F.3d 979 (3d Cir. 1997) (debtor who knew he had duty to file returns, had the wherewithal to pay the taxes due, and intentionally failed to do so had evaded taxes); *In re* Zuhone, 88 F.3d 469 (7th Cir. 1996) (court found long series of complicated transactions designed to evade taxes); *In re* Birkenstock, 87 F.3d 947 (7th Cir. 1996) (debtor husband's actions showed attempts to avoid tax liability, but debtor wife's mere failure to pay back taxes was not evasion); Dalton v. Internal Revenue Serv., 77 F.3d 1297 (10th Cir. 1996) (debtor's attempts to conceal assets in order to avoid taxes constituted evasion); *In re* Bruner, 55 F.3d 195 (5th Cir. 1995) (debtors who failed to file returns, failed to pay taxes and attempted to hide income and assets had willfully evaded taxes); *In re* Toti, 24 F.3d 806 (6th Cir. 1994) (debtor has evaded taxes if he voluntarily, consciously and intentionally failed to file returns and pay taxes while living lavish lifestyle; even if evasion was not felonious); *In re* Roper, 294 B.R. 301 (B.A.P. 8th Cir. 2003) (debtor who did not take steps to avoid taxes and who relied on advice of professionals in dealing with IRS did not evade taxes); *In re* Binkley, 242 B.R. 728 (M.D. Fla. 1999) (tax debt discharged for debtor who was not complicit in her husband's fraud); *In re* Brackin, 148 B.R. 953 (Bankr. N.D. Ala. 1992) (evidence did not show that debtor had intentionally claimed non-allowable deductions, but tax on discharge of indebtedness income that debtor never reported was nondischargeable); *In re* Jones, 116 B.R. 810 (Bankr. D. Kan. 1990) (tax debts held nondischargeable when debtor concealed assets). *See also In re* Frosch, 261 B.R. 181 (Bankr. W.D. Pa. 2001) (negligent mistakes on return not evasion); *In re* Howard, 167 B.R. 684 (Bankr. M.D. Fla. 1994) (poor judgment in using funds for purposes other than payment of taxes is not evasion); *In re* Gathwright, 102 B.R. 211 (Bankr. D. Or. 1989) (tax debt found dischargeable when errors were due to sloppiness and lack of understanding of tax code rather than fraud).

The decision in *Cassidy v. Comm'r* was revisited in *In re* Cassidy, 892 F.2d 637 (7th Cir. 1990), in which the court held that its earlier dischargeability decision in a tax court appeal was binding on the debtor in a later bankruptcy proceeding.

136 11 U.S.C. § 523(a)(1)(B)(ii).

Even if a tax is dischargeable as outside this exception, it may nevertheless be nondischargeable as an income tax for which a return is last due within three years of bankruptcy. Etheridge v. Illinois, 127 B.R. 421 (C.D. Ill. 1989).

137 *See generally In re* Lewis, 199 F.3d 249 (5th Cir. 1999) (state taxes deemed assessed when notice of assessment was given, even though state followed improper procedures); *In re* O'Connell, 246 B.R. 332 (B.A.P. 8th Cir. 2000) (state law definition of assessment was not dispositive of when tax was assessed under section 507(a)(8)(A)); *In re* Hardie, 204 B.R. 944 (S.D. Tex. 1996) (taxes assessed when IRS issued certificate of assessment, not when tax court entered judgment determining deficiency); *In re* King, 122 B.R. 383 (B.A.P. 9th Cir. 1991) (date of assessment depends on specific tax code and practices involved), *aff'd*, 961 F.2d 1423 (9th Cir. 1992); *In re*

(c) not yet assessed, but assessable after filing of the bankruptcy;[138]
- Property taxes assessed before commencement of the case and last payable without penalty less than one year before filing of the bankruptcy;[139]
- Excise taxes[140]
  (a) On transactions as to which a return was required and last due less than three years before the bankruptcy, or
  (b) On transactions, as to which no return was required, which occurred less than three years before the bankruptcy;
- Taxes required to be collected or withheld by the debtor, such as employment "trust fund" taxes (income taxes and FICA withholding) or sales taxes.[141]

A paragraph added at the end of section 523(a) in 2005 defines "return" as "a return that satisfies the requirements of applicable nonbankruptcy law (including applicable filing requirements)," and includes returns filed under Internal Revenue Code section 6020(a) or equivalent state or local law, or stipulated judgments or orders, but does not include returns made pursuant to Internal Revenue Code section 6020(b) (service-filed returns) or equivalent state or local law. Returns filed under Internal Revenue Code section 6020(a) are generally prepared by the taxing authority with the debtor's assistance based on information and documentation provided by the debtor, whereas a return filed under Internal Revenue Code section 6020(b) is prepared without the debtor's cooperation and is based on information the taxing authority has obtained on its own. This provision generally codifies the law that when a debtor participates in or signs off on a return, it is considered a return, but when the debtor does not participate in the taxing authority's creation of a return, it is not.[142] It also clarifies that if the debtor files a return after the taxing authority has already

---

Hartman, 110 B.R. 951 (D. Kan. 1990) (federal income tax deficiency not assessed immediately upon notice of tax deficiency but only after IRS had taken other steps required by Internal Revenue Code before liability could attach); *In re* Oldfield, 121 B.R. 249 (Bankr. E.D. Ark. 1990) (tax assessed when IRS entered taxes due as determined by tax court on taxpayers' master file and sent notice of deficiency to debtors); *In re* Shotwell, 120 B.R. 163 (Bankr. D. Or. 1990) (tax assessed when summary record signed by assessment officer rather than when returns are filed); *In re* King, 96 B.R. 356 (Bankr. M.D. Fla. 1989).

138 11 U.S.C. § 523(a)(1)(A) (incorporating 11 U.S.C. § 507(a)(8)(A)). *See In re* Aberl, 78 F.3d 241 (6th Cir. 1996) (offer in compromise made prior to assessment does not toll time period for priority status); *In re* King, 961 F.2d 1423 (9th Cir. 1992) (discussing different meaning of "assessment" under California law which, unlike federal law, does not involve creation of a tax lien after notice of deficiency is sent); *In re* Wines, 122 B.R. 804 (Bankr. S.D. Fla. 1991) (although no assessment usually may be made after three years from filing of tax returns, because assessment was prohibited until tax court entered final decision on debtor's petition for redetermination tax was still assessable); *In re* Crist, 85 B.R. 807 (Bankr. N.D. Iowa 1988); *In re* Carter, 74 B.R. 613 (Bankr. E.D. Pa. 1987) (discussion of assessment deadlines).

139 11 U.S.C. § 523(a)(1)(A) (incorporating 11 U.S.C. § 507(a)(8)(B)). Some property taxes may acquire lien status. When they do, they no longer constitute priority debts, nor are they nondischargeable under section 523(a)(1). However, the lien associated with the debt, if unpaid or not avoided, will pass through the bankruptcy unaffected. The penalty necessary to place a tax outside this exception need not be solely a monetary one. *In re* S. Shore Vending, Inc., 25 B.R. 111 (Bankr. D. Mass. 1982) (issuance of a warrant to sell property constitutes a penalty).

140 11 U.S.C. § 523(a)(1)(A) (incorporating 11 U.S.C. § 507(a)(8)(E)). A tax may be an excise tax in some circumstances even if it is measured by gross receipts. *In re* Groetken, 843 F.2d 1007 (7th Cir. 1988) (Illinois retailer's occupation tax). *See also In re* Grynberg, 986 F.2d 367 (10th Cir. 1993) (gift taxes were excise taxes); *In re* Suburban Motor Freight, Inc., 998 F.2d 338 (6th Cir. 1993) (unpaid workers compensation premiums, as involuntary exaction applicable to all similarly situated firms, were excise taxes); *In re* C-T of Va., 977 F.2d 137 (4th Cir. 1992) (tax imposed upon employer when pension plan assets reverted to employer upon plan's termination was excise tax); New Neighborhoods, Inc. v. W. Va. Workers Compensation Fund, 886 F.2d 714 (4th Cir. 1989) (premiums due the state Workers Compensation Fund are excise taxes under federal law); *In re* Marcucci, 256 B.R. 685 (D.N.J. 2000) (New Jersey vehicle insurance surcharge debt was not an excise tax).

141 11 U.S.C. § 523(a)(1)(A) (incorporating 11 U.S.C. § 507(a)(8)(C)). Although such taxes are usually owed by businesses, consumers who have employed others, or who were previously in business may have liabilities for such taxes. *See generally In re* Gust, 197 F.3d 1112 (1st Cir. 1999) (liability imposed on individual based on responsibility to withhold trust fund taxes is a nondischargeable tax).

A debtor may request that the bankruptcy court determine whether there is liability for withholding taxes as a "responsible person" with respect to a businesses with which the debtor has been affiliated. Adams v. Coveney, 162 F.3d 23 (1st Cir. 1998) (debtor not liable for corporation's withholding taxes under state law, which was construed to be less strict than federal law); *In re* Macagnone, 253 B.R. 99 (M.D. Fla. 2000); *In re* Newton, 260 B.R. 1 (Bankr. D. Ariz. 2000) (debtor held not liable for responsible person penalty for tax quarter when corporation had insufficient funds to pay taxes); *In re* Schwartz, 192 B.R. 90 (Bankr. D.N.J. 1996) (debtor could initiate proceeding to determine whether he was responsible person even though IRS had not yet claimed that he had such liability).

142 *See In re* Colsen, 446 F.3d 836 (8th Cir. 2005) (if face of document indicated honest and genuine attempt to satisfy tax laws, document constitutes return, even if filed after assessment); *In re* Payne, 431 F.3d 1055 (7th Cir. 2005) (when debtor gave no excuse for filing tax forms six years late and after assessment, tax forms did not constitute "returns"); *In re* Hatton, 220 F.3d 1057 (9th Cir. 2000) (neither substitute return prepared without input from debtor nor installment agreement signed by debtor constituted return); *In re* Moroney, 352 F.3d 902 (4th Cir. 2003) (income tax forms unjustifiably filed years late, when the IRS has already prepared substitute returns and assessed taxes, do not constitute "returns" for purposes of 11 U.S.C. § 523(a)(1)(B)(i)); *In re* Hindenlang, 164 F.3d 1029 (6th Cir. 1999) (tax forms filed after IRS had assessed deficiencies were not "returns" because they were filed too late to have any effect under Internal Revenue Code); *In re* Bergstrom, 949 F.2d 341 (10th Cir. 1991); *In re* Nunez, 232 B.R. 778 (B.A.P. 9th Cir. 1999) (tax forms filed after IRS assessed deficiency qualified as returns when filed in good faith); *In re* Savage, 218 B.R. 126 (B.A.P. 10th Cir. 1998) (amended returns filed after IRS filed substitute returns constituted "returns" for purposes of dischargeability provision).

The fact that a substitute return or an assessment has been completed by a taxing authority should not preclude the honest filing of a return thereafter. *In re* Izzo, 287 B.R. 158 (Bankr. E.D. Mich. 2002); *In re* Woods, 285 B.R. 284 (Bankr. S.D. Ind. 2002).

prepared one without the debtor's participation, that later return does not qualify as a return.[143]

The language requiring a return to satisfy "applicable filing requirements" could be troublesome. What requirements are included? If timeliness were included, it would render the timeliness language in section 523(a)(1)(B)(ii) superfluous. Nonetheless, some courts have held that an untimely return does not qualify as a return under this language.[144] Fortunately, it appears that the Internal Revenue Service does not contend that timeliness is one of the "applicable requirements."[145]

The 2005 amendments also added rules for calculating the time periods when they have been interrupted by a bankruptcy automatic stay or an offer in compromise. The 240-day period after an assessment in section 507(a)(8)(A) is extended by any time during which an offer in compromise was pending or in effect during the 240 days, plus thirty days.[146] It is also extended by any time during which collections were stayed in a prior bankruptcy case, plus ninety days.[147] In addition, language added at the end of section 507(a)(8) provides that all of the time periods in that paragraph are suspended for any period during which collection is stayed as a result of an appeal of a collection action, plus ninety days, plus any time during which collection was stayed in a prior bankruptcy case, plus ninety days.[148]

Any penalties related to nondischargeable taxes are also nondischargeable, unless the penalty is solely punitive in nature or relates to a transaction that occurred more than three years before the filing of the petition.[149] Erroneous refunds of non-dischargeable taxes are similarly nondischargeable.[150] The treatment of prepetition interest is not as clear; but most courts have held that it is nondischargeable.[151] Postpetition interest on nondischargeable tax debts is clearly nondischargeable.[152] And in limited situations, a party who has paid the tax claim of the debtor may become subrogated to the claim and eligible for the same priority and treatment related to dischargeability.[153]

Occasionally, it is not altogether clear whether a particular debt to a governmental entity is a tax subject to these provisions. Courts consider the debt's inherent characteristics, especially whether, or how closely, it is related to a debtor's voluntary use of a service, rather than assessed regardless of the debtor's actions. Thus, when a charge is assessed only when services are used, in proportion to their use, that charge is not a tax.[154] Similarly, if the charge is exacted as punishment for an unlawful act or omission, such as early withdrawal of individual retirement account funds, it is a penalty and not a tax.[155]

---

143 Wogoman v. IRS (*In re* Wogoman), 475 B.R. 239 (B.A.P. 10th Cir. 2012).

144 McCoy v. Miss. State Tax Comm'n (*In re* McCoy), 666 F.3d 924 (5th Cir. 2012).

145 Internal Revenue Service Chief Counsel Notice of Litigating Position CC-2010-016, *available at* www.irs.gov/pub/irs-ccdm/cc_2010_016.pdf.

146 11 U.S.C. § 507(a)(8)(A)(ii)(I).

147 11 U.S.C. § 507(a)(8)(A)(ii)(II). *See In re* Jones, 657 F.3d 921 (9th Cir. 2011) (provision was inapplicable when taxes first became due after property of estate revested in debtor upon confirmation of plan in a prior case, because there was no stay precluding collection).

148 *See In re* Jones, 657 F.3d 921 (9th Cir. 2011) (time period was not tolled for tax arising after plan confirmation in prior case, because taxing authority was not stayed from collecting from estate property that had revested in debtor); Kolve v. IRS (*In re* Kolve), 459 B.R. 376 (Bankr. W.D. Wis. 2011) (same). *See also* United States v. Montgomery, 475 B.R. 742 (D. Kan. 2012) (when there are multiple suspension periods, 90 days are added only once).

149 11 U.S.C. § 523(a)(1)(A) (incorporating 11 U.S.C. §§ 507(a)(7)(G), 726(a)(4)); Cassidy v. Comm'r, 814 F.2d 477 (7th Cir. 1987).

Actually, section 507(a)(7)(G) only applies to income, gross receipts, property, and excise taxes. McKay v. United States, 957 F.2d 689 (9th Cir. 1992) (penalties relating to transactions more than three years old are dischargeable even if underlying taxes are not); Roberts v. United States, 906 F.2d 1440 (10th Cir. 1990) (same); *In re* Burns, 887 F.2d 1541 (11th Cir. 1989) (same). *See In re* Cassidy, 983 F.2d 161 (10th Cir. 1992) (ten percent penalty for premature pension fund withdrawal was non-pecuniary penalty not entitled to priority and not a tax); *In re* Bates, 974 F.2d 1234 (10th Cir. 1992) (punitive tax penalties not entitled to priority); *In re* Hanna, 872 F.2d 829 (8th Cir. 1989) (postpetition penalties are nondischargeable); *In re* Hovan, 172 B.R. 974 (Bankr. W.D. Wash. 1994) (compensatory nature of penalty must be demonstrated by clear statutory language or legislative history), *aff'd*, 96 F.3d 1254 (9th Cir. 1996).

150 United States v. Frontone, 383 F.3d 656 (6th Cir. 2004); Bleak v. United States, 817 F.2d 1368 (9th Cir. 1987). *But see In re* Jackson, 253 B.R. 570 (M.D. Ala. 2000) (erroneous refund was dischargeable because section 507(c) applies only to priority status and not dischargeability).

151 *See In re* Johnson, 146 F.3d 252 (5th Cir. 1998) (debtor liable for postpetition interest on nondischargeable taxes, but not for interest on amounts paid by trustee accruing after such payments had been made); *In re* Hardee, 137 F.3d 337 (5th Cir. 1998) (increase in amount of interest for underpayments arising from tax-motivated transaction was interest and not penalty); *In re* Larson, 862 F.2d 112 (7th Cir. 1988) (prepetition interest on a nondischargeable tax liability is nondischargeable). *See also In re* Bates, 974 F.2d 1234 (10th Cir. 1992) (prepetition interest has same priority as underlying tax debt); *In re* Garcia, 955 F.2d 16 (5th Cir. 1992) (interest on tax debt has same priority as underlying tax debt).

But interest on dischargeable tax penalties is dischargeable even if the underlying tax debt is not. *In re* Teeslink, 165 B.R. 708 (Bankr. S.D. Ga. 1994).

152 *In re* Fullmer, 962 F.2d 1463 (10th Cir. 1992); *In re* Burns, 887 F.2d 1541 (11th Cir. 1989); *In re* Hanna, 872 F.2d 829 (8th Cir. 1989); *In re* Irvin, 129 B.R. 187 (W.D. Mo. 1990) (liability for postpetition interest survives bankruptcy even though prepetition claim was fully paid by estate). *See also* Bruning v. United States, 376 U.S. 358, 84 S. Ct. 906, 11 L. Ed. 2d 772 (1964).

153 *See In re* Fields, 926 F.2d 501 (5th Cir. 1991); W. Surety Co. v. Waite, 698 F.2d 1177 (11th Cir. 1983); *In re* Allway, 37 B.R. 420 (Bankr. E.D. Pa. 1984) (former spouse).

154 Bidart Bros. v. California Apple Comm'n, 73 F.3d 925 (9th Cir. 1996) (assessments on apple producers that were kept segregated from general revenues and used for purpose of promoting apple sales were not taxes); *In re* Jenny Lynn Mining Co., 780 F.2d 585 (6th Cir. 1986); *In re* Lorber Indus. of Cal., 675 F.2d 1062 (9th Cir. 1982); *In re* Adams, 40 B.R. 545 (E.D. Pa. 1984); *In re* Mounier, 232 B.R. 186 (Bankr. S.D. Cal. 1998) (ten percent assessment for early withdrawal from retirement plan was not a tax).

155 United States v. Reorganized Fabricators, 518 U.S. 213, 135 L. Ed. 2d 506, 116 S. Ct. 2106 (1996) (exaction imposed upon employer that fails to correct pension plan deficiency was a penalty, not an excise tax); *In re* Marcucci, 256 B.R. 685 (D.N.J. 2000) (New Jersey vehicle insurance surcharge debt was civil penalty and not an

Nor is the liability under the Internal Revenue Code of a transferee of assets from a taxpayer a tax; it is merely a method of collecting the tax owed by the taxpayer.[156] On the other hand, revenue collected on an *ad valorem* basis from all property holders or for a purpose that confers no particular benefit on the payer would be considered a tax.[157]

In addition, even if a tax is an excise tax, it must be an excise tax "on a transaction" to fall under section 507(a)(7)(E). Thus an occupation tax is dischargeable despite the fact that it may be an excise tax, because it is not a tax on a transaction.[158]

Some, but not all, of the taxes that are nondischargeable in chapter 7 are also nondischargeable in chapter 13. Under section 1328(a)(2), taxes that are described in section 507(a)(8)(C) (taxes required to be withheld or collected by the debtor), section 523(a)(1)(B) (unfiled return or late return filed within two years before petition), and section 523(a)(8)(C) (fraudulent return or evasion) are nondischargeable when the debtor receives a discharge after completion of a plan. Other taxes that are nondischargeable in chapter 7, but may be discharged in chapter 13, are priority debts in chapter 13 that are required to be paid in full through the plan unless the creditor agrees otherwise or a claim for them is not filed.[159]

In some cases, it is to the debtor's advantage to arrange the bankruptcy filing and the filing of a tax return so that a debt that is nondischargeable in chapter 13 will also be a priority debt. If such is the case, the debtor will be permitted to pay that debt, which will not be discharged, before paying other debts that will be discharged.[160] For example, a debtor may render an old nondischargeable tax debt, for which no return was filed, a priority debt if the debtor files a return shortly before the bankruptcy case and waits for the assessment to be made before filing the case. The tax is then one which was assessed within 240 days before the petition and is a priority debt, which can be separately classified and paid, with penalties and interest, before other unsecured debts. However, this strategy may not be successful if the taxing authority has already made an assessment in the case.

15.4.3.1.2 Analyzing tax debts to determine dischargeability

In view of the relative intricacy of these provisions, it is always wise to check each particular fact situation against the Code itself. In some cases, when significant amounts of money are involved, it may pay to delay filing until one or more of the time periods listed above has expired. For the purpose of calculating time limits under the various provisions, taxes are found to be payable from the date the relevant tax return is due rather than the date on which quarterly estimated payments are required.[161] It should also be remembered that, because taxes in many of the categories listed above are priority claims, a chapter 13 plan must normally provide for their full payment.[162]

In analyzing federal income tax debts, it is important to have all the facts, including precise dates, so that the relevant time

---

excise tax); *In re* Cespedes, 393 B.R. 403 (Bankr. E.D.N.C. 2008) (penalty on early individual retirement account withdrawal was not an excise tax).
156 *In re* Pert, 201 B.R. 316 (Bankr. M.D. Fla. 1996).
157 *In re* Suburban Motor Freight, Inc., 998 F.2d 338 (6th Cir. 1993) (unpaid workers compensation premiums, as involuntary exaction applicable to all similarly situated firms, were excise taxes); *In re* Dietz, 914 F.2d 161 (9th Cir. 1990) (assessment imposed by Virginia on individuals for operating uninsured vehicle is involuntary pecuniary burden and thus nondischargeable, excise tax; however, a separate service fee was intended to defray administrative costs and was not excluded from discharge); United States v. River Coal Co., 748 F.2d 1103 (6th Cir. 1984); *In re* Lorber Indus. of Cal., 675 F.2d 1062 (9th Cir. 1982).
158 *In re* Templar, 170 B.R. 562 (Bankr. M.D. Pa. 1994). *But see In re* Groetken, 843 F.2d 1007 (7th Cir. 1988) (Illinois retailer's occupation tax was excise tax).
159 11 U.S.C. § 1322(a)(2); Mich. Dep't of Treasury v. Hight (*In re* Hight), 670 F.3d 699 (6th Cir. 2012) (debtor could pay taxes for tax year ending before petition as prepetition claim even though taxes not yet due); *In re* Dixon, 218 B.R. 150 (B.A.P. 10th Cir. 1998); *In re* Senczyszyn, 444 B.R. 750 (E.D. Mich. 2011). *See In re* Joye, 578 F.3d 1070 (9th Cir. 2009) (taxes incurred before petition date were claims that were dischargeable even if they were not payable until after petition date). *But see In re* Ripley, 926 F.2d 440 (5th Cir. 1991) (taxes not claims until they were payable); *In re* Turner, 420 B.R. 711 (Bankr. E.D. Mich. 2009) (same).
160 The mere fact that a debt is nondischargeable in chapter 13 does not necessarily mean the debtor can pay it ahead of other debts. *See* § 12.4.3, *supra*.

161 *In re* Ripley, 926 F.2d 440 (5th Cir. 1991). *Cf.* Moore v. Internal Revenue Serv., 132 B.R. 533 (Bankr. W.D. Pa. 1991) (when chapter 11 debtor does not elect to divide the taxable year in which the case is filed so that prepetition taxes are the responsibility of the debtor and not the estate, the entire year's tax obligation is treated as if it arose postpetition).
162 11 U.S.C. § 1322(a)(2). *See* § 12.3.6.1, *supra*.
The holders of such tax claims may agree to different treatment. 11 U.S.C. § 1322(a)(2). *See also In re* Riley, 204 B.R. 28 (Bankr. E.D. Ark. 1996) (tax was provided for in plan when original plan proposed paying priority claim, even though modified plan, not objected to by taxing authority, did not provide for payment).
Full payment is not required on a priority claim if it is not filed by the creditor. *See In re* Joye, 578 F.3d 1070 (9th Cir. 2009); United States v. Carr, 142 B.R. 351 (D. Neb. 1992) (amended IRS proof of claim not allowed and amounts not included in original claim discharged); *In re* Tomlan, 102 B.R. 790 (E.D. Wash. 1989) (IRS's failure to file timely claim deprives it of priority status so that its claim was discharged without full payment under chapter 13 plan), *aff'd*, 907 F.2d 114 (9th Cir. 1990); *In re* Richards, 50 B.R. 339 (E.D. Tenn. 1985) (IRS claim not allowed and need not be paid when it was not timely filed); *In re* Dixon, 218 B.R. 150 (B.A.P. 10th Cir. 1998) (tax for tax year ending prior to chapter 13 petition was prepetition claim discharged because no claim filed for such tax, even though return was not yet due when chapter 13 petition was filed); *In re* Rothman, 76 B.R. 38 (Bankr. E.D.N.Y. 1987) (debtor discharged from taxes not included in taxing authorities' claim). *See also* § 15.4.2, *supra*. *But see In re* Hairopolous, 118 F.3d 1240 (8th Cir. 1997) (unfiled IRS claims not discharged due to lack of notice when only notice of bankruptcy that IRS received before claims bar date was no asset chapter 7 notice sent before conversion to chapter 13); *In re* Grynberg, 986 F.2d 367 (10th Cir. 1993).
However, the failure of the government to file a proof of claim does not affect the dischargeability of a tax debt. For this reason, it may be advisable for the debtor to file a claim on behalf of the taxing authority in such cases if assets would be distributed in payment of a nondischargeable claim.

§ 15.4.3.1.2   Consumer Bankruptcy Law and Practice

periods can be calculated accurately. The best way to ensure this is to obtain a transcript from the Internal Revenue Service (IRS). Several types of transcripts are available, such as the MFTRA-X (Account Transcript), which is fairly easily deciphered, and a more detailed MFT-30, which must be decoded. The former, unfortunately, omits information that may be important, such as whether a return listed was a substitute return not filed by the debtor, in which case it does not trigger the time periods triggered by filed returns.

The MFTRA-X and other transcripts can be obtained by mailing or faxing an IRS transcript request form to the appropriate regional IRS office.[163] If requested by the debtor's attorney, the form requesting transcripts may need be accompanied by an IRS form power of attorney signed by the debtor. Requests by the debtor's attorney can also be made by calling the IRS practitioner hotline at (866) 860-4259. The debtor can also obtain this transcript in person at the local IRS field office or by calling the IRS at (800) 908-9946.[164] In an emergency, the IRS will sometimes give some information over the phone and send a transcript more quickly if the debtor's counsel calls the tax practitioner hotline, and immediately sends a power of attorney by facsimile. The MFT-30 takes longer to obtain, usually about two weeks. In complicated cases, a Freedom of Information Act request can be sent to the appropriate IRS disclosure office, requesting the debtor's entire file, including the MFT-30, collection file, notices of deficiency, and records of assessments. However, obtaining these records can take several months.

Once counsel obtains the necessary information, the claim for each tax year must be separately analyzed.[165] First, is there a lien securing the claim? If so, to the extent that the lien is not undersecured and is properly recorded, the tax claim (including interest and penalties) is an allowed secured claim. The lien will probably not be eliminated in chapter 7,[166] even if the tax is dischargeable,[167] although a lien for penalties may be avoidable under section 724(a).[168] In chapter 13, a tax claim is not a priority claim to the extent it is an allowed secured claim. Therefore it is not subject to the requirement of section 1322(a)(2) that it be paid in full. However, if the plan provides for the claim, the taxing authority must receive the present value of its allowed secured claim under section 1325(a)(5)(ii).[169] If the plan does not provide for the secured claim, the taxing authority may seek relief from the automatic stay.[170]

If the debtor filed a tax return, the debt is dischargeable in chapter 7 if all of the following are true:

- The return was not fraudulent and was filed on time or, if the return was filed late, it was filed more than two years before the bankruptcy;
- The tax is not a priority claim (see below); and
- The debtor did not willfully evade taxes.

An unsecured tax claim for which a return has not been filed is never dischargeable in chapter 7 or in chapter 13. Similarly, a tax claim based upon a fraudulently filed return is nondischargeable in chapter 13. A chapter 13 debtor normally must pay all priority tax claims in full, probably including prepetition interest but not penalties. Whether the claim is a priority claim depends upon when the debtor's tax return was last due and when the tax was last assessable.

The tax debt is a priority claim if the tax return was last due less than three years before the date of the petition. The due date of the return is normally April 15th (but occasionally the 16th or 17th if the 15th is on a weekend) of the year after the tax year. However, if the debtor obtained an extension, the due date would be the extended deadline. If the debtor was in a prior bankruptcy case during this period, it is normally also extended by the amount of time that case was pending.[171]

A tax debt also is a priority debt if it was assessed within 240 days before the petition, or is assessable after the commencement of the case. Federal income tax is assessed on the date the IRS notifies the taxpayer of a tax claim, or perhaps, on the earlier date that an assessment officer signs a summary record of assessment (Form 23-C).[172] The date of the assessment is normally stated on the IRS transcript and when a return is timely filed it is normally around the time of the return. An assessment may be made within three years[173] of when a return is filed or of the last day the return was due, whichever was later. If an amended tax return is filed, a new 240-day period begins to run for additional taxes assessed. Therefore, if a tax is not otherwise a priority tax, no return or amended return should be filed before the bankruptcy case is filed, unless the debtor wishes to trigger a new assessment period. The assessment time period does not begin to run when a substitute return is filed by the IRS.[174] The 240 days is extended by the time during which an offer in compromise made after the assessment[175] is pending or

---

163 See Appx. H.2, *infra*, for forms and more information on obtaining tax records. The IRS form power of attorney, Form 2848, can be obtained from www.irs.ustreas.gov/forms_pubs/forms.html. In some cases it may be sufficient to supply Form 8821, a tax information authorization, which will not cause all future tax notices to be mailed to the attorney as would a power of attorney.

164 The call initiates an automatic process that results in the transcript arriving by mail in about five to ten business days at the debtor's address found on the return. Information about using the IRS call-in procedure is provided in Appx H.2, *infra*.

165 For a more detailed discussion of analyzing tax claims, see M. King, Discharging Taxes in Bankruptcy (1996).

166 See § 10.4.2.6.3, *supra*, for discussion of avoiding tax liens.

167 If the tax is dischargeable, the lien cannot attach to after-acquired property, however. *In re* Dishong, 188 B.R. 51 (Bankr. M.D. Fla. 1995).

168 See § 10.4.2.6.8, *supra*.

169 See § 11.6.1.3, *supra*.

170 *Id.*

171 11 U.S.C. § 507(a)(8).

172 Treas. Reg. § 301.6203-1.

173 The period is six years if the return omits over twenty-five percent of reportable gross income.

174 See § 15.4.3.1.1, *supra*.

175 United States v. Aberl, 175 B.R. 915 (N.D. Ohio 1994) (language in section 507(a)(8) only extends period for offers in compromise made during the 240-day period), *aff'd*, 78 F.3d 241 (6th Cir. 1996); *In re* Colish, 239 B.R. 670 (Bankr. E.D.N.Y. 1999) (same). *See In*

in effect plus thirty days.[176] If the debtor was in a prior bankruptcy case during this period it is normally also extended by the amount of time that collection was stayed in that case, plus ninety days.[177]

Once each year's taxes, interest, and penalties are analyzed, they may be categorized as allowed secured claims, unsecured priority claims, claims that are nondischargeable in chapter 7 (which overlap with priority claims), claims that are nondischargeable in chapter 13 (also overlapping with priority claims), and unsecured claims that are dischargeable in both chapter 7 and 13. The debtor's counsel can then compute the amounts that would not be discharged in chapter 7, the amounts that would not be discharged in chapter 13, and the amounts that would have to be paid in a chapter 13 case, in order to decide on the strategy that offers the debtor the greatest benefit.

15.4.3.2 Debts Incurred Through False Pretenses, Fraud, or False Financial Statements—11 U.S.C. § 523(a)(2)

15.4.3.2.1 Overview

While the exception to discharge for taxes is the exception most commonly applicable in consumer cases, the exception dealing with false pretenses, fraud and false financial statements[178] is the one that has given rise to the most litigation. Generally speaking, the Code upholds a creditor's timely-filed complaint seeking a determination that a debt is nondischargeable if the debt is for obtaining money, property, services, or an extension, renewal, or refinancing of credit, by false pretenses, a false representation, fraud, or a false financial statement.[179]

Initially after enactment of the Bankruptcy Code, litigation concerning this exception had decreased in consumer cases for two reasons. First, debts that are not dischargeable under this subsection in chapter 7 were, until 2005, dischargeable in chapter 13. And second, creditors who file nondischargeability complaints based upon this subsection and lose are often required to pay attorney fees to the debtor's counsel, as discussed below.

More recently, however, there have been periods of time during which there was an increase in claims of fraud by creditors in consumer cases. For the most part these were due to a concerted effort by various card issuers to establish that consumers who use a credit card when they do not have a present ability to make substantial payments have committed fraud. Creditors also took advantage of *pro se* debtors and poorly represented debtors who often simply settled cases because they did not want to incur the expense of defending. However, with consolidation in the credit card industry and the trend toward selling delinquent debt to third parties unfamiliar with the underlying accounts, the number of dischargeability complaints is again dropping.

The basis for many of these cases is the creditor's claim that when consumers use credit cards they make an implied representation about ability to pay. As will be discussed in more detail below, the vast majority of these cases involve consumers who intended to repay and who believed that they would be able to do so.[180] No misrepresentation was involved. Additionally, because the Supreme Court has made clear that justifiable reliance by the creditor on representations by the debtor is a prerequisite for a claim of fraud,[181] and because there is no such reliance in a credit card transaction, credit card nondischargeability cases brought on this basis should fail.[182]

15.4.3.2.2 Elements which must be proved by the creditor in cases of alleged false financial statements

15.4.3.2.2.1 Generally

Cases based on allegedly false financial statements by consumers have become more rare as consumer lending has shifted away from finance company loans and other document-based transactions. However, such cases have begun to surface in the wake of the mortgage crisis, with debt buyers who have purchased underwater junior mortgages asserting that they were obtained by fraud, often based on little or no evidence and the hope that a *pro se* or poorly represented debtor will not defend or will quickly settle. To prevail on a complaint alleging nondischargeability pertaining to a false financial statement under 11 U.S.C. § 523(a)(2)(B), a creditor must prove that the

---

re Romagnolo, 269 B.R. 63 (M.D. Fla. 2001) (discussing length of tolling for defective offer in compromise).

176 11 U.S.C. § 507(a)(8)(A)(ii). See In re Klein, 189 B.R. 505 (C.D. Cal. 1995) (letter appealing rejection of offer in compromise was not a new offer in compromise); United States v. Aberl, 175 B.R. 915 (N.D. Ohio 1994) (letter asking reconsideration of offer in compromise that was not form letter prescribed by IRS did not renew offer in compromise), aff'd, 78 F.3d 241 (6th Cir. 1996).

177 Young v. United States, 535 U.S. 43, 122 S. Ct. 1036, 152 L. Ed. 2d 79 (2002).

178 11 U.S.C. § 523(a)(2).

179 A few courts have held that a creditor may also seek a determination of the amount of liability on the underlying debt in the dischargeability action, or other relief related to collection. In re Kennedy, 108 F.3d 1015 (9th Cir. 1997) (bankruptcy court could enter money judgment on disputed state law claim it had found nondischargeable); In re McLaren, 3 F.3d 958 (6th Cir. 1993) (creditor could seek determination of amount of liability; debtor who had filed voluntary bankruptcy waived right to jury trial); Abramowitz v. Palmer, 999 F.2d 1274 (8th Cir. 1993) (court could impose constructive trust on non-debtor spouse's interest in home in connection with dischargeability case).

Note that the standard of proof to establish fraud related to the debt may be "clear and convincing evidence" under state law, while a preponderance standard applies to the issue of nondischargeability. See Grogan v. Garner, 498 U.S. 279, 111 S. Ct. 654, 112 L. Ed. 2d 755 (1991).

180 See § 15.4.3.2.3.2, infra.
181 Field v. Mans, 516 U.S. 59, 116 S. Ct. 437, 133 L. Ed. 2d 351 (1995).
182 See In re Alvi, 191 B.R. 724 (Bankr. N.D. Ill. 1996); In re Willis, 190 B.R. 866 (Bankr. W.D. Mo.), aff'd, 200 B.R. 868 (W.D. Mo. 1996); § 15.4.3.2.3.2, infra.

transaction met every element set out in that subsection.[183] All of the exceptions to discharge are to be construed narrowly.[184] The Supreme Court has held that the creditor has the burden of proof on these issues and that the preponderance of the evidence standard is applicable.[185]

15.4.3.2.2.2 The debtor obtained money, property, services, or an extension, renewal, or refinancing of credit

The first element that the creditor must allege and prove is that the debtor obtained money, property, services, or an extension, renewal, or refinancing of credit through the use of the allegedly false statement. Thus, if the creditor has given up nothing in the transaction, the exception to discharge is not applicable.[186] And the money, property, or extension, renewal, or refinancing of credit must have come from the creditor claiming its debt is nondischargeable.[187]

The exception applies to the extent that the debt arises from a fraudulent act of the debtor whereby the debtor obtained money or property. Thus, the Supreme Court has held that punitive or multiple damages which arise from such fraud are also nondischargeable.[188] It remains unclear, as it was under the prior Act, whether a transaction is covered by this provision when the money, property, and so forth, is obtained by the debtor for another.[189] It is also unclear to what extent a debtor can be held responsible for actions of a spouse or an agent that were fraudulent.[190]

The most important aspect of this element is its applicability to refinancing transactions. By adding the words "extension, renewal, or refinancing of credit, to the extent obtained," Congress intended to include the entire refinanced debt in some, but not all, refinancing transactions. This marked a change in the law that had prevailed in many bankruptcy courts; previously, only the amount of the refinanced loan that was "fresh cash" had been held nondischargeable.

The apparent original intent of the provision was to make the entire refinanced loan nondischargeable, but only in cases when the creditor agreed to refinance because of detrimental reliance on the false financial statement.[191] Thus, despite some unfortunate language in the legislative history[192] which seems at first to indicate that the entire refinanced loan is nondischargeable whenever the original loan was in default at the time of refinancing, there is still room in most cases for the argument that the creditor lost nothing, or even gained something, from refinancing.[193] Using repeated refinancing as a method of business keeps the customer "on the book," over a long period of time, and often results in greater payments of interest, application of the "hidden penalty" in the Rule of 78's,[194] and additional loan servicing charges. Thus, especially in cases in which the refinancing was initially suggested by the creditor,[195]

---

183 *In re* Cohn, 54 F.3d 1108 (3d Cir. 1995); *In re* Kimzey, 761 F.2d 421 (7th Cir. 1985).
184 *See, e.g.*, Kawaauhau v. Geiger, 523 U.S. 57, 118 S. Ct. 974, 140 L. Ed. 2d 90 (1998); Gleason v. Thaw, 236 U.S. 558, 562, 35 S. Ct. 287, 289, 59 L. Ed. 717 (1915) ("exceptions to discharge . . . should be confined to those plainly expressed"); *In re* Ward, 857 F.2d 1082 (6th Cir. 1988); *In re* Black, 787 F.2d 503 (10th Cir. 1986); *In re* Hunter, 780 F.2d 1577 (11th Cir. 1986).
185 Grogan v. Garner, 498 U.S. 279, 111 S. Ct. 654, 112 L. Ed. 2d 755 (1991).
186 *See, e.g., In re* Harlan, 7 B.R. 83 (Bankr. D. Ariz. 1980) (forbearance in suing a co-maker is not property); *In re* Kriger, 2 B.R. 19 (Bankr. D. Or. 1979) (creditor who agreed to stipulate to judgment on alleged debt did not give money or property to debtor simply because judgment was less than that which could have been obtained). *But cf. In re* Van Horne, 823 F.2d 1285 (8th Cir. 1987) (debt nondischargeable when debtor obtained renewal while concealing fact that he intended to divorce creditor's daughter).
187 Marcusen v. Glen (*In re* Glen), 639 F.3d 530 (8th Cir. 2011) (reduction of equity of creditor holding unrecorded mortgage caused by debtors granting another mortgage was not transaction in which debtors obtained money or property from creditor).
188 Cohen v. de la Cruz, 523 U.S. 213, 118 S. Ct. 1212, 130 L. Ed. 2d 341 (1998).
189 *See In re* Ashley, 903 F.2d 599 (9th Cir. 1990) (debtor who arranged loan for business in which he had financial interest considered to be recipient of the loan); *In re* Ward, 115 B.R. 532 (W.D. Mich. 1990) (debtor did not obtain benefit when shares of stock received were valueless); *In re* Jacobs, 54 B.R. 791 (Bankr. E.D.N.Y. 1985) (debtor did not share in loan proceeds to his client, so no nondischargeable debt despite fraud); 4 Collier on Bankruptcy ¶ 523.08[1] (16th ed.).
190 *See In re* Bonanzio, 91 F.3d 296 (2d Cir. 1996) (debtor responsible only if debtor knew of fraud, or should have known, and knowingly retained benefit from fraud); *In re* Tsurukawa, 258 B.R. 192 (B.A.P. 9th Cir. 2001) (husband's fraud could not be imputed to spouse unless she knowingly participated in fraud, was a business partner, or stood in agency relationship). *See generally* § 15.4.3.2.3.1, *infra*.
191 *See In re* Campbell, 159 F.3d 963 (6th Cir. 1998) (agreement to forbear from collection was an extension of credit induced by false financial statement); *In re* Siriani, 967 F.2d 302 (9th Cir. 1992) (creditor who renewed bond had to show that it relied to its detriment on false representations by giving up valuable collection remedies).
192 124 Cong. Rec. H11,096 (daily ed. Sept. 28, 1978) (remarks of Rep. Don Edwards), *reprinted in* 1978 U.S.C.C.A.N. 6453.

The passage in question states that the entire refinancing is nondischargeable "if the existing loan is in default or the creditor *otherwise* reasonably relies to his detriment" (emphasis added). This implies that if the loan was in default but the creditor did not rely to his detriment as to the refinancing aspect, only the fresh cash would be excepted from discharge. The most sensible reading of the statement in question and the actual language of the statute is that only the new money should be excepted from discharge unless the creditor can prove that it would actually have successfully pursued other remedies to recover more from the debtor, that because of the debtor's falsehoods it gave up on that planned course of action, and that it did not have another opportunity to pursue it later. Otherwise, the creditor could prove no detriment with regard to the refinancing aspect of the new transaction. *In re* Gadberry, 37 B.R. 752 (Bankr. C.D. Ill. 1984). *See also* Zaretsky, *The Fraud Exception to Discharge under the New Bankruptcy Code*, 53 Am. Bankr. L. J. 253, 266, 267 (1979).
193 *But see In re* McFarland, 84 F.3d 943, 947 (7th Cir.) (entire debt nondischargeable based on false financial statement related to refinancing); *In re* Goodrich, 999 F.2d 22 (1st Cir. 1993) (entire amount of loan, not just amount extended after false financial statement, was nondischargeable).
194 *See* Hunt, *The Rule of 78: Hidden Penalty in Consumer Credit Transactions*, 55 B.U. L. Rev. 331 (1975).
195 *See, e.g., In re* Archangeli, 6 B.R. 50 (Bankr. D. Me. 1980) (bank

or was required by state law when new funds were advanced,[196] a strong argument may be made that the refinancing itself was not detrimental to the creditor[197] and was not obtained by the consumer as a result of any alleged falsehoods.

A number of courts have adopted these arguments in holding only the "new money" or "fresh cash" nondischargeable.[198] When there has been some payment on a loan that is partially nondischargeable, the payment may, at least in some cases, be apportioned pro rata by the court between the nondischargeable and dischargeable portions.[199]

The "fresh cash" argument received a substantial boost from the 1984 amendments to the Code. Section 523(a)(2) was amended by the addition of the words "to the extent obtained" as part of the description of those obligations which are nondischargeable. This seemingly made clear that to the extent that credit had already been obtained previously without fraud or a false financial statement such obligations are not covered by the exception.[200]

A refinancing may also extinguish a basis for nondischargeability arising out of the refinanced transaction. If the refinancing is intended to eliminate the liability on the preexisting note, the debtor may be able to argue that all claims arising from that note are also extinguished.[201] However, the Supreme Court has held that, ordinarily, a settlement of a fraud case that substitutes a new contractual obligation does not eliminate the ability to claim that the underlying debt is nondischargeable due to fraud.[202] The Court did leave open the possibility that a creditor could be precluded from bringing such a claim if the settlement included a promise that the creditor would not make a claim of nondischargeability for fraud.[203]

15.4.3.2.2.3 The statement was materially false and in writing

To prevail on the false financial statement prong of section 523(a)(2), as opposed to fraud or false pretenses, a creditor cannot simply prove that a debtor's financial statement was false. The financial statement must be in writing.[204] In addition, the financial statement must be *materially* false. Credit card lenders are rarely successful in nondischargeability actions brought under this prong of section 523(a)(2)(b) because credit card applications are often taken over the phone and typically contain almost no information about the debtor's financial condition that is relied upon by the lender in granting credit.[205] Small omissions are usually insufficient to meet this materiality test.[206] Similarly, a false statement that is irrelevant to the decision about whether to grant credit is not material.[207] Thus a debtor contesting this element should be entitled to conduct discovery into the creditor's application evaluation process and credit scoring systems and methods to determine what effect the falsehood actually had.

---

desired consolidation because of its belief that debtor would be better able to make payments to it). *But see In re* McFarland, 84 F.3d 943, 947 (7th Cir. 1996) (entire debt found nondischargeable despite creditor requirement that prior debt be repaid).

196 *In re* Danns, 558 F.2d 114 (2d Cir. 1977).

The legislative history assents that section 523(a)(2)(B) codifies *Danns* and states that when state law requires a refinancing, only fresh cash is excepted from discharge, but seems to assume that such requirements only exist when there has been no default. *Id. See* 124 Cong. Rec. H11,096 (daily ed. Sept. 28, 1978) (remarks of Rep. Dan Edwards). However, such requirements also exist if the loan is in default.

197 *See In re* Gadberry, 37 B.R. 752 (Bankr. C.D. Ill. 1984). *But see In re* Liming, 797 F.2d 895 (10th Cir. 1986) (refinancing does not purge fraud in obtaining original loan).

198 *In re* Greenidge, 75 B.R. 245 (Bankr. M.D. Ga. 1987); *In re* Ojeda, 51 B.R. 91 (Bankr. D.N.M. 1985); *In re* Wright, 52 B.R. 27 (Bankr. W.D. Pa. 1985). *But see In re* McFarland, 84 F.3d 943, 947 (7th Cir. 1996); *In re* Kim, 62 F.3d 1511 (9th Cir. 1995), *aff'g* 163 B.R. 161 (B.A.P. 9th Cir. 1994) (creditor must show only that it had valuable collection remedies that it lost during the loan renewal period).

199 *In re* Hunter, 771 F.2d 1126 (8th Cir. 1985).

200 *But see In re* Gerlach, 897 F.2d 1048 (10th Cir. 1990) (fraud committed to obtain extension of credit made debt nondischargeable to extent court could reasonably estimate amount obtained by the fraud, including old debt extended, renewed or refinanced through fraud).

201 *See In re* Fischer, 116 F.3d 388 (9th Cir. 1997) (agreement that was novation of prior contract eliminated any nondischargeability claims arising out of prior contract); *In re* West, 22 F.3d 775 (7th Cir. 1994) (general release included a release of a nondischargeability claim in bankruptcy, stating, because even if the obligation arising from debtor's embezzlement would have been nondischargeable due to its fraudulent nature, no allegations of fraud surround the note, and the note substituted a contractual obligation for a tortious one). *But see* United States v. Spicer, 57 F.3d 1152 (D.C. Cir. 1995) (settlement agreement on fraud claim did not extinguish nondischargeability claims grounded in underlying debt).

202 Archer v. Warner, 538 U.S. 314, 123 S. Ct. 1462, 155 L. Ed. 2d 454 (2003). *See also In re* Detrano, 326 F.3d 319 (2d Cir. 2003).

203 Archer v. Warner, 538 U.S. 314, 322, 123 S. Ct. 1468, 155 L. Ed. 2d 463 (2003).

204 *In re* Kaspar, 125 F.3d 1358 (10th Cir. 1997) (credit card application taken over telephone not in writing, even though lender later transferred debtor's answers to a document); Blackwell v. Dabney, 702 F.2d 490 (4th Cir. 1983); *In re* Jackson, 252 B.R. 877 (Bankr. W.D.N.Y. 2000).

205 *In re* Simos, 209 B.R. 193 (Bankr. M.D.N.C. 1997) (claim under section 523(a)(2)(b) denied when lender presented no evidence that application was relied upon).

Credit card lenders usually rely upon a credit report in making credit decisions.

206 *Compare In re* Adams, 368 F. Supp. 80 (D.S.D. 1973) (small amounts omitted in proportion to total listed not material) *with In re* Harasymiw, 895 F.2d 1170 (7th Cir. 1990) (failure to disclose $128,000 mortgage on property offered as collateral for loan was material) *and In re* Barrett, 2 B.R. 296 (Bankr. E.D. Pa. 1980) (omission of $10,000 debt changed outcome in formula lender used to determine whether to extend credit).

207 *In re* Furio, 77 F.3d 622 (11th Cir. 1996) (omission of child support obligation from financial statement not materially false when support was taken into account by creditor and decision to grant credit was not affected); *In re* Bogstad, 779 F.2d 370 (7th Cir. 1985) (if lender would have made loan regardless of misrepresentation, then the misrepresentation was not material). *Cf. In re* Jordan, 927 F.2d 221 (5th Cir. 1991) (failure to disclose encumbrances on debtor's liquid assets was material omission; bank would never have approved loan if encumbrances had been revealed).

15.4.3.2.2.4 The statement concerned the financial condition of the debtor or an insider

This requirement is similar to the last. The statement must concern the debtor's financial condition. A recital of false information in a deed or contract is insufficient.[208] A statement having no bearing on the debtor's finances or an insider's[209] finances is not sufficient to bar dischargeability of the debt, no matter how false or distorted.

15.4.3.2.2.5 The creditor reasonably relied upon the false statement

Creditors often cannot meet the test requiring a showing that they reasonably relied on a false financial statement. In reality this test encompasses two elements that the creditor must prove—that the creditor in fact relied on the statement, and that such reliance was reasonable. Whether a creditor reasonably relied on a statement depends on all of the circumstances of the case.[210]

Thus, when a creditor relies on the consumer's past record of dealing with the creditor or on other information,[211] this standard is not met. If a loan or refinancing is offered and agreed to before the false financial statement is executed, no reliance can be shown.[212] Often, other information possessed by the creditor, such as a credit report, indicates that the financial statement is false, and if the creditor had reason to know that the financial statement was false, it could not have relied upon it.[213] Similarly, if the financial statement was perfunctorily completed for the file and the creditor made no real reference to it in granting credit, no reliance can be shown.[214] This may be the case in some situations in which a lien is taken and the creditor relies on the value of the property subject to the lien rather than on the debtor's ability to make payment.[215]

Even if the creditor shows that it did rely on the statement, that reliance may not have been reasonable. The reasonableness test requires consideration of whether the creditor followed its standard practices in evaluating creditworthiness, whether the creditor followed the standards or customs of the creditor's industry by conducting a commercially reasonable investigation, whether there was a "red flag" that would have alerted a prudent lender to the possibility that the debtor's statement was inaccurate, and whether even minimal investigation would have revealed the debtor's misrepresentations.[216]

If the creditor did not obtain a credit report, or check any information given by the debtor, its reliance may not have met this standard.[217] And if the creditor told the debtor not to worry

---

208 *In re* Phillips, 804 F.2d 930 (6th Cir. 1986) (misstatement of acreage in a deed is not a false written statement of debtor's financial condition).

209 "Insider" is defined in 11 U.S.C. § 101(31) and includes relatives of the debtor.

210 *In re* Coston, 987 F.2d 1096 (5th Cir. 1992) (trial court's finding of reasonable reliance based on circumstances would not be overturned unless clearly erroneous).

At least one appellate court has held that when a debt is assigned the assignee may assert reliance by the assignor, even though the assignee is now the creditor and it never relied on the debtor's statement. *In re* Boyajian, 564 F.3d 1088 (9th Cir. 2009).

211 *In re* Bruce, 214 B.R. 938 (Bankr. E.D.N.Y. 1997) (lender did not rely on loan application omission concerning $400 per month obligation as debtors were otherwise qualified for loan based on lender's debt to income ration guideline); *In re* Savich, 82 B.R. 1011 (Bankr. W.D. Mo. 1988) (bank's course of dealing with borrower established that bank ignored the debtor's financial statements which contained misrepresentations); *In re* Lacey, Bankr. L. Rep. (CCH) ¶ 67,715 (Bankr. S.D.N.Y. 1980).

212 *In re* Greene, 65 B.R. 266 (Bankr. M.D. Fla. 1986).

213 *In re* Morris, 223 F.3d 548 (7th Cir. 2000) (when creditor, based on past experience, had doubts about debtor's statements, reliance without further investigation was not reasonable); *In re* Brooks, 392 B.R. 642 (Bankr. M.D. La. 2008) (creditor did not reasonably rely on debtor's erroneous written statement of total income in credit application when along with her application debtor had also submitted pay stubs indicating what her actual income was); *In re* Baratta, 272 B.R. 501 (Bankr. M.D. Fla. 2001); *In re* Michael, 265 B.R. 593 (Bankr. W.D. Tenn. 2001) (no reliance when creditor ignored "red flags" based on its knowledge of omissions in financial statement that it helped debtors to prepare and fill out); *In re* Smith, 2 B.R. 276 (Bankr. E.D. Va. 1980); *In re* Schlickman, 6 B.R. 281 (Bankr. D. Mass. 1980); *In re* Lamb, Bankr. L. Rep. (CCH) ¶ 67,202 (Bankr. S.D.N.Y. 1979). *See also In re* Coston, 987 F.2d 1096 (5th Cir. 1992) (creditor's reliance on debtor's statement that retirement account could easily be converted to cash was not reasonable).

214 *In re* Forget, 392 B.R. 773 (Bankr. S.D. Iowa 2008) (debtors' incorrect written statements to credit union that they had never filed bankruptcy or been parties to a lawsuit were not made with intent to deceive; creditor did not show reliance); *In re* Jones, 3 B.R. 410 (Bankr. W.D. Va. 1980).

215 *But see In re* Collins, 946 F.2d 815 (11th Cir. 1991) (it is not unreasonable for creditor to fail to perfect its lien even if the security interest would have fully protected it from injury arising from debtor's false representation).

216 *In re* Cohn, 54 F.3d 1108 (3d Cir. 1995).

217 *In re* Jones, 31 F.3d 659 (8th Cir. 1994) (reliance not reasonable when "red flags" should have alerted creditor to investigate further); *In re* Kirsh, 973 F.2d 1454 (9th Cir. 1992) (attorney creditor did not show required justifiable reliance in believing debtor's representations regarding liens on property without ordering a title report); *In re* Ward, 857 F.2d 1082 (6th Cir. 1988) (bank did not reasonably rely on misrepresentation in card application when it did not even conduct superficial credit investigation); *In re* Rosel, 63 B.R. 603 (Bankr. W.D. Ky. 1986) (no effort by creditor to check accuracy of information); *In re* Breen, 13 B.R. 965 (Bankr. S.D. Ohio 1981) (creditor did not act reasonably in failing to make credit check). *But see In re* Woolum, 979 F.2d 71 (6th Cir. 1992) (lower court not clearly erroneous in finding that bank could reasonably rely on statements despite the fact that they were incomplete and contained mistakes); *In re* Watson, 958 F.2d 977 (10th Cir. 1992) (reliance without obtaining verification was reasonable when debtor had been introduced to bank by well-respected customer who verbally agreed to guarantee loan); *In re* Jordan, 927 F.2d 221 (5th Cir. 1991) (reasonable reliance found when bank failed to order credit check, because debtor was a well-known customer and bank contacted another bank to confirm accuracy of financial statements); *In re* Bonnet, 895 F.2d 1155 (7th Cir. 1989) (even if financial statements should have raised "red flags"; evidence supported conclusion that creditor reasonably relied on false financial statements); *In re* Dallam, 850 F.2d 446 (8th Cir. 1988) (misrepresentation induced action irrespective of reliance); *In re* Phillips, 804 F.2d 930 (6th Cir. 1986) (long term prior relationship may excuse a creditor's failure to check credit information); *In re* Garman, 643

about listing every single debt owed on the financial statement, it could not have reasonably relied on that statement. Some courts have even held that a creditor may not reasonably rely on a list of debts unless it includes the statement that all debts have been included.[218] In litigating a false financial statement case it is important to obtain discovery with respect to all of the persons involved in the transaction on behalf of the creditor, and what information they did and did not obtain elsewhere. Obviously, if such witnesses are no longer employed by the creditor, it will be difficult for it to prove its case.

15.4.3.2.2.6 The debtor's intent to deceive

Finally, the creditor must prove that the debtor had an actual intent to deceive it through the use of the false financial statement.[219] If the debtor's false disclosure was innocently or negligently made, the debt is dischargeable, although some courts have considered a "reckless indifference" to the truth to be equivalent to intentional falsehood.[220] Thus, debtors who failed to list debts because they thought a spouse or relative was responsible for paying them have been found to be without intent to deceive.[221] Similarly, debtors who made a good faith effort, but omitted debts such as taxes in answering ambiguous questions, were entitled to discharge of the debts involved.[222] Given good faith, even seriously inaccurate estimates of assets or liabilities do not constitute intentional deception.[223] The debtor may also have simply assumed that the creditor knew of debts from prior statements or other sources. However, it has been held that an intent to deceive can be inferred from the circumstances.[224]

One common defense on the question of intent arises out of the practices of creditors who mislead debtors about the purpose of the financial statement. It was well known, and indeed it was noted in the legislative history of the Code,[225] that some finance companies required financial statements for future use in bankruptcy proceedings rather than for making the decision to grant credit. These creditors typically provided a form that had very little space for listing debts and they orally advised the debtor not to worry if the list is not complete. Some creditors described the form as a mere formality or as a list of credit references. Such companies then retained the form for use in a bankruptcy case, in which they challenged the dischargeability of the debt,[226] hoping that the debtor would reaffirm rather than pay an attorney to litigate the matter.

In cases in which such conduct can be shown, of course, there is no intent to deceive on the part of the debtor,[227] nor is there reasonable reliance on the part of the creditor. Often, it can be helpful to conduct discovery into the company's practices, and particularly the number of cases in which it has filed complaints seeking to have debts ruled nondischargeable. Finding more than a very few such cases is usually fatal to the creditor's complaint.

15.4.3.2.3 Debts incurred through false pretenses or fraud

15.4.3.2.3.1 Generally

Very similar to cases dealing with false financial statements are complaints challenging dischargeability on the basis of false pretenses, false representations, or actual fraud.[228] These complaints are usually based upon information conveyed by the debtor, orally, in writing, or by conduct, but not in a written financial statement.[229] Indeed, it is questionable whether any statement concerning the debtor's financial condition is dischargeable under this provision, because there is a separate provision, section 523(a)(2)(B), that covers only a written financial statement.[230] To include oral or written financial statements in section 523(a)(2)(A) would render section 523(a)(2)(B) meaningless. For this reason, some courts have interpreted

---

F.2d 1252 (7th Cir. 1980) (creditor reliance reasonable despite absence of further investigation when debtor was a longtime customer); *In re* Allen, 65 B.R. 752 (E.D. Va. 1986).

The issue of reasonable reliance is reviewed on appeal as a factual finding that is not reversible unless it is clearly erroneous. *In re* Coston, 991 F.2d 257 (5th Cir. 1993) (en banc).

218 *See* Dial Fin. v. Duthu, 188 So. 2d 151 (La. Ct. App. 1966).

219 *In re* Martin, 963 F.2d 809 (5th Cir. 1992) (fraud involves moral turpitude or intentional wrong and misrepresentations must be knowingly and fraudulently made).

220 Knoxville Teachers Credit Union v. Parkey, 790 F.2d 490 (6th Cir. 1986) (misrepresentation of liabilities by $4300 was grossly reckless and satisfied the element of intentional deception); Birmingham Trust Nat'l Bank v. Case, 755 F.2d 1474 (11th Cir. 1985); *In re* Martin, 761 F.2d 1163 (6th Cir. 1985) ("grossly reckless disregard" for truth was sufficient to come within exception to discharge). *See also In re* Lansford, 822 F.2d 902 (9th Cir. 1987) (debt nondischargeable as to wife when she signed purchase documents which repeated misrepresentations in husband's financial statement).

221 *In re* Mosley, 4 B.R. 177 (Bankr. S.D. Fla. 1980); *In re* Mausser, 4 B.R. 728 (Bankr. S.D. Fla. 1980).

222 *In re* Miller, 39 F.3d 301 (11th Cir. 1994) (based upon totality of circumstances, bankruptcy court correctly held that there was no intent to deceive when assets were valued on net basis and real estate values were in flux); Gabellini v. Rega, 724 F.2d 579 (7th Cir. 1984) (accounting error not intentional deception); Firstmark Capital Corp. v. Shuback, Bankr. L. Rep. (CCH) ¶ 67,514 (Bankr. W.D. Mo. 1980).

223 *In re* Cohen, 507 F.3d 610 (7th Cir. 2007) (debtor's overly optimistic written statement of accounts given to creditor was not materially false and creditor failed to establish intent to deceive); *In re* Dorsey, 505 F.3d 395 (5th Cir. 2007) (evidence did not clearly show debtor intended to deceive lender regarding ownership of guns pledged as collateral); *In re* Rosel, 63 B.R. 603 (Bankr. W.D. Ky. 1986).

224 *In re* Young, 995 F.2d 547 (5th Cir. 1993).

225 H.R. Rep. No. 95-595, at 130 (1977).

226 *See, e.g.,* All State Credit Plan, Halihan v. Anderson, 250 So. 2d 806 (La. Ct. App. 1971).

227 *See, e.g., In re* Rosia, 4 B.R. 701 (Bankr. S.D. Fla. 1980) (debtor instructed to state falsely that she owned a home).

228 11 U.S.C. § 523(a)(2)(A).

229 Under the Federal Rules of Civil Procedure, fraud must be pleaded with particularity. A creditor's failure to do so might be grounds to dismiss the complaint. *See In re* Sibley, 71 B.R. 147 (Bankr. D. Mass. 1987) (complaint must appraise debtor of acts that form basis for claim).

230 *See In re* Gulevsky, 362 F.3d 961 (7th Cir. 2004) (writing requirement could not be circumvented by proceeding under section 523(a)(6)).

the phrase "respecting the debtor's ... financial condition" in section 523(a)(2)(B) narrowly.[231]

A debtor will be denied the discharge of a particular debt under this section if it is shown that the creditor provided money, property, services, or an extension, renewal, or refinancing of credit[232] due to an intentionally and materially false statement by the debtor[233] upon which the creditor justifiably relied.[234] This standard is basically the standard for fraud at common law.[235] However, the fraud must be actual, and not constructive or implied by law.[236]

Thus, debtors who have obtained money in their businesses through deliberate misrepresentations about security interests, or about the use that would be made of the funds, have been denied discharge on those debts.[237] Loans obtained through knowing misrepresentations about other intended activities may also be nondischargeable.[238] In addition, an intentional failure to disclose a material fact may constitute false pretenses. Debtors who fail to disclose significant facts about a transaction, or about unrecorded mortgages on real estate, have been denied discharges of debts incurred in that fashion.[239] However, other courts have held that, absent explicit representations concerning financial condition, there can be no false pretenses or false representations.[240]

Just as with false financial statements, all of the elements of the exception to discharge must be proved in each case. The creditor must prove both intent on the part of the debtor and justifiable reliance on the part of the person who was allegedly deceived.[241] Thus, it is not sufficient to show simply that the debtor wrote a bad check. It must also be shown that the check induced the transfer of money, property, or credit;[242] if it was given in payment of an antecedent debt, no false pretenses exist. Furthermore, the intent requirement is not satisfied unless the debtor knew at the time the check was issued that it would not be honored.[243] In fact, the Seventh Circuit Court of Appeals

---

231 *Compare* Bandi v. Becnel (*In re* Bandi), 683 F.3d 671 (5th Cir. 2012) (statement that debtor owned property was not statement of overall financial position, so it was covered by section 523(a)(2)(A), not (B)), *and In re* Joelson, 427 F.3d 700 (10th Cir. 2005), *with* Engler v. Van Steinburg (*In re* Van Steinburg), 744 F.2d 1060, 1060–61 (4th Cir. 1984) (debtor's representation that certain property he owned was unencumbered at the time he pledged it as collateral for a loan from the creditor was a statement regarding the debtor's financial condition).

232 See § 15.4.3.2.2.2, *supra*, for further discussion of whether debtor obtained money, property, services, extension, renewal, or refinancing.

233 The debtor may commit fraud through the agency of another person only if the debtor knew or should have known of the fraud. *See In re* Bonanzio, 91 F.3d 296 (2d Cir. 1996) (debtor responsible only if debtor knew of fraud, or should have known, and knowingly retained benefit from fraud); *In re* Allison, 960 F.2d 481 (5th Cir. 1992) (debt that was nondischargeable with respect to husband held dischargeable with respect to wife who did not participate in transaction); *In re* Walker, 726 F.2d 452 (8th Cir. 1984); *In re* Tsurukawa, 258 B.R. 192 (B.A.P. 9th Cir. 2001) (husband's fraud could not be imputed to spouse unless she knowingly participated in fraud, was a business partner, or stood in agency relationship); *In re* Allen, 65 B.R. 752 (E.D. Va. 1986) (wife who did not sign spouse's false financial statement was not denied discharge of debt). *But see In re* M.M. Winkler & Assocs., 239 F.3d 746 (5th Cir. 2001) (fraud imputed to innocent partner even if not carried out in ordinary course of business and innocent partner did not benefit from it); *In re* Ledford, 970 F.2d 1556 (6th Cir. 1992) (fraud of one partner imputed to other general partner when fraud was carried out in ordinary course of partnership's business and other partner profited from fraud); *In re* Luce, 960 F.2d 1277 (5th Cir. 1992) (fraud of one partner committed in ordinary course of partnership's business imputed to other partner).

234 Field v. Mans, 516 U.S. 59, 116 S. Ct. 437, 133 L. Ed. 2d 351 (1995).

235 Field v. Mans, 516 U.S. 59, 116 S. Ct. 437, 133 L. Ed. 2d 351 (1995) (false pretenses, false representation, and actual fraud are common law terms and "they imply elements that the common law has defined them to include").

236 *See* 124 Cong. Rec. H11,095, H11,096 (daily ed. Sept. 28, 1978); S17,412, S17,413 (daily ed. Oct. 6, 1978) (section 523(a)(2)(A) was intended to codify the holding in Neal v. Clark, 95 U.S. 704, 24 L. Ed. 586 (1877), which interpreted fraud under the Bankruptcy Act to mean actual or positive fraud rather than fraud implied by law).

237 *In re* Miller, 5 B.R. 424 (Bankr. W.D. La. 1980); *In re* Jones, 2 B.R. 46 (Bankr. N.D. Ala. 1979).

238 *In re* Milbank, 1 B.R. 150 (Bankr. S.D.N.Y. 1979) (debtor obtained loan from wife and her father upon representation that he would try to strengthen marriage; loan found nondischargeable upon proof that he was at same time engaged in affair with wife of next door neighbor).

239 *In re* Quintana, 4 B.R. 508 (Bankr. S.D. Fla. 1980); *In re* Flanzbaum, 7 B.R. 826 (Bankr. S.D. Fla. 1980).

240 *In re* Hunter, 780 F.2d 1577 (11th Cir. 1986).

241 *See In re* Slyman, 234 F.3d 1081 (9th Cir. 2000) (home owner's association did not rely on any representation by debtor in providing services which it provided as a matter of course to all home owners); *In re* Rubin, 875 F.2d 755 (9th Cir. 1989) (claimants were entitled to rely on the debtor/real estate agent's misrepresentations based on his position and apparent experience); *In re* Mullet, 817 F.2d 677 (10th Cir. 1987); *In re* Finkel, 21 B.R. 17 (B.A.P. 9th Cir. 1982); *In re* Drake, 5 B.R. 149 (Bankr. D. Idaho 1980) (debtors did not have intent to convert vehicles taken for resale even though they ultimately did not pass on proceeds to the original seller). *But see In re* Allison, 960 F.2d 481 (5th Cir. 1992) (creditor need not prove reasonable reliance under section 523(a)(2)(A)); *In re* Ophaug, 827 F.2d 340 (8th Cir. 1987) (reasonable reliance need not be shown under section 523(a)(2)(A)).

242 *But see In re* Campbell, 159 F.3d 963 (6th Cir. 1998) (agreement to forbear from collection was an extension of credit); Field v. Mans, 157 F.3d 35 (1st Cir. 1998) (fraudulent concealment of sale of property that would have permitted acceleration of mortgage induced non-acceleration which was deemed an extension of credit).

243 *In re* Davis, 246 B.R. 646 (B.A.P. 10th Cir. 2000) (debtor expected to deposit funds in account to pay check), *aff'd in part, vacated in part on other grounds*, 35 Fed. Appx. 826 (10th Cir. 2002); *In re* Burgstaler, 58 B.R.508 (Bankr. D. Minn. 1985) (even if the debtor knew there were insufficient funds to cover the check, no intent may be present if the debtor expected to be able to deposit money in the account before the check was honored); *In re* Denson, 7 B.R. 213 (Bankr. E.D. Va. 1980) (debtor believed he was entitled to draw moneys in excess of the amounts scheduled and did not conceal that excess); *In re* Wise, 6 B.R. 867 (Bankr. M.D. Fla. 1980) (creditor did not reasonably rely on NSF checks (checks returned due to insufficient funds in drawer's account) because debtor had previously submitted such checks, creditor had access to checkbook, creditor made out checks for debtor to sign, and evidence also showed debtor intended to pay). *See also In re* Sibley, 71 B.R. 147 (Bankr. D. Mass. 1987) (allegation that debtor issued check which

has held that a check, by itself, is not even a statement and therefore a bad check cannot be a false statement that gives rise to a nondischargeable claim.[244] In cases in which bad checks are involved, therefore, a creditor must prove some other false pretenses besides the check itself. The fact that a representation or promise later turns out to be one that the debtor does not fulfill is not sufficient to show intent.[245] Otherwise, almost every delinquent debt would be nondischargeable under this exception.

The requirement of justifiable reliance, which was enunciated by the Supreme Court in *Field v. Mans*,[246] is slightly different than the test for reasonable reliance used with respect to false financial statements. It judges whether the creditor's reliance on the debtor's false pretenses or false statement was justifiable based upon "the qualities and characteristics of the particular plaintiff, and the circumstances of the particular case."[247] It differs from reasonable reliance, which is an objective standard applicable to all creditors based on community norms.[248]

15.4.3.2.3.2 Credit cards and other credit use with no intent to pay

The most common allegation of false pretenses is that the debtor obtained money, goods, or services on credit with no intent to pay. As distinguished from debts that the debtor *later* finds himself or herself unable or unwilling to pay, debts incurred through false pretenses are incurred through an intentionally false representation that they would be paid. Because many courts have held that such a representation may be found to have been implied,[249] rather than expressed, it is not surprising that difficult problems of proof can arise as to intent and as to exactly when the debtor decided that the debt would not be paid.

In consumer cases, these issues arise most frequently when credit cards are involved, particularly if there is evidence of an unusual "buying spree" shortly before the bankruptcy. It is not uncommon for creditors to allege that such use of credit constitutes a knowing misrepresentation, upon which they justifiably relied, that the debt could and would be paid.

As the creditor has the burden of proof in such cases, it must produce evidence which sustains these allegations.[250] The 1984, 1994, and 2005 amendments to the Code made this burden far easier for creditors to meet in certain specified circumstances when a debtor allegedly "loaded up" prior to bankruptcy. In any case in which a debtor incurred consumer debts[251] in excess of $600 to a single creditor for luxury goods or services within ninety days prior to filing a bankruptcy, or cash advances[252] on an open end credit plan[253] totaling more than $875 within seventy days prior to a filing, there is a presumption that the debts were incurred through false pretenses.[254]

---

was dishonored is sufficient to state a claim under § 523(a)(2)(A)).

244 *In re* Scarlata, 979 F.2d 521 (7th Cir. 1992). *See also* Williams v. United States, 458 U.S. 279, 102 S. Ct. 3088, 73 L. Ed. 2d 767 (1982) (issuance of a check is not an implied representation that the payor has sufficient funds in the account to cover the check); *In re* Kucera, 373 B.R. 878 (Bankr. C.D. Ill. 2007) (mere presentation of counterfeit check did not constitute a false representation under section 523(a)(2)(A)); *In re* Trevisan, 300 B.R. 708 (Bankr. E.D. Wis. 2003) (check not representation of any kind); *In re* Coatney, 185 B.R. 546 (Bankr. N.D. Ohio 1995).

245 *In re* Ashley, 5 B.R. 262 (Bankr. E.D. Tenn. 1980) (no false representation simply because goods sold proved defective); *In re* Brooks, 4 B.R. 237 (Bankr. S.D. Fla. 1980) (no showing that debtor's implied representation that note would be paid was known to be false at time note was executed). *See also In re* Kroen, 280 B.R. 347 (Bankr. D.N.J. 2002) (alleged promise that debtor would not later seek to discharge debt in bankruptcy was invalid as matter of public policy, so creditor attorney could not have justifiably relied on it).

246 516 U.S. 59, 116 S. Ct. 437, 133 L. Ed. 2d 351 (1995).

247 *Id.*, 516 U.S. at 70, 71. *See In re* Spadoni, 316 F.3d 56 (1st Cir. 2003) (reversing bankruptcy court finding that landlord "should have known" that tenant's promises to pay overdue rent were not reasonable, court of appeals made de novo judgment that reliance was justifiable based on friendship between the parties and other circumstances); Sanford Inst. for Sav. v. Gallo, 156 F.3d 71 (1st Cir. 1998) (due to circumstances of case, creditor justifiably relied on debtor's representations even though it failed to conduct title search which would have revealed fraud).

248 Field v. Mans, 516 U.S. 59, 116 S. Ct. 437, 133 L. Ed. 2d 351 (1995).

249 *But see In re* Robinson, 340 B.R. 316 (Bankr. E.D. Va. 2006) (debtor's silence in failing to question unusually low utility bills was not an implied representation); *In re* Alvi, 191 B.R. 724 (Bankr. N.D. Ill. 1996) (use of credit card did not involve any representation, either express or implied); *In re* Cox, 182 B.R. 626 (Bankr. D. Mass. 1995) (credit card debt cannot be found nondischargeable based upon implied misrepresentation on intention to pay).

250 *See In re* McGee, 359 B.R. 764 (B.A.P. 9th Cir. 2006) (affirming refusal to enter default judgment when creditor introduced no evidence and 190% interest rate undercut creditor claim of reliance); *In re* Vee Vinhnee, 336 B.R. 437 (B.A.P. 9th Cir. 2005) (affirming refusal to enter default judgment when creditor produced no admissible evidence and offered only electronic records without proper evidentiary foundation). *See also In re* Panem, 352 B.R. 269 (Bankr. D. Colo. 2006) (refusing to approve stipulations of nondischargeability in absence of evidence when debtors were not sophisticated); *In re* Bungert, 315 B.R. 735 (Bankr. E.D. Wis. 2004) (creditor did establish prima facie case when it had not provided specific factual allegations about the debtors' conduct and had not provided evidence of fraud, other than a list of the charges and cash advances).

251 "Consumer debt" is defined at 11 U.S.C. § 101(8).

252 *See In re* Pugh, 356 B.R. 528 (Bankr. D. Colo. 2006) (refinancing of debt to same creditor not a cash advance); *In re* Manning, 280 B.R. 171 (Bankr. S.D. Ohio 2002) (balance transfer is not a cash advance).

Convenience checks are not normally considered cash advances. *See In re* Welch, 208 B.R. 107 (S.D.N.Y. 1997) (cash advance is ATM withdrawal or a check written to cash); *In re* Poor, 219 B.R. 332 (Bankr. D. Me. 1998) (balance transfer was not a "cash advance" under this section); *In re* Cameron, 219 B.R. 531 (Bankr. W.D. Mo. 1998) (same); *In re* Woods, 66 B.R. 984 (Bankr. E.D. Pa. 1986).

253 A single loan from a finance company is not an open-end credit plan. *In re* Hulbert, 150 B.R. 169 (Bankr. S.D. Tex. 1993).

254 11 U.S.C. § 523(a)(2)(C).

Pursuant to 11 U.S.C. § 104, the dollar amounts in section 523(a)(2)(c) are adjusted every three years. *See generally In re* Koch, 83 B.R. 898 (Bankr. E.D. Pa. 1988).

"Luxury goods or services" are defined in this subsection as goods and services that are not reasonably necessary for the support or maintenance of the debtor or the debtor's dependents.[255] This language was changed in 2005 from prior language which required the property to be "reasonably acquired." It is not clear whether this change will have any impact, but it may help debtors who acquired necessary items, even if it was doubtful that they could afford them.

Therefore, the presumption would not arise if the debtor purchased more than $600 worth of ordinary clothing or a necessary major appliance.[256] Similarly, when a debt is incurred to refinance an earlier debt within ninety days prior to bankruptcy, the presumption does not arise, even if the earlier debt was to purchase luxury goods or services, because those goods and services were not obtained during the ninety-day period.[257] And even when the subsection's standards are met, the presumption is rebuttable. It may be overcome if the debtor can show a sudden change in circumstances after the transaction or that bankruptcy had not been contemplated until after the transaction when the debtor consulted counsel. Indeed, it should be overcome in any case in which the court is convinced that the debtor honestly intended to pay the debt.[258]

The presumption is also not operative unless the creditor files a timely dischargeability complaint. The amendments did not alter Code section 523(c) which, as discussed above,[259] provides that a claim of nondischargeability under section 523(a)(2) is lost if not raised during the bankruptcy case.

Obviously, any anticipated problems that might be caused by the presumption may be avoided in most cases by delaying a bankruptcy until after the applicable time period has passed. However, the time period is only relevant to the automatic presumption. Debts incurred prior to that period may still be found nondischargeable for fraud or false pretenses. Eliminating the presumption means simply that the creditor has the burden of going forward, as well as the burden of proof, on all elements of the cause of action in such cases.

To show fraudulent intent, it is not sufficient to prove simply that the debt was incurred and not paid, because that much is true of all dischargeable debts.[260] Usually, absent an admission on the part of the debtor, it is almost impossible to prove the debtor's intent through direct evidence or statements that the debtor has made. These difficulties have led courts to look to circumstantial evidence.

The courts have considered several indicia as strong evidence of fraudulent intent.[261] The first of these is a surge of credit use shortly before the bankruptcy. When a debtor suddenly resigned from her job and left home to travel extensively on credit, without notifying anyone of her whereabouts, it was not hard for the court to infer intent, despite a defense that such activities were the result of mental illness.[262] A debtor who shortly before his bankruptcy charged more than $60,000 in luxury items on a trip to France, which was more than his annual income, and who had no assets other than a home that was subject to foreclosure, was found to have had no intent to repay the debt.[263] And a debtor who engaged in an elaborate

---

255 11 U.S.C. § 523(a)(2)(C). *See, e.g., In re* Zeman, 347 B.R. 28 (Bankr. W.D. Tex. 2006) (creditor has burden of showing that purchases were luxury goods and services); *In re* Shaw, 294 B.R. 652 (Bankr. W.D. Pa. 2003) (payments to divorce attorney not for luxury services); *In re* Hall, 228 B.R. 483 (Bankr. M.D. Ga. 1998) (gambling in which debtor engaged, in desperate attempt to pay off casino markers was not in the nature of a "luxury"); *In re* Vernon, 192 B.R. 165 (Bankr. N.D. Ill. 1996) (legal services for divorce proceedings were not luxury services); *In re* Claar, 72 B.R. 319 (Bankr. M.D. Fla. 1987) (lifetime membership to PTL religious theme park); *In re* Herran, 66 B.R. 323 (Bankr. S.D. Fla. 1986) ($1021 worth of giftware, cosmetics, fragrances, and clothing); *In re* Hussey, 59 B.R. 573 (Bankr. M.D. Ala. 1986) (three-wheeled vehicle).

  Cash used to pay other debts is not a luxury good. *In re* Woods, 66 B.R. 984 (Bankr. E.D. Pa. 1986). An unrestricted cash loan is also not covered by this provision, even if it is used to purchase luxury goods. *In re* Neal, 113 B.R. 607 (B.A.P. 9th Cir. 1990).

256 Chase Bank v. Turnbow (*In re* Turnbow), 430 B.R. 801 (Bankr. W.D. Ky. 2010) (lawn mower not luxury item); *In re* Park, 375 B.R. 153 (Bankr. W.D. Pa. 2007) ($3000 minivan purchased by debtor for family use using credit card within ninety days of bankruptcy filing was not purchase of a "luxury" item); *In re* Larisey, 185 B.R. 877 (Bankr. M.D. Fla. 1995) (air conditioner repair and carpet were not luxury goods or services).

257 *In re* Shurbier, 134 B.R. 922 (Bankr. W.D. Mo. 1991) (loan to repay earlier debt for goods and services did not give rise to presumption); *In re* Smith, 54 B.R. 299 (Bankr. S.D. Iowa 1985).

258 *See* Discover Bank v. Anthony, 2010 WL 2079858 (E.D. Wis. May 19, 2010) (debtor who had $3000 in cash advances in ten days was trying to get by and avoid bankruptcy, which he did not consider until after last advance); *In re* May, 428 B.R. 393 (Bankr. W.D. Mich. 2010) (unsophisticated debtor who used cash advances to make minimum payments on credit cards during period of disability considered payments part of his living expenses and intended to repay), *aff'd*, 448 B.R. 197 (W.D. Mich. 2011); *In re* Cline, 282 B.R. 493 (Bankr. W.D. Wash. 2002) (because debtor used her account for necessities, and always planned to repay, the presumption of fraud burst and burden of proof reverted to creditor); *In re* Johansen, 160 B.R. 328 (Bankr. W.D. Wis. 1993) (presumption overcome because debtor did not know, when she bought collector edition dolls, that her husband planned to file bankruptcy case and that his attorney would advise joint petition, and debtor had intended to pay for dolls even though she did not have money immediately available); *In re* McDonald, 129 B.R. 279 (Bankr. M.D. Fla. 1991) (presumption overcome by debtor's conduct); *In re* Leaird, 106 B.R. 177 (Bankr. W.D. Wis. 1989) (presumption overcome by proof that debtors made purchases impulsively and did not contemplate bankruptcy until they subsequently became aware of a different debt).

259 *See* § 15.4.2, *supra*.

260 *In re* Richards, 196 B.R. 481 (Bankr. E.D. Ark. 1996) (mere draw down of credit limit through cash advances does not prove intention to deceive). *See also In re* Bagby, 2009 WL 6498177 (Bankr. N.D. Ga. June 23, 2009) (default judgment denied when creditor made only conclusory allegations of fraud; promise to pay debt, by itself, not false representation); *In re* Sinclair, 191 B.R. 474 (Bankr. M.D. Fla. 1996) (credit card issuer denied default judgment when sole allegation was that debtor used card eight to nine months before bankruptcy case, with no specific facts indicating fraud); *In re* Roberts, 193 B.R. 828 (Bankr. W.D. Mich. 1996) (default judgment denied when bank offered no evidence of debtor's intent or any other evidence other than charges made).

261 *See generally In re* Dougherty, 84 B.R. 653 (B.A.P. 9th Cir. 1988).

262 *In re* Banasiak, 8 B.R. 171 (Bankr. M.D. Fla. 1981).

263 *In re* Hashemi, 104 F.3d 1122 (9th Cir. 1996).

scheme of "credit card kiting," using one card to make minimum payments on another, was found to have had no intent to repay.[264] Similarly, a debtor who made approximately $1000 worth of credit purchases, most of which were gift certificates used not for others but for himself, the court found such behavior more than a little suspicious.[265]

A few courts have gone so far as to say that any substantial use of credit, at least by a sophisticated debtor, at a time when the debtor should have known that he or she would be unable to pay, constitutes false pretenses.[266] But most courts have held that use of the card at a time when the debtor was unable to pay, by itself is not sufficient to show that the debtor lacked intention to repay.[267] The key issue is whether the debtor had a subjective intent, even if unrealistic, to repay. If the debtor intended to repay, the debt should be found dischargeable.[268] One of the primary purposes of credit use is to purchase items the debtor could not otherwise then afford to purchase.[269] Normally, debtors who use credit when they have little income expect their circumstances to improve so they will be able to repay.

A second indication of fraudulent intent is the use of the credit card after it is no longer permitted by the credit contract, either because the credit limit has been exceeded or because the creditor has instructed the debtor to destroy, return, or cease using the card.[270] Some courts have held that such use constitutes intentional false representation to the merchant that the card is being used in compliance with the terms of the contract and is therefore fraudulent by itself.[271] The evidence of fraud has been found stronger for a debtor who ceased to make purchases in excess of $50, the amount at which merchants at that time customarily called for credit approval.[272] And, of course, proof that the debtor consulted an attorney or other evidence that bankruptcy was contemplated at the time of the credit use is quite helpful to the creditor's cause.[273]

A debtor may raise a number of arguments in defense against such claims. Most courts have held that exceeding the credit limit, without more, is not sufficient to constitute false pretenses.[274] Especially if the creditor has acquiesced in such use of a credit card over a period of months, the creditor should be estopped from later challenging it, or it should be found that the contract was changed by the parties' conduct.[275] Indeed, the Eleventh Circuit Court of Appeals has held that debts incurred through credit card use cannot be excepted from discharge unless the use occurs after an unequivocal revocation of credit card privileges.[276] A debtor's honest belief that she could and would pay, even if that belief is ill-founded, negates any fraudulent intent.[277] An absence of fraudulent intent is also evidenced in many cases by return of the credit cards when that is finally requested.[278]

In addition, a debtor can fairly argue that there was no reliance on a representation made by the debtor at the time of the card transaction because the creditor was relying on the express agreement to repay that had occurred when the card was issued, along with its investigation at that time, and because the debtor never communicated with the creditor at the time of the transaction.[279] Justifiable reliance may also be

---

264 *In re* Eashai, 87 F.3d 1082 (9th Cir. 1996).

However, as the concurring opinion points out, the decision does not mean that a debtor commits fraud any time one credit card is used to make a payment on another. Indeed, credit card grantors encourage such "balance transfers." See FIA Card Servs. v. May (*In re* May), 448 B.R. 197 (W.D. Mich. 2011) (unsophisticated debtor who made minimum payments on other cards with cash advances was not engaged in "kiting" and had no intent to defraud because he viewed minimum payments as necessary living expenses).

265 *In re* Ratajczak, 5 B.R. 583 (Bankr. M.D. Fla. 1980).

266 *In re* Kell, 6 B.R. 695 (Bankr. D. Colo. 1980) (debtor obtained new cards after filing chapter 13 case, and after admitting he was "broke," and proceeded to incur new purchases amounting to about $2500, paying only about $600 of them). *Cf. In re* Larson, 136 B.R. 540 (Bankr. D. N.D. 1992) (credit card use even after chapter 11 filing was not fraudulent when debtor did not increase use and continued to make substantial payments on bill and reduced balance).

267 *In re* Sziel, 209 B.R. 712 (Bankr. N.D. Ill. 1997).

268 *In re* Ettell, 188 F.3d 1141 (9th Cir. 1999) (debtor had intent to repay, even if it was objectively unlikely he would be able to do so); *In re* Rembert, 141 F.3d 277 (6th Cir. 1998) (debtor had intent to repay when she took cash advances for gambling); *In re* Anastas, 94 F.3d 1280 (9th Cir. 1996) (nondischargeability determination may not be based solely upon fact that at time debts were incurred debtor was not likely to be able to repay them; additional evidence of fraudulent intent is required).

269 *In re* Hernandez, 208 B.R. 872, 879 (Bankr. W.D. Tex. 1997) (major reason consumers use credit cards is a present lack of ability to repay, and this is also primary reason lenders want consumers to use credit cards).

270 *In re* Brewster, 5 Bankr. Ct. Dec. (LRP) 783 (Bankr. E.D. Va. 1979). See *In re* Dougherty, 84 B.R. 653 (B.A.P. 9th Cir. 1988).

271 *In re* Nolan, 1 B.R. 644 (Bankr. M.D. Fla. 1979); *In re* Cushingberry, 5 Bankr. Ct. Dec. (LRP) 954 (Bankr. E.D. Mich. 1977).

272 *In re* Schartner, 7 B.R. 885 (Bankr. N.D. Ohio 1980).

Such evidence, however, is not conclusive. *In re* Dougherty, 84 B.R. 653 (B.A.P. 9th Cir. 1988).

273 But see *In re* Cacho, 137 B.R. 864 (Bankr. N.D. Fla. 1991) (fact that debtor consulted attorney concerning possible bankruptcy before cash advance was not sufficient to show fraud when debtor made numerous payments of debts after that and did not file until two months later).

274 *In re* Lyon, 8 B.R. 152 (Bankr. D. Me. 1981) (and cases cited therein); *In re* Parker, 1 B.R. 176 (Bankr. E.D. Tenn. 1979).

275 *In re* Lyon, 8 B.R. 152 (Bankr. D. Me. 1981) (and cases cited therein). See also *In re* Chincilla, 202 B.R. 1010 (Bankr. S.D. Fla. 1996) (debtor's exceeding credit limit is not indicia of fraud when lender responded by increasing credit limit with $2000 in unsolicited credit).

276 First Nat'l Bank of Mobile v. Roddenberry, 701 F.2d 927 (11th Cir. 1983).

This holding may be called into question to some extent by the 1984 addition of section 523(a)(2)(C) to the Code. But those amendments may also be seen as strengthening the argument that defining the extent to which Congress intended prebankruptcy credit card usage to be considered fraudulent. *In re* Cox, 182 B.R. 626 (Bankr. D. Mass. 1995).

277 *In re* Lyon, 8 B.R. 152 (Bankr. D. Me. 1981) (and cases cited therein); *In re* Parker, 1 B.R. 176 (Bankr. E.D. Tenn. 1979).

278 *In re* Lyon, 8 B.R. 152 (Bankr. D. Me. 1981) (and cases cited therein); *In re* Parker, 1 B.R. 176 (Bankr. E.D. Tenn. 1979).

279 *In re* Kountry Korner Store, 221 B.R. 265 (Bankr. N.D. Okla. 1998) (creditor which relied only on third party credit reports in granting

challenged based upon the credit granting investigation and standards used in a particular case. If the creditor knew the debtor had no income at the time the card was granted, or never even asked the debtor's income, a court is unlikely to find justifiable reliance.[280] As with reliance on alleged false financial statements, credit card lenders cannot ignore "red flags" that would cause a prudent lender to question the decision to extend credit.[281] If the debtor immediately begins to use the card primarily for gambling, or to make late payments, and the creditor continues to extend credit, justifiable reliance may be difficult for the creditor to prove.[282] Thus, it is important to determine the information that the creditor had when the credit was granted as well as during the time the credit card was used.

There are other factual issues related to credit card dischargeability that can be brought out by thorough discovery.[283] For example, did the creditor have a practice of encouraging consumers with large balances to make additional purchases by increasing their credit limits or by advertising products or services in their billing statements? These practices undermine a creditor's claim that it justifiably relied on the debtor's implied representations about ability to pay, particularly if an increased credit limit is typically granted without a review of the debtor's recent credit record or current income. Similarly, a creditor's practices with respect to accepting minimum payments should be reviewed. If a debtor had the ability to make anticipated minimum payments in the short term, that fact undermines circumstantial evidence which tends to establish that the debtor had no intent to repay.

When cases go to trial, it is important to make a record regarding the debtor's intent at the time of the purchase—usually through the debtor's testimony. For example, if the debtor was unemployed at the time of the purchase, did he or she expect to be reemployed shortly? Was there a reasonable belief that financial difficulties would be temporary? Were the purchases within the debtor's credit limit? Did the debtor have the ability and intent to continue to make the minimum monthly payments despite financial difficulties? Had the debtor had prior financial problems from which he or she recovered that led to a reasonable assumption that these financial difficulties would also be resolved? Had the debtor consulted a bankruptcy attorney before making the purchases? Did the debtor continue to offer partial payments to the creditor which were rejected so that bankruptcy became the only realistic option?

Virtually all debtors have had some financial problems before they file bankruptcy. Most people use credit cards fully expecting that their circumstances will improve so that their debts can be repaid. It is thus inappropriate to use past financial difficulties alone as evidence of fraudulent intent.[284]

---

credit card and had no information about debtor's solvency, budget, work history or assets could not claim justifiable reliance); *In re* Simos, 209 B.R. 188 (Bankr. M.D.N.C. 1997) (creditor who offered no evidence on justifiable reliance could not prevail under section 523(a)(2)); *In re* Christensen, 193 B.R. 863 (N.D. Ill. 1996) (creditor must show more than use of card to show reliance and justifiable nature of reliance; credit card company cannot sit back and do nothing); *In re* Feld, 203 B.R. 360 (Bankr. E.D. Pa. 1996) (AT & T Universal Card failed to prove justifiable reliance because it sent unsolicited card, took no steps to restrict debtor's use of card, and failed to present evidence on reliance issue). *See also In re* Bird, 224 B.R. 622 (Bankr. S.D. Ohio 1998) (issuance of preapproved loan checks did not involve justifiable reliance on any representation made by the debtor); *In re* Alvi, 191 B.R. 724 (Bankr. N.D. Ill. 1996) (credit card issuer failed to show actual or justifiable reliance when it passively extended credit on card; it had willingly undergone risk of nonpayment by factoring risk into finance charges); *In re* Willis, 190 B.R. 866 (Bankr. W.D. Mo.) (creditor that failed to offer evidence of justifiable reliance at time of card use did not prove all elements of case; any creditor who knew of debtor's outstanding credit card debt could not have proved justifiable reliance); *In re* Cox, 182 B.R. 626 (Bankr. D. Mass. 1995); *In re* Bui, 188 B.R. 274 (Bankr. N.D. Cal. 1995) (when debt is assigned, creditor must show reasonable reliance at every stage in chain of transactions transferring debtor's account). *But see In re* Mercer, 246 F.3d 391 (5th Cir. 2001) (en banc) (court held that each use of the card is a new contract and representation of intent to pay and that company could justifiably rely on that representation absent red flags or actual knowledge that it was untrue, essentially reducing dischargeability of credit cards to issue of whether debtor had intent to deceive and whether creditor was aware of red flags, and thus rewarding creditors who do not investigate a debtor's credit and therefore do not discover red flags).

280 *In re* Grause, 245 B.R. 95 (B.A.P. 8th Cir. 2000) (creditor that did nothing more than periodically check FICO credit scores did not justifiably rely when even a cursory look at debtor's situation should have put creditor on notice of her dire straits). *But see In re* Mercer, 246 F.3d 391 (5th Cir. 2001) (en banc) (credit card company could justifiably rely on implied representation even though decision to grant credit was based solely on credit reports and not any express representation of debtor).

281 *In re* Akins, 235 B.R. 866 (W.D. Tex. 1999) (debtor obtained approval to use a convenience check up to her full $4000 credit limit based on acceptable FICO score even though she had two other credit cards totaling approximately $30,000 in debt, or one-hundred-fifty percent of her gross income); *In re* Ellingsworth, 212 B.R. 326 (Bankr. W.D. Mo. 1997) (debtor sent a pre-approved credit card with credit limit of $4000 based on FICO score even though she had sixteen other credit cards); *In re* Briese, 196 B.R. 440 (Bankr. W.D. Wis. 1996) (debtors issued a pre-approved credit card with line of $11,500, even though bank had conducted a credit check that confirmed debtors' unsecured debt alone exceeded two-thirds of their annual income, a debt-to-income ratio of sixty-six percent). *See also In re* Hodges, 407 B.R. 415 (Bankr. D. Kan. 2009) (payday lenders, who lend to debtors in very precarious financial condition at extremely high rates, can almost never show justifiable reliance).

282 *In re* Reynolds, 221 B.R. 828 (Bankr. N.D. Ala. 1998) (no justifiable reliance when credit card was used almost exclusively for cash advances at local casino over long period); *In re* Stockard, 216 B.R. 237 (Bankr. M.D. Tenn. 1997) (first three payments were at least two weeks late and payments then ceased, but creditor did nothing to limit card use).

283 See § 15.4.3.2.4, *infra*, and form discovery in Appendix G.12, *infra*. *See generally Litigating the Dischargeability of Credit Card Debts*, 14 NCLC REPORTS Bankruptcy and Foreclosures Ed. 10 (Nov./Dec. 1995).

284 *See In re* Mercer, 246 F.3d 391 (5th Cir. 2001) (en banc); *In re* Anastas, 94 F.3d 1280 (9th Cir. 1996) (nondischargeability determination may not be based solely upon fact that at time debts were incurred debtor was not likely to be able to repay them; additional evidence of fraudulent intent is required); *In re* Cox, 182 B.R. 626 (Bankr. D. Mass. 1995) (all debtors have history of financial problems which cannot alone establish intent); FCC Bank v. Dobbins,

15.4.3.2.3.3 Public benefits overpayments

Another type of fraud problem that may arise in the cases of low-income debtors involves past overpayments of Social Security, unemployment, welfare, or other benefits. In many cases involving such overpayments, the amount that was erroneously paid is deducted from future benefits, often causing considerable hardship.

In determining whether debts for such overpayments should be discharged, the bankruptcy court applies the same standards as in other cases under section 523(a)(2). These standards may be quite different from those applied by the agency that administers the benefits; many such agencies, including the Social Security Administration, may decide to recoup erroneous payments even if the debtor was not at fault or may use a fault standard far less favorable to the debtor than that used in bankruptcy.[285]

Clearly, any overpayment that is the result of an administrative error should be discharged under the bankruptcy standard. No exception to discharge applies solely because the debt is owed to a government agency.[286] Nor would recoupment after bankruptcy be a setoff permitted under 11 U.S.C. § 553, because it would not meet the mutuality requirement, which prohibits a prepetition debt of the debtor from being setoff against monies that become due to the debtor only after the bankruptcy.[287] Following these principles, and despite the past opposition of the Social Security Administration, courts have consistently held Social Security overpayments to be dischargeable unless a successful dischargeability challenge is made under 11 U.S.C. § 523.[288] The Social Security Administration's former position that 42 U.S.C. § 407 exempts overpayments from discharge, a position it once memorialized in its claims manual,[289] has been uniformly rejected by the courts.

However, debtors who fraudulently obtain benefits by intentionally and falsely representing that they are unemployed will usually be denied a discharge of overpayments if a complaint is filed.[290] Courts are likely to extend this rule to those who do not report new employment, at least if it can be shown that they were aware of their duty to do so, under the theory that such failure constitutes a continuing misrepresentation.[291] Of course, other intentional falsehoods in the application regarding eligibility questions can also lead to an exception of an overpayment from discharge.[292] On the other hand, fraud cannot be assumed simply because a debtor has erroneously received payments while working or because the agency has incorrect information.[293]

15.4.3.2.4 Tactics in cases under 11 U.S.C. § 523(a)(2) and award of attorney fees under 11 U.S.C. § 523(d)

Some creditors file complaints alleging nondischargeability because of a false financial statement, false pretenses, or fraud in hopes that they can obtain a settlement reaffirming all or part of a debt, because some debtors' attorneys do not defend against such cases. It is important to quickly disabuse a creditor/plaintiff of such notions by making it known that the case will be vigorously defended, quite possibly at the creditor's expense.

The best way to do this is to litigate and negotiate aggressively. It should be remembered that the creditor must plead and prove every element of the case (except when the section 523(a)(2)(C) presumption applies, in which case the creditor has the burden of proof only if the presumption is rebutted). Further, the rules require fraud to be pleaded with particularity.[294] If these requirements are not met, the debtor may move for dismissal.[295] Simi-

---

151 B.R. 509 (W.D. Mo. 1992) (debtor's insolvency at time of credit card use, without more, was not sufficient to render complaint substantially justified).

285 *See In re* Chen, 227 B.R. 614 (D.N.J. 1998) (fraud standard used in state unemployment compensation proceeding was less demanding than that of section 523(a)(2), so finding in such proceeding not entitled to preclusive effect).

286 Some debts owed to government agencies for taxes, or for fines, penalties or forfeitures are nondischargeable under 11 U.S.C. § 523(a)(7). *See* § 15.4.3.1, *supra*; § 15.4.3.7, *infra*.

287 *See* § 10.4.2.6.7, *supra*, for a discussion of setoffs under section 553.

The right to recover money from a state or the federal government based on an improper setoff, however, may be limited based on sovereign immunity. *See* § 14.3.2.2, *supra*. For further discussion of such problems see § 15.5.5.4, *infra. See also In re* Soto, 667 F.2d 235 (1st Cir. 1981) (assignment of future wages not a security interest because property acquired postpetition is not subject to prepetition debts).

288 Rowan v. Morgan, 747 F.2d 1052 (6th Cir. 1984); Lee v. Schweiker, 739 F.2d 870 (3d Cir. 1984); *In re* Neavear, 674 F.2d 1201 (7th Cir. 1982). *See also* McKenney v. City of Cincinnati Retirement Sys., 2 Ohio App. 3d 42, 440 N.E.2d 619 (1981) (obligations to city retirement fund held dischargeable). *But see In re* Beaumont, 586 F.3d 776 (10th Cir. 2009) (Veterans Administration could recoup overpayment from future benefits).

289 At one time the Social Security Claims Manual instructed employees to continue recoupment proceedings and to advise claimants and attorneys that "the law requires that future benefits due a person should be withheld to recoup the overpayment." POMS § 02215.185. That is no longer current policy.

290 *In re* Kaliff, 2 B.R. 465 (Bankr. D. Ariz. 1979).

291 *Id.*; *In re* Berry, 3 B.R. 430 (Bankr. D. Or. 1980).

292 *In re* Forcier, 7 B.R. 31 (Bankr. D. Ariz. 1980) (student status concealed).

293 *See* Aboraia v. USDA Food and Nutrition Serv. (*In re* Aboraia), 2012 WL 385635 (Bankr. N.D. Ala. Feb. 6, 2012) (debtors honestly believed they did not have to report adoptive parent subsidies as unearned income). *Cf. In re* Howell, 4 B.R. 102 (Bankr. M.D. Tenn. 1980) (debt in such circumstances could not automatically be classified separately in chapter 13 plan).

294 Federal Rule of Bankruptcy Procedure 7009 incorporates Federal Rule of Civil Procedure 9(b). A motion to dismiss based on failure to plead fraud with particularity may reveal the nature of the circumstantial evidence which the creditor believes supports its claim of intent. Am. Express Travel Related Serv. Co. v. Henein, 257 B.R. 702 (E.D.N.Y. 2001) (affirming dismissal of complaint that did not plead fraud with particularity); Chase Bank v. Vanarthos (*In re* Vanarthos), 440 B.R. 67 (Bankr. S.D.N.Y. 2010) (complaint stating only dates and amounts of charges and petition date did not plead fraud with particularity).

295 *In re* Giuffrida, 302 B.R. 119 (Bankr. E.D.N.Y. 2003) (merely alleging that debtor exceeded credit limit and that debtor's debts exceeded his income when he used credit card did not state a claim under section 523(a)(2)); *In re* Herring, 191 B.R. 317 (Bankr.

larly, there may be issues regarding whether the plaintiff has standing to assert rights as a creditor.[296]

The debtor may raise counterclaims as well as defenses in answering the complaint. If the debt itself is not owed because the debtor's rights under consumer credit laws were violated, or for some other reason, dischargeability becomes a moot point.[297] Such challenges to the existence of the debt can also be useful in settling for a lower amount, if that is later desired.

Discovery should be fully pursued. The creditor's practices with respect to obtaining credit reports, credit scoring, filing other dischargeability complaints, and frequently refinancing, encouraging or making a profit from refinancing, may all be relevant. Operations manuals, standardized forms, and other internal documents setting out these practices should be sought if any of them are relevant or could lead to the discovery of relevant information. These inquiries may well serve to put the creditor on the defensive, forcing it to explain why it granted credit in the first place, why it did not obtain a credit report or did not rely on one, why it increased the debtor's credit, why it encourages refinancings and why it challenges dischargeability more than other creditors. The practitioner may also be able to find other consumers who will back up the debtor's assertion as to the creditor's practices in closing loans. Exposure of unethical practices and bad publicity are usually the last things a creditor wants.

In some cases, the creditor may be seeking a determination of nondischargeability for a debt that is not limited to the debt incurred by fraud. Issues concerning refinancings are discussed above.[298] Moreover, if the debt obtained by fraud has been replaced by a newer obligation not obtained through fraud, the newer obligation may well be dischargeable.[299] In other cases, the creditor's asserted liquidated damages can be challenged as unrelated to the alleged fraudulent conduct.[300]

In some cases, it may be appropriate to move for summary judgment. If a creditor has failed to develop through discovery any facts to support its case, given the creditor's burden of proof, the broad allegations of fraud that it may have pleaded in its complaint will be insufficient to prevent summary judgment.[301] Especially if going to trial will involve significant expense, summary judgment may be a good way to cut short the creditor's case.

Finally, the creditor should be reminded of 11 U.S.C. § 523(d) which requires it to pay attorney fees to the debtor if the latter prevails and the creditor's complaint was not "substantially justified."[302] The purpose of this provision is to prevent a creditor from bringing a questionable case to exploit the debtor's need to pay a lawyer to assert a meritorious defense to a dischargeability complaint; thus, whenever a creditor does not have significant evidence to support its claim, the creditor should be obliged to pay the debtor's attorney.[303] Otherwise, the debtor will have lost money even when the case is won.

The "substantially justified" standard was adopted from the Equal Access to Justice Act, 28 U.S.C. § 2412(d). Under that

---

E.D.N.C. 1995) (credit card issuer's conclusory allegation merely that debtor did not have ability or intention to repay not sufficiently specific because there was no mention of debtor's financial condition at relevant times).

296 See In re Pittard, 358 B.R. 457 (Bankr. N.D. Ga. 2006) (dismissing section 523(a)(2) claim because fraud claim not assignable under Georgia law); In re Wilson, 311 B.R. 566 (B.A.P. 9th Cir. 2004) (plaintiff did not have standing because it had not registered as collection agent on assigned debt), aff'd, 185 Fed. Appx. 696 (9th Cir. 2006).

297 The bankruptcy court has jurisdiction to determine the validity of the debt as well as its dischargeability. In re McLaren, 990 F.2d 850 (6th Cir. 1993). See In re Wilder, 178 B.R. 174 (Bankr. E.D. Mo. 1995) (debt that was barred by statute of limitations was not a claim and could not be nondischargeable).

298 See § 15.4.3.2.2.2, supra.

299 See In re West, 22 F.3d 775 (7th Cir. 1995) (when debtor had executed note to employer to repay embezzled funds and employer had agreed not to sue debtor on any obligation other than note, section 523(a)(4) was inapplicable). But see Archer v. Warner, 538 U.S. 314, 123 S. Ct. 1462, 155 L. Ed. 2d 454 (2003); United States v. Spicer, 57 F.3d 1152 (D.C. Cir. 1995) (debt that originated through debtor's fraud remained nondischargeable even though there was settlement agreement, regardless of whether agreement included release or waiver of fraud claim).

300 Courts have rejected creditors' attempts to collect attorney fees when they have prevailed in dischargeability cases, even when the underlying contract provides for fees incurred in collection litigation. Collingwood Grain, Inc. v. Coast Trading Co., 744 F.2d 686, 693 (9th Cir. 1984) (fees not awarded when there were no basic contract enforcement issues); In re King, 135 B.R. 734 (Bankr. W.D.N.Y. 1992) (Congress did not intend prevailing creditors to collect fees); In re LeMaster, 147 B.R. 52 (Bankr. D. Idaho 1992) (issues were not basic contract enforcement issues, citing Fabian v. W. Bank Farm Credit, 951 F.2d 1149 (9th Cir. 1991)).

301 In re Herndon, 193 B.R. 595 (M.D. Fla. 1996) (affidavits submitted by First Card Services in response to summary judgment motion, stating only that debtor did not pay on credit card accounts and restating general allegations of complaint, not sufficient to raise genuine issue of material fact). See also In re Sinclair, 191 B.R. 474 (Bankr. M.D. Fla. 1996) (credit card issuer denied default judgment when sole allegation was that debtor used card eight to nine months before bankruptcy case, with no specific facts indicating fraud); In re Roberts, 193 B.R. 828 (Bankr. W.D. Mich. 1996) (default judgment denied when bank offered no evidence of debtor's intent or any other evidence other than charges made).

302 See Bennett v. Lukens, 131 B.R. 427 (S.D. Ind. 1991) (fees awarded when creditor filed nondischargeability action in state court); In re Beam, 73 B.R. 434 (Bankr. S.D. Ohio 1987) (fees awarded when creditor pressed late dischargeability complaint without substantial justification).

Previously, fees were recoverable in all cases in which they would not be clearly inequitable, a slightly more liberal standard. The fees should be awarded for all hours reasonably expended on the litigation including appellate representation. In re Wiencek, 58 B.R. 485 (Bankr. E.D. Va. 1986). But see In re Burns, 894 F.2d 361 (10th Cir. 1990) (debtor who successfully defended nondischargeability action not entitled to fees because loan at issue used for investments, was not "consumer debt" within meaning of section 523(d)). See generally Obtaining Attorneys Fees in Dischargeability Cases, 15 NCLC REPORTS Bankruptcy and Foreclosures Ed. 21 (May/June 1997).

303 Carthage Bank v. Kirkland, 121 B.R. 496 (S.D. Miss. 1990); In re May, 428 B.R. 393 (Bankr. W.D. Mich. 2010) (awarding fees based on creditor's meager evidence even though presumption of fraud arose due to cash advances shortly before petition), aff'd, 448 B.R. 197 (W.D. Mich. 2011); In re Grayson, 199 B.R. 397 (Bankr. W.D. Mo. 1996); In re Surbier, 134 B.R. 922 (Bankr. W.D. Mo. 1991).

Act courts have held that a losing party must make a strong showing of justification for its claims;[304] there is no requirement that the prevailing party demonstrate the losing party's bad faith.[305] The same is true of 11 U.S.C. § 523(d); Congress clearly rejected creditor proposals to award fees only when bad faith could be demonstrated.[306] It is the creditor's burden to show that fees should not be awarded.[307] Although a creditor may present proof as to "special circumstances" that might warrant a denial of fees, courts have not readily accepted such justifications in light of the purpose of the statute[308]

Indeed, the fact that a creditor failed to diligently investigate the debtor's credit prior to extending credit has been held to be an important factor in deciding that fees should be awarded.[309] One useful tactic, especially if the creditor has sent a letter threatening a dischargeability complaint, is to immediately inform the creditor of the facts supporting the debtor's defense. A better argument can then be made that the creditor's proceeding was not substantially justified in light of the facts available to it either before the case was filed or before significant attorney fees had been incurred. Similarly, a creditor's failure to investigate whether it has a valid nondischargeability claim by attending the section 341 meeting or conducting an examination of the debtor under Bankruptcy Rule 2004 before filing a complaint has often been held sufficient to show that an unsuccessful action was not substantially justified.[310] The fact that the statutory "loading up" presumption exists does not excuse a lack of investigation.[311] However, absent some evidence that suggests a colorable argument for nondischargeability, a creditor does not have an unlimited right to conduct a Rule 2004 examination, which could be used to harass the debtor,[312] especially in view of the right to examine the debtor at the section 341(a) meeting of creditors.

A section 523(d) fee application should be filed within a reasonable time after conclusion of the action.[313] Fees may be awarded even if the debtor failed to specifically request costs and fees in answering the complaint, although careful practice might include the attorney fee claim as a counterclaim to the original action.[314] Fees should be awarded not only for defending the action but also for the time necessary to litigate the attorney fee issue.[315] Otherwise, creditors could render the fees insufficient simply by causing a good deal of work to obtain them. Section 523(d) has also been construed as authorizing an award of fees for appellate representation.[316]

In addition, attorney fees may be available under other statutory provisions or rules. A frivolous complaint may be grounds for sanctions under Federal Rule of Bankruptcy Procedure 9011, provided the procedures of that rule are followed.[317] And some state statutes provide for consumers to

---

304 Natural Res. Defense Council v. United States Envtl. Prot. Agency, 703 F.2d 700 (3d Cir. 1983); FCC Bank v. Dobbins, 151 B.R. 509 (W.D. Mo. 1992) (debtor's insolvency at time of credit card use, without more, was not sufficient to render complaint substantially justified).

305 See, e.g., Fed. Election Comm'n v. Rose, 806 F.2d 1081 (D.C. Cir. 1986); Blitz v. Donovan, 740 F.2d 1241 (D.C. Cir. 1984). See also In re Hingson, 954 F.2d 428 (7th Cir. 1992) (traditional equitable principles).

306 See H.R. 4786, 97th Cong. § 9(b) (1981), the creditors' proposed bill which would have allowed fees only if bad faith were shown. Cases decided prior to the 1984 amendments also rejected a bad faith requirement. In re Carmen, 723 F.2d 16 (6th Cir. 1983); In re Majewski, 7 B.R. 904 (Bankr. D. Conn. 1980); In re Schlickman, 7 B.R. 139 (Bankr. D. Mass. 1980).

307 In re Hunt, 238 F.3d 1098 (9th Cir. 2001) (creditor that presented virtually no evidence that debtor intended to commit fraud failed to meet burden of proof); In re McCarthy, 243 B.R. 203 (B.A.P. 1st Cir. 2000).

308 In re Stine, 254 B.R. 244 (B.A.P. 9th Cir. 2000) (alleged inaccuracies in schedules which were irrelevant to dischargeability case were not substantial justification, nor were they or the fact that debtor was represented by pro bono counsel special circumstances warranting denial of fees), aff'd, 19 Fed. Appx. 626 (9th Cir. 2001); Carthage Bank v. Kirkland, 121 B.R. 496 (S.D. Miss. 1990) (debtor's "hostile and furtive" attitude toward bank did not constitute "special circumstances" warranting denial of attorney fees); In re Gross, 149 B.R. 460 (Bankr. E.D. Mich. 1992).

309 In re Arroyo, 205 B.R. 984 (Bankr. S.D. Fla. 1997) (when AT & T Universal card gave preapproved and unsolicited card, granted without any evaluation for creditworthiness, no reliance was shown in "six boring hours" of trial; case would have been avoided with minimal investigation by creditor and therefore debtor's counsel awarded $12,200 in fees, including $5000 fee enhancement); In re Leonard, 158 B.R. 839 (Bankr. D. Colo. 1993); In re Cordova, 153 B.R. 352 (Bankr. M.D. Fla. 1993).

310 FIA Card Servs. v. Conant, 476 B.R. 675 (D. Mass. Aug. 16, 2012) (virtually no investigation before or after complaint); FIA Card Servs. v. Dunbar (In re Dunbar), 2012 WL 1757427 (D. Mont. May 15, 2012); In re Sales, 228 B.R. 748 (B.A.P. 10th Cir. 1999) (credit card issuer which failed to investigate prior to filing complaint and whose only basis for filing complaint was a high balance on account was not substantially justified in filing complaint); In re Flowers, 391 B.R. 178 (M.D. Ala. 2008) (attorney fees assessed pursuant to section 523(d) against credit card issuer who made fraud allegations without pre-filing investigation and without follow-up discovery); In re Stahl, 222 B.R. 497 (Bankr. W.D.N.C 1998) (dischargeability complaint used to coerce settlement found to warrant fees); In re Chinchilla, 202 B.R. 1010 (Bankr. S.D. Fla. 1996) (AT & T conducted only minimal and negligent prefiling investigation, using neither the 341 meeting or a Rule 2004 examination); In re Grayson, 199 B.R. 397 (Bankr. W.D. Mo. 1996) (AT & T never investigated case by interrogating debtor and never planned to prove its allegations if its complaints were contested and filed solely to extract settlements from debtors; debtors' attorney awarded fees after AT & T voluntarily dismissed its complaint).

311 Discover Bank v. Paintiff (In re Paintiff), 2012 WL 1466786 (Bankr. C.D. Ill. Apr. 27, 2012).

312 In re Strecker, 251 B.R. 878 (Bankr. D. Colo. 2000).

313 In re Wiencek, 58 B.R. 485 (Bankr. E.D. Va. 1986).
  Federal Rule of Civil Procedure 54(d), which sets a deadline for fee applications, is not incorporated in Federal Rule of Bankruptcy Procedure 7054.

314 In re Bernhardy, 103 B.R. 198 (Bankr. N.D. Ill. 1989).

315 In re Dayton, 306 B.R. 322 (Bankr. N.D. Cal. 2004).

316 In re Wiencek, 58 B.R. 485 (Bankr. E.D. Va. 1986). But see In re Vasseli, 5 F.3d 351 (9th Cir. 1993) (section 523(d) does not grant bankruptcy court authority to award fees for appellate representation; however appellate court may award fees under Federal Rule of Appellate Procedure 38 as sanctions for frivolous appeal).

317 Federal Rule of Bankruptcy Procedure 9011 was amended in 1997 to conform substantially to Federal Rule of Civil Procedure 11.

receive fees if they prevail against creditors who have placed attorney fees clauses in their contracts.[318]

The fact that the debtor is represented by a legal services program should not be a factor in a fees determination, because the courts have consistently held such parties to be entitled to statutory attorney fees on the same basis as all others.[319] Nor should the fact that the case was dismissed or dropped by the creditor short of a final judgment after full trial on the merits excuse liability for attorney fees.[320] However, fees awardable against certain governmental units may be limited by the provisions of section 106(a)(3) of the Code.[321]

15.4.3.3 Creditors Not Listed or Scheduled by the Debtor—11 U.S.C. § 523(a)(3)

Debts owed to some creditors that are not listed or scheduled in the bankruptcy case are excepted from the discharge. This exception[322] underscores the importance of filing a complete and accurate list of a client's debts in every case. And at least one court of appeals has held that it applies not only to the schedules themselves, but also to any mailing label matrix required by local rules.[323] Under the 2005 amendments this exception is expressly applicable to chapter 13 cases as well as to chapter 7 cases. But even before the amendment, failure to list a creditor sometimes had similar consequences in a chapter 13 case.[324] Creditors who are never listed and are thus not informed of the bankruptcy need not file a complaint during the bankruptcy case to raise this ground for nondischargeability.

Fortunately, there are a number of exceptions to this exception. The debt is discharged, even though not listed, if the creditor receives actual notice, either from the debtor or from some other source, that the bankruptcy has been filed,[325] and receives that notice in time to file a proof of claim or, if the claim is nondischargeable and a dischargeability complaint is required, in time to file such a complaint.[326] Because the deadline for claims is presently ninety days after the first date set for the meeting of creditors (or later), and in many chapter 7 cases there is no deadline under the rules,[327] most creditors can still be notified of the case even if their claims are not discovered until well after the case is filed.[328] Indeed, because under section 726(a)(2)(C) a creditor without notice can receive distributions even if the claim is not filed before the claims bar date, as long as the claim is filed in time to permit payment of

---

318 See In re Martinez, 416 F.3d 1286 (11th Cir. 2005) (debtor entitled to recover fees under Florida reciprocal fees statute for dischargeability defense); In re Baroff, 105 F.3d 439 (9th Cir. 1997) (debtor awarded fees under California statute providing for reciprocal fees); In re Mawji, 228 B.R. 321 (Bankr. M.D. Fla. 1999) (fees awarded under Florida law). See also § 16.5.3, infra.

319 See, e.g., Blum v. Stenson, 465 U.S. 886, 104 S. Ct. 1541, 79 L. Ed. 2d 891 (1984); In re Hunt, 238 F.3d 1098 (9th Cir. 2001) (fact that debtor had pro bono representation did not preclude fees); Rodriguez v. Taylor, 569 F.2d 1231 (3d Cir. 1977); Sellers v. Wollman, 510 F.2d 119 (5th Cir. 1977).

320 Discover Bank v. Ferguson (In re Ferguson), 2012 WL 3202610 (Bankr. E.D. Mich. Aug. 3, 2012) (creditor offered to dismiss suit); In re McFadyen, 192 B.R. 328 (Bankr. N.D.N.Y. 1995); In re Mull, 122 B.R. 763 (Bankr. W.D. Okla. 1991); In re Begley, 12 B.R. 839 (Bankr. D. Conn. 1981).

321 See § 14.3.2.2, supra.

322 See 11 U.S.C. § 523(a)(3).

323 In re Adams, 734 F.2d 1094 (5th Cir. 1984).

This holding is questionable in general and inapplicable when the debtor provides timely actual notice of the filing to the omitted creditor. See generally § 9.5, supra.

324 See Ellett v. Stanislaus, 506 F.3d 774 (9th Cir. 2007) (taxes not discharged when notice of chapter 13 bankruptcy contained inaccurate Social Security number); United States Small Bus. Admin. v. Bridges, 894 F.2d 108 (5th Cir. 1990) (failure to schedule debts in chapter 11 case meant they would not be discharged); Reliable Elec. Co. v. Olson Constr. Co., 726 F.2d 620 (10th Cir. 1984) (creditor who had been denied opportunity to comment on chapter 11 plan was not bound by plan); In re Pack, 105 B.R. 703 (Bankr. M.D. Fla. 1989) (debt not scheduled in chapter 13 case is not discharged). See also Broomall Indus. Inc. v. Data Design Logic Sys., Inc., 786 F.2d 401 (Fed. Cir. 1986) (failure to include potential creditor about which debtor had knowledge precludes discharge of that claim in chapter 11 case).

325 In re Barnes, 969 F.2d 526 (7th Cir. 1992) (creditor received actual notice when debtor orally informed him of bankruptcy and debt discharged even though debtor at same time had promised to repay it); Briley v. Hidalgo, 981 F.2d 246 (5th Cir. 1992) (debt to assignee of guarantor was discharged when assignee had actual notice of case).

326 See In re Smith, 582 F.3d 767 (7th Cir. 2009) (notice sent less than three weeks before deadline not sufficient); In re Medaglia, 52 F.3d 451 (2d Cir. 1995) (creditor had timely actual notice of case even though it did not have notice of deadlines); In re Dewalt, 961 F.2d 848 (9th Cir. 1992) (notice seven days before deadline was insufficient; notice at least thirty days before deadline required for debt to be discharged); In re Sam, 894 F.2d 778 (5th Cir. 1990) (notice eighteen days before deadline for dischargeability complaint was sufficient time); In re Compton, 891 F.2d 1180 (5th Cir. 1990) (creditor had actual notice of case in time to file dischargeability complaint); In re Green, 876 F.2d 854 (10th Cir. 1989); In re Schlueter, 391 B.R. 112 (B.A.P. 10th Cir. 2008) (in asset case, notice must be given early enough for creditor to file timely claim, even if notice after claims bar date but before trustee's distribution would have allowed creditor to collect distribution); In re Horlacher, 2009 WL 903620 (N.D. Fla. Mar. 31, 2009) (notice in time for creditor to file tardy claim sufficient when claim would be filed before trustee distribution); § 15.4.2, supra.

327 Fed. R. Bankr. P. 3002(c).

328 In fact, when a debt does not involve fraud, a creditor may probably be added by amendment even after closing of the case in a no-asset case when no deadline for filing of claims was ever set. In re Soult, 894 F.2d 815 (6th Cir. 1990) (debtor entitled to reopen case to add omitted creditor after bar date passed); In re Rosinski, 759 F.2d 539 (6th Cir. 1985); In re Stark, 717 F.2d 322 (7th Cir. 1983); In re Adams, 41 B.R. 933 (D. Me. 1984); In re Zablocki, 36 B.R. 779 (Bankr. D. Conn. 1984); In re Ratliff, 27 B.R. 465 (Bankr. E.D. Va. 1983); Southwest Fla. Production Credit Ass'n v. Fawl, Bankr. L. Rep. (CCH) ¶ 67,459 (Bankr. S.D. Fla. 1980). See also Colonial Surety Co. v. Weizman, 564 F.3d 526 (1st Cir. 2009) (no-asset debtors in chapter 7 could ask bankruptcy court to reopen case to belatedly list creditor who was innocently omitted and who would have received no benefit from notice of original case); In re Baitcher, 781 F.2d 1529 (11th Cir. 1986) (amendment denied if evidence of debtor's fraud or intentional omission). But see In re Laczko, 37 B.R. 676 (B.A.P. 9th Cir. 1984).

As discussed later in this section, such an amendment is usually not necessary for the debt to be discharged.

the claim, the appropriate deadline for notice when there is a bar date for claims is the last day a claim could be filed in time to receive a distribution.[329] In a chapter 13 case, a late claim is usually allowed if no party objects to the claim, which will often permit a non-scheduled creditor to receive distributions in the case.

Creditors that claim they were not informed of the time limit for filing a nondischargeability complaint must prove not only that they did not have timely notice of the case, but also that their claims are in fact nondischargeable under one of the listed exceptions.[330] If the debt is nondischargeable under one of those exceptions, section 523(a)(3) permits the creditor without timely notice to bring its dischargeability action at any time.[331]

The exception to the exception applies if the creditor receives actual notice of the case even though the debt is not duly scheduled.[332] However, it is not enough to show that the creditor receives a newspaper that lists bankruptcies, unless perhaps it is also shown that the creditor reads such lists regularly. Sometimes, but not always, notice is imputed if an agent, for example a collection agent or attorney, receives notice.[333] It is safest, therefore, to list the creditor itself in the bankruptcy schedules, though the agent or attorney may also be listed. If a creditor is not scheduled at the outset of a case, the schedules should be amended and the debtor's counsel should be sure to send a copy of the notice of the meeting of creditors to the creditor, by certified mail, to ensure actual notice.[334] If a discharge has already been granted, the debtor may still file an amendment up to the time the case is closed,[335] or even afterward.[336] Even if the schedules are not amended, actual notice sent and received within the time limits should be sufficient under the wording of section 523(a)(3).

If such notice is sent, it is a good idea to provide accurate information about the debtor's address and taxpayer identification number, as well as an account number if possible, to avoid a later dispute about and whether sufficient information was provided for effective notice. However, it is important to note that the provisions of section 342(g) pertaining to "effective notice" under section 342 do not affect the dischargeability of a debt. By its terms, section 342(g) affects only sanctions for violations of the automatic stay and turnover requirements.

In no-asset chapter 7 cases in which creditors are sent the typical notice that they should not file claims,[337] courts have held that all otherwise dischargeable claims are discharged even if they are not listed in the debtor's schedules.[338] The rationale is that the only notice that the unscheduled creditors holding such claims miss is a notice not to file a proof of claim and a notice of a deadline for dischargeability objections which such creditors do not have. They therefore are not within the

---

329 *In re* Ricks, 253 B.R. 734 (Bankr. M.D. La. 2000). *See also In re* Hatley, 2010 WL 200825 (Bankr. E.D. Tenn. Jan. 12, 2010) (even though claims deadline had run when creditor learned of case, debtor's filing of proof of claim on behalf of creditor satisfied requirement that notice permitted timely filing of claim).

330 *In re* Lochrie, 78 B.R. 257 (B.A.P. 9th Cir. 1987); *In re* Anderson, 72 B.R. 783 (Bankr. D. Minn. 1987); *In re* Barrett, 24 B.R. 682 (Bankr. M.D. Tenn. 1982).

Although there is a time limit for filing a complaint under section 523(a)(15), it was probably inadvertently omitted from the list in section 523(a)(3). *See In re* Dixon, 280 B.R. 755 (Bankr. M.D. Ga. 2002) (court must follow statute's plain language).

331 *In re* Santiago, 175 B.R. 48 (Bankr. 9th Cir. 1994).

The debtor may raise laches as a defense to a section 523 (a)(3) complaint but will have a heavy burden to prove that there has been lack of diligence by the creditor that has prejudiced the debtor. *In re* Beaty, 306 F.3d 914 (9th Cir. 2002). *See also In re* Staffer, 306 F.3d 967 (9th Cir. 2002) (motion to reopen bankruptcy case was not a prerequisite to creditor complaint under section 523(a)(3)).

Although section 523(a)(6) is listed in section 523(a)(3), presumably proof that a creditor had a claim described in that paragraph would not be sufficient in a chapter 13 case if the debtor completes the plan, because section 523(a)(6) is not applicable in such cases.

332 *In re* Presley, 288 B.R. 732 (Bankr. W.D. Va. 2003) (debt discharged, even though improperly scheduled as owed to someone else, because creditor heard about case in time to act). *But see In re* Massa, 187 F.3d 292 (2d Cir. 1999) (when creditor was notified of chapter 13 petition, but never notified that case was converted to chapter 7 or scheduled in time to file a timely dischargeability complaint, creditor had not received adequate notice to protect its rights and could challenge dischargeability for fraud under section 523(a)(3)); *In re* Brown, 267 B.R. 877 (Bankr. W.D. Okla. 2001) (knowledge of debtors' statement that they intended to file a bankruptcy case is not sufficient absent knowledge of actual filing).

333 *See In re* Schicke, 290 B.R. 792 (B.A.P. 10th Cir. 2003) (judgment creditor was properly scheduled in care of attorney who obtained judgment), *aff'd*, 97 Fed. Appx. 249 (10th Cir. 2004); *In re* Price, 79 B.R. 888 (B.A.P. 9th Cir. 1988), *aff'd*, 871 F.2d 97 (9th Cir. 1989); 4 Collier on Bankruptcy ¶ 523.09[4][a] (16th ed.). *But see* United States Small Bus. Admin. v. Bridges, 894 F.2d 108 (5th Cir. 1990) (knowledge of bankruptcy filing of government agency branch office could not be imputed to separate agency branch office); *In re* Todd, 441 B.R. 647 (Bankr. D. Ariz. 2011) (notice to attorney who obtained judgment well before bankruptcy insufficient); *In re* Gold, 375 B.R. 316 (Bankr. N.D. Tex. 2007) (notice to attorneys who had represented debtor's children in child abuse case years earlier, and had not had contact with them for at least two years, was not adequate notice).

Notice may not be imputed unless the agent's scope of authority pertains to the collection of the debt involved. Ford Motor Credit Co. v. Weaver, 680 F.2d 451 (6th Cir. 1982). Nor is notice to a creditor's attorney sufficient when there is no indication as to which of the attorney's clients might be the debtor's creditor. Maldonado v. Ramirez, 757 F.2d 48 (3d Cir. 1985).

334 See Chapter 8, *supra*, for discussion of amending schedules.

335 Fed. R. Bankr. P. 1009; *In re* Jones, 22 B.R. 416 (Bankr. M.D. Fla. 1982).

336 When the deadline for claims has never passed, it may be possible to reopen the case to add creditors. See cases cited above. *See also* 11 U.S.C. § 350. *But see In re* Smith, 21 F.3d 660 (5th Cir. 1994) (debtor could not amend schedules to add creditor four years after petition when claims bar date had passed and creditor had otherwise been prejudiced by delay).

337 *See* Official Form 9A (reprinted in Appx. D, *infra*).

338 *In re* Parker, 313 F.3d 1267 (10th Cir. 2002) (debtor's intent in failing to list claim is irrelevant); *In re* Madaj, 149 F.3d 467 (6th Cir. 1998); Judd v. Wolfe, 78 F.3d 110 (3d Cir. 1996); *In re* Beezley, 994 F.2d 1433 (9th Cir. 1993); *In re* Karras, 165 B.R. 636 (N.D. Ill. 1994) (debt dischargeable in no asset case even if debtor intentionally failed to schedule it); *In re* Anderson, 104 B.R. 427 (Bankr. N.D. Fla. 1989); *In re* Mendiola, 99 B.R. 864 (Bankr. N.D. Ill. 1989); *In re* Smolarick, 56 B.R. 720 (Bankr. W.D. Va. 1986). *But see* Colonial Sur. Co. v. Weizman, 564 F.3d 526 (1st Cir. 2009).

terms of section 523(a)(3) and suffer no prejudice from the lack of notice.[339] Many of these courts have held that in such cases there is no need to amend the schedules to add the omitted creditor because the debt is already discharged by operation of law.[340] On the other hand, if a creditor could have filed a valid dischargeability complaint under one of the sections listed in section 523(c), the debt is nondischargeable after the deadline for such complaints passes regardless of whether the schedules are amended.

In other words, under the language of the statute, a creditor in a no asset case is never denied the right to file a timely proof of claim because there is no deadline. Similar logic would suggest that when an otherwise dischargeable debt is not listed in a case involving only partial payments to unsecured creditors, the debt should be nondischargeable only to the extent of that creditor's unpaid pro rata share of the total amount distributed to unsecured creditors, because that is the only harm suffered by the creditor.[341]

If the creditor is duly scheduled, it is irrelevant whether or not it receives notice. The courts have held that minor irregularities, such as misspellings or incorrect amounts listed as due, do not render improper the listing of a particular creditor.[342] Generally, it has been held that if the creditor's identity can be reasonably ascertained, the listing is sufficient.[343] However, listing a creditor's address as that of its attorney, or in care of its attorney, may not be sufficient.[344] Moreover, if the debtor knows that the debt has been assigned, the assignee must be listed as the creditor. And if the debtor lists an incorrect address, the court may inquire whether the debtor exercised reasonable diligence in completing the schedules.[345] If the debtor does not know and cannot, with reasonable diligence, determine[346] a creditor's name or address, the unknown information need not be listed.[347] But the fact of the debt and whatever information the debtor does know should be listed, along with a statement that the supplied information is the extent of the debtor's knowledge, and perhaps a description of efforts taken to obtain the missing information.[348]

Usually, issues under this exception arise in state courts, which have concurrent jurisdiction to decide them, because the creditor without notice will simply sue to collect its debt. The action may be removed to bankruptcy court, however, once the affirmative defense of the discharge is raised.[349] Even if a default judgment is obtained by the creditor, the debtor should be able to litigate the dischargeability issue in bankruptcy court;[350] if the debtor is correct in asserting that the debt was discharged, the creditor's judgment would be void under 11 U.S.C. § 524(a).

---

339 The same lack of prejudice forms the basis of the argument supporting the reopening of no-asset cases to schedule inadvertently omitted creditors. See § 15.4.3.2.3.3, supra. See also In re Stone, 10 F.3d 285 (5th Cir. 1994) (permitting amendment of claim because no prejudice to creditor who had dischargeable claim in no asset case).

340 See, e.g., In re Parker, 313 F.3d 1267 (10th Cir. 2002) (debtor's intent in failing to list is irrelevant); In re Madaj, 149 F.3d 467 (6th Cir. 1998); In re Beezley, 994 F.2d 1433 (9th Cir. 1993); In re Stecklow, 144 B.R. 314 (Bankr. D. Md. 1992); In re Thibodeau, 136 B.R. 7 (Bankr. D. Mass. 1992).

341 In re Ladnier, 130 B.R. 335 (Bankr. S.D. Ala. 1991).

342 Kreitlin v. Ferger, 238 U.S. 21, 35 S. Ct. 685, 59 L. Ed. 1184 (1915); 4 Collier on Bankruptcy ¶ 523.09[1], [2] (16th ed.). See In re Walker, 125 B.R. 177 (Bankr. E.D. Mich. 1990) (debt properly scheduled when "North Washington St." is listed rather than "South Washington").

There is no requirement that a corporate creditor be listed at its home office or principal place of business. In re Savage, 167 B.R. 22 (Bankr. S.D.N.Y. 1994). However, listing of a totally incorrect address may render a debt not duly scheduled. Ford Motor Credit Co. v. Weaver, 680 F.2d 451 (6th Cir. 1982). See also In re Fauchier, 71 B.R. 212 (B.A.P. 9th Cir. 1987).

343 4 Collier on Bankruptcy ¶ 523.09[2] (16th ed.). But see In re Mitchell, 418 B.R. 282 (B.A.P. 8th Cir. 2009) (creditor who was minor was not properly scheduled when debtor failed to comply with Fed. Rule of Bankr. P. 1007(m) by listing name, address, and relationship of adult person).

344 However, notice to the attorney may be sufficient to constitute actual notice, particularly if there is evidence that the attorney informed his or her client about the bankruptcy. See In re Price, 79 B.R. 888 (B.A.P. 9th Cir. 1988), aff'd, 871 F.2d 97 (9th Cir. 1989). See also In re Land, 215 B.R. 398 (B.A.P. 8th Cir. 1997) (notice to attorney for creditor imputed to creditor because attorney was agent of creditor); In re Malandra, 206 B.R. 667 (Bankr. E.D.N.Y. 1997) (notice to creditor counsel who frequently represented clients in bankruptcy was sufficient).

345 See In re Faden, 96 F.3d 792 (5th Cir. 1996) (debtor's listing of creditor's parent company's address was more than mere negligence, and debtor intentionally or recklessly failed to provide correct address, so debt not discharged); In re Fauchier, 71 B.R. 212 (B.A.P. 9th Cir. 1987) (use of addresses that were two years old).

Significantly, the debtors in Faden appear to have been sophisticated investors rather than consumer debtors. The same principles should not apply to inadvertent misinformation or negligence. Moreover, the court of appeals in Faden did not adequately address why the parent corporation did not pass on the bankruptcy notice to its subsidiary.

346 See In re Gelman, 5 B.R. 230 (Bankr. S.D. Fla. 1980).

347 See Gen. Collections, Inc. v. Steward, 539 N.E.2d 981 (Ind. Ct. App. 1989) (when creditor dissolved and reformed under new name and at new address without notice to debtor, listing old name and address was sufficient and debt is discharged).

348 The names of creditors may not always be known. The debtor may have engaged in acts with unknown victims. One question which arises in some cases, mostly involving environmental torts or product liability, is whether the debt arises only when injuries manifest themselves. This is important for dischargeability purposes, both so that the injured person knows of his or her claim and so that the debtor knows of the claim in order to give proper notice. The general rule is that injuries become manifest when the claimant discovers the injury and knows or has reason to know the cause. Probably, no claim exists which can be discharged until this occurs. See In re Cent. R.R. Co. of N.J., 950 F.2d 887 (3d Cir. 1991). See also § 9.4.2, supra; § 15.5.1.1, infra.

349 See § 14.4.1, supra, for a discussion of removal to bankruptcy court. See also In re Guseck, 310 B.R. 400 (Bankr. E.D. Wis. 2004) (debtor could reopen case to seek dischargeability of nonscheduled debt in bankruptcy court).

350 See In re McGhan, 288 F.3d 1172 (9th Cir. 2002) (bankruptcy court abused its discretion in refusing to reopen case to decide whether debt was nondischargeable under section 523(a)(3) and whether discharge injunction was violated; state court's order that debt was

Of course, a claim which is not discharged solely because it was not listed in a chapter 7 case may be included and discharged in a subsequent bankruptcy.[351]

15.4.3.4 Fraud As a Fiduciary, Embezzlement, or Larceny—11 U.S.C. § 523(a)(4)

The fourth exception to discharge, applicable in both chapter 7 and chapter 13, involves fraud or defalcation while acting in a fiduciary capacity, or embezzlement or larceny even if not in a fiduciary capacity.[352] The exception based on fraud or defalcation is rarely invoked in cases involving consumers, as few consumers have acted as fiduciaries.[353]

Defalcation has been defined as failure by a trustee to properly account for funds placed in his or her trust.[354] It seems clear that for this exception to apply the trust relationship involved must be an express or technical trust, and not a constructive trust implied by law in some cases of wrongful conduct.[355] A sales employee who has misappropriated funds is thus not a fiduciary, though a consignee may be one.[356] When a true fiduciary relationship is created by statute, there is little doubt that the section applies.[357]

The terms larceny and embezzlement are also included in this exception in the Code and are applicable to non-fiduciaries

---

not discharged improperly modified bankruptcy court's discharge order).

351 *See In re* Dye, 108 B.R. 135 (Bankr. W.D. Tex. 1989). *See also In re* Samora, 117 B.R. 660 (Bankr. D.N.M. 1990) (debtors may discharge debts scheduled in previous bankruptcy case even though previous case dismissed for failure to obey court order as long as discharge was not waived or denied in previous case).

352 4 Collier on Bankruptcy ¶ 523.10 (16th ed.). *Accord In re* Kapnison, 65 B.R. 221 (Bankr. D.N.M. 1986).

353 The most common application in consumer cases may be to guardians for elderly persons and executors of estates. *See, e.g.*, *In re* Messineo, 192 B.R. 597 (Bankr. D.N.H. 1996) (son breached fiduciary duties when, as co-guardian of his elderly mother's estate, he misappropriated her funds and property for his own use).

354 *See, e.g.*, Kwiat v. Doucette, 81 B.R. 184 (D. Mass. 1987). *See also In re* Moreno, 892 F.2d 417 (5th Cir. 1990) (when debtor, while officer of debtor corporation, directed transfer of $200,000 to himself and companies in which he owned at least fifty percent interest he acted in fiduciary capacity).

Courts have disagreed regarding whether there must be some element of culpability for a defalcation to be nondischargeable or whether all defalcations by fiduciaries are nondischargeable. *Compare* Bullock v. BankChampaign (*In re* Bullock), 670 F.3d 1160 (11th Cir. 2012) (showing of recklessness required), *In re* Hyman, 502 F.3d 61 (2d Cir. 2007) (defalcation under section 523(a)(4) requires a showing of conscious misbehavior or extreme recklessness—a showing akin to the showing required for *scienter* in the securities law context), *In re* Baylis, 313 F.3d 9 (1st Cir. 2002) (defalcation requires some degree of fault, closer to fraud, without necessity of meeting a strict specific intent requirement), *and* Chao v. Rizzi, 2007 U.S. Dist. LEXIS 57773 (W.D. Pa. Aug. 8, 2007) (defalcation does not include innocent or negligent defaults), *with In re* Uwimana, 274 F.3d 806 (4th Cir. 2001) (negligence or innocent mistake may be defalcation); *In re* Lewis, 97 F.3d 198, 204 (9th Cir. 1996) (defalcation includes innocent, as well as intentional or negligent defaults), *In re* Dauterman, 156 B.R. 976 (Bankr. N.D. Ohio 1993) (defalcation need not be intentional or in bad faith), *and In re* Waters, 20 B.R. 277 (Bankr. W.D. Tex. 1982) (intent not an essential element of defalcation, and debt nondischargeable when Texas statute placed upon debtor the responsibility to account for funds).

355 Arvest Mortg. Co. v. Nail (*In re* Nail), 680 F.3d 1036, 1041 (8th Cir. 2012) (the mere use of the word "trustee," when viewed in the context of lienholder protection statute as a whole, did not reflect a legislative intent to create the kind of express or technical trust required in the strict and narrow sense under § 523(a)(4)); *In re* Banks, 263 F.3d 862 (9th Cir. 2001) (attorney was fiduciary with respect to client trust account); *In re* Garver, 116 F.3d 176 (6th Cir. 1997) (attorney-client relationship without more, such as holding of funds, is not fiduciary relationship); *In re* Gergely, 110 F.3d 1448 (9th Cir. 1997) (fiduciary duties do not arise from doctor-patient relationship); *In re* Cantrell, 88 F.3d 344 (5th Cir. 1996) (exception only applies when there is an express trust and recognizable corpus); *In re* Woldman, 92 F.3d 546 (7th Cir. 1996) (debtor attorney was not fiduciary for attorney who referred personal injury case to him with respect to referring attorney's agreed share of contingent fee; fiduciary obligation must involve substantial inequality in power or knowledge); *In re* Nicholas, 956 F.2d 110 (5th Cir. 1992) (debtor was not a fiduciary under Texas statute that deemed contractor to be "trustee" of funds due to subcontractors absent intent to defraud); *In re* Long, 774 F.2d 875 (8th Cir. 1985); *In re* Teichman, 774 F.2d 1395 (9th Cir. 1985); *In re* Schneider, 99 B.R. 974 (B.A.P. 9th Cir. 1989) (financial advisor who takes control over another's money is a fiduciary pursuant to an express trust); *In re* Schoen, 407 B.R. 420 (Bankr. W.D. Okla. 2009) (debtor who received health insurance benefits that were supposed to be paid to hospital was not a fiduciary based on agreement with hospital); *In re* Tucker, 346 B.R. 844 (Bankr. E.D. Okla. 2006) (exception inapplicable when no agreement created fiduciary relationship); *In re* Schusterman, 108 B.R. 893 (Bankr. D. Conn. 1989) (lottery sales agent had no fiduciary duty under Connecticut law); *In re* Valdes, 98 B.R. 78 (Bankr. M.D. Fla. 1989) (executor in context of a probate proceeding acts as a fiduciary); *In re* Tester, 62 B.R. 486 (Bankr. W.D. Va. 1986) (contract requiring that proceeds of a sale be held "in trust" insufficient to establish fiduciary relationship; *In re* Paley, 8 B.R. 466 (Bankr. E.D.N.Y. 1981) (contract requiring money to be held "in trust" not enough to create fiduciary relationship); *In re* Wise, 6 B.R. 867 (Bankr. M.D. Fla. 1980); *In re* Walker, 7 B.R. 563 (Bankr. M.D. Ga. 1980); *In re* Miles, 5 B.R. 458 (Bankr. E.D. Va. 1980) (contract requiring funds to be held separately not enough to create fiduciary relationship); 4 Collier on Bankruptcy ¶ 523.10[1][c] (16th ed.). *But see In re* Hayes, 183 F.3d 162 (2d Cir. 1999) (attorney-client relationship is fiduciary relationship); *In re* Lewis, 97 F.3d 1182 (9th Cir. 1996) (state law made partners fiduciaries for each other).

356 *In re* Shiller, 21 B.R. 643 (Bankr. D. Idaho 1982) (consignee's debt not dischargeable); 4 Collier on Bankruptcy ¶ 523.10[1][c] (16th ed.).

357 *In re* McGee, 353 F.3d 537 (7th Cir. 2003) (city ordinance requiring landlord to place tenant's security deposit in segregated account created a fiduciary relationship); *In re* Niles, 106 F.3d 1456 (9th Cir. 1997) (real estate broker who handled client's funds for sales, rentals and loans was a fiduciary); *In re* Short, 818 F.2d 693 (9th Cir. 1987) (debtor who had contractual and statutory duty to pay taxes, maintain books and distribute funds to joint venturers was a fiduciary); *In re* Interstate Agency Inc., 760 F.2d 121 (6th Cir. 1985); *In re* Thomas, 729 F.2d 502 (7th Cir. 1984); *In re* Johnson, 691 F.2d 249 (6th Cir. 1982); Carey Lumber Co. v. Bell, 615 F.2d 370 (5th Cir. 1980). *See* Quaif v. Johnson, 4 F.3d 950 (11th Cir. 1993) (insurance agent's statutory duty to segregate insurance premiums made him a fiduciary). *Cf. In re* Boyle, 819 F.2d 583 (5th Cir. 1987) (no true trust created by statute); Runnion v. Pedrazzini, 644 F.2d 756 (9th Cir. 1981) (same).

as well as fiduciaries. "Larceny" is not necessarily defined in bankruptcy in the same way it is defined in state law.[358] Larceny is defined as a matter of federal common law as taking property from its rightful owner willfully and with fraudulent intent.[359] Embezzlement is the fraudulent appropriation of property belonging to another by a person in lawful possession of that property.[360]

As under 11 U.S.C. § 523(a)(2), it is the creditor's burden to show actual fraudulent intent in order to prove embezzlement.[361] If the debt in question was not actually incurred with such intent, even if it replaced a debt that would have met the tests for fraud, the debt is not excepted from the discharge.[362]

In any case, for this exception to apply, a complaint must be filed during the bankruptcy case within the time limits set by the Bankruptcy Rules.[363] The amount excepted from discharge is equal to the amount misappropriated, rather than any greater amount that may be owed to the creditor.[364]

15.4.3.5 Domestic Support Obligations—11 U.S.C. § 523(a)(5)

15.4.3.5.1 In general

The Code excepts domestic support obligations from discharge in both chapter 7 and chapter 13 cases.[365] The term "domestic support obligation" is defined in section 101(14A) and encompasses what was considered alimony, maintenance, or support under former section 523(a)(5), but is broader in several respects. The definition includes both prepetition and postpetition obligations, and it includes interest that accrues on a debt under applicable nonbankruptcy law, "notwithstanding any other provision of this title."[366] It includes obligations in the nature of support owed to or recoverable by a spouse, former spouse, or child of the debtor,[367] by such child's parent,[368] legal guardian, or responsible relative, or by a governmental unit. The definition includes such obligations, whether established or subject to establishment before, on, or after the date of the order for relief, if they were established by reason of a separation agreement, divorce decree, order of a court of record, administrative determination made by a governmental unit, or property settlement.[369] It does not include obligations that have been assigned unless they were assigned to a governmental unit or voluntarily assigned for purposes of collection.

This exception does not include debts for support owed to entities not specified in the definition of domestic support obligation. Thus, debts owed under "palimony" decisions, to persons who were never validly married to the debtor, are not excepted from discharge,[370] nor are debts for support of puta-

---

358 See In re Shreve, 386 B.R. 602 (Bankr. W.D. Va. 2008) (federal common law definition, rather than expanded state definition, should be used); In re Lane, 115 B.R. 81 (Bankr. E.D. Va. 1990) (debt arising from conduct which constituted larceny under Virginia law was nevertheless dischargeable); In re Goux, 72 B.R. 355 (Bankr. N.D.N.Y. 1987) (debt not due to larceny under Code when debtor obtained possession of funds lawfully, even though debtor had plead guilty to petit larceny); In re Storms, 28 B.R. 761 (Bankr. E.D.N.C. 1983).

359 Werner v. Hoffman, 5 F.3d 1170 (8th Cir. 1993) (no larceny found with respect to failure to return creditor's property when debtor's initial possession of property was lawful); In re Rose, 934 F.2d 901 (7th Cir. 1991) (debtor took husband's funds from safe deposit box); In re Figler, 407 B.R. 181, 193 (Bankr. W.D. Pa. 2009) (theft of satellite TV services was larceny); In re Tucker, 346 B.R. 844 (Bankr. E.D. Okla. 2006) (no larceny when reimbursement check from health insurer was payable to debtor).

360 Werner v. Hoffman, 5 F.3d 1170 (8th Cir. 1993) (no embezzlement found with respect to failure to return creditor's property when debtor did not improperly use creditor's property that was lawfully in debtor's possession); In re Tucker, 346 B.R. 844 (Bankr. E.D. Okla. 2006) (exception inapplicable when reimbursement check from health insurer was payable to debtor); In re Conder, 196 B.R. 104 (Bankr. W.D. Wis. 1995) (one cannot embezzle one's own property, so creditor who held only security interest in debtor's property could not claim embezzlement); In re Trovato, 145 B.R. 575 (Bankr. N.D. Ill. 1991) (embezzlement shown when debtor saved money for his employer but then deposited funds in his own bank account). See In re Belfry, 862 F.2d 661 (8th Cir. 1988) (when creditor had only his own "understanding" that debtor would use funds for certain purpose, embezzlement had not been shown). See also In re Wallace, 840 F.2d 762 (10th Cir. 1988) (state court judgment that debtor embezzled funds collaterally estops bankruptcy court from relitigating embezzlement issue).

361 See, e.g., In re Weber, 892 F.2d 534 (7th Cir. 1989).

362 In re West, 22 F.3d 775 (7th Cir. 1995) (when debtor had executed note to employer to repay embezzled funds and employer had agreed not to sue debtor on any obligation other than note, section 523(a)(4) was inapplicable). But see Archer v. Warner, 538 U.S. 314, 123 S. Ct. 1462, 155 L. Ed. 2d 454 (2003).

363 11 U.S.C. § 523(c); Fed. R. Bankr. P. 4007(c). See § 15.4.2, supra.

364 In re Bennett, 989 F.2d 779 (5th Cir. 1993). But see In re Bugna, 33 F.3d 1054 (9th Cir. 1994) (punitive damages also not discharged).

365 11 U.S.C. §§ 523(a)(5), 1328(a).
   For a lengthy discussion of this exception, see Henry J. Sommer & Margaret Dee McGarity, Collier Family Law and the Bankruptcy Code Ch. 6 (1992). Because these debts are excepted from discharge in chapter 13, postpetition interest on them is also excepted from discharge, even if the allowed secured claim for the principal is paid in a chapter 13 plan. In re Foster, 319 F.3d 495 (9th Cir. 2003); In re Crable, 174 B.R. 62 (Bankr. W.D. Ky. 1994).

366 See In re Foster, 319 F.3d 495 (9th Cir. 2003) (chapter 13 debtor who paid support arrearages in full still owed interest at end of plan). But see In re Smith, 586 F.3d 69 (1st Cir. 2009) (late payment penalties on support payments were not domestic support obligations).

367 The child need not be a minor and "support" probably includes educational expenses. See In re Harrell, 754 F.2d 902 (11th Cir. 1985).
   However, the child must be a child of the debtor. In re White, 253 B.R. 253 (Bankr. W.D. Ark. 2000) (even though state court continued to hold him liable, debtor's debt for support of child determined not to be his by DNA test was not nondischargeable as support for a child of the debtor).

368 See In re Maddigan, 312 F.3d 589 (2d Cir. 2002) (attorney fees awarded to out-of-wedlock mother in custody case were nondischargeable support).

369 A support award entered in a court of record is nondischargeable even if it is not embodied in a divorce decree or marital separation agreement. Shine v. Shine, 802 F.2d 583 (1st Cir. 1986) (suit for separate maintenance).

370 In re Doyle, 70 B.R. 106 (B.A.P. 9th Cir. 1986).

tive spouses, for example, spouses in a void marriage.[371] Similarly, debts assigned to a former spouse's estate after her death are not included in the exception.[372] Most courts have held that claims for repayment of support overpayments or wrongfully paid support are not domestic support obligations because they are not intended to provide support.[373] And in some cases, such as divorce decrees that give the non-debtor spouse a right to pension benefits, courts have ruled that there is no debt to be discharged because the divorce decree granted a vested interest in the pension or other property to that spouse.[374]

15.4.3.5.2 Support debts owed to governmental units

Unfortunately, support rights assigned to public welfare departments in cases in which the debtor's children receive public assistance are included within this exception to discharge. The exception includes both sums owing at the time of the assignment and sums which become due thereafter.[375] All obligations within the scope of the definition of domestic support obligation are nondischargeable if they are owed to a governmental unit. As part of the amendments adopting this definition, Congress repealed section 523(a)(18) as no longer necessary.

Moreover, there need not ever have been an actual assignment of a court order for the debt to be nondischargeable. The definition of domestic support obligation includes an obligation for assistance provided by a governmental unit. In addition to the provisions of section 523(a)(5), section 456(b) of the Social Security Act, which had previously applied only to child support, provides that a debt owed to a state or municipality that is in the nature of support and that is enforceable under Part IVD of the Social Security Act is not "released" by a discharge in bankruptcy.[376]

A few courts have expanded the definition of "domestic support obligation" beyond its obvious intent to include other debts determined by an administrative agency to be owed to governmental units that have no relation to support orders or support obligations of debtors. These courts have held that if a debtor is determined to have received an overpayment of funds intended to support dependents the obligation to repay the overpayment is a domestic support obligation.[377] In so doing, they ignore the fact that the reference to administrative determinations was originally added to the Code in order to encompass non-court adjudications of family support obligations, not every decision made by any governmental agency. They also fail to recognize that the debt to the state for the overpayment of benefits is not for support of debtor's spouse, former spouse, or child of the debtor, or such child's parent. Rather, it is a debt for the return of a benefit paid to the debtor which should not have been paid in the first place.[378] By the reasoning of these courts, all sorts of debts owed to the government, if arguably they were intended for support, could be classed as nondischargeable domestic support obligations.

Thus the most a bankruptcy can do with respect to such debts is provide protection during a reasonable payment plan under chapter 13, subject to the specific requirements for payment of domestic support obligations in chapter 13.[379] This protection, however, can be very valuable in areas where overzealous prosecutors and judges harass and even incarcerate those who, because of unemployment or other problems, have allowed their dependents to become public charges.

15.4.3.5.3 Determination of whether debt is a domestic support obligation

Most of the disputes about whether a debt is a domestic support obligation concern whether the debt is for alimony, maintenance, or support as opposed to being a property settlement debt—which is covered by a different dischargeability provision,[380] is not a priority debt, and is dischargeable in chapter 13.[381] As with any exception to discharge, the burden is on the creditor to establish that the debt is nondischargeable under section 523(a)(5).[382] The legislative history makes clear that this question is to be determined as a matter of federal

---

371 See *Putative Spousal Support Rights and the Federal Bankruptcy Act*, 25 UCLA L. Rev. 69 (1977). *See also In re* Magee, 111 B.R. 359 (M.D. Fla. 1990).

372 *In re* Brunhoff, 4 B.R. 381 (Bankr. S.D. Fla. 1980). *See also In re* Fields, 23 B.R. 134 (Bankr. D. Colo. 1982) (support arrearage obligation to ex-wife who was also in bankruptcy discharged because the right to collect the arrearage had passed to ex-wife's trustee as part of her estate). *But see In re* McIntyre, 328 B.R. 356 (Bankr. D. Mass. 2005) (debt that passed to spouse's estate was not assigned for purposes of section 523(a)(5)).

However, if an assignment is only for purposes of collection, the exception still applies. *In re* Beggin, 19 B.R. 759 (Bankr. W.D. Wash. 1982). *But see In re* Silansky, 897 F.2d 743 (4th Cir. 1990) (listing divorce judgment for attorney fee as asset in bankruptcy schedules does not constitute an assignment); *In re* Combs, 101 B.R. 609 (B.A.P. 9th Cir. 1989) (when ex-wife died after bankruptcy petition filed, status of debt determined as of petition date).

373 *See In re* Vanhook, 426 B.R. 296 (Bankr. N.D. Ill. 2010) (collecting cases).

374 *See, e.g., In re* McCafferty, 96 F.3d 192 (6th Cir. 1996) (divorce decree dividing pension created separate property interest in pension for non-debtor spouse); Bush v. Taylor, 912 F.2d 989 (8th Cir. 1990) (en banc); *In re* Chandler, 805 F.2d 555 (5th Cir. 1986) (wife's right to receive portion of ex-husband's military pension was her own property and not his obligation).

375 *In re* Stovall, 721 F.2d 1133 (7th Cir. 1983).

376 42 U.S.C. § 656(b); *In re* Cervantes, 219 F.3d 955 (9th Cir. 2000)

(prejudgment support arrearages nondischargeable in chapter 13 under 42 U.S.C. § 656(b)).

377 Wisconsin Dep't of Workforce Dev. v. Ratliff, 390 B.R. 607, 616 (E.D. Wis. 2008) (food stamp benefits were intended to support debtor's children so overpayment was nondischargeable). *Cf. In re* Tinnell, 2009 WL 1664581 (Bankr. D. Neb. June 12, 2009) (no evidence that an administrative determination based on evidence had ever been made).

378 State v. Hickey (*In re* Hickey), 473 B.R. 361, 364–365 (Bankr. D. Or. 2012).

379 *See* 11 U.S.C. §§ 1307(c)(11), 1322(a)), 1325(a)(8), 1328(a); Ch. 12, *supra*; Henry J. Sommer & Margaret Dee McGarity, Collier Family Law and the Bankruptcy Code Ch. 8 (1992).

380 11 U.S.C. § 523(a)(15). *See* § 15.4.3.14, *infra*.

381 11 U.S.C. § 523(a)(15) is not included among the exceptions to a normal chapter 13 discharge listed in section 1328(a)(2).

382 Tilley v. Jessee, 789 F.2d 1074 (4th Cir. 1986).

bankruptcy law, and not state law.[383] The designation of a debt as alimony or property settlement by a state court decree or agreement is not binding in the dischargeability determination; a court can look behind such language to determine the real nature of the debt.[384] However this issue will arise less frequently now that property settlement debts are also nondischargeable in chapter 7 cases. Because state courts have concurrent jurisdiction with respect to dischargeability of such debts, a decision by a state court on a section 523(a)(5) dischargeability issue is probably binding, at least if the issue is actually litigated.[385]

The main indicators that courts will look to in determining whether the debt is in the nature of a support payment rather than a property settlement are:

- Whether the payments terminate upon death or remarriage of the spouse receiving them;[386]
- Whether payments are contingent on future earning abilities;
- Whether payments are to be periodic over a long period of time rather than in a lump sum; and
- Whether the payments are designated as being for purposes such as medical care, mortgage, or other needs of the spouse receiving them.

Each of these factors indicates that support, based upon the needs of the obligee spouse, is intended, rather than a property settlement. The existence of those needs at the time of the agreement, by itself, is often sufficient for a finding that an obligation was for the purpose of support.[387] While labels in a divorce decree or settlement are not binding on the court, at least some deference may be given to how the various obligations are labeled in the agreement.[388] Another factor that courts may find relevant is the parties' tax treatment of the payments. A spouse who has taken the benefit of treatment of marital obligations as alimony may be estopped from later contending the obligation was a property settlement.[389] Similarly, an obligee who did not report past payments as alimony income, may be estopped from later claiming the debt is in the nature of alimony.

If the intent of an agreement is to provide support, it is irrelevant whether such support is required under state law.[390] If the court finds, on the other hand, that payments are to compensate for a spouse's property interest, they will be designated as in the nature of a property settlement with dischargeability to be determined under another Code section.[391] Normally, a trial

---

383 S. Rep. No. 95-989, at 79 (1978); H.R. Rep. No. 95-595, at 364 (1977).

384 11 U.S.C. § 523(a)(5)(B); Cummings v. Cummings, 244 F.3d 1263 (11th Cir. 2001) (court must look at intent of divorce court in ordering payment labeled as equitable distribution); In re Goin, 808 F.2d 1391 (10th Cir. 1987). See also In re Norbut, 387 B.R. 199, 210 (Bankr. S.D. Ohio 2008) (debt for overpayment of support was nondischargeable because it had resulted in creditor not having sufficient funds to support himself).

Therefore, the fact that a party argued in state court that a debt was property settlement for purposes of state law did not estop that party from arguing it was in the nature of support under federal bankruptcy law. In re Dennis, 25 F.3d 274 (5th Cir. 1994).

385 In re Gross, 722 F.2d 599 (10th Cir. 1983); In re Peterman, 5 B.R. 687 (Bankr. E.D. Pa. 1980). See also In re Comer, 723 F.2d 737 (9th Cir. 1984) (res judicata also applies as to amount of support found owing by state court). But see In re Williams, 3 B.R. 401 (Bankr. N.D. Ga. 1980).

386 See In re Morel, 983 F.2d 104 (8th Cir. 1992) (when one portion of award was payable until death or remarriage and other portion was not, the portion not conditioned on the obligee continuing to live as a single person was a dischargeable property settlement).

387 In re Werthen, 329 F.3d 269 (1st Cir. 2003) (obligation to pay over percentage of debtor's bonuses, though labeled property settlement, was needed for support of children and payments were to be received roughly until children reached majority); In re Benick, 811 F.2d 943 (5th Cir. 1987) (wife needed support); In re Yeates, 807 F.2d 874 (10th Cir. 1986) (payments needed to provide basic necessities); In re Shaver, 736 F.2d 1314 (9th Cir. 1984) ("property settlement" found in nature of support when wife needed support

and divorce decree had no explicit provision for support of wife); In re Combs, 101 B.R. 609 (B.A.P. 9th Cir. 1989) (listing eight factors in finding debt for spousal support nondischargeable); In re Fox, 6 Bankr. Ct. Dec. (LRP) 709 (Bankr. N.D. Tex. 1980). See Henry J. Sommer & Margaret Dee McGarity, Collier Family Law and the Bankruptcy Code Ch. 6 (1992); Schiffer, The New Bankruptcy Reform Act: Its Implications for Family Law Practitioners, 19 J. Fam. L. 1, 21 (1980–1981).

388 See Tilley v. Jessee, 789 F.2d 1074 (4th Cir. 1986) (settlement agreement structured so as to divide property settlement from alimony given great weight in determining that debt is dischargeable); In re Long, 794 F.2d 928 (4th Cir. 1986) (characterization of monetary obligation as alimony in jury award given deference in determining that a debt is nondischargeable). See also In re Singer, 787 F.2d 1033 (6th Cir. 1986) (recital in agreement interpreted and given great weight in making determination that an obligation constituted support).

389 Robb v. Fulton, 23 F.3d 895 (4th Cir. 1994); In re Davidson, 947 F.2d 1294 (5th Cir. 1991).

Such decisions are probably erroneous in looking to this single factor, because the requirements for federal tax deductibility are not exactly the same as the indicia of support under federal bankruptcy law.

390 Richardson v. Edwards, 127 F.3d 97 (D.C. Cir. 1997) (obligation to pay support past children's age of majority in nature of support even though there was no legal duty of support); In re Sampson, 997 F.2d 717 (10th Cir. 1993) (listing variety of factors which showed true function and intent of obligation); In re Biggs, 907 F.2d 503 (5th Cir. 1990) (debtor's divorce decree obligation to former wife was nondischargeable alimony, even though Texas law did not provide for alimony awards); In re Yeates, 807 F.2d 874 (10th Cir. 1986); In re Harrell, 754 F.2d 902 (11th Cir. 1985); Boyle v. Donovan, 724 F.2d 681 (8th Cir. 1984).

391 In re Ingram, 5 B.R. 232 (Bankr. N.D. Ga. 1980).

See § 15.4.3.14, infra, for a discussion of nondischargeable property settlements. Alternatively, the debt incurred as a result of a property settlement might be found nondischargeable on some other grounds such as fraud. See, e.g., Edelkind v. Alderman, 106 B.R. 315 (N.D. Ga. 1989) (debtor fraudulently induced his former wife to accept a promissory note and then dishonored the note); In re Brasher, 20 B.R. 408 (Bankr. W.D. Tenn. 1982) (property settlement agreement found fraudulent under 11 U.S.C. § 523(a)(2) when entered into with intent to file bankruptcy after inducing wife to waive alimony).

court's findings on such issues will not be disturbed on appeal if the proper legal standards are applied.[392]

Spouses or former spouses often disagree about the nature of a "hold harmless" agreement in which one spouse agrees to pay marital debts and then later claims that they were discharged in a bankruptcy.[393] Whether the responsibility for these debts is more in the nature of a support payment or a property settlement is determined using similar criteria.[394] For these debts to be determined nondischargeable domestic support obligations, most courts have held that payment of them must be necessary to support the non-debtor spouse at the time of the agreement or order.[395] If the debtor spouse has agreed to pay current mortgage, utility, insurance, and tax payments, for example, such payments are normally deemed to be support.[396] This conclusion is bolstered if the non-debtor spouse is unemployed[397] or if the agreement provides for payment through the court, with noncompliance punishable by contempt.[398] Other cases in which courts have found an intent to provide support have involved such debts as payments for life insurance policies that name the debtor's spouse and children as beneficiaries,[399] payments for medical treatment after the divorce,[400] and debts for furniture used by the former spouse and children, when the intent was to relieve the spouse from the burden of paying them, and the spouse waived the right to periodic alimony payments.[401]

The Sixth Circuit Court of Appeals has mandated a several step analysis to determine the dischargeability of a hold harmless obligation under section 523(a)(5).[402] Under this test, the bankruptcy court must look to the intent of the family law court or the intent of the parties themselves as to each loan obligation.[403] If payments were intended as support, the bankruptcy court must then decide whether the payments have the effect of providing support and whether that support is necessary for the daily needs of the spouse and children. If these factors are present, the court must finally decide whether the payments are within the criteria for ability to pay that would normally be applied to support orders. If the amounts are unreasonably excessive, they are dischargeable.

All other circuits to address the issue have rejected the Sixth Circuit approach to the extent that approach looks to current need and the amounts of payments ordered.[404] These courts have generally held that the bankruptcy court should look only to whether the payments due were originally intended to be in the nature of support rather than a property settlement. Once the debt is determined to be one that was originally intended for support, no further inquiry is to be made and the debt must be declared a nondischargeable domestic support obligation.[405]

On the other hand, if the intent was simply to divide assets and previous liabilities, the debt is not nondischargeable under section 523(a)(5),[406] especially if there is no apparent benefit intended for the other spouse.[407] Such debts are, however, normally nondischargeable in chapter 7 cases under section 523(a)(15).[408] If such debts are discharged, as they may be in a chapter 13 case, any action to collect them is enjoined under section 524 of the Code.[409]

---

392 *In re* Brody, 3 F.3d 35 (2d Cir. 1993) (listing factors trial court found showed parties' intent to provide support); *In re* Troup, 730 F.2d 464 (6th Cir. 1984); Boyle v. Donovan, 724 F.2d 681 (8th Cir. 1984); Stout v. Prussel, 691 F.2d 859 (9th Cir. 1982).

393 Most courts hold that a hold harmless provision creates a separate obligation to the spouse protected by it. *But see* Heilman v. Heilman (*In re* Heilman), 430 B.R. 213 (B.A.P. 9th Cir. 2010) (hold harmless provision regarding community debt discharged before divorce was invalid attempt to reaffirm debt).

394 *See In re* Rice, 94 B.R. 617 (Bankr. W.D. Mo. 1988) (obligation to pay bills and attorney fees and lien on house found to be property settlement when divorce court had separately awarded spousal maintenance); *In re* Campbell, 74 B.R. 805 (Bankr. M.D. Fla. 1987) (property settlement found when debtor's obligations would not terminate on death or remarriage of ex-spouse).

395 *In re* Robinson, 921 F.2d 252 (10th Cir. 1990) (even if non-debtor spouse refinanced a mortgage the debtor agreed to pay, the debtor's obligation would survive and remain nondischargeable); *In re* Warner, 5 B.R. 434 (Bankr. D. Utah 1980). *Cf. In re* Edwards, 91 B.R. 95 (Bankr. C.D. Cal. 1988) (state court cannot order debtor to pay spouse's debts discharged in bankruptcy as alimony, support or maintenance).

396 *In re* Gianakas, 917 F.2d 759 (3d Cir. 1990); Sylvester v. Sylvester, 865 F.2d 1164 (10th Cir. 1989); *In re* Tope, 7 B.R. 422 (Bankr. S.D. Ohio 1980); *In re* Henry, 5 B.R. 342 (Bankr. M.D. Fla. 1980). *But see* Richardson v. Edwards, 127 F.3d 97 (D.C. Cir. 1997) (obligation to assume second mortgage not intended as a means of providing support).

397 *In re* Tope, 7 B.R. 422 (Bankr. S.D. Ohio 1980).

398 *In re* Henry, 5 B.R. 342 (Bankr. M.D. Fla. 1980).

399 *In re* Evans, 4 B.R. 232 (Bankr. S.D. Ala. 1980).

400 *In re* Breaux, 8 B.R. 218 (Bankr. W.D. La. 1981).

401 *In re* Coil, 680 F.2d 1170 (7th Cir. 1982); *In re* Sturgell, 7 B.R. 59 (Bankr. S.D. Ohio 1980).

402 *In re* Calhoun, 715 F.2d 1103 (6th Cir. 1983). *See also* Boyle v. Donovan, 724 F.2d 681 (8th Cir. 1984) (court looked to intent of parties, financial situation at time of agreement, and family pattern of life to find obligation in nature of support even when state law did not require support).

403 The Sixth Circuit has since held that in determining the court's intent, once it is shown that there is a direct payment obligation, labeled as maintenance, terminable on death, remarriage or receipt of Social Security, there is a conclusive presumption that it is intended as support. *In re* Sorah, 163 F.3d 397 (6th Cir. 1998).

404 *See, e.g.*, Sylvester v. Sylvester, 865 F.2d 1164 (10th Cir. 1989); Forsdick v. Turgeon, 812 F.2d 801 (2d Cir. 1987); Draper v. Draper, 790 F.2d 52 (8th Cir. 1986); *In re* Harrell, 754 F.2d 902 (11th Cir. 1985).

405 *See, e.g.*, Sylvester v. Sylvester, 865 F.2d 1164 (10th Cir. 1989); Forsdick v. Turgeon, 812 F.2d 801 (2d Cir. 1987); Draper v. Draper, 790 F.2d 52 (8th Cir. 1986); *In re* Harrell, 754 F.2d 902 (11th Cir. 1985).

406 *In re* Williams, 3 B.R. 401 (Bankr. N.D. Ga. 1980) (debtor's car payments and health club membership); *In re* Travis, Bankr. L. Rep. (CCH) ¶ 67,520 (Bankr. W.D. Okla. 1980) (agreement not enforceable by contempt order); *In re* Francisco, 1 B.R. 565 (Bankr. W.D. Va. 1980) (clause about debts distinct from paragraph on support). *But see In re* Kodel, 105 B.R. 729 (Bankr. S.D. Fla. 1989) (debtor's payments to wife from business proceeds found to be support rather than equitable division of business).

407 *In re* Diers, 7 B.R. 18 (Bankr. S.D. Ohio 1980).

408 *See* § 15.4.3.14, *infra*.

409 *In re* Jones, 38 B.R. 690 (N.D. Ohio 1983) (state proceedings to

One type of divorce debt that has usually been found to be in the nature of support and thus nondischargeable is a debt for attorney fees payable by one spouse to the other's attorney, at least when the first spouse has been awarded alimony or support.[410] The attorney fees are sometimes deemed to rise or fall with the determination on the primary debt.[411] Other courts have reasoned that the award of fees is based upon the need of one spouse[412] or the duty of the other to support.[413] Generally, pre-Code cases with such holdings[414] are still good law. However, it has also been held by a few courts that when the fees are payable directly to the attorney they constitute an assigned obligation which is dischargeable.[415] And some courts have held that the attorney may not be an appropriate party to seek the dischargeability determination.[416]

Courts have also struggled with whether attorney fees incurred in custody proceedings, including fees of attorneys appointed to represent children, are dischargeable. Most courts have found this issue to turn on whether the representation was necessary for the welfare of the child; in such cases the fees have been found nondischargeable.[417] Most of these courts have not addressed, however, the issue of whether the fees are owed to an entity listed in section 101(14A), as is also required by section 523(a)(5).[418]

Another frequent situation is that of a divorce decree which has divided the debtor's pension benefits, often through a Qualified Domestic Relations Order. Usually, such pension divisions are deemed to transfer a present interest in the pension benefits to the other spouse, so they do not create a debt that may be later discharged in bankruptcy.[419]

Naturally, bankruptcy debtors and potential debtors, as well as their spouses, will want to keep these principles in mind when negotiating marital settlements. Obtaining a large property settlement in return for reduced alimony may be a short-lived victory if obligations under the former are discharged in bankruptcy soon afterwards. Although some state courts have found discharge of property settlement obligations in bankruptcy to be changed circumstances justifying modification of alimony awards,[420] some of these cases may contravene the Bankruptcy Code's "fresh start" policy.[421]

15.4.3.6 Willful and Malicious Injury—11 U.S.C. §§ 523(a)(6), 1328(a)(4)

The sixth category of debts excepted from discharge consists of debts for willful and malicious injury by the debtor to another entity or the property of another entity.[422] This excep-

---

collect on discharged property settlement debt enjoined by bankruptcy court); *In re* Marriage of Williams, 203 Cal. Rptr. 909 (Ct. App. 1984) (attempted setoff of discharged debt).

410 *See* Macy v. Macy, 114 F.3d 1 (1st Cir. 1997); *In re* Catlow, 663 F.2d 960 (9th Cir. 1981).

When the fees are owed by the debtor to an attorney who represented the debtor in seeking an order of child support, the debt is not in the nature of support and is dischargeable. *In re* Rios, 901 F.2d 71 (7th Cir. 1990).

411 *In re* Bell, 5 B.R. 653 (Bankr. W.D. Okla. 1980); Lynn v. Lynn, 91 N.J. 510, 453 A.2d 539 (1982). *See In re* Rice, 94 B.R. 617 (Bankr. W.D. Mo. 1988).

412 *In re* Joseph, 16 F.3d 86 (5th Cir. 1994); *In re* Evans, 2 B.R. 85 (Bankr. W.D. Mo. 1979). *Cf. In re* Gibson, 103 B.R. 218 (B.A.P. 9th Cir. 1989) (attorney fee award dischargeable when state court did not appear to have considered need in making it).

413 *In re* Pelikant, 5 B.R. 404 (Bankr. N.D. Ill. 1980); *In re* Knabe, 8 B.R. 53 (Bankr. S.D. Ind. 1980). *See also In re* Strickland, 90 F.3d 444 (11th Cir. 1996) (attorney fees awarded in post-divorce custody action based on relative need and ability to pay).

414 *See, e.g., In re* Cornish, 529 F.2d 1363 (7th Cir. 1976); *In re* Nunnally, 506 F.2d 1024 (5th Cir. 1975); Damon v. Damon, 283 F.2d 571 (1st Cir. 1960).

415 *In re* Allen, 4 B.R. 617 (Bankr. E.D. Tenn. 1980). *But see In re* Hudson, 107 F.3d 355 (5th Cir. 1997) (fees nondischargeable despite fact that they were awarded directly to attorney); *In re* Spong, 661 F.2d 6 (2d Cir. 1981); *In re* Gwinn, 20 B.R. 233 (B.A.P. 9th Cir. 1982) (fees payable directly to attorney remain nondischargeable); *In re* Knabe, 8 B.R. 53 (Bankr. S.D. Ind. 1980) (holding fees not an assigned debt).

416 *In re* Delillo, 5 B.R. 692 (Bankr. D. Mass. 1980); *In re* Allen, 4 B.R. 617, (Bankr. E.D. Tenn. 1980). *But see In re* Spong, 661 F.2d 6 (2d Cir. 1981); *In re* Gwinn, 20 B.R. 233 (B.A.P. 9th Cir. 1982).

417 *In re* Maddigan, 312 F.3d 589 (2d Cir. 2002) (attorney fees awarded to out-of-wedlock mother in custody case were nondischargeable support); *In re* Chang, 163 F.3d 1138 (9th Cir. 1998) (debts for professional fees in child custody case owed to father and guardian *ad litem* were nondischargeable); Miller v. Gentry, 55 F.3d 1487 (10th Cir. 1995); *In re* Jones, 9 F.3d 878 (10th Cir. 1994) (fees were incurred on behalf of child); *In re* Peters, 964 F.2d 166 (2d Cir. 1992), *aff'g* 133 B.R. 291 (S.D. N.Y. 1991). *See also* Epstein v. Defilippi (*In re* Defilippi), 430 B.R. 1, 5 (Bankr. D. Me. 2010) (debtors required to pay fees of guardian ad litem, even though child was not their biological child, because they had been given parental rights). *Cf.* Adams v. Zentz, 963 F.2d 197 (8th Cir. 1992) (case primarily concerned mother's efforts to frustrate father's relationship with child). *But see In re* Lowther, 321 F.3d 946 (10th Cir. 2002) (attorney fee award that would compromise debtor's ability to support children presented unusual circumstances that were an exception to usual dischargeability rule in custody cases); *In re* Jones, 2010 WL 4008155 (Bankr. W.D. La. Oct. 12, 2010) (one-time assessment of fees in custody contempt order not in nature of support where support had been terminated).

418 *See* Tucker v. Oliver, 423 B.R. 378 (W.D. Okla. 2010) (visitation proceeding attorney fees owed to former daughter-in-law of debtors not within scope of definition of domestic support obligation).. *See generally* Henry J. Sommer & Margaret Dee McGarity, Collier Family Law and the Bankruptcy Code ¶ 6.03[4] (1992).

419 *In re* Gendreau, 122 F.3d 815 (9th Cir. 1997); *In re* McCafferty, 96 F.3d 192 (6th Cir. 1996) (divorce decree dividing pension created separate property interest in pension for non-debtor spouse); Bush v. Taylor, 912 F.2d 989 (8th Cir. 1990) (en banc); *In re* Chandler, 805 F.2d 555 (5th Cir. 1986). *But see In re* Reines, 142 F.3d 970 (7th Cir. 1998) (city pension could not be divided by family court and obligation to pay benefits to former spouse found to be dischargeable).

420 *In re* Myers, 773 P.2d 118 (Wash. Ct. App. 1989); Eckert v. Eckert, 424 N.W.2d 759 (Wis. Ct. App. 1988).

421 Modification issues are discussed in Henry J. Sommer & Margaret Dee McGarity, Collier Family Law and the Bankruptcy Code ¶ 6.10 (1992).

422 11 U.S.C. § 523(a)(6).

While this exception to discharge is not applicable in chapter 13 cases, the fact that such a debt is not dischargeable in chapter 7 may be found relevant to a determination of whether a chapter 13 plan

tion encompasses a narrow class of tort liabilities, in which the debtor's conduct was both intentional and such that it was intended to harm an entity or its property. If the creditor does not have an enforceable claim against the debtor based on the alleged injury, the exception does not apply.[423] In addition, if a contractual obligation has been substituted for the original alleged tort debt, the exception may not apply.[424]

A slightly different exception to discharge, added in 2005, applies in chapter 13 cases for an award of restitution or damages in a civil action against the debtor, when that award was based on willful or malicious injury by the debtor that caused personal injury or death of an individual. Debts for willful or malicious injury to property, and debts that have not yet been adjudicated and reduced to an award of restitution or damages,[425] continue to be dischargeable in chapter 13. It is not clear whether the "willful *or* malicious" requirement in this new provision will be much different than the "willful *and* malicious" test under current section 523(a)(6).[426] Most of the litigation under the chapter 7 exception has centered on whether specific conduct was willful and malicious. It is clear, at one end of the spectrum, for example, that assault and battery is willful and malicious.[427] At the other end, negligence, even gross negligence, is not.[428] Thus, few liabilities that arise out of automobile accidents are excepted from discharge under this subsection, regardless of whether the debtor was driving while intoxicated,[429] driving without insurance,[430] or violating various traffic laws.[431] Even a reckless disregard for the safety of others is not sufficient to except the debt from discharge.[432]

The Supreme Court clarified this issue in *Kawaauhau v. Geiger*.[433] The Court held that medical malpractice could not be willful and malicious injury under this section because the word "willful" modified "injury," thus requiring that the actor intended the harmful consequences of the act in question, knowing that they would occur.

Although the case law indicates that a case-by-case analysis must be made to determine whether conduct was willful and malicious, proof of an intentional tort is not enough. The ultimate outcome usually depends on the nature of the act. The intentional setting of a fire is obviously sufficient,[434] but breaches of contractual rights, even if intentional, generally fall short of the standard.[435] Most courts have adopted a definition of willful

---

proposing discharge of such a debt was proposed in good faith. *In re* Lemaire, 898 F.2d 1346 (8th Cir. 1990) (en banc). *See* §§ 12.3.3, 12.3.5, *supra*.

423 *In re* Zelis, 66 F.3d 205 (9th Cir. 1995) (creditor that had settled with joint tortfeasor had no claim against debtor and could not have claim held nondischargeable); *In re* Shapiro, 180 B.R. 37 (Bankr. E.D.N.Y. 1995) (creditor whose claim was barred by statute of limitations could not bring dischargeability action). *See also In re* Olson, 262 B.R. 18 (Bankr. D.R.I. 2001) (state victim compensation fund did not have enforceable claim because it had not made payments to victim and could not, in any case, stand in victim's shoes for nondischargeability action).

424 *But see* Archer v. Warner, 123 S. Ct. 1462, 155 L. Ed. 2d 454 (2003) (creditor not precluded from bringing a nondischargeability claim by prebankruptcy settlement of claim; court left open the possibility of preclusion if settlement includes a promise that creditor will refrain from pursuing nondischargeability action).

425 *In re* Byrd, 388 B.R. 875 (Bankr. C.D. Ill. 2007) (prepetition judgment required). *But see In re* Waag, 418 B.R. 373 (B.A.P. 9th Cir. 2009) (no prepetition award required); *In re* Taylor, 388 B.R. 115 (Bankr. M.D. Pa. 2008) (no prepetition judgment required).

426 *See* Kawaauhau v. Geiger, 523 U.S. 57, 118 S. Ct. 974, 140 L. Ed. 2d 90 (1998).

427 *In re* Miera, 926 F.2d 741 (8th Cir. 1991) (debtor judge could not discharge award of compensatory and punitive damages to court reporter for battery consisting of kissing court reporter on mouth without his consent); *In re* Dardar, 620 F.2d 39 (5th Cir. 1980). *See also In re* Braen, 900 F.2d 621 (3d Cir. 1990) (malicious prosecution judgment nondischargeable); *In re* Latch, 820 F.2d 1163 (11th Cir. 1987) (civil theft judgment nondischargeable); *In re* Moberg, 156 B.R. 810 (Bankr. D. Minn. 1993) (sexual assault was willful and malicious); *In re* Gee, 156 B.R. 291 (Bankr. W.D. Wash. 1993) (sexual harassment claim found willful and malicious), *aff'd in part*, 173 B.R. 189 (B.A.P. 9th Cir. 1994).

428 Kawaauhau v. Geiger, 523 U.S. 57, 118 S. Ct. 974, 140 L. Ed. 2d 90 (1998) (doctor's malpractice involving negligent and reckless conduct not covered by section 523(a)(6)); *In re* Kelly, 100 F.3d 110 (9th Cir. 1996), *aff'g* 182 B.R. 255 (B.A.P. 9th Cir. 1995) (showing of legal malpractice is not sufficient to prove willful and malicious conduct); *In re* Delaney, 97 F.3d 800 (5th Cir. 1996) (accidental firing of gun that debtor tapped on car window was not willful and malicious, even though debtor intentionally tapped on window).

429 Cassidy v. Minihan, 794 F.2d 340 (8th Cir. 1986); *In re* Compos, 768 F.2d 1155 (10th Cir. 1985); *In re* Wright, 66 B.R. 403 (Bankr. S.D. Ind. 1986); *In re* Naser, 7 B.R. 116 (Bankr. W.D. Wis. 1980); *In re* Bryson, 3 B.R. 593 (Bankr. N.D. Ill. 1980). *See* § 15.4.3.10, *infra*. *See also In re* Taneff, 190 B.R. 501 (Bankr. W.D.N.Y. 1996) (even high probability of producing harm by selling liquor to intoxicated driver would not be willful and malicious).

However, many of these debts are nondischargeable under 11 U.S.C. § 523(a)(9). In other situations in which the debtor argues that actions were not willful because of intoxication, there may be issues about whether the debtor was in control of his or her faculties. *See In re* Thirtyacre, 36 F.3d 697 (7th Cir. 1994) (debtor's argument that he was depressed and intoxicated rejected when he had been sober enough to operate car, track and find victim's boyfriend, and argue with boyfriend).

430 Pechar v. Moore, 98 B.R. 488 (D. Neb. 1988); *In re* Bex, 143 B.R. 835 (Bankr. E.D. Ky. 1992) (actions of debtors in allowing automobile insurance to lapse did not create willful injury to creditor injured in accident involving debtors' vehicle, because debtors had no intent or knowledge that their son would become involved in accident while they were uninsured).

431 Oregon Ford, Inc. v. Claburn, 89 B.R. 629 (N.D. Ohio 1987) (debtor had driven rented vehicle in excess of lawful speed limit); *In re* Donnelly, 6 B.R. 19 (Bankr. D. Or. 1980).

432 Kawaauhau v. Geiger, 523 U.S. 57, 118 S. Ct. 974, 140 L. Ed. 2d 90 (1998) (doctor's malpractice involving negligent and reckless conduct not covered by section 523(a)(6)); *In re* Duncan, 448 F.3d 725 (4th Cir. 2006) (state court judgment based on reckless indifference did not establish facts necessary for exception to apply); *In re* Quezada, 718 F.2d 121 (5th Cir. 1983); *In re* Warren, 7 B.R. 546 (Bankr. M.D. Ga. 1980); H.R. Rep. No. 95-595, at 363 (1977); S. Rep. No. 95-989, at 77–79 (1978).

433 523 U.S. 57, 118 S. Ct. 974, 140 L. Ed. 2d 90 (1998). *See also In re* Delaney, 97 F.3d 800 (5th Cir. 1996) (accidental firing of gun that debtor tapped on car window was not willful and malicious, even though debtor intentionally tapped on window).

434 *In re* Wuttke, 6 Bankr. Ct. Dec. (LRP) 1304 (Bankr. D.N.J. 1980).

435 *In re* Riso, 978 F.2d 1151 (9th Cir. 1992) (contract giving right of first refusal with respect to sale of property did not give rise to security interest that would constitute property; intentional breach

and malicious injury as one which involves the intentional doing of a wrongful act, which necessarily causes injury, without just cause or excuse.[436] Under the *Kawaauhau* decision, there are very good arguments that not only must the actions have been very likely to cause injury but that the debtor must also have subjectively known the injury was likely and intended to cause the injury.[437] Because mere reckless disregard as to the truth or falsity of a published statement may support a libel verdict under some circumstances, a court may have to determine whether an obligation based on libel arose from willful or malicious conduct so as to be nondischargeable.[438]

Perhaps the most common attempts to use this exception in consumer cases arise from alleged conversions of a creditor's collateral. It was probably the frequent use of such allegations in cases in which consumers innocently disposed of such property that led to the requirement that the willful and malicious exception be raised during the bankruptcy case if it is to be raised at all.[439]

It is clear, though, that the willful and malicious standard is applicable to conversion cases.[440] Although a technical conversion may occur whenever a debtor disposes of collateral, no matter how small its value, more is required to bring the discharge exception into play.[441] The debt is not excepted from discharge unless the debtor understood that a security interest existed[442] and acted with a specific intent to harm or defraud the

---

of contract not within exception unless accompanied by willful and malicious tortious conduct); *In re* Mitchell, 227 B.R. 45 (Bankr. S.D.N.Y. 1998) (obligation for past due rent dischargeable; landlord demonstrated only breach of contract); *In re* Brazington, 3 B.R. 309 (Bankr. D. Idaho 1980); *In re* Warren, 7 B.R. 546 (Bankr. M.D. Ga. 1980). *See also In re* Popa, 140 F.3d 317 (1st Cir. 1998) (employer's failure to obtain workers compensation insurance was not willful and malicious injury because there was no intent to injure); *In re* Saylor, 108 F.3d 219 (alleged fraudulent transfer of assets in which creditor did not have a property interest was not willful and malicious injury to property of creditor); *In re* Barriger, 61 B.R. 506 (Bankr. W.D. Tenn. 1986) (allowing insurance to lapse on automobile in which creditor held security interest in violation of the parties' contract not willful or malicious conduct). *But see* Lockerby v. Sierra, 535 F.3d 1038 (9th Cir. 2008) (lack of just cause for a breach of contract, standing alone, did not render a breach of contract willful and malicious injury); *In re* Bammer, 131 F.3d 788 (9th Cir. 1997) (en banc) (debtor caused willful and malicious injury by knowingly participating in scheme to make his mother's assets unavailable to creditors).

436 *See, e.g., In re* Abbo, 168 F.3d 930 (6th Cir. 1999) (debt for malicious prosecution and abuse of process nondischargeable when debtor had been found to have acted maliciously with intent to injure); *In re* Walker, 48 F.3d 1161 (11th Cir. 1995) (debtor must intend injury or intentionally take action substantially certain to cause injury); *In re* Conte, 33 F.3d 303 (3d Cir. 1994) (debtor must have personally inflicted injury or acted with substantial certainty that injury would result; knowledge that there was a high probability of harm is not sufficient); *In re* Pasek, 983 F.2d 1524 (10th Cir. 1993) (breach of covenant not to compete not willful and malicious because debtor reasonably relied on legal opinion that covenant was not enforceable; statute requires intentional or deliberate injury); *In re* Cecchini, 780 F.2d 1440 (9th Cir. 1986). *See, e.g., In re* Ormsby, 591 F.3d 1199, 1207 (9th Cir. 2010) (debtor knew that using, without permission, property which he had previously paid to lease would cause damages through loss of payments); Redd v. Lee (*In re* Lee), 2011 WL 841247 (Bankr. N.D. Cal. Mar. 7, 2011) (intentional infliction of emotional distress through harassing and intimidating phone calls). *See also In re* Karlin, 112 B.R. 319 (B.A.P. 9th Cir. 1990) (inadvertent publication of photographs without subject's permission was excusable under the circumstances and any debt arising from the invasion of privacy was dischargeable); *In re* Strybel, 105 B.R. 22 (B.A.P. 9th Cir. 1989) (conduct of psychiatrist in having sexual relations with patient did not give rise to nondischargeable debt); *In re* Meyer, 100 B.R. 301 (D.S.C. 1989) (judgment debt arising from the tort of "criminal conversation" is not dischargeable).

An act may be both fraudulent and willful and malicious. *In re* Stokes, 995 F.2d 76 (5th Cir. 1993) (unfair and deceptive practices found willful and malicious).

437 *In re* Moore, 337 F.3d 1125 (10th Cir. 2003) (state court fraud verdict against debtor for misrepresenting insurance coverage was not debt for willful and malicious injury, because debtor did not intend injury to occur); *In re* Su, 290 F.3d 1140 (9th Cir. 2002), *explaining and limiting In re* Jercich, 238 F.3d 1202 (9th Cir. 2001); Hidy v. Bullard (*In re* Bullard), 449 B.R. 379, 382 (B.A.P. 8th Cir. 2011) (criminal conviction for battery in second degree not sufficient to prove maliciousness because it could have been based on reckless conduct). *But see* Jendusa-Nicolai v. Larsen, 677 F.3d 320 (7th Cir. 2012) (loss of consortium damages were derivative of assault and battery damages and therefore nondischargeable, even though debtor had not intended to injure his ex-wife's husband and children).

438 *In re* Peck, 295 B.R. 353 (9th Cir. 2003) (false accusation of child molestation was malicious); *In re* Kennedy, 249 F.3d 576 (6th Cir. 2001) (debtors who falsely denied creditor-husband's paternity of child when they had undeniable evidence their claims were untrue committed willful and malicious injury to reputation); Wheeler v. Laudani, 783 F.2d 610 (6th Cir. 1986). *See In re* Yanks, 931 F.2d 42 (11th Cir. 1991) (defamation judgment collaterally estopped debtor in subsequent dischargeability action because malice was actually litigated and determined).

439 11 U.S.C. § 523(c).

440 Printy v. Dean Witter Reynolds, Inc., 110 F.3d 853 (1st Cir. 1997) (debtor who took advantage of broker's computer error to enrich himself at expense of broker committed willful and malicious conversion); Vulcan Coals, Inc. v. Howard, 946 F.2d 1226 (6th Cir. 1991) (allegation of conversion of collateral is sufficient to make out a case under section 523(a)(6)); *In re* Graham, 7 B.R. 5 (Bankr. D. Nev. 1980). *See also In re* Grey, 902 F.2d 1479 (10th Cir. 1990) (debtor's sale of collateral was willful and malicious even though security agreement did not use phrase "after-acquired property"); *In re* Wood, 96 B.R. 993 (B.A.P. 9th Cir. 1988) (debt found nondischargeable when debtor failed to notify spouse of early retirement and converted pension benefits in which she had an interest). *See also* Maxfield v. Jennings (*In re* Jennings), 670 F.3d 1329 (11th Cir. 2012) (debtor willfully and maliciously transferred property to put it beyond creditor's reach); Shankle v. Shankle (*In re* Shankle), 476 B.R. 908 (Bankr. N.D. Miss. 2012) (debtor willfully and maliciously withdrew money from marital accounts and refused to divide it in accordance with divorce decree).

441 Davis v. Aetna Acceptance Co., 293 U.S. 328, 55 S. Ct. 151, 79 L. Ed. 393 (1934); Werner v. Hoffman, 5 F.3d 1170 (8th Cir. 1993) (no willful and malicious injury found with respect to failure to return creditor's property caused by carelessness and poor records). *See* Chrysler Credit Corp. v. Rebhan, 842 F.2d 1257 (11th Cir. 1988) (debtor was actively engaged in management of car dealership which converted proceeds of cars in which the plaintiff had a security interest; implied or constructive malice was found).

442 *In re* Posta, 866 F.2d 364 (10th Cir. 1989) (evidence that debtors were inexperienced in business matters, had never read security

creditor.[443] It also is not excepted if the creditor was aware of the debtor's actions and failed to object to them.[444] This is especially true for retailers who know that their credit cards will often be used to purchase gifts and who fail to discourage (and in some cases encourage) that practice.[445] Moreover, if the debt is excepted, it should be nondischargeable only to the extent of the value of the collateral converted, if that value is less than the debt.[446]

In light of the Supreme Court's decision about punitive damages under section 523(a)(2),[447] there is little doubt that any punitive and multiple damages included in a debt for willful and malicious injury that is not discharged will also be nondischargeable.

Finally, it is clear under the Code that only willful and malicious acts of the debtor, and not those of agents, children, or others, can lead to a finding of nondischargeability.[448] This changes the law from that developed under the former Bankruptcy Act, which in some cases denied the discharge of debts for willful and malicious acts of partners, children, and others for whom the debtor was legally responsible under state law.[449]

15.4.3.7 Fines and Penalties—11 U.S.C. §§ 523(a)(7), 1328(a)(3)

One of the less frequently applicable exceptions is that for fines and penalties owed to governmental units and for their benefit.[450] To be nondischargeable under this provision the debt must be owed to a governmental unit.[451] By its terms, this exception is limited to purely punitive, as opposed to compensatory, assessments.[452] However, the Supreme Court in *Kelly v.*

---

agreement and intended to fulfill their loan obligation was sufficient to establish that conversion of collateral was not willful or malicious); *In re* McCune, 85 B.R. 834 (W.D. Mo. 1988) (no willful or malicious conversion when debtor did not understand breach of legal rights which occurred when property was transferred); *In re* Casselli, 4 B.R. 531 (Bankr. C.D. Cal. 1980) (debtor was unaware of security interest when she gave away collateral).

443 *In re* Peklar, 260 F.3d 1035 (9th Cir. 2001) (debtor who removed furniture from property in derogation of landlord's rights did not act willfully and maliciously); *In re* Littleton, 942 F.2d 551 (9th Cir. 1991) (conversion of collateral not willful when debtors were struggling to keep business going and there was no evidence that debtors personally benefited from the sale); *In re* Phillips, 882 F.2d 302 (8th Cir. 1989); *In re* Posta, 866 F.2d 364 (10th Cir. 1989); *In re* Cecchini, 780 F.2d 1440 (9th Cir. 1986) (substituted opinion on denial of rehearing) (debtor acted under mistaken belief in converting checks of another); *In re* Long, 774 F.2d 875 (8th Cir. 1985); St. Paul Fire & Marine Ins. Co. v. Vaughn, 779 F.2d 1003 (4th Cir. 1985); *In re* Logue, 294 B.R. 59 (B.A.P. 8th Cir. 2003) (selling cattle that secured loan was not malicious when proceeds used to feed remaining cattle); *In re* Howard, 6 B.R. 256 (Bankr. M.D. Fla. 1980); *In re* Hawkins, 6 B.R. 97 (Bankr. W.D. Ky. 1980) (debtor sold automobile after it was wrecked and remitted some of proceeds to creditor); *In re* Hodges, 4 B.R. 513 (Bankr. W.D. Va. 1980) (debtor sold equipment to raise money to pay mortgage, not to harm creditor, whom he still intended to pay). *See also In re* Porayko, 443 B.R. 419 (Bankr. N.D. Ill. 2010) (debtor had no intent to injure creditor when he used bank account for ordinary living expense in violation of creditor's citation to discover assets that prohibited transfer of nonexempt assets). *But see In re* Foust, 52 F.3d 766 (8th Cir. 1995) (debt found due to willful and malicious conversion when debtor converted crops securing loans, sold them in distant market, keeping proceeds, and fabricated reports of grain thefts to cover up scheme); *In re* Granati, 307 B.R. 827 (E.D. Va. 2002) (finding debtor converted payments from annuity that equitably belonged to factoring company without addressing issue of malice), *aff'd*, 63 Fed. Appx. 741 (4th Cir. 2003).

444 *In re* Wolfson, 56 F.3d 52 (11th Cir. 1995) (debtor's belief that creditor acquiesced in his actions, engendered by course of dealing with creditor, was reasonable and supported conclusion that conversion was not willful or malicious).

445 *In re* Goycochea, 192 B.R. 847 (Bankr. D. Md. 1996) (Sears could not claim conversion of collateral when debtor gave goods purchased to others, because Sears had knowledge that goods purchased are often given as gifts and therefore impliedly consented to transfer); *In re* Hodges, 83 B.R. 25 (Bankr. N.D. Cal. 1988) (creditor required to prove that giving away collateral as a gift is an intentional violation of the security agreement).

446 *In re* Penney, 76 B.R. 160 (Bankr. N.D. Cal. 1987). *See In re* Modicue, 926 F.2d 452 (8th Cir. 1991) (conversion of collateral renders debt nondischargeable to the extent of the value of the collateral at the time of sale). *See also* Epstein, *Collection of U.C.C. Claims in Bankruptcy*, 11 UCC L.J. 295, 303, 304 (1979).

447 Cohen v. De La Cruz, 523 U.S. 213, 118 S. Ct. 1212, 140 L. Ed. 2d 341 (1998).

448 *In re* Maltais, 202 B.R. 807 (Bankr. D. Mass. 1996); *In re* Miller, 196 B.R. 334 (Bankr. E.D. La. 1996) (acts of debtor's minor son in shooting creditor could not be imputed to debtor for purposes of discharge exception); *In re* Albano, 143 B.R. 323 (Bankr. D. Conn. 1992) (restaurant owner's liability to patron injured in altercation with employee found dischargeable). *But see In re* Cecchini, 780 F.2d 1440 (9th Cir. 1986) (partner's acts imputed to debtor).

449 *In re* Eggers, 51 B.R. 452 (Bankr. E.D. Tenn. 1985).

450 11 U.S.C. § 523(a)(7).

451 *In re* Sandoval, 541 F.3d 997 (10th Cir. 2008) (bail bond debt to nongovernment entity dischargeable); Hughes v. Sanders, 469 F.3d 475 (6th Cir. 2006) (malpractice action default judgment, though entered as a sanction, was not payable to governmental unit); *In re* Rashid, 210 F.3d 201 (3d Cir. 2000) (federal restitution payable to private victims not within discharge exception); *In re* Towers, 162 F.3d 952 (7th Cir. 1998) (restitution order payable to attorney general for benefit of fraud victims was not for benefit of a governmental unit and therefore was dischargeable, but separate $50,000 penalty was nondischargeable); *In re* Pulley, 303 B.R. 81 (D.N.J. 2003) (drunk driving surcharge collected by state for benefit of private creditors was dischargeable); *In re* Wilson, 299 B.R. 380 (Bankr. E.D. Va. 2003) (criminal restitution to pay creditor's damages determined in a civil case was dischargeable); *In re* McNabb, 287 B.R. 820 (Bankr. D. Colo. 2003) (restitution debt owed to private parties not within scope of exception; state could not pass statute to change this result); *In re* Friedman, 253 B.R. 576 (Bankr. S.D. Fla. 2000) (discovery sanction payable to a private party in compensation of pecuniary loss was dischargeable); *In re* Bailey, 202 B.R. 317 (Bankr. D.N.M. 1995) (sanction debt assigned to state university by university officials who debtor had sued found to be not for benefit of governmental unit, so it was dischargeable); *In re* Strutz, 154 B.R. 508 (Bankr. N.D. Ind. 1993) (attorney fees awarded as sanctions were dischargeable).

However, 11 U.S.C. § 523(a)(13), added in 1994, makes all federal criminal restitution orders nondischargeable in chapter 7. *See* § 15.4.3.12, *infra*.

452 *See In re* Hickman, 260 F.3d 400 (5th Cir. 2001) (bail bond

§ 15.4.3.7   Consumer Bankruptcy Law and Practice

Robinson,[453] held that a restitution order in a welfare fraud case constitutes a nondischargeable fine or penalty within the meaning of this section. Some courts, following *Kelly*, have found state criminal restitution debts dischargeable even if they are forwarded to a private victim.[454] Similar reasoning has led to some courts holding that a compensatory assessment of costs is nondischargeable.[455] But an examination of the circumstances of other judicial and administrative restitution awards may turn up grounds for distinguishing *Kelly*, which was based on the finding that the award had a penal or rehabilitative purpose.[456]

The exception may extend to fines imposed by administrative agencies as well as by courts.[457]

In a chapter 13 case, many penalties and fines are dischargeable.[458] In the past, arguments were frequently raised about whether court-imposed payments were debts within the meaning of the Bankruptcy Code. The United States Supreme Court laid most of those arguments to rest by holding that restitution orders imposed as a condition of probation in a criminal proceeding are debts dischargeable in chapter 13.[459] Shortly after it was rendered, this decision was partially overruled by Congress through an amendment creating Code section 1328(a)(3), which makes nondischargeable restitution debts included in a sentence on the debtor's conviction of a crime.[460] Other restitution debts, such as those imposed in pre-trial diversion programs, remain dischargeable in chapter 13 unless they come within the scope of section 1328(a)(4).

Certain fines, other than federal criminal fines,[461] also remain dischargeable in chapter 13. The 1994 amendments to the Bankruptcy Code made nondischargeable in that chapter fines imposed as part of a sentence upon conviction of a crime.[462]

---

forfeiture debt dischargeable); *In re* Collins, 173 F.3d 924 (4th Cir. 1999) (exception covers only fines that are penal in nature; liability of surety on forfeited bail bonds was dischargeable); S. Bend Cmty. Sch. Corp. v. Eggleston, 215 B.R. 1012 (N.D. Ind. 1997) (attorney fees and costs awarded in civil case against governmental unit were not within scope of section 523(a)(7)); *In re* Lopes, 339 B.R. 82 (Bankr. S.D.N.Y. 2006) (debt to private bail bond company was not to governmental unit and was compensation for pecuniary loss). *But see In re* Nam, 273 F.3d 281 (3d Cir. 2001) (bail bond forfeiture judgment against individual who was not a professional bail bondsman was not dischargeable under section 523(a)(7)).

453 479 U.S. 36, 107 S. Ct. 353, 93 L. Ed. 2d 216 (1986). *See also In re* Soderling, 998 F.2d 730 (9th Cir. 1993) (restitution incurred during marriage was a liability of community property under California law); *In re* Warfel, 268 B.R. 205 (B.A.P. 9th Cir. 2001) (criminal restitution, though payable to different governmental unit than the one that imposed it, was nondischargeable).

454 *In re* Troff, 488 F.3d 1237 (10th Cir. 2007) (restitution obligation is not dischargeable); *In re* Verola, 446 F.3d 1206 (11th Cir. 2006); *In re* Thompson, 418 F.3d 362 (3d Cir. 2005) (distinguishing from civil restitution orders); Williams v. Meyer (*In re* Williams), 438 B.R. 679 (B.A.P. 10th Cir. 2010) (postpetition criminal restitution order for prepetition securities fraud not barred by discharge).

455 Richmond v. New Hampshire Supreme Court Comm. on Prof'l Conduct, 542 F.3d 913 (1st Cir. 2008) (costs imposed in attorney disciplinary proceeding had a purpose to sanction and were not purely compensatory, so they were nondischargeable); Thompson v. Virginia, 16 F.3d 576 (4th Cir. 1994) (fact that punishment was contingent on costs rendered costs nondischargeable as fines, penalties or forfeitures); *In re* Hollis, 810 F.2d 106 (6th Cir. 1987); Betts v. Att'y Registration & Disciplinary Comm'n, 165 B.R. 870 (N.D. Ill. 1994) (costs imposed for attorney disciplinary proceeding not dischargeable); *In re* Cillo, 165 B.R. 46 (M.D. Fla. 1994) (same); *In re* Garvin, 84 B.R. 824 (Bankr. M.D. Fla. 1988) (cost of prosecution imposed as part of prebankruptcy criminal prosecution constitutes a nondischargeable fine). *But see In re* Schaffer, 515 F.3d 424 (5th Cir. 2008) (costs imposed in dental license revocation proceeding were dischargeable); *In re* Taggart, 249 F.3d 987 (9th Cir. 2001) (costs, but not monetary sanctions, imposed in attorney disciplinary proceedings were dischargeable); *In re* Findley, 387 B.R. 260 (B.A.P. 9th Cir. 2008) (costs imposed in attorney disciplinary proceeding were dischargeable even though legislature called them penal), *rev'd*, 593 F.3d 1048 (9th Cir. 2010) (based on changes in state statute that labeled costs as penalty); Love v. Scott (*In re* Love), 442 B.R. 868 (Bankr. M.D. Tenn. 2011) (costs in attorney disciplinary proceeding were for pecuniary losses and discharged).

456 Williams v. Motley, 925 F.2d 741 (4th Cir. 1991) (service fee imposed on uninsured motorists to defray administrative expenses found dischargeable); Smith v. Sims (*In re* Sims), 2012 WL 528156 (Bankr. S.D. Miss. Feb. 17, 2012) (restitution imposed on parent by juvenile court based on minor child's acts not shown to have penal or rehabilitative purpose, and not shown to benefit state); Basquin v. Stasson (*In re* Stasson), 472 B.R. 748 (Bankr. E.D. Mich. 2012)

(restitution ordered by attorney disciplinary board not to or for benefit of governmental unit); *In re* Bill, 90 B.R. 651 (Bankr. D.N.J. 1988) (insurance surcharge imposed for traffic violation is a dischargeable debt); *In re* Taite, 76 B.R. 764 (Bankr. C.D. Cal. 1987) (civil restitution order not within scope of section 523(a)(7) but can be within scope of section 523(a)(2)); *In re* Brown, 39 B.R. 820 (Bankr. M.D. Tenn. 1984) (restitution under pre-trial diversion program); *In re* Tauscher, 7 B.R. 918 (Bankr. E.D. Wis. 1981) (back pay portion of administrative assessment for violation of Fair Labor Standards Act was dischargeable, but penalty assessment was not). *See also In re* Caggiano, 34 B.R. 449 (Bankr. D. Mass. 1983) (parking fines not dischargeable but surcharge imposed by Registry of Motor Vehicles was dischargeable as a charge to recover pecuniary losses).

457 *See In re* Poule, 91 B.R. 83 (B.A.P. 9th Cir. 1988) (civil penalties imposed for debtor's violation of contractor licensing law are nondischargeable fines). *See also In re* Hercules Enters., 387 F.3d 1024 (9th Cir. 2004) (bankruptcy court could not order that sanction would be nondischargeable under section 523(a)(7) in future bankruptcy case).

458 Pennsylvania Dep't of Pub. Welfare v. Davenport, 495 U.S. 552, 110 S. Ct. 2126, 109 L. Ed. 2d 588 (1990); *In re* Young, 10 B.R. 17 (Bankr. S.D. Cal. 1980). *See In re* DeBaecke, 91 B.R. 3 (Bankr. D.N.J. 1988) (insurance surcharges imposed for traffic violations are dischargeable debts in chapter 13 when the offenses occurred prepetition, even if the surcharges are imposed postpetition); *In re* Colon, 102 B.R. 421 (Bankr. E.D. Pa. 1989) (prepetition traffic fines are dischargeable in chapter 13; attempts to collect them by postpetition license suspension violate the automatic stay).

459 Pennsylvania Dep't of Pub. Welfare v. Davenport, 495 U.S. 552, 110 S. Ct. 2126, 109 L. Ed. 2d 588 (1990). *See also* Lugo v. Paulsen, 886 F.2d 602 (3d Cir. 1989) (insurance surcharge levied against individuals convicted of drunk driving is a debt).

460 *See In re* Bova, 326 F.3d 300 (1st Cir. 2003) (fact that injured party sought civil judgment to enforce restitution order did not change fact that debt arose from criminal restitution order and was nondischargeable in chapter 13).

461 *See* 18 U.S.C. § 3613(f).

462 11 U.S.C. § 1328(a)(3).

In cases filed prior to the amendments, all fines were dischargeable in chapter 13. *In re* Hardenberg, 42 F.3d 986 (6th Cir. 1994).

Thus, an adjudication in a juvenile proceeding is not within the scope of this provision.[463] Similarly, costs of prosecution have been held dischargeable in chapter 13.[464]

Clearly, civil penalties are not included within this new statutory language. There may also be issues concerning whether parking tickets or traffic tickets remain dischargeable. The answer in a particular case may turn on whether parking or traffic violations are deemed "crimes" under state law. In many states they probably are not, especially if there is state law defining crimes as including only misdemeanors and felonies. There may also be issues regarding whether a "conviction" has occurred in such cases, or whether there has been a "sentence."[465]

In any case, there is no doubt that a debtor may provide for such debts in a chapter 13 plan even if they are nondischargeable. If the debtor does so, the automatic stay should bar collection efforts, such as attempts to revoke the debtor's driver's license or to incarcerate the debtor due to nonpayment. There may be issues regarding whether the debtor can separately classify such debts, similar to issues that now arise with respect to nondischargeable student loans.[466] Also, the debtor may have to file a claim on behalf of the creditor to ensure that the debt is paid.[467]

Not included in either the chapter 7 exception or the chapter 13 exception are two specific kinds of tax penalties. Those penalties relating to a tax which is dischargeable are also dischargeable, as are any tax penalties relating to a transaction or event that occurred more than three years before the filing of the petition.[468] Also not included in either exception are civil awards for multiple and punitive damages.[469] However, such awards may be nondischargeable if the underlying debt is nondischargeable under another provision of section 523(a) or section 1328(a)(4).[470]

15.4.3.8 Student Loans—11 U.S.C. § 523(a)(8)

15.4.3.8.1 In general

The exception to discharge for student loans, applicable in both chapter 7 and chapter 13, resulted from publicity over a supposed flood of bankruptcies in the early 1970s filed by students who were just finishing their education with the purpose of discharging their student loans before they started earning money. The exception has had several different wordings and, as last amended,[471] covers an "educational benefit, overpayment or loan" which is "made, insured or guaranteed by a governmental unit, or made under any program funded in whole or in part by a governmental unit or a nonprofit institution, or for an obligation to repay funds received as an educational benefit, scholarship or stipend." This language was intended to broaden the scope of the exception to cover most, if not all, student loans made or insured by nonprofit institutions or governmental units,[472] at least when the debtor is the

---

463 *In re* Sweeney, 492 F.3d 1189 (10th Cir. 2007).
464 *In re* Ryan, 389 B.R. 710 (B.A.P. 9th Cir. 2008).
465 *See In re* Wilson, 252 B.R. 739 (B.A.P. 8th Cir. 2000) (plea of guilty with deferred sentence of probation was conviction, as determined under federal law).
466 *See* § 12.4.3, *supra*; § 15.4.3.8.5, *infra*; 8 Collier on Bankruptcy ¶ 1322.05[2] (16th ed.).
467 *See* § 8.4.6, *supra*.
468 11 U.S.C. § 523(a)(7)(A), (B); McKay v. United States, 957 F.2d 689 (9th Cir. 1992) (penalties relating to transactions more than three years old are dischargeable even if underlying taxes are not); *In re* Roberts, 906 F.2d 1440 (10th Cir. 1990) (tax penalties dischargeable even if underlying tax liability is nondischargeable, if taxable period was more than three years before bankruptcy filing); *In re* Roberts, 129 B.R. 71 (C.D. Ill. 1991) (debtor need establish grounds for only one of the two exceptions and need not prove both); *In re* Polston, 239 B.R. 277 (Bankr. M.D. Pa. 1999) (penalties were incurred on date tax returns were due but not filed). *See also* § 15.4.3.1.1, *supra*. *Cf. In re* Wilson, 407 B.R. 405 (10th Cir. 2009) (three-year period on penalty for filing frivolous return ran from date of return); United States v. Amici, 197 B.R. 696 (M.D. Fla. 1996) (penalty for failure to file partnership return did not relate to a tax and therefore was not within the exception to the exception).
469 *In re* Marvin, 139 B.R. 202 (Bankr. E.D. Wis. 1992); *In re* Manley, 135 B.R. 137 (Bankr. W.D. Okla. 1992).
470 Cohen v. De La Cruz, 523 U.S. 213, 118 S. Ct. 1212, 130 L. Ed. 2d 341 (1998).
471 *See* Pub. L. No. 101-647, 104 Stat. 4789 (1990); Pub. L. No. 98-353, 98 Stat. 333 (1984); Pub. L. No. 96-56, 93 Stat. 387 (1979) (amending 11 U.S.C. § 523(a)(8)).
472 Prior to 2005, there were sometimes issues about whether the lender came within the scope of section 523(a)(8). The statutory language includes loans from a trust fund administered by a state university. *In re* Shore, 707 F.2d 1337 (11th Cir. 1983). It also includes "scholarships" under the public health service's health professions scholarship program when the student does not fulfill his or her obligation of active duty service. United States Dep't of Health & Human Servs. v. Smith, 807 F.2d 122 (8th Cir. 1986); *In re* Brown, 59 B.R. 40 (W.D. La. 1986). *See also In re* O'Brien, 419 F.3d 104 (2d Cir. 2005) (loan made by private lender but conditionally guaranteed by nonprofit entity came within scope of section); *In re* Murphy, 282 F.3d 868 (5th Cir. 2002) (entire student loan not dischargeable, including portion used for living expenses); *In re* Burks, 244 F.3d 1245 (11th Cir. 2001) (obligation to repay stipend due to failure to complete obligation to teach in "other race" institution after receiving degree was educational loan obligation); T I Fed. Credit Union v. Delbonis, 72 F.3d 921 (1st Cir. 1995) (loan from nonprofit federal credit union nondischargeable; federal credit union was instrumentality of United States); *In re* Merchant, 958 F.2d 738 (6th Cir. 1992) (loan guaranteed by nonprofit institution was nondischargeable); *In re* Bolen, 287 B.R. 127 (D. Vt. 2002) (loan from Law Access program partially funded by non-profit corporation was within scope of section); *In re* Rosen, 179 B.R. 935 (Bankr. D. Or. 1995) (loan made by union training committee was within purview of nondischargeability section); *In re* Hammerstrom, 95 B.R. 160 (Bankr. N.D. Cal. 1989) (student loan made by commercial bank with arrangement that loan was to be purchased by nonprofit guarantee agency is covered by section 523(a)(8)); *In re* Avila, 53 B.R. 933 (Bankr. W.D.N.Y. 1985). *Cf. In re* Segal, 57 F.3d 342 (3d Cir. 1995) (when nonprofit hospital paid off debtor's student loan, replacing it with new loans, those new loans were not nondischargeable under this section because they were not made under a "program" of giving educational loans); *In re* Reis, 274 B.R. 46 (Bankr. D. Mass. 2002) (educational loan made by grandparents dischargeable); *In re* Scott, 287 B.R. 470 (Bankr. E.D. Mo. 2002) (loan from for-profit truck driving school was dischargeable); *In re* Jones, 242 B.R. 441 (Bankr. W.D. Tenn. 1999) (debt to for-profit trade school was not within scope of section 523(a)(8)); *In re* Shorts, 209 B.R. 818 (Bankr. D.R.I. 1997) (same); *In re* Simmons, 175 B.R. 624 (Bankr. E.D. Va. 1994) (credit union was not a

student loan recipient rather than a co-signer.[473] It does not include debts to educational institutions for tuition, however.[474]

Generally, if a student loan debt is nondischargeable, postpetition interest on the debt is also not discharged.[475]

The exception was broadened in 2005 to also include any other education loans from for-profit lenders if they are qualified education loans as defined in section 221(d)(1) of the Internal Revenue Code.[476] The term "qualified education loan" is defined in section 221(d)(1) of the Internal Revenue Code to mean any indebtedness incurred by the taxpayer *solely* to pay qualified higher education expenses.[477] Debtors who have incurred debt for education and other purposes may argue the debt was not incurred solely to pay higher education expenses and therefore is not subject to the nondischargeability provision in section 523(a)(8).

The Internal Revenue Code also provides that the qualified higher education expenses must be incurred on behalf of the taxpayer, the taxpayer's spouse, or any dependent of the taxpayer and must be paid or incurred within a reasonable period of time before or after the indebtedness is incurred and attributable to education furnished during a period when the recipient was an eligible student.[478] Therefore, if the student for whom the loan was taken is not the debtor, the debtor's spouse, or the debtor's dependent, it is not within the definition.

In order to be considered a qualified education loan, the loan must be incurred to pay expenses for education furnished during a period when the recipient was an eligible student.[479] There are circumstances in which a student may take out a loan to attend school, but not necessarily be an eligible student. For example, aggressive proprietary schools in some cases enroll non-high-school graduates without properly administering the

---

nonprofit institution and loan was not made pursuant to a program within meaning of section 523(a)(8)); *In re* Sinclair-Ganos, 133 B.R. 382 (Bankr. W.D. Mich. 1991) (credit union not a non-profit institution within meaning of section 523(a)(8)).

Some of these cases would be decided differently after the 2005 addition of section 523(a)(8)(B).

473 *See In re* Pryor, 234 B.R. 716 (Bankr. W.D. Tenn. 1999) (exception not applicable to non-student cosigner); *In re* Behr, 80 B.R. 124 (Bankr. N.D. Iowa 1987) (exception not applicable to non-student codebtor); *In re* Meier, 85 B.R. 805 (Bankr. W.D. Wis. 1986) (exception not applicable to accommodation party); *In re* Zobel, 80 B.R. 950 (Bankr. N.D. Iowa 1986) (exception not applicable to co-maker); *In re* Bawden, 55 B.R. 459 (Bankr. M.D. Ala. 1985); *In re* Washington, 41 B.R. 211 (Bankr. E.D. Va. 1984) (exception not applicable to non-student codebtor); *In re* Boylen, 29 B.R. 924 (Bankr. N.D. Ohio 1983). *Cf.* H.R. Rep. No. 95-595, at 134 (1977) ("The proponents of an exception to discharge have argued that educational loans are different from most loans, they . . . [rely] for repayment solely on the debtor's future increased income resulting from the education."). *But see In re* Pelkowski, 990 F.2d 737 (3d Cir. 1993) (language of statute does not limit exception to discharge to exclude parent cosigners); *In re* Varma, 149 B.R. 817 (N.D. Tex. 1992); *In re* Wilcon, 143 B.R. 4 (D. Mass. 1992); *In re* Hammerstrom, 95 B.R. 160 (Bankr. N.D. Cal. 1989) (student loan signed solely by parents nondischargeable); *In re* Taylor, 95 B.R. 550 (Bankr. E.D. Tenn. 1989) (obligation of co-maker spouse who did not receive benefit of loan not dischargeable); *In re* Selmonsky, 93 B.R. 785 (Bankr. N.D. Ga. 1988) (cosigner's obligation on student loan is nondischargeable); *In re* Barth, 86 B.R. 146 (Bankr. W.D. Wis. 1988); *In re* Feenstra, 51 B.R. 107 (Bankr. W.D.N.Y. 1985) (student loan signed solely by parent nondischargeable).

474 *In re* Hawkins, 469 F.3d 1316 (9th Cir. 2006) (debt for tuition subsidy that arose when debtor did not fulfill terms of subsidy was not educational loan), *aff'g* 317 B.R. 104 (B.A.P. 9th Cir. 2004); *In re* Chambers, 348 B.R. 650 (7th Cir. 2003) (open account for unpaid tuition and fees not a loan); *In re* Mehta, 310 F.3d 308 (3d Cir. 2002); Cazenovia College v. Renshaw 222 F.3d 82 (2d Cir. 2000) (tuition debt not a loan and not part of a program); *In re* Rezendes, 324 B.R. 689 (N.D. Ind. 2004) (debt for apprenticeship training that arose under contract because debtor went to work for nonunion employer after training was not a loan; Manning v. Chambers, 290 B.R. 328 (N.D. Ill. 2003) (applying *Renshaw* and *Mehta*, tuition debt held dischargeable as there was no evidence that parties entered into loan arrangement prior to services being provided); *In re* Nelson, 188 B.R. 32 (D.S.D. 1995) (debt for tuition, room and board to university was not a loan); *In re* Moore, 407 B.R. 855 (Bankr. E.D. Va. 2009) (unpaid tuition, absent signed note and advance of funds, is not an educational loan; school held in contempt of discharge order for withholding transcript); *In re* Navarro, 284 B.R. 727 (Bankr. C.D. Cal. 2002) (agreement that student would be responsible for tuition and fees was not a promissory note for sum certain and therefore dischargeable); *In re* Johnson, 222 B.R. 783 (Bankr. E.D. Va. 1998) (debt for tuition was not obligation for funds received on a loan and there was no "program" or disbursement of "funds" that would render debt nondischargeable); *In re* Meinhart, 211 B.R. 750 (Bankr. D. Colo. 1997) (debt to school was not an obligation to repay "funds received" as required by statute); *In re* Coole, 202 B.R. 518 (Bankr. D.N.M. 1996) (debt to school for services rendered was not a loan). *But see* Busson-Sokolik v. Milwaukee Sch. of Eng'g (*In re* Busson-Sokolik), 635 F.3d 261 (7th Cir. 2011) (loan existed where debtor signed note and funds were deposited into debtor's account); *In re* McKay, 558 F.3d 888 (9th Cir. 2009) (deferred tuition payment agreement treated as loan because contract drafted as extension of credit providing for monthly billing, late fees, set due dates, and collection charges); *In re* Udell, 454 F.3d 180 (3d Cir. 2006) (obligation to pay for Air Force education when military service not completed was within scope of section); *In re* DePasquale, 225 B.R. 830 (B.A.P. 1st Cir. 1998) (payment agreement for overdue tuition constituted "loan"); *In re* Johnson, 218 B.R. 449 (B.A.P. 8th Cir. 1998) (debtor who signed promissory note to college for unpaid tuition had student loan); Capron v. Cedar Rapids Elec. Apprenticeship Training & Educ. Trust (*In re* Capron), 454 B.R. 738 (Bankr. N.D. Iowa 2011) ("scholarship loan" for union apprenticeship program was educational loan); *In re* Kesler, 401 B.R. 356 (Bankr. S.D. Ill. 2009) (debt for union apprenticeship program was a nondischargeable loan). *See generally Failure to Pay Tuition Does Not Create Nondischargeable Education Loan*, 17 NCLC REPORTS Bankruptcy and Foreclosure Ed. 17 (Mar./Apr. 1999).

475 *In re* Woods, 233 B.R. 324 (5th Cir. 2000); Leeper v. Pennsylvania Higher Educ. Assistance Agency, 49 F.3d 98 (3d Cir. 1995) (postpetition interest not discharged, even after debtor paid prepetition debt in full through chapter 13 plan); *In re* Pardee, 218 B.R. 916 (B.A.P. 9th Cir. 1998), *aff'd*, 187 F.3d 548 (9th Cir. 1999); *In re* Jordan, 146 B.R. 31 (D. Colo. 1992).

476 11 U.S.C. § 523(a)(8); *In re* LeBlanc, 404 B.R. 793 (Bankr. M.D. Pa. 2009) (when Canadian debtor had not filed a United States tax return during the relevant time period, she was not considered a taxpayer under 26 U.S.C. § 7701(a)(14), and thus the loan extended to her by a corporation could not have qualified under 26 U.S.C. § 221(d)).

477 26 U.S.C. § 221(d) (emphasis added).

478 26 U.S.C. § 221(d)(1).

479 26 U.S.C. § 221(d)(1)(C).

required "ability to benefit test."[480] Student debtors improperly enrolled in this way are eligible for a cancellation of their loans and should also be categorized as "ineligible" students for purposes of whether the loan was a qualified education loan under section 523(a)(8).

In addition, a loan is a "qualified education loan" if it is incurred solely to pay qualified higher education expenses. The term "qualified higher education expenses" means items and services considered to be "the cost of attendance," which is broadly defined in section 472 of the Higher Education Act.[481]

If an indebtedness was incurred for any purpose other than for such expenses, it is not within the exception.[482] It is intended to be limited to education loans, and not extend to other debts incurred by students, such as ordinary credit card debts.[483]

The expenses must also be for attendance at an "eligible education institution."[484] "Eligible institutions" are defined as institutions that are eligible to participate in a Title IV program, which refers to the title of the Higher Education Act that governs federal financial assistance programs.[485] Most, but not all schools, are eligible to participate in these programs. For example, numerous unaccredited schools have gone in and out of business in recent years. These unaccredited schools are not eligible to participate in the Title IV programs.[486] Other scam programs such as "diploma mills" also are not eligible to participate in Title IV programs. Borrowers with student loans from these schools should be able to discharge the loans without having to prove hardship.

Some courts have held, however, that contractually imposed liquidated damages for nonpayment of student loans are dischargeable, because the penalties are not debts for an "educational loan."[487] And student loan creditors may be denied collection costs and fees as part of their claims when no entitlement exists under relevant regulations or contract provisions.[488]

---

480 *See* National Consumer Law Center, Student Loan Law § 6.3.2 (4th ed. 2010 and Supp.).

481 Expenses for "cost of attendance" include:

(1) tuition and fees normally assessed a student carrying the same academic workload as determined by the institution, and including costs for rental or purchase of any equipment, materials, or supplies required of all students in the same course of study;

(2) an allowance for books, supplies, transportation, and miscellaneous personal expenses, including a reasonable allowance for the documented rental or purchase of a personal computer, for a student attending the institution on at least a half-time basis, as determined by the institution;

(3) an allowance (as determined by the institution) for room and board costs incurred by the student which—

(A) shall be an allowance determined by the institution for a student without dependents residing at home with parents;

(B) for students without dependents residing in institutionally owned or operated housing, shall be a standard allowance determined by the institution based on the amount normally assessed most of its residents for room and board; and

(C) for all other students shall be an allowance based on the expenses reasonably incurred by such students for room and board;

(4) for less than half-time students (as determined by the institution) tuition and fees and an allowance for only books, supplies, and transportation (as determined by the institution) and dependent care expenses (in accordance with paragraph (8));

(5) for a student engaged in a program of study by correspondence, only tuition and fees and, if required, books and supplies, travel, and room and board costs incurred specifically in fulfilling a required period of residential training;

(6) for incarcerated students only tuition and fees and, if required, books and supplies;

(7) for a student enrolled in an academic program in a program of study abroad approved for credit by the student's home institution, reasonable costs associated with such study (as determined by the institution at which such student is enrolled);

(8) for a student with one or more dependents, an allowance based on the estimated actual expenses incurred for such dependent care, based on the number and age of such dependents, except that—

(A) such allowance shall not exceed the reasonable cost in the community in which such student resides for the kind of care provided; and

(B) the period for which dependent care is required includes, but is not limited to, class-time, study-time, field work, internships, and commuting time;

(9) for a student with a disability, an allowance (as determined by the institution) for those expenses related to the student's disability, including special services, personal assistance, transportation, equipment, and supplies that are reasonably incurred and not provided for by other assisting agencies;

(10) for a student receiving all or part of the student's instruction by means of telecommunications technology, no distinction shall be made with respect to the mode of instruction in determining costs;

(11) for a student engaged in a work experience under a cooperative education program, an allowance for reasonable costs associated with such employment (as determined by the institution); and

(12) for a student who receives a loan under this or any other Federal law, or, at the option of the institution, a conventional student loan incurred by the student to cover a student's cost of attendance at the institution, an allowance for the actual cost of any loan fee, origination fee, or insurance premium charged to such student or such parent on such loan, or the average cost of any such fee or premium charged by the Secretary, lender, or guaranty agency making or insuring such loan, as the case may be.
See 20 U.S.C. § 1087*ll*.

482 *See In re* Carow, 2011 WL 802847 (Bankr. D.N.D. Mar. 2, 2011) (private loan funds covered "costs of attendance" at colleges when debtor signed notes stating that proceeds would be used for "qualified education-related expenses" and, in discharge proceeding, debtor stipulated that she used the funds for those purposes).

483 The Higher Education Opportunity Act of 2009 requires that colleges must provide a "net price calculator" on their websites. 20 U.S.C. § 1015a(a). The purpose of the calculator will be to give potential applicants an individualized estimate of how much it will cost them to attend the school. The calculator will display the full "costs of attendance" with itemized components. It will then estimate the amount of grants and scholarships the student is likely to receive. Finally, the calculator will list a net price—the amount the student would be expected to cover with savings, work, and loans. The availability of this tool will provide some guidance in determining whether a particular private loan was for a mixed use.

484 26 U.S.C. § 221(d)(2).

485 26 U.S.C. § 221(d)(2) (referring to 26 U.S.C. § 25A(f)(2)(B)).

486 *See* National Consumer Law Center, Student Loan Law Ch. 9 (4th ed. 2010 and Supp.).

487 *See, e.g., In re* Lipps, 79 B.R. 67 (Bankr. M.D. Fla. 1987).

488 *In re* McAlpin, 254 B.R. 449 (Bankr. D. Minn. 2000) (collection costs and fees disallowed based on 34 C.F.R. § 674.45(e), when creditor failed to prove they were reasonable and limited to actual or average cost incurred), *rev'd on other grounds*, 263 B.R. 881 (B.A.P. 8th Cir. 2001), *aff'd*, 278 F.3d 866 (8th Cir. 2002).

If a student loan is discharged, the lender should not accept any further payments on the loan, such as payments the lender may receive through a tax intercept program, or even money voluntarily paid by the debtor.[489] Department of Education regulations provide that if a guaranty agency receives any payments on a discharged loan on which the Department of Education previously paid a claim to the agency, the agency must return one hundred percent of those payments to the sender and notify the borrower that there is no obligation to pay the loan.[490]

15.4.3.8.2 Student loan dischargeability tests

15.4.3.8.2.1 Former seven-year test

11 U.S.C. § 523(a)(8) makes student loan debts nondischargeable in bankruptcy cases unless repayment would cause the debtor "undue hardship." This provision is incorporated in chapter 13 by section 1328(a)(2).

Prior to 1998, student loans were dischargeable if they had come due more than seven years prior to the debtor's bankruptcy filing. This exception to the exception was repealed in 1998.[491] *Therefore the seven year provision is applicable only to bankruptcy cases filed before October 7, 1998 and the discussion below applies only to such cases. It is included primarily for the purpose of analyzing whether a student loan may have been discharged in a past bankruptcy case.*

Although student loans usually first become due shortly after graduation,[492] extensions and consolidations had, on occasion, caused confusion as to whether the seven years had passed as of the date of the bankruptcy petition. Generally, the first date that payments became due was deemed the critical point of reference.[493] Later consolidations were sometimes held to start the running of a new seven year period from the date of the first payment on the consolidated loan.[494] On the other hand, a creditor's unilateral changes in the payment schedule,[495] or deferments that were retroactive and not permitted by state regulations,[496] did not change the first payment due date, nor did payment agreements that did not involve cessation of payments.[497] However, courts sometimes suspended the running of the time period when payment was deferred by re-enrollment after the initial period has begun to run.[498]

There was also some disagreement about whether the seven year period continued to run during a bankruptcy case when collection of the loan may have been stayed.[499] Department of Education regulations offered a useful clarification on this issue, providing that the Department did not consider the time a debtor is in bankruptcy to be a suspension of the repayment period if the debtor made payments during the case sufficient to meet the amount owed under the debtor's repayment schedule.[500]

If there is any dispute about whether the seven years had passed, then a strategic decision must be made about whether to seek a declaratory judgment on dischargeability in the bankruptcy court. The debtor's other potential course of action is to wait and see if the creditor recommences collection efforts following bankruptcy and then raise the discharge defensively in the applicable state or federal forum.[501]

If a bankruptcy court determination is desired, there is no time limit to commence an adversary proceeding to resolve the dischargeability issues. In fact, the applicable rule even speaks

---

489 The protections of the discharge injunction apply. 11 U.S.C. § 524(a)(2). See § 15.5, *infra*.

490 34 C.F.R. § 682.402(l).

491 Higher Education Amendments of 1998, Pub. L. No. 105-244, 112 Stat. 1581 (effective Oct. 7, 1998). See *In re* Lewis, 506 F.3d 927 (9th Cir. 2007) (amendment eliminating dischargeability of older loans did not violate due process even though it applied to loans already made).

492 See *In re* Woodcock, 45 F.3d 363 (10th Cir. 1995) (based upon language of note, debtor's payments first came due nine months after debtor ceased to be matriculated in a program leading to a degree, even though debtor continued to take courses after that).

493 *In re* Scott, 147 F.3d 788 (8th Cir. 1998).

494 Hiatt v. Indiana State Student Assistance Comm'n, 36 F.3d 21 (7th Cir. 1994) (seven years runs from date on which first payment was due on consolidation loan); *In re* McGrath, 143 B.R. 820 (D. Md. 1992), aff'd, 8 F.3d 821 (4th Cir. 1993); *In re* Martin, 137 B.R. 770 (Bankr. W.D. Mo. 1992).
   The argument that the seven-year period commences separately for each installment as it becomes due has been uniformly rejected. See, e.g., *In re* Nunn, 788 F.2d 617 (9th Cir. 1986). See also *In re* Mason, 300 B.R. 160 (Bankr. D. Conn. 2003) (consolidation loan obtained by duress held void and unenforceable, permitting debtor to obtain discharge under the former seven-year rule).

495 *In re* Woodcock, 45 F.3d 363 (10th Cir. 1995) (creditor could not unilaterally change the due date of first payment); *In re* Brinzer, 45 B.R. 831 (S.D. W. Va. 1984); *In re* Chisari, 183 B.R. 963 (Bankr. M.D. Fla. 1995) (neither debtor's failure to notify lender of withdrawal from school nor lender's failure to send repayment schedule on time extended due date); *In re* Marlewski, 168 B.R. 378 (Bankr. E.D. Wis. 1994); *In re* Whitehead, 31 B.R. 381 (Bankr. S.D. Ohio 1983). See *In re* Cramley, 21 B.R. 170 (Bankr. E.D. Tenn. 1982) (lender had no right to unilaterally suspend payment period without request of borrower). *But see In re* Woodcock, 144 F.3d 1340 (10th Cir. 1998) (extensions granted at debtor's request stopped running of repayment period, even though debtor was not legally entitled to them).

496 *In re* Manriquez, 207 B.R. 890 (B.A.P. 9th Cir. 1996) (retroactive forbearance agreement signed after seven years had already run did not render loan nondischargeable); *In re* Flynn, 190 B.R. 139 (Bankr. D.N.H. 1995); *In re* Keenam, 53 B.R. 913 (Bankr. D. Conn. 1985).

497 *In re* Salter, 207 B.R. 272 (Bankr. M.D. Fla. 1997) (stipulation changing amount of payments did not constitute a new obligation that would restart the seven-year time period); *In re* Marlewski, 168 B.R. 378 (Bankr. E.D. Wis. 1994).

498 *In re* Kaufman, 9 B.R. 755 (Bankr. E.D. Pa. 1981). See also *In re* Woodcock, 45 F.3d 363 (10th Cir. 1995) (loans became due when debtor ceased to be matriculated due to graduation, even though debtor was part-time student after that, so loans became due nine months after graduation).

499 *In re* Gibson, 184 B.R. 716 (E.D. Va. 1995) (period during which lender was stayed from taking action excluded in computing seven year period), aff'd, 86 F.3d 1150 (4th Cir. 1996).

500 34 C.F.R. § 682.402(m)(5).

501 See, e.g., Indiana Univ. v. Canganelli, 501 N.E.2d 299 (Ill. App. Ct. 1986) (discharge can be raised as a defense to collection of student loans in postbankruptcy state court proceedings).

of allowing cases to be reopened in order to obtain determinations on issues related to dischargeability.[502]

15.4.3.8.2.2 Undue hardship test

The sole exception to the nondischargeability of student loans is available when excepting the debt from discharge would cause the debtor or the debtor's dependents undue hardship. Courts have long struggled to define the term "undue hardship" found in section 523(a)(8). Although most of the published opinions on the subject agree that "undue" means more than the "garden variety" hardship that arises from the expense of future payments,[503] each judge seems to bring a unique set of values to the process of defining and implementing the applicable standard.

Several circuit courts of appeals have adopted a definition of undue hardship that employs a three-part test, known as the *Brunner* test.[504] Under this test, undue hardship exists if:

- The debtor cannot maintain, based on current income and expenses, a 'minimal' standard of living for the debtor and the debtor's dependents if forced to repay the loans;
- Additional circumstances exist indicating that this state of affairs is likely to persist for a significant portion of the repayment period of the student loans;[505] and
- The debtor has made good faith efforts to repay the loans.

Other courts have adopted a "totality of the circumstances" test, which does not necessarily conflict with the three-part Brunner test but rather expands upon the scope of factors a court may consider.[506] Under this test, the court may consider nonpecuniary effects of the loan, including the effect on the debtor's mental health.[507]

Although Congress has now defined "undue hardship" differently for a different section of the Code,[508] no court has yet relied upon that definition for the purpose of determining student loan dischargeability.

In general, low-income debtors are most likely to obtain a discharge under the *Brunner* test. Generally speaking, debtors with incomes lower than $30,000 (or more for large families)[509] are found to be at a minimal standard of living.[510] They should seek to have the court focus on their income and expenses as the basis for a determination of undue hardship, but debtors need not be at the poverty level to demonstrate undue hardship. Most debtors who have been denied an undue hardship discharge had incomes several times greater than the

---

502 Fed. R. Bankr. P. 4007(b).
503 *See, e.g.*, Brunner v. New York State Higher Educ. Serv., 831 F.2d 395 (2d Cir. 1987); *In re* Kopf, 245 B.R. 731 (Bankr. D. Me. 2000) (while "garden variety" hardship may not be sufficient, on the other extreme debtors should not be required to prove a "certainty of hopelessness" or "total incapacity").
504 *In re* Frushour, 433 F.3d 393 (4th Cir. 2005); *In re* Oyler, 397 F.3d 382 (6th Cir. 2005); Educ. Credit Mgmt. Corp. v. Polleys, 352 F.3d 1302 (10th Cir. 2004) (test does not require certainty of hopelessness for second prong; good faith prong should not allow imposition of court's values on debtor's life choices); *In re* Cox, 338 F.3d 1238 (11th Cir. 2003); *In re* Pena, 155 F.3d 1108 (9th Cir. 1998); *In re* Faish, 72 F.3d 298 (3d Cir. 1995); *In re* Roberson, 999 F.2d 1132 (7th Cir. 1993); Cheesman v. Tennessee Student Assistance Corp., 25 F.3d 356 (6th Cir. 1994); Brunner v. New York State Higher Educ. Servs., 831 F.2d 395 (2d Cir. 1987).
505 To meet this prong of the test, the debtor must simply prove that the inability to pay will continue for a substantial portion of the loan repayment period. No evidence of exceptional facts beyond that is necessary. *In re* Nys, 446 F.3d 938 (9th Cir. 2006). *See also In re* Carnduff, 367 B.R. 120 (B.A.P. 9th Cir. 2007) (under second *Brunner* prong, debtors not required to prove continuation of financial hardship with certainty but by preponderance of evidence); *In re* Jackson, 2007 WL 2295585 (Bankr. S.D.N.Y. Aug. 9, 2007) (*Brunner* test does not require a finding of "certainty of hopelessness"); *In re* King, 368 B.R. 358 (Bankr. D. Vt. 2007) ("certainty of hopelessness" standard was never adopted by court of appeals in *Brunner*; widespread use of standard by courts is based on erroneous reading of Second Circuit decision).
506 *See* Long v. Educ. Credit Mgmt. Corp., 322 F.3d 549 (8th Cir. 2003); Bronsdon v. Educ. Credit Mgmt. Corp. (*In re* Bronsdon), 435 B.R. 791 (B.A.P. 1st Cir. 2010) (adopting totality test; "undue hardship" prong of *Brunner* test lacks textual foundation); *In re* Kopf, 245 B.R. 731 (Bankr. D. Me. 2000).

   The Court of Appeals for the First Circuit allows the bankruptcy courts to develop their own standards for "undue hardship" without doctrinal adherence to either the *Brunner* or "totality of the circumstances" standards. *In re* Nash, 446 F.3d 188 (1st Cir. 2006).
507 *In re* Reynolds, 425 F.3d 526 (8th Cir. 2005).
508 11 U.S.C. § 524(m) provides that a reaffirmation agreement is presumed to be an undue hardship if the debtor's income minus the debtor's expenses is insufficient to make payments on the agreement.
509 *See, e.g., In re* Sweeney, 304 B.R. 360 (Bankr. D. Neb. 2002) (family of six needed $45,000 income for minimal standard of living). *See also In re* Doe, 325 B.R. 69 (Bankr. S.D.N.Y. 2005) (debtor's support of her mother was a reasonable expense); *In re* Cota, 298 B.R. 408 (Bankr. D. Ariz. 2003) (fact that debtor had fathered eleven children was not basis for denying student loan discharge; debtor did not agree to waive his right to procreate when he incurred the student loan obligation); *In re* Mitcham, 293 B.R. 138 (Bankr. N.D. Ohio 2003) (court should not second-guess debtor's decision to take in two grandchildren, or similar decisions such as adoption).
510 *In re* Kelly, 312 B.R. 200 (B.A.P. 1st Cir. 2004) ($30,000 income of debtor with seventeen-year-old child and two foster children justified partial discharge). *See also In re* Pena, 155 F.3d 1108 (9th Cir. 1998) (discharge granted to childless couple with income of $20,976); *In re* Hornsby, 144 F.3d 433 (6th Cir. 1998) (debtors did not need to be at poverty level to show undue hardship); *In re* Cline, 248 B.R. 347 (B.A.P. 8th Cir. 2000) (single woman in good health who earned $25,000 and is unlikely to earn more granted discharge); *In re* Nary, 253 B.R. 752 (N.D. Tex. 2000) (income of $48,000 for family of five, though 2.2 times poverty standard, would justify discharge based on family expenses if it could not be increased); *In re* Coulson, 253 B.R. 174 (W.D.N.C. 2000) (mother and two children with income of $23,975 could not repay loans); *In re* Myers, 280 B.R. 416 (Bankr. S.D. Ohio 2002) (satellite television, related school expenses, and camping expenditures were within minimum standards of living for family with children); *In re* Ivory, 269 B.R. 890 (Bankr. N.D. Ala. 2001) (citing studies showing that income far higher than poverty level is needed for minimal standard of living); *In re* Turretto, 255 B.R. 884 (Bankr. N.D. Cal. 2000) (debtor with one child in her care could not repay loans with income of over $25,000). *Cf. In re* O'Hearn, 339 F.3d 559 (7th Cir. 2003) (single debtor with no dependents who earned $43,000 per year plus benefits, which might increase to $50,000, did not meet first prong of *Brunner* test).

poverty level.[511] However, debtors must be prepared to rebut student loan creditors' nitpicking their budgets in attempts to prove that money is available for loan payments.[512] Certainly, any debtor who can demonstrate some personalized misfortune, disability, or unique underprivilege should bring that factor to the attention of the court.[513] Similarly, every effort should be made to establish lack of job skills, lack of available jobs, disabilities and other factors which make it improbable that a low-income debtor will have better prospects in the future.[514] Courts generally have not required the introduction of expert testimony to prove these factors.[515] Debtors who do not demonstrate that they are not likely to earn significantly more in the future are often denied discharge of their loans.[516] The test requiring a good faith effort to pay the loan does not require that

---

511 *See, e.g., In re* Roberson, 999 F.2d 1132 (7th Cir. 1993) (court found debtor could earn over $30,000); *In re* McGinnis, 289 B.R. 257 (Bankr. M.D. Ga. 2003) (debtor need not be at or below poverty level). *See also In re* Brown, 378 B.R. 623 (Bankr. W.D. Mo. 2007) (income significantly above Department of Health and Human Services' poverty guidelines does not preclude undue hardship discharge). *But see In re* Walker, 650 F.3d 1227 (8th Cir. 2011) (debtors had income of around $60,000 but also had five children, two of whom were autistic); *In re* Scott, 417 B.R. 623 (Bankr. W.D. Wash. 2009) (loans discharged for debtors with family of four and over $60,000 in income); *In re* Avellano, 2009 WL 2779822 (Bankr. N.D. Cal. June 16, 2009) (single debtor with Master's degree and over $40,000 in income granted discharge).

512 *See, e.g., In re* Nixon, 453 B.R. 311 (Bankr. S.D. Ohio 2011) (debtors' monthly expenses of $126 for cable television, $67 for cell phones, and $68 for land line were consistent with minimal standard of living); *In re* McLaney, 375 B.R. 666 (M.D. Ala. 2007) (rejecting creditor's argument that expenses for telephone, cell phone, cable television, religious tithe, and "other" were unnecessary and noting that other necessary expenses such as clothing were not budgeted).

513 *See, e.g., In re* Nys, 446 F.3d 938 (9th Cir. 2006) (rejecting narrow view subscribed to by some courts which require "exceptional circumstances" and instead providing a list of factors to be considered when determining the existence of "additional circumstances" under the *Brunner* test); Educ. Credit Mgmt. Corp. v. Polleys, 352 F.3d 1302 (10th Cir. 2004) (debtor had emotional problems beyond her control); *In re* Cline, 248 B.R. 347 (B.A.P. 8th Cir. 2000) (single woman unable to increase income would need decades to repay $53,000 in loans); *In re* Reynolds, 2004 WL 1745835 (D. Minn. Aug. 2, 2004) (upholding discharge of loans owed by law graduate because of debtor's mental illness even though she possibly could afford to make some payments); *In re* Johnson, 121 B.R. 91 (Bankr. N.D. Okla. 1990) (single mother of two not receiving support); *In re* Reilly, 118 B.R. 38 (Bankr. D. Md. 1990) (debtor was divorced mother of three whose ex-husband was incurably ill and therefore not contributing support); *In re* Zobel, 80 B.R. 950 (Bankr. N.D. Iowa 1986) (unemployed debtors who had made numerous unsuccessful attempts to find work); *In re* Wilcox, 57 B.R. 479 (Bankr. M.D. Ga. 1985) (debtor holding down subsistence job; wife suffering from crippling arthritis and confined to wheelchair); *In re* Dockery, 36 B.R. 41 (Bankr. D. Tenn. 1984) (debtor had suffered severe industrial injuries and several heart attacks); *In re* Diaz, 5 B.R. 253 (Bankr. W.D.N.Y. 1980) (divorced mother of four who had a series of illnesses, heart trouble, and alcoholic problem, need for future surgery, and a husband confined to a mental clinic presented "classic" hardship case); *In re* Bagley, 4 B.R. 248 (Bankr. D. Ariz. 1980) (debtor and husband lived on $560 per month earned by him as an Army private and had postpetition debts of over $4000 for hospitalization of their baby); *In re* Fonzo, 1 B.R. 722 (Bankr. S.D.N.Y. 1979) (policeman-debtor had expenses exceeding income for himself, wife, and four children).

But a debtor's choice to work in a low-paying field may not help in proving undue hardship. *In re* Oyler, 397 F.3d 382 (6th Cir. 2005) (minister could have earned more in another field); *In re* Gerhardt, 348 F.3d 89 (5th Cir. 2003) (well-educated single musician could obtain additional employment).

514 *See, e.g.,* Bene v. Educ. Credit Mgmt. Corp. (*In re* Bene), 474 B.R. 56 (Bankr. W.D.N.Y. 2012) (debtor had worked in low wage job for twelve years and had no degree, professional diploma, or license); *In re* Price, 25 B.R. 256, 258 (Bankr. W.D. Mo. 1982) (relevant considerations include "whether the education enabled or would enable the debtor to obtain substantially higher income"); *In re* Powelson, 25 B.R. 274 (Bankr. D. Neb. 1982) (vocational degree in hairstyling did not enhance debtor's job skills or employability). *See also In re* Pena, 207 B.R. 919 (B.A.P. 9th Cir. 1997) (debtors did not have to show "exceptional circumstances" to show they were unlikely to improve their financial situation in the future), *aff'd* 155 F.3d 1108 (9th Cir. 1998); *In re* Ordaz, 287 B.R. 912 (Bankr. C.D. Ill. 2002) (consolidation loan that restructured student loan with same lender at end of original ten-year term did not "restart the clock" on a new fifteen-year repayment period for purposes of considering future inability to repay).

515 *In re* Mosley, 494 F.3d 1320 (11th Cir. 2007) (debtor not required to submit independent medical evidence to corroborate his testimony about impact of psychiatric disorder on ability to work); *In re* Barrett, 487 F.3d 353 (6th Cir. 2007) (debtor did not have to introduce expert testimony to establish medical condition when he had testified about it and produced a corroborating doctor's letter); *In re* Hertzel, 329 B.R. 221 (B.A.P. 6th Cir. 2005) (court could take judicial notice of progressive nature of debtor's multiple sclerosis); Ackley v. Sallie Mae Students Loans (*In re* Ackley), 463 B.R. 146, 150 (Bankr. D. Me. 2011) (debtors' testimony concerning their aches, pains, and other symptoms, along with their accrued medical expenses and their ages of 58 and 60, demonstrated that each debtor had health problems which limited their employment prospects); *In re* Nixon, 453 B.R. 311 (Bankr. S.D. Ohio 2011) (court takes judicial notice of National Institute of Mental Health publication on bi-polar disorder); *In re* Jackson, 2007 WL 2295585 (Bankr. S.D.N.Y. Aug. 9, 2007) (no requirement that debtor provide corroborating medical testimony on effect of disability on work efforts); *In re* Hamilton, 361 B.R. 532 (Bankr. D. Mont. 2007) (creditor's vocational expert, who was not medical doctor, failed to rebut evidence of work-related health limitations established by debtor's medical records and by testimony of debtor and his wife); *In re* Denittis, 362 B.R. 57 (Bankr. D. Mass. 2007) (parties stipulated to debtor's diagnosis of multiple sclerosis; court may take judicial notice of published resources on long-term effects of condition); *In re* Jara, 2006 WL 2806556 (Bankr. D.N.J. Sept. 27, 2006) (court takes judicial notice of National Institute of Mental Health publication describing chronic nature of bi-polar disorder); *In re* Gobin, 2006 WL 3885136 (Bankr. E.D. Ky. May 15, 2006) (court takes judicial notice of National Institute of Mental Health publication on symptoms of depression).

516 *See, e.g.,* Goulet v. Educ. Credit Mgmt. Corp., 284 F.3d 773 (7th Cir. 2002) (record devoid of evidence that debtor's problems with alcoholism and a felony conviction prevented debtor from being gainfully employed); *In re* Rifino, 245 F.3d 1083 (9th Cir. 2001) (debtor had Master's degree and was already earning over $27,000 with additional increases likely); *In re* Brightful, 267 F.3d 324 (3d Cir. 2001) (debtor who did not introduce evidence showing why she could not use her skills as legal secretary to earn more income denied discharge of loan).

repayment actually occurred, although it may require some effort to deal with the loan prior to bankruptcy.[517]

In evaluating student loans that were incurred for vocational school education, two additional considerations related to discharge are appropriate. First, the student's undue hardship argument may be strengthened if the student loan arose from a private vocational school that closed down or defrauded the student. Not only do courts sense the unfairness involved in making a student repay a loan for a valueless education, but also the absence of acquired skills makes it less likely that the debtor will be able to obtain employment that could make possible future loan repayment.[518] In fact, the debtor may be excused from paying the loan, even without a bankruptcy case or may have a defense to liability on the loan.[519]

Evidence that a student obtained no benefit from the trade school education is relevant to the issue of whether the debtor will be able to pay in the future, because it suggests lack of skills necessary to obtain income for repayment.[520] It is also relevant to the debtor's payment history, because the debtor may not have had the ability to make any payments and because a valueless vocational school education is outside the Congressional concern about highly skilled professionals shedding loan obligations prior to a lucrative career.[521]

A further argument related to the dischargeability of trade school loans is that, absent discharge, the debtor may be ineligible for future government educational loans.[522] If a discharge is not granted, a low-income student will not be able to go back to school, and will not be able to obtain a decent paying job, making repayment now or in the future an undue hardship.

Sometimes, even in fairly strong hardship cases, student loan creditors offer to take very low payments. While it could be argued that the court should only look to the payments actually due under the terms of the note, such offers of low payments can make it more difficult to assert that the loan, as modified by the creditor, presents a hardship. Perhaps not surprisingly, courts have been attracted to this method of compromising on the outcome of the case, sometimes finding no hardship solely because of the reduced-payments offer. In fact, a few have even devised other solutions short of complete nondischargeability in difficult cases, by reducing the term and/or amount of the loan.[523] The Sixth Circuit Court of Appeals approved a bankruptcy court's order ruling that a debtor's loans were dischargeable, but stayed enforcement of its order for eighteen months to see if the debtor's situation improved.[524] The authority for such actions has been questioned by other courts, because this

---

517 *In re* Innes, 284 B.R. 496 (D. Kan. 2002) (failure to make payments does not prevent finding of good faith effort if debtor had no ability to make payments); *In re* Brown, 239 B.R. 204, 209 (S.D. Cal. 1999) (and cases cited therein); *In re* Naylor, 348 B.R. 680 (Bankr. W.D. Pa. 2006) (involuntary payments by seizure of debtor's tax refunds and portions of his Social Security checks effectively deprived debtor of ability to make voluntary payments on student loans; involuntary payments should be considered as loan payments for good faith determination); *In re* Ivory, 269 B.R. 890 (Bankr. N.D. Ala. 2001) (no bad faith when debtor never had ability to repay loan); *In re* Turretto, 255 B.R. 884 (Bankr. N.D. Cal. 2000); *In re* Coats, 214 B.R. 397 (Bankr. N.D. Okla. 1997); *In re* Hornsby, 201 B.R. 195 (Bankr. W.D. Tenn. 1995), *aff'd* 144 F.3d 433 (6th Cir. 1998); *In re* Maulin, 190 B.R. 153 (Bankr. W.D.N.Y. 1995). *See also In re* Lewis, 276 B.R. 912 (Bankr. C.D. Ill. 2002) (rejecting creditor arguments that only payments made on consolidation loan, and not payments on original loans, could be considered).

518 *See, e.g., In re* Law, 159 B.R. 287 (Bankr. D.S.D. 1993) (repayment of $20,000 student loan for two and a half weeks of useless flight training would be undue hardship); *In re* Evans, 131 B.R. 372 (Bankr. S.D. Ohio 1991) (trade school education in word-processing did not put debtor in a position to repay her student loans); *In re* Correll, 105 B.R. 302 (Bankr. W.D. Pa. 1989) (student loan discharged when debtor received no benefit from the education); *In re* Carter, 29 B.R. 228 (Bankr. N.D. Ohio 1983) (loan discharged when debtor did not obtain a marketable skill); *In re* Love, 28 B.R. 475 (Bankr. S.D. Ind. 1983) (college education did not provide marketable skill); *In re* Price, 25 B.R. 256, 258 (Bankr. W.D. Mo. 1982) (relevant considerations include "whether the education enabled or would enable the debtor to obtain substantially higher income"); *In re* Powelson, 25 B.R. 274 (Bankr. D. Neb. 1982) (vocational degree in hairstyling did not enhance debtor's job skills or employability); *In re* Ford, 22 B.R. 442 (Bankr. W.D.N.Y. 1982) (court considered that debtor obtained little benefit from her education); *In re* Littell, 6 B.R. 85 (Bankr. D. Or. 1980) (whether the debtor benefited economically from schooling should be a "substantial factor" in determining whether undue hardship exists).

519 *See* § 15.4.3.8.4, *infra*; National Consumer Law Center, Student Loan Law Chs. 6, 9 (4th ed. 2010 and Supp.).

This treatise should be consulted for other nonbankruptcy student loan discharges available to debtors in addition to the closed school discharge, such as those based on the debtor's permanent and total disability and a school's false certification of the debtor's eligibility.

520 *See, e.g., In re* Lewis, 276 B.R. 912 (Bankr. C.D. Ill. 2002) (lack of benefit from uncompleted junior college program considered under second prong of *Brunner* test); *In re* Powelson, 25 B.R. 274 (Bankr. D. Neb. 1982).

521 *In re* Evans, 131 B.R. 372 (Bankr. S.D. Ohio 1991). *Cf. In re* Mason, 464 F.3d 878 (9th Cir. 2006) (debtor had law degree and had only attempted to take bar exam one time). *Cf.* Educ. Credit Mgmt. Corp. v. Jesperson, 571 F.3d 775 (8th Cir. 2009) (attorney in good health denied discharge of student loans despite overwhelming amount of debt).

522 *See* National Consumer Law Center, Student Loan Law § 6.1 (4th ed. 2010 and Supp.).

523 *In re* Saxman, 325 F.3d 1168 (9th Cir. 2003) (partial discharge order is permissible); *In re* Hornsby, 144 F.3d 433 (6th Cir. 1998) (partial discharge is permitted under court's equitable powers); *In re* Andresen, 232 B.R. 127 (B.A.P. 8th Cir. 1999) (discharging two of three student loans); *In re* Griffin, 197 B.R. 144 (Bankr. E.D. Okla. 1996) (discharging accrued interest and attorney fees on loans, but not principal); *In re* Hinkle, 200 B.R. 690 (Bankr. W.D. Wash. 1996) (discharging three out of six student loans); *In re* Littell, 6 B.R. 85 (Bankr. D. Or. 1980) (each debtor ordered to pay $10 per month for remainder of five-year period after initial loan due date); *In re* Hemmen, 7 B.R. 63 (Bankr. N.D. Ala. 1980) (court conditioned discharge of loan on debtor using best efforts to find employment and paying any sums he received in excess of $3600 per year after taxes toward student loan for remainder of five years after loan matured). *See also In re* Alderete, 412 F.3d 1200 (10th Cir. 2005) (undue hardship as to portion to be discharged must be proved); *In re* Miller, 377 F.3d 616 (6th Cir. 2004) (same); *In re* Cox, 338 F.3d 1238 (11th Cir. 2003) (partial discharge may not be ordered if debtor does not show undue hardship); Blair, 291 B.R. 514 (B.A.P. 9th Cir. 2003) (partial discharge may not be ordered for debtor who did not satisfy any of the *Brunner* test's three prongs).

524 *In re* Cheesman, 25 F.3d 356 (6th Cir. 1994).

section of the statute, unlike others, does not use the phrase "to the extent" in describing whether a loan is dischargeable.[525]

In a similar vein, student loan creditors have argued in recent cases that there cannot be undue hardship because the Department of Education's regulations provide for payment relief in the form of Income Contingent Repayment Plans (ICRP) and Income-Based Repayment Plans (IBRP).[526] Several courts have found the availability of these repayment plans relevant under the various hardship tests.[527] These courts fail to apply the statute as written, which affords the debtor an opportunity to obtain an absolute discharge, and fail to consider the student loan that the debtor actually has as opposed to some modification of that loan.[528] Many courts have rejected the argument that the availability of an income contingent repayment plan is a defense to student loan dischargeability and have recognized that placing a debtor in a twenty-five-year repayment plan that is not likely to pay off, or sometimes even reduce, the loan does not mitigate the undue hardship the loan would cause.[529] At least one court has concluded that such payment plans should not present an opportunity for courts to abdicate their obligation to apply the bankruptcy law as written.[530] Under ICRPs payments must be made if the debtor's income is even slightly above poverty level, which still does not afford a minimal standard of living.[531] Furthermore, income contingent repay-

---

[525] Educ. Credit Mgmt. Corp. v. Carter, 279 B.R. 872 (M.D. Ga. 2002); In re Pincus, 280 B.R. 303 (Bankr. S.D.N.Y. 2002) (no language in section 523(a)(8) permits granting of partial discharge); In re Skaggs, 196 B.R. 865 (Bankr. W.D. Okla. 1996) (court's authority limited to determination whether entire debt is dischargeable).

[526] See 20 U.S.C. §§ 1078(m), 1087a; 34 C.F.R. § 685.209(a)(2)(i). The ICRP is still available, only in the Direct Loan Program. As of July 1, 2009, the IBR plan is available in both the Direct Loan Program and FFEL Program. See National Consumer Law Center, Student Loan Law § 3.1.3.2 (4th ed. 2010 and Supp.).

[527] See, e.g., In re Parker, 328 B.R. 548 (B.A.P. 8th Cir. 2005) (discharge denied when court determined debtor could make payments under ICRP); In re Wallace, 259 B.R. 170 (C.D. Cal. 2000) (remand for further proceedings on impact of ICRP; debtor's lack of diligence in pursing payment plans, even those presented for first time during discharge proceedings, may prove lack of good faith effort to repay the loans); In re Standfuss, 245 B.R. 356 (Bankr. E.D. Mo. 2000) ("flexibility" of an ICRP plan considered in determining debtors' ability to repay student loan). See also In re Mason, 464 F.3d 878 (9th Cir. 2006) (failure to pursue ICRP was a factor in determining lack of good faith); In re Tirch, 409 F.3d 677 (6th Cir. 2005) (while not a per se indication of a lack of good faith, decision not to take advantage of the ICRP is probative of intent to repay loans); Wieckliewicz v. Educational Credit and Mgmt. Corp., 2011 WL 607718 (S.D. Fla. Feb. 15, 2011) (affirming dismissal of debtor's dischargeability complaint when debtor refused to apply for IBRP after bankruptcy court ordered him to apply as condition to proceeding with complaint).

[528] See In re Lee, 352 B.R. 91 (B.A.P. 8th Cir. 2006) (placing too much emphasis on ICRP factor would prevent in many cases "individualized determination" of undue hardship required by section 523(a)(8)); In re Kopf, 245 B.R. 731 (Bankr. D. Me. 2000) (no matter how flexible or "humanely executed" such programs may be, they simply are not the equivalent of a discharge). See also Cagle v. Educ. Credit Mgmt. Corp. (In re Cagle), 462 B.R. 829 (Bankr. D. Kan. 2011) (denying motion to dismiss that argued debtor must exhaust administrative remedy seeking disability discharge before seeking undue hardship discharge).

[529] Bronsdon v. Educ. Credit Mgmt. Corp. (In re Bronsdon), 435 B.R. 791 (B.A.P. 1st Cir. 2010) (ICRP unrealistic in light of debtor's age, difficulty finding employment, and other burdens); In re Ford, 269 B.R. 673 (B.A.P. 8th Cir. 2001); Educ. Credit Mgmt. Corp. v. Curiston, 351 B.R. 22 (D. Conn. 2006) (failure to apply for ICRP did not preclude finding of undue hardship); In re Jesperson, 366 B.R. 908 (Bankr. D. Minn. 2007) (applying "totality of circumstances" test and finding undue hardship when ICRP would merely increase the indebtedness over the long term for forty-three-year-old debtor with over $300,000 in student loans), rev'd, 571 F.3d 775, 781 (8th Cir. 2009) (refusal to enter into ICRP is "a factor" to consider in evaluating the totality of the debtor's circumstances; no undue hardship when correct earnings calculation showed debtor had substantial excess income to make payments under ICRP); In re Smith, 442 B.R. 550, 555 (Bankr. S.D. Tex. 2010) (not bad faith for 56 year-old debtor to decline 25-year repayment plan, as "attempting repayment over 25 years would be financial folly"); In re Adler, 300 B.R. 740 (Bankr. N.D. Cal. 2003) (debtor would face an unaffordable tax liability of $18,000 at age seventy-four); In re Strand, 298 B.R. 367 (Bankr. D. Minn. 2003) (debtor would be hamstrung into poverty for the rest of his life, precluded from obtaining any credit, and perhaps even from obtaining approval of a rental application, growing hopelessly more insolvent, with no realistic possibility of ever retiring the debt until at the age of seventy-nine, the debt would be forgiven and he would be assessed an enormous income tax liability, probably nondischargeable in bankruptcy); In re Cheney, 280 B.R. 648 (N.D. Iowa 2002).

[530] In re Lee, 352 B.R. 91 (B.A.P. 8th Cir. 2006) (court must apply statutory test, which may yield different result than ICRP); In re Bronsdon, 2010 WL 147798 (Bankr. D. Mass. Jan. 8, 2010) (even though debtor would have no payments under ICRP, subjecting her to meaningless payment plan when there was little likelihood she could ever pay anything was inconsistent with court's role as the adjudicator of undue hardship), aff'd, 435 B.R. 791 (B.A.P. 1st Cir. 2010); In re Kopf, 245 B.R. 731 (Bankr. D. Me. 2000) (no matter how flexible or "humanely executed" such programs may be, they simply are not the equivalent of a discharge).

The Kopf court noted that even when a debtor's monthly payment obligation is reduced to zero under an ICRP, this will only "postpone repayment indefinitely and, unless interest is abated, permit additional interest accruals." Id. at 735. See also In re Durrani, 311 B.R. 496 (Bankr. N.D. Ill. 2004) ("[c]ourts must not turn to the ICRP as a substitute for the thoughtful and considered exercise of . . . discretion" required under the Brunner test).

An ICRP actually allows the loan balance to increase, with capitalization of some interest, and does not prevent the discharge of a remaining balance after twenty-five years from being deemed taxable income to the debtor. See also In re Durrani, 311 B.R. 496 (Bankr. N.D. Ill. 2004) (unlike discharge in bankruptcy, ICRP discharge may result in substantial nondischargeable tax liability for debtor because unpaid amount and accrued interest over twenty-five-year period treated as income), aff'd, 320 B.R. 357 (N.D. Ill. 2005); In re Korhonen, 296 B.R. 492, 496 (Bankr. D. Minn. 2003); In re Thomsen, 234 B.R. 506, 514 (Bankr. D. Mont. 1999) (debtors will simply replace nondischargeable student loans with another nondischargeable debt in form of income taxes).

See generally National Consumer Law Center, Student Loan Law § 3.1.3.1 (4th ed. 2010 and Supp.), for a discussion of the long-term consequences for borrowers making small payments under an ICRP.

[531] In re Lee, 352 B.R. 91 (B.A.P. 8th Cir. 2006) (ICRP payments of $13.03 monthly not an option for debtor whose expenses for necessities already exceed income); In re Cumberworth, 347 B.R. 652 (B.A.P. 8th Cir. 2006); In re Groves, 398 B.R. 673 (Bankr. W.D. Mo. 2008) (after imputing income as if debtor were employed at

ment plans actually allow the loan balance to go up, with capitalization of some interest, and does not prevent the discharge of a remaining balance after twenty-five years from being deemed taxable income to the debtor.[532] If Congress had intended such payment programs to meet all hardship situations, it would have repealed the undue hardship provisions.[533] It has not done so and has, in fact, amended them since those programs were enacted.

15.4.3.8.3 Procedure for dischargeability determination

A proceeding to determine dischargeability of a student loan may be brought at any time.[534] It usually must be commenced by a complaint pursuant to the adversary proceeding rules.[535] A state student loan creditor is not immune from suit under the Eleventh Amendment.[536] The debtor has at least the burden of going forward with proof in such a case, but courts have differed regarding whether the debtor has the ultimate burden of proof, because in other dischargeability proceedings the creditor bears that burden.[537] If the debtor is challenging whether the loan is covered by the exception, courts have generally placed the initial burden on the student loan creditor to establish that the debt is the type of loan that is excepted from discharge under § 523(a)(8).[538]

Although a debtor has the option of seeking a determination related to dischargeability in a nonbankruptcy forum after the bankruptcy is completed,[539] some state or nonbankruptcy federal courts may be unwilling to make a decision on what they perceive to be a bankruptcy issue, especially if the open question is "undue hardship."[540] A debtor may also seek an administrative discharge of the loan concurrently with a proceeding in bankruptcy court. Often the student loan agency will agree to stay the bankruptcy proceeding pending an administrative determination. However, if only a conditional discharge is obtained administratively, the debtor may seek full discharge in the bankruptcy case.[541] If the facts are favorable during the bankruptcy case, the better practice is to seek to have the issue decided in bankruptcy court prior to discharge.[542] If an unfavorable decision is received and circumstances subsequently change for the worse, dischargeability of student loan obligations possibly may be relitigated by reopening a prior complaint or bringing a new proceeding even if the debtor's bankruptcy case has been closed.[543]

---

work for which she was qualified, payment required by ICRP would still create undue hardship); *In re* Douglas, 366 B.R. 241 (Bankr. M.D. Ga. 2007) (debtor diagnosed with HIV who has limited employment options due to felony conviction and who could not maintain minimal standard of living under current income and expenses has reasonable basis for not considering ICRP). *See also In re* Ford, 269 B.R. 673 (B.A.P. 8th Cir. 2001) (availability of ICRP is merely one factor considered in totality of circumstances test and not determinative in case when ICRP would result in sixty-two-year-old woman with arthritic condition carrying large and increasing debt that would not be forgiven until she was eighty-seven years old); *In re* Neeson, 2008 WL 379699 (Bankr. W.D. Mo. Feb. 12, 2008) (ICRP not option for debtor who lacks funds to purchase car and who has been using credit cards to pay for clothes, utilities, and home repairs); *In re* Robbins, 371 B.R. 372 (Bankr. E.D. Ark. 2007) (there is "no point" to pursuing ICRP when payments would be zero).

532 *In re* Barrett, 487 F.3d 353 (6th Cir. 2007). *See* 34 C.F.R § 685.209(c)(5); National Consumer Law Center, Student Loan Law § 3.1.3.1 (4th ed. 2010 and Supp.). *See also In re* Durrani, 320 B.R. 357 (N.D. Ill. 2005) (unlike discharge in bankruptcy, ICRP discharge may result in substantial nondischargeable tax liability for debtor because unpaid amount and accrued interest over twenty-five year period treated as income); *In re* Korhonen, 296 B.R. 492 (Bankr. D. Minn. 2003); *In re* Thomsen, 234 B.R. 506 (Bankr. D. Mont. 1999) (debtors will simply replace nondischargeable student loans with another nondischargeable debt in form of income taxes). *But see* Educational Credit Mgmt. Corp. v. Jesperson, 571 F.3d 775, 782 (8th Cir. 2009) (tax liability from possible future debt forgiveness is speculative); *In re* Goodman, 449 B.R. 287 (Bankr. N.D. Ohio 2011) (tax consequences mitigated when creditor presents stipulation that any remaining debt owing at end of ICRP/IBRP will be considered an undue hardship and discharged in bankruptcy).

533 *See In re* Nanton-Marie, 303 B.R. 228 (Bankr. S.D. Fla. 2003) (nothing in Code requires consideration of ICRP as condition precedent to undue hardship discharge); *In re* Johnson, 299 B.R. 676 (Bankr. M.D. Ga. 2003) (if Congress had intended the question of dischargeability of student loans to be delegated to a non-judicial entity, no matter how fair its formulas and intentions may appear, it could have provided for such); *In re* Alston, 297 B.R. 410 (Bankr. E.D. Pa. 2003) (requiring income contingent repayment agreement as proof of good faith would eviscerate section 523(a)(8)).

534 Fed. R. Bankr. P. 4007(b). *See In re* Walker, 650 F.3d 1227 (8th Cir. 2011) (debtor not required to seek dischargeability determination before discharge); *In re* Smith, 442 B.R. 550 (Bankr. S.D. Tex. 2010) (no deadline for seeking an undue hardship determination).

535 Fed. R. Bankr. P. 7001–7087. United Student Aid Funds, Inc. v. Espinosa, 130 S. Ct. 1367 (2010) (improper to seek discharge of student loan based on undue hardship other than by filing adversary proceeding).

536 Tennessee Student Assistance Corp. v. Hood, 541 U.S. 440, 124 S. Ct. 1905, 158 L. Ed. 2d 764 (2004). *See* § 14.3.2.2, *supra*.

537 *In re* Fox, 163 B.R. 975 (Bankr. M.D. Pa. 1993) (debtor has burden of going forward but not burden of proof); *In re* Alliger, 78 B.R. (Bankr. E.D. Pa. 1987); *In re* Norman, 25 B.R. 545 (Bankr. S.D. Cal. 1982). *But see* Tennessee Student Assistance Corp. v. Hood, 541 U.S. 440, 124 S. Ct. 1905, 158 L. Ed. 2d 764 (2004) (student loans presumptively nondischargeable).

538 *In re* Rumer, 469 B.R. 553 (Bankr. M.D. Pa. 2012); *In re* Stone, 199 B.R. 753 (Bankr. N.D. Ala. 1996).

539 11 U.S.C. § 523(c); Standifer v. Alaska, 3 P.3d 925 (Alaska 2000) (debtor could move to vacate postbankruptcy default judgment on student loan to obtain determination of undue hardship dischargeability).

540 *See* Massachusetts Higher Educ. Assistance Corp. v. Taylor, 390 Mass. 755, 459 N.E.2d 807 (1984) (implying that if undue hardship claim not raised in bankruptcy court it is waived).

541 Pitts v. USA Servicing Co. (*In re* Pitts), 432 B.R. 866 (Bankr. M.D. Fla. 2010) (debtor who received three year conditional disability discharge not precluded from seeking undue hardship discharge).

542 Of course, if no decision is obtained in the bankruptcy court for some reason, debtors, in appropriate circumstances, should feel free to raise discharge on the basis of hardship in response to a later collection case. Alternatively, removal of the collection case to the bankruptcy court may be sought. 28 U.S.C. § 1452; Fed. R. Bankr. P. 9027. *See generally* § 14.4.1, *supra*.

543 11 U.S.C. § 350; Fed. R. Bankr. P. 4007(b); *In re* Sobh, 61 B.R. 576 (E.D. Mich. 1986). *See In re* Walker, 650 F.3d 1227 (8th Cir. 2011) (court could consider circumstances since time of discharge); Thurman v. United Student Aid Funds, Inc., 2012 WL 993412 (W.D.

The Supreme Court has stated that "unless the debtor affirmatively secures a hardship determination, the discharge order will not include a student loan debt."[544] As a practical matter, student loan creditors will continue collection efforts absent such a determination, so it is necessary in any event to obtain a court decision that the loan is dischargeable.

15.4.3.8.4 Pursuing student loan defenses and nonbankruptcy alternatives

If it is not likely that a student loan debt will be found dischargeable (and especially in chapter 13 if payments on the debt are going to be made), the debtor should consider whether there are defenses to the debt, particularly if there was a close relationship between the school and the lender. If possible, the debtor should consider bringing school-related defenses (for example, breach of contract, warranty, fraud or unfair trade practice) to the proof of claim filed by the originating lender or guarantee agency.[545] A decision disallowing the claim based on a valid defense is as good as or better than a decision that the loan is dischargeable.[546] A claim that the debt is not owing due to such defenses may also be joined with a claim that the debt is dischargeable based upon undue hardship.

Federal borrowers have choices, including different types of repayment plans, ways to postpone repayment, and even ways to get out of default through repayment. A detailed description of these options is available in NCLC's *Student Loan Law* treatise. Borrowers may also find useful self-help materials at www.studentloanborrowerassistance.org. The options for private loans are more limited; those are discussed in Ch. 11 of NCLC's *Student Loan Law*. It is possible to cancel federal student loans outside of bankruptcy without full repayment in very limited circumstances. Cancellation (also called "discharge") is the most complete way to deal with a student loan. Discharge not only makes the loan obligation go away, but in some cases, the government must also give back any payments made (whether voluntarily or involuntarily). Cancellation is available in cases where the borrower has a total and permanent disability[547] or has died.[548] There are also cancellations available for some problems with the school, such as if the school closed when the borrower was enrolled,[549] if the school falsely certified the borrower's eligibility,[550] or if the school failed to refund the borrower's tuition after withdrawing from the program.[551]

If the borrower is experiencing short term financial difficulties, a deferment or forbearance may be available to temporarily cease collection of the loan. There are many different types of deferments (i.e., economic hardship, unemployment, etc.) and forbearances depending on the type of loan and when it was taken out.[552] Generally, interest does not accrue on subsidized federal loans during a deferment but will accrue during a forebearance.

Borrowers needing longer term solutions should look at the different repayment options. These options are different depending on whether or not the borrower is in default. Borrowers not in default on their loans may be eligible for repayment plans tied to their income[553] and some borrowers are eligible for extended repayment plans.[554] Note that the monthly payment in the income-based and income contingent repayment plans can be as low as zero dollars for very low-income borrowers. Borrowers needing to cease loan payments should explore the repayment plans before choosing a deferment or forbearance.

Borrowers who are in default are not eligible for the flexible repayment plans. However, these borrowers may be able to get

---

Wash. Mar. 21, 2012) (debtor could file dischargeability proceeding fourteen years after discharge had been entered); Queen v. Educ. Credit Mgmt. Corp. (*In re* Watkins), 461 B.R. 57 (W.D. Mo. 2011) (court could consider undue hardship complaint filed long after debtor's discharge); Smith v. Wells Fargo Educ. Fin. Servs. (*In re* Smith), 442 B.R. 550 (Bankr. S.D. Tex. 2010) (debtor could obtain undue hardship discharge determination several years after case closed, even though lender had consolidated several loans into new loan), *aff'd*, 2011 WL 4625397 (S.D. Tex Sept. 30, 2011); *In re* Fisher, 223 B.R. 377 (Bankr. M.D. Fla. 1998) (debtor who had not sought discharge of student loan during bankruptcy could reopen case to seek undue hardship discharge in light of postbankruptcy accident which reduced her ability to repay). *But see In re* Bugos, 288 B.R. 435 (Bankr. E.D. Va. 2003) (refusing to reopen case to determine undue hardship based on circumstances that arose after bankruptcy petition was filed); *In re* Kapsin, 265 B.R. 778 (Bankr. N.D. Ohio 2001) (refusing to reopen case to consider changed circumstances alleged to cause undue hardship).

544 Tennessee Student Assistance Corp. v. Hood, 541 U.S. 440, 124 S. Ct. 1905, 1912, 158 L. Ed. 2d 764 (2004).

545 *See In re* Goldberg, 297 B.R. 465 (Bankr. W.D.N.C. 2003) (debtor who never received check and whose school closed one week after she enrolled received no consideration); *Raising School-Related Defenses Against GSL Collection Action*, 10 NCLC REPORTS Deceptive Practices and Warranties Ed. 29 (Sept./Oct. 1991); National Consumer Law Center, Student Loan Law § 9.6 (4th ed. 2010 and Supp.). *See also* Tipton v. Sec'y of Educ., 768 F. Supp. 540 (S.D. W. Va. 1991); *In re* Mason, 300 B.R. 160 (Bankr. D. Conn. 2003) (consolidation loan obtained by duress held void and unenforceable).

546 To the extent the claim is disallowed, the debtor would have a binding judgment that the debt is not owed. Additionally, the creditor would not be entitled to any dividend available from the estate. Finally, attorney fees might be available to counsel to the extent that a determination is based on unfair and deceptive acts or practices or another statute involving fee shifting.

547 *See* National Consumer Law Center, Student Loan Law § 9.7 (4th ed. 2010 and Supp.).

548 *See* National Consumer Law Center, Student Loan Law § 9.8 (4th ed. 2010 and Supp.).

549 *See* National Consumer Law Center, Student Loan Law § 9.3 (4th ed. 2010 and Supp.).

550 *See* National Consumer Law Center, Student Loan Law § 9.4 (4th ed. 2010 and Supp.).

551 *See* National Consumer Law Center, Student Loan Law § 9.5 (4th ed. 2010 and Supp.).

552 *See* National Consumer Law Center, Student Loan Law Ch. 4 (4th ed. 2010 and Supp.).

553 *See* National Consumer Law Center, Student Loan Law § 3.1.3 (4th ed. 2010 and Supp.).

554 *See* National Consumer Law Center, Student Loan Law § 3.1.2 (4th ed. 2010 and Supp.).

out of default through consolidation or rehabilitation.[555] Once the loan is no longer in default, the borrower will be eligible for the various repayment options. After resolving the default, the borrower will also regain eligibility for additional Title IV funds (i.e., Pell grants and federal loans).

It is important to note that federal student loans have a long period of delinquency, 270 days, before the loans go into default. During this period of delinquency, borrowers are eligible for the various repayment plans, as well as deferments and forbearances.

15.4.3.8.5 Special issues regarding student loans in chapter 13

In the past, because student loan debts were dischargeable upon completion of a chapter 13 plan, chapter 13 was an attractive option for those who sought to deal with student loan debt burdens. However, changes in the law eliminated many of the advantages of the chapter 13 option. Code section 1328(a)(2) now incorporates section 523(a)(8) by reference so that student loans that are nondischargeable in chapter 7 are also nondischargeable in chapter 13.

Nevertheless, student loan issues continue to arise in chapter 13 cases that are filed for other reasons. Additionally, in some cases a chapter 13 plan may still provide advantages during the term of the plan, even if the debt is ultimately nondischargeable.

Given that amended section 1328(a) simply incorporates section 523(a)(8), issues of dischargeability of student loans in chapter 13 cases should be treated almost identically to those arising in chapter 7 cases. For example one court addressing dischargeability in chapter 13 determined undue hardship just as if the case had proceeded under chapter 7.[556] The mere fact that the debtor can afford chapter 13 plan payments should not be dispositive of the ability to pay a student loan.[557] In many cases those payments go almost entirely to secured creditors to ensure a debtor continued shelter, transportation to work or other necessities, or are made at great sacrifices that cannot be sustained beyond the plan period.

As in chapter 7, the debtor must affirmatively request a finding of undue hardship for the debt to be found dischargeable during the bankruptcy case. Although a plan provision might provide that confirmation of the plan will constitute a finding that undue hardship exists,[558] such provisions are disfavored by many courts.[559] A few courts have even sanctioned counsel for placing such provisions in plans.[560] As discussed above, the procedure used in most cases for resolving questions related to dischargeability in bankruptcy is the one set out in Federal Rule of Bankruptcy Procedure 4007 which provides for an adversary proceeding.

As most chapter 13 cases continue for the three to five year length of the plan and because the nondischargeability of student loans can be raised at any time,[561] careful considerations of timing should be brought to bear in order to ensure that the issues are heard when the debtor faces maximum financial pressures. However, some courts may take the position that no determination on dischargeability can be made until the end of the case.[562]

In a few districts, the chapter 13 standing trustee has taken the position that nondischargeable student loan debts must be fully paid in a chapter 13 bankruptcy plan. That position is incorrect. Even if a student loan is not dischargeable, it nevertheless remains an unsecured claim during the bankruptcy case (unless the creditor holds a non-avoided judgment lien), subject to those provisions of the Code applicable to unsecured debts.

For most cases, this means that during the bankruptcy plan, the student loan creditor is entitled to the greater of what it would receive under the best interests of the creditors test[563] or the ability to pay test[564] just like any other unsecured creditor.[565] Certainly, any arguments that a case must be dismissed because the debtor's filing was made in bad faith merely in order to improperly discharge student loans should be put to rest.[566]

---

555 *See* National Consumer Law Center, Student Loan Law Ch. 6 (4th ed. 2010 and Supp.).

556 *In re* Evans, 131 B.R. 372 (Bankr. S.D. Ohio 1991).

557 *In re* Goranson, 183 B.R. 52 (Bankr. W.D.N.Y. 1995) (income used for plan payments would not be available at end of plan, because major portion of payments was for car payments and other expenses that would continue after the plan).

558 Espinosa v. United Student Aid Funds, Inc., 553 F.3d 1193 (9th Cir. 2008), *cert. granted*, 129 S. Ct. 2791 (June 15, 2009), *aff'd*, United Student Aid Funds, Inc. v. Espinosa, 130 S. Ct. 1367 (2010).

559 United Student Aid Funds, Inc. v. Espinosa, 130 S. Ct. 1367 (2010) (improper to include such provision in plan); *In re* Mammel, 221 B.R. 238 (Bankr. D. Iowa 1998); *In re* Key, 128 B.R. 742 (Bankr. S.D. Ohio 1991).

560 *See, e.g., In re* Evans, 242 B.R. 407 (Bankr. S.D. Ohio 1999).

561 Fed. R. Bankr. P. 4007(b); *In re* Coleman, 560 F.3d 1000 (9th Cir. 2009) (debtor did not need to wait until end of case to file dischargeability complaint); *In re* Cassim, 395 B.R. 907 (B.A.P. 6th Cir. 2008) (same), *aff'd*, 594 F.3d 432 (6th Cir. 2010).

562 *See, e.g., In re* Bender, 368 F.3d 846 (8th Cir. 2004) (student loan discharge determination not ripe for adjudication until conclusion of plan at time of discharge); *In re* Ekenasi, 325 F.3d 541 (4th Cir. 2003) (ordinarily dischargeability proceeding should not be brought until end of chapter 13 case unless there are circumstances under which the *Brunner* factors could be predicted with sufficient certainty earlier in case); *In re* Cleveland, 89 B.R. 69 (B.A.P. 9th Cir. 1988) (decision on dischargeability of HEAL loan cannot be made until close of chapter 13 plan); *In re* Raisor, 180 B.R. 163 (Bankr. E.D. Tex. 1995) (dischargeability based upon undue hardship cannot be determined until end of plan).

563 11 U.S.C. § 1325(a)(4). *See* § 12.3.2, *supra*.

564 11 U.S.C. § 1325(b). *See* § 12.3.4, *supra*.

565 *See In re* Owens, 82 B.R. 960 (Bankr. N.D. Ill. 1988) (potentially nondischargeable HEAL loan may be treated like other unsecured debts during chapter 13); *In re* Gronski, 65 B.R. 932 (Bankr. E.D. Pa. 1986) (same).

566 Examples of such cases include: *In re* Stewart, 109 B.R. 998 (D. Kan. 1990); *In re* Makarchuk, 76 B.R. 919 (Bankr. N.D.N.Y. 1987).

For other reasons, decisions requiring minimum payments to unsecured creditors beyond those required by the ability to pay or best interest of the creditors tests are obsolete. *See* Educ. Assistance Corp. v. Zellner, 827 F.2d 1222 (8th Cir. 1987); *In re* Owens, 82 B.R. 960 (Bankr. N.D. Ill. 1998). *See generally* § 12.3, *supra*.

Thus, the debtor can propose treatment of a student loan creditor during a bankruptcy plan that is no different than treatment of any other unsecured creditor.[567] The student loan creditor will not be entitled to additional regular payments outside the plan prior to the debtor's discharge.

However, if the student loan is nondischargeable, it is in the debtor's interest to make sure that as much of the loan as possible is paid during the bankruptcy. Frequently this means that the debtor wishes to propose a plan to separately classify the student loan and have it paid at a higher percentage than other unsecured debts.[568] Several judicial decisions have explicitly held that a separate classification in favor of a student loan creditor does not "discriminate unfairly" within the meaning of 11 U.S.C. § 1322(b)(1).[569] At least one court has held that there is a reasonable basis for the separate classification both because the debt is nondischargeable and because absent payment the debtor may be unable to return to school to obtain a degree.[570] And even if separate classification is not permitted, the debtor has the absolute right to provide in the plan for a cure of all defaulted payments and maintenance of current payments under Code section 1322(b)(5) if the loan's last payment is after the plan's last payment.[571]

15.4.3.8.6 Health education assistance loans and other special loan programs

Congress created an additional student loan exception to discharge for certain student loans in the Omnibus Budget Reconciliation Act of 1981. Section 292f(g) of title 42, U.S. Code[572] provides that no bankruptcy discharge may be granted as to a Health Education Assistance Loan (HEAL) within seven years after the date repayment is to begin. During this seven year period no hardship discharge is available for such loans.[573] Even after the seven years, the loan is dischargeable only if the bankruptcy court finds that denial of a discharge would be unconscionable.[574] This nondischargeability provision has been held to apply in chapter 13 as well as in chapter 7.[575] Because the provision contains language making discharge available after seven years based on unconscionability, a discharge should be possible in a chapter 13 case that is filed within seven years of the first repayment due date, if the discharge is not entered until after the seven-year period has expired.[576] Several courts have held that in the context of a chapter 13 plan, the student loan creditor can be treated like other unsecured creditors and that a determination as to discharge can only be made at the conclusion of the plan.[577] Moreover, based on the language of section 523(b), HEAL loans may be dischargeable in a second bankruptcy filing under the more lenient standards of section 523(a) if the prior case resulted in a discharge.[578]

As with section 523(a)(8), the provision making HEAL debts nondischargeable is self-executing. The burden is on the debtor to request and establish grounds for a court to find the loan dischargeable.[579] Courts have held that failure to discharge the loan would be unconscionable if it was "excessive, exorbitant," "lying outside the limits of what is reasonable or acceptable," "shockingly unfair, harsh, or unjust" or "outrageous."[580]

---

567 Some courts have held, however, that a nondischargeable student loan debt continues to accrue interest during the life of the plan. See § 15.4.3.8.1, *supra*.

568 See generally § 12.4, *supra*.

569 *In re* Cox, 186 B.R. 744 (Bankr. N.D. Fla. 1995); *In re* Boggan, 125 B.R. 533 (Bankr. N.D. Ill. 1991); *In re* Freshley, 69 B.R. 96 (Bankr. N.D. Ga. 1987).

Similarly, separate classification of nondischargeable debts for support arrearages have been allowed. See, e.g., *In re* Leser, 939 F.2d 669 (8th Cir. 1991); *In re* Storberg, 94 B.R. 144 (Bankr. D. Minn. 1988); *In re* Davidson, 72 B.R. 384 (Bankr. D. Colo. 1987). But see *In re* Groves, 39 F.3d 212 (8th Cir. 1994) (affirming bankruptcy court's refusal to permit separate classification).

570 *In re* Freshley, 69 B.R. 96 (Bankr. N.D. Ga. 1987).

See also § 12.4, *supra*, for additional discussion of classification of claims.

571 *In re* Truss, 404 B.R. 329 (Bankr. E.D. Wis. 2009); *In re* Chandler, 210 B.R. 898 (Bankr. D.N.H. 1997); *In re* Sullivan, 195 B.R. 649 (Bankr. W.D. Tex. 1996); *In re* Benner, 156 B.R. 631 (Bankr. D. Minn. 1993). See also *In re* Kalfayan, 415 B.R. 907 (Bankr. S.D. Fla. 2009) (classification allowed because nonpayment of student loan would jeopardize debtor's professional license); *In re* Webb, 370 B.R. 418 (Bankr. N.D. Ga. 2007) (debtor may pay general unsecured creditors a one percent dividend through plan payments while making regularly scheduled student loan payments directly to student loan creditor pursuant to section 1322(b)(5)). But see *In re* Labib-Kiyarash, 271 B.R. 189 (B.A.P. 9th Cir. 2001) (use of section 1322(b)(5) subject to debtor showing that classification is fair under section 1322(b)(1)); *In re* Thibodeau, 248 B.R. 699 (Bankr. D. Mass. 2000).

572 This section replaces the former applicable provision, 42 U.S.C. § 294f(g).

573 *In re* Hampton, 47 B.R. 47 (Bankr. N.D. Ill. 1985).

However, for bankruptcy cases commenced prior to the statute's amendment changing the five-year nondischargeability period to seven years, the five-year period is still applicable. *In re* Barrows, 159 B.R. 86 (Bankr. D.N.H. 1993).

574 42 U.S.C. § 292f(g).

575 *In re* Johnson, 787 F.2d 1179 (7th Cir. 1986).

576 *In re* Nelson, 183 B.R. 972 (Bankr. S.D. Fla. 1995) (also holding that under section 292f(g) the time period was not tolled during forbearance periods). But see Ellzey v. United States Dep't of Health & Human Services, 302 B.R. 385 (S.D. Ala. 2003) (time period tolled during prior bankruptcy case).

577 United States v. Lee, 89 B.R. 250 (N.D. Ga. 1987) (debt is conditionally dischargeable during pendency of chapter 13 plan), *aff'd*, 853 F.2d 1547 (11th Cir. 1988); *In re* Cleveland, 89 B.R. 69 (B.A.P. 9th Cir. 1988) (upon completion of chapter 13 plan, issue would be whether non-discharge of loan would be unconscionable); *In re* Battrell, 105 B.R. 65 (Bankr. D. Or. 1989); *In re* Owens, 82 B.R. 960 (Bankr. N.D. Ill. 1988). See also *In re* Gronski, 65 B.R. 932 (Bankr. E.D. Pa. 1986).

578 *In re* Tanski, 195 B.R. 408 (Bankr. E.D. Wis. 1996).

579 United States v. Rushing, 287 B.R. 343 (D.N.J. 2002); United States v. Wood, 925 F.2d 1580 (7th Cir. 1991). See also United States v. Erkard, 200 B.R. 152 (N.D. Ohio 1996) (United States, as guarantor of HEAL obligation must be made a party to dischargeability proceeding).

580 *In re* Woody, 494 F.3d 939 (10th Cir. 2007) (denying discharge, even while acknowledging debtor's problems, because he had steady income of $40,000 per year and had made little effort to pay debt); United States Dep't of Health & Human Servs. v. Smitley, 347 F.3d 109 (4th Cir. 2003) (court should determine dischargeability of

Several other health education programs have similar provisions which make debts arising in those programs nondischargeable.[581] Generally the operation of these provisions is similar to that of the HEAL provisions.

15.4.3.9 Debts Incurred Through Drunk Driving—11 U.S.C. § 523(a)(9)

As a result of increased public concern about the social problem of drunk drivers, the 1984 amendments added an exception to the chapter 7 discharge for debts incurred through drunk driving.[582] A 1990 amendment to the statute made the exception to discharge applicable in chapter 13 cases as well.[583] The same amendment broadened the exception to include unlawful driving while under the influence of a drug or other substance, but also narrowed it to include only debts for death or personal injury.[584] Thus, debts for property damage are not nondischargeable under section 523(a)(9).[585] The 1990 amendment also removed a former requirement that the debt be evidenced by a judgment to be nondischargeable. The 2005 amendments broadened the section to include operating a vessel or aircraft and also made debts within the scope of section 523(a)(9) priority debts.[586]

Therefore, the specific terms of this subsection narrow its scope somewhat. Section 523(a)(9) applies only if the debtor operated a motor vehicle, vessel, or aircraft[587] and the operation was unlawful due to intoxication. And it only applies to claims for death or personal injury. It has been held that a snowmobile is a motor vehicle.[588]

At a minimum, the language of the subsection also presumably requires that the debtor met the legal standard for intoxication in the jurisdiction where the accident occurred. These standards vary and may not even exist in every jurisdiction. When they do exist, there may be disputes about how the standard is to be applied, especially if it is not labeled "intoxication."[589] In many cases a judgment or consent decree does not specify whether or not the standard was met, and there is then a question of whether this issue may later be separately litigated to determine dischargeability under this provision.[590]

---

non-HEAL loans first and then apply HEAL standard to remainder; repayment not unconscionable when debtor could repay in twenty-five-year plan); *In re* Rice, 78 F.3d 1144 (6th Cir. 1996) (nondischarge of HEAL obligation not unconscionable when debtor and his wife had $60,000 income and payment would not reduce family's income to anything close to poverty level); Matthews v. Pineo, 19 F.3d 121 (3d Cir. 1994) (nondischarge not unconscionable when debtor chose to move to a small town and earn less than she could elsewhere as physician, rather than fulfill requirement of service in medically underserved area); *In re* Malloy, 155 B.R. 940 (E.D. Va. 1993) (nondischarge not unconscionable in case of debtor who was healthy, college educated and steadily employed); *In re* Nelson, 183 B.R. 972 (Bankr. S.D. Fla. 1995) (nondischarge would be unconscionable based on debtor's psychological and emotional health); Kline v. United States, 155 B.R. 762 (Bankr. W.D. Mo. 1993) (nondischarge would be unconscionable in view of debtor's chronic depression, anxiety and panic disorder). *See also In re* Ascue, 268 B.R. 739 (Bankr. W.D. Va. 2001) (partial discharge, eliminating $300,000 in interest on National Health Service Corps loan for debtor whose earnings were limited), *aff'd*, 2002 WL 192561 (W.D. Va. Feb. 7, 2002).

581 *In re* Brown, 79 B.R. 789 (Bankr. N.D. Ill. 1987) (National Health Services Corp. Scholarship Program—42 U.S.C. § 254o(d)). *See also* 37 U.S.C. § 302g(e) (pertaining to refund obligations of military reservist physicians who receive special pay and who terminate their service early); *In re* Simone, 375 B.R. 481 (Bankr. C.D. Ill. 2007) (unconscionability standard similar to the HEAL standard applies to determinations of dischargeability of loans under the Indian Health Service Loans Repayment Program, 25 U.S.C. § 1616a(m)(4)).

Unlike HEAL loans, these provisions have not been amended to change the five-year absolute bar on discharge to seven years. Provisions relating to such exceptions to discharge are included in Appendix A.3, *infra*.

It has been held that the fact that a loan may be dischargeable under one of these specialized provisions does not exempt it from nondischargeability under section 523(a)(8). *In re* Udell, 454 F.3d 180 (3d Cir. 2006). The provisions have been held to operate cumulatively, so that no discharge at all may be sought during the period in which a discharge is prohibited. *In re* Dunn, 325 B.R. 807 (Bankr. N.D. Iowa 2005) (dismissing complaint seeking undue hardship discharge of ROTC debt within time when discharge proscribed by 10 U.S.C. § 2005).

582 11 U.S.C. § 523(a)(9).
This provision has been applied retroactively to judgments entered prior to its effective date. *See In re* Fielder, 799 F.2d 656 (11th Cir. 1986). *See also* Leach v. Reckley, 63 B.R. 724 (S.D. Ind. 1986).

583 11 U.S.C. § 1328(a)(2).

584 *See In re* Longhenry, 246 B.R. 234 (Bankr. D. Md. 2000) (loss of consortium is a personal injury). *But see In re* Felski, 277 B.R. 732 (E.D. Mich. 2002) (statutory subrogation claim against uninsured intoxicated motorist arising from injuries in accident would be nondischargeable if accident was caused by intoxicated motorist); *In re* Delia, 353 B.R. 532 (Bankr. W.D. Mich. 2006) (indemnity judgment against debtor, obtained by bar that had been held liable under dramshop statute for personal injuries caused by debtor's driving while intoxicated, was nondischargeable).

585 *In re* Wiggins, 180 B.R. 676 (M.D. Ala. 1995); *In re* Brisson, 186 B.R. 205 (Bankr. E.D. Va. 1995); *In re* Williams, 175 B.R. 17 (Bankr. M.D. Tenn. 1994).

586 11 U.S.C. § 507(a)(10).

587 The statute does not cover vicarious liability. *In re* Lewis, 77 B.R. 972 (Bankr. S.D. Fla. 1987) (debt dischargeable when debtor's daughter drove car).

588 *In re* Dunn, 203 B.R. 414 (E.D. Mich. 1996).

589 *See, e.g.,* Whitson v. Middleton, 898 F.2d 950 (4th Cir. 1990) (evidence as a whole showed intoxication even though no drunk driving charge was made and no breath test administered); *In re* Spencer, 168 B.R. 142 (Bankr. N.D. Tex. 1994) (debt dischargeable when creditor did not show by preponderance of evidence that debtor was intoxicated as defined by Texas law); *In re* Humphrey, 102 B.R. 629 (Bankr. S.D. Ohio 1989) (debtor who had been charged with "driving under the influence" of alcohol found to have been intoxicated based on the evidence as a whole even though state accepted a plea to "reckless operation of a motor vehicle"); *In re* Tuzzolino, 70 B.R. 373 (Bankr. N.D.N.Y. 1987) (various degrees of intoxication are all "legal intoxication" under section 523(a)(9)); *In re* Dougherty, 51 B.R. 987 (Bankr. D. Colo. 1985) (conviction of "driving while ability impaired" came within discharge exception). *See also In re* Barnes, 266 B.R. 397 (B.A.P. 8th Cir. 2001) (discussing admissible evidence of intoxication).

590 *In re* Pahule, 78 B.R. 210 (E.D. Wis. 1987) (bankruptcy court could look to underlying facts of debtor's criminal conviction for driving under influence to find civil judgment within scope of section 523(a)(9)), *aff'd*, 849 F.2d 1056 (7th Cir. 1988). *See also In re*

§ 15.4.3.10   Consumer Bankruptcy Law and Practice

The state courts have concurrent jurisdiction with the bankruptcy forum over any such disputes.

This subsection closes the hole which case law created in the willful and malicious injury exception of section 523(a)(6). It makes clear that drunk driving debts do not fall within the section 523(a)(6) exception, because Congress saw fit to establish a new subsection to deal with them.[591] Thus, if such debts do not fall within the terms of section 523(a)(9), they should be dischargeable. For example, a criminal restitution debt for injuries arising out of judgment based on the debtor operating a vehicle while intoxicated was found nondischargeable under this section.[592] Additionally, one court of appeals has held that an insurance surcharge imposed by a state as a result of a drunk driving conviction is also nondischargeable under section 523(a)(9).[593] However, it is unlikely that the latter decision is still good law after section 523(a)(9) was amended to include only debts for death or personal injury.

15.4.3.10 Debts Not Discharged in Prior Bankruptcy Case—11 U.S.C. § 523(a)(10), (b)

11 U.S.C. § 523(a)(10) contains an exception to discharge which is rarely invoked. It is relevant only if the debtor has been denied a discharge in a prior bankruptcy case, which rarely occurs in consumer cases.[594] If the debtor has been denied a discharge, any debt that existed when the prior bankruptcy was filed may not be discharged in a later bankruptcy. In some cases there may be difficult issues concerning whether the circumstances existing at the time of the prior case gave rise to a "claim" as defined by section 101.[595]

This exception does not apply, however, if discharge was denied in the prior case only because of the six-year or eight-year bar to consecutive bankruptcy discharges, or because of failure to pay filing fees, or because a debtor was denied a discharge for failure to complete a credit education course.[596] Similarly, it does not apply if a discharge is revoked because the debtor failed to provide information or documents required in an audit, because such acts are not listed in section 523(a)(10).[597] Nor does it apply when a debt was reaffirmed in a prior bankruptcy case.[598] The sections creating these bars to discharge under both the Act and the Code are conspicuously omitted from the list in 11 U.S.C. § 523(a)(10) designating causes for prior denial of discharge that trigger this exception. This exception also does not apply when a previous case was dismissed, with or without prejudice, if a discharge was not waived or denied in that case.[599]

In addition to the exception to discharge for cases in which a discharge was denied or waived, a separate provision preserves the result of dischargeability determinations in a prior case for most debts in subsequent cases. Section 523(b) provides that, if a debt was excepted from a discharge in a prior case, it is not excepted from discharge in a later case unless the debt is nondischargeable under the terms of section 523(a). Thus, if a debt not discharged in a prior case, such as a tax debt, has become dischargeable due to the passage of time, it can be discharged in the later case. It is unclear whether a new dischargeability complaint must be filed for the types of debts that would ordinarily require them under section 523(c)[600] or whether such debts are remain nondischarged under principles of res judicata.[601]

15.4.3.11 Debts Emerging from Responsibilities to Federal Depository Institutions—11 U.S.C. § 523(a)(11), (12)

The two exceptions to discharge in section 523(a)(11) and (12) are rarely, if ever, applicable in consumer cases. They were added to the Code as part of the Congressional response to the savings and loan crisis in order to help the Federal Deposit Insurance Corporation (FDIC) and other regulators recover assets to pay the cost of the bailout.

Greenwasser, 269 B.R. 918 (Bankr. S.D. Fla. 2001) (denying summary judgment motion based on prior criminal adjudication); *In re* Caffey, 248 B.R. 920 (Bankr. N.D. Ga. 2000) (debt could be found nondischargeable under this section even if debtor was acquitted in criminal DUI case, because burden of proof was only a preponderance of evidence in bankruptcy proceeding); *In re* Phalen, 145 B.R. 551 (Bankr. N.D. Ohio 1992) (court could find that debtor was driving while under the influence even though debtor plead guilty to a different charge); *In re* Bennett, 80 B.R. 800 (Bankr. E.D. Va. 1988) (debt arising from default judgment entered when debtor was sued for damages resulting from drunk driving is nondischargeable).

591 *See* Cassidy v. Minihan, 794 F.2d 340 (8th Cir. 1986); *In re* Wright, 66 B.R. 403 (Bankr. S.D. Ind. 1986). *But see In re* Adams, 761 F.2d 1422 (9th Cir. 1985).

592 *See In re* Steiger, 159 B.R. 907 (B.A.P. 9th Cir. 1993) (amount of nondischargeable restitution obligation was set in criminal process based on ascertainable damages for vehicular homicide).

593 Lugo v. Paulsen, 886 F.2d 602 (3d Cir. 1989).

594 *See* § 15.2, *supra*, for discussion of denial of discharge. This section has also been applied in a case in which discharge was revoked in a prior case. *In re* Klapp, 706 F.2d 998 (9th Cir. 1983).

595 *See In re* Buckley, 404 B.R. 877 (Bankr. S.D. Ohio 2009); § 15.5.1.1, *infra* (discussing when a claim exists).

596 *See* § 15.2.2.8, *supra*.

597 *In re* Hickman, 448 B.R. 769 (Bankr. C.D. Ill. 2011).

598 *In re* Johnson, 255 B.R. 696 (Bankr. E.D. Mich. 2000) (debt reaffirmed in prior bankruptcy in settlement of dischargeability dispute was not nondischargeable under section 523(a)(10) unless written waiver of discharge approved by court in prior case provided that debt would be nondischargeable in future bankruptcy cases); *In re* Lones, 50 B.R. 801 (Bankr. W.D. Ky. 1985).

599 *In re* Samora, 117 B.R. 660 (Bankr. D.N.M. 1990). *See also In re* Logan, 145 B.R. 324 (Bankr. D. Kan. 1992) (order dismissing prior case and denying a discharge for failure to attend creditors' meeting was not a denial of discharge for cause under section 727 that gave rise to an exception to discharge in later case). *But see In re* Smith, 133 B.R. 467 (Bankr. N.D. Ind. 1991) (dismissal with prejudice automatically bars future discharge of debts existing at the time of dismissal based on 11 U.S.C. § 349(a)).

600 *See* § 15.4.2, *supra*.

601 *See In re* Moncur, 328 B.R. 183 (B.A.P. 9th Cir. 2005) (claim preclusion principles render debt nondischargeable in later case even without timely adversary proceeding).

Section 523(a)(11) excepts from discharge debts that emerged from fraud or defalcation in a fiduciary capacity[602] related to the debtor's responsibility to a depository institution or credit union when that debt is memorialized in a "final judgment, unreviewable order, consent order, decree or ... settlement agreement." Section 523(a)(12) excepts debts for malicious or reckless failure to maintain the capital of insured depository institutions, unless such responsibility has been terminated by an act of the applicable regulatory agency.

Section 523(c) was also amended to extend the deadline for regulatory agencies in some cases under sections 523(a)(2), (4) and (6).[603] The deadline was also extended for actions to determine nondischargeability under section 523(a)(11).[604]

15.4.3.12 Federal Criminal Restitution—11 U.S.C. § 523(a)(13)

Code section 523(a)(13), enacted as part of a 1994 crime bill, excepts from discharge any order of restitution issued under title 18 of the United States Code, the federal criminal code. As the Supreme Court had already held that criminal restitution generally came within the scope of section 523(a)(7)'s exception for non-compensatory fines, penalties and forfeitures payable to or for the benefit of a governmental unit,[605] this section appears to make only a few additional types of debts nondischargeable. If the federal criminal restitution debt is not payable to or for the benefit of a governmental unit, this section would make it nondischargeable nonetheless. Similarly, if the restitution were found to be compensation for actual pecuniary loss, this section would prevent it from being discharged. However, non-federal criminal restitution debts which do not fall within section 523(a)(7) are not affected by section 523(a)(13).

Section 523(a)(13) is not applicable when the debtor receives a full chapter 13 discharge under Code section 1328(a).[606] But, oddly, a separate exception to that discharge is in some ways broader than the exceptions to discharge in chapter 7. The chapter 13 exception, in section 1328(a)(3) includes all criminal restitution debts, whether state or federal, imposed in a sentence upon conviction of a crime. However, as discussed elsewhere in this treatise,[607] the chapter 13 exception may permit discharge of some restitution debts not dischargeable in chapter 7 if they are not imposed in a sentence upon conviction of a crime.

15.4.3.13 Debts Incurred to Pay Nondischargeable Taxes or to Pay Federal Election Law Fines or Penalties—11 U.S.C. § 523(a)(14A), (14B)

At the urging of the credit card industry, Congress enacted section 523(a)(14A) which, as amended and redesignated,[608] provides that a debt incurred to pay a tax that would have been nondischargeable under section 523(a)(1) is nondischargeable to the same extent as the tax debt would have been. Supposedly, this section was needed to prevent debtors anticipating a bankruptcy from using a credit card to pay nondischargeable taxes and then discharging the credit card debt. Significantly, the section does not apply in chapter 13, because it was not incorporated in Code section 1328(a). It also does not apply to debts incurred to pay secured tax debts, such as real estate taxes in many states, because section 523(a)(1) incorporates section 507(a)(8), which applies only to unsecured claims.[609]

Although the provision was intended to facilitate the payment of taxes by credit card, it is not limited to credit card payments. Any loan that a lender could show was used to pay taxes probably would be within its scope. However, lenders may not know, in many cases, whether a loan was used to pay taxes unless the loan proceeds check is made out to the tax creditor, for example to pay off a tax lien, or the debtor uses a credit card convenience check made out to the tax creditor. If a lender cannot prove that a debt was incurred to pay a tax, the section is inapplicable.[610]

The new section also creates difficult tracing problems. If taxes are paid by credit card, how are payments on the account after that to be apportioned? In view of the amendment's proponents' arguments that this provision was only to protect against debtors evading the nondischargeability of taxes by borrowing money to pay them, all payments after the credit was incurred to pay taxes should be allocated to the tax charges until those charges are paid. However, creditors undoubtedly will argue for other methods of allocating payments, such as FIFO (first-in, first-out) or prorating them. The issue could become even more confused if the debtor accepted one of the frequent solicitations by credit card companies to pay off the balance on one card using a new card. Of course, in such cases it is unlikely the new card issuer would know that the prior card was used to pay taxes.

Unfortunately, the amendment does little to deter its intended targets, while harming others who are innocent of any intent to manipulate the Code. Debtors who plan their bankruptcy cases and are intent on evading the tax discharge exception can simply obtain cash advances or incur debts to pay other expenses so they can pay their taxes with cash. Alternatively,

---

602 Presumably those terms would be defined as they are for cases under 11 U.S.C. § 523(a)(4). See § 15.4.3.4, *supra*.
603 11 U.S.C. § 523(c)(2).
    For further discussion of the procedure for determining nondischargeability of various debts, see § 15.4.2, *supra*.
604 *Id.*
605 See § 15.4.3.7, *supra*.
606 Compare 11 U.S.C. § 1328(b) to which section 523(a)(13) is applicable.
607 See § 15.4.3.7, *supra*.

608 Prior to the 2005 amendments the provision was designated as 11 U.S.C. § 523(a)(14).
609 *In re* Nguyen, 2010 WL 56075 (Bankr. E.D. Va. Jan. 6, 2010).
610 *See* Chase Bank v. Mueller (*In re* Mueller), 455 B.R. 151 (Bankr. W.D. Wis. 2011) (creditor could not prove that debt incurred in anticipation of taxes was actually paid by debtor to taxing authority).

some may seek to cover their tracks by incurring debt to pay their taxes and then incurring debt from another creditor to pay off the first debt. Because the second lender or credit card issuer will rarely be aware that the debt it paid off was used to pay nondischargeable taxes, the debtor will have achieved the precise result that section 523(a)(14A) attempts to prevent. The only debtors likely to be hurt by the nondischargeability provision are those who genuinely want to pay their taxes, incur debts to do so, and later run into financial problems before those debts are paid.

Section 523(a)(14B), added in 2005, is not likely to be invoked very often. It probably was intended to make nondischargeable debts for federal election law fines and penalties, but as drafted it excepts only debts incurred to pay such fines and penalties, which are rarely owed by consumers. If the section is utilized it will present many of the same difficulties of identifying and tracing payments that are raised by section 523(a)(14A) and discussed above.

15.4.3.14 Marital Property Settlement Debts—11 U.S.C. § 523(a)(15)

The Bankruptcy Reform Act of 1994 created a new exception to discharge for marital property settlements in limited situations. The provision was amended in 2005 to make all marital property settlements nondischargeable, eliminating both the balancing tests it had previously contained and the need for a creditor to file a proceeding in the bankruptcy court to obtain a determination of nondischargeability. Section 523(a)(15) now applies to all debts to a spouse, former spouse, or child of the debtor incurred in the course of a divorce or separation or in connection with a separation agreement, divorce decree or other order of a court of record, or a determination made in accordance with state or territorial law by a governmental unit.[611] Like most dischargeability provisions, section 523(a)(15) can be raised in a nonbankruptcy court after the bankruptcy case is concluded.

Section 523(a)(15) originally grew out of a bill that had proposed that property settlement debts "assumed or incurred" be found nondischargeable. The provision which was enacted created a more limited exception. The word "assumed" was deleted so, as the legislative history also states,[612] the only obligation that is not discharged is that which runs to the spouse, former spouse, or child of the debtor.[613] The language was further clarified in 2005 to provide that the debt must be one to a spouse, former spouse, or child of the debtor.

However, nothing in section 523(a)(15) affects the nondischargeability of debts, whether labeled alimony or property settlement, that in fact are in the nature of alimony, maintenance, or support and therefore are domestic support obligations nondischargeable under section 523(a)(5).[614] Also significant is the fact that the exception only applies in chapter 7, 11, and 12 cases and in cases of chapter 13 hardship discharges. It was not added to Code section 1328(a), the provision governing chapter 13 discharges after full compliance with a plan, so that true property settlement debts remain dischargeable for debtors who complete chapter 13 plans.

Ordinarily, as in most other dischargeability litigation, no attorney fees are awarded in litigation under section 523(a)(15). However, if a divorce decree provides that fees are to be awarded for enforcement of the decree, a prevailing non-debtor may be awarded fees, at least for litigation of the state law issues of the divorce decree's validity, amount, and enforceability.[615]

15.4.3.15 Debts for Condominium, Cooperative, or Home Owner Association Fees—11 U.S.C. § 523(a)(16)

The Bankruptcy Reform Act of 1994 also enacted a new section 523(a)(16) making nondischargeable certain condominium and cooperative fees or assessments. The provision was amended in 2005 to add fees and assessments with respect to a lot in a home owners association and to change the language concerning when fees are nondischargeable. The prior standard limiting fees to those incurred during a period that the debtor occupied the dwelling was changed to "for as long as the debtor or the trustee has a legal, equitable, or possessory ownership interest" in the property. In light of the new language, after considering any possible tax consequences, if the debtor no longer wishes to retain title to the property it may be in the debtor's interest to attempt to convey the property to the holder of the mortgage, even if the holder is not foreclosing.[616]

---

611 See Floody v. Kearney (*In re* Kearney), 433 B.R. 640 (Bankr. S.D. Tex. 2010) (whether debt arose out of divorce decree had been decided by state court contempt order enforcing debt, and that decision had issue preclusive effect); Woosley v. Woosley, 2010 WL 500423 (M.D. Tenn. Feb. 5, 2010) (modification of marital settlement agreement that occurred four months after divorce finalized was "in connection with" divorce decree and therefore nondischargeable).

612 H.R. Rep. No. 103-835, at 55 (1994), *reprinted in* 1994 U.S.C.C.A.N. 3340.

613 *In re* Wodark, 425 B.R. 834 (B.A.P. 10th Cir. 2010) (interpreting separation agreement provision obligating debtor to pay credit card debt as creating liability to her former spouse that was nondischargeable under section 523(a)(15)); *In re* Dollaga, 260 B.R. 493 (B.A.P. 9th Cir. 2001) (creditor who was not spouse, former spouse, or child of debtor lacked standing under section 523(a)(15)); Paulus v. Paulus (*In re* Paulus), 2011 WL 2560285 (Bankr. N.D. Ohio June 27, 2011); *In re* Sanders, 236 B.R. 107 (Bankr. S.D. Ga. 1999) (debt owed to debtor's former divorce attorney not within scope of section); *In re* Finaly, 190 B.R. 312 (Bankr. S.D. Ohio 1995) (creditor that was not spouse, former spouse or child of debtor did not have standing to assert exception). *See also* Corso v. Walker, 449 B.R. 838 (W.D. Pa. 2011) (debtor's former spouse could not assert that loan debtor had agreed to pay was nondischargeable under section 523(a)(8), because debtor's agreement to hold her harmless from loans was separate obligation).

614 *See* § 15.4.3.5, *supra*.

615 Renfrow v. Draper, 232 F.3d 688 (9th Cir. 2000).

616 *See* Pigg v. BAC Home Loans Servicing L.P. (*In re* Pigg), 453 B.R. 728 (Bankr. M.D. Tenn. 2011) (court fashioned remedy to end debtor's ownership and preserve fresh start).

The provision applies only to fees and assessments that become due and payable after the petition date. Notably, prepetition fees and assessments are dischargeable.[617]

Under a literal reading of the new language, a discharge does not discharge the debtor from a debt for such fees "for as long as the debtor or the trustee has a legal, equitable, or possessory ownership interest" in the property. So, quite arguably, once the debtor no longer has such an interest, the fees are discharged. Congress changed the language from reference to fees incurred during a particular period, and this change must be assumed to have meaning.

This exception originally grew out of a split in the case law regarding whether condominium fees were prepetition debts dischargeable in bankruptcy.[618] The exception does not apply in chapter 13 cases in which the debtor completes a plan, because it was not added to section 1328(a).[619]

The enactment of section 523(a)(16) resolved the disputes about whether other condominium or cooperative fees are claims that can be discharged. By specifying that some postpetition fees are claims that cannot be discharged, the provision implicitly undermines decisions holding that such fees were not prepetition claims.[620] In addition, the legislative history states that, except to the extent made nondischargeable by this section, obligations to pay postpetition fees are dischargeable, and expressly adopts the holding of In re Rosteck,[621] which held that because they arose from a prepetition contract they were prepetition claims.[622]

Lastly, the amendment contains a savings clause making clear that even if a debt was nondischargeable in a prior bankruptcy case or in a pre-conversion case, it still may be discharged in a later case or converted case filed after the debtor vacated the property, if the conditions of nondischargeability are no longer present.

15.4.3.16 Costs and Fees in Prisoner Litigation—11 U.S.C. § 523(a)(17)

Yet another exception to the chapter 7 discharge, not applicable in chapter 13, was added by the Prisoner Litigation Reform Act, part of an omnibus budget bill enacted in 1996.[623] The wording of the section was amended in 2005 to make clear that the exception is limited to costs and fees that are imposed upon prisoners who seek to file actions *in forma pauperis* in federal courts.

The exception was enacted as part of a larger bill that substantially changed the rights of prisoners to file actions *in forma pauperis* under 28 U.S.C. § 1915. The bill directed federal courts to require any prisoner filing an action to make monthly payments toward fees and costs from the prison account earned by the prisoner. Section 523(a)(17) prohibits prisoners from using chapter 7 to discharge the payments they are ordered to make.

It is this purpose that accounts for the strange wording of section 523(a)(17). The section, prohibits the discharge of "a fee imposed on a prisoner by any court for the filing of a case, motion, complaint, or appeal or for other costs and expenses assessed with respect to such filings, *regardless of an assertion of poverty by the debtor under subsection (b) or (f)(2) of title 28 (or a similar non-Federal law), or the debtor's status as a prisoner, as defined in section 1915(h) of title 28 (or a similar non-Federal law)*" (emphasis added).

15.4.3.17 Pension Loans—11 U.S.C. § 523(a)(18)

Section 523(a)(18) was transformed in 2005[624] into a provision that makes loans from pension funds and from section 403(b) and section 401(k) plans nondischargeable. The debt must be owed to a pension, profit-sharing, stock bonus, or other plan established under sections 401, 403, 408, 408A, 414, 457, or 501(c) of the Internal Revenue Code, under a loan permitted under section 408(b)(1) of the Employee Retirement Income Security Act (ERISA) or subject to section 72(p) of the Internal Revenue Code, or a loan from a thrift savings plan that satisfies the requirements of 5 U.S.C. § 8433(g).

Few debtors had ever contended that such loans, which are essentially secured by a pension account, were eliminated by bankruptcy. Curiously, section 523(a)(18) also provides that nothing in the provision is to be construed such that the loans are debts that would be subject to discharge in the first place.[625]

---

617 *In re* Moreno, 479 B.R. 553 (Bankr. E.D. Cal. 2012) (interest and attorney fees relating to prepetition fees were discharged); Fauser v. Prop. Owners Ass'n (*In re* Fauser), 2011 WL 5006508 (Bankr. S.D. Tex. Oct. 20, 2011).

618 *See* § 15.5.1.1, *infra*.

619 *In re* Colon, 465 B.R. 657 (Bankr. D. Utah 2011); *In re* Kelly, 2010 WL 1740739 (Bankr. N.D. Cal. Apr. 28, 2010) (postpetition homeowner association fees may be discharged in chapter 13 case in which debtor's confirmed plan provided for surrender of property). *But see In re* Spencer, 457 B.R. 601 (E.D. Mich. 2011); Simms-Wilson v. Linebarger Goggan Blair & Sampson L.L.P. (*In re* Simms-Wilson), 434 B.R. 452 (Bankr. S.D. Tex. 2010) (postpetition fees are postpetition claim; no discussion of legislative history).

However, a debtor who intends to retain a condominium and continue to reside in it will likely be required to provide for payment of postpetition condominium or cooperative fees in the chapter 13 plan. *See In re* Foster, 435 B.R. 650 (B.A.P. 9th Cir. 2010) (adopting "you stay, you pay" policy based on finding that requirement to pay homeowners' association dues under Washington law is covenant that runs with the land).

620 *See, e.g., In re* Rosenfeld, 23 F.3d 833 (4th Cir. 1994).

621 899 F.2d 694 (7th Cir. 1990).

622 *In re* Mattera, 203 B.R. 565 (Bankr. D.N.J. 1997) (chapter 13 discharge eliminated debtor's personal liability for postpetition condominium fees even though she remained owner of condominium after petition). *But see In re* Lozada, 214 B.R. 558 (Bankr. E.D. Va. 1997) (because section 523(a)(16) did not mention postpetition assessments by home owners' associations court was constrained to follow prior Fourth Circuit authority that they were postpetition debts).

623 Pub. L. No. 104-134, 110 Stat. 1321 (1996).

624 Prior to the 2005 amendments, section 523(a)(18) contained a now-repealed provision regarding support obligations owed to states and municipalities.

625 This reference to a loan not being construed as a debt applies to a loan made under a governmental plan under section 414(d), or a contract or account under section 403(b) of the Internal Revenue

A complementary amendment to section 362(b) permits continued collection of such loans notwithstanding the automatic stay.[626]

15.4.3.18 Debts Arising from Securities Violations—11 U.S.C. § 523(a)(19)

Section 523(a)(19) excepts from discharge debts arising from securities violations. It is not limited to cases in which judgments were entered prepetition, as it may have been prior to a 2005 clarifying amendment. This provision is virtually never applicable in consumer cases.

15.4.3.19 Debts Made Nondischargeable by Other Statutes

Congress has passed several other statutory provisions which may make debts nondischargeable in bankruptcy under either chapter 7 or 13. Two statutes making student loan debts nondischargeable in some circumstances outside section 523(a)(8) are discussed above.[627] Similarly, certain obligations arising from retention bonuses or continuation pay paid to military personnel were made nondischargeable when the discharge is entered less than five years from the date the retention or continuation agreement is terminated.[628] To the extent that these provisions contain language making them applicable when a discharge is entered within five years, they will not apply in a chapter 13 case that is filed within five years if the discharge is not entered until after the five-year period has expired.

15.4.3.20 Debts That Were Nondischargeable in a Previous Bankruptcy Case—11 U.S.C. § 523(b)

Section 523(b) provides that certain types of debts that were not discharged in a prior bankruptcy case may be discharged in a later case if they would have been dischargeable under section 523(a) in the later case. The debts enumerated include debts that were previously found nondischargeable under subsections 523(a)(1), (a)(3), and (a)(8). What these debts have in common (or at least had in common when section 523(b) was enacted)[629] is that they all turn on time periods that may have changed in the later bankruptcy case. For example, section 523(a)(1) looks to whether a return for a prior tax year was filed more than two years before the bankruptcy petition, and whether a tax return was last due less than three years before the petition.[630] While that may not have been true in the first case, it may well be true in the later case. Similarly, section 523(a)(3) looks to whether certain debts were scheduled in a case or whether the creditor otherwise had notice in time to participate. If a debt was not dischargeable due to lack of timely scheduling or notice in the first case, it may still be scheduled and therefore be dischargeable in the second case.

However, other debts that were nondischargeable in a prior case cannot be discharged in a later case, except for a case in which a debtor receives a discharge under section 1328(a).[631] In this respect, section 523(b) applies principles of res judicata.[632]

Section 523(b) may well allow a debtor with a HEAL loan that was nondischargeable in an earlier case under both section 523(a)(8) and 42 U.S.C. § 292f(g)[633] to seek an undue hardship discharge of that loan under section 523(a)(8) without meeting the stricter requirements for discharge of a HEAL loan. The debtor can argue that the plain language of section 523(b) provides that the loan, which meets the description of that subsection, is dischargeable if the loan is not nondischargeable under section 523(a)(8) in the second case.[634]

15.4.4 Res Judicata and Collateral Estoppel in Dischargeability Cases

One of the more disputed issues in dischargeability litigation has been the extent to which prior state court judgments are binding upon the parties in bankruptcy court through res judicata or collateral estoppel. At least some of the questions

---

Code. A similar provision is found in new section 362(b)(19). These provisions may have been an attempt to overrule the holding *In re* Buchferer, 216 B.R. 332 (Bankr. E.D.N.Y. 1997) (pension loan found to be non-recourse secured claim), and to codify the result in New York City Employees Retirement Sys. v. Villarie, 648 F.2d 810 (2d Cir. 1981).

626 11 U.S.C. § 362(b)(19). *See* Ch. 9, *supra*.

627 42 U.S.C. § 292f(g) (Health Education Assistance Loans—HEAL); 42 U.S.C. § 254o(d)(3) (National Health Services Scholarship Program). *See* § 15.4.3.8.6, *supra*. *See also* 42 U.S.C. § 288-5 (incorporating 42 U.S.C. § 254o).

628 37 U.S.C. § 301d(c)(3). *See also* 37 U.S.C. § 302f (obligation of reserve health specialists who fail to honor agreement to serve in armed forces to refund special bonus pay not dischargeable in bankruptcy with no exceptions); 37 U.S.C. § 317(f)(3) (five year nondischargeable provision related to obligation to refund retention bonuses of military officers who terminate agreement); 37 U.S.C. § 302g(e) (refund obligations of military reservist physicians who receive special pay and who terminate their service early not dischargeable if less than five years after termination); 37 U.S.C. §§ 301e(d)(3), 314(d)(4), 318(h)(3), 319(f)(3), 321(f)(3), 322(f)(4); Pub. L. No. 106-65, § 1705(d)(3), 113 Stat. 512 (1999).

Such statutes are reprinted in Appendix A.3, *infra*.

629 Prior versions of 11 U.S.C. § 523(a)(8) permitted discharge of student loans if the first payment was due more than five (or later seven) years before the petition.

630 *In re* Cates, 289 B.R. 389 (Bankr. E.D. Ark. 2003).

631 Section 1328(a) discharges all debts provided for by the plan, with certain exceptions. Section 1328(b) discharges all debts provided for in the plan except those provided for under section 1322(b)(5) and those that are nondischargeable under section 523(a). It does not mention section 523(b).

632 *In re* Paine, 283 B.R. 33 (B.A.P. 9th Cir. 2002).

633 *See* § 15.4.3.8.6, *supra*.

634 *See In re* Tanski, 195 B.R. 408 (Bankr. E.D. Wis. 1996).

repeatedly raised in this area have been addressed by the Supreme Court.

In *Brown v. Felsen*,[635] the debtor had entered into a judgment by stipulation in state court, and thereafter filed a bankruptcy case. The creditor then alleged that the debt was incurred through fraud, deceit, and malicious conversion, which would make it nondischargeable. The lower courts, following the rule in the Tenth Circuit, held that the state court stipulation and judgment did not mention fraud and that the bankruptcy court could not go beyond that state court record. Therefore, they held the debt was dischargeable.

The Supreme Court reversed, stating that a creditor should not be required to litigate issues of possible fraud in every state court collection suit just to guard against discharge in a possible later bankruptcy. The Court found that this would frustrate Congressional policy which intended the bankruptcy court to handle dischargeability issues, and held that when the debtor adds the new element of bankruptcy to a dispute the creditor should then have an opportunity to respond by raising dischargeability. Thus, the bankruptcy court was instructed to go outside the state court record to hear evidence on the dischargeability issue.

Brown v. Felsen thereby resolved the question of what to do when a fraud claim had been raised, but not actually litigated or resolved, in prior state litigation. Bankruptcy courts have since had little problem following its holding in that situation.[636]

Slightly different than *Brown* is the case in which the creditor pleaded all of the elements that would give rise to nondischargeability and then obtained a default judgment in state court. Does res judicata apply in this situation? The courts have held it does not, based upon *Brown v. Felsen*.[637] Res judicata is inapplicable because the dischargeability cause of action is separate and distinct from any state law cause of action.[638] Moreover, Congress intended the dischargeability cause of action to be decided (for certain types of nondischargeability complaints) only in the bankruptcy courts.[639]

The final possibility is the case in which the factual issues necessary to establish a nondischargeable debt were raised, actually litigated and determined in the state court. There the question is whether collateral estoppel, which normally precludes relitigation of factual issues actually litigated and necessarily decided in a prior case, should be applicable to dischargeability cases. In *Brown*, the Supreme Court expressly left this issue open,[640] and lower courts differed on its resolution.

A unanimous Supreme Court answered the question twelve years later, holding that collateral estoppel (also known as issue preclusion) can be applied to permit creditors, who have successfully reduced fraud claims to judgment, to exempt those claims from discharge.[641] Consequently, collateral estoppel applies when a creditor can produce a record from a nonbankruptcy court proceeding establishing fraud or willful and malicious injury.[642] Similarly, collateral estoppel can apply against

---

635 442 U.S. 127, 99 S. Ct. 2205, 60 L. Ed. 2d 767 (1979).

636 *See, e.g., In re* Daley, 776 F.2d 834 (9th Cir. 1985) (a stipulated dismissal of state court fraud claims did not bar dischargeability action); *In re* DiNoto, 46 B.R. 489 (B.A.P. 9th Cir. 1984) (bankruptcy judge free to make own determination as to dischargeability on stipulated judgment debt); *In re* Ashley, 5 B.R. 262 (Bankr. E.D. Tenn. 1980); *In re* Enterkin, Bankr. L. Rep. (CCH) ¶ 67,506 (Bankr. N.D. Ga. 1980). *See also In re* King, 103 F.3d 17 (5th Cir. 1997) (debtor failed to make record establishing that state court judgment in favor of creditor which failed to award damages on creditor's claim of fraud precluded dischargeability claim based on fraud because there was no evidence that the state court had made findings on the issue of fraud); Greenberg v. Schools, 711 F.2d 152 (11th Cir. 1983) (fact that fraud litigation had been started in state court did not bar dischargeability complaint or extinguish fraud dischargeability claim).

637 *See, e.g., In re* Eskenazi, 6 B.R. 366, 368 (B.A.P. 9th Cir. 1980); *In re* Iannelli, 12 B.R. 561, 563 (Bankr. S.D.N.Y. 1981); Franks v. Thomason, 4 B.R. 814, 821 (Bankr. N.D. Ga. 1980); *In re* McKenna, 4 B.R. 160, 162 (Bankr. N.D. Ill. 1980); *In re* Mallory, 1 B.R. 201 (Bankr. N.D. Ga. 1979). *See also In re* McMillan, 579 F.2d 289 (3d Cir. 1978).

638 *In re* Rahn, 641 F.2d 755 (9th Cir. 1981); *In re* McKenna, 4 B.R. 160 (Bankr. N.D. Ill. 1980); *In re* Richards, 7 B.R. 711 (Bankr. S.D. Fla. 1980). *See also In re* Gibbs, 107 B.R. 492 (Bankr. D.N.J. 1989) (consent judgment entered in district court prior to bankruptcy which included provision that debt would be nondischargeable is not res judicata, because district court lacked subject matter jurisdiction over bankruptcy issue before bankruptcy was filed).

639 *In re* Shuler, 722 F.2d 1253 (5th Cir. 1984); Carey Lumber Co. v. Bell, 615 F.2d 370 (5th Cir. 1980); *In re* Houtman, 568 F.2d 651 (9th Cir. 1978); *In re* Eskenazi, 6 B.R. 366 (B.A.P. 9th Cir. 1980).

640 Brown v. Felsen, 442 U.S. 127, 139 n.10, 99 S. Ct. 2205, 60 L. Ed. 2d 767 (1979).

641 Grogan v. Garner, 498 U.S. 279, 111 S. Ct. 654, 112 L. Ed. 2d 755 (1991). *See also In re* Bugna, 33 F.3d 1054 (9th Cir. 1994) (jury verdict finding fraud given collateral estoppel effect in proceeding to establish fraud as a fiduciary under section 523(a)(4)); *In re* St. Laurent, 991 F.2d 672 (11th Cir. 1993) (state court fraud judgment given collateral estoppel effect in determining dischargeability under section 523(a)(2)(A)); *In re* Miera, 926 F.2d 741 (8th Cir. 1991) (state court judgment for battery given collateral estoppel effect to preserve judgment from discharge as a willful and malicious injury); *In re* Braen, 900 F.2d 621 (3d Cir. 1990) (malicious prosecution judgment under New Jersey law given collateral estoppel effect); Cohen v. Bucci, 905 F.2d 1111 (7th Cir. 1990) (prior finding of fraudulent transfer under 11 U.S.C. § 548 precluded debtor from disputing fraudulent intent under section 727(a)(2)(A)).

Similarly, collateral estoppel may be applied to findings of fraud contained in a final award entered in an arbitration proceeding. *See In re* Khaligh, 338 B.R. 817 (B.A.P. 9th Cir. 2006) (arbitrator's findings satisfied willful and malicious standards), *aff'd*, 506 F.3d 956 (9th Cir. 2007); *In re* O'Neill, 260 B.R. 122 (Bankr. E.D. Tex. 2001).

642 *See, e.g., In re* Porter, 539 F.3d 889 (8th Cir. 2008) (issue preclusion applies to willful and malicious injury claim that had been reduced to civil judgment against debtor/employer in prepetition sexual harassment action); *In re* Nangle, 274 F.3d 481 (8th Cir. 2001) (prior court orders and jury verdict could only be interpreted as having found debtor's acts to be willful and malicious); *In re* Scarborough, 171 F.3d 638 (8th Cir. 1999) (judgment for malicious prosecution necessarily included finding that debtor acted willfully and maliciously); *In re* McNallen, 62 F.3d 619 (4th Cir. 1995); *In re* Lacy, 947 F.2d 1276 (5th Cir. 1991) (debtor's misrepresentations established in state court proceedings); *In re* Tsamasfyros, 940 F.2d 605 (10th Cir. 1991) (debtor's breach of fiduciary duty established in state court proceeding); B.B. v. Bradley (*In re* Bradley), 466 B.R. 582 (B.A.P. 1st Cir. 2012) (no evidence in record that state court judgment was based on willful and malicious injury, as opposed to

a creditor when an issue such as the debtor's malice has been actually litigated and decided in the debtor's favor.[643]

The party seeking collateral estoppel has the burden of making an evidentiary record sufficient to establish that collateral estoppel applies.[644] This would normally require filing the relevant aspects of the nonbankruptcy court record with the bankruptcy court, generally by attaching certified copies to the dischargeability complaint or to a motion for summary judgment. Moreover, for a prior judgment to preclude litigation of dischargeability, all of the elements necessary to the nondischargeability cause of action must have also been necessary to the prior cause of action. If the prior proceeding did not require proof of all of the elements necessary to obtain a judgment that a debt is nondischargeable, the creditor must prove those elements in the court deciding the dischargeability proceeding.[645]

Collateral estoppel usually has no applicability if the fraud issue was not actually litigated, that is, if a default judgment was obtained.[646] But the effect of a prior judgment has generally been held to depend on the law of the state in which it was entered.[647] Thus, some courts have given collateral estoppel

---

recklessness); *In re* Giangrosso, 145 B.R. 319 (B.A.P. 9th Cir. 1992) (state court judgment given collateral estoppel effect even though jury did not state whether it was based on fraud or conversion, because either theory would render debt nondischargeable); *In re* Smith, 128 B.R. 488 (S.D. Fla. 1991) (consent judgment and state court record used as basis for collateral estoppel).

643 Recoveredge Ltd. P'ship v. Pentecost, 44 F.3d 1284 (5th Cir. 1995) (creditor could not assert under section 523(a)(2) that debtor committed fraud after judgment in earlier action that had been entered on all of creditor's claims except fraud claim); *In re* Menna, 16 F.3d 7 (1st Cir. 1994) (broker could not obtain nondischargeability judgment against debtor after broker had been found liable in action against broker for negligently repeating debtor's fraudulent statements; negligence finding necessarily precluded the broker from arguing it had reasonably relied on debtor's statements); *In re* Picard, 133 B.R. 1 (Bankr. D. Me. 1991) (claim of shooting victim found dischargeable when victim had failed to establish malice in connection with his request for punitive damages in state court).

644 *See In re* Pancake, 106 F.3d 1242 (5th Cir. 1997) (collateral estoppel did not apply because creditor failed to present evidence that the state court held a hearing to determine facts upon entering uncontested judgment).

645 *See In re* Barboza, 545 F.3d 702 (9th Cir. 2008) (federal court judgment finding debtor liable for willful copyright infringement never addressed the maliciousness requirement of section 523(a)(6)); *In re* Gupta, 394 F.3d 347 (5th Cir. 2004) (general jury finding of breach of a partner's duties not sufficient to show breach of fiduciary duties under state law); *In re* Spigel, 260 F.3d 27 (1st Cir. 2001) (state court judgment did not encompass all of the elements required for nondischargeability); *In re* Harmon, 250 F.3d 1240 (9th Cir. 2001) (state court judgment did not necessarily decide issue of fraud when it could have been entered based on constructive fraud); *In re* Peklar, 260 F.3d 1035 (9th Cir. 2001) (conversion judgment did not establish that debtor who removed furniture from property in derogation of landlord's rights acted willfully and maliciously); *In re* Markowitz, 190 F.3d 455 (6th Cir. 1999) (legal malpractice judgment did not establish willful and malicious injury); *In re* Miller, 156 F.3d 598 (5th Cir. 1998) (state court judgment against debtor did not have collateral estoppel effect in dischargeability action for embezzlement or willful and malicious injury because state cause of action required fewer elements to be proved; conversely, state court verdict for debtor on issue of fiduciary fraud has collateral estoppel effect on dischargeability claim for fraud as a fiduciary, because elements of dischargeability claim were more demanding than state court claim); *In re* Graham, 973 F.2d 1089 (3d Cir. 1992) (tax court consent decree stating that fraud issue was "uncontested" not given collateral estoppel effect when tax court did not make specific fraud finding); *In re* Lewis, 271 B.R. 877 (B.A.P. 10th Cir. 2002) (state disciplinary proceeding against attorney did not establish all of the elements of fraud); Zohlman v. Zoldan, 226 B.R. 767 (S.D.N.Y. 1998) (prior judgment in state court did not preclude debtor from litigating elements of fiduciary defalcation under section 523); *In re* Howell, 373 B.R. 1 (Bankr. W.D. Ky. 2007) (state court judgment finding debtor liable for "wanton and reckless" conduct as business partner was not preclusive as to "willful and malicious injury" standard in bankruptcy); *In re* Sutherland-Minor, 345 B.R. 348 (Bankr. D. Colo. 2006) (although state court judgment established debtor received overpayment of child care benefits, some elements of fraud, including debtor's intent to deceive, had not been litigated).

646 Sartin v. Macik, 535 F.3d 284 (4th Cir. 2008) (default judgment does not have collateral estoppel effect under North Carolina law); *In re* Palmer, 207 F.3d 566 (9th Cir. 2000) (findings in adverse judgment of Tax Court based on facts deemed admitted because debtor did not respond to allegations did not have preclusive effect); *In re* Pancake, 106 F.3d 1242 (5th Cir. 1997) (summary judgment entered after defendant's answer was stricken did not have preclusive effect under Texas law because there was no showing that a hearing to determine facts had been held); Phillips v. Weissert (*In re* Phillips), 434 B.R. 475 (B.A.P. 6th Cir. 2010) (collateral estoppel effect not given with respect to issue of whether act was willful and malicious, which was not litigated, but was given on issue of damages, because state court held hearing on damages); *In re* Silva, 190 B.R. 889 (B.A.P. 9th Cir. 1995) (default judgment not given collateral estoppel effect when entered after unopposed summary judgment motion); Stokes v. Vierra, 185 B.R. 341 (N.D. Cal. 1995) (under majority rule of Restatement (Second) of Judgments §§ 27–29, default judgment does not meet actually litigated test; default judgment for failing to comply with discovery was not actually litigated); *In re* Pelechronis, 186 B.R. 1 (D. Mass. 1995) (default judgment not given collateral estoppel effect if debtor shows good faith excuse for allowing default to occur); Jones v. Ind. Fin. Co., 180 B.R. 531 (S.D. Ind. 1994); *In re* McArthur, 391 B.R. 453 (Bankr. D. Kan. 2008) (state court default judgment on worthless check claim not given preclusive effect on fraud dischargeability issues); *In re* Trevisan, 300 B.R. 708 (Bankr. E.D. Wis. 2003) (small claims court default judgment under bad check statute not entitled to preclusive effect); *In re* Slominski, 229 B.R. 432 (Bankr. D.N.D. 1998) (default judgment finding of conversion, drafted by plaintiff's counsel, not given collateral estoppel effect). *See also In re* Young, 91 F.3d 1367 (10th Cir. 1996) (state court consent decree did not have preclusive effect on dischargeability determination because parties did not express intent that it precluded litigation of issues in bankruptcy case); *In re* Friedman, 200 B.R. 1 (Bankr. D. Mass. 1996) (debtor's plea of guilty to charge of tax evasion not given preclusive effect when debtor maintained he pleaded guilty to avoid incarceration, but plea could be offered as evidence of evasion); *In re* Prather, 178 B.R. 501 (Bankr. W.D. Wash. 1995) (stipulated fraud judgment not given collateral estoppel effect).

647 *In re* Baylis, 217 F.3d 66 (1st Cir. 2000) (state court judgment did not have preclusive effect on issue of bad faith because under Massachusetts law a finding must have been essential to a judgment to have preclusive effect and alternative grounds for judgment not ruled upon in final appellate review were not essential to judgment); *In re* Tulloch, 373 B.R. 370 (Bankr. D. Mass. 2007) (court predicted

effect to the facts necessary to a default judgment,[648] or to a judgment entered as a discovery sanction.[649] It is not clear whether stipulated facts can be the basis for collateral estoppel. To the extent such facts are incorporated in a judgment, courts may deem them to be the equivalent of litigated findings of fact. However, a bankruptcy court (or other court deciding issues of dischargeability) is not bound by a stipulation made prior to a bankruptcy case that a debt will not be dischargeable in bankruptcy.[650]

If collateral estoppel does not apply, a creditor must litigate the factual and legal issues in the bankruptcy court.[651] And, all courts agree that collateral estoppel can never bar introduction of evidence when any element of the nondischargeability complaint has not been previously decided.[652]

Whether a creditor can bring a claim based on a whole new cause of action that relies on the same facts supporting a previously litigated dischargeable claim is unclear. That claim is probably barred by res judicata when it arises from a common nucleus of operative facts as the actually litigated claims.[653]

A different problem sometimes arises in cases in which the creditor has not yet obtained a judgment on the alleged claim. Obviously, if the claim is not valid in the first place, then the courts need not reach the dischargeability issue. Generally, this means that the court must first decide whether the debt exists,[654] and then determine whether it is dischargeable. While it is clear that bankruptcy courts have jurisdiction to do this,[655] they will occasionally let previously filed proceedings in other courts proceed to their conclusion (at least if they are not removed to bankruptcy court).[656] If the case is tried in the bankruptcy court, then any right to jury trial the debtor has on the issue of liability is preserved and a jury may be demanded in that court.[657]

---

that under Massachusetts law debtor's participation of trial, in which he invoked Fifth Amendment right to decline to testify, was sufficient to bring into effect collateral estoppel on issue of debtor's drunk driving). *See In re* Sweeney, 276 B.R. 186 (B.A.P. 6th Cir. 2002) (Ohio law permits default judgment to be given collateral estoppel effect only if court knows judgment was based on merits rather than a procedural default). *But see In re* Wald, 208 B.R. 516 (Bankr. N.D. Ala. 1997) (preclusive effect of default judgment should be based on federal collateral estoppel law, not state).

648 *In re* Catt, 368 F.3d 789 (7th Cir. 2004) (default judgment had collateral estoppel effect under Indiana law); *In re* Caton, 157 F.3d 1026 (5th Cir. 1998) (default judgment entered after debtor ceased participating in lawsuit found to have collateral estoppel effect under Illinois law); *In re* Calvert, 105 F.3d 315 (6th Cir. 1997) (default judgment given preclusive effect because it would have had that effect under California law); *In re* Nourbakhsh, 67 F.3d 798 (9th Cir. 1995). *See also* Evans v. Ottimo, 469 F.3d 278 (2d Cir. 2006) (applying collateral estoppel to default judgment based on testimony at an inquest); *In re* Cantrell, 329 F.3d 1119 (9th Cir. 2003) (default judgment does not have collateral estoppel effect under California law if defendant was not personally served and had no knowledge of action; however collateral estoppel may apply if party has actual knowledge that default judgment entered and fails to take action to set it aside); *In re* Garner, 56 F.3d 677 (5th Cir. 1995) (defendant answered complaint but failed to appear for trial); *In re* Bursack, 65 F.3d 51 (6th Cir. 1995) (defendant participated in litigation but did not defend at trial); *In re* Griego, 64 F.3d 580 (10th Cir. 1995) (defendant appeared in litigation but alleged that it was not competently represented); *In re* Thompson, 262 B.R. 407 (B.A.P. 6th Cir. 2001) (magistrate's decision without final judgment not entitled to preclusive effect under Ohio law).

649 *In re* Docteroff, 133 F.3d 210 (3d Cir. 1997) (judgment entered as discovery sanction given collateral estoppel effect); *In re* Ansari, 113 F.3d 17 (4th Cir. 1997) (judgment entered as discovery sanction had collateral estoppel effect under Virginia law); *In re* Gober, 100 F.3d 1195 (5th Cir. 1996) (preclusive effect given to judgment entered as discovery sanction); *In re* Daily, 47 F.3d 365 (9th Cir. 1995); *In re* Bush, 62 F.3d 1319 (11th Cir. 1995). *See also* Muegler v. Bening, 413 F.3d 980 (9th Cir. 2005) (debtor could not relitigate issues decided by state court, even though debtor claimed that sanctions imposed by state court had prevented full and fair opportunity to litigate).

650 *In re* Huang, 275 F.3d 1173 (9th Cir. 2002) (debtor not precluded from contesting dischargeability proceeding by prebankruptcy settlement agreement not to do so); *In re* Cole, 226 B.R. 647 (B.A.P. 9th Cir. 1998). *But see* Saler v. Saler, 217 B.R. 166 (E.D. Pa. 1998) (stipulation in earlier bankruptcy case that debt was not dischargeable given preclusive effect in later bankruptcy case); *In re* Siebert, 302 B.R. 265 (Bankr. N.D. Ohio 2003) (consent judgment in prior bankruptcy case bound debtor in later case).

651 *In re* Raynor, 922 F.2d 1146 (4th Cir. 1991); *In re* Turner, 144 B.R. 47 (Bankr. E.D. Tex. 1992); *In re* Sharp, 119 B.R. 779 (Bankr. D.

Idaho 1990). *See also In re* Johns, 158 B.R. 687 (Bankr. N.D. Ohio 1993) (*nolo contendere* plea could not be admitted in support of plaintiff's dischargeability case). *But see* Meyer v. Rigdon, 36 F.3d 1375 (7th Cir. 1994) (different rules apply under section 523(a)(11) because the language of that section makes nondischargeable *any* final judgment arising from debtor's fraud or defalcation while acting as a fiduciary for a financial institution).

652 *See* Massachusetts v. Hale, 618 F.2d 143 (1st Cir. 1980); *In re* Graham, 94 B.R. 386 (Bankr. E.D. Pa. 1987) (questions as to fraud penalty on delinquent taxes not fully litigated, collateral estoppel not applied); *In re* Rambo, 5 Bankr. Ct. Dec. (LRP) 800 (Bankr. M.D. Tenn. 1979).

653 *See In re* Heckert, 272 F.3d 253 (4th Cir. 2001) (creditor could not obtain judgment granting more relief than had already been granted in state court judgment; court could only determine dischargeability of state court judgment). *But see In re* Keller, 106 B.R. 639 (B.A.P. 9th Cir. 1989) (creditor not precluded from arguing that debt was based on willful and malicious conduct when only negligence was pleaded and tried in state court proceeding).

654 Although Grogan v. Garner, 498 U.S. 279, 111 S. Ct. 654, 112 L. Ed. 2d 755 (1991), holds that the preponderance of the evidence standard is applicable to determine nondischargeability in bankruptcy, presumably if a higher evidentiary standard is applicable under state law to establish the debt, for example, a debt for fraud, that higher standard is also applicable to that question if it arises in bankruptcy court.

655 However, there is some doubt whether the bankruptcy court has the power to enter a final judgment on a state law cause of action if not necessary to determine a creditor's claim. *See* Stern v. Marshall, 131 S. Ct. 2594, 180 L. Ed. 2d 475 (2011); § 14.2.1, *supra*.

656 *In re* Harris, 7 B.R. 284 (Bankr. S.D. Fla. 1980). *See also In re* Wardrobe, 559 F.3d 932 (9th Cir. 2009) (relief from stay order only permitted creditor to pursue claims pending at time relief was granted, so judgment on fraud claim added after relief from stay was granted was not valid and did not have preclusive effect on dischargeability issue).

657 28 U.S.C. § 1411.

However, any jury trial may have to be conducted in the district court. *See* § 14.2.7, *supra*.

Finally, res judicata principles apply when a court has made a postpetition determination of whether a debt was discharged by a bankruptcy case. Except for debts made nondischargeable by sections 523(a)(2), (4), or (6), state courts have concurrent jurisdiction to make dischargeability determinations. Once a state court has found a debt to be dischargeable or nondischargeable, that judgment cannot be challenged in the bankruptcy court.[658] Therefore, if a debtor is concerned that the state court may not fully comprehend the nuances of bankruptcy law, the debtor may wish to remove the proceeding to the bankruptcy court before a judgment is entered.[659]

15.5 The Protections of the Discharge

15.5.1 Effects on Discharged Claims

15.5.1.1 Definition of Claim for Discharge Purposes

With respect to the vast majority of debts discharged in bankruptcy cases, the protections of the discharge can only be described as sweeping. They extend to a wide range of debts—all debts that arose before the order for relief[660] in a chapter 7 case, except those made nondischargeable by a specific provision of title 11 or other federal law.

It is not always clear whether an obligation of a debtor is a prepetition claim that is discharged. "Debt" is defined as any liability on a claim[661] and "claim" is very broadly defined to include any right to payment or right to an equitable remedy if such remedy gives rise to a right to payment, whether or not such right is reduced to judgment, liquidated, unliquidated, fixed, contingent, matured, unmatured, disputed, undisputed, legal, equitable, secured, or unsecured.[662] Most courts have found, based on applicable state laws, that breach of a contract to sell real property is a right to equitable performance that gives rise to a right to payment, and therefore creates a dischargeable claim.[663]

The Supreme Court interpreted these definitions in *Ohio v. Kovacs*,[664] giving them the broad meaning intended by Congress. In *Kovacs*, an injunctive order, which as a practical matter could only be complied with through the payment of money, was found to be a dischargeable claim.[665] In other cases, however, there may still be disputes as to what constitutes a debt that may be discharged. For example, advances against retirement accounts, often recouped from an employees' wages may be considered to be use of the employee's own money, so that recoupment of wages can continue.[666] Generally, if a debt is rooted in the debtor's prebankruptcy past, it is discharged.[667] In contrast, condominium assessments which arise postpetition have been held to be claims that may discharged, at least in some circumstances, because they are contingent, unmatured debts at the time of filing.[668] Courts have differed regarding whether the right to enforce a covenant not to compete is a claim that is dischargeable.[669]

Other disputes arise in numerous contexts in which the debtor's prepetition conduct has consequences that are undiscovered, or even undiscoverable, until after a petition is filed or

---

658 *In re* Swate, 99 F.3d 1282 (5th Cir. 1996) (state court determination that support debt was nondischargeable after debtor's first bankruptcy case given res judicata effect in second bankruptcy case); *In re* Garcia, 313 B.R. 307 (B.A.P. 9th Cir. 2004) (default judgment of nondischargeability in earlier bankruptcy case was binding on issue of whether same debt was dischargeable in a later bankruptcy case, assuming facts had not changed); *In re* Whitten, 192 B.R. 10 (Bankr. D. Mass. 1996) (debtor bound by state court determination that condominium fees were not discharged). *See* 11 U.S.C. § 523(b). *See also In re* Goetzman, 91 F.3d 1173 (9th Cir. 1996) (*Rooker-Feldman* doctrine prevents relitigation of questions related to discharge resolved by state court foreclosure judgment).
659 Removal of cases to bankruptcy court is discussed in § 14.4.1, *supra*.
660 The order for relief occurs upon the filing of a voluntary case. 11 U.S.C. § 301. When a case is converted from chapter 7 to chapter 13 or vice-versa, the conversion constitutes a new order for relief under the new chapter. 11 U.S.C. § 348(b).
661 11 U.S.C. § 101(12).
662 11 U.S.C. § 101(5).
663 *In re* Nickels Midway Pier, L.L.C., 341 B.R. 486, 499 (D.N.J. 2006); *In re* Rabin, 361 B.R. 282 (Bankr. S.D. Fla. 2007).

664 469 U.S. 274, 105 S. Ct. 705, 83 L. Ed. 2d 649 (1985).
665 *Id.*
666 *See* New York City Employees Retirement Sys. v. Villarie, 648 F.2d 810 (2d Cir. 1981); *In re* Scott, 142 B.R. 126 (Bankr. E.D. Va. 1992) (debtor who borrowed from his pension plan borrowed only from himself and no "debt" existed).
  These cases should be considered overruled by Johnson v. Home State Bank, 501 U.S. 78, 111 S. Ct. 2150, 115 L. Ed. 2d 66 (1991), because they relied on the principle that the debtor did not have personal liability. *See also In re* B & L Oil Co., 782 F.2d 155 (10th Cir. 1986) (creditor may recoup overpayments made to debtor prior to filing by withholding payment for purchases made from debtor after bankruptcy). *But see In re* Buchferer, 216 B.R. 332 (Bankr. E.D.N.Y. 1997) (pension loan found to be non-recourse secured claim); Soiett v. Veteran's Admin., 92 B.R. 563 (Bankr. D. Me. 1988) (prepetition advanced sick leave and advanced annual leave gave rise to claims against the debtor which were discharged).
667 *See In re* Ybarra, 424 F.3d 1018 (9th Cir. 2005) (when debtor continued to litigate a cause of action after the bankruptcy petition, attorney fees awarded to defendant were not discharged to extent they were incurred postpetition).
668 *In re* Rosteck, 899 F.2d 694 (7th Cir. 1990); *In re* Elias, 98 B.R. 332 (N.D. Ill. 1989) (debtor entitled to award of attorney fees for enforcing discharge injunction); *In re* Wasp, 137 B.R. 71 (Bankr. M.D. Fla. 1992) (action brought by home owners association to collect fees under prepetition agreement which had been unmatured at time of bankruptcy filing constituted attempt to collect debt that was discharged); *In re* Turner, 101 B.R. 751 (Bankr. D. Utah 1989). *But see In re* Raymond, 129 B.R. 354 (Bankr. S.D.N.Y. 1991) (postpetition condominium assessments not discharged); *In re* Ryan, 100 B.R. 411 (Bankr. N.D. Ill. 1989) (in order to obtain discharge of condominium assessments debtor must relinquish ownership and possession of unit within reasonable time after filing).
  Dischargeability of condominium assessments is now specifically governed by 11 U.S.C. § 523(a)(16). *See* § 15.4.3.15, *supra*.
669 *Compare In re* Ward, 194 B.R. 703 (Bankr. D. Mass. 1996) (covenant gives right to dischargeable claim) *with* Kennedy v. Medicap Pharmacies, 267 F.3d 493 (6th Cir. 2001) (covenant not to compete was not a dischargeable claim) *and In re* Hirschorn, 156 B.R. 379 (Bankr. E.D.N.Y. 1993) (covenant is equitable remedy not within the scope of definition of claim).

a case is closed. Many courts have concluded that such circumstances create cognizable claims in bankruptcy.[670] Whether they are discharged, however, may depend on whether the creditor receives appropriate notice of the bankruptcy.[671] There can also be difficult issues regarding when a claim arises during a series of events that ultimately led to a debt.[672]

In chapter 13, the normal discharge covers all "debts," "provided for in the plan," excepting only the debts listed in section 1328(a).[673] Although it is fairly clear that an unsecured debt is "provided for" even if no payment on that debt is possible in the plan,[674] Section 1328(a) also generally discharges all claims that are disallowed in a chapter 13 case.[675] it is still probably a good idea to include at least a nominal amount for all unsecured creditors in every chapter 13 plan. In chapter 13 too, there may be disputes as to what is a "debt."[676] The Supreme Court has ruled that a restitution order in a criminal case is a "debt,"[677] although Congress thereafter made most restitution debts nondischargeable by enacting section 1328(a)(3).

15.5.1.2 Elimination of Personal Liability and Protections for Property

The discharge operates to eliminate the personal liability of the debtor. It does not eliminate valid liens against the debtor's property that have not been avoided, paid, or modified during the bankruptcy.[678] Thus, a mortgage continues to be valid after a chapter 7 case, though the creditor can no longer obtain a deficiency judgment against the debtor if the property fails to satisfy the debt. And, if a chapter 13 plan provides for the creditor to retain a lien in order to comply with 11 U.S.C. § 1325(a)(5), that lien remains valid until the full claim of the creditor is paid or a discharge under section 1328 is granted.

However, as discussed in an earlier chapter,[679] exempt property may not be reached after the case even by most creditors that hold nondischargeable claims. It is protected from any prebankruptcy "debt of the debtor," except debts for domestic support obligations, certain debts owed by parties involved in financial institutions, fraudulently incurred educational debts, and debts secured by a lien not voided in the bankruptcy.[680] As "debt" is defined as liability on a claim[681] and "claim against the debtor" includes claims against property of the debtor,[682] it appears that exempt property is also protected against any claim against property of the debtor except those secured by valid liens. In fact, these protections are granted to debtors even in completed cases that do not result in a discharge, because section 522(c) does not make them contingent upon a discharge being granted.

15.5.1.3 Voiding of Judgments

In both chapter 7 and chapter 13 cases, the discharge automatically voids any judgment obtained at any time to the extent such judgment is a determination of the debtor's personal liability on a discharged debt.[683] Thus, even if a creditor proceeded to judgment after the bankruptcy, that judgment would be void ab initio.[684] Although this means that the debtor

---

670 *See, e.g., In re* Parker, 313 F.3d 1267 (9th Cir. 2002) (legal malpractice claim arose when conduct occurred); Grady v. A.H. Robbins Co., 839 F.2d 198 (4th Cir. 1988) (Dalkon Shield inserted prior to manufacturer's bankruptcy gave rise to a claim subject to the automatic stay, even though no injury was manifested until after the bankruptcy was filed). *See* § 15.4.3.2.4, *supra. See also In re* Remington Rand Corp., 836 F.2d 825 (3d Cir. 1988) (creditor may have bankruptcy claim even though no cause of action has accrued on that claim). *But see* Epstein v. Official Comm. of Unsecured Creditors, 58 F.3d 1573 (11th Cir. 1995) (people who might be injured in accidents involving planes manufactured by debtor, but who had no relationship with debtor at time of case, did not hold claims).

671 *In re* Cent. R.R. Co. of N.J., 950 F.2d 887 (3d Cir. 1991) (claim not manifest until discovered or reasonable person would discover injury). *See* § 15.4.3.3, *supra. See also* City of New York v. N.Y., N.H. & H. R.R. Co., 344 U.S. 293, 73 S. Ct. 299, 97 L. Ed. 333 (1953) (due process requires that creditor be given an opportunity to file a claim prior to discharge).

672 *See In re* Gray, 394 B.R. 900 (Bankr. C.D. Ill. 2008) (debt for demolition costs of abandoned properties did not accrue until the city served unfitness notice on debtor, even if demolition proceedings were inevitable before then).

673 11 U.S.C. § 1328(a); *In re* Nation, 352 B.R. 656 (Bankr. E.D. Tenn. 2006) (when plan provided for payment of secured creditor through plan, underlying debt was discharged even though it was not paid in full before discharge).

Certain other provisions making government related debts nondischargeable may also be applicable. *See* § 15.4.3.12, *supra.*

674 At least one court of appeals has held that even a plan proposing to pay nothing to unsecured creditors has "provided for" those creditors, because they have notice of the possible discharge of their debts. Lawrence Tractor Co. v. Gregory, 705 F.2d 1118 (9th Cir. 1983).

Moreover, the Supreme Court has held that a debt is "provided for" if it is simply referred to or mentioned in a plan. Rake v. Wade, 508 U.S. 464, 473, 113 S. Ct. 2187, 2193, 124 L. Ed. 2d 424, 434–435 (1993).

675 *But see* Fla. Dep't of Revenue v. Diaz (*In re* Diaz), 647 F.3d 1073 (11th Cir. 2011) (discharge of disallowed claims is subject to exceptions to discharge, including exception for domestic support obligations).

676 *See* 11 U.S.C. § 101(12).

See discussion above.

677 Pennsylvania Dep't of Pub. Welfare v. Davenport, 495 U.S. 552, 110 S. Ct. 2126, 109 L. Ed. 2d 588 (1990). *See also In re* Hardenberg, 42 F.3d 986 (6th Cir. 1994) (criminal fines and court costs were debts).

678 Dewsnup v. Timm, 502 U.S. 410, 112 S. Ct. 773, 116 L. Ed. 2d 903 (1992); Chandler Bank of Lyons v. Ray, 804 F.2d 577 (10th Cir. 1986); Fed. Deposit Ins. Corp. v. Davis, 733 F.2d 1083 (4th Cir. 1983). *See* Johnson v. Home State Bank, 501 U.S. 78, 111 S. Ct. 2150, 115 L. Ed. 2d 66 (1991).

679 *See* § 10.5, *supra.*

680 Also excepted are debts found nondischargeable under section 523(a)(4) and (6) when the liability is to an agency regulating a federal depository institution, 11 U.S.C. § 522(c)(3), and certain educational debts incurred through fraud, 11 U.S.C. § 522(c)(4).

681 11 U.S.C. § 101(12).

682 11 U.S.C. § 102(2).

683 11 U.S.C. § 524(a)(1).

684 *In re* Gurrola, 328 B.R. 158 (B.A.P. 8th Cir. 2005) (equitable estoppel did not permit creditor to enforce judgment that was void under section 524(a)(1)); *In re* Fernandez-Lopez, 37 B.R. 664 (B.A.P. 9th Cir. 1984) (permitting collateral attack in bankruptcy

need take no action to protect against such a judgment, the better course would be to seek relief from the judgment as early as possible, perhaps in the bankruptcy court, because even a void judgment may cause various kinds of problems for the debtor until it is stricken. If the debtor does raise the bankruptcy discharge in the state court and is unsuccessful, it may not be possible to relitigate the issue in the bankruptcy court,[685] so it is usually better to immediately seek enforcement of the discharge in the bankruptcy court, which is more likely to be familiar with the applicable law.

The provision voiding judgments is self-effectuating, and no further action is required by the debtor with respect to judgments already entered.[686] Any diligent record search to check the status of judgments should also turn up the debtor's bankruptcy, which voids all judgments against him or her, at least if all of the proceedings occurred in the same locality. Nonetheless, in some areas it is advisable and customary to notify the court of the discharge or otherwise record its existence where a judgment is recorded.[687]

It is also important to note that the voidness of the judgment extends only to the debtor's personal liability to pay the judgment. To the extent that the judgment acts as a lien on property, that lien is not affected by the bankruptcy unless it is paid or avoided.[688] For this reason, counsel must take advantage of the opportunities in bankruptcy to avoid judgment liens[689] or otherwise to address them as secured claims.[690] However, if a lien does not exist at the time of the bankruptcy petition, a judgment for a personal liability that has been discharged cannot be the basis for a later imposition of a lien.[691]

15.5.1.4 The Discharge Injunction

Section 524(a)(2) puts into effect a broad injunction against the commencement or continuation of any action, the employment of process, or any act to collect, recover, or offset any discharged debt as a personal liability of the debtor or from property of the debtor. This section was intended to cover not only legal proceedings, but also any other acts of creditors, such as dunning, harassment, withholding of further credit, selling the discharged debt to another entity, threatening or instituting criminal proceedings, and the like, whether directed at the debtor or at anyone else.[692] For example, including the debt in a new loan, or conditioning a new loan on repayment of a discharged debt, violates the injunction.[693] Similarly, selling a

---

court on judgment obtained in violation of discharge); L.F. Rothschild & Co. v. Angier, 84 B.R. 274 (D. Mass. 1988); *In re* Dabrowski, 257 B.R. 394 (Bankr. S.D.N.Y 2001) (bankruptcy judge not required to give deference to judgment that was void under section 524(a)(1)). *See In re* Levy, 87 B.R. 107 (Bankr. N.D. Cal. 1988) (state court default judgment on claim that debt was not discharged is void when debt was, in actuality, discharged). *But see* Fed. Deposit Ins. Corp. v. Gulf Life Ins. Co., 737 F.2d 1513 (11th Cir. 1984) (bankruptcy defense rejected when it was pleaded but not proved).

685 *In re* Ferren, 203 F.3d 559 (8th Cir. 2000) (*Rooker-Feldman* doctrine prohibited bankruptcy court from reviewing state court's determination that creditor had not violated discharge injunction). *See also In re* Hamilton, 540 F.3d 367 (6th Cir. 2008) (state court judgment that modifies the debtor's discharge is void ab initio, therefore *Rooker-Feldman* doctrine did not preclude bankruptcy court from determining scope of discharge as to subject debt and refusing to enforce state court determination that debtor had waived discharge by failing to assert it as an affirmative defense). *Cf. In re* Pavelich, 229 B.R. 777 (B.A.P. 9th Cir. 1999) (*Rooker-Feldman* doctrine did not prevent enforcement of discharge injunction).

686 *See In re* Rourke, 288 B.R. 50 (Bankr. E.D.N.Y. 2003) (because prepetition judgments were voided by discharge, they could not become liens on property acquired after bankruptcy petition).

687 *See* Johnson v. Cadles of Grassy Meadows, II, L.L.C. (*In re* Johnson), 466 B.R. 67 (Bankr. E.D. Va. 2012) (creditor required by Virginia law to mark judgment as discharged in bankruptcy).

688 For a discussion of leases in chapter 13, see § 12.9, *supra*.

689 *See* § 10.4.2.3, *supra*.

690 *See* Ch. 11, *supra*.

691 *In re* Glover, 2010 Bankr. LEXIS 3165 (Bankr. M.D.N.C. Sept. 14,

2010) (judicial lien could not attach to property formerly held as tenants by entireties upon divorce of debtors because judgment had become void).

692 S. Rep. No. 95-989, at 80 (1978); H.R. Rep. No. 95-595, at 366 (1977). *See In re* Pratt, 462 F.3d 14 (1st Cir. 2006) (refusal to release lien on junked vehicle that lender refused to repossess, unless debtors agreed to pay debt, was objectively coercive); *In re* Simon, 153 F.3d 991 (9th Cir. 1998) (injunction applied to acts to collect from debtor's non-estate property in a foreign country); *In re* Lumb, 401 B.R. 1 (B.A.P. 1st Cir. 2009) (debtor stated claim for violation of discharge injunction in alleging creditor brought bad faith lawsuit against debtor's spouse to coerce payment); *In re* Andrus, 189 B.R. 413 (N.D. Ill. 1995) (creditor found in contempt for erecting signs in his yard intended to pressure debtor into paying discharged debt, notwithstanding creditor's argument that conduct was protected by First Amendment); Van Meter v. Am. State Bank, 89 B.R. 32 (W.D. Ark. 1988) (requiring former debtor to borrow additional sum to repay discharged prior loan violates discharge injunction); *In re* Jarvar, 422 B.R. 242 (Bankr. D. Mont. 2009) (filing counterclaim for discharged debt violated discharge injunction); *In re* Nassoko, 405 B.R. 515 (Bankr. S.D.N.Y. 2009) (selling discharged debt violated discharge injunction); *In re* Faust, 270 B.R. 310 (Bankr. M.D. Ga. 1998) (referring debtor's account to collection agency was willful violation of discharge injunction); *In re* Lafferty, 229 B.R. 707 (Bankr. N.D. Ohio 1998) (creditor violated discharge injunction by selling discharged accounts receivable without noting debtors' discharges in records sent to purchaser); *In re* Walker, 180 B.R. 834 (Bankr. W.D. La. 1995) (creditor violated injunction by not taking steps to terminate automatic deductions from its employee's wages for debt repayment). *See also* Greenwood Trust Co. v. Smith, 212 B.R. 599 (B.A.P. 8th Cir. 1997) (soliciting reaffirmation agreement by direct contact with a represented debtor violates state consumer credit legislation). *But see* Brown v. Pennsylvania State Employees Credit Union, 851 F.2d 81 (3d Cir. 1988) (credit union's letter telling debtor she would be denied future service unless she reaffirmed dischargeable debt does not violate discharge injunction); Canning v. Beneficial Me., Inc. (*In re* Canning), 462 B.R. 258 (B.A.P. 1st Cir. 2011) (creditor did not violate discharge injunction by refusing to either foreclose or release lien on real property); *In re* Garske, 287 B.R. 537 (B.A.P. 9th Cir. 2002) (telephone calls from secured creditor about whether debtor intended to continue payments in a ride-through jurisdiction did not violate discharge injunction).

The debtor in *Brown* might have been more successful in arguing that the credit union was a governmental unit prohibited from discriminating by section 525, an argument she abandoned below. *See In re* Trusko, 212 B.R. 819 (Bankr. D. Md. 1997) (credit union a governmental unit for purposes of a different Code section).

693 *In re* Poindexter, 376 B.R. 732 (Bankr. W.D. Mo. 2007) (requiring

discharged debt, which can only have the purpose of benefiting from the buyer's attempt to collect, is a violation of the injunction.[694] The injunction has been broadly construed to cover acts that are related only indirectly to the discharged debt but that could cause harm to the debtor because of the debt's previous existence.[695] A limited exception, contained in section 524(j) permits mortgage creditors to continue to send normal statements or coupon books,[696] as long as the actions are in the ordinary course of business between the debtor and the creditor, and no attempt is made to collect the debt against the debtor personally.[697]

Violation of the injunction is contempt, punishable by awards of damages and attorney fees.[698] If the violation is asserted against the Internal Revenue Service, the debtor may have to exhaust administrative remedies prior to seeking judicial relief.[699] Attempts to collect a discharged debt may also violate

---

debtor to sign new note and deed of trust for debt that debtor had agreed to voluntarily repay violated discharge injunction and warranted punitive damages); *In re* Watkins, 240 B.R. 668 (Bankr. E.D.N.Y. 1999) (awarding punitive damages and attorney fees against creditor that conditioned post-discharge loan on debtors agreeing to repay discharged debt); *In re* Mickens, 229 B.R. 114 (Bankr. W.D. Va. 1999) (awarding attorney fees against creditor that facilitated and permitted inclusion of discharged debt in new loan); *In re* Smurzynski, 72 B.R. 368 (Bankr. N.D. Ill. 1987) (attempt to have debtor sign papers acknowledging total indebtedness in excess of amount received in current transaction).

694 *In re* Laboy, 2010 WL 427780 (Bankr. D. P.R. Feb. 2, 2010) (selling discharged debt violated discharge injunction); McGlynn v. Credit Store, 234 B.R. 576 (D.R.I. 1999) (discussing claims against credit card issuers for practice of selling discharged debts to purchasers who would attempt to induce debtors to open new accounts that included discharged debts); *In re* Lafferty, 229 B.R. 707 (Bankr. N.D. Ohio 1998) (creditor violated discharge injunction by selling discharged accounts receivable without noting debtors' discharges in records sent to purchaser).

695 *See In re* Warren, 7 B.R. 201 (Bankr. N.D. Ala. 1980) (garnishment proceeding based on discharged debt, when employer had not answered and thus itself became liable for a debt, was enjoined because likely effect of its continuation would be firing of debtor). *But see* Hawxhurst v. Pettibone Corp., 40 F.3d 175 (7th Cir. 1994) (discharge injunction did not prevent creditor from proceeding against debtor's insurers); *In re* Siragusa, 27 F.3d 406 (9th Cir. 1994) (discharge did not prevent state court from modifying alimony order based upon changed circumstances including the discharge of property settlement obligation); *In re* Walker, 927 F.2d 1138 (10th Cir. 1991) (creditor granted relief from discharge injunction to collect debt from state real estate recovery fund; provision allowing recovery fund to suspend debtor's license found unenforceable based on section 525(a)); *In re* Jet Fla. Sys., 883 F.2d 970 (11th Cir. 1989) (creditor granted relief from discharge injunction to obtain judgment in defamation case which would be borne by debtor's insurer and have little or no effect on debtor); BUKE, L.L.C. v. Eastburg (*In re* Eastburg), 447 B.R. 624, 634 (B.A.P. 10th Cir. 2011) (affirming relief from discharge injunction to proceed up to point of trial in state court on debt, with bankruptcy court to rule on dischargeability prior to state court trial); *In re* Swain, 325 B.R. 264 (B.A.P. 8th Cir. 2003) (mere act of delivering to prosecutor debtor's motion to convert chapter 13 case to chapter 7, which instigated criminal bad check prosecution, did not violate discharge injunction).

696 In re Covel, 474 B.R. 702 (Bankr.W.D.Ark. Jul 03, 2012)(section 524(j) reflects Congress approval of the ride-through option for loans secured by the debtor's principal residence); Jones v. Bac Home Loans Servicing, L.P. (In re Jones), 2009 WL 5842122 (Bankr. S.D. Ind. Nov. 25, 2009) (creditor letter and payment coupon fell within the exception).

697 *See* Collins v. Wealthbridge Mortg. Corp. (*In re* Collins), 474 B.R. 317 (Bankr. D. Me. 2012) (letters sent to debtors who no longer owned property violated discharge injunction); *In re* Humphrey, 2012 WL 868730 (Bankr. M.D. Fla. Mar. 14, 2012) (mortgage holder's 38 collection calls to debtor violated discharge injunction); *In re* Wallace, 2011 WL 1335822 (Bankr. M.D. Fla. Apr. 5, 2011) (mortgage servicer's collection calls and demand letters violated injunction); Jones v. Bac Home Loans Servicing, L.P. (*In re* Jones), 2009 WL 5842122 (Bankr. S.D. Ind. Nov. 25, 2009) (creditor letter and payment coupon fell within the exception).

698 *In re* Hardy, 97 F.3d 1384 (11th Cir. 1996) (IRS violation of discharge injunction would be contempt and debtor could seek damages and fees, but damages and fees were limited by section 106(a)); United States v. Kolb, 161 B.R. 30 (N.D. Ill. 1993) (attorney fees awarded against Internal Revenue Service in action to remedy setoff which violated discharge injunction); *In re* DeLaFuente, 430 B.R. 764 (Bankr. S.D. Tex. 2010) (per diem fine and attorney fees imposed upon creditor as contempt sanctions for post-discharge collection efforts contrary to plan that cured default); *In re* McClure, 420 B.R. 655 (Bankr. N.D. Tex. 2009) (actual damages, punitive damages, and attorney fees awarded when bank referred discharged debt for collection and collection agency had inadequate procedures to prevent collection of discharged debts), *modified on reconsideration*, 430 B.R. 358 (Bankr. N.D. Tex. 2010); *In re* Curtis, 322 B.R. 470 (Bankr. D. Mass. 2005) (debtor awarded $15,000 emotional distress damages and $30,000 punitive damages); *In re* Gervin, 337 B.R. 854 (Bankr. W.D. Tex. 2005) (awarding $25,000 emotional distress damages); *In re* Goodfellow, 298 B.R. 358 (Bankr. N.D. Iowa 2003) (letters, telephone calls, and continued reporting of debt to credit reporting agency sanctioned by $5000 actual damages and $5000 punitive damages); *In re* Harbour Oaks Dev. Corp., 228 B.R. 801 (Bankr. M.D. Fla. 1999) (continuation of foreclosure action in violation of discharge constitutes civil contempt); *In re* Driggers, 204 B.R. 70 (Bankr. N.D. Fla. 1996) (debtors awarded fees and costs after credit card company continued to send bills and dunning letters for discharged debt, plus $500 for each future violation); *In re* Thibodaux, 201 B.R. 827 (Bankr. N.D. Ala. 1996) (debtor awarded damages, attorney fees and costs for IRS freezing of postpetition tax refunds to collect discharged taxes); *In re* Lovato, 203 B.R. 747 (Bankr. D. Wyo. 1996) (debtor awarded attorney fees and costs for IRS freezing of postpetition tax refunds to collect discharged taxes); *In re* Kiker, 98 B.R. 103 (Bankr. N.D. Ga. 1988) (IRS' continued efforts to collect discharged tax debt warranted award of attorney fees and costs); *In re* Roush, 88 B.R. 163 (Bankr. S.D. Ohio 1988) (actual damages and attorney fees when creditor did not maintain procedures adequate to prevent collection efforts on discharged debts); Behrens v. Woodhaven Ass'n, 87 B.R. 971 (Bankr. N.D. Ill. 1988) (decision to sue debtors after discharge of prepetition contract obligation constitutes contempt of court); *In re* Barbour, 77 B.R. 530 (Bankr. E.D.N.C. 1987). *See also* § 9.6, *supra* (discussion of contempt sanctions). *But see In re* Arch Wireless, Inc., 534 F.3d 76 (1st Cir. 2008) ("known creditor" of debtor not in contempt of discharge order when debtor had not given the creditor formal notice of bankruptcy filing consistent with due process); *In re* Rivera Torres, 432 F.3d 20 (1st Cir. 2005) (United States had not waived sovereign immunity with respect to emotional distress damages).

699 Kuhl v. United States, 467 F.3d 145 (2d Cir. 2006) (debtor could not recover attorney fees against IRS because she had not exhausted administrative remedies); *In re* Grewe, 4 F.3d 299 (4th Cir. 1993)

other statutes, such as the Fair Debt Collection Practices Act (FDCPA),[700] state debt collection regulations[701] or state tort law.[702] A number of courts have held that continuing to report a discharged debt to credit reporting agencies without noting that it was included in a bankruptcy and is no longer owed has a coercive effect and can violate the discharge injunction, the FDCPA, or the Fair Credit Reporting Act.[703]

However, this section does not bar the enforcement of valid liens against property of the debtor if they have not been paid, modified, or avoided in the bankruptcy.[704] These liens are limited to property acquired before the bankruptcy regardless of any clause that would otherwise cover after-acquired property.[705] For the same reason, the discharge does not affect other property interests of third parties, such as a portion of the debtor's pension awarded to a former spouse in prebankruptcy divorce proceedings.[706] Similarly, many courts have held that the discharge injunction does not bar a suit that is only nomi-

---

(attorney fees could not be awarded under 26 U.S.C. § 7430(a) in successful action against Internal Revenue Service for violation of discharge injunction because debtors had failed to exhaust administrative remedies); Kovacs v. United States Dept. of Justice, 2012 WL 3234818 (E.D. Wis. 2012) (attorney fees awarded against IRS at statutory rate where debtors exhausted administrative remedies).

[700] 15 U.S.C. §§ 1692e(2)(A)(4), (5), (10), 1692k. *See also* Randolph v. IMBS, Inc., 368 F.3d 726 (7th Cir. 2004) (no irreconcilable conflict exists between FDCPA and Bankruptcy Code, so both statutes can be enforced simultaneously); Rios v. Bakalar & Assocs., P.A., 795 F. Supp. 2d 1368 (S.D. Fla. 2011) (same); Molloy v. Primus Auto. Fin. Servs., 247 B.R. 804 (C.D. Cal. 2000) (FDCPA claim not preempted by Bankruptcy Code); *In re* Potes, 336 B.R. 731 (Bankr. E.D. Va. 2005) (creditor's actions may give rise to remedies under both section 524 and the Fair Credit Reporting Act); *In re* Gunter, 334 B.R. 900 (Bankr. S.D. Ohio 2005) (creditor's actions may give rise to remedies under both section 524 and the FDCPA). *But see* Simmons v. Roundup Funding, L.L.C., 622 F.3d 93, 96 (2d Cir. 2010) (no remedy for filing invalid proof of claim under FDCPA because Bankruptcy Code provides remedies). *See generally* National Consumer Law Center, Fair Debt Collection §§ 5.5.4, 5.5.7, 5.5.8, 5.5.13 (7th ed. 2011 and Supp.).

[701] *See also* Sears, Roebuck & Co. v. O'Brien, 178 F.3d 962 (8th Cir. 1999) (Sears violated the Iowa Consumer Credit Code prohibiting creditor contact with a debtor represented by counsel by sending a copy of a letter soliciting a reaffirmation agreement directly to the debtor); Sturm v. Providian Nat'l Bank, 242 B.R. 599 (S.D. W. Va. 1999) (creditor violated West Virginia debt collection statute); *In re* Faust, 270 B.R. 310 (Bankr. M.D. Ga. 1998) (creditor violated discharge injunction; debt collector violated FDCPA, but not discharge injunction). *Cf.* Strasters v. Weinstein & Riley, P.S., 2010 U.S. Dist. LEXIS 134976 (E.D. Wash. Dec. 21, 2010) (FDCPA violation could be asserted with respect to collection of debt where debtor agreed to pay part of debt as settlement of dischargeability proceeding). *See generally* National Consumer Law Center, Fair Debt Collection § 11.2 (7th ed. 2011 and Supp.).

[702] Miele v. Sid Bailey, Inc., 192 B.R. 611 (S.D.N.Y. 1996) (one thousand dollars in damages under FDCPA and $60,000 in damages under state tort law awarded against debt collector who repeatedly attempted to collect discharged debt).

[703] *See* Carriere v. Fed. Credit Union, 2004 WL 1638250 (W.D. La. July 12, 2004); *In re* Wynne, 422 B.R. 763 (Bankr. M.D. Fla. 2010); *In re* Winslow, 391 B.R. 212 (Bankr. D. Me. 2008); *In re* McKenzie-Gilyard, 388 B.R. 474 (Bankr. E.D.N.Y. 2007) (denying motion to dismiss complaint which alleged that creditor violated discharge order by refusing to update debtor's credit report to show zero balance owed after discharge; even though creditor had sold account it still retained a direct financial interest under sale agreement in the debtor making payments on the account); *In re* Russell, 378 B.R. 735 (Bankr. E.D.N.Y. 2007) (complaint stated valid claim of discharge order violation by alleging that refusal to update credit report was indirect attempt to secure "voluntary" payment of debt); *In re* Torres, 367 B.R. 478 (Bankr. S.D.N.Y. 2007) (reporting could violate discharge injunction; erroneous holding that bankruptcy court did not have jurisdiction to consider Fair Credit Reporting Act or defamation claims); *In re* Lohmeyer, 365 B.R. 746 (Bankr. N.D. Ohio 2007); *In re* Burgess, 2007 WL 130818 (Bankr. E.D. Va. Jan. 12, 2007); Norman v. Applied Card Sys., Inc. (*In re* Norman), 2006 WL 2818814 (Bankr. M.D. Ala. Sept. 29, 2006); Smith v. Am. Gen. Fin., Inc. (*In re* Smith), 2005 WL 3447645 (Bankr. N.D. Iowa Dec. 12, 2005); *In re* Goodfellow, 298 B.R. 358 (Bankr. N.D. Iowa 2003) (reporting of discharged debt as ninety days past due violated discharge injunction); *In re* Weinhoeft, 2000 WL 33963628 (Bankr. C.D. Ill. Aug. 1, 2000); *In re* Singley, 233 B.R. 170 (Bankr. S.D. Ga. 1999). *See also In re* Sommersdorf, 139 B.R. 700, 701 (Bankr. S.D. Ohio 1992) (bank's actions in placing notation of debt charge-off on codebtor's credit report violated automatic stay).

[704] *See, e.g., In re* Dinatale, 235 B.R. 569 (Bankr. D. Md. 1999) (IRS did not violate discharge injunction by renewing tax lien or contacting debtor about lien, but did violate injunction by attempting to garnish debtor's wages); *In re* Pendlebury, 94 B.R. 120 (Bankr. E.D. Tenn. 1988). *See In re* Beaumont, 586 F.3d 776 (10th Cir. 2009) (Veterans Administration could recoup overpayment from future benefits); § 15.5.5.4, *infra*.

However, a court may look behind an action that purports to be one to enforce a lien to determine whether the true purpose is to collect the debt as a personal liability. Houghton v. Foremost Fin. Servs., 724 F.2d 112 (10th Cir. 1983); *In re* Braun, 152 B.R. 466 (N.D. Ohio 1993) (creditor's postpetition suit against debtor violated discharge injunction and attorney held in contempt despite creditor's claim that it sought only damages for postpetition conversion of collateral when suit did not seek to obtain property or its value, but rather sought precise amount previously owed on note); *In re* Evans, 289 B.R. 813 (Bankr. E.D. Va. 2002) (replevin action brought after bank notified that car had been sold to satisfy storage lien and which sought damages and attorney fees was attempt to circumvent discharge injunction). *See also In re* Ramirez, 280 B.R. 252 (C.D. Cal. 2002) (when debtor retained automobile by continuing payments without reaffirmation, creditor did not violate discharge by mailing informational billing statements that were not intended to harass or coerce debtor into making involuntary payments).

The mutual setoff of preexisting debts may also still be allowed, because it is considered similar to a security interest under 11 U.S.C. § 553. See § 10.4.2.6.7, *supra*, for a discussion of setoffs.

Likewise, true recoupment by an entity that owes money to the debtor is allowed. *See* Terry v. Standard Ins. Co. (*In re* Terry), 443 B.R. 816 (B.A.P. 8th Cir. 2011) (right to recoupment by private disability insurer must be assessed using equitable considerations); *In re* Madigan, 270 B.R. 749 (B.A.P. 9th Cir. 2001) (long-term disability insurer did not have a right to recoupment because discharged overpayment did not arise from same transaction or occurrence as debtor's current claim); Eissa v. Aetna Life Ins. Co., 2010 WL 4942131 (D. Kan. Nov. 30, 2010) (recoupment by private disability insurer allowed).

[705] 11 U.S.C. § 552.

[706] Bush v. Taylor, 912 F.2d 989 (8th Cir. 1990) (en banc); *In re* Chandler, 805 F.2d 555 (5th Cir. 1986); *In re* Teichman, 774 F.2d 1395 (9th Cir. 1985).

nally against the debtor if that suit really seeks to recover from an insurance company, provided no recovery is sought from the debtor.[707]

For debtors with interests in community property, the discharge is even broader; it covers creditors' prebankruptcy claims against any after-acquired community property that would have been included in the bankruptcy estate, even if only one spouse has filed a bankruptcy petition.[708] The only exceptions to this broad rule are claims excepted from discharge in the debtor spouse's case and claims which would not have been discharged if the non-debtor spouse had filed.[709] Of course, these provisions also mean that all creditors of both spouses should be listed in the schedules to prevent nondischargeability problems under section 523(a)(3), which pertains to unlisted creditors.[710]

Although some courts have held otherwise, the discharge provisions should also give rise to an implied right of action for damages.[711] Unlike claims for contempt, this uniform order need not be enforced by a contempt proceeding in the court that issued it, because debtors are enforcing a statutory right rather than a unique order that requires interpretation by its maker.[712]

In addition, there is ample authority to enforce the discharge injunction by requiring disgorgement and other equitable remedies under 11 U.S.C. § 105(a).[713]

Section 524(i) makes it a violation of the discharge injunction for a creditor to fail to properly credit payments received under a confirmed plan, either during or after the case, if confirmation has not been revoked, the plan is not in default, and the creditor has received payments as required by the plan. This additional protection is discussed in an earlier chapter.[714] All of the enforcement remedies available for violations of the discharge injunction should also be available in such cases.[715]

15.5.2 Reaffirmation and Security Interests Which Survive Bankruptcy

15.5.2.1 Reaffirmation by Agreement Only

Some of the most persistent problems under the previous Bankruptcy Act were those arising through the reaffirmation of debts by consumer debtors. By using a variety of coercive levers, such as threats of repossession, collection activities directed at cosigners, and refusal to lend more money without reaffirmation, creditors routinely lured debtors into giving up the protections of their bankruptcy discharges by making new and binding promises to pay debts that had been discharged.[716]

This problem was recognized by both the Bankruptcy Commission, which proposed a total bar against reaffirmation agreements,[717] and Congress.[718] Although the Code does not completely bar reaffirmation agreements, it does restrict them significantly under the theory that reaffirmation is rarely a wise step for the debtor.[719]

Section 524(c) and (k) sets forth a number of requirements that must be followed before a reaffirmation is binding.[720] First, there must be an agreement between the debtor and the creditor

---

707 *In re* Edgeworth, 993 F.2d 51 (5th Cir. 1993); *In re* Hendrix, 986 F.2d 195 (7th Cir. 1993); Green v. Welsh, 956 F.2d 30 (2d Cir. 1992). *Contra In re* White Motor Credit, 761 F.2d 270 (6th Cir. 1985).
But see also cases cited above.
708 11 U.S.C. § 524(c); *In re* Strickland, 153 B.R. 909 (Bankr. D.N.M. 1993) (discharge acted as injunction against any act to collect discharged debt incurred by non-debtor spouse from present or future New Mexico community property, but did not prevent collection from non-debtor spouse's separate property). *See also In re* Nelson, 308 B.R. 343 (Bankr. E.D. Wis. 2004) (discussing what happens in joint case in which one debtor converts from chapter 13 to chapter 7).
Generally, section 541(a)(2) provides that community property comes into the bankruptcy estate, even if only one spouse files, if it is under the sole, equal, or joint management and control of the debtor, or to the extent it is liable for a claim against the debtor or both a claim against the debtor and a claim against the debtor's spouse. This means all community property in Arizona, Idaho, and New Mexico. *See generally* Henry J. Sommer & Margaret Dee McGarity, Collier Family Law and the Bankruptcy Code Ch. 4 (1992); Pedlar, *Community Property and the Bankruptcy Reform Act of 1978*, 11 St. Mary's L.J. 349 (1979).
709 11 U.S.C. § 524(a)(3), (b); *In re* Rollinson, 322 B.R. 879 (Bankr. D. Ariz. 2005) (wife's embezzlement debt created exception to discharge with respect to community property, but not with respect to husband's separate property).
A determination that an objection to the discharge of a non-debtor spouse would have been sustained must be sought by the creditor within the time limits for objecting to the debtor spouse's discharge, unless the non-debtor spouse has previously been denied a discharge within six years. 11 U.S.C. § 524(a)(3), (b). *See In re* Smith, 140 B.R. 904 (Bankr. D.N.M. 1992) (if wrongdoing spouse is in chapter 13 at time of other spouse's chapter 7 case, creditor may only proceed against community property after dismissal of chapter 13 case if it has timely sought a determination of dischargeability as to wrongdoing spouse in innocent spouse's chapter 7 case).
710 *See* § 15.5.5.7, *infra*.
711 *See* § 15.5.5.7, *infra*.
712 *But see* Alderwoods Group, Inc. v. Garcia, 682 F.3d 958 (11th Cir.

Fla. 2012) (discharge injunction must be enforced in court that entered discharge).
713 *In re* Mickens, 229 B.R. 114 (Bankr. W.D. Va. 1999); *In re* Vazquez, 221 B.R. 222 (Bankr. N.D. Ill. 1998) (actual and punitive damages awarded pursuant to section 105). *See* § 15.5.5.7, *infra*. *But see* Walls v. Wells Fargo Bank, 276 F.3d 502 (9th Cir. 2002).
714 *See* Ch. 13, *supra*.
715 *See* Nibbelink v. Wells Fargo Bank (*In re* Nibbelink), 403 B.R. 113 (Bankr. M.D. Fla. 2009) (awarding punitive damages and attorney fees).
716 *See* Butler Consumer Discount Co. v. Cain, 50 B.R. 388 (W.D. Pa. 1985) (new loan after bankruptcy which included prior indebtedness was a reaffirmation); *In re* Beres, 2009 WL 2916911 (Bankr. W.D. Tex. July 30, 2009) (when the obligation was an *in rem* mortgage with no personal liability, there could be no reaffirmation because no debt was discharged); § 15.5.1, *supra*.
717 Report of the Comm'n on the Bankr. Laws of the United States, H.R. Doc. No. 93-137, pt. I at 177, pt. II at 130 (1973).
718 H.R. Rep. No. 95-595, at 162–164 (1977).
719 See discussion of advisability of reaffirmation in Chapter 8, *supra*.
720 *See In re* Esposito, 154 B.R. 1011 (Bankr. N.D. Ga. 1993) (creditor violated stay by repossessing property in reliance on reaffirmation agreement negotiated by *pro se* debtor that was not approved by the court).

which is enforceable under applicable nonbankruptcy law.[721] That agreement in most cases is essentially a contract to reaffirm, but the requirements of the Code also apply to other postpetition contracts which effectively constitute a renewed obligation to pay a prepetition debt.[722] Without an agreement there can be no reaffirmation; in such a case neither the debtor nor the creditor may seek court approval of reaffirmation.[723] The agreement may alter the terms of the original contract, either in favor of the debtor or the creditor.[724] Only the debtor may actually apply to the court for approval of the reaffirmation, when that is still necessary.[725]

The reaffirmation agreement must be made prior to the discharge. By the terms of 11 U.S.C. § 524(c), a reaffirmation agreement is not enforceable unless entered into before the discharge[726] and unless the court at the discharge hearing, or the attorney who negotiated the agreement for the debtor,[727] has informed the debtor of the right not to enter into the agreement and of the legal effects of the agreement and any default thereunder.[728] Once the discharge has been granted, no reaffirmation is possible,[729] and the discharge may not be revoked to provide for one.[730]

---

[721] *See* Salyersville Nat'l Bank v. Bailey (*In re* Bailey), 664 F.3d 1026 (6th Cir. 2011) (reaffirmation agreement voided under Kentucky law because it was based on mutual mistake regarding whether debt was secured).

[722] *In re* Lopez, 345 F.3d 701 (9th Cir. 2002) ("asset retention agreement" which required debtors to pay discharged debt was void reaffirmation); Bennett v. Renwick, 298 F.3d 1059 (9th Cir. 2002) (state court settlement agreement requiring repayment of discharged debt was unenforceable reaffirmation regardless of whether new consideration had been provided); *In re* Getzoff, 180 B.R. 572 (B.A.P. 9th Cir. 1995) (new guaranty of corporate debt by principal who had obtained discharge after prior guaranty was invalid reaffirmation); *In re* Zarro, 268 B.R. 715 (Bankr. S.D.N.Y. 2001) (postpetition settlement agreement that included reaffirmation of debt was unenforceable and judgment based on agreement was void); *In re* Smith, 224 B.R. 388 (Bankr. N.D. Ill. 1998) (addition of discharged debt after discharge to new loan debt constituted invalid reaffirmation); *In re* Artzt, 145 B.R. 866 (Bankr. E.D. Tex. 1992) (absent consideration, note renewing dischargeable debt after bankruptcy filed is an invalid reaffirmation); Schneider v. Curry, 584 So. 2d 86 (Fla. Dist. Ct. App. 1991) (postpetition contract in which only consideration is debtor's prepetition debt found to be invalid reaffirmation). *But see* DuBois v. Ford Motor Credit Co., 276 F.3d 1019 (8th Cir. 2002) (creditor did not violate discharge injunction when debtors voluntarily entered into and paid new car lease that included excess usage charges from previous lease that had been discharged without any coercion by creditor; court did not address question of whether new lease was a void reaffirmation).

[723] *In re* Jamo, 283 F.3d 392 (1st Cir. 2002) (creditor cannot be required to agree to reaffirmation on terms to which it does not agree); *In re* Turner, 156 F.3d 713 (7th Cir. 1998) (reaffirmation agreements not valid without creditors' signatures); *In re* Casenove, 306 B.R. 367 (Bankr. M.D. Fla. 2004) (creditor cannot be forced to accept reaffirmation of only portion of secured debt covered by cross-collateralization clause); *In re* Vinson, 5 B.R. 32 (Bankr. N.D. Ga. 1980) (debtor may not unilaterally reaffirm); *In re* Breckenridge, 3 B.R. 141 (Bankr. N.D. Ohio 1980) (there is no agreement to approve if debtors change their minds prior to discharge hearing).

[724] *In re* Schott, 282 B.R. 1 (B.A.P. 10th Cir. 2002).

[725] *In re* Carlos, 215 B.R. 52 (Bankr. C.D. Cal. 1997); *In re* Newsome, 3 B.R. 626 (Bankr. W.D. Va. 1980). *See also In re* Parker, 193 B.R. 525 (B.A.P. 9th Cir. 1996) (creditor did not have standing to appeal bankruptcy court's disapproval of reaffirmation agreement), *aff'd*, 139 F.3d 668 (9th Cir. 1998).

[726] 11 U.S.C. § 524(c)(1); *In re* Giglio, 428 B.R. 397 (Bankr. N.D. Ohio 2009) (disapproving agreement that was not signed by creditor until after discharge); *In re* Herrera, 380 B.R. 446 (Bankr. W.D. Tex. 2007) (agreement made after discharge invalid despite order setting aside discharge for purpose of filing reaffirmation agreement); *In re* Collins, 243 B.R. 217 (Bankr. D. Conn. 2000) (agreement not made until signed by debtor); *In re* Whitmer, 142 B.R. 811 (Bankr. S.D. Ohio 1992); *In re* Eccleston, 70 B.R. 210 (Bankr. N.D.N.Y. 1986).

[727] The 1994 amendments to the Code eliminated the requirement of a discharge hearing in cases in which an attorney negotiated a reaffirmation agreement on behalf of the debtor, provided the attorney certifies that the attorney fully advised the debtor of the legal effect and consequences of reaffirmation and of a default under the agreement. 11 U.S.C. § 524(c)(3)(C).

[728] 11 U.S.C. § 524(c)(5); *In re* Roth, 43 B.R. 484 (N.D. Ill. 1984). *See* Arnhold v. Kyrus, 851 F.2d 738 (4th Cir. 1988) (absence of required admonishments by court invalidates reaffirmation); *In re* Pitts, 462 B.R. 844 (Bankr. M.D. Fla. 2012) (court admonishments at discharge hearing when agreement not signed by attorney were required for agreement's validity even if debt secured by real property); *In re* Johnson, 148 B.R. 532 (Bankr. N.D. Ill. 1992) (reaffirmation invalid when debtor did not attend discharge hearing and agreement did not advise debtor of rescission rights); *In re* Fisher, 113 B.R. 714 (Bankr. N.D. Okla. 1990) (debtor's failure to attend reaffirmation hearing rendered reaffirmation agreement for debt secured by car unenforceable; therefore, debt was discharged and monies collected by creditor had to be turned over to trustee in subsequent chapter 13 case); *In re* Saeger, 119 B.R. 184 (Bankr. D. Minn. 1990) (reaffirmation agreement not enforceable when no discharge hearing was requested or held); *In re* Churchill, 89 B.R. 878 (Bankr. D. Colo. 1988) (reaffirmation rescindable until after hearing at which court advises debtor of consequences). *But see In re* Sweet, 954 F.2d 610 (10th Cir. 1992) (reaffirmation agreement valid despite debtors' failure to attend reaffirmation hearing when debtors did not claim they did not know about hearing and hearing occurred more than sixty days after agreement was signed, so that debtors no longer had right to rescind agreement and thus hearing could not have affected their obligations); *In re* Richardson, 102 B.R. 254 (Bankr. M.D. Fla. 1989) (although no hearing was held, the debtor is estopped from denying validity of reaffirmation agreement when creditor relied on agreement by not filing timely complaint to determine dischargeability).

[729] *In re* Martin, 474 B.R. 789 (B.A.P. 6th Cir. 2012) (voluntary payments after bankruptcy did not give creditor right to enforce debt); *In re* Brown, 220 B.R. 101 (Bankr. C.D. Cal. 1998) (debtor's postbankruptcy agreement to pay creditor in return for forbearance in repossessing necklace was prohibited reaffirmation); *In re* Arnold, 206 B.R. 560 (Bankr. N.D. Ala. 1997) (debtor's postbankruptcy agreement to pay debt in exchange for promise not to garnish wife's wages was not enforceable even though there was consideration for agreement); *In re* Coots, 4 B.R. 281 (Bankr. S.D. Ohio 1980).

[730] *In re* Bellano, 456 B.R. 220 (Bankr. E.D. Pa. 2011) (refusing to reopen case to file reaffirmation involving mortgage modification, based in part on HAMP directive that debtors who file bankruptcy were intended to be eligible for HAMP without being required to reaffirm their mortgage debts); *In re* Golladay, 391 B.R. 417 (Bankr. C.D. Ill. 2008) (discharge orders will not be set aside to allow parties to enter into untimely reaffirmation agreements); *In re* McQuality, 5 B.R. 302 (Bankr. S.D. Ohio 1980). *But see In re* Eccleston, 70 B.R. 210 (Bankr. N.D.N.Y. 1986) (discharge would be vacated only upon showing of explanation for failure to obtain

15.5.2.2 Disclosure Requirements

Several other requirements for an enforceable reaffirmation agreement were added by later amendments. The agreement must contain the disclosures described in section 524(k).[731] The disclosures must be clear and conspicuous.[732] According to section 524(k)(1), the disclosures consist of a combination of the disclosure statement described in section 524(k)(3), completed as required by that paragraph, and the agreement, statement, declaration, motion, and order described in section 524(k)(4) to (k)(8). Unless all of these documents conform to statutory requirements, the disclosures required by section 524(c)(2) have not been given. Section 524(k)(1) also provides that these are the only disclosures that are required.[733]

The disclosures required by section 524(k)(3), designated as "Part A," are in some ways similar to those required for consumer credit transactions under the Truth in Lending Act, and incorporate certain concepts from that law. They require the use of particular terms and phrases, including "Amount Reaffirmed" and "Annual Percentage Rate," as well as standard statements.[734]

However, creditors are given latitude in how the disclosures are made, limiting the amount of useful information provided to debtors and making it difficult to prove inaccuracies. For example, the amount reaffirmed is described as including the total of any fees and costs that have accrued prior to the disclosure, but the creditor is not compelled to itemize the separate charges.[735] A repayment schedule may be provided "at the election of the creditor," and if provided the creditor need only describe the repayment obligation with "reasonable specificity to the extent then known by the disclosing party."[736] Despite the well-known abuses by department store creditors in coercing reaffirmations based on inflated values for secured household goods, creditors are not required to disclose the current value of the property securing the debt.[737] The statute only requires a listing of the items and "their original purchase price" for a purchase-money security interest, or the "original amount of the loan" for a non-purchase money security interest.[738]

The required disclosures are far more lengthy and confusing than the form promulgated by the Administrative Office of the United States Courts that was previously used in many courts. It is likely that many debtors will not understand them, and it is also likely that many law firms will be hired to draft forms that comply with these complicated new provisions. There is also a potential for much litigation, similar to that under the Truth in Lending Act, if creditors do not strictly comply with the disclosure requirements.

15.5.2.3 Form of the Reaffirmation Agreement

The 2005 Act sets out requirements as to the form of a reaffirmation agreement, designated as "Part B," as dictated by section 524(k)(4). The agreement must include a brief description of the credit agreement, a task that may not be easy in light of the complicated agreements utilized by consumer creditors. The creditor and the debtor(s) must both sign and date the agreement.

The agreement must then be filed with the court,[739] along with all of the attachments required by section 524(k), including a form of order approving the agreement and, if the debtor is not represented by an attorney with respect to the agreement,

---

approval of reaffirmation prior to discharge); *In re* Solomon, 15 B.R. 105 (Bankr. E.D. Pa. 1981) (in light of special equities raised, discharge vacated to allow reaffirmation three days after discharge hearing). See generally § 15.3, *supra*.

731 11 U.S.C. § 524(c)(2).

Under prior provisions requiring different disclosures, courts found reaffirmation agreements invalid when the disclosures were not properly given. *See In re* Minor, 115 B.R. 690 (D. Colo. 1990) (when debtor agreed to settle state court action by waiving dischargeability of debt, waiver not a valid reaffirmation when Code's detailed requirements were not met); *In re* Smyth, 277 B.R. 353 (Bankr. N.D. Ohio 2001) (notice of right to rescind inadequate because it did not provide sufficient information on how to rescind); *In re* Roberts, 154 B.R. 967 (Bankr. D. Neb. 1993) (reaffirmation agreement not containing conspicuous language notifying debtors of right to rescind was not valid). *But see In re* Bassett, 285 F.3d 882 (9th Cir. 2002).

The notice to the debtor of the right to rescind cannot be qualified by language in the agreement which purports to give the creditor the right to keep any payments made pursuant to the agreement before rescission. *In re* Wiley, 224 B.R. 58 (Bankr. N.D. Ill. 1998), *vacated on other grounds*, 237 B.R. 677 (Bankr. N.D. Ill. 1999). A reaffirmation agreement containing such language should be found invalid as not having properly given notice of the right to rescind.

Similarly, a reaffirmation agreement on one debt cannot provide that rescission of the agreement rescinds agreements on other debts. *In re* Ireland, 241 B.R. 539 (Bankr. E.D. Mich. 1999).

732 11 U.S.C. § 524(k)(2). *See In re* Noble, 182 B.R. 854 (Bankr. W.D. Wash. 1995) (statement in same type face, size and format as bulk of agreement was not clear and conspicuous).

733 Prior local rules and standing court orders concerning reaffirmation agreements may no longer be enforceable to the extent that they require disclosures that are inconsistent with new section 524(k). *See, e.g., In re* Kamps, 217 B.R. 836 (Bankr. C.D. Cal. 1998); *In re* Bruzzese, 214 B.R. 444 (Bankr. E.D.N.Y. 1997).

Two different reaffirmation agreement forms promulgated by the Administrative Office of United States Courts are reprinted in Appendix E.10, *infra*. The use of these forms should only be considered to comply with the statute they are is properly completed by the creditor.

734 The "Amount Reaffirmed" and "Annual Percentage Rate" must be disclosed more conspicuously than other terms. 11 U.S.C. § 524(k)(2). Several of the disclosures, such as the "Annual Percentage Rate," seem to assume that the terms of the underlying credit contract will not be renegotiated and will remain in effect upon reaffirmation.

735 11 U.S.C. § 524(k)(3)(C).

736 11 U.S.C. § 524(k)(3)(H).

737 However, Official Form 27, the Reaffirmation Agreement Cover Sheet discussed below, remedies this omission by requiring the value of collateral to be stated. In addition, one of the reaffirmation agreement forms promulgated by the Administrative Office of United States Courts, reprinted in Appendix E.10, *infra*, provides for disclosure of the current market value of collateral.

738 11 U.S.C. § 524(k)(3)(G).

739 11 U.S.C. § 524(c)(3). *See In re* Davis, 273 B.R. 152 (Bankr. S.D. Ohio 2001) (reopening case for filing of agreement because agreement need not be filed before discharge).

a motion for court approval of the agreement. Under Bankruptcy Rule 4008, the debtor must also file a reaffirmation agreement cover sheet conforming to Official Form 27, which contains additional information, including the value of any collateral, a statement of the total income and expense amounts stated in schedules I and J, and an explanation of any difference between those amounts and the amounts in the statement filed under section 524(k).[740] The court can then review this information in deciding whether to approve the agreement in cases in which the court has the power to disapprove the reaffirmation.[741] As with other requirements for the form of the agreement, the failure to comply with the requirement of filing the cover sheet should render the agreement invalid.[742]

15.5.2.4 Protective Provisions

Finally, in all debt reaffirmations, there are various protective requirements, depending upon the circumstances. In every reaffirmation the debtor must sign a form statement, designated "Part D." Except when the debtor is represented by an attorney and is reaffirming a debt to a credit union, this form requires the debtor to compute whether the debtor has sufficient disposable income to make the payments required under the reaffirmation agreement and, if not, to explain how the debtor can afford to make the payments and identify additional sources of income the debtor will use to make the payments.[743]

If an attorney has negotiated the reaffirmation, the agreement filed with the court must be accompanied by the attorney's affidavit, in the form dictated by section 524(k)(5), that the reaffirmation represents a fully informed and voluntary agreement by the debtor and will not impose an undue hardship on the debtor or the debtor's dependents.[744] The affidavit must also affirm that the attorney advised the debtor of the legal effect and consequences of the agreement and of any default under the agreement.[745] In addition, unless the creditor is a credit union, if the debtor's budget as reflected in Part D does not demonstrate adequate income to make the payments required by the reaffirmation agreement, the declaration must also state that in the attorney's opinion the debtor is able to make those payments.[746]

Because a creditor seeking a reaffirmation is attempting to collect a debt, compliance with state and federal debt collection regulations is also required.[747]

If the agreement was not negotiated by an attorney, the court must hold a discharge and reaffirmation hearing. The court must also, after informing the debtor of the legal effect and consequences of reaffirmation, decide whether to approve the agreement as not imposing an undue hardship on the debtor or the debtor's dependents and as being in the debtor's best interests.[748] The only exception in which such approval is not required is for reaffirmations of consumer debts secured by real property, to the extent they are secured by that property.[749] It is not clear whether this exception applies in cases in which the agreement is negotiated by an attorney, because the exception appears only in the subsection pertaining to reaffirmations not negotiated by an attorney. The language of section 524(c)(3) suggests that, even if the debt is secured by real property, an attorney for a debtor cannot negotiate a reaffirmation that imposes an undue hardship on the debtor or a dependent of the debtor.

In addition, the court may disapprove certain reaffirmation agreements, even in cases in which the debtor is represented by an attorney or the debt is secured by real property, although a hearing is not required in every case.[750] Except if the creditor is a credit union,[751] if the debtor's declaration shows a budget insufficient to make payments under the agreement, a presumption arises that the reaffirmation agreement is an undue hardship and the court is required to review the matter.

The debtor may submit a written explanation of how additional funds will be obtained to make the payments in order to rebut the presumption. If the presumption is not rebutted, the court "may" disapprove the agreement after notice to the debtor and creditor and a hearing concluded before the discharge.[752]

---

740 Official Form 27 is reprinted in Appx. D, *infra*.
　　The necessary documents, once signed by the debtor and, if applicable, debtor's counsel, may be filed by the debtor or the creditor. *In re* Boliaux, 422 B.R. 125 (Bankr. N.D. Ill. 2010).
741 Fed. R. Bankr. P. 4008 advisory committee's note (2009).
742 First State Bank v. Zahos (*In re* Zahos), 2012 WL 2384372 (Bankr. C.D. Ill. June 25, 2012).
743 11 U.S.C. § 524(k)(6).
744 11 U.S.C. § 524(c)(3), (k)(5). *See In re* Adams, 229 B.R. 312 (Bankr. S.D.N.Y. 1999) (unsworn declaration was not a declaration and therefore reaffirmation was void).
745 11 U.S.C. § 524(c)(3), (k)(5).
746 11 U.S.C. § 524(k)(5).
747 *See* Sears, Roebuck & Co. v. O'Brien, 178 F.3d 962 (8th Cir. 1999);

　　Greenwood Trust Co. v. Smith, 212 B.R. 599 (B.A.P. 8th Cir. 1997) (soliciting reaffirmation agreement by direct contact with a represented debtor violates state debt collection legislation). *See also In re* Machnic, 271 B.R. 789 (Bankr. S.D. W. Va. 2002) (credit card issuer violated state consumer protection law by asking in dischargeability proceeding for costs and attorney fees that were not owed under state law). *See generally* National Consumer Law Center, Fair Debt Collection (7th ed. 2011 and Supp.).
748 11 U.S.C. § 524(c)(6). *See In re* Brown, 95 B.R. 35 (Bankr. E.D. Va. 1989) (approval of reaffirmation agreement denied because creditor had threatened conduct which would violate the Code's antidiscrimination provision).
　　When the debtor is represented by counsel, the court is less likely to interject itself into these issues. *See In re* Pendlebury, 94 B.R. 120 (Bankr. E.D. Tenn. 1988). The undue hardship and best interests tests are discussed further in § 15.5.2.6, *infra*.
749 It is unclear whether a creditor has a security interest in real property for this purpose if prior liens equal or exceed the value of the property so the creditor is in reality totally undersecured.
750 11 U.S.C. § 524(m)(1).
751 11 U.S.C. § 524(m)(2). However, this exception does not apply when the court is required to approve the agreement under section 524(c)(6), because there is no certification by an attorney who negotiated the agreement that it would not impose undue hardship. *In re* Cooper, 2012 WL 566070 (Bankr. D. Kan. Feb. 21, 2012).
752 11 U.S.C. § 524(m)(1). *See In re* Morton, 410 B.R. 556 (B.A.P. 6th Cir. 2009) (court may not disapprove an attorney-certified reaffirmation agreement unless there is a presumption of undue hardship).

However the standard for approval of a reaffirmation agreement under section 524(c)(6)(A) remains unchanged.[753] The agreement must not impose an undue hardship on the debtor and must be in the debtor's best interest, which suggests that the court should never approve an agreement when the presumption of undue hardship has not been satisfactorily rebutted.[754]

In order to fully review all agreements in which the presumption arises, courts may have to delay the discharge in many cases. Bankruptcy Rule 4004(c)(1)(J) provides that the discharge shall be delayed if a presumption of undue hardship has arisen. And Bankruptcy Rule 4008 requires the debtor to file a statement of the total income and expense amounts stated in schedules I and J, as well as an explanation of any difference between those amounts and the amounts in the statement filed under section 524(k). Nothing prevents a court from requiring additional information in order to evaluate whether an agreement should be approved. But if the creditor is a credit union, court review is required only if the debtor is not represented by an attorney.[755]

To be enforceable, the agreement must not have been rescinded during the time permitted.[756]

15.5.2.5 Abusive Creditor Reaffirmation Practices

In a number of major cases, courts have found that many creditors had longstanding practices of obtaining reaffirmation agreements without filing them with the court.[757] This practice rendered the reaffirmations invalid because the agreements failed to meet the requirements of section 524(c)(3).[758] Collection based on such agreements violates the discharge injunction.[759] Other statutory remedies may be available as well.[760]

Class actions against retailers including Sears, May Department Stores, Montgomery Ward, and the Federated Department Stores were settled so that money paid on illegal reaffirmation was repaid to consumers with interest.[761] Some of the settlements also provided for compensatory or punitive damages.

Abusive reaffirmation procedures remain common. These practices undermine the fresh start and should be resisted whenever possible.[762] Some retailers have responded to court hostility to their overly aggressive reaffirmation tactics, by instead insisting that consumers redeem personal property that is subject to a security interest. As the personal property involved would have little or no value if it were repossessed, the redemption may be an unwise and expensive means for a debtor to retain the property. Creditors that encourage debtors to make this unwise choice now use the redemption process to avoid the procedural requirements and court oversight necessary to obtain a valid reaffirmation.[763] Several courts have asserted authority to review and reject redemption agreements that are unfair to a debtor.[764] Other creditors have attempted to condition reaffirmation of a secured debt on reaffirmation of an unrelated unsecured debt. Such coercive tactics may go beyond the consensual negotiation of a reaffirmation agreement permitted by the automatic stay.[765]

---

753 See § 15.5.2.6, infra.

754 See, e.g., In re Stillwell. 348 B.R. 578 (Bankr. N.D. Okla. 2006) (agreement disapproved speculation about possible overtime pay or additional employment did not overcome presumption); In re Laynas, 345 B.R. 505 (Bankr. E.D. Pa. 2006) (agreement disapproved because no evidence introduced to rebut presumption).

755 11 U.S.C. § 524(m)(2).

756 11 U.S.C. § 524(c)(4). See In re Polkus, 2008 WL 5099967 (Bankr. D. Ariz. Dec. 3, 2008) (rescission need not be in writing unless creditor has complied with section 342 requirements for written notice); In re McAuliffe, 180 B.R. 336 (Bankr. D. Me. 1995) (debtor who rescinded reaffirmation entitled to return of all payments to the mortgage company made under the agreement, but had to pay compensation for continued use of residence during period reaffirmation was in effect); In re Davis, 106 B.R. 701 (Bankr. S.D. Ala. 1989) (failure to give creditor notice of intent to rescind reaffirmation agreement within sixty days precluded such rescission). But see In re Booth, 242 B.R. 912 (B.A.P. 6th Cir. 2000) (erroneously holding that, although oral rescission normally would be sufficient under section 524(c), agreement valid even though it contained requirement that rescission be in writing).

757 See In re Latanowich, 207 B.R. 326, 336 (Bankr. D. Mass. 1997).

758 In re Gardner, 57 B.R. 609 (Bankr. D. Me. 1986) ("An agreement to reaffirm an otherwise dischargeable debt will be binding only if it is made in compliance with section 524(c) and (d)."); In re Hovestadt, 193 B.R. 382, 386 (Bankr. D. Mass. 1996). Accord In re Daily, 47 F.3d 365, 367 (9th Cir. 1995); In re Getzoff, 180 B.R. 572, 574, 575 (B.A.P. 9th Cir. 1995); In re Bowling, 116 B.R. 659, 664 (Bankr. S.D. Ind. 1990).

759 In re Latanowich, 207 B.R. 326, 336 (Bankr. D. Mass. 1997); In re Vazquez, 221 B.R. 222 (Bankr. N.D. Ill. 1998) (creditor and attorney for creditor sanctioned for collection actions on debt for which reaffirmation agreement never filed); In re Bowling, 116 B.R. 659, 664 (Bankr. S.D. Ind. 1990).

760 See § 15.5.1.4, supra.
 Unfair trade practice laws are also implicated. See National Consumer Law Center, Unfair and Deceptive Acts and Practices (7th ed. 2008 and Supp.).

761 See Mohl, Sears Admits Missteps in Collecting on Debts, The Boston Globe, Apr. 10, 1997, at A1.
 Several cases against major creditors are still pending based on appellate proceedings (in the First, Sixth, Seventh and Ninth Circuits) concerning the availability of a class-wide relief and private remedies under sections 524 and 105. See § 15.5.5.7, infra.

762 See generally Abusive Creditor Reaffirmation Practices Require Strong Response, 15 NCLC REPORTS Bankruptcy and Foreclosures Ed. 17 (Mar./Apr. 1997).

763 11 U.S.C. § 524(c), (d).

764 Fed. R. Bankr. P. 6008; In re White, 231 B.R. 551 (Bankr. D. Vt. 1999) (upholding general order that required filing of redemption agreements); In re Lopez, 224 B.R. 439 (Bankr. C.D. Cal. 1998). But see Arruda v. Sears, Roebuck & Co., 310 F.3d 13 (1st Cir. 2002) (debtor's post-discharge agreement to pay "value" of collateral in exchange for release of lien, which on its face does not impose personal liability, if not a reaffirmation, at least when debtors agreed to value of property and there was no allegation of harassment or coercion); In re Spivey, 265 B.R. 357 (E.D.N.Y. 2001).

765 But see In re Jamo, 283 F.3d 392 (1st Cir. 2002) (creditors permitted to refuse reaffirmation not made on their terms, but specific threats in connection with reaffirmation negotiations could be overly coercive), rev'g 262 B.R. 159 (B.A.P. 1st Cir. 2001).
 The Jamo decision has been undercut by the 2005 amendments to section 524. The form reaffirmation agreement prescribed by section 524(k) does not permit a creditor to cancel the reaffirmation agreement for one debt if the debtor rescinds the agreement for a second debt. In addition, section 362(h) does not grant relief from

Provisions enacted in 2005 protect creditors to some extent, but do not permit abuses of the types described above. Section 524(*l*) permits creditors to accept payments made by debtors in connection with reaffirmation agreements. A creditor may accept a voluntary payment by the debtor either before or after the filing of a reaffirmation agreement with the court.

However, the authorization to accept payments is limited to an agreement that a creditor believes in good faith to be effective. Thus, for example, if the creditor knows, or should with reasonable diligence know, that the agreement does not meet the requirements for a valid reaffirmation, the creditor is not permitted to accept payments. The provision does not authorize a creditor to retain payments after it learns that a reaffirmation agreement is invalid or has been rescinded.

Section 524(*l*)(3) provides that the disclosure requirements of section 524(c)(2) and (k) are satisfied if the required disclosures are made in good faith. This provision, too, appears to be a limitation on creditors' actions to undermine the reaffirmation requirements. If the required disclosures are made, but are not made in good faith, perhaps because the creditor has added excessive charges to the agreement or plans to change the credit terms immediately, there is no protection. The provision does not excuse a creditor from making the required disclosures simply because the creditor has acted in good faith. It operates only if the creditor has made the disclosures that are required.

15.5.2.6 The Undue Hardship and Best Interests Tests

Because the tests for approval of reaffirmation of consumer debts not secured by real property were new, the courts had to determine what circumstances are sufficient to satisfy them. To do this evaluation, they looked to a number of factors.

Principally, courts have sought to determine the debtor's reasons for wanting to reaffirm. If the debtor seeks only to satisfy a "moral obligation" or to protect a cosigner, courts have generally found that reaffirmation is not in the debtor's best interests.[766] Reaffirmation agreements in which the only benefit to the debtors is a small amount of new credit have been found to be against the debtors' best interests.[767] Similarly, a reaffirmation coerced under the threat of a nondischargeability proceeding has been found to be in bad faith.[768] The possibility of undisclosed or unfair pressure from creditors, cosigners, and others has weighed heavily in these cases, and the courts have pointed out that the absence of reaffirmation does not prevent the debtor from voluntarily making whatever payments he or she chooses.[769] It only serves to prevent the debtor from being bound by an agreement to pay should he or she become unable or unwilling to pay.

Cases in which debts are secured by the debtor's property have presented more difficult problems.[770] First, courts have often looked to whether the property was a necessity for the debtor and whether reaffirmation was necessary in order to keep the property.[771] In one case, reaffirmation was allowed on a debt secured by vehicles necessary for the debtor's employment, but denied as to a debt secured by an expensive television.[772] Even with debts secured by necessary property, courts have looked askance at reaffirmation agreements to pay more than the value of the property, absent a showing that some other method, such as redemption, was not possible.[773] Other courts have flatly refused to approve reaffirmations for amounts in excess of the value of the collateral.[774] On occasion, they have also enjoined creditors from attempting to add attorney fees or other fees to the reaffirmed debt.[775] It appears that some agreements have been proposed mainly in cases in which the debtor's counsel was lazy, incompetent, or both, in not exploring better alternatives for the debtor, and the decisions refusing reaffirmation when such alternatives are available are clearly correct.

In any event, a court should not approve a reaffirmation if the court is not convinced the debtor will be able to make the payments. If the evidence does not overcome the section 524(m) presumption of undue hardship, the court should find such hardship exists and disapprove the agreement. Similarly, in credit union cases in which the presumption does not operate,

---

the stay if the debtor offers to reaffirm a debt on its original terms and the creditor refuses.

766 *In re* Long, 3 B.R. 656 (Bankr. E.D. Va. 1980); *In re* Berkich, 7 B.R. 483 (Bankr. E.D. Pa. 1980); *In re* Avis, 3 B.R. 205 (Bankr. S.D. Ohio 1980). *See also In re* Hirte, 71 B.R. 249 (Bankr. D. Or. 1986) (reaffirmation of unsecured debt which has been discharged to settle nondischargeability claim disapproved when deadline for filing nondischargeability complaint had passed). *But see In re* Kinion, 207 F.3d 751 (5th Cir. 2000) (local rule may not provide that only secured debt can be reaffirmed).

767 *In re* Bain, 223 B.R. 343 (Bankr. N.D. Tex. 1998) (reaffirmation of a $388 debt to obtain an additional $12 in credit).
Some courts have looked to the effective annual percentage rate of the new credit in evaluating the consumer's best interests. *See, e.g., In re* Bruzzese, 214 B.R. 444 (Bankr. E.D.N.Y. 1997).

768 *In re* Iappini, 192 B.R. 8 (Bankr. D. Mass. 1995) (general statement that Sears' reaffirmation practices are coercive and in bad faith with possibility of sanctions left open in the event of a continuation of those practices).

769 *Id.*; 11 U.S.C. § 524(f). *See also In re* Griffen, 13 B.R. 591 (Bankr. S.D. Ohio 1980) (reaffirmation coerced by threat of illegal postdischarge collection activity). *But see In re* Arnold, 206 B.R. 560 (Bankr. N.D. Ala. 1997) (payments made pursuant to debtor's postbankruptcy agreement to pay debt in exchange for promise not garnish wife's wages were not voluntary payments).

770 *See also* § 8.8.2, *supra*.

771 *See* § 11.5.4, *supra*, and § 15.5.3, *infra*, for discussion of whether reaffirmation is necessary in order to retain property when payments are current. *See In re* Ezell, 269 B.R. 768 (Bankr. S.D. Ohio 2001) (refusing approval of reaffirmation of debt secured by vehicle owned by debtor's wife, from whom he was separated).

772 *In re* McGrann, 6 B.R. 612 (Bankr. E.D. Pa. 1980).

773 *In re* Delano, 6 Bankr. Ct. Dec. (LRP) 1280 (Bankr. D. Me. 1980).
The court did not mention, although it could have done so, conversion to chapter 13 for payment of the allowed secured claim in installments. *See* Ch. 11, *supra*.

774 *In re* Hoffman, 358 B.R. 839 (Bankr. W.D. Va. 2006) (reaffirming debt for twice the value of vehicle collateral not in debtors' best interest); *In re* Jenkins, 4 B.R. 651 (Bankr. E.D. Va. 1980).

775 *See, e.g., In re* Allen, 215 B.R. 503 (Bankr. N.D. Tex 1997).

the court should not approve an agreement if the debtor has not shown an ability to make the payments.

15.5.2.7 Factors to Be Considered by Attorneys Validating Reaffirmation Agreements

Attorneys should be extremely cautious in negotiating and validating reaffirmation agreements. There are serious problems of possible malpractice liability if such an agreement later causes harm to the debtor, for example, through the debtor's loss of property if the debtor does not later pay the reaffirmed debt. There is no question that many debtors enter into ill-advised reaffirmations; the numerous cases in which courts have disapproved reaffirmations suggest that attorneys have not always been as wary of reaffirmations as the courts. Although a reaffirmation in which an attorney has filed the requisite declaration no longer requires express court approval to be valid, courts nonetheless have the power, under Federal Rule of Bankruptcy Procedure 9011 and section 524(c)(3), to review such declarations and the accompanying reaffirmations.[776]

Thus, it is usually better practice to avoid reaffirmations if at all possible. It is always advisable to verify whether a creditor really has and can document any security interest it claims, as well as the amount due. A detailed letter of inquiry should be sent to any creditor claiming a security interest.[777] Many creditors cannot provide documentation of a security interest and the documentation supplied by others may be insufficient to create a security interest.[778] Courts have required detailed disclosure of the terms of the reaffirmation. If the court needs such information for reaffirmations that it approves, an attorney deciding whether a reaffirmation is in the debtor's best interest should require no less.

Very often the debtor can obtain the result desired by simply maintaining voluntary payments on a debt without reassuming the legal obligation. For example, a creditor cannot pursue a codebtor if the debtor's payments remain current. And many courts have held that property subject to a security interest may not be repossessed if payments are up to date.[779] The advisability of this course of action is especially true for debts secured by real property, because all of the provisions enacted in 2005 concerning the statement of intention that might have changed the law apply only to personal property.[780] Similarly, if a personal property lease is assumed in a chapter 7 case under section 365(p), the debtor may retain possession of the property without reaffirming.[781] If there is any doubt on this issue, a chapter 13 filing should be considered to deal with the secured claim, rather than a reaffirmation.

One way out for an attorney unsure about a possible reaffirmation, perhaps one fervently desired by a client, is to leave the question to the court. If the attorney does not negotiate the reaffirmation agreement, then the procedure for court approval must be followed,[782] relieving the attorney of responsibility for the decision. Moreover, if the debtor enters into a reaffirmation agreement on a debt secured by personal property and the court disapproves it, the debtor may thereby gain the right to retain collateral by keeping current on loan payments, because the debtor is relieved of the ramifications of sections 362(h), 521(a)(6), and 521(d).[783]

---

776 *See In re* Melendez, 235 B.R. 173 (Bankr. D. Mass. 1999) (attorneys violated their obligations under Rule 9011 by failing to make reasonable inquiry before submitting declarations); *In re* Melendez, 224 B.R. 252 (Bankr. D. Mass. 1998); *In re* Bruzzese, 214 B.R. 444 (Bankr. E.D.N.Y. 1997) (attorney found to have violated Rule 9011 and ethical obligations by signing reaffirmation agreement declaration that was not accurate and did not investigate or explain facts to client); *In re* Izzo, 197 B.R. 11 (Bankr. D.R.I. 1996) (debtor's attorney ordered to show cause why reaffirmation should not be declared void when debtor's expenses exceeded his income even without car payment provided for in agreement).

777 *See* Form 138, Appx. G.12, *infra*.

778 *See, e.g., In re* Immerfall, 216 B.R. 269 (Bankr. D. Minn. 1998) (Sears documents did not create valid security interest); *In re* Carlos, 215 B.R. 52 (Bankr. C.D. Cal. 1997) (documents did not describe collateral with necessary specificity). *See also* § 15.5.3, *infra*.

779 *See* § 11.5.4, *supra*; § 15.5.3, *infra*.

780 *See In re* Waller, 394 B.R. 111 (Bankr. D.S.C. 2008) (refusing to approve reaffirmation of mortgage because debtor had right to prevent foreclosure by keeping payments current without reaffirmation).

781 Thompson v. Credit Union Financial Group, 453 B.R. 823 (W.D. Mich. 2011); *In re* Crawford, 2010 WL 2103580 (Bankr. M.D.N.C. May 19, 2010); *In re* Eader, 426 B.R. 164 (Bankr. D. Md. 2010). *See* § 12.9.5.3, *supra*.

782 11 U.S.C. § 524(c)(6). *See In re* James, 120 B.R. 582 (Bankr. W.D. Okla. 1990) (court would not approve reaffirmation agreement when creditor held unsecured, unliquidated claim; debtor could not bifurcate claim so as to affirm it only to the extent it was secured by debtor's automobile and attorney had not certified, without qualification, that reaffirmation would impose no undue hardship on debtor). *But see In re* Jamo, 283 F.3d 392 (1st Cir. 2002) (absent counsel's approval, a represented debtor cannot reaffirm).

783 *In re* Baker, 400 B.R. 136 (D. Del. 2009) (lender held in contempt and assessed compensatory damages and attorney fees for repossessing debtor's vehicle in violation of stay after debtor and lender had entered into timely reaffirmation agreement that bankruptcy court would not approve); *In re* Perez, 2010 WL 2737187 (Bankr. D.N.M. July 12, 2010) (where debtor attempted to reaffirm, but attorney did not certify that reaffirmation would not pose undue hardship, reaffirmation was not valid, but creditor could not repossess vehicle); *In re* Chim, 381 B.R. 191 (Bankr. D. Md. 2008) (creditor cannot enforce *ipso facto* clause while debtor current in payments after debtor had entered into timely reaffirmation agreement which the court refused to approve); *In re* Bower, 2007 WL 2163472 (Bankr. D. Or. July 26, 2007) (debtor who timely entered into reaffirmation agreement that was not approved by court may retain vehicle as long as she remains current on payments); *In re* Moustafi, 371 B.R. 434 (Bankr. D. Ariz. 2007) (same); *In re* Husain, 364 B.R. 211 (Bankr. E.D. Va. 2007) (same). *See also In re* Schwass, 378 B.R. 859 (Bankr. S.D. Cal. 2007) (denying stay relief to secured automobile creditor because debtor had indicated she was willing to enter into timely reaffirmation agreement if creditor prepared one, but creditor refused to prepare one).

See Chapter 11, *supra*, for discussion of statement of intention provisions.

15.5.3 Secured Debts Without Reaffirmation

After bankruptcy, for various reasons, secured debts may exist in which neither reaffirmation nor redemption has taken place. This may occur because the debtor does not choose to be personally bound. It may also occur because the creditor refuses to agree to reaffirmation.

In such cases, the question arises whether the creditor may foreclose upon its still-existing lien on a car or a home due to a "bankruptcy clause" which creates an automatic default upon the debtor filing a bankruptcy case even absent a monetary default under the contract. Such contractual default clauses are not favored under the Code,[784] but some creditors have argued that they may still be used to foreclose upon collateral even if there has been no default in payments. The 2005 enactment of section 521(d), which preserves such clauses in certain circumstances, further complicates the analysis.[785] Other contractual clauses which generally make impairment of collateral an event of default should not be enforceable by a secured creditor solely based on the debtor's bankruptcy filing and refusal to reaffirm.[786] Similarly, failure to file the notice of election with respect to retention of secured property, required by 11 U.S.C. § 521(a)(2) does not necessarily give a secured creditor the automatic right to repossess collateral.[787]

There are several ways debtors can overcome this potential problem. The best way, usually preferable to reaffirmation, is a redemption agreement that does not provide for reaffirmation. Although it usually cannot be required to do so,[788] a creditor may enter a binding agreement not to foreclose as long as contractual payments are made.[789]

Even when creditors are not willing to enter into such agreements, many creditors will take no action against the debtor as long as payments are current. In most cases, especially when the property has little value, the creditor is better off economically if it receives continued payments from the debtor. If foreclosure or repossession is attempted, several arguments can be made by the debtor.[790] First, it can be argued that once the debtor's interest in the property had become property of the estate (later to be exempted or abandoned), it was no longer conditioned upon any bankruptcy clause, due to the operation of section 541(c) of the Code which invalidates such clauses as to all property of the estate.[791] Because the debtor is entitled to claim exemptions out of the property of the estate,[792] it follows that the interest claimed as exempt is the estate's interest, freed of the bankruptcy clause. However this argument is not available to the extent section 521(d) is applicable to the debt. In some states, such as those that have enacted the Uniform Consumer Credit Code, there must be a monetary default for the creditor to repossess, so the mere filing of a bankruptcy case is not sufficient.[793] State law arguments can also be made that the creditor waived the right to repossess based on the filing of a bankruptcy by accepting payments after the bankruptcy case was filed. It can also be argued that actions based upon such a clause are unconscionable or not in compliance with the Uniform Commercial Code's requirement of good faith.[794] Some decisions have simply stated, using various reasons, that foreclosure while the debtor is current in payments is not permissible.[795] A final alternative is to file a new chapter 13 case, under which the debtor could retain the property and cure the default.[796] Sometimes the threat of a chapter 13 case or of conversion to that chapter, in which the creditor might be paid less, or more slowly, is enough to persuade a recalcitrant creditor to agree to the debtor's continuing payment without reaffirmation.

If the debtor does fall behind on payments postpetition or post-discharge, the creditor is, of course, entitled to enforce a valid lien. State court defenses may be raised or a new bankruptcy case under chapter 13 may be available as an option. However, the costs of foreclosure, repossession or replevin are prepetition personal liabilities under the contract and may not be collected from the debtor personally because they have been discharged.[797]

A related problem that has arisen in recent years with increasing frequency concerns the rights of the debtor against credit card issuers asserting a purchase money security interest in goods purchased by credit card. Sears and several other creditors have, at various times, aggressively pursued claimed security interests in the bankruptcy process.[798] The first response to such a claim may be to seek proof of the grounds on which it is asserted. Frequently the creditor has inadequate

---

784 See 11 U.S.C. §§ 363(1), 365(b)(2), 541(c).
785 See Chapter 11, *supra*, for discussion of 11 U.S.C. § 521(d).
786 See Chapter 11, *supra*, for discussion of 11 U.S.C. § 521(d).
787 See In re Belanger, 962 F.2d 345 (4th Cir. 1992); Lowry Fed. Credit Union v. West, 882 F.2d 1543 (10th Cir. 1989). *See also In re* French, 185 B.R. 910 (Bankr. M.D. Fla. 1995) (debtor who attempted to negotiate reaffirmation agreement but who would not agree to additional attorney fees demanded by creditor had complied with statement of intentions); § 11.4, *supra*. *But see In re* Taylor, 3 F.3d 1512 (11th Cir. 1993).

The fact that the 2005 provisions only apply to personal property reinforces the holdings of these cases with respect to debts secured by real property. *See In re* Pope, 2011 WL 671972 (Bankr. E.D. Va. Feb. 17, 2011); *In re* Wilson, 372 B.R. 816 (Bankr. D.S.C. 2007).
788 See discussion of redemption in Chapter 11, *supra*.
789 *See In re* Coots, 4 B.R. 281 (Bankr. S.D. Ohio 1980).
790 *See also* § 11.5.4, *supra*.
791 *In re* Winters, 69 B.R. 145 (Bankr. D. Or. 1986); *In re* Bryant 43 B.R. 189 (Bankr. E.D. Mich. 1984).
792 11 U.S.C. § 522(b).
793 *See* Malachin v. Daimler Chrysler Fin. Servs. Ams. L.L.C., 2007 Pa. Dist. & Cnty. Dec. LEXIS 158 (Pa. County Ct. 2007) (creditor had no right under state law to accelerate and repossess when there was no monetary default); *In re* Rowe, 342 B.R. 341 (Bankr. D. Kan. 2006). *But see* Hall v. Ford Motor Credit Co. L.L.C., 254 P.3d 526, 292 Kan. 176 (Kan. 2011); Ford Motor Credit Co., L.L.C. v. Roberson, 25 A.3d 110, 420 Md. 649 (Md. 2011).
794 Unif. Commercial Code § 1-201(19).
795 State law anti-forfeiture provisions in statutes or common law may support this argument.
796 11 U.S.C. §§ 1306(b), 1322(b)(3).
797 *In re* McNeil, 128 B.R. 603 (Bankr. E.D. Pa. 1991).
798 These issues are discussed at length in *Helping Your Client Do The Wash: The Effect in Bankruptcy of PMSI Claims Created By Revolving Credit Accounts*, 12 NCLC REPORTS *Bankruptcy and Foreclosures Ed.* 37 (Jan./Feb. 1994).

documentation. Upon obtaining the purported documentation, other questions about the validity of the security interest may also be raised.[799] Finally, in most jurisdictions, a debtor may be advised that there is little risk in ignoring such possible security interests because the creditor cannot breach the peace to repossess and the debtor may refuse entry to the repossessing agent. Creditors will rarely seek state replevin remedies to obtain an order requiring surrender of the goods, because such procedures are costly in comparison to the value of the used goods. In the rare case in which such an action is undertaken, defenses to repossession may be raised in the replevin action.

A variation of this practice is the attempted use of cross-collateralization (spreader) clauses in contracts such as automobile loan contracts or mortgages which purport to make the property involved security for future advances, such as those on credit cards. There are a variety of arguments against such claims, such as arguments based on whether the debtor knew and intended to create such a security interest, especially when the original contract (which is later assigned) was entered into with a dealer who the debtor would have no reason to believe would make any future advances.[800] A failure to disclose the security interest on the later transaction would probably violate the Truth in Lending Act as well.[801] It may also be that the efforts of the creditor to procure a reaffirmation agreement have violated the automatic stay or other statutes.[802]

15.5.4 Protection Against Discrimination Based on Bankruptcy

In addition to the other protections of the discharge, the Code contains a specific provision barring some types of discrimination based upon a person's bankruptcy or a debt discharged in bankruptcy. Section 525(a) provides that, with a few uncommon exceptions, a governmental unit:[803]

> [M]ay not deny, revoke, suspend, or refuse to renew a license, permit, charter, franchise, or other similar grant to, condition such a grant to, discriminate with respect to such a grant against, deny employment to, terminate the employment of, or discriminate with respect to employment against, a person that is or has been a debtor under this title or a bankrupt or a debtor under the Bankruptcy Act, or another person with whom such bankrupt or debtor is or has been associated, solely because such bankrupt or debtor is or has been a debtor under this title or a bankrupt or a debtor under the Bankruptcy Act, has been insolvent before the commencement of the case under this title, or during the case but before the debtor is granted or denied a discharge, or has not paid a debt that is dischargeable in the case under this title or that was discharged under the Bankruptcy Act.

It is clear that this provision is directed at governmental units and that it does not cover private entities. But the legislative history also makes clear that the Code is not intended to authorize discrimination by private entities. Rather, Congress thought it best for the courts initially to develop rules with respect to such entities, and gave strong intimations that discrimination not specifically within the terms of section 525 that greatly impeded a debtor's fresh start might be prohibited.[804] To date, case law has been scarce, but the courts have been

---

799 These may include questions about whether the security interest is valid pursuant to the Uniform Commercial Code's Article 9, whether the contract is an unenforceable adhesion contract, and whether proper accounting practices were used. See In re Immerfall, 216 B.R. 269 (Bankr. D. Minn. 1998) (Sears charge slips without underlying credit agreement they purported to incorporate did not prove security interest; description of some items also inadequate); In re Carlos, 215 B.R. 52 (Bankr. C.D. Cal. 1997) (property in which Sears alleged security interest was inadequately described in charge slip); § 11.2.2, supra. See generally Helping Your Client Do The Wash: The Effect in Bankruptcy of PMSI Claims Created By Revolving Credit Accounts, 12 NCLC REPORTS Bankruptcy and Foreclosures Ed. 37 (Jan./Feb. 1994).

Moreover, no security interest is created if the person signing the charge slip is not the account holder who signed the security agreement.

800 In re Kim, 256 B.R. 793 (Bankr. S.D. Cal. 2000) (dragnet clause invalid because credit union did not rely on automobile as collateral in providing credit card); In re Gibson, 249 B.R. 645 (Bankr. E.D. Pa. 2000) (dragnet clause did not secure unrelated loans); In re Wollin, 249 B.R. 555 (Bankr. D. Or. 2000) (dragnet clause invalid because credit card debt not of same class as auto loan); In re Fassinger, 246 B.R. 513 (Bankr. W.D. Pa. 2000) (credit union dragnet clause invalid under Pennsylvania "relatedness rule"); In re Cushing, 230 B.R. 639 (Bankr. W.D. Pa. 1999) (mortgage note dragnet clause, under which lender argued that credit card debt was secured by mortgage, was invalid). See also In re Brooks, 274 B.R. 495 (Bankr. E.D. Tenn. 2002) (credit card debt owed only by wife not secured by mortgage on home owned by both debtors, based on language of mortgage); In re Merrill, 258 B.R. 750 (Bankr. W.D. Mo. 2001) (security interest based on future advances not perfected under state law if not noted on certificate of title); National Consumer Law Center, Repossessions § 3.9 (7th ed. 2010 and Supp.). But see In re Conte, 206 F.3d 536 (5th Cir. 2000) (upholding cross-collateral clause).

801 See National Consumer Law Center, Truth in Lending §§ 4.6.7.6, 5.5.5.7 (7th ed. 2011 and Supp.).

802 Sears, Roebuck & Co. v. O'Brien, 178 F.3d 962 (8th Cir. 1999) (bankruptcy law does not preempt state consumer credit code provision); In re Hurley, 215 B.R. 391 (B.A.P. 8th Cir. 1997) (sending debtors "informational copy" of letter to their attorney seeking reaffirmation violated Iowa Consumer Credit Code prohibition against creditors communicating with represented debtors). See also § 9.4.4, supra.

803 "Governmental unit" is defined in 11 U.S.C. § 101(27). See In re Trusko, 212 B.R. 819 (Bankr. D. Md. 1997) (credit union a governmental unit for purposes of a different Code section).

804 S. Rep. No. 95-989, at 81 (1978); H.R. Rep. No. 95-595, at 367 (1977). See In re Holmes, 309 B.R. 824 (M.D. Ga. 2004) (IRS ordered to consider debtor's offer in compromise under section 105 even though not required by section 525); In re Macher, 303 B.R. 798 (W.D. Va. 2003) (IRS ordered to consider debtor's offer in compromise under section 105 based on fresh start policy); In re Peterson, 321 B.R. 259 (Bankr. D. Neb. 2004) (following Holmes); In re Golliday, 216 B.R. 407 (Bankr. W.D. Mich. 1998) (although city's termination of debtor's right to sit as rent commissioner found not to violate section 525, it did violate fresh start principles enunciated by Supreme Court and was therefore enjoined).

§ 15.5.4

somewhat receptive to claims of private discrimination.[805] Probably, the strongest cases could be made against quasi-governmental entities such as state bar associations, which are specifically mentioned in the legislative history.[806]

In 1984, another legislative step in this direction was taken with the addition of section 525(b), prohibiting private employers from employment discrimination based on bankruptcy, insolvency before a bankruptcy, or nonpayment of a debt discharged or dischargeable in a bankruptcy case.[807] This section is most often helpful when employers are unhappy with court orders to deduct chapter 13 payments from a debtor's paycheck and forward them to the chapter 13 trustee. It will also help in those occasional cases in which debtors owe debts to their employers or to persons or institutions closely affiliated with their employers.[808] However, as in any employment discrimination case, there may still be difficult problems of proof as to motivation, particularly when the employer presents alternative reasons for its actions adverse to the debtor. The court may have to evaluate whether the reasons presented are the true motivations for the employer's actions and, if so, whether those reasons are valid.[809] And many courts have held that this provision does not extend to hiring decisions with respect to debtors who were not yet employees of the employer on the date of the bankruptcy petition.[810]

Yet another step was taken by a 1994 amendment that prohibits discrimination against a debtor seeking a student loan or grant. Section 525(c) prohibits a governmental unit or private entity involved in a student loan program from discriminating based upon a bankruptcy case, insolvency prior to a

---

805 *See, e.g., In re* Blackwelder Furniture Co., 7 B.R. 328 (Bankr. W.D.N.C. 1980) (preliminary injunction issued requiring private company to continue dealing with corporate debtor according to previous business relationship). *See In re* Bradley, 989 F.2d 802 (5th Cir. 1993) (bankruptcy court must take jurisdiction to determine discrimination claim if there is a potential violation of section 525). *But see* Wilson v. Harris Trust & Sav. Bank, 777 F.2d 1246 (7th Cir. 1985) (section 525 did not apply to private employer prior to 1984 Amendments).

806 *See In re* Oksentowicz, 314 B.R. 638 (Bankr. E.D. Mich. 2004) (privately owned apartment complex participating in Section 8 housing program and subject to extensive regulation by the Dep't of Housing and Urban Development was governmental unit); *In re* Marcano, 288 B.R. 324 (Bankr. S.D.N.Y. 2003) (pervasive entwinement of the city in the workings and composition of a nominally private tenant's association justified conclusion that association should be considered an instrumentality of the city and a governmental unit).

807 *See* Robinette v. WESTconsin Credit Union, 686 F. Supp. 2d 1206 (W.D. Wis. 2010) (protection extended to employee terminated because she said she intended to file bankruptcy case); Leary v. Warnaco, 251 B.R. 656 (S.D.N.Y. 2000) (provision applied both the current employees and to hiring of new employees). *But see In re* Majewski, 310 F.3d 653 (9th Cir. 2002) (section 525(b) inapplicable when debtor fired before bankruptcy case was filed, even if cause was debtor's intention to file bankruptcy case); *In re* Mayo, 322 B.R. 712 (Bankr. D. Vt. 2005) (although supervisor told debtor she would be fired if she filed bankruptcy case, section was inapplicable when debtor resigned before case was filed); Kepple v. Miller, 257 Ga. App. 784, 572 S.E.2d 687 (2002) (section 525(b) inapplicable to real estate agent who was independent contractor).

808 *See* Simms-Wilson v. Linebarger Goggan Blair & Sampson L.L.P. (*In re* Simms-Wilson), 434 B.R. 452 (Bankr. S.D. Tex. 2010) (firing attorney who had filed bankruptcy case because she owed dischargeable taxes to law firm's client violated § 525(b)); *In re* Patterson, 125 B.R. 40 (Bankr. N.D. Ala. 1990) (antidiscrimination provision applied to employer's credit union which denied services to the debtor), *aff'd*, 967 F.2d 505 (11th Cir. 1992); *In re* McNeely, 82 B.R. 628 (Bankr. S.D. Ga. 1987) (antidiscrimination provision applied to entity which refused to do business with independent contractor after claim of that entity's sister corporation was discharged in bankruptcy). *Cf.* Mangan v. Cullen, 870 F.2d 1396 (8th Cir. 1989) (district administrator in state court system has qualified official immunity against damage suit for discrimination brought by court reporter who was not given a raise after she discharged state's claim in bankruptcy). *But see* Asquino v. Fed. Deposit Ins. Corp., 196 B.R. 25 (D. Md. 1996) (provision of Federal Deposit Insurance Act precluded review of termination of employment of debtor by F.D.I.C.).

809 *See, e.g.,* White v. Kentuckiana Livestock Mkt., Inc., 397 F.3d 420 (6th Cir. 2005) (employer showed that bankruptcy was not sole reason for discharge from position); Laracuente v. Chase Manhattan Bank, 891 F.2d 17 (1st Cir. 1989) (debtor must show bankruptcy is sole reason for dismissal, bank had valid basis to dismiss bank employee who improperly processed loans for family and friends); Mangan v. Cullen, 870 F.2d 1396 (8th Cir. 1989) (state official had valid nondiscriminatory basis for treating employee differently after she discharged state's claim in bankruptcy); Bell v. Stanford-Corbitt-Bruker, Inc., Bankr. L. Rep. (CCH) ¶ 72,114 (S.D. Ga. 1987) (termination of employment is unlawful if it would not have occurred "but for" the debtor's bankruptcy); *In re* McKibben, 233 B.R. 378 (Bankr. E.D. Tex. 1999) (debtor awarded almost $90,000 in lost wages when circumstances belied employer's stated reason for termination); *In re* Sweeney, 113 B.R. 359 (Bankr. N.D. Ohio 1990) (termination from employment, though couched in terms of concern for financial imprudence, was based solely on employee's insolvency and was thus discriminatory); *In re* Vaughter, 109 B.R. 229 (Bankr. W.D. Tex. 1989) (employer's failure to allow bankruptcy debtor to participate in advancement program was discriminatory); *In re* Hopkins, 81 B.R. 491 (Bankr. W.D. Ark. 1987) (debtor reinstated with full back pay after she was fired solely for filing bankruptcy); *In re* Hicks, 65 B.R. 980 (Bankr. W.D. Ark. 1986) (bank not permitted to transfer teller due to alleged fear of customer relations problem stemming from teller's bankruptcy when bank had no valid concern about teller's honesty); *In re* Hopkins, 66 B.R. 828 (Bankr. W.D. Ark. 1986) (bank employee could not be terminated on basis of fear of public reaction to employee's bankruptcy when there was no doubt of employee's honesty). *See also* Comeaux v. Brown & Williamson Tobacco Co., 915 F.2d 1264 (9th Cir. 1990) (prospective employer did not discriminate when debtor's bankruptcy status was not sole reason for decision not to hire; employer had told debtor, before learning of chapter 13 filing, that it would not hire him because of credit history). *Cf. In re* Arentson, 126 B.R. 236 (Bankr. N.D. Miss. 1991) (bankruptcy court could decide issue of bankruptcy discrimination despite arbitration provision in employment contract).

810 Burnett v. Stewart Title, Inc. (*In re* Burnett), 635 F.3d 169 (5th Cir. 2011) (section 525(b) does not extend to hiring); Myers v. TooJay's Mgmt. Corp., 640 F.3d 1278 (11th Cir. 2011) (same); Rea v. Federated Investors, 627 F.3d 937 (3d Cir. 2010) (same); Fiorani v. Caci, 192 B.R. 401 (E.D. Va. 1996) (section 525(b) did not extend to hiring); Pastore v. Medford Sav. Bank, 186 B.R. 553 (D. Mass. 1995) (omission of words "deny employment to" in section 525(b) means that hiring decisions are not covered by that section, because those words do appear in section 525(a)).

bankruptcy case, or an unpaid debt that was discharged in a bankruptcy case.

In addition to the question of who may or may not discriminate, there is also a good deal of uncertainty about how broad the scope of section 525(a) really is. What is covered by the phrase "license, permit, charter, franchise, or other similar grant"? Clearly covered are such matters as issuance of drivers' licenses[811] and employment, but what of various public benefits, such as welfare or Social Security when the agency has been denied recoupment by the discharge.[812] What of utility service provided by public entities? May a deposit be required of debtors who have discharged debts when it is not required of others? Several courts have concluded that in some contexts it is not discriminatory for a governmental entity to deny benefits to a debtor who has discharged a debt, based on the fact that the debtor's need for government assistance is less as a result of the discharge.[813]

The answers to some of these questions can be found in the legislative history,[814] which states that the section is intended to codify the result of *Perez v. Campbell*.[815] In that case, the Supreme Court held that a state could not deny a driver's license due to a debt after that debt had been discharged in bankruptcy, because that denial would impair the debtor's fresh start. Although *Perez* dealt with a driver's license, the "fresh start" principle is equally applicable to virtually any type of public benefit or government action. As discussed below, section 525 has already been broadly interpreted to include the right to live in public housing, and the right to receive a transcript from a university to which a student loan was owed.[816] Denial of various other governmental benefits, services or privileges has also been found discriminatory.[817] It is also clear that the section extends not just to discrimination based upon the bankruptcy, but also discrimination based upon an unpaid debt that was discharged in bankruptcy.[818] Under section 525, except insofar as creditworthiness is being considered, the

---

811 *See In re* Kish, 238 B.R. 271 (Bankr. D.N.J. 1999) (license could not be denied due to nonpayment of discharged insurance "surcharges"); *In re* Brown, 244 B.R. 62 (Bankr. D.N.J. 2000) (denial of driver's license to chapter 13 debtor who was paying dischargeable traffic fines through plan violated section 525); *In re* Colon, 102 B.R. 421 (Bankr. E.D. Pa. 1989) (prepetition traffic fines are dischargeable in chapter 13; attempts to collect them by postpetition license suspension violate the automatic stay and nondiscrimination provision); *In re* Young, 10 B.R. 17 (Bankr. S.D. Cal. 1980) (state could not deny driver's license due to fine which would be discharged in chapter 13).

812 *See In re* Lech, 80 B.R. 1001 (Bankr. D. Neb. 1987) (government loan agreement with right to extend annually comes within governmental antidiscrimination provision); *In re* Latchaw, 24 B.R. 457 (Bankr. N.D. Ohio 1982) (quasi-governmental transit authority could not take disciplinary action against an employee under policy which prohibited wage garnishment when court ordered employer to pay debtor's wages to chapter 13 trustee); *In re* Rose, 23 B.R. 662 (Bankr. D. Conn. 1982) (home mortgage financing program within scope of section 525); Parker v. Contractors State License Bd., 231 Cal. Rptr. 577 (Ct. App. 1986) (contractor's license could not be suspended solely for failure to pay debt to union). *See also In re* Harris, 85 B.R. 858 (Bankr. D. Colo. 1988) (provision of state law which provides that bankruptcy discharge cannot relieve debtor of real estate license suspension violates supremacy clause). *But see* Ayes v. United States Dep't of Veterans Affairs, 473 F.3d 104 (4th Cir. 2006) (VA loan guaranty entitlement was not an "other similar grant"); Toth v. Mich. State Hous. Dev. Auth., 136 F.3d 477 (6th Cir. 1998) (section 525 did not extend to denial of credit in state home improvement loan program); Dixon v. United States, 68 F.3d 1253 (10th Cir. 1995) (debtor who did not discharge indemnity obligation to government on VA mortgage could have future eligibility for government guaranteed loans reduced; court held that denial of benefits was not attempt to collect discharged debt and did not discuss section 525(a)); *In re* Watts, 876 F.2d 1090 (3d Cir. 1989) (state mortgage assistance loans not within the scope of section 525); *In re* Goldrich, 771 F.2d 28 (2d Cir. 1985) (student loan not a license, charter or grant within meaning of statute); *In re* Begley, 46 B.R. 707 (E.D. Pa. 1984) (right to have state public utility commission mediate dispute with utility was not license, charter or grant within meaning of section 525), *aff'd*, 760 F.2d 46 (3d Cir. 1985).

This holding in *Goodrich* was legislatively overruled by the passage of 11 U.S.C. § 525(c) in 1994.

813 Lee v. Yeutter, 106 B.R. 588 (D. Minn. 1989) (debt restructuring under the Agricultural Credit Act denied), *aff'd*, 917 F.2d 1104 (8th Cir. 1990). *See also In re* Watts, 876 F.2d 1090 (3d Cir. 1989) (state mortgage assistance can be denied on the basis of bankruptcy filing, because the bankruptcy protects the debtor against foreclosure of the mortgage on which assistance is sought).

814 S. Rep. No. 95-989, at 81 (1978); H.R. Rep. No. 95-595, at 366 (1977).

815 402 U.S. 637, 91 S. Ct. 1704, 29 L. Ed. 2d 233 (1971).

816 *See* § 15.5.5, *infra*.

817 *See, e.g., In re* Bradley, 989 F.2d 802 (5th Cir. 1993) (denial of insurance license would be in violation of section 525 if retention of license was conditioned on payment of discharged debt); *In re* Ray, 355 B.R. 253 (Bankr. D. Or. 2006) (contractor's license could not be denied to debtor based on debts of corporation of which he had been principal when debtor's liability on those debts had been discharged); *In re* Jessamey, 330 B.R. 80 (Bankr. D. Mass. 2005) (section 525 violated when town denied motor vehicle registration based on nonpayment of dischargeable excise tax); *In re* Berkelhammer, 279 B.R. 660 (Bankr. S.D.N.Y. 2002) (state could not remove debtor from list of Medicaid-eligible physicians based on nonpayment of prepetition debt); *In re* Jacobs, 149 B.R. 983 (Bankr. N.D. Okla. 1993) (revocation of insurance agent license violated discharge injunction and section 525(a)); *In re* Walker, 927 F.2d 1138 (10th Cir. 1991) (denial of real estate license because of payment by real estate recovery fund to debtor's creditor would violate section 525(a)). *See also* Fed. Communications Comm'n v. NextWave Personal Communications, 537 U.S. 293, 123 S. Ct. 832, 839, 154 L. Ed. 2d 863, 874 (2003); *In re* Exquisito Servs., 823 F.2d 151 (5th Cir. 1987) (refusal to renew food service contract violated section 525); *In re* William Tell II, 38 B.R. 327 (N.D. Ill. 1983) (liquor license restored); *In re* Mills, 240 B.R. 689 (Bankr. S.D. W. Va. 1999) (Congress intended broad interpretation to assist debtor's fresh start and therefore IRS refusal to consider offers in compromise from bankruptcy debtors violated section 525); *In re* Coleman Am. Moving Servs., 8 B.R. 379 (Bankr. D. Kan. 1980) (Air Force enjoined from discriminating against chapter 11 debtor in contract bidding; term "employment" construed broadly).

818 11 U.S.C. § 525; Henry v. Heyison, 4 B.R. 437 (E.D. Pa. 1980); *In re* Goldrich, 45 B.R. 514 (Bankr. E.D.N.Y. 1984) (barring application of statute denying student loan to any student who had defaulted on previous loan), *rev'd on other grounds*, 771 F.2d 28 (2d Cir. 1985) (scope of section 525 does not include future extensions of credit such as student loans).

debtor should be treated the same as if the discharged debt never existed.[819]

The Supreme Court has interpreted section 525(a) broadly, holding that a court must look behind the alternative alleged motives of a government agency that denies a license.[820] It is not sufficient for the government to say that a license was denied for a "regulatory" purpose if the proximate cause for the denial was the failure to pay a dischargeable debt.[821] The Court made clear that the fact that licenses were also revoked for nonbankruptcy debtors who failed to pay similar debts did not change this fact.[822] The Court specifically rejected the argument, raised by the dissent, that there must be discrimination based upon the debtor's filing bankruptcy, rather than simply nonpayment of a dischargeable debt, as contrary to the clear meaning of the statutory language.[823]

One important limitation which should be noted, however, is that the section bars discrimination only when it is solely based upon the bankruptcy or upon nonpayment of a dischargeable debt. When other factors are involved, unless they can be shown to be pretextual, the debtor will have a difficult case, especially because the legislative history specifically states that factors such as future financial ability may be considered, if applied in a nondiscriminatory fashion.[824] Thus, a financial responsibility law cannot require only debtors who have filed bankruptcies to obtain insurance. However, if all persons who do not have assets sufficient to pay a judgment are required to obtain insurance, then debtors who filed bankruptcies would not be excepted under section 525(a).[825] And if a debt is not discharged in a bankruptcy, discrimination based upon that debt is not prohibited by this section.[826]

Finally, it should be remembered that in situations when section 525 is not applicable, section 524 may still prevent the challenged action.[827] Whenever it can be shown that the denial or other act directed at a client was intended to coerce payment of the discharged debt, that act is in violation of the injunction in section 524(a) and therefore should be considered a contempt of court.[828]

15.5.5 Particular Problems Relating to Discharge Protections

15.5.5.1 Drivers' Licenses

One of the more common uses of bankruptcy by low-income clients is to prevent the loss of or to regain a driver's licenses that is jeopardized by state financial responsibility laws such as the one dealt with in *Perez v. Campbell*.[829] Typically, such statutes provide that an operator's license, and sometimes vehicle registration, is suspended until a tort judgment arising out of a motor vehicle accident is paid. The Supreme Court held in *Perez* that, if the debt is discharged in bankruptcy, the license can no longer be denied.

Following *Perez*, courts have more recently held that any other discrimination based upon a discharged debt, such as a requirement that special insurance or a bond be purchased before a license can be granted, is also prohibited under the Supremacy Clause because it too would tend to frustrate the Congressional purpose of giving debtors a fresh start.[830] Similarly, a license cannot be withheld on the basis of nonpayment of traffic tickets which are dischargeable in chapter 13 cases,[831] or of other dischargeable charges arising from driving infractions.[832] In such situations, section 525 has been read to mean

---

819 H.R. Rep. No. 103-835, at 58 (1994), *reprinted in* 1994 U.S.C.C.A.N. 3340.
820 Fed. Communications Comm'n v. NextWave Personal Communications, 537 U.S. 293, 123 S. Ct. 832, 839, 154 L. Ed. 2d 863, 874 (2003).
821 537 U.S. 293, 123 S. Ct. 832, 839, 154 L. Ed. 2d 863, 874, 875 (2003).
822 123 S. Ct. at 841, 842.
823 *Id.*
824 S. Rep. No. 95-989, at 81 (1978); H.R. Rep. No. 95-595, at 367 (1977). *See In re* Smith, 259 B.R. 901 (B.A.P. 2001) (section 525 not applicable because debtor's public housing lease terminated due to fraud; dictum that there would be no protection under section 525 even if nonpayment of rent was only reason); Brookman v. State Bar of Cal., 46 Cal. 3d 1004, 760 P.2d 1023, 251 Cal. Rptr. 495 (1988) (order that suspended attorney make restitution was not solely because debt was discharged in bankruptcy or because debt not paid; purpose of order was to protect the public from professional misconduct); *In re* Anonymous, 74 N.Y.2d 938, 549 N.E.2d 472 (1989) (denial of application for admission to bar not based solely on applicant's bankruptcy filing).
825 *In re* Norton, 867 F.2d 313 (6th Cir. 1989) (no discrimination found when financial responsibility law is applied equally to every financially irresponsible driver); Henry v. Heyison, 4 B.R. 437 (E.D. Pa. 1980).
  The *Norton* holding is probably no longer good law after the Supreme Court's decision in *NextWave*.
826 Johnson v. Edinboro State College, 728 F.2d 163 (3d Cir. 1984).

827 *See* § 15.5.1, *supra*.
828 *In re* Olson, 38 B.R. 515 (Bankr. N.D. Iowa 1984) (clinic refusing medical services unless debt "voluntarily" paid after discharge found in contempt). *See* § 15.5.1.4, *supra*.
829 402 U.S. 637, 91 S. Ct. 1704, 29 L. Ed. 2d 233 (1971). *See* Form 106, Appx. G.10, *infra*.
830 Henry v. Heyison, 4 B.R. 437 (E.D. Pa. 1980). *See also In re* Young, 10 B.R. 17 (Bankr. S.D. Cal. 1980) (license could not be denied due to nonpayment of dischargeable fines). *But see* Duffey v. Dollison, 734 F.2d 265 (6th Cir. 1984) (upholding requirement of financial responsibility insurance based upon debt discharged in bankruptcy).
  The *Duffey* holding is probably no longer good law after the Supreme Court's decision in *NextWave*.
831 Smith v. Pennsylvania Dep't of Transp., 66 B.R. 244 (E.D. Pa. 1986); *In re* Brown, 244 B.R. 62 (Bankr. D.N.J. 2000) (denial of driver's license to chapter 13 debtor who was paying dischargeable traffic fines through plan violated section 525); *In re* Colon, 102 B.R. 421 (Bankr. E.D. Pa. 1989) (attempts to collect prepetition traffic fines by postpetition license suspension violate the automatic stay and nondiscrimination provision); *In re* Young, 10 B.R. 17 (Bankr. S.D. Cal. 1980).
  However, not all fines are dischargeable, even in chapter 13. *See* § 15.5.5.5, *infra*. *But see In re* Raphael, 238 B.R. 69 (D.N.J. 1999) (denying injunction against state district court on 11th Amendment grounds and because debts not yet discharged by chapter 13 debtor).
832 *In re* Kish, 238 B.R. 271 (Bankr. D.N.J. 1999) (license could not be denied due to nonpayment of discharged insurance "surcharges").

that the debtor involved should be treated as if the discharged debt never existed.[833] However, if the license has been suspended or revoked for some reason other than simply the nonpayment of money, such as points assessed after traffic violations, bankruptcy will not resolve that problem.

Thus, for a client who needs a driver's license, but cannot pay a judgment or fines, bankruptcy can be an ideal solution. Especially in areas where use of an automobile is a necessity of life, such a bankruptcy can be a vital service.

15.5.5.2 Student Loans and College Transcripts

One of the persistent problems under the prior Bankruptcy Act concerned college students and graduates who were refused transcripts from educational institutions because of discharged tuition debts or student loans. The case law that had developed under the Act seemed to make a distinction between private institutions and public ones, holding only the latter bound by the Supremacy Clause under *Perez*.[834] However, there was considerable scholarly criticism of those cases which denied transcripts as being contrary to the "fresh start" principle of bankruptcy.[835]

Assuming that a transcript can fit within the "license, permit, charter, franchise, or other grant" language, section 525(a) codifies the result of those cases holding a public institution could not deny a transcript.[836]

Similarly, the denial of further student loans by such a public entity based upon the bankruptcy is barred.[837] This principle was clarified and reemphasized by the 1994 enactment of Code section 525(c), which specifically prohibits discrimination with respect to student loans or grants based upon discharge of a prior debt.[838] The Department of Education has also made clear in regulations that students who have discharged prior student loans are eligible for new Pell grants and other non-loan assistance.[839] Following the 1994 amendment to the Code, the Department also clarified that no reaffirmation of a prior debt is required to obtain a new student loan.[840]

And, to the extent that pre-Code cases had held that withholding a transcript was a valid means for a private party to induce payment of a debt,[841] those cases are clearly no longer good law due to the prohibition in section 524 of "any act" to collect a debt after discharge.[842] Indeed, as soon as a bankruptcy case is filed, such acts to collect a debt are prohibited by the automatic stay of section 362.[843]

One additional argument a debtor might face from a private college withholding a transcript is that the school is not trying to coerce payment of the debt, but rather is simply exercising its right to refuse to enter into new transactions, such as providing a transcript, with the debtor. This argument could be attacked directly under *Perez*, as discussed above, by attempting to convince a court to extend the *Perez* doctrine to private entities.[844] It may also be shown to be a pretext to cover up an actual intent to coerce payment. Unlike a creditor who decides not to extend further credit or services, the college puts nothing new at risk in releasing a transcript. The transcript fee is normally paid in advance, and there is no chance whatsoever of harm to the creditor.[845] Finally, the debtor might argue that the

---

833 Henry v. Heyison, 4 B.R. 437 (E.D. Pa. 1980). *See also In re* Young, 10 B.R. 17 (Bankr. S.D. Cal. 1980) (license could not be denied due to nonpayment of dischargeable fines). *But see* Duffey v. Dollison, 734 F.2d 265 (6th Cir. 1984) (upholding requirement of financial responsibility insurance based upon debt discharged in bankruptcy); *In re* Geiger, 143 B.R. 30 (E.D. Pa. 1992) (restoration of license could be conditioned on payment of $25 restoration fee, which was held nondiscriminatory because it was charged whenever a license was restored to a driver), *aff'd*, 993 F.2d 224 (3d Cir. 1993).

The *Duffey* holding is probably no longer good law after the Supreme Court's decision in *NextWave*.

834 *Compare* Girardier v. Webster College, 563 F.2d 1267 (8th Cir. 1977) *with* Handsome v. Rutgers Univ., 445 F. Supp. 1362 (D.N.J. 1978).

835 *See, e.g.*, Comment, *Post Discharge Coercion of Bankrupts by Private Creditors*, 91 Harv. L. Rev. 1336 (1978); Note, *Withholding Transcripts for Non-Payment of Educational Debts: Before and After Bankruptcy*, 15 Willamette L. Rev. 563 (1979).

836 *See In re* Howren, 10 B.R. 303 (Bankr. D. Kan. 1980); *In re* Heath, 3 B.R. 351 (Bankr. N.D. Ill. 1980); Lee v. Bd. of Higher Ed. in City of New York, 1 B.R. 781 (Bankr. S.D.N.Y. 1979).

837 *But see* Richardson v. Pennsylvania Higher Educ. Assistance Agency, 27 B.R. 560 (E.D. Pa. 1982) (there could be independent reasons for denial of new loans).

838 The legislative history makes clear that this section was meant to clarify what Congress already believed the law to be. H.R. Rep. No. 103-835, at 58 (1994), *reprinted in* 1994 U.S.C.C.A.N. 3340. In addition, there would be no reason for the new section to refer to student loans discharged under the prior Bankruptcy Act, as it does, if the new section were not applicable to bankruptcy cases commenced prior to enactment of the 1994 amendments.

839 58 Fed. Reg. 32,188 (June 8, 1993) (amending 34 C.F.R. 668.7(f)(1)). *See also* 34 C.F.R. § 668.34 (student not considered to be in default if loan was discharged in bankruptcy).

840 *See* 59 Fed. Reg. 61,212 (Nov. 29, 1994) (FFEL loans); 59 Fed. Reg. 61,667 (Dec. 1, 1994) (explaining that reaffirmation no longer required for other loan programs due to change in Bankruptcy Code provisions).

A more detailed discussion of these issues is found at National Consumer Law Center, Student Loan Law Ch. 7 (4th ed. 2010 and Supp.).

841 *See* Girardier v. Webster College, 563 F.2d 1267 (8th Cir. 1977).

842 *In re* Kuehn, 563 F.3d 289 (7th Cir. 2009); Parraway v. Andrews Univ., 50 B.R. 316 (W.D. Mich. 1984); *In re* Moore, 407 B.R. 855 (Bankr. E.D. Va. 2009) (withholding transcript and degree due to unpaid tuition violated discharge injunction). *See* Op. N.Y. Att'y Gen., *reprinted in* Poverty L. Rep. (CCH) ¶ 31,093 (June 9, 1980). *But cf.* Johnson v. Edinboro State College, 728 F.2d 163 (3d Cir. 1984) (transcript may be denied when student loan debt is *not* discharged).

843 *In re* Kuehn, 563 F.3d 289 (7th Cir. 2009); Loyola Univ. v. McClarty, 234 B.R. 386 (E.D. La. 1999); *In re* Parham, 56 B.R. 531 (Bankr. E.D. Pa. 1986); *In re* Howren, 10 B.R. 303 (Bankr. D. Kan. 1980); *In re* Heath, 3 B.R. 351 (Bankr. N.D. Ill. 1980).

For discussion of the automatic stay see Chapter 9, *supra*.

844 This argument was urged, with respect to both private and public colleges under the Act, in Girardier v. Webster College, 563 F.2d 1267, 1277 (8th Cir. 1977) (Bright, J. concurring).

845 *See In re* Kuehn, 563 F.3d 289 (7th Cir. 2009); *In re* Heath, 3 B.R. 351 (Bankr. N.D. Ill. 1980); Comment, *Postdischarge Coercion of Bankrupts by Private Creditors*, 91 Harv. L. Rev. 1336, 1344 (1979).

right to a transcript is a property right that is received in conjunction with the degree or with enrollment.[846] If this is the case, and the debtor claims this right as exempt under section 522, then a good argument exists that a creditor may not withhold such property, which is also property of the estate, from the debtor.[847]

Thus, debtors are afforded significant protections with respect to college transcripts under the Code. Since its enactment the courts have largely made this problem a thing of the past.

15.5.5.3 Public and Private Housing

Many of the issues that arise with respect to student loans are also involved in disputes concerning the right to remain in public or private housing after discharge. A strong argument can be made that the right to remain in public housing is in essence a grant of the subsidy which makes possible lower rents. Further, it is well established in case law and HUD regulations that tenants may be evicted from public housing only for valid cause.[848] Thus, it is not surprising that section 525 has been found applicable to bar eviction of public housing tenants who discharged rent arrearages through bankruptcy.[849] The 2005 amendments relating to the automatic stay in eviction proceedings should not change these substantive rights.[850] In a case in which continued occupancy is conditioned upon payment of the arrearages, a valid claim may also exist that there are violations of section 524(a).[851] As the right to continued occupancy of the public housing unit derives from section 525(a) without regard to the automatic stay, an adversary action to enforce the tenant's rights under section 525(a) would be appropriate if a housing authority appears determined to proceed with an eviction when the bankruptcy stay is no longer in effect.[852]

Like private colleges, private landlords present more difficult problems. In most places, the landlord has no obligation to renew a lease, and the landlord may assert its right to evict the tenant at the end of the lease for any reason, including bankruptcy. The landlord may also argue that the lease was rejected and thus terminated if it was not assumed during the bankruptcy, although this argument should fail.[853] While it is clear that in most cases relief from the automatic stay must be obtained to evict during the pendency of the bankruptcy case,[854] after the case the debtor must find some other protection.[855] The same analysis probably applies to private landlords receiving Section 8 subsidies,[856] even though the subsidy could not be terminated by the housing authority directly.

The possible arguments to the contrary are similar to those in the student loan context. The debtor may argue for extension of *Perez* to private entities. If the debtor can show that the landlord has tried to coerce payment of the discharged debt by threatening eviction, protection may also be obtained under section 524(a). In many places the debtor can also assert a right to remain based upon state law. For example in most rent-control jurisdictions and some other jurisdictions the tenant may only be evicted for good cause. It has been held in such areas that when the discharged debt is the only possible basis for the eviction, the eviction must be seen as a means to compel payment and thus enjoined.[857] Similarly, the debtor can argue that the eviction is barred because it is in retaliation for the debtor's exercise of rights granted under the law. At least as long as the debtor posts adequate security for future rent and is otherwise complying with the lease, this argument may well be persuasive. Of course, if a problem with the debtor's landlord is anticipated, the best course of action may be to file a chapter 13 case to take advantage of the additional options under that chapter.[858]

---

846 *See* Handsome v. Rutgers Univ., 445 F. Supp. 1362 (D. N.J. 1978).
847 For a discussion of exemptions see Chapter 10, *supra*.
848 24 C.F.R. § 866.4(l)(1). *See, e.g.*, Tyson v. N.Y. City Hous. Auth., 369 F. Supp. 513 (S.D.N.Y. 1974). *See also In re* Adams, 94 B.R. 838 (Bankr. E.D. Pa. 1989) (household members remaining after lessee vacated public housing unit are entitled to the rights of public housing tenants).
849 *In re* Stolz, 315 F.3d 80 (2d Cir. 2002) (section 525 trumps any contrary language in section 365); *In re* Curry, 148 B.R. 966 (S.D. Fla. 1992); *In re* Biggs, 2007 WL 654247 (W.D. Pa. Feb. 28, 2007), *appeal vacated as moot*, 271 Fed. Appx. 286 (3d Cir. 2008); Gibbs v. Hous. Auth., 76 B.R. 257 (D. Conn. 1983), *aff'g* 9 B.R. 758 (Bankr. D. Conn. 1981); *In re* Pace, 23 Clearinghouse Rev. 1548 (Bankr. W.D. Ky. 1989); *In re* Szymecki, 87 B.R. 14 (Bankr. W.D. Pa. 1988); *In re* Sudler, 71 B.R. 780 (Bankr. E.D. Pa. 1986). *But see In re* Robinson, 54 F.3d 316 (7th Cir. 1995) (if public housing lease was terminated prior to tenant's bankruptcy, lessor was not required by section 525 to renew lease); *In re* Smith, 259 B.R. 901 (B.A.P. 8th Cir. 2001) (section 525 not applicable because debtor's public housing lease terminated due to fraud; dictum that there would be no protection under section 525 even if nonpayment of rent was only reason); *In re* Valentin, 309 B.R. 715 (Bankr. E.D. Pa. 2004) (section 525(a) protects only future right to participate in public housing program, not the lease itself); *In re* Lutz, 82 B.R. 699 (Bankr. M.D. Pa. 1988) (landlord who receives subsidy from Dep't of Housing and Urban Development toward debtor's rental is not a public entity subject to the Code's antidiscrimination provision).
850 *In re* Kelly, 356 B.R. 899 (Bankr. S.D. Fla. 2006).
851 *See* § 15.5.1, *supra*.
852 A sample complaint to enforce a public housing tenant's rights under section 525(a) can be found at Form 104, Appx. G.10, *infra*.
853 See discussion of assumption and rejection of leases in § 12.9, *supra*.
854 For a discussion of the automatic stay and the exception to the stay with respect to a lessor who has obtained a judgment for possession, see Chapter 9, *supra*.
855 *See* 187 Concourse Assocs. v. Bunting, 670 N.Y.S.2d 686 (Civ. Ct. 1997) (prebankruptcy possessory judgment for apartment not discharged or vacated by bankruptcy).
856 *In re* Lutz, 82 B.R. 699 (Bankr. M.D. Pa. 1988). *But see In re* Oksentowicz, 314 B.R. 638 (Bankr. E.D. Mich. 2004) (privately owned apartment complex participating in Section 8 housing program and subject to extensive regulation by the Dep't of Housing and Urban Development was governmental unit; discrimination found based on owner's refusal to accept debtor's rental application), *aff'd*, 2005 U.S. Dist. LEXIS 20258 (E.D. Mich. Sept. 16, 2005).
857 *In re* Malone, 19 Collier Bankr. Cas. (MB) 163 (Bankr. N.J. 1978); *In re* Smallwood, No. B-78-02468 (Bankr. D.N.J. Oct. 1978), 12 Clearinghouse Rev. 509 (Dec. 1978).
858 For a discussion of leases in chapter 13, see § 12.9, *supra*.

15.5.5.4 Social Security, Welfare, and Other Governmental Benefits

In many instances, debtors have debts to local, state or federal governmental agencies, that arise out of various public benefit programs and that they wish to discharge. These debts may arise out of a general duty to reimburse for such benefits, which exists under some state laws, or out of an overpayment which the debtor is required to repay.

In most cases these debts are dischargeable because, absent certain kinds of fraud, they do not fall within any of the exceptions to discharge.[859] It seems clear that any future denial or recoupment of benefits based upon the discharge would fall squarely within the prohibitions of sections 525(a) and/or 524(a).[860]

One situation which may sometimes arise concerns the debtor who has made an agreement to repay interim public assistance benefits received while the debtor is awaiting an award of Supplemental Security Income benefits (SSI). In such cases, federal law provides that the debtor's retroactive benefit check may be sent by the Social Security Administration to the state welfare department so that the latter may deduct the amount owed under the agreement.[861]

If a bankruptcy is filed by the debtor recipient, the debt to the welfare department should be dischargeable unless the agency successfully argues an exception to discharge.[862] (It should be remembered that certain exceptions, such as fraud and false pretenses may not be raised except in the bankruptcy court and before the deadline set by the rules.)[863] In fact, it is likely that even the contingent liability under the agreement for welfare benefits not yet received can also be discharged, because contingent claims are included in the liabilities covered by the discharge.[864]

Thus, any action taken by the state to collect the debt would be stayed during the bankruptcy case by section 362(a)[865] and afterwards by section 524(a).[866] Moreover, the Social Security Administration could not discriminate against the debtor by sending the retroactive benefit check to the local welfare office, based upon the discharged debt, without violating section 525(a).[867] Finally, to the extent that the transfer has already taken place and was of property acquired within ninety days prior to the case, it would probably constitute a preference avoidable by the debtor or trustee.[868]

15.5.5.5 Criminal Proceedings, Fines, and Incarceration

In some cases, the tricky problem of dealing with criminal or quasi-criminal proceedings during or after bankruptcy may be encountered. During the bankruptcy, such problems may sometimes be dealt with through use of the automatic stay.[869] Both during and after the case, section 525(a) may also be applicable. Assuming that the right to be free from incarceration is a

---

859 *In re* Ramirez, 795 F.2d 1494 (9th Cir. 1986) (debtor had no duty to reimburse state for welfare payments to his former spouse and children when there was no support order or court decree obligating him to provide support); Lee v. Schweiker, 739 F.2d 870 (3d Cir. 1984) (Social Security overpayment); *In re* Neavear, 674 F.2d 1201 (7th Cir. 1982) (Social Security overpayments); Baker v. United States, 100 B.R. 80 (M.D. Fla. 1989) (FECA disability benefits); *In re* Olson, 9 B.R. 52 (Bankr. E.D. Wis. 1981) (overpayment of unemployment benefits discharged); *In re* Hudson, 9 B.R. 363 (Bankr. N.D. Ill. 1981) (welfare overpayments allegedly obtained through fraud dischargeable in chapter 13). *See also In re* Malinowski, 156 F.3d 131, 135 (2d Cir. 1998) (withholding of postpetition unemployment benefits to repay prepetition overpayment was not permissible recoupment and violated automatic stay); § 15.4.3.2.3, *supra*. *But see In re* Beaumont, 586 F.3d 776 (10th Cir. 2009) (Veterans Administration could recoup overpayment from future benefits).

It should also be noted that the *Ramirez* decision may no longer be good law after the 2005 bankruptcy amendments.

860 *In re* Cost, 161 B.R. 856 (Bankr. S.D. Fla. 1993) (attorney fees and costs awarded as sanctions to remedy Social Security Administration's recovery of discharged overpayment through withholding from benefits). *But see In re* Beaumont, 586 F.3d 776 (10th Cir. 2009) (Veterans Administration could recoup overpayment from future benefits).

861 42 U.S.C. § 1383(g).
862 *See* § 15.4.3.2.3, *supra*.
863 *See* § 15.4.2, *supra*.

864 Section 727(b) provides for discharge of all "debts" which arose before the bankruptcy. Section 101(12) defines "debt" as "liability on a claim" and section 101(5) defines "claim" to include contingent claims.

865 See discussion of automatic stay under this section in § 9.4, *supra*.

866 *But see In re* Vasquez, 788 F.2d 130 (3d Cir. 1984), *rev'g* 42 B.R. 609 (Bankr. E.D. Pa. 1984).

The *Vasquez* decision ignored persuasive arguments that its finding of a common law assignment was contrary to state law. *See also* § 15.5.1, *supra*.

867 *See* § 15.5.3, *supra*.

For a discussion of possible limitations on such an action based on sovereign immunity, see § 14.3.2.2, *supra*.

868 11 U.S.C. §§ 522(h), 547.

Under section 547(e)(2) and (3), the transfer is made, for purposes of these sections only, when the debtor has acquired rights in the property transferred and the transfer takes effect. However, a debtor seeking to use section 522(h) might have to defend against the argument that the agreement was voluntary. Such an argument would probably be surmounted if the debtor could show that the alternative to signing was starving to death. See § 10.4.2.5, *supra*, for a discussion of these issues.

These sections would prove particularly helpful if the welfare department attempted to argue that it had a security interest, a rather doubtful proposition in view of the wording of the regulation and agreements involved. Even if a lien were found to exist, any property acquired after the case was commenced would not be subject to that lien. *See* 11 U.S.C. § 552(a).

Some preference actions against state or federal governments may be precluded by sovereign immunity. *See* § 14.3.2.2, *supra*.

869 *See* § 9.4.7, *supra*, for a discussion of related issues. *See generally In re* Poule, 91 B.R. 83 (B.A.P. 9th Cir. 1988) (comparison of application of automatic stay for restitution with application for fine); *In re* Coulter, 305 B.R. 748 (Bankr. D.S.C. 2003) (although automatic stay did not prohibit state court probation violation hearing, state which had filed a proof of claim for restitution and fees was bound by debtor's confirmed plan providing for their payment).

"license,"[870] then the state cannot incarcerate a debtor due to a debt that was discharged.[871] Similarly, driver's license suspensions, based on dischargeable unpaid traffic fines should be found to violate section 525(a).[872] To the extent that it can be shown that a criminal or contempt proceeding is for the purpose of collecting a discharged debt,[873] such proceedings are in violation of section 524(a) or (b).[874]

However, as discussed elsewhere in this chapter,[875] the court must first find that the fine or restitution order is a dischargeable debt. The Supreme Court has held that at least some restitution debts are not dischargeable in a chapter 7 case,[876] but such debts may be dischargeable in a chapter 13 case.[877] Similarly, fines are not generally dischargeable in chapter 7, but may be dischargeable in chapter 13.[878]

If those hurdles are overcome, along with such issues as abstention,[879] the bankruptcy forum's authority under 11 U.S.C. § 105, could give debtors significant protections in the many cases in which creditors and local authorities attempt to use criminal or contempt proceedings to coerce payments.[880] However, emotions in such cases may run high, and enforcement of the bankruptcy protections may be difficult.

15.5.5.6 Tax Consequences of the Discharge

The law is clear that, generally speaking, the discharge of a debt in bankruptcy, unlike most other types of discharge of indebtedness without payment, is excludable from gross income for tax purposes.[881] Nonetheless, some creditors believe that they are required to send a bankruptcy debtor a 1099 Form when a debt is discharged in bankruptcy.[882] Although this problem may eventually disappear as a result of clarifying tax regulations,[883] and the fact that the current version of Form 1099-C states on its reverse side that "debts canceled in bankruptcy are not includable in your income," it is likely to persist for some time.

These forms cause considerable confusion and harm to debtors. All too often, an unskilled tax preparer will see the 1099 form, assume the debtor had taxable income, and list the amount stated on the form as income on the debtor's tax return. It is also possible, but unlikely, that the Internal Revenue Service will incorrectly seek payment of taxes which are not

---

870 "License" has been defined as the "authority or liberty given to do or forbear any act," the "leave to do a thing which the licensor could prevent," and "permission to do something which without the license would not be allowable." See Black's Law Dictionary 1067 (4th ed. rev.).

871 See generally Pennsylvania Dep't of Pub. Welfare v. Davenport, 495 U.S. 552, 110 S. Ct. 2126, 109 L. Ed. 2d 588 (1990).

The Davenport decision does not fully address whether a judge could have someone imprisoned for the probation violation inherent in not paying a dischargeable restitution order. However, the court's dicta, taken together with common sense, strongly suggests that a discharge and/or the automatic stay and/or the confirmed plan must preclude the debtor's incarceration for failure to pay restitution after a chapter 13 case has been filed. In fact, the court specifically found that the exception to the automatic stay for commencement or continuation of criminal proceedings did not encompass the enforcement of obligations arising out of such proceedings. Id., 110 S. Ct. at 2132. In some instances that argument may have to be presented first to the state court sentencing judge. If necessary, emergency habeas corpus proceedings could bring the issue before a bankruptcy or other federal judge. In re Rainwater, 233 B.R. 126 (Bankr. N.D. Ala. 1999) (writ of habeas corpus granted to release debtor from imprisonment for violation of probation by not paying restitution that was provided for in chapter 13 plan), vacated, 254 B.R. 273 (N.D. Ala. 2000). See § 14.4.5, supra. But see Hucke v. Oregon, 992 F.2d 950 (9th Cir. 1993) (revocation of probation after nonpayment of restitution did not violate the automatic stay as attempt to collect debt because state court judge canceled restitution obligation when probation was revoked).

872 See In re Colon, 102 B.R. 421 (Bankr. E.D. Pa. 1989) (prepetition traffic fines are dischargeable in chapter 13; attempts to collect them by postpetition license suspension violate the automatic stay); In re Young, 10 B.R. 17 (Bankr. S.D. Cal. 1980) (state could not deny driver's license due to fine which would be discharged in chapter 13).

Many criminal fines are no longer dischargeable in chapter 13, due to a 1994 amendment to 11 U.S.C. § 1328(a). See § 15.4.3.7, supra.

873 See In re Kaping, 13 B.R. 621 (Bankr. D. Or. 1981) (prosecution of criminal nonsupport charge enjoined when principal motivation was to obtain restitution of discharged debts).

874 Burton v. Mouser (In re Burton), 2010 WL 996537 (Bankr. W.D. Ky. Mar. 16, 2010) (continuation of bad check prosecution violated discharge injunction); In re Dovell, 311 B.R. 492 (Bankr. S.D. Ohio 2004) (preliminary injunction issued when criminal proceeding would not have occurred but for actions of creditor intended to compel payment of discharged debt). See § 15.5.1, supra. See also In re Gilliam, 67 B.R. 83 (Bankr. M.D. Tenn. 1986). But see In re Daulton, 966 F.2d 1025 (6th Cir. 1992) (when creditors did not seek restitution, their signing of criminal complaint against debtor alleging fraudulent sale of collateral does not violate discharge injunction); Nash v. Clark County Dist. Atty's. Office (In re Nash), 464 B.R. 874 (B.A.P. 9th Cir. 2012) (when debtor had signed agreement with prosecutor, prior to bankruptcy, to pay gambling marker, bankruptcy court could not take action that would interfere with criminal proceeding); Williams v. Meyer (In re Williams), 438 B.R. 679 (B.A.P. 10th Cir. 2010) (once debtor has been convicted of crime, motivation of creditor not relevant).

875 See § 15.4.3.7, supra.

876 Kelly v. Robinson, 479 U.S. 36, 107 S. Ct. 353, 93 L. Ed. 2d 216 (1986).

877 Pennsylvania Dep't of Pub. Welfare v. Davenport, 495 U.S. 552, 110 S. Ct. 2126, 109 L. Ed. 2d 588 (1990).

But see 11 U.S.C. § 1328(a)(3) containing an exception to discharge in chapter 13 applicable to restitution included in a criminal sentence.

878 See § 15.4.3.7, supra.

879 See § 9.4.7, supra.

880 See In re Lenke, 249 B.R. 1 (Bankr. D. Ariz. 2000) (bankruptcy court had authority to enjoin prosecution if it was disguised effort to collect debt); In re Hudson, 9 B.R. 363 (Bankr. N.D. Ill. 1981); Rendleman, The Bankruptcy Discharge: Toward a Fresher Start, 58 N.C. L. Rev. 723, 736–741 (1980). But see § 9.4.7, supra.

881 Internal Revenue Code, 26 U.S.C. § 108(a)(1)(A).

882 Some confusion is possible because there may be tax consequences of prepetition debt forgiveness, for example, if a deficiency obligation is forgiven in connection with a deed in lieu of foreclosure, as discussed below.

883 26 C.F.R. §§ 1.6050P-0, 1.6050P-1 (indebtedness discharged in bankruptcy required to be reported only if creditor knows that the debt was incurred for business or investment purposes).

owed based on a filed 1099.[884] A debtor could thus pay taxes that are not owed, often losing a needed tax refund.

A related problem can occur when a debt was forgiven by the creditor prior to the bankruptcy. The most common example is a deficiency obligation which is forgiven in exchange for a deed in lieu of foreclosure or another type of foreclosure workout. Although the prepetition forgiveness of debt is technically a taxable event separate from the bankruptcy discharge,[885] it is generally not taxable in the event that the debtor was insolvent.[886] Tax issues can also arise when there is a foreclosure on a mortgage that was obtained after the original purchase of a property; if the mortgage was for more than the original purchase price a capital gain may be created. In most cases, however, the $500,000 capital gains exemption for sale of a debtor's principal residence will prevent any tax liability.

In view of the fact that these problems have become more common, attorneys should always advise debtors that the discharge of indebtedness in bankruptcy and most types of forgiveness of debt are not taxable. It is also helpful to recommend that a tax preparer with a question about the law on this issue should be referred to the attorney.

15.5.5.7 Enforcement of the Discharge Protections

In almost every case in which the debtor's discharge rights are being violated, it is wise to take some type of protective action. Even though a judgment obtained on a discharged debt is void,[887] that judgment could also cause illegal but harmful garnishment of the debtor's wages or seizure of the debtor's property. Thus, it is good practice to assert the protections of discharge as early as possible.

The first decision that arises in such cases is where to enforce the debtor's rights. Although they could be raised in the state forum in which a proceeding is already pending, it is usually preferable to go to the bankruptcy forum, which is likely to be more sympathetic to the debtor's concerns. The bankruptcy court clearly has jurisdiction over any proceeding relating to the debtor's bankruptcy, and in many cases a state court proceeding may be removed to federal district court.[888] If the debtor does litigate the issue in the nonbankruptcy court, there is a risk that any attempt to seek relief from the challenged actions in the bankruptcy court thereafter would be barred.[889]

Several remedies may be possible in the bankruptcy forum (in addition to simply defending a removed action). The federal court may issue a writ of habeas corpus to release a debtor incarcerated in state proceedings.[890] An injunction may be issued against private parties or state officials. If the problem is a common one, a class action should be considered, though it might be better to bring an individual case first if the law is unclear.[891] Attorney fees should be available in any action against state or local officials under section 524 or 525.[892] Finally, violators of the section 524(a) injunction can be held in contempt of court.[893] The remedies for civil contempt can include both damages and attorney fees, even if the contempt is not willful.[894]

---

884 This would obviously be an IRS error subject to dispute by the debtor.
885 26 U.S.C. § 61(a)(12).
886 26 U.S.C. § 108(a)(1)(B).
887 11 U.S.C. § 524(a)(1); *In re* Cruz, 254 B.R. 801 (Bankr. S.D.N.Y. 2000). *But see* Fed. Deposit Ins. Corp. v. Gulf Life Ins. Co., 737 F.2d 1513 (11th Cir. 1984) (bankruptcy defense rejected when it was pleaded but not proved); § 15.5.1.3, *supra*.
888 28 U.S.C. §§ 1334(b), 1452.
   See § 14.4.1, *supra*, for a discussion of removal. *See also In re* Myers, 18 B.R. 362 (Bankr. E.D. Va. 1982) (bankruptcy case reopened and creditor fined $10,000 for willful violation of discharge injunction).
889 *In re* Ferren, 203 F.3d 559 (8th Cir. 2000) (bankruptcy court lacked jurisdiction over debtor's attack on state court order disbursing foreclosure sale proceeds to judicial lienholders due to *Rooker-Feldman* doctrine). *Cf. In re* Pavelich, 229 B.R. 777 (B.A.P. 9th Cir. 1999) (*Rooker-Feldman* doctrine did not prevent enforcement of discharge injunction); *In re* Presley, 288 B.R. 732 (Bankr. W.D. Va. 2003) (litigated judgment against debtor was void even though debtor did not raise bankruptcy defense).
890 See § 14.4.5, *supra*, for a discussion of the writ of habeas corpus in bankruptcy cases.
891 See § 14.7, *supra*, for a discussion of class actions in bankruptcy.
892 See discussion of class actions in § 14.7, *supra*, and attorney fees in § 16.5, *infra*. *See also* Eastman v. Baker Recovery Servs. (*In re* Eastman), 2010 WL 5462469 (Bankr. W.D. Tex. Dec. 29, 2010) (debtor entitled to fees even if there are no other damages).
893 *In re* Hill, 222 B.R. 119 (Bankr. N.D. Ohio 1998) (creditor's calls to debtor after bankruptcy were willful and therefore in contempt of court even though creditor had procedures to prevent violations of discharge, debtor awarded attorney fees); *In re* Tardo, 145 B.R. 862 (E.D. La. 1992) (creditor's attorney found in contempt for seeking to collect attorney fees he would have received under contingent fee agreement with creditor after court rejected his argument that contingent attorney fee was a separate debt which had not been scheduled or discharged); *In re* Esposito, 119 B.R. 305 (Bankr. M.D. Fla. 1990) (unsecured creditor who tricked debtors into payment of discharged debt found in contempt of court and ordered to pay damages and attorney fees); *In re* Barrup, 51 B.R. 318 (Bankr. D. Vt. 1985); *In re* Gallagher, 47 B.R. 92 (Bankr. W.D. Wis. 1985). *See also* § 15.5.1.4, *supra*.
894 *In re* Rosteck, 899 F.2d 694 (7th Cir. 1990) (sanctions imposed against condominium association that had attempted to collect postpetition condominium assessments which were discharged); *In re* Elias, 98 B.R. 332 (N.D. Ill. 1989) (creditor found in contempt even though violation of discharge injunction was not in bad faith, when creditor has knowledge of discharge order); *In re* Slayton, 409 B.R. 897 (Bankr. N.D. Ill. 2009) (Eleventh Amendment did not bar damages against state, but section 106 barred punitive damages); *In re* Atkins, 279 B.R. 639 (Bankr. N.D.N.Y. 2002) ($30,000 damages awarded against federal government for attempts to collect discharged loan); *In re* Wasp, 137 B.R. 71 (Bankr. M.D. Fla. 1992) (action brought by home owners association to collect fees under prepetition agreement which had been unmatured at time of bankruptcy filing constituted contempt); *In re* Burson, 107 B.R. 285 (Bankr. S.D. Cal. 1989) (government violated discharge injunction when it attempted to collect serviceman's repayment obligation; though obligation matured postpetition, government had contingent right to payment at time serviceman filed bankruptcy); *In re* Barrup, 51 B.R. 318 (Bankr. D. Vt. 1985); *In re* Gallagher, 47 B.R. 92 (Bankr. W.D. Wis. 1985). *See* McComb v. Jacksonville Paper Co., 336 U.S. 187, 191 (1949); Borg-Warner Acceptance Corp. v. Hall, 685 F.2d 1306 (11th Cir. 1982); Vuitton et Fils v. Carousel Handbags, 592 F.2d 126 (2d Cir. 1979); § 9.6, *supra*.

The debtor may also assert an implied private right of action under section 524 and seek equitable relief under section 105 of the Bankruptcy Code. Under the principles set forth by the Supreme Court in *Cort v. Ash*,[895] there is every reason to find that Congress intended that such a right of action exist. These issues were well analyzed by the district court in *Malone v. Norwest Financial California, Inc.*,[896] although that decision was later overruled.[897] The *Malone* court held, first, that the enforcement of the bankruptcy discharge is not a matter typically left to state law. Second, the debtors who receive discharge are clearly the specific intended beneficiaries of section 524, not mere incidental beneficiaries. Third, there is evidence of Congressional intent that there be implied remedies: the statute provides for rescission of invalid reaffirmations, for example, and such rescission logically gives rise to actions for enforcing the rescission and restitution. The mere fact that there is an explicit private right of action for violations of section 362, enacted by a later Congress, has no bearing on remedies for violations of section 524, because Congress might have already assumed such a remedy existed based on the rescission remedies available. Indeed, the Supreme Court has held that the availability of statutory injunctive relief does not limit the corollary equitable powers to order rescission and restitution.[898] And the legislative history shows that Congress intended broad discharge protections for bankruptcy debtors; to restrict those remedies would be inconsistent with that intent. For the same reason, there is no basis for finding that Congress intended to preempt state consumer protection laws or restrict use of other federal consumer protection laws as they apply to bankruptcy debtors.[899]

A number of courts have held that there is no private right of action that allows a class of debtors to pursue relief for violations of the discharge order.[900] Some courts have also held that contempt of the discharge injunction is the only remedy for violations of the discharge and preempts state law remedies.[901] The Ninth Circuit Court of Appeals has further held that contempt must be sought by a motion rather than by an adversary proceeding.[902] As discussed above, these cases are clearly wrong given that the discharge injunction is a creation of statute. Unlike other contempt claims, this uniform order need not be enforced solely by an individual contempt proceeding in the court that issued it, because debtors are enforcing a statutory right rather than a unique order that requires interpretation by its maker.[903] Moreover, there is ample authority to enforce the discharge injunction by requiring disgorgement and other equitable remedies under 11 U.S.C. § 105(a).[904]

Reopening of the bankruptcy case may be required to address post-discharge issues, although not all courts require it as

---

Note that a subsequent statutory amendment may have overruled the *Burson* case by making such claims nondischargeable. *See* 37 U.S.C. §§ 301d(c)(3), 317(f)(3). *See also* § 15.5.1.4, *supra*. But see 26 U.S.C. § 7433(e), which appears to limit damages for violations of the discharge injunction by the Internal Revenue Service to willful violations.

Section 7433(e) also contains a statute of limitations for seeking relief. *See* Kovacs v. United States, 614 F.3d 666 (7th Cir. 2010). It also appears to require exhaustion of administrative remedies. Kovacs v. United States, 614 F.3d 666 (7th Cir. 2010); Kuhl v. United States, 467 F.3d 145 (2d Cir. 2006). *But see In re* Johnston, 2010 WL 1254882 (Bankr. D. Ariz. Mar. 22, 2010); *In re* Graham, 2003 WL 21224773 (Bankr. E.D. Va. Apr. 11, 2003). *See generally* § 15.5.1.4, note 661, *supra*.

895 422 U.S. 66, 95 S. Ct. 2080, 45 L. Ed. 2d 26 (1975).
896 245 B.R. 389 (E.D. Cal. 2000). *See also* Molloy v. Primus Auto. Fin. Servs., 247 B.R. 804 (C.D. Cal. 2000) (finding private right of action under section 524); Rogers v. Nationscredit Fin. Servs., 233 B.R. 98 (N.D. Cal. 1999).
897 Walls v. Wells Fargo Bank, 276 F.3d 502 (9th Cir. 2002).
898 *See* California v. Am. Stores, 495 U.S. 271, 110 S. Ct. 1853, 109 L. Ed. 2d 240 (1990) (injunctive relief available under Clayton Act creates power to order other equitable relief including divestiture of acquired assets); Porter v. Warner Holding Co., 328 U.S. 395, 66 S. Ct. 1086, 90 L. Ed. 1332 (1946) (grant of specific equitable powers by statute did not restrict other equitable powers unless statute explicitly so stated).
899 Randolph v. IMBS, Inc., 368 F.3d 726 (7th Cir. 2004) (no irreconcilable conflict exists between Fair Debt Collection Practices Act and Bankruptcy Code, so both statutes can be enforced simultaneously); Sears Roebuck & Co. v. O'Brien, 178 F.3d 962 (8th Cir. 1999) (state debt collection law violated by creditor sending reaffirmation solicitation letter); Molloy v. Primus Auto. Fin. Servs., 247 B.R. 804 (C.D. Cal. 2000); *In re* Padilla, 379 B.R. 643 (Bankr. S.D. Tex. 2007) (Bankruptcy Code does not immunize mortgage creditor from causes of action based on Real Estate Settlement Procedures Act); *In re* Holland, 374 B.R. 409 (Bankr. D. Mass. 2007) (no inherent conflict between Bankruptcy Code and provisions of Real Estate Settlement Procedures Act); *In re* Faust, 270 B.R. 310 (Bankr. M.D. Ga. 1998) (recommending judgment under Fair Debt Collection Practices Act for acts that violated discharge injunction).
900 *See, e.g., In re* Bassett, 285 F.3d 882 (9th Cir. 2002); Cox v. Zale Del., Inc., 239 F.3d 910 (7th Cir. 2001); Pertuso v. Ford Motor Credit Co., 233 F.3d 417 (6th Cir. 2000); Walls v. Wells Fargo Bank, 255 B.R. 38 (E.D. Cal. 2000); Bessette v. Avco Fin. Servs., 230 F.3d 439 (1st Cir. 2000) (the court of appeals found that an action could be brought to remedy discharge violations under 11 U.S.C. § 105).
901 *See, e.g.*, Cox v. Zale Del., Inc., 239 F.3d 910 (7th Cir. 2001); Pertuso v. Ford Motor Credit Co., 233 F.3d 417 (6th Cir. 2000); Walls v. Wells Fargo Bank, 255 B.R. 38 (E.D. Cal. 2000); Rogers v. Nationscredit Fin. Servs. Corp., 233 B.R. 98 (N.D. Cal. 1999), *overruled by* Walls v. Wells Fargo Bank, 276 F.3d 502 (9th Cir. 2002).
902 Barrientos v. Wells Fargo Bank, 633 F.3d 1186 (9th Cir. 2011).
903 Bessette v. Avco Fin. Servs., Inc., 230 F.3d 439 (1st Cir. 2000) (discharge injunction may be enforced in class action because statutory injunction under section 524 is a uniform order in every bankruptcy case). *But see* Alderwoods Group, Inc. v. Garcia, 682 F.3d 958 (11th Cir. Fla. 2012) (discharge injunction must be enforced in court that entered discharge).
904 Bessette v. Avco Fin. Servs., Inc., 230 F.3d 439 (1st Cir. 2000) (section 524 may be enforced through section 105); *In re* Rodriguez, 396 B.R. 436 (Bankr. S.D. Tex. 2008); *In re* Mickens, 229 B.R. 114 (Bankr. W.D. Va. 1999); *In re* Vazquez, 221 B.R. 222 (Bankr. N.D. Ill. 1998) (actual and punitive damages awarded pursuant to section 105). *See also In re* Harris, 312 B.R. 591 (N.D. Miss. 2004) (section 105 could provide remedy for improper assessment of late charges in chapter 13 cure); § 15.5.1.4, *supra. But see* Duby v. United States (*In re* Duby), 451 B.R. 664 (B.A.P. 1st Cir. 2011) (punitive sanctions not available against United States because § 106 did not waive sovereign immunity for punitive damages).

a prerequisite to enforcing the discharge.[905] Reopening should be liberally granted when necessary to afford relief for the debtor.[906]

Thus, the bankruptcy forum does not offer assistance to debtors only during their bankruptcy cases. Its expanded reach enables it to provide a full measure of protection as long as it is needed in relation to the bankruptcy and the debts discharged therein. The bankruptcy forum has become one to which consumer debtors can turn to solve many of their problems, applying a law which, unlike most, is designed principally to benefit those unfortunate people who so often find themselves victimized elsewhere.

---

[905] *See In re* Singleton, 269 B.R. 270 (Bankr. D.R.I. 2001) (see also cases cited therein), *vacated on other grounds*, 284 B.R. 322 (D.R.I. 2002).

[906] *See* Fed. R. Bankr. P. 5010.

No filing fee is required to reopen a case if the reopening is for actions related to the debtor's discharge. *See* Judicial Conference of the United States, Bankruptcy Court Miscellaneous Fee Schedule, reprinted in Appendix C.4, *infra*.

Chapter 16 Attorney Fees for Debtor's Counsel and Attorney Duties in Consumer Bankruptcy Cases

16.1 Introduction

A topic of more than passing interest to private attorneys representing consumer debtors is the matter of attorney fees. While the general factors governing decisions concerning what fees to charge and how to collect them can be very similar to those for other types of legal matters, bankruptcy attorney fees are unusual in several ways. Similarly, while the duties of debtors' attorneys are generally coextensive with those of attorneys representing other clients, there are special bankruptcy provisions of which they must be aware.

Unlike most clients of private practitioners, bankruptcy clients are always facing serious financial problems. They may have great difficulties in paying even modest fees. These difficulties require counsel to consider alternatives to the typical fee arrangements under which some amount is paid in advance with the remainder billed as services are performed. Such arrangements may be particularly disadvantageous as to unpaid balances owed when the petition is filed; any debt owed on the date of the petition is dischargeable[1] and any attempt to collect such a debt would violate the automatic stay imposed by 11 U.S.C. § 362.[2]

Another unusual aspect of bankruptcy attorney fees is the requirement that all such fees be disclosed to the court and approved by the court. While in a typical case this requirement has no impact on the ultimate receipt of fees, special circumstances, as discussed below, can render it important in a particular case.

A third key difference, in chapter 13 cases and in occasional chapter 7 cases involving the liquidation of assets, is the possibility for payment of attorney fees through the court's administration of the bankruptcy. Most typically, this means that fees may be paid as a priority claim through the debtor's chapter 13 plan, an arrangement that provides one solution for the debtor unable to pay all or even part of the fee in advance.

With respect to attorney duties, all attorneys in bankruptcy cases are subject to Federal Rule of Bankruptcy Procedure 9011, a close correlate of Federal Rule of Civil Procedure 11. However, there are additional provisions in section 707(b)(4) that slightly modify the Rule 9011 sanctions in certain circumstances,[3] and there are other provisions governing "debt relief agencies" with which attorneys should comply.[4]

16.2 Initial Fee Arrangements with Clients

16.2.1 The Basic Fee

As in any other matter, it is very important for the attorney and client to discuss and have a clear understanding of fee arrangements as early as possible. Normally, this discussion occurs at the first interview with the debtor. Many attorneys have preprinted retainer agreements or brochures, that they give to clients at this initial consultation, spelling out exactly which services are covered by the attorney's basic fee, and what charges will be made for additional services, should they prove necessary.[5] Naturally, these written materials and all fee arrangements should be consistent with any previous advertisements or representations that the attorney has made.[6]

Many attorneys, as well as some courts in their review of counsel's compensation, begin the process of setting fees by deciding upon a reasonable basic fee for those services necessary in a typical bankruptcy case.[7] This fee covers the initial

---

1 Rittenhouse v. Eisen, 404 F.3d 395 (6th Cir. 2005) (fees for filing chapter 7 bankruptcy case were discharged); *In re* Bethea, 352 F.3d 1125 (7th Cir. 2003) (postpetition collection of prepetition fees violated automatic stay); *In re* Biggar, 110 F.3d 685 (9th Cir. 1997); *In re* Newkirk, 297 B.R. 457 (Bankr. W.D.N.C. 2002) (obtaining postdated checks for prepetition fees, to be cashed postpetition, violated automatic stay and created conflict of interest with client). *See also In re* Perez, 177 B.R. 319 (Bankr. D. Neb. 1995) (any reaffirmation of prepetition debt for attorney fees must comply with all requirements for reaffirmation).

2 See Chapter 9, *supra*, for a general discussion of the automatic stay.

3 *See* § 16.7.2, *infra*.

4 *See* § 16.8.1, *infra*.

5 An attorney seeking to comply with the debt relief agency provisions must provide a contract with this information within five days after first providing "bankruptcy assistance," and before a petition is filed. 11 U.S.C. § 528(a)(1),(2). *See* § 16.8.4, *infra*.

6 *See In re* Stewart, 10 B.R. 472 (Bankr. E.D. Va. 1981) (court reduced fees agreed upon by debtors to level which had been advertised in local publications).

7 *See, e.g., In re* Stewart, 10 B.R. 472 (Bankr. E.D. Va. 1981); *In re* Hill, 5 B.R. 541 (Bankr. C.D. Cal. 1980); *In re* St. Pierre, 4 B.R. 184 (Bankr. D.R.I. 1980). *See also In re* Bancroft, 204 B.R. 548 (Bankr. C.D. Ill. 1997) (attorney who did not personally interview clients or attend meeting of creditors was not providing even minimum level of professional services and was not entitled to attorney fee).

consultation and advice to a debtor about alternatives to bankruptcy, consequences of bankruptcy, whether to file, and under what chapter to file. It also encompasses preparation of the initial papers, such as the petition, schedules, statement of affairs and chapter 13 plan, as well as any factual investigation necessary for that task. In addition, the basic fee includes compensation for attendance at the meeting of creditors, chapter 13 confirmation hearing, and discharge hearing (when a discharge hearing is required). Finally, this fee is deemed to encompass ancillary minor and routine tasks and advice to the debtor throughout the course of the case,[8] which are often listed if an applicable local rule sets a "no look" fee that will generally not be questioned. For cases that are more complex than a typical case, an attorney may charge fees higher than the usual fee. Most bankruptcy courts do not permit an attorney to "unbundle" these basic services and provide, for example, only the preparation of the papers initially filed.[9] And courts normally require that an attorney who files a case must seek permission before withdrawing from a case.[10]

However, it is clear that the basic fee is not cast in stone and serves more as a guideline for the convenience and efficiency of the court and counsel, permitting prompt approval of fees without a detailed review of the work done. Because fees in bankruptcy cases are to be awarded on the same basis as fees in other cases, counsel is entitled to request more than the court's normal fee, even in a routine case, under the lodestar method which provides for compensation at a reasonable hourly rate for time reasonably expended.[11] Nonetheless, counsel seeking to deviate from the basic fee may face a substantial burden in convincing the court that the rates and hours sought are reasonable if other attorneys in the district routinely perform the same services at a lower cost.[12]

16.2.2 Amounts Typically Charged

While there are great variations in the amounts charged to cover basic services, the range in chapter 7 cases is usually from $1000 to $2000 and many courts set an informal limit between $1500 and $2500.[13] Some attorneys and courts con-

---

8 *In re* Snyder, 445 B.R. 431 (Bankr. E.D. Pa. 2010) (chapter 13 fee agreement construed against debtor's attorney where ambiguous as to ancillary matters excluded from flat fee; fees reduced from requested $11,700 to $3500); *In re* Wesseldine, 434 B.R. 31 (Bankr. N.D.N.Y. 2010) (lien avoidance motion included in "no look" chapter 13 flat fee under local rule, precluding separate fee claim). *See In re* Kasperek, 399 B.R. 591 (Bankr. W.D.N.Y. 2009) (debtor's counsel could not demand additional fees for complying with trustee turnover requests when such tasks were not specifically excluded from services that would be rendered in exchange for basic fee).

9 *See* Hale v. United States Tr., 509 F.3d 1139 (9th Cir. 2007) (attorney sanctioned for providing only preparation of documents when debtors did not understand limitations on services and attorney refused to say which services he personally performed); *In re* Stewart, 10 B.R. 472 (Bankr. E.D. Va. 1981); *In re* Hill, 5 B.R. 541 (Bankr. C.D. Cal. 1980); *In re* St. Pierre, 4 B.R. 184 (Bankr. D.R.I. 1980). *See also In re* Bancroft, 204 B.R. 548 (Bankr. C.D. Ill. 1997).

10 *In re* Bulen, 375 B.R. 858 (Bankr. D. Minn. 2007) (it was improper for fee agreement to state that attorney would withdraw if he was not paid because local rule required attorney to handle entire case unless court gave permission for attorney to withdraw).

11 *In re* Pilgrim's Pride Corp., 690 F.3d 650 (5th Cir. 2012) (lodestar analysis for bankruptcy fees unchanged by Supreme Court decisions in fee-shifting cases); Zolfo, Cooper & Co. v. Sunbeam-Oster Co., 50 F.3d 253 (3d Cir. 1995) (baseline rule for professional fees in bankruptcy cases is for firms to receive their normal rates); *In re* Boddy, 950 F.2d 334 (6th Cir. 1991) (use of $650 "normal and customary" fee for bankruptcy case, rather than lodestar method, was abuse of discretion); *In re* Williams, 357 B.R. 434 (B.A.P. 6th Cir. 2007) (court should have conducted lodestar analysis when counsel sought amount in excess of basic fee); *In re* Dorn, 443 B.R. 555 (Bankr. M.D. Fla. 2011) (chapter 7 debtor's counsel who structured practice to emphasize role of attorneys rather than paralegals and recorded time appropriately for lodestar calculation entitled to fee substantially higher than local "no look" amount); *In re* Johnson, 331 B.R. 534 (Bankr. W.D.N.Y. 2005) (attorney seeking compensation for additional tasks above usual chapter 13 fee must submit time records for entire case); *In re* Barger, 180 B.R. 326 (Bankr. S.D. Ga. 1995) (lodestar method should be used in chapter 13 case). *See also In re* Zwern, 181 B.R. 80 (Bankr. D. Colo. 1995) (counsel seeking to use lodestar method must submit meaningful time records and task summaries). *But see In re* Eliapo, 298 B.R. 392 (B.A.P. 9th Cir. 2003) (attorney who had opted for standardized "no look" standard fee could not later seek lodestar computation of higher fee for services covered by "no look" fee); *In re* Parsons, 2010 WL 3547601 (Bankr. D.N.M. Sept. 9, 2010) (small rural practice not specializing in bankruptcy may charge chapter 7 fee higher than customary in district, but higher fee precluded because failed to keep time records).

12 *See In re* Eliapo, 468 F.3d 592 (9th Cir. 2006) (attorney who had applied for no-look fee did not show extraordinary circumstances justifying additional fees for normal case preparation tasks, but was awarded fees for other additional work; attorney should have been granted opportunity for a hearing on disputed fees); *In re* Cahill, 428 F.3d 536 (5th Cir. 2005) (case did not involve sufficient amount of work to deviate from standard fee); *In re* Peterson, 251 B.R. 359 (B.A.P. 8th Cir. 2000) (reducing hourly rate and number of hours in fee request based on court's perceptions of amounts charged by other local attorneys); *In re* Heise, 436 B.R. 143 (Bankr. D.N.M. 2010) (attorney's reputation as proficient in handling chapter 13 cases did not support fee based on higher hourly rate than other local bankruptcy attorneys); *In re* Laberge, 380 B.R. 277 (Bankr. D. Mass. 2007) ($6000 fee and involvement of two attorneys was not justified in relatively simple chapter 7 case); *In re* Finlasen, 250 B.R. 446 (Bankr. S.D. Fla. 2000) (reducing fees because time sheets did not indicate date of each entry and there was evidence that they were a form list of time entries); *In re* Thorn, 192 B.R. 52 (Bankr. N.D.N.Y. 1995) (fees reduced to amounts customarily charged when no time records or other evidence introduced to support unusually high fees requested in routine cases).

13 Attorney fees have increased substantially because of the additional services required under the 2005 amendments. *See In re* Murray, 348 B.R. 917 (Bankr. M.D. Ga. 2006) (raising no-look fee from $1500 to $2500). *See also* Lupica, Lois R., The Consumer Bankruptcy Fee Study: Final Report (Dec. 1, 2011).

For cases concerning fees decided before 2005, see *In re* Agnew, 144 F.3d 1013 (7th Cir. 1998) (presumptive fee of $575 upheld in cases in which attorney offered no evidence that his services were worth more); *In re* Geraci, 138 F.3d 314 (7th Cir. 1998) (presumptive $800 fee for no asset chapter 7 case not abuse of discretion). *See also* Jean Braucher, *Lawyers and Consumer Bankruptcy: One Code, Many Cultures*, 67 Am. Bankr. L.J. 501 (1993) (discussing range of fees and median fees charged to chapter 7 clients in four

sider it appropriate to add a small increment to this fee in joint cases[14] or when other complications make the case more difficult than average to prepare.[15] Similarly, in chapter 13 cases, basic fees generally range from $2000 to $4000,[16] but in complicated cases may be up to $5000, or more. Although the presumptive fee maximums set by courts can normally be overcome by additional evidence justifying a higher fee in particular cases, the presumptive fees and procedures for overcoming the presumptions are also subject to judicial review and may be set aside when they are arbitrary or outdated.[17]

For attorneys in doubt regarding what amounts are appropriate in a particular locale, it is usually a good idea to review the fee disclosure statements which have been filed and approved in recent cases. Often a discussion of the question with a trustee or attorney more experienced in bankruptcy can also prove helpful.

An attorney can usually predict other services that will be necessary, such as motions to avoid liens or the filing of a homestead deed, once the facts of a debtor's case are known. The fees for such services, assuming that they will proceed routinely, should also be set in advance. In some cases an agreement for a percentage contingency fee may be appropriate, but no such agreement may override the court's duty to determine whether fees are reasonable. If the agreement produces a fee in excess of the reasonable value of services rendered, the excess portion of the fee may be disallowed.[18]

Lastly, the attorney and client should agree upon an arrangement for fees, usually at an hourly rate prevalent in the community, should complications arise.[19] Such complications might include a motion for relief from the automatic stay, the need to object to a claim, or a dischargeability complaint. In every case the debtor should be advised of all costs likely to be incurred, including the necessary filing fees and costs for a credit counseling briefing and credit education course,[20] as well as possible costs for public record searches and appraisals. The attorney must bear in mind, however, that unless withdrawal from the case is permitted the attorney will, in many jurisdictions, be expected to handle all aspects of the case even if the client does not pay these fees.[21]

16.2.3 Method of Payment

In chapter 7 cases, an attorney usually wants to be paid all or most of the fee in advance of the filing. Because an attorney fee contracted for prior to the petition is a dischargeable debt and collection efforts are subject to the automatic stay, collection after filing may prove impossible.[22] It does seem clear that

---

cities studied before 2005 amendments).

14 *In re* Stewart, 10 B.R. 472 (Bankr. E.D. Va. 1981) ($85 added in joint case).

15 *In re* St. Pierre, 4 B.R. 184 (Bankr. D.R.I. 1981) ($150 added for completion of Statement of Affairs for Debtors Engaged in Business).

16 Attorney fees have increased substantially because of the additional services required under the 2005 amendments. *See* Lupica, Lois R., The Consumer Bankruptcy Fee Study: Final Report (Dec. 1, 2011) (finding that the national mean attorney fee in chapter 13 cases increased by 24% after 2005, and that the highest post-2005 mean attorney fees were in Maine, Nevada, and New Hampshire ($4950, $4335, and $4294, respectively)); Government Accountability Office, Report No. GAO-08-697, Dollar Costs Associated with the Bankruptcy Abuse Prevention and Consumer Protection Act of 2005 (2008), *available at* www.gao.gov/new.items/d08697.pdf (detailing study of increased attorney fees); *In re* McNally, 2006 WL 2348687 (Bankr. D. Colo. Aug. 10, 2006) (in discussing rise in chapter 13 fees after 2005 amendments, court noted it has allowed uncontested fee applications in the range of $1800 to $5000). *See also In re* Debtor's Attorney Fees in Chapter 13 Cases, 374 B.R. 903 (Bankr. M.D. Fla. 2007) (revising presumptively reasonable chapter 13 fee to $3300 for thirty-six-month plan and $3600 for sixty-month plan, with additional allowed charges of $250 if no hearing is required or $350 if a hearing is held for specified "*a la carte* items").

For cases concerning fees decided before 2005, see *In re* Migiano, 242 B.R. 759 (Bankr. S.D. Fla. 2000) (chapter 13 fees typically range from $1500 to $2500); *In re* Howell, 226 B.R. 279 (Bankr. M.D. Fla. 1998) ($1300 a reasonable fee for routine chapter 13 case); *In re* Yates, 217 B.R. 296 (Bankr. N.D. Okla. 1998) (detailed fee application and time records required if attorney seeks more than $1300 flat fee maximum); *In re* Roffle, 216 B.R. 290 (Bankr. D. Colo. 1998) (presumptive fee for uncomplicated chapter 13 case of $1200); *In re* Casull, 139 B.R. 525 (Bankr. D. Colo. 1992) (fee reduced to court's standard fee of $1200 because of lack of adequate documentation that higher fee was warranted); *In re* Fricker, 131 B.R. 932 (Bankr. E.D. Pa. 1991) ($1200 normal maximum charge for typical chapter 13 case). *See also* Jean Braucher, *Lawyers and Consumer Bankruptcy: One Code, Many Cultures*, 67 Am. Bankr. L.J. 501 (1993) (fees charged to most chapter 13 clients in four cities studied were Austin—$1500, San Antonio—$1300, Cincinnati—$650, Dayton—$650).

17 *In re* Kindhart, 160 F.3d 1176 (7th Cir. 1998) (bankruptcy court required to update presumptive fees, which had not been adjusted in ten years); *In re* Ingersoll, 238 B.R. 202 (D. Colo. 1999) (bankruptcy court ordered to change fee procedures which unduly restricted rights to obtain fees above presumptive amounts).

18 *In re* Yermakov, 718 F.2d 1465 (9th Cir. 1983).

19 *See In re* Apodaca, 401 B.R. 503 (Bankr. S.D. Fla. 2009) (approving additional fees provided for in retainer).

20 See Chapter 7, *supra*, for discussion of the credit counseling briefing and Chapter 8, *supra*, for discussion of the required education course. Many attorneys collect the fees for these services from the client so that the fees can be paid to the provider with the attorney's credit card, because a debtor may not use a credit card after deciding to file a bankruptcy case.

21 *See, e.g., In re* Egwim, 291 B.R. 559 (Bankr. N.D. Ga. 2003) (attorney expected to represent debtor in all contested matters and adversary proceedings and could not enter into agreement limiting representation to less); *In re* Johnson, 291 B.R. 462 (Bankr. D. Minn. 2003) (attorney could not enter into fee agreement that did not include representation at section 341 meeting).

22 Attorneys in a few jurisdictions have attempted to offer "no money down" chapter 7 cases, arguing that their fees in the bankruptcy cases were not dischargeable and could be collected postpetition. These arguments have generally, and properly, been rejected. Rittenhouse v. Eisen, 404 F.3d 395 (6th Cir. 2005) (fees for filing chapter 7 bankruptcy case were discharged); *In re* Bethea, 352 F.3d 1125 (7th Cir. 2003) (postpetition collection of prepetition fees violated automatic stay); *In re* Biggar, 110 F.3d 685 (9th Cir. 1997); *In re* Lawson, 437 B.R. 609 (Bankr. E.D. Tenn. 2010) (division of chapter 7 flat fee into small initial payment labeled for prepetition services and a larger payment labeled a "retainer" for postpetition

payment of the attorney fee prior to filing is not a preference, because the payment is not for an antecedent debt, but rather for work done substantially contemporaneously or to be done in the future.[23]

Although a few courts have held otherwise, fees paid as a prepetition retainer in advance for postpetition services that the attorney commits to provide also should not be deemed property of the bankruptcy estate.[24] The attorney fee should be deemed earned when the attorney contracts to provide future services in exchange for it.[25] The Supreme Court has generally approved of this method of payment in chapter 7 cases.[26] Alternatively, at a minimum, the fees paid should be deemed subject to a possessory lien that survives the bankruptcy.[27]

A few courts have attempted to draw a distinction between prepetition and postpetition services. These courts permit an attorney to collect fees after the petition is filed for postpetition services on the theory that the debt for such services is created only when the services are rendered.[28] At least one court has permitted an attorney to take postdated checks from a client for postpetition, but not prepetition, legal work.[29] Even assuming these courts are correct, most attorneys will not wish to be owed fees after the petition is filed because most of the work in a routine chapter 7 case is done, or should be done, before the petition is filed, and because of the procedural obstacles to withdrawing as counsel once the case is filed if fees are not paid.[30]

Generally, an attorney may not enter into an arrangement with a client to provide only prepetition services in a bankruptcy case.[31] Attempts to have clients reaffirm debts for prepetition legal work have obvious ethical ramifications, because the attorney's duty to advise the debtor about reaffirmation presents a conflict with her own interest in being paid.[32] Similarly, accepting postdated checks that are deposited after the bankruptcy petition, without advising a debtor that the debt is dischargeable will run afoul of ethical rules, the automatic stay, and discharge injunction.[33] Of course, a chapter 7 debtor faced with postpetition litigation in the bankruptcy case may pay legal fees for such litigation from postpetition earnings or

---

services and paid through post-dated checks created conflict of interest and potential violations of stay and discharge order); *In re* Symes, 174 B.R. 114 (Bankr. D. Ariz. 1994). *See also In re* Waldo, 417 B.R. 854 (Bankr. E.D. Tenn. 2009) (payment of chapter 7 attorney fees through postdated checks violated automatic stay, discharge order, and required disgorgement of fees due to counsel's failure to advise of dischargeability of debt for fees); *In re* McTyeire, 357 B.R. 898 (Bankr. M.D. Ga. 2006) (state court action to collect chapter 7 fees after discharge violated discharge injunction); *In re* Shell, 312 B.R. 431 (Bankr. M.D. Ala. 2004) (cashing postdated checks for chapter 7 fees violated stay and debt for fees was discharged); *In re* Newkirk, 297 B.R. 457 (Bankr. W.D.N.C. 2002) (obtaining postdated checks for prepetition fees, to be cashed postpetition, violated automatic stay and created conflict of interest with client); *In re* Haynes, 216 B.R. 440 (Bankr. D. Colo. 1997) (fee agreement calling for postpetition payments in chapter 7 created conflict of interest and did not reflect fact that most of attorney's work was done prepetition thereby creating a dischargeable debt); *In re* Martin, 197 B.R. 120 (Bankr. D. Colo. 1996) (fee agreement which permitted the debtor to pay fee through postpetition installments gave rise to conflict of interest and entire fee disallowed).

23 See § 10.4.2.6.4, *supra*, for discussion of avoidable preferences.
24 Barron v. Countryman, 432 F.3d 590 (5th Cir. 2005) (retainers collected by chapter 13 attorney before petition filed were earned upon receipt under attorney's retainer agreement and state law, and did not have to be escrowed or approved by bankruptcy court because they were not property of the estate); *In re* Redding, 247 B.R. 474 (B.A.P. 8th Cir. 2000) (fees paid before bankruptcy were from non-estate property absent some other proceeding which rendered funds estate property). *But see In re* Blackburn, 448 B.R. 28 (Bankr. D. Idaho 2011) (funds held as "security retainer" under which law firm held security interest in funds received prepetition for representation in postpetition adversary proceeding in chapter 7 case were estate property subject to turnover).
25 See Ruan v. Butera, Beausang, Cohen & Brennan, 193 F.3d 210 (3d Cir. 1999) (advance retainer was nonrefundable under state law and became property of attorney when paid); Indian Motorcycle Assocs. III L.P. v. Massachusetts Hous. Fin. Agency, 66 F.3d 1246, 1254, 1255 (1st Cir. 1995); *In re* Jones, 236 B.R. 38 (D. Colo. 1999) (reasonable attorney fees received prior to petition for services to be performed postpetition were not property of the estate).
26 Lamie v. United States Tr., 540 U.S. 526, 124 S. Ct. 1023, 1032 157 L. Ed. 2d 1024, 1036 (2004) ("It appears to be routine for debtors to pay reasonable fees for legal services before filing for bankruptcy to ensure compliance with statutory requirements."). *See also In re* CK Liquidation Corp., 343 B.R. 376 (D. Mass. 2006) (*Lamie*'s "retainer exception" applies only to flat fee retainers). *See generally* Collier Compensation, Employment and Appointment of Trustees and Professionals in Bankruptcy Cases ¶ 3.02[1], p. 3-2 (2002) ("In the majority of cases, the debtor's counsel will accept an individual or a joint consumer chapter 7 case only after being paid a retainer that covers the 'standard fee' and the cost of filing the petition.").
27 *In re* Century Cleaning Servs., 215 B.R. 18 (B.A.P. 9th Cir. 1997), *aff'd on other grounds*, 195 F.3d 1053 (9th Cir. 1999); *In re* Hodes, 289 B.R. 5 (D. Kan. 2003) (debtors' counsel had valid retaining liens against retainers paid prepetition for postpetition services).
28 *In re* Sanchez, 241 F.3d 1148 (9th Cir. 2001); *In re* Hines, 147 F.3d 1185 (9th Cir. 1998); Walton v. Clark & Washington, P.C., 469 B.R. 383 (Bankr. M.D. Fla. 2012) (separate contract and fee for postpetition services permissible if there is proper disclosure to client and if attorney agrees not to withdraw from case without court approval); *In re* McNickle, 274 B.R. 477 (Bankr. S.D. Ohio 2002).
29 *In re* Jastrem, 224 B.R. 125 (Bankr. E.D. Cal. 1998).
   However, this practice may violate state consumer protection laws.
30 *See In re* Cuddy, 322 B.R. 12 (Bankr. D. Mass. 2005) (denying motion to withdraw by counsel who had entered general appearance but had not been paid); *In re* Davis, 258 B.R. 510 (Bankr. M.D. Fla. 2001) (denying attorney's motion to withdraw after confirmation even though contract with debtor provided that attorney would represent them only through confirmation).
31 *But see In re* Castorena, 270 B.R. 504 (Bankr. D. Idaho 2001) (permitting fee for work done under agreement to provide prepetition work only, but reducing fee from $250 to $125).
32 *In re* Pasco, 220 B.R. 119 (Bankr. D. Colo. 1998) (reaffirmation agreement with attorney did not provide adequate disclosure to client that debt was dischargeable). *But see In re* Nidiver, 217 B.R. 581 (Bankr. D. Neb. 1998) (permitting reaffirmation of attorney fee for prepetition services due to benefits to debtors of continuing to have counsel represent them; court did not explain why payment for postpetition services would not be sufficient).
33 *In re* Waldo, 417 B.R. 854 (Bankr. E.D. Tenn. 2009).

other property that is exempted or is not property of the estate, provided those fees are properly disclosed.[34]

Practically speaking this means that a chapter 7 debtor usually should pay the entire filing fee in advance, because the debtor may not pay any additional money or property to an attorney for services in connection with the case until after the filing fee is paid in full or has been waived.[35] Often, with the increase in bankruptcy costs and fees, a debtor will have to save money for several months to afford the attorney fees—paying installments to the attorney—before the case is filed. This process can be made somewhat easier if the debtor can be advised that certain debts the debtor has been struggling to pay, but that will be discharged, need not be paid. Debtors also rely on gifts from family members or borrow money from retirement accounts or home equity lines of credit to raise funds for the fee. In some jurisdictions attorneys take assignments of debtors' expected tax refunds for all or part of the fee.[36]

The attorney fee may be paid in ways other than cash from the client. It may be paid by a third party such as a friend or relative. The debtor may also give the attorney a security interest in property or transfer property outright to the attorney. However, the potential for later problems in enforcing the security interest or establishing the fair value of transferred property may make such arrangements inadvisable. They also create the possibility of a conflict of interest between the attorney and the debtor or the estate.[37] When a bankruptcy attorney is a creditor of the estate by virtue of a debt for prepetition nonbankruptcy-related work, there may be a conflict of interest justifying denial of that attorney's bankruptcy fee.[38]

The remaining method by which an attorney may be compensated is through payment from the debtor's estate. As discussed below,[39] this arrangement is common in chapter 13 cases. It is possible in a chapter 7 case filed by a consumer only if 1) the attorney is specifically appointed by the court to represent the trustee in a particular matter[40] and 2) the debtor has sufficient nonexempt property to pay all priority administrative expenses in full. Because attorneys for chapter 7 debtors rarely are appointed to represent the estate and because debtors, if they receive good advice, normally protect their nonexempt property by converting it to exempt property[41] or by filing a chapter 13 petition,[42] this method of payment in consumer chapter 7 cases is extremely rare. Moreover, all attorney fees paid from estate property must be approved in advance.[43]

Other than the attorney for a debtor in a chapter 13 case, any attorney representing the bankruptcy estate must be appointed by the court, and this rule can sometimes create pitfalls for unsuspecting nonbankruptcy attorneys, especially attorneys in personal injury cases. When a claim is property of the estate, the estate must file an application to retain counsel to pursue the claim.[44] Often the estate will retain counsel who was handling the case prior to the bankruptcy, especially if that counsel had a fee agreement creating a lien on the proceeds of the claim. But if an attorney pursues a claim belonging to the estate without being appointed to represent the estate, that attorney may be denied all fees in connection with the matter.[45]

---

34 *See In re* Bressman, 327 F.3d 229 (3d Cir. 2003) (attorneys not required to disgorge fees paid from estate property when they had taken precautions to avoid being paid with estate assets); *In re* Griffing, 313 B.R. 757 (Bankr. N.D. Ill. 2004) (discussing fees for postpetition redemption).

35 Fed. R. Bankr. P. 1006(b)(3).

This Rule marks a change from pre-2005 practice. Under Federal Rule of Bankruptcy Procedure 1006(b)(3), no attorney fees at all could be paid until after the filing fee was paid in full. With the possibility of a fee waiver in chapter 7 cases, the rule was relaxed, and Official Forms 3A and 3B were drafted to permit debtors to pay the filing fee in installments or to seek a waiver of the fee, even if they had paid an attorney or petition preparer a fee.

36 *In re* Hunter, 2011 WL 1749933 (Bankr. D. Kan. May 5, 2011) (debtor could pay chapter 7 attorney flat fee with assignment of prepetition portion of current year's tax refund). *See* Redmond v. Lentz & Clark, Prof'l Ass'n (*In re* Wagers), 340 B.R. 391 (Bankr. D. Kan. 2006), *rev'd*, 514 F.3d 1021 (10th Cir. 2007).

The *Wagers* case was unusual in involving an extremely large refund and a fee that was not clearly earned on receipt. The use of tax refunds to pay flat fees earned on receipt is still permissible. *See In re* Carson, 374 B.R. 247 (B.A.P. 10th Cir. 2007).

37 *See In re* Martin, 62 B.R. 943 (D. Me. 1986), *aff'd*, 817 F.2d 175 (1st Cir. 1987); *In re* Automend, Inc., 85 B.R. 173 (Bankr. N.D. Ga. 1988).

38 *See In re* Pierce, 809 F.2d 1356 (8th Cir. 1987); *In re* Hargis, 73 B.R. 622 (Bankr. N.D. Tex. 1987).

39 *See* § 16.4, *infra*.

40 Lamie v. United States Tr., 540 U.S. 526, 124 S. Ct. 1023, 1032, 157 L. Ed. 2d 1024, 1036 (2004) (attorney for chapter 7 debtor who has not been appointed to represent estate cannot be paid from estate because amendment to 11 U.S.C. § 330(a) made by the Bankruptcy Reform Act of 1994 deleted reference to "the debtor's attorney" as one of the persons who could be paid professional fees).

Fortunately a new provision, section 330(a)(4)(B), makes clear that the court can award fees to debtors' attorneys in chapters 12 and 13.

41 *See* § 6.5.2.2, *supra*, for a discussion of such exemption planning.

42 *See* § 12.8.1, *supra*, for a discussion of the debtor's right to retain possession of nonexempt property in a chapter 13 case.

43 11 U.S.C. § 330(a).

44 11 U.S.C. § 327(a); Fed. R. Bankr. P. 2014(a).

Special counsel may be appointed to handle a matter on a contingent fee basis. In such cases, the bankruptcy court may not later review the agreed contingent fee to see if it is reasonable, except in cases in which it finds that unanticipated developments rendered the original agreement improvident. *In re* Reimers, 972 F.2d 1127 (9th Cir. 1992).

45 *See In re* Anderson, 936 F.2d 199 (5th Cir. 1991) (although attorney may be denied fees for all work done before attorney was appointed, court has discretion to approve employment *nunc pro tunc*); *In re* Alcala, 918 F.2d 99 (9th Cir. 1990); Tanenbaum v. Smith, Friedman & Assocs., 289 B.R. 800 (D.N.J. 2002) (bankruptcy court could void settlement of personal injury action that belonged to estate and had not been disclosed; attorney waived retaining lien by surrendering files); *In re* Alletto, 2010 WL 5124721 (Bankr. D. Conn. Dec. 8, 2010) (attorney retained by trustee with court approval who settled personal injury action and disbursed funds without court approval was required to disgorge his fee); *In re* Dooley, 399 B.R. 340 (Bankr. D. Mass. 2009) (attorney not appointed by court required to turn over attorney fees retained from postpetition settlement of prepetition claim); *In re* Moore, 312 B.R. 902 (Bankr. N.D. Ala. 2004) (attorney required to turn over to chapter 7 trustee not only fee retained from settlement but also balance of settlement

16.3 Court Supervision of Bankruptcy Attorney Fees

16.3.1 Introduction

One aspect of attorney fees in bankruptcy that is somewhat unusual is the close court supervision of the fees charged. In addition, monitoring and, when appropriate, commenting upon attorney fees applications is one of the primary duties of the United States trustee's office.[46] This supervision of attorney fees in bankruptcy arises mainly from an unfortunate history of abuse and overreaching by the bankruptcy bar.

The purpose of the monitoring is twofold. First, it was designed to prevent bankruptcies in which the debtor has significant assets from becoming boondoggles for the lawyers involved. Scandals in cases in which little, if anything, was left for creditors by the time the attorneys finished compensating themselves have left the bankruptcy courts quite sensitive to this problem. Second, the scrutiny of fees paid by the debtor is based upon a recognition that bankruptcy clients are particularly vulnerable to attorney overreaching.[47] Court oversight now prevents much of that overreaching.

16.3.2 Disclosures Required

Hence, both the Code and the Federal Rules of Bankruptcy Procedure have strict requirements for disclosure of all fees. Section 329(a) requires any attorney who represents a debtor in a bankruptcy case, or in connection with a bankruptcy case, to file a statement of all compensation paid or agreed to be paid in connection with services rendered within one year prior to filing, or to be rendered, which are related to the bankruptcy. Such a statement must be filed even if the attorney has charged only for advice or preparation of papers and has not appeared in the bankruptcy case.[48] The same section requires disclosure of the source of all such compensation.[49] If the debtor has given the attorney a lien or otherwise transferred property in connection with compensation, that must be disclosed.[50] It is important to note that the statute requires disclosure of sums already paid as well as money to be paid prospectively. It is improper to list only money which is expected from the estate.

Bankruptcy Rule 2016(b) requires the statement of compensation to be filed within fourteen days after a voluntary petition is filed or at such other time as the court may direct. In addition it must be transmitted to the United States trustee. If at a later time the debtor pays or agrees to pay any further fees not previously disclosed, the rule requires a supplemental disclosure to be filed within fourteen days thereafter. The supplemental statement should generally conform to the same standards as the original disclosures.[51]

The failure to file these forms may jeopardize an attorney's right to receive any fees at all.[52] The rule also requires a

---

proceeds paid to debtor when cause of action had not been disclosed or exempted). *Cf. In re* Chaparro Marinez, 293 B.R. 387 (Bankr. N.D. Tex. 2003) (when debtor had successfully exempted personal injury cause of action it ceased to be property of estate and attorney did not have to be appointed by court, or have fees in settlement approved by court).

46 28 U.S.C. § 586(a)(3).

47 *See generally* H.R. Rep. No. 95-595, at 329 (1977); Fed. R. Bankr. P. 2017 advisory committee's note.

48 *In re* Zepecki, 277 F.3d 1041 (8th Cir. 2002) (fees for services in connection with prepetition sale of property were fees for services in contemplation of bankruptcy which had to be disclosed); *In re* Basham, 208 B.R. 926 (B.A.P. 9th Cir. 1997) (attorney who prepared papers for debtors who filed "pro per" but did not file fee disclosure, and who charged excessive fees for services rendered, required to disgorge all fees); *In re* Garcia, 456 B.R. 361 (N.D. Ill. 2011) (bankruptcy court must consider whether attorney representing debtor in prepetition foreclosure avoidance matters provided services motivated by imminence of bankruptcy, not only whether attorney entered appearance for debtor in bankruptcy case); *In re* Ross, 2010 WL 2509939 (Bankr. N.D. Cal. June 16, 2010) (attorneys who debtors paid to provide mortgage modification services were required to file disclosure); *In re* Mayeaux, 269 B.R. 614 (Bankr. E.D. Tex. 2001) (fees paid for assistance in connection with claims of mismanagement and misappropriation were for services in contemplation of bankruptcy and had to be disclosed); *In re* Campbell, 259 B.R. 615 (Bankr. N.D. Ohio 2001) (fees for services in connection with refinancing to complete chapter 13 plan should have been disclosed); *In re* Greco, 246 B.R. 226 (Bankr. E.D. Pa. 2000) (fees for legal research paid by third party, a non-debtor spouse, were subject to review by court in assessing overall reasonableness of fees charged).

49 This section has been held to also require disclosures by non-attorneys providing services of a legal nature. *In re* Telford, 36 B.R. 92 (B.A.P. 9th Cir. 1984).

50 *In re* Alfieri, 2012 WL 642787 (Bankr. M.D. Fla. Feb. 24, 2012) (security interest is expected tax refund not disclosed).

51 *In re* Chez, 441 B.R. 724 (Bankr. D. Conn. 2010) (requiring disgorgement of fees collected for amending schedules that were not disclosed). *See In re* Hackney, 347 B.R. 432 (Bankr. M.D. Fla. 2006) (fees for work on refinancing used to pay off chapter 13 plan should have been disclosed); *In re* Jones, 356 B.R. 39 (Bankr. D. Idaho 2005) (disclosure required when debtor entered into postpetition contingent fee agreement for stay violation litigation); *In re* Miller, 312 B.R. 626 (Bankr. S.D. Ohio 2004) (one court's requirements with respect to disclosure of fees with respect to redemption motion); *In re* Lewis, 309 B.R. 597 (Bankr. N.D. Okla. 2004) (failure to disclose postpetition payments resulted in denial of all fees).

52 *In re* Kisseberth, 273 F.3d 714 (6th Cir. 2001) (affirming order requiring disgorgement of fees when disclosure requirements not met); *In re* Downs, 103 F.3d 472 (6th Cir. 1996) (disgorgement of fees is appropriate remedy when fee disclosure requirements not met); *In re* Redding, 263 B.R. 874 (B.A.P. 8th Cir. 2001) (affirming order requiring disgorgement of fees when disclosure requirements not met); *In re* Basham, 208 B.R. 926 (B.A.P. 9th Cir. 1997) (attorney who prepared papers for debtors who filed "pro per" but did not file fee disclosure, and who charged excessive fees for services rendered, required to disgorge all fees); *In re* Andreas, 373 B.R. 864 (Bankr. N.D. Ill. 2007) (attorney sanctioned for failing to disclose fees received in mortgage refinancing transactions that paid off chapter 13 plans); *In re* Bell, 212 B.R. 654 (Bankr. E.D. Cal. 1997) (attorney who failed to file timely fee disclosure, charged excessive fees and failed to disclose potential conflict of interest created by borrowing money on debtors' behalf ordered to disgorge all fees); *In re* Fricker, 131 B.R. 932 (Bankr. E.D. Pa. 1991) (court has discretion to require disgorgement of all fees when disclosure not filed). *See also In re* Park-Helena Corp., 63 F.3d 877 (9th Cir.

statement regarding whether the attorney has shared or agreed to share such compensation with any other person, and the particulars of any such sharing arrangement, except when the sharing is with another attorney in the same firm.[53] The rules make clear that any sharing in the form of referral or forwarding fees to attorneys who have not performed real service to earn their portion of the fee are not allowed, and can be the basis for the denial of fees for all attorneys involved in the transaction.[54] Similar sorts of fees to non-attorneys are also improper, and must be disclosed to the court, with respect to prebankruptcy fees at least, in response to question nine in the Statement of Financial Affairs.[55]

In addition, when compensation is sought from the estate, including payment through the chapter 13 plan, an attorney must provide a detailed statement of the services rendered and expenses incurred[56] to justify the amount requested.[57] Although such a listing is not technically required when the attorney is paid directly by the debtor (except in some jurisdictions by local rule), it is a good idea to furnish a statement of services in such cases as well.[58] Not only does the description of services support the amount of fees requested, it also makes clear to the court what services have not been included, so that there can be no later question regarding whether the attorney fee included particular activities.[59] Indeed, it is usually advisable to include in the statement a specific disclosure of the hourly rate or other arrangements which have been made for such additional services as might become necessary.[60] Finally, Rule 2016(b) requires a supplemental disclosure statement to be filed with the court after any payment or agreement not previously disclosed.

It is common for local rules (and occasionally local custom) to provide additional specifications for attorney fee disclosures, including special service requirements. Local practice should be reviewed.

16.3.3 Bankruptcy Court Review of Fee Disclosures and Requests

The Bankruptcy Code also follows the approach of the prior rules in requiring the court to review all payments or arrangements between the debtor and her attorney. All fees paid by the debtor that are related to the bankruptcy case are subject to review.[61] Any payments exceeding the reasonable value of services rendered may be ordered returned to either the debtor or the estate, whichever is appropriate.[62] And, of course once the fees are disallowed by the court they cannot be collected directly from the client.[63]

Although the Bankruptcy Rules provide that an order disallowing fees may be made on the court's own motion,[64] it most

---

1995) (fees denied completely when attorneys failed to disclose source of prepetition retainer); *In re* Ostas, 158 B.R. 312 (N.D.N.Y. 1993) (attorney ordered to disgorge $1600 in fees charged to obtain stay of foreclosure as fees that were not disclosed; fees were "in connection" with bankruptcy case).

53 See *In re* Holmes, 304 B.R. 292 (Bankr. N.D. Miss. 2004) (failing to disclose bonuses paid to non-attorney staff in connection with particular bankruptcy cases violated Rule 2016(b)).

Other fee sharing arrangements are generally prohibited under 11 U.S.C. § 504, at least if the compensation is from property of the estate. *See In re* Ferguson, 445 B.R. 744 (Bankr. N.D. Tex. 2011) (failure of attorney retained by chapter 13 trustee to disclose fee sharing agreement with another firm violated § 504 and precluded retained attorney's recovery of contingency fee); *In re* Harwell, 439 B.R. 455 (Bankr. W.D. Mich. 2010) (payment of fee to another attorney to cover 341 meeting, even though fee was not charged to debtor, made disclosure stating that there was no fee sharing inaccurate); *In re* Zuniga, 332 B.R. 760 (Bankr. S.D. Tex. 2005) (failure to disclose fee sharing with out-of-state firm violated Rule 2016(b)); *In re* Wright, 290 B.R. 145 (Bankr. C.D. Cal. 2003) (discussing rules for disclosure of payments to "appearance attorney" who attends creditors meeting or hearing); *In re* Greer, 271 B.R. 426 (Bankr. D. Mass. 2002) (it was improper fee-sharing to pay another attorney $50 to represent debtors at creditors meeting because merely listing attorney on letterhead and adding attorney to malpractice insurance did not establish "of counsel" relationship); *In re* Palladino, 267 B.R. 825 (Bankr. N.D. Ill. 2001) (disallowing fees sought in fee application for attorneys who were not part of firm hired by debtor and were not hired by debtor).

54 Fed. R. Bankr. P. 2016 advisory committee's note. *See In re* Matis, 73 B.R. 228 (Bankr. N.D.N.Y. 1987).

55 *See* Official Form 7 (reprinted in Appx. D, *infra*).

56 Costs and expenses may be recovered to the extent that they are actual and necessary. *See In re* Nat'l Paragon Corp., 76 B.R. 73 (E.D. Pa. 1987).

57 Fed. R. Bankr. P. 2016(a); Barron v. Countryman, 432 F.3d 590 (5th Cir. 2005) (fees collected from chapter 13 debtors after petition was filed had to be approved by court); *In re* Pinkins, 213 B.R. 818 (Bankr. E.D. Mich. 1997) (fees reduced for failure to submit time records).

58 *See* Form 31, Appx. G.3, *infra*.

59 See *In re* All Cases in Which Robin L. Musher Is Counsel of Record, 387 B.R. 669 (Bankr. W.D. Pa. 2008) (fees for additional work not allowed because Rule 2016(b) statement did not disclose a work carve-out or preserve the possibility that attorney might file a subsequent fee application for fees beyond the flat amount set forth).

60 *Id*.

61 *In re* Walters, 868 F.2d 665 (4th Cir. 1989) (court had power to review fees paid by debtors from exempt property in state court suits against creditor); Hearn v. Persels & Assocs., P.L.L.C. (*In re* Hearn), 2011 WL 5357849 (Bankr. M.D.N.C. Nov. 4, 2011) (bankruptcy court had power to review fees paid for prepetition debt settlement plan that had been intended to avoid bankruptcy); *In re* Woodward, 229 B.R. 468 (Bankr. N.D. Okla. 1999) (attorney required to disclose fees even if they were passed on to another attorney). *Cf. In re* Hargis, 895 F.2d 1025 (5th Cir. 1990) (court had no authority to order disgorgement of fees paid for services not related to bankruptcy case); *In re* Chaparro Martinez, 293 B.R. 387 (Bankr. N.D. Tex. 2003) (Code provisions regulating attorney fees not applicable to fees relating to debtor's personal injury claim that was not property of debtor's bankruptcy estate).

62 11 U.S.C. § 329(b); *In re* Lee, 884 F.2d 897 (5th Cir. 1989) (court ordered return of fees attorney collected under contingent fee agreement to the extent they exceeded reasonable hourly rate).

63 *See In re* Gantz, 209 B.R. 999 (B.A.P. 10th Cir. 1997) (fees which bankruptcy court denied upon application that they be paid from chapter 13 estate were never due to attorney and could not be collected by attorney directly from client).

64 Fed. R. Bankr. P. 2017(a). *See In re* Busy Beaver Bldg. Ctrs., Inc., 19 F.3d 833 (3d Cir. 1994) (bankruptcy court has power to review fees *sua sponte* even if neither U.S. trustee nor any other party objects to fees); *In re* Wyslak, 94 B.R. 540 (Bankr. N.D. Ill. 1988).

often occurs after a request by the trustee or the United States trustee. In many districts the court specifically requires the trustee to make a recommendation regarding whether an attorney fee should be approved, and it has been held that reviewing fees is part of the United States trustee's function of supervising the administration of bankruptcy cases.[65] The Executive Office for United States Trustees has announced that it considers the monitoring of debtors' attorney fees to be a very important part of the U.S. trustee's job.[66]

One aspect of reviewing fees involves the question of whether the fees charged are reasonable in relation to the services involved. Bankruptcy courts have broad discretion in determining appropriate levels of compensation.[67] As discussed above,[68] most judges have a range of rates that they consider to be fair for the basic services involved in a consumer bankruptcy case. Information as to what this range is should be easy to obtain through a review of fees approved in other cases in the public record of fees on file at the clerk's office.[69] Many judges also have let it be known what they feel is equitable for an uncontested adversary proceeding or other routine tasks.[70] Different courts have a variety of rules regarding such issues as whether fees are allowed for travel time,[71] which costs are compensable, and the rates that will be permitted for costs such as photocopying.

Counsel for debtors should not be afraid, however, to charge more than the basic fee when the work reasonably required in a case warrants a larger fee which the client agrees to pay.[72] The "basic fee" utilized by many courts is only a guideline set for the convenience of the court and counsel. Bankruptcy litigation can be lengthy and complex, and the legislative history of the Code makes clear that Congress intended bankruptcy attorneys to be compensated at the same level as other attorneys in the community handling nonbankruptcy matters of similar difficulty.[73] Previous case law[74] that held that bankruptcy cases were governed by a special "spirit of economy" that dictated lower fees was expressly disapproved.[75] The policy of the Code is to encourage quality representation in bankruptcy by allowing fees which will attract competent practitioners.

Courts also concern themselves with preventing the abuse of the bankruptcy process by attorneys at the expense of debtors or creditors. In pursuit of this goal, bankruptcy judges have remedied conduct that ranges from unfair advertising to incompetence to outright fraud.

For example, the fees of an attorney who had deceptively advertised his fees were limited in all of his cases to the low fees advertised.[76] Other attorneys who failed to attend hearings or cooperate with trustees, misrepresented their fees, and allowed their clients to be seriously prejudiced have been denied all fees and ordered to reimburse their clients for costs incurred.[77] When services rendered have been harmful or worth-

---

65 *In re* Pierce, 809 F.2d 1356 (8th Cir. 1987); *In re* Grant, 14 B.R. 567 (Bankr. S.D.N.Y. 1981); *In re* McLeon, 6 B.R. 327 (Bankr. E.D. Va. 1980).

66 Tell, *Chasing the Bankruptcy Bumblers*, Nat'l L. J., May 11, 1981, at 1, 26.

67 *See, e.g., In re* Lawler, 807 F.2d 1207 (5th Cir. 1987); *In re* McKeeman, 236 B.R. 667 (B.A.P. 8th Cir. 1999) (reduction in hourly rate to that charged by local attorneys and refusal to grant fees for travel time not an abuse of discretion).

68 *See* § 16.2.2, *supra*.

69 Such a record must be maintained by the class pursuant to Federal Rule of Bankruptcy Procedure 2013.

70 *See, e.g., In re* Ray, 314 B.R. 643 (Bankr. M.D. Tenn. 2004) ($300 fee reasonable for redemption motion); *In re* Hill, 5 B.R. 541 (Bankr. C.D. Cal. 1980) ($250 a reasonable fee for adversary proceeding to remove judicial liens).

71 *See In re* Braddy, 195 B.R. 365 (Bankr. E.D. Mich. 1996) (attorney permitted full compensation for travel time). *But see In re* Sapienza, 417 B.R. 1 (E.D. Mich. 2009) (in routine chapter 13 case where attorney's fee claim already exceeded typical "flat fee," bankruptcy court had discretion to limit attorney compensation to one hour of travel time per day).

72 *See, e.g., In re* Tuttle, 2009 WL 1789286 (Bankr. E.D. Va. June 15, 2009) (fees higher than guideline were reasonable in case likely to be complex); *In re* Buckner, 350 B.R. 874, 881–882 (Bankr. D. Idaho 2005) (enhancing fees one-and-a-half times lodestar amount in recognition of risk debtors' counsel took in pursuing stay violation proceeding); *In re* Shamburger, 189 B.R. 965 (Bankr. N.D. Ala. 1995) (attorney entitled to additional compensation for work performed on novel issues). *See generally In re* Lawler, 807 F.2d 1207 (5th Cir. 1987); *In re* Powerline Oil Co., 71 B.R. 767 (B.A.P. 9th Cir. 1986).

73 *In re* Boddy, 950 F.2d 334 (6th Cir. 1991) (use of $650 "normal and customary" fee for bankruptcy case, rather than lodestar method, was abuse of discretion); Grant v. George Schumann Tire & Battery Co., 908 F.2d 874 (11th Cir. 1990) (bankruptcy attorney fees should be calculated by lodestar method and should be no less and no more than fees received for comparable nonbankruptcy work; however, fees should not be awarded on appeal unless the appeal benefited the estate, creditors, or the debtor); Lopez v. Consejo De Titulares Del Condominio Carolina Court Apartments, 405 B.R. 24 (B.A.P. 1st Cir. 2009) (reversing fee reduction based upon minimal damages in stay violation case and holding that lodestar method should have been used).

74 *See, e.g., In re* Beverly Crest Convalescent Hosp., Inc., 548 F.2d 817 (9th Cir. 1977); *In re* Paramount Merrick, Inc., 252 F.2d 482, 485 (2d Cir. 1958).

75 124 Cong. Rec. H11,091, H11,092 (daily ed. Sept. 28, 1978) (statement of Rep. Don Edwards); H.R. Rep. No. 95-595, at 329, 330 (1977).

76 *In re* Stewart, 10 B.R. 472 (Bankr. E.D. Va. 1981).

77 *In re* Clark, 223 F.3d 859 (8th Cir. 2000) (attorney who misrepresented that he had done work that was really done by paralegal and collected flat fee designed for work done by attorneys ordered to disgorge fees); *In re* Kasperek, 399 B.R. 591 (Bankr. W.D.N.Y. 2009) (debtor's counsel who failed to comply with trustee turnover requests, when such tasks were not specifically excluded from services that would be rendered in exchange for basic fee, required to pay trustee's fees and expenses); *In re* Dean, 401 B.R. 917 (Bankr. D. Idaho 2008) (disgorgement of one-half of chapter 7 fee ordered when counsel failed to verify perfection of lien on debtor's mobile home before filing); *In re* Bost, 341 B.R. 666 (Bankr. E.D. Ark. 2006) (complete disgorgement of attorney fees ordered for series of cases in which counsel facing rush of cases filed false and disorganized schedules and statements); *In re* Taylor, 242 B.R. 549 (Bankr. S.D. Ga. 1999) (fee of attorney who failed to attend hearings reduced from $1100 to $250); *In re* Pinkins, 213 B.R. 818 (Bankr. E.D. Mich. 1997) (fees denied when attorney's legal assistant engaged in unauthorized practice of law, legal assistant signed retention letters and attorney had no contact or direct relationship with clients); *In re* Davila, 210 B.R. 727 (Bankr. S.D. Tex. 1996)

less to the debtor, all fees have been denied.[78] Similarly, when attorneys have acted unethically in other respects, their requested fees have not been allowed.[79] And when attorneys have failed to accurately disclose the fees charged, those fees have been reduced or denied.[80]

Finally, this supervisory power has been used to police the fees and conduct of non-attorneys who provide debtors with "advice" or "services" in connection with bankruptcy cases, which are then often filed *pro se*.[81] Either upon motion by the United States trustee, or upon request of disgruntled "clients," section 329 of the Code, combined with remedies available under Code section 110[82] and state unfair trade practice statutes,[83] can be an effective weapon against the unauthorized practice of law and abusive practices of these "clinics," "debt counselors," "typing services" and other operations that prey on the misfortunes of financially troubled debtors.

16.3.4 Making a Record on Fee Issues

Regardless of the way the fee request comes to the court's attention, the matter must be given the same type of careful consideration required by the rules for any other type of proceeding.[84] A final (as opposed to interim) order on fees is a final appealable order.[85] In cases likely to be appealed, all parties must be careful to ensure that there is evidence in the record to support their positions. Although written findings of fact are not necessary in the typical fee request, they are important when a substantial issue is likely to arise. If the bankruptcy court does not make such findings, it should be specifically requested to do so, in order to create an adequate record for appellate review.[86]

(fees ordered disgorged because attorney was not competent, filed inaccurate schedules, failed to disclose fees, inadequately trained and supervised employees and provided little if any accurate legal advice to clients). *See also In re* Pierce, 809 F.2d 1356 (8th Cir. 1987); *In re* Hargis, 73 B.R. 622 (Bankr. N.D. Tex. 1987).

78 *In re* West, 398 B.R. 629 (Bankr. E.D. Ark. 2009) (disgorgement of all chapter 13 fees ordered due to numerous deficiencies in representation including failure to review mortgagee claims, leaving debtor in default at end of plan); *In re* Gore, 2008 WL 5049915 (Bankr. E.D. Pa. Nov. 25, 2008) (ordering disgorgement of total fees of $3750 for two chapter 7 cases when disclosures were deficient and counsel's faulty legal work provided no real benefit to debtors); *In re* Burghoff, 374 B.R. 681 (Bankr. N.D. Iowa 2007) (debtor's counsel sanctioned for charging and collecting $5737.50 for preparation of brief with substantial plagiarized content); *In re* Vargas, 257 B.R. 157 (Bankr. D.N.J. 2001) (debtor's counsel who certified and filed "unwarranted and unsubstantiated" reaffirmation agreements ordered to disgorge fees); *In re* Rutherford, 54 B.R. 784 (Bankr. W.D. Mo. 1985); *In re* Wright, 48 B.R. 172 (Bankr. E.D.N.C. 1985); *In re* Bolton, 43 B.R. 598 (Bankr. E.D.N.Y. 1984) (fees denied for groundless third bankruptcy petition filed one week after second petition dismissed); *In re* Chin, 31 B.R. 314 (Bankr. S.D.N.Y. 1983); *In re* Crestwell, 30 B.R. 619 (Bankr. D.D.C. 1983). *See also In re* Busby, 46 B.R. 15 (Bankr. E.D.N.Y. 1984) (questioning several apparently poor decisions made by attorney who requested $3500 fee in chapter 13 case).

79 *In re* Evangeline Ref. Co., 890 F.2d 1312 (5th Cir. 1989) (when facts misrepresented in fee application, all compensation should be denied); *In re* Georgetown of Kettering Ltd., 750 F.2d 536 (6th Cir. 1984) (the application of attorney who represented conflicting interests should have been denied); *In re* McGregory, 340 B.R. 915 (B.A.P. 8th Cir. 2006) (conflict of interest in representing both debtor and lender in refinancing); *In re* Rainwater, 100 B.R. 615 (Bankr. M.D. Ga. 1989) (no compensation for deficient services and attorney sanctioned for filing petition without meeting debtor, reviewing her records, or counseling her about bankruptcy); *In re* Vivado, 94 B.R. 785 (Bankr. D.D.C. 1989) (debtors were not eligible to file case and counsel's action was therefore a sham proceeding); *In re* Costello, 95 B.R. 594 (Bankr. S.D. Ill. 1989) (conflict of interest); *In re* Whitman, 51 B.R. 502 (Bankr. D. Mass. 1985) (fee reduced when law firm overreached by taking a security interest in debtor's major asset); *In re* Smith, 24 B.R. 266 (Bankr. D.D.C. 1982) (failure to explain how the unethical conduct diminished the value of services rendered), *rev'd in part sub nom. In re* Devers, 33 B.R. 793 (D.D.C. 1983).

80 *In re* Jackson, 401 B.R. 333 (Bankr. N.D. Ill. 2009) (ordering disgorgement of fees paid in two chapter 13 cases because disclosures were false and fees well above no-look level); *In re* Henderson, 360 B.R. 477 (Bankr. D.S.C. 2006) (disgorgement ordered due to failure to file fee disclosures and other required documents); *In re* Woodward, 229 B.R. 468 (Bankr. N.D. Okla. 1999); *In re* Pair, 77 B.R. 976 (Bankr. N.D. Ga. 1987); *In re* Chambers, 76 B.R. 194 (Bankr. M.D. Fla. 1987); *In re* Whitman, 51 B.R. 502 (Bankr. D. Mass. 1985); *In re* Meyer, 50 B.R. 3 (Bankr. S.D. Fla. 1985); *In re* Weaver, 49 B.R. 190 (Bankr. N.D. Ala. 1985). *See also* Lavender v. Wood Law Firm, 785 F.2d 247 (8th Cir. 1986) (law firm which had not obtained approval for payment of fees in chapter 11 case required to reimburse estate for such fees). *But see In re* Redding, 247 B.R. 474 (B.A.P. 8th Cir. 2000) (reversing disgorgement order based on nondisclosure because only issue under section 329 is reasonableness of fees, though court left open possibility of sanctions for rule violation); *In re* Gage, 394 B.R. 184 (Bankr. N.D. Ill. 2008) (court declined to impose sanctions on chapter 13 debtor's counsel who filed false fee disclosure statement; errors were result of carelessness and not fraud, and fees had been restored to client).

81 *In re* Fleet, 95 B.R. 319 (E.D. Pa. 1989); *In re* Webster, 120 B.R. 111 (Bankr. E.D. Wis. 1990) (permanent injunction issued against lay person engaging in unauthorized practice of law and requiring return of monies paid to him by debtor when that person prepared bankruptcy papers, failed to file a statement of compensation, and received fees before the filing fees were paid in full); *In re* Bachman, 113 B.R. 769 (Bankr. S.D. Fla. 1990).

82 This provision contains special requirements for non-attorney bankruptcy petition preparers. *See* § 16.6, *infra*.

83 *In re* Fleet, 95 B.R. 319 (E.D. Pa. 1989). *See also* National Consumer Law Center, Unfair and Deceptive Acts and Practices § 6.15.1 (7th ed. 2008 and Supp.).

84 *In re* Eliapo, 468 F.3d 592 (9th Cir. 2006) (attorney should have been granted opportunity for a hearing on disputed fees); Thomas v. Bankr. Estate of Jones, 360 B.R. 624 (E.D. Mich. 2007) (bankruptcy court denied attorney due process by refusing to hold hearing before cutting fees).

85 *See In re* Spillane, 884 F.2d 642 (1st Cir. 1989). *Cf. In re* Boddy, 950 F.2d 334 (6th Cir. 1991) (interim award became final when it no longer could be modified by the court); *In re* Dahlquist, 751 F.2d 295 (8th Cir. 1985) (interim award became final when bankruptcy case was dismissed).

86 *In re* Botelho, 8 B.R. 305 (B.A.P. 1st Cir. 1981). *See also In re* Clark, 223 F.3d 859 (8th Cir. 2000) (appellant attorney did not provide reviewing court transcript or other record that supported his contentions); *In re* Boddy, 950 F.2d 334 (6th Cir. 1991) (case remanded when court had not discussed how award was calculated under lodestar method); *In re* Pfleghaar, 215 B.R. 394 (B.A.P. 8th Cir. 1997) (attorney entitled to evidentiary hearing before bank-

When the record evidences the hours reasonably spent and the bankruptcy court gives no specific reason for reducing fees below the amount requested, an appellate court may reverse the reduction of fees as an abuse of discretion.[87]

16.4 Payment of Attorney Fees Through the Chapter 13 Plan

16.4.1 Fees Which Can Be Paid Through a Plan

One important feature of chapter 13 not usually present in chapter 7 cases[88] is the possibility of paying the debtor's attorney from the property of the estate. The opportunity for the debtor to pay all or part of the fee in installments is often the only way a financially strapped client can pay the fee at all. And the fact that the attorney has some assurance, though hardly a complete guarantee, that the fee can be paid in this manner makes him or her more comfortable about taking the client's case without advance payment of all or most of the fee.

Normally the attorney for the debtor classifies her fee among the administrative expenses entitled to priority under 11 U.S.C. § 507(a)(1). Not only does this mean that the fee must be paid in full for the plan to be confirmed under section 1322(a)(2), but it usually means the fee will be paid before most other creditors receive payment.[89] It also means that, if fees have been approved, they may be paid by the trustee pursuant to section 1326(a)(2) if the case is dismissed before confirmation.[90]

Fees may have to be paid concurrently with adequate protection payments to certain secured creditors and payments on leases under section 1326(a)(1).[91] In addition, there are issues concerning whether the language in section 1325(a)(5)(B)(iii)(I) dictating that holders of allowed secured claims be paid in "equal monthly installments" requires those installments to begin before the debtor's attorney has been paid in full. The

---

ruptcy court denied his fee application); *In re* Reuber, 2011 WL 1102821 (E.D. Mich. Mar. 23, 2011) (remanding because bankruptcy court limited chapter 13 fees to "no look" amount without explaining lodestar analysis); Potter v. Bailey, 454 B.R. 715 (S.D. Tex. 2011) (remanding because bankruptcy court failed to state factors and considerations that led to drastic reduction from amount requested for representation in chapter 13 case).

87 Potter v. Bailey, 454 B.R. 715, 725 (S.D. Tex. 2011) (remand required because bankruptcy court did not explain its reasoning in reducing fees); *In re* Grunau, 376 B.R. 322 (M.D. Fla. 2007) (reversing disgorgement order because bankruptcy court failed to explain legal standard used to evaluate fee award); *In re* Paster, 119 B.R. 468 (E.D. Pa. 1990) (under "lodestar" method applicable in circuit to bankruptcy fees, when court did not specifically take issue with number of hours reasonably spent and rate was not excessive, reduction of fees was abuse of discretion). *But see* Berliner v. Pappalardo (*In re* Sullivan), 674 F.3d 65 (1st Cir. 2012) (bankruptcy court need not go line by line through time records to point out duplicative or unnecessary work; court's general finding that case was not so unusually complex as to warrant high fee was sufficient).

88 A debtor's attorney may not receive compensation from the estate for representing the debtor in a chapter 7 case. Lamie v. United States Tr., 540 U.S. 526, 124 S. Ct. 1023, 1032, 157 L. Ed. 2d 1024, 1036 (2004). *See* § 16.2.3, *supra*.

Usually a debtor with nonexempt property should be advised to convert it to exempt property or to file a chapter 13 case. Even if that did not occur, it would normally make more sense to pay the attorney from the nonexempt property prior to the case.

89 11 U.S.C. §§ 1322(a)(2), 1326(b)(1); *In re* Busetta-Silvia, 314 B.R. 218 (B.A.P. 10th Cir. 2004) (both prepetition and postpetition fees were priority administrative expenses to be paid ahead of unsecured creditors); *In re* Shorb, 101 B.R. 185 (B.A.P. 9th Cir. 1989) (fees must be paid prior to or concurrently with other claims and cannot be deferred to six months after commencement of payments to unsecured claims); *In re* Parker, 21 B.R. 692 (E.D. Tenn. 1982) (attorney fees may be paid prior to or concurrently with secured and unsecured claims), *aff'g* 15 B.R. 980 (Bankr. E.D. Tenn. 1981); *In re* Bellamy, 379 B.R. 86 (Bankr. D. Md. 2007) (attorney fees should be distributed by chapter 13 trustee before creditors are paid, except to extent fees have not yet been earned); *In re* Harris, 304 B.R. 751 (Bankr. E.D. Mich. 2004) (debtor's plan could provide for payment of priority attorney fees before other creditors). *See also In re* Meadows, 297 B.R. 671 (Bankr. E.D. Mich. 2003) (plan could require trustee to hold $2000 in reserve for thirty days after confirmation for payment of anticipated counsel fees). *But see In re* Lasica, 294 B.R. 718 (Bankr. N.D. Ill. 2003) (fees could not be paid through plan if confirmed plan made no provision for paying them). By local rule in some districts, however, attorney fees are customarily paid pro rata with other disbursements to assure the attorney's continued interest in the success of the plan. *See In re* Pedersen, 229 B.R. 445 (Bankr. E.D. Cal. 1999) (local rule required submission of waiver of right to receive fees before creditors if counsel sought to receive fees under court's fee guidelines); *In re* Pappas & Rose, Prof'l Corp., 229 B.R. 815 (Bankr. W.D. Okla. 1998) (local rule requiring payment of fees over twenty-four months); *In re* Lanigan, 101 B.R. 530 (Bankr. N.D. Ill. 1986) (bankruptcy court had authority to order payment of fees over life of plan). *See also In re* Townsend, 186 B.R. 248 (Bankr. E.D. Mo. 1994) (payment of fees before mortgage cure was improper if it caused cure to take longer than time permitted by local rule; court did not address question of whether local rule could control substantive issue of length of cure period).

Of course, deferring counsel fees until later in the plan increases the risk that the fees will not be paid in full, and courts that require counsel to defer fees must recognize that it will result in higher fees being charged due to that risk.

90 *In re* Matthews, 2012 WL 3263599 (E.D. Pa. Aug. 9, 2012) (bankruptcy court should have ruled on attorney fee request when chapter 13 case was dismissed); *In re* Hall, 296 B.R. 707 (Bankr. E.D. Va. 2002) (trustee had obligation to pay allowed fees of debtor's counsel before returning funds to debtor in dismissed case); *In re* Lampman, 276 B.R. 182 (Bankr. W.D. Tex. 2002) (attorney fees may be paid by trustee in dismissed chapter 13 case, but only if fees are allowed by court after debtor and trustee have opportunity to object); *In re* Oliver, 222 B.R. 272 (Bankr. E.D. Va. 1998). *See also In re* Lewis, 346 B.R. 89 (Bankr. E.D. Pa. 2006) (fee motion must be filed before dismissal order); *In re* Harris, 258 B.R. 8 (Bankr. D. Idaho 2000) (attorney could be paid from funds held by trustee only through request for fees to be allowed as administrative expenses and could not assert charging lien on funds). *But see In re* Fernandez, 2011 WL 1404891 (S.D. Tex. Apr. 13, 2011) (upon dismissal prior to plan confirmation trustee not required to retrieve adequate assurance payments already disbursed to mortgagee in order to pay attorney's fee claim), *aff'd*, 2012 WL 1889621 (5th Cir. May 24, 2012).

91 See Chapter 9, *supra*, for discussion of such payments.

better view is that it does not require such payments and most secured creditors will hopefully recognize that if they must share initial payments with attorney fees, their "equal monthly payments" will be smaller and it will take longer for them to be paid the full amount due to them under the plan.[92]

Fees which are not entitled to treatment as administrative expenses must be classified with other unsecured claims. They will be paid less than one hundred cents on the dollar in most plans.

Under Code section 330(a)(4)(B), services which are compensable as administrative expenses in a chapter 12 or chapter 13 case include not only services which benefit the bankruptcy estate, but also services necessary for representing the debtor's interests in connection with the bankruptcy case, based on consideration of the benefit and necessity of such services to the debtor. This language would encompass even services outside the bankruptcy court if those services were necessary to successful completion of the case.[93]

It is well established that virtually all of the basic services in a chapter 13 case do benefit the estate, for example, prepetition advice about bankruptcy, preparation of the initial papers and plan, and attendance at the creditors' meeting and the confirmation hearing. As a practical matter, courts rarely question payment of the entire basic fee as an administrative expense. It also seems quite clear that fees for other activities to preserve the estate or the functioning of the plan, such as objections to claims or modifications of the plan, warrant priority administrative expense treatment.

Because a chapter 13 debtor's attorney is not limited to compensation only for services that benefit the estate, there should be little dispute about the right to compensation for any work done in legitimate pursuit of the chapter 13 case. When it is necessary to defend against a motion for relief from the automatic stay, the court will normally find that such defense was necessary and for the debtor's benefit. Similarly, defense of a debtor's exemption rights and dischargeability litigation should clearly be compensable under the test laid out in section 330(a)(4)(B).

However, some courts find an abuse of the system when all or almost all of the debtor's plan payments go toward payment of the attorney fee. Such use of chapter 13 as simply a device for collecting fees, with little or no benefit to any creditors, may be looked upon with disfavor as little more than a disguised liquidation and akin to past abuses in which the primary beneficiaries of a bankruptcy plan were the attorneys involved.[94]

On the other hand, especially because of the increased costs of bankruptcy after the 2005 legislation, courts should not adopt a per se rule against fee-only chapter 13 cases in all situations.[95] There may be valid reasons, such as an emergency need for bankruptcy by a debtor who cannot pay fees in advance, or the possibility of ongoing medical expenses that could not soon be discharged in a later case if the debtor filed a chapter 7 case, that may make such cases a valid and necessary strategy.

16.4.2 Procedure for Obtaining Payment of Fees Through the Plan

The Bankruptcy Rules provide that an attorney who seeks compensation for services from the estate, that is, through the plan, must file an application for those fees including a detailed statement of services rendered, the time and costs expended,[96] and the amounts requested.[97] The application must also be transmitted to the United States trustee.[98] Some courts require a great deal of specificity in such statements.[99] The same rule requires that this application state all payments made or promised for legal services in connection with the case, the source of such payments made or promised, and whether such payments have been or will be shared with anyone other than an attorney in the applicant's firm.[100] Most courts allow attorney fees for

---

92 See Chapter 11, *supra*, for discussion of the "equal monthly payments" requirement.

93 *See, e.g., In re* Powell, 314 B.R. 567 (Bankr. N.D. Tex. 2004) (fees awarded to divorce counsel); *In re* Polishuk, 258 B.R. 238 (Bankr. N.D. Okla. 2001) (fees allowed for work in domestic relations court).

94 *In re* Buck, 432 B.R. 13 (Bankr. D. Mass. 2010) (cases filed in chapter 13 solely for purpose of paying attorney fees through plan were in bad faith); *In re* Molina, 420 B.R. 825 (Bankr. D.N.M. 2009); *In re* San Miguel, 40 B.R. 481 (Bankr. D. Colo. 1984). *See also* Tell, *Chasing the Bankruptcy Bumblers*, Nat'l L. J., May 11, 1981, at 1, 26.

95 *In re* Crager, 691 F.3d 671 (5th Cir. 2012) (debtor had legitimate reason for filing chapter 13 case that paid nothing to unsecured creditors); Berliner v. Pappalardo (*In re* Puffer), 674 F.3d 78 (1st Cir. Mass. 2012) (no per se rule that fee-only chapter 13 case was in bad faith simply because no unsecured creditors would be paid); *In re* Antonio, 2010 WL 1490589 (Bankr. E.D.N.C. Apr. 13, 2010) (rejecting trustee's request for blanket order denying "no-look" chapter 13 fees in all attorney fee-only chapter 13 cases).

96 Costs that are reimbursable may include photocopying, postage, long distance telephone calls, and travel expenses. *In re* Nat'l Paragon Corp., 76 B.R. 73 (E.D. Pa. 1987).

A court may not arbitrarily reject certain categories of expenses as non-compensable "overhead" when those expenses are billed to nonbankruptcy clients in the market. *In re* Hillsborough Holdings Corp., 127 F.3d 1398 (11th Cir. 1997).

97 Fed. R. Bankr. P. 2016(a).

98 *Id.*

99 *In re* Beverly Mfg. Corp., 841 F.2d 365 (11th Cir. 1988) (fee application was inadequate because there was no indication of specific nature of each service performed and some entries "lumped" together several different services in one time period); *In re* Williams, 384 B.R. 191 (Bankr. N.D. Ohio 2007) (chapter 13 fee request reduced from $2700 to $1400, with court inferring from numerous identical entries for short time periods that counsel's time records were not contemporaneous); *In re* Vermon-Williams, 377 B.R. 156 (Bankr. E.D. Va. 2007) (fee request reduced because chapter 13 counsel entered minimum time amounts for routine tasks and did not record contemporaneous time entries); *In re* Newman, 270 B.R. 845 (Bankr. S.D. Ohio 2001) (fees denied for work not documented by contemporaneous time records); *In re* Thacker, 48 B.R. 161 (Bankr. N.D. Ill. 1985); *In re* Horn & Hardart Baking Co., 30 B.R. 938 (Bankr. E.D. Pa. 1983).

100 Fed. R. Bankr. P. 2016(a).

the time spent on the fee application, at least if the time is substantial.[101] Compensation for time spent may be enhanced for exceptional results, but only if the applicant produces specific evidence showing why such enhancement is necessary to make the award commensurate with nonbankruptcy compensation.[102]

The Code provides that compensation from the estate can be awarded only after notice and hearing.[103] Given the meaning of "notice and a hearing" in the Code,[104] this does not necessarily mean that a hearing must occur. Some type of notice to all parties that fees are sought from the estate is required, giving them an opportunity to request a hearing to raise any questions they might have.[105]

As a practical matter, these provisions mean that the debtor's attorney must apply in some manner for her fees to be approved with notice to all parties interested in the case. In some districts this can be done through a combination of the disclosure statement of fees, if it lists services rendered, and a provision in the plan to be confirmed stating that fees will be paid through the plan. If this method is followed, then notice of the plan should include notice of this plan provision. In other jurisdictions, a separate application must be filed. Normally, the payment of fees through the plan is approved in conjunction with confirmation of the plan.[106]

After confirmation, there are sometimes circumstances that require the debtor's attorney to do other work not originally anticipated. When this occurs, an application for additional fees may be made if the work is compensable from the estate.[107] In many courts, an application and proposed order approving such additional fees can be attached to the pleading filed, especially when it is a fairly simple uncontested matter such as a modification of the plan.[108] However, once the plan has been confirmed, some courts may require a motion to modify the plan if additional attorney fees are requested to be paid through the plan.[109]

16.5 Other Sources of Attorney Fees in Bankruptcy Cases

16.5.1 Overview

An additional source of attorney fees often overlooked by many bankruptcy practitioners is the opposing party.[110] Most practitioners are aware of the Bankruptcy Code provisions that provide for attorney fees to be awarded to prevailing debtors in certain circumstances, such as proceedings to enforce the automatic stay,[111] certain dischargeability complaints,[112] and involuntary bankruptcy petitions.[113] But they are often less knowledgeable about the myriad of other federal and state statutes that provide for attorney fees to prevailing parties. Altogether there are nearly one-hundred such federal statutes, and many more state statutes.[114]

---

101   *In re* Nucorp Energy, Inc., 764 F.2d 655 (9th Cir. 1985); *In re* Heise, 436 B.R. 143 (Bankr. D.N.M. 2010) (allowing compensation for time spent on fee application, but limiting billable time to one hour).
102   *In re* Manoa Fin. Co., 853 F.2d 687 (9th Cir. 1988).
103   See also Federal Rule of Bankruptcy Procedure 2002(a), requiring twenty-one days' notice to the debtor, the trustee, and all creditors of an application for compensation or reimbursement of expenses in excess of $1000.
104   "After notice and a hearing" is defined at 11 U.S.C. § 102(1).
105   See Fed. R. Bankr. P. 2002(a)(7).
106   See *In re* Dewey, 237 B.R. 783 (B.A.P. 10th Cir. 1999) (affirming denial of fees sought by "corrected" application after confirmation because increase in fees sought would have made plan nonconfirmable).
      In some cases, approval of an attorney fee as proper may preclude a later malpractice action by the debtor claiming that the attorney work was inadequate. See Grausz v. Englander, 321 F.3d 467 (4th Cir. 2003).
107   *In re* Williams, 378 B.R. 811 (Bankr. E.D. Mich. 2007) (court reduced fees sought for postconfirmation legal work that consisted primarily of attempts to modify significantly underfunded chapter 13 plan, finding that the costs of protracted litigation exceeded reasonable benefit to debtor); *In re* Robinson, 368 B.R. 492 (Bankr. E.D. Va. 2007) (postconfirmation supplemental fee application seeking $13,351.20 reduced by 40% as allowance for debtor's counsel's "learning curve" on post-BAPCPA matters, and by additional 20% due to vagueness of counsel's fee contract with debtor); *In re* Hanson, 223 B.R. 775 (Bankr. D. Or. 1998) (attorney barred from collecting fees for postconfirmation work if no fee application was filed and approved). *See also In re* Phillips, 219 B.R. 1001 (Bankr. W.D. Tenn. 1998) (attorney could not file postpetition claim for consumer debt under section 1305(a)(2) for postpetition fees).
108   For one form of such an attachment, see Form 32, Appx. G.3, *infra*.
109   *In re* Hallmark, 225 B.R. 192 (Bankr. C.D. Cal. 1998) (modification must be sought when plan provided specific amount for administrative expense attorney fees). See *In re* Black, 116 B.R. 818 (Bankr. W.D. Okla. 1990) (when attorney sought fees six times higher than those provided for in confirmed plan, which would utilize all funds available to unsecured creditors, and no motion to modify plan had been filed, attorney held bound by confirmed plan and application for additional fees denied).
110   A variety of potential opportunities to shift fees are discussed in *Ten Ways to Win Attorneys Fees in Your Bankruptcy Practice (Without Taking A Penny From the Debtor)*, 12 NCLC REPORTS Bankruptcy and Foreclosures Ed. 25 (July/Aug. 1993).
111   11 U.S.C. § 362(k) (section 362(h) prior to the 2005 amendments). See, e.g., Young v. Repine (*In re* Repine), 536 F.3d 512 (5th Cir. 2008) (upholding fees awarded against creditor and attorney who sought to collect support from estate property; fees need not be paid by debtor before court can award them); Lopez v. Consejo De Titulares Del Condominio Carolina Court Apartments, 405 B.R. 24 (B.A.P. 1st Cir. 2009) ($26,680 fee reasonable for stay violation case calculated using lodestar method); *In re* Parks, 2008 WL 2003163 (Bankr. N.D. Ohio May 6, 2008) (representation of debtor pro bono did not preclude award of $3000 attorney fees for successfully representing debtor in stay violation action against utility). *See also* § 9.6, *supra*.
112   11 U.S.C. § 523(d) provides for attorney fees to many debtors who successfully defend against complaints brought under 11 U.S.C. § 523(a)(2). See § 15.4.3.2.4, *supra*.
113   11 U.S.C. § 303(i). See § 14.8, *supra*.
114   See, e.g., *In re* Hoopai, 581 F.3d 1090, 1102 (9th Cir. 2009) (debtor who set aside foreclosure sale and successfully defended on appeal bankruptcy court's decision that sale had not extinguished her rights in property entitled to fees as prevailing party under Hawaii statute regulating contract actions); *In re* Fowler, 427 B.R.1 (W.D. Ark. 2010) (fees awarded under state fee-shifting statute). *See generally*

16.5.2 The Civil Rights Attorney's Fees Awards Act of 1976

The most important of these statutes is 42 U.S.C. § 1988, the Civil Rights Attorney's Fees Awards Act of 1976. Despite its title, there are strong arguments that this law applies in every action brought under the Bankruptcy Code against state and local entities or officials.

The Civil Rights Attorney's Fees Awards Act of 1976 prescribes fee awards in every action under 42 U.S.C. § 1983, which in turn is applicable to every denial of federal statutory rights under color of law. The leading case on the subject, *Maine v. Thiboutot*,[115] held that the denial of rights granted by a federal statute, in that instance the Social Security Act, gave rise to a cause of action under section 1983. The Supreme Court held that section 1983 should be interpreted literally: the civil rights statute could be used to enforce any right created by the Constitution or laws of the United States, regardless of whether the right had a constitutional or civil rights character.[116]

Because the Bankruptcy Code is a federal statute, the *Thiboutot* holding should be applicable. Thus, any denial, under color of law, of rights granted by the Code creates a cause of action under 42 U.S.C. § 1983.[117] If the plaintiff in such a case is successful, attorney fees should be awarded under the Civil Rights Attorneys Fee's Awards Act.[118]

The ramifications of these principles are broad. In every case in which a debtor seeks to enforce bankruptcy rights (arising out of any Code section) against a county-run or municipal utility, or a state or local governmental entity, attorney fees should be available. For example, those claims may rely upon the following provisions:

- Section 525(a), prohibiting discrimination by governmental units against debtors who have filed bankruptcy cases;
- Section 362, providing for the automatic stay;
- Section 366, dealing with utility service; or
- Section 524, dealing with the protections of discharge.

Many of these claims may give rise to fees under Code section 362(k) or contempt theories, so section 1988 will not be necessary.

Damages and fees may also be sought under sections 1983 and 1988 from private parties acting under color of law in concert with government officials.[119] Although debtors' advocates can often receive fee awards under other theories, the possibility of receipt of significant fees under the civil rights acts should not be ignored.[120]

16.5.3 Consumer Protection Statutes

Also common, but all too often neglected, are opportunities in bankruptcy cases to bring actions under various consumer protection statutes providing for attorney fees. A thorough familiarity with debtors' rights under these statutes can result in substantial, additional fees for bankruptcy attorneys, not to mention important benefits for their clients.

On the federal level, the most important of these statutes is the Truth in Lending Act.[121] Section 130(a) of the Act,[122] which is applicable to every consumer credit transaction, provides for mandatory attorney fees to successful consumer litigants.[123] In view of the fact that the typical consumer debtor has entered into numerous transactions subject to the Act, an attorney handling a substantial number of bankruptcies is quite likely to find many potential Truth in Lending cases in her files.

Other federal consumer protection statutes providing for attorney fees include the Magnuson-Moss Warranty Act,[124] the Fair Debt Collection Practices Act,[125] the Equal Credit Opportunity Act,[126] and the Fair Credit Reporting Act.[127] With respect to the Fair Credit Reporting Act in particular, it is common for creditors and reporting agencies to incorrectly report debts that have been discharged in bankruptcy. Monitoring a debtor's credit report after discharge can lead to additional claims for the debtor and additional fees for the debtor's attorney.[128]

Alba Conte, Attorney Fee Awards (2d ed. 1993); Mary Francis Derfner & Arthur D. Wolf, Court Awarded Attorney Fees (1986); E. Richard Larson, Federal Court Awards of Attorney's Fees (1981).

115 448 U.S. 1, 100 S. Ct. 2502, 65 L. Ed. 2d 555 (1980).
116 *Id.*, 448 U.S. at 8.
But compare Middlesex County Sewerage Auth. v. Nat'l Sea Clammers Ass'n, 453 U.S. 1, 101 S. Ct. 2615, 69 L. Ed. 2d 435 (1981), in which this holding was modified somewhat as to some statutes.
117 Almand v. Benton County, 145 B.R. 608 (W.D. Ark. 1992) (cause of action under section 1983 for violations of automatic stay).
118 *In re* Watts, 93 B.R. 350 (E.D. Pa. 1988), *rev'd on other grounds*, 876 F.2d 1090 (3d Cir. 1989); Higgins v. Philadelphia Gas Works, 54 B.R. 928 (E.D. Pa. 1985); *In re* McKibben, 233 B.R. 378 (Bankr. E.D. Tex. 1999); *In re* Gibbs, 12 B.R. 737 (Bankr. D. Conn. 1981); *In re* Maya, 8 B.R. 202 (Bankr. E.D. Pa. 1981).
119 Almand v. Benton County, 145 B.R. 608 (W.D. Ark. 1992) (cause of action under section 1983 for violations of automatic stay against parties who participated in wrongful execution against debtor's property).
120 However, requests for fees against government entities may now be met with the argument that they must be limited to the rates set forth in 28 U.S.C. § 2412(d)(2)(A) due to the operation of 11 U.S.C. § 106(a)(3). See § 16.5.7, *infra*.
121 15 U.S.C. §§ 1601–1677.
See § 14.4.4, *supra*, for further discussion of the Truth in Lending Act in bankruptcy cases. *See* National Consumer Law Center, Truth in Lending (7th ed. 2010 and Supp.).
122 15 U.S.C. § 1640(a).
123 *See, e.g., In re* Jansen, 47 B.R. 641 (Bankr. D. Ariz. 1985) ($13,104 fee for Truth in Lending case).
124 15 U.S.C. §§ 2301–2312. *See generally* National Consumer Law Center, Consumer Warranty Law Ch. 2 (4th ed. 2010 and Supp.).
125 15 U.S.C. §§ 1692–1692*o*. *See generally* National Consumer Law Center, Fair Debt Collection (7th ed. 2010 and Supp.).
126 15 U.S.C. §§ 1691–1691f. *See generally* National Consumer Law Center, Credit Discrimination (5th ed. 2009 and Supp.).
127 15 U.S.C. §§ 1681–1681t. *See generally* National Consumer Law Center, Fair Credit Reporting (7th ed. 2010 and Supp.).
128 *See* § 8.9, *supra*.

§ 16.5.4   Consumer Bankruptcy Law and Practice

Many state laws have similar provisions. These include usury statutes,[129] laws prohibiting unfair and deceptive practices,[130] and laws regulating collection practices or landlord-tenant relationships. A number of states require that if creditors' contracts contain a clause giving them a right to fees if they prevail in litigation with the debtor then that obligation is reciprocal.[131] Bankruptcy practitioners should become familiar with all such statutes that touch so frequently upon their clients' lives.

In most cases claims under these statutes, if they arose prior to the bankruptcy, may be reserved by the debtor as exempt property and then pursued by the debtor in the bankruptcy forum or elsewhere. Even when the debtor cannot exempt such claims, the trustee in a chapter 7 case rarely has either the interest or expertise to pursue them and normally abandons them back to the debtor. In chapter 13 cases, in which the debtor retains control over all property of the estate,[132] there is no reason why such claims may not be immediately pursued if the debtor wishes.

However, counsel representing a chapter 7 debtor with respect to a prepetition cause of action must pay close attention to the rules regarding representation of the bankruptcy estate. During the bankruptcy case, or at least until the cause of action has been exempted or abandoned and the time for objecting to that treatment has passed, the cause of action belongs to the estate and cannot be pursued without the participation of the trustee and the appointment of debtor's counsel as special counsel for the estate pursuant to Code section 327.[133] In many cases, it may be easier to disclose the cause of action in the schedules and allow the cause of action to remain dormant until the bankruptcy case is over and it is clear that it has been exempted or abandoned, placing it back in the debtor's control.[134]

16.5.4 The Equal Access to Justice Act

In litigation against the federal government, an additional potential source of attorney fees is the Equal Access to Justice Act, 28 U.S.C. § 2412. This Act provides, *inter alia*, for attorney fees when the federal government takes a position, before or during litigation, that is not "substantially justified."[135] The Supreme Court has held that more than good faith is necessary for the government to meet this test; a position that is "justified in substance or in the main," "having a reasonable basis both in law and in fact," is required.[136] Similar fee provisions apply to litigation with the Internal Revenue Service.[137]

---

129 *See generally* National Consumer Law Center, Consumer Credit Regulation § 2.3 (2012).

130 *See generally* National Consumer Law Center, Unfair and Deceptive Acts and Practices (7th ed. 2008 and Supp.).

131 *See In re* Hoopai, 581 F.3d 1090, 1102 (9th Cir. 2009) (debtor who set aside foreclosure sale and successfully defended on appeal bankruptcy court's decision that sale had not extinguished her rights in property entitled to fees as prevailing party under Hawaii statute regulating contract actions); *In re* Martinez, 416 F.3d 1286 (11th Cir. 2005) (debtor awarded fees for successful dischargeability defense under Florida reciprocal fees statute); *In re* Baroff, 105 F.3d 439 (9th Cir. 1997) (debtor awarded fees under California statute providing for reciprocal fees because nondischargeability proceeding was an action on the contract); First State Bank of Crossett v. Fowler, 427 B.R. 1 (W.D. Ark. 2010) (fees for proceedings seeking disgorgement of overpayment from mortgagee arose from note and were covered by prevailing party statute's provision); *In re* Nealy, 139 B.R. 48 (D.D.C. 1992) (awarding fees incurred in dischargeability proceeding based on contract clause that provided that creditor would pay debtor's fees if debtor prevailed in collection litigation); *In re* Jerk Machine, 422 B.R. 327 (Bankr. S.D. Fla. 2010) (debtor who prevailed in fraudulent transfer proceeding against bank entitled to attorney fee award under Florida reciprocal fees statute); *In re* Guarnieri, 297 B.R. 365 (Bankr. D. Conn. 2003) (fees awarded for debtors' successful objection to mortgage lender's proof of claim), *aff'd*, 308 B.R. 122 (D. Conn. 2004); *In re* Mawji, 228 B.R. 321 (Bankr. M.D. Fla. 1999) (fee granted for successfully defending nondischargeability action based on reciprocity provision in state law); *In re* Pichardo, 186 B.R. 279 (Bankr. M.D. Fla. 1995) (fees awarded to debtor's counsel in student loan dischargeability proceeding under statute providing that, if a contract imposes fees on a debtor who loses in litigation, debtor is entitled to fees from creditor who loses in litigation). *But see In re* Sheridan, 105 F.3d 1164 (7th Cir. 1997) (chapter 11 debtor could not recover under Florida reciprocal fee statute because dischargeability action was not "action with respect to the contract"); *In re* Johnson, 756 F.2d 738 (9th Cir. 1985) (California statute providing for attorney fees to prevailing party in any action on a contract which contains an attorney fee clause not applicable to motion for relief from automatic stay).

The right to fees under such statutes is not preempted by the Bankruptcy Code when the debtor's successful litigation is based on state law claims and defenses. *See In re* Gifford, 256 B.R. 661 (Bankr. D. Conn. 2000) (debtor's claim for attorney fees under state fee-shifting statute not preempted in connection with granting of debtor's objection to mortgage lender's proof of claim based on state law).

132 11 U.S.C. § 1306(b). *See* § 12.8.1, *supra*.

133 *See* Cuevas-Segarra v. Contreras, 134 F.3d 458 (1st Cir. 1998) (attorneys who settled estate's cause of action without being appointed counsel for estate required to disgorge fees); § 16.2.3, *supra* (discussing fees paid from estate property).

134 It is crucial to disclose the cause of action fully, or the debtor may face issues of judicial estoppel. *See* §§ 3.5, 7.3.7.2.2, 10.1.2, 14.3.2.6.3, *supra*.

135 28 U.S.C. § 2412(d). *See* Dougherty v. Lehman, 711 F.2d 555 (3d Cir. 1983).

136 Pierce v. Underwood, 487 U.S. 552, 108 S. Ct. 2541, 101 L. Ed. 2d 490, 504 (1988).

137 26 U.S.C. § 7430. *See In re* Yochum, 89 F.3d 661 (9th Cir. 1996) (bankruptcy court was "court of the United States" with authority to award fees under 26 U.S.C. § 7430); *In re* Cascade Farms, 34 F.3d 756 (9th Cir. 1994) (district court could order IRS to pay fees to bankruptcy debtor under 26 U.S.C. § 7430); *In re* Germaine, 152 B.R. 619 (B.A.P. 9th Cir. 1993) (bankruptcy court was "court of the United States" for purposes of 26 U.S.C. § 7430); *In re* Chambers, 140 B.R. 233 (N.D. Ill. 1992) (bankruptcy court was "court of the United States" that could award fees under 26 U.S.C. § 7430); *In re* Seay, 369 B.R. 423 (Bankr. E.D. Ark. 2007) (in awarding fees pursuant to 26 U.S.C. § 7430, court allowed "premium" rate ranging from $30 to $75 per hour above basic statutory rate of $125 in view of lawyers' expertise in complex legal area). *But see In re* Grewe, 4 F.3d 299 (4th Cir. 1993) (fees under 26 U.S.C. § 7430 denied because debtors did not exhaust administrative remedies); *In*

However, the Act provides that fees normally must be awarded at a relatively low statutory rate.[138] This rate may be adjustable, though, at least for inflation.[139] Obviously, despite the lack of prevailing market rates, the possibility of recovering fees in litigation against federal agencies when they are otherwise unavailable can benefit both attorneys and their clients. It has been utilized in the bankruptcy courts,[140] and in view of the intransigent positions frequently taken by the federal government in bankruptcy cases, it is likely to be applied often. It should apply to the United States trustee, a component of the federal Justice Department, when that office takes a position that is not substantially justified.

16.5.5 Fees As Sanction for Violation of Bankruptcy Rules

16.5.5.1 Rule 9011

Fees may be awarded to debtor's counsel when imposed as a sanction against an opposing party or counsel for violation of Federal Rule of Bankruptcy Procedure 9011. Rule 9011 does not function primarily as a fee-shifting provision. The purpose of an award of sanctions under the Rule is to deter future litigation abuses.[141] Yet, because the abusive practices of a creditor or its counsel may have a harmful impact on bankruptcy debtors and undermine the functioning of the bankruptcy courts themselves, there are many instances when the justification for shifting fees and costs as a Rule 9011 sanction is compelling.

The securitization of mortgage obligations and other consumer debt has spawned an industry of servicers who specialize in preparing routine bankruptcy documents for creditors.[142] These "default" servicers often operate on a nationwide scale and, through their non-attorney staff, submit data electronically to local counsel for use in preparing documents for filing in the local bankruptcy court. In some instances the documents may be filed in a bankruptcy court under the electronic signature of a local attorney who has not reviewed the supporting documents.[143] Or they may be filed under the electronic signature of an attorney for a national servicer who reviews only a random sample of the filed documents.[144] A local creditor attorney may have no direct contact with his or her client or may be prohibited from having such contact, and the "client" may be nothing more than a computer database managed by a company that contracts with a major servicer.[145]

Given the lack of human oversight and separation of functions, the filings generated by these servicing systems are highly prone to error. Creditor attorneys who allow documents to be filed under their names without reviewing them expose themselves to potential sanctions. The bankruptcy courts have taken the initiative in scrutinizing the practices of these servicers, particularly as they appear in connection with routine filings such as proofs of claim and motions for relief from the stay.[146]

Rule 9011 imposes an obligation on the claimant to make a reasonable inquiry before filing a proof of claim.[147] Attorneys and unrepresented creditors who submit claims without a proper legal or factual basis are subject to sanctions, which may include an award of attorney fees and expenses to the objecting

---

re Graham, 981 F.2d 1135 (10th Cir. 1992) (fees could not be awarded under 26 U.S.C. § 7430 if government's position was not substantially unjustified ab initio); *In re* Brickell Inv. Corp., 922 F.2d 696 (11th Cir. 1991) (bankruptcy court not a "court of the United States" for purposes of awarding fees under Internal Revenue Code § 7430; however, party may seek fees under this section by following procedures for non-core proceedings to obtain judgment of the district court).

138 28 U.S.C. § 2412(d)(1).
139 28 U.S.C. § 2412(d)(2)(A).
140 O'Connor v. Dep't of Energy, 942 F.2d 771 (10th Cir. 1991) (bankruptcy court had jurisdiction to award fees under Equal Access to Justice Act); *In re* Armstead, 106 B.R. 405 (Bankr. E.D. Pa. 1989); *In re* Hagan, 44 B.R. 59 (Bankr. D.R.I. 1984) (fees awarded against Social Security Administration in case in which it pursued its uniformly rejected claim that benefits overpayments are not dischargeable in bankruptcy). *But see In re* Davis, 899 F.2d 1136 (11th Cir. 1990) (bankruptcy court did not have jurisdiction to award fees under Equal Access to Justice Act, and fee award could only be entered by district court upon recommended findings of fact and conclusions of law supplied by bankruptcy court).
141 Kirk v. Capital Corp., 16 F.3d 1485, 1490 (8th Cir. 1994); *In re* Kunstler, 914 F.2d 505, 522–523 (4th Cir. 1990); White v. Gen. Motors Corp., 908 F.2d 675, 684 (10th Cir. 1990).
142 *See* § 14.4.3.4, *supra*.

143 *In re* Parsley, 384 B.R. 138 (Bankr. S.D. Tex. 2008) ("simplified" loan histories provided by national law firm, through a separate entity employing 300–350 legal assistants, to local law firm for use in prosecuting stay relief motions are not reviewed for accuracy by attorneys for the national firm before they are provided to the local firm).
144 *In re* Taylor, 655 F.3d 274 (3d Cir. 2011) (affirming bankruptcy court order imposing Rule 9011 sanctions against law firm, one attorney, and lender).
145 *In re* Parsley, 384 B.R. 138 (Bankr. S.D. Tex. 2008) (local counsel's restricted relationship with national counsel effectively barred local counsel from communication with client, leading to filing of meritless stay relief motion).
146 *In re* Taylor, 655 F.3d 274 (3d Cir. 2011) (affirming bankruptcy court order imposing Rule 9011 sanctions against law firm, an attorney, and lender); *In re* Ulmer, 363 B.R. 777 (Bankr. D.S.C. 2008) ($33,500 sanction imposed against law firm that allowed out-of-state paralegals to prepare stay relief motions later filed electronically with court without attorney review); *In re* Rivera, 342 B.R. 435 (Bankr. D.N.J. 2006), *subsequent decision at* 369 B.R. 193 (Bankr. D.N.J. 2007), *aff'd*, 2007 WL 1946656 (D.N.J. June 27, 2007) ($125,000 penalty under Rule 9011 assessed against law firm for attaching pre-signed supporting affidavits to 250 stay relief motions). *See also In re* Woodruff, 2010 WL 386209 (Bankr. M.D. Ala. Jan. 27, 2010) (finding that debtor has sufficiently alleged an independent cause of action for "fraud on the court" based on mortgage creditor's filing of false affidavits in connection with stay relief motions).
147 *In re* Dansereau, 274 B.R. 686 (Bankr. W.D. Tex. 2002); *In re* Knox, 237 B.R. 687 (Bankr. N.D. Ill. 1999); *In re* Lenior, 231 B.R. 662 (Bankr. N.D. Ill. 1999).

The proof of claim form, Official Form 10, requires that the person signing the claim attest to the following: "I declare under penalty of perjury that the information provided is true and correct to the best of my knowledge, information and reasonable belief."

party.[148] Mortgage holders and servicers who pursue meritless stay relief motions face similar sanctions.[149] The failure to make a reasonable inquiry into the identity of the current holder of an obligation may lead to significant sanctions.[150] Courts have also sanctioned counsel and creditors who routinely assess fees against debtors that have no basis in the underlying contract.[151] A creditor may be subject to Rule 9011 sanctions without signing a pleading or court document if it has provided false information or failed to correct false information used by its attorney.[152]

A debtor seeking sanctions under Rule 9011 should take care to comply with the rule's procedural requirements. Bankruptcy Rule 9011 was amended in 1997 to conform substantially to Federal Rule of Civil Procedure 11. Except with respect to a bankruptcy petition filed in violation of the rule, a motion for sanctions may not be filed until twenty-one days have passed after it has been served on the respondent, who may withdraw or correct the challenged pleading or paper during that time.[153] If sanctions cannot be awarded under Rule 9011 because this "safe-harbor" procedure has not been followed, the court may in some instances award fees as a sanction based on the court's inherent authority.[154]

16.5.5.2 Rules 3001 and 3002.1

Some of the problems with inadequate or incorrect proofs of claims are also addressed by Bankruptcy Rule 3001. That rule requires a creditor asserting a claim based an open-end or revolving consumer credit agreement—except one for which a security interest is claimed in the debtor's real property—to file a statement specifying certain information about the claim.[155] It further requires the creditor to provide, upon request of a party in interest, a copy of the writing(s) on which the claim is based.[156] If a creditor fails to comply with this rule without cause, sanctions including attorney fees may be appropriate.[157]

In addition, Bankruptcy Rule 3002.1 addresses the frequent accounting mistakes made by mortgage servicers in chapter 13 cases curing home mortgage defaults.[158] Among the remedies for a failure to comply with the rule is the award of reasonable expenses and attorney fees caused by the failure.[159]

16.5.6 Other Fee-Shifting Provisions

Finally, it must be remembered that almost any type of action relating to the debtor's affairs may be brought under the expanded jurisdiction of the bankruptcy forum.[160] It is possible that any one of the wide array of other state and federal fee-shifting statutes could be applicable in a particular case. Even a summary discussion of these statutes is beyond the scope of this treatise, and the topic of fee awards has been well-covered elsewhere.[161] Although the courts have differed upon the question of how these fees should be determined, all agree that they must be premised upon fair hourly rates which

---

148 *In re* McAllister, 123 B.R. 393 (Bankr. D. Or. 1991) (Rule 9011 sanctions imposed against state revenue department for filing proof of claim for income taxes not owed); *In re* Hamilton, 104 B.R. 525 (Bankr. M.D. Ga. 1989) (attorney fees awarded to debtor as Rule 9011 sanction against IRS for filing claim for taxes without reasonable inquiry).

149 *In re* Koontz, 2010 WL 5625883 (Bankr. N.D. Ind. Sep. 30, 2010) (attorney fees awarded to debtor's counsel under Rule 9011 for successful standing challenge to mortgagee's proof of claim); *In re* Cabrera-Mejia, 402 B.R. 335 (Bankr. C.D. Cal. 2008) ($21,000 sanction imposed on law firm under Rule 9011 and section 105(a) for practice of filing motions for relief from stay and withdrawing them before twenty-one contested hearings); *In re* Schuessler, 386 B.R. 458 (Bankr. S.D.N.Y. 2008) (Rule 9011 sanctions, including payment of debtor's attorney fees, imposed on creditor for seeking stay relief pursuant to its policy of filing for relief whenever borrowers were two payments behind, regardless of substantial equity in property and debtors' payment history); *In re* Fagan, 376 B.R. 81 (Bankr. S.D.N.Y. 2007) (debtor's attorney fees and costs awarded for defending stay relief motion filed when creditor's own records showed debtor current in payments); *In re* Osborne, 375 B.R. 216 (Bankr. M.D. La. 2007) (damages and attorney fees awarded against creditor and its attorney for filing affidavit alleging debtor defaulted on agreement despite attorney's lack of personal knowledge; sanction imposed under 11 U.S.C. § 105 and 28 U.S.C. § 1927). *See also In re* Martinez, 393 B.R. 27 (Bankr. D. Nev. 2008) (lender and its law firm ordered to pay debtors' attorney fees related to proceeding to set aside stipulation for relief from stay entered by mutual mistake); § 9.7.3.2, *supra*.

150 *In re* Nosek, 406 B.R. 434 (D. Mass. 2009) (imposing Rule 9011 sanctions of $250,000 against mortgage loan servicer and $25,000 against law firm for failure to disclose identity of current holder of securitized mortgage obligation during course of protected litigation), *aff'd in part and modified in part*, 609 F.3d 6 (1st Cir. 2010) (affirming sanctions finding but reducing sanction from $250,000 to $5,000); *In re* Hayes, 393 B.R. 259 (Bankr. D. Mass. 2008) ("[i]naccurate representations about the moving party's status as the holder may constitute a violation of Fed. R. Bankr. P. 9011").

151 *In re* Haque, 395 B.R. 799 (Bankr. S.D. Fla. 2008) (law firm and creditor jointly and severally sanctioned $95,130.45 for routinely claiming a bogus $2114.10 penalty fee in stay relief motions); *In re* Porcheddu, 338 B.R. 729 (Bankr. S.D. Tex. 2006) (sanctioning law firm $65,000 under Rule 9011 for practice of falsely representing its time records for stay relief motions as contemporaneous).

152 *In re* Kilgore, 253 B.R. 179 (Bankr. D.S.C. 2000).

153 *See* Fed. R. Bankr. P. 9011(c)(1)(A); § 16.7, *supra*.
154 *See In re* Walker, 532 F.3d 1304 (11th Cir. 2008) (although sanctions under Rule 9011 were unavailable to movant due to non-compliance with safe harbor rule, bankruptcy court properly exercised inherent power to assess $14,000 attorney fees as sanction against creditor's attorney who filed unsubstantiated claims accusing debtor's counsel of fraud), *cert. denied*, 129 S. Ct. 1986 (2009); *In re* Jones, 2007 WL 1703673 (Bankr. E.D. Va. June 8, 2007) (although fees could not be awarded under Rule 9011 because request did not comply with safe harbor rule, court invoked its inherent equitable power to award fees to debtor who had incurred unnecessary litigation expense in proving debt was dischargeable). *See also* § 16.5.6, *infra*.
155 Fed. R. Bankr. P. 3001(c)(3)(A).
156 Fed. R. Bankr. P. 3001(c)(3)(B). *See* § 14.4.3.5, *supra*.
157 Fed. R. Bankr. P. 3001(c)(2)(D).
158 *See* § 11.6.2.8.2, *supra*.
159 Fed. R. Bankr. P. 3002(i)(2).
160 See Chapter 2, *supra*, for a discussion of bankruptcy court jurisdiction.
161 Alba Conte, Attorney Fee Awards (2d ed. 1993); Mary Francis Derfner & Arthur D. Wolf, Court Awarded Attorney Fees (1986); E. Richard Larson, Federal Court Awards of Attorney's Fees (1981).

will serve the statutes' purpose of attracting attorneys to such cases. Suffice it to say that the opportunities for financial rewards in bringing cases of great benefit to consumer clients, even when those clients cannot themselves afford sizeable attorney fees, are enormous.

When no fee-shifting statute is applicable, or when a fee-shifting statute permits an award of fees only to a prevailing plaintiff, a debtor responding to a pleading or motion filed in bad faith may still be awarded fees under the court's inherent authority. An exception to the "American Rule" under which each party bears his or her own litigation costs applies when a party has "acted in bad faith, vexatiously, wantonly, or for oppressive reasons."[162] This inherent court authority to award fees when an opposing party has needlessly increased the cost of litigation is supplemented by 28 U.S.C. § 1927, which provides that an attorney appearing in a "court of the United States" who "so multiplies the proceedings in any case unreasonably and vexatiously" may be required by the court to pay excess costs, expenses, and attorney fees reasonably incurred because of the conduct.[163]

16.5.7 Limitations on Fee Awards Against Governmental Units

Unfortunately some limitations were placed on the awarding of attorney fees against at least some governmental units by the Bankruptcy Reform Act of 1994.[164] Code section 106(a)(3) states that awards of attorney fees against a governmental unit must be "consistent with the provisions and limitations of" 28 U.S.C. § 2412(d)(2)(A), a subsection of the Equal Access to Justice Act (EAJA).[165]

It is, first of all, unclear whether this provision is simply an exception to the abrogation of sovereign immunity, or whether it goes beyond that. Some governmental units, such as municipalities, never had sovereign immunity and some attorney fees claims (for example, for contempt of court) may be awardable irrespective of sovereign immunity. The structure of the new section 106 suggests that the attorney fee language in section 106(a)(3) is designed to modify and limit the general abrogation language in section 106(a). If that is the case, then the attorney fee limitation should not be applied to situations in which the governmental unit never had sovereign immunity.

In *Central Virginia Community College v. Katz*[166] the United States Supreme Court held that certain bankruptcy proceedings are not suits against the state that implicate a state's sovereign immunity, because they are ancillary to a bankruptcy court's *in rem* jurisdiction. Essentially the Court concluded that the states never had sovereign immunity to waive with respect to certain essential bankruptcy proceedings, such as actions to remedy violations of the automatic stay. The decision may well have an impact on future interpretations of section 106 and its limits on attorney fees in actions brought against a state to enforce provisions of the Bankruptcy Code.[167]

In addition, 28 U.S.C. § 2412(d)(2)(A) limits attorney fees against the *federal government* to a rate of $125 per hour, which may be adjusted for inflation since the section's most recent amendment, so that it is currently significantly higher.[168] This provision should not affect fees awarded against state and local governments. Because 28 U.S.C. § 2412(d) only applies to the federal government, a higher fee award against a state or local government is not inconsistent with that provision.

The amendment can thus be read to make clear that the attorney fee provisions in the Code (for example, section 362(k) and section 523(d)) do not override the EAJA with respect to rates for fee awards against the federal government in cases to which the EAJA would otherwise have applied.[169] However, other governmental units may argue that the provision covers all fee awards "against any governmental unit."

16.6 Services Provided by Petition Preparers and Other Non-Attorneys

It is not surprising, given the tremendous need for bankruptcy relief among many low-income debtors and the lack of *pro bono* or affordable bankruptcy attorneys in some areas, that various types of non-attorney operations have sprung up that purport to offer debtors assistance in filing bankruptcy cases. Typically dubbed "typing services," "document preparation services," or "independent paralegals," these entities advertise that they can solve debt problems and prevent evictions and foreclosures without the necessity of an attorney.

Generally, these non-attorney operations are downright fraudulent, making promises to debtors which they cannot hope

---

162 Chambers v. NASCO, Inc., 501 U.S. 32, 45–46, 111 S. Ct. 2123, 115 L. Ed. 2d 27 (1991).

163 *See In re* Schaefer Salt Recovery, Inc., 542 F.3d 90 (3d Cir. 2008) (as unit of the district court, which is a "court of the United States," a bankruptcy court has authority to award sanctions under 28 U.S.C. § 1927); Adair v. Sherman, 230 F.3d 890, 895 n.8 (7th Cir. 2000); *In re* Cohoes Indus. Terminal, Inc., 931 F.2d 222, 230 (2d Cir. 1991). *But see In re* Courtesy Inns, Ltd., Inc., 40 F.3d 1084, 1086 (10th Cir. 1994) (no authority for bankruptcy courts to impose 28 U.S.C. § 1927 sanctions).

164 Pub. L. No. 103-394, 108 Stat. 4106 (1994).

165 *See* Jove Eng'g, Inc. v. Internal Revenue Serv., 92 F.3d 1539 (11th Cir. 1996) (attorney fees could be awarded against Internal Revenue Service for violating automatic stay, but fees had to be consistent with EAJA and 26 U.S.C. § 7430); § 16.5.4, *infra*.

166 546 U.S. 356, 126 S. Ct. 990, 163 L. Ed. 2d 945 (2006). *See* § 14.3.2.2, *supra*.

167 *See In re* Omine, 485 F.3d 1305 (11th Cir. 2007) (majority holds that constitutional abrogation of sovereign immunity does not affect attorney fees limits set in section 106; dissent holds that section 106's limitations on fees is inapplicable in light of *Katz*, and also due to state's filing of proof of claim in case). *See also In re* Slayton, 409 B.R. 897 (Bankr. N.D. Ill. 2009) (debtors may pursue action for compensatory damages, injunction, costs, and fees against state for violation of discharge injunction and section 525(a) related to refusal to issue driver's licenses).

168 *See* § 16.5.4, *supra*.

169 The "substantial justification" test which must be met for fees under EAJA is in a separate portion of EAJA that is not referenced in the new section 106(a). Therefore, it is not applicable unless fees are being sought solely under EAJA.

to keep and extracting fees which far exceed the value of the work performed. These entities engage in the worst type of consumer fraud, because they are aimed at vulnerable low and moderate income individuals facing financial distress who are desperate for honest help. By promising to stop a foreclosure or eviction, for example, without any real plan for long-term relief, these operators take money which could more appropriately be used to address the consumer's debt problems directly.

The "assistance" provided by even the best non-attorney petition preparer is, in fact, the unauthorized practice of law.[170] It is virtually impossible to properly help someone prepare bankruptcy schedules without giving substantial legal advice.[171] If no legal advice is proffered, then there is little value to the service, schedules are likely to be improperly prepared, and a fee is charged which exceeds the value of inputting information into a computer.

Usually, the advice given is also incorrect or incomplete. Debtors are sent to file bankruptcy petitions with papers that are inadequate or defective, leading to quick dismissals, loss of property that could have been protected or, at best, a bankruptcy case that does not give the debtor all the relief to which the debtor is entitled. In the worst cases, debtors are not even aware that bankruptcy cases have been filed on their behalf; their signatures are forged by the non-attorney preparer. In some schemes, the only assistance offered by the entity advertising that it can solve debt problems is a referral to a bankruptcy attorney, after the debtor is charged a fee of two hundred dollars or more.[172] And in yet one more variation, an attorney is hired by the non-attorneys with no supervisory responsibilities other than to act as a figurehead and sign papers prepared by the non-attorneys.[173]

The courts have been plagued by the problems caused by these operations for some time. In some areas, such as southern California, they have reached epidemic proportions. They are remedied only when the United States trustee, the court, or consumers take affirmative action to stop them. When challenges are raised, the court can enjoin unlawful practices[174] and require disgorgement of funds and damages, either as unlawful fees under the Bankruptcy Code[175] or as damages for unfair and deceptive trade practices.[176] Once such an order is entered, and without being able to engage in unauthorized practice of law or unfair and deceptive practices, few of the non-attorney operations can remain in business without risking contempt sanctions for violation of a court order.[177]

---

170 *In re* Doser, 412 F.3d 1056 (9th Cir. 2005) (giving debtors an incomplete and inaccurate "bankruptcy overview" prepared by franchisor, "We the People," and telling them that it was reliable was practice of law); Taub v. Weber, 366 F.3d 966 (9th Cir. 2004) (petition preparer's advice regarding the meaning of terms "market value" and "secured claim or exemption" was unauthorized practice of law); *In re* Agyekum, 225 B.R. 695 (B.A.P. 9th Cir. 1998) (preprinted bankruptcy guide and questionnaire used by preparer to assist debtors constituted practice of law); *In re* Langford, 2007 WL 3376664 (M.D.N.C. Nov. 2, 2007) (petition preparer's use of a bankruptcy forms workbook constituted the unauthorized practice of law; preparer ordered to refrain from continued use of book); *In re* Sanchez, 446 B.R. 531 (Bankr. D.N.M. 2011) (petition preparer's use of software for selection of exemptions, decision on which chapter to file under, and advice on dischargeability of debts constituted unauthorized practice of law); *In re* Jay, 446 B.R. 227 (Bankr. E.D. Va. 2010) (petition preparer's provision of exemption list, preparation of homestead deed, and assistance in preparing answers to motions violated prohibition under § 110 against giving legal advice); United States Tr. v. Lopano (*In re* Bagley), 433 B.R. 325 (Bankr. D. Mont. 2010) (information on preparer's website was legal advice and preparer's changes in information supplied by debtor constituted practice of law); *In re* Evans, 413 B.R. 315 (Bankr. E.D. Va. 2009) (looking to state law to find unauthorized practice of law by petition preparer, rejecting constitutional challenges to section 110 based on vagueness and due process); *In re* Powell, 266 B.R. 450 (Bankr. N.D. Cal. 2001) (actions in connection with lien avoidance motion were unauthorized practice of law).

"We the People" agreed to an injunction prohibiting the unauthorized practice of law in Martini v. We the People Forms & Serv. Ctrs., USA, Inc. (*In re* Barcelo), 2005 Bankr. LEXIS 2148 (Bankr. E.D.N.Y. Oct. 24, 2005). Whether this injunction will change the practices of this petition preparer remains to be seen.

171 *See In re* Flowers, 2010 WL 381880 (Bankr. M.D. Ga. Jan. 26, 2010) (discussing impossibility of completing bankruptcy documents without making legal decisions).

172 *See In re* Fleet, 95 B.R. 319 (E.D. Pa. 1989) (finding that such practices were unfair and deceptive).

173 *In re* Hessinger & Assocs., 171 B.R. 366 (Bankr. N.D. Cal. 1994), *vacated on other grounds*, 192 B.R. 211 (N.D. Cal. 1996).

174 *In re* Skobinsky, 167 B.R. 45 (E.D. Pa. 1994); *In re* Jay, 446 B.R. 227 (Bankr. E.D. Va. 2010) (enjoining petition preparer from engaging in list of specific practices violating § 110); *In re* Harris, 152 B.R. 440 (Bankr. W.D. Pa. 1993) ("legal technician" who engaged in unauthorized practice of law enjoined from completing bankruptcy forms for clients); *In re* McCarthy, 149 B.R. 162 (Bankr. S.D. Cal. 1992) (owner of paralegal and typing service enjoined from continuing unauthorized practice of law and from advertising under heading "Legal Clinics" in telephone directory).

175 *In re* Cochran, 164 B.R. 366 (Bankr. M.D. Fla. 1994) (typing service required to disgorge all fees in excess of $50 per case, which was deemed to be value of services provided); *In re* Robinson, 162 B.R. 319 (Bankr. D. Kan. 1993) (individuals engaged in unauthorized practice of law required to disgorge all fees received); *In re* Evans, 153 B.R. 960 (Bankr. E.D. Pa. 1993) (legal self-help company required to disgorge all fees in excess of $100 value of its services and enjoined from collecting fees of over $100 in future; company also ordered to provide all present and future customers with copy of court's opinion); *In re* Harris, 152 B.R. 440 (Bankr. W.D. Pa. 1993) ("legal technician" who engaged in unauthorized practice of law ordered to disgorge all sums received for services); *In re* McCarthy, 149 B.R. 162 (Bankr. S.D. Cal. 1992) (order to remit all fees in case); *In re* Herren, 138 B.R. 989 (Bankr. D. Wyo. 1992) (all fees ordered remitted to debtor); O'Connell v. David, 35 B.R. 141 (Bankr. E.D. Pa. 1983), *modified* 35 B.R. 146 (E.D. Pa. 1983), *aff'd*, 740 F.2d 958 (3d Cir. 1990). *See also In re* Fleet, 95 B.R. 319 (E.D. Pa. 1989) (court has authority to regulate fees paid to non-attorneys in scheme whereby non-attorneys collected fees for referring debtors to a bankruptcy attorney after numerous deceptive advertisements and statements).

176 *In re* Fleet, 95 B.R. 319 (E.D. Pa. 1989) (triple damages awarded to debtors who had paid money to non-attorneys who deceptively promised to solve debt problems); *In re* Samuels, 176 B.R. 616 (Bankr. M.D. Fla. 1994).

177 *See In re* Guttierez, 248 B.R. 287 (Bankr. W.D. Tex. 2000) (fine for contempt of prior order); *In re* Repp, 218 B.R. 518 (Bankr. D. Ariz. 1998) ($1 million fine for contempt of injunction and failure to pay previous fines).

Efforts to regulate the provision of bankruptcy services by non-attorneys received a major boost from the enactment of Code section 110,[178] as well as criminal penalties,[179] to deal specifically with the issue of non-attorney petition preparers. This section was strengthened by amendments enacted in 2005.

Section 110(a) defines a bankruptcy petition preparer as a person other than an attorney for the debtor or an employee of such attorney under the direct supervision of such attorney who prepares for compensation a petition or other documents in a bankruptcy case.[180] This definition thus excludes law students and *pro bono* volunteers who are not compensated. The provisions also apply to the operators of Internet websites that produce bankruptcy documents based on information provided by the debtor electronically.[181] They apply to franchisors who participate in operating the petition preparation service.[182] They supplement, but do not displace, other laws that protect consumers.[183]

The section creates a paper trail to identify and monitor petition preparers. All documents filed must have the preparer's signature, printed name, address, and Social Security number, as well as the Social Security numbers of all other people who assisted in preparing the document.[184] The Official Forms have been amended to include a space for this information on each form.[185] The preparer must also provide a notice to the debtor disclosing that the preparer is not an attorney and cannot give legal advice, with examples of legal advice that cannot be given.[186] In addition, the preparer must, within ten days after the filing of a petition, file a declaration under penalty of perjury of any fees received from or on behalf of the debtor and fees yet to be paid.[187] The Supreme Court and the Judicial Conference of the United States are authorized to promulgate rules or guidelines for setting maximum allowable fees chargeable by bankruptcy petition preparers.[188] They have not done so and thus, in the absence of rules from these sources, bankruptcy courts in some districts have promulgated their own guidelines limiting petition preparer fees.[189]

The section also contains prohibitions of the most common abuses, including cases in which debtors were not even aware a bankruptcy had been filed on their behalf. The preparer must furnish copies of all documents to the debtor.[190] The preparer may not execute a document on behalf of the debtor or offer any legal advice to the debtor.[191] This provision was amended in 2005 to include a nonexclusive list of the types of activities that are considered to be legal advice.[192] The preparer may not use the word "legal" or similar terms in advertisements.[193] Use of

---

178 11 U.S.C. § 110.
179 18 U.S.C. § 156.
180 *See In re* Crowe, 243 B.R. 43 (B.A.P. 9th Cir. 2000) (individual who sold self-help book and then prepared bankruptcy petitions for those who had purchased book was preparing petitions for compensation); *In re* Fraga, 210 B.R. 812 (B.A.P. 9th Cir. 1997) (corporation that prepared documents for *pro se* petitions was a petition preparer within definition even though it was owned by an attorney); McDow v. Am. Debt Free Ass'n (*In re* Spence), 411 B.R. 230 (Bankr. D. Md. 2009) (entity that prepared papers that mirrored the schedules and statement of financial affairs, which could then be used by law firm to which it referred clients, was a bankruptcy petition preparer); *In re* Moore, 290 B.R. 287 (Bankr. E.D.N.C. 2003) (franchisor, "We the People," was petition preparer when petition preparer did business under franchisor's name and paid percentage of fees to franchisor); *In re* France, 271 B.R. 748 (Bankr. E.D.N.Y. 2002) (real estate broker who assisted debtor in filing petitions was petition preparer). *See also In re* Desilets, 291 F.3d 925 (6th Cir. 2002) (attorney admitted to federal district court bar could practice in bankruptcy court even if not admitted to state bar for court's jurisdiction so he was not a petition preparer).
    Related practices that do not involve the provision of bankruptcy services may be subject to state law regulation. *See In re* McNeal, 286 B.R. 910 (Bankr. N.D. Cal. 2002) (treble damages awarded to debtor for foreclosure consultant's violation of state law).
181 *In re* Reynoso, 315 B.R. 544 (B.A.P. 9th Cir. 2004), *aff'd*, 477 F.3d 1117 (9th Cir. 2007); Wiggins v. Housely (*In re* Wiggins), 2012 WL 3597656 (Bankr. N.D. Cal. Aug. 20, 2012) (person need not have directly prepared bankruptcy papers to be subject to section 110); United States Tr. v. Lopano (*In re* Bagley), 433 B.R. 325 (Bankr. D. Mont. 2010); *In re* Thomas, 315 B.R. 697 (Bankr. N.D. Ohio 2004).
182 Gould v. Clippard, 340 B.R. 861 (M.D. Tenn. 2006) (franchisor "We the People U.S.A." found to be petition preparer).
183 *In re* Bankruptcy Petition Preparers, 307 B.R. 134 (B.A.P. 9th Cir. 2004) (upholding local rule requiring that petition preparers must be certified as legal document preparers under Arizona law).
184 11 U.S.C. § 110(b), (c); *In re* Flowers, 2010 WL 381880 (Bankr. M.D. Ga. Jan. 26, 2010) (petition preparer fined for failing to include Social Security number and enjoined from preparing further cases due to unauthorized practice of law). *See In re* Bohman, 202 B.R. 179 (Bankr. S.D. Fla. 1996) (preparer fined for failing to sign dischargeability complaint prepared for debtor; preparation of complaint held to be unauthorized practice); *In re* Paskel, 201 B.R. 511 (Bankr. E.D. Ark. 1996) (preparer fined $1500 for failing to place name and address on three documents). *See also In re* Crawford, 194 F.3d 954 (9th Cir. 1999) (requirement of Social Security number disclosure not unconstitutional).
185 *See* Official Forms 1, 3, 6, 7, 8 (reprinted in Appx. D, *infra*).
186 11 U.S.C. § 110(b)(2). *See In re* Clarke, 426 B.R. 443 (Bankr. E.D.N.Y. 2009), *aff'd*, Wynns v. Davis, 435 Fed. Appx. 27 (2d Cir. 2011) (preparer may not delay making this disclosure until after papers are prepared).
187 11 U.S.C. § 110(h).
188 11 U.S.C. § 110(h)(1).
189 For example, the Bankruptcy Court for the Northern District of California limits charges for preparers' services to $150. The Bankruptcy Court for the Eastern District of California set a maximum fee for petition preparer services of $125, unless the court specifically approves a higher fee. *See In re* Hill, 450 B.R. 885 (B.A.P. 9th Cir. 2011) (rejecting challenge to Arizona district's $200 presumptive ceiling for petition preparer charges, analogizing hourly value of services to those of a typist); Kuhns v. United States, 2010 WL 1990558 (N.D. W. Va. May 18, 2010) (upholding $150 limit on petition preparer fees set by bankruptcy court based on value of typing services).
190 11 U.S.C. § 110(d).
191 11 U.S.C. § 110(e).
192 11 U.S.C. § 110(e)(2)(b). *See In re* Bernales, 345 B.R. 206 (Bankr. C.D. Cal. 2006) (by adding examples of legal advice, the 2005 amendments did not change the section's general prohibition against the unauthorized practice of law).
193 11 U.S.C. § 110(f); *In re* Hennerman, 351 B.R. 143 (Bankr. D. Colo. 2006) (website was an advertisement); *In re* Moffett, 263 B.R. 805 (Bankr. W.D. Ky. 2001) (use of "paralegal" in advertisement violated section 110); *In re* Brokenbrough, 197 B.R. 839 (Bankr. S.D. Ohio 1996) (use of word "legal" in telephone listings violated statute); *In re* Burdick, 191 B.R. 529 (Bankr. N.D.N.Y. 1996) (use

language in an advertisement that implies that legal services will be offered also violates this provision.[194] The court must disallow and order disgorgement of any fees in excess of the value of services provided.[195] Sometimes, even a small fee is excessive, because petition preparer services, without more, may do the debtor more harm than good. If the services have no value, or a negative value, the entire fee should be disgorged.[196] The preparer may not collect any payment for court fees.[197]

Each violation of these provisions, including failure to disgorge excessive fees, is subject to a fine of not more than $500.[198]

To encourage enforcement of its provisions, the section creates a cause of action for damages and injunctive relief in addition to the potential fines.[199] The debtor, trustee, United States trustee, or bankruptcy administrator may file a motion for damages, payable to the debtor, if the preparer violates any of the provisions of section 110, or commits any unfair, deceptive or fraudulent act.[200] This permits private parties to bring violations to the attention of the court. In a successful action, the debtor is to be awarded actual damages plus the greater of $2000 or twice the amount paid to the petition preparer.[201] A trustee or creditor moving for damages is entitled to an additional $1000 in statutory damages.[202]

---

of word "paralegal" in an advertisement for a petition preparer ruled improper as a similar term to "legal").

194 *In re* Johnson, 2012 WL 1438236 (Bankr. E.D.N.C. Apr. 25, 2012) (term "legal aid alternatives" used in advertising); *In re* Ali, 230 B.R. 477 (Bankr. E.D.N.Y. 1999) (use of term "by law" in flyer describing bankruptcy rights gives debtors the impression that legal services will be offered).

195 11 U.S.C. § 110(h); *In re* Agyekum, 225 B.R. 695 (B.A.P. 9th Cir. 1998) ($173 fee excessive, reasonable value of service only $125); Gould v. Clippard, 340 B.R. 861 (M.D. Tenn. 2006) (value of typing services provided by "We the People" was $30); *In re* Moore, 290 B.R. 287 (Bankr. E.D.N.C. 2003) (fee of $199 was excessive and only $80 was permitted); *In re* Pavlis, 264 B.R. 57 (Bankr. D.R.I. 2001) (presumed reasonable fee was $30 per hour for no more than five hours); *In re* Moffett, 263 B.R. 805 (Bankr. W.D. Ky. 2001) (preparer enjoined from charging more than $20 per hour with maximum of $100); *In re* Guttierez, 248 B.R. 287 (Bankr. W.D. Tex. 2000) (reasonable fee for typing services was $50); *In re* Mullikin, 231 B.R. 750 (Bankr. W.D. Mo. 1999) (reasonable value of petition preparer services found to be $150; preparer required to disgorge entire $404 fee as sanction); *In re* Ali, 230 B.R. 477 (Bankr. E.D.N.Y. 1999) (reasonable value of preparing skeleton petition without balance of forms necessary to complete case is $25); *In re* Burdick, 191 B.R. 529 (Bankr. N.D.N.Y. 1996) (because value of typing a bankruptcy petition is $50, fee in excess of that amount ordered returned to debtors). *See also In re* Moore, 232 B.R. 1 (Bankr. D. Me. 1999) (maximum flat fee should be $75; paralegal could seek a larger fee if circumstances warrant); *In re* Hartman, 208 B.R. 768 (Bankr. D. Mass. 1997) (fee of $100—$20 per hour—permissible if schedules competently prepared; incompetence required disgorgement of $625 of $675 fee).

196 *In re* Sam's Enterprises, Inc., 2011 WL 1696681 (Bankr. N.D. Ga. Mar. 28, 2011) (order directing preparer to disgorge $800 in fees and to pay to debtors damages in the amount of $4000 and to the U.S. Trustee fines in the amount of $3000); *In re* Jay, 446 B.R. 227 (Bankr. E.D. Va. 2010) (disgorgement of all fees charged in nine cases); *In re* Amstutz, 427 B.R. 636 (Bankr. N.D. Ohio 2010) (disgorgement of full fee ordered where petition preparer engaged in unauthorized practice of law); *In re* Pillot, 286 B.R. 157 (Bankr. C.D. Cal. 2002) (value of services which constituted unauthorized practice of law was zero); *In re* Bradshaw, 233 B.R. 315 (Bankr. D.N.J. 1999) (value of defendants' services was "negative" because innocent people relied on defendants' empty promises to their detriment and paid $300 for the privilege; entire fee ordered disgorged); *In re* Stacy, 193 B.R. 31 (Bankr. D. Or. 1996) (dismissed petition had no value to debtor).

197 11 U.S.C. § 110(g); *In re* Buck, 307 B.R. 157 (C.D. Cal. 2004) (acceptance, for delivery to court, of cashier's check made payable to bankruptcy court violated statute); *In re* McDaniel, 232 B.R. 674 (Bankr. N.D. Tex. 1999); *In re* Green, 197 B.R. 878 (Bankr. D. Ariz. 1996) (preparer fined for delivering money order for filing fee to court). *See In re* Wallace, 227 B.R. 826 (Bankr. S.D. Ind. 1998) (preparer could neither collect fees nor deliver petition to court because by latter action preparer is controlling the timing of filing because case cannot be filed without fees).

198 11 U.S.C. § 110(l). *See In re* Bradshaw, 233 B.R. 315 (Bankr. D.N.J. 1999) (maximum fine of $500 for each document filed without required language); *In re* Cordero, 185 B.R. 882 (Bankr. M.D. Fla. 1995) (fine of $250 for each violation of statute).

199 *In re* Alloway, 401 B.R. 43 (Bankr. D. Mass. 2009) (assessing treble maximum penalties and ordering disgorgement when petition preparer repeatedly failed to disclose role in filings); *In re* Vlcek, 307 B.R. 615 (Bankr. N.D. Ill. 2004) (damages are awarded in addition to fines in order to give debtors incentive to help remedy violations).

200 11 U.S.C. § 110(i). *See In re* Doser, 412 F.3d 1056 (9th Cir. 2005) (inviting debtors to "chat" with a supervising attorney for "We the People" but not informing them that they cannot rely on that attorney's advice and that attorney does not represent them, was unfair and deceptive); *In re* Baugh, 2012 WL 1570026 (Bankr. W.D. Tex. May 3, 2012) (awarding debtor $2500 in damages plus the return of the petition preparer fee, because the preparer's advice to file the petition but not the required schedules, statements, and chapter 13 plan resulted in debtor's case being dismissed); *In re* Tomlinson, 343 B.R. 400 (E.D.N.Y. 2006) ("We the People" telling debtors they were not receiving legal advice, when in fact they were, was deceptive); *In re* Moore, 290 B.R. 287 (Bankr. E.D.N.C. 2003) (inviting debtors to "chat" with a supervising attorney for "We the People" but not informing them that they cannot rely on that attorney's advice and that attorney does not represent them, was unfair and deceptive); *In re* Landry, 250 B.R. 441 (Bankr. M.D. Fla. 2000) (calling a portion of fee a "membership fee" in a "document preparation club" and failing to disclose that fee was fraudulent and deceptive act).

201 11 U.S.C. § 110(i)(1). *See* Wynns v. Adams, 426 B.R. 457 (E.D.N.Y. 2010), *aff'd*, 435 Fed. Appx. 27, 2011 WL 2519550 (2d Cir. June 27, 2011) ($2000 statutory damages mandatory upon finding of violation of § 110(i)(1); no showing of actual damages required); *In re* Gavin, 184 B.R. 670 (E.D. Pa. 1995); *In re* Kangarloo, 250 B.R. 115 (Bankr. C.D. Cal. 2000) (recommending $2050 actual damages for cost of proper bankruptcy filing plus $2000 statutory damages and plus $1500 attorney fees); *In re* Murray, 194 B.R. 651 (Bankr. D. Ariz. 1996) (recommending that debtors be awarded actual damages, statutory damages and attorney fees for unfair and deceptive acts of preparer).

The damages must be awarded by the district court, after the bankruptcy court certifies the underlying facts to that court and the moving party then moves for the award in district court. *See* Order Interpreting 11 U.S.C. § 110, 198 B.R. 604 (C.D. Cal. 1996).

202 11 U.S.C. § 110(i)(2). *See In re* Landry, 250 B.R. 441 (Bankr. M.D. Fla. 2000) (awarding $1000 minimum damages and attorney fees to trustee).

The language of this provision was not changed despite the fact that creditors are no longer listed as parties who can bring motions in section 110(i)(1).

The "unfair and deceptive" language is from the Federal Trade Commission Act and state unfair and deceptive practices laws, so case law under those statutes should be used in judging preparers' activities.[203] The damage provisions are modeled on the federal Truth in Lending Act damage provisions.[204] As under Truth in Lending, class actions are possible and will be easy to bring for violations giving rise to strict liability, because the proof will consist of the forms filed by the preparer.

The party that brings a successful action is also entitled to attorney fees and costs,[205] which should provide an incentive for attorneys to bring such actions. The court may also enter injunctive relief against specific unfair or deceptive acts by petition preparers.[206] If the court finds that such an injunction would not be sufficient to prevent such conduct, or if the preparer has not paid a fine imposed under section 110, the court may enjoin the person from acting as a petition preparer.[207] Courts have held that evidence of unauthorized practice of law is sufficient to establish unfair and deceptive conduct in violation of section 110(i) or to justify injunctive relief under section 110(j).[208] A debtor, trustee or creditor may also be awarded attorney fees and costs for successfully seeking injunctive relief.[209]

Petition preparers who violate any of the provisions of section 110 can be fined up to $500 for each violation.[210] These fines must be tripled if the preparer advised the debtor to omit assets or income from the schedules or to use a false Social Security number. The fine must also be tripled if the preparer failed to inform the debtor that the debtor was filing a bankruptcy case or failed to disclose the preparer's identity on any document prepared for filing.[211] A debtor, trustee, creditor, United States trustee, or bankruptcy administrator may seek the imposition of such fines, but debtors will usually prefer to seek damages under section 110(i) and perhaps injunctive relief under section 110(j), along with attorney fees.

Fraudulent or misleading advertisements to tenants facing eviction—petition preparers promising that tenants legally can remain in their apartments rent free—have been a recurrent problem in many jurisdictions. Often, the victims of this scam don't know that the bankruptcy only temporarily prevents eviction. In some cases, the tenants are not even told that they are filing bankruptcy. In one such case, a New Jersey court sanctioned and permanently enjoined a ring of petition preparers that repeatedly engaged in these practices from directly or indirectly operating as petition preparers anywhere in the United States.[212]

Finally, to prevent any implication that section 110 authorizes non-attorneys to give legal advice or services, section 110(k) states that nothing in the section shall be construed to permit activities otherwise prohibited by law.

Courts and United States trustees have brought numerous actions under these provisions. In view of the widespread nature of the petition preparer business, section 110 also offers debtors' attorneys an opportunity to earn attorney fees while at the same time putting an end to unfair and deceptive practices that cause substantial harm to consumer debtors.

It is important to note that bankruptcy petition preparers are explicitly included in the definition of "debt relief agency." They routinely fail to comply with the debt relief agency provisions, giving yet another remedy that can be invoked against them.[213]

---

203 See generally National Consumer Law Center, Unfair and Deceptive Acts and Practices (7th ed. 2008 and Supp.).
204 15 U.S.C. § 1640.
205 11 U.S.C. § 110(i)(1)(C). See In re Tomlinson, 343 B.R. 400 (E.D.N.Y. 2006) (awarding fees to trustee, debtor's attorney, and fines and compensation for lost work time to debtor).
206 11 U.S.C. § 110(j)(2)(A).
207 11 U.S.C. § 110(j)(2). See In re Order Certifying Cases to Dist. Court for Finding of Crim. Contempt, 2012 U.S. Dist. LEXIS 50437 (S.D. Ind. Apr. 6, 2012) (criminal contempt proceedings for violation of earlier injunction); Bartok v. DeAngelis, 2012 WL 664928 (D.N.J. Feb. 29, 2012) (upholding bankruptcy court decision to enjoin preparers on a nationwide basis after they continued to engage in unlawful activity); In re Kuch, 2012 WL 837232 (Bankr. D. Colo. Mar. 12, 2012) (permanently enjoining preparer from providing any services related to bankruptcy and assessing more than $26,000 in fines); In re Schweitzer, 196 B.R. 620 (Bankr. M.D. Fla. 1996) (statewide injunction entered precluding preparer from acting as preparer in other bankruptcy cases due to numerous violations); In re Gavin, 181 B.R. 814 (Bankr. E.D. Pa. 1995) (injunction against individual acting as a petition preparer in any jurisdiction); In re Lyvers, 179 B.R. 837 (Bankr. W.D. Ky. 1995) (injunction against filing any petition or other papers in bankruptcy court for district).
208 See, e.g., In re Sanchez, 446 B.R. 531 (Bankr. D. N.M. 2010) (providing legal advice was unauthorized practice of law and constituted "fraudulent, unfair, or deceptive" practice mandating $2,000 statutory damages); McDow v. Mayton, 379 B.R. 601 (E.D. Va. 2007) (permanent injunction entered to stop broad range of petition preparer activities held to be the unauthorized practice of law; court also orders penalties and disgorgement of fees); In re McDaniel, 232 B.R. 674 (Bankr. N.D. Tex. 1999); In re Moore, 232 B.R. 1 (Bankr. D. Me. 1999). See also In re Graves, 279 B.R. 266 (B.A.P. 9th Cir. 2002) (court could issue injunction sua sponte, but petition preparer must be given notice and opportunity to be heard on issuance of injunction); In re Bonarrigo, 282 B.R. 101 (D. Mass. 2002) (violation of previous agreed order delineating what petition preparer could do justified injunction against acting as petition preparers in court's jurisdiction).

One court concluded that preparation of a chapter 13 plan by a petition preparer necessarily involves unauthorized practice of law. In re Hobbs, 213 B.R. 207 (Bankr. D. Me. 1997).
209 11 U.S.C. § 110(j)(4).
210 11 U.S.C. § 110(l)(1).
211 Hills v. McDermott (In re Wicker), 2012 WL 580481 (E.D. Mich. Feb. 22, 2012) (fines tripled where preparer concealed his participation); In re Martin, 424 B.R. 496 (Bankr. D.N.M. 2010) (multiple $500 fines trebled in ten cases because petition preparer failed to disclose identity); In re Sanchez, 446 B.R. 531 (Bankr. D.N.M. 2011) (trebling of penalties mandatory upon finding of violation enumerated in § 110(l)(2)).
212 In re Bradshaw, 233 B.R. 315 (Bankr. D.N.J. 1999).
213 McDow v. Am. Debt Free Ass'n (In re Spence), 411 B.R. 230 (Bankr. D. Md. 2009).

16.7 Duties of Debtors' Counsel Under Bankruptcy Rule 9011 and Related Provisions

16.7.1 Federal Rule of Bankruptcy Procedure 9011

All attorneys and other parties filing or submitting documents to the court in bankruptcy cases are subject to Federal Rule of Bankruptcy Procedure 9011. Every document must be signed by at least one attorney of record.[214] A *pro se* party must sign all papers. The signer must also list her address and telephone number.[215]

The only exception to this rule is that a list, schedule, statement, or amendment to one of these documents need not be signed by the attorney who submits it. This exception raises issues about whether these documents are subject to the strictures of Rule 9011(b), although that paragraph refers not only to documents that are signed, but also to documents presented by filing, submitting, or advocating.[216] The issue is further clouded by section 319 of the 2005 amendments, which states a sense of Congress that Rule 9011 should be amended to provide that documents submitted to the court or to a trustee (including schedules) be submitted only after reasonable inquiry to verify that the information therein is well grounded in fact and warranted by existing law or a good faith argument for the extension, modification, or reversal of existing law.[217] And, as discussed below, section 707(b)(4)(D) states yet a third, slightly different, standard for schedules.

Rule 9011(b) provides that by presenting a paper to the court, an attorney or unrepresented party certifies to the best of that person's knowledge, information, and belief, formed after an inquiry reasonable under the circumstances, that:

- It is not being presented for any improper purpose, such as to harass, cause unnecessary delay, or needlessly increase litigation costs;
- The claims, defenses and other legal contentions are warranted by existing law or a nonfrivolous argument for the extension, modification, or reversal of existing law or establishment of new law;
- The allegations and factual contentions have evidentiary support or, if specifically so identified, are likely to have evidentiary support after further investigation or discovery; and
- The denials of factual contentions are warranted on the evidence or, if specifically so identified, are reasonably based on a lack of information.

Sanctions for violation of these standards can be sought by a separate motion, served as provided in Rule 7004. However, the motion for sanctions normally cannot be filed until twenty-one days after it is served, a "safe harbor" period during which time the party against whom sanctions are sought is given an opportunity to withdraw or correct the challenged paper. If the motion is ultimately filed, the court may award the prevailing party attorney fees. Sanctions can include non-monetary penalties, a penalty paid to the court or, if a motion is filed, an order to pay some or all of the expenses caused by the violation of Rule 9011. The court may also initiate sanctions for violation of Rule 9011(b).

However, an important exception to the "safe harbor" rule provides that it does not apply to the bankruptcy petition itself. Because the filing of a bankruptcy petition can have such immediate and powerful effects, including the automatic stay, the party filing it cannot later withdraw it to avoid sanctions.[218]

There is ample case law and other authority interpreting Rule 9011 and much more interpreting Federal Rule of Civil Procedure 11, upon which Rule 9011 is based. For further research, these sources can be consulted.

16.7.2 Section 707(b)(4)

16.7.2.1 Costs and Attorney Fees for Successful Section 707(b) Motions—§ 707(b)(4)(A)

Under section 707(b)(4)(A) of the Bankruptcy Code, costs and attorney fees incurred in prosecuting a successful section 707(b) motion to dismiss the case may be assessed against the debtor's attorney, but only in certain circumstances. Fees and costs may be awarded only if a debtor's attorney violates Rule 9011 of the Federal Rules of Bankruptcy Procedure in filing the bankruptcy case itself.[219] Moreover, the procedures contained in Bankruptcy Rule 9011 for awarding costs and fees must be followed.

In fact, the only real change brought about by this provision is that costs and fees may be awarded to the trustee even if the court initiates a proceeding to show cause.[220] However, this provision only applies to a section 707(b) motion brought by a trustee, not the United States trustee or bankruptcy administrator. This limitation means that a debtor's attorney may not be assessed liability under this provision if the debtor's income is below the state's median family income, because only the judge, United States trustee, or bankruptcy administrator may file a motion under section 707(b) in cases filed by a debtor whose income is below the median.[221]

The original purpose of the provision apparently was to give trustees an incentive to file section 707(b) motions, but since

---

214 Fed. R. Bankr. P. 9011(a).
215 *Id.*
216 *In re* Withrow, 405 B.R. 505 (B.A.P. 1st Cir. 2009) (Rule 9011 applies to documents that are submitted, even if not signed by attorney).
217 Pub. L. No. 109-8, § 319, 119 Stat. 23 (2005) (available on this treatise's companion website).

218 *See* Fed. R. Bankr. P. 9011 advisory committee's note (1997).
219 11 U.S.C. § 707(b)(4)(A).
220 Under Bankruptcy Rule 9011(c)(2), if the court initiates a proceeding the monetary sanction must be payable to the court.
221 11 U.S.C. § 707(b)(6). *See* Ch. 13, *supra*.

the provision was originally introduced[222] the standard under section 707(b)(4)(A) was changed to the same standard as under Bankruptcy Rule 9011, which is unlikely to entice trustees to expend great efforts in litigating under the section.

16.7.2.2 Civil Penalties Under Bankruptcy Rule 9011—§ 707(b)(4)(B)

Under section 707(b)(4)(B), a court may also assess a civil penalty against a debtor's attorney who violates Bankruptcy Rule 9011. But courts already possess the authority to assess civil penalties under Bankruptcy Rule 9011(c).[223] The only difference is that this penalty, unlike the penalties under Bankruptcy Rule 9011, may be payable to the trustee, the United States trustee, or the bankruptcy administrator, and may be paid to them even if the penalty is assessed on motion of another party or on the court's own initiative.[224]

16.7.2.3 Attorney Certifications—§ 707(b)(4)(C)

Section 707(b)(4)(C) provides that the signature of an attorney on a petition, pleading, or written motion is a certification that the attorney has:

- Performed a reasonable investigation into the circumstances giving rise to the petition, pleading, or written motion;
- Determined that it is well-grounded in fact;
- Determined that it is warranted by existing law or a good faith argument for the extension, modification, or reversal of existing law; and
- Determined that it does not constitute an "abuse" under paragraph (707)(b)(1).[225]

This provision applies to all attorneys, not just those representing debtors, and is applicable to all motions and pleadings filed in chapter 7 cases.[226] For example, it applies to frivolous motions for relief from the automatic stay filed in chapter 7 cases, and requires the attorney to reasonably investigate amounts asserted in such motions. On the other hand, the certification does not apply to schedules or statements.

The language of this provision is quite similar to the former language of Bankruptcy Rule 9011 and it is not clear that it adds anything to current Bankruptcy Rule 9011. One difference is the use of the phrase "reasonable investigation" rather than "reasonable inquiry." But it is unclear whether this change in wording makes any difference. The existing texts of both *Moore's Federal Practice* when discussing Rule 11 of the Federal Rules of Civil Procedure and *Collier on Bankruptcy* when discussing Rule 9011 of the Federal Rules of Bankruptcy Procedure use the words "inquiry" and "investigation" interchangeably.[227] Moreover, in discussing the duty to investigate, *Moore's* states: "[a]n attorney may rely on objectively reasonable representations of his or her client."[228] It states further that "[a]ll *available* documents that are relevant to the case should be examined."[229] Such a standard would certainly include all documents in the possession of the client, but does not appear to require an attorney to obtain documents that are not easily accessible.

In view of this section's similarities to Bankruptcy Rule 9011, it is unlikely that courts will draw a distinction between the certification requirement under section 707(b)(4)(C) and Bankruptcy Rule 9011. Courts will likely, at most, use this section as an additional basis on which to sanction bad conduct that would have been punishable in any event.[230]

Section 707(b)(4)(C) also provides that an attorney filing a petition certifies that the attorney has determined that the petition is not an abuse under section 707(b)(1). Based on its placement in the context of an attorney's "determination" with respect to other similar Bankruptcy Rule 9011 conclusions, courts are likely to look to analogous provisions in current and former Bankruptcy Rule 9011 and interpret this language to require a good faith determination, after reasonable inquiry under the circumstances. Importantly, the provision does not require an attorney to certify that the petition is not an abuse, but only that the attorney determined that it was not an abuse. In any event no remedies are provided for violations of this provision, which presumably means that the standards of Bankruptcy Rule 9011 would apply.

16.7.2.4 Attorney Certification As to Schedules—§ 707(b)(4)(D)

Section 707(b)(4)(D) provides that the signature of an attorney for the debtor also certifies that the attorney has no knowledge, after an inquiry, that the schedules are incorrect.[231] This standard is a pretty low one, requiring actual knowledge, not

---

222 *See* S.625, 106th Cong. § 102 (1999) (as reported from the Senate Judiciary Committee).
223 Fed. R. Bankr. P. 9011(c)(2) (court may order penalty paid into court).
224 *See In re* Withrow, 405 B.R. 505, 510 (B.A.P. 1st Cir. 2009) (fees awarded to trustee for violations of Rule 9011 and section 707(b)(4)). *See also In re* Kayne, 453 B.R. 372 (B.A.P. 9th Cir. 2011) (imposing $20,000 sanction payable to trustee against debtor's attorney under § 707(b)(4) and Rule 9011(b) for knowing omission of asset from schedules).
   Bankruptcy Rule 9011 provides that a sanction imposed for violation of the rule may include attorney fees and other expenses to a party only if imposed on a motion by that party. *See* Fed. R. Bankr. P. 9011(c)(2).
225 11 U.S.C. § 707(b)(4)(C).
226 *See* 11 U.S.C. § 103(b) (provisions of chapter 7 apply only in chapter 7 cases).
227 2 Moore's Federal Practice § 11.11[2] (3d ed. 2004); 10 Collier on Bankruptcy ¶ 9011.04[2] (16th ed.).
228 2 Moore's Federal Practice § 11.11[2] (3d ed. 2004).
229 2 Moore's Federal Practice § 11.11[2] (3d ed. 2004) (emphasis added).
230 *See, e.g., In re* Withrow, 391 B.R. 217 (Bankr. D. Mass. 2008) (court discusses similar standards under Rule 9011 and section 707(b)(4)(C) and (D) for assessing what constitutes reasonable attorney investigation of facts in connection with preparation of debtors' schedules and statements).
231 11 U.S.C. § 707(b)(4)(D).

just a belief or suspicion, that the schedules are inaccurate. It requires an inquiry, which should be no greater than for other pleadings, perhaps less, because it does not use the word "reasonable."

Quite arguably this more specific, and less stringent, standard for schedules overrides any other standard.[232] However, as with the other standards, courts are unlikely to look to the nuances of the language and will simply continue to penalize those whom they believe to be engaged in seriously deficient conduct.[233]

16.8 Debt Relief Agency Provisions

16.8.1 Applicability of Debt Relief Agency Provisions to Debtor's Attorney

16.8.1.1 Definition of Debt Relief Agency

More confusing, if not absurd, are the provisions setting out requirements for "debt relief agencies." The determination of whether a person is a debt relief agency turns on the interrelated definitions in section 101 of "assisted person," "bankruptcy assistance," and "debt relief agency."

An "assisted person" is defined in section 101 as any person whose debts are primarily consumer debts and whose nonexempt property is worth less than $175,750.[234] This definition encompasses the vast majority of consumers because there is no requirement that an assisted person be a bankruptcy debtor.

"Bankruptcy assistance" is defined as goods or services sold or otherwise provided to an "assisted person" with the purpose of providing advice, document preparation, or representation in a bankruptcy case or proceeding, regardless of the chapter.[235] The advice or representation need not be in connection with a case in which the assisted person is a debtor, nor need it be in connection with a consumer bankruptcy case.

A "debt relief agency" is defined as any person who provides bankruptcy assistance to an assisted person in return for compensation, or who is a bankruptcy petition preparer as defined in section 110 of the Code.[236] The Supreme Court has held that the definition of a debt relief agency includes attorneys,[237] but that the provisions of sections 526, 527, and 528 cover only attorneys who offer bankruptcy-related services to consumer debtors.[238] Although the Court did not specifically deal with the issue, the logical corollary of this holding is that they would not apply in a situation in which an attorney who might have been a debt relief agency in another case is not providing bankruptcy assistance services for compensation. Therefore, the provisions should apply only when a consumer debtor is a client, the services relate to that consumer's bankruptcy case, and the services are provided for compensation. Moreover, it is clear that if a person never accepts compensation for providing bankruptcy assistance to an assisted person, that person is not a debt relief agency. Thus attorneys cannot become debt relief agencies by rendering assistance in *pro bono* cases.[239]

Because "person" is defined to include partnerships and corporations, presumably the entire law firm could be a debt relief agency, even if only one of the members handles bankruptcy matters or otherwise meets the definition for providing bankruptcy assistance.

16.8.1.2 Persons Specifically Excluded from the Definition of Debt Relief Agency

The definition of "debt relief agency" includes several specific exemptions. As mentioned above, a person is not a debt relief agency if the bankruptcy assistance provided is not "in return for the payment of money or other valuable assistance."[240] In addition, the following persons or entities are excluded from the definition:

- Any person who is an officer, employee, director, or agent of a debt relief agency or petition preparer;
- A nonprofit organization that is exempt from taxation under section 501(c)(3) of the Internal Revenue Code;
- A creditor of the assisted person to the extent the creditor is assisting the person in restructuring a debt owed to the creditor (this exemption would not include a new mortgage broker arranging a loan to pay off a chapter 13 case);
- A depository institution or credit union or affiliate or subsidiary thereof; and
- An author, publisher, distributor, or seller of copyrighted works, when acting in that capacity.[241]

By excluding officers, employees, directors, or agents of debt relief agencies or petition preparers, an attorney employed by a firm or by the attorney's own professional corporation (of which she is an officer), or by any entity providing bankruptcy assistance, is not a "debt relief agency" even though the attorney's employer is. This exclusion could seemingly allow thinly capitalized petition preparers and their officers, and perhaps thinly capitalized professional corporations or other entities employing attorneys, to escape liability under the remedy provision found in section 526(c) of the Code.

---

232 *See* 28 U.S.C. § 2075 (rules shall not modify, enlarge, or abridge substantive rights).
233 *See In re* Kayne, 453 B.R. 372 (B.A.P. 9th Cir. 2011) (attorney who failed to schedule promissory note as asset sanctioned over $20,000 for violations of § 707(b)(4)(D)); *In re* Withrow, 405 B.R. 505 (B.A.P. 1st Cir. 2009) (general drift of requirements is that counsel should exercise significant care).
234 11 U.S.C. § 101(3).
235 11 U.S.C. § 101(4A).
236 11 U.S.C. § 101(12A).
237 Milavetz, Gallop & Milavetz, P.A. v. United States, 130 S. Ct. 1324, 176 L. Ed. 2d 79 (2010).
238 Milavetz, Gallop & Milavetz, P.A. v. United States, 130 S. Ct. 1324, 1341, 176 L. Ed. 2d 79 (2010).

239 *In re* Reyes, 2007 WL 6082567 (S.D. Fla. Dec. 17, 2007) (*pro bono* credit from state bar was not valuable consideration).
240 11 U.S.C. § 101(12A).
241 11 U.S.C. § 101(12A).

The exemption for nonprofit organizations will assist many legal services organizations and their attorneys by excluding them from the debt relief agency requirements. However, the exemption includes not only legitimate nonprofits but also operations masquerading as nonprofits, such as some of the new credit counseling agencies.

16.8.2 Restrictions on Debt Relief Agencies

Mostly, the debt relief agency restrictions prohibit practices already considered improper, such as failing to perform services as promised, making untrue or misleading statements, or advising clients to make statements that an agency should know are misleading.[242] Although the latter restriction, by itself, might appear to be a strict liability provision for any untrue or misleading statements, the section's remedy provisions speak of negligence or intentional misconduct,[243] for which remedies exist under current law. Courts are unlikely to hold attorneys responsible for untruths they could not, with reasonable care, have discovered.

Section 526(a)(3) of the Code also prohibits debt relief agencies from misrepresenting the services to be provided to an assisted person or the benefits and risks of bankruptcy.[244] Again, these actions generally are improper under current law.

Section 526(a)(4) prohibits an attorney who is a debt relief agency from advising an assisted person to incur *more* debt in contemplation of filing a bankruptcy case or in order to pay bankruptcy fees to an attorney or petition preparer.[245] This provision arguably departs from current law as it may be perfectly proper to advise a debtor to incur a debt that the debtor plans to pay or that will not be affected by a bankruptcy. Indeed, if a debtor needs to pay attorney fees through a chapter 13 plan,[246] that debtor must incur a debt to the attorney for fees and is unlikely to be aware of the procedure unless advised about it by an attorney. If applied to attorneys, the restriction on such lawful and proper advice would infringe on the First Amendment rights of attorneys and their clients.[247]

The Constitutional problems with section 526(a)(4) were evaded by the Supreme Court in *Milavetz, Gallop & Milavetz, P.A. v. United States*,[248] a case in which the Court interpreted the section so narrowly that it does not prohibit any conduct other than conduct that would have been improper under previously existing law. The Court limited the proscribed advice to only that which is impelled principally by the prospect of filing a bankruptcy case and obtaining a discharge of such debts or is motivated by an attempt to game the means test. In other words, only advice to incur debt for a clearly improper purpose is prohibited.

The Court specifically found that "advice to refinance a mortgage or purchase a reliable car prior to filing because doing so will reduce the debtor's interest rates or improve his ability to repay is not prohibited, as the promise of enhanced financial prospects, rather than the anticipated filing, is the impelling cause. Advice to incur additional debt to buy groceries, pay medical bills, or make other purchases 'reasonably necessary for the support or maintenance of the debtor or a dependent of the debtor,' is similarly permissible,"[249] perhaps even if it might later be discharged. Furthermore, the Court held that, although an attorney cannot advise a debtor to incur more debt for an impermissible purpose, "a lawyer may discuss the legal consequences of any proposed course of conduct with a client and may counsel or assist a client to make a good faith effort to determine the validity, scope, meaning or application of the law."[250]

16.8.3 Disclosures Required of Debt Relief Agencies

16.8.3.1 Relationship Between Section 527 and Section 342(b)(1) Disclosures

Section 527 of the Bankruptcy Code sets out a series of "disclosures" that debt relief agencies must make to all assisted persons being provided bankruptcy assistance. Section 527(a)(1) also states that the agency must provide the assisted person with the written notice required by section 342(b)(1) of the Code, despite the fact that section 342 requires that the notice be given by the clerk of the court.[251] Confusingly, section 527(a)(1) only mentions a portion of the notice required under section 342, omitting the portion that section 342(b)(2) requires.[252]

---

242 11 U.S.C. § 526(a)(1), (2).
243 11 U.S.C. § 526(c). See § 3.8, *infra*.
244 11 U.S.C. § 526(a)(3).
245 11 U.S.C. § 526(a)(4).
246 See § 15.4, *supra*.
247 Milavetz, Gallop & Milavetz, Prof'l Ass'n v. United States, 541 F.3d 785 (8th Cir. 2008) (advice restrictions of section 526(a)(4) are substantially overbroad and unconstitutional, but notice/advertisement provisions of section 528(a)(4) and (b)(2) pass "rational basis" constitutionality test), *cert. granted*, 129 S. Ct. 2766 (2009), *and cert. granted*, 129 S. Ct. 2769 (2009); Conn. Bar Ass'n v. United States, 394 B.R. 274 (D. Conn. 2008) (section 526(a)(4)'s restrictions on advice about incurring new debt are unconstitutionally broad; applying advertising requirements to attorneys who do not represent consumer debtors violates First Amendment); Zelotes v. Martini, 352 B.R. 17 (D. Conn. 2006), *aff'd on reconsideration*, 363 B.R. 660 (D. Conn. 2007); Olsen v. Gonzalez, 350 B.R. 906 (D. Or. 2006), *as amended by* 368 B.R. 886 (D. Or. 2007). See also Samuel L. Bufford & Erwin Chmerinsky, *Constitutional Problems in the 2005 Bankruptcy Amendments*, 82 Am. Bankr. L.J. 1 (2008) (discussing First Amendment concerns related to BAPCPA provi-

sions regulating lawyer advertising and legal advice). *But see* Hersh v. United States, 553 F.3d 743 (5th Cir. 2008) (construing provision to prohibit only advice to engage in undefined "abuse").
248 130 S. Ct. 1324 (2010).
249 *Id.* at 1339, n.6.
250 *Id.* at 1337–38.
251 Section 342(b)(1) requires that the clerk of the court provide a notice containing: (1) a brief description of different chapters and their purpose, benefits, and costs, and (2) a brief description of the services provided by credit counseling agencies.
252 Section 342(b)(2) requires that the clerk of the court provide a notice containing: (1) a statement specifying that a person who

16.8.3.2 Disclosures Concerning the Bankruptcy Process

To the extent not covered by the section 342(b)(1) notice, and within three days after the agency first offers to provide bankruptcy assistance services to an assisted person (including a creditor or landlord), the agency must provide a clear and conspicuous notice that:

- All information provided in a bankruptcy case is required to be complete, accurate, and truthful;
- All assets and liabilities must be completely and accurately disclosed in documents filed to commence a case;
- Current monthly income, amounts for means test calculations and, in chapter 13 cases, disposable income must be stated after a reasonable inquiry; and
- Information provided in a case may be audited and failure to provide such information may lead to the case's dismissal or to sanctions, including criminal sanctions.[253]

In addition, the debtor must be informed that the replacement value of each asset, as defined in section 506 of the Code, must be stated when requested in the "documents filed to commence the case" after reasonable inquiry to establish that value.[254] However the document filed to commence the case is the petition, which requires no property valuation. Even if the provision is read to mean the schedules, those documents do not "request" replacement value[255] and it is not relevant to at least some purposes of the schedules. While the required statement may be misleading, few debtors will understand it anyway.

A debt relief agency must retain copies of the notices required under section 527(a) for two years after the date when the notices are given to an assisted person.[256]

16.8.3.3 Required Statement About Bankruptcy Assistance Services

A debt relief agency must also provide the assisted person with a statement about "bankruptcy assistance services."[257] This statement must be provided at the time the notice under section 527(a)(1) is given, but no time requirement is set in section 527(a)(1), which refers to the clerk's notice under section 342(b)(1). The clerk is required to give this notice before commencement of the case; so if a creditor, who is an assisted person, first consults a debt relief agency after the commencement of the case, it may be impossible to give timely notice to the creditor. This conundrum could lead attorneys to refuse to represent individual creditors because they cannot comply with the notice provision's requirements.

The required statement must be clear and conspicuous and must be provided in a separate document. In addition it must be given verbatim, or in substantially similar language to the extent applicable, even though it includes information that may be incorrect. For example, it states: "You will have to pay a filing fee to the bankruptcy court," which is not always true because the court may waive the fee,[258] or no fee may be charged for a particular proceeding. It also states: "The following information helps you understand what must be done in a routine bankruptcy case to help you evaluate how much service you need." In fact, the statement provides no such information. Finally, it proceeds to "inform" the assisted person that "you can hire an attorney to represent you, or you can get help in some localities from a bankruptcy petition preparer who is not an attorney," a statement that implies petition preparers are competent to help bankruptcy debtors and which may promote petition preparers' unauthorized practice of law. To the extent this provision is applicable to attorneys, it compels speech that is false, that the attorney does not believe, and that serves no substantial governmental need and therefore probably violates the First Amendment. However, at least one appellate court has upheld the provision, because an attorney can modify the language and is only required to give the disclosures that are substantially similar to those in the statute and that are applicable.[259]

The full text of the statement is reprinted below.

Statement Required Under Section 527(b)

IMPORTANT INFORMATION ABOUT BANKRUPTCY ASSISTANCE SERVICES FROM AN ATTORNEY OR BANKRUPTCY PETITION PREPARER.

If you decide to seek bankruptcy relief, you can represent yourself, you can hire an attorney to represent you, or you can get help in some localities from a bankruptcy petition preparer who is not an attorney. THE LAW REQUIRES AN ATTORNEY OR BANKRUPTCY PETITION PREPARER TO GIVE YOU A WRITTEN CONTRACT SPECIFYING WHAT THE ATTORNEY OR BANKRUPTCY PETITION PREPARER WILL DO FOR YOU AND HOW MUCH IT WILL COST. Ask to see the contract before you hire anyone.

The following information helps you understand what must be done in a routine bankruptcy case to help you evaluate how much service you need. Although bankruptcy can be complex, many cases are routine.

Before filing a bankruptcy case, either you or your attorney should analyze your eligibility for different forms of debt relief available under the Bankruptcy Code and which

---

knowingly and fraudulently conceals assets or makes a false oath or statement under penalty of perjury in a bankruptcy case shall be subject to fine and imprisonment, and (2) a statement specifying that all information supplied by a debtor in connection with a bankruptcy case is subject to examination by the attorney general.

253 11 U.S.C. § 527(a)(2). *See* Form 5, Appx. G.2, *infra* (sample notice).
254 11 U.S.C. § 527(a)(2)(B).
255 The information may be requested in the form chapter 13 plans used in some districts.
256 11 U.S.C. § 527(d).
257 11 U.S.C. § 527(b). *See* Form 6, Appx. G.2, *infra* (sample notice).
258 *See* 28 U.S.C. § 1930(f).
259 Conn. Bar Ass'n v. United States, 620 F.3d 81 (2d Cir. 2010).

form of relief is most likely to be beneficial for you. Be sure you understand the relief you can obtain and its limitations. To file a bankruptcy case, documents called a Petition, Schedules and Statement of Financial Affairs, as well as in some cases a Statement of Intention need to be prepared correctly and filed with the bankruptcy court. You will have to pay a filing fee to the bankruptcy court. Once your case starts, you will have to attend the required first meeting of creditors where you may be questioned by a court official called a 'trustee' and by creditors.

If you choose to file a chapter 7 case, you may be asked by a creditor to reaffirm a debt. You may want help deciding whether to do so. A creditor is not permitted to coerce you into reaffirming your debts.

If you choose to file a chapter 13 case in which you repay your creditors what you can afford over 3 to 5 years, you may also want help with preparing your chapter 13 plan and with the confirmation hearing on your plan which will be before a bankruptcy judge.

If you select another type of relief under the Bankruptcy Code other than chapter 7 or chapter 13, you will want to find out what should be done from someone familiar with that type of relief.

Your bankruptcy case may also involve litigation. You are generally permitted to represent yourself in litigation in bankruptcy court, but only attorneys, not bankruptcy petition preparers, can give you legal advice.

16.8.3.4 Disclosures Required of Non-Attorney Agencies That Prepare Bankruptcy Documents

Debt relief agencies, but not attorneys who prepare bankruptcy petitions, schedules, and statements for debtors, are required to provide clear and conspicuous written notice to an assisted person giving "reasonably sufficient information" on how to provide the information required to file for bankruptcy.[260] To the extent that the debt relief agency does not provide the required information itself, the notice must explain such unsettled questions of law as:

- How to determine replacement value of assets;
- How to determine current monthly income and perform means test calculations;
- How to determine disposable income in a chapter 13 case;
- How to list creditors, determine the amount owed, and determine the proper address for the creditor; and
- How to determine what property is exempt and to value exempt property at replacement value as defined in section 506 of the Code (which has nothing to do with valuing property for exemption purposes).

A debt relief agency may give this information only to the extent allowed by applicable nonbankruptcy law. Because all of these subjects constitute legal advice about very complicated issues, no petition preparer can properly give such advice and the provision is essentially applicable to no one, or it will compel petition preparers to engage in the unauthorized practice of law.[261]

16.8.4 Written Contract Under Section 528(a)

A debt relief agency must execute a written contract with an assisted person within five days after the date the agency first provides bankruptcy assistance to the assisted person, and prior to filing a petition.[262] Fulfilling this obligation may be impossible because the assisted person may not wish to sign a contract, and obviously there is no way to force the assisted person to sign. In such cases, the debt relief agency's obligation should be satisfied by tendering the contract. Alternatively, a debt relief agency, even before rendering any advice or providing a free consultation, could tender a contract that states the services that would be provided if the debtor chooses to pursue a case, but gives the debtor the option to pursue a case or not, with little or no fee for services if the debtor chooses not to proceed.[263]

In light of this requirement attorneys may choose to be careful not to give advice in an initial telephone call, which is often good practice in any event. Telephone tape recordings and other general information provided to the public probably would not be considered bankruptcy assistance, because it is not provided "in a case or proceeding on behalf of another," especially in light of other provisions regulating advertising.[264] However, in emergency cases or when debtors live in rural areas, are homebound, or have transportation problems, the requirement of a written contract may mean that attorneys will be able to give urgently necessary advice and information only at the risk of noncompliance with the statute. The provision will also be likely to interfere with bar association information hotlines and other efforts to provide information to consumers. Thus this provision, too, raises serious constitutional issues about access to courts and the First Amendment. However, at least one appellate court has upheld the provision, because an attorney can only be sanctioned for intentional or negligent failure provision of services in violation of the section and therefore cannot be sanctioned for a client's refusal to sign a

---

260 11 U.S.C. § 527(c).

261 *See, e.g., In re* Doser, 412 F.3d 1056 (9th Cir. 2005) (giving debtors an incomplete and inaccurate "bankruptcy overview" prepared by franchisor "We the People," and telling the debtors that it was reliable, constituted the practice of law); Taub v. Weber, 366 F.3d 966 (9th Cir. 2004) (petition preparer's advice regarding the meaning of terms "market value" and "secured claim or exemption" was unauthorized practice of law). *See also* § 16.6, *supra*.

262 11 U.S.C. § 528(a)(1).

263 *See* Form 4, Appx G.2, *infra* (sample initial consultation agreement).

264 *See* 11 U.S.C. § 528(a)(3); § 3.7, *infra*.

contract.[265] This holding suggests that if the attorney has provided a contract to the client after providing emergency services and the client does not return it, the attorney will not be in danger of sanctions.

The written contract must explain, clearly and conspicuously, the services that will be provided and the fees, charges, and terms of payment.[266] The assisted person must be provided a copy of the executed and completed contract.[267] These requirements apply to all attorneys acting as debt relief agencies.

16.8.5 Advertising Requirements Under Section 528(a)

If a debt relief agency advertises bankruptcy assistance services or the benefits of bankruptcy it must disclose that the services or benefits are with respect to bankruptcy relief under title 11.[268] The agency must also clearly and conspicuously use the following statement, or a substantially similar statement, in such advertisements: "We are a debt relief agency. We help people file for relief under the Bankruptcy Code."[269]

Advertising is defined to include "general media, seminars, mailings, telephonic or electronic messages," but only if directed to the general public.[270] It appears that mailings to particular individuals facing foreclosure may not be included, if they are not sent to the general public. Similarly, it is not clear that business cards or letterheads need to contain the information if they are not distributed to the general public. The term advertising is also defined to include:

- Descriptions of bankruptcy assistance in chapter 13, whether or not chapter 13 is mentioned in the advertisement;
- Statements such as "federally supervised repayment plans," or "federal debt restructuring help," or other similar statements that might lead a consumer to believe credit counseling is being offered when, in fact, bankruptcy services are being offered; and
- Advertisements to the general public indicating that a debt relief agency provides assistance with respect to credit defaults, mortgage foreclosures, evictions, excessive debt, debt collection pressure, or the inability to pay consumer debts.[271]

The advertising requirements apply to any advertisement offering assistance with respect to credit defaults, mortgage foreclosures, or evictions. The requirements also blur the distinction between attorneys and petition preparers, which will cause more people to fall prey to petition preparers.

It is unclear how much leeway is given by the right to use "substantially similar" language. May an attorney omit the phrase "debt relief agency" if the attorney makes clear that bankruptcy services are offered? This change should be allowed, as the supposed purpose of the requirement is to prevent attorneys from "luring" clients in by not mentioning that the service they offer is bankruptcy.

Constitutional problems with section 526(a)(4) were avoided by the Supreme Court in *Milavetz, Gallop & Milavetz, P.A. v. United States*,[272] which held that the advertising requirements apply only to attorneys advertising bankruptcy services to consumer debtors. The Court also held that attorneys may further identify themselves as law firms or attorneys to avoid being confused with non-attorney petition preparers and that section 528 also gives them flexibility to tailor the disclosures to individual circumstances, as long as the resulting statements are "substantially similar" to the statutory examples.[273]

16.8.6 Remedies for Failure to Comply with Debt Relief Agency Provisions

The 2005 Act specifies remedies for failure to comply with the debt relief provisions. Contracts not complying with the requirements in sections 527 or 528 of the Code are void, and may not be enforced by any court or any other person, other than the assisted person (though it is unclear how even the assisted person can enforce a void contract, especially if a court cannot enforce it).[274] Any waiver by an assisted person of rights under section 526 is not enforceable against a debtor,[275] which leaves a question about whether it can be enforced against an assisted person who is not a debtor.

A debt relief agency is liable to an assisted person for any fees or charges in connection with bankruptcy assistance, plus actual damages, attorney fees, and costs, if the debt relief agency:

- Intentionally or negligently failed to comply with any provision of sections 526, 527, or 528 with respect to a bankruptcy case for such assisted person;
- Provided bankruptcy assistance in a case dismissed or converted to another chapter because of the agency's intentional or negligent failure to file documents; or

---

265 Conn. Bar Ass'n v. United States, 620 F.3d 81 (2d Cir. 2010).
266 11 U.S.C. § 528(a)(1)(A), (B).
267 11 U.S.C. § 528(a)(2).
268 11 U.S.C. § 528(a)(3).
269 11 U.S.C. § 528(a)(4).
270 11 U.S.C. § 528(a)(3).
271 11 U.S.C. § 528(b)(1), (2).

272 130 S. Ct. 1324 (2010).
273 *Id.* at 1341.
274 11 U.S.C. § 526(c)(1).
    This provision does not provide a cause of action for disgorgement of fees. *In re* Gutierrez, 356 B.R. 496 (Bankr. N.D. Cal. 2006).
    The statute provides for voiding of the contract only if the contents of the contract do not comply with the statute. Violation of the 5-day requirement in section 528(a)(1) does not cause the contract to be void. B.O.C. Law Group, P.C. v. Carroll (*In re* Galloway), 2011 WL 2148603 (E.D. Mich. May 30, 2011); *In re* Humphries, 453 B.R. 261 (E.D. Mich. 2011) (violation of the 5-day written contract requirement does not render fee contract signed more than five days after initial consultation void).
275 11 U.S.C. § 526(b).

- Intentionally or negligently disregarded material requirements of the Code or the Bankruptcy Rules applicable to the agency.[276]

The main effect of these provisions is to add statutory damages (in the amount of the fees paid to the agency), to the extent they exceed actual damages, and attorney fees, to the amount that could be recovered in malpractice and unfair and deceptive practices claims that already exist.

State attorneys general are given authority to enforce the provisions in state or federal court, and to seek injunctive relief, actual damages for assisted persons, and attorney fees.[277] In addition, the bankruptcy court on its own motion may enjoin and sanction debt relief agencies that intentionally violate or engage in a pattern of violating section 526.[278]

Nothing in sections 526, 527, or 528 exempts any person from complying with state law, except to the extent state law is inconsistent.[279] State regulations on lawyer advertising, however, may be preempted by these provisions. Nothing in sections 526, 527, or 528 limits the ability of a state or federal court to enforce qualifications for the practice of law.[280]

The debt relief agency provisions provide an additional tool for pursuing nonattorneys who attempt to give advice about bankruptcy. In addition to petition preparers, this may include entities that simply advise a debtor to file bankruptcy cases on their own[281] and debt settlement companies that provide advice about bankruptcy. Thus, the provisions may provide a new cause of action enabling debtors or trustees to recover damages.

---

276 11 U.S.C. § 526(c)(2). *See, e.g.*, *In re* Irons, 379 B.R. 680 (Bankr. S.D. Tex. 2007) (court utilizes section 526 in reviewing basic competency of counsel whose failure to file documents in timely fashion led to dismissal of chapter 13 case; no specific sanction imposed); *In re* Gutierrez, 356 B.R. 496 (Bankr. N.D. Cal. 2006) (attorney who did nothing to attempt to comply was negligent; attorney did not argue he was not a debt relief agency).

277 11 U.S.C. § 526(c)(3).

278 11 U.S.C. § 526(c)(5). *See In re* Fahey, 2009 WL 2855728 (Bankr. S.D. Tex. Sept. 1, 2009) (applying section 526(c)(5) to bar attorney from practicing before bankruptcy court based on long history of cases dismissed for failure to comply with basic Code standards).

279 11 U.S.C. § 526(d).

280 11 U.S.C. § 526(d)(2).

281 *In re* Valdez, 2011 WL 3704716 (Bankr. S.D. Tex. Aug. 22, 2011) ("Financial Hope for America" advised debtor to file bankruptcy cases).

Chapter 17 Chapter 12 Bankruptcy: Family Farmer and Family Fisherman Reorganization

17.1 Overview

17.1.1 Evolution and Historical Background of Chapter 12

17.1.1.1 Current Status of Chapter 12

Chapter 12 has provided an opportunity for reorganization for a limited category of family farmers for over twenty years. In 2005, this opportunity was expanded to include a limited category of family fisherman. This Chapter discusses chapter 12 reorganization, focusing primarily on the original focus of chapter 12—family farmers. This focus, however, can be applied as well to family fisherman.

Chapter 12 is a blend of consumer and commercial bankruptcy concepts designed to provide family farmers with an opportunity for successful bankruptcy reorganization. It was first enacted in 1986 as a temporary provision of the Bankruptcy Code and was renewed numerous times, each time as another temporary extension.[1] Renewals, however, sometimes came months after chapter 12 had expired, creating frustrating gaps in its availability.[2] The Bankruptcy Abuse Prevention and Consumer Protection Act of 2005 (the 2005 Act) remedied this problem by making chapter 12 a permanent part of the Bankruptcy Code.[3]

17.1.1.2 Purpose of Chapter 12

Chapter 12 is a powerful reorganization tool for eligible debtors, providing authority for debt reduction that exceeds what can be accomplished in either a Chapter 11 or 13 bankruptcy. However, it is not a panacea for family farmers' or fishermen's economic woes. It provides a specific limited remedy which will help some but not all of those eligible. Attorneys must analyze each situation to determine if their client is eligible for chapter 12 and, if so, whether filing is the most appropriate remedy.

Chapter 12's legislative history is instructive in understanding its design and its mechanics.[4] A bankruptcy chapter exclusively for family farmers has its roots in the Frazier-Lemke Acts which created special bankruptcy provisions for farmers in the 1930s and early 1940s.[5] Both in creating chapter 12 and in

---

1 Bankruptcy Judges, United States Trustees, and Family Bankruptcy Act of 1986, Pub. L. No. 99-554, § 302, 100 Stat. 3103. *See* Jerome M. Stam & Bruce L. Dixon, *Farmer Bankruptcies and Farm Exits in the United States, 1899–2002*, United States Dep't of Agric., Econ. Research Serv., Agric. Info. Bull. No. AIB788, app. 31–32 (Mar. 2004) (legislative history of chapter 12 bankruptcy). *See also* Susan A. Schneider, *History of Chapter 12 Bankruptcy: On Again, Off Again*, Agric. L. Update, Aug. 2001, at 1.

2 Although originally limited to seven years as emergency legislation for family farmers in a time of economic crisis, see 132 Cong. Rec. S17,075–S17,093 (daily ed. Oct. 3, 1986), chapter 12 has been extended several times. *See, e.g.*, Pub. L. No. 103-65, 107 Stat. 311 (1993); Pub. L. No. 106-5, 113 Stat. 9 (1999) (extended chapter 12 through October 1, 1999). In 1999 Congress extended chapter 12 temporarily, but declined to make it permanent. The extension ran through July 1, 2000. Pub. L. No. 106-70, 113 Stat. 1031 (1999) (became effective at the close of the previous extension on October 1, 1999). On July 1, 2000, chapter 12 expired. However, on May 11, 2001, Congress passed an eleven-month extension of chapter 12. Pub. L. No. 107-8, 115 Stat. 10 (2001). The eleven months ran retroactively from July 1, 2000 through June 1, 2001. At that point, chapter 12 again expired. Then, on June 26, 2001, Congress passed an additional four-month extension, again running partly retroactively from June 1, 2001, through October 1, 2001. Pub. L. No. 107-17, 115 Stat. 151 (2001). Congress then passed another two extensions: one running from September 30, 2001, through June 1, 2002, passed on May 7, 2002, Pub. L. No. 107-170, 116 Stat. 133 (2002), and another extension running from May 31, 2002 through January 1, 2003, passed on May 13, 2002, Pub. L. No. 107-171, 116 Stat. 134 (2002). Following those enactments, Congress then passed another two six-month extensions: one extension running from December 31, 2002, through July 1, 2003, and the other running from June 30, 2003, through January 1, 2004. Pub. L. No. 107-377, 115 Stat. 3115 (2002); Pub. L. No. 108-73, 117 Stat. 891 (2003). Once again, Congress allowed chapter 12 to expire. Then, on October 25, 2004, Congress passed another extension, again running retroactively, from January 1, 2004 through June 30, 2005. Pub. L. No. 108-369, 118 Stat. 1749 (2004). As these laws reenacted chapter 12 retroactively, presumably cases filed in the gap period under other chapters were eligible for conversion.

3 Pub. L. No. 109-8, § 1001, 119 Stat. 23, 185–186 (2005).

4 Compare H.R. 5316 with Senate amendments. *See* 132 Cong. Rec. (daily ed. May 6, 1986). What emerged as chapter 12 is different from both proposals in some respects. *See also* H.R. Conf. Rep. No. 99-958 (1986), *reprinted in* 1986 U.S.C.C.A.N. 5247–5252.

5 Frazier-Lemke Farm Mortgage Acts Ch. 869, 48 Stat. 1289 (1924); Ch. 792, 49 Stat. 942 (1935); Ch. 39, §§ 1, 2, 54 Stat. 40 (1940); Norton, *The New Family Farmer Bankruptcy Act*, 3 Prac. Real Estate Lawyer No. 4, 37–44 (July 1987).

The earlier Frazier-Lemke Acts had constitutional problems concerning impairment of property rights under the Fifth Amendment. It has been intimated that the Fifth Amendment problems may also infect chapter 12. *See* United States v. Sec. Indus. Bank, 459 U.S. 70, 103 S. Ct. 407, 74 L. Ed. 2d 235 (1982). However, the cases

making it permanent, Congress recognized the financial problems encountered by the traditional family farm and the inability of the other chapters of the Bankruptcy Code to furnish these farmers with an opportunity for a successful reorganization.[6]

The problems that support the need for chapter 12 in substantial measure arise from factors beyond farmers' control. There is always significant risk involved in farming, due to its dependency upon weather conditions and upon the market. For example, the natural disasters inherent in crop production can make profits and losses highly unpredictable. In addition farmers are typically unable to negotiate the price at which their products are sold but are subject to market forces beyond their control. Finally, there are fundamental changes that continue to occur in American agriculture that individual farmers have little opportunity to influence. These changes include the industrialization of production, the greater concentration of resources, the concentration of markets, the increasing use of production contracts, the increasing influence of foreign trade, developments in agricultural biotechnology, environmental regulation, and changes in federal farm policies. Such dramatic change can result in financial stress for those struggling to adapt to the changing business climate.

17.1.2 Special Bankruptcy Code Protections Outside of Chapter 12

Early on, Congress acknowledged special circumstances that justify at least minimal protection for farmers experiencing financial distress. This protection initially came in the form of a limitation on a creditor's right to force the farmer-debtor into bankruptcy. As early as the Bankruptcy Act of 1898 creditors of a "person engaged chiefly in farming or in tillage of soil" were prevented from forcing that person into an involuntary bankruptcy.[7] This protection against involuntary bankruptcy remains the law today.

Section 303(a) of the Bankruptcy Code allows a creditor to commence an involuntary chapter 7 or chapter 11 bankruptcy case against a debtor, but an exception to this power protects "farmers," "family farmers," and certain corporations.[8] Two distinct definitions apply to these terms. A person is a "farmer" under section 101(20) if eighty percent or more of the person's gross income came from a farming operation owned or operated by that person in the tax year immediately preceding the commencement of the case.[9] A person is a "family farmer" if the person is engaged in a farming operation, the person's debts do not exceed $3,792,650,[10] at least fifty percent of the person's debts arise out of the farming operation (excluding debt on a principal residence), and more than fifty percent of the person's gross income comes from farming.[11] Certain "family farm corporations" also fit within the definition of "family farmer" if more than fifty percent of the outstanding stock or equity is held by the family that operates the farm, more than eighty percent of the value of the corporate assets relate to the farming operation, and the debts do not exceed $3,792,650.[12] Neither farmers nor family farmers can be forced into an involuntary bankruptcy.[13]

The protection granted to farmers and family farmers by section 303 has been held not to be jurisdictional. "Farmer" or "family farmer" status must be affirmatively raised as a defense to the commencement of an involuntary bankruptcy proceeding.[14]

Another form of protection is that a farmer reorganization case under either chapter 11 or chapter 13 cannot be converted, without the farmer's consent, to a liquidation case under chapter 7.[15] And, absent a finding of fraud,[16] a family farmer reorganization under chapter 12 cannot be converted to chapter 7.[17] Despite these Code prohibitions on involuntary case commencement and conversion, some circuit courts of appeal allow creditors to propose plans which liquidate the debtor under chapter 11 when the farmer's reorganization efforts stall.[18]

---

addressing this issue to date find that chapter 12 passes constitutional muster: Albaugh v. Terrell, 93 B.R. 115 (E.D. Mich. 1988); *In re* Kloberdanz, 83 B.R. 767 n.6 (Bankr. D. Colo. 1988); *In re* Bullington, 80 B.R. 590 (Bankr. M.D. Ga. 1987), *aff'd sub nom.* Travelers Ins. Co. v. Bullington, 89 B.R. 1010 (M.D. Ga. 1988), *aff'd*, 878 F.2d 354 (11th Cir. 1989).

6 H.R. Conf. Rep. No. 99-958, at 48 (1986), *reprinted in* 1986 U.S.C.C.A.N. 5246, 5249 (noting that most family farmers have too much debt to be eligible for chapter 13 and that chapter 11 is often too complicated, too expensive, and unworkable).

7 Bankruptcy Act of 1898, ch. 541, § 4(b), 30 Stat. 544.

8 11 U.S.C. § 303(a).

This protection is not extended to family fisherman. Note that an involuntary bankruptcy cannot be commenced against any debtor under chapter 13. *In re* KZK Livestock, Inc., 147 B.R. 452 (Bankr. C.D. Ill. 1992). Presumably the same is true for chapter 12, as the Code does not provide creditors with any such power.

9 11 U.S.C. § 101(20). *See, e.g., In re* Sharp, 361 B.R. 559 (B.A.P. 10th Cir. Okla. 2007) (affirming bankruptcy court's dismissal of involuntary bankruptcy brought against farmer and holding that evidence supported finding that debtor was a farmer under section 101(20)).

"Farming operation" is defined in 11 U.S.C. § 101(21). *See* § 17.2.2.3, *infra*.

10 11 U.S.C. § 101(18).

This amount is adjusted every three years to reflect changes in the Consumer Price Index. 11 U.S.C. § 104.

11 11 U.S.C. § 101(18)(A).

The definition of "family farmer" is discussed in greater detail in § 17.2.2.4, *infra*.

12 11 U.S.C. § 101(18)(B).

This debt ceiling is adjusted every three years to reflect changes in the Consumer Price Index. 11 U.S.C. § 104. The definition of "family farmer" is discussed in greater detail in § 17.2.2.4, *infra*.

13 11 U.S.C. § 303(a).

14 *See In re* McCloy, 296 F.3d 370 (5th Cir. 2002) (farmer status must be affirmatively raised as a defense to involuntary bankruptcy; farmer status does not impact the court's jurisdiction over the matter); *In re* Frusher, 124 B.R. 331 (D. Kan. 1991) (same).

15 11 U.S.C. §§ 1112(c), 1307(f).

16 Graven v. Fink, 936 F.2d 378 (8th Cir. 1991).

17 11 U.S.C. § 1208.

18 Button Hook Cattle Co. v. Commercial Nat'l Bank & Trust Co. (*In re* Button Hook Cattle Co.), 747 F.2d 483 (8th Cir. 1984) (confirming the liquidation plan proposed by the creditor after the debtor's

The Bankruptcy Code also recognizes that farmers may be entitled to special protection when they are involved in the production of grain and a grain storage facility that they have done business with files for relief in bankruptcy. Similarly, fishermen who sell their fish to a storage or processing facility that files bankruptcy may also be entitled to special protection. Section 507(a)(6) gives each group sixth priority, up to $5775 per individual, for their allowed unsecured claims.[19] For farmers, section 557 provides for an expedited determination of the rights to grain assets when a grain storage facility files for bankruptcy.[20]

17.1.3 Farmer Reorganizations Under Chapters Other Than Chapter 12

17.1.3.1 Overview

Before the creation of chapter 12, family farmer reorganization options were limited to chapters 11 and 13. These two options are still available to family farmers who qualify; family farmers are not compelled to use chapter 12 to reorganize.[21] In most cases, however, chapter 12 is the preferred option. Chapters 11 and 13 were not constructed with the special needs of the farmer debtor in mind and both provide significant barriers to farmer reorganization.

17.1.3.2 Problems Under Chapter 13 for Farmers

Chapter 13 provides the template for chapter 12; chapter 13's "automatic cramdown" feature is its cornerstone.[22] However, chapter 13's ceiling for eligibility of no more than $1,081,400 in liquidated, noncontingent secured debt and no more than $360,475 in liquidated, noncontingent unsecured debt[23] makes chapter 13 unavailable for many farming operations.[24]

Chapter 13 also requires that the debtor be an "individual with a regular income."[25] Farms owned by family partnerships and family-owned corporations are ineligible. In addition, the "regular income" criteria has sometimes been interpreted to disqualify farming operations in which the major source of income is crop farming because of the irregularity and infrequence of income. Chapter 13 cases are customarily set up with payments due on a monthly or other relatively frequent basis.[26]

Confirmation of chapter 13 plans also typically do not depend on such reorganizational strategies as sales and recovery of property, strategies that may be very useful in reorganizing a farming operation.[27] There are limits posed on the chapter 13 debtor's ability to restructure certain debts.[28] And, unless otherwise ordered by the bankruptcy court, chapter 13 plan payments must begin in all cases within thirty days after filing of the plan, a requirement that may be problematic for a farmer.[29]

Some of the most significant advantages for farmers for chapter 12 over chapter 13 are:

- There is a higher debt ceiling for chapter 12 eligibility than under chapter 13;[30]
- Indebtedness secured by residential real property and/or the farm homestead can be restructured and the payments thereupon modified and changed from those originally provided by contract;[31]
- All secured indebtedness can be—if appropriate—reamortized and repaid over a length of time exceeding the three to five year life of the chapter 12 plan;[32]
- Payments can be scheduled to coincide with farm income production periods.

However, certain debts may be dischargeable in chapter 13, but not in chapter 12.[33] Occasionally this may be a reason to choose chapter 13 over chapter 12.

120-day exclusive plan filing period had passed).

19 11 U.S.C. § 507(a)(6). The priority maximum is adjusted every three years to reflect changes in the Consumer Price Index. 11 U.S.C. § 104.
20 11 U.S.C. § 557.
21 The option of orderly liquidation and removal of debt is also open to a farmer under chapter 7, and the chapter 7 remedy is an important option for farmers whose reorganization is impossible.
22 11 U.S.C. § 1325(a). See § 11.6, supra.
23 11 U.S.C. § 109(e).
  This debt ceiling is adjusted every three years to reflect changes in the Consumer Price Index. 11 U.S.C. § 104.
24 The restrictive chapter 13 format has been best utilized by small dairy and livestock operations with a continuous cash flow. See Bromley, *The Chapter 12 Family Farm Bankruptcy Law*, 60 Wis. B. Bull. No. 1, at 18–20 (Jan. 1987); Comment, *Chapter 13 and the Family Farm*, 3 Bankr. Dev. J. 599 (1986); Bruce H. Matson, *Understanding the New Family Farmer Bankruptcy Act*, 21 U. Rich. L. Rev. 521 (1987); Steven Shapiro, *An Analysis of the Family Farmer Bankruptcy Act of 1986*, 15 Hofstra L. Rev. 353 (1987).
25 11 U.S.C. § 109(e).

26 There have been instances in which crop farm operation plans have been confirmed in chapter 13. See In re Fiegi, 61 B.R. 994 (Bankr. D. Or. 1986); In re Hines, 7 B.R. 415 (Bankr. D.S.D. 1980).
27 Such strategies are useful tools of chapter 7 trustees and are available to chapter 11 and chapter 12 debtors-in-possession. See 11 U.S.C. §§ 1107, 1203. See also § 10.4.2, supra; §§ 17.3, 17.4.3.5, infra.
28 For example, see 11 U.S.C. § 1322(b)(2), which restricts the modification of debts secured only by the debtor's principal residence. In addition, chapter 13 does not contain a provision allowing for the continued payment of secured claims after the term of the plan, a central feature of chapter 12. 11 U.S.C. § 1222(b)(9).
29 11 U.S.C. § 1326(a)(1). But see In re Westenberg, 365 B.R. 895 (Bankr. D. Wis. 2007) (debtors were entitled to discharge at end of their chapter 13 three-year plan term, despite fact that plan provided for direct payments to secured creditors beyond that term and enforcing the plan as confirmed).
30 See 11 U.S.C. §§ 101(18), 109(f).
31 11 U.S.C. § 1222(b)(2); Harmon v. United States, 101 F.3d 574 (8th Cir. 1996) (lien stripping permitted in chapter 12); In re Zabel, 249 B.R. 764 (Bankr. E.D. Wis. 2000). But see In re Anderson, 305 B.R. 861, 866 (B.A.P. 8th Cir. 1994) (debtor must bring affirmative lien avoidance action to avoid valueless lien; plan provision alone is insufficient).
  Contrast chapter 13 requirements. Nobelman v. Am. Sav. Bank, 508 U.S. 324, 113 S. Ct. 2106, 124 L. Ed. 2d 228 (1993).
32 11 U.S.C. § 1222(b)(9).
33 The exceptions to discharge contained in 11 U.S.C. § 523(a) are applicable to all discharges under chapter 12, but not to a discharge

17.1.3.3 Problems Under Chapter 11 for Farmers

Before enactment of chapter 12, most farmers attempted reorganization under chapter 11, even though this chapter is generally ill suited to family farm reorganization. Chapter 11 presents both practical and substantive problems for family farms.[34]

As a practical matter, chapter 11 is designed as a commercial remedy for large investor-owned corporations, and it is a costly and cumbersome tool for an unsophisticated small business. Chapter 11 requires relatively complex disclosure statements and reorganization plans, and it anticipates a lengthy confirmation process.[35] The result is that much time (both for the attorney and the farmer) and money is spent producing paperwork and making court appearances. The filing fee of $200 in chapter 12 versus $1000 for chapter 11 also makes chapter 11 unattractive for an already cash poor farming operation.[36]

Substantively it may be very difficult for a family farmer to obtain confirmation of his or her reorganization plan. Chapter 11 provides a dual route for confirmation under either section 1129(a) or 1129(b), both of which present obstacles for farmer reorganization.

Section 1129(a) provides for creditor approval or rejection by voting on a plan of reorganization. Creditors in classes impaired by the plan and who are not promised a one-hundred percent repayment of their claims can vote against the plan and thereby block its confirmation. In addition, in most cases, an undersecured creditor can elect to have its claim treated and repaid as if *fully* secured.[37] Most farm creditors are undersecured, and repaying these creditors in full, instead of merely the value of their collateral, would make plan feasibility and confirmation virtually impossible.

The second route available for confirmation is the section 1129(b) "cram down." While this route allows for confirmation of plans over creditor objection and for payment of secured creditors at the value of their collateral rather than the face amount of their claims,[38] plan confirmation must follow the "absolute priority" rule. The "absolute priority" rule does not allow owners of property to keep their ownership interest after confirmation if creditors in all classes ahead of them, for example, secured and general unsecured creditors, receive less than one-hundred percent of their claims.[39] The absolute priority rule still serves as a barrier to chapter 11 reorganization unless sale of the farm is part of the plan.[40]

Another disadvantage of chapter 11 farm reorganization is that a creditor may propose a liquidation plan if the farmer has not been successful in his or her reorganization efforts.[41]

As a result of these disadvantages, relatively few effective bankruptcy reorganizations for family farmers have occurred in chapter 11 cases without the cooperation of a farmer's major creditors.

17.1.4 The Unique Nature of Farm Finance

17.1.4.1 Overview

An attorney who undertakes representation of farmers in financial difficulty should become familiar with some of the unique aspects of farm finance. Historically, farms have benefited from special laws that reflect Americans' support for family farms, and farm finance exemplifies this support. For example, state law should be consulted as there may be special protections that are available to farmers that face foreclosure.[42]

Federal government policy also reflects this special support for farmers. There are two major institutional lenders created to provide farm finance, the Farm Credit System and the Farm Service Agency. Despite their similar sounding names, they are very different entities. In addition to these lenders, the federal government also has created a wide array of federal farm programs, most of which provide additional income to farmers.

17.1.4.2 The Farm Credit System

The Farm Credit System (FCS) is a network of federally chartered borrower-owned cooperatives that was specifically created to provide a competitive source of agricultural credit.[43]

---

under section 1328(a). *Compare* 11 U.S.C. § 1228(a) *with* 11 U.S.C. § 1328(a). *See generally* § 15.4.1, *supra*.

34 Norwest Bank v. Ahlers, 485 U.S. 197, 108 S. Ct. 963, 99 L. Ed. 2d 169 (1988). *See generally* Randy Rogers & Lawrence P. King, Collier Farm Bankruptcy Guide ¶ 2.05[2] (1999); Frasier, *The New Bankruptcy Code Chapter 12: Friend of the Family Farmer?* 41 Wash. State B. News 29 (Aug. 1987); Bruce H. Matson, *Understanding the New Family Farmer Bankruptcy Act*, 21 U. Rich. L. Rev. 521 (1987); Norton, *The New Family Farmer Bankruptcy Act*, 3 Prac. Real Estate Law. 37 (July 1987); Steven Shapiro, *An Analysis of the Family Farmer Bankruptcy Act of 1986*, 15 Hofstra L. Rev. 353 (1987); H.R. Conf. Rep. No. 99-958, at 48 (1986).

35 Randy Rogers & Lawrence P. King, Collier Farm Bankruptcy Guide ¶ 2.05[2] (1999).

36 28 U.S.C. § 1930(a).

37 11 U.S.C. §§ 1111(b)(2), 1129(a). *See, e.g., In re* Baxley, 72 B.R. 195 (Bankr. D.S.C. 1986) (farmer chapter 11); *In re* Hallum, 29 B.R. 343 (Bankr. E.D. Tenn. 1983); *In re* Griffiths, 27 B.R. 873 (Bankr. D. Kan. 1983).

38 11 U.S.C. § 1129(b)(2)(A).

39 11 U.S.C. § 1129(b)(2)(B)(ii), (b)(2)(C)(ii). *See* 7 Collier on Bankruptcy ¶ 1129.03[e] (15th ed. rev.).

40 The Eighth Circuit attempted to find a way around this barrier in the farm case of *In re* Ahlers, 794 F.2d 388 (8th Cir. 1986), but the Supreme Court reversed, finding that the farmer's contribution of labor and expertise was not a sufficient contribution to alter the absolute priority rule. Norwest Bank v. Ahlers, 485 U.S. 197, 108 S. Ct. 963, 99 L. Ed. 2d 169 (1988). For a helpful discussion of chapter 11 confirmation requirements, see Randy Rogers & Lawrence P. King, Collier Farm Bankruptcy Guide ¶ 2.05[2] (1999).

41 11 U.S.C. § 1121(c). *See* Button Hook Cattle Co. v. Commercial Nat'l Bank & Trust Co. (*In re* Button Hook Cattle Co.), 747 F.2d 483 (8th Cir. 1984) (confirming the liquidation plan proposed by the creditor after the debtor's 120-day exclusive plan filing period had passed).

42 For example, before a farm debt may be foreclosed Iowa law requires mediation. Iowa Code § 654A.

43 *See* 12 U.S.C. § 2001. The system was created in 1916 to provide agricultural loans "because rural banks were unable or unwilling to risk doing so."

It now stands as the largest competitor to commercial banks, holding the second largest portfolio of outstanding agricultural loans. FCS lenders include Agricultural Credit Associations (ACAs) which make short, intermediate, and long-term loans; Federal Land Credit Associations (FLCAs) or Federal Land Banks (FLBs) which make only long-term loans; and Production Credit Associations (PCAs), which make only short and intermediate-term loans.

The FCS is a Government Sponsored Enterprise (GSE) characterized by three distinct attributes. First, lenders within the FCS system are federally chartered entities that are not under the control of the usual financial regulators, but rather, are subject to regulation by the Farm Credit Administration, an independent federal agency. Second, it is the only GSE that is organized as a borrower-cooperative. The FCS institutions are not owned or managed by either the federal government or private investors—they are owned on a cooperative basis by the member-borrowers. Third, FCS lenders must operate exclusively within the confines of the lending authority granted to them by Congress. Federal statutes and regulations govern their lending practices and establish a variety of "borrowers rights."[44]

17.1.4.3 The Farm Service Agency Loan Programs

The Farm Service Agency (FSA), formerly the Farmers Home Administration (FmHA), is a federal agency within the United States Department of Agriculture (USDA) that was created expressly for the purpose of providing loans to family farmers that are unable to obtain credit from conventional sources.[45] FSA farm loan programs also target certain groups by reserving a portion of loan funding for use by socially disadvantaged (SDA) family farmers and beginning farmers.[46] FSA's mission recognizes imperfections in credit markets and attempts to address concerns about social equity in access to agricultural credit.

FSA serves its special mission through two separate lending programs: the direct loan program and the guaranteed loan program. Direct loans are strictly regulated and are available to eligible borrowers, subject to funding availability, for farm ownership, operating, conservation, and emergency purposes.[47]

Specific loan servicing rights are mandated by statute and must be offered to distressed borrowers.[48] In some cases, the loan servicing options available to farmers under the FSA direct loan programs may offer a farmer a better chance to reorganize than bankruptcy. Once a farmer has received a discharge in bankruptcy, however, these programs may no longer be available.[49]

Guaranteed loans are originated and serviced by qualified participating lenders and then guaranteed by the government. Under a guarantee, FSA covers up to ninety percent (in certain cases, ninety-five percent) of the losses sustained if the loan defaults. Both commercial banks and FCS lenders participate in the guaranteed loan program. There are federal regulatory guidelines that govern lenders who participate in the guaranteed loan programs.[50] Borrowers have limited rights under these guidelines, and whatever rights they may have can be difficult to enforce.[51]

If a borrower defaults and the USDA honors the lender's subsequent loss claim under the guarantee, the USDA will have a right to pursue the borrower for whatever loss claim was paid. For this reason, borrowers with a guaranteed loan who file for relief in bankruptcy should always list both their primary lender and the FSA as creditors in order to prevent the FSA from attempting to collect on the guarantee as a postpetition obligation.

17.1.4.4 The Federal Farm Programs

17.1.4.4.1 Treatment in bankruptcy

Federal farm programs provide an important source of income for most farming operations, and maintaining this income may be critical to the success of reorganization under chapter 12. The legal questions at issue include:

- Can a farm program payment be exempted?
- Is a farm program contract an executory contract that must be assumed under section 365?
- Can the government set off the farm program payment due to the farmer against any debt that the farmer may owe to the federal government?

---

44 12 U.S.C. §§ 2199–2202e; 12 C.F.R. pt. 617. *See also* Christopher R. Kelley & Barbara J. Hoekstra, *A Guide to Borrower Litigation Against the Farm Credit System and the Rights of Farm Credit Borrowers*, 66 N.D. L. Rev. 127, 130–149 (1990).

45 7 U.S.C. § 1922.
For a history of the FSA loan programs and the FSA's predecessor agency, the Farmers Home Administration, see Curry v. Block, 541 F. Supp. 506 (D. Ga. 1982). Current program information is available at www.fsa.usda.gov/FSA/webapp?area=home&subject=fmlp&topic=landing.

46 FSA information regarding its loan programs for socially disadvantaged farmers can be found at www.fsa.usda.gov/FSA/webapp?area=home&subject=fmlp&topic=sdl.

47 7 U.S.C. §§ 1921, 1941, 1961; 7 C.F.R. pt. 764. USDA FSA administrative handbooks and official notices also guide the administration of these loan programs. Both are available on the USDA's website at www.fsa.usda.gov/FSA/webapp?area=home&subject=lare&topic=landing. FSA has an overview of its loan programs available on the USDA's website at www.fsa.usda.gov/FSA/webapp?area=home&subject=fmlp&topic=landing.

48 7 U.S.C. § 2001; 7 C.F.R. pt. 766.
Note also that adverse decisions by the FSA are appealable to the National Appeals Division of the USDA. 7 U.S.C. §§ 6991, 6996; 7 C.F.R. § 11.3. Information is available on the USDA NAD website at www.nad.usda.gov/.

49 *See* Lee v. Yeutter, 917 F.2d 1104 (8th Cir. 1990) (upholding FSA regulation that provides that a farmer is no longer a "borrower" and is thus ineligible for FSA administrative debt restructuring after discharge).

50 7 C.F.R. pt. 762.

51 FSA takes the position that its contract is with the lender, not the borrower. *See* Parker v. United States Dep't of Agric., 879 F.2d 1362 (6th Cir. 1989) (FSA guaranteed loan borrower is not a party to the guaranty contract and is not a third party beneficiary of this contract). *But see* Schuerman v. United States, 30 Fed. Cl. 420 (Fed. Cl. 1994) (farmer may be a third party beneficiary).

- Does a creditor's security interest attach to the government farm program payment and, if so, can it be cut off under section 552?

These issues will be discussed in the sections below that address exemptions, executory contracts, setoff, and lien dissolution.[52] In most cases, these issues will turn on an assessment of the nature of the farmer's rights under the program and the time that these rights attached. Therefore some background on the nature of the various federal farm programs is critical.

17.1.4.4.2 Basic attributes of federal farm programs

Federal farm programs share basic attributes that are critical to an understanding of their special role as a source of farm income. First, each farm program is specifically created by statute, either as part of a comprehensive farm bill[53] or as a separate statutory enactment.[54] Statutory provisions and the regulations promulgated thereunder control all aspects of the programs.[55]

Second, in addition to being created by Congress, a farm program must also be funded by Congress. Funding, or a lack thereof, may be an issue whenever rights to a federal program payment are considered.[56]

Third, each individual farm program is implemented by the USDA (usually the FSA) through the promulgation of specific regulations[57] and the development of internal administrative rules and procedures.[58]

Fourth, each program is based on the voluntary participation of the farmer. Although economically farmers may have great incentive to participate, they are never required to do so. The voluntary decision to participate in a specific program will bind the farmer to specific statutory and regulatory requirements that may or may not be related to the specific program.[59]

Fifth, if a farmer chooses to enroll in a federal farm program, the farmer is required to sign a contract with the Commodity Credit Corp. (CCC).[60] Typically, the contract recites the primary obligations of the farmer and the government and incorporates by reference the regulations governing the particular program.[61] The terms of the contract are not negotiated by the parties. Instead, they are dictated by the applicable statutes and regulations. The "sign-up" process occurs when the farmer and a representative of the CCC each sign a contract that binds both parties to the terms of the contract.[62]

Federal farm programs can also be analyzed according to a series of distinguishing characteristics that separate one program from another.

The first distinction concerns the farm program's connection or lack thereof to current commodity production. Some programs, most notably the traditional disaster assistance programs, are directly connected to production. The farmer's eligibility for the program and the amount of payment that the farmer will receive under the program is tied to what the farmer did or did not produce.[63]

In contrast, many current farm programs are decoupled from production. These programs "separate the linkage between

---

52 Exemptions are discussed in § 17.4.3.1, *infra*; executory contracts are discussed in § 17.4.7, *infra*; set off is discussed in § 17.4.12, *infra*; and lien dissolution is discussed in § 17.4.3.4, *infra*.

53 Congress typically enacts comprehensive legislation setting forth farm policy every four or five years. This legislation is termed the "farm bill." *See, e.g.*, The Food, Conservation, and Energy Act of 2008, Pub. L. No. 110-246, 122 Stat. 1651 (codified in scattered sections of 7, 15, 16, and 21 U.S.C.) (setting forth the provisions of the most recently enacted farm bill). *See also* Christopher R. Kelley, *Resolving Federal Farm Program Disputes*, 19 Wm. Mitchell L. Rev. 283, 288 (1993).

54 *See, e.g.*, The Agricultural Assistance Act of 2003, Pub. L. No. 108-7, 117 Stat. 11 (codified at 16 U.S.C. § 3801 note) (authorizing crop loss disaster assistance for prior crop losses).

55 Provisions in the program regulations confirm that the statutory and regulatory provisions will prevail over conflicting provisions in the contract. *See, e.g.*, 7 C.F.R. § 1410.53 (providing that "[i]f, after a CRP contract is approved by CCC, it is discovered that such CRP contract is not in conformity with this part, these regulations shall prevail, and CCC may, at its sole discretion, terminate or modify the CRP contract, effective immediately or at a later date as CCC determines appropriate").

56 *See, e.g.*, United States v. Thomas (*In re* Thomas), 91 B.R. 731, 732–733 (N.D. Tex. 1988), *modified by* 93 B.R. 475 (N.D. Tex. 1988) (explaining the supplemental appropriation that was needed to fully fund disaster payments under the Agriculture, Rural Development, and Related Agencies Appropriations Act of 1987).

57 *See, e.g.*, Grains and Similarly Handled Commodities—Marketing Assistance Loans and Loan Deficiency Payments for the 2008 Through 2012 Crop Years, 7 C.F.R. pt. 1421.

58 The Handbooks are available on the USDA website at www.fsa.usda.gov/FSA/webapp?area=home&subject=lare&topic=landing. *See generally* Christopher R. Kelley, *Federal Farm Program Payment-Limitations Law: A Lawyer's Guide*, 17 Wm. Mitchell L. Rev. 199, 210–215 (1993) (explaining the origin and importance of the administrative handbooks in implementing federal farm programs).

59 Christopher R. Kelley, *Federal Farm Program Payment-Limitations Law: A Lawyer's Guide*, 17 Wm. Mitchell L. Rev. 199, 289 (1993).

60 The CCC is a federally chartered corporation created and governed by the CCC Charter Act. 15 U.S.C. §§ 714–714p. It is "an agency and instrumentality of the United States, within the Department of Agriculture, subject to the general supervision and direction of the Secretary of Agriculture." 15 U.S.C. § 714. The CCC serves as the fiscal agency for the commodity program and other farm programs. *See* Rainwater v. United States, 356 U.S. 590, 592, 78 S. Ct. 946, 2 L. Ed. 2d 996 (1958) (describing the CCC as "simply an administrative device established by Congress for the purpose of carrying out federal farm programs with federal funds").

61 For example, in order to receive Direct Payments under a current farm program, a producer must complete and sign the Direct and Counter-Cyclical Program Contract, Form CCC-509. A representative of the CCC will sign when the producer is accepted into the program, committing the government to the contract. This contract, along with the Appendix to Form CCC-509, which "sets forth additional terms and conditions" and specifically incorporates the program regulations into the contract, governs the duties of the parties.

62 Most federal farm program contracts are available on the USDA website, e-forms service, at http://forms.sc.egov.usda.gov/eForms/welcomeAction.do?Home.

63 *See, e.g.*, 7 C.F.R. pt. 1416 (explaining Emergency Agricultural Disaster Assistance Programs).

government payments to producers and the quantity of a commodity produced or marketed."[64] Thus, they are made irrespective of any particular crop currently grown by the farmer.[65] Although the production *history* of the acreage that the farmer enrolls in the program may be factored into the amount of payments received, the payment bears no relation to the crops grown during the contract period. For example, the Direct Payment Program provides a decoupled payment, as payments are not tied to current production nor are they tied to market price. Payments are based on rates specified by statute and the producer's historic payment acres and payment yields. Not only does it not matter how much the farmer grows during the program year, with very limited exceptions, it does not even matter what crop is grown, or if a commercial crop is produced at all.[66]

A second distinguishing factor is the underlying goal of the program. On this basis federal farm programs can be divided into three categories: price support, conservation, and disaster assistance. Price support programs are enacted with the goal of increasing farm income.[67] Conservation programs seek to minimize the negative environmental consequences of farming and encourage conservation practices.[68] Disaster assistance programs are enacted in response to crop and livestock damage caused by natural forces.[69] Like the price support programs, disaster assistance programs seek to increase farm income, but only insofar as there have been offsetting losses incurred as a result of a natural disaster. These diverse underlying goals may be significant if it is necessary to determine congressional intent when interpreting farm program provisions.

Third, how closely is the program associated with a specific tract of farm property? While many programs have a connection with the production history of a particular tract of farmland,[70] certain specific programs have a more direct connection with a particular tract of real estate. The Conservation Reserve Program (CRP) is a clear example of this type of program.[71]

Under the CRP program eligible acreage must be assessed to be highly "erodible," and the producer receives payments for taking it out of production. The payments are often referred to as rental payments.[72]

The fourth distinguishing factor concerns the obligations that are required of the farmer under the program. Under some programs few obligations are placed on the farmer. In contrast, under other programs, the farmer is contractually bound to detailed and specific ongoing obligations required by the statute and regulations that implement the program.

Finally, the length of the contract term can be an important distinguishing factor. Farm program contracts can run as long as ten years,[73] although one year or one crop season is more frequently the duration.[74]

Each of these factors can be important in assessing the legal obligations of the parties and, by extension, rights to the payments in the bankruptcy case.

17.1.5 Timing a Chapter 12 Filing

The most obvious consideration in making a chapter 12 filing is to forestall a crisis event—for example, foreclosure, repossession—that will destroy the farming operation. The new credit counseling requirement applies to all individual debtors, so fulfilling this obligation must be built into prebankruptcy planning.[75] Other factors may bear on the timing of a chapter 12 bankruptcy and should factor into the filing decision too. For example:

- Eligibility for chapter 12 is limited to those with more than fifty percent of their gross income from farming.[76] This computation must be made either in the tax year immediately preceding the bankruptcy filing or in each of the second and third years preceding the filing.[77] Given the importance of off-farm income in sustaining family farm operations, a family farmer may be eligible one year but not another.

- The avoidance of a security interest in crops will be fully effective only if they have not yet been planted.[78] It may be advantageous to either accelerate or forestall filing based on planting dates.

---

64 For definitions of these types of farm program terms, see the USDA ERS Glossary at www.ers.usda.gov/topics/farm-economy/farm-commodity-policy/glossary.aspx.

65 *See* Mary E. Burfisher & Jeffrey Hopkins, *Decoupled Payments in a Changing Policy Setting,* Agric. Econ. Rep. 838, United States Dep't of Agric., Econ. Research Serv. (Nov. 2004). Note that the farmer's right to a particular level of payment may, however, be based on historical production figures.

66 *See, e.g.,* 7 C.F.R. pt. 1412.

67 *See* 7 U.S.C. § 1421 (authorizing the Secretary to provide price support to farm producers through the CCC).

68 *See, e.g.,* 16 U.S.C. § 3831 (authorizing the Conservation Reserve Program "to assist owners and operators of land . . . to conserve and improve the soil, water, and wildlife resources of such land").

69 See, for example, the Crop Loss Disaster Assistance Program, created by the Omnibus Consolidated and Emergency Supplemental Appropriations Act, Pub. L. No. 105-277, § 1101(a), 112 Stat. 2681 (1999).

70 The production history of a specific acreage is memorialized in the determination of "base." *See, e.g.,* 7 U.S.C. § 7911 (determining base acres for purposes of the Direct Payment Program). Base acres help to determine that amount of future payments received.

71 *See* 7 C.F.R. pt. 1412.

72 7 C.F.R. § 1410.42.
   Courts that have evaluated the nature of CRP payments have split on their legal designation, with some finding them to be rental payments and others finding that they are not. *See, e.g.,* Fed. Deposit Ins. Corp. v. Hartwig, 463 N.W.2d 2, 5 (Iowa 1990) (CRP payments constitute rent under a mortgage "rents and profits" clause). *Contra* Brown v. Farmers Home Admin. (*In re* Koerkenmeier), 107 B.R. 195, 198 (W.D. Mo. 1989) (CRP program does not create an interest in real estate sufficient for a characterization of the payments as rent).

73 *See, e.g.,* 7 C.F.R. § 1410.7 (providing that CRP contracts are for a ten-year term).

74 *See, e.g.,* 7 C.F.R. § 1412.1.

75 11 U.S.C. § 109(h).

76 11 U.S.C. § 101(18)(A).

77 11 U.S.C. § 101(18)(A).

78 *See* § 17.4.3.4, *infra.*

- If crops will be harvested preconfirmation, their harvest value (rather than input value) may have to be accounted for in the liquidation analysis, requiring payments to be significantly higher to unsecured creditors.[79]
- Benefits under farm program contracts may be subject to offset, subject to a security interest, or accounted for in the liquidation analysis if the contract is signed prepetition. Filing prior to entering into these contracts may be advantageous.[80]
- Some property can only be retrieved under 11 U.S.C. §§ 547 and 548, or time limitations expanded under 11 U.S.C. § 108, if the bankruptcy case is properly timed to use the powers of the Code effectively.

17.2 Commencement of a Case

17.2.1 Introduction

Chapter 12 is only available to a "family farmer" or a "family fisherman" with "regular annual income." Each of these terms is specifically defined in the Code. Not every farmer and not every fisherman has chapter 12 as an option.[81]

17.2.2 Eligibility for Chapter 12 Relief

17.2.2.1 In General

All individuals are subject to the prepetition credit counseling requirement at section 109(h) in order to be eligible for bankruptcy.[82] This eligibility requirement applies to individuals who are farmers, family farmers, or family fishermen and, it applies in chapter 12 cases.[83] The credit counseling requirement does not apply, however, to corporations or partnerships that are otherwise eligible for chapter 12.[84] However, individual family farm or family fisherman corporation stockholders and/or partners are likely to need to file as individuals in addition to the business filing in order to address their personal liability. These individuals will need to meet the credit counseling requirement.[85]

Section 109(f) limits the availability of chapter 12 to "family farmers," as defined in section 101(18), engaged in a farming operation and "family fishermen," as defined in section 101(19A), engaged in a commercial fishing operation. For individual debtors, these definitions each include a debt ceiling, a minimum percentage debt from farming or fishing, and a minimum percentage of income from farming or fishing. Each allows for corporate or partnership structure, but excludes large family and investor-owned operations.[86] Eligibility is further restricted to those with "regular annual income."[87]

As chapter 12 offers powerful reorganization tools to debtors, eligibility for chapter 12 relief is frequently challenged.[88] A challenge can be brought by creditors or by the chapter 12 trustee through a motion to dismiss or as an objection to confirmation. Farmers who are found to be ineligible for chapter 12 are likely to be dismissed from bankruptcy, although a creditor may also use the farmer's ineligibility to support a finding of bad faith in a motion for relief from the automatic stay.[89] Eligibility is determined as of the filing date of the chapter 12 petition.[90] The burden of proving eligibility rests with the debtor.[91] These eligibility requirements are the subject of inquiry by the chapter 12 trustee at the section 341 meeting of creditors. Some courts have held that these requirements are jurisdictional and subject to strict construction.[92] At least two courts have held that an estate in probate cannot be a debtor under chapter 12.[93]

---

79 *See, e.g., In re* Musil, 99 B.R. 448 (Bankr. D. Kan. 1988).
80 *See, e.g.,* Schneider v. Nazar (*In re* Schneider), 864 F.2d 683 (10th Cir. 1988).
81 Chapter 12 is not the exclusive remedy for a farmer who falls within its ambit of eligibility. A family farmer can file for bankruptcy under any chapter for which he or she may be eligible.
82 11 U.S.C. § 109(h). *See* § 7.3.5, *supra*.
83 *See* Bogedain v. Eisen (*In re* Bogedain), 2006 WL 2471939 (E.D. Mich. Aug. 24, 2006) (the credit counseling requirement in section 109(h) applies to all individuals, including individual family farmers who file for relief under chapter 12).
84 11 U.S.C. § 109(h).
85 11 U.S.C. § 109(h). *See* § 7.3.5, *supra*.
86 11 U.S.C. §§ 101(18)(B), 101(19A)(B) (defining eligibility criteria for corporations and partnerships). *See In re* Burke, 81 B.R. 971 (Bankr. S.D. Iowa 1987); *In re* Easton, 79 B.R. 836 (Bankr. N.D. Iowa 1987), *aff'd*, 104 B.R. 111 (N.D. Iowa 1988), *vacated*, 883 F.2d 630 (8th Cir. 1989), *on remand*, 118 B.R. 676 (Bankr. N.D. Iowa 1990).
87 11 U.S.C. § 109(f).
88 For recent decisions on Chapter 12 eligibility challenges, *see, In re* Woods, 465 B.R. 196 (B.A.P. 10th Cir. 2012); *In re* Meadows, 2012 WL 2411905 (Bankr. E.D. Ky. June 26, 2012); *In re* Allen, 2012 WL 1207233 (Bankr. D. Ariz. Apr. 10, 2012); *In re* Fuentes, No. EDCV 10–01419 DDP, 2011 WL 6294489 (D. C.D. Cal. Dec. 16, 2011); *In re* Cooper, 2011 WL 3882278 (Bankr. D. Or. Sept. 2, 2011); *In re* Powers, 2011 WL 3663948 (Bankr. N.D. Cal. Aug.12, 2011); *In re* Jones, 2011 WL 3320504 (Bankr. D. Or. Aug. 2, 2011).
89 *See, e.g., In re* Gibson, 355 B.R. 807 (Bankr. E.D. Cal. 2006).
90 *In re* Cross Timbers Ranch, Inc., 151 B.R. 923 (Bankr. W.D. Mo. 1993); *In re* Grey, 145 B.R. 86 (Bankr. D. Kan. 1992) (cannot gain eligibility by filing adversary to capture farm funds to credit for earlier tax years when not otherwise eligible; must be eligible from income data available at filing); *In re* Watford, 92 B.R. 557 (M.D. Ga. 1988), *aff'd in part, vacated in part on other grounds*, 898 F.2d 1525 (11th Cir. 1990); *In re* Williams Land Co., 91 B.R. 923 (Bankr. D. Or. 1988).
91 Cottonport Bank v. Dichara, 193 B.R. 798 (W.D. La. 1996); *In re* Voelker, 123 B.R. 749 (Bankr. E.D. Mich. 1990); *In re* Snider, 99 B.R. 374 (Bankr. S.D. Ohio 1989); *In re* Plafcan, 93 B.R. 177 (Bankr. E.D. Ark. 1988).
92 Whaley v. United States, 76 B.R. 95 (N.D. Miss. 1987); *In re* Johnson, 73 B.R. 107 (Bankr. S.D. Ohio 1987); *In re* Stedman, 72 B.R. 49 (Bankr. D.N.D. 1987); *In re* Orr, 71 B.R. 639 (Bankr. E.D.N.C. 1987).

 The bankruptcy court may also raise the issue of eligibility *sua sponte*. 11 U.S.C. § 105; *In re* Lerch, 85 B.R. 491 (Bankr. N.D. Ill. 1988), *aff'd*, 94 B.R. 998 (N.D. Ill. 1989). *Contra* First Brandon Nat'l Bank v. Kerwin-White, 109 B.R. 626 (D. Vt. 1990) (eligibility is not jurisdictional; it is a defense which is waived if not raised in a timely fashion by a creditor); *In re* Hettinger, 95 B.R. 110 (Bankr. E.D. Mo. 1989); *In re* Reak, 92 B.R. 804 (Bankr. E.D. Wis. 1988); §§ 17.2.2.4.3, 17.4.6.3, *infra*.
93 *In re* Estate of Grassman, 91 B.R. 928 (Bankr. D. Or. 1988) (and

17.2.2.2 The Regular Annual Income Requirement

Section 109(f) limits the availability of chapter 12 to a "family farmer or family fisherman with regular annual income,"[94] paralleling a chapter 13 requirement of "regular income,"[95] but modifying it with the annual time frame. The Code provides that this requirement limits eligibility to a "family farmer whose annual income is sufficiently stable and regular to enable such family farmer to make payments under a plan under chapter 12 of this title."[96] The definition of this requirement for "family fisherman" mirrors this provision.[97] The emphasis is on having a sufficient annual income to fund the plan and not on the regularity of that income during the year.[98] As such, the "regular annual income" requirement is closely linked to the feasibility requirement for confirmation.[99]

The "regular annual income" requirement makes no reference to the source of that income.[100] When revenue is from sources outside the debtor's control, such as accounts receivable or promissory notes, regularity and stability may be lacking.[101] However, several courts have taken into positive account gratuitous payments and income from family members, particularly when those non-debtor family members have property at risk in the bankruptcy proceeding.[102]

The regularity and sufficiency of annual income necessary for chapter 12 eligibility can be enhanced by the presence of either off-farm income—provided it does not endanger the income eligibility percentage—or livestock operations which produce relatively predictable income at regular intervals.[103]

17.2.2.3 The "Engaged in a Farming Operation" Requirement

A family farmer must be engaged in a "farming operation."[104] Similarly, a family fisherman must be "engaged in a commercial fishing operation."[105] As both are also defined according to the income they receive from farming/fishing and their debts from farming/fishing, the "engaged in farming" and "engaged in a commercial fishing operation" requirements will overlap extensively with the determination of whether income and debts relate to the operation.

"Farming operation" is a term in the Code that predates the enactment of chapter 12, as it was previously defined with respect to the definition of "farmer." The term "includes farming, tillage of the soil, dairy farming, ranching, production or raising of crops, poultry, or livestock, and production of poultry or livestock products in an unmanufactured state."[106] The legislative history indicates that this definition should be interpreted broadly.[107] The listing of items with the use of the term "includes" indicates that the list provides examples, but is not exhaustive.[108]

In assessing whether a debtor has a true farming operation, courts have looked to the actual physical presence and involvement of family members, the ownership of traditional farm assets by the debtor, the permanent cessation of all or part of the farming operation, the type of product and its market, and most importantly, if the operation is subject to traditional farm risk.[109] The totality of the circumstances must reflect a farm

---

cases cited therein; although the court takes no position on whether the heirs may file their own partnership case under chapter 12). *See also In re* Erickson, 183 B.R. 189 (Bankr. D. Minn. 1995) (dismissal of case warranted upon debtor's death).

94 *See* 11 U.S.C. § 109(f).
95 *See* 11 U.S.C. § 109(e).
96 11 U.S.C. § 101(19).
97 11 U.S.C. § 101(19B).
98 Randy Rogers & Lawrence P. King, Collier Farm Bankruptcy Guide ¶ 4.03[1] (1999).
99 *See* 11 U.S.C. § 1225(a)(6). *See also* Randy Rogers & Lawrence P. King, Collier Farm Bankruptcy Guide ¶ 4.03[1] (1999).
100 *See In re* Mikkelsen Farms, Inc., 74 B.R. 280 (Bankr. D. Or. 1987); *In re* Hoskins, 74 B.R. 51 (Bankr. C.D. Ill. 1987) (chapter 12); Randy Rogers & Lawrence P. King, Collier Farm Bankruptcy Guide ¶ 4.03[1] (1999).
101 *In re* Van Fossen, 82 B.R. 77 (Bankr. W.D. Ark. 1987).
102 *In re* Cheatham, 78 B.R. 104 (Bankr. E.D.N.C. 1987); *In re* Hoskins, 74 B.R. 51 (Bankr. C.D. Ill. 1987); *In re* Campbell, 38 B.R. 193 (Bankr. E.D.N.Y. 1984) (chapter 13); *In re* Cohen, 13 B.R. 350 (Bankr. E.D.N.Y. 1981) (chapter 13) (non-debtor spouse contribution).
103 *In re* Sandifer, 448 B.R. 382 (Bankr. D.S.C. 2011) (finding that the "annual income" requirements for eligibility for Chapter 12, must be treated broadly and clearly include off farm income); *In re* Hoskins, 74 B.R. 51 (Bankr. C.D. Ill. 1987).

104 *See* 11 U.S.C. § 101(18)(A),(B).
105 *See* 11 U.S.C. § 101(19A).
106 11 U.S.C. § 101(21).
107 *See In re* KZK Livestock, Inc., 147 B.R. 452 (Bankr. C.D. Ill. 1992) and *In re* Blanton Smith Corp., 7 B.R. 410 (Bankr. M.D. Tenn. 1980) for a good discussion of this legislative history.
    See also In re Buchanan, 2006 WL 2090213 (M.D. Tenn. July 25, 2006); *In re* Glenn, 181 B.R. 105 (Bankr. E.D. Okla. 1995); *In re* Sugar Pine Ranch, 100 B.R. 28 (Bankr. D. Or. 1989); *In re* Maike, 77 B.R. 832 (Bankr. D. Kan. 1987); *In re* Wolline, 74 B.R. 208 (Bankr. E.D. Wis. 1987).
108 11 U.S.C. § 102(3). *See In re* Shepherd, 75 B.R. 501 (Bankr. N.D. Ohio 1987); *In re* Stedman, 72 B.R. 49 (Bankr. D.N.D. 1987). *Compare In re* Wolline, 74 B.R. 208 (Bankr. E.D. Wis. 1987) *with In re* Maike, 77 B.R. 832 (Bankr. D. Kan. 1987).
109 Fed. Land Bank of Columbia v. McNeal, 77 B.R. 315 (S.D. Ga. 1987), *aff'd*, 848 F.2d 170 (11th Cir. 1988); *In re* Howard, 212 B.R. 864 (Bankr. E.D. Tenn. 1997) (non-debtor sons living on farm and owning some part of the farm livestock does not undermine qualification of operation as family farm); *In re* Glenn, 181 B.R. 105 (Bankr. E.D. Okla. 1995); *In re* French, 139 B.R. 476 (Bankr. D.S.D. 1992); *In re* Voelker, 123 B.R. 749 (Bankr. E.D. Mich. 1990) (active involvement in management decisions and shared labor); *In re* Sugar Pine Ranch, 100 B.R. 28 (Bankr. D. Or. 1989); *In re* Easton, 79 B.R. 836 (Bankr. N.D. Iowa 1987), *aff'd*, 104 B.R. 111 (N.D. Iowa 1988), *vacated*, 883 F.2d 630 (8th Cir. 1989), *on remand* 118 B.R. 676 (Bankr. N.D. Iowa 1990); *In re* Maike, 77 B.R. 832 (Bankr. D. Kan. 1987); *In re* Mikkelsen Farms, Inc., 74 B.R. 280 (Bankr. D. Or. 1987); *In re* Rott, 73 B.R. 366 (Bankr. D.N.D. 1987); *In re* Tart, 73 B.R. 78 (Bankr. E.D.N.C. 1987). *See also In re* Garako Farms, Inc., 89 B.R. 506 (Bankr. E.D. Cal. 1988) (assessing corporate eligibility, cites additional factors: (1) is the farming opera-

operation.[110] Operations that involve service activities or retail sales without the production of a product may be found ineligible.[111] Cases decided under 11 U.S.C. §§ 101(21) and 303 concerning the definition of "farming operation" may be relevant in determining what is a "farming operation" for the purposes of chapter 12.[112]

While some nontraditional farms may be within the scope of chapter 12,[113] other operations may be barred.[114] Service occupations, in which crop growing and other traditional forms of farming are absent or relatively incidental to the business, or when the farm work is primarily performed for other farmers, generally may not be considered "farming operations," and the income generated may not be considered "farm income" sufficient to qualify for chapter 12 relief.[115]

The question of whether a debtor is "engaged in a farming operation" also arises in the circumstance of farmers who have discontinued or significantly dismantled their farming operation. Some courts have found that such actions may make the debtor ineligible for chapter 12, regardless of the farmer's history.[116] Others have held that the level of activity of the farmer should not be dispositive of eligibility, so long as all statutory eligibility requirements are met.[117]

Mirroring the farming operation requirement, the definition of family fisherman requires that the debtor be "engaged in a commercial fishing operation."[118] A commercial fishing operation is defined as:

(A) the catching or harvesting of fish, shrimp, lobsters, urchins, seaweed, shellfish, or other aquatic species or products of such species; or
(B) for purposes of section 109 and chapter 12, aquaculture activities consisting of raising for market any species or product described in subparagraph (A);[119]

Thus, catfish farmers who meet the family fisherman eligibility requirements will be eligible for chapter 12 relief as "family fisherman." Under prior law, some courts assumed that they fit within the definition of family farmer under section 101(18),[120] but it now appears that they will be defined as fishermen instead of farmers and may need to adhere to the eligibility provisions associated with that category.

---

tion the principal source of income for the debtor; (2) does the debtor (or corporate officer) live on the property; (3) is the debtor involved in other businesses from which income is received; (4) is the debtor trying to offset income from some other source; (5) is the debtor involved in farming as a tax shelter; (6) does the debtor own or lease the subject property).

110 *In re* Buchanan, 2006 WL 2090213 (M.D. Tenn. July 25, 2006) (applying "totality of the circumstances" test, court held that debtors' horse boarding and training business was a farming operation for purposes of chapter 12). *But see In re* Jones, 2011 WL 3320504 (Bankr. D. Or. Aug. 2, 2011) (horse training and boarding does not constitute a "farming operation").

111 *In re* Cooper, 2011 WL 3882278 (Bankr. D. Or. Sept. 2, 2011); *In re* Jones, 2011 WL 3320504 (Bankr. D. Or. Aug. 2, 2011) (horse training and boarding does not constitute a "farming operation").

112 *In re* Maschhoff, 89 B.R. 768 (Bankr. S.D. Ill. 1988); *In re* Seabloom, 78 B.R. 543 (Bankr. D. Ill. 1987); *In re* McKillips, 72 B.R. 565 (Bankr. N.D. Ill. 1987).

One court has even stretched its analysis to embrace cases defining "farmer" under 11 U.S.C. § 522(f)(2) in assessing eligibility. *See In re* Hettinger, 95 B.R. 110 (Bankr. E.D. Mo. 1989).

113 *In re* Watford, 92 B.R. 557 (M.D. Ga. 1988) (catfish farming, by reference to other cases); *In re* Teolis, 419 B.R. 151 (Bankr. D.R.I. 2009) (nursery operation that was involved in growing of flowering plants, trees, and shrubs was involved in "farming operation" for purposes of chapter 12 eligibility); *In re* Sugar Pine Ranch, 100 B.R. 28 (Bankr. D. Or. 1989) (harvesting of merchantable timber on a sustained yield basis); *In re* Borg, 88 B.R. 288 (Bankr. D. Mont. 1988) (fox pelting part of farm operation); *In re* Hill, 83 B.R. 522 (Bankr. E.D. Tenn. 1988) (plant nursery operation); *In re* SWF, Inc., 83 B.R. 27 (Bankr. S.D. Cal. 1988) (shellfish cultivation operation); *In re* Maike, 77 B.R. 832 (Bankr. D. Kan. 1987) (game farm and kennel operation); *In re* Wolline, 74 B.R. 208 (Bankr. E.D. Wis. 1987) (riding horse operation which provided financing for traditional farm operation).

114 *In re* Watford, 92 B.R. 557 (M.D. Ga. 1988) (catching and selling stone crabs' claws/development of ponds for recreational use), *aff'd in part, vacated in part*, 898 F.2d 1525 (11th Cir. 1990); Fed. Land Bank of Columbia v. McNeal, 77 B.R. 315 (S.D. Ga. 1987), *aff'd*, 848 F.2d 170 (11th Cir. 1988); *In re* McKillips, 72 B.R. 565 (Bankr. N.D. Ill. 1987).

115 Fed. Land Bank of Columbia v. McNeal, 77 B.R. 315 (S.D. Ga. 1987), *aff'd*, 848 F.2d 170 (11th Cir. 1988); *In re* Blackwelder Harvesting Co., 106 B.R. 301 (Bankr. M.D. Fla. 1989) (citrus harvesting services company ineligible); *In re* Cluck, 101 B.R. 691 (Bankr. E.D. Okla. 1989) (horse breeding, training and boarding operation ineligible); *In re* Faber, 78 B.R. 934 (Bankr. S.D. Iowa 1987); *In re* Maike, 77 B.R. 832 (Bankr. D. Kan. 1987); *In re* Haschke, 77 B.R. 223 (Bankr. D. Neb. 1987); *In re* McKillips, 72 B.R. 565 (Bankr. N.D. Ill. 1987). Recent unpublished cases on this issue include: *In re* Cooper, 2011 WL 3882278 (Bankr. D. Or. Sept. 2, 2011) (purchase and retail sale of Christmas trees not farming); *In re* Jones, 2011 WL 3320504 (Bankr. D. Or. Aug. 2, 2011) (horse boarding and training not farming).

116 *In re* Lloyd, 37 F.3d 271 (7th Cir. 1994) (no substantial farming activities); *In re* Buchanan, 2010 WL 1039981 (D. Del. Mar. 22, 2010) (debtor who no longer owned his farm property at the time his petition was filed could not be engaged in farming for purposes of chapter 12 eligibility); *In re* Lawless, 79 B.R. 850 (W.D. Mo. 1987); *In re* Tart, 73 B.R. 78 (Bankr. E.D.N.C. 1987).

The court in *In re* Burke, 81 B.R. 971 (Bankr. S.D. Iowa 1987) opined that the focus of chapter 12 is to continue, not revive, farming operations.

117 Cottonport Bank v. Dichara, 193 B.R. 798 (W.D. La. 1996); *In re* Hettinger, 95 B.R. 110 (Bankr. E.D. Mo. 1989); *In re* Fogle, 87 B.R. 493 (Bankr. N.D. Ohio 1988); *In re* Land, 82 B.R. 572 (Bankr. D. Colo. 1988); *In re* Easton, 79 B.R. 836 (Bankr. N.D. Iowa 1987), *aff'd*, 104 B.R. 111 (N.D. Iowa 1988), *vacated*, 883 F.2d 630 (8th Cir. 1989), *on remand*, 118 B.R. 676 (Bankr. N.D. Iowa 1990); *In re* Maike, 77 B.R. 832 (Bankr. D. Kan. 1987); *In re* Indreland, 77 B.R. 268 (Bankr. D. Mont. 1987); *In re* Mikkelsen Farms, Inc., 74 B.R. 280 (Bankr. D. Or. 1987) (leased farm caused by economic conditions can be farming operation). *Cf. In re* Paul, 83 B.R. 709 (Bankr. D.N.D. 1988).

118 11 U.S.C. § 101(19A).

119 11 U.S.C. § 101(7A).

120 *See, e.g.*, Watford v. Fed. Land Bank of Columbia (*In re* Watford), 898 F.2d 1525, 1528–1529 (11th Cir. 1990) (reversing lower court's rejection of debtors' eligibility for chapter 12 and holding debtors' intent to establish commercial catfish ponds on their farm land should have been considered in determining status as "family farmer").

The "engaged in a commercial fishing operation" requirement relates directly to the income and debt requirements that apply to an operation that is "owned or operated" by the debtors. This requirement was used to find a fisherman ineligible because his work on a commercial fishing vessel was found to be seasonal employment, without evidence of ownership or management interest.[121]

17.2.2.4 Definition of "Family Farmer" and "Family Fisherman"

17.2.2.4.1 Overview

The terms "family farmer" and "family fisherman" for individual debtors are defined according to a maximum debt ceiling, a percentage of farm income, and a percentage of farm debt.

17.2.2.4.2 Debt ceiling

A family farmer's aggregate debts cannot exceed $3,792,650.[122] This maximum amount increases with the Consumer Price Index.[123] The same debt ceiling applies to family farm corporations and partnerships.[124] In a joint case the aggregate debt ceiling applies to both an individual and his or her spouse *together*. Separate petitions cannot be filed by spouses under chapter 12 to escape this debt ceiling limitation, except when liabilities are not joint.[125] Eligibility is generally determined from the debtor's good faith indication of debts in the schedules, not claims filed, although the presumption of the reasonable accuracy of a debtor's schedules is rebuttable.[126]

Unlike chapter 13, the chapter 12 debt limit applies to all debts, including guarantees and contingent debts, and not just noncontingent liquidated debts.[127] Consequently, disputed, contingent and unliquidated indebtedness may either eliminate eligibility or may require, if permitted by the court, swift litigation at a preliminary stage of the bankruptcy proceeding to weed out such claims that may bar eligibility.[128] Courts have intimated that prepetition compromise of debts to achieve chapter 12 eligibility may be acceptable, if done in a legally enforceable and provable manner,[129] but that postpetition compromise[130] or an attempt to credit collateral that will be surrendered postpetition to achieve eligibility is ineffective.[131]

"Family fishermen" are limited to maximum aggregate debts of $1,757,475 although, like the similar eligibility limitation for family farmers, this amount is indexed.[132] The same maximum applies to individuals, corporations, and partnerships.[133]

17.2.2.4.3 Debt arising from the farm operation or commercial fishing operation

Another requirement for individual "family farmer" status is that at least fifty percent of the debtor's aggregate noncontingent liquidated debt must arise from the farming operation owned or operated by the farmer.[134] A debt for the debtor's

---

121 *In re* Allen, 2012 WL 1207233 (Bankr. D. Ariz. Apr. 10, 2012).
122 11 U.S.C. § 101(19).
123 11 U.S.C. § 104.
124 11 U.S.C. § 101(18)(B).
125 If, under state law, liability cannot be apportioned between parties, it cannot be done under chapter 12 as an artifice to meet eligibility requirements. *See, e.g., In re* Marchetto, 24 B.R. 967 (B.A.P. 1st Cir. 1982); *In re* Walton, 95 B.R. 514 (Bankr. S.D. Ohio 1989); *In re* Welch, 74 B.R. 401 (Bankr. S.D. Ohio 1987); *In re* Johnson, 73 B.R. 107 (Bankr. S.D. Ohio 1987); *In re* Anderson, 51 B.R. 532 (Bankr. D.S.D. 1985); *In re* Cronkleton, 18 B.R. 792 (Bankr. S.D. Ohio 1982).
126 *In re* Pearson, 773 F.2d 751 (6th Cir. 1985) (chapter 13); *In re* Williams Land Co., 91 B.R. 923 (Bankr. D. Or. 1988) (under Federal Rule of Bankruptcy Procedure 3001(f), proofs of claim may also be considered for debt amounts when evaluating eligibility); *In re* Carpenter, 79 B.R. 316 (Bankr. S.D. Ohio 1987); *In re* Labig, 74 B.R. 507 (Bankr. S.D. Ohio 1987) (twenty-seven percent debt understatement excessive).
127 *See In re* Reiners, 846 F.2d 1012 (5th Cir. 1988); *In re* Quintana, 107 B.R. 234 (B.A.P. 9th Cir. 1989) (counterclaims cannot be used to reduce indebtedness amount for eligibility purposes); *In re* Vaughn, 100 B.R. 423 (Bankr. S.D. Ill. 1989). *Compare* 11 U.S.C. § 101(18)(A), (B) *with* 11 U.S.C. §§ 109(e), 303(a).
But see the approach taken by the court in *In re* Williams Land Co., 91 B.R. 923 (Bankr. D. Or. 1988), which follows chapter 13 elimination for consideration of disputed, precautionarily scheduled, and intracorporate claims. *In re* Lands, 85 B.R. 83 (Bankr. E.D. Ark. 1988), finds no-recourse loans are not counted for eligibility purposes. *Contra In re* Lindsey, Stephenson & Lindsey, 995 F.2d 626 (5th Cir. 1993) (no-recourse obligation is debt for chapter 12 eligibility determination).
128 *See* § 12.2.2, *supra*; Quintana v. Comm'r of Internal Revenue Serv., 915 F.2d 513 (9th Cir. 1990); *In re* Quintana, 107 B.R. 234 (B.A.P. 9th Cir. 1989) (counterclaims cannot be used to reduce indebtedness amount for eligibility purposes); Whaley v. United States, 76 B.R. 95 (N.D. Miss. 1987); *In re* Cross Timbers Ranch, Inc., 151 B.R. 923 (Bankr. W.D. Mo. 1993); *In re* Vaughn, 100 B.R. 423 (Bankr. S.D. Ill. 1989); *In re* Carpenter, 79 B.R. 316 (Bankr. S.D. Ohio 1987); *In re* Budde, 79 B.R. 35 (Bankr. D. Colo. 1987).
At least one chapter 13 case suggests that offsets, counterclaims or disputes are not sufficient to change the character of a debt amount for eligibility purposes. *See In re* Sylvester, 19 B.R. 671 (B.A.P. 9th Cir. 1982).
129 *In re* Budde, 79 B.R. 35 (Bankr. D. Colo. 1987); *In re* Labig, 74 B.R. 507 (Bankr. S.D. Ohio 1987).
130 *In re* Cross Timbers Ranch, Inc., 151 B.R. 923 (Bankr. W.D. Mo. 1993); *In re* Carpenter, 79 B.R. 316 (Bankr. S.D. Ohio 1987); *In re* Labig, 74 B.R. 507 (Bankr. S.D. Ohio 1987).
131 Quintana v. Comm'r of Internal Revenue Serv., 915 F.2d 513 (9th Cir. 1990); *In re* Cross Timbers Ranch, Inc., 151 B.R. 923 (Bankr. W.D. Mo. 1993); *In re* Stedman, 72 B.R. 49 (Bankr. D.N.D. 1987).
As one court indicated, the labeling of debt as "disputed" cannot be used to shoehorn a farm operation into eligibility for chapter 12. *In re* Labig, 74 B.R. 507 (Bankr. S.D. Ohio 1987).
132 11 U.S.C. §§ 101(19A), 104.
133 11 U.S.C. § 101(19A)(B).
134 11 U.S.C. § 101(18)(A). *See In re* Haarmann, 387 B.R. 216 (Bankr. S.D. Ill. 2008) (obligation for misappropriation of trade secrets was not contingent nor unliquidated even though debtor filed for bankruptcy before the judgment could be formally entered; therefore the obligation had to be included with debtor's other noncontingent, liquidated debt in assessing his eligibility for chapter 12 relief); *In re* Saunders, 377 B.R. 772 (Bankr. M.D. Ga. 2007) (non-farm debt does not become farm debt solely because farm real estate is offered as collateral; dismissing debtor's case on eligibility grounds).

principal residence is excluded from this computation unless the debt arises out of the farming operation.[135] The same requirement applies to partnerships and corporations.[136]

In order to qualify as a family fisherman, at least eighty percent of the debtor's aggregate noncontingent liquidated debt must arise out of the commercial fishing operation owned or operated by the fisherman.[137] A debt for the debtor's principal residence is also excluded from this computation unless the debt arises out of the fishing operation.[138] The same requirement applies to partnerships and corporations.[139]

Mortgage debt, tax indebtedness, and indebtedness arising from the settlement of litigation, when necessary to keep the farm operation, have been held to arise from the farm operation.[140] Indebtedness may be considered as arising from the farming operation under the proper circumstances even if collateralized with non-farm property if: (1) the reason for which the debt was incurred is directly related to the farm operation; and (2) the use of the funds obtained was directly related to the farm operation.[141]

17.2.2.4.4 Income arising from the farming operation or the commercial fishing operation

In order to be a "family farmer," an individual or husband and wife must have received at least fifty percent of their gross income from the farming operation, either in the taxable year immediately preceding the tax year in which the bankruptcy petition is filed or in each of the second and third taxable years preceding the year of filing.[142] This fifty percent income requirement does not apply to farm partnerships or corporations.[143]

In order to be a "family fisherman" an individual or husband and wife must have received at least fifty percent of their gross income from the commercial fishing operation in the taxable year immediately preceding the tax year in which the bankruptcy petition is filed.[144] There is no provision for looking back to the second and third years prior to filing. As with family farmers, this requirement does not apply to fishing partnerships of corporations.[145]

Not all income received by a farmer qualifies as arising from the farming operation. The question of what constitutes income from the "farming operation" has been extensively litigated since the advent of chapter 12. Some courts have accepted the tax characterization of gross income included on a farmer's tax return as dispositive, finding "gross income" to have the same meaning in bankruptcy as in tax laws.[146] Other courts have decided that a straight tax characterization is inappropriate.[147] Some courts have approached it from a middle ground, concluding that the tax approach is acceptable when compatible with chapter 12, but should be abandoned when irreconcilable.[148] All reported cases find that gross farm income is

---

135 11 U.S.C. § 101(18)(A), (B). A recent case considered whether home construction debt could be included as farm debt and held that it could so long as it had "some connection to the debtor's farming activity." *In re* Woods, 465 B.R. 196, 203–4 (B.A.P. 10th Cir. 2012).

136 11 U.S.C. § 101(18)(B).

137 11 U.S.C. § 101(19A)(A).

138 11 U.S.C. § 101(19A)(A), (B).

139 11 U.S.C. § 101(19A)(B).

140 *In re* Woods, 465 B.R. 196 (B.A.P. 10th Cir. 2012); *In re* Marlett, 116 B.R. 703 (Bankr. D. Neb. 1990); *In re* Roberts, 78 B.R. 536 (Bankr. C.D. Ill. 1987); *In re* Rinker, 75 B.R. 65 (Bankr. S.D. Iowa 1987).

141 *In re* Kan Corp., 101 B.R. 726 (Bankr. W.D. Okla. 1988) (whether a debt incurred from a loan "arises out of a farming operation" as required by 11 U.S.C. § 101(18)(B)(ii) is determined by the use made of the loan proceeds, not nature of the collateral or motive of the debtor); *In re* Reak, 92 B.R. 804 (Bankr. E.D. Wis. 1988); *In re* Douglass, 77 B.R. 714 (Bankr. W.D. Mo. 1987).

142 11 U.S.C. § 101(18)(A).

The determination is made from the tax year immediately preceding filing, regardless of whether the current tax year would indicate eligibility or ineligibility. *In re* Nelson, 291 B.R. 861 (Bankr. D. Idaho 2003) (debtors who were no longer operating dairy farm at time of confirmation still eligible for chapter 12 relief); *In re* Clark, 288 B.R. 237 (Bankr. D. Kan. 2003) (debtors need only meet income test for taxable year preceding filing and will remain family farmers even if plan is to cease farming operations postconfirmation and enroll in government conservation reserve program); *In re* Fogle, 87 B.R. 493 (Bankr. N.D. Ohio 1988); *In re* Paul, 83 B.R. 709 (Bankr. D.N.D. 1988); *In re* Bergmann, 78 B.R. 911 (Bankr. S.D. Ill. 1987); *In re* Indreland, 77 B.R. 268 (Bankr. D. Mont. 1987).

The income must have been actually received, not simply earned, during that tax year examined for eligibility. *In re* Bergmann, 78 B.R. 911 (Bankr. S.D. Ill. 1987).

143 11 U.S.C. § 101(18)(B).

144 11 U.S.C. § 101(19A)(A).

145 11 U.S.C. § 101(19A)(B).

146 *In re* Wagner, 808 F.2d 542 (7th Cir. 1986); *In re* Francks, 251 B.R. 441 (B.A.P. 10th Cir. 1999); United States v. Lawless, 79 B.R. 850 (W.D. Mo. 1987); *In re* Lamb, 209 B.R. 759 (Bankr. M.D. Ga. 1997) (partnership income); *In re* Gossett, 86 B.R. 941 (Bankr. S.D. Ohio 1988); *In re* Bergmann, 78 B.R. 911 (Bankr. S.D. Ill. 1987); *In re* Martin, 78 B.R. 593 (Bankr. D. Mont. 1987); *In re* Pratt, 78 B.R. 277 (Bankr. D. Mont. 1987); *In re* Shepherd, 75 B.R. 501 (Bankr. N.D. Ohio 1987); *In re* Nelson, 73 B.R. 363 (Bankr. D. Kan. 1987). See also *In re* Meadows, 2012 WL 2411905 (Bankr. E.D. Ky. June 26, 2012) ("gross income" for Chapter 12 eligibility purposes has the same meaning as in the Internal Revenue Code); *In re* Fuentes, 2011 WL 6294489 (C.D. Cal. Dec. 16, 2011) (social security and military benefits cannot be excluded; Internal Revenue Code definition of gross income applies).

See analysis in *In re* Brown, 95 B.R. 800 (Bankr. N.D. Okla. 1989) as to applicable tax provisions and non-agricultural businesses. The tax regulations addressed therein indicate that gross farm income does not contemplate reduction for expenses, but that nonagricultural businesses must deduct cost of goods sold from gross sales to reach the gross income figure. 26 U.S.C. § 61(a)(2); Treas. Reg. §§ 1.61-3, 1.61-4.

147 *In re* Sandifer, 448 B.R. 382 (Bankr. D.S.C. 2011) (addressing the income requirements for eligibility for chapter 12, the court went beyond the individual debtors' income tax reporting to allow attribution of farm income from the debtors' L.L.C. to help them qualify for chapter 12 relief); *In re* Barnett, 162 B.R. 535 (Bankr. W.D. Mo. 1993); *In re* Sugar Pine Ranch, 100 B.R. 28 (Bankr. D. Or. 1989); *In re* Burke, 81 B.R. 971 (Bankr. S.D. Iowa. 1987); *In re* Wolline, 74 B.R. 208 (Bankr. E.D. Wis. 1987); *In re* Guinnane, 73 B.R. 129 (Bankr. D. Mont. 1987).

148 *In re* Vantiger-Witte, 2006 WL 3861108 (Bankr. N.D. Iowa Dec. 20,

income before deductions for expenses.[149] One court determined that grain held as inventory, representing potential income, but as yet unliquidated, cannot be counted as income for purposes of eligibility.[150] However, proceeds from the sale of equipment and personal property, if directly related to the farm operation and not done as an independent business activity, has been considered to be income from the farm operation.[151] At least one court has held that sale of land is not income from the farming operation unless it can be "shown to be an inherent part of active farming."[152]

The cases are divided on whether rents derived from leases of farm property constitute income from the farming operation. While crop share leases, with their attendant risks result in farm income, cash leases are problematic.[153] The courts have generally found that when the farmer has no involvement with the land rented and is not subject to the regular risks of farming, the rental income is not income from the farm operation.[154] However, if the rent payment is subject to traditional farm risks, it can be considered income from the farming operation for eligibility purposes.[155] Income from rented land when the debtor has played a significant role in, or had ownership interest in, its crop production will generally be classified as farm income.[156]

Farmers have traditionally performed some farming-related work for other farmers and family members, referred to as "custom work." The majority of courts have found that payment for this type of work, when a part of the entirety and customary operation of a farmer's operation, to be income from the farming operation.[157] However, marketing and storing, or exclusive provision of trucking or services when not part of the farmer's actual crop production, generally is not.[158] Wages earned by farmers in chapter 12 from corporate family farm operations have been held to be farm income for chapter 12 eligibility purposes.[159]

Various other sources of income have been considered by the courts under chapter 12 to determine whether they constitute income from the "farming operation" for eligibility purposes. Reimbursement for preparation of ground, and seed and fertilizer expenses have been found to be farm income, as have crop share income,[160] deficiency payments, and payments from FSA

2006); *In re* Smith, 109 B.R. 241 (Bankr. W.D. Ky. 1989); *In re* Snider, 99 B.R. 374 (Bankr. S.D. Ohio 1989); *In re* Faber, 78 B.R. 934 (Bankr. S.D. Iowa 1987).

In re Creviston, 157 B.R. 380 (Bankr. S.D. Ohio 1993) uses the following considerations in evaluating whether income is "farm income" for purposes of eligibility: (1) extent to which debtor is involved in operations which produced farm income; (2) historical source of debtor's income; (3) whether challenged income as non-farm is departure from norm (for example, sales, off-farm income to shore up existing operation, and so forth); (4) degree of farming risk; (5) degree to which income producing farm assets are owned by third parties; (6) characterization of challenged income on tax return.

149 Gross income from non-farm business generally means gross profits and not gross receipts. *See In re* Gossett, 86 B.R. 941 (Bankr. S.D. Ohio 1988).

150 *In re* Snider, 99 B.R. 374 (Bankr. S.D. Ohio 1989).

151 *In re* Armstrong, 812 F.2d 1024 (7th Cir. 1987) (ruling with respect to farmer protection from involuntary bankruptcy); Cottonport Bank v. Dichara, 193 B.R. 798 (W.D. La. 1996); *In re* Wilson, 2007 Bankr. LEXIS 359 (Bankr. D. Mont. Feb. 7, 2007); *In re* Barnett, 162 B.R. 535 (Bankr. W.D. Mo. 1993); *In re* Burke, 81 B.R. 971 (Bankr. S.D. Iowa 1987); *In re* Haschke, 77 B.R. 223 (Bankr. D. Neb. 1987); *In re* Shepherd, 75 B.R. 501 (Bankr. N.D. Ohio 1987); *In re* Welch, 74 B.R. 401 (Bankr. S.D. Ohio 1987).

152 *In re* Powers, 2011 WL 3663948 (Bankr. N.D. Cal. Aug. 12, 2011).

153 The Seventh Circuit has adopted a strict risk-based test, holding that cash rent cannot be considered to be farm income. *In re* Armstrong, 812 F.2d 1024, 1027 (7th Cir. 1987). A sharp dissent in *Armstrong* advocated a "totality of the circumstances" test that is frequently cited in other circuits. *Id.* at 1030–1031 (concurring in part and dissenting in part). The Eighth Circuit rejected both the majority and the dissenting positions in *Armstrong*, holding that in order for cash rent to be income from farming, the farmer must maintain a significant degree of engagement in and a significant operational role in the production of the crops on the rented land. Otoe County Nat'l Bank v. Easton (*In re* Easton), 883 F.2d 630, 634 (8th Cir. 1989).

154 *In re* Armstrong, 812 F.2d 1024 (7th Cir. 1987). *See also In re* Swanson, 289 B.R. 372 (Bankr. C.D. Ill. 2003); *In re* Krueger, 104 B.R. 223 (Bankr. D. Neb. 1988); *In re* Maschhoff, 89 B.R. 768 (Bankr. S.D. Ill. 1988) (rents from farm houses not considered income from farm operation); *In re* Seabloom, 78 B.R. 543 (Bankr. C.D. Ill. 1987); *In re* Haschke, 77 B.R. 223 (Bankr. D. Neb. 1987); *In re* Tim Wargo & Sons, Inc., 74 B.R. 469 (Bankr. E.D. Ark. 1987),

aff'd, 869 F.2d 1128 (8th Cir. 1989); *In re* Mary Freese Farms, Inc., 73 B.R. 508 (Bankr. N.D. Iowa 1987).

155 *In re* Maynard, 295 B.R. 437 (Bankr. S.D.N.Y. 2003); *In re* Howard, 212 B.R. 864 (Bankr. E.D. Tenn. 1997); *In re* Voelker, 123 B.R. 749 (Bankr. E.D. Mich. 1990); *In re* Krueger, 104 B.R. 223 (Bankr. D. Neb. 1988); *In re* Jessen, 82 B.R. 490 (Bankr. S.D. Iowa 1988); *In re* Burke, 81 B.R. 971 (Bankr. S.D. Iowa 1987); *In re* Easton, 79 B.R. 836 (Bankr. N.D. Iowa 1987), aff'd, 104 B.R. 111 (N.D. Iowa 1988), vacated, 883 F.2d 630 (8th Cir. 1989), on remand, 118 B.R. 676 (Bankr. N.D. Iowa 1990); *In re* Welch, 74 B.R. 401 (Bankr. S.D. Ohio 1987); *In re* Mikkelsen Farms, Inc., 74 B.R. 280 (Bankr. D. Or. 1987); *In re* Rott, 73 B.R. 366 (Bankr. D.N.D. 1987).

156 *In re* Edwards, 924 F.2d 798 (8th Cir. 1991); *In re* Easton, 118 B.R. 676 (Bankr. N.D. Iowa 1990), after remand from 883 F.2d 630 (8th Cir. 1989) (for example, "walked" land during growth, helped to determine how farmed, base also rented, helped to seed, sow and fertilize).

157 *In re* Barnett, 162 B.R. 535 (Bankr. W.D. Mo. 1993); *In re* Maschhoff, 89 B.R. 768 (Bankr. S.D. Ill. 1988) (rents from farm houses not considered income from farm operation); *In re* Martin, 78 B.R. 593 (Bankr. D. Mont. 1987); *In re* Welch, 74 B.R. 401 (Bankr. S.D. Ohio 1987); *In re* Guinnane, 73 B.R. 129 (Bankr. D. Mont. 1987). *Contra In re* Watford, 92 B.R. 557 (M.D. Ga. 1988); *In re* Sugar Pine Ranch, 100 B.R. 28 (Bankr. D. Or. 1989) (citing *In re* Hampton, 100 B.R. 535 (Bankr. D. Or. 1987) in *dicta*).

158 *In re* Van Air Flying Serv., Inc., 146 B.R. 816 (Bankr. E.D. Ark. 1992); *In re* Watford, 92 B.R. 557 (M.D. Ga. 1988); *In re* Haschke, 77 B.R. 223 (Bankr. D. Neb. 1987).

159 *In re* Lamb, 209 B.R. 759 (Bankr. M.D. Ga. 1997) (partnership income); *In re* Pierce 175 B.R. 153 (Bankr. D. Conn. 1994) (partnership income); *In re* Schafroth, 81 B.R. 509 (Bankr. S.D. Iowa 1988) (Subchapter S corporation); *In re* Burke, 81 B.R. 970 (Bankr. S.D. Iowa 1987). *Contra In re* Way, 120 B.R. 81 (Bankr. S.D. Tex. 1990) (director's fees for managing two other farms is not farm income because no risk and farming for others); *In re* Hampton, 100 B.R. 535 (Bankr. D. Or. 1987).

160 *In re* Burke, 81 B.R. 970 (Bankr. S.D. Iowa 1987); *In re* Welch, 74 B.R. 401 (Bankr. S.D. Ohio 1987). *Contra* Tim Wargo & Sons, Inc.

programs.[161] By contrast, loan income, debt forgiveness, business losses, Social Security payments, barter value of goods received from other farms, and IRA withdrawals are not part of farm income.[162] One court has gone so far as to find that both cash rent from farm leasing, although not imbued with traditional farming risk, and hourly wages should still be considered farm income for eligibility purposes based upon the debtor's showing of: (1) active farming history and intent to salvage farm operation for future use; (2) clear and convincing evidence that the renting and liquidation are based on sound business judgment aimed at saving farming business; (3) payment of farm debt with wages.[163]

Unfortunately, too much reliance on non-farm income, even if income is generated in order to save the farm, will leave some genuine family farmers ineligible for chapter 12.

17.2.2.4.5 Eligibility requirements for partnerships and corporate farmers

A corporation or partnership that engages in a farming operation can also be eligible for chapter 12 relief if it meets the following eligibility requirements:

- More than fifty percent of the outstanding stock or equity in the partnership or corporation must be held by one family, or by one family and the relatives of the members of that family;
- This family or their relatives must conduct the farming operation;
- More than eighty percent of the value of the corporation or partnership must be related to the farming operation;
- The debts of the corporation or partnership must not be greater than $3,544,525, although this limit will increase in future years in tandem with the Consumer Price Index;
- Not less than fifty percent of the corporation or partnership debts must arise out of the farming operation that is owned or operated by the corporation or partnership; and
- If a corporation issues stock, its stock must not be not publicly traded.[164]

A corporation or partnership engaged in a commercial fishing operation must meet similar but more restrictive requirements in order to be eligible for chapter 12 relief. More than fifty percent of the outstanding stock or equity must be held by the family and the family must conduct the commercial fishing operation. More than eighty percent of the value of the corporation or partnership's assets must be related to the commercial fishing operation. The corporation or partnership's total debts must not exceed $1,642,500 and not less than eighty percent of the debt must arise out of the commercial fishing operation. If the corporation issues stock, the stock must not be publicly traded.[165]

Many farming operations have existed as loose or informal joint enterprises, but may not exist as legal partnerships under the relevant law. The clearest indicia of a partnership eligible for chapter 12 relief are written partnership agreements and partnership tax returns.[166] Any partnership seeking chapter 12 relief must clearly distinguish between the assets and obligations of the partnership itself and those of the individual partners.[167]

17.2.2.5 Joint Chapter 12 Filings

Joint filings under chapter 12 by both spouses are permitted.[168] A debtor may also file an individual case without including a spouse; or spouses may file individual cases and move for joint administration of the cases, provided each individually meets the eligibility requirements.[169] Many farm loans will have both husband and wife as signatories, making a joint filing desirable.[170]

When only one spouse files for chapter 12 relief, the court may assess the income eligibility and apportion income earned based upon state law, or in its absence, upon such basis as is equitable and fair. When wages or salaries are clearly attributable to one person, for eligibility purposes those wages or salary must be so credited solely to the earning spouse regardless of joint tax filing. However, when both spouses are active family farmers, this may mean a fifty-fifty split of income earned in the requisite tax year for eligibility purposes.[171]

---

v. Equitable Life Assurance Soc'y of the U.S., 869 F.2d 1128 (8th Cir. 1989).
161 *In re* Way, 120 B.R. 81 (Bankr. S.D. Tex. 1990); *In re* Fenske, 96 B.R. 244 (Bankr. D.N.D. 1988); *In re* Paul, 83 B.R. 709 (Bankr. D.N.D. 1988); *In re* Jessen, 82 B.R. 490 (Bankr. S.D. Iowa 1988); *In re* Shepherd, 75 B.R. 501 (Bankr. N.D. Ohio 1987); *In re* Welch, 74 B.R. 401 (Bankr. S.D. Ohio 1987).
162 *In re* Wagner, 808 F.2d 542 (7th Cir. 1986); *In re* Francks, 1999 WL 565893 (B.A.P. 10th Cir. Aug. 2, 1999) (loan income); *In re* Koenegstein, 130 B.R. 281 (Bankr. S.D. Ill. 1991); *In re* Smith, 109 B.R. 241 (Bankr. W.D. Ky. 1989) (insurance proceeds/capital gain from destruction of property is not farm income when debtors would not otherwise be eligible for chapter 12); *In re* Dutton, 86 B.R. 651 (Bankr. D. Colo. 1988); *In re* Rott, 73 B.R. 366 (Bankr. D.N.D. 1987).
163 *In re* Hettinger, 95 B.R. 110 (Bankr. E.D. Mo. 1989).
164 11 U.S.C. § 101(18)(B).
165 11 U.S.C. § 101(19A)(B).
166 *In re* LLL Farms, 111 B.R. 1016 (Bankr. M.D. Ga. 1990) (good discussion of the informal partnership as eligible for chapter 12 relief); *In re* Schauer Agric. Enters., 82 B.R. 911 (Bankr. S.D. Ohio 1988); *In re* Seabloom, 78 B.R. 543 (Bankr. C.D. Ill. 1987).
167 *In re* Eber-Acres Farm, 82 B.R. 889 (Bankr. S.D. Ohio 1987).
168 11 U.S.C. § 101(18)(A).
169 *In re* Welch, 74 B.R. 401 (Bankr. S.D. Ohio 1987).
170 Because the codebtor stay applies in chapter 12 only to consumer debts, a creditor may pursue a cosigning spouse who does not participate in a joint filing. However, when the liabilities of the spouses are not joint and when the eligibility ceilings are a problem, separate filings or a single filing may be desirable. See §§ 12.2.3.1, 17.2.2.4.2, 17.2.2.4.3, *supra*.
  Even in joint cases, however, note that all farm assets might not be jointly owned by both spouses. Property interests and secured status should be evaluated carefully. See, e.g., *In re* Snyder, 436 B.R. 81 (Bankr. C.D. Ill. 2010) (holding that farm debtor wife had one-half interest in crops grown, and that she had not granted security interest in her share).
171 *In re* Dutton, 86 B.R. 651 (Bankr. D. Colo. 1988).

Joint filings are not permitted for other individuals, although they may be working together in the family farming operation. Unless the operations fall within chapter 12's partnership eligibility criteria, individual chapter 12 cases will be required for each farmer.[172] However, partnerships and corporations may have their cases consolidated for joint administration either procedurally or substantively with other chapter 12 debtors, provided that all debtor entities are separately eligible for relief under chapter 12.[173]

17.2.3 Initial Schedules, Forms, and Fees

17.2.3.1 Schedules

The schedules for chapter 12 filings must conform to the Official Forms which are reproduced in Appendix D to this treatise. Skeletal or abbreviated filings may be used in certain emergency situations.[174] All of the new disclosure requirements and debtor responsibilities imposed by the 2005 amendments will apply to chapter 12 filings unless specifically exempted.[175]

Insofar as it is possible and consistent with existing facts, the preparation of the schedules should be done with an eye toward their harmony with other documentation produced by the debtor for creditors, for example, financial statements and loan applications.[176]

17.2.3.2 Appointment of Counsel

Because the debtor in chapter 12 operates as a debtor-in-possession and because of the amount of the fees which may be involved, the Code requires the same application process for chapter 12 cases as for chapter 11, with application for appointment of counsel and an order approving the application.[177] Such appointment should be routinely granted unless some conflict of interest or perceived inability competently to represent a debtor due to time constraints or past unacceptable performances is apparent.[178]

Application for appointment as counsel for a family farmer should be done with the initial schedules; otherwise a court may decline compensation for work performed prior to approval of the application or question the ability of counsel to appear on behalf of the debtor.[179] Care should also be taken to obtain court approval for the employment and compensation of all professionals and nonbankruptcy counsel working for debtors.[180]

17.2.3.3 Costs and Attorney Fees

The non-waivable filing fee for a chapter 12 case, whether individual, joint, corporate, or partnership, is $200.[181] There is also a $39 administrative fee due in every case. Counsel for the chapter 12 debtor should check the local rules and orders of the applicable court for imposition of other charges attendant to a chapter 12 filing. (Fees for the chapter 12 trustee arising from payments under a confirmed chapter 12 plan are discussed in § 17.4.1.2, *infra*.)

Attorney fees for a chapter 12 case are another factor in determining the costs of a filing. Attorney fees arrangements in chapter 12 cases, both as to fees paid prepetition and postpetition expectations, must be fully and accurately disclosed to the court, as in all other types of bankruptcy cases.[182] These fees are gauged by federal fee standards,[183] and must be consonant with fees charged in the appropriate legal community and with the number of hours actually expended by the attorney.[184] All fees are subject to review and all postpetition

---

Whether both spouses are "family farmers" may also be raised as an eligibility issue. Farm spouses who hold off-farm employment or whose contribution to the farming operation is not salaried are sometimes challenged as not being "farmers." *See In re* Teolis, 419 B.R. 151 (Bankr. D.R.I. 2009) (finding wife eligible for chapter 12 relief).

172 However, separate cases of family members involved in a single farming operation may be consolidated for joint administration by the court. *See In re* Plafcan, 93 B.R. 177 (Bankr. E.D. Ark. 1988); *In re* Bullington, 80 B.R. 590 (Bankr. M.D. Ga. 1987) (debtors had farmed together as a farm partnership for several years, had commonly owed debts and commonly owned assets, so separately filed cases meshed for coordination of payments), *aff'd sub nom.* Travelers Ins. Co. v. Bullington, 89 B.R. 1010 (M.D. Ga. 1988).

173 *In re* Plafcan, 93 B.R. 177 (Bankr. E.D. Ark. 1988); *In re* Williams Land Co., 91 B.R. 923 (Bankr. D. Or. 1988).

174 *See* § 7.2.2, *supra*.

175 11 U.S.C. § 521.

176 A discrepancy between a previous financial statement and the bankruptcy schedules can result in a nondischargeability finding under section 523(s)(B). *See, e.g.,* John Deere Co. v. Myers (*In re* Myers), 124 B.R. 735 (Bankr. S.D. Ohio 1991), *aff'd*, 61 F.2d 1577 (6th Cir. 1992).

177 *See* 11 U.S.C. §§ 327, 1203; Fed. R. Bankr. P. 2016; *In re* Fulton, 80 B.R. 1009 (Bankr. D. Neb. 1988); *In re* Slack, 73 B.R. 382 (Bankr. W.D. Mo. 1987).

Fee disclosure is also required. Fed. R. Bankr. P. 2016(b).

178 *See, e.g., In re* Brown, 354 B.R. 535 (Bankr. N.D. Okla. 2006) (admonishing attorney with conflict of interest who served as "ghost-writer" of debtors' pleadings). *See also In re* Brown, 371 B.R. 486 (Bankr. N.D. Okla. 2007) (attorney required to disgorge fees).

179 *See, e.g., In re* Samford, 102 B.R. 724 (Bankr. E.D. Mo. 1989); *In re* Stacy Farms, 78 B.R. 494 (Bankr. S.D. Ohio 1987); *In re* Willamette Timber Sys., Inc., 54 B.R. 485 (Bankr. D. Or. 1985); *In re* Wolsky, 35 B.R. 481 (Bankr. D.N.D. 1983); *In re* Ladycliff College, 35 B.R. 111 (Bankr. S.D.N.Y. 1983); *In re* Lewis, 30 B.R. 404 (Bankr. E.D. Pa. 1983).

180 11 U.S.C. §§ 327, 328; *In re* Samford, 102 B.R. 724 (Bankr. E.D. Mo. 1989).

181 28 U.S.C. § 1930(a)(5).

182 11 U.S.C. § 329; Fed. R. Bankr. P. 2014, 2016. *See also* Ch. 16, *supra*.

However, fees in commercial and quasi-commercial cases will—and are expected to—run higher than in consumer cases.

183 *See, e.g., In re* Yermakov, 718 F.2d 1465 (9th Cir. 1983); Barber v. Kimbrell's, Inc., 577 F.2d 216 (4th Cir. 1978); Johnson v. Ga. Highway Express, Inc., 488 F.2d 714 (5th Cir. 1974); *In re* Casco Bay Lines, Inc., 25 B.R. 747 (B.A.P. 1st Cir. 1982); *In re* Heller, 105 B.R. 434 (Bankr. N.D. Ill. 1989).

184 *In re* Miller, 288 B.R. 879 (B.A.P. 10th Cir. 2003) (evidence of attorney fee rates in local area supported reduction of attorney's hourly rate); *In re* Coy, 417 B.R. 17 (Bankr. N.D. Ohio 2009) (creditor's attorney compensation that was added to creditor's se-

fees are subject to the application process and review by the bankruptcy court.[185] Any fees received postpetition must be reported to the bankruptcy court within fifteen (15) days; however, no fees should be received postpetition without court approval.[186]

17.2.3.4 Other Reports and Documentation

The chapter 12 trustee is likely to require submission of supplemental information prior to the first meeting of creditors.[187] Information submitted will assist the trustee in making a preliminary assessment of eligibility and feasibility.

As in chapter 11 cases, the United States trustee or chapter 12 trustee will require monthly or other periodic reports showing income, expenditures, and changes in the farm operation during the case.[188] These reports should be filed accurately and in a timely manner consistent with the trustee's expectations. They should be reflective of *all* transactions of the debtor. Failure to file these reports can result in dismissal of the chapter 12 case.[189] The trustee may also request and require from time to time other reports, documentation, or information from the debtor, including proof of insurance coverage.[190]

17.2.4 Voluntary Conversion from Other Chapters to Chapter 12

Chapter 7: Section 706(a) provides an absolute right to convert from a chapter 7 bankruptcy to one under chapter 12, provided there has been no previous conversion.

Chapter 11: Section 1112(d) allows conversion from a chapter 11 case to one under chapter 12 at the request of the debtor if the debtor has not received a discharge under section 1141(d) and the conversion is found to be "equitable."

Chapter 13: Section 1307(d) allows conversion from chapter 13 to chapter 12 after notice and a hearing, unless the case is dismissed or converted to chapter 7 under section 1307(e).[191] Unlike the absolute right to convert between chapters 7 and 12, the provision for notice and hearing gives creditors and trustees the opportunity to oppose conversion from chapter 13.[192]

At minimum, a debtor must be eligible for relief under chapter 12 for conversion to be allowed.[193] If conversion is considered, eligibility will be measured as of the date of the original filing, not the date of conversion.[194]

17.2.5 What to Expect at the Meeting of Creditors

The meeting of creditors is conducted by the standing chapter 12 trustee or the United States trustee. Creditors may well appear and submit questions.

The debtor will be required to disclose information under oath concerning the nature of the operation, the assets owned, and what may be anticipated in the plan proposal. The trustee and secured creditors should be apprised of the status of secured collateral and insurance thereon. Financing arrangements for the coming year need to be disclosed, either as filed or anticipated to be filed. If sale, return or abandonment of land or equipment is in process or anticipated, that also should be disclosed.

Creditors may use the meeting of creditors as an opportunity to develop evidence leading to nondischargeability complaints and/or objections to confirmation. If there are significant inconsistencies between previous statements or documents created by the debtor and his or her bankruptcy schedules, this may come out at the meeting. If the debtor has given little thought to the actual mechanics of reorganization or is vague about matters bearing on feasibility, this may also be scrutinized at the meeting.

The meeting of creditors can used as an occasion to confer with and appraise the positions of the creditors and the trustee, ferret out potential problems, to agree to valuations of collateral and/or plan treatment (if possible), and to make creditors and the trustee as comfortable as possible with the debtor's situation and case. All reports and documents should be filed before the meeting, for example, monthly reports due, documents required by the chapter 12 trustee, and any amendments to schedules.

---

cured claim must be based on hours billed and reasonable hourly rate, not contingency agreement).

185 Fed. R. Bankr. P. 2016(a); *In re* Brooks, 2010 WL 2044933 (Bankr. C.D. Ill. May 24, 2010) (attorney compensation claim reduced based on improper claim of hourly compensation for paraprofessional and quality of service performed); *In re* Fox, 140 B.R. 761 (Bankr. D.S.D. 1992); *In re* Fulton, 80 B.R. 1009 (Bankr. D. Neb. 1988). *See In re* Combe Farms, Inc., 257 B.R. 48 (Bankr. D. Idaho 2001) (fees reduced because attorney failed to make disclosures required by Rule 2014).

186 Fed. R. Bankr. P. 2016(b); *In re* Brandenburger, 145 B.R. 624 (Bankr. D.S.D. 1992); *In re* Fox, 140 B.R. 761 (Bankr. D.S.D. 1992) (retention of jurisdiction to determine fees after dismissal).

187 United States Trustee Program, Guidelines for Supervision of Chapter 12 Cases.

188 *Id.*

189 United States Trustee Program, Guidelines for Supervision of Chapter 12 Cases. *See In re* Goza, 142 B.R. 766 (Bankr. S.D. Miss. 1992) (court can prevent debtor's voluntary dismissal if necessary reports and accounting lacking); *In re* Wickersheim, 107 B.R. 177 (Bankr. E.D. Wis. 1989).

190 United States Trustee Program, Guidelines for Supervision of Chapter 12 cases.

---

191 *In re* Land, 82 B.R. 572 (Bankr. D. Colo. 1988).

192 *See, e.g., In re* Wulf, 62 B.R. 155 (Bankr. D. Neb. 1986); *In re* Collins, 19 B.R. 209 (Bankr. S.D. Fla. 1982).

193 *In re* Walker, 77 B.R. 803 (Bankr. D. Nev. 1987).

194 11 U.S.C. § 348(a); State Bank of Waubay v. Bisgard, 80 B.R. 491 (D.S.D. 1987); *In re* Cobb, 76 B.R. 557 (Bankr. N.D. Miss. 1987).

17.3 The Family Farmer As Debtor-in-Possession

17.3.1 What Is a Debtor-in-Possession?

The filing of a chapter 12 petition establishes the family farmer debtor as a debtor-in-possession.[195] A debtor-in-possession, often termed a DIP, is a legal fiction created by the Bankruptcy Code, originally under chapter 11.[196] Although it is the individual who operates the farming operation as a DIP, a DIP is a legal entity separate and apart from the actual debtor.

It is the debtor as DIP who operates the debtor's farming operation, applies to the court concerning all operating decisions which require court approval, challenges claims of creditors, controls the property of the estate, and proposes a chapter 12 plan.[197] A DIP has the powers, duties and fiduciary responsibilities of a bankruptcy trustee.[198] Because the DIP is a separate legal entity distinct from the original debtor, the DIP can use all of the avoiding powers bestowed upon a chapter 7 trustee without regard to whether the prebankruptcy debtor took any actions or made any transfers voluntarily.[199] A DIP has all of a trustee's avoidance powers to recover and recapture property for reorganization.[200]

The DIP also has a trustee's responsibilities in bankruptcy and a fiduciary obligation to creditors to protect and preserve the estate.[201] The DIP must account for all monies and property which are in or come into its possession or control, and must also account for all sums expended by it. The DIP is obligated to make accurate periodic reports to the court and the chapter 12 trustee concerning income, cash flow and expenditures.[202] In addition, a chapter 12 DIP may be required to submit other reports and information to the court, trustee or creditors.[203] A DIP is required to open new bank accounts upon filing, and all income and expenditures must be funneled through that account; the account should be labeled so that, in addition to the debtor's name, it indicates that the debtor is a chapter 12 debtor-in-possession.[204] In addition, the DIP must be certain to apprise the trustee of all activity in the chapter 12 case.[205]

17.3.2 Removal of the Farmer As a Debtor-in-Possession

The bankruptcy court, upon request of a party in interest, and after notice and a hearing, may remove a family farmer from operating the farm as a debtor-in-possession for cause—including fraud, dishonesty, incompetence or gross mismanagement, occurring either before or after the commencement of the case.[206] Removal is, however, considered to be an extraordinary remedy.[207]

Upon the debtor's removal, the standing chapter 12 trustee or an appointee of the United States trustee will operate the farm or recommend that the court dismiss or convert the chapter 12 case as circumstances warrant.[208] The trustee may continue the farm operation with the farmer debtor as an employee, but the trustee is not compelled to do so. The trustee may hire a farmer/manager if one is needed, requesting permission under section 327, and may promptly petition the court for plan modification under section 1229 to reflect additional costs.[209]

Once removed a debtor-in-possession can be restored to DIP status and operation of the farm, although this outcome is rare.[210]

17.4 General Principles

17.4.1 The Chapter 12 Trustee

17.4.1.1 Role and Standing of the Trustee

The chapter 12 trustee is an administrative officer with duties similar to those of chapter 13 trustees. The chapter 12 trustee may be the United States trustee, a standing chapter 12 trustee appointed by the United States trustee who serves in all chapter 12 cases, or a disinterested person appointed by the United States trustee.[211] Most districts have appointed a special stand-

---

195 11 U.S.C. § 1203.
196 11 U.S.C. §§ 1107, 1108.
197 11 U.S.C. § 1203.
198 *In re* WWG Indus., Inc., 772 F.2d 810 (11th Cir. 1985); Georgia Pac. Corp. v. Sigma Serv. Corp., 712 F.2d 962 (5th Cir. 1983); *In re* Hartman, 102 B.R. 90 (Bankr. N.D. Tex. 1989); *In re* Hollinrake, 93 B.R. 183 (Bankr. S.D. Iowa 1988); *In re* Russell, 60 B.R. 42 (Bankr. W.D. Ark. 1985); *In re* Diamond, 49 B.R. 754 (Bankr. S.D.N.Y. 1985).
199 *Cf.* 11 U.S.C. § 522(g).
200 8 Collier on Bankruptcy ¶ 1203.02[2] (15th ed. rev.).
201 *In re* Halux, Inc., 665 F.2d 213 (8th Cir. 1981); *In re* J.A.V. Ag., Inc., 154 B.R. 923 (Bankr. W.D. Tex. 1993); *In re* Russell, 60 B.R. 42 (Bankr. W.D. Ark. 1985).
202 *In re* Lawless, 74 B.R. 54 (Bankr. W.D. Mo. 1987), *aff'd*, 79 B.R. 850 (W.D. Mo. 1987); *In re* Paolina, 53 B.R. 399 (Bankr. W.D. Pa. 1985), *aff'd*, 60 B.R. 828 (W.D. Pa. 1986); *In re* Diamond, 49 B.R. 754 (Bankr. S.D.N.Y. 1985).
203 Many trustees require other information to be furnished beyond the schedules so that a clearer picture of the debtor's predicted income and plans can be discerned.
204 This idea may be good practice. However, the United States trustee does not have power to require that the letters "D.I.P." be printed on checks. *See, e.g., In re* Young, 205 B.R. 894 (Bankr. W.D. Tenn. 1997).
205 *Cf.* 11 U.S.C. § 1302(b).
206 11 U.S.C. § 1204(a).
    Compare the conversion provisions of 11 U.S.C. § 1208(d). *See generally* Bruce H. Matson, *Understanding the New Family Farmer Bankruptcy Act*, 21 U. Rich. L. Rev. 521 (1987).
207 *In re* Jessen, 82 B.R. 490 (Bankr. S.D. Iowa 1988); *In re* H & S Transp. Co., 55 B.R. 786 (Bankr. M.D. Tenn. 1985); *In re* Diamond, 49 B.R. 754 (Bankr. S.D.N.Y. 1985).
208 11 U.S.C. § 1204(b)(5).
    However, the trustee cannot propose a plan under chapter 12. *See also* United States Trustee Program, Guidelines For Supervision of Chapter 12 Cases.
209 United States Trustee Program, Guidelines For Supervision of Chapter 12 Cases.
210 11 U.S.C. § 1204(b).
211 11 U.S.C. § 1202; Robiner v. Demczyk, 269 B.R. 167 (N.D. Ohio

ing chapter 12 trustee for administration of family farmer cases. In other districts with modest chapter 12 activity, the standing chapter 13 trustee also serves as the standing chapter 12 trustee although the administration and distribution of funds are segregated from the chapter 13 operation.

The duties of the chapter 12 trustee closely resemble those of a chapter 13 trustee,[212] but the chapter 12 trustee does not have the express duty to investigate the debtor's affairs,[213] unless the court so orders.[214] However, the chapter 12 trustee is empowered to inquire into and examine the affairs of the family farmer debtor to the extent necessary to determine the debtor's eligibility for chapter 12 relief and confirmability of any proposed plan or modified plan.[215] The chapter 12 trustee customarily examines the debtors at the meetings of creditors[216] and also participates in hearings concerning valuation of property subject to lien, confirmation, plan modification, and sale of property.[217] The trustee may also object to creditors' claims and assist in defining and clarifying issues for the parties and the court.[218]

The chapter 12 trustee, like the chapter 13 trustee, is charged by statute with the duty to monitor plan payments.[219] The failure to make payments under a chapter 12 plan is a default which can result in the trustee's filing of a motion to dismiss.[220] The trustee's duties also include periodic reports to the court and solicitation of reports from the debtor for information which bears on eligibility and the plan's confirmability.[221]

When a plan so provides, the debtor and affected creditor(s) consent, and the court approves, the chapter 12 trustee may act as a liquidating agent for property of the estate.[222]

The role of the trustee postconfirmation may be limited. While the trustee can address fraud under 11 U.S.C. §§ 1202(b)(2), 1228(d), 1230 and 1208(d), any examination must have substantial evidence to generate such a duty after confirmation.[223]

17.4.1.2 Payments Made Through the Chapter 12 Trustee and Trustee Compensation

17.4.1.2.1 General

The compensation of chapter 12 trustees and their offices, like those administering chapter 13 cases, is derived from payments made through the chapter 12 plan.[224] A percentage fee is charged against "all payments received by such individual" under the chapter 12 plan. The Code sets out maximum fees to be paid to chapter 12 trustees appointed by the court independent of United States trustees: ten percent of the first $450,000 and no more than three percent of any additional payments.[225] Many districts have set the trustee's surcharge at the ten percent maximum.[226] A chapter 12 trustee may also be allowed additional administrative fees as awarded by the bankruptcy court.[227]

17.4.1.2.2 Challenges to variations in trustee costs paid by different debtors

A number of farmers have raised challenges to the overall chapter 12 trustee compensation scheme.[228] These challenges have generally been rejected. For example, the debtors in an Illinois chapter 12 case asked the court to review the reasonableness of the ten percent commission set for their trustee.[229] The debtors argued that the "longstanding policy of the judicial involvement in compensation paid out of a bankruptcy" autho-

---

2001) (United States trustee must appoint the chapter 12 trustee, but the chapter 12 trustee may not resign from particular cases without permission from the court; submission of resignation to United States trustee is insufficient).

212 *See In re* Teigen, 142 B.R. 397 (Bankr. D. Mont. 1992). *Compare* 11 U.S.C. § 1202 *with* 11 U.S.C. § 1302.

213 *See* 11 U.S.C. § 1302(c) (requiring the trustee to assume investigation duties as described in § 1106(a)(3) and (a)(4) if the debtor is engaged in business).

This provision is not contained in Chapter 12.

214 11 U.S.C. § 1202(b)(2).

Such examination may be ordered *sua sponte* by the court or upon motion of a creditor. *See, e.g., In re* Graven, 84 B.R. 630 (Bankr. W.D. Mo. 1988).

215 *See also* United States Trustee Program, Guidelines for Supervision of Chapter 12 Cases, No. 5; *In re* Roesner, 153 B.R. 328 (Bankr. D. Kan. 1993); *In re* Martens, 98 B.R. 530 (Bankr. D. Colo. 1989). *Compare* 11 U.S.C. § 1202(b) *with* 11 U.S.C. § 704(7). But the trustee's power to object may be limited. *See In re* Teigen, 142 B.R. 397 (Bankr. D. Mont. 1992) (trustee cannot object to claims treatment on behalf of creditors which accept plan or fail to object).

216 United States Trustee Program, Guidelines for Supervision of Chapter 12 Cases, No. 5. 11 U.S.C. § 341 indicates that the United States trustee convenes and presides over the meeting but, in fact, it is usually his designee, the chapter 12 trustee, who conducts the meeting.

217 *In re* Roesner, 153 B.R. 328 (Bankr. D. Kan. 1993); *In re* Martens, 98 B.R. 530 (Bankr. D. Colo. 1989).

218 11 U.S.C. § 1202(b)(3); *In re* Beard, 45 F.3d 113 (6th Cir. 1995); *In re* Jennings, 190 B.R. 863 (Bankr. W.D. Mo. 1995); *In re* Martens, 98 B.R. 530 (Bankr. D. Colo. 1989).

219 11 U.S.C. §§ 1202(b)(4), 1208(c)(6).

220 The trustee is a party in interest under 11 U.S.C. § 1208(c), with standing to bring a motion to dismiss. *See, e.g., In re* A-1 Trash Pick-Up, Inc., 802 F.2d 774 (4th Cir. 1986); *In re* Tiana Queen Motel, Inc., 749 B.R. 146 (2d Cir. 1984).

221 11 U.S.C. § 1202(b)(3); United States Trustee Program, Guidelines for Supervision of Chapter 12 Cases.

See discussion of trustee's duties and responsibilities in *In re* Mouser, 99 B.R. 803 (Bankr. S.D. Ohio 1989).

222 *In re* Lindsay, 142 B.R. 447 (Bankr. W.D. Okla. 1992); *In re* Tyndall, 97 B.R. 266 (Bankr. E.D.N.C. 1989).

223 *In re* Gross, 121 B.R. 587 (Bankr. D.S.D. 1990).

224 28 U.S.C. § 586(e).

225 28 U.S.C. § 586(e)(1)(B)(2).

In some circumstances, however, the trustee can also receive fees in a case even if there is not a confirmed plan. *See* Stahn v. Haeckel, 920 F.2d 555 (8th Cir. 1990).

226 If a district has numerous chapter 12 cases with successful plans filed, it can be anticipated that the percentage there will be lowered.

227 *See* § 17.2.4, *supra*.

228 *See, e.g.,* Greseth v. Fed. Land Bank (*In re* Greseth), 78 B.R. 936 (D. Minn. 1987).

229 *In re* Marriott, 156 B.R. 803 (Bankr. S.D. Ill. 1993).

rized the court to conduct this review.[230] The debtors further argued that payment of the commission would affect their ability to reorganize and was inconsistent with the legislative intent underlying chapter 12.[231] The court rejected the debtors' request, holding that Congress had vested the executive branch with the authority to set fees and had "eliminated the judiciary's role in overseeing compensation for such trustees."[232] Accordingly the court held that it had "no authority to review the reasonableness" of the fee.[233]

The fee system has also been challenged as unconstitutional under the uniformity of laws provision of Article I, Section 8, of the United States Constitution.[234] This challenge focused on the practical effect of the statutory maximum, under which some debtors may have to pay a ten percent trustee's fee and others may pay less. The debtors argued that trustee's fees vary between the states, the United States trustee regions and even between different trustees in the same region.[235]

This challenge, however, was also rejected.[236] The court held that the compensation system is "designed to award the trustee reasonable compensation for the services rendered in each case."[237] The court reasoned that historically trustee's fees have always been judged on a reasonableness basis, with no guarantee of uniformity on a debtor-by-debtor basis. The court stated, "easonableness, and not uniformity, is the criterion for expenses of administration."[238]

17.4.1.2.3 Avoiding the trustee commission for certain payments

While farm debtors have been unsuccessful in challenging the specific percentage fee applied, there has been some success in challenging the application of the fee to all payments made by the debtor. Section 586(e)(2) provides that the trustee is to collect her percentage fee from "all payments *received by such individual* [the trustee] *under plans* in the cases under chapter 12 or 13."[239] Some debtors have argued that if they make a payment directly to the creditor, without using the trustee, the trustee's percentage fee should not be assessed. This issue, referred to herein as the direct payment issue, has produced numerous reported decisions, with the result being three lines of cases with conflicting holdings.

One line of cases holds that a debtor is not allowed to make direct payments to impaired creditors, and therefore there is no option of using direct payments to avoid the trustee's fee.[240] However, even under this line of cases, a debtor would be allowed to make direct payments to an unimpaired creditor.[241] One case offered an extension of this approach in holding that a voluntary agreement with a creditor did not constitute an impaired claim for purposes of determining the trustee's fee. Because the agreement was voluntary, and because the claim was not provided for in the plan, the debtor did not need to apply the trustee's percentage fee to payments made to that creditor.[242] A second line of cases holds that although certain payments to impaired creditors can be made directly by the debtor, the trustee's fee must still be assessed on these payments.[243]

A third line of cases finds that direct payments to certain creditors with impaired claims can be made and that the trustee's fee does not apply to these direct payments.[244] In jurisdictions that have adopted this reasoning, debtors may propose paying some of their creditors directly in order to minimize the amount paid to the trustee. This issue is discussed further in § 17.5.7.3, *infra*.

17.4.1.2.4 Does the trustee receive a fee on its fee?

Another trustee compensation issue producing significant litigation and causing a split in authority is whether the chapter 12 trustee should receive her ten percent commission only on payments made by the debtors to their creditors, or whether the ten percent fee also should be computed on the money paid to the trustee herself. It again turns on an interpretation of section 586(e), which provides that the trustee shall collect "such percentage fee from all payments received."[245]

The Tenth Circuit addressed this issue in *Foulston v. BDT Farms*.[246] The United States trustee's office argued that the standing trustee was to be paid an amount equal to ten percent of all money received by the trustee, that is, ten percent of the amount to be paid to creditors plus ten percent of the trustee's fee itself. This results in a trustee's fee of 11.1111%. The

---

230 *Id.* at 804.
231 *Id.*
232 *Id.* at 805.
233 *Id.* (relying on *In re* Schollett, 980 F.2d 639, 645 (10th Cir. 1992); *In re* Savage, 67 B.R. 700, 705, 706 (D.R.I. 1986); *In re* Citrowski, 72 B.R. 613, 615 (Bankr. D. Minn. 1987)). *But see In re* Melita, 91 B.R. 358, 363 (Bankr. E.D. Pa. 1988); *In re* Sousa, 46 B.R. 343, 346, 347 (Bankr. D.R.I. 1985) ("effectively overruled" by *Savage*).
234 *In re* Westpfahl, 168 B.R. 337 (Bankr. C.D. Ill. 1994).
235 The debtors in *Westpfahl* reported fees of five percent in Nebraska, seven percent in the Northern District of Iowa, and ten percent in the Central District of Illinois. They further alleged that once a standing trustee reaches her statutory maximum compensation, the percentage fee will be reduced, to the advantage of debtors filing subsequently but not debtors who filed previously.
236 *Westpfahl*, 168 B.R. at 360.
237 *Id.*
238 *Id.*
239 28 U.S.C. § 586(e)(2) (emphasis added).

240 *In re* Williams, 408 B.R. 709 (Bankr. W.D. Tenn. 2009) (check in possession of debtor at commencement of case jointly payable to debtor and creditor for prepetition sale of secured crops would be turned over to creditor, with debtor required to pay a trustee fee). *See, e.g.*, Fulkrod v. Savage (*In re* Fulkrod), 973 F.2d 801 (9th Cir. 1992); *In re* C.A. Jackson Ranch Co., 181 B.R. 552 (Bankr. E.D. Okla. 1995).
241 *See, e.g.*, *In re* Finkbine, 94 B.R. 461, 464 (Bankr. S.D. Ohio 1988).
242 *In re* Kosmicki, 161 B.R. 828 (Bankr. D. Neb. 1993).
243 *See, e.g.*, *In re* Marriott, 161 B.R. 816 (Bankr. S.D. Ill. 1993).
244 *See, e.g.*, Michel v. Beard (*In re* Beard), 45 F.3d 113 (6th Cir. 1995); Wagner v. Armstrong (*In re* Armstrong), 36 F.3d 723 (8th Cir. 1994); *In re* McCann, 202 B.R. 824 (Bankr. N.D.N.Y. 1996); Westpfahl v. Clark (*In re* Westpfahl), 168 B.R. 337 (Bankr. C.D. Ill. 1994).
245 28 U.S.C. § 586(e).
246 21 F.3d 1019 (10th Cir. 1994).

debtors argued that the trustee should receive fees in an amount equal to ten percent of the payments made under the plan to creditors. The Tenth Circuit reversed the lower courts, and gave deference under the *Chevron* standard to the interpretation of the United States trustee's office.

The *BDT Farms* decision has received significant criticism and has been specifically and adamantly rejected by the Court of Appeals for the Eighth Circuit in *Pelofsky v. Wallace*.[247]

17.4.1.3 Role of the Chapter 12 Trustee upon Removal of the Family Farmer As a Debtor-in-Possession

If the bankruptcy court removes the family farmer as the debtor-in-possession,[248] the chapter 12 trustee has all the powers of a chapter 7 trustee or trustee appointed in a chapter 11 case concerning operation of the business.[249] This issue is discussed in § 17.3.1, *supra*.

17.4.2 What Constitutes Property of the Estate

"Property of the estate" in chapter 12 cases is similar to that in chapter 13 cases.[250] In chapter 12, property of the estate subject to administration in the case includes, in addition to all of the debtor's property acquired prepetition:

- All property which the debtor acquires after the commencement of the case but before the case is closed, dismissed, or converted to a case under chapter 7, whichever happens first;[251] and
- Earnings from services performed by the debtor after the commencement of the case but before the case is closed, dismissed or converted to a case under chapter 7, whichever occurs first.[252]

The debtor remains in possession of all his or her property, except under the following circumstances:

- If the debtor is removed as a debtor-in-possession;
- If a confirmed plan or order confirming a plan otherwise provides;
- If relief from the automatic stay is obtained which may allow removal of property from the debtor by state process; or
- If the debtor affirmatively abandons property preconfirmation pursuant to section 554.

The property of an active family farmer's estate usually contains types of property with which an attorney who does not work primarily with farmers will be unfamiliar and may overlook. For example, the farmer may:

- Be entitled to payments under government programs;[253]
- Have crop or dairy base, crop allotments, or other price support entitlements which have value, and may be sold or increased;[254]
- Own shares in farmers' cooperatives;
- Participate in conservation, reforestation or loan programs with concomitant obligations for debtor performance;[255]
- Be entitled to payments on contracts or rental arrangements due both prepetition and postpetition.[256]

All may have value; all are property of the estate which must be accounted for in the debtor's schedules and for plan and confirmation purposes.

17.4.3 Exemptions, Lien Avoidance, and Recapture Powers

17.4.3.1 Exemptions Available to Family Farmers Under Chapter 12

The exemptions available to individual family farmers under chapter 12 include those available in other bankruptcy chapters.[257] In addition, some farm states have specific exemption laws that apply specifically to farmers. For example, Minnesota law provides that a farmer is entitled to exemption in "farm machines and implements used in farming operations" not exceeding $13,000 in value.[258] State law may, however, also provide that exemptions are only available to individuals, eliminating the ability of partnership or corporate owned property to be exempted.

---

247 102 F.3d 350 (8th Cir. 1996). *See also In re* Westpfahl, 168 B.R. 337 (Bankr. C.D. Ill. 1994); *In re* Wallace, 167 B.R. 531 (Bankr. E.D. Mo. 1994). *Cf.* Kathleen A. Laughron, *The Standing Chapter 13 Trustee's Percentage Fee: Solving Algebraic Equation*, 24 Creighton L. Rev. 823 (1991).
248 11 U.S.C. § 1204.
249 11 U.S.C. § 1202(b)(5). *See* § 17.3.1, *supra*.
250 *See* § 2.6, *supra*. Compare 11 U.S.C. §§ 541, 1207 *with* 11 U.S.C. § 1306.
251 Included are postpetition inheritances and life insurance proceeds. *In re* Hart, 151 B.R. 84 (Bankr. W.D. Tex. 1993); *In re* Cook, 148 B.R. 273 (Bankr. W.D. Mich. 1992) (inheritances and lottery winnings); *In re* Martin, 130 B.R. 951 (Bankr. N.D. Iowa 1991); *In re* Cornell, 95 B.R. 219 (Bankr. W.D. Okla. 1989).
252 11 U.S.C. § 1207(a); *In re* Clark, 186 B.R. 249 (Bankr. W.D. Mo. 1995); *In re* White, 151 B.R. 247 (Bankr. D.N.M. 1993).
253 *See, e.g., In re* Winterroth, 97 B.R. 454 (Bankr. C.D. Ill. 1988) (PIK certificates). *See* FarmPro Servs., Inc. v. Brown, 276 B.R. 620 (D.N.D. 2002) (property of the estate includes crop disaster payments received postpetition by chapter 12 debtors); *In re* Boyett, 250 B.R. 817 (Bankr. S.D. Ga. 2000) (FSA payments under disaster relief program as property of the estate in chapter 7). *But see In re* Stallings, 290 B.R. 777 (Bankr. D. Idaho 2003) (disaster relief payment received postpetition under program that did not exist until after debtor filed bankruptcy was not property of the estate).
254 *See In re* Kocher, 78 B.R. 844 (Bankr. S.D. Ohio 1987).
255 *See In re* Bremer, 104 B.R. 999 (Bankr. W.D. Mo. 1989) (CRP payments and unharvested crops are property of the estate); *In re* Hunerdosse, 85 B.R. 999 (Bankr. S.D. Iowa 1988); *In re* Claeys, 81 B.R. 985 (Bankr. D.N.D. 1987); *In re* Dunning, 77 B.R. 789 (Bankr. D. Mont. 1987).
256 *In re* Winterroth, 97 B.R. 454 (Bankr. C.D. Ill. 1988).
257 11 U.S.C. § 522(b). *See* Ch. 10, *supra*.
258 Minn. Stat. § 550.37(5).

Because most farm indebtedness has been incurred by both farmer and spouse, or has been cosigned by the spouse, many chapter 12 petitions will be joint petitions,[259] permitting the use of two sets of exemptions.[260] Moreover, most courts consider spouses who participate to some degree in the farming operation, either physically or as a record-keeper, a farmer for purposes of exemption.[261] Similarly, the fact that a farmer or spouse may have other occupations as well as farming may not preclude the exemption and subsequent lien avoidance of farm property as tools of the trade.[262]

Most attempts to exempt farm program payments have been rejected.[263] However, in the recent case of *In re Wilson*,[264] the court held that the farmer debtor's payments under the Direct Payment Program could be exempted under Iowa Code § 627.6(8)(a), which allows an exemption for "any public assistance benefit." Program payments that are closely tied to exempt homestead property may also be considered exempt as arising from the homestead property.[265]

Putting farm operations into the name of a legal entity instead of the farmer's name can affect the farmer's ability to exercise his or her exemption rights. For example, under some state laws, property that is owned by a corporation or limited liability entity cannot be claimed by the individual farmer as a homestead.[266]

17.4.3.2 Exemptions for "Tools of Trade" and "Livestock"

The federal exemptions and almost all state-formulated exemptions provide protection for "tools of trade."[267] This category is of special interest to farmers, allowing exemption of the tools utilized in the farming operation.[268] A minority of courts exempt farm implements as "tools of trade" only if they are smaller, hand-held tools,[269] but the majority view is that farm equipment and implements may be exempted under a functional or "use" test subject to dollar value limitations.[270]

A number of courts have addressed the issue of whether a tools of the trade exemption allows for the exemption of certain types of livestock. The Seventh Circuit did not allow the exemption of a dairy herd as well as a tractor, holding that large capital assets could not be tools of the trade; the exemption was limited to small items, "tools" in the ordinary sense.[271] But the Second Circuit has held that bulls used in a dairy operation fell under the Vermont state "tools of the trade" exemption.[272] Similarly, the Tenth Circuit has held that breeding stock could be "tools of the trade."[273]

Another federal and common state exemption of special interest to farmers is for livestock retained by the farmer for personal and family use, for example, consumption or production for the debtor and his or her dependents alone. The emphasis is upon the exclusive family use of the livestock. Livestock which is part of the farming operation in general thus cannot be exempted under this limited provision.[274]

---

259 As allowed by 11 U.S.C. § 302.
260 11 U.S.C. § 522(b).
   However, two sets of exemptions may not be available when a state exemption, if chosen or mandated, allows only one set of exemptions for joint petitioners. *See, e.g.*, *In re* Talmadge, 832 F.2d 1120 (9th Cir. 1987) (Calif. law); Stevens v. Pike County Bank, 829 F.2d 693 (8th Cir. 1987) (Ark. law).
261 *See, e.g.*, *In re* Zimmel, 185 B.R. 786 (Bankr. D. Minn. 1995); *In re* Schroeder, 62 B.R. 604 (Bankr. D. Kan. 1986); Middleton v. Farmers State Bank, 45 B.R. 744 (Bankr. D. Minn. 1985); *In re* Decker, 34 B.R. 640 (Bankr. N.D. Ind. 1983); *In re* Flake, 32 B.R. 360 (Bankr. W.D. Wis. 1983); Thorp Credit & Thrift Co. v. Pommerer, 10 B.R. 935 (Bankr. D. Minn. 1981). *See also* Susan A. Schneider, *Who Owns the Family Farm: The Struggle to Determine the Property Rights of Farm Wives*, 14 N. Ill. U. L. Rev. 689 (1994). *Contra In re* Indvik, 118 B.R. 993 (Bankr. N.D. Iowa 1990).
262 *See, e.g.*, Production Credit Ass'n of St. Cloud v. LaFond (*In re* LaFond), 791 F.2d 623 (8th Cir. 1986); *In re* Lampe, 278 B.R. 205 (B.A.P. 10th Cir. 2002); *In re* Meadows, 75 B.R. 357 (W.D. Va. 1987); *In re* Schley, 2011 WL 13445 (Bankr. N.D. Iowa 2011) (finding farm wife, a school principal, was farmer for purposes of lien avoidance, based on her long time involvement with farming operation); *In re* Smith, 78 B.R. 922 (Bankr. S.D. Iowa 1987); *In re* Rasmussen, 54 B.R. 965 (Bankr. W.D. Mo. 1985); *In re* Weinbrenner, 53 B.R. 571 (Bankr. W.D. Wis. 1985). *Contra In re* Samuel, 36 B.R. 312 (Bankr. E.D. Va. 1984). *See generally* §§ 10.2.2.7, 10.4.2.4, *supra*; § 17.4.3.3, *infra*.
263 *See, e.g.*, *In re* Pritchard, 75 B.R. 877, 878 (Bankr. D. Minn. 1987) (rejecting claim that federal program payments were exempt under nonbankruptcy federal law); *In re* Weyland, 63 B.R. 854 (Bankr. E.D. Wis. 1986) (rejecting claim that Dairy Termination Program payments were exempt earnings).
264 305 B.R. 4 (N.D. Iowa 2004).
265 *In re* Hardage, 69 B.R. 681 (Bankr. N.D. Tex. 1987) (exempting a land-based payment tied to the debtor's exempt homestead), *rev'd on other grounds*, 837 F.2d 1319 (5th Cir. 1988).
266 *See In re* Arnhoelter, 431 B.R. 453 (Bankr. E.D. Wis. 2010) (debtor who did not personally own the home occupied at the time that a judgment was docketed, given that ownership was in debtor's limited liability company, could not claim a homestead exemption under Wisconsin law, even though he later dissolved the limited liability company and acquired title).
267 *See* § 10.2.2.7, *supra*.
268 Production Credit Ass'n of St. Cloud v. LaFond, 791 F.2d 623 (8th Cir. 1986); Augustine v. United States, 675 F.2d 582 (3d Cir. 1982); *In re* Hrncirik, 138 B.R. 835 (Bankr. N.D. Tex. 1992); *In re* Weinbrenner, 53 B.R. 571 (Bankr. W.D. Wis. 1985) (and cases cited therein); Middleton v. Farmers State Bank, 45 B.R. 744 (Bankr. D. Minn. 1985).
269 *See, e.g.*, *In re* Patterson, 825 F.2d 1140 (7th Cir. 1987) (addressing exemption under federal 11 U.S.C. § 522(d) only); O'Neal v. United States, 20 B.R. 12 (Bankr. E.D. Mo. 1982); Yparrea v. Roswell Production Credit Ass'n, 16 B.R. 33 (Bankr. D.N.M. 1981).
270 Production Credit Ass'n of St. Cloud v. LaFond, 791 F.2d 623 (8th Cir. 1986); Augustine v. United States, 675 F.2d 582 (3d Cir. 1982); *In re* Mutchler, 95 B.R. 748 (Bankr. D. Mont. 1989); *In re* Thompson, 82 B.R. 985 (Bankr. W.D. Wis. 1988); *In re* Duss, 79 B.R. 821 (Bankr. W.D. Wis. 1987); *In re* Schyma, 68 B.R. 52 (Bankr. D. Minn. 1985); *In re* Brzezinski, 65 B.R. 336 (Bankr. W.D. Wis. 1985) (farm function); *In re* Yoder, 32 B.R. 777 (Bankr. W.D. Pa. 1983); *In re* Liming, 22 B.R. 740 (Bankr. W.D. Okla. 1982), *rev'd sub nom.* Cent. Nat'l Bank & Trust Co. v. Liming, 797 F.2d 895 (10th Cir. 1986).
271 *In re* Patterson, 825 F.2d 1140 (7th Cir. 1987).
272 Parrotte v. Sensenich (*In re* Parrotte), 22 F.3d 472 (2d Cir. 1994).
273 *In re* Heape, 886 F.2d 280, 283 (10th Cir. 1989).
274 *In re* Thompson, 750 F.2d 628 (8th Cir. 1984); Patterson v. Abbotsford State Bank, 64 B.R. 120 (W.D. Wis. 1986), *aff'd*, 825 F.2d 1140 (7th Cir. 1987); *In re* Meadows, 75 B.R. 357 (W.D. Va. 1987); *In re*

17.4.3.3 Lien Avoidance Under Section 522(f)[275]

Section 522(f) lien avoidance provisions for exempt property and tools of trade impaired by judicial liens and non-possessory, non-purchase money security interests are available for farmers under *all* bankruptcy chapters.[276] In many cases, a farmer will be able to recapture some farm equipment and reduce the amount of repayment to a secured creditor because a blanket non-purchase money interest covers the equipment.[277] Debtors may also be able to avoid liens under these provisions in proceeds after postpetition sale of equipment.[278] Lien avoidance may also free property for needed sale or trade. Consequently it is important for the farmer's attorney to check security agreements and Uniform Commercial Code (UCC) filings to ascertain whether the security interest is purchase money.[279]

Whenever possible chapter 12 lien avoidance should be undertaken at the outset of the case, because the avoidance of liens can have an effect upon the amount and nature of repayment to creditors and enhance feasibility.[280] However, the Code contains no time limit on such debtor action. In some jurisdictions avoidance of judicial liens may also be accomplished by valuations and provisions in the chapter 12 plan which reduce judgment creditors to unsecured creditors, provided all such creditors have notice of those provisions, an opportunity to object, and the plan is confirmed.[281]

17.4.3.4 Section 552 Lien Dissolution

Section 552 governs the postpetition effect of a security interest, dissolving that interest with respect to most collateral obtained after filing. This protection is particularly important in farm bankruptcy in that most farm security agreements include an "after-acquired" property clause that provides that the security interest will attach to property that the debtor acquires in the future. Section 552 automatically cuts off the creditor's security interest in certain after-acquired property.

While the general rule is that the after-acquired clause of the security agreement does not apply after filing, a very significant exception applies to collateral that falls into the categories "proceeds, product, offspring, or profits of" property covered by the security agreement and existing at the time of filing.

For family farmers, this lien dissolution means that creditors' security interests in the future production of certain types of farm products are automatically eliminated. For example, most farm creditors who take blanket security interests have liens on future crop production. Section 552(a) automatically dissolves security interests in future crops and proceeds therefrom.[282] However, section 552 does not apply to crops which are in the ground at the time the bankruptcy petition is filed,[283] nor does it apply to the proceeds of prepetition crops—it only applies to crops planted after filing and their proceeds.[284]

Section 552(a) also can dissolve security interests in after-acquired equipment.[285] However, postpetition rents may still be subject to a security interest unless a debtor can show an appropriate equitable basis for their dissolution; if the creditor

---

Wiford, 105 B.R. 992 (Bankr. N.D. Okla. 1989); *In re* Simmons, 86 B.R. 160 (Bankr. S.D. Iowa 1988); *In re* Duss, 79 B.R. 821 (Bankr. W.D. Wis. 1987) (hay not household good or tool of trade for exemption purposes); *In re* Eakes, 69 B.R. 497 (Bankr. W.D. Mo. 1987); *In re* Sticha, 60 B.R. 717 (Bankr. D. Minn. 1986); *In re* Newbury, 70 B.R. 1 (Bankr. D. Kan. 1985); *In re* Yoder, 32 B.R. 777 (Bankr. W.D. Pa. 1983). *See In re* Wilson, 738 So. 2d 17 (La. 1999) (answering question certified by the Court of Appeals for the Fifth Circuit, 162 F.3d 378 (1998), the state Supreme Court applied a functional test; animals used for farm work such as a draft horse may be exempt, but animals which produce the product of the farming operation such as dairy cows are not). *Contra In re* Cook, 66 B.R. 3 (Bankr. W.D. Wis. 1985) (cows specialized tools of trade with hay to feed for one year); *In re* Walkington, 42 B.R. 67 (Bankr. W.D. Mich. 1984) (dairy cattle as tools of trade).

275 For a more complete discussion of these lien avoidance provisions, see § 10.4.2, *supra*.

276 Augustine v. United States, 675 F.2d 582 n.3 (3d Cir. 1982); *In re* Currie, 34 B.R. 745 (D. Kan. 1983); *In re* Simmons, 86 B.R. 160 (Bankr. S.D. Iowa 1988); *In re* Hunerdosse, 85 B.R. 999 (Bankr. S.D. Iowa 1988); *In re* Dykstra, 80 B.R. 128 (Bankr. N.D. Iowa 1987) (chapter 12); *In re* Ptacek, 78 B.R. 986 (Bankr. D.N.D. 1987) (chapter 12). *But see* Farmers State Bank of Oakley v. Schroeder, 62 B.R. 604 (Bankr. D. Kan. 1986).

277 Production Credit Ass'n of St. Cloud v. LaFond, 791 F.2d 623 (8th Cir. 1986) (chapter 7); *In re* Hall, 752 F.2d 582 (11th Cir. 1985) (chapter 13); *In re* Thompson, 750 F.2d 628 (8th Cir. 1984) (chapter 11); *In re* Ptacek, 78 B.R. 986 (Bankr. D.N.D. 1987). *See* § 10.4.2.4, *supra*.

Because lien avoidance is tied to eligibility for the underlying exemption, if the law governing the exemption claim limits the availability of exemptions to individuals, then corporations and partnerships may not be able to accomplish lien avoidance.

278 *In re* Brzezinski, 65 B.R. 336 (Bankr. W.D. Wis. 1985).

279 The typical security interest taken by Farm Service Agency is a good example of a blanket security interest which usually is largely non-purchase money, non-possessory. Sovereign immunity does not apply to the federal government for lien avoidance. 11 U.S.C. § 106; Flick v. United States, 47 B.R. 440 (W.D. Pa. 1985).

280 One court has allowed the effect of section 522(f) lien avoidance to take place only upon entry of discharge in the chapter 12 case. *In re* Simmons, 86 B.R. 160 (Bankr. S.D. Iowa 1988); *In re* Hunerdosse,

85 B.R. 999 (Bankr. S.D. Iowa 1988).

Failure to reserve rights to pursue lien avoidance in negotiated settlements incorporated into chapter 12 plans might result in their loss. *In re* Wickersheim, 107 B.R. 177 (Bankr. E.D. Wis. 1989).

281 *See* § 10.4.2.4, *supra*.

282 *In re* Borg, 88 B.R. 288 (Bankr. D. Mont. 1988); *In re* Hill, 83 B.R. 522 (Bankr. E.D. Tenn. 1988); Randall v. Bank of Viola, 58 B.R. 289 (Bankr. C.D. Ill. 1986); *In re* Lorenz, 57 B.R. 734 (Bankr. N.D. Ill. 1986); *In re* Liebe, 41 B.R. 965 (Bankr. N.D. Iowa 1984) (postpetition PIK payments); *In re* Sheehan, 38 B.R. 859 (Bankr. D.S.D. 1984).

283 *In re* Klaus, 247 B.R. 761 (Bankr. C.D. Ill. 2000); *In re* Vanasdale, 64 B.R. 92 (Bankr. N.D. Ohio 1986); Randall v. Bank of Viola, 58 B.R. 289 (Bankr. C.D. Ill. 1986); *In re* Beck, 61 B.R. 671 (Bankr. D. Neb. 1985).

284 *In re* Smith, 72 B.R. 344 (Bankr. S.D. Ohio 1987); *In re* Wallman, 71 B.R. 125 (Bankr. D.S.D. 1987); *In re* Lorenz, 57 B.R. 734 (Bankr. N.D. Ill. 1986); *In re* Sheehan, 38 B.R. 859 (Bankr. D.S.D. 1984). *But see* Fed. Deposit Ins. Corp. v. Coones, 954 F.2d 596 (10th Cir. 1992) (postpetition crops produced with prepetition crop funds equal postpetition crops still secured under section 552(b)).

285 *In re* Butler, 97 B.R. 508 (Bankr. E.D. Ark. 1988).

is oversecured, the court might consider this dissolution proper under section 552(b).[286]

Two decisions in northern states apply section 552(a) lien dissolution to milk and proceeds.[287] However, most courts, relying on the language of section 552(b), hold that section 552(a) does not apply to the proceeds, products, offspring, rents, or profits of property in which a valid prepetition security interest attached.[288] Instead, section 552(b) applies, which holds such security interests valid unless the court, based on the equity of the case, orders otherwise.[289]

Another issue which has been litigated is how section 552 applies to farm program payments.[290] Critical to this issue is a determination of whether the debtor had an interest in the farm program at the time of filing. If so, arguably, the security interest attached, and after-acquired postpetition property is not at issue.

In other contexts, when deciding at what time a farmer has a cognizable interest in a federal farm program, most courts have considered whether or not the contract was signed prepetition. If it was, it can be argued that the debtor had a right to payment at that point in time.[291] With respect to disaster assistance, the courts have not looked to the date that the contract was signed, but considered whether the disaster legislation was enacted prepetition.[292] If it was, courts have held that the debtor had at least a contingent right to the assistance at that time.[293] For additional discussion of the federal farm programs at issue, see § 17.4.11, *infra*.

---

286   11 U.S.C. § 552(b); *In re* Hollinrake, 93 B.R. 183 (Bankr. S.D. Iowa 1988).
287   *In re* Lawrence, 56 B.R. 727 (D. Minn. 1984); *In re* Pigeon, 49 B.R. 657 (Bankr. D.N.D. 1985).
288   Smith v. Dairymen, Inc., 790 F.2d 1107 (4th Cir. 1986); *In re* Neilson, 48 B.R. 273 (D.N.D. 1985); *In re* Rankin, 49 B.R. 565 (Bankr. W.D. Mo. 1985); United States v. Hollie, 42 B.R. 111 (Bankr. M.D. Ga. 1984).
289   Some courts have used the language of section 552(b) which allows the lien dissolution even as to those security interests outlined therein upon "equitable" grounds to dissolve milk assignment liens. *See, e.g., In re* Delbridge, 61 B.R. 484 (Bankr. E.D. Mich. 1986). *See also* United Va. Bank v. Slab Fork Coastal Co., 784 F.2d 1188 (4th Cir. 1986) (*dicta*).
      At least two cases have addressed this "equitable" exception and found it to have application when the debtor uses assets which would otherwise be available to unsecured creditors to enhance the value of a secured creditor's collateral. J. Catton Farms, Inc. v. First Nat'l Bank of Chicago, 779 F.2d 1242 (7th Cir. 1985); *In re* Vill. Properties, Ltd., 723 F.2d 441 (5th Cir. 1984).
290   In the 1970s and 1980s, courts struggled with the proper characterization of rights under federal farm programs and what description is needed in order for attachment and perfection of an Article 9 security interest. *See, e.g., In re* Kingsley, 865 F.2d 975, 979 (8th Cir. 1989). The prevailing trend is for farm program payments to be considered "general intangibles," "contract rights," or "accounts." *Id.* Because most lenders now include these categories in their security agreements, in addition to "crops and proceeds of crops," the proper description is not often at issue.
291   *See, e.g.,* Schneider v. Nazar (*In re* Schneider), 864 F.2d 683 (10th Cir. 1988).
292   *See, e.g.,* Drewes v. Vote (*In re* Vote), 276 F.3d 1024 (8th Cir. 2002).
293   Most of the litigation in this area has involved the question of

Section 552(a) releases collateral from a security agreement so that:

- The collateral may be repledged to another creditor to secure new financing for the coming crop year;
- The debtor need not get permission to use the proceeds or cash collateral from the sale of the crops;
- The debtor need not provide adequate protection upon the freed crops; and
- The value of crops will not be counted in the calculation of the value of the secured creditor's claim.

17.4.3.5 Other Avoidance and Recapture Powers of the Family Farmer Debtor-in-Possession

17.4.3.5.1 In general

A chapter 12 debtor-in-possession has the same powers to avoid liens and recapture property as trustees under chapter 7 and 11 and debtors-in-possession under chapter 11.[294] These avoidance and recapture abilities are analyzed elsewhere in this treatise.[295] This subsection concentrates on avoidance and recapture issues of special interest to farmers. It should be remembered that, unlike the situation in consumer bankruptcies, because the family farmer is characterized as a debtor-in-possession, transfers and liens can be avoided for the benefit of the chapter 12 estate without regard to the voluntariness of the transfer or the property involved's eligibility for exemption.[296] However, when a debtor has pledged property to enable the use of cash collateral during the pendency of chapter 12 case, it may be subsequently impermissible to recapture that property by a form of lien avoidance.[297]

17.4.3.5.2 Recovery of property as a fraudulent transfer[298]

In limited circumstances, farm property which has been lost by forced sale can be recaptured under section 548(a)(2) if its transfer was made for less than reasonably equivalent value; *and*:

- The debtor was insolvent or made insolvent by the transfer;[299] *or*

---

      whether the farm program payment is property of a chapter 7 estate. *See* Susan A. Schneider, *Who Gets the Check: Determining When Federal Farm Program Payments are Property of the Bankruptcy Estate*, 84 Neb. L. Rev. 469 (2005).
294   11 U.S.C. § 1203; *In re* Teigen, 123 B.R. 887 (Bankr. D. Mont. 1991). *See also* 8 Collier on Bankruptcy ¶ 1203.02[2] (15th ed. rev.). *See generally* Thomas H. Jackson, *Avoiding Powers in Bankruptcy*, 36 Stan. L. Rev. 725 (Feb. 1984).
295   *See* § 10.4.2.6, *supra*.
296   *Cf.* 11 U.S.C. § 522(g), (h).
297   *In re* Gilbert, 147 B.R. 801 (Bankr. W.D. Okla. 1992).
298   *See also* § 10.4.2.6.5, *supra*.
299   11 U.S.C. § 548(a)(1)(B).
      Insolvency is a modified balance sheet test. *See* 11 U.S.C. § 101(32). In most cases there is no contest concerning the debtor's insolvency; it is readily apparent from the schedules and circumstances. However, when it is not readily apparent, the debtor-in-

- The debtor was engaged in business or was about to engage in business or a transaction for which any property remaining with the debtor was an unreasonably small capital;[300] or
- The debtor intended to incur debt that would be beyond the debtor's ability to pay.[301]

An additional basis for the recovery of property may be found if a transfer was made for the benefit of an insider or an obligation was incurred for the benefit of an insider, under an employment contract and not in the ordinary course of business.[302] Refer to § 10.4.2.6.5, *supra*, for a discussion of setting aside fraudulent transfers.

17.4.3.5.3 Preferential transfers[303]

Several kinds of transfers to farm creditors may be preferential, subject to recapture under section 547(b). Recovery of preferences can provide the farmer with needed working capital, can redistribute the debtor's assets more equitably among creditors, or can go to satisfy secured debts. Payments made to undersecured creditors, when it can be demonstrated that the payments were applied to the unsecured portion of the indebtedness, may also be recoverable.[304] In addition, the debtor may be able to avoid as a preference extra security granted within ninety days prior to the bankruptcy filing. For example, there may be a preference when a creditor adds as security government payments due the farmer, but not in existence until the ninety-day preference period.[305] Postpetition transfers may also be recovered by the chapter 12 trustee.[306]

Transfers to "insider creditors" made for a full year before the bankruptcy filing are vulnerable to recapture.[307] This situation is likely to arise in a family farm bankruptcy, as there is often reliance on relatives for financial assistance. A debtor who made preferential payments to relatives classified as insiders may be forced to recapture the funds as a preference. Failure to do so could violate the debtor's fiduciary duty as trustee and could be used as evidence of fraud.

Refer to § 10.4.2.6.4, *supra*, for a further discussion of preferences.

17.4.3.5.4 Avoidance of improperly perfected security interests[308]

The chapter 12 debtor-in-possession also is entitled to use the "strong-arm powers" of a trustee, including the power to avoid unperfected security interests.[309] Attorneys for farmers are well advised to check all creditors' security interests to determine whether they have properly attached and were perfected.[310]

Refer to §§ 10.4.2.6.2, 10.4.2.6.3, *supra*, for a further discussion of the strong arm powers that may be available.

17.4.3.5.5 Redemption and cure

After the commencement of a bankruptcy case, there is a breathing spell when all deadlines are temporarily suspended, and when the debtor-in-possession is given an opportunity to examine the estate, its assets, and any choses in action. Section 108(b) provides that if nonbankruptcy law, an order issued in a nonbankruptcy proceeding, or an agreement fixes the time within which the debtor may file a pleading, demand, notice, proof of claim or loss, cure a default, or perform any similar act, *and* that period has not expired before the filing of the debtor's petition, the debtor-in-possession may be given sixty days from the bankruptcy filing to act. This "breathing spell" may extend the debtor-in-possession's time to act. However if, as of the date of filing, the period remaining under the nonbankruptcy law, order, or agreement is longer than sixty days, the debtor-in-possession can act within that time period and section 108(b) will not operate to extend the period for performance.[311]

---

possession can either demonstrate that the debtor was insolvent at the time of transfer or show such insolvency existed before and after the transfer by retrogression. See, e.g., Kanasky v. Randolph, 27 B.R. 953 (Bankr. D. Conn. 1983).

However, it must be remembered that any debt satisfaction by the transfer must be subtracted from the debtor's liabilities for the balance sheet test of insolvency pursuant to 11 U.S.C. § 548(d)(2)(A).

300 11 U.S.C. § 548(a)(1)(B). *See, e.g.*, Jacobson v. First State Bank of Benson, 48 B.R. 497 (Bankr. D. Minn. 1985).
301 11 U.S.C. § 548(a)(1)(B).
302 11 U.S.C. § 548(a)(1)(B)(IV).
303 *See generally* § 10.4.2.6.4, *supra*.
304 Small v. Williams, 313 F.2d 29 (4th Cir. 1963); Azar v. Morgan, 301 F.2d 78 (5th Cir. 1962); Mazer v. Aetna Fin. Co., 6 B.R. 449 (Bankr. D.N.M. 1980).

Generally, payments are first applied to the unsecured portion of an undersecured debt, but proof of how payments were applied will be necessary when there is cross-collateralization. United States v. Beattie, 31 B.R. 703 (Bankr. W.D.N.C. 1984). However, prepetition set-offs which have arisen under government liens may not always be regarded as preferential and therefore avoidable. See, e.g., *In re* Remillong, 131 B.R. 727 (Bankr. D. Mont. 1991); *In re* Stall, 125 B.R. 754 (Bankr. S.D. Ohio 1991). Contra *In re* Hankerson, 133 B.R. 711 (Bankr. E.D. Pa. 1991).

305 *In re* Miller, 428 B.R. 437 (Bankr. N.D. Ohio 2010) (preference not found even though FDIC re-perfected lapsed security interest during 90-day period prior to bankruptcy filing); *In re* Lemley Estate Bus. Trust, 65 B.R. 185 (Bankr. N.D. Tex. 1986).
306 11 U.S.C. § 549. *See In re* Martin, 78 B.R. 599 (Bankr. D. Mont.

1987). *See generally* § 10.4.2.6.6, *supra*.
307 11 U.S.C. § 547(b)(4)(B).
308 *See generally* §§ 10.4.2.6.2, 10.4.2.6.3, *supra*.
309 11 U.S.C. §§ 544, 545. *See, e.g.*, *In re* Marshall, 239 B.R. 193 (Bankr. S.D. Ill. 1999) (landlord's statutory lien on crops found avoidable); *In re* Ladd, 106 B.R. 174 (Bankr. C.D. Ill. 1989); *In re* Hartman, 102 B.R. 90 (Bankr. N.D. Tex. 1989).
310 For example, some courts have found government program payments under the PIK program to be general intangibles, not proceeds. A financing statement which failed to reserve a security interest in general intangibles, although expressly including proceeds, would be insufficient and the creditor's security interest unperfected. *See In re* Ladd, 106 B.R. 174 (Bankr. C.D. Ill. 1989); *In re* Winterroth, 97 B.R. 454 (Bankr. C.D. Ill. 1988); *In re* Kingsley, 73 B.R. 767 (Bankr. D.N.D. 1987); *In re* Bindl, 13 B.R. 148 (Bankr. W.D. Wis. 1982); § 17.1.1.4, *infra*.
311 11 U.S.C. § 108.

Moreover, if the time period for performance has expired prior to the filing of the bankruptcy petition, the bankruptcy case will *not* revive any right forfeited by inaction; section 108(b) will not operate to extend or recreate any right to perform.[312]

In a farm context, section 108(b) can be used to forestall the running of a statutory redemption period. If, however, under state law the only property right that the debtor had as of filing is the right to redeem the property, section 108(b) will not enlarge this right. Although redemption could be made, it is likely that the underlying debt will not be able to be restructured under chapter 12.[313]

17.4.4 The Automatic Stay and Codebtor Stay in Chapter 12 Cases

17.4.4.1 The Automatic Stay

The automatic stay[314] applies in all respects to chapter 12 cases with little variation from its application in other chapters.[315] For a general discussion of the automatic stay, see Chapter 9, *supra*.

The automatic stay is invaluable in stopping foreclosure actions, a primary source of farmer crisis. Because, as a practical matter, the beginning of the foreclosure process alerts other creditors in rural communities to a farmer's problems, who will often immediately move to repossess, attach, levy or set-off, the power of the automatic stay accompanying chapter 12 filing *before* the eleventh hour can prevent unnecessary—and sometimes irreversible—complications.

The automatic stay should also prevent the use of set-off by any creditor under 11 U.S.C. § 553. The most common set-off in farm bankruptcy is when the government retains a farm program payment, setting off that money against a prepetition debt owed to the government by the farmer. The government must seek relief from the stay before undertaking this set-off.[316]

17.4.4.2 The Codebtor Stay

The chapter 12 stay for codebtors of family farmers is drawn verbatim from the chapter 13 codebtor stay.[317] It is limited to consumer debts not incurred in the ordinary course of a farmer's business, and lasts only so long as the chapter 12 case is active.[318]

When the stay is lifted to allow pursuit of a codebtor for repayment, the court may subrogate the claim to avoid overpayment and allow the codebtor to stand in the place of the original creditor for payment for the chapter 12 debtor to the extent the debt is paid by the codebtor.[319]

When motivation for a loan or guarantee/cosigning is for business profit, such as continuation of the family farming operation, and/or the collateral is farm land, that cannot be considered a debt within the protection of the section 1201 codebtor stay.[320] By definition, a family farm corporation can not incur consumer debt because all debt is of a corporate nature.[321] Absent payment, or a binding provision in a confirmed plan relieving codebtors of liability, valid claims against non-filing codebtors will survive the bankruptcy to the extent that they are not paid.[322]

17.4.4.3 Grounds for Relief from the Automatic Stay[323]

The grounds for stay relief under section 362(d) are applicable to cases under chapter 12:

- Lack of adequate protection or other cause; and
- Lack of equity coupled with a finding that the property at issue is not necessary for effective reorganization and rehabilitation of the debtor.

Lack of adequate protection has been the easiest grounds in chapter 11 for a secured creditor to assert to obtain stay relief, or at minimum to obtain payment from debtors preconfirmation. Two factors in chapter 12 have made this creditor assertion more difficult: (1) the time from filing to plan promulgation and confirmation is short, so that the court is not as concerned with prejudice to the creditor by passage of time; and (2) the concept of adequate protection for creditors has been altered by section 1205.

Adequate protection in section 1205 is tied to the concept of diminution in value of the collateral, rather than assuring the

---

312 *See, e.g., In re* Tynan, 773 F.2d 177 (7th Cir. 1985); *In re* Glenn, 760 F.2d 1428 (6th Cir. 1985) (chapter 13); *In re* Heiserman, 78 B.R. 899 (Bankr. C.D. Ill. 1987).

313 Johnson v. First Nat'l Bank of Montevideo, 719 F.2d 270 (8th Cir. 1983). *See also In re* Smith, 85 F.3d 1555 (11th Cir. 1996); *In re* Martinson, 731 F.2d 542 (8th Cir. 1984); *In re* Monfortson, 75 B.R. 121 (Bankr. D. Mont. 1987); *In re* Liddell, 75 B.R. 41 (Bankr. D. Mont. 1987).

  Note that some states may well have redemption periods that extend for a long time. Compare the state-mandated redemption times of one year post-foreclosure in Minnesota and North Dakota with the statutes discussed in Sun Bank/Suncoast v. Constr. Leasing & Inv. Corp., 20 B.R. 546 (Bankr. M.D. Fla. 1982).

314 11 U.S.C. § 362(h).

315 11 U.S.C. § 103(a).

  As in non-farm cases, it may be possible for a debtor to receive damages for a creditor's willful violation of the automatic stay. *See* Graham v. Graham, 2010 WL 3894451 (C.D. Ga. Sept. 29, 2010).

316 Winchester v. Commodity Credit Corp. (*In re* Winchester), 191 B.R. 93 (Bankr. N.D. Miss. 1995).

317 *Compare* 11 U.S.C. § 1202 *with* 11 U.S.C. § 1301. See § 9.4.5, *infra*.

318 11 U.S.C. § 1201(a)(1), (a)(2).

319 *In re* Binstock, 78 B.R. 994 (Bankr. D.N.D. 1987).

320 *In re* Smith, 189 B.R. 11 (Bankr. C.D. Ill. 1995); *In re* SWF, Inc., 83 B.R. 27 (Bankr. S.D. Cal. 1988); *In re* Circle Five, Inc., 75 B.R. 686 (Bankr. D. Idaho 1987); *In re* Bigalk, 75 B.R. 561 (Bankr. D. Minn. 1987).

321 *In re* SWF, Inc., 83 B.R. 27 (Bankr. S.D. Cal. 1988); *In re* Circle Five, Inc., 75 B.R. 686 (Bankr. D. Idaho 1987).

322 *In re* Lazy D Diamond Ranch, Inc., 4 Fed. Appx. 418 (9th Cir. 2001).

323 *See generally* § 9.7, *supra*.

creditor the benefit of its bargain (anticipated profits), so the threshold which the debtor must meet to retain property in the face of an adequate protection argument for stay relief is smaller. In many cases the creditor may not be entitled to any adequate protection payment.[324]

At its outer limit adequate protection requires the fair rental value of the property at issue; however, property which is stable in value may require no further protection.[325] For further discussion of adequate protection under chapter 12, see § 17.4.11, *infra*.

However, there are other issues which may be placed under the adequate protection umbrella which can lead to stay relief. Most prominent in farmer cases is the misuse or failure to get permission to use cash collateral.[326] Similarly, conversion of collateral during the pendency of the case is grounds for stay relief.

The alternative ground for relief from stay is for the secured creditor to show a lack of equity in the collateral, but that showing *must* be coupled with a showing that the property is not necessary for an effective reorganization and rehabilitation of the debtor.[327]

Whether the property is necessary for the farming operation may depend upon whether the property is an intrinsic part of the farming operation or whether comparable property can be rented or procured for equal or less expenditure.[328] The debtor should attempt to demonstrate both the role of the property in the farming operation and its advantage upon retention. The debtor should also probably address the feasibility of the chapter 12 plan, although on stay motion that showing need not be as extensive as that required for confirmation. To that end, a showing of feasibility with cash flows, projections, and farm history may be required. However, because of the short time frame for confirmation, the consideration of stay relief may be deferred until confirmation.[329]

Relief from the automatic stay for "cause" is a catch-all category for both unsecured and secured creditors showing equitable grounds for relief. Stay relief may be granted after confirmation for plan default affecting secured creditors.[330] Stay relief may be granted an individual creditor for grounds which might also militate for dismissal under section 1208.[331] When stay relief is granted on this or any other grounds, and an appeal is contemplated, a stay pending appeal may be necessary to prevent mootness. If the property at issue is sold pursuant to relief from stay, the appellate court will be usually powerless to reverse the foreclosure.[332]

The 2005 amendments added a provision to section 362 that authorizes the lifting or modification of the automatic stay when a debtor has filed a bankruptcy that is dismissed and then refiles under chapter 7, 11, or 13.[333] Chapter 12 is notably absent from the list of included chapters, so a debtor may be able to refile under chapter 12 without concern for this provision. However, if a debtor files a chapter 12 case that is dismissed, and the debtor refiles under chapter 7, 11, or 13, then section 362(c)(3) may be triggered. In one recent case the court held, however, that the dismissal of a chapter 12 case due to ineligibility, followed by a good faith filing under chapter 11, did not trigger the provisions of section 362(c)(3).[334]

17.4.5 Objections to Discharge[335]

As in chapter 13, the chapter 12 debtor is granted a discharge at such time as the debtor has completed making all of the payments called for by the plan, other than payments made extending beyond the plan period.[336] The scope of the chapter 12 discharge, however, is similar to that available in chapter 11.[337]

---

324 *See* Randy Rogers & Lawrence P. King, Collier Farm Bankruptcy Guide ¶¶ 2.05[3][a], 4.02[5] (1999).

325 11 U.S.C. § 1205.
The concept that an equity cushion can provide adequate protection is applicable to 11 U.S.C. § 361 as well as to section 1205. *In re* Novak, 95 B.R. 24 (Bankr. E.D.N.Y. 1989).

326 *See, e.g., In re* Williams, 61 B.R. 567 (Bankr. N.D. Tex. 1986); *In re* Krisle, 54 B.R. 330 (Bankr. D.S.D. 1985).

327 *In re* Glenn, 181 B.R. 105 (Bankr. E.D. Okla. 1995); *In re* Gore, 113 B.R. 504 (Bankr. E.D. Ark. 1989); *In re* Lewis, 83 B.R. 682 (Bankr. W.D. Mo. 1988).
A showing of lack of equity alone is not sufficient. *See, e.g., In re* W.S. Sheppley & Co., 45 B.R. 473 (Bankr. D. Iowa 1984).

328 The showing is that the property will contribute to the reorganization, but need not be that it is irreplaceable. *In re* Saypol, 31 B.R. 796 (Bankr. S.D.N.Y. 1983). The leasing of a family farm in years previous to the bankruptcy can demonstrate lack of need for reorganization. *In re* Hutton, 45 B.R. 558 (Bankr. D.N.D. 1984).

329 A plan must be proposed within ninety days after filing under chapter 12 (absent extensions); a confirmation hearing must be held not less than forty-five days thereafter. However, courts have granted stay relief preconfirmation for lack of good faith and lack of feasibility. *In re* Ouverson, 79 B.R. 830 (Bankr. N.D. Iowa 1987); *In re* Welsh, 78 B.R. 984 (Bankr. W.D. Mo. 1987).

330 Reinbold v. Dewey County Bank, 942 F.2d 1304 (8th Cir. 1991).

331 *See, e.g., In re* Kennedy, 181 B.R. 418 (Bankr. D. Neb. 1995); *In re* Fern Acres, Ltd., 180 B.R. 554 (Bankr. D. Neb. 1995); *In re* Novak, 103 B.R. 403 (Bankr. E.D.N.Y. 1989); *In re* Novak, 95 B.R. 24 (Bankr. E.D.N.Y. 1989); *In re* Ouverson, 79 B.R. 830 (Bankr. N.D. Iowa 1987); *In re* Welsh, 78 B.R. 984 (Bankr. W.D. Mo. 1987); *In re* McMartin Indus., 62 B.R. 718 (Bankr. D. Neb. 1986). *See also In re* Wald, 211 B.R. 359 (Bankr. D.N.D. 1997) (stay relief granted for cause based on chapter 12 debtor's lack of good faith).

332 *See, e.g., In re* Riley, 122 F. Supp. 2d 684 (W.D. Va. 2000) (appeal moot after property sold pursuant to grant of relief from stay and dismissal of chapter 12 case), *aff'd*, 25 Fed. Appx. 149 (4th Cir. 2002). *See generally* § 14.9.5, *supra*.

333 11 U.S.C. § 362(c)(3); § 9.3.3, *supra*.
Note, however, that under section 362(c)(4) if two more cases are filed and dismissed within a year, the automatic stay will not go into effect if a third case is filed. This provision applies to any bankruptcy filed by an individual. *In re* Benefield, 438 B.R. 706 (Bankr. D.N.M. 2010) (holding that no stay went into effect due to debtors' two prior dismissed Chapter 12 cases pending within one year of their current case). *See also In re* Benefield, 438 B.R. 709 (Bankr. D.N.M. 2010) (denying debtors' motion to reinstate stay).

334 *In re* McKinnon, 378 B.R. 405 (Bankr. S.D. Ga. 2007).

335 *See generally* Ch. 15, *supra*.

336 *See* § 17.7, *infra*.

337 *Compare* 11 U.S.C. § 727(b) *with* 11 U.S.C. § 1141(d). *See generally* Bruce H. Matson, *Understanding the New Family Farmer Bankruptcy Act*, 21 U. Rich. L. Rev. 521 (1987).

Unlike the broader chapter 13 discharge,[338] the confirmation and consummation of a chapter 12 plan will not discharge debts which would be nondischargeable under section 523(a).[339]

During the chapter 12 proceedings, creditors can raise objections to discharge or dischargeability under either section 523 or section 727. Attorneys representing a family farmer should carefully review past transactions with their clients to determine if either section poses a problem. The presence of a substantial nondischargeable debt may have serious ramifications for the success of the chapter 12 plan. Counsel should review Chapter 15, *supra*, particularly § 15.4, *supra*, for a further discussion of the types of debt that may be nondischargeable and for the procedures governing determinations of nondischargeability.

There are, however, special issues that arise in farm bankruptcies that are different from those that arise in consumer bankruptcies. For example, because farmers are in the business of selling their products, the sale of secured property may arise as the subject of a discharge or dischargeability action.[340] Similarly, technical and complex patent infringement lawsuits may transition into nondischargeability cases when the farmer seeks relief in bankruptcy. Monsanto, for example, has been very aggressive in pursuing farmers that it believes have infringed their patent on "Round-up Ready" seed, and this pursuit continues into bankruptcy court.[341]

17.4.6 Dismissal and Conversion

17.4.6.1 Voluntary Dismissal

Chapter 12 allows the family farmer debtor, upon his or her own request, to dismiss a chapter 12 proceeding at any time without permission of the court, unless the case is in chapter 12 as a result of a conversion from either chapter 7 or 11.[342] Any waiver of that right of conversion is unenforceable.[343] If the case is a conversion to chapter 12 from either chapter 7 or chapter 11, then court approval upon notice and hearing is required prior to dismissal.

Several courts have disregarded the clear language of 11 U.S.C. § 1208(b) allowing dismissal of a chapter 12 case at any time by the debtor. In *In re Tyndall*,[344] the bankruptcy court declined to permit voluntary dismissal under section 1208(b) after a default under a plan that provided for mandatory liquidation of collateral by the chapter 12 trustee upon default and election by the creditor. In spite of the provisions of section 1208(b) making waiver of dismissal unenforceable, that court found the right to dismiss less than absolute when rights gained in reliance upon the bankruptcy are involved.[345] State court judgments for fraud, intentional misrepresentation, and the like can sometimes result in nondischargeable debts that cannot be relitigated in bankruptcy.[346]

Courts also decline to permit dismissal when the court finds fraud at the time a motion to convert under 11 U.S.C. § 1208(d) is pending.[347]

Unless the bankruptcy court orders otherwise for "cause," the dismissal of a case will reinstate avoided transfers or voided liens, vacate certain types of orders made during the case, and revest estate property in the entity that owned it prior to the commencement of the case.[348] A more difficult question arises with respect to payments held or received by the trustee and whether they should be distributed according to the confirmed plan as provided by section 1226(a) or whether, after administrative expenses are paid pursuant to section 1226(a), the remainder should go back to the debtor.[349]

---

338 11 U.S.C. § 1328(a).
339 11 U.S.C. § 1228(a).
340 Southeast Neb. Coop. Corp. v. Schnuelle, 441 B.R. 616 (B.A.P. 8th Cir. 2011) (affirming bankruptcy court's finding that certain farm debts were non-dischargeable under § 523(a)(2)(A) and (B)); *In re* Schnuelle, 441 B.R. 616 (8th Cir. B.A.P. 2011) (debt was excepted from discharge under both §§ 523(a)(2)(A) and (B); debtor fed secured grain crop to his cattle and presented false financial information in writing). *See, e.g., In re* Marklin, 429 B.R. 880 (Bankr. W.D. Ky. 2010) (debt excepted from discharge under § 523(a)(6) because debtor sold secured crop and deposited proceeds in personal bank account rather than remitting them to secured creditor); Guar. Bank & Trust Co. v. Sandford (*In re* Sanford), 362 B.R. 743 (Bankr. M.D. La. 2007) (in ruling on creditor's complaint charging its debt was nondischargeable under section 523(a) and seeking the denial of discharge under section 727(a), the court found that the debtor's sale of secured cattle without remitting or accounting for the proceeds, combined with his failure to maintain business records and appear for examination, supported the denial of his discharge).
341 *See, e.g.*, Monsanto Co. v. Trantham (*In re* Trantham), 304 B.R. 298 (B.A.P. 6th Cir. 2004) (patent infringement judgment held by Monsanto was nondischargeable); *In re* Henderson, 352 B.R. 439 (Bankr. N.D. Tex. 2006) (rejecting Monsanto's relief from stay motion and holding that its patent infringement claims could be litigated in its pending nondischargeability action).

342 11 U.S.C. § 1208(b); *In re* Lerch, 85 B.R. 491 (Bankr. N.D. Ill. 1988). *See In re* Cotton, 992 F.2d 311 (11th Cir. 1993); *In re* Davenport, 175 B.R. 355 (Bankr. E.D. Cal. 1994) (section 105 available to sanction debtor rather than prevention of dismissal).
343 11 U.S.C. § 1208(b).
344 97 B.R. 266 (Bankr. E.D.N.C. 1989).
345 The court distinguishes the circumstances in *In re Tyndall* from those in the unreported case *In re* Allen, No. 87-00185-MO8 (Bankr. E.D.N.C. 1988), in which the plan provisions apparently provided for possible (but not mandatory) liquidation by the trustee upon default. *In re* Goza, 142 B.R. 766 (Bankr. S.D. Miss. 1992) (voluntary dismissal not allowed until accounting and reports of income and expense produced for trustee).
346 *In re* Marek, 468 B.R. 406 (D. Idaho 2012).
347 Graven v. Fink (*In re* Estate of Gravan), 936 F.2d 378 (8th Cir. 1991). *See also In re* Molitor, 76 F.3d 218 (8th Cir. 1996) (chapter 13 debtor not allowed to voluntarily dismiss based on bad faith and pending motion by creditors to convert to chapter 7); Neal v. W. Credit Bank, 181 B.R. 560 (D. Utah 1995); *In re* Cotton, 136 B.R. 888 (M.D. Ga. 1992); *In re* Foster, 121 B.R. 961 (N.D. Tex. 1990), aff'd, 945 F.2d 400 (5th Cir. 1991); § 13.9, *supra*. *But see In re* Barbieri, 182 F.3d 319 (2d Cir. 1999) (right to dismiss is absolute and cannot be overridden even to prevent fraud).
348 11 U.S.C. § 349(b). *See, e.g.*, Wiese v. Cmty. Bank of Cent. Wis., 526 F.3d 584 (7th Cir. 2009).
349 The facts of the case and the circumstances surrounding dismissal will be critical to the result. In one extreme case, the federal government creditor prevailed upon the district court to issue a

17.4.6.2 Involuntary Dismissal

As in chapters 7, 11, and 13, any party in interest, including the United States trustee, may move to dismiss a chapter 12 case; the court may also consider dismissal *sua sponte*.[350] Notice and hearing upon such motion is required.[351]

The court may dismiss the case for cause, including:

(1) Unreasonable delay or gross mismanagement by the debtor that is prejudicial to creditors;[352]

(2) Nonpayment of filing fees or case charges;

(3) Failure to file timely a reorganization plan;[353]

(4) Failure to make timely payments under a confirmed plan;[354]

(5) Denial of plan confirmation and denial of additional time for filing of an additional plan or modification;[355]

(6) Material default in a confirmed plan;

(7) Revocation of confirmation or denial of confirmation of a plan modified after initial conformation;

(8) Termination of a confirmed plan by the plan's terms;

(9) Continuing loss to or diminution of the estate and absence of a reasonable likelihood of rehabilitation;

(10) Failure to pay a domestic support obligation that first became payable after filing;[356]

(11) Commission of fraud by the debtor in connection with the chapter 12 case.[357]

In addition, since the 2005 amendments, on the request of a party in interest a chapter 12 debtor's case may be dismissed by the court if the debtor fails to pay any domestic support obligation that first becomes due after the filing of the petition.[358]

Other grounds for dismissal that have been found to be for "cause" include lack of good faith,[359] abusive refiling,[360] failure to comply with court orders or statutory directives,[361] overlapping bankruptcy case filings,[362] failure to make timely filings and performance,[363] and lack of eligibility for chapter 12 relief.[364] The failure of a debtor to pay disposable income under the plan during its life has been used as a foundation for a trustee's motion to dismiss under section 1208(d).[365]

Dismissals for abusive refiling and/or lack of good faith have been made in some cases with prejudice, either for the period of 180 days specified in section 109(g) or such longer period as the bankruptcy court chooses to impose pursuant to section 105.[366] Abusive refilings have also generated assessment by the

---

prejudgment attachment upon the funds held by the trustee after dismissal to prevent their return to the debtor. *In re* Ethington, 150 B.R. 48 (Bankr. D. Idaho 1993). *See also In re* Samford, 102 B.R. 724 (Bankr. E.D. Mo. 1989).

In chapter 13 cases the Ninth Circuit has held that payments go back to the debtor. *In re* Nash, 765 F.2d 1410 (9th Cir. 1985). *See also In re* Plata, 958 F.2d 918 (9th Cir. 1992) (over a strong dissent).

350 *In re* Henderson Ranches, 75 B.R. 225 (Bankr. D. Idaho 1987).

351 11 U.S.C. § 1208(c). *See generally* Bruce H. Matson, *Understanding the New Family Farmer Bankruptcy Act*, 21 U. Rich. L. Rev. 521 (1987).

352 *See In re* Suthers, 173 B.R. 570 (W.D. Va. 1994); *In re* Fern Acres, Ltd., 180 B.R. 554 (Bankr. D. Neb. 1995); *In re* Hoffman, 168 B.R. 608 (Bankr. N.D. Ohio 1994); *In re* French, 139 B.R. 476 (Bankr. D.S.D. 1992); *In re* Beswick, 98 B.R. 900 (Bankr. N.D. Ill. 1989), *stay on appeal denied*, 98 B.R. 904 (N.D. Ill. 1989); *In re* Rivera Sanchez, 80 B.R. 6 (Bankr. D. P.R. 1987); *In re* Lubbers, 73 B.R. 440 (Bankr. D. Kan. 1987).

353 *In re* Braxton, 121 B.R. 632 (Bankr. N.D. Fla. 1990); *In re* Lawless, 74 B.R. 54 (Bankr. W.D. Mo. 1987), *aff'd*, 79 B.R. 850 (W.D. Mo. 1987).

354 *In re* Gribbins, 242 B.R. 637 (Bankr. W.D. Ky. 1999).

355 *In re* Hoffman, 168 B.R. 608 (Bankr. N.D. Ohio 1994); *In re* Rivera Sanchez, 80 B.R. 6 (Bankr. D. P.R. 1987).

356 11 U.S.C. § 1208(c), (d).

357 11 U.S.C. § 1208(c).

358 11 U.S.C. § 1208(c)(10).

359 *In re* Euerle Farms, Inc., 861 F.2d 1089 (8th Cir. 1988); *In re* Burger, 254 B.R. 692 (S.D. Ohio 2000) (lack of good faith included effort to misrepresent ownership of property of the estate to obtain the automatic stay, and minimal need for reorganization); *In re* @Vantage.com, 2007 WL 2688815 (Bankr. N.D. Cal. Sept. 13, 2007) (dismissing chapter 12 bankruptcy case of an organic farming corporation due to bad faith); *In re* Fern Acres, Ltd., 180 B.R. 554 (Bankr. D. Neb. 1995); *In re* Hoffman, 168 B.R. 608 (Bankr. N.D. Ohio 1994); *In re* Beswick, 98 B.R. 900 (Bankr. N.D. Ill. 1989), *stay on appeal denied*, 98 B.R. 904 (N.D. Ill. 1989); *In re* Hyman, 82 B.R. 23 (Bankr. D.S.C. 1987); *In re* Guglielmo, 30 B.R. 102 (Bankr. M.D. La. 1983) (chapter 13).

360 *In re* Bisso, 225 F.3d 661 (9th Cir. 2000) (dismissal based on history of prior filings found within the discretion of the bankruptcy court); Lerch v. Fed. Land Bank of St. Louis, 94 B.R. 998 (N.D. Ill. 1989); *In re* Borg, 105 B.R. 56 (Bankr. D. Mont. 1989); *In re* Walton, 95 B.R. 514 (Bankr. S.D. Ohio 1989); *In re* Hyman, 82 B.R. 23 (Bankr. D.S.C. 1987); *In re* McDermott, 77 B.R. 394 (Bankr. N.D.N.Y. 1987) (chapter 11); *In re* Galloway Farms, Inc., 82 B.R. 486 (Bankr. S.D. Iowa 1987); *In re* Ouverson, 79 B.R. 830 (Bankr. N.D. Iowa 1987); *In re* Welsh, 78 B.R. 984 (Bankr. W.D. Mo. 1987); *In re* S Farms One, Inc., 73 B.R. 103 (Bankr. D. Colo. 1987); *In re* Turner, 71 B.R. 120 (Bankr. D. Mont. 1987).

361 *In re* Walton, 95 B.R. 514 (Bankr. S.D. Ohio 1989). *See In re* Gahm, 229 F.3d 1151 (6th Cir. Aug. 31, 2000) (failure to comply with terms of order vacating dismissal is grounds for involuntary redismissal).

362 *In re* Borg, 105 B.R. 56 (Bankr. D. Mont. 1989).

363 *In re* Novak, 934 F.2d 401 (2d Cir. 1991); *In re* French, 139 B.R. 476 (Bankr. D.S.D. 1992).

364 *See* § 17.2.2.1, *supra*; *In re* Snider, 99 B.R. 374 (Bankr. S.D. Ohio 1989); *In re* Lawless, 74 B.R. 54 (Bankr. W.D. Mo. 1987), *aff'd*, 79 B.R. 850 (W.D. Mo. 1987).

365 *In re* Kuhlman, 118 B.R. 731 (Bankr. D.S.D. 1990).

366 *In re* Hildreth, 165 B.R. 429 (Bankr. N.D. Ohio 1994) (failure to provide financial information and to attend confirmation hearing is willfulness under section 109(g)); *In re* Walton, 116 B.R. 536 (Bankr. N.D. Ohio 1990) (dismissal with prejudice for two years when abusive refiling, delay of foreclosure, and ineligibility for relief shown on face of schedules); *In re* Walton, 95 B.R. 514 (Bankr. S.D. Ohio 1989); *In re* Lerch, 85 B.R. 491 (Bankr. N.D. Ill. 1988), *aff'd*, 94 B.R. 998 (N.D. Ill. 1989); *In re* Wilson, 85 B.R. 72 (Bankr. N.D. Ill. 1988) (chapter 13); *In re* Hyman, 82 B.R. 23 (Bankr. D.S.C. 1987); *In re* McDermott, 77 B.R. 394 (Bankr. N.D.N.Y. 1987) (chapter 11); *In re* Dyke, 58 B.R. 714 (Bankr. N.D. Ill. 1986) (chapter 13).

It is not clear how these cases are reconciled with section 349(a).

bankruptcy court against debtors for costs and expenses of creditors in appropriate circumstances.[367]

17.4.6.3 Voluntary Conversion from Chapter 12 to Other Chapters

Conversion of a case from chapter 12 to another chapter is conditioned upon the premise that the debtor seeking conversion is entitled to be a debtor under the chapter to which conversion is sought.[368] A chapter 12 debtor has an absolute right to convert a pending case to one under chapter 7 for liquidation.[369] Any waiver of that right is unenforceable.[370]

There are no specific provisions allowing the conversion of a chapter 12 case to one under either chapters 11 or 13. Debtors who have filed chapter 12 cases, but find themselves ineligible because of income or debt restrictions, may want to request conversion to chapter 11. Arguably, section 1208(e) anticipates the possibility of such conversion, although the absence of specific provision as contained in other sections[371] can also be interpreted as precluding or limiting such conversion.[372]

Those courts which have considered this conversion question have not reached a uniform answer. Some have approved the option of conversion from chapter 12 to chapter 11 within the discretion of the bankruptcy judge;[373] others have prohibited such conversion.[374]

The authority of the farmer DIP to operate his or her business ends if and when the order of conversion is entered changing the form of bankruptcy to one under chapter 7.[375] Nevertheless, the debtor continues to have the obligation of safeguarding the estate, turning over property, cooperating with the trustee and court, furnishing information, and appearing at examinations and hearings.[376]

There may also be situations in which a chapter 12 debtor seeks to convert to chapter 13, seeking either the broader discharge of debt or simply a more suitable framework. In one recent case a chapter 12 debtor sold the farm real estate through the chapter 12 plan, essentially ending the farming operation, and then moved to convert to chapter 13 and proposed to fund that plan with non-farm income. The court allowed the conversion.[377]

17.4.6.4 Involuntary Conversion from Chapter 12 to Chapter 7

Chapter 12 provides that upon the request of a party in interest, after notice and a hearing, a court may convert a chapter 12 case to one under chapter 7 "upon a showing that the debtor has committed fraud in connection with the case."[378]

Grounds used to justify conversion under section 1208(d) have included willful failure to pay over all disposable income during plan life,[379] conversion of collateral and fraud in dealing with an individual creditor,[380] and material misrepresentations.[381]

In some instances, the court may find that the evidence of fraud that supports the conversion of the case from chapter 12 to chapter 7 is sufficient for a denial of discharge under section 727, even without relitigating the issue.[382]

17.4.7 Executory Contracts and Unexpired Leases[383]

17.4.7.1 Overview

The chapter 12 debtor-in-possession has the power to assume or reject executory contracts and unexpired leases under section 365 of the Code. Refer to the discussion of this topic in the context of chapter 13 in § 12.9, *supra*, for a general understanding of section 365.

There are two executory contract issues and two unexpired lease issues that are particularly important in chapter 12 cases.

---

367 *In re* Fern Acres, Ltd., 180 B.R. 554 (Bankr. D. Neb. 1995); *In re* Hyman, 82 B.R. 23 (Bankr. D.S.C. 1987) (chapter 12); *In re* McDermott, 77 B.R. 384 (Bankr. N.D.N.Y. 1987); *In re* Kinney, 51 B.R. 840 (Bankr. C.D. Cal. 1985) (chapter 13); *In re* Jones, 41 B.R. 263 (Bankr. C.D. Cal. 1984) (chapter 13).
368 11 U.S.C. § 1208(e).
369 11 U.S.C. § 1208(a).
370 11 U.S.C. § 1208(a).
371 *See* 11 U.S.C. §§ 1112(d), 1307(d), 1307(e), 706(a).
372 *Compare* 11 U.S.C. § 1307(d), (e) *with* 11 U.S.C. § 1208.
373 *See, e.g., In re* Lawless, 79 B.R. 850 (W.D. Mo. 1987) (although circumstances in this case persuaded the court to deny permission to convert); *In re* Miller, 177 B.R. 551 (Bankr. N.D. Ohio 1994); *In re* Vaughn, 100 B.R. 423 (Bankr. S.D. Ill. 1989) (over chapter 12 debt limit: allow conversion prejudice to creditors, and otherwise not inequitable); *In re* Bird, 80 B.R. 861 (Bankr. W.D. Mich. 1987); *In re* Baldwin Farms, 78 B.R. 143 (Bankr. N.D. Ohio 1987).
374 *See In re* Roeder Land & Cattle Co., 82 B.R. 536 (Bankr. D. Neb. 1988); *In re* Christy, 80 B.R. 361 (Bankr. E.D. Va. 1987); *In re* Johnson, 73 B.R. 107 (Bankr. S.D. Ohio 1987).
375 Vregdenhil v. Hoekstra, 773 F.2d 213 (8th Cir. 1985); *In re* J.A.V. Ag., Inc., 154 B.R. 923 (Bankr. W.D. Tex. 1993).
376 *In re* J.A.V. Ag., Inc., 154 B.R. 923 (Bankr. W.D. Tex. 1993).
377 *In re* Vantiger-Witte, 2007 WL 3287105 (Bankr. N.D. Iowa Nov. 6, 2007) (allowing conversion of a chapter 12 case to chapter 13).
378 11 U.S.C. § 1208(d); Reinbold v. Dewey County Bank, 942 F.2d 1304 (8th Cir. 1991) (constitutionality); *In re* Nichols, 447 B.R. 97 (Bankr. N.D.N.Y. 2010) (denying creditor's motion to convert chapter 12 case to chapter 7; holding that debtor did not act with requisite fraudulent intent when equipment was transferred to L.L.C. as part of estate planning efforts). *See* § 16.1.2, *supra*.
379 *In re* Kuhlman, 118 B.R. 731 (Bankr. D.S.D. 1990).
380 Reinbold v. Dewey County Bank, 942 F.2d 1304 (8th Cir. 1991).
381 *In re* Yates, 429 B.R. 675 (Bankr. E.D. Mo. 2010) (debtor's chapter 12 case was converted to chapter 7 based on a variety of grounds, including withholding and concealing assets, failing to keep adequate records, failing to explain loss of assets, and failing to follow court orders); *In re* Kingsley, 162 B.R. 249 (Bankr. W.D. Mo. 1994). *See also In re* Bange, 2010 WL 1418410 (Bankr. D. Kan. Apr. 5, 2010) (damages and reliance on part of creditor are not required to permit finding of fraud under § 1208; "damage to the bankruptcy process is sufficient").
382 *See In re* Williamson, 414 B.R. 895 (Bankr. S.D. Ga. 2009) (chapter 12 court's finding of fraud precluded relitigation of that issue for discharge purposes under doctrine of collateral estoppel).
383 *See generally* § 12.9, *supra*.

17.4.7.2 Federal Farm Program Contracts As Executory Contracts

Farmers will frequently participate in one or more federal farm programs. As these contracts, in particular those that extend beyond one year, have been held to be executory contracts, it may be necessary for the farmer to reaffirm the program contract in order to continue participation in the program. On the other hand, if the farmer has defaulted in his obligation under the program and risks penalties, rejection of the contract may be in order.

17.4.7.3 Installment Land Contracts As Executory Contracts

A significant amount of farmland is conveyed through an installment land contract or "contract for deed." Although the parties to the contract may view it as a simplified mortgage transaction, as is noted in § 12.9.1, *supra*, such a contract may be considered an executory contract under section 365. If it is, the debtor's rights to modify that contract are severely limited, generally allowing only the opportunity to affirm or reject the contract as written.

In deciding whether such a contract should be considered to be a security device or an executory contract, most courts have looked to state law in analyzing the contract.[384] Although the state law trend appears to favor treatment of these contracts as security devices, that may not always be the case.

The Eighth Circuit has addressed this issue in a farm context in three cases. In each case, the court held that state law was determinative to the characterization. In two cases it held that a contract for deed is executory. In *In re Speck*,[385] the Eighth Circuit interpreted the character of a contract for deed under South Dakota law and found it to be an executory contract. In *Brown v. First Nat'l Bank in Lenox*,[386] the court applied Iowa law and reached the same conclusion. In both cases, the debtors were not allowed to restructure the contracts in their bankruptcy cases, but were forced to either assume or reject the contract as written. In the third case, *Heartline Farms v. Daly*,[387] however, the court applied Nebraska law and found the contract to be a "security device" that could be restructured.

As is apparent, there is a split of authority on this important issue, and attorneys must consult state law to assess the rights of their clients.[388]

17.4.7.4 Unexpired Equipment Leases

Rejection of farm equipment leases can be particularly helpful in the chapter 12 paring down process. Most long-term leases are more expensive than either purchasing the equipment outright or leasing services or equipment short-term on an "as needed" basis. This rejection of long term leases should be done at an early stage to avoid unnecessary administrative expenses.[389]

17.4.7.5 Unexpired Farmland Rental Agreements

Many family farmers depend on rented land for a significant part of their operation. Family farmers with rented acreage should pay particular attention to section 365(d)(4) which requires that leases upon non-residential real property must be assumed within sixty days of the filing of the original petition or that an extension of that period be arranged prior to its expiration.[390] Failure to assume non-residential real property leases within that time means the leases will be deemed rejected and possession must return to the lessor.[391]

17.4.8 Use of Cash Collateral

The typical consumer debtor is not concerned with the use of cash collateral except for the consumer's use of checking or

---

384 *In re* Streets & Beard Farm P'ship, 882 F.2d 233 (7th Cir. 1989).
  For a somewhat different approach, see *In re* Terrell, 892 F.2d 469 (6th Cir. 1989) (calling for a combined federal and state law analysis).
385 798 F.2d 279 (8th Cir. 1986).
386 844 F.2d 580 (8th Cir. 1988), *aff'd*, 487 U.S. 1260 (1988).
387 934 F.2d 985 (8th Cir. 1991).
388 *Bankruptcy cases holding that a contract for deed is an executory contract include*: *In re* Pogue, 130 B.R. 297 (Bankr. E.D. Mo. 1990); *In re* Bellamah Cmty. Dev., 107 B.R. 337 (Bankr. D.N.M. 1989); *In re* Larsen, 122 B.R. 733 (Bankr. D.S.D. 1988); *In re* Coffman, 104 B.R. 958 (Bankr. S.D. Ind. 1988); *In re* Aslan, 65 B.R. 826 (Bankr. C.D. Cal. 1986), *aff'd*, 909 F.2d 367 (9th Cir.

1990); *In re* Anderson, 36 B.R. 120 (Bankr. D. Haw. 1983); Shaw v. Dawson, 48 B.R. 857 (Bankr. D.N.M. 1985).
  Bankruptcy cases holding that a contract for deed is a security device include: *In re* Wilcox, 201 B.R. 334 (Bankr. N.D.N.Y. 1996); *In re* Fitch, 174 B.R. 96 (Bankr. S.D. Ill. 1994); *In re* Kratz, 96 B.R. 127 (Bankr. S.D. Ohio 1988); *In re* McDaniel, 89 B.R. 861 (Bankr. E.D. Wash. 1988); *In re* Fox, 83 B.R. 290 (Bankr. E.D. Pa. 1988); *In re* Sennhenn, 80 B.R. 89 (Bankr. S.D. Ohio 1987); *In re* Pribonic, 70 B.R. 596 (Bankr. W.D. Pa. 1987); *In re* Booth, 19 B.R. 53 (Bankr. D. Utah 1982).
389 11 U.S.C. §§ 503(b)(1)(A), 507(a)(1). See, e.g., Union Leasing Co. v. Peninsula Gunite, Inc., 24 B.R. 593 (B.A.P. 9th Cir. 1982); *In re* Templeton, 154 B.R. 930 (Bankr. W.D. Tex. 1993); *In re* Xonics, Inc., 65 B.R. 69 (Bankr. N.D. Ill. 1986). See also 11 U.S.C. § 1222(a)(2).
  Note that some purchase agreements are disguised as equipment leases, and the character of the contract can be litigated before the bankruptcy court. See *In re* Del-Maur Farms, Inc., 2011 WL 2847709 (Bankr. D. Neb. July 14, 2011) (holding that agreement between farmer and CoBank Farm Leasing Servs. Corp. for use of hog equipment was not a lease as creditor claimed but was a secured transaction for sale of equipment under U.C.C. § 1-203).
390 The courts are divided on the timing of § 365(d)(4) and extensions. A minority indicate that the motion for assumption or the motion for extension must be *heard and decided* within sixty days. See, e.g., *In re* Condo. Admin. Servs., Inc., 55 B.R. 792 (Bankr. M.D. Fla. 1985); *In re* Southwest Aircraft Servs., Inc., 53 B.R. 805 (Bankr. C.D. Cal. 1985).
  The majority hold that a motion for extension filed within the sixty-day period, whether resolved or not in that period, is sufficient. See, e.g., *In re* Am. Health Care Mgmt., 900 F.2d 827 (5th Cir. 1990). See generally 3 Collier on Bankruptcy ¶ 365.04[3][c] (15th ed. rev.).
391 11 U.S.C. § 365(d)(4).

savings accounts at creditor institutions.[392] However, the source of a farmer's income for living and operating expenses is often derived directly from sources in which secured creditors have a continuing, postpetition security interest. Moreover, in chapter 12 an ongoing business is at issue, and this business is likely to need funds for its continuation, which may involve the use of "cash collateral."

Chapter 12 does not change the section 363 requirements for use of cash collateral in which a creditor has a security interest: the debtor must obtain the creditor's permission to use the cash collateral or the court must determine that the debtor is entitled to use the cash collateral in the farming operation subject to the provision of adequate protection for the creditor.[393] Debtor's application to use cash collateral must be served upon all creditors and a hearing set thereupon.[394] Because the typical family farmer debtor will need to use cash collateral almost immediately,[395] the application should be filed with the petition or as soon thereafter as practicable. A hearing can be set upon short notice.[396]

What may serve as adequate protection for use of cash collateral will differ from case to case, but it should be remembered that adequate protection means prevention of diminution of value of the collateral, not benefit of the bargain.[397] For a more in depth discussion of adequate protection under chapter 12, see § 17.4.11, *infra*. The following is a list of factors contributing to a finding of adequate protection with regard to use of cash collateral:

- Current payments, interest and/or insurance on the collateral;[398]
- Additional security in unencumbered property or second liens;[399]
- First distribution under plan of a larger plan payment for cash collateral used;
- Severance of part of property and its conveyance or abandonment to creditor for payment; sale or culling of animals with proceeds to creditor as an immediate payment;
- Additional security interest in property or grain, particularly that upon which the previous lien had dissipated under 11 U.S.C. § 552;
- Continuation of the business itself and livestock maintenance can provide adequate protection, because the collateral may immediately devalue (such as dairy cows) if left unattended and because some collateral will replenish only upon continuation of the farming operation;[400]
- Periodic reports to the individual creditor whose cash collateral is being used;[401]
- Payment of creditor by another party with greater financial stability than the debtor;
- Showing that cash infusion from financing will contribute to a concomitant enhancement in the creditor's interest in secured property;
- Use of the cash collateral to feed and keep live collateral;
- Equity cushion between creditor's interest and value of pledged property;[402]
- Right of inspection to secured creditor to determine levels of security;
- Deposit of cash collateral in interest-bearing account in insured institution.[403]

17.4.9 New Financing and Its Approval

It is likely that the farmer will need to obtain financing to fund the continuing farm operation. Section 363 governs the use or sale of property of the estate,[404] including cash collateral, and section 364 governs efforts to obtain new financing.[405]

---

392 See § 11.3.5, *supra*.
393 11 U.S.C. §§ 363(c)(2), 1205; *In re* Stacy Farms, 78 B.R. 494 (Bankr. S.D. Ohio 1987).
394 Fed. R. Bankr. P. 2002(a)(2), 6004(a).
395 The proceeds from cash collateral are the majority of the general operating revenues of a debtor with a dairy or livestock operation and farmers whose crops are not subject to section 552 lien dissolution. A farmer whose loans have been accelerated by the Farmers Home Administration has also had his ability to use proceeds of his farm for living expenses cut off, so that immediate relief is essential.
396 That notice can be as little as seventy-two hours in emergency situations. *See, e.g., In re* Sheehan, 38 B.R. 859 (Bankr. D.S.D. 1984).
     Some hearings have been conducted by telephone. *See, e.g., In re* Halls, 79 B.R. 417 (Bankr. S.D. Iowa 1987).
     Some courts have local rules which provide for emergency hearings concerning cash collateral. Chapter 12 as originally conceived in the Senate had a provision for emergency hearing on cash collateral *ex parte*, but that provision was deleted in conference committee.
397 11 U.S.C. § 1205.
398 *In re* Rennich, 70 B.R. 69 (Bankr. D.S.D. 1987).
399 *See In re* TNT Farms, 226 B.R. 436 (Bankr. D. Idaho 1998) (discussion of priority of adequate protection liens issued in connection with cash collateral order).
     The replacement lien must be comparable to the lien dissipated. For example, bankruptcy courts are split as to whether replacement lien in forthcoming crops (even with crop insurance) is an adequate replacement lien for the use of proceeds from the sale of a previous crop. *See, e.g., In re* Berens, 41 B.R. 524 (Bankr. D. Minn. 1984). *Contra In re* Wiesler, 45 B.R. 871 (D.S.D. 1985) (chapter 11); *In re* Berg, 42 B.R. 335 (D.N.D. 1984) (chapter 11); *In re* Gilbert, 147 B.R. 801 (Bankr. W.D. Okla. 1992); *In re* Westcamp, 78 B.R. 834 (Bankr. S.D. Ohio 1987) (chapter 12); *In re* Stacy Farms, 78 B.R. 494 (Bankr. S.D. Ohio 1987) (chapter 12); *In re* Hoff, 54 B.R. 746 (Bankr. D.N.D. 1985) (chapter 11).
400 *In re* Underwood, 87 B.R. 594 (Bankr. D. Neb. 1988); *In re* Milleson, 83 B.R. 696 (Bankr. D. Neb. 1988); *In re* Wobig, 73 B.R. 292 (Bankr. D. Neb. 1987); *In re* Hoff, 54 B.R. 746 (Bankr. D.N.D. 1985) (chapter 11).
401 *In re* Watford, 159 B.R. 597 (M.D. Ga. 1993); *In re* Wobig, 73 B.R. 292 (Bankr. D. Neb. 1987).
402 *In re* Fischer, 2008 WL 583444 (Bankr. D. Neb. Feb. 28, 2008) (allowing use of cash collateral in the amount of $22,000 when the net value of the collateral was $511,000 and the secured creditor was owed $311,000, leaving equity of approximately $200,000); *accord In re* Wilson, 378 B.R. 862 (Bankr. D. Mont. 2007) (equity cushion protected oversecured creditor; use of cash collateral allowed).
403 11 U.S.C. § 1205. *See In re* Gore, 113 B.R. 504 (Bankr. E.D. Ark. 1989); *In re* Westcamp, 78 B.R. 834 (Bankr. S.D. Ohio 1987).
404 11 U.S.C. § 363.
405 11 U.S.C. § 364.

Both require the approval of the bankruptcy court. For example, court approval is necessary whenever the debtor seeks to incur:

- New secured indebtedness;
- Unsecured indebtedness outside the ordinary course of business; or
- Unsecured indebtedness to which a superpriority would apply.[406]

The debtor should make application as soon as practicable for such approval. The application should recite:

- All terms and conditions of the arrangements sought;
- The fact that similar or better terms and conditions cannot be obtained elsewhere for this farmer debtor;
- The necessity of the arrangement for the continuation of the farming operation;
- Proposed treatment of the creditor providing new financing under the debtor's plan; and
- Whether the arrangement encroaches upon the interests of any other creditors' interests.

In this latter event, court permission and/or creditor permission will be needed to subordinate the original creditor to the new one. The original creditor's interest will need to be adequately protected. For further discussion of the adequate protection requirement under chapter 12, see § 17.4.11, *infra*.

17.4.10 Sale of Property Free and Clear of Liens

Chapter 12 includes a provision[407] allowing the chapter 12 trustee and the debtor-in-possession[408] to sell farmland or farm equipment free and clear of liens regardless of creditor consent.[409] Any lien affected by the sale attaches to the proceeds.[410] As with all sales of secure property under section 363, the trustee or debtor-in-possession must make application for sale free and clear of liens, and notice must be given to all creditors and parties in interest. In practical terms, a sale free and clear can be utilized to:

- Sell unnecessary property;
- Reduce debt service to a secured creditor by applying the proceeds of a sale to the creditor's allowed secured claim;
- Allow sale to friendly entities or relatives of the debtor at a fair value;
- Allow sale to only a portion of farmland rather than an entire parcel.[411]

17.4.11 Adequate Protection Under Chapter 12

Instead of utilizing the adequate protection definition applicable to other bankruptcy chapters,[412] section 1205 creates a special chapter 12 definition of adequate protection for secured creditors.[413] Section 1205 applies to chapter 12 cases whenever reference is made to adequate protection under sections 362 (automatic stay and relief therefrom), 363 (sale, use and lease of property and use of cash collateral), and 364 (obtaining credit).

The theme of section 1205 is diminution in value of collateral, not benefit of bargain.[414] As the legislative history expressly indicates, section 1205 does not require the debtor to provide lost opportunity costs.[415]

Adequate protection under chapter 12 can be provided by several methods:

- Cash payments to the extent that the automatic stay or any activity of the debtor results in decrease in the value of property securing a claim or of an entity's ownership interest in property;[416]

---

406 11 U.S.C. § 364(b)–(d); *In re* Stacy Farms, 78 B.R. 494 (Bankr. S.D. Ohio 1987).

    Although section 364 allows the debtor to incur unsecured credit in the ordinary course of business without court approval, every sizable extension of credit to farmers should be submitted to the bankruptcy court for approval.

407 11 U.S.C. § 1206.

408 Although section 1206 is couched in terms of sale by the trustee, the debtor-in-possession should be able to exercise this same power with court approval by virtue of 11 U.S.C. § 1203 and Congress' admonition in the legislative history. See H.R. Conf. Rep. No. 99-958, at 50 (1986), *reprinted in* 1986 U.S.C.C.A.N. 5251.

409 11 U.S.C. §§ 363(b), (c), 1206. *See also* §§ 17.5.4.4, 17.5.4.5, *infra*.

410 11 U.S.C. §§ 363(b), 363(c), 1206. *See also* §§ 17.5.4.4, 17.5.4.5, *infra*.

    A creditor is also allowed to bid at any sale, unless forbidden to do so by the court, and if the creditor purchases the property, the successful bid price may be offset against the creditor's claim. *See* H.R. Conf. Rep. No. 99-958, at 50 (1986), *reprinted in* 1986 U.S.C.C.A.N. 5251.

411 *See* H.R. Conf. Rep. No. 99-959, at 50 (1986), *reprinted in* 1986 U.S.C.C.A.N. 5251.

    "Most family farmer reorganizations, to be successful, will involve the sale of unnecessary property. This section of the Conference Report allows Chapter 12 debtors to scale down the size of their farming operations by selling unnecessary property." *Id.* The same goals may also be accomplished in some circumstances by surrender of all or a portion of the property back to the secured creditor. *See also* § 17.5.4.4, *infra*.

412 11 U.S.C. § 361.

413 11 U.S.C. § 1205(a). *See also* H.R. Conf. Rep. No. 99-958, at 49–50 (1986), *reprinted in* 1986 U.S.C.C.A.N. 5251.

414 *In re* Shouse, 95 B.R. 470 (Bankr. W.D. Ky. 1988); *In re* Pretzer, 91 B.R. 428 (Bankr. N.D. Ohio 1988); *In re* Turner, 82 B.R. 465 (Bankr. W.D. Tenn. 1988); *In re* Kocher, 78 B.R. 844 (Bankr. S.D. Ohio 1987); *In re* Westcamp, 78 B.R. 834 (Bankr. S.D. Ohio 1987); *In re* Mikkelsen Farms, Inc., 74 B.R. 280 (Bankr. D. Or. 1987); *In re* Rennich, 70 B.R. 69 (Bankr. D.S.D. 1987).

415 H.R. Conf. Rep. No. 99-958, at 49 (1986), *reprinted in* 1986 U.S.C.C.A.N. 5250.

    It expressly eliminated application in chapter 12 of the holdings in *In re* Am. Mariner Indus., Inc., 734 F.2d 426 (9th Cir. 1984) and Grundy Nat'l Bank v. Tandem Mining Corp., 754 F.2d 1436 (4th Cir. 1985). Subsequently, in United Sav. Ass'n of Tex. v. Timbers of Inwood Forest Assocs., Ltd., 484 U.S. 365, 108 S. Ct. 626, 98 L. Ed. 2d 740 (1988), the Supreme Court overruled *Am. Mariner* and *Grundy*, holding that undersecured creditors are not entitled to lost opportunity costs. *See also In re* Anderson, 88 B.R. 877 (Bankr. N.D. Ind. 1988).

416 11 U.S.C. § 1205(b)(1). *Cf.* 11 U.S.C. § 361(1).

- Provision of additional or replacement liens to the extent that the automatic stay or any activity of the debtor results in decrease in the value of property securing a claim or of an entity's ownership interest in property;[417]
- Paying for the use of farmland the reasonable rent customary in the community where the land is located, based upon the rental value, net income and earning capacity of the property;[418]
- Other relief, other than granting of an administrative priority as will adequately protect the value of collateral or property used.[419]

This concept of adequate protection implicitly codifies the concept that an equity cushion alone may serve as adequate protection for a creditor under proper circumstances.[420] There may be times when no additional adequate protection is required, such as when there is a sufficient equity cushion or when the collateral will not decline in value over time.[421] However, insurance coverage is generally required for adequate protection regardless of value, stability or decline.[422]

17.4.12 Creditors' Right to Set Off

Under section 553, a creditor may claim or set off against its indebtedness any benefits or property in the creditor's possession or control if: (1) the debt owed to the creditor by the debtor arose before commencement of the bankruptcy case; (2) the claim of the creditor against the debtor also arose before commencement of the bankruptcy case; and (3) the debt and claim are mutual obligations.[423] The provisions of section 553 do not expand the rights of creditors; the creditor claiming a right to set off must be entitled so to do under existing non-bankruptcy law.[424] The ability of a creditor to exercise any right to set off is tempered by the automatic stay, which prohibits set-off without stay relief or court permission. To attempt set-off without relief or permission subjects a creditor to those penalties available under sections 362(h) and 105.[425]

Moreover, the set off of mutual debts or claims may not be mandatory; some courts have held that the bankruptcy court can exercise discretion in whether to allow set-off.[426] Particularly when the property is needed for reorganization, some courts have been willing to deny a creditor its right to set off.[427] Other courts, however, have held that they do not have the power to deny a set-off that meets the requirements of section 553.[428]

In many chapter 12 cases, debtors owe government creditors including perhaps the Internal Revenue Service (IRS), yet they are due benefits from federal farm programs. It is common for the USDA to assert a right to set off against benefits due a

---

417 11 U.S.C. § 1205(b)(2). *See In re* TNT Farms, 226 B.R. 436 (Bankr. D. Idaho 1998) (discussion of priority of adequate protection liens issued in connection with cash collateral order). *Cf.* 11 U.S.C. § 361(2); *In re* Pretzer, 91 B.R. 428 (Bankr. N.D. Ohio 1988).

418 11 U.S.C. § 1205(b)(3).
However, rent is not required; the right to rental payment is limited to any demonstrable decrease in value. *In re* Anderson, 88 B.R. 877 (Bankr. N.D. Ind. 1988). For a discussion of rent as a form of adequate protection, see *In re* Kocher, 78 B.R. 844 (Bankr. S.D. Ohio 1987).

419 11 U.S.C. § 1205(b)(4). *See also* H.R. Conf. Rep. No. 99-958, at 49, 50 (1986), *reprinted in* 1986 U.S.C.C.A.N. 5250, 5251. *Cf.* 11 U.S.C. § 361(3).

420 *See, e.g.*, Walker v. Johnson, 38 B.R. 34 (Bankr. D. Vt. 1983) (and cases cited therein); Aegean Fare, Inc. v. Massachusetts, 33 B.R. 745 (Bankr. D. Mass. 1983). *See also In re* Monnier Bros., 755 F.2d 1336 (8th Cir. 1985); *In re* Turner, 82 B.R. 465 (Bankr. W.D. Tenn. 1988); *In re* Mikkelsen Farms, Inc., 74 B.R. 280 (Bankr. D. Or. 1987); *In re* Raylyn Ag, Inc., 72 B.R. 523 (Bankr. S.D. Iowa 1987); *In re* Rennich, 70 B.R. 69 (Bankr. D.S.D. 1987).

421 *In re* Anderson, 137 B.R. 820 (Bankr. D. Colo. 1992); *In re* Shouse, 95 B.R. 470 (Bankr. W.D. Ky. 1988); *In re* Pretzer, 91 B.R. 428 (Bankr. N.D. Ohio 1988); *In re* Anderson, 88 B.R. 877 (Bankr. N.D. Ind. 1988); *In re* Turner, 82 B.R. 465 (Bankr. W.D. Tenn. 1988); *In re* Rennich, 70 B.R. 69 (Bankr. D.S.D. 1987).

422 *In re* Pretzer, 91 B.R. 428 (Bankr. N.D. Ohio 1988).

423 *In re* Marshall, 240 B.R. 302 (Bankr. S.D. Ill. 1999) (creditor may not set off debt for purchase of goods and services against unearned portion of advance payment for storing grain); *In re* Hazelton, 85 B.R. 400 (Bankr. E.D. Mich. 1988), *rev'd*, 96 B.R. 111 (E.D. Mich. 1988); *In re* Brooks Farms, 70 B.R. 368 (Bankr. E.D. Wis. 1987); *In re* Fred Sanders Co., 33 B.R. 310 (Bankr. E.D. Mich. 1983). *See generally* § 10.4.2.6.7, *supra*.

424 *In re* Bergman, 2007 WL 2693641 (Bankr. D. Kan. Sept. 10, 2007) (co-operative was not allowed to set off against ledger credits because it was unable to prove right to do so under co-operative bylaws); *In re* Hazelton, 85 B.R. 400 (Bankr. E.D. Mich. 1988), *rev'd*, 96 B.R. 111 (E.D. Mich. 1988). *See also In re* Myers, 282 B.R. 478 (B.A.P. 10th Cir. 2002) (federal government denied right of set-off because its claim against debtors had been discharged in prior chapter 7 case).

425 United States v. Ketelsen, 104 B.R. 242 (D.S.D. 1988), *aff'd*, 880 F.2d 990 (9th Cir. 1989); *In re* Hazelton, 85 B.R. 400 (Bankr. E.D. Mich. 1988), *rev'd*, 96 B.R. 111 (E.D. Mich. 1988); *In re* Britton, 83 B.R. 914 (Bankr. E.D.N.C. 1988); *In re* Rinehart, 76 B.R. 746 (Bankr. D.S.D. 1987) (chapter 11), *aff'd*, 88 B.R. 1014 (D.S.D. 1988), *aff'd sub nom.* Small Bus. Admin. v. Rinehart, 887 F.2d 165 (8th Cir. 1989); *In re* Woloschak Farms, 74 B.R. 261 (Bankr. N.D. Ohio 1987). *Cf.* Citizens Bank of Md. v. Strumpf, 516 U.S. 16, 116 S. Ct. 286, 133 L. Ed. 2d 258 (1995) (an administrative freeze does not violate the automatic stay).

426 *See* Riggs v. Gov't Employees Fin. Corp., 623 F.2d 68 (9th Cir. 1980); *In re* Diplomat Elec., Inc., 499 F.2d 342 (5th Cir. 1974); *In re* Julien Co., 116 B.R. 623 (Bankr. W.D. Tenn. 1990), *In re* Nielson, 90 B.R. 172 (Bankr. W.D.N.C. 1988); *In re* Hazelton, 85 B.R. 400 (Bankr. E.D. Mich. 1988) (chapter 12), *rev'd*, 96 B.R. 111 (E.D. Mich. 1988); Artus v. Alaska Dep't of Labor, 16 B.R. 308 (Bankr. D. Alaska 1981).

427 *See In re* Butz, 104 B.R. 128 (Bankr. S.D. Iowa 1989); *In re* Nielson, 90 B.R. 172 (Bankr. W.D.N.C. 1988); *In re* Hazelton, 85 B.R. 400 (Bankr. E.D. Mich. 1988) (chapter 12), *rev'd*, 96 B.R. 111 (E.D. Mich. 1988); *In re* Rinehart, 76 B.R. 746 (Bankr. D.S.D. 1987) (chapter 11), *aff'd*, 88 B.R. 1014 (D.S.D. 1988), *aff'd sub nom.* Small Bus. Admin. v. Rinehart, 887 F.2d 165 (8th Cir. 1989); Allbrand Appliance & Television Co. v. Merdav Trucking Co., 16 B.R. 10 nn.29–31 (Bankr. S.D.N.Y. 1981).

428 *See, e.g.*, N.J. Nat'l Bank v. Gutterman (*In re* Applied Logic Corp.), 576 F.2d 952, 957, 958 (2d Cir. 1978); *In re* Kraus, 261 B.R. 218, 223 (B.A.P. 8th Cir. 2001).
Collier on Bankruptcy adheres to this strict interpretation of section 553 rights, stating, "[t]he Bankruptcy Code provides no general equitable mechanism for disallowing rights of setoff that are expressly preserved by section 553." 5 Collier on Bankruptcy ¶ 553.02[3] (15th ed. rev.).

bankruptcy debtor and necessary for the funding of the chapter 12 plan. For additional discussion of the federal farm programs at issue, see § 17.1.4.4, supra.

Although early on, some courts held that a set-off requested by a government agency lacked mutuality either: (1) because the creditor agency making the claim for set-off is not the same agency providing the benefits;[429] or (2) because the debtor-in-possession (DIP) is not the same entity as the original debtor.[430] The majority of courts, however, have now concluded that the various agencies of the United States are one entity for set-off purposes, as is the debtor and the debtor-in-possession.[431]

The critical issue in farm program set-off cases is likely to involve a determination of when the farmer had a right to the farm program payment. If this right did not attach prior to the bankruptcy filing, that is, if it is not a prepetition right, then it cannot be offset against a prepetition debt.

In deciding when a farmer has a cognizable interest in a federal farm program for purposes of set off, most courts have looked to the date that the contract was signed. If it was before the date of the bankruptcy filing, the majority of courts have held that the debtor had a prepetition right to payment.[432] When set-off is allowed, one response is to provide in the plan for repayment of the creditor involved by allowing the set-off to occur automatically from benefits.[433] The plan may also provide for continuing payment of the creditor via set-off by specific grant of that right in postpetition benefits not otherwise subject to set-off. Another response may be to increase the allowed secured claim of the creditor to include the value of the set-off, and request court permission to have present use of the benefits and repayment or reimbursement under the plan pursuant to 11 U.S.C. § 1225(a)(5).[434] However, when a plan is confirmed providing for treatment of a creditor and that creditor has failed to seek set-off prior to confirmation, or a creditor has failed to assert a right to set off in its proof of claim, some courts have determined that the creditor has waived any right or claim to set off.[435]

17.5 The Chapter 12 Reorganization Process

17.5.1 Introduction

Sections 1222 and 1225 provide the requirements for the chapter 12 debtor's reorganization plan. If the debtor can convince the court that the proposed plan meets these requirements, the court "shall" confirm the plan, even in the face of creditor objection.

17.5.2 Procedure and Timing in Chapter 12 Cases

Only a debtor may propose a plan under a chapter 12.[436] The deadline for a chapter 12 plan proposal is ninety days from the date of the filing of the chapter 12 petition.[437] Attorneys must not miss this deadline, unless they first obtain express court approval for the extension of time. Failure to timely file a plan may result in dismissal or conversion.[438] However, chapter 12 has a special provision allowing the ninety-day period to be extended if such extension is "substantially justified."[439] It is thus important to make any request for an extension *before* the ninety-day period has expired. Courts have varied significantly

---

429 In re Butz, 86 B.R. 595 (Bankr. S.D. Iowa 1988), rev'd, No. 88-366-A (S.D. Iowa 1988), on remand, 104 B.R. 128 (Bankr. S.D. Iowa 1989) (the court denied the right to set off to the Farmers Home Administration as inconsistent with the rehabilitative purposes and intent of the Bankruptcy Code and chapter 12 in particular); In re Hunerdosse, 85 B.R. 999 (Bankr. S.D. Iowa 1988); In re Rinehart, 76 B.R. 746 (Bankr. D.S.D. 1987) (chapter 11), aff'd, 88 B.R. 1014 (D.S.D. 1988), aff'd sub nom. Small Bus. Admin. v. Rinehart, 887 F.2d 165 (8th Cir. 1989); Hill v. Farmers Home Admin., 19 B.R. 375 (Bankr. N.D. Tex. 1982).

430 In re Gore, 124 B.R. 75 (Bankr. E.D. Ark. 1990); In re Hill, 19 B.R. 375 (Bankr. N.D. Tex. 1982).

431 United States v. Maxwell, 157 F.3d 1099 (7th Cir. 1998) (federal government a single entity for set-off purposes); In re Turner, 84 F.3d 1294 (10th Cir. 1996) (en banc); In re Greseth 78 B.R. 936 (D. Minn. 1987); In re Parrish, 75 B.R. 14 (N.D. Tex 1987); In re Matthieson, 63 B.R. 56 (D. Minn. 1986); In re Julien Co., 116 B.R. 623 (Bankr. W.D. Tenn. 1990); In re Ratliff, 79 B.R. 930 (Bankr. D. Colo. 1987); In re Woloschak Farms, 74 B.R. 261 (Bankr. N.D. Ohio 1987).

432 See, e.g., In re Kraus, 261 B.R. 218 (B.A.P. 8th Cir. 2001); In re Matthieson, 63 B.R. 56 (D. Minn. 1986).

Most of the litigation in this area has involved the question of whether the farm program payment is property of a chapter 7 estate. See Susan A. Schneider, Who Gets the Check: Determining When Federal Farm Program Payments are Property of the Bankruptcy Estate, 84 Neb. L. Rev. 469 (2005).

433 In re Greseth, 78 B.R. 936 (D. Minn. 1987).

434 In re Thomas, 84 B.R. 438 (Bankr. N.D. Tex. 1988) (chapter 7) (treatment of set-off as secured claim), aff'd in part, rev'd in part, 91 B.R. 731 (N.D. Tex. 1988) (appeal did not involve mutuality issue).

435 In re Stephenson, 84 B.R. 74 (Bankr. N.D. Tex. 1988); In re Britton, 83 B.R. 914 (Bankr. E.D.N.C. 1988).

436 11 U.S.C. § 1221; In re Roesner, 153 B.R. 328 (Bankr. D. Kan. 1993).

437 11 U.S.C. § 1221.

438 11 U.S.C. § 1208(c)(3); Pertuset v. Am. Sav. Bank, 438 B.R. 354 (B.A.P. 6th Cir. 2010) (affirming Bankruptcy Court's dismissal of debtors' case on grounds that debtor failed to file timely plan); In re Lawless, 79 B.R. 850 (W.D. Mo. 1987); In re Rivera Sanchez, 80 B.R. 6 (Bankr. D. P.R. 1987); In re Offield, 77 B.R. 223 (Bankr. W.D. Mo. 1987); In re Lubbers, 73 B.R. 440 (Bankr. D. Kan. 1987).

However, even cases which dismiss for untimely filing find the ninety-day time requirement is not jurisdictional. See In re Land, 82 B.R. 572 (Bankr. D. Colo. 1988); In re Raylyn Ag, Inc., 72 B.R. 523 (Bankr. S.D. Iowa 1987) (plan filed in ninety-two days; no dismissal). Conversion can only occur in chapter 12 with debtor consent or under the limited circumstance of fraud under 11 U.S.C. § 1208(d).

439 11 U.S.C. § 1221. See, e.g., In re Erickson, 2012 WL 1453967 (Bankr. D. Wyo. 2012) (allowing debtors 14 days to amend their third proposed plan, and noting that the case had been open for 16 months).

in their willingness to allow additional time for the development of a proposed plan.[440]

The chapter 12 plan may be modified up to the time of confirmation;[441] and a second plan may be proposed, with the court's permission, if the first is denied confirmation.[442]

A hearing on confirmation must be held within forty-five days after the filing of the chapter 12 plan.[443] The court may extend the time for the confirmation hearing beyond the forty-five days if circumstances so require.[444]

17.5.3 Determining the Value of the Creditor's Claims: The Allowed Secured Claim

Section 1225 contains specific and distinct requirements for the treatment of secured claims and unsecured claims under the debtor's plan. In most chapter 12 cases the debtor will have at least one major secured creditor that is undersecured, that is, the debt to that creditor is more than the amount of valid security. In this situation, chapter 12 provides for the bifurcation of the debt to the creditor into the allowed secured claim (generally equal to the value of the security) and an unsecured claim equal to the remaining obligation. In order to be confirmed, the debtor's plan must adhere to the secured claim requirements for that portion of the debt and the unsecured claim requirements for the remaining portion of the debt. However, it is the secured claim that will be most critical to an effective reorganization.

Therefore, the core of many chapter 12 confirmations has been valuation of the security held by secured creditors, that is, the valuation of the allowed secured claims of those creditors. It is necessary for the debtor's attorney to review the valuation claimed by the secured creditor. The valuation can be obtained either through discovery, informal disclosure, or it may have been previously disclosed to the debtor as part of any proffer of voluntary liquidation or buy out prior to filing. In any event, such valuation is in the creditor's files and should be accessible upon request. If the creditor's valuation appears high, as it probably will, the debtor should have an appraisal done of both real and personal property subject to the security interest prior to filing under chapter 12.

While it may be desirable to come up with a valuation which maximizes the value of the collateral for some purposes such as defense of automatic stay motions, in chapter 12 confirmation, as in chapter 13, the perspective is the reduction of the secured creditor's claim to its optimal low for the one-hundred percent repayment and interest calculation. There may be times, however, when a low valuation should be partially compromised for the sake of expeditious or unopposed confirmation. Section 1225(a)(5)(A) specifically contemplates this course.[445]

The valuation of a security interest in chapter 12 under 11 U.S.C. § 506 is at a "going concern" or fair market value, not liquidation value (unless property sale or surrender is proposed), because reorganization and use of the property is contemplated.[446] The point in time at which valuation of the amount of the allowed secured claim—the value of the collateral pledged to the creditor—is determined has been addressed in various ways by the bankruptcy courts. Some freeze the valuation of the allowed secured claim as of the date of the petition's filing;[447] most place valuation as of the effective date of the plan, that is, the date of the confirmation order.[448] Again, the statute specifically states "value, as of the effective date of the plan."[449] Valuation must be based upon actual use, not highest and best use.[450] Possible increase or appreciation in the

---

440 Compare In re Erickson, 2012 WL 1453967 (Bankr. D. Wyo. 2012), with In re Marek, 2012 WL 2153648 (Bankr. D. Idaho 2012) (noting the "firmness of the 90-day plan filing requirement" and dismissing the debtors' case).

441 11 U.S.C. § 1223. See, e.g., In re Erickson, 2012 WL 1453967 (Bankr. D. Wyo. 2012) (rejecting the debtors' proposed plan on several grounds, but allowing debtors 14 days to amend the proposed plan, while noting that the case had been open for 16 months).

442 11 U.S.C. § 1208(c)(5); In re Bentson, 74 B.R. 56 (Bankr. D. Minn. 1987). See § 17.6, infra.

443 11 U.S.C. § 1224.

444 In re Ivy, 76 B.R. 147 (Bankr. W.D. Mo. 1987); In re O'Farrell, 74 B.R. 421 (Bankr. N.D. Fla. 1987).

However, the court in In re Ryan, 69 B.R. 599 (Bankr. M.D. Fla. 1987), found that a request for extension of the forty-five-day period to "work out problems with creditors" and to file a second amended plan if necessary were insufficient cause for extension of the time frame of section 1224. In re Braxton, 121 B.R. 632 (Bankr. N.D. Fla. 1990) (debtor's delay in obtaining valuation was not sufficient grounds for extending time for plan proposal). See also In re Thao, 2006 WL 4449684 (Bankr. W.D. Mo. Oct. 19, 2006) (refusing to grant continuance of debtors' plan confirmation hearing and stating that "the Chapter 12 process is to move forward as expeditiously as possible").

445 In re Weldin-Lynn, Inc., 79 B.R. 409 (Bankr. E.D. Ark. 1987); In re Durr, 78 B.R. 221 (Bankr. D.S.D. 1987); In re Hansen, 77 B.R. 722 (Bankr. D.N.D. 1987).

446 In re Felten, 95 B.R. 629 (Bankr. N.D. Iowa 1988) (cannot use valuation formula in Agricultural Credit Act of 1987); In re Foster, 79 B.R. 906 (Bankr. D. Mont. 1987); In re Weldin-Lynn, Inc., 79 B.R. 409 (Bankr. E.D. Ark. 1987); In re Robinson Ranch, Inc., 75 B.R. 606 (Bankr. D. Mont. 1987) (good discussion of all appraisal methods); In re Citrowske, 72 B.R. 613 (Bankr. D. Minn. 1987).

One court concluded that going concern value for a farm, under the proper circumstances, may be less than liquidation value because of use. In re Snider Farms, Inc., 79 B.R. 801 (Bankr. N.D. Ind. 1987). See Assocs. Commercial Corp. v. Rash, 520 U.S. 953, 117 S. Ct. 1879, 138 L. Ed. 2d 148 (1997) (replacement value is appropriate valuation standard for automobile in chapter 13 if debtor intends to use the property). See generally § 11.2.2.3, supra; In re Winthrop Old Farm Nurseries, Inc., 50 F.3d 72 (1st Cir. 1995); In re McClurkin, 31 F.3d 401 (6th Cir. 1994); In re Coker, 973 F.2d 258 (4th Cir. 1992).

447 In re Big Hook Land & Cattle Co., 81 B.R. 1001 (Bankr. D. Mont. 1988).

448 In re Tunnissen, 216 B.R. 834 (Bankr. D.S.D. 1996); In re Rice, 171 B.R. 399 (Bankr. N.D. Ala. 1994); In re Braxton, 124 B.R. 870 (Bankr. N.D. Fla. 1991) (value can exclude nursing animals when unmarketable or when they would die absent continuation of the farming operation).

449 11 U.S.C. § 1225(a)(5)(B)(ii).

450 In re McElwee, 449 B.R. 669 (Bankr. M.D. Pa. 2011) (applying Assocs. Commercial Corp. v. Rash, 520 U.S. 953, 117 S. Ct. 1879 (1997) to chapter 12 real estate valuation; using two step approach to valuation that first considered debtor's proposed use of property

value of the property over the plan's life is not recoverable as part of a creditor's allowed secured claim.[451]

Valuation of real property may be made by a number of approaches: comparable sales or market value approach, cost approach, and/or income approach. Most bankruptcy courts have deemed the comparable sales or market value approach as the most reliable indicia of real property value.[452] However, some courts have found that the lack of recent real property sales in an area and/or the skew attributable to the declining farm economy and increasing foreclosures which affects market value have made the income approach more reliable under the circumstances of a case.[453] Several courts endorse the market value approach, but consider other appraisal approaches to test its efficacy.[454] Although rental may be a component of the basis for the income appraisal approach, courts have indicated that the espousal of a different adequate protection standard in section 1205(b)(3) cannot justify a straight rental value approach to real property valuation.[455]

Appraisals should be sure to contain consideration of *all* items of value. In the case of real property, this must include valuation—or at least consideration—of all base or allotments that run with the land and any contracts which may affect value.[456] Courts may take judicial notice of land values if appropriate documents and publications exist for their geographic areas.[457] In some areas state law may bear on farm land values.[458]

Contested valuation will require expert testimony and may involve documentary evidence and indices involving both the appraisal and typical farm practices and sales. It should also be remembered that the owner of property is competent to testify as to its value.[459] Any previous offers to purchase the property undergoing valuation are also relevant.[460]

Finding reputable and competent farm appraisers for both real and personal property at a cost the debtor can bear may be difficult, particularly when many have been employed on a regular basis by the creditors usually involved in farm bankruptcies.[461] Any critical valuation should be done prepetition, if possible, to allow counsel to evaluate the amount of cramdown possible and to prepare the outline of a plan. Any appraiser and arrangement for compensation made by the debtor postpetition must be approved by the bankruptcy court under 11 U.S.C. § 327.

Finally, in addition to considering the value of the security, section 506 provides that a secured claim may also include the value of any right to set off that the creditor may have. Thus, a recognized right to set off may enhance a creditor's secured claim and thereby increase the amount required to be paid under the debtor's reorganization plan.[462]

17.5.4 Chapter 12 Plan Requirements: Secured Claims

17.5.4.1 In General

Section 1225(a)(5) sets out three alternatives for the treatment of secured claims under chapter 12. First, the secured creditor can agree to its treatment under the plan. Second, the plan can provide that the secured creditor receive the "present value" of its secured claim and keep its lien on its collateral.

---

under the plan and then looked to value of property); Farmers & Merchants Bank v. Southall, 2012 WL 2886419 (M.D. Ga. 2012); Cent. State Bank v. Volas, 2012 WL 3069947 (Bankr. W.D. Mich. 2012); *In re* Caraway, 95 B.R. 466 (Bankr. W.D. Ky. 1988); *In re* Hollinrake, 93 B.R. 183 (Bankr. S.D. Iowa 1988); *In re* Anderson, 88 B.R. 877 (Bankr. W.D. Ind. 1988); S. Rep. No. 95-989 (1978), *reprinted in* 1978 U.S.C.C.A.N. 5787 (legislative history).

451 *In re* C.R. Druse, Sr., Ltd., 82 B.R. 1013 (Bankr. D. Neb. 1988); *In re* Big Hook Land & Cattle Co., 81 B.R. 1001 (Bankr. D. Mont. 1988); *In re* Wobig, 73 B.R. 292 (Bankr. D. Neb. 1987).

This principle should be remembered when valuing replenishing collateral, for example, livestock and dairy. *In re* Borg, 88 B.R. 288 (Bankr. D. Mont. 1988) (replenishing collateral; no value added for increase in livestock).

452 *In re* Hudson, 2011 WL 1004630 (Bankr. M.D. Tenn. 2011) (determining value of debtors' land and poultry houses, court was persuaded by appraiser who reconciled market, cost, and income valuations; finding that market conditions made income approach the most appropriate of the three methods of assessing value); *In re* Hollinrake, 93 B.R. 183 (Bankr. S.D. Iowa 1988); *In re* Anderson, 88 B.R. 877 (Bankr. W.D. Ind. 1988) (market value approach should consider adjustments for: (1) any undue "suburbia and urban collar influence"; (2) any excessive disparity between the income approach and the market approach; and (3) any adjustment in location, size/shape, soil/topography, time of sale, and percent of tillable land; (4) downward adjustments for size of parcel; (5) evidence of poor yields based on soil); *In re* Borg, 88 B.R. 288 (Bankr. D. Mont. 1988); *In re* Chaney, 87 B.R. 131 (Bankr. D. Mont. 1988); *In re* Snider Farms, Inc., 79 B.R. 801 (Bankr. N.D. Ind. 1987).

453 *In re* Cool, 81 B.R. 614 (Bankr. D. Mont. 1987); *In re* McKeag, 77 B.R. 716 (Bankr. D. Neb. 1987); *In re* Danelson, 77 B.R. 261 (Bankr. D. Mont. 1987).

454 *In re* Hollinrake, 93 B.R. 183 (Bankr. S.D. Iowa 1988); *In re* Borg, 88 B.R. 288 (Bankr. D. Mont. 1988).

455 *In re* Snider Farms, Inc., 79 B.R. 801 (Bankr. N.D. Ind. 1987); *In re* Beyer, 72 B.R. 525 (Bankr. D. Colo. 1987).

456 See § 16.4.3, *supra*. See also *In re* Townsend, 90 B.R. 498 (Bankr. M.D. Fla. 1988) (tobacco allotments); *In re* Borg, 88 B.R. 288 (Bankr. D. Mont. 1988) (add value of royalty-producing leases); *In re* Claeys, 81 B.R. 985 (Bankr. D.N.D. 1987); *In re* Ratliff, 79 B.R. 930 (Bankr. D. Colo. 1987); *In re* Dunning, 77 B.R. 789 (Bankr. D. Mont. 1987).

457 Ahlers v. Norwest Bank of Worthington, 794 F.2d 388 (8th Cir. 1986); *In re* Anderson, 88 B.R. 877 (Bankr. N.D. Ind. 1988); *In re* Snider Farms, Inc., 83 B.R. 977 (Bankr. N.D. Ind. 1988) (judicial notice of land values and interest rates).

458 *In re* Kocher, 78 B.R. 844 (Bankr. S.D. Ohio 1987).

459 *See, e.g.*, Robinson v. Watts Detective Agency, 685 F.2d 729 (1st Cir. 1982); S. Ctr. Livestock Dealer, Inc. v. Sec. State Bank of Hedley, 614 F.2d 1056 (5th Cir. 1980).

460 *In re* Weldin-Lynn, Inc., 79 B.R. 409 (Bankr. E.D. Ark. 1987).

461 The Rural Appraisal Manual of the American Society of Farm Managers and Rural Appraisers, Inc. is a good source of information and the society may be a source of appraisal talent if debtor has difficulty in locating an appraiser.

462 United States v. Krause (*In re* Krause), 261 B.R. 218 (B.A.P. 8th Cir. 2001).

Note, however, that the court should consider the present value of a set-off claim that extends over a period of time. See also § 17.4.12, *supra*, regarding set-off under section 553.

This second alternative is the one that is used most often by chapter 12 debtors. In general terms, it means that the creditor will be paid an amount equal to the fair market value of the collateral. This amount can be paid over time, often for as long a period as would be appropriate for a new loan of that type. The creditor will be entitled receive interest at market rate. The third alternative is that the plan can provide that the secured property is surrendered to the creditor in satisfaction of the secured claim.

Unless a secured creditor agrees to a lesser amount,[463] each secured creditor must be paid one-hundred percent of its allowed secured claims under a chapter 12 plan and be accorded the "present value" of their claim, which means addition of an interest or discount rate over the period for repayment.[464] Present value calculation allows flexibility within recognized farm lending practices. The debtor is expected to keep collateral adequately insured and to pay required taxes.[465]

Based upon chapter 12's language and case law in chapters 12 and 13 secured indebtedness which has been accelerated prepetition can be deaccelerated by the chapter 12 plan.[466] The decisions which have addressed either balloon notes or fully matured notes in the chapter 12 context have found that they may be spread for long-term repayment over a reasonable amortization as if ballooning or maturity had not occurred or would not occur, so long as the creditor retains its lien, in light of section 1222(b)(9).[467]

Chapter 12, however, contains two important departures from chapter 13's treatment of secured creditors:

(1) Chapter 12 allows the repayment of secured creditors, if appropriate, over a period longer than the life of the chapter 12 plan even though the original indebtedness is not so amortized; and

(2) Chapter 12 allows modification of the rights of holders of security interests in *all* real and personal property without regard to its residential nature, so that secured creditors collateralized by the farmstead can be reamortized without the need for cure of default.[468]

The valuation of allowed secured claims proposed by debtor or agreed upon by debtor and creditors must be disclosed in the plan for court evaluation of feasibility and compliance with section 1225(a)(5).[469]

17.5.4.2 Amortization and Extending Plan Payments Beyond the Plan's Life

In chapter 12, as in chapter 13, the life of a plan is three to five years. Secured creditors may be paid the value of their allowed secured claim over the life of the plan. As in chapter 13, chapter 12 allows cure of default on all secured indebtedness the term for repayment of which is longer than the plan's life over such longer period as is scheduled for this indebtedness.[470] However, unlike chapter 13, chapter 12 also allows the extension of repayment of secured indebtedness, regardless of original amortization, over a period beyond the life of the chapter 12 plan.[471]

The period of time over which a secured debt can be reamortized or spread must be determined in light of what is commercially reasonable in similar circumstances in the farm economic sector.[472] The following factors are helpful in this determination:

1. *What kind of property collateralizes the original loan?* Repayment on debt collateralized by real property typically can be spread over more lengthy periods, while debts secured by personal property require a shorter repayment period.

2. *How long is the useful life (depreciation schedule) of the personal property? How long has the debtor had the property?* The term should be compared with the value of

---

463 11 U.S.C. § 1225(a)(5)(A).
   The provisions of section 1225(a)(5)(A) allow the debtor and a secured creditor to consent to treatment, regardless of whether such treatment may be authorized under the Code or whether it is similar to prepetition treatment. *In re* Lyon, 161 B.R. 1013 (Bankr. D. Kan. 1993).
464 11 U.S.C. § 1225(a)(5). *See In re* Woerner, 214 B.R. 208 (Bankr. D. Neb. 1997) (plan cannot deprive creditor of the value of its lien); *In re* Claeys, 81 B.R. 985 (Bankr. D.N.D. 1987); *In re* Weldin-Lynn, Inc., 79 B.R. 409 (Bankr. E.D. Ark. 1987) (and cases cited therein).
465 *In re* Ames, 973 F.2d 849 (10th Cir. 1992) (plan to pay secured creditor only through results of litigation rejected); *In re* Pretzer, 91 B.R. 428 (Bankr. N.D. Ohio 1988); *In re* Pond, 43 B.R. 522 (Bankr. D.N.D. 1984); *In re* Abbott, 23 B.R. 484 (Bankr. W.D. Okla. 1982).
   The 1994 amendments to the Code added 11 U.S.C. § 362(b)(18), an exception to the automatic stay, which allows for postpetition and *ad valorem* taxes to attach to a debtor's property.
466 *In re* Terry, 780 F.2d 894 (11th Cir. 1985) (and cases cited therein); *In re* Taddeo, 685 F.2d 24 (2d Cir. 1982); *In re* Davis, 77 B.R. 312 (Bankr. M.D. Ga. 1987).
   However, see limitations discussed in § 17.4.3.5.5, *supra*.
467 11 U.S.C. § 1222(b)(2), (b)(5), (b)(9); *In re* Beard, 134 B.R. 239 (Bankr. S.D. Ohio 1991); *In re* Foster, 79 B.R. 906 (Bankr. D. Mont. 1987); *In re* Martin, 78 B.R. 598 (Bankr. D. Mont. 1987); *In re* Dunning, 77 B.R. 789 (Bankr. D. Mont. 1987). *See* § 17.5.4.2, *infra*.
468 This is also now a departure from chapter 11 as changed by the 1994 amendments which limits modification of debts secured by residential real property which serves as the debtor's principal residence in much the same manner as chapter 13. *See* 11 U.S.C. § 1123(b)(5); 11 U.S.C. § 1322(b)(2).
469 *In re* Kloberdanz, 83 B.R. 767 (Bankr. D. Colo. 1988); *In re* Rivera Sanchez, 80 B.R. 6 (Bankr. D.R.I. 1987).
470 11 U.S.C. § 1222(b)(5).
471 11 U.S.C. § 1222(b)(9); *In re* Tognini, 2011 WL 2650598 (Bankr. E.D. Va. July 6, 2011) (confirming distinction between chapter 13 and chapter 12, with latter allowing payments to extend beyond plan term); *In re* Beard, 134 B.R. 239 (Bankr. S.D. Ohio 1991); *In re* Mouser, 99 B.R. 803 (Bankr. S.D. Ohio 1989); *In re* Miller, 98 B.R. 311 (Bankr. N.D. Ohio 1989); *In re* Kline, 94 B.R. 557 (Bankr. N.D. Ind. 1988).
472 *See In re* Woods, 465 B.R. 196 (B.A.P. 10th Cir. 2012) (noting that "courts have generally been lenient in allowing debtors the maximum time to pay their claims"); *In re* Rose, 135 B.R. 603 (Bankr. N.D. Ind. 1991); *In re* Indreland, 77 B.R. 268 (Bankr. D. Mont. 1987).

the collateral over time, so that no additional adequate protection for depreciation need be allowed for under the plan.[473]

3. *Is the loan purchase money or non-purchase money?* The more commercially reasonable approach is shorter terms for purchase money than for non-purchase money.

4. *What is the original term on the loan?* How long does the plan propose to extend repayment to the creditor beyond its original bargain? Is the original amortization as good for the debtor as any reamortization would be.

5. *How long can it be anticipated that the debtor will remain farming?* The age of the debtor can be a factor although courts have not found it controlling when approving amortizations which will extend beyond the reasonable life expectancy of the debtor.[474]

6. *How long is the repayment period for loans in the private sector currently being made with the same or similar collateral? How long for government or Farm Credit System lenders?* What are the maximum and minimum periods typically given?

7. *Are the payments under the chapter 12 plan to be made in equal payments, or does the Plan propose a front or end advantage by larger payments?* Can a debtor compensate for a longer, less reasonable term by some advantage for the affected creditor?

8. *What are the policies of the actual lender involved?* Does the creditor have the capacity to reamortize, reschedule or defer payments itself? Does it typically restructure loans or have the capacity to do so? What are its typical terms for lending? Is the lender a private individual or an institution?[475]

9. *Are balloon notes or notes with disproportionate payments typical for the type of loan being reamortized and rescheduled?* The reamortization can contain a balloon, or can amortize the payments on the loan over a long period of time with a balloon due at a point in time before the end of the scheduled amortization.[476]

10. *Is the creditor willing to agree to a reasonable and feasible amortization period?*

While the following should be viewed only as a rough indicator, generally real estate loans can be amortized over fifteen to twenty years, although under the proper circumstances thirty to forty years may be appropriate.[477] A balloon payment either affecting repayment term and/or both repayment term and amortization (for example, a twenty-year amortization with payoff at ten years) may be proposed if typical and feasible.[478]

Personal property such as farm equipment may have an outer limit for reamortization of seven years, although circumstances may dictate a shorter or longer period.[479] Livestock may vary with its useful life; dairy cattle, for example, may be as long as seven years, while feeder operations may be less. Continuous replacement and upgrading of a livestock operation may militate for a longer period for repayment.[480]

B.R. 355 (B.A.P. 9th Cir. 1997) (evaluation of chapter 12 plan involving negative amortization of secured debt, feasibility is overriding concern).

477 *In re* Prescott, 2011 WL 7268057 (Bankr. S.D. Ga. 2011) (approving 25 year repayment plan for real estate claim); *In re* John V. Francks Turkey Co., 251 B.R. 441 (B.A.P. 10th Cir. 1999) (twenty-five years allowed); *In re* Zerr, 167 B.R. 953 (Bankr. D. Kan. 1994) (thirty years allowed); *In re* Miller, 98 B.R. 311 (Bankr. N.D. Ohio 1989); *In re* Hagen, 95 B.R. 708 (Bankr. D.N.D. 1989) (thirty-year amortization in plan as originally confirmed); *In re* Schaal, 93 B.R. 644 (Bankr. W.D. Ark. 1988); *In re* Hart, 90 B.R. 150 (Bankr. E.D.N.C. 1988) (thirty-year amortization under original plan and modification); *In re* Chaney, 87 B.R. 131 (Bankr. D. Mont. 1988) (forty-year amortization, *dicta*); *In re* Bar L O Farms, West, 87 B.R. 125 (Bankr. D. Idaho 1988) (forty-year amortization); *In re* Simmons, 86 B.R. 160 (Bankr. S.D. Iowa 1988) (*dicta*); *In re* Bullington, 80 B.R. 590 (Bankr. M.D. Ga. 1987) (allowed thirty-year amortization on land authorized by section 1225(a)(5)(B) as construed *in pari materia* with section 1222(b)(9)), *aff'd sub nom.* Travelers Ins. Co. v. Bullington, 89 B.R. 1010 (M.D. Ga. 1988), *aff'd*, 878 F.2d 354 (11th Cir. 1989); *In re* Snider Farms, Inc., 79 B.R. 801 and 83 B.R. 1003 (Bankr. N.D. Ind. 1987 and 1988); *In re* Smith, 78 B.R. 491 (Bankr. N.D. Tex. 1987); *In re* O'Farrell, 74 B.R. 421 (Bankr. N.D. Fla. 1987); *In re* Lenz, 74 B.R. 413 (Bankr. C.D. Ill. 1987); *In re* Hagensick, 73 B.R. 710 (Bankr. N.D. Iowa 1987); *In re* Janssen Charolais Ranch, Inc., 73 B.R. 125 (Bankr. D. Mont. 1987). But see *In re* Rose, 135 B.R. 603 (Bankr. N.D. Ind. 1991) (thirty-year amortization inappropriate based on age and income); *In re* Koch, 131 B.R. 128 (Bankr. N.D. Iowa 1991) (thirty years too long); *In re* Lupfer Bros., 120 B.R. 1002 (Bankr. W.D. Mo. 1990) (twenty-five-year amortization too long).

478 *See In re* Koch, 131 B.R. 128 (Bankr. N.D. Iowa 1991) (thirty-year amortization with balloon at fifteen years); *In re* LLL Farms, 111 B.R. 1016 (Bankr. M.D. Ga. 1990) (thirty-year amortization with balloon at twenty years).

479 *In re* Butler, 97 B.R. 508 (Bankr. E.D. Ark. 1988) (twenty years on equipment unacceptable); *In re* Fenske, 96 B.R. 244 (Bankr. D.N.D. 1988) (seven to ten year amortization on equipment, *dicta*); *In re* Adam, 92 B.R. 732 (Bankr. E.D. Mich. 1988) (nine-year amortization on equipment when first lien paid off, excellent maintenance record and sufficient budgeting for repair); *In re* Townsend, 90 B.R. 498 (Bankr. M.D. Fla. 1988) (three-year amortization on equipment).

480 *In re* Simmons, 86 B.R. 160 (Bankr. S.D. Iowa 1988) (seven to

---

473 *In re* Rice, 171 B.R. 399 (Bankr. N.D. Ala. 1994); *In re* Borg, 88 B.R. 288 (Bankr. D. Mont. 1988) (repayment of principal upon collateralized loan must follow depreciation or section 1225(a)(5)(B)(i) lien retention not complied with).

474 *In re* John v. Francks Turkey Co., 251 B.R. 441 (B.A.P. 10th Cir. 1999) (twenty-five years allowed although debtor was sixty-two based on commitment of debtor's son to plan); *In re* Howard, 212 B.R. 864 (Bankr. E.D. Tenn. 1997) (twenty-year payment plan too long for debtors who were sixty-two and fifty-seven at time of confirmation). *See, e.g.,* Mulberry Agric. Enters., Inc., 113 B.R. 30 (D. Kan. 1990); *In re* Foster, 79 B.R. 906 (Bankr. D. Mont. 1987). Contra *In re* Rose, 135 B.R. 603 (Bankr. N.D. Ind. 1991).

475 *In re* Rose, 135 B.R. 603 (Bankr. N.D. Ind. 1991) (individual lender should be treated differently on amortization than institutional lender); *In re* Koch, 131 B.R. 128 (Bankr. N.D. Iowa 1991).

476 *In re* Foster, 79 B.R. 906 (Bankr. D. Mont. 1987) (contract for deed maturing postpetition; norm found to be ten to fifteen years or twenty years with balloon at ten years; thirty-year amortization with balloon at fifteen years acceptable); *In re* Smith, 78 B.R. 491 (Bankr. N.D. Tex. 1987) (thirty-year amortization with balloon at twenty years for Federal Land Bank). *See, e.g., In re* Nauman, 213

17.5.4.3 Interest Rates for Secured Creditors

Secured creditors in chapter 12 cases are entitled to an interest or discount rate to assure them the present value of their claim when it is paid over time.[481] In the past, although courts have agreed that a "market rate" was generally appropriate, different courts have taken diverse approaches to determining what the market rate might be.

Some courts in chapter 12 cases had followed an approach that considered the market rate for the type and quality of loan, not specific to the individual creditor at issue.[482] Other courts preferred to use a "formula" approach that would typically use as a starting point the risk free cost of money, that is, the rate for treasury bills or the prime rate.[483] These courts often added a consideration of a risk factor in addition to market rate, if appropriate to the individual case considering the collateralization and other factors contributing to risk of subsequent default.[484]

The Supreme Court largely resolved this dispute in *Till v. SCS Credit Corp.*[485] The Court held that a formula method is to be used, with the prime rate of interest[486] as the starting point, adjusted by a factor for risk. Although not setting any specific amount for the risk factor, the Court cited cases adding one to three percent to the interest rate, and noted that the rate selected should be "high enough to compensate the creditor for its risk but not so high as to doom the plan."[487] The Court also held that an objecting creditor has the burden of going forward with evidence that the interest rate proposed by the debtor is inadequate.[488]

The preconfirmation and postconfirmation periods should be distinguished for oversecured farm creditors for interest rates under the rationale in *United States v. Ron Pair Enterprises, Inc.*[489] Oversecured creditors may be entitled to their contract rates during the preconfirmation period, although not thereafter, as well as reasonable attorney fees under section 506(b).[490]

17.5.4.4 Return or Surrender of Property to Secured Creditors

One of the most effective tools of reorganization is the paring down of the farm operation by reduction of collateral and its accompanying debt service. One of the primary methods of accomplishing this is return, relinquishment or abandonment to the secured creditor of all or a portion of the creditor's collateral. Such a return or relinquishment operates to reduce the allowed secured claim by the value of the collateral. Chapter 12 permits such relinquishment and credit.[491] How much credit is given to reduce the allowed secured claim of a creditor depends upon the consent of the creditor or the valuation of the collateral by the court.[492] Such return may include surrender of stock or shares owned by the debtor in cooperatives, Federal Land Banks, and Production Credit Associations for credit against the secured claim of those creditors; however, generally, surrender to Farm Credit lenders requires their permission under the Agricultural Credit Act of 1987.[493]

---

fifteen years on livestock if replaced) (*dicta*); *In re* Foster, 79 B.R. 906 (Bankr. D. Mont. 1987); *In re* Dunning, 77 B.R. 789 (Bankr. D. Mont. 1987).

481 11 U.S.C. § 1225(a)(5)(B)(ii); *In re* Batchelor, 97 B.R. 993 (Bankr. E.D. Ark. 1988); *In re* Weldin-Lynn, Inc., 79 B.R. 409 (Bankr. E.D. Ark. 1987).

This is true whether the lien is consensual or by operation of law (and unavoidable). United States v. Ron Pair Enters., Inc., 489 U.S. 235, 109 S. Ct. 1026, 103 L. Ed. 2d 290 (1989).

482 *In re* Fisher, 930 F.2d 1361 (8th Cir. 1991) (finding FmHA entitled to market rate, not lower blended, weighted rate under existing contracts); *In re* Hardzog, 901 F.2d 858 (10th Cir. 1990).

483 *In re* Fowler, 903 F.2d 694 (9th Cir. 1990) (prime rate plus risk factor method approved in chapter 12 case); United States v. Doud, 869 F.2d 1144 (8th Cir. 1989) (chapter 12 case upholding treasury bond plus two percent risk factor as providing a "market rate").

484 United States v. Neal Pharmacal Co., 789 F.2d 1283 (8th Cir. 1986); *In re* Monnier Bros., 755 F.2d 1336 (8th Cir. 1985); *In re* S. States Motor Homes, 709 F.2d 647 (11th Cir. 1983); *In re* Davenport, 158 B.R. 832 (Bankr. E.D. Cal. 1992) (finds chapter 12 should reduce risk factors).

485 541 U.S. 465, 124 S. Ct. 1951, 158 L. Ed. 2d 787 (2004).

Although *Till* was a chapter 13 case, the statutory provisions entitling secured creditors to interest are virtually identical in chapters 11, 12, and 13. *See In re* Woods, 465 B.R. 196 (B.A.P. 10th Cir. 2012) (holding that *Till* overrules *Hardzog* and applying the prime plus risk test adopted in *Till*). Accord *In re* Prescott, 2011 WL 7268057 (Bankr. S.D. Ga. 2011); *In re* Wilson, 378 B.R. 862 (Bankr. D. Mont. 2007).

486 The prime rate of interest may be found on the Internet at: http://federalreserve.gov/releases/h15/data.htm#top.

487 124 S. Ct. at 1962; *In re* Hudson, 2011 WL 1004630 (Bankr. M.D. Tenn. 2011) (confirming debtors' chapter 12 plan with 5% interest rate for long term real estate debt; citing *Till v. SCS Credit Corp.* for use of prime rate (3.25%) plus risk factor of 1.75%).

See § 11.6.1.3.3.6, *supra*, for a discussion of the risk factor.

488 124 S. Ct. at 1961.
489 489 U.S. 235, 109 S. Ct. 1026, 103 L. Ed. 2d 290 (1989).
490 *In re* Foertsch, 167 B.R. 555 (Bankr. D.N.D. 1994).
491 The legislative history clearly contemplates such paring down. *See* 11 U.S.C. §§ 1225(a)(5)(C), 1222(b)(7), 1222(b)(8), 1222(b)(10); *In re* B & G Farms, Inc., 82 B.R. 549 (Bankr. D. Mont. 1988); *In re* Indreland, 77 B.R. 268 (Bankr. D. Mont. 1987); *In re* Robinson Ranch, Inc., 75 B.R. 606 (Bankr. D. Mont. 1987); *In re* O'Farrell, 74 B.R. 421 (Bankr. N.D. Fla. 1987); *In re* Mikkelsen Farms, Inc., 74 B.R. 280 (Bankr. D. Or. 1987); Randy Rogers & Lawrence P. King, Collier Farm Bankruptcy Guide ¶ 4.08[2][d], at 4-114 (1992).

492 *In re* Branch, 127 B.R. 891 (Bankr. N.D. Fla. 1991) (valuation to be made on surrendered property according to disposition and value without remaining property); *In re* Butler, 97 B.R. 508 (Bankr. E.D. Ark. 1988); *In re* Caraway, 95 B.R. 466 (Bankr. W.D. Ky. 1988). *See In re* Grimm, 145 B.R. 994 (Bankr. D.S.D. 1992) (stay relief and disposition of collateral after default does not result of itself in debt satisfaction).

493 *In re* Davenport, 153 B.R. 551 (B.A.P. 9th Cir. 1993); *In re* Carter, 165 B.R. 518 (Bankr. M.D. Fla. 1994) (allows surrender); *In re* Wright, 103 B.R. 905 (Bankr. M.D. Tenn. 1989); *In re* Cansler, 99 B.R. 758 (Bankr. W.D. Ky. 1989); *In re* Neff, 89 B.R. 672 (Bankr. S.D. Ohio 1988) (Agricultural Credit Act of 1987 provisions require cancellation of all but one share of a borrower's statutory stock on a dollar for dollar basis equal to the amount of principal forgiven in any restructuring agreement between the borrower and Federal Land Bank; 12 U.S.C. § 2202(b)); *In re* Ivy, 86 B.R. 623 (Bankr. W.D. Mo. 1988); *In re* Arthur, 86 B.R. 98 (Bankr. W.D. Mich. 1988); *In re* Greseth, 78 B.R. 936 (D. Minn. 1987); *In re* Massengill, 73 B.R. 1008 (Bankr. E.D.N.C. 1987).

Valuation of the reduction of the allowed secured claim of the creditor by collateral surrender must be determined by the court or by consent among the parties. That value need not be set by the subsequent sale of the property, although that method can be used. While the value attributed to the property by the creditor itself may help determine value, it will generally not be dispositive and a valuation hearing may be necessary.[494] Offer of return or surrender must be made in good faith.[495]

Chapter 12 apparently also allows debt reduction and satisfaction under a plan by surrender to a secured creditor of property of value which is *not* pledged to the creditor as security.[496] This parallels a debtor's ability to offer a secured creditor a replacement lien on unpledged collateral.[497] In one case, the debtor was allowed to surrender part of the property in full payment of the debt. This is a powerful tool, but one that might not be approved in all situations.[498]

When tangible property is surrendered to a creditor as payment under a plan, the plan should provide both for the disposition of any surplus after sale by the creditor and for treatment of the creditor's claim in the event of shortfall.[499] However, recent case law indicates that if an undersecured creditor files only a secured claim and fails to amend or seek valuation, then after surrender to the creditor of its collateral there may be no remaining unsecured claim regardless of any deficiency after sale.[500]

17.5.4.5 Sale of Property Free and Clear of Liens

Chapter 12 allows the sale of collateral in a debtor's estate free and clear of liens regardless of whether the consent of the secured creditor is granted and of whether the sale will bring sufficient funds to satisfy the entirety of the secured creditor's claim.[501] By contrast, sale free and clear of liens can only take place in other bankruptcy chapters under certain more restrictive conditions.[502] Although section 1206 is couched in terms of sale by the trustee, the debtor can sell conditioned upon court permission.[503] Any liens existing on the property before sale will attach to the sale proceeds.[504]

17.5.4.6 Replacement Liens

Because confirmation of a chapter 12 plan revests property in the debtor, and the secured creditor is bound by the plan after confirmation, under chapter 12 a debtor may be able to propose the substitution of other collateral for existing collateral if that is beneficial for the debtor and non-prejudicial to the creditor.[505] Situations in which replacement liens or substitution of different collateral may be appropriate are:

- When the debtor needs to sell equipment and replace it with new or better used equipment;
- When such substitution will allow payment of the allowed secured claim over a period of time longer than consonant with the existing collateral;
- When the creditor has agreed to replacement; or
- When additional or replacement collateral will obviate the problem of diminution of collateral value faster than scheduled repayment.[506]

Surrender has generally not been allowed under chapter 11. *See, e.g.*, *In re* Eisenbarth, 77 B.R. 235 (Bankr. D.N.D. 1987); *In re* Walker, 48 B.R. 668 (Bankr. D.S.D. 1985).

The courts in *In re Ivy* and *In re Massengill* indicated that FLB/PCA stock is to be retired and credited at book value not to exceed par or the face amount pursuant to 12 U.S.C. § 2034(a). *In re Massengill*, which has been cited in most chapter 12 cases allowing stock surrender, was reversed on appeal. Fed. Land Bank of Columbia v. Massengill, 100 B.R. 276 (W.D.N.C. 1989). This decision holds that surrender of stock in Federal Land Banks and Production Credit Associations for credit upon the secured claim is impermissible, refusing to allow bankruptcy law to override certain stock ownership requirements of the Farm Credit Act of 1971. *See also In re* Overholt, 125 B.R. 202 (S.D. Ohio 1990); *In re* Miller, 106 B.R. 136 (Bankr. N.D. Ohio 1989) (reconsidering and reversing decision at 98 B.R. 311 (1989) which had permitted stock surrender); *In re* Shannon, 100 B.R. 913 (S.D. Ohio 1989).

494 *In re* Fobian, 951 F.2d 1149 (9th Cir. 1991) (provision for revaluation after confirmation); *In re* Caraway, 95 B.R. 466 (Bankr. W.D. Ky. 1988).

495 *In re* Kerwin, 996 F.2d 552 (2d Cir. 1993) (details considerations re valuation for purposes of surrender and satisfaction); *In re* Gray-Bailey, 427 B.R. 536 (D. Idaho 2010) (promise not to oppose creditor's foreclosure action does not meet requirement for "surrender" under § 1225(a)(5)(C) for purposes of chapter 12 confirmation); *In re* Braxton, 124 B.R. 870 (Bankr. N.D. Fla. 1991) (scattered, landlocked swamp land parcels proffered for return indicated lack of good faith).

496 11 U.S.C. § 1222(b)(7); *In re* Durr, 78 B.R. 221 (Bankr. D.S.D. 1987); *In re* Indreland, 77 B.R. 268 (Bankr. D. Mont. 1987); *In re* Mikkelsen Farms, Inc. 74 B.R. 280 (Bankr. D. Or. 1987).

497 *See* § 17.5.4.6, *infra*.

498 *In re* Kerwin, 996 F.2d 552 (2d Cir. 1993).

499 *In re* Kerwin, 996 F.2d 552 (2d Cir. 1993) (surrender may be full debt satisfaction under section 1225(a)(5)(B)(ii)); *In re* Fobian, 951 F.2d 1149 (9th Cir. 1991); *In re* Gore, 113 B.R. 504 (Bankr. E.D. Ark. 1989).

500 *In re* Harrison, 987 F.2d 677 (10th Cir. 1993); *In re* Padget, 119 B.R. 793 (Bankr. D. Colo. 1990) (chapter 13). *Cf. In re* Grimm, 145 B.R. 994 (Bankr. D.S.D. 1992).

501 *See* 11 U.S.C. § 1206; *In re* Brileya, 108 B.R. 444 (Bankr. D. Vt. 1989).

502 *See* 11 U.S.C. § 363(f).

503 *In re* Webb, 932 F.2d 155 (2d Cir. 1991); *In re* Brileya, 108 B.R. 444 (Bankr. D. Vt. 1989).

504 *In re* Brileya, 108 B.R. 444 (Bankr. D. Vt. 1989).

505 11 U.S.C. §§ 1205(b)(2), 1222(b)(2). *See, e.g., In re* Lairmore, 101 B.R. 681 (Bankr. E.D. Okla. 1988); *In re* Durr, 78 B.R. 221 (Bankr. D.S.D. 1987); *In re* Indreland, 77 B.R. 268 (Bankr. D. Mont. 1987). *But see* 11 U.S.C. § 1225(a)(5)(B); *In re* Stallings, 290 B.R. 777 (Bankr. D. Idaho 2003).

The lien retention requirement of section 1225(a)(5)(B)(ii) presents special problems in reorganizing secured debt when the security is livestock that will be sold. This problem is discussed and resolved somewhat in Abbott Bank-Thedford v. Hanna (*In re* Hanna), 912 F.2d 945 (8th Cir. 1990).

506 The ability to substitute collateral appears to hinge upon: (1) the liquidity of the replacement collateral in comparison to the original collateral; and (2) the risk involved in the replacement collateral in

Replacement liens or collateral may be made part of a chapter 12 plan or such replacement may be undertaken prior to plan proposal or confirmation.

17.5.5 Chapter 12 Plan Requirements: Unsecured Claims

17.5.5.1 In General

Section 1225 also sets forth specific confirmation requirements that apply to the debtor's unsecured claims. There are two such requirements, the "liquidation test" and the "disposable income requirement." The debtor's plan must meet each of these different tests with regard to each of his or her unsecured creditors. Note that a secured creditor may have both a secured and an unsecured claim, so all of the relevant tests must be applied to that creditor.

17.5.5.2 The Liquidation Test

Chapter 12 requires that unsecured creditors under a plan receive at least as much or more than they would have received if the debtor had undergone liquidation.[507] This test is discussed elsewhere in this treatise.[508] In many farmer bankruptcies, virtually all equity has been pledged to one or more creditors as security; unpledged property is usually exempt. In such cases, unsecured creditors would receive little or nothing upon liquidation.

In some cases, however, debtors have property—particularly real property—which is not part of the exempt farmstead and which has remained unpledged. This property must be included for purposes of the liquidation analysis.[509] Moreover, if a plan proposes the sale of property, secured creditors must be protected in a way that matches their rights upon liquidation.[510]

Liquidation analysis is determined "as of the effective date of the plan."[511] Courts have keyed it to the projected effective date of the plan[512] or of the order confirming the plan.[513] The liquidation analysis may include certain postpetition property and program payments, depending upon the timing of the debtor's entitlement to them.[514] If the court recognizes the presence of fraudulent transfers, then it may require the liquidation analysis to include the value of those transfers in its calculation.[515]

Some chapter 12 trustees insist on some payment to the unsecured creditors for confirmation. However, the courts that have addressed the issue of zero percent or nominal unsecured distribution plans have clearly indicated that if they truly represent the outcome of the liquidation analysis and the disposable income test, such plans may be confirmed.[516]

17.5.5.3 The Disposable Income Requirement

The second confirmation requirement applicable to unsecured claims is the disposable income requirement. The 2005 Act made very significant changes to this requirement. These changes can best be understood in the context of prior interpretations of this requirement, even though this case law should not be binding under the new provisions.

The chapter 12 disposable income requirement precisely mirrors the provisions of chapter 13.[517] To obtain confirmation over the objection of the chapter 12 trustee or the holder of an allowed unsecured claim to treatment of the unsecured creditors, a chapter 12 plan must require that the family farmer debtor devote *all* of his or her disposable income for at least

---

comparison to the original collateral. *See, e.g., In re* Frank, 27 B.R. 748 (Bankr. S.D. Ohio 1983).

Concepts which have evolved from evaluating replacement collateral in the adequate protection context are also useful. *See, e.g., In re* O'Connor, 808 F.2d 1393 (10th Cir. 1987); *In re* Schaller, 27 B.R. 959 (W.D. Wis. 1983); *In re* Bear River Orchards, 56 B.R. 976 (Bankr. E.D. Cal. 1986).

507 11 U.S.C. § 1225(a)(4); *In re* Fortney, 36 F.3d 701 (7th Cir. 1994); Rice v. Dunbar (*In re* Rice), 357 B.R. 514 (B.A.P. 8th Cir. 2006) (denying debtors' request for a continuance and affirming dismissal of the case, finding that the debtors' plan did not meet the liquidation test), *aff'd*, 271 Fed. Appx. 538 (8th Cir. 2008) (per curiam); *In re* Fischer, 2008 WL 2788456 (Bankr. D. Neb. July 15, 2008) (denying confirmation of the debtor's plan in part because it did not meet the liquidation test); *In re* Rott, 94 B.R. 163 (Bankr. D.N.D. 1988); *In re* Nielsen, 86 B.R. 177 (Bankr. E.D. Mo. 1988) (citing Holytex Carpet Mills v. Tedford, 691 F.2d 392 (8th Cir. 1982)).

508 *See* § 12.3.1, *supra*. *See generally* Bruce H. Matson, *Understanding the New Family Farmer Bankruptcy Act*, 21 U. Rich. L. Rev. 521 (1987) (sample calculation).

For an interesting discussion on valuing stock in closely held family farm corporations for liquidation analysis purposes, see *In re* Harper, 156 B.R. 858 (Bankr. E.D. Ark. 1993).

509 *See, e.g., In re* Ayers, 137 B.R. 397 (Bankr. D. Mont. 1992).

510 *In re* Erickson, 2012 WL 1453967 (Bankr. D. Wyo. 2012).

511 11 U.S.C. 1225(a)(4).

512 *In re* Dawes, 423 B.R. 550 (Bankr. D. Kan. 2010) ("effective date of the plan" cannot be earlier than date of first confirmation hearing on plan); *In re* Hopwood, 124 B.R. 82 (Bankr. E.D. Mo. 1991); *In re* Lupfer Bros., 120 B.R. 1002 (Bankr. W.D. Mo. 1990); *In re* Musil, 99 B.R. 448 (Bankr. D. Kan. 1988) (debtors cannot redefine effective date; effective date cannot be earlier than the date the first confirmation plan heard); *In re* Perdue, 95 B.R. 475 (Bankr. W.D. Ky. 1988). *Contra In re* Nielsen, 86 B.R. 177 (Bankr. E.D. Mo. 1988) (determined from date of petition).

513 Gribbons v. Fed. Land Bank of Louisville, 106 B.R. 113 (W.D. Ky. 1989) (*dicta*); *In re* Foos, 121 B.R. 778 (Bankr. S.D. Ohio 1990); *In re* Bremer, 104 B.R. 999 (Bankr. W.D. Mo. 1989); *In re* Milleson, 83 B.R. 696 (Bankr. D. Neb. 1988).

514 Gribbons v. Fed. Land Bank of Louisville, 106 B.R. 113 (W.D. Ky. 1989) (in *dicta*); *In re* Foos, 121 B.R. 778 (Bankr. S.D. Ohio 1990) (restricted to post-filing but preconfirmation property; acceptable to exclude growing crops; exclusion of government payments depends on present entitlement to them); *In re* Lupfer Bros., 120 B.R. 1002 (Bankr. W.D. Mo. 1990); *In re* Bremer, 104 B.R. 999 (Bankr. W.D. Mo. 1989); *In re* Perdue, 95 B.R. 475 (Bankr. W.D. Ky. 1988).

515 *In re* Zurface, 95 B.R. 527 (Bankr. S.D. Ohio 1989). *But see In re* Winterroth, 97 B.R. 454 (Bankr. C.D. Ill. 1988) (absent the pendency of an adversary proceeding to recover a fraudulent conveyance, court cannot rule on its validity or impact).

516 *See In re* Kjerulf, 82 B.R. 123 (Bankr. D. Or. 1987); *In re* Big Hook Land & Cattle Co., 77 B.R. 793, 795 (Bankr. D. Mont. 1987); *In re* Danelson, 77 B.R. 261 (Bankr. D. Mont. 1987).

517 *Compare* 11 U.S.C. § 1225(b)(1) *with* 11 U.S.C. § 1325(b)(1). *See* § 12.3.4, *supra*.

three years to repayment under the plan.[518] Although an objection is needed to trigger this requirement, the trustee or any unsecured creditor has the right to object, and it should be presumed that someone will do so.[519]

Case law reveals a very significant difference, however, between how the identical disposable income language has been interpreted in chapter 12 and chapter 13.[520] Considering the identical language in section 1325, courts have held that, in the context of a chapter 13 case, projected disposable income is determined as of plan confirmation. The debtor includes reference to disposable income in the proposed plan, and if there is an objection, the debtor is required to "make a best effort" at a three-year projection of disposable income. This "best effort" may become a factor in the good faith analysis required for confirmation. Under these chapter 13 cases, once the plan has been confirmed, it has a binding effect on the debtor and the creditors. The potential for increases in income beyond that which is projected is handled with a specific provision in the plan addressing this event. The actual amount of projected disposable income cannot be relitigated as a basis for determining dischargeability.[521]

Some courts have not interpreted the disposable income requirement in chapter 12 this way, however. Without addressing the chapter 13 interpretation, these courts have allowed the issue of disposable income to be raised as an objection to discharge, even when the debtor had met the projections contained in a confirmed plan. Debtors who can be shown to have had *actual* disposable income over the term of the plan that has not been turned over to unsecured creditors have been denied discharge for failing to fulfill the requirements of the plan as required under section 1225.[522]

This interpretation of the disposable income requirement presented serious difficulties for family farmers on the verge of emerging from a successful bankruptcy. It forced farm debtors to go back and account for all income and expenses throughout the plan term, litigating a wide variety of issues, including whether expenses were actually "necessary for the continuation, preservation, and operation" of the farm.[523] As major undersecured creditors as well as the chapter 12 trustee viewed discharge as their last chance to increase payments from the debtor, aggressive investigations were conducted.[524] Moreover, particularly harsh judicial rulings raised concerns that farmers' otherwise successful reorganizations would fail due to the imposition of significant obligations at the end of the plan term.[525] There was also concern that farmers were not being left with sufficient liquid assets to keep the farm operating after discharge.[526]

The 2005 Act amended the disposable income requirement, section 1225(b), in a direct effort to resolve these problems.[527] Three alternatives are now offered to the debtor for confirmation. The first two alternatives remain unchanged. The debtor can pay the full value of the unsecured claims under section 1225(b)(1)(A). As a second alternative, the original "projected disposable income" language is retained as section 1225(b)(1)(B). A new third alternative is provided: the debtor's plan may provide that the "value of the property to be distributed under the plan . . . is not less than the debtor's projected disposable income."[528]

This change, and particularly the difference between the second and third alternatives, requires an understanding of the history of farm debtors' prior problems with the courts' interpretation of the disposable income requirement. Under a literal interpretation of the unchanged second alternative, the payment of projected disposable income is all that was ever required of the debtor. Drafters of the changes were faced with the odd task

---

518 11 U.S.C. § 1225(b)(1)(B); *In re* Fortney, 36 F.3d 701 (7th Cir. 1994); *In re* Sandifer, 2011 WL 2118863 (Bankr. D.S.C. 2011) (denying confirmation of chapter 12 plan because it failed to commit all disposable income as required under § 1225(b)(1)(B)); *In re* Winterroth, 97 B.R. 454 (Bankr. C.D. Ill. 1988).

Spousal income *may* be included in disposable income calculations for feasibility purposes; it is unresolved whether it *must* be. *In re* Soper, 152 B.R. 984 (Bankr. D. Kan. 1993).

519 Farm Credit Bank v. Hurd, 108 B.R. 430 (W.D. Tenn. 1989); *In re* Rowley, 143 B.R. 547 (Bankr. D.S.D. 1992), *aff'd*, 22 F.3d 190 (8th Cir. 1994); *In re* Dues, 98 B.R. 434 (Bankr. N.D. Ind. 1989); *In re* Coffman, 90 B.R. 878 (Bankr. W.D. Tenn. 1988).

Failure of a creditor to object upon this basis at confirmation will preclude any subsequent objection upon subsequent modification, unless the debtor proposes a modification prejudicial to the creditor. *In re* Coffman, 90 B.R. 878 (Bankr. W.D. Tenn. 1988).

520 For a detailed and critical look at judicial interpretations of disposable income as well as a discussion of recent changes, see Susan A. Schneider, *Bankruptcy Reform and Family Farmers: Correcting the Disposable Income Problem*, 38 Tex. Tech L. Rev. 309 (2006).

521 *See, e.g.*, Anderson v. Satterlee (*In re* Anderson), 21 F.3d 355 (9th Cir. 1994).

522 *See, e.g.*, Hammrich v. Lovald, 98 F.3d 388 (8th Cir. 1996); Broken Bow Ranch, Inc. v. Farmers Home Admin., 33 F.3d 1005 (8th Cir. 1994); Rowley v. Yarnall, 22 F.3d 190 (8th Cir. 1994); *In re* Schmidt, 145 B.R. 983 (Bankr. D.S.D. 1991); *In re* Coffman, 90 B.R. 878 (Bankr. W.D. Tenn. 1988).

523 *See, e.g., In re* Wood, 122 B.R. 107, 115 (Bankr. D. Idaho 1990) (the disposable income test requires the court to conduct a subjective analysis of the debtor's expenditures to determine if they were reasonably necessary).

524 *See, e.g., id.* at 116 (categorizing trustee's "microscopic examination" of debtor's records as "extreme" and finding that no disposable income was owed).

In *In re Wood*, the trustee claimed that the debtor owed over $218,000 in disposable income. In reaching that sum, he included non-cash items such as depreciation deductions and a net operating loss carryover as items of income. *Id.*

525 *See, e.g.*, Hammrich v. Lovald (*In re* Hammrich), 98 F.3d 388, 389 (8th Cir. 1996) (debtors required to pay $95,885.86 in order to receive discharge); Broken Bow Ranch v. Farmers Home Admin. (*In re* Broken Bow), 33 F.3d 1005, 1007 (8th Cir. 1994) (debtors required to pay $81,862 in order to receive discharge).

526 *See, e.g., Hammrich*, 98 F.3d at 390 (the value of calves that were not yet ready for market were "marketable commodities" that should be included in disposable income calculations); *Broken Bow Ranch*, 33 F.3d at 1009 (computation of disposable income can require debtor to obtain borrowed financing for crop input expenses).

527 Pub. L. No. 109-8, § 1006, 119 Stat. 23, 187 (codified at 11 U.S.C. § 1225(b)).

528 11 U.S.C. § 1225(b).

of forcing compliance with the projected income requirement in chapter 12 to bring it in line with chapter 13 interpretations of the same language. Faced with this dilemma, the third alternative provides a workable solution. It allows the debtor's plan to provide that the value of property distributed under the plan will not be less than the projected amount of disposable income as determined at confirmation.[529] This affirms the reliance upon projected income, mirroring the language used to address secured claims under section 1225(a)(5)(B)(ii): "the value . . . of property to be distributed . . . under the plan . . . is not less than the allowed amount of such claim." By using the term "value," it offers the debtor the ability to provide for payment of the projected amount through a property distribution. And it allows the debtor to provide value that should essentially eliminate any future concern about the obligation.

As further protection for debtors, section 1229—modification of plan after confirmation—was amended to restrict changes to the plan once it has been confirmed.[530] This provision provides that a debtor's obligations under a confirmed chapter 12 plan may not be modified "to increase the amount of any payment due before the plan as modified becomes the plan." Under this provision, modifications should be allowed only to create new obligations for the future, capturing future income that is greater than that anticipated when the plan was originally confirmed. This change should prevent courts from looking back to retroactively assess past disposable income obligations.

The 2005 Act provided that no party except for the debtor can call for any increase based on disposable income that would "increase the amount of payments to unsecured creditors required for a particular month so that the aggregate of such payments exceeds the debtor's disposable income for such month."[531] This provision also prevents the court from being able to go back into the debtor's past, either at a discharge hearing or during the plan term, to impose a new obligation that is greater than what the individual can presently afford to pay from disposable income that month.

Finally, the 2005 Act provided that the plan may not be modified "in the last year of the plan by anyone except the debtor, to require payments that would leave the debtor with insufficient funds to carry on the farming operation after the plan is completed."[532] This provision emphasizes the importance of allowing the debtor sufficient income for the continuation of the farming operation, consistent with the definition of disposable income.

These provisions should prohibit the type of retroactive accounting that has been undertaken by courts at discharge when courts have attempted to reconcile early projections with what the trustee or creditors argue was actual disposable income at the time of discharge.[533]

Given the changes to chapter 12, debtors should propose chapter 12 plans that reflect the literal interpretation of the projected disposable income requirement. Whenever possible, all disputes regarding disposable income should be raised at the plan confirmation hearing, and a reasonable disposable income payment should be determined at that time. Attention should be directed to the courts that have made such disposable income determinations in chapter 13 cases involving farm debtors.[534] Similarly, feasibility analysis that is already required for confirmation can be used as a model for assessing projected income and expenses.[535] The fixing of a certain sum as an obligation provides the debtor with a clear benchmark and the creditors with a defined expectation of payment. Changes in income or expenses that occur during the plan term and that are significant should be addressed according to the modification provisions set forth in section 1229. As shown by the difficulty presented with determining actual disposable income, the courts should find that the literal interpretation of the projected disposable income requirement now mandated by the 2005 amendments will in fact be an easier and fairer standard to apply.

Minimal investment in chemicals, fertilizer, feed, seed, and the like may result in substandard crop and livestock production that will be inadequate to support a chapter 12 plan. Similarly, minimization of critical farm expenses in chapter 12 will result in early plan failure and bad business planning. Budgeting for operating expenses should therefore take into account reasonable—neither optimal nor minimal—expenditures consonant with good farming practices and yields necessary for chapter 12

---

529 11 U.S.C. § 1225(b)(1)(c)).

530 Pub. L. No. 109-8, § 1006, 119 Stat. 23, 187 (codified at 11 U.S.C. § 1229(d)(1)).

531 Pub. L. No. 109-8, § 1006, 119 Stat. 23, 187 (codified at 11 U.S.C.§ 1229(d)(2)).

532 Pub. L. No. 109-8, § 1006, 119 Stat. 23, 187 (codified at 11 U.S.C.§ 1229(d)(3)).

533 This issue has been complicated by the proposal and confirmation of plans that require the debtor to pay actual disposable income. Although these plans have been the direct result of judicial interpretation of the disposable income requirement as requiring actual accounting at discharge, if this is what the debtor's plan provides, the debtor will be bound to its terms regardless of the statutory change. Given the evidence that Congress intended to correct an erroneous interpretation of the law, one can argue that preexisting plans that were silent as to the issue of actual or projected disposable income should be interpreted in a manner consistent with the new law. Taking this a step further, it might be possible for debtors to argue that they should be allowed to modify a plan calling for actual disposable income to bring it into conformance with the new language.

534 See, e.g., In re Edwards, 2004 WL 316418, at *12 (Bankr. D. Vt. Feb. 13, 2004) (mem.) (the farm debtor's proposed chapter 13 plan did not commit all of his projected disposable income to plan payments and denying confirmation); In re Schyma, 68 B.R. 52, 63 (Bankr. D. Minn. 1985) (the farm debtors' proposed chapter 13 plan committed all of their projected disposable income to plan payments, but denying confirmation on other grounds).

In both cases, the courts were able to consider the financial information presented and make a reasonable assessment of projected disposable income. See Edwards, 2004 WL 316418, at *12; Schyma, 68 B.R. at 63.

535 See, e.g., In re Novak, 252 B.R. 487, 492 (Bankr. D.N.D. 2000) (considering the debtor's cash flow and finding that the debtors' plan was not feasible).

17.5.5.4 Treatment of Priority Unsecured Creditors

Section 507 sets forth several categories of unsecured indebtedness which are accorded priority treatment. Attorneys should always review this section for applicability to their client's individual situation. Section 1222 sets forth the appropriate treatment of these claims in a chapter 12 bankruptcy, with the general rule being that such claims are entitled to full payment.

The 2005 Act amended section 1222 to provide an exception for certain tax claims related to capital gains. This provision now provides that a "claim owed to a governmental unit that arises as the result of a sale, transfer, or exchange or other disposition of any farm asset used in the debtor's farming operation . . . is not entitled to priority under section 507" so long the debtor receives a discharge of debt.[536] The provision was added to reflect the problem of huge capital gain taxes that might result from the downsizing of farming operations as part of the Chapter 12 reorganization process.

This tax advantage produced significant litigation regarding the scope of the debtor's ability to treat tax obligations as nonpriority unsecured claims, with debtors arguing that the favorable tax treatment extends to gains from all assets sold prepetition or postpetition, and the Internal Revenue Service arguing that it was limited to liabilities that existed prepetition and limited to gains from the sale of capital assets.[537]

The U.S. Supreme Court resolved the split in the circuits on this issue in In re Hall, holding that the sale of property postpetition does not produce a tax liability "incurred by the estate" under section 503(b), and thus is not an obligation of the estate. It is "neither collectible nor dischargeable" as part of the Chapter 12 plan.[538] The Court is correct in noting that the drafters of Chapter 12 modeled it after Chapter 13 instead of Chapter 11. As such, the Chapter 12 estate is not a separate entity for taxable purposes.

The Supreme Court interpretation in Hall presents a significant problem for debtors who need to sell assets as part of their Chapter 12 plan. Since Hall, Senators Chuck Grassley (R-IA) and Al Franken (D-MN) have introduced the Family Farmer Bankruptcy Tax Clarification Act of 2012 (S.3545) to resolve this problem. Under this proposed Act, any unsecured claim owed to a "governmental unit" by either the farmer debtor or the bankruptcy estate that arises as a result of the sale, transfer, exchange, or other disposition of any farm asset used in the debtor's farming operation would qualify as an unsecured dischargeable claim, without regard to whether the disposition of the farm assets occurred before or after the farmer filed a petition for bankruptcy. The Act also establishes a process for governmental units to a file a postpetition claim for taxes under Chapter 12. Until this or similar legislation is passed, however, the Hall problem remains.

By statutory definition, priority debts must be unsecured.[539] If a tax claim qualifies as a secured claim, it does not qualify for priority treatment, so the discussion above is irrelevant. A tax debt is secured in bankruptcy to the extent a lien securing the debt arises under state or federal law and the lien is unavoidable in bankruptcy.[540] If a tax creditor has a secured claim that is provided for in the plan, it is subject to section 1225(a)(5).

Domestic support obligations are included in the list of priority obligations in section 507.[541] The repayment of priority debts may occur over the course of five years, if the plan so provides and is confirmed.[542] Specifically with regard to domestic support obligations, however, section 1222(4), provides that "notwithstanding any other provision of this section, a plan may provide for less than full payment of all amounts owed for a claim entitled to priority under section 507(a)(1)(B) only if the plan provides that all of the debtor's projected disposable income for a five-year period beginning on the date that the first payment is due under the plan will be applied to make payments under the plan."[543]

Unlike the provisions of chapter 11,[544] and in contrast to the language used in section 1225(a)(5)(B)(ii) with regard to allowed secured claims, the language of section 1222(a)(2) does not provide for payment of the "present value" of the priority unsecured claim. As a result, interest or discount value need not be added to the repayment of a priority claim.[545] Also in

---

536 11 U.S.C. § 1222(a)(2)(A).
537 The Eighth Circuit ruled that the ability to strip a tax claim of its priority under § 1222(a)(2)(A) applies to postpetition sales of farm assets as well as prepetition sales. Knudsen v. Internal Revenue Serv., 581 F.3d 696 (8th Cir. 2009). See also In re Ficken, 430 B.R. 663 (B.A.P. 10th Cir. 2010); In re Schilke, 379 B.R. 899 (Bankr. D. Neb. 2007). However, the Ninth Circuit held that § 1222(a)(2)(A) does not apply to postpetition sales of farm assets, because a chapter 12 estate is not a separate entity for tax purposes, and thus it cannot "incur" a tax. Therefore it cannot take advantage of the special tax treatment allowed under § 1222(a)(2)(A). U.S. v. Hall, 617 F.3d 1161 (9th Cir. 2010). Accord In re Dawes, 652 F.3d 1236 (10th Cir. 2011); Smith v. Internal Revenue Serv., 447 B.R. 435 (Bankr. W.D. Pa. 2011).
538 U.S. v. Hall, 132 S. Ct. 1882 (2012).
539 In re Stanford, 826 F.2d 353 (5th Cir. 1987); United States v. Neal Pharmacal Co., 789 F.2d 1283 (8th Cir. 1986); In re Wrigley, 195 B.R. 914 (Bankr. E.D. Ark. 1996) (county tax liability creates a lien under state law and therefore tax claim is not a priority claim).
540 11 U.S.C. § 101(37), (53); In re Stanford, 826 F.2d 353 (5th Cir. 1987); In re Krump, 89 B.R. 821 (Bankr. D.S.D. 1988).
541 11 U.S.C. § 507(a)(1).
542 11 U.S.C. § 1222(c).
  One court has allowed a debtor to grant a tax lien on unencumbered property, subject to objection by other creditors, for payment as a secured claim over a longer period while providing for interest. See In re Palombo, 144 B.R. 516 (Bankr. D. Colo. 1992); In re Teigen, 142 B.R. 397 (Bankr. D. Mont. 1992); In re C.R. Druse, Sr., Ltd., 82 B.R. 1013 (Bankr. D. Neb. 1988).
543 11 U.S.C. § 1222(4).
544 11 U.S.C. § 1129(a)(9)(B), (C).
545 In re Mitchell, 210 B.R. 978 (Bankr. N.D. Tex. 1997) (priority income tax debt); In re Bossert, 201 B.R. 553 (Bankr. E.D. Wash. 1996) (same). See In re Wakehill Farms, 123 B.R. 774 (Bankr. N.D. Ohio 1990); In re Krump, 89 B.R. 821 (Bankr. D.S.D. 1988); In re Herr, 80 B.R. 135 (Bankr. S.D. Iowa 1987).

contrast to chapter 11, the payment of priority administrative expenses is not required immediately upon confirmation or on the effective date of the chapter 12 plan.[546]

17.5.6 Classification of Claims

17.5.6.1 Introduction

Generally claims of equal rank concerning the same property (whether as collateral or as distribution upon or in lieu of liquidation from general assets) should be included in the same class. Claims of different rank or of the same rank concerning different property should be separately classified. Classification of claims should not be arbitrary, should not do substantial violence to the nature and rights inherent in the claims, and should not uselessly increase the number of classes of creditors.[547]

17.5.6.2 Classification of Codebtor Claims

Chapter 12, like chapter 13, specifically allows the different treatment of unsecured claims on consumer debts with codebtors.[548] Those debts can be placed, for more favorable treatment, in a separate class apart from the general unsecured claims.[549] Debts in such a class are the same debts to which the automatic codebtor stay of section 1201 applies.[550]

Congress did not extend this provision in chapter 12 to encompass business indebtedness. The codebtor classification should not prove very useful in chapter 12 because most consumer debt for farmers is not joint except with a spouse.[551]

17.5.6.3 Classification of the Claims of Unsecured Creditors

Unsecured claims may be classified into different classes for separate treatment in a chapter 12 plan.[552] There is no requirement in the Code that all similar creditors must be grouped into the same class.[553] Another general rule is that unsecured creditors may bear discrimination by classification, but not unfair discrimination.[554]

In addition, section 1222(a)(2) creates at least two classes of unsecured creditors: unsecured creditors entitled to priority treatment under section 507 and other unsecured creditors. Creditors in the priority class of creditors must be paid 100 cents on the dollar on their claims over the life of the plan, unless any creditor consents to different treatment.[555] For most farmer bankruptcies, this class will contain certain tax claims and administrative expenses.[556] Although all priority creditors must receive one-hundred cents on the dollar, it is possible to break out separate classes of priority creditors without impermissible discriminatory treatment. For example, certain administrative expenses may be paid out of the first distribution under the plan (for example, repayment of crop financing, attorney fees), and other priority claims spread over the plan's life (for example, taxes).

The general unsecured creditors include all remaining creditors in the family farmer's bankruptcy, including the undersecured portion of indebtedness of creditors with collateral.[557] As a general rule, all unsecured claims and the unsecured claims of creditors holding collateral worth less than their indebtedness are placed in one class.[558] However, there may be compelling reasons for breaking some claims into separate classes for different treatment, so long as the plan does not discriminate unfairly among the classes of unsecured creditors.

Unsecured creditors may be divided into separate classes based upon their interplay with the bankruptcy.[559] Chapter 11, with its commercial context and discharge provisions similar to chapter 12, offers a closer analogy than chapter 13 consumer

---

546 *In re* Mosbrucker, 227 B.R. 434 (B.A.P. 8th Cir. 1998) (unpaid employee withholding taxes are nondischargeable priority trust fund taxes though labeled penalties by the Internal Revenue Service), *aff'd*, 198 F.3d 250 (8th Cir. 1999). *See In re* Palombo, 144 B.R. 516 (Bankr. D. Colo. 1992); *In re* Teigen, 142 B.R. 397 (Bankr. D. Mont. 1992); *In re* Citrowske, 72 B.R. 613 (Bankr. D. Minn. 1987). *Cf.* 11 U.S.C. § 1129(a)(9)(A).
See also discussion of treatment of priority debts in § 17.5.5.4, *infra*.
547 *See* Anderson, *Classification of Claims and Interests in Reorganization Cases Under the New Bankruptcy Code*, 58 Am. Bankr. L.J. 99 (1984).
548 11 U.S.C. § 1222(b)(1); 11 U.S.C. § 1322(b)(1).
See § 9.4.5, *supra*, for a discussion of the codebtor stay in chapter 13.
549 *See, e.g.*, Barnes v. Whelan, 689 F.2d 193 (D.C. Cir. 1982); *In re* Dondero, 58 B.R. 847 (Bankr. D. Or. 1986); *In re* Perkins, 55 B.R. 422 (Bankr. N.D. Okla. 1985).
550 For a discussion of the types of debts which may be properly placed in such a codebtor class or must be excluded, see § 17.4.4.2, *supra*.
551 In most cases, this joint debt is farm operation debt which would not be subject to the codebtor stay and which would compel a joint petition under 11 U.S.C. § 302.

552 11 U.S.C. §§ 1222(a)(3), (b)(1).
553 Teamsters Nat'l Freight Indus. Negotiating Comm. v. U.S. Truck Co., 800 F.2d 581 (6th Cir. 1986); *In re* Planes, Inc., 48 B.R. 698 (Bankr. N.D. Ga. 1985).
554 *See* § 12.4, *supra*.
555 11 U.S.C. § 1222(a)(2).
Unlike cases under chapter 11, administrative expenses need not be paid at confirmation but can be paid over time. *In re* Citrowske, 72 B.R. 613 (Bankr. D. Minn. 1987).
556 11 U.S.C. §§ 507(a)(1), 503, 547(b).
557 11 U.S.C. § 506(a); *In re* Hollinrake, 93 B.R. 183 (Bankr. S.D. Iowa 1988).
558 3 Norton Bankr. L. & Prac. § 60.05; *In re* Pine Lake Vill., 19 B.R. 819 (Bankr. S.D.N.Y. 1982). *See* First Nat'l Bank v. Allen, 118 F.3d 1289 (8th Cir. 1997) (failure to object to plan which provided for banks' secured claims, but not their unsecured claims constitutes waiver of the unsecured claims).
559 *See* Anderson, *Classification of Claims and Interests in Reorganization Cases Under the New Bankruptcy Code*, 58 Am. Bankr. L.J. 99 (1984); Blair, *Classification of Unsecured Claims in Chapter 11 Reorganizations*, 58 Am. Bankr. L.J. 197 (1984).

cases. Permitted chapter 11 classes may include trade creditors and creditors upon which the debtor—particularly a rural debtor—must depend for continued credit or services,[560] certain nondischargeable debts,[561] and unsecured portions of the debts of otherwise secured creditors.[562] Yet greater flexibility in claims classification should be available in chapter 12, because there is no voting and thus less incentive for a court to condemn creative classes for supposed gerrymandering.[563]

17.5.6.4 Classification of the Claims of Secured Creditors

The classification of secured creditors in chapter 12 should follow the same procedure generally used in chapter 11, rather than chapter 13: each secured creditor should be placed in a separate class.[564] This approach is in keeping with the general admonition concerning claims classification that only creditors of equal rank should be placed within the same class. Because there are differences in the collateral or the position of a creditor with regard to its interest in the collateral, each secured creditor's claim will be fundamentally different. Segregation of each secured creditor is advisable because each secured claim will probably differ in its treatment according to:

- Term over which repayment will be effectuated;[565]
- Interest rate;[566]
- Collateralization and lien retention;[567]
- Creditor agreement to a particular treatment;
- Surrender of collateral in whole or part to the creditor.

Because there is no balloting procedure in chapter 12, as there is in chapter 11, this breakout presents no hazard for purposes of balloting or the section 1111(b)(2) election. Remember that creditors that are undersecured have allowed secured claims only to the extent of the value of their collateral.[568] As a result, such creditors must also have a part of their claims classified with the unsecured creditors.[569] A secured creditor with more than one variety of claim, for example, a security interest in farmstead property and a security interest in equipment, may be placed in one class for treatment, or two or more classes based upon different periods for repayment dictated by different collateral.

Although most courts find the anti-discrimination test of 11 U.S.C. § 1222(a)(3), to be generally inapplicable to secured claims,[570] at least one court has determined that it also forbids vastly disproportionate interest and term treatment among secured creditors with similar claims.[571] However, the satisfaction of different secured creditors by partial surrender of collateral with repayment[572] or complete surrender of collateral[573] while other secured creditors are paid over time has not been found to be impermissible discrimination among secured creditors.

A statutory lien may be avoidable under 11 U.S.C. §§ 545(3) and 544(a). Hence, like liens avoidable under section 522(f), failure to reduce such a lien to unsecured status can result in more favorable treatment to that creditor when unsecured creditors are not paid in full. This may discriminate unfairly against a class or classes of unsecured creditors in derogation of section 1222(b)(1).[574]

17.5.7 Other Chapter 12 Plan Requirements

17.5.7.1 Good Faith Test

Section 1225 also includes a "good faith" test for plan confirmation. The plan must have been proposed in good faith, that is, the debtor must have a sincere intention to reorganize the farming operation according to the plan. Chapter 12 is not to be used solely to delay creditors from enforcing their legal rights.[575]

Courts which have addressed good faith in chapter 12 cases have found evidence of lack of good faith when there has been: (1) failure to disclose material assets, transfers, and indebtedness;[576] (2) abusive refiling and filing for purposes of delay;[577]

---

560 Brinkley v. Chase Manhattan Mortgage & Realty Trust, 622 F.2d 872 (5th Cir. 1980); In re Sutherland, 3 B.R. 420 (Bankr. W.D. Ark. 1980).
561 In re Haag, 3 B.R. 649 (Bankr. D. Or. 1980) (child support). But see In re May, 1999 Bankr. LEXIS 1750 (Bankr. D. Kan. Nov. 22, 1999) (separate classification of debt incurred by fraud was not fair).
562 These may be placed in a different class, but different treatment may be prohibited unless the interests of these creditors are dissimilar to unsecured creditors in general.
563 Compare In re Greystone III Joint Venture, 948 F.2d 134 (5th Cir. 1991) with In re ZRM-Oklahoma P'ship, 156 B.R. 67 (Bankr. W.D. Okla. 1993).
564 In re Robinson Ranch, Inc., 75 B.R. 606 (Bankr. D. Mont. 1987); In re Citrowske, 72 B.R. 613 (Bankr. D. Minn. 1987); In re Martin, 66 B.R. 921 (Bankr. D. Mont. 1986) (chapter 11).
565 See § 17.5.4.2, supra.
566 See § 17.5.4.3, supra.
567 See §§ 17.5.3, 16.5.4, supra.
568 11 U.S.C. § 506(a); Harmon v. United States, 101 F.3d 574 (8th Cir. 1996) (lien stripping permitted in chapter 12); In re Zabel, 249 B.R. 764 (Bankr. E.D. Wis. 2000). See § 11.2, supra.
569 See First Nat'l Bank v. Allen, 118 F.3d 1289 (8th Cir. 1997) (failure to object to plan which provided for banks' secured claims, but not their unsecured claims constitutes waiver of the unsecured claims).
570 In re Fortney, 36 F.3d 701 (7th Cir. 1994) (treatment of tax lien can be different from mortgages and on short amortization even if longer treatment would result in increased payments to unsecured creditors); In re Harper, 157 B.R. 858 (Bankr. E.D. Ark. 1993); In re Bland, 149 B.R. 980 (Bankr. D. Kan. 1992) (cure and restructuring allowed).
571 In re Weldin-Lynn, Inc., 79 B.R. 409 (Bankr. E.D. Ark. 1987).
572 In re Indreland, 77 B.R. 268 (Bankr. D. Mont. 1987); In re Robinson Ranch, 75 B.R. 606 (Bankr. D. Mont. 1987).
573 In re B & G Farms, Inc., 82 B.R. 549 (Bankr. D. Mont. 1988).
574 In re Arnold, 88 B.R. 917 (Bankr. N.D. Iowa 1988).
575 11 U.S.C. § 1225(a)(3).
576 In re Luchenbill, 112 B.R. 204 (Bankr. E.D. Mich. 1990); In re Welsh, 78 B.R. 984 (Bankr. W.D. Mo. 1987).
  Not every such failure constitutes bad faith, however. In re Nelson, 291 B.R. 861 (Bankr. D. Idaho 2003) (debtors' prepetition sale of cattle without advising secured creditor reflected poor judgment but was not bad faith that would preclude plan confirmation).
577 In re Beswick, 98 B.R. 900 (Bankr. N.D. Ill. 1989); In re Galloway

(3) transfer of assets to debtor controlled entity prepetition to avoid foreclosure;[578] (4) failure to file timely schedules and obey court orders[579] (5) filing of a petition without intent or ability to reorganize;[580] and (6) inadequate claim valuation.[581] Abusive refiling with lack of good faith can cause subsequent dismissal *with* prejudice, and in extreme cases potential liability for costs, expenses, and attorney fees.[582]

By contrast, courts have not generally found evidence of a lack of good faith from: (1) creating exempt assets from nonexempt assets prepetition;[583] (2) zero or nominal distribution to unsecured creditors;[584] or (3) surrender of collateral to secured creditors.[585]

Some indicia of good faith in farm cases, as observed in the case of In re Kloberdanz,[586] appear to be: (1) a substantially leaner farm operation pared down prepetition; (2) relatively short payout to principal secured creditors; (3) sharing with secured creditors any upside gain or sales proceeds of farm if sold during plan; (4) demonstrably frugal lifestyle and modest living expenses; and (5) substantial work and personal involvement of both debtors in management and day-to-day farm operation.

17.5.7.2 The Feasibility Requirement

17.5.7.2.1 *General observations*

Section 1225 also contains a feasibility requirement.[587] The debtor must be able to show the court that the plan is feasible, that is, that he or she can afford to make all of the payments that are required under the plan. This requirement is independent of the requirements for secured and unsecured claims, implying that courts can make an independent inquiry even if creditors do not raise an objection. Demonstrating the plan's feasibility is likely to require carefully prepared cash flow projections for the full term of the plan and may require debtor testimony. Non-farm income can be used to make plan payments.

It is the debtor's burden to demonstrate feasibility at confirmation,[588] although the debtor is given the benefit of the doubt.[589] Although the debtor is not expected to be able to guarantee the success of the plan, the debtor must provide "reasonable assurance that the plan can be effectuated."[590]

The bankruptcy court is charged with the responsibility to make an informed, independent judgment based upon information and estimates embracing all relevant facts.[591] The court can

---

Farms, Inc., 82 B.R. 486 (Bankr. S.D. Iowa 1987); *In re* McDermott, 77 B.R. 384 (Bankr. N.D.N.Y. 1987).

578 *In re* S Farms One, Inc., 73 B.R. 103 (Bankr. D. Colo. 1987).
   However filing immediately pre-foreclosure is not in itself bad faith. *See In re* Euerle Farms, Inc., 861 F.2d 1089 (8th Cir. 1988); *In re* Marshall, 108 B.R. 195 (Bankr. C.D. Ill. 1989); *In re* Snider, 99 B.R. 374 (Bankr. S.D. Ohio 1989); *In re* Zurface, 95 B.R. 527 (Bankr. S.D. Ohio 1989); *In re* Land, 82 B.R. 572 (Bankr. D. Colo. 1988); *In re* Ouverson, 79 B.R. 830 (Bankr. N.D. Iowa 1987) (but can be with other factors); *In re* Weldin-Lynn, Inc., 79 B.R. 409 (Bankr. E.D. Ark. 1987); *In re* Route 202 Corp., 37 B.R. 367 (Bankr. E.D. Pa. 1984) (chapter 11).

579 Lerch v. Fed. Land Bank of St. Louis, 94 B.R. 998 (N.D. Ill. 1989); *In re* S Farms One, Inc., 73 B.R. 103 (Bankr. D. Colo. 1987); *In re* Turner, 71 B.R. 120 (Bankr. D. Mont. 1987).

580 *In re* Euerle Farms, Inc., 861 F.2d 1089 (8th Cir. 1988); *In re* Gibson, 355 B.R. 807 (Bankr. E.D. Cal. 2006). *See also In re* Wald, 211 B.R. 359 (Bankr. D.N.D. 1997) (lack of good faith found based on prior unsuccessful cases and lack of meaningful change in circumstances).

581 *In re* Euerle Farms, Inc., 861 F.2d 1089 (8th Cir. 1988); *In re* Melcher, 416 B.R. 666 (D. Neb. 2009) (confirmation of chapter 12 plan was denied, as it unfairly discriminated against claim of debtor's ex-wife and thus was not proposed in good faith with respect to her claim).

582 *In re* Borg, 105 B.R. 56 (Bankr. D. Mont. 1989); *In re* McDermott, 77 B.R. 384 (Bankr. N.D.N.Y. 1987).
   Absent court order for cause, however, dismissals are without prejudice except to the extent of limitations in 11 U.S.C. § 109(g). 11 U.S.C. § 349(a). *See* §§ 13.2, 17.4.6, *supra*.

583 *In re* McKeag, 77 B.R. 716 (Bankr. D. Neb. 1987) (but court also found that converting nonexempt assets to exempt assets immediately prepetition may militate for some plan repayment based upon value of such converted assets).

584 *See In re* Kjerulf, 82 B.R. 123 (Bankr. D. Or. 1987); *In re* Big Hook Land & Cattle Co., 77 B.R. 793, 795 (Bankr. D. Mont. 1987); *In re* Citrowske, 72 B.R. 613 (Bankr. D. Minn. 1987).

585 *In re* Kjerulf, 82 B.R. 123 (Bankr. D. Or. 1987).
   However transfer of collateral back to creditors to help guarantors can be bad faith in a corporate context. *In re* Sandy Ridge Dev. Corp., 77 B.R. 69 (Bankr. M.D. La. 1987).

586 83 B.R. 767 (Bankr. D. Colo. 1988).

587 11 U.S.C. § 1225(a)(6).

588 *In re* Ames, 973 F.2d 849 (10th Cir. 1992); *In re* Wilson, 378 B.R. 862 (Bankr. D. Mont. 2007); *In re* Gough, 190 B.R. 455 (Bankr. M.D. Fla. 1996); *In re* Foertsch, 167 B.R. 555 (Bankr. D.N.D. 1994); *In re* Zurface, 95 B.R. 527 (Bankr. S.D. Ohio 1989); *In re* Adam, 92 B.R. 732 (Bankr. E.D. Mich. 1988); *In re* Crowley, 85 B.R. 76 (Bankr. W.D. Wis. 1988); *In re* Snider Farms, Inc., 83 B.R. 1003 (Bankr. N.D. Ind. 1988); *In re* Eber-Acres Farm, 82 B.R. 889 (Bankr. S.D. Ohio 1987).

589 *In re* Rape, 104 B.R. 741 (W.D.N.C. 1989); *In re* Hudson, 2011 WL 1004630 (Bankr. M.D. Tenn. 2011) (finding debtors' plan to be feasible, discussing feasibility requirement, debtor's burden of proof for showing feasibility, and purposes of chapter that lead to giving debtor "the benefit of the doubt"); *In re* Wilson, 378 B.R. 862 (Bankr. D. Mont. 2007); *In re* Volker Farms, 2007 WL 626042 (Bankr. D. Or. Feb. 23, 2007); *In re* Tofsrud, 230 B.R. 862 (Bankr. D.N.D. 1999); *In re* Tate, 217 B.R. 518 (Bankr. E.D. Tex. 1997) (lack of feasibility found even after debtors are given the benefit of the doubt); *In re* Foertsch, 167 B.R. 555 (Bankr. D.N.D. 1994); *In re* Harper, 157 B.R. 858 (Bankr. E.D. Ark. 1993).

590 *In re* Ames, 973 F.2d 849, 851 (10th Cir. 1992) (finding that debtors' plan was not feasible; quoting *In re* Hopwood, 124 B.R. 82, 86 (E.D. Mo. 1991)); *In re* Melcher, 416 B.R. 666 (D. Neb. 2009) (insufficient evidence was shown to establish feasibility; revenue projections were higher than historical earnings without changes in the operation). *See also In re* Wilson, 378 B.R. 862 (Bankr. D. Mont. 2007); *In re* Hermesch Entities, 2007 WL 781938 (Bankr. E.D. Okla. Mar. 13, 2007).

591 Consol. Rock Prods. Co. v. DuBois, 312 U.S. 510, 61 S. Ct. 675, 85 L. Ed. 2d 982 (1941); *In re* Braxton, 124 B.R. 870 (Bankr. N.D. Fla. 1991); *In re* Butler, 97 B.R. 508 (Bankr. E.D. Ark. 1988); *In re* Eber-Acres Farm, 82 B.R. 889 (Bankr. S.D. Ohio 1987); *In re* Weldin-Lynn, Inc., 79 B.R. 409 (Bankr. E.D. Ark. 1987); *In re* Timber Tracts, Inc. 70 B.R. 773 (Bankr. D. Mont. 1987) (chapter 11); *In re* Martin, 66 B.R. 921 (Bankr. D. Mont. 1986) (chapter 11);

make substantial inquiry into feasibility even when parties in interest remain silent. In early chapter 12 cases, many courts took the approach of minimizing the feasibility inquiry when creditors have leveled no objections based upon section 1225(a)(6), preferring to allow the debtor to have his or her opportunity at repayment and rehabilitation, and considering shortfall only in the event of default. Yet even these courts expect some debtor showing of evidence concerning plan feasibility.[592]

Bankruptcy courts have recognized that feasibility is more difficult to gauge and projections are more speculative in farm cases because of the high degree of risk and variability of market factors and government subsidy/payment programs.[593] Courts generally only require that projections of both performance and expenditures fall within "reasonable ranges," rather than tight constraints.[594] The debtor is "required only to provide reasonable assurance, not a guarantee" of success.[595]

17.5.7.2.2 Determination of feasibility

The determination of feasibility for a chapter 12 plan requires an evaluation of the best indicia of plan success—or failure—available to the decision-maker at the time plan confirmation is sought. It is an issue for consideration at confirmation; consideration prior to confirmation would be premature even though a plan's lack of feasibility may be grounds for a chapter 12 case's dismissal.[596]

Confirmation determinations in farm cases under chapters 11 and 13 prior to the advent of chapter 12 provided insight into the courts' analysis of feasibility in early chapter 12 cases.[597] The following list details factors which have influenced courts concerning feasibility specifically in farm cases. The degree to which inquiry is necessary into these factors is proportionate to the degree of creditor/court interest; certainly not all are anticipated or required to be positive. These factors also provide a good preliminary checklist for inquiry into a debtor's operation prepetition to determine the likelihood of success in chapter 12.[598]

(1) Debtor's historic cash flow;
(2) Historic and present levels of production and expense;[599]
(3) Earning capacity of the debtor and immediate family;[600]
(4) Inclusion of all expenses in budgeting, including property and other taxes and utilities;[601]
(5) Ability to project realistically, based upon historical performance, crop and/or livestock yields and prices and timetable for realization from sale;[602]
(6) Whether debtor's projections of expenses and income fall within reasonable ranges as gauged by standard studies and measures of same, expert and debtor testimony, and the debtor's and court's experience;[603]
(7) Demonstration of continued sources of economical, financing and feed, seed, custom work (if own equipment is not used), and so forth;[604]
(8) Circumstance(s) which led to previous poor performance or cash flow, and evidence of elimination or mitigation of same;[605]
(9) Maintenance of stability of operation and historic stability record (particularly important in livestock and dairy operations);

In re Fursman Ranch, 38 B.R. 907 (Bankr. W.D. Mo. 1984).

592 This can be done through the testimony of the debtor at confirmation, through a simple series of questions directed at eligibility, intentions, reorganizational efforts, understanding of the plan, and ability to meet payments. *In re* Braxton, 124 B.R. 870 (Bankr. N.D. Fla. 1991); *In re* Hagen, 95 B.R. 708 (Bankr. D.N.D. 1989).

593 *See, e.g., In re* Fursman Ranch, 38 B.R. 907, 912 (Bankr. W.D. Mo. 1984).

594 *In re* Rape, 104 B.R. 741 (W.D.N.C. 1989); *In re* Dittmer, 82 B.R. 1019 (Bankr. D.N.D. 1988); *In re* Fowler, 83 B.R. 39 (Bankr. D. Mont. 1987); *In re* Reitz, 79 B.R. 934 (Bankr. D. Kan. 1987); *In re* Hochmuth Farms, Inc., 79 B.R. 266 (Bankr. D. Md. 1987); *In re* Konzak, 78 B.R. 990 (Bankr. D.N.D. 1987); *In re* Big Hook Land & Cattle Co., 77 B.R. 793 (Bankr. D. Mont. 1987); *In re* Hansen, 77 B.R. 722 (Bankr. D.N.D. 1987); *In re* Douglass, 77 B.R. 714 (Bankr. W.D. Mo. 1987).

595 *In re* Woods, 465 B.R. 196 (B.A.P. 10th Cir. 2012).

596 11 U.S.C. § 1208(c)(5). *See, e.g., In re* Woloschak, 70 B.R. 498 (Bankr. N.D. Ohio 1987).

597 *See, e.g., In re* Bartlett, 92 B.R. 142 (E.D.N.C. 1988); *In re* Snider Farms, Inc. 83 B.R. 1003 (Bankr. N.D. Ind. 1988); *In re* Gibson, 61 B.R. 997 (Bankr. D.N.H. 1986); *In re* Neff, 60 B.R. 448 (Bankr. N.D. Tex. 1985); *In re* Hoff, 54 B.R. 746 (Bankr. D.N.D. 1985); *In re* Cott, 49 B.R. 570 (Bankr. W.D. Mo. 1985); *In re* Fursman Ranch, 38 B.R. 907 (Bankr. W.D. Mo. 1984).

598 *See generally* Clarkson v. Cooke Sales & Serv. Co., 767 F.2d 417 (8th Cir. 1985) (chapter 11); *In re* Nauman, 213 B.R. 355 (B.A.P. 9th Cir. 1997) (application of various factors to plan involving negative amortization of secured debt); *In re* Snider Farms, Inc., 83 B.R. 1003 (Bankr. N.D. Ind. 1988).

599 *In re* Melcher, 416 B.R. 666 (D. Neb. 2009) (revenue projections that exceed historical earnings must be supported by demonstrated changes in operation); *In re* Rape, 104 B.R. 741 (W.D.N.C. 1989); *In re* Foertsch, 167 B.R. 555 (Bankr. D.N.D. 1994); *In re* Creviston, 157 B.R. 380 (Bankr. S.D. Ohio 1993); *In re* Butler, 101 B.R. 566 (Bankr. E.D. Ark. 1989); *In re* Crowley, 85 B.R. 76 (Bankr. W.D. Wis. 1988); *In re* Snider Farms, Inc., 83 B.R. 1003 (Bankr. N.D. Ind. 1988); *In re* Kloberdanz, 83 B.R. 767 (Bankr. D. Colo. 1988).

600 *In re* Soper, 152 B.R. 984 (Bankr. D. Kan. 1993).

601 *In re* Alvstad, 223 B.R. 733 (Bankr. D.N.D. 1998) (debtor could not establish that cash flow would meet farm expenses together with projected meager living expenses). *See, e.g., In re* Oster, 152 B.R. 960 (Bankr. D.N.D. 1993); *In re* Hagen, 95 B.R. 708 (Bankr. D.N.D. 1989) (modification); *In re* Hochmuth Farms, Inc., 79 B.R. 266 (Bankr. D. Md. 1987); *In re* Big Hook Land & Cattle Co., 77 B.R. 793 (Bankr. D. Mont. 1987); *In re* Hansen, 77 B.R. 722 (Bankr. D.N.D. 1987).

602 *In re* Harper, 157 B.R. 858 (Bankr. E.D. Ark. 1993). *See also In re* Oster, 152 B.R. 960 (Bankr. D.N.D. 1993); *In re* Rott, 94 B.R. 163 (Bankr. D.N.D. 1988); *In re* Douglass, 77 B.R. 714 (Bankr. W.D. Mo. 1987).

603 *See In re* Weber, 297 B.R. 567 (Bankr. N.D. Iowa 2003); *In re* Gough, 190 B.R. 455 (Bankr. M.D. Fla. 1996); *In re* Oster, 152 B.R. 960 (Bankr. D.N.D. 1993); *In re* Adam, 92 B.R. 732 (Bankr. E.D. Mich. 1988); *In re* Townsend, 90 B.R. 498 (Bankr. M.D. Fla. 1988).

604 *In re* Foertsch, 167 B.R. 555 (Bankr. D.N.D. 1994) (written leases versus oral leases as assurance of continuity of operation); *In re* Big Hook Land & Cattle Co., 77 B.R. 793 (Bankr. D. Mont. 1987).

605 *See, e.g., In re* Dittmer, 82 B.R. 1019 (Bankr. D.N.D. 1988).

(10) Whether debtor's debt and operational burdens have been reduced by sale of property or paring down of farm operation;
(11) Condition of operating equipment and livestock;
(12) Prospects of refinancing all or part of the operation, and/or continued financing for successive years of operation;
(13) Substantial payments made in the past to creditors, particularly secured creditors;[606]
(14) Use of accepted farming methods and characterization of the debtor as a "good" or "poor" manager;[607]
(15) Expectancy and interplay of family donations and donations of money, labor and expertise of money and/or property (seed, feed, livestock, and so forth) during the plan's life;[608]
(16) Labor donation to the farm effort;
(17) Income from outside sources;
(18) Income from government payments, contracts and/or subsidies (PIK, ASCS certificates, and so forth);[609]
(19) Presence, maintenance and/or increase of base or allotments to support product prices;
(20) Presence or absence of crop and other insurance, both for income protection and as an item of expense properly projected;[610]
(21) Presence of accounting for next year's crop expenses and reasonable cushion for risk;[611]
(22) Utilization of farm production to minimize family living expenses;[612]
(23) Evidence of maintenance and/or upgrading livestock/dairy herds by introduction or acquisition of new animals;
(24) Monitoring and treatment of operation for peak efficiency, for example, DHIA testing for dairy herds;
(25) Realistic valuation of secured claims and reasonable interest or discount rates for their repayment;[613]
(26) Presence of plan provisions which protect creditors when feasibility is marginal, for example, recapture provisions for return of collateral to a creditor upon plan default;[614]
(27) Resolution or projected resolution of adversary proceedings which have an impact upon plan operation;[615]
(28) Ability to meet lump sum payments or balloon provisions in plan;[616]
(29) Postpetition performance under protection of chapter 12 stay;[617]
(30) Ability to pay postpetition administrative expenses;[618]
(31) Presence or absence of nondischargeable debts;[619]
(32) Impact of trustee's surcharges.[620]

Some indicia of feasibility are more persuasive than others. For example, crop insurance and outside income provide the kind of stability that minimizes risk. A positive cash flow history and a history of substantial payments to creditors are convincing, but not many farmers have such a recent history. Meaningful reduction of the size of the farming operation, with a concomitant reduction in expenses, is a plus not only for feasibility, but as a demonstration of genuine good faith in attempting reorganization;[621] the operation which has been failing in the past generally needs change above debt reduction to accomplish reorganization and lasting viability.[622] Stricter proof of feasibility may be required when long-term payments are proposed.[623]

To present an effective case on feasibility, the debtor's testimony and available documentary evidence can be proffered. If the plan relies on the efforts of persons other than the debtor, those persons may also be called to testify. Documentary evidence might include appraisals, cash flow statements, and other materials from the farm's records or that of its creditors. Discovery procedures are available under the Rules to enhance access to creditor's records including to obtain familiarity with documents which may be used by creditors to undermine the debtor's case. The court may also take judicial

---

606 In re Gough, 190 B.R. 455 (Bankr. M.D. Fla. 1996); In re Fursman Ranch, 38 B.R. 907 (Bankr. W.D. Mo. 1984).
607 In re Cluck, 101 B.R. 691 (Bankr. E.D. Okla. 1989).
608 See, e.g., In re Cheatham, 78 B.R. 104 (Bankr. E.D.N.C. 1987); In re Edwardson, 74 B.R. 831 (Bankr. D.N.D. 1987). Contra In re Rott, 94 B.R. 163 (Bankr. D.N.D. 1988).
609 In re Kloberdanz, 83 B.R. 767 (Bankr. D. Colo. 1988).
610 In re Martin, 66 B.R. 921 (Bankr. D. Mont. 1986) (chapter 11).
611 In re Coffman, 90 B.R. 878 (Bankr. W.D. Tenn. 1988); In re Townsend, 90 B.R. 498 (Bankr. M.D. Fla. 1988) (lack of reserves affects feasibility); In re Snider Farms, Inc., 83 B.R. 1003 (Bankr. N.D. Ind. 1988); In re Fowler, 83 B.R. 39 (Bankr. D. Mont. 1987); In re Reitz, 79 B.R. 934 (Bankr. D. Kan. 1987); In re Hochmuth Farms, Inc., 79 B.R. 266 (Bankr. D. Md. 1987); In re Konzak, 78 B.R. 990 (Bankr. D.N.D. 1987); In re Kocher, 78 B.R. 844 (Bankr. S.D. Ohio 1987); In re Big Hook Land & Cattle Co., 77 B.R. 793 (Bankr. D. Mont. 1987); In re Hansen, 77 B.R. 722 (Bankr. D.N.D. 1987); In re Douglass, 77 B.R. 714 (Bankr. W.D. Mo. 1987). Contra In re Dues, 98 B.R. 434 (Bankr. N.D. Ind. 1989) (failure to build cushion into budget acceptable; an accurate cash flow based on history probably already has some cushion).
612 In re Oster, 152 B.R. 960 (Bankr. D.N.D. 1993).
613 In re Ames, 973 F.2d 849 (10th Cir. 1992); In re Cool, 81 B.R. 614 (Bankr. D. Mont. 1987); In re Beyer, 72 B.R. 525 (Bankr. D. Colo. 1987).
614 In re Barnett, 162 B.R. 535 (Bankr. W.D. Mo. 1993). See, e.g., In re O'Farrell, 74 B.R. 421 (Bankr. N.D. Fla. 1987).
615 See, e.g., In re Martin, 78 B.R. 593 (Bankr. D. Mont. 1987); In re Edwardson, 74 B.R. 831 (Bankr. D.N.D. 1987); In re Bentson, 74 B.R. 56 (Bankr. D. Minn. 1987).
616 In re Foertsch, 167 B.R. 555 (Bankr. D.N.D. 1994); In re Kuether, 158 B.R. 151 (Bankr. D.N.D. 1993); In re Borg, 88 B.R. 288 (Bankr. D. Mont. 1988).
617 In re Creviston, 157 B.R. 380 (Bankr. S.D. Ohio 1993); In re Cluck, 101 B.R. 691 (Bankr. E.D. Okla. 1989).
618 In re Winter, 151 B.R. 278 (Bankr. W.D. Okla. 1993).
619 In re Oster, 152 B.R. 960 (Bankr. D.N.D. 1993).
620 Id.
621 In re Kloberdanz, 83 B.R. 767 (Bankr. D. Colo. 1988).
622 Care must be taken to include *all* anticipated and foreseeable expenses. A court cannot confirm a plan with an admitted negative cash flow. In re Bartlett, 92 B.R. 142 (E.D.N.C. 1988). See also In re Adam, 92 B.R. 732 (Bankr. E.D. Mich. 1988).
623 In re Snider Farms, Inc., 83 B.R. 1003 (Bankr. N.D. Ind. 1988).

notice of reliable publications which indicate interest rates[624] or land values.[625]

17.5.7.3 Trustee Fees and the Direct Payment Issue

Payments due under the chapter 12 plan generally must be paid through the office of the chapter 12 trustee for disbursement according to the plan. In the first years under chapter 12 the courts almost uniformly mandated that most payments be funneled through the trustee, because of the start-up costs for new chapter 12 cases and trustees and because of the nature of the chapter 12 plan restructuring of secured and unsecured debt.[626] In those cases, the trustee surcharge in chapter 12 placed a significant burden upon the family farmer debtor because many districts allowed the maximum percentage (ten percent) for trustee's fees.

One approach to reducing this burden is to make some payments due in chapter 12 direct payments without administration by the chapter 12 trustee.[627] Sections 1226(c), 1222(a)(1) and 1225(a)(5)(B)(ii) clearly contemplate this possibility.[628] It should also be remembered that no surcharge will attach to the portion of those secured debts amortized beyond the plan's three to five year life for that period when payment continues after discharge.[629]

The case law has been mixed as to the success of direct payments as a means of avoiding the trustee's fee. This issue is discussed in § 17.4.1.2, *supra*, and the cases cited there should be consulted. Whether the debtor can make the payments directly and whether they are subject to the surcharge has largely been worked out by either controlling district or circuit court precedent.[630]

If direct payments are allowed as a means of avoiding application of the fee, attorneys should consider using direct payment for some, but not all, of their client's plan obligations. Some kinds of payments and circumstances lend themselves readily to allowance for direct payment during the life of the plan. For example:

Attorney Fees: Arrangements for the payment of attorney fees for work performed after filing *and* duly approved by the bankruptcy court upon application should be paid directly. There is a compelling argument that cost of representation should bear no surcharge for administration.[631]

Postpetition Debt Repayment: When the debtor has received postpetition new financing which will be paid entirely out of the proceeds of harvest, it makes more sense administratively for the sale proceeds check to be cut to the debtor and creditor, reported to the trustee contemporaneously, but distributed to that creditor directly without trustee administration. The chapter 12 trustee has no expectation of surcharge from such a postpetition debt at the creation of the chapter 12 case, nor is payment made under the plan.

Lump Sum Creditor Payment(s): There may be occasions when a creditor or creditors will be paid a large sum upon a claim or claims all at once through a sale free and clear of lien.[632] When this happens, the chapter 12 trustee's office normally will have had only minimal participation in the sale and the proceeds will be distributed to one or a limited number of creditors holding pre-sale liens. Such a payment is more representative of liquidation than administration, and the chapter 12 trustee has not functioned as a liquidating agent.[633]

Balloon Payments: As in cases involving sales free and clear of lien, there may be some creditors who, because of the structure of their indebtedness going into the bankruptcy, or by plan choice, will be paid with a one-time distribution soon after the plan is confirmed. While these will generally be paid out of the debtor's regular operating revenues, the administration required is disproportionate to the trustee's fee.

---

624 *In re* Neff, 89 B.R. 672 (Bankr. S.D. Ohio 1988) (Federal Reserve Bank's Quarterly Survey of Agricultural Credit Conditions at Commercial Banks); *In re* Crane Auto., Inc., 88 B.R. 81 (Bankr. W.D. Pa. 1988) (chapter 11 non-farm case; uses Wall Street Journal).

625 *See* § 17.5.3, *supra*.

626 *See, e.g., In re* Greseth, 78 B.R. 936 (D. Minn. 1987); *In re* Hildebrandt, 79 B.R. 427 (Bankr. D. Minn. 1987); *In re* Hagensick, 73 B.R. 710 (Bankr. N.D. Iowa 1987) (while some direct payments can be made, they will still be subject to the trustee's surcharge); *In re* Meyer, 73 B.R. 457 (Bankr. E.D. Mo. 1987).

Most real property in chapter 12 will be rescheduled and reamortized, so that the direct payment to creditors holding mortgages, deeds to secure debt, or contracts for deed will be different from the original contract; the primary rationale for allowing direct payment to a creditor in chapter 13 was to avoid modification of the rights of such holders. Also, most chapter 12 plans would pay little, if anything, to unsecured creditors so that the percentage payable to compensate the trustee will be minuscule if assessed only upon repayment to unsecured creditors.

627 *See* § 12.4.4, *supra*.

628 *In re* Kline, 94 B.R. 557 (Bankr. N.D. Ind. 1988); *In re* Finkbine, 94 B.R. 461 (Bankr. S.D. Ohio 1988); *In re* Pianowski, 92 B.R. 225 (Bankr. W.D. Mich. 1988); *In re* Sutton, 91 B.R. 184 (Bankr. M.D. Ga. 1988).

The Ninth Circuit has held that direct payments may not be made to impaired creditors. *See* Fulkrod v. Barmettler, 126 B.R. 584 (B.A.P. 9th Cir. 1991), *aff'd*, 973 F.2d 801 (9th Cir. 1992).

629 However, chapter 12 plans should make specific provision for this in their treatment of such debts.

630 *See, e.g.,* Wagner v. Armstrong (*In re* Wagner), 36 F.3d 723 (8th Cir. 1994) (direct payments allowed within limits, with no trustee commission thereon); *In re* Fulkrod, 973 F.2d 801 (9th Cir. 1992) (no direct payments allowed). *See also* § 17.4.1.2, *supra*.

631 *In re* Pianowski, 92 B.R. 225 (Bankr. W.D. Mich. 1988). *But see In re* Beard, 134 B.R. 239 (Bankr. S.D. Ohio 1991) (attorney fees must be paid through plan); *In re* Heller, 105 B.R. 434 (Bankr. N.D. Ill. 1988) (except in rare instances, attorney fees should be paid through trustee because of duty to monitor administrative expenses of estate).

632 11 U.S.C. § 1205; *In re* Schneekloth, 186 B.R. 713 (Bankr. D. Mont. 1995).

In fact, this was the rationale in *In re* Sousa, 61 B.R. 105 (D.R.I. 1986), for a reduced trustee surcharge.

633 However, in some cases the sale will not satisfy all liens or there will be disputes over the claims to the proceeds of sale. In that event, the court should probably order the chapter 12 trustee to become the repository of the disputed funds, so that some administrative tending by the trustee will be necessary. *See, e.g., In re* McClintock, 75 B.R. 612 (Bankr. W.D. Mo. 1987).

Transfers in Kind to Creditors: When debt satisfaction is effectuated under the plan by the transfer or surrender either of collateral or unencumbered property other than cash, the lack of trustee involvement should allow direct transfer without attachment of a trustee's fee.[634]

Some courts have required, when evaluating the allowance of direct payment and claims classification, that direct payments cannot be allowed for some creditors and not others when the claims are substantially similar.[635] Tax and administrative claims, exclusive of fees, should be paid under the plan by the trustee.[636] Generally no direct payments have been permitted to general unsecured creditors.[637] Some courts may restrict cure of defaults and arrearages to payments through the trustee.[638]

The most thorough consideration of direct payments and what policies and factors may be considered in their allowance has come from the bankruptcy court in *In re Pianowski*.[639] The court detailed a variety of appropriate factors which may justify direct payments. The court in *Pianowski* also required the monitoring of direct payments by inclusion of the following provisions: (a) debtors shall keep accurate records reflecting all direct payments to secured creditors and attorneys, making them available to the trustee and all interested parties during the plan's life; (b) direct payments to creditors must be made by check or other method whereby debtors can conclusively demonstrate timely making; (c) debtors shall file an annual report on a date certain of each year which discloses the amounts, check numbers and dates when direct payments were made, and if a direct payment has not been timely made; (d) in the event debtors fail, neglect or refuse to report, debtors shall be deemed in plan default; upon default, unpaid creditors, trustee or any other interested entity may file appropriate motions.

17.5.8 Additional Protections for Domestic Support Obligations

The 2005 Act provided a number of new protections to encourage the payment of domestic support obligations, defined to include child support, alimony, and maintenance. In cases in which these obligations are present, these provisions should be carefully built into the chapter 12 plan. These protections may be summarized as follows:

- A new first priority status for prepetition unsecured claims for domestic support obligations was created under section 507(a)(1)(B).
- Under section 1222(b), the debtor will not be allowed to reduce the amount of a domestic support obligation that has section 507(a)(1)(B) priority unless the debtor's plan commits to paying all of the debtor's projected disposable income for a five-year period.
- Section 1225 includes a new confirmation requirement requiring the debtor to be current on all postpetition domestic support obligations.[640]
- Failure to pay a postpetition domestic support obligation is included as a ground for dismissal of the bankruptcy.[641]
- The debtor who has a domestic support obligation will not be entitled to a discharge unless he or she is current with respect to this obligation and files a certification of this fact. The obligations included in this requirement are all postpetition obligations and prepetition obligations, but only to the extent that they are provided for by the plan.[642]

The amendments also made a change to section 1222 that appears to be intended to apply to domestic support obligations but may have larger implications. A new provision is added to require that a chapter 12 plan must "provide for the payment of interest accruing after the date of filing of the petition on unsecured claims that are nondischargeable under § 1228(a)."[643] A limitation is placed on this requirement so that interest is to be paid only to the extent that the debtor has disposable income available after providing for all allowed secured claims. Debts that are nondischargeable under section 1228(a) include domestic support obligations but also include debts provided for under section 1222(b)(5), section 1222(b)(9), or specified in section 523(a).[644]

17.5.9 Other Plan Provisions

Section 1222(b)(11) specifically authorizes the inclusion of any appropriate provision in a chapter 12 plan so long as it does not contravene the confirmation standards of sections 1222 and 1225.[645] This allows for quite a bit of creativity in fashioning a workable chapter 12 plan. Nevertheless, counsel should never let this creativity obscure the primary—and pragmatic—goal of confirmation.

---

634 *In re* Mikkelsen Farms, Inc., 74 B.R. 280 (Bankr. D. Or. 1987).
635 *In re* Hildebrandt, 79 B.R. 427 (Bankr. D. Minn. 1987).
636 *In re* Greseth, 78 B.R. 936 (D. Minn. 1987); *In re* Beard, 134 B.R. 239 (Bankr. S.D. Ohio 1991); *In re* Mouser, 99 B.R. 803 (Bankr. S.D. Ohio 1989); *In re* Kline, 94 B.R. 557 (Bankr. N.D. Ind. 1988); *In re* Rott, 94 B.R. 163 (Bankr. D.N.D. 1988).
637 *In re* Erickson P'ship, 83 B.R. 725 (D.S.D. 1988); *In re* Cross, 182 B.R. 42 (Bankr. D Neb. 1995) (however, there may be exceptions when unsecured creditors can be paid directly); *In re* Marriott, 161 B.R. 816 (Bankr. S.D. Ill. 1993); *In re* Mouser, 99 B.R. 803 (Bankr. S.D. Ohio 1989); *In re* Kline, 94 B.R. 557 (Bankr. N.D. Ind. 1988). Compare 11 U.S.C. § 1225(a)(4) *with* 11 U.S.C. § 1225(a)(5)(B)(ii).
638 *In re* Kline, 94 B.R. 557 (Bankr. N.D. Ind. 1988).
639 92 B.R. 225 (Bankr. W.D. Mich. 1988).
640 11 U.S.C. § 1225(a)(7).
641 11 U.S.C. § 1208(c)(8).
642 11 U.S.C. § 1228(a); *In re* Melcher, 416 B.R. 666 (D. Neb. 2009) (confirmation of chapter 12 plan was denied; claims of debtor's ex-wife and her attorney were domestic support obligations that could not be delayed for one year as proposed in proposed plan).
643 11 U.S.C. § 1222(b)(11).
644 11 U.S.C. § 1228(a).
645 *In re* Davenport, 153 B.R. 551 (B.A.P. 9th Cir. 1993) (chapter 12 contemplates maximum flexibility in restructuring); *In re* Butler, 97 B.R. 508 (Bankr. E.D. Ark. 1988); *In re* Neff, 89 B.R. 672 (Bankr. S.D. Ohio 1988).

In addition to potential plan treatment of creditors outlined in §§ 17.5.4, 17.5.5, *supra*, some plan provisions which may or should be included under appropriate circumstances are suggested below:

Assumption or Rejection of Executory Contracts. Section 365 provides that, in chapter 12, leases and executory contracts shall be assumed or rejected by the time of confirmation.[646] The plan should specifically reject or assume any leases and executory contracts of the debtors, if they have not already being rejected or assumed by specific action preconfirmation. If any contracts have been rejected or assumed preconfirmation, the plan should contain a recitation of that occurrence.

Provisions for New Financing in Future Plan Years. The legislative history of chapter 12 specifically contemplates that a plan can anticipate and provide for the incurring of new debt for financing of the farm operation under section 364 and payment of the same under the plan.[647] A plan which provides for yearly distribution, for example, may provide that the financing for each year, as approved by the court, be paid from that distribution as an administrative expense, secured claim, or possibly by direct payment. Similarly, if money is used for capital improvements rather than creditor repayment, a monitoring provision should be included in the plan.[648]

Provision for Payment of Attorney Fees Through the Plan. Attorney fees may be treated as an administrative expense under the plan or possibly allowed for direct payment. However, any request for fees to be placed under the plan needs to be accompanied by an application for award of fees and an enumeration of time and work performed to authorize such plan treatment.

Revesting of Estate Property in Debtor. Section 1227(b) provides that an order of confirmation will vest property of the estate in the debtor unless the order or plan provides differently. Any distribution or disposition of property which does not vest in the debtor must be enumerated in the plan. The plan may also reiterate the vesting provisions of section 1227(b).

Payments Through the Trustee and Fees. Any provisions which seek to have payment to creditors permitted directly rather than through the chapter 12 trustee must be identified. The plan must specify and explain any request to reduce the chapter 12 trustee's fee in the case, either across the board or concerning selected creditors or transactions.

Provisions for Use of Cash Collateral During the Life of the Plan. A plan can provide for the continued use of cash collateral by a debtor during the life of a plan without the continual approval process of section 363, if sale of farm products is in the ordinary course of the debtor's business, for example, dairy, feeder pigs, and so forth. However, the plan should provide for the manner in which the collateral will be sold and the proceeds used, and for the maintenance of preconfirmation levels of replenishing collateral.[649]

Disposition of Any Farm Program Attributes or Benefits. A farmer may be entitled to any number of benefits as a result of federal or other programs. Some of those benefits may be peculiar to the farmer, his or her land, or his or her operation,[650] such as base, allotments, termination program benefits, diversion program benefits, Payment-in-Kind (PIK) program benefits, storage benefits, conservation program contacts, or other kinds of assets. These all have value to the estate and to creditors. If the disposition of those attributes or benefits will be different from complete vesting in the debtor, (for example, allowance of setoff of program benefits for creditor payment during the plan) then the plan should provide for such disposition.[651]

Recapture or Drop Dead Provisions. Some plans contain a provision that, in the event of plan default, collateral will be relinquished to the secured creditor without further need for action in the federal or state courts. Such a provision was fairly common in chapter 11 cases prior to chapter 12 because many of those cases depended upon the agreement of the secured creditors for confirmation; chapter 12 cases do not so depend. Because of such a provision's drastic—and terminal—effect, such a provision should be agreed to only in exceptional circumstances, only when confirmation cannot be otherwise obtained, and with full knowledge and agreement of the debtor(s).[652] Such provisions may be difficult or impossible to modify under section 1229 because they anticipate default.[653] When a confirmed plan has a recapture provision with mandatory liquidation by the trustee upon default, one court has not allowed voluntary dismissal under section 1208(b) without curing of the default.[654]

Graduated Payments or Deferral. In limited cases, particularly when there has been a disaster or other exceptional loss, it may be possible to propose a plan with either a graduated repayment schedule or deferred payments during the initial period of the chapter 12 plan. Similarly, interest-only payments (usually one to three years for servicing on major secured indebtedness) could be designed to increase cash flow for building or rebuilding farm operations for later increases in income production, usually in livestock or dairy operations.

---

646 11 U.S.C. § 365(d)(2).
    This section also allows debtors-in-possession those powers by reference to 11 U.S.C. § 1203.
647 H.R. Conf. Rep. No. 99-958, at 48 (1986), *reprinted in* 1986 U.S.C.C.A.N. 5249.
648 *In re* Hansen, 77 B.R. 722 (Bankr. D.N.D. 1987).
649 *See* §§ 17.4.8, 17.4.11, *supra*.
650 *See* § 17.4.3.4, *supra*.
651 *In re* Greseth, 78 B.R. 936 (D. Minn. 1987).
652 *See, e.g., In re* Gore, 113 B.R. 504 (Bankr. E.D. Ark. 1989) (but such a provision must contain a lifting of the stay); *In re* Hagen, 95 B.R. 708 (Bankr. D.N.D. 1989); *In re* Martens, 98 B.R. 530 (Bankr. D. Colo. 1989); *In re* Grogg Farms, Inc., 91 B.R. 482 (Bankr. N.D. Ind. 1988); *In re* Dittmer, 82 B.R. 1019 (Bankr. D.N.D. 1988); *In re* Erickson P'ship, 77 B.R. 738 (Bankr. D.S.D. 1987); *In re* O'Farrell, 74 B.R. 421 (Bankr. N.D. Fla. 1987).
653 *In re* Grogg Farms, Inc., 91 B.R. 482 (Bankr. N.D. Ind. 1988).
654 *In re* Tyndall, 97 B.R. 266 (Bankr. E.D.N.C. 1989). *See* § 17.4.6.3, *supra*.

While not a usual approach to repayment, in limited circumstances and particularly with creditor approval, such provisions could be confirmed.[655]

Reservation of Issues and Alternative Plan Treatment of Creditors. In some circumstances, confirmation may go forward with some issues unresolved—particularly nondischargeability of individual debts, property surrender, a cause of action such as lender liability, or lien avoidance. Because confirmation can set the rights of the debtor and creditors, when issues must survive for resolution after confirmation, the plan should provide for reservation of the issues and alternative treatments of the creditor(s) involved based upon the probable outcomes once the open issues are resolved.[656] Similarly, a plan may minimize the effect of res judicata by specifically and expressly preserving claims not intrinsic to the contractual relationship between debtor and a creditor.[657]

Right of First Refusal Upon Sale. If property is surrendered by consent of default, the debtor may retain the right to redeem such property by matching the bid accepted by the creditor for sale, if the plan so provides.[658]

Provisions Rejected by the Courts. The bankruptcy courts in Arkansas and Kansas have rejected as unacceptable, provisions which have attempted to: provide for *ex parte* application and granting of moratoria and payment extensions due to unforeseeable circumstances;[659] provide for an "effective date" of the plan significantly different than that provided by statute and case law;[660] include sale provisions for collateral which provide for consent to sale and partial payment of proceeds;[661] provide for full claim satisfaction (both secured and unsecured) from collateral surrender at any time during the plan's life without a valuation hearing.[662]

17.6 Denial of Confirmation

In the event confirmation of a chapter 12 plan is denied, the court may dismiss the case under 11 U.S.C. § 1208(c)(5).[663] This is the anticipated route when it appears to the court that no feasible plan can be constructed or when confirmation standards cannot possibly be met given the factual circumstances of a case.

However, at its discretion, the court can allow additional time within which the debtor may propose another plan under chapter 12 or modify the rejected plan to meet confirmation standards and creditor or trustee objection.[664] The court may look to the following factors to determine whether to allow additional time for proposing another plan: (1) when the original plan was filed; (2) how comprehensive and complete the original plan was; (3) reasons for denial of confirmation; (4) likelihood of successful confirmation of new plan and prima facie showing that reorganization is possible; (5) length of time requested to propose another plan;[665] and (6) prior proposal of multiple plans which were not confirmable.[666] A request for additional time will not be routinely granted, and all efforts to meet the time requirements should be made.

17.7 The Chapter 12 Discharge and Its Operation

17.7.1 Scope of the Chapter 12 Discharge

The chapter 12 discharge is a hybrid of some of the discharge provisions available in other chapters.[667] Like chapters 7 and 11, but unlike chapter 13, the discharge in chapter 12 excepts debts which are nondischargeable pursuant to section 523(a).[668] Like chapter 13, the chapter 12 discharge excepts long-term indebtedness when the maturity date is beyond the life of the chapter 12 plan.[669] The chapter 12 discharge also excepts secured indebtedness upon which repayment exceeds the life of the chapter 12 plan.[670] With these exceptions, the chapter 12

---

655 *See, e.g., In re* Craven, 97 B.R. 549 (Bankr. W.D. Mo. 1989); *In re* Fowler, 83 B.R. 39 (Bankr. D. Mont. 1987); *In re* Big Hook Land & Cattle Co., 77 B.R. 793 (Bankr. D. Mont. 1987) (plan determined to be not feasible in this decision for other reasons); *In re* Martin, 66 B.R. 921 (Bankr. D. Mont. 1986) (chapter 11). *Contra In re* Cool, 81 B.R. 614 (Bankr. D. Mont. 1987) (no interest deferral).

Yet built-in modifications based upon default yet to be experienced which do not provide for notice and hearing to creditors may not be permitted. *In re* Gore, 113 B.R. 504 (Bankr. E.D. Ark. 1989).

656 *See, e.g., In re* Arthur, 86 B.R. 98 (Bankr. W.D. Mich. 1988); *In re* Bentson, 74 B.R. 56 (Bankr. D. Minn. 1987).

657 *In re* Mass Farms, Inc., 917 F.2d 1210 (9th Cir. 1990). *Cf. In re* Howe, 913 F.2d 1138 (5th Cir. 1990).

658 *In re* Coleman, 125 B.R. 621 (Bankr. D. Mont. 1991).

659 *In re* Gore, 113 B.R. 504 (Bankr. E.D. Ark. 1989); *In re* Butler, 97 B.R. 508 (Bankr. E.D. Ark. 1988).

Yet at least one court has found that a consensual drop-dead provision will not prevent modification under section 1229. *In re* Mader, 108 B.R. 643 (N.D. Ill. 1989).

660 *In re* Musil, 99 B.R. 448 (Bankr. D. Kan. 1988).

661 *In re* Gore, 113 B.R. 504 (Bankr. E.D. Ark. 1989); *In re* Butler, 97 B.R. 508 (Bankr. E.D. Ark. 1988).

662 *In re* Gore, 113 B.R. 504 (Bankr. E.D. Ark. 1989); *In re* Butler, 97 B.R. 508 (Bankr. E.D. Ark. 1988).

663 *See, e.g., In re* Merek, 2012 WL 2153648 (Bankr. D. Idaho 2012).

664 11 U.S.C. § 1208(c)(5). *See §§* 17.4.6.2, 17.5.2, *supra. See also, In re* Pertuset, 2010 WL 3422455 (B.A.P. 6th Cir. Aug. 24, 2010) (chapter 12 case was dismissed under section 1208(c)(3) and (c)(9) for failure to file timely plan and continuing diminution of estate); *In re* Greseth, 78 B.R. 936 (D. Minn. 1987); *In re* Bentson, 74 B.R. 56 (Bankr. D. Minn. 1987). *But see In re* Weber, 297 B.R. 567 (Bankr. N.D. Iowa 2003) (dismissal appropriate as debtors unable to obtain confirmation after submitting four plans over one-year period).

665 *In re* Bentson, 74 B.R. 56 (Bankr. D. Minn. 1987).

666 *In re* Luchenbill, 112 B.R. 204 (Bankr. E.D. Mich. 1990).

667 11 U.S.C. §§ 524, 727(b), 1141(d)(1)(A), 1228(a), 1328(a).

668 11 U.S.C. §§ 727(b), 1141(d)(2). *See In re* Nelson, 255 B.R. 314 (Bankr. D.N.D. 2000) (debt found nondischargeable under section 523(a)(4) for defalcation in a fiduciary capacity when farmer as trustee farmed and earned profits on trust land without paying rent).

669 11 U.S.C. § 1328(a)(1).

670 11 U.S.C. § 1228(a)(1).

The section appears to except debts treated under 11 U.S.C. § 1222(b)(5) and (b)(10) from discharge; however, it appears that is

discharge covers all other indebtedness included in the petition and addressed by the plan.[671] Like the chapter 13 discharge,[672] the chapter 12 discharge is granted to the debtor only after completion of the plan provisions and payments.[673] Particular attention must be paid to counseling debtors concerning unpaid nondischargeable tax debts. Postpetition interest may have continued to accrue thereby creating ongoing risk to an otherwise successfully reorganized farming endeavor.[674]

The Federal Rules of Bankruptcy Procedure provide guidelines for filing of claims in chapter 12 cases. The debtor should address all claims in the plan; in order for a debt to be discharged, it must be provided for by the plan.[675]

17.7.2 The Hardship Discharge

Like chapter 13,[676] chapter 12 provides for a hardship discharge in the event a debtor cannot reasonably consummate a chapter 12 plan because of circumstances beyond the debtor's control.[677] A debtor seeking a hardship discharge must make affirmative application for it. Notice and a hearing are required for granting of a hardship discharge.[678] The hardship discharge provisions of chapters 12 and 13 are identical, so that case law which has arisen under chapter 13 should be applicable to chapter 12 cases.

At any time after the confirmation of a plan and before the debtor has completed payments under the plan, the court may grant a hardship discharge if the debtor and the aggregate of plan payments already made meet the following three requirements:

1. The debtor has failed to complete plan payments due to circumstances for which the debtor should not be held accountable;
2. The value as of the effective date of the plan of property actually distributed under the plan on account of each allowed unsecured claim is not less than would have been paid under a hypothetical liquidation case; *and*
3. Postconfirmation modification of the plan is not practicable.[679]

The scope of the hardship discharge is the same as the general discharge provided in section 1228(a) and is generally co-extensive with the discharge granted in chapter 7 cases.[680] All unsecured debts are discharged except those: (1) excepted from discharge under section 523(a) as nondischargeable; (2) in which the cure of default or the time for payment of the debt under the plan extends beyond the time of the last payment of the plan as confirmed as provided by section 1222(b)(9); and/or (3) designed to result in the vesting of property in the debtor upon their completion under section 1222(b)(10).[681]

A hardship discharge can be granted prior to the running of the three years of plan life contemplated under chapter 12.[682] Little case law has evolved upon the issue of hardship discharge. However, a hardship discharge is unlikely to be available for a debtor whose conscious choice or decision results in the inability to consummate a chapter 12 plan.[683] The courts are likely to look to the effort that the debtor has put forth during the duration of the chapter 12 plan in considering the merit of granting a hardship discharge.

17.7.3 Revocation of Discharge

Revocation of discharge in chapter 12 cases is addressed by 11 U.S.C. § 1228(d). On request of a party in interest and notice and hearing within one year after discharge under this section, the court may revoke such discharge only if such discharge was obtained by the debtor through fraud, and the requesting party did not learn of such fraud until after the discharge was granted. Unlike chapter 11, in which the discharge is issued at confirmation, the discharge in a chapter 12 case is issued at the end of the case. Therefore, the knowledge of fraud *must* arise post-discharge and be material to the issuance of the discharge in the case.[684]

---

a typographical error and the correct citation concerning long-term indebtedness as structured by the plan is 11 U.S.C. § 1222(b)(9). *In re* Eber-Acres Farm, 82 B.R. 889 (Bankr. S.D. Ohio 1987).

671 11 U.S.C. § 1228(a). *But see* § 17.8.2, *infra*.
672 11 U.S.C. § 1328(a).
673 11 U.S.C. § 1228(a).
    A discharge is to be granted "as soon as practicable after completion by the debtor of all payments under the plan." The payments referred to in section 1228(a) are payments during the plan's life, not long-term secured indebtedness. *In re* Weber, 25 F.3d 413 (7th Cir. 1994); *In re* Gage, 159 B.R. 272 (Bankr. D.S.D. 1993); *In re* Grimm, 145 B.R. 994 (Bankr. D.S.D. 1992); *In re* Butler, 97 B.R. 508 (Bankr. E.D. Ark. 1988).
674 *See generally In re* Cousins, 209 F.3d 38 (1st Cir. 2000) (discussion of nondischargeable tax debts in chapter 12 context).
675 See § 14.4.3, *supra*, for a discussion of time deadlines and late filed claim.
676 11 U.S.C. § 1328(b), (c). *See* § 4.7.2, *supra*.
677 11 U.S.C. § 1228(b), (c); *In re* Roesner, 153 B.R. 328 (Bankr. D. Kan. 1993).
678 11 U.S.C. § 1228(b).

679 *See* 11 U.S.C. § 1229; § 17.8.1, *infra*.
680 11 U.S.C. § 727(b).
681 The literal reading of the 1986 Act excepts from discharge debts under 11 U.S.C. § 1222(b)(5) and (b)(10). However, that construction makes no sense and is undoubtedly a typographical error. Commentary, Collier Special Supplement, The Bankruptcy Judges, United States Trustees, and Family Farmer Bankruptcy Act of 1986, at C-7. The hardship discharge is designed to except long-term secured indebtedness, whether originating as such ((b)(5)) or as restructured by the confirmed plan ((b)(9)).
682 *See, e.g., In re* Thornton, 21 B.R. 462 (Bankr. W.D. Va. 1982).
683 *See, e.g., In re* Linden, 174 B.R. 769 (C.D. Ill. 1994) (hardship discharge requires the presence of catastrophic circumstances, more economic hardship causing inability to complete plan is not sufficient); *In re* Fenning, 174 B.R. 475 (Bankr. N.D. Ohio 1994); *In re* Fischer, 23 B.R. 432 (Bankr. W.D. Ky. 1982).
684 *See, e.g., In re* Gross, 121 B.R. 587 (Bankr. D.S.D. 1990). *See generally* § 15.3, *supra*.

17.8 Postconfirmation Issues

17.8.1 Postconfirmation Modification of the Chapter 12 Plan

The confirmation of a chapter 12 plan marks the court's approval of the undertaking of reorganization by the family farmer. It is only the beginning. The attorney's responsibility for representation, advice and action does not end at confirmation, but continues throughout the life of the plan.

Section 1229 allows modification of a chapter 12 plan after confirmation.[685] The debtor is *not* the exclusive party who can offer a postconfirmation modification; section 1229(a) allows the trustee and any holder of an allowed unsecured claim to propose a modification after confirmation.[686] Postconfirmation modification is conditioned upon several requirements, some of which are new restrictions imposed by the 2005 amendments:

(1) Any modification of the plan after confirmation must occur before completion of the payments called for under the plan;[687]

(2) The modification can: increase or reduce the amount of payments on claims of a particular class provided for by the plan; extend or reduce the time for payments; or alter the amount of the distribution to a creditor whose claim is provided for by the plan to the extent necessary to take account of any payment of such claim other than under the plan;[688]

(3) Modification must meet the plan confirmation standard of section 1222(a) and 1225(a);[689]

(4) Modification must meet any standards applicable to the modification in section 1222(b);[690]

(5) If the modification does not alter the rights of secured creditors, then a creditor's acceptance or rejection of the original plan is deemed to apply to the modification, unless the secured creditor affirmatively changes its acceptance or rejection upon notification of proposed modification;[691]

(6) The modified plan cannot provide for payments which extend beyond three years from the due date of the first payment under the original plan, although for cause the court can allow extension for up to five years;[692]

(7) A plan may not be modified: (1) to increase the amount of any payment due before the plan as modified becomes the plan; (2) by anyone except the debtor, based on an increase in the debtor's disposable income, to increase the amount of payments to unsecured creditors required for a particular month so that the aggregate of such payments exceeds the debtor's disposable income for such month; or (3) in the last year of the plan by anyone except the debtor, to require payments that would leave the debtor with insufficient funds to carry on the farming operation after the plan is completed.[693]

Notice and a hearing are required for modification; however, if no objection to modification is lodged, the plan can be implemented as modified as a matter of course without the necessity of formal hearing.[694]

Reasons for modification include illness of the debtor and unforeseen financial difficulties.[695] In the farm context, drought

---

685 11 U.S.C. § 1329; *In re* Hagen, 95 B.R. 708 (Bankr. D.N.D. 1989).
   Modification is initiated by motion under Bankruptcy Rule 9013, not by application. *In re* Hart, 90 B.R. 150 (Bankr. E.D.N.C. 1988). See §§ 4.6, 4.7.3, *supra*.

686 11 U.S.C. § 1229(a); *In re* Wiest, 446 B.R. 441 (Bankr. D. Mont. 2011) (rejecting chapter 12 trustee's attempt to modify chapter 12 plan and holding that trustee was bound by confirmed plan and could not use modification to remedy defects that he failed to notice prior to confirmation).
   These holders of undersecured or partially secured claims are included. *In re* Cook, 148 B.R. 273 (Bankr. W.D. Mich. 1992). See *In re* Roesner, 153 B.R. 328 (Bankr. D. Kan. 1993); *In re* Koonce, 54 B.R. 643 (Bankr. D.S.C. 1985). However, a modification proposed by any party must meet the same standards for approval of the modification set forth in section 1229.

687 11 U.S.C. § 1229(a); *In re* Cook, 148 B.R. 273 (Bankr. W.D. Mich. 1992); *In re* Moss, 91 B.R. 562 (Bankr. E.D. Cal. 1988) (chapter 13); *In re* Pritchett, 55 B.R. 557 (Bankr. W.D. Va. 1985).
   This period apparently can extend beyond the three to five year plan life, if secured debt has been amortized by the plan beyond that time period. See *In re* Schnakenberg, 195 B.R. 435 (Bankr. D. Neb. 1996).

688 11 U.S.C. § 1229(a)(1); *In re* Hart, 90 B.R. 150 (Bankr. E.D.N.C. 1988); *In re* DeMoss, 59 B.R. 90 (Bankr. W.D. La. 1986); *In re* Davis, 34 B.R. 319 (Bankr. E.D. Va. 1983).
   One court has held that these are the exclusive grounds for modification. Section 1229 cannot be used to make modifications on other bases. *In re* Wruck, 183 B.R. 862 (Bankr. D.N.D. 1995) (cannot change disbursement method by modification).

689 11 U.S.C. § 1229(b)(1); *In re* Roesner, 153 B.R. 328 (Bankr. D. Kan. 1993); *In re* Hagen, 95 B.R. 708 (Bankr. D.N.D. 1989); *In re* Hart, 90 B.R. 150 (Bankr. E.D.N.C. 1988) (feasibility).

690 11 U.S.C. § 1229(b)(1).

691 11 U.S.C. § 1229(b)(1) (with reference to 11 U.S.C. § 1223(c)).
   This requirement concerning acceptance and rejection is actually a holdover from the balloting procedure and the acceptance and rejection necessary in the confirmation route for chapter 11 plans under 11 U.S.C. § 1129(a). Rejection does not occur in chapters 12 and 13 because of cramdown; however, initial express acceptance by a secured creditor of treatment which does not comport with chapter 12 confirmation standards certainly can occur.

692 11 U.S.C. § 1229(c); *In re* Whitby, 146 B.R. 19 (Bankr. D. Idaho 1992); *In re* Hart, 90 B.R. 150 (Bankr. E.D.N.C. 1988).
   This limitation does not apply to debts which are reamortized or reamortizable under 11 U.S.C. § 1222(b)(5) and (b)(9). The calculation of the time runs from the date the first payment under the original plan was due. *In re* Eves, 67 B.R. 964 (Bankr. N.D. Ohio 1986). The requirement that extension can be had "for cause" to a five-year repayment schedule is taken lightly by some districts, but scrutinized more strictly by others.

693 Connor v. First Nat'l Bank-Haskell, 2008 WL 2714243 (N.D. Tex. July 11, 2008) (allowing modification of the debtors' plan to provide for payment of a postconfirmation condemnation award to unsecured creditors), *aff'd*, 2009 WL 270046 (5th Cir. Feb. 5, 2009) (per curiam).

694 11 U.S.C. § 102(1); *In re* Eves, 67 B.R. 964 (Bankr. N.D. Ohio 1986).

695 *See, e.g., In re* DeMoss, 59 B.R. 90 (Bankr. W.D. La. 1986).
   The change of circumstances need not be egregious, but should be material and substantial. *In re* Pritchett, 55 B.R. 557 (Bankr. W.D. Va. 1985).

or unexpected damage to crops or livestock outside the control of the debtor may provide justification for modification.[696] The court can, under appropriate circumstances, permit a moratorium on plan payments under such compelling circumstances.[697]

Early case law, summarized below, sheds light both upon the acceptance of modification upon default and construction of initial plans under chapter 12. However, these cases do not address any new interpretation of plan modification in light of the changes to the disposable income requirement.

Most courts have found that no special circumstances are necessary for request of modification; the presence or possibility of default is circumstance enough.[698] For these courts, there is no particular threshold, only a proper showing of changed circumstances.[699]

However, postconfirmation modification is a method of addressing unforeseen difficulties.[700] Circumstances warranting modification must be *unanticipated*.[701] If the debtor proposes modification (in contrast to the trustee or a creditor), the burden of proving that the modification meets confirmation requirements rests with the debtor.[702]

The nature of the circumstances giving rise to the need for modification bears upon the feasibility of any proposed modification.[703] The debtor may have to show that the default was the product of circumstances outside the control of the debtor, not likely to reoccur, and thus likely to be amenable to remedy by modification.[704] Although droughts can recur, they must be viewed as unanticipated and anomalous,[705] justifying modification. Prepetition defaults cannot be considered upon modification because of the res judicata effect of the initial confirmation.[706] A sale or abandonment that could not be consummated under an original plan, when all other plan provisions have been complied with, may be modified.[707]

Postpetition defaults brought about solely by climatic conditions or by failure to consummate a plan provision unrelated to crop or livestock performance (for example, sale of property) must be distinguished from those produced by initial sloppiness (for example failure to do initial valuations correctly, as above) or budget overruns somewhat within the debtor's control. If the postconfirmation default has been occasioned by budget overruns, doubt may be resolved against the debtor.[708] Efforts to satisfy the feasibility requirement on modification must be accompanied by accurate financial data sufficient to overcome the prejudicial effect of preceding year's budget experience.[709]

The nature of bankruptcy proceedings can lead to the inclusion of plan provisions arrived at by consent, which neither the creditor nor debtor could legally insist upon as products of negotiation. When terms are negotiated, courts may approach modification with caution.[710] A "drop dead" or recapture provision may be just such a term.[711] As circumstances warranting modification should be *unanticipated*, if the plan anticipates default, the debtor may not be able to modify the plan to avoid the consequences of that default over the objection of the affected creditor.[712]

One case has determined that because section 1229(b)(1) makes section 1222(b) applicable to modifications, to restrict modification to the three to five year plan life would be contrary to the intent of chapter 12 and would make its provisions significantly inferior to the modification provisions under chapter 11.[713] As a result, the modification in the *Hart* case could extend the life of the plan as modified beyond the original time frame of the plan as initially proposed.

17.8.2 Postconfirmation Indebtedness

Indebtedness incurred by the debtor after confirmation of a chapter 12 plan must be paid by the debtor separate and apart from the plan and not as a part of the chapter 12 proceeding.[714] Unlike chapter 13, chapter 12 does not have a provision to allow postpetition indebtedness accrued for taxes, approved by the trustee, or incurred upon an emergency basis to be folded back into the plan.[715]

However, due to the special purposes and the rehabilitative nature of chapter 12, it is conceivable that a postconfirmation modification could be proposed under section 1229 which includes postpetition indebtedness so long as undue prejudice did not result to prepetition creditors.[716] Thus, a debtor may not

---

696 *In re* Craven, 97 B.R. 549 (Bankr. W.D. Mo. 1989) (drought).
697 *See, e.g.*, Johnson v. Vanguard Holding Co., 708 F.2d 865 (2d Cir. 1983).
698 *In re* Hagen, 95 B.R. 708 (Bankr. D.N.D. 1989).
699 *In re* Grogg Farms, Inc., 91 B.R. 482 (Bankr. N.D. Ind. 1988).
700 *Id.*; *In re* Hart, 90 B.R. 150 (Bankr. E.D.N.C. 1988).
701 *In re* Cook, 148 B.R. 273 (Bankr. W.D. Mich. 1992) (discussion of modification bases: unforeseeability versus change alone); *In re* Wickersheim, 107 B.R. 177 (Bankr. E.D. Wis. 1989); *In re* Cooper, 94 B.R. 550 (Bankr. S.D. Ill. 1989); *In re* Grogg Farms, Inc., 91 B.R. 482 (Bankr. N.D. Ind. 1988).
702 *In re* Hart, 90 B.R. 150 (Bankr. E.D.N.C. 1988); *In re* Dittmer, 82 B.R. 1019 (Bankr. D.N.D. 1988).
703 *In re* Hagen, 95 B.R. 708 (Bankr. D.N.D. 1989).
704 *Id.*
705 *Id.*
706 *In re* Craven, 97 B.R. 549 (Bankr. W.D. Mo. 1989).
  Yet that effect might cut both ways—one court has determined that a debtor cannot redo valuations to change the amount due unsecured creditors postconfirmation, based upon failure to do a liquidation analysis properly prior to the confirmation of the initial plan. *In re* Cooper, 94 B.R. 550 (Bankr. S.D. Ill. 1989).
707 *In re* Webb, 932 F.2d 155 (2d Cir. 1991) (modification to allow sale permitted); *In re* Hart, 90 B.R. 150 (Bankr. E.D.N.C. 1988).

708 *In re* Hagen, 95 B.R. 708 (Bankr. D.N.D. 1989).
709 *Id.*
710 *In re* Grogg Farms, Inc., 91 B.R. 482 (Bankr. N.D. Ind. 1988).
711 *Id.*
712 *Id. But see In re* Mader, 108 B.R. 643 (N.D. Ill. 1989).
  Plan had expedited default remedies provision or "drop dead" clause (at option of FLB: conversion, trustee sale or deed delivery). The *Mader* court concluded as a matter of law that its presence in a confirmed plan does not preclude the possibility of modification under section 1229.
713 *In re* Hart, 90 B.R. 150 (Bankr. E.D.N.C. 1988).
714 *See, e.g., In re* Winter, 151 B.R. 278 (Bankr. W.D. Okla. 1993); *In re* Hester, 63 B.R. 607, 609 (Bankr. E.D. Tenn. 1986).
715 *See* 11 U.S.C. § 1305.
716 For example, it might be allowed when the postpetition debt helps bring benefits or revenue back into the estate for payment to

borrow postconfirmation on a super-priority basis and subordinate the preconfirmation debt.[717]

If the incurring of postpetition indebtedness can be foreseen prior to confirmation, then it can be placed within the chapter 12 plan itself for original confirmation. For example, if the debtor has been allowed to incur credit preconfirmation under section 364, to be repaid by the first annual distribution under the plan, the plan can provide that the debtor can incur similar debt in future years subject to court approval, and if approved, such debt will be treated and repaid in the same manner as the initial postpetition/preconfirmation debt.[718]

17.8.3 Revocation of Confirmation

The confirmation of a chapter 12 plan may be revoked if the order of confirmation was procured by fraud.[719] Revocation must be requested by a party in interest within one-hundred-eighty days of the entry of the order confirming the plan.[720] Notice and a hearing are required prior to revocation.[721] If confirmation is revoked, then the court will dispose of the chapter 12 case by dismissal, or, if appropriate, by conversion to chapter 7, unless the court allows additional time and the debtor proposes and the court confirms a plan modification.[722]

The provision for confirmation revocation in chapter 12 is drawn verbatim from chapter 13,[723] so that case law developed under chapter 13 should be equally applicable to chapter 12 cases. Chapter 11 also has a provision for revocation of confirmation based upon fraud.[724] As fraud is the sole ground for confirmation revocation in chapter 12 cases, fraud sufficient to warrant revocation should also be sufficient to justify conversion under section 1208(d).[725]

In defining the parameters of fraud which will suffice for confirmation revocation, courts have likened it to fraud sufficient to revoke an individual discharge[726] and fraud under section 523(a)(2).[727] The fraud must be directly connected with procurement of confirmation, as contrasted with other aspects of the case.[728]

The burden upon a party seeking revocation of a confirmation order appears to be to prove that:

- Movant is a party in interest;
- Application to revoke confirmation has been filed within 180 days of entry of the confirmation order;
- There exists fraud in procurement of the plan confirmation, demonstrated by:
  - the debtor made a representation regarding compliance with section 1225 which was materially false;
  - the representation was either known by the debtor to be false, was made without belief in its truth, or was made with reckless disregard for the truth;[729]
  - the representation was made to induce the court to rely upon it;
  - the court did rely upon it; and
  - as a consequence of such reliance, the court entered the confirmation order.[730]

The question of whether knowledge of the fraud preconfirmation and failure to object preconfirmation upon those grounds will bar later attempts to raise fraud to revoke discharge has

---

prepetition creditors, or when the postpetition expense itself can be paid from benefits unforeseen at confirmation and arising postconfirmation.

717   *In re* Les Ruggles & Sons, Inc., 222 B.R. 344 (Bankr. D. Neb. 1998).
718   In fact, the legislative history of chapter 12 specifically contemplates that future financing may be anticipated in a chapter 12 plan. *See* H.R. Conf. Rep. 99-958, at 50, 51 (1986), *reprinted in* 1986 U.S.C.C.A.N. 5251, 5252.

> Because Section 1227 is modeled after Section 1327, family farmers may provide in their plans for postconfirmation financing secured by assets that have revested in the debtor. The debtor may also use revested property to the extent it is not encumbered by the plan or order of confirmation to secure post-confirmation credit.

Id.
719   11 U.S.C. § 1230(a).
720   11 U.S.C. § 1230(a); Combs v. Combs, 34 B.R. 597 (Bankr. S.D. Ohio 1983).
      The court may also initiate revocation *sua sponte* under the 1986 amendments to 11 U.S.C. § 105. *In re* Davis, 68 B.R. 205 (Bankr. S.D. Ohio 1986). *See also* Chinichian v. Campolongo, 784 F.2d 1440 (9th Cir. 1986) (in a chapter 13 case, partial confirmation could be revoked for bad faith under 11 U.S.C. § 1325); *In re* Gross, 121 B.R. 587 (Bankr. D.S.D. 1990) (strict construction on time period).
721   11 U.S.C. § 1230(a).
722   11 U.S.C. § 1230(b).
      Conversion would only be appropriate if the debtor requested conversion or if fraud were present; however, the fraud necessary for revocation of confirmation mirrors the fraud sufficient to justify conversion under 11 U.S.C. § 1208(d).
723   *See* 11 U.S.C. § 1330.
724   *See* 11 U.S.C. § 1144.
      Revocation of confirmation under chapter 11 also revokes discharge.
725   *See, e.g., In re* Krisle, 54 B.R. 330 (Bankr. D.S.C. 1985) (no voluntary dismissal of a chapter 11 case when gross misuse of cash collateral found); Paccar Fin. Corp. v. Pappas, 17 B.R. 662 (Bankr. D. Mass. 1982) (although the court couched its order directing conversion on grounds of bad faith, its findings supporting that approach have fraud etched into them).
726   *See* 11 U.S.C. §§ 727(d)(1), 1144.
727   Stamford Mun. Employees Credit Union, Inc. v. Edwards, 67 B.R. 1008 (Bankr. D. Conn. 1986).
728   *In re* Courson, 243 B.R. 288 (Bankr. E.D. Tex. 1999) (failure of creditor to understand plan is insufficient ground for revocation of confirmation).
      For grounds for revocation see generally *In re* Hicks, 79 B.R. 45 (Bankr. N.D. Ala. 1987); *In re* Scott, 77 B.R. 636 (Bankr. N.D. Ohio 1987); *In re* Moseley, 74 B.R. 791 (Bankr. C.D. Cal. 1987) (and cases surveyed therein); *In re* Braten Apparel Corp., 21 B.R. 239 (Bankr. S.D.N.Y. 1982), *aff'd*, 742 F.2d 1435 (2d Cir. 1983).
729   Actual, affirmative fraud is required. Stamford Mun. Employees Credit Union, Inc. v. Edwards, 67 B.R. 1008 (Bankr. D. Conn. 1986); *In re* Braten Apparel Corp., 21 B.R. 239 (Bankr. S.D.N.Y. 1982), *aff'd*, 742 F.2d 1435 (2d Cir. 1983).
730   Stamford Mun. Employees Credit Union, Inc. v. Edwards, 67 B.R. 1008 (Bankr. D. Conn. 1986).

§ 17.8.3   Consumer Bankruptcy Law and Practice

been decided both ways under the Code.[731]

---

[731] *In re* Braten Apparel Corp., 21 B.R. 239 (Bankr. S.D.N.Y. 1982), aff'd, 742 F.2d 1435 (2d Cir. 1983), specifically finds that the language of 11 U.S.C. § 1144 for chapter 11 cases on confirmation revocation eliminates the requirements under the old Bankruptcy Act that knowledge of the grounds for revocation must come to the moving party's knowledge after confirmation. *See also* Stamford Mun. Employees Credit Union, Inc. v. Edwards, 67 B.R. 1008 (Bankr. D. Conn. 1986); Official Equity Sec. Holders' Comm. v. Wilson Foods Corp., 45 B.R. 776 (Bankr. W.D. Okla. 1985); *In re* DFD, Inc., 43 B.R. 393 (Bankr. E.D. Pa. 1984).

Chapter 18 — Consumers As Creditors in Bankruptcy: Selected Topics

18.1 Introduction

Frequently, consumers have claims against businesses or individuals who file bankruptcy. Sometimes litigation by a consumer or a class of consumers may even motivate a retailer, service provider, finance company, or others to seek shelter in the bankruptcy system. Similarly, tenants may discover that their landlord has filed bankruptcy and services to their building have stopped. A consumer may also be a creditor in the bankruptcy of a separated or former spouse.[1]

Several finance company lenders, holding hundreds of thousands of mortgages on the homes of low-income debtors, have recently filed bankruptcy.[2] As many of the affected home owners have claims or defenses to those mortgages, advocates need to understand how bankruptcy can affect these claims and defenses and what tools are available to protect them.[3]

Representing consumers in bankruptcy when they are not debtors involves different perspectives and different legal issues than those that arise when representing consumer debtors. This Chapter presents selected topics and discusses some of the issues consumers may face as creditors or parties in interest.

There is voluminous literature on representation of creditors.[4] Most of that literature concerns representation of commercial interests. This Chapter focuses on basic concepts and on topics of special importance to consumer creditors. When topics overlap those discussed earlier in this treatise, there are cross references rather than a repetition of the material.

18.2 Prebankruptcy Strategy

18.2.1 Preparing for the Debtor's Voluntary Bankruptcy

When consumers have claims against persons or entities that are financially shaky, the possibility that the person or entity may file bankruptcy should be considered when pursuing claims and collection of the claims. In many instances, lawyers who have obtained large judgments against an abusive business or landlord find they have merely wasted their time or falsely raised their client's hopes when the judgment debtor files for bankruptcy. The clients become unsecured creditors in a chapter 7 or 11 bankruptcy, and any distribution to them is nominal or nonexistent. While there is no way to assure collection in the face of a threatened bankruptcy, there are steps that may help in some cases.

The best approach is to name a defendant in the original suit who is a "deep pocket" and unlikely to file bankruptcy. In pursuing claims against landlords or other businesses, determine if, in addition to the corporate entity that conducts the business, there is potential liability on the part of individuals involved, parent companies, secured lenders, lawyers, franchisors and others.[5] Also consider what third parties may have obligations to make good on a consumer's claim, such as officer and director liability policy insurers or state recovery funds[6] for licensed real estate agents or attorneys. A consumer who obtains a judgment should be sure to insist on filing of an appeal bond if the defendant appeals; the bond surety will then be liable in the event of the defendant's bankruptcy.[7]

Another protective strategy when pursuing claims against individuals (not corporations) is to include claims that could be nondischargeable if the individual subsequently files for bankruptcy.[8] A finding of nondischargeability will permit the consumer to collect from the debtor's future income and assets acquired postpetition, even in the event of the debtor's bankruptcy. Nondischargeable claims include those based on fraud

---

1 While this chapter will cover some topics relevant to spouses of debtors, a more comprehensive treatment can be found in Henry J. Sommer & Margaret Dee McGarity, Collier Family Law and the Bankruptcy Code (2009).
2 See § 18.9, infra.
3 Id.
4 See texts discussed in § 1.5.3, supra. Another text which may be helpful to those new to representation of creditors, although it is oriented to the representation of commercial interests, is LoPucki, Strategies For Creditors in Bankruptcy Proceedings (2d ed. 1991), published by Little Brown and Co.
5 See § 18.5.7, infra; National Consumer Law Center, Unfair and Deceptive Acts and Practices § 11.1 (7th ed. 2008 and Supp.).
6 See, e.g., Ariz. Rev. Stat. Ann. § 32-2186; Cal. Bus. & Prof. Code § 10471 (West) (Chapter 6.5 Real Estate Recovery Program); 63 Pa. Cons. Stat. § 455.801 (Real Estate Licensing Act, Real Estate Recovery Fund).
7 See, e.g., Fed. R. App. P. 8(b).
8 See § 18.5.4, infra.

or false pretenses,[9] breach of fiduciary duty, embezzlement or larceny,[10] for willful and malicious injury,[11] or injury incurred through drunk driving.[12]

While holdings in other courts are not binding as res judicata to determine dischargeability in bankruptcy court, they may be given effect under the doctrine of collateral estoppel, and in any event, will be persuasive evidence in the bankruptcy court.[13] Care should be taken to have the court make factual findings that could later be used in a bankruptcy proceeding.

When settling potentially nondischargeable claims, care should be taken to have the settlement agreement and, if possible, any order confirming the settlement, recite grounds establishing nondischargeability. For example, in consumer cases involving fraud and other claims, a settlement agreement will be useful in a later nondischargeability case only if the defendant admits liability for fraud. If the plaintiff explicitly releases liability on fraud-based claims in exchange for an admission of liability on other claims that are dischargeable in bankruptcy, that release may undermine the consumer's position if the defendant later files bankruptcy.[14] Similarly, because it is easier to have family support debts found nondischargeable than property settlement obligations,[15] care should be taken in drafting marital separation and divorce agreements. These concerns should be addressed aggressively in settlement negotiations.

If a judgment has been obtained or liability admitted, the consumer should collect the debt or at least obtain a lien in the debtor's property to secure the debt as quickly as possible before a possible bankruptcy filing can occur. Speedy collection can be complicated, however, by the trustee's power to avoid as preferences many "transfers" to creditors (in this case the consumer) ninety days prior to the bankruptcy filing that would put the creditor (the consumer) in a better position than other creditors if the bankruptcy were filed as a chapter 7 and the transfer had not been made.[16]

For example, if a cash payment is made in full or partial settlement of the debt and the debtor files within ninety days of the payment, the trustee or the debtor in possession may be able to recover the cash from the consumer creditor. Similarly, because "transfer" is broadly defined,[17] the trustee may be able to void a security interest granted to secure the debt within the ninety days, may recover property levied upon in execution of the judgment, and may recover the proceeds from the sale of the levied goods. As a result, collection efforts may have to tread a fine line between obtaining as much as possible as quickly as possible and not pushing the debtor into bankruptcy.

To avoid the situation in which a transfer is recoverable as a preference, explore whether there is a third party who may be required (or willing) to make payment of the debt.[18]

Any settlement for less than the full amount of the debt should include a condition that the reduction in the amount owed only becomes effective at the end of the preference period and that if the payment is recovered as a preference the consumer will be owed the full amount of the debt plus costs and attorney fees.[19]

Similar issues arise when judgment liens are potentially avoidable because they impair a debtor's exemptions.[20] If an individual debtor has more than one attachable parcel of real estate, the lien should be attached to the parcel that would not be eligible for a homestead exemption in a later bankruptcy. The simplest rule of thumb is to make sure that any judgment lien attaches to as much property as possible.

18.2.2 Putting the Debtor into Involuntary Bankruptcy

Bankruptcy is a favorable collection forum in certain circumstances. When consumer creditors have obtained a large judgment against an abusive business or landlord that appears to exceed the judgment debtor's assets, an involuntary bankruptcy petition can serve as an effective collection mechanism.[21]

An involuntary petition may be filed under chapter 7 or chapter 11 by three or more creditors with liquidated, non-contingent, undisputed,[22] and unsecured claims aggregating at least $14,425.[23] If the petition is opposed, the bankruptcy court

---

9 11 U.S.C. § 532(a)(2). See § 15.4.3.2, supra.
10 11 U.S.C. § 523(a)(4). See § 15.4.3.4, supra.
11 11 U.S.C. § 523(a)(6). See § 15.4.3.6, supra.
12 11 U.S.C. § 523(a)(9). See § 15.4.3.9, supra.
13 See § 15.4.4, supra.
14 See § 15.4.4, supra.
15 See §§ 15.4.3.5, 15.4.3.14, supra.
16 11 U.S.C. § 547(b). See § 10.4.2.6.4, supra.
　For an excellent, more detailed discussion of the implications of section 547(b) for the unsecured creditor prior to bankruptcy upon which the following paragraphs draw heavily, see LoPucki, Strategies For Creditors In Bankruptcy Proceedings Ch. 2 (2d ed. 1991) (Representing Unsecured Creditors in the Shadow of Bankruptcy).
17 "Transfer" is defined in 11 U.S.C. § 101(54). Transfer includes granting of security interests and involuntary transfers.

18 See, e.g., In re Sun Railings, 5 B.R. 538 (Bankr. S.D. Fla. 1980) (payment was found not be an avoidable preference because the payment was borrowed as an unsecured loan from a third party and paid directly by the third party to the creditor).
　The limits of this doctrine are discussed in In re Neponset River Paper Co., 231 B.R. 829 (B.A.P. 1st Cir. 1999).
19 For an example of such a clause, see LoPucki, Strategies For Creditors In Bankruptcy Proceedings § 2.14.3 (2d ed. 1991).
20 11 U.S.C. § 522(f). See § 10.4.2.3, supra.
21 11 U.S.C. § 303.
　For a more complete discussion of involuntary bankruptcy, see § 14.8, supra.
22 On the question of whether the creditor's claims are subject to a bona fide dispute, the bankruptcy court should be willing to give the consumers' earlier judgment effect under the doctrine of collateral estoppel. In re DEF Invs., Inc., 186 B.R. 671 (Bankr. D. Minn. 1995). However, the dispute may be as to either liability or the amount of the debt.
23 11 U.S.C. § 303(b).
　The $14,425 amount is adjusted periodically for inflation, under 11 U.S.C. § 104. If the debtor has fewer than twelve qualifying creditors, one or more creditors with over $14,425 in qualifying claims may file the petition.

will hold a hearing, and will enter an order for relief if the debtor is failing to pay its debt(s) as they become due.[24]

An involuntary order for chapter 7 relief can provide many benefits for consumer creditors. It results, among other things, in the appointment of a trustee to take control of the debtor's assets.[25] Creditors can elect a trustee of their own choosing at the meeting of creditors.[26] Forcing an involuntary bankruptcy can trigger useful disclosure requirements as well as other asset discovery procedures.[27] It can also prevent a dishonest debtor from transferring away assets that might have been available to satisfy a judgment and from otherwise mismanaging the business. Similarly, an involuntary case can be used to recover assets that have already been fraudulently transferred.[28] There may also be the possibility, based on the limitations on state homestead exemptions enacted in 2005,[29] that a debtor's homestead property which would be protected under applicable nonbankruptcy law may be liquidated in an involuntary bankruptcy. Two other potentially useful powers in an involuntary bankruptcy are the trustee's power to avoid any preferential transfers the debtor has made within the previous ninety days (or within one year to insiders)[30] and the court's power to appoint new management for the debtor.[31] An involuntary bankruptcy may also be used to bring related parties and their assets before the bankruptcy court when there has been a voluntary bankruptcy by only one of several related parties (partners, spouses, subsidiaries and affiliated corporations, joint owners of real estate, and so forth).

In one case, consumer creditors filed an involuntary petition against a rent-to-own company against which consumers had obtained a judgment for usury.[32] Several other unreported cases involved large mismanaged apartment complexes in which tenants had judgments requiring damage payments and substantial repairs. An involuntary bankruptcy case in the latter situation may force a change of ownership if the debtor has effectively abandoned the building. It may also create opportunities to commence discussions about the future of the building with secured creditors.

However, advocates should remember that there are substantial risks to an involuntary bankruptcy strategy. The bankruptcy court may require petitioners to post a bond for the debtor's expenses and potential damages.[33] An involuntary petition that is dismissed can result in compensatory and punitive damages, as well as attorney fees and costs.[34]

18.3 The Automatic Stay

18.3.1 Introduction

In pursuing claims on behalf of consumers, the consumer's attorney must be aware that as soon as an entity has filed a bankruptcy petition, the consumer and the consumer's attorney[35] are subject to the far-reaching impact of the automatic stay.[36] Virtually all legal proceedings against the debtor and other collection efforts must cease until relief is granted by the bankruptcy court. Violators of the stay risk being subject to contempt, actual damages, costs, attorney fees and punitive damages.[37] Moreover, actions taken in violation of the stay are void or at least voidable, even absent notice of the stay.[38] The scope of the stay is discussed in detail in Chapter 9, *supra*.

Formal notice of the filing is *not* required to subject an attorney or creditor to the automatic stay.[39] Once an attorney has received any indication that a bankruptcy has been filed, she should assume the stay is in effect unless the absence of a filing has been verified by inquiry to the bankruptcy court or the PACER electronic document system.[40] Upon receipt of notice, the creditor or its attorney is generally obligated to inform any state court in which litigation is pending of the existence of the stay.[41]

---

24 11 U.S.C. § 303(h)(1).
    There is a second, alternative basis for entry of an involuntary order for relief that applies in the following, very limited circumstances: when a custodian was appointed for the debtor's assets, or took possession of the debtor's assets, within 120 days before the petition filing, *and* the custodian was *not* a trustee, receiver or agent taking charge of "less than substantially all" of the debtor's assets to enforce a lien. 11 U.S.C. § 303(h)(2).
    For example, if all of a landlord's buildings were in control of a receiver or liquidator, creditors could seek to preempt the self-help or state law process and obtain the benefits of the bankruptcy law. Appointment of a receiver for only one of a landlord's many buildings, on the other hand, would not meet this criterion.
25 11 U.S.C. § 701.
26 11 U.S.C. § 702.
27 An order for relief in an involuntary case triggers the requirement that schedules and a statement of affairs be filed within fourteen days. Fed. R. Bankr. P. 1007(c). Debtor's examinations are also available under Federal Rule of Bankruptcy Procedure 2004. An involuntary debtor will not necessarily be cooperative in filing schedules and appearing for questioning, however. *See* § 18.5.8, *infra*.
28 The trustee's powers to avoid transfers are discussed in Chapter 15, *supra*.
29 See Chapter 10, *supra*, for discussion of homestead exemption limitations.
30 11 U.S.C. § 547. *See* § 10.4.2.6.4, *supra*.
31 11 U.S.C. § 303(g).
32 *In re* DEF Invs., Inc., 186 B.R. 671 (Bankr. D. Minn. 1995).

33 11 U.S.C. § 303(e).
34 11 U.S.C. § 303(i). *See* § 14.8, *supra*.
35 *See, e.g., In re* Carter, 691 F.2d 390, 391, 392 (8th Cir. 1982) (landlord's attorney in contempt for continuing eviction after receiving notice of the stay).
36 11 U.S.C. § 362. *See* Ch. 9, *supra*.
37 11 U.S.C. § 362(k). *See* § 9.6, *supra*.
38 *See* § 9.6, *supra*.
39 *In re* Carter, 691 F.2d 390 (8th Cir. 1982); Fid. Mortgage Investors v. Camelia Builders, Inc., 550 F.2d 47 (2d Cir. 1976). *See also* § 9.6.3, *supra*.
40 *See, e.g., In re* Carter, 16 B.R. 481 (W.D. Mo. 1981) (when creditor's counsel had doubts about representations of debtor's counsel that filing had been made it was incumbent upon creditor's counsel to verify the filing with the bankruptcy court), *aff'd*, 691 F.2d 390 (8th Cir. 1982).
41 Sternberg v. Johnston, 595 F.3d 937 (9th Cir. 2010), *cert denied* 131 S. Ct. 102 (2010) (creditor's attorney willfully violated stay by not taking corrective action within reasonable time to vacate contempt

§ 18.3.2 Consumer Bankruptcy Law and Practice

A number of new exceptions and limitations to the automatic stay were added to the Code by the 2005 amendments, and are discussed in detail in Chapter 9, *supra*. In some cases, these amendments may permit a consumer creditor to proceed with certain litigation or collection efforts without seeking relief from the stay, particularly against an individual debtor who has had prior dismissed bankruptcy cases.

18.3.2 Relief from the Stay

In most instances the bankruptcy court must grant relief from the stay before any litigation or collection action against the debtor may be taken. Grounds for relief from stay are discussed in detail elsewhere in this treatise.[42] This section addresses issues that are specifically applicable to consumers as creditors.

In cases in which state or federal (nonbankruptcy) litigation is well advanced, consumers may seek relief from the stay, or abstention, to continue the litigation in the state court for the limited purpose of liquidating the claim.[43] A bankruptcy court may also grant stay relief to allow a consumer creditor to enforce an order granting injunctive relief in the court that issued it.[44]

Stay relief may be readily granted when a consumer creditor possesses a secured claim that is not being adequately protected.[45] Consumers may be secured by judgment liens or, in some cases, by a state law right to set off mutual claims.

Government agency actions for equitable relief under their police and regulatory powers are not subject to the automatic stay.[46] For example, public agencies may continue to enforce consumer protection laws,[47] rent regulations,[48] and laws against discrimination.[49] However, public agencies are stayed from enforcing money judgments, or taking control of the debtor's property through state law liquidation or receivership proceedings.[50]

---

order against debtor for nonpayment of spousal support from estate property; instead attorney defended order in state court in its entirety); Eskanos & Adler, Prof'l Corp. v. Leetien, 309 F.3d 1210 (9th Cir. 2002) (failure to dismiss or stay pending collection action against debtor was willful violation of stay); In re Soares, 107 F.3d 969, 978 (1st Cir. 1997); In re Braught, 307 B.R. 399 (Bankr. S.D.N.Y. 2004) (creditor willfully violated stay by failing to take affirmative action to vacate state court judgment entered in violation of stay).

42 In re Bison Res., Inc., 230 B.R. 611 (Bankr. N.D. Okla. 1999) (discussing standards applicable to this type of motion). See § 9.7, *supra*.

43 See §§ 9.7.3.2.1, 14.5, *supra*. See also Davis v. Life Investors Ins. Co., 282 B.R. 186 (S.D. Miss. 2002) (court exercised discretionary abstention because consumer's action against auto dealer and insurance carrier for wrongful denial of credit disability insurance claim was not core proceeding in auto dealer's chapter 11); In re Ice Cream Liquidation, Inc., 281 B.R. 154 (Bankr. D. Conn. 2002) (sexual harassment and discrimination claims based on liability of successor corporation were "personal injury tort claims" within meaning of 28 U.S.C. § 157(b) and therefore could not be tried in bankruptcy court; court exercised discretion to lift stay and abstain as to remaining claims); In re Pac. Gas & Elec. Co., 279 B.R. 561 (Bankr. N.D. Cal. 2002) (bankruptcy court, not district court, has jurisdiction to decide whether to abstain; abstention and stay relief granted as to 1250 personal injury claims).

44 See, e.g., In re Veit, 227 B.R. 873 (Bankr. S.D. Ind. 1998).

45 See § 9.7.3.2.2, *infra*.

46 11 U.S.C. § 362(b)(4).

47 In re Halo Wireless, Inc., 684 F.3d 581 (5th Cir. 2012) (although initiated by private parties seeking to vindicate their own pecuniary interests, state public utility commission proceedings are excepted from stay because they further the state's regulatory and police powers); Solis v. SCA Restaurant Corp., 463 B.R. 248 (E.D.N.Y. 2011) (U.S. Dept. of Labor's proceeding to enforce Fair Labor Standards Act against debtor employer not stayed); State of California v. Villalobos, 453 B.R. 404 (D. Nev. 2011) (§ 362(b)(4) permits State to continue its state court action raising claims of unfair competition, securities fraud, and licensing violations against chapter 11 debtor); In re First Alliance Mortgage Co., 263 B.R. 99 (B.A.P. 9th Cir. 2001) (state may continue to prosecute state court consumer protection action so as to obtain a money judgment for restitution, civil penalties and attorney fees, but enforcement of such judgment would be stayed); United States EEOC v. CTI Global Solutions, Inc., 422 B.R. 49 (D. Md. 2010) (EEOC could pursue discrimination action against debtor/employer and seek judgment of compensatory and punitive damages, back pay, and injunctive relief); EEOC v. Wildwood Indus., Inc., 2009 WL 2050992 (D. Ill. July 8, 2009) (same); Iams Funeral Home, Inc. v. West Virginia, 392 B.R. 218 (N.D. W. Va. 2008) (state action to enjoin debtor from making and enforcing funeral servicer's contracts in violation of state consumer protection laws was not stayed); In re Fed. Trade Comm'n v. AmeriDebt, Inc., 343 F. Supp. 2d 451 (D. Md. 2004) (section 364(b)(4) allows Federal Trade Commission (FTC) to proceed with action against fraudulent debt counseling agency for rescission of consumers' contracts, restitution, and disgorgement, but not enforcement of money judgment); In re First Alliance Mortgage Co., 264 B.R. 634 (C.D. Cal. 2001) (bankruptcy court order enjoining FTC and state attorneys general from proceeding with consumer protection actions reversed; actions exempt from automatic stay); In re Clifton, 441 B.R. 44 (Bankr. E.D. Cal. 2010) (Secretary of Labor did not violate automatic stay by pursuing federal ERISA action for injunctive relief and monetary award against debtor-employer); In re Fitness Mgmt. Group, Inc., 2009 WL 4230075 (Bankr. W.D.N.C. Nov. 23, 2009) (automatic stay does not bar action to enforce consumer protection statute regulating health clubs); In re Dolen, 265 B.R. 471 (Bankr. M.D. Fla. 2001) (exception to automatic stay under section 362(b)(4) permits FTC to continue prosecution of consumer fraud action against chapter 13 debtor and to enforce preliminary injunction obtained in that action but does not allow use of the injunction to enjoin debtor's use of postpetition earnings); In re Nelson, 240 B.R. 802 (Bankr. D. Me. 1999) (state could pursue court action against debtor under consumer protection statutes); In re Liss, 59 B.R. 556 (Bankr. N.D. Ill. 1986).

48 In re Berry Estates, Inc. 812 F.2d 67 (2d Cir. 1987).

49 Equal Employment Opportunity Comm'n v. Le Bar Bat, Inc., 274 B.R. 66 (S.D.N.Y. 2002) (EEOC enforcement action under Title VII not subject to automatic stay based on section 362(b)(4) to extent that agency acts in the public interest and not simply to benefit individual employees); In re Mohawk Greenfield Motel Corp., 239 B.R. 1 (Bankr. D. Mass. 1999).

50 In re WinPar Hospitality Chattanooga, L.L.C., 404 B.R. 291 (Bankr. E.D. Tenn. 2009) (refusing to enjoin civil forfeiture action against proceeds of sale of debtor's property acquired through fraudulent scheme even if government ultimately decides to use proceeds to compensate victims of scheme). Compare In re NextWave Personal Communications, Inc., 244 B.R. 253 (Bankr. S.D.N.Y. 2000) (FCC

If the state court litigation is or was commenced by the debtor—for example, by a bankrupt finance company seeking to foreclose a mortgage, or by a bankrupt landlord seeking to evict a tenant—the creditor may raise defenses, because the stay applies to actions *against* the debtor and not actions initiated by the debtor.[51] However, pursuit of counterclaims does require relief from the stay as discussed in more detail in connection with rights of tenants below.[52]

The 2005 amendments expanded the Code's provisions exempting most domestic relations litigation from the scope of the automatic stay.[53] Revised section 362(b)(2) excepts from the automatic stay the commencement or continuation of an action to establish or modify child support, alimony, or maintenance.[54] The exception applies to creditors' actions on or after the date of the order for relief and applies to debts owed to or payable to a spouse, former spouse, child, or a governmental unit.[55] Proceedings to establish paternity and to modify or establish child custody and visitation are excepted, as are divorce proceedings (but not division of property that is property of the bankruptcy estate).[56] Proceedings for protection from domestic violence are specifically excepted.[57] Creditors' actions to collect court-ordered child support by wage withholding from estate property or property of the debtor are excepted, as are acts to collect child support through tax intercepts, credit agency reporting, and license suspension.[58]

The domestic relations creditor is bound by the terms of a confirmed chapter 13 plan.[59] However, several provisions of chapter 13 specifically promote child support collection. In addition to the priority for prepetition domestic support debts, the plan must provide for payment of postpetition domestic support obligations as a condition of confirmation.[60] The confirmed plan will be subject to dismissal if postpetition domestic support obligations are not being paid.[61]

An exception to the automatic stay is also available for collection of a domestic support obligation from property that is not property of the estate.[62] Thus, in a chapter 7 case, postpetition income can be collected by a support creditor, but property of the estate is not reachable (at least until it has "left" the estate because it is exempt or abandoned).[63] In a chapter 13 case, because all property acquired by the debtor is property of the estate, all actions to collect domestic support obligations are usually stayed,[64] unless permitted by another specific provision of section 362(b)(2). Notably, section 362(b)(2)(B) does not permit the commencement or continuation of a proceeding to enforce a domestic support obligation, even with respect to property that is not property of the estate. It permits only the collection of payments.

Some judicial proceedings with respect to domestic support obligations are excepted from the automatic stay under a more narrow provision. Section 362(b)(2)(A) of the Code provides an exception to the stay for the commencement or continuation of proceedings to establish paternity or to establish or modify a domestic support obligations.[65] This exception is carefully worded so that it does not permit proceedings to enforce such orders. However, once a state family court enters an order for current support, the bankruptcy court is likely to permit relief from the stay in most cases in which the debtor does not comply with it.[66]

If actions are inadvertently taken which violate the stay, the court is empowered in limited circumstances to "annul" the stay, that is, to grant retroactive relief from the stay.[67] Such relief is granted only in limited circumstances and usually involves duplicitous or bad faith conduct by the debtor that prejudices the interests of a creditor.[68]

---

actions as creditor to collect debt are stayed although FCC has power to take regulatory actions), *with In re* Fed. Communications Comm'n, 217 F.3d 125 (2d Cir. 2000) (court of appeals issues mandamus to require bankruptcy court to allow FCC to resell debtor's radio spectrum licenses). *See generally In re* Mystic Tank Lines Corp., 544 F.3d 524 (3d Cir. 2008) (state does not violate stay in reducing to judgment its claim for costs it expended in prepetition environmental cleanup).

51 Martin-Trigona v. Champion Fed. Sav., 892 F.2d 575 (7th Cir. 1989); *In re* Way, 229 B.R. 11 (B.A.P. 9th Cir. 1998). *See* § 9.4.2, *supra*.
52 *See* § 18.3.4, *infra*.
   See also sample forms in Appendix G.14, *infra*.
53 *See* § 9.4.6.3, *supra*.
54 11 U.S.C. § 362(b)(2)(A)(ii) (referencing 11 U.S.C. § 101(14A) (definition of "domestic support obligation").
55 11 U.S.C. § 101(14A).
56 11 U.S.C. § 362(b)(2)(A)(iii)–(iv).
57 11 U.S.C. § 362(b)(2)(A)(v).
58 11 U.S.C. § 362(b)(2)(C)–(F). *See generally In re* Penaran, 424 B.R. 868 (Bankr. D. Kan. 2010) (withholding of income that is property of debtor or estate to pay domestic support obligation under judicial order is excepted from stay); *In re* Fort, 412 B.R. 840 (Bankr. W.D. Va. 2009) (same).
59 *See, e.g., In re* Rodriguez, 367 Fed. Appx. 25 (11th Cir. 2010) (state violated plan confirmation order by sending dunning letters for child support arrears to debtor after plan confirmed); *In re* Schroeder, 2009 WL 3526504 (Bankr. D. Nev. Oct. 23, 2009) (same). *But see In re* McGrahan, 459 B.R. 869 (B.A.P. 1st Cir. 2011) (despite exception to automatic stay under § 362(b)(2)(f), terms of confirmed plan may explicitly bar tax intercepts to collect prepetition child support debt provided for in plan, however language of plan at issue here did not expressly and conspicuously prohibit the intercepts).
60 11 U.S.C. § 1325(a)(8). *See* Ch. 12, *supra*.
61 11 U.S.C. § 1307(c).
62 11 U.S.C. § 362(b)(2)(B). *See generally* Henry J. Sommer & Margaret Dee McGarity, Collier Family Law and the Bankruptcy Code (2009).
63 11 U.S.C. § 522(c)(1) allows exempt property to be pursued for these debts.
64 11 U.S.C. § 1306(a); Carver v. Carver, 954 F.2d 1573 (11th Cir. 1992) (action seeking to collect divorce obligations from chapter 13 debtor's wages violated automatic stay); *In re* Farmer, 150 B.R. 68 (Bankr. N.D. Ala. 1991) (state court order to incarcerate chapter 13 debtor for failing to pay support would violate automatic stay).
65 11 U.S.C. § 362(b)(2)(A).
66 *See generally* Henry J. Sommer & Margaret Dee McGarity, Collier Family Law and the Bankruptcy Code (2009).
67 11 U.S.C. § 362(d).
68 *See also* Franklin v. Office of Thrift Supervision, 31 F.3d 1020 (10th Cir. 1994) (power to annul stay should rarely be used, probably only in cases of claimants who were honestly ignorant of stay). *See generally In re* Soares, 107 F.3d 969 (1st Cir. 1997) (annulment

The stay does not bar litigation against co-defendants who are not bankruptcy debtors[69] except certain co-debtors in cases under chapter 12[70] or chapter 13.[71] A consumer plaintiff may wish to add parties, or dismiss the debtor as a party, or both, in order to proceed with litigation that would otherwise be subject to the stay.[72]

18.3.3 Practical Considerations Applicable to Stay Relief Issues

In deciding whether to seek stay relief in order to litigate in another forum, it is helpful to consider whether the consumer creditor can obtain better relief elsewhere. In certain cases bankruptcy court may be as good, or better than, state or federal court.[73] For example, a tenant whose necessary services have been terminated may prefer bankruptcy court because the debtor in chapter 11 or 13 is required to oversee estate property and may make special accommodations with the tenant in order to avoid dismissal of the case or the appointment of a trustee to manage the property.[74] More generally, bankruptcy provides a good opportunity to cost-effectively investigate the debtor's assets and maximize their use for the benefit of creditors.[75] Moreover, the proof of claim process and other bankruptcy remedies discussed below may make it easier, rather than harder, to find assets of a recalcitrant debtor.

Once a decision is made that relief from stay is the desired remedy, there is a $176 filing fee to make that motion.[76] No fee is required if the motion is filed by a child support creditor.[77] This fee is waivable upon filing a motion to proceed *in forma pauperis*.[78] The considerations for granting *in forma pauperis* relief are especially valid for low-income creditors because they were dragged involuntarily into the bankruptcy process.[79]

18.3.4 Tenants' Counterclaims Against a Bankrupt Landlord

One common problem affecting tenants whose landlords file bankruptcy is the need to raise counterclaims to a state court eviction case brought by the landlord. For these purposes it is necessary to distinguish between defenses and counterclaims. A tenant is not prevented by the automatic stay from raising defenses against a landlord's eviction action.[80] However, relief from the automatic stay is probably required in order to pursue

---

should not be granted when creditor knew of bankruptcy and failed to inform state court); *In re* Siciliano, 13 F.3d 748 (3d Cir. 1994) (bankruptcy court should not have denied motion for relief from stay applicable retroactively without considering whether grounds for annulment exist); *In re* Albany Partners, Ltd., 749 F.2d 670 (11th Cir. 1984) (lack of good faith on filing may constitute sufficient grounds to annul the stay); *In re* Bright 338 B.R. 530 (B.A.P. 1st Cir. 2006) (upholding finding of "unusual and unusually compelling circumstances" to justify retroactive annulment of stay when debtor's schedules had not disclosed her ownership interest in the subject property, an innocent third party had purchased the property at foreclosure sale, and the debtor delayed in objecting to the sale); *In re* WorldCom, Inc., 325 B.R. 511 (Bankr. S.D.N.Y. 2005) (denying creditor's request for retroactive annulment of stay and noting significant differences in legal tests for retroactive annulment of stay and termination of stay by motion under section 362(d)).

69 *In re* Excel Innovations, Inc., 502 F.3d 1086 (9th Cir. 2007) (bankruptcy court abused discretion in extending stay to non-debtor companies in chapter 11 case); Queenie, Ltd. v. Nygard Int'l, 321 F.3d 282 (2d Cir. 2003) (appeal stayed as to defendant who filed bankruptcy and his wholly owned corporation, but not as to other defendants); *In re* Cont'l Airlines, 203 F.3d 203 (3d Cir. 2000) (bankruptcy court's injunction of shareholders' lawsuits against non-debtor directors and officers found insupportable); Credit Alliance Corp. v. Williams, 851 F.2d 119 (4th Cir. 1988); Fortier v. Dona Anna Plaza Partners, 747 F.2d 1324 (10th Cir. 1984); Austin v. Unarco Indus., Inc., 705 F.2d 1 (1st Cir. 1983); Pitts v. Unarco Indus., Inc., 698 F.2d 313 (7th Cir. 1983); Wedgeworth v. Fibreboard Corp., 706 F.2d 541 (5th Cir. 1983); Williford v. Armstrong World Indus., 715 F.2d 124 (4th Cir. 1983); Rimco Acquisition Co. v. Johnson, 68 F. Supp. 2d 793 (E.D. Mich. 1999) (parent company's bankruptcy does not stay action against wholly owned subsidiary); *In re* Irwin, 457 B.R. 413 (Bankr. E.D. Pa. 2011) (neither automatic stay nor discretionary stay under § 105(a) prevent receiver from proceeding in state court under constructive trust theory against debtor's family members to recover proceeds of Ponzi scheme orchestrated by debtor); *In re* Bora Bora, 424 B.R. 17 (Bankr. D. P.R. 2010) (expense of defending litigation is not unusual circumstance warranting extension of stay to chapter 11 debtor's corporate principal); Dixie Aire Title Servs., Inc. v. SPW, L.L.C., 389 B.R. 222 (Bankr. W.D. Okla. 2008) (automatic stay will not extend to non-debtor entities for whose actions debtor could potentially be liable. *See also In re* Paul, 534 F.3d 1303 (10th Cir. 2008) (creditor's ongoing state court litigation against business partners of former debtors, including pursuit of discovery against debtors, does not violate discharge order unless conducted to harass debtors or coerce them to pay prepetition debts); *In re* Am. Hardwoods, Inc., 885 F.2d 621 (9th Cir. 1989) (court lacks power to institute non-automatic stay pursuant to 11 U.S.C. § 105 to protect non-debtor guarantors); *In re* St. Petersburg Hotel Assocs., Ltd., 37 B.R. 380 (Bankr. M.D. Fla. 1984) (discussing cases on scope of section 105 to protect non-debtors).

70 11 U.S.C. § 1202. *See* § 17.4.4.2, *supra*.
71 11 U.S.C. § 1301. *See* § 9.4.5, *supra*.
72 *See* § 18.5.7, *infra*.

73 *See* Ch. 14, *supra*.
74 *See* §§ 18.7.4, 18.8.2, *infra*.
75 In addition to the debtor's schedules and other disclosure obligations, § 18.5.8, *infra*, discusses special discovery rights available against a bankruptcy debtor.
76 *See* Judicial Conference of the United States, Bankruptcy Court Miscellaneous Fee Schedule ¶ 21 (reprinted in Appx. C.3, *infra*).
77 *See* Judicial Conference of the United States, Bankruptcy Court Miscellaneous Fee Schedule ¶ 21 (reprinted in Appx. C.3, *infra*).

A child support creditor or a representative of that creditor must file Form B281 in order to qualify for the exemption. A copy of the form is reprinted in Appendix E, *infra*.
78 *See* § 18.6.2, *infra*.

Form pleadings are available in Forms 162 and 163, Appendix G.14, *infra*.
79 *See* § 18.6.2, *infra*. *See also* Tripati v. United States Bankruptcy Court for E.D. Texas, 180 B.R. 160 (E.D. Tex. 1995) (constitution requires that an indigent creditor "be afforded an opportunity to be heard before his claims are disposed of").
80 *See, e.g.*, Martin-Trigona v. Champion Fed. Sav., 892 F.2d 575 (7th Cir. 1989); *In re* Way, 229 B.R. 11 (B.A.P. 9th Cir. 1998). *See* § 18.3.2, *supra*.

counterclaims that arose before the petition was filed.[81]

Generally, a two-part process will be necessary to raise counterclaims. First, as eviction cases can proceed quickly, the tenant should seek time from the state court in order to obtain stay relief in the bankruptcy court. This is not usually a problem because state court judges realize that tenants cannot be expected to fight an eviction without raising their available counterclaims. However, some showing that the counterclaim is not frivolous may be necessary. Second, the tenant should seek simultaneous relief from stay in the bankruptcy court.[82] This should be done on an expedited basis, if necessary, to satisfy the state court schedule.

Courts have recognized that litigants must be afforded the opportunity to raise counterclaims in actions brought by the debtor.[83] Stay relief will usually be granted to litigate the debtor's liability on the counterclaims and allow the counterclaims to be set off against any rent owed by the tenant—but not to enforce any resulting judgment in favor of the tenant against property belonging to the estate.

One further point related to eviction cases brought by bankrupt landlords is that in chapter 7, and occasionally in chapter 11, property passes to a trustee.[84] In some cases, the landlord/debtor will nevertheless assert a right to pursue eviction actions against tenants. However, the debtor is no longer the real party in interest and therefore cannot bring an eviction action.[85] The bankruptcy trustee must bring all eviction actions until the property is sold or abandoned.[86]

18.4 Filing a Proof of Claim

18.4.1 For Individual Consumer Creditors

Generally speaking, a creditor must file a proof of claim to share in the distribution of the bankruptcy estate. The concept of a "claim" in the Bankruptcy Code is very broad.[87]

As a result, a claim may and should be filed even if the consumer has no judgment against the debtor, has not begun litigation or is not certain of the exact amount of the claim. Even if litigation has begun or a judgment has been obtained outside the bankruptcy proceeding, a proof of claim must still be filed in the bankruptcy court.

The claim must be made on Official Form 10[88] or a substantially similar document.[89] The form is relatively simple and self-explanatory. It may be filed by the consumer's attorney[90] and should be filed with the court[91] (not with the trustee) unless there is a local rule to the contrary.

In cases under chapters 7, 12, or 13, the proof of claim must be filed within ninety days after the first date set for the meeting of creditors under section 341(a) of the Code.[92] In 1994, Congressional action reinforced the importance of timely filing. Untimely claims are no longer permitted in any jurisdiction.[93]

The first date set for the meeting of creditors, which sets the clock running for the chapter 7, 12 and 13 proofs of claim, is from twenty-one to fifty days after the filing of the bankruptcy petition.[94] If the debtor listed the consumer as a creditor, the consumer should receive notices of the meeting from the court. Otherwise, the court files must be checked to determine the date.

In a chapter 11 case, the court sets the time for filing of proofs of claim and may extend the time for cause.[95] The time for filing may be set in the chapter 11 plan and will become an order of the court upon confirmation of the plan, rather than a separate court order. A creditor whose claim is listed in the schedule of liabilities in a chapter 11 and not listed as disputed, contingent, or unliquidated does not have to file a claim in a chapter 11 case.[96]

Chapter 11 debtors must make reasonable efforts consistent with due process to identify creditors for purposes of giving notice of the claims bar date.[97] What constitutes reasonable efforts can vary widely depending on the nature of the debtor's business. For example, when the company that owned Borders

---

81 In re Way, 229 B.R. 11 (B.A.P. 9th Cir. 1998).
82 A form pleading is available in Form 161, Appendix G.14, *infra*.
    An alternative strategy might be to remove the eviction case to the bankruptcy court and to have it heard in conjunction with proceedings on the tenant's proof of claim for damages. See § 14.4.1, *supra*.
83 *See, e.g., In re* Countryside Manor, Inc., 188 B.R. 489 (Bankr. D. Conn. 1995) (relief from stay granted to allow creditor to file counterclaim in case commenced prepetition by debtor); *In re* Pro Football Weekly, Inc., 60 B.R. 824 (N.D. Ill. 1986). *See also* Pursifull v. Eakin, 814 F.2d 1501 (10th Cir. 1987) (stay lifted to allow determination in state court of matters related to lease).
84 For a discussion of additional issues facing tenants subject to eviction during their landlord's chapter 11 and chapter 13 cases, see § 18.8.4, *infra*.
85 11 U.S.C. § 363(b), (c). *See* § 2.6, *supra*.
86 11 U.S.C. § 554.
    For a discussion of abandonment see § 18.8.2, *infra*.
87 11 U.S.C. § 101(5).
88 Reprinted in Appendix D, *infra*.
89 Fed. R. Bankr. P. 3001(a).
90 Fed. R. Bankr. P. 3000(b).
91 Fed. R. Bankr. P. 3002(b), 5005(a).
92 Fed. R. Bankr. P. 3002(c).
93 11 U.S.C. § 502(b)(9). *See In re* marchFIRST, Inc., 573 F.3d 414 (7th Cir. 2009) (disallowing proof of claim filed without authorization by fax and received by court clerk forty-three minutes after deadline); *In re* Stone, 473 B.R. 465 (Bankr. M.D. Fla. 2012) (summarizing legislative history of § 502(b)(9), court cannot exercise its equitable powers to allow proof of claim filed one day after bar date). Case law to the contrary has thus been legislatively overruled. *See, e.g., In re* Hausladen, 146 B.R. 557 (Bankr. D. Minn. 1992).
94 Fed. R. Bankr. P. 2003(a).
95 Fed. R. Bankr. P. 3003(c)(3).
    Late filed claims are allowable in chapter 11 cases in the event of "excusable neglect." Fed. R. Bankr. P. 9006(b)(1). The Supreme Court has defined excusable neglect fairly liberally, to include inadvertence, mistake, or carelessness, in the context of filing a late claim in a chapter 11 case. Pioneer Inv. Servs. Co. v. Brunswick Assocs., 507 U.S. 380, 113 S. Ct. 1489, 123 L. Ed. 2d 74 (1993).
96 Fed. R. Bankr. P. 3003(b)(1). *See In re* FirstPlus Fin., Inc., 248 B.R. 60, 71 (Bankr. N.D. Tex. 2000) (unscheduled creditor must file a claim).
97 City of New York v. New York N.H & H.R. Co., 344 U.S. 293 (1953); Clementron Corp. v. Jones, 72 F.3d 341 (3d Cir. 1995).

book stores recently liquidated under chapter 11, it was liable on 17.7 million store gift cards with outstanding unredeemed balances aggregating $210.5 million.[98] Two weeks after the claims bar date had passed, a proposed class of Borders' gift card holders sought to file a claim in the chapter 11 case. The card holders claimed that notice of the bar date published once in the New York Times failed to meet minimal standards of due process. However, evidence from discovery revealed that Borders never maintained databases of contact information for all gift card holders, as it did for purchasers of certain store promotions. While any "known" creditors would have been entitled to direct, actual notice of the claims bar date,[99] the movants before the court represented truly "unknown" card holders. For these creditors, the constructive publication notice sufficed.[100] The mortgage lender New Century prevailed with similar arguments in its chapter 11 case.[101] Newspaper publication sufficed to notify potential consumer creditors of New Century of the bar date for claims related to its unfair loan origination practices.

Filing a claim is still advisable. In many cases, the debtor will not have valued the claim as high as the creditor would have or given it the priority that the creditor may assert. Further, if the case is converted to a chapter 7, as many chapter 11 cases are, only claims actually filed by the creditor in the chapter 11 are deemed to be filed in the superseding case.[102] At the time of conversion, a new claim date will be set for those who have not previously filed claims.

There are a few exceptions to the timing requirement.[103] The one most likely to be encountered is a "no asset" notice. In a chapter 7 case, if it appears that there will be no assets to be distributed, the notice of the meeting of creditors may indicate that proofs of claim need not be filed, that creditors will be notified if it later appears that there will be assets for distribution, and that notice of a time for filing will then be given.[104]

Certain claims are entitled to priority.[105] They are paid in the order of priority set by the Code before payment to general unsecured creditors.[106] In making a proof of claim, take care to claim any available priorities. Priority status is extremely important in a chapter 11 or chapter 13 case. The debtor will not be able to confirm a plan unless all priority claims are paid in full—immediately in a chapter 11 case[107] and over the life of the plan in a chapter 13 case.[108] Even when the debtor has no assets that are unencumbered by liens, priority unsecured creditors get paid in full. For example, the holder of a mortgage on a building may want to sell the building through a chapter 11 plan process, in which case funds must be set aside to pay priority creditors.[109]

A proof of claim is deemed allowed unless there is an objection.[110] Therefore, the claim should be for as high an amount and with as high a priority as good faith will permit.[111]

18.4.2 Class Proofs of Claim

The filing of a class proof of claim should be considered when large numbers of consumers are involved, such as in the bankruptcy of a retailer or a large apartment building.[112] A class claim may also be appropriate when employees have priority

---

98 In re BGI, Inc., 476 B.R. 812 (Bankr. S.D.N.Y. 2012).
99 Tulsa Professional Collection Serv., Inc. v. Pope, 485 U.S. 478, 490 (1988) (a "known" creditor is one whose identity is "reasonably ascertainable by the debtor"); In re Circuit City Stores, Inc., 439 B.R. 652 (E.D. Va. 2010), aff'd 668 F.3d 83 (4th Cir. 2012).
100 In re BGI, Inc., 476 B.R. 812 (Bankr. S.D.N.Y. 2012).
101 In re New Century Holdings, Inc., 465 B.R. 38 (Bankr. D. Del. 2012).
102 Fed. R. Bankr. P. 1019(3).
    See Advisory Committee Note noting that paragraph three of Federal Rule of Bankruptcy Procedure 1019 reverses the holding in In re Crouthamel Potato Chip Co., 786 F.2d 141 (3d Cir. 1986) which held, under an earlier version of the rule, that all claims scheduled in a chapter 11 were deemed filed in the superseding case.
103 The exceptions are set out in Federal Rule of Bankruptcy Procedure 3002(c).
104 Fed. R. Bankr. P. 3002(c)(5). See also In re Kendavis Holding Co., 249 F.3d 383 (5th Cir. 2001) (employee's claim for pension benefits not discharged even though he had actual knowledge of employer's bankruptcy and did not file claim because employer violated the employee's due process rights by sending letter advising that pension rights would not be affected by the bankruptcy proceeding).
105 11 U.S.C. § 507.
106 The most likely priorities for consumer creditors are administrative expenses for postpetition claims discussed in § 18.5.3, infra, the consumer priority discussed in § 18.5.5, infra, claims for wages, salaries, or commissions pursuant to 11 U.S.C. § 507(a)(4), and claims for contributions to employee benefit plans pursuant to 11 U.S.C. § 507(a)(5).
107 11 U.S.C. § 1129(a)(9)(B)(ii).
108 11 U.S.C. § 1322(a)(2).
    A limited exception, added by the 2005 Act, provides that less than full payment may be made on a domestic support obligation assigned to a governmental unit if certain conditions are met. See 11 U.S.C. § 1322(a)(4).
109 On the other hand, if the secured creditor obtains relief from the stay and sells a building under state foreclosure rules, there is no protection for priority claim holders.
110 11 U.S.C. § 502(a); In re DeAngelis Tangibles, 238 B.R. 96 (Bankr. M.D. Pa. 1999).
    For a discussion of objections to proofs of claim, see § 14.4.3, supra. In some situations, it may be advisable for claimants to seek a withdrawal of the reference so that an objection to the claim may be heard by the district court. See In re First Alliance Mortgage Co., 282 B.R. 894 (C.D. Cal. 2001) (permissive withdrawal of reference granted as to 2000 individual borrower claims against debtor-lender because district court had previously withdrawn reference as to government claims). For discussion of withdrawal of reference, see § 14.2.5, supra.
111 See, e.g., In re Partners Group Fin., L.L.C., 394 B.R. 68 (Bankr. E.D. Pa. 2008) (consumer's proof of claim against mortgage broker properly included treble damages based on unliquidated UDAP claim and attorney fees; portion of claim that included consequential damages for lost income and profits due to debtor's breach of contract disallowed contract).
112 See In re Longo, 144 B.R. 305 (Bankr. D. Md. 1992) (state education code and regulations give state higher education commission parens patriae standing to file proofs of claim against bankrupt vocational school for refunds owed to former students). See generally § 14.7, supra.

wage claims.[113] A series of recent cases has now approved class proofs of claim in the Sixth,[114] Seventh,[115] Ninth[116] and Eleventh[117] Circuits, as well as in several district and bankruptcy courts.[118] These cases seem to signal a reversal of an earlier judicial hostility toward such claims.[119] Courts continue to take a variety of approaches to these cases based on the circumstances.[120] It may be particularly appropriate to allow a class claim or other class treatment in bankruptcy for victims of fraud when there are insufficient assets to satisfy investors in a Ponzi scheme.[121] Class certification should be available, without a class proof claim, in an adversary proceeding seeking class-wide relief such as imposition of a constructive trust on the debtors' assets.[122] The courts have also recognized the effectiveness of defendant classes in pursuing transferees of assets belonging to the estate.[123]

In preparing a class proof of claim it is prudent to set out factors that fulfill the requirements of Rule 23 of the Federal Rules of Civil Procedure regarding class actions. The claim should be filed in the name of a representative or representatives of the class and not in the name of an attorney purporting to represent the class.[124] Authorization of individual class members is not needed.[125] A class proof of claim, however,

---

113 *In re* Birting Fisheries, Inc., 178 B.R. 849 (W.D. Wash. 1995), *aff'd*, 92 F.3d 939 (9th Cir. 1996) (per curiam).

114 Reid v. White Motor Corp., 886 F.2d 1462 (6th Cir. 1989). *See also In re* Commonpoint Mortgage Co., 283 B.R. 469 (Bankr. W.D. Mich. 2002) (borrowers' class proof of claim certified alleging UDAP and other state law claims against originating lender).

115 *In re* Am. Reserve Corp., 840 F.2d 487 (7th Cir. 1988).

116 *In re* Birting Fisheries, Inc., 92 F.3d 939 (9th Cir. 1996). *See also In re* First Alliance Mortgage Co., 269 B.R. 428 (C.D. Cal. 2001) (class certification granted based on borrowers' class proof of claim for TILA and UDAP claims against debtor-lender).

117 *In re* Charter Co., 876 F.2d 866 (11th Cir. 1989).

118 *In re* Chateaugay Corp., 104 B.R. 626 (S.D.N.Y. 1989); *In re* Zenith Laboratories, Inc., 104 B.R. 659 (D.N.J. 1989); *In re* Craft, 321 B.R. 189, 192–193 (Bankr. N.D. Tex. 2005) (summarizing cases and recognizing allowance of class claims as majority view); *In re* Kaiser Group Int'l, Inc., 278 B.R. 58 (Bankr. D. Del. 2002) (noting that overwhelming majority of courts permit class claims and allowing class of forty-seven shareholder claimants alleging common violation of securities laws); *In re* United Companies Fin. Corp., Inc., 276 B.R. 368 (Bankr. D. Del. 2002) (certification of class proof of claim based on debtor's failure to comply with state loan broker law avoids burden of conducting 291 separate claim hearings); *In re* First Interregional Equity Corp., 227 B.R. 358, 366 (Bankr. D.N.J. 1998). *See also* Gentry v. Siegel, 668 F.3d 83, 91 (4th Cir. 2012) (joining circuits allowing class proofs of claim, but disallowing class claim in particular case); *In re* Friedman's, Inc., 356 B.R. 766 (Bankr. S.D. Ga. 2006) (class claim for violation of UDAP statute could not be disallowed on basis that it included statutory damages). *But see In re* United Companies Fin. Corp., Inc., 277 B.R. 596 (Bankr. D. Del. 2002) (class proof of claim based on lender's ECOA violations not certified when individual questions of law and fact predominate).

119 *See In re* Standard Metals, 817 F.2d 625 (10th Cir. 1987), *vacated and reversed on other grounds sub nom.* Sheftelman v. Standard Metals Corp., 839 F.2d 1383 (1987); *In re* Charter Co., 876 F.2d 866, 869 n.3 (11th Cir. 1989) (and cases cited therein); *In re* FirstPlus Fin., Inc. 248 B.R. 60 (Bankr. N.D. Tex 2000) (class certification denied for consumer claims against finance company, supporting minority view that Rule 3001(b) does not allow class claims). *Cf. In re* Edmond, 934 F.2d 1304 (4th Cir. 1991) (state consumer protection act gives state's consumer protection agency *parens patriae* standing to bring nondischargeability action on behalf of group of injured consumers without satisfying requisites of a class action).

120 *See In re* Trebol Motors Distrib. Corp., 211 B.R. 785 (Bankr. D. P.R. 1997) (class proof of claim to enforce prepetition RICO judgment allowed; appropriate class mirrors that already approved by federal district court in underlying class action), *aff'd*, 220 B.R. 500 (B.A.P. 1st Cir. 1998); *In re* Sacred Heart Hosp. of Norristown, 177 B.R. 16 (Bankr. E.D. Pa. 1995) (court would allow class proof of claim in an appropriate context, but a variety of factors must be considered and allowance should be granted sparingly); *In re* Retirement Builders, Inc., 96 B.R. 390 (Bankr. S.D. Fla. 1988) (important factor is that class certification was previously granted in a nonbankruptcy forum).

121 *See, e.g.*, *In re* First Interregional Equity Corp., 227 B.R. 358 (Bankr. D.N.J. 1998) (investors buying a similar fraudulent investment satisfy commonality prerequisite to class action proceeding). *See also In re* Four Star Fin. Servs., Inc., 444 B.R. 428 (Bankr. C.D. Cal. 2011) (refusing to strike class proof of claim based on prior state court class action judgment against perpetrator of Ponzi scheme).

122 *In re* Partsearch Technologies, Inc., 453 B.R. 84 (Bankr. S.D.N.Y. 2011) (approving class for settlement of adversary action under WARN Act); *In re* Taylor Bean & Whitaker, 2010 WL 4025873 (Bankr. M.D. Fla. Sept. 27, 2010) (class for WARN Act adversary proceeding certified, finding class action adversary proceeding appropriate and preferable to class claim mechanism); *In re* ABMD Ltd., 439 B.R. 475 (Bankr. S.D. Ohio 2010) (certifying class under WARN Act). *See In re* Bill Heard Enters., 400 B.R. 795 (Bankr. N.D. Ala. 2009) (class of WARN Act claimants certified for adversary proceeding; need not rely on claims process); *In re* Protected Vehicles, Inc., 392 B.R. 633 (Bankr. D.S.C. 2008), *subsequent decision*, 397 B.R. 339 (Bankr. D.S.C. 2008) (same); *In re* Johnson, 80 B.R. 791 (Bankr. E.D. Va.) (class certified and constructive trust imposed), *aff'd*, 960 F.2d 396 (4th Cir. 1992). *See also In re* United Artists Theatre Co., 410 B.R. 385 (Bankr. D. Del. 2009) (class certified under Rule 23(b)(2) so that claimants could obtain determination that discharge of debt should be voided because they had not received adequate notice prior to discharge). *But see In re* Bally Total Fitness of Greater N.Y., Inc., 411 B.R. 142 (S.D.N.Y. 2009) (class claim based on state wage-and-hour claims rejected; claims could be resolved effectively by individual determinations with appropriate notice; also, common questions did not predominate).

123 *In re* Dehon Inc., 298 B.R. 206 (Bankr. D. Mass 2003) (certifying mandatory defendant class under Federal Rule of Civil Procedure 23(b)(1)); *In re* Integra Res., Inc., 179 B.R. 264 (Bankr. D. Colo. 1995), *aff'd*, 262 F.2d 1089 (10th Cir. 2001), *later decision at* 354 F.3d 1246 (10th Cir. 2004) (certifying defendant class of stock transferees in action challenging transfer as fraudulent conveyance).

124 *See, e.g.*, Reid v. White Motor Corp., 886 F.2d 1462 (6th Cir. 1989) (permitting class proof of claim but denying claim in that case because it was filed by and in name of attorney who was not a representative of the class and who did not file proof that he represented class). *See also In re* First Alliance Mortgage Co., 269 B.R. 428 (C.D. Cal. 2001) (private parties asserting a "representative" claim under California unfair competition law may file class proof of claim on behalf of public, which should be treated same as claim filed by attorney general under *parens patriae* doctrine).

125 *See also In re* W.R. Grace & Co., 2007 WL 4333817 (D. Del. Dec. 6, 2007) (claimants could not ratify proofs of claim filed and signed on their behalf by law firm when written authorization was obtained after expiration of claims bar date). *But see In re* W.R. Grace & Co., 316 Fed. Appx. 134 (3d Cir. 2009) (attorney's role as class counsel

probably requires a separate motion to certify the class under the relevant rules, although such a motion may not be necessary if no objection to the claim is filed.[126] Some or all of the elements required to certify the class can be established by collateral estoppel if a class has been certified outside the bankruptcy process.[127]

Exclusive reliance on the filing of a class proof of claim can present some dangers. The language of section 502(a) certainly supports the position that a class claim is deemed allowed unless and until a party objects to it. Yet problems may arise when an objection to the class claim surfaces late in the proceedings. If this occurs, the class claimant may move for certification of a class under Federal Rule of Civil Procedure 23 and point out any delay was the fault of the objecting party, not the class claimant. However, courts in some recent decisions have not reacted favorably to these arguments. These courts emphasized the discretionary nature of allowing class certification in bankruptcy and exercised this discretion against the class claimants who could have filed motions for class certification earlier in the proceeding.[128] The better practice in most cases is to file the class proof of claim and a formal motion for class certification or class adversary action as soon as possible after commencement of the case.[129]

To safeguard the rights of individual claimants in the event that class certification is denied, all individuals who can easily be identified should be named in their individual and representative capacities. Following up on a class proof of claim may involve additional litigation on behalf of the class. This litigation may include responding to an objection to the claim,[130] moving for stay relief, challenging dischargeability,[131] or any other activities appropriate for bankruptcy creditors. To the extent that class litigation occurs by adversary proceeding, the formalities of Rule 23 will separately apply.[132] To the extent litigation is commenced by motion, the court has discretion to apply Rule 23.[133]

---

in related state court case did not constitute authority to sign for and file individual claims for claimants in bankruptcy case); *In re* Bally Total Fitness of Greater N.Y., Inc., 411 B.R. 142 (S.D.N.Y. 2009) (authorization of unnamed/absent class members must be by express authority from each class member or through timely class certification order entered pursuant to Rule 23(g)(1), incorporated by Federal Rule of Bankruptcy Procedure 7023); *In re* FirstPlus Fin., Inc. 248 B.R. 60 (Bankr. N.D. Tex 2000) (minority position that Rules 2019 and 3001(b) require authorization).

126 *See* Reid v. White Motor Corp., 886 F.2d 1462 (6th Cir. 1989) (bankruptcy rules permit filing of class proofs of claim, however, claim may be denied for failure to follow procedural requirements of Federal Rule of Civil Procedure 23 as made applicable by Federal Rule of Bankruptcy Procedure 7023); *In re* Charter Co., 876 F.2d 866 (11th Cir. 1989) (no motion for class certification is required unless an objection to class proof of claim is filed).

Better practice would probably be to file a motion for class certification at or near the time of filing the proof of claim.

127 *In re* Lebner, 197 B.R. 180 (Bankr. D. Mass. 1996).

Similarly, denial of class status in bankruptcy may be based on denial of certification of the same class in a different court before the debtor filed bankruptcy. *In re* Keck, Mahin & Cate, 253 B.R. 530 (N.D. Ill. 2000); *In re* Blockbuster, Inc., 441 B.R. 239 (Bankr. S.D.N.Y. 2011) (adopting findings of prior state court ruling denying certification of same proposed class).

128 *In re* W.R. Grace & Co., 316 Fed. Appx. 134 (3d Cir. 2009) (class members cannot "ratify" claims after bar date has passed and class claim had not been approved before bar date); *In re* Motors Liquidation Co., 447 B.R. 150 (S.D.N.Y. 2011) (denying motion to certify class claims where motion filed 8 months after claim bar date and Rule 23 requirements not satisfied); *In re* Ephedra Prods. Liab. Litig., 329 B.R. 1 (S.D.N.Y. 2005) (consideration of class certification motion would interfere with timely distribution under plan already submitted for a vote); *In re* Tarragon Corp., 2010 WL 3842409 (Bankr. D.N.J. Sept. 24 2010) (striking class proof of claim where claimants did not move for class certification until after confirmation of chapter 11 plan); *In re* Tronox, Inc., 2010 WL 1849394 (Bankr. S.D.N.Y. May 6, 2010) (refusing to extend claim bar date when class counsel who had been seeking to represent claimants prepetition in related U.S. District Court securities action delayed without reasonable cause to seek extension until five months after bar date); *In re* Adam Aircraft Indus., Inc., 2009 WL 2100929 (Bankr. D. Colo. Mar. 20, 2009) (agreeing that Code and rules authorize class claim but rejecting claim under WARN Act because filed after bar date; claimants also unable to show they met numerosity requirement), *motion for leave to appeal denied*, 2010 WL 717841 (D. Colo. Feb. 23, 2010); *In re* Computer Learning Ctrs., Inc., 344 B.R. 79 (Bankr. E.D. Va. 2006) (class treatment denied when timely class proof of claim had been filed, but no formal motion for class certification filed until more than four years after commencement of case); *In re* WorldCom, Inc., 343 B.R. 412 (Bankr. S.D.N.Y. 2006); *In re* Craft, 321 B.R. 189 (Bankr. N.D. Tex. 2005) (noting the usefulness of class clams in general, but finding that consideration of class motion at late stage in proceedings would prejudice debtor and other creditors). *But see* Gentry v. Siegel, 668 F.3d 83, 92 (4th Cir. 2012) (class proof of claim may be approved despite filing motion to apply Rule 7023 after claim bar date, denying class claim on other grounds); *In re* Spring Ford Indus., 2004 WL 231010 (Bankr. E.D. Pa. Jan. 20, 2004) (finding no prejudice, granting class certification despite one-year delay in bringing motion).

129 *See In re* Quantegy, Inc., 343 B.R. 689 (Bankr. M.D. Ala. 2006) (approving class claim when claimant filed class adversary action nine days after commencement of case).

130 One court has held that absent a class proof of claim it is inappropriate for individual creditors to respond to objections to their claims by a class response. *In re* Gen. Dev. Corp., 154 B.R. 601 (Bankr. S.D. Fla. 1993).

131 Several courts have allowed class dischargeability proceedings. Anderson v. Cohen (*In re* Cohen), 1995 WL 346948 (Bankr. E.D. Pa. June 5, 1995) (dischargeability determination amounts to declaratory relief, so Federal Rule of Civil Procedure 23(b)(2) standards apply, rather than Rule 23(b)(3)); *In re* Iommazzo, 149 B.R. 767 (Bankr. D.N.J. 1993); *In re* Livaditis, 132 B.R. 897 (Bankr. N.D. Ill. 1991); *In re* Duck, 122 B.R. 403 (Bankr. N.D. Cal. 1990). *See also In re* Lebner, 197 B.R. 180 (Bankr. D. Mass. 1996) (class treatment denied only because not all creditors could have brought timely dischargeability proceedings); *In re* Gen. Dev. Corp., 154 B.R. 601 (Bankr. S.D. Fla. 1993) (finding that class treatment is inappropriate in fraud related dischargeability case only because of factual distinctions between each creditor's claims). *But see In re* Hanson, 104 B.R. 261 (Bankr. N.D. Cal. 1989) (class dischargeability proceeding not allowed).

132 Fed. R. Bankr. P. 7023. *See, e.g., In re* BGI, Inc., 465 B.R. 365 (Bankr. S.D.N.Y. 2012) (applying Rule 7023 to certify class and approve class action settlement of WARN Act claimants).

133 *See* Fed. R. Bankr. P. 9014 (granting the court discretion to apply various adversary rules to a contested matter). *See also In re* Gen. Dev. Corp., 154 B.R. 601 (Bankr. S.D. Fla. 1993).

18.5 Strategies to Increase the Chance of Recovery

18.5.1 General

Unsecured creditors without priority claims are in the worst position of all creditors in a bankruptcy proceeding. Only in the rarest instance will they receive the full amount of their claim. In most chapter 7 cases, they will receive nothing. Without aggressive advocacy, this may be true even if the consumer creditors were victims of egregious fraud.[134]

Attorneys for consumers whose interests are affected by another party's bankruptcy should seek, wherever possible, to characterize their claims to avoid general unsecured creditor status. Some claims may be secured. Others may be claims to property that is not a part of the bankruptcy estate, such as trust funds. Still other claims may be not be dischargeable against individuals in bankruptcy. Some claims may have priority, such as the consumer priority, or be postpetition claims, which can be claimed as part of the administrative expenses of the bankruptcy estate. Or inequitable conduct by other claimants toward the debtor or the consumer creditors may warrant the subordination of their claims to the consumers' claims.[135] Finally, claims against the entity in bankruptcy may also be pursued against others not in bankruptcy.[136]

18.5.2 Property Which Is Not Part of the Bankruptcy Estate—Trust Funds

18.5.2.1 General

If property held by the entity in bankruptcy is treated as being held in trust for the consumer, it will not be part of the bankruptcy estate, nor will it be subject to the Code's distribution rules. Instead, the consumer can recover the property directly. Trust theories apply not only to property subject to a formal trust agreement, but also in situations in which the court may impose a trust, such as when a debtor holds deposits from a consumer or when the debtor has obtained the property by fraud.[137]

"Property of the estate"[138] although broadly defined,[139] does not encompass property held in trust by the debtor for another beneficiary. Subsection 541(d) states that when the debtor holds only legal title and not an equitable interest in property, the equitable interest is not property of the estate. Courts have consistently held under 541(d) that property subject to a trust is excluded from the estate.[140]

If a trust exists, the consumer should be able to have the trust's funds or property[141] separated out of the bankruptcy estate. A court order confirming the existence of a trust and setting it aside for the beneficiary should probably be sought in an adversary proceeding, presumably for a declaratory judgment.[142] As trust property does not belong to the estate, relief from stay, for cause, may also be available.[143] Due to the potentially binding impact a confirmed plan, claims that property is held in trust should be raised in chapter 11, 12 or 13 cases before confirmation, including, if necessary, by objecting to the plan.[144] A proof of claim may also be filed reserving all

---

134 *See generally* Vukowich, *Civil Remedies in Bankruptcy for Corporate Fraud*, 6 Am. Bankr. Inst. L.J. 439 (1998).

135 *See* § 18.5.6, *infra*.

136 These issues are discussed in § 18.5.7, *infra*. No stay would apply automatically to such claims except as to codebtors in chapter 12 and 13. *See* § 9.4.5, *supra*. Requests for non-automatic stays as to non-debtor parties in such situations are normally denied. *See* § 9.4.7, *supra*. In some cases an effort must be made to pierce the corporate veil. Such actions can potentially be brought in bankruptcy court. *In re* Haugen Constr. Servs., Inc., 104 B.R. 1013, 1019 (D.N.D. 1989). *See In re* Simplified Info. Sys., Inc., 89 B.R. 538, 540 (W.D. Pa. 1988). *See also In re* Lee Way Holding Co., 105 B.R. 404, 412 (Bankr. S.D. Ohio 1989).

137 In *Cunningham v. Brown*, 265 U.S. 1, 44 S. Ct. 424, 68 L. Ed. 873 (1924), the Supreme Court held that a trust may be imposed in bankruptcy to recover funds belonging to any plaintiff, if those funds are adequately traced to a fraudulent investment scheme. (The case is notable because it emerged out of the original "Ponzi" investment scam.) Despite its age, the case remains good law. *See In re* Johnson, 80 B.R. 791 (Bankr. E.D. Va.) (constructive trust imposed on debtor's assets on behalf of defrauded investors), *aff'd*, 960 F.2d 396 (4th Cir. 1992). *See also* Hoxworth v. Blinder, 74 F.3d 205 (10th Cir. 1996) (constructive trust imposed in favor of a class of investors defrauded by the "penny stock" king of Colorado.) *See generally* Kull, *Restitution in Bankruptcy: Reclamation and Constructive Trust*, 72 Am. Bankr. L.J. 265 (1998); Vukowich, *Consumer and Fraud Victims' Claims in Bankruptcy: Constructive Trusts and the Consumer Priority*, 1988 Ann. Survey of Bankr. Law 129 (criticizing use of constructive trusts in bankruptcy).

138 11 U.S.C. § 541.

139 *See* § 2.5, *supra*.

140 *See, e.g., In re* Gen. Coffee Corp., 828 F.2d 699 (11th Cir. 1987) (assets held in constructive trust by debtor for another do not come into bankruptcy estate); Mid-Atlantic Supply v. Three Rivers Aluminum Co., 790 F.2d 1121 (4th Cir. 1986) (property held in trust belongs to beneficiary); *In re* N.S. Garrott & Sons, 772 F.2d 462 (8th Cir. 1985) (estate's interest in property subject to constructive trust). *See also* United States v. Whiting Pools, Inc., 462 U.S. 198, 103 S. Ct. 2309, 2313 n.10, 76 L. Ed. 515 (1983) ("Congress plainly excluded property of others held by the debtor in trust at the time of filing of the petition"); *In re* McCafferty, 96 F.3d 192 (6th Cir. 1996) (divorce decree created an identifiable prepetition constructive trust in favor of wife on debtor's pension distribution so that the distribution was not part of husband's bankruptcy estate); *In re* Jeter, 73 F.3d 205 (8th Cir. 1996) (general unsecured creditors not entitled to a finding of constructive trust based on a loan transaction when funds lent were not used for their intended purpose); *In re* B.I. Fin. Servs. Group, Inc., 854 F.2d 351 (9th Cir. 1988); Conn. Gen. Life Ins. v. Universal Ins. Co., 838 F.2d 612 (1st Cir. 1988). *But see In re* Omegas Group, Inc., 16 F.3d 1443 (6th Cir. 1994) (bankruptcy court cannot impose a constructive trust which was not identified prepetition).

141 However, if the consumer interest is in real estate or other property for which interests must be recorded, the trustee may be able to avoid the trust under section 544. *See* § 10.4.2.6.2, *supra*.

142 Fed. R. Bankr. P. 7001.

143 *In re* Newpower, 233 F.3d 922 (6th Cir. 2000). *See generally* § 18.3, *supra*.

144 *See* Nugent v. Am. Broad. Sys., 1 Fed. Appx. 633 (9th Cir. 2001) (constructive trust claim lost due to confirmation of plan).

rights to the property and claiming the right to assert alternative remedies as a creditor, if a trust is not ultimately declared.

Low-income consumers have sometimes been victimized when money order sellers have filed bankruptcy after the consumer purchased a money order, but before its intended recipient cashed the money order. Consumer advocates argued aggressively and with some success that money paid for a money order is held in trust for the purpose of paying the intended recipient upon presentation. However, because of the delays in recovering funds based on a trust theory, many consumers experienced hardship when their landlords, mortgage holders or other creditors were not paid.

In 1994 Congress fixed this problem, in part, by excluding from the estate, in most instances, proceeds of sale of a money order sold fourteen days or less before filing bankruptcy.[145] The remedy is only partial because money orders are often purchased long before they are cashed and the purchaser may have no control over how long a money order is held by its recipient. Additionally, in cases involving serious misuse of funds, it is unclear how quickly a remedy can be fashioned to have the money orders paid.

18.5.2.2 Determining the Existence of a Trust

Under section 541, courts look to state law to determine if property is subject to a trust.[146] As one of the standard works on the law of trusts explains:

> Trusts are classified with respect to the manner of their origin. When based upon the expressed intent of the settlor (creator of the trust) they are called express trusts; when they come into existence because of presumed or inferred intent they are given the name of resulting trusts; and when they are created by court action in order to work out justice, without regard to the intent of the parties, they are denominated constructive trusts.[147]

In some cases, the facts may establish an express trust in the consumer's favor. To establish an express trust, the bankruptcy court will look to state law and must find that the consumers as beneficiaries and the debtor as trustee intended to establish an express trust.[148] Intent can be inferred from conduct, although the establishment of a segregated fund is not sufficient alone to prove intent to establish an express trust.[149]

The most useful of the trust classifications for consumer creditors is more likely to be the equitable remedy of constructive trust, which allows courts to impose a trust on property initially held by a debtor or even held by a trustee in bankruptcy. For example, when money or property has been taken from a consumer by fraud, the court may treat the property as being held in trust and not as part of the bankruptcy estate.[150]

As an equitable doctrine, constructive trusts can cover a wide range of situations beyond blatant fraud. "The constructive trust may be defined as a device used by [the courts] to compel one who unfairly holds a property interest to convey that interest to another to whom it justly belongs."[151] Accordingly, a court's willingness to impose a constructive trust is a fact-sensitive process with different fact patterns being stressed as important in different jurisdictions. However, simple failure to repay a debt or misapplication of loaned funds, by itself, is insufficient to create a trust.[152]

A constructive trust may also be imposed on property purchased with funds traced to a defendant's wrongful conduct.[153] This is true even if the wrongfully obtained funds are commingled with legitimate funds to purchase the property.[154] When wrongfully obtained funds, or property bought with such funds, are transferred to a third party, a constructive trust may be imposed unless the third party is a bona fide purchaser for value.[155] The source of the funds must, of course, be traced to the wrongdoer.

---

145 11 U.S.C. § 541(b)(5). *See In re* Supermarkets of Cheltenham, Inc., 1998 WL 386381 (Bankr. E.D. Pa. July 7, 1998) (turnover ordered of commingled funds paid to money order company by supermarket).

146 *See, e.g., In re* B.I. Fin. Servs. Group, Inc., 854 F.2d 351 (9th Cir. 1988); *In re* N.S. Garrott & Sons, 772 F.2d 462 (8th Cir. 1985).

147 George Bogert, Bogert's Trusts and Trustees § 1, at 11 (2d ed. 1984).

148 Elliot v. Bumb, 356 F.2d 749 (9th Cir. 1966) (express trust established by agreement); *In re* U.S. Lan Sys. Corp., 235 B.R. 847 (Bankr. E.D. Va. 1999) (wages withheld to pay into 401(k) plan were subject to express statutory trust under ERISA, and when funds were moved to operating account, constructive trust would be imposed).

149 *In re* Tele-Tone Radio Corp., 133 F. Supp. 739 (D.N.J. 1955); Van Denbergh v. Walker, 47 F. Supp. 549 (E.D. Pa. 1942), *aff'd*, 138 F.2d 1023 (3d Cir. 1943); Equitable Life Assurance Soc'y v. Stewart, 12 F. Supp. 186 (W.D.S.C. 1935).

150 *See In re* Johnson, 80 B.R. 791 (Bankr. E.D. Va.) (constructive trust imposed on debtor's assets on behalf of defrauded investors), *aff'd*, 960 F.2d 396 (4th Cir. 1992); *In re* Teltronics Ltd., 649 F.2d 1236 (7th Cir. 1981).

151 George Bogert, Bogert's Trusts and Trustees § 471, at 3 (2d ed. 1982).

152 *In re* Jeter, 73 F.3d 205 (8th Cir. 1996) (general unsecured creditors not entitled to a finding of constructive trust based on a loan transaction when funds lent were not used for their intended purpose).

153 *In re* Linsey, 296 B.R. 582 (Bankr. D. Mass. 2003) (imposing trust on two cars and the value of home improvements (in the form of an equitable lien on debtor's exempt homestead) when debtor had purchased car and home improvements with embezzled funds).

154 *See, e.g.*, Church v. Bailey, 90 Cal. App. 2d 501, 203 P.2d 547 (1949).

155 *See, e.g.*, Church of Jesus Christ of Latter Day Saints v. Jolley, 24 Utah 2d 187 (1970). *See In re* Newpower, 233 F.3d 922 (6th Cir. 2000) (embezzled property belongs to the person(s) from whom it was embezzled; however, if embezzled property is transferred to third parties, constructive trust may be imposed). *See also* Dyll v. Adams, 167 F.3d 945 (5th Cir. 1999) (constructive trust may be imposed on entirely innocent beneficiaries of fraudulent conduct). *See generally* Annotation, *Imposition of Constructive Trust in Property Bought With Stolen or Embezzled Funds*, 38 A.L.R. 3d 1354 (1997).

> This principle is useful if the transferee files bankruptcy, because the constructive trust keeps the assets out of the estate in that instance. The principle also may be used as an alternative to

Potential available underlying causes of action justifying imposition of a constructive trust include statutory claims under RICO,[156] or UDAP,[157] and common law claims for fraud,[158] or conversion.[159] A constructive trust can also be imposed, absent wrongful conduct, simply to prevent unjust enrichment.[160]

By way of illustration of some of the principles discussed here, the plaintiffs in *In re Johnson*,[161] had a class certified and a constructive trust imposed on the defendant's property held by the bankruptcy estate. The debtor, Johnson, had sold shares in an industrial wine import venture that did not exist. The scheme ran for six years, through seventeen different limited partnerships and raised about $26 million from more than 400 investors. Proceeds of the scheme, were used, in part, to pay off the early investors.[162]

By the time a bankruptcy case was filed against Johnson, available assets consisted of only approximately 1.6 million dollars. The bankruptcy court certified a class of defrauded investors and imposed a constructive trust on the assets (except for $129,000 that could not be traced to the fraudulent scheme). Imposing the trust kept the assets out of the bankruptcy estate. The court found that the plaintiffs were seeking recovery of their own funds, rather than assets belonging to Johnson.

Recently a split of authority has developed about whether constructive trusts (as opposed to express trusts) can be created after a bankruptcy filing. Some courts have concluded that a constructive trust is cognizable only if it is impressed upon assets of the estate, by a court or by operation of statutory law, prior to bankruptcy filing.[163] However, one of the leading courts taking that position has mitigated it somewhat by concluding that relief from the automatic stay may be available to continue a prepetition action seeking imposition of a constructive trust.[164] Presumably, a constructive trust, if imposed in the nonbankruptcy court could then be recognized by the bankruptcy court.[165] Other courts conclude that the state law of constructive trusts creates the trust from the time of the action giving rise to the trust—so that the trust is in existence before the bankruptcy filing whether it has been judicially identified or not.[166] The latter courts would entertain the possibility of declaring a constructive trust by a determination made after bankruptcy is filed.

This split of authority militates in favor of seeking the imposition of a constructive trust, whenever possible, before a bankruptcy case is filed. In appropriate cases, perhaps even preliminary injunctive relief in the form of a declaration of a trust should be sought in order to prevent a loss to the consumer beneficiary in the event that the wrongdoer files bankruptcy.

If the bankruptcy court is willing to impose a constructive trust postpetition, it will look to state law[167] to find the elements necessary.[168] For example, the Supreme Court of Tennessee has

---

fraudulent transfer theories when the original constructive trustee files bankruptcy after transferring trust assets for less than their value. One potential advantage may be that recovery of fraudulently transferred assets under the Bankruptcy Code would require sharing those assets with other creditors, while imposition of a constructive trust on behalf of consumers would not. *Cf. In re* Nat'l Liquidators, Inc., 232 B.R. 915 (Bankr. S.D. Ohio 1998) (false profits transferred to early investors in Ponzi scheme recovered as fraudulently transferred and shared among all creditors).

156 County of Cook v. Lynch, 560 F. Supp. 136 (N.D. Ill. 1982).
157 *In re* Teltronics, Ltd., 649 F.2d 1236 (7th Cir. 1981).
158 *In re* Johnson, 80 B.R. 791 (Bankr. E.D. Va.), *aff'd*, 960 F.2d 396 (4th Cir. 1992).
159 Chiu v. Wong, 16 F.3d 306 (8th Cir. 1994).
160 *See, e.g., In re* Brook Valley VII, Joint Venture, 496 F.3d 892 (8th Cir. 2007) (constructive trust imposed on proceeds of fraudulent foreclosure sale orchestrated by debtors' principals); Clark v. Tibbetts, 167 F.2d 397 (2d Cir. 1948); *In re* Wells, 296 B.R. 728 (Bankr. E.D. Va. 2003) (court invalidated oral purchase agreement but imposed constructive trust in favor of purchaser for payments made towards purchase price); *In re* Indian River Estates, 293 B.R. 429 (Bankr. N.D. Ohio 2003) (prepetition specific performance decree directing debtor/developer to convey properties to non-profit creditor for low-income housing development created a constructive trust removing properties from the estate).
161 80 B.R. 791 (Bankr. E.D. Va.), *aff'd*, 960 F.2d 396 (4th Cir. 1992).
162 *In re* Johnson, 55 B.R. 800 (Bankr. E.D. Va. 1985).
163 *In re* Union §Mortgage Co., 25 F.3d 338 (6th Cir. 1994); *In re* Omegas Group, Inc., 16 F.3d 1443 (6th Cir. 1994).

Alternatively, courts have held that the trustee can use the strong-arm powers as a hypothetical bona fide purchaser under 11 U.S.C. § 544 to avoid transfer to a constructive trust, especially if such trust was not created prior to bankruptcy. *See In re* N. Am. Coin & Currency Ltd., 767 F.2d 1573 (9th Cir. 1985); Mullins v. Burtch, 249 B.R. 360 (D. Del. 2000). *But see In re* Morris, 260 F.3d 654 (6th Cir. 2001) (limiting the holding in *Omegas Group, Inc.*).
164 *In re* Newpower, 233 F.3d 922 (6th Cir. 2000).
165 *Id. See also In re* Morris, 260 F.3d 654 (6th Cir. 2001) (explaining *Newpower*).
166 Chiu v. Wong, 16 F.3d 306 (8th Cir. 1994); *In re* Unicom Computer Corp., 13 F.3d 321 (9th Cir. 1994). *See In re* McCafferty, 96 F.3d 192 (6th Cir. 1996) (divorce decree created an identifiable prepetition constructive trust in favor of wife on debtor's pension distribution so that the distribution was not part of husband's bankruptcy estate); Belisle v. Plunkett, 877 F.2d 512 (7th Cir. 1989) (a constructive trust may survive bankruptcy); *In re* Quality Holstein Leasing, 752 F.2d 1009 (5th Cir. 1985) (same); *In re* Pitchford, 410 B.R. 416 (Bankr. W.D. Pa. 2009) (state court's prepetition imposition of constructive trust was not a transfer that could be avoided as a preference).

These cases are supported to some extent by legislative history which refers to at least one instance in which Congress believed that a constructive trust would survive in bankruptcy. H.R. Rep. No. 95-595, at 368 (1977). *See In re* Dameron, 206 B.R. 394 (Bankr. E.D. Va. 1997) (funds received by debtors and placed in accounts pursuant to escrow agreements are not property of the bankruptcy estate), *aff'd*, 155 F.3d 718 (1998).
167 *In re* Longhorn Oil & Gas Co., 64 B.R. 263 (Bankr. S.D. Tex. 1986); Daniel R. Cowans, Cowans Bankruptcy Law and Practice § 9.6, at 73 (1989).
168 *In re* Bernard L. Madoff Inv. L.L.C., 458 B.R. 87, 131–32 (Bankr. S.D.N.Y. 2011) (sustaining constructive trust claim under New York law, voiding transfers to family members who served as officers in enterprise formed up to conduct Ponzi scheme); *In re* Magna Entertainment Corp., 438 B.R. 380 (Bankr. D. Del. 2010) (applying state and federal law, court imposes constructive trust over betting proceeds held by debtor racetrack operator); *In re* LaLonde, 431 B.R. 199, 208 (Bankr. D. Wis. 2010) (Wisconsin law applies constructive trust under a flexible standard that looks to whether party acquired property "by some form of wrongful conduct"). *See, e.g., In re* Auto-Train Corp., 53 B.R. 990 (Bankr. D.C. 1985) (breach of fiduciary duty), *aff'd*, 810 F.2d 270 (D.C. Cir. 1987); *In*

declared the constructive trust to be a doctrine of equity under which the courts work out justice in the most efficient manner;[169] and according to recent commentary, a showing of constructive fraud need not be made as a prerequisite for establishing a constructive trust in Tennessee.[170] North Carolina courts are willing to impose constructive trusts when constructive fraud, fiduciary relationships, family relationships or mistake are established.[171] The legislature in South Dakota has codified constructive trusts as an equitable duty to convey property back to an aggrieved party in order to avoid unjust enrichment.[172]

Consumer protection statutes can be used to persuade the court to recognize a constructive trust.[173] When the debtor has violated such a statute, the consumer could argue that a constructive trust should be imposed to further the legislature's consumer protection policy.[174] For example, some statutes require a merchant to deliver goods or services to prepaid consumers within the time specified by contract or within thirty days if the merchant's time for performance was unspecified.[175] When a merchant's intervening bankruptcy has halted performance, a constructive trust should be imposed on the funds paid to the merchant by the consumer in order to accomplish the goals of the consumer protection legislation.

In some instances, courts find grounds for imposing a trust in the statutes and regulations that authorized funding for the debtor's prebankruptcy operations. The financial resources are considered held in trust for a public purpose and not part of the bankruptcy estate.[176] Because the debtor is viewed as a "conduit" for government funds, a showing of breach of fiduciary duty or fraud is not required in order to impose the trust.[177] In view of the restrictions imposed on use of the funds under the government program, the courts apply a less exacting tracing requirement than in other constructive trust situations.[178]

In many instances the courts have recognized constructive trusts arising out of domestic relations obligations. For example, in *Davis v. Cox*[179] an ex-husband withdrew a portion of his individual retirement account (IRA) account during the pendency of divorce proceedings, in violation of orders of the Maine family court. He later filed for bankruptcy relief. During the bankruptcy the family court awarded a significant portion of the IRA funds remaining in the account to the creditor's former spouse. The court of appeals eventually affirmed the bankruptcy court's imposition of a constructive trust for the former spouse in the funds in the IRA account, equal to the amount the family court awarded her.[180] In the court of appeals' view, the state family court would have considered the funds in the

---

re Richmond Children's Ctr., Inc., 49 B.R. 262, 267 (S.D.N.Y. 1985) (trust avoids unjust enrichment), *rev'd on other grounds*, 58 B.R. 980 (S.D.N.Y. 1986); *In re* Butts, 46 B.R. 292, 296 (Bankr. N.D. 1985) (confidential relationship breached); *In re* Vt. Real Estate Inv. Trust, 25 B.R. 813, 816 (Bankr. D. Vt. 1982) (honesty and fair dealing standard).

For descriptions of the elements necessary to have the courts impose constructive trusts in various jurisdictions, see Banks, *A Survey of the Constructive Trust in Tennessee*, 12 Mem. St. U.L. Rev. 71 (1981); Jennings & Shapiro, *The Minnesota Law of Constructive Trusts & Analogous Equitable Remedies*, 25 Minn. L. Rev. 667 (1941); Lacy, *Constructive Trusts and Equitable Liens in Iowa*, 40 Iowa L. Rev. 107 (1954); Lauerman, *Constructive Trusts and Restitutionary Liens in North Carolina*, 45 N.C. L. Rev. 424 (1966); Schuerenberg, *Constructive Trust in Texas*, 21 Baylor L. Rev. 59 (1969); Vanneman, *The Constructive Trust: A Neglected Remedy in Ohio*, 10 U. Cin. L. Rev. 366 (1936); Notes, *Constructive Trusts in Real Property—Review of Oregon Cases*, 11 Or. L. Rev. 393 (1931); Note, *Imposition of a Constructive Trust in New England*, 41 B.U. L. Rev. 78 (1961); Comment, *The Status of Implied Trusts in South Dakota*, 8 S.D. L. Rev. 93 (1958).

169 *See* Banks, *A Survey of the Constructive Trust in Tennessee*, 12 Mem. St. U.L. Rev. 71, 79 (1981).
170 *Id.*
171 *In re* Brokers, Inc., 396 B.R. 146 (Bankr. M.D.N.C. 2008) (constructive trust imposed as remedy for company president's breach of fiduciary obligations). *See also* Lauerman, *Constructive Trusts and Restitutionary Liens in North Carolina*, 45 N.C. L. Rev. 424, 428–439, 444 (1966).
172 *See* Comment, *The Status of Implied Trusts in South Dakota*, 8 S.D. L. Rev. 93 (1958).
173 *See* Schrag & Ratner, *Caveat Emptor—Empty Coffer: The Bankruptcy Law Has Nothing to Offer*, 72 Colum. L. Rev. 1147, 1152 (1972).
174 *In re* Washington Mut., Inc., 450 B.R. 490 (Bankr. D. Del. 2011) (constructive trust imposed on employee compensation plan funds that chapter 11 debtor failed to disburse to employees in violation of ERISA); 5 Collier on Bankruptcy ¶ 541.11 (16th ed.); Daniel R. Cowans, Cowans Bankruptcy Law and Practice § 9.6, at 75 (1989). *See, e.g.*, Huffman v. Farros, 275 F.2d 350 (9th Cir. 1960) (constructive trust imposed on license held by trustee in bankruptcy); *In re* D. & B. Elec., Inc., 4 B.R. 263 (Bankr. W.D. Ky. 1980) (state statute creates trust in favor of materialmen). *See also In re* Frosty Morn Meats, 7 B.R. 988 (M.D. Tex. 1980) (federal statute creates express trust for stock breeders).
175 *See, e.g.*, Ala. Code § 8-19-5.
    For a general discussion of such prohibitions, see National Consumer Law Center, Unfair and Deceptive Acts and Practices § 5.7.2 (7th ed. 2008 and Supp.).
176 *In re* Lan Tamers, Inc., 329 F.3d 204 (1st Cir. 2003) (constructive trust applied to funds held as reimbursement for work performed under a federal grant program that funded school renovations); *In re* Columbia Gas Syss., Inc., 997 F.2d 1039 (3d Cir. 1993); *In re* Joliet-Will Cmty. Action Agency, 847 F.2d 430 (7th Cir. 1988); *In re* W. Cent. Hous. Dev. Org., 338 B.R. 482 (Bankr. D. Colo. 2005) (comprehensive regulatory obligations in contracts between debtor nonprofit housing developer and governmental agencies created a trust in loan funds and deeds of trust held by debtor for the benefit of participants in low income housing programs); *In re* Lexington Healthcare Group, Inc., 335 B.R. 570 (Bankr. D. Del. 2005) (under ERISA a statutory trust attached to portion of employee wages withheld for contribution to employees' 401(k) plans).
177 *In re* Lan Tamers, 329 F.3d 204 (1st Cir. 2003) (court considered following factors in finding a trust: (1) the role the debtor was intended to play under the federal grant program as a mere delivery vehicle of funds; (2) strict federal regulatory controls limited the debtor's use of the funds; (3) diversion of the funds to benefit general creditors would thwart the government's overall regulatory scheme; and (4) transmitting the funds to creditors would grant them a windfall).
178 *In re* Lexington Healthcare Group, Inc., 335 B.R. 570 (Bankr. D. Del. 2005) (tracing requirement met by showing some "nexus" between funds withheld from employee wages for 401(k) contributions and an escrow account set up later by the employer).
179 356 F.3d 76 (1st Cir. 2004).
180 *Id.*, 356 F.3d at 89.

account held in trust for the spouse at the time of the bankruptcy filing. In similar instances the bankruptcy courts have looked to state law and orders from the debtor's domestic relations litigation to remove property from the bankruptcy estate for the benefit of a non-debtor former spouses or children.[181]

Constructive trusts could be imposed when statutes require the merchant debtor to return the consumer's property.[182] For example, a constructive trust could be imposed on consumer payments that must be returned after a consumer's rescission under the federal Truth in Lending Act,[183] state home solicitation sales acts,[184] or state unfair and deceptive practices statutes.[185] Arguments for a constructive trust also apply when tenants retain an interest in security deposits misappropriated by their landlords.[186]

18.5.2.3 Tracing Trust Funds

Consumers attempting to have trusts imposed on funds paid or entrusted are often required to trace the specific funds being claimed.[187] The tracing requirement is considered to be a matter of federal law rather than state law.[188]

The tracing requirement may be a major obstacle to recovering funds when the funds have been commingled and then partially drawn down. Even when those accounts have been replenished with additional deposits, the courts generally apply a "lowest intermediate balance test" which limits any claimant to an amount equal to the lowest balance ever reached in the account after the claimant's funds had been commingled.[189] If the funds have been converted into other property, the claimant can trace the disbursed funds into the new property.[190]

This requirement for tracing the trust funds and allowing a trust to be imposed on only the lowest balance of funds reached in the trust after a claimant's funds went into the debtor's account, obviously works a hardship on claimants either unable to trace the payments made to a debtor or unfortunate enough to have made their payments prior to a substantial or even total dissipation of funds.[191]

Courts have recognized that in appropriate circumstances, based on the equitable powers under the Code,[192] they can abandon the usual strict tracing requirements of the trust doctrine.[193] Thus, the Seventh Circuit has held that consumers defrauded by a merchant need not trace their funds in the debtor's accounts in order to have the court impose a constructive trust on the funds remaining in the debtor's accounts.[194]

---

181 McCafferty v. McCafferty, 96 F.3d 192 (6th Cir. 1996) (based on terms of prepetition divorce decree, one-half of debtor's pension benefits held in constructive trust for non-debtor former spouse); *In re* Mayer, 451 B.R. 702 (E.D. Mich. 2011) (constructive trust imposed based on terms of prepetition divorce decree requiring payment of attorney fees out of marital property awarded to debtor); *In re* Combs, 435 B.R. 467 (Bankr. E.D. Mich. 2010) (constructive trust created in portion of debtor's pension fund ordered paid to former spouse under prepetition divorce decree); *In re* Pardee, 433 B.R. 377 (Bankr. N.D. Okla. 2010) (interest in debtor's IRA funds identified in divorce order as awarded to ex-spouse is held in constructive trust for ex-spouse and is not property of estate); *In re* Petty, 333 B.R. 472 (Bankr. M.D. Fla. 2005) (prepetition divorce judgment granting ex-wife portion of debtor's military pension vested property right in ex-wife at time of judgment); *In re* Forant, 331 B.R. 151 (Bankr. D. Vt. 2004) (divorce order granting wife rights in debtor husband's retirement account removed her interest from bankruptcy estate under constructive trust); *In re* Palidora, 310 B.R. 164 (Bankr. D. Ariz. 2004) (child support payments made pursuant to court order are held in constructive trust for benefit of child and are not part of parent's bankruptcy estate); *In re* Reider, 177 B.R. 412 (Bankr. D. Me. 1994) (wife, who was to receive half of proceeds of sale of marital residence under divorce decree, is beneficiary of constructive trust in proceeds of fire insurance resulting from loss of home before it could be sold).

182 5 Collier on Bankruptcy ¶ 541.11 (16th ed.). *See, e.g., In re* Goldberger Inc., 32 F. Supp. 615 (E.D.N.Y. 1940) (sales tax paid to debtor was held by debtor as trustee and therefore did not become property of the estate).

183 15 U.S.C. § 1635. *See* National Consumer Law Center, Truth in Lending Ch. 6 (8th ed. 2012).

184 *See* National Consumer Law Center, Unfair and Deceptive Acts and Practices Ch. 9 (7th ed. 2008 and Supp.).

185 *See, e.g.*, Ohio Rev. Code Ann § 1345.09 (West). *See generally* National Consumer Law Center, Unfair and Deceptive Acts and Practices § 13.7 (7th ed. 2008 and Supp.).

186 This issue is discussed further below.

187 Cunningham v. Brown, 265 U.S. 1, 44 S. Ct. 424, 68 L. Ed. 873 (1923); Schuyler v. Littlefield, 232 U.S. 707, 34 S. Ct. 466, 58 L. Ed. 806 (1914).

188 Conn. Gen. Life Ins. v. Universal Ins. Co., 838 F.2d 612 (1st Cir. 1988).

189 Schuyler v. Littlefield, 232 U.S. 707, 710, 34 S. Ct. 466, 58 L. Ed. 806 (1914); First Fed. of Mich. v. Barrow, 878 F.2d 912 (6th Cir. 1989); 5 Collier on Bankruptcy ¶ 541.11 (16th ed.). *See In re* Dameron, 206 B.R. 394 (Bankr. E.D. Va. 1997) (funds received by debtors and placed in accounts pursuant to escrow agreements are not property of the bankruptcy estate, despite commingling, to the extent of the lowest intermediate balance in the debtor's account), *aff'd*, 155 F.3d 718 (4th Cir. 1998). *See also In re* Mushroom Transp., 227 B.R. 244, 255 (Bankr. E.D. Pa. 1998) (extended discussion of common law rules applicable to tracing funds).

190 Schuyler v. Littlefield, 232 U.S. 707, 710, 34 S. Ct. 466, 58 L. Ed. 806 (1914); Chiu v. Wong, 16 F.3d 306 (8th Cir. 1994) (constructive trust in property converted from partnership assets traced to homestead); Johnson v. Morris, 175 F.2d 65, 68 (10th Cir. 1949); Kim v. Nyce, 807 F. Supp. 2d 442 (D. Md. 2011) (constructive trust in real property purchased with funds from defrauded investors); *In re* Brown, 427 B.R. 715 (D. Minn. 2010) (debtor's use of funds misappropriated from victims of investment scheme to pay down his home mortgage and deposit in his retirement account warranted placing constructive trust on equity in home and on account funds, setting aside any exemption otherwise applicable to the property); *In re* De Steph, 2010 WL 2206983 (Bankr. D.N.H. May 26, 2010) (tracing satisfied when debtor, an investment advisor, admitted he purchased vehicle with deceptively acquired funds). *See generally* J.A. Bryant, Jr., Annotation, *Imposition of Constructive Trust in Property Bought With Stolen or Embezzled Funds*, 38 A.L.R.3d 1354 (1997).

191 Conn. Gen. Life Ins. v. Universal Ins. Co., 838 F.2d 612 (1st Cir. 1988).

192 11 U.S.C. § 105.

193 *See, e.g., In re* Mahan & Rowsey Inc., 62 B.R. 46, 48 (W.D. Okla. 1985), *aff'd*, 817 F.2d 682 (10th Cir. 1987).

194 *In re* Teltronics Ltd., 649 F.2d 1236 (7th Cir. 1981).
  Although this case was decided prior to the enactment of the Bankruptcy Code in 1978, none of the changes affected the tracing

Similarly, in those circumstances in which the debtor draws down an account to a balance well below the amount of the claimant's payment to the debtor, but the debtor subsequently replenishes the account from other sources, the bankruptcy court might use its equitable powers to adopt the trust revival doctrine which allows a constructive trust to be imposed on those subsequently deposited funds.[195]

Finally, between competing claimants to the same commingled account, the majority position holds that the most recent contributors to the account have claims superior to the earlier contributors to the account.[196] However, a state law minority position allows distribution among claimants in a commingled account to distribution pro rata regardless of the time of deposit.[197]

18.5.3 Postpetition Claims As Administrative Expenses

Most consumer claims against businesses in bankruptcy will have arisen before the filing of that bankruptcy petition. But some claims, especially torts which may be of a continuing nature such as debt collection harassment or those involving illegal housing conditions, may continue after the bankruptcy filing or may arise after the filing.[198]

After the filing, not only the property of the debtor, but the proceeds, rents and profits from that property become part of the bankruptcy estate.[199] During the pendency of the bankruptcy case, the business will be operated either by a trustee or more likely by the corporate entity as a "debtor in possession" in a chapter 11[200] or chapter 12[201] or by the individual debtor as a "debtor in possession" in a chapter 12[202] or chapter 13 case.[203] Claims arising after the filing of the petition and prior to confirmation are thus claims against the bankruptcy estate and are considered administrative expenses as a cost or expense of preserving the estate.[204] For example, the postpetition right to return of a security deposit, absent rejection of the lease, has been held to be an administrative expense entitled to priority.[205] Administrative expenses receive the second highest priority and are paid before all other unsecured claims except certain domestic support obligations.[206]

A proof of claim should be filed indicating that the claim arose postpetition, both by setting out the date that the claim accrued and by labeling the claim "administrative" in parentheses. The claim should also indicate that it is a priority claim under section 507(a)(2). A motion or application should then be filed requesting an order designating the claim as an administrative expense under section 503 and ordering payment.

Even administrative expenses, however, are ordinarily paid after secured claims.[207] If, for example, the bankruptcy estate principally consists of an apartment building, and sale of the building does not generate enough funds to pay off the mortgage holders, then neither the administrative expenses nor the unsecured claims will be paid. An exception to this rule exists under section 506(c), which allows certain expenses of preserving and disposing of the secured property to be paid before the secured claim is paid.[208]

Section 506(c) provides that the reasonable and necessary costs of preserving and disposing of property securing an allowed secured claim may be recovered by the trustee, to the extent the expenditure benefits the secured creditor.[209] Claims are made most commonly for continued utility services, other costs of maintaining the business as a going concern, costs of storage of the property and costs of selling the property.[210]

---

requirements developed by the courts prior to 1978. Thus, this case and those cited below remain good precedents.

195 *See, e.g., In re* Teltronics Ltd., 649 F.2d 1236 (7th Cir. 1981); *In re* Gottfried Baking Co., 312 F. Supp. 643 (S.D.N.Y. 1970). *But see In re* Dameron, 206 B.R. 394, 403 (Bankr. E.D. Va. 1997) (lowest intermediate balance rule precludes replenishing trust funds with later deposits).

196 *In re* Schmidt, 298 F. 314, 316 (S.D.N.Y. 1923) (Learned Hand, in district court considering a bankruptcy case, holds that most recent depositors withdraw from trust *res* first).

197 People v. Cal. Safe Deposit & Trust Co., 167 P. 388 (Cal. 1917) (state banking liquidation actions); Gibbs v. Gerberich, 203 N.E.2d 851, 856 (Mass. 1964) (trust case).

198 As to whether a tort claim is prepetition or postpetition, compare *In re* M. Frenville Co., 744 F.2d 332 (3d Cir. 1984) (when acts occurred prepetition but cause of action arose postpetition, the claim is postpetition) with *In re* A.H. Robins Co., 63 B.R. 986 (Bankr. E.D. Va. 1986) (contra), *aff'd*, 839 F.2d 198 (4th Cir. 1988). *See also In re* Wheeler, 137 F.3d 299 (5th Cir. 1998) (attorney's malpractice in preparing the bankruptcy petition occurred before the bankruptcy filing so that claim for malpractice claim became property of the estate). *But see In re* Philadelphia Newspapers, L.L.C., 690 F.3d 161 (3d Cir. 2012) (debtor newspaper's postpetition publication of internet link to an alleged defamatory article published prepetition could not be basis for administrative claim).

199 11 U.S.C. § 541(b).

200 *See* 11 U.S.C. §§ 1107, 1108 (unless trustee is appointed, debtor has power of trustee including the operation of the debtor's business).

201 11 U.S.C. § 1203 (debtor in possession has functions and duties of trustee including operating the debtor's farm).

202 11 U.S.C. § 1203.

203 11 U.S.C. § 1304 ("Unless the court orders otherwise a [chapter 13] debtor engaged in business may operate the business of the debtor. . . .").

204 11 U.S.C. § 503(b)(1); *In re* Charlesbank Laundry, Inc., 755 F.2d 200 (1st Cir. 1985) (civil fine based on debtor's postpetition conduct granted administrative expense status). *See, e.g., In re* Friendship College Inc., 737 F.2d 430 (4th Cir. 1987) (the term "estate" as used in section 503(b)(1)(B)(i) implies postpetition liabilities. *See also* Reading Co. v. Brown, 391 U.S. 471, 482, 88 S. Ct. 1759, 20 L. Ed. 2d 751 (1968) (postpetition tort claim is administrative expense).

205 *In re* Boston Post Road L.P., 21 F.3d 477 (2d Cir. 1994) (tenants who are owed security deposits have administrative claims which are entitled to priority); *In re* Cantonwood Assocs. L.P., 138 B.R. 648 (Bankr. D. Mass. 1992) (same).

206 11 U.S.C. § 507(a)(1), (2).

207 *In re* Trim-X, Inc., 695 F.2d 296 (7th Cir. 1982); *In re* Delta Towers, Ltd., 924 F.2d 74 (5th Cir. 1991).

208 *See* 11 U.S.C. § 506(c).

209 *See* 11 U.S.C. § 506(c).

210 *In re* Spa at Sunset Isles Condo. Ass'n, Inc., 454 B.R. 898 (Bankr. S.D. Fla. 2011) (in connection with implementation of condo-

Three elements must be shown before an expense qualifies to be paid under section 506(c): 1) the expenditure must be necessary, 2) the amounts expended are reasonable, and 3) the secured creditor benefits from the expenditure.[211]

The usefulness of this provision is limited, however, by the fact that only the trustee may seek to "tax" a secured creditor for expenses of preserving collateral.[212] Earlier cases allowing the party who provided the service or incurred the expense to recover under section 506(c) from the secured creditor are no longer good law.[213] In a case in which, for example, tenants have claims for reimbursement of repairs, or utility expenditures, recovery from the secured creditor will require cooperation of the trustee, who might be willing to invoke 506(c) to reimburse the tenants, if doing so will preserve or increase the value of the estate. Still, this provision can be useful to tenants in persuading the trustee to pay for utilities and essential services to the property out of the secured creditor's funds.

18.5.4 Challenging Dischargeability

18.5.4.1 General

In some circumstances, particular debts may be declared nondischargeable. Such debts remain legally in effect after the bankruptcy and are not subject to the Code's prohibitions on collecting discharged debts.[214] The creditor is free to collect the debt from the future income or later acquired property of the debtor.[215] Whether a particular debt is nondischargeable depends on whether the debtor is an individual or a corporation and the Bankruptcy Code chapter under which the debtor has filed.

18.5.4.2 Individual Debtors in Chapters 7, 11, and 12

18.5.4.2.1 Grounds for a finding of nondischargeability

When the debtor is an individual who has filed under chapters 7, 11, or 12 or receives a hardship discharge under section 1328(b) of chapter 13,[216] certain categories of debts, set out in section 523(a), are not dischargeable. Generally, those most relevant to cases involving consumers as creditors would be claims based on fraud or false pretenses,[217] fraud as a fiduciary, embezzlement or larceny,[218] domestic support obligations (alimony, maintenance, or support),[219] additional obligations related to dissolution of a marriage under some conditions,[220] willful and malicious injury,[221] or drunk driving.[222] When there has been government enforcement of consumer claims, additional grounds for nondischargeability may apply.[223] And several courts have concluded that dischargeability issues can be raised by a governmental agency on behalf of individual consumers through standing conferred by the *parens patriae* doctrine.[224]

---

minium association's chapter 11 plan, mortgagee must pay condominium maintenance fees under § 506 (c) despite contrary provision of state law). *See, e.g., In re* Delta Towers, Ltd., 924 F.2d 74 (5th Cir. 1991) (utility service); *In re* P.C. Ltd., 929 F.2d 203 (5th Cir. 1991) (keeping business going); *In re* McKeesport Steel Castings, Co., 799 F.2d 91 (3d Cir. 1986) (utility service); *In re* Trim-X, Inc., 695 F.2d 296 (7th Cir. 1982) (storage costs).

211 *In re* Delta Towers, Ltd., 924 F.2d 74 (5th Cir. 1991); *In re* Trim-X, Inc., 695 F.2d 296 (7th Cir. 1982).
212 Hartford Underwriters Ins. Co. v. Union Planters Bank, 530 U.S. 1, 120 S. Ct. 1942, 147 L. Ed. 2d 1 (2000).
213 *See, e.g., In re* Parque Forrestal, Inc., 949 F.2d 504 (1st Cir. 1991).
214 11 U.S.C. § 524. *See* § 15.5, *supra*.
215 Property exempted in the bankruptcy court, however, retains its protection and cannot be seized to satisfy most nondischargeable debts. 11 U.S.C. § 522(c).
216 11 U.S.C. § 1328(b).
217 11 U.S.C. § 532(a)(2). *See* Stokes v. Ferris, 150 B.R. 388 (W.D. Tex. 1992) (state unfair trade practice judgment found to give rise to nondischargeable debt based on fraud, false pretenses and willful and malicious injury), *aff'd*, 995 F.2d 76 (5th Cir. 1993); § 15.4.3.2, *supra*.
218 11 U.S.C. § 523(a)(4). *See In re* Messineo, 192 B.R. 597 (Bankr. D.N.H. 1996) (son breached fiduciary duties when, as co-guardian of his elderly mother's estate, he misappropriated her funds and property for his own use); § 15.4.3.4, *supra*.
219 11 U.S.C. §§ 101(14A), 523(a)(5), 1141(d)(2), 1328(a)(2).
  In chapter 7 and chapter 13 cases, and for individuals in chapter 11, the domestic support obligation discharge exception now applies to alimony, maintenance, and support debts that accrue before, on, or after the date of the order for relief, including debts owed to a governmental unit. *See* § 15.4.3.5, *supra*.
220 11 U.S.C. § 523(a)(15) (property settlement debts incurred in divorce or separation decrees are not dischargeable under any circumstances in chapters 7, 11, or 12, but are dischargeable in chapter 13). *See* § 15.4.3.14, *supra*.
221 11 U.S.C. §§ 523(a)(6), 1328(a)(4) (willful and malicious injury to individuals, not property). *See* § 15.4.3.6, *supra*.
222 11 U.S.C. § 523(a)(9). *See* § 15.4.3.9, *supra*.
223 11 U.S.C. § 523(a)(7), (13); *In re* Horras, 443 B.R. 159 (B.A.P. 8th Cir. 2011) (fines and penalties debtor must pay to Dept. of HHS for knowingly presenting false Medicare and Medicaid billings nondischargeable under § 523(a)(2) and (7)). *See* §§ 15.4.3.7, 15.4.3.18, *supra*. *See also* United States Dep't of Hous. & Urban Dev. v. Cost Control Mktg. & Sales of Va., 64 F.3d 920 (4th Cir. 1995) (judgment owed to HUD nondischargeable under section 523(a)(7) as long as damages assessed were penal even though damages were measured by consumer's losses and even if some part of judgment would repay consumers for their losses); *In re* Jensen, 395 B.R. 472 (Bankr. D. Colo. 2008) (civil penalties assessed in state attorney general action against debtor who ran credit repair business are nondischargeable under section 523(a)(7)).
224 *In re* Taibbi, 213 B.R. 261 (Bankr. E.D.N.Y. 1997) (county consumer protection agency has *parens patriae* standing to raise dischargeability claims on behalf of consumers). *See also In re* Asif, 455 B.R. 768 (Bankr. D. Kan. 2011) (Dept. of Labor can bring dischargeability action on behalf of alien workers entitled to back pay awards); *In re* Abeyta, 387 B.R. 846 (Bankr. D.N.M. 2008) (Federal Trade Commission has standing on behalf of itself and affected consumers to pursue nondischargeability action based on its prepetition fraud judgment against debtor); *In re* Gorski, 272 B.R. 59 (Bankr. D. Conn. 2002) (state human rights agency having duty to enforce civil rights laws has standing in nondischargeability action involving its award in housing discrimination proceeding even though it is not recipient of award); § 18.4.2, *supra*.

§ 18.5.4.2.1   Consumer Bankruptcy Law and Practice

In certain cases more than one ground for nondischargeability will apply.[225] When a consumer has been the victim of an unfair trade practice or outright fraud, nondischargeability claims may be raised under the provision based on fraud,[226] breach of fiduciary duty,[227] willful or malicious injury[228] or all three.

---

225 See In re Stokes, 995 F.2d 76 (5th Cir. 1993) (damages under the Texas consumer protection act found nondischargeable based on both subsections 523(a)(2)(A) and 523(a)(6)); In re Dobrayel, 287 B.R. 3 (Bankr. S.D.N.Y. 2002) (court sua sponte found debt owed by contractor to be nondischargeable as incurred from defalcation while acting in fiduciary capacity, although creditor pleaded only fraud and false pretenses).

226 11 U.S.C. § 523(a)(2). See, e.g., Cohen v. de la Cruz, 523 U.S. 213, 118 S. Ct. 1212, 140 L. Ed. 2d 341 (1998) (actual and punitive damages awarded to tenants based on UDAP for rent overcharges nondischargeable under section 523(a)(2)(A)); In re Goguen, 691 F.3d 62 (1st Cir. 2012) (debtor contractor's false representations about his licensed status were factual and legal causes of consumer's entering into homebuilding transaction, debt arising from failure to complete work non-dischargeable); In re Alport, 144 F.3d 1163 (8th Cir. 1998) (home purchasers claim due to builder's failure to pay subcontractors fell within fraud exception to discharge); Morlang v. Cox, 222 B.R. 83 (W.D. Va. 1998) (debt for money obtained by unlicensed home improvement contractor through misrepresentation that he was authorized to do home improvement work was nondischargeable under 11 U.S.C. § 523(a)(2)); In re Hernandez, 452 B.R. 709 (Bankr. N.D. Ill. 2011) (fraudulent conduct by home improvement contractor); In re Davis, 377 B.R. 827 (Bankr. E.D. Tex. 2007) (debt based on debtor's violations of state deceptive practices and debt collection statutes for conduct in foreclosing on home owner after acting as realtor for same individual held to be nondischargeable); In re Hurst, 337 B.R. 125 (Bankr. N.D. Tex. 2005) (auto auctioneer who overcharged based on rigged bids incurred nondischargeable debt based on false representations); In re Logan, 313 B.R. 745 (Bankr. S.D. Ohio 2004) (debt based on deceptive conduct of home improvement contractor); In re Santos, 304 B.R. 639 (Bankr. D.N.J. 2004) (debt based on debtor medical service provider's false representations about quality of services was nondischargeable); In re Rebarchek, 293 B.R. 400 (Bankr. N.D. Ohio 2002) (state UDAP judgment given collateral estoppel effect and found nondischargeable based on fraud); In re Fuselier, 211 B.R. 540 (Bankr. W.D. La. 1997) (state fraud and breach of contract damages found nondischargeable under section 523(a)(2)(A) when contractor secured job by falsifying license number and his plan for use of home owners' payments); In re Bottone, 209 B.R. 257 (Bankr. D. Mass. 1997) (debtor/home inspector denied summary judgment in nondischargeability case alleging that he knowingly misrepresented condition of home); In re George, 205 B.R. 679 (Bankr. D. Conn. 1997) (investment "advisor" who convinced creditors to invest in coins, a condominium and mutual fund could not discharge a state UDAP debt because he had falsely represented his qualifications and objectivity); In re Tallant, 207 B.R. 923 (Bankr. E.D. Cal. 1997) (lawyers' misrepresentations in context of attorney/client business transaction found to preclude discharge of debt based on fraud), aff'd. in part and rev'd. on other grounds, 218 B.R. 58 (B.A.P. 9th Cir. 1998); In re Bebber, 192 B.R. 120 (W.D.N.C. 1995) (false promise that construction project was secured by fraud gave rise to nondischargeable unfair trade practices judgment); In re Friedlander, 170 B.R. 472 (Bankr. D. Mass. 1994) (state UDAP damages including multiple (punitive) damages found nondischargeable based on fraud); In re Cornner, 191 B.R. 199 (Bankr. N.D. Ala. 1995) (loan broker fraud debt found nondischargeable when deposit was made but no loan was procured). See also Kearns v. Tempe Technical Inst., 993 F. Supp. 714 (D. Ariz. 1997) (negligent supervision insufficient basis to find debt of trade school's president nondischargeable for fraud).

227 11 U.S.C. § 523(a)(4). See, e.g., In re McGee, 353 F.3d 537 (7th Cir. 2003) (debtor-landlord guilty of defalcation in fiduciary duty by not complying with city ordinance requiring landlords to segregate tenant security deposits in interest bearing accounts); In re Niles, 106 F.3d 1456 (9th Cir. 1997) (application of section 523(a)(4)); In re Storie, 216 B.R. 283, 285 (B.A.P. 10th Cir. 1997) (chapter 7 debtors-general contractors committed defalcation by negligently failing to pay suppliers with money received from creditors-property owners); In re Mullarkey, 410 B.R. 338 (Bankr. D. Mass. 2009) (equity skimming scheme reversed, and reconveyance to victimized creditor ordered, with creditor's interest a nondischargeable claim under section 523(a)(4)); In re Jacobs, 403 B.R. 565 (Bankr. N.D. Ill. 2009) (employer breaches fiduciary duty in surreptitiously withdrawing funds from employee's ERISA-qualified profit sharing plan); In re O'Quinn, 374 B.R. 171 (Bankr. M.D.N.C. 2007) (former employees stated valid claim under section 523(a)(4) that discharge exception applied to debtor-employer's breach of fiduciary duties under ERISA and COBRA statutes); In re Suarez, 367 B.R. 332 (Bankr. E.D.N.Y. 2007) (health club owner committed defalcation by not complying with New York law requiring deposit of membership fees in an escrow account); In re Donlevy, 342 B.R. 774 (Bankr. N.D. Ill. 2006) (debt based on debtor's defalcation relating to deposit on home improvement contract); In re West, 339 B.R. 557 (Bankr. E.D.N.Y. 2006) (debt based on prepetition judgment against debtor for conduct in foreclosure rescue scheme); In re Duncan, 331 B.R. 70 (Bankr. E.D.N.Y. 2005) (debtor's self-dealing in managing employees' retirement plan was defalcation in fiduciary capacity); In re Gunter, 304 B.R. 458 (Bankr. D. Colo. 2003) (same); In re Ardolino, 298 B.R. 541 (Bankr. W.D. Pa. 2003) (debt for security deposit owed by former landlord to former tenant is not debt from fraud or from defalcation while acting in fiduciary capacity, but is nondischargeable as arising from embezzlement under section 523(a)(4)); In re Kohler, 255 B.R. 666 (Bankr. E.D. Pa. 2000) (debt related to abuse of a confidential relationship with an elder found to be a nondischargeable breach of fiduciary duty by collateral estoppel); In re Heilman, 241 B.R. 137 (Bankr. D. Md. 1999) (custom home builder was not a fiduciary with respect to home buyer's deposit; opinion includes exhaustive list of cases on whether attorneys, directors, partners, property managers, insurance agents, contractors and homebuilders are "fiduciaries" for purposes of section 523(a)(4)); In re Young, 208 B.R. 189 (Bankr. S.D. Cal. 1997) (real estate broker had fiduciary duties once funds were entrusted by clients to his care). But see In re Bucci, 493 F.3d 635 (6th Cir. 2007) (debtor-employer's obligation to make monthly contributions to employees' benefit funds under collective bargaining agreement did not satisfy fiduciary relation requirement under section 523(a)(4)). See generally In re Bullock, 670 F.3d 1160 (11th Cir. 2012) (creditor's unclean hands not defense available to debtor in defending action to declare debt nondischargeable under § 523(a)(4)).

228 11 U.S.C. § 523(a)(6); In re Nangle, 274 F.3d 481 (8th Cir. 2001) (jury verdict awarding punitive damages under state consumer protection act based on repeated debt collection contacts established that debtor caused willful and malicious injury); In re Kennedy, 249 F.3d 576 (6th Cir. 2001) (defamation judgment found nondischargeable on grounds of collateral estoppel); Piccicuto v. Dwyer, 39 F.3d 37 (1st Cir. 1994) (enhanced damages awarded under state unfair trade practice law for willful conduct found nondischargeable on grounds of collateral estoppel under section 523(a)(6)); In re Cottingham, 473 B.R. 703 (B.A.P. 6th Cir. 2012) (debtor-husband's knowledge of wife's ongoing embezzlement of funds from her employer made him a conspirator in activities and liable on debt found nondischargeable under § 523(a)(6)); In re Jones, 300 B.R. 133 (B.A.P. 1st Cir. 2003) (state agency damage award against

However, the Supreme Court has ruled that only intentional torts can be found nondischargeable for willful and malicious injury.[229] Torts based on reckless or negligent conduct are not within the scope of the exception.[230]

Punitive damages and attorney fees awarded for fraud are nondischargeable, together with actual damages, under 11 U.S.C. § 523(a)(2).[231] The Supreme Court's definitive ruling on the punitive damages dischargeability issue arose in the context of a consumer protection claim by tenants against their landlord. The tenants had pleaded and proved an unfair trade practice claim for illegal rent overcharges, which led to an award of treble damages and attorney fees. The Supreme Court held that section 523(a)(2)(A) "prevents the discharge of all liability arising from fraud and that an award of treble damages therefore falls within the scope of the exception."[232] By this reading, the Court extends protection from discharge not just to multiple and punitive damages, but also to claims for litigation fees and costs and to other foreseeable consequential damages of fraud.[233]

While the *Cohen* ruling will be helpful to creditors with consumer protection claims against an individual that files bankruptcy, it would be incorrect to assume that establishing unfair or deceptive practices under state law will be sufficient to guarantee nondischargeability in bankruptcy, because a bankruptcy debtor may argue that a practice was unfair or deceptive, but not fraudulent.[234] Good practice will continue to require that fraud claims be brought alongside UDAP claims and proved whenever possible. A nonbankruptcy court resolving UDAP claims should be encouraged to find fraud explicitly when the facts support that outcome. Absent such a finding, there may be a problem trying to use collateral estoppel in a dischargeability case based on the prior judgment.

It is also important to keep in mind that when settling cases with any individual who might later file bankruptcy, language in the settlement agreement absolving them of fraud may preclude a later dischargeability claim. However, the Supreme Court has held that, ordinarily, a settlement of a fraud case that substitutes a new contractual obligation does not eliminate the ability to claim that the underlying debt is nondischargeable due to fraud.[235] At a minimum, the settlement agreement should be neutral on this issue so that it can be litigated, if necessary, in bankruptcy court. If possible, write into the agreement that the settlement is based on fraud, or better yet, that all amounts to be paid are damages for fraud that are not dischargeable in bankruptcy.

---

employer based on sexual harassment found nondischargeable on grounds of collateral estoppel under section 523(a)(6)); Zygulski v. Daugherty, 236 B.R. 646 (N.D. Ind. 1999) (husband willfully and maliciously dissipated assets from wife's illegal pyramid scheme, so his debt to victims was found nondischargeable—conversion fulfills the malice requirement); *In re* Ma, 375 B.R. 387 (Bankr. N.D. Ohio 2007) (debt found nondischargeable under "willful and malicious injury" exception due to mortgage broker's deceptive loan origination practices); *In re* Busch, 311 B.R. 657 (Bankr. N.D.N.Y. 2004) (judgment debt entered in favor of employee in Title VII sexual harassment action excepted from discharge under section 523(a)(6)); *In re* Guillory, 285 B.R. 307 (Bankr. C.D. Cal. 2002) (debtor's wrongful repossession of truck found to be conversion resulting in willful and malicious injury); *In re* Foushee, 283 B.R. 278 (Bankr. N.D. Iowa 2002) (judgment against debtor-employer for firing employee in violation of whistleblower statute found nondischargeable on grounds of collateral estoppel under section 523(a)(6)); *In re* Paeplow, 217 B.R. 705 (Bankr. D. Vt. 1998) (conversion of security deposit could be willful and malicious injury); *In re* Topakas, 202 B.R. 850 (Bankr. E.D. Pa. 1996) (sexual harassment claim was for willful and malicious injury), *aff'd*, 1997 WL 158197 4107 (E.D. Pa. Mar. 31, 1997); Littlefield v. McGuffey, 145 B.R. 582 (Bankr. N.D. Ill. 1992) (judgment for compensatory and punitive damages based on findings that debtor-landlord engaged in racial discrimination in violation of Fair Housing Act is nondischargeable as willful and malicious injury). *See generally* Blake, *Debts Non-Dischargeable for "Willful and Malicious Injury": Applicability of Bankruptcy Code § 523(a)(6) in a Commercial Setting*, 104 Com. L.J. 64 (Spring 1999).

229 Kawaauhau v. Geiger, 523 U.S. 57, 118 S. Ct. 974, 140 L. Ed. 2d 90 (1998). *See In re* Sarbaz, 227 B.R. 298 (B.A.P. 9th Cir. 1998) (*Geiger* standard applies retroactively); *In re* Thomason, 288 B.R. 812 (Bankr. S.D. Ill. 2002) (sexual harassment involving both physical and verbal abuse excepted from discharge); *In re* Mode, 231 B.R. 295 (Bankr. E.D. Ark. 1999) (large judgment against repossessor found to create nondischargeable debt in bankruptcy, when the repossessor had deliberately run over the automobile owner during the repossession attempt).

In determining whether an act is willful, courts generally hold a business person to a higher standard than a consumer debtor. *See In re* Penton, 299 B.R. 701 (Bankr. S.D. Ga. 2003) (debt based on conversion of property subject to security interest held nondischargeable under section 523(a)(6)).

230 *See In re* Popa, 140 F.3d 317 (1st Cir. 1998) (employer's failure to obtain workers' compensation insurance is not willful because it was not done with the actual intent to cause injury as required by the *Geiger* standard); *In re* Martino, 220 B.R. 129 (Bankr. M.D. Fla. 1998) (employer was not discharged from paying an employee-damages grounded in sexual harassment, sex discrimination and defamation because his actions were intended to injure).

231 Cohen v. de la Cruz, 523 U.S. 213, 118 S. Ct. 1212, 140 L. Ed. 2d 341 (1998). *See also In re* Nangle, 274 F.3d 481 (8th Cir. 2001) (state court contempt judgment based on debt collector's failure to comply with prior judgment held nondischargeable under section 523(a)(6)); Scarborough v. Fischer 171 F.3d 638 (8th Cir. 1999) (punitive damages for willful and malicious injury also nondischargeable under section 523(a)(6)); *In re* Smith, 321 B.R. 542 (Bankr. D. Colo. 2005) (bankruptcy court will not review amount of attorney fees awarded as part of prepetition judgment when debt is found nondischargeable based on prior judicial finding of willful and malicious injury).

232 Cohen v. de la Cruz, 523 U.S. 213, 118 S. Ct. 1212, 140 L. Ed. 2d 341 (1998).

233 For example, payments owed to third parties to correct problems caused by the debtor's fraud may be nondischargeable. *In re* Pleasants, 219 F.3d 372 (4th Cir. 2000) (debtor who misrepresented himself as architect may not discharge consequential damage claims).

234 *See, e.g., In re* Davis, 638 F.3d 549 (7th Cir. 2011) (prepetition state court finding that debtor-contractor engaged in deceptive practices did not satisfy fraudulent intent element of § 523(a)(2)(A)). *See* National Consumer Law Center, Unfair and Deceptive Acts and Practices § 4.2.3 (7th ed. 2008 and Supp.). *See also* note 250, *infra* (collecting bankruptcy court non-dischargeability decisions applying collateral estoppel from nonbankruptcy courts' findings in UDAP cases).

235 Archer v. Warner, 538 U.S. 314, 123 S. Ct. 1462, 155 L. Ed. 2d 454 (2003). *See also In re* Detrano, 326 F.3d 319 (2d Cir. 2003).

§ 18.5.4.2.2   Consumer Bankruptcy Law and Practice

Consumer protection claims also give rise to nondischargeability arguments under 11 U.S.C. § 523(a)(4) and (6), provisions which do not require proof of fraud.[236] It is usually prudent to raise these claims together with one based on fraud when litigating the dischargeability of a UDAP claims.

More detail on many issues related to nondischargeability is provided elsewhere in this treatise.[237]

18.5.4.2.2 Procedures for obtaining a determination of nondischargeability

The Bankruptcy Code makes an important distinction between two categories of exceptions to discharge. The first category consists of debts that are excepted from the discharge regardless of whether the issue is raised during the bankruptcy case. Debts in this first category include domestic support obligations, certain debts incurred through drunk driving, and debts when a discharge was denied or waived in a prior bankruptcy.[238] Creditors holding claims covered by these exceptions are free to assert them against the debtor after the bankruptcy, without the permission of the bankruptcy court.

The second category of exceptions consists of debts that are excluded from the discharge only if their nondischargeability is raised and determined during the bankruptcy case. The debts falling into this category are those specified in subsections (a)(2), (a)(4), and, in a chapter 7, 11, or 12 case, (a)(6) of section 523.[239] These subsections deal with debts incurred by false pretenses or false financial statements, claims for breach of fiduciary duty, embezzlement, larceny,[240] and claims for willful and malicious injuries. The Bankruptcy Rules require consumers and other creditors to raise such nondischargeability issues by an adversary proceeding during the bankruptcy case.[241] The deadline for commencing such a proceeding is sixty days after the first date set for the section 341 meeting of creditors.[242] While the Supreme Court has ruled that the filing deadline is not jurisdictional,[243] the Court's ruling did not specifically address whether principles of equitable tolling may apply to the filing deadline.[244] In every case, the court will give at least thirty days' notice of this deadline, which may be extended upon motion for cause only if such motion is filed before the deadline passes.[245] Normally, this notice is combined with the notice of the meeting of creditors.[246]

If a complaint alleging nondischargeability is not filed before this deadline, or any extension, then the claim is permanently discharged, and the deadline may be raised as a complete defense to any later dischargeability or court action, even if the creditor did not receive proper notice of the deadline.[247] The potentially harsh consequences of the time limit in a consumer case were illustrated in *In re Towers*.[248] The Illinois attorney

---

236 *See* Stokes v. Ferris, 150 B.R. 388 (W.D. Tex. 1992) (state unfair trade practice judgment found to give rise to nondischargeable debt based on willful and malicious injury as well as fraud), *aff'd*, 995 F.2d 76 (5th Cir. 1993).

237 *See* § 15.4, *supra*. *See also* National Consumer Law Center, Unfair and Deceptive Acts and Practices § 11.9 (7th ed. 2008 and Supp.).

238 *See* § 15.4.2, *supra*.

239 11 U.S.C. § 523(c).

240 Some consumer scams may come under theft by deception, a form of larceny in many states.

241 Fed. R. Bankr. P. 7001.

242 Fed. R. Bankr. P. 4007(c).

The deadline is extended to the next workday following a Saturday, Sunday, or holiday. *In re* Burns, 102 B.R. 750 (B.A.P. 9th Cir. 1989). The complaint must be properly filed by the deadline. Mere mailing by the deadline is not sufficient. *See In re* Strickland, 50 B.R. 16 (Bankr. M.D. Ala. 1985). Nor, perhaps, is filing without paying the necessary filing fee sufficient. *See In re* Smolen, 48 B.R. 633 (Bankr. N.D. Ill. 1985); § 15.4.2, *supra*.

When a bankruptcy case is dismissed and reinstated, one court has held that the sixty-day limitation period recommences on the first date, following reinstatement, set for creditors' meeting. *In re* Dunlap, 217 F.3d 311 (5th Cir. 2000).

243 Kontrick v. Ryan, 540 U.S. 443, 124 S. Ct. 906, 157 L. Ed. 2d 867 (2004) (debtor who failed to raise timeliness objection to late-filed dischargeability complaint waived the objection).

244 *See, e.g., In re* Maughan, 340 F.3d 337 (6th Cir. 2003) (bankruptcy court did not abuse its discretion in allowing creditor to file complaint three days after bar date when debtor had refused to comply with discovery); *In re* Crawford, 347 B.R. 42 (Bankr. S.D. Tex. 2006) (clerk's sending out a second scheduling notice listing erroneous bar date extended time for creditor to file complaint); *In re* Phillips, 288 B.R. 585 (Bankr. M.D. Ga. 2002) (creditor who learned after case closed that debt had been incurred by using a forged document may file dischargeability complaint after bar date); *In re* Linzer, 64 B.R. 243 (Bankr. E.D.N.Y. 2001) (granting motion to file complaint beyond bar date when debtor first gave notice of bankruptcy to creditor by mailing notice to creditor's nonbankruptcy attorney nine days before the bar date).

245 Fed. R. Bankr. P. 4007(c); *In re* Taibbi, 213 B.R. 261 (Bankr. E.D.N.Y. 1997) (county consumer protection agency that levied fine against debtor for deceptive trade practices established cause to extend filing deadline based on need to investigate more than sixty recently filed complaints).

Only a creditor, and not the trustee, is a party in interest entitled to request an extension of the deadline. *In re* Farmer, 786 F.2d 618 (4th Cir. 1986). Such a request must set forth a specific and satisfactory explanation why the creditor is unable to file a timely complaint. *In re* Englander, 92 B.R. 425 (B.A.P. 9th Cir. 1988) (complaint which failed to allege specific grounds for nondischargeability permitted when cured by amended complaint after bar date; but plaintiff's attorney sanctioned); *In re* Littell, 58 B.R. 937 (Bankr. S.D. Tex. 1986).

The court has no discretion to extend the time limit once the deadline has passed. *In re* Hill, 811 F.2d 484 (9th Cir. 1987); *In re* Brown, 102 B.R. 187 (B.A.P. 9th Cir. 1989) (court has no discretion to extend the deadline even for extraordinary circumstances such as natural disasters); *In re* Neese, 87 B.R. 609 (B.A.P. 9th Cir. 1988); *In re* Beam, 73 B.R. 434 (Bankr. S.D. Ohio 1987) (court cannot extend deadline even though an objection was timely, but erroneously, filed in an unrelated case). *But see In re* Kontrick, 295 F.3d 724 (7th Cir. 2002) (deadline subject to equitable tolling).

246 *See* Official Forms 9A–9I (reprinted in Appx. D, *infra*).

247 *In re* Green, 876 F.2d 854 (10th Cir. 1989) (actual notice of the bankruptcy filing is sufficient); *In re* Price, 871 F.2d 97 (9th Cir. 1989) (knowledge of the bankruptcy is sufficient); *In re* Alton, 837 F.2d 457 (11th Cir. 1988); Neeley v. Murchison, 815 F.2d 345 (5th Cir. 1987); *In re* Bucknum, 105 B.R. 25 (B.A.P. 9th Cir. 1989); *In re* Ricketts, 80 B.R. 495 (B.A.P. 9th Cir. 1987), *aff'd*, 951 F.2d 204 (9th Cir. 1991). *But see In re* Eliscu, 85 B.R. 480 (Bankr. N.D. Ill. 1988) (creditor with no notice of case at all not subject to deadline).

248 162 F.3d 952 (7th Cir. 1998).

general failed to raise viable nondischargeability claims based on a state UDAP judgment in a timely way. The court found that nondischargeability arguments under sections (a)(2), (4) and (6) were barred. The court also rejected the state's last ditch attempt to have the debt found nondischargeable on the alternative basis that a civil restitution order was issued under UDAP which could be found nondischargeable under section 523(a)(7) without a time limit.[249]

State court findings of fact or conclusions of law may provide a basis to collaterally estop the debtor from litigating many of the issues required to establish nondischargeability.[250]

Bankruptcy courts must frequently evaluate the degree to which a nonbankruptcy court's finding in prebankruptcy litigation addressed an element of a nondischargeability exception, such as intent to deceive or the malice behind an action.[251]

If the debt owed to the consumer is unliquidated, the bankruptcy court has jurisdiction not only to find the debt nondischargeable, but also to liquidate the debt and enter judgment.[252]

---

249 The court found that the restitution order was not payable for the benefit of a governmental unit, as required under section 523(a)(7). *See also In re* Audley, 268 B.R. 279 (Bankr. D. Kan. 2001) (judgment debt for civil penalties payable to state fund for violations of consumer protection statute nondischargeable under section 523(a)(7)), *aff'd on other grounds*, 275 B.R. 383 (B.A.P. 10th Cir. 2002).

250 *In re* Ormsby, 591 F.3d 1199 (9th Cir. 2010) (state court's finding that debtor converted office records held by title insurer was sufficient to support finding of nondischargeability for fiduciary fraud); *In re* Porter, 539 F.3d 889 (8th Cir. 2008) (willful and malicious injury nondischargeability finding based on collateral estoppel effect of prepetition sexual harassment judgment); *In re* Pancake, 106 F.3d 1242 (5th Cir. 1997) (collateral estoppel not available for Texas default judgment based on breach of fiduciary duty absent evidence of state court hearing at which creditor carried its evidentiary burden); Piccicuto v. Dwyer, 39 F.3d 37 (1st Cir. 1994) (unfair trade practice judgment under state law found nondischargeable on grounds of collateral estoppel under section 523(a)(6)); *In re* Zwanziger, 467 B.R. 475 (B.A.P. 10th Cir. 2012) (issue preclusion applied to bar creditor's claim for emotional distress damages against debtor, based on finding in prebankruptcy litigation that debtor waived claim for emotional distress damages); *In re* Stanley-Snow, 405 B.R. 11 (B.A.P. 1st Cir. 2009) (collateral estoppel applied to state court default judgment in UDAP action, conclusive on nondischargeability under section 523(a)(2)(A)); *In re* Audley, 275 B.R. 383 (B.A.P. 10th Cir. 2002) (unfair trade practice judgment based on false representations that goods were made by handicapped workers found nondischargeable on grounds of collateral estoppel under section 523(a)(2)(A)); *In re* Markarian, 228 B.R. 34 (B.A.P. 1st Cir. 1998) (finding of fraud in RICO case could be basis for collateral estoppel in dischargeability proceeding); *In re* Krishnamurthy, 209 B.R. 714, 721, 722 (B.A.P. 9th Cir. 1997) (state court judgment for fraud which included punitive damages collaterally estopped debtors defending nondischargeability claim under section 523(a)(6), because punitive damages could only be awarded in California based on wrongful acts under standard akin to section 523(a)(6)), *aff'd*, 125 F.3d 858 (9th Cir. 1997); *In re* Quansah, 2011 WL 1363992 (Bankr. E.D. Va. Apr. 11, 2011) (because prepetition punitive damages award to creditor under Virginia consumer fraud statute had to be based on finding of willfulness, award established element of intent for purposes of § 523(a)(2)(A)); *In re* Jones, 2011 WL 204326 (Bankr. E.D. Tenn. Jan. 21, 2011) (state court's finding of willful and knowing violation of Tennessee UDAP statute satisfied elements of § 523(a)(2)(A)); *In re* Peckham, 442 B.R. 62 (Bankr. D. Mass. 2010) (collateral estoppel applied to debtor's liability based upon prepetition state court judgment against debtor, but judgment not conclusive as to claim for treble damages under state UDAP law because judgment was entered by default); *In re* Miller, 403 B.R. 804 (Bankr. W.D. Mo. 2009) (finding in prebankruptcy ruling in racial discrimination action that debtor intended to cause severe emotional distress to claimant satisfied willful and malicious injury standard for nondischargeability). *See also In re* Easterberg, 2010 WL 3371091 (Bankr. D.N.M. Aug. 23, 2010) (for purposes of establishing collateral estoppel, creditor may pursue consumer claims pending in prepetition state court action; state court action involved same issues as the willful and malicious injury dischargeability action creditor brought in bankruptcy court); *In re* Porcelli, 325 B.R. 868 (Bankr. M.D. Fla. 2005) (in nondischargeability action against individual debtor, collateral estoppel effect given to judgment entered in Federal Trade Commission enforcement action for deceptive telemarketing acts against corporation controlled by debtor); *In re* Dawson, 270 B.R. 729 (Bankr. N.D. Iowa 2001) (state court judgment against debtor and her boyfriend contractor based on home improvement fraud given collateral estoppel effect); *In re* Busick, 264 B.R. 518 (Bankr. N.D. Ind. 2001) (state court findings under home improvement fraud statute sufficient to prove nondischargeability for purposes of section 523(a)(2)(A); *In re* Mannie, 258 B.R. 440 (Bankr. N.D. Cal. 2001) (judgment for wrongful employment termination nondischargeable under section 523(a)(6) based on collateral estoppel doctrine). *See* § 15.4.4, *supra*.

State agency decisions may also be given collateral estoppel effect. *See In re* Jones, 300 B.R. 133 (B.A.P. 1st Cir. 2003) (discrimination complaint resulting in state agency damage award against employer based on sexual harassment found nondischargeable on grounds of collateral estoppel under section 523(a)(6)). *But see In re* Barboza, 545 F.3d 702 (9th Cir. 2008) (prepetition judgment did not address maliciousness element separately from willfulness, so not preclusive for section 523(a)(6) purposes); *In re* Mater, 335 B.R. 264 (Bankr. D.N.H. 2005) (state agency employment discrimination decision is not equivalent of a finding under section 523(a)(6) of willful and malicious injury).

251 *See, e.g., In re* Bradley, 446 B.R. 582 (B.A.P. 1st Cir. 2012) (record from prebankruptcy state court proceeding did not establish intent to cause injury, an element of § 523(a)(6) discharge exception).

252 *In re* Ungar, 633 F.3d 675 (8th Cir. 2011) (circuit courts have "unanimously" concluded that in addition to declaring a debt nondischargeable, a bankruptcy court has jurisdiction to liquidate a debt and enter a monetary judgment against the debtor); *In re* Riebesell, 586 F.3d 782 (10th Cir. 2009) (bankruptcy court had jurisdiction to enter money judgment against debtor attorney for amount of debt owed to client and to find debt nondischargeable); *In re* Morrison, 555 F.3d 473 (5th Cir. 2009) (bankruptcy court has authority to declare debt nondischargeable because incurred through false financial statements, to liquidate debt, and to enter judgment); *In re* Sasson, 424 F.3d 864 (9th Cir. 2005) (bankruptcy court had jurisdiction to enter money judgment in nondischargeability adversary proceeding even though no prepetition judgment had been entered on debt in state court proceeding); *In re* Kennedy, 108 F.3d 1015 (9th Cir. 1997) (fraud debt owed to consumer creditors by real estate broker properly liquidated and reduced to judgment in the bankruptcy court); *In re* McLaren, 3 F.3d 958 (6th Cir. 1993); *In re* Deitz, 469 B.R. 11 (B.A.P. 9th Cir. 2012) (rejecting argument that Supreme Court's *Stern v. Marshall* ruling affected bankruptcy courts' authority to enter a money judgment in a nondischargeability proceeding. *See* Cohen v. de la Cruz, 523 U.S. 213, 118 S. Ct. 1212, 140 L. Ed. 21d 341 (1998) (bankruptcy court found rent overcharge

When there is a basis for fee-shifting under nonbankruptcy law related to enforcement of the underlying claim, some courts have held that this fee-shifting should apply to an action to obtain a determination of nondischargeability of the claim in bankruptcy court.[253]

Sometimes complex procedural issues arise because a debt may be nondischargeable if it is not scheduled by the debtor.[254] This is a limited exception to the discharge that is covered in another section of this treatise.[255] Failure to list consumer claims based on fraud or breach of fiduciary duty or failure to notify consumers of a bankruptcy case is a common problem that may impede protecting consumer rights. Nevertheless, if the consumer has actual notice of the bankruptcy, the deadlines for objecting to discharge discussed above will apply and the exception to discharge for unscheduled claims will not.[256]

18.5.4.3 Chapter 13

The 2005 amendments eliminated several of the advantages that the chapter 13 discharge formerly held over its chapter 7 counterpart. Debts incurred through fraud or false pretenses[257] and debts arising from fraud as a fiduciary, embezzlement, or larceny[258] are now nondischargeable in chapter 13. However, the creditor must still seek a formal determination of nondischargeability within sixty days after the first date set for meeting of creditors, or these debts will be discharged. The chapter 13 discharge of debts for willful and malicious injury[259] has been limited. Under new section 1328(a)(4), the discharge will not apply to debts for restitution or damages awarded in a civil action against the debtor as a result of willful or malicious personal injury or death the debtor caused to an individual.[260] Thus, debts for willful and malicious injury to property are still dischargeable in chapter 13, as are debts for personal injury that have not been liquidated in a civil action. The other significant category of debts that are nondischargeable in chapter 7 but that will be discharged as provided for in the chapter 13 plan are debts incurred in a divorce or separation as a property settlement or division of marital property.[261]

If obtaining a determination of nondischargeability is not possible for some reason, another possible consumer strategy when someone is using a chapter 13 filing to discharge particularly heinous conduct, is to move for dismissal[262] or object to confirmation of the chapter 13 plan on the basis of the absence of good faith.[263] In *In re Smith*,[264] a home repair operator, who had fleeced senior citizens by making unnecessary repairs and had been found liable subsequently for more than $40,000, filed under chapter 13. While the judgment debts would not have been dischargeable in a chapter 7 because of the home repair operator's fraudulent conduct, they would have been dischargeable in this pre-2005 chapter 13 case. The debts from the judgments amounted to about half of his total indebtedness. In the chapter 13 plan, Smith proposed to pay $600 over a five-year period toward his total unsecured obligations of about $80,000 (including the $40,000 owed the consumers he bilked). In reversing confirmation of Smith's chapter 13 plan, the court held that the nature of the debts and the timing of the bankruptcy could be considered in determining the good faith of the filing. The decision recommended that the debts arising from illegal activity be required to have a higher payout.[265]

Any party in interest may object to confirmation of a chapter 13 plan.[266] Creditors will receive at least twenty-eight days' notice of the time in which to file objections to the plan.[267] Objections to confirmation must be filed with the court and served on the debtor, the trustee and any other entity designated by the court.[268] Objections are considered contested matters.[269]

18.5.4.4 Corporate or Partnership Debtors

Corporations or partnerships in chapter 7 are not granted a discharge.[270] This exception to discharge is rarely of any value to creditors because a corporation or partnership is unlikely to start up again after going through a chapter 7. However, state law rules concerning successor liability of corporations should be carefully scrutinized. In some cases when corporations are merged or sold in the liquidation process, the successor entity

---

claim of tenants was nondischargeable, and liquidated the claim for treble damages and attorney fees, findings were affirmed by the Court of Appeals for the Third Circuit; the Supreme Court did not review the issue of liquidating the claim amount). *See also In re* Santos, 304 B.R. 639 (Bankr. D.N.J. 2004) (finding district and state courts have greater expertise in evaluating damages in personal injury matters, court declined to liquidate nondischargeable debt).

253 *In re* Haun, 396 B.R. 522 (Bankr. D. Idaho 2008). *See also In re* Dinan, 448 B.R. 775 (B.A.P. 9th Cir. 2011) (applying nonbankruptcy law, prevailing creditor entitled to award of attorney's fees and costs incurred in dischargeability action). *But see In re* Wilkerson, 2010 WL 432252 (Bankr. D. Ill. Feb. 1, 2010) (state law fee-shifting statute does not control assessment of fees to prevailing party in dischargeability action).
254 11 U.S.C. § 523(a)(3).
255 *See* § 15.4.3, *supra*.
256 *See id.*
257 11 U.S.C. § 523(a)(2).
258 11 U.S.C. § 523(a)(4).
259 11 U.S.C. § 523(a)(6).
260 11 U.S.C. § 1328(a)(4). *See generally In re* Chacon, 438 B.R. 725 (Bankr. D.N.M. 2010) (allowing state court civil action for sexual assault to proceed against debtor in order to determine whether claim subject to § 1328(a)(4) existed).
261 11 U.S.C. § 523(a)(15).
262 *In re* Mattson, 241 B.R. 629 (Bankr. D. Minn. 1999) (landlord's chapter 13 dismissed for bad faith, in light of prepetition race discrimination, and fact that bankruptcy was intended primarily to delay payment of nondischargeable judgment in favor of tenants).
263 *See* §§ 12.3.3–12.3.5, *supra*.
264 848 F.2d 813 (7th Cir. 1988). *See also In re* Goddard, 212 B.R. 233 (D.N.J. 1997) (bankruptcy court erred by failing to treat debtor's pre-filing misconduct as relevant to a determination of good faith based on the totality of the circumstances).
265 848 F.2d 813 (7th Cir. 1988).
266 11 U.S.C. § 1324.
267 Fed. R. Bankr. P. 2002(b).
268 Fed. R. Bankr. P. 3020(b)(1).
269 Fed. R. Bankr. P. 3020(b)(1), 9014. *See* § 1.4.2, *supra*.
270 11 U.S.C. § 727(a)(1).

will have some liability on the prior corporation's undischarged obligations.[271]

Corporate or partnership debtors in chapter 12 are treated the same as individual debtors.[272] They are thus subject to the exceptions from discharge of section 523. Corporations or partnerships may be granted a discharge in chapter 11 and generally are not subject to the exceptions of section 523.[273] The 2005 amendments created a limited exception to the corporate discharge. It applies to debts for fraud as defined by section 523(a)(2)(A) (false pretenses, false representations, or actual fraud) or section 523(a)(2)(B) (materially false written financial statements) owed to a "domestic governmental unit" and for debts owed to any "person" for a fraud debt owed under the Federal False Claims Act or similar state statute.[274] Individual debtors in chapter 11 are subject to the discharge exceptions of section 523(a).[275]

An increasingly common issue is whether liability for an undiscovered tort arises prepetition even if there is no manifestation of injury until after the case is filed or completed. Although there is a split of authority, several courts have held that such liability may not be discharged as a prepetition claim under the Code's definition of claim, especially when the injured parties could have had no knowledge of their relationship to the debtor while the bankruptcy case was pending.[276]

Related issues arise when a debtor engages in a pattern of conduct that results in separate prepetition and postpetition claims. One court has held in a case evaluating claims under the Americans with Disabilities Act, that an employer's postbankruptcy denials of accommodation may be actionable even though the initial denial of accommodation took place prior to bankruptcy and gave rise to a discharged claim.[277]

In the meantime, Congress has ratified the practice of some courts that had confirmed plans transferring liability for undiscovered claims in certain circumstances to trusts for the benefit of potential claimants established under the plan.[278] The circumstances in which such trusts tend to be established are those in which a corporation files bankruptcy knowing of significant potential liabilities, such as asbestos related health claims, before all potential claimants may have manifest symptoms.

18.5.5 The Consumer Priority

Section 507(a)(7) of the Bankruptcy Code provides certain consumers with priority as creditors in bankruptcy proceedings.[279] Consumer creditors are given a seventh priority after claims made by six other categories of preferred creditors.[280] The consumer priority gives individual creditors priority for claims in the amount of $2600 for any prebankruptcy deposit of money made in connection with the purchase, lease or rental of property or services intended for personal, family or household use, when the goods or services were not delivered or provided.[281] The priority is only available to individuals and is not available for corporations or partnerships.[282] Priority status is

---

271 *See, e.g.*, Lemelle v. Universal Mfg. Corp., 18 F.3d 1268 (5th Cir. 1994) (successor corporation found to have liability under both Alabama and Delaware law). *Cf. In re* Nat'l Gypsum Co., 219 F.3d 478 (5th Cir. 2000) (successor corporation not liable).

272 11 U.S.C. § 1228.
   See § 17.7, *supra*, for a discussion of the chapter 12 discharge.

273 11 U.S.C. § 1141 (d)(1); Rederford v. U.S. Airways, Inc., 589 F.3d 30 (1st Cir. 2009) (discharge order from employer's chapter 11 case bars former employee's ADA action for equitable relief in the form of job reinstatement even though she was not seeking monetary damages); Jaurdon v. Cricket Communications, Inc., 412 F.3d 1156 (10th Cir. 2005) (employees who failed to file proofs of claim after receiving notice of employer's chapter 11 case and whose race discrimination claims were therefore discharged by the confirmation order could not proceed with appeal in discrimination case). *But see In re* Sanchez, 659 F.3d 671 (8th Cir. 2011) (employment discrimination claim against chapter 11 debtor accruing after deadline for submission of non-administrative expense claims not discharged under confirmation order).
   However, no discharge is granted if the plan amounts to a liquidation, close of business, or if the debtor could have been denied a discharge if the case had been filed under chapter 7. 11 U.S.C. § 1141(d)(3). A fuller discussion of chapter 11 procedures together with some potential opportunities to protect the rights of consumer creditors in chapter 11 cases can be found in § 18.7, *infra*.

274 11 U.S.C. § 1141(d)(6).
275 11 U.S.C. § 1141(d)(2).
276 *In re* Grossman's, Inc., 607 F.3d 114 (3d Cir. 2010) (asbestos-related claim arose when individual was exposed prepetition, even though injury manifested itself postpetition); *In re* SNTL Corp., 571 F.3d 26 (9th Cir. 2009) (claim arises when claimant can fairly or reasonably contemplate the claim's existence, even if claim not yet accrued under nonbankruptcy law); Lemelle v. Universal Mfg. Corp., 18 F.3d 1268 (5th Cir. 1994). *See also In re* Wheeler, 137 F.3d 299 (5th Cir. 1998) (attorney's malpractice in preparing the bankruptcy petition occurred before the bankruptcy filing so that claim for malpractice was property of the estate); Republic Bank & Trust Co., 444 B.R. 728 (W.D. Ky. 2011) (legal malpractice claim against debtor attorney discharged where malpractice occurred prepetition but injury to claimant occurred postpetition). *Cf.* Jones v. Chemetron Corp., 212 F.3d 199 (3d Cir. 2000); Grady v. A.H. Robins Co., 839 F.2d 198 (4th Cir. 1988) (prepetition claim arises when the conduct giving rise to the tort occurs even if there is no manifestation prepetition). *But see* Wright v. Owens Corning, 679 F.3d 101 (3d Cir. 2012) (*Grossman* ruling applicable only to cases confirmed after date of the decision, clarifying ruling to mean that a claim arises when a party is exposed to the product or conduct of the debtor at any time up to date of plan confirmation). *See generally In re* Huffy Corp., 424 B.R. 295 (Bankr. S.D. Ohio 2010) (noting three current approaches to treatment of time of accrual of bankruptcy claim: (1) when right to payment arose under state law; (2) a "time of the conduct" approach, which disregards when claimant detected the injury; and (3) the approach adopted by the court—the "relationship/fair contemplation approach" which looks at the conduct plus some relationship or contact with claimant such that injury was fairly contemplated by the parties at the time); § 15.5.1, *supra*.

277 O'Loghlin v. County of Orange, 229 F.3d 871 (9th Cir. 2000).
278 11 U.S.C. § 524(g)(1).
279 11 U.S.C. § 507(a)(7).
280 11 U.S.C. § 507(a)(1)–(6).
281 11 U.S.C. § 507(a)(7).
   The amount of the consumer priority is adjusted for inflation every three years. 11 U.S.C. § 104. For cases filed between April 1, 2001 and March 31, 2004, the amount of the priority was $2100.
282 Lawyers Edition, Bankruptcy Serv. § 21.265 at 87 (1981); *In re* Carolina Sales Corp., 43 B.R. 596, 597 (Bankr. E.D.N.C. 1984). *See also In re* Elsinghorst Bros. Co., 180 B.R. 52 (individual members'

especially important in chapter 11, 12 or 13 cases because the plan must pay priority claims in full.[283]

Prior to the adoption of the Code, consumer creditors who could not persuade the bankruptcy court to return deposits paid to bankrupt retailers on some theory such as constructive trust were relegated to unsecured creditor status.[284] The bankruptcies of large retailers such as W.T. Grant, which gave rise to numerous claims by consumers who had given the debtor deposits without being aware that those deposits were not specifically held by the retailer for refund, prompted Congress to act.[285] Commentary by consumer advocates earlier in the decade brought this problem to the attention of the public and Congress.[286] Subsequent commentary explained that a consumer priority was necessary because consumers who did not have the resources to conduct credit checks on retailers before making consumer deposits could not have avoided losses in the bankruptcy of large retailers.[287] Congress met these problems by providing for a consumer priority.[288]

The few reported cases to consider issues pertaining to the consumer priority provisions of the Bankruptcy Code have read section 507(a)(7) broadly.[289] Each member of a household or family has a separate $2600 maximum; the family or household is not limited to one priority claim.[290] Courts have interpreted the term "deposit" broadly, to include any payment of money by consumers who had not yet received full performance from the bankrupt seller. This includes situations in which the consumer paid in full, rather than in part,[291] and cases in which the consumer received some of the goods or services.[292] Arguably the priority could also extend to payments by consumers when the merchant attempted delivery of goods or services, but when the consumer has substantial warranty or contract claims such that the merchant's "delivery" could be considered defective or invalid.[293]

Courts have found this priority applicable to a wide variety of transactions, encompassing even transactions that would not ordinarily be considered consumer transactions. The purchase of a yacht for personal use in a lease/purchase transaction has been held to give rise to a consumer priority.[294] Similarly, a transaction in which a wholesale distributor of appliances promoted sales by arranging free trips for participating retailers and allowing individuals to participate in the trips by purchasing tickets, has also been held to fall within section 507(a)(7) (formerly section 506(a)(6)).[295] In yet another case, in recognizing a consumer priority for deposits given to a residential home builder, the court concluded that Congress did not intend to limit section 507(a)(7) to transactions with retail merchants.[296] And courts have held that the consumer deposit priority applies to security deposits posted by residential tenants.[297] This is likely to be the best potential result if the

---

claims asserted on their behalf by a religious society treated as a priority).

283 11 U.S.C. §§ 1129(a)(9)(B), 1222(a)(2), 1322(a)(2).

284 *Proposed Amendments to the Bankruptcy Act: Hearings on H.R. 31 and 32 Before the Subcomm. on Civil & Constitutional Rights of the House Comm. on the Judiciary*, 94th Cong., Series 27, pt. 3, at 1188 (1976).

285 *Id.*; 4 Collier on Bankruptcy ¶ 507.08[1] (16th ed.); H.R. Rep. No. 95-595, at 188 (1977).

286 *See, e.g.*, Schrag & Ratner, *Caveat Emptor—Empty Coffer: The Bankruptcy Law Has Nothing to Offer*, 72 Colum. L. Rev. 1147 (1972).

287 *See, e.g.*, Carroll, *Priorities & Subordination*, 17 Hous. L. Rev. 223, 235 (1979).

288 4 Collier on Bankruptcy ¶ 507.08[1] (16th ed.); H.R. Rep. No. 95-595, at 188 (1977).

289 *In re* Tart's T.V., Furniture & Appliance Co., 165 B.R. 171 (Bankr. E.D.N.C. 1994) (lump sum payments made for unfulfilled extended warranties give rise to consumer priority claims to the extent of covered repairs as limited by the amount of the available priority); *In re* Terra Distrib. Co., 148 B.R. 598 (Bankr. D. Idaho) (same). *See also In re* Utility Craft, Inc., 2008 WL 5429667 (Bankr. M.D.N.C. Dec. 29, 2008) (store credit given customer who returned defective furniture not entitled to consumer priority under section 507(a)(7)). *But see In re* Four Star Fin. Servs., 469 B.R. 30 (C.D. Cal. 2012) (reversing allowance of class consumer priority claim for payments for campground membership fees; initial fee purchased membership and was not a deposit to be applied toward payment for future services); *In re* Palmas del Mar Country Club, Inc., 443 B.R. 569 (Bankr. D. P.R. 2010) (fee for membership in country club, although labeled "deposit" in agreement, not analogous to deposit to be applied to purchase of item within purview of consumer priority); *In re* Heritage Vill. Church, 137 B.R. 888 (Bankr. D.S.C. 1991) (donator/purchasers of time-share at Heritage U.S.A. not entitled to consumer priority status because, having already satisfied their obligation by completing the purchases, their funds were not "deposits" under section 507(a)(6) (now section 507(a)(7))).

290 *In re* Cont'l Country Club, 64 B.R. 177 (Bankr. M.D. Fla. 1986); *In re* James R. Corbitt Co., 48 B.R. 937 (Bankr. E.D. Va. 1985).

291 *In re* Salazar, 430 F.3d 992 (9th Cir. 2005) (customer who paid full price in advance for swimming pool construction that was never completed prepetition paid a "deposit" entitled to the consumer priority); *In re* Deangelis Tangibles, Inc., 238 B.R. 96 (M.D. Pa. 1999); *In re* Kuers, 409 B.R. 768 (Bankr. E.D.N.C. 2009) (priority for deposit paid toward purchase of car through eBay); *In re* WW Warehouse, Inc., 313 B.R. 588 (Bankr. D. Del. 2004) (priority applied to claims against debtor who sold gift certificates for its business, then filed for bankruptcy before the certificates were redeemed); *In re* Terra Distrib., Inc., 148 B.R. 598 (Bankr. D. Idaho 1992); *In re* Longo, 144 B.R. 305 (Bankr. D. Md. 1992); *In re* Carolina Sales Corp., 43 B.R. 596 (Bankr. E.D.N.C. 1984).

292 *In re* River Vill. Assocs., 161 B.R. 127 (Bankr. E.D. Pa. 1993), *aff'd*, 181 B.R. 795 (E.D. Pa. 1995); *In re* Longo 144 B.R. 305 (Bankr. D. Md. 1992).

293 *See In re* Longo, 144 B.R. 305 (Bankr. D. Md. 1992) (trade school students who did not receive training they paid for).

294 *In re* CSY Yacht Corp., 34 B.R. 215 (Bankr. M.D. Fla. 1983).

295 *In re* Carolina Sales Corp., 43 B.R. 596 (Bankr. E.D.N.C. 1984).

296 *See also In re* Cont'l Country Club, 64 B.R. 177 (Bankr. M.D. Fla. 1986) (down payment on purchase of a mobile home entitled to priority); *In re* James R. Corbitt Co., 48 B.R. 937 (Bankr. E.D. Va. 1985). *Cf. In re* Mickelson, 192 B.R. 516 (Bankr. D.N.D. 1996) (purchase of grain drying equipment from seed company is not for personal, family or household use), *aff'd*, 205 B.R. 190 (D.N.D. 1996). *But see In re* Glass, 203 B.R. 61 (Bankr. W.D. Va. 1996) (advance payment on purchase of real property structured by the consumer in the form of a loan to the sellers does not qualify as a deposit).

297 Guarracino v. Hoffman, 246 B.R. 130 (D. Mass. 2000) (security deposit entitled to priority; damages related to mishandling security deposit are not); *In re* River Vill. Assocs., 161 B.R. 127 (Bankr. E.D. Pa. 1993), *aff'd on other grounds*, 181 B.R. 795 (E.D. Pa.

deposits have not been segregated and cannot be considered property that is not property of the estate, as discussed above.[298] Finally, students at a vocational school are considered consumers whose contract for lessons is a purchase of services under section 507(a)(7).[299]

A consumer claims a section 507(a)(7) priority at the time the proof of claim is filed.[300] The claim is then deemed allowed unless the debtor in possession, trustee, or a party in interest, such as another creditor, objects to the claim.[301] Upon such objection, after notice and hearing, the court rules on the objection.[302]

18.5.6 Equitable Subordination

Bankruptcy courts possess the power to prevent the consummation of a claimant's fraudulent or otherwise inequitable course of conduct by subordinating that creditor's claims to the claims of other creditors.[303] This principle of equitable subordination is now codified in 11 U.S.C. § 510(c), but it was first developed by the courts.[304] Consumer creditors may be able to use these principles to get their claims paid before the claims of secured or priority creditors in some situations.

Three conditions must be generally be satisfied before equitable subordination of a claim is justified.[305] First, the creditor against whom subordination is sought must have engaged in some sort of inequitable conduct.[306] Transferring assets out of the bankrupt corporation without a fair return to the corporation, undercapitalizing the corporation, or insider selling of property to the corporation at inflated prices are all examples of such conduct. Claims of officers, directors, principal shareholders and other fiduciaries, and their immediate families are subject to special scrutiny, because of the potential for abuse of these positions.[307] If an objection to a fiduciary's claim has some substantial factual basis, then the fiduciary has the burden to show the transaction's good faith and its benefit to the corporation.[308] The inequitable conduct need not be related to the claim asserted; rather, any unfair act by the claimant that decreases the other creditors' recovery in the bankruptcy may warrant equitable subordination.[309] Given the active market in transfer of claims related to many corporate liquidations, the subordination doctrine has been applied to assignees of claims despite their assertions that they took the assignments in good faith.[310]

The second condition that must be shown is that the misconduct resulted in injury to the other creditors or conferred an unfair advantage on the claimant.[311] The claim should be subordinated to the extent necessary to offset the harm caused to the debtor and other creditors.[312] But if the amount of the claim exceeds the harm caused, then only part of the claim will

---

1995). *See also* Gaertner v. Romanus (*In re* Romanus), 1998 Bankr. LEXIS 397 (Bankr. W.D. Pa. Apr. 3, 1998) (security deposit and first month rent payment entitled to consumer priority when the debtor/landlord failed to deliver the property in habitable condition). *But see In re* Cimaglia, 50 B.R. 9 (Bankr. S.D. Fla. 1985) (security deposits not within scope of priority for consumer deposits).

298 *See* § 18.5.2, *supra*.
299 *In re* Longo, 144 B.R. 305 (Bankr. D. Md. 1992).
    For discussion of class proofs of claim in this and other cases, see § 18.4.2, *supra*.
300 11 U.S.C. § 501; Fed. R. Bankr. P. 3001.
301 11 U.S.C. § 502; Fed. R. Bankr. P. 3007.
302 11 U.S.C. § 502(b). *See In re* CSY Yacht Corp., 34 B.R. 215 (Bankr. M.D. Fla. 1983).
303 11 U.S.C. § 510(c); Heiser v. Woodruff, 327 U.S. 726, 66 S. Ct. 853, 90 L. Ed. 970 (1946); Pepper v. Litton, 308 U.S. 295, 60 S. Ct. 238, 84 L. Ed. 281 (1939).
304 4 Collier on Bankruptcy ¶ 510.05 (16th ed.). *See* 11 U.S.C. § 510(c).
305 *See In re* Mobile Steel Co., 563 F.2d 692 (5th Cir. 1977); 4 Collier on Bankruptcy ¶ 510.05 (16th ed.).
306 *In re* Mobile Steel Co., 563 F.2d 692 (5th Cir. 1977); *In re* Forest Street, L.L.C., 409 B.R. 543 (Bankr. D. Mass. 2009) (creditor/lender's misrepresentations in leading debtor into loans with onerous terms constituted inequitable conduct, justifying subordination of lender's claim to those of all general unsecured creditors). *See also In re* Sentinel Mgmt. Group, Inc., 689 F.3d 855 (7th Cir. 2012) (non-insider bank that made undercapitalized prepetition loan to debtor did not engage in sufficiently egregious conduct to trigger equitable subordination of its secured claim); *In re* Rabex of Colo., Inc., 226 B.R. 905 (D. Colo. 1998) (claim based on veil piercing theory against debtor could not be equitably subordinated to claims of other creditors because creditor that pierced corporate veil to obtain claim committed no inequitable conduct). *See generally In re*

QuVis, 446 B.R. 490 (Bankr. D. Kan. 2011) (discussing standard for inequitable conduct required to support claim for subordination, rejecting effort to subordinate insider's claim), *aff'd*, 469 B.R. 353 (D. Kan. 2012).

307 *In re* Racing Servs., 571 F.3d 729 (8th Cir. 2009) (applying equitable subordination to administrative expense claim of sole shareholder of debtor company after her criminal conviction resulted in forfeiture and seizure of company assets); *In re* Advanced Modular Power Sys., Inc., 413 B.R. 643, 677 (Bankr. S.D. Tex. 2009) (equitable subordination applied based on finding of stockholder's breach of fiduciary duty in conversion of debtor corporation's assets), *aff'd*, 2009 WL 7760300 (S.D. Tex. Dec. 30, 2009); *In re* Kreisler, 331 B.R. 364 (Bankr. N.D. Ill. 2005) (equitable subordination applied to claim filed by new corporation set up by insiders and family members of principles seeking to maximize their recovery from bankruptcy estate). *See also* Pepper v. Litton, 308 U.S. 295, 60 S. Ct. 238, 84 L. Ed. 281 (1939); *In re* Multipanics, Inc., 622 F.2d 709 (5th Cir. 1980); *In re* Southwest Equip. Rental, Inc., 193 B.R. 276 (E.D. Tenn. 1996) (finding special obligations of insider officers and directors when employees suffer the harm).

308 *In re* Mobile Steel Co., 563 F.2d 692 (5th Cir. 1977); *In re* Broadstripe, L.L.C., 444 B.R. 51 (Bankr. D. Del. 2010) (creditor failed to rebut claims of inequitable conduct as insider).

309 *Id.*; *In re* Herby's Foods, Inc., 2 F.3d 128 (5th Cir. 1993) (insider creditors' conduct in seeking to buy out undercapitalized company to their own advantage warranted equitable subordination to other unsecured creditor's claims); *In re* Mahan, 373 B.R. 177 (Bankr. M.D. Fla. 2007) (equitable subordination applied to claim for loan repayment that debtors had assigned to insiders to the detriment of other creditors).

310 *In re* Enron Corp., 333 B.R. 205 (Bankr. S.D.N.Y. 2005).

311 *In re* Mobile Steel Co., 563 F.2d 692 (5th Cir. 1977); *In re* Westgate-California Corp., 642 F.2d 1174 (9th Cir. 1981); *In re* Northstar Dev. Corp., 465 B.R. 6 (Bankr. W.D.N.Y. 2012) (equitable subordination applied to corporate officer whose claim for his contributions to corporation would have represented over 95% of all unsecured claims filed).

312 *In re* Mobile Steel Co., 563 F.2d 692 (5th Cir. 1977).

be subordinated, as the purpose of equitable subordination is to do justice among the creditors, not to punish the wrongdoer.[313]

Finally, courts have held that equitable subordination of the claim must not be inconsistent with other provisions of the Bankruptcy Code.[314] Two Supreme Court cases concluded that courts are not authorized to adjust claims of creditors who have not engaged in inequitable conduct in contravention of the scheme of priorities outlined by Congress.[315] This overrules a line of cases in which IRS penalty claims were subordinated, without fault, to claims of other creditors that had suffered actual losses.[316]

A related but distinct equitable remedy, the "recharacterization" of a claim, has been utilized by a number of courts to correct the inequities generated by questionable lending practices in troubled companies headed for chapter 11.[317] Under this judicially created doctrine the courts deny "claim" status to certain insider loans, treating them instead as equity investments in the debtor company. The recharacterization effectively deprives the claimant of any priority and, most likely, of any distribution at all. If the alleged debt is recharacterized as an equity contribution, equitable subordination does not come into play. There is no "claim" to subordinate.[318]

18.5.7 Seeking Defendants Not in Bankruptcy

In addition to pursuing claims against the party in bankruptcy, the consumer's attorney should explore whether there may be other parties not in bankruptcy who can be held liable.[319] Whether the consumer's claims involve torts, contracts or violations of consumer protection statutes, there are a variety of theories for holding the following liable:

- Agents, such as sales personnel and advertising agencies;[320]
- Principals and co-venturers, such as corporations and other business entities;[321]
- Directors, officers, and owners, parent corporations, franchisors;
- Third parties offering the means or assisting in tortious or deceptive schemes;[322]
- Assignees in sales and service transactions and related third-party creditors;
- Secured creditors or investors who financed the venture;[323]
- Bonding companies and other insurers.[324]

Consumer advocates have employed a number of these theories to hold accountable various parties involved in mortgage lending abuses that led to the recent foreclosure crisis.[325] When tenants' claims are concerned, it is possible in some circumstances to hold a non-bankrupt secured creditor responsible for essential services or for injuries due to failure to maintain the property. This should always be possible after foreclosure if the secured creditor has become the owner,[326] but also if the lender has status as mortgagee in possession under state law or if the facts establish that the landlord has control over the property.[327]

---

313 *In re* Westgate-California Corp., 642 F.2d 1174 (9th Cir. 1981).
314 *In re* Mobile Steel Co., 563 F.2d 692 (5th Cir. 1977).
315 United States v. Reorganized CF & I Fabricators of Utah, Inc., 518 U.S. 213, 116 S. Ct. 2106, 135 L. Ed. 2d 506 (1996); United States v. Noland, 517 U.S. 535, 116 S. Ct. 1524, 134 L. Ed. 2d 748 (1996).
316 *See* 4 Collier on Bankruptcy ¶ 510.05[2], at 510–15 (16th ed.). *See also In re* Friedman's, Inc., 356 B.R. 766 (Bankr. S.D. Ga. 2006) (class claim for violation of UDAP statute which sought penalty damages was subject to binding chapter 11 plan which subordinated such claims, but would not be equitably subordinated to the extent it sought statutory minimum damages of $200 per consumer).
317 *In re* Lothian Oil, Inc., 650 F.3d 539 (5th Cir. 2011) (bankruptcy courts have authority under § 502(b) to apply state law to recharacterize claim, and can recharacterize claim of non-insider); *In re* Airadigm Communications, Inc., 616 F.3d 642 (7th Cir. 2010) (because recharacterization addresses whether claim exists at all, analysis for recharacterization precedes consideration of equitable subordination of claim). *See* Official Comm. of Unsecured Creditors for Dorneir Aviation, Inc. v. Plan Monitoring Comm., 453 F.3d 225 (4th Cir. 2006); *In re* Submicron Corp., 432 F.3d 448 (3d Cir. 2006); *In re* Repository Technologies, Inc., 381 B.R. 852 (N.D. Ill. 2008) (recharacterization imposed on portion of chief executive officer's claim for repayment of unauthorized advances he made to debtor company). *But see* Daewoo Motor Am., Inc., 471 B.R. 721 (Bankr. C.D. Cal. 2012) (denying recharacterization where loan from insiders included fixed maturity date and rate of interest, indicating this was not a disguised equity contribution).
318 *In re* AutoStyle Plastics, Inc., 269 F.3d 726, 748 (6th Cir. 2001).
319 No stay would apply automatically to such claims except as to codebtors in chapter 12 and 13. *See* § 9.4.5, *supra*. Requests for non-automatic stays as to non-debtor parties in such situations are normally denied. *See* § 9.4.7, *supra*.
320 *See* Dewitt v. Daley, 336 B.R. 552 (S.D. Fla. 2006) (former employees could pursue Fair Labor Standards Act claim for overtime pay against debtor employer's manager, a non-debtor, who was liable under labor statute and not subject to protection of bankruptcy stay).
321 In such cases involving corporations it may be necessary to pierce the corporate veil. *See* § 18.5.2.1, *supra*.
322 *See, e.g., In re* Irwin, 457 B.R. 413 (Bankr. E.D. Pa. 2011) (automatic stay does not bar receiver from proceeding in state court against debtor's family members who received proceeds from Ponzi scheme organized by debtor). A civil conspiracy claim may be a useful tool to pursue such third parties. *See* Williams v. Aetna Fin. Co., 700 N.E.3d 859 (Ohio 1998); National Consumer Law Center Foreclosures Ch. 6 (4th ed. 2012) (discussing theories for liability of various participants in schemes related to securitization of predatory mortgage loans).
323 *See Case History: Recovering Consumer Deposits From a Bankrupt Furniture Store*, 10 NCLC REPORTS *Bankruptcy and Foreclosures Ed.* 41 (Mar./Apr. 1992).
324 These theories are discussed in National Consumer Law Center, Unfair and Deceptive Acts and Practices Ch. 11 (7th ed. 2008 and Supp.). *See also* Golann, *In Search of Deeper Pockets: Theories of Extended Liability*, 17 Mass. L. Rev. 114 (1986).
325 *See* National Consumer Law Center, Unfair and Deceptive Acts and Practices Ch. 11 (7th ed. 2008 and Supp.); National Consumer Law Center, Mortgage Lending Ch. 10 (1st ed. 2012); National Consumer Law Center, Foreclosures Ch. 4 (4th ed. 2012).
326 *See* National Consumer Law Center, Foreclosures § 16.8 (4th ed. 2012).
327 *See, e.g.*, McCorristin v. Salmon Signs, 582 A.2d 1271 (N.J. Super. Ct. App. Div. 1990) (mortgagee in possession steps into shoes of landlord); Thornhill v. Ronnie's I-45 Truck Stop, Inc., 944 S.W.2d

A related strategy for making a secured creditor responsible for building maintenance in the bankruptcy process is to assert an administrative claim for payment ahead of the secured creditor. This strategy is discussed in § 18.5.3, *supra*.

18.5.8 Rule 2004 Examinations

Section 343 of the Code provides for examination of the debtor at the meeting of creditors. Federal Rule of Bankruptcy Procedure 2004 goes beyond this provision, and allows the examination of *any entity* on motion of any party in interest,[328] as well as the production of documents. Rule 2004 examinations may help consumer creditors discover hidden assets or challenge dischargeability.

The scope of Rule 2004 is the same as section 343: examination must relate to the "acts, conduct or property or to the financial condition of the debtor," to "any matter which may effect the administration of the debtor's estate," or to "the debtor's right to a discharge."[329] Information is subject to discovery if it "fairly tends to establish something which may become important in the administration of the estate."[330] Local practice for requesting a Rule 2004 examination varies. In some courts it is requested *ex parte*, with the party to be examined having a right to quash the subpoena. In other courts, it is requested by a noticed motion.[331] United States Trustees have used Rule 2004 examinations with increasing frequency as a tool to investigate collection practices of mortgage servicers. The courts have consistently rejected the servicers' attempts to oppose these examinations.[332]

Depending on the thoroughness of the debtor's schedules and the examination of the debtor at the meeting of creditors, a Rule 2004 deposition may be useful in discovering hidden assets of the debtor. Some consumer creditors, such as tenants, may be aware of assets that the debtor has failed to disclose. Consumers should go over the debtor's schedules carefully and look for assets that might not be accurately reported. A consumer may also use Rule 2004 to see if trust funds have been converted to other property.[333]

An important aspect of Bankruptcy Rule 2004 is its application to "any entity," rather than just the debtor. Thus, in a chapter 11 proceeding, any officer of a debtor corporation is subject to deposition. Another important use is establishing fraudulent conduct necessary to challenge dischargeability. For instance, while the schedules may reveal the debtor's financial condition at the time the petition was filed, Rule 2004 makes it possible to discover the debtor's prepetition finances. This may enable a consumer to show that the debtor incurred a debt by fraud.[334] Finally, Rule 2004 may be useful in investigating grounds for equitable subordination of claims.[335]

18.6 In Forma Pauperis

18.6.1 Need for Consumers As Creditors to Proceed In Forma Pauperis

Once a bankruptcy petition is filed, there is no fee for debtors to file motions or adversary proceedings in bankruptcy court.[336] For creditors and other parties who are not debtors, however, there are fees—$293 to file a complaint, and $176 for a motion for relief from the stay.[337] When low-income persons are creditors or are otherwise parties in bankruptcy proceedings, such as when a landlord is in bankruptcy, they may need to proceed *in forma pauperis*.

18.6.2 Seeking In Forma Pauperis Relief

While former 28 U.S.C. § 1930(a) was not a model of clarity, most courts had held that its restriction on *in forma pauperis* filings applied only to starting a bankruptcy case, and that the regular federal *in forma pauperis* statute, 28 U.S.C. § 1915, applied to other proceedings.[338] In addition to removing the restriction on fee waivers for chapter 7 filing fees, the 2005 amendments to the Code also clarified that the courts may waive other filing fees imposed under any part of 28 U.S.C. § 1930 for other debtors and creditors, in accordance with

---

780 (Tex. App. 1997) (secured lender exercising control over property held responsible for injuries due to fire at premises).

328 *See generally In re* Summit Corp., 891 F.2d 1 (1st Cir. 1989) (broad interpretation appropriate in evaluating who can be examined); *In re* M4 Enters. Inc., 190 B.R. 471 (Bankr. N.D. Ga. 1996) (trustee is party in interest that can be examined).

329 Fed. R. Bankr. P. 2004(b).

330 Ulmer v. United States, 219 F. 641 (6th Cir. 1915).

The scope of the permitted examination is very broad. The only restriction is that the examination may not be used to harass the debtor or frivolously waste assets of the estate. *In re* M4 Enters. Inc., 190 B.R. 471 (Bankr. N.D. Ga. 1996).

331 Note that Rule 2004 is not applicable in the context of an adversary proceeding or contested matter, in which the formal discovery process is available. *See* Fed. R. Bankr. P. 7026, 9014.

332 *In re* Youk-See, 450 B.R. 312 (Bankr. D. Mass. 2011) (U.S. Trustee has standing to conduct Rule 2004 examination regarding Bank of America's loan modification practices that involved specific debtor); *In re* Michalski, 449 B.R. 273 (Bankr. N.D. Ohio 2011) (denying Wells Fargo's motion to quash subpoena and granting motion for examination focused on servicer's fees); *In re* Subpoena Duces Tecum, 461 B.R. 823 (Bankr. C.D. Cal. 2011) (Bank of America); *In re* Davis, 452 B.R. 610 (Bankr. E.D. Mich. 2011) (Bank of America); *In re* Davis, 452 B.R. 610 (Bankr. E.D. Mich. 2011); *In re* DeShetler, 453 B.R. 295 (Bankr. S.D. Ohio 2011); *In re* Countrywide Home Loans, Inc., 384 B.R. 373 (Bankr. W.D. Pa. 2008). Some courts have limited the scope of Rule 2004 examinations to the circumstances of a particular debtor, rather than allow inquiry into the full range of the servicer's nationwide practices. Bank of America v. Landis, 2011 WL 6104495 (D. Nev. Dec. 7, 2011) (U.S. Trustee has standing to conduct Rule 2004 examination over mortgage servicer's practices, but scope limited to specific debtor); *In re* Underwood, 457 B.R. 635 (Bankr. S.D. Ohio 2011).

333 *See* § 18.5.2.3, *supra*.

334 *See* § 18.5.4, *supra*.

335 *See* § 18.5.6, *supra*.

336 Judicial Conference of the United States, Bankruptcy Court Miscellaneous Fee Schedule (reprinted in Appendix C.4, *infra*).

337 *Id.*

338 *See* § 14.6, *supra*.

§ 18.6.2

Judicial Conference policy.[339] No such policy has been adopted with respect to such fees, so courts will presumably continue to waive fees for indigents as they had generally been doing prior to the amendments.

Nevertheless in many jurisdictions, the clerk's office will be unfamiliar with *in forma pauperis* filings and may not accept them as a matter of course. A sample motion, certification of indigency and order are set out in Appendix G, *infra*.[340] Until local practice is settled, a supporting memorandum should probably be filed whenever a low-income individual seeks *in forma pauperis* relief.

The points to be made in a supporting memorandum are straightforward. 28 U.S.C. § 1915 permits "Any court of the United States" to:

> authorize the commencement, prosecution or defense of any suit, action or proceeding, civil or criminal, or appeal therein, without prepayment of fees and costs or security therefor, by a person who makes affidavit that includes a statement of all assets such prisoner possesses that the person is unable to pay such fees or give security therefor.[341]

Courts have regularly held that 28 U.S.C. § 1915 applies to fees for proceedings in bankruptcy court other than filing fees. Thus in *In re Shumate*,[342] in which a debtor sought leave to appeal a court order *in forma pauperis*, the court held that a bankruptcy court was a "court of the United States" for the purposes of 28 U.S.C. § 1915. The court held further that the former limitation of 28 U.S.C. § 1930(a) requiring payment notwithstanding section 1915 applies only, as the statutory language sets out, to "parties commencing a case." The court in *Shumate* followed similar holdings in *In re Moore*,[343] *In re Palestino*,[344] and *In re Sarah Allen Home, Inc.*[345] Other courts have reached the same conclusion.[346] Thus, 28 U.S.C. § 1930 does not prohibit other bankruptcy proceedings from proceeding *in forma pauperis*.[347]

Additionally, important due process arguments are available concerning many fees, particularly for indigent creditors.[348] Indigent creditors, such as tenants seeking to preserve a security deposit or other property right, have a due process right of access to court to preserve their property, which is distinguishable from the issues addressed by the Supreme Court in *United States v. Kras*.[349]

Moreover, 28 U.S.C. § 773(c), dealing with appeals from the bankruptcy court, expressly contemplates appeals *in forma pauperis*.[350] The House Report on the Bankruptcy Reform Act of 1978 specifically included, as a subject as to which procedural rules would have to be drafted, "provisions for *in forma pauperis* proceedings."[351]

In jurisdictions where *in forma pauperis* relief is available, applicable procedural requirements must be met. At a minimum, this includes filing an affidavit containing sufficient facts to establish lack of financial resources to pay the filing fee. Such an affidavit might include a household budget. An evidentiary hearing may be available in appropriate circumstances.[352] An application may be denied if it is not accompanied by an affidavit setting forth the creditor's financial circumstances.[353] Additionally, some courts will examine the

---

339 Bernegger v. King, 2011 WL 1743880 (E.D. Wis. May 6, 2011) (construing amended 28 U.S.C. § 1930(f)(3) to authorize bankruptcy and district courts to consider debtors' motions to appeal *in forma pauperis*).

340 *See* Forms 101, 102, Appx. G.10, *infra*.

341 The current version of 28 U.S.C. § 1915(a)(1), amended by the Prison Litigation Reform Act of 1996, refers to "assets such prisoner possesses." Courts agree that this wording is a typographical error and that the word "prisoner" should be "person." *See* Martinez v. Kristi Kleaners, 364 F.3d 1305 (11th Cir. 2004) (acknowledging that individuals not incarcerated may proceed *in forma pauperis*); Haynes v. Scott, 116 F.3d 137 (5th Cir. 1997) (concluding that section 1915(a)(1) applies both to prisoners and non-prisoners); Floyd v. U.S. Postal Serv., 105 F.3d 274, 275 (6th Cir. 1997) (superseded on other grounds) (term "prisoner possesses" was erroneously substituted for "person possesses"); Leonard v. Lacy, 88 F.3d 181, 183 (2d Cir. 1996) (indicating that "prisoner possesses" is an error by use of [sic]).

342 91 B.R. 23 (Bankr. W.D. Va. 1988).

343 86 B.R. 249 (Bankr. W.D. Okla. 1988) (leave to appeal).

344 4 B.R. 721 (Bankr. M.D. Fla. 1980) (leave to initiate adversary proceeding).

345 4 B.R. 724 (Bankr. E.D. Pa. 1980) (leave to initiate adversary proceeding).

346 *See, e.g., In re* Minh Vu Hoang, 2011 WL 6180408 (D. Md. Dec. 12, 2011) (granting *in forma pauperis* application for appeal, but dismissing appeal as frivolous); *In re* McGinnis, 155 B.R. 294 (Bankr. D.N.H. 1993); *In re* Jackson, 86 B.R. 251 (Bankr. N.D. Fla. 1988) (appeal *in forma pauperis* permitted); *In re* Weakland, 4 B.R. 114 (Bankr. D. Del 1980) (fee in adversary proceeding; section 1930(a) limitation on section 1915 applies only to filing fees). *See also In re* Richmond, 247 Fed Appx. 831 (7th Cir. 2007) (reversing lower court rulings that held bankruptcy courts lacked authority to waive filing fee for creditor's adversary proceeding (decided under pre-2005 law)). *But see In re* Price, 410 B.R. 51 (Bankr. E.D. Cal. 2009) (noting Ninth Circuit's continuing position that bankruptcy courts are not "courts of the United States" within contemplation of section 1915).

347 *In re* Shumate, 91 B.R. 23 (Bankr. W.D. Va. 1988); *In re* Weakland, 4 B.R. 114 (Bankr. D. Del 1980).

348 *See, e.g.*, Tripati v. United States Bankruptcy Court for the E. Dist. of Texas, 180 B.R. 160 (E.D. Tex. 1995) (Constitution requires that an indigent creditor "be afforded an opportunity to be heard before his claims are disposed of"); *In re* Lassina, 261 B.R. 614 (Bankr. E.D. Pa. 2001) (creditor has right to fee waiver that can be denied for lack of proper evidence of indigency); *In re* Sarah Allen Home Inc., 4 B.R. 724 (Bankr. E.D. Pa. 1980).

349 *See* § 18.5.4.2.1, *supra*.

350 Note, however, that 28 U.S.C. § 773(c) has since been repealed.

351 H.R. Rep. No. 95-595, at 307 (1977).

352 *See In re* Lassina, 261 B.R. 614 (Bankr. E.D. Pa. 2001) (creditor's affidavit did not support finding of indigency; *in forma pauperis* request denied for lack of evidence with leave to seek evidentiary hearing).

353 *In re* Hall, 2008 WL 2714413 (Bankr. W.D. Tex. July 10, 2010) (recognizing that *in forma pauperis* appeals are permitted, but denying applications here because they failed to provide supporting affidavits and underlying claims deemed frivolous); *In re* Fitzgerald, 192 B.R. 861 (Bankr. E.D. Va. 1996) (although creditors may proceed *in forma pauperis* in bankruptcy litigation, application denied for failure to file necessary affidavit); *In re* Barham, 197 B.R. 319 (Bankr. W.D. Mo. 1996).

merits of the creditor's claim and deny *in forma pauperis* treatment if it concludes that the creditor's position is meritless.[354]

18.7 Chapter 11

18.7.1 Introduction

Consumer attorneys accustomed to using chapters 7 and 13 for their clients may be less familiar with chapter 11, the chapter likely to be utilized by a landlord, retailer or other party against whom consumers have claims. While a chapter 11 case, in theory, is a reorganization,[355] which suggests that at least some of the consumer claims will be paid, in most cases the debtor goes out of business and no payments are made to unsecured creditors.

At the outset of the case, the attorney representing a consumer creditor or group of consumer creditors must assess not only the strength of her clients' claims but also the debtor's financial position and prospects. The initial source of information on the debtor will be the schedules and statement of financial affairs. Other potentially useful sources of information are: (1) the debtor's answers to questions posed at the meeting of creditors[356] and (2) the monthly operating reports which a debtor still operating its business must file with the court.[357] Based on the attorney's assessment of the value of the assets which may be available to creditors from either liquidation of the debtor or the debtor's potential future operating profits, the attorney will want to set realistic goals for the representation of her consumer creditor clients and plot an appropriate strategy.

While not as pervasive as the changes to the consumer sections of the Code, the 2005 amendments made some significant changes to chapter 11. In amending chapter 11 Congress was reacting to two developments. The first was the spate of well-publicized large corporate bankruptcies involving pervasive financial irregularities and insider abuse. The other impetus for change was the acknowledgment of general trends in chapter 11 cases over recent years. Specifically, many scholars and practitioners had been noting the fundamental shift in the nature of chapter 11 cases.[358] For many years the trend has been that plans of reorganization are confirmed and completed in only a small percentage of chapter 11 cases. The businesses seldom reorganize and continue as going concerns. In the majority of chapter 11 cases the courts have either been overseeing sales of assets, dismissing the cases, or converting them to chapter 7. In many chapter 11 liquidations the courts simply implement preexisting deals orchestrated by a few savvy creditors.

The 2005 amendments responded to these developments in two ways. First, the amendments to chapter 11 impose new paperwork requirements on debtors and tightened time frames, particularly for small business debtors. The amendments set stricter controls over insider compensation and strengthened the supervisory roles of the United States trustee and the courts. Second, to address the concerns about too many cases being in chapter 11 that did not belong there, the amendments created new standards in section 1112(b) that make it easier to convert or dismiss a chapter 11 case. Section 1112(b) now permits the court, in its discretion, to convert or dismiss a chapter 11 case—whatever is in the best interests of creditors and the estate—for cause.[359] As any party in interest may move for a remedy under this section, it represents a strong leverage point for consumer creditors.

From the perspective of consumer creditors, the more extensive documentation requirements and the increased authority of the trustee should be helpful tools in pursuing claims against debtors who have injured consumers. The amendments should help consumers get cases out of chapter 11 when more effective remedies exist elsewhere. To the extent that these amendments were enacted in response to public outrage over widespread corporate misconduct, consumer advocates should do everything they can to insist that those remedial purposes are not forgotten.

The filing of a chapter 11 case presents a number of leverage points for consumer creditors. This section sets out some selected chapter 11 issues of special interest to attorneys representing consumer creditors.[360]

Local rules may apply. When there is no local bankruptcy rule, courts may expect that the local district court rules be met.

354 *In re* Heghmann, 324 B.R. 415, 420 (B.A.P. 1st Cir. 2005) (*in forma pauperis* motion should be granted for qualifying applicant if there is "any nonfrivolous or colorable issue on appeal," but finds instant appeal duplicative of others by same party; dissent finds genuine issues of law and would grant motion); *In re* Merritt, 186 B.R. 924 (Bankr. S.D. Ill. 1995) (appeal cannot be filed *in forma pauperis* if court concludes that appeal has no merit).

355 The Code, however, does provide for "liquidating" chapter 11 cases in which the debtor sells all or nearly all of its assets. 11 U.S.C. § 1123(b)(4).

356 This opportunity to ask questions of the debtor may be supplemented by a deposition pursuant to Federal Rule of Bankruptcy Procedure 2004. *See* § 18.5.8, *supra*. The meeting of creditors involves less costs and expense for consumer creditors, but it may not allow for the type of detailed questioning that is available under Rule 2004.

357 The monthly operating report should include a monthly cash flow statement and updated balance sheet. The monthly operating report is required by the United States trustee's office in each bankruptcy district pursuant to its powers to "monitor" the administration of bankruptcy cases. For a discussion of the United States trustee, see § 18.7.2.2, *infra*.

358 *See, e.g.*, Douglas G. Baird & Robert K. Rasmussen, *Chapter 11 at Twilight*, 56 Stan. L. Rev. 673 (2003); Thomas E. Carlson & Jennifer Frasier Hayes, *The Small Business Provisions of the 2005 Bankruptcy Amendments*, 79 Am. Bankr. L.J. 645 (2005); Richard Levin & Alesia Ranney-Marinelli, *The Creeping Repeal of Chapter 11: The Significant Business Provisions of the Bankruptcy Abuse Prevention and Consumer Protection Act of 2005*, 79 Am. Bankr. L.J. 603 (2005).

359 *See* § 18.7.11, *infra*.

360 *See also* § 6.3.4, *supra*.

18.7.2 General Role of Creditors and the United States Trustee

18.7.2.1 Creditors' Right to Vote on the Debtor's Plan

In a chapter 11 case, as in a chapter 13 case, the debtor's fundamental goal is to obtain confirmation of a plan which will favorably adjust the debtor's obligations to prebankruptcy creditors. However, there is a fundamental difference between chapter 13 and chapter 11 in the process leading to plan confirmation.

In a chapter 13 case, the debtor is legally entitled to confirmation of the plan if the plan meets certain statutory criteria that are set forth in 11 U.S.C. §§ 1322 and 1325. If these criteria are met, the plan must be confirmed. Ordinarily, creditors do not act collectively in a chapter 13 case. Each creditor individually receives notice and opportunity to be heard concerning the substance of the plan, but can prevent confirmation only by showing that a legal condition under section 1322 or 1325 has not been satisfied.

In a chapter 11 case, creditors vote on the plan of reorganization. Once a plan has been approved by the creditors, it is normally confirmed by the court. Confirmed plans can be consensual or nonconsensual, and the Code gives certain protections to dissenting creditors. A creditor may voluntarily waive its right to vote on the plan as a strategic matter. For example, a creditor might agree to less than full payment of its claim and support a plan because it will receive more in reorganization than in liquidation under chapter 7.

Creditors are placed into classes with other creditors with similarly substantial claims or interests,[361] and creditors vote by class.[362] Examples of classes include secured creditors, unsecured creditors holding priority claims for employees' wages or taxes, and general unsecured creditors.[363] A creditor is denied the ability to vote on the plan of reorganization if its claim is "unimpaired"—that is, if the proposed treatment of the claim under the plan "leaves unaltered the legal, equitable and contractual rights to which such claim or interest entitles" the creditor.[364] If a claim has been objected to, the creditor may request that it be temporarily allowed for purposes of plan voting.[365]

If each class consents to the plan, the court will almost certainly confirm the plan. If one or more classes of creditors votes against confirmation of the plan, the plan can still be confirmed under a procedure known as a "cramdown," which offers protections to dissenting creditors, including the "absolute priority" rule.[366] Alternatively, the court may approve dismissal or conversion of the case to chapter 7.[367]

18.7.2.2 Creditors' Right to Participate in the Chapter 11 Plan

Because confirmation is ordinarily based on creditor "consent," chapter 11 has enhanced provisions for creditor participation in the case as compared to chapter 13. As under chapter 13, creditors in a chapter 11 case may act individually to protect their interests or otherwise contest the debtor's actions in the chapter 11 case.[368] Any party in interest may seek appointment of a trustee or examiner,[369] move to convert the case to a chapter 7 liquidation,[370] or simply object to the plan.[371] An individual creditor can receive notice of significant motions or other matters in the chapter 11 case by filing with the court and serving on the debtor's counsel a request for notice pursuant to Federal Rule of Bankruptcy Procedure 2002(i).

In addition, chapter 11 explicitly provides a mechanism for creditors to act collectively through an official creditors' committee.[372] The creditors' committee is empowered to participate in virtually every phase of the chapter 11 case,[373] representing the interests of its constituent class of creditors. The committee is explicitly empowered to inquire into the acts, conduct, assets, liabilities and financial condition of the debtor, as well as to investigate the operation of the debtor's business.[374] The creditors' committee may seek court approval to hire counsel, accountants, or other professionals to provide necessary assistance in performing its function.[375] The fees and expenses of committee lawyers and accountants are paid by the debtor as administrative expenses.[376]

18.7.2.3 The United States Trustee

In 1986, after a period of experimentation, Congress established a permanent United States trustee system, covering every state except Alabama and North Carolina.[377] The United States Attorney General appoints United States trustees for twenty-two regions around the country, each region composed of one

---

361 11 U.S.C. § 1122(a).
362 11 U.S.C. § 1126(c).
363 The Code provides little guidance as to the composition of classes. Classes may be grouped for administrative convenience, 11 U.S.C. § 1122(b), and creditors must have similar interests. 11 U.S.C. § 1122(a).
364 11 U.S.C. § 1124(1).
365 Fed. R. Bankr. P. 3018(a) (final sentence).
366 See 11 U.S.C. § 1129(b).
367 11 U.S.C. § 1112.
368 See 11 U.S.C. § 1109(b) (any "party in interest" has the right to "appear and be heard on any issue" in a chapter 11 case).
369 11 U.S.C. § 1104.
370 11 U.S.C. § 1112.
371 11 U.S.C. § 1128.
372 See § 18.7.3, infra.
373 See 11 U.S.C. § 1103.
374 11 U.S.C. § 1103(c).
375 See 11 U.S.C. § 328(a).
376 11 U.S.C. §§ 330(a), 503(b)(2), 507(a)(2).
377 The Bankruptcy Judges, United States Trustees, and Family Farm Bankruptcy Act of 1986, Pub. L. No. 99-554, 100 Stat. 3088.
   The provisions concerning the United States Trustee System are codified at 28 U.S.C. §§ 581–589a. See also § 2.7, supra, for another discussion of the United States Trustee System.

or more judicial districts.[378] Assistant United States trustees may also be appointed.[379]

The United States trustee is required to "supervise the administration of cases and trustees in cases under chapter 7, 11, or 13."[380] The role of the United States trustee's office is crucial in many chapter 11 cases. It usually monitors the progress of chapter 11 cases to assure that they are properly handled and progress to some conclusion.[381]

The United States trustee convenes and presides at the section 341 meeting of creditors,[382] appoints the creditor committees,[383] may request the appointment of a chapter 11 trustee or examiner, and makes the appointment if one is ordered by the court,[384] and may request the dismissal or conversion of a chapter 11 case.[385] The United States trustee may monitor and comment on plans and disclosure statements in chapter 11.[386] More generally, the United States trustee may raise claims and may appear and be heard in any case or proceeding under chapter 11 (except the United States trustee may not file a chapter 11 plan).[387] The United States trustee will generally require regular cash flow and profit and loss statements from chapter 11 debtors.

With all these powers and the close relationship to the bankruptcy court, the United States trustee can be an important source of information and a critical ally. At the section 341 meeting, the consumer's attorney should be sure to establish contact with the assistant United States trustee assigned to the case, explain the consumer's view, and express an interest, if any, in serving on the creditors' committee, or in forming a separate consumer or tenant committee.[388] Thereafter, contact with the United States Trustee's Office should be maintained and the United States trustee should be provided with copies of information crucial to the consumer's case.

18.7.3 Appointment of a Creditors' Committee

At the meeting of creditors,[389] or perhaps at a separate meeting of creditors holding the largest unsecured claims, the creditors will determine if they wish to form an official creditors' committee. The United States trustee usually offers membership on the committee to the holders of the largest unsecured claims against the debtor.[390] However, if consumer claims are a significant issue in the case, the United States trustee may be willing to appoint a consumer creditor (or her attorney acting as agent) to the committee. As the creditors' committee may seek court approval to hire counsel, accountants, or other professionals to provide necessary assistance to the committee at the estate's expense,[391] there may be some jockeying over who will represent the committee as counsel. If a consumer is appointed to the committee, she may suggest and advocate for a particular attorney to be hired as counsel to the committee. One provision of the 2005 amendments authorizes the court, on request of a party in interest, to order the United States trustee to change the membership of a committee if the court determines that the change is necessary to ensure adequate representation of creditors.[392] The provision appears to have been designed to facilitate participation by small businesses, but there is no reason why consumer creditors may not use the procedure as well.

For consumer creditors and their attorneys, there are both potential advantages and disadvantages to participating in a creditors' committee. A potentially significant, albeit intangible, benefit is the increased status that counsel to the committee has in court proceedings. The position taken on an issue by counsel to the creditors' committee is not simply that of an individual creditor but rather that of the entire class of unsecured creditors and, as such, may be given great weight by the court. Committee members and counsel have access to timely information about the debtor's activities and plan formulation, and a real opportunity to negotiate with the debtor. In addition, counsel to the committee, once approved by the court, may seek compensation for their services from the estate, that is, the debtor, as an administrative expense.[393] Of course, counsel will only be paid if there are assets in the estate, so there is necessarily some risk of nonpayment to the attorney.

A drawback of committee status is that the consumer creditor, in her capacity as a committee member, and counsel to the committee undertakes a responsibility to protect the interests of other unsecured creditors. Another drawback is that consumer representatives may be continually outvoted or drowned out by large creditors, typically commercial lenders and bondholders. For these reasons, depending upon the circumstances in the case, a consumer creditor may decide that it is not worthwhile

---

378 28 U.S.C. § 581.
379 28 U.S.C. § 582.
380 28 U.S.C. § 586a(3).
  For a complete compilation of the statutory duties of the United States trustee beyond those set out in 28 U.S.C. §§ 581–589a, see 1 Collier on Bankruptcy ¶ 6.22 (16th ed.).
381 See 28 U.S.C. § 586a(3)(G) (United States trustee may monitor progress of cases and take appropriate action to prevent undue delay).
382 11 U.S.C. § 341.
383 11 U.S.C. § 1102.
  See § 18.7.3, infra, for a discussion of the appointment of a creditors' committee in chapter 11.
384 11 U.S.C. § 1104.
  See § 18.7.4, infra, for a discussion of the appointment of a trustee or examiner in chapter 11.
385 11 U.S.C. § 1112.
386 28 U.S.C. § 586a(3)(B).
387 11 U.S.C. § 307.
388 See § 18.7.3, infra.

389 11 U.S.C. § 341; Fed. R. Bankr. P. 2003.
390 11 U.S.C. § 1102(b)(1).
391 11 U.S.C. § 328(a).
392 11 U.S.C. § 1102(a)(4).
393 11 U.S.C. § 503(b)(4). Cf. In re FirstPlus Fin., Inc., 254 B.R. 888 (Bankr. N.D. Tex. 2000) (attorney fees of individual creditors serving on committee are not compensable).

to help form or participate on a committee and that her interest is better served by acting in an individual capacity.

Another alternative, at least when the attorney is representing a substantial number of consumer creditors with similar claims against the debtor, is to request that the court authorize the appointment of a special committee of creditors.[394] This may be appropriate in a case in which the consumers have claims that are distinct from those of the other unsecured creditors such as deposit claims with priority status.[395] Although the court may be reluctant to authorize a special committee when another committee of unsecured creditors has already been appointed due to the added administrative expenses involved, the decision is within the court's discretion.[396] Especially when consumer claims may have a significant impact on the outcome of the case, the court may be willing to appoint a special committee of consumer creditors. At least one court has authorized the creation of a formal employees subcommittee empowered to designate a representative to sit on the creditors' committee.[397]

Another amendment enacted in 2005 directs creditors' committees to provide "access to information" to creditors who have not been appointed to the committee but who hold claims of the kind represented by the committee.[398] The committee must "solicit and receive comments" from these non-appointed creditors,[399] and the court may order further disclosures from the committee.[400] Initial judicial responses to this amendment were receptive to the committees' concerns about confidentiality and interpreted the new disclosure duties narrowly.[401] In some instances, this provision has improved access to information in chapter 11 cases by requiring creditors' committees to maintain public websites.[402]

18.7.4 Appointment of a Trustee or an Examiner

18.7.4.1 Introduction

When a chapter 11 case is filed, the debtor ordinarily remains in control of the business as a "debtor in possession."[403] Section 1104(a), however, authorizes the court in some circumstances to appoint a trustee to take over and manage the debtor's affairs.[404] This provision gives consumers powerful leverage against businesses that are mismanaged after filing under chapter 11. For example, tenants may force the appointment of a trustee when a landlord-debtor failed to maintain a building in compliance with state sanitary codes. When a community hospital went into bankruptcy, community groups and others obtained appointment of a trustee.[405] More recently, trustees have been appointed in cases involving Ponzi schemes.[406] Even if unsuccessful, the good faith filing of a

---

394 11 U.S.C. § 1102(a)(2).
395 11 U.S.C. § 507(a)(7).
Form pleadings are available in Forms 164 and 165, Appendix G.14, infra. See generally Case History: Recovering Consumer Deposits From a Bankrupt Furniture Store, 10 NCLC REPORTS Bankruptcy and Foreclosures Ed. 41 (Mar./Apr. 1992).
396 11 U.S.C. § 1102(a)(2). But see In re Ctr. Apartments, Ltd., 277 B.R. 747 (Bankr. S.D. Ohio 2001) (court refused to appoint official tenants' committee because named tenants could not establish that they were creditors of debtor-landlord, but encouraged tenants to participate in proceedings as parties in interest pursuant to section 1109(b)).
397 See In re County of Orange, 179 B.R. 195 (Bankr. C.D. Cal. 1995) (appointing bondholders' and employees' subcommittees entitled to compensation for a "substantial contribution" to the case). But see In re Salant Corp., 53 B.R. 158 (Bankr. S.D.N.Y. 1985) (separate employees' committee unnecessary).
398 11 U.S.C. § 1102(b)(3).
399 11 U.S.C. § 1102(b)(3)(B).
400 11 U.S.C. § 1102(b)(3)(C).
401 In re S&B Surgery Ctr., Inc., 421 B.R. 546 (Bankr. C.D. Cal. 2009) (to comply with duty under section 1102(b)(3), chapter 11 debtor must establish and maintain a website to provide non-confidential information to unsecured creditors); In re REFCO, 336 B.R. 187, 198 (Bankr. S.D.N.Y. 2006) (section 1102(b)(3)(A) does not require creditors' committee to release information that could reasonably be determined to be confidential and non-public, proprietary, privileged, or whose disclosure could violate an agreement, order, or law).

402 See, e.g., In re MF Global Holdings Ltd., 2012 WL 734195 (Bankr. S.D.N.Y. Mar. 6, 2012) (improving access to information by establishing a website for customers to submit questions to the committee and by requiring that the committee respond to any general unsecured creditor's request for information within 30 days); In re S & B Surgery Ctr., Inc., 421 B.R. 546 (Bankr. C.D. Cal. 2009) (requiring unsecured creditors' committee to establish and maintain Internet website to provide non-confidential information for unsecured creditors regarding debtor's Chapter 11 case).
403 See 11 U.S.C. §§ 1101(1) (defining "debtor in possession"), 1107 (giving the debtor in possession most of the powers of a trustee), 1108 (giving a trustee authorization to operate the debtor's business).
404 11 U.S.C. § 1104(a) states:

> At any time after the commencement of the case but before confirmation of a plan, on request of a party in interest or the United States trustee, and after notice and a hearing, the court shall order the appointment of a trustee—
> (1) for cause, including fraud, dishonesty, incompetence, or gross mismanagement of the affairs of the debtor by current management either before or after the commencement of the case, or similar cause, but not including the number of holders of securities of the debtor or the amount of assets or liabilities of the debtor; or
> (2) if such appointment is in the interests of creditors, any equity security holders, and other interests of the estate, without regard to the number of holders of securities of the debtor or the amount of assets or liabilities of the debtor; or
> (3) if grounds exist to convert or dismiss the case under section 1112, but the court determines that the appointment of a trustee or an examiner is in the best interests of the creditors and the estate.

405 In re St. Mary Hosp., 89 B.R. 503, 504 n.1 (Bankr. E.D. Pa. 1988).
406 See, e.g., Picard v. JPMorgan Chase & Co., 460 B.R. 84, 88 (S.D.N.Y. 2011) (trustee appointed in the Securities Investor Pro-

motion for a trustee may produce a marked change in the debtor's behavior.

18.7.4.2 General Standards

Section 1104 permits the court on the request of a party in interest or the United States trustee to order the appointment of a trustee "[f]or cause, including fraud, dishonesty, incompetence, or gross mismanagement of the affairs of the debtor by current management either before or after the commencement of the case, or similar cause"; or in the (best) interests of the creditors.[407]

Chapter 11 is designed to allow the debtor-in-possession to retain management and control of the debtor's business operation unless a party in interest can prove that the appointment of a trustee is justified.[408] As the trustee appointment is an extraordinary remedy, a strong presumption exists that the debtor should be permitted to remain in possession absent a showing of need for the appointment of a trustee.[409] But the decision to appoint a trustee under section 1104(a) must be made on a case-by-case basis.[410] Although appointment of a trustee is the exception rather than the rule, the decision to appoint a trustee is within the discretion of the bankruptcy court.[411]

18.7.4.3 Grounds for Appointment of a Trustee Under Section 1104(a)(1)

Section 1104(a)(1) allows appointment of a trustee for "cause," which includes "fraud, dishonesty, incompetence or gross mismanagement," but nothing in the section requires that cause be limited to only those four transgressions. Cases have held that the examples of cause enumerated in section 1104(a)(1) are not exhaustive and the court may thus find that cause exists for a reason not specifically set forth in the statute.[412]

Moreover, paragraphs (1) and (2) of subsection (a) can also be applied together in the absence of any enumerated element and the best interest test can be added.[413]

Appointment of a trustee for fraud generally requires a misrepresentation and breach of the "duty of each to refrain from even attempted deceit of another with whom he deals and the right of the latter to assume he will do so."[414] Fraud is determined by a fact-sensitive and case-by-case inquiry but usually involves a blatant attempt by the debtor to deceive the creditors to the profit of the debtor and the detriment of the creditors. Examples of fraud include when the assets are sold just prior to the filing of the petition with the knowledge that the transfer would be avoided,[415] when assets are siphoned out of the estate by means of a kickback scheme,[416] or when a complete conversion of corporate assets has occurred.[417] Dishonesty is regarded as a lesser form of fraud, that is, a lesser degree of misrepresentation or breach of fiduciary duty.[418]

Incompetence is related to mismanagement, requiring a showing of a lack of business acumen and ability. However, the mere fact of filing a case under chapter 11 is insufficient to show incompetence.[419]

Gross mismanagement suggests some extreme ineptitude on the part of management,[420] above and beyond simple misman-

---

tection Act liquidation of Bernard L. Madoff).

407 11 U.S.C. § 1104(a).

408 *See, e.g., In re* Bayou Group, L.L.C., 363 B.R. 674, 687 (S.D.N.Y. 2007), *aff'd* 564 F.3d 541 (2d Cir. 2009) (affirming the bankruptcy court's refusal to appoint trustee based on the strong presumption that the debtor should be permitted to continue operations); *In re* Ionosphere Clubs, Inc., 113 B.R. 164, 167 (Bankr. S.D.N.Y. 1990).

409 *Id.*

410 *In re* Sharon Steel Corp., 871 F.2d 1217, 1226 (3d Cir. 1989).

411 *Compare In re* Keeley & Grabanski Land P'ship, 455 B.R. 153, 163 (B.A.P. 8th Cir. 2011) (proper standard for a party seeking the appointment of a chapter 11 trustee is preponderance of the evidence), *and In re* G-I Holdings, Inc., 385 F.3d 313, 317–18 (3d Cir. 2004) (party moving for the appointment of a trustee must prove its necessity by clear and convincing evidence).

412 *In re* Veblen W. Dairy, L.L.P., 434 B.R. 550 (Bankr. D.S.D. 2010) (finding cause to appoint trustee because of debtor in possession's continuing suspicious dealings with parties subject to transfer actions); *In re* Nartron Corp., 330 B.R. 573 (Bankr. W.D. Mich. 2005) (approving the appointment of a trustee with limited powers to oversee debtor's financial management; noting conflicts within management); *In re* Suncruz Casinos, 298 B.R. 821 (Bankr. S.D. Fla. 2003) (finding no fraud, dishonesty, incompetence, or gross mismanagement, but directing appointment of trustee due to internal conflicts within debtor's management); *In re* Cardinal Indus.,

109 B.R. 755, 765 (Bankr. S.D. Ohio 1990); *In re* V. Savino Oil & Heating Co., 99 B.R. 518, 525 (Bankr. E.D.N.Y. 1989). *See In re* Ngan Gung Restaurant, Inc., 195 B.R. 593 (S.D.N.Y. 1996) (court has power to appoint a trustee to sanction conduct abusive of the judicial process). *But see In re* Bayou Group, L.L.C., 564 F.3d 541 (2d Cir. 2009) (affirming denial of motion to appoint trustee for cause when there was no allegation of fraud, dishonesty, or gross mismanagement and no showing how appointment of trustee would facilitate bankruptcy proceedings).

413 7 Collier on Bankruptcy ¶ 1104.02[3][d] (16th ed.).

414 *In re* Garman, 643 F.2d 1252, 1260 (7th Cir. 1980). *See generally In re* Vaughn, 429 B.R. 14 (Bankr. D.N.M. 2010) (grounds to appoint trustee when debtor had engaged in prepetition Ponzi scheme and took Fifth Amendment at creditors' meeting. *See also In re* McGhee, 993 F.2d 228, n.1 (4th Cir. 1993).

415 *In re* Russell, 60 B.R. 42 (Bankr. W.D. Ark. 1985).

416 *In re* Bibo, 76 F.3d 256 (9th Cir. 1996); *In re* PRS Ins. Group, Inc., 274 B.R. 381, 387 (Bankr. D. Del. 2001).

417 *In re* V. Savino Oil & Heating Co., 99 B.R. 518, 524 (Bankr. E.D.N.Y. 1989); *In re* Colby Constr. Inc., 51 B.R. 113, 116 (Bankr. S.D.N.Y. 1985).

418 *See id.*

419 *In re* LaSherene, Inc., 3 B.R. 169, 174–176 (Bankr. N.D. Ga. 1980). *See generally In re* New Towne Dev., L.L.C., 404 B.R. 140 (Bankr. M.D. La. 2009) (court required to appoint trustee for cause due to internal management disputes).

420 *In re* Keeley & Grabanski Land P'ship, 455 B.R. 153, 164 (B.A.P. 8th Cir. 2011) (trustee appointed due to debtor's gross mismanagement, which included significant unexplained operating losses, leasing land on which debt is due for less than market value, and inability to service debt); *In re* Euro-Am. Lodging Corp., 365 B.R. 421 (Bankr. S.D.N.Y. 2007) (trustee appointed due to debtor's gross mismanagement which included failure to pay substantial ongoing tax obligations); *In re* Brown, 31 B.R. 583, 585–86 (D.D.C. 1983). *But see In re* Sundale, Ltd., 400 B.R. 890 (Bankr. S.D. Fla. 2009) (gross mismanagement standard not met despite nonpayment of taxes and poor maintenance of hotel owned by debtor; gross mis-

agement.[421] Courts generally recognize that some mismanagement exists in every insolvency case.[422] Postpetition mismanagement of the debtor's affairs is evidence of the need for an appointment of a trustee.[423] In addition, prepetition mismanagement can be ground for appointment of a trustee.[424]

Cause may take a variety of forms. The Tenth Circuit in *In re Oklahoma Refining Co.*,[425] affirmed the bankruptcy court's appointment of a trustee because of the failure to keep adequate records and to file reports, and the existence of a history of transactions with affiliated companies. The Third Circuit found cause under section 1104(a)(1) for appointment of a trustee when there was systematic siphoning of the debtor's assets to other companies under common control on the eve of bankruptcy, and continuing postpetition mismanagement.[426] And a New York bankruptcy court[427] found debtor's prepetition conduct, postpetition nondisclosures and misrepresentations, and noncompliance with statutory requirements relating to a second corporation which took over the business of the debtor's corporation constituted cause for appointment of a trustee pursuant to section 1104(a)(1). The Fifth Circuit considered whether there are grounds to appoint a trustee when the interests of an electric cooperative's consumer board members (lower utility rates) conflicts with the interests of the cooperative's creditors.[428]

18.7.4.4 Grounds for Appointment of a Trustee Under Section 1104(a)(2)

Even absent a finding of cause under subsection 1104(a)(1), the court may appoint a trustee if it is in the best interests of the parties.[429] Subsection 1104(a)(2) provides a flexible standard for the appointment of a trustee,[430] allowing the court to exercise *equity* powers to appoint a trustee to protect the interests of creditors, equity security holders, and other interests in the debtor's estate.[431] Unlike the "cause" standard, the "best interests" standard entails the exercise of discretionary powers and equitable considerations; a cost-benefit analysis of the cost of a trustee to the estate compared with the benefits sought to be derived will be a significant aspect of this determination.[432] For example, courts have appointed trustees under the best interests standard when fees paid by management created a possible conflict of interest.[433]

Bankruptcy courts applying the best interests standard eschew rigid absolutes and look to the practical realities and necessities, considering such factors (in addition to the cost-benefit analysis) as: (1) trustworthiness of the debtor; (2) debtor-in-possession's past and present performance and prospects for the debtor's rehabilitation; (3) debtor's justification for its actions; (4) reliance and harm to other parties; (5) conclusive evidence of detriment to the estate; and (6) business community and creditors' confidence (or lack thereof) in present management.[434] In some cases the court finds the appointment of a trustee was proper under either section 1104(a)(1) or (2).[435]

Several cases have held that a debtor's breach of fiduciary duty (which is constructive fraud as well) is grounds for a trustee appointment under subsection (a)(2) because a debtor-in-possession is a fiduciary for the creditors of the estate and has the same duties as trustees appointed by the court.[436]

---

management must be extreme ineptitude, not simple mismanagement).

421 Schuster v. Dragone, 266 B.R. 268, 272 (D. Conn. 2001) (court must find something more aggravated than simple mismanagement in order to appoint a trustee); *In re* Anchorage Boat Sales, Inc., 4 B.R. 635, 645 (Bankr. E.D.N.Y. 1980).

422 *In re* LaSherene, Inc., 3 B.R. 169 (Bankr. N.D. Ga. 1980).

423 *In re* Ionosphere Clubs, Inc., 113 B.R. 164, 168 (Bankr. S.D.N.Y. 1990); *In re* Colby Constr. Inc., 51 B.R. 113, 117 (Bankr. S.D.N.Y. 1985).

424 *In re* Intercat, Inc., 247 B.R. 911 (Bankr. S.D. Ga. 2000) (evidence of willful infringement of patent rights of another company); *In re* Russell, 60 B.R. 42 (Bankr. W.D. Ark. 1985); *In re* Ford, 36 B.R. 501, 504 (Bankr. W.D. Ky. 1983).

425 838 F.2d 1133 (10th Cir. 1988).

426 *In re* Sharon Steel Corp., 871 F.2d 1217 (3d Cir. 1989).

427 *In re* V. Savino Oil & Heating Co., 99 B.R. 518, 526–528 (Bankr. E.D.N.Y. 1989).

428 *See In re* Cajun Elec. Power Coop., Inc., 69 F.3d 746 (5th Cir. 1995), *modified after reh'g*, 74 F.3d 599 (5th Cir. 1996) (conflict of interest found to go beyond that which is inherent in the structure of rural electrical cooperative).

429 11 U.S.C. § 1104(a)(2); *In re* Eurospark Indus., Inc., 424 B.R. 621, 627 (Bankr. E.D.N.Y. 2010); *In re* Cardinal Indus., 109 B.R. 755, 765, 766 (Bankr. S.D. Ohio 1990).

430 *In re* Parker Grande Dev., 64 B.R. 557, 561 (Bankr. S.D. Ind. 1986);

In re Anchorage Boat Sales, Inc., 4 B.R. 635, 644 (Bankr. E.D.N.Y. 1980).

431 *In re* Nautilus of N.M., Inc., 83 B.R. 784, 789 (Bankr. D.N.M. 1988).

432 *In re* Taub, 427 B.R. 208 (Bankr. E.D.N.Y. 2010) (appointment of trustee in best interests of creditors when case had been mismanaged for twenty-one months since filing), *aff'd*, 2011 WL 1322390 (E.D.N.Y. Mar. 31, 2011); *In re* Plaza de Retiro, Inc., 417 B.R. 632 (Bankr. D.N.M. 2009) (appointment of trustee under section 1104(a)(2) and 1104(a)(1) when debtor's practices in operating retirement community "verge on the fraudulent"); *In re* Cardinal Indus., Inc., 109 B.R. 755, 766 (Bankr. S.D. Ohio 1990); *In re* V. Savino Oil & Heating Co., 99 B.R. 518, 525 (Bankr. E.D.N.Y. 1989); *In re* Stein & Day, Inc., 87 B.R. 290, 295 (Bankr. S.D.N.Y. 1988).

433 *In re* Taub, 427 B.R. 208, 230 (Bankr. E.D.N.Y. 2010), *aff'd*, 2011 WL 1322390 (E.D.N.Y. Mar. 31, 2011); *In re* Eurospark Indus., Inc., 424 B.R. 621 (Bankr. E.D.N.Y. 2010) (movant established by clear and convincing evidence that trustee appointment warranted for best interests of creditors due to debtor's refusal to settle lawsuits for benefit of estate); *In re* L.S. Good & Co., 8 B.R. 312 (Bankr. N.D. W. Va. 1980).

434 *In re* Ionosphere Clubs, Inc., 113 B.R. 164, 168 (Bankr. S.D.N.Y. 1990); *In re* Evans, 48 B.R. 46, 48 (Bankr. W.D. Tex. 1985).

435 *In re* Celeritas Technologies, L.L.C., 446 B.R. 514 (Bankr. D. Kan. 2011) (acrimony between debtor and major creditor met standard for appointment of trustee, both under cause standard and as evidence of debtor's dereliction of fiduciary duties); *In re* Brown, 31 B.R. 583, 585 (Bankr. D.D.C. 1983).

436 *In re* Nautilus of N.M., Inc., 83 B.R. 784, 789 (Bankr. D.N.M. 1988); *In re* Parker Grande Dev., 64 B.R. 557, 561 (Bankr. S.D. Ind. 1986) (breach of fiduciary duty because debtor-in-possession has such poor skills, ability, training and experience in land management and business acumen, he could not protect and conserve property for the benefit of the creditors); *In re* Russell, 60 B.R. 42, 47 (Bankr. W.D. Ark. 1985); *In re* Ford, 36 B.R. 501, 504 (Bankr.

18.7.4.5 Appointment of a Trustee for Fraud, Dishonesty or Criminal Conduct by Insiders

Section 1104(e), added by the 2005 amendments, directs the United States trustee to move for the appointment of a trustee if there are reasonable grounds to suspect that officers or insiders of the debtor participated in "actual fraud, dishonesty, or criminal conduct" in managing the entity or in preparing its financial reports.[437] The 2005 amendments also specify that any conduct which would be a basis for a court to order conversion or dismissal of the case under section 1112 may also be a ground for the court to appoint a trustee or examiner in lieu of conversion or dismissal.[438] A court may exercise its discretion to appoint a trustee or examiner rather than dismiss the case when it determines that the appointment will be in the best interests of the creditors and the estate.[439]

18.7.4.6 Appointment of an Examiner

Another mechanism available to creditors under chapter 11 is to move for appointment of an examiner. An examiner is directed to conduct an investigation and report the results of the investigation, but does not take over and manage the debtor's affairs.[440] Appointment of an examiner may be particularly useful in cases in which there is some evidence of wrongdoing or mismanagement by the debtor but the evidence of fraud or mismanagement is insufficient to convince the court to appoint a trustee.

Section 1104(c) permits the court on request of a party in interest or the United States trustee, to order the appointment of an examiner to investigate "allegations of fraud, dishonesty, incompetence, misconduct, mismanagement, or irregularity in the management of the affairs of the debtor," if the appointment is in the best interests of the creditors or the debtor's fixed unsecured debt exceeds $5 million.[441] Unsupported allegations of wrongdoing or mismanagement are not generally sufficient to support appointment of an examiner. The courts require that there be a factual basis underlying the need for an independent investigation.[442] However, if the debtor's unsecured debt exceeds $5 million, the court is required to appoint an examiner.[443] If the debtor's unsecured debt is less than $5 million, appointment is discretionary and the court will weigh the same equitable considerations used to determine whether to appoint a trustee under section 1104(a)(2).[444] Although the standard is the same, the results of the court's cost-benefit analysis under the two provisions may be different, as the costs of employing an examiner are much less than the costs of a trustee, and the nature, extent and duration of the examiner's investigation may be limited by the court.[445]

Examiners are usually appointed to investigate particular subjects or allegations, and to report their findings to the court and the parties in interest.[446] On occasion the courts appoint examiners to perform other tasks, such as to mediate between the debtor and creditors or to prosecute causes of action on the debtor's behalf.[447] The practices and procedure for appointing

---

W.D. Ky. 1983) (co-owner president of debtor was incapable of dealing with debtor as fiduciary, and appointed a trustee pursuant to (a)(2)). *Cf. In re* Cardinal Indus., 109 B.R. 755, 766–768 (Bankr. S.D. Ohio 1990) (debtors had not addressed serious deficiencies in recordkeeping processes; evidence established the Unsecured Creditor's Committees' loss of faith in debtors' intentions and abilities to reorganize their affairs; and the cost-benefit analysis was met).

437 11 U.S.C. § 1104(e). *See In re* The 1031 Tax Group, L.L.C., 374 B.R. 78 (Bankr. S.D.N.Y. 2007) (appointment of trustee denied because current management not tainted by fraud of former member of debtor's management).

438 11 U.S.C. § 1104(a)(3).

439 11 U.S.C. § 1104(a)(3).

440 *See* 11 U.S.C. § 1106(b). *See generally In re* Prosser, 2009 WL 2424409 (Bankr. D. V.I. July 31, 2009), *aff'd in part, dismissed in part,* 469 B.R. 228 (D. V.I. 2012) (discussing the limited role of an examiner).

441 11 U.S.C. § 1104(c).

442 *In re* Hardy, 319 B.R. 5 (Bankr. M.D. Fla. 2004) (appointing examiner based on record of debtor's testimony at creditors' meeting, lack of full disclosure in schedules, and complex nature of debtor's financial affairs); *In re* Mechem of Ohio, Inc., 92 B.R. 760 (Bankr. N.D. Ohio 1988); *In re* Gilman Serv., Inc., 46 B.R. 322 (Bankr. D. Mass. 1985); *In re* 1243 20th St., Inc., 6 B.R. 683 (Bankr. D.D.C. 1980); *In re* Leniham, 4 B.R. 209 (Bankr. D.R.I. 1980); *In re* Bel Air Assocs. Ltd., 4 B.R. 168 (Bankr. W.D. Okla. 1980).

443 *In re* Revco D.S., Inc., 898 F.2d 498 (6th Cir. 1990); Walton v. Cornerstone Ministries Investors, Inc., 398 B.R. 77 (N.D. Ga. 2008) (reversing bankruptcy court's denial of motion to appoint examiner for debtor with $143 million in unsecured claims; appointment mandatory for debtor with debts of this magnitude). *But see In re* Residential Capital, L.L.C., 474 B.R. 112, 121 (Bankr. S.D.N.Y. 2012) (recognizing the split of authority on whether an examiner is required in every case where unsecured debts exceed $5 million); *In re* Erickson Retirement Communities, L.L.C., 425 B.R. 309 (Bankr. N.D. Tex. 2010) (although appointment of examiner mandatory if debts exceed threshold amount, courts have discretion in defining scope of examiner's duties); *In re* Spansion, Inc., 426 B.R. 114 (Bankr. D. Del. 2010) (denying motion for appointment of examiner despite apparent mandate based on debt amount; costs would burden estate, not further administration of the case, and restricting examiner's role would be meaningless).

444 *In re* West End Fin. Advisors, L.L.C., 2012 WL 2590613 (Bankr. S.D.N.Y. 2012); *In re* Gilman Serv., Inc., 46 B.R. 322 (Bankr. D. Mass. 1985); *In re* Leniham, 4 B.R. 209 (Bankr. D.R.I. 1980).

445 *See In re* Gliatech, Inc., 305 B.R. 832, 835 (Bankr. N.D. Ohio 2004) (noting that an examiner typically investigates the debtor's business but does not replace the debtor in possession in handling the day-to-day affairs of the business); *In re* Mako, Inc., 102 B.R. 809 (Bankr. E.D. Okla. 1988); *In re* Gilman Serv., Inc., 46 B.R. 322 (Bankr. D. Mass. 1985); 7 Collier on Bankruptcy ¶ 1104.03[3] (16th ed.). *See also In re* Revco D.S., Inc., 898 F.2d 498 (6th Cir. 1990) (court has authority to limit scope of examiner's authority).

446 *See, e.g., In re* Carnegie Int'l Corp., 51 B.R. 252 (Bankr. S.D. Ind. 1984) (law professor appointed examiner to investigate debtor causes of action); *In re* 1243 20th St., Inc., 6 B.R. 683 (Bankr. D.D.C. 1980) (examiner appointed to investigate a prepetition transfer by debtor to a related corporation). *See also In re* Fibermark, 339 B.R. 321 (Bankr. D. Vt. 2006) (examiner's report available to parties to make substantive decisions about their respective rights, but report itself, other than its conclusions, not admissible in evidence over hearsay objection).

447 *See, e.g., In re* Pub. Serv. Co. of N.H., 99 B.R. 177 (Bankr. D.N.H.

an examiner are similar to those required for the appointment of a trustee. An examiner's report may provide excellent objective evidence to support subsequent appointment of a trustee, but the Code prohibits appointment of an examiner and a trustee at the same time.[448]

18.7.4.7 Practice and Procedure

An application for appointment of a trustee or an examiner is by motion and may be made by any party in interest or by the United States trustee.[449] Although the motion can be filed at any time, the court may be reluctant to appoint a trustee or an examiner based on prepetition mismanagement. It may therefore, be preferable to wait for evidence of postpetition misconduct. Once a plan is confirmed, however, the court may lose the power to appoint a trustee, because such an appointment would be inconsistent with the terms of the plan.[450]

Ordinarily, before filing the motion, a record should be built of the debtor's mismanagement. Communications with the debtor or debtor's attorney should be in writing or followed up by confirming letters. Wherever possible, "objective" evidence other than the consumer's experience should be gathered so that the court can be convinced that this is more than a quarrel between the consumer creditor and the debtor. For example, if the debtor is a landlord and the issue is the management of the building, reports should be obtained from state or local housing inspectors documenting the conditions of the building.

The cooperation of the United States trustee can be critical in the success of the motion. Ideally, the United States trustee's office will join in the motion or file a separate supporting motion, but in any event the court is very likely to ask for the opinion of the United States trustee and to give significant weight to that opinion.

As soon as a chapter 11 is filed, the consumer's attorney should make contact with the United States trustee's office, find out which person in the office has been assigned to the case, alert him or her that difficulty is anticipated with the debtor and a motion for appointment of a trustee may be filed. Copies of all correspondence should be sent to the United States trustee's office. Prior to filing the motion, the consumer's attorney should sit down with the United States trustee to present the reasons for filing the motion and request that the United States trustee join in the motion or file a supporting motion.

In considering the motion for appointment of a trustee, the court is not required to conduct a full evidentiary hearing, at least when the record already contains undisputed facts showing that cause exists.[451] The party moving for the appointment has the burden of proof showing "cause" and at least one court has said the evidence supporting the motion must be clear and convincing.[452] Once the court has found that "cause" exists under section 1104, it has no discretion but to appoint a trustee.[453]

Numerous courts have held that appointment of a trustee in a chapter 11 case is an extraordinary remedy.[454] There is generally a bias in favor of allowing the debtor to continue managing the estate, absent a strong showing of fraud, incompetence or mismanagement.[455] Courts often express concern about protecting the interests of creditors by avoiding the administrative costs which appointment a trustee necessarily generates.[456] For these reasons, a request for a trustee will not be appropriate for every case.

The United States trustee's office is required to maintain a panel of persons willing to serve as trustees in chapter 11 cases.[457] Thus, unlike many state court actions for appointment of a receiver in which, as a practical matter, the moving party must be prepared to locate a suitable receiver, the aggrieved consumer creditor does not have to recommend a trustee for a chapter 11 bankruptcy. Ordinarily the court will order that the United States trustee appoint a trustee. Ordinarily the trustee will be selected from the United States trustee's panel, but the trustee does not have to be from that panel, and the consumer's attorney may suggest someone else who is suitable.

Finally, although some courts have held an order appointing a trustee in bankruptcy is a procedural order, and thus not a final substantive order that may be reviewed immediately,[458] more recent decisions have held otherwise. In *Committee of Dalkon*

1989) (examiner appointed to mediate and break deadlock in reorganization plan negotiations).

448 11 U.S.C. § 1104(c). *See also In re* Int'l Distrib. Ctrs., Inc., 74 B.R. 221 (S.D.N.Y. 1987) (an examiner may not subsequently be made trustee in the same case).

449 11 U.S.C. § 1104(a).

A trustee may also be appointed by the court *sua sponte*. *In re* Bibo, 76 F.3d 256 (9th Cir. 1996); Allen v. King, 461 B.R. 709, 710 (D. Mass. 2011).

450 *In re* Am. Preferred Prescription, Inc., 250 B.R. 11 (E.D.N.Y. 2000), *rev'd on other grounds*, 255 F.3d 87 (2d Cir. 2001).

451 *In re* Casco Bay Lines, Inc., 17 B.R. 946, 950 (B.A.P. 1st Cir. 1982).

452 *In re* G-I Holdings, Inc., 385 F.3d 313, 317–18 (3d Cir. 2004) (party moving for the appointment of a trustee must prove its necessity by clear and convincing evidence). *See also In re* Tradex Corp., 339 B.R. 823 (D. Mass. 2006) (preponderance of the evidence standard applies in appointing chapter 11 trustee). *But see In re* Keeley & Grabanski Land P'ship, 455 B.R. 153, 163 (B.A.P. 8th Cir. 2011) (proper standard for a party seeking the appointment of a chapter 11 trustee is preponderance of the evidence); *In re* Sundale, Ltd., 400 B.R. 890, 900 (Bankr. S.D. Fla. 2009) (collecting cases, concluding that majority of courts addressing issue have applied clear and convincing evidence standard in ruling on motion to appoint trustee).

453 *In re* Okla. Ref. Co., 838 F.2d 1133, 1136 (10th Cir. 1988). *See also In re* Basil St. Partners, L.L.C., 477 B.R. 856 (Bankr. M.D. Fla. 2012).

454 *See, e.g., In re* Adelphia Communications Corp., 336 B.R. 610, 655 (Bankr. S.D.N.Y. 2006) (collecting cases); *In re* McCorhill Publ'g, Inc., 73 B.R. 1013 (Bankr. S.D.N.Y. 1987).

455 *See, e.g., In re* Sharon Steel Corp., 871 F.2d 1217 (3d Cir. 1989); *In re* Natron Corp., 330 B.R. 573 (Bankr. W.D. Mich. 2005) (finding wasteful expenditures by management engaged in longstanding "vendetta" litigation, court appoints trustee with limited powers).

456 *See, e.g., In re* Costa Bonita Beach Resort Inc., 2012 WL 3716842 (Bankr. D. P.R. Aug. 27, 2012) (moving party failed to provide a cost-benefit analysis of how appointment of a trustee outweighed detriment to the estate); *In re* McCorhill Publ'g, Inc., 73 B.R. 1013 (Bankr. S.D.N.Y. 1987).

457 28 U.S.C. § 586(a)(1).

458 Albrecht v. Robison, 36 B.R. 913, 915, 916 (D. Utah 1983).

Shield Claimants v. A.H. Robins Co.,[459] the Fourth Circuit found an order denying the request for an appointment of a trustee pursuant to section 1104(a) was immediately reviewable as a final decision, even though the order may not have been final in a technical sense. The court also held that as the determination of cause is within the discretion of the fact finder; in the absence of an abuse of discretion, the appellate court will not disturb the lower court's findings.[460]

18.7.5 Objection to Compensation Paid to Debtor's Principals

When a business files a chapter 11 bankruptcy, the debtor may continue to pay its employees their salary for the postpetition services rendered. In fact, such employees' right to payment is an administrative expense claim entitled to priority payment.[461] However, there is also the potential for the debtor's principal shareholders, partners, or proprietors to continue to pay a substantial salary to themselves during postpetition operations, thereby dissipating the remaining assets that would otherwise be available to creditors.

A number of courts have held that the bankruptcy court has the power to determine the propriety of the continued employment of the debtor's principals and to fix the level of their compensation.[462] In some jurisdictions, local rules govern the procedure by which a debtor may obtain authority to continue to pay its principals for postpetition services rendered to the debtor.[463] In evaluating creditor objections to the salaries being paid to officers or principals of the debtor, the general standard employed by the court is the value, in the open market, of the services being provided. This, in turn, requires an evaluation of the salaries paid for equivalent positions in equivalent businesses.[464]

The 2005 amendments added section 503(c), which imposes significant limitations on compensation packages paid to retain insiders and officers of the debtor.[465] The provisions severely limit retention and severance payments to insiders, with the effect that few such compensation packages will be approved in a chapter 11 case. The provisions prohibit administrative expense priority for transfers that are not in the ordinary course of business or justified by the facts and circumstances of the case.[466] However, some courts have approved compensation if the compensation is labeled as "incentive" payments as opposed to "retention" payments.[467] The court may approve severance packages or "golden parachute" deals only under limited circumstances now specified in the Code.[468]

The possibility of a creditor objection to the salary which may be paid to principals of the "opposing party" (the debtor) is an obvious leverage point.[469] Aside from the possibility that

---

459 828 F.2d 239, 241, 242 (4th Cir. 1987). *See also In re* Walker, 515 F.3d 1204, 1211 (11th Cir. 2008) (agreeing with Third and Fourth Circuits that order approving, denying, removing trustee is final order for purposes of appeal).

460 Dalkon Shield Claimants, 828 F.2d 239 (4th Cir. 1987).*See also* Byrd v. Johnson, 467 B.R. 832, 842 (D. Md. 2012) *cf. In re* Sharon Steel Corp., 871 F.2d 1217, 1225 (3d Cir. 1989).

461 11 U.S.C. §§ 503(b), 507(a)(2).

462 *See, e.g., In re* Lynx Transp., Inc., 1999 WL 615366 (Bankr. E.D. Pa. Aug. 11, 1999); *In re* Holly's Inc. 140 B.R. 643, 690, 691 (Bankr. W.D. Mich. 1992); *In re* Zerodec Mega Corp., 39 B.R. 932 (Bankr. E.D. Pa. 1984) (grounding the court's authority in 11 U.S.C. §§ 327 and 105).

463 *See, e.g.,* Local Rule 4002-1 (Bankr. E.D. Pa.) (requiring notice to creditors of the level of compensation to the debtor's principal and providing for a procedure for creditors to object).

464 *See, e.g., In re* Quigley Co., 437 B.R. 102, 156 (Bankr. S.D.N.Y. 2010); *In re* Athos Steel & Aluminum, Inc., 69 B.R. 515 (Bankr. E.D. Pa. 1987).

465 11 U.S.C. § 503(c); *In re* Pilgrim's Pride Corp., 401 B.R. 229 (Bankr. N.D. Tex. 2009) (section 503(c)(3) sets stricter standard than prior "business judgment" test under section 363(b)(1) for compensation packages that benefit managers hired after date of petition). *See In re* Nellson Nutraceutical, Inc., 369 B.R. 787 (Bankr. D. Del. 2007) (bonus and incentive payment plan not restricted by section 503(c) limits on retention payments to insiders); *In re* Global Home Prods., L.L.C., 369 B.R. 778 (Bankr. D. Del. 2007) (section 503(c) did not apply because debtors sought approval of incentive, not retention plans); *In re* Dana Corp., 358 B.R. 567 (Bankr. S.D.N.Y. 2006). *See generally* Bethany C. Suhreptz, *Note: Key Employee Retention Plans, Executive Compensation, and BAPCPA: No Rest for Congress, No More for Execs*, 35 Wm. Mitchell L. Rev. 1194 (2009) (discussing legislative background and recent decisions on section 503(c)).

466 11 U.S.C. § 503(c) (focusing on necessity of retaining the employee, existence of bona fide offers from other potential employers, and establishing compensation limits in relation to salaries and wages paid to debtor's non-management staff); *In re* Fieldstone Mortgage Co., 427 B.R. 357 (Bankr. D. Md. 2010) (debtor failed to show that a distinct and separate business organization had made bona fide offer with same or greater compensation than retention plan it was offering to insider); *In re* Foothills Tex., Inc., 408 B.R. 573 (Bankr. D. Del. 2009) (rejecting debtor's assumption of prepetition contracts obligating it to make retention payments to statutory insiders). *See generally In re* Borders Group, Inc., 453 B.R. 459 (Bankr. S.D.N.Y. 2011) (under subsection (3) of § 503(c), although debtor's postpetition employee retention plan did not apply to insiders, it had to be justified under facts and circumstances presented); *In re* Mesa Air Group, Inc., 2010 WL 3810899 (Bankr. S.D.N.Y. Sept. 24, 2010) (approving retention plan as complying with § 503(c)(3)).

467 *In re* QuVIS, 2009 WL 4262077 (Bankr. D. Kan. Nov. 23, 2009) (section 503(c) not applicable to compensation program not designed and intended primarily for inducing employee to remain with company); *In re* Nellson Nutraceutical, 369 B.R. 787, 801–803 (Bankr. D. Del. 2007) (permitting payments to insiders because primarily motivational and not "retentive").

468 11 U.S.C. § 503(c)(2) (severance package for insider must be part of program made generally available to all employees and not exceed ten times the value of similar benefits paid to non-management employees during that calendar year). *See generally In re* Forum Health, 427 B.R. 650 (Bankr. N.D. Ohio 2010) (striking CEO's severance pay provision when not part of program generally applicable to all full-time employees; program was not applicable to union employees who were majority of debtor's work force).

469 *In re* Benard Technologies, Inc., 342 B.R. 174 (Bankr. D. Del. 2006) (rejecting administrative expense claim of chief executive officer who sought three times his prepetition salary); *In re* Appliedtheory Corp., 312 B.R. 225 (Bankr. S.D.N.Y. 2004) (rejecting executives' "golden parachute" claims for amounts several times greater than their pre-termination salaries. *Cf. In re* Forum Group, Inc., 82 F.3d 159 (7th Cir. 1996) (outgoing directors' golden parachute payments

the creditor can hit the debtor's principals directly in their "pocketbook," in a hearing on compensation, the court will necessarily consider evidence regarding the debtor's business operations and the principals' responsibilities and conduct. If such evidence puts the debtor in a bad light, it may be useful to present it to the court early in the case as an objection to the principals' compensation, particularly if the evidence may not be sufficient to satisfy the more onerous requirements for the appointment of a trustee.

18.7.6 Transfer Avoidance Actions

As a debtor in possession, a chapter 11 debtor has, generally speaking, the same powers as a chapter 7 trustee.[470] These powers include the right to set aside certain prepetition transfers, including preferences,[471] fraudulent conveyances[472] and transfers avoidable under the "strong-arm" powers.[473]

A creditor actively participating in a chapter 11 case may learn that there are potential transfer avoidance claims that the debtor is not pursuing. This occurs with some regularity because prosecution of the claims would require that the principals or their relatives or other closely connected parties return money or other assets to the debtor for the benefit of all creditors.

For example, a review of the debtor's books and bank records might reveal a pattern of payment by the debtor of the personal expenses (for example, home mortgage) of the principals. Similarly, valuable property may have been transferred for little or no consideration to a family member or to a corporate principal.[474] Such payments and conveyances may be avoidable as fraudulent transfers. Or, in the two year period prior to bankruptcy, the principals may have withdrawn cash from the company in excess of their usual salaries, ostensibly as repayment of "loans" advanced to the debtor. Such transfers may be avoidable as either fraudulent conveyances or preferences. The debtor may have made substantial payments in the two year period prior to bankruptcy to lenders who held claims guaranteed by the debtors' principals. Such payments, too, may be avoidable as preferences.[475]

The investigation and discovery of the existence of these claims, by itself, may lead the chapter 11 debtor to quickly seek a settlement with the active creditor. In the absence of a settlement, if the debtor (as trustee) does not act to recover the transfer, the court can authorize a creditors' committee or individual creditor to prosecute the avoidance action on behalf of the debtor's estate if satisfied that the debtor is not inclined to pursue a potentially meritorious claim.[476] If successful, the creditor's attorney may seek reasonable counsel fees from the estate.[477] Alternatively, failure to seek recovery of potentially avoidable transfers can be grounds for appointment of an independent trustee.[478] A court-appointed trustee is much more likely than the debtor in possession to investigate and seek relief for abusive transfers of corporate property. If such a trustee has been appointed, information about abusive transfer should be brought to her attention.

18.7.7 Objections to the Debtor's Disclosure Statement

As part of confirmation process the proponent of a chapter 11 plan must file and obtain court approval of a disclosure statement.[479] The disclosure statement is usually filed simultaneously with or shortly after the filing of the plan of reorganization.[480]

The purpose of a disclosure statement is to provide sufficient information to enable creditors to make an informed judgment

---

invalidated because outgoing directors recommended new directors so that there was no actual relinquishment of control as required by the golden parachute agreements).

470 11 U.S.C. § 1107(a).
    For a detailed discussion of trustee avoidance powers, see § 10.4.2.6, *supra*.
471 11 U.S.C. § 547.
    The 2005 amendments added a limitation that a transfer by a business debtor of less than $5000 cannot be avoided as a preference. 11 U.S.C. § 547(c)(9). The amendments also lighten the transferee's burden in arguing that the "ordinary course of business" defense applies to block avoidance of a preference. 11 U.S.C. § 547(c)(2). 28 U.S.C. § 1409(b) was also amended to require certain trustee litigation to recover money from consumers and other non-insiders to be commenced in the district where the defendant resides.
472 11 U.S.C. § 548.
473 11 U.S.C. § 544.
474 *See generally In re* Blatstein, 260 B.R. 698 (E.D. Pa. 2001) (exploring scope of transfers to debtor's wife that may be avoided).
475 Levit v. Ingersoll Rand Fin. Corp., 874 F.2d 1186 (7th Cir. 1989).
476 *In re* The Gibson Group, Inc., 66 F.3d 1436 (6th Cir. 1995) (creditor has standing to bring preference and fraudulent transfer actions after making demand on debtor in possession to bring those actions and having the demand refused); *In re* S.T.N. Enters., 779 F.2d 901 (2d Cir. 1985); *In re* Philadelphia Light Supply Co., 39 B.R. 51 (Bankr. E.D. Pa. 1984). *See generally In re* Racing Servs., Inc., 540 F.3d 892, 898 (8th Cir. 2008) (approving derivative standing to creditors to pursue avoidance actions when trustee or debtor in possession is unable or unwilling to do so; collecting cases on issue of derivative standing); *In re* Terra Bentley II, L.L.C., 2011 WL 808190, *4 (Bankr. D. Kan. Mar. 2, 2011) (collecting cases on creditor's derivative standing to bring transfer avoidance action).
    Intervention in a pending case which is not being aggressively prosecuted may also be possible. 11 U.S.C. § 1109(b). *See generally In re* Chalk Line Mfg., 184 B.R. 828 (Bankr. N.D. Ala. 1995) (and cases cited therein). *But cf.* Hartford Underwriters Ins. Co. v. Union Planters Bank, 530 U.S. 1, 120 S. Ct. 1942, 147 L. Ed. 2d 1 (2000) (denying a creditor remedy under an analogous Code section; recognizing but not deciding the connection between the issues).
    The question of the "derivative standing" of creditors' committees to pursue avoidance actions has recently divided the courts. *Compare* Official Comm. of Unsecured Creditors of Cybergenics Corp. v. Chinery, 330 F.3d 548 (3d Cir. 2003) (en banc) (approving standing) *with* United Phosphorous Ltd. v. Fox, 305 B.R. 912 (B.A.P. 10th Cir. 2004) (rejecting standing).
477 11 U.S.C. § 503(b)(3)(B).
478 *See* § 18.7.4, *supra*.
479 11 U.S.C. § 1125(b).
480 Fed. R. Bankr. R. 3016(c).

about the proposed plan.[481] The type of information ordinarily provided in a narrative form in the disclosure statement includes: a brief history of the debtor and its financial operations; a description of the circumstances which resulted in the debtor's financial distress and bankruptcy filing; a summary of the legal and financial events which have occurred since the bankruptcy filing; a chapter 7-type liquidation analysis; a summary of the contents of the plan and the treatment of the different creditor classes; and an explanation of the means by which the debtor expects to carry out the provisions of the plan.[482] As the disclosure statement must be approved by the court upon notice and hearing, the debtor must file a motion seeking court approval and give notice of the motion to all creditors.[483]

A creditor may file objections to the proposed disclosure statement.[484] The disclosure statement hearing is another juncture in the confirmation process when a creditor may oppose the debtor and thus acquire leverage for more favorable treatment for its claim. This leverage may be limited because the debtor is usually willing to amend or supplement the disclosure statement to neutralize objections. In some cases, the court might consider objections to the disclosure statement that are based on the alleged legal defects in the substance of the plan itself.[485]

18.7.8 Objections to the Debtor's Plan of Reorganization

After the disclosure statement is approved, the court will issue an order directing the debtor to send out ballots to the creditors for voting on the plan. The court will also schedule a confirmation hearing and set a deadline by which creditors may file objections to the plan. Notice of the confirmation hearing and objection deadline is given to all creditors.[486]

Section 1129(a) of the Code sets out thirteen requirements that must be met for consensual confirmation of a chapter 11 plan. Perhaps the most significant requirement is found in section 1129(a)(8) which provides that every class must either accept the plan or be unimpaired.[487] If this requirement is not met, the plan may not be confirmed under section 1129(a). Thus, the importance of the plan voting is self-evident.

Separate and apart from plan voting, however, any creditor can object to confirmation on any of the other twelve grounds found in section 1129(a), even if the class to which that creditor belongs has voted to accept the plan.[488] It is beyond the scope of this discussion to discuss comprehensively all of the requirements for confirmation under section 1129(a). However, for a consumer creditor with a consumer priority claim,[489] a prepetition wage claim,[490] or an employee benefits claim,[491] there are at least two potential objections that may be available.

First, if the consumer's claim is a consumer deposit claim entitled to priority under section 507(a)(7) or for certain prepetition wages or benefits,[492] it must either be: (1) paid in full with interest over the length of the plan even if the consumer's class has accepted a plan containing less favorable treatment or (2) paid in full on the effective date[493] of the plan if the consumer's class has not accepted the plan.[494] Absent this treatment, the plan is not confirmable. Second, if there is reason to question the debtor's financial ability to make the payments required by the plan, the debtor may assert objections under section 1129(a)(2)[495] and (a)(11)[496] at the confirmation hearing.

If a plan cannot be confirmed under section 1129(a), a debtor may request confirmation under the chapter 11 "cramdown" provision, section 1129(b). Cramdown requires that at least one impaired class of creditors has accepted the plan.[497] The plan is confirmable only if it does not discriminate unfairly and is "fair and equitable" as to each class of dissenting creditors.[498] Thus, even if the consumer creditor's class does not accept the plan, the debtor may seek confirmation under section 1129(b).

Section 1129 sets out separate tests for the fair and equitable standard for secured and unsecured creditors. For a plan to be

---

481   11 U.S.C. § 1125(a).
482   As discussed in § 18.7.10, *infra*, a court may determine in a small business case that the debtor's plan itself may be the disclosure statement.
483   11 U.S.C. § 1125(b); Fed. R. Bankr. P. 3017(a).
484   See Form 167, Appendix G.14, *infra*, for an example of an objection to a disclosure statement.
485   *In re* Monroe Well Serv., 80 B.R. 324 (Bankr. E.D. Pa. 1987).
486   Fed. R. Bankr. P. 3020(b)(2).
487   Another significant subsection is section 1129(a)(7). Section 1129(a)(7) provides that if a class of claims is impaired, the plan cannot be confirmed unless either every claimant in the class accepts the plan or the distribution to the class under the plan provides the same value that the class would receive in a chapter 7 liquidation. This hypothetical liquidation test, or "best interests of the creditors" test is also found in chapter 13. *See* 11 U.S.C. § 1325(a)(4); *In re* Barakat, 99 F.3d 1520 (9th Cir. 1996) (tenant security deposit claimants were not "impaired" class after debtor assumed leases, because their claims became postpetition priority claims payable in full).

488   A class of creditors has accepted the plan if creditors holding at least two-thirds in amount and more than one-half in number of the allowed claims of the class have voted to accept the plan. 11 U.S.C. § 1126(c). See Form 168, Appendix G.14, *infra*, for an example of an objection to confirmation of a chapter 11 plan.
489   Section 507(a)(7) grants seventh priority to consumer claims arising from the deposit of money in connection with executory contracts related to property or services.
490   Section 507(a)(4) grants fourth priority to wage claims, including vacation, severance, and sick leave pay.
491   Section 507(a)(5) grants fifth priority to unpaid contributions to employee benefits plans.
492   11 U.S.C. § 507(a)(4).
493   The effective date of the plan is the date that distributions to creditors or other significant actions are scheduled to begin. The term is usually defined in the plan itself, often as shortly after the confirmation order becomes final and unappealable.
494   11 U.S.C. § 1129(a)(9)(B).
495   11 U.S.C. § 1129(a)(2) requires that the plan comply with the applicable provisions of the Code. Section 1123(a)(5) requires that a plan "shall . . . provide adequate means for the plan's implementation."
496   11 U.S.C. § 1129(a)(11) requires that confirmation "is not likely to be followed by the liquidation, or the need for further financial reorganization" unless the plan itself proposes liquidation.
497   *See* 11 U.S.C. § 1129(b)(1).
498   *See* 11 U.S.C. § 1129(b)(1).

fair and equitable as to secured creditors, the plan must provide for the creditor to retain its lien and receive in deferred cash payments the present value, as of the effective date (that is, confirmation date) of the plan of its allowed secured claim.[499] This is essentially the same requirement as is found under chapter 13.[500]

Usually a consumer creditor will be unsecured. For the plan to be fair and equitable as to a dissenting class of unsecured claims that will not receive a distribution equal to the present value of the allowed unsecured claims, the creditors must receive the same distribution as they would receive in a chapter 7 liquidation and no junior class of creditors or interests can receive any distribution.[501] This last requirement, known as the "absolute priority rule," means that the dissenting class of creditors must receive full payment of their allowed claims before the debtor or the owners of the debtor can retain any nonexempt property.[502]

18.7.9 Creditor's Plan of Reorganization

The Bankruptcy Code grants a chapter 11 debtor a time period of 120 days from the entry of the order for relief during which the debtor has the exclusive right to file a plan of reorganization.[503] If the debtor does not file a plan within the 120-day period or if a plan is not confirmed within a 180-day time period following the entry of the order for relief, any party in interest may propose a plan of reorganization.[504] This time limit is intended to give the debtor a reasonable period of time to negotiate a consensual plan with its creditors while at the same time imposing a deadline so that the debtor does not have undue leverage in the negotiations.

It is not uncommon for a debtor to move for an extension of the exclusivity period.[505] Such extensions may be permitted, after notice and hearing, "for cause."[506] Congress responded to concerns about the duration of extensions by setting time limits. For non-small business cases the exclusivity period may not be extended for cause beyond eighteen months from the date of the order for relief.[507] The debtor's plan must be accepted within twenty months of the date of the order for relief.[508]

Objection to the debtor's motion to extend the exclusivity period can be fertile ground for creditors. The decision by the court on exclusivity is discretionary and often quite fact-specific.[509] The willingness of courts to extend the exclusivity period can vary substantially in different jurisdictions. Active creditor opposition to the debtor may be grounds for denial of the extension of the exclusivity period, if the objecting creditors can show that further negotiations are unlikely to result in a confirmable consensual plan.[510]

After the exclusivity period has expired, any creditor is permitted to propose a plan. This option can be a useful strategy when the debtor is no longer operating and the creditors and the debtor cannot agree on the most profitable way of liquidating the debtor's assets. An operating debtor will be reluctant to implement a plan proposed by creditors, and it may thus be necessary that the plan provide for new management. A "creditor plan" may make sense if the creditors prefer that debtor's operations cease and that the assets be liquidated.[511] In at least one instance, a tenant ownership plan was filed and confirmed with the aid of community development groups experienced in property management and turnarounds of troubled buildings.[512]

A plan proposed by creditors must meet all of the same procedural and substantive requirements of a debtor's plan:

---

499 The amount of the allowed secured claim can be based upon the stripping of an undersecured claim under 11 U.S.C. § 506(a). However, in chapter 11, an undersecured creditor may have the right to elect to be treated as fully secured. 11 U.S.C. § 1111(b). *See generally* RadLAX Gateway Hotel, L.L.C. v. Amalgamated Bank, 132 S. Ct. 2065, 2067 (2012) (settling a circuit split in favor of undersecured creditors, holding that § 1129(b)(2)(A)(iii) does not allow confirmation of plan that proposes sale of assets free and clear without allowance for credit bidding).

500 *Compare* 11 U.S.C. § 1129(b)(2)(A) *with* 11 U.S.C. § 1325(a)(5)(B).

501 11 U.S.C. § 1129(b)(2)(B).

502 Without definitively resolving the issue, the Supreme Court has ruled on whether there is an exception to the absolute priority rule in favor of creditors that contribute "new value" to the reorganizing debtor. Bank of Am. Nat'l Trust & Sav. Ass'n v. 203 N. LaSalle St. P'ship, 526 U.S. 434, 119 S. Ct. 1411, 143 L. Ed. 2d 607 (1999). The Court concluded that the opportunity to contribute new value (and avoid the effect of the absolute priority rule) cannot be limited exclusively to one group of creditors or equity holders in a reorganizing company. The implication of the opinion is that there is a "new value" exception available once all parties are given a full and fair opportunity to compete to obtain it.

The absolute priority rule was held not to apply to prevent approved rate decreases for member/owners of a rural electric cooperative. *In re* Cajun Elec. Coop., Inc., 185 F.3d 446 (5th Cir. 1999).

503 11 U.S.C. § 1121(b). *See In re* Clamp-All Corp., 233 B.R. 198 (Bankr. D. Mass. 1999) (creditor's claim subordinated as a remedy for violating the exclusivity period by mailing out a proposed alternative plan in the 120-day period).

504 11 U.S.C. § 1121(c)(2), (3).

505 Creditors can also seek to have the exclusivity period shortened. 11 U.S.C. § 1121(d). *See In re* Geriatrics Nursing Home, Inc., 187 B.R. 128 (D.N.J. 1995) (creditor bears heavy burden in seeking premature termination of exclusivity period).

506 11 U.S.C. § 1121(d). *See In re* Express One Int'l, Inc., 194 B.R. 98 (Bankr. E.D. Tex. 1996) (list of factors which courts have identified as relevant to determining whether cause exists).

507 11 U.S.C. § 1121(d)(2)(A).

508 11 U.S.C. § 1121(d)(2)(B).

509 *In re* Borders Group, Inc., 460 B.R. 818 (Bankr. S.D.N.Y. 2011) (rejecting creditors' opposition to extension of exclusivity period, reviewing factors that indicate adequacy of debtor's efforts to submit plan). *See, e.g., In re* Friedman's, Inc., 336 B.R. 884 (Bankr. S.D. Ga. 2005) (balance of harm to creditors favored granting extension); *In re* Mid-State Raceway, Inc., 323 B.R. 63 (Bankr. N.D.N.Y. 2005) (seasonal nature of debtor's business weighed against further delays); *In re* Express One Int'l, Inc., 194 B.R. 98 (Bankr. E.D. Tex. 1996) (enumerating grounds for extensions).

510 *See, e.g., In re* Gagel & Gagel, 24 B.R. 674 (Bankr. S.D. Ohio 1982).

511 An alternative way to get to a similar result would be by a motion seeking conversion of the case to chapter 7. 11 U.S.C. § 1112(b).

512 *See Showdown in Minneapolis: How a Member of the Bankruptcy Bar Foiled a Notorious Slumlord*, Consumer Bankr. News (Sept. 3, 1992).

compliance with the provisions of section 1123(a);[513] approval of a disclosure statement; voting by the creditors; and satisfaction of the confirmation requirements of section 1129.[514] A consumer creditor should give careful thought before undertaking to propose a plan as there can be considerable time and expense involved in shepherding a plan through the confirmation process. At the same time, however, the prospect of a creditor's plan may be extremely helpful in negotiations with the debtor.

18.7.10 Special Provisions Applicable to Small Business Bankruptcies

The 2005 amendments established new procedures and modified some existing standards applicable to chapter 11 cases involving small businesses.[515] Debtors who meet the statutory definition of a "small business" can no longer opt out of coverage under the small business provisions.[516] The amendments establish expedited proceedings in certain areas and mandate new reporting requirements at various stages of the case. The exclusivity period in small business cases runs for 180 days from the order for relief.[517] If the debtor has not filed a plan by the expiration of the exclusivity period, all parties then have 120 days to file a plan.[518] The statute states that a plan must be filed within this 300-day period.[519] Extensions beyond the 300-day limit are to be granted under a standard that is stricter than the one applicable to non-small business chapter 11 cases.[520] The plan must be confirmed within forty-five days after filing unless the time is extended, again applying the tightened standard for consideration of any extensions.[521] Failure to comply with the time deadlines for filing and confirming a plan is cause for dismissal or conversion of the case.[522]

In an attempt to simplify procedures the amendments allow a small business debtor, subject to court approval, to include the disclosure statement information in the plan, and the court may hold a combined hearing on approving the disclosure statement and confirming the plan.[523] The amendments authorize the development of standard disclosure statements for small business cases.[524]

The small business debtor must file specified documents and disclosures with the petition. These include the debtor's "most recent balance sheet, statement of operations, cash flow statement, and Federal income tax return."[525] Absent "extraordinary and compelling circumstances," the small business debtor must file all schedules and statements of financial affairs by thirty days after the date of the order for relief, unless the court grants an extension.[526] Thereafter the debtor must submit ongoing periodic financial reports.[527] "Senior management personnel" of the debtor must appear at scheduling conferences, meetings with the trustee, and the section 341 meeting of creditors.[528] A new provision requires that the United States trustee interview the debtor before the meeting of creditors,[529] and the debtor must allow the trustee or a designated representative to inspect the debtor's business premises, books, and records at reasonable times, after reasonable prior notice.[530] As with the plan filing deadlines, failure to comply in a timely manner with any of these reporting, documentation, and appearance provisions is cause for dismissal or conversion of the case.[531] Finally, the amendments create a special automatic stay exception applicable to repeat filers of small business chapter 11 cases.[532]

---

513 11 U.S.C. § 1123(a).
514 11 U.S.C. § 1129.
515 See 11 U.S.C. § 101(51D), generally defining "small business debtor" as a person engaged in non-real estate business activities and who has less than $2,343,300 in non-contingent liquidated secured and unsecured debts as of date of the petition or order for relief. Debts owed to affiliates and insiders are excluded from this total. The debts owed by affiliated entities are included in the total. See also Fed. R. Bankr. P. 1020. See generally Thomas E. Carlson & Jennifer Frasier Hayes, *The Small Business Provisions of the 2005 Bankruptcy Amendments*, 79 Am. Bankr. L.J. 645 (2005).
516 The definition recognizes that the United States trustee may appoint a committee of unsecured creditors in the case of an otherwise qualifying small business debtor. 11 U.S.C. § 101(51D)(A).
517 11 U.S.C. § 1121(e)(1).
518 11 U.S.C. § 1121(e)(2).
519 11 U.S.C. § 1121(e)(2).
520 11 U.S.C. § 1121(e)(3). *See In re* Roots Rents, Inc., 420 B.R. 28 (Bankr. D. Idaho 2009) (small business plan confirmation deadline may only be extended if all three requirements of section 1121(e)(3) have been met).
521 11 U.S.C. §§ 1129(e), 1121(e)(3). *See In re* Save Our Springs (S.O.S.) Alliance, Inc., 388 B.R. 202 (Bankr. W.D. Tex. 2008) (refusing to grant extension of plan confirmation deadline under small business provisions). *See also In re* Crossroads Fords, Inc., 453 B.R. 764 (Bankr. D. Neb. 2011) (if plan not confirmed within 45 days, debtor can withdraw it, file another plan, and not run afoul of 45-day limit); *In re* Darby Gen. Contracting, Inc., 410 B.R. 136 (Bankr. E.D.N.Y. 2009) (denying small business debtor's motion to extend time to confirm plan because debtor failed to show it was more likely than not plan would be confirmed in a reasonable time). *See generally In re* Maxx Towing, Inc., 2011 WL 3267937 (Bankr. E.D. Mich. July 27, 2011) (summarizing split in decisions as to whether case must be dismissed if plan not confirmed within 45 day and no timely extension was sought, holding courts have authority not to dismiss under particular circumstances); *In re* AMAP Sales & Collision, Inc., 403 B.R. 244 (Bankr. E.D.N.Y. 2009) (to grant extension for confirmation in chapter 11 small business case, court need find it is more likely than not it would confirm some plan, not necessarily the current one, within a reasonable period of time).
522 11 U.S.C. § 1112(b)(4)(J); *In re* Sanchez, 429 B.R. 393 (Bankr. D. P.R. 2010) (granting trustee's motion to dismiss case when small business debtor failed to file plan and disclosures or seek extension within 300 days).
523 11 U.S.C. § 1125(f).
524 11 U.S.C. § 1125(f)(2).
525 11 U.S.C. § 1116(1)(A) (in lieu of the documents the debtor can file a verification that it does not have such documents).
526 11 U.S.C. § 1116(3).
527 11 U.S.C. § 308(b).
528 11 U.S.C. § 1116(2).
529 28 U.S.C. § 586(a)(7); 11 U.S.C. § 1116(2).
530 11 U.S.C. § 1116(7).
531 *See* 11 U.S.C. § 1112(b)(4)(E)–(H), (J).
532 11 U.S.C. § 362(n) (generally, the automatic stay will not apply in a new case if the debtor has a small business case pending or was a debtor in a small business case that was dismissed or in which a

18.7.11 Seeking Dismissal or Conversion of a Chapter 11 Case

On request of a party in interest (including any consumer creditors), a chapter 11 case may be dismissed or converted to a case under chapter 7, pursuant to 11 U.S.C. § 1112(b).[533] This section was revised in 2005 primarily to limit the court's discretion in determining whether or not a particular case should be dismissed or converted. The statute attempts to achieve this goal by mandating a judicial review involving some initial presumptions and a shifting burden of proof.[534] The court must first determine whether one or more of the sixteen specified "causes" enumerated in section 1112(b)(4) exist. These include substantial or continuing loss to or diminution of the estate and the absence of a reasonable likelihood of rehabilitation; gross mismanagement; failure to comply with any court order; an unexcused failure to satisfy timely filing, reporting, and documentation requirements; failure to attend hearings; and failure to pay taxes or postpetition child support.[535]

If a movant establishes that one or more of these conditions exist, the court has limited discretion to refrain from ordering conversion or dismissal. Ultimately, the court must find "unusual circumstances" which establish that a continuation of the chapter 11 case would be in the best interests of the creditors and the estate.[536] The debtor has a limited ability to override the effect of the finding of "cause" for dismissal or conversion by establishing that: (1) a plan will be confirmed within a reasonable time, and (2) there were reasonable justifications for any acts of the debtor that gave rise to the "cause," and the deficiency will be cured within a reasonable time.[537] As under the prior version of the section, despite an apparent drafting error,[538] the list of circumstances that constitute "cause" for conversion or dismissal in section 1112(b) is nonexclusive, and the court should be willing to consider other grounds including lack of good faith.[539]

If cause exists and "unusual circumstances" as defined by the statute are absent, the court may either convert or dismiss the case, depending on the best interests of the creditors and the estate.[540] Generally the choice between conversion or dismissal is considered discretionary, but there are limits on a court's discretion.[541]

Pursuit of a motion to convert or dismiss is a strategic decision that must be made based on the circumstances of the individual case. Such motions should not be undertaken lightly.

---

533 Cases may not be converted to chapter 12 or 13 unless the debtor so requests. 11 U.S.C. § 1112(d).

534 See generally Thomas E. Carlson & Jennifer Frasier Hayes, The Small Business Provisions of the 2005 Bankruptcy Amendments, 79 Am. Bankr. L.J. 645 (2005).

535 11 U.S.C. § 1112(b)(4); In re Om Shivi, Inc., 447 B.R. 459 (Bankr. D.S.C. 2011) (dismissal required where record showed pattern of negative income from debtor's motel business and lack of funds for repairs); In re Babayoff, 445 B.R. 64 (Bankr. E.D.N.Y. 2011) (conversion ordered as in best interest of creditors and estate due to debtor's inability to confirm plan, failure to file adequate disclosures, and non-compliance with court orders); In re Vaughn, 429 B.R. 14 (Bankr. D.N.M. 2010) (court must convert to chapter 7 when debtor refused to testify at creditors' meeting, all creditors and trustee favored conversion, no prospect for improvement, and no unusual circumstances meriting otherwise); In re Van Eck, 425 B.R. 54 (Bankr. D. Conn. 2010) (failure to maintain insurance on real property assets of estate is a cause for dismissal). See, e.g., In re Pittsfield Weaving Co., 393 B.R. 271 (Bankr. D.N.H. 2008) (cause found for dismissal of chapter 11 case, including failure to file timely reports, nonpayment of taxes, failure to pay employee insurance benefits, and lack of confirmable plan two years after filing of petition).

536 11 U.S.C. § 1112(b)(1),(2). See, e.g., In re Gateway Access Solutions, Inc., 374 B.R. 556 (Bankr. M.D. 2007) (chapter 11 debtor failed to show any "unusual circumstances"; case ordered converted to chapter 7 due to continuing diminution of estate attributed to director's unauthorized postpetition loans).

537 11 U.S.C. § 1112(b)(2).

538 Prior to the 2005 amendments, section 1112(b)(4) contained a list of ten factors a moving party could rely upon in establishing "cause." Because the conjunction "or" was used in joining the list of factors, the court could dismiss or convert the case if only one of the listed factors for cause was proven. The statute was amended in 2005 to expand the list to sixteen factors and the disjunctive "or" was replaced with the conjunctive "and." One court has found that this change was a drafting error. In re TCR of Denver, Inc., 338 B.R. 494 (Bankr. D. Colo. 2006) (requiring proof of all sixteen factors, some of which apply only to individual chapter 11 debtors, would render the provision meaningless as virtually no corporate chapter 11 case could ever be dismissed for cause).

539 In re Integrated Telecom Express, Inc., 384 F.3d 122 (3d Cir. 2004) (dismissal for bad faith appropriate when debtor, a commercial tenant, filed for chapter 11 relief in order to take technical advantage of the cap on damages for breaking lease, with no intention of reorganizing or liquidating); In re Wallace, 2011 WL 1230535 (D. Idaho Mar. 30, 2011) (affirming Bankr. D. Idaho Jan. 26, 2010) (dismissal citing failure to document basis for continuing substantial diminution of business's resources); Singer Furniture Acquisition Corp. v. SSMC, Inc., 254 B.R. 46 (M.D. Fla. 2000) (Bilzerian bankruptcy dismissed based on evidence of bad faith including primary motivation of thwarting litigation by secured creditors in another jurisdiction); Quarles v. United States Tr., 194 B.R. 94 (W.D. Va.), aff'd, 86 F.3d 55 (4th Cir. 1996); In re Forum Health, 444 B.R. 848 (Bankr. N.D. Ohio 2011) (debtor's ability to pay creditors in full outside of bankruptcy after sale of certain assets is proper ground to dismiss chapter 11 case); In re Milford Conn. Assocs., L.P., 389 B.R. 303 (Bankr. D. Conn. 2008) (cause existed to convert chapter 11 case to chapter 7 based on debtor's intention to "park" case in chapter 11 for nineteen months until market conditions improved for sale of property); In re Boughton, 243 B.R. 830 (Bankr. M.D. Fla. 1999).

540 The grounds to dismiss or convert under section 1112(b)(4) are also referenced in section 1104(a)(3) as grounds for appointment of a trustee or examiner. Thus the court has the option to appoint a trustee or examiner as an alternative disposition in any proceeding in which it considers dismissal or conversion for cause. See, e.g., In re USA Commercial Mortg. Co., 452 Fed. Appx. 715, 724 (9th Cir. 2011) (affirming district court's grant of lender's motion to convert servicer's chapter 11 case to chapter 7 because servicer had "a negative cash flow and could not reasonably depend on future fees" for reorganization).

541 See In re Super. Siding & Window, Inc., 14 F.3d 240 (4th Cir. 1994) (choice should not be made solely by counting the votes of unsecured creditors).

Most judges are reluctant to convert or dismiss chapter 11 cases early on, absent a showing of extreme misconduct or complete inability to reorganize.[542] When possible, if there are major secured or unsecured creditors whose claims dwarf those of the affected consumers, their position should be solicited in advance of filing a motion. Judges are unlikely to convert or dismiss in the face of opposition to such a motion by the major creditors.

A motion to convert or dismiss is often useful when a case has been pending for a long time without movement toward a confirmable plan. At a minimum, the motion will wake up the debtor and/or the court in order to get the case moving. Alternatively, a motion to dismiss may be a good idea if the creditor can establish inequitable postpetition conduct by the debtor that suggests improper motives in the reorganization process. Often the same conduct that would give rise to a motion to appoint a trustee is also a proper basis for seeking conversion or dismissal under section 1112(b).[543]

Another ground for dismissal of a chapter 11 case is offered by the recent decision of the Court of Appeals for the Third Circuit in *SGL Carbon Corp.*[544] When a solvent company files chapter 11 not to reorganize any debt, but simply to gain a tactical advantage in pending litigation, the bankruptcy may be dismissed on the basis that it was not filed in good faith. The Third Circuit distinguished other chapter 11 cases filed by companies facing mass tort liabilities, on the basis that SGL Carbon Corp. was not facing any prospect of crippling liabilities, or even major disruption to its operations, as a result of the threatened litigation.

18.7.12 Representing Employees and Other Industrial Stakeholders in Chapter 11 Proceedings

18.7.12.1 Introduction

As companies face increased pressure to restructure in order to remain competitive, many are turning to chapter 11 filings as a means of doing so. A chapter 11 filing enables a struggling company to shed less profitable operations and burdensome obligations. This not only affects the company's suppliers, customers, secondary lenders, tort claimants, and so forth, but it can be devastating to the livelihoods of its employees and the economic vitality of its local community. This subsection discusses some of the remedies available to a chapter 11 debtor's employees and community residents, with an emphasis on possible strategies for keeping the debtor's manufacturing facilities operable and for preserving employees' jobs and the local community's economic base.

18.7.12.2 Employee Priority Claims

Section 507(a) provides that certain prepetition employee wage and benefit claims will be treated with priority. Section 507(a)(4) gives fourth priority to claims for wages, salaries, and commissions earned within 180 days before either the petition filing date or the date of cessation of the debtor's business, whichever occurs first.[545] The maximum amount entitled to priority under this section is $11,725.[546] This priority extends to vacation, severance and sick leave pay.[547] (Prepetition "trust

---

542 *In re* Macon Prestressed Concrete Co., 61 B.R. 432 (Bankr. M.D. Ga. 1986) (reorganization is the preferred outcome whenever possible).

However, when there is evidence that the debtor is using the bankruptcy process for an improper purpose, some courts have found that the case may be dismissed at the outset for lack of good faith. *In re* Albany Partners, Ltd., 749 F.2d 670 (11th Cir. 1984) (lack of good faith on filing is "cause" under section 1112(b)). *Cf. In re* Madison Hotel Assocs., 749 F.2d 410 (7th Cir. 1984) (good faith prerequisite to plan confirmation is different from good faith requirement on filing).

543 *In re* SI Grand Traverse L.L.C., 450 B.R. 703 (Bankr. W.D. Mich. 2011) (although grounds existed to dismiss case, court directs appointment of trustee as alternative best serving interests of creditors and estate); *In re* Snydor, 431 B.R. 584 (Bankr. D. Md. 2010) (in deciding whether to dismiss or convert case, court can exercise discretion to appoint trustee, selecting remedy that is in the best interest of creditors and the estate). *See In re* Starmark Clinics, L.P., 388 B.R. 729 (Bankr. S.D. Tex. 2008) (in considering motion to appoint trustee court may *sua sponte* dismiss chapter 11 case); § 18.7.4.3, *supra*.

544 *In re* South Beach Sec., 606 F.3d 366 (7th Cir. 2010) (dismissal for bad faith when sole creditor of solvent debtor is insider; debtor merely seeking tax benefit); *In re* SGL Carbon Corp., 200 F.3d 154 (3d Cir. 1999). *See also In re* Blumenberg, 263 B.R. 704 (Bankr. E.D. N.Y. 2001) (chapter 11 petition filed with no intention of reorganizing and for sole purpose of attacking state court judgment was in bad faith and warranted dismissal of converted chapter 7 case). *Cf. In re* Muralo Co., 301 B.R. 690 (Bankr. D.N.J. 2003) (refusing to dismiss as bad faith filing, court distinguished *SGL Carbon*).

545 The 2005 amendments redesignated sections 507(a)(3) and 507(a)(4) as sections 507(a)(4) and 507(a)(5), respectively. The priority "look-back" period for wages, salaries, and commissions increased from 90 to 180 days under the 2005 Act, and the maximum amount increased from $4925 to $10,000. As with wage claims, the entire amount of postpetition benefit claims are entitled to administrative priority under 11 U.S.C. § 507(a)(2). *See* § 18.5.3, *supra*.

546 11 U.S.C. § 507(a)(4). *But see* Meyers v. Heffernan, 740 F. Supp. 2d 637 (D. Del. 2010) (former employees who filed priority claim for commissions under § 507(a)(4) in employer corporation's chapter 11 case not barred from pursuing amounts in excess of capped claim in later state court proceeding against principals of corporation).

The amount of the employee priority is adjusted for inflation every three years. 11 U.S.C. § 104. For cases filed between April 1, 2001 and March 31, 2004, the amount of the priority was $4650. *See generally In re* Organogenesis Inc., 316 B.R. 574 (Bankr. D. Mass. 2004) (priority given up to first $4650 (the wage priority amount at that time) of allowed claims for damages based on WARN Act violations, balance of damage awards treated as general unsecured claims); *In re* Myer, 197 B.R. 875 (Bankr. W.D. Mo. 1996) (priority applies to earned commissions, but not to damages for lost opportunity to earn commissions awarded in court case for breach of employment contract).

547 11 U.S.C. § 507(a)(4). *See In re* Crafts Precision Indus., Inc., 244 B.R. 178 (B.A.P. 1st Cir. 2000) (vacation pay is covered by section 507(a)(3), but is not a contribution to an employee benefit plan covered by what is now section 507(a)(5)); *In re* Powermate Holding Corp., 394 B.R. 765 (Bankr. D. Del. 2008) (WARN Act damages payable to former employees receive priority for prepetition wage claim under section 507(a)(4)); *In re* First Magnus Fin.

fund" taxes—that is, employer-withheld income taxes and the employee's share of Social Security taxes as well as the employer's share—are entitled to eighth priority under section 507(a)(8)).[548] Courts, pursuant to section 105(a), normally permit debtors to pay prepetition wage claims in the ordinary course in response to a motion filed at the beginning of the chapter 11 case. The priority is not limited to subordinate employees and may be asserted by officers, directors, stockholders, partners, or independent contractors of the debtor.[549]

Some state laws provide for an automatic lien to secure unpaid wages in certain circumstances.[550] When such a statutory lien has not been avoided under section 545,[551] the claim will be paid before distribution to unsecured priority creditors. Otherwise, any claim for wages earned outside the 180-day time period or in excess of the statutory amount is treated as an unsecured, non-priority claim.

Section 507(a)(5) gives a fifth priority to claims for contributions to an employee benefit plan (for example, pension, health, or life insurance plans), arising from services rendered within 180 days before either the petition filing date or the date of cessation of the debtor's business, whichever occurs first.[552] The maximum amount allowed for *all claims under each benefit plan* is calculated according to the following formula: (1) multiply the total number of employees covered by the plan by $11,725, (2) subtract any priority wage claims paid to those employees pursuant to section 507(a)(4), and (3) subtract any other priority benefit claims paid to those employees pursuant to section 507(a)(5).[553] Each claimant is entitled to a pro rata share of the total.

Employer contributions to a trust established for payment of employees' medical benefits are entitled to priority under section 507(a)(5),[554] as are premiums to privately administered employee group insurance plans.[555] The Supreme Court has ruled that a debt owed by an employer to a worker's compensation insurance plan is not in the nature of a contribution to an employee benefit plan entitled to priority under section 507(a)(5).[556] There is a split of authority concerning workers' compensation premiums.[557] In addition to the claims process, section 1114 of the Code creates certain procedural and substantive protections for retiree benefits during chapter 11 proceedings.[558] Before seeking to modify retiree benefits, the trustee must negotiate over the changes in good faith with employee representatives. Section 1114 authorizes an administrative expense priority for retiree benefits payments during the chapter 11 proceeding.

An employee asserts priority by filing a proof of claim, and the claim is deemed allowed unless an objection is made and a hearing held.[559] Employees may want to consider filing a class proof of claim,[560] especially for benefit claims under section 507(a)(4).

Corp., 390 B.R. 667 (Bankr. D. Ariz. 2008) (WARN Act claims of former employees not an administrative priority claim under section 507(a)(2)); *In re* Ground Round, Inc., 316 B.R. 423 (Bankr. D. Mass. 2004) (vacation pay is covered by wage priority, but will be calculated only as accruing during the applicable time period). *See also In re* Metro Fulfillment, Inc., 294 B.R. 306 (B.A.P. 9th Cir. 2003) (penalty wage claims entitled to administrative expense priority). *But see In re* LandAmerica Fin. Group, Inc., 435 B.R. 343 (Bankr. E.D. Va. 2010) (severance pay entitled to priority and calculated as total earned as of termination date, not only as the pro-rated portion earned over 180-day period prior to termination), *aff'd sub nom.* Matson v. Alacron, 651 F.3d 404 (4th Cir. 2011).

548 11 U.S.C. § 507(a)(8).
549 *See In re* Jade W. Corp., 53 B.R. 16 (Bankr. D. Or. 1985) (officers and directors of debtor entitled to assert wage priority). *See also In re* Wang Laboratories, Inc., 164 B.R. 404, 408 (Bankr. D. Mass. 1994) (independent contractors of debtor also entitled to assert wage priority).
550 *See, e.g.*, Cal. Civ. Proc. Code §§ 1204–1208 (West).
551 *See In re* Edgar B, Inc., 200 B.R. 119 (M.D.N.C. 1996) (limit in priority is on the aggregate dollar claim for all employees to the plan; there is no $4000 limit for individual employees); *In re* C & S Cartage and Leasing Co., 204 B.R. 565 (Bankr. D. Neb. 1996) (because limit on priority is an aggregate for all employees, individual claim is not barred solely because the individual had already received a priority claim to the extent of $4000 for unpaid wages); § 10.4.2.6.3, *supra*.
552 As with wage claims, the entire amount of postpetition benefit claims is entitled to administrative priority under 11 U.S.C. § 507(a)(2). *See In re* Consol. Freightways Corp. of Del., 564 F.3d 1161 (9th Cir. 2009) (priority for employee benefit plan contributions under section 507(a)(5) applied to retirees as well as current employees at time of petition filing, as long as claimant rendered services during the 180-day prepetition period); § 18.5.3, *supra*.

553 11 U.S.C. § 507(a)(4).
554 *In re* Structurelite Plastics Corp., 86 B.R. 922 (Bankr. S.D. Ohio 1988). *But see In re* Louis Jones Enters., Inc., 442 B.R. 126 (Bankr. N.D. Ill. 2010) (§ 507(a)(5) priority applies despite employer's failure to segregate funds withheld from employees' paychecks to pay for employees' health insurance premiums).
555 *In re* Saco Local Dev. Corp., 711 F.2d 441 (1st Cir. 1983). *See also In re* Qualia Clinical Serv., Inc., 2010 WL 1430234 (Bankr. D. Neb. Feb. 12, 2010) (employer's payment of debtor/doctor's medical malpractice insurance premiums was benefit covered by section 523(a)(5)).
556 Howard Delivery Serv., Inc. v. Zurich Am. Ins. Co., 126 S. Ct. 2105, 165 L. Ed. 2d 110 (2006) (an insurance plan paid for by the employer in order to comply with the worker's compensation laws is different from the bargained-for employee fringe benefits that are within the intended scope of section 507(a)(5)).
557 *Compare* Employers Ins. of Wausau v. Plaid Pantries, Inc., 10 F.3d 605 (9th Cir. 1993) (workers compensation premium claims entitled to priority) *with In re* Birmingham-Nashville Express, Inc., 224 F.3d 511 (6th Cir. 2000); *In re* HLM Corp., 62 F.3d 224 (8th Cir. 1995) (contra); *In re* S. Star Foods, 144 F.3d 712 (10th Cir. 1998) *and In re* Allentown Moving and Storage, 208 B.R. 835 (Bankr. E.D. Pa.), *aff'd*, 214 B.R. 761 (E.D. Pa. 1997).

  The latter courts have found that these premiums are typically paid to state insurance funds rather than to plans which benefit employees directly so that they are not contributions to an employee benefit plan.

558 11 U.S.C. § 1114. *See In re* Visteon Corp., 612 F.3d 210 (3d Cir. 2010) (§ 1114 takes precedence over conflicting provisions of non-bankruptcy law).
559 *See* § 18.5.5, *supra*.
560 *In re* Taylor Bean & Whitaker, 2010 WL 4025873 (Bankr. M.D. Fla. Sept. 27, 2010) (certifying class of former employees to assert priority claims under § 507(a)(4) in adversary proceeding as alternative to class claim). *See* § 18.4.2, *supra*. *See also In re* Birting Fisheries, Inc., 178 B.R. 849 (W.D. Wash. 1995), *aff'd* 92 F.3d 939 (9th Cir. 1996); *In re* Powermate Holding Corp., 394 B.R. 765

18.7.12.3 Job Retention Strategies in Chapter 11 Proceedings

18.7.12.3.1 Introduction

When a major employer files for protection under chapter 11, employees and members of the local community will be primarily interested in the prospects for continued operation of the debtor's business. Even employees with wage and benefit claims will usually be more concerned with whether they will have a job to go back to than with whether their prepetition claims will be fully paid. The job retention strategies available to employees and other interested parties in a chapter 11 proceeding will vary according to the circumstances of each case. A few possibilities are discussed below.

18.7.12.3.2 Right to intervene

Section 1109(b) states that "[a] party in interest . . . may raise and may appear and be heard on any issue in a case under this chapter."[561] Creditors, such as employees with wage or benefit claims, are specifically authorized under section 1109 to be heard.[562] A more difficult question is whether non-creditor employees, laid-off employees and representatives of the local community have a sufficient interest to justify intervention.

A party is a "party in interest" if it has a sufficient stake in the outcome of the proceeding to require representation, and the Code's list of who may be a party in interest is illustrative and non-exhaustive.[563] A party who is not a creditor or shareholder is typically entitled to intervene if it has a significant economic or similar interest in the outcome of a chapter 11 case.[564] The term "party in interest" should be interpreted in light of the legislative history and purposes of the Bankruptcy Code.[565] The legislative history of chapter 11 indicates that Congress sought to encourage greater participation in reorganization cases.[566] Section 1109(b) should be construed liberally so as to effectuate that purpose.[567]

Current and former employees have a clear economic interest in the survival of their employer's business: Their livelihood is at stake. The local community has a similar interest: The local economy suffers through the loss of payroll and a "ripple effect" job loss. As local tax revenues decrease, schools deteriorate, public services are reduced, and residential taxes may increase. Social problems—alcoholism and drug use, divorce, domestic violence, mental health problems—all increase as a result of a large plant shutdown.[568] There is a strong argument that the economic impact of a plant shutdown on the surrounding community creates a sufficient economic interest to allow a representative group of individuals to intervene on behalf of the community at large.

18.7.12.3.3 Opposing a chapter 11 liquidation

Occasionally, the debtor and its major secured creditors will seek court permission to sell assets in order to satisfy secured claims. A sale of all or substantially all of a debtor's assets is known as a liquidating chapter 11. As a business may be worth considerably more as a going concern than in a piecemeal liquidation, holders of junior secured claims, priority claims (such as wages, benefits, and local tax obligations), and unsecured claims may be disadvantaged.[569] Moreover, the sale of even some of a business' assets may have an adverse effect on the likelihood of a successful reorganization, and therefore threaten the number and quality of jobs that will be retained.

Other than in the ordinary course of business, the chapter 11 debtor in possession may sell property of the estate only after notice and a hearing.[570] If no interested party files a timely objection to a notice of sale, court approval is not required.[571] Such an objection must be filed at least seven days prior to any scheduled sale.[572] In ruling on a proposed sale, the court must consider the effect of the property's disposition on future plans

---

(Bankr. D. Del. 2008) (certifying class of claimants for WARN Act damages under section 507(a)(4)).

561   11 U.S.C. § 1109(b).

   Note that this section provides the right to be heard in a bankruptcy "case." Whether a party is entitled to intervene in an adversary proceeding is governed by Federal Rule of Civil Procedure 24, made applicable to bankruptcy proceedings by Federal Rule of Bankruptcy Procedure 7024. Presumably, the right to be heard pursuant to section 1109(b) is more expansive than the right to intervene under Rule 24. *See In re* Caldor Corp., 303 F.3d 161 (2d Cir. 2002) (finding the right to intervene under section 1109(b) extends to adversary actions).

562   Labor unions and other employee associations also have limited authorization to be heard on the economic soundness of a reorganization plan under Federal Rule of Bankruptcy Procedure 2018(d).

563   *In re* Kaiser Steel Corp., 998 F.2d 783 (10th Cir. 1993); *In re* Amatex Corp., 755 F.2d 1034 (3d Cir. 1985).

564   *In re* Amatex Corp., 755 F.2d 1034 (3d Cir. 1985) (future tort claimants allowed to intervene in order to preserve estate for payment of future claims); *In re* Brown Transp., 118 B.R. 889 (Bankr. N.D. Ga. 1990) (third party allowed to intervene in order to challenge transfer of estate property to competitor); *In re* Hathaway Ranch P'ship, 116 B.R. 208 (Bankr. C.D. Cal. 1990) (debtor's limited partner allowed to intervene); *In re* Wilson, 94 B.R. 886 (Bankr. E.D. Va. 1989) (defendant in civil suit brought by trustee may intervene to challenge abandonment of suit).

565   *In re* Ionosphere Clubs, Inc., 101 B.R. 844 (Bankr. S.D.N.Y. 1989).

   See also In re Ctr. Apartments, Ltd., 277 B.R. 747 (Bankr. S.D. Ohio 2001) (tenants not authorized to serve on creditor's committee nevertheless have right under section 1109(b) to be heard on objection to sale of property and other issues that arise).

566   *In re* Amatex Corp., 755 F.2d 1034 (3d Cir. 1985).

567   *Id.*

   The right to intervene in a "case" as provided for under section 1109(b) has been construed to include intervention in adversary proceedings. *See In re* Caldor Corp., 303 F.3d 161 (2d Cir. 2002) (section 1109(b) confers on parties in interest an unconditional right to intervene in adversary proceedings).

568   For a modest fee, the Midwest Center for Labor Research (Chicago: (773) 278-5418) can prepare a social costs assessment that will estimate the anticipated monetary cost of a particular plant shutdown on the local community.

569   Anderson & Wright, *Liquidating Plans of Reorganization*, 56 Am. Bankr. L.J. 29 (1982).

570   11 U.S.C. § 363(b).

571   11 U.S.C. § 363(b).

572   Fed. R. Bankr. P. 6004(b).

of reorganization.[573] Property of the estate should not be sold if it is necessary to an effective reorganization.[574]

The preconfirmation sale of all or substantially all of a debtor's assets is disfavored. The basic policy behind chapter 11 is that it is generally preferable to allow a business to continue to operate than to liquidate its assets.[575] Only if revival of the business is impossible should liquidation proceed and only then does maximum recovery for creditors become of primary importance.[576] Moreover, such sales potentially circumvent the disclosure and voting requirements that are the very essence of the chapter 11 scheme.[577]

The general rule is that the preconfirmation sale of all or substantially all of a debtor's assets can take place only when there is a "sound business reason."[578] Implicit in this standard are the following factors: (1) the proportionate value of the asset to the estate as a whole, (2) the amount of time that has elapsed since filing, (3) the likelihood that a plan will be proposed and confirmed in the near future, (4) the effect of the proposed sale on future reorganization, (5) the adequacy of the sale price, (6) whether a sale or lease is proposed, and (7) most importantly, whether the asset is increasing or decreasing in value.[579] Other courts have also required that there be adequate and reasonable notice of the sale and that the sale be conducted in good faith.[580] In no case should a sale be confirmed merely to appease major creditors.[581]

18.7.12.3.4 Placing conditions upon approval of a sale of the debtor's business

A court of equity may grant or deny relief upon performance of a condition that will safeguard the public interest.[582] If an interested party files an objection, a sale of the debtor's business requires court approval under section 363(b). This is certainly true of preconfirmation sales and of auctions held pursuant to a confirmed plan. It is questionable whether a court has discretion to impose conditions upon a sale to a specific purchaser pursuant to a reorganization plan that otherwise meets the requirements for confirmation under section 1129.[583] It could be argued that any such purchaser may only be approved in accordance with public policy considerations under section 1123(a)(7). In any case, whenever a sale of a chapter 11 debtor's business is proposed, interested parties should seek to intervene and ask the court to impose conditions upon that sale in order to safeguard the public interest. One such condition might be a requirement that the property be sold to an entity that intends to keep the business in operation.[584]

In a chapter 11 proceeding, property of the estate need not be sold to the highest bidder.[585] A court may accept a lower bid for a debtor's business, if the higher bidder indicates it would shut the business down. With appropriate proof, the court may consider other issues beyond the money involved.

18.7.12.3.5 Other job retention strategies

In addition to those outlined above, other strategies may be available depending upon the circumstances of a particular case. For instance, if the debtor-in-possession is not operating the business in a sound manner, employees or other interested parties may wish to file a motion to appoint a trustee or examiner.[586] If the debtor has not filed a reorganization plan, it may be possible to file a creditor's plan.[587] Finally, it may be possible for the employees and/or local community to obtain financing to purchase the debtor's business.[588]

18.8 Special Problems of Tenants

18.8.1 General

When real estate markets decline, owners of private housing[589] occupied by low-income tenants may file bankruptcy. Often, tenants receive no official notice. They may come to their lawyer to complain that the building is no longer receiving services such as utilities, trash pick-up and repairs and also to report that no one is collecting the rent. A call to the landlord or the landlord's attorney reveals that the landlord has filed a petition in bankruptcy. This subsection discusses steps to be taken by the tenants' lawyer to protect tenants' rights, with an emphasis on assuring the continuation of needed services.

---

573 *In re* Lionel Corp., 722 F.2d 1063 (2d Cir. 1983).
574 The standards for relief from the automatic stay should be analogous. *See* § 9.7.3.2.3, *supra*.
575 7 Collier on Bankruptcy ¶ 1100.01 (16th ed.).
576 John C. Anderson, Chapter 11 Reorganizations § 1.01, at 1-1, 1-2 (1983); Anderson & Wright, *Liquidating Plans of Reorganization*, 56 Am. Bankr. L.J. 29 (1982).
577 *See In re* Braniff Airways, Inc., 700 F.2d 935 (5th Cir. 1985); *In re* Air Beds, Inc., 92 B.R. 419 (B.A.P. 9th Cir. 1988).
578 *In re* Lionel Corp., 722 F.2d 1063 (2d Cir. 1983); *In re* Westpoint Stevens, Inc., 333 B.R. 30 (S.D.N.Y. 2005) (reversing bankruptcy court's decision to allow preconfirmation sale of assets to satisfy debt owed to secured creditor).
579 *In re* Lionel Corp., 722 F.2d 1063 (2d Cir. 1983).
580 *In re* Titusville Country Club, 128 B.R. 396 (Bankr. W.D. Pa. 1991).
581 *In re* Lionel Corp., 722 F.2d 1063 (2d Cir. 1983).
582 Am. United Mut. Life Ins. Co. v. City of Avon Park, 311 U.S. 138, 61 S. Ct. 157, 85 L. Ed. 91 (1940).
   Bankruptcy courts are courts of equity, and their proceedings are proceedings in equity. Pepper v. Litton, 308 U.S. 295, 60 S. Ct. 238, 84 L. Ed. 281 (1939).

583 *See* § 18.7.8, *supra*.
584 A creditor whose claim is impaired may also be able to obtain commitments from the debtor in exchange for voting to approve the plan.
585 *In re* Karpe, 84 B.R. 926 (Bankr. M.D. Pa. 1988). *See also* 3 Collier on Bankruptcy ¶ 363.02(1)(g) (16th ed.).
586 *See* § 18.7.4, *supra*.
587 *See* § 18.7.9, *supra*.
588 *See, e.g.*, § 18.8.3, *infra*.
589 When the building has been constructed with the aid of federal or state programs which earmark some or all units for low or moderate income tenants, tenants may have other rights beyond those discussed in this subsection.

18.8.2 Maintaining Services When Private Landlords File Chapter 7 Bankruptcy

18.8.2.1 Abandonment by a Chapter 7 Trustee

When the owner believes the building is no longer financially viable, a chapter 7 bankruptcy may be filed.[590] If title to the building is in a corporation or other legal entity which the owner believes insulates him or her from personal liability, the bankruptcy will be in the name of the entity holding title and that entity will the "debtor" in the bankruptcy proceeding. A landlord holding property in her own name may also file under chapter 7, although this will expose all of the landlord's assets to the bankruptcy process and not just the real estate holdings.

Upon the filing of the bankruptcy petition, the property of the debtor, with some inconsequential exceptions, becomes the property of the bankruptcy estate.[591] In theory, the chapter 7 trustee takes over management of the assets of the estate and liquidates them for the benefit of the unsecured creditors.[592] In practice, in a typical apartment building bankruptcy, the only assets of the entity filing bankruptcy will be the building and the land on which it is situated. The real estate will frequently be mortgaged well beyond its value so there is no equity remaining for the unsecured creditors.

Section 554 of the Bankruptcy Code[593] permits the trustee to "abandon" property that is burdensome to the estate or is of inconsequential value and benefit to the estate. Because the building will usually have no equity from which the estate will benefit upon foreclosure and because the rents will be insufficient to meet the mortgage payments and other expenses, the trustee is likely to conclude that the building meets the statutory tests for abandonment.

In theory, abandonment means turning the property back to the debtor.[594] In an apartment building bankruptcy, as a practical matter, abandonment means relieving the trustee of any obligation and clearing the way for the secured lenders to foreclose.

The filing of the chapter 7 bankruptcy is likely to have been an act of desperation on the part of the landlord, brought on by a final realization that the building or buildings are not economically viable, by the threat or actuality of litigation from the tenants, or by all of these factors. As a result, upon filing, the owner may make no arrangement for the continuation of utility or other services or for the management of the building. If the building has low-income tenants, is in bad condition and perhaps is already the subject of dispute between the tenant and the landlord, the trustee's instinct will be to have nothing to do with it.[595] She may immediately file a motion for abandonment and in any event may do nothing about providing services.

Abandonment by the trustee has the potential for leaving the tenants in legal limbo. The foreclosing creditors may do nothing until they have completed state foreclosure proceedings which, depending on state practice, may take from several weeks to several months. The creditors may believe they have no legal right to manage the building prior to the foreclosure, or may wish to avoid responsibility for building maintenance and housing code compliance. The debtor in theory remains responsible until the foreclosure but, by filing bankruptcy, the debtor has renounced any intention of continuing management and will have no interest or incentive to continue. Further, continued involvement by the debtor may be the last thing the tenants want.

18.8.2.2 Legal Theories to Prevent Abandonment

The tenants' attorney has some tools to protect the tenants' interests in this situation. In *Midlantic National Bank v. New Jersey Department of Environmental Protection*,[596] the United States Supreme Court held that a trustee could not abandon property even though it was burdensome to the estate when abandonment would be "in contravention of a state statute or regulation that is reasonably designed to protect the public health or safety from identified hazards."[597] In a footnote the court added that the violation could not be speculative or indeterminate but must involve "imminent and identifiable harm."[598]

Courts have looked at two factors in evaluating claims under the *Midlantic* doctrine. First, the opposing party must establish that the danger resulting from abandonment is imminent[599] and

---

590 For a general discussion of chapter 7 bankruptcy see Chapter 3, *supra*.
591 11 U.S.C. § 541.
592 11 U.S.C. § 704.
593 11 U.S.C. § 554.
594 *See, e.g.*, *In re* Franklin Signal Corp., 65 B.R. 268 (D. Minn. 1986) (effect of abandonment is that ownership and control of the asset is reinstated in the debtor with all rights and obligations as before filing a petition in bankruptcy); *In re* Cruseturner, 8 B.R. 581, 591, 592 (Bankr. D. Utah 1981).
595 Among other things, in a deteriorating situation, the trustee may be concerned about personal legal liability as well as the liability of the estate. Although the trustee is generally not personally liable for actions taken in an official capacity, some exposure to liability exists. *See, e.g.*, Yadkin Valley Bank & Trust Co. v. McGee, 819 F.2d 74 (4th Cir. 1987) (trustee may be individually liable for negligence if actions are outside the bounds of the trustee authority and liable within his official capacity when actions are willfully and deliberately in violation of his duties); *In re* Rigden, 795 F.2d 727 (9th Cir. 1986) (trustee liable for negligent violations of duties imposed upon him by law).
   The expense for short-term liability and other insurance for the building involved may be prohibitive. One possibility is to have the lender cover the building and the trustee under its insurance coverage.
596 474 U.S. 494, 106 S. Ct. 755, 88 L. Ed. 2d 859 (1986).
597 *Id.*, 474 U.S. at 507.
598 *Id.*, 474 U.S. at n.9.
599 *In re* Vel Rey Properties, 174 B.R. 859 (Bankr. D.D.C. 1994) (trustee could abandon apartment building because public danger from housing code violations was not imminent); *In re* Smith-Douglass, Inc., 856 F.2d 12 (4th Cir. 1988) (allowing abandonment of fertilizer plant despite presence of environmental violations because the danger was not "imminent"); *In re* Armstrong, 96 B.R. 55 (Bankr. E.D.N.C. 1989) (upon finding of imminent danger, abandonment only permitted conditional upon the debtor setting

in violation of law.[600] Second, some courts have stressed there must be resources available to the trustee to alleviate the danger.[601] When these two factors can be shown, courts will not permit the trustee to abandon the property.[602]

While the *Midlantic* case involved the ownership of a dump containing toxic materials and most of the cases following *Midlantic* have involved some sort of environmental hazard, nothing in the language of the case limits its holding to such hazards. In an unreported West Virginia case,[603] for example, a legal services attorney, arguing on the basis of *Midlantic* and section 959, discussed below, obtained an order requiring the trustee to accept payments from the tenants and Section 8 payments from the public housing authority[604] to restore utility service and to continue to manage the property until such time as the secured party presented an acceptable plan for taking over the management.

Related to the *Midlantic* doctrine are the trustee's obligations under 28 U.S.C. § 959(b):

[A] trustee, ... appointed ... in any court of the United States, ... shall manage and operate the property in his possession ... according to the requirements of the valid laws of the State in which such property is situated, in the same manner that the owner or possessor thereof would be bound to do if in possession thereof.

While the Supreme Court in *Midlantic* suggested that section 959(b) might not apply in liquidation, that is, chapter 7 cases, it nevertheless based its decision in part on the policy of section 959(b) that the trustee is bound by local law.[605] In the West Virginia case,[606] the court used section 959(b) as the basis for its authority to order the chapter 7 trustee to manage the building and provide services.

Section 959(b) may also be enforced against a landlord who is a debtor in a chapter 13 case. The chapter 13 debtor retains possession and control of property of the estate and is subject to obligations the Code imposes upon a trustee. In *In re Gollnitz*,[607] the court considered what remedies to impose when a chapter 13 debtor sought to abandon real property that was subject to a state environmental enforcement action. The court found two options available. Pursuant to section 363(e), the court conditioned the debtor's abandonment of the property on the debtor's compliance with state environmental laws. As an alternative, if the debtor retained possession, the court acknowledged that the state enforcement action could proceed against the debtor.

18.8.2.3 Loss of Services Without Abandonment

When the trustee has not abandoned the property, she may nevertheless not supply needed service. This situation arose in *Saravia v. 1736 18th Street, N.W. Limited Partnership*.[608] *Saravia* involved a chapter 11 case in which the debtor in possession,[609] having rejected the tenant leases under section 365(a) of the Bankruptcy Code,[610] attempted to cut off municipal services arguing that because the leases were voided, there was no obligation to provide the services required under the lease. The District of Columbia Circuit flatly rejected the debtor's argument. The court ruled that so long as the District of Columbia, where the housing was located, required the provision of heat and other utility services to tenants under its housing regulations, then, especially in light of the Supreme Court's discussion of section 959(b) in the *Midlantic* case, section 959(b) required the debtor in possession, as trustee, to comply with the District of Columbia housing regulations and provide the required services. While the trustee in a chapter 7 is unlikely to reject tenant leases,[611] the *Saravia* case is an important precedent illustrating that the principles of *Midlantic*

---

aside $250,000 for the cleanup); *In re* Purco, 76 B.R. 523 (Bankr. W.D. Pa. 1987) (court adopts a clear and imminent danger test and finds such danger not present); *In re* Franklin Signal Corp., 65 B.R. 268 (Bankr. D. Minn. 1986) (abandonment of contaminated property permitted because, among other reasons, the danger was not immediate); *In re* Okla. Ref. Co., 63 B.R. 562 (Bankr. W.D. Okla. 1986) (same).

600 *See, e.g., In re* Brio Ref., Inc., 86 B.R. 487 (N.D. Tex. 1988) (upholding abandonment because no known violation of law at the time of abandonment).

601 *See, e.g., In re* Franklin Signal Corp., 65 B.R. 268 (Bankr. D. Minn. 1986) (abandonment of contaminated property permitted because among other reasons trustee had no funds for clean-up); *In re* Okla. Ref. Co., 63 B.R. 562 (Bankr. W.D. Okla. 1986) (abandonment of contaminated property permitted in part because estate had no funds for cleanup); *In re* A & T Trailer Park, Inc., 53 B.R. 144 (Bankr. D. Wyo. 1985) (trustee permitted to abandon trailer park not in compliance with environmental laws when estate had no assets to pay for needed expenses). *Cf. In re* Smith-Douglass, Inc., 856 F.2d 12 (4th Cir. 1988) (court in dicta disagrees with lower court holding that resources of the estate are irrelevant in determining propriety of abandonment under *Midlantic*).

602 *In re* Am. Coastal Energy, Inc., 399 B.R. 805 (Bankr. S.D. Tex. 2009) (chapter 11 trustee may not abandon contaminated estate property, has duty to bring property into compliance with environmental and safety laws). *See, e.g., In re* Stevens, 68 B.R. 774 (D. Me. 1987) (chapter 7 trustee could not abandon drums of contaminated oil, cleanup expenses are priority administrative expenses); *In re* Peerless Plating Co., 70 B.R. 943 (Bankr. W.D. Mich. 1987) (chapter 7 trustee could not abandon metal plating shop over objections of the Environmental Protection Agency). *But see In re* Vel Rey Properties, 174 B.R. 859 (Bankr. D.D.C. 1994) (trustee not permitted to operate apartment building without compliance with building code in order to maximize return to creditors, but could abandon the property because public danger from the housing code violations was not imminent). *Cf. In re* Armstrong, 96 B.R. 55 (Bankr. E.D.N.C. 1989) (debtor in possession in chapter 11 could abandon polluted property only if $250,000 set aside for cleanup).

603 Hemetek v. Standish (*In re* Bush), Clearinghouse No. 44,839 (Bankr. S.D. W. Va. 1990).

604 *See* § 18.8.2.4, *infra*.

605 Midlantic Nat'l Bank v. N.J. Dep't of Envtl. Prot., 474 U.S. 494, 505, 106 S. Ct. 755, 761, 762, 88 L. Ed. 2d 859, 868 (1986).

606 *See* Hemetek v. Standish (*In re* Bush), Clearinghouse No. 44,839 (Bankr. S.D. W. Va. 1990).

607 456 B.R. 733 (Bankr. W.D.N.Y. 2011).

608 844 F.2d 823 (D.C. Cir. 1988).

609 *See* § 18.7.4.1, *supra*.

610 11 U.S.C. § 365(a).

611 See the discussion of rejection of leases in § 18.8.4, *infra*.

may apply to tenants' rights in housing.[612]

Another useful case in states that allow a debtor to recoup money expended to cure a landlord's default on an obligation to repair and maintain the premises is *In re Flagstaff Realty Trust*.[613] In *Flagstaff*, the Third Circuit concluded that a tenant that had performed prepetition repairs could recoup any amounts expended from rent even after the debtor filed bankruptcy and rejected the lease. A similar outcome should be possible under 11 U.S.C. § 365(h) for postpetition expenditures for which recoupment is allowed under state law. It may also be possible to work with local government regulatory authorities to enforce building and fire codes. Such enforcement of police and regulatory powers is not stayed by the bankruptcy case.[614]

18.8.2.4 Steps to Take

The clients' immediate concern will be to assure themselves of services to the building. Ordinarily, in a chapter 7 case in which the building has been privately developed, there is no reason to oppose foreclosure and sale.[615] The major concern will be to assure that services continue in any interim period and perhaps to assist in the smooth transfer of ownership.

When the tenants' attorney finds that the landlord has filed a chapter 7 bankruptcy petition and services are not being provided, the first thing to do is to call the trustee and discuss the situation.[616] The trustee may well be unaware of what has happened and be willing to cooperate.

The trustee, however, is unlikely to regard the opportunity to manage a building of low-income tenants as a bonanza. The tenants' attorney should stress that the tenants are only asking for assistance in the interim period between the filing and the expected foreclosure on the property and, if it is the case, that they will have no objection to relief from the stay to permit foreclosure.[617]

If the trustee does cooperate, the tenants' attorney may be in the unfamiliar, but nevertheless vital, position of assisting in collecting the rent so that the resources are available to maintain services. The attorney may be able to guide the trustee through the intricacies of Section 8 vouchers and certificates,[618] and LIHEAP[619] payments with which the trustee is unlikely to be familiar. The attorney should also assure her clients and other tenants that it is appropriate to pay their rent to the trustee or the trustee's property manager or designee.

The tenants' attorney should also quickly contact the lender holding the senior security. Like the trustee, the lender's first instincts will not be to join in a quest to provide services to this troubled property. The lender will by now have realized its loan is in trouble and that it is unlikely to recover its money at the foreclosure sale. It will likely consider substantial involvement to be throwing good money after bad and to be exposing itself to needless liability.[620]

Nevertheless, it may be possible to convince the lender that it is in its interest to assist the tenants. If the building is in danger of deterioration because tenants are likely to start moving out, or in danger of vandalism from inadequate security, the value of the building will almost certainly decrease if nothing is done. Keeping the building maintained and fully occupied, the tenants' attorney should argue, will help the lenders as much as the tenants.

---

612 *But see In re* Vel Rey Properties, 174 B.R. 859 (Bankr. D.D.C. 1994) (trustee not permitted to operate apartment building without compliance with building code in order to maximize return to creditors, but could abandon the property because public danger from the housing code violations was not imminent).

613 60 F.3d 1031 (3d Cir. 1995).

614 11 U.S.C. § 362(b)(4), (5). *See In re* 1820–1838 Amsterdam Equities, Inc., 191 B.R. 18 (S.D.N.Y. 1996) (bankruptcy court could not interfere with code enforcement by city against debtor's property).

615 If the building has been developed with the aid of federal or state programs which require making some or all units available to low-income tenants, other issues may arise about the status of the subsidy agreements. The tenants may wish to take advantage of the opportunity to gain site control in order to implement a tenant ownership plan, with help from the local community development agency. In such cases, tactics may differ.

616 The trustee in a chapter 7 is more akin to a party in a lawsuit than a court official, so advocates need not be concerned about the propriety of *ex parte* communications.

617 While it will normally be in the tenants' interest to move the foreclosure proceedings along as fast as possible, if there is a possibility that the tenants themselves or a nonprofit community development group might be interested in purchasing the building, tenants may then wish to delay while the feasibility of other ownership is explored.

618 Under Section 8 of the Housing Act of 1937, 42 U.S.C. § 1437f, and the implementing regulations, 24 C.F.R. pt. 800, Section 8 eligible low-income tenants receive rent subsidies. These payments are issued by the local housing authority and paid directly to the landlord so that the landlord receives two checks, one from the tenant and the other from the housing authority. The trustee will have to arrange to be named payee by the housing authority in place of the landlord. For a detailed explanation of the Section 8 program, see National Housing Law Project, HUD Housing Programs: Tenants' Rights (1981 and 1985 Supp.).

619 Under the federal Low Income Home Energy Assistance Program (LIHEAP) agencies administering the program in some states may arrange direct payment of energy assistance benefits to landlords, when heat or electric services are included as part of the rent. *See* 42 U.S.C. § 8624(b)(7). When landlords are receiving LIHEAP payments directly, the trustee will have to arrange to receive the payments in place of the landlord. For an explanation of the LIHEAP program, see National Consumer Law Center, Access to Utility Service Ch. 7 (5th ed. 2011).

620 As discussed earlier in this Chapter, a secured creditor in some cases may be forced to pay expenses which maintain the value of its security. The trustee might therefore pay for necessary upkeep and force payment of these costs from the secured creditor. *See* § 18.5.3, *supra*. This can provide some leverage to force the secured creditor to participate in reasonably maintaining the property. In addition, state law theories for holding a secured lender responsible may apply. For example, in many states a mortgagee which has constructive possession of a property or which has exercised substantial control over property is potentially liable to tenants. *See, e.g.*, McCorristin v. Salmon Signs, 582 A.2d 1271 (N.J. Super. Ct. App. Div. 1990) (mortgagee in possession steps into shoes of landlord); Thornhill v. Ronnie's I-45 Truck Stop, Inc., 944 S.W.2d 780 (Tex. App. 1997) (secured lender exercising control over property held responsible for injuries due to fire at premises).

If the lender does express some interest, the tenants' attorney should try to get the lender talking to the trustee quickly. Among other things, the lender could arrange for building management, cover the trustee under its liability policy, and post any deposits that might be required to restore utility service or make any needed emergency repairs. Even if no cooperation is anticipated from the lender, it will be helpful at subsequent hearings to know what the lender's approach is going to be.

If the trustee will not cooperate, or has filed and will not withdraw a motion for abandonment, then the tenants must seek relief from the bankruptcy court. While most of the issues could be raised in opposition to a motion for abandonment, the tenants will be in a stronger and clearer position by not only opposing the abandonment, but also asking for affirmative relief in the form of an order enjoining the trustee from failing to provide the needed services. Because the request will be for equitable relief, the tenants must file an adversary proceeding.[621] When services have already been cut off, tenants may need to ask for a temporary restraining order or for a preliminary injunction.[622]

In preparing for the hearing, it will probably be useful to have the appropriate local health or safety agency inspect the building. That authority should be prepared to testify that no heat or electricity is available and that their absence violates local ordinances or state statutes and poses an imminent threat to health and safety. While most judges would probably be willing to take judicial notice that absence of heat and light is a threat to safety, the inspector's testimony about what building or health codes are being violated will satisfy the *Midlantic* violation of law requirement.

In addition to proving imminent danger, tenants may also have to prove that the resources are available for the trustee to remedy the situation. Tenants should testify about willingness to pay rent. If possible, statements from the local housing authority, the public assistance agency and the local energy assistance agency about the availability of Section 8 payments, public assistance payments and LIHEAP payments, respectively, should be presented.[623] If the trustee has expressed a reluctance to become involved in the management, it will also be helpful to obtain a statement from a commercial or nonprofit management group expressing a willingness to manage the property and an analysis that the cash flow from the building will be sufficient to provide services and remedy violations.

It is important that the imminent danger part of the tenant's case not prove too much. Testimony that the building is falling down and needs major structural repairs could potentially be harmful because the trustee is then likely to argue that the resources are not available to manage the building.[624]

The judge and the trustee will probably both be wary of any long-term involvement by the trustee. If that is the case, at the hearing the tenants' attorney should stress that the tenants have no objection to the lenders obtaining relief from the stay for the purpose of the foreclosure, and that the tenants are only seeking to assure an orderly transition to new ownership.

Given the relatively informal nature of bankruptcy hearings and the request for equitable relief, the tenants' attorney should be prepared to enter into discussions to fashion some agreement among the tenants, the trustee and the lender.[625] For example, if management of the building is an issue, the tenants might locate a community housing group that would be willing to be hired by the trustee as an interim manager.

If the judge does not grant the relief the tenants seek, the tenants may appeal the decision to the district court or the bankruptcy appellate panel.[626] Before appealing, consider the other alternative of proceeding in state court. For example, if there is a possibility of having a sympathetic state housing court appoint a receiver for the building, that may be better than having the district court judge force an unwilling bankruptcy court judge and trustee to oversee the building. If the decision is to proceed in state court, the tenants should seek an order from the bankruptcy court granting the tenants relief from the automatic stay[627] for that purpose. Even though the building has been abandoned, it is probably still subject to the automatic stay.[628]

18.8.2.5 Forcing Abandonment to the Lender

When there is only one lienholder, another tactic may be to have the court order the property abandoned directly to the lender. Such an order may immediately transfer title to the lender, making the lender responsible for applicable health and safety codes.

Under section 554, the court has authority to order that abandonment be to a party other than the debtor.[629] Tenants

---

621 For an example, see Hemetek v. Standish (*In re* Bush), Clearinghouse No. 44,839A (Bankr. S.D. W. Va. 1990).
622 *Id.*
623 See discussion above.
624 *See* § 18.8.2.1, *supra.*

625 See, for example, the order in the *Hemetek* case discussed in § 18.8.2.2, *supra*, and *In re* Armstrong, 96 B.R. 55 (Bankr. E.D.N.C. 1989) (abandonment only permitted conditional upon the debtor setting aside $250,000 for cleanup of hazard).
626 See § 14.9, *supra*, for an explanation of appeals from the bankruptcy court. In some situations, a direct appeal to the court of appeals may be possible.
627 11 U.S.C. § 362. *See* Ch. 9, § 18.3, *supra.*
628 H.R. Rep. No. 95-595, at 343 (1977), *reprinted in* 1978 U.S.C.C.A.N. 5787, 6299 (property no longer in the estate still subject to the stay if it goes to the debtor); *In re* Cruseturner, 8 B.R. 581 (Bankr. D. Utah 1981) (same).
629 11 U.S.C. § 554(c). *See* Dominion Bank of Cumberlands v. Nuckolls, 71 B.R. 593 (W.D. Va. 1987) (after hearing property could be abandoned to creditor); *In re* Maropa Marine Sales Serv. & Storage, Inc., 92 B.R. 547 (Bankr. S.D. Fla. 1988) (property should be abandoned to undersecured creditor, not sold at auction by trustee); *In re* Ware, 59 B.R. 549 (Bankr. N.D. Ohio 1986) (property abandoned to secured creditor); H.R. Rep. No. 95-595, at 377 (1977); Sen. Rep. No. 95-989, at 92 (1978) ("Abandonment may be to any party with a possessory interest in the property abandoned."; cited with approval in Ohio v. Kovacs, 469 U.S. 274, 284 n.12, 105 S. Ct.

could propose abandonment to the lender as an alternative resolution when objecting to the trustee's motion to abandon. Tenants as parties in interest may also bring their own motion for abandonment to the lender.[630] Abandonment to the lender could be proposed as alternative relief to forcing administration of the building by the trustee as discussed in previous subsections. Requesting alternative relief will make it clear to the court that the tenants only interest is assuring that there is a responsible party to manage the building.

The lender may argue that while it may wish to foreclose, it should not be forced to take title to the property. In many cases, the owner will have been in default on the building for many months or even years. Tenants should point out to the court that the lender had ample opportunity to foreclose.

18.8.2.6 Maintaining Services in the Event the Property Has Been Abandoned

Even if the trustee has abandoned the property, there are steps the tenants can take to maintain services. These include forcing the debtor to continue to maintain the property, forming a tenant association to collect voluntary rent and to assume direct responsibility for services, and petitioning to have the property placed under receivership pursuant to state law.

The filing of a bankruptcy petition does not absolve a debtor from the responsibility to maintain rental property on an ongoing basis. The trustee may deem the property abandoned at the end of the case under section 554(c) in which case it reverts to the debtor, unless the court orders otherwise. Once in possession of the abandoned property, the debtor must comply with applicable state laws regarding the use of that property.[631] Even though the debtor may have rejected the lease agreements,[632] if nonbankruptcy requirements for their termination have not been met, a landlord-tenant relationship still exists.[633] The debtor's bankruptcy filing should therefore have no effect on the tenants' ability to use the remedies normally available to them under state law to compel their landlord to maintain services.[634]

If the debtor has rejected the lease agreements, the tenants may also assume management of the rental property themselves, at least until foreclosure. Once the property has been abandoned, there is nothing to prevent the tenants from forming their own association, collecting voluntary rent, and contracting with utility companies for continued services.[635] Many states have laws that prevent utilities from terminating service to rental property without first giving tenants notice and an opportunity to avoid termination by assuming payments.[636]

Finally, the tenants can file a petition in state court to have the rental property placed in receivership. At a minimum, a receiver would collect rent and maintain necessary services to the property. In some states, tenants are given specific statutory authority to petition for receivership.[637] Even in the absence of statutory authority, however, a court in equity can order receivership. For instance, tenants who seek to enjoin their landlord from maintaining rental property in an uninhabitable condition, and who can demonstrate that their landlord is prospectively unable or unwilling to comply with such an injunction, can request that the court appoint a receiver for the property so that compliance is assured. As receivership is an act against the property, rather than the debtor, there is probably no need to seek relief from the automatic stay before pursuing this remedy after the property has been abandoned and is no longer property of the estate.[638]

18.8.3 Pursuing Opportunities for Tenant Ownership in a Chapter 7 Bankruptcy

Aside from assuring that services to the rental property are maintained, the tenants may wish to consider what steps they can take to improve their long-term situation. With one absentee landlord in bankruptcy, the tenants may understandably be less than eager to see another absentee landlord buy the property out of foreclosure. If that is the case, tenant ownership strategies should be explored. Chances are, when a residential landlord files for bankruptcy, the rental property has been allowed to deteriorate for some time. Because tenant owners are far more likely to reinvest rent money in the property, tenant ownership may offer the best chance to improve tenants' living conditions.

In some cases, the debtor will not be interested in continued ownership, and the primary mortgage holder will not want to proceed to foreclosure unless it believes there is a potential buyer for the property.[639] Rental property with code violations and organized tenants does not present a very attractive investment opportunity. These circumstances are ripe for tenant ownership. The challenge, of course, is to come up with the financing.

705, 83 L. Ed. 2d 649, 659 (1985)). *But see In re* Manchester Heights Assocs., L.P., 165 B.R. 42 (Bankr. W.D. Mo. 1994); *In re* Caron, 50 B.R. 27 (Bankr. N.D. Ga. 1984) ("the procedures of § 554 and Rule 6007 cannot be used to effect turnover, recovery or legal title or possession to any particular creditor").

630 11 U.S.C. § 554(b); Fed. R. Bankr. P. 6007(b).

631 *See* Ohio v. Kovacs, 469 U.S. 274, 105 S. Ct. 705, 83 L. Ed. 2d 649 (1985).

632 *See* § 12.9, *supra*.

633 11 U.S.C. § 365(h)(1)(A)(ii). *See* § 18.8.4, *infra*.

634 *See generally* National Consumer Law Center, Tenants' Rights to Utility Service Ch. 7 (1994).

635 *Id.*; § 6.2, *supra*.

636 *See generally* National Consumer Law Center, Tenants' Rights to Utility Service Ch. 7 (1994); § 18.5.3, *supra*.

637 See, for example, Mass. Gen. Laws ch. 111, § 127(I), which authorizes tenants to petition the courts to enforce the state sanitary code, and specifies various injunctive remedies, including receivership.

638 If the property has not been abandoned, relief from the automatic stay is necessary. *See* 11 U.S.C. § 362(a)(3).

639 A secured lender who assumes any management function (such as collecting rent) or who obtains title to the property through its foreclosure proceeding risks being thrown into a landlord-tenant relationship as a mortgagee in possession. *See, e.g.*, McCorristin v. Salmon Signs, 582 A.2d 1271 (N.J. Super. Ct. App. Div. 1990).

The first step in securing financing for a tenant buyout is to prove that tenants can manage the property at a profit. The best way to do this is to actually manage the property. There are a variety of opportunities for this in a chapter 7 bankruptcy.[640] First, if the trustee has not abandoned the property pursuant to section 554, the tenants can ask the trustee to hire a tenant association to manage it. Alternatively, they could petition the court to abandon the property to such an association.[641] If the property has already been abandoned (and if the leases have been rejected), a tenant association could collect voluntary rent and assume management functions pending foreclosure.[642]

Once the tenants prove they can viably manage the property, the next step is to prepare a business plan and seek financing for a buyout. The primary mortgage holder should be approached. Depending on its chances of finding a commercial buyer for the property, it may be willing to finance a tenant buyout. Local community development corporations (CDCs) should also be approached. CDCs make good partners for exploring financing for low-income housing development. Finally, it might be possible to find a community development loan fund that exists specifically to finance such ventures.

After financing is secured, there are various ways to go about purchasing the property. The first step should be to contact the debtor and secured creditor(s). If the trustee has not abandoned the property, either of them could propose that the bankruptcy court conduct a sale pursuant to section 363. The secured creditor could also seek relief from the automatic stay in order to pursue foreclosure. The tenants may bid on the property at the foreclosure sale or buy the property from the lender if the lender (as is most often the case) is the high bidder at the foreclosure auction.[643]

18.8.4 Preventing Evictions in Chapter 11 and 13 Proceedings

If the owner believes, however unrealistically, that the property may continue to be economically viable, then the owner may file under chapter 11, or in the case of a small building, under chapter 13.[644] The strategy for tenants may differ when faced with proceedings under chapter 11 or 13.

In a chapter 11 reorganization bankruptcy, the debtor generally continues to operate the business as a "debtor in possession" with the rights and duties of a trustee.[645] A chapter 13 debtor owning a business is similarly treated.[646] In those cases, abandonment is not likely.

In potential "gentrification" situations, landlords in bankruptcy may wish to evict low-income tenants in hopes of replacing them with those of higher income. Tenants whose landlord is in chapter 11 or 13, or conceivably in chapter 7, bankruptcy and who are faced with a rejection of their unexpired leases as defined under section 365 are given important rights by section 365(h).

If the trustee or debtor-in-possession rejects the lease, the lessee has two options under section 365(h): (1) retain the estate and appurtenant rights, including the right to sublet or assign, or (2) elect to treat the lease as terminated and assert a claim against the estate for damages flowing from the breach.[647] Note that rejection of the lease relieves the bankrupt lessor from duties contained in the lease, such as the duties to provide heat or trash disposal, except to the extent such an obligation is imposed on a breaching lessor by applicable nonbankruptcy law.

The tenant may retain possession and continue to remain in possession as long as the tenant would have had the right to unilaterally renew the lease under relevant nonbankruptcy law.[648] Section 8 tenants, tenants in rent-controlled housing, or tenants under statutes such as New Jersey's, which requires "cause" for eviction[649] have a right to continued occupancy so long as their rent payments are maintained and other lease provisions not breached. Section 365(h) thus protects tenants from eviction despite a section 365 rejection of their lease. Moreover, if the landlord rejects the lease, section 365(h) provides that the tenant can set off the lease payments up to their full value against the tenant's damages resulting from the rejection.[650] If the lessee so elects, it may not seek damages based on rejection of the lease as a claim against the estate.

The 1994 amendments to the Bankruptcy Code provided new protections for tenants when a debtor rejects a lease. The provision makes clear that the tenant may not only retain possession, but also that rights appurtenant to that possession are protected.[651] This legislatively overrules cases that had held that possession after lease rejection did not include a variety of ancillary tenant rights under the lease.[652] The Second Circuit in

---

640 In addition to the strategies discussed here, tenants in a chapter 11 case may be able to file a creditors' plan providing for tenant management. See § 18.7.9, supra.
641 See § 18.8.2.5, supra.
642 See § 18.8.2.6, supra.
643 Tenants in a chapter 11 case could also file a creditors' plan providing for tenant ownership. See § 18.7.9, supra.
644 Chapter 13 is only available to individuals with less than $1,081,400 in secured debt. 11 U.S.C. § 109(e).
645 11 U.S.C. § 1107. See generally § 18.7, supra.
646 11 U.S.C. § 1304.
647 11 U.S.C. § 365(h)(1).
648 See Green Tree Servicing, L.L.C. v. DBSI Landmark Towers, L.L.C., 652 F.3d 910, 913 (8th Cir. 2011); In re Scharp, 463 B.R. 123, 132 (Bankr. C.D. Ill. 2011) (section 365(h) clarifies that neither landlord's bankruptcy filing nor rejection of lease terminates the lease unilaterally); In re Churchill Properties III, L.P., 197 B.R. 283 (Bankr. N.D. Ill. 1996) (tenant with rejected lease had right to remain in possession even if real property was sold by lessor's trustee).
649 N.J. Stat. Ann. § 2A-18:61.3 (West).
650 In re Milstead, 197 B.R. 33 (Bankr. E.D. Va. 1996) (tenant's claim for relocation damages resulting from debtor's rejection of lease allowed because tenant's duty to mitigate did not require it to remain in possession rather than vacate premises in order to reduce damages).
651 11 U.S.C. § 365(h)(1)(A)(ii). See In re Flagstaff Realty Assocs., 60 F.3d 1031 (3d Cir. 1995) (debtor retains right of recoupment under lease for improvements made prior to debtor's rejection of lease).
652 See, e.g., In re Carlton Restaurant, Inc., 151 B.R. 353 (Bankr. E.D.

In re Berry Estates, Inc.,[653] has held that filing bankruptcy does not protect a landlord debtor from rent control regulations because the regulations are an exercise of the state police power.

In cases under any chapter, the landlord may be seeking eviction of a tenant/creditor in state court for cause. When the tenant has counterclaims based, for example, on conditions in the property, relief from stay to raise those claims may be necessary.[654]

A related problem can occur when the trustee or landlord as debtor in possession elects to reject the lease and also sell the rental property under a section 363 asset sale free and clear of the tenants' possessory or other interests in the property.[655] In this situation, section 365(h) should preserve the tenants' benefits under the lease at least for the balance of the lease term, thereby preventing the tenants from being evicted by the new owner and requiring services to be maintained. However, one circuit court of appeals has held that an asset sale under section 363(f) can operate to cut off a tenant's possessory interest notwithstanding the rights provided to tenants under section 365(h).[656] Tenants may seek to avoid the holding in *Qualitech Steel* by arguing that the asset sale has not met the requirements for approval set out in section 363(f). For example, because a free and clear sale cannot be approved by the bankruptcy court if it would not be permitted under applicable nonbankruptcy law,[657] residential tenants may be able to point to state or federal housing law that prohibits a purchaser from repudiating an existing lease.[658] In addition, the court in *Qualitech Steel* noted that a section 363 asset sale should not be approved if the tenants are not provided with adequate protection of their interests.[659] Unfortunately, this puts the burden on tenants to file an objection to the sale and affirmatively request that their interests be adequately protected. In a recent bankruptcy court decision, the tenants prevailed in blocking a proposed sale by asserting both the debtor-landlord's failure to satisfy one of the conditions for allowance of sale under section 363(f) and the landlord's failure to offer adequate protection under section 363(e).[660]

18.8.5 Security Deposits

In addition to an interest in having services continue despite the initiation of bankruptcy proceedings, the tenants may have an interest in security deposits that the landlord obtained from the tenant at the commencement of the tenancy. As the assets of the estate are stretched to reach the claims of the landlord's creditors, the status of the tenants' security deposits may well become points of contention.

When tenants have left the building before or during the bankruptcy, the tenants' claim for return of security may be met by countervailing claims that security deposits are property of the debtor's estate. Even when the tenants remain, the trustee may take the position that security deposits commingled with the debtor's funds, or used by the debtor for its own purposes, ceased to be security deposits. In either situation, the tenants risk becoming unsecured creditors for the amount of the security deposit unless the bankruptcy court accepts the tenants' argument that security deposits are entitled to a different status. Tenants may be able to have the deposits treated as not the landlord's property or as property held in trust by the landlord. At the least, they should be able to assert the consumer priority.[661] If the lease is not rejected, the right to the return of a security deposit should be an administrative expense, which is entitled to priority status.[662]

Pa. 1993) (preventing a tenant from assigning a lease after lease rejection).

653 812 F.2d 67 (2d Cir. 1987).

654 The process for obtaining that relief is discussed in § 18.3, *supra*.

655 11 U.S.C. § 363(f). See 18.9.3, *infra*.

656 Precision Indus., Inc. v. Qualitech Steel SBQ, L.L.C., 327 F.3d 537 (7th Cir. 2003). See also *In re* Hill, 307 B.R. 821 (Bankr. W.D. Pa. 2004) (following *Qualitech*).

657 11 U.S.C. § 363(f)(1).

658 See, e.g., *In re* Welker, 163 B.R. 488 (Bankr. N.D. Tex. 1994) (trustee may sell property only after compliance with the Dep't of Housing and Urban Development's statutory and regulatory procedures as section 363(f) does not trump federal housing acts).

Because section 363(f) is drafted in the disjunctive, tenants may need to show that each of the five listed statutory conditions has not been satisfied in order to stop a free and clear sale. See *In re* Dundee Equity Corp., 1992 WL 53743 (Bankr. S.D.N.Y. Mar. 6, 1992) (conditions not met because applicable nonbankruptcy law did not permit sale, section 363(f)(1); tenants did not consent to sale, section 363(f)(2); tenants' interest not a lien, section 363(f)(3); trustee did not dispute validity of lease, section 363(f)(4); and no provision of New York law compelled tenants, under circumstances of case, to accept a money satisfaction in lieu of performance, section 363(f)(5)).

659 See 11 U.S.C. § 363(e).

660 *In re* Haskell, 321 B.R. 1 (Bankr. D. Mass. 2005).

In *Haskell* the landlord argued that it satisfied one of the five conditions for allowance of a sale of the tenants' leasehold interest under section 363(f) because the tenants could be compelled "to accept a money satisfaction of such interest." 11 U.S.C. § 363(f)(5). In support of this contention the landlord referred to the possibility that, under an eminent domain takeover, the lessee's interest could be given a monetary value. The court rejected the analogy as too speculative. The landlord also asserted that adequate protection would be available from the sale proceeds as compensation for the tenants' interest. Again the court rejected this contention as speculative, particularly given the likelihood that there would be no proceeds from a sale left over to pay anything for the tenants' interest.

661 Guarracino v. Hoffman, 246 B.R. 130 (D. Mass. 2000) (security deposit entitled to priority; damages related to mishandling security deposit are not); *In re* River Vill. Assocs., 161 B.R. 127 (Bankr. E.D. Pa. 1993), *aff'd on other grounds*, 181 B.R. 795 (E.D. Pa. 1995); *In re* Wise, 120 B.R. 537 (Bankr. D. Ala. 1990). See § 18.5.5, *supra*. See also Gaertner v. Romanus (*In re* Romanus), 1998 Bankr. LEXIS 397 (Bankr. W.D. Pa. Apr. 3, 1998) (prepaid security deposit and first month rent payment entitled to consumer priority when the debtor/landlord failed to deliver the property in habitable condition).

662 *In re* Boston Post Road L.P., 21 F.3d 477 (2d Cir. 1994) (tenants who are owed security deposits have administrative claims which are entitled to priority); *In re* Cantonwood Assocs. L.P., 138 B.R. 648 (Bankr. D. Mass. 1992) (same).

See § 12.9, *supra*, for a discussion of assumption or rejection of

§ 18.8.5 Consumer Bankruptcy Law and Practice

The tenant's best hope for success is to have the bankruptcy court find that the security deposits are not assets of the bankruptcy estate because the deposits were never the landlord's property. A trustee in bankruptcy only succeeds to the debtor's right and title in property.[663] If a claimant challenges the debtor's right to property, the claimant bears the burden of proof on the issue of ownership.[664] The bankruptcy court looks to state law to determine the debtor's right in contested property.[665] Few bankruptcy cases have addressed the issue of whether the security deposits held by a debtor/landlord are assets of the debtor's bankruptcy estate.[666]

State statutory provisions which mandate that landlords maintain security deposits given by residential tenants in escrow accounts specifically established to hold such funds during the term of residential leases offer the best grounds for having security deposits separated from the debtor's property. Some state statutes regulating the collection of deposits from residential tenants explicitly provide that these deposits must be maintained in separate escrow accounts that remain the property of the tenants.[667] A few statutes go further and specifically provide that these escrow deposits remain tenants' property even against claims of a trustee in bankruptcy.[668] A minority of states have taken no legislative action to control the collection of security deposits[669] or have adopted bare-bones statutes which do not specify how the security deposits are to be maintained, but merely mandate that the deposits be returned at the end of the lease term.[670]

The stronger statutes should assure the tenants of recovery. For example, in a New York case in which the lessee was a debtor in bankruptcy and had defaulted under the terms of the lease, the landlord sought to reach the tenant's security deposit ahead of the debtor's general creditors.[671] There the court looked to the state statute that required the maintenance of segregated escrow accounts for tenants' security deposits and found that the deposits remained the tenants' property.[672]

Certain lease provisions may support the argument that a security deposit is not an asset of the debtor's estate. Many forms of residential leases provide for the payment of security by the tenant at the commencement of the lease and the establishment of segregated escrow accounts by the landlord to hold those funds. Based on such provisions, tenants can argue that, by contract, the security deposits paid to a landlord pursuant to such lease provisions never become the property of the landlord.[673]

Even in those jurisdictions in which state statutes require that landlords hold security deposits in trust or the lease provides for such accounts, cases are certain to arise when a financially pressed landlord has invaded the trust and dissipated the security deposits. Section 523(a)(4) of the Bankruptcy Code provides that an individual debtor cannot be discharged from a debt arising out of a debtor's embezzlement, larceny, or fraud or defalcation while acting in a fiduciary capacity.[674] This remedy is limited to individual debtors[675] and applies most commonly to a landlord's dissipation of an express trust.[676]

Arguments can be made, based on many states' statutory or common law, that a transfer of property to be held as security creates an express trust within the meaning of section 523(a)(4).[677] The transfer of a security deposit pursuant to a lease

---

executory contracts and § 18.5.3, *supra*, for a discussion of postpetition claims as administrative expenses.

663 5 Collier on Bankruptcy ¶ 541.11 (16th ed.). See § 18.5.2, *supra*.

664 5 Collier on Bankruptcy ¶ 541.11 (16th ed.).

665 *Id.*; *In re* Contractors Equip. Supply Co., 861 F.2d 241 (9th Cir. 1988) (status of payment of account receivable determined under state law).

666 One adverse case is *In re* Dilberts Leasing & Dev. Corp., 345 F.2d 172 (2d Cir. 1965) (in commercial case in which lease did not require segregation of security deposit, tenant held to be general creditor).

One helpful case, though decided in another context, held that tenants were not creditors of a debtor-landlord solely based on the latter holding their security deposits because the tenants held title to the deposits under state law. *In re* Ctr. Apartments, Ltd., 277 B.R. 747 (Bankr. S.D. Ohio 2001). *See also In re* Coomer, 375 B.R. 800 (Bankr. N.D. Ohio 2007) (debtor-tenant's security deposit not estate property under state law, rejecting trustee's turnover motion).

667 *See, e.g.*, Fla. Stat. § 83.49; Ga. Code Ann. § 44-7-31; Mass. Gen. Laws ch. 186, § 15B(1)(E); N.Y. Gen. ObLig. Law § 7-103 (McKinney).

668 *See, e.g.*, Me. Rev. Stat. tit. 14, § 6038; Mass. Gen. Laws ch. 186, § 15B(1)(E).

669 Alabama and Mississippi are examples of states not adopting security deposit legislation.

670 *See, e.g.*, Ark. Code Ann. § 18-16-301; Ind. Code § 32-7-5-1.

671 *In re* Pal-Playwell Inc., 334 F.2d 389 (2d Cir. 1964).

672 *Id.* at 391.

673 Courts construing commercial leases frequently find that the contract terms related to the security deposit create an express trust or security interest. *See, e.g., In re* Verus Inv. Mgmt., L.L.C., 344 B.R. 536, 542–543 (Bankr. N.D. Ohio 2006) (lease terms created security interest in tenant deposit under state law); *In re* Timothy Dean Restaurant & Bar, 324 B.R. 1 (Bankr. D.D.C. 2006) (lease term created express trust in tenant security deposit).

674 11 U.S.C. § 523(a)(4); *In re* Christian, 172 B.R. 490 (Bankr. D. Mass. 1994); *In re* Wise, 120 B.R. 537 (Bankr. D. Alaska 1990).

See § 15.4.3.4, *supra*, for a detailed discussion of dischargeability.

675 An individual debtor may be found responsible in some circumstances for a defalcation by a trust entity or a corporation. *See In re* Lebner, 197 B.R. 180 (Bankr. D. Mass. 1996) (trial necessary to determine if realty trust beneficiary is responsible for actions of trust). *See generally* § 18.5.7, *supra*.

676 *In re* Niles, 106 F.3d 1456 (9th Cir. 1997) (discussing application of section 523(a)(4)); *In re* Angelle, 610 F.2d 1335 (5th Cir. 1980); *In re* Dloogoff, 600 F.2d. 166 (8th Cir. 1979); 4 Collier on Bankruptcy ¶ 523.10[1][c] (16th ed.).

677 *In re* McGee, 353 F.3d 537 (7th Cir. 2003) (city ordinance requiring security deposit be held in insured bank account and not commingled with other assets, and providing that funds were to remain property of tenant, created a fiduciary relationship arising from a trust); *In re* Frempong, 460 B.R. 189 (Bankr. N.D. Ill. 2011) (nondischargeable debt under § 523(a)(4) can include security deposit withheld in violation of city ordinance as well as interest and penalties assessed under ordinance). *See also In re* Alomari, 2011 WL 3648630 (Bankr. N.D. Ill. Aug. 15, 2011) (although no local law created fiduciary relationship, specific nature of landlord's alleged promise to protect lessee's security deposit stated claim for nondischargeability under § 523(a)(4)). *See generally* United States v. Miell, 661 F.3d 995 (8th Cir. 2011) (trust relationship created

agreement creates a trust *res* to be held for the particular purpose of providing security if the tenant violates the lease.[678] Use of those funds for other purposes is then a defalcation within the meaning of the statute.[679] When such an action is available, it often offers good potential for class certification and class relief.[680] If there is a prior state court judgment establishing a violation of a state law protecting security deposits, that judgment may collaterally estop the debtor on many of the issues required to establish nondischargeability.[681] Tenants may succeed in a nondischargeability action under section 523(a)(4) even if defalcation is not proven when a landlord's misappropriation of the security deposit amounts to embezzlement.[682]

If there is a claim available under a state UDAP statute for misappropriation of security deposits,[683] that claim may create a basis to argue nondischargeability not only under section 523(a)(4), but also under sections 523(a)(2)(A) and 523(a)(6) as well. Section 523(a)(2)(A) covers debts based on fraud or false pretenses and section 523(a)(6) covers willful and malicious injury such as conversion.[684]

Another approach to solving the problem of the depleted trust would be under 28 U.S.C. § 959(b). That statute requires that trustees appointed in federal court comply with state laws affecting any property held by the trustee. In *Saravia v. 1736 18th Street, N.W. Limited Partnership*,[685] the D.C. Circuit held a debtor in possession to compliance with local housing regulations based on the obligations imposed on bankruptcy trustees under section 959(b).

No bankruptcy case has yet to hold that either a trustee or debtor in possession must comply with security deposit escrow requirements of state statutes after those escrow funds had been wrongful disbursed. But, based on section 959(b) and *Saravia*, the legal basis for extending the trustees' obligation to a duty to replace dissipated security deposits seems to be within reach and is certainly worth arguing.

In a few jurisdictions, statutes specifically provide that any successors to a landlord that collected security deposits have an obligation to return those deposits to tenants or compensate the tenant with rent credits.[686] Other state statutes impose bonding requirements on landlords that collect statutory established levels of aggregate security deposits.[687] Section 959(b) should require the trustee to return deposits or collect from the bonding company in jurisdictions with this type of legislation. The tenants would also have a claim against the bonding company, which would not be subject to the automatic stay.

Without either a statutory or contractual basis for persuading the bankruptcy court that a tenant's security deposits were not a landlord-debtor's property, an effort may be made to have a constructive trust impressed on the debtor's funds.[688] Landlord-tenant statutes or lease provisions requiring separate accounting for deposits may provide a basis for imposition of a constructive trust even if they fall short of the requirements of an express trust. Even the enactment of a less than adequate state security deposit statute might provide the grounds for a constructive trust. A state statute, for example, might not specify that the security deposits held by the landlord remained the property of the tenant.[689] One could nevertheless argue that a constructive trust ought to be imposed to implement the protection the statute sought to provide. Similarly, a lease provision providing for an escrow or payment of interest on the deposit might supply the basis for arguing that a trust relationship was actually created or implied.

Procedurally, the tenants' attempt to have security deposits excluded from the debtor's estate as property belonging to the tenant, and not property to which the debtor has a right, should be by an adversary proceeding.[690] Proceeding directly in state court with an action to recover the security deposit will almost invariably violate the automatic stay.[691]

---

through landlord's holding of tenant's security deposit is basis for enhancement of landlord's sentence for mail fraud under sentence enhancement guideline for abuse of trust).

Courts may refer to a trust imposed pursuant to state common law or statute as a "technical" trust. *See, e.g., In re* Paeplow, 217 B.R. 705 (Bankr. D. Vt. 1998).

678 *See In re* Christian, 172 B.R. 490 (Bankr. D. Mass. 1994) (security deposit claims and punitive damages award entered against landlord under state law found to be nondischargeable under section 523(a)(4)); *In re* Wise, 120 B.R. 537 (Bankr. D. Alaska 1990). *See also In re* Morgan, 2010 WL 1416991 (Bankr. S.D. Fla. Apr. 7, 2010) (denying motion to dismiss consumer's action seeking declaration of nondischargeability of debt for security deposit under 11 U.S.C. § 523(a)(4)). *Cf. In re* Lebner, 197 B.R. 180 (Bankr. D. Mass. 1996) (security deposit creates express trust under Massachusetts law, but payment of last month's rent does not).

679 *See In re* McGee, 353 F.3d 537 (7th Cir. 2003) (landlord's unlawful retention of security deposit was defalcation for purposes of section 523(a)(4)); *In re* Bologna, 206 B.R. 628 (D. Mass. 1997) (security deposit law creates fiduciary responsibilities for landlord, but state court judgment which does not address whether landlord was at fault in misappropriating funds cannot collaterally estop landlord on question of whether defalcation occurred); § 15.4.3.4, *supra*.

680 *See* §§ 14.7, 18.4.2, *supra*.

681 *See In re* Christian, 172 B.R. 490 (Bankr. D. Mass. 1994) (collateral estoppel found). *Cf. In re* Lebner, 197 B.R. 180 (Bankr. D. Mass. 1996) (discussing limits of collateral estoppel).

682 *In re* Ardolino, 298 B.R. 541 (Bankr. W.D. Pa. 2003) (although no trust established because state law did not require security deposit to be held in escrow account until third year of lease, landlord's misappropriation of funds with fraudulent and deceptive intent was embezzlement for purposes of section 523(a)(4)).

683 See generally National Consumer Law Center, Unfair and Deceptive Acts and Practices § 2.2.6 (7th ed. 2008 and Supp.) for discussion of the application of UDAP laws to residential leases.

684 *See* § 18.5.4, *supra*; *In re* Cohen, 106 F.3d 52 (3d Cir. 1997) (actual and punitive damages awarded to tenants based on UDAP for rent overcharges nondischargeable under section 523(a)(2)(A)), *aff'd*, 523 U.S. 213 (1998).

685 844 F.2d 823 (D.C. Cir. 1988).

686 *See, e.g.*, Mass. Gen. Laws ch. 186, § 15B(c).

687 Fla. Stat. § 83.49.

688 *See* § 18.5.2, *supra*; 5 Collier on Bankruptcy ¶ 541.11 (16th ed.). *But see In re* Cimaglia, 50 B.R. 9 (Bankr. S.D. Fla. 1985) (putting security deposits into segregated accounts not sufficient evidence alone to find a trust).

689 *See, e.g.*, Ind. Code § 32-7-5-1.

690 *See* ¶ 11.3.2, *supra*.

691 *In re* Kline, 424 B.R. 516 (Bankr. D.N.M. 2010) (former tenants'

Care should be taken that a proof of claim is also filed. The proof of claim should have a statement reserving all rights to the property and claiming the right to assert alternate remedies. A priority should be asserted under the consumer priority section of the Code[692] when the tenants' proof of claim is filed. This section gives individuals a $2600 priority for deposits made in connection with the lease or rental of property.

18.9 Representing Consumers When Lenders File Bankruptcy

18.9.1 Lender Bankruptcies

In recent years, a number of large non-bank lending companies and mortgage servicers have filed chapter 11 bankruptcy cases,[693] giving rise to numerous new issues in applying bankruptcy law to the anomalous situation in which the lender is the debtor, and the borrowers are creditors. Several of these cases involve "subprime" mortgage lenders and servicers involved in predatory lending practices, who were defendants in various consumer class actions and government enforcement actions. In at least some cases, the bankruptcy filing appeared to have been filed for the purpose of "laundering" the loans by discharging consumer claims and defenses and selling the loan portfolios or servicing rights to new entities.[694]

Consumer advocates should not be prematurely discouraged when a lender files for bankruptcy. The amounts still payable on all the lender's loans are "assets,"[695] and those funds will come under the supervision of the bankruptcy court and will be distributed according to the rules of the Code. If the lender plans to reorganize, consumer borrowers may have an opportunity to assert claims that must be paid or settled before the reorganization can succeed. A lender bankruptcy may present unexpected opportunities for consumers to receive restitution, or at least some debt reduction relief.

18.9.2 Automatic Stay Issues for Consumer Borrowers

The automatic stay arising when a lender or servicer files a bankruptcy petition affects only legal proceedings against the lender or servicer; it does not stay legal proceedings in which the lender or servicer is plaintiff, such as mortgage foreclosures.[696] The consumer borrower is stayed from asserting counterclaims but may assert defenses, including affirmative defenses and recoupment claims up to the amount of the asserted debt.[697] Nothing in section 362 bars a consumer defendant from pursuing discovery, filing motions, and taking any other steps necessary to assert defenses in litigation initiated by a bankrupt lender or servicer. However, it is advisable to cease all litigation against the lender or servicer, including discovery, until stay relief has been obtained from the bankruptcy court.

One difficult situation arises in states where non-judicial foreclosure is permitted. Ordinarily, a mortgage holder or servicer sends a written notice of sale, and the consumer asserts defenses by filing an action seeking an injunction barring or delaying the foreclosure sale. However, if the mortgage holder or servicer has filed for bankruptcy, such an action against that party is barred by the automatic stay. The best practice would be to seek relief from the stay in bankruptcy court. The consumer may file a motion in the mortgage holder's or servicer's bankruptcy case to lift the stay, which would almost invariably be granted.[698] Such a case would present very strong "cause," under 11 U.S.C. § 362(d)(1), for lifting or modifying the stay to

---

pursuit of security deposit claim in state court against landlord violated automatic stay in chapter 13 case).

692 11 U.S.C. § 507(a)(7). See § 18.5.5, supra.

693 Bankrupt loan companies have included GMAC (Residential Capital, L.L.C.), Accredited Home Lender, Mortgage Lender Network USA, Aegis Mortgage Corp., American Home Mortgage Holding, New Century Financial Corp., BNC Mortgage L.L.C., Delta Financial Corp., Fieldstone Mortgage Corp., First Magnus Financial, OWNIT Mortgage Corp., People's Choice Home Loan, Fremont General, Quality Home Loans, Southstar Funding, HomeBanc Funding Corp., Conseco Financial, United Companies Lending, Conti Mortgage, First Alliance Mortgage (FAMCO), FirstPlus Financial, Empire Funding, and Washington Mutual, Inc. (WAMU). Links to the significant documents in many of these cases, including petitions, plans, confirmation orders, and sale orders can be found at NCLC's "Lender Bankruptcies" website at: www.nclc.org/bankrupt-lenders-failed-banks/lender-bankruptcies.html. *See also In re* Conseco, Inc., 299 B.R. 875 (N.D. Ill. 2003); *In re* First Alliance Mortg. Co., 269 B.R. 428 (C.D. Cal. 2001); *In re* Conti Mortg. Co., Bky 00-12184 (Bankr. S.D.N.Y. 2000); *In re* FirstPlus Fin., 248 B.R. 60 (Bankr. N.D. Tex. 2000); *In re* Empire Funding Corp., No. 00-11478 (Bankr. W.D. Tex. 2000); *In re* United Co. Fin. Corp., 241 B.R. 521 (Bankr. D. Del. 1999). *See also* Cathy Lesser Mansfield, *The Road to Subprime "HEL" Was Paved with Good Congressional Intentions: Usury Deregulation and the Subprime Home Equity Market*, 51 S.C. L. Rev. 473, 530 n.355 (2000); Diane Henriquez, *Troubled Lender Seeks Protection*, New York Times, Mar. 24, 2000, at A-1.

694 Diane Henriquez, *Troubled Lender Seeks Protection*, New York Times, Mar. 24, 2000, at A-1 (noting that First Alliance Mortgage Co. was solvent, and filed primarily to deal with consumer lawsuits). *Cf. In re* SGL Carbon Corp., 200 F.3d 154 (3d Cir. 1999) (chapter 11 dismissed because it was filed by solvent company, solely to gain tactical advantage in antitrust litigation).

695 Some loan companies sell their loans on the secondary market, or securitize them. The bankrupt lender may only retain the right to service the loans or a portion of the excess interest paid by borrowers.

696 Martin-Trigona v. Champion Fed. Sav., 892 F.2d 575, 577 (7th Cir. 1989). See § 18.3, *supra*.

697 *In re* TLC Hospitals, Inc., 224 F.3d 1008, 1011 (9th Cir. 2000) (recoupment claims exempt from automatic stay); Martin-Trigona v. Champion Fed. Sav., 892 F.2d 575, 577 (7th Cir. 1989) ("There is, in contrast, no policy of preventing persons whom the bankrupt has sued from protecting their legal rights...."). *See also* Bill Heard Chevrolet Corp. v. Histle, 2006 WL 328125 (M.D. Tenn. Feb. 10, 2006) (creditor did not violate stay by moving to dismiss prepetition action brought by debtor), *aff'd*, 221 Fed. Appx. 434 (6th Cir. 2007).

698 *See In re* Millsap, 141 B.R. 732, 733 (Bankr. D. Idaho 1992) (creditor entitled as a matter of right to stay relief to assert compulsory counterclaim in suit be debtor). *See also* § 18.3, *supra*.

allow the consumer to assert defenses to the foreclosure sale. The motion may be filed *in forma pauperis*.[699] Because a lender or servicer in bankruptcy may face hundreds, or even thousands, of individual borrower claims related to pending foreclosures, the bankruptcy court may address issues related to borrowers' stay relief claims in a general order. For example, the bankruptcy court presiding over the bankruptcy of GMAC Mortgage (Residential Capital, L.L.C.) issued an order that specifically addressed eviction and foreclosure proceedings involving consumer borrowers.[700] The court's order exempted from the automatic stay certain claims and counterclaims of borrowers related exclusively to the secured property. For example, under the order the automatic stay would not prohibit a borrower from taking legal actions to stop or set aside a foreclosure, whether in a judicial or non-judicial foreclosure jurisdiction. A borrower could plead a claim for monetary relief when necessary to defend a foreclosure or eviction. However, the borrower would be required to seek formal relief from the automatic stay to pursue a monetary damages claim against the debtor that was not essential to defending a foreclosure or eviction.[701]

Consumer borrowers with non-purchase money mortgage loans may have a right to rescind their loans under the Truth in Lending Act,[702] under other consumer protection laws, or on common law grounds such as fraud. No court has addressed the issue of whether the sending of a written demand to rescind a loan by a bankrupt debtor is a violation of the automatic stay.

It is very plausible to argue that a rescission demand, standing alone, does not violate the automatic stay. The transmission of a written rescission notice is necessary to prevent the consumer's rights from expiring,[703] and is equivalent to any party to a contract simply stating the party's belief as to the party's rights under a contract.[704] Ordinarily, outside of bankruptcy, when the lender disagrees with the borrower and believes the loan should not be rescinded, the borrower's next step is to file suit to enforce the rescission. It is that next step, of suing for rescission, which is stayed by the lender's bankruptcy. The statute of limitations to file such a suit for court enforcement of the rescission would be tolled by the bankruptcy.[705] The best practice is to follow up the rescission demand with a motion for relief from stay to enforce the rescission, file a proof of claim based on the rescission, and/or assert the rescission as a defense in any foreclosure action.

A bankrupt lender might argue that a rescission demand would amount to an "act to exercise control over property of the estate," that is, the loan, or an "act to collect a claim against the debtor."[706] Terminating a contract with the debtor is in some cases a violation of the stay.[707] A debtor loan company might therefore argue that a rescission notice was equivalent to contract termination, or to an action to set off mutual debts, both of which are prohibited by the automatic stay. The most cautious approach would therefore be to either file a motion for stay relief that includes a rescission demand or to file a proof of claim with the rescission demand. Either action ought to be sufficient to protect the consumer from expiration of the right to rescind.

In some cases the automatic stay will not affect a borrower's efforts to vindicate consumer protection claims, because the debtor loan company does not own the loan outright, but is merely a servicer. This is most common when the consumer's loan has been "securitized," which means that it has been transferred to a trust, along with a large pool of similar loans, and is owned by a trustee on behalf of various investors.[708] The debtor loan company with whom the consumer is dealing is a servicer, and is paid some portion of the monthly interest as a servicing fee. The servicing loan company may also retain a subordinate interest in a portion of the consumer's loan payments, typically the right to receive excess interest after the trust investors have been paid a guaranteed fixed rate.[709]

---

699 *See* § 18.6, *supra*.

700 *See In re* Residential Capital, L.L.C., 2012 WL 3423285 (Bankr. S.D.N.Y Aug. 14, 2012) (interpreting court's general order to permit state court to determine whether borrower's counterclaims against GMAC, including those for monetary damages, constituted a defense to foreclosure, and if found to be defense to foreclosure, bankruptcy court may permit state court to adjudicate claim as part of foreclosure action).

701 *In re* Residential Capital, L.L.C., 2012 WL 355584 (Bankr. S.D.N.Y. Aug. 16, 2012) (denying stay relief for action in Mississippi court seeking only monetary damages; court notes possession not at issue and if it were, state court would be appropriate forum in which to resolve possession issue); *In re* Residential Capital, L.L.C., 2012 WL 3556912 (Bankr. S.D. N.Y. Aug. 16, 2012) (stay relief denied for Minnesota class action over forced place insurance practices of GMAC, lender agreeing not to foreclose); *In re* Residential Capital, L.L.C., 2012 WL 3860586 (Bankr. S.D.N.Y. Aug. 8, 2012) (automatic stay bars pursuit of damages claim against debtor in North Carolina court, parties agreed stay would not bar defense of foreclosure proceeding).

702 15 U.S.C. § 1635. *See* National Consumer Law Center, Truth in Lending Ch. 6 (8th ed. 2012).

703 Beach v. Ocwen Fed. Bank, 523 U.S. 410, 118 S. Ct. 1408, 140 L. Ed. 2d 566 (1998).

704 *Cf.* Citizens Bank of Md. v. Strumpf, 516 U.S. 16, 21, 116 S. Ct. 286, 133 L. Ed. 2d 258 (1995) ("temporary refusal to pay [by Bank that held debtor deposits] was neither a taking of possession of respondent's property nor an exercising of control over it, but merely a refusal to perform its promise"); *In re* Smith 737 F.2d 1549 (11th Cir. 1984) (creditor could respond to debtor's rescission demand without violating the stay protecting the consumer debtor).

705 11 U.S.C. § 108(c).

However, the borrower should not allow the rescission right to expire. *See In re* Williams, 276 B.R. 394 (Bankr. E.D. Pa. 2002) (lender's bankruptcy does not extend time for borrower to rescind loan under TILA because section 108(c) applies only to filing of action and not exercise of rescission right).

706 11 U.S.C. § 362(a)(3), (6). *See* § 9.4.3, *supra*.

707 *See* § 9.4.3, *supra*.

708 *See* Cathy Lesser Mansfield, *The Road to "HEL" Was Paved with Good Congressional Intentions: Usury Deregulation and the Subprime Home Equity Market*, 51 S.C. L. Rev. 473, 531, 532 (2000) (growing use of securitization by subprime mortgage lenders in 1990s).

709 *See* Chandler v. Norwest Bank of Minn., 137 F.3d 1053 (8th Cir. 1998) (describes roles of loan originator, loan purchaser, trustee for loan pool, and servicer, noting that the trust itself owns the securitized loans).

The rights of the loan company as servicer, and the trust as owner of the loans, are spelled out in a pooling and servicing agreement (PSA). In many cases, the PSA does not require that the assignment of the consumer loans be perfected (such as by recording a mortgage assignment to the trustee). The originating lender and/or servicer will appear from public records to still be the owner of the loan, and in the case of a mortgage, may foreclose in its own name. Nevertheless, the true owner of the loan is not the servicer, it is the trustee for the investors in the mortgage-backed securities. The servicer's contractual rights do not rise to the level of an ownership interest in the loan.[710]

For this reason, a consumer borrower is free to take legal action against the trustee as owner of her loan. The automatic stay has no effect on legal action against other parties who are not debtors in bankruptcy.[711] Even if the servicer is bound by the PSA to repurchase a consumer's loan in the event the mortgage is found unenforceable in whole or in part, the loan owner has either a right of contribution against the bankrupt lender, or at best a guarantee. The automatic stay does not ordinarily protect a principal obligor in the guarantor's bankruptcy.[712] If the consumer has initiated legal action against the loan company prior to a bankruptcy, it may be worthwhile to determine whether a trustee or other assignee should be substituted as the defendant, so that the consumer's litigation can go forward against a party not in bankruptcy. In an action against parties other than the debtor lender or servicer, a consumer may find it advantageous or necessary to pursue discovery against the debtor. Early cases addressing the issue of pursuing discovery against bankrupt entities while litigating against other parties assumed that the automatic stay applied to the debtor as a third-party witness. These cases articulated a balancing test to determine whether or not the automatic stay should be lifted.[713] However, more recent cases suggest that the automatic stay may not apply to the pursuit of discovery against the debtor as a non-party witness.[714]

In summary, relief from the stay is probably not necessary to:

- Pursue legal action (including counterclaims) against other parties who are not in bankruptcy;
- Assert defenses in litigation brought by the bankrupt lender;
- Notify the lender of the exercise of a valid right to rescind.

Consumer attorneys should also consider the merits of filing a proof of claim, and/or waiting until the consumer's loan is sold by the debtor, as alternatives to immediately seeking relief from the stay. However, when in doubt about the applicability of the stay, the best practice is to move for relief under section 362(d).

---

710 *In re* Litenda Mortgage Corp., 246 B.R. 185, 193, 194 (Bankr. D.N.J. 1999).

711 *See* Queenie, Ltd. v. Nygard Int'l, 321 F.3d 282 (2d Cir. 2003) (appeal stayed as to defendant who had filed bankruptcy and his wholly owned corporation, but not as to other defendants); Credit Alliance Corp. v. Williams, 851 F.2d 119 (4th Cir. 1988) (automatic stay did not protect guarantor); Fortier v. Dona Anna Plaza Partners, 747 F.2d 1324 (10th Cir. 1984); Williford v. Armstrong World Indus., 715 F.2d 124 (4th Cir. 1983); Wedgeworth v. Fibreboard Corp., 706 F.2d 541 (5th Cir. 1983); Austin v. Unarco Indus., 705 F.2d 1 (1st Cir. 1983); §§ 9.4.2, 18.3, *supra*. *See also In re* Am. Hardwoods, Inc., 885 F.2d 621 (9th Cir. 1989) (court lacks power to institute non-automatic stay pursuant to 11 U.S.C. § 105 to protect non-debtor guarantors). *See generally In re* Thornburg Mortgage, Inc. Sec. Litig., 824 F. Supp. 2d 1214 (D.N.M. 2011) (investors' class action alleging SEC Act violations; automatic stay does not bar court from considering liability of principals who organized marketing of mortgage-backed securities through corporation now in bankruptcy).

A primary objective of the parties to the securitization process is that the loans being securitized will not become property of the originating lender's estate if the lender files bankruptcy. To accomplish this, the loans are transferred to a "special purpose entity" (also referred to as a "bankruptcy remote entity") and ultimately held by the trust. The structure of these transactions is carefully designed so that the transfer of assets will be treated as a "true sale" and not reachable by a bankruptcy trustee if the lender files bankruptcy. *See In re* LTV Steel Co., 274 B.R. 278 (Bankr. N.D. Ohio 2001).

This supports a consumer borrower's position that the automatic stay issued in the originating lender's bankruptcy should not preclude claims brought against the trustee as owner of the borrower's loan. The bankrupt lender might, however, seek an injunction from the bankruptcy court under 11 U.S.C. § 105. *See* § 9.4.7, *supra*.

712 *See* McCartney v. Integra Nat'l Bank N., 106 F.3d 506, 509, 510 (3d Cir. 1997) (noting that in exceptional circumstances bankruptcy court may enjoin action against third party if non-debtor party has no assets, and the action will in effect be against the debtor.); § 18.3.2, *supra*.

713 *See In re* Johns-Manville Corp., 41 B.R. 926 (S.D.N.Y. 1984) (reversing denial of motion for stay relief to conduct discovery); *In re* Johns-Manville Corp. (Norton), 39 B.R. 659 (S.D.N.Y. 1984) (allowing non-debtor party to depose debtor and stating that lifting stay to allow limited discovery was proper to avoid "devastating prejudice" to litigants).

714 *See In re* Miller, 262 B.R. 499 (B.A.P. 9th Cir. 2001) (automatic stay does not preclude discovery against debtor to gather information for claims against non-debtor parties); Peter Rosenbaum Photography Corp. v. Otto Doosan Mail Order Ltd., 2004 WL 2973822 (N.D. Ill. Nov. 30, 2004) (automatic stay did not prevent discovery against debtor who was not defendant, but simply an "interested non-litigant," and discovery sought related to defenses raised by non-debtor defendants); *In re* Hillsborough Holdings Corp., 130 B.R. 603 (Bankr. M.D. Fla. 1991) (automatic stay inapplicable to discovery aimed at debtor as long as discovery pertained to claims and defenses of non-debtor party). *See also In re* Paul, 534 F.3d 1303 (10th Cir. 2008) (creditor's ongoing state court litigation against business partners of former debtors, including pursuit of discovery against debtors, does not violate discharge order unless conducted to harass debtors or coerce them to pay prepetition debts); Kovacs v. Koot, 2007 WL 604927 (S.D. Fla. Feb. 22, 2007) (plaintiff creditor may subpoena debtor as witness in aid of execution of judgment against non-debtor party); *In re* Richard B. Vance and Co., 289 B.R. 692 (Bankr. C.D. Ill. 2003) (discovery pertaining to claims against debtor's codefendants, even if discovery requires response from debtor, is not stayed). *But see In re* Residential Capital, L.L.C. __ B.R. __, 2012 WL 4867399 (Bankr. S.D.N.Y. Oct. 12, 2012) (acting under 11 U.S.C. § 105(a), bankruptcy court orders stay of discovery involving debtor GMAC in connection with federal court action against non-debtor affiliates of GMAC and underwriters, citing burdens that extensive discovery would impose on GMAC's reorganization efforts).

18.9.3 Loan Company Sales of Assets Under 11 U.S.C. § 363

In both chapter 7 and chapter 11 cases, but more commonly in the latter, the rights of creditors may be determined not by a liquidation or plan confirmation process, but rather through a sale of some or all of the debtor's assets, free and clear of interests in the property, under 11 U.S.C. § 363(b) and (f).

Although the Bankruptcy Code does not provide for corporate debtors to receive a discharge in chapter 7,[715] and a discharge does not affect the liability of co-defendants,[716] some motions for asset sales under section 363 seek very broad injunctive relief resembling a discharge, and barring creditors from pursuing claims against purchasers and other successors to the debtor. A sale of all or nearly all of the debtor's assets may render the remainder of the bankruptcy proceeding inconsequential. There will be little left to the case apart from distributing the proceeds of the sale (cash or securities in the buyer, typically). More significantly, the purchaser of the assets of a lender may contend that consumers are barred from asserting claims as a result of a section 363 sale.

In one of the very few positive changes for consumers made by the 2005 amendments, section 362(*o*) was added to ensure that consumer claims and defenses are preserved following a section 363 sale. The purchaser under a section 363 sale of any interest in a consumer credit transaction that is subject to the Truth in Lending Act or any interest in a consumer credit contract as defined by the Federal Trade Commission's Preservation of Claims Trade Regulation (FTC Holder Rule),[717] remains subject to all claims and defenses that are related to the consumer credit transaction or contract, to the same extent the purchaser would be subject to such claims and defenses of the consumer had the interest been purchased at a sale not under section 363. By incorporating the definition and coverage sections of the Truth in Lending Act and the FTC Holder Rule, section 362(*o*) should apply to virtually all consumer credit transactions. Unlike the doctrine of recoupment discussed below, section 363(*o*) will permit the consumer to assert affirmative claims against the purchaser as well as defenses, to the extent that such claims may be raised under applicable non-bankruptcy law against a purchaser at a nonbankruptcy sale. In addition, because the provision preserves all claims and defenses that "are related to" the consumer credit transaction or contract, it should apply to claims and defenses involving not only the origination of the credit transaction but also any subsequent servicing of the loan, if the servicing rights are being sold in the section 363 sale. To date, no court has interpreted this new provision of the Code.[718]

Because section 363(*o*) preserves claims and defenses to the extent they may be asserted against a purchaser at a nonbankruptcy sale, questions may arise concerning successor liability, which is ordinarily a question of state law.[719] Section 363(*o*), however, should make clear that bankruptcy court orders protecting purchasers of consumer credit transactions at section 363 sales from successor liability[720] are no longer permitted. Even if section 363(*o*) does not apply, some courts have questioned the authority under the Bankruptcy Code for such orders, especially with regard to claims that were unknown at the time of the bankruptcy, such as product liability claims.[721]

To the extent that section 363(*o*) does not apply and a consumer has a claim that arises from the same transaction as the bankruptcy debtor's claim against the consumer, a section 363 sale of assets should not affect the consumer's rights. A consumer borrower's defenses to payment of a delinquent loan owed to a bankrupt loan company should not be affected by a sale of the loan under section 363. The consumer's defenses, so long as they are in the nature of recoupment, define the "property" being sold (for example, the loan) and are therefore not an "interest" in the property divested by the sale.[722] Thus, a consumer may assert claims defensively, up to the amount of the debt owed by the consumer, against a purchaser of assets, despite a sale "free and clear" under 11 U.S.C. § 363.

18.9.4 Filing a Proof of Claim for a Consumer Borrower

While a consumer's defenses to a loan may be viewed as recoupment defenses, and therefore not a "claim" in the bankruptcy sense, it is still advisable to file a proof of claim in a lender's bankruptcy. For bankruptcy cases of large financial institutions, websites are often set up to provide information on filing claims. Otherwise, the Code and Bankruptcy Rule pro-

---

715 11 U.S.C. § 727(a)(1).

716 11 U.S.C. § 524(e).

717 16 C.F.R. § 433.1.
    For a detailed discussion of the coverage of the FTC holder rule, see National Consumer Law Center, Unfair and Deceptive Acts and Practices (7th ed. 2008 and Supp.).

718 *See In re* Am. Home Mortgage, 402 B.R. 87 (Bankr. D. Del. 2009) (transfer of loan servicing rights allowed independently of loans).

719 3 Collier on Bankruptcy ¶ 363.02[3], at 363-16 through 363-17 (16th ed.). *See generally* § 18.5.4.4, *supra*.

720 *See, e.g., In re* Trans World Airlines, Inc., 322 F.3d 283 (3d Cir. 2003) (successor airline not liable for flight attendants' employment discrimination claims that were covered by section 363(f) asset sale order); *In re* Gen. Motors Corp., 407 B.R. 463, 505 (S.D.N.Y. 2009) (permitting old corporation's assets to pass to new corporation free and clear of successor liability claims); *In re* All Am. of Ashburn, 56 B.R. 186 (Bankr. N.D. Ga. 1986) (section 363(f) sale precluded mobile home owners from bringing product liability claims against purchaser of debtor-manufacturer's assets), *aff'd on other grounds*, 805 F.2d 1515 (11th Cir. 1986).

721 3 Collier on Bankruptcy § 363.02[3], at 363-17 (16th ed.). *See* Nelson v. Tiffany Indus., Inc., 778 F.2d 533 (9th Cir. 1985) (material issues of fact existed, precluding summary judgment, as to whether there was collusive agreement under which successor corporation induced predecessor to file bankruptcy to avoid future tort liability). *See generally In re* Trans World Airlines, Inc., 2001 WL 1820325 (Bankr. D. Del. Mar. 27, 2001), *aff'd*, 322 F.3d 283 (3d Cir. 2003) (property of airline can be sold free and clear of employment discrimination claims).

722 Folger Adam Sec., Inc. v. DeMatteis/MacGregor, 209 F.3d 252, 260–261 (3d Cir. 2000); EMC Mortgage Corp. v. Atkinson, 888 N.E.2d 456 (Ohio Ct. App. 2008) (bankruptcy sale did not preclude consumer's assertion of defenses against purchaser of loan).

cedures for filing proofs of claim, discussed earlier in this chapter, must be followed.[723] The claim, unless objected to, will in some cases allow the consumer to vote on a plan, and/or receive payment from the liquidation or reorganization of the lender. If the lender is not the current holder of the consumer's loan, the consumer can still file any claim arising out of the loan origination for which the lender is individually or jointly liable. However, the consumer should carefully evaluate whether to accept any distribution on the claim if the lender's confirmed chapter 11 plan provides for a release of claims the consumer may have against non-debtor third parties.[724]

A consumer borrower may assert secured status, based on a right of set-off, to the extent the consumer still owes a balance to the lender. If the consumer has affirmative claims against the lender, for example for statutory or punitive damages, state law may allow those claims to be set off against the consumer's loan debt. Setoff rights are protected by section 553 of the Code, and are secured claims under section 506(a).

Under a confirmed chapter 11 plan, the consumer's secured claim, if allowed, should be paid in full, by immediately reducing the debt owed by the consumer to the lender, by payment of the claim in deferred cash payments, or by having the consumer's claim "attach" to the loan if the loan is sold, that is, allowing the consumer to assert the setoff against the purchaser of the loan.[725] The setoff right should not be adversely affected by a confirmed plan, discharge, or sale of assets.[726]

Some consumer borrowers have priority claims arising from a loan transaction. If the consumer has had payments or loan proceeds set aside in escrow as a deposit for future payments of taxes, insurance, or home repairs, the escrow deposit amounts should come within the consumer deposit priority.[727] Similarly, if part of a loan was applied to a credit insurance premium, the unearned portion of the premium for future months could be regarded as a deposit for which services have not yet been delivered. Arguably, other amounts paid from loan proceeds by the consumer for services that were of no value or were not actually rendered could come within the section 507(a)(7) priority, such as spurious broker or appraisal fees.

18.9.5 Third-Party and Successor Releases and Injunctions

Chapter 11 plans often include provisions in their fine print that attempt to enjoin creditors from pursuing claims against the debtor's potential codefendants in litigation. These third-party release and injunction provisions can leave consumers unable to pursue the otherwise useful strategy of "sidestepping" the lender's bankruptcy by asserting claims against agents, successors, assignees, and other liable third parties. The Bankruptcy Code does not authorize a discharge of a party who is not a debtor,[728] and the courts have generally taken a dim view of chapter 11 plan provisions that appear to result in such a discharge. In addition, such orders are prohibited if the third party is a purchaser at a section 363 sale that is subject to section 363(*o*).[729]

For example, in *In re Continental Airlines*, the Third Circuit Court of Appeals refused to enforce a chapter 11 plan provision that would have enjoined a shareholder class action against officers and directors of the bankrupt airline company.[730] The Third Circuit declined to hold that third-party releases are always per se invalid unless consensual, as other courts have done.[731] Courts that do allow third-party release provisions will consider factors such as whether the third parties have contributed funds to the reorganization, whether the claims are being paid in full or nearly in full, whether the terms of the release have been fully disclosed, and whether the affected creditors have agreed to accept the plan treatment.[732]

The approach adopted by the Seventh Circuit to this "knotty problem" has been to emphasize that non-debtor releases should be "consensual and non-coercive."[733] In approving the release in *In re Specialty Equipment Companies, Inc.*, the Seventh Circuit noted that the debtor's plan permitted each creditor to choose whether to be bound by the release and that only creditors who affirmatively voted to accept the plan would have claims released; a creditor who voted to reject the plan or who abstained from voting could still pursue claims against third-party non-debtors.[734]

---

723 See § 18.4, *supra*.
724 See § 18.9.5, *infra*.
725 See 11 U.S.C. § 1129(b)(2)(A).
  Less favorable treatment is possible only if the class of secured creditors agrees to it, that is, accepts the plan. See § 1129(a)(8), 1129(b).
726 See 3 Collier on Bankruptcy ¶ 363.06[7] (16th ed.).
727 See § 18.5.5, *supra*.
  Also keep in mind the discussion of trust fund theories in § 18.5.2, *supra*.

728 11 U.S.C. § 524(e).
729 See § 18.9.3, *supra*.
730 *In re* Cont'l Airlines, 203 F.3d 203 (3d Cir. 2000). See also § 18.3.2, *supra*.
731 See, e.g., *In re* Lowenschuss, 67 F.3d 1394 (9th Cir. 1995) (chapter 11 plan that released claims against non-debtors could not be confirmed); *In re* Zenith Elecs. Corp., 241 B.R. 92 (Bankr. D. Del. 1999). See also Peter E. Meltzer, *Getting out of Jail Free: Can the Bankruptcy Plan Process Be Used to Release Nondebtor Parties?*, 71 Am. Bankr. L.J. 1 (1997).
732 *In re* Cont'l Airlines, 203 F.3d at 212, 213.
733 *In re* Specialty Equip. Companies, Inc., 3 F.3d 1043, 1045, 1046 (7th Cir. 1993). See also *In re* Artra Group, Inc., 300 B.R. 699 (Bankr. N.D. Ill. 2003) (court rejected proposed adversary proceeding settlement that included broad injunctive provision seeking to enjoin any entity from pursuing claims in any way related to debtor).
734 *In re* Specialty Equip. Companies, Inc., 3 F.3d 1043, 1045, 1046 (7th Cir. 1993).
  Although mere acceptance of a plan distribution without an affirmative assent to be bound by a release provision should not cut off further pursuit of claims, a consumer borrower who has filed a proof of claim in a lender's bankruptcy should carefully review any conditions relating to acceptance of a distribution. See *In re* Conseco, Inc., 301 B.R. 525 (Bankr. N.D. Ill. 2003) (court confirmed plan only after third party release was modified to provide that it would bind only those creditors who agreed to be bound, either by

As a further limitation on broad releases and injunctions protecting third parties, some courts have held that such orders are permissible only if they are limited to property of the debtor's estate.[735] This should prevent a bankruptcy court from approving an order that releases non-debtor trustee owners of securitized loans from borrower claims. In addition, the bankruptcy court may lack jurisdiction to enjoin an action between non-debtor parties in which one of the parties claims to be protected by a plan release or similar order.[736] In a similar vein, a state court action against a non-debtor party that is removed to federal court based on the purported effect of a third-party release should be remanded if the debtor is not a party to the action and if the action will have little or no effect on the debtor's bankruptcy.[737]

In one very limited group of cases, Congress added a special provision to authorize injunctions to protect third parties, including purchasers of the assets of the debtor corporation. This special provision is limited to asbestos claims in chapter 11 cases when a trust has been established to pay off present and future injury claims.[738] The existence of this limited exception suggests that Congress knows how to authorize discharge-like injunctions to protect third parties, and that courts should leave it to Congress to define other circumstances in which such discharge provisions might be appropriate.[739]

By way of illustration of some of the principles discussed here, the plaintiff in *Bailey v. Green Tree Servicing Limited Liability Co.*[740] brought an action in state court against the mortgage servicer that had purchased the servicing rights to her mortgage in a section 363(f) asset sale, and against the trustee owner of her securitized mortgage.[741] The servicer and trustee removed the action to federal court and argued in response to a remand motion that the home owner's claims were barred by orders entered in the originating lender's bankruptcy and that the federal court had jurisdiction over the matter as a "core proceeding" based on the originating lender's bankruptcy.[742] The court held that because the alleged servicing misconduct occurred after the section 363(f) sale, the bankruptcy court's sale order could not possibly protect the servicer from claims based on its future, post-acquisition conduct.[743] The court also found that the sale order did not protect the trustee from claims that the loan was unconscionable.[744] Finally, as the plaintiff's state law claims related solely to her mortgage, which was not part of the originating lender's bankruptcy because it had been sold well before the lender filed bankruptcy, the court found that the matter was not a "core proceeding" in the originating lender's bankruptcy and was not within the federal court's jurisdiction, and therefore remanded the case to state court.[745]

The Supreme Court's decision in *Travelers Indemnity Co. v. Bailey*[746] did not fundamentally alter the debate over the authority of bankruptcy courts to approve third-party releases. In *Travelers* the Court upheld an injunction entered as part of a chapter 11 confirmation order barring suits against Travelers, a non-debtor insurance company. Travelers had provided coverage to the debtor, the asbestos manufacturer Johns-Manville. The Court found that the terms of the confirmation order were unambiguous in barring a broad range of litigation, including suits alleging independent wrongdoing by Travelers related to insurance coverage of the debtor. The Court's holding, however, was a narrow one. Res judicata applied to the final plan confirmation order entered more than twenty years earlier. The finality that must be afforded the order precluded indirect attacks on it through state court actions brought decades later. The Court did not address the issue of whether the bankruptcy court had jurisdiction to approve the release in the confirmation order in the first place. Nor did the court reach the question of the applicability of Code section 524(g), which expressly au-

---

voting for the plan or by receiving a distribution under the plan and choosing not to opt out of release); *In re* Arrowmill Dev. Corp., 211 B.R. 497, (Bankr. D.N.J. 1997) (non-debtor must affirmatively assent to release of claim).

735 *See, e.g.*, Fogel v. Zell, 221 F.3d 955 (7th Cir. 2000); *In re* Artra Group, Inc., 300 B.R. 699 (Bankr. N.D. Ill. 2003).

736 Zerand-Bernal Group, Inc. v. Cox, 23 F.3d 159 (7th Cir. 1994) (bankruptcy court lacked jurisdiction to enjoin product liability suit against purchaser of debtor's assets); *In re* Conseco, Inc., 305 B.R. 281 (Bankr. N.D. Ill. 2004) (court refused to exercise jurisdiction over declaratory judgment action relating to binding effect of release provisions in chapter 11 plan it had confirmed).

737 *See In re* Hotel Mt. Lassen, Inc., 207 B.R. 935 (Bankr. E.D. Cal. 1997) (court held that removed actions are not "related to" debtor's bankruptcy case within meaning of 28 U.S.C. § 1334(b) and must be remanded). *See also* § 14.4.1, *supra*.

738 11 U.S.C. § 524(g).

739 *In re* Lowenschuss, 67 F.3d 1394 (9th Cir. 1995) (amendment adding section 524(g) supports conclusion that section 524(e) does not permit third-party injunctions in non-asbestos cases).

See also § 9.4.7, *supra*, regarding limited circumstances when bankruptcy courts may extend automatic stay to non-debtor parties under section 105(a) of the Code.

740 Bailey v. Green Tree Servicing L.L.C., 2004 WL 2347585 (S.D. W. Va. July 23, 2004).

This case was decided before the enactment of section 363(*o*).

741 The original lender, Conseco Finance, sold the plaintiff's mortgage to a trust, and retained the right to service the loan. Conseco then filed bankruptcy. Conseco sold the servicing rights to Green Tree Servicing in a section 363(f) sale, approved by the bankruptcy court.

742 The defendants alleged that the federal court in West Virginia had jurisdiction over the West Virginia state court action, pursuant to 28 U.S.C. § 1334(b) and § 1452, based on the originating lender Conseco's bankruptcy filing in a bankruptcy court in Illinois.

743 *See also* Lucas v. Green Tree Servicing L.L.C., 2006 WL 1896612 (S.D. W. Va. July 10, 2006) (motion to dismiss denied because plaintiff's complaint asserted servicing claims arising after sale order).

744 A different result was reached in *In re* Mayer-Myers, 2007 WL 790839 (Bankr. D. Vt. Mar. 14, 2007), in which the court found that the plaintiff's recoupment claim was clearly barred by the same *Conseco* free and clear asset sale order and that the plaintiff could not collaterally attack the validity of the order. *See also* Sowell v. U.S. Bank Trust, 317 B.R. 319 (E.D.N.C. 2004) (action against securitization trustee dismissed because challenge to *Conseco* bankruptcy order must be made in court that issued it).

745 Because the court found that it did not have subject matter jurisdiction, it did not reach the plaintiff's argument that the matter should have been remanded on equitable grounds pursuant to 28 U.S.C. § 1452(b).

746 557 U.S. 137, 129 S. Ct. 2195, 174 L. Ed. 2d 99 (2009).

thorizes bankruptcy courts in chapter 11 cases to bar future asbestos-related claims against non-debtors.[747] In the Court's view, the bankruptcy court's original determination that it had jurisdiction to enter the order was an aspect of the final judgment that could not be challenged by collateral attack long after the order became final.

Two lessons can be gleaned from the *Travelers* ruling. First, the decision highlights the importance of raising timely objections to third-party releases before a plan confirmation order becomes final. Second, claimants must ensure that releases and injunctions against future litigation against non-debtors are drafted as narrowly as possible.[748]

18.10 Other Mechanisms to Protect Consumers in Business Bankruptcies

The 2005 amendments created two new mechanisms to protect consumers in business bankruptcies. The first relates to the sale or lease of certain consumer information by the debtor.[749] When a debtor seeks to sell or lease "personally identifiable information"[750] outside of the ordinary course of business,[751] to entities not affiliated with the debtor, the transaction must be (1) consistent with the debtor's privacy policy in effect at the time of filing,[752] or (2) the court must approve the transaction after the appointment a consumer privacy ombudsman. Section 332 sets forth the procedures for the appointment of and the duties of the consumer privacy ombudsman. In general, the ombudsman assists the court in its consideration of the facts and circumstances of the proposed sale or lease of information including the potential losses or gains of consumer privacy, potential costs and benefits to consumers, and potential alternatives that would mitigate privacy losses or potential costs.[753]

A second mechanism allows the court to appoint a patient care ombudsman in any bankruptcy case filed by a health care business.[754] "Health care business" is defined broadly and includes facilities offering the diagnoses or treatment of injury, deformity, or disease, surgical services, drug treatment, psychiatric or obstetric care, skilled nursing facilities, intermediate care facilities, assisted living facilities, and homes for the aged.[755] The role of the patient care ombudsman is to "monitor the quality of patient care and to represent the interests of the patients of the health care business."[756] The patient care ombudsman is authorized to interview patients and physicians.[757] In addition, the patient care ombudsman must file a report with the court at least every sixty days.[758]

Another new section added by the 2005 amendments details the procedures for the disposal of patient records if a health care business provider files for bankruptcy and if the trustee is unable to pay for storage of patient records as required by federal law.[759]

---

747 *Id.*, 129 S. Ct. at 2207.
748 *See, e.g., In re* Davis Offshore, L.P., 644 F.3d 259 (5th Cir. 2011) (although terms of release and exculpatory clause in confirmation order were broad and could be subject to conflicting interpretations, clause enforced where parties involved had access to sophisticated legal and financial assistance when order entered).
749 11 U.S.C. § 363(b).
750 "Personally identifiable information" is defined in new section 101(41A).
751 For example, the limitation is not applicable to businesses that ordinarily lease customer lists. *See* 11 U.S.C. § 363(a).
752 The provisions of section 363(b) only appear to be applicable if the debtor in fact had a privacy policy which had previously been disclosed to consumers. *See* 11 U.S.C. § 363(b)(1).
753 11 U.S.C. § 332(b).
754 11 U.S.C. § 333.
755 11 U.S.C. § 101(27A). *See also* Fed. R. Bankr. P. 1021, 2007.2, 2015.1, 2015.2.
756 11 U.S.C. § 333(a). *See generally In re* Renaissance Hospital-Grand Prairie, Inc., 2008 WL 5746904 (Bankr. N.D. Tex. Dec. 31, 2008) (authorizing ombudsman to hire attorney and other professionals).
757 11 U.S.C. § 333(b)(1).
758 11 U.S.C. § 333(b)(2).
759 11 U.S.C. § 351.

Bibliography

Ackerly, *Tenants by the Entirety Property and the Bankruptcy Reform Act*, 21 Wm. & Mary L. Rev. 701 (1980).

Alan M. Ahart, *Enforcing Nondischargeable Money Judgments: The Bankruptcy Courts' Dubious Jurisdiction*, 74 Am. Bankr. L.J. 115 (2000).

Alan M. Ahart, *The Inefficacy of the New Eviction Exceptions to the Automatic Stay*, 80 Am. Bankr. L.J. 125 (2006).

Alan M. Ahart, *The Liability of Property Exempted in Bankruptcy for Pre-Petition Domestic Support Obligations After BAPCPA: Debtors Beware*, 81 Am. Bankr. L.J. 233 (2007).

Alan M. Ahart, *The Limited Scope of Implied Powers of a Bankruptcy Judge: A Statutory Court of Bankruptcy, Not a Court of Equity*, 79 Am. Bankr. L.J. 1 (2005).

Peter C. Alexander & Kelly Jo Slone, *Thinking About the Private Matters in Public Documents: Bankruptcy Privacy in an Electronic Age*, 75 Am. Bankr. L.J. 437 (2001).

Am. Bar Ass'n, *Working Paper: Best Practices for Debtors' Attorneys*, 64 Bus. Law. 79 (Nov. 2008).

Laura B. Bartell, *From Debtors' Prisons to Prisoner Debtors: Credit Counseling for the Incarcerated*, 24 Bankr. Dev. J. 15 (2008).

Laura B. Bartell, *The Appeal of Direct Appeal—Use of the New 28 U.S.C. § 158(d)(2)*, 84 Am. Bankr. L.J. 145 (2010).

Eric G. Behrens, *Stern v. Marshall: The Supreme Court's Continuing Erosion of Bankruptcy Court Jurisdiction and Article I Courts*, 85 Am. Bankr. L.J. 387 (2011).

Susan Block-Lieb, *A Comparison of Pro Bono Representation Programs for Consumer Debtors*, 2 Am. Bankr. Inst. L. Rev. 37 (1994).

Douglass G. Boshkoff, *Bankruptcy-Based Discrimination*, 66 Am. Bankr. L.J. 387 (1992).

Jean Braucher, *The Challenges to the Bench and Bar Presented by the 2005 Bankruptcy Act: Resistance Need Not Be Futile*, 2007 U. Ill. L. Rev. 93 (2007).

Jean Braucher, *An Empirical Study of Debtor Education in Bankruptcy: Impact on Chapter 13 Completion Not Shown*, 9 Am. Bankr. Inst. L. Rev. 557 (2001).

Jean Braucher, *Lawyers and Consumer Bankruptcy: One Code, Many Cultures*, 67 Am. Bankr. L.J. 501 (1993).

William Houston Brown, *Taking Exception to a Debtor's Discharge: The 2005 Bankruptcy Amendments Make It Easier*, 79 Am. Bankr. L.J. 419 (2005).

Samuel L. Bufford & Erwin Chemerinsky, *Constitutional Problems in the 2005 Bankruptcy Amendments*, 82 Am. Bankr. L.J. 1 (2008).

Butler, *A Congressman's Reflections on the Drafting of the Bankruptcy Code of 1978*, 21 Wm. & Mary L. Rev. 557 (1980).

David Gray Carlson, *Modified Plans of Reorganization and the Basic Chapter 13 Bargain*, 83 Am. Bankr. L.J. 585 (2009).

Erwin Chemerinsky, *Constitutional Issues Posed in the Bankruptcy Abuse and Consumer Protection Act of 2005*, 79 Am. Bankr. L.J. 571 (2005).

Marianne B. Culhane & Michaela M. White, *Catching Can-Pay Debtors: Is the Means Test the Only Way?*, 13 Am. Bankr. Inst. L. Rev. 665 (2005).

Marianne B. Culhane & Michaela M. White, *Debt After Discharge: An Empirical Study of Reaffirmation*, 73 Am. Bankr. L.J. 709 (1999).

Conrad K. Cyr, *The Chapter 13 "Good Faith" Tempest: An Analysis and Proposal for Change*, 55 Am. Bankr. L.J. 271 (1981).

Susan L. DeJarnatt, *In re McCrate: Using Consumer Bankruptcy as a Context for Learning in Advanced Legal Writing*, 50 J. Legal Educ. 50 (2000).

Gregory M Duhl, Divided Loyalties: The Attorney's Role in Bankruptcy Reaffirmations, 84 Am. Bankr. L. J. 361 (2010).

Richard H. Fallon, *Of Legislative Courts, Administrative Agencies, and Article III*, 101 Harv. L. Rev. 916 (1988).

Jeffrey T. Ferriell, *The Constitutionality of the Bankruptcy Amendments and Federal Judgeship Act of 1984*, 63 Am. Bankr. L.J. 109 (Spring 1989).

Martin D. Gelfand, *How a Community Saved Their Hospitals from Unnecessary Liquidation*, 75 Am. Bankr. L.J. 3 (2001).

Seth J. Gerson, Note, *Separate Classification of Student Loans in Chapter 13*, 73 Wash. U. L.Q. 269 (1995).

Karen Gross, Failure and Forgiveness: Rebalancing the Bankruptcy System (1999).

Charles R. Haywood, *The Power of Bankruptcy Courts to Shift Fees under the Equal Access to Justice Act*, 61 U. Chi. L. Rev. 985 (1994).

Henry E. Hildebrand, III, *Impact of the Bankruptcy Abuse and Consumer Protection Act of 2005 on Chapter 13 Trustees*, 79 Am. Bankr. L.J. 373 (2005).
Christopher M. Hogan, Note, *Will the Ride-Through Ride Again?*, 108 Colum. L. Rev. 882 (2008).
Margaret Howard, *Exemptions Under the 2005 Amendments: An Opportunity Lost*, 79 Am. Bankr. L.J. 397 (2005).
Margaret Howard, *Shifting Risk and Fixing Blame, The Vexing Problem of Credit Card Obligations in Bankruptcy*, 75 Am. Bankr. L.J. 63 (2001).
R.L. Hughes, *Code Exemptions: Far Reaching Achievement*, 28 DePaul L. Rev. 1025 (1979).
Thomas H. Jackson, The Logic and Limits of Bankruptcy Law (1986).
Melissa B. Jacoby & Mirya Holman, *Managing Medical Bills on the Brink of Bankruptcy*, 10 Yale J. Health Pol'y L. & Ethics 239 (2010).
Susan Jensen, *A Legislative History of the Bankruptcy Abuse and Consumer Protection Act of 2005*, 79 Am. Bankr. L.J. 485 (2005).
Lawrence P. King, *The History and Development of the Bankruptcy Rules*, 70 Am. Bankr. L.J. 217 (1996).
Kenneth N. Klee, *Legislative History of the New Bankruptcy Code*, 54 Am. Bankr. L.J. 275 (1980).
Christopher M. Klein, *Bankruptcy Rules Made Easy (2001): A Guide to the Federal Rules of Civil Procedure That Apply in Bankruptcy*, 75 Am. Bankr. L.J. 35 (2001).
Robert M. Lawless, et al., *Did Bankruptcy Reform Fail? An Empirical Study of Consumer Debtors*, 82 Am. Bankr. L.J. 349 (2008).
Lois R. Lupica, The Costs of BAPCPA: Report of the Pilot Study of Consumer Bankruptcy Cases, 18 ABI L. Rev. 43 (2010).
Bruce H. Mann, Republic of Debtors: Bankruptcy in the Age of American Independence (2002).
Ronald J. Mann & Katherine Porter, *Saving Up for Bankruptcy*, 98 Geo. L.J. 289 (2010).
Leslie R. Masterson, *Rolling the Dice: The Risks Awaiting Compulsive Gamblers in Bankruptcy Court*, 83 Am. Bankr. L.J. 749 (2009).
Geraldine Mund, *Appointed or Anointed: Judges, Congress, and the Passage of the Bankruptcy Act of 1978 Part Three: On the Hill, Beware*, 81 Am. Bankr. L.J. 341 (2007).
Lisa A. Napoli, *Reaffirmation After the Bankruptcy Abuse Prevention and Consumer Protection Act of 2005: Many Questions, Some Answers, Beware*, 81 Am. Bankr. L.J. 259 (2007).
Jonathan Remy Nash & Rafael I. Pardo, *Does Ideology Matter in Bankruptcy? Voting Behavior on the Courts of Appeals*, 53 Wm. & Mary L. Rev. 919 (2012).
Scott Norberg & Nadja Schrieber Compo, *Report on an Empirical Study of District Variations, and the Roles of Judges, Trustees, and Debtors' Attorneys in Chapter 13 Cases*, 81 Am. Bankr. L.J. 431 (2007).
Chrystin Ondersma, *Are Debtors Rational Actors? An Experiment*, 13 Lewis & Clark L. Rev. 279 (2010).
Joseph Pace, *Bankruptcy As Constitutional Property: Using Statutory Entitlement Theory to Abrogate State Sovereign Immunity*, 119 Yale L.J. 1568 (2010).
Rafael I. Pardo, *The Real Student Loan Scandal: Undue Hardship Discharge Litigation*, 83 Am. Bankr. L.J. 179 (2009).
Alan Pedlar, *Community Property and the Bankruptcy Reform Act of 1978*, 11 St. Mary's L.J. 349 (1979).
Katherine M. Porter, Broke: How Debt Bankrupts the Middle Class (Studies in Social Inequality) (2012).
Katherine M. Porter, *Life After Debt: Understanding The Credit Restraint of Bankruptcy Debtors*, 18 Am. Bankr. Inst. L. Rev. 1 (2010).
Katherine M. Porter, *Misbehavior and Mistake in Bankruptcy Mortgage Claims*, 87 Tex. L. Rev. 121 (2008).
John Rao, *Fresh Look at Curing Mortgage Defaults in Chapter 13*, 27 Am. Bankr. Inst. J. 14 (2008).
John Rao, *Impact of Marrama on Case Conversions: Addressing the Unanswered Questions*, 15 Am. Bankr. Inst. L. Rev. 585 (2007).
Alan N. Resnick, *The Bankruptcy Rulemaking Process*, 70 Am. Bankr. L.J. 245 (1996).
Stefan A. Riesenfeld, *Classification of Claims and Interests in Chapter 11 and 13 Cases*, 75 Calif. L. Rev. 391 (1987).
Susan A. Schneider, *Bankruptcy Reform and Family Farmers: Correcting the Disposable Income Problem*, 38 Tex. Tech L. Rev. 309 (2006).
Susan A. Schneider, *Who Gets the Check: Determining When Federal Farm Program Payments Are Property of the Bankruptcy Estate*, 84 Neb. L. Rev. 469 (2005).
David A. Scholl, *Bankruptcy Court: The Ultimate Consumer Law Forum?*, 44 Bus. Law. 935 (1989).
Stephen L. Sepinuck, *Rethinking Unfair Discrimination in Chapter 13*, 74 Am. Bankr. L.J. 341 (2000).
Michael Simkovic, *The Effect of BAPCPA on Credit Card Industry Profits and Practices*, 83 Am. Bankr. L.J. 1 (2009).
David A. Skeel, Jr., Debt's Dominion: A History of Bankruptcy Law in America (2001)
David A. Skeel, Jr., *Vern Countryman and the Path of Progressive (and Populist) Bankruptcy Scholarship*, 113 Harv. L. Rev. 1075 (2000).
Daniel L. Skoler, *The Status and Protection of Social Security Benefits in Bankruptcy Cases*, 67 Am. Bankr. L.J. 585 (1993).
David F. Snow, *The Dischargeability of Credit Card Debt: New Developments and the Need for a New Direction*, 72 Am. Bankr. L.J. 63 (1998).
Henry J. Sommer, *In Forma Pauperis in Bankruptcy: The Time Has Long Since Come*, 2 Am. Bankr. Inst. L. Rev. 93 (1994).

Henry J. Sommer, *The New Law of Bankruptcy: A Fresh Start for Legal Services Lawyers*, 13 Clearinghouse Rev. 1 (1979).

Henry J. Sommer, *Trying to Make Sense Out of Nonsense: Representing Consumers Under the "Bankruptcy Abuse and Consumer Protection Act of 2005"*, 79 Am. Bankr. L.J. 191 (2005).

Henry J. Sommer & Margaret Dee McGarity, Collier Family Law and the Bankruptcy Code (1991).

David T. Stanley & M. Girth, Bankruptcy: Problem, Process, Reform (1971).

Wiliam F. Stone, Jr. & Bryan A. Stark, *The Treatment of Attorney's Fee Retainers in Chapter 7 Bankruptcy and the Problem of Denying Compensation to Debtors' Attorneys for Post-Petition Legal Services They Are Obliged to Render*, 82 Am. Bankr. L. J. 551 (2008).

Terasa A. Sullivan, Elizabeth Warren & Jay Lawrence Westbrook, As We Forgive Our Debtors: Bankruptcy and Consumer Credit in America (1989).

Teresa A. Sullivan, Elizabeth Warren & Jay Lawrence Westbrook, The Fragile Middle Class: Americans in Debt (2000).

Teresa A. Sullivan, Elizabeth Warren & Jay Lawrence Westbrook, *From Golden Years to Bankruptcy Years*, Norton Bankr. L. Advisor (July 1998).

Charles Jordan Tabb, *The History of the Bankruptcy Laws in the United States*, 3 Am. Bankr. Inst. L. Rev. 5 (1995).

Philip Tedesco, *In Forma Pauperis in Bankruptcy*, 84 Am. Bankr. L.J. 79 (2010).

United States Government Accountability Office, Dollar Costs Associated with the Bankruptcy Abuse Prevention and Consumer Protection Act of 2005, Report No. GAO-08-697 (2008), *available at* http://www.gao.gov/new.items/d08697.pdf.

United States Government Accountability Office, Bankruptcy Reform: Dollar Costs Associated with the Bankruptcy Abuse Prevention and Consumer Protection Act of 2005 (June 2008), *available at* www.gao.gov/new.items/d08697.pdf.

Rory Van Loo, *A Tale of Two Debtors: Bankruptcy Disparities by Race*, 72 Albany L. Rev. 231 (2009).

Thomas F. Waldron & Neil M. Berman, *Principled Principles of Statutory Interpretation: A Judicial Perspective After Two Years of BAPCPA*, 81 Am. Bankr. L.J. 195 (2007).

Eilzabeth Warren, *Bankrupt Children*, 86 Minn. L. Rev. 1003 (2002).

Elizabeth Warren, *The Bankruptcy Crisis*, 73 Ind. L.J. 1079 (1998).

Elizabeth Warren, *Bankruptcy Policy*, 54 U. Chi. L. Rev. 775 (1987).

Elizabeth Warren, *The Changing Politics of American Bankruptcy Reform*, 37 Osgoode Hall L.J. 189 (1999).

Elizabeth Warren, *The Market for Data: The Changing Role of Social Sciences in Shaping the Law*, 2002 Wis. L. Rev. 1.

Elizabeth Warren, *What is a Women's Issue? Bankruptcy, Commercial Law, and Other Gender-Neutral Topics*, 25 Harv. Women's L.J. 19 (2002).

Elizabeth Warren & A. Tyagi, The Two Income Trap: Why Middle Class Mothers and Fathers are Going Broke (2003).

Jay Lawrence Westbrook, *Empirical Research in Consumer Bankruptcy*, 80 Tex. L. Rev. 2123 (2002).

Yen, *Bankruptcy and the Low Income Client*, 34 Clearinghouse Rev. 709 (2001).

Index and Quick Reference

Quick Reference to the Consumer Law Practice Series

The Quick Reference to the Consumer Law Practice Series pinpoints where to find specific topics analyzed in any of the twenty NCLC treatises. The Quick Reference is now available at www.nclc.org/qr. Placing the Quick Reference on a website ensures that readers have the most up-to-date version, including any revised section numbering.

Another way to locate topics is to go to www.nclc.org/keyword and perform keyword searches within individual treatises or across all NCLC publications. This function allows for compound searches such as "identity theft (near) punitive damages," and shows results in context, with the appropriate book title and page number where the reference is found.

Pleadings related just to *Consumer Bankruptcy Law and Practice* can be found on the companion website to this title and can be located using different search functions, including the "Pleading Finder." For more information, see page ix, *supra*.

NCLC also has over 2000 additional sample pleadings on websites accompanying our other titles. The best way to locate and access a pleading among this broader group is to use NCLC's *Consumer Law Pleadings Index Guide* or the finding aids on its companion website.

More information on individual treatises in this series is available at What Your Library Should Contain on page v, *supra*, or by going to www.nclc.org/shop.

Index

ABANDONMENT OF PROPERTY
apartment buildings, 18.8.2.1, 18.8.2.2, 18.8.2.5, 18.8.2.6
automatic stay, effect, 11.3.3
irrevocable decision, 3.5.1
no significant nonexempt equity, 3.5.1, 8.3.11
prohibition by court, 11.3.3
request by debtor, 3.5.1
request by secured creditor, 11.3.3
right of redemption, *see* RIGHT OF REDEMPTION

ABILITY TO PAY TEST
see also CURRENT MONTHLY INCOME; DISPOSABLE INCOME
bad faith and, 13.4.7.4
chapter 13 plan, 12.3.4
  change in circumstances, 12.3.4.5
  disposable income test, 12.3.4.4
  full payment test, 12.3.4.3
  generally, 7.3.12.3, 12.3.4.1
  incomes below threshold, 13.4.7.1
  objections, 12.3.4.2

ABSTENTION
discretionary abstention, 14.5.3
generally, 14.5.1
mandatory abstention, 14.5.2

ABUSE OF CHAPTER 7
attorney certification, 16.7.2.3
changes to standard, 13.4.7
dismissal of case, 3.2.1.5, 13.4

consumer debts, 13.4.2
discretionary dismissal, 13.4.6.3
generally, 13.4.1
incomes above threshold, 13.4.3, 13.4.7.1
procedure, 13.4.8
safe harbor, 13.4.4
means test, *see* MEANS TEST
presumption of abuse, *see* PRESUMPTION OF ABUSE

ACTIONS
see also CIVIL PROCEEDINGS
automatic stay, *see* AUTOMATIC STAY
bankruptcy petition preparers, against, 16.6
class actions, *see* CLASS ACTIONS
consumer protection actions, 16.5.3
damages, *see* DAMAGES
discharge protections, enforcement, 15.5.1.4, 15.5.5.7
postpetition claims
  consumers as creditors, 18.5.3
  discharge, 4.6, 8.7.2, 13.7.2
  utilities, 9.8.2.2.4
prepetition causes of action
  listing in schedule, 7.3.7.2.2
  pursuing, 16.5.3
  standing, 14.3.2.6.2
  unlisted, judicial estoppel, 14.3.2.6.3

ADDRESSES
change of address, duty to notify, 8.2
creditors, for notice purposes, 9.6.3.2.3, 9.6.3.2.4

ADEQUATE ASSURANCE
lease or executory contract, 12.9.2
utilities, 9.8.2.2
  amount necessary, 9.8.2.2.3
  local practice, 9.8.2.1
  methods of assurance, 9.8.2.2.1
  when required, 9.8.2.2.2

ADEQUATE PROTECTION
automatic stay, 9.7.3.2.2, 12.8.2.3
  chapter 12, 17.4.4.3, 17.4.11
automatic turnover, 9.9.3
cash collateral use, 17.4.8
property in possession of debtor, 12.8.2
secured creditors
  chapter 12, 17.4.11
  chapter 13 payments, 8.3.12.2, 11.6.1.3.3.2, 12.8.2.2
  first steps after chapter 13 filing, 4.3

ADVANTAGES AND DISADVANTAGES OF BANKRUPTCY
see also BANKRUPTCY
advantages
  automatic stay, 6.2.1.4
  discharge of most debts, 6.2.1.1
  litigation advantages, 6.2.1.6
  other protections, 6.2.1.5
  secured debts, regarding, 6.2.1.3
  unsecured creditors, protection from, 6.2.1.2

ADVANTAGES AND DISADVANTAGES OF BANKRUPTCY (cont.)
disadvantages
  cost of filing, 6.2.2.6
  credit and reputation, effect on, 6.2.2.3
  discharge unavailable, 6.2.2.8.2
  feelings of moral obligation, 6.2.2.5
  loss of property, 6.2.2.2
  possible discrimination, 6.2.2.4
  situations when wrong tool, 6.2.2.8.1
  weighing, 6.2.2.7
joint filings, 6.4
type of case
  chapter 7 advantages, 6.3.2
  chapter 11 situations, 6.3.4
  chapter 13 advantages, 6.3.3

ADVERSARY PROCEEDINGS
see under BANKRUPTCY PROCEEDINGS

ADVERTISEMENTS
debt relief agencies, 16.8.5

ALIMONY
see DOMESTIC SUPPORT OBLIGATIONS

ALLOWED SECURED CLAIMS
see also CLAIMS BY CREDITORS; SECURED CREDITORS
adequate protection payments, 11.6.1.3.3.2, 12.8.2.2
bifurcation of claims, 11.7
  chapter 7, 11.2.1.2
  chapter 12, 11.2.1.3, 17.5.3
  chapter 13, 11.2.1.3, 12.2.3.1
chapter 12 cramdown, 17.5.4
chapter 13 conversion to chapter 7, 13.7.3
chapter 13 cramdown, 11.6.1, 11.7
chapter 13 plans, payment through, 11.6.1.3
collateral, statement of intention, 11.4
defined, 11.1, 11.4.2.4.2
determination, 11.2
  chapter 12, 17.5.3
  chapter 13, 11.6.1.3.3.5, 11.6.1.4
  procedure, 11.2.2
family farmer reorganizations, see CHAPTER 12 PLANS (FAMILY FARMERS AND FISHERMEN)
general principles, 11.2.1.1
government liens, 11.2.1.1
hardship discharge, 4.7.2
interest and fees, 11.6.1.3.3.6
means test deductions, 13.4.5.3.2
objections, 11.2.2.1, 11.6.1.3.3.5
reaffirmation, 11.5.4
recent purchases, 11.6.1.4
reconsideration, 14.4.3.7
right of redemption, see RIGHT OF REDEMPTION
valuation
  appraisal, necessity, 11.2.2.3.4
  chapter 12, 17.5.3
  converted cases, 13.7.3
  date, 11.2.2.2
  exempt property, inclusion, 11.2.2.3.4
  generally, 11.2.2.1, 11.6.1.3.3.5
  method, 11.2.2.3
  present value, 11.6.1.3.3.1, 11.6.1.3.3.6

APPEALS
abstention decision, 14.5.1, 14.5.2
appellate panel service
  see also BANKRUPTCY APPELLATE PANEL (BAP)
  from, 2.4.3, 14.9.3
  to, 2.4.3, 14.9.1
automatic stay relief, 9.7.3.3.3
bankruptcy court, from, 2.4.3, 14.9.1
consumer awards, 18.2.1
court of appeals, to, 2.4.3, 14.9.2
  certification, Official Form 24, Appx. D.3
district court
  from, 2.4.3, 14.9.3
  to, 2.4.3, 14.9.1
final orders, 14.9.4
in forma pauperis, 14.6.1
notice of appeal, Official Form 17, Appx. D.3
procedures, time, 14.9.5
stay pending, 9.7.3.3.3, 14.9.5

APPRAISALS
see also VALUATION
allowed secured claims, necessity, 11.2.2.3.3

ARBITRATION CLAUSES
avoiding, 14.3.2.5

ASSETS
see also PROPERTY
concealment, effect, 15.2.2.2
distribution to creditors, 3.5.4
loss or deficiency, failure to explain, 15.2.2.5
no-asset case, defined, 3.1
nominal asset cases, 3.5, 8.3.11

ATTORNEY-CLIENT PRIVILEGE
trustees in bankruptcy, claiming debtor's, 2.6

ATTORNEY FEES AND COSTS
see also ATTORNEYS
amounts typically charged, 16.2.2
automatic stay violations, 9.6.2
bankruptcy petition preparers, 16.6
bankruptcy rule violations, sanctions, 16.5.5
basic fee, 16.2.1, 16.3.3
chapter 12 reorganizations
  disclosure, 17.2.3.3
  payment through plan, 17.5.7.3, 17.5.9
chapter 13 plans
  collection means, 6.3.3
  deduction from disposable income, 12.3.4.4.4
  payment under, 7.3.12.3, 16.4
  priority claim, 12.3.6.1
civil rights awards, 16.5.2
consumer protection awards, 16.5.3
court supervision, 16.3
creditors' committees, 18.7.2.2
dischargeability complaints, 15.4.3.2.4
disclosure form, 7.3.13.2, Appx. E.4
  filing, 7.2.1
disclosure requirements, 7.3.13.2, 16.3.2
dismissed cases, liability, 16.7.2.1
divorce proceedings, dischargeability, 15.4.3.5.3
equal access to justice awards, 16.5.4
estate property, payment from, 16.2.3
fee-shifting provisions, 16.5.6
governmental units, awards against, 16.5.7
initial arrangements, 16.2
method of payment, 16.2.3
motion to dismiss, 16.7.2.1
non-attorney services, 16.3.2, 16.3.3, 16.6
nonpayment, effect, 16.2.2
postpetition services, 16.2.3
prepetition services, 16.2.3
prevailing debtors, 16.5
record on fee issues, 16.3.4
right to cure, allowable, 11.6.2.7.1
Rule 3001 and Rule 3002.1 sanctions, 11.6.2.8.2.6, 16.5.5.2
Rule 9011 sanctions, 16.5.5.1
statement of fees charged, 16.3.2, Appx. E.3
tax refunds, assignment to pay, 2.5.5
unusual aspects, 16.1

ATTORNEYS
bankruptcy petitions, filing on behalf of debtor, 3.2.1.1
  signature, 16.7.2.3, 16.7.2.4
chapter 11, appointment, 17.2.3.2
chapter 12, appointment, 17.2.3.2
confirmation hearings, attendance, 8.6
costs, see ATTORNEY FEES AND COSTS
counseling the debtor, 6.1, Appx. K
  see also COUNSELING THE CONSUMER DEBTOR; PRACTICE AIDS
creditor's attorney, listing in schedule, 7.3.7.3.4
debt relief agencies, as
  advertising requirements, 16.8.5
  disclosure requirements, 16.8.3.2
  failure to comply with provisions, 16.8.6
  restrictions on advice, 16.8.2
  statement about services, 16.8.3.3
  status, 16.8.1
  written contract requirement, 16.8.4
declaration on petition, 7.3.2, 7.3.6, 7.4
duties
  debt relief agency provisions, 16.8
  Federal Rule of Bankruptcy Procedure 9011, 16.7
Federal Rule of Bankruptcy Procedure 9011
  duties, 16.7.1
  sanctions, 16.5.5.1
  violations, 16.7.2.2
fees, see ATTORNEY FEES AND COSTS
privilege, see ATTORNEY-CLIENT PRIVILEGE
reaffirmation agreements, validating, 15.5.2.4, 15.5.2.7

BANKRUPTCY

Index and Quick Reference

References are to sections

ATTORNEYS (*cont.*)
role of non-attorneys, *see* BANKRUPTCY PETITION PREPARERS
signature as certification, 16.7.2.3
   schedules, 16.7.2.4
statement about bankruptcy assistance services, 16.8.3.3
unbundling services, 16.2.1

AUDITS
debtor audits, 8.3.15.1, Appx. C.2

AUTOMATIC STAY
abandoned property, effect, 11.3.3
adequate protection, 9.7.3.2.2, 12.8.2.2.3
advantage of bankruptcy, 6.2.1.4
advice to clients, 8.2
appeal pending, effect, 9.7.3.3.3
bankruptcy monitoring fees, 14.4.3.4.5
chapter 7, 3.3
chapter 12
   adequate protection, 17.4.4.3, 17.4.11
   application, generally, 17.4.4.1
   codebtor stay, 17.4.4.2
   relief, grounds, 17.4.4.3
chapter 13, 4.3
   inability to complete plan, 8.7.5
codebtor stay, 6.2.1.4, 9.3.3.5, 9.4.5, 17.4.4.2
consumers as creditors, 18.3, 18.9.2
disputes that may arise, 8.3.10
duration, 9.3
   no prior case dismissed in year prior, 9.3.2
   prior case dismissed in year prior, 9.3.3
enforcement, 9.6
exceptions, 9.4.6
   criminal proceedings, 9.4.6.2
   family law exceptions, 9.4.6.3
   in rem orders, 9.4.6.5.2
   non-avoidable transfers, 9.4.6.7
   other exceptions, 9.4.6.9
   repeat filers, 9.4.6.5
   residential tenant evictions, 9.4.6.6
   retirement fund loan repayments, 9.4.6.4
   tax refund intercepts, 9.4.6.8
generally, 9.1
lender bankruptcies, 18.9.2
notice to creditors
   effective notice, 9.6.3.3
   giving notice, 8.3.1, 9.5, 9.6.3.1
   requirements of notice, 9.6.3.2
personal property leases, 12.9.5.2
purpose, 9.2
reinstitution, 9.4.7
relief from the stay
   appeals from, 9.7.3.3.3
   burden of proof, 9.7.3.1.4
   chapter 12, 17.4.4.3
   chapter 13, 8.7.5
   commencement by motion, 9.7.1
   consumers as creditors, 18.3.2–18.3.4, 18.9.2
   counterclaims and defenses, 9.7.3.1.3
   discovery, 9.7.3.1.2
   grounds for relief, 9.7.3.2, 12.8.2.2.3
   lender bankruptcies, 18.9.2
   loss mitigation programs, 9.7.2
   modification, 9.7.3.3.2
   in rem orders, 9.4.6.5.2
   parties, 9.7.3.1.1
   prior bankruptcy proceedings, effect, 9.4.6.5, 9.7.3.1.5
   standing, 9.7.3.1.1
   tactics, 9.7.3.3
   time limits, 9.7.2
   unassumed leases, 12.9.4
repetitive filings, effect, 9.4.6.5, 9.7.3.1.5
   chapter 12, 17.4.4.3
   timing considerations, 6.5.3.7
scope
   codebtors, 9.4.5, 17.4.4.2
   debtor's actions, 9.4.2, 14.4.2
   debtor's property, 9.4.3
   exceptions, 9.4.6
   legal proceedings, 9.4.2, 9.4.6.2
   non-automatic stays, 9.4.7
   other prohibitions, 9.4.4
sovereign immunity, effect, 9.6.6
tax intercepts, 9.4.4
termination, order confirming, 9.3.3.4
utility services, 9.8
violations
   contempt remedies, 9.6.4
   damages, 8.3.1, 9.6.2
   effect, 9.6.1
   governmental units, 9.6.6
   jurisdiction, 9.6.5
   notice issues, 9.6.3
   procedural issues, 9.6.7
   UDAP violation, as, 9.6.5

AUTOMATIC TURNOVER
adequate protection, 9.9.3
application, 9.9, 9.9.1
chapter 7, 3.3
chapter 13, 4.3
general rule, 9.9.1
notice to property-holders, 8.3.1
possession after turnover, 9.9.4
procedure, 9.9.3
secured parties in possession, scope, 9.9.2

AUTOMOBILE TITLE PAWNS
bankruptcy, effect, 11.9

AUTOMOBILES
see MOTOR VEHICLES

AVOIDANCE OF LIENS AND TRANSFERS
see also POSTPETITION TRANSFERS; PREBANKRUPTCY TRANSFERS
chapter 12, 17.4.3.3, 17.4.3.5
chapter 13 plans, 11.7
divorce-related liens, 10.4.2.3.1, 10.4.2.3.2
exempt property, 3.5.1, 8.3.6, 10.4.2
foreclosure sales, 10.4.2.6.5
fraudulent transfers
   chapter 11, 18.7.6
   chapter 12, 17.4.3.5.2
generally, 10.4.2.6.2, 10.4.2.6.5
joint property, 10.4.2.3.3
liens, 10.4.2
   exempt property, 8.3.6, 10.4.2.1, 10.4.2.2, 10.4.2.3
   family farmers, 17.4.3.3, 17.4.3.5.1, 17.4.3.5.4
   joint property, 10.4.2.3.3
   judicial liens, 10.4.2.3, 10.4.2.10, 17.4.3.3
   non-purchase money security interests, 10.4.2.4
   pre-Code liens, 10.4.2.10
   preservation, 10.4.2.9
   statement of intention, 7.3.11
   trustee's powers, 10.4.2.6
non-avoidable transfers, automatic stay, application, 9.4.6.7
powers of debtor, 10.4.2
preferences
   chapter 11, 18.7.6
   debtor use of powers, 10.4.2.6.4.3
   exceptions to avoidance, 10.4.2.6.4.2
   family farmers, 17.4.3.5.3
   generally, 10.4.2.6.4.1
   prebankruptcy, 6.5.2.1, 6.5.3.2
preservation of property, 10.4.2.9
procedures, 8.3.6, 10.4.2.2
property recovered by trustee, 10.4.2.5
recovery of property after, 10.4.2.8
trustee's powers, 10.4.2.6, 10.4.2.7

BAD FAITH
see also GOOD FAITH TEST
attorney fee awards re, 16.5.6
conversion of proceedings, 13.7.1, 13.7.2, 13.7.3
dismissal of case, 13.4.7.1, 13.4.7.4
relief from stay, 9.7.3.2.1

BANK ACCOUNTS
freezes on, 9.4.4, 11.3.5
listing in schedule, 7.3.7.2.2
statements, source of information, 5.3.4

BANKRUPTCY
advantages, *see* ADVANTAGES AND DISADVANTAGES OF BANKRUPTCY
alternatives, 6.2.2.8.2
auto pawn transactions and, 11.9
business bankruptcies, *see* BUSINESS BANKRUPTCIES
case
   definition, 1.4.2
   venue, 3.2.3
case law, *see* CASE LAW
chapter 7, *see* CHAPTER 7 LIQUIDATIONS
chapter 11, *see* CHAPTER 11 REORGANIZATIONS
chapter 12, *see* CHAPTER 12 REORGANIZATIONS (FAMILY FARMERS AND FISHERMEN)
chapter 13, *see* CHAPTER 13 REORGANIZATIONS

BANKRUPTCY (cont.)
common questions, client handout, Appx. K.2
consumers as creditors, *see* CONSUMERS AS CREDITORS
counseling the debtor, 6.1, Appx. K
   see also COUNSELING THE CONSUMER DEBTOR
debt relief agency provisions, 16.8
defined, 2.1
disadvantages, *see* ADVANTAGES AND DISADVANTAGES OF BANKRUPTCY
discharges, *see* DISCHARGE OF DEBTS IN BANKRUPTCY
discrimination regarding, 6.2.2.4, 15.5.4, 15.5.5
dismissal, *see* DISMISSAL OF CASE
documents, *see* BANKRUPTCY FORMS
emergency situations, 7.2.2
farmers, *see* FARMERS
federal code, *see* BANKRUPTCY CODE
federal rules, *see* FEDERAL RULES OF BANKRUPTCY PROCEDURE
filing, *see* BANKRUPTCY PETITIONS
forms, *see* BANKRUPTCY FORMS; OFFICIAL BANKRUPTCY FORMS
governing law, 1.4
health care businesses, 18.10
involuntary, *see* INVOLUNTARY BANKRUPTCIES
ipso facto default, *see* BANKRUPTCY CLAUSES
jurisdiction, 2.4.2, 14.2
landlords, 18.3.4, 18.8
lenders, 18.9
liquidations, *see* CHAPTER 7 LIQUIDATIONS; CHAPTER 11 LIQUIDATIONS
local rules, 1.4.2, 1.4.4.2
monitoring fees, 14.4.3.4.5
NCLC treatise
   companion website, 1.3.2, 5.1.3, Appx. M
   focus, 1.2
   organization, 1.3.2
   practice guide chapters, 5.1.1
   purpose, 1.3.1
   use of materials, 5.1.3
   using as research tool, 1.3.4
   web-based text searching, 1.3.3, Appx. M.6
necessity, weighing, 6.2.2.7
neglected remedy, 1.1.3
no-asset cases, defined, 3.1
overview, 1.1.1
papers, *see* BANKRUPTCY FORMS; OFFICIAL BANKRUPTCY FORMS
petitions, *see* BANKRUPTCY PETITIONS
practice aids, *see* PRACTICE AIDS
proceedings, *see* BANKRUPTCY PROCEEDINGS
property administered, *see* BANKRUPTCY ESTATE
purposes, 2.3
questionnaire, 5.3.2, Appx. F
recoupment claims, 14.3.2.4
related statutes, text, Appx. A
relief available, 2.2
remedial value, 1.1
rent-to-own transactions and, 11.8
reorganizations, *see* CHAPTER 11 REORGANIZATIONS; CHAPTER 12 REORGANIZATIONS (FAMILY FARMERS AND FISHERMEN); CHAPTER 13 REORGANIZATIONS
reporting services, 1.5.4
research aids, *see* RESEARCH AIDS
rules, *see* FEDERAL RULES OF BANKRUPTCY PROCEDURE
straight bankruptcies, *see* CHAPTER 7 LIQUIDATIONS
title pawn transactions and, 11.9
treatises and texts, 1.5.3
trustees in bankruptcy, *see* TRUSTEES IN BANKRUPTCY
U.S. trustee, *see* UNITED STATES TRUSTEE PROGRAM
using remedy, 1.1.4
voluntary, *see* VOLUNTARY BANKRUPTCIES
wrong tool situations, 6.2.2.8.1

BANKRUPTCY ABUSE PREVENTION AND CONSUMER PROTECTION ACT OF 2005
see also BANKRUPTCY CODE
changes enacted, 1.1.2.5
legislative history, 1.5.1.5
poor drafting, 1.1.2.5
selected provisions, Appx. A.4.9

BANKRUPTCY APPELLATE PANEL (BAP)
see also APPEALS; BANKRUPTCY COURT
appeals from, 2.4.3, 14.9.3
appeals to, 2.4.3, 14.9.1
establishment, 1.1.2.4, 14.9.1

BANKRUPTCY ASSISTANCE SERVICES
see ATTORNEYS; BANKRUPTCY PETITION PREPARERS; DEBT RELIEF AGENCIES

BANKRUPTCY CLAUSES
validity, 8.8.2, 11.5.4, 15.5.3

BANKRUPTCY CODE
see also BANKRUPTCY; FEDERAL RULES OF BANKRUPTCY PROCEDURE
amendments to
   1978 Bankruptcy Reform Act, 1.1.2.1, 1.5.1.1, Appx. A.4.1
   1984 consumer amendments, 1.1.2.2, 1.5.1.2, Appx. A.4.2
   1986 changes, 1.1.2.3, 1.5.1.3, Appx. A.4.3
   1994 Bankruptcy Reform Act, 1.1.2.4, 1.5.1.4, Appx. A.4.6
   2005 amendments, 1.1.2.5, 1.5.1.5, 9.6.3.2, 17.1.1.1, Appx. A.4.9
   chapter 12 enactment, 17.1.1.1
   other amendments, 1.1.2.6
   pending legislation, 1.4.4.1
case law, 1.4.4.3
debt relief agency provisions, 16.8
definitions, 1.4.1
exemption provisions, importance, 10.1.1
legislative history, 1.5.1
National Bankruptcy Review Commission, 1.1.2.4
rules of construction, 1.4.1
structure, 1.4.1
text, Appx. A.1
transitional provisions, Appx. A.4.1–Appx. A.4.3

BANKRUPTCY COURT
see also BANKRUPTCY APPELLATE PANEL (BAP); BANKRUPTCY JUDGES
abstention
   discretionary, 14.5.3
   mandatory, 14.5.2
   right to, 14.5.1
advantages
   fairer results, 14.3.1
   federal court access, 14.3.2.3
   sovereign immunity waiver, 14.3.2.2
   venue, 14.3.2.1
appeals, 2.4.3, 14.9
   bankruptcy appellate panel, 2.4.3, 14.9.1
   direct appeal to court of appeals, 14.9.2
   district court, 14.9.1
attorney fees, *see* ATTORNEY FEES AND COSTS
bringing matter before
   claims by debtor, 14.4.2, 14.4.4
   example, 14.4.4
   habeas corpus, 14.4.5, 15.5.5.7
   objections to claims, 14.4.3.1
   removal to, 14.4.1, 14.4.4
case docket listing, 2.4.1
case law, binding effect, 1.4.4.3
claims docket listing, 2.4.1
class actions, 14.7
contempt of court, 14.2.8
discharge protections, enforcement, 15.5.5.7
dischargeability determinations, 15.4.2, 15.4.4
dismissal of cases
   involuntary dismissal, 13.3, 13.4
   voluntary dismissal, 13.2
dockets, access, 2.4.1
filing fees, *see* FILING FEES
final orders, 14.9.4
generally, 14.1
in forma pauperis litigation, 14.6, 18.6.2
in personam jurisdiction, 14.3.2.1
involuntary cases, 14.8
jurisdiction, 2.4.2, 9.6.5, 14.2, 15.5.5.7

Index and Quick Reference **BANKRUPTCY**

References are to sections

BANKRUPTCY COURT (*cont.*)
jury trials, 14.2.7
loss mitigation programs, 9.7.2
notice by clerk of available relief, 7.3.6
reaffirmation agreements, approval, 15.5.2.4, 15.5.2.6
records, 2.4.1
related provisions, Appx. A.2
removal to, 14.4.1
   generally, 14.4.1.1
   procedure after removal, 14.4.1.3
   procedure for removal, 14.4.1.2
   remand of removed actions, 14.4.1.4
reporting services, 1.5.4
rules of procedure, *see* FEDERAL RULES OF BANKRUPTCY PROCEDURE
status, 2.4.1
supervision and review of fees, 16.3.3
tax returns, filing with, 8.3.4.2
venue, 14.3.2.1

BANKRUPTCY ESTATE
see also PROPERTY
attorney fees, payments from, 16.2.3, 16.4.2
automatic stay, effect, 9.4.3
chapter 12 reorganizations
   composition, 17.4.2
   possession, 17.4.2
   vesting in debtor, 17.5.9
chapter 13 plans
   possession, 12.8.1
   vesting in debtor, 12.8.5
contents
   education savings accounts, 2.5.3
   generally, 2.5.1
   pawned personal property, 2.5.4
   pensions and spendthrift trusts, 2.5.2
   tax refunds and credits, 2.5.5
defined, 2.5.1
exempt property, *see* EXEMPT PROPERTY
money orders, exclusion, 18.5.2.1
nonexempt property, retention, 8.3.11
postpetition property, inclusion, 8.2
potential claims, property of, 14.3.2.6.2
security deposits, status, 18.8.5
substantive consolidation of cases, 6.4

BANKRUPTCY FORMS
additional time to file, 7.3.13.5
amending, 7.1.1, 8.3.2
attorneys, duties, 16.7
bankruptcy petition preparers, 7.3.1, 7.3.13.2, 7.4
chapter 7, 3.2.2
chapter 12, 17.2.3
chapter 13, 4.2.2
   discharge, 8.8.1
commercial forms, 7.1.2
completing, 1.3.2, 7.3.1
computer software, 5.1.3, 7.1.3, Appx. D.1.2
credit counseling certificate, 7.2.1, 7.3.5
current monthly income statement, 7.3.9
deficiencies, 13.3.1, 13.3.2
disclosure of fees, 7.3.13.2

electronic filing, 7.1.4
emergency bankruptcies, 7.2.2
filing, 7.2.1
   electronic filing, 7.1.4, Appx. D.1.4
filing deadlines, *see* TIME LIMITS
filing fees, *see* FILING FEES
financial affairs, *see* STATEMENT OF FINANCIAL AFFAIRS
format, 7.3.1
general principles, 7.1.1
intentions, *see* STATEMENT OF INTENTION
list of creditors, codebtors, executory contracts, 7.3.4
local rules or practice, 7.3.13.6
non-attorney preparers, *see* BANKRUPTCY PETITION PREPARERS
non-official forms, 7.3.1
obtaining forms, 1.4.3, 7.1.2
official forms, *see* OFFICIAL BANKRUPTCY FORMS
other forms, 7.3.13, Appx. E
notice of available relief, 7.3.6
personal financial management course certificate, 8.3.3
petition, *see* BANKRUPTCY PETITIONS
preprinted forms, 1.3.2, 1.4.3, 7.1.2
sample completed forms, Appx. D.2
sample pleadings and forms, Appx. G
   NCLC companion website, 1.3.2, 5.1.3, Appx. M
schedules, *see* SCHEDULES
signing and verification, 7.4, 16.7.1
   attorney certification, 16.7.2.3
Social Security number, *see* STATEMENT OF SOCIAL SECURITY NUMBER
standardized forms, 7.3.1
statistical summary of certain liabilities, 7.3.7.8
substantial compliance with official forms, 1.4.3, 7.3.1
   computer programs, 7.1.3, Appx. D.1.2
   permitted alterations, Appx. D.1.3
   precise compliance not necessary, 7.3.1
summary of schedules, 7.3.7.8
unofficial forms, 7.3.1

BANKRUPTCY JUDGES
see also BANKRUPTCY COURT
additional 1986 judgeships, 1.1.2.3
contempt powers, 14.2.8
expertise, 14.3.1
jury trials, conducting, 14.2.7
related provisions, Appx. A.2, Appx. A.4.2, Appx. A.4.3

BANKRUPTCY PETITION PREPARERS
see also DEBT RELIEF AGENCIES; NON-ATTORNEYS
actions against, 16.6
advertisements, 16.6, 16.8.5
assistance from, 16.6
defined, 16.6
disclosure requirements, 16.8.3.4

compensation disclosure, 7.3.13.2, Appx. E.9
fees, 7.3.13.2, 16.3.3, 16.6
generally, 16.6
information requirements, 7.3.13.2, 7.4, 16.6
   forms include space for, 7.3.1, 16.6
Official Forms
   declaration and signature, Form 19A, Appx. D.3
   notice to debtors, Form 19B, Appx. D.3
notice to debtor, 16.6, Appx. D.3
regulation as debt relief agency, 16.6, 16.8.1.1
   disclosure requirements, 16.8.3.4
   failure to comply, 16.8.6
regulation under s. 110, 16.6
restrictions on, 16.6, 16.8.2
signing of documents, 7.4
statement about bankruptcy assistance services, 16.8.3.3
unauthorized practice of law, 16.6
written contract requirement, 16.8.4

BANKRUPTCY PETITIONS
see also BANKRUPTCY FORMS
advice to clients after filing, 8.2
amendments to initial papers, 8.3.2
annotated and completed forms, Appx. D.2
audits, 8.3.15.1
chapter 7
   declaration of attorney, 7.3.2
   declaration of understanding, 7.3.2, 7.3.6
   eligibility, 3.2.1
   filing, effect, 3.3
   filing, forms and fees, 3.2.2, 7.2.1
chapter 13
   filing, effect, 4.3
   filing, forms and fees, 4.2.2, 7.2.1
   filing when discharge unavailable, 12.10.3
   postpetition claims, 4.6, 8.7.2
electronic filing, 7.1.4, Appx. D.1.4
filing costs
   see also FILING FEES
   amendments, 8.3.2
   chapter 7, 3.2.2, 14.6.2.1
   chapter 13, 4.2.2
   generally, 6.2.2.6, 7.2.1
   installment payments, 7.3.13.3
   joint filings, 6.4
   waiver, 14.6
format, 7.1.2, 7.3.2
forms, 7.2.1
   Official Form 1, 7.3.2, Appx. D.2
   sample forms, Appx. D.2
good faith filing, 9.3.3.2.2, 9.3.3.2.3
involuntary, 14.8, 17.1.2
joint filings, 6.4, 7.3.7.3, 7.3.7.6, 7.3.8, 10.2.1.1, 10.2.2.1
national database, 2.4.1, 5.3.4
non-attorney preparers, *see* BANKRUPTCY PETITION PREPARERS
notice by clerk prior to filing, 7.3.6
PACER system, 2.4.1, 5.3.4
preparing, 7.3.2

699

BANKRUPTCY *Consumer Bankruptcy Law and Practice*

References are to sections

BANKRUPTCY PETITIONS (*cont.*)
prior filings
    effect on eligibility, 3.2.1.2, 12.10
    information on, 2.4.1, 5.3.4
signing, 7.4, 16.7.1
    attorney certification, 16.7.2.3
successive filings, 3.2.1.2, 4.2.1.4, 6.2.2.8.2, 12.10
    effect on automatic stay, 9.4.6.5, 9.7.3.1.5, 17.4.4.3
timing considerations, 6.5
venue, 3.2.3

BANKRUPTCY PROCEEDINGS
see also CORE PROCEEDINGS; NON-CORE PROCEEDINGS
abstention, 14.5
adversary proceedings
    caption, Appx. D.3
    cover sheet, Appx. E.5
    described, 14.2.4.1
    rules, 1.4.2
    subpoena, Appx. E.7.2
    summons, Appx. E.6
applications, 14.2.4.1
case, distinction, 1.4.2
categories, 1.4.2, 14.2.4
contested matters, 14.2.4.1
    rules, 1.4.2
conversion of proceedings, *see* CONVERSION OF PROCEEDINGS
defined, 1.4.2, 14.2.4.1
disputes that arise
    generally, 8.3.10
    resolving, 3.4, 4.4
forms, *see* BANKRUPTCY FORMS
in forma pauperis, 14.6
    bankruptcy court, powers, 14.6.2
    generally, 14.6.1
jurisdiction, 14.2.4, 14.2.5
notice requirements, 9.6.3.2, 14.3.2.1
prior proceedings, information on, 2.4.1, 5.3.4
rules, *see* FEDERAL RULES OF BANKRUPTCY PROCEDURE
sample pleadings, Appx. G
service requirements, 14.3.2.1
withdrawal to district court, 14.2.5
venue, 3.2.3, 14.3.2.1

BANKRUPTCY REFORM ACT OF 1994
see also BANKRUPTCY CODE
changes enacted, 1.1.2.4
legislative history, 1.5.1.4
National Bankruptcy Review Commission, 1.1.2.4
selected provisions, Appx. A.4.6

BANKRUPTCY RULES
see FEDERAL RULES OF BANKRUPTCY PROCEDURE

BAPS
see BANKRUPTCY APPELLATE PANEL (BAP)

BENEFICIARIES
see also TRUSTS
chapter 7 filings, 3.2.1.1

BENEFITS REPLACING WAGES
see also PUBLIC BENEFITS; SOCIAL SECURITY BENEFITS
federal exemption, 10.2.2.11
wage orders, attachment, 12.6.1

BOOKS
see RECORDS

BUDGET COUNSELING
see CREDIT COUNSELING

BURDEN OF PROOF
allowed secured claims
    fees and charges, 11.6.1.3.3.5
    present value interest, 11.6.1.3.3.6
attorney fees, 15.4.3.2.4
collateral estoppel, 15.4.4
dischargeability proceedings, 15.4.3.2.4
    domestic support obligations, 15.4.3.5.3
    false financial statements, 15.4.3.2.2.1
    false pretenses or fraud, 15.4.3.2.3.1
    no intent to pay, 15.4.3.2.3.2
    student loans, 15.4.3.8.3
HEAL debts, dischargeability, 15.4.3.8.6
proof of claim, 11.2.2.3.2, 14.4.3.3

BUSINESS BANKRUPTCIES
see also CHAPTER 11 REORGANIZATIONS; CONSUMERS AS CREDITORS
employees, representing, 18.7.12
    see also EMPLOYER BANKRUPTCY
health care businesses, 18.10
landlords, *see* LANDLORD BANKRUPTCIES
lenders, *see* LENDER BANKRUPTCIES
privacy protections, 18.10
small businesses, *see* SMALL BUSINESS BANKRUPTCIES

CAPITAL GAINS
foreclosure sales, liability, 11.3.4
income treatment, 13.4.3.2.5

CASE LAW
see also RESEARCH AIDS
citator, 1.5.6
computer-assisted research, 1.5.7
NCLC consulting service, 1.3.4.2
NCLC treatise, 1.3.4.1
overview, 1.4.4.3
reporting services, 1.5.4

CASH COLLATERAL
see also COLLATERAL
family farmer reorganizations
    adequate protection, 17.4.11
    special provisions, 17.5.9
    use, generally, 17.4.8
holding by creditors, 11.3.5

CAUSES OF ACTION
see also ACTIONS; CLAIMS BY DEBTORS
prepetition causes of action
    consumer protection statutes, 16.5.3
    listing in schedule, 7.3.7.2.2
    standing, 14.3.2.6.2
    unlisted, judicial estoppel, 14.3.2.6.3

CHAPTER 7 LIQUIDATIONS
see also BANKRUPTCY
abandonment of property, 3.5.1, 8.3.11, 11.3.3
abuse of provisions, *see* ABUSE OF CHAPTER 7
addition of creditors, 8.5
amendments to statement or schedules, 8.3.2
attorney fees, *see* ATTORNEY FEES AND COSTS
audits of debtor, 8.3.15.1
automatic stay, *see* AUTOMATIC STAY
claims filed by creditors, 3.3, 3.5.3, 8.4.6
claims filed by debtor on behalf of creditor, 8.4.6
considerations favoring, 6.3.2
consumers as creditors, 18.2.2, 18.5.4.2, 18.8.2
conversion
    bad faith, 13.7.1, 13.7.2, 13.7.3
    chapter 11, from, 17.1.2
    chapter 11, to, 18.7.11
    chapter 12, from, 17.1.2, 17.4.6.3, 17.4.6.4
    chapter 12, to, 17.2.4
    chapter 13, from, 4.2.3, 4.7.4, 8.7.5.4, 13.3.1, 13.7.2, 17.1.2
    chapter 13, to, 4.2.3, 13.7.1
    exempt property, effect, 10.1.2
credit counseling prerequisite, 3.2.1.1, 3.2.1.4
dischargeability complaints, 3.3
discharges, *see* DISCHARGE OF DEBTS IN BANKRUPTCY
dismissal, *see* DISMISSAL OF CASE
distribution to creditors, order, 3.5.4
eligibility, 3.2.1
farmers, involuntary, 17.1.2
filing deadlines, *see* TIME LIMITS
filing requirements, 3.2.2, 7.2.1
financial management course requirement, 8.3.3, 15.2.2.11
first steps, 3.3
forms, *see* BANKRUPTCY FORMS; OFFICIAL BANKRUPTCY FORMS
interim trustee, appointment, 3.3
involuntary, 17.1.2
landlords, 18.8.2
liquidation of estate, 3.5.2
meeting of creditors, *see* MEETING OF CREDITORS (SECTION 341(a))
nominal asset cases, 3.5.1, 8.3.11
non-recourse loans, stripdown, 11.2.1.2
objections, filing, 3.3
overview, 2.2, 3.1

700

Index and Quick Reference
References are to sections

CHAPTER 7 LIQUIDATIONS (*cont.*)
personal property leases, assumption or rejection, 8.3.7.2, 12.9.5
petition, *see* BANKRUPTCY PETITIONS
procedures after meeting of creditors, 3.5, 8.5
retaining nonexempt property, 8.3.11
right of redemption, *see* RIGHT OF REDEMPTION
sale of assets, 18.9.3
statement of intention, *see* STATEMENT OF INTENTION
student loans, dischargeability, 15.4.3.8.5
successive filings, 3.2.1.2, 6.2.2.8.2, 15.2.2.8, 15.2.2.9
tenant ownership, 18.8.3
tenants, maintaining services, 18.8.2
timing considerations
    anticipation of further debt, 6.5.3.1
    means test calculations, 6.5.3.6
    prebankruptcy transfers, 6.5.2.1
    presumption of abuse, 6.5.3.6
trustee, *see* TRUSTEES IN BANKRUPTCY

CHAPTER 11 LIQUIDATIONS
see also CHAPTER 11 REORGANIZATIONS
code provision for, 18.7.1
imposing conditions, 18.7.12.3.4
involuntary, 17.1.2
lender bankruptcies, 18.9.3
opposing, 18.7.12.3.3
sale of assets, 18.9.3

CHAPTER 11 REORGANIZATIONS
see also BANKRUPTCY
appointment of counsel, requirement, 17.2.3.2
classification of creditors, 18.7.2.1
compensation to debtor's principal, objections, 18.7.5
consumers as creditors, 18.2.2, 18.5.4.2, 18.7.12, 18.8.4, 18.9
conversion from chapter 12, 17.4.6.3
conversion to chapter 7, 18.7.11
    farmers, 17.1.2
conversion to chapter 12, 17.2.4
creditors' committee, 18.7.2.2, 18.7.3
creditors' rights, 18.7.2.1, 18.7.2.2, 18.7.9
disclosure statement, objections, 18.7.7
dismissal, 18.7.11
employees, representing, 18.7.12
examiner, appointment, 18.7.4.6, 18.7.4.7
farmers, use by, 17.1.3.1
    problems with, 17.1.3.3
generally, 18.7.1
industrial stakeholders, representing, 18.7.12
lender bankruptcies, 18.9.1
notice to creditors, 18.4.1
plan of reorganization
    creditor plan, 18.7.9
    filing, time, 18.7.9
    objections to, 18.7.8
    third party releases, 18.9.5

voting by creditors, 18.7.2.1
procedures, 2.2
recharacterization of claims, 18.5.6
sale of assets, *see* CHAPTER 11 LIQUIDATIONS
small business reorganizations, 18.7.10
successive filings, restrictions, 15.2.2.8
successor releases and injunctions, 18.9.5
tenants, preventing eviction, 18.8.4
third party releases and injunctions, 18.9.5
transfer avoidance actions, 18.7.6
trustee appointment
    cause, grounds, 18.7.4.3, 18.7.4.5
    equitable considerations, 18.7.4.4
    general standards, 18.7.4.2
    introduction, 18.7.4.1
    practice and procedure, 18.7.4.7
U.S. trustee, role, 18.7.2.3
use by consumer debtors, 6.3.4

CHAPTER 12 PLANS (FAMILY FARMERS AND FISHERMEN)
see also CHAPTER 12 REORGANIZATIONS (FAMILY FARMERS AND FISHERMEN)
adequate protection, 17.4.11
allowed secured claims, treatment, 17.5.4
    amortization, 17.5.4.2
    interest rates, 17.5.4.3
    reduction, 17.5.4.4
    valuation, 17.5.3
classification of claims
    codebtors, 17.5.6.2
    direct payments, 17.5.7.3
    generally, 17.5.6.1
    secured creditors, 17.5.6.4
    unsecured creditors, 17.5.6.3
collateral, substitution, 17.5.4.6
confirmation
    denial, 17.6
    postconfirmation issues, 17.8.1
    reservation of issues, 17.5.9
    revocation, 17.8.3
    time frame, 17.5.2
default cure, 17.5.4.2
disposable income commitment, 17.5.4.2, 17.5.5.3
domestic support obligations, 17.5.8
feasibility requirement, 17.5.7.2
    determination, 17.5.7.2.2
    generally, 17.5.7.2.1
good faith test, 17.5.7.1
liquidation test, 17.5.5.2
modification
    generally, time, 17.5.2
    postconfirmation, 17.5.5.3, 17.8.1
other provisions, suggestions, 17.5.9
payments
    deferral, 17.5.9
    direct payments, 17.5.7.3, 17.5.9
    extensions beyond plan life, 17.5.4.2
    trustee, through, 17.4.1.2.1, 17.5.7.3
postpetition indebtedness, 17.8.2
    tax liabilities, 17.5.5.4

priority unsecured creditors, 17.5.5.4
proposal, 17.5.2
replacement liens, 17.5.4.6
setoffs, provision for, 17.4.12
special provisions, 17.5.9
surrender of property, 17.5.4.4
tax claims, 17.5.5.4
time limits, 17.5.2
trustee compensation, 17.4.1.2
unsecured claims, treatment, 17.5.5

CHAPTER 12 REORGANIZATIONS (FAMILY FARMERS AND FISHERMEN)
see also BANKRUPTCY; FARMERS; FISHERMEN
adequate protection concept, 17.4.11
advantages over chapter 11, 17.1.3.3
advantages over chapter 13, 17.1.3.2
appointment of counsel, requirement, 17.2.3.2
attorney fees, disclosure, 17.2.3.3
automatic stay, application, 17.4.4.1
cash collateral, use, *see* CASH COLLATERAL
consumers as creditors, 18.5.4.2
conversion from other chapters, 17.2.4
conversion to other chapters
    involuntary, 17.1.2, 17.4.6.4
    voluntary, 17.4.6.3
credit counseling requirement, 17.2.2.1
current status, 17.1.1.1
DIP, *see* DEBTOR-IN-POSSESSION (DIP)
discharges
    see also DISCHARGE OF DEBTS IN BANKRUPTCY
    discharge issues, 17.4.5, 17.7
    discharge orders, forms, Appx. E.8.5, Appx. E.8.6
dismissal
    involuntary, 17.4.6.2
    voluntary, 17.4.6.1
eligibility, 17.2.2
    commercial fishing operation, 17.2.2.3
    corporations, 17.2.2.4.5
    debt ceiling, 17.2.2.4.2
    family farmer, 17.2.2.4
    family fisherman, 17.2.2.4
    farming operation, 17.2.2.3
    generally, 17.2.2.1
    partnerships, 17.2.2.4.5
    nature of debt, 17.2.2.4.3
    nature of income, 17.2.2.4.4
    regular annual income, 17.2.2.2
executory contracts, assumption, 17.4.7
evolution of, 17.1.1
filing fees, 17.2.3.3
historical background, 1.1.2.3, 17.1.1
initial documentation, 17.2.3.4
liens
    automatic dissolution, 17.4.3.4
    avoidance, 17.4.3.3, 17.4.3.5
    sales free and clear, 17.4.10, 17.5.4.5
meeting of creditors, 17.2.5

701

CHAPTER 12 REORGANIZATIONS (FAMILY FARMERS AND FISHERMEN) *(cont.)*
new financing, approval, 17.4.9
other options, problems with use, 17.1.3
overview, 17.1
periodic reports, 17.2.3.4
permanent status, 17.1.1.1
plans, *see* CHAPTER 12 PLANS (FAMILY FARMERS AND FISHERMEN)
postpetition dispositions, tax liability, 17.5.5.4
procedures, 17.5.2
property of the estate, 17.4.2
provisions, creation, 1.1.2.3, 1.5.1.3
purpose, 17.1.1.2
recapture of property, 17.4.3.5
redemption rights, 17.4.3.5.5
related provisions, Appx. A.4.3
right to cure, 17.4.3.5.5
schedules, 17.2.3.1
secured creditors, treatment, 17.5.4
  valuation of claims, 17.5.3
supplemental information, 17.2.3.4
tax claims, 17.5.5.4
timing, 17.1.5, 17.5.2
trustee, *see* TRUSTEES IN BANKRUPTCY
unexpired leases, assumption, 17.4.7
unsecured creditors, treatment, 17.5.5

CHAPTER 13 PLANS
see also CHAPTER 13 REORGANIZATIONS
ability to pay test, *see* ABILITY TO PAY TEST
adequate protection of property, 12.8.2
adequate protection payments, 8.3.12.2, 12.8.2.2
administration, 8.7
advice to clients, 8.2
allowed secured claims, 8.3.12.1, 8.3.12.2, 11.6.1.3, 11.6.2
attorney fees, payment through, 7.3.12.3, 16.4
binding effect, 12.11
classification of claims
  claims by former chapter 7 trustees, 12.4.5
  claims with cosigners, 12.4.2
  generally, 12.4.1
  others, 12.4.3
  payments directly to creditors, 12.4.4
  practical considerations, 12.4.6
confirmation
  application for, 8.6
  considerations, 4.3, 4.5, 12.7
  denial, effect, 8.3.12
  distribution of payments, 8.3.12
  effect, 4.5
  hearing, 4.5, 8.6
  mandatory, 12.7
  modified plans, 8.6
  res judicata effect, 9.7.3.2.1, 12.7, 12.11
  revocation, 4.5
  standards, 7.3.12.3
  vesting of property after, 12.8.5
debtors below medium income, 12.3.4.4.5
disposable income, 12.3.4.4
  commitment of, 7.3.12.3, 12.3.4.1, 12.3.4.4.6
distributions in equal monthly payments, 11.6.1.3.3.2
executory contracts, 12.9
  assumption, 12.9.2
  rejection, 12.9.3.1, 12.9.3.3
failure to complete, 4.7
  conversion to chapter 7, 4.7.4, 8.7.5.4, 13.7.2
  dismissal, 4.7.5, 8.7.5.5, 13.6
  generally, 8.7.5.1
  hardship discharge, 4.7.2, 8.7.5.3
  modification, 4.7.3, 8.7.5.2
  options, 4.7.1
feasibility of plan, 12.5
filing requirement, 4.2.2, 7.2.1
form plans, 7.3.12.2
format, 7.3.12
formulating the plan, 7.3.12.5
generally, 7.3.12
hardship discharge, 4.7.2, 8.7.5.3
income and expenses, estimating, 7.3.7.6
income payments to trustee, 12.6.1
interest and penalty payments, 12.6.2
landlords, 18.8.2.2
late payment charges, 14.4.3.4.4
leases, 12.9
  assumption, 12.9.2
  rejection, 12.9.3.2
length of plan, 12.3.4.4.6
  maximum, 12.6.3
lien retention, 11.6.1.3.3.1
liquidation of property under, 12.6.5
loan modification
  involuntary, 11.6.1
  voluntary, 11.6.1.5
long-term debts, 11.6.2, 15.4.1
modification
  change in circumstances, 12.3.4.5
  confirmation hearing, 8.6
  generally, 4.7.3, 8.7.4, 12.11
  inability to complete plan, 8.7.5.2
  objections, 4.6
  postpetition transactions, 4.6, 8.7.2
  time, 4.6, 12.3.4.5
mortgage refinancings, 12.6.6
objections, grounds, 4.4, 8.6, 12.3.4.2
payments
  adequate protection payments, 8.3.12.2, 11.6.1.3.3.2, 12.8.2.2
  automatic increases, 12.3.4.5
  commencement, time, 4.3, 8.3.12.1
  crediting mistakes, 14.4.3.4.4, 14.4.3.4.8, 15.5.1.4
  directly to creditors, 11.6.2.6, 12.4.4, 12.4.6
  disposable income, effect, 12.3.4.1
  graduated payments, 8.3.12.3
  modification, 12.3.4.5
  outside plan, 11.6.2.6, 12.4.4, 12.4.6
  personal property leases, 8.3.12.2, 12.8.2.2
  postpetition support obligations, 12.3.6.3
  present value, 11.6.1.3.3.1
  priority creditors, 12.3.6
  schedules, 7.3.12
  tracking, 2.6, 8.7.1
  trustee, payment through, 8.7.1
  wage deductions, 8.3.12
percentage plans, 7.3.12.5
permissible provisions, 7.3.12.4
possession of property, 12.8.1
postpetition transactions, 4.6
  claims, 8.7.2
  mortgage payments, 8.7.3
pot plans, 7.3.12.5
priority claims, 12.3.6
requirements, 7.3.12.3, 12.7
signing, 7.4
standards, 7.3.12.3, 11.6.1.3, 12.3–12.7
student loans, 15.4.3.8.3
summarization, filing, 7.2.1
tax claims, 7.3.7.3.3, 12.3.6.1
trustee's charges, adjustments, 12.6.4
trustee's duties, 2.6
undersecured claims, 11.7
unexpired leases, 12.9
  assumption, 12.9.2
  rejection, 12.9.3.2
unsecured creditors, 12.3
  ability to pay test, 12.3.4
  best interests test, 12.3.2
  good faith test, 12.3.3, 12.3.5
  priority creditors, 12.3.6
use of property, 12.8.1
zero payment plans, 12.3.4.1

CHAPTER 13 REORGANIZATIONS
see also BANKRUPTCY
adequate protection payments, 8.3.12.2, 12.8.2.2
administrative expenses, 12.3.4.4.4, 12.3.6.1
  means test deduction, 13.4.5.3.7
amendments to statement or schedules, 8.3.2
attorney fees, *see* ATTORNEY FEES AND COSTS
audits of debtor, 8.3.15.1
automatic stay, *see* AUTOMATIC STAY
claims filed by creditors, 4.3, 4.4, 8.4.6
claims filed by debtor on behalf of creditor, 8.4.6
commencement of case, 4.2
considerations favoring, 6.2.2.8.2, 6.3.3
consumers as creditors
  evictions, preventing, 18.8.4
  generally, 18.5.4.3
conversion
  bad faith, 13.7.1, 13.7.2, 13.7.3
  chapter 7, from, 4.2.3, 13.7.1
  chapter 7, to, 4.2.3, 4.7.4, 8.7.5.4, 13.3.1, 13.7.2, 17.1.2
  chapter 12, to, 17.2.4
  exempt property, effect, 10.1.2

CHAPTER 13
REORGANIZATIONS (cont.)
cramdown, 11.6
credit counseling prerequisite, 4.2.1.1
discharges, see DISCHARGE OF DEBTS IN BANKRUPTCY
dismissal, see DISMISSAL OF CASE
domestic support obligations
   certification, 4.8, 8.8.1, Appx. E.14
   classification, 12.3.6.1, 12.4.3
   postpetition, 12.3.6.3
eligibility, 4.2.1
   debt limitations, 4.2.1.3, 12.2.3
   generally, 4.2.1.1, 12.2.1
   partners, 12.2.2
   regular income, 4.2.1.2, 12.2.2
farmers, use by, 17.1.3.1
   problems with, 17.1.3.2
filing deadlines, see TIME LIMITS
filing requirements, 4.2.2
first steps, 4.3
forms, see BANKRUPTCY FORMS; OFFICIAL BANKRUPTCY FORMS
good faith use, 12.3.3, 12.3.5
issues, generally, 12.1
joint cases, 4.2.1.2
liens, voiding, 11.7
long-term debts, right to cure, 11.6.2, 15.4.1
meeting of creditors, see MEETING OF CREDITORS (SECTION 341(a))
overview, 4.1
personal financial management course requirement, 8.3.3
personal property lease payments, 8.3.12.2, 12.8.2.2
petition, see BANKRUPTCY PETITIONS
plans, see CHAPTER 13 PLANS
postpetition claims, 4.6, 4.7.4, 8.7.2
postpetition support obligations must be met, 12.3.6.3
preconfirmation activities, 4.4
prior bankruptcies, effect, 12.10
reasons for filing, 6.3.3
secured creditors
   adequate protection, 8.3.12.2, 11.6.1.3.3.2, 12.8.2.2
   debtor's right to cure, 11.6.2
   modification of rights, 11.6.1
   principal residences, 11.6.1.2
   purchase money security interests, 11.6.1.4
   standards under plan, 11.6.1.3
statement of income and expenses, annual filings, 8.3.5
statement of intention, necessity, 7.3.11
student loan issues, 12.4.3, 15.4.3.8.5
successive filings, restrictions, 4.2.1.4, 6.2.2.8.2, 15.2.2.9
tax return filing, prerequisite, 8.3.14, 12.3.6.2
timing considerations
   disposable income, 6.5.3.6
   purchase money security interests, 6.5.3.5
   tax debts, 6.5.3.4

trustee, see TRUSTEES IN BANKRUPTCY

CHARITABLE CONTRIBUTIONS
avoidance status, 10.4.2.6.2, 10.4.2.6.5
defined, 10.4.2.6.5
donations after bankruptcy, 1.1.2.6, 12.3.4.4.5
means test deduction, 12.3.4.4.5, 13.4.5.3.9
protection for donations, 1.1.2.6, 10.4.2.6.5
reasonable expenses, 5.3.3.4, 12.3.4.4.5

CHECKS
transfer date, 10.4.2.6.6

CHILD SUPPORT
see DOMESTIC SUPPORT OBLIGATIONS

CHILDREN
see MINORS

CIVIL PROCEEDINGS
see also ACTIONS; LEGAL PROCEEDINGS
damages or restitution, dischargeability, 15.4.3.6
delay of discharge pending, 10.2.3.4.5.6, 15.2.2.12

CIVIL RIGHTS AWARDS
attorney fees, bankruptcy, application, 16.5.2

CLAIMS BY CREDITORS
see also CREDITORS
allowed secured claims, see ALLOWED SECURED CLAIMS
baseless, 14.4.3.3
claim, defined, 15.5.1.1, 18.4.1
classification
   chapter 12, 17.5.6
   chapter 13, 12.4
consumers as creditors, 18.4
debt buyers, 14.4.3.5
discharge, effect on, 15.5.1
disputes, resolving, 3.4, 4.4
equitable subordination, 18.5.4
escrow overcharges, 14.4.3.4.2
filing by debtor, 8.4.6
   chapter 13, 4.4
government claims, see GOVERNMENT CLAIMS
inadequate documentation, 14.4.3.5
interest overcharges, 14.4.3.4.3
late charge abuses, 14.4.3.4.4
late filing, 14.4.3.2
monitoring and other fees, 14.4.3.4.5
mortgage overcharges, 14.4.3.4
no legal or factual basis, 16.5.5.1
objections to, 3.5.3, 4.4, 8.3.9, 14.3.2.4, 14.4.3
   Official Form 20B, Appx. D.3
postpetition claims, see POSTPETITION CLAIMS
prepetition settlement attempts, effect, 14.4.3.6

proof of claim, see PROOF OF CLAIM
recharacterization, 18.5.4
reconsideration of claims, 14.4.3.7
Rule 3001 sanctions, 16.5.5.2
Rule 9011 sanctions, 16.5.5.1
tax claims, see TAX CLAIMS

CLAIMS BY DEBTORS
automatic stay, effect, 9.4.2, 14.4.2
prepetition causes of action, 16.5.3
   listing in schedule, 7.3.7.2.2
   standing, 14.3.2.6.2
   unlisted, judicial estoppel, 14.3.2.6.3

CLASS ACTIONS
bankruptcy court, 14.7
bankruptcy petition preparers, against, 16.6
consumers as creditors, 18.4.2
discharge protections, enforcement, 15.5.5.7

CLIENT HANDOUTS
see also PRACTICE AIDS
common bankruptcy questions, Appx. K.2
legal rights, Appx. K.3
using credit wisely, Appx. K.4

CODEBTORS
see also SPOUSES
automatic stay
   advantages, 6.2.1.4
   effect, 9.4.2
   prior dismissed cases, effect, 9.3.3.5
   scope, 9.4.5, 17.4.4.2
chapter 12 reorganizations
   automatic stay, application, 17.4.4.2
   special classification, 17.5.6.2
claims with, chapter 13 priority, 12.4.2
credit report of bankruptcy, 9.4.5
listing
   filing of list, 7.3.4
   schedule, Sch. H, 7.3.7.3, 7.3.7.5

COLLATERAL
see also SECURITY INTERESTS
cash collateral, see CASH COLLATERAL
chapter 12 reorganizations
   return to creditor, 17.5.4.4
   sale payments, 17.5.7.3
   sales free and clear, 17.4.10, 17.5.4.5
   substitutions, 17.5.4.6
chapter 13 cramdown, 11.6.1
conversion, see CONVERSION OF PROPERTY
credit card debts, 5.3.3.3
distribution to creditors, 3.5.4
finance company loans, 5.3.3.3
gathering information regarding, 5.3.3.3
retention, 11.4.2
right of redemption, see RIGHT OF REDEMPTION
statement of intention, see STATEMENT OF INTENTION
valuation, see VALUATION

COLLATERAL ESTOPPEL
dischargeability issues, application, 15.4.4, 18.5.4.2.2

COLLECTION · *Consumer Bankruptcy Law and Practice*

References are to sections

COLLECTION AGENCIES
automatic stay, notice, effect, 8.3.1, 9.4.4
listing as creditor in schedule, 7.3.7.3.4
payments to, avoidance as preference, 10.4.2.6.4.3
regulation, 6.2.1.1

COLLEGE TRANSCRIPTS
discharge protections, 15.5.5.2

COMMERCIAL FISHING OPERATIONS
see also FISHERMEN
chapter 12 eligibility, 17.2.2
   corporations, 17.2.2.4.5
   debt ceiling, 17.2.2.4.2
   nature of debt, 17.2.2.4.3
   nature of income, 17.2.2.4.4
   partnerships, 17.2.2.4.5
defined, 17.2.2.3

COMMUNITY PROPERTY
see JOINT PROPERTY

COMPENSATION PAYMENTS
federal exemption, 10.2.2.12

COMPUTERIZATION
see also WEB RESOURCES
bankruptcy forms, 5.1.3, 7.1.3, 7.3.1, Appx. D.1.2
bankruptcy practice, 7.1.3
computer-assisted research, 1.5.7
electronic filing, *see* ELECTRONIC FILING
web-based text searches, 1.3.3, Appx. M.6

CONDOMINIUM OR COOPERATIVE FEES
dischargeability, 15.4.3.15, 15.5.1.1
   listing in schedule, 7.3.7.3.4
means test deduction, 13.4.5.3.2

CONFIRMATION OF PLAN
see CHAPTER 12 PLANS (FAMILY FARMERS AND FISHERMEN); CHAPTER 13 PLANS

CONSOLIDATION OF CASES
joint bankruptcies, differences, 6.4

CONSTRUCTIVE TRUSTS
see also TRUSTS
existence, determination, 18.5.2.2

CONSUMER DEBTORS
see DEBTORS

CONSUMER DEBTS
see also DEBTORS; LIABILITIES
anticipation of further debt, 6.5.3.1
automatic stay, *see* AUTOMATIC STAY
bankruptcy advantages, 6.2.1
bankruptcy disadvantages, 6.2.2
buyers of debt, claims by, 14.4.3.5
chapter 13 limitations, 12.2.3
codebtors, *see* CODEBTORS
collateral, *see* COLLATERAL
contingent debts, 7.3.7.3.1, 7.3.7.3.4

definition, 11.5.2, 13.4.2
   debt, defined, 15.5.1.1
discharge, *see* DISCHARGE OF DEBTS IN BANKRUPTCY
dischargeability, *see* DISCHARGEABILITY
intention regarding collateral, *see* STATEMENT OF INTENTION
listing in schedules, 7.3.7.3
   disputed debts, 7.3.7.3, 14.4.3.5
long-term debts, *see* LONG-TERM DEBTS
means test deductions
   priority debts, 13.4.5.3.3
   secured debts, 13.4.5.3.2
medical debts, *see* MEDICAL DEBTS
mutual debts, *see* MUTUAL DEBTS
NCLC Guide to Surviving Debt, 6.1.2
nonbankruptcy approaches, 6.2.2.8.2
procedures after meeting of creditors, 3.5
reaffirmation, *see* REAFFIRMATION AGREEMENTS
repayment plans, avoidance of preferences, 10.4.2.6.4.2
resulting from wrongful conduct, homestead exemption cap, 10.2.3.4.5
statement of financial affairs, 7.3.8
unliquidated debts, 7.3.7.3

CONSUMER PRIVACY OMBUDSMAN
business bankruptcies, 18.10

CONSUMER PROTECTION STATUTES
attorney fees, 16.5.3
automatic stay issues, 9.7.3.3.2, 18.9.2

CONSUMERS AS CREDITORS
see also CREDITORS
automatic stay, 18.3
chapter 11 overview, 18.7
circumstances, 18.1
consumer priority, 18.5.5
dischargeability issues, 18.2.1, 18.5.4
equitable subordination, 18.5.6
in forma pauperis, 18.6
increased recovery strategies
   generally, 18.5.1
   trust claims, 18.5.2
involuntary bankruptcy, forcing, 18.2.2
lender bankruptcies, 18.9
money orders, 18.5.2.1
postpetition claims, 18.5.3
prebankruptcy strategy, 18.2
preparing for voluntary bankruptcy, 18.2.1
proof of claim
   class claims, 18.4.2
   individual consumers, 18.4.1
Rule 2004 examinations, 18.5.8
seeking defendants not in bankruptcy, 18.5.7
tenants, special problems, 18.8

CONTEMPT OF COURT
automatic stay violations, 9.6.4
bankruptcy court powers, 14.2.8
discharge, denial, 15.2.2.6
discharge protections, 15.5.5.7
utility companies, 9.8.2.1

CONTRACTS
arbitration clauses, avoiding, 14.3.2.3
bankruptcy clauses, validity, 8.8.2, 11.5.4, 15.5.3
cross-collateralization clauses, 15.5.3
debt relief agencies, requirement, 16.8.4
executory, *see* EXECUTORY CONTRACTS
rent-to-own, *see* RENT-TO-OWN TRANSACTIONS
spreader clauses, 15.5.3

CONVERSION OF PROCEEDINGS
see also BANKRUPTCY PROCEEDINGS
bad faith, 13.7.1, 13.7.2, 13.7.3
chapter 7 to chapter 12, 17.2.4
chapter 7 to chapter 13, 4.2.3, 13.7.1
chapter 11 to chapter 7, 17.1.2, 18.7.11
chapter 11 to chapter 12, 17.2.4
chapter 12 to chapter 7, 17.1.2, 17.4.6.3, 17.4.6.4
chapter 12 to chapter 11, 17.4.6.3
chapter 12 to chapter 13, 17.4.6.3
chapter 13 to chapter 7, 4.2.3, 4.7.4, 8.7.5.4, 13.3.1, 13.7.2, 17.1.2
chapter 13 to chapter 12, 17.2.4
effect of conversion, 13.7.3
involuntary, 13.3.1, 13.7.2, 17.1.2, 17.4.6.4

CONVERSION OF PROPERTY
see also FRAUDULENT TRANSFERS
discharge bar, willful and malicious injury, 15.4.3.6

CONVEYANCES
see FRAUDULENT TRANSFERS; PREBANKRUPTCY TRANSFERS

CORE PROCEEDINGS
see also BANKRUPTCY PROCEEDINGS
determination by court, 14.2.4.3
exceptions, 14.2.6
mandatory abstention, application, 14.5.2
mandatory withdrawal, 14.2.5.2
non-core, distinction, 14.2.4.2, 14.2.4.3
procedures, 14.2.4.2

CORPORATIONS
see also BUSINESS BANKRUPTCIES
chapter 7 eligibility, 3.2.1.1
chapter 12 eligibility, 17.2.2.1, 17.2.2.4.5
discharges, 15.2.2.1, 18.5.4.4
farm corporations, *see* FARM CORPORATIONS

COSIGNERS
see also CODEBTORS
claims with, chapter 13 priority, 12.4.2

COST OF LIVING ADJUSTMENTS
federal exemptions, 10.2.2.1

COSTS
see ATTORNEY FEES AND COSTS; FILING FEES

COUNSEL
see ATTORNEYS; DEBT RELIEF AGENCIES

704

COUNSELING THE CONSUMER DEBTOR
see also PRACTICE AIDS
advantages of bankruptcy, 6.2.1
answers to common questions, Appx. K.2
bankruptcy discharge, Appx. K.3
choosing the type of bankruptcy case, 6.3
client handouts, Appx. K
credit counseling requirement, *see* CREDIT COUNSELING
debt relief agencies, *see* DEBT RELIEF AGENCIES
delaying petition, reasons for
  exemption planning, 6.5.2.2
  other reasons, 6.5.3
  prebankruptcy transfers, 6.5.2.1
disadvantages of bankruptcy, 6.2.2
exemption planning, 6.5.2.2
explaining bankruptcy, 6.1.2
options, explaining, 6.1.1
paying favored creditors, 6.5.3.2
quick filings, considerations, 6.5.1
spouses, filing by both, 6.4
using credit wisely, Appx. K.4

COUNTERCLAIMS
see also SETOFFS
automatic stay litigation, raising, 9.7.3.1.3, 9.7.3.3.2
eviction proceedings, 18.3.4
jurisdiction of Bankruptcy Court, 14.2.1, 14.2.4.2

COURT OF APPEALS
appeals to, 2.4.3, 14.9.2
  certification, Official Form 24, Appx. D.3

COVENANT NOT TO COMPETE
executory contract status, 12.9.1

CRAMDOWN
see also STRIPDOWN
chapter 12, 17.5.4
chapter 13, 11.6
defined, 11.6.1.1

CREDIT AGREEMENTS
bankruptcy clauses, validity, 8.8.2, 15.5.3
spreader clauses, 15.5.3

CREDIT CARDS
balance transfers, status as preference, 10.4.2.6.4.1
debts
  documentation, 14.4.3.5
  listing in schedule, Sch. F, 7.3.7.3.4
fraud, Rule 2004 examinations, 8.3.15.2
security interests created by, enforceability, 5.3.3.3, 15.5.3
surrender by debtor, 8.4.3
taxes paid with, dischargeability, 15.4.3.13
use without intent to pay, 15.4.3.2.3.1, 15.4.3.2.3.2
using wisely after bankruptcy, Appx. K.4

CREDIT COUNSELING
see also COUNSELING THE CONSUMER DEBTOR
approved agencies, 3.2.1.4
  criteria for approval, Appx. C.1
certification of counseling, filing, 7.2.1, 7.3.5
cost of briefing, 3.2.1.4, 6.2.2.6
debt relief agencies, *see* DEBT RELIEF AGENCIES
deferment, 3.2.1.4, 7.2.2
involuntary bankruptcies, 14.8
overview, 3.2.1.4
prepetition attempts at repayment plan, effect, 14.4.3.6
prerequisite to filing, 7.3.5
  chapter 7, 3.2.1.1, 3.2.1.4
  chapter 12, 17.2.2.1
  chapter 13, 4.2.1.1
  effect on ability to file quickly, 6.5.1
statement of compliance, 7.3.2, 7.3.5
waiver, 3.2.1.4

CREDIT HISTORY
see also CREDIT REPORTS
bankruptcy effect, 6.2.2.3

CREDIT INSURANCE
chapter 13 plans, rejection, 12.9.3.3

CREDIT REPORTS
see also CREDIT HISTORY
discharged debts, 8.9
dismissed petitions, 14.8
disputed debts, listing in schedule, 7.3.7.3.1
source of information, 5.3.4

CREDITORS
addition after first meeting, 8.5
address for notice, 9.6.3.2.3, 9.6.3.2.4
adequate protection, 9.7.3.2.2
automatic stay, notification, 8.3.1
bankruptcy of, *see* LENDER BANKRUPTCIES
best interests of creditors' test, 7.3.12.3
chapter 11 plans
  classification, 18.7.2.1
  creditors' committee, 18.7.2.2, 18.7.3
  plan proposal, 18.7.9
  voting on, 18.7.2.1
claims, *see* CLAIMS BY CREDITORS
classification in chapter 13 plans, 7.3.12.3
consumers as, *see* CONSUMERS AS CREDITORS
distribution of assets in chapter 7, 3.5.4
equitable subordination, use of doctrine against, 18.5.6
filing deadlines, 3.3, 15.4.3.3
first meeting, *see* MEETING OF CREDITORS (SECTION 341(a))
government, *see* GOVERNMENT CLAIMS; GOVERNMENTAL UNITS
list of creditors
  failure to list, effect, 15.4.3.3
  filing, 7.3.4
mailing matrix, 7.2.1, 15.4.3.3
schedules, Sch. D–Sch. F, 7.3.7.3
meeting, *see* MEETING OF CREDITORS (SECTION 341(a))
notification of case, 15.4.3.3
objections to exemptions, 8.5, 10.3.3, 10.3.4
preferences, *see* PREFERENCES
priority unsecured creditors, *see* PRIORITY UNSECURED CREDITORS
secured creditors, *see* SECURED CREDITORS
setoffs, *see* SETOFFS
tax returns, provision to, 8.3.4.1
turnover of property to trustee, *see* AUTOMATIC TURNOVER
unsecured creditors, *see* UNSECURED CREDITORS

CRIMINAL FINES
see FINES AND PENALTIES

CRIMINAL PROCEEDINGS
see also LEGAL PROCEEDINGS
automatic stay, application, 9.4.6.2, 9.4.7
delay of discharge pending, 10.2.3.4.5.6, 15.2.2.12
discharge protections, 15.5.5.5
homestead exemption cap, 10.2.3.4.5

CRIMINAL RESTITUTION
see RESTITUTION DEBTS

CROSS-COLLATERALIZATION CLAUSES
validity, 15.5.3

CURING DEFAULT
see RIGHT TO CURE

CURRENT MONTHLY INCOME
see also INCOME
deductions from, 13.4.5
defined, 12.3.4.4.1, 13.4.3.2.1
determination, 13.4.3.2
  six-month average, 13.4.3.2.1
  statutory exemptions, 13.4.3.2.7
disposable income, *see* DISPOSABLE INCOME
means test, *see* MEANS TEST
presumption of abuse, 13.4.6.1
statement of, *see* STATEMENT OF CURRENT MONTHLY INCOME

CUSTODIAN
definition, 9.9

CUSTODY PROCEEDINGS
see also DOMESTIC SUPPORT OBLIGATIONS; FAMILY LAW PROCEEDINGS
attorney fees, dischargeability, 15.4.3.5.3

DAMAGES
see also RESTITUTION DEBTS
automatic stay violations, 8.3.1, 9.6.2
  notice requirements, 9.6.3.3
bankruptcy petition preparers, violations, 16.6

DAMAGES (cont.)
discharge injunction violations, 15.5.1.4
dischargeability, 15.4.3.6, 18.5.4.2.1

DEBT BUYERS
proof of claim, 14.4.3.4.7, 14.4.3.5

DEBT CEILING
chapter 12 eligibility, 17.2.2.4.2

DEBT COLLECTORS
see also COLLECTION AGENCIES
regulation, 6.2.1.1

DEBT MANAGEMENT PLANS
filing with certificate of credit counseling, 7.3.5

DEBT RELIEF AGENCIES
see also BANKRUPTCY PETITION PREPARERS
advertisements, 16.8.5
bankruptcy petition preparers, status, 16.6
defined, 16.8.1.1
   exclusions, 16.8.1.2
disclosure requirements, 16.8.3
provisions
   application to attorneys, 16.8.1
   failure to comply, 16.8.6
restrictions on, 16.8.2
statement about bankruptcy assistance services, 16.8.3.3
written contract requirement, 16.8.4

DEBTOR-IN-POSSESSION (DIP)
chapter 11 reorganizations
   operation of business, 18.8.4
   removal, 18.7.4
chapter 12 farm reorganizations
   see also FARMERS
   avoidance actions, pursuance, 17.4.1.1
   lien avoidance powers, 17.4.3.5
   recapture powers, 17.4.3.5
   reinstatement, 17.3.2
   removal, 17.3.2, 17.4.1.3
   separate legal entity, powers, 17.3.1
chapter 13, 18.8.4

DEBTOR PLANS
see CHAPTER 12 PLANS (FAMILY FARMERS AND FISHERMEN); CHAPTER 13 PLANS

DEBTORS
see also CONSUMER DEBTS
ability to pay test, see ABILITY TO PAY TEST
actions against, automatic stay, see AUTOMATIC STAY
actions brought by, automatic stay, effect, 9.4.2, 14.4.2
assistance to, debt relief agency provisions, 16.8
attendance at hearings
   confirmation, 8.6
   discharge, 8.8
   meeting of creditors, 8.4.3
audits, 8.3.15.1, Appx. C.2
available relief, notice by clerk of bankruptcy court, 7.3.6
awareness of bankruptcy information, 8.4.5
causes of action, listing in schedule, 7.3.7.2.2
counseling, 6.1, Appx. K
   see also COUNSELING THE CONSUMER DEBTOR
court orders, refusal to obey, 15.2.2.6, 15.3
credit and reputation, bankruptcy effect on, 6.2.2.3, 6.3.3
credit cards, surrender, 8.4.3
creditors, as, see CONSUMERS AS CREDITORS; LENDER BANKRUPTCIES
death of debtor, effect on case, 13.3.1
DIP, see DEBTOR-IN-POSSESSION (DIP)
discrimination after bankruptcy, 6.2.2.4, 15.5.4, 15.5.5
dishonesty, denial of discharge, 15.2.2.4, 15.2.2.5
examination of
   additional examination, Rule 2004, 8.3.15.2
   awareness of bankruptcy information, 8.4.5
   meeting of creditors, at, 1.1.2.4, 3.4, 4.4, 8.4.3, 8.4.5
expenses of, 5.3.3.4
farmers, see FARMERS
feelings of moral obligation, 6.2.2.5
filing of creditor claims, 8.4.6
financial affairs, see STATEMENT OF FINANCIAL AFFAIRS
fishermen, see FISHERMEN
fraudulent conduct, see FRAUD
gathering information, 5.3.3
identification, 8.4.2, 8.4.3
imprisonment, habeas corpus, 14.4.5, 15.5.5.7
income, see INCOME
intention regarding collateral, see STATEMENT OF INTENTION
material misstatement, 8.3.15.1
NCLC bankruptcy treatise, focus, 1.2, 1.3.4.1
NCLC Guide to Surviving Debt, 6.1.2
nonbankruptcy approaches, 6.2.2.8.2
personal liability, elimination, 15.5.1.2
personal property leases, assumption, 12.9.5.3
property, see BANKRUPTCY ESTATE; PROPERTY
sale of assets, 18.9.3
small businesses, 18.7.10
testify, refusal, 15.2.2.6
using credit wisely, Appx. K.4

DEBTS
see also LIABILITIES
consumer as creditor, see CONSUMERS AS CREDITORS
consumer debts, see CONSUMER DEBTS
dischargeability, see DISCHARGEABILITY
family farmers and fishermen, chapter 12 eligibility
   arising from operation, 17.2.2.4.3
   ceiling, 17.2.2.4.2
reaffirmation, see REAFFIRMATION AGREEMENTS
student loans, see STUDENT LOANS

DECEPTIVE PRACTICES
see UNFAIR TRADE PRACTICES

DECLARATIONS
attorneys, requirement on petition, 7.3.2, 7.3.6
bankruptcy petition, 7.3.2
bankruptcy petition preparers, 16.6
   Form 19A, Appx. D.3
debtors, truth of schedules, 7.3.7.7, 7.4
statement of financial affairs, 7.3.8, 7.4

DECLARATORY RELIEF
issues in dispute, 8.3.10

DEFAULT, CURING
see RIGHT TO CURE

DEFENSES
see also COUNTERCLAIMS
automatic stay, motions for relief, 9.7.3
student loan debts, 15.4.3.8.4

DEFERRED PAYMENT CONTRACTS
listing in schedules, 7.3.7.3.4

DEFINITIONS
adequate assurance, 9.8.2.2.1, 12.9.2
adversary proceeding, 14.2.4.1
advertising, 16.8.5
allowed secured claim, 11.1, 11.4.2.4.2
bankruptcy, 2.1
bankruptcy estate, 2.5
bankruptcy petition preparer, 16.6
case, 1.4.2
cause, 18.7.11
charitable contribution, 10.4.2.6.5
claim, 15.5.1.1
claim against the debtor, 11.6.2.4
commercial fishing operation, 17.2.2.3
consumer debt, 3.5, 11.5.2, 13.4.2
contingent debt, 7.3.7.3, 12.2.3.2
cramdown, 11.6.1.1
creditor, 10.2.3.4.3
current monthly income, 12.3.4.4.1, 13.4.3.2.1
custodian, 9.9
debt, 12.2.3.1, 15.5.1.1
debt relief agency, 16.8.1.1
dependent, 13.4.5.2.1
disposable income, 7.3.12.3, 12.3.4.1
domestic support obligations, 15.4.3.5.2, 17.5.8
domicile, 10.2.1.2
effective notice, 9.6.3.3
embezzlement, 15.4.3.4
entity, 9.9
executory contract, 7.3.7.4, 12.9.1
exempt property, 10.1.2

Index and Quick Reference **DISCHARGE**

References are to sections

DEFINITIONS (*cont.*)
family farmer, 17.1.2, 17.2.2.4
family fisherman, 17.2.2.4
farmer, 17.1.2
farming operation, 17.2.2.3
fraudulent transfers, 10.4.2.6.5
good faith, 9.3.3.2.3, 12.3.3
good faith purchaser, 9.4.6.7
health care business, 18.10
household, 13.4.3.3
household goods, 10.4.2.4
incidental property, 11.6.1.2.2.4
income, 13.4.3.2.8
individual with regular income, 4.2.1.2, 12.2.2
insider, 15.2.2.7
insolvent, 10.4.2.6.5
insufficiency, 10.4.2.6.7
item, 10.2.2.4
judicial lien, 10.4.2.3
larceny, 15.4.3.4
liquidated debt, 12.2.3.2
luxury goods or services, 12.3.4.4.5, 15.4.3.2.3.2
median family income, 13.4.3.3
modify, 11.6.1
no-asset case, 3.1
primarily, 13.4.2
principal residence, 11.6.1.2.2.6
proceedings, 1.4.2, 14.2.4.1
public assistance, 10.2.2.11
purchaser, 9.4.6.7, 10.4.2.6.6
qualified education loans, 15.4.3.8.1
regular annual income, 17.2.2.2
return, 15.4.3.1.1
secured debt, 12.2.3.1
security interest, 10.4.2.6.4.3, 11.6.1.2.2.6
substantially contemporaneous, 10.4.2.6.4.2
transfer, 9.4.6.7, 10.4.2.1, 10.4.2.6.6
undue hardship, 15.4.3.8.2.2
unexpired lease, 7.3.7.4
unliquidated debt, 7.3.7.3
value, 10.4.2.6.5

DEPENDENTS
exemption claims
 exemption planning, 10.4.1
 filing deadline, 10.3.1
IRS definition, 13.4.5.2.1
means test deduction, 13.4.5.2.1, 13.4.5.3.6

DISABILITY BENEFITS
see also BENEFITS REPLACING WAGES
federal exemption, 10.2.2.11

DISABLED PERSONS
credit counseling, waiver of requirement, 3.2.1.4
financial management course, waiver, 8.3.3
support expenses, means test deduction, 13.4.5.3.6
veterans, means test exemption, 13.4.4

DISASTER SITUATIONS
federal farm programs, 17.1.4.4.2

DISCHARGE INJUNCTION
enforcement of discharge, 15.5.1.4, 15.5.5.7
incorrect crediting of payments as violation, 14.4.3.4.8

DISCHARGE OF DEBTS IN BANKRUPTCY
see also DISCHARGEABILITY
bars to
 chapter 13, 4.2.1.5
 dishonesty, 15.2.2.4
 excepted debts, 15.4
 failure to complete financial management course, 8.3.3, 15.2.2.11
 failure to explain loss or deficiency, 15.2.2.5
 failure to pay support obligations, 12.3.6.3, 17.5.8
 fraud, 15.4.3.2, 15.4.3.4
 intentional concealment, 15.2.2.2
 non-individuals, 15.2.2.1
 prior discharge, 12.10.1, 15.2.2.8, 15.2.2.9
 prohibited acts in another case, 15.2.2.7
 refusal to obey court orders, 15.2.2.6
 unjustified failure to keep books or records, 15.2.2.3
chapter 7
 denial, effect, 15.2.1
 discharge order, 8.8.1
 distinguishing from chapter 13, 12.10.2
 forms, Appx. E.8.1, Appx. E.8.2
 hearing, 3.6, 8.8.3
 notice of discharge, 3.6
 objections, grounds, 15.2.2
 postpetition debts, 4.7.4, 13.7.2
 prior discharge, effect, 12.10.1
 requirements, meeting, 3.2.1.3
 scope, 3.6
chapter 12
 forms, Appx. E.8.5, Appx. E.8.6
 hardship discharge, 17.7.2
 objections to, 17.4.5
 revocation, 17.7.3
 scope, 17.4.5, 17.7.1
chapter 13
 consumers as creditors, 18.5.4.3
 distinguishing from chapter 7, 12.10.2
 forms, Appx. E.8.3, Appx. E.8.4
 hardship discharge, 4.7.2, 8.7.5.3
 hearing, 4.8, 8.8.3
 notice of discharge, 4.8
 postpetition claims, 4.6, 8.7.2
 prior discharges, effect, 12.10
 priority unsecured debts, 12.3.6.1
 reopening after, 4.8
 revocation, 4.8
 right to, 4.2.1.5, 4.8
 scope, 4.8
 support obligations, 12.3.6.1, 12.3.6.3
 tax debts, 12.3.6.1, 12.3.6.2
client handout, Appx. K.3
corporate or partnership debtors, 18.5.4.4
criminal penalties, 15.4.3.7, 15.4.3.12

delay due to presumption of undue hardship, 15.5.2.4
delay to determine homestead exemption, 10.2.3.4.5.6, 15.2.2.12
denial prior bankruptcy, effect, 15.4.3.10
domestic support obligations, 15.4.3.5
drivers' licenses, return after, 15.5.5.1
effect on discharged claims, 15.5.1
enforcement of discharge, 15.5.5.7
exceptions to discharge, *see* DISCHARGEABILITY
exempt property, protection after, 10.5
fines and penalties, 15.4.3.7, 15.5.5.5
hardship discharge
 chapter 12, 17.7.2
 chapter 13, 4.7.2, 8.7.5.3
 exceptions, 15.4.1
 student loans, 15.4.3.8.2.2, 15.4.3.8.3
hearings
 attendance of debtor, 8.8.1
 chapter 7, 3.6
 chapter 13, 4.8
 circumstances, 8.8.1
 discretionary nature, 1.1.2.3, 8.8.1
 procedure at, 8.8.3
 reaffirmation of debt, 3.6, 8.8.2
incorrect crediting of payments as violation of, 14.4.3.4.8
injunctive enforcement, *see* DISCHARGE INJUNCTION
listing of debts, requirement, 7.3.7.3
objections in chapter 7 cases, 15.2
 grounds, 15.2.2
 how they arise, 15.2.1
 voluntary dismissal, 15.2.1
order for, 8.8.1
 forms, Appx. E.8
 Official Form 18, Appx. D.3
overview, 8.8.1
parking tickets, 15.4.3.7
personal financial management course prerequisite, 8.3.3
postpetition debts, 4.6, 4.7.4, 8.7.2, 13.7.2
presumption in favor, elimination, 13.4.7.3
prior discharges, effect, 12.10, 15.2.2.8, 15.2.2.9
protections
 discrimination, 15.5.4, 15.5.5
 enforcement, 15.5.5.7
 problems regarding, 15.5.5
 reaffirmation, 15.5.2
 scope, 15.5.1
 secured debts, 15.5.3
reaffirmation after, restriction, 15.5.2.1
revocation, grounds, 15.3
selected provisions, Appx. A.3
steps after discharge, 8.9
student loans, 15.4.3.8
tax claims, 6.5.3.4, 7.3.7.3.3, 12.3.6.1
tax consequences, 15.5.5.6
unsecured debts, advantage of bankruptcy, 6.2.1.1
written waiver, 15.2.2.10

707

DISCHARGEABILITY
see also DISCHARGE OF DEBTS IN BANKRUPTCY
chapter 7, 3.6
chapter 12, 17.4.5
chapter 13, 4.8
chapter 13 differences, 15.4.1
collateral estoppel, application, 15.4.4
condominium fees, 15.4.3.15
consumers as creditors
   chapter 13, 18.5.4.3
   chapters 7, 11, and 12, 18.5.4.2
   claims, 18.2.1, 18.5.4.1
   corporate or partnership debtors, 18.5.4.4
criminal fines, 15.4.3.7
criminal restitution, 15.4.3.12
debts incurred through fraud, 15.4.3.2
debts not listed or scheduled, 15.4.3.3
determination
   complaints by creditor, 8.3.10, 15.4
   complaints by debtor, 8.3.8
   forum, 15.4.2, 15.4.4
   jurisdiction, 15.4.4
   raising issue, time, 15.4.2
domestic support obligations, 15.4.3.5
drunk driving debts, 15.4.3.9
embezzled funds, 15.4.3.4
federal depository responsibilities, 15.4.3.11
federal tax paid by credit card, 15.4.3.13
fiduciaries committing fraud, 15.4.3.4
fines and penalties, 15.4.3.7
   election law fines, 15.4.3.13
fraudulently incurred debts, 15.4.3.2, 15.4.3.4
governmental units, support debts, 15.4.3.5.2
home owner association fees, 15.4.3.15
larcenous funds, 15.4.3.4
marital property settlements, 15.4.3.5.3, 15.4.3.14
military retention bonuses, 15.4.3.19
pension loans, 15.4.3.17
prior bankruptcy debts, 15.4.3.10, 15.4.3.20
prisoner litigation, costs and fees, 15.4.3.16
public benefit debts, 15.5.5.4
public benefit overpayments, 15.4.3.2.3.3
res judicata, application, 15.4.3.20, 15.4.4
restitution obligations, 9.4.6.2, 15.4.3.12
securities violation debts, 15.4.3.18
student loans, 15.4.3.8
   undue hardship test, 15.4.3.8.2.2
taxes, 6.5.3.4, 15.4.3.1, 15.4.3.13
willful and malicious injury, 15.4.3.6

DISCLOSURES
attorney compensation, 7.2.1, 7.3.13.2
   form, Appx. E.4
bankruptcy petition preparers, 16.8.3.4
   compensation disclosure, 7.3.13.2, Appx. E.9
debt relief agencies, 16.8.3
   advertisements, 16.8.5
reaffirmation agreements, 15.5.2.2, 15.5.2.5

DISCOVERY
automatic stay, effect, 9.4.2, 18.9.2
automatic stay relief
   expedited discovery, 9.7.3.3.2
   generally, 9.7.3.1.2
   valuation issues, 9.7.3.3.1
mortgage overcharges, 14.4.3.4.1
valuation issues
   equity in property, 9.7.3.3.1
   secured claims, 11.2.2.1

DISCRIMINATION
bankruptcy regarding, protections, 6.2.2.4, 15.5.4, 15.5.5

DISMISSAL OF CASE
attorney fees and costs, 16.7.2.1
chapter 7
   abuse of provisions, 3.2.1.5, 13.4
   bad faith, 13.4.7.4
   crimes, dismissal based on, 13.5
   involuntary dismissal, 13.3, 13.4
   motion to dismiss, 13.4.8
   rejection of executory contract, 13.4.7.5
   voluntary dismissal, 13.2
chapter 11, 18.7.11
chapter 12
   involuntary, 17.4.6.2
   voluntary, 17.4.6.1
chapter 13
   involuntary dismissal, 13.3
   voluntary dismissal, 4.7.5, 8.7.5.5, 13.2
effect of dismissal, 13.6
generally, 13.1
involuntary dismissal
   grounds, 13.3, 13.4, 13.5, 17.4.6.2
   motion to dismiss, 8.3.10, 13.3.1
prior case in year before petition, effect on stay, 9.3.3
voluntary dismissal, 13.2, 17.4.6.1
with prejudice, 3.2.1.2
without prejudice, 13.4.8

DISPOSABLE INCOME
see also ABILITY TO PAY TEST; INCOME
chapter 12 plans, 17.5.5.3
chapter 13 plans, 7.3.12.3, 12.3.4.4
   deduction of administrative expenses, 12.3.4.4.4
   exclusions, 12.3.4.4.2
current monthly income, see CURRENT MONTHLY INCOME
defined, 7.3.12.3, 12.3.4.1
means test formula, 12.3.4.4.3, 13.4.5
Official Form 22C, Appx. D.2
projected disposable income, 12.3.4.4.1
refinancing proceeds, status, 12.6.6
statement of current monthly income, 7.3.9
timing petition to lower, 6.5.3.6

DISTRICT COURT
appeals from, 14.9.3
appeals to, 14.9.1

DIVIDENDS
payments to creditors, 3.5.4

DIVORCE PROCEEDINGS
see also DOMESTIC SUPPORT OBLIGATIONS; FAMILY LAW PROCEEDINGS; MARITAL PROPERTY SETTLEMENTS
attorney fees, dischargeability, 10.4.3.5.3
automatic stay exemption, 9.4.6.3
debts related to, dischargeability, 10.4.3.5
related obligations, avoidance, 10.4.2.3.1, 10.4.2.3.2, 10.4.2.6.4.2

DOCUMENTS
see also BANKRUPTCY FORMS; PRODUCTION OF DOCUMENTS
failure to provide, involuntary dismissal, 13.3.2
meeting of creditors, 8.4.2
   chapter 7, 3.4
   chapter 13, 4.4
trustee requests for, Appx. H.7

DOMESTIC SUPPORT OBLIGATIONS
see also DIVORCE PROCEEDINGS; MARITAL PROPERTY SETTLEMENTS
additional protections, 17.5.8
automatic stay, application, 9.4.6.3, 18.3.2
avoidance, 10.4.2.3.1, 10.4.2.3.2, 10.4.2.6.4.2
chapter 7 distribution, 3.5.4
chapter 12 plans, 17.5.8
   postpetition obligations, 17.4.6.2
chapter 13 certification, 4.8
   form, Appx. E.14
   prior to discharge, 8.8.1
chapter 13 classification, 12.3.6.1, 12.4.3
chapter 13, postpetition, 12.3.6.3
creditor appearance form, Appx. E.11
defined, 15.4.3.5.1, 17.5.8
dischargeability, 15.4.1, 15.4.3.5
   chapter 7, 3.6
   chapter 13, 4.8
federal exemption, 10.2.2.11
governmental institutions, rights assigned to, 15.4.3.5.2
means test deductions, 13.4.5.3.3
payments excluded from disposable income, 12.3.4.4.2.2, 12.3.4.4.2.3
property settlement distinguished, 15.4.3.5.3

DOMESTIC VIOLENCE
expenses to maintain safety from, means test deduction, 13.4.5.3.5

DONATIONS
see CHARITABLE CONTRIBUTIONS

DRIVERS' LICENSES
discharge protections, 15.5.5.1, 15.5.5.5

DRUNK DRIVING DEBTS
see IMPAIRED DRIVING DEBTS

DUE PROCESS
notice to creditors, 18.4.1

EDUCATION SAVINGS TRUSTS
bankruptcy estate, exclusion, 2.5.3
 timing considerations, 6.5.3.8
listing in schedule, 7.3.7.2.2

EDUCATIONAL EXPENSES
means test deduction, 13.4.5.3.8
reasonable expenses, 5.3.3.4

EDUCATIONAL LOANS
see HEALTH EDUCATION ASSISTANCE LOANS (HEAL); QUALIFIED EDUCATION LOANS; STUDENT LOANS

ELECTION LAW FINES
dischargeability, 15.4.3.13

ELECTRONIC FILING
bankruptcy forms, 7.1.4
 chapter 7, 3.2.2
 chapter 13, 4.2.2
 computer programs, 7.1.3, 7.1.4
 converting documents to PDF format, Appx. D.1.4.2
 overview, Appx. D.1.4.1

ELIGIBILITY CONSIDERATIONS
chapter 7, 3.2.1
chapter 12, 17.2.2
chapter 13, 4.2.1, 12.2

EMBEZZLEMENT
see also FRAUD
discharge exception, 15.4.3.4

EMERGENCY BANKRUPTCIES
see also BANKRUPTCY
procedures, 7.2.2

EMPLOYEE BENEFIT PLANS
bankruptcy estate, exclusion, 2.5.2, 10.2.2.11
contributions, priority claims, 18.7.12.2

EMPLOYEE RETIREMENT INCOME SECURITY ACT (ERISA)
see ERISA PENSION PLANS

EMPLOYER BANKRUPTCY
employee priority claims, 18.7.12.2
job retention strategies, 18.7.12.3
representing employees and other stakeholders, 18.7.12
right to intervene, 18.7.12.3.2
sale of assets
 imposing conditions, 18.7.12.3.4
 opposing, 18.7.12.3.3

EMPLOYMENT CONTRACTS
listing in schedule, 7.3.7.4

EMPLOYMENT INCOME
see also INCOME
payment advices, filing, 7.3.10

ENCUMBERED PROPERTY
see COLLATERAL; LIENS; SECURITY INTERESTS

ENTITY
definition, 9.9

EQUAL ACCESS TO JUSTICE ACT
attorney fee awards, 15.4.3.2.4, 16.5.4, 16.5.7

EQUITABLE SUBORDINATION
bankruptcy, application, 18.5.6

ERISA PENSION PLANS
see also PENSIONS
bankruptcy estate, exclusion, 2.5.2, 10.2.2.11

ESCROW OVERCHARGES
bankruptcy monitoring fees, 14.4.3.4.5
objecting to, 14.4.3.4.2

ESSENTIAL SERVICES
see UTILITY SERVICES

ESTATE
see BANKRUPTCY ESTATE

ESTOPPEL
unlisted causes of action, 14.3.2.6.3

EVICTIONS
see also RESIDENTIAL TENANCIES; UNEXPIRED LEASES
automatic stay
 effect, 9.4.3
 exceptions to stay, 9.4.6.6
 special problems, 9.7.3.2.4
 timing the petition, 6.5.3.7
landlord bankruptcy, preventing, 18.3.4, 18.8.4
petition preparers, misleading advertising, 16.6
prepetition judgments, 9.4.6.6.2, 9.7.3.2.4, 12.9.2

EXAMINATION OF DEBTOR
audits, 8.3.15.1
chapter 7, 3.4
 awareness of bankruptcy information sheet, 8.4.5
chapter 13, 4.4
meeting of creditors, 1.1.2.4, 8.4.3, 8.4.5
Rule 2004 examinations, *see* RULE 2004 EXAMINATIONS

EXAMINERS
chapter 11, appointment, 18.7.4.6, 18.7.4.7

EXECUTORS
see PERSONAL REPRESENTATIVES

EXECUTORY CONTRACTS
adequate assurance, 12.9.2
chapter 12
 assumption, 17.4.7
 provisions, 17.5.9
chapter 13 plans, 12.9
 assumption, 12.9.2
 classification, 12.4.3
 procedure and tactics, 12.9.4
 rejection, 12.9.3.1, 12.9.3.3
definition, 12.9.1

federal farm programs, 17.4.7.2
installment land contracts, 17.4.7.3
listing
 filing of list, 7.3.4
 schedule, Sch. G, 7.3.7.4
personal services, abusive rejection, 13.4.7.5

EXEMPT PROPERTY
automatic allowance, 10.3.4
avoidance of transfers, 10.4.2
 see also AVOIDANCE OF LIENS AND TRANSFERS
choice of state or federal exemptions, 10.2.1
conversion, effect, 13.7.3
cost of living adjustments, 10.2.2.1
definition, 10.1.2
dependent claims, 10.3.1, 10.4.1
determination date, 10.1.2, 10.3.3
discharge protections, 10.5, 15.5.1.2
earned tax credits, 2.5.5
education savings accounts, 2.5.3
employee benefit plans, 2.5.2
family farmers, 17.4.3
federal exemptions
 see also FEDERAL EXEMPTIONS
 application, 10.2.1.1, 10.2.1.2
 cost of living adjustments, 10.2.2.1
 nonbankruptcy exemptions, 10.2.3
 specific exemptions, 10.2.2
 state opt out, 10.2.1.1
 wild card, 10.2.2.6
future benefits, 10.2.2.11
health aids, 10.2.2.10
homesteads, 10.2.2.2
household goods, 10.2.2.4
importance to debtor, 10.1.1
injury or loss payments, 10.2.2.12
item, definition, 10.2.2.4
jewelry, 10.2.2.5
joint filings, 10.2.1.1, 10.2.2.1, 10.2.3.1, 10.2.3.2
life insurance
 accrued value, 10.2.2.9
 matured, 10.2.2.8
listing in schedule, Sch. C, 7.3.7.2.3
livestock, 17.4.3.2
money orders, 18.5.2.1
motor vehicles, 10.2.2.3
objections, filing, 8.5, 10.3.3, 10.3.4
pawned personal property, 2.5.4
possession issues, 3.5.1, 9.9.4, 10.1.2
prebankruptcy planning, 6.5.2.2, 10.4.1, 15.2.2.2
procedure for claiming
 amending claim, 10.3.2
 initial claim, 10.1.2, 10.3.1
 Official Form 6, Sch. C, Appx. D.2
purpose of exemptions, 10.1.3
recovered by trustee, 10.4.2.5
recovery after avoidance, 10.4.2.8
retirement funds, 2.5.2, 10.2.2.13, 10.2.3.3
right of redemption, *see* RIGHT OF REDEMPTION
Schedule C, 7.3.7.2.3, Appx. D.2

EXEMPT PROPERTY (cont.)
spendthrift trusts, 2.5.2
state exemptions
see also STATE EXEMPTIONS
application, 6.5.2.2, 10.2.1.2
domiciliary requirements, 10.2.1.2
federal modification, 10.2.3.1
joint property, 10.2.3.2
property not subject to process, 10.2.3.2
retirement funds, 10.2.3.3
summaries, Appx. J
statement of intention, 7.3.11
tools of the trade, 10.2.2.7, 17.4.3.2
trust funds, 18.5.2
valuation, 10.1.2, 10.3.3
waiver, prohibition, 10.4

EXPENSES
see also FINANCIAL STATEMENTS
gathering information, 5.3.3.4
IRS local standards
housing and utilities, 13.4.5.2.5, Appx. I.2.3
transportation, 13.4.5.2.4, Appx. I.2.4
IRS National Standards
heath care expenses, 13.4.5.2.3, Appx. I.2.5
living expenses, 13.4.5.2.2, Appx. I.2.2
IRS other necessary expenses, 13.4.5.2.6
listing in schedule, Sch. J, 7.3.7.6
means test, deductions, 13.4.5.2, 13.4.5.3, Appx. I.2

FAIR CREDIT REPORTING ACT
attorney fees, 16.5.3
bankruptcy effect on credit, 6.2.2.3
discharged debts, reporting, 8.9

FAIR DEBT COLLECTION PRACTICES ACT
attorney fees, 16.5.3
debtor harassment, stopping, 6.2.1.1

FAMILY FARMERS
see FARMERS

FAMILY FISHERMEN
see FISHERMEN

FAMILY LAW PROCEEDINGS
see also CUSTODY PROCEEDINGS; DIVORCE PROCEEDINGS; DOMESTIC SUPPORT OBLIGATIONS; MARITAL PROPERTY SETTLEMENTS
attorney fees, dischargeability, 15.4.3.5.3
automatic stay exemption, 9.4.6.3, 18.3.2
debts pertaining to, dischargeability, 15.4.3.5.3

FARM BENEFITS
see FARM PROGRAMS

FARM CORPORATIONS
chapter 12 eligibility, 17.2.2.1, 17.2.2.4.5
family farmer, inclusion in definition, 17.1.2

FARM CREDIT SYSTEM (FCS)
described, 17.1.4.2

FARM EQUIPMENT
see also COLLATERAL
redemption, 17.4.3.5.5
sales free and clear, 17.4.10, 17.5.4.5
tools of the trade exemption, application, 10.2.2.7, 17.4.3.2
unexpired leases, rejection, 17.4.7.4

FARM LAND
installment contracts as executory contracts, 17.4.7.3
recovery as fraudulent transfer, 17.4.3.5.2
sales free and clear, 17.4.10, 17.5.4.5
unexpired rental agreements, assumption, 17.4.7.5

FARM PROGRAMS
basic attributes, 17.1.4.4.2
disposition of benefits through plan, 17.5.9
executory contract issues, 17.4.7.2
exemption status, 17.4.3.1
Farm Credit System, 17.1.4.2
Farm Service Agency loan programs, 17.1.4.3
security interests, dissolution, 17.4.3.4
set-offs against government claims, 17.4.4.1, 17.4.12
treatment in bankruptcy, 17.1.4.4.1

FARM SERVICE AGENCY
loan programs, 17.1.4.3

FARMERS
appointment of counsel, 17.2.3.2
bankruptcies
see also CHAPTER 12 REORGANIZATIONS (FAMILY FARMERS AND FISHERMEN)
chapter 11 problems, 17.1.3.3
chapter 12 availability, 17.2.2
chapter 13 problems, 17.1.3.2
federal farm programs, treatment, 17.1.4.4.1, 17.4.3.1
involuntary bankruptcies, protections, 17.1.2
involuntary conversions, protections, 17.1.2
benefit programs, *see* FARM BENEFITS
cash collateral, use, 17.4.8
corporations, *see* FARM CORPORATIONS
crops, security interests, 17.4.3.4
defined, 17.1.2
DIP, *see* DEBTOR-IN-POSSESSION (DIP)
disposable income, 17.5.5.3
family farmer, defined, 17.1.2, 17.2.2.4
farming operation
debts arising from, 17.2.2.4.3
defined, 17.2.2.3
income arising from, 17.2.2.4.4
new financing
approval, 17.4.9
direct payments, 17.5.7.3
plan provisions, 17.5.9

1986 legislation, selected provisions, Appx. A.4.3
partnerships, 17.2.2.1, 17.2.2.4.5
property sales free and clear, 17.4.10, 17.5.4.5
regular annual income, defined, 17.2.2.2
reorganizations
chapter 11 problems, 17.1.3.3
chapter 12, *see* CHAPTER 12 REORGANIZATIONS (FAMILY FARMERS AND FISHERMEN)
chapter 13 problems, 17.1.3.2
options, 17.1.3.1
special protections, 17.1.2, 17.1.4.1
unique nature of farm finance, 17.1.4
economic problems specific to farmers, 17.1.1.2
Farm Credit System, 17.1.4.2
Farm Service Agency loan programs, 17.1.4.3
federal farm programs, 17.1.4.4

FARMING OPERATIONS
see also FARMERS
chapter 12 eligibility, 17.2.2
corporations, 17.2.2.4.5
debt ceiling, 17.2.2.4.2
nature of debt, 17.2.2.4.3
nature of income, 17.2.2.4.4
partnerships, 17.2.2.4.5
defined, 17.2.2.3

FEDERAL AGENCIES
see also GOVERNMENTAL UNITS
Farm Credit Administration, 17.1.4.2
Farm Service Agency, 17.1.4.3

FEDERAL COURT
bankruptcy cases, access, 14.3.2.3

FEDERAL COURTS IMPROVEMENT ACT OF 2000
selected text, Appx. A.4.8

FEDERAL DEPOSITORY INSTITUTIONS
responsibilities regarding, dischargeability, 15.4.3.11

FEDERAL EXEMPTIONS
see also EXEMPT PROPERTY
application, 10.2.1.1, 10.2.1.2
choosing, 10.2.1
cost of living adjustments, 10.2.2.1
nonbankruptcy exemptions, 10.2.3
specific exemptions, 10.2.2
state opt out, 10.2.1.1
wild card, 10.2.2.6

FEDERAL FARM PROGRAMS
see FARM PROGRAMS

FEDERAL RULES OF BANKRUPTCY PROCEDURE
see also BANKRUPTCY CODE
adversary proceedings, 1.4.2
advisory committee notes, 1.5.2
amendments to, 1.4.2, 1.4.4.1

Index and Quick Reference
References are to sections

FRAUDULENT

FEDERAL RULES OF BANKRUPTCY PROCEDURE (*cont.*)
appeals, 2.4.3
contested matters, 1.4.2
conversion, 8.7.5.4
dismissal of bankruptcy, 8.7.5.5
duties of counsel, 16.7.1
generally, 1.4.2, Appx. B
hardship discharge, 8.7.5.3
lien avoidance, application, 8.3.6, 10.4.2.2
local rules, effect, 1.4.2, 1.4.4.2
military members, means testing, 1.4.2
objections to claims, application, 8.3.9
official forms, 1.4.3, 7.1.2, Appx. D
   see also OFFICIAL BANKRUPTCY FORMS
overview, 1.4.2
proceedings, 14.2.4
relief from automatic stay, 9.7.1
Rule 2004 examinations, *see* RULE 2004 EXAMINATIONS
Rule 3001, *see* RULE 3001
Rule 3002.1, *see* RULE 3002.1
Rule 9011, *see* RULE 9011
text, Appx. B
violations, 16.7.2.2

FEES
administrative fees, chapter 13, 12.3.4.4.4, 12.3.6.1
   means test deduction, 13.4.5.3.7
attorney fees, *see* ATTORNEY FEES AND COSTS
bankruptcy monitoring fees, 14.4.3.4.5
bankruptcy petition preparers, 7.3.13.2, 16.3.3, 16.6
condominium fees, *see* CONDOMINIUM OR COOPERATIVE FEES
credit counseling, 6.2.2.6
electronic public access fees, Appx. C.4
filing, *see* FILING FEES
fines and penalties, *see* FINES AND PENALTIES
home owners associations, *see* HOME OWNERS ASSOCIATION FEES
miscellaneous fees, Appx. C.3
mortgage servicer abuses, 14.4.3.4
personal financial management course, 6.2.2.6
postpetition fees
   dispute procedure, 8.7.3, 11.6.2.8.2.4
   notice requirements, 8.7.3, 11.6.2.8.2.3
trustee compensation, chapter 13, 6.2.2.6
trustee surcharge, chapter 7, 7.2.1
wage orders, validity, 12.6.1
waiver of fees, *see under* FILING FEES; WAIVER

FELONS
homestead exemption cap, 10.2.3.4.5

FIDUCIARIES
see TRUSTEES

FILING FEES
see also FEES

chapter 7, 3.2.2
   waiver, 7.3.13.4, 14.6.2.1, Appx. H.6
chapter 12, 17.2.3.3, 14.6.2.2
chapter 13, 4.2.2, 14.6.2.2
generally, 6.2.2.6, 7.2.1
in forma pauperis filings, 14.6
   bankruptcy court, powers, 14.6.2, 18.6.2
   consumers as creditors, 18.6
   general principles, 14.6.1
installment payments
   application for, 7.2.1, 7.3.13.3
   attorney fees, effect, 7.3.13.3, 16.2.3
   Official Form 3A, Appx. D.2
   rejected waiver applications, 7.3.13.4
noticing fee, 7.2.1
trustee compensation, 6.2.2.6, 7.2.1
waiver, 6.2.2.6, 14.6
   application for, 7.2.1, 7.3.13.4
   bankruptcy court, powers, 14.6.2, 18.6.2
   chapter 7, 3.2.2, 14.6.2.1
   chapter 12, 14.6.2.2, 17.2.3.3
   chapter 13, 4.2.2, 14.6.2.2
   consumer as creditor, 18.6.2
   general principles, 14.6.1
   Official Form 3B, Appx. D.2
   statutory authority, 14.6.2

FINANCE COMPANY LOANS
bankruptcy of lender, *see* LENDER BANKRUPTCIES
personal property collateral, 5.3.3.3

FINANCIAL MANAGEMENT COURSE
see PERSONAL FINANCIAL MANAGEMENT COURSE

FINANCIAL STATEMENTS
chapter 13, annual filing, 8.3.5
false use, discharge bar, 15.4.3.2.2
statement of financial affairs, *see* STATEMENT OF FINANCIAL AFFAIRS

FINANCING
chapter 12 plans
   approval, 17.4.9
   direct payments, 17.5.7.3
   plan provisions, 17.5.9
chapter 13 cases, refinancing during, 12.6.6

FINES AND PENALTIES
see also RESTITUTION DEBTS
Bankruptcy Rule 9011 violations, 16.7.2.2
discharge protections, 15.5.5.5
dischargeability, 15.4.3.7
   chapter 13, 4.8
liens securing, avoidance, 10.4.2.6.8
related provisions, Appx. A.3

FIRST MEETING OF CREDITORS
see MEETING OF CREDITORS (SECTION 341(a))

FISHERMEN
appointment of counsel, 17.2.3.2
commercial fishing operation
   corporations, 17.2.2.1, 17.2.2.4.5

debts arising from, 17.2.2.4.3
defined, 17.2.2.3
income arising from, 17.2.2.4.4
partnerships, 17.2.2.1, 17.2.2.4.5
family fisherman, defined, 17.2.2.4
regular annual income, defined, 17.2.2.2
reorganizations
   see also CHAPTER 12 REORGANIZATIONS (FAMILY FARMERS AND FISHERMEN)
   chapter 12 eligibility, 17.2.2

FORECLOSURE
automatic stay, effect, 8.3.1, 9.4.2, 9.4.3
   repeat filers, 9.3.3.6, 9.4.6.5.1
avoidance of transfers, 10.4.2.6.5
bankrupt lenders, 18.9.2
capital gains liability, 11.3.4
chapter 13 filing to prevent, 6.3.3
discharge, after, validity, 15.5.3
escrow overcharges, 14.4.3.4.2
fraudulent transfer status, 10.4.2.6.5
   farm land, 17.4.3.5.2
notice of filing to forestall, 8.3.1
right to cure after, 11.6.2.2

FORMA PAUPERIS
see IN FORMA PAUPERIS

FORMS
see BANKRUPTCY FORMS

FORUM
bringing matters before bankruptcy forum, 14.4
discharge protections, enforcement, 15.5.5.7
dischargeability determinations, 15.4.2, 15.4.4

FRAUD
see also EMBEZZLEMENT; LARCENY
confirmation revocation
   chapter 12 plans, 17.8.3
   chapter 13 plans, 4.5
credit card fraud, Rule 2004 examinations, 8.3.15.2
credit use with no intent to pay, 15.4.3.2.3.2
discharge bar
   claims based on, 18.5.4.2.1
   debts incurred through, 15.4.3.2
   fiduciary fraud, 15.4.3.4
   intentional concealment, 15.2.2.2
   prohibited acts in another case, 15.2.2.7
discharge revocation, 15.3
luxury goods or services within 60 days, 6.5.2.1, 15.4.3.2.3.2
spouse or agent, liability of debtor, 15.4.3.2.2.2

FRAUDULENT CONVERSION
nonexempt property into exempt property, 10.2.3.4.3

FRAUDULENT TRANSFERS
avoidance
   chapter 11, 18.7.6
   generally, 10.4.2.6.2, 10.4.2.6.5

711

FRAUDULENT TRANSFERS (*cont.*)
charitable donations, status, 1.1.2.6,
　10.4.2.6.2, 10.4.2.6.5
discharge bar, circumstances, 15.2.2.2
exemption planning not, 6.5.2.2, 15.2.2.2
farm land, foreclosed, recapture, 17.4.3.5.2
gambling losses, status, 10.4.2.6.5
prebankruptcy transfers, 6.5.2.1

GAMBLING LOSSES
avoidance status, 10.4.2.6.5

GARNISHMENTS
see WAGE GARNISHMENTS

GIFTS
reasonable expenses, 5.3.3.4

GOOD FAITH TEST
ability to pay, 13.4.7.1, 13.4.7.4
automatic stay extension where prior case
　dismissal, 9.3.3.2.2
chapter 12, 17.5.7.1
chapter 13, 12.3.3, 12.3.5
presumption of not good faith, 9.3.3.2.2
　overcoming, 9.3.3.2.3

GOVERNMENT BENEFITS
see FARM PROGRAMS; PUBLIC
　BENEFITS

GOVERNMENT CLAIMS
allowed secured claims, 11.2.1.1
automatic stay, 9.4.4
chapter 12 reorganizations, setoff rights,
　17.4.12
proof of claim, filing, time, 14.4.3.2
register of addresses, 7.3.7.3.1
sovereign immunity
　abrogation, 9.6.6, 14.3.2.2
　stripdown, effect, 11.2.1.1
support obligations, 15.4.3.5.2
tax claims, *see* TAX CLAIMS

GOVERNMENTAL UNITS
address register, 7.3.7.3.1
automatic stay violations, 9.6.6
bankruptcy filing, notification, 7.3.7.3
claims by, *see* GOVERNMENT CLAIMS
discrimination by, prohibited, 6.2.2.4, 15.5.4
fee awards against, 16.5.7
raising claims on behalf of consumers,
　18.5.4.2.1
sovereign immunity, abrogation, 9.6.6,
　14.3.2.2
support obligations owed to, dischargeability, 15.4.3.5.2
utilities as, 9.8.2.2.5

GUARANTORS
see COSIGNERS

GUARDIANS
bankruptcy petitions, filing, 3.2.1.1

GUIDE TO SURVIVING DEBT (NCLC)
counseling consumer debtors, 6.1.2

HABEAS CORPUS
bankruptcy court, powers, 14.4.5
incarcerated debtors, 14.4.5, 15.5.5.7

HARASSMENT BY CREDITORS
notice of automatic stay, 8.3.1
restrictions, 6.2.1.1

HARDSHIP DISCHARGE
see also DISCHARGE OF DEBTS IN
　BANKRUPTCY
chapter 12, 17.7.2
chapter 13, 4.7.2, 8.7.5.3
exceptions, 15.4.1
HEAL debts, 15.4.3.8.6

HEALTH AIDS
federal exemption, 10.2.2.10
non-purchase money liens, avoidance,
　10.4.2.4, 10.4.2.10

HEALTH CARE BUSINESSES
bankruptcies, patient protections, 18.10

HEALTH CARE EXPENSES
IRS National Standards, 13.4.5.2.3, Appx.
　I.2.5

**HEALTH EDUCATION ASSISTANCE
　LOANS (HEAL)**
see also STUDENT LOANS
dischargeability, 15.4.3.8.6, 15.4.3.20

HEALTH INSURANCE
chapter 13 plans, modification to purchase,
　4.6, 12.3.4.5
means test deduction, 13.4.5.3.4

HEARINGS
abandonment of property, 11.3.3
automatic stay relief
　continuation, 9.7.3.3.2
　right to, 9.7.1
　time limits, 9.7.2
chapter 12 plans
　confirmation, 17.5.2
　postconfirmation modifications, 17.8.1
　revocation of confirmation, 17.8.3
chapter 13 eligibility, determination,
　12.2.3.3
confirmation hearings
　attendance, 8.6
　chapter 12, 17.5.2
　chapter 13, 4.5, 8.6
discharge hearing
　attendance, 8.8.1
　chapter 7, 3.6
　chapter 13, 4.8
　discretionary nature, 1.1.2.3, 8.8.1
　procedure at, 8.8.3
　reaffirmation of debt, 8.8.2
disposition by trustee, 11.3.4
objections to exemptions, 8.5, 10.3.3

**HOME AFFORDABLE
　MODIFICATION PROGRAM
　(HAMP)**
voluntary loan modification, 11.6.1.5

HOME OFFICE EQUIPMENT
tools of the trade exemption, 10.2.2.7

HOME OWNERS ASSOCIATION FEES
dischargeability, 15.4.3.15

HOMESTEAD EXEMPTION
see also PRINCIPAL RESIDENCE
chapter 13 discharge, statement prior to,
　8.8.1
discharge delay to determine, 10.2.3.4.5.6,
　15.2.2.12
exemption pourover, 10.2.2.6
federal exemption, 10.2.2.2
limitations on, 10.2.3.4
listing in schedule, 7.3.7.2.3
objections, time, 10.3.3
state exemptions, 6.5.2.2, 10.2.3.4

HOUSEHOLD GOODS
see also JEWELRY; PERSONAL
　PROPERTY
definition, 10.4.2.4
federal exemption, 10.2.2.4, 10.2.2.6
luxury goods, *see* LUXURY GOODS OR
　SERVICES
means test expense deduction, 13.4.5.2.2
　IRS standards, Appx. I.2.2
non-purchase money liens, avoidance,
　10.4.2.4, 10.4.2.10
right of redemption, use, 11.5.5
valuation, 11.2.2.3.3
　date, 11.2.2.2.2
　replacement value, 11.2.2.3.1

HOUSING
see also RESIDENTIAL TENANCIES
discharge protections, 15.5.5.3
means test expense deduction, 13.4.5.2.5
　IRS standards, Appx. I.2.3

IDENTIFICATION
debtors at meeting of creditors, 8.4.2, 8.4.3

IMPAIRED DRIVING DEBTS
see also PERSONAL INJURY CLAIMS;
　WRONGFUL DEATH CLAIMS
dischargeability, 15.4.1, 15.4.3.6, 15.4.3.9

IMPRISONMENT
debtors, habeas corpus, 14.4.5, 15.5.5.7
discharged debts, protections, 15.5.5.5

IN FORMA PAUPERIS
consumers as creditors, 18.6
　need to proceed as, 18.6.1
　seeking relief, 18.6.2
debtors proceeding as, 14.6
prisoner litigation, 15.4.3.16
waiver of filing fees, 6.2.2.6, 14.6, 18.6.2
　general principles, 14.6.1
　Official Form 3B, 7.2.1, 7.3.13.4, Appx.
　　D.2
　statutory authority, 14.6.2

***IN REM* ORDERS**
automatic stay relief, 9.4.6.5.2, 9.7.3.1.5

INCAPACITATED PERSONS
credit counseling, waiver, 3.2.1.4
financial management course, waiver, 8.3.3

INCOME
see also DISPOSABLE INCOME
chapter 7, abuse of provisions, 13.4
chapter 12 plans
 disposable income, 17.5.5.3
 eligibility, 6.2.2.3
chapter 13 plans
 disposable income, 7.3.12.3
 annual statement of income and expenses, 8.3.5
 submission to trustee, 7.3.12.3, 12.6.1
current monthly income, see CURRENT MONTHLY INCOME
definition, 13.4.3.2.8
expenses, 5.3.3.4, 13.4.5.2, 13.4.5.3
family farmers and fishermen
 arising from operation, 17.2.2.4.4
 regular annual income, 17.2.2.2
listing in schedule, Sch. I, 7.3.7.6
payment advices, filing, 7.3.10
statements
 see also FINANCIAL STATEMENTS
 current monthly income, 7.3.9, 13.4.3.2.1
 financial affairs, 7.3.8

INCOME TAX CREDITS
see TAX CREDITS

INCOME TAX REFUNDS
see TAX REFUNDS

INCOME TAX RETURNS
see TAX RETURNS

INCOMPETENT PERSONS
bankruptcy filings
 chapter 7, 3.2.1.1
 chapter 13, 4.2.1.1

INDEPENDENT PARALEGALS
see BANKRUPTCY PETITION PREPARERS; NON-ATTORNEYS

INDIAN TRIBAL LAW
exemptions, 10.2.3.1

INDIVIDUAL RETIREMENT ACCOUNTS (IRAs)
see also PENSIONS
bankruptcy estate, exclusion, 2.5.2
federal exemption, 10.2.2.13.1
 cap, 10.2.2.13.3
withdrawals, income treatment, 13.4.3.2.6

INDIVIDUAL WITH REGULAR INCOME
definition, 4.2.1.2, 12.2.2

INFANTS
see MINORS

INHERITANCES
bankruptcy estate, inclusion, 8.2

INJUNCTIVE RELIEF
automatic stay, enforcement, 9.6.5

bankruptcy petition preparers, against, 16.6
chapter 11 plan provisions providing, 18.9.5
discharge protections, see DISCHARGE INJUNCTION
proceeding not covered by automatic stay, 9.4.7

INJURY
personal injury claims, see PERSONAL INJURY CLAIMS
willful and malicious, dischargeability, 15.4.3.6

INSTALLMENT LAND CONTRACTS
executory contract issues, 17.4.7.3

INSURANCE
see also CREDIT INSURANCE; LIFE INSURANCE
gathering information regarding
 assets, 5.3.3.2
 expenses, 5.3.3.4
personal property, proof in chapter 13 cases, 8.3.13, 12.8.4

INTEREST OVERCHARGES
objecting to, 14.4.3.4.3

INTEREST PAYMENTS
allowed secured claims, 11.6.1.3.3.6
chapter 12 plans, 17.5.4.3
chapter 13 plans, 12.6.2
long-term debts, right to cure, 11.6.2.7.2

INTERNAL REVENUE SERVICE
see also GOVERNMENTAL UNITS
automatic stay, 9.4.4, 9.5
living expense standards, 7.3.9, 13.4.5.2, Appx. I.2
practice aids, Appx. H
tax claims, see TAX CLAIMS
tax refunds, see TAX REFUNDS
transcripts from, 15.4.3.1.2, Appx. H.2

INTERNET RESOURCES
see WEB RESOURCES

INVOLUNTARY BANKRUPTCIES
see also BANKRUPTCY
consumers as creditors, 18.2.2
farmers, restrictions, 17.1.2
frivolous petitions, protections, 14.8
generally, 14.8

***IPSO FACTO* CLAUSES**
see BANKRUPTCY CLAUSES

JEWELRY
see also HOUSEHOLD GOODS; LUXURY GOODS OR SERVICES; PERSONAL PROPERTY
federal exemption, 10.2.2.5
non-purchase money liens, avoidance, 10.4.2.4, 10.4.2.10

JOINT BANKRUPTCIES
see also BANKRUPTCY; CODEBTORS; SPOUSES
advantages, 6.4

attorney fees, 16.2.2
chapter 12 reorganizations
 debt ceiling, 17.2.2.4.2
 exempt property, 17.4.3.1
 filings, generally, 17.2.2.5
consolidation of cases, 6.4
current monthly income, 13.4.3.2.3
exempt property, 10.2.1.1, 10.2.2.1, 10.2.3.1, 10.2.3.2
 homestead caps, application, 10.2.3.4.5.7
federal exemptions, 10.2.2.1
filing costs, 6.4
financial management course, 8.3.3
involuntary, validity, 14.8
prior individual filings, effect, 9.3.3.2.1, 9.3.3.3
schedules, filing, 7.3.7.3, 7.3.7.6
statement of financial affairs, 7.3.8
substantive consolidation, differences, 6.4

JOINT PROPERTY
see also SPOUSES
automatic stay, effect, 9.4.3
discharge, effect on, 15.5.1.4
distribution of community property, 3.5.4
effect of bankruptcy, 2.5
exemption provisions
 application, 10.2.1.1, 10.2.2.1
 homestead exemption,, 10.2.2.2
 state exemptions, 10.2.3.2
joint filings, see JOINT BANKRUPTCIES
judicial liens, avoidance, 10.4.2.3.3
listing in schedules, 7.3.7.2.1

JUDGMENTS
see also JUDICIAL LIENS
consumers as creditors, 18.2.1, 18.2.2
discharge, effect on, 15.5.1.3
landlords, prepetition
 chapter 13 plan confirmation, effect, 12.9.2
stay exemption, 9.4.6.6.2, 9.7.3.2.4

JUDICIAL ESTOPPEL
unscheduled claims, 14.3.2.6.3

JUDICIAL IMPROVEMENTS ACT OF 1990
selected provisions, Appx. A.4.5

JUDICIAL LIENS
see also JUDGMENTS; LIENS
avoidance
 divorce related liens, 10.4.2.3.1, 10.4.2.3.2
 exempt property, 10.4.2.3, 10.4.2.10
 extent of power to avoid, 10.4.2.3.1
 family farmers, 17.4.3.3, 17.4.3.5
 joint property, 10.4.2.3.3
 judgments, 15.5.1.3
 limitations on, 10.4.2.3.2
chapter 13 cramdown, application, 11.6.1.2.2.6
definition, 10.4.2.3.1

JUDICIAL SALES
fraudulent transfer status, 10.4.2.6.5

JURISDICTION
abstention, 14.5.1
automatic stay
  relief from stay, 9.7.1
  violations, 9.6.5
bankruptcy court, 2.4.2, 14.2
bringing matters before bankruptcy forum, 14.4
constitutionality, 14.2.1
contempt powers, 14.2.8
core and non-core proceedings, 14.2.4.2
counterclaims, 14.2.1, 14.2.4.2
discharge protections, enforcement, 15.5.5.7
dischargeability issues, 15.4.4
district court, 14.2.2
generally, 14.1
history, 14.2.1
in personam jurisdiction, 14.3.2.1
jury trials, 14.2.7
personal injury claims, 14.2.6
referral to bankruptcy court, 14.2.2
related proceedings, 14.2.1
withdrawal to district court, 14.2.5
wrongful death claims, 14.2.6

JURY TRIALS
bankruptcy court, 14.2.7

LAND INSTALLMENT SALES
as executory contract, 12.9.1
right to cure, *see* RIGHT TO CURE

LANDLORD BANKRUPTCIES
see also CONSUMERS AS CREDITORS
eviction proceedings, counterclaims, 18.3.4
special problems, 18.8

LANDLORD-TENANT PROCEEDINGS
see EVICTIONS

LARCENY
see also FRAUD
discharge exception, 15.4.3.4

LATE CHARGE ABUSES
postpetition payments, 14.4.3.4.4

LEASES
see UNEXPIRED LEASES

LEGAL PROCEEDINGS
see also ACTIONS; CIVIL PROCEEDINGS; CRIMINAL PROCEEDINGS
automatic stay, *see* AUTOMATIC STAY
bankruptcy court, removal to, 14.4.1
remand of removed actions, 14.4.1.4

LENDER BANKRUPTCIES
see also CONSUMERS AS CREDITORS
automatic stay issues, 18.9.2
generally, 18.9.1
proof of claim, filing, 18.9.4
sales of assets, 18.9.3
third party and successor releases, 18.9.5

LIABILITIES
see also CONSUMER DEBTS
gathering information regarding, 5.3.3.3, 5.3.4

LIENS
see also REPOSSESSIONS; SECURITY INTERESTS
allowed secured claims, validity, 11.2.1, 11.7
automatic stay, effect, 9.4.3
  real property of repeat filers, 9.3.3.6, 9.4.6.5
avoidance, *see* AVOIDANCE OF LIENS AND TRANSFERS
chapter 12 reorganizations
  automatic dissolution, 17.4.3.4
  avoidance, 17.4.3.3, 17.4.3.5
  replacement liens, 17.5.4.6
  sales free and clear of, 17.4.10, 17.5.4.5
chapter 13, retention until payment or discharge, 11.6.1.3.3.1
discharge, effect on, 15.5.1.3
  chapter 13, 4.8
enforcement after discharge, 3.6, 4.8, 15.5.3
exempt property, 3.5.1
government liens, *see* GOVERNMENT CLAIMS; STATUTORY LIENS
judicial liens, *see* JUDICIAL LIENS
listing as exempt in schedule, 7.3.7.2.3
listing in schedule, Sch. D, 7.3.7.3.2
modification of records after discharge, 8.9
redemption of personal property
  generally, 8.3.7.1
  statement of intentions, 7.3.11
searching to gather information, 5.3.4
statutory liens, *see* STATUTORY LIENS
truth in lending claims regarding, 14.4.4
turnover of property to trustee, *see* AUTOMATIC TURNOVER
valuation, 11.2.2.3

LIFE INSURANCE
see also INSURANCE
bankruptcy estate, inclusion, 8.2
federal exemption
  accrued value, 10.2.2.9
  dependent payments, 10.2.2.12
  unmatured, 10.2.2.8
gathering information
  reasonable expense, 5.3.3.4
  value, 5.3.3.2

LIMITATIONS
see STATUTE OF LIMITATIONS; TIME LIMITS

LIQUIDATED DEBTS
determination, 12.2.3.2

LIQUIDATION
chapter 7, *see* CHAPTER 7 LIQUIDATIONS
chapter 11, *see* CHAPTER 11 LIQUIDATIONS
chapter 13, circumstances, 12.6.5
procedures, 2.2

LITIGATION AIDS
see PRACTICE AIDS

LITIGATING IN BANKRUPTCY COURT
see also BANKRUPTCY COURT
abstention, 14.5
advantages, 14.3
appeals, *see* APPEALS
class actions, 14.7
in forma pauperis, 14.6
involuntary bankruptcy cases, 14.8
jurisdiction, *see* JURISDICTION
jury trials, 14.2.7
procedure, 14.4

"LITTLE TUCKER ACT"
sovereign immunity, application, 14.3.2.2

LIVESTOCK
tools of the trade status, 10.2.2.7, 17.4.3.2

LOAN COMPANIES
see CREDITORS; LENDER BANKRUPTCIES

LONG-TERM DEBTS
see also CONSUMER DEBTS; MORTGAGES
chapter 13 plans, right to cure, 11.6.2, 15.4.1

LUXURY GOODS OR SERVICES
see also JEWELRY
ability to pay test, application, 12.3.4.4.5
defined, 12.3.4.4.5, 15.4.3.2.3.2
prebankruptcy transfers, 6.5.2.1, 15.4.3.2.3.2

MAILING MATRIX
filing requirements, 7.2.1, 15.4.3.3
form, 7.3.4
list of creditors
  chapter 7, 3.2.2
  chapter 13, 4.2.2

MAINTENANCE
see DOMESTIC SUPPORT OBLIGATIONS

MARITAL PROPERTY SETTLEMENTS
see also DIVORCE PROCEEDINGS; FAMILY LAW PROCEEDINGS
bankruptcy estate, inclusion, 8.2
constructive trusts, 18.5.2.2
dischargeability, 15.4.3.5.3, 15.4.3.14
support payments distinguished, 15.4.3.5.3

MARRIED COUPLES
see JOINT BANKRUPTCIES; JOINT PROPERTY; SPOUSES; SUBSTANTIVE CONSOLIDATION

MATRIX (MAILING LABELS)
see MAILING MATRIX

MEANS TEST
see also ABUSE OF CHAPTER 7
ability to pay, effect, 13.4.7.4
data, Appx. I

Index and Quick Reference

References are to sections

MEANS TEST (*cont.*)
formula, 13.4.5
　application of formula, 13.4.6
　deduction of IRS expense allowances, 13.4.5.2, Appx. I.2
　deduction of other expenses, 13.4.5.3
Official Form 22A, Appx. D.2
presumption of abuse, 3.2.1.5, 13.4.6
procedures, 13.4.8
safe harbor
　disabled veterans, 13.4.4
　incomes below threshold, 13.4.3, 13.4.7.1
　military reservists, 13.4.4
statement of current monthly income, 7.3.9, 13.4.3.2.1
timing of petition, 6.5.3.6

MEDICAL AIDS
see HEALTH AIDS

MEDICAL DEBTS
see also CONSUMER DEBTS
bankruptcy, effect, 6.2.2.4.2
further debt, anticipation, 6.5.3.1

MEDICAL EXPENSES
see HEALTH CARE EXPENSES

MEETING OF CREDITORS (SECTION 341(a))
adjournments, 10.3.4
advice to clients, 8.2, 8.4.1
attendance, 8.4.3
　creditors seeking reaffirmation, 8.4.4
chapter 7 bankruptcies
　after meeting, 3.5, 8.5
　examination of debtor, 8.4.5
　notice, 3.3
　procedures, 3.4
chapter 12 bankruptcies, 17.2.5
chapter 13 bankruptcies
　notice, 4.3
　procedures, 4.4
claims, checking, 8.4.6
disputes, resolving, 8.4.3
　chapter 7, 3.4
　chapter 13, 4.4
document requirements, 8.4.2
　chapter 7, 3.4
　chapter 13, 4.4
examination of debtor by trustee, 8.4.3
　chapter 7, 3.4, 8.4.5
　chapter 13, 4.4
events prior or after meeting, 8.3
notice, Official Form 9, Appx. D.3
preparation for, 8.4.1
procedure at, 8.4.3
　chapter 7, 3.4
　chapter 13, 4.4

MILITARY PERSONNEL
credit counseling requirement, waiver, 3.2.1.4
financial management course, waiver, 8.3.3
means test exemption, 13.4.4
statement of military service, Appx. E.12

MILITARY RETENTION BONUSES
dischargeability, 15.4.3.19

MINORS
bankruptcy filing
　chapter 7, 3.2.1.1
　chapter 13, 4.2.1.1

MOBILE HOMES
chapter 13 cramdown exemption, application, 11.6.1.2.2.6
real or personal property, 7.3.7.2.1

MODIFICATION
chapter 12 plans, *see* CHAPTER 12 PLANS (FAMILY FARMERS AND FISHERMEN)
chapter 13 plans, *see* CHAPTER 13 PLANS
cure, status as, 11.6.1.2.3
secured claims, *see* CRAMDOWN
voluntary loan modification programs, 11.6.1.5

MONEY ORDER COMPANIES
bankruptcy, effect on consumers, 18.5.2.1

MONITORING FEES
challenging, 14.4.3.4.5

MORTGAGES
see also LIENS; SECURITY INTERESTS
bankrupt lenders, 18.9
bankruptcy monitoring fees, 14.4.3.4.5
chapter 13 cramdown, application, 11.6.1
chapter 13 right to cure, 11.6.2
escrow overcharges, 14.4.3.4.2
foreclosures, *see* FORECLOSURES
holder of mortgage, determination, 9.7.3.1.1
means test deductions, 13.4.5.2.5, 13.4.5.3.2
modification, 11.6.1.2, 11.6.1.5
objecting to overcharges, 14.4.3.4
postpetition payments, 8.7.3
proof of claim, requirements, 14.4.3.4.1, 14.4.3.4.2, 14.4.3.5
refinancing during chapter 13, 12.6.6
Rule 3001 requirements, 14.4.3.4.2, 14.4.3.5
Rule 3002.1 requirements, 11.6.2.8.2, 14.4.3.4.1, 14.4.3.4.6
　final cure payment, 11.6.2.8.2.5
　payment changes, 8.7.3, 11.6.2.8.2.2
　postpetitition fees, 11.6.2.8.2.3, 11.6.2.8.2.4
securitized mortgages, 9.7.3.1.1, 14.4.3.4.7
servicer abuses, 14.4.3.4, 16.5.5
spreader clauses, 15.5.3
undisclosed fees, 14.4.3.4.6

MOTOR VEHICLES
federal exemption, 10.2.2.1, 10.2.2.3
impaired driving debts, 15.4.3.9
means test deductions
　expenses, 13.4.5.2.4
　loan payments, 13.4.5.3.2
purchase money security interests, chapter 13 treatment, 6.5.3.5, 11.6.1.4, 12.8.2.2

right of redemption, use, 11.5.5
reaffirmation agreements, 11.4.2.8, 11.5.4
"retain and pay" option, 11.4.2.8
snowmobiles, status, 15.4.3.9
title pawn transactions, 11.9
valuation, 5.3.4, 11.2.2.3.2

MUTUAL DEBTS
setoffs, 10.4.2.6.7

NATIONAL BANKRUPTCY REVIEW COMMISSION
establishment, 1.1.2.4

NATIONAL CONSUMER LAW CENTER (NCLC)
Bankruptcy Basics, guide for attorneys, 1.3.4.2
bankruptcy treatise, 1.2, 1.3
consulting service, 1.3.4.2
initial forms software, Appx. D.1.2
NCLC Guide to Surviving Debt, 6.1.2

NATIONAL DEFENSE AUTHORIZATION ACT 2000
selected provisions, Appx. A.4.7

NON-ATTORNEYS
see also BANKRUPTCY PETITION PREPARERS; DEBT RELIEF AGENCIES
fees to, disclosure, 16.3.2, 16.3.3, 16.6
role in bankruptcy case, 5.1.2, 16.6
unauthorized practice of law, 16.6

NON-CORE PROCEEDINGS
see also BANKRUPTCY PROCEEDINGS
core proceedings, distinction, 14.2.4.2, 14.2.4.3
procedures, 14.2.4.4

NON-PURCHASE MONEY SECURITY INTERESTS
see also SECURITY INTERESTS
avoidance, 10.4.2.4, 10.4.2.10

NOTICE
automatic stay
　effective notice, 9.6.3.3
　giving notice, 8.3.1, 9.5, 9.6.3.1
　requirements, 9.6.3.2
automatic turnover, 9.9.3
bankruptcy case, Official Form 9, Appx. D.3
bankruptcy petition preparers to debtor, 16.6
　Official Form 19B, Appx. D.3
clerk of bankruptcy court, available relief, 7.3.6
form, Appx. E.2
creditors, to, 14.3.2.1, 15.4.3.3
　effective notice, 9.6.3.3, 9.9.3
　mailing label matrix, *see* MATRIX (MAILING LABELS)
　Official Form 9, Appx. D.3
　reasonable efforts, 18.4.1
debt relief agencies, requirements, 16.8.3
motion or objection, Official Form 20A, Appx. D.3

715

NOTICE (*cont.*)
objection to claim, Official Form 20B, Appx. D.3
removal to bankruptcy court, 14.4.1.2

OBJECTIONS
barred claims, 14.4.3.2
chapter 7, discharge, 15.2
chapter 7, time limits, 3.3
chapter 13, time limits, 4.3
chapter 13 plans, 4.4, 8.6, 11.6.1.3.3.7, 12.3.4.2
claims by creditors, 3.5.3, 4.4, 8.3.9, 8.4.6, 14.3.2.4, 14.4.3
  Official Form 20B, Appx. D.3
exemptions claimed, 8.5, 10.3.3, 10.3.4
failure to raise, effect, 14.4.3.1
inadequate documentation, 14.4.3.4.7, 14.4.3.5
mortgage overcharges, 14.4.3.4
other objections, Official Form 20A, Appx. D.3
prepetition settlement attempts, based on, 14.4.3.6
recoupment claims, raising as, 14.3.2.4
secured claims, 11.2.2.1, 11.6.1.3.3.5
unenforceable claims, 14.4.3.3

OFFICIAL BANKRUPTCY FORMS
see also BANKRUPTCY FORMS
amendments to, 1.4.3, 1.4.4.1
annotations, Appx. D.2
bankruptcy petition preparers, information on, 16.6
chapter 12, application, 17.2.3.1
commercial forms, 7.1.2
completing, 1.3.2, 7.3.1, Appx. D.1
computer software, 7.1.3, 7.3.1, Appx. D.1.2
general principles, 7.1.1
initial forms
  amendments to, 8.3.2
  chapter 7, 3.2.2
  chapter 13, 4.2.2
  preparing, 7.3
  sample forms, Appx. D.2
obtaining, 1.4.3, 5.1.3, 7.1.2
Official Form 1 (voluntary petition), 7.3.2
  see also BANKRUPTCY PETITIONS
  annotations and completed form, Appx. D.2
Official Form 3A (filing fee by installment), 7.2.1
  annotations and completed form, Appx. D.2
Official Form 3B (waiver of filing fee), 7.3.13.4
  annotations and completed form, Appx. D.2
Official Form 6 (schedules), 7.3.7
  see also SCHEDULES
  annotations and completed form, Appx. D.2
Official Form 7 (financial affairs), 7.3.8

  see also STATEMENT OF FINANCIAL AFFAIRS
  annotations and completed form, Appx. D.2
Official Form 8 (intentions), 7.3.11
  see also STATEMENT OF INTENTION
  annotations and completed form, Appx. D.2
Official Form 21 (Social Security number), 7.3.3
  see also STATEMENT OF SOCIAL SECURITY NUMBER
  annotations and completed form, Appx. D.2
Official Form 22 (current monthly income), 7.3.9
  see also STATEMENT OF CURRENT MONTHLY INCOME
  annotations and completed form, Appx. D.2
Official Form 23 (financial management course), 8.3.3
  annotations and completed form, Appx. D.2
other Official Forms, Appx. D.3
reproducible forms, 1.4.3, 7.1.2, Appx. D, Appx. E
sample completed forms, Appx. D.2
substantial compliance, 1.4.3, 7.3.1
  computer programs, 7.1.3
  permitted alterations, Appx. D.1.3
  precise compliance not necessary, 7.3.1

OMBUDSMAN
consumer privacy ombudsman, 18.10
patient care ombudsman, 18.10

PACER SYSTEM
bankruptcy court dockets, access, 2.4.1, 5.3.4
fee schedule, Appx. C.4

PAPERS
see BANKRUPTCY FORMS

PARALEGALS
see BANKRUPTCY PETITION PREPARERS; NON-ATTORNEYS

PARKING TICKETS
dischargeability, 15.4.3.7

PARTNERSHIPS
chapter 12 eligibility, 17.2.2.1, 17.2.2.4.5
chapter 13 eligibility, 12.2.2
discharges, 15.2.2.1, 18.5.4.4

PATIENT CARE OMBUDSMAN
health care business bankruptcies, 18.10

PAUPERIS
see IN FORMA PAUPERIS

PAWNED PERSONAL PROPERTY
automatic stay, effect, 9.4.3
bankruptcy estate, exclusion, 2.5.4

PAYMENT ADVICES
filing, 7.3.10

PAYMENT PLANS
see CHAPTER 12 PLANS (FAMILY FARMERS AND FISHERMEN); CHAPTER 13 PLANS

PENALTIES
see FINES AND PENALTIES

PENSIONS
bankruptcy estate, exclusion, 2.5.2, 10.2.2.11
contributions, priority claim, 18.7.12.2
ERISA, *see* ERISA PENSION PLANS
federal exemption, 10.2.2.13
IRAs, *see* INDIVIDUAL RETIREMENT ACCOUNTS (IRAs)
listing in schedules, 7.3.7.2.2
loans from debtor's plan, repayment
  automatic stay exemption, 9.4.6.4
  dischargeability, 15.4.3.17
  disposable income exclusion, 12.3.4.4.2.4
  monthly income, exemption or inclusion, 13.4.3.2.7
Qualified Domestic Relations Order, 15.4.3.5.3
withdrawals, income treatment, 13.4.3.2.6

PERSONAL FINANCIAL MANAGEMENT COURSE
advice to clients, 8.2
approved courses, 8.3.3
certificate of completion, filing
  chapter 7, 15.2.2.11
  chapter 13, 8.8.1
  Official Form 23, Appx. D.2
  time limits, 8.3.3
cost of course, 6.2.2.6
discharge prerequisite, 8.3.3, 15.2.2.11
  chapter 7, 3.2.1.3, 3.6
  chapter 13, 4.8
requirements, 8.3.3

PERSONAL INJURY CLAIMS
bankruptcy court
  jurisdiction, 14.2.6
  mandatory abstention, application, 14.5.2
dischargeability
  drunk driving, 15.4.3.9
  generally, 15.4.3.6

PERSONAL PROPERTY
see also PROPERTY
exempt, *see* EXEMPT PROPERTY
household goods, *see* HOUSEHOLD GOODS
leases
  adequate protection, 8.3.12.2, 12.8.2.2
  chapter 7, assumption or rejection, 8.3.7.2, 12.9.5
  chapter 13, assumption or rejection, 12.9
  chapter 13 payments, 8.3.12.2, 12.8.3
  proof of insurance, 8.3.13, 12.8.4
  statement of intention, 7.3.11, 11.4
listing in schedule, Sch. B, 7.3.7.2.2
motor vehicles, *see* MOTOR VEHICLES

PERSONAL PROPERTY (*cont.*)
non-purchase money liens, avoidance, 10.4.2.4, 10.4.2.10
purchase money security interests, *see* PURCHASE MONEY SECURITY INTERESTS
right of redemption, 8.3.7.1
   see also RIGHT OF REDEMPTION
secured, *see* COLLATERAL
valuation, 7.3.7.2.2, 11.2.2.3.3
   converted cases, 13.7.2, 13.7.3
   date, 11.2.2.2.2
   replacement value, 11.2.2.3.1

PERSONAL REPRESENTATIVES
bankruptcy estate, representing, 3.2.1.1
bankruptcy petitions, filing, 3.2.1.1

PETITION PREPARERS
see BANKRUPTCY PETITION PREPARERS

PETITIONS IN BANKRUPTCY
see BANKRUPTCY PETITIONS

PLEADINGS
see also BANKRUPTCY FORMS
sample pleadings and forms, Appx. G
   computer programs, 7.1.3
   NCLC companion website, 1.3.2, 5.1.3, Appx. M

POSSESSION
creditor remedies, *see* RECLAMATION OF PROPERTY; REPOSSESSION
debtor-in-possession, *see* DEBTOR-IN-POSSESSION (DIP)
exempt property, 3.5, 10.1.2
landlords, prepetition judgment
   chapter 13 plan confirmation, effect, 12.9.2
   stay exemption, 9.4.6.6.2, 9.7.3.2.4
property of the estate
   chapter 12 plans, 17.4.2
   chapter 13 plans, 12.8.1
   retention by debtor, 8.3.11
property turned over to trustee, 9.9.4

POSTPETITION CLAIMS
chapter 13, conversion from, 4.7.4, 13.7.2
consumers as creditors, 18.5.3
discharge, 4.6, 8.7.2
   converted cases, 13.7.3
domestic support obligations, 12.3.6.3
utilities, 9.8.2.2.4

POSTPETITION FEES
Rule 3002.1
   dispute procedure, 11.6.2.8.2.4
   notice requirements, 11.6.2.8.2.3
   sanctions, 11.6.2.8.2.6

POSTPETITION TRANSACTIONS
chapter 7 conversion, inclusion, 4.7.4, 13.7.2
utility usage, 9.8.2.2.4
chapter 12 dispositions, tax liability, 17.5.5.4

chapter 13 plans
   modification, 4.6, 8.7.2
   mortgage payments, 8.7.3

POSTPETITION TRANSFERS
see also AVOIDANCE OF LIENS AND TRANSFERS
automatic stay, application, 9.4.6.7
avoidance, 10.4.2.6.6, 10.4.2.9
check, by, date of transfer, 10.4.2.6.6
definition of transfer, 9.4.6.7, 10.4.2.6.6
religious and charitable donations, 1.1.2.6, 12.3.4.4.5
setoffs, 10.4.2.6.7

POWER OF ATTORNEY
bankruptcy filing by, 3.2.1.1

PRACTICE AIDS
see also RESEARCH AIDS; WEB RESOURCES
advice after discharge, 8.9
advice after papers filed, 8.2
attorney fees, *see* ATTORNEY FEES AND COSTS
automatic stay litigation
   other tactics, 9.7.3.3.2
   stays pending appeal, 9.7.3.3.3
   valuation problems, 9.7.3.3.1
bankruptcy court advantages, 14.3
best practices, 5.1.3, Appx. H.5, Appx. H.7
chapter 7 fee waiver, 14.6.2.1, Appx. H.6
chapter 12 plans
   direct payments, 17.5.7.3
   feasibility, 17.5.7.2.2
   provisions, 17.5.9
chapter 13 plans
   successive filings, 12.10.3
   unexpired leases or executory contracts, 12.9.4
client handouts, Appx. K
client questionnaire, 5.3.2, Appx. F
computerization, 7.1.3, Appx. D.1.2
counseling the debtor, 6
   see also COUNSELING THE CONSUMER DEBTOR
   advantages and disadvantages of bankruptcy, 6.2
   choosing type of bankruptcy, 6.3
   exemption planning, 6.5.2.2
   explaining bankruptcy, 6.1.2, Appx. K
   explaining options 6.1.1
   prebankruptcy transfers, 6.5.2.1, 6.5.3.2
   spousal filing, 6.4
   timing, 6.5
   using credit wisely, Appx. K.4
date calculator, Appx. H.1
declaration concerning schedules, 7.3.7.7
delay of petition as tactic, 6.5.3.3
discharge orders, retention, 8.8.1
dischargeability complaints, 15.4.3.2.4
division of labor, 5.1.3
document production requests, Appx. H.7
electronic case filing, Appx. D.1.4
exemption claims, 10.3

exemption planning, 6.5.2.2, 10.4.1
facts and information, 5
   frequently missed info, 5.3.3
   full and accurate, need for, 5.4
   importance of getting, 5.2
   methods of gathering, 5.3
   other sources, 5.3.4
   questionnaire, 5.3.2, Appx. F
   web resources, 5.3.4
involuntary bankruptcies, generally, 14.8
landlord bankruptcy
   maintaining services, 18.8.2
   preventing abandonment, 18.8.2.2
   tenant ownership, 18.8.3
litigation advantages of bankruptcy, 6.2.1.6
meeting of creditors, 8.4
multiple cases, 7.2.3
NCLC *Bankruptcy Basics*, 1.3.4.2
NCLC bankruptcy treatise, using, 1.3, 5.1.1, 5.1.3
NCLC companion website, 1.3.2, 5.1.3, Appx. M
NCLC consulting service, 1.3.4.2
NCLC Guide to Surviving Debt, 6.1.2
NCLC web-based text search feature, 1.3.3, Appx. M.6
non-attorneys, role, 5.1.2, 5.1.3
preparing and filing papers, 7
   fees, 7.2.1
   forms, 7.2.1, 7.3
   generally, 7.1
   signing and verification, 7.4
   time considerations, 7.2
reaffirmation agreements, 15.5.2.6
sample pleadings and forms, Appx. G
   NCLC companion website, 1.3.2, 5.1.3, Appx. M
secured property, retention, 11.4.2.8, 11.5.4
subsequent to filing, 8
   administration of chapter 13 plans, 8.7
   advice to clients, 8.2
   after discharge, 8.9
   after meeting of creditors, 8.5, 8.6
   confirmation hearings, 8.6
   discharge and discharge hearing, 8.8
   events prior to meeting of creditors, 8.3
   generally, 8.1
   meeting of creditors, 8.4
tax information, interim guidance, Appx. H.3
tax returns or transcripts, obtaining, Appx. H.2
timing the petition, 6.5
United States Trustee Program, Appx. H.4
websites, helpful, Appx. L

PREBANKRUPTCY TRANSFERS
see also AVOIDANCE OF LIENS AND TRANSFERS
avoidance by debtor
   consumer as creditor, chapter 11, 18.7.6
   exempt property, principles, 10.4.2.1
   farmers, 17.4.3.5
   judicial liens, 10.4.2.3

PREBANKRUPTCY TRANSFERS (*cont.*)
avoidance by debtor (*cont.*)
   non-purchase money security interests, 10.4.2.4
   pre-Code liens, 10.4.2.10
   preferences, 10.4.2.6.4.3
   procedures, 8.3.6, 10.4.2.2
   property recovered by trustee, 10.4.2.5
   trustee's powers, use, 10.4.2.6, 10.4.2.7
avoidance by trustee
   fraudulent transfers, 10.4.2.6.5
   liens securing penalties, 10.4.2.6.8
   preferences, 10.4.2.6.4.1, 10.4.2.6.4.2
   setoffs, 10.4.2.6.7
   statutory liens, 10.4.2.6.3
   strong-arm clause, 10.4.2.6.2
   voluntary transfers, 10.4.2.6.1
avoided transfers, preservation, 10.4.2.9
cash advances, 6.5.2.1
charitable donations, 1.1.2.6, 10.4.2.6.2, 10.4.2.6.5
check, by, date of transfer, 10.4.2.6.6
definition of transfer, 10.4.2.1
discharge, denial, 15.2.2.2
exempt property, avoidance, 8.3.6
exemption planning, 6.5.2.2
fraudulent conveyances, 6.5.2.1
luxury goods or services, 6.5.2.1
preferences, 6.5.2.1, 6.5.3.2

PREFERENCES
attorney fees paid in advance, status, 16.2.3
avoidance
   chapter 11, 18.7.6
   chapter 12, 17.4.3.5.3
   exceptions, 10.4.2.6.4.2
   generally, 10.4.2.6.4.1
   prebankruptcy, 6.5.2.1, 6.5.3.2
consumers as creditors, 18.2.1
exceptions, 10.4.2.6.4.2
security interests, status, 10.4.2.6.4.2, 10.4.2.6.4.3

PRESUMPTION OF ABUSE
see also ABUSE OF CHAPTER 7
avoiding through chapter 13, 6.3.3
generally, 3.2.1.5, 13.4.6.1
incomes below threshold, 13.4.3, 13.4.7.1
means test, *see* MEANS TEST
rebutting, 13.4.6.2
statement of current monthly income, 7.3.9, 13.4.3.2.1
   determining current monthly income, 13.4.3.2
   median income test, 13.4.3.3
   timing considerations, 6.5.3.6

PRINCIPAL RESIDENCE
see also HOMESTEAD EXEMPTION; MORTGAGES
capital gains exemption, 11.3.4
chapter 13 cramdown, exemption, 11.6.1.2
defined, 11.6.1.2.2.6
right to cure default, 11.6.1.1, 11.6.1.2.3, 11.6.2

PRIOR BANKRUPTCIES
automatic stay, effect, 9.4.6.5, 9.7.3.1.5
chapter 7, 3.2.1.2, 6.2.2.8.2, 15.2.2.8, 15.2.2.9
chapter 12, 17.4.4.3
chapter 13, 4.2.1.4, 6.2.2.8.2, 12.10, 15.2.2.9
information gathering, 2.4.1, 5.3.4
in rem orders, 9.4.6.5.2, 9.7.3.1.5
prior discharges, effect, 15.2.2.8, 15.2.2.9, 15.4.3.10

PRIORITY UNSECURED CREDITORS
see also CREDITORS; UNSECURED CREDITORS
administrative expenses, 12.3.4.4.4
attorneys, fees, 16.4.1
categories, 7.3.7.3.3
chapter 12 plans
   classification, 17.5.6.3
   treatment, 17.5.5.4
chapter 13 plans, payment, 7.3.12.3, 7.3.12.5, 12.3.6
consumers as, 18.5.5, 18.7.12.2, 18.9.4
distribution to, 3.5.4
domestic support obligations, 17.5.8
employees, 18.7.12.2
listing in schedule, Sch. E, 7.3.7.3.3
means test deductions, 13.4.5.3.3
tax claims, 12.3.6.1, 15.4.3.1.2

PRISONER LITIGATION
costs and fees, dischargeability, 15.4.3.16

PRIVACY ISSUES
business bankruptcies, 18.10
income tax returns, 8.3.4.3
   disclosure by trustee, 8.3.4.1

PROBATE PROCEEDINGS
automatic stay, effect, 9.4.3

PROCEEDINGS IN BANKRUPTCY
see BANKRUPTCY PROCEEDINGS

PRODUCTION OF DOCUMENTS
best practices, Appx. H.7
meeting of creditors, 8.4.2
   chapter 7, 3.4
   chapter 13, 4.4
identification, 8.4.2, 8.4.3

PROOF OF CLAIM
see also CLAIMS BY CREDITORS
allowing, chapter 7, 3.5.3
burden of proof, 11.2.2.3.2, 14.4.3.3
consumers as creditors
   class claims, 18.4.2
   individual consumers, 18.4.1
   lender bankruptcies, 18.9.4
   trust funds, 18.5.2.1
debt buyers, 14.4.3.5
false information, 16.5.5.1, 16.5.5.2
filing, time, 3.3, 4.4, 14.4.3.2, 15.4.3.3
filing by debtor, 8.4.6
government claims, 14.4.3.2
inadequate documentation, 14.4.3.4.7, 14.4.3.5
mortgage overcharges, 14.4.3.4
Official Form 10, Appx. D.3
reasonable inquiry prior to, 16.5.5.1
securitized debt, 14.4.3.4.7, 14.4.3.5

PROPERTY
see also ASSETS; COLLATERAL; PERSONAL PROPERTY; REAL PROPERTY
abandonment by trustee, *see* ABANDONMENT OF PROPERTY
after filing, advice to clients, 8.2
automatic stay, effect, 9.4.3, 9.7.3.2.3
bankruptcy estate, *see* BANKRUPTCY ESTATE
chapter 13
   adequate protection, 12.8.2
   continued use, 12.8.1
discharge protections, 15.5.1.2
disposition by trustee, 11.3.4
exempt, *see* EXEMPT PROPERTY
gathering information, frequently missed, 5.3.3.2
harmful property, indicating on petition, 7.3.2
incidental property, defined, 11.6.1.2.2.4
joint, *see* JOINT PROPERTY
liquidation, *see* LIQUIDATION
listing in schedules, 7.3.7.2
loss in bankruptcy, 6.2.2.2
possession, *see* POSSESSION
protection from unsecured creditors, 6.2.1.2
reclamation, *see* RECLAMATION OF PROPERTY
recovery after transfer avoidance, 10.4.2.8
right of redemption, *see* RIGHT OF REDEMPTION
transfers, *see* POSTPETITION TRANSFERS; PREBANKRUPTCY TRANSFERS
turnover to trustee, *see* AUTOMATIC TURNOVER
valuation, *see* VALUATION
willful and malicious injury, dischargeability, 15.4.3.6

PROPERTY SETTLEMENTS
see MARITAL PROPERTY SETTLEMENTS

PUBLIC BENEFITS
see also BENEFITS REPLACING WAGES; FARM BENEFITS; SOCIAL SECURITY BENEFITS; WELFARE BENEFITS
discharge protections, 15.5.5.4
federal exemption, 10.2.2.11
overpayments, dischargeability, 15.4.3.2.3.3

PUBLIC UTILITIES
see UTILITY SERVICES

PUNITIVE DAMAGES
see also DAMAGES

PUNITIVE DAMAGES (*cont.*)
automatic stay violations, 9.6.2
  notice requirements, 9.6.3.3
dischargeability, 15.4.3.6, 18.5.4.2.1

PURCHASE AND SALE AGREEMENTS
pending, listing in schedule, 7.3.7.4

PURCHASE MONEY SECURITY INTERESTS
see also SECURED CREDITORS; SECURITY INTERESTS
chapter 13 filing
  adequate protection payments, 4.3, 8.3.12.2, 12.8.2.2
  proof of insurance, 8.3.13, 12.8.4
  recent purchases, 11.6.1.4
  timing considerations, 6.5.3.5

QUALIFIED EDUCATION LOANS
see also STUDENT LOANS
defined, 15.4.3.8.1
dischargeability, 15.4.3.8.1

REAFFIRMATION AGREEMENTS
see also CONSUMER DEBTS
agreement, necessity, 15.5.2.1
attorneys, validation, 15.5.2.4, 15.5.2.7
best interests test, 15.5.2.6
consequences, 8.8.2
court approval, 8.8.2, 8.8.3, 15.5.2.4, 15.5.2.6
  chapter 7, 3.6
  chapter 13, 4.8
debtors not represented by attorneys, 3.6, 8.4.4, 8.8.1, 15.5.2.4
disadvantages, 8.8.2
disclosure requirements, 15.5.2.2, 15.5.2.5
factors to be considered, 15.5.2.7
form, 15.5.2.3, 15.5.2.4, Appx. E.10
  Official Form, Appx. D.3
invalid agreements, 15.5.2.5
meeting of creditors, 8.4.4
payments, acceptance, 15.5.2.5
prepetition legal fees, 16.2.3
pressure from creditors, 8.4.4, 15.5.2.1, 15.5.2.5
protective provisions, 15.5.2.4
redemption as alternative, 11.5.5, 15.5.2.5
requirements, 15.5.2
secured debts, 11.5.4
statement of intention, 3.5, 7.3.11
student loans, 15.5.5.2
undue hardship
  presumption, 15.5.2.4
  test, 15.5.2.6

REAL ESTATE SETTLEMENT PROCEDURES ACT (RESPA)
mortgage errors
  annual escrow account review, 14.4.3.4.2
  informal discovery, 14.4.3.4.1

REAL PROPERTY
see also PROPERTY
chapter 13 cramdown

application, 11.6.1.2.1
  right to cure default, 11.6.2
chapter 13, sales under, 12.6.5
in rem orders, 9.4.6.5.2, 9.7.3.1.5
leasehold interests, *see* UNEXPIRED LEASES
lien enforcement, automatic stay exception, 9.3.3.6, 9.4.6.5
listing in schedule, Sch. A, 7.3.7.2.1
pending sale agreements, listing in schedule, 7.3.7.4
postpetition transfers, 10.4.2.6.6
security interests, *see* MORTGAGES
valuation, 5.3.4, 11.2.2.3.3
  date, 11.2.2.2.2
  timing of petition, 6.5.3.8

RECLAMATION OF PROPERTY
see also REPOSSESSION
complaints seeking, 8.3.10
family farmer plans, provision in, 17.5.9
postpetition actions by secured creditors, 11.3.2

RECORDS
claims by creditors, inadequate documentation, 14.4.3.5
failure to keep, denial of discharge, 15.2.2.3

RECOUPMENT CLAIMS
raising, 14.3.2.4
setoffs, effect, 10.4.2.6.7

REDEMPTION OF PROPERTY
see RIGHT OF REDEMPTION

REFINANCING
chapter 13 cases, during, 12.6.6

RELIEF FROM STAY
see AUTOMATIC STAY

RELIGIOUS LIBERTY AND CHARITABLE DONATION PROTECTION ACT
see also CHARITABLE CONTRIBUTIONS
donations after bankruptcy, 1.1.2.6, 12.3.4.4.5
protection for donations, 1.1.2.6, 10.4.2.6.2, 10.4.2.6.5

RENT-TO-OWN TRANSACTIONS
bankruptcy, effect, 11.8
listing in schedule, 7.3.7.2.2, 7.3.7.3.2, 7.3.7.4

REORGANIZATIONS
chapter 11, *see* CHAPTER 11 REORGANIZATIONS
chapter 12, *see* CHAPTER 12 REORGANIZATIONS (FAMILY FARMERS AND FISHERMEN)
chapter 13, *see* CHAPTER 13 REORGANIZATIONS
term of art, 2.2

REPOSSESSION
see also POSSESSION; RECLAMATION OF PROPERTY

automatic stay, effect, 9.4.3
automatic turnover, application, 9.9.2
chapter 13 filing to prevent, 6.3.3
discharge, after, validity, 15.5.3
personal property, threats, 8.4.3
postpetition by secured creditors, 11.3.2, 11.4.2.8, 11.5.4
preference, status as, 10.4.2.6.4.3

RES JUDICATA
automatic stay litigation, application, 9.7.3.1.5
chapter 12 plans, provisions minimizing, 17.5.9
chapter 13 plans, confirmation as, 9.7.3.2.2, 12.7, 12.11
claims, failure to object, effect, 14.4.3.1
dischargeability issues, 15.4.2, 15.4.3.20, 15.4.4

RESEARCH AIDS
see also PRACTICE AIDS
bibliography, Bibliography
citator, 1.5.6
computer-assisted research, 1.5.7
  NCLC companion website, 1.3.2, 5.1.3, Appx. M
  NCLC web-based text searches, 1.3.3, Appx. M.6
information gathering, 5.3.4
legislative history, 1.5.1
periodicals, 1.5.5
reporting services, 1.5.4
rules advisory committee notes, 1.5.2
sources of law, 1.4
treatises and texts, 1.5.3
  NCLC Guide to Surviving Debt, 6.1.2
  NCLC treatises, 1.3.2, 1.3.4

RESIDENTIAL TENANCIES
see also EVICTIONS; UNEXPIRED LEASES
automatic stay, application, 9.4.6.6, 9.7.3.2.4
bankruptcy of landlord
  liability of secured creditors, 18.5.7
  maintaining services, 18.5.7, 18.8.2
  preventing evictions, 18.8.4
  security deposits, 18.8.5
  tenant ownership, 18.8.3
discharge protections, 15.5.5.3
homestead exemption, 10.2.2.6
judgment for possession, prepetition
  chapter 13 plan confirmation, effect, 12.9.2
  indication on petition, 7.3.2
  stay exemption, 9.4.6.6.2, 9.7.3.2.4
listing in schedule, 7.3.7.4

RESTITUTION DEBTS
see also DAMAGES; FINES AND PENALTIES
automatic stay, 9.4.6.2
avoidance as preference, 10.4.2.6.4.3
criminal proceedings, status, 9.4.6.2, 15.5.1.1
discharge protections, 15.5.5.5

RESTITUTION DEBTS (*cont.*)
dischargeability, 15.4.1, 15.4.3.6, 15.4.3.7, 15.4.3.12, 15.5.1.1

RETIREMENT FUNDS
see PENSIONS

RETURNS
defined, 15.4.3.1.1
tax returns, *see* TAX RETURNS

RIGHT OF REDEMPTION
agreements regarding, court review, 8.3.7.1, 11.5.5, 15.5.2.5
automatic stay, effect, 8.3.7.1, 9.4.3
chapter 12
    plan provisions, 17.5.9
    rights, 17.4.3.5.5
enforcement, 8.3.7.1
limits on right, 11.5.2
listing property as exempt, 7.3.7.2.3
payment in installments, 11.5.3, 11.5.4
personal property, 8.3.7.1
purpose, 11.5.1
reaffirmation alternative, 11.5.5, 15.5.2.5
statement of intention, 7.3.11
stipulated settlements, 8.3.7.1
time limits, 8.3.7.1
uses in practice, 11.5.5

RIGHT TO CURE
amount required, 11.6.2.7
chapter 12, 17.4.3.5.5, 17.5.4.2
chapter 13, 11.6.2
current payments outside plan, 11.6.2.6
effect of cure, 11.6.2.8.1
effectuating cure, 11.6.2.8.2, 14.4.3.4.6
executory contracts, 12.9.2
final payment, notice, 11.6.2.8.2.5
interest on arrears, 11.6.2.7.2
land installment sales, 11.6.2
long-term debts, 11.6.2, 15.4.1
modification status, 11.6.1.2.3
mortgages after acceleration, 11.6.2.2, 11.6.2.3
mortgages maturing before end of plan, 11.6.2.3
principal residence, 11.6.1.2.3, 11.6.2
reasonable time, 11.6.2.5
Rule 3002.1, use, 11.6.2.8.2, 14.4.3.4.6
unexpired leases, 12.9.2

RULE 2004 EXAMINATIONS
see also FEDERAL RULES OF BANKRUPTCY PROCEDURE
circumstances, 8.3.15.2
consumers as creditors, 18.5.8
failure to conduct, effect, 8.3.15.2
scope, 8.3.15.2
subpoena, Appx. E.7.1

RULE 3001
see also FEDERAL RULES OF BANKRUPTCY PROCEDURE
proof of claim, documentation, 14.4.3.5
    escrow account statement, 14.4.3.4.2
sanctions, 16.5.5.2

RULE 3002.1
see also FEDERAL RULES OF BANKRUPTCY PROCEDURE
background, 14.4.3.4.6
fee dispute procedure, 11.6.2.8.2.4
major mortgage servicers, compliance settlement, 11.6.2.8.2.7
notice of postpetition fees, 8.7.3, 11.6.2.8.2.3
notice of final cure payment, 11.6.2.8.2.5
notice of payment change, 8.7.3, 11.6.2.8.2.2
overview, 11.6.2.8.2.1
sanctions, 11.6.2.8.2.6, 14.4.3.4.1, 16.5.5.2

RULE 9011
see also FEDERAL RULES OF BANKRUPTCY PROCEDURE
attorney certifications, 16.7.2.3, 16.7.2.4
overview, 16.7.1
sanctions
    attorneys, against, 16.7.2.2
    creditors, against, 16.5.5.1
    debtors, against, 16.7.2.1

RULES OF BANKRUPTCY PROCEDURE
see FEDERAL RULES OF BANKRUPTCY PROCEDURE

SCHEDULES
see also BANKRUPTCY FORMS
amending, 8.3.2
annotations, Appx. D.2
attorney certification, 16.7.2.4
audits, 8.3.15.1
chapter 12, 17.2.3.1
codebtors, Sch. H, 7.3.7.5
creditor information, Sch. D–Sch. F, 7.3.7.3
debtor's property, Sch. A–Sch. C, 7.3.7.2
declaration of truth, 7.3.7.7
executory contracts, Sch. G, 7.3.7.4
exempt property, Sch. C, 7.3.7.2.3
expenses, Sch. J, 7.3.7.6
failure to file, dismissal of case, 13.3.1, 13.3.2
generally, 7.3.7
income, Sch. I, 7.3.7.6
Official Form 6, 7.3.7, Appx. D.2
overview, 7.3.7.1
personal property, Sch. B, 7.3.7.2.2
priority debts, Sch. E, 7.3.7.3.3
real property, Sch. A, 7.3.7.2.1
sample completed schedules, Appx. D.2
secured debts, Sch. D, 7.3.7.3.2
summary of schedules, 7.3.7.8
unexpired leases, Sch. G, 7.3.7.4
unsecured debts, Sch. F, 7.3.7.3.4

SECTION 341(a) MEETING OF CREDITORS
see MEETING OF CREDITORS (SECTION 341(a))

SECURED CLAIMS
see ALLOWED SECURED CLAIMS

SECURED CREDITORS
see also CREDITORS; SECURITY INTERESTS
allowed secured claims, *see* ALLOWED SECURED CLAIMS
avoidance of liens and transfers, 8.3.6, 10.4.2
bankruptcy clauses, validity, 11.5.4, 15.5.3
chapter 7 distribution, 3.5.4
chapter 12 reorganizations
    adequate protection, 17.4.4.3, 17.4.11
    classification, 17.5.6.4
    good faith test, 17.5.7.1
    treatment, 17.5.4
chapter 13 cramdown
    adequate protection, 4.3, 11.6.1.3.3.2
    limits on, 11.6.1.2
    modification of rights, 11.6.1
    payment, 7.3.12.3, 7.3.12.5
    standards under plan, 11.6.1.3
dealing with
    bankruptcy tools, 6.2.1.3
    generally, 11.1
determination, 12.2.3.1
gathering information regarding, 5.3.3.3
listing in schedule, Sch. D, 7.3.7.3.2
postpetition actions
    abandonment by trustee, 11.3.3
    automatic stay, relief, 9.7
    cash collateral, holding, 11.3.5
    disposition by trustee, 11.3.4
    reclamation of property, 11.3.2
redemption by debtor, *see* RIGHT OF REDEMPTION
statement of debtor's intentions, *see* STATEMENT OF INTENTION

SECURED DEBTS
see ALLOWED SECURED CLAIMS; SECURITY INTERESTS

SECURED PROPERTY
see COLLATERAL

SECURITIES VIOLATIONS
debts arising from, dischargeability, 15.4.3.18

SECURITIZED LOANS
automatic stay relief, 9.7.3.1.1
lender bankruptcy, effect, 18.9.5
proof of claim, 14.4.3.4.7, 14.4.3.5

SECURITY DEPOSITS
landlord bankruptcy, recovery, 18.8.5
listing in schedule, 7.3.7.2.2

SECURITY INTERESTS
see also COLLATERAL; LIENS; REPOSSESSIONS; SECURED CREDITORS
allowed secured claims, *see* ALLOWED SECURED CLAIMS
avoidance, *see* AVOIDANCE OF LIENS AND TRANSFERS
bankruptcy clauses, 11.5.4
bifurcation, 11.7

SECURITY INTERESTS (cont.)
bifurcation (cont.)
   chapter 7, 11.2.1.2
   chapter 12, 11.2.1.3, 17.5.3
   chapter 13, 11.2.1.3, 12.2.3.1
cash collateral, *see* CASH COLLATERAL
chapter 12
   automatic dissolution, 17.4.3.4
   avoidance, 17.4.3.3, 17.4.3.5
   determination, 17.5.3
chapter 13 cramdown, 11.6
chapter 13 limitations, 12.2.3.1
cross-collateral clauses, 15.5.3
definition, 10.4.2.6.4.3, 11.6.1.2.2.6
elimination, various means, 11.1
enforcement after discharge, 15.5.1.4, 15.5.2, 15.5.3
gathering information regarding, 5.3.3.3
hardship discharges, effect, 4.7.2
listing as exempt in schedule, 7.3.7.2.3
listing in schedule, Sch. D, 7.3.7.3.2
partial encumbrances, 3.5.4
personal property
   adequate protection payments, 8.3.12.2, 12.8.2.2
   proof of insurance, 8.3.13, 12.8.4
   "retain and pay" option, 11.4.2
   validity, 8.4.3
preferences, *see* PREFERENCES
purchase money, *see* PURCHASE MONEY SECURITY INTERESTS
real property, *see* MORTGAGES
redemption, *see* RIGHT OF REDEMPTION
spreader clauses, 15.5.3
statement of intention regarding, *see* STATEMENT OF INTENTION

SERVICE
bankruptcy proceedings, 14.3.2.1

SERVICERS
abuses, 14.4.3.4
   sanctions, 16.5.5.1, 16.5.5.2
Rule 3002.1 requirements, 11.6.2.8.2
voluntary loan modifications, 11.6.1.5

SETOFFS
see also COUNTERCLAIMS
allowed secured claims, 11.2.1
automatic stay, effect, 9.4.4
avoidance, 10.4.2.6.7
bank account freezes, 11.3.5
chapter 12, government creditors, 17.4.12
governmental units, 14.3.2.2
lender bankruptcies, 18.9.4
mutual debts, 10.4.2.6.7, 17.4.12
post discharge, 10.5
recoupment claims, 10.4.2.6.7, 14.3.2.4
right to, 10.4.2.6.7, 17.4.12
tax claims, 9.4.4, 9.4.6.8, 17.4.12

SETTLEMENT
prepetition attempts, effect on creditor's claim, 14.4.3.6

SMALL BUSINESSES
chapter 11 reorganizations, 18.7.10

SOCIAL SECURITY BENEFITS
see also PUBLIC BENEFITS
current monthly income, exclusion, 13.4.3.2.7
discharge protections, 15.5.5.4
federal exemption, 10.2.2.11
overpayments, dischargeability, 15.4.3.2.3.3
wage orders, attachment, 12.6.1

SOCIAL SECURITY NUMBERS
production at meeting of creditors, 8.4.2, 8.4.3
statement of, *see* STATEMENT OF SOCIAL SECURITY NUMBER

SOVEREIGN IMMUNITY
attorney fee awards, relationship, 16.5.7
Bankruptcy Code, abrogation, 1.1.2.4, 9.6.6, 14.3.2.2
stripdown not violation of, 11.2.1.1
Tucker Act, application, 14.3.2.2

SPENDTHRIFT TRUSTS
bankruptcy estate, exclusion, 2.5.2

SPOUSES
see also CODEBTORS; JOINT BANKRUPTCIES; JOINT PROPERTY
chapter 13 eligibility, 4.2.1.2, 6.3.2, 12.2.2
considerations favoring chapter 7, 6.3.2
financial management course, completion, 8.3.3
fraudulent actions, liability of debtor, 15.4.3.2.2.2
income, treatment for bankruptcy purposes, 13.4.3.2.3
joint filings, considerations, 6.4
listing in schedule, 7.3.7.5
marital property settlements, *see* MARITAL PROPERTY SETTLEMENTS
prior filing by, effect, 9.3.3.2.1, 9.3.3.3, 12.10.3
statement of financial affairs, 7.3.8
support obligations, *see* DOMESTIC SUPPORT OBLIGATIONS

SPREADER CLAUSES
validity, 15.5.3

STANDING
prepetition causes of action, 14.3.2.6.2
securitized debts, 9.7.3.1.1, 14.4.3.4.7

STATE EXEMPTIONS
see also EXEMPT PROPERTY
choosing, 10.2.1
domiciliary requirements, 10.2.1.2
   exemption planning, 6.5.2.2
farmers, 17.4.3.1
federal modification, 10.2.3.1
homestead exemptions, 10.2.3.4
joint property, 10.2.3.2
property not subject to process, 10.2.3.2

retirement funds, 10.2.3.3
summaries, Appx. J

STATEMENT ABOUT BANKRUPTCY ASSISTANCE SERVICES
required statement, 16.8.3.3

STATEMENT OF ATTORNEY COMPENSATION
form, Appx. E.3
requirement, 16.3.2

STATEMENT OF CURRENT MONTHLY INCOME
see also BANKRUPTCY FORMS; CURRENT MONTHLY INCOME
filing, 7.3.9, 13.4.3.2.1
Official Form 22, Appx. D.2

STATEMENT OF FINANCIAL AFFAIRS
see also BANKRUPTCY FORMS; FINANCIAL STATEMENTS
filing, 7.2.1
generally, 7.3.8
Official Form 7, Appx. D.2

STATEMENT OF INTENTION
see also BANKRUPTCY FORMS
conversion from chapter 13, 4.7.4
filing requirement, 7.2.1
generally, 7.3.11, 11.4
Official Form 8, Appx. D.2
performance, 3.5, 11.4.1
retention of property, 11.4.2

STATEMENT OF SOCIAL SECURITY NUMBER
see also BANKRUPTCY FORMS
chapter 7, 3.4
chapter 13, 4.4
emergency bankruptcies, 7.2.2
filing, 7.2.1, 7.3.3
Official Form 21, Appx. D.2
privacy issues, 7.3.3

STATISTICAL SUMMARY OF CERTAIN LIABILITIES
required form, 7.3.7.8

STATUTE OF LIMITATIONS
see also TIME LIMITS
avoidance actions, 10.4.2.2, 10.4.2.7
bankruptcy stay violations, 9.6.2
fraudulent conveyances, 10.4.2.6.5
recovery actions, 10.4.2.2, 10.4.2.8
student loans, 15.4.3.8.2
tax reach backs, 6.5.3.4
TIL claims, 14.4.4
tolling, 10.4.2.7

STATUTORY LIENS
see also LIENS
avoidance, 10.4.2.6.3
chapter 13 cramdown, application, 11.6.1.2.2.6
preferences, exception, 10.4.2.6.4.2
valuation of property, 11.2.2.3.4

STAY OF PROCEEDINGS
see AUTOMATIC STAY

STRAIGHT BANKRUPTCY
see CHAPTER 7 LIQUIDATIONS

STRIPDOWN
see also CRAMDOWN
chapter 13 plans, 11.2.1.3, 11.2.2
government claims, 11.2.1.1
limitations on, 11.6.1.2
non-recourse loans, 11.2.1.2

STUDENT LOANS
administrative discharge, 15.4.3.8.3, 15.4.3.8.4
chapter 13 classification, 12.4.3
chapter 13 issues, 15.4.3.8.5
defenses, raising, 15.4.3.8.4
dischargeability, 15.4.1, 15.4.3.8
   chapter 7, 3.6
   chapter 13, 4.8
   procedure, 15.4.3.8.3
discharge issues
   discharge protections, 15.5.5.2
   hardship discharge, 15.4.3.8.2.2, 15.4.3.8.3
   related provisions, Appx. A.4.4
HEAL debts, 15.4.3.8.6
nonbankruptcy alternatives, 15.4.3.8.4
qualified education loans, defined, 15.4.3.8.1
reaffirmation agreements, 15.5.5.2
related provisions, Appx. A.3, Appx. A.4.4

SUBPOENAS
forms, Appx. E.7

SUBSTANTIAL ABUSE
see also ABUSE OF CHAPTER 7
standard changed, 13.4.7.2

SUBSTANTIVE CONSOLIDATION
joint bankruptcy, differences, 6.4

SUMMARY OF SCHEDULES
required form, 7.3.7.8

SUMMONS
forms, Appx. E.6

SUPPORT OBLIGATIONS
see DOMESTIC SUPPORT OBLIGATIONS

TAX CLAIMS
see also GOVERNMENT CLAIMS
allowed secured claims, 11.2.1.1
automatic stay
   effect, 9.4.4, 9.4.6.8
   violations, 9.6.6
burden of proof, 14.4.3.3
chapter 12 dispositions, 17.5.5.4
chapter 13 classification, 12.3.6.1, 12.4.3
dischargeability, 15.4.3.1
   analyzing to determine, 15.4.3.1.2
   chapter 13, 4.8, 15.4.3.1.1
   generally, 7.3.7.3.3, 15.4.3.1.1
   reach back periods, 6.5.3.4
federal taxes paid by credit card, 15.4.3.13
government claims, status as, 15.4.3.1.1
listing in schedules, 7.3.7.3.3
litigating in bankruptcy court, 14.3.2.3
means test deductions, 13.4.5.3.3
objections to, 14.4.3.2
priority status, 7.3.7.3.3, 17.5.5.4
proof of claim, filing, time, 14.4.3.2
set-off rights
   automatic stay, application, 9.4.4, 9.4.6.8
   chapter 12, 17.4.12

TAX CONSEQUENCES
discharge, 15.5.5.6

TAX CREDITS
bankruptcy estate, exclusion, 2.5.5
   federal exemption, application, 10.2.2.11

TAX LIENS
avoidance, 10.4.2.6.3

TAX REFUNDS
assignment for attorney fees, 2.5.5
bankruptcy estate, inclusion, 2.5.5, 7.3.7.2.2
chapter 13 plan issues, 12.3.4.4.3, 12.3.4.4.5
expected, effect on waiver of filing fee, 14.6.2.1
intercepts
   automatic stay, application, 9.4.4, 9.4.6.8
   avoidance as preference, 10.4.2.6.4.3

TAX RETURNS
chapter 13 prerequisite, 4.3, 8.3.14, 12.3.6.2
failure to file, effect, 15.4.3.1.1
obtaining, Appx. H.2
production, 8.3.4
   court, filing with, 8.3.4.2
   privacy concerns, 8.3.4.3
   trustee and creditors, to, 8.3.4.1
source of information, 5.3.4

TENANTS
see also RESIDENTIAL TENANCIES; UNEXPIRED LEASES
evictions, see EVICTIONS
landlord bankruptcies, see LANDLORD BANKRUPTCIES

TIME LIMITS
see also STATUTE OF LIMITATIONS
appeals, 2.4.3, 14.9.5
attorney fee applications, 15.4.3.2.4
automatic stay litigation, 9.7.2
avoidance of liens, 10.4.2.2
bankruptcy petition preparers, disclosures, 16.6
chapter 7, 3.3
chapter 11 plans, 18.7.9
chapter 12 reorganizations
   generally, 17.5.2
   plan proposals, 17.5.2
   revocation of discharge, 17.7.3
   unexpired farmland leases, assumption, 17.4.7.5
chapter 13 reorganizations
   claims and objections, 4.3
   commencement of plan payments, 8.3.12
dischargeability, raising, 15.4.2, 18.5.4.2.2
emergency bankruptcies, filings, 7.2.2
exempt property
   amending claim, 10.3.2
   dependent claims, 10.3.1
extensions, 7.3.13.5
financial management course, 8.3.3
fraudulent conveyances, 6.5.2.1
jury trials, filing of consents, 14.2.7
objections to claims, 8.3.9, 8.4.6, 14.4.3.1
objections to discharge, 3.3, 15.2.1
objections to exemptions, 3.3, 8.5, 10.3.3, 10.3.4
preferences, 6.5.2.1
proof of claim
   consumers as creditors, 18.4.1
   filing, 3.3, 14.4.3.2, 15.4.3.3
   filing by debtor, 8.4.6
redemption of personal property, 8.3.7.1
removal to bankruptcy court, 14.4.1.2
small business reorganizations, 18.7.10
stated intentions, following through, 7.3.11
statement of compensation, filing, 16.3.2
statement of intention, filing, 7.3.11, 11.4.1
tax intercept, 9.4.4
utility services, adequate assurance, 9.8.2

TITLE PAWNS
bankruptcy, effect, 11.9

TOOLS OF THE TRADE
family farmers
   exemption, 17.4.3.2
   redemption, 17.4.3.5.5
federal exemption, 10.2.2.7
livestock, status as, 17.4.3.2
non-purchase money liens, avoidance, 10.4.2.4, 10.4.2.10

TORT CLAIMS
see also PERSONAL INJURY CLAIMS; WRONGFUL DEATH CLAIMS
bankruptcy court, jurisdiction, 14.2.6, 14.5.2
dischargeability, 15.4.3.6, 18.5.4.2.1, 18.5.4.4
undiscovered prepetition, 18.5.4.4

TRANSCRIPTS
educational institutions, discharge protections, 15.5.5.2
IRS, 15.4.3.1.2

TRANSFERS
avoidance, see AVOIDANCE OF LIENS AND TRANSFERS
donations, see CHARITABLE CONTRIBUTIONS
fraudulent, see FRAUDULENT TRANSFERS
postpetition, see POSTPETITION TRANSFERS
prebankruptcy, see PREBANKRUPTCY TRANSFERS

TRANSPORTATION EXPENSES
means test deduction, 13.4.5.2.4
   IRS standard, Appx. I.2.4

Index and Quick Reference   **UNSECURED**

References are to sections

TRUST FUNDS
see also TRUSTS
bankruptcy estate
   exempt from, 18.5.2.1
   existence of trust, 18.5.2.2
   tracing trust funds, 18.5.2.3
constructive trusts, 18.5.2.2
self-settled trusts, avoidance of transfers, 10.4.2.6.5

TRUSTEES
see also TRUSTS
bankruptcy trustees, *see* TRUSTEES IN BANKRUPTCY
chapter 7 filings, restrictions, 3.2.1.1, 6.2.2.8.1
fraud by, discharge bar, 15.4.3.4, 15.4.3.11
U.S. trustee, *see* UNITED STATES TRUSTEE PROGRAM

TRUSTEES IN BANKRUPTCY
see also UNITED STATES TRUSTEE PROGRAM
appointment and duties, 2.6
automatic stay, motions for relief, party, 9.7.3.1.1
automatic turnover of property to, *see* AUTOMATIC TURNOVER
avoidance powers
   fraudulent transfers, 10.4.2.6.5
   liens securing penalties, 10.4.2.6.8
   postpetition transfers, 10.4.2.6.6
   preferences, 10.4.2.6.4.1, 10.4.2.6.4.2
   preservation of property, 10.4.2.9
   setoffs, 10.4.2.6.7
   statutory liens, 10.4.2.6.3
   strong-arm clause, 10.4.2.6.2
chapter 7 liquidations
   abandonment of property, 3.5, 8.3.11, 11.3.3, 18.8.2.1
   administration of property, 3.5, 14.3.2.6.2
   compensation surcharge, 7.2.1
   disposition of property, 11.3.4
   disputes, powers, 3.4
   distribution to creditors, 3.5.4
   final report, 3.5.4
   interim trustee, appointment, 3.3
   liquidation of estate, 3.5.2
   objections, 8.5
   oral examination of debtor, 3.4
   unpaid compensation, payment in chapter 13, 12.4.5
chapter 11, appointment, 18.7.4
chapter 12 reorganizations
   additional to DIP, 17.3.1
   appointment, 17.4.1.1
   compensation, 17.4.1.2
   plan payments through, 17.4.1.2.1, 17.5.7.3, 17.5.9
   removal of DIP, operation of farm, 17.3.2, 17.4.1.3
   role and standing, 17.4.1.1
chapter 13 reorganizations
   appointment, 4.3
   charges, adjustments, 12.6.4

commission, amount, 6.2.2.6
commission, payment under plan, 7.3.12.3, 11.6.1.3.3.6
fees, priority claim, 12.3.6.1
form plans, promulgation, 7.3.12.2
income payments to, 12.6.1
objections to claims, 4.4
oral examination of debtor, 4.4
plans, administration, 4.4, 8.7.1
secured creditors, standing regarding, 11.6.1.3.3.6
standing trustee, 2.6, 4.3
document production requests, Appx. H.7
meeting of creditors, powers, 8.4.3
   oral examination of chapter 7 debtor, 8.4.5
minimum commission, 7.3.12.3
motion to dismiss, costs, 16.7.2.1
objections to exemptions, 10.3.3, 10.3.4
prepetition causes of action, administration, 14.3.2.6.2
property recovered by, exemption claim, 10.4.2.5
tax returns, provision to, 8.3.4.1

TRUSTS
see also TRUST FUNDS; TRUSTEES
bankruptcy petitions, restrictions on filing, 3.2.1.1, 6.2.2.8.1
constructive trusts, *see* CONSTRUCTIVE TRUSTS
spendthrift trusts, *see* SPENDTHRIFT TRUSTS

TRUTH IN LENDING CLAIMS
attorney fees, 16.5.3
automatic stay issues, 9.7.3.3.2, 18.9.2
bankruptcy court, bringing before, 14.4.4

TUCKER ACT
sovereign immunity application, 14.3.2.2

TURNOVER OF PROPERTY
see AUTOMATIC TURNOVER

TYPING SERVICES
see BANKRUPTCY PETITION PREPARERS; NON-ATTORNEYS

UNAUTHORIZED PRACTICE OF LAW
non-attorney operations, 16.6

UNEXPIRED LEASES
see also EVICTION; RESIDENTIAL TENANCIES
adequate protection, 12.8.2.2
assumption
   chapter 7, 8.3.7.2, 12.9.5.3
   chapter 12, 17.4.7.1, 17.4.7.5
   chapter 13, 12.9.2, 12.9.4
automatic stay relief
   personal property leases, 12.9.4, 12.9.5.2
   residential leases, 9.7.3.2.4
chapter 12, assumption or rejection, 17.4.7
   equipment leases, 17.4.7.4
   farmland rental agreements, 17.4.7.5
chapter 13 plans

adequate protection, 12.8.2.2
assumption, 12.9.2
classification, 12.4.3
payments, 12.8.3
procedure and tactics, 12.9.4
proof of insurance, 12.8.4
rejection, 12.9.3.2
default, curing, 12.9.2
discharge protections, 15.5.5.3
listing
   filing of list, 7.3.4
   schedule, Sch. G, 7.3.7.4
personal property leases
   automatic stay relief, 12.9.4, 12.9.5.2
   chapter 7, assumption or rejection, 8.3.7.2, 12.9.5
   chapter 12, assumption or rejection, 17.4.7.1, 17.4.7.4
   chapter 13, assumption or rejection, 12.9
   chapter 13 payments, 8.3.12.2, 12.8.2.2, 12.8.3
   deemed rejection, 12.9.5.2
   proof of insurance, 8.3.13, 12.8.4
   statement of intention, 7.3.11, 11.4
rejection
   chapter 7, 12.9.5.2
   chapter 12, 17.4.7.1, 17.4.7.4
   chapter 13, 12.9.3, 12.9.4
rent-to-own transactions, *see* RENT-TO-OWN TRANSACTIONS
residential leases, 9.7.3.2.4

UNFAIR TRADE PRACTICES
attorney fee awards, 16.5.3
automatic stay violations, 9.6.5
non-attorney services, 16.3.3, 16.6
non-possessory, non-purchase money liens, 10.4.2.4, 10.4.2.10
security deposit misappropriation, 18.8.5

UNITED STATES CODE
selected provisions, Appx. A.2, Appx. A.3
title 11, *see* BANKRUPTCY CODE

UNITED STATES TRUSTEE PROGRAM
see also TRUSTEES IN BANKRUPTCY
approved financial management courses, 8.3.3
attorney fees, monitoring, 16.3.1, 16.3.3, 16.4.2
chapter 11, role, 18.7.2.3, 18.7.4.7
function, generally, 2.7
helpful resources, Appx. H.4
institution of system, 1.1.2.3, 1.5.1.3
motion for dismissal, bringing, 13.4
phase-in of operation, 1.4.1
related provisions, Appx. A.4.3
trustees in bankruptcy, appointment, 2.6

UNSECURED CREDITORS
see also CREDITORS
bankruptcy as protection from, 6.2.1.2
chapter 12 plans, 17.5.5
   classification, 17.5.6.3
   disposable income commitment, 17.5.5.3

UNSECURED CREDITORS (cont.)
chapter 12 plans (cont.)
    good faith test, 17.5.7.1
    liquidation test, 17.5.5.2
chapter 13 plans, 12.3
    best interests test, 7.3.12.3, 7.3.12.5, 12.3.2
    classification, 12.4
    objections, 12.3.4.2
determination, 12.2.3.1
discharge, effect on, 15.5.1
listing in schedule, Sch. F, 7.3.7.3.4
priority creditors, see PRIORITY UNSECURED CREDITORS

UTILITY SERVICES
adequate assurance of payment, 9.8.2
denial of service, restrictions, 9.8.1
governmental utilities, 9.8.2.2.5
landlord bankruptcy
    maintaining service, 18.5.7, 18.8.2
    taxing of secured creditor, 18.5.3
means test deduction, 13.4.5.2.5
    IRS standards, Appx. I.2.3
postpetition shut-offs, 9.8.2.2.4
reinstatement, 9.8.1, 9.8.2

VALUATION
allowed secured claims
    appraisal, necessity, 11.2.2.3.4
    chapter 12 reorganizations, 17.5.3
    conversion from chapter 13 to 7, 13.7.2, 13.7.3
    date, 11.2.2.2
    exempt property, inclusion, 11.2.2.3.4
    generally, 11.2.2.1, 11.6.1.3.3.5
    method, 11.2.2.3
    present value, 11.6.1.3.3.1, 11.6.1.3.3.6
causes of action, 7.3.7.2.2
equity in property
    exemption claims, 10.3.3
    stay litigation, 9.7.3.3.1

exempt property, 10.1.2, 10.3.3
motor vehicles, 5.3.4, 11.2.2.3.2
personal property, 7.3.7.2.2, 11.2.2.3.3
    converted cases, 13.7.2
    date, 11.2.2.2.2
    replacement value, 11.2.2.3.1
private market value, 11.2.2.3.2
real property, 5.3.4, 7.3.7.2.1
    date, 11.2.2.2.2
    timing of petition, 6.5.3.8
replacement cost, 11.2.2.3.1, 11.2.2.3.2
right of redemption, 11.5.5
web resources, 5.3.4

VENUE
bankruptcy matters, 3.2.3, 14.3.2.1

VETERANS
see also MILITARY PERSONNEL
disabled veterans, means test exemption, 13.4.4

VOLUNTARY BANKRUPTCIES
see also BANKRUPTCY; INVOLUNTARY BANKRUPTCIES
consumers as creditors, preparing for, 18.2.1
defined, 2.1
petitions, see BANKRUPTCY PETITIONS

WAGE GARNISHMENTS
avoidance as preference, 10.4.2.6.4.2, 10.4.2.6.4.3

WAGE ORDERS
chapter 13 cases, 8.3.12, 12.6.1

WAGES
priority claims, 18.7.12.2
withholding for retirement fund loans
    automatic stay exemption, 9.4.6.4
    disposable income exclusion, 12.3.4.4.2.4

WAIVER
credit counseling requirement, 3.2.1.4
default, see RIGHT TO CURE

filing fees, 6.2.2.6, 14.6, 18.6.2
see also IN FORMA PAUPERIS
application for, 7.2.1, 7.3.13.4
chapter 7, 14.6.2.1, Appx. H.6
chapter 12, 17.2.3.3
consumers as creditors, 18.6.2
general principles, 14.6.1
Official Form 3B, 7.2.1, 7.3.13.4, Appx. D.2
statutory authority, 14.6.2
financial management course, 8.3.3
setoff rights, 10.4.2.6.7

WEB RESOURCES
see also COMPUTERIZATION; RESEARCH AIDS
bankruptcy court documents, 2.4.1, 5.3.4
bankruptcy forms, 1.3.2, 1.4.3, 7.1.2
bankruptcy research, 1.5.7
bankruptcy, understanding, 6.1.2
helpful websites, Appx. L
NCLC companion website, 1.3.2, 5.1.3, Appx. M
NCLC web-based text searches, 1.3.3, Appx. M.6
PACER, 2.4.1, 5.3.4, Appx. C.4
valuation issues, 5.3.4

WELFARE BENEFITS
see also PUBLIC BENEFITS
discharge protections, 15.5.5.4
federal exemption, 10.2.2.11

WRONGFUL CONDUCT
homestead exemption cap, 10.2.3.4.5

WRONGFUL DEATH CLAIMS
see also PERSONAL INJURY CLAIMS
bankruptcy court
    jurisdiction, 14.2.6
    mandatory abstention, application, 14.5.2
drunk driving, dischargeability, 15.4.3.9

NOTES

NOTES

NOTES

NOTES

NOTES

NOTES